THE ROUGH GUIDE TO
SOUTHEAST ASIA
ON A BUDGET

This fifth edition updated by
Stuart Butler, Meera Dattani, Tom Deas, Nick Edwards,
Marco Ferrarese, Esme Fox, Paul Gray, Anthon Jackson,
Daniel Jacobs, Joanna James, Richard Lim, Mike
MacEacheran, Shafik Meghji, Rachel Mills, Sarah Reid,
Daniel Stables, Iain Stewart, Gavin Thomas and Martin
Zatko

ROUGH
GUIDES

Contents

Introduction to
Southeast Asia

With its tempting mix of volcanoes, rainforest, rice fields, beaches and coral reefs, Southeast Asia is one of the most stimulating and accessible regions for independent travel in the world. You can spend the day exploring thousand-year-old Hindu ruins and the night at a rave on the beach; attend a Buddhist alms-giving ceremony at dawn and go whitewater rafting in the afternoon; chill out in a bamboo beach hut one week and hike through the jungle looking for orang-utans the next.

In short, there is enough here to keep anyone hooked for months, and the average cost of living is so low that many travellers find they can afford to take their time. The region comprises Brunei, Cambodia, Indonesia, Laos, Malaysia, Myanmar, the Philippines, Singapore, Thailand and Vietnam. As useful gateways to the region, we have also included Southeast Asian neighbours **Hong Kong and Macau**. Though the region has long been on the travellers' trail, it doesn't take too much to get off the beaten track – whether it's to discover that perfect beach or to delve into the lush rainforest.

The **beaches** here are some of the finest in the world, and you'll find the cream of the crop in Thailand, the Philippines and Malaysia, all of which boast postcard-pretty, white-sand bays, complete with azure waters and wooden beach shacks dotted along their palm-fringed shores. The clear tropical waters also offer supreme diving opportunities for novices and seasoned divers alike.

Southeast Asia's myriad **temple complexes** are another of the region's best-known attractions. The Khmers left a string of magnificent constructions across the region, the most impressive of which can be seen at Angkor in Cambodia, while the colossal ninth-century stupa of Borobudur in Indonesia and the temple-strewn plain of Bagan in Myanmar are impressive Buddhist monuments.

Almost every visitor to the region makes an effort to climb one of the spectacular **mountains**, whether getting up before dawn to watch the sun rise from Indonesia's Mount Bromo or embarking on the two-day trek to scale Mount Kinabalu in Malaysia.

ABOVE MONKS, CAMBODIA **OPPOSITE** SNORKELLING IN PALAWAN, THE PHILIPPINES

Witnessing **tribal culture** is a highlight for many visitors to less explored areas, and among the most approachable communities are the tribal groups around Sa Pa in Vietnam, the Torjan of Sulawesi in Indonesia, known for their intriguing architecture and burial rituals, and the ethnic minority villages surrounding Hsipaw in Myanmar.

Where to go

Many travellers begin their trip in **Thailand**, which remains the most popular destination in Southeast Asia, with its long, tropical coast, atmospheric temples and sophisticated cuisine. First stop for most is the capital Bangkok, which can overwhelm the senses with its bustle and traffic, but retains beautiful palaces and pockets of traditional Thai life. Travelling north will take you to ancient capitals, elegant hill towns and the cultural hub of Chiang Mai; travel south and you have thousands of islands to explore, from established beach resorts and party islands to diving centres and secluded idylls.

Neighbouring **Laos**, with its burgeoning tourist industry, is still perhaps the best country to explore if you're looking to escape the crowds, and for many people a slow boat down the Mekong here is still the quintessential Southeast Asian experience; journey's end is the exquisite former royal capital of Luang Prabang, the undoubted jewel of the country. To the west, **Myanmar** (Burma) is seeing something of a visitor boom, as travellers flocking to explore the country's remarkable pagodas, landscapes and culture. Start at the historic former capital of Yangon, before venturing to the stilt villages of Inle Lake and the temple-strewn plain at Bagan.

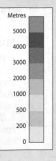

Metres
5000
4000
3000
2000
1000
500
200
0

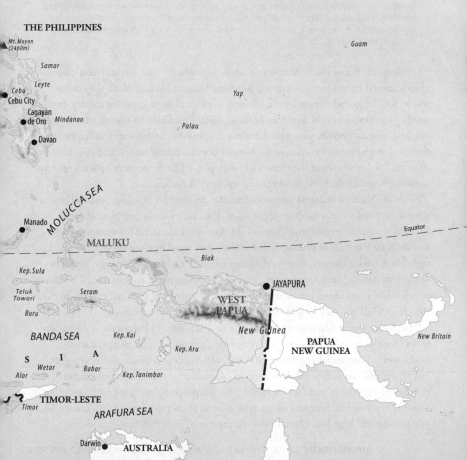

JAPAN

PHILIPPINE
SEA

PACIFIC
OCEAN

THE PHILIPPINES

Mt. Mayon
(2460m)

Samar

Leyte

Cebu
Cebu City

Cagayan
de Oro   Mindanao

Davao

Guam

Yap

Palau

Manado

MOLUCCA SEA

MALUKU

Biak

Equator

JAYAPURA

Kep. Sula

Teluk
Towori   Seram

Buru

BANDA SEA   Kep. Kai

WEST
PAPUA

New   Guinea

PAPUA
NEW GUINEA

New Britain

Kep. Aru

S   I   A

Wetar   Babar

Alor

Timor

TIMOR-LESTE

Kep. Tanimbar

ARAFURA SEA

Darwin   AUSTRALIA

FIVE TIPS FOR PLANNING YOUR SOUTHEAST ASIAN ADVENTURE

1. Plan around the weather Tropical Southeast Asia has two monsoons, which affect different coasts (see p.10). Plan your route to take this into account – and consider each country's regional variations.

2. Budget carefully – but have the odd splurge You can live on as little as $20 a day in some countries, if you're prepared to stay in very basic accommodation, eat at food stalls and travel on local buses, but think about where paying a little more will really enrich your trip.

3. Take local transport You might be able to buy a budget flight – and even grab an Uber in the big cities – but don't discount local transport. It's good value, and is often one of the highlights of a trip, not least because of the chance to meet local people. Overland transport between neighbouring countries is also fairly straightforward so long as you have the right paperwork and are prepared to be patient.

4. Try the street food… This is the home of the world's tastiest cuisines, and the really good news is that the cheapest is often the best, with markets and roadside hawkers unbeatable places to try the many local specialities. Night markets, in particular, are great for tasting different dishes at extremely low prices – with sizzling woks full of frying noodles, swirling clouds of spice-infused smoke and even rows of glistening fried insects.

5. …But stay healthy Like most travellers, you'll most likely suffer nothing more than an upset stomach, so long as you observe basic precautions about food and water hygiene, and research pre-trip vaccination and malaria prophylactic requirements – but arrange health insurance before you leave home. Some of the illnesses you can pick up may also not show themselves immediately, so if you become ill within a year of returning home, tell your doctor where you have been (see p.36).

Heading east brings you to **Vietnam**, with its two vibrant, and very different cities, with elegant capital Hanoi to the north and headlong frenetic Ho Chi Minh City in the south. You'll also find impressive old Chinese towns and some stunning scenery, from the northern mountains to the southern Mekong delta. From here it's easy to cross into neighbouring **Cambodia**, where the fabulous temple ruins at Angkor remain a major draw – though Phnom Penh's appeal grows (as does its dining scene), and you shouldn't miss the low-key charm of river towns like Kampot, while the country's pocket of coast around Sihanoukville draws in increasing numbers of backpackers.

South of Thailand, **Malaysia** deserves a leisurely exploration, boasting beautiful beaches, good diving and some rewarding jungle hikes. The east Malaysia provinces of Sabah and Sarawak – which share the large island of Borneo with Indonesia's Kalimantan province and the little kingdom of **Brunei** – offer adventurous travel by river through the jungle, nights in tribal longhouses, and the challenge of climbing Mount Kinabalu. **Singapore**, along with Bangkok and Hong Kong, is a major gateway to the region; though relatively pricey, it has a fascinating mix of tradition and modernity, and after you've been on the road for a while you may find its more Westernized feel quite appealing.

From Singapore or Malaysia it's a boat ride or short flight to **Indonesia**. It could take you a lifetime to explore this vast and varied archipelago, with fantastic volcanic landscapes, an unparalleled diversity of tribal cultures, decent beaches and diving, and lots of arts and crafts. Beyond the capital of Jakarta, Java offers the ancient, culturally rich city of Yogyakarta and the vast Borobudur temple complex, along with volcanoes and surf beaches. Vast Sumatra would take months to do justice to – but is known for its orang-utans and huge lake Danau Toba. To the east of Java, Bali barely needs an

introduction as the premier vacation destination in the archipelago, with throbbing resorts to the south and the sophisticated cultural hub Ubud at its centre. To escape the crowds, continue east to discover coastal idylls on Lombok and the Gili Islands, and then on again to far-flung islands like Sulawesi and Maluku.

Northeast of Indonesia, a flight away from mainland Southeast Asia, and consequently less visited, **the Philippines** has some of the best beaches and most dramatic diving in the whole region, along with some wonderful Spanish architecture, incredible rice terraces and unique wildlife, making it well worth the detour from the main tourist trail.

When to go

Southeast Asia sits entirely within the tropics and so is broadly characterized by a hot and humid climate that varies little throughout the year, except during the two annual monsoons. Bear in mind, however, that each country has myriad microclimates; for more detail, consult the introduction to each chapter.

Architectural wonders

 1 BOROBUDUR, INDONESIA
Page 200
The biggest Buddhist stupa in the world, covered in delicately sculpted reliefs.

2 SINGAPORE'S MARINA BAY
Page 688
Strikingly modern architecture creates a spectacular cityscape, dominated by *Marina Bay Sands*, while the Esplanade Theatres complex has been dubbed the "durians" locally.

 3 BAGAN, MYANMAR
Page 557
Few vistas match the sight of Bagan's two thousand temples, stupas and monasteries.

4 LUANG PRABANG, LAOS
Page 372
Luang Prabang's colonial houses and red-roofed Buddhist temples have won it a place on the UNESCO World Heritage list.

5 ROYAL CITY OF HUE, VIETNAM
Page 875
A majestic citadel and grand imperial mausoleums dotted along the Perfume River.

 6 ANGKOR WAT, CAMBODIA
Page 93
This immense temple complex is nothing short of magnificent.

7 CITY SKYLINE, HONG KONG
Page 140
One of the most impressive urban vistas in the world.

The **southwest monsoon** arrives in west-coast regions at around the end of May and brings daily rainfall to most of Southeast Asia by mid-July – excepting certain east-coast areas, with Malaysia, for example sheltered from it. From then on you can expect overcast skies and regular downpours until October or November. This is not the best time to travel in Southeast Asia, as west-coast seas are often too rough for swimming, some islands become inaccessible, and poorly maintained roads may get washed out. However, rain showers often last just a couple of hours a day and many airlines and guesthouses offer decent discounts at this time.

The **northeast monsoon** brings drier, slightly cooler weather to most of Southeast Asia (east-coast areas excepted) between November and February, making this period the best overall time to travel in the region. The main exceptions to the above pattern are the east-facing coasts of Vietnam, Thailand and Peninsular Malaysia, which get rain when the rest of tropical Asia is having its driest period, but stay dry during the southwest monsoon. If you're planning a long trip to Southeast Asia, this means you can often escape the worst weather by hopping across to the other coast. Indonesia and Singapore are hit by both monsoons, attracting the west-coast rains from May through to October, and the east-coast rains from November to February.

AVERAGE DAILY TEMPERATURES AND RAINFALL

This climate chart lists average maximum daily temperatures and average monthly rainfall for the capital cities of Southeast Asia. Bear in mind, however, that each country has myriad microclimates, determined by altitude and proximity to the east or west coast among other factors; for more detail, see the "when to go" box in the introduction of each chapter.

	Jan	Feb	March	April	May	June	July	Aug	Sept	Oct	Nov	Dec
BANGKOK, THAILAND												
max (°C)	32	33	34	35	34	33	32	32	32	31	31	31
max (°F)	89.5	91.5	93	95	93	91.5	89.5	89.5	89.5	88	88	86
Rainfall (mm)	8	20	36	58	198	160	160	175	305	206	66	5
HANOI, VIETNAM												
max (°C)	20	21	23	28	32	33	33	32	31	29	26	22
max (°F)	68	69.5	73.5	82.5	89.5	91.5	91.5	89.5	88	84	78.5	71.5
Rainfall (mm)	18	28	38	81	196	239	323	343	254	99	43	20
HONG KONG & MACAU												
max (°C)	18	17	19	24	28	29	31	31	29	27	23	20
max (°F)	64.5	62.5	66	75	82.5	84	88	88	84	80.5	73.5	68
Rainfall (mm)	33	46	74	137	292	394	381	367	257	114	43	31
JAKARTA, INDONESIA												
max (°C)	29	29	30	31	31	31	31	31	31	31	30	29
max (°F)	84	84	86	88	88	88	88	88	88	88	86	84
Rainfall (mm)	300	300	211	147	114	97	64	43	66	112	142	203
KUALA LUMPUR, MALAYSIA												
max (°C)	32	33	33	33	33	33	32	32	32	32	32	32
max (°F)	89.5	91.5	91.5	91.5	91.5	91.5	89.5	89.5	89.5	89.5	89.5	89.5
Rainfall (mm)	159	154	223	276	182	119	120	133	173	258	263	223
MANILA, THE PHILIPPINES												
max (°C)	30	30	31	33	34	34	33	31	31	31	31	31
max (°F)	86	86	88	91.5	93	93	91.5	88	88	88	88	88
Rainfall (mm)	23	23	13	18	33	130	254	432	422	356	193	145
NAYPYITAW, MYANMAR (BURMA)												
max (°C)	30	32	36	39	37	34	34	33	33	33	30	28
max (°F)	86	90	97	102	99	93	93	91	91	91	86	82
Rainfall (mm)	5	2	9	33	154	160	198	229	186	131	37	7
PHNOM PENH, CAMBODIA												
max (°C)	31	32	34	35	34	33	32	32	31	30	30	30
max (°F)	88	89.5	93	95	93	91.5	89.5	89.5	88	86	86	86
Rainfall (mm)	7	10	40	77	134	155	171	160	224	257	127	45
SINGAPORE												
max (°C)	30	31	31	31	32	31	31	31	31	31	31	31
max (°F)	86	88	88	88	89.5	88	88	88	88	88	88	88
Rainfall (mm)	252	173	193	188	173	173	170	196	178	208	254	257
VIENTIANE, LAOS												
max (°C)	28	30	33	34	32	32	31	31	31	31	29	28
max (°F)	82.5	86	91.5	93	89.5	89.5	88	88	88	88	84	82.5
Rainfall (mm)	5	15	38	99	267	302	267	292	302	109	15	3

Southeast Asia's best beaches

Offshore islands, Sihanoukville (Cambodia)
The coastal waters off Sihanoukville (p.108) are peppered with tropical islands lapped by clear, balmy seas, many graced with white-sand beaches. Offering peaceful stretches of sand, they're great places to hole up in for a few days and drink in the idyllic surroundings.

Beaches near Kuta, Lombok (Indonesia) The main development on Lombok's south coast, the quiet fishing town of Kuta (p.300) is an excellent base to kick back by the sea. The surrounding coastline is utterly spectacular, a series of giant headlands separating astonishing white-sand beaches such as Mawun and Selong Belanak.

Pulau Perhentian (Malaysia) Malaysia's most beautiful beaches are found on the twin islands of Pulau Perhentian – Perhentian Kecil and Perhentian Besar (p.463) – where crystal-clear waters lap against secluded, white-sand strands. Offshore wreck dives and snorkel sites offer opportunities for beginners and pros.

El Nido (Philippines) Though El Nido's main beach (p.668) is a little scruffy, the surroundings are truly inspirational – this iridescent bay is the jumping-off point for the enchanting Bacuit archipelago, 45 jungle-smothered outcrops of limestone riddled with karst cliffs, sinkholes and lagoons.

Ko Tao (Thailand) Ko Tao (Turtle Island), so named because its outline resembles a turtle nose-diving towards Ko Pha Ngan, is home to a clutch of beautiful beaches (p.801). The rugged shell of the turtle is crenellated with secluded coves, while Hat Sai Ree, the turtle's underbelly, is a long curve of classic beach backed by palm trees.

Phu Quoc (Vietnam) Vietnam's largest offshore island, Phu Quoc (p.919) rises from its slender southern tip like a genie released from a bottle. It has now cast on enough visitors to challenge Nha Trang as Vietnam's top beach destination.

OPPOSITE GUNUNG MULU NATIONAL PARK, MALAYSIA (P.495)
FROM TOP EL NIDO, THE PHILIPPINES; KO TAO, THAILAND; MAWUN, NEAR KUTA, LOMBOK, INDONESIA

Eat like a local

1 NASI GORENG, INDONESIA
Page 170
You'll find many variants of this classic snack: fried rice with shredded meat and vegetables.

2 DIM SUM, HONG KONG
Page 126
Dim sum – a selection of little dumplings and dishes – is the classic Cantonese way to start the day.

3 MOHINGAR, MYANMAR
Page 527
Breakfast on catfish soup with vermicelli, onions, lemongrass, garlic, chilli and lime.

4 AMOK DTREI, CAMBODIA
Page 70
In this mild Cambodian curry, fish is mixed with coconut milk and seasonings before being wrapped in banana leaves and baked.

5 CHILLI CRAB, SINGAPORE
Page 675
Try the quintessential Singaporean dish, stir-fried crab in a sweet, sour and spicy tomato chilli, at one of the city's numerous hawker centres.

6 PHO, VIETNAM
Page 835
You'll find steaming bowls of pho, pronounced "fur", across Vietnam.

5

6

The great outdoors

1 G-LAND, INDONESIA
Page 213
Indonesia's world-class surf is best tackled from April to October.

2 THE NORTHWESTERN CIRCUIT, VIETNAM
Page 862
Take a motorbike tour of Vietnam's mountainous far north.

3 LUANG NAMTHA, LAOS
Page 388
Strike out into the wild highlands on a tour from Luang Namtha, visiting hill-tribe villages en route.

4 THE VISAYAS, THE PHILIPPINES
Page 635
Meet loggerhead turtles or whale sharks on a marine exploration of the Visayas.

5 MOUNT KINABALU, MALAYSIA
Page 506
Southeast Asia's highest peak is a challenging but straightforward two-day hike.

6 BUKIT LAWANG, INDONESIA
Page 220
See orang-utans in the wild at Bukit Lawang in Sumatra.

7 KRABI, THAILAND
Page 814
Discover your own lonely bays and mysterious lagoons on a sea-kayak tour of Krabi.

1

2

Get away from it all

1 BANDA ISLANDS, INDONESIA
Page 342
Travel to these far-flung islands for their sublime diving.

2 TREKKING AROUND SA PA, VIETNAM
Page 865
See a different side to Vietnam on a hike to ethnic-minority villages around Sa Pa.

3 WAT PHOU, CHAMPASAK, LAOS
Page 401
Explore the spellbinding pre-Angkorian ruins of Wat Phou.

4 BANAUE RICE TERRACES, THE PHILIPPINES
Page 625
The stairways to heaven; for the best view, trek through them to Batad.

5 KHAO SOK NATIONAL PARK, THAILAND
Page 808
Kayak through the humid jungle, then spend the night in a lakeside rafthouse.

6 HSIPAW, MYANMAR
Page 586
Set out on a trek from this once sleepy backwater in Shan State.

Itineraries

You can't expect to fit everything Southeast Asia has to offer into one trip, and we don't suggest you try. On the following pages is a selection of itineraries that guide you through the different countries, picking out a few of the best places and major attractions along the way. For those taking a big trip through the region you could join a few together – across from northern Thailand into Laos and down the mighty Mekong, for example. There is, of course, much to discover off the beaten track, so if you have the time it's worth exploring the smaller towns and villages further afield, finding your own deserted island, perfect hill town or just a place you love to rest up and chill out.

VIETNAM

Few countries have changed so much over such a short time as Vietnam. Many visitors find a vast number of places to visit that intrigue and excite them in Hanoi, Ho Chi Minh City and the other major centres; despite the cities' allure, it's the country's striking landscape that most impresses.

❶ **Hanoi** Vietnam's historical, political and cultural capital, Hanoi is an animated maze of old merchant streets and grand French-colonial architecture. **See p.842**

❷ **Ha Long Bay** Sail around this UNESCO World Heritage Site, where two thousand limestone karsts jut out of the shimmering turquoise waters. **See p.857**

❸ **Sa Pa** This bustling market town nestled in the northern mountains is a popular base for tours to ethnic minority villages, and visits to Bac Ha market. From here you can set out to explore the dramatic landscape of Vietnam's northwestern circuit, before doubling back to Hanoi to continue south. **See p.863**

❹ **Hue** A tranquil yet engaging city, Hue is famous for its nineteenth-century imperial architecture. **See p.875**

❺ **Hoi An** This charmingly seductive sixteenth-century merchant town offers excellent shopping opportunities and an attractive beach. **See p.883**

ABOVE FLOATING MARKET, VIETNAM; RICE PADDIES, BALI

6 Nha Trang The country's pre-eminent party town, Nha Trang has a popular municipal beach, plus boat trips to nearby islands, diving, snorkelling and nearby Cham architecture. **See p.889**

7 Mui Ne Watersports hub with a vast stretch of golden, palm-shaded beach, laidback backpacker hangouts and sand dunes. **See p.893**

8 Da Lat Vietnam's premier hill station and the gateway to the Central Highlands. **See p.898**

9 Ho Chi Minh City Vietnam's bustling second city and an effervescent collusion of French colonial style and brash, cosmopolitan youth. See p.903

10 Mekong Delta Interconnecting canals and rivers cut through lush rice paddies; hop on a boat to visit one of the region's floating markets. See p.912

11 Phu Quoc Vietnam's largest island, a restful place fringed with sandy beaches and an offshore archipelago perfect for diving and snorkelling. **See p.919**

MYANMAR (BURMA)

This is a fascinating time to discover Myanmar, as it reinvents itself after being cut off from the Western world for decades. You'll find rice paddies, temples and beautiful mountain scenery, and a population eager to introduce foreigners to their country and culture.

1 Yangon Start your trip exploring the colonial-era buildings, street markets and glorious Shwedagon Pagoda in the former capital, Yangon. **See p.534**

2 Mawlamyine Once the capital of British Lower Burma, this is now Myanmar's third-largest city. **See p.551**

3 Hpa-an Take the boat from Mawlamyine to Hpa-an where you can watch the sun rise over the serene Kan Thar Yar Lake. **See p.553**

4 Kyaiktiyo The precariously balanced Golden Rock at Kyaiktiyo is one of the holiest Buddhist sites in the country. **See p.550**

5 Kalaw Use Kalaw as a base for one- or two-day treks to visit ethnic-minority villages. See p.567

6 Inle Lake Sample traditional life (or try your luck "leg rowing") on this stunning stretch of water. **See p.570**

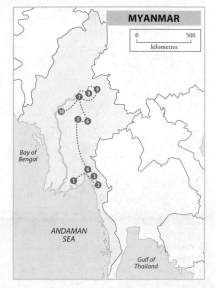

7 Mandalay Watch the sun set over the commercial hub of northern Myanmar from Mandalay Hill. **See p.573**

8 Pyin Oo Lwin Botanical gardens beckon at this former hill station. **See p.583**

9 Hsipaw Ride the train across Gokteik viaduct to reach Hsipaw, an increasingly popular trekking base. **See p.586**

10 Bagan Take a boat from Mandalay to visit these awe-inspiring temples. **See p.557**

LAOS AND CAMBODIA

Laos and Cambodia are now firmly established on the Southeast Asian tourist trail. From forest-clad hills and impenetrable jungle to white-sand beaches and relaxed offshore islands, Cambodia packs a lot into a small area. Landlocked Laos remains one of Southeast Asia's most beguiling destinations; its people are undoubtedly one of the highlights of any visit.

1 Houayxai to Luang Prabang The unmissable two-day trip down the Mekong River ends in beguiling Luang Prabang, the city of golden spires. **See box, p.391**

2 Vang Vieng A natural playground with stunning scenery; the perfect place for cycling, caving, and floating down the river on an inner tube. **See p.368**

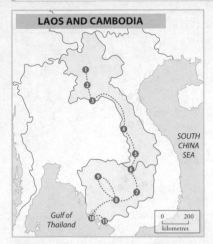

LAOS AND CAMBODIA

SOUTH CHINA SEA

Gulf of Thailand

0   200
kilometres

❸ Vientiane A charming capital boasting a number of interesting temples, good restaurants and the chance to indulge in a relaxing herbal sauna. **See p.360**

❹ Savannakhet The draws at this provincial capital are its lovely French-colonial architecture, narrow lanes and pretty shophouses. **See p.393**

❺ Champasak This sleepy little town makes the perfect base to explore the atmospheric Khmer ruins of Wat Phou. **See p.400**

❻ Si Phan Don Spend your days chilling out in a hammock on one of the four thousand islands scattered across the Mekong, before picking up a minibus to Stung Treng in Cambodia. **See p.404**

❼ Kratie The unassuming town of Kratie is home to a colony of rare freshwater Irrawaddy dolphins. **See p.115**

❽ Phnom Penh A pleasant sprawl of shophouses and boulevards, lustrous palaces and engrossing museums. **See p.76**

❾ Angkor An easy bus ride takes you to Siem Reap and the world-famous temples of Angkor. From here it's a straightforward journey to Bangkok or back to Phnom Penh. **See p.87**

❿ Sihanoukville Cambodia's only proper beach resort provides travel-worn tourists with a chance to relax, party and sun-worship on its sandy beaches. The offshore islands have a delightful Robinson Crusoe appeal. **See p.104**

⓫ Kampot A lazy riverside town surrounded by fields and in the shadow of the abandoned French hill station on Bokor Mountain, it makes a peaceful spot before heading on to Vietnam. **See p.111**

BANGKOK AND NORTHERN THAILAND

The clash of tradition and modernity in Thailand is most intense in Bangkok, the first stop on almost any itinerary. Within its historic core you'll find resplendent temples, canalside markets, a forest of skyscrapers and some achingly hip bars and clubs. The forested mountains of the north, meanwhile, are set apart from the rest of the country by their art, architecture, exuberant festivals and Burmese-influenced cuisine.

❶ Bangkok Immerse yourself in Thailand's frenetic capital, with its grand palaces, noisy tuk-tuks and thriving, crowded markets. **See p.716**

❷ Kanchanaburi A mix of charming rafthouses, waterfalls and lush hills, this place is a popular and chilled-out backpackers' haunt. **See p.734**

❸ Ayutthaya Rent a bicycle and explore the remarkable, extensive ruins of this ancient capital. **See p.739**

❹ Sukhothai The elegant temple remains in Old Sukhothai attest to its former glory. **See p.745**

❺ Umphang If you fancy breaking free of the tourist route, head for this lovely, isolated place surrounded by majestic mountains that are perfect for trekking. **See p.749**

❻ Chiang Mai The complete backpacker package: vibrant markets, hill treks to ethnic minority villages, glorious temples and delectable cuisine. **See p.750**

❼ Pai Amble through Pai's arty night market and finish the evening in one of the town's excellent live-music bars. **See p.764**

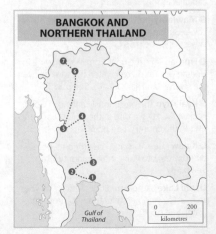

BANGKOK AND NORTHERN THAILAND

Gulf of Thailand

0   200
kilometres

THAILAND'S BEACHES AND ISLANDS

Sand and sea are what many Thai holidays are about, and with over 3000km of tropical coastline, there are plenty of white-sand beaches to choose from. You can dive, swim and sunbathe year-round, for when the monsoon rains are battering one coast you merely have to cross to the other to escape them.

❶ **Phetchaburi** Retains an old-world charm with its historic shophouses, fascinating wats and Rama IV's fabulous hilltop palace. **See p.789**

❷ **Ko Tao** Rough, mountainous, jungle interiors, secluded east-coast beaches, a tastefully developed west-coast beach life and numerous dive schools to choose from. **See p.801**

❸ **Ko Pha Ngan** Famous for its pre-, post-, in-between and actual full-moon parties, Ko Pha Ngan also offers a few, as yet untainted, paradise beaches. **See p.797**

❹ **Khao Sok National Park** Tropical jungle, dotted with dramatic limestone crags, this is one of the most bio-diverse places on the planet. **See p.808**

❺ **Ko Phi Phi** An ugly tourist village that's host to undeniably fun late-night parties is offset by beautiful (yet crowded) Long Beach, great snorkelling and diving, and the magnificent Maya Bay. **See p.817**

❻ **Ko Lanta** Manages to combine a relaxed island getaway experience with spectacular sunsets and good nightlife. **See p.819**

❼ **Ko Lipe** While rapidly becoming overdeveloped, you will still find pockets of paradise here, and the stunning Ko Tarutao National Marine Park is yours to explore. **See p.824**

THAILAND'S BEACHES AND ISLANDS

INDIAN OCEAN

Gulf of Thailand

0 200 kilometres

SINGAPORE AND MALAYSIA

From the fast-paced capital and charming colonial towns to the laidback Perhentian Islands and remote national parks, Malaysia is a varied country that warrants several weeks of exploration. Singapore is a useful gateway to the region, but don't be surprised if this futuristic, captivating city waylays you for longer than you expected.

❶ **Singapore** An easy introduction to Southeast Asia, with an array of tourist-friendly pleasures: shopping, markets, zoos, temples and delicious food. **See p.671**

❷ **Malacca** This old colonial town with a fascinating mix of cultures makes an ideal first stop in Malaysia from either Singapore or Indonesia. **See p.470**

❸ **Kuala Lumpur** Visit the thriving capital, packed with modern architecture, monuments, galleries and markets. **See p.425**

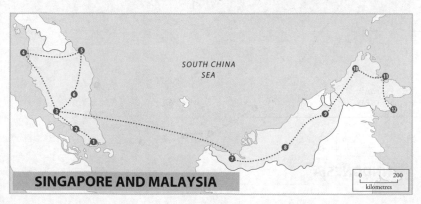

SOUTH CHINA SEA

SINGAPORE AND MALAYSIA

0 200 kilometres

❹ George Town With thriving food and arts scenes, this beautiful former-colonial town has plenty to draw you in and encourage you to linger. **See p.443**

❺ Perhentian Islands A pair of stunning small islands, with white-sand beaches and buckets of charm, this is the perfect place to kick back and relax. **See p.463**

❻ Taman Negara National Park Explore the spectacular and ancient rainforests of Malaysia's interior. **See p.456**

❼ Kuching Sarawak's capital is an attractive, relaxed city that makes a good base for visits to Iban longhouses. **See p.481**

❽ The Batang Rajang A journey along this 560km river takes you past isolated forts and logging wharfs, and through little-visited towns and longhouses into the true heart of Sarawak. **See p.490**

❾ Gunung Mulu National Park Sarawak's premier national park bursts with flora and fauna, and is home to the impressive limestone spikes of the Pinnacles. **See p.495**

❿ Kinabalu National Park An exhausting, exhilarating trek up Mount Kinabalu, the highest peak in Southeast Asia, is rewarded with breathtaking views from the summit at sunrise. **See p.506**

⓫ Sandakan and around While not an appealing city in itself, Sandakan makes a great base to discover Sabah's rich wildlife at Sepilok's Orang-utan Rehabilitation Centre, Turtle Islands National Park and along the Kinabatangan River. **See p.510**

⓬ Pulau Sipadan One of the top dive sites in the world, the waters around here teem with spectacular marine life. **See p.517**

INDONESIA

Travel across the Indonesian archipelago is pretty unforgettable, in tiny fragile planes, rusty ferries and careering buses. Give yourself plenty of time to cover the large distances, taking in the country's soaring volcanoes, awe-inspiring dive sites, memorable wildlife and laidback island retreats.

❶ Bukit Lawang and Danau Toba There's plenty to discover among the beautiful scenery of northern Sumatra: Bukit Lawang is home to orang-utans, while further south lies the vast lake Danau Toba, with pleasant island resorts and fascinating traditional villages. **See p.220 & p.225**

❷ Jakarta Whether you're travelling from Sumatra or Singapore, you may end up in the frenetic capital, where it's worth taking time to explore the interesting museums and enjoy the vibrant nightlife. **See p.177**

❸ Yogyakarta The cultural heart of Java, with a fascinating walled royal city, Yogya is a centre for Javanese arts and also the best place to base yourself for visiting the magnificent temples of Borobudur and Prambanan. **See p.192**

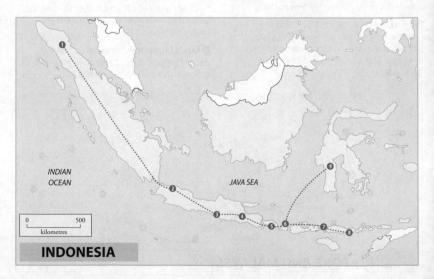

④ Gunung Bromo A vast volcanic crater, with the still-smoking Gunung Bromo rising up from its base; the pre-dawn hike up to the crater rim is well worth the effort for the dramatic sunrise views over a spectacular landscape. **See p.210**

⑤ Bali The beautiful Hindu island is still the most popular destination in the archipelago, with great nightlife, perfect surf and the chilled-out cultural centre of Ubud. **See p.243**

⑥ Lombok Just a short hop from Bali, head to the awesome Gunung Rinjani for a few days' trekking, or to the Gili Islands, just off the northwest coast, for some fabulous diving. **See p.284**

⑦ Komodo and Rinca Enjoy close encounters with the fearsome Komodo dragon. Overnight trips can be organized from Labuanbajo on Flores, or from Lombok. **See p.306**

⑧ Flores A fertile, mountainous island, Flores has one of the most alluring landscapes in the country. The three craters of Kelimutu each contain a lake of vibrantly different colours. **See p.307**

⑨ Tanah Toraja You'll probably have to backtrack to Bali before travelling up to Sulawesi, where the major attraction is the highlands of Tanah Toraja, home to a fascinating culture and flamboyant festivals. **See p.329**

THE PHILIPPINES

Graced by dazzling beaches, year-round sun and numerous opportunities for diving, island-hopping and surfing, the Philippines has long attracted a steady stream of foreign visitors. Yet there's far more to these islands than sand and snorkelling. Beyond the coastline are places to visit of a different nature; mystical tribal villages, ancient rice terraces, jungle-smothered peaks and crumbling Spanish churches.

① Manila The Philippine capital can appear sprawling and seedy, but it has a compelling energy all of its own. It's also the most convenient gateway to some of the country's more inaccessible areas. **See p.601**

② Palawan A prehistoric landscape of underground rivers, giant lizards, shockingly

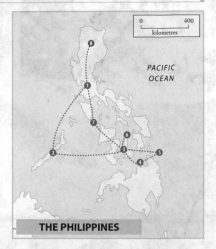

THE PHILIPPINES

beautiful limestone islands and some of the best wreck-diving in the world. **See p.664**

③ Cebu City The Philippines' second city is nearly as frenetic as Manila, and an inevitable stop as you island-hop around the Visayas. **See p.649**

④ Camiguin Easily reached from Cebu City, this small volcanic island offers some of the country's most appealing adventure activities and a laidback, bohemian arts scene. **See p.661**

⑤ Siargao This small teardrop-shaped island located off the northeastern coast of Cagayan de Oro draws crowds of enthusiastic surfers eager to ride Cloud 9, one of the world's most acclaimed reef breaks. **See p.663**

⑥ Malapascua and Bantayan For a slice of island living complete with limited electricity and captivating sunsets, these islands off the tip of Cebu are the Visayas at their best. **See p.656 & p.655**

⑦ Boracay One of the world's most beautiful beaches, with nightlife to rival Manila, Boracay is still an unmissable stop on any trip to the Philippines. **See p.635**

⑧ The Cordilleras For a Philippine experience a world away from the sun-drenched beaches of the south, head north to the cool mountain villages of the Igorot tribes, nestled among jaw-dropping rice-terrace scenery. **See p.619**

NONG KHAI, THAILAND

Basics

Getting there

The quickest and easiest way to get to Southeast Asia is by air. One of the cheapest options is to buy a flight to one of the region's gateway cities, such as Singapore or Bangkok, and make onward travel arrangements from there. If you're keen to combine your trip with a visit to India or China, you could consider a stopover or open-jaw ticket, which flies you into one country and out of another, allowing you to explore overland in between. If you're planning a multi-stop trip, then a round-the-world or Circle Asia/Pacific ticket offers good value; the least expensive and most popular routes include one or more "surface sectors" where you have to make your way between point A and point B by road, rail or sea or by a locally bought flight. As an alternative to air travel, you could consider taking one of the world's classic overland trips, the Trans-Siberian Railway, through Russia and Mongolia to China, and continue from there to Indochina.

The biggest factor affecting the price of a ticket is the time of year you wish to travel. **High season** for many Asian destinations is over Christmas (when much of the region is at its driest), during the UK summer holidays, and over Chinese New Year. As such, you should book well in advance during these periods. Some airlines and travel agents charge more than others, so it's always good to shop around. Compare fares online using a site like Skyscanner (W skyscanner.net), and check out discount-flight agents. You can also get good deals if you are a **student** or are **under 26** with discount agents such as STA Travel and the Canadian company Travel Cuts (see p.31).

Flying into Southeast Asia on a one-way ticket is fairly inexpensive and gives you plenty of options for onward travel, but it could cause **problems at immigration**, for example in Indonesia (see p.166). Stricter officials might ask to see proof of your onward

or return transport, while others will be more satisfied if you can give details of a convincing onward route, with dates. Showing proof of sufficient funds to keep you going (even if this just means flashing a couple of credit/debit cards) will also placate immigration officials. It's pretty rare for you to be asked for this information, but there's no harm in being prepared.

In some countries, you may have to apply for a **visa** in advance if arriving on a one-way ticket, rather than being granted one automatically at immigration, so always check with the relevant embassy before you leave. If you are continuing overland, you should research visa requirements at the border crossings before leaving home. Details on **overland transport** from neighbouring Southeast Asian countries are given in the introduction to each chapter.

Flights from the UK and Ireland

It's usually more expensive to fly **from the UK and Ireland** nonstop than to change planes in Europe, the Middle East or Asia en route. Some European airlines offer competitive fares to Asia from **regional airports** such as Glasgow, Manchester, Dublin and Belfast, although prices may often be higher than flights from London; Manchester is currently the only regional airport from where you can fly direct to destinations like Singapore and Hong Kong.

One of the cheapest and most useful **gateways** to Southeast Asia is **Bangkok**. London–Bangkok flights start at about £400 return, rising 30–50 per cent during peak times (July, Aug, Dec), and take a minimum of twelve hours. Another competitively priced and popular gateway city is **Singapore**. London–Singapore flights start at around £450 return, again rising during peak times (mid-July to Sept), and take at least twelve hours; flights to Hanoi/Ho Chi Minh City and Kuala Lumpur are similarly priced.

If you want to go to China as well as Southeast Asia, consider buying a flight to **Hong Kong**. Direct London–Hong Kong flights start at about £425 return, and take at least eleven hours. Hong Kong gives you easy and inexpensive local transport options into Guangdong province, from where you could continue west into Vietnam, and on into Laos.

A BETTER KIND OF TRAVEL

At Rough Guides we are passionately committed to travel. We believe it helps us understand the world we live in and the people we share it with – and of course tourism is vital to many developing economies. But the scale of modern tourism has also damaged some places irreparably, and climate change is accelerated by most forms of transport, especially flying. All Rough Guides' flights are carbon-offset, and every year we donate money to a variety of environmental charities.

Vietnam Airlines flies direct from London to **Ho Chi Minh City** and **Hanoi**, while Philippine Airlines now has nonstop services from London to **Manila**.

If you're planning to fly from London to Vientiane, Phnom Penh or Yangon, you will have to change planes in Bangkok, Hanoi/Ho Chi Minh City, Singapore or Dubai, as there are currently no direct flights to these destinations.

A one-year open RTW ticket from London, taking in Bangkok (with surface travel to Phuket), Kuala Lumpur, Borneo, Bali and Manila, costs from £1100; more basic options are around £600, while more elaborate routes can cost up to £2000. The cheapest time to begin your RTW trip is usually post-Easter to mid-June. Check out STA Travel and ⓦ roundtheworldflights.com for good deals.

Flights from the US and Canada

There's no way around it: **flights from North America** to Southeast Asia are long. With the exception of nonstop services to Singapore, Bangkok and Hong Kong from the US West Coast, all flights, including so-called "direct flights", will require a stop somewhere along the way. But this means you can take advantage of the **stopovers** offered by many airlines.

Numerous airlines run daily flights to **Bangkok** from major East and West Coast cities, usually making one stop, though it is possible to fly direct from Los Angeles. Flying time from both the West Coast via northern Asia and from New York via Europe is around eighteen hours. Departing from the West Coast, expect to pay from US$800 return, a bit more from the East Coast. From Canada, the flight takes around seventeen hours (from Vancouver via Hong Kong) or around twenty (from Toronto via Europe). Prices start from around Can$900 from either Vancouver or Toronto. **Singapore** is served from New York, Los Angeles (nonstop) and San Francisco; flying eastbound is more direct but still involves at least 22 hours' travelling time. Prices start around US$900 from New York; or US$800 from Los Angeles and San Francisco. From Toronto or Montreal, prices start at Can$1100 and, from Vancouver, Can$950.

Fly via **Hong Kong** if you wish to visit mainland Asia. The cheapest low-season fare from the US West Coast is around US$550 for the round trip and typically includes a connection in Taiwan or Korea. A direct flight costs more and takes at least fourteen hours. From the East Coast, direct flights to Hong Kong take at least fifteen hours and the cheapest fares from New York start from around US$600. The best options for flights **from Canada** to Hong Kong

include nonstop flights from Vancouver (13hr) and Toronto (15hr). Fares from Canada's west coast start at around CAN$650.

An RTW itinerary might be LA to Bangkok (make your own way to Phuket), Kuala Lumpur, Borneo, Bali and Manila for around US$1800.

Flights from Australia and New Zealand

The cheapest way to get to Southeast Asia **from Australia and New Zealand** is to buy a one-way flight to one of the region's gateways such as Bali, Jakarta, Singapore, Kuala Lumpur, Bangkok or Hong Kong, and carry on from there by air, sea or overland.

Airfares from east coast **Australian gateways** are all pretty similar, although nonstop flights are generally cheaper from Darwin and Perth (one-way flights from the former to Bali cost less than Aus$100, for example). **From New Zealand**, you can expect to pay about NZ$200–400 more from Christchurch and Wellington than from Auckland. Return fares to Indonesia, Malaysia, the Philippines and Brunei can be as little as Aus$350/NZ$550, while to Thailand, Indochina and Hong Kong you can expect to pay from Aus$450/NZ$800.

A RTW ticket from Sydney to Singapore, taking in Bangkok, London, Oslo, New York and Los Angeles, starts at around Aus$1700; one from Auckland to Hong Kong, taking in Shanghai, Munich, Rome and Vancouver, costs from NZ$1999.

Agents and operators

AGENTS

Flight Centre UK ☎ 0844 800 8660, Australia ☎ 133 133, Canada ☎ 1877 967 5302, New Zealand ☎ 0800 243 544, South Africa ☎ 0860 400 727, US ☎ 1 877 992 4732, ⓦ flightcentre.com. Discounted flights, tours, packages and hotel bookings.

North South Travel UK ☎ 01245 608291, ⓦ northsouthtravel .co.uk. Friendly, competitive travel agency, offering discounted fares worldwide. Profits are used to support projects in the developing world, especially the promotion of sustainable tourism.

STA Travel Australia ☎ 134 782, New Zealand ☎ 0800 474 400, South Africa ☎ 0861 781 781, UK ☎ 0871 230 0040, US ☎ 1 800 781 4040; ⓦ statravel.com. Worldwide specialists in independent travel; also student IDs, travel insurance, car rental, rail passes and more. Good discounts for students and under-26s.

Student Flights Australia ☎ 1800 046 462, ⓦ studentflights.com .au. Flights and round-the-world tickets, plus adventure travel, hotel bookings, rail passes and TEFL placements, for students and budget travellers.

Trailfinders UK ☎ 020 7368 1200, Ireland ☎ 01 677 7888, Australia ☎ 1300 780 212; ⓦ trailfinders.com. One of the best-informed and most efficient agents for independent travellers.

Travel Cuts Canada ☎ 1800 667 2887, ⓦ travelcuts.com. Flight and hotel bookings, with good discounts for younger travellers.

Tour operators

An organized tour is worth considering if you're after a more energetic holiday, have ambitious sight-seeing plans and limited time, are uneasy with the language and customs, or just don't like travelling alone. The specialists listed below can also help you get to more remote areas and organize activities that may be difficult to arrange yourself, such as extended, multi-country tours, rafting, diving, cycling and trekking. Some also arrange volunteering opportunities. Unless stated otherwise, the prices refer to the land tour only, so you'll need to factor in extra for flights.

FROM THE UK AND IRELAND

Earthwatch Institute UK ☎ 01865 318838, ⓦ earthwatch.org. A wide range of opportunities to assist archeologists, biologists and community workers in homestays. Prices start at around £2400 for twelve days.
Exodus UK ☎ 020 8675 5550, ⓦ exodus.co.uk. Overland trips aimed at 18–45-year-olds, including the sixteen-day "Cycle Indochina and Angkor" (from £2249 including flights from London).
Explore UK ☎ 0845 013 1537, ⓦ explore.co.uk. Heaps of options throughout Southeast Asia, including tours that explore the Angkor ruins in Cambodia and the jungles of Borneo.
Imaginative Traveller UK ☎ 0845 287 2949, ⓦ imaginative-traveller.com. Broad selection of tours to less-travelled parts of Asia, including walking, cycling, camping, cooking and snorkelling. Their "Java and Bali Explorer" tour costs £1324 for 22 days.
Intrepid Travel UK ☎ 0800 781 1660, ⓦ intrepidtravel.com. A wide range of holidays, including adventure and overland, plus a "basics" range for more budget-conscious travellers.
Rickshaw Travel UK ☎ 0127 322 399, ⓦ rickshawtravel.co.uk. Recommended agency specializing in mix-and-match, bite-sized activities and trips, including kayaking on the Mekong.
Symbiosis UK ☎ 01845 123 2844, ⓦ symbiosis-travel.com. Environmentally aware outfit that offers specialist-interest holidays in Southeast Asia, cycling trips, and trekking through jungles and longhouse communities of Sarawak and Sabah.
TravelLocal UK ☎ 01865 242 709, ⓦ travellocal.com. An innovative agency that enables you to create tailor-made holidays through Laos travel experts based in Laos (and around the world).

FROM THE US AND CANADA

Adventures Abroad US & Canada ☎ 1 800 665 3998, ⓦ adventures-abroad.com. Specializing in small-group tours, including a sixteen-day trip taking in Thailand, Vietnam, Laos and Cambodia for around US$4500.
Geographic Expeditions US ☎ 1 800 777 8183, ⓦ geoex.com. Specialists in "responsible tourism" with a range of customized tours and/or set packages, their trips are perhaps a bit more demanding of the traveller than the average specialist.

Mountain Travel-Sobek US ☎ 1 888 831 7526, ⓦ mtsobek.com. Both group and private custom-made tours to Laos, Vietnam, Thailand, Malaysia, Indonesia and Cambodia.
Pacific Holidays US ☎ 1800 355 8025, ⓦ pacificholidaysinc.com. Economical tour group, with trips including a ten-day "Wonders of the Orient" sightseeing tour of Singapore, Bangkok and Hong Kong from US$2755.

FROM AUSTRALIA AND NEW ZEALAND

The Adventure Travel Company New Zealand ☎ 03 364 3400 or ☎ 04 494 7180, ⓦ adventuretravel.co.nz. New Zealand's one-stop shop for adventure travel and agents for Intrepid, Peregrine, Guerba Expeditions and a host of others.
Adventure World Australia ☎ 1300 295 049, ⓦ adventureworld.com.au, New Zealand ☎ 0800 238 368, ⓦ adventureworld.co.nz. Agents for a vast array of international adventure travel companies.
Allways Dive Expeditions Australia ☎ 1800 33 82 39, ⓦ allwaysdive.com.au. All-inclusive dive packages with a choice of accommodation for every budget to prime locations throughout Southeast Asia.
Earthwatch ☎ 03 9682 6828, ⓦ earthwatch.org/australia. Volunteer work on projects in Borneo, Cambodia and Thailand.
Gecko's Grassroots Adventures ☎ 03 8601 4444, ⓦ geckosadventures.com. Numerous tours of Southeast Asia, including nine days in the south of Thailand from Aus$660.
Intrepid Travel Australia ☎ 1300 018 871, ⓦ intrepidtravel.com. Small-group tours to China and Southeast Asia with an emphasis on cross-cultural contact and low-impact tourism.
Stray Travel Australia ☎ 1300 733 048; New Zealand ☎ 09 526 2140, ⓦ straytravel.asia. This backpacker-oriented company runs a network of hop-on, hop-off bus services covering Cambodia, Laos, Thailand and Vietnam.
The Surf Travel Co Australia ☎ 02 9222 8870; ⓦ surftravel.com.au. A well-established surf travel company that can arrange accommodation and yacht charters in Indonesia, as well as give the lowdown on the best surf beaches in the region.
World Expeditions Australia ☎ 1300 720 000, New Zealand ☎ 0800 350 354; ⓦ worldexpeditions.com. Committed to responsible travel and sustainable tourism, World Expeditions are specialists in small-group treks and adventure holidays.

Getting around

Local transport across Southeast Asia is uniformly good value compared to public transport in the West, and is often one of the highlights of a trip, not least because of the chance to fraternize with local travellers. Overland transport between neighbouring Southeast Asian countries is generally fairly straightforward so long as you have the right paperwork and are patient; full details

on cross-border transport options are given throughout the Guide. Travelling between countries by bus, train or boat is obviously more time-consuming than flying, but it's also cheaper and can be more satisfying.

Local transport

Not surprisingly, the ultra-modern enclaves of Singapore and Hong Kong boast the fastest, sleekest and most efficient transport systems in the region. Elsewhere, **long-distance buses** are the

MAJOR BORDER CROSSINGS, OVERLAND AND SEA ROUTES

The following is an overview of those land and sea crossings that are both legal and straightforward ways for tourists to travel between the countries of Southeast Asia. The information is fleshed out in the accounts of relevant border towns within this book. Long-distance tourist buses often run between major destinations, making cross-border travel simpler and quicker, but there are also numerous options by local transport.

TO BRUNEI

From Malaysia Boats to Brunei depart daily from Lawas and Limbang in northern Sarawak, and from Pulau Labuan in Sabah, itself connected by boat to Kota Kinabalu. From Miri in Sarawak, many buses travel daily to the capital, Bandar Seri Begawan.

TO CAMBODIA

From Vietnam Six main border crossings: at Moc Bai to Bavet (buses run from HCMC to Phnom Penh); two crossings just north of Chau Doc on the Bassac River (by bus and boat); and from near Ha Tien over the border (Prek Chang) to Kep (by *xe om* only); plus two little-used crossings in Cambodia's east.
From Thailand Six border crossings: the key routes are from Aranyaprathet to Poipet (with connections to Siem Reap and Phnom Penh); the coastal crossing at Hat Lek, near Trat, then to Cham Yeam; and two crossings from northeast Thailand – the Chong Chom–O'Smach border pass near Kap Choeng in Thailand's Surin province and the little-used Sa Ngam–Choam crossing.
From Laos One border crossing, at Trapaeng Kriel–Nong Nok Khiene, on the route between Stung Treng and Si Phan Don.

TO HONG KONG AND MACAU

From China By train from Beijing to Hong Kong (via Guangzhou in Canton). Boats from China dock at China Ferry Terminal in Hong Kong and the Terminal Maritimo in Macau.

TO INDONESIA

From Malaysia and Singapore Several routes by boat from Malaysia and Singapore to ports in Sumatra including: Penang to Medan; Melaka to Dumai or Pekanbaru; Johor Bahru and Singapore to Pulau Batam and Pulau Bintan, in Indonesia's Riau archipelago (and on to Sumatra); and from Port Klang, near Kuala Lumpur, to Dumai. By bus from Kuching (Sarawak) to Pontianak (Kalimantan). By ferry from Tawau (Sabah) to Pulau Nunukan and Pulau Tarakan in northeastern Kalimantan.

TO LAOS

From Thailand Six main border crossings (by various combinations of road and rail transport): Chiang Khong to Houayxai; Nong Khai to Vientiane; Nakhon Phanom to Thakhek; Mukdahan to Savannakhet; Chong Mek to Pakse; and Beung Khan to Paksan.
From Vietnam Six main border crossings: the Lao Bao–Dasavanh, 240km from Savannakhet (buses from Hue and Da Nang to Savannakhet); at Cau Treo, 105km from Vinh (buses from Da Nang to Savannakhet and Vientiane); the Bo Y crossing 80km from Kon Tum (buses to Attapu); Tay Trang crossing, near Dien Bien Phu, to Muang Khoua (buses from Dien Bien Phu to Muang Khoua); Nam Can to Nong Het, east of Phonsavan in Laos (buses from Vinh to Phonsavan); and the more remote Na Meo, east of Sam Neua.
From China By bus from Jinghong in China's southwestern Yunnan province to Oudomxai and Luang Namtha, via the border crossing at Boten.
From Cambodia One crossing, at Trapaeng Kriel–Nong Nok Khiene.

chief mode of travel in Southeast Asia, which, though often frequent, can be fairly uncomfortable and sometimes nerve-wracking. Standards vary across the region, and often between different companies that cover the same route. At the bottom end seats are usually cramped and the

whole experience is often uncomfortable, so wherever possible, try to book a pricier but more comfortable a/c bus for overnight journeys – or take the train. Shorter bus journeys can be very enjoyable, however, and are often the only way to get between places. Buses come in various shapes

TO MALAYSIA AND SINGAPORE

From Thailand Though there are buses and trains from Bangkok via Hat Yai into Malaysia, these routes are currently advised against because of political unrest in southern Thailand; check the latest situation before travelling (see box, p.826). The western routes are safer, particularly from Satun, from where you can take local transport to Kuala Perlis and Pulau Langkawi or Alor Setar; also by ferry from Ko Lipe to Pulau Langkawi.

From Indonesia Several routes by boat from Sumatra including: Medan to Penang; Dumai to Melaka; Tanjung Balai to Port Klang; from Pulau Batam and Pulau Bintan in the Riau archipelago to Johor Bahru and Singapore. From Kalimantan, you can take a bus from Pontianak to Kuching (12hr) in Sarawak. Or you can cross into Sabah on a ferry from either Pulau Tarakan (3hr) or Pulau Nunukan (1hr) to Tawau – a day's bus ride southeast of Kota Kinabalu.

From Brunei Direct boats from Bandar Seri Begawan to Limbang and Lawas (Sarawak), and Pulau Labuan (just off Sabah). Also, direct buses from Bandar Seri Begawan to Miri in Sarawak (via Seria and Kuala Belait) and Kota Kinabalu in Sabah (8hr).

TO MYANMAR (BURMA)

Check the status of border crossings before you travel.

From Thailand There are five border crossings: Ranong–Kawthaung, Three Pagodas Pass (Sangkhlaburi–Payathonzu; day-trips only), Ban Phu Nam Ron–Htee Kee, Mae Sot–Myawaddy and Mae Sai–Tachileik.

TO THAILAND

From Malaysia and Singapore Travel to some areas of southern Thailand (such as Hat Yai) is not recommended (see box, p.826); check the latest situation before travelling. The safest routes are by minibus from Kangar to Satun, and by boat from Kuala Perlis and Pulau Langkawi to Satun, and from Langkawi to Ko Lipe.

From Laos There are six border crossings: Houayxai to Chiang Khong; Vientiane across the first Friendship Bridge to Nong Khai; Thakhek to Nakhon Phanom; Savannakhet to Mukdahan; Pakse to Chong Mek and Paksan–Beung Khan.

From Cambodia Six border crossings: Poipet to Aranyaprathet; by bus from Sihanoukville via Koh Kong and Hat Lek to Trat in east Thailand; across the two border crossings from Pailin (easiest at Phsa Prom and one further north at Daung Lem) to Chanthaburi province in northeast Thailand; via the Chong Chom–O'Smach border pass to Surin; and the little-used Sa Ngam–Choam crossing.

From Vietnam By bus from Vietnam, via the Lao Bao Pass, Savannakhet in Laos and then across the Second Friendship Bridge to Thailand.

From Myanmar There are five border crossings: Kawthaung– Ranong, Three Pagodas Pass (Sangkhlaburi–Payathonzu; day-trips only), Htee Kee–Ban Phu Nam Ron, Mae Sot–Myawaddy and Tachileik–Mae Sai.

TO VIETNAM

From Laos Six border crossings: the Lao Bao pass and the Cau Treo pass, near Vinh (buses via both from Vientiane and Savannakhet to Da Nang or Hue); the Bo Y crossing (from Attapeu to Kon Tum in Vietnam's Central Highlands); Tay Trang (from Muang Ngoi to Dien Bien Phu); Nong Het Nam Can (from Phonsavan to Vinh); and the remote, seldom-used Na Meo crossing (east of Sam Neua).

From Cambodia Four main crossings including: Moc Bai (buses from Phnom Penh, and from Moc Bai on to Ho Chi Minh City); two crossings north of Chau Doc in the Mekong Delta (boat or bus); and the Xa Xia/Ha Tien border crossing near Kep and Kampot in Cambodia to Ha Tien in Vietnam.

From China Three crossings: Lao Cai (from Kunming in China by bus, or by direct train from Beijing to Hanoi); Mong Cai (by bus from Guangzhou); and the Huu Nghi border crossing (by bus or train from Pingxiang or Nanning).

and sizes; full details of all these idiosyncrasies are given in each chapter.

Trains are generally the most comfortable way to travel any distance. Thailand and Peninsular Malaysia both have decent train networks and rolling stock, while Indonesia's is a notch below them, but still a better option than buses on Java. Vietnam's train system is also good for some journeys, and again it's often worth paying extra for more comfort on longer routes.

Taxis come in many forms, including the infamous **tuk-tuk** (three-wheeled buggies with deafening two-stroke engines), rickshaws powered by a man on a bicycle, or simply a bloke on a motorbike (usually wearing a numbered vest); only conventional taxis in the major cities have meters, so all prices must be bargained for and fixed before you set off. In many riverine towns and regions, it's also common to travel by taxi boat. Taxi and ride-share app Uber (W uber .com) and Singapore-based rival Grab (W grab.com) operate in an increasing number of Southeast Asian destinations (mainly cities), including Bangkok, Singapore, Bali, Kuala Lumpur and Hanoi.

Regular **ferries** connect all major tourist islands with the mainland, and often depart several times a day, though some islands become inaccessible during the monsoon. In some areas, **flying** may be the only practical way to get around. Tickets are usually reasonably priced, especially if the route is covered by two or more of the region's growing number of airlines (see below).

In most countries, **timetables** for any transport other than trains and planes are vague or non-existent; the vehicle simply leaves when there are enough passengers to make the journey profitable for the driver. The best strategy is to turn up early in the morning when most local people begin their journeys. For an idea of frequency and duration of transport services between the main towns, check the "Arrival and departure" details in each chapter. **Security** is an important consideration on public transport (see p.44).

Throughout Southeast Asia it's possible to rent your own transport, though in Vietnam and Myanmar you can't rent self-drive cars. **Cars** are available in all major tourist centres, and range from flimsy Jimnys to a/c 4WDs; you will need your international driver's licence. If you can't face the traffic yourself, you can often hire a **car with driver** for a small extra fee. One of the best ways to explore the countryside is to rent a **motorbike**. They vary from small 100cc Yamahas to more robust trail bikes and can be rented from guesthouses, shops or tour agencies. Check the small print on your insurance

policy, and if you're renting a bigger bike (125cc and above), make sure your licence covers it. **Bicycles** are also a good way to travel, and are readily available to rent. Don't forget to check that the bicycle's in working order before you set off.

Regional airlines

The airlines listed below are good options for travelling within countries, and from country to country.

AirAsia Kuala Lumpur T 600 85 9999, W airasia.com. AirAsia flies extensively to many places throughout the region and even to India, Japan and Australia. Frequent daily flights leave from their Kuala Lumpur hub to popular destinations such as Bali, Bangkok, Brunei, Ho Chi Minh City, Hong Kong, Jakarta, Kota Kinabalu, Manila, Phnom Penh, Phuket, Vientiane and Yangon; and a number of flights also leave from Bangkok to places including Bali, Chiang Mai, Hanoi, Hong Kong, Jakarta, Krabi and Singapore.

Bangkok Airways Bangkok T 02 270 6699, W bangkokair.com. Regular flights from Bangkok to Chiang Mai, Da Nang, Hong Kong, Luang Prabang, Phnom Penh, Phuket, Siam Reap, Singapore and Vientiane.

Cathay Dragon Hong Kong T 3193 3888, W cathaypacific.com. A subsidiary of Cathay Pacific, Cathay Dragon (formerly Dragonair) flies to destinations across the Asia Pacific region including Hanoi, Kota Kinabalu, Phnom Penh, Manila and Phuket.

Cebu Pacific Air Philippines T 2702 2888, W cebupacificair.com. Flights to most domestic locations within the Philippines plus regular services to all main Asian cities including Bangkok, Bandar Seri Bagawan, Hong Kong, Kuala Lumpur, Singapore and Bangkok.

Garuda Jakarta T 021 2351 9999, W garuda-indonesia.com. Indonesia's national airline. Frequent flights from Denpasar (Bali) and its hub at Jakarta to Kuala Lumpur and Singapore, plus numerous other domestic and regional destinations.

Jet Star Asia Singapore T 800 6161 977, W jetstar.com. Daily flights from Singapore to Bangkok, Bali, Ho Chi Minh City, Hong Kong, Jakarta, Kuala Lumpur, Macau, Manila and Phnom Penh, and less frequent flights to Siem Reap.

Lao Airlines Vientiane T 021 212 057, W laoairlines.com. Frequent flights from Vientiane and Luang Prabang to Bangkok, Chiang Mai, Hanoi, Ho Chi Minh, and Siem Reap, as well as flights to Phnom Penh and Singapore, and within Laos.

Malaysia Airlines Kuala Lumpur T 1300 883000, W malaysiaairlines.com. Flights from KL to destinations across Malaysia and throughout Southeast Asia (and beyond), including Bangkok, Brunei, Hong Kong, Singapore and Yangon.

MASwings Sabah and Sarawak T 1300 883 000, W maswings .com.my. The best-value fares to the biggest variety of destinations within Malaysian Borneo.

Nokair Bangkok T 02 627 2000, W nokair.com. Frequent daily flights from Bangkok across Thailand, including to Chiang Mai, Krabi, Koh Phi Phi and Phuket, plus a handful to neighbouring countries.

Silk Air Singapore T 6223 8888, W silkair.com. Daily flights from Singapore to Kota Kinabalu, Kuala Lumpur, Kuching, Phnom Penh, Phuket, Siem Reap and Yangon, and less frequent flights to Chiang Mai, Lombok and Balikpapan, plus destinations in India, China and Australia.

Thai Airways Bangkok ☎ 02 545 3690, Ⓦ thaiairways.com. Frequent daily flights from Bangkok to Bali, Hanoi, Ho Chi Minh City, Hong Kong, Kuala Lumpur, Luang Prabang, Macau, Manila, Penang, Phnom Penh, Phuket, Singapore and Vientiane.

Tiger Airways Singapore ☎ 65 680 84437, Ⓦ tigerairways.com. Regular flights from Singapore to Bangkok, Hanoi, Ho Chi Minh City, Jakarta, Kuala Lumpur, Kuching, Macau, Penang, Phuket and Yangon.

Vietnam Airlines Hanoi ☎ 04 3832 0320, Ⓦ vietnamairlines .com. Frequent flights from Hanoi and Ho Chi Minh City to Siem Reap and Vientiane, plus daily flights to Bangkok, Hong Kong, Kuala Lumpur, Luang Prabang, Manila, Phnom Penh, Sihanoukville and Singapore.

Accommodation

You'll rarely have a problem finding inexpensive accommodation in Southeast Asia, particularly if you stick to the main tourist areas. The mainstays of the travellers' scene are guesthouses (which are sometimes known as "bungalows" or "backpackers"), which can be anything from a bamboo hut to a three-storey concrete block.

Guesthouses and hotels

A standard **guesthouse** room will be a simple place with one or two beds, hard mattresses, thin walls and a fan – some, but not all, have a window (usually screened against mosquitoes), and the cheapest ones share a bathroom. Always ask to see several rooms before opting for one, as standards can vary widely within the same establishment. For a **hostel bed** or **basic double room** with shared bathroom in a guesthouse that's in a capital city or tourist centre, rates start at about US$3–5 in Cambodia, US$6 in Thailand and Indonesia, US$8 in Laos, Malaysia and Vietnam, US$10 in Myanmar, US$15 in the Philippines, and US$25 in Brunei, Hong Kong and Singapore.

In smaller towns and beach resorts, rates can be significantly lower, and prices everywhere are usually negotiable during low season. **Single rooms** tend to cost about two-thirds the price of a double, but many guesthouses also offer dorm beds, which can cost as little as US$3.50 a night. Many places provide useful **facilities**, such as restaurants, travellers' notice boards, wi-fi, safes for valuables, left-luggage, laundry and tour-operator desks. At most guesthouses, **check-out time** is noon; during high season it's worth arriving as early as possible to ensure you get a room, unless you've got one booked already. Although some hostels

and guesthouses still don't accept telephone bookings (language is also a barrier), an increasing number now allow you to book your accommodation online, either directly or via a site like Ⓦ booking.com or Ⓦ agoda.com.

If you venture to towns that are completely off the tourist circuit, you'll find that the cheapest accommodation is usually the bland and sometimes seedy **cheap urban hotels** located near bus and train stations. These places are designed for local businesspeople rather than tourists and may double as brothels; they tend to be rather soulless, but are usually inexpensive and clean enough.

For around US$15–40 almost anywhere in Southeast Asia except Singapore and Hong Kong, you can get yourself a comfortable room in a smart guesthouse or small **mid-range hotel**. These are often very good value, offering pleasantly furnished rooms, with private hot-water bathroom, and possibly a/c, a fridge and a TV as well. Some also have a swimming pool.

Hostels

Hostels are common in major destinations throughout the region, and many are more stylish, sociable and secure than their guesthouse counterparts.

Village accommodation

In the more remote and rural parts of Southeast Asia, you may get the chance to stay in **village accommodation**, be it the headman's house, a family home, or a traditional longhouse. Accommodation in these places usually consists of a mattress on the floor in a communal room, perhaps with a blanket and mosquito net, but it's often advisable to take your own net and blanket or sleeping bag. As a sign of appreciation, your hosts will welcome gifts, and a donation may be in order, too. But in reality, the chance of encountering this kind of arrangement is quite rare. Some countries such as Laos forbid tourists from sleeping in homes that aren't approved by the government as tourist accommodation.

> ### ACCOMMODATION PRICES
> All accommodation prices in this Guide represent the cost of the cheapest double room or dorm bed available in high season, unless otherwise stated.

THE JOY OF BED BUGS

A bugbear of travellers all over the world is that an inexpensive place to lay your head sometimes equals a cosy night with small, scurrying strangers. **Bed bugs** are pesky little biters that lie uninvited in your bed, sealed into the creases and seams of the mattress. Tell-tale signs are small spots of dry blood on the mattress or sheet, or you may even see the small, pinhead-sized bugs themselves in the sides of the mattress. The joy of bed bugs is their ability to be transported from place to place. They'll worm their way into sleeping bags, sheets and even clothing, ensuring that wherever you lay your hat is their home too.

Homestays

A good way to meet the locals – and, in many cases, ensure that your spending actually benefits the local community you're visiting – is to stay in a homestay, which are springing up across the region; ⓦhomestay.com has a good range.

Camping

Given that accommodation is (generally) so inexpensive in Southeast Asia and that there are few campsites, there's no point taking a tent with you. The only times when you may need to **camp** are in the national parks or when trekking, and you may be able to rent gear locally. Bungalow owners usually take a dim view of beach campers. Beaches, especially in tourist areas, are often unsafe at night, particularly for women.

Bathrooms

In most places in Southeast Asia, you can expect bathrooms with Western-style facilities such as sit-down toilets and either hot- or cold-water showers. In rural areas, on beaches, and in some of the most basic accommodation, however, you'll be using a **traditional Asian bathroom**, often referred to as a **mandi**, where you wash using the scoop-and-slosh method. This entails dipping a plastic scoop or bucket into a huge vat or basin of water and then sloshing the water over yourself. The basin functions as a water supply only and not a bath; all washing is done outside it and the basin should not be contaminated by soap or shampoo. **Toilets** in these places will be Asian-style squat affairs, flushed manually with water scooped from the pail that stands alongside; **toilet paper** tends to clog these things up, so if you want to avoid an embarrassing situation, learn to wash yourself like the locals do.

Health

The vast majority of travellers to Southeast Asia suffer nothing more than an upset stomach, so long as they observe basic precautions about food and water hygiene (see p.39), and research pre-trip vaccination and malaria prophylactic requirements.

The standard of **local healthcare** varies across the region, with Cambodia, Laos and Myanmar having the least advanced systems (it is best to get across the border and go to a Thai hospital) and Singapore boasting world-class medical care. If you have a minor ailment, it's usually best to head for a pharmacy – most have a decent idea of how to treat common ailments and can provide many medicines without prescription. Otherwise, ask for the nearest doctor or hospital. Details of major hospitals are given throughout each chapter. If you have a serious accident or illness, you may need to be evacuated home or to Singapore, so it's vital to arrange **health insurance** before you leave home.

When planning your trip, **visit a doctor** at least two months before you leave, to allow time to complete any recommended courses of vaccinations or anti-malarial tablets. For up-to-the-minute **information**, visit the NHS's Fit For Travel website (ⓦwww.fitfortravel.nhs.uk). There are also several other helpful websites (see p.40).

General precautions

Bacteria thrive in the tropics, and the best way to combat them is to keep up standards of personal hygiene. Frequent **bathing** is essential and hands should be washed before eating, especially in countries where cutlery is not traditionally used. Cuts or scratches can become infected very easily and should be thoroughly cleaned, disinfected and bandaged to keep dirt out.

Ask locally before **swimming** in freshwater lakes and rivers, including the Mekong River, as tiny worms carrying diseases such as bilharzia infect some tracts of fresh water in Southeast Asia. The worm enters through the skin and may cause a high fever after some weeks, but the recognizable symptoms of stomach pain and blood in the urine only appear after the disease is established, which may take months or even years. At this point, some damage to internal organs may have occurred.

Inoculations

No compulsory vaccinations are required for entry into any part of Southeast Asia, but health professionals strongly recommend that travellers to the region get **inoculations** against the following common and debilitating diseases: typhoid, hepatitis A, tetanus and polio. In addition, you may be advised to have some of the following vaccinations, for example, if travelling during the rainy season or if planning to stay in remote rural areas: rabies, hepatitis B, Japanese encephalitis, diphtheria, meningitis and TB. If you're only going to Hong Kong and Macau, you may not have to get any inoculations. If you've been in an area infected with yellow fever during the fourteen days before your arrival in Southeast Asia, you will need to bring your yellow fever certificate with you to prove you've been vaccinated against the disease.

Malaria

All of Southeast Asia lies within a **malarial zone**, although in many urban and developed tourist areas there is little risk (see box, p.38). Most doctors advise travellers on a multi-country trip through Southeast Asia to take full precautions against malaria, which is very dangerous and potentially fatal. Information regarding malaria is constantly being updated, so make sure you seek medical advice before you travel.

Malaria is caused by a parasite in the saliva of the anopheles mosquito that is passed into the human when bitten by the mosquito. There are many strains and some are resistant to particular prophylactic drugs. The most common anti-malarials are: chloroquine (Avloclor or Nivaquine) and proguanil (Paludrine), mefloquine (Lariam), doxycycline (Vibramycin) and Malarone (atovaquone-proguanil). It's absolutely essential to finish your course of

anti-malarials, as there is some time delay between being bitten and the parasites emerging into the blood. Note that some anti-malarials can have nasty side-effects. Mefloquine, in particular, can sometimes cause dizziness, extreme fatigue, nausea and nightmares.

No drug is one hundred percent effective, and it is equally important to stop the mosquitoes biting you. Mosquitoes are mainly active from dusk until dawn, and during this time you should wear trousers, long-sleeved shirts and socks, and smother yourself and your clothes in mosquito repellent containing DEET. DEET is strong stuff, and if you have sensitive skin a natural alternative is citronella (sold as Mosi-guard in the UK). At night, you should sleep either under a mosquito net sprayed with DEET or in a room with screens across the windows. Accommodation in tourist spots nearly always provides screens or a net (check both for holes), but if you're heading off the beaten track, take a net with you. Mosquito coils – widely available in Southeast Asia – also help keep the insects at bay.

Malaria symptoms include fever, headache and shivering, similar to a severe dose of flu and often coming in cycles, but a lot of people have additional symptoms. You will need a blood test to confirm the illness, and the doctor will prescribe the most effective treatment locally. If you develop flu-like symptoms any time up to a year after returning home, inform a doctor that you have been to a country where malaria is present and ask for a blood test.

Dengue fever

A nasty disease that's become increasingly widespread in recent years, **dengue fever** is a virus carried by mosquitoes that bite day and night. There's no vaccine or tablet available to prevent the illness, which causes fever, headache and joint and muscle pains, as well as possible internal bleeding and circulatory-system failure. There is no specific drug to cure it, and the only treatment is lots of rest, liquids and Panadol (or any other acetaminophen painkiller, *not* aspirin, which can increase chances of haemorrhaging), though more serious cases may require hospitalization. It is vital to get an early medical diagnosis and get treatment.

Heat problems

Travellers unused to tropical climates regularly suffer from **sunburn** and **dehydration**. The important thing is to make sure that you drink enough water,

> ### TELL YOUR DOCTOR WHERE YOU'VE BEEN
> Some of the **illnesses** you can pick up in Southeast Asia may not show themselves immediately. If you become ill within a year of returning home, tell your doctor where you have been.

MALARIAL OR NOT?

Areas infected with malaria are constantly changing, so find out what the current situation is from your doctor before travelling.

Brunei Extremely low malarial risk.
Cambodia Malarial in all forested and hilly rural areas, in Siem Reap and along the Thai and Laos borders. Phnom Penh, Sihanoukville and Battambang have a very low malarial risk.
Hong Kong and Macau Extremely low malarial risk outside of northern rural areas.
Indonesia Very malarial, though low risk on the tourist resorts of Bali and Java.
Laos Very malarial, though risk is minimal in Vientiane.
Malaysia Malarial, especially in Sabah and Sarawak, but very low risk on the Peninsula.

Myanmar High risk of malaria across the country, apart from Mandalay and Yangon.
Philippines Malarial except on the majority of the Visayas Islands (except Romblon Island).
Singapore Extremely low malarial risk.
Thailand Generally low malaria risk, but very high risk along the borders with Cambodia, Laos and Myanmar, as well as northern Kanchanaburi province, and parts of Trat province (but low risk on Ko Chang).
Vietnam Malarial, but low risk in Hanoi, Ho Chi Minh City, the coastal plains between them and the northern Red River Delta.

wear suntan lotion and limit your exposure to the sun. As you sweat in the heat you lose salt, so you may want to add some extra to your food. A more serious result of the heat is **heatstroke**, indicated by high temperature, dry red skin and a fast, erratic pulse. As an emergency measure, try to cool the patient off by covering them in sheets or sarongs soaked in cold water and turn the fan on them; they may need to go to hospital, though. **Heat rashes**, **prickly heat** and **fungal infections** are also common: wear loose cotton clothing, dry yourself carefully after bathing and use medicated talcum powder.

Stomach problems

Most health problems experienced by travellers are a direct result of food they've eaten. Avoid eating uncooked vegetables and fruits that cannot be peeled, and be warned that you risk ingesting worms and other parasites from dishes containing raw meat or fish. Cooked food that has been sitting out for an undetermined period of time should also be treated with suspicion. Avoid sharing glasses and utensils. The amount of money you pay for a meal is no guarantee of its safety; in fact, food in top hotels has often been hanging around longer than food cooked at busy roadside stalls. Use your common sense – eat in places that look clean, avoid reheated food and be wary of shellfish.

If you travel in Asia for an extended period of time, though, you are likely to come down with some kind of stomach bug. For most, this is just a case of **diarrhoea**, caught through bad hygiene, or unfamiliar or affected food, and is generally over in

a couple of days. **Dehydration** is one of the main concerns if you have diarrhoea, so rehydration salts dissolved in clean water provide the best treatment. **Gastroenteritis** is a more extreme version, but can still be cured with the same blend of rest and rehydration. You should be able to find a local brand of **rehydration salts** in pharmacies in most Southeast Asian towns, but you can also make up your own by mixing three teaspoons of sugar and one of salt to a litre of water. You will need to drink as much as three litres a day to stave off dehydration. Eat non-spicy, non-greasy **foods**, such as young coconut, dry toast, rice, bananas and noodles, and steer clear of alcohol, coffee, milk and most fruits. Since diarrhoea purges the body of the bugs, taking blocking **medicines** such as Imodium is not recommended unless you have to travel.

The next step up from gastroenteritis is **dysentery**, diagnosable from blood and mucus in the (often blackened) stool. Dysentery is either amoebic or bacillary, with the latter characterized by high fever and vomiting. Serious attacks will require antibiotics, and hospitalization.

Giardia can be identified by foul-smelling wind and burps, abdominal distension, evil-smelling stools that float, and diarrhoea without blood or pus. Don't be over-eager with your diagnosis though, and treat it as normal diarrhoea for at least 24 hours before resorting to flagyl antibiotics.

Viruses

The frequency with which travellers suffer from these infectious diseases makes a very strong case for inoculation (see p.37). **Hepatitis A** is a water-borne viral infection spread through water and food. It causes jaundice, loss of appetite, and nausea, and can leave you feeling wiped out for months. Seek immediate medical help if you think you may have contracted it. Havrix is a vaccination against hepatitis A, which can last for over 20 years provided you have had a booster 6–12 months after your first jab. You can also vaccinate against **hepatitis B**, which is transmitted by bodily fluids during unprotected sex or by intravenous drug use.

Cholera and **typhoid** are generally spread when communities rely on sparse water supplies. The initial symptoms of cholera are a sudden onset of watery, but painless, diarrhoea. Later, nausea, vomiting and muscle cramps set in. Cholera can be fatal if adequate fluid intake is not maintained. Copious amounts of liquids, including oral rehydration solution, should be consumed and medical treatment should be sought immediately. Like cholera, typhoid is also spread in small, localized epidemics. Symptoms can vary widely, but generally include headaches, fever and constipation, followed by diarrhoea. Vaccination against typhoid is recommended for all travellers to Southeast Asia.

Many countries in Southeast Asia have significant **AIDS** problems. Condoms are available at pharmacies throughout the region, though the quality is not always reliable: it's best to bring a supply with you, take special care with expiry dates and bear in mind that condoms don't last as long when kept in the heat. Blood transfusions, intravenous drug use, acupuncture, dentistry, tattooing and body piercing are also high-risk.

Another virus to be aware of is rabies (see p.40).

Bites and stings

The most common irritations for travellers come from tiny pests and the danger of infection is to or via the bitten area, so keep bites clean. **Fleas**, **lice** and **bed bugs** (see box, p.36) adore grimy sheets, so examine your bedding carefully, air and beat the offending articles and then coat yourself liberally in insect repellent. Scabies, which cause severe itching by burrowing under the skin and laying eggs, might affect travellers who stay in hill-tribe villages.

Ticks are nasty pea-shaped bloodsuckers that attach themselves to you if you walk through long grass. A dab of petrol, alcohol, Tiger Balm or insect repellent, or a lit cigarette, should make them let loose and drop off; whatever you do, don't pull them off, as their heads can remain under the skin, and cause infection. Bloodsucking **leeches** can be a problem in the jungle and in fresh water. Get rid of them by rubbing them with salt, though anti-tick treatments also work. Apply **DEET** or **Dettol** to the tops of your boots and around the lace-holes. Specially woven leech socks are also available to buy in specialist travel shops back home and often locally in leech-infested areas; recommended for the squeamish.

Southeast Asia has many species of both land and sea **snakes**, so wear boots and socks when hiking. If **bitten**, the number one rule is not to panic. Stay still in order to slow the venom's entry into the bloodstream. Wash and disinfect the wound, apply a pressure bandage as tightly as you would for a sprain, splint the affected limb, keep it below the level of the heart and get to hospital as soon as possible. **Scorpion** stings are very painful

---

THINK BEFORE YOU DRINK

Most **water** that comes out of taps in Southeast Asia has had very little treatment, and can contain a whole range of bacteria and viruses – always stick to bottled, boiled or sterilized water. Except in the furthest-flung corners, **bottled water** is on sale everywhere. Be wary of salads and vegetables that have been washed in tap water, and note that **ice** is not always made from sterilized water. The only time you're likely to be out of reach of bottled water is when trekking into remote areas, in which case you must boil or sterilize your water.

The major drawback with bottle water is the waste it causes. Visualize the size of the pile of plastic you'd leave behind after getting through a couple of bottles per day, then imagine that multiplied by millions and you have something along the lines of the amount of non-biodegradable landfill waste generated each year by tourists alone.

The best solution is to purify your own water. Chemical sterilization using chlorine is completely effective, fast and inexpensive (remove the nasty taste it leaves with neutralizing tablets or lemon juice). Alternatively, invest in some kind of purifying filter incorporating chemical sterilization to kill even the smallest viruses. An array of compact products is available, but pregnant women or anyone with thyroid problems should check that iodine isn't used as the chemical sterilizer.

but usually not fatal; swelling usually disappears after a few hours.

If stung by a **jellyfish**, the priority treatment is to remove the fragments of tentacles from the skin – without causing further discharge of venom – which is most easily done by applying vinegar to deactivate the stinging capsules. The best way to minimize the risk of stepping on the toxic spines of sea urchins, sting rays and stone fish is to wear thick-soled shoes, though these cannot provide total protection; sea-urchin spikes should be removed after softening the skin with a special ointment (like Tiger Balm), though some people recommend applying urine to help dissolve the spines. For sting-ray and stone-fish stings, alleviate the pain by immersing the wound in very hot water – just under 50°C – while waiting for help.

Rabies is transmitted to humans by the bite of infected animals; **tetanus** is an additional danger from such bites. All animals should be treated with caution, particularly monkeys, cats and dogs. Be extremely cautious with wild animals that seem inexplicably tame, as this can be a symptom. If you do get bitten, scrub the wound with a strong antiseptic and then alcohol and get to a hospital as soon as possible. Do not attempt to close the wound. The incubation period for the disease can be as much as a year or as little as a few days; once the disease has taken hold, it will be fatal.

Medical resources for travellers

AUSTRALIA AND NEW ZEALAND

Travellers' Medical and Vaccination Centre ☎ 1300 658 844, **Ⓦ** traveldoctor.com.au. Lists travel clinics in Australia, New Zealand and South Africa.

UK AND IRELAND

Fit For Travel Ⓦ fitfortravel.nhs.uk. Up-to-date travel health information from the NHS.

Hospital for Tropical Diseases Travel Clinic, 2nd floor, Mortimer Market Building, Capper St, London WC1E 6JB **☎** 020 3447 5999, **Ⓦ** thehtd.org.

MASTA (Medical Advisory Service for Travellers Abroad) ☎ 020 7731 8080, **Ⓦ** masta-travel-health.com. Details of the nearest travel clinic.

Tropical Medical Bureau Ireland **☎** 1850 487 674, **Ⓦ** tmb.ie.

US AND CANADA

Canadian Society for International Health Ⓦ csih.org. This site has an extensive list of travel health centres in Canada.

Centers for Disease Control and Prevention Ⓦ cdc.gov/travel. Official US government's site for travel health.

International Society for Travel Medicine ☎ 1 404 373 8282, **Ⓦ** istm.org. Has a full list of travel health clinics.

Travel Medicine ☎ 1800 872 8633, **Ⓦ** travmed.com. Sells first-aid kits, mosquito netting, water filters, reference books and other health-related travel products; the website has a list of US travel clinics.

Culture and etiquette

Although the peoples of Southeast Asia come from a huge variety of ethnic backgrounds and practise a spread of religions, they share many social practices and taboos, many unfamiliar to Westerners. You will get a much friendlier reception if you do your best to be sensitive to local mores, particularly regarding dress. Country-specific social and religious customs are dealt with in the relevant chapters.

Dress

Appearance is very important in Southeast Asian society, and dressing neatly is akin to showing respect. Clothing – or the lack of it – is generally what bothers Southeast Asians most about tourist behaviour. You need to **dress modestly** whenever you are outside a tourist resort, and in particular when entering homes and religious buildings, and when dealing with people in authority, especially when applying for visa extensions. For women, that means below-knee-length skirts or trousers, a bra and sleeved tops; for men, long trousers. "Immodest" clothing includes thong bikinis, shorts, vests, and anything that leaves you with bare shoulders. Most Southeast Asian people find **topless** and nude bathing extremely unpalatable. If you wash your own clothes, hang out your **underwear** discreetly.

Visiting temples, mosques and shrines

Besides dressing conservatively, always take your **shoes** off when entering temples, pagodas and mosques. **Monks** are forbidden from having close contact with women, which means that as a female, you mustn't sit or stand next to a monk, even on a bus, nor brush against his robes, or hand objects directly to him. When giving something to a monk, the object should be placed on a nearby table or passed via a layman. All **Buddha images** are sacred, and should never be clambered over. When sitting on the floor of a monastery building that has a Buddha image, never point your feet in the direction of the image.

When visiting a **mosque**, women must cover their shoulders and possibly their heads as well (bring a scarf or shawl). Many religions prohibit **women** from engaging in certain activities – or even entering a place of worship – during menstruation. If attending a **religious festival**, find out beforehand whether a dress code applies.

Social practices and taboos

In Buddhist, Islamic and Hindu cultures, various parts of the body are accorded a particular status. The **head** is considered the most sacred part of the body and the **feet** the most unclean. This means that it's very rude to touch another person's head – even to affectionately ruffle a child's hair – or to point your feet either at a human being or at a sacred image. Be careful not to step over any part of people who are sitting or lying on the floor (or the deck of a boat), as this is also considered rude. If you do accidentally kick or brush someone with your feet, apologize immediately and smile as you do so.

Public displays of sexual affection like kissing or cuddling are frowned upon across the region, though friends (rather than lovers) of the same sex often hold hands or hug in public.

Most Asians dislike **confrontational behaviour**, such as arguing or shouting, and will rarely outwardly display irritation of any kind.

Religion

Religion pervades every aspect of life in most Southeast Asian communities, dictating social practices to a much greater extent than in the West. All of the world's major faiths are represented in the region, but characteristic across much of Southeast Asia is the syncretic nature of belief, so that many Buddhists, Hindus and Muslims incorporate animist rituals into their daily devotions as well as occasional elements of other major faiths.

Buddhism

Buddhists follow the teachings of Gautama Buddha who, in his five-hundredth incarnation, was born in present-day Nepal as **Prince Gautama Siddhartha**, to a wealthy family during the sixth century BC. At an early age, Siddhartha renounced his life of luxury to seek the ultimate deliverance from worldly suffering and strive to reach **Nirvana**, an indefinable, blissful state. After several years he attained enlightenment and then devoted the rest of his life to teaching the Middle Way that leads to Nirvana.

His **philosophy** was built on the Hindu theory of perpetual reincarnation in the pursuit of perfection, introducing the notion that desire is the root cause of all suffering and can be extinguished only by following the eightfold path or Middle Way. This **Middle Way** is a highly moral mode of life that encourages compassion and moderation and eschews self-indulgence and antisocial behaviour. But the key is an acknowledgement that the physical world is impermanent and ever changing, and that all things – including the self – are therefore not worth craving. Only by pursuing a condition of complete detachment can human beings transcend earthly suffering.

In practice, rather than set their sights on Nirvana most Buddhists aim only to be **reborn** higher up the incarnation scale. Each reincarnation marks a move up a kind of ladder, with animals at the bottom, women figuring lower down than men, and monks coming at the top. The rank of the reincarnation is directly related to the good and bad actions performed in the previous life, which accumulate to determine one's **karma** or destiny – hence the obsession with "**making merit**". Merit making can be done in all sorts of ways, including giving alms to a monk or, for a man, becoming a monk for a short period.

Schools of Buddhism

After the Buddha passed into Nirvana in 543 BC, his doctrine spread relatively quickly across India. His teachings, the Tripitaka, were written down in the Pali language and became known as the **Theravada School of Buddhism** or "The Doctrine of the Elders". Theravada is an ascetic form of Buddhism, based on the principle that each individual is wholly responsible for his or her own accumulation of merit or sin and subsequent enlightenment; it is prevalent in **Thailand**, **Laos**, **Cambodia** and **Myanmar** as well as in Sri Lanka.

The other main school of Buddhism practised in Southeast Asia is **Mahayana Buddhism**, which is current in **Vietnam**, and in **ethnic Chinese communities** throughout the region, as well as in China itself, and in Japan and Korea. The ideological rift between the Theravada and Mahayana

Buddhists is comparable in scale to the one that divides Catholicism and Protestantism. Mahayana Buddhism attempts to make Buddhism more accessible to the average devotee, easing the struggle towards enlightenment with a pantheon of Buddhist saints or bodhisattva who have postponed their own entry into Nirvana in order to work for the salvation of all humanity.

Chinese religions

The **Chinese communities** of Singapore, Hong Kong, Macau, Malaysia, Vietnam and Thailand generally adhere to a system of belief that fuses Mahayana Buddhist, Taoist and Confucianist tenets, alongside the all-important ancestor worship.

Ancestor worship

One of the oldest cults practised among both city dwellers and hill-tribes people who migrated into Southeast Asia from China is that of **ancestor worship**, based on the fundamental principles of filial piety and of obligation to the past, present and future generations. Practices vary, but all believe that the spirits of deceased ancestors have the ability to affect the lives of their living descendants, rewarding those who remember them with offerings, but causing upset if neglected. At funerals and subsequent anniversaries, paper money and other **votive offerings** are burnt, and special food is regularly placed on the ancestral altar.

Confucianism

The teachings of **Confucius** provide a guiding set of moral principles based on piety, loyalty, humanitarianism and familial devotion, which permeate every aspect of Chinese life. Confucius is the Latinized name of K'ung-Fu-Tzu, who was born into a minor aristocratic family in China in 551 BC and worked for many years as a court official. At the age of 50, he set off around the country to spread his ideas on social and political reform. His central tenet was the importance of **correct behaviour**, namely selflessness, respectfulness and non-violence, and loyal service, reinforced by ceremonial rites and frequent offerings to heaven and to the ancestors.

After the death of Confucius in 478 BC, the doctrine was developed by his disciples, and by the first century AD, Confucianism had absorbed elements of Taoism and evolved into a **state ideology** whereby kings ruled under the Mandate of Heaven. Social stability was maintained through a fixed hierarchy of relationships encapsulated in the notion of filial piety. Thus children must obey their parents without question, wives their husbands, students their teacher, and subjects their ruler.

Taoism

Taoism is based on the **Tao-te-ching**, the "Book of the Way", traditionally attributed to **Lao Tzu** ("Old Master"), who is thought to have lived in China in the sixth century BC. A philosophical movement, it advocates that people follow a central path or truth, known as Tao or "The Way", and cultivate an understanding of the nature of things. The Tao emphasizes effortless action, intuition and spontaneity; it cannot be taught, nor can it be expressed in words, but can be embraced by virtuous behaviour. Central to the Tao is the duality inherent in nature, a tension of complementary opposites defined as **yin** and **yang**, the female and male principles. Harmony is the balance between the two, and experiencing that harmony is the Tao.

In its pure form Taoism has no gods, but in the first century AD it corrupted into an organized religion venerating a deified Lao Tzu, and developed highly complex rituals. The vast, eclectic pantheon of Taoist **gods** is presided over by the Jade Emperor, who is assisted by the southern star, the north star and the God of the Hearth. Then there is a collection of immortals, genies and guardian deities, including legendary and historic warriors, statesmen and scholars. Confucius is also honoured as a Taoist saint.

Islam

Islam is the youngest of all the major religions, and in Southeast Asia is practised mainly in **Indonesia**, **Malaysia**, **Singapore** and **Brunei**. It was founded by **Mohammed** (570–630 AD), a merchant from Mecca in Arabia, who began, at the age of forty, to receive messages from Allah (God). On these revelations Mohammed began to build a new religion: Islam or "Submission", as the faith required people to submit to God's will. Islam quickly gained in popularity in Southeast Asia, not least because its revolutionary concepts of equality in subordination to Allah freed people from the feudal Hindu caste system that had previously dominated parts of the region.

The Islamic religion is founded on the **Five Pillars**, the essential tenets revealed by Allah to Mohammed and collected in the **Quran**, the holy book that Mohammed dictated before he died. The first is that all Muslims should profess their faith in Allah with the phrase "There is no God but Allah and

Mohammed is his prophet". The act of praying is the second pillar. Five daily prayers can be done anywhere, though Muslims should always face Mecca when praying, cover the head, and ritually wash feet and hands. The third pillar demands that the faithful should always give a percentage of their income to charity, while the fourth states that all Muslims must observe the fasting month of **Ramadan**. This is the ninth month of the Muslim lunar calendar, when the majority of Muslims fast from the break of dawn to dusk, and also abstain from drinking and smoking. The reason for the fast is to intensify awareness of the plight of the poor. The fifth pillar demands that every Muslim should make a pilgrimage to Mecca at least once in their lifetime.

Hinduism

Hinduism was introduced to Southeast Asia by Indian traders more than a thousand years ago, and spread across the region by the Khmers of Cambodia who left a string of magnificent castle-temples throughout northeast Thailand, Laos, and most strikingly at Angkor in Cambodia. The most active contemporary Hindu communities live in **Singapore** and **Malaysia**, and the Indonesian island of **Bali** is also a very vibrant, if idiosyncratic, Hindu enclave.

Central to Hinduism is the belief that life is a series of reincarnations that eventually leads to spiritual release. The aim of every Hindu is to attain **enlightenment** (*moksa*), which brings with it the union of the individual and the divine, and liberation from the painful cycle of death and rebirth. *Moksa* is only attainable by pure souls, and can take hundreds of lifetimes to achieve. Hindus believe that everybody is reincarnated according to their **karma**, this being a kind of account book that registers all the good and bad deeds performed in the past lives of a soul. Karma is closely bound up with caste and the notion that an individual should accept rather than challenge their destiny.

A whole variety of **deities** are worshipped, the most ubiquitous being Brahma, Vishnu and Shiva. **Brahma** is the Creator, represented by the colour red and often depicted riding on a bull. As the Preserver, **Vishnu** is associated with life-giving waters; he rides the garuda (half-man, half-bird) and is honoured by the colour black. Vishnu also has several avatars, including Buddha – a neat way of incorporating Buddhist elements into the Hindu faith – and Rama, hero of the Ramayana story. **Shiva**, the Destroyer or, more accurately, the Dissolver, is associated with death and rebirth, and

with the colour white. He is sometimes represented as a phallic pillar or lingam. He is the father of the elephant-headed deity **Ganesh**, generally worshipped as the remover of obstacles.

Christianity

Christianity is more widely spread in Southeast Asia than you might expect, with communities found right across the region. Catholicism is the dominant faith in the **Philippines** (Protestantism is also practised by a much smaller percentage of the population), and there are also small but significant Christian communities in Singapore, Hong Kong, Malaysia, Indonesia and Vietnam.

Animism

Animism is the belief that all living things – including plants and trees – and some non-living natural features, such as rocks and waterfalls, have **spirits**. It is practised right across Southeast Asia, by everyone from the Dayaks of Sarawak and the hill tribes of Laos to the city dwellers of Bangkok and Singapore, though rituals and beliefs vary significantly. As with Hinduism, the animistic faiths teach that it is necessary to live in harmony with the spirits; disturb this harmonious balance, by upsetting a spirit for example, and you risk bringing misfortune upon yourself, your household or your village. For this reason, animists consult, or at least consider, the spirits before almost everything they do, and you'll often see small **offerings** of flowers or food left by a tree or river to appease the spirits that live within.

Travel essentials

Costs

Your **daily budget** in Southeast Asia depends both on where you're travelling and on how comfortable you want to be. You can survive on £16/US$20 a day in most parts of Cambodia, Indonesia, Malaysia, Thailand and Vietnam, around £17/US$22 a day in the Philippines, £20/US$25 a day in Laos and Myanmar, £28/US$35 in Hong Kong, and on £32/US$40 in Singapore, but for this money you'll be sleeping in very basic accommodation, eating at simple food stalls, and travelling on local buses. We outline each country's costs in more detail at the start of each chapter.

In some countries, prices for tourist accommodation and foreigners' restaurants are quoted in

US dollars, though the local equivalent is always acceptable.

Travellers soon get so used to the low cost of living in Southeast Asia that they start **bargaining** at every available opportunity, much as local people do. Most buyers start their counterbid at about 25 percent of the vendor's opening price, and the bartering continues from there. But never forget that the few pennies you're making such a fuss over will go a lot further in a local person's hands than in your own.

Price tiering exists in parts of Southeast Asia, with foreigners paying more than locals for public transport, hotels and entry fees to museums and historical sites. Remember that prices vary within individual countries, especially when you enter more remote areas. Very few **student discounts** are offered on entry prices.

Tipping isn't a Southeast Asian custom, although some smarter restaurants expect a gratuity, and most expensive hotels/guesthouses add service taxes. Guides, particularly on multi-day tours, also expect tips (generally around US$10/day).

Crime and personal safety

Travelling in Southeast Asia is generally safe and unthreatening, though, as in any unfamiliar environment, you should keep your wits about you. The most common hazard is opportunistic theft, which can easily be avoided with a few sensible precautions. Occasionally, political trouble flares in the region, so before you travel you may want to check the official government advice on international trouble spots (see box opposite). Most experienced travellers find this official advice less helpful than that offered by other travellers. In some countries, there are specific year-round dangers such as kidnapping (southern Philippines), and unexploded ordnance (Laos, Cambodia, Vietnam); details of these and how to avoid them are described in the introduction to the relevant country.

General precautions

As a tourist, you are an obvious target for opportunistic **thieves** (who may include your fellow travellers), so don't flash expensive cameras or watches around. Carry cash and important documents (airline tickets, credit cards and passport) under your clothing in a **money belt**. It's a good idea to keep $100 cash or so, photocopies of the relevant pages of your passport and insurance details separate from the rest of your valuables. Another good tip is to scan your passport and valuable documents, email them to yourself and save them on your smartphone/tablet, so you can access them offline.

Ensure that **luggage** is lockable and keep important documents on your person rather than in outer pockets. A **padlock** and chain, or a cable lock, is useful for doors and windows at inexpensive guesthouses and beach bungalows, and for securing your pack on **buses**, where you're often separated from your belongings. If your pack is on the top of the bus or boat, make sure it is attached securely, and keep an eye on it whenever the bus or boat pulls into a station, jetty or port. Be especially aware of pickpockets on buses, who usually operate in pairs: one will distract you while another does the job. On **trains**, either cable-lock your pack or put it under the bottom bench-seat, out of public view. Be wary of accepting food and drink from strangers on long overnight bus or train journeys: there is a rare possibility that it's drugged in order to knock you out while your bags are stolen.

Some guesthouses and hotels have **safe-deposit boxes** or lockers, which solve the problem of what to do with your valuables while you go swimming. The safest lockers are those that require your own padlock, as valuables sometimes get lifted by hotel staff. Padlock your luggage when leaving it in hotel or guesthouse rooms.

Violent crime against tourists is not common in Southeast Asia, but it does occur. Obvious precautions include securing locks at night, and not travelling alone at night in an unlicensed taxi, tuk-tuk or rickshaw. Think carefully about motorbiking alone in sparsely inhabited and politically sensitive border regions. If you're going hiking on your own for a day, inform hotel staff of your route so that they can look for you if you don't return when planned.

Con artists and scams

Con artists are usually fairly easy to spot. Always treat **touts** with suspicion – if they offer to take you to a great guesthouse/jewellery shop/untouristed village, you can be sure there'll be a huge commission in it for them, and you may end up being taken somewhere against your will. A variation involves taxi drivers assuring you that a major sight is closed for the day, so encouraging you to go with them on their own special tour.

Some, but by no means all, **travel agencies** in the backpackers' centres of Southeast Asia are fly-by-night operations. Although it's not necessarily incriminating if a travel agent's office seems to be the proverbial hole in the wall, it may be a good idea to reject those that look too temporary in favour of something permanent and thriving. In Vietnam in particular, travel agents and guesthouses will often copy the name of a successful and reputable company, so always double-check the address to ascertain that it is actually the place that's recommended.

Reporting a crime

If you are a victim of theft or violent crime, you'll need a **police report** for insurance purposes. Try to take someone along with you to the police station to translate, though police will generally do their best to find an English-speaker. Allow plenty of time for any involvement with the police, whose offices often wallow in bureaucracy; you may also be charged "administration fees" for enlisting their help, the cost of which is open to sensitive negotiations. You may also want to contact your **embassy** – listed in the "Directory" section of the capital cities in the Guide. In the case of a medical emergency, you will also need to alert your **insurance company**.

Drugs

Drugs penalties are tough throughout the region – in many countries there's even the possibility of being sentenced to death – and you won't get any sympathy from consular officials. Beware of drug scams: either being shopped by a dealer or having substances slipped into your luggage. If you are arrested, or end up on the wrong side of the law for whatever reason, you should ring the consular officer at your embassy immediately.

Electricity

In most parts of the region, electricity is supplied at an almost equal balance of 220 and 230V, though socket type varies from country to country, so you should bring a travel plug with several adaptors. Power cuts are common, so bring a torch.

Insurance

Wherever you're travelling to in Southeast Asia, you must have adequate travel insurance. Before buying a policy, check that you're not already covered: student health coverage often extends during holidays and for one term beyond the date of last enrolment, and your home insurance policy may cover your possessions against loss or theft even when overseas.

Most policies exclude so-called dangerous sports unless an extra premium is paid: in Southeast Asia, this can mean scuba diving, whitewater rafting and bungee jumping, though probably not trekking. Read the small print and benefits tables of prospective policies carefully.

You should definitely take **medical coverage** that includes both hospital treatment and medical evacuation; be sure to ask for the 24-hour medical emergency number. Keep all medical bills and, if possible, contact the insurance company before making any major outlay. Very few insurers will arrange on-the-spot payments in the event of a major expense – you will usually be reimbursed only after going home, so a credit/debit card could be useful to tide you over.

When securing **baggage cover**, make sure that the per-article limit will cover your most valuable possession. If you have anything stolen, get a copy of the police report, otherwise you won't be able to claim. Always make a note of the policy details and leave them with someone at home in case you lose the original. If you don't have a digital copy of the documents, it is worth scanning them, emailing them to yourself and then downloading a copy onto your smartphone, tablet or laptop.

OFFICIAL ADVICE ON INTERNATIONAL TROUBLE SPOTS

The following sites provide useful advice on travelling in countries that are considered unstable or unsafe for foreigners.

Australian Department of Foreign Affairs Ⓦ dfat.gov.au. Advice and reports on unstable countries and regions.

British Foreign and Commonwealth Office Ⓦ fco.gov.uk. Constantly updated advice for travellers on circumstances affecting safety in more than 130 countries.

Canadian Foreign Affairs Department Ⓦ international.gc.ca. Country-by-country travel advisories.

US State Department Travel Advisories Ⓦ travel.state.gov. Website providing "consular information sheets" detailing the dangers of travelling in most countries of the world.

ROUGH GUIDES TRAVEL INSURANCE

Rough Guides has teamed up with WorldNomads.com to offer great **travel insurance** deals. Policies are available to residents of more than 150 countries, with cover for a wide range of **adventure sports**, 24hr emergency assistance, high levels of medical and evacuation cover and a stream of **travel safety information**. Roughguides.com users can take advantage of their policies online 24/7, from anywhere in the world – even if you're already travelling. And since plans often change when you're on the road, you can extend your policy and even claim online. Roughguides.com users who buy travel insurance with WorldNomads.com can also leave a positive footprint and donate to a community development project. For more information go to ⓦ roughguides.com/travel-insurance.

Internet

Internet access is widespread in Southeast Asia, and connection speeds are getting quicker, particularly in the cities. Wi-fi is often offered for free by hotels, hostels, cafés, restaurants and bars, as well as some airports and city malls.

Language

In touristy areas across the region it is generally fairly easy to find someone who speaks English, particularly if they work for a travel agency or hotel. Bus and taxi drivers, shopkeepers, and so on, may not, however, particularly in rural areas. It is well worth learning a few words – "hello", "thanks", "sorry", and so on – in the local language(s) to ease the process and to be polite.

Laundry

There are few coin-operated laundries in Southeast Asia, but most guesthouses and hotels will wash your clothes for a reasonable price.

Left luggage

Most guesthouses and hotels will store luggage for you, though sometimes only if you make a reservation for your anticipated return; major train stations and airports also have left-luggage facilities.

LGBT travellers

Homosexuality is broadly tolerated in much of Southeast Asia, if not exactly accepted. Thailand and the Philippines have the most public and developed **LGBT scenes** in the region, and gay travellers are generally made to feel welcome in both places. Indonesia, Cambodia, Laos and Vietnam all have less visible gay communities, but they do exist and homosexuality is legal in all four

countries. The situation is far less positive in more conservative Malaysia, and LGBT travellers there should be especially discreet. Despite this, there are gay bars and meeting places in Kuala Lumpur and Penang. In Singapore, though there is a discreet gay scene, sex between men is illegal; however, the law is not generally enforced. Homosexuality is also illegal in Myanmar and discrimination widespread, though again enforcement of the law is rare.

The tourist-oriented gay sex industry is a tiny but highly visible part of Southeast Asia's gay scene, and is most obvious in Thailand where gay venues are often nothing more than brothels.

For detailed **information** on the LGBT scene in Southeast Asia, check out the **websites** ⓦ utopia-asia.com, which is an excellent resource for gay travellers to all regions of Asia and has travellers' reports on gay scenes across the region, and ⓦ fridae.asia, which lists LGBT city guides within Asia.

Contacts for LGBT travellers

UK

Gay Travel ⓦ gaytravel.co.uk. Online gay and lesbian travel agent with listings.

THE US AND CANADA

Damron ☎ 1 800 462 6654 or ☎ 415 255 0404, ⓦ damron.com. Publishes guides with hundreds of LGBT-friendly accommodation options. **International Gay & Lesbian Travel Association** ☎ 1 954 630 1637, ⓦ iglta.org. Its website has a list of LGBT-friendly travel agents, worldwide, plus accommodation.

AUSTRALIA AND NEW ZEALAND

Gay Travel ☎ 1800 429 8728, ⓦ gaytravel.com. Advice on trip-planning and bookings. **Rainbow Travel** Australia ☎ 02 9191 2979, New Zealand ☎ 0800 123 669, ⓦ rainbowtourism.com. Works with regional LGBT travel agencies to offer tours as well as accommodation throughout Southeast Asia, including homestays.

Mail

Travellers can receive mail in any country in Southeast Asia via **poste restante**. The system is universally fairly efficient, but tends only to be available at the main post office in cities and popular tourist destinations. Most post offices hold letters for a maximum of one month, though some hold them for up to three, and others seem to hold them forever. Mail should be addressed: Name (family name underlined or capitalized), Poste Restante, GPO, Town or City, Country. It will be filed by family name, though it's always wise to check under your first initial as well. To collect mail, you'll need to show your passport and may have to pay a small fee.

Money

The easiest way to carry your money is in the form of plastic; ATMs are fairly widespread, except in the smallest towns and most rural areas. Banks charge a handling fee of about 1.5 percent per transaction when you use your debit card at overseas ATMs.

Growing numbers of hotels, restaurants, shops and travel agents allow you to pay with debit or credit cards, with Visa and MasterCard the most widely accepted. Pre-paid cash cards such as Travelex's "cash passport" (Ⓦ travelex.com), which are used in the same way as debit/credit cards, are also a useful thing to have.

Note, however, that surcharging of up to five percent is rife, and theft and forgery are major industries – always demand the carbon copies and destroy them immediately. It's sensible not to rely on plastic alone; consider taking more than one card with you, as well as a stash of cash (in US dollars and/or the local currency). Most **international airports** have exchange counters, which is useful, as you can't always buy Southeast Asian currencies before leaving home (though rates are generally poor). Tourist centres also have convenient **exchange counters** where rates can compare favourably with those offered by the banks, but always establish any **commission** first – the places that display promising rates may charge a hefty fee, and be careful of some common scams, including miscalculating amounts (especially when there are lots of zeros involved), using a rigged calculator, folding over notes to make the amount look twice as great and removing a pile of notes after the money has been counted.

Sharing economy sites like WeSwap (Ⓦ weswap .com) have been a useful development in recent years, allowing travellers to exchange foreign currency (often at good rates).

Wiring money

Wiring money through a specialist agent is fast but expensive. The money wired should be available for collection, usually in local currency, from the company's local agent within twenty minutes of being sent via Western Union (Ⓦ westernunion .com) or MoneyGram (Ⓦ moneygram.com); both charge on a sliding scale, so sending larger amounts of cash is better value. Better value than either of these, though currently only available for certain Southeast Asian countries (including Vietnam and Indonesia), is TransferWise (Ⓦ transfer wise.com).

Phones

You can **phone** home from any city or large town in Southeast Asia. One of the most convenient ways of doing so is over the internet, with a provider such as Skype (Ⓦ skype.com), enabling you to make free internet calls. An expensive alternative is to take a **telephone charge card** from your phone company back home, to charge calls to your account.

In most places national telecommunications offices or post offices tend to charge less than private telephone offices and guesthouses for international calls. In phone centres where there's no facility for reverse-charge calls, you can almost always get a **"call-back"**. Ask the operator for a minimum (one-minute) call abroad and get the phone number of the place you're calling from; you can then be called back directly at the phone centre.

Mobile phones

Generally speaking, UK, Australian and New Zealand mobile phones should work fine in Southeast Asia. However, with US mobiles only multi-band models are likely to function abroad. Check with your provider what the call charges will be before setting off.

You are likely to be charged extra for incoming calls when abroad, as the people calling you will be paying the usual rate. For further information about using your phone abroad, check out Ⓦ telecomsadvice.org.uk/features/using_your_ mobile_phone_abroad_roaming.htm. If you're in a country for a while it's worth buying a local pre-pay SIM card, but you'll need to get your phone "unlocked" before you leave home.

IDD CODES

To phone abroad from the following countries, first dial the international access code, then the IDD country code, then the area code (usually without the first zero), then the phone number:

INTERNATIONAL ACCESS CODES WHEN DIALLING FROM:

Australia ☎ 0011
Brunei ☎ 00
Cambodia ☎ 00
Canada ☎ 011
Hong Kong ☎ 001
Indonesia ☎ 001, 008
Ireland ☎ 00
Laos ☎ 14
Macau ☎ 00
Malaysia ☎ 00

Myanmar ☎ 00
New Zealand ☎ 00
Northern Ireland ☎ 048
The Philippines ☎ 00
Singapore ☎ 001, 002
South Africa ☎ 00
Thailand ☎ 001
UK ☎ 00
US ☎ 011
Vietnam ☎ 00

IDD COUNTRY CODES

Australia ☎ 61
Brunei ☎ 673
Cambodia ☎ 855
Canada ☎ 1
Hong Kong ☎ 852
Indonesia ☎ 62
Ireland ☎ 353
Laos ☎ 856
Macau ☎ 853
Malaysia ☎ 60

Myanmar ☎ 95
New Zealand ☎ 64
The Philippines ☎ 63
Singapore ☎ 65
South Africa ☎ 27
Thailand ☎ 66
UK ☎ 44
US ☎ 1
Vietnam ☎ 84

Tourist information

Although some Southeast Asian countries have no dedicated tourist information offices abroad, there's plenty of information available online.

Tourist offices abroad

Local tourist information services are described in the introduction to each chapter.

Brunei ⓦ bruneitourism.travel.

Cambodia ⓦ tourismcambodia.org. UK & Ireland ☎ 020 8451 7850.

Hong Kong and Macau ⓦ discoverhongkong.com; Australia and New Zealand ☎ 02 9283 3083; Canada ☎ 416 366-2389; UK and Ireland ☎ 020 7432 7700; US: New York ☎ 212 421 3382, Los Angeles ☎ 323 938 4582, ⓦ en.macautourism.gov.mo; Australia ☎ 02 9264 1488; New Zealand ☎ 09 308 5206; UK and Ireland ☎ 020 8334 8325; US ☎ 310 545 3464; US: California ☎ 310 545 3464, New York ☎ 646 227 0690.

Indonesia ⓦ indonesia.travel.

Laos ⓦ tourismlaos.org.

Malaysia ⓦ tourism.gov.my; Australia: Sydney ☎ 02 9299 4441, Perth ☎ 08 9481 0400; Canada ☎ 604 689 8899; South Africa ☎ 011 268 0292; UK and Ireland ☎ 020 7930 7932; US: Los Angeles ☎ 213 689 9702, New York ☎ 212 754 1113.

Myanmar ⓦ myanmartourism.org.

The Philippines ⓦ tourism.gov.ph; Australia and New Zealand ☎ 02 9279 3380; UK and Ireland ☎ 020 7835 1100; US: Los Angeles ☎ 213 487 4525, New York ☎ 212 575 7915, San Francisco ☎ 415 956-4060.

Singapore ⓦ yoursingapore.com; Australia ☎ 02 9290 2888; New Zealand ☎ 0800 608 506; UK and Ireland ☎ 020 7484 2710; US: Los Angeles ☎ 323 677 0808, New York ☎ 212 302 4861.

Thailand ⓦ tourismthailand.org; Australia and New Zealand ☎ 02 9247 7549; UK and Ireland ☎ 020 925 2511; US: Los Angeles ☎ 323 461 9814, New York ☎ 212 432 0433.

Vietnam ⓦ vietnamtourism.com.

Useful websites

For country-specific websites see the relevant country introduction.

AsianDiver ⓦ uw3some.com. Online version of the divers' magazine, with good coverage of Southeast Asia's diving sites, including recommendations and first-hand diving stories.

Open Directory Project ⓦ dmoz.org/Recreation/Travel. Scores of backpacker-oriented links, including many Asia-specific ones, plus travelogues and message boards.

Rough Guides ⓦ roughguides.com. Award-winning site for independent travellers, with destination guides and features.

Tourism Concern ⓦ tourismconcern.org.uk. Website of the British organization that campaigns for responsible tourism. Plenty of useful links to politically and environmentally aware organizations across the world, and particularly good sections on issues such as human rights and tourism.

TravelFish ⓦ travelfish.org. A frequently updated online resource on eight of the most popular Southeast Asian countries, dedicated to backpackers. There's a useful message board, plus you can read travellers' reviews and get advice on specific trip planning.

Time zones

The region is covered by four time zones. Cambodia, west Indonesia (Java, Sumatra, Kalimantan Barat and Kalimantan Tengah), Laos, Thailand and Vietnam are **7 hours ahead of GMT**, 12 hours ahead of New York, 15 hours ahead of LA, 3 hours behind Sydney and 5 hours behind Auckland. Brunei, Hong Kong and Macau, central Indonesia (Bali, Lombok, Nusa Tenggara, Sulawesi and south and east Kalimantan), Malaysia, the Philippines and Singapore are all **8 hours ahead of GMT**, 13 hours ahead of New York, 16 hours ahead of LA, 2 hours behind Sydney and 4 hours behind Auckland. Eastern Indonesia (Irian Jaya and Maluku) is **9 hours ahead of GMT**, 14 hours ahead of New York, 17 hours ahead of LA, 1 hour behind Sydney and 3 hours behind Auckland. Myanmar is six-and-a-half hours ahead of GMT. No countries in the region use daylight saving time.

Visas

Country-specific advice about visas, entry requirements, border formalities and visa extensions is given in the introduction at the beginning of each chapter. As a broad guide, the only countries in Southeast Asia for which citizens of the EU, the US, Canada, Australia and New Zealand need to buy a visa in advance are: **Vietnam** (a pre-arranged "visa-on-arrival" can be sourced from a Vietnamese travel agency, but it's better to get one from a Vietnamese embassy/consulate; from US$25), though they may change in the future – check before travelling (there was limited visa-free travel in 2016, since retracted); and **Myanmar** – purchase online (see p.524) or in advance at an embassy or consulate; $50). In **Indonesia** you can now get a thirty-day visa on arrival at major airports and seaports (see p.166), but the situation is prone to change, so it's worth checking

Different rules usually apply if you're staying more than thirty days or arriving overland, and as all visa requirements, prices and processing times are subject to change, it's always worth double-checking with embassies. Most countries require your passport to be valid for at least six months from your date of entry. Some also demand proof of onward travel or sufficient funds to buy a ticket.

Travellers with disabilities

Aside from Hong Kong and Singapore, which have wheelchair-accessible public transport, most Southeast Asian countries make few provisions for people with disabilities. Pavements are usually high, uneven, and lack dropped kerbs, and public transport is not wheelchair-friendly. On the positive side, however, most disabled travellers report that help is never in short supply, and wheelchair-users with collapsible chairs may be able to take cycle rickshaws and tuk-tuks, balancing their chair in front of them. Also, services in much of Southeast Asia are very inexpensive for Western travellers, so you should be able to afford to hire a car or minibus with driver for a few days, stay at better-equipped hotels, and take some internal flights. You might also consider hiring a local tour guide to accompany you on sightseeing trips – a native speaker can facilitate access to temples and museums, or perhaps book a package holiday. Carry a doctor's letter with you about any drug prescriptions you have for when you're passing through airport customs, as this will ensure that you don't get hauled up for narcotics transgressions.

Contacts for travellers with disabilities

AUSTRALIA AND NEW ZEALAND

Disabled Persons Assembly 4/173–175 Victoria St, Wellington, New Zealand ☎ 048 019100, ⓦ dpa.org.nz. Resource centre with lists of travel agencies and tour operators for people with disabilities.
National Disability Services P33 Thesiger Court, Deakin, ACT, 2600 ☎ 02 6283 3200, ⓦ nds.org.au. Provides lists of travel agencies and tour operators for people with disabilities.

UK AND IRELAND

Irish Wheelchair Association Blackheath Drive, Clontarf, Dublin 3 ☎ 018 186400, ⓦ iwa.ie. Useful information provided about travelling abroad with a wheelchair.
Tourism For All Shap Road Industrial Estate, Shap Road, Kendal, Cumbria LA9 6NZ ☎ 0845 124 9971, ⓦ tourismforall.org.uk. Provides general advice and information for disabled travellers.

US AND CANADA

Access-Able ⓦ access-able.com. Rather outdated, but still useful resource for travellers with disabilities.
Mobility International 451 Broadway, Eugene, OR 97401, voice and TDD ☎ 541 343 1284, ⓦ miusa.org. Information and referral services, access guides, tours and exchange programmes.
Society for Accessible Travel and Hospitality (SATH) 347 5th Ave, New York, NY 10016 ☎ 212 447 7284, ⓦ sath.org. Non-profit educational organization that has actively represented travellers with disabilities for over 40 years.

Women travellers

Southeast Asia is generally a safe region for women to travel around alone. That said, it pays to take the normal precautions, especially late at night when there are few people around on the streets; after dark, take licensed taxis rather than cycle rickshaws and tuk-tuks; and during large events such as full-moon parties.

Be aware that a common Asian perception of Western female travellers is of sexual availability and promiscuity. This is particularly the case in the traditional Muslim areas of Indonesia and Malaysia, as well as southern Thailand and the southern Philippines, where lone foreign women can get treated contemptuously however decently attired. Most Southeast Asian women **dress modestly** and it usually helps to do the same, avoiding skimpy shorts and vests, which are considered offensive (see p.40). Some Asian women travelling with white men have reported cases of serious harassment – something attributed to the tendency of Southeast Asian men (particularly in Vietnam) to automatically label all such women as sex workers. Be wary of invitations to drink with a man or group of men if there are no other women present. To many Southeast Asian men, simply accepting such an invitation will be perceived as tacit agreement to have sex, and some will see it as their "right" to rape a woman who has "led them on" by accepting such an invitation. Women should also take care around Buddhist monks. It should go without saying that monks who touch women (something strictly against the Buddhist precepts) or who suggest showing you around some isolated site – such as a cave – should be politely but firmly rebuffed. The key is to stay aware without being paranoid.

OMAR ALI SAIFUDDIEN MOSQUE

Brunei

HIGHLIGHTS

❶ **Ambuyat** Get your chopsticks around Brunei's slithery national dish. **See p.54**

❷ **Omar Ali Saifuddien Mosque** Admire Brunei's most photogenic mosque reflected in its own private lagoon. **See p.56**

❸ **Kampong Ayer** Visit the largest stilt village in the world. **See p.57**

❹ **Royal Regalia Museum** See the presents given to one of the world's richest men. **See p.58**

❺ **Ulu Temburong National Park** Go wildlife-spotting and climb above the jungle canopy. **See p.61**

HIGHLIGHTS ARE MARKED ON THE MAP ON P.53

ROUGH COSTS

Daily budget Basic US$50, occasional treat US$70
Drink Watermelon juice US$4.50
Food *Ambuyat* for two US$12
Hostel/budget hotel US$14/US$55
Travel Bus: BSB–Kota Kinabalu (172km; 8–9hr) US$32

FACT FILE

Population 412,238
Language Bahasa Malaysia, though English is also widely spoken
Religion Muslim, with Buddhist and Christian minorities
Currency Brunei dollars (B$)
Capital Bandar Seri Begawan
International phone code ☏ + 673
Time zone GMT + 8hr

1

Introduction

Surrounded by Sarawak on Borneo's northern coast, the tiny but thriving sultanate of Brunei combines rampant consumerism and notable wealth with Islamic conservatism. Most famous as the home of one of the world's richest men, for those with a bit of time and some cash to spend, the state offers a few hidden surprises. With its decorative architecture and streets flooded with brand-new cars, the capital, Bandar Seri Begawan, can often feel a world away from its Malaysian neighbours. Further afield, the remote Ulu Temburong National Park offers untouched virgin rainforest teeming with flora and fauna.

Budget travel is harder here; accommodation is more expensive than in Sarawak and Sabah, and if you wish to travel outside of the capital, your only options are renting a car (though petrol is cheap) or joining a tour. Many of Brunei's attractions can be found on a much grander scale, for a fraction of the cost, in the neighbouring Malaysian states. But for those looking for a sense of serenity off the beaten track, Brunei is a good stopover.

Resident Bruneians experience a quality of life that is unlike anywhere else in Southeast Asia: education and healthcare are free; houses, cars and even pilgrimages to Mecca are subsidized; and taxation on personal income is unheard of. You won't see any scooters here, and all the cars look as if they've just rolled out of a showroom. The explanation for this is simple: oil, first discovered in 1929 at the site of the town of Seria. Brunei's wealth is all down to the natural resources pumping through its veins, so it will be interesting to see how the county fares when the "black gold" runs out in twenty years' time.

CHRONOLOGY

c. Seventh century Chinese records suggest that a forerunner to the Brunei state – referred to as "Po ni" – has trading relations with China, exporting birds' nests, hornbill ivory and timber.

1370 Sultan Mohammed becomes the first sultan.

Mid-1400 Sultan Awang Alak der Tabar marries a princess from Melaka and converts to Islam. By the end of the century Brunei is independent and trade with Malacca flourishes.

Fifteenth century After the fall of Malacca in 1511, many wealthy Muslim merchants decamp to Brunei, accelerating its conversion to Islam, and bolstering its position as a trading centre.

1526 The Portuguese establish a trading post in Brunei.

1578 Spain's forces take the capital of Brunei, only to be chased out days later by a cholera epidemic.

1588 & 1645 Brunei raided by the Spanish again.

1660s Feuding between the princes results in civil war. Brunei languishes in obscurity for more than 150 years.

1839 Fortune-seeker James Brooke arrives near Kuching, helps the sultan to quell a rebellion, and demands the governorship of Sarawak in return. Brooke and his successors take Brunei's former territories to create the present-day territory of Sarawak.

January 1846 British gunboats quell a court coup; in return Pulau Labuan is ceded to the British Crown.

1888 The British declare Brunei a protected state, with responsibility for its foreign affairs.

WHEN TO GO

The **climate** is hot and humid, with average temperatures in the high 20s to early 30s all year round. Lying 440km north of the equator, Brunei has a tropical weather system so, even if you visit outside the wet season (usually Nov–March), there's every chance you'll get caught in some rain. If you wish to meet the **sultan** himself, the best time to come is at the end of Ramadan (see p.56) when the palace throws open its doors for four days.

1890 The cession of the Limbang region, literally splitting Brunei in two.

1906 The British set up a Residency in Brunei.

1929 The discovery of the Seria oilfield; extraction begins.

1941–45 The Japanese occupation; after their defeat Brunei becomes a British Protectorate again.

1959 The British withdraw – but still control defence and foreign affairs – and a new constitution enshrining Islam as the state religion is established.

1962 Left-wing Brunei People's Party win the election but the sultan refuses to let them form a government. The ensuing violence is crushed with the assistance of the British Army. The sultan starts ruling by decree under emergency powers that largely remain in place today.

1963 Brunei is the only Malay state that chooses to remain a British dependency rather than join the Malaysian Federation.

October 5, 1967 Following the voluntary abdication of his father, the current sultan, Sultan Hassanal Bolkiah (see box, p.58), takes the throne.

1970s As oil prices escalate, Bruneians – especially the sultan – grow rich.

January 1, 1984 Brunei gains full independence from Britain and is declared a "democratic monarchy".

1991 A conservative, religious ideology is introduced, which presents the sultan as defender of the faith; the sale of alcohol is banned.

1998 The sultan's playboy brother (and finance minister) Jefri is sued for embezzling US$14.8bn of state funds: the court reduces his living expenses to a meagre US$300,000 a month.

2004 The sultan revives Brunei's twenty-seat legislative council after two decades.

2007 Brunei, Indonesia and Malaysia sign a "Rainforest Declaration" designed to protect the natural habitats of Borneo's rare species.

2009 Brunei celebrates 25 years of independence.

2011 Brunei stages its biggest energy exhibition ever, with exhibitors at the Energy Expo including energy-efficient technology, biofuels and oil and gas.

2013 The Sultan announces the implementation of Sharia law from 2014 onwards, with adulterers to be stoned and public flogging for Muslim consumers of alcohol.

ARRIVAL AND DEPARTURE

Brunei can be reached by air, land or sea. Some long-haul **flights** (principally between the UK and Australia) have stopovers at Brunei International Airport, while Royal Brunei Airlines, Malaysia Airlines and AirAsia run

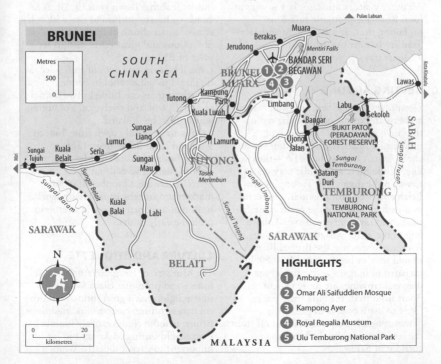

BRUNEI

Metres
500
0

SOUTH CHINA SEA

Pulau Labuan

Muara

Berakas

Jerudong

Mentiri Falls

BRUNEI MUARA

BANDAR SERI BEGAWAN

Kota Kinabalu

Lawas

Tutong

Kampung Parit

Kuala Lurah

Limbang

Labu

Sekoloh

SABAH

Sungai Liang

Lumut

Seria

Sungai Mau

Lamunin

Bangar

Ujong Jalan

BUKIT PATOI (PERADAYAN) FOREST RESERVE

Sungai Trusan

Sungai Tujuh

Kuala Belait

TUTONG

Tasek Merimbun

Sungai Temburong

Miri

Sungai Baram

Sungai Belait

Kuala Balai

Labi

BELAIT

Sungai Tutong

Sungai Limbang

Batang Duri

SARAWAK

TEMBURONG

ULU TEMBURONG NATIONAL PARK

SARAWAK

N

0   20
kilometres

MALAYSIA

HIGHLIGHTS

1 Ambuyat
2 Omar Ali Saifuddien Mosque
3 Kampong Ayer
4 Royal Regalia Museum
5 Ulu Temburong National Park

1

connecting flights from surrounding Sabah and Sarawak; there are also regular flights to other regional hubs, including Singapore, Kuala Lumpur, Bangkok, Hong Kong, Jakarta, Ho Chi Minh City and Manila, with AirAsia, Singapore Airlines, Malaysia Airlines, Thai Airways and Philippines Airlines. **Boats** to Brunei depart daily from Labuan, Lawas and Limbang (see p.59) in Malaysia. Travelling overland, you can reach Bandar Seri Begawan by direct **bus** from Miri in Sarawak (see p.493), and Kota Kinabalu in Sabah. There is even a direct bus service that links the city with Pontianak in Kalimantan.

VISAS

US citizens, New Zealanders, British and most other European travellers are granted ninety days in Brunei without charge, while Canadian nationals are allowed fourteen days. Australians must apply for a visa on arrival (VOA), which costs B$20 for up to thirty days. All other visitors must apply for visas at local Brunei diplomatic missions or, failing that, at a British consulate. Transit visas are available for 72-hour stays.

GETTING AROUND

Downtown Bandar Seri Begawan is small and easy to explore on foot; the rest of the city is covered by a network of inexpensive buses (B$1 per ride). For a cheap "tour", hop on bus #1A – the circle line. While there are regular services to towns in the districts of Tutong, Kuala Belait and Seria from Bandar, buses are non-existent south of the main coastal roads, and **taxis** are expensive. A short hop to the water village of Kampong Ayer, straight across the Brunei River, should set you back around B$0.50; be prepared to bargain and consider that diagonal crossings are more expensive. Apart from that, the only time you're likely to use a **boat** is to get to the Temburong district, which is cut off from the rest of Brunei by the Limbang corridor of Sarawak.

ACCOMMODATION

Accommodation in Brunei is more expensive than in Sabah and Sarawak, and the country is not well set up for backpackers, though there are hostels in both Bandar and Bangar. There are some areas, however, where local Malay and Murut villages and Iban longhouses offer fledgling **homestay programmes** – speak to Brunei Tourism (see p.60) about current ones to visit.

FOOD AND DRINK

The **food** in Brunei is very similar to that of Malaysia; you'll find many Indian, Pakistani and Bangladeshi dishes here, as well as some excellent international food. Brunei does have its own signature dish, *ambuyat* – a tasteless, glutinous, sticky mass, which is made from the pith of the sago tree mixed with water and eaten with special chopsticks called *chandas* after being dunked in a variety of sauces. It can be found at night markets and on some restaurant menus; don't chew it; just let it slither down your throat. *Nasi katok* – a hearty portion of rice with spicy *sambal* and a chunk of fried chicken – is ubiquitous and great value with its set price of B$1.

You'll be drinking a lot of fruit juice, as it's illegal to sell **alcohol** in Brunei, though tourists can bring in two bottles of wine/spirits and twelve cans of beer, which must be declared.

Cafés are generally open from 7am to 9pm and **restaurants** from 11am to 10pm, but around Jalan Sultan in Bandar's centre several stay open 24 hours. There are a number of **night markets** around the capital, with hawker stalls that are open from late afternoon until the early hours.

CULTURE AND ETIQUETTE

The Ministry of Religious Affairs actively fosters and promotes **Islam**, which as a state religion has a great influence on the country's culture, customs and traditions. Brunei is more conservatively Islamic than neighbouring Malaysia and it's important to dress modestly. Women should cover their shoulders and legs – ensure skirts and shorts are below knee-length. For men, T-shirts with sleeves and long shorts or trousers are considered respectable. However, travellers are generally excused and rarely experience any trouble.

SPORTS AND ACTIVITIES

Some seventy percent of Brunei's land area is covered by primary rainforests, much of it protected. The best area for **trekking** is the Temburong district, an area of pristine jungle largely undiscovered by tourists. The principal national park, Ulu Temburong, can be visited independently, though most people choose the easy option of visiting as part of an expensive tour from Bandar (see p.60). Tasek Lama park in Bandar is a free alternative with a lake, waterfalls and several kilometres of interesting rainforest trails.

COMMUNICATIONS

There are numerous cafés with free wi-fi scattered about town, plus a number of **internet cafés** around Bandar, most with headsets for Skype, charging around B$3/hr. Otherwise, **International** (IDD) **calls** can be made from call centres using the 095 access code for B$0.30–0.50/min. Local prepaid SIM cards with either DST or Progresif Cellular cost B$30 and **local calls** cost B$0.05–0.30. To phone abroad from Brunei, dial ❶00 + IDD country code + area code minus first 0 + subscriber number. Brunei has an efficient **postal system**; it takes around a week for postcards to reach Europe and the USA.

BRUNEI ONLINE

ⓦ **brudirect.com** Daily local and international news.
ⓦ **bruneitourism.travel** Brunei Tourism's website has a wealth of information – from seven-star hotels to local markets – though it is a little out of date.
ⓦ **thanislim.com** Brunei's premier food blogger reviews the country's best eats.

EMERGENCY NUMBERS

Ambulance ❶ **991**
Fire brigade ❶ **995**
Police ❶ **993**

CRIME AND SAFETY

Brunei in general has very little crime and travellers rarely experience any trouble. Note that the possession of **drugs** – whether hard or soft – carries a hefty prison sentence, trafficking is punishable by death by hanging, and Sharia law could be applied to tourists for petty crime.

MEDICAL CARE AND EMERGENCIES

Medical services in Brunei are modern and excellent, and staff speak good English. Tourists must pay for medical services upfront, and the cost depends upon the level of treatment required. The main **hospital** is RIPAS Hospital in Bandar (see p.61), which has modern facilities and Western-trained staff.

Oral **contraceptives** and condoms are available at pharmacies; tampons can be found at the Yayasan Complex shopping mall or at many smaller South Asian grocery stores.

INFORMATION AND MAPS

In addition to Brunei Tourism's offices (see p.60), look out also for the glossy quarterly *Borneo Insider's Guide* (ⓦborneoinsidersguide.com) magazine.

Nelles East Malaysia **map** has the best coverage of Brunei, while the free *Official Map of Brunei Darussalam* is sometimes found in the tourist offices.

MONEY AND BANKS

Brunei's **currency** is the Brunei dollar, which is divided into 100 cents; you'll see it written as B$, or simply as $. The Brunei dollar is tied to the Singapore dollar, the two currencies used interchangeably in both countries with the exception of the S$2. Notes come in B$1, B$5, B$10, B$50 and B$100 denominations; coins are in

1

denominations of 1, 5, 10, 20 and 50 cents (c). At the time of writing, the **exchange rate** was B$1.75 to the British pound, B$1.52 to the euro, and B$1.43 to the US dollar.

There's no shortage of **ATMs** in BSB; many accept all types of credit and debit card. Money-changing outfits offer better exchange rates than banks.

Major **credit cards** are accepted in most hotels and large shops. Banks will **advance cash** against MasterCard, Visa, American Express or other Maestro, Plus or Cirrus cards.

OPENING HOURS AND HOLIDAYS

Government offices in Brunei open Monday to Thursday and Saturday 7.45am to 12.15pm and 1.30pm to 4.30pm; **shopping centres** open daily 10am to 9pm. **Banking hours** are Monday to Friday 9am to 4pm and Saturday 9am to 11am. **Post offices** are open Monday to Thursday and Saturday 8am to 4.30pm, and 8am to 11am and 2pm to 4pm on Fridays.

Most of Brunei's **public holidays** are based on the Islamic calendar and change annually according to the lunar calendar, so check with the tourist office. During **Ramadan**, Muslims spend the ninth month of the Islamic calendar fasting in the daytime; during this time it is culturally sensitive for tourists not to eat or smoke blatantly in public during daylight hours.

PUBLIC HOLIDAYS

January 1 New Year's Day
January/February Chinese New Year
Feb 24 Brunei National Day
April Israk Mikraj (Ascension of the Prophet)
May 31 Royal Brunei Armed Forces' Day
May First day of Ramadan
June Nuzulul Quran (Revelation of the Quran day)
Usually June Hari Raya Aidil Fitri (End of Ramadan)
July 15 Sultan's Birthday
August/September Hari Raya Aidil Adha (Festival of Sacrifice)
Usually September Hijrah (Islamic New Year)
Usually November Maulidur Rasul (Prophet Mohammad's Birthday)
Dec 25 Christmas Day

FESTIVALS

Brunei National Day The sultan and 35,000 other Bruneians watch parades and fireworks at the Sultan Hassanal Bolkiah National Stadium, just outside Bandar.
Brunei Royal Armed Forces' Day Bandar's square hosts parades and displays.
Sultan's Birthday A fortnight of parades, lantern processions, traditional sports competitions and fireworks.
Hari Raya Aidil Fitri The sultan declares his home, the Istana Nurul Iman, open to the public for four days. All visitors meet the man himself and receive gifts.

Bandar Seri Begawan

The capital of Brunei is **BANDAR SERI BEGAWAN**, also known as BSB or simply Bandar. There is a striking contrast here between the modern buildings and wide, quiet streets of downtown and the lively, colourful, traditional stilt houses across the river in Kampong Ayer, the world's largest water village and home to nearly a quarter of the sultanate's population. The city's main sights can easily be covered in a couple of days. However, central BSB's peace at night and sense of space provide a welcome contrast to the chaos of most Southeast Asian cities.

As recently as the middle of the nineteenth century, BSB was little more than a sleepy water village, but with the discovery of oil came its evolution into the modern waterfront city of today.

WHAT TO SEE AND DO

Downtown Bandar is hemmed in by water. To the east is Sungai Kiangggeh; to the south, the wide Sungai Brunei; and to the west, Sungai Kedayan, which runs up to the Edinburgh Bridge. The **Omar Ali Saifuddien Mosque** is Bandar's most obvious point of reference. Central BSB is a fairly small place and easily navigable on foot. Sundays are car-free days, and the city centre comes alive with pop-up stalls, zumba dancing and outdoor activities.

The Omar Ali Saifuddien Mosque

At the very heart of the city is the white, golden-domed **Omar Ali Saifuddien**

Mosque (non-Muslim visitors: Mon–
Wed, Sat & Sun 8.30am–noon, 1.30–
3pm & 4.30–5.30pm, Fri 4.30–5.30pm).
Built in classical Islamic style, it was
commissioned by and named after the
father of the present sultan, and
completed in 1958. The floors and walls
of the sumptuous interior are made of fine
Italian marble; the UK is responsible for
the stained-glass windows and
chandeliers, while Saudi Arabia has
provided the finest carpets. Topping the
cream-coloured building is a golden
dome, adorned inside with a mosaic
comprising more than three million pieces
of Venetian glass. Its 44m-high minaret is
the tallest building in central BSB; no
other building is allowed to top that.

The mosque is surrounded by an
artificial lagoon; the stone boat sitting in
the water is a replica of a sixteenth-
century *mahligai* (royal barge).

Kampong Ayer
Kampong Ayer's stilt villages have
occupied this stretch of the Sungai Brunei

for hundreds of years. This "Venice of the
East" – the largest water village in the
world – is home to an estimated thirty
thousand people, their dwellings
connected by a maze of wooden
promenades. These villages have their
own clinics, mosques, schools, a fire
brigade and a police station; the homes
have piped water, electricity and TV. The
waters, however, are distinctly unsanitary,
and the houses susceptible to fire.

There is far more life in the villages
than in central Bandar, and the
meandering pathways make it an
intriguing place to explore on foot; enter
via the bridge just behind the Yayasan
Complex, or pay one of the boatmen to
ferry you across the choppy grey waters
on a speedboat (from B$1).

Visit the **Kampong Ayer Cultural and
Tourism Gallery** (Mon–Thurs, Sat & Sun
9am–5pm, Fri 9–11.30am & 2.30–5pm;
free) across the river for an insight into
the history of Kampong Ayer and displays
on its cottage industries, such as weaving,
woodwork and pottery. Climb the

1

observation tower for panoramic views of the stilt village and speedboats whizzing across the chocolate-coloured water.

Boat tours

Boatmen hanging around the waterfront will do their best to convince you to take a **boat tour**, which is the best way to see the water village, as well as the Istana (see below) and the mangroves beyond, where there's an excellent chance of seeing proboscis monkeys, monitor lizards and even crocodiles. You'll need to negotiate the length and price of your tour; standard tours are around B$35–40 and take an hour or so. To get the most out of it, it's best to pay a bit more and go with Danny (see p.60), as he's good at spotting wildlife and will also be able to tell you the history of the city – something that's beyond the reach of many boatmen with their limited English.

Royal Regalia Museum

The centrally located **Royal Regalia Museum** (Mon–Thurs & Sun 9am–5pm, Fri 9–11.30am & 2.30–5pm, Sat 9.45am–5pm; free) is dedicated almost entirely to the Sultan of Brunei and is the most entertaining museum in Bandar. A series of captioned photos of the sultan traces his path from jug-eared child to absolute monarch via a stint at the Sandhurst Military Academy, painting a rather flattering portrait of his life. Standout exhibits include the sultan's enormous, gold-winged Royal Chariot in the main hall; and a golden throne, crown, keris (ceremonial dagger) and

gold hand, used to support the sultan's chin during the coronation, behind glass on the first floor. Other first-floor galleries are filled with **exotic objects** given to the sultan as gifts by foreign heads of state; spot the bronze falcon from Ukraine, Nazca lines pins from Peru and framed calligraphy resembling a boat.

The Jame 'Asr Hassanil Bolkiah Mosque

It's an ongoing debate whether the **Jame 'Asr Hassanil Bolkiah (State) Mosque** (also known as the Kiarong Mosque; Mon–Wed & Sat 8am–noon, 2–3pm; Sun 10.30am–noon, 2–3pm; closed Thurs & Fri), set in harmonious gardens near the commercial suburb of Gadong, has a distinct edge over the Omar Ali Saifuddien Mosque. With its sea-blue roof, 29 golden domes representing Brunei's 29 sultans, and slender minarets, this is Brunei's largest mosque, constructed to commemorate the silver jubilee of the sultan's reign in 1992.

Buses #01A and #23 skirt the grounds of the mosque, 3km from the centre en route to the shopping area of Gadong.

The Istana Nurul Iman

The official residence of the sultan is sited along the banks of the Sungai Brunei, 4km west of the capital. Bigger than either Buckingham Palace or the Vatican, the Istana is a monument to self-indulgence, with 1788 rooms, including a staggering 257 bathrooms and a royal banquet hall that can seat four thousand. Designed by Filipino architect Leanrdo Locsin, it is a

---

THE SULTAN OF BRUNEI

Brunei's 29th sultan, **Hassanal Bolkiah**, is reported to be one of the world's richest monarchs, worth a cool US$22 billion. His list of assets includes: the 1788-room Istana Nurul Iman (see above); family homes in London, LA, New York and Paris; two Boeings; five aircraft hangars to house his five thousand cars; and climate-controlled stables for his two hundred polo ponies. His yearly expenditure at one time listed US$2.52m on badminton lessons, US$2.5m on masseuses and acupuncturists and nearly US$100,000 on guards for his exotic-bird cages.

This information all became public after he accused his younger brother, Prince Jefri, of siphoning off US$14.8bn during his thirteen years as finance minister. A court battle ensued, and after fifteen years it ruled in the sultan's favour. Jefri was dealt a crushing blow and ordered to hand over two hotels, three houses, diamonds, cherished paintings and cash. But when your older brother is the Prime Minister, Defence Minister, Supreme Commander of the Armed Forces, Supreme Head of Islam and Chief of Police, as well as sultan, who was he to argue?

blend of traditional and modern, with Islamic motifs, such as arches and domes, and sloping roofs fashioned on traditional longhouse designs, combined with all the mod cons you'd expect of a homeowner whose fortune is estimated at US$22 billion. Still, from the outside it looks remarkably like an airport terminal. The palace is open to the general public for four days after Ramadan, when you get to shake hands with the sultan himself and get a goodie bag.

Empire Hotel & Country Club

Ever wondered what a US$1.1 billion folly looks like? If so, it's worth taking a bus to this beyond-extravagant **hotel** (☎02 418888, ☎theempirehotel.com), built on the orders of less-than-prudent Prince Jefri as lodging for the guests of the royal family. The hotel is now a luxurious resort with touches such as the US$500,000 gold-and-Baccarat crystal lamps in the lobby and the B$17,000-a-night Emperor Suite (home to Michael Jackson during his reclusive period), though it's not available to the general public. Twin rooms are a more reasonable B$270, but you don't have to stay here in order to bask in the opulence; a flying visit and an inexpensive cup of tea in the lounge suffices. Since bus #57 runs only three times daily, plan a leisurely visit or arrange a taxi back (B$35).

ARRIVAL AND DEPARTURE

By plane Brunei International Airport (Lapangan Terbang Antarabangsa; ☎02 331747) is 8km north of the city. There are free public phones beyond passport control, a tourist information booth and ATMs. Taxis to the centre cost around B$30 (around B$40 after 9pm). Alternatively, bear right as you exit arrivals into the free parking zone where you can catch a bus (#23, #24, #36 or #38; every 15min; 6.30am–6pm; B$1) into town. Brunei airport departure tax is B$5 for flights to east Malaysia, Indonesia and the Philippines, and B$12 to all other destinations.
Destinations Bangkok, Thailand (daily; 4hr); Ho Chi Minh City, Vietnam (4 weekly; 1hr 55min); Hong Kong (daily; 3hr 30min); Kota Kinabalu, Sabah (daily; 40min); Kuala Lumpur, Malaysia (daily; 2hr 20min); Jakarta, Indonesia (5 weekly; 2hr 20min); Manila, Philippines (several daily; 2hr); Singapore (daily; 2hr).
By boat "Flying coffin" boats (thus named because of their shape and because of the occasional accidents that have killed some passengers) run between the Jalan

Residency jetty 2km east of the centre of Bandar and Bangar.
Destinations Bangar (roughly hourly 6am–4.30pm; 45min).
By bus Long-distance buses from Sabah and Sarawak arrive at and depart along the waterfront on Jl McArthur. Jesselton Express (☎071 45734, ☎sipitangexpress.com .my) runs to Kota Kinabalu, Sabah via Limbang, Bangar and Lawas (see box below), while PHLS Express (☎02 771668, ☎phls38.com) serves Miri, Sarawak via Seria and Kuala Belait. For a marginally pricier but more convenient option for Miri, it's possible to arrange door-to-door pick-up via Mrs Lee of *Dillenia Guesthouse* (see p.494). S. J. S. Executive Bus (☎071 30686, ☎sjsbus.wordpress .com) runs to Pontianak, Kalimantan.
Destinations Kota Kinabalu, Sabah (daily at 8am; 9hr); Miri, Sarawak, via Kuala Belait (5 daily; 4hr); Pontianak (daily at 9am; 26hr).

GETTING AROUND

By bus Local buses leave from the bus station on Jl Cator, right in the centre of town (daily 6.30am–6pm; from B$1). There are six lines – Northern, Circle, Southern, Central,

> ### INTO MALAYSIA: KOTA KINABALU
> You can take a direct air-conditioned bus from Bandar to **Kota Kinabalu** in Sabah, but be prepared to sacrifice several passport pages, as this bus must cross eight immigration posts along the way – the first as you leave Brunei, the second on entering Sarawak at Kuala Lurah and the third departing Sarawak, which is followed by number four, re-entering Brunei at Ujong Jalan. The remaining four stops are upon departing Brunei again, re-entering Sarawak at Labu, departing Sarawak, and then on entering Sabah at Pantai.
>
> A quicker, cheaper and less passport-consuming alternative is to take the Eastern Line bus from BSB bus terminal to the **Serasa ferry terminal** in Muara (every 2hr 6.45–7pm; 1hr; B$1) and catch a speed boat to **Labuan** island in Sabah (6 daily at 8am, 8.30am, 9.30am, 12.30pm, 1pm & 4.40pm; 1hr; B$17). There's one daily direct boat from Labuan to Kota Kinabalu at 1pm (3hr; RM39), but it's quicker to take one of the frequent fibreglass dinghies to the tiny port of **Menumbok** (30min; RM15) from where buses continue to Kota Kinabalu (hourly; 2hr 30min; RM18).

1

Western and Eastern – and routes are clearly displayed in the bus station, with an explanatory map. Frequency varies.

By taxi Taxis use the meter, starting at B$3.50 and increasing by B$0.50 each 250m. After 10pm, the meter starts at B$5.25 and goes up by B$0.20 every 20 seconds. A taxi from the city centre to Gadong costs around B$13; B$17 to the airport; B$35 to the Serasa Wharf in Muara and B$30 to the *Empire Hotel*. Taxis wait outside the bus station on Jl Cator, or you can call one on ☎02 222214.

By water taxi The jetty below the intersection of Jl Roberts and Jl McArthur is the best place to catch a motorized canoe across the river to Kampong Ayer (B$1).

INFORMATION AND TOURS

Tourist information You can pick up information and decent maps from the information counter at the airport (daily 8am–noon & 1.30–5pm) and the Kampong Ayer Cultural & Tourism Gallery (see p.57).

Tour operators Danny (☎073 880 1180) is a freelance tour guide who usually hangs around the Jl Cator bus station wearing a beret and waistcoat with a Confederate-flag design; he is a treasure-trove of local information who can arrange onward travel and excellent boat tours (see p.58). Sunshine Borneo Tours (☎02 446509, ⊚exploreborneo .com), an offshoot of the Kuching-based Borneo Adventure (see p.484), run tours to Ulu Temburong National Park – both day-trips and overnight stays. Borneo Guide (☎02 426923, ⊚borneoguide.com) specializes in eco-programmes around Brunei and beyond; day-trips to Ulu Temburong National Park cost B$150 and include meals, the canopy walk, a jungle hike to the Sumbiling eco-village and a visit to a longhouse; three-day/two-night visits (B$325) are also available.

ACCOMMODATION

There's not a lot of choice when it comes to central accommodation, budget or otherwise, but unless you have your own wheels, it's not particularly convenient to be based anywhere else.

Jubilee Hotel Jl Kampung Kianggeh ☎02 228070, ⊚jubileehotelbrunei.com. This central high-rise was recently renovated but lacks the *Terrace's* swimming pool, but has clean and functional rooms. Family suites come with kitchenettes, and the rate includes breakfast and airport pick-up. The downstairs restaurant serves good local dishes. Doubles B$78

MSS Mega Rest House 1st floor, 27 Jl Sultan ☎02 222384. A central budget option, offering a clean but windowless eight-bed dorm catered to backpackers and several good-value twins and doubles. Breakfast is included. Dorms B$20, doubles B$38

New KHS Hotel 140 Jl Pemancha ☎02 222052, ⊚khsoon-resthouse.tripod.com. Taken over by Borneo Guide's management, Bandar's oldest budget guesthouse

was being renovated at the time of writing. Expect pleasant new rooms with linoleum floors and modern en-suite bathrooms, which should take over the former three floors of ageing and tatty doubles and dorms. Dorms B$20, doubles B$50

Pusat Belia Jl Sungei Kianggeh ☎0887 3066 or ☎0872 0301, ⊚facebook.com/hostelyouthcentre. By far the cheapest and best option for backpackers, this youth centre has sparklingly clean singles and four- and ten-bed dorms with a few facilities. The rarely staffed reception is open between 7.45am and 4.30pm, with staff supposedly on call until 10pm. It's best to call ahead or contact the staff on their Facebook page. Dorms B$10

★**Terrace Hotel** Jl Tasek Lama ☎02 243554, ⊚terracebrunei.com. Though the compact rooms at this central hotel are a little musty, they come with double beds, cable TV, in-room kettles and free use of the swimming pool. There's wi-fi in the lobby; the gym is an extra B$5/hr and the restaurant serves tasty Chinese and Malay dishes. Doubles B$65

EATING

Bandar has a decent eating scene that ranges from excellent night markets and street stalls serving local specialities to a wealth of international cuisine.

Al-hilal Restaurant 45 Jl Sultan ☎02 230003. This central and inexpensive restaurant serves all the curries and Malaysian staples you need, including Penang-style *kuey teow* (fried flat noodles with beansprouts and prawns; B$4) and zesty *ayam penyet* (fried chicken with spicy *sambal*, fried tofu and soy-based *tempe*; B$4), and is a good choice for non-alcoholic nightcaps. Daily 24hr.

Aminah Arif Unit 2–3, Block B, Rahman Building, Spg 88, Kiulap ⊚aminaharif.com.bn; bus #20 to the Kg Kiulap stop. Don't want to leave without sampling Brunei's signature dish? This is one of the best places to try it. Bring a friend and go for the "*ambuyat* special" (B$16 for two). If sago gloop just isn't for you, there are plenty of noodle, rice and soupy dishes to choose from. Daily noon–10pm.

★**Chop Jing Chew** Simpang 5, 10 Jl Gadong ☎02 424132. It's worth taking a taxi to Bandar's oldest Chinese *kopitiam* in Gadong to sample one of the city's best breakfasts. Their Sino-Malay specialities, like the delicious *roti kacang khawin* (a soft hot bun filled with butter, coconut jam and crushed peanut), will satisfy any sweet-tooth cravings. Mon–Sat 5.30am–7pm, Sun 5.30am–noon.

De-Royall Café 38 Jl Sultan ☎02 232519. This inviting small café brews strong coffees, spills leopard-skinned lounge chairs and tables on the curb, and is part of Bandar's new breed of 24-hour joints. The free wi-fi is a convenient perk while sipping soft drinks (B$2.5) and sampling their Western and Asian mains (from B$8.90). Daily 24hr.

★**Pasar Malam Gadong** Jl Pasar Gadong. Not far from The Mall in Gadong, this neatly organized night market is a feast for the senses and the best place to try Malay-style noodle and rice dishes, as well as Brunei's national dish – *ambuyat*. There are few places to sit down, though, as most folks get takeaway. Dishes from B$1. Daily 4–10pm.

Semporna Enak Waterfront, Jl McArthur. Sheltered by the Arts Museum and set right on the waterfront, this restaurant is good for casual meals and coffee with Kampung Ayer's views. Come for the glowing sunsets, fresh seafood and inexpensive western dishes – the B$8.50 grilled lamb shoulder with chips is a steal. Daily 8am–4.30am.

Taman Selera Jl Tasek Lama & Jl Stoney. Located in a park opposite the *Terrace* hotel, this night market is home to more than twenty stalls serving a mix of Malay and international food. *Roti john* (omelette sandwich with or without meat) is a popular snack among locals, and the satay and seafood dishes are excellent. Daily 5–10pm.

Tamu Kianggeh Jl Sungai Kianggeh. The food stalls at this colourful produce market across a bridge serve good, cheap *soto ayam* (spicy chicken noodle soup), satay, *nasi campur* (mixed rice), *kelupis* (glutinous rice steamed in a leaf) and other Malay staples. Mains from B$2. It's at its busiest and best at weekends. Daily from 5pm.

SHOPPING

Shopping malls include Yayasan Complex (Jl Pretty; daily 10am–10pm, closed Fri noon–2pm), a department store with some fast-food franchises; Centrepoint and The Mall complexes (same hours) in Gadong are Bandar's shopping and entertainment areas, and include the huge *Centrepoint* hotel, a convention area, a cineplex and places to eat.

Paul & Elizabeth Book Services 2nd floor, Yayasan Complex, Jl Pretty ☎02 220958, ⓦfacebook.com /paulandelizabethbookservices/. Stocks a selection of English-language paperbacks, maps and books on Brunei. Daily 9am–9pm.

DIRECTORY

Embassies and consulates Australia, Level 6, DAR Takaful IBB Utama, Jl Pemancha (☎02 229435); Canada, 5th floor, Jl McArthur Building 1, Jl McArthur (☎02 220043); Indonesia, Lot 4498, Simpang 528, Kg Sungei Hanching Baru, Jl Muara (☎02 330180); New Zealand, c/o Deloitte & Touche, 5th floor, Wisma Hajjah Fatimah, 22–23 Jl Sultan (☎02 222422); UK, Level 2, Block D, Yayasan Complex, Sultan Hassanal Bolkiah, Jl Pretty (☎02 222231); US, Simpang 336-52-16-9, Jl Duta (☎02 238 4616).

Exchange There are many cash-only moneychangers on Jl McArthur with identical rates, and a variety of banks with ATMs on Jl Sultan.

Hospital The RIPAS Hospital (☎02 242424), across Edinburgh Bridge on Jl Putera Al-Muhtadee Billah, has the

best equipment, 24hr emergency services and English-speaking staff.

Laundry Maxiclean, opposite *Brunei Hotel*, Jl Pemancha (Mon–Thurs, Sat & Sun 9am–6pm).

Pharmacies Yin Chee Dispensary, Jl Bunga Kuning; Khong Lin Dispensary, G3A, Wisma Jaya, Jl Pemancha.

Post office The GPO (Mon–Thurs & Sat 7.45am–12.15pm & 1.30–4.30pm; Fri 8–11am & 2–4pm) is at the intersection of Jl Elizabeth Dua and Jl Sultan.

Temburong District

The sparsely populated and seldom visited **Temburong** district is Brunei's great expanse of untouched jungle, and the country's greatest natural attraction. Temburong's nondescript main town, **Bangar**, is the gateway to the pristine forest that lies within – protected in **Ulu Temburong National Park**, easily visited as a day-trip or overnight with one of Bandar's tour companies (see opposite).

ULU TEMBURONG NATIONAL PARK

Undoubtedly one of Brunei's highlights, the lowland rainforest of **Ulu Temburong National Park** is home to rich flora and fauna, with Borneo's famous proboscis monkey a guaranteed sight on any trip. The park consists of 500 square kilometres of pristine rainforest, with only a tiny fraction of it open to visitors, who come here for short jungle hikes, swimming in a waterfall and a canopy walk.

Until the bridge between Bandar and Temburong district is completed in 2018, day-trips to the park typically start with a hair-raising "flying coffin" journey from Bandar to Bangar. Boats scream through narrow mangrove estuaries that are home to crocodiles and proboscis monkeys, swooping around corners at a 45-degree angle. From the Bangar jetty, it's a twenty-minute drive south to the jetty at the small kampung of **Batang Duri**. From here you make your way upstream to **Ulu Temburong Park Headquarters** along Sungai Temburong; this stretch is very

1

shallow in dry season, and when the water level is low you may have to get out and help pull the boat over rocks. Otherwise, it's an exhilarating thirty-minute trip, with the boatman deftly propelling the *temuai* (Iban longboat) around the submerged logs and rocks and riding the rapids.

Canopy Walk

After you register at the Park Headquarters, it's another short trip upriver to where a long, steep set of stairs, followed by often muddy steps with rope handrails, leads up to the base of the **Canopy Walk**. The park's main attraction consists of an aluminium walkway suspended between towers – the highest rising 60m above the jungle floor. The view from the top is breathtaking: you can see Brunei Bay to the north and Gunung Mulu Park in Sarawak to the south.

If your guide speaks good English, it's a bonus since they can explain the workings of the canopy ecosystem, which supports insects, birds, snakes and more. The walkway and towers are a bit wobbly in the wind, but perfectly sturdy; sunscreen and a hat are important, as you're exposed to the elements up there.

If you're on a day-trip, as opposed to staying overnight, you're at a bit of a disadvantage, since you'll be on the canopy walk at the hottest time of day, when animals and birds are hiding; the best time to go up is early in the morning or late in the afternoon.

Waterfall

After the canopy walk, the longboat whisks you off back past the park headquarters and along a series of bouncy river rapids to a little side stream, which you wade through for a few minutes before reaching an idyllic little waterfall. The pool beneath the waterfall is deep enough to splash around in, and if you stay still, you will feel a tickling sensation as the small fish living in that pool nibble on the dead skin of your feet, giving you a natural pedicure.

The waterfall trip is followed by lunch and a return trip to Bandar in a "flying coffin", possibly stopping at a modern longhouse along the way. If you stay overnight, you can take part in jungle hikes and river-related activities.

ACCOMMODATION

Sumbiling Eco Village ☎ 02 426923, ⓦ borneoguide .com/ecovillage. A few minutes downstream from Batang Duri, this rustic eco-camp is run by Borneo Guide (see p.60) in conjunction with the local Iban community. The rooms are basic but have fans and mosquito nets. The Iban food on offer is delicious. Apart from visiting the Ulu Temburong Park nearby, you can also go inner-tubing on the river and trekking in the jungle. Two days & one night (minimum 2 people) including meals. Per person **B$195**

Ulu Ulu Resort ☎ 02 441791, ⓦ uluuluresort.com. This riverside lodge, built of sturdy hardwood, is the only place to stay in the park itself, with a mix of doubles and chalets, as well as its own cinema. Price includes transport from Bandar and full board; activities cost extra. Two days and one night **B$330**

ANGKOR WAT

Cambodia

HIGHLIGHTS

❶ **Royal Palace** The golden spires, landscaped gardens and Silver Pagoda make up the capital's most appealing sight. **See p.76**

❷ **Choeung Ek** Infamous killing fields featuring a memorial temple containing thousands of human skulls. **See p.85**

❸ **Angkor Wat** Unforgettable temple, crowned with soaring towers. **See p.93**

❹ **Angkor Thom** Walled city crammed with ancient monuments. **See p.95**

❺ **Tonle Sap lake** Miniature inland sea dotted with dozens of floating villages. **See p.98**

❻ **Island hopping** Cambodia's southern islands are a picture of pure shores, turquoise seas and tranquillity. **See p.108**

HIGHLIGHTS ARE MARKED ON THE MAP ON P.65

ROUGH COSTS

Daily budget Basic US$20–25, occasional US$40
Drink Angkor beer US$1
Food Khmer mains US$4–5
Hostel/budget hotel US$3–5/US$7–8
Travel Phnom Penh–Siem Reap: bus/share taxi 6–8hr, US$6–8

FACT FILE

Population 16 million
Language Khmer
Religions Theravada Buddhism (97 percent), Islam, Christianity, Animism
Currency Riel (r), US dollar
Capital Phnom Penh
International phone code ☎ + 855
Time zone GMT +7hr

Introduction

Having left its troubled past largely behind, Cambodia has established itself as one of Southeast Asia's most enjoyable destinations, offering a quieter, less developed and considerably more laidback taste of Indochina than neighbouring Thailand and Vietnam. Infrastructure has improved massively too, with new roads bringing once remote destinations within increasingly easy reach – although getting around is still a time-consuming affair. The temples of Angkor are very much on the tourist mainstream, attracting some two million visitors a year, but away from the temples and parts of the coast, most of the country remains relatively untouched and little visited, guaranteeing a warm welcome from the country's irrepressibly friendly inhabitants, and with plentiful attractions ranging from unspoilt beaches and colonial townscapes through to dense forests and majestic rivers and lakes. Go now, before the coach parties arrive.

The Kingdom of Cambodia occupies a modest wedge of land, almost completely hemmed in by Vietnam, Laos and Thailand. Most visitors head straight for the stunning **Angkor ruins**, a collection of more than one hundred temples dating back to the ninth century. Once the seat of power of the Khmer Empire, Angkor is royal extravagance on a grand scale, its imposing features enhanced by a dramatic setting amid lush jungle and verdant fields.

The capital, **Phnom Penh**, is also an alluring attraction in its own right. Wide, sweeping boulevards and elegant, if neglected, French colonial-style facades lend the city a romantic appeal. However,

there's also stark evidence that you're visiting one of the world's poorest countries. Halfway between Angkor and Phnom Penh, it's worth stopping off for a day at **Kompong Thom** to make a side-trip to the pre-Angkor ruins of **Sambor Prei Kuk** where there is scarcely another tourist in sight.

Miles of **unspoilt beaches** and remote islands offer sandy seclusion along the southern coastline. Although **Sihanoukville** is the main port of call, it's easy enough to discover nearby hidden coves and offshore islands. **Ratanakiri** province in the northeastern corner of the country, with its hill tribes and volcanic scenery, is also becoming increasingly popular with visitors, while neighbouring **Mondulkiri** is less well known, but equally impressive, offering dramatic woodlands, villages and mountains. **Battambang** in the central plains, Cambodia's second city, is a sleepy provincial capital, and the gateway to a region steeped in Khmer Rouge history.

WHEN TO GO

Cambodia's **monsoon climate** creates two distinct seasons. The southwesterly monsoon from May to October brings heavy rain, humidity and strong winds – especially in the latter two months – while the northeasterly monsoon from November to April produces dry, hot weather, with average temperatures rising from 25°C in November to around 32°C in April. The best months to visit are December and January, as it's dry and relatively cool, though Angkor is at its most stunning during the lush rainy season.

CHRONOLOGY

First century AD The area to the west of the Mekong Delta, along the trading route from India to China, begins to become an important commercial settlement, known by the Chinese as Funan.

Sixth century Now known as Chenla, the region is occupied by small, disparate fiefdoms operating independently. The temples of Sambor Prei Kuk date from this time.

Early ninth century Rival Chenla kingdoms are united by Jayavarman II, and the Khmer Empire's greatest period, known as the Angkorian period, begins. Jayavarman II establishes the religious cult of the *devaraja* (god-king). The empire lasts for 39 successive kings.

c.1181–1219 The reign of Jayavarman VII, the last major Angkor king. After reclaiming Angkor from the Champa Empire he embarks on a massive programme of construction, culminating in the creation of Angkor Thom.

Fourteenth century The Thai army mounts raids on Cambodian territory, virtually destroying Angkor Thom.

Mid-fifteenth century The capital of Angkor is abandoned in favour of more secure locations to the south; the Khmer Empire is in irreversible decline.

1594 The Khmer capital falls to the Thais; vast swathes of land are lost in tribute payments to both Siam and Vietnam.

1863 King Norodom, wanting to reduce Thai control and secure his own position, exchanges mineral and timber rights with the French in return for military protection.

1904 King Norodom dies; the following three kings are chosen by the French.

1941 18-year-old Prince Norodom Sihanouk succeeds King Monivong; World War II interrupts French control and Japan invades.

1945 Following the Japanese surrender, King Sihanouk campaigns for independence; France, preoccupied by Vietnam, grants it.

May 1954 Independence is formally recognized by the Geneva Conference. Sihanouk abdicates, installing his father Norodom Suramarit as king, to fight in the elections.

1955 Sihanouk's party, The People's Socialist Community, wins every seat in the newly formed parliament. Political opposition is ruthlessly repressed, and communist elements, the "Khmer Rouge", flee to the countryside.

1960 Sihanouk's father dies and Sihanouk appoints himself Chief of State, in a further gesture of despotic power.

1960s Despite publicly declaring neutrality over the Vietnam conflict, Sihanouk allows the North Vietnamese to use Cambodian soil for supplying the Viet Cong.

1969–73 The US covertly bombs Cambodia's eastern provinces where they believe Viet Cong guerrillas are hiding. Thousands of Cambodian civilians are killed or maimed.

1970 General Lon Nol and Prince Sisowath Matak depose Sihanouk. The Viet Cong are ordered to leave, but instead push deeper into Cambodia, pursued by US and South Vietnamese troops. As the country turns into a battlefield, the Khmer Rouge regroup and begin taking control of large areas.

HIGHLIGHTS
1 Royal Palace
2 Choeung Ek
3 Angkor Wat
4 Angkor Thom
5 Tonle Sap lake
6 Island hopping

2

April 17, 1975 Khmer Rouge forces march into Phnom Penh to the cheers of the Cambodian people – but subsequently institute a brutal regime to eradicate all perceived opposition, killing between one and two million people.

1978 Invading Vietnamese forces reach Phnom Penh and a Vietnamese-backed government led by Hun Sen is established; the Khmer Rouge flee to the jungle near the Thai border. A rival Chinese-backed government-in-exile is created, dominated by the Khmer Rouge, and headed by Sihanouk; the international community recognizes this in opposition to Vietnam.

1987 Negotiations between the Hun Sen's government and the coalition led by Sihanouk begin, and the Vietnamese agree to start withdrawing troops.

1991 The Paris Peace Accords are signed. Sweeping powers are granted to the UN Transitional Authority in Cambodia (UNTAC) to supervise control of the country and implement free elections, although little disarmament is achieved.

1993 Despite assassinations and intimidation tactics, there is a nearly ninety-percent turnout at the elections; a fragile coalition between the royalist FUNCINPEC party and Hun Sen's Cambodian People's Party (CPP) is agreed.

1994 The Khmer Rouge are outlawed, and though they still control the north and northwest, an amnesty begins to attract some defections.

1996 Notorious senior Khmer Rouge commander Ta Mok arrests Pol Pot and sentences him to life imprisonment; more defections follow.

1998 As Cambodian troops encroach on the last Khmer Rouge strongholds, Pol Pot dies, possibly of a heart attack, or possibly executed by his own cadres.

2004 King Sihanouk abdicates and invites one of his sons, Norodom Sihamoni, to replace him as king.

2008 Hun Sen wins another election. UN-backed war crime trials of former Khmer Rouge leaders begin. The first to stand trial is Duch, head of S21 prison in Phnom Penh (see p.80) – he is eventually sentenced to life in prison.

2008–11 Repeated clashes between Cambodian and Thai troops around the disputed border temple of Preah Vihear.

June 2012 The trials of top-ranking Khmer Rouge leaders Nuon Chea, Khieu Samphan, Ieng Sary and his wife, Ieng Thirith, commence amid allegations that the court is bowing to government pressure to act favourably towards powerful and wealthy Khmers who were previously mid-level Khmer Rouge commanders. Ieng Sary dies in early 2013, while his wife is declared mentally unfit to stand trial.

October 2012 Norodom Sihanouk, Cambodia's "King-Father", dies of a heart attack aged 89. His son Norodom Sihamouni succeeds him.

July 2013 In fresh elections, Hun Sen's CCP wins a narrow victory over Sam Rainsy's Cambodian National Rescue Party, amid allegations of electoral fraud. Widespread protests erupt sporadically during 2013 and 2014.

August 2014 Khmer Rouge leaders Nuon Chea and Khieu Samphan are sentenced to life imprisonment.

November 2015 Opposition leader Sam Rainsy goes into self-imposed exile after Hun Sen brings defamation charges against him.

July 2016 Killing of leading anti-government journalist Kem Ley.

THE KHMER ROUGE

Born of radical communism and wartime opportunism, the **Khmer Rouge** defined the darkest period in Cambodia's history, leaving a legacy that will last for generations. The ragtag band of communist guerrillas, led by French-educated Saloth Sar (subsequently known as **Pol Pot**), first began to garner popular support during the American bombings of eastern Cambodia. After King Sihanouk was deposed (see above), the Khmer Rouge took advantage of the chaos to seize territory, eventually marching into Phnom Penh to the cheers of Cambodians longing for peace. But the party, known simply as **Angkar**, immediately began to act on their deranged designs to create a socialist utopia by transforming the country into an agrarian collective. The entire population of Phnom Penh and other provincial capitals was forcibly removed to the countryside to begin new lives as peasants working on the land. They were the lucky ones. Pol Pot ordered the mass extermination of intellectuals, teachers, writers, educated people, and their families. Even wearing glasses was an indication of intelligence, a "crime" punishable by death. The brutal regime lasted four years before invading Vietnamese forces captured Phnom Penh in 1978; by this time, between one and three million Cambodians had perished in the genocide.

Driven into the jungle, the Khmer Rouge installed themselves near the Thai border and continued to wage guerrilla warfare against the occupation government, supported by an international community fearful of communist expansionism. It wasn't until Ieng Sary, one of Pol Pot's trusted inner circle, defected in 1996, causing a split in the Khmer Rouge ranks, that the tide began to turn. Pol Pot himself was dead of heart failure within two years, having been convicted by his own troops of murder.

ARRIVAL AND DEPARTURE

There are **flights** to Phnom Penh from Kuala Lumpur, Singapore, Seoul, Bangkok, Vientiane, Ho Chi Minh City, Dubai (via Yangon) and several cities in China including frequent connections with Hong Kong. Siem Reap's international airport is also reached from most of these cities. Travelling **overland** into Cambodia is possible from neighbouring Thailand, Vietnam and Laos.

OVERLAND FROM LAOS

It's possible to cross from Laos at the **Trapaeng Kriel–Nong Nok Khiene** crossing between Stung Treng and Si Phan Don (see p.408).

OVERLAND FROM THAILAND

There are six entry points from Thailand: the border crossing at **Aranyaprathet**, near **Poipet** (see box, p.781); two crossings at **Pailin** (see p.104); the coastal border at **Hat Lek** to Cham Yeam, west of Koh Kong (see box, p.785); two crossings in northeast Thailand: the little-used crossing at the **Chong Chom–O'Smach**, near Kap Choeng in Thailand's Surin province (see box, p.775); and at **Chong Sa Ngam–Choam** border between Si Saket province in Thailand and the Cambodian town of Anlong Veng.

OVERLAND FROM VIETNAM

From Vietnam, seven crossings are open to foreigners. The busiest (on the main highway between Ho Chi Minh City and Phnom Penh) is at **Moc Bai–Bavet** (see box, p.912). There are three border posts in southern Cambodia, including two near the Vietnamese town of **Chau Doc** (see box, p.916) and one at **Ha Tien** (see box, p.918), east of Kep on the coast. There are three further, although little-used, crossings in eastern Cambodia, including the **O Yadaw–Le Tanh** border post between Banlung and Pkeiku.

VISAS

All foreign nationals except those from certain Southeast Asian countries need a **visa** to enter Cambodia. **Tourist visas**, valid for thirty days, cost US$35 and are issued on arrival at all border crossings and airports; two passport photos are required. You may be able to pay an extra $2 to have the one from your passport copied, depending on the mood of the official. However, there have been reports of people being denied visas for not having a photo. Cambodian visa officials are notoriously unfriendly as well as corrupt, and Cambodian border officials at land crossings have been known to inflate the price. To avoid the risk, you may prefer to take care of your tourist visa online in advance (ⓦevisa.gov.kh), though these e-visas are valid only at the airports and at the Koh Kong, Bavet and Poipet land crossings – check the website for details. **E-visas** cost $30 for the visa plus an additional $7 administrative charge and take three days to process; you'll need to provide a digital photograph.

Extending a tourist visa is officially done at the Department of Immigration, Pochentong Road, opposite the airport in Phnom Penh (Mon–Fri 8–11am & 2–4pm). You'll need one passport photo and next-day service costs $60. Given the location of the offices, it's easier to take advantage of the extension services offered by travel agents and guesthouses; they can do the running around for you for a $5–10 commission. A tourist visa can only be extended once, for one month. If you wish to stay longer you'll need a business visa. You are charged $5/day for overstaying your visa.

GETTING AROUND

Transport in Cambodia is all part of the adventure. Massive improvements to the national highway network in the past five years have made getting around the country much easier than it once was, with many formerly dirt roads surfaced and new highways built. Even so, getting from A to B remains a time-consuming process: roads are still narrow and bumpy, while regular wet-season inundations play havoc with transport (and often wash away large sections of tarmac in their wake). Regular **boats** run between Phnom Penh, Siem Reap and Battambang, and there are also **trains** between Phnom Penh

2

and Sihanoukville. Fortunately, Cambodia isn't a big country, and most journeys between major centres take no more than a few hours – even the trip between Phnom Penh and Siem Reap can now be done in as little as five hours.

The **bus** system provides connections between all major towns and is likely to be your standard means of transport. **Minibuses** and **share taxis** can be useful if you want to get somewhere not served by bus, though buses are generally preferable unless you're in a serious rush – in which case you probably shouldn't be in Cambodia at all.

BUSES

Buses are the cheapest (and usually the most convenient and comfortable) way to get around, connecting all major cities and towns. Some smaller places aren't yet on the bus network, and others – Banlung, Sen Monorom and Pailin, for example – have only one or two services a day.

All buses are privately run, operated by a growing number of companies. Phnom Penh Sorya are the biggest; others include Rith Mony, GST, Paramount Angkor and Capitol Tours, while other companies like Giant Ibis and Mekong Express operate luxury express buses on the most popular routes.

Buses generally arrive at and depart from their respective company offices. Unfortunately, this means there are no bus stations or suchlike in which to get centralized information about the timetables and fares of all the services available. Some guesthouses or tour operators can provide this; otherwise you'll have to visit all the individual bus company offices. Fares are generally much of a muchness on all but luxury buses.

MINIBUSES

Minibuses provide the main alternative to buses, at a similar price. These generally serve the same routes as buses, and also go to smaller destinations. They also tend to be slightly faster. On the downside, most get absolutely packed and can be horribly uncomfortable, especially for taller travellers (there's little legroom at the best of times, unlike the buses, which are relatively luxurious in comparison). There are also a few "luxury minibus" services on the main inter-city and international routes (Mekong Express's "limousine bus" services, for example), although these get mixed reviews, and you can never be entirely certain of what you're getting until it's possibly too late.

SHARE TAXIS

Share taxis are generally slightly more expensive but also slightly quicker than buses and minibuses; they also serve local destinations off the bus and minibus network. On the downside, like minibuses they get absurdly packed. Three or even four people on the front passenger seat is the norm – although you can pay roughly double the standard fare to have it to yourself, or indeed pay to hire the entire taxi. The driving can often be slightly hair-raising too. Share taxis usually leave from the local transport stop. There are no fixed schedules, although most run in the morning, leaving when (very) full.

LOCAL TRANSPORT

Motorcycle taxis, commonly called **motos**, are the most convenient way of getting around town and are inexpensive – short journeys cost around $1. English-speaking drivers can usually be found outside hotels, guesthouses and other tourist spots. Non-English-speaking drivers will often nod enthusiastically in a show of understanding, only to proceed to the nearest guesthouse or tourist site. You can hire a moto for the day to visit sights in and around towns all over the country. For trips within a 20km radius, a daily rate of around $15 is the norm.

Three-wheeled **cyclos** (cycle rickshaws) are a more relaxing way to trundle around Phnom Penh, but are only practical for shorter trips. Cyclo fares are subject to negotiation, usually costing a little more than motos ($2–3). Faster and more comfortable are **tuk-tuks**, motorbike-drawn rickshaws that ply the roads of most major cities. These can comfortably carry up to four people – although the under-powered engines tend to struggle with more than a couple of people on board. Fares are usually around $1–3 for short trips around town. With motos, cyclos and tuk-tuks, agree a fare in advance.

Taxis aren't really used for short hops around town. There are only a few metered taxi services in Phnom Penh. Otherwise, cars are rented by the day, or by the journey.

VEHICLE RENTAL

Renting a **motorbike** is the most practical self-drive option for Cambodia's backcountry roads. At the rental shops in Phnom Penh, you can pick up a fairly good 250cc bike ($11/day), which should be able to handle most terrain, while elsewhere basic bikes can go for as little as $6–7/day. **Cars** tend to come with a driver and cost around $60–100 per day depending on mileage.

If you do intend to **self-drive** any vehicle in Cambodia, bear in mind that road conditions are unpredictable. Really, it's only practical if you've had experience of driving in Southeast Asia already.

Officially, vehicles drive on the right, but **traffic regulations** in Cambodia are flexible and you may encounter people driving on the left. Traffic on the roads from Phnom Penh to Sihanoukville and Kompong Cham is heavy and hectic, but much lighter elsewhere.

Bicycles are available to rent cheaply (usually about $1–3/day), and except in Phnom Penh, where traffic is intimidating, cycling is a pleasant way to explore.

TRAINS

The **railway** line between Phnom Penh and Sihanoukville reopened in 2016, with stops at Takeo and Kampot. Two trains with comfortable modern carriages currently operate on this route on Fridays, Saturdays, Sundays and public holidays (from Phnom Penh to Sihanoukville on Fridays, and in both directions on Saturdays and Sundays). The journey takes around 7hr and costs $7. As yet, tickets aren't sold in town, so advance purchase is at the station (☎078 888582, ⓦroyal-railway.com).

BOATS

Regular **ferries** run between Phnom Penh and Siem Reap, and Siem Reap and

Battambang. Conditions are fairly cramped so don't expect the luxury that the foreigner prices imply. Many tourists opt to sit on the roof for the views and sunbathing.

PLANES

Cambodia Angkor Air (ⓦcambodiaangkorair.com), Cambodia Bayon Airlines (ⓦbayonairlines.com), Sky Angkor (ⓦskyangkorair.com) and Bassaka Air (ⓦbassakaair.com) fly between Phnom Penh, Siem Reap and Sihanoukville. Fares on all airlines are broadly similar, with flights between Phnom Penh, Siem Reap and Sihanoukville for around $60–80 one-way, although (except for the Siem Reap–Sihanoukville route) by the time you've got to and from the airports it's not an awful lot quicker than going by bus. There is a US$6 departure tax on domestic flights, although this is usually included in the price.

ACCOMMODATION

There are basic hotels in every provincial town, usually in fairly featureless modern concrete blocks. In general, expect to have an en-suite shower (sometimes, but not always, with hot water). The cheapest **hotel** rooms go for a bargain $7–8 or so. Most hotel rooms have double beds as standard – ask for a twin if you want separate beds.

Tourist-oriented **budget guesthouses** are springing up in towns across the country, though you'll find most of them in Phnom Penh, Siem Reap and Sihanoukville. In some places it's possible to get a bed for as little as $5 if you don't mind basic facilities or the lack of a window. Throughout the country, you'll pay around $5–7 more per night for air-conditioning, which is a bargain considering the high price of electricity. Phnom Penh, Siem Reap and Sihanoukville also have a growing number of **hostels** with cheap dorm beds for as little as $2/night. Prices given refer to the cost of a dorm bed or cheapest double room, but most establishments will offer more luxurious rooms as well. **Camping** is theoretically illegal in Cambodia, but is a possibility in some places – for example, on the beaches and islands of the south coast.

2

2

Electricity is usually supplied at 220 volts, through plugs of the two-flat-pin variety. Power cuts and surges are much less common than they once were, but not unknown.

FOOD AND DRINK

Cambodian food is similar to Thai cuisine, although usually considerably milder, with herbs being used for flavouring rather than spices, and chilli served on the side rather than being blended into the dish. Even **curry dishes**, such as the delicious coconut milk and fish **amok**, tend to be served very mild. **Stir-fries**, introduced by the Chinese, also feature on most menus, while local variations on common Vietnamese dishes can also be found, and French influence can be seen in the universal love of coffee and baguettes. **Rice** is the staple food, while **noodles** are eaten more for breakfast – when they're served as a soup – and as a snack. Hygiene standards may not match what you're used to, but produce is always fresh. At street stalls though, given the lack of refrigeration, it's as well to make sure that the food is piping hot. If you have a choice, pick somewhere that's busy.

WHERE TO EAT

The cheapest Khmer cuisine is found at **street stalls** and **markets**, which is where you'll find dishes more like the ones the locals eat at home. There are usually one or two dishes on offer at each stall. If you're ordering soup, you can pick and choose the ingredients to taste. These stalls are dirt-cheap – you can get a meal for around $1 – though the portions tend to be on

the small side. Some baguette and noodle stalls are open throughout the day, but many more crop up around sunset.

Khmer restaurants are the next step up, recognizable by their beer signs outside. In the evenings, the better ones fill up early on, and most places close soon after 9pm. Buying a selection of dishes to share is the norm: dishes typically cost $1.50–3. Some places have an English-language menu, although most don't, in which case you'll just have to practise your Khmer or point at what other diners are eating.

Tourist restaurants are plentiful in Phnom Penh, Siem Reap, Sihanoukville and many other places, though standards vary enormously. Menus generally feature Khmer dishes alongside a range of Western offerings (not always resembling what you might expect to be served back home). These places generally cost a little more than local restaurants, with mains at around $4–5 (or $7–15 in more upmarket restaurants). Western-oriented restaurants tend to stay open later, usually closing around 10–11pm, or later if they double as bars.

KHMER FOOD

A standard **meal** in Cambodia consists of rice, plus two or three other dishes, either a fish or meat dish, and a steaming bowl of soup. Flavours are dominated by fish sauce, herbs – especially lemon grass (particularly in soup) – coconut milk, galangal and tamarind.

Cambodia's national dish, **amok**, features in various forms on virtually every menu in the country – a mild yellow curry with a rich coconut-milk sauce traditionally baked in banana leaves. The classic version of amok is served with fish (**amok dtrei**), although chicken amok is now equally common.

Fish turns up in many other dishes, particularly around the Tonle Sap, where freshwater fish are abundant. Popular dishes include **dtrei chorm hoy** (steamed fish), **dtrei aing** (grilled fish) and **somlar mjew groueng dtrei** (Cambodian fish soup with herbs).

For snacks, try **noam enseum j'rook** (sticky rice, soy beans and pork served in a bamboo tube) or **noam enseum jake** (sticky rice and banana). Baguettes (**noam pang**) are always a handy snack food. Vendors have a selection of fillings, normally pork pâté, sardines, pickled vegetables and salad.

There are some surprisingly tasty **desserts** to be found at street stalls, markets and some restaurants, many of them made from rice and coconut milk. They're very cheap, so you could try a selection. Succulent **fruits** are widely available at the markets. Rambutan, papaya, pineapple, mangosteen and dragonfruit are delicious, and bananas incredibly cheap. Durians grow in abundance in Kampot, and are, according to Cambodians, the world's finest; they're in season from late March.

DRINKS

If you want to reduce the chance of stomach problems, don't drink **tap water** and don't take **ice** out on the streets, although it's generally safe in tourist bars and restaurants. Bottled, sealed water is available everywhere. Other thirst-quenchers are the standard international **soft drinks** brands and a few local variants. Freshly squeezed sugar-cane juice is another healthy roadside favourite, although the tastiest Khmer beverage has to be **dteuk krolok**, a sweet, milky fruit shake, to which locals add an egg for extra nutrition.

Cambodian **coffee** is quite unlike anything you'll have tasted back home. Beans are traditionally roasted with butter and sugar, plus various other ingredients which might include anything from rum to pork fat, giving the beverage a strange, sometimes faintly chocolatey, aroma – something of an acquired taste. It's often served (and generally tastes better) iced. If you order it white, it comes with a slug of condensed milk already in the glass. Chinese-style **tea** is commonly drunk with meals, and is served free in most restaurants. You'll only find Western tea in tourist restaurants.

The most popular local brew is **Angkor beer**, a fairly good lager, owing in part to the use of Australian technology at the Sihanoukville brewery, although there are numerous other brands available, including the confusingly soundalike (and very similar-tasting) Anchor beer.

CULTURE AND ETIQUETTE

Cambodians are extremely conservative, and regardless of their means do their very best to keep clean; you'll gain more respect if you're well turned out and modest in your dress. Men should wear tops and women avoid skimpy tops and tight shorts. Particularly offensive to Cambodians is any display of public affection between men and women: even seeing foreigners holding hands can be a source of embarrassment. Cambodia shares many of the same attitudes to **dress** and **social taboos** as other Southeast Asian cultures (see p.40).

Tipping is common only in Western restaurants – a dollar or two is generally adequate, and much appreciated.

SPORTS AND OUTDOOR ACTIVITIES

Cambodia's lack of tourist infrastructure, combined with the continuing danger of landmines, has made trekking and mountain biking difficult (if not downright dangerous) in the past. However, an increasing number of opportunities are appearing for travellers hankering to get outdoors.

For **trekking**, the place to be is the northeast, particularly Banlung and Sen Monorom, where local guides can lead groups or individuals on treks into the surrounding jungle and Virachey National Park (p.119) lasting anything from a day to a week. Another good place to hike is in the forested hills around Koh Kong, gateway to the pristine Cardamom Mountains (see p.110).

For **diving**, there are a number of PADI dive shops in Sihanoukville and nearby islands, which offer certification courses, fun dives and "discover diving" outings for beginners (see p.105).

Cycling and **kayaking** are slowly taking off in the northeast around the Mekong. Kratie and Stung Treng are the best places to organize trips. **Mountain biking** is more difficult and expensive to organize,

2

2

although several companies in Phnom Penh and Siem Reap organize bike trips from half-day tours to a couple of weeks. Grasshopper Adventures at Vicious Cycles (23 St 144; ☎012 462165, ⓦgrasshopperadventures.com) offer a six-day trip around Angkor's temples, while Spice Roads' (296 Krous Village; ☎063 964323, ⓦspiceroads.com) tours include the Cardamom Mountains.

COMMUNICATIONS

To send anything by **mail** it's best to use the main post office in Phnom Penh, as all mail from the provinces is consolidated here anyway. International post is often delivered in around a week, but can take up to a month, depending on the destination.

To **phone abroad** from Cambodia, dial ☎001 + IDD country code + area code minus first 0 + subscriber number. You can make international calls from most post offices, although these are usually expensive, as are calls made from hotel and guesthouse phones. Phone shops (which can be found around most Cambodian markets) offer cheaper calls, often using a mobile rather than a landline. It's also easy to pick up a local SIM card to access cheap international phone-call rates.

Wi-fi is widely available even in fairly out-of-the-way places; all the hotels and guesthouses listed offer it for free, as do many restaurants and cafés. There are **internet cafés** in all major towns; prices vary considerably, but are usually $0.50–1/hr.

CRIME AND SAFETY

The **security situation** in Cambodia has improved significantly over the last few years and all areas covered in this Guide are safe to travel in, but be very aware of the fact that Cambodia is one of the most heavily mined countries in the world, and also has significant quantities of unexploded ordnance (UXO) lying around.

Mines and ordnance apart, there is still a culture of guns in Cambodia, and there have been incidents of armed robbery

> ### CAMBODIA ONLINE
> ⓦ**mekong.net/cambodia** Documents the dark side of Cambodia's recent history, and contains a photo gallery and biographies of some of those who survived the Khmer Rouge atrocities, as well as some travelogues.
> ⓦ**canbypublications.com** Online version of the free tourist guides available in Phnom Penh, Sihanoukville and Siem Reap, full of up-to-date information about food, lodging and transport.
> ⓦ**phnompenhpost.com** Website of Cambodia's leading daily English-language newspaper.

against locals and tourists alike. **Gun crime** is a regular occurrence in Phnom Penh (although considerably less common elsewhere in the country), usually reaching a peak at festival times, most notably Khmer New Year. Don't be paranoid, but, equally, be aware that a small but significant number of visitors continue to be mugged at gunpoint (and occasionally shot), even in busy and touristed areas. Given this, it's a very good idea to keep all valuables well out of sight. If you are unfortunate enough to find yourself being robbed, on no account resist – the consequences if you do so could possibly be fatal. It's also worth making sure that all bags are hidden between your legs if travelling by moto – snatch-and-grab robberies have also been reported, with victims occasionally being pulled off the back of motos by the straps of their bags during attempted grabs.

There are no countrywide **emergency numbers** in Cambodia – every town or district has its own set of numbers for emergency police, fire and ambulance services (where such services are available). In an emergency the best thing to do is recruit the help of staff at your guesthouse or hotel and let them guide you.

There are plenty of civilian and military **police** hanging around, whose main function appears to be imposing arbitrary fines or tolls for motoring "offences". Of the two, the **civilian police**, who wear blue or khaki uniforms, are more helpful. Military police wear black-and-white armbands. If find yourself in need of actual police assistance, your best bet is the **tourist police** offices in major cities; they generally speak some English.

LANDMINES

The war has ended, but the killing continues. Years of guerrilla conflict have left Cambodia the most densely mined country in the world. The statistics are horrendous: up to six million **landmines** in the country; more than forty thousand amputees; and hundreds of further mine victims every year. The worst affected areas are the province of Battambang and the border regions adjacent to Thailand in the northwest, namely Banteay Meanchey, Pailin and Preah Vihear provinces.

Although the risk is very real for those who work in the fields, the threat to tourists is minimal. The main **tourist areas** are clear of mines, and even in the heavily mined areas, towns and roads are safe. The main danger occurs when striking off into fields or forests, so stick to known safe paths. If you must cross a dubious area, use a local guide, or at least ask the locals "**mee-un meen dtay?**" ("Are there mines here?"). Look out for the red mine-warning signs, and on no account touch anything suspicious.

MEDICAL CARE AND EMERGENCIES

Clinics and hospitals in Phnom Penh and Siem Reap are equipped to deal with most ailments, but generally medical facilities are poor. For serious **medical emergencies**, it's best to try to get your insurance company to transfer you to Bangkok. In a crisis it's best to enlist the help of your hotel, and secondly to immediately contact your travel insurance company back home for additional back-up and support.

Street-corner **pharmacies** are well stocked with basic supplies, and money rather than a prescription gives easy access to anything available, though beware of out-of-date medication. Standard shop hours (see p.74) apply at most places, but some stay open in the evening. More reputable operations with English- and French-speaking pharmacists can be found in Phnom Penh and Siem Reap, where a wider variety of specialized drugs is available.

INFORMATION AND MAPS

Cambodia has a network of basic **tourist offices**, although they're starved of resources and generally don't have much information (even if they're open, which often they're not), so it's better to ask at local guesthouses.

Most **maps** of Cambodia are horribly inaccurate and/or out of date. Far and away the best is Reise Know-How's Kambodscha map (that's "Cambodia" in German), beautifully drawn on un-rippable waterproof paper, and as detailed and up to date as you could hope for, given Cambodia's ever-developing road network.

MONEY AND BANKS

Cambodia's official unit of currency is the **riel**, abbreviated to "r". **Notes** come in denominations of 100, 200, 500, 1000, 2000, 5000, 10,000, 20,000, 50,000 and 100,000. US dollars are used throughout the country as a second currency, interchangeable with riel at an almost universally recognized rate of $1 = 4000r. Prices are quoted in a mix of dollars and riel (or sometimes both). In practice, it's absolutely fine to pay in either dollars or riel (calculated according to the $1 = 4000r exchange rate), or even in a combination of the two (equally, you'll often be given change in a mix of currencies). It's a bit of a headspin to start with, but worth getting to grips with as soon as you can in order to avoid rip-offs or misunderstandings. Note too that the Cambodian economy runs entirely on paper. There are no riel **coins** in circulation, and US coins aren't recognized either. In addition, **Thai baht**, abbreviated to "B", are widely used in the border areas.

The easiest way of accessing funds in Cambodia is via the country's good network of **ATMs** (money is dispensed in dollars). You'll find Canadia and Acleda ATMs in every town of any consequence (both accept foreign Visa and

2

KHMER

Khmer is the national language of Cambodia. Unusually for the region, it is not a tonal language, which theoretically makes it easier to master. However, the difficulty lies with pronunciation, as there are both vowels and consonant clusters that are pronounced unlike any sounds in English. What follows here is a phonetic approximation widely used for teaching Khmer. (People and places throughout this chapter follow the commonly used romanized spellings rather than the phonetic system used below.)

PRONUNCIATION

Most consonants follow English pronunciation, except the following:

bp a sharp "p" sound, between the English "b" and "p"
dt a sharp "t" sound, between the English "d" and "t"
hs soft "h"
n'y/ñ as in "canyon"
a as in "ago"
aa as in "bar"
ai as in "Thai"
ao as in "Lao"

ay as in "pay"
ee as in "see"
eu as in the expression of disgust "uugh"
i as in "fin"
o as in "long"
oa as in "moan"
oo as in "shoot"
ou similar to "cow"
OO as in "look"
u as in "fun"

GREETINGS AND BASIC PHRASES

Hello	soo-a s'day	Car	laan toit
How are you?	sok sa-bai jee-a dtay?	Bicycle	gong
		Bank	tor-nee-a-gee-a
Fine, thanks	sok sa-bai jee-a dtay	Post office	bprai-sa-nee
Goodbye	lee-a hou-ee	Passport	li-keut ch'lorng dain
Excuse me	som dtoh	Hotel	son-ta-gee-a
Please	som	Motorbike taxi	moto/motodub
Thank you	or-kOOn	Restaurant	poa-cha-nee-ya-taan
Can you speak English?	nee'ak jeh ni-yee-ay reu dtay?		
I don't understand	k'nyom s'dup meun baan dtay	Please stop here	soam chOOp tee neeh
Yes (male)	baht	Left/right	ch'wayng/s'dam
Yes (female)	jahs	Do you have any rooms?	nee'ak mee-un bon-dtOOp dtay?
No	dtay	How much is it?	t'lai bpon maan?
Where is the ...?	... noo-ee- naa?	Cheap/expensive	taok/t'lai
Ticket	som-bot	Single room	bon-dtOOp
Airport	jom nort yoo-un hoh/aa-gaah-sa-yee-un-taan	A/c	graiy moo-ay maa-seen dtro-chey-at
		Electric fan	dong-harl
Boat (no engine)	dtook	Mosquito net	mOOng
Boat (with engine)	karnowt	Toilet paper	gra-daah
Bus/coach	laan tom/laan krong	Telephone	dtoo-ra-sup
Taxi	dtak-see		

MasterCards), plus various other ATMs in larger places. Note, however, that all charge a commission fee of up to $5. **Credit-card advances** are available in Phnom Penh, Siem Reap, Sihanoukville and Battambang, but don't rely on them as a source of cash, as systems are unreliable.

OPENING HOURS AND HOLIDAYS

Opening hours vary, and even posted "official" times tend to be flexible. In theory, **office hours** are Monday to Saturday 7.30am to 5.30pm, with a siesta of at least two hours from around 11.30am. **Banking hours** are generally Monday to Friday 8.30am to 3.30pm, and many banks

EMERGENCIES

Help!	*choo-ee!*
Are there any mines here?	*mee-un meen dtay?*
Accident	*kroo-ah t'nak*
Please call a doctor	*soam hao kroo bphet moak*
Hospital	*moo-un dtee bphet*
Police station	*bpohs bpoli*

NUMBERS

1	*moi*	11, 12, 13, etc	*dop moi/moi don dop, dop bpee/ bpee don dop, dop bai/bai don-dop*
2	*bpee*		
3	*bpai*		
4	*bpoo-oun*	20	*m'pay*
5	*bprahm*	30, 40, 50, etc	*saam seup, sai seup, haa seup*
6	*bprahm-moi*	100	*moi roy*
7	*bprahm bpee/ bprahm bpeul*	101	*moi roy moi*
8	*bprahm-bai*	200, 300, 400, etc	*bpee roy, bai roy, bpoo-oun roy*
9	*bprahm-bpoo -oun*	1000	*moi bpoa-un*
10	*dop*	10,000	*moi meun*

FOOD AND DRINKS GLOSSARY

lerk gai-o	Cheers!
dtai bon-lai soam	Only vegetables, please
k'nyom niam sait dtey, sait dt'ray	I don't eat meat or fish
k'nyom chong …	I'd like …

Rice and noodles

geautiev	noodle soup
mee chaa	fried noodles
bai	cooked rice
bai chaa	fried rice

Fish, meat and vegetables

bong-kong	shrimp/prawn
bon-lai	vegetables
bpayng boh	tomato
bpoat	corn
dom-loang barang	potato
dtee-a	fish
dt'ray	duck
dtray-meuk	squid
g'daam	crab
moa-un	chicken
sait	meat

sait goa	beef
sait j'rook	pork

Basics

bpong	egg
bpong moa-un chien	fried eggs
dtao-oo	tofu
m'tayh	chilli
nOOm-bpung	bread
om-beul	salt
plai cher	fruit
s'gor	sugar

Drinks

bee-yair	beer
dteuk dtai	tea
dteuk groatch-grobaight	orange juice
dteuk doing	coconut milk
dteuk k'nai choo	palm wine
dteuk sot moi dorb	bottle of water
dteuk om bpow	sugar-cane juice
dteuk sot	drinking water
ka-fei dteuk doh goa	coffee with milk
gaa-fay khmao	coffee (black)
ot dak dteuk kork	no ice

are also open on Saturday morning. **Post offices** (7am–5pm, or later), markets, **shops** (7am–8pm, or later), travel agents and many tourist offices open every day.

PUBLIC HOLIDAYS

January 1 International New Year's Day
January 7 Victory Day, celebrating the liberation of Phnom Penh in 1979 from the Khmer Rouge
February (variable) Meak Mochea, celebrating Buddhist teachings and precepts
March 8 International Women's Day
April 13/14 (variable) Choul Chhnam (Khmer New Year)
April/May (variable) Visaka Bochea, celebrating the birth, enlightenment and passing into nirvana of the Buddha

2

May 1 Labour Day
May (variable) Bon Chroat Preah Nongkoal, the "Royal Ploughing Ceremony"
May 13–15 (variable) King Sihamoni's Birthday
June 1 International Children's Day
June 18 The Queen Mother's Birthday
September 24 Constitution Day
Late Sept/early Oct (variable) Pchum Ben, "Ancestors' Day"
October 15 King Father's Commemoration Day, celebrating the memory of Norodom Sihanouk
October 23 Anniversary of the Paris Peace Accords
October 30–November 1 (variable) King Sihanouk's Birthday
November 9 Independence Day
Early November Bon Om Toeuk, "Water Festival"
December 10 UN Human Rights Day

FESTIVALS

Festivals tend to be fixed by the lunar calendar, so dates vary from year to year.
Choul Chhnam (April 13 or 14) Khmer New Year is the most significant festival of the year, a time when families get together, homes are spring-cleaned and people flock to the temples with elaborate offerings.
Pchum Ben (late Sept/early Oct) "Ancestors' Day" is one of the most important events in the festive calendar. Families make offerings to their ancestors in the fifteen days leading up to it, and celebrations take place in temples on the day itself.
Bon Om Toeuk (early Nov) The "Water Festival" is celebrated every year when the current of the Tonle Sap, which swells so much during the rainy season that it actually pushes water upstream, reverses and flows back into the Mekong River. The centre of festivities is Phnom Penh's riverbank, where everyone gathers to watch boat racing, an illuminated boat parade and fireworks.

Phnom Penh and around

It's easy to dismiss Cambodia's capital, **PHNOM PENH**, as a one-night stopover, but don't. The city sprawls west from the confluence of the Mekong and Tonle Sap rivers, and first impressions of trafficky boulevards and generic low-rise, concrete blocks can be disheartening. But the centre of Phnom Penh has huge appeal, its French influence evident in the

open-fronted colonial shophouses lining the streets, the occasional majestic monument or public building animating the cityscape, and a mind-boggling number of bars, restaurants and cafés. The Phnom Penhois are open and friendly, and the city is small enough to get to know quickly. Phnom Penh may not be rich in world-class tourist attractions – the main sights can be covered in a couple of days – but many visitors end up lingering, for its food and drink scene, surprisingly good shopping, Mekong river setting and laidback atmosphere.

WHAT TO SEE AND DO

Phnom Penh **city centre** can be loosely defined as the area between Monivong Boulevard to its west the Tonle Sap River to the east, and stretching north to Chroy Chung Va Bridge and south to Boueng Keng Kang (BKK) neighbourhood, below Sihanouk Boulevard. Its tourist hub is scenic Sisowath Quay, from where most sights and monuments are easily accessible, while a short tuk-tuk ride south is the up-and-coming Russian Market district.

Sisowath Quay and around

Marking the eastern edge of Phnom Penh, Sisowath Quay, which runs north and south of the centre, is lined with tall palms on one side, and bars, cafés and restaurants on the other. Always lively, it becomes the city's social centre by evening, with aerobics classes, food vendors and an atmospheric **night market** at the northern end by the Tourist Docks. Here, numerous boat companies offer **sunset cruises** along the Tonle Sap, or boats can be rented along the shore. The small, fairly nondescript square of land at the junction of **Sisowath Quay** and Street 184, in front of the Royal Palace, is where Cambodians used to congregate to listen to declarations and speeches from the monarch, and where Khmer families still gather at evenings and weekends, with picnics, games, kite-flying and beer the order of the day.

The Royal Palace

Behind the park, set back from the riverbank on Sothearos Boulevard, stand the **Royal Palace** and adjacent **Silver**

Pagoda (daily 8–11am & 2–5pm; $10, English-speaking guide $10), the city's finest examples of twentieth-century Khmer-influenced architecture. Both are one-storey structures – until the Europeans arrived, standing above another's head (the most sacred part of the body) was strictly prohibited.

The **palace** is itself off-limits, but it's possible to visit several buildings within the compound, even when the king is around. A blue flag flies when he is in residence.

At the entrance, visitors are directed to the palace complex first, an oasis of order and calm. Head straight for the central main building, the exquisite **Throne Hall**, guarded on either side by seven-headed naga (serpents). Inside, the ceiling is adorned with colourful murals recounting the Reamker, Cambodia's version of the Hindu legend Ramayana.

As you leave the Throne Hall via the main stairs, on your left you'll see the **Royal Waiting Room** where the king waited on coronation day and mounted his elephant for the ceremonial procession. A similar building on the right, the **Royal Treasury**, houses the crown jewels, royal regalia and other valuable items. In front and to the left, bordering Sothearos Boulevard, is the **Dancing** or **Moonlight Pavilion**, built for dancing performances and where the king could address his subjects.

Across the complex, back towards the Silver Pagoda, stands the quaint, grey **Pavilion of Napoleon III** (currently closed to the public). Originally erected at the residence of Empress Eugénie in Egypt, it was packed up and transported to Cambodia as a gift to King Norodom, who constructed the first palace here in 1866. The internal wall of the **Silver Pagoda courtyard** is decorated with a richly coloured and detailed mural of the Ramayana myth, painted in 1903–4 by forty Khmer artists. The Silver Pagoda takes its name from the floor of the temple, completely covered with silver tiles – 5329, to be exact – although a protective carpet covers most of it. It's also known as Wat Preah Keo Morakot ("Temple of the Emerald Buddha"), after the famous **Emerald Buddha** statue, made from Baccarat crystal, which resides here.

Returning to the stupa-filled courtyard, seek out the artificial Mount Mondap to see a huge Buddha footprint (Buddhapada), a gift from Sri Lanka.

The National Museum
Just north of the Royal Palace on Street 13, at the corner of Street 178, the grand, red-painted structure that houses the **National Museum** (daily 8am–5pm, last admission 4.30pm; $5, audioguide $5, camera/video (courtyard only) $1/$3; English-speaking guides $6; ☎023 211753, @cambodiamuseum.info) is a combination of twentieth-century French design and Cambodian craftsmanship. Its four galleries, set around a tranquil courtyard, shelter an impressive array of relics, art and sculpture covering Cambodian history from the sixth century to the present day – remarkable considering it was abandoned during the Khmer Rouge years, its contents looted and the museum director murdered. Highlights include a tenth-century sandstone garuda (mythical bird), over 2m high, a 3m-tall eight-armed Vishnu and intricate bas-reliefs depicting Buddha incarnations.

A more recent exhibit is the cabin of a nineteenth-century royal boat. Also look out for a wall panel looted, then recovered, from the twelfth-century Angkor temple Banteay Chhmar.

South to Independence Monument
On Sothearos Boulevard, just south of the Royal Palace, you'll come to a park, in the middle of which stands the **Cambodia–Vietnam Friendship Monument**, commemorating the defeat of the Khmer Rouge in 1979. The southern tip of the park, just after **Wat Botum**, is crossed by Sihanouk Boulevard, lined with colonial-era buildings. Following Sihanouk Boulevard west brings you to **Independence Monument**, on the roundabout at the junction with Norodom Boulevard, built in 1958 to celebrate Cambodia's independence from France. Just southwest is **Wat Langka** and the start of Boueng Keng Kang, or **BKK**, a neighbourhood popular with expats and home to an increasing number of hotels, bars and restaurants.

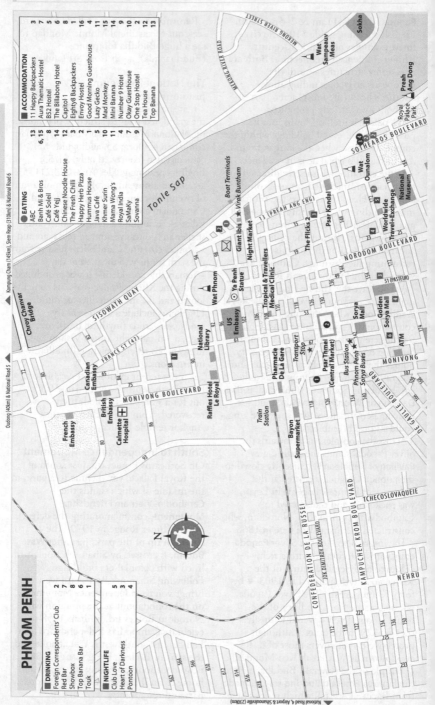

PHNOM PENH

■ DRINKING
Foreign Correspondents' Club	2
Red Bar	7
Showbox	8
Top Banana Bar	6
Touk	1

■ NIGHTLIFE
Club Love	5
Heart of Darkness	3
Pontoon	4

● EATING
ABC	13
Banh Mi & Bros	6, 15
Café Soleil	8
Café Yejj	12
Chinese Noodle House	14
The Fresh Chilli	3
Happy Herb Pizza	2
Hummus House	1
Java Café	5
Khmer Surin	10
Mama Wong's	11
Royal India	4
SaMaKy	7
Sovanna	9

■ ACCOMMODATION
11 Happy Backpackers	3
Aura Thematic Hostel	7
B52 Hostel	5
The Billabong Hotel	8
Capitol 1	1
Eighty8 Backpackers	16
Envoy Hostel	1
Good Morning Guesthouse	4
Lazy Gecko	11
Mad Monkey	15
Mini Banana	14
Number 9 Hotel	9
Okay Guesthouse	10
One Stop Hostel	2
Tea House	12
Top Banana	13

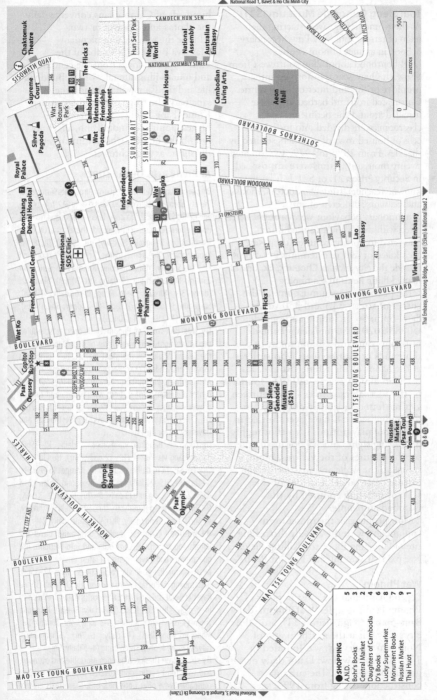

National Road 1, Bavet & Ho Chi Minh City

SAMDECH HUN SEN

Chaktomuk
Theatre

SISOWATH QUAY

The Flicks 3

246

Hun Sen Park

Naga
World

National
Assembly

Australian
Embassy

NATIONAL ASSEMBLY STREET

Supreme
Court

258

Wat
Botum
Park

Cambodian-
Vietnamese
Friendship
Monument

Meta House

Cambodian
Living Arts

Aeon
Mall

Wat
Botum

SURAMARIT

SIHANOUK BVD

SOTHEAROS BOULEVARD

Silver
Pagoda

Royal
Palace

Roomchang
Dental Hospital

Independence
Monument

Wat
Langka

NORODOM BOULEVARD

S1 (PASTEUR)

Lao
Embassy

Vietnamese Embassy

International
SOS Clinic

Help+
Pharmacy

French Cultural Centre

MONIVONG BOULEVARD

The Flicks 1

MONIVONG BOULEVARD

Wat Ko

Thai Embassy, Monivong Bridge, Tonle Bati (35km) & National Road 2

BOULEVARD

Capitol
Bus Stop

SIHANOUK BOULEVARD

MAO TSE TOUNG BOULEVARD

Psar
Orussey

NOUKAN

JOSEPH BROZ TITO

YOUGOSLAVIE

Toul Sleng
Genocide
Museum
(S21)

Russian
Market
(Psar Toul
Tom Poung)

CHARLES

Olympic
Stadium

Psar
Olympic

MONIREITH BOULEVARD

BOULEVARD

LA7 (TEP ANI)

MAO TSE TOUNG BOULEVARD

MAO TSE TOUNG BOULEVARD

Psar
Damkor

National Road 3, Kampot & Choeung Ek (12km)

0   500
metres

2

Toul Sleng Genocide Museum (S21)

As the Khmer Rouge were starting their reign of terror, Toul Svay Prey Secondary School, in a quiet Phnom Penh neighbourhood about 2km southwest from Sisowath Quay, was transformed into a primitive prison and interrogation centre. Corrugated iron and barbed wire were installed around the perimeter, and classrooms were divided into individual cells or housed rows of prisoners secured by shackles. From 1975 to 1979, an estimated twenty thousand victims were imprisoned in **Security Prison 21**, or S21 as it became known. Teachers, students, doctors, monks and peasants suspected of anti-revolutionary behaviour were brought here, often with their spouses and children. Subjected to horrific tortures, they were then killed or sent to extermination camps outside the city such as **Choeung Ek**, one of many killing fields in Cambodia.

The prison is now a **museum**, at the corner of streets 113 and 350 (daily 8am–5pm; $6 including audioguide; ☏088 8202037, ⊛tuolslenggenocide museum.com) and a monument to the thousands of Cambodians who suffered at the hands of the Khmer Rouge. It's been left almost exactly as it was found by the Vietnamese forces – the fourteen victims found hideously disfigured in the individual cells have been buried in the school playground. It's a thoroughly depressing sight, and it's not until you see the pictures of the victims, blood stains on the walls and instruments of torture that you get any idea of the scale of suffering endured by the Cambodian people.

Most people visit the museum in conjunction with the equally distressing site of Choeung Ek or the Killing Fields, (see p.85), 12km outside Phnom Penh.

Wat Phnom

Legend has it that the most popular of Phnom Penh's temples, **Wat Phnom** (daily 8am–5pm; foreign visitors $1), atop the city's only hill at the northern end of Norodom Boulevard, was founded in 1373 by a local widow, Daun (lady or grandmother) Penh. The current construction, dating from 1926, sees hundreds of Cambodians converge daily for photos and a prayer or two.

Inside the temple, a resplendent Maitreya Buddha ("Buddha of the Future") looks down from the central dais, and murals illustrate tales of the Buddha's life and the Ramayana. Behind the main sanctuary, the stupa of fifteenth-century Khmer King Ponhea Yat remains the highest point in Phnom Penh, a fact not lost on the French, who commandeered the shrine as a watchtower.

ARRIVAL AND DEPARTURE

By plane Phnom Penh International Airport lies 9km west of the city, about 30–60min away. Taxis charge $12, tuk-tuks $9 and motos $3–5 for the journey. Licensed taxis and tuk-tuks operate from a counter directly outside the terminal building.
Destinations Bangkok (10 daily; 1hr 10min); Dubai via Yangon (daily; 9hr); Hanoi (daily; 3hr 10min); Ho Chi Minh City (4–5 daily; 45min); Hong Kong (1–2 daily; 2hr 25min); Kuala Lumpur (4 daily; 1hr 50min); Shanghai (daily; 3hr 40min); Siem Reap (5–6 daily; 45min); Singapore (4 daily; 2hr); Tapei (1–2 daily; 3hr 15min); Vientiane (1–2 daily; 1hr 20min).
By bus Buses out of Phnom Penh operate scheduled departures from their own offices or depots located near the Central Market or the night market. Bus companies usually send a tuk-tuk to collect you from your guesthouse. Arriving into town, most buses draw up near the southwest corner of Central Market, from where moto and tuk-tuk drivers are eager to drive you into the centre of town. Bus schedules change frequently; ask at guesthouses and travel agents for the latest.
Destinations Bangkok via Poipet (6 daily; 12–15hr); Battambang via Pursat (10–12 daily; 6hr); Ho Chi Minh City via Bavet (16 daily; around 6hr); Kampot (5–7 daily; 3–4hr); Kep (5–7 daily; 4–5hr); Kompong Cham (2–4 daily; 2–3hr); Koh Kong (3 daily; 6–7hr); Kratie (2–3 daily; 6–7hr); Siem Reap (hourly; 6–7hr); Sihanoukville (hourly; 4–5hr); Stung Treng (daily; 9hr); Vientiane (daily; 24hr).
By minibus Countless minibus companies travel the length and breadth of Cambodia and into Vietnam. Ask guesthouses and travel agents for latest times.
Destinations Bangkok via Poipet (4–5 daily; 12–15hr); Battambang via Pursat (5–6 daily; 6hr); Ho Chi Minh City via Bavet (several daily; 6–7hr); Kampot (8 daily; 3–4hr); Kep (4–5 daily; 4hr); Koh Kong (2–3 daily; 5–6hr); Kompong Thom (3 daily; 4hr); Kratie (2–3 daily; 4hr 30min); Sen Monorom/Mondulkiri (4 daily; 6–7hr); Sihanoukville (several daily; 4–5hr); Stung Treng (4–5 daily; 9hr).
By share taxi These can be uncomfortable and cramped, and with most destinations covered by bus and minibus companies who offer hotel pick-ups, share taxis are not

necessary. If want to travel by share taxi and are going a long way, get to Central Market early, as drivers like to complete the trip in daylight.

By boat Boats dock at the terminals just east of the post office on Sisowath Quay. Boats leave at 7.30am for Siem Reap. At $35, it's pricier than the bus, but for many, the experience is worth it. Journey times vary slightly, subject to variations in river flow. To Chau Doc, for Vietnam, tickets cost $25–29. Boats have allocated seating; several companies operate the routes so buy tickets in advance at the dock or via a guesthouse/travel agent.

Destinations Chau Doc (3 daily; 4hr 30min); Siem Reap (1 daily; 7hr).

By train An enjoyable, reasonably punctual, if limited, train service travels between Phnom Penh and Sihanoukville and stops in Takeo and Kampot. At the time of writing, it leaves Phnom Penh once a day Fri–Sun with extra services during public holidays; buy tickets at the train station (closed Tues), near *Raffles* hotel.

Destinations Kampot (1 daily Fri–Sun; 4hr 30min–5hr); Sihanoukville (I daily Fri–Sun; 7hr); Takeo (1 daily Fri–Sun; 1hr 30 min–2hr).

INFORMATION

Tourist information The airport has a tourist information desk (variable hours), with a list of accommodation and travel agents. There's a tourist information office (daily 8am–6.30pm) near Chaktomuk Theatre; although friendly, it mainly touts city tours. Most guesthouses and hotels provide reliable information.

Publications The free quarterly *Phnom Penh Visitors' Guide* (@ canbypublications.com) and *Phnom Penh Pocket Guide* (@ cambodiapocketguide.com) have a wealth of information on activities and sights around the city, plus a useful map. You'll find them at numerous restaurants, guesthouses and bars.

Tour agencies There is a wealth of tour agencies around Phnom Penh. While some are geared towards large groups, independent budget travellers can try Worldwide Travel & Exchange (cnr St 19 & St 172; @ 010 305094, @ info.wwte@gmail.com). Alternatively, arrange tours through a backpacker guesthouse such as *B52, Capitol 1, Mad Monkey* or *Top Banana*, which all have travel desks.

GETTING AROUND

By moto Motorcycle taxis, or motos, are inexpensive and the quickest and most convenient way of getting around the city. Expect to pay $1–2 for a short hop, or up to $3 for a longer journey within the city. You can also hire a moto driver for a day – explain to the driver exactly where you want to go and negotiate a price beforehand. A good English-speaker will charge around $20–30/day for his services as driver and guide.

By taxi Taxis are not hailed on the street – you can either book them over the phone or pick one up at Monivong Boulevard near Central Market/Psar Thmei, where they tend to gather. Negotiate the fare in advance. Taxis are also available for hire for the day: expect to pay $30–70 depending on distance travelled. Taxi DCP Phnom Penh (@ 010 900150, (@ taxidcpphnompenh.com) offers a 24hr taxi service with reliable English-speaking, and female, drivers.

By tuk-tuk Tuk-tuks are everywhere in Phnom Penh, relatively zippy and, for groups of two or more, usually the cheapest way to get around. Negotiate the fare in advance, and expect to pay around $2–4 per trip within the city centre.

By bike and motorbike The many bike rental outlets near *Capitol Guesthouse* charge around $3/day. Lucky! Lucky! (413 Monivong Blvd; @ 023 212788) charges $5/day for a 110cc moped, $11/day for a 250cc off-road bike, with discounts on longer rentals. Helmets are provided but no insurance. It's worth paying the token amount ($0.50/2000r) to park in the many moto compounds around the city; thieves are rather partial to unattended Hondas.

By cyclo Unique to Phnom Penh, cyclos are a relaxing way to get around. You'll find a few along St 158 near *Billabong Hotel* near Sorya Mall, and around Central Market.

ACCOMMODATION

The backpacker vibe can be found predominantly around St 258 and St 172 in central Phnom Penh and increasingly around St 278 in the BKK neighbourhood.

CENTRAL PHNOM PENH

11 Happy Backpackers 87–89 St 136 @ 088 777 7421, @ 11happybackpackers.com. Big, friendly place with over forty rooms and fifty dorm beds, a mix of no-bunk, a/c dorms and simple en-suite fan and a/c rooms (some without windows) plus a spacious, leafy rooftop restaurant-bar with pool table, comfy chairs and lots of nooks for hiding away. It also houses the community-run Flicks 2 cinema, and the tour desk can organize visas and tickets. Dorms $5, doubles $10

Aura Thematic Hostel 205A St 19 @ 023 986211, @ aurahostel.com. Behind the Royal Palace, this immaculate hostel has male, female and mixed dorms, all en suite and with a/c, each individually designed – think Japanese art to jungle prints. Beds are pod-style, single or double, and there's a private four-bed VIP room too. Upstairs the *Eluvium Rooftop Lounge* is open from 5pm to non-guests, with happy hours (5–8pm) and daily events. $1 breakfasts. Dorms $5

B52 Hostel 52 St 172 @ 070 323285, @ lb52 .phnompenh@gmail.com. A breath of fresh air on St 172, this new backpackers has two ten-bed dorms, one with a balcony, a six-bed female dorm (all with lockers) and a handful of private rooms. All are en suite and with hot water. There's a sociable and cheap bar-restaurant below, and a helpful travel desk. Dorms $5, doubles $18

2

★**The Billabong Hotel** 5 St 158 ☎023 223703, ⓦ thebillabonghotel.com. Five minutes from Central Market, this hybrid hotel-hostel with a big pool has a great selection of single, double and superior private rooms (breakfast included), plus spotless, spacious dorms, including a female-only one, all en-suite with a/c, balcony, lockers and free towels. The sociable poolside bar and restaurant serves good Western and local food (breakfast from $2, fried rice $3.50). Dorms $6, doubles $35

Capitol 1 14 St 182 ☎023 548409, ⓦ capitoltourscambodia .com. The *Capitol* empire is a backpacking institution in Phnom Penh. Backpackers come here (entrance on St 107) for the cheap accommodation, food and tours. Staff can help with onward travel. They have one of the most comprehensive selections of inexpensive tours, but check they're not cramming too many sights into one day. Rooms are a bit cell-like but are plentiful, and the cheapest come with shared bathrooms (a/c rooms $10). Doubles $5

★**Eighty8 Backpackers** St 88 just off Monivong Blvd ☎023 500 2440, ⓦ 88backpackers.com. In a slightly out-the-way location, but still within walking distance of Wat Phnom and the riverside, this boutique backpackers has a pool and stylish open bar and restaurant with an extensive menu. Five dorm rooms include one with sliding metal doors for a private sleeping space, a female dorm, and cheaper beds in the "above bar" mixed dorm. Double and family rooms all have a/c and hot water, some with balconies. Dorms $6.40, doubles $24

Good Morning Guesthouse 42 St 23 ☎093 866999, ⓦ goodmorningguesthouse.com. This new, family-run guesthouse in a quiet but central spot near the palace, with a lovely garden and private rooms, some with a/c. Cheapest have shared bathrooms, $10 gets you an en-suite fan double, $13 with a/c, and the $20 quad room is great value; all have hot water. There's a great restaurant, particularly for Cambodian food plus rice wine made by one of the owner's mothers, and a free drink with meals during happy hour (4–7pm). Helpful travel desk and free pick-up for bus arrivals; airport pick-up $7 (airport price $9). Doubles $7

★**Lazy Gecko Guesthouse** 1D St 258 ☎078 786025, ⓦ lazygecko.asia. Recently revamped, this long-standing backpacker guesthouse is a top pick. Mixed and female-only dorms have king-sized beds and en-suite hot water bathrooms, and they have private fan and a/c rooms. The buzzing café below serves gastro pub food (mac'n'cheese $4, Greek salad $3.50) and hosts DJ nights and barbecues, with a microbrewery on the cards. Dorms $5, doubles $12

Number 9 Hotel 7C St 258 ☎023 984999, ⓦ number9hotel. com. One of Phnom Penh's first "boutique" backpackers, with a sleek and modern bar-restaurant, a/c rooms and rooftop hot tub and pool table on the first floor. Doubles $20

Okay Guesthouse 3BE St 258 ☎012 300804, ⓦ okay-guesthouse.com. A friendly, family-run hostel and

lively backpacker restaurant. Rooms are basic but clean, and they run a useful travel desk. *Same Same* next door has similar prices, and a nice communal area but far less appealing rooms. Doubles $12

One Stop Hostel 85 Sisowath Quay ☎098 991184, ⓦ onederz.com/phnom-penh. Scrupulously clean, friendly hostel facing the Tonle Sap River with a variety of a/c dorms, with and without windows, and two female dorms. All have large lockers and comfy beds with personal socket, and lamp. Free tea and coffee in the lounge. Dorms $7

BOUENG KENG KANG (BKK)

★**Envoy Hostel** 32 St 322 ☎023 220840, ⓦ envoyhostel .com/phnompenh. Super-clean a/c dorms and private bunk and double rooms, modern bathrooms, a rooftop terrace and helpful staff give this hostel, in a converted villa, an edge in the increasingly popular BKK neighbourhood. With a large communal area, kitchen facilities and several balcony chill-out areas, it's sociable and relaxed. Dorms $7, doubles $24

Mad Monkey 26 St 302 ☎023 987091, ⓦ madmonkey hostels.com. This flashpacker hostel occupies two buildings across from each other and has gained a rep for its party pool, chill-out areas and lively bar and restaurant. The a/c en-suite dorms have extra-large bunk beds and private rooms are smart. Dorms $7, doubles $18

Mini Banana 135 St 51 ☎023 726854, ⓦ mini-banana .asia. Tucked away off St 51, this has one of the best hostel restaurants in town, with a French chef rustling up gourmet burgers and more. A sixteen-bed a/c dorm has three bathrooms, and seven private rooms include two with a/c. Dorms $7, doubles $13

Top Banana 9E St 278 ☎012 885572, ⓦ topbanana.biz. An original Phnom Penh party haunt, *Top Banana* remains a backpacker favourite. Rooms and dorms have been upgraded, and the newly designed bar and lounge area continues to attract non-guests. Dorms $6, doubles $14

EATING

Street stalls, where you can fill up on noodle dishes or filled baguettes, spring up in different places at various times of day: markets are a good place for a daytime selection, and later, the riverside and night market. Phnom Penh also has plenty of reasonably priced restaurants aimed at expats and tourists, with more opening up all the time; expect to pay $4–7 for a simple main course.

CENTRAL PHNOM PENH & RIVERFRONT
The Fresh Chilli 4 St 172 ☎077 787864. It's Cambodian food only at this locally run restaurant whose tagline is "We support Khmer food". From fried tarantulas to delicious stir-fried fish with ginger ($4.75), it's a welcome addition to busy St 172. Daily 9am–11pm.

Happy Herb Pizza 345 Sisowath Quay ☎012 921915, ⓦhappyherbpizza.com. Cheap breakfasts, burgers and Cambodian food as well as pizzas and pastas in this riverfront restaurant. Pizzas start from $4.50 and can be made "happy" with a marijuana-infused base. Daily 8am–11pm.

Hummus House 95 Sisowath Quay, near the night market ☎092 483759, ⓦfacebook.com/hummushousecambodia. This popular Lebanese joint is the go-to place for kebabs, meaty *shawarmas*, hummus wraps ($3) and delicious home-made bread. Daily 10.30am–10.30pm.

★**Java Café** 56 Sihanouk Blvd ☎023 987420, ⓦjavacambodia.com. Fill up on soups, salads and home-made muffins ($2) in a/c cool or unwind on the balcony overlooking the Independence Monument; the upper level also has a gallery with changing exhibitions. Daily 7am–10pm.

Royal India 21 St 111, just south of *Capitol I* guesthouse ☎012 855651. Consistently good north Indian food at economical prices is served with a smile at this simple restaurant. The halal menu is comprehensive and includes chicken and mutton curries from $3, dhal for $2 and tasty sweet and salty lassis. Daily 9.30am–9.30pm.

★**Sovanna** 2C St 21 ☎011 840055. A local favourite, with an extensive menu including grilled pork ribs ($3), stir-fried dishes like beef *lok-lak* ($4.50) and fried rice with crab ($3). Its sister restaurant, *Sovanna II*, is a few doors along. Daily 6–11am & 4–11pm.

BOUENG KENG KANG (BKK)
Café Soleil 22 St 278 ☎012 923371. This vegetarian restaurant serves both local and Western food with a menu that includes breakfast pancakes ($2.75), sandwiches from $1.75 and fruit shakes and smoothies for $2. Daily 7am–10pm.

Chinese Noodle House 553 Monivong Blvd ☎012 937805. Freshly pulled noodles, sunk into soups or fried ($2), are standouts at this no-frills food joint, and the pork and chive dumplings ($1.80) are divine. Daily 10am–10pm.

Khmer Surin 9 St 57 ☎012 887320, ⓦkhmersurin.com. kh. Stunning Khmer-Thai restaurant with walkways leading over little ponds, fountains, and romantic tables tucked away in corners. The food lives up to the decor; try the seafood *amok* ($6). Daily 10am–10pm.

★**Mama Wong's** 41 St 308 ☎097 850 8383, ⓦmamawongs.com. Dumpling and noodle house on bustling St 308. The menu is universally good, particularly the spring onion pancakes ($2) and prawn and chive dumplings ($4.50). Most mains $5. Daily 11am–11pm.

SaMaKy 9E St 51 & 278 ☎070 600017, ⓦfacebook.com/samakyrestaurant. At this friendly open-sided restaurant opposite Wat Langka, chefs serve up a good mix of Western salads and Asian fusion dishes such as roast duck and noodles ($6). Daily 7am–11pm.

RUSSIAN MARKET
ABC St 360, near Tuol Sleng Prison Museum ☎015 909898. Choose which vegetables, noodles (from $.0.50/2000r) and meat (from $1.50) you want and cook it yourself at tabletop barbecues. Great fun and a local favourite. Daily 4–11pm.

Banh Mi & Bros 78 St 450 ☎085 400880, ⓦfacebook.com/banhmiandbros/. Fill up on *banh mi* (Vietnamese sandwiches) with fillings from bacon and egg ($2.20) to a packed veggie roll ($3.50). Combos with drink and dessert for $2 extra. There's another branch on 173 St 63 in BKK. Daily 10am–10pm.

Café Yejj 170 St 450, corner of market ☎092 600750, ⓦfacebook.com/CafeYejj. Social enterprise café training vulnerable youth and women, and serving everything from breakfast (from $2.75) to green curry ($5.25) and a particularly good selection of Middle Eastern dishes (falafel $4.50). Daily 8am–9pm.

DRINKING
For most Khmers, nightlife centres around an early evening meal out, followed by a burst of karaoke: you'll see plenty of karaoke restaurants around town. However, other nightlife tastes are more than catered for. You'll always find a crowd in established backpacker favourites such as *Top Banana*, *Mad Monkey* and *Pontoon*, often well into the wee hours. Street 51, between streets 174 and 154, has numerous dive bars, including outlets at the Golden Sorya Mall which serve cheap food and drinks 24hr a day. Street 308 in BKK has a more upmarket vibe, and just off the street are Bassac Lane's atmospheric if slightly pricier bars.

★**Foreign Correspondents' Club (FCC)** 363 Sisowath Quay ☎069 253222, ⓦfcccambodia.com. The balmy air, whirring ceiling fans, rooftop views and spacious armchairs invite one to spend a hot afternoon on the G&Ts (happy hour 5–7pm) in this atmospheric historic bar. Upper terrace open 4–11pm. Daily 6am–midnight.

Red Bar St 308, BKK ☎010 729655. Lively place on bar-lined St 308, there's always a good atmosphere here with $1 draught beer and $2.50 mixers during the 5–8pm happy hour. Daily 5pm–1am.

Showbox 11 St 330, near Tuol Sleng Museum ☎017 275824, ⓦfacebook.com/showboxphnompenh. In the

2

developing Toul Sleng neighbourhood, 1km from the Russian Market, this fun bar hosts live music, open-mic and comedy nights. Buy a beer before 6.30pm to enjoy free beer 6.30–7pm. Food is good value – toasties and fried rice from $2.50, or get a sausage roll and pie fix from $5. Daily 11am–midnight.

★**Top Banana Bar** 9E St 278 ☎012 885572, ⓦtopbanana.biz. If you're after a lively drink and want to meet fellow backpackers, this rooftop guesthouse bar is just the spot. Live music, beer pong, 4–8pm happy hour and dancing on the furniture are standard behaviour until the early hours. Sound like a regular and order the house speciality cocktail, wingman (dark rum and lemonade), for $2.75. Daily 8am–3am.

Touk 1st Floor, cnr Sisowath Quay and St 178 ☎012 248694. Serves cheaper drinks than its neighbour, the *FCC*, yet the river views from its wraparound balcony are every bit as good; their daily two-for-one happy hour (4.30–7.30pm) is a steal, given the riverfront setting. Daily 8am–midnight.

NIGHTLIFE

Club Love St 278, opposite *Top Banana* ⓦfacebook.com/lovephnompenh. Late-night club with guest DJs, special events and cheap drinks (happy hour 11pm–midnight) including free shots at this party favourite on St 278. It's handily air-conditioned too. Daily 11pm–4am.

Heart of Darkness 26 St 51. Overrated, but it's been here for ages and is one of those places everybody has to visit once. It can be borderline unbearably loud inside. Daily 9pm–5am.

★**Pontoon** 10 St 172, cnr St 51 ☎0101 300400, ⓦpontoonclub.com.com. Phnom Penh's largest club is a perennial favourite with the local and expat crowd, with visiting DJs (Goldie once played here), a beautiful amber bar, an intriguing range of cocktails and comfy couches to lose yourself in. They also host a popular drag show, Shameless, every Wednesday. Daily 10pm–sunrise.

ENTERTAINMENT

CINEMAS

The Flicks ⓦtheflicks.asia. Volunteer-staffed community movie houses screening Western, arthouse and Cambodian films ($3.50/person) in intimate sofa-filled a/c rooms with food to order. Flicks 1 is at 39b St 95 in BKK3, Flicks 2 is at 90 St 136 (inside *11 Happy Backpackers*).

Meta House 37 Sothearos Blvd ⓦmeta-house.com. Offers free afternoon Cambodian documentary screenings (4pm) and more mainstream nightly films (7pm; $2), as well as live music, visual poetry and art exhibitions.

TRADITIONAL ARTS

Cambodian Living Arts ☎017 998570, ⓦcambodianlivingarts.org. Traditional dance show every

night at the National Museum $15 (7pm; Oct–March Mon–Sat).

Chaktomuk Theatre Sisowath Quay ☎023 725119, ⓦfacebook.com/ChaktomukTheatre. Performances here are infrequent – check the listings in the Friday edition of the *Cambodia Daily*. The theatre also occasionally hosts Khmer plays and musical shows. Sovanna Phum, 166 St 99, a little way south of town (☎023 987564, ⓔsovannaarts @yahoo.com), promote Khmer arts and host traditional performances on Friday and Saturday evenings.

SHOPPING

BOOKSHOPS

Bohr's Books 3 Sothearos Blvd ☎012 929148, ⓦfacebook.com/bohrsbooks. New and used titles, and a decent selection of Cambodian and Southeast Asia-related guides. Daily 8am–8pm.

D's Books 79 St 240 ☎092 527028, ⓦfacebook.com/ds.books.shops. An excellent place to stock up on secondhand books (both fiction and non-fiction) in many languages. Daily 9am–9pm.

Monument Books 111 Norodom Blvd, near St 240 ☎023 223622, ⓦmonument-books.com. Huge stock of English books, papers and magazines. Additional branches at the airport and Aeon Mall. Daily 8.30am–8.30pm

MARKETS

A trip to one of the capital's numerous markets is essential, if only to buy the red-checked *krama* (traditional chequered scarf). The markets are liveliest in the morning; many vendors have a snooze at midday for a couple of hours and things wind down by 5pm.

Central Market (Psar Thmei). Expect to barter with savvy vendors at the Art Deco Central Market/Psar Thmei. Electronic goods, T-shirts, shoes and wigs are all in abundance here and it's airy and bright inside.

Russian Market (Psar Toul Tom Poung) Cnr 163 & 440 streets. A stroll around this market in the southern end of town is a colourful and often more rewarding experience, a good balance of tourist-oriented curios and stalls for locals, with jewellery, gems, food, souvenirs and furniture.

SOUVENIRS

A.N.D. 52 St 240 ☎023 224713, ⓦfacebook.com/artisandesigners. Pick up stylish fairtrade fashion made from vintage fabrics by local designers; there's another store across the road. Tree-lined St 240 is lined with similar shops, mainly selling clothes and homewares, almost all with an ethical slant. Daily 8am–8pm.

Daughters of Cambodia 321 Sisowath Quay, ⓦdaughtersofcambodia.org. Providing employment to men and women who were trafficked into the sex industry, the Daughters of Cambodia visitor centre has a ground-floor boutique selling clothes, jewellery, homewares and children's toys made by staff. There's a great riverview café and nail spa upstairs. Daily 9am–5.30pm.

SUPERMARKETS
Lucky Supermarket 160 Sihanouk Blvd ☎081 222028, ⓦluckymarketgroup.com. Vast choice of food items from cheese to chorizo at this popular chain store. Daily 8am–9.30pm.
Thai Huot 99–105 Monivong Blvd ☎023 724623, ⓦthaihuot.com. This large store is one of the best for spices, and European products. A second store is in BKK1 214 St, 63 cnr St 352. Daily 7.30am–8.30pm.

DIRECTORY
Banks and exchange There are a few ATMs at the airport and many more downtown. The best rates for changing foreign currency into riel can be found with the moneychangers around Psar Thmei. ABA, ANZ and Canadia Bank all have branches along Sihanouk Blvd between St 63 and the Olympic Stadium.
Dentists Roomchang Dental Hospital, 4 St 184 (☎023 211338, ⓦroomchang.com) offers free consultations, is reasonably priced and has English-speaking staff.
Embassies and consulates Australia, National Assembly St (☎023 213470, ⓦcambodia.embassy.gov .au); Canada, 27–29 St 75 (☎023 430813, ⓦcambodia .gc.ca); Laos, 15–17 Mao Tse Toung Blvd (☎023 997931); Thailand, 196 Norodom Blvd (☎023 726306, ⓦwww .thaiembassy.org/phnompenh); UK, 27–29 St 75 (☎023 427124; US 1 St 96 (☎023 728000, ⓦkh.usembassy.gov); Vietnam, 436 Monivong Blvd (☎023 726274, ⓦwww .vietnamembassy-cambodia.org).
Hospitals and clinics International SOS Clinic at 161 St 51 (☎023 816911) or the Tropical & Travellers' Medical Clinic, 88 St 108 (☎023 306802, ⓦtravellersmedicalclinic .com).
Pharmacies English-speaking pharmacists are available at Pharmacie de la Gare, 124 Monivong Blvd (daily Mon–Sat 7am–7pm, Sun 7am–5pm; ☎023 430205, ⓦpharmacie-delagare.com/en), which stocks a good selection of international medicines. There are numerous branches of U-Care (daily 8am–10pm; ☎023 224199 ⓦu-carepharmacy .com) around town; Help+ Pharmacy at 322 Monivong Blvd, cnr St 252, is open 24hr (☎023 210338).
Post office The main post office is east of Wat Phnom, on St 13 between sts 98 and 102 (Mon–Fri 7.30am–5pm, Sat 7am–noon).
Tourist police ☎012 942484 or ☎097 778 0002 (English, French and Italian spoken).
Visas For visa extensions, it's easier to go through a travel agent or your guesthouse, usually with no more than a $5 commission. The Department of Immigration (☎017

812763) is out of town on Russian Blvd opposite the airport, and it's not worth the hassle or expense.

CHOEUNG EK (THE KILLING FIELDS)

A visit to **CHOEUNG EK**, 12km southwest of Phnom Penh, is a sobering experience (daily 7.30am–5.30pm; $6 including audioguide; ☎023 211753, ⓦkillingfieldsmuseum.com). It was here in 1980 that the bodies of 8985 people, victims of Pol Pot and his Khmer Rouge comrades, were exhumed from 86 mass graves. A further 43 graves have been left untouched. Many of those buried had suffered prolonged torture at S21 prison (see p.80), before being led to their deaths. Men, women, children and babies were beaten to death, shot, beheaded, or tied up and buried alive. It's best visited with a guide, or use the excellent, if harrowing, audioguide included in the ticket price.

The site is dominated by a tall, white, hollow stupa that commemorates all those who died from 1975 to 1979, displaying thousands of unearthed skulls on glass shelves. A pile of the victims' ragged clothing lies scattered underneath. A pavilion has a small display of the excavation of the burial pits, and a handwritten sign nearby (in Khmer and English) outlines the Khmer Rouge atrocities, a period described as "a desert of great destruction which overturned Kampuchean society and drove it back to the Stone Age". Although Choeung Ek is by far the most notorious of the killing fields, scores of similar plots can be found all over Cambodia, many with no more than a pile of skulls and bones as a memorial.

It costs approximately $15 return to reach Choeung Ek by moto/tuk-tuk, and excursions are run by various Phnom Penh guesthouses and agents. You could even cycle if you're prepared to brave the traffic (and dust); find Monireth Blvd, southwest of Central Market, and follow it south, forking left at the large petrol station after the Acleda and ANZ banks, from where it's about 5km to Choeung Ek.

2

INTO VIETNAM

The popular 280km trip from Phnom Penh to HCMC is possible via **public transport**. Several companies operate full-sized buses or express a/c minibuses all the way to HCMC for $10–15 (until 1.30pm). The alternative is to take a share taxi ($5) to the **Bavet–Moc Bai border**, then find a minibus to HCMC (US$4) after crossing the border (a 500m or so walk); there are plenty of touts at Bavet to help you out. However you get to the border, allow time to clear **immigration** – the border is open 7am–8pm. The city-to-city trip takes about six to seven hours, including immigration formalities. Some nationalities including UK and several European ones are currently exempt from **visas** for stays in Vietnam of up to fifteen days. It's free but you can't extend your stay or re-enter Vietnam within thirty days of departure. If need be, arrange visas at the Vietnamese Embassy at the southern end of Monivong Boulevard in Phnom Penh (Mon–Fri 8–11.30am & 2–5pm) for around $60, depending on your nationality and how quickly you need it. Guesthouses and travel agents can organize it for a few dollars more.

You can also cross the border by boat at **Chau Doc**, but it's longer and more expensive, albeit an adventure. Book ahead for the express boat to Chau Doc from Sisowath Quay ($25–29). In both cases, check your visa requirements.

Central Cambodia

Central Cambodia is a largely forgotten territory, stretching from northwest of Phnom Penh through endless miles of sparsely populated countryside before arriving suddenly at the bright lights of Siem Reap. The region remains largely off the tourist trail, although major road improvements have made some of its impressive but formerly remote temples more easily accessible. These are rewarding destinations if you're itching to get off the tourist trail and, compared to Angkor Wat, they're practically deserted. Centrepiece of the region is **Kompong Thom**, the only town of any size hereabouts. It's no major expedition if you want to see the impressive brick temples of **Sambor Prei Kuk**, some of the most ancient in the country.

KOMPONG THOM

Located roughly midway between Phnom Penh and Siem Reap on National Route 6, **KOMPONG THOM** is the gateway to the pre-Angkor temple ruins of **Sambor Prei Kuk**, 30km northeast. The town itself is little more than a busy transport stop, but it's a friendly place, and with a passable selection of inexpensive accommodation and food. The main features are a **double-bridge** over the Sen River – where the old one has been left alongside the new one, built with Australian assistance (hence the kangaroos at each end) – and gaudy Wat Kompong Thom, the local **temple**, with its massive leopard and rhino statues standing guard outside.

ARRIVAL AND DEPARTURE

By bus Buses generally stop opposite the market on the main road, not far from the taxi transport stop. Most transport is just passing through, so make sure your driver knows you want to get off here. You won't have to walk more than 500m from here to reach a hotel or guesthouse, but there are plenty of moto and tuk-tuk drivers around if you need one.
Destinations Phnom Penh (hourly; 5–6hr); Siem Reap (8 daily; 3hr).

By share taxi or minibus These leave between around 6am and 2pm. The transport stop is in the square one block east of the main road opposite the *Arunras Hotel*. Share taxis cost around $8/6 to Phnom Penh and Siem Reap respectively.
Destinations Kompong Cham (2hr 30min); Phnom Penh (4–5hr); Siem Reap (2hr 30min).

ACCOMMODATION

Arunras Hotel and Guesthouse NR 6 ☎ 012 961294. Housed in adjoining buildings, with the hotel rooms slightly more modern and expensive; the building has Kompong Thom's only elevator, a fact about which the proprietors are immensely proud. Both offer clean, good-value rooms ($5 extra for a/c), with guesthouse doubles from $8 and hotel rooms starting a dollar cheaper. Doubles $7
Stung Sen Royal Garden Hotel NR 6 ☎ 062 961228, ✉ stungsen_hotel@yahoo.com. A slightly more upmarket alternative to the *Arunras Hotel*, set in a shady garden overlooking the river, with spacious and comfy modern

rooms (with a/c and hot water) at a very competitive price. Doubles $13

Vimean Sovann Guesthouse St 7 ☏078 220 333, ⓦ vimeansovannguesthouse.com. In a quiet side street a 5min walk south of the centre, this friendly, efficiently run guesthouse offers bright, spacious, attractively furnished and spotlessly clean modern rooms (with hot water; a/c $5 extra) at giveaway rates, plus free bikes and a small restaurant. Doubles $7

EATING

Inexpensive food stalls at the market, on the main road just south of the bridge, are open from early morning to mid-afternoon, and the night market sets up outside the east entrance to the market from late afternoon.

Arunras Hotel NR 6 ☏062 961294. Lively hotel restaurant, busy with both locals and tourists, in a large mirror-walled dining room stuffed with wooden furniture. The menu features a substantial range of good Chinese and Khmer dishes (mains $3.50–4.50) served in large portions. Daily 7am–10pm.

SAMBOR PREI KUK

The site of the major seventh-century Chenla capital known as Ishanapura, **Sambor Prei Kuk** once boasted hundreds of temples, although most have crumbled or been smothered by the encroaching forest. Three fine sets of towers remain, however – well worth the excursion and modest entrance fee ($3).

The site is divided into three groups: north, central and south. The north group (closest to the car park), known as **Prasat Sambor Prei Kuk**, is distinguished by the reliefs of the central sanctuary tower. These depict **flying palaces**, said to be the homes of the gods who guard the temples. In spite of their age, you can make out figures and the floors of the palace. Also look out for the cute reliefs of winged horses and tiny human faces.

The central group is the latest, dating from the ninth century, although only the main sanctuary tower, **Prasat Tao**, remains – particularly photogenic, with sprouting vegetation and lions flanking the entrance steps. Intricate foliage carvings are visible on the south lintel.

The south group, **Prasat Neak Pean**, was the most important temple at Ishanapura. Inside the brick-walled enclosure stand several unusual octagonal towers decorated

with further flying palaces and (on the west side of the inner wall) some elaborate but eroded bas-reliefs in a line of roundels.

Look out, too, for the small shrine just north of the entrance road, almost completely gobbled up by the roots of an enormous **strangler fig**, which seems to sprout from the crumbling walls as if out of some enormous pot.

ARRIVAL AND DEPARTURE

By moto or tuk-tuk The site is about 15km east of NR 64, about 1hr from Kompong Thom. Motos and tuk-tuks cost around $8–10/$12–15 return.

Angkor

The world-renowned temples of **Angkor**, in northwest Cambodia, stand as an impressive monument to the greatest ancient civilization in Southeast Asia. Spiritually, politically and geographically, Angkor was at the heart of the great Khmer Empire. During the Angkorian period, the ruling god-kings (*devarajas*) built imposing temples as a way of asserting their divinity, leaving a legacy of more than one hundred temples built between the ninth and fifteenth centuries.

The nearest town to the temples is **Siem Reap**, which has established itself as the base from which to make your way round Angkor, a tradition begun by an American, Frank Vincent Jr, who borrowed three elephants from the governor of Siem Reap in 1872 to explore the ruins. These days, there are plenty of motos, tuk-tuks and taxis on hand for the journey.

Southeast from Siem Reap stretches the vast **Tonle Sap** lake, home to dozens of picturesque floating villages, which swells to more than 8000 square kilometres during the rainy season before contracting spectacularly once again during the dry.

Further ancient temple complexes can be found dotted around the region, most of them seeing only a fraction of the crowds that flock to Angkor's headline attractions. East of Angkor, jungle-smothered **Beng Melea** and majestic **Koh Ker** can easily be combined in a day-trip from Siem Reap, while further afield are the vast ruined

2

complex of **Banteay Chhmar** and dramatic **Preah Vihear**, perched high on a mountain-top above the Thai border.

SIEM REAP

SIEM REAP is far and away Cambodia's most touristy town, and the hordes of foreign visitors can come as a bit of a culture shock if you've spent long in other parts of the country – although you'll enjoy the incredible range of tourist-friendly facilities and brilliant collection of restaurants and bars. Despite the number of tourists, it's retained a surprising amount of its original small-town charm.

Psar Chas

The old colonial heart of Siem Reap around the riverfront and lively **Psar Chas** market remains the most interesting part of town, still sporting many of its original French-era shophouses – transformed into buzzing cafés, bars and shops. Just north is the main tourist area, centred on the raucous **Pub St**, as it's now known, for obvious reasons, thronged with crowds of sun-crazed funseekers day and (particularly) night and looking more like a scene from downtown Bangkok than anything remotely Cambodian.

Artisans d'Angkor

A short walk west of Psar Chas, **Artisans d'Angkor** (daily 7.30am–6.30pm; free; ☎092 777462, ⌨artisansdangkor.com) offers a fascinating snapshot of Cambodian arts and crafts collected under one roof, with artisans producing gorgeous (but very pricey) wood and stone carvings, lacquer-work, gilding and silverwork. The centre also produces its own silk at the Angkor Silk Farm (daily 8am–5pm; free), 16km west of Siem Reap. Free buses run from Artisans d'Angkor to the farm (daily 9.30am & 1.30pm).

Angkor National Museum

A visit to Siem Reap's **Angkor National Museum** (Angkor Wat Rd, 1.5km north of the centre; daily 8.30am–6.30pm; $12; ⌨angkornationalmuseum.com) is an essential adjunct to a visit to the temples themselves – the only downside is the over-the-top entrance fee. Choice pieces of ancient Khmer sculpture are beautifully exhibited in vast galleries, while multimedia presentations provide background on Cambodian history and religion.

ARRIVAL AND DEPARTURE

By plane Besides flights to Phnom Penh, there are an increasing number of international connections. Transport between the town and airport costs around $7; some hotels and guesthouses pick you up or take you there for free.
Destinations Bangkok (1hr 10min); Hanoi (2hr); HCMC (1hr 20min); Kuala Lumpur (3hr); Phnom Penh (40min); Sihanoukville (1hr 10min); Singapore (3hr 20min); Vientiane (3hr).

By bus Buses arrive at/leave from the Chong Kov Sou bus station 3km east of town, although some also pick up/drop off at one of the various bus company offices along the south end of Sivatha Boulevard near Psar Chas, or at the junction of National Route 6 and Pokambor Ave, just north of the centre.
Destinations Bangkok (12 daily; 9–12hr); Battambang (8 daily; 4hr); Kompong Cham (5 daily; 6hr); Kompong Thom (20 daily; 3hr); Phnom Penh (20 daily; 6–8hr); Poipet (10 daily; 3hr); Sihanoukville (3 daily; 10hr).

By share taxi or pick-up Share taxis arrive and depart from the market, Psar Leu, to the east of the city, a hectic transport hub from where you can easily catch a tuk-tuk or moto into town ($4).

By boat Boats cruise into the port, around 12km south of Siem Reap (the exact distance varies with the level of the lake), passing the touristy floating village of Kompong Khneas en route. Guesthouse reps will be keen to offer a free ride into town, so it's a good idea to decide beforehand where you want to stay; otherwise, there are plenty of motos ($4) and tuk-tuks ($5). Boats leave from the port at 7am for Phnom Penh ($35) and at 8am for Battambang ($25). When the water level is really low (Feb–May) the express boats for Phnom Penh moor some way out, and you'll be taken out to them on a smaller craft. You'll need to book your ticket at

> ### INTO THAILAND AT POIPET
> From Siem Reap it's a three-hour bus or taxi ride to the busy border crossing at **Poipet** (around 10 buses/minibuses daily; $7–10). Thai visas are issued on the spot. Once in Thailand, you can take a tuk-tuk to Aranyaprathet (see box, p.781), from where you can head on to Bangkok by bus (every 30min, last one 6pm; 5hr) or train (2 daily leaving at 6.40am & 1.55pm, arriving Bangkok 12.05pm & 11.30pm; ⌨thairailways.com).

Cambodian Cultural Village (2km), War Museum (4km), Airport (6km), Sisophon & Poipet — Angkor National Museum & The Temples of Angkor

Psar Leu (2km), Transport stop and Bus Station, Rolous & Phnom Penh

SIEM REAP

0 — 250 metres

■ DRINKING & NIGHTLIFE	
Asana	2
Miss Wong	3
Red Piano	5
Siem Reap Brewpub	1
Temple Bar	4

■ ACCOMMODATION				● EATING			
Blossoming Romduol Lodge	14	Onederz Hostel	9	The Blue Pumpkin	7, 14	Khmer Kitchen	12, 13
Bou Savy	1	One Stop Hostel	11	Bugs Café	5	Marum	1
European	3	Mom's	2	Butterflies Garden	11	New Leaf Eatery	10
Golden Takeo	5	The Siem Reap Hostel	12	Currywala	3	Sugar Palm	2
Happy Guest House	4	Two Dragons	6	Footprint Cafés	15	The Veg "G" Table Café	4
Hi Siem Reap Deluxe Hostel	15	U-Dara Inn Guesthouse	7	For Life	6	Viva	8, 9
Ivy Guest House	8	Viroth's Villa	10	Genevieve's	16		
Mingalar Inn	13			Haven	17		

least a day ahead (two days ahead March–Nov when often just one boat runs on each route). If you buy your ticket from a guesthouse or hotel, a minibus will collect you, although this may mean setting out as early as 5.30am; otherwise, you'll have to make your own way to the port.

Destinations Battambang (daily; 6hr wet season, up to 8hr in the dry); Phnom Penh (daily; 5–6hr).

GETTING AROUND

The town is small enough to walk across from top to bottom in not much more than 20min or so. There are also plentiful motos and tuk-tuks (both $1–2 for shorter/longer trips around the centre), plus bicycles for rental (from $2–5/day) at numerous places.

INFORMATION AND TOURS

Government-licensed temple guides ($35/day) can be hired at any of the city's three tourist offices.

Tourist offices In the southwest corner of the Royal Gardens (daily 7.30am–5.30pm); on Sivatha Blvd near Psar Chas (Mon–Fri 8am–9pm, Sat & Sun 8am–5pm); and on Vithei Charles de Gaulle (Angkor Wat Rd) on the way to

2

the temples. Guesthouses are generally a much better source of information.

Publications The useful *Siem Reap Angkor Visitors Guide*, published three times a year and available from some hotels, guesthouses and the tourist offices, contains listings of places to stay, eat and drink. It's also available at ⓦ canbypublications.com.

ACCOMMODATION

Most budget accommodation is concentrated in two areas: in and around Psar Chas, and in the various streets running east of the river (particularly around St 20 near Wat Bo). There's an excellent selection, and standards are generally good, although prices are a bit higher than elsewhere in Cambodia, with many places offering a/c rooms only.

AROUND PSAR CHAS

Blossoming Romduol Lodge Psakrom St ☎ 012 545811, ⓦ blossomingromduolsiemreap.com. Efficient modern hotel with big bright tiled a/c rooms with balcony plus a good-sized pool and neat pavilion restaurant out the front – although a bit too much piped muzak. Excellent value at current rates. Includes breakfast. Doubles $18

Hi Siem Reap Deluxe Hostel River Rd ☎ 063 765569, ⓦ hisiemreap.com. More intimate and less institutional than most other hostels in town, in a riverside house just south of the centre, with a mix of ten- and (for $1 extra) eight-bed dorms all with individual bed-sockets and reading lights, a few spacious, colourfully painted rooms, plus nice swimming pool and small bar, pool table, café, and free tea and coffee. Dorms $7, doubles $20

Ivy Guest House Kandal Village ☎ 012 380516, ⓦ ivy -guesthouse.com. In a rustic old ivy-clad wooden house, this is a Siem Reap guesthouse of the old school – basic, but with bags of character. Downstairs is a laidback café with bar and pool table, upstairs is a nice little verandah; accommodation is in a mix of simple fan rooms (with cold water) and slightly posher a/c rooms (with hot water; $15). Doubles $8

Mingalar Inn (formerly the *Mandalay Inn*) Psakrom St ☎ 093 798079, ⓦ mingalarinn.com. Long-running Siem Reap stalwart, and still one of the best cheapies in the city centre, with a range of comfortable fan and a/c rooms (all with hot water; a/c $5 extra), although some are beginning to look their age. The helpful staff can arrange tours, and there's a small gym and a good little restaurant. Excellent

---

★**TREAT YOURSELF**

Viroth's Villa St 23 ☎ 063 761720, ⓦ viroth-villa.com. Super-cool boutique retreat sporting modern rooms with minimalist white decor and all mod cons, plus tranquil grounds with a spa and tiny swimming pool. Doubles $75

---

single rates, with rooms from just $8. Doubles $15

Onederz Hostel Next to Angkor Night Market ☎ 063 963525, ⓔ onestophostelsr2@gmail.com. One of Siem Reap's nicest hostels, in a very central location in a big cool white and glass building with spacious, light-filled downstairs lounge and café, rooftop pool and a mix of twelve- and (for $1 extra) six-bed dorms, all a/c and with individual bed-lights and sockets. Dorms $8

One Stop Hostel Sivatha Blvd ☎ 063 963 625, ⓔ onestophostelsr@gmail.com. One of the town's better and more modern hostels, with a selection of dorms, all a/c, with beds equipped with individual sockets and lights, plus hot water in all bathrooms. Choose between standard ten-bed dorms and smaller four- or six-bed dorms for an extra $1. There's also a women-only dorm. Dorms $7

U-Dara Inn Guesthouse Kandal Village ☎ 063 760980, ⓦ u-darainn.com. In a colonial-era shophouse in cool but quiet Kandal Village, this place has bags of old-fashioned character plus neat and cosy wood-panelled rooms (all a/c with hot water). Doubles $15

NORTH OF THE CENTRE

Bou Savy Off Airport Rd ☎ 063 964967, ⓦ bousavyguesthouse.com. Excellent – despite the inconvenient location – family-run guesthouse. There's a mix of rooms (all with hot water and fridge; some a/c for $25) spread over two buildings, so you might want to have a look at a few before you choose. The sociable plant-strewn courtyard café is a nice place to hang, and there's also a pretty little pool. Advance bookings recommended; rates include free pickup and breakfast. Doubles $18

EAST OF THE RIVER

European Off St 20 ☎ 012 582237, ⓦ european -guesthouse.com. Quiet guesthouse with large, spotless rooms (all with a/c and hot water) set around an attractive, shady garden, plus a small but rather unappetizing-looking pool. Excellent value, if you don't mind the slightly moribund atmosphere. Doubles $12

Golden Takeo Off St 20 ☎ 012 785424, ⓦ goldentakeoguesthouse.com. Near Wat Bo, this backpacker place offers comfortable accommodation at cut-throat prices. Rooms (with a/c and hot water for $4 extra) are nicely decorated with wall paintings and well equipped with TVs, desk and kettle. Excellent value, although the whole place is singularly lacking in atmosphere. Doubles $8

Happy Guest House Off St 20 ☎ 063 963815, ⓦ www .happyangkorguesthouse.com. The liveliest of the Wat Bo backpacker places, centred on a sociable and shady pavilion restaurant out front. Rooms aren't quite as nice as in some nearby places but are acceptable, and decent value – albeit a bit bare and past their best. Fan rooms come with cold water only, a/c ones with hot (for $12). Doubles $9

Mom's Wat Bo St ☎ 012 630170, ⓦ momguesthouse.com.

Long-running place, more of a hotel now than a guesthouse, but still owned by the same friendly family and with super service. Rooms (all with hot water, a/c, safe and fridge) are spacious and spotless, and there's also a medium-sized saltwater pool out the back. Doubles $20

The Siem Reap Hostel 7 Makara ☎ 063 964660, ⓦ thesiemreaphostel.com. The oldest hostel in town and still going strong, despite burgeoning competition. All dorms are a/c with individual bed-lights and sockets; choose between standard dorms with eight or ten beds and outside bathrooms or nicer six-bed deluxe dorms with in-dorm bathrooms and little balconies ($2 extra) – but don't bother with the overpriced and unappealing rooms. There's also a small spa, pool table, yoga classes, tour desk, a rather drab little pool and a brilliant little a/c mini-cinema for movie screenings. Dorms $8, doubles $30

★**Two Dragons** St 20 ☎ 063 965107, ⓦ twodragons -asia.com. There's a real home-from-home feel at this old Siem Reap stalwart, with friendly and efficient service, cosy and nicely furnished rooms (all with a/c, hot water and cable TV) and a small restaurant out front serving a good range of Thai, Khmer and Western food. Doubles $18

EATING

Siem Reap has a huge selection of restaurants catering to tourist tastes; for something more authentic and affordable, head for the markets and the cheap fruit stalls on the eastern side of the river near National Route 6.

The Blue Pumpkin Hospital St. The original branch of this hugely popular café-cum-bakery (now with outlets all round town). Construct your own snack or picnic from a wide selection of freshly baked breads, sandwiches, cakes, shakes and ice creams – and there's even a fair selection of alcoholic beverages, served in the "Cool Lounge" upstairs. There's a branch nearby on Sivatha Blvd. Daily 6am–11pm.

Bugs Café Angkor Night Market St ☎ 017 764560, ⓦ bugs -cafe.e-monsite.com. The ultimate Cambodian challenge for have-a-go-food heroes, serving up a largely insect-based menu, plus scorpion, snake and crocodile, all fashioned into neatly crafted tapas ($4–9). The fresh ants salad or cupcakes garnished with silkworms offer a (relatively) gentle introduction, after which you might brave an insect skewer (spiders, grasshoppers and waterbugs), a tarantula samosa or the signature "Bug Mac", perhaps rounded off with a slice of cricket cheesecake. Daily 5–11pm.

Butterflies Garden St 25 ☎ 063 761211, ⓦ butterfliesofangkor.com. Tranquil garden café with colourful butterflies (bought from local children) flitting between the tables. The menu features the usual Khmer ($5–6) and Western ($6–8) mains – the quality's pretty good, although service can be a bit hit and miss. Profits help support local community projects. Daily 6am–10pm.

Currywala Sivatha Blvd ☎ 092 459 723. Looking a bit like a 1980s curry house in Brick Lane, this decor-impaired venue is a good spot for solid subcontinental food spiced with attitude and served in truly heroic portions. The choice of North Indian classics (mains $5–8) ticks all the usual boxes and there's a good vegetarian selection too (although many vegetarian options are more expensive than their meat counterparts). Daily 11am–10.30pm.

Footprint Cafés St 26 ☎ 017 594644, ⓦ footprintcafes .org. Chic little café with lots of books to browse and buy and a good selection of food including all-day breakfasts and loads of salads alongside inexpensive international and Asian mains ($3–6.50) ranging from burgers and fish 'n' chips to chicken satay. All profits support local community projects. Mon & Wed–Sun 6.30am–10pm.

For Life The Lane ☎ 012 545426. A local expat favourite, and usually a haven of calm amid the madness of Psar Char, serving excellent Khmer food (mains $4.50–5) including loads of authentic dishes including *prahok ktis* (minced pork in fish sauce), *bobor* (porridge) and all sorts of soups and salads. Daily 11am–11pm.

Genevieve's Sok San Rd ☎ 081 410783, ⓦ facebook.com/ GenevievesRestaurant. Wildly popular restaurant serving up a great selection of Khmer and international dishes (including good vegetarian options; mains $5–7). Varied Western options include comfort food like lasagne and fish 'n' chips, alongside fancier creations like pan-fried duck breast and slow-cooked pork belly, while Khmer dishes are an explosion of Asian flavours – the chicken *amok* is a triumph. Reservations strongly advised, particularly for dinner. Mon–Sat noon–2pm & 5.30–9.30pm.

Haven Chocolate Rd ☎ 078 342404, ⓦ havencambodia .com. Peaceful expat-run training restaurant for local kids serving up well-prepared and -presented Khmer and Asian classics ($7–8) plus a small but judicious selection of Western dishes, including good vegetarian and a couple of Swiss options. Choose between a seat in the lovely rambling garden or indoors. Booking is usually essential, although you might get lucky at lunch during the low season. Mon–Sat 11.30am–3pm & 5.30–10pm.

Khmer Kitchen Cnr Hospital St & St 9 ☎ 012 763468, ⓦ khmerkitchens.com. Excellent, inexpensive Khmer food (mains $4.50–5) in an atmospheric old shophouse, plus a few Thai dishes and cheap beer. There's a second (smaller) branch at the corner of St 11 and Alley West (☎ 012 349501). Daily 9am–11pm.

Marum Near Wat Po Lanka ☎ 017 363284. Attractive garden restaurant set around a traditional-style wooden house, run as a training restaurant by Friends International. The excellent Asian-inspired fusion menu includes plenty of inventive and unusual creations, like lotus, jackfruit and coriander hummus, alongside locally inspired offerings including mini crocodile burger with banana crisps, or beef and red tree ants stir-fried with kaffir lime. Dishes ($4– 6.50) are served in smallish, almost tapas-sized portions – you may want to order three or four between two

2

people. Popular with tour parties so worth reserving, especially for dinner. Daily 11am–10.30pm.

New Leaf Eatery Off Pokambor Ave ☎ 063 766016, ⓦ newleafeatery.com. Good-looking and sociable café – one of the nicest places in the centre to hang out, and there's an extensive selection of secondhand books for sale. Good coffee and drinks, served in recycled jars with bamboo straws, plus snacks, sandwiches, all-day breakfasts and other comforting café food. All profits go to support local causes. Daily 7.30am–9.30pm.

★ **Sugar Palm** Taphul St ☎ 012 818143, ⓦ thesugarpalm .com. Attractively rustic pavilion restaurant under a huge wooden house – perfect for a romantic candlelit dinner. The menu focuses on authentic Khmer food with a short but inventive selection of dishes (mains $7–8) – frogs' legs with basil, for example, or squid with black Kampot pepper, plus flavoursome pomelo and green mango salads. Mon–Sat 11.30am–3pm & 5.30–10pm.

The Veg "G" Table Café Wat Bo Rd ☎ 088 642 3753, ⓦ theveggtablecafe.com. Homey little café serving up excellent and inventive vegetarian dishes (some of which can also be adapted for vegans; mains $5.50) including veggie burgers, falafel, beetroot carpaccio, assorted salads and Siem Reap's most spectacular potato croquettes. Mon–Sat 11am–3pm & 6–9pm, Sun 11am–3pm.

Viva Hospital St ☎ 092 209154, ⓦ vivasiemreap.com. Wildly popular Mexican restaurant serving tasty versions of all the usual Tex-Mex classics (mains $5–7) including quesadillas, nachos, enchiladas, tacos and burritos. The restaurant's signature margaritas are cheap and very popular. There's a second branch on St 11. Daily 6.30am–midnight.

DRINKING AND NIGHTLIFE

Siem Reap is a bustling place, with bars targeted at foreigners opening up all over town, especially on the notorious "Pub Street".

★ **Asana** Between St 7 & The Lane ☎ 092 987801, ⓦ asana-cambodia.com. Occupying the last surviving wooden house in central Siem Reap, *Asana* is what a traditional Cambodian village house would look like if you put a chic urban bar inside it. Piles of rice and flour sacks double as seats upstairs, while downstairs there's a swinging hammock-bed to lounge in. Slightly above-average prices, but well worth it, particularly for the moreish *sombai* and Asian-style cocktails ($4.50). Daily 11am– midnight.

Miss Wong The Lane ☎ 092 428332, ⓦ misswong.net. Alluring little retro-Shanghai-style bar – one of central Siem Reap's most enjoyable places to linger of an evening. The excellent cocktails (around $4.50) come with a pronounced Asian twist – Singapore slings, lemongrass Collins, apricot and kaffir lime martinis and so on – and there's excellent food too. Daily 6pm–1am.

Red Piano Pub St ☎ 092 477730. One of Pub Street's more civilized drinking spots, especially if you can bag one of the coveted streetside wicker armchairs. The good drinks list includes lots of Belgian beers (Duvel, Hoegaarden, Chimay and Leffe), or try the signature "Tomb Raider" cocktail, still going strong after well over a decade. Daily 6.30am–midnight.

Siem Reap Brewpub Cnr St 5 & Shinta Mani ☎ 080 888555, ⓦ siemreapbrewpub.asia. Stylish modern restaurant and microbrewery serving up quality beers by brewmaster Neo Say Wee using German malts, Australian hops and craft yeast from New Zealand. Choose from blond, golden, dark and Indian pale ales, the Honey Weiss wheat-beer or the lemongrass- and pepper-scented Saison Ale. Daily 11am–11pm.

Temple Bar Pub St ☎ 015 999922. A granddaddy of the Siem Reap nightlife scene, sprawling over three levels at the heart of the Pub St action. The middle floor is the nicest – and where a popular free *apsara* show is also staged nightly – with cheap beer, spangly red-and-gold Oriental decor and cushioned balcony perches for bird's-eye views of the mayhem below. Daily 7am–3.30am.

DIRECTORY

Banks and exchange There are plenty of banks and ATMs throughout Siem Reap – the Canadia Bank at the junction of Sivatha Blvd and Hospital Rd is particularly convenient, and commission-free.

Hospitals The Royal Angkor International Hospital, NR 6 (2km from the airport; ☎ 063 761888, ⓦ royalangkorhospital.com), has some of the better medical services including call-out service, 24hr emergency care, ambulance, translation and evacuation to Bangkok. The government-run Siem Reap Provincial Hospital, 500m north of Psar Chas (☎ 063 963111), is basic and to be used only as a last resort.

Internet Try the big (but nameless) place on Sok San St, just west of Psar Chas (24hr; 3000 riel/hr).

Post and couriers The post office is on Pokambor Ave (daily 7am–5.30pm).

Supermarkets For basic provisions, there are numerous mini-markets dotted around the centre including a useful cluster along Sivatha Blvd opposite the western end of Pub St. There's a well-stocked supermarket in the Angkor Trade Centre on Pokambor Ave just north of Psar Chas.

DANCE AND MUSIC

Siem Reap is a good place to take in a cultural **Khmer** performance of classical dance, often known as "Apsara dancing", packaged with dinner by several of the hotels and bars around town; there's a good free show nightly at 7pm in the *Temple Bar*, plus more upmarket productions at the *Angkor Village Hotel*.

★ **TREAT YOURSELF**

Siem Reap is a great place to try an inexpensive **spa treatment** featuring Khmer or other types of massage. **Lemon Grass Garden** (Sivatha Blvd, near the *Park Hyatt* hotel, second branch further south on Sivatha Blvd next to *Khmer Touch* restaurant; ☎ 012 387385, ⊕ lemongrassgarden.com) offers excellent spa treatments at bargain prices, including traditional Khmer body, foot, head, shoulder and neck massages (most also available as "twin-touch" four-hand massages), facials and body scrubs along with manicures, pedicures and waxing (from $15/hr).

Tourist police North of town at Mondul 3 Village, Slorkram Commune ☎ 063 760215.

THE TEMPLES OF ANGKOR

In 802, Jayavarman II declared himself universal god-king, becoming the first of a succession of 39 monarchs to reign over what would eventually become the most powerful kingdom in Southeast Asia. So the **Angkor era** was born, a period marked by gargantuan building projects, the design and construction of inspirational **temples** and palaces, the creation of complex irrigation systems and the development of magnificent walled cities. However, as resources were channelled into ever more ambitious construction projects, Angkor became a target for attacks from neighbouring **Siam**. Successive invasions culminated in the sacking of Angkor in the fifteenth century and the city was abandoned to the jungle. Although Khmers knew of the lost city, it wasn't until the West's "discovery" of Angkor by a French missionary in the nineteenth century that international interest was aroused.

WHAT TO SEE AND DO

More than one hundred Angkorian monuments lie spread over some 3000 square kilometres of countryside around Siem Reap. The best-known monuments are the vast temple of **Angkor Wat** and the walled city of **Angkor Thom**, while jungle-ravaged **Ta Phrom** and exquisitely

decorated **Banteay Srei** are also popular sites. The **Roluos** ruins are significant as the site of the empire's first capital city and as a point of comparison with later architectural styles. Many of the artefacts on display at the temples of Angkor are not originals – **thefts** of the valuable treasures have been a problem since the 1970s and the majority are now copies.

Angkor Wat

Built in the twelfth century as a temple (and subsequently mausoleum) for Suryavarman II, **Angkor Wat** represents the height of Khmer art, combining architectural harmony, grand proportions and detailed artistry. Approaching along the sandstone causeway across a broad moat and through the western gate, you're teased with glimpses of the central towers, but it's not until you're through the gate that the full magnificence of the temple comes into view. The causeway, extending 300m across the flat, open compound, directs the eye to the proud temple and its most memorable feature, the five distinctive conical towers, designed to look like lotus buds.

Continuing east along the causeway, you'll pass between the wat's library buildings and two ponds, and mount a flight of steps to the **Terrace of Honour**. The terrace is the gateway to the extraordinary **Gallery of Bas Reliefs**, a covered gallery which extends around the perimeter of the first level. The carvings cover almost the entire wall – 700m long, 2m high – depicting religious narratives, battle scenes and Hindu epics. The best-known carving, **the Churning of the Ocean of Milk**, covering the southern half of the East Gallery, depicts the myth of creation: gods (*devas*) and evil spirits (*asuras*) churn the ocean for a thousand years to produce the elixir of immortality, creating order out of chaos. The detail and sharpness of the images make this one of the greatest stone sculptures ever created.

Returning to the Terrace of Honour and walking towards the central chamber, you'll pass through the cruciform galleries linking the first and second levels. On the right-hand side is the **Gallery of One Thousand Buddhas**, though only a handful of figures now remain. The walls of the courtyard on the next level are decorated with the figures of some 1800 *apsaras* (celestial nymphs), each individually carved with

their own uniquely detailed features. A neck-wrenchingly steep staircase leads up to the topmost third level (you'll probably have to queue to get up), from where various Buddha images look down from the central sanctuary on the temple below.

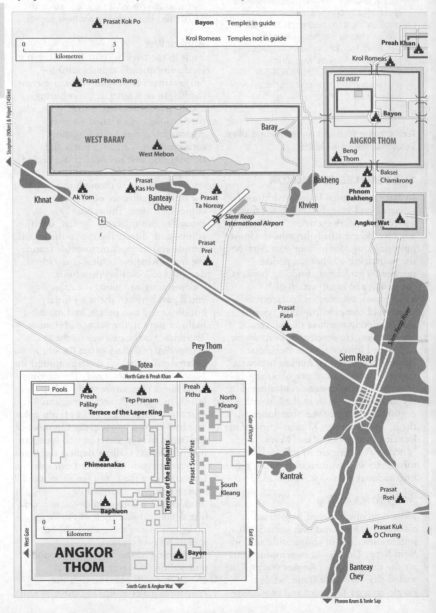

Angkor Thom

Angkor Thom, 2km north of Angkor Wat, was the last and greatest capital of the Angkor era, built during the late twelfth and early thirteenth centuries. The immense city is enclosed within a square of defensive walls, 8m high and 3km long on each side, themselves surrounded in turn by a 100m-wide moat – although of the original wooden houses which once filled the space inside the walls no trace remains. Certainly more spectacular and extravagant than any Western city at the time, Angkor Thom was an architectural

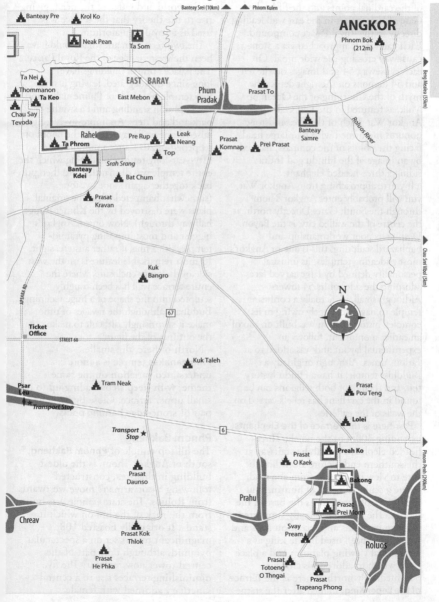

ANGKOR

Banteay Srei (10km) ▲   ▲ Phnom Kulen

Banteay Pre ▲   Krol Ko ▲

Neak Pean ▲

Ta Som ▲

Phnom Bok (212m) ▲

Ta Nei ▲

EAST BARAY

Thommanon ▲   Ta Keo ▲

East Mebon ▲

Phum Pradak ▲

Prasat To ▲

Chau Say Tevoda ▲

Rahel   Pre Rup ▲   Leak Neang ▲   Prasat Komnap ▲   Prei Prasat ▲

Banteay Samre ▲

Ta Phrom ▲

Srah Srang   Top ▲

Banteay Kdei ▲   Bat Chum ▲

Prasat Kravan ▲

Roluos River

Kuk Bangro ▲

Ticket Office

67

N

STREET 60

Kuk Taleh ▲

Psar Leu
★ Transport Stop

Tram Neak ▲

Prasat Pou Teng ▲

Lolei ▲

Transport Stop ★

6

Prasat O Kaek ▲

Preah Ko ▲

Prasat Daunso ▲

Bakong ▲

Prahu

Prasat Prei Monti ▲

Chreav

Prasat Kok Thlok ▲

Svay Pream ▲

Roluos

Prasat He Phka ▲

Prasat Totoeng O Thngai ▲

Prasat Trapeang Phong ▲

Beng Mealea (55km) ▶
Chau Srei Vibol (5km) ▶
Phnom Penh (290km) ▶

2

masterpiece, home to perhaps 150,000 inhabitants. Now only the city's great religious monuments, built in imperishable stone, remain as a testament to the city's former grandeur.

There are five gateways set in the walls around Angkor Thom, four covering each of the cardinal points and the fifth, the Gate of Victory, set in the east wall leading directly to the Royal Palace compound. Each gateway is approached via a **stone causeway** crossing the wide moat. On each causeway, 54 god images on the left and 54 demons on the right depict the myth of the Churning of the Ocean of Milk, as featured in the East Gallery of Angkor Wat. Each of the five sandstone **gopuras** is crowned with four large heads, facing the points of the compass, flanked by an image of the Hindu god Indra riding a three-headed elephant.

If you're approaching from Angkor Wat, you will probably enter Angkor Thom through the South Gate. Directly north, at the centre of the walled city, is the **Bayon**. Despite its poor workmanship and haphazard sculpting, this is one of Angkor's most endearing temples, its unusual personality defined by large carved faces adorning the sides of its 54 towers. Although small, it's actually a confusing temple to navigate, largely owing to its complex history. Bayon was built on top of an earlier monument, follows an experimental layout and was added to at various times. Although originally a Buddhist temple, it has a Hindu history too, and themes of both religions can be found in the excellent bas-reliefs carved on the walls of the galleries.

Past here is the **Terrace of the Elephants**, extending 300m to the north. Three-headed elephants guard the stairway at the southern end; before ascending, be sure to view the terrace from the road, where a sculpted frieze of hunting and fighting elephants adorns the base of the terrace. The terrace originally supported wooden pavilions and reception halls and would have been used by the king as a ceremonial viewing platform and a place from which to address his citizens.

Immediately north of here is the **Terrace of the Leper King**, named after the statue

of a naked figure discovered here (now in Phnom Penh's National Museum – a copy stands on top of the terrace). It's uncertain who the Leper King was or even where the name originates, though an inscription on the statue suggests that it may represent Yama, the god of the underworld and judge of the dead, giving rise to the theory that the terrace was used as a royal crematorium.

The two terraces mark what would have been the western edge of the Royal Palace. The palace's timber buildings have long-since disintegrated, leaving just the two temple pyramids of Phimeanakas and the Baphuon standing amid a swathe of parkland and trees. An impressively long raised stone walkway leads to the **Baphuon**, reopened in 2011 after a monumental fifty-year-long restoration during which the entire temple was dismantled and then put back together again stone by stone (somewhat hampered when the original plans were destroyed by the Khmer Rouge halfway through). Now one of Angkor's biggest and most imposing pyramid-temples, it's a fine, if rather austere, sight. Its most remarkable feature is on the west side of the outer enclosure, where the entire terrace wall has been roughly sculpted into the shape of a huge reclining Buddha – although the ravages of time make it surprisingly difficult to make out the outlines of the figure.

North of here, the smaller **Phimeanakas** temple is a more understated variation on the same theme, with steep steps leading up to its small upper terrace. Close by lies a fine pair of stone-edge **bathing pools**.

Phnom Bakheng

The hilltop temple of **Phnom Bakheng**, south of Angkor Thom, is the oldest building in this area, constructed following Yasorvarman's move westwards from Roluos. The state temple was built from the rock of the hill on which it stands. It originally boasted 108 magnificent towers set on a spectacular pyramid, although only part of the central tower now remains. The five diminishing terraces rise to a central sanctuary adorned with female

VISITING THE TEMPLES

Most of the temples are open daily 7.30am–5.30pm. Angkor Wat and Sra Srang open for sunrise at 5am, while Pre Rup and Phnom Bakheng are open sunrise to sunset (5am–7pm).

TRANSPORT

There are a number of **transport options** to get to and around Angkor Wat from Siem Reap: your choice will depend on your time frame, your budget and which temples you intend to visit. Hiring a tuk-tuk is the best way to get around (tours of the Grand and Petit Circuit temples, each lasting a day, can be had for just $15). For one person, a moto tour can cost as little as $12, but is obviously less comfortable. If you have time to spare, renting a bicycle (around $2–5/day from numerous outlets in Siem Reap) is perhaps the most enjoyable way to explore the temples. Distances are manageable, and the terrain is almost completely flat, although be aware that exploring the temples, with their endless steps, can be pretty tiring, so don't try to cover too many in a day.

ENTRY PASSES

Entry passes are required to enter the Angkor area, and must also be shown at all the temples. The main ticket office is at the junction of Apsara Road and Street 60. Three categories of pass are available: one day ($37), three days ($62, to be used within one week) or seven days ($72, to be used within one month). Most people find it adequate to buy the three-day pass, which gives enough time to see all the temples in the central area and to visit the outlying temples at Roluos and Banteay Srei. If you're short on time, you can cover Angkor Wat, the Bayon, Ta Phrom and Banteay Srei in one (very) full day.

divinities, which once housed the lingam of the god Yashodhareshvara. Bakheng, however, is visited less for its temple than for the view from the hilltop; Angkor Wat soars upwards from its jungle hideout to the east. At sunset, the best time to visit for great views of Angkor, it becomes a circus of tourists and vendors, with elephant rides on offer and souvenir T-shirts piled up on the ancient stones.

Preah Khan

Just beyond the northeast corner of Angkor Thom's perimeter wall stands **Preah Khan**, a tranquil site surrounded by dense foliage. The twelfth-century temple served as the temporary residence of King Jayavarman VII while he was rebuilding Angkor Thom, damaged in an attack by the Siamese. At the southern end of the east **gopura**, a photogenic battle of wood and stone is being fought as an encroaching tree grows through the ruins: the tree appears to be winning.

Ta Keo

About 2km east of the Bayon, **Ta Keo** scores well on the height points, but is awarded nothing for decoration. This towering replica of Mount Meru, which

was never finished, is bereft of the usual Angkor refinements. It's commonly believed that it was struck by lightning, a truly bad omen.

Ta Phrom

The stunning twelfth-century temple-monastery of **Ta Phrom**, 1km southeast of Ta Keo, has a magical appeal (although it is also spectacularly crowded during the morning and early afternoon). Rather than being cleared and restored like most of the other Angkor monuments, it's been left to the jungle and appears roughly as it did to the Europeans who rediscovered these ruins in the nineteenth century. Roots and trunks intermingle with the stones and seem almost part of the structure, and the temple's cramped corridors reveal half-hidden reliefs, while valuable carvings litter the floor.

Jayavarman VII originally built Ta Phrom as a Buddhist monastery, although Hindu purists have since defaced the Buddhist imagery. The temple was once surrounded by an enclosed city. An inscription found at the site testifies to its importance: more than twelve thousand people lived at the monastery, maintained by almost eighty thousand people in the surrounding villages.

2

Banteay Kdei

Southeast of Ta Phrom and one of the quieter sites in this area, **Banteay Kdei** is a huge twelfth-century Buddhist temple, constructed under Jayavarman VII. It's in a pretty poor state of repair, but the crumbling stones create an interesting architecture of their own. Highlights are the carvings of female divinities and other figures in the niches of the second enclosure, and a frieze of Buddhas in the interior court. Opposite the east entrance to Banteay Kdei is the **Srah Srang** or "Royal Bath", a large lake which was probably used for ritual ablutions.

Roluos group

Due east of Siem Reap close to the small town of **Roluos** are three of Angkor's oldest temples: **Bakong**, **Preah Ko** and **Lolei**. The relics date from the late ninth century, the dawn of the Angkorian era, and a time when the emphasis was on detail rather than size.

South of National Route 6, the first temple you come to is **Preah Ko**, built by Indravarman I as a funerary temple for his ancestors. It's in poor condition, but is charming; the highlights are the six brick towers of the central sanctuary, which sit on a low platform at the centre of the inner enclosure.

Cambodia's earliest temple-mountain, **Bakong** is made up of five tiers of solid sandstone surrounded by brick towers. Entering from the east across the balustraded causeway, you'll come into the inner enclosure through a ruined **gopura**; originally eight brick towers surrounded the central sanctuary, but only five remain standing. In the heart of the enclosure is a five-tiered pyramid. Twelve small sanctuaries are arranged symmetrically around the fourth tier, and above you on the summit is the well-preserved central sanctuary – if you're wondering why it's in such good condition, it's because it was rebuilt in 1941.

Return to the main road for the sanctuary of **Lolei**, built by Yashovarman I on an artificial island. Its four collapsing brick-and-sandstone towers are only worth visiting for the Sanskrit inscriptions in the door jambs that detail the work rosters of the temple slaves; a few carvings remain but are badly eroded.

Banteay Srei

Further afield, the pretty tenth-century temple of **Banteay Srei** is unique among its Angkorian peers. Its miniature proportions, unusual pinkish sandstone and intricate ornamentation create a surreal effect, enhanced by its astonishingly well-preserved state. The journey to the site, about 30km northeast of Angkor Wat, takes about an hour. Tour groups start arriving en masse from 8.30am, and because of its small size, it gets crowded quickly – arriving earlier than this, or later in the afternoon (after 3/4pm), helps avoid the crowds.

From the entry tower, across the moat, the tops of the three intricate central towers and two libraries are visible over the low enclosure wall, their rose-pink sandstone a surreal sight against the green backdrop of the jungle. Inside, the enclosure is a riot of intricate decoration and architecture, with wall-niches housing guardian divinities enclosed in carved foliage and panels extravagantly decorated with scenes from Hindu mythology.

TONLE SAP LAKE

Temples aside, you shouldn't leave Siem Reap without exploring the fascinating string of **lakeside villages** on the nearby **Tonle Sap**, the massive freshwater lake that dominates the map of Cambodia. The majority of these lake's inhabitants are fishermen, mostly stateless ethnic **Vietnamese** who have been here for decades, despite being widely distrusted by the Khmer.

Lakeside villages

The closest of the lakeside villages to Siem Reap (about 18km south of the centre), **CHONG KHNEAS** pulls in regular crowds of coach parties on whistlestop tours looking for a quick taste of lakeside life but is perhaps worth a look if you can't make it to any of the more peaceful villages further afield. Tourism notwithstanding, Chong Khneas remains a genuine **floating village**, with houses (most of them little better than floating shacks) built on bamboo rafts, lashed together to keep them from drifting apart.

KOMPONG PHLUK (around 35km from Siem Reap) is more authentic and more relaxed, although it is embracing tourism. This is a **stilted** rather than a floating village, its buildings raised upon high wooden pillars. At the height of the **wet season** in September water levels can rise

2

ANGKORIAN TEMPLES FURTHER AFIELD

There are a number of other major Angkor-era temple complexes within striking distance of Siem Reap, most (just about) reachable within a day-trip.

BENG MEALEA

Easily visited as a longish half-day trip from Siem Reap (1hr 30min; about $35/55 by tuk-tuk/car), the largely unrestored temple of **Beng Mealea** ($5) gives a good idea of what French archeologists found when they first arrived at Angkor, with huge piles of mossy masonry tumbled between trees and glimpses of intricate carvings peeping from amid the jungle-smothered ruins. Occupying a strategic location roughly midway between Angkor and Koh Ker, the temple was most likely built during the mid-twelfth century by Suryavarman II, creator of Angkor Wat, and follows a very similar layout, although it's tricky to make out the ground plan, not helped by the efforts of the Khmer Rouge, who blew up the central tower while hunting for buried treasure.

KOH KER

Some 125km northeast of Siem Reap (and easily combined with Beng Mealea in a day-trip; 1hr from Beng Mealea; about $85 by car for both), **Koh Ker** ($10) was briefly capital of the Khmer Empire in the tenth century and boasts more than forty major monuments spread across eighty square kilometres, although many have been neglected, looted and largely engulfed by jungle. The major surviving temple complex is **Prasat Thom**, consisting of three enclosures laid out in a row. Next door is the former capital's most memorable sight, the remarkable **Prang**, a 35m-high, seven-tiered sandstone ziggurat looking oddly like one of the great Mayan monuments of Central America. Numerous other temples dot the surrounding area.

BANTEAY CHHMAR

The huge Angkorian-era temple of **Banteay Chhmar** ($5) is one of Cambodia's most memorable destinations, as fine as almost anything in Angkor but attracting only a trickle of visitors. The temple is best known for its magnificent **carvings**, once rivalling those at the Bayon and Angkor Wat. Many have been looted, although the meticulously reconstructed **eastern gallery** gives a good sense of what the temple originally looked like, while the remains of further carvings, including a spectacular 32-armed Avalokitesvara, survive amid the great piles of tree-choked masonry.

To get here by public transport you'll need to catch a bus to Sisophon (2hr from Siem Reap). From here it's a 1hr drive to Banteay Chhmar (roughly $25 by moto, or $30 by tuk-tuk return). You'll struggle to do the round trip in a day – best to spend the night in the excellent Banteay Chhmar **village homestay** (w visitbanteaychhmar.org), next to the temple.

PREAH VIHEAR

Right on the border with Thailand, the magnificent mountaintop temple of **Preah Vihear** ($10) makes maximum use of its spectacular setting overlooking the plains of Cambodia and Thailand below. Long squabbled over by the two countries, tensions erupted in 2011, although the situation has now stabilized and the site is safe to visit. Fronted by a magnificent triumphal staircase, the temple boasts spectacular views along the jagged line of the **Dangkrek Mountains**.

To reach Preah Vihear by public transport catch a share taxi to the small town of Sra Em. From here take a moto (around $15 return, including waiting time) to the ticket office, where you'll be obliged to hire another moto for the short ride to the temple ($5 return). There are several inexpensive guesthouses in Sra Em. To do it as a day-trip you'll need to take a tour (at least $100 per vehicle).

2

well above 10m, completely drowning the surrounding patches of forest and sometimes flooding the village buildings. During the **dry season**, lake levels fall progressively, and between March and May the waters usually vanish completely, leaving the village houses stranded atop their huge stilts amid an expanse of mud.

Some 15km southwest of Siem Reap, the smaller floating village of **BANTEAY MECHREY** is emerging as a popular, slightly quieter alternative. The village is strung out along a small river just off the Tonle Sap itself, complete with an impressive pagoda. The nearby **Prek Toal Biosphere Reserve** serves as a sanctuary for waterbirds, including three endangered species – spot-billed pelicans, greater adjutant storks and white-winged ducks.

Around 20km further down the lake from Kompong Phluk is **KOMPONG KHLEANG**. This was a major centre of lake trade in the French colonial period and remains the most sizeable settlement hereabouts, with around sixteen thousand inhabitants living in a mixture of stilted and floating houses. It's the largest but also the least touristed of the four main Tonle Sap villages, and remains surrounded by water year-round.

ARRIVAL AND TOURS

By rickshaw It's easy to pick up a rickshaw from Siem Reap to Chong Khneas and arrange your own boat trip when you arrive at the village. For the more remote lake villages you could also make your own way independently by rickshaw and then arrange your own boat, although it probably won't work out an awful lot cheaper than taking an organized tour.

Tour operators Tours of the lake can be arranged through numerous operators around Siem Reap, including Beyond Unique Escapes (☎ 063 969269, ⊛ beyonduniqueescapes .com), Osmose Nature Tours (⊛ osmosetonlesap.net) and Tara River Boat (☎ 092 957765, ⊛ taraboat.com).

Western Cambodia

The flat plains fanning out from Phnom Penh and stretching all the way to the border with Thailand are the nation's agricultural heartland – Battambang province is popularly known as the "rice-bowl" of Cambodia on account of its fertile rice-paddies and other tropical produce. Centrepiece of the region (and Cambodia's second city) is **Battambang**, an agreeable town, home to some of the country's finest surviving French-colonial architecture, and an enjoyably relaxed place to hang out for a few days.

The region is sandwiched between the **Cardamom Mountains** in the southwestern corner of the country and the **Dangrek Range** in the north. A perfect hideout, these frontier hills were home to the fugitive but still powerful leaders and soldiers of the Khmer Rouge for nearly twenty years after they were ousted from power in 1979. The towns within these formerly Khmer Rouge-occupied territories, such as the remote frontier outpost of **Pailin**, are not particularly attractive, as you might expect after twenty years of war and isolation, but the countryside is stunning in places and has a Wild West appeal. The Khmer Rouge legacy lives on here, not least in myriad mines that still dot the countryside – on no account wander from clearly marked paths.

BATTAMBANG

BATTAMBANG is Cambodia's second-biggest city, though you wouldn't think so from its laidback atmosphere, and it's a world apart from Phnom Penh's urban bustle. It's keen to move up in the world, however – and the French-colonial-era shophouses now sport an increasing array of fancy restaurants and bars. That said, the unhurried central market, Psar Nat, is still the busiest Battambang gets.

WHAT TO SEE AND DO

There are two pleasant **temples** within walking distance of the town centre – **Wat Piphithearam** and **Wat Dhum Rey Sor**. Further afield are **Phnom Sampeu** and **Wat Banan**, which make lovely day-trips out of the city – a tuk-tuk/moto will take you to both for about $20/15.

Also worth a visit is the quirky "**Bamboo Railway**", running along a stretch of disused track just outside Battambang. A dozen or so "trains" run up and down the line on demand, each consisting of a small bamboo platform set on top of a metal undercarriage and powered by motorbike engines – a fun way to get a glimpse of Battambang's lush hinterlands. The line starts 7km from Battambang (return by moto/tuk-tuk $4/5), with twenty- to thirty-minute trips up and down the line costing $5 per person.

Phnom Sampeu

Some 15km southwest of Battambang, a large temple complex squats atop the lopsided hill of **Phnom Sampeu** ($1), said to resemble a sinking boat when seen in profile with nearby **Phnom G'daong**. It's a colourful sight, although nowadays better known for its tragic associations with the Khmer Rouge, who used it as a prison, many of whose inmates were killed on the mountaintop.

A breathless twenty-minute hike up steep steps takes you to the top of the hill, dotted with a sprawling cluster of assorted modern shrines and stupas. Directly below the summit of the hill and the main vihara, steps lead down to the sombre, bat-infested **Laang Lacaun** ("Theatre Cave"), gloomy even at midday beneath its vast slab of overhanging rock. Thousands of people were killed here, thrown to their deaths by Khmer Rouge cadres through an opening in the rocks above. A few of the victims' smashed skulls and bones have been collected in an ornate metal cage as a memorial to Khmer Rouge atrocities.

Wat Banan

Reached from Phnom Sampeu via a ferociously bumpy back-country road, the modest temple of **Wat Banan** ($2) looks almost like a dilapidated miniature of Angkor Wat, with its five conical towers rising out of the trees at the summit of a 70m-high hill. It's a steep clamber up to the top but worth it to see the detailed lintels, beheaded *apsaras*, and views out over endless paddies, with Phnom Sampeu visible to the north.

ARRIVAL AND DEPARTURE

By bus Buses arrive at and depart from various bus company offices near the transport stop in the northwest of town, just off National Route 5. Bus tickets can be bought through hotels and guesthouses, which can also arrange to have you picked up and taken to your bus.
Destinations Pailin (2 daily; 2hr); Phnom Penh (15 daily; 6hr 30min); Poipet (4 daily; 3hr); Siem Reap (8 daily; 4hr).
By share taxi and minibus These leave from the transport stop unless you're going to Pailin, in which case you should join a share taxi in the south of town, near the start of Route 10 at Psar Leu ($6). They leave from early morning until noon.
Destinations Pailin (1hr 30min); Phnom Penh (6hr); Poipet (2hr 30min); Siem Reap (3hr 30min).
By boat The river boat dock is a few hundred metres north of the town centre; hotel reps and English-speaking moto drivers meet the boats, so you'll have no trouble getting to your accommodation. Boats depart daily at 7am for Siem Reap (6hr in the wet season, up to 8hr in dry) and cost $25.

ACCOMMODATION

Asia North of the market ☎053 953523, ⓦasiahotelbattambang.com. Spotless modern hotel offering a wide variety of very comfortably furnished rooms at ultra-competitive prices, although the very cheapest lack windows and come with cold water only. A/c available for an extra $5. Doubles $\overline{6}$
Here Be Dragons East of the river ☎089 264895, ⓦherebedragonsbattambang.com. Inexpensive waterfront accommodation in a mix of bright and colourful fan rooms and comfortable dorms – choose between the six-bed dorm with fan or the eight-bed dorm with a/c ($5). The lively programme of events includes yoga sessions, movie screenings, cocktail and barbecue nights, and a popular quiz every Wednesday evening. Dorms $\overline{3}$, doubles $\overline{10}$
Hostel Cambodia Preah Vihea St ☎017 728038. Acceptable if uninspiring budget lodgings in a selection of functional but comfortable dorms, the cheapest with fourteen beds (six-bed ones $4), all with a/c and hot water, plus individual lockers and bed-sockets. Dorms $\overline{3.25}$
Royal Hotel 100m west of Psar Nat ☎053 952522, ⓦroyalhotelbattambang.com. Long-running travellers' favourite, set around an airy atrium and with a wide range of accommodation ranging from small fan rooms with cold

---

★ TREAT YOURSELF

Battambang Resort Wat Ko Village, 5km south of the centre ☎012 510100, ⓦbattambangresort.com. Idyllic resort a short drive south of the city, with spacious rooms set among gorgeous gardens dotted with coconut palms and mango trees. Facilities include a big pool and an attractive pavilion-style restaurant, and there's a good range of tours on offer – or just lounge on a hammock or cruise the lake on a pedalo. Doubles $\overline{60}$

2

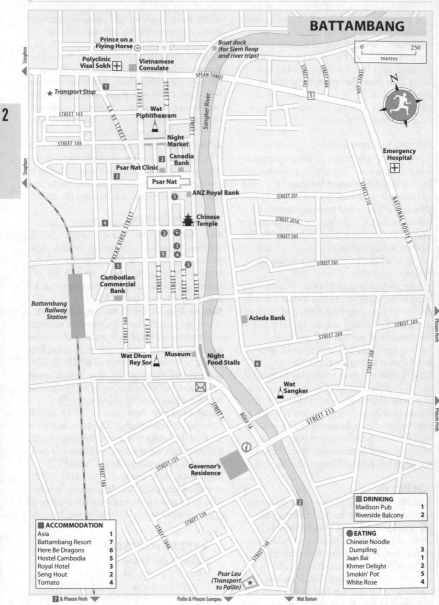

BATTAMBANG

Prince on a Flying Horse

Boat dock (for Siem Reap and river trips)

Polyclinic Visal Sokh

Vietnamese Consulate

SPEAN THMEI

Transport Stop

STREET 103

STREET 109

LA HE STREET

STREET 3

STREET 1

Wat Piphithearum

Night Market

Psar Nat Clinic

Canadia Bank

Psar Nat

ANZ Royal Bank

Chinese Temple

STREET 201

STREET 201A

STREET 203

STREET 205

Emergency Hospital

NATIONAL ROUTE 5

STREET 210

Cambodian Commercial Bank

PREAH VIHEA STREET

STREET 2.5

STREET 2

STREET 1.5

STREET 1

Battambang Railway Station

STREET 100

STREET 3

Acleda Bank

STREET 209

STREET 209

STREET 208

Wat Dhum Rey Sor

Museum

Night Food Stalls

Wat Sangker

STREET 1

ROAD 1A

STREET 213

STREET 135

Governor's Residence

STREET 106

STREET 139

STREET 164A

STREET 149

Psar Leu (Transport to Pailin)

Sangker River

STREET 602

STREET 604

STREET 606

5

0   250
metres

N

Sisophon

Sisophon

Phnom Penh

Phnom Penh

7 & Phnom Penh   Pailin & Phnom Sampeu   Wat Banan

DRINKING

| Madison Pub | 1 |
| Riverside Balcony | 2 |

ACCOMMODATION

Asia	1
Battambang Resort	7
Here Be Dragons	6
Hostel Cambodia	5
Royal Hotel	3
Seng Hout	2
Tomato	4

EATING

Chinese Noodle Dumpling	3
Jaan Bai	1
Khmer Delight	2
Smokin' Pot	5
White Rose	4

water to spacious a/c rooms with hot ($13). It's not quite as smart as other places in town in this price range, although the super-central location and helpful staff more than compensate, and it's a good place to sort out trips, tours and onward transport. Doubles $8

Seng Hout 50m north of Psar Nat ☎053 952900, ⓦ senghouthotel.com. Comfortable and very competitively

priced mid-range hotel in a pair of buildings just north of the market. Choose between comfortable rooms in the older building (where you'll also find the hotel's pool and gym) and slightly smarter but more sterile rooms (some windowless) in the new wing (same price) to the south. A/c costs an extra $5. Doubles $10

Tomato West of Psar Nat ☎095 647766. The cheapest

option in town, in an attractive shophouse-style building with a pretty ground-floor terrace shaded by enormous potted plants, plus a second building over the road. Rooms themselves are not much more than spartan boxes but reasonably clean and quiet – and given the price you really can't complain. There's also a basic but very cheap dorm. Dorms $2, doubles $3

EATING AND DRINKING

In the evening, a buzzing night-market opens up on the street south of Wat Piphithearam. For delicious noodle dishes, desserts and fruit shakes, head down to the riverfront opposite the post office, where street stalls set up in the afternoon and serve late into the evening.

Chinese Noodle Dumpling (Lan Chov Khorko Miteanh) St 2 ☎ 092 589639. A local institution and a popular breakfast stop, serving up great noodles and the best dumplings (steamed or fried) in town at giveaway prices. Mains $2. Daily 9am–9pm.

Jaan Bai St 2, cnr St 1.5 ☎ 097 398 7815. Battambang's most innovative restaurant (with a menu supervised by Australian Thai-food guru David Thompson) serving up top-notch Khmer, Thai and Vietnamese dishes in tapas-size portions (small plates $3–5, large plates $5–7) using seasonal organic produce. Daily 11am–9pm (last orders).

Khmer Delight One block south of Psar Nat, between St 2 & St 2.5 ☎ 053 953195. One of the nicest-looking restaurants in town, with a wide-ranging menu of Khmer standards alongside Western dishes such as spaghetti bolognese and fish'n'chips and some Indian and Asian classics– a mite expensive (most mains around $5–6) but good quality, and served in big portions. Daily 9.30am–10pm.

Smokin' Pot Two blocks south of Psar Nat ☎ 012 821400. Simple café-restaurant dishing up reliable Khmer food, plus a good Thai selection (mains $3–4), at bargain prices. Also runs good cookery classes. Daily 7am–10pm.

White Rose St 2 ☎ 012 691213. This long-running local restaurant attracts a cross-over crowd of tourists and locals, with a long menu of inexpensive Khmer and Chinese dishes (mains $2–3.50), plus a good selection of Western breakfasts and shakes. Daily 8am–10pm.

DRINKING

Madison Pub St 2.5 ☎ 053 650 2189. No-frills little corner bar, popular with the city's Francophone expat crowd, offering one of the city's better selections of tipples plus ice cream, crêpes and a good selection of breakfasts. Daily 7am–midnight.

Riverside Balcony Riverfront, south of the centre ☎ 010 337862. Great place for a sundowner, occupying the upstairs terrace of a fine old wooden house in a lovely riverside setting, with soft lighting, good music and a great drinks list, including plenty of cocktails. Good pizzas, too ($4–8.50). Happy hour 5–7pm. Tues–Sun 4–11pm.

DIRECTORY

Health Polyclinique Visal Sokh (☎ 012 843415), next to the Vietnamese Consulate north of the centre.
Internet World Net, between streets 2 and 1.5 (daily 7am–8pm; 2000 riel/hr).
Post office St 1 in the south of town (Mon–Fri 7–11am & 2–5pm).

PAILIN

Some 80km southwest of Battambang, **PAILIN** is a dusty little frontier town. The only link to the rest of the country is National Route 57 from Battambang, and once you arrive there's really no reason to be here unless you're crossing the border into Thailand. The town has a wild and edgy atmosphere, and remains one of the most heavily mined regions in the country: high up and surrounded by jungle, it was long a Khmer Rouge stronghold, supplied with food and weapons from the nearby Thai border.

WHAT TO SEE AND DO

Pailin was once famous for its **gem mining**, though the land is now pretty much mined out. All you're likely to see today are a few dealers in the **market**, ready to hand over cash for rough, uncut stones pulled from the ground.

The hill of **Phnom Yat** houses a small pagoda, its outer wall decorated with startling images of people being tortured in hell – tongues are pulled out with pliers, women drowned, people stabbed with forks and heads chopped off.

ARRIVAL AND DEPARTURE

By bus There are just two buses daily to Pailin from Battambang (run by Paramount Angkor; 2hr), which continue to the border crossing at Psar Pruhm. The transport stop is at the central market.
By share taxi Share taxis arrive at and depart from the market in the centre of town. Most only go to Battambang (1hr 30min), from where you'll probably have to change to get transport elsewhere.

ACCOMMODATION AND EATING

Bamboo Guesthouse 4km out of town on the road towards the border ☎ 012 405818. A pleasant refuge from central Pailin with a range of wooden bungalows in an

2

attractive garden, all with hot water and a/c. The restaurant is one of the best in town, serving Khmer and Thai food, plus a few Western options. Doubles $15

Pailin Ruby West of the traffic circle on the main road through town ☏ 055 636 3603. The best and least unruly (Pailin attracts a lot of truckers) place to stay in town. Rooms are clean and pleasant enough, with en-suite bathrooms, TV and chunky wood furniture; hot water and a/c are available for an extra $5. Doubles $7

The southwest

To the southwest of Phnom Penh, the Cardamom and Elephant mountains rise up imposingly from the plains, as if shielding Cambodia's only stretch of coast from the world. Indeed, only a few places along the coast are accessible by road. The most popular destination is the beach resort of **Sihanoukville**, whose sandy shores are the launching point for trips to **Ream National Park** and the idyllic **islands** in the Gulf of Thailand. Eastwards is the beguiling riverside town of **Kampot** and, further along, the resurgent seaside resort of **Kep**. On Cambodia's western border, **Koh Kong** is a transit point for visitors arriving from or leaving for Thailand, but it's also the gateway into the lush jungle of the Cardamoms.

These areas are well served by public **transport**. National Routes 3, 4 and 48 are in good condition, and fast ferries and boats service the islands.

SIHANOUKVILLE

Cambodia's only full-blown beach resort, **SIHANOUKVILLE** is a sprawling affair where new developments are a frequent sight amid the swaying palms. While Ochheuteal Beach and Serendipity Beach Road justify the party town reputation, there are quieter spots too, particularly around Otres, 6km away. Sihanoukville is also the entry point to the islands of Koh Rong, Koh Rong Samloem and Koh Ta Kiev.

Sihanoukville may not be the prettiest place, but its plentiful restaurants serving fresh seafood, lively bars and decent sandy beaches (albeit unspectacular by Southeast Asian standards) make it a good place to refuel, unwind or party, though it can get crowded during high season or holiday weekends.

WHAT TO SEE AND DO

Spread over a large peninsula and ringed by beaches, the town centre, or **downtown**, lies inland, centred around the bustling local market, **Psar Leu**. There's plenty to do nearby: exploring beaches, day-trips to **Ream National Park**, island-hopping (see p.109), and diving and snorkelling off the mainland.

Beaches

Closest to town are **Serendipity** and **Ochheuteal** beaches (essentially the same beach, the latter the main hub of activity), where you'll find the busiest backpacker vibe. There's a huge range of accommodation, bars and restaurants, plus sunbeds, beach bars and watersports. Some 6km southeast is the mellow beach scene at **Otres 1** and **Otres 2**, the nicest of Sihanoukville's seaside offerings, and 1km inland on the estuary at **Otres Village**, home to numerous guesthouses and a growing artistic community where activities include yoga, horseriding and kayaking. West of downtown is **Victory Hill** or Weather Station Hill, a backpacker hub now eclipsed by Serendipity Beach Road. Its seedy reputation, where middle-aged gentleman look for "hired company", doesn't extend to its quieter hassle-free shoreline at **Victory Beach**; beyond is **Hawaii Beach**, a favourite with Khmer families. Further around the peninsula is **Independence Beach**, named after the seven-storey 1960s **Independence Hotel**, a luxury resort at its western end. The bay curves gently, with a line of drinks stalls and shaded huts, and rocks and small coves offer privacy. Continuing east is pretty **Sokha Beach**, mostly reserved for guests of the huge *Sokha Resort*.

ARRIVAL AND DEPARTURE

By plane Sihanoukville Airport is 23km southeast of town. Taxis cost $20, tuk-tuks $15, minibus $6. Cambodia Angkor Air (☏ 023 666 6786, ⟨w⟩ cambodiaangkorair.com), Cambodia Bayon Airlines (☏ 078 231 5553, ⟨w⟩ bayonairlines.com) and Sky Angkor Bayon Airlines (☏ 063 967300, ⟨w⟩ skyangkorair.com) run daily flights to and from Siem Reap. Cambodia Angkor Air/Vietnam Airlines (☏ 023 990840, ⟨w⟩ vietnamairlines.com) operate a joint route to HCMC.

By bus The bus park currently occupies a temporary spot near Psar Leu market. Most companies offer hotel pick-up or leave/arrive at their offices, mostly around Ekareach St. Destinations Bangkok (5 daily; 12hr); Battambang (2 daily; 11 hr); HCMC (6 daily; 10–12hr); Koh Kong (2 daily; 4–5hr); Phnom Penh (12 daily; 4–5hr); Siem Reap (6 daily; 10hr).

By share taxi or minibus Minibuses and taxis usually terminate at/near the transport hub by Psar Leu market. Routes are operated by numerous companies. A tuk-tuk to Serendipity Beach Rd costs $2–3.
Destinations Ha Tien (5 daily; 5hr); Kampot (10 daily; 2hr); Kep (5 daily; 3–4hr); Koh Kong (4 daily; 4hr); Phnom Penh (20 daily; 4hr); Siem Reap (6 daily; 10hr).

By boat Ferries and fast boats connect to the nearby islands (see p.108).

By train Trains run between Phnom Penh and Sihanoukville via Takeo and Kampot on Fri, Sat, Sun, and public holidays. Phnom Penh (7hr), Kampot (1hr 40min–2hr 40min), Takeo (5hr 30min); tickets $4–7. Tickets available at station; you can usually buy on the day (☏ 078 888582, ⟨w⟩ royal-railway.com).

GETTING AROUND

By moto and tuk-tuk Motos and tuk-tuks are the main form of local transport. Motos cost $2–3 between Serendipity Beach Rd/Ochheuteal Beach and downtown/Victory Hill; tuk-tuks $3. A moto/tuk-tuk to Otres costs $3/$5.

Motorbike rental Guesthouses and travel agents can arrange motorbike rental. A 125cc bike goes for about $5/day and a 250cc for $12. It's common to request passports as security. Wear a helmet, and lock your moto when you leave it.

INFORMATION AND ACTIVITIES

Tourist information *Sihanoukville Visitors' Guide* (⟨w⟩ canbypublications.com), *Sihanoukville Advertiser* (⟨w⟩ sihanoukvilleadvertiser.com) and *Coastal* (⟨w⟩ coastal -cambodia.com) list new places to sleep, eat and drink; they're available free in bars, restaurants and guesthouses. There's a small tourist office midway up Serendipity Beach Rd (daily 7am–10pm).

Travel agents Ana Travel, Serendipity Beach Rd, next to *Beach Road Hotel* (daily 8.30am–8.30pm; ☏ 012 915301, ⟨w⟩ anatravelandtours.com), and Mottah Travel, 193 Ekareach St downtown opposite Canadia Bank (daily 8.30am–9pm; ☏ 012 996604, ⟨w⟩ mottah.com), are both excellent.

Diving EcoSea Dive (☏ 034 934631, ⟨w⟩ ecoseadive.com), Scuba Nation (☏ 012 604680, ⟨w⟩ divecambodia.com) and Koh Rong Dive Centre (☏ 034 934744, ⟨w⟩ kohrong-divecenter .com) have offices on Serendipity Beach Rd; The Dive Shop (☏ 034 933664, ⟨w⟩ diveshopcambodia.com) is on 14 Mithona St. Prices from $320 for PADI Open Water, two fun dives $80, and introductory dives $95. On Koh Rong Samloem, EcoSea Dive has a base at M'Pai Bai, as does Cambodian Diving Group (☏ 096 224 5474, ⟨w⟩ cambodiandivinggroup.com), while The Dive Shop is on Sunset Beach. Koh Rong Dive Center is also at Koh Toch on Koh Rong.

ACCOMMODATION

Budget accommodation is plentiful. Downtown is quieter, but proximity to the beach gives Serendipity Beach Rd and Otres the edge; inland Otres Village is increasingly popular. Late-night girlie bars in Victory Hill may be off-putting to some, but the area remains lively.

DOWNTOWN

Gekozy St 203, two blocks southeast of Caltex petrol station off Ekareach St ☏ 012 495825, ✉ mailme@geckozy -guesthouse.com. Small, friendly guesthouse in a local part of town with ten en-suite rooms (two with hot water) garden, communal areas and DVDs aplenty. Doubles $7

WEATHER STATION/VICTORY HILL

★**Backpacker Heaven** Ekareach St opposite *Marina Hotel* ☏ 010 237539, ⟨w⟩ facebook.com/backpackerheaven. Lovely pool and sociable setup in a converted villa. Clean dorms, chill-out areas and travel desk. Dorms $5, doubles $27

2

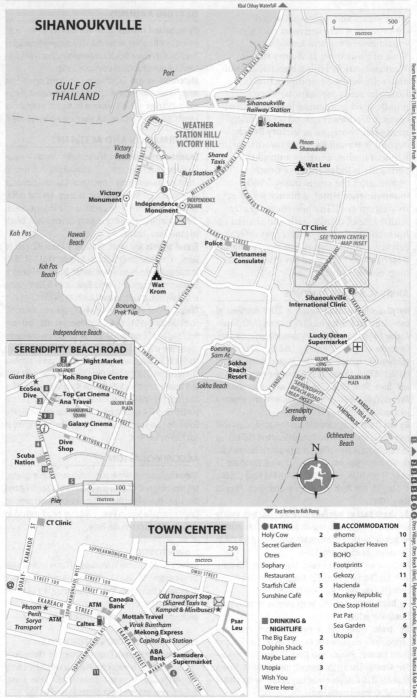

SIHANOUKVILLE

Kbal Chhay Waterfall

0 — 500 metres

Ream National Park (18km); Kampot & Phnom Penh

GULF OF THAILAND

Port

Victory Beach

Sihanoukville Railway Station

WEATHER STATION HILL/ VICTORY HILL

Sokimex

Phnom Sihanoukville

Wat Leu

Shared Taxis

Bus Station

Victory Monument

Independence Monument

INDEPENDENCE SQUARE

Koh Pos

Hawaii Beach

CT Clinic

Police

SEE 'TOWN CENTRE' MAP INSET

EKAREACH STREET

Vietnamese Consulate

Koh Pos Beach

Wat Krom

Sihanoukville International Clinic

Boeung Prek Tup

Lucky Ocean Supermarket

GOLDEN LIONS ROUNDABOUT

Independence Beach

SERENDIPITY BEACH ROAD

Boeung Sam At

Sokha Beach Resort

GOLDEN LION PLAZA

SEE SERENDIPITY BEACH ROAD MAP INSET

Night Market

GOLDEN LIONS RNDBT

Sokha Beach

Serendipity Beach

Giant Ibis

Koh Rong Dive Centre

EcoSea Dive

Top Cat Cinema

Ana Travel

GOLDEN LION PLAZA

SIHANOUKVILLE SQUARE

Galaxy Cinema

Ochheuteal Beach

Dive Shop

Scuba Nation

0 — 100 metres

Pier

Fast ferries to Koh Rong

TOWN CENTRE

CT Clinic

0 — 250 metres

SOPHEAKMONGKOL NORTH

OMUI STREET

STREET 109

STREET 108

STREET 109

Canadia Bank

Old Transport Stop (Shared Taxis to Kampot & Minibuses)

EKAREACH STREET

ATM

Psar Leu

Phnom Penh Sorya Transport

ATM

Caltex

Mottah Travel

Virak Buntham

Mekong Express

Capitol Bus Station

ABA Bank

Samudera Supermarket

EATING
Holy Cow	2
Secret Garden Otres	3
Sophary Restaurant	1
Starfish Café	5
Sunshine Café	4

DRINKING & NIGHTLIFE
The Big Easy	2
Dolphin Shack	5
Maybe Later	4
Utopia	3
Wish You Were Here	1

ACCOMMODATION
@home	10
Backpacker Heaven	1
BOHO	2
Footprints	3
Gekozy	11
Hacienda	4
Monkey Republic	8
One Stop Hostel	7
Pat Pat	5
Sea Garden	6
Utopia	9

Otres Village; Otres Beach (6km); Flyboarding Cambodia; Hurricane; Otres Nautica & Koh Ta Kiev

SERENDIPITY BEACH ROAD & OCHHEUTEAL BEACH

@home Serendipity Beach Rd ☎034 934898, ⓦhome-cambodia.com. Spacious fan and a/c rooms with TV and hot-water showers. Restaurant serves Swiss and Khmer dishes. Doubles $15

Monkey Republic Serendipity Beach Rd ☎012 490290, ⓦmonkeyrepublic.info. Backpacker favourite with pool, a/c dorms and private rooms, some with a/c and hot water. The pub-style bar-restaurant (daily 8am–midnight) is a good place to start the night. Dorms $5, doubles $10

★One Stop Hostel Off Golden Lions roundabout ☎034 933433, ⓦonederz.com/sihanoukville. Sparkling dorms and bathrooms are set around an open-air pool, plus there's a sociable lounge area and cheap food; breakfast from $2. Dorms $8

Utopia Serendipity Beach Rd ☎034 933586, ⓦutopia-cambodia.com. The $2 fan dorms at this 130-bed party hostel are a big draw for backpackers. A/c dorms ($3) were scheduled to open and they have basic, private rooms. The hostel is known for its Saturday pool parties and the 25-person hot tub. Dorms $2, doubles $8

OTRES BEACH AND OTRES VILLAGE

★BOHO Off the main road before *Kub Club*, Otres Village ☎090 780993, ⓦfacebook.com/bohocambodia. A beachy-boho vibe prevails at this cool hostel with en-suite a/c and fan dorms. Rooftop terrace and friendly bar-restaurant and 75c beers during happy hour (6–9pm); breakfast from $2.50. Dorms $6

Footprints Otres 2 ☎097 2621598, ⓦfootprintsotres.wixsite.com/footprintsotres. Free beer at check-in at the only backpacker hostel (dorms and rooms) on quieter Otres 2. They also have an open-air mattress dorm above the beach bar. Dorms $5, doubles $20

Hacienda Otres Village, opposite Otres market ☎070 814643, ⓦfacebook.com/haciendaotres. Super-sociable hostel with a ten-bed "freedom" dorm ($3 first night, free thereafter if you spend money in their bar/restaurant) and garden bungalows. Dorms $3, doubles $12

Pat Pat Otres 1 ☎069 411574, ⓦpat-patguesthouse.com. The a/c fourteen-bed dorm with two en-suite hot-water bathrooms is excellent value. There's also a pool, gym, boules area and bar-restaurant, and friendly owners. Dorms $6, doubles $25

SeaGarden Otres 1 ☎096 253 8131, ⓦfacebook.com/seagarden.otres. Eleven seafront bungalows with shared bathrooms at the eastern end of Otres 1. Excellent bar-restaurant too, which is great for breakfast. Doubles $15

EATING

Sihanoukville has a good selection of restaurants, around Ekareach St in downtown, Serendipity Beach Rd and Otres. The best-value Khmer food is found at the cluster of food stalls to the eastern side of Golden Lions roundabout. Many bars on Ochheuteal Beach offer $4 barbecues.

★Holy Cow Ekareach St ☎012 478510. This laidback spot in an old wooden house has a varied, inexpensive Khmer and Western menu (cottage pie $3.25). Daily 9am–10pm.

★Secret Garden Otres Otres 2 ☎097 649 5131, ⓦsecretgardenotres.com. Rooms are pricey but the beach bar is one of the best, with 75c happy-hour beers, excellent food (salads $5, stuffed squid $7) and good vegetarian options. Kitchen closes 9.30pm. Daily 7am–11.30pm.

Sophary Restaurant Victory Hill ☎012 976107. Super-cheap breakfasts (pancakes/eggs $1, fruit salad $1.25) and mains $2–3 at this locally run restaurant. It also has a travel desk. Daily 8am–9pm.

Starfish Café St 208, 100m off 7 Makara behind Samudera Supermarket ☎012 828432, ⓦstarfishcambodia.org. Delicious bread, cakes ($2) and scones served in a garden. A shop sells fairtrade arts and crafts and there's a massage place across the courtyard. Profits go to *Starfish*'s grassroots charity, supporting projects in Cambodia. Daily 7am–5.30pm.

Sunshine Café Otres 1 ☎012 828432, ⓦfacebook.com/SunshineCafeOtres. The $5 barbecue, fried fish sandwiches ($4) and Khmer specialities including *ban chaev*, savoury pancakes ($3.50), are favourites at this beach restaurant. Daily 8am–10pm.

DRINKING AND NIGHTLIFE

Numerous bars line Serendipity Beach Road and Ochheuteal Beach, while Otres 1 offers a laidback party vibe. On Saturdays, there's live music, food stalls and crafts at Otres Market in Otres Village (6pm–late).

The Big Easy Serendipity Rd ☎017 827677, ⓦthebigeasycambodia.com. Starting point for Friday's Sihanoukville Pub Crawl. Live bands, party tunes and good food (mac'n'cheese $3, Thai curry $3.25) make this hostel bar a favourite drinking spot. Daily 6.30am–midnight.

Dolphin Shack Start of Ochheuteal Beach ⓦfacebook.com/dolphinshackbeachclub. Loud, lively beach bar with nightly parties, fire shows and Khmer and Western DJs; think vodka buckets, beer pong, 50c beer and booze cruises. Open 24hr.

Maybe Later Serendipity Beach Rd ☎097 869 5264, ⓦfacebook.com/maybelatercambodia. Lively joint with an eye-popping range of rum and tequila, and top-notch Mexican food. Daily 11am–2am.

Utopia Serendipity Beach Rd ☎034 933586, ⓦutopia-cambodia.com. Popular late-night bar with pool and huge hot tub. People flock for the 50c beer, $1 shots and $2.50 cocktails. Things can get rowdy; be smart and watch your belongings. Daily 10am–late.

★Wish You Were Here Otres 1 ☎097 241 5884, ⓦfacebook.com/OtresBeachCambodia. A super-long happy hour (4–10pm) draws people to this Otres hangout.

Tasty dishes (curry $3, breakfasts $1.50) and good-value dorms ($6) too. Daily 7am–late.

DIRECTORY

Banks and exchange ATMs are plentiful on Serendipity Beach Rd and along Ekareach St. Canadia Bank, ANZ, Acleda and ABA are all between Caltex petrol station and 7 Makara St. Otres 1 and 2 each have an ATM; there are none on the islands.

Hospitals and clinics Sihanoukville International Clinic (☎ 034 933911) on Ekareach St, and CT Clinic on Boray Kamakor St (☎ 081 886666), both downtown, have 24hr emergency service, English-speaking doctors and accept credit cards. On Koh Rong, there's a volunteer-staffed clinic (ⓦ facebook.com/Kohrongemergency) in Koh Toch.

Police 316 Ekareach St between Independence Square and the town centre on the first hill. The 24hr tourist police number is ☎ 097 7780008.

Post office The main post office is opposite the Independence Monument (Mon–Sat 7.30am–noon & 2–5.30pm).

ISLANDS NEAR SIHANOUKVILLE

As the crowds swell and developments get out of hand in Sihanoukville, many use it as a jumping-off point to the appealing nearby islands. The largest and most developed is **KOH RONG** where a buzzing backpacker strip has emerged on the southeast corner at **Koh Toch** (Koh Tui) village; activities include boat tours, pub crawls and High Point ropes park (☎ 016 839993, ⓦ high-point.asia). It's more laidback at **Long Set** (4K) beach, just north of Koh Toch, and positively horizontal at **Sok San village** on the west coast's Long Beach.

Neighbouring **KOH RONG SAMLOEM** has a growing number of enticing options along its beautiful bays – Saracen, Sunset and M'Pai Bai – while peaceful **KOH TA KIEV** retains a real castaway vibe and has several, atmospheric places to stay. Take cash; no island has an ATM and cash advances are pricey.

Most Sihanoukville guesthouses can organize island-hopping day-trips, such as to **Bamboo Island** for around $15 including barbecue and snorkelling. Dive shops in town and on the islands offer **diving trips** (see p.105) including for first-timers.

ARRIVAL AND DEPARTURE

By boat Ferries and fast boats connect Sihanoukville to Koh Toch on Koh Rong, Saracen Bay on Koh Rong Samloem, and selected bays. Many properties arrange their own transfers ($10–12 return). Schedules change frequently; it can be easier to book with an agent. Prices are currently fixed ($15/$12 for ferry/fast boat).

ACCOMMODATION

KOH RONG

Most budget options on Koh Rong are in Koh Toch village. Quieter Sok San village on westerly Long Beach also has a handful of cheap bungalows.

Bong's Guesthouse Koh Toch village, main drag ⓦ 019 3924856, ⓦ bongsguesthouse.com. All-day happy hour, free breakfast and sociable atmosphere make *Bong's* a favourite. Dorms and private rooms, some en suite. Dorms $7, doubles $14

Lonely Beach North of island ☎ 097 685840, ⓦ lonely-beach.net. Rustic getaway with an open-sided dorm and simple bungalows on one of Koh Rong's quietest beaches. Dorms $10, bungalows $25

Prek Svay Homestay Northeast coast. Stay with a family in a fishing village at this homestay run by local organizer Johnny. The easiest way to book and get there is via Adventure Adam's boat tour (☎ 010 354002, ⓦ adventureadam.org). All meals included. Per person $17

KOH RONG SAMLOEM

Beach Island Resort Saracen Bay north of Orchid Pier ☎ 077 765069, ⓦ thebeachresort.asia. The open, two-tier seaview dorm is good value. Mattresses can sleep two and come with a safe, charging point and mosquito net. There are also a variety of bungalows and a well-priced menu (noodles $3.50, breakfast from $2.50). Dorms $10, bungalows $24

The Chill Inn M'Pai Bai ☎ 016 824211 ⓦ facebook.com/ chillinncambodia. Great-value breezy dorms including two loft rooms. Sociable bar (7.30am–midnight), with activities that include barbecues and beach games. Dorms $6.50, doubles $15

★**Huba Huba** Sunset Beach ☎ 088 5545619, ⓦ huba-huba-cambodia.com. Sunset Beach accommodation is universally good, but *Huba Huba's* dorms, spacious tents and bungalows are particularly inviting. Excellent food with a French twist, and late-night beach bar. No wi-fi. Dorms $5, tents $20, bungalows $30

KO TA KIEV

A castaway experience beckons on Ko Ta Kiev. Note most places don't have 24hr electricity or wi-fi.

★**Crusoe Island** Top of Long Beach ☎ 093 549239, ⓦ crusoeisland.asia. Camp, pitch your hammock over the sand or kip down in a bungalow at this sociable, family-run spot. Excellent food and they organize island treks and boat trips. Boat transfer from Otres 1 $10 return. Electricity evenings only. Own tent/person $\overline{3}$, dome tent $\overline{\$10}$, bungalows $\overline{\$15}$

The Last Point East coast ☎088 5026930, ⓦ lastpointisland.com. This solar-powered place has a private beach, and the sunrise views from the two-level dorm are a winner; they also have hammocks, tents and bungalows, some in the jungle ("jungalows"). A circular beach bar serves good food and wood-fired pizzas. Boat $12 return from *SeaGarden* on Otres 1. Camping $\overline{\$2}$, dorms $\overline{\$5}$, bungalows $\overline{\$20}$

EATING AND DRINKING

KOH TOCH

3 Brothers Koh Toch main drag ⓦ facebook.com/ ThreeBrothersGuesthouse. Free beer with selected dishes such as rice with chicken ($2) and *amok* ($3) make this exceptional value. Western food from $1.50. Daily 7am–9pm.

Dragon Den Pub Koh Toch, side street after *Bong's* ⓦ facebook.com/DragonDenPub. The island's first "pub", serving fifty-plus beers including Sihanoukville-brewed Five Men. Free popcorn. Daily 9.30am–2am.

Island Boys Koh Toch, two doors up from *Bong's* ☎070 240154, ⓦ kohrongislandboys.com. Cheap beds aside (dorms $7, doubles $16), you'll always find a party here. Happy hour 6–9pm. Daily 7.30am–late.

KOH RONG SAMLOEM

Most resorts double up as bars and restaurants. For late-night drinks on Saracen Bay, head to *Tree Bar* or *Octopussy Bar*.

★**Fishing Hook** M'Pai Bai boat pier. The $6 all-you-can-eat buffet is a hit with vegans, vegetarians, meat-lovers and seafood fans. Book in advance. Leftovers aren't wasted; locals join for dinner later. Good for breakfast and lunch too. Daily 7am–10.30pm.

REAM NATIONAL PARK

Ream National Park, or Preah Sihanouk National Park, 18km east of Sihanoukville, is one of Cambodia's most accessible national parks, and a great place to explore the country's unspoilt natural environment. Some sections have been leased to developers, with plans for a resort and even a port, but for now it remains a pristine spot. Its 210 square kilometres include evergreen and mangrove forests, sandy beaches, coral reefs, offshore islands and a rich diversity of flora and fauna.

Park rangers at its headquarters (daily 7.30–11.30am & 2–5pm; ☎012 875096) are helpful, and can arrange **boat trips**

($50 per boat, or $10 per person for large groups) along the Prek Teuk Sap estuary to Mangrove Island, Thmor Tom fishing village and Koh Sam Pouch Beach. The river is bordered by mangroves, and you're likely to see kingfishers, eagles and monkeys. Two-hour guided walks along forested nature trails cost $8 per person, or book a day tour.

ARRIVAL AND DEPARTURE

To get to the park headquarters from Sihanoukville, head along National Route 4 to Ream village, turning right down the track next to the airport.

By moto or tuk-tuk A moto/tuk-tuk costs $10/$15 from Sihanoukville.

On a tour Joining a group costs about $20–25 per person including lunch.

ACCOMMODATION AND EATING

★**Monkey Maya** Ream Beach ☎016 767686 ⓦ monkeymayaream.com. Part of the Monkey Republic brand, secluded, sociable *Monkey Maya* is idyllically perched above Ream Beach. The airy sixteen-bed dorm and sea-facing bungalows (some sleep four) are excellent value. Friendly staff and delicious food. Dorms $\overline{\$10}$, bungalows $\overline{\$45}$

KOH S'DACH

The small island of **KOH S'DACH** (King's Island) is the fishing capital of Cambodian waters, just off Koh Kong province in the Gulf of Thailand. If you've time for a detour, it's highly recommended.

Off the north shore of Koh S'Dach you'll find brilliantly coloured coral within paddling distance while the cluster of **islands** nearby – Koh Samai, Koh Samot, Koh Chan and Koh Totang – offer good reefs for snorkelling. You can charter a fishing boat for around $30 a day or book with dive outfit Octopuses Garden (☎086 412432, ⓦ octopuscambodia.com). Alternatively, hop in a small, fibreglass boat to the mainland (around $2) and explore the deserted beaches. Thai **Baht** is accepted on the island.

ARRIVAL AND DEPARTURE

By bus and boat Take a Koh Kong-bound bus from Sihanoukville or Phnom Penh and alight at Andoung Tuek where motos and minivans head to Poi Yopon, the mainland fishing village facing the archipelago. Alternatively, ask to be dropped at *Café Sok Srei*, 6km after Andoung Tek; the café owner will arrange the minivan to Poi Yopon. Some share taxis also go direct to Poi Yopon. From Poi Yopon fishing boats regularly depart for Ko S'Dach (10min).

ACCOMMODATION AND EATING

You can buy snacks and food at the market, and shops sell beer, snacks and sundries.

May's Kitchen Main St. Helpful owner Mai prepares mouth-watering Thai and Khmer dishes at this simple streetside restaurant. Try the *pad thai* and spicy salads. Daily 7.30am–8.30pm.

Octopuses Garden Near the pier ☎086 412432, ⓦoctopuscambodia.com Over-water dive centre with an airy four-bed mezzanine dorm and treehouse bungalow (shared bathroom). Breakfast included, dinner $6. Dorms $15, bungalow $35

Yvonne's Western tip of island ☎071 245 4648. Best known for its tasty fish, pasta and pizza (restaurant daily 9am–9pm), the owner has recently added six bright-blue shared-bathroom bungalows with seaview terraces. Bungalows $10

KOH KONG

Previously, boat schedules and border opening times made an overnight stop in **KOH KONG** a necessity. Since the Thai border post extended its hours to 10pm, there's no need to stay, but this region of pristine mangrove forest, serene **Tatai River** and jungle-clad **Cardamom Mountains** is worth a stop. Islands include **Koh Kong Island** (separate to the mainland town Koh Kong), with seven beautiful beaches on the seaward side (although sandflies can be a problem). You can charter a six-person boat for around $100 (or $25 per person on day-trips with local operators) for the two-hour trip. Avoid the rough seas between June and October.

ECO ADVENTURES IN KOH KONG

Koh Kong is an emerging ecotourism destination; day-trips to waterfalls and treks into the lush jungle of the Cardamoms are offered by the reliable Ritthy at Koh Kong Eco Adventure Tours (☎012 707719, ⓦkohkongecoadventure.com). For kayaking and other activities, try Neptune (☎088 777 0576, ⓦneptuneadventure-cambodia.com), whose base is a chilled-out guesthouse on the Tatai River, 20km east of town, itself a lovely place to stay ($25).

INTO THAILAND: KOH KONG

From **Koh Kong**, it's a 12km moto/tuk-tuk ride ($3/$6) to the border crossing at Cham Yeam (daily 6am–10pm). Fifteen-day Thai visas for most passports are arranged on the spot. From **Hat Lek**, on the Thai side of the border, minibuses leave for Trat (see p.785), 91km northwest, roughly every forty minutes (daily 7am–5pm; 1hr–1hr 30min; B120); Trat has regular connections to Bangkok and Koh Chang.

Situated on the eastern bank of the Kah Bpow River, Koh Kong was historically an insular outpost, its prosperity based on fishing, logging and smuggling. These days, the border brings in the trade. A 2km-long bridge crosses the river, and a left turn shortly after the bridge takes you to **Koh Yor Beach**, a pretty strip of sand lined with low-key restaurants. Despite the fact that much of the rich sandalwood forest has been felled and transported to Thailand, the surrounding area is beautiful and remains largely unspoilt.

ARRIVAL AND INFORMATION

By bus Buses usually drop off east of town near the Acleda Bank, a $1–2 moto ride into town.

Destinations Phnom Penh (4 daily; 6hr); Sihanoukville (4 daily; 4hr).

By share taxi or minibus Most companies will drop you off by the market or the port, an easy walk to most guesthouses. Frequent services to Phnom Penh and Sihanoukville, and a few to Kep and Kampot.

Services Koh Kong town is walkable, but motos are inexpensive at $1 a trip. ATMs include Acleda near the bus station, Canadia Bank on the riverfront and Bank of Cambodia by the market.

ACCOMMODATION

Moto drivers take commissions, so know where you're going or book ahead.

Kaing Kaing Guesthouse Riverfront, near the old boat dock ☎089 836073. This friendly Khmer-run guesthouse on the riverfront has eighteen fan and a/c rooms with hot-water bathrooms. Limited English spoken. Doubles $20

Paddy's Bamboo Guesthouse Chicken Farm Rd, 350m from Fat Sam's/roundabout ☎015 533223, ⓔppkohkong @gmail.com. The hammock option here is one of the cheapest places in town. Rooms are better value than the stuffy dorms and there's a sociable bar-restaurant and travel desk. Hammocks $2, dorms $8, doubles $6

Ritthy's Retreat Riverfront ☎012 707719, ✉ritthy
.info@gmail.com. Welcoming guesthouse run by
knowledgeable Ritthy (of Koh Kong Eco Adventure Tours),
with en-suite dorms and rooms, some with a/c ($14) and
hot water. Good restaurant. Dorms $\overline{\$4}$, doubles $\overline{\$7}$

EATING AND DRINKING

Baan Peakmai *Asian Hotel*, riverside ☎035 936667.
What this hotel restaurant lacks in atmosphere, it makes
up for with tasty Thai and Khmer dishes, including
vegetarian ones, for around $5. Daily 6.30–9.30am,
11am–2pm & 5–10pm.
Fat Sam's High St, near the roundabout ☎097 737 0707.
Filling English breakfasts ($6), comfort food and 75c beer
are on the menu, plus pool table and motorbike rental.
Mon–Sat 9am–9.30pm, Sun 4–9.30pm.
★**Wood House** South of roundabout ☎087 269620.
French and Khmer owners serve up delicious plates of local
and European cuisine, including breakfasts; the burger is
exceptional ($6.25). Daily 8.30am–10.30pm.

KAMPOT

KAMPOT, with its riverside location,
backdrop of misty Bokor Mountains and
terraces of French shophouses, is one of
Cambodia's most appealing towns, with
an excellent choice of accommodation
and restaurants. It's also the staging post
for side-trips to Kep, and a pleasant place
to spend an afternoon browsing the
market, strolling along the Teuk Chhou
River, heading into the mountains to
explore caves and visiting pepper
plantations, or pottering along the river
for a swim or sunset cruise, plus activities
such as kiteboarding and kayaking. The
river marks the town's western boundary,
with the new market to the north.

The somewhat eerie French-colonial hill
station in **Bokor National Park** is perched
high in the mountains above Kampot,
home to an abandoned 1920s hotel and
casino and crumbling royal residences. A
$100-million development may change the
fate of Bokor, not necessarily to the benefit
of the ecosystem; a plush hotel and casino
have opened, with plans for villas, golf
courses, water parks and cable car. A 32km
road makes access easy. All guesthouses and
travel agents (such as All Tours Cambodia
by *Captain Chim's* on Old Market Rd, and
Sok Lim Tours and Mr Bison Tours on
Guesthouse St) organize trips ($8).

ARRIVAL AND INFORMATION

By bus Several buses, including Giant Ibis, travel to and
from Phnom Penh (6 daily; 3hr 30min–5hr). Avoid the
circuitous route via Kep, which can take up to 5hr.
By moto or tuk-tuk A moto to Kep costs $10, tuk-tuk
$15, taxi $20; the journey takes 30–45min.
By share taxi or minibus Regular departures from the
market or the transport stop by Total petrol station (top of
Old Market Rd). Most offer hotel pick-ups.
Destinations Kep (7 daily; 1hr); Koh Kong (2 daily: 5hr);
Phnom Penh (10 daily; 3–4hr); Sihanoukville (10 daily;
2hr 30min).
By train A pleasant if limited train service operates
between Phnom Penh and Sihanoukville via Takeo and
Kampot. Leaves Fri, Sat, Sun and public holidays.
Phnom Penh (5hr), Sihanoukville (1hr 40min–2hr
40min), Takeo (3hr); tickets $4–7. Tickets only from the
station; you can usually buy on the day (☎078 888582,
⊛ royal-railway.com).
Publications Free booklets *Coastal* (⊛ coasta
l-cambodia.com) and *Kampot Survival Guide*
(⊛ kampotsurvivalguide.com) have up-to-date listings.

ACCOMMODATION

IN TOWN

Billabong 250m from the market ☎096 767 2977,
⊛ billabongguesthouse.com. A pool, swim-up bar and
poolside restaurant make this a backpacker favourite.
Clean, en-suite ten-bed fan dorm plus private rooms
(some with a/c; $18). It also hosts Sunday live music
sessions. Dorms $\overline{\$5}$, doubles $\overline{\$12}$
Captain Chim's Guesthouse Old Market Rd ☎012
321043. Kampot stalwart with cheap-and-cheerful fan
and cold-water rooms; a/c ones have hot water ($15). Free
laundry, good-value restaurant (breakfasts $1.25) and
travel desk. Doubles $\overline{\$7}$
Kampot Dorm St 730/Guesthouse St, off Salt Workers
Roundabout ☎012 719872, ⊛ facebook.com/
KampotDorms. No-frills sixteen-bed dorm run by a local
travel-pro whose restaurant and bar (next door) and travel
company Sok Lim Tours are well regarded. Dorms $\overline{\$2.50}$
Mad Monkey Riverside Rd after Kampot Museum
☎096 739 0284, ⊛ madmonkeyhostels.com/kampot.
Laidback party hostel with a pool, bar and numerous
options from female dorms to family rooms (a/c rooms
£24). Food is great; most dishes under $5. Dorms $\overline{\$7}$,
doubles $\overline{\$15}$
Magic Sponge St 730/Guesthouse St off Salt Workers
roundabout ☎017 946428, ⊛ magicspongekampot.com.
Book ahead for the six-bed "penthouse" dorm, with
padded mattresses, en-suite hot-water bathroom and
balcony. Refurbished private rooms are excellent value (a/c
$17). Happy hour noon–5pm, breakfasts from $1. Dorms
$\overline{\$5}$, doubles $\overline{\$12}$

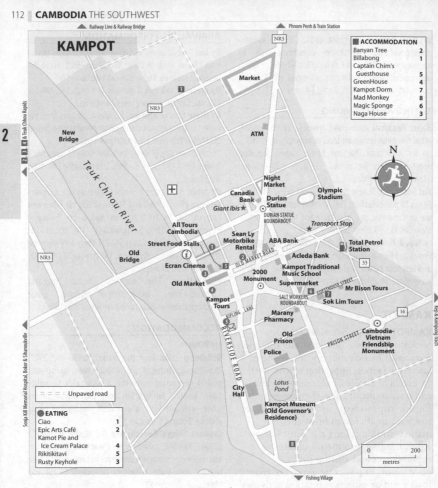

KAMPOT

■ ACCOMMODATION
Banyan Tree	2
Billabong	1
Captain Chim's Guesthouse	5
GreenHouse	4
Kampot Dorm	7
Mad Monkey	8
Magic Sponge	6
Naga House	3

Market

New Bridge

ATM

Teuk Chhou River

Night Market

Canadia Bank

Durian Statue

Olympic Stadium

Giant Ibis ★

DURIAN STATUE ROUNDABOUT

★ *Transport Stop*

All Tours Cambodia

Sean Ly Motorbike Rental

ABA Bank

Total Petrol Station

Street Food Stalls

OLD MARKET ROAD

Acleda Bank

33

Old Bridge

NR3

Ecran Cinema

2000 Monument

Kampot Traditional Music School

Old Market

Supermarket

GUESTHOUSE STREET

Mr Bison Tours

SALT WORKERS ROUNDABOUT

Sok Lim Tours

Kampot Tours

KIPLING LANE

Marany Pharmacy

16

RIVERSIDE ROAD

Old Prison

PRISON STREET

Cambodia-Vietnam Friendship Monument

Police

= = = Unpaved road

Lotus Pond

City Hall

Kampot Museum (Old Governor's Residence)

0   200
metres

▼ Fishing Village

●EATING
Ciao	1
Epic Arts Café	2
Kamot Pie and Ice Cream Palace	4
Rikitikitavi	5
Rusty Keyhole	3

(Map margin labels: Sonja Kill Memorial Hospital, Bokor & Sihanoukville; & Teuk Chhou Rapids; Kep & Kampong Trach)

ON THE RIVER

Banyan Tree Teuk Chhou Rd, 2km north of town ☎ 078 665094, ⓦ banyantreekampot.com. Formerly *Bodhi Villa*, this jungle garden guesthouse is popular for its variety of dorms, bungalows and rooms (shared bathrooms) and for its Friday-night parties. Dorms $\overline{\$3}$, doubles $\overline{\$6}$, bungalows $\overline{\$8}$

★**GreenHouse** 6km west of town, off Teuk Chhou Rd ☎ 088 886 3071, ⓦ greenhousekampot.com. Rustic riverview bungalows with modern bathrooms in a tropical garden are a steal, plus there are delicious French-inspired, Kampot pepper dishes on offer. Over-12s only because of jetty. Bungalows $\overline{\$25}$

Naga House Teuk Chhou Rd, 2km north of town ☎ 012 289916, ⓦ facebook.com/nagahousekampot. Known for its Saturday parties, *Naga House* has a sociable set-up with shared-bathroom bungalows and an impressive menu. Dorms $\overline{\$4}$, bungalows $\overline{\$7}$

EATING AND DRINKING

The best street food is found between the Old Bridge and up to the night market by the Durian roundabout, where stalls appear in the evenings. Kampot nightlife is fun and laidback, with late and lively Friday nights at *Banyan Tree* and Saturdays at *Naga House*, on the river.

Ciao St 722, between Old Bridge and Old Market. Find Diego at his street-food stand, where he prepares home-made pasta and pizza from $3. Daily 6–10pm.

★**Epic Arts Café** Old Market St ☎ 092 922069, ⓦ epicarts .org.uk. Part of a project benefiting people with disabilities and staffed by deaf people, this inviting café serves home-made baked goods (scones $2) and full meals. Daily 7am–4pm.

Kampot Pie and Ice Cream Palace Riverfront Rd, near old market ☎ 099 657826. Home-baked pastries (from $1) and ice creams are served up at this riverfront spot. *Mary's Snack Shack* outside serves breakfasts ($2.75) and snacks such as hot dogs for $1.75. Daily 6.30am–8.30pm.

Rikitikitavi Riverfront Rd ☏017 306557, ⓦrikitikitavi
-kampot.com. Happy-hour cocktails and top-notch Khmer
and Western mains such as amok curry ($6.75) are on offer
at this riverview restaurant; leave room for the apple pie
($3.25). Daily 7am–10pm.
Rusty Keyhole Riverfront Rd ☏012 679607. Popular
spot with a long happy hour 11am–7pm (75c beer, $1.50
spirits), and a menu that includes spare ribs and Sunday
roasts. Daily 8.30am–11.30pm.

KEP

Some 25km southeast of Kampot, **KEP**
may not have the most spectacular beach,
but its breezy seaside character and
palm-shaded walks remain seductive,
while empty, strangely evocative prewar
colonial villas are reminders of the havoc
wreaked by the Khmer Rouge. Now, Kep
is renowned throughout Cambodia for its
delicious, inexpensive seafood, freshly
plucked from the ocean. It's a favourite
with expats and Cambodians who
descend at the weekend, attracted by
seaside picnic huts, the relaxed vibe and
excellent accommodation.

Approaching Kep from Kampot, you'll
go past the crab market, Psar Kdam,
around the headland and see the large
Vietnamese island of **Phu Quoc** rising
offshore in the Gulf of Thailand.

Highlights include exploring the lush
national park ($1) behind the town. Access
is via **Veranda Natural Resort** (☏036 638
8588, ⓦveranda-resort.com). It's worth
stopping for a beer or home-made cake,
and non-guests can use the pool ($8).

You can also go on island boat tours,
the most popular being to **Koh Tonsay** or
Rabbit Island, with its palm-fringed
beach, massage pavilions and restaurants.
Boat trips can be arranged at guesthouses
in Kep or Kampot, or on Kep beach
(from $7 or $25 for a private charter).
You can stay overnight in rustic off-grid
bamboo cottages ($5).

ARRIVAL AND DEPARTURE

By bus Phnom Penh Sorya travel via Kep from Phnom
Penh to Kampot; check if they stop in Kep, otherwise it
can be a long journey.
Destinations Kampot (2 daily; 45min); Phnom Penh (3
daily; 4hr).
By share taxi or minibus You'll be dropped off and

picked up at Kep beach; motos and tuk-tuks will take you
to your guesthouse.
Destinations Kampot (4 daily; 1hr); Phnom Penh (4–5
daily; 4hr); Sihanoukville (5 daily; 3–4hr).
By moto or tuk-tuk A moto/tuk-tuk to Kampot costs
$10/$15 (45min).

ACCOMMODATION

Bacoma St 33A, 200m south of the Vishnu statue
☏088 411 2424, ⓦbacoma.weebly.com. The squeaky-
clean rooms and stone-walled thatched bungalows here,
set in tranquil gardens, are superb value. There's a chill-
out area, good food and helpful owners. Bungalows **$15**,
doubles **$18**
Kepmandou 200m east of Rabbit Island Pier ☏097 795
8723. This lively sea-facing hostel has quirky rooms, some
without windows, an open-sided first-floor communal
area, pool table and kitchen. Hammocks **$3**, dorms **$4**,
doubles **$4**
★ Khmer House Bungalow North of Rabbit Island Pier
☏097 367 7745, ✉cheamsamoeun@gmail.com. Excellent-
value stilted bungalows with hot water and fans at this
family-run place. There are lovely views of the countryside
from the restaurant, which uses ingredients from the organic
garden. Doubles **$10**

2

EATING

Kep is heaven for seafood connoisseurs. Try the crab market on the western seafront for cheap dishes, or the stalls by Kep Beach for grilled fish and chicken.

Beachside Tacos Kep Beach, by *Chan Vanna Guest House*. Three tacos for $3, burritos for $5 and Khmer dishes for $1.50–2.50 at this streetside stand near Kep Beach. Daily 6.30am–10.30pm.

The Crab Kitchen Halfway along crab market strip ☎ 016 789994, ⓦ facebook.com/thecrabkitchen.kep. Friendly owners serve up crab with Kampot pepper ($7.50) and other local dishes. Happy hour 4–8pm; 75c beer and $2.50 cocktails. Daily 9am–11pm.

★ **Sailing Club** Next to *Knai Bang Chatt* hotel on the coast, 5min walk from crab market ☎ 078 333685, ⓦ knaibangchatt.com/the-sailing-club. Happy-hour cocktails (5–7pm) are a must at this swish sunset bar. Their new cocktail bar next door offers tapas and late-night opening (4pm–late). Daily 7am–10pm.

Eastern Cambodia

Running south from Laos, the mighty **Mekong** forms a natural boundary between eastern Cambodia and the rest of the country.

Many travellers pass through eastern Cambodia en route to or from Laos, although the serene riverside towns of **Kompong Cham** and **Kratie** are increasingly attracting visitors in their own right, while the latter also offers the chance of spotting rare Irrawaddy dolphins frolicking amid the Mekong waters. Cambodia's remote **eastern uplands** remain largely untouched by the march of development (although the region's forests have suffered from uncontrolled logging). If you like nature and wildlife, this is the place to be, and significant patches of dense, unspoilt rainforest remain. Tucked away in the far northeast, the sleepy capital of Ratanakiri province, **Banlung**, is surrounded by peaceful countryside dotted with waterfalls, lakes and the occasional impromptu gem mine. It's also the starting point for rewarding visits to local **chunchiet** (indigenous hill tribe) villages and for treks into the pristine jungle of the **Virachey National Park**, with the chance of

spotting gibbons and rare birdlife.

South of here the laidback little town of **Sen Monorom** (capital of Mondulkiri province) has emerged as a major centre for **ethical elephant tourism**, offering the chance to walk with and observe elephants in their natural jungle habitat.

KOMPONG CHAM AND AROUND

The east's largest city and capital of the province of the same name, **KOMPONG CHAM** was one of Cambodia's most cosmopolitan cities during the colonial era but is now something of a sleepy backwater. All routes into the east pass through here, and although there's no overwhelming reason to stop, it's a nice place to do so.

The **waterfront** is particularly attractive, with a string of time-warped colonial buildings lined up along the Mekong (about 1.5km wide here). On the riverbank around 1km south of here, **Wat Dei Doh** is fronted by a huge standing Buddha and surrounded by grounds scattered with intriguing statues of people and animals, while a forest of miniature stupas stabs up into the sky. Roughly opposite the wat, a remarkable **bamboo bridge** ($1), rebuilt from scratch every year as the river waters subside, leads during the dry season over to the idyllic island of Koh Paen.

Wat Nokor

The most interesting sight around town is **Wat Nokor** ($2, ticket also valid for Phnom Pros and Phnom Srei), about 2km north of the centre just off National Route 7. Much of the original eleventh-century temple survives, with a garishly coloured modern vihara now inserted rudely into the heart of the ancient ruins. It's an art historian's nightmare but has a certain gruesome fascination, with luminous modern murals and columns framed by ancient laterite walls, still showing traces of the black paint applied during the days of Khmer Rouge occupation.

Phnom Pros and Phnom Srei

About 12km further out of town past Wat Nokor rise the twin temple hills of **Phnom**

Pros and **Phnom Srei** ($2, ticket also valid for Wat Nokor), "Man and Woman Mountains". According to legend, in ancient times women had to ask men to marry them. Fed up with this, the women challenged the men to see who could build the best temple by daybreak – the winners would win the right to be proposed to. When the women realized they were lagging behind, they built a huge fire, which the men took to be the rising sun. The men headed for bed while the women carried on building, producing a magnificent temple and winning the right to receive proposals.

ARRIVAL AND DEPARTURE

By bus Buses arrive and depart from their various offices in the centre of town, all within a 10min walk of the riverfront and guesthouses.
Destinations Banlung (2 daily; 8hr); Kratie (3 daily; 3hr); Phnom Penh (12 daily; 4hr); Siem Reap (5 daily; 6hr); Stung Treng (1 daily; 6hr).
By share taxi or minibus Taxis and minibuses are found at the market and are especially quick if heading north to Kratie and beyond.
Destinations Kratie (2hr 30min); Phnom Penh (3hr 30min); Stung Treng (5hr).

ACCOMMODATION

Mekong Riverfront ☎042 941536. One of the town's oldest hotels, showing its age but still a reasonable choice for its cheap and comfortable fan rooms (with hot water) despite the rather institutional atmosphere, although the a/c rooms are drab and overpriced (at $15). Doubles $8
Moon River Riverfront ☎016 788973. Chic riverfront restaurant (daily 6am–10pm) serving up a good selection of Western and Asian cuisine including flavoursome Khmer fish and meat *amoks* and curries (mains around $3). Also has a mixed bag of rooms upstairs (optional a/c for $4 extra) of various sizes and standards. Doubles $11

EATING

There's an excellent string of tourist-oriented places to eat and drink along the riverfront. Around the market, you'll find some decent food stalls and noodle shops.
Destiny Coffee Shop Pasteur St, just off the riverfront. This chic café is more Phnom Penh than Kompong Cham, serving up good coffee and shakes plus snacks and light meals and a short selection of Western and Asian mains (around $4). Daily 7am–5pm, Fri & Sat until 8pm.
Mekong Crossing Riverfront ☎017 801788. Always lively, this bar-restaurant is the town's best place for a drink, either in the cosy interior or lounging on a wicker

chair on the terrace outside. There's also a decent menu of cheap Asian and Khmer staples (mains $2.50–3.50) plus pricier Western dishes. Daily 6am–10pm.
Smile Riverfront ☎017 997709. The top restaurant in town, run as a training centre for orphans and vulnerable children and serving excellent Khmer food, bursting with flavour, plus a decent range of Western dishes, salads, sandwiches and snacks. Mains $4–5. Daily 6am–10pm.

KRATIE AND AROUND

Life ticks by slowly in **KRATIE** (pronounced "Kracheh"). This indolent town on the Mekong is an unexpected delight, with a wonderful hotchpotch of colonial terraces and a fine old **Governor's Residence**, on the waterfront just south of the centre. There's not much to do in the town itself, which stretches lazily along the west bank of the river, but it makes a good base for exploring the surrounding countryside.

About 11km north of Kratie along the river is peaceful **Phnom Sambok**, a lushly forested twin-peaked hill. The dense trees hide a meditation commune and a small temple on the higher summit.

Around 10km further north along the same road, **Kampie** provides the best riverside vantage point from which to view a pod of rare freshwater **Irrawaddy dolphins**, of which it's thought that only around eighty remain in the entire Mekong. A small group of these snub-nosed dolphins lives in this area of rapids, with virtually guaranteed sightings if you take the official boat trip ($9, or $7 in a group of three or more).

The easiest way to visit these places is to hire a moto ($5 return) or tuk-tuk ($10), although you could easily cycle along the beautiful riverside road. If you can spare a full day, you could also include a visit to **Sambor**, some 35km north of Kratie, the site of an ancient pre-Angkorian capital (moto $15, tuk-tuk $20).

ARRIVAL AND DEPARTURE

By bus Most buses to and from Kratie are run by Phnom Penh Sorya, departing/terminating at their offices just west of the market. Tickets for buses and minibuses can be bought through many of the town's guesthouses.
Destinations Banlung (1 daily; 5hr); Kompong Cham (3 daily; 3hr); Phnom Penh (3 daily; 7hr); Stung Treng (1 daily; 2hr 30min).

2

By share taxi or minibus Taxis will usually drop you off en route; otherwise, the transport stop is one block north of the market. Share taxis and minibuses leave from the transport stop and are the quickest way to travel between Kratie and Kompong Cham ($6), and are also quicker to Phnom Penh ($7). Heading south, most share taxis and minivans also save time by taking the rougher but much more direct route along the river; buses take a much more roundabout route inland via Snoul.

Destinations Banlung (5hr); Kompong Cham (2hr 30min); Phnom Penh (6hr); Sen Monorom (5hr); Stung Treng (2hr 30min).

ACCOMMODATION

Balcony Riverfront, north of the centre ☎ 097 760 6393, ⊛ balconyguesthouse.net. Large and rather institutional concrete box of a guesthouse offering a mish-mash of fan and a/c rooms (cold water only; en suite $12; a/c $15). There's also a basic dorm and a sunny river-facing balcony. Dorms $5, doubles $10

Heng Heng II Riverfront, near the market ☎ 012 929943. Right in the centre, this cosy little hotel is Kratie town's best option if you can't snag a bed at *Le Tonle*, with a helpful English-speaking owner and comfortable fan and slightly plusher a/c rooms (all with hot water; $13) kitted out with chintzy wooden furniture. Doubles $7

★**Le Tonle Tourism Training Centre** Just off the riverfront north of the centre ☎ 072 210505, ⊛ letonle .org. Kratie's stand-out accommodation option, run as a tourism training school for local youngsters. Accommodation is in a handful of attractive wood-panelled rooms all sharing a couple of immaculate bathrooms. Fills up fast, so advance reservations generally essential; a/c rooms $15. Doubles $10

Star Backpackers St 10, opposite the market ☎ 097 339 1285. Crammed into microscopic premises above the *Tokae* restaurant with ultra-cheap accommodation in a very basic ten-bed dorm plus small and simple but inexpensive fan rooms. Right in the thick of the town-centre action, with noise levels to match. Dorms $2.50, doubles $5

EATING AND DRINKING

Snack and drink stalls set up every evening by the riverside.

★**Le Tonle Tourism Training Centre** Just off the riverfront north of the centre ☎ 072 210505, ⊛ letonle .org. Lovely open-air restaurant serving up quality Khmer and Western food (mains $3–4) – try the signature *amok* or pomelo salad. Good for breakfast too. Daily 6.30am–9.30pm.

Pete's Pizza Pasta & Café (aka *Sorya Café*) Riverfront, north of the centre ☎ 090 241148, ⊛ petescafekratie.com. Attractive café serving up excellent pizza, pasta and salads (mains around $5) plus bakery items including the signature pumpkin bread. Daily 7am–9pm.

Red Sun Falling Riverfront ☎ 011 285806. This cosy café is a good place to start or end your day, with a big selection of Western breakfasts (carb-up with the "Super Full Monty", $6), good, cheap Asian mains ($2–2.50), plus comforting Western favourites including chicken and chips, salads and shakes. Daily 7am–9pm.

STUNG TRENG

For most people, **STUNG TRENG** is just a staging post on the way to Laos, but the surrounding countryside is beautiful and can be explored by boat, moto or bicycle. Hotel and guesthouse owners can arrange visits to a silk weaving centre, fruit orchards, lakes and waterfalls, and boat trips to remote villages.

One of the most popular outings is a Mekong trip to the **Laos border** (the border crossing itself is at Trapaeng Kriel), offering the possibility of some dolphin-spotting and a glimpse at the waterfalls that make the river impassable here.

INTO LAOS: TRAPAENG KRIEL – NONG NOK KHIENE

Cambodia's only border crossing into Laos is at **Trapaeng Kriel** (near Veun Kham on the Lao side of the border) 57km north of Stung Treng. The journey takes just over one hour. The border itself is open daily 7am–5pm; Laos visas (roughly $30–40 depending on nationality) are issued on the spot if you don't have one already. Several companies run through-buses from Cambodia to destinations in Laos including Don Det (around $11) and Pakse ($15), while some minibuses also cover the same routes. Tickets for buses and minibuses can be bought at guesthouses in Stung Treng, Banlung and elsewhere.

Entering Cambodia, visas are issued on arrival (roughly $30–40, depending on your nationality). If you're not arriving on a through-bus, you can pick up onward transport in share taxis and minibuses from the border to Stung Treng, and possibly further south to Kratie, Kompong Cham and even Phnom Penh, depending on how early you are and how lucky you get.

ARRIVAL AND DEPARTURE

By bus All road transport arrives at and leaves from the transport stop on the riverfront, apart from Phnom Penh Sorya buses, which arrive at and depart from their office by the market. Tickets can be bought through the *Riverside Guesthouse* and *Ponika's Palace*.

Destinations Kompong Cham (1 daily; 6hr); Kratie (1 daily; 2hr 30min); Phnom Penh (1 daily; 10hr).

By share taxi or minibus Share taxis and pick-ups leave from the transport stop at around 7.30am and then intermittently through the day, depending on demand.

Destinations Banlung (2hr); Kompong Cham (5hr 30min); Kratie (2hr 30min); Laos border, 1hr (see box opposite); Phnom Penh (9hr).

ACCOMMODATION AND EATING

Ponika's Palace Just northeast of the market ☎ 012 916441. There's nothing particularly palatial about this simple little family-run, tourist-oriented café, offering economical Khmer food (mains $3–4) alongside pizza, pasta and other Western and Asian standards. Decent Western breakfasts too. Daily 6am–9pm.

Riverside Guesthouse By the transport stop ☎ 012 257207. The centre of Stung Treng's very modest travellers' scene. Rooms are basic and past their best, but alright at the price (a/c twice the price), and owner Mr T is a great source of information about local tours and onward travel. The passable café (daily 6.30am–9.30pm) downstairs has a big, traveller-friendly menu featuring lots of Asian mains ($3–3.50) and Western staples. Doubles $6

BANLUNG AND AROUND

The sprawling town of **Banlung**, almost 600km northeast of Phnom Penh, only became the provincial capital in 1979, replacing the Khmer Rouge capital of Voen Sai (which had in turn replaced

▲ Voen Sai & Virachey National Park

BANLUNG

Boeung Kamsan

■ ACCOMMODATION	
Banlung Balcony Guesthouse	2
The Courtyard Guesthouse	4
Flashpacker/Backpacker Pad	3
Terres Rouges Lodge	1
Tree Top Eco Lodge	5

● EATING	
Banlung Balcony Guesthouse	1
Café Alee	3
Green Carrot	2

Boeung Kansaing

N

Stadium

Police

Virachey National Park HQ

Independence Monument

Acleda Bank

NATIONAL ROUTE 78

Lucky Tours

Canadia Bank

Transport Stop

Highland Tours

NATIONAL ROUTE 78

Wat Eisay Patamak

Airfield

Market

Phnom Svay, Waterfalls, Lumphat, Chum Rai Bai Srok & Stung Treng

Yeak Laom

0   200
metres

2

Lumphat, which had been devastated by American bombs). The town is a good base for trips and treks into the surrounding area to visit *chunchiet* villages and the forests of the nearby Virachey National Park.

WHAT TO SEE AND DO

Banlung may be the provincial capital, but not a lot happens here. At its heart is the **market**, especially lively in the early morning when local *chunchiet* come in to sell fresh produce and forest foods, setting out their wares on the pavement in front of the market building.

Yeak Laom Lake

Banlung's best-known sight is the dramatic **Yeak Laom Lake** ($2), 4km east of town ($5 return by moto), created by a volcanic eruption many thousands of years ago. It's a 3km walk around the beautiful lakeside path, through stands of bamboo and dense green forest, the tranquillity interrupted only by the occasional bird call. A swim in the clean, turquoise waters is a good way to cleanse yourself of the penetrating dust from Banlung's red dirt roads.

Phnom Svay

On the western edge of Banlung, the easy ten-minute climb up **Phnom Svay**, behind the pretty **Wat Eisay Patamak**, is well worth it for the glorious views of the O Traw Mountains. All of this is lost on the 5m-long Reclining Buddha, which lies at the summit, his eyes closed.

★TREAT YOURSELF

Terres Rouges Lodge Boeung Kansaing ☏012 660902, ⓦratanakiri-lodge.com. Luxurious boutique hotel in lush gardens near the lake. The lodge's wooden buildings look a bit like a miniature Khmer village given a cool modern makeover, with beautifully designed colonial-style rooms in the main building, plus even more stylish suites in private bungalows arranged around the beautiful grounds. There's also a top-notch restaurant and a good-sized pool, plus small spa. Doubles $65

The waterfalls

East of Banlung the countryside is dotted with a trio of impressive waterfalls: Ka Chhang and Katieng (roughly 4km from Banlung), and Chha Ong (8km). At **Chha Ong** (2000r) water sprays from a rock overhang into a small jungle clearing. There's nowhere to swim, but brave visitors shower under the smaller column of water. **Ka Chhang** (2000r) and **Katieng** (3000r) are pretty but rather less impressive.

ARRIVAL AND DEPARTURE

Hotels and guesthouses are the best places for sorting out onward transport; minibuses will usually come and pick you up from your accommodation. Share taxis arrive at the transport stop near the market.
By bus There are very few buses to or from Banlung – most transport is by minibus or share taxi.
Destinations Kompong Cham (1 daily; 8hr); Kratie (1 daily; 5hr); Phnom Penh (1 daily; 10hr).
By share taxi and minibus Transport goes to Stung Treng ($9) and then on to Kratie (another $7).
Destinations Kratie (4hr); Stung Treng (2hr).

ACCOMMODATION

Banlung Balcony Guesthouse Boeung Kansaing ☏097 809 7036, ⓦbalconyguesthouse.net. Large and rather institutional guesthouse in a peaceful location near Boeung Kansaing lake offering a range of spacious and good-value – if slightly knackered-looking – tiled fan rooms (some with shared bathroom; en suite $8) plus a handful of nicer wood-panelled rooms upstairs ($12, or $15 with a/c). There's also a good attached restaurant. Doubles $5
The Courtyard Guesthouse Town centre ☏097 333 4626, ⓔthecourtyardguesthouse@gmail.com. Cut-price town-centre lodgings offering big, basic rooms (cold water only) and a small dorm. The helpful owners also run the excellent Lucky Tours and can arrange all sorts of tours and treks. Dorms $2.50, doubles $5
Flashpacker/Backpacker Pad Boeung Kansaing ☏031 666 5213. Two-in-one accommodation with neat, cosy and very good-value modern rooms (a/c $3 extra) in the main building and super-cheap mosquito-netted beds ($2 per person) in an airy seven-bed hot-water dorm in the building next door. Doubles $8
★Tree Top Eco Lodge East of the centre ☏012 490333, ⓦtreetop-ecolodge.com. Banlung's oldest – and still its best – ecolodge, with accommodation in bungalows scattered across a thickly wooded hillside and connected by a picturesque network of raised walkways. The bungalows themselves are surprisingly smart and comfortable, nicely furnished and with big

French windows through which to enjoy the views, plus hammocks for lounging and quaint pebbled bathrooms (some with hot water for $3 extra). Small restaurant attached. Doubles $12

EATING

Banlung Balcony Guesthouse Boeung Kansaing ✆ 097 809 7036. A prime location overlooking the lake is the main draw at this attractive open-air restaurant, and the food's pretty good too, with a decent selection of Western mains ($5–7) including good burgers and an above-average choice of authentic Khmer food ($3–4) including good soups and stir-fries. Daily 7am–9pm, bar open until 11pm.

★ **Café Alee** East of the centre ✆ 089 473767. This attractive wooden pavilion-style restaurant is one of the nicest places to eat in Banlung, with a wide-ranging menu stuffed with all the usual Western and Khmer favourites (mains $4–6) along with a truckload of other home-from-home comforts – anything from cookies and fruit bread to pancakes and popcorn, plus an interesting selection of local coffees. Daily 7am–10pm.

Green Carrot East of the centre ✆ 098 909453. Cosy little café with crisp service, cool music and good food, including Khmer favourites (mains $3–4) plus a smattering of slightly more Western dishes such as pizza and pasta – while veggies will appreciate the great range of Western and Asian-style salads and tofu dishes. Daily 9am–10pm.

VOEN SAI AND VIRACHEY NATIONAL PARK

The road north of Banlung wends its way past numerous *chunchiet* villages until, after around 38km, it reaches the village of **VOEN SAI**, located on the San River, the headquarters of Virachey National Park and one of the most accessible villages in the region.

Covering more than 800,000 acres, **Virachey National Park** is a haven for a variety of endangered species, including deer, rare hornbills and kouprey, the almost-extinct jungle cow. There's also a healthy gibbon population, while tigers are also said to lurk here, although most sightings appear to have occurred after a few too many bottles of Angkor beer. The only way of getting into the park is on one of the various **treks** (1–7 nights) organized by a number of operators around town. Prices start from around $35 per person per day in a group of two (cheaper in larger groups). Many treks feature a visit to a *chunchiet* village, a night or two in a

hammock and a ride downriver on a bamboo raft. Reliable **local operators** include Parrot Tours (✆ 097 403 5884, ✇ jungletrek.wix.com/parrot-tours), Highland Tours (✆ 097 658 3841, ✉ highland.tour@yahoo.com) and Lucky Tours (✆ 097 333 4626, ✇ luckytours4u .blogspot.com), all with offices in the area northeast of the market in Banlung.

If you want to explore the countryside but don't want to trek, all these operators can also organize interesting **tours**, usually combining trips to waterfalls with visits to *chunchiet* villages and a boat trip or to see local elephants.

SEN MONOROM AND AROUND

The smallest of all Cambodia's provincial capitals, **SEN MONOROM** (420km from Phnom Penh) has transformed over the past few years into one of Asia's leading centres for **ethical elephant tourism**, inspired by the example of the ground-breaking Elephant Valley Project. There's also some good **trekking** and interesting indigenous villages in the surrounding countryside, while the town itself, set amid rolling green hills, is a pleasant place to hang out for a day or two, with a good selection of places to eat and stay.

WHAT TO SEE AND DO

Locals will direct you to the **Monorom Falls** (aka Sihanouk Falls), a peaceful nook on the edge of the jungle where a 10m-high cascade drops into a swirling plunge pool. You can either walk the few kilometres here or hire a moto along the easy road. The more distant but spectacular **Bou Sraa Falls**, about 40km northeast from Sen Monorom, can be reached by moto by way of a stunningly beautiful forest trail. The falls are a dramatic two-tiered affair, with more than 30m of water gushing into a jungle-clad gorge. For the ultimate view of the falls and the surrounding jungle canopy, buckle up for the new **Mayura Zipline** (✇ mondulkresort.com; $69), with treetop ziplines and viewing platforms culminating in a spectacular 100m-zipline ride high over the falls themselves.

2

Elephant projects

For most visitors Sen Monorom's stand-out attraction is its string of **elephant projects**, all offering the chance to walk and interact with elephants and observe them in their natural jungle habitat – but not to ride them. The pioneering **Elephant Valley Project** (10km northwest of Sen Monorom; Mon–Fri; day-visit $85, or $55 including a half day's volunteer work; 📞099 696041, 🖥elephantvalleyproject .org), remains the best – albeit the most expensive.

The success of the project has inspired a string of similar initiatives around town, all offering similar tours and activities (and also including bathing with the elephants, something the Elephant Valley Project doesn't allow). Reputable organizations include the **Bunong Elephant Project Office** ($35; 📞097 816 2770, 🖥bunongelephant project.org); the **Elephant Community Project** ($35; 📞097 362 6644, 🖥elephantcommunityproject.org); the **Mondulkiri Project** ($50; 📞097 723 4177, 🖥mondulkiriproject.org) and the **Mondulkiri Elephant and Wildlife Sanctuary Office** ($40; 📞097 659 1101, 🖥mondulkirisanctuary.org). A couple of these places also combine an elephant visit with a second day spent trekking in the jungle, while some include a Bunong village visit in their programmes.

ARRIVAL AND DEPARTURE

By bus There are a couple of buses daily between Sen Monorom and Phnom Penh ($12) via Kompong Cham, run by Phnom Penh Sorya and Rith Mony.

Destinations Kompong Cham (4hr 30min); Phnom Penh (8hr).

By share taxi or pick-up These run either direct from Phnom Penh (7hr; $15) or Kompong Cham (4hr). You will get *very* dusty in a pick-up, unless you sit in the cab.

ACTIVITIES

Trekking and tours As well as the various elephant projects, for trekking and tours, the long-running Green House Tours on Banlung Rd, about 1km from the centre (📞097 362644, 🖥greenhouse-tour.blogspot.co.uk), is a good option.

ACCOMMODATION

Chantha Srey Pich 500m west of the centre 📞011 550388. Good new cheapie with small, functional fan rooms (cold water only) – nothing much to look at but neat, comfortable and spotlessly clean (although windows may be lacking). There's also a basic thirteen-bed dorm, plus attached restaurant. Dorms __$2.50__, doubles __$6__

★**Nature Lodge** 2km east of the centre 📞012 230272, 🖥naturelodgecambodia.com. Idyllic little ecolodge, tucked away in the countryside outside town, with accommodation in simple but comfortable stilted wooden cabins (with hot water) widely scattered around very spacious grounds, plus an attractively rustic little restaurant and bar. Doubles __$15__

Phanyro Town centre 📞017 770867. Attractive guesthouse with accommodation in a cluster of neat and cosy wooden chalets (with hot water and nice bathrooms) set around attractive leafy gardens on the edge of a hill (although no views). Excellent value. Doubles __$8__

Pich Kiri Main Rd (NR76) 📞012 282370, ✉pichkiri @gmail.com. One of Sen Monorom's best mid-range options, in a brilliantly central location and with spacious, good-value and very comfortable rooms (a/c $5 extra) kitted out with chintzy wooden furniture. Doubles __$10__

EATING

The Hangout Town centre 📞088 721 9991. Good all-round travellers' caff run by a Khmer-Australian couple and serving up a decent selection of Khmer dishes (mains $3) and more expensive Western options ($4.50–6) including lots of comfort food like bangers and mash, chicken parmigiano and fish 'n' chips. Good breakfasts, too. Daily 7am–10pm.

Hefalump Café Main Rd (NR76) 📞099 696041. Run by a quartet of conservation and development NGOs, this convivial little garden café serves as the nerve hub of Sen Monorom's expat and ecotourism scene and is also a great place for coffee, breakfasts and cake, including Mondulkiri's best – indeed, probably only – lemon meringue pie. Mon–Fri 7am–6pm, Sat 11am–4pm, Sun noon–4pm.

Khmer Kitchen Main Road (NR76) 📞092 963243. Local restaurant given a makeover for the tourist trade with attractive wooden decor and wide-ranging menu (mains $3–4) of authentic Khmer staples including banana flower salad, *lok lak* (spicy stir-fried beef) and *samlor ktis* (a refreshingly tart sour soup). Daily 6am–10pm.

Mondulkiri Pizza South of the centre 📞097 522 2219. Rustic restaurant in a cute little bamboo pavilion serving up 22 varieties of excellent thin-crust pizza (around $6) – the best Italian you could reasonably expect in the wilds of Mondulkiri. Daily 10am–9pm.

SUNSET FROM VICTORIA PEAK

Hong Kong & Macau

HIGHLIGHTS

❶ **Victoria Peak** Take the Peak Tram and admire Hong Kong's skyline from above. **See p.135**

❷ **Star Ferry** The cheapest tour of Victoria Harbour is on one of Hong Kong's iconic ferries. **See p.138**

❸ **Outlying islands** Visit the world's largest seated bronze Buddha and go hiking. **See p.141**

❹ **Dining scene** Gorge yourself on any cuisine imaginable in Kowloon and Central. **See p.149**

❺ **Old Macau** Explore the candy-coloured remains of Macau's colonial past. **See p.152**

❻ **Macanese food** Try the Portuguese classics with a Chinese twist. **See p.159**

HIGHLIGHTS ARE MARKED ON THE MAPS ON P.123 & P.153

ROUGH COSTS

Daily budget Basic US$45, occasional treat US$75
Food Noodle soup, fried rice US$5–7
Drink Tsingtao US$5.50–7
Hostel/budget hotel US$20/65
Travel Bus: Central–Stanley US$1–1.50; MTR: Tsim Sha Tsui–Central US$0.70

FACT FILE

Population 7.2 million in Hong Kong; 566,400 in Macau

Language Cantonese and English in Hong Kong; Cantonese and some Portuguese in Macau

Currency Hong Kong dollar (HK$); pataca (MOP$) in Macau

International phone code ☏852 in Hong Kong (☏01 from Macau); ☏853 in Macau

Time zone GMT + 8hr

Introduction

An extraordinary, vibrant and crowded territory of more than seven million people, Hong Kong is undoubtedly one of the world's great cities. The view of Hong Kong Island's skyscrapers from across the harbour makes a stunning urban panorama, and this insomniac metropolis buzzes with energy day and night. Beyond the modern cityscape, Hong Kong also offers traditional temples with smouldering incense and fortune-tellers; rugged rural escapism with waterfalls and pristine beaches; and an eating and drinking scene that ranges from streetside noodle shacks to Michelin-starred haute cuisine. Its compact size and enviably efficient transport system make it perfect for a brief stopoff, but there's enough to keep you hooked for weeks. Tiny Macau, meanwhile, offers a unique fusion of Portuguese and Chinese traditions surviving amid an onslaught of casino-led development.

In the decades since their **handover** to China, in 1997 for Hong Kong and 1999 for Macau, the people of both cities have found themselves in a unique position: subject to the ultimate rule of Beijing, they live in semi-democratic capitalist enclaves, or "Special Administrative Regions" (SAR). Hong Kong has largely benefited from this arrangement, with high-spending mainland tourists flocking to the city in growing numbers, though calls for greater independence have created tension with the Chinese authorities. The influx of mainlanders' money has also exacerbated the staggering inequality of incomes here: the conspicuous consumption of the few hundred super-rich (all Cantonese), for which Hong Kong is famous, tends to mask the fact that most people work long hours and live in crowded, tiny apartments – Hong Kong is vastly more expensive than its Southeast Asian neighbours.

Sixty kilometres west from Hong Kong across the Pearl River Delta, the formerly Portuguese colony of **Macau** may seem a geographic and economic midget compared to its high-rise cousin but the city punches well above its weight – thanks largely to a recent, rapid and vast expansion of gambling in the territory. Development has already changed the character of this formerly sleepy colonial backwater beyond recognition (and construction of a land link to Hong Kong – a series of bridges and tunnels – is due to be completed in late 2017), but old Macau is still very much in evidence and the historic centre boasts UNESCO World Heritage status. With a colonial past pre-dating that of Hong Kong by nearly three hundred years, Macau's historic buildings – from

WHEN TO GO

Hong Kong and Macau's **climate** is subtropical. The best time to visit is between late October and April, when the weather is cooler, humidity levels drop and the flowers are in bloom. Between December and February, it can get quite cool but the skies are generally clear. The temperature and humidity start to pick up in mid-April, and between late June and early October readings of over 30°C and 95 percent humidity or more are the norm. During **typhoon season**, from May to September, ferry and airline timetables can be disrupted by bad weather. If a category T8 typhoon is on its way, offices and shops will close and public transport will shut down. Fortunately, typhoons usually don't last too long.

old fortresses to Baroque churches to faded mansion houses – are plentiful, and almost every tiny backstreet holds a surprise. South of the main city, on **Taipa** and **Coloane**, are beaches, parks and quiet villages where you can sample a unique cuisine blending Asian, European and African influences.

CHRONOLOGY

HONG KONG

4000–2500 BC The earliest inhabitants of the Hong Kong area are Neolithic hunter-gatherers and fishermen.

214 BC The region is conquered by Chinese emperor Qin Shi Huang and incorporated into imperial China for the first time.

1000–1400 AD The Five Clans – Tang, Hau, Pang, Liu and Man – build their walled villages in what is now the New Territories.

1557 Dutch and French traders come to the region, following the Portuguese traders in Macau.

1683 British East India Company establishes a base in China's Guangzhou province, and trades for silk, porcelain and tea.

1773 British shiploads of opium arrive from India and demand for the drug explodes in China.

1839 The first Opium War starts. Commissioner of Guangzhou, Lin Zexu, forces the British to surrender their opium, before ceremonially burning it.

1840 A naval expeditionary force is dispatched from London; it blockades ports and seizes assets up and down the Chinese coast for a year.

1841 British naval landing party plants the Union Jack at Possession Point on Hong Kong Island.

1842 The Treaty of Nanking cedes to Britain "in perpetuity" a small offshore island called Hong Kong, opens five ports to foreign trade, abolishes the monopoly system of trade and exempts British nationals from Chinese law.

1856–60 Second Opium War: after more blockades and a march on Beijing, China cedes Britain the Kowloon peninsula and Stonecutters Island.

1898 As the Qing dynasty declines, Britain secures a 99-year lease on one thousand square kilometres of land north of Kowloon, known as the New Territories.

1907 The drug trade is voluntarily dropped as Hong Kong merchants switch from trade to manufacturing.

1941–45 Japanese forces occupy Hong Kong along with the rest of eastern China.

1949 As mainland China falls to the communists, many merchants, particularly from Shanghai, move to Hong Kong.

1966–67 With the Cultural Revolution in full flow on the mainland, pro-Red Guard riots break out in Hong Kong. However, there is little support from Mao's regime and they fizzle out.

HONG KONG

HIGHLIGHTS
1 Victoria Peak
2 Star Ferry
3 Outlying islands
4 Dining scene

1984 The Sino-British Joint Declaration is signed. Britain agrees to relinquish the territory as long as Hong Kong maintains a capitalist system for at least fifty years.

1988 The Basic Law is published as the constitutional framework for the one country, two systems policy.

1989 The Tiananmen Square massacre occurs in Beijing. In the biggest demonstration in Hong Kong in modern times, a million people take to the streets in protest.

1992 Chris Patten becomes the last Governor and introduces a series of reforms, including increasing the voting franchise for the 1995 Legislative Council elections (Legco) from 200,000 to 2.7 million people.

1997 Britain hands Hong Kong over to China. Beijing disbands Legco, and Tung Chee Hwa, a shipping billionaire, becomes the first Chief Executive of the Hong Kong Special Administrative Region (SAR) of the People's Republic of China. Within days, the Asian Financial Crisis begins and Hong Kong's economy goes into recession.

2003 The SARS outbreak causes widespread panic and disruption, and leads to just under three hundred deaths.

2005 Chief Executive Tung Chee Hwa resigns; Donald Tsang succeeds him.

2007 Hong Kong's first contested election for Chief Executive is won by Tsang.

2010 Formal talks held between Chinese officials and the Opposition Democratic Party – habitually hostile to Beijing – are the first since the 1997 handover.

2012 C.Y. Leung is appointed Chief Executive.

August 2014 Beijing rules out a fully democratic election for Chief Executive in 2017, saying that only pre-approved candidates will be allowed to run.

Sept–Dec 2014 Pro-democracy protesters occupy areas of Admiralty, Causeway Bay and Mong Kok, closing several major roads for almost three months in what has become known as the "Umbrella Movement".

2016 Riots break out over Chinese New Year, targeting police as social tension in the city worsens; In September a handful of pro-independence activists win Legco seats amid the highest voter turnout since 1997, igniting debate when they pledge loyalty to the "Hong Kong nation" during their swearing in.

MACAU

500 AD Macau is part of the Maritime Silk Road between Guangzhou and Southeast Asia.

1513 The Portuguese arrive in China's Pearl River Delta.

1557 The Portuguese persuade local Chinese officials to rent them a strategically placed peninsula at the mouth of the delta, which they call Macao. As the only foreigners permitted to trade with China, the Portuguese become sole agents for merchants across a whole swathe of east Asia and grow immensely wealthy.

1641 The Portuguese lose Melaka in Malaysia to the Dutch; Macau's trading links are cut and its fortunes wane.

1842 Once the British have claimed Hong Kong to the east, Macau's status as a backwater is definitively settled.

1847 Licensed gambling is introduced as a desperate means of securing some kind of income.

1848–1870s Macau is the centre of the "coolie" slave trade, with slave ships departing for South America with slaves kidnapped in southern China.

1851 & 1864 Portugal occupies Taipa and Coloane.

1966 Violent riots erupt, but China does not want the Portuguese to leave because of potential economic shock to Hong Kong.

1974 Fascist dictatorship ends in Portugal, and all Portuguese colonies are relinquished, but China turns down the Portuguese offer to leave Macau.

1984 After agreement with Britain over Hong Kong, China agrees to negotiate the return of Macau as well.

1987 The Sino-Portuguese Joint Declaration is signed, making Macau a "Special Administrative Region" (SAR) of China, effectively a semi-democratic capitalist enclave subject to Beijing.

1999 China assumes formal sovereignty of Macau; it is the last European colony in Asia to be handed back.

2002 Hong Kong tycoon Stanley Ho's monopoly on casinos ends and Macau's gambling industry booms as mainlanders are given greater freedom to travel.

2004 The opening of Las Vegas Sands Casino ushers in a new style of super casino, and a new era of increased foreign investment.

2006 Macau overtakes Las Vegas as the world's most lucrative casino market and the first casino opens on the Cotai Strip.

2013 Annual gaming revenues hit US$45 billion, six times that of Las Vegas.

2015 Macau's economy contracts twenty percent over the year as the Chinese economy slows and mainland tourists head to other destinations.

ARRIVAL AND DEPARTURE

Hong Kong can be reached by land, sea or air. It is a major regional hub for flights from the US, Europe and Asia. **Trains** from Guangzhou, Beijing and Shanghai in China arrive at Hung Hom station on the Kowloon peninsula. You can take a bus from here to Hong Kong Island, or else to the Tsim Sha Tsui Star Ferry terminus, where you can catch a ferry over to Central on Hong Kong Island.

Boats from mainland China and Macau arrive at the China Ferry Terminal on Canton Road, in downtown Kowloon. Ferries from Macau also arrive at the

Hong Kong–Macau Ferry Terminal in Sheung Wan, just west of Central on Hong Kong Island. From here you can catch a bus, underground train or tram to other parts of Hong Kong.

Hong Kong international **airport** (ⓦhongkongairport.com) is situated on Lantau Island. It is linked to Hong Kong Island and Kowloon by the high-speed Airport Express train and buses. There are direct bus services from the airport to Shenzhen and Guangzhou in mainland China, as well as cities in the Pearl River Delta, the latter also served by fast Skypier ferry connections.

You can also fly directly to Macau (see p.158).

VISAS

Most nationalities need only a valid passport to enter **Hong Kong**, although the length of stay varies. British citizens get 180 days, whereas citizens of the EU, Canada, Australia, New Zealand and the US can stay for up to 90 days, and South Africans are allowed 30 days. Check the latest visa requirements at ⓦimmd.gov.hk. The easiest way to **extend your stay** is to go to Macau and come back.

To enter **Macau**, citizens of the UK, EU, Australia, New Zealand, South Africa, Canada and the US need only a valid passport and can stay for a period between 30 and 90 days. The simplest way to **extend your stay** is to go to Hong Kong and re-enter Macau at a later date.

GETTING AROUND

Hong Kong's public transport system is efficient, extensive and inexpensive, although crowded during rush hour. The MTR (Mass Transit Railway) system – overground, underground and light rail – and the main bus routes are easy to use. Few taxi drivers are fluent in English, however, so get someone to write down your destination in Chinese characters. The same goes for taking taxis in Macau (see p.159), although the city is easy to tackle on foot and by bus.

ACCOMMODATION

Hong Kong has plenty of budget accommodation, most of which is located in Kowloon. The lion's share of the budget market is taken up by **guesthouses** – flats converted to hold as many tiny private rooms (singles, doubles, triples and quads) as possible. These typically come with equally tiny bathrooms where you can shower while sitting on the loo, as well as a/c, TVs, kettles and telephones. Tall Westerners may discover that the majority of beds will be too short for them. Solo travellers won't have trouble finding rooms, but may find that the price of a single is mostly more than half the price of a double. Doubles cost around HK$300–700, while singles are around HK$200–450. The majority of the guesthouses are located in high-rises, the names of which tend to end with "… Mansions" and thus unrealistically raise your expectations.

A handful of great backpacker **hostels** have recently started to give the guesthouses a run for their money. Most of these are also located in high-rises, though you do get a few in more peaceful, out-of-the-way locations. These typically come with a common area, lockers and a plethora of information on the city. Dorm prices can be as low as HK$150. Free wi-fi is standard.

Accommodation in **Macau** is generally more expensive, as there is a dearth of cheap lodgings, and tends to consist of guesthouses rather than hostels. As most cater for mainland tourists, many staff won't speak English. Prices often shoot up at weekends. To get the best rates for many guesthouses, book your room through an external website in advance.

FOOD AND DRINK

One of the great culinary capitals of the world, Hong Kong offers not only superb, native Cantonese cooking but the full gamut of regional Chinese cuisines and perhaps the widest range of international restaurants of any city outside Europe or North America. This is due in part to the cosmopolitan nature of

3

the population, but also, perhaps more importantly, to the incredible seriousness attached to dining by the local Chinese. Hong Kong residents eat out regularly, and foodie culture thrives.

In Macau, Macanese food is a tempting blend of Portuguese and Asian, and Portuguese and Chinese restaurants also abound. In both Hong Kong and Macau, the **water** is fit for drinking.

HONG KONG

As well as the joys of dim sum – a Hong Kong speciality meaning "little eats", and other Cantonese dishes – the city offers everything from fiery Sichuan cookery to veggie-friendly Buddhist cuisine. You'll also find excellent Indian and Malaysian curry houses, sushi bars, Vietnamese, Italian, French and Korean restaurants, British pub-style food and varied cheap **street stalls** (*dai pai dongs*). All budgets are catered for; many restaurants also offer limited lunchtime menus which are around half the price of eating out at dinnertime. English or picture **menus** are widely available. Most restaurants will add a ten percent **service charge** to your bill.

The kind of **snacks** you'll find at the *dai pai dongs* and many indoor food halls and canteens (called *cha chan tengs*) include seafood, noodle soups, *congee* (savoury rice porridge) and buns stuffed with *char siu* pork; they shouldn't cost more than HK$50 for a large meal. **Milk tea** (strong black tea with evaporated or condensed milk strained through a large "tea sock") is a signature Hong Kong beverage and most street stalls sell this steaming brew from dawn.

The most common Chinese food in Hong Kong is **Cantonese**, from China's southern Guangdong province. Dishes consist of extremely fresh food, quickly cooked and only lightly seasoned. Popular ingredients are fruit and vegetables, fish and shellfish, though the cuisine is also known for more unusual ingredients such as fish maw and chicken's feet.

Other Chinese regional cuisines are well represented in Hong Kong, and adventurous diners will find boiled dumplings from **Beijing**, delicately flavoured **Shanghai-style** seafood dishes and mouth-numbingly spicy stir-fries from **Sichuan** without too much trouble.

In most Chinese restaurants, the usual **drink** with your meal is **tea**, often brought to your table as a matter of course. **Beer** is also popular. All restaurants and bars are non-smoking.

Drinking can be expensive, so it's best to make good use of happy hours to avoid drifting into insolvency. Bars stay open until 2 or 3am.

MACAU

The Portuguese elements of **Macanese food** include fresh bread, cheap imported wine and good coffee, as well as an array of dishes ranging from *caldo verde* (vegetable soup) to *bacalhau* (dried salted cod). One of Macau's most interesting Portuguese colonial dishes is **African chicken**, a concoction of Goan and east African influences, comprising grilled chicken smothered in a mildly spiced peanut and coconut sauce. Macau is also justly acknowledged for the exceptional quality of its sweet, flaky custard tarts or *natas*. Straightforward **Cantonese restaurants**, often serving dim sum for breakfast and lunch, are also plentiful.

Most restaurants in Macau don't open as late as they do in Hong Kong – although bars do. If you want to eat later than 10pm, you'll probably end up either in a hotel (many of which have 24hr coffee bars that also serve snacks) or in the NAPE (Novos Aterros do Porto Exterior) bar-restaurant area.

DIM SUM

A veritable institution, **dim sum** is a breakfast or midday meal consisting of small savoury buns, dumplings, pancakes and other small dishes, all washed down with copious amounts of tea. Traditionally these delicious eats are wheeled through the restaurant on trolleys, with punters choosing whichever takes their fancy. There are only a couple of trolley *dim sum* places left in Hong Kong, one of which is *Lin Heung Tea House* (see p.149). Most dishes cost HK$13–50, and dumplings and buns usually come in portions of three or four.

Drinking is not quite as expensive as in Hong Kong, but not far off. Most drinking takes place in the casinos, and bars can often feel empty even at weekends, although some stay open till dawn.

CULTURE AND ETIQUETTE

Generally speaking, Hong Kong and Macau people are not as concerned as other Asian cultures about covering the skin – girls often wear skirts as short as those in the West. However, **bathing topless** on any of Hong Kong's beaches is illegal. To avoid faux pas, point with your palm rather than your index finger, avoid wearing white in a social setting as it's the colour of mourning, and don't feel obliged to leave a tip (though some restaurants add ten-percent gratuity to the bill). If you're invited to someone's house, bring a gift (not a clock, anything white or in a set of four – a very unlucky number) and present it with both hands. If you're given a gift, refuse it first before accepting, as accepting straight away makes you look greedy. If out to dinner with Hong Kongers, try to serve others first and don't take the last bit of food on a serving plate, which is considered impolite.

SPORTS AND ACTIVITIES

Hong Kong residents are keen sporting spectators. **Horse racing**, inseparable from gambling and therefore illegal in mainland China, is a popular pastime, and both Sha Tin and Happy Valley racecourses have weekly meets during the season (see p.134). The other huge sporting draw is the **Rugby Sevens**, which takes place over three days at the end of March. This international tournament, where teams have seven players instead of fifteen, is a major fixture in Hong Kong's calendar.

Hong Kong also offers some amazing **outdoor activities**, from hiking and scuba diving to windsurfing on the tiny island of Cheung Chau, while the Macau Tower offers the highest commercial **bungee** platform in the world (see p.156).

COMMUNICATIONS

From Hong Kong, **airmail** takes three days to a week to reach Europe or North America; from Macau between five days and a week.

Local calls from private phones in **Hong Kong** are free, public **phones** are cheap (HK$1/5min) and **phonecards** (HK$10–100) are widely available (try 7-Eleven). You can make **international calls** from International Direct Dialling (IDD) phones. Hong Kong SIM cards can be bought for less than HK$50 and local calls from mobiles are inexpensive.

In Macau, local calls are free from **private phones**, MOP$1 from payphones. Instructions tend to be in both Portuguese and English.

Internet access, particularly free wi-fi, is available in most hostels and guesthouses. Purchase a CSL prepaid SIM card to access more than 15,000 wi-fi hotspots in Hong Kong. In Macau, you can access free wi-fi in touristy areas using the user name and password "wifigo"; you have to reconnect after 45-minute sessions.

CRIME AND SAFETY

You're very unlikely to encounter any trouble in Hong Kong or Macau. To avoid **pickpockets**, keep money and wallets in hard-to-reach places and be careful when getting on and off packed public transport. Men should avoid strip bars where the Neanderthals at the door will make sure you fork out for hugely expensive drinks for the "girls".

HONG KONG AND MACAU ONLINE

Ⓦ**discoverhongkong.com** The Hong Kong Tourist Board's fantastic website is packed with information, and an interactive itinerary planner. Free mobile apps include My Hong Kong and Hong Kong Insider's Guide.
Ⓦ**hkoutdoors.com** Information on mountain biking, sea kayaking, birdwatching, hiking and more.
Ⓦ**www.macautourism.gov.mo** Macau tourist website with travel information, lists of guesthouses and suggested tours.

3

Carrying some form of **identification** is a legal requirement: for a traveller this means your passport. Most police officers speak some English, and will quickly radio help for you if they can't understand and you have a major problem. **Drug possession** carries stiff penalties in both Hong Kong and Macau.

MEDICAL CARE AND EMERGENCIES

Pharmacies (daily 9am–6pm or 24hr in hospitals) are marked with a red-and-white cross and sell many medications

---

EMERGENCY NUMBERS

In both Hong Kong and Macau, dial ☎ **999** for fire, police and ambulance.

---

over the counter without a prescription. Contraceptives and antibiotics are also available over the counter. Hong Kong pharmacies have a registered pharmacist on-site who usually speaks English.

Medical care in Hong Kong (see p.151) is generally of an excellent standard, but does not come cheap. If you need a doctor, you'll have to pay for any treatment or medicines prescribed, so

---

CANTONESE

Cantonese is the official language of Hong Kong, with Mandarin a fast-growing second. English is widely spoken among the well educated and many in the tourist trade (although not many taxi drivers), otherwise, people speak only basic English. The vast majority of people in Macau speak Cantonese and some also speak Portuguese and English. Cantonese is a tonal language, which means that the tone a speaker gives to a word will determine its meaning. As even the simplest two-letter word can have up to nine different meanings depending on the pitch of the voice, the Romanized word is really only an approximation of the Chinese sound.

PRONUNCIATION

oy as in b**oy**
ai as in f**i**ne
i as in s**ee**
er as in **ur**n
o as in p**o**t
ow as in n**ow**
oe as in **oh**
or as in l**aw**

WORDS AND PHRASES

Good morning	*Joe sun*
Hello/how are you?	*Lay hoe ma?*
Thank you/excuse me	*M goy*
Goodnight	*Joe tow*
Goodbye	*Joy geen*
I'm sorry	*Doy m joot*
Can you speak English?	*Lay sik m sik gong ying man?*
Yes	*Yow*
No	*Mo*

I don't understand	*Ngor m ming bat*
What is your name?	*Lay gew mut yeh meng?*
My name is …	*Ngor gew …*
I am from England /America	*Ngor hai Ying /May gwok yan*
Where are these places? (while pointing to the place name or map)	*Ching mun, leedi day fong hai been do ah?*
Train	*For chair*
Bus	*Ba-see*
Ferry	*Do lun schoon*
Taxi	*Dik-see*
Airport	*Fay gay cherng*
Hotel	*Jow deem*
Hostel	*Loy gwun*
Restaurant	*Charn Teng*
Toilets	*Chee saw*
Police	*Ging chat*

NUMBERS

The number two changes when asking for two of something – **lerng wei** (a table for two) – or stating something other than counting – **lerng mun** (two dollars).

1	*yat*
2	*yee*
3	*saam*
4	*say*
5	*mm*
6	*lok*
7	*chat*
8	*bat*
9	*gow*
10	*sap*
11, 12, 13, etc	*sap yat, sap yee, sap saam*

make sure you have adequate travel insurance. Macau's hospitals (see p.160) offer 24hr emergency services.

MONEY AND BANKS

ATMs throughout Hong Kong and Macau accept international cards.

Hong Kong's unit of **currency** is the Hong Kong dollar (HK$); it is divided into one hundred cents. Bills come in denominations of $10, $20, $50, $100, $500 and $1000, and there are 10 cent, 20 cent, 50 cent, $1, $2, $5 and $10 coins. At the time of writing, the exchange rate was around HK$9.5 to the **pound sterling**, HK$8.4 to the euro, and it's pegged at HK$7.76 to the US dollar. There are no restrictions on taking any currency in and out of Hong Kong.

The unit of **currency** in Macau is the pataca (abbreviated to MOP$; often seen as M$, MOP or ptca), which consists of one hundred avos. At the time of writing, the **exchange rate** was £1 to MOP$9.75, US$1 to MOP$8 and €1 to MOP$8.7. Bills come in MOP$10, $20, $50, $100, $500 and $1000 denominations, and there are 10-, 20- and 50-avo coins, as well as MOP$1, $2, $5 and $10 coins.

3

20, 21, 22, 23, etc	yee sap, yee sap yat, yee sap yee, yee sap saam
30, 40, 50, etc	saam sap, say sap, mm sap
100	yat bat
1000	yat cheen

FOOD AND DRINKS GLOSSARY

Ordering food

Mai daan	Bill/check
Fai tzee	Chopsticks
La sow ho choy	House speciality
Gay dor cheen?	How much is that?
Ngor hai fut gow toe /ngor tzee sik soe	I'm a Buddhist/ vegetarian
Ngor serng yew …	I would like …
Choy daan/toe choy /Ying man choy daan	Main/set menu/ English menu

Drinks

Beh tsow	Beer
Ga fay	Coffee
Char	Tea
Kong tuen soy	Mineral water
Poe toe tsow	Wine

Staple foods

Ah choy	Bean sprouts
Ow yok	Beef
Dou si jerng	Black bean sauce
Gai	Chicken
Lat jew	Chilli
Hai	Crab
Daan chow faan	Egg fried rice
Yue	Fish
Soe choy	Green leafy vegetables
For war	Hotpot
Yok choon	Kebab

Meen tew	Noodles
Tong meen	Noodle soup
Jew yok	Pork
Ha	Prawns
Bak faan	Rice (boiled)
Chow fann	Rice (fried)
Jok	Rice porridge congee
How aap	Roast duck
Dow foo	Tofu
Wun tun meen	Wonton noodle soup

Vegetables and eggs

Dun herng goo	Braised mountain fungus
Dow foo soe choy	Fried beancurd with vegetables
Herng la ke tzee tew	Spicy braised aubergine
Soe choy tong	Vegetable soup

Dim Sum (Yum Cha)

Char syew bao	Barbecue pork bun
Daan tat	Custard tart
Faan sue woo gau	Fried taro and mince dumpling
Gau tzee	Jiaozi steamed pork dumpling
Leen yong bao	Lotus paste bun
Yuet beng	Moon cake – sweet bean paste in flaky pastry
Ha peen	Prawn crackers
Ha gow	Prawn dumpling
Tzee ma ha dor si	Prawn paste on fried toast
Wo teet	Shanghai fried vegetable dumpling
Chun goon	Spring roll

The pataca is pegged to the Hong Kong dollar at the rate of MOP$103 to HK$100, and the two currencies are interchangeable in Macau, though you get slightly less for your Hong Kong dollars. Try to get rid of your patacas before heading to Hong Kong.

All the **major credit cards** are accepted in the larger hotels, but most guesthouses and restaurants still expect payment in cash.

OPENING HOURS

In Hong Kong and Macau, **offices** are generally open Monday to Friday 9am–5.30pm, with lunch hour 1–2pm; **shops** are open daily 10am–8pm or later in busy tourist areas like Causeway Bay and Tsim Sha Tsui. **Banks** are open Monday to Friday 9am–4.30pm and Saturday 9am–12.30pm; **post offices** are open Monday to Friday 9.30am–5pm and Saturday 9.30am–1pm, and **restaurants** tend to be open 11am–3pm & 6–11pm or else 11am–11pm. **Government offices** close on public holidays and some religious festivals.

PUBLIC HOLIDAYS

The following public holidays are observed – Sundays are also classed as public holidays. Macau observes the same holidays, with the exception of the HKSAR Establishment Day.

January 1 New Year
February 16–20, 2018; February 5–7, 2019 Chinese New Year
March 30–April 2, 2018; April 19–22, 2019 Easter (holidays on Good Friday, Easter Saturday and Easter Monday)
April 5 Ching Ming
May 1 Labour Day
May 22, 2018; May 12, 2019 Buddha's birthday
June 18, 2018; June 7, 2019 Tuen Ng (Dragon Boat) Festival
July 1 Hong Kong SAR Establishment Day
September 24, 2018; September 13, 2019 Mid-Autumn Festival
October 1 China National Day
October 28, 2017; October 17, 2018; October 7, 2019 Chung Yeung
November 2 All Souls' Day (Macau only)

December 8 Feast of Immaculate Conception (Macau)
December 20 Macau SAR Establishment Day (Macau)
December 25 Christmas Day
December 26 Boxing Day

FESTIVALS

With roots going back hundreds (even thousands) of years, many of Hong Kong's festivals are highly symbolic and are often a mixture of secular and religious displays and devotions. On these occasions, there are dances and Chinese opera performances at temples, with plenty of noise and offerings – food and paper goods that are burned as gifts to the dead. The normal Chinese holidays are celebrated in Macau, plus some Catholic festivals introduced from Portugal, such as the procession of Our Lady of Fatima from São Domingos Church annually on May 13 (although this is not a public holiday).

As the Chinese use the lunar calendar, many festivals fall on different days, even different months, from year to year; for exact details, contact the Hong Kong or Macau tourist offices.

Chinese New Year (Feb 16, 2018; Feb 5, 2019). The most important festival celebrated in Hong Kong and Macau; the entire population participates and there are spectacular firework displays over the harbour; festivities last for a fortnight.

Tin Hau Festival (May 8, 2018; April 27, 2019). Particular to Hong Kong in honour of the Goddess of Fishermen, large seaborne festivities take place at Joss House Bay near Clearwater Bay.

Tuen Ng (Dragon Boat) Festival (June 18, 2018; June 7, 2019). In Hong Kong, with races along the coast in long, narrow boats.

Yu Lan (Hungry Ghost) Festival (Aug 24, 2018; Aug 14, 2019) Hong Kong's Chiu Chow community appease evil spirits by burning fake money, cooking up sacrifices and performing live Chinese operas and dramas in public parks all around the Territory.

Mid-Autumn Festival (Sept 24, 2018; Sept 13, 2019). Chinese festival, almost as popular as Chinese New Year. Celebrations are more public in Hong Kong and Macau.

Wine and Dine Festival (Oct/Nov). A four-day epicurean festival to kick off November's annual wine and dine month, featuring restaurant promotions, street carnivals and wine-tasting events.

Hong Kong

The territory of **HONG KONG**, whose name means "fragrant harbour", comprises an irregularly shaped peninsula abutting the Pearl River Delta to the west, and a number of offshore islands, which cover more than a thousand square kilometres in total. The southern part of the peninsula, **Kowloon**, and the island immediately south of it, **Hong Kong Island**, are the principal urban areas of Hong Kong. They were ceded to Britain "in perpetuity", but were returned to China at midnight on June 30, 1997. Since then, it has been renamed the **Hong Kong Special Administrative Region (SAR)** of the People's Republic of China.

The island of Hong Kong offers traces of the old colony – from English place names to ancient trams trundling along what was once the shore – among superb modern architecture and futuristic cityscapes, as well as rural corners for **hiking** and bathing on the **beaches** of its southern shore. Kowloon, in particular its southernmost tip, **Tsim Sha Tsui**, is the budget accommodation centre, and offers fantastic shopping, from lofty international designers to traditional markets. The **offshore islands**, including **Lamma** and **Lantau**, are locally famous for their fresh fish restaurants, scenery and tranquillity, while the **New Territories**, north of Kowloon, is where you find remnants of ancient walled villages, splendid temples and some great hiking and biking terrain.

HONG KONG ISLAND

As the oldest colonized part of Hong Kong, its administrative and business centre and site of some of the most expensive real estate in the world, **Hong Kong Island** is, in every sense, the heart of the territory. Despite its size, just 15km from east to west and 11km from north to south, the island encompasses the best the territory has to offer in one heady hit: lavish temples to consumer excess, the vivid sights and smells of a Chinese wet market and (away from the north shore's steel and concrete mountains) surprising expanses of sandy beach and forested nature reserves.

WHAT TO SEE AND DO

The territory's major financial and commercial quarter, **Central**, lies on the northern shore of Hong Kong Island overlooking Victoria Harbour. East of Central are **Wan Chai** and lively **Causeway Bay**, while in the opposite direction is **Sheung Wan**, rather older and more traditional in character. Towering over the city, **The Peak** is a highlight of any trip to the city, offering magnificent views and great walking opportunities.

On its south side, Hong Kong Island straggles into the sea in a series of dangling peninsulas and inlets. The atmosphere is quieter here than on the north shore. You'll find not only separate seafront suburbs such as **Aberdeen**, its busy bay full of boats and sampans, and **Stanley**, with its waterfront bazaar, but also beaches, such as **Repulse Bay** and **Deep Water Bay**, the **Ocean Park** amusement park, and, further east, the remote and pretty village of **Shek O**.

3

CENTRAL'S ELEVATED WALKWAYS

Inland from the shore, the main west–east roads are Connaught Road, Des Voeux Road and Queen's Road respectively. However, it's not possible to cross many of the roads at street level, so pedestrians are better off concentrating on the extensive system of **elevated walkways**. Coming off the Star Ferry upper deck will lead you straight into the walkways. First off to your right is the entrance to the **IFC Mall**, while carrying straight on takes you inland. **Hong Kong MTR Station** is under the IFC Mall; **Central Station** is reached by heading in a straight line then dropping down to Pedder Street just before World-Wide House, while **Exchange Square**'s three marble-and-tinted-glass towers sit atop the **Bus Station**. A further branch of the elevated walkway runs northwest from here, parallel with the shore and along the northern edge of Connaught Road all the way to the Macau Ferry Terminal and Sheung Wan MTR.

3

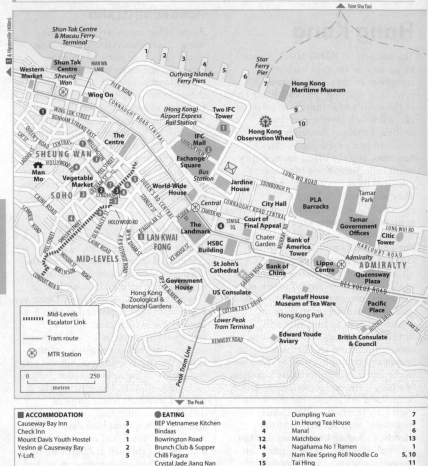

▊ ACCOMMODATION		● EATING		Dumpling Yuan	7
Causeway Bay Inn	3	BEP Vietnamese Kitchen	8	Lin Heung Tea House	3
Check Inn	4	Bindaas	4	Mana!	6
Mount Davis Youth Hostel	1	Bowrington Road	12	Matchbox	13
YesInn @ Causeway Bay	2	Brunch Club & Supper	14	Nagahama No 1 Ramen	1
Y-Loft	5	Chilli Fagara	9	Nam Kee Spring Roll Noodle Co	5, 10
		Crystal Jade Jiang Nan	15	Tai Hing	11

Buses are plentiful to all destinations on the southern shore, and Aberdeen is linked to Central by a tunnel under The Peak. Nowhere is more than an hour from Central.

Central
Central extends out from the Star Ferry Pier a few hundred metres in all directions. Right next to the Star Ferry Pier is the engrossing **Hong Kong Maritime Museum** (Mon–Fri 9.30am–5.30pm, Sat & Sun 10am–7pm; HK$30; ⊕hkmaritimemuseum.org), its three floors subtly lit to resemble a ship's interior and its partly interactive exhibitions ranging from an overview of

China's maritime history to the creation of Victoria Harbour, with a wealth of period objects, paintings, nautical instruments, boat models and photography.

Easily recognizable from the tramlines that run up and down here, **Des Voeux Road** used to mark Hong Kong's seafront before the days of reclamation. East along Des Voeux Road, you'll find Statue Square on your left towards the shore, and, immediately south, the magnificently high-tech, "inside-out" **HSBC Building**, designed by Sir Norman Foster in 1985 – at the time of construction one of the most expensive office blocks ever built (US$1 billion). A

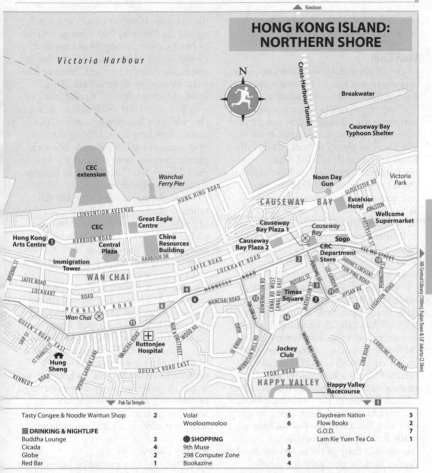

HONG KONG ISLAND: NORTHERN SHORE

Tasty Congee & Noodle Wantun Shop	2	Volar	5	Daydream Nation	5
		Wooloomooloo	6	Flow Books	2
DRINKING & NIGHTLIFE				G.O.D.	7
Buddha Lounge	3	**SHOPPING**		Lam Kie Yuen Tea Co.	1
Cicada	4	9th Muse	3		
Globe	2	298 Computer Zone	6		
Red Bar	1	Bookazine	4		

few hundred metres east is the 300m-high blue glass geometric shard of the **Bank of China** tower, designed by Chinese-American architect I.M. Pei.

South of Queen's Road the land begins to run uphill. The **Mid-Levels Escalator** is a giant series of escalators that runs 800m straight up the hill (downwards only 6–10am; upwards 10.20am–midnight) servicing the expensive **Mid-Levels** residential area, favoured by expats, as well as the thriving restaurant district of **SoHo**, with the steep pedestrian stretch of **Graham Street market** lined with stalls overflowing with fresh produce. Nearby **Lan Kwai Fong** is equally good for eating and drinking, with long queues of Hong

Kongers in business attire snaking their way to the flavour-of-the-moment restaurants at lunchtimes and drinking after work.

A short but steep walk away are the **Hong Kong Zoological and Botanical Gardens** (daily 6am–7pm; free), one of the oldest zoos in the world, founded in 1864 and home to more than 160 species of birds in well-kept aviaries. From the eastern exit, a ten-minute walk along Garden Road brings you to **Hong Kong Park** (daily 6am–11pm; free); The highlight here is the wonderful **Edward Youde Aviary** (daily 9am–5pm; free), with ninety species of birds in a rainforest setting; look out also for a museum showcasing tea ware (Mon & Wed–Sun 10am–6pm; free).

Wan Chai

In the 1950s and 1960s, **Wan Chai** – the area stretching east of Central – was known throughout east Asia as a thriving red-light district, catering in particular for US soldiers on leave from Korea and Vietnam. Lockhart Road is still home to plenty of **bars**, while Jaffe Road to the north is lined with **restaurants**. Local hipsters have claimed the area comprising St Francis, Moon and Star streets and, further east, Ship Street, but most of the area retains a busy, workaday vibe – especially in the stall-filled lanes surrounding Wan Chai Market. When it comes to shopping, Wan Chai is one of the best places in town to stock up on electronics.

Just north of Gloucester Road is the **Hong Kong Arts Centre** (2 Harbour Road; daily 10am–6pm; free; ⓦhkac.org.hk; ⓜWan Chai, exit C), featuring a cinema and art galleries that host interesting exhibitions, such as a recent retrospective on the city's comics, and other cultural events. Pick up a free copy of the monthly listings magazine *ArtsLink* here.

South of Queens Rd East, along Stone Nullah Lane, is the largest Taoist temple on Hong Kong Island – **Pak Tai Temple** (daily 8am–5pm), honouring its namesake, a deity of the sea whose 3m-tall copper likeness graces the main hall.

Causeway Bay

East of Wan Chai, **Causeway Bay** is a lively district packed with shops and restaurants. It's centred between the eastern end of Lockhart Road and the western edge of Victoria Park – Hong Kong's largest swath of urban greenery. Trams run here along Yee Wo Street, a continuation of Hennessy Road from Wan Chai.

The main activity in Causeway Bay is shopping – for fashion, electronics and homewares. Near the eponymous MTR station you'll find **Jardine's Crescent**, a narrow alleyway packed with market stalls selling cheap clothes, jewellery and knick-knacks. On the shore, in front of the *Excelsior Hotel* on Gloucester Road, stands the **Noonday Gun** – immortalized in Noël Coward's song *Mad Dogs and Englishmen* – which is fired every day at noon. The eastern part of Causeway Bay is dominated by **Victoria Park** (daily 24hr). On weekdays it's a good place to watch nimble local residents practising tai chi, while on Sundays Indonesian maids come picnicking here. During the mid-autumn festival the park fills with people carrying lanterns, and just before the Chinese New Year the place becomes an immense flower market.

Out in the bay is the Causeway Bay **typhoon shelter** that used to protect fleets of junks and sampans – these days the yachts that replaced them have been shunted down the coast to Shau Kei Wan to make way for major engineering work in the Causeway Bay shelter.

Inland from Hennessy Road, on the corner of Matheson and Russell streets, is Causeway Bay's most famous shopping plaza, the half-moon-shaped **Times Square**, fronted by a huge video screen. Just to the west of Times Square lies one of the city's best wet markets – **Bowrington Road Market** – where you can watch the sellers expertly dismembering poultry, fish and meat in the mornings and then grab a bite to eat at the food stalls that stay open until the evening.

Happy Valley

The low-lying area extending inland from the shore south of Wan Chai and Causeway Bay is known as Happy Valley, and means only one thing for the people of Hong Kong: horse racing or, more precisely, gambling. The **Happy Valley Racecourse** (Sept–June Wed 7–11pm; HK$10; ⓦhkjc.com), reachable by tram, dates back to 1846. Immense fortunes have been won and lost here over the past 170 years and Wednesday night at the races is a quintessential Hong Kong experience, the stands packed with cheering punters. HK$10 will buy you standing room only at the race track level, but you can also stump up for a Tourist Badge (present your passport at the members' entrance; HK$130–190) to gain entry to the Members' Enclosure.

Across Wong Nai Chung Road from the racecourse is the **Hong Kong Cemetery** (daily 7am–6pm), which gives you an insight into the city's colourful history. Dating back to the mid-nineteenth century, it features the gravestones of colonialists, film stars and naval officers. St Michael's Catholic cemetery, with its soot-stained stone angels, is next door, and Jewish, Hindu, Muslim and Parsee graves are also found nearby.

Western District

The site of Hong Kong's original Chinese settlement, Western District's crowded residential streets and traditional shops form a striking contrast to Central. **Sheung Wan** spreads south up the hill from the seafront at the modern Shun Tak Centre, a fifteen-minute walk along the elevated walkway from Exchange Square in Central, though you'll get more flavour of the district by hopping on a "ding ding" (the local term for the city's trams) along Des Voeux Road. Head south to the area around **Bonham Strand East** for an intriguing range of specialist shops selling traditional Chinese medicine, all manner of dried sea creatures and personalized stone seals (along Man Wa Lane).

Running from partway up the Mid-Levels escalator to the Western District is **Hollywood Road**, lined with antique and curio shops. The antique shops extend into the small alley, Upper Lascar Row, commonly known as **Cat Street**, where you'll find stalls selling posters of Chairman Mao, the "little red book", carvings, jewellery, "ancient" coins and brass door knockers. Nearby **Ladder Street**, which runs north–south across Hollywood Road, is a relic from the nineteenth century when a number of such stepped streets existed to help sedan-chair carriers get their loads up the steep hillsides.

On Hollywood Road, adjacent to Ladder Street, the 170-year-old **Man Mo Temple** (daily 8am–6pm) is one of Hong Kong's most atmospheric, with twisting coils of smouldering incense hanging from the rafters and worshippers waving fragrant clumps of incense sticks.

Branching off northwards from Hollywood Road is **Possession Street**, where Commodore Gordon Bremmer, and the British marines under his command, planted the Union Jack in 1841 to take possession of Hong Kong Island for the British Crown; there are no plaques to commemorate this.

The Peak

The uppermost levels of the 552m hill that towers over Central and Victoria Harbour have long been known as Victoria Peak (or simply "The Peak"), and, in colonial days, the area was populated by upper-class expats. Today The Peak offers some extraordinary panoramic views over the city and harbour below, as well as pleasant, leisurely walks. See ⓦthepeak.com.hk for more information.

The Peak Tram (see box below) drops you at the terminal in the **Peak Tower**. This building and the **Peak Galleria** across the road are full of souvenir shops and pricey bars and restaurants, some with spectacular views. The Peak Tower charges HK$48 to access its **Sky Terrace 428** viewing gallery (Mon–Fri 10am–11pm; Sat & Sun 8am–11pm), or you can buy a ticket that combines the tram and the terrace (HK$75 one-way, HK$88 return). The **view** from the top of the Peak Galleria is almost as good, and is

> ### RIDING THE PEAK TRAM
>
> Half the fun of The Peak is the ascent on the **Peak Tram**, a cable-hauled funicular that's been climbing 396 vertical metres to the terminus since 1888 in just eight minutes – a remarkable piece of engineering. To find the Lower Peak Tram Terminal in Central, catch bus #15C (HK$4.20) from the Central Bus Terminus near the Star Ferry (10am–11.40pm), or walk up Garden Road – it's a little way up the hill from St John's Cathedral. The Peak Tram itself (daily 7am–midnight; HK$32 one-way, HK$45 return; ⓦthepeak.com.hk) runs every ten to fifteen minutes. If you want to see the sunset from up high, start queuing no later than 4pm; Sundays and public holidays are the busiest times and best avoided.

free of charge. For more great vistas, follow Mount Austin Road to Victoria Peak Garden, formerly the site of the Governor's residence, burnt down to the ground by the Japanese in World War II. Another great alternative is to circumambulate The Peak along the 3.5km loop formed by the Harlech Road, due west of the Peak Terminal, and Lugard Road on the northern slope, which sweeps around The Peak before curving back to the terminal.

An excellent way to descend The Peak is to **walk**, the simplest route being to follow the sign pointing to Hatton Road, from opposite the picnic area on Harlech Road. A very clear path leads all the way through trees, eventually emerging after about 45 minutes in Mid-Levels, near the junction between Kotewall Road and Conduit Road. Catch bus #13 or minibus #3 from Kotewall Road to Central, or you can walk east for about 1.5km along Conduit Road until you reach the top end of the Mid-Levels Escalator (see p.133), and follow that down into Central. The tourist office supplies useful maps (see p.147).

Aberdeen

Situated on the quieter south side of Hong Kong Island, **Aberdeen** is where Hong Kongers come for a seafood lunch. A tiny minority of Aberdeen's residents still live on **sampans** (small motorized boats) in the narrow harbour that lies between the main island and the offshore island of Ap Lei Chau – a tradition that certainly preceded the arrival of the British in Hong Kong, and a way of life that is now facing extinction. A time-honoured and enjoyable tourist activity in Aberdeen is to take a **sampan tour** around the harbour (around HK$68 for 30min). The trip offers great photo opportunities of the old houseboats jammed together, complete with dogs, drying laundry and outdoor kitchens. You'll also pass boat yards and floating restaurants, especially spectacular when lit up at night. The most famous is *Jumbo Floating Restaurant*, created by Stanley Ho in the style of a giant floating

OCEAN PARK

Ocean Park (daily 10am–6pm in winter, 10am–8pm in summer; HK$385; ⓦoceanpark.com.hk), Hong Kong's gigantic **theme and adventure park**, combines the rollercoasters of Thrill Mountain with a host of animal attractions. Waterfront's Grand Aquarium – the world's largest aquarium dome – features an impressive collection of marine life, including sharks and jellyfish, while you can catch dolphin and killer whale shows at Marine World, on the Summit headland, reachable from the main Waterfront entrance by cable car and funicular. The stars of Amazing Asian Animals are four giant pandas and rare red pandas, and there are aviaries, a rainforest and Polar World to explore. The park is also active in wildlife conservation. It's situated just east of Aberdeen; take bus #629 from Admiralty MTR station, #70 or #75 from Central, #72 or #92 from Causeway Bay, or #973 from Tsim Sha Tsui. Get off just after you exit the Aberdeen tunnel.

imperial palace; Dragon Court is overpriced but the 3rd-floor dim sum is great. To reach Aberdeen, catch **bus** #7 or #70 from Central, #72 from Causeway Bay, or #73 or #973 from Stanley. There are also regular **boat** connections between Aberdeen and nearby Lamma Island (see p.141).

Repulse Bay and around

The wide, sandy beach of **Repulse Bay**, an upmarket suburb on the southern coast of Hong Kong Island, is very popular with locals. The bay's unusual English name may stem from the British fleet's repulsion of pirates there in 1841. Near the southeast end of the beach is a **Kwun Yam Shrine** (daily 8am–8pm), dedicated to the goddess of the sea and surrounded by a wide variety of deity and animal statues. In front of the shrine is **Longevity Bridge**, the crossing of which is said to add three days to your life. Several kilometres northwest of Repulse Bay is **Deep Water Bay**, a smaller bay with a beach and a wakeboarding centre, and without Repulse Bay's crowds. You can reach both Repulse Bay and Deep Water Bay on **buses** #6, #6X or #260 from Central, minibus #40 from Causeway Bay, or bus #973 from Tsim Sha Tsui East.

Stanley

Straddling the neck of Hong Kong's southernmost peninsula is **Stanley**, a moderately sized residential village, with a sweeping European-style promenade and large numbers of pubs, bars and restaurants. A little way to the north of the bus stop is **Stanley Main Beach**, popular with windsurfers. Walk downhill from the bus stop and you'll soon find kitschy **Stanley Market** (open during daylight hours) and, beyond, a seafront promenade. Strolling west along the seafront, you'll come to **Tin Hau Temple** (daily 8am–8pm), completely rebuilt since it was established in 1767. Inside, there's a large, blackened tiger skin, the remains of an animal shot near here in 1942.

Next to the temple stands the colonnaded **Murray House**, an officers' barracks dating back to 1844 that's been reconstructed here, brick by brick, after being moved from its spot in Central where the Bank of China Tower stands today.

If you follow Wong Ma Kok Road south from the bus station, you'll reach the **Stanley Military Cemetery** (daily 8am–5pm; bus #6A); its graves from the 1840s and 1940s give you some idea of the toll that diseases and the Japanese invasion took on Hong Kong respectively. Buses #73 and #973 run between Aberdeen and Stanley. All the buses that go to Repulse Bay also go to Stanley.

Shek O

In the far east of the island, **Shek O** is Hong Kong's most remote and exclusive settlement – house numbers on Shek O Road refer not to location but to when the owner became a member of the golf club and therefore allowed to build here. A strong surf pounds the wide, white **beach**, and during the week the small village is more or less deserted.

Big Wave Bay, a thirty-minute walk from Shek O, past the Shek O Golf & Country Club, offers windsurfing, and on the headland above the bay is one of Hong Kong's **prehistoric rock carvings**.

To get to Shek O, catch bus #9 (30min; HK$6.90) from the bus terminal outside the **Shau Kei Wan** MTR station (exit A3) on the northeastern shore of Hong Kong Island. It's a picturesque journey over hills during which you'll spot first the sparkling waters of the Tai Tam Reservoir, then Stanley (to the southwest) and finally Shek O itself, appearing below.

Alternatively, jump off at Cape Collinson near To Tei Wan Village, and walk to Shek O along the **Dragon's Back** ridge, one of Hong Kong's most famous hikes (2–3hr), which boasts spectacular views and is part of the 50km Hong Kong Trail (see box, p.143); you can also paraglide and abseil from here. To reach the trail, head into Shek O Country Park and follow signs to Shek O Peak. The tourist office brochure (⋓discoverhongkong.com), *The Inside Guide to Hikes and Walks in Hong Kong*, has full details.

KOWLOON

A 4km strip of the mainland grabbed by the British in 1860 to add to their offshore island, **Kowloon** was part of the territory ceded to Britain "in perpetuity" and was accordingly developed with gusto and confidence. With the help of

---

THE LAST JUNK IN HONG KONG

Most travellers hold romantic images of Victoria Harbour filled with traditional Chinese wooden junks rigged with scarlet sails – the old workhorses of the waves – but these have long been decommissioned. Today just a single one remains: the lovingly restored **Duk Ling** (☏3759 7070, ⋓dukling.com.hk), typical of junks built in the mid-twentieth century, which now offers trips around the harbour. You can choose to sail from either Kowloon's public pier in Tsim Sha Tsui (hourly, 2.30–8.30pm), or Central Pier 9 on Hong Kong Island (hourly 2.45–8.45pm; HK$230–280); book your spot in advance.

3

land reclamation and the diminishing significance of the border between Kowloon and the New Territories at Boundary Street, Kowloon has, over the years, just about managed to accommodate the vast numbers of people who have squeezed into it. Today, areas such as Mong Kok, jammed with soaring tenements, are among the most densely populated urban areas in the world (in places shoehorning 100,000 people into each square kilometre).

Kowloon is more down to earth and ethnically diverse than the financial playground of Hong Kong Island's northern shore. The view from the Tsim Sha Tsui East Promenade towards the wall of skyscrapers across the harbour is one of the most unforgettable city panoramas, especially at night.

WHAT TO SEE AND DO

Tsim Sha Tsui is the tourist heart of Hong Kong, complete with ethnic enclaves, and **Nathan Road** – lined with shops and budget hotels – is its main artery, leading down to the harbour. Hong Kong's major museums (ⓦmuseums.gov.hk) are also all here.

The part of Kowloon north of Tsim Sha Tsui – encompassing **Yau Ma Tei** and **Mong Kok** – is rewarding to walk around, with authentic Chinese neighbourhoods and interesting markets.

Tsim Sha Tsui

The **Star Ferry Pier**, for ferries to Hong Kong Island (see box below), is right on the southwestern tip of the **Tsim Sha Tsui** peninsula. The **Hong Kong Cultural Centre**, about 100m east of the Star Ferry

Pier, contains concert halls, theatres and galleries, including, in an adjacent wing, the **Museum of Art** (closed for major renovation work until 2019).

Just to the north, at 10 Salisbury Road, the domed **Hong Kong Space Museum** (Mon & Wed–Fri 1–9pm, Sat & Sun 10am–9pm; HK$10; ⓦmuseums.gov.hk) was also undergoing a revamp at the time of research. The new exhibition halls promise plenty of interactive exhibits to explain our current understanding of the universe, including a "virtual space station" to demonstrate what zero gravity feels like. The attached **Space Theatre** presents IMAX-style shows for an additional fee (HK$24–32).

Salisbury Road runs parallel to the waterfront and is dominated by large hotels, such as the iconic *Peninsula Hotel* that dates back to 1928. Running north from Salisbury Road, neon-lit **Nathan Road** boasts Hong Kong's most concentrated collection of electronics shops, tailors, jewellery stores and fashion boutiques. The nearby **Kowloon Park** (Nathan Rd & Austin Rd; daily 5am–midnight) is a sprawling green space dotted with enormous banyan trees; on Sunday afternoons you can catch Kung Fu Corner displays here.

Over on Chatham Road South, east of Nathan Road, is one superbly presented museum that no visitor should miss: the **Hong Kong Museum of History** (daily except Tues 10am–6pm, Sun 10am–7pm; free; ⓦhk.history.museum). While the permanent collection is slated for renovation, for now, the "Hong Kong Story" walks you through the territory's history, from prehistoric times, through

---

THE STAR FERRY

Dating back to 1888, the **Star Ferry**, with its legendary fleet of vessels such as the *Twinkling Star* that ply Victoria Harbour, is a beloved part of the city's history. It was a Star Ferry that brought governor Sir Mark Aitchinson Young to Tsim Sha Tsui in 1941, to surrender to the Japanese, and it was at the Tsim Sha Tsui pier that rioters gathered in 1966 to protest a five-cent hike in ticket prices. The Star Ferry was founded by Dorabjee Nowrojee, a Parsi from Bombay who bought a steamboat for his family's use, at a time when the locals were crossing the harbour in sampans. Riding one of the boats today is a quintessential Hong Kong experience, and the cheapest way to get a tour of one of the world's most spectacular harbours (HK$3.40) as you make the ten-minute journey between Kowloon and Central; photos are best taken from the bottom deck.

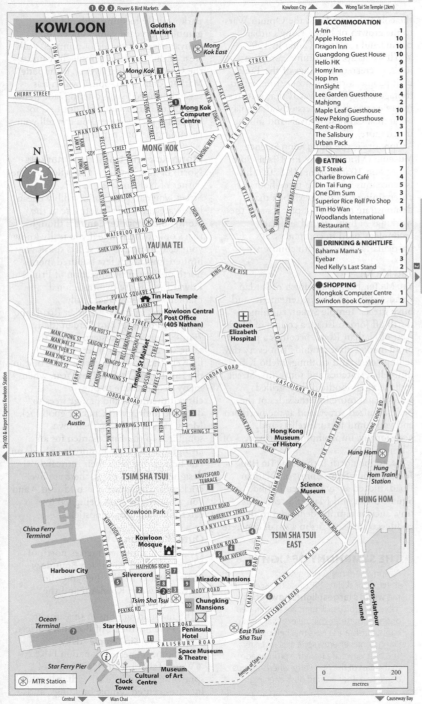

KOWLOON

① ② ③ , Flower & Bird Markets

Kowloon City ◣   ◣ Wong Tai Sin Temple (2km)

Goldfish Market

Mong Kok East

MONGKOK ROAD
FIFE STREET
TONG MEI ROAD

Mong Kok

ARGYLE STREET

ARGYLE STREET

CHERRY STREET

VICTORY AVE
PEARL AVE
WATERLOO ROAD

NELSON ST

SAI YEUNG CHOI STREET
TUNG CHOI STREET
FA YUEN STREET
SAI YEE STREET

KWONG WA ST

① Mong Kok Computer Centre

SHANTUNG STREET

NATHAN ROAD

KAM LAM ST
SOY ST
RECLAMATION STREET
PORTLAND STREET
SHANGHAI ST
CANTON ROAD
FERRY STREET
KANSU STREET

MONG KOK

DUNDAS STREET

HAMILTON ST

PITT STREET

Yau Ma Tei

WATERLOO ROAD

YAU MA TEI

WYLIE ROAD
MARTIN HILL RD
PRINCESS MARGARET RD
HO

SHEK LUNG ST

MAN LING LA

TUNG KUN ST

WING SING LA

KING'S PARK RISE

PUBLIC SQUARE ST
MARKET ST

Tin Hau Temple

Jade Market

Kowloon Central Post Office (405 Nathan)

Queen Elizabeth Hospital

MAN CHONG ST
MAN WAI ST
MAN YUEN ST
MAN YING ST
MAN WUI ST

PAK HOI ST
SAIGON ST
BATTERY ST
NINGPO ST
NANKING ST
PARKES ST
WOOSUNG ST
SHANGHAI ST
RECLAMATION ST

Temple St Market

CHI WO ST

NATHAN ROAD

FERRY STREET
WATERLOO RD
CANTON RD

JORDAN ROAD

JORDAN ROAD

GASCOIGNE ROAD

Austin

Jordan ③

BOWRING STREET

KWUN CHUNG ST
PILKEM ST
TAK KING ST
TAK SHING ST
COX'S ROAD
JORDAN PATH
JORDAN ROAD

Hong Kong Museum of History

Hung Hom

HO MAN TIN HILL RD
CHEONG WAN RD
LUK CHUI ROAD
HONG CHONG RD

AUSTIN ROAD WEST

AUSTIN ROAD

AUSTIN ROAD

Hung Hom Train Station

HUNG HOM

TSIM SHA TSUI

HILLWOOD ROAD

KNUTSFORD TERRACE ①

OBSERVATORY ROAD

Science Museum

CHATHAM ROAD
SCIENCE MUSEUM ROAD

Kowloon Park

KIMBERLEY ROAD

KIMBERLEY STREET

GRANVILLE ROAD

CAMERON ROAD ④

TSIM SHA TSUI EAST

China Ferry Terminal

Kowloon Mosque

PRAT AVENUE ⑤

GRANVILLE RD ⑥

MODY ROAD

Harbour City

Silvercord ⑤

HAIPHONG ROAD ⑦

KOWLOON PARK DRIVE
CANTON ROAD
LOCK RD
HANKOW RD
MODY ROAD

② ⑧ ⑨
Mirador Mansions

CHATHAM ROAD SOUTH

Cross-Harbour Tunnel

Tsim Sha Tsui ②

PEKING RD

MIDDLE ROAD

Chungking Mansions ⑩

SALISBURY ROAD

Ocean Terminal ⑦

Star House

Peninsula Hotel

East Tsim Sha Tsui

Avenue of Stars

①
i

SALISBURY ROAD

Space Museum & Theatre

Star Ferry Pier

Clock Tower

Cultural Centre

Museum of Art

MTR Station

0   200
metres

Central ▽   ▽ Wan Chai

Causeway Bay ▽

Sky100 & Airport Express Kowloon Station

3
2

the colonial period and the Opium Wars to the growth of Hong Kong's urban culture and return to China in 1997. You'll see national costume, a replica junk, re-created dwellings of the Tanka boat people, a retro grocery store, video footage from World War II that features interviews with prisoners of war, displays on annual Chinese festivals and much, much more.

Opposite is the **Hong Kong Science Museum** (Mon–Wed & Fri 10am–9pm, Sat & Sun 10am–9pm; HK$20; ⓦhk .science.museum), with three floors of entertaining hands-on exhibits that demonstrate the laws of physics and the workings of light, sound and the technology used in computers. It's particularly popular with children.

Yau Ma Tei
Yau Ma Tei, beginning north of Jordan Road, is full of high-rise tenements and busy streets. **Temple Street**, running north off Jordan Road, a couple of blocks west of Nathan Road, becomes a packed **night market** after around 7pm every day, selling fake brand clothing, Hello Kitty umbrellas, watches and souvenirs. Street stalls serving noodle dishes, grilled seafood and more line the sides of the pedestrianized street, and at the northern end you'll find fortune-tellers and, occasionally, impromptu performances of Chinese opera.

Just to the north is the local **Tin Hau Temple** (daily 8am–8pm), off Nathan Road, tucked away between Public Square Street and Market Street. This tiny, ancient temple, dedicated to the goddess of the sea, sits in a small concrete

park, usually teeming with old men gambling on card games under the banyan trees. A couple of minutes' walk west of the Tin Hau Temple, just under the Gascoigne Road flyover, is the **Jade Market** (daily 9am–6pm), which has several hundred stalls offering jade items; be sure to barter hard and don't go for expensive pieces unless you can tell your jadeite from your nephrite.

Mong Kok and traditional markets
North of Yau Ma Tei is **Mong Kok**. At the corner of Nelson Street and Fa Yuen Street, you can pick up incredibly cheap hardware and bargain software at the **Mong Kok Computer Centre** – though that's only worthwhile if you really know your electronics, as the sellers speak very limited English. A few hundred metres north of here in the direction of Prince Edward MTR are two traditional markets: **Flower Market** (daily 7am–7pm), in Flower Market Road, and the **Yuen Po Street Bird Garden** (daily 7am–8pm), at the eastern end of the same street, where it meets the MTR flyover. The flower market is at its best in the run-up to Chinese New Year, when many people come to buy chrysanthemums and orange trees to decorate their apartments for good luck. Many local men bring their own songbirds to the Bird Garden for an airing; as well as the hundreds of birds on sale here, along with their intricately designed bamboo cages, there are live crickets – whose fate is as bird-feed – and you may see the birds being fed live caterpillars held by chopsticks.

Outer Kowloon
Head a few hundred metres north of Mong Kok and you reach **Boundary Street**, which marks the symbolic border between Kowloon and the New Territories.

The main attractions in this area are well to the northeast of Boundary Street. The **Wong Tai Sin Temple** (daily 7am–5pm; suggested donation HK$2; ⓦWong Tai Sin, exit B2) consists of sprawling grounds filled with colourful, incense-scented temple buildings, and

---

THE SYMPHONY OF LIGHTS

At 8pm every night Hong Kong's spectacular skyline becomes the scene of the **world's largest light show**, when more than forty buildings are illuminated during a fourteen-minute extravaganza of lights, music and lasers that celebrates Hong Kong's energy, spirit and diversity. The best views are from the promenade to the east of the Star Ferry, where crowds begin to gather around dusk each night.

GETTING HIGH IN HONG KONG

For some of Hong Kong's best panoramas, head for the **Sky100** observation deck (1 Austin Rd West; daily 10am–9pm; HK$168; ⓦsky100.com.hk; ⓜKowloon Station) at the International Commerce Centre – Hong Kong's highest skyscraper. It sits on the building's 100th floor (nearly 400m up) and the 360-degree views, supplemented by maps and interactive exhibits, are particularly striking at night.

throngs of worshippers practising Taoism, Buddhism and Confucianism – more than any other temple in Hong Kong (especially during Chinese New Year). Big, bright and colourful, it offers a glimpse into the practices of modern Chinese religions: solemn devotees kneel and pray, wave lighted incense sticks, present food and drink to images of deities, or have their fortune read with *chim* (bamboo sticks), which are shaken out of boxes onto the ground and interpreted by on-site fortune-tellers.

One stop further east, Diamond Hill MTR takes you to the tranquil **Chi Lin Nunnery** (daily 9am–4.30pm; free) and **Nan Lian Garden** (daily 7am–9pm; free). The nunnery is a Tang Dynasty reproduction and is built of wood, without the use of a single nail, in striking contrast to the tower blocks looming all around it. The serene Nan Lian Garden has a circular walk (around 1hr) that takes in a carp pond, golden pagoda and a small bonsai tree collection. There's an excellent vegetarian restaurant here, specializing in mushroom and vegetable dishes (lunch from HK$100).

The New Territories

They make up 86 percent of Hong Kong's territory, yet the vast **New Territories** are little explored by visitors, most of whom stick to Hong Kong Island and Kowloon. There is so much to see here, from temples, monasteries and the remains of the original walled villages to pristine beaches, marshlands for birdwatching and hiking around the Plover Cove Reservoir (see box, p.143).

Take the MTR northwest along the West Rail Line to Tuen Mun, then switch to Light Rail lines #610 or #615 and alight at Tsing Shan Tsuen to hike up to the **Tsing Shan Monastery** (daily 6am–6pm), Hong Kong's oldest temple,

founded 1500 years ago, rebuilt in 1926 and accessible by a thirty-minute steep walk uphill. Parts of the iconic Bruce Lee film *Enter the Dragon* were shot here, and there's a slightly creepy charm to the more decayed shrines.

Tin Shui Wai MTR station is the starting point for the 1.6km-long **Ping Shan heritage trail** that takes you past Hong Kong's only surviving ancient pagoda and through three partially walled villages. At the other end of the trail, near Ping Shan Light Rail station, stop by the **Ping Shan Tang Clan Gallery** (follow the signs and walk uphill; Tues–Sun 10am–5pm; free), a museum dedicated to the Tang clan – the first to settle in Hong Kong five hundred years ago. You'll also find the impressive **Tang Ancestral Hall** and the **Yu Kiu Ancestral Hall** here – the largest of their kind in the city.

You can also take the MTR East Rail Line to Tai Po to visit the lively **Tai Po Market** or head one stop further to Tai Wo MTR station to visit the bustling Farmers' Market (Sun 9am–5pm), or take bus #64K to Ng Tung Chai for a hike through the bamboo groves to **Man Tak Monastery** (30min) and the **Ng Tung Chai Waterfalls**, a twenty-minute walk further uphill.

THE OUTLYING ISLANDS

Hong Kong's **outlying islands** offer a striking contrast to the nonstop buzz of the city in the form of peaceful seascapes, old fishing villages, hilly hikes and relative rural calm, almost entirely free of motor vehicles.

Lamma Island

Lying just to the southwest of Aberdeen, **Lamma** is the closest island to Hong Kong Island, with a spine of green-clad hills, a few sandy beaches, and lots of seafood restaurants, particularly at Yung Shue Wan village. There are two possible **ferry** crossing points, from Central direct to either Yung Shue Wan or Sok Kwu Wan, and from Aberdeen to Yung Shue Wan via Pak Kok Tsuen, or to Sok Kwu Wan via Mo Tat Wan. The best way to appreciate much of the island is to take a boat to Pak Kok Tsuen or Mo Tat Wan, then hike from one to the other (3hr or so) to catch the boat back. Bring plenty of drinking water; the well-signposted, paved hiking trails that run up and down the hills are relatively steep and there's little shade.

Mo Tat Wan Beach is wide and peaceful and located on the eastern spur of the island. A twenty-minute walk along the coast takes you to **Sok Kwu Wan**, its row of seafood restaurants built out over the water and fish farms in the harbour. The trail continues to the main village of **Yung Shue Wan** (1hr 15min), passing the **kamikaze caves**, where the Japanese stored boats filled with explosives during World War II, and the wide crescent of **Hung Shing Yeh Beach**, good for swimming and sunbathing. This stretch is particularly popular with local hikers, but you don't have to go far to find yourself in blissful solitude, especially if you continue to Pak Kok Tsuen, where the last stretch of the trail passes through a lovely bamboo grove, or take a detour from Sok Kwu Wan to deserted Tung O beach along a trail that branches off before you reach the kamikaze caves.

Cheung Chau Island

Cheung Chau is just south of Lantau and an hour from Hong Kong by ferry. Despite its minuscule size of 2.5 square kilometres, Cheung Chau is the most heavily populated of all the outer islands, and the narrow strip between its two headlands is jam-packed with tiny shops, markets and seafront restaurants.

As well as delicious alfresco meals, the island offers some good **walks** and several temples, the most important being the colourful two-hundred-year-old **Pak Tai Temple** (daily 7am–5pm), a few hundred metres northwest of the ferry pier. For a few days in May the temple is the site of one of Hong Kong's liveliest and most unusual events, the **Tai Ping Ching Chiu (Bun) Festival**, which culminates in a race up a 20m-high bamboo tower covered with buns.

FERRIES TO THE ISLANDS

Three separate companies operate ferries from Central to the outlying islands: New World First Ferry (ⓦwww.nwff.com.hk), Hong Kong & Kowloon Ferry Co (ⓦhkkf.com.hk) and Discovery Bay Transportation Services (ⓦhkri.com). The following is a selection of the most useful island **ferry services**. Schedules differ slightly on Sundays and public holidays, when prices also rise.

TO CHEUNG CHAU
From Outlying Islands Ferry Piers (Pier 5) 24hr service (every 30min; 35min–1hr; HK$13.20/slow, HK$25.80/fast). There are also nine sailings daily between Mui Wo on Lantau and Cheung Chau.
From Aberdeen Pier Operated by Maris Ferry. First boat out 7.10am, last boat back 9.30pm (7 daily Mon–Fri, 12 daily Sat & Sun; 55min; HK$30 Mon–Fri, HK$32 Sat & Sun; ⓦmarisferry.com.hk).

TO YUNG SHUE WAN, LAMMA ISLAND
From Outlying Islands Ferry Piers (Pier 4) First boat out 6.30am, last boat back 11.30pm (roughly every 20–30min; 30min; HK$17.10).
From Aberdeen (via Pak Kok Tsuen) Operated by Tsui Wah Ferry Service. First boat out 6am, last boat back 9.20pm (11 daily; 45min; HK$19; ⓦtraway.com.hk).

TO SOK KWU WAN, LAMMA ISLAND
From Outlying Islands Ferry Piers (Pier 4) First boat out 7.20am, last boat back 10.40pm (11 daily; 45min; HK$21).
From Aberdeen (via Mo Tat Wan) Operated by Chuen Kee Ferry. First boat out 6am, last boat back 10.10pm (13 daily; 45min; HK$12; ⓦferry.com.hk).

TO MUI WO (SILVERMINE BAY), LANTAU ISLAND
From Outlying Islands Ferry Piers (Pier 6) First boat out 6.10am, last boat back 11.30pm (every 30–40min; 30–60min; HK$15.20 slow, HK$25.40 fast).

HONG KONG OUTDOORS

Hong Kong is not just a heaving metropolis, and there are ample opportunities for hiking and biking. The islands of **Lamma** and **Cheung Chau** provide easy, paved walks around headlands, while **Lantau**, especially in the southwest corner, offers spectacular mountains, sea views and camping. Hong Kong Island is bisected by the 50km-long **Hong Kong Trail**: passing through five country parks, it's best done in segments. Further afield, the area around **Plover Cove Reservoir** in the New Territories, reachable by taking East Rail Line MTR to Tai Po Market stop and then by bus #75K, is prime hiking and biking country, with rugged trails of varying lengths and difficulty ratings. **Sai Kung Peninsula**, affectionately known as the "back garden", also has tremendous outdoor appeal, boasting watersports, surfing, trekking and the Territory's second-tallest mountain – Ma On Shan – which peaks at a challenging 702m.

The free Hong Kong Tourist Board brochure **The Inside Guide to Hikes and Walks in Hong Kong** provides basic maps and information on walks around Hong Kong, and the helpful Discover Hong Kong website (🌐discoverhongkong.com) provides detailed info on hikes, including e-books. You can also consider investing in Pete Spurrier's thorough *Serious Hiker's Guide to Hong Kong* (available in most bookshops). Decent trainers are enough for most walks, but do make sure to take plenty of **water** with you (stores are few and far between), and a hat as many of the trails are quite exposed.

If you don't fancy heading off into the wilderness alone, try **Walk Hong Kong** (🌐walkhongkong.com); they offer excellent, highly informative guided walks in English or German, while **Kayak and Hike** (🌐kayak-and-hike.com) explore Sai Kung by kayak and on foot.

The main beach on the island, the scenic but crowded **Tung Wan Beach**, is due west of the ferry pier. Windsurf boards (from HK$90/hr) and kayaks (from HK$80/hr) are available for rent during the summer months at the nearby **Windsurfing Centre** (🌐ccwindc.com.hk). To walk round the southern half of the island, follow signs from here for the **Mini Great Wall**, which is actually a ridge leading past some interesting rock formations. As a general rule, paths branching off to the right take you back towards the village, while left forks keep you going round the coast. Past the cemetery, follow signs down to **Pak Tso Wan** for a peaceful, secluded beach. It's also worth detouring to the **Cheung Po Tsai cave** on the island's westernmost tip; pirates used it to stash their booty in the eighteenth century – queues to enter the cave are common, after it featured in a local television series. A similar signposted circular walk covers the smaller northern half of the island. Each loop takes about three hours.

Lantau Island

With wild countryside, monasteries, old fishing villages and secluded beaches, **Lantau Island** – twice the size of Hong Kong Island – offers the best quick escape

from the city. Former governor Crawford Murray MacLehose declared all areas of Lantau more than 200m above sea level a country park, so Lantau remains relatively peaceful.

The island's biggest attraction is found high up on the Ngong Ping Plateau, in the western part of the island. The **Po Lin Monastery** (daily 8am–6pm; free) is the largest temple in the whole territory of Hong Kong, though it's more of a tourist draw than a spiritual retreat these days. Hundreds of visitors ascend the 268 steps to pay their respects to the 26m-high bronze **Tian Tan Buddha** (daily 10am–5.30pm), the largest seated bronze outdoor representation of Lord Gautama in the world, weighing in at 250 tonnes. The monastery makes for a particularly lively spectacle around Buddha's birthday. The monastery's *Po Lin Vegetarian Restaurant* (daily 11.30am–4.30pm) serves filling multi-course meals (from HK$60).

The most spectacular way of reaching the "Big Buddha" is to take the **Ngong Ping 360 cable car** (Mon–Fri 10am–6pm, Sat & Sun 10am–6.30pm; HK$130 one-way, HK$185 return; 🌐np360 .com.hk). The ride takes about half an hour, and presents sweeping views over northern Lantau, although its popularity makes for long queues (regularly 1hr

3

plus) in each direction. The Po Lin Monastery (Ngong Ping in bus schedules) can also be reached by bus #2 from Mui Wo, bus #23 from Tung Chung (the town by the cable-car terminus) and bus #21 from Tai O.

Right on the far northwestern shore of Lantau, the little fishing village of **Tai O** specializes in processing salt fish (hence the smell), and you'll find dried seafood heaped on tables in the little market area. Constructed over salt flats and a tiny offshore island, this community of stilt houses and quiet narrow lanes has become a weekend outing spot for Hong Kongers. The picturesque walk to **Lung Ngam Monastery** across the Sun Kei bridge takes you past houses built out of old boats and on to hillside views and mangroves. You can reach Tai O by bus #1 from Mui Wo, #21 from the Po Lin Monastery or #11 from Tung Chung.

If you take the ferry to Lantau from Pier 6 at the Outlying Islands ferry terminal in Central or the inter-island ferry from Cheung Chau island, you arrive at the sleepy town of **Mui Wo**, which has a decent enough beach at Silvermine Bay just to the northwest of town. Buses #1, #2 and #4 run from Mui Wo past several more beaches along the south coast, the **Cheung Sha Beach** being the most appealing.

ARRIVAL AND DEPARTURE

BY PLANE

Hong Kong International Airport (☎2181 8888, ⓦhongkongairport.com) is 34km west of Central on the north coast of Lantau Island and is served by more than 100 airlines from more than 160 destinations worldwide, including numerous cities in mainland China.

Destinations Bangkok (18 daily; 2hr 30min); Beijing (18 daily; 3hr 30min); Chengdu (5 daily; 2hr 30min); Guangzhou (2 daily; 50min); Ho Chi Minh City (4 daily; 2hr 45min); Jakarta (7 daily; 4hr 30min); Kuala Lumpur (11 daily; 2hr); Kuching (2 weekly; 3hr 45min); Manila (15 daily; 2hr); Nanjing (3 daily; 2hr); Phnom Penh (2 daily; 2hr 30min); Phuket (4 daily; 3hr 30min); Seoul (19 daily; 3hr 30min); Shanghai (30 daily; 2hr 30min); Singapore (20 daily; 4hr); Sydney (5 daily; 9hr); Tokyo (21 daily; 3hr 55min); Xian (2 daily; 2hr 45min).

Airport Express The quickest (and priciest) way to get to and from the airport is via the high-speed Airport Express line (daily 5.50am–12.45am; ⓦmtr.com.hk), which stops at Central (24min; HK$100), Kowloon (22min; HK$90) and

Tsing Yi (12min; HK$60) MTR stations and runs every 10–12min. If taking the Airport Express, it's worth getting the Airport Express Travel Pass (see box, p.146).

Airbuses Frequent Airbuses (daily 6am–midnight) are cheaper than the Airport Express; buy tickets on board or from airport customer service counters. The #A11 goes to Causeway Bay on Hong Kong Island via Sheung Wan, Central, Admiralty and Wan Chai (70min; HK$40), the #A12 goes direct to Central (50min; HK$45) and the #A21 goes to Hung Hom MTR Station via Tsim Sha Tsui, Jordan, Yau Ma Tei and Mong Kok (75min; HK$33). All buses have equivalent (though much less regular) night services and none gives change; this is available from the transport centre at the airport, as are Octopus cards (see box, p.146).

Taxis Taxis into the city are metered and reliable, but it's a good idea to have the name of your lodgings written down in Chinese characters to show the driver. It costs roughly HK$300 to get to Tsim Sha Tsui (20–30min) and about HK$350 for Hong Kong Island (30–50min). There's a HK$5 surcharge for every piece of luggage in the boot, and you may need to pay a tunnel toll too – on some cross-harbour trips the passenger pays the return charge as well.

BY TRAIN

The simplest way to reach mainland China is by direct train from Hung Hom train station or by taking the East Rail MTR line to the pedestrian border crossings at Lo Wu or Lok Ma Chau. Train tickets are obtainable in advance from CTS offices or on the same day from Hung Hom station. For more information, check ⓦwww.it3.mtr.com.hk.

Hung Hom station Located to the east of Tsim Sha Tsui. You can transfer to the West Rail MTR line for one stop to East Tsim Sha Tsui MTR Station, a short walk from Nathan Rd.

Destinations Beijing (on alternate days; 3.15pm; 24hr; from HK$600); Guangzhou East (hourly 7.25am–8.01pm; 2hr; from HK$210); Shanghai (on alternate days; 3.15pm; 19hr; from HK$550).

Lo Wu/Lok Ma Chau MTR stations The furthest MTR stations along the East Rail Line are easy gateways to Shenzhen. The border crossing at Lok Ma Chau is open 24hr, while the Lo Wu crossing operates between 6.30am and midnight.

BY BUS

There are regular daily bus services to Guangzhou and Shenzhen operated by China Travel Service (CTS; ⓦctshk .com); these take about one hour longer than the direct train and pick up and drop off at Hung Hom, Sheung Wan, Wan Chai and Causeway Bay (frequent 7am–10.45pm; 3hr–3hr 30min; HK$110).

BY FERRY

You can travel to a number of Chinese cities directly from Hong Kong. Tickets can be bought in advance from a

3

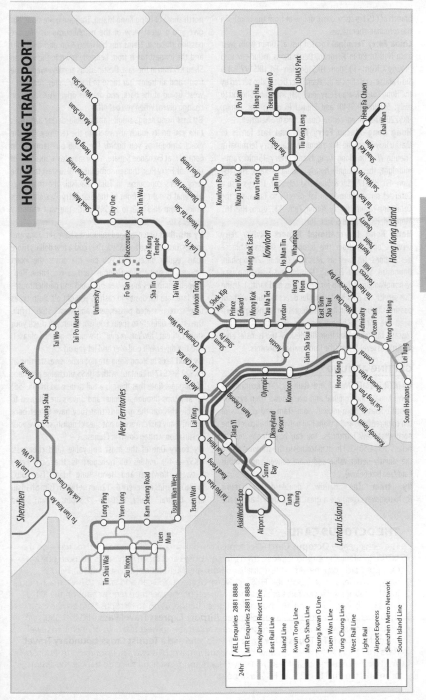

HONG KONG TRANSPORT

New Territories

Shenzhen

Kowloon

Hong Kong Island

Lantau Island

Wu Kai Sha
Ma On Shan
Heng On
Tai Shui Hang
Shek Mun
City One
Sha Tin Wai
Che Kung Temple
Racecourse
Fo Tan
Sha Tin
Tai Wai
University
Tai Po Market
Tai Wo
Fanling
Sheung Shui
Lo Wu
Lok Ma Chau
Fu Tian Kou An
Long Ping
Yuen Long
Kam Sheung Road
Tin Shui Wai
Siu Hong
Tuen Mun
Tsuen Wan West
Tsuen Wan
Tai Wo Hau
Kwai Hing
Kwai Fong
Lai King
Lai Chi Kok
Mei Foo
Nam Cheong
Tsing Yi
Sunny Bay
Disneyland Resort
Tung Chung
AsiaWorld-Expo
Airport
Olympic
Kowloon
Hong Kong

Po Lam
Hang Hau
Tseung Kwan O
LOHAS Park
Tiu Keng Leng
Yau Tong
Lam Tin
Kwun Tong
Ngau Tau Kok
Kowloon Bay
Choi Hung
Diamond Hill
Wong Tai Sin
Lok Fu
Kowloon Tong
Shek Kip Mei
Prince Edward
Mong Kok East
Mong Kok
Yau Ma Tei
Jordan
Austin
Sham Shui Po
Cheung Sha Wan
Tsim Sha Tsui
East Tsim Sha Tsui
Hung Hom
Ho Man Tin
Whampoa

Heng Fa Chuen
Chai Wan
Shau Kei Wan
Sai Wan Ho
Tai Koo
Quarry Bay
North Point
Fortress Hill
Tin Hau
Causeway Bay
Wan Chai
Admiralty
Central
Sheung Wan
HKU
Sai Ying Pun
Kennedy Town
Ocean Park
Wong Chuk Hang
Lei Tung
South Horizons

Legend

24hr	AEL Enquiries 2881 8888
	MTR Enquiries 2881 8888
	Disneyland Resort Line
	East Rail Line
	Island Line
	Kwun Tong Line
	Ma On Shan Line
	Tseung Kwan O Line
	Tsuen Wan Line
	Tung Chung Line
	West Rail Line
	Light Rail
	Airport Express
	Shenzhen Metro Network
	South Island Line

branch of CTS (ⓦctshk.com), online or from the booths in the terminals themselves.

China Ferry Terminal Located just a 10min walk west from Nathan Rd in Kowloon. Destinations include Macau (hourly 7.30am–10.30pm; HK$164 Mon–Fri, HK$177 Sat & Sun) and several stops in the Pearl River Delta (also served by the Hong Kong–Macau Ferry Terminal), including Shekou (6 daily; 50min; HK$140) and Zhuhai (6 daily; 1hr 10min; HK$220), though not central Guangzhou or Shenzhen.

Hong Kong–Macau Ferry Terminal Fast ferries to Macau leave from the Hong Kong–Macau Ferry Terminal in Sheung Wan on Hong Kong Island (every 15min 7am–midnight, then roughly hourly midnight–7am; HK$164 Mon–Fri, HK$177 Sat & Sun) and take 1hr. There's also a Cotai Jet service from Shun Tak directly to Taipa, for the Cotai Strip casinos (every 30min; 7am–11.30pm; HK$165 Mon–Fri, HK$177 Sat & Sun; 1hr).

Hong Kong International Airport SkyPier ferry services operate from the airport to several Chinese destinations (as well as Macau): Zhuhai, Zhongshan, Dongguan, Shekou, Fuyong, Nansha and Shenzhen (see ⓦhongkongairport.com for timetables and tariffs). Using this service, it's possible to transfer direct to China without passing through Hong Kong immigration (although you'll need the correct Chinese visa for all destinations bar Macau). Buy your ticket from the desks in the transfer area on Arrivals level 5, near the immigration counters.

GETTING AROUND

By MTR The MTR (Mass Transit Railway; ⓦmtr.com.hk) is Hong Kong's underground and overground train system, which operates from roughly 6am–1am and consists of ten coloured lines and a Light Rail network that covers the northwest New Territories. You can buy single-journey tickets (HK$4.50–30) from machines in the stations, or use the slightly better value and more convenient Octopus Card (see box below).

By tram The narrow, double-decker trams (ⓦhktramways.com) are a great way to travel along the north shore of Hong Kong Island. They are quite slow, but give you a great view of the neighbourhoods you are passing through. Trams run between 6am and midnight and the longest run is from Kennedy Town in the west to Shau Kei Wan in the east. Destinations are displayed at the front, and all trams, bar those to Happy Valley, run east–west. Board at the back, and pay the driver (HK$2.30; no change given) when you get off.

By bus Hong Kong's single- and double-decker a/c buses take you pretty much anywhere in the territory. Pay the exact amount as you board. The main bus terminal in Central is at Exchange Square, a few minutes' walk south of the Star Ferry Pier, though some buses also start from the ferry pier's concourse. In Tsim Sha Tsui, the main bus terminal is right in front of the Star Ferry Pier. Bus fares range from HK$3.50 to HK$45, with the vast majority under $10.

By minibus Green-topped minibuses have set stops and routes, but can also be hailed. They cost a few dollars more than regular buses, and you pay the driver the exact amount or swipe your Octopus Card as you enter. Red-topped minibuses are owner-operated and neither routes nor fares are fixed; pay in cash as you get off. Both types take sixteen seated passengers, and won't stop if full. Drivers are unlikely to speak English; when you reach your stop, call out "*Yau lok, m'goi!*" (I want to get off, please!) and the driver will pull over and let you off.

By taxi Taxis in Hong Kong are not expensive, starting at HK$22 (HK$17 in Lantau), with a HK$5 surcharge per piece of luggage. Note that there is a toll to be paid (HK$5–55) on any trips through a tunnel and drivers are allowed to double this, on the grounds that they have to get back again. Many taxi drivers do not speak English, so have your destination written down in Chinese.

By ferry One of the most enjoyable (and cheapest: HK$2–3.40) modes of transport is the Star Ferry between Kowloon and Hong Kong Island (see box, p.138). Ferries run every 6–12min between Tsim Sha Tsui and Central (daily 6.30am–11.30pm; 9min), and

THE OCTOPUS CARD

The rechargeable **Octopus Card** (ⓦoctopus.com.hk) "smart card" can be used for travel on the MTR, Light Rail, the Airport Express, trams, ferries, buses and green minibuses. You can buy an Octopus Card from the airport terminal and from any MTR station; it costs HK$150, with a refundable deposit of HK$50 and HK$100 worth of credit. You can add value to it via machines in MTR stations. Octopus fares are around five percent cheaper than regular fares on the MTR, and since buses, trams and minibuses don't give change, using an Octopus Card ensures you don't overpay. The card is also available as an **Airport Express Travel Pass** (HK$250/350, including one/two trips on the Airport Express and three consecutive days of unlimited travel on the MTR), an **MTR Tourist Day Pass** (HK$65/24hr) and a **Tourist Cross-boundary Travel Pass** (HK$100/140 for one/two days of consecutive travel plus two single journeys to/from Lo Wu/Lok Ma Chau stations). When you leave Hong Kong, just hand the card back at the airport or an MTR terminal to get your HK$50 deposit.

between Tsim Sha Tsui and Wan Chai (daily 7.20am–10.50pm; 8min). Regular ferries also run to the outlying islands (see box, p.142).

INFORMATION AND TOURS

Tourist information The super-efficient Hong Kong Tourism Board (HKTB; ✺discoverhongkong.com) has several handy offices: one in the arrivals area of the airport (daily 8am–9pm), at the Star Ferry Concourse in Tsim Sha Tsui (daily 8am–8pm) and in the Peak Piazza on Hong Kong Island (daily 11am–8pm). There's also a HKTB multilingual telephone service (daily 9am–6pm, ☎ 2508 1234).

Listings publications Countless leaflets on what to do can be picked up at HKTB outlets. *Time Out magazine* ($18; ✺timeout.com.hk) publishes a fortnightly Hong Kong edition, containing up-to-date information on restaurants, bars, happy hours, clubs, concerts and exhibitions.

Walking tours There are some excellent themed tours run by individual companies but bookable through HKTB. Walk In Hong Kong (✺walkin.hk) organize outstanding specialized walking tours for small groups, taking you off the beaten path to the city's cemeteries, venerable traditional Chinese medicine shops, North Point and other characterful neighbourhoods; tours typically last 3hr and cost from HK$480. If that seems a little steep, try HK Free Walk (✺hkfreewalk.com) where guides work for tips on their 2–3hr walks through Tsim Sha Tsui.

Harbour cruises Two outfits run nightly 45min harbour cruises aboard traditional red-sailed junks; 1950s-built Duk Ling (HK$230; ✺dukling.com.hk) and the more modern Aqua Luna (HK$195; ✺aqualuna.com.hk), both including a complimentary drink. Wild Hong Kong (✺wildhongkong .com) organize adventurous hikes, kayaking excursions and canyoning trips in Hong Kong's country parks (from HK$300/person depending on group size).

ACCOMMODATION

HONG KONG ISLAND

The budget rooms on Hong Kong Island are mostly in Causeway Bay, some near Sogo and others towards Leighton Rd. They tend to be more expensive than Kowloon, but comparatively quieter.

Causeway Bay Inn Flat A, 1/F, Percival House, 77–83 Percival St ✺causewaybayinn.com; ⓜCauseway Bay; map pp.132–133. Just three comfortable, modern en-suite rooms – two with twin beds and one a double – decorated in pastel shades, with TVs, a/c and mini fridges. You get an entrance code for your room as there doesn't tend to be anyone manning the reception. Perfect for a quiet stay. Doubles HK$390

Check Inn 2/F, 269–273 Hennessy Rd ☎ 2155 0175, ✺checkinnhk.com; ⓜWan Chai; map pp.132–133. Friendly, colourful hostel that's perfect for night owls who like pub crawls and socializing. Lockers are on the small side, luggage space is at a premium and getting up on the top bunks requires a certain degree of acrobatic skill, but the staff are very helpful. Dorms HK$200

Mount Davis Youth Hostel 123 Mount Davis Path ☎ 2817 5715, ✺yha.org.hk; map pp.132–133. Perched on the top of a mountain above Kennedy Town, this self-catering retreat has superb, peaceful views over the harbour. Extra-friendly staff and spotless rooms go a good way towards compensating for the slightly grotty bathroom facilities. Getting here can be a major expedition, unless you catch the infrequent shuttle bus from the ground floor of the Shun Tak Centre – phone the hostel for times. Dorms HK$160, doubles HK$330

★**YesInn @ Causeway Bay** 2/F, Nan Yip Bldg, 472 Hennessy Rd ☎ 2213 4567, ✺yesinn.com; ⓜCauseway Bay; map pp.132–133. Bright and colourful, with a chill-out area and rooftop garden that encourage mingling, a good mix of single-sex and mixed dorms and private rooms, and beds big enough for Westerners, *YesInn* wins points for comfort and efficiency. Nice extras include iPads that you can borrow and 24hr tea and coffee. Dorms HK$150, doubles HK$500

Y-Loft 238 Chai Wan Rd ☎ 3721 8989, ✺youthsquare.hk; ⓜChai Wan; map pp.132–133. Don't be put off by the rather remote location at the end of the MTR: the area is blissfully untouristy and you're well positioned to explore Shek O and the south side of Hong Kong Island. The doubles and triples are immense by Hong Kong standards and all come with giant flat-screen TVs and wheelchair access. Doubles HK$770

KOWLOON

Most of the accommodation listed is within a 15min walk of the Star Ferry Pier – conveniently central, though very touristy.

A-Inn 8/F, Sincere House, 83 Argyle St ☎ 9533 6817, ✺ainnhongkong.hostel.com; ⓜMong Kok; map p.139. More like a budget hotel than a hostel, *A-Inn* has compact doubles, triples and quads with plasma-screen TVs. There's no common room, so it's good for a quiet stay rather than for meeting fellow travellers. Very convenient location right next to the MTR station. Doubles HK$450

Hello HK A7, 6/F, Mirador Mansions, 54–56 Nathan Rd ☎ 3995 4171, ✺helloinn.blogbus.com; ⓜTsim Sha Tsui; map p.139. Run by the ever-smiling Ivan, this is one of the best guesthouses in the area – though with only six rooms, you must book ahead. Rooms are clean, bright and have bathrooms (with shower cubicles) and LCD TVs, though only two have windows. DVD players are available on request and there's a Chinese visa outlet next door. Doubles HK$300

Homy Inn 8/F, Block C, Union Mansion, 33–35 Chatham Rd South ☎ 8100 0189, ✺homyinn.com.hk; ⓜTsim Sha Tsui; map p.139. In spite of the misspelled name, this place is, in fact, very homey and the staff get top marks for going out of their way to ensure your Hong Kong stay is a good one. There are clean, functional singles, doubles and family rooms, all with crisp white linens. Doubles HK$300

★ **Hop Inn** 9/F, James S. Lee Mansion, 33–35 Carnarvon Rd ☎ 2881 7331, ⊚ hopinn.hk; ⓜ Tsim Sha Tsui; map p.139. Colourful little en-suite rooms, each one individually decorated by a local artist, glass-walled bathrooms and extra-helpful staff. No common room but a friendly, sociable vibe prevails, as it does in their other two branches. Dorms HK$150, doubles HK$540

InnSight 3/F 9 Lock Rd ☎ 2369 1151, ⊚ innsight.hk; ⓜ Tsim Sha Tsui; map p.139. Just eight individually decorated en-suite rooms with a/c and TVs in a great location and with very helpful owners. Their only single room costs HK$510. Doubles HK$630

Lee Garden Guest House Block A, 8/F, Fook Kiu Mansion, 36 Cameron Rd ☎ 2367 2284, ⊚ starguesthouse .com.hk; ⓜ Tsim Sha Tsui; map p.139. Friendly owner Charlie Chan and his son Raymond offer a comfortable range of clean, small singles, doubles and triples (all with windows), that feel more like a hotel than a guesthouse. Cheaper rooms share facilities. The Chans also own the similar *Star Guest House* (6/F, 21 Cameron Rd; ☎ 2723 8951). Doubles HK$430

★ **Mahjong** 1/F, Pak Tai Mansion, 2A–2B Ma Hang Chung, To Kwa Wan ☎ 2705 1869, ⊚ themahjonghk.com; bus #11 from ⓜ Kowloon and ⓜ Jordan; map p.139. A hip new hostel offering dorm accommodation with nice details including hotel-grade mattresses and in-built black-out screens. The staff's enthusiasm about their neighbourhood makes the out-of-the-way location seem like an advantage, and there are female-only (HK$220) and potentially awkward but apparently popular double-bed dorms (HK$399) available too. Dorms HK$180

Rent-a-Room Flat A, 2/F, Knight Garden, 7–8 Tak Hing St ☎ 2366 3011, ⊚ rentaroomhk.com; ⓜ Jordan; map p.139. This clean hotel offers two floors of decent-sized rooms – singles, doubles, triples and quads – as well as a whole range of facilities including money-changing and laundry. Rooms are a bit featureless but come with phones, a/c, fridges and kitchenettes. Discounts available for longer stays and security is top-notch. Doubles HK$700

The Salisbury 41 Salisbury Rd ☎ 2268 7888, ⊚ ymcahk .org.hk; ⓜ Tsim Sha Tsui; map p.139. *The Salisbury* is all about location. The dorm rooms are basic and pricey, but the comfortable harbour-view rooms offer the same vista as the venerable *Peninsula Hotel* next door for a fraction of the price. Other perks include a tour desk, helpful staff and self-service laundry. Dorms HK$400, doubles HK$1540

Urban Pack 14/F, Hai Phong Mansion, 53–55 Haiphong Rd ☎ 2732 2271, ⊚ urban-pack.com; ⓜ Tsim Sha Tsui; map p.139. Cool "designer hostel" decorated with fun murals, where the staff make you feel like family. The

dorms might be a little cramped, but the place is super-clean and you may find yourself extending your stay because of the welcoming vibe. Dorms HK$150

CHUNGKING MANSIONS

Chungking Mansions is an apartment block at 36–44 Nathan Rd with the highest concentration of budget guesthouses in Kowloon. It's an ethnic enclave of immigrants from India and Africa and has an unforgettable atmosphere: on the ground floor, you can visit an internet café, eat a great curry, get a haircut, buy a mobile phone, change money and buy clothes. Above the second floor, the building is divided into five blocks, lettered A to E, each served by two lifts, and usually attended by long queues. The building may feel a bit like a firetrap, but fire safety is at acceptable levels these days, and there's CCTV. Guesthouses vary widely – from dingy flophouses to spotless little places – and there are usually young men loitering at the entrance, dishing out business cards and trying to entice you to stay at their guesthouse. Below are several recommended places; if you arrive without a reservation, never agree to stay without inspecting the rooms first, and beware that the less scrupulous touts may try to tell you that your reserved guesthouse is dirty/has closed down, so take it with a pinch of salt.

Apple Hostel B-7, 10/F, Block B ☎ 2369 9802, ⊚ applehostel.com.hk; ⓜ Tsim Sha Tsui; map p.139. Friendly place with tiny singles and doubles and minuscule bathrooms where you can shower while sitting on the loo. That said, everything is spotless, towels are changed daily and every room comes with a phone and kettle. Wi-fi is semi-reliable. Doubles HK$400

Dragon Inn B-2, 3/F, Block B ☎ 2367 7071, ⊚ www .dragoninn.info; ⓜ Tsim Sha Tsui; map p.139. Well-organized, friendly and secure hostel-cum-travel agent with singles, doubles and triples. The newer rooms verge on the luxurious and there's even a "honeymoon room", though you have to wonder who'd spend their honeymoon at Chungking Mansions. Doubles HK$360

Guangdong Guest House B-2, 5/F, Block B, ⊚ guangdonghostel.com; ⓜ Tsim Sha Tsui; map p.139. Friendly, helpful Simon oversees various configurations of compact rooms: singles, doubles, triples and quads. All are clean and come with a/c and phones, but, as elsewhere in Chungking Mansions, the rooms tend to be curry-scented during the day. Doubles HK$600

Maple Leaf Guesthouse E-4, 12/F, Block E ☎ 9325 6152, ⊚ mapleleafguesthouse.hostel.com; ⓜ Tsim Sha Tsui; map p.139. Welcoming, secure guesthouse with compact, well-lit rooms and equally compact bathrooms. Doubles HK$320

New Peking Guest House A1, 12/F, Block A ☎ 2723 8320, ⊚ www.chungking-mansions.hk/A12-2.htm; ⓜ Tsim Sha Tsui; map p.139. Spotless guesthouse with toothbrushes, fridge and electrical converters provided by the friendly management. Take your pick from singles, doubles, triples and quads. Doubles HK$380

EATING

CENTRAL

Most cheap eating in Central can be found along Wellington St and along either side of the Mid-Levels Escalator. Further east, you'll find plenty of choice on Jaffe Rd and in the streets near Times Square. If you want to eat during peak lunch and dinnertime hours, be prepared to queue.

★**BÊP Vietnamese Kitchen** 88–90 Wellington St Ⓜ Central; map pp.132–133. Part of a small, locally run Vietnamese chain, whose crisp, clean and sharp flavours make a nice break from Chinese food. The *banh mi* sandwiches (HK$58), rice-skin rolls (HK$78) and poached chicken salad (HK$78) are excellent, and two can eat very well for HK$300. No reservations; expect to queue at lunchtime. Daily noon–4.30pm & 6–11pm.

Bindaas LG/F 33 Aberdeen St Ⓜ Central or Sheung Wan; map pp.132–133. Great modern Indian food, this is Hong Kong's take on Mumbai street food. Their snacks and small plates (from HK$68) are the stars here – the *pao* (filled buns) and "NaanZa" (naan crossed with pizza) are especially popular, and there's a good drinks menu too. The set lunch costs a reasonable HK$98. Mon–Sat noon–3pm & 6.30–11pm, Sun noon–11pm.

★**Chilli Fagara** 7 Old Bailey St Ⓜ Central or Sheung Wan; map pp.132–133. The crimson decor at this thimble-sized Sichuan restaurant gives you some idea of what to expect: beautiful, heat-laden dishes, such as tender chunks of fish in a sweet chilli sauce and red hot chilli prawns that'll bring a tear to your eye – a challenge even to the brave. Set lunch HK$98. Daily 11.30am–3pm & 5–11.30pm.

Dumpling Yuan 69 Wellington St Ⓜ Central; map pp.132–133. This efficient Pekinese restaurant lists a good mix of meaty and veggie choices among its dumpling offerings. Tuck into pork and leek or beef and celery (HK$55) or opt for cold sesame noodles. Daily 10am–11pm.

Lin Heung Tea House 160–164 Wellington St Ⓜ Sheung Wan; map pp.132–133. One of the last surviving dim sum places in Hong Kong where the tiny bites are brought round on trolleys, *Lin Heung* is barely controlled bedlam spread over several floors. Just point at the steamed dumplings, buns, pork ribs, rice with chicken and fish maw and other dishes as the trolleys pass by. Best enjoyed with a group of friends. Dishes from HK$15. Daily 6am–11pm.

Mana! 92 Wellington St Ⓜ Central; map pp.132–133. The self-described "fast slow food" at this organic vegetarian and vegan café consists of flatbreads topped with grilled tofu and roast vegetables, mezze platters of hummus and olives, hearty soup of the day and portobello mushroom and halloumi burgers. Mains from HK$78. Daily 10am–10pm.

Nagahama No 1 Ramen 14 Kau U Fong Ⓜ Sheung Wan; map pp.132–133. One of many super-popular ramen noodle joints, *Nagahama* uses a pork bone soup base that gives its chunky, slurpable noodles their distinctive flavour. Large portions, tiny place, so put on your queuing shoes. Mains from HK$80. Daily 11.30am–10pm.

Tasty Congee & Noodle Wantun Shop Shops 3016–3018, IFC Mall, 1 Harbour View St Ⓜ Hong Kong, exit E1; map pp.132–133. Shoppers at the luxury IFC Mall pile into this simple restaurant to feast on the signature prawn wontons, noodle soup, prawn congee and flat rice noodles stir-fried with beef; less standard offerings include boiled jellyfish strips and stewed pork feet. Mains from HK$38. Daily 11am–11pm.

WAN CHAI AND CAUSEWAY BAY

Bowrington Road Ⓜ Causeway Bay; map pp.132–133. This tiny alley boasts two culinary treats. The "Cooked Food Centre" (daily 6am–2am) has a dozen open kitchens serving great authentic food at rock-bottom prices (Hainan chicken with rice and soup; HK$40), but you'll need to point for your dinner as little English is spoken. In the evening, locals perch on plastic stools to enjoy deliciously fresh and varied seafood dishes from the hole-in-the-wall restaurants. Prices are reasonable – razor clams in black bean sauce HK$75.

Brunch Club & Supper 1st floor, 13 Leighton Rd Ⓜ Causeway Bay; map pp.132–133. Cosy and relaxed, this is a great place for the morning after the night before, with brunch sets ranging from muesli and yogurt (HK$48) to eggs with smoked salmon and parmesan (HK$95). It's worth getting out of bed for the chocolate truffle tart alone. Happy hour 6–9pm daily. Also at 70 Peel St (Ⓜ Central). Mon–Thurs & Sun 9am–11pm, Fri & Sat 8.30am–11pm.

Crystal Jade Jiang Nan Shop 310, 3/F, Tai Yau Plaza, 181 Johnston Rd Ⓜ Wan Chai; map pp.132–133. Shanghainese diner specializing in steamed dumplings and noodle dishes. The more unusual dishes include smoked duck with tea leaves. Mains from HK$70. Daily 11am–11pm.

Matchbox 2 Sun Wui Rd Ⓜ Causeway Bay; map pp.132–133. Come to this retro *cha chaan teng* for good-quality Hong Kong standards such as baked pork chop rice or their glorious deep-fried French toast. A meal and drink will come to under HK$100, and their "nostalgic" afternoon tea set is great value at HK$46 for noodles, tea and eggs on toast. Daily 7am–11pm.

Nam Kee Spring Roll Noodle Co 1/F, San Kei Tower, 56–58 Yee Wo St Ⓜ Causeway Bay; map pp.132–133. Choose from eight meat options for a perfect bowl of steaming-hot noodles in aromatic broth – delicious pork belly noodles cost HK$34. Also at 66–72 Stanley St (Ⓜ Central). Mon–Sat 7.30am–11pm & Sun 11am–11pm.

★**Tai Hing** 73 Lee Garden Rd Ⓜ Causeway Bay; map pp.132–133. Busy *siu-mei* (roast) specialist with roast duck, goose and pork glistening in the window. The friendly staff don't speak much English but they're helpful, and succulent dishes, including hunks of roast pork, crispy crackling, rice and *kankun* (HK$59), are served up in no time at all. Daily 7.30am–3.30am.

KOWLOON

You can take your pick from a multitude of stalls and cafés on Temple St and the surrounding area. Prat Ave has a wide variety of Asian choices, while Knutsford Terrace is good for international food – albeit slightly pricey. Chungking Mansions (see p.148) is the place for inexpensive curries – just follow your nose.

BLT Steak Shop G62, G/F, Ocean Terminal Ⓜ Tsim Sha Tsui; map p.139. *Bistro Laurent Tourondel* is all about beef – porterhouse, New York strip, ribeye, you name it. Lighter options available for the less carnivorous (though not a vegetarian option in sight) and lunch sets start from HK$138. Daily noon–11pm.

Charlie Brown Café 58–60 Cameron Rd Ⓜ Tsim Sha Tsui, Exit B2; map p.139. The world's first (though not the only) Charlie Brown-themed café. The food – pasta, burgers, salads and sandwiches – won't wow your tastebuds, but where else can you get your rice shaped into a Snoopy? Mains from HK$80. Mon–Thurs & Sun 8.30am–11pm, Fri & Sat 8.30am–12.30am.

Din Tai Fung Shop 130, 3rd floor, Silvercord, Canton Rd Ⓜ Tsim Sha Tsui; map p.139. Large, bright Taiwanese restaurant focusing mostly on dumplings. The speciality is the *xiao long bao* (from HK$60), but it's hard to go wrong with noodle soup or pork and truffle dumplings. Also at G/F, 68 Yee Woo St (Ⓜ Causeway Bay). Daily 11.30am–10pm.

★**One Dim Sum** Kenwood Mansion, 15 Playing Field Rd Ⓜ Prince Edward, exit A; map p.139. One of two Michelin-starred cheapies in Hong Kong, this compact dim sum joint is perpetually packed with punters who come for the *chiu chow* dumplings, the rice rolls with prawns and barbecued pork, chicken rice and congee. Look for the line of stools by the door; queues move quickly. Dishes HK$13–20. Mon–Fri 11am–midnight, Sat & Sun 10am–midnight.

Superior Rice Roll Pro Shop 384 Portland St Ⓜ Prince Edward; map p.139. Small joint popular with locals that specializes in eight types of rice rolls: barbecued pork, dried shrimp, vegetable and a few other select flavours. Ask for an English menu. Rice rolls from HK$22. Daily 8am–11.30pm.

Tim Ho Wan 9–11 Fuk Wing St Ⓜ Sham Shui Po; map p.139. Hong Kong's cheapest Michelin-starred restaurant. Now with branches across town, the dim sum's the star at this establishment; everything is freshly made in house, and the *char siew bao* (barbecue pork buns; HK$16) and the *chiu chow* dumplings are renowned. Queues can be lengthy around mealtimes, so go late morning or early afternoon when there are fewer people. Daily 10am–9.15pm.

Woodlands International Restaurant Wing On Plaza, 62 Mody Rd Ⓜ Tsim Sha Tsui or East Tsim Sha Tsui, exit J; map p.139. This unpretentious South Indian vegetarian restaurant has been serving up delicious, filling thalis (HK$90) and crisp dosas (from HK$55) in the same location for 35 years, quite a feat on Hong Kong's dining scene. Daily noon–3.30pm & 6.30–10.30pm.

DRINKING AND NIGHTLIFE

Drinking in Hong Kong is expensive and a beer will normally set you back at least HK$50; however, most bars operate happy hours with drinks discounted by as much as fifty percent. Many bars have "ladies' nights", usually Wednesday or Thursday, where women can easily stay out all night without spending anything. The most concentrated collection of bars is in Central, spreading from the long-standing, popular Lan Kwai Fong to the network of streets leading into and including the more upmarket Soho area. Rubbing shoulders with the "hostess bars" in Jaffe and Lockhart roads in Wan Chai are a dozen or more regular clubs and bars. Tsim Sha Tsui's nightlife scene is somewhat sparse compared to Hong Kong Island, but there are a few bars, lounges and clubs found near the harbour and Jordan. Check out Ⓦ hkclubbing.com for what's hot at the moment.

HONG KONG ISLAND

Buddha Lounge L/G Amber Lodge, 23 Hollywood Rd, Central Ⓜ Central; map pp.132–133. Small and cosy after-hours bar decorated with Buddha images, with a superb sound system and DJ sets until the very early hours. Nightly drinks specials, Tuesday ladies' night and a happy hour 4–10pm. Mon–Sat 1pm–late.

Cicada 47A Elgin St, Soho Ⓜ Central; map pp.132–133. Delicious Asian tapas such as minted lamb and potato balls (HK$88) perfectly complement lychee bellinis and other happy-hour cocktails (HK$30; 3–7.30pm) at this wine bar-cum-restaurant. Daily noon–1am.

Globe 45–53 Graham St, Soho Ⓜ Central; map pp.132–133. Immense bar known for one of the longest lists of local and imported beers in the city, plus solid comfort food (set lunch from HK$140). Happy hour 10am–8pm, with pints from HK$46. Mon–Sat 10am–2am.

Red Bar 4th floor, IFC Mall, 8 Finance St, Ⓜ Central; map pp.132–133. Fabulous rooftop bar facing out over the harbour and the Kowloon skyline, with a good cocktail menu (from HK$95) and nightly DJ sets. The deck area is public, so you can also bring drinks from elsewhere to enjoy the view. Happy hour 6–9pm. Daily 11.30am–late.

Volar Basement, 38–44 D'Aguilar St Ⓜ Central, exit D2; map pp.132–133. With an interior that looks like the set of *Tron*, this busy club has two rooms playing music that ranges from commercial pop to hard house. Cover charges free–HK$200 depending on what's on. Dress nicely and get there before 1am. Tues–Sat 6pm–5am.

★ **Wooloomooloo** 31/F, 256 Hennessy Rd ⓜ Wan Chai; map pp.132–133. Situated above the acclaimed steakhouse of the same name, this rooftop bar has fantastic 270-degree views over Victoria Harbour and Happy Valley, comfy rattan sofas and friendly staff. Cocktails from HK$95. Daily 3pm–late.

KOWLOON
Bahama Mama's 4–5 Knutsford Terrace ⓜ Tsim Sha Tsui, exit B1; map p.139. The beach-bar theme here, complete with surfboards and an outdoor terrace, prompts party-crowd antics. DJs on Fridays and Saturdays and a young, exuberant crowd. Happy hour 5–9pm. Daily 4pm till late.

Eyebar 30/F iSquare, 63 Nathan Rd ⓜ Tsim Sha Tsui, exit L5; map p.139. Fantastic views over Hong Kong Island make the roof terrace here a brilliant sunset spot. With cocktails from HK$80, the prices are reasonable for Hong Kong, though do be aware that there's a swingeing HK$500/person minimum charge at the best tables. Happy hour 6–9pm with free bar snacks. Daily 11.30am–late.

Ned Kelly's Last Stand 11a Ashley Rd ⓜ Tsim Sha Tsui, exit L5; map p.139. Decked out with Oz-related paraphernalia and named after a gun-slinging Australian convict, this lively pub is a favourite with expats and tourists. Happy hour 11.30am–9pm. Daily 11.30am–late.

SHOPPING

BOOKSHOPS
Bookazine 3F, Prince's Building, Chater Rd ⓦ bookazine .com.hk; ⓜ Central; map pp.132–133. Excellent English-language bookshop with a good range of popular fiction and local interest. Several other branches around town. Mon–Sat 9.30am–7.30pm, Sun 10am–7pm.

Flow Books 2F, Lyndhurst Building, 29 Lyndhurst Terrace ⓦ flowbooks.net; ⓜ Central; map pp.132–133. Secondhand bookshop crammed to the rafters with pre-loved books on a mind-boggling range of subjects. Daily noon–7pm.

Swindon Book Company 13–15 Lock Rd ⓦ swindonbooks.com; ⓜ Tsim Sha Tsui map p.139. Hong Kong's oldest English-language bookshop, with a solid range of works on Hong Kong and China, and a wide range of other titles. Mon–Sat 10am–8pm, Sun 12.30–6.30pm.

CLOTHES AND ACCESSORIES
Local casual-wear chain stores, including Giordano, Wanko and Bossini, have branches all over the city. For something less generic, head to Granville Rd in Tsim Sha Tsui, which is packed with small boutiques.

9th Muse 12/F, One Lyndhurst Tower, 1 Lyndhurst Terrace ⓦ the9thmuse.com; ⓜ Central; map pp.132–133. Stocking hand-crafted handbags and striking jewellery, designs from this boutique have been tempting local fashionistas for years, and it's not too expensive. Daily 10.30am–7.30pm.

Daydream Nation 2/F, Hong Kong Arts Centre, 2 Harbour Rd ⓦ daydream-nation.com; ⓜ Wan Chai; map pp.132–133. Everything here is designed by a local brother-and-sister team who produce creative clothing and bold accessories aimed at a youthful audience. Daily 12.30–8.30pm.

ELECTRONICS
298 Computer Zone 298 Hennessy Rd ⓜ Wan Chai; map pp.132–133. A disconcerting maze of shops crammed into three levels, with a well-concealed entrance despite the huge sign. Discounted computers and accessories, plus a vast collection of novelty USB drives. Daily 11am–9pm.

Mong Kok Computer Centre Cnr Nelson St & Fa Yuen sts ⓜ Mong Kok; map p.139. A one-stop shop for anything electronic, but there's a language barrier, and you need to know exactly what you're looking for. Daily 10am–10pm.

GIFTS
G.O.D. 9 Sharp St East ⓦ god.com.hk; ⓜ Causeway Bay; map pp.132–133. With several branches across the city, G.O.D. stands for "goods of desire" and specializes in retro-styled gifts with a twist. Daily 11am–10pm.

Lam Kie Yuen Tea Co. 105–107 Bonham Strand East ⓦ lkytea.com; ⓜ Sheung Wan; map pp.132–133. Something of an institution, this *cha hong* has been selling tea since 1955. The choice is immense and includes pricey fermented varieties for connoisseurs; you can try before you buy. Mon–Sat 9am–6pm.

DIRECTORY

Banks and exchanges Banks and ATMs are found throughout Hong Kong. Banks offer good exchange rates; if you need to change money outside of banking hours, try the moneychangers in Chungking Mansions and Central's Worldwide House.

Embassies and consulates Australia, 23/F, Harbour Centre, 25 Harbour Rd, Wan Chai (☎ 2827 8881); Canada, 9/F, Berkshire House, 25 Westlands Rd, Quarry Bay (☎ 3719 4700); China, 7/F, Lower Block, China Resources Building, 26 Harbour Rd, Wan Chai (☎ 3413 2300); New Zealand, Rm 6501, Central Plaza, 18 Harbour Rd, Wan Chai (☎ 2525 5044); South Africa, Rm 1906, Central Plaza, 18 Harbour Rd, Wan Chai (☎ 3926 4300); UK, 1 Supreme Court Rd, Admiralty (☎ 2901 3000); US, 26 Garden Rd, Central (☎ 2523 9011).

Hospitals Emergency care is excellent in both public and private hospitals, though foreign visitors have to pay hefty fees even in public hospitals (from HK$990 for basic treatment in casualty to HK$23,000 for a day in intensive care), so make sure you have travel insurance. Ambulances (dial ☎ 999) take you to a public hospital; Ruttonjee Hospital (266 Queen's Rd East, Wan Chai; ☎ 2291 2000) and the Queen Elizabeth Hospital (30 Gascoigne Rd, Kowloon; ☎ 3506 8888) are the most centrally located major public hospitals.

3

CHINESE VISAS

To enter China, you'll need a pre-arranged **visa**. The official consular website states that all visas are required to be processed in your home country, though travel agencies and hotels, even the cheapest hostels, in Hong Kong offer this service. However, it's best to check before you travel. A **single-entry visa** costs from HK$200 with a four-day wait, HK$400 if you want it within three days (express) or HK$500 for the rush two-day service. Some passport-holders, including British and US, may have to pay significantly more (HK$360 and HK$1100 respectively) for the standard four-day service). The Ministry of Foreign Affairs **visa office** is on the 7/F, Lower Block, China Resources Building, 26 Harbour Rd, Wan Chai (Mon–Fri 9am–noon & 2–5pm; ☎3413 2300, ⓦwww.fmcoprc.gov.hk).

Internet Free wi-fi is available at the vast majority of lodgings, as well as MTR stations (15min limit per session), public libraries, parks and numerous cafés and bars.

Laundry Various in Kowloon, including on the ground floor of Golden Crown Court, Nathan Rd (one block north of *Mirador Mansions*; red entrance). Sunshine Laundry on Sharp St West, just under the flyover from Times Square in Causeway Bay, is friendly, efficient and open 24hr.

Left luggage In the departure lounge at the airport (daily 5.30am–1.30am), at Airport Express stations and in the Hong Kong-China Ferry Terminal in Tsim Sha Tsui. Most lodgings will store your luggage for a few days, though some may charge for this.

Post office The General Post Office is at 2 Connaught Place, Central (Mon–Sat 8am–6pm, Sun 9am–5pm), just south of the Star Ferry Pier. The Kowloon main post office is at 10 Middle Rd, Tsim Sha Tsui (Mon–Sat 9am–6pm).

Macau

Macau is a city with a split personality: its UNESCO World Heritage Portuguese fortresses and crumbling churches jostle for space with ultramodern casinos in the only city in China where gambling is legal. The melange of Portuguese and Chinese food, winding historic lanes, Taoist temples and modern skyscrapers gives it a character distinct from nearby Hong Kong.

Macau comprises three parts: the **peninsula**, linked by bridge to the island of **Taipa**, and beyond that the former island of **Coloane**, now joined to Taipa by an ever-widening strip of land reclamation and home to the majority of the casinos.

The peninsula of Macau, the location of the original old city and most of the historic sights (as well as the city amenities), is entirely developed right up to the border with China in the north. Taipa and Coloane used to be mere dots of land supporting a few small fishing villages, and although Coloane is still relatively tranquil, the expanding airport, a third bridge from the mainland and a huge reclamation and casino-building programme mean that much of Taipa, barring its historical centre, has become a rather soulless city suburb.

Although many travellers base themselves in Hong Kong and cover Macau on a day-trip, a short visit means running yourself ragged; it's well worth staying overnight and allowing yourself at least a couple of days to explore at leisure.

MACAU PENINSULA

The peninsula is compact and it's possible to get around most of it on foot; handy buses ply several main routes. The town of Macau was born in the south of the peninsula, around the bay-front road known as the **Avenida de Praia Grande**, and spread north from there. The most important road today, **Avenida de Almeida Ribeiro**, cuts across the peninsula from southeast (where it's known as Avenida do Infante Dom Henrique) to west, taking in the *Hotel Lisboa*, one of Macau's most famous landmarks. The road ends at the **Porto Interior** (Inner Harbour), near the old docking port, from which foreigners can still depart for the mainland city of Zhuhai in Guangdong. The western part of Almeida Ribeiro is also the budget-hotel area, and some of the streets immediately inland from here are worth poking around. **Rua da Felicidade**, hung with red lanterns, is where part of *Indiana Jones and the Temple of Doom* was shot and is now full of discreet guesthouses, restaurants, aromatic *pastelarias* (pastry shops) and colourful stalls.

The northern part of the peninsula up to the border with China is largely residential, though there are a couple of interesting temples.

Largo do Senado
The attractive **Largo do Senado** (Senate Square) marks the downtown area and bears the unmistakeable influence of southern Europe. At the northern end of the square stands the imposing sixteenth-century Baroque church, **São Domingos** (daily 10am–6pm; free), while to the south, across the main road, stands the **Leal Senado** (Tues–Sun 9am–9pm; free), generally considered the finest Portuguese building in the city. Step into the interior courtyard here to see blue-and-white Portuguese tiles around the walls; upstairs you will find the richly decorated **senate chamber** itself. In the late sixteenth century, all of the colony's citizens would cram into this hall to debate issues of importance. The senate's title, *leal* (loyal), was earned during the period when Spain occupied the Portuguese throne and Macau became the final stronghold of those loyal to the true king. Today, the senate chamber is still used by the municipal government of Macau. Adjacent to the chamber is the wood-carved **Senate Library** (Mon–Sat 1–7pm), whose collection includes many fifteenth- and sixteenth-century books, which visitors are free to browse.

Tak Seng On Pawnshop Museum
A short walk northwest from Largo do Senado, the carefully restored premises of former pawnbroker **Tak Seng On** (daily 10.30am–7pm; free) offer a fascinating glimpse behind the scenes of an early twentieth-century pawnshop, with its thick-walled, slit-windowed depository standing behind it. The shape of Tak Seng On's red and gold sign is still used by **pawnbrokers** in Macau and Hong Kong, and symbolizes a bat holding a coin – "bat" is a homonym for good fortune in Chinese.

São Paulo
A few hundred metres north of Largo do Senado stands Macau's most famous

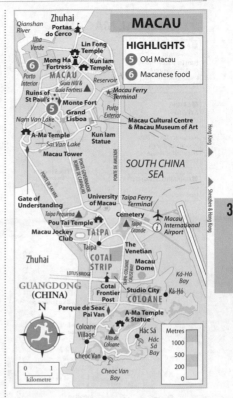

landmark, the **church of São Paulo**, once hailed as the greatest Christian monument in east Asia. Constructed at the beginning of the seventeenth century, it dominated the city for two hundred years until its untimely destruction by fire in 1835. Luckily, however, the facade did not collapse – richly carved and laden with statuary, the cracked stone still presents an imposing sight from the bottom of the steps leading up from the Rua de São Paulo. Behind the facade are the **Na Tcha Temple** (daily 8am–5pm), dedicated to the child god of war in 1888 to fight an outbreak of cholera in the city, and a small section of the old city walls, built nearly five hundred years ago.

Fortaleza do Monte and Museum of Macau
Immediately east of São Paulo looms another early seventeenth-century monument, the impressive **Fortaleza do**

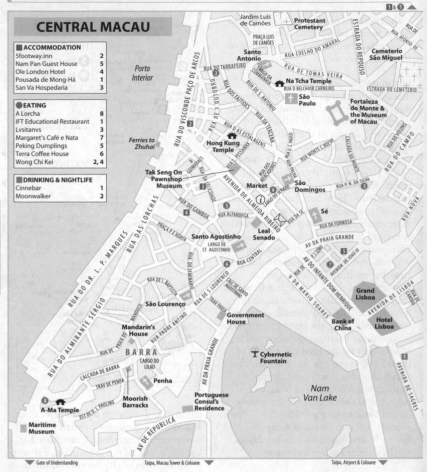

CENTRAL MACAU

■ ACCOMMODATION

5footway.inn	2
Nam Pan Guest House	5
Ole London Hotel	4
Pousada de Mong-Há	1
San Va Hospedaria	3

● EATING

A Lorcha	8
IFT Educational Restaurant	1
Lvsitanvs	3
Margaret's Café e Nata	7
Peking Dumplings	5
Terra Coffee House	6
Wong Chi Kei	2, 4

■ DRINKING & NIGHTLIFE

Cinnebar	1
Moonwalker	2

Porto Interior

Ferries to Zhuhai

Jardim Luís de Camões

Protestant Cemetery

PRAÇA LUÍS DE CAMÕES

Santo Antonio

RUA COELHO DO AMARAL

Cemeterio São Miguel

Na Tcha Temple

São Paulo

Fortaleza do Monte & the Museum of Macau

Hong Kung Temple

Tak Seng On Pawnshop Museum

Market

São Domingos

Sé

Leal Senado

Santo Agostinho

AVENIDA DE ALMEIDA RIBEIRO

AV. DA PRAIA GRANDE

Grand Lisboa

Hotel Lisboa

Bank of China

São Lourenço

Government House

Mandarin's House

BARRA

LARGO DO LILAU

Penha

Moorish Barracks

Cybernetic Fountain

Portuguese Consul's Residence

Nam Van Lake

A-Ma Temple

Maritime Museum

▼ Gate of Understanding   Taipa, Macau Tower & Coloane ▼   Taipa, Airport & Coloane ▼

Monte (daily 7am–7pm; free), which presents a startling contrast to the bristling modernity of Macau. Built between 1617 and 1626, this imposing fortress covers an area of 10,000 square metres. It was only once used in a military capacity: to repel the Dutch in 1622, when a lucky shot succeeded in blowing up the Dutch magazine. It also houses the excellent **Museum of Macau** (Tues–Sun 10am–6pm; MOP$15; ⓦ www.macaumuseum.gov.mo), which provides a wonderful introduction to the territory, with the two cultures – Chinese and Portuguese – presented side by side, from early oracle bone script and China's unique inventions

(gunpowder, paper, printing and compass-making) to Portugal's maritime achievements. You can press buttons to hear the cries of different street hawkers, learn about firework-making and check out the latest architecture in the contemporary Macau gallery.

Praça Luís de Camões

One of the nicest parts of Macau lies a few hundred metres northwest of São Paulo around **Praça Luís de Camões**. North, facing the square, is the **Jardim Luís de Camões** (daily 6am–10pm; free), a shady park full of tai chi enthusiasts and built in honour of the great sixteenth-century Portuguese poet, Luís de

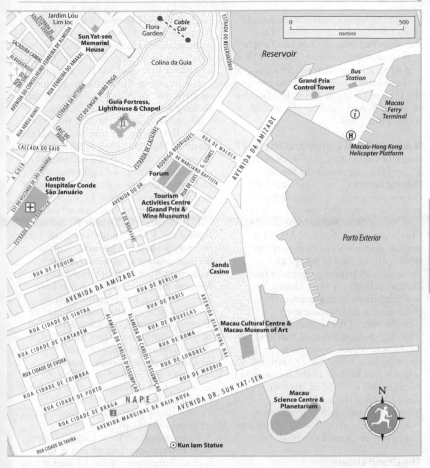

3

Camões, who is thought to have been banished here for part of his life. Immediately east of the square lies the **Protestant Cemetery** (daily 8.30am–5.30pm; free), where all the non-Catholic traders, visitors, sailors and adventurers who happened to die in Macau in the early part of the nineteenth century are seeing out eternity.

Colina da Guia and around

Colina da Guia is Macau's highest hill, and its summit is crowned by the seventeenth-century **Guia Fortress** (daily 9am–5.30pm), the dominant feature of which is a charming whitewashed **lighthouse**, added in 1865 and the oldest

anywhere on the Chinese coast. It's still in operation, and the different typhoon warning signals are displayed inside the fort. Next to the lighthouse is the **Guia Chapel**, its walls decorated with frescoes combining Catholic and Chinese motifs, which were uncovered during routine conservation work in 1998. You can take a **cable car** (Tues–Sun 8am–6pm; MOP$3 return) up the hill from the Flora Garden or climb the steps underneath it. At the top there are some superb views over the whole peninsula, including, on a clear day, a glimpse of Lantau Island far to the east. Buses #2, #17, #19 and #22 stop near the cable car.

Several blocks away, along Avenida do

3

Coronel Mesquita, look for the round stone table inside the grounds of the four-hundred-year-old **Kun Iam Temple** (daily 7am–6pm; buses #12, #17, #18 and #23); it is here that the first treaty of trade and friendship was signed between the US and China in 1844. The Goddess of Mercy herself stands in the incense-scented main hall.

Macau Cultural Centre and the NAPE
South of Colina da Guia, overlooking the Outer Harbour, stands the **Macau Cultural Centre** (Tues–Sun 9am–7pm; ⓦwww.ccm.gov.mo), the city's prime venue for theatre and opera. Inside you'll find the excellent **Macau Museum of Art** (Tues–Sun 10am–6.30pm; MOP$5; ⓦwww.mam.gov.mo), its five storeys filled with the likes of Ming- and Qing-dynasty painting, ceramics from Shiwan, calligraphy from Guangdong and exhibitions of contemporary photography and Macanese art.

To the west of the Cultural Centre, the 20m-high bronze statue of **Kun Iam**, the Goddess of Mercy, emerges from a 7m-high lotus in the Outer Harbour. The seafront area in front of the statue, along Avenida Dr Sun Yat-Sen (accessible by bus #3A, #8, #10A and #12), has become Macau's main entertainment area, **the NAPE**, with its array of bars and restaurants open until the small hours.

The Grand Lisboa
A major landmark and gambling institution, the **Grand Lisboa** (ⓦgrandlisboa.com) is Macau's tallest building. Resembling a psychedelically lit pineapple by night and with more than 800 slot machines and 370 gaming tables spread over four floors, the casino is the peninsula's largest. Its predecessor, **Hotel Lisboa**, stands across the street. The city's glitziest casino in the 1970s and 80s, its orange and white facade looks decidedly low-key today.

The Barra district
The southwestern side of the Macau peninsula is known as the **Barra district**. Situated underneath Barra Hill overlooking the Inner Harbour, the celebrated **A-Ma Temple** (daily 7am–6pm; free) may be six hundred years old in some sections. Dedicated to the goddess A-Ma, whose identity blurs from Queen of Heaven into Goddess of the Sea (who is also known as Tin Hau), the temple is an attractive jumble of altars among the rocks, greenery and coils of incense.

Immediately across the road from the A-Ma Temple, on the seafront, stands the **Maritime Museum** (Mon & Wed–Sun 10am–6pm; MOP$10), a well-presented collection covering old explorers, seafaring techniques, equipment, models and dragon boats. Buses #1, #2, #5, #7 and #10A swing by here, among others.

If you walk up Calçada de Barra from behind the A-Ma Temple, you'll reach the fortress-like **Moorish barracks**, built to accommodate two hundred Muslim policemen from Goa and inspired by Moorish architecture. Turn left at leafy Largo do Lilau, just after the barracks, and duck into the **Mandarin's House** (10 Travessa de Antonio da Silva; Mon, Tues & Thurs–Sun 10am–6pm; free). This elegant and surprisingly tranquil nineteenth-century abode – once the home of Chinese wordsmith Zheng Guanying – is the largest private residence in Macau. Access the courtyards via the circular moon gate; its many rooms retain an elegant simplicity and symmetry. Running northeast from Largo do Lilau, **Rua Central** passes through one of the earliest Portuguese residential areas, where you'll find the 1860 **Teatro Dom Pedro V**, China's first Western-style theatre.

Macau Tower
The futuristic spike rising 338m at the southern end of the peninsula is the **Macau Tower** (ⓦmacautower.com.mo), which offers impressive views out to sea and over China. It's also the site of the world's highest bungee jump (233m), operated by A.J. Hackett (from MOP$3288; ☎8988 8656, ⓦajhackett.com) – jumpers free fall at an eye-wateringly fast 200km per hour. They also offer an exhilarating sky walk (from MOP$788) around the outside of the tower, tower climb (MOP$1888) and night-time bungee and night walk for nocturnal daredevils. For the less

adventurous, there are two observation decks (Mon–Fri 10am–9pm, Sat & Sun 9am–9pm; MOP$135). The road north from here up to the Praia Grande takes about fifteen minutes on foot, or take bus #9A, #18, #23, #26 or #32.

TAIPA

Until the eighteenth century, **Taipa** was two islands separated by a channel, the silting up of which caused the two to merge into one. The same fate has now befallen Taipa and Coloane, except that this time land reclamation is the culprit – the two islands have been fused to make space for large-scale development. Much of Taipa is covered with ageing high-rise apartment buildings, which might cause you to overlook two pockets of interest: the small village and former waterfront promenade.

Taipa Village

Taipa Village on the southern shore, with its old colonial promenade, is a pleasant place to wander. There isn't much more than a few streets to the modern village, where the buses stop, though you'll find some great restaurants around the central north–south alley, **Rua do Cunha**, and, to the west – on the right as you face the shore – a couple of ancient temples in the vicinity of a quiet old square, which has benches perfectly sited for people-watching. Along Rua Correia da Silva, the **Museum of Taipa & Coloane History** (Tues–Sun 10am–6pm; MOP$5) features excavated relics from the two villages, as well as scale models of buildings.

The village is reachable by buses #22, #25, #26A, #28A and #33. Buses #25 and #33 also stop at the **Pou Tai Temple** (daily 9am–6pm), north of the village, Macau's largest temple complex, with an enormous statue of Lord Gautama.

Avenida da Praia

The island's real interest lies a few minutes' walk to the east of Taipa Village, in the former waterfront area. Here, as though frozen in time, is a superb old colonial promenade, the **Avenida da Praia**, complete with its original pale-green houses, public benches and street lamps. The beautifully restored mansions overlook what was the sea – but is now the back of *The Venetian*. The five mansions are open to the public as the **Taipa Houses Museum** (Tues–Sun 10am–7pm; free). Most of the mansions host temporary exhibitions, but the westernmost building has been refitted as it would have been in the 1920s to offer a fascinating glimpse of early twentieth-century Macanese life.

The Cotai Strip

An area of reclaimed land billed as "Asia's Las Vegas", the **Cotai Strip**, lined with immense casinos, sits between Taipa and Coloane, with its own ferry service and, in practice, its own border crossing. The biggest, busiest and brashest of the casinos is The Venetian (ⓦvenetianmacao.com), its interior decorated with three million sheets of gold leaf and featuring a gondola ride on the canal past rows of plasticky Venetian buildings. Games include blackjack, roulette, baccarat and Sands stud poker. Newer additions to the strip include movie-themed Studio City (ⓦstudiocity-macau.com), notable for its figure-of-eight Ferris wheel – the world's first.

COLOANE

Coloane island is considerably bigger than Taipa, yet the village is smaller, leaving you with plenty of forested hills to explore and beaches to relax on.

A-Ma Temple and around

The first attraction is the **Parque de Seac Pai Van** (daily 8am–6pm; free), a large park with a **Giant Panda Pavilion** (Tues–Sun 10am–1pm & 2–5pm; MOP$10; ☏2833 7676, ⓦwww .macaupanda.org.mo). The Pavilion's cute panda pair was gifted to Macau by the Chinese government in December 2009 in honour of its tenth anniversary of reunification. On top of the nearby hill, **Alto de Coloane**, is a 20m-tall white marble **statue** of the goddess A-Ma who gave Macau its name. Just below lies the impressive **A-Ma Temple** (daily 8am–6pm) with its multi-tiered roofs and crowds of worshippers lighting incense under

3

strings of red lanterns. The temple is part of the A-Ma Cultural Village, which includes a good vegetarian restaurant, museum and retreat. Any bus heading to/from Coloane Village will drop you here (#15, #21A, #25, #26, #26A or #50).

From behind the small eating area opposite the temple you can join up with the **Coloane trail**, part of a network of well-signposted walks around the peninsula. Follow the signs and a half-hour walk will take you down to **Hác Sá Reservoir**; the path then continues across the road and down to the eponymous black-sand beach (see below).

Coloane Village

The buses all stop at the roundabout in pretty **Coloane Village** on the western shore, overlooking mainland China just across the water. In the shore-side mud you'll see old men fishing with nets, and it's a pleasant spot for a coffee and a scrumptious Portuguese custard tart from *Lord Stow's Bakery* (see p.160). Along the seafront you'll also find the unexpected yellow-and-white **St Francis Xavier Chapel** (daily 10am–8pm), which is fronted by a plaza flanked by appealing alfresco restaurants. A few hundred metres beyond this is the **Tam Kong Temple** (daily 8.30am–5.30pm) housing a metre-long whale bone, carved into the shape of a dragon boat, to the right of the main altar.

Beaches

Coloane's beaches are pleasant and not usually crowded, although the murky water can make the public pools (both May–Oct Mon 1–9pm, Tues–Sun 8am–noon & 1–9pm; MOP$15) beside each beach a more appealing option for a swim. Tree-lined, black-sand **Hác Sá Beach** on the eastern shore is the most popular and reachable by buses #21A, #25 and #26A from Almeida Ribeiro; you could stop off at **Cheoc Van Beach** to the south on your way. It's also possible to walk most of the way round the headland between the two. Both beaches have good facilities, including showers, toilets and street barbecue stalls, as well as some decent, though pricey, restaurants nearby.

ARRIVAL AND DEPARTURE

By plane Macau International Airport is a mini-hub mostly used by budget airlines operating limited routes around Southeast Asia. It's perched on Taipa (ⓦ macau -airport.com) and connected by airport bus #AP1 (MOP$4.20) to the ferry terminal and the Chinese border. Destinations Bangkok (6 daily; 3hr); Beijing (3 daily; 3hr); Chiang Mai (daily; 3hr); Kuala Lumpur (daily, 3hr 45min); Manila (2 daily; 2hr 15min); Osaka (daily; 3hr 45min); Seoul (5 daily; 3hr 30min); Shanghai (8 daily; 2hr 15min); Singapore (daily; 4hr); Taipei (10 daily; 1hr 30min); Tokyo (daily; 4hr); Xiamen (1 daily; 1hr 20min); as well as an increasing number of other Chinese and Asian cities.

By ferry Every day, large numbers of vessels make the 1hr journey between the Macau Ferry Terminal (Terminal Marítimo) in the Outer Harbour and Hong Kong – both Central and Kowloon. The terminal is connected to the budget-hotel area on Almeida Ribeiro by #3A, #10 and #10A buses. Allow 40min before departure for queues with luggage and passport control. Daytime tickets are valid on all boats earlier than the stated time. The main boat service is the 24hr Turbojet route (every 15min, 7am–midnight, then roughly every 30–60min; ⓦ www .turbojet.com.hk) from the Hong Kong–Macau Ferry Terminal and the China Ferry Terminal in Hong Kong. Tickets cost from HK$164 one-way; prices rise at weekends, during public holidays and on night boats (5.45pm–6.30am) when you should book ahead. Cotai Jet (ⓦ cotaiwaterjet.com) also run high-speed catamarans from the Hong Kong–Macau Ferry Terminal to the Macau Ferry Terminal and the Taipa Temporary Ferry Terminal near the Cotai Strip (every 30min, 7am–11.30pm; HK$165), from where there are complimentary buses to all the major casinos. Carry-on luggage allowance is 10kg in economy class but large bags can be checked in.

By bus You can walk across the Chinese border (daily 6am–1am) at the Portas do Cerco border gate in the far north of the peninsula, into Zhuhai Special Economic Zone; buses #3, #5 and #9 connect the border gate with Avenida de Almeida Ribeiro and Rua da Praia Grande. Once in mainland China, you can easily pick up a bus to Guangzhou; there are also direct buses from Macau Airport. Alternatively, cross via the Lotus Bridge at the Cotai Frontier Post (24hr) on the block of reclaimed land joining Taipa and Coloane; buses #15, #21A, #25 and #26A stop here.

GETTING AROUND

By bus Buses operate from 6am until just after midnight. The flat bus fare on the peninsula is MOP$3.20; MOP$4.20 to Taipa; MOP$5 to Coloane Village and MOP$6.20 to Hác Sá Beach; only exact fares are accepted, so hoard your small change or get the rechargeable MACAUPass, available from numerous supermarkets and convenience stores (MOP$130, including the refundable MOP$30 deposit). The *Macau Tourist Map*, available from Macau Government Tourist Office outlets, shows all the bus routes. Buses #3 and #3A run between the ferry and the city centre; both also run to the border crossing, as does bus #5. Buses #21A, #25 and #26A are the most convenient routes to Taipa and Coloane, while the airport is served by buses #AP1, #26, #MT1 and #MT2.

By taxi Flag fall for the first 1.6km is MOP$17, with MOP$2 for each 200m thereafter. Surcharges include: MOP$5 if you're coming from the airport or heading to Coloane, MOP$2 if you're crossing to Taipa, and MOP$3 for each item of luggage in the boot. Taxi drivers speak little English.

INFORMATION

Tourist information The Macau Government Tourist Office (MGTO; ⓣ 2833 3000, ⓦ en.macautourism.gov.mo) has offices in several locations, the most useful being the Macau Ferry Terminal (daily 9am–10pm; ⓣ 2872 6416), at Macau International Airport (daily 9am–1.30pm, 2.15–7.30pm & 8.15–10pm; ⓣ 2886 1436) and in Hong Kong at the Hong Kong-Macau Ferry Terminal, Room 336–337, Shun Tak Centre, 20 Connaught Rd (daily 9am–8pm; ⓣ 2857 2287). All dish out free maps and plenty of pamphlets on attractions, and the website is useful for events listings.

ACCOMMODATION

Guesthouses and cheap hotels are clustered at the western end of Almeida Ribeiro, spreading out from the Porto Interior. Prices usually go up by at least MOP$50 at weekends when places get booked up, and all hotels charge fifteen percent tax, so make sure that's included in the price. Booking online tends to be cheaper than walk-ins.

MACAU PENINSULA

5footway.inn 8 Rua da Constantino Brito ⓣ 2892 3118; bus #3. This boutique guesthouse is a Singapore export, and a welcome one at that. Expect spotless rooms with crisp linens, wooden floors, a/c, touches of modern art and lightning-fast wi-fi. Doubles, triples and quads available; great value if travelling with friends. Doubles **MOP$680**

Nam Pan Guest House 2/F, 8 Avda de D Joao IV ⓣ 2848 2842, ⓦ www.cnmacauhotel.com; buses #3, #5, #10. The central location is a winner here, and the eight wi-fi enabled rooms are clean and decent. The downsides are that you'll have to lug your luggage up to the 3rd floor via a narrow staircase, and the staff are uninterested at best. Doubles **MOP$580**

Ole London Hotel 4–6 Rua Praça de Ponte e Horta 4–6 ⓣ 2893 7761, ⓦ olelondonhotel.com; buses #3A, #7, #10A. A 5min trot from Largo do Senado, this ambitious hotel offers bright, compact rooms, with wi-fi and room service in a convenient location near the Porto Interior, though the cheapest doubles are windowless. Doubles **MOP$750**

★**Pousada de Mong-Há** Colina de Mong-Há ⓣ 2851 5222, ⓦ www.ift.edu.mo/pousada; buses #8, #8A, #12, #18A. The pousada's awkward hilltop location can be forgiven on account of its helpful English-speaking staff, individually decorated en-suite rooms (all non-smoking) with Oriental art and fixtures, and delicious buffet breakfasts. There's a peaceful rooftop garden, two good restaurants, and it's within Mong-Há Park, site of an old Portuguese fort. Doubles **MOP$700**

San Va Hospedaria 65–67 Rua da Felicidade ⓦ sanvahotel.com; buses #3, #3A, #10, #10A. *San Va*'s rooms are basic, in a traditional wooden house with shared facilities, but it has a fantastic location and wi-fi. Walls don't quite meet the ceiling, so you may feel as if you're in bed with your neighbours, and some rooms are windowless. The staff speak no English, but are friendly and have a list of useful questions on the desk for you to point at. Book at least two days in advance. Doubles **MOP$260**

3

EATING

Most restaurants in Macau serve Chinese and Portuguese food. If you want something different head to the NAPE, although it will be pricier than anywhere else on Macau.

MACAU PENINSULA

IFT Educational Restaurant Colina de Mong-Há; buses #8, #8A, #12, #18A. The trainee chefs at this establishment really deliver when it comes to good Macanese and Portuguese food. Feast on the likes of *bacalhau* risotto and African chicken, with mains from MOP$110 and a MOP$200 fixed menu at lunchtime. Mon–Fri 12.30–3pm & 7–10.30pm.

Lvsitanvs 28 Rua Pedro Nolasco da Silva; buses #2, #2A, #12, #22. Opposite the Portuguese Consulate, this low-key café draws a crowd of regulars with its good-value Portuguese food. Toasted sandwiches (from MOP$10) are served all day, and the lunch menu includes *bacalhau* croquettes (MOP$40 with rice and salad), and pan-fried *chouriço* sausage (MOP$50). Mon–Fri 10am–7pm, Sat 10am–5pm.

Margaret's Café e Nata Rua Comandante Mata e Oliveira. A Macau institution, with street-side benches where you can tuck into inexpensive, chunky sandwiches, pizzas, home-baked quiches and muffins. Macau's creamy custard tarts (*natas:* MOP$10) don't get any better, as the queues outside attest to. Mon, Tues & Thurs–Sun 8.30am–6pm.

Peking Dumplings 5 Travessa do Atero Novo; buses #3, #3A, #10. This tiny, informal eatery serves many kinds of dumplings to a loyal local crowd. Choose from steamed meaty dumplings, dumplings in soup, fried dumplings and more. Set meals (MOP$24) are particularly good value. Daily 11am–midnight.

Terra Coffee House 20 Rua Central; buses #6B, #9, #9A, #16. Fantastic little coffee house where the baristas really know their beans. They also serve light meals and cakes,

★ TREAT YOURSELF

Less than two percent of the population speaks Portuguese, but Macanese food is still heavily influenced by its colonial past, blending Asian, European and African influences. Here are two of the most famous places worth splashing out on:

A Lorcha 289 Rua do Almirante Sérgio ☎ 2831 3193; buses #1, #5, #10. A local institution, "The Sailboat" serves an extensive menu of expertly cooked Macanese dishes, such as oxtail stew and seafood rice. Standouts include the heart-stopping *serradura*, a spectacular cream-and-biscuit dessert. Book ahead on weekends and expect MOP$200–300/ person. Mon & Wed–Sun 12.30–3pm & 6.30–11pm.

Fernando's 9 Praia de Hác Sá, Coloane. An institution among local expats with the casual, cheerful atmosphere of a Mediterranean bistro and great Portuguese dishes such as garlic prawns, pork ribs and grilled chicken (mains from MOP$88). They don't take reservations, and even if you get there early (essential at weekends) you may still have to wait for a table. Situated just 50m from the Hác Sá Beach bus stop; there's no sign, so follow your nose. Daily noon–9.30pm.

and – for those in search of a different kind of pick-me-up – a decent selection of craft ales. Mon–Sat noon–11.45pm, Sun noon–8pm.

Wong Chi Kei 51 Rua Cinco de Outubro; buses #8A, #18A, #19, #26. At the original location of this smart noodle shop you can munch on shrimp roe noodles, crab congee, wonton noodle soup and more. The beer is also cheap (from MOP$16) and there's a history of noodles on the place mat to educate you while you wait. Mains start from MOP$40. There's another branch at 17 Largo do Senado. Mon–Sat 8.30am–1.30am, Sun 8.30am–midnight.

TAIPA AND COLOANE

Galo 45 Rua do Cunha, Taipa; buses #11, #15, #22, #30, #33. A good place to sample tasty Portuguese food right in the middle of Taipa Village; go for the fish in tomato sauce, African chicken or the clams in garlic, and skip the oily steak. They have another, more expensive, branch called *Dom Galo* in the NAPE. Mains from MOP$78. Daily 11am–11pm.

Lord Stow's Bakery Coloane Town Square; buses #21A, #25, #26A. A leading contender for Macau's best egg

custard tart (MOP$10). Either luxuriate in the a/c at one of the three *Lord Stow's Cafés* in Coloane, or head down to the waterfront with your tarts, still warm from the oven. Daily: bakery 7am–10pm; cafés 9am–6pm.

Nga Tim 1 Rua Caetano, Coloane; buses #21A, #25, #26A. A busy family restaurant with gingham tablecloths opposite St Francis Xavier Chapel, serving delicious Chinese-Portuguese food. Service is slow but the owner is quite a character. Mains around MOP$70. Daily noon–1am.

Pou Tai Restaurants Inside the Pou Tai temple; buses #25, #33. There are two restaurants here; the one on the ground floor is the smarter of the two and boasts an English menu (mains from MOP$40), while the first floor serves a fixed set menu (MOP$90/head). Whichever you pick, expect generous helpings of strictly vegetarian dishes. Mon–Sat 11am–8pm, Sun 9am–9pm.

DRINKING AND NIGHTLIFE

Although drinking isn't a major pastime in Macau and can be expensive, a cluster of bars and night-time cafés lies in the stretch of reclaimed land just southwest of the ferry terminal and in front of the new Kun Iam statue (follow signs to NAPE).

Cinnebar *Wynn Macau*, Rua Cidade de Sintra, NAPE; buses #8, #10A, #23. Amiable bar serving decent cocktails and malt whiskies; choose from the refined indoor setting or the relaxed outdoor area in the garden. Daily 3pm–late.

Moonwalker NAPE Lot 13, Avda Marginal da Baia Nova; buses #8, #10A, #23. This is one of the larger bars on the waterfront, with action spread over two floors and live music every night except Tues from 10pm; open until 6am at the weekends. Daily happy hour 4–8pm; beer MOP$50. Daily 4pm–late.

Old Taipa Tavern 21 Rua dos Negociantes, Taipa Village; buses #11, #15, #22, #30, #33. Despite being known as "OTT", this pub makes a pleasant, low-key spot for a drink (from MOP$45), with outside seating set on a quiet square in Taipa Village. Food served. Daily noon–1am.

DIRECTORY

Hospital and pharmacies There is a 24hr emergency department at the public Centro Hospitalar Conde São Januário, Estrada do Visconde São Januário (☎ 2831 3731; English spoken), and several pharmacies in Largo do Senado.

Police The main police station (24hr) is on Calcada do Gamboa, a few hundred metres west of Largo do Senado. In an emergency, call ☎ 999. There's also an SOS Tourist Hotline on ☎ 112.

Post office Macau's General Post Office is on the east side of Largo do Senado (Mon–Fri 9am–6pm, Sat 9am–1pm).

BOROBUDUR

Indonesia

HIGHLIGHTS

❶ **Borobudur** The biggest Buddhist stupa in the world. **See p.200**

❷ **Orang-utans** See these enchanting creatures at Bukit Lawang. **See p.220**

❸ **Ubud** Bali's cultural capital, with art galleries, dance performances and festivals. **See p.260**

❹ **Gunung Rinjani** Climb one of Indonesia's highest mountains. **See p.297**

❺ **Tanah Toraja, Sulawesi** Gorgeous scenery, traditional architecture and vibrant festivals. **See p.329**

❻ **Banda Islands** Pristine diving off these far-flung volcanic isles. **See p.342**

HIGHLIGHTS ARE MARKED ON THE MAP ON PP.164–165

ROUGH COSTS

Daily budget Basic US$25–30/occasional treat US$35–55

Drink Bintang beer US$2.25

Food *Nasi goreng* US$1

Hostel/budget hotel US$12

Travel Shuttle bus: Kuta–Ubud (1hr 30min) US$6; Flight: Jakarta–Denpasar (1hr 40min) US$50

FACT FILE

Population 255 million

Language Bahasa Indonesia

Currency Indonesian rupiah (Rp)

Capital Jakarta

International phone code ☏ + 62

Time zone GMT + 7–9hr. Bali is one hour ahead of Java

Introduction

The Indonesian archipelago spreads over 5200km between the Asian mainland and Australia, all of it within the tropics, and comprises 17,000 islands to explore. Its ethnic, cultural and linguistic diversity is correspondingly great – more than 500 languages and dialects are spoken by its 255 million people, whose fascinating customs and lifestyles are a major attraction.

Highlights are scattered widely across the archipelago, beginning in **Medan** on Sumatra's northeast coast. From here, the classic itinerary runs to the thick jungles and **orang-utan sanctuary** at Bukit Lawang and down towards the lakeside resorts on Pulau Samosir in Southeast Asia's largest lake, **Danau Toba**. Further south, the area around the laidback town of **Bukittinggi** appeals because of its flamboyant Minangkabau architecture, the beautiful scenery around Danau Maninjau and the rafflesia reserves in the hills. Many travellers then hurtle through to **Java**, probably spending no more than a night or two in the traffic-clogged capital **Jakarta** in their rush to the ancient cultural capital of **Yogyakarta** – the best base for exploring the huge **Borobudur** (Buddhist) and **Prambanan** (Hindu) temples. Java's biggest natural attractions are its volcanoes, most famously Gunung Merapi on the outskirts of Yogya and East Java's **Gunung Bromo**, where travellers brave a sunrise climb to the summit.

Just across the water from Java sits **Bali**, the long-time jewel in the crown of Indonesian tourism, a tiny island of elegant temples, verdant landscape and fine surf. The biggest resorts are in the party conurbation of **Kuta-Legian-Seminyak**, with the more subdued beaches at **Lovina** and **Candidasa** appealing to travellers not hellbent on nightlife. Most visitors also spend time in Bali's cultural centre **Ubud**, whose lifeblood continues to be painting, carving, dancing and music-making. The islands east of Bali – collectively known as **Nusa Tenggara** – are attracting increasing numbers of travellers, particularly neighbouring **Lombok**, with its beautiful beaches and temples. East again, the **Komodo dragons** draw travellers to **Komodo** and **Rinca**, and then it's an easy hop across to **Flores**, which has the unforgettable coloured crater lakes of **Kelimutu**. South of Flores, **Sumba** is famous for its intricate fabrics, grand funeral ceremonies and extraordinary annual ritual war, the pasola.

North of Flores, **Sulawesi** is renowned for the idiosyncratic architecture and impressively ghoulish burial rituals of the highland Torajans. West of Sulawesi, the island of Borneo plays host to the Indonesian state of **Kalimantan**, with opportunities for river travel in remote jungle. Across the Molucca Sea to the east of Sulawesi are the **Maluku islands**, a smattering of mostly unexplored volcanic

---

WHEN TO GO

The whole Indonesian archipelago is tropical, with **temperatures** at sea level always between 21°C and 33°C, although cooler in the mountains. In theory, the year divides into a wet and dry season, though it's often hard to tell the difference – increasingly so with the effects of climate change, which has already altered seasonal patterns, sometimes shortening and concentrating wet seasons. Very roughly, in much of the country, November to April are the **wet** months (Jan and Feb the wettest) and May through to October is **dry**. The **peak tourist season** is between mid-June and mid-September and again over Christmas and New Year. This is particularly relevant in the major resorts, where prices rocket and rooms can be fully booked for days, and sometimes weeks, on end.

SAFETY IN INDONESIA

While Indonesia has often appeared in international news for the wrong reasons, there is no need to be more alarmed here than you would be in most other parts of Southeast Asia. Communal violence continues to rear its ugly head on occasion, particularly along the fault lines between heavily Muslim and Christian areas, but there has been nothing approaching the internecine warfare of the turn of the twenty-first century – which left thousands dead in central **Sulawesi** and the **Maluku Islands**. And since the 2005 ceasefire in **Aceh**, over a decade of peace has followed the long and deadly insurgency. Calm has returned to these far-flung provinces, and travellers have been trickling back for years.

Remote and little-visited **West Papua** (formerly known as Irian Jaya) remains the country's least settled area largely due to the ongoing separatist struggle of Organisasi Papua Merdeka (Free Papua Movement). However, it is safer and more accessible today than ever along its burgeoning tourist trail. Make sure you are fully aware of the latest situation, and heed any warnings given out by your foreign office (see box, p.45) as well as the local people who, along with your fellow travellers, are usually the best source of up-to-date information.

Though extremely rare, **terror attacks** have targeted venues frequented by foreigners, and there are frequent reports of terror plots being foiled by police. The militant Islamic Jemaah Islamiyah terrorist group has been responsible for numerous bombs in Indonesia, most notably the Bali bomb of 2002, which killed more than two hundred people. Subsequently there were bombings at the *Marriott* hotel in Jakarta in August 2003, the Australian embassy in Jakarta in September 2004, Bali again in October 2005 and Jakarta's *JW Marriott* and *Ritz-Carlton* hotels in July 2009. The Jemaah Islamiyah network was dealt a seemingly crushing blow in 2010 with a police raid in Aceh, but its ideology has continued to garner a following. In 2014 the group pledged allegiance to ISIS, which claimed responsibility for the January 2016 attacks near the Sarinah shopping centre in downtown Jakarta.

4

islands with a rich historical legacy and vibrant reefs, while still further east is **Papua**, Indonesia's wild, final frontier, spectacularly diverse in both cultures and landscapes.

CHRONOLOGY

c. 800,000 BC Java Man, whose skull fragments were found near Solo in 1893, is one of the earliest pieces of evidence of hominoids in the region.

Fifth century AD Numerous small Hindu kingdoms pepper the islands.

Seventh century The Buddhist Srivijaya kingdom, based in Palembang in South Sumatra, controls the Melaka straits for the next four hundred years. Its empire extends as far as Thailand and West Borneo.

Ninth century In central Java, it's an age of spectacular, competitive temple building: the Buddhist Sailendra kingdom erects the magnificent temple of Borobudur, while the rival Sanjaya empire builds the Hindu Prambanan temple complex.

1292–1389 The Hindu Majapahit empire, based in East Java, rules over a vast area from Sumatra to Timor, the first time the archipelago's major islands are united.

Fourteenth century Islam, which had been introduced to Sumatra centuries earlier, spreads eastwards into Java as small coastal sultanates grow after the collapse of the Majapahit empire.

Early sixteenth century The Portuguese establish a virtual monopoly over the lucrative spice trade, taking control of the Moluccas (Maluku or Spice Islands).

1602 The Dutch, who had arrived at the end of the sixteenth century, establish the Dutch East India Company (VOC), which gains a monopoly over trade with the Moluccas. It starts building a loose, lucrative empire across the archipelago.

1619 The VOC builds a fortress in Jakarta. The local population responds angrily, and the Dutch retaliate by razing the city and renaming it Batavia.

Eighteenth century The plains of Central Java, ruled by the Islamic Mataram empire, are riven by dynastic disputes, known as the Three Wars of Succession. The last one (1746–57) divides the empire into three sultanates, two at Solo and one at Yogyakarta. The Dutch then subjugate the entire territory.

1799 The VOC folds and the Dutch government (under a French Protectorate) takes possession of its territories.

1811 The British, under Sir Thomas Stamford Raffles, attack and pick off the islands one by one, landing at Batavia in 1811.

1816 With the end of the Napoleonic Wars, the territories return to the Dutch, who are soon embroiled in bloody disputes with opponents of their rule.

1830 The Dutch devise the Cultural System whereby Javanese farmers must grow cash crops for sale in Europe at a huge profit. Java becomes one giant plantation, to the detriment of indigenous farmers.

1870 onwards The Dutch gradually implement more progressive policies, but this coincides with some devastating natural disasters. Later, irrigation, healthcare and education programmes are started.

1894–1920 The Dutch expand into previously independent territories: Lombok in 1894, Bali in 1906 and Aceh in 1908. By 1910 the Dutch have conquered nearly all of Indonesia; West Papua is the last to fall, in 1920.

1927 Achmed Sukarno founds the pro-independence Partai Nasional Indonesia (PNI). The Dutch outlaw the party and imprison Sukarno in 1931, later exiling him.

1942–45 Indonesia is occupied by the Japanese.

August 17, 1945 Sukarno reads a Declaration of Independence, but it is not recognized by the Allies, who return the territory to the Dutch.

1946–49 War with the Dutch, who withdraw in December 1949. The new Republic of Indonesia is established, with Sukarno as president.

1949–65 Sukarno presides over a system he calls guided democracy – in reality authoritarian rule. He forges ties with the Soviet Union, and is sympathetic to the communist party, against the Indonesian army.

September 30, 1965 A group of communists (with whom Sukarno is thought to be in cahoots) abduct and execute a number of leading generals, claiming they are preventing an army-led coup. General Suharto eventually seizes control from them.

1965–67 Suharto launches a purge against the communists, during which it's thought at least 500,000 people die. He restores relations with the West and aid pours into Indonesia. In 1967 Suharto is named acting president.

1970s Indonesia benefits from rising oil prices – its biggest export.

December 1975 Indonesia invades East Timor, which had been granted independence by Portugal the previous year.

1997 Southeast Asia's currency crisis. The value of the rupiah plummets. There are widespread demonstrations, and riots take place in major cities.

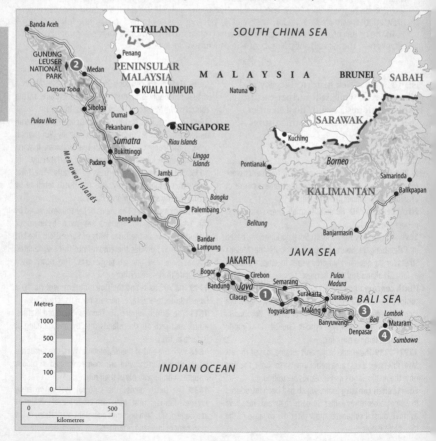

May 21, 1998 Suharto steps down after 32 years and his vice-president, B.J. Habibie, takes over. In early November there's more rioting, with demands that Suharto be tried on charges of mismanagement and corruption.

1999 Though the Indonesian Democratic Party of Struggle, led by Megawati Sukarnoputri, Sukarno's daughter, wins the elections, Indonesia's parliament chooses Gus Dur as president, with Megawati vice-president.

1999 East Timor gains independence. Other far-flung Indonesian provinces begin to become more vocal – and violent – in their struggle for sovereignty.

2002–05 There is a series of bombings – first in a nightclub and Irish bar in Kuta, Bali, in 2002, and next at the *Marriott* in Jakarta in August 2003, the Australian Embassy in September 2004, and Bali again in October 2005.

December 26, 2004 Indonesia is the hardest-hit country in the devastating Boxing Day Tsunami, with more than 160,000 dead or missing in Northern Sumatra.

August 15, 2005 A peace deal is signed between the Indonesian government and separatist Free Aceh Movement (GAM), ending three decades of fighting.

January 2008 Suharto dies. His legacy is mixed: he oversaw the country's economic growth, but was accused of – and evaded prosecution for – massive corruption, and many human rights abuses, including the deaths of hundreds of thousands.

July 17, 2009 The bombings of the *Ritz-Carlton* and *JW Marriott* hotels in Jakarta kill nine people and injure more than fifty.

September 2009 An earthquake with a magnitude of 7.6 rocks the city of Padang in West Sumatra; more than 1300 people are killed and more than one million left homeless.

October 25, 2010 The eruption of Mount Merapi in Java kills 353 people and causes the evacuation of 350,000 while covering Borobudur in volcanic ash.

June 2013 Government fuel price hikes spark violent protests.

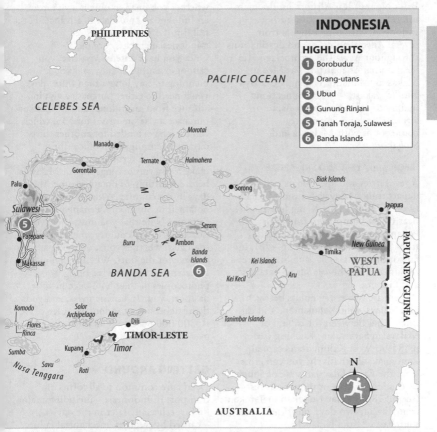

INDONESIA

HIGHLIGHTS

1. Borobudur
2. Orang-utans
3. Ubud
4. Gunung Rinjani
5. Tanah Toraja, Sulawesi
6. Banda Islands

4

October 20, 2014 Political outsider Joko Widodo, widely considered a champion of the poor, becomes Indonesia's seventh president.

January 14, 2016 Terrorist attacks at Sarinah shopping centre in central Jakarta kill four and injure 23; Islamic State media claim responsibility.

November 4, 2016 Blasphemy allegations against Jakarta's Chinese and Christian mayor draws hundreds of thousands of conservative Muslim protesters to the capital, injuring dozens and fuelling debate over religious toleration in Indonesia.

December 7, 2016 Earthquake strikes Aceh Province, leaving 104 dead and over a thousand injured.

December 2016 The Netherlands agrees to fund investigations into the killing of roughly 100,000 Indonesians at the end of its colonial rule.

ARRIVAL AND DEPARTURE

Jakarta's Sukarno-Hatta Airport and Bali's Ngurah Rai Airport are the main international air gateways into Indonesia, with direct flights from several Australian cities and destinations throughout Asia. The archipelago also has international airports at Medan, Makassar, Manado, Padang, Surabaya and Yogyakarta – with connections mainly to other Southeast Asian airports. Indonesia has ferry connections with Malaysia and Singapore.

FROM MALAYSIA AND SINGAPORE

A few ferries and speedboats still depart from Malaysia – from Malacca (see p.473) and Port Klang (see p.432), near Kuala Lumpur, to **Dumai** or **Pekanbaru**. You can also take ferries from Johor Bahru (see box, p.478), in far southern Malaysia, and Singapore to Sumatra via the islands of **Batam** and **Bintan**.

There are two entry points between **East Malaysia and Kalimantan**. You can catch a bus between the capital of Malaysian **Sarawak** at Kuching (see p.484) to West Kalimantan's capital, Pontianak; alternatively, you can cross from the East Malaysian state of **Sabah** by catching a two- or three-hour ferry (see p.518) to **Pulau Nunukan** or **Tarakan** from Tawau, two days' bus ride southeast of Kota Kinabalu.

VISAS

As of 2016, citizens from most of the world – 169 countries, including all of Europe as well as Australia, New Zealand, Canada and the US – can enter Indonesia visa-free at any of Indonesia's **official immigration gateways** and stay for thirty days. However, Indonesian visa regulations are notoriously prone to change, so it's worth checking before you travel. Official gateways include major international airports – such as Jakarta, Denpasar (Bali), Yogyakarta, Solo, Surabaya and Medan – and several seaports, including Padang Bai in Bali, Tanjung Priok for Jakarta, Pulau Batam and Pulau Bintan (between Singapore and Sumatra), and Medan on Sumatra. If you're arriving in Indonesia through a more remote air- or seaport, check whether you need to obtain a visa from an Indonesian consulate in advance. For a full list of official gateways see ⓦindonesianembassy.org.uk.

Once you have entered visa-free, you cannot extend your stay, so if you are planning to stay longer than thirty days, you'll need to either purchase a visa in advance from an Indonesian consulate or purchase a visa on arrival for $35, which can then be extended for another thirty days at an immigration office (for Rp250,000). Alternatively, you could make a visa run to Singapore or Malaysia before returning to obtain another thirty days in the country. A visa is most easily obtained in Singapore, Penang or Kuala Lumpur. Note that you must show your ticket out of the country when applying for a visa, whether you're applying at the embassy or the port. When applying for an extension of your visa, bring photocopies of the photo page in your passport, your Indonesian visa, and your flight ticket out of Indonesia. A fee of Rp300,000 per day is incurred if you overstay your visa.

GETTING AROUND

Delays are common to all forms of transport in Indonesia – including major flights, especially later in the day – caused by weather, mechanical failure, or simply not enough passengers turning up, so you'll save yourself a good deal of stress if you keep your schedule as flexible as possible.

BUSES, MINIBUSES AND TRAINS

Buses are inexpensive, easy to book and leave roughly on time. But they're also slow, cramped and often plain terrifying. Where there's a choice of operators on any particular route, ask local people which bus company they recommend. **Tickets** are sold a day or more in advance from the point of departure or bus company offices – which are not necessarily near the relevant **bus station** (*terminal*). Where services are infrequent it's a good idea to buy tickets as early as possible. Tell the driver your exact destination, as it may be possible to get delivered right to the door of your hotel. The average **long-distance bus** has padded seats but little leg- or headroom; it's worth forking out for a luxury bus, if available, which costs roughly twice as much but will have reclining seats. You'll get regular meal stops at roadhouses along the way. On shorter routes, you'll use minibuses, known widely as angkot – or by their Balinese tag, bemo. Other names for local transport include *taksi* (angkot in Kalimantan), pete-pete (Sulawesi) and labi labi (Aceh). Once on their way, they're faster than buses and cheaper; fares are handed over on board, and rarely advertised. You may also have to pay for any space your luggage occupies. It's almost impossible to give the **frequency** with which angkots and public buses run; if no frequency is given in the text, they are frequent, roughly hourly. Journey times given are the minimum you can reasonably expect.

A more pleasant alternative to big buses and angkots is **tourist shuttle buses** – though far more expensive than local services, these will take you between points as quickly as possible. Fitted with air-conditioning, these are often simply called *travel* (share taxis in Flores as well as northern Sumatra). The longest-established firm of tourist shuttle buses on Bali and Lombok is **Perama** (⦿peramatour.com), who have offices in most major tourist

destinations and produce a useful leaflet outlining their routes.

In Java, **trains**, run by PT Kereta API, are often more comfortable and reliable than buses, and train stations are generally far more centrally situated than the far-flung bus terminals. You're also less likely to get ripped off at the train ticket window (*loket*). If you have a local SIM card, you can save the trip to the station by dialling ⦿121 for train information and bookings; you will receive a confirmation code via SMS, which you then take to the nearest Indomaret or Alfamart to pay and get a receipt. Some of these convenience stores have self-service ticket machines. If you can work with Bahasa Indonesia, you can search and book tickets on the railway's official website, ⦿tiket.kereta-api.co.id; a more user-friendly agent is ⦿tiket.com – often worth the small commission. Get to the station at least one hour early to exchange booking receipts for boarding passes.

BOATS AND FERRIES

While the rise of affordable airlines has dealt a huge blow to sea travel, there remain plenty of boat connections between islands. Where other services haven't taken over – particularly the far east of the archipelago – ships continue to retain their relevance. **Public ferries** run regularly on the shorter crossings between neighbouring islands, such as between Sumatra and Java, Java and Bali, and Bali and Lombok, for example. In more visited areas you'll find **tourist boat services**, and combined long-distance bus and boat options. However, with the advent of cheap domestic flights, ferry services have become much less frequent and poorer value.

Pelni (⦿pelni.co.id), the national carrier, currently operates 28 **passenger liners**, most of which run on weekly or monthly circuits to serve a total of 92 ports between Sumatra and Papua. The best place for up-to-date information on routes is the **local Pelni office**, which should have timetables for relevant ferries serving their ports. Comprehensive timetables for Pelni's coverage across the whole country can be picked up from their head office in Jakarta. The vessels are well maintained, and as safe and punctual as any transport in Indonesia can be. **Tickets** are available from Pelni offices two or three days before departure, but it's best to pay an agent to reserve these as early as possible. You can only buy tickets for services that depart locally. Accommodation on board is usually divided into two or four classes, the most expensive of these complete with double bed, washroom, air-conditioning and large lockers to store your luggage. If all classes are full, then the only option is to sleep in the corridors, stairwells or on deck (buy a rattan mat, and get to the port early to stake out your spot on the floor). Lock luggage and chain it to something immovable. Fourth-class food is edible at best and "lines" in the canteen are extremely long at mealtimes, so stock up in advance.

PLANES

Flying is increasingly a top choice for both visitors and a skyrocketing number of Indonesian passengers. As well as saving time, flights often save money if you take into account en route costs aboard long-haul buses and boats. In some remote parts of the country, it may be the only practical way to get around. As airlines have competed fiercely for booming business, safety standards have lagged behind. However, there has been slow improvement: in August 2016, foreign air safety regulators upgraded the country's rating, ending a nine-year ban on entering Europe and the United States. State-operated **Garuda** (🅦garuda-indonesia.com) is the most reputable, handling a range of international flights (though you might also use them for transport within Indonesia), as does Air Asia (🅦airasia .com/id/en), while airlines providing domestic services include Lion, Merpati and Sriwijaya. **Reconfirm** your seat, as waiting lists can be long and being bumped off a flight isn't unheard of; get a computer printout of the reconfirmation if possible. Arrive at the airport **early**, as seats on overbooked flights are allocated on a first-come,

first-served basis. At other times, "fully booked" planes can be almost empty, so if you really have to get somewhere it's always worth going to the airport to check. Fares are typically good value: a flight between Bali and Jakarta, for example, costs around $55. Departure tax is included in the ticket price.

RENTAL VEHICLES

Car-rental agencies abound in tourist hot spots such as Bali. Local operators offer a range of cars, from mini MPVs like the Toyota Avanza to mini SUVs like the Suzuki Jimny (from around Rp250,000–400,000/day). You'll need to produce an **international drivers' licence** before you rent (in some cases these can be purchased for around Rp200,000). Rental motorbikes vary from small 100cc Yamahas to trail bikes. Prices start at around Rp50,000 per day without insurance. Conditions are not suitable for inexperienced drivers, with heavy traffic on major routes; there are increasing numbers of **accidents** involving tourists, so don't take risks.

Traffic in Indonesia **drives on the left** and drivers must always carry an international driving licence and the vehicle registration documents. Passengers in the front of a vehicle must wear a seatbelt by law, and all motorcyclists must wear a helmet. The **police** carry out regular spot checks, and you'll be **fined** for any infringements.

URBAN TRANSPORT

In cities, colour-coded or numbered minibuses known as **angkots** (also called bemos, oplets or microlets) run fixed circuits, although routes are often adaptable according to their customers. Rides through the city usually cost Rp3000–5000, depending on the distance travelled, but fares are never displayed and are typically collected upon exiting; visitors are frequently overcharged. Other standbys include **ojek**, single-passenger motorbikes, and **becak**, cycle-rickshaws capable of squeezing in two or even three passengers. Jakarta also has motorized *becak*, called **bajaj**. Negotiating **fares** for these vehicles requires a balance of firmness and tact. Taxis are generally cheaper than a *bajaj*, and in most cities use a meter (*argo*), though *bajaj* can prove useful when in a hurry during the peak-hour mess. The latest addition to urban transport comes from rideshare **apps** like Uber (ⓦuber.com), which has drivers in Jakarta, Bali, Bandung, Surabaya and Yogyakarta. More popular for finding cars is Grab (ⓦgrab.com/id), and there's Gojek (ⓦgo-jek.com) for ojeks.

ACCOMMODATION

Prices for the simplest double room start at around $5 (more in touristy areas like Bali), and in all categories are at their **most expensive** from mid-June through to August, and in December and January. Single rooms are a rarity; the best lone travellers can usually hope for is a 25 percent discount or so on a double.

Check-out time is usually noon. The most basic accommodation has shared, cold-water **bathrooms**, where you wash using a mandi (see p.36). Toilets in these places are generally squat affairs, flushed manually with water scooped from the pail that stands alongside, so you'll have to provide toilet paper yourself.

The bottom end of Indonesia's accommodation market is provided by homestays and hostels. *Penginapan*, or **inns**, are often simply spare bedrooms in the family home, and there's often not much difference between these and *losmen*, *pondok* and *wisma*, which are also family-run operations. Rooms vary from whitewashed concrete cubes to artful bamboo structures – some are even set in their own walled gardens. Hard beds and bolsters are the norm, and you may be provided with a light blanket. Most *losmen* rooms have fans and cold-water bathrooms, though some offer air-conditioning and hot water in select rooms.

Almost any place calling itself a **hotel** will include at least a basic breakfast in the price of a room. Most of the mid-range and top-end places add a service-and-tax surcharge of between 10 and 22 percent to your bill, and smarter establishments quote prices – and often prefer foreigners to pay – in dollars, though they accept plastic or a rupiah equivalent. In popular areas such as Bali and Tanah Toraja, it's worth booking ahead during the peak seasons. Typically bland and anonymous, inexpensive urban hotels are designed for local businesspeople rather than tourists, though fierce competition in recent years has led to some great-value options at moderate prices, most with air-conditioning and hot water. Some of the cheapest can be found through regional booking websites such as ⓦnidarooms.com and ⓦzenrooms.com.

In remote, rural Indonesia, you may end up **staying in villages** without formal lodgings, in a bed in a family house. First ask permission from the local police or the *kepala desa* (village head). In exchange for accommodation and meals, you should offer cash or useful gifts, such as rice, salt, cigarettes or food, to the value of about $2 at the very least. The only bathroom might be the nearest river. With such readily available and inexpensive alternatives, **camping** is only necessary when trekking.

Usually, **electricity** is supplied at 220–240 volts AC, but outlying areas may still use 110 volts. Most outlets take plugs with two rounded pins.

FOOD AND DRINK

At first glance Indonesian food may appear to lack variety, and the ubiquity of *nasi* (fried rice) may indeed cause some travellers to despair. However, regional specialities from across the archipelago – as well as far beyond, with influences from Chinese, Middle Eastern, Malay, Indian and Polynesian cuisines – contribute to a surprising diversity in Indonesian cuisine. Rice (*nasi*) is the favoured staple across much of the country, an essential, three-times-a-day fuel. Noodles (*mie*) are also widely popular. Chicken, goat and beef are the main meats in this predominantly Muslim country, though there's often excellent seafood, and plenty of pork options in Christian areas. **Vegetarians** can eat well in Indonesia, with many

4

restaurants offering at least a few reliable options, including *cap cay* (fried mixed vegetables), *tahu* (tofu), and *tempe* (pressed, fermented soya beans), a Javanese speciality.

INDONESIAN FOOD

Spices, the backbone of all Indonesian cooking, are ground and chopped together then fried to form a paste, which is either used as the flavour-base for curries, or rubbed over ingredients prior to frying or grilling. Chillies always feature, along with *terasi* (also known as *belacan*), a fermented shrimp paste. Meals are often served with *sambal*, a blisteringly hot blend of chillies and spices. Vegetarians should be aware that *krecek*, a type of sambal, contains cow skin.

Light meals and snacks include various rice dishes such as **nasi goreng**, a plate of fried rice with shreds of meat and vegetables and topped with a fried egg, and **nasi campur**, boiled rice served with a small range of side dishes. Noodle equivalents are also commonly available, as are **gado-gado**, steamed vegetables dressed in a peanut sauce, and **sate**, small kebabs of meat or fish, barbecued over a fire and again served with spicy peanut sauce. Indonesian bread (*roti*) is made from sweetened dough, and usually accompanies a morning cup of coffee.

Sumatran **Padang restaurants** are found right across Indonesia, the typically fiery food pre-cooked and displayed cold on platters piled up in a pyramid shape inside a glass-fronted cabinet. It's not the most hygienic eating style, and there are no menus, but it's a wonderful way to sample new dishes. You only pay for what you consume. You may encounter boiled *kangkung* (water spinach); *tempe*; egg, vegetable, meat or seafood curry; fried whole fish; potato cakes; fried cow's lung; and, last but not least, *rendang* (slow-cooked and caramelized beef in a gravy of coconut milk and spices).

WHERE TO EAT

The cheapest places to eat in Indonesia are at the **mobile stalls** (*kaki lima*, or "five legs"), which ply their wares around the streets and bus stations during the day,

and congregate at night markets after dark. You simply place your order and they cook it up on the spot. **Warung** are the bottom line in Indonesian restaurants, usually just a few tables, and offering much the same food as *kaki lima* for under a dollar a dish. **Rumah makan** are bigger, offer a wider range of dishes and comfort, and may even have a menu, while places labelled as **restaurants** are likely to cater to the upper class, with fully-fledged service and often international food. Most warung, *rumah makan* and restaurants are open from around 10/11am until 10pm, though few operate to strict timings. Many of the moderate and all of the expensive establishments will add up to 21 percent service tax to the bill.

DRINKS

Most tap **water** in Indonesia has had very little treatment, and can contain a whole range of bacteria and viruses. Drink only bottled, boiled or sterilized water. Boiled water (*air putih*) can be requested at accommodation and restaurants, and dozens of brands of **bottled water** (*air minum*) are sold throughout the islands. Indonesian **coffee** is among the world's best, and drunk with copious amounts of sugar (*gula*) and, occasionally, condensed milk (*susu manis*).

Alcohol is often a touchy subject in Indonesia, where public drunkenness may incur serious trouble. There's no need to be paranoid about this in cities, however, and the locally produced **beers**, Anker and Bintang, are good, and widely available at Chinese restaurants and bigger hotels. In non-Islamic regions, even small warung sell beer. **Spirits** are less publicly consumed, and may be technically illegal, so indulge with caution. Nonetheless, home-produced brews are often sold openly in villages. *Tuak* (also known as *balok*) or palm wine, made by tapping a suitable tree for its sap, comes in plain milky white or pale red varieties, and varies in strength. Far more potent are rice wine (*arak* or *brem*), and *sopi*, a distillation of *tuak*, either of which can leave you incapacitated after a heavy session.

CULTURE AND ETIQUETTE

Indonesia is the world's most populous Muslim country, but the practice of **Islam** across the archipelago has been shaped by centuries of interaction with Hinduism, Buddhism and other faiths, as well as traditional animist practices. As a result, Islam in Indonesia has historically been buffered against the more austere, exclusivist ideologies of certain Middle Eastern states. While Islamists have made advances in recent decades, the majority of Indonesians – including the largest Muslim organizations in the country – remain relatively open and tolerant in line with the state philosophy of *Pancasila*, which grants followers of all religions equal rights. Although there are regional variations in accepted social norms, with Aceh among the most conservative provinces and Bali the most liberal, there are also differences within provinces. Outside the main tourist resorts, dress conservatively, especially when visiting religious sites, to avoid giving offence. Be especially sensitive during the Muslim fasting month of Ramadan.

Visitors to **Balinese temples** (*pura*) show respect to the shrines and dress modestly – no skimpy clothing, bare shoulders or shorts. Often you'll be required to wear a sarong and a ceremonial sash around your waist (usually provided by the most-visited temples).

Indonesia shares the same **attitudes to dress and social taboos** as other Southeast Asian cultures (see p.40). In addition, Indonesians are generally very sociable, and dislike doing anything alone. It's normal for complete strangers engaged in some common enterprise – catching a bus, for instance – to introduce themselves and start up a friendship. **Sharing cigarettes** between men is in these circumstances a way of establishing a bond, and Westerners who don't smoke should be genuinely apologetic about refusing; it's worth carrying a packet to share around even if you save your own "for later".

SPORTS AND OUTDOOR ACTIVITIES

DIVING

4

Indonesia has many of the world's best **diving sites**, among the finest of which are Pulau Bunaken off **Sulawesi**, **Pulau Weh** off northern Aceh in Sumatra, the **Bandas** in the Maluku Islands, and **Raja Ampat** to the west of Papua. **Bali** has many good sites, including the famous *Liberty* wreck, and reputable tour operators at all major

---

TRADITIONAL DANCE AND MUSIC

Given Indonesia's enormous cultural and ethnic mix, it's hardly surprising that the range of traditional music and dance across the archipelago is so vast.

DANCE

Best known are the highly stylized and mannered **classical dance performances** in Java and Bali, accompanied by the gamelan orchestra. Every step is minutely orchestrated, and the merest wink of an eye or arch of an eyebrow has significance. Ubud on Bali and Yogyakarta on Java are the centres for these dances. Yogya is also the main place to catch a performance of **wayang kulit**, shadow puppet plays.

GAMELAN

A gamelan is an ensemble of tuned percussion, consisting mainly of gongs, metallophones and drums, made of bronze, iron, brass, wood or bamboo, with wooden frames, which are often intricately carved and painted. The full ensemble also includes vocalists and is led by the drummer in the centre. A large gamelan may be played by as many as thirty musicians, and is a communal form of music-making – there are no soloists or virtuosos.

Sundanese (West Javanese) *degung* is the most accessible gamelan music for Western ears. Its musical structures are clear and well defined, and it is played by a small ensemble, but includes the usual range of gongs and metallophones found in all gamelan.

By Jenny Heaton and Simon Steptoe

beach resorts. The best time for diving is between late April and early October. Most major beach resorts have dive centres, but once you get further afield you'll probably have to rely on live-aboard cruises or even on having your own gear. A day's diving costs anything from $45 to upwards of $100. Ask about the reputation of the dive operators before signing up, check their PADI or equivalent accreditation and, if possible, get first-hand recommendations from other divers. Be aware that it is down to you to check your equipment, and that the purity of an air tank can be suspect, and could cause serious injury. Also check your guide's credentials carefully, and bear in mind that you may be a long way from a decompression chamber.

SURFING

Indonesia is also one of the world's premier surfing destinations, with an enormous variety of first-class waves and perfect breaks. The best-known waves are found on **Bali**, **G-Land** (Grajagan) on Java and around **Krui** in southern Sumatra; further afield, **Sumba**, the **Mentawai Islands**, and **Lhoknga** in Aceh are also increasingly popular.

In June and July, during the best and most consistent surf, you can expect waves to be crowded, especially in Java and Bali. Several surf companies in Bali offer all-in surf safaris to other destinations in Indonesia. Try to bring your own board, though in the popular surf spots you can rent some decent boards on the beach. Most public transport charges extra for boards, but many surfers simply rent motorbikes with board-carrying attachments.

For detailed reviews of surf breaks, see the book *Indo Surf and Lingo*, available from ⓦindosurf.com.au and from surfshops and bookshops in Bali. Good surf websites include ⓦbaliwaves.com, ⓦindosurflife.com, ⓦwannasurf.com and ⓦwavehunters.com.

TREKKING

There are endless **trekking** opportunities in Indonesia. The most popular **volcano treks** include Gunung Batur on Bali and

Gunung Bromo and Gunung Merapi on Java; more taxing favourites include Gunung Rinjani on Lombok and Gunung Sinabung in Sumatra. Also in Sumatra, the **Gunung Leuser National Park** is Southeast Asia's largest, and includes the famous Bukit Lawang orang-utan sanctuary. The long haul to **Gunung Leuser** itself from Ketambe as well as many routes heading into the park from Bukit Lawang require **guides**, and not just to find the paths: turning up at a remote village unannounced can cause trouble, as people may mistrust outsiders, let alone Westerners. Guides are always available from local villages and tourist centres, at a cost of about Rp250,000–300,000 per day.

COMMUNICATIONS

Mobile phone coverage is improving fast across Java, Sumatra and Bali, but elsewhere is confined largely to the main cities and populated areas only. If you're staying longer than a week or so in Indonesia, it can be highly useful to purchase an Indonesian SIM card for around Rp100,000. The dominant operators are Telkomsel, Three and Indosat. There's a somewhat complicated registration process, so ask the sales assistant for help to set up your phone. You shouldn't have to pay to receive calls. Dial *808# to check your phone number, and *889# to check your remaining balance. A SIM card is increasingly handy as internet cafés are becoming less common. **Wi-fi** is widespread at hotels and restaurants, and there are still plenty of internet cafés in towns and cities; prices vary widely from Rp3000 to Rp30,000/hr.

To **call abroad** from Indonesia, dial ☏001 or ☏008 + country code + area code (minus the first 0) + number. For international directory enquiries call ☏102; the international operator is ☏101.

Indonesia's **poste restante** system is fairly efficient, but only in the cities. In larger post offices, the parcels section is usually in a separate part of the building; sending one is expensive and time-consuming. The cheapest way of sending mail home is by surface (under 10kg only). Don't seal the parcel before staff at the post office have checked its contents; in larger towns there is usually a parcel-wrapping service nearby.

CRIME AND SAFETY

Indonesia has endured a torrid time over the past decade or so, most recently with the January 2016 terror attacks in downtown Jakarta, killing eight including the four assailants. Together with the July 2009 bombings of Jakarta's *Ritz-Carlton* and *JW Marriott* hotels, the 2002 Bali bombings which left more than 200 (mostly foreigners) dead and the violence that surrounded the political and religious upheavals of the past decade, it undermines the idea that Indonesia is a safe place to travel. Considering the scale of Indonesia and the vast number of international travellers, incidents involving Westerners are rare. **Petty theft**, however, is a fact of life, so don't flash around expensive computer equipment, jewellery or watches. Don't hesitate to check that doors and windows – including those in the bathroom – are secure before accepting **accommodation**; if the management seems offended by this, you probably don't want to stay there anyway. Some guesthouses and hotels have safe-deposit boxes.

If you're unlucky enough to get **mugged**, never resist and, if you disturb a thief, raise the alarm rather than try to take them on. Be especially aware of **pickpockets** on ferries, buses or bemos, who usually operate in pairs: one will distract you while another does the job. Afterwards, you'll need a **police report** for insurance purposes. Try to take along someone to translate, though police will generally do their best to find an English-speaker. You may also be charged "administration fees", the cost of which is open to sensitive negotiations. Have

EMERGENCY NUMBERS

Police ☎110
Ambulance ☎118/☎119
Fire ☎113

nothing to do with **drugs** in Indonesia: the penalties are extremely tough, and you won't get any sympathy from consular officials.

MEDICAL CARE AND EMERGENCIES

If you have a minor ailment, head to a **pharmacy** (*apotek* or *apotik*), which can provide many medicines without prescription. Condoms (*kondom*) are available from pharmacists and convenience stores. If you need an English-speaking doctor (*doktor*) or dentist (*doktor gigi*), seek advice at your accommodation or at the local tourist office. You'll find a **public hospital** (*rumah sakit*) in major cities and towns, and in some places these are supplemented by **private hospitals**, many of which operate an accident and emergency department. If you have a serious accident or illness, you will need to be evacuated home or to Singapore, which has Asia's best medical provision. It is, therefore, vital to arrange **health insurance** before you leave home.

INFORMATION AND MAPS

There's a range of **tourist offices** in Indonesia, including government-run organizations, normally called **Dinas** (or Kantor) Pariwisata (Diparda). However, many tourist information centres in Indonesia are little more than pamphlet outlets. Good hostels are often the best sources of information.

Good all-round maps include GeoCentre's 1:2,000,000 series and the Nelles Indonesia series. In the same league is the Periplus (⊕periplus.com) range of user-friendly city and provincial maps.

MONEY AND BANKS

The Indonesian currency is the **rupiah** (abbreviated to "Rp"). **Notes** come in denominations of Rp500 (very rare), Rp1000, Rp5000, Rp10,000, Rp20,000, Rp50,000 and Rp100,000; **coins**, mainly used for bemos, come in Rp25 (rare), Rp50, Rp100, Rp500 and Rp1000 denominations. Officially, rupiah are

4

BAHASA INDONESIA

Although there are also more than 250 native languages spoken throughout the archipelago, Indonesia's national language is Bahasa Indonesia, a form of Bahasa Malay. Because it's written in Roman script, has no tones and uses a fairly straightforward grammar, it's relatively easy to learn.

PRONUNCIATION

a as in a cross between father and cup
e sometimes as in along; or as in pay; or as in get; or sometimes omitted (*selamat* pronounced "slamat")
i either as in boutique; or as in pit
o either as in hot; or as in cold
u as in boot

ai as in fine
au as in how
c as in cheap
g always hard, as in girl
k hard, as in English, except at the end of the word, when you should stop just short of pronouncing it

GREETINGS AND BASIC PHRASES

Good morning	*Selamat pagi*	city/city centre	*kota*
Good day	*Selamat siang*	hospital	*rumah sakit*
Good afternoon	*Selamat sore*	hotel	*losmen*
Good evening	*Selamat malam*	market	*pasar*
Goodbye	*Selamat tinggal*	pharmacy	*apotek*
Please (requesting)	*Tolong*	police station	*kantor polisi*
Please (offering)	*Silakan*	post office	*kantor pos*
Thank you (very much)	*Terima kasih (banyak)*	shop	*toko*
		telephone office	*wartel/kantor telkom*
You're welcome	*Sama sama*		
Sorry/Excuse me	*Ma'af*	bicycle	*sepeda*
No worries/Never mind	*Tidak apa apa*	bus	*bis*
Yes	*Ya*	car	*mobil*
No (with verb)	*Tidak* (sometimes pronounced "*tak*")	entrance/exit	*masuk/keluar*
		ferry	*feri*
Do you speak English?	*Bisa bicara bahasa Inggris?*	motorbike	*sepeda motor*
		taxi	*taksi*
I don't understand	*Saya tidak mengerti*	ticket	*karcis*
I want/would like …	*Saya mau …*	Stop!	*Estop!*
I don't want it/No thanks	*Tidak mau*	air-conditioning	*AC* (pronounced "*ah say*")
open/closed	*Buka/tutup*		
Where is the …?	*Di mana …?*	bathroom	*kamar mandi*
How much/many?	*Berapa?*	fan	*kipas*
What is the price for this?	*Berapa harga ini?*	hot water	*air panas*
airport	*Bandara*	mosquito net	*kelambu nyamuk*
bank	*Bank*	toilet	*kamar kecil/wc* (pronounced "*way say*")
beach	*Pantai*		
bemo/bus station	*terminal*		

NUMBERS

Zero	*Nol/kosong*	11, 12, 13, etc	*Sebelas, duabelas, tigabelas*
1	*Satu*		
2	*Dua*	20	*Duapuluh*
3	*Tiga*	21, 22, etc	*Duapuluh satu, duapuluh dua, duapuluh tiga, etc*
4	*Empat*		
5	*Lima*		
6	*Enam*	30, 40, etc	*Tigapuluh, Empatpuluh, Limapuluh*
7	*Tujuh*		
8	*Delapan*		
9	*Sembilan*	100	*Seratus*
10	*Sepuluh*	200	*Duaratus*
		1000	*Seribu*

FOOD AND DRINKS GLOSSARY

daftar makanan	menu
dingin	cold
enak	delicious
goreng	fried
makan malam	dinner
makan pagi	breakfast
makan siang	lunch
panas	hot (temperature)
pedas	hot (spicy)
saya ingin bayar	I want to pay
saya seorang vegetaris	I'm a vegetarian
saya tidak makan daging	I don't eat meat
sayur saja	Only vegetables

Meat, fish and basic foods

anjing	dog
ayam	chicken
babi	pork
bakmi	noodles
buah	fruit
es	ice
ikan	fish
itik	duck
jaja	rice cakes
jus	juice
kambing	goat
kari	curry
kepiting	crab
nasi	rice
sambal	hot chilli sauce
sapi	beef
soto	soup
telur	egg
tikkus	rat
udang	prawn

everyday dishes

ayam bakar	fried chicken
bakmi goreng	fried noodles and meat
bakso	meat balls
bubur ayam	rice porridge with chicken (breakfast food)
cap cay	mixed fried vegetables
gado-gado	steamed vegetables served with a spicy peanut sauce
kwetiau	Singaporean stir-fry of flat rice noodles and meat
lumpia	spring rolls

murtabak	thick dough pancake, often filled with meat
nasi ayam	boiled rice with chicken
nasi campur	boiled rice served with small amounts of vegetable, meat, fish and sometimes egg
nasi goreng	fried rice
nasi gudeg	rice with jackfruit and coconut-milk curry
nasi pecel	rice with vegetables, peanut sauce, and often tempe
nasi putih	plain boiled rice
nasi soto ayam	chicken-and-rice soup
pisang goreng	fried bananas
rendang	dry-fried beef and coconut-milk curry
rijsttaffel	Dutch/Indonesian buffet of six to ten meat, fish and vegetable dishes with rice
sate	meat or fish kebabs served with a spicy peanut sauce
tahu goreng telur	tofu omelette
urap-urap/urap timum	vegetables with coconut and chilli

Drinks

jus jeruk	orange juice
jus jeruk nipis	lemon juice
air minum	drinking water
arak	palm or rice spirit
bir	beer
brem	local rice beer
kopi	coffee
kopi susu	coffee with milk
sopi	palm spirit
susu	milk
the	tea
tuak	palm wine

4

available outside Indonesia, but the currency's volatile value means that few banks carry it. At the time of writing, the exchange rate was Rp16,100 to £1 and Rp13,350 to US$1.

Sometimes prices for tourist services, such as diving or organized trips, are quoted in **dollars** or **euros**, but you can pay in rupiah at the exchange rate at that time.

You'll find **banks** capable of handling foreign exchange in provincial capitals and bigger cities throughout Indonesia, and almost every town has at least one or two **ATMs**, which are also found within most Indomaret and Alfamart convenience stores. These generally accept at least one from Visa, MasterCard or Cirrus-Maestro. There are also privately run **moneychangers** in major tourist centres. Always count your money carefully, as unscrupulous dealers can rip you off, either by folding notes over to make it look as if you're getting twice as much, or by distracting you and then whipping away a few notes from your pile.

OPENING HOURS AND HOLIDAYS

As a rough outline, businesses such as airline offices open Monday to Friday 8am to 5pm and Saturday 8am to noon. Banking hours are Monday to Friday 8am to 3pm and Saturday 8am to 1pm, but banks may not handle foreign exchange in the afternoons or at weekends. Post offices operate roughly Monday to Thursday 8am to 2pm, Friday 8 to 11am and Saturday 8am to 1pm, though in the larger cities the hours are much longer. Muslim businesses, including **government offices**, may also close at 11.30am on Fridays, the main day of prayer, and national **public holidays** see all commerce compulsorily curtailed.

Ramadan, a month of fasting during daylight hours, falls during the ninth Muslim month (see box below). Even in non-Islamic areas, Muslim restaurants and businesses shut down during the day, and in the more staunchly Islamic parts of rural Lombok, Sumatra and North Maluku, you should not eat, drink or smoke in public at this time.

TIMING RAMADAN

Local religious authorities across the Muslim world use the new moon to calculate the timing of **Ramadan**. The exact day of celebration varies from place to place, and Ramadan slides slowly forward from year to year in relation to the Gregorian calendar. The first day of the following month is **Eid al Fitr**, the most important date in the Islamic calendar, marking the end of Ramadan. Tentative dates for upcoming years are as follows: May 16–June 14, 2018; May 6–June 5, 2019; April 24–May 24, 2020.

PUBLIC HOLIDAYS

Most of the national public holidays fall on different dates of the Western calendar each year, as they are calculated according to Islamic or local calendars.
January 1 New Year's Day (*Tahun Baru*)
January/February Chinese New Year
March/April *Nyepi*, Balinese New Year
March/April Good Friday and Easter Sunday
April Isra Miraj (Ascension Day of Muhammed)
May/June *Waisak* Day. Anniversary of the birth, death and enlightenment of Buddha
May/June Ascension Day of Jesus
Usually June Idul Fitri. The celebration of the end of Ramadan
August 17 Independence Day (*Hari Proklamasi Kemerdekaan*)
Usually September Muharam, Islamic New Year
Usually August Idul Adha Feast of Sacrifice
Usually November Maulid Nabi Muhammad. Anniversary of the birth of Muhammed Lailat
December 25 Christmas Day

FESTIVALS

In addition to national public holidays, there are frequent **religious festivals** throughout Indonesia's Muslim, Hindu, Chinese and indigenous communities. Each of Bali's twenty thousand temples has an anniversary celebration, for instance, and other ethnic groups may host elaborate marriages or funerals, along with more secular holidays. Many of these festivals change annually against the Western **calendar**.
Galungun Bali. Takes place for ten days every 210 days to celebrate the victory of good over evil.

Pasola West Sumba. Held four times in February and March, this festival to balance the upper sphere of the heavens culminates with a frenetic pitched battle between two villages of spear-wielding horsemen.

Nyepi Throughout Bali. End of March or beginning of April. The major purification ritual of the year.

Sekaten Central Java. March or April. The celebration of the birthday of the prophet Muhammed includes a month-long festival of fairs, gamelan recitals and performances.

Erau Festival Tenggarong, Kalimantan. September. A big display of indigenous Dayak skills and dancing.

Funerals Tanah Toraja, Sulawesi. Mostly May to September. With buffalo slaughter, bullfights and *sisemba* kick-boxing tournaments.

Krakatau Festival Lampung, Sumatra. October. Five days of events highlighting Lampung's cultural heritage, including Tuping Karnaval (Lampung Mask Carnival); part of the celebration occurs on the island of Anak Krakatau itself.

Kora Kora Festival Traditional longboat races in the Maluku Islands, held in Ternate and the Banda Islands in mid-November.

Kasada Bromo, East Java. Offerings are made to the gods and thrown into the crater. Held on the fourteenth day of Kasada, the twelfth month in the Tenggerese calendar year (Dec).

Java

One of the most densely populated places in all of Asia, **JAVA** is also characterized by great natural beauty. This island's central spine is dominated by volcanoes, over forty of which remain active, their fertile slopes supporting a landscape of glimmering rice fields dotted with countless villages. To the south of this mountainous backbone is the homeland of the ethnic Javanese and the centre of their arts, culture and language, epitomized by the royal courts of **Yogyakarta** and **Solo**. Still steeped in traditional dance, music and art, these two cities are the mainstay of Java's tourist industry, providing excellent bases from which to explore the sublime Buddhist temple of **Borobudur**, as well as the equally fascinating Hindu complex of **Prambanan**. To the east, the volcanic massif of **Gunung Bromo** is another major stop on most travellers' itineraries, not least for the sunrise walk to its summit. And there are plenty more volcanic landscapes to explore,

including the turquoise lake of **Kawah Ijen**, the ancient temples and coloured lakes of the windswept **Dieng Plateau,** and the world's most famous – and destructive – volcano, **Krakatau**, off the west coast of Java. There is also a good share of pretty beaches, some of the best set around the palm-fringed resort of **Pangandaran** on the southern coast.

Java's cities tend to prove less enticing to many travellers, though these frenetic sprawls certainly have their own allure. None can compare with **Jakarta**, the capital and modern face of Indonesia, boasting fascinating ethnic and historical quarters, interesting museums, a host of gargantuan new malls and the best nightlife on the island. Moving on to Java's neighbouring islands is easily done – Bali is just a forty-minute ferry from Banyuwangi in the east, as is Sumatra from Merak in the west.

JAKARTA

Bounded to the north by the Java Sea and to the south by the low Bogor Hills, **JAKARTA** is Indonesia's unrivalled megalopolis. Home to almost thirty million people (including the greater, official metropolitan area known as Jabodetabek), it comprises almost 700 square kilometres of concrete sprawl, an amalgam of glamorous shopping malls, colonial-era relics, exclusive enclaves and slums spread beneath a soaring skyline. Notorious for noise, congestion and pollution, many travellers don't give it a second glance – thereby missing out on the many charms of the national capital. Indeed, there's nowhere better to experience Indonesia's pulsing dynamism and its heart-rending contrasts than in the "Big Durian".

Among the city's highlights are **Kota** in the north, former heart of the colonial Dutch city, along with its neighbouring **Sunda Kelapa**, the bustling old port, and just to the south, the city's fascinating Glodok area – Jakarta's Chinatown. Each of these districts is dotted with historic buildings, including a few of the country's finest museums, among them the **Museum Bank Indonesia**, the

4

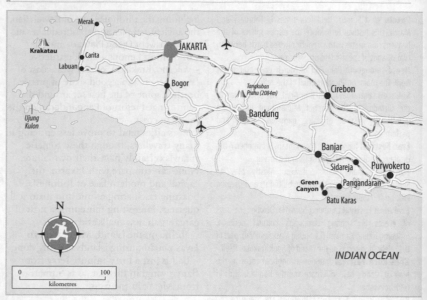

INDIAN OCEAN

4

Maritime Museum, the **Wayang Museum** and the **Jakarta History Museum**. The city centre is marked with more monuments and museums, most notably **Monas Tower** and the **National History Museum**, while mega-shopping complexes, some of them attractions in their own right, are scattered throughout the city.

WHAT TO SEE AND DO

To head from north to south through the centre of Jakarta is to go forward in time, from the quaint old Dutch area of **Kota** in the north to modern golf courses and amusement parks in the south. **Medan Merdeka**, a giant, threadbare patch of grass, marks the spiritual centre of Jakarta, if not exactly its geographical one, bordered to the west by the city's major north–south thoroughfare. The main commercial district and the budget accommodation enclave of **Jalan Jaksa** lie just a short distance to the south of Medan Merdeka.

Kota (Old Batavia)

Formerly known as **Batavia**, the quaint old district of **Kota** was once the administrative centre of the Dutch trading empire. To reach Kota, take the Trans Jakarta from Sarinah (Rp3500), which ends up in front of the Art Deco-style **Kota train station**, built in 1929. North of the station along Jalan Lada, past the Politeknik Swadharma, you enter the formerly walled city of Batavia, whose centre, **Taman Fatahillah**, an attractive cobbled square hemmed in by museums, lies 300m to the north of the train station. On the south side, the **Jakarta History Museum** (Tues–Sun 9am–3pm; Rp5000) traces the region's history back to the Stone Age; most displays are accompanied by English descriptions. The finest exhibit is the ornate **Cannon Si Jagur**, which previously stood in the square and was built by the Portuguese to defend Malacca. It is emblazoned with sexual imagery, from the clenched fist (a suggestive gesture in Southeast Asia) to the barrel itself, a potent phallic symbol in Indonesia.

To the west of the square is the small but worthwhile **Wayang Museum** (Tues–Sun 9am–3pm; Rp5000), dedicated to the Javanese art of puppetry and housed in one of the oldest buildings in the city. Although some of its exhibits are poorly maintained, the museum has puppets from right across the archipelago,

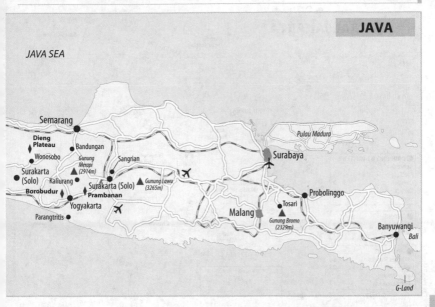

JAVA

JAVA SEA

Semarang

Dieng Plateau

Bandungan

Wonosobo

Gunung Merapi (2914m)

Sangrian

Surakarta (Solo)

Kaliurang

Surakarta (Solo)

Gunung Lawu (3265m)

Borobudur

Prambanan

Yogyakarta

Parangtritis

Pulau Madura

Surabaya

Probolinggo

Tosari

Malang

Gunung Bromo (2329m)

Banyuwangi

Bali

G-Land

4

and there is a free bi-monthly **wayang show** (2nd & 4th Sun at 10am). To the east of the square, the **Balai Seni Rupa** (Tues–Sun 9am–3pm; Rp5000), Jakarta's fine arts and ceramics museum, houses works by Indonesia's most illustrious artists. While in the area, don't miss the chance to luxuriate in the stylish surroundings of the historic *Café Batavia*, on the northwestern corner of Taman Fatahillah. A couple of blocks south of the square, just beside Kota station, lies the area's best-executed museum, the **Museum Bank Indonesia** (Mon–Fri 8am–3.30pm; Sat & Sun 8am–4pm; Rp5000), with excellent displays tracing the country's history through an economic lens, as well as an impressive collection of old bank-notes from around the world.

Sunda Kelapa and around

About 1km north of Kota lies the historic harbour of **Sunda Kelapa** (Rp2500), the most important foreign port of the entire Dutch empire. Although the bulk of the sea traffic docks at Tanjung Priok these days, a few of the smaller vessels, particularly some picturesque wooden schooners, still call in at this eight-hundred-year-old port. You can walk here

from Kota (about 20min), hail an ojek (Rp15,000) or take the pale blue #15 angkot from just west of the Kota busway stop (Rp5000).

From Sunda Kelapa, cross over the bridge to the west (on the right as you exit the port) and turn right at the nineteenth-century watchtower, the **Uitkijk**, built to direct shipping traffic to the port. Here, buried in the chaotic Pasar Ikan (fish market) that occupies this promontory, is the entrance to the **Museum Bahari**, or **Maritime Museum** (Tues–Sun 9am–3pm; Rp5000), housed in a warehouse dating from 1652. All kinds of sea craft are on display, from the Buginese *pinisi* to the *kora-kora* war boat from the Moluccas.

Head towards the *VOC Galangan* restaurant, keeping the Kali Besar canal on your left until you come to the ornate wooden drawbridge, **Jembatan Pasar Ayam**, which is in immaculate condition. The grand Dutch terraced houses on the streets south of here were once the smartest addresses in Batavia, the most famous being the Chinese-style **Toko Merah** (Red Shop) at 11 Jalan Kali Besar Barat – the former home of Dutch governor-general, Van Imhoff.

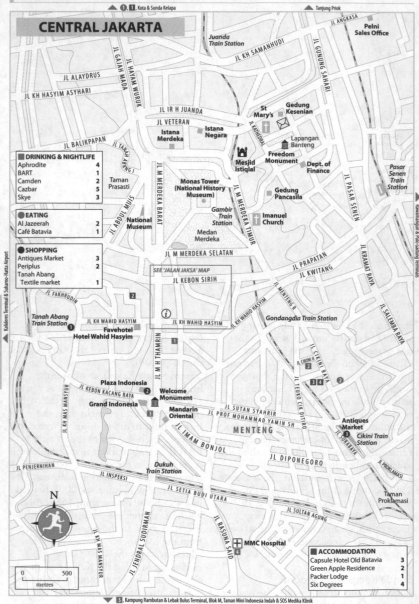

Glodok

The buzzing markets and temples of Jakarta's **Glodok** neighbourhood – Chinatown – are among the city's better-kept secrets. Longtime predecessors of the Dutch, Chinese shopkeepers continue to dominate this colourful area about 1km south of Old Batavia. The most interesting part is the open-air fresh produce market of **Petak Sembilan**, with fruit-and-vegetable stands alongside crates of eels, frogs, turtles and sea cucumbers leaving little room to navigate Jalan Kemenangan, its busiest stretch. Heading south from here, you'll pass the area's oldest Buddhist temple, the seventeenth-century **Vihara Jin de Yuan**, marked by swooping rooftops and guarded by phoenixes and dragons. Although damaged in a 2015 fire, it's as evocative as ever, filled with candles and clouded with incense smoke. You're welcome to enter and take photos, but take care to do so in a respectful fashion. The entire neighbourhood comes especially alive from December until late January during Chinese New Year festivities. To reach the area take busway #1 to the Glodok stop, set just to the west of Petak Sembilan.

Medan Merdeka

The heart and lungs of Jakarta, **Medan Merdeka** is a square kilometre of sun-scorched grass and pleasant manicured gardens in the middle of the city. At its centre stands the **Monas Tower**, a soaring 137m marble, bronze and gold torch, commissioned by Sukarno in 1962 to symbolize the indomitable spirit of the Indonesian people, and known as "Sukarno's last erection" in recognition of his world-famous philandering. Beneath the tower's square base, known as the Goblet Yard, is the **National History Museum** (Tues–Sun 8am–2pm & 7–10pm; Rp5000; ticket must be paid using JakCard – Rp40,000 with Rp20,000 credit), a series of 52 dioramas that depict the history of Jakarta and Indonesia's struggle for independence. You can take a lift up to the top of the tower for an impressive city view (an additional Rp10,000).

The **National Museum** (Tues–Fri 8am–4pm, Sat & Sun 8am–5pm; Rp10,000; ☎021 386 8172), on the western side of Medan Merdeka, is an interesting detour and a great introduction to Indonesia. Many of the country's top ruins have been plundered for their statues, which now sit, unmarked, in the museum courtyard. Other highlights include huge Dongson kettledrums, the skull and thigh bone of Java Man, found near Solo in 1936, and

the cache of golden artefacts discovered at the foot of Mount Merapi in 1990.

The dazzling white, if rather unprepossessing, **Mesjid Istiqlal** looms over the northeastern corner of Medan Merdeka. Completed in 1978, it is the largest mosque in Southeast Asia and can hold up to 250,000 people. For a small donation, and providing you're conservatively dressed, the security guards will take you on an informal tour. At the foot of the minaret sits a 2.5-tonne wooden drum from east Kalimantan, the only traditional feature in this otherwise state-of-the-art mosque.

Mini Indonesia

Eighteen kilometres south of Medan Merdeka, on the road to Bogor, is the **Taman Mini Indonesia Indah** theme park, (Tues–Sun 9am–4pm; Rp15,000; Trans Jakarta from Sarinah to Semanggi, then switch buses to Garuda Taman Mini). This peculiar oasis is like an Indonesian Neverland celebrating the archipelago's rich ethnic and cultural diversity, with gondolas offering the best view of the sprawling complex. At its centre is a man-made lake, around which are 26 houses, each built in the traditional style of Indonesia's provinces.

The park also contains a reptile garden, bird park, 4D cinema, IMAX theatre and several museums. Among these are the **Museum of Indonesia**, which has displays on the country's people, geography, flora and fauna, and the neighbouring **Museum Purna Bhakti Pertiwi**, which displays a fabulously opulent collection of gifts presented to President Suharto, including a whole gamelan orchestra made of old Balinese coins, a series of carved wooden panels depicting Suharto's life story, and an enormous rubber-tree root decorated with the nine gods of Balinese Hinduism.

ARRIVAL AND DEPARTURE

BY PLANE
Jakarta's Sukarno-Hatta Airport (☎021 550 5000) is 13km west of the city centre and connects with virtually all of Indonesia's major cities. The airport has a small tourist office in Terminal 2D (☎021 550 7088) and a handful of

4

exchange booths, most of which close at 10pm; rates at these are significantly lower than in the city centre. Terminal 1 serves domestic flights from all but Air Asia and Garuda; Terminal 2 serves most international flights, as well as domestic flights for Air Asia and Sriwijaya; and the new, state-of-the-art Terminal 3 is reserved for all Garuda flights. Free yellow shuttle buses link the terminals, running roughly every 20min. DAMRI buses connect the airport to Gambir train station (every 15min 4am–last flight, from Gambir to airport 3am–9pm; 45min; Rp40,000). DAMRI services also link Bogor (1hr 40min; Rp55,000). Upon arrival, turn left out of the gate and walk about 200m to the bus stand. Taxis between the airport and Jl Jaksa cost about Rp180,000, including Rp35,000 in toll fees. Blue Bird (blue cabs) and Express (white cabs) are the most reliable firms. Flights to Pangandaran depart from Halim Perdana Kusumua Airport in the south of the city.

Destinations Ambon (5 daily; 3hr 30min); Banda Aceh (3 daily; 2hr 50min); Balikpapan (23 daily; 2hr); Bangkok (7 daily; 3hr 30min); Denpasar (44 daily; 1hr 50min); Jayapura (4 daily; 5hr 30min); Makassar (46 daily; 2hr 20min); Manado (10 daily; 3hr 15min); Medan (38 daily; 2hr 20min); Pangandaran (daily; 1hr); Pekanbaru (20 daily; 1hr 45min); Singapore (37 daily; 1hr 50min); Solo/Surakarta (18 daily; 1hr 10min); Sorong (2 daily; 4hr 5min); Surabaya (60 daily; 1hr 25min); Ternate (1–2 daily; 4hr 15min); Yogyakarta (33 daily; 1hr 10min).

BY BUS

Buses connect Jakarta to all points in Java as well as many cities on neighbouring islands. All of Jakarta's major bus terminals are linked by Trans Jakarta buses to Jl Jaksa. Bus tickets are cheaper from the bus stations than from agencies in town, although tickets bought from agencies often include free connections to the far-flung terminals. Allow at least 1hr 30min to get from the city centre to any bus station. Due to crowds it's advisable not to attempt bus travel at the end of Ramadan.

Pulogebang terminal New terminal 18km to the east, with the most buses heading to east Java and Bali.

Kampung Rambutan 20km south, has the most frequent departures to Bogor and Bandung.

Lebak Bulus, 18km to the southwest, and **Kalideres**, 17km west, have frequent departures for all points west in both Java and Sumatra, including Labuan and Merak.

Destinations Frequent departures for Bandung (4hr 30min); Bogor (1–2hr); Bukittinggi (30hr); Denpasar (24hr); Labuan (3hr 30min); Medan (2 days); Merak (3hr); Padang (31hr); Pangandaran (12hr); Solo (13hr); Surabaya (15hr); Yogya (12hr).

BY FERRY

All Pelni ferries dock at Tanjung Priok harbour in the northeast of the city. There is a Trans Jakarta bus stop about 500m south

MERAK AND FERRIES TO SUMATRA

Near the northwestern tip of Java, **Merak** is the port for ferries across the Sunda Straits to Bakauheni on Sumatra. Regular ferries **to Sumatra** leave roughly every hour throughout the day and less frequently at night (2hr 20min; Rp15,000). Crowds of buses connect with the ferries to take you on to Bandar Lampung (1hr 30min; Rp30,000). To avoid any hassle in Merak, consider the DAMRI's convenient bus-boat-bus combination tickets (from Rp155,000; 6–7hr), with several morning departures from Gambir.

of the harbour, connecting to Jl Jaksa's Sarinah stop (take the #12 corridor then switch to #1 at Kota), while taxis should cost around Rp120,000 in bad traffic. The Pelni booking office (☎021 6385 0960) is at Jl Gajah Mada 14, about 200m south of the Sawah Besar stop on the #1 busway route. Tickets can be bought from numerous agents around town.

Destinations Ambon (fortnightly; 4 days); Belawan (for Medan; weekly; 2 days); Makassar (2 weekly; 2 days); Pontianak (2 monthly; 4 days); Pulau Batam (weekly; 30hr); Surabaya (2 fortnightly; 22hr); Ternate (monthly; 5 days).

BY TRAIN

There are four central train stations (and dozens of minor suburban ones). All train stations are linked by the Trans Jakarta network to Jl Jaksa (Sarinah stop). Tickets can be booked at the station's ticket window, the nearest Indomaret or Alfamart, or online at ⊛tiket.kereta-api.co.id (Bahasa Indonesia) or a more user-friendly agent such as ⊛tiket.com. **Gambir** (☎021 386 2363) is the most popular and convenient, with executive and business-class trains heading all across West and Central Java – including Yogya, Surakarta (Solo), Bogor and Bandung. The office at the north end of Gambir (daily 7.30am–7pm) sells tickets for the *Parahyangan Express* to Bandung and the *Argolawu Express* to Yogya and Solo. The walk from Gambir to Jl Jaksa takes 20min, while taxis are also available for around Rp25,000 from Gambir to Jaksa; avoid the touts and head for the Blue Bird or Express taxi ranks. Ojeks outside Gambir are especially handy during peak hours (around Rp20,000).

Pasar Senen The most useful of the other stations (☎021 421 0006), east of the city centre, serving economy-class trains heading to all points east.

Destinations From Gambir station unless stated otherwise: Bandung (7 daily; 3hr); Banjar (for Pangandaran, from Pasar Senen; 2 daily; 8hr); Bogor (every 20min; 1hr 30min); Purwokerto (Gambir and Pasar Senen; 12 daily; 5–6hr); Solobapan, Solo (5 daily; 7hr–10hr 25min); Surabaya (5 daily; 9hr–14hr 30min); Yogyakarta (Gambir and Pasar Senen; 9 daily; 6hr 50min–8hr 40min).

INFORMATION

Tourist office Jakarta's Visitor Information Centre is inside the Jakarta Theatre building next to *Burger King*, opposite Sarinah's department store on Jl Wahid Hasyim, near Jl Jaksa (Mon–Fri 7.30am–6pm, Sat 9am–2pm; ☎021 314 2067). Useful maps and brochures covering Jakarta are available here, and the English-speaking staff are friendly.

GETTING AROUND

BY BUS

Trans Jakarta busway system The only bus service (daily 5am–10pm) in Jakarta with designated stops and by far the easiest and most useful service for tourists. It runs from the Harmoni Central Busway to Kalideres, Ancol, Pulo Gadung, Rawamangun, Rambutan, Ragunan and Blok M, with other useful stops being Sarinah (for Jl Jaksa) and Kota (for Old Batavia). With its own designated bus lane, it's also quicker than other transport services. In order to pay the fare (Rp3500 one-way; flat fare), you'll need to pick up a "Jakcard" (Rp40,000, including Rp20,000 credit) from the ticket office at the station and then scan it at the turnstile.

Other buses In recent years, Jakarta's other bus lines have been pulled back to minimize overlap with the Trans Jakarta system, and thus their usefulness for travellers has greatly diminished. Among those remaining relevant are the small, pale-blue angkots (minivans; minimum fare Rp3000) that operate out of Kota bus station. Large coaches found all over the city charge Rp4000–7000 (Rp8000 for a/c buses). To alight, hail the driver or conductor with "*kiri!*" (left) or rap the overhead rail with a coin.

BY BAJAJ

The two-stroke motorized rickshaws, or *bajaj* (pronounced "ba-jais"), monopolize the city's backstreets. *Bajaj* are banned from major thoroughfares such as Jl Thamrin, so you might get dropped off in an inconvenient spot for your final destination. A journey from Jl Jaksa to the post office should cost about Rp20,000, and from Jl Jaksa to Gambir should cost Rp15,000. Bargain hard.

BY TAXI

Jakarta's taxis are numerous and, providing you know your way around the city, inexpensive. Many taxi drivers will take the "scenic route" to your destination if you seem unsure. Recommended firms are Blue Bird (☎021 798 9000) and Express (☎021 2650 9000). Most drivers speak little to no English, but will usually use the meter ("*argo*") without being asked; fares depend on how long you spend stuck in Jakarta's infamous traffic jams (a half-hour ride should cost about Rp120,000). Although meters begin at Rp6500, the minimum fare is around Rp10,000. Women should avoid travelling in taxis alone at night as there have been reports of assaults and robberies. Alternatively, you can download the Uber or Grab apps to find a car to your destination, or Gojek to find an ojek (see p.168).

ACCOMMODATION

Jakarta's cluster of backpacker-oriented lodgings fills up fast and should be booked ahead. Most budget places are on or around Jl Jaksa, the city's old travellers' enclave to the south of Medan Merdeka, though good alternatives are popping up elsewhere, particularly in the Cikini Raya area, 2km southeast of Jaksa.

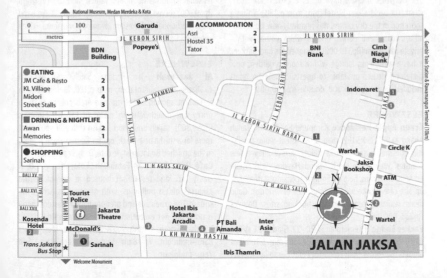

JALAN JAKSA

JALAN JAKSA

Asri Jl Kebon Sirih Barat I Gang 10/18 ☎ 021 314 7684; map p.183. Hidden down a narrow lane across from *Hostel 35*, this homestay is a quiet retreat from the noise of Jaksa, with spotless rooms at a bargain price, each with a/c and attached mandi and some with cable TV (Rp170,000). Complimentary coffee and tea around the clock. Doubles **Rp150,000**

Hostel 35 Jl Kebon Sirih Barat 35 ☎ 021 392 0331; map p.183. One of the more welcoming hostels around Jaksa, this refurbished hostel has a good range on offer, including a/c rooms (Rp250,000) with new fittings and widescreen TVs. Even the somewhat scruffy cheaper rooms come with inside bathrooms and breakfast. Doubles **Rp150,000**

Tator Jl Jaksa 37 ☎ 021 3192 3940; map p.183. This cool and quiet family-run hotel is a travellers' favourite and is often fully booked. Aside from the cell-like fan singles on the top floor (Rp100,000), all the ageing but well-kept rooms have a/c and inside bathrooms, including a few singles (Rp180,000). Breakfast is included in the price and there is a lovely seating area at the front. Doubles **Rp200,000**

CIKINI RAYA

Capsule Hotel Old Batavia Jl Cikini Raya 60 Z ☎ 021 390 5123, ✉ book.batavia.mch@gmail.com; map p.180. Welcoming new hostel with spotless pod-style, state-of-the-art dorms that come with lockers, duvets and no fewer than four electric sockets. There are also a few cramped but stylish doubles, helpful staff and a simple breakfast. Cosy ambience in the common areas – excellent for sharing a Bintang with fellow travellers. Dorms **Rp180,000**, doubles **Rp380,000**

Six Degrees Jl Cikini Raya 60 B–C ☎ 021 314 1657, 🌐 jakarta-backpackers-hostel.com; map p.180. Within a short hop of the city centre, this relatively new hostel has all-a/c rooms and dorms, one of which comes with a private bathroom (Rp310,000). Designed for backpackers, it has a welcoming lounge with a rooftop garden, pool table and kitchen available to guests. Simple breakfast included. Dorms **Rp115,000**, doubles **Rp280,000**

ELSEWHERE

Green Apple Residence Kampung Bali X 14A, Tanah Abang ☎ 021 390 5192; map p.180. Great-value family-run guesthouse set down a quiet, narrow alley a few minutes' walk from Jl KH Wahid Hasyim, with clean en-suite a/c rooms, helpful, English-speaking staff and an on-site café (in the works at the time of writing). Good deals available through online booking sites. Doubles **Rp235,000**

Packer Lodge Jl Kemurnian IV 20–22, Glodok 21 ☎ 021 629 0162, 🌐 jakarta.thepackerlodge.com; map p.180. Just around the corner from colourful Petak Sembilan market

and the Vihara Jin de Yuan, and a 15min walk from Old Batavia, with well-appointed a/c rooms and pod-style dorms fitted with lockers. There's a cosy common area and kitchen, and breakfast is included. Dorms **Rp140,000**, Doubles **Rp280,000**

EATING

There is a great deal more variation to the cuisine here than elsewhere in the country, from a wealth of affordable fine dining options to a thriving street food scene.

JALAN JAKSA

Some of the best-value street food in the city can be found at the stalls crammed along Jl HA Salim around its intersection with Jl KH Wahid Hasyim.

JM Cafe & Resto Jl Jaksa 41; map p.183. Great place for a beef or mutton curry (Rp40,000) at the quieter southern end of Jl Jaksa, which supplements its Indian dishes with live European football and is a popular travellers' hangout day and night. Bintang Rp45,000. Daily 8.30am–4am.

KL Village Jl Jaksa 21–23; map p.183. The best value on the street and deservedly the most popular with both locals and travellers, serving cheap Indonesian food (*nasi goreng* Rp13,500) and a good range of Chinese, Indian, Malay and Thai cuisine (including *roti canai* from Rp8000 and an amazing *tom yum* soup for Rp23,500). Packed in the evenings, so be prepared to wait for your meal. Daily 8am–2am.

Midori Jl KH Wahid Hasyim 106 ☎ 021 314 8957, 🌐 restoranmidori.com; map p.183. Hidden down a small alley off the busy main road, this Japanese restaurant offers a pleasant escape from the bustle of Jaksa, with reasonably authentic udon, ramen and bento (from Rp50,000) served in classy, dim-lit surrounds. A live band plays traditional Indonesian *keroncong* music on Friday evenings. Daily 10am–10pm.

ELSEWHERE

Al Jazeerah Jl Raden Saleh 58, Cikini 🌐 aljazeerahrestaurant.com; map p.180. Middle Eastern restaurant serving authentic pan-Arab cuisine, with a pricey but mouthwatering menu of kebabs, hummus (Rp58,300), salads and good Turkish coffee. If you're just there for a shisha or a snack, opt for floor-cushion seating in the attached Bedouin-style café. Daily 9am–2am.

Café Batavia Taman Fatahillah, Kota; map p.180. A classy café and restaurant housed in one of central Jakarta's oldest buildings, with great views across the square. The expensive and predominantly Western menu is good but not exceptional (club sandwich Rp79,000); it's the historic setting you're paying for. Mon–Thurs 8am–midnight, Fri 8am–1am, Sat 7am–1am, Sun 7am–midnight.

DRINKING AND NIGHTLIFE

Though many travellers passing through don't leave Jl Jaksa in the evening, preferring to hang out in one of the low-key bars along the road, Jakarta has much else to offer at night, including hundreds of bars and nightclubs and a wide range of entertainment.

Aphrodite Bar & Restaurant Jl HR Rasuna Said Kav 22 Ⓦ aphroditebar.com; map p.180. Featuring cold beer, finger foods, a couple of pool tables and a slew of flatscreen TVs, this sports bar near the Australian embassy draws a mixed crowd of locals and expats. Mon–Thurs 6am–2am, Fri & Sat 6am–3am, Sun 6am–12.30am.

Camden Jl Gandaria I 336 ☎021 722 9737; map p.180. Perhaps Jakarta's best approximation of an English pub (though the red telephone box might be a touch of overkill), with a cool, dark-wood interior and a pleasant beer garden outside – a good mix of locals and Cikini-based backpackers. Mon–Thurs & Sun 5pm–2am, Fri & Sat 5pm–3am.

Cazbar Jl Mega Kuningan Ⓦ thecazbar.com; map p.180. Very popular with expats, *Cazbar* has a sports bar upstairs with a pool table, darts and screenings of English premier league football, as well as occasional live music downstairs (check website for schedule). Free wi-fi. Daily 7am–2am.

Memories Jl Jaksa 17 ☎0812 9022 1355; map p.183. The most popular evening drinking den on Jl Jaksa and a great place to meet fellow travellers. There is a huge menu of Western and Indonesian dishes, though most patrons don't come for the food, which is on the expensive side (*cap cai* Rp30,000). It also has one of Jaksa's largest libraries, as well as some decent rooms (fan or a/c Rp120,000/175,000). Daily 8am–2am.

SHOPPING

While Jakarta has no particular indigenous craft of its own, the capital isn't a bad place to go souvenir shopping.

Antiques Market Jl Surabaya, Pasar Cikini; map p.180. Set one block west of Cikini Station in Jakarta's Menteng district, this strip of small shops is a great place to find all manner of trinkets and souvenirs, from wooden carvings and jewellery to old Dutch banknotes. Daily 10am–6pm.

Periplus Plaza Indonesia; map p.180. There are a couple of bookshops in the basement of the smart Indonesia Plaza, but the best by far is this branch of the excellent Periplus chain, with a good selection of English titles. Daily 10am–10pm.

Sarinah Jl KH Wahid Hasyim 11, map p.183. The fourth and fifth floors of this department store are given over to souvenirs, with *wayang kulit* and *wayang golek* puppets, leather bags and woodcarvings. Batik fabrics are sold on the fourth floor. Daily 9am–10pm.

Tanah Abang Textile Market Jl Fachrudin 5; map p.180. A few blocks west of Sarinah at the end of Jl KH Wahid Hasyim, this multi-block complex is the oldest

wholesale market in Indonesia (dating from 1735) and the largest of its kind in Southeast Asia. Packed with shoppers at weekends. Daily 8.30am–4.30pm.

DIRECTORY

Banks and exchange Banks with ATMs are available throughout the city. Cimb Niaga, near the northern end of Jl Jaksa on Jl Kebon Siri, offers the best exchange rates in town.

Embassies Australia, Jl H Rasuna Said Kav 15–16 (☎021 2550 5555); Canada, World Trade Centre, 6th Floor, Jl Jend Sudirman Kav 29 (☎021 2550 7800); Malaysia, Jl Rasuna Said Kav 1–3, Kuningan (☎021 522 4947); New Zealand, 10th Floor, Jl Asia Afrika 8 (☎021 2995 5800); Singapore, Jl Rasuna Said 2, Kuningan (☎021 2995 0400); South Africa, Wisma GKBI, 7th Floor, Jl Jend Sudirman Kav 28 (☎021 2991 2500); Thailand, Jl Imam Bonjol 74 (☎021 390 4055); UK, Jl Patra Kuningan Raya Blok L5–6 (☎021 2356 5200); US, Jl Medan Merdeka Selatan 5 (☎021 3435 9000).

Hospitals and clinics The best in town are the MMC hospital on Jl Rasuna Said (☎021 520 3435) and the SOS Medika Klinik (☎021 5794 8600) on Jl Lingkar

4

★ TREAT YOURSELF: ROOFTOP BARS

Rooftop bars and lounges have swept Jakarta, making the most of the booming skyline with their unbeatable views and plush, sophisticated surrounds. It's worth the splurge to check out at least one of these venues, where a cocktail will set you back about Rp75,000–120,000. Some of the best spots are within easy reach of Jaksa:

Awan *Kosenda Hotel*, Jl KH Wahid Hasyim 127 ☎021 3193 6868; map p.183. Relatively tiny ninth-floor bar, which is laidback and good value and tastefully adorned with lush greenery.

BART *Artotel*, Jl Sunda 3 ☎021 3192 5888; map p.180. On the top floor of the *Artotel* behind Sarinah is a sleek, spacious lounge with pretty views, a broad cocktail selection and no strict dress code.

Skye BCA Tower, Grand Indonesia Mall ☎021 2358 6996; map p.180. Jakarta's highest rooftop lounge, occupying the 56th floor of the BCA Tower and entered through the Grand Indonesia Mall. Enforces a smart-casual dress code (no shorts, tanktops or sandals) and has hefty minimum charges for tables (upwards of Rp2,000,000), though you can stand or sit at the bar for a minimum charge of around Rp200,000.

Mega, both in Kuningan. Any *Praktek Umum* (public clinic) will treat foreigners cheaply. Dial ☎118 or ☎119 for an ambulance.

Immigration office Jl Pos Kota 4 RT 04/RW 06, Pinangsia, Taman Sari, West Jakarta (☎021 690 4845).

Internet There are cheap internet cafés along Jl Jaksa, among them Greenet (daily 24hr; Rp6000/hr), just north of Tator. Many restaurants have free wi-fi.

Post office The GPO lies to the north of Lapangan Benteng (Mon–Sat 8am–8pm, Sun 9am–5pm), northeast of Medan Merdeka.

Tourist police Jl Wahid Hasyim 9 (2nd Floor of Jakarta Theatre) ☎021 526 4073. For emergencies, dial ☎110.

KRAKATAU

At 10am on August 27, 1883, an explosion equivalent to ten thousand Hiroshima atomic bombs tore apart **KRAKATAU ISLAND**; the boom was heard as far away as Sri Lanka. As the eruption column towered 40km into the atmosphere, a thick mud rain began to fall over the area and the temperature plunged by 5°C. One single **tsunami** as tall as a seven-storey building raced outwards, erasing three hundred towns and villages and killing more than 36,000 people. Once into the open sea, the waves travelled at up to 700km/hr, reaching South Africa and scuttling ships in Auckland harbour. Two-thirds of Krakatau had vanished for good, and on those parts that remained, not so much as a seed or an insect survived.

Today, the crumbled caldera is clearly visible west of the beaches near Merak and Carita, its sheer northern cliff face soaring 800m straight out of the sea. But it is the glassy black cone of **Anak Krakatau**, the child of Krakatau volcano, that visitors come to see, a barren wasteland that's still growing and still very much active. It first reared its head from the seas in 1930, and now sits angrily smoking among the remains of the older peaks. To get here requires a several-hour **motorboat trip**, then a half-hour walk up to the crater, from where you can see black lava flows, sulphurous fumaroles and smoke. The most convenient way to visit the volcano is from **Carita**, although tours tend to be cheaper from Sumatra.

Carita

Boasting one of the most sheltered stretches of sea in the western reaches of Java, Carita is the island's best spot to arrange **tours to Krakatau** as well as to **Ujung Kulon National Park**. When you arrive in town, be wary of unlicensed guides. Krakatau Tour (☎0813 8666 8811, ⓦkrakatau-tour.com) is a reputable company that offers day-trips from Rp5,000,000 for groups of three and Rp5,500,000 for groups of up to seven people, with discounts on weekdays.

ARRIVAL AND DEPARTURE

By bus and angkot Buses run from the Kalideres bus station in Jakarta to Labuan (3hr 30min); from here you can catch an angkot to Carita – don't get conned into taking transport to the angkot stop, which is just a 2min walk towards the seafront and to the right.

ACCOMMODATION AND EATING

All accommodation in Carita is on or close to the main seaside road, known as Jl Carita Raya or Jl Pantai Carita. Prices shoot up at the weekend, when the town is invaded by jet-skiers. The public parts of the beach in Carita are lined with food carts selling *murtabak*, *sate* and *soto* (traditional soup).

The Sunset View Jl Pantai Carita ☎0253 801075, ⓦaugusta-ind.com. One of the best-value places in town, with a pool, a good location near the marina and up to 40 percent discounts outside peak season. Doubles **Rp380,000**

BOGOR

Located 300m above sea level and just over an hour's train journey south of Jakarta, **BOGOR** is home to the famously lush **Kebun Raya Bogor** or **Botanical Gardens** (daily 7.30am–5pm; Rp25,000), founded by Sir Stamford Raffles in 1811. Worth a day-trip from Jakarta, the magnificent gardens offer respite from the congested streets of Bogor, and it is a delight to wander the shady pathways between towering bamboo stands, climbing bougainvillea, tropical rainforest and ponds full of water lilies and fountains. Near the gardens' main entrance is the **Zoological Museum** (daily 8am–4pm; included in ticket), which houses some 30,000 specimens, including a complete skeleton of a blue whale, a stuffed Javan rhino and, most impressively, the remains of a huge coconut crab.

Bogor is also an ideal base for hiking in **Mount Halimun Salak National Park**, as well as whitewater rafting and visiting hot springs, waterfalls and some of Java's most picturesque terraced rice paddies.

ARRIVAL AND DEPARTURE

By bus The Bogor bus terminal is about 500m southeast of the gardens.

Destinations Bandung (every 20min; 3–4hr); Jakarta (every 15min; 1–2hr).

By train The train station is about 500m northwest of the Botanical Gardens, with Commuterline connections to Jakarta's Cikini Station (every 20min; 1hr 30min).

By bemo The main bemo stop is behind the bus terminal, but the best place to pick up bemos is by the train station. Bemo #2 runs between the station and the Botanical Gardens; #3 runs between the station and the bus terminal.

INFORMATION

Tourist office A useful tourist information centre lies about 50m to the right on Jl Kapten Muslihat 51 when exiting the train station at Taman Topi (daily 8am–5pm; ☎0813 8393 1844, ✉rswandi@yahoo.com). Eco-tours to Mount Halimun Salak National Park can be arranged here.

ACCOMMODATION AND EATING

Night stalls along Jl Pengadillan set up after 6pm. There are also busy daytime stalls along Jl Kaptan Muslihat.

Abu Pensione Jl Mayor Oking 15 ☎0251 832 2893 or ☎0815 8626 5324. With friendly staff, tidy rooms, river views and good breakfasts (Rp35,000), this is the best budget place by the train station. The pricier rooms have hot water and a/c (Rp300,000), and the staff can help with travel bookings. Manager Selfi leads interesting 3–4hr walking tours along the river (Rp250,000). To get here, turn right out of the station then take your first right down Jl Mayor Oking. Doubles Rp150,000

Hostel Bogor Jl Narasoma 3/5 ☎0251 831 9020, ⊕hostelbogor.com. Cosy, converted home in the quiet backstreets 3km north of the gardens. Simple rooms are clean and come with shared bathrooms and terraces. Friendly owner Ika cooks a good Indonesian breakfast and allows free use of the kitchen, which is stocked with tea, coffee, beers and soft drinks. Doubles Rp200,000

BANDUNG AND AROUND

Set 750m above sea level, and protected by a fortress of watchful volcanoes 190km southeast of Jakarta, **BANDUNG** is a centre of industry and traditional arts. Sundanese culture has remained intact here since the fifth century when the first Hindu Sundanese settled in this part of West Java. Modern Bandung, although teeming with noise and traffic and certainly far removed from its quaint colonial days, remains one of the nation's cultural and intellectual hubs, bubbling with life in its myriad cafés, restaurants, bars, open markets and flashy new malls. Still, the top attraction for most visitors to the area is the nearby **Tangkuban Prahu volcano**.

WHAT TO SEE AND DO

On Jalan Asia-Afrika, northeast of the *alun-alun* (town square), is the **Gedung Merdeka** building, host of the first Asia-Afrika Conference in 1955 and known as the Asia-Afrika or Liberty Building. Inside, a small museum (Tues–Thurs 8am–4pm, Fri 2–4pm, Sat & Sun 9am–4pm; free) commemorates the conference. Running north from here is **Jalan Braga**, the chic shopping boulevard of 1920s Bandung. The side streets that run off Jalan Braga were notorious for their raucous bars and brothels. The seediness remains today, as this historic district comes alive each night with its slew of lively bars and pubs.

A twenty-minute walk to the northeast takes you to the impressive 1920s **Gedung Sate Building**, Jl Diponegoro 22, which gets its name from the regular globules on its gold-leaf spire, resembling meat on a skewer. The excellent **Geographical Museum** (Mon–Thurs 8am–4pm, Sat & Sun 8am–2pm; Rp10,000) is nearby at Jl Diponegoro 57, and displays mountains of fossils, as well as the skeletons of dinosaurs and a 4m mammoth.

ARRIVAL AND DEPARTURE

By plane The airport is 5km northwest of the city centre (taxi Rp80,000).

Destinations Balikpapan (2 daily; 2hr 5min); Denpasar (6 daily; 1hr 40min); Kuala Lumpur (3 daily; 2hr 10min); Makassar (daily; 2hr 10min); Pangandaran (daily; 35min); Singapore (daily; 1hr 45min); Solo (daily; 1hr 10min); Surabaya (6 daily; 1hr 15min).

By bus The main terminal is Leuwi Panjang, 5km south of the city centre, with buses heading west to Bogor and Jakarta; Cicaheum terminal on the eastern edge of town is for those heading to central and east Java. Both terminals

BANDUNG

N

ACCOMMODATION
By Moritz	1
Chez Bon	2
De Halimun	3

EATING
Bandung Suki	2
Braga Permai	3
Paskal Food Market	1

DRINKING & NIGHTLIFE
Amnesia	1
Beer Express	3
Classic Rock	2

SHOPPING
| Jeans Street | 1 |
| Trans Studio Mal | 2 |

Map labels: Lembang & Tangkuban Prahu; Bandung Zoo; Bemo Stop & Dago; JL PASUPATI; JL CIPAGANTI; JL CHAMPELAS; JEANS STI; JL PASTEUR; Geographical Museum; JL DIPONEGORO; Gedung Sate; Airport (2.5km); Istana Plaza; JL PASIR KALIKI; JL PAJAJARAN; JL UANDA; JL MARTADINATA; JL SUMBAWA; Bandung Indah Plaza; JL CICENDO; Taman Lalu Lintas; JL MERDEKA; JL SUMATRA; JL KEBON KAWUNG; Kebun Raya; Train & Bemo Station; PASKAL HYPER SQUARE; Santosa Hospital; Angkot Station; Arcade Braga City Walk; JL LEMBONG; Grand Royal Panghegar; JL KEBON JATI; JL GARDUJATI; JL BRAGA; Ciaheum Bus Terminal (4km); JL JEND SUDIRMAN; Gedung Merdeka; JL NARIPAN; JL VETERAN; ALUN-ALUN; JL ASIA-AFRIKA; JL DALEM KAUM; JL LENG KECIL; JL ASTANA ANYER; JL OTISTA; Jeans Street; Leuwi Panjang Bus Terminal; Kebun Kelapa Bus Terminal; 0 250 metres; 3 & 2 (2km)

are connected to one another and to the city centre by local DAMRI buses (every 15min; Rp3000).

Destinations Frequent departures unless otherwise stated: Banyuwangi (2 daily; 24hr); Bogor (4hr); Jakarta (4–5hr); Pangandaran (5hr); Yogyakarta (9hr).

By train The train station is located near the city centre, within walking distance of most budget accommodation. The *Argo Willis* (daily 7.30am) is recommended for the scenic ride eastward to Yogyakarta and Surabaya.

Destinations Jakarta (6 daily; 3hr); Surabaya (3 daily; 12–13hr); Yogyakarta (6 daily; 7–8hr).

INFORMATION

Tourist office 227 Jl Ahmad Yani (Mon–Fri 8am–4.30pm; ☏ 022 721 0761, ⓦ bandungtourism.com), on the road to Cicaheum terminal, with friendly, eager staff and a good website covering upcoming events.

GETTING AROUND

Buses and minibuses Bandung's white-and-blue DAMRI buses cost Rp3800 for non-a/c and Rp5000 for a/c. The buses ply routes between the bus terminals through the centre of town. Red angkots (minibuses)

also run a useful circular route, via the train station and the *alun-alun* (town square), to the Kebun Kelapa bus terminal, which serves Cicaheum bus terminal, Dago, Ledeng and Lembang.

Becaks and taxis Becaks line the major streets and are useful for short journeys where the numerous one-way streets can make an otherwise simple taxi journey expensive. Regardless of meters, the minimum taxi charge is usually Rp25,000. Blue Bird (☏ 022 756 1234) is recommended.

ACCOMMODATION

Bandung has some good-value budget accommodation right in the centre, with most options only a 10- to 15min walk from the train station.

By Moritz Jl Belakang Pasar/Luxor Permai 35 ☏ 022 420 5788. One of the longest-standing backpacker-oriented places in Bandung, this remains a great place to meet other travellers. The friendly staff can arrange tours and onward travel, and the bright rooms, with hot water and breakfast included, are a bargain. Doubles Rp130,000

Chez Bon Jl Braga 45 ☏ 022 426 0600, ⓦ chez-bon.com. Opened by culinary celebrity Bondan Winarno in 2013, this shiny but sterile hostel is set right in the heart of Braga, with clean, a/c dorm rooms with two to sixteen beds. Hot-water showers, private lockers and complimentary breakfasts on the rooftop. Dorms Rp150,000

De Halimun Jl Halimun 12 ☎022 730 2260, ⓦhalimunhotel.com. Welcoming guesthouse in the quiet leafy suburbs 2km southeast of Braga, with all a/c rooms with hot-water showers, centred around an attractive courtyard, with a good restaurant and pleasant sitting areas. Doubles Rp325,000

EATING

Bandung Suki Jl Braga 70. Serves an affordable selection of Chinese, Thai, Korean and seafood dishes in a welcoming setting with minimalist decor. The speciality is dim sum and spring rolls (Rp20,000 for three), and there are regular discounts and promotions. Daily 10am–10pm.

Braga Permai Jl Braga 58 ☎022 423 3778, ⓦbragapermai .com. Local and expat favourite with nearly a century of history and plenty of outdoor seating right in the thick of Braga's action. Despite its popularity it remains one of the street's cheapest options, with a large Sundanese and Italian menu (margherita pizza Rp40,000). Daily 9am–midnight.

★**Paskal Food Market** Paskal Hyper Square, Jl Pasirkaliki 25–27. Huge and pleasant open-air food court offering over a thousand dishes from Southeast Asia (meals from Rp10,000). It's one of the most popular evening hangout spots in Bandung, with live music at weekends. Order from as many stalls as you like, then take a receipt from the main cashier and wait for each dish to arrive at your table. Mon–Fri 11am–11.30pm, Sat & Sun 10am–midnight.

DRINKING AND NIGHTLIFE

Bandung's liveliest (and seediest) nightlife centres around the Jl Braga area, although dozens of other bars, pubs and entertainment venues are scattered across town.

Amnesia Pascal Hyper Square, Jl Pasirkaliki. Flashy nightclub with a spacious dance floor often packed at weekends with hundreds of patrons that include students, businessmen and expats. There's a blend of house and remixed chart tunes and karaoke upstairs. Tues–Sun 10pm–4am.

Beer Express Jl Braga 42. Dark, smoky drinking hall open to the street right in the heart of Braga, with beer towers, waterpipes and live DJs blaring technopop and drawing a young, mostly student, crowd. Large Bintang Rp50,000. Daily 3pm–4am.

Classic Rock Jl. Lembong 1. Tightly packed venue at the north end of Jl Braga where fans of the genre come to revel in old-school musical nostalgia as Bandung's best rock bands blast covers and just jam. Music starts at 8pm, and there is good finger food and interesting cocktails. Daily 6pm–12.30am.

ENTERTAINMENT

Pick up the *Jakarta and Java Kini* magazine from the tourist information office or check out ⓦwhatsnewjakarta.com to find out about special performances.

Ram fighting Though held less frequently these days, *adu domba* (ram fighting) still takes place about once a month on Sunday mornings near the Sari Ater hot spring, 30km from the city. Check ahead at the tourist office, then take a Subang minibus from the train station to Ciater (Rp15,000). To the sound of Sundanese flutes and drums, the magnificently presented rams lunge at each other until one of them fades; there's no blood, just flying wool and clouds of dust.

Saung Angklung Jl Padasuka 118 ☎022 727 1714, ⓦangklung-udjo.co.id. *Angklung* (bamboo instrument) musical performances are held at this venue east of town near Cicaheum bus terminal (daily 3.30–5pm; weekday/weekend Rp100,000/110,000).

SHOPPING

Shoppers flock to Bandung from all across the region for its clothing markets and flashy malls.

Jeans Street Jl Cihampelas. Jalan Cihampelas, known to Westerners as Jeans Street, is set to the north of the city centre, lined with shops and factory outlets selling cheap T-shirts, bags, shoes and jeans.

Trans Studio Mall Jl Gatot Subroto. The largest of Bandung's many malls, complete with an indoor theme park. Daily 10am–10pm.

DIRECTORY

Banks and ATMs are all over town, and two Golden Megacorp moneychangers, at Jl Juanda 89 opposite the Telkom building and at Jl Oto Iskandardinata 180, have excellent rates.

Hospital Santosa Hospital is just next to the train station at Jl Kebonjati 38 (☎022 4248 333).

Police station Central Bandung Station (Polresta Bandung Tengah), Jl Jend Ahmad Yani 282 ☎022 720 0058. Dial ☎110 for emergencies.

Post office Jl Asia-Afrika 49 at Jl Banceuy (Mon–Sat 8am–9pm).

TANGKUBAN PRAHU VOLCANO

The mountainous region to the north of Bandung is the heart of the Parahyangan Highlands – the "Home of the Gods" – a highly volcanic area considered by the Sundanese to be the nucleus of their spiritual world. A pleasant day out from Bandung on public transport takes you first to the 2084m-high **Tangkuban Prahu** (daily 7am–5pm; Mon–Fri Rp200,000

Sat & Sun Rp300,000), the most visited volcano in West Java, 29km north of Bandung. To get here from Bandung, take a Subang minibus from the train station to the turn-off for the volcano (30min; Rp15,000), then either take an ojek (40,000; 10min) or it's a 5km hike.

After decades of dormancy, the volcano erupted several times in October 2013, and continues to spew out vast quantities of sulphurous gases. The **information booth** at the summit car park has details about crater walks; guides will offer their services, but it's pretty obvious where you should and shouldn't go – just be sure to wear strong hiking boots. The main crater, **Kawah Ratu**, is the one you can see down into from the end of the summit road, a huge, dull, grey cauldron with a few coloured lakes. From the summit you can trek down to **Domas Crater**, site of a small working sulphur mine.

PANGANDARAN

Once a humble fishing village, **PANGANDARAN** has become West Java's top beach resort, with sweeping stretches of black, volcanic sand and a smattering of nearby natural wonders – most notably the spectacular **Green Canyon**. Set between two long, arching bays, the town is a cluster of hotels funnelled into a narrow isthmus, rising above it a lush, bulky headland that makes up the **National Park**. Pangandaran fills up at weekends and during holidays, while at other times it can be a bit of a ghost town, with plenty of room to relax on its beaches.

WHAT TO SEE AND DO

There are some wonderful hikes within easy striking distance of town, the nearest being inside **Pangandaran National Park** (Mon–Fri Rp210,000, Sat & Sun Rp310,000), just across the channel at the south end of town. A guide (from Rp100,000 for 2hr) is highly recommended to lead you through the caves and spot most of the resident wildlife, which includes black monkeys, macaques, porcupines, monitor lizards and bats. Within the park are also a handful of pristine beaches, the most popular being **Pasir Putih**. Its white strip of sand is visible from Pangandaran Beach, from where boats shuttle day-trippers, bypassing the hike (and the hefty national park fee) for Rp40,000 per person (minimum of four people). There's good surfing at the main beach, and it's a suitable place for learners. Two-hour lessons run at about Rp200,000.

Green Canyon

Well worth the 30km trip west from Pangandaran, the **Green Canyon** (Mon–Thurs, Sat & Sun 7.30am–5pm, Fri 1–5pm; Rp12,500; 45min boat excursion Rp200,000 for a maximum of five passengers) – known in Sundanese as Cukang Taneuh – is a series of spectacular bends in the Cijulang River as it passes through the sheer walls of an old cave system. From the small docks by the ticket office, you ride up the river in small boats, keeping an eye out for snakes and monitor lizards and then pausing at the canyon's deepest point for a swim.

Green Valley

Seventeen kilometres northwest of Pangandaran, the lazy stretch of the Citumang River known as the **Green Valley** is broken up by pretty cascades in a lush, narrow valley. Caves, cliffs and rope swings line the river, and you can body surf most of the way to the dam at the end (daily 7.30am–5pm; Rp20,000, required guide Rp150,000/person, including life-jacket). Most travellers reach both the Green Valley and the Green Canyon on all-inclusive day-tours (Rp350,000), offered widely in Pangandaran – going it alone is almost as expensive. At the entrance, a guide is required if you intend to float the river, which is at least half the fun. Navigating the route from Pangandaran can be tricky, especially the more direct routes that traverse mud trails through rice paddies. The simplest route runs west about 12km out of town along the main road, then taking a right at the town of Cibenda, from where the Green Valley (known locally as Citumang) is about 3km up the road.

ARRIVAL AND DEPARTURE

Pangandaran has a city admission charge of Rp5500, collected at the gates outside town.

By plane The airport is about 30km west of town. Susi Air operates one daily flight each to Jakarta (1hr) and Bandung (35min). An ojek from here costs about Rp100,000 and a shared taxi (four people) about Rp250,000. Susi Air's booking office is just across from the bus station.

By bus Pangandaran's bus station is a 20min walk (or a Rp10,000 becak ride) north of the town centre.

Destinations Unless otherwise specified, hourly departures to the following: Bandung (6hr); Banjar (2hr); Jakarta (8 daily; 9hr); Sidareja (1hr 30min).

By train The nearest train stations are at Sidareja to the northeast and Banjar to the northwest – both linked by buses. Although closer to Pangandaran by bus, Sidareja has fewer connections, including just one daily train to Yogyakarta (11.55am; 3hr 15min).

Destinations From Banjar: Bandung (6 daily; 4hr); Jakarta (Pasar Senen station; 2 daily; 8hr 30min); Yogyakarta (6 daily; 4hr).

INFORMATION AND ACTIVITIES

Tourist office The head of the local surfing club runs an unofficial tourist office (☎ 0813 1376 4535) beside *Bamboo Beach Bar & Café*.

Surfing Pangandaran Surf (☎ 0821 3044 4007, ⊛ pangandaransurf.net), based at *Mini Tiga*, offers lessons (one-day/two-days Rp250,000/Rp450,000) and board rental (Rp100,000/day).

Tours For day-trips to Green Valley, Green Canyon and the national park, the experienced guides at Dindin Tours (☎ 0812 2376 0776) are recommended.

ACCOMMODATION AND EATING

There are a few warung and plenty of restaurants lining the beach, while most accommodation is set in the alleys just across the coastal road.

Bamboo Café & Resto Jl Pa ☎ 0813 1371 8567. Laidback bar and restaurant in a central spot along the beach, with seafood and Javanese specialities like *nasi uduk* (yellow rice with tofu, *tempe* and fried chicken; Rp30,000). This and the neighbouring *Bamboo Beach Bar & Café* are run by brothers, and both are popular spots at weekends when there's live music. Mon–Fri 8am–1am, Sat & Sun until 3am.

Mini Tiga Jl Pamugaran Bulak Laut ☎ 0265 639436, ⊛ minitigahomestay.weebly.com. Welcoming place up an alley from the coastal road across from *Beach Break Bar*. Upstairs rooms come with a/c and spacious bathrooms (Rp200,000), and breakfast is served in the beautiful sitting areas, great for meeting fellow travellers – especially when staff are sharing *arak*. Surfing lessons on offer (Rp200,000; 2hr). Doubles Rp150,000

Panorama à la Plage Jl Pamugaran 1 ☎ 0813 7057. One of Pangandaran's best bargains, set 50m from the beach at the end of the main road to the bus station. The rattan-walled rooms include fan-equipped doubles and singles (Rp75,000), and you can bump up to a/c for Rp150,000. Doubles Rp120,000

THE DIENG PLATEAU

The moody expanse of the **Dieng Plateau** northwest of Yogya lies in a volcanic caldera 2093m above sea level and holds a rewarding mix of multicoloured sulphurous **lakes**, craters that spew pungent sulphuric gases and some of the oldest **Hindu temples** in Java. The volcano is still active – clouds of poisonous gases killed 149 people in 1979 and forced the evacuation of 1200 people in 2011 – and the landscape up on this misty, temperate plain is terraced on nearly every surface with cabbage and potato plantations clinging to the edges of impossible slopes. There are dozens of simple homestays in **Dieng village** and an increasing number of multilingual guides in both Dieng and nearby **Wonosobo**. Though many travellers arrive on day-trips from Yogya, it is worthy of an overnight visit (not least because of the 4hr journey from Yogya). The temples here are interesting and the plateau offers a different, more temperate side to Java.

WHAT TO SEE AND DO

There are numerous trekking options available on the plateau and further afield, as well as sunrise trips to **Sikunir Hill** and **Cebong Lake** (departing from town around 2.30am). All the main attractions can be reached on foot from the village of **Dieng**, just across the fields from the plateau's main temple complex.

The temples

It is believed that the Dieng Plateau was once a fully self-contained **retreat** for priests and pilgrims. Unfortunately, it soon became waterlogged, and the plateau was abandoned in the thirteenth century, only to be rediscovered, drained and restored some six hundred years later by the Dutch. The eight temples left on Dieng are a tiny fraction of what was once a huge complex built by the Sanjayas in the seventh and eighth centuries.

Of these temples, the five that make up the **Arjuna complex** (daily 6.15am–5.15pm; Rp25,000), standing in fields opposite Dieng village, are believed to be the oldest. The northernmost of these two-storey temples, the **Arjuna Temple**, is the oldest on Java (c.680 AD), and was dedicated to Shiva. Next to Arjuna stands **Candi Srikandi**, the exterior of which is adorned with reliefs of Vishnu (on the north wall), Shiva (east) and Brahma (south). **Candi Gatutkaca** overlooks the Arjuna complex 300m to the southwest, and twenty minutes' walk (1km) south of here stands the peculiar-looking **Candi Bima**, its roof adorned with Shiva heads framed in lotus petals.

The lakes

From Candi Bima, you can continue down the road on foot for 1km or so to **Telaga Warna** (coloured lake; daily 8am–5pm; Mon–Fri Rp100,000, Sat & Sun Rp150,000), the best example of Dieng's coloured lakes, where sulphurous deposits shade the water blue, from turquoise to azure. Adjacent to the lake is crystal-clear **Telaga Pengilon**, which makes for beautiful photos in nice weather.

The craters

Around 2km from Candi Gatutkaca is **Sikidang Crater**. This volcanic bowl has numerous hot springs that have appeared through the bubbling mud. Behind the black spring is a walking path that has a great vantage point of the area. There are no safety rails and the path can get slippery when it rains, so take care not to fall into the scalding mud ponds.

ARRIVAL AND DEPARTURE

By bus Buses connect the Dieng Plateau with Yogya, for which you'll need to change buses several times. From Yogya's Jombor terminal, first head to Magelang (Rp25,000), then to Wonosobo (Rp35,000), and finally to Dieng itself (Rp30,000). The complete journey takes roughly 4–5hr. From Jakarta, head west to Purwokerto (5–6hr by train; 9hr by bus), from where frequent buses connect to Wonosobo (Rp20,000).

ACCOMMODATION AND EATING

The tiny village of Dieng skirts Jl Raya Dieng, which runs along the plateau's eastern edge. There are a few warung in the square behind *Hotel Bu Djono*, serving *nasi goreng* (Rp10,000) and the hot herbal drink *purwaceng* (Rp10,000), which locals call the "Javanese Viagra".

Gunung Mas Jl Raya Dieng 42 ☏ 0813 2702 7929. Spotless, if spartan, rooms with hot water and breakfast. The shared, second-storey balcony overlooks a small courtyard removed from the noise from the main road (but not the call to prayer from the adjacent mosque). Doubles Rp200,000

Homestay Bougenville Jl Raya Dieng ☏ 0813 2707 2112. Friendly little place in the centre of town, near the entrance to the Arjuna temple complex. There are five well-kept rooms with comfy beds and decent hot showers on the second floor of the owner's home, tea and coffee on tap and a cosy shared sitting room and balcony. Doubles Rp150,000

DIRECTORY

Bank There's a BNI with an ATM just north of Gunung Mas.

Internet Clinic Computer, just north of Bougenville, has an internet connection (Rp3000/hr).

YOGYAKARTA

YOGYAKARTA (pronounced "Jogjakarta" and often just shortened to Yogya, or "Jogja") ranks as one of the best-preserved and most attractive cities in Java, and is a major centre for the classical **Javanese arts** of batik, ballet, drama, music, poetry and puppet shows. It is also the perfect base from which to explore the temples of Borobudur and Prambanan, or take an early morning hike up **Gunung Merapi**. Tourists flock here, attracted not only by the city's courtly splendour, but also by the cuisine and shopping, and the various language and cultural courses on offer. As a result there are more tourist-oriented hotels in Yogya than anywhere else in Java and, unfortunately, a correspondingly high number of touts, pickpockets and con artists.

Sultan Hamengkubuwono I (also known as **Mangkubumi**) established his court here in 1755, spending the next 37 years building the new capital, with the Kraton as the centrepiece and the court at Solo as the blueprint. In 1946, the capital of the newly declared Republic of Indonesia was moved to Yogya from Jakarta, and the **Kraton** became the unofficial headquarters for the republican movement. The royal household of Yogya continues to enjoy almost slavish devotion from its subjects. After winning the gubernatorial election in 1998, the current sultan – Hamengkubuwono X – worked to negotiate a 2012 ruling that ensured future sultans will inherit the position of governor, with the position of vice-governor going to the sultan of Paku Alam. In what was perhaps a more controversial move, in 2015 the septuagenarian sultan tapped his eldest daughter, Gusti Kanjeng Ratu Pembayun, to become his heir and Yogya's first female sultan.

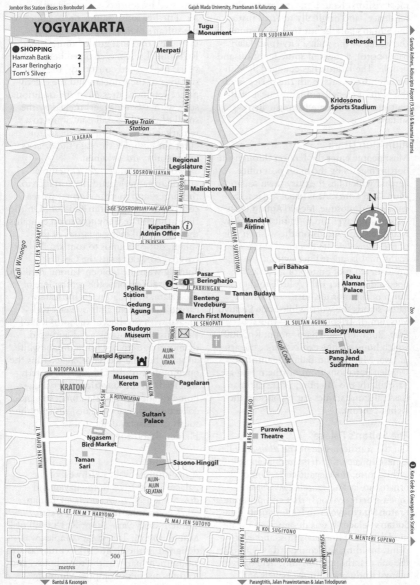

Jombor Bus Station (Buses to Borobudur)

Gajah Mada University, Prambanan & Kaliurang

YOGYAKARTA

● SHOPPING	
Hamzah Batik	2
Pasar Beringharjo	1
Tom's Silver	3

Tugu Monument
JL JEN SUDIRMAN
Bethesda
Merpati
Kridosono Sports Stadium

Tugu Train Station
JL JLAGRAN
JL P MANGKUBUMI

Regional Legislature
JL SOSROWIJAYAN
Maliboro Mall
JL MALIOBORO
JL MATARAM

SEE 'SOSROWIJAYAN' MAP

Mandala Airline
Kepatihan Admin Office ℹ️
JL PAJEKSAN
JL MAYOR SURYOTOMO

Kali Winongo
JL LET JEN SUPRAPTO

Puri Bahasa
Paku Alaman Palace

Pasar Beringharjo
JL A YANI
JL PABRINGAN
Police Station
Taman Budaya
Gedung Agung
Benteng Vredeburg
March First Monument
JL SENOPATI

Sono Budoyo Museum
TRIKORA
Biology Museum

Kali Code
Sasmita Loka Pang Jend Sudirman

Mesjid Agung
ALUN-ALUN UTARA
JL SULTAN AGUNG
JL NOTOPRAJAN

KRATON
Museum Kereta
JL NGASEM
JL ROTOWIJAYAN
ALUN ALUN
Pagelaran
JL BRIG JEN KATAMSO

JL WAHID HASYIM
Sultan's Palace
Purawisata Theatre

Ngasem Bird Market
Taman Sari
Sasono Hinggil
ALUN-ALUN SELATAN

JL LET JEN M T HARYONO
JL MAJ JEN SUTOYO
JL KOL SUGIYONO
JL MENTERI SUPENO
JL PARANGTRITIS
SSINGAMANGARAJA

SEE 'PRAWIROTAMAN' MAP

0 ___ 500
metres

Bantul & Kasongan

Parangtritis, Jalan Prawirotaman & Jalan Tirtodipuran

Garuda Airlines, Adisucipto Airport (9.5km) & Nanamia Pizzeria

Zoo

Kota Gede & Giwangan Bus Station

4

N

The layout of Yogya reflects its character: frenetic, modern and brash on the outside, but with a tranquil, ancient and traditional heart in the **Kraton**, the walled city. Set in a 2km-wide strip of land between the rivers Kali Winongo and Kali Code, this is the focus of interest for most visitors. Kraton means "royal residence" and originally referred just to the **Sultan's Palace**, but today it denotes the whole of the walled city (plus Jalan Malioboro), a town of some ten thousand people. The Kraton has changed little in two hundred years; both the palace, and the 5km of crenellated icing-sugar walls that surround it, date from the first sultan's reign.

Alun-alun Utara

Most people enter the Kraton through the northern gates by the main post office, beyond which lies the busy town square, Alun-alun Utara. As is usual in Java, the city's grand mosque, **Mesjid Agung** (visit outside of prayer times), built in 1773 by Mangkubumi, stands on the western side of the *alun-alun*. It's designed along traditional Javanese lines, with a multi-tiered roof on top of an airy, open-sided prayer hall. A little to the north of the mosque, just by the main gates, stands the worthwhile **Sono Budoyo Museum**, Jl Trikora 6 (Tues–Thurs 8am–2pm, Fri–Sun 8am–noon; Rp5000), which houses a fine exhibition of the arts of Java, Madura and Bali. The intricate wooden partitions from northern Java are particularly eye-catching, as are the many classical stone statues dating back to the eighth century.

The Sultan's Palace

On the southern side of the *alun-alun* lies a masterpiece of understated Javanese architecture, the elegant collection of ornate kiosks and graceful *pendopos* (open-sided pavilions) that comprise the **Kraton Ngayogyokarto Hadiningrat** – the **Sultan's Palace**. It was designed as a scale model of the Hindu cosmos, and every plant, building and courtyard is symbolic; the sultans, though Muslim, held on to many Hindu and animist beliefs and

thought that this design would ensure the prosperity of the royal house.

The palace (Mon–Thurs, Sat & Sun 8.30am–2pm, Fri 8.30am–noon) is split into two parts. The first section, the **Pagelaran** (Rp5000), lies immediately south of the *alun-alun*. Belonging to the monarch's brother, this section is often bypassed by tourists as there is little to see. Further south stands the entrance to the sultan's **main palace** (Rp12,500, including optional guided tour; camera Rp1000). Little has changed here in 250 years: the hushed courtyards, the faint stirrings of the gamelan and the elderly palace retainers, dressed in the traditional style with a *kris* (dagger) tucked by the small of their back, all contribute to a remarkable sense of timelessness. You enter the complex through the palace's outer courtyard or **keben**.

Two silver-painted *raksasa* (temple guardian statues) guard the entrance to the largest and most important palace courtyard, the **Pelataran Kedaton**. On the right, the ornate **Gedung Kuning** contains the offices and living quarters of the sultan, out of bounds to tourists. A covered corridor joins the Gedung Kuning with the Golden Throne Pavilion, or **Bangsal Kencono**, the centrepiece of the Pelataran Kedaton. Its intricately carved roof is held aloft by hefty teak pillars, with carvings of the lotus leaf of Buddhism supporting a red-and-gold diamond pattern of Hindu origin, while around the pillar's circumference runs the opening line of the Quran. The eastern wall leads to the **Kesatrian** courtyard, home to another gamelan orchestra and a collection of royal portraits, while to the south is a display dedicated to Hamengkubuwono IX.

Taman Sari

A five-minute walk southwest of the palace, along Jalan Rotowijayan and down Jalan Ngasem and Jalan Taman, takes you to the **Taman Sari** (Water Garden; daily 9am–3pm; Rp15,000) of Mangkubumi. This giant complex was designed in the eighteenth century as an amusement park for the royal house, and features a series of empty swimming pools and fountains, an underground mosque and a large boating lake. Unfortunately, it fell into disrepair and most of what you see today is a concrete reconstruction, financed by UNESCO.

Jalan Malioboro

The 2km stretch of road heading north from the *alun-alun* was designed as a **ceremonial boulevard** by Mangkubumi, along which the royal cavalcade would proceed on its way to Mount Merapi. Today it is as lively as ever, with becaks, horse-drawn carriages and tinted SUVs sharing the pavement that leads towards the palace, with batik and jewellery shops shoulder to shoulder nearly all the way down. The road changes name three times along its length, beginning as Jalan A Yani in the south, continuing as Jalan Malioboro, and then finally ending as Jalan Mangkubumi. At the southern end of the street stands the **Benteng Vredeburg**, Jl A Yani 6 (Tues–Sun 7.30am–4pm; Rp10,000), a fort ordered by the Dutch, and built by Mangkubumi in the late eighteenth century. This relic of Dutch imperialism has been restored to its former glory, and now houses a series of informative dioramas recounting the end of colonialism in Indonesia.

Paku Alaman Palace

Yogyakarta's second court, **Paku Alaman Palace** (Tues, Thurs & Sat 9.30am–2pm; Rp12,500), was built in 1813, set on the north side of Jalan Sultan Agung. As is traditional, the minor court of the city faces south as a mark of subservience to the main palace.

ARRIVAL AND DEPARTURE

By plane Adisucipto Airport (@0274 484261) lies 10km east of the city centre, connected with Jl Malioboro in Yogya by Trans Jogja #1A (daily 6am–7.30pm; 30–45min; Rp4000); for Prawirotaman, transfer to #2A or #3A. A taxi in either direction costs around Rp70,000.

Destinations Balikpapan (6 daily; 1hr 50min); Bandung (2 daily; 1hr 5min); Denpasar (8 daily; 1hr 15min); Jakarta (33 daily; 1hr 15min); Makassar (4 daily; 1hr 50min); Surabaya (7 daily; 1hr 15min).

By bus Intercity buses arrive at and depart from Giwangan terminal, about 5km southeast of the city centre. Those arriving from Borobudur or elsewhere in the north or west

can alight at Jombor terminal, around 3km north of the city centre, from where Trans Jogja #2A links to the main post office. Trans Jogja buses #3A and #3B link Giwangan with both Prawirotaman and Malioboro.

Destinations Frequent departures to Bandung (9hr 30min); Bogor (10hr 30min); Borobudur (2hr); Cilacap (5hr); Denpasar (15hr); Jakarta (11hr 30min); Magelang (1hr 30min); Prambanan (45min); Probolinggo (9hr); Solo (2hr); Surabaya (7hr 30min).

By train Tugu train station (@0274 514270) is one block north of Jl Sosrowijayan, on Jl Pasar Kembang. A taxi to Jl Prawirotaman costs Rp35,000; or catch southbound bus #2A along Jl Malioboro from the Trans Jogya station.

Destinations Bandung (6 daily; 8hr); Jakarta (12 daily; 8hr 30min); Malang (5 daily; 7hr 15min); Sidareja (for Pangandaran; 2 daily; 3hr); Solo (16 daily; 1hr); Surabaya (7 daily; 4hr 50min).

INFORMATION

Tourist information Jl Malioboro 16 (Mon–Thurs 7.30am–7pm, Fri & Sat 7.30am–6pm; @0274 566000, @visitingjogja.com). Plenty of information on local events, language and meditation courses and up-to-date transport information. Also check @gudeg.net (Bahasa Indonesia only) for information on events and attractions.

Intras Tour Jl Malioboro 131 @0274 561972. Probably the most respected and reliable of Yogya's travel agents, set just a few metres south of the eastern end of Jl Sosro.

TOUR OPERATORS

Yogya tour companies number in the hundreds, most offering trips to the nearby temples (from Rp100,000 for a tour of both Prambanan and Borobudur, not including entrance fees), as well as further afield. Trips to Bali with overnight stops at Bromo and Ijen are most popular (three-day tours Rp650,000 excluding meals and entrance fees).

Cecko Trans Jl Sosro Gang II 63 @0274 560966. Friendly guide offering some of the cheapest deals around, including interesting mountain-bike trips to Merapi (Rp300,000 each for two people; Rp275,000 each in groups of three or more).

Via Via Café Jl Prawirotaman 30 @0274 372874, @viaviajogja.com. The most innovative of Yogya's operators. Tours include cycling, motorbiking, hiking, rock climbing, sandboarding, caving and rafting trips, as well as a five-day trip to Bali taking in Bromo, the hill town of Kalibaru and the Meru Betiri National Park (€450 each for two people; €420 for 3–4 people).

GETTING AROUND

By bus Convenient Trans Jogya buses run eight set routes linking important points in the city (Rp4000). Route maps are displayed at most stops (*halte*).

By becak Becak are the most convenient form of transport, and there are plenty of them around. It should cost no more than Rp10,000 from Jl Sosro to the main post office (Rp15,000 from Jl Prawirotaman).

By horse-drawn carriage Known as *andong*, they tend to queue up along Jl Malioboro, and are quite a bit pricier than becak (starting at around Rp40,000 for a ride from Jl Sosro to the palace).

By taxi Good value (Rp6500 minimum). You can usually find them hanging around the main post office, or phone Citra Taksi (☎ 0274 373737).

By bike and motorbike Bikes start at Rp20,000/day and motorbikes at Rp50,000/day. In Malioboro, try Cecko Trans, on Jl Sosro Gang II, or Wanderlust on Jl Sosro G I 92 (☎ 081 802 707573); in Prawirotaman, head to Satu Dunia, Jl Prawirotaman 44 (☎ 0851 274 414 431), or Mahdi, Jl Tirtodipuran 51 (☎ 0274 2672386, ✉ itseasy51@yahoo.com). Orange-suited parking attendants throughout the city will look after your bike for around Rp1000.

ACCOMMODATION

A kilometre north of the Kraton, Jl Sosrowijayan (known as Jl Sosro) is Yogyakarta's answer to the Khao San Road in Bangkok. A slightly more upmarket alternative is around Jl Prawirotaman, in the suburbs southeast of the Kraton.

JALAN PRAWIROTAMAN AND AROUND

Agung Inn Jl Prawirotaman 30 ☎ 0274 383577; map opposite. Small, friendly hotel next to *Via Via*, offering seven squeeky-clean rooms with a/c, hot showers and breakfasts, as well as coffee, tea and mineral water on tap around the clock in the shared kitchen area. Doubles Rp250,000

Delta Homestay Jl Prawirotaman II MGIII/597A ☎ 0274 372051, ⊕ dutagardenhotel.com; map opposite. This cheap and welcoming homestay has basic, somewhat worn rooms, though the ones with a/c and private bathrooms (Rp300,000) are pleasant enough. Most have small patios facing the pool. Doubles Rp150,000

Elton Homestay Jl Tirtodipuran 27 ☎ 0877 5990 2981, ✉ eltonhomestay@gmail.com; map opposite. Friendly homestay in an old, stately home with a range of rooms, from the cramped, dingy former servants' quarters (now fan-equipped singles; Rp100,000) with shared bathrooms to the echoing old masters' chamber (Rp350,000). Guests have kitchen access and breakfast is included. Doubles Rp150,000

Kampoeng Djawa Guesthouse Jl Prawirotaman 40 ☎ 0274 378318, ⊕ kampoengdjawahotel.com; map opposite. Popular among backpackers, *Kampoeng Djawa* has tidy rooms with hot and cold water, fan or a/c (Rp200,000), and self-service tea and coffee, afternoon snacks and breakfast in a lush sitting area. Book ahead. Doubles Rp100,000

4

● SHOPPING
The Lucky Boomerang	1
Periplus	2

SOSROWIJAYAN (SOSRO)

Tugu Train Station

JL JLAGRAN LOR

JL PASAR KEMBANG

Hotel Neo Malioboro

JL JOYOREGARAN

GANG II

Cecko Trans

GANG I

Pop Hotel

Food Market

Satu Dunia

JL SOSROWIJAYAN

Malioboro Inn

Intras Tour

JL SOSRODIPURAN GTI

N

JL MALIOBORO

Malioboro Mall

● EATING
Batik Resto	3
Bedhot	1
Jaba Jero	4
Superman	2

■ DRINKING & NIGHTLIFE
Lucifer	2
Oxen Free	1

■ ACCOMMODATION
Anda	2
Bladok	4
Pawon Cokelat	1
Wakeup Homestay	3

JL DAGEN

0   100
metres

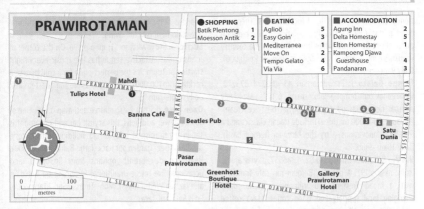

Pandanaran Jl Prawirotaman 38 ☎0274 458 0077, ⓦpandanaranjogja.com; map above. This giant newcomer to Prawirotaman has clean and compact budget rooms with a/c, hot showers and comfortable beds. Pricier rooms have much bigger windows and plenty more space, and there's an attractive pool and rooftop café that has great views across the entire valley. Doubles **Rp325,000**

JALAN SOSRO AND AROUND

Anda Jl Sosro Gang II; map opposite. This friendly losmen is one of the cheapest places on Jl Sosro. The simple rooms have attached mandis and a pleasant outdoor sitting area and very little else. No breakfast, no wi-fi and no reservations: rooms go on a strictly first-come-first-served basis. Doubles **Rp100,000**

★**Bladok** Jl Sosro 76 ☎0274 560452, ⓦbladok.web.id; map opposite. Whitewashed hotel with clean, comfortable rooms, all en suite, and a brilliant pool with a waterfall in the back. VIP rooms come with poolside terrace, hot water, a/c, fridge and TV (Rp320,000), and the open-air restaurant and café out front is one of the most popular spots on the street. Doubles **Rp238,000**

Pawon Cokelat Jl Sosro Gang I/102 ☎0274 292 4232, ⓦpawoncokelat.com; map opposite. Hidden away in the back alleys of Sosro, this attractive, modern-style guesthouse offers a refreshing change from the generally dark and gloomy surrounding losmen. It's set in an open, concrete building lavished in greenery, with nice sitting areas scattered around, including in the small rooftop garden. All ten of its spotless rooms come with a/c, LED TVs and breakfast in the downstairs chalkboard-menu café. Doubles **Rp300,000**

Wakeup Homestay Jl Gandekan Lor 44 ☎0274 514762, ⓦwakeuphomestay.com; map opposite. Bright, modern new hostel just across from *Lucifer* at the west end of Sosro, offering some of the best-value dorms in town: clean, pod-style and fitted with a/c and lockers. There's a common lounge, a simple Indonesian breakfast included and helpful staff. Dorms **Rp135,000**

EATING

Yogya's specialities are *ayam goreng* (fried chicken) and *nasi gudeg* (rice and jackfruit), and many food stalls serve nothing else. Every evening a food market sets up on Jl Malioboro and by 8pm the entire street is thronged with diners.

JALAN PRAWIROTAMAN

This area has some of Yogya's best restaurants as well as a solid string of bars and pubs along Jl Parangtritis.

Aglioö Jl Prawirotaman 43 ☎0274 388934; map above. Cosy Italian restaurant with a warm, candlelit ambience serving delicious pizzas (margherita Rp59,000) cooked in a wood-fired oven, as well as pasta (from Rp36,000) and a good selection of Indonesian food. Al-fresco dining, with generous portions, friendly service and free wi-fi. Daily 8am–11pm.

Easy Goin' Jl Prawirotaman 12 ☎0274 384092, ⓦeasygoingresto.com; map above. True to its name, this laidback café, bar and restaurant is open to the street, has a cosy sitting area out back, an epic happy hour (10am–7pm) and a broad menu of tasty Western, Indonesian and Mexican dishes, from beef burritos (Rp65,000) and burgers (Rp45,000) to *nasi tumpeng* (yellow rice with *tempe* and fried chicken; Rp55,000). Daily 10am–after midnight.

★**Mediterranea** Jl Tirtodipuran 24A ☎0274 371052, ⓦrestobykamil.com; map above. Fanciest spot on the street, and arguably the best non-Indonesian restaurant in Yogya, with a broad, eclectic menu centred around Italian and French cuisine (duck burger with sauce bearnaise Rp69,000) and a warm, inviting ambience, particularly in the covered, candle-lit patio out back. Save room for dessert (tiramisu Rp35,000). Tues–Sun 8.30am–11pm.

Move On Jl Prawirotaman 6–8 ☎0274 287 2815, ⓦfacebook.com/moveon.yogya; map above. Sleek, a/c addition to Prawirotaman's café scene, with lofty ceilings, trendy decor and a clientele of local hipsters. There are good pastas (*aglio e olio* Rp25,000) and black-dough pizzas (Rp40,000), and coffee from all across the country (barista's daily selection Rp15,000; *kopi luwak* Rp40,000). Daily 9am–midnight.

Tempo Gelato Jl Prawirotaman 43 ☎0274 373272, ✆facebook.com/tempogelato; map p.197. Massively popular new gelateria serving Yogya's best ice cream. Flavours (Rp40,000 for three) include Italian classics and a few local innovations – try the *kemangi* (lemon basil). Daily 10am–9pm.

Via Via Jl Prawirotaman 30 ☎0274 386557, ✆viaviajogja .com; map p.197. A popular, Belgian-run café franchise with a broad Western and Indonesian menu, daily changing local specials and good coffee (Java coffee Rp12,000), as well as a decent selection of local and imported beers (Hoegaarden Rp78,000). A range of worthwhile tours and courses is on offer in cooking, batik, and Bahasa Indonesia (see opposite), and there's live jazz on Friday evenings starting at 8pm. Sat–Thurs 7.30am–11pm, Fri 7.30am–midnight.

JALAN SOSRO

Batik Resto Jl Sosro 10; map p.196. This central bar and restaurant is a longtime favourite, with pleasant seating areas both on and away from the street, a range of Indonesian and Western dishes (beef *sate* Rp52,000; margherita pizza Rp55,000), as well as Sosro's longest happy hour (1–8pm). Daily 7am–1am.

Bedhot Jl Sosro Gang II/127 ✆bedhots.com; map p.196. Central and friendly place serving Indonesian, Chinese and decent interpretations of Western food in a dimly lit, bohemian setting. Try the tasty *tempe* (soya bean) burgers (Rp35,000), *arak* (rice wine; Rp30,000) or *sayur lodeh* (vegetables in coconut sauce; Rp20,000), a Javan speciality. Daily 8am–11pm.

Jaba Jero Jl Suryowijayan 45; map p.196. A replacement of the old, popular *Bintang Café*, this bar and restaurant has much of the same staff and a classic Sosro blend of local and Western dishes. There are nice vantages over the street from its cosy upstairs seating, great for people-watching, a romantic evening or just an ice-cold Bintang (large Rp45,000). Daily 7am–1am.

Superman Jl Sosro Gang I/71; map p.196. Spacious, thatched-roof restaurant down a pokey side street. In business for over four decades, it's popular for its relaxed vibe and broad international menu, with delicious pancakes (from Rp10,000), ice-cold beer (large Bintang Rp35,000), regular screenings of European football and free wi-fi. Daily 8am–10pm.

DRINKING AND NIGHTLIFE

Yogya's nightlife is really an early-evening affair; very few places stay open beyond midnight, and most of the action

happens between 7 and 11pm, when the city's cultural entertainment is in full swing.

Lucifer Jl Suryowijayan 71; map p.196. On the corner of Jl Sosro, this attractive venue has live music every night starting at 10pm. It's the perfect place for a cold beer or a cocktail (Rp100,000) after a day exploring the temples. Daily 6pm–2am.

Oxen Free Jl Sosro 2 ✆oxenfree.net; map p.196. One of Sosro's newer additions, this stylish bar and restaurant is set in a refurbished colonial-era building with a cosy, candle-lit beer garden out back (large Bali Hai Rp45,000). Hearty all-day brunch options from Rp30,000, and occasional live music (traditional *keroncong* on Tuesdays and jazz on Wednesdays). Mon–Thurs & Sun 11am–2am, Fri & Sat until 3am.

TRADITIONAL CULTURAL PERFORMANCES

WAYING KULIT AND WAYANG GOLEK

Wayang kulit (shadow puppetry) is the epitome of Javanese culture, and it's worth catching a show, although *wayang golek*, where wooden puppets are used, tends to be easier to follow, as the figures are more dynamic and expressive. With one honourable exception, all of the performances listed are aimed at tourists, and only two hours long. For up-to-date events, check ✆visitingjogja .com.

Sasono Hinggil Alun-alun Selatan. Yogya's only genuine, full-length *wayang kulit* performance runs from 9pm to 5am on the second Saturday of every month (Rp20,000).

Sono Budoyo Museum Jl Trikora 1. The most professional and popular abridged *wayang kulit* show (Mon–Thurs & Sat 8–10pm; Rp20,000).

Sultan's Palace On Saturday mornings (10am–noon), there's a practice-cum-performance of *wayang kulit* in the Sri Manganti courtyard, and every Wednesday (10am–noon) a free *wayang golek* show. On Monday, Tuesday and Thursday mornings between 10am and noon there are free gamelan performances.

JAVANESE DANCING

The Ramayana dance drama is a modern extension of the court dances of the nineteenth century, which tended to use that other Indian epic, the *Mahabharata*, as the source of their story lines.

Prambanan Jl Raya Yogya-Solo km16 ☎0274 497771. The indoor Trimurti Theatre at Prambanan holds seasonal Ramayana ballet performances (Nov–April; Tues, Thurs & Sat 7.30–9.30pm; ☎0274 496408), while the Open Air Theatre puts on the full story during summer months (May–Oct 3–4 times weekly; 7.30–9.30pm) and individual episodes at sporadic intervals the rest of the year. Tickets for both performances (Rp125,000–400,000 depending on where you sit) are available at the door or from the tourist office in Yogya, where you can check the complete schedule.

Purawisata Theatre Jl Brig Jen Katamso ☎0274 375705, ⓦamazingramayanaballet.com. Every night the Purawisata Theatre (also called the Mandira Baruga) puts on a 1hr 30min performance of the Ramayana (8–9.30pm; Rp300,000; including dinner Rp420,000); the story is split into two episodes, each performed on alternate nights.

Sultan's Palace The Kraton Classical Dance School holds weekly public rehearsals (Sun 10am–noon). No additional fee once you've paid to get into the palace. Very worthwhile.

COURSES

Batik courses Basic courses are offered at many hotels, including *Via Via* (daily 9am–1pm; Rp200,000).

Cookery courses *Via Via* (see opposite) runs morning and afternoon courses (from Rp160,000).

Language courses Yogya is the place to learn Bahasa Indonesia. The most established schools are Alam Bahasa Indonesia by the northern ring road at Jl Sarirejo RT 06 RW 47 (☎0851 0900 1577, ⓦalambahasa.com); Puri Bahasa Indonesia, Jl Purwanggan 15 (☎0274 588192, ⓦpuribahasa.com); and Wisma Bahasa, Jl Affandi, Gang Bromo No. 15A (☎0274 561627, ⓦwisma-bahasa.com). One-to-one tuition typically costs US$10/hr. *Via Via* (see opposite) offers a daily 3hr course starting at 9am (Rp100,000).

SHOPPING

Yogya is Java's souvenir centre, with keepsakes and mementos from all over the archipelago finding their way into the city's shops and street stalls.

ANTIQUES, PUPPETS AND CURIOS

There are a number of cavernous antique shops near Jl Prawirotaman dealing mainly in teak furniture from Jepara and the north, but they also sell woodcarvings, *wayang kulit* puppets and *keris* daggers.

Moesson Antik Jl Prawirotaman 27 ⓦmoessongallery .com; map p.197. This shop's collection ranges from simple tat to genuine antiques – great for a rummage even if you have no intention of buying.

BATIK AND SOUVENIRS

With the huge influx of tourists over recent decades, Yogya has evolved a batik style that increasingly panders to Western tastes. However, there is still plenty of the traditional indigo-and-brown batik clothing for sale, especially on Jl Malioboro. For the best-quality and most expensive batiks, head to Jl Tirtodipuran, west of Jl Prawirotaman. Be aware of the "batik exposition", a common tout that simply brings you to a particular gallery in hopes of commission.

Batik Plentong Jl Tirtodipuran 48; map p.197. Large shop with friendly staff that stocks a wide selection of good-quality batik fabrics. Free tours of the batik-making process are offered, allowing you a peek into the batik workshop out back. Daily 8am–6pm.

Hamzah Batik Jl A Yani 9; map p.193. One of the most reputable outlets in town, the first floor of this a/c complex is filled with fine batik, all at fixed prices. A range of other souvenirs fills the second storey. Daily 8am–9pm.

Pasar Beringharjo Jl A Yani 16; map p.193. Densely packed three-storey market at the southern end of Malioboro – batiks are found throughout the upper levels, where haggling skills come in handy. Worth a look even if you're not looking to buy. Daily 9am–5pm.

BOOKS

The Lucky Boomerang Jl Sosro Gang I; map p.196. The Lucky Boomerang stocks new and secondhand English-language novels and a good selection of multilingual books. Mon–Sat 9am–10pm, Sun 9am–10pm.

Periplus Lower ground floor of Malioboro Mall; map p.196. Has a wide selection of English-language novels and histories of Indonesia, as well as guidebooks and maps. Daily 10am–10pm.

LEATHER AND POTTERY

All around Yogya, and particularly in the markets, and some of the shops along Jl Malioboro, hand-stitched, good-quality leather bags, suitcases, belts and shoes are for sale extremely cheaply. Javanese pottery is widely available throughout Yogya. The markets along Jl Malioboro sell ochre pottery, including decorative bowls, erotic statues, whistles, flutes and other pottery instruments.

SILVER

The Kota Gede suburb is the home of the silver industry in Central Java, famous for its fine filigree work. Jl Kemasan is the "silver street" of Yogya and there is a huge selection of jewellery and trinkets. If your budget is limited, note that the stallholders along Jl Malioboro sell perfectly reasonable silver jewellery, much of it from East Java or Bali. To reach Kota Gede, take the Trans Jogja 3A from Malioboro or the 2A from Prawirotaman.

Tom's Silver Jl Ngeksi Gondo 60; map p.193. This huge workshop produces great work and you can wander around and watch the smiths at work. Daily 8.30am–4.30pm.

DIRECTORY

Banks and exchange There are many banks with ATMs across the city centre. To exchange money, head to PT Gajahmas Mulyosakti, Jl A Yani 86A, offering competitive rates.

Hospitals and clinics The nearest hospital to the centre is Bethesda at Jl Jend Sudirman 70 (☎ 0274 586688). Gading Clinic, south of the Alun-alun Selatan at Jl Maj Jen Panjaitan 25, has English-speaking doctors (☎ 0274 375396).
Internet Wi-fi is available in most cafés across town and at least a couple *warnets* in each area (Rp7000/hr).
Police station Jl Reksobayan 1, near the Benteng Vredeburg Museum (☎ 274 512511 or ☎ 274 512940). Dial ☎ 110 for emergencies.
Post office Jl Senopati 2, at the southern end of Jl Malioboro (Mon–Sat 6am–10pm, Sun 6am–8pm). There's a small branch near *Bladok* on Jl Sosro 55 (Mon–Fri 8am–2pm, Sat 8am–noon).

GUNUNG MERAPI AND KALIURANG

Marking the northern limit of the Daerah Istimewa Yogyakarta, symmetrical, smoke-plumed **Gunung Merapi** (Giving Fire) is an awesome 2914m presence in the centre of Java, visible from Yogyakarta, 25km away. This is one of Indonesia's most volatile volcanoes, and some volcanologists consider it the most consistently active volcano on earth. Through the centuries its ability to annihilate has frequently been demonstrated – as recently as 2010 an entire mountain village was destroyed, killing more than 350 people.

Nearly 1km up on Merapi's southern slopes is the misty and ramshackle hill village of **KALIURANG**. Bemos here cost Rp15,000 from Jalan Simanjutak in Yogya. In Kaliurang, you can join a trekking group to reach high on the barren flanks of Merapi, organized by *Vogel's Hostel* for $25 (see below), a fairly arduous five-hour scramble, much of it through the humid jungle that beards Merapi's lower slopes. During the dry season (April–Oct), it's possible to climb all the way to the top, but at other times, or when the volcano is active, you may have to settle for a distant view from the observation platform (entry Rp25,000), a Rp10,000 ojek ride from Kaliurang. Alternatively, the northern approach via the village of Selo (reachable from Yogyakarta by a string of minibuses to Boyolali and then Selo) is much tougher, taking around four hours up and three back down. Guides are essential, and can be found in Selo (Rp200,000). From both the southern and northern entrances, hikers will have to pay the Gunung Merapi National Park fee (Mon–Fri Rp100,000, Sat & Sun Rp155,000). All treks typically begin in the dark between 3 and 5am. Bring warm clothes, a torch or headlamp and a sturdy pair of shoes.

ACCOMMODATION

★**Vogel's Hostel** Jl Astya Mulya 76, Kaliurang ☎ 0274 895208, ⓦ vogelshostel.net. This is a great budget hostel, split into several parts: the rooms in the newer green and white bungalows are beautiful (from Rp125,000), while those in the old building are more spartan but good value. The food is delicious (try the *paniki*, bat soup; Rp30,000), and there's a decent travellers' library. The staff can organize various treks, and the owner, Christian Awuy, a Manado-native, is a bona fide expert on Merapi. Dorms <u>Rp30,000</u>, doubles <u>Rp70,000</u>

BOROBUDUR

Forty kilometres west of Yogya, surrounded on three sides by volcanoes and on the fourth by jagged limestone cliffs, is the largest Buddhist monument in the southern hemisphere. This is the temple of **Borobudur**, the greatest single piece of classical architecture in the archipelago. The temple is actually a colossal multi-tiered Buddhist stupa lying at the western end of a 4km-long chain of temples (one of which, the nearby **Candi Mendut**, is also worth visiting), built in the ninth century by the Saliendra dynasty. At 34.5m tall, however, and covering an area of some 200 square metres, Borobudur is on a different scale altogether, dwarfing all the other *candi* in the chain. Abandoned and neglected for almost a thousand years, Borobudur was "rediscovered" by the English in 1815, though nothing much was done until 1973, when UNESCO began to take the temple apart, block by block, in order to replace the waterlogged hill with a concrete substitute.

WHAT TO SEE AND DO

Borobudur is pregnant with symbolism, and precisely oriented so that its four sides face the four points of the compass; the **ticket office** lies to the southeast of the complex (daily 6am–5.30pm;

Rp270,000; 15 percent discount for guests of *Rajasa, Lotus I, II*; package ticket for Borobudur and Prambanan Rp416,000; sunrise admission Rp450,000, only via *Manohara Hotel*; ☏0293 788 131, ⊛manoharaborobudur .com; guided tour Rp75,000).

The stupa

Unlike most temples, Borobudur was not built as a dwelling for the gods, but rather as a representation of the Buddhist cosmic mountain, Meru. Accordingly, at the base is the real, earthly world, a world of desires and passions, and at the summit is nirvana. Thus, as you make your way around the temple passages and slowly spiral to the summit, you are symbolically following the path to enlightenment.

The first five levels – the square terraces – are covered with three thousand **reliefs** representing man's earthly existence. As you might expect, the lowest, subterranean level has carvings depicting the basest desires, best seen at the southeast corner. The reliefs on the **first four levels above ground** cover the beginning of man's path to enlightenment. Each of the ten series (one on each level on the outer wall and one on the inner wall) tells a story, beginning by the eastern stairway and continuing clockwise. Follow all the stories, and you will have circled the temple ten times – a distance of almost 5km. Buddha's own path to enlightenment is told in the upper panels on the inner wall of the first gallery. As you enter the **fifth level**, the walls fall away to reveal a breathtaking view of the surrounding fields and volcanoes. You are now in the Sphere of Formlessness, the realm of enlightenment: below is the chaos of the world, above is nirvana, represented by a huge empty stupa almost 10m in diameter. Surrounding this stupa are 72 smaller ones, most of which are occupied by statues of Buddha.

Candi Mendut

Originally Borobudur was part of a chain of four temples joined by a sacred path. Two of the other three temples have been restored, and at least one, **Candi Mendut**

(daily 7am–5pm; Rp3500; ☏0911 341652) 4km east of Borobudur, is worth visiting. Buses between Yogya and Borobudur drive right past Mendut (1hr 20min from Yogya, Rp20,000; 10min from Borobudur, Rp5000). Built in 800 AD, Mendut was restored at the end of the nineteenth century. The exterior is unremarkable, but the three giant **statues** sitting inside – of Buddha and the Bodhisattvas Avalokitesvara and Vajrapani – are exquisitely carved and startling in their intricacy. Across the valley is the **Mendut Buddhist Monastery** (daily 7am–8pm; free), its immaculate grounds of lotus and lily ponds containing a wide variety of Buddhist architecture, including laughing, starving and reclining Buddhas, a Tibetan-style dharma wheel and a miniature Angkor Thom.

ARRIVAL AND DEPARTURE

Most choose to see the site on a day-trip from Yogya, with plenty of agencies offering all-inclusive tours (from Rp75,000); these are only slightly more expensive than reaching the sites by public transport, which involves multiple changes. Motorbike rental is a cheaper option (Rp50,000), allowing the freedom to explore the scenic countryside around Borobudur.

By bus Numerous buses depart from Yogya's Giwangan Station and call in at Jombor bus station (handy for Jl Sosro, connected by Trans Jogya 2A) before heading off to Borobudur village bus station (1hr–1hr 30min; Rp25,000); your bus may stop briefly in Muntilan. The entrance to the temple lies about 750m southwest of the bus stop, and the last bus back to Yogya leaves Borobudur around 6pm.

ACCOMMODATION AND EATING

Most people who stay in Borobudur overnight choose to eat in their hotel, though there are a couple of inexpensive Padang places and the usual warung opposite the entrance to the temple grounds.

Cempaka Jl Medang Kamulan 8B ☏0293 789393, ⊜cempakavilla.borobudur@hotmail.com. Just past *Lotus Guesthouse* and down a narrow dirt road to the right, about 10min walk from the temple entrance, *Cempaka Guesthouse* (not to be confused with the more upscale *Cempaka Villa*) has a quiet setting away from the road, friendly staff and tidy rooms with a/c and somewhat cramped bathrooms, all set around a gravel courtyard. Breakfast included. Doubles <u>Rp275,000</u>

Lotus II Jl Balaputradewa 54 ☏0293 788845, ⊜jackpriyana@yahoo.com.sg. Owned by the family that runs *Lotus Guesthouse*, the popular sequel is set slightly further from the temple and has larger rooms with hot water, some featuring patios and balconies overlooking the rice fields. Be prepared for an early wake-up call from the mosque next door. Friendly staff provide excellent local information and a range of tours, including sunrise views of Borobudur from a nearby hilltop and meditation at Mendut Monastery. Doubles Rp275,000

Lotus Guesthouse Jl Medang Kamulan 2 ☎ 0293 788281. This old stalwart, set near the temple entrance, is looking a little worse for wear, though rooms are cheap and sufficiently clean. The better ones have hot water and a/c (Rp250,000), and there are great views from the rooftop. Doubles Rp125,000

Rajasa Jl Badrawati 2 ☎ 0293 788276, ✉ rajasaborobudur @gmail.com. Just south of the temple, this peaceful hotel has beautiful views over the rice fields and the Menora Hills in the distance, although the beds are a little lumpy. Rooms with hot water and a/c are available for Rp400,000, and all rooms come with breakfast. Doubles Rp200,000

DIRECTORY

Banks There are several ATMs at the northeast corner of the complex, including a BNI, BRI and Mandiri.
Motorbikes Available at *Rajasa* for Rp100,000/day.

THE PRAMBANAN PLAIN

Nourished by the volcanic detritus of Mount Merapi and washed by innumerable small rivers, the verdant **Prambanan Plain** lies 18km east of Yogya, a patchwork blanket of sun-spangled paddy fields and vast plantations sweeping down from the southern slopes of the volcano. As well as being one of the most fertile regions in Java, the plain is home to the largest concentration of ancient ruins on the island. Over thirty **temples** and **palaces**

RAMAYANA BALLET PERFORMANCES

The highlights of the dancing year in Central Java are the phenomenal Ramayana ballets held each summer at **Prambanan's Open-Air Theatre**, to the west of the complex. From May to October, the timeless Hindu epic is performed in its entirety, with the magnificent Shiva, Vishnu and Brahma temples serving as a backdrop. Individual episodes are performed sporadically outside this time.

lie scattered over a thirty-square-kilometre area, most built during the eighth and ninth centuries by two rival kingdoms, the Buddhist Saliendra and the Hindu Sanjaya dynasties.

Prambanan

Heading east from Yogya along Jalan Adisucipto, you'll catch sight of three giant, rocket-shaped temples looming up by the side of the highway, each of them smothered in intricate narrative carvings. This is the **Prambanan Archeological Park** (daily 6am–6pm; Rp243,000; two-day package including Borobudur Rp416,000; guided tours Rp75,000; Trans Jogja bus #1A), the largest Hindu temple compound in all of Indonesia and a worthy rival to Borobudur. The complex consists of six temples in a raised **inner courtyard**, surrounded by **224 minor temples** which now lie in ruins. The three largest temples are dedicated to the Hindu triad: Shiva, whose 47m temple is the tallest of the three, Brahma (to the south of the Shiva temple) and Vishnu (north). Facing these are three smaller temples housing the animal statues – or "chariots" – that would accompany the gods: Hamsa the swan, Nandi the bull and Garuda the sunbird, respectively.

The **Shiva Temple** is decorated with exceptional carvings, including a series along the inner wall of the first terrace walkway that recounts the first half of the Ramayana epic. At the top of the steps is the temple's inner sanctuary, whose eastern chamber contains a statue of Shiva, while in the west chamber is Shiva's elephant-headed son, Ganesh. A beautiful sculpture of Nandi the bull stands inside the temple of Shiva's chariot. Just as painstakingly decorated, the first terrace of the **Brahma Temple** takes up the Ramayana epic where the Shiva Temple left off, while the carvings on the terrace of Vishnu's temple recount stories of **Krishna**, the eighth of Vishnu's nine earthly incarnations.

North of Prambanan

Just north through the trees from the Prambanan Temple are three ancient Buddhist temples (daily 6am–6pm;

entrance included in Prambanan ticket), built in the late eighth century and therefore predating Borobudur. Though not as grand as the Shiva Temple, visitors will share these sites with much thinner crowds – sometimes only the sheep that graze in the ruins' shade. After passing the crumbling ruins of **Candi Lumbung** and **Candi Bubrah**, the last temple you'll reach is **Candi Sewu** (1km north of Shiva Temple), the most intact and impressive of Prambanan's Buddhist temples. Laid out in a mandala pattern and guarded at each entrance by a pair of burly dwarapala statues, the complex includes more than 240 structures, many adorned with beautifully carved bodhisattvas.

South of Prambanan

About 3km south of Prambanan and perched on a hill rising 200m over the Prambanan Plain is the ninth-century **Kraton Ratu Boko** (daily 6am–6pm; entrance Rp125,000, combined with Prambanan Rp360,000). The ruins are in two parts: the ceremonial gate that adorns most advertising posters, and, 400m to the east, a series of bathing pools. The views from the kraton are wonderful, and on a clear day the restaurant has wonderful vistas of Merapi. It's roughly an hour's walk from Prambanan, though there is also a shuttle bus (included in combined ticket). Still less-visited is **Candi Sojiwan**, a plain, square temple, sparingly decorated with scenes from Buddhist folklore and set about 1km southeast of Prambanan village, just off the route to Ratu Boko.

West of Prambanan

A short hop to the west of Prambanan are several more worthwhile temples (daily 6am–6pm; Rp5000 for each) near the village of Kalasan, reached by a short angkot ride or thirty-minute walk. The first one you'll reach heading west is the eighth-century **Candi Sari** just north of the main road after about 3km. With an unusual, house-like design capped with stupas resembling those of Borobudur, the temple features elaborate carvings of various goddesses and bodhisattvas. About 150m southwest amid rice fields just across

the main road is the artfully crumbling spire of **Candi Kalasan**. An inscription here bears the date of 778 AD, and both of these Buddhist temples are believed to be among the very oldest of the entire Prambanan plain. Just over 2km north of the main road is the ninth-century **Candi Sambisari**, a small Shiva temple complex adorned with statues of Hindu gods. Buried in 5m of soil and volcanic ash until its excavation in the 1980s, it has sparked curiosity over how much yet remains undiscovered in the Prambanan plain.

ARRIVAL AND DEPARTURE

The Prambanan temple complex is easily visited on a day-trip from Yogya.

By bus Prambanan is linked to Malioboro in Yogya by Trans Jogya #1A (40min; Rp4000). Buses also link Solo's Tirtonadi terminal (Rp15,000; 1hr 30min).

By bike Some visitors cycle here from Yogya, to then easily visit more of the plain's far-flung ruins. Fume-choked Jl Adisucipto is the most straightforward route, but there's a quieter alternative that begins by heading north along Yogya's Jl Simanjutak and Jl Kaliurang until you reach the Mataram Canal, just past the main Gajah Mada University compound. Follow the canal path east for 12km (1hr), and you'll eventually come out near Candi Sari on Jl Adisucipto. *Via Via* (see p.198) also organizes bike rides to Prambanan.

SURAKARTA (SOLO)

Sixty-five kilometres northeast of Yogya stands quiet, leafy low-rise **SURAKARTA**, or, as it's more commonly known, **SOLO**. This is the older of the two royal cities in Central Java, and its ruling family can lay claim to being the rightful heirs to the Mataram dynasty.

Not long after their establishment – in 1745 and 1757 respectively – Solo's two royal houses wisely stopped fighting and instead threw their energies into the arts, developing a highly sophisticated and graceful court culture. The gamelan pavilions became the new theatres of war, with each city competing to produce the more refined court culture – a situation that continues to this day.

WHAT TO SEE AND DO

Like Yogya, Solo has two **royal palaces** and a number of museums, yet its tourist industry has lagged behind. The city's

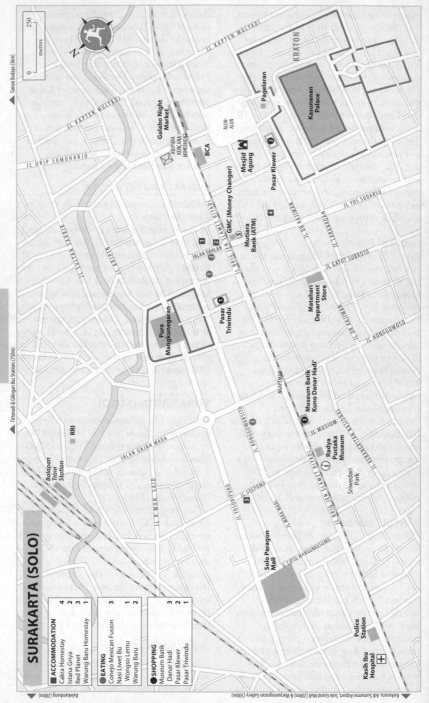

SURAKARTA (SOLO)

ACCOMMODATION
Cakra Homestay	4
Istana Griya	2
Red Planet	3
Warung Baru Homestay	1

EATING
Conejo Mexican Fusion	3
Nasi Liwet Bu Wongso Lemu	1
Warung Baru	2

SHOPPING
Museum Batik Danar Hadi	3
Pasar Klewer	2
Pasar Triwindu	1

KRATON

Kasunanan Palace

Pagelaran

ALUN-ALUN

Galabo Night Market

ADIPURA KENCANA MONUMENT

BCA

Mesjid Agung

Pasar Klewer

GMC (Money Changer)

Mutiara Bank (ATM)

JALAN DAHLAN

Pura Mangkunegaran

Pasar Triwindu

Matahari Department Store

Museum Batik Kuno Danar Hadi

Radya Pustaka Museum

Sriwedari Park

RRI

JALAN GAJAH MADA

Balapan Train Station

Solo Paragon Mall

Police Station

Kasih Ibu Hospital

JL KAPTEN MULYADI
JL KAPTEN MULYADI
JL URIP SUMOHARJO
JL YOS SUDARSO
JL GATOT SUBROTO
JL HONGGOWOSO
JL MUSIUM
JL SULTAN SAHRIR
JL TRIPIN
JL BRIG JEN SLAMET RIYADI
JL DR RADJIMAN
NGAPEMAN
JL RONGGOWARSITO
JL MOH. SAID
JL YOSODIPURO
JL SOEPOMO
JL WORA MARI
JL CIPTO MANGUNKUSUMO
JL BRIG JEN SLAMET RIYADI
JL KEMBANGAN RATULANGI KARTASURA

Taman Budaya (3km)

Tirtonadi & Gilingan Bus Stations (750m)

Balekambang (200m)

Kartasura, Adi Sumarmo Airport, Solo Grand Mall (200m) & Waryaningratan Gallery (500m)

0 — 250 metres

main source of income is from textiles, and Solo has the biggest **batik market** on Java. Solo also makes an ideal base from which to visit the home of Java Man at Sangiran, as well as the intriguing temples Candi Ceto and Candi Sukuh, each about 35km to the northeast.

Kasunanan Palace
Brought from Kartasura by Pakubuwono II in one huge day-long procession in 1745, the **Kasunanan Palace** (Mon–Fri 8.30am–2pm, Sat & Sun 8.30am–3pm; Rp15,000; guide Rp50,000) is Solo's largest and most important royal house. It stands within the kraton, just south of the *alun-alun*. Non-royals must enter the main body of the palace by the eastern entrance. This opens out into a large courtyard whose surrounding buildings house the palace's **kris** (dagger) collection, as well as a number of chariots, silver ornaments and other royal knick-knacks. An archway to the west leads into the Susuhunan's living quarters. Many of the buildings in this courtyard are modern copies, the originals having burnt down in 1985.

Pura Mangkunegaran
The second royal house in Solo, the **Pura Mangkunegaran**, on Jl Ronggowarsito (Mon–Wed & Fri, Sat 8am–3pm, Thurs & Sun 9am–2.30pm; Rp20,000, mandatory guide Rp50,000), faces south towards the Kasunanan Palace as a mark of respect. However, with its fine collection of antiques and curios, in many ways the Pura Mangkunegaran is the more interesting one. It was built in 1757 to placate the rebellious Prince Mas Said (Mangkunegara I), a nephew of Pakubuwono II, who was given a royal title, a court in Solo and leadership over four thousand of Solo's households in a peace deal. The palace hides behind a high white wall, entered through the gateway to the south. The vast **pendopo** (the largest in Indonesia) that fronts the palace shields four gamelan orchestras underneath its rafters, three of which can only be played on very special occasions. The *pendopo*'s vibrantly painted roof features Javanese zodiac figures

surrounding the main batik centrepiece that took three years to complete. A portrait of the current resident, Mangkunegara IX, hangs by the entrance to the **Dalam Agung**, or living quarters, whose reception room has been turned into a good museum, displaying ancient coins, ballet masks and chastity preservers. Visits last roughly an hour, and the dress code prohibits sleeveless shirts – but only for men.

Radya Pustaka Museum
A kilometre west along Jalan Brig Jen Slamet Riyadi from Pura Mangkunegaran brings you to the well-kept **Radya Pustaka Museum** (Tues–Sun 8.30am–1pm; Rp10,000, camera charge Rp5000). Built by the Dutch in 1890, this is one of the oldest and largest museums in Java, housing an extensive Dutch and Javanese library as well as dusty collections of *wayang kulit* puppets, *kris* and scale models of the mosque at Demak and the cemetery at Imogiri.

Museum Batik Kuno Danar Hadi
One of Solo's newest attractions, this fine batik museum is housed in the elegant nineteenth-century **Ndalem Wuryoningratan** building, just east of the Radya Pustaka Museum at Jl Slamet Riyadi 261 (daily 9am–4pm; Rp35,000 including 1hr guided tour; ☎0271 714326). Along the tour you'll learn the elaborate process behind the Javanese art and see some of its finest specimens, both traditional and contemporary.

ARRIVAL AND DEPARTURE
By plane Adi Sumarmo Airport is 10km west of Solo and just 2km north of Kartasura. The Batik Solo Trans (BST) bus service links the city centre (every 15min; 1hr; Rp7000). A taxi (30min) will cost about Rp75,000 from the airport to Solo, and Rp60,000 in the opposite direction.
Destinations Denpasar (daily; 1hr 15min); Jakarta (20 daily; 1hr 10min); Kuala Lumpur (3 weekly; 2hr 25min).
By bus Buses terminate at the Tirtonadi bus station in the north of the city. Just across the crossroads by the northeastern corner of Tirtonadi is the minibus terminal, Gilingan. From the front of the *Hotel Surya*, overlooking Tirtonadi, orange angkot #6 (Rp5000) departs for the town centre, stopping at Ngapeman, the junction of Jl Gajah Mada and Jl Brig Jen Slamet Riyadi. To reach the bus

station from the centre, catch a #05 orange bus from Matahari department store.

Destinations Frequent buses to Bandung (12hr); Banyuwangi (12hr); Jakarta (13hr); Malang (7hr); Surabaya (6hr); Yogyakarta (2hr).

By train You'll pay about Rp20,000 for a becak from outside the Balapan train station, 300m south of Tirtonadi, to Jl Dahlan.

Destinations Bandung (6 daily; 9hr); Jakarta (5 daily; 8hr 30min); Malang (6 daily; 6hr 25min); Surabaya (7 daily; 4–5hr); Yogya (16 daily; 1hr).

INFORMATION AND TOURS

Tourist office Behind the Radya Pustaka Museum at Jl Brig Jen Slamet Riyadi 275 (daily 8am–5pm; ☎0271 711435, ⏿pariwisatasolo.surakarta.go.id). It has details of events, a reasonable range of brochures and maps, and – when Patrick Orlando is around – English-speaking staff.

Tours Several hotels in Solo organize a range of excursions. Cycling tours are popular, among the most rewarding organized by *Istana Griya* (Rp175,000) and *Warung Baru* (Rp200,000); each runs about 5hr including a visit to a gamelan factory, bakery, tofu factory and a manufacturer of *arak*. The same hotels also offer excursions to take in both Candi Ceto and Candi Sukuh, stopping en route at the picturesque Jumog waterfall (around Rp300,000/person). For Bromo or Ijen, tours from Yogya are a better bet.

GETTING AROUND

By becak Unlike the ones in Yogya, Solo's becak do not charge a higher rate if there is more than one person in the carriage. As ever, bargain hard.

By taxi The main taxi stand is situated by the Matahari department store; they are metered, though the minimum fare is Rp35,000.

By bus The BST bus service can ease trips across town: #1 runs from the airport to Palur bus terminal in the east, passing all the way down Slamet Riyadi (5am–6pm; Rp4500).

By bike Being flat and, for a Javanese city, relatively free of traffic, cycling is an excellent way to get around. Most homestays rent out bikes for Rp20,000–35,000/day and motorbikes for Rp100,000/day.

ACCOMMODATION

The backpacker enclave is around Jl Dahlan, while there are several good-value mid-range options further west along Jl Slamet Riyadhi.

Cakra Homestay Jl Cakra II/15, Kauman ☎0271 634743, ⏨hotelcakrahomestay@yahoo.com. In a peaceful setting tucked away behind high walls just off busy Jl Baki Solo, with traditional Javanese furnishings, a pretty pool, and a gamelan orchestra where practices are held on Mondays and Thursdays. Rooms are simple but comfortable, a few with a/c (Rp200,000). Doubles `Rp125,000`

Istana Griya Jl Dahlan 22 ☎0271 632667. Highly efficient homestay with good-value though somewhat worn rooms, some with a/c and hot water (Rp175,000) – including one built for families (Rp250,000). Breakfast included. The friendly English-speaking owner organizes a range of tours and rents out bikes and motorbikes. Doubles `Rp125,000`

Red Planet Jl Dr Soepomo 49 ☎021 2949 8888, ⏿redplanethotels.com/hotel/solo. Solo's branch of this international, Thailand-based hotel chain is the best-value mid-range option in town, with ten floors of bright, clean rooms with a/c and flat-screen TVs. There are also English-speaking staff and great city views from the upper floors. Doubles `Rp275,000`

Warung Baru Homestay Off Jl Dahlan ☎0271 656369 or ☎0813 2901 1942, ⏨dodynz@gmail.com. A neat and friendly little place down a quiet alley off Jl Dahlan. There is a wonderful garden and sitting area out the front of five colourful rooms with comfy beds, two equipped with fan and three with a/c (Rp150,000). Doubles `Rp125,000`

EATING

Solo's warung are renowned for local specialities such as *nasi liwet* (chicken or vegetables and rice drenched in coconut milk and served on a banana leaf) and *nasi gudeg* (jackfruit curry). For dessert, try *kue putu* (coconut cakes) or *srabi*, a rice flour and coconut milk pancake served with a variety of fruit toppings. Most of these are found along Jl Brig Jen Slamet Riyadi and at the Galabo night market.

Conejo Mexican Fusion Jl Ronggowarsito 151. A new and surprising addition to Solo's restaurant scene, with some of the best Mexican food on Java, most dishes with a local spin (beef rendang taco Rp40,000). Special deals on Taco Tuesday. Mon–Sat 11am–11pm, Sun 10am–10pm.

Nasi Liwet Bu Wongso Lemu Jl Teuku Umar 34. In business since 1950, this humble street stall with cramped seating draws crowds after dusk for its speciality of *nasi liwet* (from Rp17,000) – locals swear it's among Solo's very best. Daily 4pm–1am.

Warung Baru Jl Dahlan 23. Solo's longtime backpacker favourite, with delicious and very inexpensive Solonese food such as *nasi liwet* and *nasi pecel* (vegetable and peanut sauce; Rp10,000 each) plus excellent home-made bread. Bike tours and batik courses can be organized here too. Daily 8am–9pm.

PERFORMING ARTS

For the last two centuries, the royal houses of Solo have developed highly individual styles for the traditional Javanese arts of gamelan and wayang. *Wayang orang*, which features human performers rather than the leather shadow puppets used in *wayang kulit*, is something of a local speciality. It combines dance, vocal and character performances to evoke scenes from the Mahabharata and Ramayana.

Balekambang Jl Balekambang 1. A pleasant park in the northeast of town hosting free Ramayana performances on the third Friday of the month (7.30–10pm).

Puro Mangkunegaran The practice gamelan performances are given (Wed 10am–noon) in the beautiful surroundings of the palace.

Taman Budaya This theatre to the northwest of town hosts free, all-night Ramayana performances beginning Thursday evenings (9pm–4am).

Sriwedari Park Two-hour performances of *wayang orang* (Mon–Sat 8–11pm; Rp5000).

SHOPPING

Museum Batik Danar Hadi Jl Slamet Riyadi 261 ⊕0271 713140. Upmarket batik galleries are numerous in Solo, the best-known being the one at this museum. Daily 9am–3pm.

Pasar Klewer Just to the north of Kasunanan Palace. One of Indonesia's largest textile markets, with some of the best bargains in Solo. Ravaged by a fire in 2014, the new complex reopened in 2017. Daily 10am–4pm.

Pasar Triwindu A block south of Pura Mangkunegaran. An antique market with a wide range of old trinkets, from porcelain pieces to brass batik stamps to car parts. Daily 10am–4pm.

DIRECTORY

Banks and exchange Most banks are found at and around the eastern end of Jl Riyadi, with ATMs and moneychangers.

Batik courses Solo is the cheapest and arguably the best place to try your hand at batik. Homestays and restaurants such as *Istana Griya* and *Warung Baru* can set you up with a number of courses. Some of the best are offered by Kampung Batik Lawayan (⊕kampoengbatiklaweyan.org) on Jl Dr Rajiman 521, west of the centre.

Hospital Rumah Sakit Kasih Ibu, on Jl Brig Jen Slamet Riyadi 404, has English-speaking doctors.

Internet Wi-fi is available in some restaurants and cafés as well as in Solo Grand Mall.

Police Station Jl Slamet Riyadi 376 ⊕0271 740683 or ⊕0271 713003. Dial ⊕110 for emergencies.

Post office Jl Jend Sudirman (daily 6am–10pm).

SURABAYA

Chaotic, noisy and sweltering, **SURABAYA** is Indonesia's second-largest city and the major port of East Java. Although to most tourists it's little more than a place to switch buses or trains between Yogya and Bromo, Surabaya isn't without its charms. Dubbed the "City of Heroes," the city is heralded among Indonesians as the birthplace of the national independence movement, and its leafy boulevards are lined with statues and monuments honouring that heritage.

WHAT TO SEE AND DO

Rich in contrasts and diversity, modern Surabaya boasts bazaars, mega-malls, chic cafés and ancient relics as well as some of the country's most colourful ethnic minority neighbourhoods, particularly its vibrant Chinese and Arab quarters.

Chinese Quarter

Surabaya's **Chinese Quarter** – centred roughly around Jalan Songoyudan and Jalan Kembang Jepun to the north of the city centre – hums with activity and an abundance of traditional two-storey shophouses that line its narrow streets. Minuscule red-and-gold altars glint in shops and houses, while Buddhist, Confucian and Hindu effigies adorn the three-hundred-year-old **Hong Tiek Hian Temple**, east of the canal on Jalan Dukuh. Stretching westward from Jalan Songoyudan to Jalan Panggung is the sprawling, covered **Pasar Pabean**, Surabaya's largest produce market, with endless crates stacked with fish, vegetables and spices in tightly packed stalls.

Kampung Arab

Just a short walk north of the Chinese Quarter is the most interesting part of Surabaya – **Kampung Arab** or **Qubah**, the Arab area. Here you will find the oldest and most famous mosque in Surabaya, **Mesjid Ampel**, originally erected in 1421. The whole kampung – bounded by Jalan Nyanplungan, Jalan KH Mas Mansur, Jalan Sultan Iskandar Muda and Jalan Pabean Pasar – was settled by Arab traders and sailors who arrived in Kali Mas harbour more than five hundred years ago. Resembling an Arab souk, its maze of tidy, well-kept alleyways is crammed cheek by jowl with stalls selling flowers, dates, shawls, beads, perfumes, prayer caps and headscarves. Dress conservatively when visiting the area – women will be asked to wear headscarves.

4

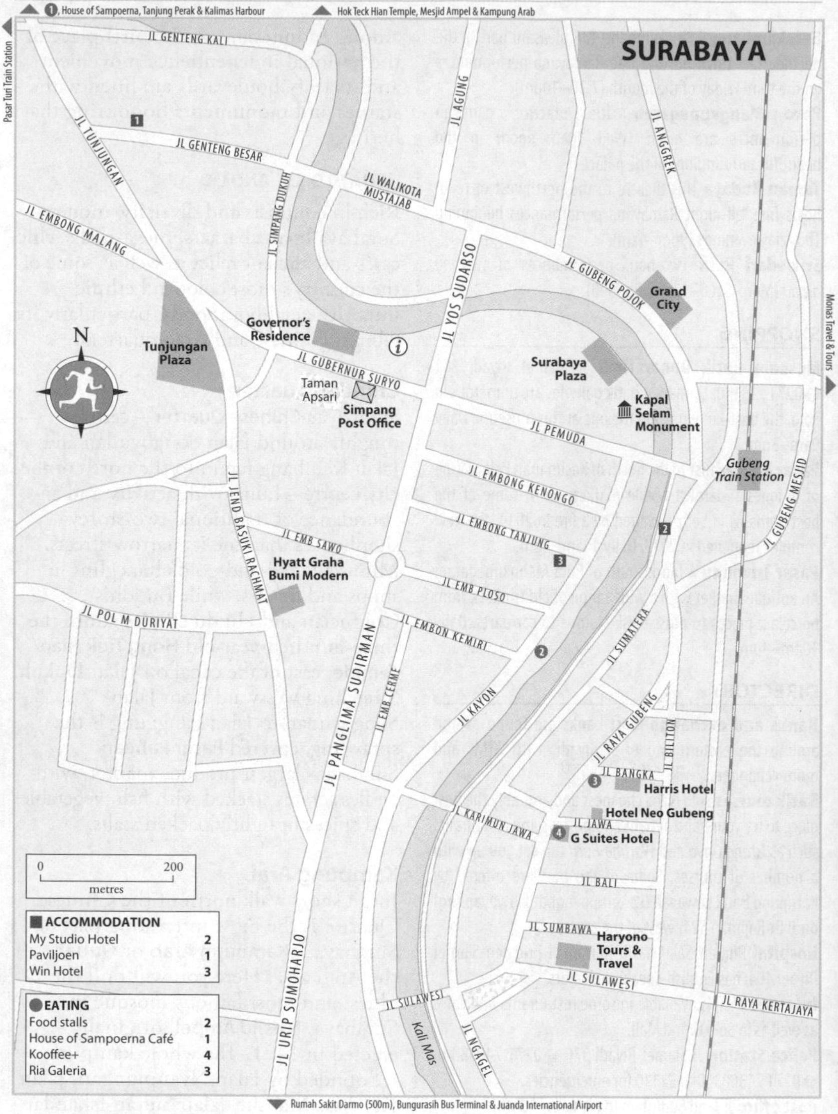

SURABAYA
1, House of Sampoerna, Tanjung Perak & Kalimas Harbour
Hok Teck Hian Temple, Mesjid Ampel & Kampung Arab
Pasar Turi Train Station
Monas Travel & Tours
Rumah Sakit Darmo (500m), Bungurasih Bus Terminal & Juanda International Airport
JL GENTENG KALI
JL TUNJUNGAN
JL GENTENG BESAR
JL AGUNG
JL ANGGREK
JL WALIKOTA MUSTAJAB
JL SIMPANG DUKUH
JL EMBONG MALANG
JL YOS SUDARSO
JL GUBENG POJOK
Grand City
Governor's Residence
Tunjungan Plaza
N
JL GUBERNUR SURYO
Taman Apsari
Simpang Post Office
Surabaya Plaza
Kapal Selam Monument
JL PEMUDA
Gubeng Train Station
JL GUBENG MESJID
JL EMBONG KENONGO
JL EMBONG TANJUNG
JL JEND BASUKI RACHMAT
JL EMB SAWO
Hyatt Graha Bumi Modern
JL EMB PLOSO
JL POL M DURIYAT
JL EMBON KEMIRI
JL SUMATERA
JL PANGLIMA SUDIRMAN
JL EMB CERME
JL KAYON
JL RAYA GUBENG
JL BILITON
JL BANGKA
Harris Hotel
Hotel Neo Gubeng
JL KARIMUN JAWA
JL JAWA
G Suites Hotel
JL BALI
JL SUMBAWA
Haryono Tours & Travel
JL SULAWESI
JL RAYA KERTAJAYA
JL URIP SUMOHARJO
Kali Mas
JL NGAGEL
0 200 metres
ACCOMMODATION
My Studio Hotel 2
Paviljoen 1
Win Hotel 3
EATING
Food stalls 2
House of Sampoerna Café 1
Kooffee+ 4
Ria Galeria 3

House of Sampoerna

Whether or not you're a fan of *kreteks* (clove cigarettes), the **House of Sampoerna**, Jl Taman Sampoerna 6 (daily 9am–10pm; free; ⓣ 031 353 9000, ⓦ houseofsampoerna.museum), a museum across the Mas River to the west of both the Chinese Quarter and the Qubah, makes a worthwhile stop. This stately Dutch compound, restored and opened to the public, was built in 1862 and later transformed into one of Indonesia's biggest *kretek* cigarette factories. It once employed 2900 workers rolling 325 cigarettes each per hour, though there are far fewer workers around today. If you come during working hours (Mon–Fri 9am–2pm, Sat 9am–noon), you can glimpse the workers hand-rolling the ever-popular Dji Sam Soe.

Downtown

Near the city centre, you can take a walk through the steel belly of **Kapal Selam Monument**, Jl Pemuda 39 (daily 8am–10pm; Rp10,000; ☎031 549 0410), a Russian-built submarine acquired by the Indonesian Navy. Up the street is the Joko Dolog, an ancient Buddha statue of dubious origin set just south of **Taman Apsari Park**, across from the governor's residence on Jalan Gubernor Suryo.

ARRIVAL AND DEPARTURE

By plane Surabaya's Juanda International Airport (☎031 298 6343) lies 18km south of the city. No public bus connects with the town centre directly, but DAMRI buses connect with Purabaya bus station (every 15min; 20min; Rp25,000), from where the #P1 service (Rp5000) connects with the city centre at the intersection of Jl Tunjungan and Jl Pemuda, continuing to the harbour; the #A2 heads right past Gubeng Station (Rp6000). There's a rank for fixed-price taxis (Rp120,000).
Destinations Ambon (2 daily; 2hr 30min); Balikpapan (16 daily; 1hr 30min); Bandung (6 daily; 1hr 20min); Denpasar (12 daily; 55min); Jakarta (61 daily; 1hr 25min); Makassar (22 daily; 1hr 30min); Manado (3 daily; 2hr 35min); Medan (2 daily; 3hr); Yogyakarta (7 daily; 1hr 10min).
By bus The main bus station is Terminal Purabaya, 6km south of the city, better known locally as Bungurasih. All long-distance and inter-island buses start and finish here, plus many of the city buses and bemos. Local buses into the city leave from the far end of the Bungurasih terminal: follow the signs for "Kota" and take the #P1 service (Rp5000), which can be hailed from the city centre along Jl Panglima Sudirman just after the intersection with Jl Pemuda. Bungurasih also has a huge taxi rank – minimum fare of Rp15,000; expect to pay at least Rp50,000 to get anywhere in the city centre. Bus tickets are available from the offices within the bus station as well as from agents on Jl Basuki Rahmat in the city centre. Book ahead. For Jakarta, use Lorena & Karina (☎031 534 5152, ☜lorena-karina.com), and for Yogya take EKA (☎031 8819 8899, ☜ekamirabus.com).
Destinations Banyuwangi (every 30min; 6–7hr); Denpasar (4 daily; 11hr); Jakarta (15 daily; 14hr); Probolinggo (every 30min; 2hr); Solo (hourly; 6hr); Yogyakarta (hourly; 8hr).
By ferry Pelni ferries dock at Tanjung Perak in the far north of the city, served by #P1 buses. The main Pelni office is at Jl Pahlawan 112 (Mon–Thurs 9am–noon & 1–3pm, Fri & Sat 9am–noon; ☎031 353 9048).
Destinations Jakarta (2 weekly; 21–24hr); Jayapura (Mon & Wed; 5–6 days); Makassar (twice weekly; 24hr).

By train Surabaya has three main train stations. Most useful to travellers are Gubeng, in the centre of town near most accommodation, serving the routes to Banyaungi and Yogyakarta; and Pasar Turi, west of the city centre, serving the faster, northerly route to Jakarta.
Destinations Banyuwangi (4 daily; 7hr); Jakarta (5 daily; 9hr–10hr 30min); Probolinggo (6 daily; 2hr); Solo (10 daily; 4hr); Yogyakarta (6 daily; 5hr).

INFORMATION

Tourist information The extremely helpful tourist office is at Jl Gubenor Suryo 15 (daily 8am–8pm; ☎031 534 0444, ☜sparkling.surabaya.go.id), with English-speaking staff and good maps and brochures.
Tours The House of Sampoerna has a free sightseeing bus that plies multiple routes (Tues–Sun 9–10am, 1–2pm, 3–4.30pm), and there's a shopping and culinary tour starting at the tourist office (Tues, Sat & Sun 9am–2pm; Rp20,500). In addition to international travel, many agents in Surabaya offer all-inclusive tours to the sights of the region, either day-trips or longer. Among the largest, best-established setups are Haryono Tours and Travel, Jl Sulawesi 27–29 (☎0858 9512 1008, ☜haryonotours.com), and Monas Tours and Travel, Jl Dharahusada Utara 6 (☎031 596 5696).

GETTING AROUND

By becak Especially useful in the north by the Kampung Arab, charging around Rp15,000 for a 10min ride.
By taxi Blue Bird is recommended (☎031 372 1234; flagfall Rp700, minimum fare Rp15,000).

ACCOMMODATION

My Studio Hotel Jl Sumatra 20 C ☎031 504 2111, ☜mystudiohotel.com. Good-value, spotless dormitories with a/c, lockers, hot breakfast, and a free shuttle service to Gubeng station, 1km to the north. Both single and double pods (Rp150,000) as well as mixed and female-only dorms available. Dorms **Rp100,000**
Paviljoen Jl Genteng Besar 94–98 ☎031 534 3449. Clean and centrally located colonial bungalows, all with attached cold-water mandi and some with a/c (Rp200,000), set around a lush courtyard. Friendly Dutch- and English-speaking staff can help with onward travel. Southbound buses #P1 and #P2 stop just at the end of the street on Jl Tunjungan. Doubles **Rp150,000**
Win Hotel Jl Embong Tanjung ☎031 545 9111, ☜thewinhotelsurabaya.com. The best-value pick of the many flashy new business hotels clustered to the south and west of Gubeng on both sides of the river, the *Win* is worth the splurge, with comfortable a/c rooms, a sleek, futuristic design and a pleasant downstairs café. English-speaking staff are as cheery as the motivational quotes plastered to the walls. Significant discounts offered on booking sites. Doubles **Rp400,000**

4

EATING AND DRINKING

There is a good selection of cheap food stalls by the river, past the flower market on Jl Kalun, serving Indonesian coffee, grilled fish and chicken dishes for the mainly local clientele. One of the local favourites is *rawon*, a thick, black beef soup served throughout the night at Surabaya's warung. Tunjungan plaza's giant top-floor food court has even more options.

House of Sampoerna Café Jl Taman Sampoerna. Set in an elegant colonial building attached to the famous cigarette factory of the same name, this posh café's menu features Western and Indonesian cuisine (barbecue beef soup Rp35,000), as well as smoking and non-smoking sections. Daily 11am–10pm.

Kooffee+ *G Suites Hotel*, 11th floor, Jl Raya Gubeng 43 ☎031 501 1001, ⊛kooffeeplus.co.id. Stylish café and restaurant with skilled, charming baristas and a smattering of local and Western cuisine (pizzas from Rp75,000) as well as cold beers (large Bintang Rp70,000). It's well worth the inflated prices for the spectacular views of Surabaya's burgeoning skyline from the eleventh storey of the *G Suites Hotel*. Mon–Fri 2–10pm, Sat & Sun noon–midnight.

Ria Galeria Jl Bangka 2–4 ☎031 503 3737. This beautifully decorated Javanese restaurant has long been a favourite dining spot for dignitaries, offering a wide sampling of Indonesian specialities like *sop buntut* (oxtail soup Rp70,000) and *gado gado* (Rp35,000) at reasonable prices. Daily 11am–9.30pm.

DIRECTORY

Banks and exchange All major Indonesian banks have huge branches in Surabaya, with exchange facilities.

Consulates US, Jl Citra Raya Niaga 2 (☎031 297 5300); UK and Australian consulates closed.

Hospital Rumah Sakit Darmo, Jl Raya Darmo 90 (☎031 567 6253).

Immigration office Jl Jend S Parman 58A (☎031 853 1785).

Internet All the big plazas have at least one internet café (from Rp5000/hr).

Police station In north Surabaya on Jl Raden Saleh (☎031 568 8099). For emergencies, call ☎031 199.

Post office The most central office is at Jl Taman Apsaril 1 (Mon–Thurs 8am–12.30pm, Fri 8–11am, Sat 8am–noon), beside Taman Apsari Park.

THE BROMO REGION

The **Bromo region** is best known for its awesome scenery. At its heart is a vast, ancient volcanic crater with sheer walls over 300m high, within which the dramatic, still-smoking **Gunung Bromo** (2329m) – one of three volcanoes in the crater – rises up from the Sea of Sand, a desolate plain at the crater's base. Hundreds of thousands visit each year to glimpse Bromo at sunrise.

WHAT TO SEE AND DO

This unique landscape now comprises the Bromo-Tengger-Semeru National Park, whose highlights are the dramatic smoking crater of **Gunung Bromo**, **Gunung Penanjakan** – on the outside crater's edge and one of the favourite sunrise spots – and **Cemoro Lawang**, with its brilliant panoramic view of the crater, at its best during the dry season. The park also contains the highest mountain in Java, **Gunung Semeru**, which can be climbed by experienced trekkers.

The most popular approach to the Bromo region is to head inland from **Probolinggo** – 100km southeast of Surabaya on the north coast – to the crater's edge at Cemoro Lawang, where most people stay in order to make the dawn trip to Gunung Bromo as easy as possible. A much less common approach involves heading inland from Pasuruan, 60km southeast of Surabaya, in order to reach the villages of Tosari and Wonokitri, also linked by road to Gunung Penanjakan.

Gunung Bromo

The climb to the top of **Gunung Bromo** (2392m) is the most popular excursion from Cemoro Lawang; if you're lucky with the clouds, there may be an absolutely spellbinding sunrise that's well worth the steep entry fee (Mon–Fri Rp220,000, Sat & Sun Rp320,000). To get to the base of Gunung Bromo, you can walk (1hr; bring a torch and follow the white pillars through the Sea of Sand), get a horse (Rp70,000), or hire a jeep for the morning to take in both Gunung Bromo and Gunung Penanjakan (Rp450,000). However you get there, you'll still have to manage the 249 concrete stairs up to the crater rim, from where there are great views down into the smoking crater and back across the Sea of Sand. Dress warmly.

Gunung Penanjakan

The best spot for postcard-perfect sunrise views, taking in the entire

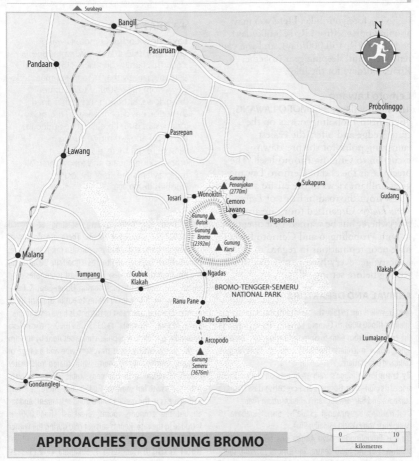

APPROACHES TO GUNUNG BROMO

Bromo area, is **Gunung Penanjakan** (2770m). The whole crater area lies below, Bromo smoking and Semeru puffing up regular plumes while the sun rises dramatically in the east. You can **camp** up here if you wish, but you'll be invaded before dawn by the hordes. Most visitors take the jeep tour from Cemoro Lawang at around 4am that will then drive across the Sea of Sand to Bromo before returning to Cemoro Lawang (Rp450,000).

Gunung Semeru
Essentially a dry-season expedition (June–Sept or possibly Oct), the climb up **Gunung Semeru** (3676m), Java's highest mountain, is a three-day hike for fit, experienced trekkers only and requires good preparation and equipment. The volcano has been in a state of continuous eruption since 1967, and over twenty thousand seismic events are typically recorded each year; it's a good idea to take a guide (ask at the PHPA office or your hotel) and heed local advice. The path starts at the village of **Ranu Pane** (2117m) to the north of the mountain, accessible from Cemoro Lawang by ojek (Rp60,000) or via a four-hour path across the Sea of Sand to Jemplang, from where it's another 6km to the village. Ranu Pane has several basic homestays (Rp80,000) and the **PHPA office** (☏0335 541038), where you must

register before your hike. Here you may also find porters (from Rp120,000/day) and guides (Rp150,000/day), and you can rent a tent and sleeping gear (together Rp50,000/day) for the hike.

Cemoro Lawang

The small village of **CEMORO LAWANG**, 46km from Probolinggo, sits on the crater's edge and offers the easiest launching point for the pre-dawn excursion to Gunung Bromo itself. The precipice at the end of Cemoro Lawang gives brilliant views of the entire area – best from the road in front of *Lava View Lodge*. Organized tours are available everywhere, but be warned that operators in both Probolinggo and Cemoro Lawang have poor reputations in regard to honesty; get everything you've paid for in writing before setting off.

ARRIVAL AND DEPARTURE

Most travellers opt to take the train to Probolinggo, then a minibus (Rp40,000) to Cemoro Lawang. These run up to the crater rim from 6am to 5pm, returning from 8am till 4pm. Yellow microlets (Rp6000) connect Probolinggo's train and bus stations.

By train Probolinggo's train station is on the northern side of its *alun-alun*. Business and Executive class trains to Surabaya and Banyuwangi are called *Mutiara Timur*.

Destinations Banyuwangi (5 daily; 5hr); Surabaya (6 daily; 2hr); Yogyakarta (3 daily; 9hr).

By bus Probolinggo's Bayu Angga bus terminal is 6km southwest of the town centre. To Cemoro Lawang, there are two daily buses – labelled "Sukapura" and "Ngadisari" on the front – as well as frequent minibuses from just outside the terminal, running until 4pm (Rp40,000).

Destinations Banyuwangi (hourly; 5hr); Surabaya (every 30min; 2hr); Yogyakarta (3 daily; 9hr).

INFORMATION

Tourist information Probolinggo has a helpful tourist information office in front of the train station (☎0335 432420, ✉pip_kotaprob@yahoo.co.id). In Cemoro Lawang, the national park office (daily 24hr) has displays about the area, while *Hotel Yoschi* is good for local information, especially if you want to trek. There's a BNI ATM near *Lava View Lodge*.

ACCOMMODATION

For such a small place, there is plenty of accommodation to choose from in Cemoro Lawang, Ngadisari (3km from the rim) and Wonokerto (5km). Rooms are pricier and poorer

---

Lava View Lodge Cemoro Lawang ☎0335 541009, ✇lavaview.lavaindonesia .com. This family-run place is in high demand, largely thanks to the unmatched views from the restaurant and upper bungalows. Although somewhat aged, the lodge has decent en-suite rooms, an Indonesian buffet breakfast (included in the price) and live music during high season. To get there, go past the drab-looking square and follow the main track towards the lip of the crater. Doubles **Rp700,000**

---

value than elsewhere in Java, starting at around Rp100,000 for ultra-basic rooms. There are dozens of nondescript homestays, and you can also camp anywhere: Penanjakan is popular, and there's a good site 200m along the rim from the *Lava View Lodge*. Most room rates drop significantly out of the high season (June–Sept & Dec–Jan). There are a few small places to eat in the vicinity of Cemoro Lawang, and most of the hotels have restaurants.

Café Lava Hostel ☎0335 541020, ✇cafelava .lavaindonesia.com. A popular choice set right by the rim of the crater, with a great travellers' vibe and a range of options, from economy rooms with shared cold-water mandi to rooms with big beds, cable TV and private bathrooms with hot showers (Rp450,000). There are lovely sitting areas in the garden and a good restaurant, and for all but the economy rooms, breakfast (Rp40,000) is included in the rate. Rooms can get cold during the winter months. Doubles **Rp175,000**

Hotel Yoschi Jl Wonokerto 1, Sukapura ☎0813 3129 8881, ✇yoschihotel.com. A cosy place with eclectic decor and a great garden for relaxing. Moving up from the economy rooms with shared bathrooms, you'll pay a hefty price for rooms with private bathrooms (Rp540,000) and hot water (Rp900,000). Staff provide good information on the area, and also book bus tickets, arrange local guides, charter transport and rent warm jackets (Rp25,000). Good discounts during quiet periods, and breakfast is included. Doubles **Rp300,000**

BANYUWANGI

On the easternmost shores of Java, the pleasant town of **BANYUWANGI** serves as a base for the hike to Kawah Crater, while **Ketapang**, 8km to the north, is the port for ferries to Gilimanuk in Bali. Buses travelling to or from Bali head straight to the ferry terminal, bypassing the town.

ARRIVAL AND DEPARTURE

By ferry The ferry terminal is situated 8km north at Ketapang. Bemos #6 (yellow) and #12 (blue) link the town centre (Rp10,000). The 24hr service to Bali (50min; Rp7000) departs every 20min.

By bus Two bus terminals serve Banyuwangi. Most useful long-distance routes depart from Sri Tanjung, situated 2km north of Ketapang and connecting Probolinggo, Surabaya and Yogyakarta, among other Javan cities, via the northern road. Brawijaya terminal, from where buses head south before curving west into Java, is 4km to the south of town.

Destinations Bandung (daily; 21hr); Jakarta (daily; 22hr); Probolinggo (5 hourly; 5hr); Solo (hourly; 11–13hr); Surabaya (every 30min; 6–7hr); Yogyakarta (hourly; 13–14hr).

By train The *Mutiara Timur* is the most comfortable way to travel. The main train station is in Ketapang, 300m west of the ferry terminal.

Destinations Probolinggo (3 daily; 5hr); Surabaya (3 daily; 7hr).

INFORMATION

Tourist office The tourist information office (Mon–Fri 7am–3.30pm; ⊕0335 424172) is near the town centre at Jl A Yani 78.

ACCOMMODATION AND EATING

Street stalls and warung are plentiful in the city centre, especially along the corner of Jl Wahid Hasyim and Jl MT Haryono.

Dormitory Tourism Jl Ahmad Yani 110 ⊕0859 0413 3742. Aptly named and centrally situated right on the main square, with three storeys of clean, all a/c four- and six-bed dorms fitted with lockers. Close proximity to a large mosque means an early wake-up call. Dorms **Rp150,000**

Kampung Osing Inn Jl Lingkungan Watu Ulo RT 02 ⊕0878 5273 8711, ⓦkampungosing.com. Simple, fan rooms in a cosy, quiet neighbourhood 5km west of the town centre and less than 2km east of Karangasem station (free pick-up service on arrival). Friendly resident guide Jin is a former mine worker. Indonesian breakfast included. Doubles **Rp140,000**

DIRECTORY

Banks and exchange For exchange, go to BCA at Jl Jend Sudirman 85–87 or BNI at Jl Banetrang 46.

Hospital Yasmin Hospital, Jl Letkol Istikqlah 80–84 (⊕0333 424671).

Internet There are hotspots all over the city, and warnets charging around Rp4000/hr.

Post office Jl Diponegoro 1 (Mon–Thurs 8am–3pm, Fri 8–11am, Sat 8am–1pm, Sun & hols 8am–noon), west of the sports field.

KAWAH IJEN

The view from the rim of **Kawah Ijen** (Ijen Crater; 2386m) is among the most spectacular to be found in all of Indonesia. Set within a 20km-wide caldera and bounded by sheer cliffs, the steaming crater holds a 200m-deep, 1km-wide, turquoise lake of highly acidic waters, the sulphuric shoreline striped in bright yellow. As well as otherworldly vistas, some of the planet's toughest workers may be seen in action here, battling toxic fumes and treacherous terrain while hauling 70kg sacks brimming with sulphur deposits.

Ijen can be reached from either Banyuwangi or Bondowoso, although most choose the former route, entailing a slightly shorter drive (1hr 15min) through forests and coffee plantations to the trailhead at Pos Paltuding. There, hikers must register their names at the **PHKA Office** and pay the admission fee (Mon–Fri Rp100,000, Sat & Sun Rp150,000) before making the one- to one-and-a-half-hour hike to the lip of the crater. Guides are not necessary during the day, but prove helpful when making the thirty-minute descent into the crater itself, which is challenging because of both toxic fumes and a steep and sometimes unclear path. Guides are certainly recommended for the increasingly popular night-time hike, where hikers reach the base of the crater in the predawn darkness in order to glimpse the **blue flames** – jets of sulphur gas that burn bright blue – before climbing back to the crater's rim for glorious sunrise views. The relatively dry months from April to October are ideal for the hike.

Transportation to Pos Paltuding is easily arranged in Banyuwangi from around Rp150,000 per person in a car or the same on the back of an ojek, including waiting time and excluding entrance fee. Along with six other people, it will cost around Rp350,000 to throw in the entrance fee, a gas mask and guide – many of them former mine workers.

GRAJAGAN: G-LAND

On the borders of Alas Purwo National Park in the far southeastern corner of Java, the fishing village of **GRAJAGAN** has

4

become famous for its world-class surf. Better known as **G-Land**, it boasts awesomely long right- and left-handers and many kilometres of pristine beach. The ideal surfing season here is during the dry season, roughly from April to October. Several tour operators on Bali and Lombok run all-inclusive trips. Prices start from $640 for an all-inclusive three-day, three-night surfing package. A recommended G-Land operator based in Kuta is G-Land Bobby's Surf Camp (☎0361 755588, ⓦgrajagan.com).

Sumatra

An explorer's paradise, much of Sumatra – an island larger than Japan – remains undiscovered. The main highlights on the beaten path are situated along the old Trans-Sumatran highway, which spans from Banda Aceh in the far north to Bandar Lampung at the island's southern tip. Of these, most are clustered in the north: the misty jungles of **Bukit Lawang**, offering the best chance in Indonesia to see orang-utans in the wild; the ancient crater lake of **Danau Toba**, spiritual heartland of the fascinating Batak tribe; the twin volcanoes of **Berastagi**, a charming hill town and ideal trekking base; and the top-notch dive spots of Aceh's laidback **Pulau Weh**, situated at Indonesia's kilometre zero. Meanwhile, within easy reach of steamy Padang on the west coast lies a wealth of attractions: **Bukittinggi**, the bustling, cultural capital of the stunning Minangkabau Highlands; **Danau Maninjau**, a palm-fringed lake surrounded by jungle-covered cliffs; and the remote **Mentawai**, a surfer's paradise.

Although getting around Sumatra on **public transport** can be gruelling – distances are vast, the roads tortuous and the driving hair-raising – it's certainly an adventure, and one best experienced sooner than later: since late 2013, a brand-new Trans-Sumatran highway has been in the works, slated for completion over the next twelve years. Meanwhile, the many safe, low-cost airlines that now link all the island's major hubs have effectively phased out the old Sumatran sea routes favoured by travellers in decades past.

MEDAN

Indonesia's third-largest city, **MEDAN** is the gateway to North Sumatra. Often railed against by fast-transiting tourists as one of Southeast Asia's least charming cities, Medan makes a better impression on visitors who stick around a bit longer. Chaotic as any Indonesian metropolis, it certainly has its fair share of pollution and traffic jams, but also boasts more urban comforts than anywhere else in Sumatra. Medan has a diverse population hailing from all across the archipelago and beyond, including substantial Indian and Chinese minorities whose roots in the city predate the arrival of the Dutch, the latter having left a few graceful examples of colonial architecture – evidence of the wealth generated from the vast plantations that to this day stretch up the slopes of the Bukit Barisan to the west of the city.

WHAT TO SEE AND DO

Most travellers spend no more than a day or so in Medan, using it as a transit point to Bukit Lawang, Berastagi, Danau Toba or Malaysia.

Museum of North Sumatra

The large, informative **Museum of North Sumatra**, Jl Joni 51, 500m east of Jalan SM Raja (Tues–Sun 9am–4pm; Rp10,000), on the southern side of the Bukit Barisan cemetery near the stadium, tells the history of North Sumatra, and includes a couple of Arabic gravestones from 8 AD and some ancient stone Buddhist sculptures.

Mesjid Raya

One of the most recognizable buildings in Sumatra, the black-domed **Mesjid Raya**, Jalan SM Raja (daily 9am–5pm, except prayer times; donation), commissioned by the sultan in 1906, was designed by Dutch architect and photographer Theodoor van Erp, who also designed the nearby Maimun Palace.

Its striking exterior consists of North African-style arched windows, blue-tiled walls and vivid stained-glass windows.

Colonial Medan

Jalan Brig Jend A Yani, at the northern end of Jalan Pemuda, was the centre of colonial Medan, and a few early twentieth-century buildings remain. The weathered **Mansion of Tjong A Fie** at no. 105 is a beautiful green and yellow two-storey house built in 1900 for the head of the Chinese community in Medan (daily 9am–5pm; entrance & English-speaking guide Rp35,000; Ⓦ tjongafiemansion.org). Beyond the striking, dragon-topped gateway, the mansion has uniquely appointed rooms well worth a gander, including a lavish reception hall, Taoist prayer rooms and a spacious upstairs ballroom now hosting local exhibits.

The fine 1920s **Harrison-Crossfield Building** (now labelled "London, Sumatra, Indonesia TBK"), at the road's northern end, was the former headquarters of a rubber exporter. Continuing north along Jalan Balai Kota and taking a left, you reach the grand, dazzlingly white headquarters of **PT Perkebunan IX** (a government-run tobacco company), on narrow Jalan Tembakau Deli, 200m north of the *Inna Dharma Deli* hotel, which was commissioned by Jacob Nienhuys in 1869.

Indian Quarter

In the west of the city, on Jalan H Zainul Arifin, is the **Sri Mariamman Temple** (daily 6am–noon & 4–9pm; donation), Medan's oldest and most venerated Hindu shrine. It was built in 1884 and is devoted to the goddess Kali. The temple marks the beginning of the Indian Quarter, the **Kampung Keling**, which is the largest of its kind in Indonesia. In recent decades, the shrinking Indian population has been offset by an increasing number of Chinese, whose presence is made known by the nearby **Vihara Gunung Timur** (Temple of the Eastern Mountain; daily 7am–5pm; donation), the largest Taoist temple in

Sumatra, adorned with a multitude of dragons, wizards, warriors and lotus petals. It's tucked away at the west end of Jalan Hang Tuah, about 800m south of Sri Mariamman.

ARRIVAL AND DEPARTURE

By plane Medan's Kuala Namu International Airport, the second largest in the country, is about 30km east of the city. The airport is linked with the city by rail and bus. By rail, the trip is quicker but pricier (20 daily in each direction, 4.45am–11.45pm from the airport, 4am–9.15pm from Medan; 40min; Rp100,000), and becaks connect Medan's train station to the Mesjid Raya area (Rp20,000). DAMRI buses connect the airport to several spots in the city (every 30min 5am–10pm): Amplas Terminal (1hr; Rp15,000); Pusat Kota (city centre by Medan Fair Plaza; 1hr; Rp20,000), from where you may alight at the junction of Jl SM Raja for Mesjid Raya; and Binjai (1hr–1hr 30min; Rp40,000), about 30km west of Medan, for buses to Bukit Lawang (2hr; Rp30,000) or to be dropped off along the way at Padang Bulan (for Berastagi; 1hr 30min; Rp25,000), and near Pinang Baris Terminal. Recommended taxis are Blue Bird and Express, charging around Rp140,000 for the trip between the airport and city centre.

Destinations Banda Aceh (4 daily; 1hr 5min); Jakarta (38 daily; 2hr 20min); Kuala Lumpur (8 daily; 1hr); Padang (3 daily; 1hr 5min); Penang (6 daily; 50min); Singapore (4 daily; 1hr 25min).

By bus Medan has two main bus stations. The sprawling Amplas station, 5km southeast of the city centre, serves buses for all points south, including Bukittinggi and Danau Toba. DAMRI buses (Rp7000) link Amplas terminal to Medan Mall on Jl Letjen MT Haryono, and white MRX buses (Rp5000) run from Amplas to Mesjid Raya via Jl Pemuda and Deli Plaza. The Pinang Baris bus station, 10km west of the city centre, serves buses for destinations to the north or west of the city, including Bukit Lawang, Berastagi and Aceh. Yellow minivan #64 travelling north past the Maimoon Palace up Jl Pemuda shuttles back and forth from Pinang Baris (Rp5000), as do DAMRI buses from Medan Mall. For Aceh buses, head to Jl Gagak Hitam near the city centre, where nearly a dozen bus companies operate regular trips to Banda Aceh, providing free shuttles to their respective terminals (recommended is PMTOH ☎ 061 847 4839). Connecting Amplas to Pinang Baris is the #64 minivan "Koperasi" (Rp7000). Another important transit point is Padang Bulan, a lay-in by the southwestern corner of the city, from where minibuses from several companies (Sinabung Jaya, Sutra and Karsima) depart for Berastagi. Padang Bulan is linked to the city centre by angkot #41 from the Mesjid Raya area (either Jl RH Juanda or Jl SM

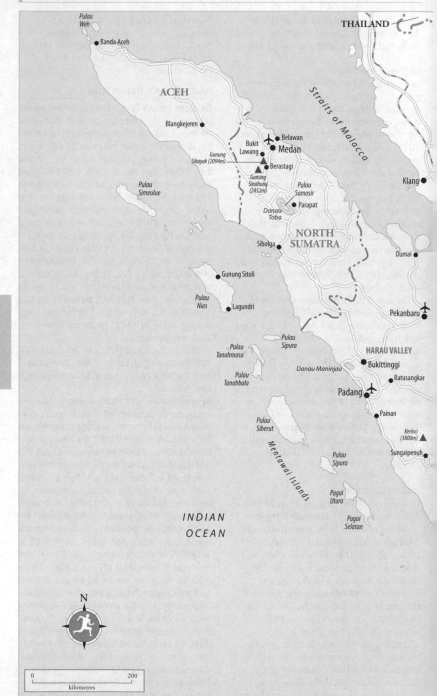

THAILAND

Pulau Weh

Banda Aceh

ACEH

Straits of Malacca

Blangkejeren

Belawan

Bukit Lawang

Medan

Gunung Sibayak (2094m)

Berastagi

Gunung Sinabung (2452m)

Pulau Samosir

Parapat

Danau Toba

Klang

NORTH SUMATRA

Pulau Simeulue

Sibolga

Dumai

Gunung Sitoli

Pulau Nias

Lagundri

Pekanbaru

Pulau Sipura

Pulau Tanahmasa

HARAU VALLEY

Bukittinggi

Danau Maninjau

Batusangkar

Pulau Tanahbala

Padang

Pulau Siberut

Painan

Kerinci (3800m)

Pulau Sipura

Sungaipenuh

Mentawai Islands

Pagai Utara

INDIAN OCEAN

Pagai Selatan

N

0   200
kilometres

4

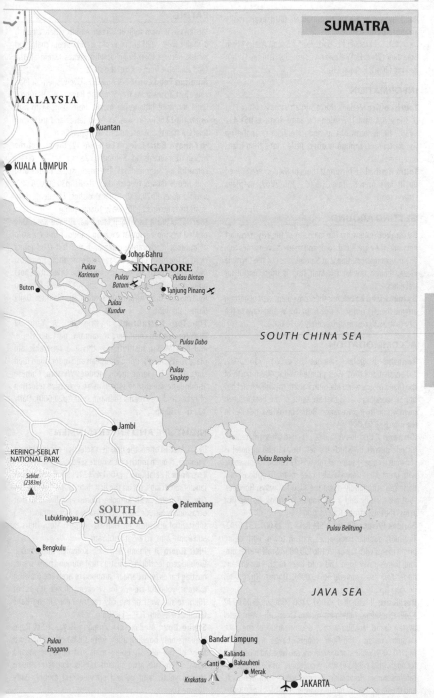

SUMATRA

MALAYSIA

Kuantan

KUALA LUMPUR

Johor Bahru
Pulau Karimun
SINGAPORE
Pulau Batam
Pulau Bintan
Buton
Tanjung Pinang
Pulau Kundur

SOUTH CHINA SEA

Pulau Dabo

Pulau Singkep

Jambi

Pulau Bangka

KERINCI-SEBLAT NATIONAL PARK

Seblat (2383m)

Lubuklinggau
SOUTH SUMATRA
Palembang

Pulau Belitung

Bengkulu

JAVA SEA

Pulau Enggano

Bandar Lampung
Kalianda
Canti
Bakauheni
Merak
Krakatau
JAKARTA

4

Raja). Bypassing the bus terminals are tourist cars, easily arranged by most hotels.

Destinations Frequent departures for Banda Aceh (12hr); Berastagi (2hr); Bukit Lawang (3hr); Bukittinggi (18hr); Padang (20hr); Parapat (3hr).

INFORMATION

Tourist office Medan's North Sumatra tourist office is at Jl Brig Jen A Yani 107 (Mon–Fri 8am–4pm; ☎061 452 8436), 400m south of Lapangan Merdeka near the *Tip Top Restaurant*, though it offers little more than maps and pamphlets.

Tours Worthwhile historical tours of Medan are offered by Tri Jaya Tour & Travel (☎061 703 2967, ⊕trijaya -travel.com).

GETTING AROUND

By angkot (minivans) The mainstay of the city transport network; they are numbered, and many have names too. The main angkot station is at Sambu, west of the Olympia Plaza, though the Medan Mall stop is more useful for travellers.

By motorized becak Another convenient way of getting around the city centre. A ride from the Mesjid Raya to the city centre will cost approximately Rp10,000.

ACCOMMODATION

Kanasha Jl Dolok Sanggul 8 ☎061 736 7932, ⊕kanashahotel.com. Well situated about 400m north of the Grand Mosque and Maimun Palace, this new hotel has bright, sparkling rooms that are some of the best value in town within their price range. Buffet breakfast included in the rate. Rp350,000

Kesawan Jl Brig Jen A Yani 97. Named after the central, historic district in which it's set, this rambling hotel is showing its age – some of the widely varied rooms come with grubby bathrooms (ask to see multiple options) and noise can echo loudly down the tiled hallways. However, staff are friendly and a few rooms overlook *Tip Top* just across the busy street. Rp275,000

Pondok Wisata Angel Jl SM Raja 70 ☎061 732 0702. The most popular backpacker spot in town, with clean, bright rooms with fan or a/c (Rp150,000). Staff are helpful, and there's tasty food and cold beer in the downstairs *Angel Café* (nasi goreng Rp10,000). Dorms Rp70,000, doubles Rp130,000

Residence Jl Tengah 1 ☎061 7760 0980 or ☎061 732 1249, ⊕residencehotelmedan.com. Clean, all-green hotel by the Grand Mosque with a decent range of compact, en-suite rooms: top-floor rooms have a/c and TV (Rp160,000), while standard rooms can be a tad musty (ask for one with a window) with a cramped, inside mandi. The café/restaurant downstairs is good value with free wi-fi, and there's a pleasant rooftop garden. Doubles Rp80,000

EATING

Medan has its own style of alfresco eating, where a bunch of stall-owners gather in one place and put out chairs and tables. Servers then bring around menus listing all the food available from each of the stalls.

Amaliun Food Court 3 Jl Amaliun. Lively, open-air food court just across from Yuki Simpang Raya mall, offering a wide range of Indonesian meals, from seafood to *nasi ayam* (Rp22,000), as well as fresh juices and ice-cream floats. A handful of restaurants stay open 24hr.

★**Cahaya Baru** Jl Teuku Cik Ditiro 12. The best of the Indian restaurants in Kampung Keling, set in clean, colourful a/c surroundings. The menu spans from North and South Indian (veg/chicken thali Rp30,000/38,000; *masala dosai* Rp20,000) to local dishes. Excellent, thick lassis (mango Rp30,000). Daily 10am–10pm.

Merdeka Walk Lapangan Merdeka, Jl Balai Kota. One of Medan's most popular evening hangout spots, a strip of outdoor restaurants, cafés and and fast-food joints right in the heart of the city serving everything from *nasi liwet* (Rp20,000) to durian pancakes. Favourite spots among locals include *Batiks Urban Kaffe*, *Jala-Jala* and *Nelayan* for their affordable seafood specialities. Daily 9am–midnight.

Tip Top Restaurant Jl Brig Jen A Yani 92 ⊕tiptop-medan.com. Part restaurant, part patisserie, and part Medan institution – this is a venerable old place that's been serving European and Indonesian food since 1934. The large menu includes Western, Chinese and Indonesian dishes as well as an extensive selection of cakes and ice creams (banana split Rp20,000). Daily 10am–9.30pm.

NIGHTLIFE AND ENTERTAINMENT

By far, Medan offers the broadest selection of nightlife on Sumatra, though much of it is quite seedy.

Entrance Jl Balai Kota 1 ☎061 457 3900. Among Medan's fancier nightclubs, set on the first floor of the *Grand Aston City Hall Hotel*, with karaoke rooms and live DJs that occasionally include big regional names. Free entrance and substantial discounts on Thursday nights. Mon–Thurs & Sun 9pm–2am, Fri & Sat until 5am.

Pitu Room Jl Pinang Baris 29, Komplek Imperium I. Ground zero for North Sumatra's underground punk scene, hosting bands from Bandar Lampung to Aceh and drawing raucous, youthful crowds for weekend shows. It's about 10km to the west of the city centre, near Pinang Baris terminal. Fri–Sun 7.30–11.30pm.

Strike Bowl Medan Yuki Simpang Raya, Jl SM Raja. Medan's only bowling alley, with six lanes on the third floor of this old shopping mall just opposite Mesjid Raya. There are also billiard tables. Popular among Medan youth, and packed on weekend nights. Daily 10am–10pm.

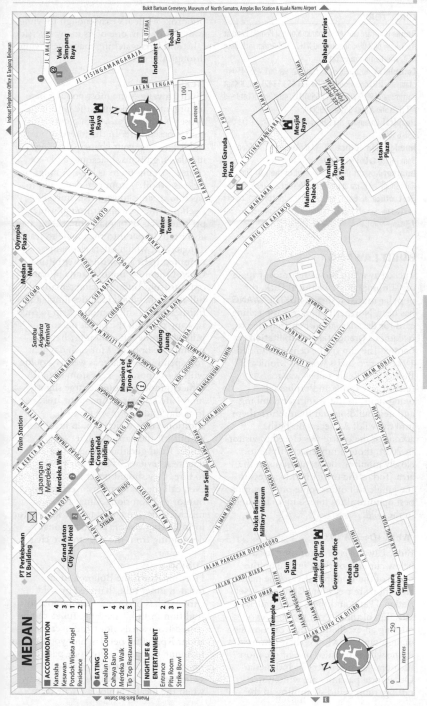

Bukit Barisan Cemetery, Museum of North Sumatra, Amplas Bus Station & Kuala Namu Airport

Indosat Telephone Office & Tanjung Belawan

Pinang Baris Bus Station

MEDAN

■ ACCOMMODATION
Kanasha	4
Kesawan	3
Pondok Wisata Angel	1
Residence	2

■ EATING
Amaliun Food Court	1
Cahaya Baru	4
Merdeka Walk	2
Tip Top Restaurant	3

■ NIGHTLIFE & ENTERTAINMENT
Entrance	2
Pitu Room	3
Strike Bowl	1

4

DIRECTORY

Banks There are clusters of banks along Jl Pemuda and at the corner of Jl Diponegoro and Jl H Zainul Arifin, including BCA, which offers good rates.

Consulates Australia, Jl Kartini 32 (☎061 455 4504); Malaysia, Jl P Diponegoro 43 (☎061 453 1342); UK, Jl Kapt Pattimura 459B (☎061 821 0559); US, 4th floor, Jl Let Jend MT Haryono A1 (☎061 451 9000).

Hospital Columbia Asia Hospital, Jl Listrik 2A (☎061 456 6368).

Immigration Office Jl Mangkubumi 2 (Mon–Fri 8am–4pm; ☎061 453 3117).

Internet Nusanet in the basement of the Yuki Simpang Raya shopping plaza opposite the Mesjid Raya (Rp4000/hr).

Post office Jl Balai Kota, on the northwest corner of Lapan-gan Merdeka (Mon–Fri 7.30am–6pm, Sat 7.30am–6pm).

BUKIT LAWANG

Tucked away on the easternmost fringes of Gunung Leuser National Park, the popular tourist resort of **BUKIT LAWANG** has been Northern Sumatra's top calling card for decades, almost entirely due to its famous **Orangutan Rehabilitation Centre**. The aim of the centre, founded in 1973 by two Swiss women, Monica Borner and Regina Frey, was to re-educate captive and orphaned orang-utans in the art of tree climbing and nest building and then return them into the wild. A success on both accounts, the centre was closed to visitors in 2014, though rangers continue to closely monitor the orang-utans in the area. Today, the town's handy access to the jungle still offers some of the world's best opportunities for seeing orang-utans in the wild.

WHAT TO SEE AND DO

Bukit Lawang is in a stunning location below curtains of thick jungle on the banks of the Bohorok River. The main attraction are treks into **Gunung Leuser National Park**, and there is a wonderful selection of these, even the shorter ones offering an excellent chance of glimpsing orang-utans. To witness their gymnastics in the wild is to enjoy one of the most memorable experiences in Indonesia. Other local pastimes are whitewater rafting, tubing and swimming in the

Bohorok, while it's easy enough to while away the days in one of its many riverside cafés and bars watching macaques swing through the trees.

Trekking

Bukit Lawang is the most popular base for organizing **treks** into the Gunung Leuser National Park, with plenty of guides based here. In the forests around Bukit Lawang, your chance of seeing monkeys, gibbons, macaques and – of course – orang-utans is high. A range of treks is on offer, from one-day walks to week-long slogs towards Ketambe in Aceh province, passing through some pristine tracts of primary forest. You may also head deeper into the jungle to reach Tangkahan, which offers elephant-mounted treks and whitewater rafting. One of the most popular and enjoyable options from Bukit Lawang remains the full-day trek, which includes lunch and finishes with a thirty-minute trip to Bukit Lawang through the rapids on an inflatable tube raft. You must have a **permit** (see opposite) for each day that you spend in the park, as well as a **guide** with IGA approval. Fees from the IGA Office (guides in hotels charge slightly more) are €35 for a three-hour trek, €45 for a day and €25 more for each additional day, which should include a permit for the park, food, tent and a guide. Read guestbook logs for up-to-date trek reviews. Whomever you decide to hire, they should never feed, touch or even call the orang-utans. Keep an eye out for the notorious Mina, a mischievous, semi-wild female known for intimidating visitors and occasionally descending from the trees to give chase.

Tubing

Hurtling down the Bohorok in an inflated inner tube, battered by wild currents, has become a time-honoured tradition in Bukit Lawang. **Tubes** can be rented from sheds along the river for about Rp20,000 per day, and you can put in about 1km up the riverside path from *Jungle Inn*. If you're not a strong swimmer, consider tubing on a Sunday, when the locals employ a rescue team along the more dangerous stretches of the river. The rapids can be quite extreme after heavy rain: proceed with caution, especially if you are without a guide, and avoid the section just before the town centre. There is a bridge 12km downstream of the village (2–3hr) just outside the town of Bohorok, from where you can catch a bus back (Rp15,000), strapping your tube to the roof.

ARRIVAL AND DEPARTURE

By bus Bukit Lawang's bus terminal is about 1km from the Bohorok Visitor Centre (Rp5000 by motorized becak). The only buses are to Medan's Pinang Baris Terminal (every 20min 5.30am–3.30pm daily; 4hr; Rp40,000).

By private minibus or car You may book a seat in a tourist car or minibus at numerous travel offices around town, among them Tobali (set near the parking area ☎ 0813 7018 9501). These depart in the morning for Medan (4hr; Rp120,000), Berastagi (5hr; Rp170,000) and Danau Toba (7hr; Rp230,000). Some charter trips to Danau Toba take in scenic spots along the way, such as Sipisopiso waterfall at the north end of the lake. For Tangkahan (3hr), you can go by ojek (Rp200,000) or 4WD (Rp550,000). Compare prices and don't be afraid to bargain.

INFORMATION

Tourist information and permits The permit office is part of the informative Bohorok Visitor Centre (daily 7.30am–3pm), packed with information about the park. Gunung Leuser National Park fees (Rp150,000/day) from the Visitor Centre and separate trekking permits (Rp12,000 for one day; plus Rp2000 for each additional day) from the IGA (Indonesian Guide Association; daily 7am–1.30pm) Office are always included in the trekking fee with organized hikes.

ACCOMMODATION AND EATING

The best accommodation in Bukit Lawang is clustered along the Bohorok's north shore. The best places to eat are the restaurants attached to each guesthouse, and most have live music on Saturday nights.

Garden Inn and Restaurant ☎ 0813 9600 0571, ⊛ bukitlawang-garden-inn.com. Simple rooms and bungalows (Rp200,000) by the river, with an attached, cosy restaurant serving Sumatran family meals (Rp20,000) and surrounded by gardens. It has a small library, friendly staff, a French-speaking owner and a pair of hammocks that are great for relaxing in with a cold beer. Doubles Rp150,000

Green Hill Café and Guest House ☎ 0813 7034 9124 or ☎ 0823 7061 6357, ⊛ greenhillbukitlawang.com. In a fantastic location overlooking the water, offering treetop bungalows with balconies, hammocks and even jungle

bathrooms with sit-down toilets (from Rp200,000). There's a cheaper room with a shared squat toilet and mandi. Attached restaurant and café downstairs with live acoustic music at night. Doubles Rp150,000

★**Indra Valley Inn** ☎ 0852 0718 2234, ⊛ indravalleyinn-bukitlawang.com. Small, laidback place right on the river with simple but charming rooms and a shared terrace decked with hammocks. The newest and nicest ones have private balconies and hot water (Rp450,000). The attached *Valley Café* is also popular, featuring regular acoustic sing-alongs. Ask owner and third-generation trekking guide Obiwan about the "jungle-style surfing" out back. Doubles Rp250,000

Jungle Inn ☎ 0813 7016 0173. The last guesthouse along the trail from the village, this is also the most organized and well-maintained spot in Bukit Lawang. There's a wide selection of rooms, all with private bathrooms – from good-value standard doubles to gigantic honeymoon suites with four-poster beds, jungle bathrooms and unbeatable views over the Bohorok (from Rp450,000). Doubles Rp300,000

Rain Forest ☎ 0813 6207 0656, ✉ nora_in2003 @mailyahoo.com. This cheap little guesthouse overlooking the Bohorok has some ultra-basic rooms consisting of a mattress on the floor, a mosquito net, flimsy rattan walls and shared bathrooms, as well as clean, comfortable doubles (Rp100,000). Fantastic meals (and cooking lessons for Rp100,000) prepared by Nora. Doubles Rp50,000

DIRECTORY

Banks and money The nearest ATM accepts only Mastercard and is 11km away in Bohorok village (Rp5000 by bus; Rp50,000 return by ojek), though at the time of writing an Indomaret had opened 3km away (Rp20,000 return by ojek), with an ATM coming soon; best to bring sufficient cash for your stay. There are exchange facilities, though rates are lower than in Medan.

BERASTAGI

Lying 1330m above sea level, 70km southwest of Medan and 25km due north of the shores of Danau Toba, **BERASTAGI** is a cold and scruffy hill station in the centre of the Karo Highlands. It was founded by the Dutch in the 1920s as a retreat from the sweltering heat of Medan, and has been popular with tourists ever since. The town is set among rolling farmland bookended by two huge but climbable **volcanoes**, Gunung Sibayak and dangerously active Gunung Sinabung (see p.224), and provides a perfect base for **trekking**. It's little more than a one-street town, with most accommodation running north of the bus station on Jalan Veteran.

WHAT TO SEE AND DO

Aside from the volcanoes, Berastagi has a handful of attractions; there are lively fresh produce markets behind the bus station and across from the war memorial, and a **Sunday market** (8am–7pm) is held on top of Gundaling Hill, a 2km walk from town or a Rp4000 angkot from just in front of the tourist office, from where there are great views of Gunung Sinabung when the weather clears. There is also a handful of scenic waterfalls in the vicinity, by far the most impressive being the 120m-high **Sipisopiso**, a few minutes off the main road running south of Kabanjahe. Meanwhile, the surrounding area boasts a smattering of **Karo heritage villages**.

The Karo villages

During the Dutch invasion of 1904, most of the towns in the Karo Highlands were razed by the Karonese themselves to prevent the Dutch from appropriating them. But there are villages where you can still see the **traditional wooden houses** with their striking palm-frond gables.

The most accessible is **Peceren** (donation), 2km northeast of Berastagi. If you're coming from the town, take the road to Medan and turn down the lane on your right after the *Green Garden*

hotel. There are three traditional houses here, though the village is probably the least picturesque example. There are three more villages to the south of Berastagi, but many of the houses are slipping into a terrible state of repair. **Lingga** (donation) is the best-known Karo village in the area, with ten traditional houses in various states of disrepair. It is possible to walk or cycle here (*Losmen Sibayak* has good maps), otherwise take a yellow Karya minibus (Rp5000) from the bus station in Berastagi to Kabenjahe, then another minibus to Lingga (Rp4000). Coming back, there are red Sigantangsira minibuses departing infrequently direct to Berastagi (Rp5000). One of the last villages built in the old style, **Dokan** (donation), is a pleasant alternative to Lingga. Set another 16km south of Kabanjahe (Rp7000 by angkot), this village has less hassle and is in better shape than Lingga, its traditional homes still occupied.

ARRIVAL AND DEPARTURE

By bus Buses to Padang Bulan in Medan (around every 30min 6am–8pm; Rp15,000; 3hr) leave every day from the bus station at the southern end of Jl Veteran and can be hailed from anywhere along the main street.

By private minibus or car Sibayak Trans Tour & Travel, in the entrance of *Losmen Sibayak* at Jl Veteran 119 (☏ 0629 91122), arranges direct tourist buses, as do most other hotels.

Destinations Bukit Lawang (4hr 30min; Rp150,000); Medan (2hr; Rp100,000); Medan airport (2hr 45min; Rp150,000); and Parapat (for Danau Toba; 4hr 30min;

THE KARO

Covering an area of almost five thousand square kilometres, from the northern tip of Danau Toba to the border of Aceh, the **Karo Highlands** comprise an extremely fertile volcanic plateau at the heart of the Bukit Barisan mountains. The plateau is home to more than two hundred farming villages and two main towns: the regional capital, Kabanjahe, and the popular market town and tourist resort of **Berastagi**.

According to local legend, the Karo people were the first of the Batak groups to settle in the highlands of North Sumatra, and, as with all Batak groups, the strongly patrilineal Karo have their own language, customs and rituals, most of which have survived, at least in a modified form, to this day. These include convoluted wedding and funeral ceremonies, both of which can go on for days, and the **reburial ceremony**, held every few years, when deceased relatives are exhumed and their bones are washed with a mixture of water and orange juice.

Today, the vast majority of the Karo are Christian, with minorities adhering to Islam and the traditional Karo religion. However, all members of Karonese society are bound by obligations to the clan, which are seen as more important than any religious duties.

Rp150,000), which is also linked by public buses (5hr): from Berastagi, the first minibus gets you to Kabenjahe (Rp5000; 25min), the second to Siantar (Rp30,000; 3hr) and the third to the jetty at Parapat (Rp25,000; 1hr 15min; last departure 4pm).

INFORMATION

Tourist office The friendly tourist office at Jl Gundaling 1 (Mon–Sat 8am–5pm; ☎ 0628 91084) is just over the road from the post office, and offers scale-challenged maps, though information at most hotels tends to be at least as helpful.

Trekking The *Losmen Sibayak* and *Wisma Sibayak* can set you up with good guides for trekking, or call Awan, a veteran guide often found at *Talitha* (☎ 0813 7072 1793, ✉ awan072@hotmail.com).

ACCOMMODATION

Losmen Sibayak Jl Veteran 119 ☎ 0628 91122. Entered through a busy travel office in the centre of town, this friendly, no-frills hotel is set back from the noise of the main road. The rooms are a bit worn, but the best of them come with squat toilets and cold showers (Rp75,000). There's wi-fi in the restaurant downstairs, which serves delicious pizzas (from Rp45,000) and other travellers' favourites. Doubles Rp60,000

Talitha Guest House Jl Kolam Renang 60B ☎ 0813 7066 4252, ⓦ facebook.com/GuesthouseTalitha. Near the 4-star *Sinabung Hotel*, reached by yellow Karya (KT) angkots heading up past the fruit market from the war memorial (Rp3000), *Talitha* has six spotless rooms attached to the Dutch-speaking owner's home, set amid manicured lawns away from the bustle and noise of the city centre. The bigger rooms come with hot water, while tea and coffee are provided around the clock. Breakfasts Rp25,000. Doubles Rp100,000

Wisma Sibayak Jl Udara 1 ☎ 0628 91104, ✉ morina _pelawi@yahoo.co.id. One of Sumatra's longest-established hostels, with a homey feel and spacious, simple rooms with private balconies, bathrooms and hot showers (Rp150,000). There's wi-fi until 10pm, a pleasant grassy sitting area and a cosy restaurant (*tempe* and guacamole sandwich Rp35,000). It's worthwhile perusing the worn travellers' comment books here, and be aware that local children drop in regularly for English practice with guests. Doubles Rp60,000

EATING

Every evening (7pm–3am), rows of street stalls pop up along Jl Veteran serving everything from *ikan bakar* (grilled fish) to hamburgers.

Asia Jl Veteran 9–10 ☎ 0628 91678. A few steps from the war memorial, this unassuming place is one of Berastagi's only established restaurants, with a blend of Chinese and Indonesian food (*kwetiau goreng* Rp30,000) served on lazy Susans, and cold beers (large Bintang Rp40,000). Daily 7am–11pm.

Mexico Coffee Resto Jl Veteran 18 ☎ 0628 92707. Long, cavernous café and restaurant off the main street with Berastagi's best fresh-brewed coffee. A good chunk of the menu is fried chicken (from Rp60,000) and Indonesian dishes (*gado gado* Rp20,000). An attached hotel has simple, overpriced rooms with hot water (Rp250,000) that are alright for a night in case the other options are full. Daily 7.30am–11pm.

Raymond Café Jl Veteran ☎ 0812 6096 9066. Tiny tourist café just beside *Wisma Sibayak*, with a few seats upstairs and a mix of Western and Indonesian dishes as well as steaks and curries (Rp20,000). The friendly owner arranges transport in shared cars and minivans, and it's a good place for cheap drinks (chai tea Rp10,000). Daily 7am–11pm.

DIRECTORY

Banks There's a BNI and BRI bank, each with ATM, on either side of *Losmen Sibayak*, which is the best place to change US dollars or travellers' cheques.

Internet Rhido Adino (Rp3000/hr), across from *Losmen Sibayak* on Jl Veteran, is one of the few internet cafés not completely taken over by gamers.

Pharmacy There are several health centres on Jl Veteran, including Dharma Bakti Apotek (no. 148).

Police The police station is situated by the war memorial, just off Jl Veteran.

Post office Next to the police station (Mon–Thurs 7.30am–3pm, Fri 7.30am–noon & Sat 7.30am–1pm).

VOLCANOES AROUND BERASTAGI

There are two active volcanoes more than 2000m high in the immediate vicinity of Berastagi: **Sibayak** (2094m), to the north of town, is possibly the most accessible volcano in the whole of Indonesia, and takes just two hours to climb up and two hours down, while the hike up **Sinabung** (2452m) – which has seen dramatic eruptions of late – to the southwest of town, is less straightforward. The mountain has mostly been off limits recently, though when open to hikers it's a longer and tougher climb requiring a bus or taxi to the trailhead. The long lists of missing trekkers plastered all around Berastagi prove that these climbs are not as easy as they may at first seem. The tourist office and losmen urge climbers always to take a guide – though for Sibayak a guide is unnecessary provided there's good visibility and you're climbing with someone else. For both volcanoes, set off early in the morning. Pick up a map from *Wisma Sibayak* or *Losmen Sibayak* and bring some trail food, warm clothing, and – if you're looking to take advantage of the hot springs at the foot of Sibayak – your swimming costume and a towel, too.

Gunung Sibayak

Although it's the easier of Berastagi's volcanoes, it's wise to get an early start or else consider taking along a guide: plenty of hikers have become lost on this route. Most hikers get an early start in order to reach the summit for sunrise. For this option, most hotels offer transport to the trail near the top (departing around 4am; Rp400,000/car). Otherwise, you can simply walk from town or take a green Kama van (Rp4000; starting 6.30am) to the coffee shop by the trailhead, where you must register your name and pay the hiking fee (Rp4000). From here, walk past the angkot station and you'll begin the series of up-and-down dips along a rough road leading to the summit. Before the end of the tarmac is a strip of stalls and some rough steps cut into the embankment rising to the left. From here, the path takes around forty minutes, eventually curving anticlockwise around the small crater lake to the summit, marked with a pair of iron antennae shafts mounted into a concrete block.

Most hikers return the way they came, though those who wish to visit the hot springs can follow a rough trail that winds down the other side of the crater rim. Facing the crater from the concrete platform at the summit, head back down along the rim to its lowest point. From here, look to the left for the scant remains of a decades-old set of concrete steps, visible about 50m along. As you follow the steps – little more than concrete strips at this stage – you'll descend through a forest and pass a grove of bamboo before emerging at a geothermal plant. Below this is a series of **hot springs** (Rp8000) – a great reward for a hard trek.

Angkots from the springs leave occasionally for Berastagi (Rp12,000; last one departs 5pm); otherwise you'll have to continue along the road for several kilometres to the junction with the main road and pick one up from there (Rp5000).

Gunung Sinabung

Indonesia's latest volcanic surprise, **Gunung Sinabung** rumbled to life with a dramatic eruption in 2010 that came after several centuries of silence, killing two people and forcing 30,000 to evacuate. In September 2013, more eruptions rocked the region, forcing over 20,000 to evacuate and a few months later the volcano ejected 9km-high ash plumes and caused disruption as far afield as Medan, where visibility was reduced to just 20m. Sinabung has rumbled on since then, occasionally sprinkling the town with a dusting of ash, and at the time of writing, the highest level of alert was still in place.

The roughly eight-hour return hike to the summit begins beside a restaurant to the north of **Danau Kawar** (Rp8000 hiking fee). Continue through cabbage fields for approximately an hour before entering fairly thick jungle, after which the hike becomes relentlessly tough. Having left the jungle, you soon find yourself scrambling up some steep and treacherous rocky gullies. A couple of hours later, you'll be standing on the edge of a cliff looking down into Gunung Sinabung's pair of craters. Take care when walking around up here, as the paths are crumbling and it's a long way down. A guide is highly recommended for this trip (around Rp400,000).

To reach Danau Kawar, take either a bus (Rp10,000; hourly departures from the bus station starting 7.30am; 45min) or taxi (Rp600,000 return for up to seven people, including the driver's long wait by the lake). Unless you're very fit, the latter option is recommended as the last bus from Danau Kawar heads back to town at 4pm.

PARAPAT

Sprawled along the eastern shores of Danau Toba, the bustling town of **PARAPAT** offers wonderful views across the lake. It's used primarily as a stopover, with most visitors staying just long enough to catch the ferry to the island of Samosir. The town is divided in two – the **resort**, crammed with ageing hotels and souvenir shops by the water, and the commercial sector to the east, in the hills away from the lake.

ARRIVAL AND DEPARTURE

By bus Buses arriving in Parapat drive through the resort to Tigaraja harbour before heading back to the bus station, 2km east of town. Frequent angkots connect the harbour with the bus station (Rp4000).

Destinations Berastagi (5hr; via Siantar 1hr 15min) and Kabenjahe (3hr), from which buses link Berastagi until 8pm (25min); Bukittinggi (several daily; 16hr); Medan (every 45min; 5hr); Padang (2 daily; 18hr); Sibolga (daily; 6hr).

By private minibus or car Private tourist transport services are faster, have a/c and break down much less often. Call to book ahead during high season. Offices are clustered just beside Tigaraja harbour, including Bagus Taxi (☎0813 6239 7309) and Raja Taxi Trans (☎0852 7005 5172). All charge roughly the same: Bukittinggi (Rp270,000; 13hr); Berastagi (Rp150,000; 4hr); Bukit Lawang (Rp200,000; 7hr); Medan (Rp100,000; 4hr); Medan airport (Rp80,000).

By ferry Daily ferries connect Tigaraja harbour with Tuk Tuk on Pulau Samosir (hourly in each direction, departing from Tigaraja 6.45am–5.10pm; departing from Tuk Tuk 8.30am–7pm; Rp15,000; 30min). Arriving in Tuk Tuk, ferries usually stop at several quays around the peninsula: name your chosen hotel and you'll be instructed where to disembark. When leaving Tuk Tuk, wave down a ferry from any hotel's quay.

ACCOMMODATION AND EATING

There are several budget hotels right around the harbour and plenty of cheap *rumah makan* along Jl Haranggaol.

Hong Kong Jl Haranggaol 9–11 ☎0625 41395. Still the busiest place in town, with spotless surroundings and a comprehensive Chinese menu, offering everything from sweet-and-sour pork to fried pig liver (both Rp60,000). Daily 8am–10pm.

Soloh Jaya Jl Haranggaol 51 ☎0625 41617. Among the best-value digs near the harbour, with tidy rooms, pleasant courtyards and a spacious terrace offering good views of the town. The brighter rooms at the top have big windows and bathrooms with cold showers, and are worth the extra rupiahs (Rp120,000). Doubles <u>Rp70,000</u>

DIRECTORY

Banks There's a BRI ATM on Jl Sisingamangaraja and a Mandiri by the bus station, a 5–10min angkot ride from Tigaraja (Rp4000).

Internet Several warnets are spread along Jl Haranggaol (daily 10am–midnight; Rp3000/hr) by the harbour.

Pharmacy Robika on Jl Haranggaol 83 (daily 7am–10pm) supplies basic medicines.

Post office Jl Sisingamangaraja, opposite the BRI ATM (Mon–Fri 7.30am–4pm, Sat 7.30am–2pm).

DANAU TOBA AND PULAU SAMOSIR

Lying right in the middle of the province at 900m, jewel-like **DANAU TOBA** is Southeast Asia's largest freshwater lake, stretching 100km long and 30km wide. It was formed about 80,000 years ago in the wake of a colossal volcanic eruption, the resulting caldera eventually buckling under massive pressure and collapsing in on itself to create the steep-walled basin now occupied by the lake. A second, smaller, volcanic eruption, 50,000 years after the first, created the Singapore-sized island in the middle of the lake, **Pulau Samosir**. Connected by ferry from **Parapat** on the lake's eastern shore, this island is the cultural and spiritual heartland of the Toba Batak people and one of the most pleasant and fascinating destinations in Indonesia.

4

WHAT TO SEE AND DO

Pulau Samosir is arguably the best spot in Sumatra in which to relax for a few days on a hammock by the azure water. Most tourists make for the eastern shores, directly across the lake from Parapat, where there's a string of enjoyable resorts, the main one being **Tuk Tuk**, with plenty of hotels, restaurants and bars. From here, you can trek into the deforested hills in the centre of the island or circle the coastline by motorbike, calling in at tiny Batak villages that have flamboyant tombs and distinctive concave-roofed houses, as well as the island's cultural centre of **Simanindo**, on Samosir's northern shore.

Tuk Tuk

The waters that lap the shores of **Tuk Tuk** are safe for **swimming**, though they can be dirty; the roped-off section of the lake by *Carolina's*, complete with pontoons, canoes and a diving board, is the most popular place. There are also a few activities on offer in Tuk Tuk, including guided treks through the interior of the island (Rp750,000) and speedboat trips to Tomok, Ambarita and Simanindo (Rp650,000/hr). You can also rent **bicycles** and **motorbikes**, should you want to visit the more far-flung reaches of the island.

Tomok

Tomok, 3km south of Tuk Tuk, is the most southerly of the resorts on the east coast; dozens of virtually identical souvenir stalls line the main street. Its main calling card is the early nineteenth-century stone **tomb of Raja Sidabutar** (daily 7am–7pm; donation), the chief of the first tribe to migrate to the island. You'll be asked to drape an *ulos* (traditional Batak scarf) across your shoulder as a mark of respect before

entering. The sarcophagus has a Singa face – a part-elephant, part-buffalo creature of Toban legend – carved into one end, and a small stone effigy of the king's wife on top of the lid. On the way to Ambarita from Tomok, due west of Tuk Tuk, is the tiny village of **Garoga**, from where you can hike to the spectacular waterfall of the same name (after rainfall). Ask locals for directions.

Ambarita

At the foot of a small banyan in **Ambarita** lies a curious collection of stone chairs (daily 6.30am–6pm; Rp6000), one of which is mysteriously occupied by a stone statue. Most of the villagers will tell you that two centuries ago, this site played host to royal conferences and the beheadings of criminals; others say the chairs are actually less than fifty years old,

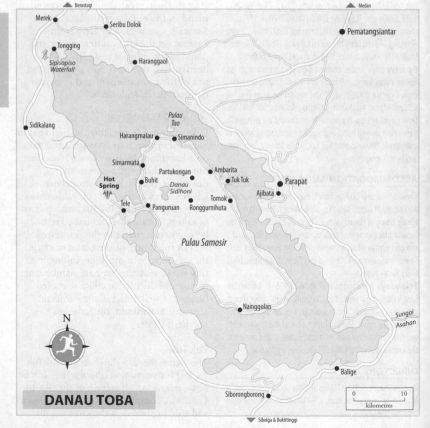

DANAU TOBA

the work of a local mason who copied drawings of the original.

Simanindo

Simanindo lies at the northern end of the island, 15km beyond the town of Ambarita. The **Museum Huta Bolon Simanindo** (daily 9am–5pm; Rp10,000) is housed in the former longhouse of Raja Simalungun, a Batak king, and showcases a range of historic artefacts, including spears, Chinese porcelain, magical charms, a wooden *guri guri* (ashes urn) and the royal boat. There are daily Batak puppet dance performances (Mon–Sat 10.30am, Sun 11.35am; Rp50,000).

Pangururan

Continuing around to the western side of the island offers superb shoreline views of the northern caldera as well as a few striking clusters of old Batak homes along the road to **Pangururan** (20km). There's little to see in the town itself, though there's a hot spring on the opposite side of the isthmus in the village of Tele (entry Rp2000). *Rico Melati*, a restaurant at the top of the hill, has great views and the nicest hot-spring pools in the area (free for diners; Rp10,000 if you just want to swim), though they're separated into a men's and women's section. *Melati* has a smaller, mixed-gender pool (same price) at the next spot down the hill.

GETTING AROUND AND TOURS

By bike and motorbike Motorbikes are ideal for hitting Samosir's highlights; they are available from almost all of Tuk Tuk's hotels (bikes/motorbikes Rp50,000/100,000), though the cheapest motorbikes are at *Bagus Bay* (Rp60,000).

By angkot Run between Tomok and Pangururan (roughly every 45min until 5pm; Rp20,000; 1hr).

Tours Many of the guesthouses, in particular *Bagus Bay Homestay* and *Carolina's*, have their own travel agencies, which can book transport and tours.

ACCOMMODATION AND EATING

Most accommodation on Samosir is on the Tuk Tuk peninsula. Tell the ferryman which hotel you're going to and he'll drop you off at the nearest quay (water levels permitting). Most guesthouses offer substantial low-season discounts (Oct to mid-Dec & mid-Jan to April).

Bagus Bay Homestay ☎0625 451287, ⓦbagusbay .com. One of the best budget options in Tuk Tuk for over 25 years, with ultra-cheap boxy rooms sharing a grubby latrine (a bargain for single travellers at Rp60,000), comfortable deluxe rooms with cosy terraces and hot water (Rp300,000), and more options in between. It also has an internet café, billiards, volleyball, bike rental, in-house massage, a bar and a lengthy menu in the restaurant, which hosts Batak performances (Wed & Sat 8pm). Doubles Rp75,000

Carolina's ☎0625 451210, ⓦcarolina-cottages.com. The Batak-style bungalows here are the first you'll see when arriving from Parapat. Though somewhat worn, rooms are good value, some set on the hill and others with lakeside views and a small slice of beach (Rp400,000). There's a huge, breezy restaurant with wi-fi, and a range of information on the island at the reception. Doubles Rp200,000

Jenny's ☎0877 6620 5859. The food is worth the wait at this small, family-run restaurant beside *Anju Cottages*, with fresh grilled fish (Rp60,000) and excellent *tempe* curry (Rp25,000) as well as a few Western favourites. Daily noon–10pm.

Liberta Homestay ☎0625 451035, ⓔliberta _homestay@yahoo.co.id. Cheap, simple rooms in Batak-style cottages with an attached restaurant and a friendly owner. Rooms with hot water from Rp77,000. Liberta lies on the southwest side of the peninsula – get off the ferry at *Bagus Bay* harbour. Doubles Rp55,000

Mas Cottages ☎0625 451051, ⓔmascottages@yahoo .com. A good-value, mid-range option about 3km north of Tuk Tuk, with a peaceful setting and spacious tile-floored rooms with hot water and verandahs overlooking the water. The new deluxe rooms (Rp485,000) are worth the splurge in the off-season when prices are slashed by up to thirty percent. Doubles Rp315,000

Merlyn Guesthouse ☎0813 6116 9130, ⓔmerlynguesthouse@mail.com. Run by a German-Indonesian couple, this centrally located little cheapie has a great backpacker vibe. All of its smart, simple rooms come with hot water, somewhat dim bathrooms and great lake views. It's an easy swim straight out from here to a rocky little island. The attached café is also good value. Doubles Rp100,000

Romlan's ☎0625 451386, ⓦromlantuktuk.com. A wonderful isolated location gives this scruffy little guesthouse its charm. The cheapest rooms are in traditional bungalows overlooking the water to Parapat, all rooms come with hot water, and there's a pleasant open-air restaurant with free wi-fi. Doubles Rp100,000

NIGHTLIFE

Anju Karaoke ☎0813 9797 9757. Three sofa-decked karaoke rooms in a roadside annexe of *Anju Cottages*, along with a simple menu of bar food and drinks. Book ahead on Sat nights (afternoon Rp70,000/hr, evening Rp90,000/hr). Daily 1–6pm & 7pm–1am.

Brando's Blues Bar Just a 2min walk from *Samosir Cottages*, this is Tuk Tuk's most happening nightlife venue, mixing reggae beats with thumping dance music and packing its spacious dance floor with a local crowd at weekends. Pool tables, cocktails and ice-cold Bintang (bottle Rp45,000). Daily 8pm–2am.

DIRECTORY

Banks Guesthouses and a handful of moneychangers offer exchange services at generally poor rates. The nearest ATM is at the BRI in Ambarita, accepting only Mastercard, while Tomok's Indomaret has another (Cimb Niaga).

Books Penny's Bookstore (daily 8am–10pm) in Tuk Tuk has a huge range of novels, DVDs, guidebooks and maps for rent, buy or exchange.

Cooking classes Kiki Andrea, the friendly owner of *Juwita Café* (☎0625 451217, ✉kikiandrea07@yahoo .com), set just north of *Carolina's*, offers Batak cooking lessons (Rp385,000 for three dishes; 2hr).

Health centre There's a 24hr health centre near Penny's Bookstore (☎0625 451075).

Internet There is wi-fi at most cafés and guesthouses, and computers at *Bagus Bay* (Rp10,000/hr).

Massage *Bagus Bay Homestay* in Tuk Tuk has an on-site massage therapist (Rp100,000).

Post office The nearest post office is in Ambarita, but you can ask to use the postboxes at local shops.

BANDA ACEH

Capital of Aceh, **BANDA ACEH** is the transit point for **Pulau Weh**, and the gateway to the wonders of Sumatra's most far-flung province. As the crow flies, the city sits closer to India than to the Indonesian capital, and the relatively few foreigners who make it up this far along the spine of Sumatra are rewarded with a vastness of primate-packed rainforests, volcanic peaks, empty beaches, eye-popping dive sites and a welcoming population of predominantly devout Muslims. Since Islam's first landing in the region (see box, p.230), Aceh's proud history was shaped by the sultans of this capital city, strategically set at the entrance to the Straits of Malacca. Recent decades have been turbulent, to say the least, with deadly conflict engulfing the province as the separatist Free Aceh Movement battled with Indonesian forces from 1976 right up until the heart-wrenching devastation of

the 2004 Boxing Day tsunami. The waves (see box below) changed everything, taking more than 70,000 lives in Banda Aceh alone, while bringing an end to the violence. When the waters receded, a massive influx of NGOs and an unprecedented amount of international aid money helped put the city back on its feet, and successful peace talks in 2005 brought much-needed stability. Now, over a decade since the calamity, the doors to both city and province are wide open to intrepid explorers.

WHAT TO SEE AND DO

Although most travellers breeze through Banda Aceh to catch the ferry to Pulau Weh, there are enough attractions around town to keep you busy for a day, and some pretty beaches with great waves nearby that can keep you around much longer.

Mesjid Raya Baiturrahman

The most prominent survivor of the 2004 earthquake and tsunami, Banda Aceh's stunning central mosque (Mon–Thurs, Sat & Sun 7–11am & 1.30–5.30pm; donation) is widely held by locals as evidence of divine intervention, and has become a symbol of Acehnese resilience. Italian-designed and Dutch-built in 1881, the mosque

THE BOXING DAY TSUNAMI

On the peaceful Sunday morning of **December 26, 2004**, 10m-tall waves raced towards the shores of Aceh at speeds of up to 500km/hr, triggered by a whopping magnitude 9.1 tremor off the Sumatran coast. The waves obliterated coastal settlements before reaching up to several kilometres inland. When the black, debris-strewn waters receded, the Acehnese were left to assess the damage: 140,000 homes destroyed, 500,000 homeless and 160,000 dead in Indonesia, mainly in Aceh. The NGOs left years ago, all projects are complete and the aid money has finally been spent – US$7 billion – on over a hundred thousand new homes, thousands of kilometres of roads as well as bridges, schools and other infrastructural projects.

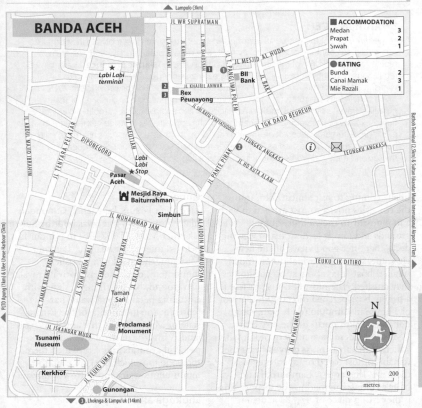

blends Mughal and colonial styles, and has expanded over the last century to include seven black, teardrop domes that cap an ornate, whitewashed facade. The adjacent square is a great spot for people-watching, particularly during the Friday prayers. Under extensive renovation at the time of writing, the marble square facing the mosque is set to feature giant mechanical umbrellas – *à la* Prophet's Mosque in Medina. In addition to wearing long trousers and long sleeves, women must don a headscarf before entering the grounds.

Tsunami Museum

Opened in 2009, Banda Aceh's controversial, ship-shaped **Tsunami Museum** (daily 9am–noon & 2–4.15pm; free) is the result of US$6.7 million from the Aceh Reconstruction Fund. Its four rambling storeys feature collections of photos and clay models, as well as an electronic simulation of the earthquake and tsunami and an "escape hill", built for refuge in the event of another tsunami. The ambitiously designed structure is as much a symbolic monument as it is a museum, with a roof that resembles a tidal wave, walls that depict a traditional Acehnese dance, and a dark, narrow entrance corridor set between 10m-tall walls of water.

Tsunami landmarks

Around town are several prominent reminders of the tsunami. By far the largest of these is the 2600-tonne **PLTD Apung** (Mon–Thurs, Sat & Sun 9am–noon & 2–5.30pm, Fri 2–5pm; donation), 1km west of the Tsunami Museum. Formerly an electricity generator docked in Ulee Lheue Harbour, it was swept inland by the giant wave,

SHARIA IN ACEH

Towards the end of the thirteenth century, Aceh became Islam's first foothold in Southeast Asia, a religious heritage of which many Acehnese remain proud. Today, Aceh maintains a reputation as the "Porch of Mecca," Indonesia's most strictly **Islamic province**. Sharia-based regulations were introduced in 2001, then greatly expanded in 2009, amounting to a widespread enforcement of Islamic laws and customs in much of the province. In 2015, an 11pm curfew was instituted for Muslim women unaccompanied by a husband or male guardian. Travellers in Aceh should dress modestly and avoid alcohol, gambling, overt homosexuality or fraternizing with members of the opposite sex (outside of marriage) in public areas, the official penalty for which can be up to 60 lashes. The rules are much relaxed, however, in tourist areas such as Palau Weh, where bars serve alcohol, beach-goers bathe in the sun and men and women mix without fear of flogging.

finally coming to rest almost 3km from the coast. It's now a tourist attraction with a monument to the victims, quaint grounds and ramps leading up to viewing decks that offer good views of the new cityscape, shared by several other (much smaller) boats that also rest on the homes they crushed. The most famous of these is a fishing boat perched directly on the roof of a house in **Lampulo** (daily 9am–5pm; donation), 3km north of the city centre.

Most Acehnese have no way of knowing which of the area's **mass graves** bears the remains of lost loved ones, so they visit them all. The largest, Lambaro, lies halfway along the road to the airport, and is the resting place of 47,781 tsunami victims. The second-largest and most famous mass grave site is Meuraxa, beside the ruins of a hospital in Ulee Lheue and just a few hundred metres from the signposted Tsunami Zero Point.

Dutch Cemetery

Stretching behind the Tsunami Museum is yet another solemn sight, known locally as **Kerkhof** (Dutch for cemetery; daily 7am–6pm; free). Here lie around 2200 soldiers killed in the Aceh War (1873–1904), hailing from the Netherlands as well as from all across Indonesia, from Java to Ambon. It is the largest Dutch graveyard outside of the Netherlands, and worth a stroll to scan the names inscribed on whitewashed tombstones and large tablets set beside the entrance gate. Local guide Muhammad Razi (☎0853 6166 9123, ✉razi25101998@gmail.com) lives beside the gate and offers complimentary tours of the grounds.

Gunongan

Like Shah Jahan's Taj Mahal, **Gunongan** (daily 7am–6pm; free) was built by Sultan Iskandar Muda (1607–36) to honour his beloved queen. Set near the Tsunami Museum, the small, whitewashed monument, once used as a private royal playground, has a striking design, with cascading petal-shaped walls that represent the mountains of the Pahang state of Malaysia, queen Kamaliah's native land. Visitors can stroll around the peaceful grounds and – provided there's someone to unlock the gate – up the monument's stairs and narrow walkways.

Lhoknga and Lampu'uk

Among the hardest-hit by the tsunami were the coastal villages of **Lhoknga** and **Lampu'uk**, about 2km apart and 15km southwest of Banda Aceh. Both have world-class waves in season (Nov–March), but Lampu'uk's beach, bounded to the north by cliffs, is the more attractive spot for swimming. Kitesurfing season (May–Oct) is also becoming a popular time to visit. The beaches remain blissfully quiet on weekdays and fill up with escapees from Banda Aceh at weekends. A fast-growing number of homestays and bungalows cater to surfers, among the best of them *Eddie's* and *Yudi's* (see opposite).

ARRIVAL AND DEPARTURE

By plane Banda Aceh's dome-capped Sultan Iskandar Muda International Airport lies 18km east of the city centre. It is linked by taxi (Rp100,000 to the city centre; Rp140,000 to Ulee Lheue Harbour; Rp170,000 to Lhoknga) and DAMRI buses (to and from Simbun supermarket, beside Mesjid Raya, Rp20,000).

Destinations Jakarta (3 daily; 2hr 50min); Kuala Lumpur (daily; 1hr 35min); Medan (5 daily; 1hr 5min); Penang (4 weekly; 1hr 40min); Surabaya (weekly; 3hr 30min).

By bus Bathoh Terminal is 3km south of the city centre along Jl Teuku M Hasan (Rp15,000 by becak), with regular daily departures for Medan (every 40min 7am–11pm; 10hr). There are about a dozen companies; among the better ones is PMTOH (☎0651 635392).

By ferry Boats to Pulau Weh depart from Ulee Lheue Harbour, about 6km northwest of the city centre (Rp50,000 by taxi and Rp25,000 by becak) – and connect to Pulau Weh's Balohan Harbour (see p.232).

INFORMATION

Tourist information The tourist information office (Jl Tgk Chik Kuta Karang 3; Mon–Fri 8am–5pm; ☎0651 26206, ⊚acehtourism.travel) is centrally located, with helpful, English-speaking staff, as well as useful brochures and maps. For new attractions and upcoming events, visit ⊚bandaacehtourism.com.

GETTING AROUND

Banda Aceh's important sites are spread out, and using local transportation can be challenging.

By labi labi Called angkots or oplets elsewhere in Indonesia, the packed minibuses of Aceh are known as labi labi. Minibuses through town stop on Jl Diponegoro, by the central Pasar Aceh, and connect the harbour (15– 20min; Rp5000) and both Lhoknga and Lampu'uk (both 20min; Rp10,000).

By becak The most pleasant way to get around town, becaks generally charge Rp4000/km. Negotiate a price before setting off. For a reliable English-speaking becak driver who can double as an excellent guide, call Firman (☎0812 5396 0980).

ACCOMMODATION

There is a dearth of good-value accommodation in Banda Aceh, and many travellers head straight for the ferry to Pulau Weh or to nearby Lhoknga or Lampu'uk. In the city centre, couples may be asked to produce proof of marriage in order to share a hotel room.

BANDA ACEH CITY CENTRE

Medan Jl Ahmad Yani 17 ☎0651 21501, ⊚hotel-medan .com. Pushed up against the river near the centre of town, just across from the popular hawker stalls of *Rex Peunayong*, this ageing business hotel has clean, white-tiled a/c rooms with TVs, hot water, a very basic breakfast buffet and wi-fi that works occasionally in the lobby. Doubles Rp300,000

Prapat Jl Ahmad Yani 19 ☎0651 22159. Next door to the *Medan*, this is among the very cheapest spots in the

city centre – a pair of drab three-storey blocks facing each other across a parking lot. The grubby fan rooms with attached bathrooms are okay for a one-night stopover. There are also a/c rooms (Rp260,000), though you'll get more for your money elsewhere. Doubles Rp110,000

Siwah Jl Twk Muhammad Daudsyah 18–20 ☎0651 21128. Though rooms are a little worn, they're well kept and all come with a/c, hot showers and an Acehnese breakfast, as well as slippers and a toiletry set. Combined with its central location, *Siwah* is still one of the best-value options in town. Doubles Rp252,000

LHOKNGA

Eddie's Off Jl Lapangan Golf, Lhoknga ☎0811 688682 or ☎0813 6031 9126, ⊜eddie_homestay@yahoo.com. Ever helpful, energetic and friendly, Eddie has recently opened an annexe with spacious a/c doubles fitted with private porches and hammocks (Rp250,000). The homestay is set about 500m from the beach with a good restaurant, a fridge stocked with beers, and smaller, fan rooms in the main, older building – including cheap singles (Rp100,000). Motorbikes and surfboards available for rent (Rp60,000/day). Doubles Rp130,000

Yudi's Off Jl Lapangan Golf, Lhoknga ☎0812 694 2879, ⊚yudisplace.com. One of the closest guesthouses to the beach, *Yudi's* has nine spotless en-suite rooms, some with a/c (from Rp250,000), set around a pleasant garden café and restaurant. Surfing lessons are on offer (2hr, Rp300,000), as well as surfboard rental (Rp70,000). Doubles Rp200,000

EATING

Ultra-cheap Acehnese food (*mie aceh* Rp10,000), as well as more familiar Indonesian favourites, are easily found at the food stalls that pop up each night all around the city centre. The biggest grouping is at Pasar Malam Rek, in a lot by the junction between Jl SM Raja and Jl Khairil Anwar (daily dusk–2am).

Bunda Jl Pante Pirak 7. A Banda Aceh institution set right in the city centre, *Bunda* has a bright, breezy dining space, friendly service and the city's best Minang (Padang) food (*nasi pakai ayam* Rp18,000). The table is filled with dishes and you pay for what you eat. Best to go with company. Daily 9am–11pm.

Canai Mamak Jl Teuku Umar 51 ☎0651 45471. The best Malay restaurant in town, with KL-style *nasi goreng* (Rp15,000), *roti canai* (Rp18,000) and sweet *canai boom* served with ice cream (Rp18,000). Both inside and outside seating on the busy main road from the city to Lhoknga. Daily 11am–11pm.

Mie Razali Jl Panglima Polem 83 ☎0651 636116. A long-standing favourite among both locals and foreigners, this unassuming little street-side restaurant opened its doors

4

in 1967 and is today as popular as ever for its tasty Acehnese noodles. Choose from boiled or fried noodles, served dry or in a soup with mushrooms, squid, shrimp (Rp20,000), crab (Rp30,000), or any combination. Daily 10am–10.30pm.

DIRECTORY

Banks and exchange There are many ATMs around the city centre, including a BII, BNI and Mandiri along Jl Panglima Polim. Belangi at Jl T Cut Ali 68 changes money (Mon–Sat 9am–5pm).

Hospital The state-of-the-art, German-built general hospital (Rumah Sakit Umum Dr Zainal Abidin) is 5km east of the city centre at Jl Tgk Daud Beureueh 108 (☎ 0651 34565).

Internet Most hotels and some restaurants have wi-fi, while there are a few internet cafés across the river on Jl Cut Meutiah charging Rp6000/hr.

Post office Near the city centre on Jl H Bendahara 33 (Mon–Thurs 8am–5pm, Fri 8am–noon & 2–5pm).

PULAU WEH

A tiny volcanic island 15km off the northern tip of Sumatra and at the very southern edge of the Andaman Sea, **PULAU WEH** is one of Southeast Asia's very best diving spots. The clear waters around Weh include a pair of protected areas, **Pulau Weh Marine Park** (26 square kilometres) and **Iboih Recreation Park** (13 square kilometres), each featuring a kaleidoscope of reef life and a plenitude of bigger fish. Among the larger pelagics easily spotted here are morays, dolphins, sharks, Napoleon (maori) wrasse, stingrays and barracuda, while in season, divers may also share the waters with manta rays and whale sharks. There are about twenty dive sites scattered around the island, with highlights including the calm, shallow **Rubiah Sea Garden**, the gorgonian-rich caves and arches of **The Canyon**, and the 134m German-built **Sophie Rickmers wreck**. Offering a refreshing respite from the noise, congestion and chaos of mainland Sumatra, Pulau Weh's slow island pace tends to keep travellers around longer than planned.

Known among foreigners as Pulau Weh, it's known locally by the same name as the principal town, **Sabang**, situated on the island's northeast corner. The main tourist areas are spread along the beaches of **Iboih** and **Gapang** to the northeast, as well as palm-fringed **Sumur Tiga**, a short hop south of the town on the east coast. Diving is year-round, although conditions are optimal during the relatively dry months from October to April.

WHAT TO SEE AND DO

The bulk of Weh's allure lies offshore, but there are a number of worthwhile excursions out of the water. Beyond relaxing on the island's handful of small beaches, popular activities include circling the island's well-kept roads by motorbike, delving into the jungle-clad interior to reach the island's small semi-active volcano, swimming at the pretty **Pria Laot waterfall**, or trekking to the remote **Kilometre Nol marker**, a whitewashed, 22m monument marking the far northwest edge of the archipelago.

Iboih

Most backpackers make a beeline for **Iboih**, the small beach on the island's northwest shore. A base for both diving and snorkelling, its long, spread-out bungalow strip faces directly across from the small, jungle-covered rock of **Pulau Rubiah**, about 100m offshore. The stunning coral reefs in the turquoise waters ringing the island are known as the **Sea Garden**, and offer some of the best snorkelling around Weh.

ARRIVAL AND DEPARTURE

By ferry Fast and slow ferries connect Banda Aceh's Ulee Lheue Harbour (Rp2000 to enter the terminal) with Weh's Balohan Harbour, on the southeast of the island. Plan to arrive at either port at least 45min before departure. Slow ASDP ferries (1hr 30min; economy/business/executive Rp22,400/42,000/53,000) depart in each direction Mon–Thurs, Sat & Sun (10am, 4pm & 10pm from Ulee Lheue; 7am, 1pm & 7pm from Balohan), and Fri (10am, 5pm & 11pm from Ulee Lheue; 7am, 2pm & 8pm from Balohan). Fast ferries are operated by Express Bahari (45min; executive/VIP Rp80,000/100,000; ☎ 0852 7054 6464), which has ticket windows at each harbour. These depart 2–3 times daily (Mon & Wed–Sun 8am, 10am & 4pm from Ulee Lheue, 8am, 2.30pm & 4pm from Balohan; Tues 9.30am & 4pm from Ulee Lheue; 8am & 2.30pm from Balohan).

INFORMATION

Tourist office The friendly tourism office (Mon–Fri 8am–noon & 2–5pm; ☎0652 21513), located just above the town of Sabang on Jl Diponegoro, has good maps and information on the island's attractions.

DIVE OPERATORS

There is a handful of dive centres on Weh, with the two mainstays located at Iboih and Gapang, each offering experienced instructors and PADI courses from Scuba Diver to Divemaster.

Lumba Lumba Diving Centre Gapang Beach ☎0811 682787, ⓦlumbalumba.com. Dutch-Indonesian diving outfit that offers top-notch equipment and the best reputation for safety on the island. €31 for one dive and €57 for two (including all gear).

Rubiah Tirta Iboih Beach ☎0652 332 4555, ⓦrubiahdivers.com. Started up in the 1970s, this family-run diving centre is the oldest on Weh, and continues to offer bargain prices and considerable discounts to experienced divers. Rp320,000 for one dive and Rp600,000 for two (gear included).

GETTING AROUND

Shared taxis connect all corners of the island, most importantly Balohan to Sabang (Rp40,000; 15min), Balohan to Gapang and Iboih (Rp55,000; 30min), Balohan to Sumur Tiga (Rp30,000; 15min) and Sabang to Gapang and Iboih (Rp50,000; 25min).

ACCOMMODATION AND EATING

Weh's most popular backpacker accommodation strip fans out along the beach at Iboih. Nearby Gapang Beach has a wider range of accommodation, from basic huts (Rp50,000) to upmarket bungalows catering to divers. Book ahead in high season.

IBOIH

Iboih Inn ☎0811 841570, ⓦiboihinn.com. Friendly place towards the end of the trail from the beach, with a good range of rooms, all with sea views and breakfast included in the rate. Small fan huts are situated above the main trail, while the pricier options are among the most luxurious in Iboih: waterfront cottages with hot showers and a/c (Rp400,000). The restaurant is set on a spacious deck over the water, and there's a pier pointing out towards Pulau Rubiah. There's free pick-up service by boat from Iboih village. Payment at check-in. Doubles Rp200,000

Olala ☎0852 6060 7311. Good-value bungalows a 5min walk from the parking lot. Choose between bungalows on the hill and over the water, each with private balcony and hammock. The restaurant is among the most popular in Iboih thanks to Eka's specials (roast chicken and potatoes

Rp55,000), and it's a good spot for meeting fellow travellers. Doubles Rp50,000

AROUND THE ISLAND

★**Bixio** Jl Kilometer Nol, Long Beach ☎0821 6430 1071, ⓦbixiowehbungalows.com. Sharing a pretty stretch of white sand with the exclusive *Pulau Weh Resort and Diving Centre*, about 3km up the road from Iboih Beach, Eva and Luca's impossibly laidback café and restaurant serves up top-notch Italian dishes, including superb home-made *gnocchi ai frutti di mare* (Rp50,000) and tiramisu. Luca also has a few bungalows out back, fitted with verandahs, hammocks and mosquito nets. Doubles Rp250,000

★**Freddie's** Jl KHA Salim, Pantai Sumur Tiga ☎0813 6025 5001, ⓦsantai-sabang.com. A worthy splurge on Weh's northeast coast, *Freddie's* makes the most of its rocky, palm-strewn setting overlooking the white sand of Sumur Tiga Beach. Varnished wooden walkways connect its en-suite bungalows, each equipped with hammocks, hot showers and sea views from private balconies. Breakfast and dinner are prepared by friendly owner Freddie Rousseau and served buffet-style in the restaurant. Doubles Rp315,000

Lumba Lumba Gapang Beach ☎0811 682787, ⓦlumbalumba.com/staying.html. Accompanying the popular diving centre is the most comfortable place on Gapang Beach, with a range of options, from simple rooms with shared bathrooms to plush cottages with fridges, baths and broad, sea-facing verandahs with hammocks (Rp470,000). Non-diving guests are welcome as long as there's a spare room. Doubles Rp200,000

DIRECTORY

Banks There are several banks with ATMs along Jl Perdagangan in Sabang, including Mandiri (no. 80), where you can also change money.

Internet There's wi-fi in most guesthouses and computers with internet access at the post office.

Motorbike rental Available from all guesthouses for Rp100,000/day; or head to Master Rental (daily 8am–10pm; ☎0853 6171 0553), in the parking lot at Iboih.

Pharmacy Bunda Farma at Jl Perdagangan 104, Sabang (daily 9am–2pm & 5–10pm).

Post office Jl Perdagangan 53, Sabang (Mon–Thurs 8am–3pm, Fri 8am–noon).

Snorkelling rental Masks and fins are available all over the island (Rp30,000/day).

PADANG

The seaside city of **PADANG** is an important transport hub for West Sumatra. Famous for its spicy local cuisine, **Makanan Padang** (Padang food), the city's climate is equally extreme: hot and humid, with the highest rainfall in Indonesia at 4508mm a year. For most travellers, Padang is little more than a transit point for Bukittinggi or the nearby Mentawai Islands. Its main attraction is the **Adityawarman Museum** (Mon–Sat 9am–4pm; Rp2000), with exhibits on Minangkabau culture and the aftermath of 2009's devastating 7.9-magnitude earthquake. Traces of the earthquake are still discernible in the buzzing central market (Pasar Raya) around Jalan Pasar Baru, also worth wandering. Beyond Padang's leafy boulevards and café-lined coast are plenty of white sandy beaches, pretty

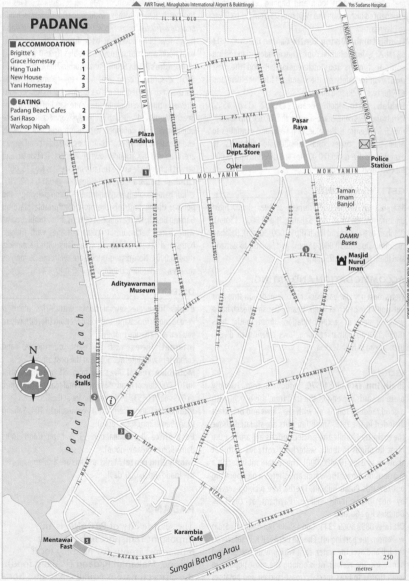

PADANG

■ ACCOMMODATION	
Brigitte's	4
Grace Homestay	5
Hang Tuah	1
New House	2
Yani Homestay	3

● EATING	
Padang Beach Cafes	2
Sari Raso	1
Warkop Nipah	3

4

waterfalls like Air Terjun Tiga Tingkat, and idyllic **islands** such as Pagang to the south, making the city a handy base.

ARRIVAL AND DEPARTURE

By plane Padang's Minangkabau International Airport is 23km north of the city centre. The 30min taxi ride to the city centre should cost around Rp120,000. DAMRI buses also run between the airport and Imam Bonjol Square (hourly 6am–6pm except 9am; Rp23,500).

Destinations Jakarta (29 daily; 1hr 45min); Kuala Lumpur (2 daily; 1hr 10min); Medan (4 daily; 1hr 5min).

By ferry Pelni boats arrive at the port of Teluk Bayur, 7km south of town, from where blue angkots #432, #433 and #434 connect Taman Imam Bonjol to the city centre, passing Jl Nipah on the way. The Pelni ticket office is located at Jl Tanjung Priok 32 in Teluk Bayur (☎0751 61624). For Pagang island, boats depart from both Port Muara and Bungus Bay, 21km south of Padang (linked by angkots; Rp10,000), the latter being closer to the island (daily 10am, returning 4.30pm; 1hr). Mentawai boats also depart from both points: the Mentawai Fast from Port Muara and slow boats from Bungus Bay (see box, p.236).

Destinations Gunung Sitoli (Nias; monthly; 21hr); Tanjung Priok (monthly; 2.5 days).

By bus Arrival and departure points for buses from Padang are numerous. Minibuses – known as "travel" – depart for regional destinations such as Bukittinggi and Payakumbuh from the north of the city at the Tranex Mandiri hub in Ulak Karang, connected to the centre by white and orange oplets (Rp3000). More convenient are private cars arranged by numerous travel agents – among them AWR (Jl Veteran 29A ☎0751 812508) – scattered along Jl Pemuda and Jl Veteran, linking most destinations (Rp40,000 for Bukittinggi; 2hr) and offering door-to-door service. For long-haul buses, use ALS on Jl Bypass Baru Km 6 (☎0751 776 2291).

Destinations Frequent daily departures for Bandar Lampung (25hr); Bukittinggi (2hr 30min); Medan (20hr); Pekanbaru (8hr); Parapat (18hr).

INFORMATION

Tourist office Jl Samudra 1 (Mon–Fri 7.30am–4pm, Sat & Sun 9am–3pm; ☎0751 34186, ✉narsyamza0609 @yahoo.com). Helpful English-speaking staff and plenty of maps and brochures.

GETTING AROUND

By bus and angkot Local angkots (Rp3000–4000) run from 6am to 9pm daily. Angkots run from Jl Moh Yamin, in the market area. Look out for the route number and destination signs suspended high above the oplet waiting area.

By bendi Stacks of horse-drawn carriages hang out by the central market, just east of the oplet terminal. Short hops around town will cost around Rp15,000.

ACCOMMODATION

Brigitte's Jl Kampung Sebelah I 14D ☎0751 36099 or ☎0813 7425 7162, ⊛brigitteshouse.padanghostel.com. Popular among surfers, with spotless rooms with fan and a/c (Rp270,000), communal breakfasts and wi-fi. There are a couple of cheap single rooms on the roof (Rp120,000). Brigitte and her pleasant staff are particularly knowledgeable about the Mentawai, and provide a range of travel services. Doubles **Rp200,000**

Grace Homestay Jl Batang Arau 88 ☎0812 6737 7988, ✉gracehomestay88@yahoo.com. Welcoming place just a few steps from the Mentawai Fast office and departure point, with basic rooms with a/c and shared bathrooms, some with balconies overlooking the river. A few larger rooms sleep six people (Rp400,000). Breakfast included. Doubles **Rp150,000**

Hang Tuah Jl Pemuda 1 ☎0751 26556, ⊛hotelhangtuah .com. A professionally run business hotel in a central location, this is one of Padang's best-value mid-range hotels. Rooms are ageing but well kept with a/c and inside bathrooms, while the pleasant balcony rooms (Rp410,280) also come with hot water. Sumatran breakfast included. Doubles **Rp260,150**

New House Jl HOS Cokroaminoto 104 ☎0751 25982, ⊛newhouse.padanghostel.com. One of Padang's newer options, set near the beach in a converted mansion fitted with high ceilings, a billiard table and a pleasant patio. All rooms are a/c, including the three- and four-bed dorm rooms, and staff are helpful with onward travel. Dorms **Rp100,000**, doubles **Rp250,000**

Yani Homestay Jl Nipah Berok 1 ☎0852 6380 1686, ✉yuliuz.caesar@gmail.com. Good-value spot beside the Buddhist temple and just a 2min walk to the beach, Yani has tidy a/c rooms, some en suite (Rp175,000). In the front there's a common area equipped with a DVD player and Xbox, and as a result the rooms upstairs or at the back are worth requesting for light sleepers. Doubles **Rp150,000**

EATING

At the southern end of Jl Pondok, due south of the market area towards the river, you'll find a wonderful night market of *sate* stalls, and another on Jl Imam Bonjol, a few hundred metres south of the junction with Jl Moh Yamin. Meanwhile, the small restaurants on Jl Moh Yamin, near the junction with Jl Pemuda, serve cheap, filling *martabaks* and sweet *roti canai*. Along Jl Pemuda things can get somewhat seedy at night.

Padang beach cafés Jl Samudra. The beach has a collection of nondescript cafés and restaurants serving simple Indonesian food and drinks (*nasi goreng* Rp10,000). The tables on the sand are the best spot in the city to enjoy a cold beverage and watch the sunset. Daily 8am–after midnight.

Sari Raso Jl Karya 3 4B–E. It makes little sense to visit the homeland of Padang food without experiencing a Padang

4

restaurant, and this may be the city's best. Up to a dozen small plates are spread across your table, and you pay only for what you eat. Very popular, and often run out of food by 8pm, so get there early. Daily 9am–9pm.

Warkop Nipah Jl Nipah 1D ☎0811 611 948. Bright and spacious whitewashed café two doors down from *Yani*. A popular breakfast and lunch-time hangout, it features a range of Indonesian favourites cooked just off the roadside (*nasi goreng* Rp12,000). Daily 6.30am–1.30pm.

DIRECTORY

Banks and exchange Bank of Central Asia, Jl H Agus Salim 10A; Bank Negara Indonesia, Jl Dobi 1, 3rd floor. ATMs are all over the city centre, though the cluster at the intersection south of the Adityawarman Museum is the nearest to most accommodation options.

Hospital Yos Sudarso Hospital, Jl Situjuh 1 (☎0751 33230).

Internet There are plenty of warnets around town. Warnet Tropic on Jl Blk Olo, 500m north of Plaza Andalus (Rp4000hr), has a good connection.

Post office The main post office is conveniently located at Jl Bagindo Azizchan 7, just north of the junction with Jl Moh Yamin (Mon–Fri 7.30am–6pm, Sat & Sun 9am–3pm).

BUKITTINGGI AND AROUND

Situated on the eastern edge of Ngarai Sianok Canyon with the conical peaks of Merapi and Singgalang rising to the south, the bustling town of **BUKITTINGGI** is a wonderful base for exploring the Minangkabau Highlands. Although the town is chaotic and sprawling, its centre, which is of most interest to visitors, is relatively compact and easy to negotiate. The most useful **landmark** is Djam Gadang, a clock tower built by the Dutch in 1926, at the junction of Jalan A Yani (the main thoroughfare) and Jalan Sudirman (the main road leading out of town to the south). Bukittinggi's **Pasar Atas** (Upper Market) stretches to the northeast of the tower, while down the hill to the north and west lies **Pasar Bawah** (Lower Market), both of which swell to bursting point on Wednesdays, Saturdays and Sundays. Jalan A Yani, 1km from north to south, is the tourist hub of Bukittinggi, and most of the sights, hotels, restaurants and shops that

THE MENTAWAI ISLANDS

A world apart from the mainland, the enticing jungle-clad **Mentawai islands** lie 150km off the west Sumatran coast from which they were separated half a million years ago. These days, the islands are at least as famous for their world-class waves as for being home to a unique tribal culture and a wealth of endemic flora and fauna – including langurs, macaques and the long-armed Mentawai (Kloss' gibbon). Both are under serious threat, from illegal logging and a government seeking to integrate the Mentawaian tribes into the Indonesian mainstream.

The islanders' traditional culture is based on communal dwelling in longhouses (*uma*) and subsistence agriculture, while their religious beliefs centre on the importance of coexisting with the invisible spirits that inhabit the world. With the advent of Christian missionaries and the colonial administration in the early twentieth century, many of the islanders' religious practices were banned, but plenty of beliefs and rituals have survived and some villages have built new *uma*.

Generally, Mentawai people welcome tourism as a way of validating and preserving their own culture, although due to the mainland's longtime monopoly on Mentawai tours, locals have received little financial benefit from it. Fortunately, independent travel has become increasingly feasible. There is a handful of homestays at the port of **Siberut**, the largest island (4000 square kilometres), where local guides may be hired, and surfers may choose from numerous all-inclusive surf camps that charge as little as Rp250,000/day. To the south, the island of **Sipora** is even cheaper, with homestays charging as little as Rp50,000 per night.

Boat schedules are subject to change, and departures are sometimes cancelled without warning. From Padang, the most convenient option is the Mentawai Fast (☎0751 893489, ⓦmentawaifast.com), with speedboats operating out of Port Muara to Siberut (Tues, Thurs & Sat at 7am; returning 3pm the same day; 3hr 10min) and Sipora (Mon, Wed, Fri & Sun at 7am; returning 3pm the same day; 3hr 10min). From Bungus Bay, the Ambu-Ambu departs for Sipora (Wed 8pm; returning Fri 8pm; 10hr), while the newer KMP Gambolo departs for Siberut (Wed & Fri at 7pm; returning Thurs & Sat eve; 11hr) and Sipora (Sun 8pm; returning Mon 8pm; 10hr). Pack some anti-seasickness tablets if big waves make you queasy.

serve the tourist trade are on this street or close by. This is one of Sumatra's most pleasant towns in which to spend a few days, with plenty of good accommodation and restaurants and lots to do in the surrounding area, which includes the rafflesia reserve at **Batang Palupah**, the spectacular **Harau Valley** and the impressive palace of **Pagaruyung**.

WHAT TO SEE AND DO

A few hundred metres to the north of the clock tower, **Fort de Kock** (daily 8am–6pm; Rp20,000) was built by the Dutch in 1825 near the end of the Padri War. There's little left of the original structure but some old cannons and parts of the moats. The fort is linked by a footbridge over Jalan A Yani to the park, **Taman Bundo Kanduang**, which has a depressing zoo (entry included in the fort ticket) and a Minangkabau museum (daily 8am–5pm; Rp15,000) housed in a beautiful *rumah gadang* constructed in 1934. Displays include a thirteenth-century Quran, some curious two-headed taxidermal specimens, and traditianl Minangkabau clothing – locals like to put

on rented sets of wedding clothes (Rp20,000) for photos.

Much more pleasant is a stroll around **Panorama Park** (daily 7.30am–5.30pm; Rp5000), perched on a lip of land overlooking the sheer cliff walls down into Ngarai Sianok Canyon, the best sight in Bukittinggi town by far, especially just before and after sunset, when bats fly overhead. Beneath the park stretch 1400m of **Japanese tunnels** (Lubang Jepang; daily 8am–6pm; Rp15,000) and rooms built by local slave labour for ammunition storage during World War II. If you choose to venture down into these dank, miserable depths, consider hiring a guide (from Rp60,000). The **Ngarai Sianok Canyon** is part of a rift valley that runs the full length of Sumatra – the canyon here is 15km long and around 100m deep, with a glistening river wending its way along the bottom.

Koto Gadang

Just beyond the western edge of the **Ngarai Sianok Canyon** lies **Koto Gadang**, a small and dwindling Minangkabau village of silversmiths. Though linked by

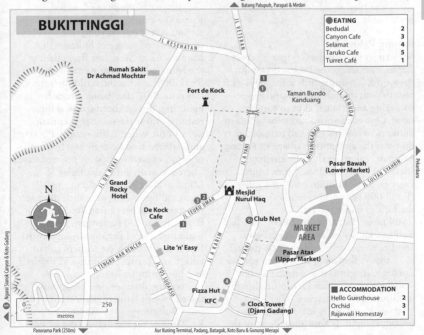

BUKITTINGGI

Batang Palupuh, Parapat & Medan

JL VETERAN

JL KESEHATAN

Rumah Sakit Dr Achmad Mochtar

Fort de Kock

Taman Bundo Kanduang

JL PEMUDA

N

JL DR RIVAI

JL A YANI

JL MINANGKABAU

Pasar Bawah (Lower Market)

JL SULTAN SYAHRIR

Pekanbaru

Grand Rocky Hotel

De Kock Cafe

Mesjid Nurul Haq

JL TEUKU UMAR

@ **Club Net**

MARKET AREA

Lite 'n' Easy

JL KARIM

JL A YANI

Pasar Atas (Upper Market)

JL TENGKU NAN RENCEH

JL YOS SUDARSO

Pizza Hut

KFC

Clock Tower (Djam Gadang)

0 — 250 metres

Ngarai Sianok Canyon & Koto Gadang

Panorama Park (250m)

Aur Kuning Terminal, Padang, Batagak, Koto Baru & Gunung Merapi

● EATING	
Bedudal	2
Canyon Cafe	3
Selamat	4
Taruko Cafe	5
Turret Café	1

■ ACCOMMODATION	
Hello Guesthouse	2
Orchid	3
Rajawali Homestay	1

4

THE MINANG HIGHLANDS

The gorgeous mountainous landscape of the **Minang Highlands** features soaring rice terraces and easily accessible traditional culture. The highlands around Bukittinggi are the cultural heartland of the **Minangkabau** (Minang) people. The Minang are staunchly matrilineal, one of the largest such societies extant, and Muslim. The most visible aspect of their culture is the distinctive architecture of their homes, with massive roofs soaring skywards at either end (representing the horns of a buffalo). Typically, three or four generations of one family would live in one large house built on stilts, the *rumah gadang* (big house) or *rumah adat* (traditional house), a wood-and-thatch structure often decorated with fabulous wooden carvings.

occasional oplets (15min; Rp3000), it's a pleasant and scenic walk from Bukittinggi. From Jalan Tengku Umar continue along up and over the top, passing the Japanese tunnels on your left as you descend the canyon. Alternatively, start at Panorama Park and emerge from the tunnels themselves. Continuing down about 50m from the tunnels is a U-bend in the road where a footpath leads down the canyon, eventually crossing a suspension bridge before climbing to the opposite ridge along the **Great Wall of Koto Gadang** (free), a curious, 1km-long structure opened in 2013. After taking in the views looking back across the canyon, continue along the road another 1km to reach Koto Gadang.

Batang Palupuh

Sometimes spanning a full metre across, *Rafflesia arnoldi* is the largest flower in the world, blooming only a few days each month with remarkable red-and-white colouring and a smell akin to rotting meat. One of the most accessible spots in Sumatra to see this rare and extraordinary flower is the enchanting village of **Batang Palupuh**, 13km north of Bukittinggi (Rp8000 by regular local buses from Pasar Bawah). Enquire here for a guide (Rp50,000 per person) to lead you into the hills to find a rafflesia.

Still more elusive is the *Amorphophallus titanum*, locally called "*bunga bangkai*", another rare, smelly and gigantic flower: *A. titanum*'s flowering stem often reaches 2m high. Its genus name describes it as "misshapen penis", and it blooms briefly just once every four years.

Yet another worthy reason to visit Batang Palupuh is **kopi luwak**, one of the world's rarest and most expensive brews. Made from digested coffee beans picked out from the droppings of palm civets, the coffee has an earthy, caramel taste – try it at Umul Khairi's home (100g bag Rp200,000; ☎0813 7417 8971, ✉umulross@yahoo.com) next to the Taqwa Mosque (see box, p.240).

Tanah Datar Valley

The Minang court of the fourteenth to nineteenth centuries was based in the valley and the entire area is awash with cultural relics, megaliths and places of interest. The largest town in the valley is **Batusangkar**, 39km southeast of Bukittinggi. Just a few kilometres away is the village of Silinduang (around Rp8000 by ojek), which houses the elegant **Istana Pagaruyung**, the reconstructed palace of Sultan Arifin Muning Alam Syah, last Raja Alam of the Minangkabau (daily 8am–5.30pm; Rp12,000). Sadly, the building burned down in 2007 after being struck by lightning, but has been painstakingly restored and is the most resplendent sight in the valley, with intricately carved and painted wood panels and five layers of giant, curved roofs with pointed eaves. There are many other examples of Minangkabau *rumah adat* in the surrounding countryside, including at the scenic villages of **Rao Rao**, north of Batusangkar, and **Pariangan**, between Batusangkar and Padangpanjang, which is said to be the oldest Minangkabau village and boasts centuries-old tombs and hot springs.

Given the distances involved, most travellers visit Batusangkar on a day-trip from Bukittinggi (1hr 30min; Rp20,000), via Padangpanjang or Baso.

Harau Valley

A fertile expanse of rice paddies and palm trees hemmed in by sheer vertical cliffs of 100m, the **Harau Valley** is one of West Sumatra's most visually stunning destinations. During the rainy season there are waterfalls, some with crystal-clear pools at their base, scattered along the valley floor where tapir, boar and siamang (tailless, black-furred gibbons) are rumoured to roam. The valley (entry Rp5000) begins just over an hour along the road from Bukittinggi to Pekanbaru, and about fifteen minutes past the city of Payakumbuh. Most people still visit Harau on day-trips, though if you'd like to linger longer you can stay at one of a handful of accommodation options, among them the ultra-basic *Abdi Homestay* (☏0852 6378 1842, ⓦabdihomestay.blogspot.com; Rp60,000), set in a tranquil spot near a 50m waterfall.

Although the trip from Bukittinggi is far more convenient on your own two wheels, public transport is an option: first, take a bus to Payakumbuh (1hr; Rp20,000), an angkot to the gate (15min; Rp4000), then an ojek to Harau (10min; Rp10,000). If you miss the last bus returning from Payakumbuh, wave down one of the many buses coming along the main road from Pekanbaru.

ARRIVAL AND DEPARTURE

By bus Long-distance buses dock at the Aur Kuning terminal, 3km southeast of the town centre. If you're coming from Padang ask the bus to stop at the Jambu Air crossing on the southern outskirts of town before turning off for the terminal; you can get a red #14 bemo (Rp3000) into the town centre from this junction. There are frequent local buses from Aur Kuning terminal (daily 7.30am–5pm) for Maninjau, Batusangkar, Payakumbuh and Padang, as well as long-distance buses (book ahead). A nightly bus links Dumai (7pm; 12hr) in time for the daily ferry to Malacca.

Destinations Unless otherwise noted, frequent departures: Batusangkar (1hr 30min); Maninjau (1hr 30min); Medan (several daily; 20hr); Padang (3hr); Pekanbaru (7 daily; 6hr); Parapat (3 daily, including 5pm ALS [a/c]; 14hr); Sibolga (daily; 11hr).

By travel Tourist minivans link Pekanbaru, Padang, Parapat (for Danau Toba) and Maninjau, and may be booked through travel agents around town, among them AWR (☏0752 32420).

CLIMBING GUNUNG MERAPI

Access to 2890m **Gunung Merapi** (Fire Mountain) is from Koto Baru, 12km south of Bukittinggi. Typically, the climb, which is strenuous rather than gruelling if you're reasonably fit, takes five hours up and four down; most people start at around 11pm in order to arrive for sunrise at the smoking crater on the summit plateau. You may spot bats, gibbons and squirrels in the forest, but the main draw is the view across to Gunung Singgalang. Bring sturdy footwear and warm clothes for the top. Roni's (☏0812 675 0688) in Bukittinggi provides experienced guides for the hike for Rp400,000/person.

INFORMATION

Tourist Information *Rajawali Homestay (JI A Yani 152)* is the best option for maps and local activities. Tour operators are also useful.

Tours The top tour operators are based in Bukittinggi's popular hotels and cafés. Among the best of these are Lite 'n' Easy (Fikar ☏813 7453 7413, ⓦliteneasy.co.id), based around the corner from *De Kock Cafe* at JI Yos Sudarso 12; Roni's Tour & Travel (☏812 675 0688, ⓦronistours.com), based at *Orchid*; and AdvenCulture (☏0852 7881 2345) at *Bedudal*; all run group tours as well as individual motorbike tours.

GETTING AROUND

By angkot scurry around town in a circular route (Rp3000). For the bus terminal, stop any red angkot heading north on JI A Yani, which will circle to the east of town and pass the main post office before turning for Aur Kuning.

Car and motorbike rental Enquire at your accommodation or any of the travel agents in town (generally Rp80,000/day).

ACCOMMODATION

Most accommodation is clustered within close earshot of Mesjid Nurul Haq at the intersection of JI A Yani and JI Teuku Umar.

★ **Hello Guesthouse** JI Teuku Umar 6B ☏0752 21542, ⓦhelloguesthouse.net. Offering excellent value and a great location, this is Bukittinggi's most popular backpacker lodgings. Helpful owner Ling offers a range of simple, clean rooms with hot water, including dorms and single rooms (Rp125,000). There's self-service tea and coffee, and a good Indonesian or Western breakfast is included in the rate. Dorms Rp75,000, doubles Rp160,000

KOPI LUWAK: THE CAT POO COFFEE

Some find it delicious and others repulsive, but all pay a pretty price for *kopi luwak*. One of the world's most expensive coffees, the unique beverage is brewed from beans fermented within the stomachs of **palm civets**, arboreal creatures that look more like weasels than cats. The palm civets tend to pick only the ripest and sweetest of red coffee cherries from the plantations of West Sumatra and their stomach enzymes go to work breaking down the proteins that give coffee its bitter taste. Following defecation, the civets' excrement strings are picked from the jungle floor bordering the plantations to be cleaned, sun-dried, roasted over cinnamon wood and finally hand-pounded into a fine powder. Thanks to the civet cats' digestive tracts, no filter is necessary when serving: simply stir in a teaspoon of the coffee powder, wait a few minutes and decide for yourself whether *kopi luwak* is worth its hefty price tag.

Orchid Jl Teuku Umar 11 ☎ 0752 32634. Well-kept rooms, most of which sleep three and come with balconies and hot water (Rp150,000). Ask for a room facing west (to the right when entering), both for the sunset views and to dampen the wake-up call from the mosque to the east. Friendly owner Roni provides excellent information on local and regional activities in the downstairs café. Doubles Rp120,000

Rajawali Homestay Jl A Yani 152 ☎ 0752 31905, ☎ ulrich.rudolph@web.de. This unassuming place on the corner has worn, spartan rooms upstairs with grimy inside mandi and a pleasant rooftop sitting area that's great for meeting fellow travellers. Owner Ulrich offers a veritable wealth of information on local activities, including a number of original, GPS-mapped trekking and motorbiking routes. Doubles Rp80,000

EATING

Dozens of nameless food stalls set up shop each night along Jl A Yani junction (7.30pm–3am), offering *sate*, *nasi goreng* and other staples.

Bedudal Café Jl A Yani 95. The hippest traveller hangout on Jl A Yani, featuring reggae, live music at weekends and a good selection of Western and Indonesian dishes (*tempe* sandwich Rp30,000; large Bintang Rp45,000). Daily 8am–midnight.

Canyon Café Jl Teuku Umar 8. There's a pleasant outdoor seating area and knowledgeable staff at this quiet place just beside *Hello Guesthouse*. Super-cheap meals (*nasi goreng* Rp15,000; veggie taco Rp20,000; chicken sandwich Rp20,000) are worth the wait and come in generous portions. Daily 8am–10pm.

Selamat Jl A Yani 19. One of the best Padang restaurants in town; they usually have eggs in coconut sauce – especially good for vegetarians – and beef *rendang* (Rp15,000 per portion), and staff are used to Westerners. Daily 8am–10pm.

Taruko Café Jl Taruko. Set 6km west of town along the scenic road to Koto Gadang, *Taruko* is a splendid place to while away an afternoon. Seated under a large Minangkaban-style thatched roof, you'll have a breathtaking

view of Tabiang Takuruang, a lone spire projecting from a bend in Sianok Canyon, with Gunung Singgalang rising in the background. Attracting a hip, young local crowd, there's a varied menu of local, Chinese and Italian cuisine (spaghetti bolognese Rp37,000). Daily 8am–6.30pm.

Turret Café Jl A Yani 140–142 ☎ 0752 625956. Breezy open café and bar next door to *Rajawali* with friendly, English-speaking staff serving modestly priced Western and Indonesian dishes and a flatscreen TV airing football matches. Affable owner Anita makes the most delicious beef *rendang* in town (Rp45,000). The friendly Lite'n'Easy crew is often found here. Daily 8am–11.30pm.

TRADITIONAL ENTERTAINMENT

Bull-racing and bullfighting *Pacu jawi* (bull racing) is held every year on September 30 in the muddy rice fields around Batusangkar. Another Minangkabau tradition is *adu kerbau* (bullfighting), held on Wednesday in Batagak (9km south of Bukittinggi), an event that stems from the legend of an invading Javanese king whose campaign ended in defeat after he wagered the outcome on a bullfight.

DIRECTORY

Banks and exchange There are plenty of banks with ATMs along Jl A Yani, including Bank Negara Indonesia, Mandiri and BNI.

Hospital Rumah Sakit Dr Achmad Mochtar is on Jl Dr Rivai (☎ 0752 21013 or ☎ 0752 33825).

Internet Club Net, Jl A Yani 25 (daily 10am–10pm), has good machines and a fast connection (Rp3000/hr).

Pharmacy Apotek Yani Baru, Jl A Yani 87 (daily 8am–8pm), offers basic medical supplies.

Post office The main post office is inconveniently far from the town centre on Jl Sudirman.

DANAU MANINJAU

A palm-fringed crater lake surrounded by 400m-high jungle-covered walls, **DANAU MANINJAU** (Lake Maninjau) lies just 15km west of Bukittinggi as the crow flies. The actual journey spans 37km through rice paddies and lush forests, and gangs of monkeys look on as you slip over the rim of the caldera and snake downwards to the lake, notching 44 hairpin turns – each one signposted. At an altitude of 500m high, the lake is 17km long and 8km wide, the area of interest for tourists stretching from the village of **MANINJAU**, where the road from Bukittinggi reaches the lakeside, to the village of **Bayur**, 4km north.

WHAT TO SEE AND DO

Most visitors come to Maninjau simply to relax and swim in the lake, though more energetic souls may like to hike into the jungle-clad hills behind the village. Popular activities include tracking down a **rafflesia** flower, hiking to the nearby **waterfall**, known locally as "sarasa" (20min), or all the way to Puncak Lawang, the highest vantage point above the lake (2hr). For any of these excursions, try *Bagoes Café*, which runs tours as well as trekking and Sunday pig-hunting with dogs, a traditional local activity. Cycling along the lakeside is also popular, but motorbikes are just about essential if you want to circumnavigate the entire lake.

ARRIVAL AND DEPARTURE

By bus Buses from Bukittinggi make a stop in the small square at the foot of the mountain road before continuing along the lakeside road to Bayur – ask the conductor to drop you at your hotel. For the return trip, daily buses depart from the square in Maninjau (8 daily; 6am–5pm; 1hr 30min). There is no direct bus to Padang: either head back to Bukittinggi or board an oplet to Lubukbasung (every 30min; 45min), from where you can hail a bus to Padang (infrequent; 2hr).

By car Departuring more frequently than buses, seven-seater "travel" cars to Bukittinggi are easily hailed from anywhere along the main road. Cars for Padang and Pekanbaru leave from Maninjau's main square.

Destinations Bukittinggi (every 10min; 1hr 30min; Rp30,000); Padang (every 2hr 7am–3pm; 3hr; Rp75,000); Pekanbaru (daily 9am & 5pm; 8hr; Rp120,000).

INFORMATION

Tourist information Local information is generally available at hotels, most reliably at *Beach Guest House*. At PT Kesuma Mekar Jaya (☎ 0812 6699 6610, ⓦ magicalsumatra.blogspot.com), just north of the BRI Bank and across the road, the ever-present Muhammad Ali is a fount of knowledge on local activities.

ACCOMMODATION AND EATING

Accommodation options are dotted along the lake's eastern shore, from about 500m south of the Bukittinggi road junction to a couple kilometres past Bayur to the north.

Arlen Nova's Paradise ☎ 0813 7408 0485, ⓦ nova-maninjau.id.or.id. A couple of hundred metres along a narrow trail through the rice paddies 2km north of Bayur and 5km north of the Bukittinggi road junction, *Arlen Nova's* enjoys a peaceful lakeside setting free of fish farms. There are large bungalows with mosquito nets, hot water and comfortable beds, and a pleasant café with delicious food (*tempe* tofu curry Rp16,000) and one of the lake's few sandy beaches. Doubles Rp200,000

Bagoes Café Jl Raya Maninjau. Set within *Beach Guest House*, this café and restaurant about 500m north of the Bukittinggi junction is the most popular traveller's hangout in town, with seating right along the water, a small library and a range of tours. The restaurant offers some of Maninjau's best Western and Indonesian food (green veg curry Rp22,000; beef *rendang* Rp35,000). Daily 7.30am–10pm.

Beach Guest House Jl Raya Maninjau ☎ 0752 861799 or ☎ 0813 6379 7005, ⓦ beachguesthousemaninjau.com. Friendly little guesthouse sharing a waterfront location with *Bagoes Café*. Simple rooms have great views from the verandahs, while out front there is a small beach and a tangled banyan tree hanging over the water, handy for launching into the lake. Doubles Rp150,000

Tan Dirih Jl Raya Maninjau ☎ 0752 61263. Just over 1km north of the Bukittinggi junction, this is the lake's romantic option, offering a bit more comfort. Room service is available and all four rooms have TV, hot water and tubs while sharing a broad porch. Unfortunately, the outlook across the water is partly obstructed by fishing platforms. Pancake breakfasts included. Doubles Rp300,000

Zalino ☎ 0812 6649 5103. Well poised for arching shoreline views from seating in a covered jetty about 650m north of the junction, this is one of the lake's top stand-alone restaurants, with an assortment of Western and Padang food, and a house speciality of locally hunted *kijang* – deer (*sate kijang* Rp30,000; *nasi rendang kijang* Rp40,000). Daily 7am–9pm.

DIRECTORY

Bank The BRI Bank just north of the Bukittinggi junction has an ATM, although VISA cards are not accepted.
Bike rental Bicycles can be rented from *Beach Guest House* or PT Kesuma Mekar Jaya (Rp50,000/day); the latter also rents motorbikes (Rp80,000/day).

Bookshop *Bagoes Café* has the largest range of books in Maninjau.

Internet All hotels offer wi-fi, while *Bagoes Café* offers customers free use of an in-house computer.

Post office The post office is a short hop towards the lake from the junction on Jl Telaga Biru Tanjung Raya (Mon–Thurs 8am–4pm, Fri 8am–noon & 2–4pm).

BANDAR LAMPUNG

Occupying a stunning location in the hills overlooking Lampung Bay, from where you can see as far as Krakatau on a clear day, **BANDAR LAMPUNG** is an amalgamation of Teluk Betung, the traditional port, and Tanjung Karang, the administrative centre on the hills behind. When you're coming here from other parts of Sumatra your destination will usually be referred to as Rajabasa, the name of the bus terminal.

Travellers rarely stay long in Lampung, instead heading south for the ferry to Java or climbing into long-haul buses to move north. However, there are numerous off-the-beaten-path activities to keep visitors around, among them jungle trekking through swampy Way Kambas, river trips in Way Kanan, boat charters to check out dolphins in Kiluan Bay and the white sandy beaches and frontal views of Krakatau in Sebuku and Sebesi islands. Surfers often head straight to **Krui** on the west coast, one of the best year-round surf spots in the country (see box below).

SURFING IN SOUTHERN SUMATRA

Bandar Lampung is a base from which to access the coastal town of **Krui**, one of Indonesia's best surfing destinations. Most surf camps offer to arrange your transfer from Bandar Lampung, but you can also take the Krui Express bus (3–4hr) from Rajabasa terminal. Several local operators offer **surfing expeditions** in the area. Check out *Lovina Krui Surf* (☎0853 7780 2212, ⒲lovinakruisurf.com), which has beautiful, pitched-roof cottages facing the waves, with full-board rates starting at Rp385,000 (a/c Rp450,000).

KRAKATAU ON A BUDGET

Although tours to **Krakatau** can be arranged through Bandar Lampung's Tourist Information Centre (see below), it's much cheaper to head south to Kalianda (1hr 30min; bemo Rp15,000), then 6km further south to Canti (ojek Rp10,000), the closest port to Krakatau. Here you can join other travellers in chartering a boat to Krakatau (2hr 30min; Rp1,500,000 for up to 20 people).

ARRIVAL AND DEPARTURE

By plane Raden Intan II Airport is 22km northwest of the city, linked by hourly Trans Lampung buses to the city centre, stopping on Jl Ahmed Yani and Jl Sudirman (from the airport 6am until the last flight arrival; to the airport 5am–5pm; Rp20,000). Fixed-price taxis from the airport into town will cost Rp110,000.

Destinations Bandung (3 daily; 1hr); Jakarta (21 daily; 50min).

By bus Long-distance buses arrive at and depart from the Rajabasa terminal (the DAMRI terminal is a 10min walk to the north of Rajabasa), 7km north of the city, though when arriving from the south you can ask to hop off as they pass Jl Sudirman in the city centre. From Jl Sudirman, green angkots (Rp4000) head northwest to Pasar Bawah, from where blue angkots (Rp4000) connect Rajabasa terminal. Hourly Trans Lampung buses also connect Jl Sudirman to Rajabasa.

Destinations Frequent daily departures for Bakauheni (2–3hr); Bukittinggi (24hr); Jakarta (7–8hr); Kalianda (1hr 30min); Padang (24hr); Pekanbaru (24hr).

By train Bandar Lampung marks the southern end of southern Sumatra's modest rail network, extending north to Palembang. The train station is on Jl Kotoraja, about 100m from Pasar Bawah.

Destination Palembang (2 daily; 9hr).

INFORMATION

Tourist office The useful tourist office is at Jl Jend Sudirman 29 (Mon–Fri 7.30am–3.30pm; ☎0721 261430, ⒲pariwisatalampung.com).

GETTING AROUND

By bus and bemo DAMRI bus services (daily 6am–9pm) run up and down Jl Randen Intan and Jl Diponegoro. Bemo routes are less fixed than buses: tell them your destination as you enter. The big green buses of the new Trans Bandar Lampung service (Rp3500) run between Rajabasa and Sukaraja in Teluk Betung.

By taxi Drivers are reluctant to use meters, so negotiate a fare first (across town should cost Rp20,000–30,000).

FERRIES TO JAVA

Around 30km southeast of Kalianda, and 90km southeast of Bandar Lampung, lies the Bakauheni ferry port, the departure point for ferries to Merak (see box, p.182), on Java's northwest tip. There are regular buses to Bakauheni from the Rajabasa terminal in Bandar Lampung (1hr 30min; Rp30,000) and bemos from Kalianda – there's no reason to stay in Bakauheni itself. **Ferries** from Bakauheni operate round the clock (2hr 20min; Rp15,000), leaving roughly hourly during the day and less frequently at night. From Merak, it's another two hours by bus to Jakarta (Rp28,000). DAMRI offers convenient **bus-boat-bus** combination tickets (from Rp155,000; 6–7hr), with several departures in the morning from Rajabasa terminal and from just beside the train station.

ACCOMMODATION AND EATING

Pasar Mambo, the night market, is at the southern end of Jl Hassanudin (dusk–midnight).

Arnes Central Hotel Jl Cut Nyak 20 ☏0721 263339, ⓦarinashotel.com/our-groups/arnes-central-hotel.html. Great-value one-star hotel with big, beautiful rooms that come with a/c, cable TV, mini-bar and a modest breakfast buffet. Convenient location next to *Central Plaza* and just across the road from the purple bemo route. Doubles Rp295,000

Begadang II Jl Diponegoro 164. Huge, busy Padang restaurant loved by locals that serves cheap seafood dishes (beef *rendang* portion Rp17,000). It's a popular place, and owner Haji Dasril has opened five of these restaurants around town, this one next to the Harley Davidson club and on the purple bemo route. Closed for Ramadan. Daily 7am–10pm.

Palapa Jl Diponegoro 154 ☏0721 261617. Offering some of the very cheapest lodgings in the city centre, this friendly hotel has somewhat grubby rooms – all a/c, some single (Rp100,000) and some with attached bathrooms (Rp200,000). Access is through a driveway off busy Jl Diponegoro, and breakfast is included. Doubles Rp150,000

DIRECTORY

Hospital Rumah Sakit Bumi Waras, Jl Wolter Moginsidi (☏0721 255032).

Immigration Jl Haniah 3, Cut Mutia (☏0721 482828).

Internet There are several internet cafés along Jl Raden Intan and Jl Sudirman (Rp5000/hr).

Police station Jl Mayor Jend Haryono (☏0721 253110).

Post office Jl KH Ahmad Dahlan 21 (Mon–Thurs 8am–5pm, Fri 8am–noon & 2–5pm).

Bali

With its pounding surf, emerald-green rice terraces and exceptionally artistic culture, the small volcanic island of

Bali – population around 4.4 million and Southeast Asia's only Hindu society – has long been Indonesia's premier tourist destination. Although congested and commercialized in the south of the island, Bali's original charm is still much in evidence, its distinctive temples and elaborate festivals set off by the mountainous, river-rich landscape of the interior.

Bali's most famous and crowded resort is the **Kuta-Legian-Seminyak** strip, an 8km sweep of golden sand and surf, with a congested strip of accommodation, shopping and nightlife. Neighbouring **Canggu** is less urbanized and its beaches have more of a wild beauty, while experienced wave-riders head for the beaches on the Bukit peninsula. **Sanur** is a fairly sedate southern beach resort, but most backpackers prefer the tranquil island of **Nusa Lembongan** and the beaches of peaceful east-coast **Amed** and **Padang Bai**. Immensely rich sea life means that snorkelling and diving are big draws at all these resorts. The mellow beach resort of **Lovina** on the north coast also has its appeal, while Bali's major cultural destination is **Ubud**, where traditional dances are staged every night and the streets are full of organic cafés, yoga studios and art galleries. In addition, there are numerous elegant Hindu temples to visit, particularly **Uluwatu**, **Tanah Lot** and **Besakih**, and a good number of volcano hikes: the most popular is the route up **Gunung Batur**, with **Gunung Agung** only for the very fit.

Transport to and from Bali is efficient: the island is served by hundreds of international and domestic flights, which all land at Ngurah Rai Airport

4

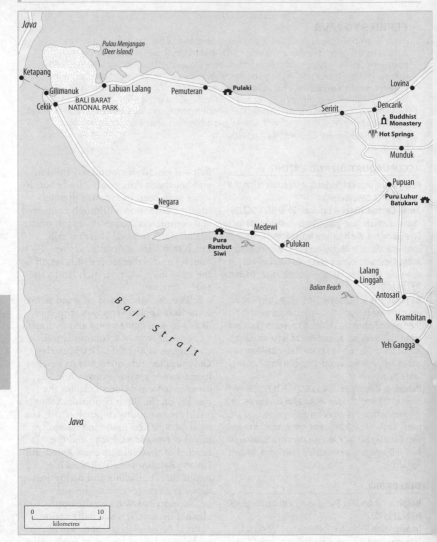

Java

Pulau Menjangan
(Deer Island)

Ketapang

Gilimanuk
Labuan Lalang
Pemuteran
Pulaki

Cekik
BALI BARAT
NATIONAL PARK

Lovina

Seririt
Dencarik

Buddhist
Monastery

Hot Springs

Munduk

Pupuan

Puru Luhur
Batukaru

Negara

Medewi

Pura
Rambut
Siwi

Pulukan

Lalang
Linggah

Balian Beach

Antosari

Krambitan

Yeh Gangga

B a l i   S t r a i t

Java

0   10
kilometres

4

just south of Kuta, as well as ferries from Java and Lombok. Pelni ferries from ports across Indonesia call at Benoa harbour (see p.246).

DENPASAR

Bali's capital city, **DENPASAR** (sometimes still known by its old name Badung), has a museum and several lively markets, but lacks the tourist accommodation and other facilities of Kuta, Legian and

Seminyak. Virtually no one stays here: travellers simply come for the day, or use it as a transport interchange.

WHAT TO SEE AND DO

Puputan Square marks the heart of the downtown area. It commemorates the ritual fight to the death (*puputan*) on September 20, 1906, when the raja of Badung and hundreds of his subjects stabbed themselves to death rather than submit to the Dutch invaders.

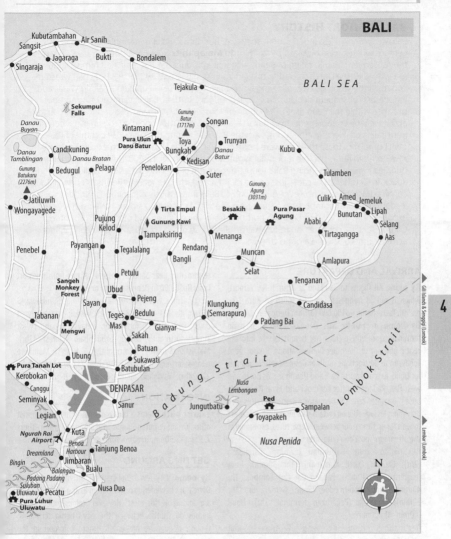

BALI

Kubutambahan
Air Sanih
Sangsit
Jagaraga
Bukti
Bondalem
Singaraja

BALI SEA

Tejakula

Sekumpul
Falls

Danau
Buyan

Gunung
Batur
(1717m)
Kintamani
Songan
Pura Ulun
Danu Batur
Toya
Bungkah
Trunyan
Candikuning
Danau
Batur
Kubu
Danau
Tamblingan
Danau Bratan
Kedisan
Gunung
Batukaru
(2276m)
Bedugul
Pelaga
Penelokan
Tulamben
Suter

Jatiluwih
Wongayagede
Gunung
Agung
(3031m)
Culik
Amed
Jemeluk
Tirta Empul
Besakih
Pura Pasar
Agung
Lipah
Bunutan
Pujung
Kelod
Gunung Kawi
Ababi
Selang
Penebel
Payangan
Tampaksiring
Menanga
Tirtagangga
Aas
Tegalalang
Rendang
Muncan
Amlapura
Bangli
Petulu
Selat
Sangeh
Monkey
Forest
Ubud
Pejeng
Tenganan
Sayan
Teges
Bedulu
Klungkung
(Semarapura)
Candidasa
Tabanan
Mas
Gianyar
Padang Bai
Mengwi
Sakah
Batuan
Sukawati
Ubung
Batubulan

Pura Tanah Lot
Kerobokan
DENPASAR
Nusa
Lembongan
Ped
Canggu
Sanur
Jungutbatu
Sampalan
Seminyak
Toyapakeh
Legian
Kuta
Ngurah Rai
Airport
Benoa
Harbour
Tanjung Benoa
Nusa Penida
Dreamland
Jimbaran
Bingin
Balangan
Bualu
Padang Padang
Suluban
Uluwatu
Pecatu
Nusa Dua
Pura Luhur
Uluwatu

Badung Strait

Lombok Strait

Gili Islands & Senggigi (Lombok)

Lembar (Lombok)

4

N

Overlooking the square on Jalan Mayor
Wisnu, the **Bali Museum** (Museum
Negeri Propinsi Bali; Mon–Thurs, Sat &
Sun 7.30am–3.30pm, Fri 7.30am–1pm;
Rp20,000; on the turquoise Kereneng–
Ubung bemo route) has displays on
prehistory, textiles and theatrical
costumes as well as an interesting exhibit
on spiritual rituals in the Gedung
Karangasem building. Alongside the Bali
Museum stands the modern state temple
of **Pura Agung Jagatnatha**, built in 1953.

Pasar Badung and Pasar Kumbasari

The biggest of Denpasar's markets is Pasar
Badung, which trades day and night from
the three-storey covered stone-and-brick
pasar (market) beside the Badung River,
just off Jalan Gajah Mada. Its top-floor art
market is crammed with good-value
sarongs, batik cloth and ceremonial gear.
The four-storey **Pasar Kumbasari** is across
on the west bank of the river just south
off Jalan Gajah Mada, and is another
good source of inexpensive handicrafts.

BALI: A SHORT HISTORY

Bali was a more or less independent society of Buddhists and Hindus until the fourteenth century, when it was colonized by the **Hindu Majapahits** from neighbouring Java. Despite the subsequent Islamicization of nearly all her neighbours, Bali has remained firmly Hindu ever since. In 1849, the Dutch started to take an interest in Bali, and by January 1909 had wrested control of the whole island. Following a short-lived Japanese occupation in World War II, and Indonesia's subsequent declaration of independence in 1945, Bali became an autonomous province within the Republic in 1949. But tensions with Java are ongoing and there is concern about wealthy entrepreneurs from Jakarta (and the West) monopolizing the financial benefits from Bali's considerable attractions, with the Balinese fearing they may lose control of their own homeland. These tensions were horrifically highlighted when Muslim extremists from Java bombed Kuta's two most popular nightclubs on October 12, 2002, killing more than two hundred people and sending Bali's tourist-dependent economy into severe decline. A second attack, in October 2005, came just as the island was starting to recover. Reprisals and religious conflict did not ensue, however, due in part to Bali's impressively equanimous Hindu leadership. Tourist numbers have since recovered, and since 2010 arrivals have risen exponentially, fuelled by a boom in numbers from China, Russia and other Asian countries. Consequently, a construction frenzy has resulted in an urban sprawl and traffic congestion across southern Bali and around Ubud.

ARRIVAL AND DEPARTURE

By plane All flights to Bali land at Ngurah Rai Airport, which is not in Denpasar, but just south of Kuta (see p.250). Taxis charge Rp100,000 to/from Denpasar.

By bemo or public bus Denpasar has four main terminals, from where trans-city bemos beetle into the centre and out to the other bemo stations. Bemos from Tegal run to destinations south of Denpasar; Batubulan is for Ubud, east and north Bali; and Ubung serves north and west Bali, Padang Bai (for Lombok) and Java. No shuttle buses operate out of Denpasar. Bemo services are becoming less reliable on certain shorter routes, so expect to wait for up to an hour between departures, especially in the afternoon; most don't run after 5pm.

Destinations from Batubulan terminal Candidasa (2hr); Gianyar (1hr); Kintamani (1hr 30min); Kuta (eastern edge; 40min); Padang Bai (for Lombok; 1hr 40min); Sanur (western edge; 25min); Semarapura (1hr 20min); Singaraja (Penarukan terminal; 3hr); Ubud (40min–1hr 20min).

Destinations from Kereneng terminal Sanur (15–25min).

Destinations from Tegal terminal Kuta (25min); Ngurah Rai Airport (40min); Sanur (25min).

Destinations from Ubung terminal Bedugul (2hr); Cekik (3hr); Gilimanuk (4hr); Jakarta (24hr); Kediri (40min); Medewi (1hr 30min); Singaraja (Sukasada terminal; 3hr 15min); Surabaya (10hr); Yogyakarta (15hr).

By boat All Pelni ships from the rest of Indonesia dock at Benoa harbour (Pelabuhan Benoa), 10km southeast. Pelni boat tickets for long-distance ferries can be bought from Pelni offices at Jl Diponegoro 165 (☎0361 234680, ⓦpelni.co.id) and at Benoa harbour (☎0361 723689). Bemos meet the ships and take passengers into Denpasar,

terminating near Sanglah hospital. A taxi from the port costs Rp50,000 to Denpasar, Kuta or Sanur.

Destinations from Benoa harbour Bima (Sumbawa; 3 fortnightly; 21–32hr); Bitung (Sulawesi; fortnightly; 4 days); Ende (Flores; fortnightly; 2 days); Kupang (West Timor; fortnightly; 26hr); Labuanbajo (Flores; 32hr); Makassar (Sulawesi; 2 fortnightly; 2–4 days); Maumere (Flores; fortnightly; 3 days); Surabaya (Java; 2 fortnightly; 22–24hr); Waingapu (Sumba; fortnightly; 26hr).

INFORMATION

Tourist offce There's a (not particularly helpful) tourist office just off Puputan Square, at Jl Surapati 7 (Mon–Thurs 7.30am–3.30pm, Fri 8am–1pm; ☎0361 234569).

GETTING AROUND

By bemo Very few travellers ever attempt to take on Denpasar's bewildering bemo system as app-taxis like Uber are affordable for most. However, colour-coded public bemos do shuttle between the city's bemo terminals, though frequencies are erratic (more common in the morning). Turquoise Kereneng–Ubung bemos go past the tourist office; both the dark blue Tegal–Sanur bemos and the beige Kereneng–Tegal bemos will take you close to the downtown department stores on Jl Dewi Sartika.

By taxi Metered taxis circulate around the city; short rides are Rp12,000. Bluebird are the most reliable, while app-taxis like Uber and Grab are also available.

ACCOMMODATION

★**Nakula Familiar Inn** Jl Nakula 4 ☎0361 226446, ⓦnakulafamiliarinn.com. Eight well-maintained rooms with a balcony and either a fan or a/c in a welcoming family-style losmen. It's less than a 10min walk from the

DENPASAR

ACCOMMODATION

Nakula Familiar Inn	2
Niki Rusdi	1

SHOPPING

Mega Art Shop	1
Matahari	3
Pasar Kumbasari	2

EATING

Babi Guling	1
Bhineka Jaya Kopi Bali	2
Cak Asm	4
Pasar Malam Kereneng	3

Bali Museum and about a 15min walk from Tegal bemo terminal. The only downside is traffic noise during rush hour. Doubles Rp200,000

Niki Rusdi Jl Pidada, just behind Ubung bus and bemo terminal ☎0361 416397. This little hotel has clean fan and a/c rooms and is handily located for Ubung bus departures/arrivals, though a bit noisy. Doubles Rp150,000

EATING

Babi Guling Jl Sutomo 20. They serve just one dish – roast suckling pig (*babi guling*) – but it's considered by some to be the best in the city and is only Rp30,000/plate. Best for lunch as they sometimes run out by mid-afternoon. There's no sign, but it's just north of Pura Maospahit. Daily 10am–5pm.

Bhineka Jaya Kopi Bali Jl Gajah Mada 80 ☎0361 224016, ⊛kopibali.com. At this modest-looking outlet of Indonesia's Butterfly Globe Brand coffee you can sample a

cup of Bali coffee, including a cappuccino or island coffee (Rp6000), then choose which grade of island beans to take home. Mon–Sat 9am–4pm.

Cak Asm Jl Tukad Gangga. The setting is basic, but the food, particularly the seafood, is delicious and extremely good value (from around Rp15,000). As a result, this simple little café is always buzzing with customers. Daily 11am–9pm.

Pasar Malam Kereneng Off Jl Hayam Wuruk, next to Kereneng bemo terminal. Night market with over fifty hot-food vendors, dishing out super-cheap soups, noodle and rice dishes from Rp15,000, including *babi guling*, fresh fruit juices and cold beers. Daily roughly 6pm–4am.

SHOPPING

Matahari Jl Dewi Sartika 4 (Tegal–Sanur bemo). Department store that stocks traditional batik shirts and sarongs as well as clothing from Western brands. Daily 9am–9pm.

Mega Art Shop Jl Gajah Mada 36. Good-quality crafts including textiles and carvings from across the archipeligo. Mon–Sat 9am–5.30pm.

Pasar Kumbasari, Jl Gajah Mada. Head to this market for clothes, souvenirs, textiles, woodcarvings, paintings and sarongs. Daily 7am–5pm.

DIRECTORY

Banks and exchange There are ATMs on all main shopping streets and exchange at most central banks.

Embassies and consulates Most foreign embassies are in Jakarta (see p.185), but residents of Australia, Canada and New Zealand should apply for help in the first instance to Bali's Australian consulate at Jl Letda Tantular 32 in the Renon district of Denpasar (☎0361 200 0100, ⓦbali .indonesia.embassy.gov.au). The US consulate is at Jl Hayam Wuruk 188 in Renon (☎0361 233605, ⓔCABali @state.gov). The UK consulate is in Sanur (see p.258).

Hospitals Sanglah Public Hospital (Rumah Sakit Umum Propinsi Sanglah, or RSUP Sanglah) at Jl Kesehatan Selatan 1, Sanglah (☎0361 227911, ⓦsanglahhospitalbali.com; Kereneng–Tegal bemo and Tegal–Sanur bemo) is the main provincial public hospital.

Immigration office Jl Panjaitan at Jl Raya Puputan, Renon (Mon–Thurs 8am–4pm, Fri 8–11am, Sat 8am–12.30pm; ☎0361 227828; Sanur–Tegal bemo).

Internet There are internet cafés inside the main shopping centres including the Ramayana Mal Bali on Jl Diponegoro.

Pharmacies Several along Jl Gajah Mada and inside all the major shopping centres.

Police There are police stations on Jl Patimura and Jl Diponegoro. The main police station is in the far west of the city on Jl Gunung Sanghiang (☎0361 424346).

Post offices The most central post office is on Jl Rambutan, north of Puputan Square. Poste restante (Mon–Fri 8am–7pm & Sat 8am–6pm; Sanur–Tegal bemo) arrives at the GPO on Jl Raya Puputan in Renon.

KUTA, LEGIAN, SEMINYAK AND CANGGU

Crammed with hotels, restaurants, bars, clubs, tour agencies and shops, the **KUTA–LEGIAN–SEMINYAK** conurbation, 10km southwest of Denpasar, is Bali's biggest, brashest beach resort. The beach itself is one of the finest on the island, its gentle curve of golden sand stretching for 8km, and lashed by huge breakers – be wary of the strong undertow. Everyone else comes to shop and party, fuelled by a pumping nightlife that ranges from the trashy in Kuta to the chic in Seminyak and Petitenget, though drugs, prostitution and gigolos (known as "Kuta cowboys") are part of the scene. Although the resort's party atmosphere was shattered in 2002, when Islamic extremists from Java bombed Kuta's two most popular clubs, and again when Kuta Square was attacked in 2005, the good-time vibe has resurfaced. A Monument of Human Tragedy now occupies the 2002 "Ground Zero" site.

It's a hectic place: noisy, full of touts and busy with constant building work. Prepare yourself for the horrific traffic, as the area's road network is totally insufficient: all the main routes are rammed with cars, motorbikes and fumes, and the pollution can be punishing. It's often quicker to walk.

Kuta stretches north from the Matahari department store in Kuta Square to Jalan Melasti, while its southern fringes, extending south from Matahari to the airport, are defined as **Tuban**. **Legian** runs from Jalan Melasti as far as Jalan Double Six (Jalan Pantai Arjuna); Seminyak goes from Jalan Double Six up to the *Oberoi Hotel*, where **Petitenget** begins. Accommodation, shopping and restaurant options broadly fit the same geographical pattern, with Kuta the destination of party-going travellers, Legian the choice for families and couples, and Seminyak favoured by those with more money. The **Kuta Karnival** is held in October and features parades, surfing and skate-boarding competitions and gigs by local bands

For more peace head to **CANGGU**, a further 7km or so up the coast, a loosely defined region, which encompasses the beaches of Batubelig, Berewa, Batu Bolong, Echo Beach (Batu Mejan) and Pererenan, with wild surf beaches, narrow lanes, luxe villas in rice fields, yoga and pilates studios and an epidemic of hipster barber shops. It's seen as the happening, alternative place, popular with long-term visitors, but budget beds are few here, and as public transport is virtually nonexistent you'll need a scooter to get around.

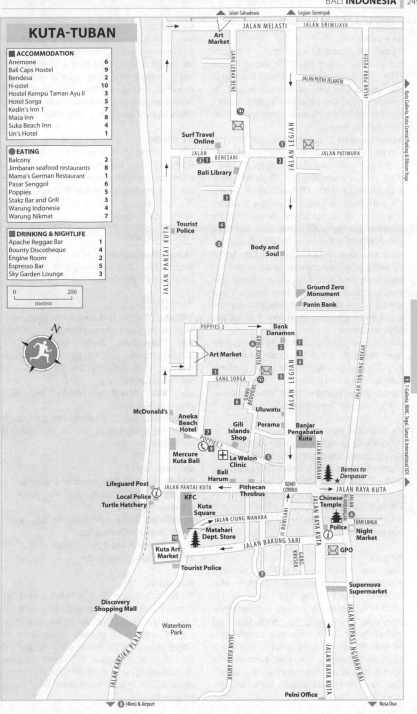

KUTA-TUBAN

■ ACCOMMODATION	
Anemone	6
Bali Caps Hostel	9
Bendesa	2
H-ostel	10
Hostel Kempu Taman Ayu II	3
Hotel Sorga	5
Kedin's Inn 1	7
Masa Inn	8
Suka Beach Inn	4
Un's Hotel	1

● EATING	
Balcony	2
Jimbaran seafood restaurants	8
Mama's German Restaurant	1
Pasar Senggol	6
Poppies	5
Stakz Bar and Grill	3
Warung Indonesia	4
Warung Nikmat	7

■ DRINKING & NIGHTLIFE	
Apache Reggae Bar	1
Bounty Discotheque	4
Engine Room	2
Espresso Bar	5
Sky Garden Lounge	3

0 ————— 200
metres

N

4

4

ARRIVAL AND DEPARTURE

BY PLANE

Ngurah Rai Airport All international and domestic flights use the modern Ngurah Rai Airport (☎0361 751011, ⓦngurahrai-airport.co.id), which is 3km south of Kuta Square and has ATMs and currency exchanges. The domestic terminal is in the adjacent building. There's a 24hr left-luggage office outside international arrivals (from Rp25,000/item/day).

Airport transport The easiest transport from the airport is by pre-paid taxi: rates are fixed and are payable at the counter just beyond the customs exit doors: Rp55,000–80,000 to Tuban or Kuta, Rp95,000–110,000 to Legian or Seminyak and Rp175,000–225,000 to Canggu. Metered taxis and app-taxis are cheaper, but you have to walk out of the airport compound to hail one. Cheaper still are the infrequent dark-blue public bemos (daily 5am–6pm; around Rp10,000 to Kuta/Legian, double with luggage), whose route takes in Jl Raya Tuban, about 700m beyond the airport gates. The northbound bemos go via Kuta's Bemo Corner and Jl Pantai Kuta as far as Jl Melasti, then travel back down Jl Legian and on to Denpasar's Tegal terminal for cross-city and onward connections. Any hotel will arrange transport to the airport (about Rp65,000 from Kuta), or take a taxi.

Domestic destinations Bima (2 daily; 1hr 15min); Jakarta (every 30min; 1hr 45min–2hr); Kupang (4 daily; 1hr 45min); Labuanbajo (6 daily; 1hr–1hr 30min); Lombok (7 daily; 30min); Makassar (6 daily; 1hr 10min); Maumere (3 daily; 2hr 20min); Surabaya (11 daily; 45min); Tambolaka (2 daily; 1hr 45min); Yogyakarta (8 daily; 1hr 20min).

BY SHUTTLE BUS

The easiest way to reach the main tourist destinations on Bali and Lombok is by tourist shuttle bus, and the most reliable service is provided by Perama (daily 6am–10pm; ☎0361 751875, ⓦperamatour.com), who pick up and drop off from their office at Jl Legian 39. Typical fares include Rp35,000 to Sanur, Rp60,000 to Ubud, Rp125,000 to Lovina and Rp450,000 to the Gili Islands (including boat transfer).

BY BUS

There are two useful bus services. Kura Kura (ⓦkura2bus .com) runs a/c minibuses (with wi-fi) across southern Bali (Rp50,000) and to Ubud (Rp 70,000) via its depot in T-Galleria, Jl By Pass Ngurah (east Kuta); from here regular buses arrive from/depart for Kuta beach, Legian and Seminyak (all Rp20,000). Alternatively, Trans Sarbagita buses do not have a great reputation for reliability or punctuality but operate a useful route: Batubulan bemo terminal–Sanur Bypass–Kuta Central Parking–Jimbaran–Nusa Dua. In theory buses run every 30min 5am–9pm. Current flat-rate fares are Rp3500.

BY BEMO

Very few travellers bother with bemos anymore, but there are a few surviving routes. From Denpasar's Tegal terminal, you can get off at any point on their round-Kuta loop, which runs via Bemo Corner, west and then north along Jl Pantai Kuta, east along Jl Melasti before heading north up Jl Legian only as far as Jl Padma, before turning round and continuing south down Jl Legian as far as Bemo Corner.

BY FERRY

Many Kuta travel agents sell boat tickets to Lombok (see p.285) and Nusa Lembongan (see p.258), and these include transfers to the relevant port. Pelni long-distance boat tickets to other islands are available from Jl Raya Kuta 299, 500m south of Supernova in Tuban Supermarket (☎0361 763963, ⓦpelni.co.id).

INFORMATION

Tourist office There's an official tourist office at Jl Raya Kuta 2 (in theory Mon–Sat 9am–7pm; ☎0361 766188), but it's not particularly helpful.

ACTIVITIES

TREKKING, CYCLING AND KAYAKING

All provide free transfers from southern Bali.

Bali Adventure Tours ☎0361 721480, ⓦbaliadventuretours.com. Adventure activities operator that offers mountain-bike trips from the rim of Gunung Batur volcano, plus trekking.

See Bali Adventures ☎0361 794 9693, ⓦseebaliadventures.com.

Sobek ☎0361 768050, ⓦbalisobek.com. Specializes in cycling and rafting/kayaking tours on the Grade II–III rapids of the Ayung River.

DIVING

The following run dive trips to southern Bali sites such as Nusa Penida, and include transport from the Kuta–Legian–Seminyak area.

AquaMarine Diving Jl Petitenget 2A, Kuta ☎0361 738020, ⓦaquamarinediving.com.

Manta Manta Diving Jl Padma, Legian ☎0812 3787 0200, ⓦmantamanta-diving.com.

SURFING

The best time of year for surfing off Kuta is April–Oct. Poppies 2, Poppies 1 and Jl Benesari are crammed with board rental (around Rp100,000/day) and repair shops, surfwear outlets and surfers' bars. Surfing lessons are offered throughout the resort, prices average $45 for a half-day introduction in a group. Freelance instructors hang out on all the main beaches, charging around $15/hr including board rental. These schools are recommended:

CURRENCY EXCHANGE SCAMS

Be extremely careful when **changing money** at currency exchange counters in Kuta as many places short-change tourists by using well-known **rip-offs** including rigged calculators and folded notes. One chain of **recommended moneychangers** is PT Central Kuta (Ⓦcentralkutabali.com), which has numerous branches including on Jalan Legian, Jalan Melasti, the Seminyak Square complex and Canggu. If you do get caught in a money-changing scam, contact the community police (see p.256).

Pro Surf School Jl Pantai Kuta ☎0361 744 1466, Ⓦprosurfschool.com. Accommodation (including dorms) is available on site.

Rip Curl School of Surf *Blue Ocean* hotel, Jl Pantai Arjuna, Legian ☎0361 750459, Ⓦripcurlschoolofsurf.com. Also offers wakeboarding, kitesurfing, windsurfing and stand-up paddleboard lessons.

Surf Travel Online Jl Benesari 29 ☎0361 750550, Ⓦsurftravelonline.com. Surfaris around Bali and beyond.

UP2U Surf School Jl Pantai Kuta, Legian ☎0812 3699 7504, Ⓦup2usurfschool.com. Beginner group lessons cost Rp300,000.

YOGA AND PILATES

Desa Seni hotel Jl Subak Sari 13, Canggu ☎0361 844 6392, Ⓦdesaseni.com. In Canggu, with up to five drop-in sessions a day in numerous styles.

The Island hotel Gang IX, off Jl Legian ☎0361 762722, Ⓦtheislandhotelbali.com. Offers daily classes of hatha and "surf" yoga.

Umalas Pilates Jl Umalas Klecung 33, Kerobokan ☎0818 1918 0630, Ⓦfacebook.com/Umalaspilatesstudio. A professional studio equipped with reformers.

GETTING AROUND

As the traffic is horrendous day and night, walking is the best way to get around.

By bemo With public bemos in decline (see opposite), unless you're on a very tight budget or bloody-minded enough to wait, a taxi is often easier. Kuta bemos are dark blue. Local trips cost around Rp5000.

By taxi The most reliable taxis are the light-blue Blue Bird taxis (☎0361 701111, Ⓦbluebirdgroup.com), which you can order online or via their app. Uber and Grab app-taxis also operate in this part of Bali. Taxis touts hang around every street corner offering transport; their rates are usually very expensive but you may have no choice late at

night; expect to pay at least Rp80,000 to get home no matter how short the distance.

By car, bike or motorbike Countless tour agents offer car (from Rp220,000) and motorbike (Rp50,000) rental. Many also offer bicycles (Rp20,000). Such is the traffic that a car is more hassle than it's worth within the resort.

ACCOMMODATION

The biggest concentration of inexpensive accommodation is in Kuta, along Poppies 1, Poppies 2 and Jl Benesari. Legian has good-value places with pools and a/c; Seminyak is pricier and Canggu expensive.

KUTA

Anemone Gang Sorga ☎0361 754683; map p.249. Spick-and-span rooms, all with a/c and hot water, in a quiet family compound with a tiny pool. Breakfast not included. Doubles Rp180,000

Bali Caps Hostel Jl Bypass Ngurah Rai 9A ☎0361 849 6665, Ⓦbalicaps.com; map p.249. Large, well-designed hostel, which feels more like a minimalist hotel; cleanliness is excellent and the modern dorm (with single or double beds) are spacious and supremely comfortable. There's a pool table and dart board, free breakfast and shuttle service to the beach and airport. Dorms Rp110,000

Bendesa Jl Legian ☎0361 754 366, Ⓦbendesa accommodation.com; map p.249. A cut above most of the competition, with a range of decent-sized rooms in a large, leafy complex around a pleasant pool and friendly staff. Doubles Rp200,000

★**H-ostel** Kuta Square E8 ☎0361 475 2387, Ⓦh-ostel.com; map p.249. Very centrally located, this contemporary hostel is close to vibrant nightlife and shopping and is only 200m from the beach. All dorms (mixed and female-only) are a/c, and bunks are equipped with charging sockets, reading lights and lockers. There's a great roof terrace, café, speedy wi-fi and breakfast is included. Dorms Rp150,000

Hostel Kempu Taman Ayu II Jl Benesari ☎0361 754376, Ⓦhomestaykempu.com; map p.249. As basic as it gets in the cheapest fan-only rooms – there's a bed, a rudimentary bathroom with hot water and outside seating – and things are a mite shabby, if clean. But if you want a rock-bottom price, it fits the bill. Doubles Rp170,000

Hotel Sorga Gang Sorga, off Poppies 1 ☎0361 751897, Ⓦhotelsorgakuta.com; map p.249. On a quiet alley, yet within firing range of the clubs on Jl Legian, these dated-but-decent rooms are comfortable, if something of an 1980s timewarp. There's a small pool and restaurant. Doubles Rp265,000

Kedin's Inn 1 Poppies 1 ☎0361 758507, Ⓦkedins-inn.com; map p.249. Backpackers' favourite, with simple rooms arranged around quiet gardens and a pool. It's in the thick of the action, though you'd never know it. A/c costs an extra Rp50,000, hot water more still. Doubles Rp250,000

4

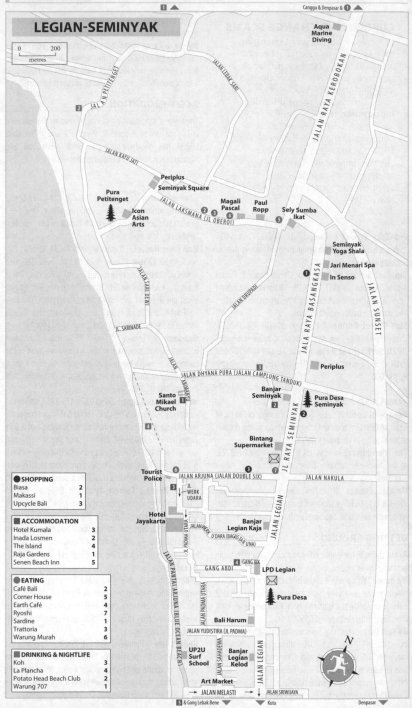

LEGIAN-SEMINYAK

0 — 200
metres

Canggu & Denpasar &

Aqua Marine Diving

JALAN N PETITENGET

JALAN LEBAK SARI

JALAN RAYA KEROBOKAN

JALAN KAYU JATI

Periplus
Seminyak Square

Pura Petitenget

Icon Asian Arts

JALAN LAKSMANA (JL OBEROI)

Magali Pascal

Paul Ropp

Sely Sumba Ikat

JALAN SARI DEWI

JALAN DRUPADI

Seminyak Yoga Shala

Jari Menari Spa

In Senso

JALA RAYA BASANGKASA

JALAN SUNSET

JL SARINADE

JALAN

Periplus

JALAN DHYANA PURA (JALAN CAMPLUNG TANDUK)

JALAN BIAWANU

Santo Mikael Church

Banjar Seminyak

Pura Desa Seminyak

JL RAYA SEMINYAK

Bintang Supermarket

Tourist Police

JALAN ARJUNA (JALAN DOUBLE SIX)

JALAN NAKULA

JL WERK UDARA

Hotel Jayakarta

JALAN PANTAI ARJUNA (BLUE OCEAN BEACH)

JALAN WERK U'DARA (BAGUS FER UNA)

Banjar Legian Kaja

JALAN LEGIAN

JALAN PADMA UTARA

GANG ABDI

GANG XIX

LPD Legian

Pura Desa

JALAN PADMA UTARA

JALAN YUDISTIRA (JL PADMA)

Bali Harum

UP2U Surf School

JALAN SAHADEWA

Banjar Legian Kelod

JALAN LEGIAN

Art Market

JALAN MELASTI

JALAN SRIWIJAYA

& Gang Lebak Bene

Kuta

Denpasar

N

● SHOPPING
Biasa	2
Makassi	1
Upcycle Bali	3

■ ACCOMMODATION
Hotel Kumala	3
Inada Losmen	2
The Island	4
Raja Gardens	1
Senen Beach Inn	5

● EATING
Café Bali	2
Corner House	5
Earth Café	4
Ryoshi	7
Sardine	1
Trattoria	3
Warung Murah	6

■ DRINKING & NIGHTLIFE
Koh	3
La Plancha	4
Potato Head Beach Club	2
Warung 707	1

Masa Inn 31 Poppies 1 ☎ 0361 758507, ⓦ masainn .com; map p.249. If you're looking for a touch more comfort, but don't want to break the bank, *Masa Inn* is a good choice for a/c, mid-range rooms, with two pools and a restaurant. Good-value singles (Rp325,000) too. Doubles Rp500,000

Suka Beach Inn Jl Benesari, off Poppies 2 ☎ 0861 752793; map p.249. This backpacker lodge offers spartan fan-cooled rooms (though don't expect "luxuries" such as towels) with dated bathrooms in blocks surrounding a large pool. Doubles Rp160,000

Un's Hotel Jl Benesari ☎ 0361 757409, ⓦ unshotel.com; map p.249. Antique furnishings, art and traditional architecture plus a lovely small garden with pool combine to provide some real Balinese character at this good-value place to stay. All rooms have hot-water en-suites but you'll pay about Rp40,000 more for a/c. Doubles Rp457,000

LEGIAN AND SEMINYAK

Hotel Kumala Jl Werk Udara ☎ 0361 732186, ⓦ hotelkumala.com; map opposite. A 5min walk from the beach, and with lots of cafés and restaurants close by, this fine-value hotel has a real Balinese flavour. Note that there are some economy rooms (Rp325,000) which are very plain; it's worth paying more for standard rooms (Rp375,000) or above, which are all spacious and well furnished, with a/c, hot water and modern bathrooms. There's a pool and restaurant. Doubles Rp325,000

Inada Losmen Gang Bima 9, off Jl Camplung Tanduk and Jl Raya Seminyak ☎ 0361 732269, ⓔ putuinada@hotmail .com; map opposite. This cheapie run by a helpful Indonesian/ Japanese couple is excellent value for the location. Its dozen basic rooms have a bed, a desk, a fan, a bathroom with hot water and that's your lot. Doubles Rp180,000

★ **The Island** Gang XIX, off Jl Legian ☎ 0361 762722, ⓦ theislandhotelbali.com; map opposite. Great little place tucked in an alley that has the feel of a secret retreat. Nine small, stylish rooms are set around a little pool, along with two of the poshest dorms in town. The atmosphere is chilled and friendly and there's a nice lounge to hang out in. Dorms Rp227,000, doubles Rp552,000

Raja Gardens Jl Abimanyu, off Jl Camplung Tanduk ☎ 0361 730494, ⓔ jdw@eksadata.com; map opposite. A real haven, this small setup has nine rooms in a beautiful garden a moment's walk from the beach. The brick bungalows are all white rattan and bleached-wood furnishings, some with open bathrooms. Peaceful, family run and good value. Rp475,000

Senen Beach Inn Gang Senen no.2, off Gang Lebak Bene ☎ 0361 755470; map opposite. Situated in a tranquil little lane and run by a friendly group of young Indonesian guys, *Senen Beach Inn* has basic, cleanish rooms with outdoor bathrooms. Breakfast costs extra. Doubles Rp160,000

CANGGU

Pondok Nyoman Bagus Pantai Pererenan ☎ 0361 848 2925, ⓦ pondokwisatanyoman.baliklik.com. Just behind the Pererenan surf break, this friendly, family-run beachside losmen has been pepped up with cheerful bright linen and modern bathrooms in rooms, all with a/c. Deluxe options have sea views, and you can check out the waves from a rooftop infinity pool. Doubles Rp480,000

Serenity Jl Nelayan, Pantai Batu Balong ☎ 0361 747 4625, ⓦ serenityecoguesthouse.com. An easy-going base built of bamboo – nicely ramshackle and nicely rambling in several areas, with a backpackers' annexe down the road. It's good value too: the homey rooms have fan or a/c, and massage and yoga are on offer. Free tea and coffee, bikes for rent and horseriding can be arranged. Dorms Rp160,000, doubles Rp200,000

EATING

KUTA AND TUBAN

Balcony *Un's Hotel*, Jl Benesari 16 ☎ 0361 750655, ⓦ thebalconybali.com; map p.249. This airy place segues from good breakfasts (like Swiss bircher muesli or herb omelette) to mains (from Rp49,000) like pork rib burger, grills and Indonesian dishes. Browse the photos of famous surfers on the walls while you dine, or there are also magazines to flick through. Daily 7am–midnight.

Jimbaran seafood restaurants Jimbaran Beach, 4km south of Kuta (about Rp60,000 by taxi); map p.249. More than fifty seafood warung barbecue the day's catch at tables on the beach here (from around Rp70,000 with trimmings); they open from noon but are best by candlelight at night.

Mama's German Restaurant Jl Legian ⓦ bali-mamas .com; map p.249. Open all day, every day, serving all manner of German specialities, notably sausages (from Rp65,000) and pork knuckle as well as German bottled beers and draught brews. There's an open kitchen, and an a/c dining room upstairs. Daily 24hr.

Pasar Senggol Jl Blambangan; map p.249. Kuta's main night market is busy with hot-food stalls serving inexpensive Indonesian food (from Rp15,000) to locals and thrifty travellers. Daily 5pm–late.

Poppies Poppies 1 ☎ 0361 751059, ⓦ poppiesbali.com; map p.249. A Kuta institution, this haven from the hustle packs 'em in for its Indonesian (*gado gado* Rp43,000; *nasi goreng* Rp65,000) and international menu (Rp50,000 and up) of well-cooked and well-presented food. The dining area is lovely, with seating beneath bougainvillea-draped pergolas. Daily 8am–11pm.

Stakz Bar and Grill Jl Benesari ⓦ stakzbarandgrill.com; map p.249. Run by a pair of Australians, this joint serves the best burgers in Kuta (Rp45,000–65,000) including veggie options with chickpeas: try the classic Aussie beef version. Daily 7am–1am.

4

Warung Indonesia Gang Ronta ☎0361 759817; map p.249. In the thick of things, this relaxed warung is more authentic than most in the area, and attracts Indonesians too – always a good sign. Pick and mix your own veg and non-veg *nasi campur* (Rp30,000 will fill up most people) or order Indonesian staples and great-value juices (around Rp15,000). Daily noon–midnight.

Warung Nikmat Gang Biduri 6A (off Jl Kubu Anyar) ☎0361 764678; map p.249. Javanese warung of the plastic stools persuasion where you can assemble a terrific *nasi campur* from around thirty spicy dishes – fried fish, beans with chilli, curried eggs, *urap* (steamed vegetables with spiced coconut), tempeh and much more for around Rp28,000. Daily 8am–9am.

LEGIAN AND SEMINYAK

Café Bali Jl Laksmana ☎0361 736484; map p.252. With mildly distressed furniture, pretty lampshades and lace tablecloths, this place has more charm than its cooler neighbours. The long, eclectic menu includes quesadillas and sushi rolls, pasta and grills, Indian and Indonesian favourites. Daily 7am–midnight.

Corner House Jl Laksmana 10A ☎0361 730276, ⍵cornerhousebali.com; map p.252. Stunning café-restaurant in an a/c loft-like space that's great for brunch, grilled meats and salads (virtually all dishes are Rp70,000–90,000) and there's a kids' menu. Daily 7am–11pm.

Earth Café Jl Laksmana ☎0361 736645; map p.252. This vegetarian-, vegan-, gluten-intolerant- and raw-foodie-friendly café/shop serves up restorative dishes such as quinoa pancakes, Arabic salad with tahini (Rp55,000) and delicious smoothies and juices in a buzzy environment. Daily 7am–11pm.

Ryoshi Jl Seminyak 17 ☎0361 731152, ⍵ryoshibali.com; map p.252. As well as serving great Japanese food (sushi sets are from Rp65,000), *Ryoshi* also hosts massively popular jazz and live music nights. Delivery service available. Daily noon–11pm.

Sardine Jl Petitenget 21 ☎0361 738202, ⍵sardinebali.com; map p.252. Destination restaurant serving gorgeous imaginative cuisine in a bamboo *bale*-style structure beside a rice field. Fish and seafood dominate the menu, with the dishes changing daily depending on the catch – miso-grilled mahi-mahi (Rp180,000), Jimbaran-style fish and organic salads are typical. Daily 11.30am–11pm.

Trattoria Jl Laksmana ☎0361 737082, ⍵trattoriaasia.com; map p.252. Flavoursome home-style Italian cuisine; the pizzas (Rp56,000–78,000) and the daily specials are the best-value options, though save some room for their yummy pannacotta. It gets very busy in the evening, so book ahead. Daily noon–10pm.

Warung Murah Jl Camplung Tanduk ☎0361 732082; map p.252. Hits the mark for thrifty diners, especially for lunch: select a *nasi campur* medley from curries, *tempe*,

fritters and vegetable dishes (from Rp20,000), or choose from the small menu featuring the usual Indo-Chinese suspects (from Rp25,000). Daily 8am–11pm.

CANGGU

Betel Nut Café Jl Batu Bolong 60 ☎0821 4680 7233 (SMS only). Popular travellers' café split between a small a/c interior and an airy upper deck. Either way, you're here for a tasty menu: fresh juices, salads, wraps and a great selection of burgers (Rp50,000). Tues–Sun 7am–10pm.

Warung Varuna Jl Batu Bolong 89. Surfers' hangout with chunky wooden tables and paint-smeared walls. Serves up a mean *nasi campur* for about Rp24,000, depending on dishes selected. There's a useful noticeboard for yoga classes and community events. Daily 8am–10pm.

DRINKING AND NIGHTLIFE

For gigs and nightlife listings see the free fortnightly magazine *The Beat* (⍵thebeatbali.com). If you're planning a big night out in Kuta, nothing really gets going until about midnight. Entrance is generally free unless there's a special event or party (when it can become pretty pricey). Check *The Beat* or look out for posters on the beach for details.

KUTA

Apache Reggae Bar Jl Legian 146 ⍵0361 761213; map p.249. Tucked away in what seems to be a Balinese barn, Kuta's reggae spot is all heavy bass and tuff riddims. Features talented live bands every night, and resident DJs. Daily 8pm–3am.

Bounty Discotheque Jl Legian ☎0361 752529; map p.249. Infamous hub of Australian excess, housed in a replica of Captain Bligh's eighteenth-century galleon. Expect mainstream dance, covers bands, themed foam parties and much drunkenness. A love-it-or-loathe-it experience. Daily 8pm–4am.

Engine Room Jl Legian ⍵engineroombali.com; map p.249. On several levels, this established club is the place for pumping r'n'b, hip-hop and house. Drinks are cheap and it's popular with a party-loving international crowd. Daily 9pm–3am.

Espresso Bar Jl Legian; map p.249. Local covers bands make a decent attempt at all the classics in this small but very popular rock bar. Drinks specials include two-for-one mojitos. Cocktails around Rp50,000. Daily 7pm–3am.

Sky Garden Jl Legian 61, across from Poppies 2 ⓦ skygardenbali.com; map p.249. Spread over four floors, this multi-bar/club venue is loud, lively and fun, with various rooms pumping out different sounds and terraces with views across the resort. Draws top DJs like Afrojack. Daily 5pm–3am.

LEGIAN AND SEMINYAK

★ **Koh** Jl Camplung Tanduk 15X, Seminyak ⓦ facebook.com/kohbali; map p.252. For more of an underground vibe this credible club has tech house, deep house and progressive DJs, a mean sound system and industrial feel. Artists who have performed here include Bushwacka!, Skream and Ralph Lawson. Thurs 10am–4am, Fri & Sat 11pm–5am.

La Plancha Beachfront, north of Jl Arjuna; map p.252. A terraced beachside café with colourful beanbags and umbrellas strewn across the sand. It gets packed at sunset with people enjoying a beer or cocktail (around Rp100,000) overlooking the sea. Daily 7am–1am.

★ **Warung 707** Batu Belig Beach; map p.252. The perfect beach hangout with beanbags and a shack for a bar serving simple drinks. Musically it's far more sophisticated than some of the mega beach clubs, with DJs playing deep house, reggae and funk to a boho clientele. Daily 10am–8pm.

CANGGU

★ **Old Man's** Jl Batu Bolong, Canggu ☏ 0361 846 9158, ⓦ oldmans.net. A no-nonsense, wildly popular Canggu

---

★ **TREAT YOURSELF**

Potato Head Beach Club Jl Petitenget, Seminyak ☏ 0361 473 7979, ⓦ ptthead.com; map p.252. Arguably Bali's hottest venue: the curved exterior, designed as a modern take on the Colosseum and clad in vintage teak shutters, shelters an oasis of beachside infinity pools. You can lounge on designer furniture with a cocktail (around Rp130,000) among Seminyak's most fashionable by day, or dance the night away to resident DJs and guest acts (Snoop Dogg, Fatboy Slim and Grace Jones have all performed here). Daily 11am–2am.

---

beach bar with tables by the waves that draws an eclectic, incongruous crowd of surfers, expats, boozers, boozing surfer expats, yogis and even the odd local. Check out its Dirty Wednesday parties, live music on Fridays and regular events. Beer is cheap and the ambience is social and relaxed. Daily 7am–11pm.

SHOPPING

Kuta–Legian–Seminyak is retail dreamland, especially for clothes, surfing gear and souvenirs. In Kuta, there are several secondhand bookshops on Poppies 1, Poppies 2, Jl Benesari and Jl Padma Utara. The 6km strip from Bemo Corner up Jl Legian into Seminyak takes in everything from cheap, mass-market stuff to style and substance around Seminyak where Jl Kayu Aya has several designer stores. Things get quirkier and more independent the further north you go: Kerobokan and Canggu have many intriguing little stores selling unusual clothing and craft products.

Biasa Jl Raya Seminyak 36, Jl Raya Seminyak 34 ☏ 0361 730308, ⓦ biasagroup.com; map p.252. Two adjacent stores with elegant, tasteful clothing from natural fabrics for men and women, plus scarves and a sophisticated take on Indonesian jewellery. Daily 9am–9pm.

Deus ex Machina Jl Batu Mejan 8, Canggu ☏ 0361 217 1076, ⓦ deuscustoms.com. Way-of-life store-café-hangout which sells surfboards, skatewear, art and the coolest customized motorcycles in Asia. Grab a coffee or a bite while you browse. Daily 8am–10.30pm.

★ **Makassi** Jl Raya Basangkasa ☏ 0361 733764 or ☏ 0361 754955, ⓦ makassi.com; map p.252. Colourful, kitsch bags, clutches, gifts and some clothing. Items can be customized to your own design from a photo, for example. Daily 9am–8pm.

Upcycle Bali Jl Arjuna, Seminyak ☏ 0813 9674 9986, ⓦ navehmilo.com; map p.252. Styling itself as a "green museum shop", this delightfully offbeat store stocks bags made from playing cards and wrappers, hats from measuring tape and lots of other curios. Daily 9am–7pm.

DIRECTORY

Dentist Bali Dental Clinic 911, Mal Bali Galleria, Simpang Siur roundabout, Jl Bypass Ngurah Rai (☏ 0361 766254, ⓦ bali911dentalclinic.com).

Embassies and consulates In Denpasar (see p.248).

Hospitals, clinics and pharmacies Two reputable, private 24hr hospitals on the outskirts of Kuta have English-speaking staff, A&E facilities, ambulance and medical evacuation services: Bali International Medical Centre (BIMC), Jl Bypass Ngurah Rai 100X (☏ 0361 761263, ⓦ bimcbali.com); and International SOS, Jl Bypass Ngurah Rai 505X (☏ 0361 710505, ⓦ internationalsos.com). For quicker (and cheaper) consultations, Legian Clinic, Jl Benesari, Kuta (☏ 0361 758503), offers 24hr services and

4

consultations from Rp575,000. There are pharmacies on every major shopping street.

Internet There are countless internet cafés; most charge around Rp15,000–20,000/hr.

Police The English-speaking community police, Satgas Pantai Desa Adat Kuta, have a 24hr office on the beach in front of *Inna Kuta Beach Hotel* (☎0361 762871). The government police station is at Jl Raya Kuta 141, south Kuta (☎0361 751598).

Post office Kuta's GPO and poste restante is on unsignposted Gang Selamat, between Jl Raya Kuta and Jl Blambangan (Mon–Sat 8am–5pm).

Spas and massage Murano Spa, Jl Dewi Saraswati III, Seminyak (daily 10am–8pm; ☎0361 738140, ⓦmuranospa.com), is a well-regarded, excellent-value spa with a free pick-up service. Massages (from Rp100,000/hr), reflexology and packages are available.

THE BUKIT

Just south of Kuta, southern Bali bulges out into **the Bukit** ("hill"), a harsh, infertile limestone plateau whose craggy coastline challenges surfers with its world-class breaks, most famously at Uluwatu and Padang Padang. Where once only hardcore wave-riders would endure the potholed tracks to get to its secluded little **surf beaches**, increasing numbers of independent travellers are now following suit as the roads have improved and new hotels and homestays open their doors. The **Bingin** and **Uluwatu** areas are where most travellers base themselves, both with a good choice of places to stay. Take local advice on where it's safe to swim as currents can be treacherous round here.

There's almost no public transport south of Jimbaran, so you'll need to rent a car or scooter, or take a taxi.

Surf beaches

Balangan Beach, the northernmost bay, has a long stretch of golden sand, with a shallow offshore reef that powers a speedy left-hand break at high tide but can make swimming dicey. Above the beach are some ramshackle surfer warung and a cluster of guesthouses, with new accommodation opening all the time in the hills around. Next up is **Dreamland**, now home to a monstrous hotel complex, golf and condo project, popular with

domestic tourists. Accessed by a separate road to the south, lively **Bingin** enjoys great coastal scenery and a laidback surfer vibe, with budget accommodation nestled into the cliff face and seafood warung on the sand. **Impossibles**, to the south of Bingin, is another small surf beach, while the break at neighbouring **Padang Padang** is considered to be one of the most exciting in Indonesia. Accommodation and restaurants are dotted around the side lanes and main road that stretches between Bingin and the mini-resort of **Uluwatu** (home to another world-class surf break) in the south.

Pura Luhur Uluwatu

Revered since the tenth century as one of Bali's most important temples, **Pura Luhur Uluwatu** (daily sunrise–sunset; Rp30,000 including sarong rental) commands a superb position on a rocky promontory 70m above the surging breakers, at the far southwestern tip of Bali. Views over the serrated coastline are staggering, and despite the crowds at sunset this is still a stunning setting. As a directional temple, or *kayangan jagat*, Pura Luhur Uluwatu is the guardian of the southwest and is dedicated to the spirits of the sea; it's also a state rather than a village temple and so has influence over all the people of Bali. However, the temple structure itself is fairly modest, and its greyish-white coral bricks are for the most part unadorned. Watch out for thieving monkeys, which snatch sunglasses and smartphones. Most tourists come here at sunset, when there's a performance of the **Kecak and Fire Dance** (daily 6–7pm; Rp80,000); consider visiting in the morning when it's much quieter.

ACCOMMODATION

Real cheapies are not that easy to find in the Bukit, where most accommodation is towards the upper end of the budget category, or mid-range and beyond.

Flower Bud Bungalows I and II Balangan ☎0361 857 2062, ⓦflowerbudbalangan.com. In lush gardens, this Balinese-owned spot ticks all the boxes for rustic escapism. You stay in traditional bungalows with large verandahs; the cheapest are cold water only. *Flowerbud II* has family-sized accommodation and a pool. Doubles **Rp570,000**

★ TREAT YOURSELF

The Temple Lodge Bingin ☎ 0857 3901 1572, ⓦ thetemplelodge.com. Perched at the top of Bingin cliff, The *Temple Lodge* is well worth a splurge for its gorgeous suites, all with antiques and many with great views. Perks include an infinity pool, daily yoga classes, spa, and a delightful restaurant serving healthy Mediterranean and Balinese dishes. Doubles **$95**

The Gong Uluwatu roadside ☎ 0361 769976, ⓔ thegongacc@yahoo.com. This chilled and friendly surfers' favourite has twelve fan-cooled rooms, some with distant sea views, rents scooters and surfboards, and sells warung-style food and travellers' breakfasts. Doubles **Rp220,000**

Kelly's Warung Bingin cliff ☎ 0813 3705 8284, ⓦ facebook.com/kellys.warung. Surfers' hostel with stylish beachfront rooms above a juice bar and surf shop. It's worth paying a little extra for the rooms at the front, which have massive balconies overlooking the waves. Doubles **Rp150,000**

Medori Putih Homestay Jl Pemutih 1A, Padang Padang ☎ 0361 895 7377, ⓦ medoriputihhomestay.com. A 10min walk from the beach, this fine-value place has twenty clean, orderly rooms, all with a/c and hot-water en-suite bathrooms and a small pool for chilling. Breakfast is not included. Doubles **Rp300,000**

Pondok Indah Gung Bingin clifftop ☎ 0361 847 0933. Family-run, this welcoming lodge has a really Balinese feel. There's a dozen rather tasteful fan-cooled rooms set round a leafy compound, some of them in pretty coconut-wood-and-thatch bungalows. Doubles **Rp320,000**

SANUR

Nicknamed "Snore" because it lacks the clubs and all-night party venues of Kuta, **SANUR** is a sedate resort popular with older visitors, and has a distinct village atmosphere, a fairly decent, 5km-long sandy beach, and some attractive budget accommodation. It's the main departure point for boats to Nusa Lembongan, plus it's only 15km to Kuta and forty minutes' drive to Ubud.

Though the sea here is only properly swimmable at high tide (a big expanse of shore gets exposed at low tide, and the currents beyond the reef are dangerously strong), there are lots of inviting

restaurants along the beach and you can walk or cycle the entire 5km from the *Inna Grand Bali Beach* in the north to the *Prama Sanur Beach Bali* in the south along a seafront esplanade.

ARRIVAL AND DEPARTURE

By shuttle bus Perama shuttle buses stop at Warung Pojok mini-market, Jl Hang Tuah 31, north Sanur; bemos run from near here to Jl Danau Tamblingan, or you can pay an extra Rp15,000 for a drop-off at your hotel.

Destinations Amed (daily; 3hr), Bedugul (daily; 2hr–2hr 30min); Candidasa (4 daily; 2hr 30min–3hr); Gili Islands (daily; 9hr); Kuta/Ngurah Rai Airport (7 daily; 40min–1hr); Lovina (daily; 3–4hr); Padang Bai (4 daily; 2hr–2hr 30min); Senggigi, Lombok (daily; 8hr 30min); Ubud (7 daily; 45min–1hr).

By bus Kura Kura minibuses (ⓦ kura2bus.com) connect Sanur with Kuta (4 daily 10am–4pm; Rs50,000). You can change at their depot in Kuta's T-Galleria mall for services to Seminyak. Or Trans Sarbagita buses run from Batubulan bemo terminal–Sanur Jl Bypass–Kuta Central Parking–Jimbaran–Nusa Dua. In theory these buses (Rs3500) run every 30min 5am–9pm.

By bemo There's a direct bemo between Sanur and Denpasar terminals at Kereneng (green; 15min; around Rp7000) and Tegal (blue; 30min; around Rp8000). Both routes cover north Sanur's Jl Bypass/Jl Hang Tuah junction, dropping passengers just outside the *Inna Grand Bali Beach* compound, before continuing via Jl Danau Beratan and Jl Danau Buyan and running south down Jl Danau Tamblingan.

By boat Sanur is the main departure point for boats to Nusa Lembongan. From a jetty in north Sanur public and private boats run to Jungutbatu (around 20 daily; 30min–2hr) and Mushroom Bay (8 daily; 40min–1hr) in Lembongan.

By taxi A taxi ride from central Kuta or Denpasar should cost about Rp110,000, or Rp65,000 in an Uber/Grab.

INFORMATION

Online There's no tourist office, but ⓦ sanurweekly.com is useful.

GETTING AROUND

By bemo The Denpasar–Sanur bemos are useful for getting around Sanur; a local ride costs around Rp5000.

By taxi Bluebird cars (☎ 0361 701111) are reliable, or try an Uber/Grab. Negotiate with transport touts for longer rides and day-trips.

By car and motorbike Easily arranged through transport touts and tour agencies.

By bike Countless outlets along Jl Danau Tamblingan (from Rp20,000/day).

4

WATERSPORTS AND DIVING

Sanur's reef dives are only really of interest to beginners or as a refresher. The coral is unspectacular, visibility so-so, and dives rarely descend beneath 12m. However, dive trips to Nusa Penida (around $125) and Amed ($110) are offered by several schools, and snorkelling trips (around $25/person/hr, including gear) are also popular.

AquaMarine Diving Jl Petitenget 2A ☎0361 738020, ⊛aquamarinediving.com. UK-run PADI five-star resort.

Blue Season Bali Gang Wanasari, off Jl Danau Poso ☎0361 270852, ⊛baliocean.com. PADI CDC centre. UK-Japanese run.

Crystal Divers Jl Danau Tamblingan 168, Batujimbar ☎0361 286737, ⊛crystal-divers.com. PADI CDC centre. Runs tailored dive safaris all over Bali.

ACCOMMODATION

Flashbacks Jl Danau Tamblingan 110, central Sanur ☎0361 281682, ⊛flashbacks-chb.com. Nine beautifully decorated rooms (some have a/c, the cheapest have shared bathrooms) and bungalows, run by friendly and professional staff. The attached *Porch Café* has divine espressos. Doubles Rp270,000

Little Pond Homestay Jl Danau Tamblingan 19, Sindhu ☎0361 289902, ⊛littlepondbali.com. The fifteen small, bright rooms grouped around a pool have a choice of fan or a/c, each with verandahs, hot water bathrooms and a homely feel. The location is quiet and close to the main beach. Doubles Rp175,000

★**Ning Homestay** Gang 3, off Jl Kesari 1 ☎0823 3910 7639, ✉ningtyas.homestay@gmail.com. Sanur's best hostel is well organized, with clean accommodation and a sociable vibe: the eight-bed dorm has a/c while the double room is fine value for Sanur. There are plenty of spots to relax and chat, a restaurant and free drinking water. Dorms Rp100,000, doubles Rp200,000

Yulia Homestay 1 Jl Danau Tamblingan 38, central Sanur ☎0361 288089, ⊛facebook.com/yulia1homestay. Attractive, terraced, fan-cooled bungalows in a homestay compound filled with the owner's prize-winning songbirds. Doubles Rp200,000

EATING AND DRINKING

The night market, inside the Sindhu Market at the Jl Danau Tamblingan/Jl Danau Toba intersection, central Sanur, is good for inexpensive local eats from around 5pm through to the early hours. Nightlife is limited – mainly covers bands and expat pubs.

★**Juicy & Crispy** Jl Tirta Nadi 5 ☎0812 3615 3336, ⊛juicyandcrispy.com. A meat feast *par excellence* – buzzing, busy *J&C* has a mercifully short menu, specializing in super-succulent spare ribs (from 5pm only) and rotisserrie chicken (from Rp42,000). It's a tiny,

cramped space, so book ahead for seating, or grab and go. Daily noon–9pm.

Little Bird Jl Danau Tamblingan 34 ☎0361 745968. Hugely likeable little warung, partly thanks to a mellow vibe, partly because of the good Indonesian food that's more zingy than most in Sanur and comes at lower prices (around Rp35,000). Daily 8am–11pm.

Warung Kecil Jl Duyung ☎0361 202 0002. Tiny, modern warung with both Indonesian and Western food. Grab a panini, salad or a *nasi campur* (Rp27,000) and slurp on a fresh juice. There are a few books to browse, too. Daily 8am–9.30pm.

Warung Sunrise Jl Hang Tuah. Beachside bar with chairs on the sand, live reggae three nights a week, gregarious staff and strong cocktails (from around Rp40,000). Daily 10am–late.

DIRECTORY

Banks and exchange There are ATMs and exchange facilities all over the resort.

Bookshops Ganesha Books, Jl Danau Tamblingan 42, central Sanur (daily 8am–10pm; ⊛ganeshabooksbali .com).

Embassies and consulates UK consulate at Jl Tirta Nadi 20A, Sanur (☎0361 270601, ⊛british-consulate .net/Bali.html). US and Australian consulates in Denpasar (see p.248).

Hospitals and clinics Head to Kuta (see p.255) or Denpasar (p.248).

Police The police station is on Jl Bypass in north Sanur, just south of the *Paradise Plaza* hotel (☎0361 288597).

Post office The main post office is on Jl Danau Buyan, north-central Sanur.

NUSA LEMBONGAN

Southeast across the Badung Strait, encircled by a mixture of white-sand beaches and mangrove, the tiny island of **NUSA LEMBONGAN** (4km by 3km) is an ideal escape from the bustle of the south. Until recently, seaweed farming was the major occupation, but tourist income is now the mainstay of the economy. The island draws backpackers, divers, snorkellers and surfers and is perfect for a bit of gentle exploring.

WHAT TO SEE AND DO

Ranged along the west coast, the low-key, slightly scruffy beachside village of **Jungutbatu** has plenty of hotels, guesthouses and restaurants. Its golden sandy beach is lovely, though the sea here is too shallow for good swimming. **Coconut Beach, Chelegimbai** and **Mushroom Bay** (Tanjung Sanghyang) to the southwest and **Dream Beach** on the south coast offer more upmarket accommodation.

You can walk around the island in three to four hours. Motorbikes and bicycles are widely available for rent in Jungutbatu, though you will have to dismount and push the latter up some of the very steep hills.

Three **surf breaks**, aptly named Shipwrecks, Lacerations and Playground, are all reached from Jungutbatu. You can paddle out to Shipwrecks from the northern end of the beach, and access the other two from Coconut Beach around the cliffs to the south of Jungutbatu.

There are several sites for snorkelling around the island, and virtually every guesthouse can organize a boat trip (Rp175,000–225,000/person for a half-day, including equipment). Further away, the Penida Wall and Crystal Bay, close to the neighbouring island of Nusa Penida, are also popular snorkelling spots. Nusa Penida offers the most spectacular diving in Bali, although the sea can be cold with treacherous currents so it is important to dive with operators familiar with the area. Manta Point off the south coast of Nusa Penida is, as the name suggests, famous for manta rays (which are encountered all year round here) and pelagic fish. Giant sunfish (*mola mola*) also frequent sites around the island at dive sites including Crystal Bay.

ARRIVAL AND DEPARTURE

By boat Eleven operators run boats from Sanur to Lembongan. These include Scoot (☎ 0361 285522, ⓦ scootcruise.com) and Rocky (☎ 0361 801 2324, ⓦ rockyfastcruise.com), which both run four times a day in each direction (30min; around Rp285,000/Rp450,000 one-way/return). Scoot also has a combination ticket with Gili Trawangan and Lombok (Rp600,000/one-way). Perama (☎ 0361 751875, ⓦ peramatour.com) operates a shuttle boat from Sanur that connects with its island-wide shuttle bus services from Sanur, Kuta and Ubud. It runs to Jungutbatu (daily at 10.30am; 90min; Rp140,000); book a day in advance. Note that you'll have to wade ashore wherever you land.

DIVING

World Diving Lembongan ☎ 0812 390 0686, ⓦ world -diving.com. The most established company on the island, this is a PADI five-star centre, based at Pondok Baruna resort in Jungutbatu. Two-dive packages are Rp1,300,000.

ACCOMMODATION

JUNGUTBATU

Bunga Bungalo ☎ 0828 9760 8691, ⓦ bleucitron.net /bunga. French-owned place full of eccentric touches, with chairs made of giant clam shells and a cute little garden. Rooms on the upper floor have sea views, and there's a restaurant. Doubles **Rp305,000**

Bungalo No. 7 ☎ 0366 559 6421, ⓦ bungalo-no7.com. Sixteen good-value rooms beside the beach in the heart of the village. Gathered around a pool, they all have en-suite bathrooms and verandahs; splash out extra for a/c, hot water and a sea view. The Bali Dive Academy dive centre is here. **Rp275,000**

★**Chillhouse Lembongan** Jl Dusun Kelod 1 ☎ 0821 4500 6892, ⓦ facebook.com/chillhouselembongan. Set back from the shore in the village, these neat, very clean and well-presented a/c rooms have good king-sized beds, hot-water bathrooms, flatscreen TVs and verandahs. The owner, Gede, is super-helpful. Doubles **Rp230,000**

Pondok Baruna ☎ 0812 390 0686, ⓦ world-diving.com. The basic fan rooms overlooking the beach are small but prettier than some of the other budget options in Jungutbatu. More expensive a/c rooms (Rp450,000) surround a pool at the back and are decked out with marble tiles and heavy wooden furniture. Rates include breakfast. World Diving Lembongan is based here. Doubles **Rp350,000**

★**Secret Garden** ☎ 0813 5313 6861, ⓦ bigfishdiving .com/stay. A relaxed hideaway, this small, peaceful place has nine spacious fan-cooled bungalows spaced around a pool in the garden, 100m from the beach. Also hosts the YogaShack and conservation-focused Big Fish Diving. Great value. Doubles **Rp250,000**

Suka Nusa ☎ 0878 6002 3778, ⓔ sukanusa@yahoo.com. These ten simple but elegant two-storey *lumbung* (traditional thatched rice-barn) bungalows are built around a small pool and have outdoor bathrooms and huge verandahs for gazing over the sea. Doubles **Rp800,000**

EATING AND DRINKING

Most hotels have restaurants (mostly open daily 8am–10pm) right on the beach.

Maria's Boemboe Bali Jungutbatu. Bamboo benches, feet in the sand and home-style cooking – this basic warung is very popular. The signature dish is Boemboe Bali – tuna, calamari or prawns cooked with herbs (Rp33,000). Daily 7am–8pm.

4

DIRECTORY

Banks and exchange There are several ATMs.
Clinic The island's health centre (*klinik*) is on the main road in Jungutbatu.

PURA TANAH LOT

Dramatically marooned on a craggy, wave-lashed rock just off the coast about 30km northwest of Kuta, **Pura Tanah Lot** (daily sunrise–sunset; Rp60,000) is Bali's most photographed sight. Framed by frothing white surf and glistening black sand, its elegant multi-tiered shrines have become Bali's unofficial symbol and attract huge crowds of visitors every day, particularly around sunset.

Unfortunately this has brought all the joys of tourism with it, and now the temple sits against a background of stalls and overenthusiastic hawkers. The temple is said to have been founded in the sixteenth century by the wandering Hindu priest Nirartha and is one of the most holy places on Bali. Only bona fide devotees are allowed to climb the stairway carved out of the rock face and enter the compounds; everyone else is confined to the base of the rock.

Pura Tanah Lot is easiest to visit by tour (from Rp60,000 from Kuta), as public transport links are poor.

SOUTHWEST SURF BEACHES

West of Tabanan, the Denpasar–Gilimanuk coast road passes a couple of appealingly low-key black-sand surf beaches, both of them served by Denpasar (Ubung)–Gilimanuk bemos. The current can be severe all along this coast, so check locally before swimming.

About 26km west of Tabanan, the village of **Lalang Linggah** gives access to the austere black sand of Balian beach, which is known for its consistent surf breaks. There's an expanding accommodation scene here.

Twenty-five kilometres further west, **Medewi** beach (about 2hr 30min by bemo from Ubung) is known for its light current and fairly benign waves, making it a popular spot for novice surfers.

ACCOMMODATION

CSB Beach Inn Medewi ☎0813 3866 7288. Family-run place with a good number of large, well-kept fan rooms and four a/c options (Rp275,000); there are great views over the shorefront rice fields. Doubles Rp150,000
Surya Homestay Lalang Linggah ☎0813 3868 5643, ✉wayan.suratni@gmail.com. A good choice on Lalang Linggah with fan-cooled rooms, all with verandahs and modern(ish) cold-water bathrooms. Doubles Rp180,000

UBUD AND AROUND

UBUD is Bali's cultural hub, a seductive town set amid terraced rice paddies and known for its talented classical dancers and musicians, and for its prolific painters and artisans. Tradition is particularly important here and temple festivals happen almost daily. However, although it's fashionable to characterize Ubud as the real Bali, especially in contrast with Kuta, it's a major tourist destination and bears little resemblance to a typical Balinese town – there's even a *Starbucks* here now.

WHAT TO SEE AND DO

Arty, high-minded Ubud has Bali's best art museums and commercial galleries, and is also a recognized centre for **spiritual tourism**, with many opportunities to try out indigenous and imported healing therapies. Organic cafés, riverside bungalows and craft shops crowd its central marketplace, while the surrounding countryside is ideal for walks and cycle rides, and there's easy access to the northern volcanoes.

There is major (mostly tasteful) development along the central Jalan Monkey Forest, and Ubud's peripheries encompass the neighbouring hamlets of Campuhan, Sanggingan, Penestanan, Nyuhkuning, Peliatan, Pengosekan and Padang Tegal.

Central Ubud

Ubud's oldest and most central art collection is the **Museum Puri Lukisan** on Jalan Raya (daily 9am–6pm; Rp85,000; ☎0361 971159, ⓦmuseumpurilukisan .com), which, though set in prettily landscaped grounds, suffers from poor labelling. Still, there are some good prewar

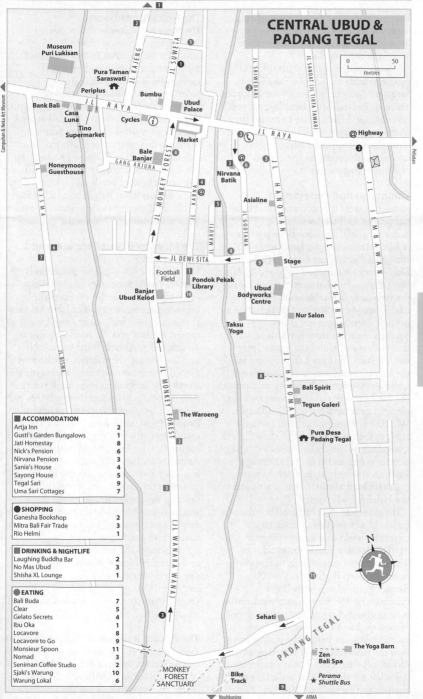

Balinese paintings, mostly monochrome, depicting local scenes, woodcarvings and impressive works in a naive expressionist style from the Ubud area.

A water garden fronts central Ubud's most atmospheric temple, **Pura Taman Saraswati** (generally sunrise–sunset; free). Through the red-brick temple gate, you'll find various shrines dotted around the temple courtyards, including a towering lotus throne sculpted with a riot of carvings and resting on the cosmic turtle and sacred naga serpents.

Campuhan and Penestanan

Extending west from central Ubud, the hamlet of **CAMPUHAN** is famous as the home of several charismatic expatriate painters, including the late Antonio Blanco, a flamboyant Catalan ("the Bali Dali") whose house and gallery on Jalan Raya Campuhan has been turned into the enjoyably camp **Museum Blanco** (daily 9am–5pm; Rp50,000 including a drink; ʬblancomuseum.com).

Across the road from here, the track that runs north along the grassy spine behind Pura Gunung Lebah forms part of the very pleasant ninety-minute circular **Campuhan Ridge walk**, taking you around the rural outskirts of Campuhan via the elevated spur between the Wos Barat and Wos Timor river valleys. You leave the ridge at the northern end of the village of Bangkiang Sidem, taking a sealed road that forks left and continues through Payogan and Lungsiakan before hitting the main road about 1.5km northwest of the Neka Art Museum.

The side road that turns off southwest beside Museum Blanco leads to the charmingly old-fashioned village of **PENESTANAN**, a centre for beadwork. The more scenic approach to the village is via the steep flight of steps 400m further north along Jalan Raya Campuhan. The steps climb the hillside to a westbound track that passes several arterial paths to panoramic hilltop accommodation before dropping down into the next valley and reaching a crossroads with Penestanan's main street. Turn left for the 1500m walk through the village and back to Museum Blanco.

The Neka Art Museum

The Neka Art Museum (Mon–Sat 9am–5pm, Sun noon–5pm; Rp75,000; ʬmuseumneka.com) boasts the island's most comprehensive collection of traditional and modern Balinese paintings. It's housed in a series of pavilions set high on a hill in Sanggingan, about 2.5km northwest of Ubud central market; all westbound bemos from the market pass the entrance. The pavilions include exhibits of Balinese painting from the seventeenth century to the present day, an archive of black-and-white photographs from Bali in the 1930s and 1940s, and contemporary works by artists from other parts of Indonesia.

The Monkey Forest Sanctuary and Nyuhkuning

Ubud's best-known tourist attraction is the **Monkey Forest Sanctuary** (daily 8.30am–6pm; Rp40,000), which occupies the land between the southern end of Jalan Monkey Forest (a 15min walk south from Ubud's central market) and the northern edge of Nyuhkuning. Although the forest itself is nothing special, the resident monkeys are playful and almost alarmingly tame (they'll snatch any items of food or drink you've got with you, so beware). Five minutes into the forest, you reach **Pura Dalem Agung Padang Tegal** (same hours; included with sanctuary entry fee), the temple of the dead for the Padang Tegal neighbourhood. *Pura dalem* are traditionally places of strong magical power and the preserve of evil spirits; in this temple you'll find half a dozen stone-carved images of the witch-widow Rangda sporting a hideous fanged face, unkempt hair, a metre-long tongue and pendulous breasts.

South from the temple, the track enters the village of **Nyuhkuning**, a respected centre for woodcarving – you can buy carvings and take lessons at several workshops – with a few cafés and small hotels.

The Agung Rai Museum of Art (ARMA)

Ubud's other major art museum is the **Agung Rai Museum of Art**, or **ARMA** (daily 9am–6pm; Rp80,000; ʬarmabali.com), in Pengosekan, on the southern

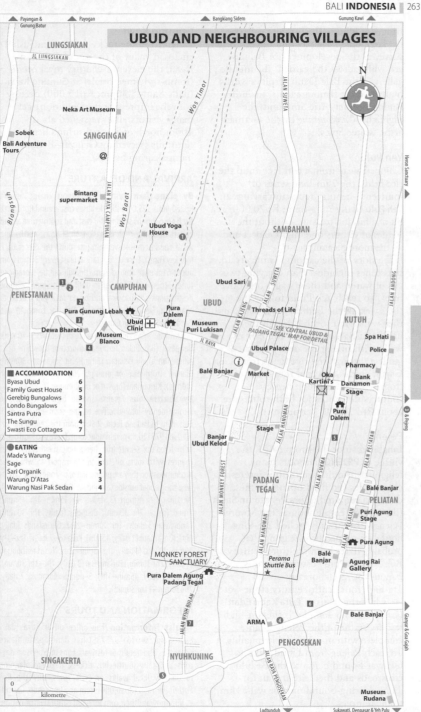

UBUD AND NEIGHBOURING VILLAGES

ACCOMMODATION

Byasa Ubud	6
Family Guest House	5
Gerebig Bungalows	3
Londo Bungalows	2
Santra Putra	1
The Sungu	4
Swasti Eco Cottages	7

EATING

Made's Warung	2
Sage	5
Sari Organik	1
Warung D'Atas	3
Warung Nasi Pak Sedan	4

fringes of Ubud. The upstairs gallery of the large Bale Daja pavilion offers a brief survey of the development of Balinese art, while across the garden, the middle gallery of the Bale Dauh displays works by Bali's most famous expats, including Rudolf Bonnet, Arie Smit and, the highlight, *Calonnarang* by the German artist Walter Spies.

Yeh Pulu

Chipped away from a cliff face amid the rice fields, the 25m-long series of fourteenth-century rock-cut carvings at **Yeh Pulu** (daily 7am–6pm; Rp20,000) is a bit of a hidden treasure, without the hordes of visitors one might expect and all the more pleasant for it.

The story of the carvings is uncertain, but scenes include a man carrying two jars of water, and three stages of a boar hunt. To reach Yeh Pulu, follow the signs west of the Bedulu crossroads, and then walk 1km south through the hamlet of Batulumbang. You can also walk (with one of the ever-present guides) through the rice fields from Goa Gajah; guides also lead four-hour treks from Yeh Pulu through nearby countryside (prices for both routes are about Rp220,000 per person).

Pejeng

Inhabited since the Bronze Age, the village of **PEJENG** harbours many religious antiquities and three interesting old temples (no fixed opening times; donation required). **Pura Penataran Sasih** (the Moon Temple) houses the Moon of Pejeng, a beautifully etched 2m-long hourglass-shaped bronze gong that probably dates from the third century BC. Nearby **Pura Pusering Jagat** is famous for its elaborately carved 1m-high fourteenth-century stone water jar, while the focus of **Pura Kebo Edan** (Crazy Buffalo Temple) is the 4m-high fertility statue of the Pejeng Giant, complete with massive lifelike phallus. To reach Pejeng from Ubud, take a Gianyar-bound bemo to the Bedulu crossroads and then either wait for a Tampaksiring-bound one, or walk 1km to the temples.

Gunung Kawi

Hewn from the rocky walls of the lush, enclosed valley of the sacred Pakrisan River, the eleventh-century royal *candi* (tomb-style memorials) at **Gunung Kawi** (daily 8am–5.30pm; Rp15,000) occupy a lovely, impressive spot and don't get many visitors. They're signed about 400m north of Tampaksiring's bemo terminus (served by Gianyar–Bedulu–Tampaksiring bemos).

ARRIVAL AND DEPARTURE

By plane Taxis to/from the airport charge around Rp280,000–325,000; shuttle buses cost around Rp60,000.

By bemo Bemos serving the east and south arrive at and depart from the central market on Jl Raya; north- and westbound bemos leave from just round the corner on Jl Monkey Forest. Services operate at least every 30min from about 6am until around 2pm (though can be sporadic at times), then every hour or so until about 5pm. For some destinations south, west and on to Java you'll need to change in Denpasar. For Padang Bai (for Lombok) and Candidasa, change in Gianyar.

Destinations Campuhan/Sanggingan (yellow; 5–10min); Denpasar (Batubulan terminal; chocolate brown or light blue; 50min) via Peliatan (5min) and Sukawati (30min); Gianyar (turquoise or orange; 20min) via Goa Gajah (10min); Kintamani (brown or bright blue; 1hr).

By shuttle bus Perama shuttle buses stop at the inconveniently located office at the southern end of Jl Hanoman in Padang Tegal, 2.5km from the central market (☎0361 973316, ⊛peramatour.com). There's no local bemo or metered taxi service from here; you can either take your chances with touts offering free transport to whichever accommodation they are promoting or pay one of the drivers who hang about outside (around Rp50,000 to central Ubud).

Destinations Airport (3 daily; 1hr 15min–1hr 45min); Amed (daily; 2hr 30min); Bedugul (daily; 1hr 30min); Candidasa (3 daily; 1hr 30min–2hr); Gili Islands (daily; 8hr); Kintamani (1 daily; 45min); Kuta (6–7 daily; 1hr–1hr 30min); Lovina (1 daily; 1hr 45min–2hr); Nusa Lembongan (1 daily; 2hr 30min); Padang Bai (3 daily; 1hr–1hr 30min); Sanur (6 daily; 45min–1hr); Senggigi (Lombok; 2 daily; 7hr 30min–11hr 30min).

INFORMATION AND TOURS

Tourist information The office on Jl Raya (daily 8am–8pm; ☎0361 973285) has dance performance schedules and details of festivals, runs inexpensive day-trips and sells shuttle-bus tickets. If you're planning to do any local walks or cycle rides, buy the *Bali Pathfinder* map (Rp50,000) from any bookshop. Consult ⊛ubudnowandthen.com for good cultural information.

Tours Walking, trekking and cycling tours are offered by: Banyan Tree Bike Tours (☎0813 3879 8516, ⓦbanyantreebiketours.com); Greenbike Tour (☎0851 0169 9692, ⓦgreenbiketour.com); and Keep Walking Tours (☎0361 973361, ⓦbalispirit.com/tours). Sunrise treks up Gunung Batur and Gunung Agung with Bali Sunrise Tours, Jl Raya Tegalalang 88 (☎0818 552669, ⓦbalisunrisetours.com).

GETTING AROUND

By bemo You can use the public bemos for short hops around the area (around Rp5000): for Campuhan/ Sanggingan, just flag down any bemo heading west, such as the turquoise ones going to Payangan.

By bike From Rp25,000/day from numerous street-side outlets along Jl Monkey Forest.

By car and motorbike Numerous places on Jl Monkey Forest rent out motorbikes (from Rp50,000/day) and cars (from Rp200,000/day). Reputable car rental, plus optional third-party insurance, from Ary's Business and Travel Service (☎0361 973130, ⓦarys_tour@yahoo.com) on Jl Raya Ubud.

Transport touts and drivers There are no metered taxis as the local transport cartel prevents Bluebird and Uber/Grab from operating in Ubud. You'll need to negotiate with the ubiquitous transport touts. Expect to pay around Rp30,000/50,000 for local rides on a motorbike/car.

ACCOMMODATION

Accommodation on the lanes around Jl Monkey Forest is both central and peaceful. Peliatan, Penestanan, Campuhan/Sanggingan and Nyuhkuning have better views but are more remote.

CENTRAL UBUD AND PADANG TEGAL

Artja Inn Jl Kajeng 9 ☎0856 379 4777; map p.261. Behind a family compound in a cute garden, this family-run place offers a handful of neat, inviting rooms in a modern block and older, spartan bamboo-walled cottages. The owners are very hospitable here. Doubles **Rp175,000**

Gusti's Garden Bungalows Jl Kajeng 27 ☎0812 465 1441, ⓦgustigardenbungalows.com; map p.261. Sixteen pleasant rooms, with fan or a/c, set around a small swimming pool in a peaceful location. The same owners run the nearby and equally good *Gusti's Garden 2*. Doubles **Rp325,000**

Jati Homestay Jl Hanoman ☎0361 977701, ⓦjatihs.com; map p.261. Run by a family of painters, this cheerful homestay has comfortable bungalows with hot water and private terraces facing the rice paddies. Doubles **Rp250,000**

Nick's Pension Jl Bisma ☎0361 975636, ⓦnickshotels-ubud.com; map p.261. Efficiently run place with a wide choice of rooms (all with private bathrooms, verandahs and plenty of space); you pay more for a rice-paddy view. There's a decent pool, and the same owners also run a couple of other hotels in Ubud (see website for details). Doubles **Rp600,000**

Nirvana Pension Jl Gootama 10 ☎0361 975415, ⓦnirvanaku.com; map p.261. Comfortably furnished and artistically decorated rooms, all with fan and hot water, in the traditional house compound of painter and batik teacher Nyoman Suradnya (see p.267). **Rp350,000**

Sania's House Jl Karna 7 ☎0361 970003, ✉sania_house@yahoo.com; map p.261. Well-maintained fan and a/c rooms (some in multistorey buildings) close to the market, and there's a small pool. Doubles **Rp250,000**

Sayong House Jl Maruti ☎0361 973305, ✉sayong_ubud@yahoo.com; map p.261. Ten simply furnished rooms, all with hot water, terraces and either fans or a/c, set around a garden. There's also a swimming pool just across the road. Doubles **Rp340,000**

★**Tegal Sari** Jl Hanoman ☎0361 973318, ⓦtegalsari-ubud.com; map p.261. Exceptionally appealing, tastefully furnished rooms, all with both fan and a/c, strung out alongside the paddy fields. There's thoughtful service, massage facilities and a pool, and cookery classes, free local transport, day-treks and village visits are all offered. Book well ahead. Doubles **Rp330,000**

Uma Sari Cottages Jl Bisma ☎0361 972964, ⓦumasaricottages.com; map p.261. Uma Sari has comfortable rooms with fans or a/c in two-storey buildings in a quiet but convenient spot. All have terraces or verandahs overlooking the rice fields, and there's a small pool. Doubles **Rp450,000**

THE OUTSKIRTS

Byasa Ubud Jl Made Lebah ☎0813 3842 9363, ⓦbyasa-ubud.com; map p.263. Set off the road, this small hotel has nine plush rooms in a delightfully peaceful location overlooking paddy fields and a lovely pool. Staff really go the extra mile here. Doubles **Rp550,000**

★**Family Guest House** Jl Sukma 39, Tebesaya, Peliatan ☎0361 974054, ⓦfamilyubud.com; map p.263. Friendly place offering well-maintained, fan-cooled bungalows in the family compound, all of them with stylish furniture,

> ★**TREAT YOURSELF**
>
> **The Sungu** Penestanan Kelod ☎0361 975719, ⓦthesunguresort.com; map p.263. A fine selection of spacious rooms and villas in pretty, leafy grounds with a pool. They serve excellent breakfasts and there's a free shuttle service to central Ubud. Check their website for special offers and package deals. Doubles **Rp950,000**

hot water and large verandahs. Rates include breakfast, tea/coffee and an afternoon snack. Doubles Rp300,000

Gerebig Bungalows Penestanan Kelod ☎ 0813 3701 9757, ⊛ gerebig.com; map p.263. Appealing rooms and bungalows, all with fan, fridge and some with kitchen facilities, set a short distance from the road amid local rice fields. The swimming pool is a bit further out in the fields. Doubles Rp460,000

Londo Bungalows Southern ridgetop, Penestanan ☎ 0361 976548, ⊛ londobungalows.com; map p.263. Ultra-friendly, family-run little place up on the ridge offering five large two-storey west-facing cottages; each sleeps four and has a kitchenette. Rp275,000

Santra Putra Jl Raya Campuhan, Campuhan ☎ 0361 977810, ⓔ karjabali@yahoo.com; map p.263. A mix of traditional thatched and modern concrete bungalows, complete with kitchenettes, panoramic rice-field views and a fabulously relaxed atmosphere. The owner offers painting and drawing classes, so you can happily spend a few days just pottering around the guesthouse. Doubles Rp375,000

Swasti Eco Cottages Nyuhkuning ☎ 0361 974079, ⊛ baliswasti.com; map p.263. Eco-hideaway with spacious, tastefully decorated accommodation in rooms (with either fans or a/c) and delightful Javanese Joglo-style cottages. There's a pool and spa, yoga sessions, and an excellent organic restaurant (which offers French, Thai, Indian and Indonesian cuisine). Doubles Rp480,000

EATING

If you like your food vegan, organic and raw, Ubud will be heaven: it's probably the centre of Asia's healthy eating scene.

CENTRAL UBUD

Bali Buda Jl Jembawan 1 ☎ 0361 844 5935, ⊛ balibuda .com; map p.261. Offers a vast menu of healthy drinks (most Rp22,000–34,000), sandwiches made with traditional or rye, spelt and red-rice breads, raw-food meals, pizza and salads, soups and main courses (Rp28,000–78,000), as well as cakes and pastries. There's a shop around the corner, plus a noticeboard for yoga and language classes and houses for rent. Daily 7am–10pm.

Clear Jl Hanoman ☎ 0361 889 4437, ⊛ facebook.com/ ClearCafeUbud; map p.261. *Clear* offers an excellent range of organic raw, vegan, vegetarian and seafood dishes, drawing culinary inspiration from across the globe (though many ingredients are sourced in Bali). The decor is eye-catching, and mains are around Rp50,000. Daily 8am–11pm.

Gelato Secrets Jl Monkey Forest ⊛ gelatosecrets.com; map p.261. Serving the best ice creams and sorbets in central Ubud, this gelateria sources its ingredients from across the Indonesian archipelago and makes its cones in house. Daily 10am–10.30pm.

Ibu Oka Just off Jl Suweta; map p.261. This open-sided warung attracts queues of diners for its *babi guling* (roast suckling pig), which is cooked fresh every day (Rp55,000 with rice and *sambal*), though the crackling could be crispier. There are a couple of other branches around town too. Daily 11am–5.30pm (or until the *babi guling* runs out).

Monsieur Spoon Jl Hanoman 10 ☎ 0361 973263, ⊛ monsieurspoon.com/shops; map p.261. Perhaps Ubud's best continental-style café, serving perfectly baked pastries, brioches and cakes (try the salted caramel), as well as breakfasts, quiches and great coffee in all the combinations you could care for. There are well-chosen tunes on the stereo. Daily 7am–9pm.

Nomad Jl Raya Ubud 35 ☎ 0361 977169; map p.261. Serves local, Asian fusion and international dishes with style from a small but inviting menu (mains from Rp42,000) including satay, Malaysian *laksa* and Balinese-style tapas. Daily 10am–11pm.

★ **Seniman Coffee Studio** Jl Sriwedari ☎ 0361 972085, ⊛ senimancoffee.com; map p.261. Coffee (Rp21,000– 28,000) is elevated to an art form at this hip café/roastery/ design shop, which has a range of equipment that would look more in place in a science lab. The menu features five regular, single-origin coffees, plus weekly "guest beans". British- and Indonesian-style breakfasts and top cakes are available too. Daily 8am–7pm.

Sjaki's Warung Off Jl Dewi Sita ☎ 0813 5718 1122, ⊛ sjakitarius.nl; map p.261. Overlooking the football field, this warung serves up cheap, good-quality Indonesian mainstays and some international dishes (around Rp30,000). Daily 10am–10pm.

Warung Lokal Jl Gootama 7; map p.261. A Balinese warung selling *cap cai*, *nasi campur*, *nasi goreng* and the like at good prices (main meals mostly Rp15,000–20,000) that attracts a clientele of savvy foreigners and locals. Daily 10am–10pm.

★ TREAT YOURSELF

Locavore Jl Dewi Sita ☎ 0361 977733, ⊛ www.locavore.co.id; map p.261. A serious gastronomic experience, this acclaimed restaurant (with an open kitchen) has really raised the bar in Ubud with its highly innovative (and expensive) Modern European cuisine. Their five- or seven-course tasting menus (from Rp575,000) change every month and include a veggie option; there's no à la carte menu. The more casual *Locavore to Go* across the street is open all day and serves posh comfort grub including the best burgers in town. Mon–Sat noon–2.30pm & 6–11pm.

THE OUTSKIRTS

Made's Warung Penestanan ridge ☎ 0361 977885; map p.263. One of several excellent options along the Penestanan ridge, serving well-priced travellers' favourites (from Rp25,000), including inexpensive juices, good *nasi campur* and (with 24hr notice) Balinese smoked duck (Rp195,000 for two). Daily 8am–10pm.

★**Sage** Jl Nyuh Bulan, Nyuhjuning ☎ 0361 976528, ⓦ facebook.com/sagerestobali; map p.263. Located on a corner plot, this vegan place has an outstanding selection of healthy dishes including "Go Jolly Green salad" (with kale, spinach and *tempe*, Rp70,000), great jackfruit tacos (Rp60,000) and wonderful juices. The attractive premises are light and airy and staff are sweet. Daily 8am–9.30pm.

Sari Organik Off Jl Abangan, about 800m walk north from the aqueduct on western Jl Raya Ubud ☎ 0361 972087; map p.263. About 20min into the Ubud Kaja rice-field walk, this café has gorgeous views and good home-grown organic produce. The menu (most dishes Rp45,000–70,000) includes great veggie kebabs, chicken and salads. Expect to wait a while. Daily 8am–8pm.

Warung D'Atas Jl Gunung Sari 777, Peliatan ☎ 0361 908 0345; map p.263. Sizzling up a storm, this unpretentious, open-sided place is a carnivore's delight with expertly spiced pork ribs, home-made sausages and kebabs at moderate prices. Their meat combo plate (Rp100,000) is almost enough for two. Daily 9.30am–10pm.

Warung Nasi Pak Sedan Jl Raya Pengosekan; map p.263. Some of the most economical food (dishes from Rp12,000) around Ubud is served at the low-key *Warung Nasi Pak Sedan*: try the tasty house speciality, *nasi campur ayam*. Daily 7.30am–5pm.

DRINKING AND NIGHTLIFE

The bar scene can be very quiet, so choose a live-music night to ensure a decent crowd. Most places outside the centre offer a free pick-up service if you phone ahead.

CENTRAL UBUD

Laughing Buddha Bar Jl Monkey Forest ☎ 0361 970928, ⓦ laughingbuddhabali.com; map p.261. There's live music (from blues to reggae) every night at this small, relaxed bar in the heart of Jl Monkey Forest. You'll find a long drinks menu plus plenty of nibbles and tapas. Happy hour stretches from 4pm to 7pm. Daily 8am–midnight.

No Mas Ubud Jl Monkey Forest ☎ 0361 908 0800, ⓦ nomasubud.com; map p.261. Stylish bar with a social vibe, vintage decor, live bands, DJs and killer cocktails (try a Pickleback – whisky and home-made juice, Rp60,000). Daily 5pm–1am.

Shisha XL Lounge Off Jl Monkey Forest; map p.261. Chilled place overlooking the football field that stays open late and features DJs and live music. Daily 10am–2am.

SHOPPING

Shopping for arts and crafts is a major pastime in Ubud: there are outlets in all its neighbourhoods, but if you're short on time the market in central Ubud is a good one-stop venue and overflows with stalls. Also worthwhile are Sukawati art market, 8km south of Ubud (served by Ubud–Batubulan bemos), and the handicraft outlets that line the 12km Ubud–Tegalalang–Pujung road (best with own transport).

Ganesha Bookshop Jl Raya Ubud, cnr Jl Jembawan ☎ 0361 970320, ⓦ ganeshabooksbali.com; map p.261. The best bookshop in Ubud, with a huge stock of new books on all things Balinese and Indonesian, maps and fiction. Daily 9am–9pm.

Mitra Bali Fair Trade Jl Monkey Forest ☎ 0361 972108, ⓦ mitrabali.com; map p.261. You can support local craftspeople at this little shop, where a changing range of crafts is on offer. Daily 9am–8pm.

Rio Helmi Jl Suweta 6B ☎ 0361 972304, ⓦ riohelmi.com; map p.261. Gallery of the respected Indonesian photographer. Limited-edition prints cost $125–2250, while mass-market prints start at around $5. There's a good a/c veggie café here too. Daily 7am–7pm.

TRADITIONAL DANCE

Up to nine different traditional dance and music shows are staged every night in the Ubud area; the tourist office publishes the weekly schedule and arranges free transport to outlying venues. Tickets (Rp80,000–120,000) can be bought at the tourist office, from touts, or at the door. If you have only one evening to catch a show, either choose the lively Kecak (Monkey Dance), or go for whatever is playing at the Ubud Palace (Puri Saren Agung), central Ubud's most atmospheric venue.

COURSES

Batik Nirvana Batik, Jl Gootama 10 (☎ 0361 975415, ⓦ nirvanaku.com; Rp485,000/day).

Cooking *Casa Luna* restaurant, Jl Raya Ubud (☎ 0361 977409, ⓦ casalunabali.com; Rp400,000/day). Excellent Balinese cookery courses in which you learn to prepare several dishes.

Crafts ARMA, JL Raya Pengosekan, Pengosekan (☎ 0361 976659, ⓦ armabali.com) offers courses (Rp300,000–600,000) in Balinese painting, woodcarving, batik, gamelan, dance and theatre, jewellery-making, basket weaving, traditional architecture, Hinduism, astrology and making offerings. Studio Perak, Jl Hanoman (☎ 0361 974244, ⓦ studioperak.com), runs courses in silversmithing: in half a day you can produce your own ring or pendant (Rp350,000 inclusive of 5g of silver).

Music and dance Sehati, Jl Monkey Forest (☎ 0361 976341, ⓦ sehati-guesthouse.com; from Rp100,000/hr).

4

MIND, BODY AND SPIRIT

Ubud is home to one of Southeast Asia's foremost yoga communities, with many resident and visiting devotees. You'll find over a dozen schools in the area and there are possibly hundreds of instructors.

Honeymoon Guesthouse Jl Bisma ☎ 0361 973282, ⊛ casalunabali.com. Offers beginners' and intermediate sessions in the morning that are a blend of Hatha and Vinyasa yoga.

Taksu Yoga Jl Goutama Selatan ☎ 0361 971490, ⊛ taksuyoga.com. Offers Vinyasa, Hatha gentle yoga and private classes. Their drop-in rate is Rp120,000. Daily 9am–5.30pm.

Ubud Yoga House Jl Subak Sokwayah ☎ 0821 4418

1058, ⊛ ubudyogahouse.com. A busy programme of Hatha, Vinyasa flow and gentle yoga sessions. Guided meditation classes are also available.

The Yoga Barn Southern Jl Hanoman, Padang Tegal ☎ 0361 971236, ⊛ theyogabarn.com. Runs a big programme of yoga classes (Rp110,000) in various disciplines, along with pilates, capoeira, dance and meditation. It also offers yoga retreats and yoga teacher training. Daily 7am–9pm.

DIRECTORY

Banks and exchange There are ATMs throughout Ubud and its environs. Many tour agents offer exchange services, but there are some common scams to be aware of (see box, p.251).

Hospitals, clinics and dentists Ubud Clinic, at Jl Raya Campuhan 36 (☎ 0361 974911, ⊛ ubudclinic.co.id), is open 24hr, staffed by English-speakers and will respond to emergency call-outs; it also has a dental service. For anything serious, the nearest hospitals are in Denpasar (see p.248).

Pharmacies There are several pharmacies on Jl Raya Ubud, Jl Monkey Forest and Jl Peliatan.

Police The main police station is on the eastern edge of town, on Jl Andong, and there is a more central police booth at the Jl Raya and Jl Monkey Forest crossroads.

Post office The GPO on Jl Jembawan (Mon–Sat 8am–5pm, Sun & hols 9am–4pm) keeps poste restante; there are postal agents throughout Ubud.

Spas and massage At Nur Salon, Jl Hanoman 28 (☎ 0361 975352, ⊛ nursalonubud.com; massage from Rp175,000), and Ubud Bodyworks Centre, Jl Hanoman 25 (☎ 0361 975720, ⊛ ubudbodyworkscentre.com; massages from Rp125,000).

BESAKIH

The major tourist draw in the east of Bali is undoubtedly the **Besakih temple complex** (daily 6am–7pm; Rp10,000), situated on the slopes of Gunung Agung, the holiest and highest mountain on the island.

Besakih is the most venerated site on Bali for Balinese Hindus, who believe that the gods occasionally descend to reside in the temple, during which times worshippers don their finery and bring them elaborate offerings. The complex's sheer scale is impressive, and on a clear day, with Agung towering dramatically behind, and with ceremonies in full swing, it's beautiful. However, Besakih has also evolved the habit of separating foreign tourists from their money as quickly as possible, which can make for a frustrating experience.

WHAT TO SEE AND DO

The complex consists of more than twenty separate temples spread over a site stretching for more than 3km. The central temple is **Pura Penataran Agung**, the largest on the island, built on seven ascending terraces, and comprising more than fifty structures. Start by following the path just outside Pura Penataran Agung's wall, and then wander at will: the *meru* (multi-tiered shrine roofs) of Pura Batu Madeg, rising among the trees to the north, are enticing. Pura Pengubengan, the most far-flung of the temples, is a couple of kilometres through the forest.

Unless you're praying or making offerings, you're forbidden to enter the temples, and most remain locked unless there's a ceremony going on. However, a lot is visible through the gateways and over walls. You'll need to wear a sarong and sash, which are available for rent, or purchase.

There are huge numbers of local guides at Besakih hoping to be engaged by visitors, but you don't need one to explore the complex; stick to the paths running

CLIMBING GUNUNG AGUNG

At 3031m, **Gunung Agung** is the highest Balinese peak and visible from throughout eastern Bali. The spiritual centre of Bali, it is believed that the spirits of the ancestors of the Balinese people dwell there. Climbing is forbidden at certain times because of **religious festivals**. Weather-wise, the **dry season** (April to mid-Oct) is best; don't contemplate it during January and February, the wettest months. You'll need walking boots, a torch, water and snacks; for the descent, a stout stick is handy.

ROUTES

There are two main routes. From **Pura Pasar Agung**, it's at least a three-hour climb with an ascent of almost 2000m, so you'll need to set out at 3am or earlier to get to the top for sunrise. From Besakih, the climb is longer (5–7hr) and much more challenging; you'll need to leave between 10pm and midnight. A third, less-used, route, from **Dukuh Bujangga Sakti**, inland from Kubu on the north coast, involves starting out in the afternoon, camping on the mountain and completing the three hours to the summit pre-dawn.

GUIDES

It's strongly advised to climb with an established trekking guide; the freelance guides who hang round Pura Pasar Agung and Besakih tend not be that safety-conscious.
Dartha Mount Agung Trekking Selat ☏0852 3700 8513, ⓦdarthamountagungtrekking .com. A guide association offering four routes and employing professional guides.
Gung Bawa Jl Tukad Pancoran IV/E 7, Denpasar ☏0812 387 8168, ⓦgungbawatrekking.com. Gung Bawa is a young, good-humoured, highly experienced and dependable guide who speaks excellent English. He charges Rp700,000/person (minimum two people) for a hiking package including guiding, food and drinks, accommodation and transport from your hotel in southern Bali.

4

along the walls outside the temples. If you do hire a guide, Rp30,000–50,000 is reasonable. Note that if you're escorted into one of the temples to receive a blessing from a priest you'll be expected to make a "donation" to the priest.

ARRIVAL AND DEPARTURE

By tour Without your own transport, the easiest way of getting to Besakih is to take an organized tour, available from any of the tourist centres (from Rp200,000/person), but anything offering less than an hour at the temple isn't worth it. If you're in a group, it's more economical to charter a car and driver for the day (around Rp500,000) and put together your own itinerary.
By public transport Bemos from Semarapura (also known as Klungkung) go as far as Menanga from where there are ojek to the temple. Bemos also run from Amlapura to Rendang, with some continuing to Menanga. Most bemos run in the morning. There are no bemos north of Menanga to Penelokan, or between Rendang and Bangli.

INFORMATION

Tourist office The Besakih tourist office (daily 7am–6pm), on the right just beyond the car park, is staffed by the local organization of guides who will pressure you to make a donation and engage their services, both of which are unnecessary.

PADANG BAI

PADANG BAI, the port for Lombok ferries, nestles in a small white-sand cove lined with fishing boats. Many travellers stay a night or two and the tiny village has developed into a laidback resort with cool cafés, cheap accommodation and live music bars. Jalan Silayukti is the main seafront road at the eastern end of the bay, while all the small roads leading from the seafront to the road across the top of the village are named, from west to east, Jalan Segara 1, Jalan Segara 2 and so on.

WHAT TO SEE AND DO

If you find the main beach too busy, head to the bay of **Bias Tugal** (also known as Pantai Kecil), to the west, which is quieter; follow the road past the post office and, just as it begins to climb, take the roadway to the left. Alternatively, if you head east over the headland from the main beach, and take a left fork just east of Topi Inn, you'll reach the pretty but miniature cove of **Blue Lagoon**, not much more than 100m long. You can snorkel here at high tide but beware the serious undertow and watch the coral (which is just below the surface). The two restaurants rent snorkelling gear (from Rp25,000) as well as sunloungers (around Rp40,000), and you're sure to find a couple of massage women in attendance. There's also a big volleyball pitch just behind the harbour, with a permanent game going on that anyone can join.

Padang Bai is a good base for diving, and the sites at Blue Lagoon attract eels, wrasses, turtles and lion fish. The operators also arrange dive trips further afield to Nusa Penida, Amed, Tulamben, Candidasa and Gili Selang.

ARRIVAL AND DEPARTURE

By plane A taxi to/from Ngurah Rai Airport is around Rp340,000.

By bemo Bemos from Semarapura and Amlapura stop at the port entrance at the western end of the bay, and everything is within easy walking distance.

Destinations Amlapura (45min); Candidasa (20min); Denpasar (Batubulan terminal; 2hr); Semarapura (30min).

By ferry The public ferry from Lembar on Lombok arrives at the port, and departs every 90min around the clock (4hr–4hr 30min; Rp40,000).

By speedboat Speedboats to the Gili Islands and mainland Lombok (see p.291) arrive at and depart from the jetty in the bay.

By shuttle bus Perama buses stop at their office near the port entrance (daily 7am–7pm; ☎0363 41419, ⊛peramatour.com).

Destinations Candidasa (3 daily; 30min); Kuta/Ngurah Rai Airport (3 daily; 2hr 30min); Sanur (3 daily; 1hr 30min); Tirta Gannga (daily; 1hr); Ubud (3 daily; 2hr).

DIVE OPERATORS

Dive trips from $70; PADI courses are available including tech diving.

Geko Dive Jl Silayukti ☎0363 41516, ⊛gekodive.com.

OK Divers Jl Silayukti 6 ☎0811 385 8830, ⊛okdiversbali.com.

Water Worx Close to Geko on Jl Silayukti ☎0363 41220, ⊛waterworxbali.com.

ACCOMMODATION

★**Bamboo Paradise** Jl Penataran Agung ☎0822 6630 4330, ⊛facebook.com/pg/bambooparadisebali. A cosy hostel and homestay with good fan-cooled dorms and a variety of basic private rooms. There's a great lounge for socializing. Dorms Rp120,000, doubles Rp230,000

Fat Barracuda Jl Segara ☎0822 3797 1212, ⊛fatbarracuda.com. A zany-looking, very well set up hostel with an excellent a/c ten-bed mixed dorm that has a hot-water en suite. The (one) private room upstairs is fan-cooled and has a balcony. Chill out in the lounge, which is loaded with beanbags. Dorms Rp95,000, doubles Rp290,000

Kembar Inn Jl Segara 6 ☎0363 41364, ⊛kembarinn .com. Old-school guesthouse with nice staff, decent rooms on several floors and a generous breakfast. There are common sitting areas for socializing. Doubles Rp175,000

Lemon House Gang Melanting 5 ☎0812 4637 1575, ⊛lemonhousebali.com. Hike up a steep flight of steps to this welcoming guesthouse with spick-and-span accommodation (the deluxe rooms are a steal). There are amazing views of the bay from the communal terrace, but noise from ferries can be an issue. Dorms Rp125,000, doubles Rp175,000

Topi Inn Jl Silayukti 99 ☎0363 41424, ⊛topiinn.net. Long-running cheapo, social guesthouse and restaurant with simple rooms (some en suite) plus a common area that doubles as an open-plan dorm with mattresses and mosquito nets (security boxes are available). Breakfast is not included. Dorms Rp65,000, doubles Rp170,000

EATING AND NIGHTLIFE

Babylon Reggae Bar Jl Segara. Tiny, perennially busy late-night drinking and music venue with local musos playing covers every Tuesday, Thursday and Friday. Small Bintangs are Rp22,000, or try one of their cocktails. Daily 5pm–3am.

Grand Café Padang Bai Harbour Jl Pantai Segara ☎0363 434 5043. Classy and popular harbour-view place offering a dozen "bio" health juices and cappuccinos. The food is good and includes pizzas, sate campur, grilled fish with garlic sauce, kebabs and steaks. Mains from Rp35,000. Daily 7am–10pm.

★**Martini's** Jl Segara ☎0818 0559 0450. The best warung in town, run by former beach hawker Martini. Famous for its chicken sate, which comes with wonderfully rich peanut sauce, it also serves good seafood dishes (from Rp35,000) and soups (from Rp25,000). Facing the car park. Daily 7am–11pm.

Ozone Café Jl Silayukti ☎0817 470 8597. This lively bar-restaurant attracts a regular clientele of beer sluggers and has live music some nights. Also serves tasty food, and fruit and soya shakes and smoothies. Daily 11am–11pm.

Topi Inn Jl Silayukti 99 ☎0363 41424, ⊛topiinn.net. Classic travellers' café with great home-baked bread, cakes, cappuccinos and a ton of imaginative vegetarian dishes – including Mediterranean salads. Mains cost from Rp45,000; water refills are available too. Keep an eye out for the regular movie and party nights. Daily 7.30am–10pm.

DIRECTORY

Banks and exchange There are exchange counters and several ATMs, two near the Perama office.

Bookshop Ryan, Jl Segara, with fiction and non-fiction including some good Indonesian titles.

Doctor Dr Nisa (☎ 0811 380645) is a highly regarded, English-speaking local doctor who will visit sick tourists privately. He can also be contacted at Water Worx dive centre on the seafront. The nearest hospitals are in Amlapura and Denpasar.

Police ☎ 0363 41388. Near the port entrance.

CANDIDASA

At the eastern end of Amuk Bay is **CANDIDASA**, a relaxed resort that appeals mostly to older visitors. The main beach has suffered serious erosion in recent decades due to over-construction in the area – the offshore coral reefs were harvested to provide lime for building tourist resorts in the 1980s – but there are small pockets of white sand. It's a good base for snorkelling, diving and exploring the east.

The pretty lagoon in the centre of Candidasa is a useful landmark.

WHAT TO SEE AND DO

The group of tiny islands lying just off the coast (Gili Tepekong, Gili Biaha and Gili Mimpang) offers excellent sites for experienced divers (currents can be strong), including walls, a pinnacle and the dramatic Tepekong Canyon. All the operators also arrange trips further afield to Padang Bai, Nusa Penida, Amed, Tulamben and Gili Selang.

For fantastic views over the coastline, follow the headland trail that forks off the road leading east in the direction of Amlapura. Beyond the headland there are some pretty beaches, with wide stretches of sand.

The reef along the coast is gradually rejuvenating and there is some decent **snorkelling** just offshore, stretching for about 1km westwards from the area in front of *Puri Bagus Candidasa* hotel. Take care not to venture too far out, and be aware of your position as the currents can be hazardous. Local boatmen and dive schools offer snorkelling trips (around Rp220,000/person for half-day trips).

ARRIVAL AND DEPARTURE

By plane Taxis to/from Ngurah Rai Airport (see p.250) cost around Rp350,000 (around 2hr).

By bus and bemo Public transport services stop anywhere along the main road through Candidasa.
Destinations Amlapura (20min); Denpasar (Batubulan terminal; 2hr); Gianyar (1hr); Padang Bai (20min).
By shuttle bus Perama (daily 8am–9pm; ☎ 0363 41114, ⓦ peramatour.com) stop at their office at the western end of the central area.
Destinations Amed (daily; 1hr 30min); Kuta/Ngurah Rai Airport (3 daily; 3hr); Lovina (daily; 3hr 30min); Padang Bai (3 daily; 30min); Sanur (3 daily; 2hr); Tirtagangga (daily; 1hr); Tulamben (daily; 2hr); Ubud (3 daily; 1hr 30min).
Information *Candidasa Network* (ⓦ candidasanetwork .com) is a free magazine with useful features and information available widely in the resort.

DIVE OPERATORS

Dive trips cost from $75; PADI Open Water courses cost around $450.
Bambu Divers ☎ 0363 41534, ⓦ bambudivers.com. Dutch-run dive school at the *Pondok Bambu*.
Shangrila Scuba Divers ☎ 0812 398 9239, ⓦ shangrilascubadivers.com. British-run centre at *Bali Palm Resort*.
Zen Dive Jl Raya Candidasa ☎ 0363 41411, ⓦ zendivebali .com. Five-star PADI dive centre.

ACCOMMODATION

Ari Homestay Jl Raya Candidasa ☎ 0817 970 7339, ⓦ arihomestaycandidasa.com. Classic budget guesthouse with well-priced en-suites and bungalows, a book exchange and a tiny hot-dog café. Pay for a "superior double" (Rp320,000) and you'll get a/c and hot water. Doubles `Rp150,000`

Gedong Gandhi Ashram Jl Raya Candidasa ☎ 0363 41108, ⓦ ashramgandhi.com. Ashram which occupies a gorgeous location between the lagoon and the ocean and rents out a few simple, attractive bungalows. Guests can take part in the daily *puja*, yoga and meditation. There's no smoking or drinking, and unmarried couples can't share a room. Volunteer placements (Rp100,000/night) are also possible. Rates include three vegetarian or fish meals a day. Doubles `Rp450,000`

Ida's Homestay Jl Raya Candidasa ☎ 0363 41096, ⓦ facebook.com/Idas.Homestay.Candidasa. Old school travellers' lodge in a coconut grove with six good-sized timber-and-thatch bungalows with mosquito nets, fans and cold-water garden bathrooms. There's a lovely shorefront deck plus a tiny patch of sandy beach. Doubles `Rp250,000`

★ **Lumbung Damuh** Jl Pantai Buitan, Manggis ☎ 0363 41553. A totally chilled little Balinese/European-owned hideaway of creatively designed *lumbung* beside a tiny patch of shore, 4km west of Candidasa. Bedrooms are upstairs, with sitting areas and hot-water garden

4

ACCOMMODATION

Ari Homestay	2
Gedong Gandhi Ashram	5
Ida's Homestay	4
Lumbung Damuh	1
Temple Café and Seaside Cottages	3

Amuk Bay

bathrooms below. A good breakfast is included; no restaurant, but there are local warung. Doubles Rp250,000

Temple Café and Seaside Cottages Jl Raya Candidasa ☎0363 41629, ⊛balibeachfront-cottages.com. The well-furnished bungalows here come in a range of standards and prices, from fan and cold-water versions to those with a/c, sea view, kitchenettes and very good hot-water bathrooms. Guests can use the pool at the *Watergarden* hotel opposite. Doubles Rp200,000

EATING

For an inexpensive meal, head to the food stalls on the waterfront opposite the police station to the north of town (11am–9pm).

Loaf Café Jl Raya Candidasa ☎0813 4629 9878. Excellent, buzzing a/c café with fine pies, sandwiches (with home-made bread), great cakes and all the coffee combinations you could wish for, as well as fresh juices and smoothies. Daily 8am–6pm.

Warung Astawa Jl Raya Candidasa ☎0363 41363. Fine-value streetfront place, with set three-course meals of Indonesian favourites, sizzling *sate* (served over charcoal coals) and flavoursome pork, chicken and fish dishes (mains from Rp45,000). Daily 7am–10pm.

DRINKING

New Queen Jl Raya Candidasa ☎0812 3653 1832, ⊛newqueen.biz.nf. Popular tourist bar and restaurant (there are daily specials) with regular reggae and rock bands and draught Bintang. Daily 9am–midnight.

DIRECTORY

Banks and exchange There are many ATMs in the central area, as well as a few moneychangers.

Doctor The Pentamedica clinic (Jl Raya Manggis 88; ☎0363 41909, ⊛pentamedica.com) is open 24hr. The nearest hospitals are in Amlapura, Semarapura and Denpasar.

Spa and massage Try Salon & Accessories (☎0363 41834; massage from Rp125,000), opposite the *Watergarden* hotel.

AMED, JEMELUK AND THE FAR EAST COAST

The stretch of coast in the far east of Bali from Culik to Aas is known as **AMED**, although this is just one village here. Accommodation is mushrooming along the 11km stretch from Amed to Aas, as people come here to enjoy the peace and quiet, the clifftop views of the glorious coastline and black beaches, and to take in the stunning underwater attractions.

Access to Amed is from the small junction village of **Culik**, 3km away, just over 9km north of Tirtagangga on the Amlapura–Singaraja road. In Amed, life centres on fishing and salt production, which you can see at close quarters. A kilometre east is the hamlet of Congkang, then **Jemeluk**, 6km from Culik, which attracts divers and snorkellers for the offshore coral terrace leading to a wall dropping to a depth of more than 40m. There's a high density of fish, with sharks, wrasses and parrotfish in the outer parts. From Jemeluk lies headland after headland: the beaches and villages of Bunutan and Lipah Beach are the most developed areas, though they remain low-key, leading on to Lehan Beach, Selang, Ibus, Banyuning and eventually Aas, almost 15km from Culik.

As well as at Jemeluk, there's excellent **diving** at a wreck at Lipah Beach and a

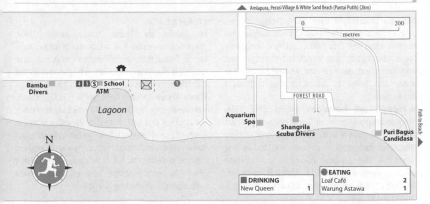

Amlapura, Perasi Village & White Sand Beach (Pantai Putih) (2km)

0   200 metres

Bambu Divers

4 5 $ School ATM

Lagoon

FOREST ROAD

Aquarium Spa

Shangrila Scuba Divers

Puri Bagus Candidasa

Path to Beach

N

■ **DRINKING**
New Queen   1

● **EATING**
Loaf Café   2
Warung Astawa   1

drift dive at Bunutan, with the chance to see schools of barracuda and giant barrel sponges. Advanced divers can explore Gili Selang, the eastern tip of Bali, where a pristine reef, pelagics and exciting currents are the draw. Good **snorkelling** spots include Jemeluk, the Lipah Beach wreck and a Japanese wreck near the coast at Banyuning.

ARRIVAL AND DEPARTURE

By shuttle bus Perama (ⓦ peramatour.com) have regular minibuses to several destinations in Bali from their office in Amed village.

Destinations Airport (daily; 2hr 45min); Candidasa (daily; 1hr 15min); Padang Bai (daily; 1hr 30min); Tirtagangga (2 daily, 30min); Ubud (daily; 2hr).

By bemo All public transport between Amlapura and Singaraja passes through Culik. Bemos are rare in the Amed area, but the odd service runs via Amed to Aas in the morning.

Destinations (from Culik only) Aas (1hr 30min); Amed (10min); Amlapura (45min); Bunutan (45min); Jemeluk (30min); Singaraja (Penarukan terminal; 2hr 30min); Tirtagangga (20min); Tulamben (20min).

By boat Fast boats run direct from Amed to the Gili Islands and Lombok (1hr–1hr 30min; Rp350,000–550,000 depending on demand). Note that both of these two services have a poor reputation for overcrowding, and safety standards may be questionable. Amed Sea Express (ⓣ 0878 6306 4799, ⓦ gili-sea-express.com) or Kuda Hitam (ⓣ 0817 471 4503, ⓦ kudahitam.com).

GETTING AROUND

By car or motorbike Transport along the Amed coast is scant. You'll either need to rent your own motorbike, available for Rp50,000/day, or use an ojek/driver.

Tours The most popular tours are the sightseeing loop via the spectacular coast road, Pura Lempuyang Luhur and inland

hikes. Prices range from Rp275,000/person for a tour on the back of a motorbike to around Rp550,000 for a car plus driver.

DIVE OPERATORS

PADI Open Water courses are around $400, and fun dives cost from $75. Most guesthouses have snorkel gear for rent (from Rp25,000/day). There are also freediving schools for breath-holding athletic types who hate underwater bubbles.

Apneista Bali Freediving and Yoga School Jemeluk ⓣ 0812 3826 7356, ⓦ apneista.com.

Bali Reef Divers *Puri Wirata* hotel, Bunutan ⓣ 0363 23523, ⓦ diveamed.com.

Eco-Dive Jemeluk ⓣ 0363 23482, ⓦ ecodivebali.com.

Euro Dive Lipah ⓣ 0363 23605, ⓦ eurodivebali.com.

Jukung Dive Congkang ⓣ 0363 23469, ⓦ jukungdivebali .com.

Ocean Prana Freediving and Yoga School Jemeluk ⓣ 0363 430 1587, ⓦ oceanprana.com.

ACCOMMODATION AND EATING

All accommodation and restaurants line the main road along the coast. There are plenty of inexpensive homestays in Amed and Jemeluk; those inland rather than beachfront are cheaper.

AMED, CONGKANG AND JEMELUK

Amed Café Hotel Jemeluk ⓣ 0363 23473, ⓦ amedcafe .com. This popular spot has 39 rooms plus a pool, dive centre, restaurant and minimarket. Rooms in all categories are spacious and nicely furnished; a/c is available, but the cheapest have fans and cold water and are right by the road. Doubles Rp350,000

Ganesh Amed Jemeluk ⓣ 0859 3516 2475, ⓦ ganeshamed.com. As well as economical fan-cooled rooms (and more expensive a/c rooms with private verandahs), *Ganesh Amed* has a small pool and direct beach access. Yoga and meditation classes (Rp120,000) are available too. Cash only. Doubles Rp350,000

4

Geria Giri Shanti ☎0819 1665 4874, ⊛geriagirishanti
.com. A tropical garden hideaway, this well-run place has
spacious, clean and thoughtfully outfitted bungalows
(good mosquito nets, nice fabrics, lots of hangers and
long mirrors) just above the road. All have fans and hot
water. Also home to Adventure Divers. Doubles
Rp385,000

★**Pondok Laut Bungalows** ☎0813 3817 7324,
✉pondoklautamed@gmail.com Quirky, unusual beachfront
place with selection of lovely rooms that boast carefully
mismatched furnishings – ceramics, ikat textiles and
furniture – that combine Indonesian and Japanese
influences. There's a small pool, breakfast is home-cooked,
nutritious and delicious and the genial owners are helpful.
Doubles Rp450,000

Sunrise Café and Bungalows Jemeluk ☎0363 23477,
✉sunrisejem@yahoo.com. Beachside rooms run by an
accommodating family, with comfy beds, crisp white
sheets and colourful embroidered tapestries on the walls
(upstairs rooms have huge verandahs with bay views).
Great low-season rates and discounts for solo travellers. As
the name suggests, there's a top café too. Doubles
Rp250,000

Warung Family Beside *Sunrise Café*, Jemeluk. The cheapest
tourist warung in the area, with fresh juices and *nasi* or *mie
goreng* with barracuda or tuna for around Rp22,000. The
highlight, though, is the delicious coconut satay shrimp. Most
dishes are under Rp30,000. Daily 11am–10pm.

BUNUTAN

Aiona Garden of Health West end of Bunutan ☎0813
3816 1730, ⊛aionabali.com. Eco-friendly hotel with
charming cottages constructed from natural materials
(rates include a delicious breakfast). There's also a lovely
vegetarian/vegan restaurant, open for lunch (noon–3pm)
and dinner (6–10pm). The menu changes daily, but expect
dishes such as home-made falafel and hummus, crisp
salads and wholemeal bread (dishes from Rp35,000). No
alcohol. They also offer yoga and meditation classes for
groups of four or more. Doubles Rp400,000

★**Galanga** ☎0819 1662 5048. The sign outside says
"fusion food", but don't let that put you off – this is an
outstanding café-restaurant serving great global food. Try
a *nangka* curry (jackfruit cooked with coconut, Rp45,000),
the perfectly cooked samosas or one of their memorable
cakes and desserts. There's great (though pricey) coffee
and tea too. Daily 9am–9.30pm.

Om Shanti ☎0878 6135 6039, ⊛omshantibali.com.
Offering fine value for money, these four very attractive
hillside cottages are supremely spacious with great
terraces and contemporary bathrooms, while their four-
poster beds boast posh linen. It's about a 10min stroll
down to the beach, there's a small pool and the spa has an
excellent reputation. Doubles Rp400,000

LIPAH BEACH

Le Jardin de Marie Lipah ☎0363 23507,
⊛lejardindemarie.sitew.fr. In a lush tropical garden, these
four good-value, thatch-roofed fan and a/c bungalows are an
excellent deal and the French owner is helpful and informed
about the region. Book well ahead. Doubles Rp400,000

Wawa Wewe In the village ☎0363 23522, ⊛bali-
wawawewe.com. The closest thing Amed has to nightlife
– a large bar that gets busy for its live music nights on
Wednesdays and Saturdays. There are two large a/c rooms
to rent (though don't expect much in the way of sleep) and
the food is decent too. Not to be confused with *Wawa
Wewe 2* (or any of their other ventures), which is much
more expensive. Doubles Rp250,000

LEHAN, SELANG, BANYUNING AND AAS

Café Indah Lipah ☎0363 23437. Use the pedestrian
bridge at EuroDive to reach this neat warung right on the
beach. *Indah* does excellent seafood, including great
grilled mahi mahi as well as the usual Indonesian and
European dishes. Daily 10am–10pm.

Eka Purnama Banyuning ☎0828 372 2642, ⊛eka-
purnama.com. Family-run, this is an excellent budget
choice, especially for snorkellers, with robust bamboo
bungalows from whose verandahs you can practically see
the reef fish across the road. Bungalows each have a single
and double bed, fan, mossie net and hot-water bathroom.
Bungalows Rp400,000

Meditasi Aas ☎0828 372 2738, ⊛meditasibungalows
.blogspot.com.au. Isolated, lovely place with a social vibe
(daily yoga classes at 5pm, cooking classes at 11am). There
are eight large bamboo fan-cooled, simply decorated
bungalows with huge sliding screens and private
verandahs and four new luxury rooms with gorgeous
wooden furniture. There's an excellent on-site organic
restaurant, *The Smiling Buddha*. No wi-fi, phone signal or
TVs. Doubles Rp400,000

★TREAT YOURSELF

Aquaterrace Selang ☎0813 3791 1096,
⊛bbamed.exblog.jp. Run by a Japanese-
Balinese couple, this place has three
immaculately minimalist rooms, in a cool,
white, chic bungalow fronted by a
gorgeous pool. As it is set on the corner of
the cliff at Selang, the panoramic views
are spectacular and the food in the
restaurant, including Japanese specialities
like *okonomiyaki* (savoury pancakes,
Rp39,000), sushi and terayaki dishes, as
well as Balinese and international food, is
excellent. Book the rooms well in advance.
Doubles Rp680,000

DIRECTORY

Banks and exchange There are two ATMs in Jemeluk, one in Congkang and moneychangers in the other settlements.

Bicycle and motorbike rental Ask at your accommodation (generally around Rp35,000/day for a bicycle; around Rp50,000/day for a motorbike). The gradients over some of the headlands are quite extreme.

Massage and spa Beach massages for Rp60,000/hr. For more pampering, try the D and J spa, with facials from Rp65,000, across the road from *Three Brothers Bungalows* in Amed (☎ 0818 0555 5484).

TULAMBEN

The small village of **TULAMBEN**, about 10km northwest of Culik, is mainly a destination for diving and snorkelling. It's the site of the most popular dive in Bali, the **Liberty wreck**, attracting over a hundred divers a day. The wreck lies about 30m offshore and is encrusted with hard and soft coral, gorgonians and hydrozoans, providing a wonderful habitat for around three hundred species of fish that live on it, and more than a hundred species that visit from deeper water. The wreck is pretty broken up and there are plenty of entrances letting you explore inside. Parts of it are in shallow water, making this a good snorkelling site, too.

Tulamben beach is black sand and stony and the village is pretty dreary, so if you are not diving or snorkelling there is little else to do. There are ATMs on the main drag.

ARRIVAL AND DEPARTURE

By bus Buses and minibuses between Amlapura and Singaraja pass through the village and will stop where you want.

By shuttle bus Perama (☎ 0363 41114, ☜ peramatour .com) shuttle buses from Candidasa (Rp100,000, minimum two people).

DIVE OPERATORS

Scuba dive centres in the area charge from $75 for two local dives and offer dive-and-accommodation packages as well as trips further afield, to Amed, Pemuteran and Nusa Penida. There's also a freediving school. The following centres are well established:

Apnea Bali ☎ 0822 6612 5814, ☜ apneabali.com. Freediving school.

Tauch Terminal ☎ 0361 774504, ☜ tulamben.com.

Tulamben Wreck Divers ☎ 0363 23400, ☜ tulambenwreckdivers.com.

Werner Lau *Siddhartha* resort ☎ 0363 23034, ☜ wernerlau.com.

ACCOMMODATION AND EATING

Liberty Dive Resort Central Tulamben ☎ 0813 3776 2206, ☜ libertydiveresort.com. Just 200m up the lane from the *Liberty* wreck, the 32 rooms and cottages here have a/c, with large balconies and hot water throughout, plus a small pool and energetic staff. Doubles Rp650,000

Puri Madha Central Tulamben ☎ 0363 22921, ☜ purimadhabeachhotel.weebly.com. Set around an expansive shoreside garden right in front of the *Liberty* wreck. The priciest of the fifteen rooms (Rp500,000) are attractively furnished, with a/c and hot water as well as ocean views; the fan rooms are quite basic. There's a pool and shoreside restaurant too. Doubles Rp200,000

Safety-Stop Central Tulamben ☎ 0812 4629 6152, ☜ safety-stop-tulamben.com. This German-owned restaurant is very popular for its great grilled meat dishes, schnitzel, pasta (from Rp47,000), burgers (from Rp65,000) and huge portions. Daily 10am–10pm.

GUNUNG BATUR AND DANAU BATUR

On a clear day, no scenery in Bali can match that of the **BATUR** area. With its volcanic peaks and silver-turquoise crater lake, the scale and spectacle of this landscape are unrivalled, so much so that UNESCO listed it as a geopark in 2012. It was formed thirty thousand years ago when the eruption of a gigantic volcano created a vast outer caldera that spans 13.5km.

Rising from the floor of this huge crater is **Gunung Batur** (1717m), an active volcano with four minor peaks of its own – wisps of sulphurous smoke drift across its slopes – and **Danau Batur** lake nestled beside it. Many visitors come to the region to climb Gunung Batur, usually for the sunrise.

There's an admission charge to the area (Rp10,000), collected at gateways as you approach the mountain.

The crater rim

The touristy villages of **Penelokan**, **Batur** and **Kintamani** are spread for 11km along the rim of the vast ancient crater and virtually merge. The views across the stark volcanic landscape from Penelokan (1450m) are majestic. Danau Batur lies far below, while the peaks of Gunung Batur and Gunung Abang (2153m) tower on either side of the lake. An entourage of hawkers accompanies the hordes of day-trippers who pass through Penelokan.

About 4km north of Penelokan, **Pura Ulun Danu Batur** (daily sunrise–sunset; Rp35,000; sarong rental available) is the second most important temple on the island after Besakih. It's a fascinating place to visit at any time as there are usually pilgrims making offerings and praying, and the mist that frequently shrouds the area adds to the atmosphere. The aggressive hawkers here spoil the experience for many, however.

Danau Batur and around

Situated at the bottom of the ancient crater, 500m below its rim, **Danau Batur** is the largest lake in Bali, 8km long and 3km wide, and one of the most glorious. Home of Dewi Danu, the goddess of the crater lake, it is especially sacred to the Balinese, and its waters are believed to percolate through the earth and reappear as springs in other parts of the island. Several villages line the lake's shore, notably Kedisan, Buahan and Toya Bungkah, which have tourist accommodation, and Songan, site of an important temple and a footpath up the mountain. Nowadays, villagers survive on tourism and the simple things the gods provide: vegetables which grow in the fertile soils along the shore, and fish.

Toya Bungkah also has a couple of hot springs for soaking stiff limbs; the garden pools in Toya Devasya (daily 8am–7pm; Rp180,000; ⓦtoyadevasya.com) are blissful.

ARRIVAL AND DEPARTURE

By bemo The lakeside villages of Kedisan and Toya Bungkah are linked by bemo to Ubud and Penelokan.

By bus The main road through Penelokan, Batur and Kintamani is on the bus route between Singaraja (Penarukan) and Denpasar (Batubulan). Buses pass through every 30min or so.

Hotel transport Some lakeside hotels offer free pick-ups from the crater rim.

By shuttle bus Perama (☎0361 750808, ⓦperamatour .com) charter service (minmum two people) runs from Ubud (daily; 1hr 30min), Sanur (daily; 2hr) or Kuta (daily; 2hr 30min).

CLIMBING GUNUNG BATUR

Batur remains active and the authorities sometimes close the mountain. Check the current situation at ⓦvsi.esdm.go.id – it's mostly in Indonesian but it is clear if any mountain is on alert. The dry season (April–Oct) is best for climbing.

Anyone who climbs Batur is put under pressure to engage a **guide** from the Association of Mount Batur Trekking Guides, or HPPGB (daily 3am–3.30pm; ☎0366 52362), which has offices in Toya Bungkah and at Pura Jati, 2km southeast of there. A guide is essential for all sunrise treks, which require route-finding in the dark – one solo foreign walker fell to his death in 2010 – and hugely advisable for longer hikes or less well-trodden paths. These routes are tricky and it's important to stay away from the most active parts of the volcano. If you are doing the climb in daylight either from Serongga or to Batur I from Toya Bungkah or Pura Jati, you don't really need a guide, but you will get intensely hassled, perhaps even intimidated, into hiring one anyway. On the plus side, a good guide will provide historical and cultural context to a walk.

Guide prices are displayed in the association's offices: Rp350,000 per person for a 4hr sunrise trek; Rp500,000 to the main crater, Batur I (5hr); Rp800,000 up Gunung Agung (6hr) or up Gunung Abang (10hr). You'll probably have to pay extra for breakfast on the mountain – usually the novelty of boiled eggs cooked by geothermal energy – and transport to the trailhead, if required. Be absolutely clear which route you are doing.

Many tour agencies around Bali run sunrise hikes with pick-ups from hotels, albeit at times no tourist should have to see. Try Bali Sunrise Tours (ⓦbalisunrisetours.com), Pineh Bali Tours (ⓦpinehbalitours.com) or Mudi Goes to the Mountain (ⓦmudigoestothemountain.com).

However you ascend, you'll need sturdy footwear for the rough track and warm clothing for dawn treks.

ACCOMMODATION AND EATING

There's plenty of losmen, hotels and warung along the main road that hugs the crater rim, but as the settlements are scruffy and suffer traffic noise you're far better off staying in the lakeside villages. All the following places are located by the lake and have restaurants.

Black Lava Hostel Toya Bunkah ☎0813 3755 8998, ⓦfacebook.com/blacklavahostel123/info. Owned by a local trekking guide, this impressive, rustic hostel has two mixed dorms (four- and six-bed, with lockers but shared bathrooms) and decent private rooms with en suites. The restaurant serves affordable local food and has sweeping lake views. Dorms Rp150,000, doubles Rp375,000

Hotel Astra Dana 500m west of the T-junction, Kedisan ☎0366 52091, ✉astradana_kintamani@yahoo.com. Well located on the lakeshore, this friendly small place has two options: bright, comfy bungalows with floor-to-ceiling windows in the garden (Rp500,000) or a dozen ultra-basic rooms in the main losmen, with cold-water bathrooms but great views from the first floor. Doubles Rp300,000

Hotel Segara 300m west of the T-junction, Kedisan ☎0366 51136, ⓦbatur-segarahotel.com. Large place, set round a yard, with various grades of comfort, from basic cold-water economy rooms, via standards with hot water (Rp300,000), to smart, newly renovated superiors and deluxes which are worth the extra rupiah if you have the budget. Traffic noise is an issue, however. Doubles Rp250,000

★**Volcano Terrace** Toya Bungkah ☎0822 3744 4410, ⓦfacebook.com/VolcanoTerraceBali. Beautifully designed new place with wonderful lake views from its four spacious minimalist rooms that boast comfort and imaginative decorative touches. It's run by a friendly local family who provide good meals and can arrange guides for the Batur hike and exploring the area. Doubles Rp400,000

DIRECTORY

Banks and exchange There are several ATMs on the main road around the crater rim but none by the lakeshore.

DANAU BRATAN AND CANDIKUNING

Neither as big nor as dramatic as the Batur region, the **Danau Bratan** (Lake Bratan) area, sometimes just known as Bedugul, has impressive mountains, beautiful lakes, quiet walks and attractive and important temples. The area generally caters for domestic rather than foreign tourists, and is pleasantly cool compared with the rest of Bali.

Situated at 1200m above sea level and thought to be 35m deep in places, Danau Bratan is surrounded by forested hills and, like Danau Batur, is revered by Balinese farmers as the source of freshwater springs across a wide area of the island. The lake and its goddess are worshipped in the temple of **Pura Ulun Danu Bratan** (daily 7am–5pm; Rp30,000), one of the most photographed temples in Bali, which consists of several shrines, some dramatically situated on small islands that appear to float on the surface of the lake.

The lake nestles in the lee of Gunung Catur, on the main Denpasar–Mengwi–Singaraja road 53km north of Denpasar and 30km south of Singaraja; no direct route links it to Batur. There are the smaller, quieter lakes of Buyan and Tamblingan about 5km to the northwest, both worth exploring if you have time.

Candikuning

The small village of **CANDIKUNING**, which sits above the southern shores of Danau Bratan, is home to one of the gems of central Bali, the **Bali Botanical Gardens** (Kebun Raya Eka Karya Bali; daily 7am–6pm; Rp18,000), with more than two thousand species of plant, including trees, bamboo and orchids, and a rich area for birdwatching. The entrance is a short walk from the market area, along a small side road. Inside the gardens is the wonderful **Bali Treetop Adventure Park** (daily 9.30am–6pm; $24; ☎0361 934 0009, ⓦbalitreetop.com), with seven circuits of ropeways, bridges, platforms and ziplines constructed up to 20m off the ground. Booking is recommended, weekends and holidays are best avoided, and packages are available from the southern resorts.

Candikuning's daily **market**, Bukit Mungsu, offers a vast range of fruit, spices and plants, including orchids.

ARRIVAL AND DEPARTURE

By bus Candikuning is on the bus route between Denpasar (Ubung; 1hr 30min) and Singaraja (Sukasada; 1hr 30min).
By shuttle bus Perama services drop you at the *Sari Artha Inn* (☎0368 21011), just below Bukit Mungsu market on the main road in Candikuning. There's one daily service to the north of the island and one to the south. All destinations cost Rp75,000.

4

Destinations Kuta (daily; 2hr 30min–3hr); Lovina (daily; 1hr 30min); Sanur (daily; 2hr–2hr 30min); Ubud (daily; 1hr 30min).

ACCOMMODATION AND EATING

Ashram ☎0361 21450. There are rooms of varying standards here, set on a grassy hillside overlooking the lake. The nicest are the ones higher up, which have hot water and great views. Doubles <u>Rp175,000</u>

Roti Bedugul On the main road near Bukit Mungsu market. This café-bakery makes fabulous home-baked bread, sweet buns and cookies, all for around Rp5000. Daily 8am–4pm.

Strawberry Hill Hotel Km 48, Bedugul ☎0368 21265, ⓦstrawberryhillbali.com. This lovely lodge has seventeen stylish little bungalows kitted out with batik prints and attractive furnishings, while the brilliant pub-like bar-restaurant has a pool table, dart board, books to browse and even a log fire. You'll find Western and Indonesian favourites on the menu (dishes Rp22,000–70,000) and you can pick your own strawberries here too. Doubles <u>Rp550,000</u>

SINGARAJA AND AROUND

The second-largest Balinese city after Denpasar, **SINGARAJA** (population 140,000) has an airy spaciousness created by broad avenues, large monuments and colonial bungalows set in attractive gardens. However, it's not exactly a cultural hotbed and of little interest to travellers, but if you're visiting the north you'll probably pass through at some point.

ARRIVAL AND DEPARTURE

By bus The city's public bus and bemo terminals are in the outskirts: Sukasada (aka Sangket) south of the city; Banyuasri in its western edge; and Penarukan in the east. Singaraja is a major transit hub for travel to Java as well as Bali.

Destinations from Sukasada Gitgit (30min); Bedugul (1hr 30min); Denpasar (Ubung terminal; 3hr 15min).

Destinations from Banyuasri Lovina (20min); Pemuteran, Seririt (40min); Gilimanuk (2hr 30min).

Destinations from Penarukan Amlapura (via Tulamben; 3hr); Culik (2hr 30min); Gianyar (2hr 20min); Kintamani, Kubutambahan (20min); Penelokan (1hr 30min; for the Batur area); Tirtagangga (2hr 30min); Tulamben (1hr).

By long-distance bus These buses leave from the offices listed. Most buses leave at night for Java. Menggala, Jl Jen Achmad Yani 76 (☎0362 24374), operates daily night-buses to Surabaya (10hr) and other cities in Java; book

ahead. Puspa Rama, Jl Jen Achmad Yani 90 (☎0362 22696), runs daily night-buses to Surabaya and Malang (10–11hr).

ACCOMMODATION

Wijaya Jl Sudiman 74 ☎0362 21915. Located conveniently close to Banyuasri terminal, *Wijaya* has clean rooms, some with a/c and hot water, and a restaurant. Doubles <u>Rp125,000</u>

EATING

There's a night market in the Jl Durian area, between Jl Dr Sutomo and the main market, Pasar Anyar, in the city centre. Kampung Tinggi, just east of the bridge on the main road east out of Singaraja, is lined with stalls every afternoon (2–8pm).

Gandi Jl Jen Achmad Yani 25 ☎0362 21163. A dependable, venerable, inexpensive Chinese place where the decor could redefine the word "plain". The menu (dishes are Rp15,000–45,000) has dozens of options; try the seafood dishes like *cap cay udang* (shrimp with stir-fried veggies). Daily 8am–8pm.

DIRECTORY

Hospitals Rumah Sakit Umum (the public hospital) is on Jl Ngurah Rai ☎0362 41046.

Post office The main post office and poste restante is at Jl Gajah Made 156 (Mon–Thurs 8am–4pm, Fri 8am–1pm & Sat 8am–noon).

LOVINA

LOVINA stretches along 8km of black-sand beach, the largest resort in Bali outside the Kuta–Legian–Seminyak conurbation. Its shoreline is not startlingly attractive (the dark sand is not most people's vision of a tropical dream beach and there's some rubbish about), but Lovina does have a decidedly Balinese, non-international feel and this ensures an enjoyably mellow, local vibe. The peak season (June–Aug & Dec) is busy, but the rest of the year Lovina is pretty quiet. Snorkelling, diving and dolphin-watching are diversions, and the resort is also a decent base for exploring the north coast and the volcanic areas inland.

The resort encompasses a string of villages. **Kalibukbuk** is the centre of Lovina and full of accommodation, restaurants and tourist facilities. Heading east of Kalibukbuk, there's more of a backpacker vibe in **Anturan**, with most places on or very close to the village beach and a snorkellable reef offshore. Anturan peters out and rice fields take over and you're officially in the village of **Pemaron**.

West of Kalibukbuk, restaurants and accommodation line the roadside in the villages of **Kaliasem** and **Temukus**. Road noise is the enemy here; only consider accommodation set far enough back to block it out.

Brahma Viahara Ashrama and hot springs

One popular outing from Lovina is to the Buddhist monastery, **Brahma Vihara Ashrama** (no fixed opening hours, but rarely closed; donation includes sarong rental), 10km southwest of Lovina, a colourful confection in a wonderful hillside setting and with a glorious gold Buddha as the centrepiece in the main temple. Catch any westbound bemo to Dencarik, where a sign points inland to the monastery, and ojek wait to take you the last few steep kilometres. From the temple you can walk to the **hot springs** (daily 8am–6pm; Rp10,000): head back downhill from the monastery and take the first road to the left. After a few hundred metres you'll reach a major crossroads and marketplace at the village of Banjar Tega. Turn left, and after about 200m you'll see a sign for the "Air Panas Holy Hot Spring", from where it's a 1km walk. Come in the morning to avoid the crowds; weekends are especially busy.

ARRIVAL AND DEPARTURE

By plane Taxis to/from Ngurah Rai Airport cost around Rp500,000.

By bemo To get around the resort, you can pick up the frequent bemos (daily 4am–6pm) that zip between Singaraja and Seririt.

By bus Inter-island buses from Java to Singaraja pass through Lovina, as do Gilimanuk–Singaraja and Amlapura–Gilimanuk services and all buses from the west of the island. The Denpasar (Ubung)–Singaraja services via Pupuan also stop in Lovina. Services to and from east Bali stop at Singaraja's Banyuasri terminal, a short bemo ride from Lovina. As the accommodation is so spread out, it's worth knowing where you want to be dropped off when you arrive.

Destinations Gilimanuk (2hr 45min); Pemuteran (1hr 15min); Seririt (20min); Singaraja (Banyuasri terminal; 20min).

By shuttle bus Perama tourist shuttle buses connect Lovina with tourist centres across Bali; their office is in Anturan (daily 8am–10pm; ☏ 0362 41161, ⊛ peramatour .com), but for an additional Rp15,000 you can be dropped off elsewhere.

Destinations All the following Perama services leave at 9am daily: Bedugul (1hr 30min); Candidasa (3hr–3hr 30min); Gili Islands, Lombok (8hr); Kuta/Ngurah Rai Airport (3hr 15min); Padang Bai (2hr 45min); Sanur (2hr 30min–3hr); Ubud (3hr 30min–4hr).

INFORMATION AND GETTING AROUND

Tourist office Lovina's tourist office (officially Mon–Sat 8am–8pm; ☏ 0362 41910) is on the main road in Kalibukbuk, but only erratically open. The useful community website ⊛ lovina.net has travel tips and accommodation and restaurant listings.

Bicycle rental Several places on Jl Mawar (from Rp20,000/day).

Car and motorbike rental Scooters/cars are around Rp50,000/220,000 per day and available throughout the resort. Established companies include Yuli Transport (☏ 036 41184), on Jl Mawar. To charter a vehicle and driver, you'll be looking at around Rp450,000/day.

ACTIVITIES

DIVING AND SNORKELLING

The local reef is pretty pedestrian for experienced divers, though there's a decent fish life, a small wooden wreck and an artificial reef that's encouraging coral growth. Local dive shops run trips to Pulau Menjangan, Tulamben and Amed, but these involve a lot of time on the road.

Spice Dive Kaliasem beachfront & Jl Bina Ria ☏ 0362 41512, ⊛ balispicedive.com. A Five-star PADI dive centre. It charges from $30 for local dives or $65–80 for trips to Menjangan, Tulamben or Amed.

Snorkelling Can be arranged through any hotel, with boat skippers on the beach (around Rp90,000/person for up to 2hr) or with dive centres. Spice Dive runs snorkelling day-trips to Menjangan and Tulamben.

DOLPHIN TRIPS

Lovina is famous (or should that be infamous) for its dawn trips to spot the resident dolphins. And depending on whom you talk to, they're either grossly overrated or one of the best things on Bali. A flotilla of traditional *prahu* head out to sea at sunrise, until one skipper spots a dolphin or two. On bad days the entire fleet (dozens of boats) chases after them – and despite regulations many boat owners harass the mammals by driving boats right through the pods and approaching far too close. On good days there

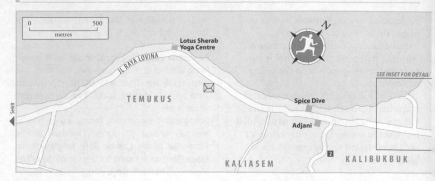

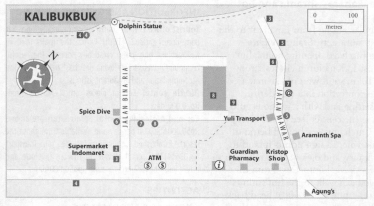

4

may be so many dolphins that the atmosphere is less frenetic and the hunt less aggressive. Boatmen charge around Rp60,000/person for the 2hr excursion, more if you want some snorkelling too; book directly with skippers on the beach or through your accommodation.

SCOOTER TOURS

Bali Vespa tours Jl Kibarak 99, Anturan ☎0877 6245 7772, ⓦbali-vespa-tour.com. Offer fun excursions (half-day from Rp370,000) that take in waterfalls, some hiking and superb scenery.

TREKKING

The most interesting trek is the hike to Sekumpul Falls and nearby villages, 30km east of Lovina. Any number of guides will be more than happy to provide a full-day outing for Rp320,000–450,000/person including lunch, depending on distances. Try Maha Nara (☎0362 27080, ⓦmahanara.com).

COOKERY CLASSES

Lovina has more than its share of cookery classes; most include transport to the morning market in Singaraja plus lunch (obviously).

Adjani ☎0812 3623 2019, ⓦadjanibali.com. Runs classes in Kaliasem, including vegetarian cooking ($35–40).

Warung Bambu Pemaron ☎0362 31455, ⓦwarung -bambu.mahanara.com. Offers various classes ($30), including one all about sweets.

YOGA

Lotus Sherab Yoga Centre Jl Raya Lovina, Kaliasem ☎0339 128680, ⓦlotussherabyoga.com. Runs morning and evening sessions on the beach; the drop-in price is Rp128,000.

SPAS AND MASSAGES

There are plenty of spas in addition to beach massages. These two Kalibukbuk places are recommended:

Agung's Jl Damai ☎0362 42018, ⓦagungs.com. Rp145,000/hr for foot massages.

Araminth Spa Jl Mawar (☎0362 41901). Full body massages are Rp120,000/hr.

ACCOMMODATION

Most of the accommodation is on side roads leading to the beach, with a few places right behind the beach. There are a few hotels on the main road, though they

■ ACCOMMODATION		● EATING		■ DRINKING & NIGHTLIFE	
Angsoka	8	Akar	6	Kantin 21	4
Harris Homestay	9	Bakery Lovina	3	Poco Bar	3
Kubu Beach	1	Jasmine Kitchen	7	Spunky's Bar and	
Rambutan	7	Le Madre	5	Restaurant	1
Rini	5	My Greek Taverna	1	Zigiz	2
Santhika Bed & Breakfast	2	Sea Breeze	4		
Sea Breeze Cottages	4	Seju	8		
Taman Lily's	6	Warung Bambu	2		
Villa Taman Ganesh	3				

are best avoided due to high traffic volumes along here at all hours.

Angsoka Off Jl Bina Ria, Kalibukbuk ☎0362 41841, ⓦangsoka.com. The brown floor tiles, nylon curtains and leatherette chairs do little for the look of the basic bungalows here, but they are spacious and clean, and there's a large pool shaded by mango trees. **Rp165,000**

★**Harris Homestay** Off Jl Bin Ria, Kalibukbuk ☎0362 41152. Sparklingly clean, exceptionally good-value German-run backpackers' accommodation with a real home-from-home, welcoming ambience. The five spacious rooms (solo travellers pay Rp120,000) in the tiny compound are attractively simple and well maintained, with fans and cold-water bathrooms. Reservations recommended. Doubles **Rp150,000**

Kubu Beach Jl Seririt, Tukadmungga ☎0362 336 1159. About halfway between Kalibukbuk and Singaraja, this wonderful beachfront place is outstanding value for money. Gorgeous contemporary rooms have high-quality wooden furniture, deep mattresses and lovely linen, minibar and TV, and tea- and coffee-making facilities. Generous balconies or terraces overlook the Java Sea and rice fields. There's a large pool and restaurant too. Doubles **Rp350,000**

Rambutan Jl Mawar, Kalibukbuk ☎0362 41388, ⓦrambutan.org. Impressive facilities – two pools, a spa, fitness centre, kids' areas and yoga room – give this UK-Balinese hotel real appeal. Rooms are in Balinese-style buildings and there are three spacious villas suitable for families or groups sharing. Standard fan-only rooms are less inviting, however. Doubles **Rp450,000**, villas **Rp950,000**

Rini Jl Mawar, Kalibukbuk ☎0362 41386, ⓦrinihotel.com. Garden hotel with a range of rooms, including budget fan-cooled ones with cold water, as well as a decent pool and restaurant. Doubles **Rp350,000**

Santhika Bed & Breakfast Jl Pandji Tisna, Kaliasem ☎0817 359 993, ⓦfacebook.com/santhikabnb. A quirky, sociable travellers' base with artistic decor and lots of little zones for chilling and chatting. The dorm is mixed and fan-cooled, and there are on-site yoga classes, a small spa and tiny pool for cooling off. All guests are welcomed with a drink, some fruit and a free foot massage. Dorms **Rp150,000**, doubles **Rp300,000**

Sea Breeze Cottages Beachfront, Kalibukbuk ☎0362 41138. In a great beachside position, this small outfit has seven rooms, five of them back-to-basics wooden cottages, all dark wood, bamboo walls and lazy days on the deck. All have hot water, and the best are beside the small pool, with sea views. Doubles Rp430,000

Taman Lily's Jl Mawar, Kalibukbuk ☎0362 41307. Small Dutch/Balinese-run place with a row of six cute, clean and comfortably furnished bungalows in a lush garden. No pool, but all have hot water and minibars. Rooms are fan-cooled or have a/c (Rp280,000). Doubles Rp240,000

Villa Taman Ganesh Jl Kartika 45, Kalibukbuk ☎0362 41272, ⓦtaman-ganesha-lovina.com. In a residential area, this intimate homestay is owned by an accommodating and informed German artist (they're his paintings on the walls). There are four self-contained units, from a cosy studio to sweet family bungalows. All are beautifully furnished and set around a pool in gardens of frangipani trees. Doubles Rp500,000

EATING

Lovina has some excellent places to eat. Restaurants are concentrated in Kalibukbuk; in the other areas, guesthouses offer meals.

Akar Café Jl Bina Ria, Kalibukbuk ☎0362 343 5636. Green in decor and ethics, this cute vegetarian café has a varied menu of imaginative food that includes Middle Eastern meze plates (Rp58,000), outstanding salads, plus juices (try a "Greenpeace" with mint, lemon and honey), teas and ice creams. There's a garden terrace with river views at the rear. Daily 7am–10pm.

Bakery Lovina Main road and Jl Kartika, Kalibukbuk ☎0362 42225, ⓦbakery-lovina.com. If you're feeling homesick, this German-run bakery is the place to come: as well as fifteen types of bread, there are cakes and pastries, and imported cheese, hams and salami. Sandwiches from Rp40,000. Daily 7am–10pm.

Jasmine Kitchen Off Jl Bina Ria, Kalibukbuk ☎0362 41565. Dishes like Penang curry with prawns or red duck curry with pineapple and sticky rice typify the above average Thai food in this small, classy place. Most mains are Rp45,000–70,000. It's also a pleasant spot to enjoy a cappuccino or coconut ice cream. Daily 9am–11pm.

Le Madre Jl Mawar, Kalibukbuk ☎0362 343 5553. This small garden restaurant serves great home-made bruschetta and foccacia sandwiches, authentic pizzas and

---

★ TREAT YOURSELF

Seju Just off Jl Bina Ria, Kalibukbuk ☎0362 706 1888, ⓦseyulovina.com. Splash out on some top-notch sushi and sashimi from this authentic little Japanese restaurant tucked away on a side street. There are also excellent bento boxes, gyoza, terriyaki and yakitori. Sushi sets from Rp55,000, shrimp tempura is Rp49,000. Daily 10am–10pm.

---

pasta (Rp35,000–65,000), plus great breakfasts: try the eggs Benedict. Daily 9am–10pm.

My Greek Taverna Jl Bina Ria, Kalibukbuk ☎0362 339 1503. With Aegean blue-and-white paintwork and a really hospitable ambience, this lively Greek-owned place has great salads (Rp30,000–45,000), lamb kebabs (Rp70,000), grilled fish, seafood specials and super-tasty meze. Daily noon–10pm.

Sea Breeze On the beach, just off Jl Bina Ria. A prime beachside spot for sunset drinks, with an excellent menu of Western, Indonesian and seafood dishes (mains from Rp30,000), plus good cakes and desserts. Acoustic music regularly accompanies the setting sun. Daily 8am–9pm.

★ **Warung Bambu** Jl Hotel Puri Bagus, Pemaron ☎0362 27080. Overlooking rice fields, this bamboo-built restaurant serves fine Balinese and Indonesian dishes – zingy curries as hot as you request, lots of seafood, traditional "Betutu style" Balinese duck or, for a blow-out, a twelve-dish *rijsttafel* (Rp195,000). There's Balinese dancing every Wednesday and Sunday evening, and free transport in the Lovina area. Contact them about cooking classes. Daily 11am–11pm.

DRINKING AND NIGHTLIFE

Kantin 21 Jl Raya, Kalibukbuk ☎0362 343 5635. The bar "where the party never ends", apparently. Either way it's a nicely scruffy, laidback place that gets progressively more boozy (blame the cheap *arak* cocktails) as the night goes on. There are live bands every night in high season. Daily 6pm–1am.

Poco Bar Jl Bina Ria, Kalibukbuk ☎0362 41535. Raucous bar with live cover bands virtually every night, a dancefloor and moderate drinks prices: small beers are Rp30,000 and the happy hour ends at 9pm. Daily 6pm–1.30am.

Spunky's Bar and Restaurant Jl Starlight, Banyualit ☎0337 365094. The bar that sundowners are made for, thanks to a superb shoreside location: settle into a bleached-wood chair and sip a juice, a chilled Bintang or *arak* cocktail. Daily noon–10.30pm.

Zigiz Jl Pantai Bina Ria, Kalibukbuk ☎0857 3844 6086, ⓦalbe.net/de/zigiz/home.htm. A tiny, lively bar over two levels – upstairs provides a nice lounge area – with live acoustic music most evenings plus cocktails (with local/imported spirits around Rp40,000/70,000) and wine by the glass. Also shows major sports events. Daily 4pm–midnight.

DIRECTORY

Banks and exchange There are ATMs and moneychangers throughout the resort.

Hospital The closest hospital is in Singaraja (see p.278).

Police Jl Raya Banyualit (☎0362 41010).

Post office The post office is about 1km west of Kalibukbuk.

BALI BARAT NATIONAL PARK

Bali's only national park, **Bali Barat National Park** (Taman Nasional Bali Barat), protects some 190 square kilometres of savannah, forest and reef 70km west of Lovina and is home to 160 species of bird, including the endangered Bali starling, Bali's one true endemic creature. A few trails are open to the public, but most visitors come to dive and snorkel the spectacular **Pulau Menjangan** reefs. However, be aware that hefty park admission charges and steep fees for guides (which are mandatory) add up to a costly visit.

All visitors must buy a permit (Rp200,000) and hire a guide either through the **National Park headquarters** (daily 8am–4pm) in **CEKIK**, 3km south of Gilimanuk, or at the Pulau Menjangan jetty. Guides charge Rp400,000–750,000 for a two- to seven-hour hike.

If your main interest is birdwatching, opt for the Prapat Agung Peninsula trek (1–2hr) or the Teluk Terima trail (2hr). The Gunung Klatakan–Gunung Bakingan rainforest trail (7hr) is more strenuous but lacking in wildlife.

Pulau Menjangan (Deer Island)

By far the most popular part of Bali Barat is **Pulau Menjangan** (Deer Island), a tiny uninhabited island 8km off the north coast, whose shoreline is encircled by fabulous coral reefs, with drop-offs of up to 60m, first-class wall dives and superb visibility.

Guides, permits and boat transport should be arranged at the jetty in **Labuan Lalang**, 13km east of Cekik, on the Gilimanuk–Singaraja bemo route (30min

from Gilimanuk or 2hr from Lovina). There's a small national park office here (daily 8am–3pm), and several warung. Boats to Pulau Menjangan can be hired any time up to 3pm; they hold ten people and cost around Rp600,000 for a four-hour snorkelling tour – it takes thirty minutes to reach the island. You'll also have to pay Rp75,000 for your guide (one per boat), plus Rp200,000 per person for the national park permit. There are occasional reports of thefts from the boats while snorkellers are underwater, so leave your valuables elsewhere. Pulau Menjangan also features on day and overnight tours for dive companies based across Bali.

ARRIVAL AND DEPARTURE

By bemo All Denpasar (Ubung)–Gilimanuk bemos pass the park headquarters, as do all Singaraja–Gilimanuk bemos.

ACCOMMODATION

The most pleasant place to stay is the lovely little beach haven of Pemuteran, 28km east of Cekik, served by Gilimanuk–Singaraja bemos. Camping is forbidden in most of the park, but you can ask to pitch your tent on Labuan Lalang's beach or at the Cekik headquarters, though there are few facilities at either.

Jubawa Homestay Pemuteran ☎0362 94745, ⊛jubawa-pemuteran.com. Friendly guesthouse with bright and airy rooms, plus a decent restaurant and a pool. Staff can organize snorkelling and diving trips to Menjangan. Doubles **Rp280,000**

Pondok Wisata Lestari 1.5km north of the park headquarters on the road to Gilimanuk ☎0365 61504. The nearest hotel and restaurant to the park, and the cheapest acceptable option in the area, though very basic. Doubles **Rp100,000**

Rare Angon Main road, Pemuteran ☎0362 94747, ⊕rareangon@yahoo.co.id. Indonesian crafts, outdoor

---

DIVING IN BALI BARAT NATIONAL PARK

The clear, shallow water between the mainland and Pulau Menjangan is protected from excessive winds and strong currents by the Prapat Agung Peninsula, and its **reefs** are in pretty good health, despite some damage. The reefs form a band 100–150m wide around the coastline, offering plenty of **dive sites** with drop-offs of 40–60m and first-class wall dives. Visibility is superb, ranging from 15–50m – and as so many of the walls top out near the surface, the snorkelling is good too. While larger pelagic species aren't common visitors, the area is phenomenally rich in sea fans, barrel sponges, sea corals and all manner of soft and hard corals, and is a haven for masses of **reef fish**, nudibranchs, moray eels and other reef dwellers. Reef sharks are regularly seen. Popular sites include **Garden Eel Point** and **Pos II**, or **Anker Wreck**, an old wooden *prahu* at 45m, for more experienced divers.

bathrooms and traditional cottages (with fan or pricier a/c options) lend more Balinese character than usual to this garden homestay. Although across the main road, it is just 200m from the beach. Doubles Rp373,000

GILIMANUK

Situated on the westernmost tip of Bali, about 17km west of Labuan Lalang, the small, ribbon-like port town of **GILIMANUK** is of interest only for its ferry connections to East Java less than 3km away. There are several ATMs in town.

ARRIVAL AND DEPARTURE

By boat The ferry terminal is a 100m walk northwest of the bus terminal to the north of town.
Destinations Ketapang, East Java (24hr service, every 20min; 45min).
By bus and bemo Buses and bemos depart when full from the transport depot across the road from the ferry terminus.
Destinations Cekik (10min); Denpasar (Ubung terminal; 4hr); Kediri (for Tanah Lot; 2hr 45min); Labuan Lalang (25min); Lovina (2hr 30min); Medewi (2hr); Padang Bai (5hr 15min); Pemuteran (1hr); Singaraja (Banyuasri terminal; 3hr).

ACCOMMODATION

Accommodation in Gilimanuk is grim, so avoid staying overnight unless absolutely necessary.
Hotel Sari Jl Raya Gilimanuk, about 800m south of the ferry terminal ☎ 0365 61264. The best of a bad bunch, despite the wailing from the karaoke bar next door. Rooms are big and clean enough. Doubles Rp160,000

Lombok and the Gili Islands

Thirty-five kilometres east of Bali at its closest point, Islamic **Lombok** (80km by 70km) is populated by Sasak people. It differs considerably from its Hindu neighbour, with lots of wide-open spaces and unspoilt beaches, and much less traffic and pollution. Visually it's stunning, with the awesome bulk of **Gunung Rinjani** (3726m) defining the north of the island, offering superb trekking from the villages of Senaru and Sembalun Lawang. But Lombok's

number one draw is undoubtedly its fabled **Gili Islands**, three tropical specks of land ringed by dazzling coral reefs which are a paradise for divers and snorkellers. Gili Trawangan is famous for its nightlife and party scene, but visit Gili Air or Meno for a mellower vibe. Down south, surrounding the small resort of **Kuta**, there's a staggering coastline dotted with largely untouched surf beaches that is a revelation to explore. Lombok's capital, the humdrum **Mataram** conurbation, is rarely visited by travellers except to change buses or visit a shopping mall, while the nearby resort of **Sengiggi** is a tad bland for most tastes, though it does have good tourist facilities.

MATARAM

The **MATARAM** conurbation of around a million inhabitants comprises four now-merged towns (Ampenan, Mataram, Cakranegara and Sweta) and stretches over 8km from west to east. At the western end of the city is the bustling old port town of **Ampenan**, the jumping-off point for Senggigi a few kilometres up the coast. Merging into Ampenan to the east, **Mataram** is the capital of West Nusa Tenggara province and full of offices and government buildings. East again, **Cakranegara**, usually known as Cakra (pronounced "Chakra"), is the commercial heart of the island, with shopping centres, markets and workshops. **Sweta**, on the eastern edge of the city area, is the location of the island's main bus station. Few tourists bother to visit the city at all, but there are some authentic Sasak restaurants and good street markets.

WHAT TO SEE AND DO

The vibrant **markets** offer a great chance to see local life. The Kebon Roek market in Ampenan and the market near the Sweta bus terminal are both worth wandering around, but the friendliest is Cakranegara market behind the Jalan Gede Ngurah/Jalan Pejanggik crossroads.
The best one-stop craft centre is the Sayang Sayang Art Market (daily 9am–6pm), on Jalan Jend Sudirman, with handicraft stalls.

4

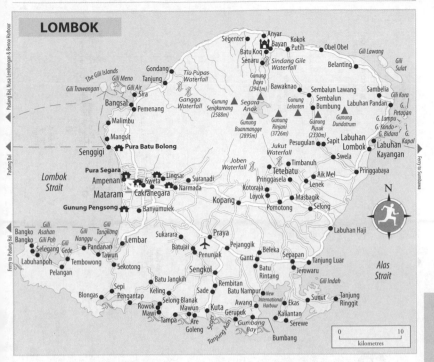

LOMBOK

Lombok pottery has an international reputation, and the Lombok Pottery Centre, Jl Sriwijaya 111A (Mon–Fri 9am–5pm; ☎0370 640351, ⊛lombokpotterycentre.com), stocks a range of products (from Rp35,000) from kitchenware to vases.

If browsing stores in the comfort of air-conditioning is more appealing, check out Mataram Mall, Jalan Pejanggik in Cakranegara, or the huge new Epicentrum, Jalan Sriwijaya, 1km south of the city centre, which has a good food court, cinema and lots of clothing and electronic stores.

ARRIVAL AND DEPARTURE

By plane All domestic and international flights operate out of Lombok International Airport (Bandara Internasional Lombok) at Praya, 35km southeast of Mataram. There are ATMs and currency exchanges here. The airport taxi counters charge Rp90,000 to get to Mataram. Every 60–90min, DAMRI public buses run from the airport via Mataram to Senggigi (stopping at the Mandalika bus terminal; Rp20,000).

By inter-island bus Buy tickets for inter-island departures at the Bertais/Mandalika/Sweta terminal.

Destinations Bima (Sumbawa; 2–3 daily; 12hr); Denpasar (Bali; hourly; 7–8hr); Dompu (Sumbawa; 2–3 daily; 10hr); Labuanbajo (Flores; 2–3 daily; 24hr); Sumbawa Besar (Sumbawa; 7–8 daily; 6hr).

By public bus and bemo Services to and from Senggigi use the Kebon Roek terminal. All other Lombok destinations depart from and arrive at the Sweta terminal (confusingly also called Bertais or Mandalika).

Destinations Bayan (for Gunung Rinjani; 2hr 30min); Labuhan Lombok (2hr); Lembar (30min); Pemenang (for the Gili Islands; 1hr 20min); Pomotong (for Tetebatu; 1hr 15min); Praya (for Kuta; 40min).

By ferry To find out about services and book tickets, head to the Pelni office at Jl Industri 1, Ampenan (Mon–Fri 8am–3pm, Sat 8am–1pm; ☎0370 637212, ⊛pelni.co.id).

INFORMATION

Tourist office The regional tourist office, Jl Langko 70, Ampenan (Mon–Fri 7am–7pm; ☎0370 640471) is unfortunately of limited use.

GETTING AROUND

By bemos Yellow bemos (around Rp3000) ply numerous routes between Kebon Roek terminal in Ampenan and the Sweta terminal. Most follow the Jl Langko–Jl Pejanggik–Jl Selaparang route heading west to east, and Jl Tumpang

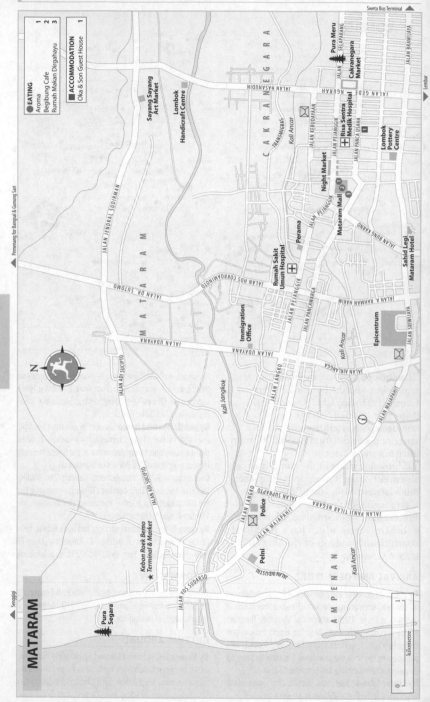

MATARAM

● **EATING**
Aroma — 1
Begibung Cafe — 2
Rumah Makan Dirgahayu — 3

■ **ACCOMMODATION**
Oka & Son Guest House — 1

Sweta Bus Terminal

Pura Meru
Cakranegara Market
Lombok Pottery Centre
Sahid Legi Mataram Hotel
Epicentrum
Risa Sentra Medik Hospital
Night Market
Mataram Mall
Perama
Rumah Sakit Umun Hospital
Immigration Office
Lombok Handicraft Centre
Sayang Sayang Art Market
Police
Pelni
Kebon Roek Bemo Terminal & Market
Pura Segara

Pemenang for Bangsal & Gunung Sari
Senggigi
Lembar

CAKRANEGARA
MATARAM
AMPENAN

JALAN SELAPARANG
JALAN BRAWIJAYA
JALAN HASANUDDIN
JALAN GEDE NGURAH
JALAN KEBUDAYAN
JALAN PANCA USAHA
JALAN PEJANGGIK
JALAN BUNG KARNO
JALAN PEJANGGIK
TRANSMIGRASI
Kali Ancar
JALAN HOS COKROAMINOTO
JALAN PEJANGGIK
JALAN PANCAWARGA
JALAN A. RAHMAN HAKIM
JALAN SRIWIJAYA
JALAN AIRLANGGA
JALAN MAJAPAHIT
JALAN UDAYANA
JALAN UDAYANA
JALAN DR. SUTOMO
JALAN JENDRAL SUDIRMAN
JALAN LANGKO
JALAN LANGKO
JALAN PANJI TILAR NEGARA
JALAN SUPRAPTO
JALAN MAJAPAHIT
JALAN TILAR NEGARA
JALAN ADI SUCIPTO
JALAN ADI SUCIPTO
JALAN YOS SUDARSO
JALAN INDUSTRI
Kali Jangkok
Kali Ancar

N

0   1
kilometre

Sari–Jl Panca Usaha–Jl Pancawarga–Jl Pendidikan heading east to west, although there are many variations.
By taxi Blue Bird taxis (☏ 0370 627000, ⦿ bluebirdgroup .com) are plentiful; the initial pick-up charge is Rp5000.
By cidomo These horse-drawn carts cover the back routes; around Rp10,000/km is reasonable.

ACCOMMODATION

Oka & Son Guest House Jl Repatmaja 5 ☏ 0819 1600 3637. A decent, if dated, budget option, on a quiet street halfway between Pura Mera and the Mataram Mall. A small Balinese-style courtyard has two rows of rooms, some of them with hot water. Doubles Rp160,000

EATING

The night market along Jl Pejanggik, just east of Mataram Mall, comes to life as darkness falls.
Aroma Jl Pejanggik 22A, Cakranegara. Popular Chinese restaurant where the decor is simple and the food (dishes around Rp40,000) is hot and fresh – try the fried squid with chilli sauce. Daily 11am–9/10pm.
Begibung Café Mataram Mall, Jl Pejanggik. Serves up fine Sasak food including spicy *ayam goreng taliwang* (huge portion is Rp48,500), veggie dishes for around Rp16,000 and fruit juices. Daily 10am–9pm.
Rumah Makan Dirgahayu Jl Cilinaya 19 ☏ 0370 637559. A large local restaurant near the Mataram Mall with a big Indonesian menu. Excellent for cheap eats; try the chicken *sate* with *lontong* rice cake for Rp20,000. Daily 7am–9pm.

DIRECTORY

Banks and exchange ATMs can be found in the malls and all along Jl Pejanggik.
Consulates The closest consulates are on Bali (see p.248).
Dentist Dr Darmono, at Jl Kebudayan 108, speaks English (Mon–Fri 8am–noon & 5–9pm; ☏ 0818 367749).
Hospital The best hospital is the private Risa Sentra Medik Hospital, close to Mataram Mall at Jl Pejanggik 115 (☏ 0370 625560). The public hospital, Rumah Sakit Umum, Jl Pejanggik 6, has a daily tourist clinic (9–11am; ☏ 0370 623498).
Immigration office Kantor Imigrasi, Jl Udayana 2, Mataram (Mon–Fri 8.30am–3pm; ☏ 0370 632520). Expect to have to make two visits for your extension to be finalized; the process can take up to a week.
Post office Lombok's main office is at Jl Sriwijaya 37, Mataram (Mon–Sat 8am–5pm, Sun 8am–noon).

LEMBAR

Boats to and from Bali and Pelni ferries dock at **LEMBAR**, 31km south of Mataram. There's little accommodation here and no reason to stay.

ARRIVAL AND DEPARTURE

By bus/bemo Bemos (around Rp15,000) run between Mataram and Lembar.
By ferry Tickets for Pelni ferries are for sale from the Pelni office in Mataram on Jl Industri 1 (Mon–Fri 9am–4pm, Sat 9am–noon; ☏ 0370 637212, ⦿ pelni.co.id).
Destinations (Pelni) The following are fortnightly services unless otherwise stated: Baubau (Sulawesi; 60hr); Benoa (Bali; 4hr); Bima (Flores; 15hr); Bitung (Sulawesi; every 4 days; 21hr); Ende (Flores; 32hr); Kalabahi (Alor; 57hr); Kupang (Timor; 42hr); Labuanbajo (Flores; 24hr); Lewoleba (Lembata; 64hr); Makassar (Sulawesi; weekly; 38hr or 95hr); Maumere (Flores; 72hr); Nunukan (Kalimantan; every 6 days; 20hr); Parepare (Sulawesi; every 4 days; 18hr); Raha (Sulawesi; 66hr); Tarakan (Kalimantan; every 6 days; 13hr); Waingapu (Sumba; 24hr).
Destinations (other operators) Padang Bai (Bali; hourly; 24hr/day; 4hr–4hr 30min). Buy tickets from the office at the port.
By taxi Metered taxis are available at the port or just outside the gates 24 hours a day. Typical fares include Rp85,000 to Mataram or Rp230,000 to Senggigi.

SENGGIGI

Covering a lengthy stretch of coastline, **SENGGIGI**, with sweeping bays separated by towering headlands, is a sleepy beach resort built along the main road. Its plethora of smart resorts attracts older visitors and families, but there are several budget hotels, homestays and traveller restaurants catering for younger backpackers, and a low-key nightlife. The beach in central Senggigi is separated into two parts by a peninsula. The southern beach, to the east of the peninsula, is much calmer than the beach to its west, which is full of locals on dates, food stalls and splashing children. There are, however, plenty of hawkers – keeping your cool and getting to know them is the best approach.

Plenty of operators cater for people who want to dive in the Gili Islands, and operators also take snorkellers on trips (around Rp200,000 per half-day), though if you plan to travel to the Gilis you'd be better off saving your diving for then, when you won't have to pay for transport.

Tour operators along the main strip also offer cycling tours (from around Rp400,000 per day) that take you to the picturesque Sekotong Beach and Pengsong Hill.

4

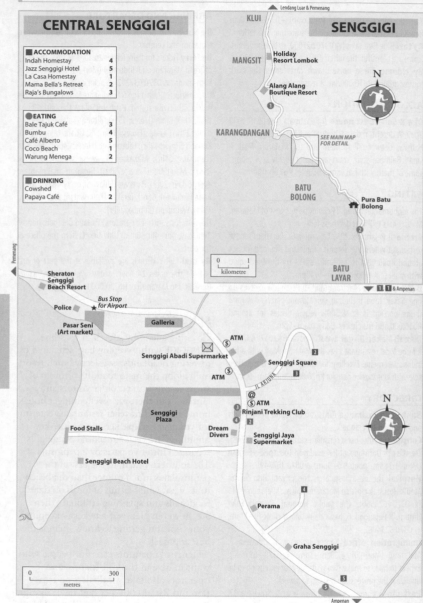

CENTRAL SENGGIGI

■ ACCOMMODATION
Indah Homestay	4
Jazz Senggigi Hotel	5
La Casa Homestay	1
Mama Bella's Retreat	2
Raja's Bungalows	3

● EATING
Bale Tajuk Café	3
Bumbu	4
Café Alberto	5
Coco Beach	1
Warung Menega	2

■ DRINKING
Cowshed	1
Papaya Café	2

SENGGIGI

Lendang Luar & Pemenang

KLUI

MANGSIT — Holiday Resort Lombok

Alang Alang Boutique Resort

KARANGDANGAN

SEE MAIN MAP FOR DETAIL

BATU BOLONG

Pura Batu Bolong

BATU LAYAR

0   1 kilometre

& Ampenan

Pemenang

Sheraton Senggigi Beach Resort

Bus Stop for Airport

Police

Pasar Seni (Art market)

Galleria

ATM

Senggigi Abadi Supermarket

Senggigi Square

ATM

JL ARJUNA

ATM

Rinjani Trekking Club

Senggigi Plaza

Dream Divers

Senggigi Jaya Supermarket

Food Stalls

Senggigi Beach Hotel

Perama

Graha Senggigi

0   300 metres

Ampenan

ARRIVAL AND DEPARTURE

By plane From the airport, a metered taxi will cost about Rp225,000. A DAMRI airport bus (Rp30,000) departs every 90min from outside the Art Market on Jl Raya Senggigi (3am–8pm).

By shuttle bus For travel to/from Senggigi and tourist centres in Bali and Lombok (including the Gili Islands) tourist shuttle buses and boat/bus combinations are often the most economical option. Perama (☎ 0370 693007, ⓦ peramatour.com) offer a good service but do not always run if business is slow. Guesthouses club together with shuttle-bus operators to share rides. Sample fares are Senggigi to Mataram Rp25,000; to Bangsal Rp60,000; to the airport, Kuta (Lombok) or Tetebatu Rp125,000.

TRIPS TO SUMBAWA, KOMODO AND FLORES

Travel agencies on Lombok and the Gili Islands advertise boat trips to **Flores** via **Sumbawa**, **Komodo** and **Rinca**, including snorkelling, trekking, sightseeing and a visit to see the Komodo dragons, with some including diving. Conditions on board are pretty basic and comforts limited. Prices vary, starting at around Rp2,000,000 per person (less for deck class) for a three- to four-day trip. Note that during the rainy season (mid-Oct to March) heavy seas may make sailings uncomfortable, and even dangerous. Be clear where the trip ends and how you'll move on (air transport out of Labuanbajo on Flores should be booked well ahead). Tour operators include Perama (w peramatour.com; contact any office) and Kencana Adventure (☎ 0370 693432, w kencanaadventure.com). **Dive centres** in Senggigi (see below) also run live-aboard trips that call in at Sumbawa, Komodo and Flores.

By bemo Bemos to and from Ampenan run throughout the day (every 15–20min) along the main road as far as Lendang Luar.

By boat The speedboats from Bali to the Gili Islands drop passengers at Teluk Nara, north of Senggigi, but the majority of companies include a shuttle-bus service to central Senggigi in the price. If not, note that there's a taxi desk by the jetty where you can buy a voucher for a share taxi to central Senggigi. Schedules change frequently and are best checked locally in Senggigi or online at w gilibookings.com. Operators include Gili Getaway (☎ 0813 3707 4147, w giligetaway.com) and Scoot Cruise (☎ 0361 285522, w scootcruise.com), which also has a direct fast boat to Nusa Lembongan and Sanur (2.30pm). Tickets to the Gili Islands cost from Rp200,000; to Bali it's Rp375,000–700,000 depending on the company and season.

ACTIVITIES

Trekking and cycling Rinjani Trekking Club, Jl Raya Senggigi Km 8 (☎ 0370 693202, w info2lombok.com), organize various cycle day-trips, taking in villages, beaches, forests and rice fields, from $25–65/person, and is a reputable agent for Rinjani trekking packages.

Diving and snorkelling There's no diving near Senggigi so all dive centres ship their clients to the Gili Islands. A two-dive package costs around $80. Reputable local dive centres include Blue Marlin (☎ 0370 693719, w bluemarlindive.com) at *Holiday Resort Lombok* on Mangsit Beach, and Dream Divers, in central Senggigi (Jl Raya Senggigi; ☎ 0370 693738, w dreamdivers.com).

ACCOMMODATION

Noise from local mosques and bars is an issue in central Senggigi, so bring earplugs.

Indah Homestay 500m off Jl Raya Senggigi, Kampung Loco ☎ 0813 3710 3930, e indah.homestay.lombok @gmail.com. Tucked away down a lane, this quiet homestay has six very neat, clean fan-cooled rooms and is run by a friendly Dutch/Indonesian couple who can arrange transport, motorbikes and laundry. Doubles **Rp200,000**

Jazz Senggigi Hotel Jl Palem Raja 2A ☎ 0370 692323, w jazzsenggigihotel.com. Just inland from the beach, this modern hotel has a/c accommodation including a clean dorm and budget twin room (both with shared bathrooms) as well as posher doubles with en-suites and a verandah. There's a bar-restaurant and pool, and staff are helpful. Dorms **Rp200,000**, twin **Rp400,000**

★**La Casa Homestay** Gang Pura Melase, Tanah Embet, Batu Layar ☎ 0370 692105, e lacasa.lombok@yahoo.com. Welcoming, very inexpensive French-run budget option, set amid coconut groves and paddy fields, 300m inland from the main road. The simple rooms grouped around a pretty garden have fans and cold-water bathrooms. Doubles **Rp140,000**

Raja's Bungalows Off Jl Arjuna ☎ 0812 373 4171, e rajas22@yahoo.com. *Raja's* has five pretty and clean, budget bungalows with fans and attached cold-water bathrooms set in a lush garden. Doubles **Rp260,000**

EATING

The beach at the end of the road to *Senggigi Beach Hotel* comes alive in the afternoons with *sate* sellers.

Bale Tajuk Café Jl Raya Senggigi. Cheerful central place with a big menu of Indonesian, Sasak and Western food (most mains around Rp35,000–60,000); try the *ayam taliwang* (spicy Sasak-style chicken, Rp55,000). Daily 10am–10pm.

Bumbu Jl Raya Senggigi. Small, popular place in central Senggigi. The Thai food (curries around Rp55,000) is

TREAT YOURSELF

Mama Bella's Retreat Jl Arjuna Tiga 11 ☎ 0370 692293, w mamabellaslombokre treat.com. A short walk from the centre, but a world away in ambience, this delightful garden hideaway has gorgeous, very well-presented a/c rooms with minibars, satellite TV and verandahs that face a central pool. It's run by a welcoming Australian couple. Doubles **Rp560,000**

excellent, but tell the waiters if you can't cope with industrial quantities of chilli. There are plenty of other options, including steaks and sandwiches. Daily 9am–11pm.

Café Alberto Jl Raya Batu Bolong ☎ 0370 693039. Beachfront Italian restaurant with its own swimming pool and fantastic sunset views. The menu includes home-made seafood spaghetti (Rp75,000), pizzas, good bread and desserts. Round off your meal with a sip of complimentary limoncello. Daily 7.30am–midnight.

★ **Coco Beach** Waroeng Karandangan beach ☎ 0817 578 0055. Excellent Indonesian home-style cooking, using many ingredients that are freshly picked from the adjacent garden. Highlights include *kare singkong* (tapioca leaf in coconut milk, Rp30,000) and squid. Food is served on banana leaves or from earthenware bowls. Free transport weekdays 6–8pm. Daily noon–10pm.

Warung Menega 3km south of Senggigi. A simple place on the coast, easily spotted by the sign on the main road, with delectable seafood sold by weight or in good-value set meals (from Rp100,000 including drinks). Daily 10am–11pm.

DRINKING AND NIGHTLIFE

Senggigi's nightlife is very sedate, in keeping with local sensibilities: think covers bands singing MOR.

Cowshed Jl Raya Senggigi ☎ 0370 693909. Big barn of a pub, ideal for Aussie comfort grub like pies or really meaty burgers (Rp70,000). Doubles as a drinking den and is a good venue to watch sports events. Call for a free pick-up, and they'll also subsidize your taxi home at the end of the night. Daily 8am–11.45pm.

Papaya Café Jl Raya Senggigi. Lively, friendly bar with live music from 8pm every night, geared at an expat audience. Daily noon until late.

DIRECTORY

Banks and exchange There are many ATMs along Jl Raya Senggigi.

Car and motorbike rental Plenty of places rent vehicles with and without drivers. Check the insurance at the time of renting. Cars from around Rp200,000/day, motorbikes from Rp50,000/day, bicycles from Rp30,000/day. Chartering a car with a driver costs around Rp450,000/day.

Doctor *Senggigi Beach Hotel* (24hr; ☎ 0370 693210) can put you in touch with one. For a hospital, head to Mataram (see p.287).

Police The tourist police (☎ 0370 632733) are on the main road.

Post office In the centre of Senggigi (Mon–Thurs 7.30am–5pm, Fri & Sat 7.30am–4pm).

Shopping The main road has several good-quality craft shops. The art market, Pasar Seni, at the north end of the main road in central Senggigi, is full of souvenir stalls but little art.

THE GILI ISLANDS

Strikingly beautiful, with glorious white-sand beaches lapped by warm, brilliant-blue waters, the three **Gili Islands** just off the northwest coast of Lombok are a magnet for visitors. Of the three, **Gili Trawangan** best fits the image of "party island", with heaps of accommodation, restaurants and nightlife. The smallest of the islands, **Gili Meno**, is very chilled indeed and something of a honeymoon escape. Closest to the mainland, **Gili Air** offers a mix of the two, with plenty of facilities in the south and more peace elsewhere. It's worth noting that there's no fresh water on any of the islands – showers are salinated, except in the more upmarket resorts which transport the water by boat from the mainland.

Accommodation prices vary dramatically depending on the season, increasing by anything up to 100 percent from June to September and in December. Reservations are near-essential in the high season.

Women should take care during and after the Gili Trawangan parties – don't leave these alone. You'll inevitably be offered drugs on the islands, but remember Indonesia has extremely tough anti-drugs laws. There are no police; it's the role of the *kepala desa*, the headman who looks after Gili Air and Gili Meno, and the *kepala kampung* on Gili Trawangan, to deal with any problems, so report any incidents to them initially. If you need to make a police report, go to the police on the mainland (at Tanjung or Ampenan).

Gili Trawangan

Furthest from the mainland, the largest of the islands, **GILI TRAWANGAN**, attracts the greatest number of visitors and is the most developed. The east coast of the island is wall-to-wall guesthouses, restaurants and dive shops. For quieter surroundings, head to the north or west coasts.

Island transport is by *cidomo* (horse and cart), or you can rent bicycles (from Rp20,000 per day) – particularly popular at sunset for reaching the west coast. A

TRAVEL TO AND FROM THE GILI ISLANDS

Most boats to the Gili Islands anchor in the shallows and passengers wade to and fro, so expect to get your feet wet.

FROM BANGSAL

The access port for public boats to the Gili Islands is the hassle-prone town of **Bangsal**, 25km north of Senggigi, a *cidomo* (horse-drawn cart) ride or a shadeless 1.5km walk from **Pemenang**, and served by buses from Sweta terminal. There is no bemo service along the coastal road north from Senggigi to Pemenang.

The ticket office (daily 8am–4.30pm) is right on the seafront; there's a printed price list covering public boats, shuttles and charters. Buy your ticket only from there; ignore anybody who tries to persuade you otherwise. Ignore the persistent hawkers in Bangsal.

Public boats run between Bangsal and Gili Air, Gili Meno and Gili Trawangan, leaving when full (daily 7am–5pm; 20–45min; Rp9000–12,000).

SENGGIGI AND ELSEWHERE ON LOMBOK AND BALI

Combination tickets for tourist shuttle buses and public ferries between the Gili Islands and all main tourist destinations on Bali and Lombok are widely advertised. Perama customers can use the Perama boat between Padang Bai and Senggigi/Gili Islands.

Fast boats depart from several harbours around south and east Bali – Benoa, Sanur, Padang Bai, Nusa Lembongan and Amed – and tickets usually include transfers from hotels all over southern Bali. The sea crossing takes 1hr 30min–2hr in a fast boat, and all-inclusive tickets average Rp675,000; in low season prices go down to around Rp450,000.

Tickets can be bought online or at any tour agent in any tourist centre. Alternatively, the websites ⓦ gilibookings.com and ⓦ gili-fastboat.com have links to most companies. Reliable fast-boat companies include: Blue Water Express (☎0361 895 1111, ⓦ bluewater-express.com); Gili Getaway (☎0813 3707 4147, ⓦ giligetaway.com), Gili Gili (☎0361 763306, ⓦ giligilifastboat .com) and Scoot Cruise (☎0361 271030, ⓦ scootcruise.com).

ISLAND HOPPING

The **"hopping island"** boat service is handy for day-trips to other islands. It does one circuit – Air–Meno–Trawangan–Meno–Air – in the morning, and one in the afternoon. It's conveniently timetabled, picking people up between 8.30 and 9.30am, and returning between 2.30 and 4pm. A return journey costs Rp25,000–35,000, depending which islands you want to travel between. Prices and times are posted in ticket offices on the islands.

4

walk around the island, less than 3km long by 2km at its widest part, takes a couple of hours. The northern end of the east coast is popular for snorkelling: most people hang out here during the day, and there are plenty of restaurants nearby.

ARRIVAL AND DEPARTURE

Perama (daily 7am–10pm) is near the jetty, and many other companies also have stalls by the harbour (see box above).

ACCOMMODATION

If you're struggling to find a cheap place to stay, head inland to the village behind the east coast where there are numerous losmen (guesthouses). Note that hostels are officially banned in Gili T, because of opposition from locals, though some places remain hostels in all but name. Dorms are permitted, but with no more than three beds in one room.

EAST COAST AND VILLAGE

Edy Homestay ☎ 087865624445, ✉ ebungalowsbanana leaf@yahoo.com. A good budget choice with eight neat, clean rooms, some designed in *lumbung* style, in a friendly compound in the village. Hot water and a/c are available. Check out *Maulana* (similar price) across the road if they are full. Doubles Rp275,000

Flush ☎0819 1725 1532. Yes, this place has an unappealing name, but it does have a central location with presentable rooms, either with fan or a/c. Very close to the mosque, though, so not the quietest. Doubles Rp350,000

Gili Beach Bum Hotel ☎0877 6526 7037, ⓦ gilibeachbum.com. Popular backpackers' lodge, by the beach and close to all the action. The very spacious a/c en-suite dorms have good security (doors are secured by a pin-coded lock), lockers and clean facilities, and there's a rooftop bar with regular movie screenings and parties. A decent breakfast buffet is included. Dorms Rp200,000

Gili Nyepi ☎0853 3749 1996, ⓦ gilinyepi.com. Just a short stroll from the harbour, these four delightful

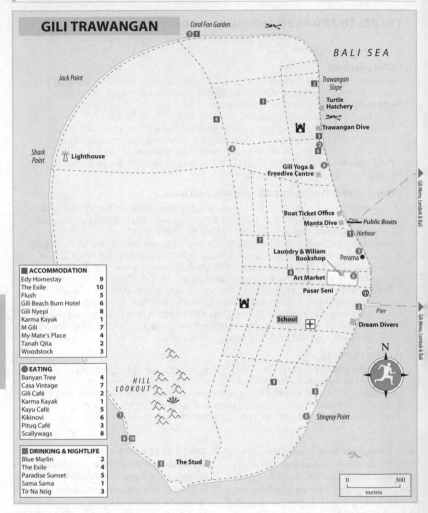

GILI TRAWANGAN

Coral Fan Garden

BALI SEA

Jack Point

Trawangan Slope

Turtle Hatchery

Trawangan Dive

Shark Point

⚓ Lighthouse

Gili Yoga & Freedive Centre

Gili Meno, Lombok & Bali

Boat Ticket Office

Manta Dive → Public Boats

Harbour

Laundry & Wiliam Bookshop

Perama

Art Market

Pasar Seni

School

Dream Divers

Gili Meno, Lombok & Bali

Pier

HILL LOOKOUT

Stingray Point

The Stud

N

0   300
metres

■ ACCOMMODATION

Edy Homestay	9
The Exile	10
Flush	5
Gili Beach Bum Hotel	6
Gili Nyepi	8
Karma Kayak	1
M Gili	7
My Mate's Place	4
Tanah Qita	2
Woodstock	3

● EATING

Banyan Tree	4
Casa Vintage	7
Gili Café	2
Karma Kayak	1
Kayu Café	5
Kikinovi	6
Pituq Café	3
Scallywags	8

■ DRINKING & NIGHTLIFE

Blue Marlin	2
The Exile	4
Paradise Sunset	5
Sama Sama	1
Tír Na Nóg	3

bungalows are set in a pretty garden and have private verandahs, a/c, attractive furnishings and spacious bathrooms. It's owned by a welcoming Dutch-Indonesian couple who look after their guests well. Doubles **Rp650,000**

M Gili ☎ 0822 4765 3384, ⓦ m-gili.com. In the heart of the village, this well-designed hostel has a small pool and its dorms are all in muted colours, with thick mattresses, ample plug sockets, good a/c and with clean hot-water en-suites. In terms of atmosphere it's more laidback than party hard. Dorms **Rp180,000**

My Mate's Place ☎ 0818 0577 9466, ⓦ mymatesplacegili .com. This party hostel is the largest in the island, with a social zone strewn with beanbags, lively bar and fun vibe

(though no pool). Dorms are a/c and have big lockers. Draws a young crowd and its snorkelling trips are popular. Dorms **Rp200,000**

Tanah Qita ☎ 0370 639159, ⓔ tanahqita@yahoo.de. A narrow limestone path winds its way among colourful overhanging flowers, leading to modern wooden *lumbung* with a/c and four-poster beds, and two "backpacker" bamboo versions with basic outdoor bathrooms. Doubles **Rp460,000**

Woodstock ☎ 0821 4765 5877, ⓦ woodstockgili.com. Eco-conscious, 1960s-focused complex of bungalows (each named after a rock'n'roll icon and powered by solar energy) set around a pool and surrounded by fruit trees. Doubles **Rp600,000**

NORTH AND WEST COASTS

The Exile ☎0819 0722 9053, ⓦtheexilegilit.com. Affordable accommodation on the quiet side of the island is in short supply, but *The Exile* offers fine value for money with an eclectic collection of huts, bungalows and rooms dotted around a large plot, all with outdoor bathrooms and some with a/c. Doubles Rp450,000

Karma Kayak ☎0818 0559 3710, ⓦkarmakayak.com. Run by two welcoming Dutch women (one a champion kayaker), this place has attractive, individually styled rooms with hot fresh-water showers. It's across from the beach, with loungers and beanbags on the sand, and kayaking trips are available. The beachside restaurant is beautifully set up, and serves great tapas and sangría. Doubles Rp825,000

EATING

The night market near the pier heaves every evening with stalls serving barbecued meat and seafood; there are also numerous low-cost warung in and around the village.

Banyan Tree East coast ☎0878 6239 1308. A great spot for a budget-friendly feed, with an excellent *nasi campur* (Rp25,000) and salad bar. The (more pricey) healthy-eating menu features dishes including dip platters and smoothie bowls (from Rp55,000) that include lots of berry goodness. Daily 7am–8pm.

Casa Vintage West coast ☎0819 1724 3808. Wonderful boho-chic beach café with painted driftwood furniture and a barefoot vibe. The menu has a strong Carib character: jerk chicken, Jamaican fried dumplings and Kingston kebab, all around Rp80,000. You'll find excellent fresh juices, and there are racks of vintage clothes to browse. Daily 8am–10pm.

Gili Café East coast ☎0813 1694 4000. Appealing place with good breakfast options (from Rp28,000) from Israel, France, Sweden, Mexico, Italy and the UK, as well as salads, sandwiches, seafood and pasta. Daily 8am–11pm.

Karma Kayak North coast ⓦkarmakayak.com. A delightful spot on the beach with excellent, imaginative tapas and meze (Rp20,000–35,000ish), plus sangría. From May to mid-Sept, this is a prime sunset-viewing destination. Daily 8am–10pm.

Kayu Café East coast ☎0878 6547 2260, ⓦfacebook .com/kayucafe. Charming café with panini, salads, pasta, healthy juices and snacks plus some of the best bread and cakes in the Gilis – try their Oreo cheesecake. There's fine coffee, and the interior is a/c. Daily 7am–8pm.

Kikinovi The village ☎0819 1592 5729. A vivacious grey-haired lady cooks up ten pots or so of cheap local food every lunchtime and sells it from her small cornershop warung by the art market. There are plenty of vegetarian choices; a veggie *campur* is just Rp20,000. Daily 10am–4pm.

Pituq Café The Village ☎0812 3677 5161, ⓦfacebook .com/Pituqcafe. This modest-looking backstreet vegan

place has a terrific global menu, with lots of Indonesian influence. Expect creations like *sesamia* (soy-rice noodles with oyster mushrooms, pak choy and baby aubergine). Most dishes are Rp45,000–60,000, and the desserts are also excellent. Daily 9am–10pm.

Scallywags Southeast coast ☎0370 614 5301, ⓦscallywagsresort.com. Fantastic seafood barbecues in the evenings – buy the fish at market price and get potatoes and unlimited salad to go with it (from Rp90,000) – plus open sandwiches, innovative salads, good tapas platters and ribs. Daily 7am–1am.

DRINKING AND NIGHTLIFE

Gili Trawangan is renowned for its parties, which alternate between venues depending on the day, and full-moon parties in the low season. All get going at about 10pm. The southwestern coast is wildly popular for drinks around sunset when big crowds gather for photos at the beach swing near *The Exile*.

Blue Marlin East coast ☎0370 613 2424, ⓦbluemarlindive.com. The big upstairs dancefloor above the dive centre is the popular Monday-night party venue. There are several bars, and DJs play deep house and trance. Daily 7am–midnight.

★ **The Exile** ☎0819 0707 7475, ⓦtheexilegilit.com. This cool west-coast reggae joint has a relaxed feel with potent mojitos, plenty of spots to lounge around on the beach and well-priced food too. Join the drum circle at sunset. Daily 8am–midnight.

Paradise Sunset One of Gili T's favourite sunset-viewing points, where a beach bar sells good mocktails, cocktails (Rp60,000) and Bintang as well as tapas, snacks and rotisserie chicken. Daily 8am–10pm.

Sama Sama East coast ☎0370 621106. One of the liveliest bars on the island, with parties most nights, often featuring reggae acts (check the posters and flyers around Gili T to see what's on). Daily noon–late.

Tír Na Nóg ☎0370 613 9463, ⓦtirnanoggili.com. Somewhat clichéd Irish bar, but perennially popular. It's a barn of a place, with bottled Guinness, darts, movies and

4

BOOTLEG BOOZE

After some bad accidents with tainted alcohol containing poisonous methanol – including several deaths – the bars and restaurants that are members of Gili Trawangan's entrepreneur association APGT have tightened purchasing policies for alcoholic drinks, only buying from trusted suppliers; look for the acronym on the menu. It's still wise to be wary of cocktails that are too cheap to be true – or simply stick to beer, which is always safe.

sports TV plus pub grub. There are nightly DJs (usually cheesy) from 10pm and it's the main party venue every Wednesday. Daily 8am–1am.

DIRECTORY

Banks and exchange There are ATMs and moneychangers all around the coast (every 50m at the southern end of the strip). Dive companies offer advances on Visa and MasterCard.

Books Several places sell and exchange secondhand books, including Wiliam Bookshop (daily 8am–8pm) behind the market.

Health There are several clinics, including Blue Island Clinic (☎ 0819 990 5701, ⓦ blueislandclinic.com) at *Vila Ombak*.

Post There's a postal agent in the Pasar Seni area.

Yoga Excellent daily yoga classes are offered at Gili Yoga, located at Freedive Gili (Rp90,000; ☎ 0878 6579 4884, ⓦ giliyoga.com).

Gili Meno

A similar oval shape to Gili Trawangan, **GILI MENO** is much smaller, about 2km long and just over 1km wide. This is the most tranquil island of the three, with a small local population, no nightlife (except a couple of low-key bars) and arguably the best beaches, as less space is taken up by fishing boats and hawkers.

SNORKELLING AND DIVING ON THE GILI ISLANDS

The **snorkelling and diving** around the Gili Islands is some of the best and most accessible in Lombok, and despite years of destructive fishing practices in the 1990s the reefs remain in pretty good condition. Indeed, there's been good regrowth thanks to a pioneering Biorock scheme which uses low-voltage electric currents to stimulate coral reproduction along steel bars placed in the ocean (at up to six times faster than normal). All the islands are fringed by reefs and visibility is generally 15–25m. The fish life includes white-tip and black-tip reef sharks, lots of sea turtles and bumphead parrotfish.

There are good snorkelling spots just off all the islands' beaches. Snorkel gear is widely available from around Rp30,000 per day, but the condition does vary. Dive companies take snorkellers further afield for about $10–20, and half-day tours of the three islands in a glass-bottomed boat (around Rp100,000 per person) are commonly advertised. The **offshore currents** around the islands are strong and can be seriously hazardous. Dive operators are aware of this, but if you're snorkelling or swimming off the beach it's easy to get carried out further than you intend and then be unable to get back to land. There have been drownings in recent years.

The best **dive sites** involve short boat trips. There are plenty of **dive operators** on the islands, and there's a loose price agreement, so prices are pretty similar. Prices include: $35 for a fun dive (for qualified divers) or $380 for a PADI Open Water course. All divers pay a one-off **reef tax** of Rp50,000 (snorkellers pay Rp25,000) to the Gili Eco Trust, which works to protect the reefs around the islands.

There are also some **freediving** schools. Breath-hold diving (without tanks or scuba gear) is an exhilarating sport, with no bubbles between you and the fish, though you should always take a course with professionals before attempting it yourself.

The nearest hospital is in Mataram, where there is also a **decompression chamber** at Jl Adi Sucipto 13B (24hr hotline ☎ 0370 660 0333).

DIVE OPERATORS

Blue Marlin Dive shops in all three islands ☎ 0370 613 2424 (Gili Trawangan), ☎ 0370 639980 (Gili Meno), ☎ 0811 391636 (Gili Air) ⓦ bluemarlindive.com. The Gili's original dive school, known for technical diving.

Divine Divers Gili Meno ☎ 0852 4057 0777, ⓦ divinedivers.com. In a great, quiet spot on the west coast; offers PADI courses up to Divemaster.

Freedive Gili Gili Trawangan ☎ 0370 619 7180, ⓦ freedivegili.com. Asia's foremost freediving school with SSI courses from $285. Has a 25m-long practice pool and is also home to Gili Yoga.

Lutwala Dive ☎ 0877 6549 2615, ⓦ lutwala.com. Based on the north coast of Trawangan, this 5-star PADI centre has small groups and does lots of instructor training.

Manta Dive Gili Trawangan and Gili Air ☎ 0878 6555 6914, ⓦ manta-dive.com. Offers both PADI and SSI courses.

Trawangan Dive Gili Trawangan ☎ 0370 614 9220, ⓦ trawangandive.com. Works with the Gili Eco Trust and can offer conservation specialities.

The snorkelling is good along the east coast; start at Royal Reef and drift down to Kontiki in the south. Take care – boats come in and out of the harbour along here. The other option is to start at the yellow light beacon in the north of the island; swim left and the current will take you round to the west coast over the Meno Wall and you can get out at the old Bounty jetty, part of the way down the west coast. Always take care if swimming offshore as currents can be strong at times.

Snorkellers can venture further afield by boat: ask on the beach (about Rp250,000 per person for a minimum of two people off Gili Meno; around Rp400,000 for all three islands). Expect to pay Rp30,000–50,000 for snorkelling gear per day. For boat trips, search out Dean (☎0813 3950 9859), one of the boat captains. He'll take you on fishing trips and to see dolphins (best March–Aug & Nov) in the sea off the north coast of Lombok (around Rp400,000 per person). There are also several dive operators on the island (see box opposite).

ARRIVAL AND DEPARTURE

The ferry office is under a tree in the harbour area of the east coast (see box, p.291), and the Perama agent is at the *Kontiki* hotel in the south of the island.

ACCOMMODATION

Gili Gila ☎0812 9149 1843, ⓦfacebook.com/gilimenohostel. Quirky bamboo, thatch and stick hostel-style set-up in the middle of the island that uses lots of recycled timber and original design touches including a sunken eating area and cool social zone with beanbags. There are fan and a/c dorms as well as private rooms; it's run by a fun French crew. Dorms **Rp110,000**, doubles **Rp220,000**

Mallias Bungalows ☎0879 1732 3327, ⓦmalliasgili .com. Centrally located, the beach-shack bungalows here, with fans and cold water, are right on the sand, enjoying unparalleled sea views though they are somewhat dated. Inland there are a few garden-view *lumbung* bungalows; also has a popular restaurant. Doubles **Rp630,000**

★**Sunset Gecko** ☎0813 5356 6774, ⓦthesunsetgecko .com. An inspiring, eco-conscious one-off, with strikingly innovative wood-and-bamboo architecture by the beach on the northwest coast. There are a few basic single rooms in the house and some cheap A-frame bungalows (all sharing bathrooms) plus some standout two-room, two-storey "big huts" with awesome sea views. Minimum two nights. Doubles **Rp280,000**

★**TREAT YOURSELF**

Villa Ottalia ☎0361 736384, ⓦlesvillasottaliagili.com. The best address on the northern side of the island, the wonderful bungalows and villas here have been fashioned from recycled timber and bamboo yet boast all the luxury a sybarite could desire: DVD/TV, fast wi-fi, a/c and minibar. There are free bikes for guests, a huge pool and good restaurant too. Doubles **Rp1,386,000**

EATING AND DRINKING

Diana Café ☎0813 5355 6612. A totally chilled feet-in-the-sand experience with hammocks, cushions and fine views on the west coast. The basic menu of Indonesian standards has good seafood and tasty *olah-olah* (vegetables, coconut and water spinach, Rp35,000) as well as cocktails with local liquor (Rp35,000). Daily 8am–10pm.

★**Pojok No Five Star** Inland off east coast ☎0821 4448 8331. Tiny rustic place with just five tables where the chef cooks up a storm with well-seasoned, delicious local dishes (seafood fried rice is Rp25,000) at very modest prices. You'll almost certainly have to wait for a table in the evening. Mon–Wed & Fri–Sun noon–10pm.

Sasak Café This reggae bar and restaurant on the west coast is a perfect spot to lounge the day away and snorkel on the reef right in front. The food (curries, sandwiches) is not remarkable, but the cocktail list (most are Rp35,000) is worth dipping into. Daily 8am–11pm.

Yaya Warung Just north of the harbour area. Simple shack serving up economical juices, smoothies and warung staples (Rp25,000ish) such as *nasi goreng* and *nasi campur*, as well as grilled fish in the evening. Daily 9am–9pm.

DIRECTORY

Banks and exchange There are a few ATMs on the island, and you can change money in the harbour area, where *Blue Marlin* also does credit-card cash advances.

Gili Air

GILI AIR stretches about 1.5km in each direction and has the largest permanent population of the three islands (around 2000 people). It's a pleasant cross between lively, social Gili Trawangan and peaceful Gili Meno. Tourism is important here, and increasingly so, but village life dominates the heart of the island, giving Gili Air a more Indonesian atmosphere. Although accommodation is spread around most of the coast, it's concentrated on the southeast and northeast corners.

The beach in the southeast corner is popular, with good snorkelling. For snorkelling further afield, boat trips are advertised pretty much everywhere (around Rp100,000 per person including equipment; 9.30am–2.30pm) and take in sites off all three islands. There are several dive operators (see box, p.294).

ARRIVAL AND DEPARTURE

The Perama office (daily 7am–1pm & 2–6pm; ☎0370 637816 or ☎0818 0527 2735) is next to *Villa Karang* hotel (see box, p.291).

ACCOMMODATION

7Seas Backpackers Southeast corner of the island ☎0811 385 1212, ⓦ7seas-cottages.com. The dorms and private rooms here are good value and generally well kept. There's a gym, pool, dive school and restaurant by the beach. Dorms Rp100,000, doubles Rp450,000

Abdi Fantastik ☎0370 636421. A long-running rustic place in a fine location on the east coast; the mainly wood-and-thatch bungalows are basic but have fans and sea views, and there are sitting areas overlooking the water. Doubles Rp375,000

Banana Cottages East coast ☎0181 037 0640. These cheerful fan-cooled, bright-yellow bungalows have comfy beds and lovely outdoor bathrooms (with cold water). There's a small book swap, and rental bikes are available. Doubles Rp300,000

Begadang Backpackers ☎0857 7275 5287, ⓦbegadangbackpackers.com. A well-organized new hostel located inland (off the northwest coast) well away from the bustle of the harbour. Choose from deluxe dorms with four or eight beds, a/c and hot-water, en-suite bathrooms (from Rp200,000), fan-cooled budget dorms or (tiny) bamboo huts. Best of all, there's a superb (mushroom-shaped) pool, surrounded by decking. Dorms Rp180,000, huts Rp250,000

Coconut Cottages ☎0370 635365. A lovely Scottish/Indonesian-run hideaway, 80m from the sea, whose

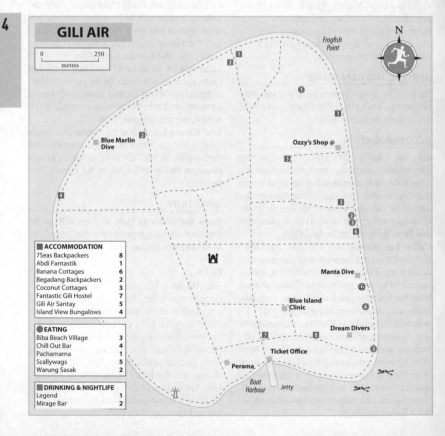

4

GILI AIR

0 — 250 metres

N

Frogfish Point

Blue Marlin Dive

Ozzy's Shop @

Manta Dive @

Blue Island Clinic

Dream Divers

Ticket Office

Perama

Boat Harbour   Jetty

■ ACCOMMODATION	
7Seas Backpackers	8
Abdi Fantastik	1
Banana Cottages	6
Begadang Backpackers	2
Coconut Cottages	3
Fantastic Gili Hostel	7
Gili Air Santay	5
Island View Bungalows	4

● EATING	
Biba Beach Village	3
Chill Out Bar	4
Pachamama	1
Scallywags	5
Warung Sasak	2

■ DRINKING & NIGHTLIFE	
Legend	1
Mirage Bar	2

comfortable fan and a/c bungalows (all with hot-water bathrooms) are secreted among a delightful tropical garden, with hammocks for enjoying the birds and butterflies. Doubles Rp440,000

Fantastic Gili Hostel ☎0877 2966 6957, ⓦfantasticgiligroup.com. Built almost entirely from bamboo, this popular hostel has smallish ceiling fan-cooled dorms (with four or five beds) and mossie nets. It's a short walk from the harbour, and the staff running the place are helpful and offer good island information. Dorms Rp125,000

Gili Air Santay ⓦgiliair-santay.com. A popular family-run spot with good-quality traditional thatched cottages (and newer a/c options) in a shady garden 100m from the central east coast, plus *berugaq* on the beach for relaxing. Doubles Rp400,000

Island View Bungalows West coast ☎0877 6526 5737. If you're after isolation, this rustic family-run place is perfect. Set in a coconut grove facing the beach on the quiet western side of the island, these bungalows come with fans or a/c, private verandahs and hot-water bathrooms. Note that the sea here is very shallow and only really swimmable at high tide. Rp525,000

EATING

Visitors flock to the northeast corner of the island to enjoy sunset cocktails on the beach. Opening hours vary depending on the season, but most places serve food from 8/9am until at least 9.30pm.

Biba Beach Village East coast ☎0819 1727 4648, ⓦbibabeach.com. Attached to the hotel of the same name, this restaurant serves quality Italian cuisine (most mains from Rp60,000) such as home-made pasta, gnocchi and ravioli, plus wood-fired pizzas and focaccia. Daily 7.30am–10pm.

Chill Out Bar Southeast coast ⓦchilloutbargiliair.com. A great spot to hang out during the day between forays into the water. Serves breakfasts (from Rp60,000), pasta, salads, Indonesian favourites and fresh seafood. A small beer is Rp30,000 and happy hour is 4–6.30pm. Daily 8am–11pm.

★**Pachamama** Inland, northeast of island ☎0878 641 5210, ⓦfacebook.com/pachamamagiliair. A lot of effort and love goes into the cooking and presentation at this terrific, pretty café. Its healthy eating menu (reckon on Rp40,000–50,000 a feed) features global classics including Vietnamese-style rice-paper rolls and mushroom burritos, while the *tempe* rice bowls have more of a local flavour. You'll also find superb smoothies, juices and coffee. Daily 10am–9pm.

Scallywags Southeast coast ⓦscallywagsresort.com. *Scallywags* enjoys a prime beach plot and has the island's best seafood barbecues (from Rp75,000, including jacket potato/rice and salad bar), plus great desserts and drinks. Daily 8am–11pm.

Warung Sasak East coast. One of the last locally owned shorefront places on the island. Most dishes are Rp25,000–50,000: try *ikan parapek*, fish with spicy yellow curry, or barbecued snapper. Daily 7am–10pm.

DRINKING AND NIGHTLIFE

Legend North coast. Expect reggae music at *Legend*, which also hosts weekly parties on Wednesdays with live music from 7 to 11pm and then a deep house or trance DJ until 3am. There's hearty portions of Indonesian and European standards, including an especially good *nasi goreng* (Rp35,000). Mon, Tues & Thurs–Sun 8am–11pm, Wed 8am–4am.

Mirage Bar North coast. There's good sunset viewing at this beach bar, with beanbags and seating angled for the best panoramas. Musically they keep things subtle and relaxed with ambient soundscapes and electronica. Also has a pool table. Mon–Thurs, Sat & Sun 9am–11pm, Fri 9am–3am.

DIRECTORY

Banks and exchange There are several ATMs by the harbour and moneychangers dotted around the coastline.

Bicycle rental Ozzy's Shop, on the east coast, rents bicycles from Rp30,000/day.

Clinic The Blue Island Clinic is just inland from the harbour (24hr; ☎0819 9970 5703, ⓦblueislandclinic.com); the closest hospital is in Mataram.

Yoga H20 Yoga (☎0877 6103 8836, ⓦh2oyogaand meditation.com) run daily yoga and meditation classes (Rp100,000). Four- and eight-day packages are available.

GUNUNG RINJANI AND AROUND

From a distance, **Gunung Rinjani** (3726m) appears to rise in solitary glory from the plains, but in fact the entire area is a throng of bare summits, wreathed in dense forest. The climb up Rinjani, taking in Danau Segara Anak, the magnificent crater lake, with the perfect cone of Gunung Baru rising from it, is the most energetic and rewarding trek on either Bali or Lombok. Climbs start from either Senaru to the north of the mountain or Sembalun Lawang to the northeast.

Trekking on Rinjani is not for the unfit. A guide is essential (see box, p.299) and you must register at the Rinjani Trek Centres at Senaru or Sembalun Lawang and pay the National Park admission fee (Rp150,000; ⓦrinjaninationalpark.com). You'll need equipment; bring your own walking boots, a torch, and food and drink (take loads of snacks even if food is provided). If you haven't got a seriously warm, windproof jacket with you, rent one. The Rinjani Trek Centres rent out radios, but increasingly mobile phones are being relied on as emergency back-up; make sure your party has one or the other.

Gunung Rinjani

There are several possible **climbs** around Rinjani, and few trekkers reach the summit – most are satisfied with shorter, less arduous trips. All treks are dependent on how active the volcano is, so check the website (see p.297) before planning a trip.

The shortest trek is from Senaru to the crater rim, from where there are spectacular views across Segara Anak to Gunung Baru, and back to Senaru (two days, one night). For a longer trek (three days/two nights), a path continues from the crater rim (2hr) and descends into the crater to the lake, at 2050m. It is steep and scary at the top, with metal handrails and some ropes, but it gets better further down. You can bathe in the lakeside hot springs, and from the lake you return the same way to Senaru.

The shortest route to the summit of Rinjani is to climb from Sembalun Lawang on the northeast side of the mountain, starting on the track next to the Rinjani Trek Centre. It takes seven or so hours to reach the overnight campsite, *Plawangan II*, and you then attack the summit the next morning. It's an extraordinarily steep haul up to the summit (3hr up; 2hr back down to *Plawangan II*). You then descend to the lake to ease tired muscles in the **hot springs** and return to Sembalun Lawang (three days/two nights).

The most complete exploration of the mountain involves a one-way trip, ascending from Sembalun Lawang, taking in the summit, then the lake and descending to Senaru – this has the advantage of getting the most exhausting ascent over while you are fresh; it's usually a four-day/three-night trek.

Batu Koq and Senaru

The small villages of **BATU KOQ** and **SENARU** (about 86km from Mataram) are south of Bayan, a small town in northern Lombok. There's an ATM in Senaru.

Just south of Pondok Senaru, a small path heads east to the river and **Sindang Gile waterfall** (no fixed opening times; Rp115,000/up to four people, including mandatory guide). The main fall is about 25m high. **Tiu Kelep** is another waterfall a further hour beyond the first; your guide fee includes the walk here too. It's a fine place for a dip; the local belief is that you become a year younger every time you swim behind the falls.

If you are not up to climbing Rinjani, you can instead take part in a half-day panoramic walking tour of the area, organized by Rinjani Trek Centres with a female guide, which includes a visit to a local village (from Rp120,000 per person; 4hr).

ARRIVAL AND DEPARTURE

By bus and bemo Buses from the Sweta terminal in Mataram and Labuhan Lombok terminate in Bayan, from where you can catch another bemo (roughly hourly, Rp7000) or ojek (around Rp20,000) up to Senaru.

ACCOMMODATION AND EATING

All accommodation listed is spread for several kilometres along the road through Batu Koq and Senaru. Bemos go all the way so you can stop outside any of them. All offer luggage storage and have small restaurants attached, serving simple food.

Pondok Indah ☏ 0878 6543 3344, ⊛ greenrinjani.com/ pondok-indah-senaru.htm. A row of basic rooms set in a pleasant garden overlooking a rambutan fruit plantation. Base for Green Rinjani treks, which plants a tree on the mountain during every hike. Doubles **Rp200,000**

Pondok Senaru ☏ 0370 622868, ✉ tiwipondoksenaru@ yahoo.com. The biggest place in the area, with a range of decent bungalows, some with hot water, in a pretty garden with good views and easy access to the waterfalls. Has a large restaurant with panoramic views too. Doubles **Rp240,000**

Simar Selaran Jl Pariwisata, Senaru ☏ 0818 540673, ✉ sinar_selatan@hotmail.com. Basic but good-value rooms, including a decent breakfast to fuel your trek. The manager, Jul, is also a rep for the RTC, so you can book treks from here, with one free night's accommodation and onward transport included in the price. Doubles **Rp125,000**

Sembalun Lawang and Sembalun Bumbung

Set in countryside that is unique in Lombok, the **Sembalun** area is a high, flat-bottomed mountain valley surrounded by hills. **SEMBALUN LAWANG**

ORGANIZING THE TREK

The mountain is **closed to trekkers** during the wettest months of the year, usually from late December to late March, and may be out of bounds at other times if the authorities consider conditions to be too risky. Trekking at any time of year is not for the frail or unfit. Most people sign up to an organized trek in advance with a trekking company.

If you want to organize your own trek, an extremely useful first stop is one of the **Rinjani Trek Centres** (**RTCs**): at the top of the village in Senaru, and in the centre of Sembalun Lawang (June–Sept daily 7am–5pm; at other times opening hours are more hit and miss). They provide information about climbing routes, can arrange all-inclusive trips, and they register and collect the fee from everyone entering the National Park. RTC guides cost around Rp250,000/day and porters around Rp200,000. You can rent equipment, though you'll need to buy your own food, and food for the porter and guide. Be aware that you'll need to start trekking in the morning, so you should organize everything the day before.

Don't forget to bring warm clothes, as it's freezing at the top, particularly when you're trying to sleep, and extra water, as the guides almost invariably don't bring enough.

TOUR PRICES

Prices largely depend on your bargaining ability (though everyone quotes "published prices", you should still negotiate). They should include guide, porters, equipment (including sleeping bags and tents) and meals. Return transport should be included in treks arranged in Senggigi or from the Gilis. Most people pay from Rp1,300,000 for a budget two-day/one-night crater-rim trek including transport to and from either Senggigi or the Gilis (you can often secure cheaper deals).

QUESTIONS TO ASK

What exactly is included in the price?
How many porters and guides are included?
What is the menu? Will snacks be provided?
Will the person you are talking to be going with you?
Will your group be part of a larger group or going independently?

TREKKING COMPANIES

The number of trekking **agencies** arranging all-inclusive treks is bewildering. It is also possible to organize a trip from Senggigi, the Gilis or even Kuta.
The following outfits are recommended:
John's Adventures Senaru ☎0817 578 8018, ⓦrinjanimaster.com.
Rudy Trekker Senaru ☎0818 0365 2874, ⓦrudytrekker.com.
Rinjani Trekking Club Senggigi ☎0370 693202, ⓦinfo2lombok.com.
STT Rinjani Sembalun ☎0819 1777 4082, ⓦrinjanisttlombok.com.

is accessed via a steep 16km road from Kokok Putih (by minibuses, pick-ups or ojek) or an equally steep 16km road north from Sapit on the other side of the mountains. Kokok Putih is accessible by bemo or minibus from Bayan or Labuhan Lombok.

The village of **SEMBALUN BUMBUNG** is 4km south of Sembalun Lawang, with houses clustered around the mosque.

ARRIVAL AND DEPARTURE

By bus Buses run through Sembalun Bumbung between Sembalun Lawang and Aik Mel; all buses between Labuhan Lombok and the Sweta bus terminal pass through Aik Mel.

ACCOMMODATION

Lembah Rinjani On the start of the track to Rinjani beside the Rinjani Trek Centre in Sembalun Lawang ☎0818 0365 2511, ⓦsites.google.com/site/lembahrinjani. Well-established place with simple, clean rooms with verandahs facing Rinjani. The cheaper cold-water rooms are supplied with hot-water buckets for bathing. There's a restaurant too; give them notice and they'll provide cold beers so you can celebrate the end of your trek. Doubles **Rp300,000**

TETEBATU

Set amid picturesque scenery of terraced fields lush with rice in the rainy season and tobacco in the dry, the small village of **TETEBATU**, 47km east of Mataram, is a temperate, tranquil spot for a few days of relaxation. Red-brick towers for drying tobacco are visible at every turn, and there are fine views of Gunung Rinjani to the north. From here you can rent motorcycles and hire guides for local treks; the most popular walk is through rice paddies and the local monkey forest to **Jukut Waterfall** (Rp100,000 per person; 4–6hr). There's no ATM in the village but several on the main cross-island highway close by.

ARRIVAL AND DEPARTURE

By bus and bemo If you're travelling here by public transport, get off at Pomotong on the main road and take either a bemo or an ojek to Tetebatu.

ACCOMMODATION AND EATING

Accommodation is on the main road north through the village and the road off to the east, Waterfall St. Most places have restaurants attached.

Hakiki Inn Jl Air Terjun ☏0818 0373 7407, ⓦhakiki-inn .com. A rustic set-up with eight basic *lumbung*-style bungalows and a few single huts set in a garden encircled by paddy fields. The food here is good and can be enjoyed on platforms surrounded by rice paddies. About 1km from the village centre. Doubles Rp150,000

★ **Les Rizieres** Jl Raya Tetebatu ☏0859 0313 8111, ⓦles-rizieres.com. Charming new French guesthouse that offers fine value and a warm ambience. Rooms are simple yet attractive with colourful bedspreads, the owners serve delicious meals and there's a large garden and views of rice fields and Rinjani. Dorms Rp150,000, doubles Rp270,000

Tetebatu Indah Homestay North side of village ☏0822 3653 4942. A very welcoming homestay owned by Bram, an English-speaking local, and his family, who really look after guests and organize meals and tours at fair rates. Rooms are clean, with mandi-style hot-water bathrooms. Doubles Rp160,000

LABUHAN LOMBOK

The port town of **LABUHAN LOMBOK** on the northeast coast is merely a transport hub on the way to Sumbawa.

ARRIVAL AND DEPARTURE

By ferry Ferries to Sumbawa run every 45min (1hr 45min–2hr) from the terminal, Labuhan Kayangan, at the far end of the promontory, 3km around the south side of the bay (accessed by bemo or ojek).

By bus Very regular buses run along the cross-island road between Labuhan Lombok and the Sweta terminal in Mataram, with some continuing on to the ferry terminal, and there are also infrequent buses between Labuhan Lombok and Bayan; change at Kokok Putih for the Sembalun valley. Travelling between Kuta and Labuhan Lombok involves changing at Praya and then Kopang, on the main road.

ACCOMMODATION

Hotel Melati Lima Tiga Jl Kayangan 14 ☏0376 23316. There are no good places in Labuhan Lombok itself, so it's best to push on elsewhere, but this place on the road to the ferry terminal has rudimentary rooms. Doubles Rp160,000

KUTA AND AROUND

The only tourist development on the south coast is **KUTA**, 49km from Mataram, a scruffy fishing village that's steadily metamorphosing into a busy little resort thanks to a recent influx of surfers and backpackers. The sheer scale of Kuta's main beach, a sweeping expanse of white sand, is certainly impressive, but it's very shallow and poor for swimming. Most visitors use Kuta a base for forays to the utterly spectacular bays east and west of the town. This region of wild coastal scenery and turbulent surf is a delight to explore – best with your own transport (renting a motorbike is ideal).

Kuta is a watersports centre. You can rent surfboards or book surf lessons and tours at Kimen Surf (☏0370 655064, ⓦkuta-lombok.net), while Whats Sup (☏0878 6597 8701, ⓦwhatsuplombok. com) is the place for all your stand-up paddleboard and kitesurfing needs. Dive operator Scuba Froggy (☏0878 6426 5958, ⓦscubafroggy.com) charges from $70 for two all-inclusive local dives. *Mimpi Manis* (see opposite) organizes fishing trips (Rp1,200,000/4–5hr for up to three people). There's also a good yoga school at the *Ashtari* restaurant (☏0877 6549 7625, ⓦashtarilombok.com), with up to five daily yoga classes (Rp100,000/75min).

Around Kuta

The glorious beaches of **Seger** and **Tanjung Aan** to the east of Kuta are, at a push, walkable, though bicycles and scooters are a better idea. Past Tanjung Aan (where a large new Club Med is planned to open by 2019), the small fishing village of **Gerupuk**, just under 8km from Kuta, perches on the western shores of Gumbang Bay. There are some good surf waves here, and boatmen will ferry you out for around Rp80,000 per boat including waiting time. From Gerupuk, there are fine views across the bay to **Bumbang** on the eastern shore, and you can rent a canoe or motorboat to take you across.

Along the coast west of Kuta you can explore half a dozen or more astonishing beaches. The closest is the tiny (but lovely) **Are Goleng**, a couple of kilometres out of Kuta, and heading west you come to **Mawun**, a gorgeous curve of golden sand with calm waters which are good for swimming, **Tampa**, **Mawi** (recommended for surfing) and **Rowok**.

Some 19km from Kuta you reach idyllic **Selong Blanak**, a giant bay with powdery pale sand, good swimming and safe surfing for novices, who appreciate its sandy bottom; local instructors rent boards (from Rp80,000) and offer lessons (Rp150,000/hr). There are refreshment shacks too, so you can happily spend the whole day there. Take a decent road map if you're exploring any further west from Selong Blanak, and be aware that the road deteriorates badly the further west you go.

ARRIVAL AND DEPARTURE

By shuttle bus Perama (agency in the *Segare Anak* hotel; ⓦperamatour.com) operates a shuttle service to Kuta from the Gili Islands, Senggigi and Mataram (minimum two people; Rp275,000 from all destinations). Other travel agency bus transfers are widely advertised in Kuta; a trip to the airport is Rp160,000. Bali destinations including fast boat cost Rp600,000–750,000.

By bemo Coming from the west, buses run to Praya from the Sweta terminal in Mataram. From Praya, bemos go to Kuta. From the east of Lombok, bemos run to Praya from Kopang on the main cross-island road.

By charter transport Ask at your accommodation. Most people use charters for one-way drops: around Rp250,000 to Mataram or Rp350,000 to Bangsal.

ACCOMMODATION

Most accommodation is spread along the road behind the beach or in the village itself; options are expanding quickly, with many new places under construction.

Bombora Jl Pantai Kuta ☎0370 615 8056, ⓔbomborabungalows@yahoo.com. A really attractive place with six pretty wooden bungalows (with fan or a/c) and a large deluxe bungalow with kitchen. All rooms are dotted around a small pool, with decking, and shaded by coconut palms. The owners lead surf trips around Indonesia. Doubles **Rp400,000**

Lamancha Homestay Jl Pantai Kuta ☎0370 615 5186. Ten-room place run by a welcoming village family. The simplest have bamboo walls and squat toilets; newer, pricier ones with a/c are more robust and nicely furnished. Doubles **Rp170,000**

Mimpi Manis Jl Pariwisata ☎0818 369950, ⓦmimpimanis.com. Owned by a very welcoming Balinese-English family, this tiny, spotless homestay, 2km north of the beach (with free daytime transport), is very good value – though it is on a busy junction. There's a fan-cooled dorm with five beds, and choice of private rooms (one has a/c), all (except the dorm) with DVD players. Dorms **Rp100,000**, doubles **Rp150,000**

Segare Anak Jl Pantai Kuta ☎0370 654846, ⓦkutalombok.com. Long-established place with selection of rooms in many different styles and standards. Bottom-end options are very basic (with squat toilets), but some of the mid-priced ones are good quality and a few have a/c. There's a dinky pool and travel services. Doubles **Rp170,000**

Sekar Kuning Jl Pariwisata ☎0370 654856. A cheapie with basic rooms with fans and cold-water bathrooms and some a/c options (Rp250,000). The decor isn't fancy and rooms (in two-storey blocks) could be a tad cleaner, but they are a good size and some of the upstairs ones have partial sea views. Doubles **Rp150,000**

The Spot ☎0370 615 8100, ⓦthespotbungalows.com. Small, attractive bamboo-and-thatch bungalows (each with a private deck and hammock), as well as a grassy communal area for socializing and a small bar-restaurant. Doubles **Rp180,000**

★**Yuli's Homestay** Jl Pariwisata ☎0819 1710 0983, ⓦyulishomestay.com. An extremely well-run and popular place owned by a charming New Zealand-Lombok couple. Its spotless rooms – all with a/c and cold-water bathrooms – are dotted around a huge grassy plot with two pools. There's a shared hot shower block and a communal kitchen too. Doubles **Rp400,000**

EATING AND NIGHTLIFE

The village has plenty of generic pizza joints and traveller cafés to choose from. The beach road is lined with candlelit warung that have nightly barbecues and inexpensive seafood; all serve until about 10pm. Nightlife mostly consists of a couple of local bands that play at one or other of the restaurant bars several nights a week.

★**Ashtari** ☎0877 6549 7625, ⓦashtarilombok.com. Occupying a spectacular panoramic hilltop position 3km west of central Kuta on the Mawun road, with breathtaking views over the Kuta coastline, this boho hangout is a great place to chill. The (fairly healthy) menu lists fine breakfasts, focaccia sandwiches (Rp50,000), grilled fish and salads, juices and cake. They also run excellent yoga sessions here (see p.300). Daily 6.30am–8.30pm.

Café 7 JI Pantai Kuta ☎0817 575 5808. Good, hearty servings of pasta, plus pizzas, deep-fried prawns (Rp45,000) and cocktails (Rp50,000). There's often a nice relaxed buzz in the evening, with shisha pipes and live music on Monday and Friday. Daily noon–11pm.

★ **El Bazaar** JI Raya Kuta 5 ☎0819 9911 3026. Offering excellent Middle Eastern food including tagines and kebabs as well as an outstanding meze platter (Rp75,000) which takes in pita bread, hummus, couscous, carrots with honey and mustard dressing, cumin potatoes in olive oil and baba ganoush, and is almost enough for two. Also serves espresso coffee. Daily 7.30am–11pm.

Nana's JI Mawun 16. Recommended for excellent, affordable Indonesian food, including vegetarian *nasi pecel* (tofu, rice, *tempe*, veg and peanut sauce) and a killer "banana beng beng" dessert, prepared with a Beng Beng chocolate bar. Daily 8am–11pm.

Sonya's ☎0819 1717 2941. This beach warung serves up great chicken satay, fish curry and *nasi campur* (all around Rp25,000–30,000) and has customers returning night after night. They also refill water bottles and have an all-you-can-eat seafood barbecue every Friday night. Daily 8am–10pm.

Warung Jawa 1 JI Pantai Kuta. A simple open-fronted warung serving great, cheap Javanese food and Indo classics. Try their grilled mahi mahi or village chicken (both Rp30,000). Daily 8am–11pm.

DIRECTORY

Banks and exchange There are several ATMs.
Bicycle rental From Rp30,000/day from guesthouses.
Motorcycle rental From Rp50,000/day from most guesthouses.

Sumbawa

Most travellers crossing the scorched, mountainous island of **SUMBAWA**, east of Lombok, experience it solely through the window of a long-distance bus. But transit travel doesn't do justice to this friendly, laidback island, with its fine beaches and surfing, offshore islands and traditional villages.

Historically, Sumbawa was divided between east and west, with the western

---

GETTING TO SUMBAWA

Ferries to and from **Lombok** (every 45min; 1hr 45min–2hr) run all day and all night and dock at Poto Tano; buses meet all incoming ferries and run south from the harbour to Sumbawa Besar (2hr 30min), and sometimes all the way to Bima (9hr); it's easy to change at Sumbawa Besar if not. Ferries to and from **Flores** (2 daily; 6–9hr) and **Sumba** (2 weekly; 9–12hr) use the port at Sape. Pelni ferries dock at Bima. Lion Air/Wings Air fly twice daily from Denpasar to Bima. From Lombok there are around six **flights** per day to Sumbawa Besar, courtesy of Garuda Indonesia or Lion Air/Wings Air.

Sumbawans influenced by the Balinese and Sasaks of Lombok, and the eastern Bimans sharing linguistic and cultural similarities with the Makarese of Sulawesi and the peoples of Flores and Sumba. The whole island is Muslim, however, and conservative dress is recommended.

Sumbawa has been a bit unsettled in recent years, with riots in Sumbawa Besar in 2013 and 2015, so check the security situation before your trip.

SUMBAWA BESAR

SUMBAWA BESAR, usually referred to simply as Sumbawa, is the island's capital, although it sprawls without a real centre. The main streets run on a one-way loop, forming a convenient racetrack for ojek drivers in the evenings, although the side streets are quiet and leafy. The area around the Sultan's Palace, to the south of town, is a particularly pleasant place to wander, where luxurious modern mansions sit side by side with old wooden huts on tiny, colourful alleys. You're welcome to walk through the palace itself, an elaborate stilted wooden mansion at Jalan Dalam Loka 1; ask the guard to unlock it for you (daily 8am–5pm; free).

Moyo Island

The main attraction around Sumbawa Besar is **MOYO ISLAND**, home to deer, buffalo, wild pigs and vast numbers of bird species. The island sits in a nature

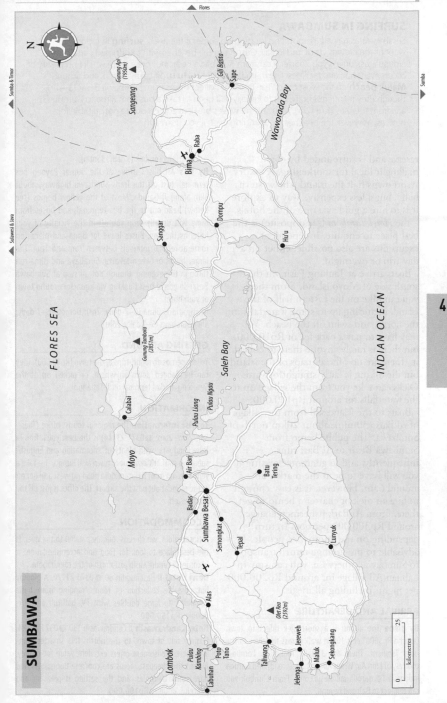

SUMBAWA

Flores

N

Gunung Api
(1950m)
Sangeang

Gili Banta
Sape

Waworada Bay

Raba
Bima

FLORES SEA

Dompu

Sanggar

Hu'u

Gunung Tambora
(2851m)

Pulau Liang
Pulau Ngau

Saleh Bay

INDIAN OCEAN

Calabai

Moyo

Air Bari

Badas

Sumbawa Besar
Semongkat
Tepal

Batu
Tering

Lunyuk

Alas

Olet Ifea
(2592m)

Pulau
Kambing

Poto
Tano

Taliwang

Jereweh
Maluk
Sekongkang

Lombok

Labuhan

Jelenga

4

Sumba & Timor

Sulawesi & Java

Sumba

0   25
kilometres

SURFING IN SUMBAWA

Sumbawa has gained a reputation for offering some of the finest **surfing** in Indonesia, without the crowds you'll find in Bali. Getting to the beaches with a surfboard can be an arduous task unless you charter a car from Sumbawa Besar, but once there you'll find plenty of accommodation and facilities. The main breaks are at **Hu'u**, off Lakey beach, and around **Maluk beach** on the west coast. The latter has direct buses from Sumbawa Besar (3–4hr), though they're infrequent. To get to Hu'u, you'll need to take a bus from Bima to Dompu (3hr), and from there to Hu'u (2hr). Many of the waves break over reefs, so are not suitable for novices; however, the beaches are stunning even if you don't surf.

reserve and is surrounded by coral, making it ideal for snorkelling. A luxury resort owns half the island (the western half), but a less expensive way to explore it is to hire a guide via one of the hotels – the *Hotel Tambora* (see opposite) is the best place to enquire. Independent excursions are also possible, either on a day-trip or overnight.

Boats arrive at Tanjung Pasir, on the south side of Moyo Island. From there you can hike on the eastern half of the island, including up to some waterfalls in the north, and swim off the beach. You may have to pay a park fee of Rp10,000, but there is rarely anyone there to collect it. There are no official maps of the island, but the hiking is fairly straightforward. Ojeks can take you from the village up to the waterfalls for around Rp100,000.

Boats to the island sail from the village of Ai Bari (30min), about 20km north of Sumbawa. The public bemo from Sumbawa Besar to Ai Bari runs infrequently, and to guarantee getting it you will have to be at the market at around 6am. However, it is easy enough to hire an ojek or charter a bemo to get there. From Ai Bari, fishermen charge around Rp300,000 per boat (return), depending on the number of people. It's advisable to pre-arrange return transport to Sumbawa; otherwise, you can stay in Labuan Aji village for around Rp200,000 per night, including all meals.

ARRIVAL AND DEPARTURE

By plane The airport is a short ojek ride into town (around Rp5000) or a 10min walk across the river to the *Hotel Tambora*. There are 3 daily flights to Lombok, courtesy of Lion Air/Wings Air (🌐 lionair.co.id) and Garuda Indonesia (🌐 garuda-indonesia.com). From Lombok you can connect to Bali and beyond.

Destinations Lombok (3 daily; 35min).

By bus All buses arrive at the Sumer Payong bus terminal, just off the Trans-Sumbawa highway, about 3km along Jl Garuda. Most of the yellow bemos (see below) head out to the bus terminal, and buses from Bima will usually drop you off in the vicinity of your hotel as they go. Buses leave for Bima and places en route at regular intervals between 7am and 1pm. The larger buses between Jakarta, Surabaya and Bima run through the evening, though not all stop at Sumbawa Besar so you're best booking via agencies around town or your hotel.

Destinations Bima (6–7 daily; 7hr); Dompu (6–7 daily; 5hr); Surabaya (5–7 daily; 26hr).

GETTING AROUND

Yellow bemos do round-trips of the town (Rp10,000). They can be flagged down anywhere, or picked up at the Seketeng market terminal on Jl Setiabudi.

INFORMATION

Tourist information The regional tourist office (Tues–Sun 7am–2pm; ☎ 0371 23714) is the best you'll find in Nusa Tenggara, with plenty of information and English-speaking staff. It's 2km out of town at Jl Bungur 1 – take a yellow bemo from Jl Hasanuddin heading west and get off at the roundabout past the airport. The office is just off the left turn-off.

ACCOMMODATION

Jl Hasanuddin, which runs roughly parallel to the river, is the best place to look for food and accommodation; it becomes Jl Cendrawasih just north of the roundabout.

Dewi Hotel Jl Hasanuddin 60 ☎ 0371 21170. A gloomy but passable collection of rooms ranging from basic "*ekonomi*" to large doubles with TV, bathtub and a/c. Doubles **Rp150,000**

Hotel Cendrawasih Jl Cendrawasih 130 ☎ 0371 24184. Slightly out of town, to the north, this smarter-than-average establishment offers excellent value for money. All but the cheapest rooms are concrete bungalows and have small balconies, and the setting is pleasant and peaceful. Doubles **Rp100,000**

★**Hotel Tambora** Jl Kebayan ☎ 0371 21555. The best option in town, with rooms ranging from basic to mid-range. Bizarrely, the cheapest rooms have Western toilets and a quiet location at the back, while the mid-range ones, with squat toilets, face the busy reception. The friendly staff are an excellent source of information. Doubles **Rp150,000**

EATING

Jl Hasanuddin is lined with restaurants, and you can also find plenty of warung around town, with the main cluster next to the stadium.

Laros Janis Jl Kebayan 2. This friendly restaurant, tucked away from the main road, serves up classic Indonesian fare like *lalapan*, *bakso* and *soto daging*, accompanied by fiery *sambals*. Dishes from Rp15,000. Daily 8am–10pm.

DIRECTORY

Banks BNI bank on Jl Kartini is the best place to change foreign currency or travellers' cheques; it offers better rates than most banks further east in Nusa Tenggara. There's another BNI beside the roundabout and several ATMs around town, including outside the *Hotel Tambora*.
Internet Yours.net, Jl Garuda 162 (Rp6000/hr).
Pharmacy Kimia Farma, Jl Cendrawasih 1.
Post office Jl Yos Sudarso 101 (Mon–Thurs 8am–3pm, Fri 8–11am & Sat 8am–1pm).

BIMA

The rather sleepy port of **BIMA** is the largest town on Sumbawa. Its people have a strong sense of Bimanese identity, offering an insight into the patchwork of ethnicities you'll find throughout Nusa Tenggara. The town is centred around the market on Jalan Flores; most of the accommodation lies to the west of the **Sultan's Palace**, whose museum (Mon–Sat 8am–5pm; Rp3000) houses a collection of traditional costumes, weapons and royal paraphernalia. The area around Bima, Wawo, boasts a distinct style of traditional thatched house; examples can be seen at Maria and Sambori, both on the Bima–Sape bus route. If you need to relax on the beach after a hard day's travel, charter a boat (15min; around Rp80,000–100,000 return) from the harbour out to the island of **Pulau Kambing**, where you'll find relative seclusion.

ARRIVAL AND DEPARTURE

By plane The airport is 20km away on the main road to Sumbawa Besar. Buses stop in both directions, and taxis meet arrivals. Lion Air/Wings Air (☎ lionair.co.id) has 2 daily flights to Bali and Lombok. Garuda Indonesia (☎ garuda-indonesia.com) also has 2 daily flights to Lombok.
Destinations Bali (2 daily; 1hr 15min); Lombok (2 daily; 1hr).
By bus Most buses to Bima arrive at the bus terminal just south of town, a short walk or bemo ride to the centre. There are several night-bus agents on Jl Pasar that offer a/c and standard buses to all major destinations, including Mataram and Sumbawa Besar. Buses to Sape leave roughly hourly from the main bus terminal.
Destinations Mataram via Sumbawa Besar (1–2 daily; 12hr); Sape (hourly; 1hr 30min); Sumbawa Besar (6–7 daily; 7hr).
By ferry Pelni ferries dock at the harbour, 2km west of Bima and served by dokar and bemo. The Pelni office is about 1.5km out of the centre at Jl Kesatria 2 (☎ 0374 42046, ☎ pelni.co.id), by the port, though you can also book tickets in town through the agent at Jl Kaharuddin 36. If you need to catch one of the early-morning ferries from Sape to Labuanbajo, tell your hotel the night before and the bus to Sape should pick you up at 4am.
Destinations Makassar (2 weekly; 28hr); Surabaya (Sun; 49hr); Waingapu (Fri; 13hr); Kupang (2 weekly; 39hr).

INFORMATION

Tourist office Jl Gajah Mada, about 2km east of town just before the bridge (Mon–Sat 8am–2pm; ☎ 0374 44331). English-speaking and helpful; to get here, catch a blue bemo heading east from the BNI bank on Jl Hasanuddin.

ACCOMMODATION AND EATING

Bima is distinctly lacking in proper restaurants, but there are plenty of warung and Padang places, especially around the market. Be warned that it's hard to find anything to eat after 9pm.
Hotel Favorit Jl Pahlawan Dara ☎ 0374 45285. Conveniently if noisily located next to the bus station, with clean rooms at very low rates – even the cheapest have showers. Doubles **Rp100,000**
Hotel Lambitu Jl Sumbawa 4 ☎ 0374 42222. By far the best budget option in town, with large clean rooms in a cool, airy building, and small suites available from Rp350,000. Doubles **Rp160,000**
Lila Graha Jl Lombok 20 ☎ 0374 42740. Dingy and old-fashioned, this is nevertheless an acceptable option in the mire of Bima's accommodation choices; it's worth spending a bit extra to get one of the a/c rooms with TVs. Decent restaurant too. Doubles **Rp200,000**

DIRECTORY

Banks The BNI on Jl Hasanuddin changes foreign currency and travellers' cheques. There are lots of ATMs along Jl Sumbawa and Jl Soekarno Hatta.

4

Internet There's a Warnet at Jl Monginsidi 8 (Rp12,000/hr).
Pharmacy Kimia Farma, Jl Soekarno Hatta 20.
Post office Jl Hasanuddin, cnr Jl Datuk Dibanta (Mon–Sat 8am–3pm).

SAPE

SAPE, Sumbawa's gateway to Flores, is a quiet, dusty town where livestock wander the streets and local fishermen ply the harbour at dusk. There isn't much to see, but it is a pleasant enough place to stay the night. Nearby **Gili Banta** makes a good day-trip, with nice beaches and a burgeoning turtle population; if you get a group together, you can charter a boat there from the harbour for around Rp100,000–150,000 per person. Otherwise, there's the dark-sand Papa Beach, 10km out of town, which is a peaceful spot for a picnic; take an ojek. Most of the town's facilities, including the post office and an ATM, are on the main road down to the port.

ARRIVAL AND DEPARTURE

By bus Buses to and from Bima (hourly till 3pm; 2hr; Rp30,000) operate from Sape harbour; from Bima it's easy enough to catch onward transport to Sumbawa Besar or Lombok.
By ferry The ASDP ferry office is at the harbour, about 2km east of the centre (☏0374 71075). There are two daily ferry services to Labuanbajo on Flores (8am & 4pm; 6–9hr), and daily services to Waikelo on Sumba (10pm; 9–12hr).

ACCOMMODATION AND EATING

Arema Jl Yos Sudarso, next to *Losmen Mutiara*. The best place to eat, with rice and noodle dishes from Rp15,000 and internet access. Daily 9am–9pm.
Losmen Mutiara Jl Yos Sudarso ☏0374 71337. Right next to the harbour gate, this is the best-established hotel in town and the one that most travellers head to, but rooms are average and staff can be apathetic. Doubles <u>Rp70,000</u>

Komodo and Rinca

Off the west coast of Flores lies **Komodo National Park**, a group of parched but majestic islands that are home to the Komodo dragon – or *ora*, as it is known

locally – which lives nowhere else. The south coast of the main island is lined with impressive, mostly dormant, volcanoes; the north is covered mainly in dusty plains, irrigated to create rice paddies around the major settlements. The two most-visited islands in the national park are **Komodo** and **Rinca**.

KOMODO

Most visitors to **Komodo Island** offload at the PHPA (park service) camp at **LOH LIANG**, where you'll find all the facilities. Although the practice of feeding live goats to the dragons stopped a long time ago, you may still feel as if you've stepped straight into *Jurassic Park* if your visit coincides with big tour groups. The longer treks around the island, especially out of high season, should guarantee you some peace and quiet, and with a good guide you can enjoy the full primordial experience. Received wisdom has it that the dragons on Komodo are bigger than on Rinca, but harder to spot.

Treks and excursions

The full-day's walk from the PHPA camp to the top of **Gunung Ara**, the highest point on the island, doesn't promise dragon sightings, but it is absolutely extraordinary. It's an arduous, excruciatingly hot march, but you'll see scores of unusual plants, animals and birdlife, such as sulphur-crested cockatoos, brush turkeys and the

---

THE KOMODO DRAGON

Varanus komodoensis, the **Komodo dragon**, is the largest extant lizard in the world. The biggest recorded specimen was well over 3m long and weighed a mammoth 150kg, but most fully grown males are around 2m and 60kg. The dragon usually strikes down prey with its immensely powerful tail or slices the leg tendons with scalpel-sharp fangs. Once the animal is incapacitated, the dragon eviscerates it, feeding on its intestines while it slowly dies. With larger prey, the dragon may simply bite the animal, then trail it until the wound becomes fatally infected from the reptile's toxic saliva.

VISITING KOMODO AND RINCA

The best way to reach Komodo and Rinca is by organizing a trip **from Labuanbajo on Flores** (see p.308), although there are also cruises to Sumbawa, Komodo and Flores **from Lombok** (see box, p.308). A host of agencies compete for tourists, so it's worth shopping around or asking for recommendations. Most people are content with a **day-trip** to Rinca, which costs from Rp400,000 per person, not including park entry fees. A **two-day trip**, including both Komodo and Rinca, snorkelling, meals and a night on the boat, costs from Rp800,000 per person. It's also possible to visit both islands independently by chartering a boat from Labuanbajo (around Rp800,000 return), though rough waters can make small fishing boats a bit risky.

The PHPA charges foreigners Rp150,000 for **entry** to the park between Monday and Saturday, and Rp220,000 on Sundays; in addition, there are additional fees for conservation (Rp20,000), camera (Rp50,000) and, if you want to explore beyond the short, free guided tour, guide (Rp50,000 per person, extra if you want to trek for more than one hour). These fees are rarely included in the price negotiated with the boat owner/travel agent, so bring enough money and plenty of small change. On all excursions around the islands a guide is necessary. Treks around the national park should reward you with sightings of wild horses, deer, wild pigs and, on Rinca, macaques, but trekking on both islands can be hot and tiring, so bring decent footwear and plenty of water.

There is a handful of simple rooms (Rp150,000) on Rinca and a basic homestay (Rp110,000) on Komodo; both are spartan, to say the least. Both islands have basic cafés at the PHPA camps, serving rice and noodle dishes, omelettes and pancakes.

megapode bird, which builds huge ground nests where its eggs are incubated in warm dung. Bring water and wear decent boots.

There are also regular guided walks from the PHPA camp to the **Banunggulung** river bed and to **Sebita**, one of the mangrove forests that are vital for providing shelter and food for the island's populations of bats, birds, crabs and fish.

The seas around Komodo, though home to spectacular coral reefs and an abundance of fish, are laced with riptides, whirlpools, sea snakes, sea-wasp jellyfish and a healthy shark population, so stick to recommended snorkelling locations such as the excellent **Pantai Merah**. Many boat operators will include at least one snorkelling stop on visits to the island. If you visit between October and January, you may be lucky enough to catch sight of migrating whales.

RINCA

Its proximity to Labuanbajo means **Rinca** receives as many visitors as Komodo, if not more, and given that the dragon populations are denser and there's less cover, you're much more likely to catch

sight of them here. Rinca consists mostly of parched grassland covering steep slopes, drought-resistant lontar palms and huge patches of flowering cacti and other hardy shrubs. The PHPA camp at **LOH BUAYA** has just four rooms and a small café. There are a couple of well-trodden treks, and at the right time (mornings and late afternoons) you shouldn't have any problems spotting dragons, monkeys, buffalo, deer and wild pigs.

Flores

A fertile, mountainous barrier between the Savu and Flores seas, **Flores** comprises one of the most alluring landscapes in the archipelago. The volcanic spine of the island soars to 2500m, and torrential wet seasons result in a lushness that marks Flores apart from its scorched neighbours. It also differs religiously – 95 percent of islanders are Catholic. The most spectacular sight in Flores is magnificent **Kelimutu**, near Moni, northeast of **Ende**. The three craters of this extinct volcano each contain a lake of different, vibrant and gradually changing colours. In the east of Flores, high-quality **ikat weaving**

4

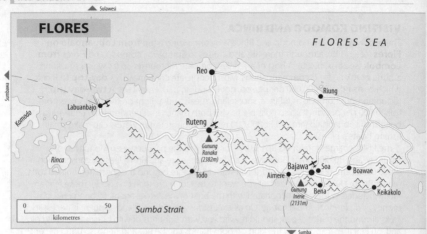

still thrives. At the extreme west end of the island, **Labuanbajo** has some fine **coral gardens** and is also the port for ferries to and **from Sumbawa**. All of Flores's major towns are linked by bus, but these can be slow, crowded and unpleasant. A number of private operators, including the recommended Gunung Mas, run faster, more comfortable *travels* (cars and minibuses) around the island, to strictly observed schedules, with hotel pick-ups – well worth the few extra rupiah.

A useful source of information on Flores is ⓦflorestourism.com.

LABUANBAJO

The charming port town of **LABUANBAJO** is experiencing a boom in tourism, serving as the gateway to Flores and the main departure point for trips to **Komodo National Park** (see box, p.307), but it nevertheless retains a laidback village feel. You can stay in town or at one of the nearby island hotels – these offer a quiet getaway with unspoilt beaches and decent snorkelling, although they tend to be overpriced. You can also easily organize **dive trips** from one of the many dive shops in town.

ARRIVAL AND DEPARTURE

By plane The airport is about 2km away from the waterfront; bemos run into town. Garuda (ⓣ080 4180 7807, ⓦgaruda-indonesia.com), Lion Air/Wings Air (ⓣ080 4177 8899, ⓦlionair.co.id) and Nam Air (ⓣ021 6471 7999, ⓦflynamair.com) have direct daily flights to Bali and Jakarta, and fluctuating services to other destinations.

Destinations Bali (8 daily; 1hr–1hr 35min); Ende (2 daily; 45min); Jakarta (daily; 2hr 10min).

By bus Your hotel can reserve you a place in a *travel*, which will come and pick you up. Public buses drop off along Jl Sokarno on their way into town; they leave from the bus station next to the harbour.

Destinations Bajawa (2 daily; 10hr); Ende (daily; 14hr); Ruteng (2 daily, 4–5hr).

By ferry Ferries from Sumbawa dock at the passenger harbour near the northern end of main Jl Sokarno, along which almost all of the town's tourist shops and restaurants are situated. The Pelni agent (ⓣ0385 41141, ⓦpelni.co.id) is up a dirt track behind the sports field; the ASDP office (ⓣ0385 41396, ⓦwww.indonesiaferry.co.id) is at the harbour. Timetables change frequently, so make sure you check the latest information on the ground.

Destinations Benoa (2 monthly; 36hr); Bira (Fri; 24hr); Makassar (fortnightly; 20hr); Sape (2 daily; 8hr).

INFORMATION

Tourist office Jl Gabriel Gampur (Mon–Fri 8am–2pm; ⓣ0385 41170). A 15min walk out of town, but they're friendly and helpful. To get here, head up the hill opposite the supermarket.

ACCOMMODATION

IN TOWN

There are also a handful of basic homestays just south of the harbour on Jl Sokarno (around Rp80,000/person).

Bayview Gardens Jl Ande Bole ⓣ0385 41549, ⓦbayview-gardens.com. Run by a Dutch-Indonesian family, this charming hotel has a lush, tropical feel, with

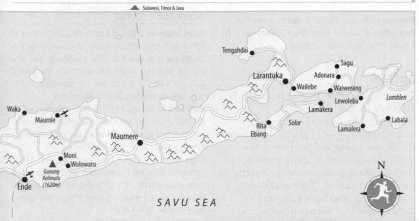

beautiful grounds, great views and well-appointed a/c rooms. Doubles Rp500,000

Gardena Hotel Jl Sokarno ☎0385 41258, ⓦ gardenaflores.com. A mainstay of Labuanbajo's budget options, this collection of shabby wooden cottages has a great location in the heart of town and offers decent value, though the rooms are looking slightly tired. An a/c bungalow will cost you Rp375,000. Doubles Rp180,000

★**Golo Hilltop** Up a dirt road at the northern end of town ☎0385 41337, ⓦ golohilltop.com. Heavenly Dutch-run place, with spacious, immaculate rooms, a swimming pool and a small restaurant; perks include free wi-fi, coffee and tea. Well worth the walk or ojek ride up the hill, if only for the views. They also run the nearby *Paradise Bar*, a fun spot with live music and the best sunset views in town. Doubles Rp475,000

Green Hill Boutique Hotel Jl Sokarno Hatta ☎0385 41289, ⓦ greenhillboutiquehotel.com. A lovely collection of bungalows staggered down the hillside, *Green Hill* has a stylish, rustic feel with minimalist rooms and beautiful harbour views. There's a popular café downstairs serving great coffee and breakfast, and a decent restaurant offering a range of reasonably priced Indonesian and Western dishes. Doubles Rp450,000

L Bajo Jl Kasimo 99 ☎0385 42151, ⓦ lbajohotel.com. This spotlessly white hotel block offers deluxe a/c rooms for Rp425,000 and fan-cooled rooms for less than half that. Bordering on the sterile, this isn't bursting with character but offers decent value. Doubles Rp200,000

ON THE BEACH

There are various island beach resorts in the area, though they're relatively expensive given that running water and electricity may not always be available, and an increasing number are rebranding as luxury resorts. Rates include transport from Labuanbajo.

Kanawa Hotel Office on Jl Sokarno ☎0385 41252, ⓦ kanawaresort.com. Standing on its own island north of Labuanbajo (1hr by boat), this hotel has reasonable bungalows set back from the beach in a beautiful setting, although service can be indifferent. You'll save money by booking your excursions around Komodo in Labuanbajo rather than at the resort. Doubles Rp500,000

EATING

Bajo Bakery Jl Sokarno. A cosy little café serving delicious home-baked bread, sandwiches, brownies, muffins, pastries, cakes and ice cream, plus fine coffee. Snacks from Rp10,000. Mon–Sat 7am–7pm.

Café in Hit Jl Sokarno. Beneath *Green Hill Boutique*, this trendy coffee bar offers a welcome respite from the heat and is constantly packed with expats, travellers and locals. You'll find the best coffee in Labuanbajo, free, fast wi-fi, and decent healthy breakfasts from Rp40,000. Daily 7am–10pm.

Made in Italy Jl Pantai Pede ⓦ miirestaurants.com. Labuanbajo's top Italian restaurant, 15min walk south of the harbour, serves authentic wood-fired, thin-crust pizzas, superior risotto and pasta dishes, as well as great coffee. Dishes from Rp90,000. Daily 11am–11pm.

Mediterraneo Jl Sokarno ⓦ mediterraneo.co.id. Sink into one of the beanbags strewn across the waterfront deck and while away the hours with a cold beer (around Rp30,000) and delicious grilled seafood, pizza or pasta. Daily 8am–11pm.

DIRECTORY

Banks There are several ATMs along Jl Sokarno; the BRI next to the post office changes most common currencies.

Diving Blue Marlin Komodo, Jl Sokarno (☎0812 3766 496, ⓦ bluemarlinkomodo.com).

Internet There's an internet café where Jl Sokarno meets Jl Bidadari south of the post office. Most hotels and restaurants provide free wi-fi.

4

Pharmacy Several on Jl Sokarno, past the post office.
Post office Jl Sokarno (Mon–Thurs 7.30am–3pm, Fri 7.30am–noon, Sat 7.30am–12.30pm).

RUTENG

The first large town after Labuanbajo is RUTENG, 140km to the east. Surrounded by forested volcanic hills and rolling rice-paddy plains, it's a cool, if dull, place. The market just to the south is the central meeting point for the local **Manggarai** people, as Ruteng is their district capital. They speak their own language and have a distinctive culture most in evidence in villages on the south coast. Their traditional houses are conical and arranged in concentric circles around a circular sacrificial arena; even the rice paddies are round, divided up like spiders' webs, with each clan receiving a slice. Most of these formations are no longer used, but a good example can still be seen at **Golo Cara**, thirty minutes by bemo from the central bus station, and traces of them are visible from the bus to Bajawa.

Around 15km north of Ruteng is **Liang Bua**, a limestone cave (Rp40,000, including a short tour) in which the skeleton of a potentially new species of human – the diminutive **Homo floresiensis**, nicknamed the "hobbit" – was discovered in 2003.

ARRIVAL AND DEPARTURE

By plane The airport is 2km from the centre, served by bemos to and from the central bus terminal. Nam Air (📞021 6471 7999, 🌐flynamair.com) operates daily flights to Kupang (daily; 1hr 45min).
By bus Buses from Labuanbajo arrive at the Mena terminal, 3km out of town. Buses from the east (apart from through buses to Labuanbajo, which go into town) will drop you at the Puspasari terminal, 4km from the centre. Bemos will take you into town from either station. When you leave Ruteng, your hotel can arrange for the bus to pick you up to save you the hassle of getting back out to the terminal.
Destinations Bajawa (several daily; 5hr); Ende (2 daily; 9hr); Labuanbajo (several daily; 4–5hr); Maumere (2 daily; 14hr).
By shared taxi The *Rima Hotel* runs a travel service to Bajawa, Ende, Labuanbajo and Maumere.

ACCOMMODATION

Hotel Susteran Jl Ahmed Yani 📞0385 22834. A ray of light amid Ruteng's dismal accommodation offerings, this guesthouse (also known as "MBC") is actually part of a convent. Rooms are simple, but immaculate. The convent choir starts early, a strange but not unpleasant way to wake up in the morning. Doubles Rp200,000
Ranaka Jl Yos Sudarso 2 📞0385 21353. Gloomy place in the town centre, with just a few rudimentary rooms, some with their own bathroom. Prices are low and the staff are friendly enough. Doubles Rp100,000
Rima Hotel Jl Ruteng-Benteng Jawa 26 📞0385 22196. Somewhat dingy, but this wooden hotel is passable for a night or two. Staff are very helpful when it comes to arranging onward transport, even if you're not staying there. Doubles Rp160,000

EATING

Ruteng shuts down at 9pm, so eat well before then.
Agape Coffee House & Café Jl Bhayangkara 8. This large, friendly café offers a wide selection of hot drinks and sweet snacks (from Rp15,000), as well as Indonesian and Western mains from Rp25,000. Daily 8am–10pm.
Ruma Makan Chacha Jl Diponegoro 12. The best eats in town, with traditional Indonesian dishes served up starting at Rp15,000, and a warm welcome courtesy of friendly owner Jofar. Daily noon–11pm.

DIRECTORY

Bank There are lots of ATMs in town, particularly along Jl Yos Sudarso and Jl Ruteng-Benteng Jawa.
Internet Most hotels, cafés and restaurants offer free wi-fi; *Kopi Mane Inspiration* has the quickest connection in town.
Post office Jl Dewi Sartika 6, behind the replica traditional house (Mon–Thurs 8am–4pm, Fri & Sat 8am–noon).

BAJAWA AND THE NGADA VILLAGES

The hill town of **BAJAWA** is one of the most popular tourist destinations in Flores, surrounded by lush slopes and striking volcanoes. **Gunung Inerie** (2245m) is just one of the active volcanoes near Bajawa: it's an arduous but rewarding hike, and if it's clear you can see all the way to Sumba from the summit.

Bajawa is the largest town in the **Ngada district**, an area that maintains its status as the spiritual heartland of Flores. Here, despite the growing encroachment of tour groups, indigenous animist religions flourish and the villages maintain traditional houses, megalithic stones and interesting totemic structures. Up to sixty thousand people in the Ngada district speak the distinct Ngada language, and a good proportion of the older generation don't understand basic Bahasa Indonesia.

Not for the faint-hearted are the local specialities of **moke**, a type of wine that tastes like methylated spirits, and **raerate** or "**rw**" (pronounced "air-vay"), dog meat marinated in coconut milk and then boiled in its own blood.

WHAT TO SEE AND DO

The influx of tourists to the Ngada region has led to a booming **guide** industry in Bajawa, with a corresponding hike in prices. A one-day village tour with an ojek (motorbike with driver) costs from Rp150,000 plus donations for the villages – Rp20,000–25,000 each. Often a traditional Bajawan meal will be thrown into the bargain. For mountain treks, guides charge from Rp300,000 a day. A day-tour should cover at least **Bena** and **Wogo**, as well as the hot springs at **Soa**, but many also include a trip to **Wawo Muda**, one of Indonesia's newest volcanoes. If you don't get approached by a licensed guide at your hotel, try the guide association, which operates an information office opposite the *Hotel Edelweis*, though it's only open sporadically.

Soa, Wogo and Bena are all accessible by public transport from Bajawa (though Bena only has one bemo a day); it can be hard to find accurate information about

NGADA ARCHITECTURE

In the centre of most villages in this district stand several **ceremonial edifices**, which represent the ancestral protection of, and presence in, the village. These include the **Ngadhu**, which resembles a man in a huge hula skirt, the thatched skirt sitting atop a crudely carved, phallic forked tree trunk, which is imbued with the power of a male ancestor. The female part of the pairing, the **Bhaga**, is a symbol of the womb, a miniature house. The symbolic coupling is supplemented by a carved stake called a **Peo**, to which animals are tied before being sacrificed.

this, and guides will often inflate prices to discourage you from independent visits, so ask bemo drivers directly. Alternatively, you can **rent a motorbike** and explore the region for yourself; *Hotel Happy Happy* charges Rp100,000 per day. Ojeks can be found around town for Rp150,000 per day, though female travellers should exercise caution as there have been several reports of indecent behaviour by ojek drivers in the area.

Ngada villages

BENA is the prettiest and most traditional of the Ngada villages, lying about 13km south of Bajawa. To reach it, take the turn-off past the large church at Mangulewa, 5km east of Bajawa. Here they have nine different clans, in a village built on nine levels with nine Ngadhu/ Bhaga couplings (see box below). It's the central village for the local area's religions and traditions, and one of the best places to see **festivals** such as weddings, planting and harvest celebrations.

Some of the finest megaliths and Ngadhu are at the twin villages of **WOGO BARU** and **WOGO LAMA**, the former lying 1km south of Mataloko (30min by bemo from Bajawa). Wogo Baru is a typically charming Ngada village, but the main attraction lies about 1.5km further down the road at Wogo Lama, where some apparently neglected megaliths sit in a clearing. All of the above villages ask visitors to give a donation, but the amount is up to you; Rp20,000–25,000 per person is reasonable, although more is always appreciated.

Hot springs and Wawo Muda

The most popular destination near Bajawa is the **hot springs** at **SOA** (Rp14,000). The springs are set in peaceful surroundings, and a small but powerful waterfall provides the cheapest hot shower on Flores. **Bemos** from Bajawa market run to Soa village, from where you can pick up an ojek for the remaining 6km to the springs – you'll need to ask your driver to wait if you don't want to walk back. There are some quieter, though equally seductive, hot springs at Malanage, 3km south of Bena.

In the first few months of 2001 a new **volcano** erupted above the small village of Ngoranale, about 10km to the north of Bajawa, leaving a blackened crater. In the rainy season the crater fills with several small lakes, variously red, orange and gold. There are no bemos to **Wawo Muda**, so you'll need private transport to Ngoranale, where you can ask a villager to show you the start of the wide and easy-to-follow trail, which takes about an hour and a half to meander up to the summit.

ARRIVAL AND DEPARTURE

By plane Bajawa airport is around 20km out of town. If you're lucky there may be a bemo to Bajawa waiting, otherwise you'll have to walk to the main road (turn right as you leave the terminal) and catch one there. If you're going to the airport, either catch a bemo from Bajawa, or take one to Soa and walk the last 2km. Lion Air/Wings Air (℡080 4177 8899, ⌨lionair.co.id) and Nam Air (℡021 6471 7999, ⌨flynamair.com) have daily flights to Kupang (1hr).

By bus The bus terminal is 3km out of town at Watujaji. Regular bemos connect the terminal with the town. Some buses come into town to look for passengers who are leaving Bajawa, but it's best to be on the safe side and go out to the terminal to pick them up.

Destinations Ende (several daily; 4hr); Labuanbajo (2 daily; 10hr); Moni (daily; 6hr); Ruteng (several daily; 5hr).

By shared taxi *Travels* cluster outside the *Hotel Virgo* opposite *Credo Café*, running daily services to Ende (4hr) and Ruteng (4hr).

ACCOMMODATION

The increase in tourism means, unfortunately, that almost every option in Bajawa is overpriced. It is also possible to stay in some of the villages around Bajawa; contact the guide association (see p.311) for information about two-day treks including an overnight in Bena, or you can ask directly at the village (around Rp250,000/person including meals).

Hotel Edelweis Jl Yani 76 ℡0384 21345. The ever-popular *Edelweis* is crumbling somewhat, but renovations were under way at the time of research. Rp275,000 will get you a grubby but acceptable en-suite room; bizarrely, though, much nicer rooms are available for almost half that in their "homestay" across the street. Doubles Rp150,000

★**Hotel Happy Happy** Jl Sudirman ℡0384 21763, ⌨hotelhappyhappy.com. The best place to stay in Bajawa, with friendly staff and sumptuous breakfasts: cooked Indonesian and Western options accompanied by fresh fruit and home-made bread. Tours of the area are on offer from Rp600,000. Rooms facing the road are noisy. Doubles Rp325,000

Hotel Nusantara II Jl Soegiopranoto ℡081 3392 38860. Friendly, spotless and good value, this town-centre hotel has plenty of tourist information available, and owner Marcelina will advise you on day-trips in the surrounding area. Doubles Rp200,000

EATING

Bajawa has a decent range of dining options, mostly along Jl Yani.

Camellia Jl Yani. The decor's a bit clinical, with white tiled floors and plastic-covered tables and chairs, but the food more than makes up for it, with delicious Indonesian dishes from Rp30,000. Daily 8am–10pm.

Credo Café Jl D.I. Panjaitan. A cosy joint across the road from *Hotel Virgo*, *Credo Café* serves simple, cheap Indonesian dishes (from Rp15,000) washed down with local coffee, Bintang and – if you're feeling brave – *arak*. Daily 8am–10pm.

Milonari Jl Yani. A small wood-walled restaurant on the main drag serving delicious Indonesian cuisine – special mention goes to the *cap cai*. From Rp25,000. Daily 9am–10pm.

DIRECTORY

Banks BNI off Jl Basoeki Rahmat changes money. ATMs line Jl Yani and Jl Sokarno-Hatta.

Internet Delta Permai, Jl M.T. Haryono.

Post office The main post office is up on the hill at the Jl Sokarno-Hatta crossroads (Mon–Thurs 7.30am–3pm, Fri 7.30am–noon & Sat 7.30am–12.30pm).

ENDE

Situated on a narrow peninsula with flat-topped Gunung Meja and the active volcano Gunung Ipi at its sea end, the port of **ENDE** is the largest town on Flores and provides access to Kelimutu and Moni (see opposite), though there is little in town to attract tourists other than banks and **ferries** to other destinations. Black-sand **beaches** stretch down both east and west coasts: the Bajawa road runs right along the seafront, so just catch a bemo out to Ndao bus terminal and the beach begins right there. The area around Ende is known for its **ikat** weaving. **NGELLA** is a weaving village about 30km east from Wolowana bus terminal in Ende, near the coast.

The cheaper losmen and some restaurants are spread out along Jalan Yani and around the airport roundabout, while the rest are down in the old town; travelling between the two areas is easily done by bemo or ojek.

ARRIVAL AND DEPARTURE

By plane The airport is just north of the town, on Jl Yani; you can walk into town, or catch an ojek. Garuda (☎080 4180 7807, ⓦgaruda-indonesia.com), Kalstar (☎021 2934 3400, ⓦkalstaronline.com), Lion Air/Wings Air (☎080 4177 8899, ⓦlionair.co.id) and Nam Air (☎021 6471 7999, ⓦflynamair.com) have regular flights across Flores and beyond.

Destinations Denpasar (4 weekly; 1hr 30min); Kupang (daily; 50min); Labuanbajo (daily; 45min); Tambolaka (daily; 50min).

By bus Buses from the east arrive 4km further on from the airport at the Wolowana bus terminal, where you'll be mobbed by ojek drivers who will take you to town. Buses from the west arrive at Ndao bus terminal, about 2km west of town; bemos are in plentiful supply.

Destinations Bajawa (several daily; 4hr); Labuanbajo (daily; 14hr); Maumere (several daily; 5hr); Moni (several daily; 1hr 30min); Ruteng (several daily; 9hr).

By ferry Ipi harbour in the old town is used for all long-distance boats; the ferry and harbour masters' offices are on the road that leads down to the harbour. Pelni ferries stop here, and there are also ASDP ferries serving Waingapu on Sumba once a week. The Pelni office at Jl Kathedral 2 (☎0381 21043, ⓦpelni.co.id) can help with Pelni and ASDP tickets.

Destinations Denpasar (fortnightly; 50hr); Kupang (2 fortnightly; 25–29hr); Sape (fortnightly; 16hr); Surabaya (fortnightly; 79hr); Waingapu (Wed; 13hr).

INFORMATION

Tourist information The headquarters of Tourism Flores, at Jl Bhakti 1, is a helpful source of maps and information about Ende and the whole of the island. Staff are very friendly and speak good English (Mon–Fri 8am–5pm; ☎0381 23141).

ACCOMMODATION

Grand Hotel Wisata Jl Kelimutu 32 ☎0381 22974, ⓦgrandwisatahotel-ende.com. Close to the airport and easily the classiest option in town, *Wisata*'s rooms are stylish and spotless. There's also a nice pool and a good restaurant next door. Doubles Rp550,000
Ikhlas Jl Yani 69 ☎0381 21695. An erstwhile backpacker option, *Ikhlas* has rested on its laurels somewhat, but it's cheap and conveniently located. An acceptable alternative if you can't get a room at *Safari* next door. Doubles Rp90,000

Safari Jl Yani 65 ☎0381 21997. The best of Ende's budget options, *Safari* is bright and airy, with basic but clean rooms set around a nice courtyard; higher-priced options will get you hot water, a/c and TV. There's also a restaurant and even a little shop. Good value. Doubles Rp100,000

EATING

Padang Roda Baru Jl Kelimutu. Spicy pick-and-mix Padang cuisine, from Rp30,000. Specializes in seafood, but it's very popular, so nothing should have been sitting around for too long. Daily 8am–10pm.
Restaurant Edelweis Jl Kelimutu 32. Connected to the *Grand Hotel Wisata*, this has a similarly classy atmosphere without the high prices. A range of delicious Indonesian, Chinese and Western dishes is on offer, starting from Rp25,000. Daily 7am–11pm.

DIRECTORY

Banks Jl Hatta and Jl Soekarno, down by the waterfront, each have several ATMs.
Internet There is a *warnet* on Jl Ahmed Yani opposite the Roxy Market.
Pharmacy Jl Kelimutu, opposite *Grand Hotel Wisata*.
Post office Jl Yos Soedarso (Mon–Fri 8am–3pm).

KELIMUTU AND MONI

Stunning **Kelimutu** volcano, with its three strangely coloured crater lakes, is without doubt one of the most startling natural phenomena in Indonesia. The picturesque village of **Moni**, 40km northeast of Ende, stretches along the road from the lower slopes of the volcano down to the valley floor, and makes a great base from which to hike up to Kelimutu and around.

Kelimutu

The summit of **Kelimutu** (1620m) forms a barren lunar landscape with, to the east, two vast turquoise pools separated by a narrow ridge. A few hundred metres to the west, settled in a deep depression, lies a dark khaki lake. The lakes' colours are due partly to the levels of certain **minerals** that dissolve in them. As the sulphurous waters erode the caldera they lie in, they uncover bands of different compounds and, as the levels of these compounds are in constant flux, so are the colours. Just as important, however, is the level of oxygen dissolved in the water. When their supply is low, the lakes look green. Conversely, when they are rich in oxygen, they range from deep red to black. In the 1960s, the lakes were red, white and blue.

Every morning at around 4am tourists ride by ojek (around Rp150,000 return) from their hotel in Moni to Kelimutu, making it to the top in time to see the sun rise hazily over the mountains; make sure you organize this early departure the night before, though you can also go later if you prefer. Just before the car park near the summit you need to pay an entrance fee of Rp150,000. There are two vantage points – you can only see two lakes from the first one, so most tourists and all the local coffee-sellers head to the second. The **walk** back down to Moni, which takes about two and a half hours, is a joy, especially in fine weather, providing views over rolling hills down to the sea. There's a path to the right at the two white pillars around the 6km mark, which cuts a good 4km off the road route, taking you through some charming local villages and past the **waterfall** (*air terjun*) on the edge of Moni – a great spot for a dip. If you take this route you'll need good shoes, as it gets very narrow and steep. Following the road, you'll pass some hot springs in which to soak your tired feet. Be sure to take plenty of water, as even going downhill you'll warm up quickly.

Moni

Nestling among lush rice paddies, the village of **MONI** exudes a lazy charm. Full of homestays and little family-run cafés, it's a relaxed place to spend a few days, with great walking in the surrounding hills. There is no bank or post office in Moni, despite the increasing number of tourists, but you can make phone calls at the tiny **wartel** off the main road, and most restaurants and cafés offer internet access. There's a branch of Flores Tourism on the main road, next to Bintang Lodge.

ARRIVAL AND DEPARTURE

By bus Buses from Ende (1hr 30min) and Maumere (3hr 30min) stop here regularly throughout the day, and *kijangs* pass through regularly. There's one bus daily to Bajawa, though you should ask your homestay to book it, otherwise it may be full by the time it gets to Moni.

ACCOMMODATION

Antoneri Lodge Next to *Mama Moni's Inn* ☎ 0822 4759 9545, ✉ willylokawoda@yahoo.com. With a selection of basic twin and double rooms set around a bright blue courtyard, *Antoneri* offers the best value in town. Rooms are no frills but spotless, and all have hot water. Doubles <u>Rp150,000</u>

Estevania Lodge On the main road ☎ 0821 4799 5023. A lovely option for those willing to splash out a bit more, *Estevania* is a friendly, family-run lodge on the main road. Rooms are spacious and tastefully decorated; there's no need to splash out for a/c. Doubles <u>Rp350,000</u>

Mama Moni's Inn Opposite the market ☎ 0821 4607 0423. An ageing but acceptable selection of rooms, with three more attractive bungalows out front. The elderly couple who run it speak good English. Doubles <u>Rp200,000</u>

EATING

There are more cafés than you'd think a town this size could merit, all along the main road.

Mopi's Place At the top of the village. Impossibly trendy by Moni's standards, *Mopi's Place* has a classic rock soundtrack, upturned barrels for tables and a range of Western and Indonesian dishes on offer all day, starting at Rp25,000. There's also great coffee, and a book exchange. Mon–Sat 7.30am–midnight, Sun 3pm–midnight.

Rainbow Café At the top of the village. The menu is limited to Indonesian staples and some Western-style pasta dishes (from Rp20,000), but it's tasty, and there's plenty of it. Daily 9am–10pm.

MAUMERE

On the north coast of Flores, roughly equidistant between Ende and Larantuka, **MAUMERE** was once the tourism centre of the island and its best diving resort. In 1992, a devastating earthquake and tsunami destroyed most of the town, as well as the coral, though this is slowly recovering. Improved transport links and regular air services are steadily making it one of the main stops on trips around Nusa Tenggara; from here, you can organize tours that take in all of Flores's attractions. Maumere is the capital of the Sikka district, especially renowned for its **weaving**, which incorporates maroon, white and blue geometric patterns in horizontal rows on a black or dark-blue background.

ARRIVAL AND DEPARTURE

By plane The airport is 15min outside town; taxis from here cost Rp100,000, or take an ojek from the main road. Garuda (☎080 4180 7807, ⓦgaruda-indonesia.com), Lion Air/Wings Air (☎080 4177 8899, ⓦlionair.co.id) and Nam Air (☎021 6471 7999, ⓦflynamair.com) fly to/from Bali and Kupang.

Destinations Bali (3 daily; 2hr); Kupang (2 daily; 40min).

By bus Buses to and from Ende, Moni and other destinations in the west are served by the Ende bus terminal, several kilometres down Jl Gajah Mada southwest of town. Bemos run from here to the centre. For onward travel, note that buses depart from the terminal but meander around town before leaving.

Destinations Bajawa (daily; 9hr); Ende (several daily; 5hr); Moni (several daily; 3hr 30min); Ruteng (daily; 14hr).

By ferry The harbour is at the northern end of town, a 15min walk or quick ojek ride to the centre. Tickets for Pelni services to Kupang and Makassar can be bought at the office at Jl Sikokoru 2 by the harbour (☎0382 21013, ⓦpelni.co.id).

Destinations Kupang (Wed; 12hr); Makassar (Wed; 17hr); Surabaya (monthly; 56hr).

By shared taxi *Travels* can be arranged by your hotel and cost around Rp50,000 to Moni.

INFORMATION

Tourist information Located south of the stadium on Jl Wairklau (Mon–Thurs 8am–2pm, Fri 8–11am; ☎0382 21652), they can provide a map and some local information.

ACCOMMODATION

Maumere itself offers a selection of decent accommodation, but you may prefer to take advantage of the beaches and stay out of town, from where you can also go snorkelling or diving.

MAUMERE

Gardena Jl Patirangga 28 ☎0382 21489. Newly renovated *Gardena* remains the best budget option in Maumere by a distance, with acceptable rooms on a quiet corner near the centre of town. Wi-fi, hot water and motorbike rental all on offer. Doubles Rp150,000

Pantai Paris Homestay Jl Nasional Larantuka 6 ☎08135 301 4229, ⓔpantai.paris.homestay@gmail.com. Homey accommodation in a bamboo-roofed villa. Owners Susi and Hermann are very friendly and run an NGO focusing on community education and sustainability. Direct access to the beach without the price tag of the luxury resorts. Dorms Rp140,000

Wini Rai II Jl Soetomo 7 ☎0382 21362. Slightly aged and pretty dingy, the rooms at *Wini Rai II* are nonetheless a cheap option in central Maumere, fine if you're just looking for a quick stopover. Doubles Rp100,000

ON THE COAST

There are a few pleasant beachside options outside Maumere.

Coconut Garden Beach Resort Jl Nasional Larantuka ☎0821 4426 0185, ⓦcoconutgardenbeachresort.com. This beautiful beach hotel is unusual in offering more affordable "backpacker" rooms, which are compact but spotlessly clean and have mosquito nets. Doubles Rp370,000

Gading Beach Hotel Around 7km outside Maumere ☎0852 3900 4490. These peaceful bungalows are owned by the same people as the *Gardena*, and offer easily the most affordable beach option. Room rates include transport from Maumere, and they can organize diving and snorkelling trips. Doubles Rp220,000

EATING

The harbour is the best place to find seafood, with a number of places offering grilled fish, priced by weight, for around Rp40,000/person. There are also some warung along the dry riverbed near the harbour, and a supermarket east of the sports field.

Golden Fish Jl Sultan Hasanuddin 30. This restaurant above an angling shop is relatively pricey but you get what you pay for: beautiful fresh seafood, hand-picked from the tank, cooked in a variety of Indonesian and Chinese styles and served in generous portions. Mains from Rp100,000. Daily 9am–10pm.

Surya Indah Jl Raja Centis. This Padang joint near the market serves the best beef *rendang* in town, as well as good *sate soto*. Dishes cost Rp17,000–20,000. Daily 11am–10pm.

DIRECTORY

Banks BRI on Jl A Yani and BNI on Jl Sukarno Hatta both change money; there are lots of ATMs around town.

Internet Flobamora near the *Sylvia Hotel* has lots of terminals and a fast connection.

Post office Jl A Yani, near the *Hotel Gardena* (Mon–Thurs 8am–3pm, Fri & Sat 8am–1pm).

Sumba

Sumba is among the most enigmatic of Indonesia's major islands. The east is made up of arid grasslands and limestone plateaux, while the west is fertile and green, with rolling hills and a long rainy season. **Waingapu**, the capital, is well known for producing the finest *ikat* fabric in Indonesia. A little further out at **Rende** and **Melolo** sit stone tombs with bizarre carvings, and in other villages on the east coast you'll find quality weaving, traditional structures and deserted beaches. The main town in the west is **Waikabubak**, where characteristic houses with thatched roofs soar to an apex over 15m above the ground.

Access to Sumba is either by **ferry** from Ende in Flores to Waingapu or from Sape in Sumbawa to Waikelo, or by **air** to either Waingapu or Waikabubak. Most people choose to fly out of **Waingapu** rather than Waikabubak, which has a very chequered record for reliability and cancellations.

WAINGAPU

It may be the largest port and town on Sumba, but **WAINGAPU** is far from a modern metropolis. Goats wander along the main road, horses are stabled in front porches, and locals still walk around barefoot, with *ikat* tied around their heads and waists. The older half of the hourglass-shaped town is centred around the port, the newer part around the market. It's only a fifteen-minute walk

between the two, but every passing ojek will assume you need a lift. The bay to the west of town has a harbour at the extreme point of either shore; all ferries dock at the **western harbour**, requiring an 8km journey around the bay to town. The eastern harbour in the old town is now just used for fishing boats, and can be picturesque, especially at sunset.

WHAT TO SEE AND DO

PRAILU is the most visited of the local **ikat-weaving villages**, and is an easy 2km walk from the hotels near the market. After signing in at the large, traditional house (no fixed opening hours but generally daily 10/11am–5/6pm; Rp10,000), you can inspect weavings that weren't good enough to be bought by the traders. The **ikat** blankets of east Sumba are ablaze with symbolic dragons, animals, gods and head-hunting images. The cloth worn by men is called the **hinggi**, and is made from two identical panels sewn together into a symmetrical blanket. These are the most popular souvenirs, as

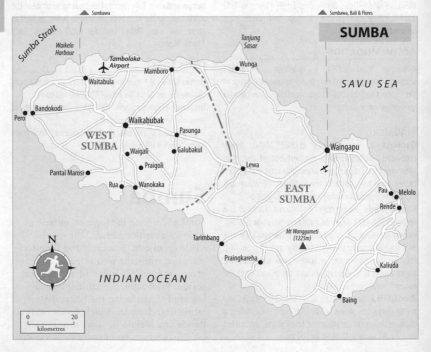

they make great wall hangings. Small blankets of medium quality usually retail for under $50, but will mainly use only chemical dye. For larger, high-quality pieces, you can pay anything from $100 to $1000. A tight weave, clean precise motifs and sharp edges between different colours are all signs of a good piece. Dealers in the towns will often give you better prices and more choice than those in the villages.

ARRIVAL AND DEPARTURE

By plane The airport is about 10km to the southeast on the road to Rende. Representatives from the main hotels are usually on hand to ferry tourists into town – as long as you agree to look at their hotel first; if they're not there, take a taxi (Rp100,000), or step outside and flag down an ojek. Lion Air/Wings Air (☎ 080 4177 8899, ⊛ lionair.co.id) and Nam Air (☎ 021 6471 7999, ⊛ flynamair.com) have flights to/from Bali and Kupang.

Destinations Bali (daily; 1hr 35min); Kupang (2 daily; 1hr).

By bus All buses will stop at the terminal west of town, but most also drive into and around town to pick up passengers for the return journey, so you should get dropped off at the market if not right at your hotel.

Destinations Melolo and Rende (several daily; 2hr); Waikabubak (several daily; 4hr 30min).

By ferry Passengers arriving at the main western harbour can get any bemo to drop them at the hotel of their choice.

The Pelni office (☎ 0387 61665, ⊛ pelni.co.id) is down at the bottom of the hill near the old harbour. Ferries leave from the western harbour; an ojek will take you there. Head to the harbour for information about ASDP ferries.

Destinations (Pelni) Denpasar (monthly; 38hr); Ende (fortnightly; 10hr); Sape (fortnightly; 14hr); Kupang (fortnightly; 33–42hr).

Destinations (other) Aimere (Fri; 9hr); Ende (Wed; 13hr).

ACCOMMODATION

All the accommodation below is in the newer part of town near the market. Hotels can arrange transport to the airport if required.

Hotel Kaliuda Jl W.J. Lalamentik 3 ☎ 0387 62806. This modest, duck-egg-colour hotel has a good central location and clean, good-value fan rooms around a nice courtyard. Doubles Rp160,000

Hotel Merlyn Jl Dil Panjaitan 25 ☎ 0387 61300. A professionally run place in the centre of town, rooms are clean with high ceilings, and have a somewhat faded elegance. Doubles Rp198,000

Hotel Sandlewood Jl Dil Panjaitan 23 ☎ 0387 61887. Homey place right by the market, pleasantly quiet and good value for money. Single rooms with a shared bathroom are only Rp66,000, and an en-suite standard room is Rp165,000. Doubles Rp99,000

EATING

Warung line the main road linking the old and new towns; anything fancier is harder to come by.

SUMBA'S TRADITIONS AND CUSTOMS

One of the main reasons to visit Sumba is to experience the extraordinary agrarian **animist cultures** in the villages. These villages, or kampung, comprise huge clan houses set on fortified hills, centred around megalithic graves and topped by a totem made from a petrified tree, from which villagers would hang the heads of conquered enemies. The national government insisted that all totems be removed back in the 1970s, and though some do remain, many have disappeared.

The most important part of life for the Sumbanese is death, when the mortal soul makes the journey into the spirit world. Sumbanese **funerals** can be extremely impressive spectacles, inspiring several days of slaughter and feasting, the corpse wrapped in hundreds of exquisite *ikat* cloths.

Ostensibly, visiting the villages often involves nothing more than renting a motorbike (available from town from around Rp80,000/day; your hotel is the best place to ask), but the difficulty for **Western visitors** to Sumba is that traditions and taboos in Sumbanese village life are still very powerful and sit ill at ease with the demands of modern tourism. A visitor to a Sumbanese village should first take the time to share *sirih pinang* (**betel nut**) with both the *kepala desa* (village headman) and his hosts. Bringing betel nut is seen as a peace offering (enemies would rarely turn up brandishing gifts), while its use is a sign of unity; Sumbanese ritual culture sets great store by returning blood to the earth, and the bright-red gobs of saliva produced by chewing *sirih* represent this. Similarly, the central purpose of the Pasola festivals is to return blood to the soil (see box, p.319). Many villages that are on the regular trail for tourists have supplanted the tradition of sharing betel with a simple request for money, but if you come with gifts (betel nuts, cigarettes, or anything else that can be shared) you'll be far more welcome.

Mr Café Jl U.T. Marisi. Bright, modern café with a/c and a delicious and extensive Indonesian menu; *soto ayam* from just Rp12,000. Daily 7am–10pm.

Rumah Makan Jawa Jl Ahmad Yani. Basic Javanese restaurant, near the turning to *Mr Café*, specializng in fried chicken dishes. Daily 8am–10pm.

Warung Ikar Bakan Enjoy Aja Pelabuhan. This fish restaurant by the harbour is highly regarded locally, and serves generous portions of freshly grilled seafood for around Rp20,000. Daily 7pm–midnight.

DIRECTORY

Banks BNI on Jl Palapa changes cash and travellers' cheques; ATMs can be found throughout town.

Internet There's a 24hr warnet in the market on Jl Palapa.

Pharmacy Jl Yani, across from the *Elvin*.

Post office Jl Dr Sutomo 2, in the old town (Mon–Thurs 8am–4pm, Fri & Sat 8am–2pm).

WAIKABUBAK

Surrounded by lush green meadows and forested hills, tiny **WAIKABUBAK** encloses several kampung with slanting thatched roofs and megalithic **stone graves**, where life proceeds according to the laws of the spirits. Kampung **Tarung**, on a hilltop just west of the main street, has some excellent megalithic graves and is regarded as one of the most significant spiritual centres on the island. The **ratu** (king) of Tarung is responsible for the annual **wula padu** ceremony, which lasts for a month at the beginning of the Merapu New Year in November. The ceremony commemorates the visiting spirits of important ancestors, who are honoured with animal sacrifices and entertained by singing and dancing. Kampung **Praijiang** is a fine five-tiered village on a hilltop surrounded by rice paddies, several kilometres east of town. You can catch a bemo (around Rp5000) to the bottom of the hill. Waikabubak enjoys an extended rainy season lasting well into May, with daily downpours and chilly nights. Most things you need in Waikabubak are either on the main street of Jalan Sudirman, which becomes Jalan Bhayangkara, or not far from it. *Ikat* traders come from all over the island to Waikabubak's daily market.

ARRIVAL AND DEPARTURE

By plane Tambolaka Airport is a good 1hr 30min north of town, though like many of Indonesia's smaller airports, it has a patchy safety record; buses (around Rp20,000) meet arriving planes. In Pasola season (see box opposite), flights are more reliable than at other times, but you'll need to book months in advance. Garuda (☎080 4180 7807, ⓦgaruda-indonesia.com) has services to Denpasar and Kupang, and Lion Air/ Wings Air (☎080 4177 8899, ⓦlionair.co.id) to Denpasar, Ende and Kupang.

Destinations Denpasar (2 daily; 1hr 20min); Ende (daily; 50min); Kupang (2 daily; 1hr 10min).

By bus The bus terminal is in the southwest of the town; bemos also stop here.

Destinations Waingapu (several daily; 4hr 30min); Waitabula (several daily; 1hr).

By ferry The daily ferry from Sape in Sumbawa arrives in Waikelo harbour; buses run to Waikabubak (1hr 15min). The ferry to Sape runs every evening (9hr).

INFORMATION

Tourist information Jl Teratai 1, near hotel *Artha* (Mon–Fri 7am–2.30pm; ☎0387 21880). Friendly, helpful staff and a small selection of brochures and maps.

ACCOMMODATION

For such a small town, the choice of places to stay is pretty good.

★**Artha** Jl Veteran 11 ☎0387 21112. A little out of town, but slightly nicer rooms for the standard price. Owner Timo is helpful and speaks good English. Doubles **Rp200,000**

Hotel Aloha Jl Sudirman 26 ☎0387 22227, ⓔyosafat .aloha@gmail.com. Spotless rooms, some with a/c, and a friendly welcome at this laidback family-run hotel. Doubles **Rp200,000**

Pelita Jl A Yani 2 ☎0387 21104. This labyrinthine collection of rooms in the centre of town is clean and perfectly serviceable, but somewhat overpriced. Doubles **Rp250,000**

EATING

There are also a handful of warung scattered around town.

★**D'Sumba Ate** Jl Ahmad Yani 148. Easily the best among Waikabubak's meagre dining options, this wood-carved restaurant serves delicious Indonesian classics (from Rp30,000) and a range of Western options. Occasional live music too. Daily 10.30am–11pm.

Manandang Resto Jl Permuda 4. Attached to the hotel of the same name, this is a decent option in the centre of town with Indonesian staples from Rp25,000. There's a selection of *ikat* on sale, too. Daily 7am–11pm.

THE PASOLA

By far the best-known and most dazzling festival in Nusa Tenggara, the **Pasola** is one of those rare spectacles that actually surpasses all expectations. It takes place in **Kodi** and **Lamboya** in February and in **Wanokaka** and **Gaura** in March; most hotels can give you a rough idea of the date. This brilliant pageant of several hundred colourfully attired, spear-wielding horsemen in a frenetic and lethal pitched battle is truly unforgettable. It occurs within the first two moons of the year, and is set off by the mass appearance of a type of sea worm which, for two days a year, turns the shores into a maelstrom of luminous red, yellow and blue. The event is a rite to balance the upper sphere of the heavens and the lower sphere of the seas. The Pasola places the men of each village into two teams in direct opposition; the spilling of their blood placates the spirits and restores balance between the two spheres. The proceedings begin several weeks before the main event, with villagers hurling abuse and insults at their neighbours in order to get their blood up. The actual fighting takes place on special Pasola fields where the battle has been fought for centuries.

DIRECTORY

Banks The BNI bank at the junction of Jl A Yani and Jl Sudirman and the BRI bank on Jl Gajah Mada both change money and have ATMs.

Internet There's a warnet on Jl Pemuda, next door to *Hotel Manandang*. Wi-fi connections at hotels and restaurants are patchy to nonexistent.

Post office Jl Bhayangkara 1, just west of the BNI bank (Mon–Thurs 8am–3pm, Fri 8–11.30am & Sat 8am–1pm).

KODI AND PERO

In the extreme west of Sumba lies the popular Kodi district. Its centre is the village of **Bandokodi**, well known for the towering roofs that top its traditional houses. It is also one of the main **Pasola** venues in west Sumba (see box above). With your own transport, you can explore the area from Waikabubak, or you can stay in **Pero**.

Pero

The only place to stay in Kodi is **PERO**, a seaside village with a solitary losmen. The village is not constructed in traditional Sumbanese style, but has a quiet charm. Numerous kampung with teetering high roofs and mossy stone tombs dot the surrounding countryside, some only a short walk away. The main surfers' beach, a desolate long stretch where high waves crash onto the steeply sloping sand, is to the right, but the currents and undertow are ferocious. There's a more sheltered beach to the left over the river, with a vantage point above for local crowds to gather and gawp as you swim.

ARRIVAL AND DEPARTURE

By bus There is one direct bus per day from Waikabubak to Bandokodi, but it can be easier to take a bus to Waitabula in the north and then connect to a Kodi service, which should take you all the way to Pero – check the price with a local, as drivers optimistically overcharge travellers. Direct buses back to Waikabubak leave Pero around 6am – you should be able to connect back to Waingapu the same day if necessary.

ACCOMMODATION

Mercy Homestay Pero ☏ 0813 375 57272. Has clean new rooms and a lovely garden. There are a lot of mosquitoes; bring a net. Full-board **Rp250,000**

Kalimantan

Dense tropical jungle, murky village-lined rivers teeming with traffic and with wildlife so abundant it becomes the norm, jungle-cloaked Kalimantan appeals to those looking to venture into undiscovered territory. Occupying the southern two-thirds of the island of Borneo, **KALIMANTAN** remains largely untouched by tourism. With few roads, the interior's **great rivers** are its highways and a trip up one of them will give you a taste of traditional Dayak life and introduce you to lush areas of dense jungle. More intrepid explorers can spend weeks on end navigating their way through seldom-ventured parts, and a visit to one of the national parks could bring you face to face with wild **orang-utans** (see box, p.323). The urban centres of **Pontianak, Balikpapan,**

Banjarmasin and Samarinda are sprawling, dusty towns which offer little aside from their services. However, once out of the crowded, populated areas, Kalimantan's character starts to unfold.

For the independent traveller, Kalimantan can be expensive and a bit of a mission; time, patience, knowledge of Bahasa and effort are certainly required. But if you're looking for a true sense of Borneo, then these obstacles are a small price to pay.

PONTIANAK

The capital of West Kalimantan, or Kalbar (short for "Kalimantan Barat"), **PONTIANAK** is a grey industrial city of more than half a million people. Lying right at the equator on the confluence of the Landak and Kapuas Kecil rivers, it is a hot and noisy place, often smoky from the vast forest fires that recurrently rage inland. Among the most interesting things about the city is its name, which translates roughly as "the vampire ghost of a woman who dies in childbirth". Most travellers stay just long enough to stock up on supplies before moving on to Kuching (see p.481) in Malaysia, Gunung Palung, Tanjung Puting or Putussibau to explore the upper reaches of the **Sungai Kapuas**, Indonesia's longest river.

WHAT TO SEE AND DO

To get your bearings, take a **boat** up the river (around Rp180,000/hr) from the Seng Hie harbour, near the ferry

4

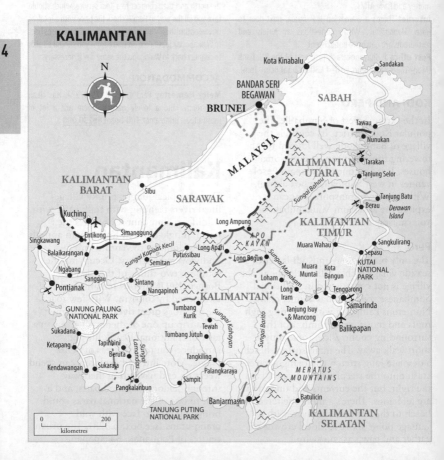

terminal. Along the river, there are still several old buildings of interest: the eye-catching **Istana Kadriyah**, built in 1771, and the traditional Javanese four-tiered roof of **Mesjid Jami** stand near each other on the eastern side of the Kapuas Kecil, just over the Kapuas bridge from the main part of town. Just over 500m north of the harbour along the river is the colourful **Vihara Bodhisattva Karaniya Metta**, the oldest Buddhist temple in West Kalimantan.

On Jalan Jend A Yani, 1.5km south of the town centre (Rp2500 by oplet), is the worthwhile **Museum Kalimantan Barat** (Tues–Sun 8am–3pm; Rp10,000), which contains a comprehensive collection of Dayak tribal masks, tattoo blocks, musical instruments, weapons and circumcision tools, as well as a worthwhile selection of Chinese and Japanese ceramics. Just round the corner from the museum, on Jalan Sutoyo, is an impressive replica of a **Dayak longhouse**.

ARRIVAL AND DEPARTURE

By plane Supadio Airport lies 20km south of the city centre, linked by taxi (Rp100,000) and DAMRI buses (Rp35,000), departing every other hour (5am–5pm). For most destinations in Kalimantan you'll have to transit through Jakarta.

Destinations Balikpapan (8 daily via Jakarta or Surabaya; 5hr with transit); Jakarta (21 daily; 1hr 25min); Ketapang (8 daily; 35min); Kuching (daily; 45min); Pangkalan Bun (3–4 weekly via Ketapang; 2hr 20min with transit); Putussibau (2 daily; 1hr).

By bus International buses arrive at and depart from Ambawang bus terminal, connected to town by DAMRI minibus (Rp35,000) or taxi (Rp150,000). Reliable

VISAS

Visiting Kalimantan from outside of Indonesia has never been easier. Visa-free facilities are available at Balikpapan, Pontianak and Tarakan airports, as well as at the Entikong border post between Kuching and Pontianak, and at the Tarakan seaport for those travelling by ferry from Tawau. If you intend to stay longer than thirty days, you can purchase a visa of the same length at any of these entry points for $35 and then extend at the nearest immigration office (Rp250,000).

TAXI OR TAKSI?

In Kalimantan there are two forms of transport; a **taxi** is a traditional taxi cab, while a **taksi**, which is often an overcrowded minibus known as an angkot, an oplet or a bemo elsewhere in Indonesia, has different colours, numbers or letters to indicate its route.

companies include DAMRI (Jl Pahlawan 226/3; ☎0561 744859) and Bintang Jaya (Jl Tanjung Pura 310A; ☎0561 659 7402).

Destinations Bandar Seri Begawan (daily 7am; 26hr); Kota Kinabalu (daily; 38hr); Kuching (several daily; 9hr); Pangkalan Bun (daily 7am; 14hr); Putussibau (2 daily via Sintang; 17hr).

By ferry The main ferry port where Pelni and other passenger boats arrive is just north of the city centre on Jl P Kasih, but you'll have to buy Pelni tickets at their office at Jl Sultan Abdul Rahman 17 (☎0561 748124). Comfortable a/c express boats run regularly to Ketapang on the west coast.

Destinations Ketapang (daily; 6hr); Surubaya (fortnightly; 44hr).

INFORMATION

Tourist information The tourist information office is just beyond the museum at Jl Sutoyo 17 (Mon–Fri 7.15am–3pm; ☎0561 742838), with English-speaking staff and loads of colourful brochures. For the most in-depth information around, contact Alex Afdhal (☎0812 576 8066, ✉alexafdhal@yahoo.com) at Borneo Access Adventurer on Jl Tanjung Harapan Gang HD Usman 46 (🖥borneoaccessadventurer.com). Alex arranges numerous adventure-based tours, including overnight Dayak Longhouse visits ($75/person) and three-day excursions to Tanjung Puting's rehabilitation centre ($300/person).

ACCOMMODATION

Ateng House 201 Jl Gajah Mada (above Ateng Tours) ☎0561 732683, 🖥atengtravel.com. Bright, clean a/c rooms with free wi-fi characterize this central budget option; the twin rooms are on the small side. Singles Rp150,000, twins Rp175,000

Hosanna Inn Jl Pahlawan 224/2 ☎0561 735052, 🖥hotelhosannainn.com. Set right beside the DAMRI ticket office where buses stop for Kuching, this little stalwart remains one of the best budget options in town. The cheaper ones have grubby shared bathrooms, but rooms themselves are all tidy and a/c. Rates include a very simple breakfast. Singles Rp135,000, twins Rp145,000

4

EATING

There are plenty of street stalls around town, especially near the market and harbour.

Beringin Jl Diponegoro 113. This is the largest of four locations around town. The friendly owner offers good West Sumatran food at low prices; the *sate* Pedang and *sambal sotong* (squid in chilli sauce) really stand out. Mains from Rp20,000. Daily 9am–10pm.

Gajah Mada Jl Gaja Madah 202. Large, upmarket Chinese restaurant famous for its excellent seafood and freshwater fish dishes (Rp150,000/kg). Chinese and regional specialities come in large portions – try the *jelawat* (West Kalimantan river fish; Rp50,000). Daily 11am–11pm.

DIRECTORY

Banks and exchange The bigger banks and money-changers have branches near the junction of Jl Tanjungpura and Jl Diponegoro. There are ATMs all over the centre.

Hospital RSU Santo Antonius, Jl KH Wahid Hasyim 249 (☎0561 732101).

Immigration office Jl Sutoyo 122 (☎0561 765576).

Post office Jl Sultan Abdul Rahman 49 (Mon–Fri 7.30am–7pm, Sat 7.30am–6pm).

BALIKPAPAN

Built around a huge petroleum complex, **BALIKPAPAN** is Kalimantan's wealthiest city, its residents enjoying a high standard of living thanks to massive offshore oil reserves that shed a dim orange glow on the surrounding waters at night. For the traveller, Balikpapan is a transit point en route to Samarinda, Banjarmasin or the Mahakam River. The intersection of the main roads Jalan Ahmed Yani and Jalan Sudirman serves as the city's core, where you'll find hotels, restaurants and the best shops, but, as almost everything is imported from Java or Sumatra, prices are generally much higher here than in the rest of Kalimantan.

ARRIVAL AND DEPARTURE

By plane Sepinggang Airport (☎0542 766886), 10km east of the city centre, is linked by taxi (15min; Rp55,000) and taksi (from the airport, take green #7, and switch at

■ ACCOMMODATION		● EATING	
Aida	3	Balikpapan Plaza	
Aiqo	4	Pacifica Foodcourt	2
Ayu	1	Depot Cendrawasih	1
San Francisco	2	Ocean's	3

THE DAYAK

Dayak is an umbrella name for all of Borneo's indigenous peoples. In Dayak religions, evil is kept at bay by attracting the presence of helpful spirits, or scared away by protective tattoos, carved spirit posts (*patong*) and lavish funerals. Shamans also intercede with spirits on behalf of the living. Although now you'll often find ostensibly Christian communities with inhabitants clutching mobile phones and watching satellite TV, the Dayak are still well respected for their jungle skills and deep-rooted traditions.

Traditionally, **head-hunting** was an important method of exerting power and settling disputes. It was believed that when cutting off someone's head the victim's soul was forced into the service of its captor. It is not practised now, but in 1997, West Kalimantan's Dayak exacted fearsome revenge against Madurese transmigrants. An estimated 1400 people were killed in a horrific purge of ethnic cleansing which involved head-hunting and cannibalism. Similar violence reoccurred between the Malays and the Madurese in the Sampit region of South Kalimantan in 2001. The situation has been peaceful for some time now, with head-hunting once again relegated to the past.

the Damai taksi terminal to a blue #5 or #6 into town; each Rp5000). Kangaroo (☎0812 555 1199, �🌐kangaroo.co.id) runs a direct a/c shuttle to Samarinda every 10min until 11.10pm (Rp135,000; 3hr).

Destinations Berau (8 daily; 1hr 5min); Jakarta (23 daily; 2hr); Makassar (7 daily; 1hr 5min); Manado (2 daily; 1hr 35min); Pontianak (daily; 1hr 30min); Singapore (4 weekly; 2hr 25min); Surabaya (17 daily; 1hr 30min).

By ferry The Pelni docks are at Semayang Harbour, 2.5km west of the centre on Jl Sudirman. Taksis #3 and #6 both go here. Tickets are available from the Pelni office (Jl Yos Sudarso 1; ☎0542 424171) at the harbour or from one of the many travel agents in the centre.

Destinations Makassar (weekly; 21hr); Nunukan (weekly; 32hr); Tarakan (weekly; 23hr).

By bus Terminal Batu Ampar, 6km north of the centre, serves long-distance destinations such as Samarinda (daily every 20min 6am–7pm; 2hr 30min) and Banjarmasin (several daily; 14hr). Take blue taksi #3 (Rp5000) to get into town. Deluxe, a/c minibuses run by Kangaroo shuttle to and from Samarinda every 10min (Rp135,000; 3hr).

AT HOME WITH THE ORANG-UTANS

Over the past few decades, Indonesia has lost about eighty percent of its original forest habitat. Illegal logging is still the number one culprit but expanding palm-oil plantations are a huge problem as well. This means the loss of the natural habitat of the stunning redhead of the simian world, the **orang-utan**. Kalimantan is one of the few areas where orang-utans still roam free; **Tanjung Puting National Park** in southern Kalimantan, **Gunung Palung National Park** in West Kalimantan, and **Kutai National Park** in East Kalimantan offer the best opportunities for seeing them in the wild. Time, money, knowledge of Bahasa and determination are definite requirements for independent visitors, though if you have all three it's worth the effort. Daily admission to each park is Rp150,000 per person (weekends and holidays Rp225,000).

GUNUNG PALUNG NATIONAL PARK

In recent decades the forest surrounding this 108,000-hectare national park has been almost completely replaced with palm oil plantations, leaving it an island of natural habitat for its substantial populations of proposcis monkeys, helmeted hornbills, and over 2000 wild orang-utans. It is also the site of an established research centre, the Gunung Palung Orang-utan Project (🌐savegporangutans.org). At the time of writing, Nasalis Tour & Travel (Jl Gajah Mada 34, Kalinilam, Ketapang; ☎0534 772 2701, 🌐nasalistour.com) still held a virtual monopoly on the park's tourism, offering three-day, two-night excursions from Rp2,600,000 per person in a group of three. Starting points are in either Ketapang or Sukadana, each accessible from Pontianak. Bring your own sleeping bag, waterproof gear, mosquito net and torch.

KUTAI NATIONAL PARK

East Kalimantan suffered from prolific logging back in the 1970s, and the 3000-square-kilometre Kutai National Park was established in 1982 to try and prevent further decline, but fires then destroyed sixty percent of the protected area. Nowadays the forest is recovering and reasonably accessible. **From Samarinda**, signing up for a tour is currently the only way of visiting the park. A recommended operator is De'Gigant Tours (Jl Martadinata 21; ☎0541 709 1536, 🌐borneotourgigant.com), run by Dutchman Lucas who has more than two decades of tour-leading experience in the region.

TANJUNG PUTING NATIONAL PARK

The 4000-square-kilometre Tanjung Puting National Park, comprising swamp forest, lowland rainforest and heath forest, is home to Malaysian sun bears, proboscis monkeys, clouded leopards, gharials and 6000 wild orang-utans. It was founded in the early 1970s by the legendary Dr Biruté Mary Galdikas. Part of the park, Camp Leakey (🌐orangutan.org/our-projects/research/camp-leakey), is less touristy than similar establishments in Sarawak and Sabah but shares their goal of rehabilitating orphaned or rescued orang-utans before reintroducing them to the wild. All-inclusive three-days and two-nights *klotok* (riverboat) tours can be arranged for around Rp2,000,000 per person from Kumai, easily accessible from Pangkalan Bun, which has daily flights to and from Pontianak, Jakarta and Surabaya with Kal Star and Trigana Air. Be Borneo Tours (☎0856 5120 2195, 🌐beborneo.com) is among the best and most competitively priced options, arranging open *klotok* tours and taking care of everything once you've arrived in Pangkalan Bun.

4

INFORMATION

Tourist office (Mon–Thurs 7.30am–4pm, Fri 7.30–11.30am; ☎ 0542 876033). On Jl MR Iswahyudi 121, near the airport, with English-speaking staff though little more than maps and brochures to offer.

ACCOMMODATION

Accommodation is mainly clustered into two groups: at the central intersection of Jl Jend A Yani and Jl Sudirman, and a few kilometres north up Jl A Yani. Decent budget accommodation is scarce.

Aida Jl Jend A Yani 12 ☎ 0542 421006. At the north end of the street, this sprawling yet friendly place has clean, decent-sized rooms, though some are dark. All rooms have cable TV and inside mandi, and some have a/c (Rp205,000). Breakfast and wi-fi in the lobby. Doubles **Rp180,000**

Aiqo Jl APT Pranoto 9 ☎ 0542 750288, ⊛ aiqohotel .com. Snazzy, bright place with compact spick-and-span rooms, with a/c, cable TV, reliable hot water, and wi-fi in the lobby. Ask for a room with a window (Rp248,000). Breakfast included. Doubles **Rp198,000**

Ayu Jl Pangeran Antasari 18 ☎ 0542 425290. Offers some of the best value in town, with small but clean fan and a/c rooms (Rp200,000) upstairs, all with attached bathrooms, set about 100m off busy Jl A Yani. Free wi-fi reaches to the second floor. Doubles **Rp150,000**

San Francisco Jl Pangeran Antasari 39 ☎ 0542 791619, ✉ sanfrancisco.bpn@gmail.com. New family-run business hotel across the street from *Ayu* that's worth the extra rupiahs, offering bright, clean rooms with a/c, hot showers, attached bathrooms and a buffet breakfast served in a pleasant rooftop restaurant. Doubles **Rp295,000**

EATING

There are cheap warung along the coastal road, at the Pelni harbour, next to the post office west on Jl Sudirman, and on the north side of Taman Bakapai.

Balikpapan Plaza Pacifica Foodcourt Jl Sudirman. In the basement of the giant Balikpapan Plaza. Great for those who struggle with Bahasa, this food court has pretty pictures of the food on offer. It's cheap and serves good *gado-gado* (Rp22,000). Daily 10am–10pm.

Depot Cendrawasih Jl Jend A Yani 1. Though you could easily walk right past this tiny restaurant along the busy main road, a few minutes' walk north of *Aida* hotel, it's a Balikpapan institution that draws local crowds for its tasty *soto banjar* (chicken soup with potatoes and eggs; Rp22,000), a South Kalimantan speciality, as well as its cakes and *es campur* (shaved ice dessert with fruits and condensed milk). Daily 11am–10pm.

Ocean's Jl Jend Sudirman. Sleek seafood restaurant with seating on a breezy wooden deck overlooking the sea. The attached bar is a great spot for a sundowner (large Bintang Rp60,000), and the wide selection of Indian dishes would warrant their own restaurant (chicken tikka masala Rp59,000). Daily 10am–2am.

DIRECTORY

Banks and exchange There are scores of ATMs, and big branches of BNI, BCA and BRI, on Jl Sudirman and Jl A Yani. For exchange, use PT Marazavalas (Jl A Yani 5).

Hospital International SOS Jl Papuk Raya 54 (☎ 0542 765966).

Immigration Office Jl Sudirman 23 (☎ 0542 421175).

Internet There are several internet cafés along Jl Ahmad Yani and one on Jl P Antasari to the north. Rates are around Rp6000/hr.

Pharmacies The Kimia Farma has two 24hr pharmacies, one at Jl Sudirman 4 and the other at Jl A Yani 95.

Post office The main post office with EMS counters is at Jl Sudirman 31 (Mon–Sat 8am–8pm, Sun 9am–5pm).

SAMARINDA AND THE SUNGAI MAHAKAM

Borneo's second-longest river, the **Mahakam**, winds southeast for over 900km from its source far inside the central ranges on the Malaysian border, before emptying into the Makassar Straits through a multi-channelled delta. An established three-day circuit begins from the lively port town of **Samarinda**, where the Mahakam is 1km wide and navigable by ocean-going ships, taking in historic **Tenggarong** and the Benuaq Dayak settlements at **Tanjung Isuy** and adjacent **Mancong**. With a week to spare, scanty forest and communities inland from the Middle Mahakam townships of **Melak** and **Long Iram** are within range; ten days is enough to include a host of Kenyah and Benuaq villages, as you venture up the changing Mahakam through the rapids towards **Long Iram** and **Long Bagun**. Especially if your Bahasa skills are lacking, consider picking up a guide in Samarinda – these tend to congregate around *Hidayah 1*, *Hidayah 2* and *Aida* hotels and start from Rp200,000 per day. The most established group in Samarinda is De'Gigant Tours (☎ 0541 777 8648, ⊛ borneotourgigant.com), though they're also a bit pricey. Samarinda is well connected by buses to Balikpapan's Batu Ampar terminal (2hr 30min).

Sulawesi

Sulawesi sprawls in the centre of the Indonesian archipelago, a tortuous outline resembling a 1000km letter "K", and one of the country's most compelling regions. Nowhere in Sulawesi is much more than 100km from the sea, though an almost complete covering of mountains isolates its four separate peninsulas from one another and from the outside world. Invaders were hard pushed to colonize beyond

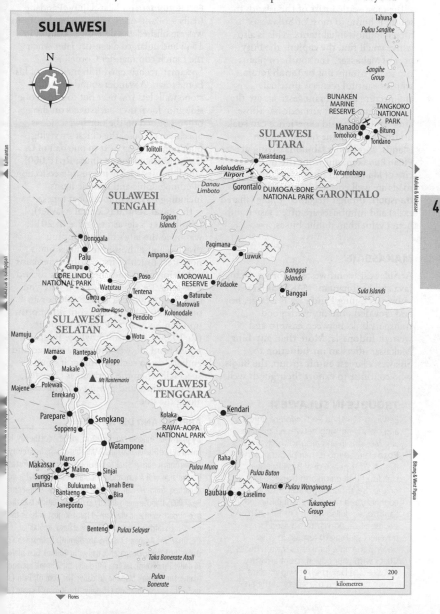

SULAWESI

N

Tahuna
Pulau Sangihe

Sangihe
Group

BUNAKEN
MARINE
RESERVE

TANGKOKO
NATIONAL
PARK

Manado
Tomohon   Bitung
Tondano

SULAWESI
UTARA

Tolitoli   Kwandang

Jalaluddin
Airport

Danau
Limboto   Gorontalo   DUMOGA-BONE
NATIONAL PARK   GARONTALO

Kotamobagu

SULAWESI
TENGAH

Togian
Islands

Donggala

Palu   Ampana   Pagimana
Gimpu   Luwuk
LORE LINDU
NATIONAL PARK   Poso   MOROWALI   Banggai
Watutau   RESERVE   Padaoke   Islands
Gintu   Tentena   Baturube   Banggai   Sula Islands
Danau Poso   Morowali
SULAWESI   Pendolo   Kolonodale
SELATAN
Mamuju   Wotu

Mamasa   Rantepao
Makale   Palopo

Majene   Polewali   ▲ Mt Rantemario   SULAWESI
Enrekang   TENGGARA

Parepare   Kolaka   Kendari
Sengkang
Soppeng   RAWA-AOPA
NATIONAL PARK
Watampone

Makassar   Maros   Raha
Sungg-   Malino   Sinjai   Pulau Muna   Pulau Buton
uminasa   Bulukumba   Tanah Beru   Wanci   Pulau Wangiwangi
Bantaeng   Bira   Baubau   Laselimo
Janeponto   Tukangbesi
Group

Benteng   Pulau Selayar

Taka Bonerate Atoll

Pulau
Bonerate

Flores

Kalimantan

Makassar & Balikpapan

Maluku & Makassar

Bitung & West Papua

4

0   200
kilometres

the coast, and a unique blend of cultures and habitats developed. The south is split between the highland **Torajans** and the lowland **Bugis**, there are various isolated tribes in the central highlands, and the Filipino-descended **Minahasans** reside in the far north.

The most settled part of the island, the south, is home to most of Sulawesi's fifteen million inhabitants. This is also where you'll find the capital, the busy port of **Makassar**. The southern plains rise to the mountains of **Tanah Toraja**, whose beautiful scenery, unusual architecture and vibrant festivals are the island's chief tourist attractions. Those after a more languid experience can soak up tropical sunshine on the **Togian Islands**, and there's fabulous diving at **Pulau Bunaken**, out from the northern city of **Manado**. In most areas, Sulawesi's roads are well covered by **public transport**, though freelance *kijang* (shared taxis) and minibuses are often faster and better value than public buses.

MAKASSAR

At Sulawesi's southwestern corner, facing Java and Kalimantan, **MAKASSAR** (also known as Ujung Pandang) is a large, hot and crowded port city with good transport links between eastern and western Indonesia. More than anything, Makassar offers an introduction to Sulawesi's largest ethnic group, the **Bugis**, who continue to export their goods well

TROUBLE IN SULAWESI

Between 1998 and 2001, violent unrest and bloody fighting between Christians and Muslims in and around the town of **Poso** claimed more than two thousand lives. A 2001 peace deal has largely stabilized the region and tourism is finally on the rise, though sporadic attacks continue, and notorious Mujahidin leader Santoso was killed nearby in July 2016. A degree of caution is still advised for travellers wishing to remain in Poso beyond the time it takes to switch buses. Check with your government advisory website (see box, p.45) for up-to-date information about the safety of the area.

beyond Sulawesi in *prahu*, distinctive vessels with steep, curved prows. The city has a long and distinguished history as a crucial trading port and coastal defence.

WHAT TO SEE AND DO

A monument to Sulawesi's colonial era, **Fort Rotterdam** on Jalan Ujung Pandang (daily 7.30am–6pm; entrance by donation) was established as a defensive position in 1545 and enlarged a century later when the Dutch commander Cornelius Speelman rechristened it in memory of his home town. A wander round the thick stone walls lets you peer out to sea on one side and down over backstreets on the other. Located on the northwest side is Speelman's House, the oldest surviving building, standing next to one half of **La Galigo Museum** (same times; Rp10,000), which houses a fairly interesting collection of ethnographic and historic items, including models of local boat types.

The **Pasar Sentral** (Central Market), rebuilt after a devastating fire in 2011, was once the city's main shopping district, and although the mega malls now steal much of its custom, it remains a thriving place and the best spot to find *pete-petes* (local bemos). From here you can pick up a becak (Rp25,000) or an ojek (Rp20,000) to take you 3km north up Jalan Sudarso to **Paotere harbour** (Rp10,000 admission), where Bugis *prahu* from all over Indonesia unload and embark cargo each morning; it's quite a spectacle when the harbour is crowded, the red, white and green *prahu* lined up along the dock.

ARRIVAL AND DEPARTURE

By plane Hasanuddin Airport, 20km northeast of the city, is linked by taxi (Rp100,000) and DAMRI buses, which run every 30min from the arrivals hall to the city, ending near the fort at the junction of Jl A Yani and Jl Riburane (daily 6am–10pm, departing from Medan Karebosi in the city 7am–8pm; Rp27,000). If you're going directly to the bus station, take the free airport shuttle (daily 5am–11pm) to just outside the gates, then catch a *pete-pete* to Terminal Daya (Rp5000).
Destinations Ambon (3 daily; 1hr 50min); Balikpapan (7 daily; 1hr 10min); Denpasar (6 daily; 1hr 20min); Gorontalo (6 daily; 1hr 30min); Jakarta (36 daily; 2hr 20min); Kupang (daily; 1hr 15min); Manado (6 daily; 1hr 50min); Palu (3 daily; 1hr 5min); Surabaya (15 daily; 1hr 30min); Ternate (2

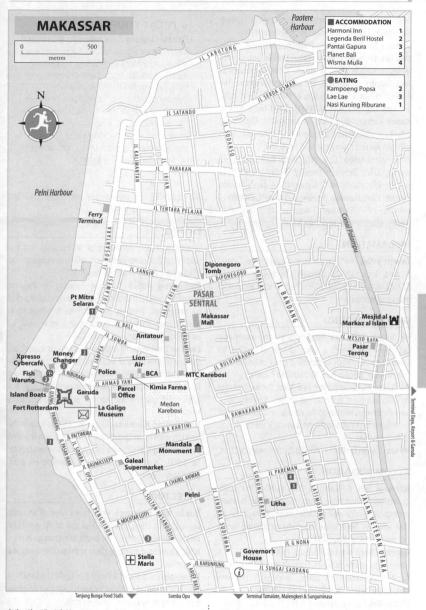

MAKASSAR

0 — 500
metres

N

Paotere
Harbour

Pelni Harbour

JL SABUTUNG
JL SERDA USMAN
JL SATANDO
JL SUDARSO
JL PARAKAN
JL IRIAN
JL TENTARA PELAJAR
Ferry Terminal
JL NUSANTARA
JL KALIMANTAN
JL SULAWESI
JL SANGIR
JALAN IRIAN
Diponegoro Tomb
JL DIPONEGORO
Pt Mitra Selaras
PASAR SENTRAL
JL BALI
Makassar Mall
JL SUMBA
Antatour
JL KOERDOMINOTO
JL BULUSARAUNG
JL ANDALAS
JL BANDANG
Canal Palompu
Mesjid al Markaz al Islam
JL MESJID RAYA
Pasar Terong
Xpresso Cybercafé
Money Changer
Lion Air
Fish Warung
JL RIBURANE
Police
BCA
MTC Karebosi
JL AHMAD YANI
Island Boats
Garuda
Parcel Office
Kimia Farma
JL TIMFEA
Fort Rotterdam
La Galigo Museum
Medan Karebosi
JL PANDANG
JL PATIMURA
JL R A KARTINI
JL BAWAKARAENG
Mandala Monument
JL SOMBA
JL PASAR IKAN
JL BAUMASSEPE
Galeal Supermarket
JL CHAIRUL ANWAR
JL OPU
Pelni
JL SULTAN HASANUDDIN
JL JENDRAL SUDIRMAN
JL GUNUNG MERAPI
JL PAREMAN
JL GUNUNG LATIMOJONG
Litha
JL PENGHIBUR
JL MOCHTAR LUTFI
JL G NONA
Governor's House
JALAN VETERAN UTARA
Stella Maris
JL KARUNRUNG
JL ARIEF RATE
JL SUNGAI SADDANG

Tanjung Bunga Food Stalls ▼   Somba Opu ▼   ▼ Terminal Tamalate, Malengkeri & Sunguminasa

Terminal Daya, Airport & Garuda

4

ACCOMMODATION
Harmoni Inn	1
Legenda Beril Hostel	2
Pantai Gapura	3
Planet Bali	5
Wisma Mulia	4

EATING
Kampoeng Popsa	2
Lae Lae	3
Nasi Kuning Riburane	1

daily; 1hr 45min); Yogyakarta (4 daily; 2hr).

By bus Both day and night buses for Rantepao dock at the huge Terminal Daya, 14km to the east on the way to the airport, from where you can catch a metered taxi (around Rp50,000) or *pete-pete* (Rp5000) into the centre; in the other direction, *pete-petes* depart from Medan Karebosi. Buses heading south use Terminal Malengkeri, 7km south

of the centre, or Sungguminasa, another 4km southeast of Malengkeri; both are linked by red *pete-pete* to Jl Jend Sudirman in the city (Rp5000). Relatively comfortable a/c bus operators such as Litha (Jl Gunung Merapi 135; ☎0411 4642262) and Bintang Prima (Ruko Tello Blok B6; ☎0411 4772888), each charging around Rp140,000 per seat, will pick you up in town.

Destinations Daily departures for Ampana (28hr); Manado (2–3 days); Rantepao (8hr); Tentena (19hr).

By ferry The Pelni harbour, Pelabuhan Makassar, is less than 1km northwest of Pasar Sentral on Jl Nusantara, with ferries running to ports all around Sulawesi, as well as Java, Sumatra, Kalimantan, Bali and Nusa Tenggara. The Pelni office is at Jl Sawerigading 14 (Mon–Fri 9am–3pm, Sat 9am–noon; ☎0411 3614861). Other boats dock at Paotere harbour, 3km north of the centre; their ticket offices are across from the harbour on Jl Nusantara. Ojeks will take you into town for around Rp20,000.

Destinations Ambon (2 weekly; 36hr); Balikpapan (1–2 weekly; 22hr); Denpasar (weekly; 2 days); Jakarta (2 weekly; 48hr); Jayapura (2 fortnightly; 4 days); Kupang (weekly; 35hr); Nunukan (weekly; 2–3 days); Larantuka (3 monthly; 24hr); Surabaya (3 weekly; 24hr); Tarakan (3 weekly; 48hr); Ternate (monthly; 62hr).

INFORMATION

Tourist office The Sulawesi Tourist Information Centre, Jl Jend Sudirman 23 (Mon–Fri 8am–4pm; ☎0411 872366 or ☎0411 878912), has helpful staff and useful maps and brochures.

GETTING AROUND

By becak Makassar's becak drivers are annoyingly persistent, and there's a good chance of ending up somewhere completely unexpected; a fare of Rp8000/km is reasonable. Bargain hard. Rp20,000 to Paotere.

By bemo Makassar's blue *pete-petes* (bemos) charge Rp5000, and most terminate at or near Karebosi. They have their routes written on the windscreen, colour-coded for different destinations; the most useful is the purple one to Terminal Daya.

By taxi Bosowa (☎0411 454545) is the recommended firm.

ACCOMMODATION

Harmoni Inn Jl Nusantara 114 ☎0411 362 2259, ⓦhotelharmoniinn.com. Central harbourfront location, impeccable service and spotless rooms, though not all have windows. Great value, especially considering there's hot water. Doubles Rp200,000

Legenda Beril Hostel Jl Sarui 2 ☎0853 4263 3633. A hostel only in name and price, *Legenda Beril* offers brilliant value, with modern a/c rooms, quick wi-fi and very friendly and helpful staff. Doubles Rp150,000

Planet Bali Jl Sungai Pareman III 15–17 ☎0411 362 0071. Although large and anonymous, this is a good option if *Wisma Mulia* just down the road is full, and even the cheapest rooms have windows. Breakfast and wi-fi are included; expect to pay a deposit upon check-in. Doubles Rp195,000

Wisma Mulia Jl Sungai Pareman III 1 ☎0411 365 0967. Friendly and immaculate, this is the best value for money in town. The cheaper rooms lack windows, but are large,

★ **TREAT YOURSELF**

Pantai Gapura Jl Pasar Ikan 10 ☎0411 368 0222, ⓦpantaigapura.com. Even if you can't afford to stay for the night, it provides an excellent shelter from the heat and hurly-burly outside. Wend your way through the maze of bungalows, perched on stilts above the sea, to the sunset bar in the far right corner, where you can enjoy a meal or drink overlooking the sea. There's also a lovely pool available to non-guests for Rp30,000. Doubles Rp760,000

with cable TV, a/c and en-suite bathrooms. Breakfast included. Doubles Rp150,000

EATING

Wander past Fort Rotterdam of an evening, and the shabby patch of concrete opposite will have woken up and filled with warung, mostly serving fish.

Kampoeng Popsa Jl Ujung Pandang 4. Pleasant waterfront patio just opposite Fort Rotterdam, surrounded by Indonesian, Western and Japanese fast-food stalls (dishes from Rp20,000), featuring live rock music at weekends. Daily 10am–midnight.

Lae Lae Jl Datamuseng 8. In a city famous for its seafood, *Lae Lae* is something of an institution, and always busy with locals and tourists. A one-person fish comes to about Rp50,000. The main doors are permanently closed, but follow the painted fish to the side entrance. Daily noon–10pm.

Nasi Kuning Riburane Jl Riburane 11. This hole in the wall is named for its speciality, yellow rice, which is served in industrial quantities with meat, egg and vegetables for Rp25,000. Come before hungry office workers eat it all. Daily 7am–1pm.

DIRECTORY

Banks and exchange Most banks have ATMs, with many located along Jl Jend A Yani and at the northeast corner of Medan Karebosi. The best moneychanger in town is Haji La Tunrung, by the seafront at the southern end of Jl Nusantara.

Hospitals Stella Maris, Jl Penghibur (☎0411 854341), is your best chance in southern Sulawesi for correct diagnosis and treatment by English-speaking staff.

Immigration Jl Perintis Kemerdekaan Km 13, Tamalanrea (Mon–Fri 8am–4pm; ☎0411 584559). Northeast of town towards the airport; not the easiest place in Indonesia for a visa extension.

Internet There's wi-fi in many hotels and restaurants, while Xpresso Cybercafé at Jl Ujung Pandang 12A has terminals (Rp5000/hr).

Pharmacy Kimia Farma on Jl Ahmad Yani.

Police Jl Ahmad Yani.

Post office Jl Slamet Riyadi near Fort Rotterdam (Mon–Sat 8am–9pm).

Shopping The huge MTC Karebosi on the northeast corner of Medan Karebosi is a good place to cool off and shop for bargains.

Travel agents The most efficient agent is AntaVaya on Jl Dr Wahidin Sudirohusodo 35 (☎0411 361 8648, ⓦ antatour.com).

TANAH TORAJA

Some 250km north of Makassar, a steep wall of mountains marks the limits of Bugis territory and the start of **Tanah Toraja's highlands**, a beautiful spread of hills and valleys where sleek buffalo wallow in lush green paddy fields. Known as **Tator** in the local idiom, Tanah Toraja is home to one of Indonesia's most confident and vivid cultures, and is planted firmly on the agenda of every visitor to Sulawesi. There's a morbid attraction to many of the region's sights, which feature ceremonial animal slaughter, decaying coffins and dank mausoleums spilling bones. Tour groups tend to concentrate on key sites, so it's not hard to find more secluded corners. Grave sites charge an entry fee of around Rp20,000.

Tanah Toraja's main town, at least as far as tourists are concerned, is **Rantepao**, 18km north of the regional capital,

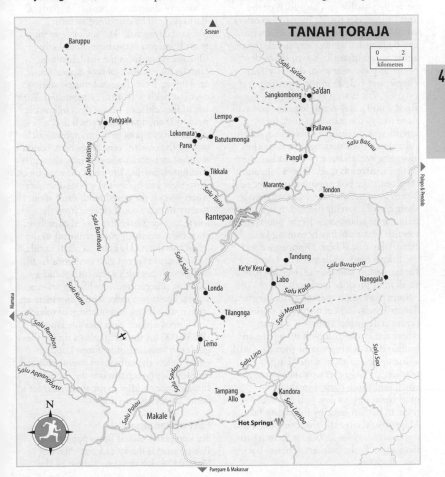

Makale. It's a popular base for travellers, most of whom descend for the major **festival season** between July and September. Expect hot days and cool nights; there is a "dry" season between April and October, but this is relative only to the amount of rain at other times, so bring non-slip walking boots and rainwear.

Rantepao

A prosperous market town on the rocky banks of **Sungai Sadan Valley**, RANTEPAO is home to the Sadan Toraja. With an abundance of good-value accommodation and worthwhile excursions in every direction, it makes an ideal base for exploring Tanah Toraja. And though it's perfectly possible to visit much of the area independently, Rantepao also offers a whole host of experienced guides who can be found at almost any hotel, travel agent or restaurant in town; if you'd prefer to pick your own, drop by *Pia's Poppies* (see p.332) in the morning or evening. Prices start at around Rp350,000 a day per guide, but you will need to pay for transport and, for attending a ceremony, gifts on top of this.

The town itself stretches just over 1km along the eastern bank of the Sadan, the central **crossroads** marked by a miniature *tongkonan* (see box opposite) on a pedestal. North from here is Jalan Mappanyuki, a short run of souvenir shops, bus agents and restaurants; Jalan Ahmad Yani points south towards Makale before becoming Jalan Pong Tiku; east is Jalan Diponegoro and the Palopo road, while westerly Jalan Landorundun leads to the riverside past a small fresh-produce market.

Rantepao's main **market** – the biggest in Tanah Toraja, 2.5km northeast of the centre at Terminal Bolu – is a must: where else could you pick up a bargain buffalo then celebrate your purchase with a litre or two of palm wine? Large markets are held every six days, though you'll find some traders in the marketplace every day. You can walk there in half an hour by following Jalan Mappanyuki over the river, passing a few impressive *tongkonan* before crossing the river again to the market. A bemo back costs Rp5000.

South of Rantepao

Makale is the administrative capital of Tanah Toraja, and the most famous sites lie off the road running south from Rantepao to Makale. The route is plied all day long by bemos running in both directions (20min; Rp7000). Just south of Rantepao, a concrete statue of a buffalo marks the turn-off to four much-restored *tongkonan* at Ke'te' Kesu (4km), the central part of which is said to be the oldest in the district. An adjacent *rante* (ceremonial ground) sports a dozen megaliths, the tallest about 3m high. A path leads up the hill past hanging and no-longer-hanging coffins mortised into the side of the truncated peak.

Some of the other sights to the south of Rantepao can be combined to form a pleasant day's stroll. The walk begins 9km from Rantepao at the turn-off to Lemo. One kilometre from the road, **Lemo** is famous for its much-photographed *tau-tau*, set 10m up a cliff face and mutely staring over the fields with arms outstretched. Turn left in the centre of Lemo, then follow the road to **Tilangnga**, where you'll find a pleasant rocky pool to swim in, but watch out for the resident eels. From here, **Londa** is about an hour's walk: continue through Tilangnga, bearing left when the road forks. Turn right just before the school, then left when you hit the paved road. After about twenty minutes you'll emerge from the forest and see a large red-roofed church on your right, at which point strike off to the left across the paddy fields to reach Londa. Set in a shaded green glen underneath tall cliffs, overhung with a few coffins and a fantastic collection of very lifelike *tau-tau*, Londa boasts two caves whose entrances are strewn with bones and offerings of tobacco. You'll need a guide with pressure lamps (Rp30,000 for the lamp, plus a tip for the guide) to venture inside. From Londa, either follow the tarmac for twenty minutes or ask villagers to point out the short cut through rice paddies to the main road for a bemo back to Rantepao.

East of Rantepao

Six kilometres east of Rantepao on the Palopo road is the spread-out village of **Marante**, which contains almost all the main features of Tanah Toraja. Close to the road is a fine row of *tongkonan*; behind, a path leads to where *tau-tau* and weathered coffins face out over a river. A few kilometres further on, look out for a group of megaliths in a field at **Tondon**. **Nanggala**, about another 6km along the Palopo road from Marante, then 2km south, is a stately village with a dozen brilliantly finished *tongkonan*, and a large flying-fox colony in the neighbouring trees.

There's a very pleasant five-hour walk due west to **Ke'te' Kesu'** from here, though the network of paths around Nanggala means you really need a map or, better still, a guide.

North of Rantepao

If you're more interested in the living than the dead, it's worth venturing north from Terminal Bolu in Rantepao to **Sa'dan**. Bemos along this road are reasonably frequent, or you can walk between sites. Seven kilometres from Rantepao you reach **Pangli**, famed for its *balok* (palm wine). Not much further, a signed road off to the left leads past some megaliths to **Pallawa**, whose *tongkonan* are embellished with scores of buffalo horns. For the more active, it's possible to walk a large loop from here to Sa'dan, though again you'll need a map. Back on the main road, another 4km brings you

---

TORAJAN CULTURE AND FESTIVALS

Anthropologists place Torajan **origins** as part of the Bronze Age exodus from Vietnam; Torajans say that their ancestors descended from heaven by way of a stone staircase, which was later angrily smashed by the creator Puang Matua after his laws were broken. These laws became the root of **aluk todolo**, the way of the ancestors. Only a fraction of Torajans now follow the old religion, the strict practice of which was prohibited after head-hunting and raunchy life-rites proved unacceptable to colonial and nationalist administrations. But its trappings remain: everywhere you'll see extraordinary **tongkonan** and **alang**, traditional houses and rice-barns, and the Torajan social calendar remains ringed with exuberant ceremonies involving pig and buffalo sacrifices. Torajans are masters at promoting their culture, positively encouraging outsiders to experience their way of life.

TORAJAN FESTIVALS

Ceremonies are divided into *rambu tuka*, or smoke ascending (associated with the east and life), and *rambu solo*, smoke descending (associated with the west and death). A typical *rambu tuka* ceremony is the **dedication of a new tongkonan**.

The biggest of all Torajan ceremonies are **funerals**, the epitome of a *rambu solo* occasion. Held over several days, it begins with the parading of the oval coffin, and traditionally, the first afternoon ends with **buffalo fights**. The following day – or days, if it's a big funeral – is spent welcoming guests, who troop village by village into the ceremonial field, led by a noblewoman dressed in orange and gold, bearing gifts of *balok* (palm wine), pigs trussed on poles and buffalo. The next day, the **major sacrifice** takes place: the nobility must sacrifice at least 24 buffalo, with one hundred needed to see a high-ranking chieftain on his way. Finally, the coffin is laid to rest in a west-oriented house-grave or rock-face mausoleum, with a **tau-tau**, a life-sized wooden effigy of the deceased, positioned in a nearby gallery facing outwards, and – for the highest-ranking nobles – a megalith raised in the village ground.

ATTENDING TORAJAN CEREMONIES

Witnessing a traditional ceremony is what draws most visitors to Tanah Toraja, particularly during the "peak festival season" in the agriculturally quiet period from June to September. To visit a ceremony outsiders should really have an **invitation**, via a guide. As more participants means greater honour, however, it's also possible to turn up at an event and hang around the sidelines until somebody offers to act as your host. You are highly unlikely to be the only foreigner attending; snap-happy tourists are part of the scenery, with each sacrifice a photographic feeding frenzy. Make sure you take a **gift** for your hosts – a carton of cigarettes, or a jerry can of *balok* – and hand it over when they invite you to sit down with them. Do not sit down uninvited; dress modestly and wear **dark clothing** for funerals – a black T-shirt with blue jeans is perfectly acceptable, as are thong sandals.

to a fork in the road: east is **Sa'dan** itself, with a bizarre array of mausoleums and an *ikat* market every six days; west is **Sangkombong**, where local women will demonstrate their weaving skills before making their sales pitch.

ARRIVAL AND DEPARTURE

By bus Terminal Bolu is 2.5km northeast of town and linked by bemos (Rp5000), though buses from Makassar can drop you off at your accommodation or in the vicinity of the crossroads. Bus companies are set along Jl Andi Mappanyuki in the town centre, and buses leave from just outside their offices. Buses to Makassar run day and night, with luxury a/c options available from a number of companies (Rp100,000–150,000). For Tentena and Poso, the best companies are Ketty (Jl Mappanyuki 49; ☏0813 4372 7230) and Rappan Marannu (Jl Mappanyuki 52; ☏0423 25193), each with daily departures at 8am (Rp170,000).

Destinations Makassar (8hr); Pendolo (10hr); Poso (14hr); Tentena (12hr).

By bemo Bemos leave Jl Ahmad Yani every few minutes for Makale (Rp7000), and just as often from Jl Diponegoro for Terminal Bolu.

INFORMATION

Tourist information The government tourist office (Mon–Sat 7am–1pm; ☏0423 25455) is just past the hospital at Jl Ahmad Yani 62A; however, the friendly tourist services at the Tora Tora gallery, Jl Mappanyuki 64, are open longer hours (daily 9am–6.30pm).

ACCOMMODATION

Accommodation is scattered across town, with some offering excellent value for money.

Duta 88 Jl Sawerigading 12, signposted off Jl Mappanyuki ☏0423 23477. Seven beautiful, if slightly gloomy, traditional bungalows, all with hot water, in a lovely garden. Very central, but the road outside is noisy. Doubles `Rp250,000`

Hotel Pison I Jl Pong Tiku GII 8, opposite *Pia's Poppies* ☏0423 21344. Central and good value, this friendly place offers a range of prices (up to Rp220,000) according to room size, location and water temperature. Everything is kept immaculate, though the cheapest rooms suffer slightly from damp. Doubles `Rp150,000`

★**Pia's Poppies** Jl Lorong Merpati 4, off Jl Pong Tiku ☏0423 21121. This backpacker stalwart, featuring a new wing, remains a beautiful and tranquil place to stay. The stylish rooms feature rock-pool bathtubs with hot water. Breakfast is extra (Rp25,000), but the food is fantastic. Doubles `Rp198,000`

Wisma Irama Jl Abdul Gani 16 ☏0423 21371, ✉wisma .irama@yahoo.co.id. Housed in a lovely terracotta Torajan villa, this guesthouse offers unremarkable, slightly ageing

rooms, with hot water, in a decent location in the centre of town. Doubles `Rp200,000`

EATING AND DRINKING

Most restaurants offer local Torajan dishes such as *piong* (chicken, fish, pork or buffalo cooked over an open fire in bamboo shoots with coconut, herbs and spices) and *pamarassan* (again chicken, fish, pork or buffalo cooked in black Torajan spice), though you should give at least two hours' notice.

Café Aras Jl Mappanyuki 64. Lovely bamboo-walled place with local artwork (for sale) adorning the walls and live music out back. Delicious Indonesian dishes start from Rp30,000; good pasta and pizza are available too. Mon–Sat 10am–10pm, Sun 3–10pm.

Saruran Jl Mappanyuki 119. Bright, cheerful Chinese-Indonesian joint, popular with young locals and soundtracked by saccharine Indo-pop. Delicious mains start at a very reasonable Rp15,000. Daily 7.30am–10pm.

DIRECTORY

Banks and exchange There are several ATMs along Jl Mappanyuki and Jl Diponegoro.

Hospital The best doctors are at Elim Hospital, Jl Ahmad Yani (☏0423 21258).

Internet There are many internet cafés around town, including several on Jl Mappanyuki; all charge Rp4000–6000/hr.

Motorbike rental Lebonna, Jl Monginsidi 102 (☏0423 23520), rents out motorbikes, as do most hotels and tour agents in town, for Rp80,000/day.

Pharmacy Azhar Farma, Jl Mappanyukki 92.

Post office Jl Ahmad Yani 111, just south of the main crossroads (Mon–Thurs 8am–3.30pm, Fri 8am–4pm, Sat 8am–12.30pm).

Travel agencies Metro Permai, at Jl Mappanyuki 15 (☏0423 21785).

TENTENA

Straddling the northern shores of Danau Poso, Indonesia's third-deepest lake, the charming Christian town of **TENTENA** offers a welcome rest on the road between the Togians and Tanah Toraja. It's also a decent base for excursions to the pristine forests and mystifying megaliths of **Lore Lindu National Park**. A pleasant motorbike ride through Tentena's countryside passes dozens of churches, cacao plantations and wonderful vistas across the lake, eventually reaching **Saluopa** (Rp20,000), a spectacular set of falls set in the jungle 14km west of town.

ARRIVAL AND INFORMATION

By bus The bus terminal is 4km northeast of the town's accommodation hub (ojeks cost Rp10,000). There are daily bemos to Poso (10am; 2hr; Rp40,000), from where buses connect Ampana (2 daily; 5hr); and night buses to Rantepao (daily 6pm; 12hr), run by Ketty and Rappan Marannu.

Information The friendly tourist office (daily 8am–6pm; ⓣ0458 21484) is just east of the new bridge, offering maps and arranging tours. Good maps and information are also available from *Hotel Victory*.

ACCOMMODATION AND EATING

The warung near the bridges serve the local speciality, *sogili bakar* (grilled freshwater eel).

Tandolala Cottages Jl Poros Tentena-Peura Km 3 ⓣ08525 5151 593. 3km south of town, this set of private (Rp300,000) and duplex cottages sits on stilts over the lake, each equipped with a mosquito net and balcony. Further out on the water, the restaurant serves set lunches and dinners (Rp60,000/80,000). Friendly owner Simon has plenty of helpful advice and can pick you up from the bus station with advance notice. Doubles Rp200,000

Victory Jl Diponegoro 18 ⓣ0458 21392, ⓦvictorytentena.com. The most popular spot in town, set on a quiet street not far from the pair of bridges. Rooms are basic and clean, some with hot water (Rp250,000) and all set around a small garden. Friendly, English-speaking staff double as excellent guides, leading treks in Lore Lindu. Doubles Rp175,000

DIRECTORY

Banks There's a Mandiri Bank ATM at the bus terminal.

Internet Shiawase Café on Jl Diponegoro (daily 8am–9.30pm) near *Hotel Victory*, with free wi-fi for customers, and computers for Rp5000/hr.

AMPANA

Small but reasonably tourist-friendly **AMPANA** is the southern access point for the Togian Islands. There are plenty of warung spread along the coastal road and a handful of decent accommodation options for those awaiting ferries, as well as most services lacking in the islands. Internet cafés are scattered around town, and there are BRI and Mandiri ATMs along Jalan Moh Hatta.

ARRIVAL AND DEPARTURE

By bus There are 2 daily buses to Ampana from Poso (5hr).

By car A seat in a shared taxi from Tentena to Ampana costs around Rp100,000.

By boat Boats to Wakai (for Kadidiri) leave from the main port, just north of Oasis, while boats to Bomba depart from the port of Labuhan, 3km east near Marina Cottages.

ACCOMMODATION

Irama Jl RA Kartini 11 ⓣ0464 21055. Just up the road from *Oasis*, this losmen is among the cheapest in town, with friendly staff and ageing, slightly grimy rooms that come with TVs and are adequate for a night. Doubles Rp110,000

Marina Cottages Jl Tanjung Api 33, Labuhan ⓣ0464 21280, ⓦmarina-cottages.com. Handy for the boats to Bomba, *Marina* is in Labuhan, 3km east of the town centre (Rp7000 by ojek). It has generously sized bungalows, some with a/c (Rp300,000) and all with terraces facing a black pebble beach. Staff are helpful, there's wi-fi in the spacious restaurant and breakfast is included. Doubles Rp150,000

Oasis Jl RA Kartini 5 ⓣ0464 21058. Just 100m from the port and run by the same management as *Kadidiri Paradise* (see p.334), this is the most popular backpacker hotel in town, with clean, simple rooms set around a lovely garden. Great for organizing onward travel to the Togians; on the downside, the karaoke next door goes on until midnight. Doubles Rp160,000

4

THE TOGIAN ISLANDS

The **TOGIAN ISLANDS** form a fragmented, 120km-long crescent across the shallow blue waters of Tomini Bay, their steep grey sides weathered into sharp ridges capped by coconut palms and hardwoods. The exceptional **snorkelling and diving** around the islands features turtles, sharks, octopus, garden eels, and a mixed bag of reef and pelagic fish species. On the downside, there are also nine depots in the Togians dealing in the live export of seafood to restaurants in Asia; many of these operations employ cyanide sprays, which stun large fish but kill everything else – including coral.

From west to east, **Batu Daka**, **Togian** and **Talata Koh** are the Togians' three main islands, with **Walea Kodi** and **Walea Bahi** further east. The main settlements are **Bomba** and **Wakai** on Batu Daka, and **Katupat** on Togian. Wakai is something of a regional hub, with transport out to smaller islands. There are no vehicle roads or widespread electricity in the Togians and you'll find it pays not to be on too tight a schedule; most accommodation places offer day-trips and shared transfers. Tourism in the islands is budget-oriented but good, and prices include meals. July through to September are the coolest months, when winds can interrupt ferries. Diving is usually good all year round, though visibility in December can be variable.

Bomba

Four hours from Ampana and at the western end of Batu Daka, **BOMBA** comprises a few dozen houses and a mosque facing north across a pleasant bay. There's a long beach 5km west of town, but it's the sea that warrants a visit here, with the Togians' best snorkelling an hour away at **Catherine reef**. The coast near here is interesting, too, offering the possibility of seeing crocodiles in remote inlets; some islets east of Bomba are completely covered by villages, their boundaries reinforced with hand-cut coral ramparts.

Wakai and Kadidiri

At the eastern end of Batu Daka, about five hours from Ampana and two from Bomba, **WAKAI** is only of interest as a transport hub. Half an hour by motorized outrigger from Wakai, 3km-long **Kadidiri**, with its fine beaches, is one of the nicest of the islands.

ARRIVAL AND DEPARTURE

FROM THE SOUTH

Boats to Wakai leave from Ampana's main port, just north of *Oasis Hotel*, while boats to Bomba depart from 3km to the east near *Marina Cottages*. Boats from Ampana to Wakai (for Kadidiri) depart daily except Fri (Mon–Thurs 10am, Sun 9am; 5hr; Rp60,000 one-way), and return from Wakai to Ampana daily except Mon & Fri (Tues, Thurs & Sun 10am, Wed 7am; 4–7hr). On Mon, Tues, Wed & Sat, boats continue from Wakai to Katupat (for Bolilanga; 1hr; Rp60,000 from Ampana), returning Sun, Tues & Thurs at 6.45am. Boats from Ampana to Bomba depart Sun, Tues & Fri (9am; 3hr; Rp25,000), returning from Bomba to Ampana on Mon, Thurs & Sat (9am; 3hr).

FROM THE NORTH

From the port of Gorontalo, the KM Tuna Tomini departs for Wakai every Tues & Fri (5pm; 12–13hr), returning from Wakai on Mon & Thurs (4pm; 12–13hr; Rp63,000/Rp90,000 a/c).

GETTING AROUND

Getting around the Togians is a slow process, and schedules are constantly changing. Your best bet is to get to Wakai, Bomba or Kadidiri, and assess your options from there, as even in Ampana and Gorontalo everyone's schedules tend to differ slightly. If time is of the essence, or if you're in a group, there is always the option of chartering local boats, though make sure you see the vessel first. The hotels on Kadidiri will pick you up from Wakai, and the hotels on Bomba can hail the passing public boats that head between Wakai and Ampana five days a week.

ACCOMMODATION

Phone reception on the islands is notoriously bad, so the numbers below might not always work. All prices include meals.

BOMBA

★**Island Retreat** ☎ 0852 4115 8853, ⓦ togianisland retreat.com. This smart American-run place to the south of Bomba sits on one of the best beaches in the Togians, most of its basic cottages only a few metres from the water. The food is fantastic, and they run a competitively priced diving operation as well (from $31/dive, plus $6 for equipment rental). Contact them at least two weeks in advance to arrange for a pick-up. Per person **Rp450,000**

Poya Lisa Cottages ☎ 0823 4995 1833, ⓦ poyalisa -bomba.com. A handful of very basic cottages set on their own idyllic island just off Bomba, a location that makes up for the lack of facilities. Friendly staff organize snorkelling trips, but for diving and equipment rental you'll need to go through *Island Retreat*. Per person **Rp135,000**

KADIDIRI

Three sets of cottages share a single beach, though only *Black Marlin* and *Paradise* organize diving.

Black Marlin ☎ 0856 5720 2004, ⓦ blackmarlindiving .com. The best-equipped dive centre on the island, with smart cottages and fantastic food; staff are unattentive, though, and non-divers should certainly look elsewhere. €30/dive. Per person **Rp250,000**

Kadidiri Paradise Contact the *Oasis* in Ampana ☎ 0813 4372 2072, ⓔ kadidiriparadise@gmail.com. Beautiful dark-wood bungalows, a lively bar and a picturesque jetty that's perfect for a sundowner. The best place to stay on Kadidiri. Rp450,000/dive. Per person **Rp250,000**

Lestari ☎ 0821 9144 4503, ⓔ teteng.lestari@yahoo .com. On the western edge of the beach, and separated from the others for half the day by high tide, *Lestari* is the smallest of Kadidiri's options, and offers good-value bungalows each with a private bathroom. Per person **Rp200,000**

BOLILANGA

About an hour away from Kadidiri, tiny Bolilanga Island is relatively un-touristy, the perfect spot if you're after complete seclusion. There's only one place to stay, and the owners can arrange a free pick-up from Katupat on Togian Island if you call ahead. From Wakai, they'll charter a boat for you for Rp300,000.

Bolilanga Island Resort ☏0852 4100 3685, ⓦbolilangaresort.com. An intimate place offering adjoining and freestanding (Rp350,000) beachfront bungalows with a wonderfully relaxing, end-of-the-world feel and good food. Inexpensive snorkelling and fishing trips are available, and guests can paddle a small boat around the tiny island for free. Per person Rp250,000

GORONTALO

GORONTALO is a quiet but well-equipped town, not an unpleasant place to get stranded should you be unlucky with Togian boat schedules. Its streets are laid out on a grid system, making it easy to navigate. The main north–south road is Jalan A Yani, where you'll find ATMs at the BNI and Danamon banks. Crossing it east–west is Jalan 23 Januari, with the post office at the junction and the Pelni office a short way further along. Wi-fi is available at the *New Melati Hotel* next to the sportsground. There are plenty of warung around, and a lively night market.

ARRIVAL AND DEPARTURE

By plane Jalaluddin Airport is 32km north of town. A seat in a shared taxi costs around Rp70,000.
Destinations Luwuk (3 weekly; 40min); Makassar (7 daily; 1hr 30min); Manado (2–3 daily; 50min).
By bus Terminal Andalas is 3km to the north of town, Rp10,000 by bentur (motorized rickshaw), with buses to Manado (daily 5.30am; 10hr) and Palu (17hr).
By car Faster and more comfortable for the trip to Manado, *kijangs* meet ferries arriving from the Togians. You can also book these at their offices north past the bus terminal on Jl Andalas, among them PO Garuda (☏0435 823192). Tickets are priced according to your seat (back/front Rp175,000/Rp200,000), and they can pick you up at your hotel.
By ferry The harbour is a 15min bentur ride from town (Rp10,000). The Pelni office is in town on Jl 23 Januari 31 (☏0435 21089).
Destinations Bitung (3 monthly; 15hr); Denpasar (monthly; 5 days); Makassar (2 monthly; 72hr).

ACCOMMODATION

Karina Jl A Yani 28 ☏0435 828411. The best-value accommodation in town, in a conveniently central position. Smart, sparkling clean and very friendly, it offers a/c, hot-water showers, TV and Western-style toilets in all rooms. Doubles Rp190,000

New Melati Jl Walter Monginsidi 1 ☏0435 822934, ⓦnewmelatihotel.com. Remains a favourite among backpackers, with decent budget rooms set around a pleasant garden beyond the posh entrance. All rooms come with worn bathrooms, and some have a/c (Rp180,000) and hot water (Rp300,000). Friendly staff are expert at helping with onward travel. Wi-fi and breakfast included. Doubles Rp130,000

EATING

There are plenty of warung around town, including in the park in front of the *New Melati*.
Magic Pan Pizzeria Jl A Yani 55 ☏0435 829619. The first port of call for many of those freshly arrived from the Togians. Set in attractive, a/c surroundings, it serves a range of thin-crust pizzas (medium Rp50,000), pastas (from Rp35,000) and a few Indonesian favourites. There's wi-fi, and they deliver (Rp7000). Daily 7am–10pm.

MANADO

Capital of Sulawesi Utara, **MANADO** is mainly used by travellers as a launching point for spectacular **diving and snorkelling** in the Bunaken Marine Reserve. You can either base yourself in Manado and do day-trips to the reefs, or stay on the island itself, where there are plenty of accommodation and dive operators to choose from.

Manado is busy, noisy, hot and in a permanent state of near-gridlock, but it also exudes a bustling energy, which can be refreshing for those feeling deprived of civilization after a trip to the Togians. The town's old hub lies in the north, where you'll find the harbour and the fresh produce **market**, Pasar Bersehati, although the area's popularity has been overtaken by the vast strip of new shopping centres known collectively as the Manado Boulevard, stretching south between Jalan Pierre Tendean and the rapidly expanding coastline. Microlets, many of which turn into mobile discos at night – complete with flashing lights, thumping bass and sometimes even LCD TVs – swarm along both this road and parallel Jalan Sam Ratulangi to the east.

Manado was flattened in 1844 by a devastating **earthquake**, and tremors measuring up to 5.0 on the Richter scale continue to rattle the town for a few seconds every three months or so.

ARRIVAL AND DEPARTURE

By plane Sam Ratulangi Airport is 12km northeast of the centre. Taxis to town cost around Rp80,000, and microlets connect terminal Paal Dua (Rp6000). Some of the bigger dive centres have representatives on hand to answer questions and help book trips.

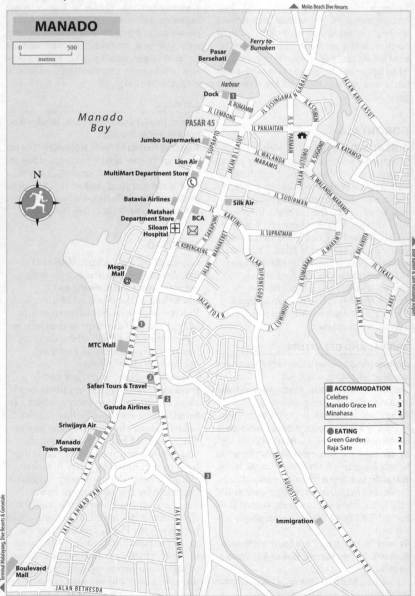

MANADO

0 — 500 metres

Molas Beach Dive Resorts

Ferry to Bunaken

Pasar Bersehati

Harbour

Dock

JL RUMAMBI

JL SISINGAN GARAJA

JL KS TUBUN

JALAN ARIE LASUT

Manado Bay

JL LEMBONG

PASAR 45

JL PANJAITAN

JL S PARMAN

JL KATAMSO

N

Jumbo Supermarket

JL SUPRAPTO

JL D LASUT

JL WALANDA MARAMIS

JALAN SUTOMO

JL SUGONO

JL WALANDA MARAMIS

Lion Air

MultiMart Department Store

Batavia Airlines

Matahari Department Store

Siloam Hospital

BCA

Silk Air

JL KARTINI

JL SARAPUNG

JL SUDIRMAN

JL SUPRATMAN

JL KORENGKENG

JALAN MAHAKERET

JALAN DIPONEGORO

JL KUMARAKA

JL MARAMIS

JL KOTAMOBAGU

JL TIKALA

JALAN TI

JL ARES

Mega Mall
@

JALAN TOAR

JL LUMIMUUT

MTC Mall

TENDEAN

JALAN SAM RATULANGI

Safari Tours & Travel

Garuda Airlines

Sriwijaya Air

Manado Town Square

JALAN PIERRE

JALAN 17 AGUSTUS

JALAN 14 FEBRUARI

JALAN AHMAD YAMI

JALAN PRAMUKA

Immigration

Boulevard Mall

JALAN BETHESDA

Terminal Malalayang, Dive Resorts & Gorontalo

Blue Banter & Sam Ratulangi Airport

4

■ ACCOMMODATION	
Celebes	1
Manado Grace Inn	3
Minahasa	2

● EATING	
Green Garden	2
Raja Sate	1

Destinations Jakarta (11 daily; 3hr 15min); Makassar (6 daily; 1hr 50min); Singapore (4 weekly; 3hr 20min); Surabaya (3 daily; 2hr 30min).

By bus Long-distance buses serving Gorontalo, Palu and Makassar use Terminal Malalayang, about 6km south along the coast, linked by microlets to the centre (Rp5000). Buses for the Minahasa Highlands use Terminal Karombasan, also to the south (microlets Rp5000). Paal Dua in the east (microlet Rp3500) connects to Bitung. Buses for Gorontalo leave at about 5.30am; those going further afield leave around lunchtime.

Destinations Gorontalo (daily; 8hr); Makassar (daily; 2–3 days); Palu (daily; 24hr).

By car For Gorontalo, the more comfortable option is by *kijang* (private car). They depart from the PO Garuda office on Jl Kartini (☏ 0431 846867; before 10am; Rp150,000–200,000 depending on seat).

By ferry The regional Pelni ferry port is in Bitung on the southern coast (Rp7500 from Terminal Paal Dua), where the nearest Pelni office is (☏ 0438 36352). Ferries to Bunaken (Rp50,000) run from the river behind the warung at Pasar Bersehati.

Destinations Bunaken (2pm Mon–Sat; 1hr); Makassar (2 weekly; 48–72hr).

DIVING AND TOURS

Day-trips from the mainland to Bunaken start at around Rp650,000/person. Safari Tours provide return transport from your hotel (☏ 0431 857637, ⓦ manadosafaris.com) and offer flights and tours; their office is at Jl Sam Ratulangi 176, almost opposite the *Minahasa*.

ACCOMMODATION

Celebes Jl Rumambi 8A ☏ 0431 859 069, ⓦ hotelcelebesmdo.com. This expansive hotel has everything from tiny singles to luxurious rooms with views over the harbour, though the cheapest rooms are poky and windowless and there's a noisy market nearby; this isn't the nicest part of town. Doubles Rp135,000

Manado Grace Inn Jl Sam Ratulangi 113, 2km south of the centre ☏ 0431 888 0288, ⓦ manadograceinn.com. It's a little out of town, but this collection of new, clean rooms in the south of the city offers great value. Even the cheapest have a/c, TV and private bathrooms. Doubles Rp170,000

★ **Minahasa** Jl Sam Ratulangi 199, 1.5km south of the centre ☏ 0431 874869, ⓦ hotelminahasa.com. The best place in town by a long shot. Most rooms are set along a pretty garden path leading up to the swimming pool, which offers superb views over Manado Bay. All rooms have hot water, a/c and wi-fi, and there's a good breakfast buffet. Doubles Rp280,000

EATING

Minahasan cooking features dog (*rintek wuuk*, usually shortened to *rw*, or "airvay"), rat (*tikkus*) and fruit bat (*paniki*), generally unceremoniously stewed with blistering quantities of chillies.

Green Garden Jl Sam Ratulangi 170. A bright, colourful Chinese restaurant, with a large menu of tasty dishes (mains from Rp30,000) including, as ever, fantastic fresh seafood. Mon–Fri 8am–midnight, Sat noon–midnight, Sun 11am–midnight.

★ **Raja Sate** Jl Pierre Tendean 39 ☏ 0431 852398. This atmospheric bamboo-and-red-brick place serves a range of Indonesian and Minahasan specialities, from simple rice and noodle dishes to mouth-watering seafood *sates*. A classier option, but it not an expensive one – mains start at Rp30,000. Mon–Sat 11.30am–11pm, Sun 6–10.30pm.

DIRECTORY

Banks and exchange There are ATMs all over town. The best place to change cash is the BCA on Jl Sam Ratulangi.
Hospital Siloam Hospital, Jl Sam Ratulangi 22 (☏ 0431 729 0900).

THE TARSIERS OF TANGKOKO

A popular trip from Manado is to the **Tangkoko National Park**, home of the world's smallest primate, the **tarsier**. These nocturnal tree-dwelling creatures resemble bush babies or aye-ayes with their large saucer eyes and long, thin fingers. The beachside forest of Tangkoko is also home to troops of black macaque, hornbills and cuscus, all of which you should be able to spot. The park entrance fee is Rp100,000, and a range of guided walks of varying duration departs throughout the day (from Rp100,000).

  Getting to Tangkoko by public transport requires a few changes. Take a microlet from town to Paal Dua (Rp3500), then a bus to Bitung (Rp15,000). Another microlet will get you to Girian (Rp5000), where a *kijang* will take you to Batuputih at the entrance to Tangkoko (Rp20,000). Alternatively, charters from Manado cost around Rp350,000. There are a handful of basic homestays opposite the park entrance, among the better options being *Tarsius* (☏ 0812 440 4882; full board only; Rp200,000) and *Ranger Homestay* (☏ 0821 9510 9661; meals not included; Rp125,000).

Immigration Jl 17 Augustus (Mon–Fri 7.30am–4pm; ☎ 0431 863491).

Internet *Warstation* on the ground floor of the Mega Mall (daily 10am–3am; Rp6000/hr).

Post office Jl Sam Ratulangi 23 (Mon–Fri 8am–6.30pm, Sat 8am–5.30pm; Sun 10am–3pm).

BUNAKEN MARINE RESERVE

Bunaken Marine Reserve, a 75-square-kilometre patch of sea northwest of Manado, is one of Indonesia's premier diving destinations. Coral reefs around the reserve's four major islands drop to a 40m shelf before plunging to depths of 200m and more, creating stupendous reef walls abounding with Napoleon (maori) wrasse, barracuda, trevally, tuna, turtles, manta rays, whales and dolphin. Set aside concerns about snakes and sharks and avoid instead the 1m-long titan triggerfish, sharp beaked and notoriously pugnacious when guarding its nest; and small, fluorescent-red anemone fish, which are apt to give divers a painful nip.

Diving is well established in Bunaken, with high-quality operators both in Manado and within the reserve on Pulau Bunaken. The island makes for an infinitely more pleasant base, with a wide range of accommodation. Experienced divers will also find plenty of budget operators on the island, though you must check the **reliability** of rental gear and **air quality**, the two biggest causes for concern here.

Off the island's west beach, between Bunaken village and Liang beach, are **Lekuan 1**, **2** and **3**, exceptionally steep deep walls, where you'll find everything from gobies and moray eels to black-tip reef sharks. There are giant clams and stingrays at Fukui, on the far western end of the island, while **Mandolin** is good for turtles and occasional mantas, and **Mike's Point** attracts sharks and sea snakes. Non-divers can snorkel straight from the beach, or ask to join a diving boat.

The best **weather conditions** are between June and November, with light breezes, calm seas and visibility underwater averaging 25m and peaking beyond 50m. Try to avoid the westerly storms between December and February and less severe, easterly winds from March until June.

Pulau Bunaken

About an hour by ferry out from Manado, **Pulau Bunaken** is a low-backed, 5km-long comma covered in coconut trees and ringed by sand and mangroves. Entry into the national park costs Rp150,000, which buys a tag valid for one year, or Rp50,000 for a day. The cheaper hotels often don't bother charging you, but do ask as the money goes toward maintaining the park. If you book in advance your homestay will usually arrange your transport. The main alternative is to take a **public ferry** to Bunaken village from the river behind the warung at Pasar Bersehati in Manado (Mon–Sat at 2pm but get there a good hour early; return 8am; Rp50,000). A wander round the main harbour will also get you a plethora of offers, usually from homestays who will charge around Rp35,000 for the journey to Bunaken if you stay with them, or Rp50,000 if you don't.

DIVE OPERATORS

All operators below are part of the North Sulawesi Watersports Association (🖥 divenorthsulawesi.com), which promotes environmentally responsible diving in Bunaken.

★ **Froggies** (see opposite). Popular place with high standards and a good reputation with experienced divers. Rp1,147,000 for two dives.

Immanuel's Part of *Daniel's* homestay on Pangalisang Beach. Friendly and popular with budget divers. €60 for two dives.

Living Colours Pangalisang Beach ☎ 0812 430 6063, 🖥 livingcoloursdiving.com. Large, efficient operator with a good reputation for both equipment and environmental awareness. €65 for two dives.

Two Fish Divers (see opposite). Pangalisang-based, UK-run outfit with good equipment and high standards. Rp1,170,000 for two dives.

ACCOMMODATION

There is plenty of accommodation on the island, though with the exception of *Daniel's* all the places listed are a fair walk from the village – ask anyone with a scooter to take you (Rp10,000). All rates are per person for three meals a day.

PANGALISANG
★**Daniel's** ☎ 0823 4949 0270, ⓦ immanueldiver.com. One of the first you come to from the village, though it can be hard to spot – look for the *Immanuel Divers* sign. Friendly, sociable, justifiably popular and the best value on the island. Unlimited wi-fi, tea and coffee included. Per person <u>Rp230,000</u>

Lorenso's Beach Garden Cottages ☎ 0852 5697 3345, ⓦ lorensobunaken.com. Friendly place with basic bungalows made of bamboo, palm bark or gleaming wood, all set in a tropical garden. Lorenso and his family of musicians serenade guests in the restaurant with guitars and a drum set of tin cans. Sizeable off-season discounts. Per person <u>Rp350,000</u>

Two Fish Divers ☎ 0813 5687 0384, ⓦ twofishdivers .com. Efficient, friendly place set in pleasant sandy gardens. There is a range of rooms, some with attached bathrooms (Rp525,000 per person), and a swimming pool, book exchange and wi-fi connection in the lounge/ restaurant. Per person <u>Rp375,000</u>

LIANG BEACH
On the other side of the island from Bunaken village, Liang fronts a beach rather than mangroves.

Froggies ☎ 0812 430 1356, ⓦ divefroggies.com. Comfortable rooms in beautiful bungalows with showers, hot water and Western bathrooms throughout. It's a bit of a climb to the upper bungalows, but the sea views are worth it. Free wi-fi and laundry. Per person <u>Rp682,000</u>

Happy Gecko ☎ 0852 9806 4906, ⓦ happygeckoresort .com. This little gem has six spacious, two-room wooden bungalows, each tastefully furnished and with a private verandah looking out towards Manado. Run by a Dutch-Indonesian couple, it also offers some of the island's most affordable diving at Gecko Dive Centre. Per person <u>Rp400,000</u>

Maluku

Scattered wide across the sea from Sulawesi to the western edge of Papua, **Maluku** – formerly known as the Moluccas – constitutes the original Spice Islands, where the exclusive production of cloves, nutmeg and mace helped fuel the expansion of colonial powers half a world away. These thousand-odd islands are roughly divided into two main clusters. **North Maluku** is centred around the largely untouched, Sulawesi-shaped island of Halmahera, though its urban hub lies on the tiny, overwhelmingly

Muslim island of **Ternate**, once the capital of the clove trade. **South Maluku**'s largest island – **Pulau Seram** – is similarly pristine and little explored, while its lively capital is set on the much smaller **Pulau Ambon**, home to a mixture of Christians and Muslims. Gruesome sectarian conflict spread from here throughout the region around the turn of the twenty-first century, though since a 2002 peace deal the islands have stayed for the most part blissfully calm. Maluku's tourism potential remains largely untapped, but the word is out on Ambon's beaches, forts and superb diving (particularly in the relatively dry months of Sept–April), and even more so on the region's jewel destination, the remote **Banda Islands**.

KOTA AMBON
The original headquarters of the Dutch East India Company (from 1610 to 1619), **KOTA AMBON** is Maluku's capital city, and host to a quarter of the islands' population. During World War II, this was a major Japanese naval base, and its colonial architecture was largely razed in Allied bombing campaigns. Nearing two decades ago, this was ground zero for inter-religious fighting, though today it looks in most respects like any other midsize Indonesian city. It's an unavoidable transit point for the Banda Islands, and most travellers spend little more time than is necessary to catch an onward ferry or flight. However, there are a few sites of interest.

WHAT TO SEE AND DO
Nestled among rolling hills around a picturesque bay, Kota Ambon combines urban comforts with a touch of laidback island charm, and its hip cafés and restaurants are particularly appealing for those returning from the quiet Bandas. In a stroll through town you'll pass dozens of impressive churches and mosques, the most striking of these the golden-domed **Masjid Al-Fatah** on Jalan AM Sangaji. A short walk to the northeast of here, the curious **World Peace Gong** – built in 2009 and decked with world flags and religious symbols – marks the city's centre, while

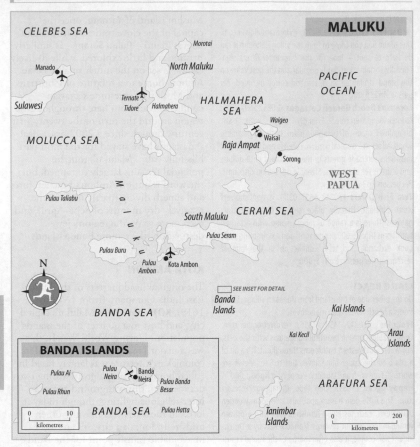

MALUKU

CELEBES SEA

Morotai

North Maluku

Manado

Sulawesi

PACIFIC OCEAN

Ternate
Tidore   Halmahera

HALMAHERA SEA

Waigeo

Waisai

Raja Ampat

Sorong

WEST PAPUA

MOLUCCA SEA

M a l u k u

CERAM SEA

South Maluku

Pulau Taliabu

Pulau Seram

Pulau Buru

Pulau Ambon

Kota Ambon

N

SEE INSET FOR DETAIL

Banda Islands

Kai Islands

Kai Kecil

Arau Islands

BANDA SEA

ARAFURA SEA

BANDA ISLANDS

Pulau Ai

Pulau Neira

Banda Neira

Pulau Rhun

Pulau Banda Besar

Pulau Hatta

BANDA SEA

0   10
kilometres

Tanimbar Islands

0   200
kilometres

just north of here is **Benteng Victoria**, the Dutch fort where national hero Pattimura (pictured on the Rp1000 note) was hanged in 1817. Though off limits to visitors at the time of writing, the city has plans to open the fort to the public.

Just offshore, Ambon's bay boasts world-class **muck diving**, with an extraordinary diversity of camouflaged critters.

Commonwealth War Cemetery

The manicured lawns of the **Commonwealth War Cemetery** (Pandan Kasturi, 2km north of centre; 24hr; free) are the resting place of more than two thousand Allied troops, most of them Australian. The site housed a POW camp during the war, and its inmates were subjected to some of the most brutal treatment of prisoners anywhere. When the camp was liberated by Americans in 1945, there were only a few hundred emaciated survivors.

Museum Siwalima

Set on a hill overlooking the bay, this old **museum** on Jalan Dr Malaiholo, Taman Makmur, 5km south of the city centre (Mon–Fri 8am–4.30pm, Sat & Sun 10am–3pm; Rp10,000; ☎0911 341652), is worth the small entry fee, though a lack of English signage means your visit might not last very long. Its ethnographic section provides a glimpse of Maluku's cultural heritage, with traditional Malukan clothing, weapons, musical instruments and jewellery. There's also a collection of specimens from the sea, including a few whale skeletons, the largest of them measuring 19m.

ARRIVAL AND DEPARTURE

By plane Pattimura airport is 20km west of the city, connected by ojek (Rp80,000), taxi (Rp150,000) and DAMRI buses (departing from Kota Ambon beside the World Peace Gong at 5am, 10am, 1pm; from the airport following most flight arrivals; Rp35,000). Batik (w batikair.com), Lion (w lionair.co.id) and Garuda have flights to/from Jakarta and Makassar, while Garuda and Sriwijaya (w sriwijayaair .co.id) have flights to/from Ternate and Sorong.

Destinations Jakarta (5 daily; 3hr 30min); Makassar (6 daily; 1hr 40min); Manado (4 weekly; 1hr 15min); Sorong (2 daily; 1hr 10min); Surabaya (2 daily; 2hr 30min).

By ferry Pelni ships use the harbour just beside the city centre, while fast ferries to the Banda Islands use Tulehu harbour 25km northeast of Kota Ambon (ojek/taxi Rp100,000/180,000). Express Bahari fast ferries to the Banda Islands (6hr; regular/executive Rp415,000/600,000) depart 9am Tues and Sat, returning at the same time on Wed & Sun mornings. Tickets for these must be bought at the harbour: arrive at least 1hr early. The Pelni office is at Jl DI Panjaiitan 19 (☎ 0911 348219, w pelni.co.id), and agents all over town sell tickets.

Destinations (Pelni) Banda Neira (1–2 monthly; 8–12hr); Sorong (2 monthly; 32hr); Ternate (2 monthly; 18hr).

DIVE OPERATOR

Dive Bluemotion Laha, just south of the airport ☎ 0812 3871 9813, w dive-bluemotion.com. Highly reputable and one of the most affordable on the island (from Rp270,000 per dive).

ACCOMMODATION

Asri Jl Baru 33 ☎ 0911 311217. Rambling old cheapie, about 10m down a narrow road just off Jl AM Sangadji, with four storeys of worn rooms – most with fan, but some with a/c (Rp135,000) – that come with grubby private bathrooms, squat toilets and a breakfast snack. There's a good view of the Al-Fatah Mosque from the shared balcony. Doubles $\overline{\text{Rp115,000}}$

Budget Jl Sirimau 12 ☎ 0851 0531 1311. Clean, all a/c hotel with small, simple rooms about 500m southeast of the centre and friendly, English-speaking staff. Most rooms are windowless (and relatively quiet), while a few have windows overlooking the noisy street. Doubles $\overline{\text{Rp300,000}}$

Le Green Jl Sam Ratulangi 93 ☎ 0911 321090, w le-green.com. One of the newest and best-value options in the centre of town, about 500m from the Pelni harbour, with helpful staff and spacious, spotlessly clean a/c rooms. Breakfast included. Doubles $\overline{\text{Rp325,000}}$

EATING

Joas Jl Said Perintah. A longtime local favourite right in the heart of the city, offering an escape from the hectic surrounding streets, coffee from across the archipelago (Rp10,000–17,000), and some of the best people-watching to be had in town. Daily 7.30am–8.30pm.

★**Sari Gurih** Jl Dana Kopra 14 ☎ 0911 341888. Set behind a smoky grill station off the street, this modest, fan-cooled dining hall has become Ambon's top catering

4

RAJA AMPAT

As pristine as they are remote, **Raja Ampat** – a cluster of islands scattered off the western tip of Papua – comprises one of the country's most sought-after destinations. If you've spent any time in Indonesia over recent years you'll have seen plenty of alluring adverts picturing the islands' impossibly idyllic karst peaks and turquoise bays. Stunning as they are, however, the islands themselves are just the tip of the iceberg, and the real reason for the visitor spike of recent years lies offshore. The word is out that Raja Ampat has some of the world's richest **coral reefs** and a whopping 1400 species of fish, from pygmy seahorses and dugongs to giant mantas. It's become a wildly popular live-aboard dive destination, while staying on the islands themselves has never been easier, with dozens of local homestays that can be arranged through the conservation-minded *Stay Raja Ampat* (w stayrajaampat.com). Neither option is cheap, however. Some budget travellers may be put off just by the costs of reaching **Sorong**, the port of entry on the west coast of Papua, let alone the Rp1,000,000 entry fee levied upon arrival. Live-aboards and higher-end accommodation will usually pick you up in Sorong's harbour, while for most others you'll have to head to **Waisai**, Raj Ampat's biggest town, to arrange onward diving and boat trips. Daily ferries make the trip (slow/fast 4hr/2hr).

Sorong is well linked **by plane** to the rest of the country, including to Ambon (1–2 daily; 1hr 10min); Jakarta (2 daily; 3hr 55min); Makassar (8 daily; 2hr 15min); and Manado (3 daily; 1hr 30min), while Marinda Raja Ampat, the new airport near Waisai, now serves direct, daily flights to/from both Sorong (daily; 30min) and Manado (2hr 5min), operated by Wings, a subsidiary of Lion Air (w lionair.co.id).

choice for visiting dignitaries, with a good selection of seafood-heavy Malukan specialities (squid and shrimp dishes all Rp80,000). Try the delicious *ikan kuah kuning* (yellow fish sauce with basil, lime, lemongrass and kenari) served with *popeda* (sago congee; Rp20,000). Daily 9am–11pm.

Sibu-Sibu Jl Said Perintah 47 A. Ambon's original café, this is a popular evening hangout with live music and karaoke. The walls are smothered in film posters, and it's one of the city's most charming spots for a drink (large Bintang Rp50,000). Daily 6am–11pm.

DIRECTORY

Banks There are banks with ATMS all over the city centre – those headed to the Bandas should stock up.
Internet Metro, just southwest of Trikora Monument at Jl Dr Soetomo 4, has computers with internet (Rp5000/hr).
Post office Jl Raya Pattimura 20 (Mon–Fri 8am–9pm, Sat until 6pm, Sun until 3pm).

BANDA ISLANDS

Clustered about 150km southeast of Ambon in the remote Banda Sea, the **BANDA ISLANDS** centre on the perfectly conical peak of **Gunung Api** (640m) – rising 4000m from the sea floor and visible from almost all corners of the islands. For centuries, nutmeg and mace – worth more than their weight in gold – made these ten steamy islands the most valuable pieces of real estate on earth. These days it's their offshore assets that are attracting visitors from halfway around the world: pristine and spectacular underwater landscapes where it's not uncommon to spot sea turtles, black marlins and hammerhead sharks. Although the operation of planes and speedboats from Ambon has enabled something of a tourism spike in recent years, the big crowds are still put off by the long journey, meaning that, at least for now, the Bandas enjoy that relished, end-of-the-world feel that's well worth the long journey.

WHAT TO SEE AND DO

For most travellers, **diving** is the pastime of choice, and there are almost always more dive sites than time. **Pulau Hatta** and **Pulau Ai** are worth the daily marine park fee (Rp50,000) for the spectacular drop-offs just beyond their white sandy beaches. On the shore is a handful of nutmeg plantations and, just across from town, **Gunung Api**, a two-hour hike to the summit through nutmeg, palm and cinnamon trees.

Banda Neira

Banda Neira is the most convenient base for the Bandas, with all links to the outside world and the best array of accommodation. Aside from mornings in the two-street town centre's humming market, almost everything here moves at a lazy, island pace. Towering over the town to the east is the pentagonal hulk of **Benteng Belgica** (donation), its ramparts and towers offering postcard-worthy views across to Gunung Api. The fort was completed in 1662 to replace the lower, less-defensible and now overgrown **Benteng Nassau**, built in 1609 on the foundations of an earlier Portuguese structure. There is a handful of colonial-era buildings scattered around town, including stately mansions, several of which housed political exiles, an old **Chinese temple** and a whitewashed **Dutch church**, its floor lined with elaborately carved VOC tombstones. The latter was vandalized during the regional wave of sectarian violence in 1999, but has been restored, now holding Sunday services for the island's tiny remaining Christian population.

Banda Besar

By far the largest of the Bandas, **Banda Besar** is one of the closest to Banda Neira, making for an easy day-trip to see its nutmeg plantations, lonely beaches and Dutch forts. Set a short hike up the steps from the sleepy village of Lonthoir, **Benteng Hollandia** (donation) – built in 1624 and abandoned for nearly the last three centuries – is the most worthwhile, offering a gorgeous vantage across to Gunung Api and Banda Neira from its overgrown walls. Boats for Banda Besar depart to Lonthoir from the jetty near *Bintang Laut* (Rp50,000/boat; Rp5000 each when full). In case Banda Neira isn't quiet enough for you, locals Usman and Yani run *Leiden* (☎0852 4401 2394; full-board Rp250,000), a tiny, basic homestay at the bottom of the steps.

Rhun Island

The most remote of the Bandas is this chilli-shaped island about 25km west of **Banda Neira**. The British controlled the outpost until 1667, when they traded it to the Dutch in a historic – and fortuitous – deal. In exchange, the Dutch let go of Manhattan. Most visit on day-trips for the sheer diving wall off its northwest coast and the pretty desert island of **Nailaka** to the east, virtually walkable from Rhun at low tide. *Manhattan Guesthouse* (☎05298 764275; full-board Rp300,000) has a handful of simple rooms by the port. A boat heads from Banda Neira to Rhun daily at 9am, returning at 2pm (2hr; Rp30,000 each way).

ARRIVAL AND DEPARTURE

By plane There are two flights weekly to Banda Neira's landing strip, year-round (except Jan & July), but the route's appointed carrier changes from year to year. Your chosen accommodation can update you with the latest schedule and book tickets, which should be done at least three weeks in advance.

By ferry Pelni ferries depart every 10 days to Ambon (8 or 12hr). Get tickets at the Pelni office on Jl Kujali (☎0910 21196), on the coast south of the post office. Express Bahari fast ferries (regular/executive Rp415,000/600,000; 6hr) to Ambon's Teluhu harbour depart from Banda Neira at 9am Wed and Sun.

INFORMATION

Tourist information The local office is at Jl Imam Bonjol (Mon–Fri 8am–2pm; ☎0914 21426), but the listed hotels are more useful, particularly if you'd like information in English.

DIVE OPERATOR

Diving season is year-round, with the exception of January and July.

Dive Bluemotion Jl Pelabuhan, 200m north of the harbour ☎0812 4714 3922, ⓦ dive-bluemotion.com. Best reputation on the island, with experienced staff and top-notch gear (from Rp425,000 per dive). Comfortable, on-site lodgings available (*Baba Lagoon Hotel*; Rp300,000).

ACCOMMODATION AND EATING

Bintang Laut Jl Pante Sarua ☎0910 20149 or ☎0822 4830 7056. Close to the local ferry dock, with a strip of simple, all a/c rooms and a friendly English-speaking owner. The communal waterfront deck is a good place to meet fellow travellers, and offers a stunning frontal view of Gunung Api. If full, try the similarly priced *Vita* next door. Doubles Rp300,000

★**Cilu Bintang Estate** Jl Benteng Belgica ☎0910 21604 or ☎0813 3034 3377, ⓦ cilubintang.com. The most luxurious option in town, this stately pavilion sits between the two forts, with bright and breezy rooms, some of them looking over the ruins of Benteng Nassau. It also hosts nightly barbecues and the Bandas' widest array of island excursions. Doubles Rp300,000

Mutiara Banda Neira ☎0813 3034 3377, ⓦ banda-mutiara.com. Comfortable, well-kept a/c rooms with spacious bathrooms and complimentary coffee around the clock in a pleasant garden area. It's set on a quiet backstreet running north from *Nutmeg Café*, and the rate includes breakfast at the nearby *Cilu Bintang* – both are run by the ever-helpful, German-speaking Abba Rizal. Doubles Rp250,000

Nutmeg Café Beside Benteng Belgica. Friendly little café between the town and Benteng Belgica, serving good juices (nutmeg syrup Rp20,000), coffee (with nutmeg Rp15,000), and pancakes (Rp15,000), from classic banana to kenari nut, cinnamon, and yes – nutmeg. Good spot for people-watching. Daily 7am–9pm.

DIRECTORY

Banks BRI has Banda Neira's very first and – at the time of writing, only – ATM towards the south end of town, though it only accepts MasterCard. It's still advisable to withdraw a sufficient amount in Ambon.

Internet There's wi-fi in all of the island's hotels, and 3G coverage for those with SIM cards.

Bike and motorbike rental *Cilu Bintang* rents both (bike/motorbike Rp75,000/Rp125,000 per day).

Post office Just south of *Cilu Bintang Estate* on Jl Benteng Belgika.

TERNATE AND NORTH MALUKU

Even less developed for tourism than their southern counterparts, the islands of **North Maluku** offer plenty of adventure. The launching point for travellers is **Pulau Ternate**, a volcanic cone rising from the sea about about 15km west of **Halmahera** – the province's largest island. Fanned along the eastern slopes of the active **Gunung Gamalama** (1715m), Pulau Ternate has been the region's beating heart since the days of the spice trade, when a virtual monopoly on clove production brought immense wealth to its sultanate. Unlike neighbouring sultanates, the dynasty has survived uninterrupted to this day, and while a

4

slew of European forts – Portuguese, Dutch and Spanish – is a testament to the island's historical importance, the bustling modern city and international airport attest its regional status.

Pulau Ternate

TERNATE is one of Indonesia's most devoutly Muslim islands, a fact that becomes most palpable around prayer times, and hosts some of Maluku's most impressive mosques. Among these, there are the **Sultan's Mosque**, with its traditional, multi-tiered roof, and the giant new green- and yellow-domed **Masjid al-Munawwar**, towering over the water just south of the lively fish market – best to avoid the mosque on Friday afternoons, though.

Beyond the city, Pulau Ternate's smattering of attractions are well worth circling the island on a motorbike, taking the coastal road and steering around mats of drying nutmeg and cloves to reach pretty beaches and coves, petrified lava fields, colonial-era ruins and the striking **Danau Tolire Besar** (Rp6000), a turquoise crater lake with steep, jungle-covered walls and – at least according to some locals – crocodiles.

Tidore

The neighbouring island sultanate of **Tidore** makes for another good day-trip, with its pair of facing Spanish forts – Benteng Tahula and Benteng Torre – outside the sleepy town of Soasio on the southeast coast. The island's picturesque **Gunung Kiematubu** – pictured on the Rp1000 note – is a three-hour hike from the village of Garabunga (Rp30,000 ojek up the slope from Saosio), and offers spectacular views of Gamalama, Halmahera. To reach Tidore, take a small boat from Ternate's Bastiong Harbour to Rum (Rp15,000; leave when full), then an angkot to Saosio (Rp25,000). The last boat returning to Ternate leaves at 5pm.

ARRIVAL AND DEPARTURE

By plane Ternate's Babullah Airport (☎ 921 312 1797), about 5km north of the city centre, serves daily flights to Jakarta and Ambon with Garuda (ⓦ garuda-indonesia .com) and Sriwijaya (ⓦ sriwijayaair.co.id). Getting there and back costs Rp30,000 by ojek or Rp50,000 per person in a shared taxi (three people).

ACCOMMODATION

Budget accommodation is limited.

Kurnia Homestay BTN BLock G 8 ☎ 0821 8823 5032. A good budget option 1.5km west of the centre, with a couple of clean fan rooms, a kitchen, motorbike rental (Rp100,000) and a helpful host, Aty. Doubles Rp250,000

Muara Jl Merdeka 19 ☎ 0813 7297 5646. The best-value spot in the city centre, situated on the upper floors of a busy mall. Though a bit worn, all rooms are clean and a/c, some with balconies overlooking the city. Doubles Rp460,000

Rumah Ngade Jl Ngade 40 ☎ 0813 4064 2369, ☒ rumahngadeguesthouse@gmail.com. New, family-run, all a/c hotel about 5km southwest of the city centre, hugging the walls of a small crater lake, Danau Ngade. Worth the splurge for the wonderful views from the shared terrace and private balconies. Doubles Rp530,000

MONK, LUANG PRABANG

Laos

HIGHLIGHTS

❶ **Vang Vieng** Enjoy a great range of adventure sports at this spectacular natural playground. See p.368

❷ **Luang Prabang** Explore this fabulous UNESCO World Heritage-listed city, the hub of the country's tourist scene. See p.372

❸ **Nong Khiaw** Soak up the stunning limestone karsts from a riverside bungalow. See p.385

❹ **Slow boat on the Mekong** Chug down the river on an atmospheric cargo boat. See p.391

❺ **Wat Phou** Seek serenity among sun-warmed Khmer ruins. See p.401

❻ **Si Phan Don** Kick back with a Beerlao on these laidback Mekong islands. See p.404

HIGHLIGHTS ARE MARKED ON THE MAP ON P.347

ROUGH COSTS

Daily budget Basic US$25/Occasional treat US$35–50

Drink Beerlao US$1.50

Food Noodle soup US$1.25

Hostel/budget hotel US$4–10

Travel Bus: Vientiane–Luang Prabang (390km; 10–12hr, US$14); Slow boat: Houayxai–Luang Prabang (300km; 2 days, US$28)

FACT FILE

Population 6.9 million

Language Lao

Religion Theravada Buddhism

Currency Kip (K)

Capital Vientiane

International phone code ☎856

Time zone GMT + 7hr

5

Introduction

Until the 1990s, Laos remained shut off from the outside world, and largely unknown to Western travellers. Since then, more and more visitors have come to discover that this landlocked country – ruled by the same communist regime since 1975 – offers some of Southeast Asia's most enchanting natural landscapes, a fascinating diversity of cultures and a remarkably warm welcome. Although much less developed than neighbouring Thailand and Vietnam, tourist facilities are steadily expanding. For many travellers a journey through Laos consists of a whistle-stop tour through the two main cities of Vientiane and Luang Prabang, with a stop in Vang Vieng, and perhaps a brief detour to the mysterious Plain of Jars or idyllic Si Phan Don. But those willing to explore further and brave bumpy, often frustratingly long, bus journeys and basic accommodation will still find the Laos of old, where people lead traditional, rural lifestyles little changed in centuries.

Laos's lifeline is the **Mekong River**, which runs the length of the country and in places serves as a boundary with Thailand. Set on a broad curve of the Mekong, **Vientiane** is Southeast Asia's most modest capital city and provides a gentle introduction to Laos, with a string of cosmopolitan cafés, restaurants and bars to compensate for a relative lack of sights. From here, most travellers dash north to the notorious tubing capital **Vang Vieng**, set in a striking position among limestone karsts, for a few days of adventure sports and – despite attempts to reinvent the town's image – partying. From here, one of the most dramatic roads in the country curves through mountains to cultured **Luang Prabang**, once the heart and soul of the ancient

kingdom of Lane Xang and now the country's most enticing cityscape, with its spellbinding panoply of gilded temples and weathered shophouses.

The wild highlands of the **far north** are the best for trekking: **Luang Namtha** remains the most popular base from which to arrange treks to nearby hill-tribe villages. From here, you can travel by bus to **Houayxai**, an entry point popular with travellers arriving from Thailand in search of a slow boat for the picturesque journey south to Luang Prabang. Some of the most dramatic scenery in Laos is in the northeast, especially round the towns of **Nong Khiaw** and **Muang Ngoi Neua**. Following routes 6 and 7 south brings you to the **Plain of Jars**, a war-scarred plateau dotted with ancient funerary urns. In the south, the vast majority of travellers zip down Route 13, stopping off in the major southern towns: genial **Savannakhet**, and the important transport hub of **Pakse**. Further south, near the charming small town of **Champasak**, lie the atmospheric ruins of **Wat Phou**, one of the most important Khmer temples outside Cambodia. South again, the lazy river islands of **Si Phan Don** lie scattered across the Mekong, home to traditional fishing communities, thunderous waterfalls and rare Irrawaddy dolphins.

WHEN TO GO

November to February are the most pleasant months to travel in lowland Laos, when daytime **temperatures** are agreeably warm and evenings slightly chilly; at higher elevations, temperatures can drop to freezing point. In March, temperatures begin to climb, peaking in April, when the lowlands are baking hot and humid. The **rains** begin in May and last until September.

CHRONOLOGY

Iron Age The Plain of Jars in the northeast dates from around 2000 years ago, and is the earliest known indigenous culture in Laos.

First century AD Indian traders introduce Buddhism to Southeast Asia; between the sixth and ninth centuries, upper Laos is dominated by the Theravada Buddhist culture of the Mon people, known as Dvaravati.

Ninth century The Hindu Khmer Empire of Angkor expands across the whole region, building dozens of Angkor-style temples.

1353 With Khmer support, exiled prince Fa Ngum takes Luang Prabang (then called Xieng Dong Xieng Thong). He establishes the Lane Xang Hom Khao Empire, the "Kingdom of a Million Elephants and the White Parasol", and extends its borders.

1512 The golden Buddha image, the Pha Bang, is brought to Xieng Dong Xieng Thong from Vientiane by King Visoun (1500–20), establishing it as the symbol of a unified Buddhist kingdom.

1563 With the Burmese Empire encroaching, the capital is moved to Vientiane, but the Pha Bang statue is left, and

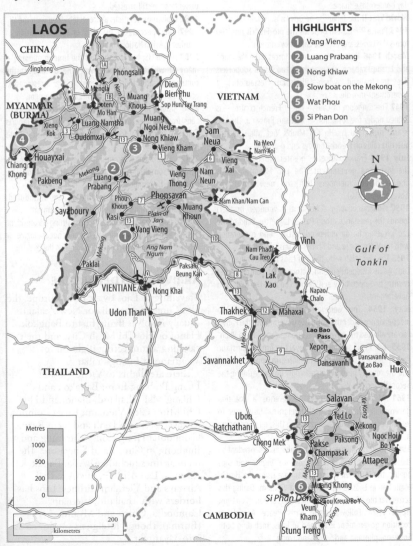

LAOS

HIGHLIGHTS
1. Vang Vieng
2. Luang Prabang
3. Nong Khiaw
4. Slow boat on the Mekong
5. Wat Phou
6. Si Phan Don

5

Luang Prabang is renamed after it. Burmese warrior-kings reduce the kingdom of Lane Xang to vassalage.

1637–94 The reign of Sourinyavongsa, and the Golden Age of Lane Xang. After his death the region divides into three principalities.

1778 The kingdom of Siam takes Vientiane, capturing the precious Pha Bang statue. Over the next century, Siam and Vietnam compete to control fragmented Lao principalities.

1893 The French vice-consul in Luang Prabang persuades the northern kingdom to pay tribute to France. For half a century, Laos is a French colony, and the country's present-day borders take shape.

World War II The Japanese occupy Laos.

1945 Prince Phetsarath deposes the pro-French king and forms the Lao Issara, or "Free Laos" government.

March 1946 French reoccupation forces take Vientiane and Luang Prabang. Thousands of Lao Issara supporters flee to Thailand, where Phetsarath establishes a government-in-exile.

1947 The Kingdom of Laos – under French control – is unified under the royal house of Luang Prabang. The Lao Issara, supported by Ho Chi Minh's Viet Minh, launch guerrilla raids on French convoys and garrisons.

July 1949 France concedes greater independence to the Vientiane government. The Lao Issara disbands and moderate members join the new Royal Lao Government (RLG).

1950 Souphanouvong (Phetsarath's younger brother) founds the resistance group Pathet Lao ("the Land of the Lao"), calling for an independent Laos and cooperation with the Vietnamese and Khmer against the French.

1953 The Viet Minh seize parts of Laos for the Pathet Lao. Laos gains independence in October, but control of the country is divided between Pathet Lao and the Royal Lao Government.

May 1954 The Geneva conference reaffirms Lao independence under the Royal Lao Government; the Pathet Lao are allotted the provinces of Phongsali and Houa Phan.

1955–60 The US supports the Royal Lao Army against the Pathet Lao. The US and Soviet Union arm opposing sides, and the country becomes increasingly unstable during the Second Indochina War.

1961 At a second Geneva conference a coalition government is formed and all foreign military agree to leave Laos; while publicly supporting this, all sides ignore it, keeping Laos at war.

1964–73 Prime minister Souvannaphouma, dependent on the US, permits "armed reconnaissance" flights over Laos against the North Vietnamese, who are using the Ho Chi Minh Trail in Laos to infiltrate South Vietnam. During this secret war the US drops 2,093,100 tonnes of bombs on Laos.

April 1974 Following the Paris Peace Accords, a coalition government is formed in Laos, including both Souvannaphouma and Souphanouvong.

1975 After communist victories in Phnom Penh and Saigon, Pathet Lao forces take Vientiane in a bloodless coup on August 23, and the Lao People's Democratic Republic (PDR) is proclaimed on December 2. A socialist regime is established and up to fifty thousand royalists are sent to labour camps.

1977 The royal family are arrested and exiled to Houa Phan province, ending the centuries-old Lao monarchy.

1986 Prime minister Kaysone Phomvihane implements the New Economic Mechanism, essentially a market economy, though there are no political reforms and dissenters are still arrested.

1992 Diplomatic relations are re-established with the US.

1997 Laos becomes a member of the Association of Southeast Asian Nations (ASEAN).

2007 In the US, ten members of the Hmong minority – many of whom had fought with the US against the communists and then emigrated – are arrested and accused of trying to overthrow the Lao government.

2009 Around four thousand Hmong are deported back to Laos from refugee camps in northern Thailand; reports follow of retribution for their involvement in the second Indochina War.

2012 Prominent community development worker Sombath Somphone is abducted in Vientiane. At the time of writing, he remains missing.

2014 Draconian internet controls are introduced, criminalizing online criticism of the government.

2016 Barack Obama becomes the first sitting US president to visit Laos. He acknowledges – but does not apologize for – the devastating impact of US bombing on the country.

ARRIVAL AND DEPARTURE

Travelling to Laos **by air** from Europe, the US, Canada, Australia or New Zealand usually involves flying first to Bangkok, Hanoi or Ho Chi Minh City, and then catching a connecting flight on to Vientiane or Luang Prabang.

There are flights to Vientiane and Luang Prabang from: Bangkok and Chiang Mai, Thailand; Hanoi and Ho Chi Minh City, Vietnam; Kuala Lumpur, Malaysia; Phnom Penh and Siem Reap, Cambodia; Hong Kong, Kunming and Jinghong in China; and Singapore. The main airlines include AirAsia, Bangkok Airways, Lao Airlines, Silk Air, Thai Airways and Vietnam Airlines. Laos has **borders** with Thailand, Vietnam, Cambodia, China and Myanmar (Burma), though foreigners cannot cross into Myanmar.

OVERLAND FROM CAMBODIA

The **Nong Nok Khiene-Trapaeng Kriel** crossing is currently the only point at which you can cross overland from Cambodia. You can get a Lao visa on arrival here (see p.116), and may have to pay a small fee of a dollar or two to immigration officials, as well as the visa fee.

OVERLAND FROM CHINA

From the town of Jinghong in China's southwestern Yunnan province, daily buses travel to and from Oudomxai and Luang Namtha. The last town on the Chinese side is the village of Mo Han and the first Lao village you come to is Boten. It's not currently possible to cross into Laos on the river.

OVERLAND FROM THAILAND

There are six main points along the Thai border where Westerners can cross into Laos: Chiang Khong (see box, p.771) to Houayxai; Nong Khai (see box, p.777) to Vientiane; Nakhon Phanom (see p.777) to Thakhek; Mukdahan (see box, p.777) to Savannakhet; Chong Mek (see box, p.777) to Pakse; and Beung Khan to Paksan. At the time of writing, visas on arrival were available at all except the last crossing (see below); check locally for the most up-to-date information before you travel. It's also possible to get a visa in advance from the Lao embassy in Bangkok.

OVERLAND FROM VIETNAM

There are six main border crossings into/ out of Vietnam: Tay Trang–Sop Hun (see box, p.869); Nam Xoi–Na Meo (see box, p.838); Nong Het–Nam Can (see box, p.875); Cau Treo–Nam Phao (see box, p.875); Lao Bao–Dansavanh (see box, p.875); Bo Y–Pho Keau (see box, p.896). Lao visas on arrival are available at all of these crossings.

VISAS

Unless you hold a passport from Japan, Russia, Switzerland or an ASEAN member state, you'll need a visa to enter Laos. Thirty-day visas are available on arrival at most international borders – all visitors must hold a passport that is valid for at least six months from the time of entry into Laos.

Visas on arrival take a few minutes to process, cost around US$30–42 (depending on nationality), and are available to passengers flying into Luang Prabang, Pakse and Vientiane. Overland travellers to Laos from Thailand can pick up visas on arrival at any of the border crossings open to foreign tourists (except, at present, at Paksan), as can those entering from Vietnam (at Nam Khan, Na Meo, Bo Y, Tay Trang, Cau Treo and Lao Bao) and Cambodia (Nong Nok Khiene-Trapaeng Kriel). From China it's possible to pick up a visa at the Mo Han crossing, but not currently at Meng Kang. Only US dollars are accepted as payment and a passport-sized photo is required. If you forget the photo, border officials will usually turn a blind eye for an extra $1. To cross into Laos from all other points, you'll need to arrange a visa in advance. Like visas on arrival, **pre-arranged tourist visas** allow for a stay of up to thirty days. Prices are generally a little higher though – especially if you pay a tour operator to help you out – so avoid buying one unless your border crossing demands it. If it does, visas can be obtained directly from Lao embassies and consulates.

Visa **extensions** are fairly easy to obtain, but you'll need to plan ahead if you want to avoid overstaying your visa (there's a $10 penalty for each extra day you overstay). The cheapest option is to visit the immigration office in Vientiane before your visa expires, where extensions are issued for $2 per day, to a maximum of sixty days, plus a 3000K application fee. Alternatively, you could leave the country and enter again or pay a local travel agent to arrange the visa extension for you.

GETTING AROUND

Boats, the traditional means of travel in Laos, still ply the Mekong and its tributaries, but **buses** are now the predominant form of transport in most areas. Regardless of whether you go by

5

road or river, you only need to travel for a week or two in Laos before realizing that timetables are flexible and estimated times of arrival pointless. It is also possible to fly, although this is obviously not the most economic mode of transport. Considering the scenery you'd be missing and the chances for interaction with locals, it's usually worth taking the time to travel by road or river instead.

PLANES

The government-owned **Lao Airlines** (ⓦlaoairlines.com) is the country's main domestic carrier. Its safety record is patchy, to say the least; in 2013, a Lao Airlines turboprop travelling from Vientiane hit bad weather, plunging into the Mekong as it approached Pakse, killing all 49 people on board. Since the accident the airline has continued to operate as normal, and it still has the most comprehensive domestic schedule by far, with flights from Vientiane to Oudomxai, Luang Namtha, Luang Prabang, Houayxai, Pakse and Phonsavan (for the Plain of Jars). Laos' first private airline, **Lao Central Airlines** (ⓦflylaocentral.com), has a small fleet flying between Vientiane, Luang Prabang and Bangkok, and has been joined by **Lao Skyway** (ⓦlaoskyway.com), who operate flights between Vientiane and several northern destinations including Luang Prabang, Houayxai, Luang Namtha and Oudomxai.

BOATS

The main boat **route** is along the Mekong River between Houayxai and Luang Prabang; smaller passenger **boats** normally also cruise up the Nam Ou River, linking Nong Khiaw to Muang Ngoi and points north. As infrastructure improves and hydroelectric dam projects block traditional river routes, more and more Lao are opting to travel by road.

The **slow boats** (*heua sa*) that ply the Houayxai to Luang Prabang route are fitted with seats for passengers – these can be anything from cushioned wooden benches to seats that appear to have been lifted from a minibus. Some boats are kitted out with a small shop selling basic

provisions (including Beerlao). An overnight stop is made (in both directions) at Pakbeng (see p.391), where you can stock up on supplies.

Parts of the Mekong are also plied by a dwindling number of **speedboats** (*heua wai*), which are a more costly but faster alternative to the slow boats. Connecting towns along the river all the way to the Chinese border, these 5m terrors accommodate up to eight passengers and can shave hours off a river journey. Fares for speedboats cost two to three times the slow-boat fare. Crash helmets are handed out before journeys and life jackets are occasionally available. Think twice about taking a speedboat, however: the Mekong has some tricky stretches, and can be particularly rough late in the rainy season. Fatal accidents occur with an alarming frequency. You should insist on a life jacket and helmet.

BUSES

Buses in Laos range from air-conditioned coaches to rattling wrecks; cramped, overloaded and extremely slow, the latter can be profound tests of endurance and patience – however, until you get on the bus, there's often no way to tell in advance which you'll get.

Scheduled toilet stops are few and far between, so it's usual to ask the driver to stop when nature calls; passengers usually relieve themselves by the side of the road. Keep in mind that some areas are still littered with unexploded ordnance (see box, p.384), so it's not a good idea to go too far off the road.

Ordinary buses run between major towns, and often link provincial hubs with their surrounding areas. In most cases, tickets should be bought from the bus station before boarding; if you're picking up a bus in the middle of its route, however, you pay on board. It's a good idea to turn up at the bus station at least half an hour before your bus's scheduled departure, especially in major transport centres where buses may leave as soon as they're full. **Timetables** are usually posted near the ticket office, though published times should be taken with a pinch of salt. Most buses leave in the morning – usually between 7am and 9am – but popular routes may have a lunchtime departure, and some tourist-focused nightbuses run between major towns and on long-distance routes (for example, Vientiane–Pakse). Despite road improvements, travelling around Laos by bus is often still painfully slow – your bus might only depart when there are enough passengers, it may stop numerous times to pick up people (and food) along the road, and you'll often find yourself crammed in with more people (and occasionally animals) than you would think could fit into the space. Be patient and good-humoured, however, and the experience will be more than worthwhile.

MINIBUSES

In major tourist centres it's also possible to travel to your next destination by **minibus**. These are popular with locals and tourists, though depending on the number of people on board (drivers love to fill their seats), they may not actually be any more comfortable than travelling by local bus. Tickets can be bought from guesthouses, travel agents and minibus stations, and usually include pick-up from your accommodation. Travelling by minibus is generally a little quicker (and more dangerous) than travelling by local bus, and you will normally have to pay a small premium for the privilege – usually 10,000–50,000K extra per journey.

SAWNGTHAEWS

In most provinces, the local bus network is complemented by **sawngthaews** – converted pick-up trucks – into which drivers cram as many passengers as they can get onto two benches in the back. They usually depart from the regular bus station and, though they will have scheduled hours, often only leave when there are enough passengers to make the trip worthwhile. Sometimes the fare is paid towards the end of the ride, but if you get on at a bus station you will often be asked to pay before you leave. To catch a sawngthaew in remote areas simply flag it down from the side of the road and tell the driver where you're headed.

JUMBOS AND TUK-TUKS

Transport within Lao towns is by motorized samlors (literally "three wheels"), which function as shared taxis for up to four or five passengers. There are two types of samlor: **jumbos** and **tuk-tuks**. Jumbos are home-made three-wheelers consisting of a two-wheeled carriage welded to the side of a motorcycle; these days, they're seen rather infrequently outside Pakse. Tuk-tuks are just bigger, sturdier jumbos, with up to eight passengers crammed into the back. To catch one, flag it down and tell the driver where you're going. You pay at the end of the ride, but make sure you agree the fare before you get in. Rates vary according to the number of passengers, the distance travelled and your bargaining skills.

VEHICLE RENTAL

Renting a car can be prohibitively expensive, and though self-drive car rental is possible in Laos, it's easier (and safer) to hire a **car and driver**. In most major towns, tour agencies have air-conditioned vans and 4WD pick-up trucks, and can provide drivers as well. Expect to pay US$80–120 per day, plus fuel. Always clarify who pays for petrol and repairs, as well as the driver's food and lodging, and be sure to ask what happens in case of a major breakdown or accident. A much cheaper alternative for short distances or day-trips is to charter a tuk-tuk or sawngthaew.

Renting a **motorbike** costs 50,000–120,000K per day, depending on the quality of the bike. A licence is not required and insurance is not available, so make sure you have travel insurance coverage. Before zooming off, check the

STREET NAMES

Only a handful of cities in Laos have street names, signs are rare, and many roads change names from block to block. Use street names to find a hotel on a map in the guide text, but when asking directions or telling a tuk-tuk driver where to go, it's usually best to refer to a landmark, monastery or prominent hotel.

5

bike thoroughly for any damage and take it for a test run. Few rental places will have a helmet on offer, but it doesn't hurt to ask; don't leave your passport as a deposit. **Bicycles** can be rented from guesthouses and tourist-oriented shops in most towns for around 10,000–40,000K per day, depending on the quality.

ACCOMMODATION

Inexpensive **accommodation** can be found all over Laos. For a basic double room, prices start at around 50,000K in smaller towns, but in Vientiane and Luang Prabang you can expect to pay 80,000–120,000K. We have quoted prices up to 250,000K in kip; anything above is quoted in US$. Large Lao cities have an increasing number of **dorm beds**, going for as little as 35,000K per night. Elsewhere, a very simple double or single room with a shared bathroom will be the cheapest option.

Standards and room types can vary widely within the same establishment, so it's worth looking at several rooms before choosing one. **Electricity** is supplied at 220 volts AC; two-pin sockets are the norm. En-suite showers and flush toilets are now found in almost every hotel, though a dying breed of very cheap places still have communal facilities and squat toilets. Note that most guesthouses and hotels will advertise hot water, but "hot" can often be less than lukewarm, and may depend on the time of day and how many other people are showering at the same time.

The distinction between a **guesthouse** and a **hotel** is blurred in Laos. Either can denote anything ranging from a bamboo-and-thatch hut to a multistorey concrete building. An increasing number of guesthouses take advance bookings through sites like ⓦagoda.com and ⓦbooking.com, though they tend to charge more than walk-in rates.

Mid-range hotels are common in medium-sized towns and are mostly four- or five-storey affairs, offering large rooms with en-suite bathrooms from around 140,000K. The beds are usually hard but the sheets and quilts are clean, and often you'll get TV and air-conditioning thrown in too.

Free **wi-fi** is provided in virtually all guesthouses/hotels.

FOOD AND DRINK

Fiery and fragrant, with a touch of sour, **Lao food** owes its distinctive taste to fermented fish sauces, lemongrass, coriander leaves, chillies and lime juice and is closely related to Thai cuisine. Eaten with the hands along with the staple sticky rice, much of traditional Lao cuisine is roasted over an open fire and served with fresh herbs and vegetables. Pork, chicken, duck and water buffalo all end up in the kitchen, but freshwater fish is the main source of protein. An ingredient in many recipes is *nâm pa*, or fish sauce, which is used like salt. Most Lao cooking includes fish sauce, so you may want to order "*baw sai nâm pa*" ("without fish sauce") if you are a vegetarian.

Vientiane and Luang Prabang have the country's best food, with excellent Lao food and international cuisine, but in remote towns you'll be faced with trying some of the more daring local dishes, such as ant egg soup, or sticking to noodle soups and fried rice. Although Laos is a Buddhist country, very few Lao are **vegetarian**. It's fairly easy, however, to get a vegetable dish or vegetable fried rice. As for **hygiene**, Laos kitchens are often nothing more than shacks without proper lighting or even running water. Sticking to well-frequented places is the safest bet, but it is by no means a guarantee that you won't get an upset stomach. In any case, do not drink tap water, try to avoid cooked food that has been left standing, and only eat fruit that you can peel.

WHERE TO EAT

The **cheapest** places for food are markets, street stalls and noodle shops. Despite their name, **morning markets** (*talat sào*) remain open all day and provide a focal point for noodle stalls (*hân khãi fõe*), coffee vendors, fruit stands and sellers of crusty French loaves. In Luang Prabang and Vientiane, vendors hawking pre-made dishes gather in **evening markets** (*talat láeng*) towards late afternoon. Takeaways such as grilled chicken (*pîng kai*), spicy papaya salad (*tam màk hung*) and minced pork salad (*larp mu*) are commonly available.

Some **noodle shops** and street stalls feature a makeshift kitchen surrounded by a handful of tables and stools. Most stalls will specialize in only one general food type, or even only one dish; for example, a stall with a mortar and pestle, unripe papayas and plastic bags full of pork rinds will only offer spicy papaya salads. Similarly, a noodle shop will generally only prepare noodles with or without broth. A step up from street stalls and noodle shops are *hân kin deum*, literally "eat-drink shops", where you'll find a somewhat greater variety of dishes, along with beer and whisky.

The concept of eating out is relatively new in Laos, so the majority of **restaurants** (*hân ahān*) are aimed at tourists; for a more local experience, it's best to head to the places mentioned above. Most proper restaurants that are frequented by locals are usually run by ethnic Vietnamese and Chinese, and may have a limited (or no) English-language menu.

LAO FOOD

Most Lao meals feature **sticky rice** (*khào niaw*), which is served in a lidded wicker basket (*típ khào*) and eaten with the hands. Typically, the rice will be accompanied by a fish or meat dish and soup, with a plate of fresh vegetables, such as string beans, lettuce, basil and mint, served on the side. Grab a small chunk of rice from the basket, squeeze it into a firm wad and then dip it into one of the dishes. It's thought to be bad luck not to replace the lid at the end of your meal. Plain, steamed, white rice (*khào jâo*) is eaten with a fork and spoon; chopsticks (*mâi thu*) are reserved for noodles.

So that a variety of tastes can be enjoyed during the course of a meal, Lao meals are eaten **communally**, with each dish, including the soup, being served at once rather than in courses. For two of you, order two or three dishes, plus rice.

If Laos were to nominate a **national dish**, a strong contender would be *larp*, a "salad" of minced meat mixed with garlic, chillies, shallots, galangal, fish sauce and ground sticky rice. Another quintessentially Lao dish is *tam màk hung* (or *tam sòm*), a spicy salad made with shredded green papaya, garlic, chillies, lime juice and fish paste (*pa dàek*). Usually not too far away from any *tam màk hung* vendor, you'll find someone selling *pîng kai* (basted grilled chicken). Grilled fish (*pîng pa*) is another favourite, with the whole fish skewered and barbecued.

Fŏe, the ubiquitous **noodle soup**, is primarily eaten for breakfast, though usually found in markets throughout the day. The basic bowl of *fŏe* consists of a light broth, to which is added thin rice noodles and slices of meat (usually beef or water buffalo). It is usually served with a plate of lettuce, mint, coriander leaves and bean sprouts, which you add to your dish alongside table condiments like fish- and chilli sauce. Also on offer at many noodle shops is *mi*, a yellow wheat noodle served in broth with slices of meat and a few vegetables.

The best way to round off a meal is with **fresh fruit** (*màk mâi*), as the country offers a wide variety including guava, lychee, rambutan, mangosteen and pomelo. Markets often have a food stall specializing in inexpensive **coconut-milk desserts**, generally called *nâm wān* – look for a stall displaying a dozen bowls containing everything from water chestnuts to fluorescent green and pink jellies.

DRINKS

The Lao don't drink **water** straight from the tap and nor should you; contaminated water is a major cause of sickness. Plastic bottles of drinking water (*nâm deum*) are sold countrywide; many guesthouses and restaurants in touristy areas offer free or inexpensive refills. Noodle shops and inexpensive restaurants generally serve free pitchers of weak tea or boiled water (*nâm tóm*), which is fine, although perhaps not as foolproof. Most **ice** you'll encounter in Laos is produced in large blocks under hygienic conditions, but it can become

5

less pure in transit or storage, so be wary. Brand-name soft drinks are widely available; more refreshing are the **fruit shakes** (*màk mâi pan*) available in larger towns, which consist of your choice of fruit blended with ice, liquid sugar and sweetened condensed milk.

The Lao drink strong **coffee**, or *kafeh hâwn*, which is served with sweetened condensed milk and sugar. If you prefer your coffee black and without sugar, ask for *kafeh dam baw sai nâm tan*. Black **tea** is available at most coffee vendors and is mixed with sweetened condensed milk, when you request *sá hâwn*.

Beerlao (*Bia Lao*) is a very enjoyable, cheap brew sold throughout the country for 10,000–15,000K for a large bottle. In Vientiane and Luang Prabang, draught Beerlao known as *bia sót* is often available at bargain prices by the litre. Drunk with equal gusto is *lào-láo*, a clear **rice alcohol** with the fire of a blinding Mississippi moonshine. *Làо-láo* is usually sold in whatever bottle the distiller had at the time (look twice before you buy that bottle of Pepsi) and is sold at drink shops and general stores.

CULTURE AND ETIQUETTE

Laos by and large shares the same attitudes to dress and **social taboos** as other Theravada Buddhist Southeast Asian cultures (see p.40). The lowland Lao traditionally **greet** each other with a *nop* – bringing their hands together in a prayer-like gesture. The status of the persons giving and returning the *nop* determines how they will execute it, so most Lao prefer to shake hands with Westerners. If you do receive a *nop* as a gesture of greeting or thank you, it is best to reply with a smile and nod of the head.

Take care to respect Lao attitudes to religion by sticking to basic temple etiquette: don't dress too provocatively, and always remove your shoes before entering the temple. It can also cause offence to photograph monks and images of the Buddha. It's important that women should never touch Buddhist monks, novices, or their clothes, and should also not hand objects directly to them.

SPORTS AND OUTDOOR ACTIVITIES

Laos's landscape is a sports haven: mountainous highlands and ethnic villages for trekkers; well-paved, relatively traffic-free routes for bike enthusiasts; and rivers for rafters and kayakers. Outdoor activities and adventure companies include **Green Discovery** (Ⓦgreendiscoverylaos .com), **Tiger Trail** (Ⓦlaos-adventures.com), and **Exo Travel** (Ⓦexotravel.com), which organize kayaking, rafting, trekking and cycling trips.

TREKKING

Trekking is gaining popularity in Laos, especially in the northern part of the country, though in recent years there has been an increase in trekking opportunities in the south. The main centres are Luang Prabang (see p.372) and Luang Namtha (see p.389), where it's easy to arrange a few days' hiking through forests and sleeping at village homestays, offering the opportunity to experience authentic Lao life.

Companies like Green Discovery, Tiger Trail and Exo Travel will lead you through spectacular wildlife on ecotours that cross through national parks called **National Biodiversity Conservation Areas (NBCA)**, which are host to a wealth of diverse flora and fauna. Despite these areas being officially protected, poaching remains a problem and habitats continue to be destroyed.

CYCLING

Cycling is an increasingly popular way to explore Laos. Organized trips are provided by companies such as London-based Red Spokes (Ⓣ0207 502 7252, Ⓦredspokes .co.uk), which runs a popular two-week tour that takes in Luang Prabang, Vang Vieng and Vientiane, as well as some rural stretches with spectacular scenery. It's also possible to rent fairly good mountain bikes in towns like Vang Vieng (see p.368) and set off on your own adventure around the countryside.

WATERSPORTS

Watersports fans can opt for **whitewater rafting** trips out of Luang Prabang on the northern rivers such as the Nam Ou, the

Nam Xeuang and the Nam Ming. Those who prefer a more relaxed paddle can **kayak** downriver at a slower pace while taking in the lovely views of Vang Vieng (see p.368), Muang Ngoi Neua (see p.387) and Si Phan Don (see p.404), among others. **Tubing** on the Nam Song in Vang Vieng (see p.368) remains popular.

CAVING AND ROCK CLIMBING

Caving and **rock climbing** are best at Vang Vieng, where Laos's first bolted cliff face has several routes for all abilities. With so many limestone karsts, Laos offers plenty of opportunities for caving, from Vang Vieng to the area just east of Thakhek in South Central Laos. For any caving excursion, remember to take a head torch and some good footwear.

COMMUNICATIONS

Most foreign smartphones can be used in Laos, though call, text and data charges are high, so if you're planning on using your phone it's worth buying a local SIM card. These are readily available from shops and markets, and for around 40,000K you'll be able to buy a package with enough data to last you several weeks of daily use. Local network Unitel has good 3G coverage in even mid-sized towns. Top-up cards can be purchased in villages across Laos that have even the most basic shop – just look for the flag displaying the network's name. **Regional codes** are given throughout the chapter: the "0" must be dialled before all long-distance calls.

Internet cafés are found all over the country; charges are around 5000–10,000K/hr. In tourist areas especially, **free wi-fi** is widespread.

CRIME AND SAFETY

Laos is a relatively **safe country** for travellers. For the most part, if you keep your wits about you, you shouldn't have any problems. Theft – especially among travellers and around major festivals – is likely to be your greatest worry, aside from UXO (see box, p.384). If you have anything stolen, you'll need to get the police to write up a report for your

LAOS ONLINE

Ⓦ vientianetimes.com Features news, accommodation listings and links to hundreds of other websites on Laos.
Ⓦ laoembassy.com Website of the Lao embassy to the US features tourist info and the latest visa regulations.
Ⓦ ecotourismlaos.com An informative website by the Lao National Tourism Administration that features helpful tips on exploring Laos's national parks.
Ⓦ laos-guide-999.com Clunky but useful site with information on transport, visas and Lao culture.
Ⓦ luangnamtha.laopdr.com An excellent site on travel in northern Laos, with info on independent trekking and ecotourism.
Ⓦ eatdrinklaos.com An excellent blog on where to eat and drink in Laos (particularly Vientiane).

insurance; bring along someone to interpret if you can.

UNEXPLODED ORDNANCE

The Second Indochina War left Laos with a legacy of **bombs**, **land mines** and **mortar shells** that will haunt the country for decades to come, despite the efforts of de-mining organizations. Round, tennis-ball-sized anti-personnel bomblets, known as "bombies", are the most common type of **unexploded ordnance** (UXO). Larger bombs, ranging in size from 100kg to 1000kg, also abound.

Although most towns and tourist sites are free of UXO, 25 percent of villages remain contaminated. As accidents often occur while people are tending their fields, the risk faced by the average visitor is extremely limited. Nonetheless, the number one rule is: don't be a trailblazer. When in rural areas, always stay on well-worn paths, even when passing through a village, and don't pick up or kick at anything if you don't know what it is.

DRUGS

It is **illegal** to smoke ganja and opium in Laos, although these and other drugs (including magic mushrooms) are still

5

LAO

The main language of Laos is Lao. The spoken Lao of Vientiane is very similar to the Thai spoken in Bangkok, though there are pockets of Laos where no dialect of Lao, much less the Vientiane version, will be heard. Since economic liberalization, English has become the preferred foreign tongue, and it's quite possible to get by without Lao in the towns. Out in the countryside, you will need some Lao phrases.

PRONUNCIATION

The dialect of Lao spoken in Vientiane, which has been deemed the official language of Laos, has six tones. Thus, depending on its tone, the word "*sang*" can mean either "elephant", "craftsman", "granary", "laryngitis", a species of bamboo, or "to build".

a as the "ah" in "autobahn"
ae as the "a" in "cat"
ai as in "Thai"
aw as in "jaw"
ao as in "Lao"
e as in "pen"
eu as in French "fleur"
i as in "mimi"
ia as in "India"
o as in "flow"
oe as in "Goethe"
u (or ou) as the "ou" in "you"
ua (or oua) as the "ua" in "truant"

b as in "big"
d as in "dog"
f as in "fun"
h as in "hello"
j (or ch) as in "jar"
k as in "skin" (unaspirated)
kh as the "k" in "kiss"
l as in "luck"
m as in "more"
n as in "now"
ng as in "singer" (this combination sometimes appears at the beginning of a word)
ny as in the Russian "nyet"
p as in "speak" (unaspirated)
ph as the "p" in "pill"
s (or x) as in "same"
t as in "stop" (unaspirated)
th as the "t" in "tin"
w (or v) as in "wish"
y as in "yes"

WORDS AND PHRASES IN LAO

Questions in Lao are not normally answered with a yes or no. Instead the verb used in the question is repeated for the answer. For example: "Do you have a room?" ("*mí hàwng wàng baw*"), would be answered "Have" ("*mí*") in the affirmative or "No have" ("*baw mí*") in the negative.

GREETINGS AND BASIC PHRASES

Hello	*Sabai di*	Where are you from?	*Jâo má tae sãi?*
Goodbye	*Lá kawn*	Hospital	*Dae*
Goodbye (in reply)	*Sok di*	I need a doctor	*Khói tâwng kan hã mãw*
How are you?	*Sabai di baw?*		
I'm fine	*Sabai di*	Where is the …?	*… yu sãi?*
Please (rarely used)	*Kaluna*	Can you help me?	*Jâo suay khói dâi baw?*
Thank you (very much)	*Khop jai (lai lai)*		
Do you speak English?	*Jâo wâo phasã angkit dâi baw?*	Police station	*Sathani tamluat*
		Do you have any rooms?	*Mí hàwng wàng baw?*
I don't understand	*Khói baw khào jai*		
Yes	*Lâew*	Can I have the bill?	*Khãw sek dae*
No	*Baw*	How much is this?	*An nî thao dai?*
Right/Left	*Khwã/Sâi*	Foreigner	*Falang*

NUMBERS

0	*sun*	5	*hà*
1	*neung*	6	*hók*
2	*sãwng*	7	*jét*
3	*sãm*	8	*pàet*
4	*si*	9	*kâo*

10	síp	30, 40, 50, etc	sãm síp, si síp, hà síp
11, 12, etc	síp ét, síp sãwng	100	hôi
20	sao	1000	phán
21, 22, 23, etc	sao ét, sao sãwng, sao sãm		

FOOD AND DRINKS GLOSSARY

I can't eat meat	khói kin sîn baw dâi
No ice	baw sai nâm kâwn

Meat, fish and basic foods

jeun khai	omelette
kai	chicken
khào jâo	rice, steamed
khào ji	bread
khào niaw	rice, sticky
kûng	shrimp
màk phét	chilli
mu	pork
nâm kat	coconut milk
nâm pa	fish sauce
nâm tan	sugar
nóm sòm	yoghurt
pa	fish
pa dàek	fish paste
pét	duck
phák	vegetables
pu	crab
sìn ngúa	beef
tâo hû	bean curd

Fruit

màk kûay	banana
màk mî	jackfruit
màk mo	watermelon
màk muang	mango
màk náo	lime/lemon
màk nat	pineapple
màk phom	apple

Noodles

fõe	rice noodle soup
fõe hàeng	rice noodle soup without broth
fõe khùa	fried rice noodles
khào piak sèn	rice noodle soup, served in chicken broth
khào pûn	flour noodles with sauce
mi hàeng	yellow wheat noodles without broth
mi nâm	yellow wheat noodle soup

Everyday dishes

khào ji pateh	bread with Lao-style pâté and vegetables
khào khùa or khào phát	fried rice
khào khùa sai kai	fried rice with chicken
khùa khing kai	chicken with ginger
khùa phák baw sai sìn	stir-fried vegetables
larp mu	minced pork
mu phát bai hólapha	pork with basil over rice
pîng kai	grilled chicken
pîng pa or jeun pa	grilled fish
tam màk hung	spicy papaya salad
tôm yam pa	spicy fish soup with lemon grass
yam sìn ngúa	spicy beef salad
yáw díp	spring rolls, fresh
yáw jeun	spring rolls, fried

Desserts

khào lãm	sticky rice in coconut milk cooked in bamboo
khào niaw màk muang	sticky rice with mango

Drinks

bia	beer
bia sót	beer, draught
kafeh	coffee
kafeh dam	black coffee
kafeh nóm hawn	hot Lao coffee (with milk and sugar)
kafeh nóm yén	iced coffee (with milk and sugar)
lào-láo	rice whisky
màk kûay pan	banana shake
màk mai pan	fruit shake
nâm deum	water
nâm kâwn	ice
nâm sá	tea
nóm	milk, usually sweetened condensed
sá jin	tea, Chinese

5

available in some places. Tourists who use illegal drugs risk substantial "fines" if caught by police, who do not need a warrant to search you or your room. Wide-scale government crackdowns on drug tourism have been effective, especially in Vang Vieng, but drugs are still (relatively) openly sold in other areas, such as the touristy islands of Si Phan Don.

MEDICAL CARE AND EMERGENCIES

You'll find **pharmacies** in all the major towns and cities. Pharmacists in Vientiane and Luang Prabang are quite knowledgeable and have a decent supply of medicines.

Otherwise, healthcare in Laos is so poor as to be virtually nonexistent. The nearest **medical care** of any competence is in neighbouring Thailand, and if you find yourself afflicted by anything more serious than travellers' diarrhoea, it's best to head for the closest Thai border crossing and check into a hospital. If you're in Vientiane and the problem is not urgent, you could also try the Alliance International Medical Centre, Honda Complex, Souphanuvong Road (☎021 513095).

INFORMATION AND MAPS

The **Lao National Tourism Administration** (LNTA; ⓦwww.tourismlaos.org) operates offices in most major towns, and the staff are generally well trained and knowledgeable, though the level of English spoken varies from office to office. Green Discovery, which has offices in most major towns, can also provide reliable information. Word-of-mouth information from other travellers is often the best source, as conditions in Laos change with astonishing rapidity.

EMERGENCY NUMBERS

In **Vientiane** dial the following numbers: Dial ❶190 in case of fire, ❶195 for an ambulance, or ❶1191 for police.

Good **maps** for Laos are difficult to find. The best road map of the country is the *Laos PDR Map*, published by Golden Triangle Rider and available in Vientiane or online at ⓦgt-rider.com. Other detailed maps of the country are also available from bookshops in Vientiane (see p.367). For town maps, in addition to those in this book, Hobo Maps (ⓦhobomaps.com) provide easy-to-use maps of various tourist towns, which are available online or from local bookshops.

MONEY AND BANKS

Lao currency is the **kip** and is available in 100,000K, 50,000K, 20,000K, 10,000K, 5000K, 2000K, 1000K and 500K notes. There are no coins in circulation. Although a 1990 law technically forbids the use of foreign currencies to pay for local goods and services, some hotels, restaurants and tour operators (usually when the price is over 200,000K) actually quote their prices in dollars and accept payment in either **baht**, **dollars** or **kip**.

At the time of writing, the official **exchange rate** was around 8000K to US$1, 10,000K to £1 and 220K to the Thai baht.

You can find ATMs in almost every large Lao town, and most will accept both Visa and MasterCard. Withdrawals usually incur a local charge (around 20,000K), though there are machines that will dispense money without charging (your bank may still charge you). It's a good idea to have a decent supply of US dollars or Thai baht in **cash** if you intend to spend time in the remoter parts of the country, or if you wish to leave Laos and re-enter (the visa on arrival fee is only payable in dollars). Major **credit cards** are accepted at many hotels, upmarket restaurants and shops in Vientiane and Luang Prabang, and most tour operators will accept card payments. **Cash advances** on Visa cards and, less frequently, MasterCard are possible in most major towns. Bear in mind that you cannot change kip back into dollars or baht once you have left the country. Travellers' cheques are no longer accepted by any banks in Laos.

COSTS

Given the potential volatility of the kip, some mid-range hotels and tour agencies have opted to fix their rates to the dollar. However, prices for guesthouses, transport and entrance fees will almost always be quoted in kip. Some of these places will also accept dollars and Thai baht, but the rate will always be more favourable if you pay in kip, and most local businesses prefer it.

While restaurants and some shops have fixed prices, you should always **bargain** in markets and when chartering transport (fares on long-distance passenger vehicles are fixed). Room rates can often be bargained for in low season. **Price tiering** does exist in Laos, with foreigners paying more than locals for entry to museums and famous sites.

OPENING HOURS AND HOLIDAYS

While official hours for **government offices** are 8am to noon and 1 to 5pm Monday to Friday, very little gets done between 11am and 2pm.

Post office hours are variable, but they are generally open Monday to Friday 8am to 4pm, often with a lunch break of an hour or two in the middle. **Banking hours** are usually 8.30am to noon and 1 to 3.30pm, Monday to Friday nationwide; exchange kiosks often keep longer hours. All government businesses close on public holidays, though some shops and restaurants may stay open. The only time when many private businesses do close – for three to seven days – is during Chinese New Year (new moon in late Jan to mid-Feb), when the ethnic-Vietnamese and Chinese populations of Vientiane, Thakhek, Savannakhet and Pakse celebrate with parties and temple visits.

Morning food and drink **stalls** are up and running at about 7am, while night stalls are usually open from 6 to 9pm. Most **restaurants** are open daily until about 10pm.

PEOPLE

The **Lao Loum** (or lowland Lao) make up the majority in Laos: between fifty percent and sixty percent of the population. They prefer to inhabit river valleys and practise Theravada Buddhism as well as some animist rituals. Of all the ethnicities found in Laos, the culture of the lowland Lao is dominant, mainly because it is they who hold political power. Their language is the official language, their religion is the state religion and their holy days are the official holidays.

MON-KHMER GROUPS

The **Khamu** of northern Laos, speakers of a Mon-Khmer language, are the most numerous of the indigenes, and have assimilated to a high degree.

Another Mon-Khmer-speaking group that inhabits the north are the **Htin**. Owing to a partial cultural ban on the use of any kind of metal, the Htin excel at fashioning bamboo baskets and fish traps.

HIGHLAND GROUPS

The **Lao Soung** (literally the "high Lao") live at the highest elevations and include the Hmong, Mien, Lahu and Akha.

The **Hmong** are the most numerous, with a population of approximately 200,000. Hmong apparel is among the most colourful to be found in Laos and their silver jewellery is prized by collectors. Their written language uses Roman letters and was devised by Western missionaries.

SOUTHERN PEOPLES

The Bolaven Plateau in southern Laos is named for the **Laven** people, a Mon-Khmer-speaking group whose presence pre-dates that of the Lao. The Laven were very quick to assimilate the ways of the southern Lao. Other Mon-Khmer-speaking minorities found in the south, particularly in Savannakhet and Salavan, include the **Bru**, who are skilled builders of animal traps; the **Gie-Trieng**, who are expert basket weavers; the **Nge**, who produce textiles featuring stylized bombs and fighter planes; and the **Katu**, a very warlike people.

5

PUBLIC HOLIDAYS

January 1 New Year's Day
January 6 Pathet Lao Day
January 20 Army Day
March 8 Women's Day
March 22 Lao People's Party Day
April 13–15 Lao New Year
May 1 International Labour Day
June 1 Children's Day
August 13 Lao Issara
August 23 Liberation Day
October 12 Freedom from France Day
December 2 National Day

FESTIVALS

All major **festivals**, whether Buddhist or animist, feature parades, music and dancing, not to mention the copious consumption of *lào-láo*. Because the Lao calendar is dictated by both solar and lunar rhythms, the dates of festivals change from year to year. Tourists are usually welcome to participate in the more public Buddhist festivals, but at hill-tribe festivals you should only watch from a distance.

Festivals of most interest to tourists include:

Makkha Busa Feb. Buddhist holy day, observed under a full moon in February, which commemorates a legendary sermon given by the Buddha.

Lao New Year or **Pi Mai Lao** Mid-April. Celebrated all over Laos, most stunningly in Luang Prabang, where the town's namesake Buddha image is ritually bathed.

Bun Bang Fai May. Also known as the rocket festival, during which crude projectiles are made from stout bamboo poles stuffed with gunpowder and fired skywards. It's hoped the thunderous noise will encourage the spirits to make it rain after months of dry weather.

Lai Heau Fai Oct. On the full moon in October, this festival of lights is most magically celebrated in Luang Prabang. Residents build large floats and festoon them with lights.

That Luang Festival Nov. Takes place in Vientiane in the days leading up to the full moon, and kicks off with a colourful procession around the country's most famous stupa as locals seek to make merit.

Bun Pha Wet Dec–Jan. Commemorates the Jataka tale of the Buddha's second-to-last incarnation as Pha Wet, or Prince Vessantara, and takes place at local monasteries on various dates throughout December or January. In larger towns, expect live bands and dancing.

Vientiane and around

Hugging a bend of the Mekong River, the capital is a quaint and easy-going place. Arriving in **VIENTIANE** from other cities in the region, your first impression is likely to be of a small, pleasant and fairly quiet town; arrive from elsewhere in Laos, however, and the city feels very much like a buzzing metropolis. Since Laos reopened its doors to foreign visitors, Vientiane has changed with dizzying rapidity. Today, with foreign investment continuing to pour in and a significant international NGO presence, the city is growing fast, and swish SUVs easily outnumber rusting tuk-tuks. Along with new shopping malls and luxurious high-rise developments, the city has a thriving tourist economy and some excellent places to stay and eat. That said, it remains one of Southeast Asia's most peaceful and easily navigable capital cities.

A few hours north of the capital is **Vang Vieng**, a once-notorious backpacker hangout set amid spectacular scenery on the road to Luang Prabang. The authorities are attempting to reinvent the town as an outdoor destination – with some success – but it remains a favourite stop on the backpacker route through Laos, and for many, tubing (and drinking) on the scenic Nam Song River is still the biggest draw.

VIENTIANE

Two days is sufficient to see Vientiane's main sights, though those who stick around longer will find plenty to keep them occupied. The impressive collection of Lao art at **Haw Pha Kaew** should be high on any visitor's list, as should the placid Buddhist monastery known as **Wat Sisaket**. At sunset, it's worth taking a ride out to **That Luang**, Laos's most important religious building, to admire the shimmer of warm sunrays across its golden surface. The city's most eye-opening attractions are the **COPE** and **Mines Advisory Group** visitor centres, which highlight some of the challenges faced by ordinary Lao people whose lives continue to be affected by ordnance dropped during the Second Indochina War. A more light-hearted day-trip destination is **Xieng Khuan** or the "**Buddha Park**", a Hindu-Buddhist fantasy in ferro-concrete on the banks of the Mekong.

WHAT TO SEE AND DO

The plaza surrounding **Nam Phou Fountain** marks the heart of tourist Vientiane, near which you'll find the greatest concentration of accommodation, restaurants and souvenir shops. The fountain, which once created a pleasant public space for locals and foreigners to cool off after the sun goes down, has now been converted into a tacky outdoor food court.

The Lao National Museum

North of Nam Phou, on Samsenthai Road, the dingy **Lao National Museum** (Mon–Fri daily 8am–noon & 1–4pm, Sat & Sun 8.30am–noon & 1–4pm; 10,000K, camera 10,000K) is haphazardly laid out, but contains some fascinating artefacts. In the early "pre-history" rooms there are dinosaur bones, stone tools, spearheads and pottery fragments. The following displays trace the country's history to the present day (or, at least, to the early 2000s, after which the exhibits peter out). Among the highlights are displays on Wat Phou (see p.401), traditional instruments, Buddhist iconography, the Lane Xang period, French colonization, the Second Indochina War, and the "inevitable victory" of the proletariat in 1975. There are plans to move the museum to a new location outside the city centre.

Wat Sisaket

Towards the southeastern end of Setthathilat Road, the street running parallel to and just south of Samsenthai Road, stands **Wat Sisaket** (daily 8am–noon & 1–4pm; 5000K), the oldest wat in Vientiane. Constructed by King Anouvong (Chao Anou) in 1818, it was the only monastery to survive the Siamese sacking ten years later. Surrounded by a tile-roofed cloister, the *sim* (building housing the main Buddha image) contains some charming, though badly deteriorating, murals. A splendidly ornate candle-holder of carved wood situated before the altar is a fine example of nineteenth-century Lao woodcarving. Outside, the cloister holds countless niches with diminutive Buddhas peering out from them.

The Presidential Palace and Haw Pha Kaew

Opposite Wat Sisaket stands the **Presidential Palace**, an impressive French Beaux Arts-style building built to house the French colonial governor, now used mainly for government ceremonies. Next to the palace, **Haw Pha Kaew** (daily 8am–noon & 1–4pm; 5000K), once the king's personal Buddhist temple, now functions as a museum of art and antiquities. The temple is named for the Emerald Buddha, or Pha Kaew, which was pilfered by the Siamese in 1779 and carried off to their capital where it remains to this day. The museum houses the finest collection of Lao art in the country, one of the most striking works being a Buddha in the "Beckoning Rain" pose (standing with arms to the sides and fingers pointing to the ground) and sporting a jewel-encrusted navel.

Lane Xang Avenue and Patouxai

Lane Xang Avenue, leading off north from Setthathilat Road, is reputedly modelled on France's Champs Élysées, and **Patouxai**, standing at one end, on the Arc de Triomphe. Popularly known as *anusawali* (Lao for "monument"), this massive concrete victory gateway topped with elaborate towers (daily 8am–4.30pm; 3000K), 1km from the Presidential Palace, was built in the late 1950s to commemorate casualties of war on the side of the Royal Lao Government. The view of Vientiane from the top is worth the climb. A handful of hawkers gather under the archway, which has a ceiling adorned with reliefs of the Hindu deities; the walls depict characters from the Ramayana, the epic Hindu story of battles between good and evil.

5

Mines Advisory Group (MAG) Information Centre

A ten-minute walk northwest of Patouxai, the new **Mines Advisory Group (MAG) Information Centre** (Tues–Sat noon–6pm; donations appreciated; ☎021 252004, ⓦmaginternational.org) is an essential visit for anyone keen to understand the human impact of Laos being the most bombed-per-capita country in the world. The secret US bombing campaigns during the "Vietnam" War left the country littered with unexploded "bombies". Between 1964 and 1973, more than two million tons of ordnance were dropped on Laos. Around thirty percent of the cluster munitions dropped failed to explode, and

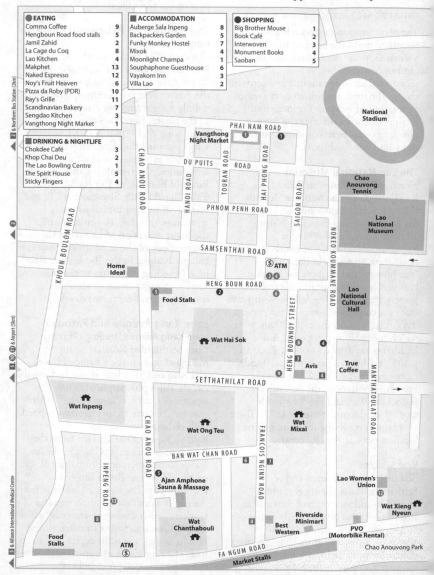

● EATING	
Comma Coffee	9
Hengboun Road food stalls	5
Jamil Zahid	2
La Cage du Coq	8
Lao Kitchen	4
Makphet	13
Naked Espresso	12
Noy's Fruit Heaven	6
Pizza da Roby (PDR)	10
Ray's Grille	11
Scandinavian Bakery	7
Sengdao Kitchen	3
Vangthong Night Market	1

■ ACCOMMODATION	
Auberge Sala Inpeng	8
Backpackers Garden	5
Funky Monkey Hostel	7
Mixok	4
Moonlight Champa	3
Souphaphone Guesthouse	6
Vayakorn Inn	1
Villa Lao	2

● SHOPPING	
Big Brother Mouse	1
Book Café	2
Interwoven	3
Monument Books	4
Saoban	5

■ DRINKING & NIGHTLIFE	
Chokdee Café	3
Khop Chai Deu	2
The Lao Bowling Centre	1
The Spirit House	5
Sticky Fingers	4

National Stadium

PHAI NAM ROAD

Vangthong Night Market

CHAO ANOU ROAD

DU PUITS ROAD

HANOI ROAD

TOURAN ROAD

HAI PHONG ROAD

SAIGON ROAD

PHNOM PENH ROAD

Chao Anouvong Tennis

Lao National Museum

KHOUN BOULOM ROAD

SAMSENTHAI ROAD

$ ATM

NOKEO KOUMMANE ROAD

Home Ideal

HENG BOUN ROAD

Lao National Cultural Hall

Food Stalls

Wat Hai Sok

HENG BOUNNOY STREET

Avis

True Coffee

SETTHATHILAT ROAD

MANTHATOULAT ROAD

Wat Inpeng

CHAO ANOU ROAD

Wat Ong Teu

Wat Mixai

FRANCOIS NGINN ROAD

BAN WAT CHAN ROAD

Ajan Amphone Sauna & Massage

Lao Women's Union

Wat Xieng Nyeun

INPENG ROAD

Wat Chanthabouli

Best Western

Riverside Minimart

PVO (Motorbike Rental)

Food Stalls

ATM $

FA NGUM ROAD

Market Stalls

Chao Anouvong Park

◀ ❷ & Northern Bus Station (2km)

◀ ❷

◀ ❺ 🏥 ⑪ & Airport (5km)

◀ 🏥 & Alliance International Medical Centre

even today, 25 percent of Lao villages are contaminated by unexploded ordnance (UXO). The tragic result is that since the end of the war, at least 20,000 people have been killed or maimed. MAG carries out vital work deactivating UXO and educating people about the ongoing dangers. MAG has another centre in Phonsavan (see p.384).

COPE Visitor Centre

Around 1km southeast of the Talat Sao bus station is the **COPE Visitor Centre** (daily 9am–6pm; donations appreciated; ☏021 241972, ⓦcopelaos.org), set up by an NGO to document the devastating effects of UXO left over from the Second Indochina War. Some of those affected tell their stories on TV screens around the

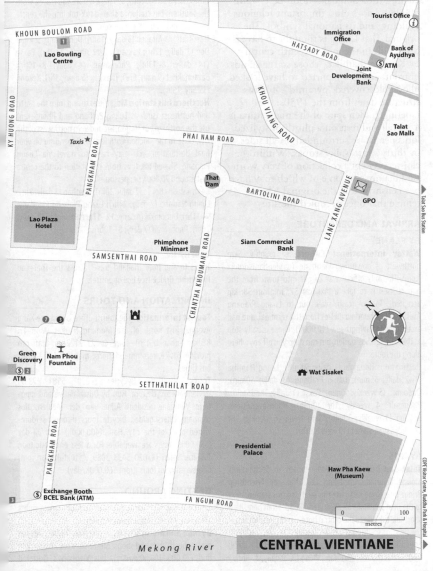

Mines Advisory Group Information centre, Patouxai (500m), That Luang (2km) & Southern Bus Station (9km)

KHOUN BOULOM ROAD

Lao Bowling Centre

KY HUONG ROAD

Tourist Office

Immigration Office

HATSADY ROAD

Bank of Ayudhya

ATM

Joint Development Bank

KHOU VIANG ROAD

Talat Sao Malls

PHAI NAM ROAD

Taxis

PANGKHAM ROAD

That Dam

BARTOLINI ROAD

LANE XANG AVENUE

GPO

Lao Plaza Hotel

Phimphone Minimart

Siam Commercial Bank

CHANTHA KHOUMANE ROAD

SAMSENTHAI ROAD

Green Discovery
ATM

Nam Phou Fountain

N

Wat Sisaket

SETTHATHILAT ROAD

PANGKHAM ROAD

Presidential Palace

Haw Pha Kaew (Museum)

Exchange Booth BCEL Bank (ATM)

FA NGUM ROAD

0   100
metres

Mekong River

CENTRAL VIENTIANE

Talat Sao Bus Station

COPE Visitor Centre, Buddha Park & Hospital

5

exhibition. But the centre isn't only about looking back; here you can find out how prosthetic limbs and rehabilitation programmes are giving victims another chance at life.

That Luang

One and a half kilometres northeast of Patouxai stands the Buddhist stupa, **That Luang** (Tues–Sun 8am–noon & 1–4pm; 5000K), Laos's most important religious building, and its national symbol. The original That Luang is thought to have been built in the mid-sixteenth century by King Setthathilat, whose statue stands in front, and was reported to have looked like a gold-covered "pyramid". Today's structure dates from the 1930s: the tapering golden spire of the main stupa is 45m tall and rests on a plinth of stylized lotus petals; it's surrounded on all sides by thirty short, spiky stupas. Within the cloisters is kept a collection of very worn Buddha images, some of which may have been enshrined in the original Khmer temple that once occupied the site.

ARRIVAL AND DEPARTURE

BY PLANE

Wattay International Airport is roughly 5km northwest of downtown Vientiane (W vientianeairport .com). The only official way to get into town from the airport itself is to take a taxi (car $7, minivan $8; kip accepted). To save cash, walk out to Luang Prabang Avenue, a few hundred metres from the terminal, and hail an eastbound sawngthaew (10,000K). These usually stop at the Talat Sao bus station, but can drop you off anywhere along the route.

Destinations Houayxai (1 daily; 50min); Luang Namtha (1–2 daily; 55min); Luang Prabang (3 daily; 50min); Oudomxai (5 weekly; 50min); Pakse (1 daily; 1hr 15min); Phongsali (4 weekly; 1hr 40min); Phonsavan/Xieng Khuang (4 weekly; 30min); Sam Neua (6 weekly; 1hr 20min); Savannakhet (10 weekly; 1hr).

BY BUS

Talat Sao bus station Public buses to destinations around Vientiane (including the Thai–Lao Friendship Bridge near Nong Khai) use the Talat Sao bus station, next to the Talat Sao Malls on Khou Vieng Road. From here, it's a short tuk-tuk ride to the central hotels and guesthouses.

Destinations Buddha Park (every 15min; 40min); Friendship Bridge (every 15min; 30min); Kasi (1 daily; 6hr); Thalat (hourly; 2hr); Vang Vieng (8–9 daily; 3–4hr).

Southern bus station Buses to and from the south tend to use the southern bus station, about 9km northeast of the centre on Rte 13; when leaving, it's a good idea to book tickets a day ahead with your guesthouse. Daily buses for Hanoi leave from here at 7pm and 7.30pm, and should arrive 24hr later (around 230,000K). There are also daily buses to Vinh, Hue and Da Nang at the same time, but buses to Ho Chi Minh City only run on Mondays, Thursdays and Saturdays; departure times change frequently, so check before you travel. From the southern bus station, a shared tuk-tuk into the centre costs around 20,000K per person.

Destinations Attapeu (3 daily; 16hr); Don Khong, Si Phan Don (1 daily; 17hr); Paksan (every 30min; 1–2hr); Pakse (14 daily; 8–13hr); Phonsavan (4 daily; 8–10hr); Savannakhet (9 daily; 8hr); Thakhek (5 daily; 5hr); Xekong (3 daily; 15hr).

Northern bus station Most buses to and from the north and northeast (such as Luang Prabang and Phonsavan) use the northern bus station, around 9km northwest of the city, close to the junction with Rte 13. Depending on your final destination, you may have to travel via Luang Prabang. Shared tuk-tuks from the station to the centre cost around 20,000K per person.

Destinations Bokeo (2 daily; 30hr); Kenthao (1 daily; 7hr); Luang Namtha (2 daily; 24hr); Luang Prabang (15 daily; 9–11hr); Oudomxai (4 daily; 12–17hr); Phongsali (2 daily; 26hr); Phonsavan (7 daily; 8–10hr).

BY TRAIN

Trains to and from Thailand travel across the Thai–Lao Friendship Bridge (see box opposite).

INFORMATION AND TOURS

Tourist information The tourist office is on Lane Xang Avenue, just north of the Morning Market (Mon–Fri 8.30am–noon & 1.30–4pm; T 021 212251). Staff can provide advice, recommendations, maps and the latest bus times.

Tours Vientiane ByCycle T 020 5581 2337, W vientianebycycle.com. Run by Dutch native and long-term Vientiane resident Aline van der Meulen, this company offers guided bicycle tours through seldom-visited parts of the city. Half- (400,000K) and full-day (550,000K) tours are available. For a less energetic tour, Tuk Tuk Safari (T 020 5433 3089, W tuktuksafari.com) offers a range of tours (from 560,000K/day).

GETTING AROUND

Central Vientiane is easily explored on foot – most sights are an easy walk from accommodation.

By bike and motorbike Bikes cost from 10,000K/day at many guesthouses and shops. Motorbikes are also easy to find (70,000–100,000K/day), but Vientiane's cluttered

TO AND FROM THAILAND: THE FIRST THAI–LAO FRIENDSHIP BRIDGE

The major crossing into Laos is the **First Thai–Lao Friendship Bridge** (daily 6am–10pm), which spans the Mekong River at a point 5km west of **Nong Khai** in Thailand and around 20km east of Vientiane. Daily **buses** leave Vientiane's Talat Sao station for the Friendship Bridge (every 15min), Nong Khai (6 daily) and Udon Thani (8 daily). From Nong Khai, you can catch a bus or **train** to Bangkok (5 trains daily; 10hr to Bangkok). You can take a train to Nong Khai from Tha Naleng (2 daily; 15min), in Laos, near the Friendship Bridge. Another option is to take the bus to the Friendship Bridge and cross using the public bus (see opposite); once on the Thai side, hire a share taxi to the train station (around 20–25 baht). Tour agencies and guesthouses in Vientiane sell train tickets, which include transfers across the border to the train station.

Entering Laos from Thailand, buses shuttle passengers across the bridge (every 15–20min). The buses start beyond Thai immigration control at the base of the bridge. You will need to clear Thai customs before boarding the bus and continuing on to Lao immigration on the opposite side of the river, where a thirty-day visa on arrival is available. An "overtime fee" of $1 may be charged if you cross at the weekend or after 4.30pm. After crossing, the cheapest way into Vientiane is by bus. Ignore the tuk-tuk drivers waiting on the Lao side and walk towards the market stalls on your right-hand side. The #14 bus leaves frequently from here, pulling up at the Talat Sao bus station.

roads take some getting used to. A well-established place in the city centre that accepts a cash deposit of around $30–50 (don't leave your passport as a deposit) is PVO on Fa Ngum Road (⚀021 254354, ✉laopvo@hotmail.com).

By tuk-tuk Shared tuk-tuks generally ply frequently travelled routes, such as Lane Xang Avenue between the Morning Market and That Luang, and along Setthathilat and Fa Ngum roads, and charge around 10,000K/person for destinations within the city. There are usually a few tuk-tuks parked and waiting for foreign passengers near Nam Phou; note that the prices the drivers have listed on laminated sheets are inflated for tourists.

ACCOMMODATION

★**Auberge Sala Inpeng** 63 Inpeng Rd ⚀021 242021, ⓦsalalao.com. These traditional-style, a/c bungalows, on a secluded plot between much larger buildings, offer a chance to escape the hustle of Vientiane's streets without moving too far from the action. You can enjoy breakfast on your own balcony overlooking the serene gardens. Doubles $30

Backpackers Garden 56 Sihome Rd, halfway between the two petrol stations ⚀020 9551 2668, ✉backpackersgarden@gmail.com. Formerly known both as *Sihome Backpackers* and *Sihome Backpackers Garden*, this hostel remains one of the most popular places for backpackers. The dorms are pretty cramped and the private rooms way overpriced, but there's a sociable bar area, a TV lounge, and friendly staff. Dorms 60,000K, doubles $34

Funky Monkey Hostel François Ngin Rd ⚀021 254181, ⓦfunkymonkeyhostel.com. Very simple private rooms and rather claustrophobic eight- and sixteen-bed dorms in a tired-looking building a quick stroll up from the Mekong.

Low prices attract young backpackers, who wind up drinking around the lobby's pool table most evenings. Dorms 40,000K, doubles 140,000K

Mixok 189 Setthathilat Rd ⚀021 251606. Popular and inexpensive backpacker digs, above the restaurant of the same name and with a travel agency on site. The simple a/c rooms are reasonable value, though you should expect some noise from the busy road outside. Doubles 150,000K

Moonlight Champa 13 Pangkham Rd ⚀021 264114, ⓦmoonlight-champa.com. A solid option in the upper budget/lower mid-range price bracket, *Moonlight Champa* has simple but clean and bright rooms with TVs and en-suite bathrooms. It is a short walk to the city-centre action, and discounts are available for longer stays. Doubles 240,000K

Souphaphone Guesthouse Ban Wat Chan Rd ⚀021 261468, ⓦsouphaphone.net. In a handsome building, behind a wat, *Souphaphone* is an economical choice. The wood-floored, en-suite rooms feel rather spare, but are still comfortable (except for the handful without outside windows, which are claustrophobic). Doubles 180,000K

★**Vayakorn Inn** 19 Heng Bounnoy St ⚀021 215348, ⓦvayakorn.biz. Not to be confused with the *Vayakorn House*, which is owned by the same people (and is also a good choice; doubles $29), this newer hotel is more luxurious. There are beautiful wooden floors and furnishings throughout, and the rooms feature a/c, TV and big corner showers. Doubles $35

Villa Lao Nongdouang Rd ⚀020 2221 7588, ⓦvillalaos .com. Located a 20min walk from the city centre, this friendly guesthouse has simple, clean – though rather cramped – rooms (those with attached bathrooms cost around $5 extra), plus a restaurant and communal TV lounge. Doubles 222,000K

5

EATING

In addition to authentically Lao markets and noodle stands, Vientiane also has a large concentration of Western restaurants, catering to virtually every taste, from sausage and sauerkraut to Korean barbecue.

MARKETS

Hengboun Road food stalls Cnr Heng Boun & Chao Anou roads. For inexpensive and tasty snacks throughout the day and into late evening, try the food carts near the Home Ideal shop on Heng Boun Rd: here you'll find good Lao-style *khào pûn* (noodles with sauce). Daily 7am–8pm.

Vangthong Night Market Phai Nam Rd, near the National Stadium. This narrow, food-focused night market sets up in the early evening, selling fresh fruit, sweet coconut desserts and *ping kai* (grilled chicken). Daily sunset–around 10pm.

BREAKFAST, BAKERIES AND CAFÉS

Comma Coffee Setthathilat Rd ☎020 5819 9566. Charming little coffee shop, whose exposed brick walls are covered by the names and home towns of past visitors. As well as great flat whites and espressos (10,000–22,000K), bubble and herbal teas, juices and shakes are on offer. There's extra seating upstairs. Daily 8am–9pm.

Naked Espresso Manthatoulat Rd ☎021 454631. A popular expat haunt, this Australian-style coffee shop serves some of the best long blacks and flat whites (14,000–25,000K) in town. Quick wi-fi, and a handy noticeboard, too. Mon–Fri 7am–5pm, Sat & Sun 8am–5pm.

Noy's Fruit Heaven Heng Boun Rd ☎030 996 0913. Need a fresh fruit fix? This relaxed joint makes great shakes, smoothies and juices (15,000–25,000K), blending in plenty of sweet coconuts and bananas, as well as various green vegetables for those on a health kick. Also does decent Western breakfasts, lunches and snacks (around 25,000K). Daily 7am–7pm.

Scandinavian Bakery On the northern edge of Nam Phou Place ☎021 215199, ⊛scandinavianbakerylaos .com. Vientiane's first European bakery is still going strong, selling huge sandwiches and traditional Swedish cakes (cinnamon roll 9000K) and breads. Sadly, the views of the fountain have been all but obscured by new buildings. Daily 7am–9pm.

ASIAN FOOD

Jamil Zahid Off Khoun Boulom Rd ☎030 990 9456, ⊛facebook.com/JamilZahidRestaurant. Tucked down an alley near the western end of Heng Boun Road, this shed-like Indian place does superb Punjabi curries, plus tandoor-cooked naans and tasty dhals (dishes 15,000–40,000K). Daily 10am–10pm.

★Lao Kitchen Heng Boun Rd ☎021 254332, ⊛lao-kitchen.com. An excellent option for visitors who want to experiment with Lao food (mains 20,000–60,000K). The menu is filled with specialities from across the country, with clear descriptions in English. Choose from a range of *larps* and *jeows*, and dishes like Pakse-style spicy sausages, deep-fried quail and grilled catfish. If you're an adventurous eater, try the "chicken knees and elbows", which is tastier than it sounds. Daily 11am–10pm.

★Makphet Ipeng Rd ☎021 260587, ⊛facebook.com/makphet. Smart, not-for-profit restaurant – the name means "chilli" in Lao – on a quiet backstreet in the centre of town, offering a modern take on classic Lao dishes (45,000–82,000K). The place is run by former street kids who were trained up for the job. Hugely popular, especially with business crowds, and it's not unusual for all the tables to be full, even at lunchtime. Bookings advised. Daily 11am–10.30pm.

Sengdao Kitchen Heng Boun Rd ☎020 5888 7791, ⊛facebook.com/sengdaokitchen. Next door to *Lao Kitchen*, and with a similar menu, this little restaurant is a cheaper option for Lao and Thai dishes. It has over forty main courses priced at 20,000K (including rice). Try the yellow curry. Daily 11am–10pm.

WESTERN FOOD

La Cage du Coq Heng Bounnoy St ☎020 5467 6065. A little slice of France in the heart of Vientiane, the charming *La Cage du Coq* has an excellent two-course set lunch (59,000K), while for dinner you can choose from classic mains (95,000–125,000K) like *coq au vin*. Mon & Wed–Sun 10am–2.30pm & 5.30–9.30pm.

Pizza da Roby (PDR) Sihom Rd ☎020 5998 9926. Probably the finest pizzas (42,000–75,000K) in Vientiane are rustled up at this joint, commonly known as *PDR*. Among the options are calzone; speck, cream and walnuts; and salami and blue cheese. Opening times can be erratic. Mon–Sat 11am–2.30pm & 5.30–10.30pm.

Ray's Grille 17/1 Sihom Rd, west of the petrol station ☎020 5896 6866, ⊛facebook.com/raysgrilleLaopdr. This no-frills American burger joint has attained legendary status (burgers around 40,000K). The house special – a whopping philly cheese steak dripping with gooey cheddar – has tourists and expats coming back for multiple visits. Microbrew beers and potent margaritas, too. The owner recently opened a US-style breakfast joint on the 10th floor of the nearby *Capitol Residence* hotel (Mon–Fri 6.30–10.30am, Sat & Sun 6.30am–1.30pm). Mon–Fri & Sun 11am–3pm & 6–9.30pm.

DRINKING AND NIGHTLIFE

Vientiane is not a great city for partying. Frequent government crackdowns have hamstrung the development of Vientiane's clubbing scene, especially when it comes to late-night places that appeal to Western visitors. The locals' favourite spots for drinking and dancing are a quick tuk-tuk ride west of the town centre along Luang Prabang Avenue.

Chokdee Café Fa Ngum Rd ☎ 020 5610 3434. A statue of Tintin points travellers and expats into this sociable Belgian bar/restaurant. The drinks list features more than forty imported beers (from 40,000K), and on Friday and Saturday evenings, *moules* are added to the extensive menu. Mon 4.30–11pm, Tues–Sun 8am–11pm.

Khop Chai Deu Setthathilat Rd ☎ 021 263829, ⓦ facebook.com/KhopChaiDeu. This big, French-period house is by far the most popular hangout for foreign tourists. Downstairs in the patio bar you can get cheap glasses of draught beer (10,000K for a glass; 78,000K for a 3l "tower"); up the big spiral staircase you'll find another very pleasant terrace bar, and then a third on the one above. Daily 9am–11pm.

The Lao Bowling Centre Khoun Boulom Rd ☎ 021 223219. This bowling alley, somewhat incongruously, is one of the few places where late-night drinking is possible. Games cost 13,000K. Daily 8am–late.

The Spirit House Fa Ngum Rd, right next to the *Beau Rivage Mekong* ☎ 021 243795, ⓦ thespirithouselaos.com. This bar is one of the best spots to watch the sunset over Thailand, with delectable cocktails (around 30,000–40,000K) and views over the river, broken only by a narrow road. Daily 7am–midnight.

Sticky Fingers François Nginn Rd ☎ 021 215972, ⓦ facebook.com/StickyFingersLaos. This small Australian-run bar (beer around 15,000K) has a loyal expat following. A good crowd is almost guaranteed between 6 and 8pm on Wednesdays and Fridays, when the famously good cocktails are half-price. Mon–Fri 5–11pm, Sat & Sun 10am–11pm.

SHOPPING

The Talat Sao area just off Lane Xang Avenue is the best place to begin a shopping tour of the capital. Although there are still covered market stalls here selling Chinese electronics and cheap consumer goods, most of these have been swallowed up by the imposing Talat Sao Malls (daily 8am–5pm), which are merging into one big shopping outlet.

At some stage, most tourists end up browsing the market stalls that occupy the new riverbank area just west of Chao Anouvong Park, marked by dozens of red gazebos. T-shirts, toys, paintings, shoes and gadgets are available, though nearly everything is mass-produced and plasticky, and true bargains are impossible to find. The more interesting textile, souvenir and antique shops are found on Samsenthai and Setthathilat roads and along the lanes running between them.

BOOKS

Big Brother Mouse Phai Nam Rd, just west of the National Stadium ☎ 021 264513, ⓦ bigbrothermouse .com. The Vientiane branch of Big Brother Mouse is run with the same idea as the main shop in Luang Prabang (see p.381). Here you can buy colourful, lightweight children's books and then give them away to Lao children when you visit remote villages. Mon–Sat 8am–4pm.

Book Café Heng Boun Rd. This small shop has a whole section devoted to learning Lao, plus plenty of English-language novels set in Laos. The proceeds from some of the books sold go to victims of UXO. Daily 8am–8pm.

Monument Books Nokeo Koummane Rd ☎ 021 243708. Stocks Vientiane's largest selection of English-language fiction and non-fiction, as well as magazines, newspapers and a wide range of detailed maps. There's also a small branch at the airport. Mon–Fri 9am–8pm, Sat & Sun 9am–6pm.

HANDICRAFTS AND JEWELLERY

Interwoven Northern edge of Nam Phou Place ☎ 021 5220 4409, ⓦ interwovenasia.com. Near the *Scandinavian Bakery*, this tiny shop has a small but sweet selection of contemporary jewellery at fair prices. Profits support women's development projects in Laos. Mon–Fri noon–8pm, Sat 10am–8pm.

★**Saoban** Chao Anou Rd ☎ 020 5510 0034, ⓦ saobancrafts.com. The Vientiane outlet of Saoban, the social development project founded by Lao activist Sombath Somphone (see p.348), provides an outlet for over 300 local artisans. High-quality and reasonably priced textiles, jewellery, teas and coffees, bags, and items fashioned from UXO are all on offer. Profits go towards empowering disadvantaged communities, so your money will be well spent. Mon–Sat 9am–8pm.

DIRECTORY

Banks and exchange Banks throughout town, especially on Lane Xang Avenue, can organize cash advances on Visa and MasterCard; a few local banks and independent moneychangers also maintain exchange booths around the city centre. ATMs are found on street corners throughout the city.

Embassies and consulates Australia, Thadua Rd (☎ 021 353800); Cambodia, near That Khao, Thadua Rd ☎ 021 314952); Canada, c/o embassy in Bangkok (☎ +66 2 636 0540); China, near Wat Nak Noi, Wat Nak Noi Rd (☎ 021 315100); Indonesia, Kaysone Phomvihane Ave (☎ 021 413909 or ☎ 021 413910); Ireland, c/o embassy in Kuala Lumpur (☎ +60 3 2161 2963); Malaysia, That Luang Rd ☎ 021 414205 or ☎ 021 414206); Myanmar (Burma), Lao-Thai Rd, Ban Wat Nak (☎ 021 314910); New Zealand, c/o embassy in Bangkok (☎ +66 2 254 2530); Philippines, Phonthan Rd (☎ 021 452490); Singapore, Thadua Rd (☎ 021 353939); Thailand, Kaysone Phomvihane Ave (☎ 021 214580); UK, J. Nehru Rd (☎ 030 770 0000); US, Thadua Rd (☎ 021 267000, ⓦ la.usembassy.gov); Vietnam, near Wat Phaxai, That Luang Rd (☎ 021 413400–4).

5

Hospitals and clinics Australian Clinic, Thadua Rd, in the Australian Embassy building (Mon–Fri 8.30am–12.30pm & 1.30–5pm; ☏ 021 353840); French Clinic, Khou Vieng Rd (☏ 021 214150); Alliance International Medical Centre, Honda Complex, Souphanuvong Rd (☏ 021 513095).
Immigration Hatsady Rd, not far from the tourist office (daily 8am–noon & 1–4pm; ☏ 021 212520). Here you can extend your visa for $2/day. Travel agents in town tend to charge around $3/day for the same service.

BUDDHA PARK

Located on the Mekong River 25km from downtown Vientiane, **Xieng Khouan** or the "**Buddha Park**" (daily 8am–5pm; 5000K, plus 3000K for cameras) is Laos's quirkiest attraction. This collection of massive ferro-concrete sculptures, which lie dotted around a wide riverside meadow, was created under the direction of Luang Phu Boonlua Surirat, a self-styled holy man who claimed to have been the disciple of a cave-dwelling Hindu hermit in Vietnam. Upon returning to Laos, Boonlua began the sculpture garden in the late 1950s as a means of spreading his philosophy of life and his ideas about the cosmos. Besides the brontosaurian reclining Buddha that dominates the park, there are concrete statues of every conceivable deity in the Hindu-Buddhist pantheon. After the revolution, Boonlua was forced to flee across the Mekong to Nong Khai in Thailand, where he established an even more elaborate version of his philosophy in concrete at Sala Kaeo Kou (also known as Wat Khaek). The cheapest way to **get to the park** is to take bus #14 from Vientiane's central bus station (every 15min). Although the bus is scheduled to run all the way to the Buddha Park, we've had reports of the bus stopping at the Friendship Bridge, only for tourists to be coaxed into buying an (overpriced) tuk-tuk ride for the last part of the journey. If this happens, walk back to the main road and flag down a shared tuk-tuk heading east; it shouldn't cost more than 5000K/person.

VANG VIENG

Just 155km north of the capital among spectacular limestone karsts, **VANG VIENG** has undergone enormous changes over the past few decades. It was once a sleepy town, with a potholed main street and a handful of guesthouses. Then, within a few years, thousands of party-hungry backpackers started to descend on the self-styled "tubing capital of the world". In 2012, following the deaths of dozens of foreign tourists – mostly as a result of them taking to the river while drunk or high – the government took action. The bars and nightclubs that had grown up around the river were torn down, their vertiginous rope swings and slides dismantled, and tubing all but stopped. When word got out, backpacker numbers plunged.

Today the place is undergoing an uneven transition to a more respectable form of tourism, with an attempt to refocus on trekking and adventure sports. There has also been a surge in Korean tourism, following the visit of a famous K-pop star a couple of years back. The days of happy shakes and opium pizzas are largely gone, though some bars have reopened along the river. **Tubing** undoubtedly remains a big draw, but as the jaw-droppingly beautiful landscape around town opens up to tourists, and more visitors see the appeal of spending a week here cycling, caving, rafting and hiking, there may be another, more positive, way for the place to move forward.

WHAT TO SEE AND DO

Vang Vieng is a small town that would be unremarkable except for its beautiful riverside position. As such, there's little to see and do in the centre; the real attraction lies beyond the town, on the river and in the caves.

Tubing

Love or hate what it's done to the place, **tubing** remains Vang Vieng's premier attraction. In fact, for some people, it's the very reason they ended up in Laos. What started as an inventive way to spend a lazy afternoon floating down the **Nam Song** rapidly evolved into an all-you-can-drink party on the river. However, these days the tubing – and the partying – is more relaxed. Only a few bars now dot the river, and drugs are seldom seen. For many, drinking is still a big part of the experience, though it's still risky, so take care and, if you're a weak swimmer, ask for a **life jacket**.

To avoid getting back after dark, it's best to start tubing early. **Tubes** are available from the lock-up near the post office. Just turn up, pay the fee (55,000K; deposit 60,000K; fines for late returns) and a tuk-tuk will drive you to the starting point, 3km north of town near the *Organic Farm* (see p.371). Tuk-tuks will only depart with at least four people on board, so on quiet days you may have to wait for others to arrive.

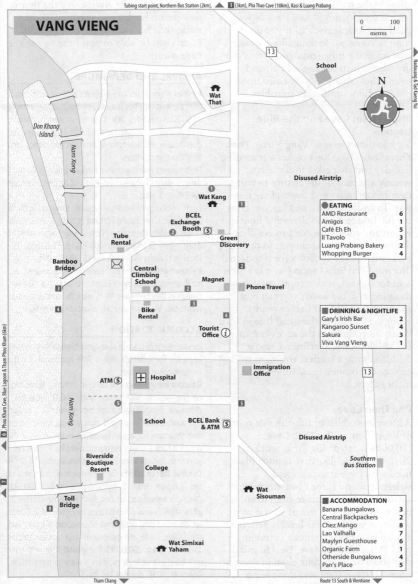

Tubing start point, Northern Bus Station (2km), 13 (3km), Pha Thao Cave (10km), Kasi & Luang Prabang

Nadouang & Tad Kaeng Yui

VANG VIENG

0   100
metres

N

School

Don Khang Island

Nam Xong

Wat That

Disused Airstrip

Wat Kang

BCEL Exchange Booth $

Tube Rental

Green Discovery

Bamboo Bridge

Central Climbing School

Magnet

Phone Travel

Bike Rental

Tourist Office ⓘ

ATM $

Hospital

Immigration Office

13

Nam Xong

School

BCEL Bank & ATM $

Disused Airstrip

Southern Bus Station

Riverside Boutique Resort

College

Toll Bridge

Wat Sisouman

Wat Simixai Yaham

Phou Kham Cave, Blue Lagoon & Tham Phou Kham (6km)

Tham Chang

Route 13 South & Vientiane

● EATING
AMD Restaurant	6
Amigos	1
Café Eh Eh	5
Il Tavolo	3
Luang Prabang Bakery	2
Whopping Burger	4

■ DRINKING & NIGHTLIFE
Gary's Irish Bar	2
Kangaroo Sunset	4
Sakura	3
Viva Vang Vieng	1

■ ACCOMMODATION
Banana Bungalows	3
Central Backpackers	2
Chez Mango	8
Lao Valhalla	7
Maylyn Guesthouse	6
Organic Farm	1
Otherside Bungalows	4
Pan's Place	5

5

A float back into town should take two or three hours from here, but you could easily spend the whole day dancing, drinking and playing mud volleyball at the bars along the way. It's important to leave enough time to get back before dark, however, as it gets cold and it becomes almost impossible to see where you're going in the fast-flowing water. Arrive back late and you will lose your deposit. A good sunblock is essential if you don't want to come out looking like a lobster. And while the tube rental place rents out dry bags (which are also sold around town), these should not be relied upon to protect phones and other valuables.

Phou Kham Cave and the Blue Lagoon

Six kilometres west of Vang Vieng, **Phou Kham Cave** (10,000K) makes a rewarding half-day trip that takes in some fine scenery and affords the chance to visit a cave and enjoy a good swim along the way. To reach the cave and lagoon, cross the toll bridge next to Riverside Boutique Resort and follow the road to Na Thong, 4km west. Signs will lead you to the car park, where the admission fee is collected. The fish-filled **Blue Lagoon** here is a great spot for a swim, with a rope swing dangling over the water; you can buy snacks, beer and fruit shakes nearby. From the far side of the small lagoon it's a short, steep climb to the cave's entrance. In the main cavern reclines a bronze Buddha; bring a torch if you want to explore the tunnels branching off the main gallery.

Pha Thao Cave

A short motorbike or tuk-tuk ride north of Vang Vieng is **Pha Thao Cave** (10,000K). Stretching for more than 2km, the tunnel-like cave is pitch black, filled with huge stalactites and stalagmites, and is the most satisfying caving trip you can make from town. It's best visited near the end of the rainy season, when the water level is perfect for a swim in the subterranean swimming pool 800m into the cave. Bear in mind that you'll be up to your chest in water at times, so travel light and don't bring anything valuable. In the height of the dry season, it's possible to go beyond the pool and explore the full length of the cave. The cave is near the Hmong village of **Pha Thao**, which lies 13km north of Vang Vieng. Turn left after the bridge just beyond the Km10 marker on Route 13 – a road sign points the way to the cave – and head for the river. Cross the skinny suspension bridge and you'll reach the village of Pha Thao at the base of a cliff. Locals will be able to point the way to the cave mouth.

ARRIVAL AND DEPARTURE

By bus Many buses and minivans arrive at and depart from the northern bus station, 2km north of the centre (a 20,000K tuk-tuk ride). Others use the southern bus station, east of the old airstrip, just off Rte 13. Agencies and guesthouses sell tickets to destinations across Laos (and neighbouring countries).

Destinations (northern bus station) Luang Prabang (3 daily; 5–6hr); Phonsavan (at least 1 daily; 6hr); Vientiane (5–6 daily; 3–4hr).

Destinations (southern bus station) Bangkok, Thailand (1–2 daily; 12hr); Luang Prabang (3 daily; 5–6hr); Pakse (1 daily; 16hr); Phonsavan (1 daily; 6hr); Savannakhet (1 daily; 10hr); Si Phan Don/4000 islands (1 daily; 11hr); Thakhek (1 daily; 9hr); Vientiane (3 daily; 3–4hr).

By sawngthaew Sawngthaews for Vientiane leave the northern bus station every 20min or so throughout the day, though as they take over 4hr to reach the capital, you'd do well to take a quicker, similarly priced minivan instead.

ACCOMMODATION

Inexpensive rooms are in abundance, though they're rarely inspiring. For quietude and a little more soul, try the western side of the river.

Banana Bungalows Just north of *Otherside Bungalows*, on the western side of the river ☏020 5501 4937, ✉banana_bungalow@hotmail.com. If you're on a budget and want relative peace and quiet without being too far from the action, these plain bungalows do the job nicely. The cheapest have a shared bathroom, while for 30,000K extra you can upgrade to an en-suite bungalow. Doubles <u>50,000K</u>

Central Backpackers On the main road, just south of the junction with Kangmuong St ☏023 511593, ⓦvangviengbackpackers.com. With an in-the-thick-of-it-all location, *Central Backpackers* is very good value. Dorms are clean and tidy, with single beds instead of bunks, and the double, triple and quad rooms feel spacious (triples 150,000K, quads 200,000K). The ground-floor restaurant isn't great but at least provides a place to meet others. Dorms <u>40,000K</u>, doubles <u>100,000K</u>

Chez Mango West of the river, just south of the toll bridge ☎ 020 5443 5747, ⓦ chezmango.com. Set in a garden filled with mango and papaya trees, these simple but appealing bungalows are a great budget choice (add 20,000K for a private bathroom). The French owner also offers tours in a battered old jeep. Doubles 60,000K

Lao Valhalla 1km west of the toll bridge, on the road to the Blue Lagoon ☎ 02 0804 2733, ✉ laovalhalla@gmail .com. One of the new breed of boutique hotels/ guesthouses in Vang Vieng, with six cute en-suite cabins (each sleeping up to two people), a good restaurant-bar, a lush, peaceful garden far away from the bustle of the town centre and a welcoming owner. Doubles $30

★**Maylyn Guesthouse** On the western side of the Nam Song ☎ 020 5560 4095, ⓦ facebook.com/ maylynguesthouse. Rustic bamboo bungalows set around a peaceful, flower-filled garden on the west side of the river, far from the noise of any late-night parties. The cheapest bungalows have shared bathrooms; en-suite ones cost from 80,000K. There's a sociable little chill-out area at the front, and there are several caves nearby. Doubles 50,000K

Organic Farm 3km north of town ☎ 020 5510 1166, ⓦ laofarm.org. It's said that tubing started here when the owner, who is known as "Mr T", encouraged his volunteers to explore the river in a new way. Today this farm is a bucolic place to stay, with dorms, simple rooms, bungalows (180,000K) and even (rather fancy) mud huts ($31). There are plenty of volunteering opportunities and a good restaurant. Dorms 35,000K, doubles 70,000K

Otherside Bungalows Just south of *Banana Bungalows*, on the western side of the river ☎ 020 5610 6070. The en-suite rooms here are slightly cheaper than those next door at *Banana Bungalows*, but feel a little damp and drab. Even so, the staff are friendly, and free tea and coffee helps to sweeten the deal. Doubles 60,000K

Pan's Place At the southern end of the main road ☎ 023 511484, ⓦ facebook.com/pansplacevangvieng. A rightly popular budget pick, *Pan's Place* has a good restaurant-bar, chilled-out TV lounge and an economical selection of small dorms and private rooms (for the latter, if you want an en-suite, expect to pay around 20,000K extra). Dorms 40,000K, doubles 90,000K

EATING

The restaurant scene is uninspired, with most places offering the same mix of international and local dishes. The sandwich and pancake stalls around town (most items 10,000–20,000K) are an economical alternative.

★**AMD Restaurant** South of the hospital along the main river road ☎ 020 5530 1238. Pint-sized, family-run restaurant serving some of the best food (mains 20,000–50,000K) in town. The tangy *tom yam* soup is reason enough to make the walk south from the centre, but the tiny open kitchen also turns out good curries, stir-fries and steaks. Daily 7.30am–10pm.

Amigos Near Wat Kang, just off the main river road ☎ 020 5878 0574. On a quiet side street, this appealing Lao/ Canadian/Australian-run Mexican restaurant delivers the goods, with tasty – and sizeable – burritos, enchiladas, tacos and quesadillas (30,000–65,000K) served up to a Cafe del Mar-heavy soundtrack. Mon–Sat 9am–1pm & 5–10pm.

Café Eh Eh Opposite the school ☎ 030 507 4369, ⓦ facebook.com/cafeeheh. Cute little coffee shop serving quality espressos, cappuccinos and lattes (10,000–20,000K) to drink in or take away, plus a selection of sandwiches and cakes. Coffee beans, organic lotions and Art Deco-style prints are also for sale. Daily 7.30am–7pm.

Il Tavolo Rte 13 ☎ 020 2345 4321, ⓦ facebook.com/ iltavolorestaurant. It's well worth crossing the disused airstrip in the evening to visit this Italian-run restaurant, which dishes up authentic pizzas (40,000–85,000K), pasta and risottos with the minimum of fuss. After your meal give the home-made limoncello a try (10,000K). Daily 5–11pm.

Luang Prabang Bakery One road north of *Gary's Irish Bar*. Right in the centre of town, this is a popular spot for a break. The menu features decent coffee, juices, milkshakes and – of course – cakes and pastries, as well as an extensive range of sandwiches (27,000–59,000K) that are ideal for picnics. Daily 7am–10pm.

Whopping Burger Next door to the Central Climbing School in the centre of town. Spartan, Japanese-run restaurant serving tasty burgers (around 50,000K) while 1960s and 70s tracks blare out. Try the samurai chicken burger, which comes with chunky chips and bundles of fresh coriander. Daily 6–11pm.

DRUGS IN VANG VIENG

Buying **drugs** in Vang Vieng used to be as easy as buying lunch – literally. Many of the town's restaurants kept whole sections of their menus reserved for pizzas and shakes made using opium or mushrooms, plus pre-rolled joints of all shapes and sizes.

When backpackers began to die with alarming regularity (not so much through the drugs, but what they did when they were on them), the government could no longer turn a blind eye. Nowadays drugs are harder to spot, although nitrous oxide balloons are sold openly in bars and weed still does the rounds. Having a smoke may be tempting, especially given the tranquil setting, but consider the consequences of getting caught. Plain-clothes police officers routinely issue heavy fines ($500 is not unheard of) if they catch a whiff of anything suspicious.

5

DRINKING AND NIGHTLIFE

Since the closure of the clubs on the island in the Nam Song, parties have migrated to the town centre. There are two main late-night venues: *Viva Vang Vieng* (see below) and *Room 101*. They're opposite each other on the main drag, and host cheesy club nights on alternate days. Regardless of which club's night it is, things get lively at around midnight when the other bars close.

Gary's Irish Bar In the centre of town ☎ 030 940 7039, ⊛ garysirishbar.com. This Irish-owned bar stands out from its cookie-cutter competitors in the town centre. There's football on the TVs, live music, a dartboard and two pool tables, pub grub, and a good selection of drinks, including Kilkenny (30,000K). Buy two cocktails/shots, get one free during the 6–10pm happy hour. Daily 9am–midnight.

Kangaroo Sunset Just north of the tourist office in the centre of town. One of the post-tubing spots for young backpackers, offering a rowdy atmosphere, inexpensive drinks (beers from 10,000K), frequent promotions, free pool and beer pong. You'll either love it or hate it. Daily noon–midnight.

Sakura Opposite *Gary's Irish Bar* in the centre of town ☎ 020 2345 4321, ⊛ facebook.com/sakurabarvv. One of the liveliest backpacker bars in town, thanks to its low prices (beers from 10,000K), frequent happy hours (noon–1pm, 5–6pm & 9–10pm; all day Sun) and friendly staff. Daily 11am–midnight.

Viva Vang Vieng Opposite *Room 101* on the main drag. There's little in it between Vang Vieng's two late-night clubs, which both play loud chart hits from the past couple of years. Of the two, *Viva* is bigger and tends to fill up more quickly. Open until around 2am most nights.

Luang Prabang and around

Nestling in a slim valley shaped by lofty green mountains and cut by the swift Mekong and Khan rivers, **LUANG PRABANG** is northern Laos's major tourist draw. Designated a World Heritage Site in 1995, the city is endowed with a legacy of ancient, red-roofed temples and French-Indochinese architecture, not to mention some of the country's most refined cuisine, its richest culture and most sacred Buddha image. Yet for all its undeniable beauty and charm, there's no doubt Luang Prabang has been transformed by its ever-growing popularity with international

visitors, with almost every property in the historic centre serving the travel industry in some form or another, and foreigners outnumbering locals across much of the old city. All the more reason, once you've had your fill of the good life, to strike out on foot, by bike or by boat to the city's outlying sights and beautiful hinterland.

WHAT TO SEE AND DO

Luang Prabang's **old city** is largely concentrated on a tongue of land, approximately 1km long and 250m wide, with the confluence of the Mekong and Nam Khan rivers at its tip. This peninsula is dominated by a steep and forested hill, **Phousi**. Most of Luang Prabang's architecture of merit is to be found on and around the main thoroughfare, **Sisavangvong/Sakkaline Road**, between the tip of the peninsula and Inthasone/Kitsalat Road to the west. Beyond here, near the Mekong, lies the old silversmithing district of Ban Wat That, which is now host to some of the city's best-value accommodation. Few travellers make the short journey across the Mekong to **Xieng Men**, but it's well worth taking a boat taxi over here to experience traditional Lao village life, just minutes from the old city.

Phousi

Crowned with a Buddhist stupa that can be seen for many kilometres around, **Phousi** ("Sacred Hill"; daily 7am–6pm; 20,000K) is both the geographical and spiritual centre of Luang Prabang. Best climbed in the early morning, before the tourist hordes arrive, the hill's peak affords a stunning panorama of the city, and can be reached by several different routes. The most straightforward is via the stairway directly opposite the main gate of the Royal Palace Museum. It's worth stopping first at the adjacent *sim* (main temple building) of **Wat Pa Houak** (donation recommended), a fine little temple that contains some fascinating murals.

An alternative approach is via **Wat Pa Siphoutthabat** near Phousi's northern foot (entrances on Sisavanvatthani Road, next to *Ikon Klub*, and via a path roughly opposite *Thanaboun* on Sisavangvong Road). There are actually three

ALMS-GIVING

The daily dawn procession of saffron-robed monks through the streets of the old city is one of Luang Prabang's biggest tourist "attractions". There's no denying the serene beauty of the alms-giving ceremony (*Tak Bat*) as kneeled locals place sticky rice into the baskets of the passing monks. However, if you do wish to see it, it's important to behave properly – in particular, dress modestly and keep a respectful distance from the monks. It is possible to join the alms-giving, but locals request that you only do so if it would be meaningful to you. Etiquette dictates you purchase sticky rice from the morning market beforehand rather than from the street vendors who congregate along Sisavangvong Road.

monasteries in this temple compound, the most interesting structure being the *sim* of **Wat Pa Khe**, a tall, imposing building with an unusual inward-leaning facade. Behind the *sim* is a stairway leading to a shrine housing a larger-than-life, stylized "**Buddha's footprint**". Above here, the path meanders steeply past a cornucopia of gilded new Buddhas up to the summit.

The Royal Palace Museum

The former **Royal Palace** (daily 8–11.30am & 1.30–4pm; 30,000K; conservative dress required) was constructed in 1904 and is now a museum preserving the paraphernalia of Laos's extinguished monarchy. The most impressive room is the dazzling **Throne Hall**, its high walls spangled with mosaics of multicoloured mirrors. On display here are rare articles of royal regalia.

Outside the palace, to the right of the main entrance to the compound, an ornate, newish temple houses the **Pha Bang**, the most sacred Buddha image in Laos. Enshrined on a richly ornamented gilded platform, the Pha Bang is believed to possess miraculous powers that safeguard the country.

Wat Mai

A little west of the museum along Sisavangvong Road, Wat Mai Suwannaphumaham, or **Wat Mai** (daily sunrise–sunset; 10,000K), dates from the late eighteenth or early nineteenth century, but it is the *sim*'s relatively modern facade with its gilt stucco reliefs that is the main focus of attention.

Wat Pa Phai and Wat Sene

Lined with restaurants and travel agents, the commercial neighbourhood just east

of the Royal Palace Museum along Sisavangvong Road contains some fine examples of traditional Chinese shophouse architecture, given a Franco-Lao treatment. A left turn down Sisavangvatthani Road will take you to **Wat Pa Phai**, the "Bamboo Forest Monastery"; its *sim* is painted and lavishly embellished with stylized *naga* (water serpents) and peacocks.

Double back up to the corner, turn left and continue down Sakkaline Road and you'll reach **Wat Sene**, where an ornate boat shed houses the monastery's two longboats used in the annual boat race festival. Held at the end of the rainy season in late August or early September, the boat races are believed to lure Luang Prabang's guardian *naga* back into the rivers after high waters and flooded rice paddies have allowed them to escape.

Wat Xieng Thong

Probably the most historic and enchanting Buddhist monastery in the entire country, **Wat Xieng Thong** (daily 6am–6pm; 20,000K), near the northernmost tip of the peninsula, is unmissable. The graceful main *sim* was built in 1560 and a recent extensive US-funded project has vividly restored much of its intricate gold stencilling and mosaic work. You'll need to stand at a distance to get a view of the roof, the *sim*'s most outstanding feature. Elegant lines curve and overlap, sweeping nearly to the ground, and evoke a bird with outstretched wings or, as the locals say, a mother hen sheltering her brood.

Across the monastery grounds is the **Funerary Carriage Hall**. The hall's wide teakwood panels are deeply carved with depictions of characters from the Lao

5

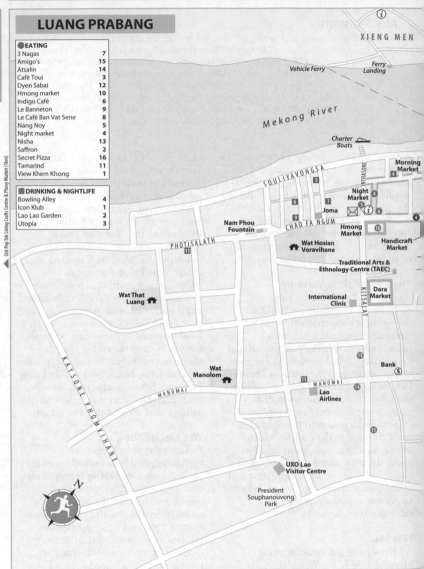

LUANG PRABANG

●EATING	
3 Nagas	7
Amigo's	15
Atsalin	14
Café Toui	3
Dyen Sabai	12
Hmong market	10
Indigo Café	6
Le Banneton	9
Le Café Ban Vat Sene	8
Nang Noy	5
Night market	4
Nisha	13
Saffron	2
Secret Pizza	16
Tamarind	11
View Khem Khong	1

■ DRINKING & NIGHTLIFE	
Bowling Alley	4
Icon Klub	1
Lao Lao Garden	2
Utopia	3

XIENG MEN

Vehicle Ferry

Ferry Landing

Mekong River

Charter Boats

SOULIYAVONGSA

Morning Market

Night Market

NITHASONE

Joma

Nam Phou Fountain

CHAO FA NGUM

Hmong Market

Wat Hosian Voravihane

Handicraft Market

PHOTISALATH

Traditional Arts & Ethnology Centre (TAEC)

Dara Market

International Clinic

Wat That Luang

KITSALAT

Wat Manolom

MANOMAI

Lao Airlines

Bank $

MANOMAI

KAYSONE PHOMVIHANE

UXO Lao Visitor Centre

President Souphanouvong Park

N

Ock Pop Tok Living Crafts Centre & Phosy Market (1km)

▼ Southern Bus Station and Naluang Tourist Bus (Minibus) Station (1km), 16 (1.2km), 4 (2.5km), Provincial Hospital (2.5km) & Kuang Si Waterfall (23km)

version of the Ramayana. Inside, the principal article on display is the *latsalot*, the royal funerary carriage, used to transport the mortal remains of King Sisavong Vong, the penultimate monarch of Laos, to cremation. The vehicle is built in the form of several bodies of parallel *naga*, with jagged fangs and dripping tongues.

Traditional Arts and Ethnology Centre (TAEC)

Situated up a steep road off Kitsalat Road, the small **Traditional Arts and Ethnology Centre** (Tues–Sun 9am–6pm; 25,000K; ☎071 253364, �🌐taeclaos.org) offers a fascinating insight into Laos's hill tribes and their customs. Exhibits include numerous items of clothing, such as an

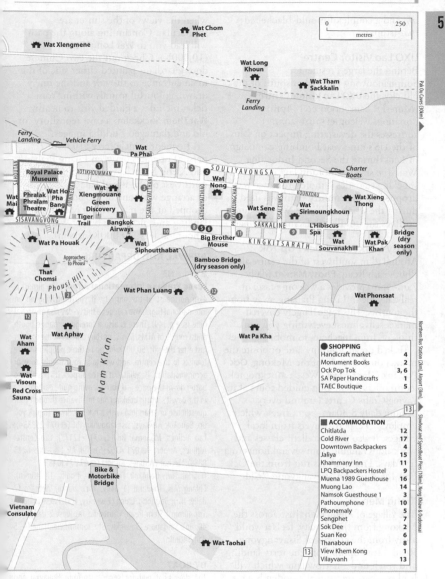

amazing Akha Pouly Nyai woman's headdress made up of over three hundred silver ornaments, as well as household objects and religious artefacts. There's also an excellent shop and a small café here.

Wat Visoun and Wat Aham

The older parts of the city may have a higher concentration of monasteries and historic buildings, but there is plenty to see beyond its confines. **Wat Visoun** and **Wat Aham** (20,000K for both) share a parcel of land on the opposite side of Phousi from the Royal Palace Museum. Wat Visoun has a bulbous, finial-topped stupa, while half-hidden behind a pair of huge banyan trees, neighbouring Wat Aham features a delightfully diminutive

5

sim and a couple of mould-blackened *that* (stupa).

UXO Lao Visitor Centre

Behind the large President Souphanouvong Park, 1km south of the old city, the **UXO Lao Visitor Centre** (Mon–Fri 8am–noon & 1–4pm; donations welcome; ⓦuxolao.org) addresses the devastating impact on Laos of the US's nine-year bombing campaign of Laos during the Second Indochina War. The small exhibition lays out the shocking statistics – more ordnance was dropped on the country than was used during the whole of World War II – and outlines the uphill task facing UXO Lao.

Phosy Market and Ock Pop Tok

Around 2km southwest of the centre along Photisalath Road, **Phosy Market** (daily 7am–5pm) provides a welcome taste of real daily life in Luang Prabang away from the tourists. This huge, largely covered market sells almost everything you can think of, from machetes to mobile phones.

Tucked down a bumpy lane opposite the market on the banks of the Mekong, **Ock Pop Tok** ("East Meets West"; ⓦockpoptok.com) offers fascinating guided tours of its Living Crafts Centre (around every 30min: daily 8.30am–5pm; free), which employs 25 expert weavers from local villages. It also runs excellent classes and workshops ranging from several hours to a few days. Free tuk-tuks run from the Ock Pop Tok shops on Sisavangvong Road.

Xieng Men

The village of **Xieng Men**, just across the Mekong from the old city, feels a world away from the crowds of Sisavangvong Road. Head uphill from the ferry landing and you'll find a narrow lane which will lead you past traditional wooden houses to the first of the temples, **Wat Xiengmene** (10,000K), built in 1592. Much of what you now see dates from modern times, though its *sim* retains its beautifully carved doors. Further on, a short but steep climb up steps to the left brings you to the timeworn *sim* and stupas of **Wat Chom Phet** (10,000K), a disused monastery best visited at dusk

when the views of the sunset are spectacular. Continuing along the path will lead you to **Wat Long Khoun** (10,000K). Check out the two Chinese door guardians painted either side of the main entrance to the *sim* and the finely drawn, colourful murals within. Your ticket includes a guided visit to nearby **Wat Tham Sackkalin**, a cave repository for old and damaged Buddha images.

A frequent vehicle ferry (10,000K/person) operates between Luang Prabang and Xieng Men, leaving from the landing northwest of the Royal Palace Museum, or arrange with one of the boatmen to be dropped at the main Xieng Men ferry landing and picked up below Wat Long Khoun (at least 20,000K/person).

ARRIVAL AND DEPARTURE

BY PLANE

Luang Prabang International Airport The airport is 4km northeast of the old city. If you're arriving on an international flight, you can get a thirty-day visa on arrival here (see p.349). There is also a foreign exchange booth and a couple of ATMs. Minivans (buy a ticket at the counter just after the exit; 50,000K for up to three people) shuttle tourists to the centre, and will take you straight to your accommodation. Heading out to the airport, it's possible to barter down the price – if you're leaving quite early or late in the day, it's worth booking one in advance through your guesthouse or arranging with a tuk-tuk driver to pick you up. Bangkok Airways, Sisavangvong Rd (☎071 253334); Lao Airlines, Manomai Rd (☎071 212172); Lao Central Airlines, Airport (☎071 410215); Silk Air (☎+065 6223 8888); Vietnam Airlines, Airport (☎071 213048).

Destinations Bangkok, Thailand (3–4 daily; 1hr 40min); Chiang Mai, Thailand (1 daily; 1hr); Hanoi, Vietnam (2 daily; 1hr); Jinghong, China (2 weekly; 1hr); Pakse (1 daily; 1hr 40min); Siem Reap, Cambodia (at least 2 daily; 1hr 40min); Singapore (3 weekly; 3hr 15min); Vientiane (4–5 daily; 40min).

BY BOAT

The slow boat pier for services to/from Houayxai and Pakbeng is in Ban Don, 10km east of the old city; speedboats arrive at the same place. Sawngthaews to town (50,000K/person) should drop you at your accommodation once you've bought a ticket at the booth at the top of the landing. At the time of writing, boat services running on the Nam Ou to Nong Khiaw had been put on hold due to a dam project. Slow boats depart daily for Pakbeng (110,000K) at 8.30am. While you can buy tickets at the navigation office in Ban Don, northwest of the Royal Palace (arrive at least

30min early; ☎071 212237), it's much easier to pick one up from the tourist office or a travel agent in town. Prices are much higher (190,000K to Pakbeng is typical), but will include pick-up from your accommodation; otherwise, a sawngthaew to the pier will cost around 60,000K (for the vehicle). You can continue on to Houayxai from Pakbeng (8hr; 110,000K), but you'll have to stay overnight in Pakbeng. The eight-seater speedboats to Pakbeng (190,000K) and Houayxai (320,000K) theoretically depart at 9am (arrive early to secure a seat), though, as they'll only set off when full, often leave (much) later; since there's no guarantee they'll run, some travel agents are reluctant to sell tickets in advance.

Destinations Houayxai (speedboat 1 daily; 6–7hr); Pakbeng (1 daily: slow boat 9hr; speedboat 3–4hr).

BY BUS

Luang Prabang has two public bus stations, plus a third for faster and pricier tourist minibuses and "VIP" international coaches; tuk-tuks to any of the stations from town cost around 20,000K. Buses from points north arrive at the Northern bus station, 3km northeast of town, near the airport. Buses from Vang Vieng, Vientiane and other points south along Rte 13 stop at the Southern bus station, 3km south of the centre. Naluang tourist bus station (aka minibus station) is opposite the Southern bus station. Tourist buses will normally drop you centrally – often at a guesthouse that the driver has links to, though you're not obliged to stay there. You can buy tickets at the bus stations, but it's usually easier (if more expensive) to get them from one of the tour agencies on Sisavangvong Road, which will include a transfer from your guesthouse. For tourist buses, you'll save money if you book direct with the bus station itself (☎071 212979, ⓦnaluangstation.com); its tickets are cheaper than the agencies in town but still include transfer.

Destinations from Northern bus station Houayxai (Borkeo; 2 daily; 13hr); Luang Namtha (2 daily; 10hr); Nong Khiaw (3 daily; 4hr); Oudomxai (3 daily; 7hr); Phongsali (1 daily; 14hr); Sam Neua (2 daily; 13hr).

Destinations from Southern bus station Phonsavan (1 daily; 9hr); Sayaboury (2 daily; 4hr); Vang Vieng (2 daily; 7hr); Vientiane (11 daily; 10–12hr).

Destinations from Naluang tourist bus station Chiang Mai, Thailand (1 daily; 18hr); Hanoi, Vietnam (1 daily; 24hr); Jinghong, China (1 daily; 14hr); Kunming, China (1 daily; 24hr); Loei, Thailand (1 daily; 8hr); Luang Namtha (1 daily; 8hr); Nong Khiaw (1 daily; 3hr); Phonsavan (1 daily; 6hr); Vang Vieng (5 daily; 5hr); Vientiane (3 daily; 7hr); Vinh, Vietnam (2 weekly; 24hr).

INFORMATION AND TOURS

Tourist information Offices at Cnr Sisavangvong & Inthasone roads (Mon–Fri 8–11.30am & 1.30–4pm; Jan–April also Sat & Sun 9–11.30am & 1–3.30pm; ☎071 212487,

ⓦtourismluangprabang.org); and Ban Natha, Chomphet, a 5min walk north of the Xieng Men boat landing (Mon–Fri 8–11.30am & 1.30 4pm; ☎020 5435 9232).

Tour agencies Sisavangvong Rd is lined with tour agencies offering day and overnight treks, mountain biking, kayaking, white-water rafting (in season), elephant interactions (see box, p.382) – and myriad combinations thereof. Though they're a little pricier than the competition, Green Discovery (☎071 212093, ⓦgreendiscoverylaos.com) and Tiger Trail (☎071 252655, ⓦlaos-adventures.com) can be relied on for both the quality and ethics of their tours.

GETTING AROUND

By bike Many guesthouses, and various shops along Sakkaline/Sisavangvong Road, rent bicycles for 20,000K/day, and you can also find motorbikes for rent on Sisavangvong Rd (from 120,000K/day).

By tuk-tuk Tuk-tuks can be surprisingly hard to find when you need one; there are always congregations outside the tourist office and above the vehicle ferry pier. Tuk-tuk journeys around the city are priced at a flat rate of 20,000K for foreigners, but you'll probably be quoted a higher price and be expected to haggle.

ACCOMMODATION

Accommodation in Luang Prabang is significantly more expensive than elsewhere in the country, and it can be hard to find much below 100,000K in high season. While the old city is still home to a dwindling number of budget options, the nicest area to stay for penny-pinching travellers is in the narrow lanes behind *Joma* café, a short stroll west from the old city between Chao Fa Ngum Rd and the Mekong, though for a bit more nightlife (such as it is) you may prefer one of the guesthouses within stumbling distance of *Utopia*, southeast of Phousi. Prices tend to rise around November, but you can get good discounts in low season (May–Sept). All places listed have free, if often unreliable, wi-fi.

THE OLD CITY

★**Downtown Backpackers** ☎020 9529 3928. Tucked behind the morning market, the six- to ten-bed a/c dorms (all the same price) at this wonderfully located hostel have comfy beds with personal lamps, power points and lockers, and the shared bathrooms are kept equally clean. Travellers congregate around the long tables on the ground floor at breakfast time (included). Dorms **57,000K**

★**Namsok Guesthouse 1** Sisavangvatthani Rd ☎071 212251. One of the few guesthouses in this part of the old town that still offers rooms for around $10, this friendly place is excellent value, with big and spotless, if rather sparse, wood-floored rooms. For a/c and a bit more style (and cash) you can go for one in the newer block behind. Doubles **100,000K**

5

Pathoumphone Kingkitsarat Rd ☎071 212946. A real bargain, especially considering its location right opposite the Nam Khan, with very friendly owners. Fan rooms have shared bathrooms and verge on dingy, but you'll be lucky to find cheaper. Ask for room 2, which has a small balcony and views over the river. Doubles 60,000K

Sok Dee Off Souliyavongsa Rd ☎071 252555. A few steps up a brick lane off the Mekong road, this popular guesthouse is a great choice for somewhere a little quieter but still central. There are bright a/c rooms (with thin walls) upstairs, though the four-bed dorms on the ground floor are the best deal. Staff put on free dinners (whisky included), making it a great place to meet other travellers. Dorms 60,000K, doubles 160,000K

Thanaboun Sisavangvong Rd ☎071 212866, ✉thanaboun.gh@gmail.com. It's more about location than atmosphere here, with plain but attractive rooms set back from the main drag. The most atmospheric, yet also the smallest and cheapest, are those off the small courtyard at the back. There's an internet café (50,000K/10min) in the foyer. Doubles 150,000K

View Khem Khong Souliyavongsa Rd ☎071 213032, ⓦviewkhemkhongguesthouse.wordpress.com. The cheapest rooms here may be rather cramped and viewless, but you won't find many better priced on the Mekong road. French manager Eric is a fantastic host, and the attached restaurant (see p.380) is quite good. Doubles $25

SOUTHWEST OF THE OLD CITY

Jaliya Manomai Rd ☎071 252154. Facing onto a lovely private garden and tucked well away from the road, the rooms at this old-fashioned, peaceful place are all very clean and comfortable, with a/c (add 40,000K) and TVs. Doubles 80,000K

Khammany Inn Photisalath Rd ☎020 9531 1579. A 10min walk from the old city, *Khammany* offers some of the cheapest dorm beds in town, but be warned: the mattresses are *very* thin. Ask for one of the smaller basement dorms – from the first-floor sixteen-bedder there's a two-storey walk down to the bathroom. Simple breakfast included. Dorms 35,000K, doubles 150,000K

LPQ Backpackers Hostel Off Chao Fa Ngum Rd ☎020 9113 8686. On the nicest of the little lanes leading to the river, this natty hostel's slightly squished eight-bed a/c dorms and whiffy bathrooms are compensated for by strong wi-fi, a pool table, and easy access to the night market. Avoid the box-like private rooms, and check for bed bugs before committing to a bed. Breakfast included. Dorms 50,000K, doubles 160,000K

Phonemaly Off Chao Fa Ngum Rd ☎071 253504. Two charming wooden buildings, lit at night with lanterns, provide some of the most atmospheric accommodation on a lane full of guesthouses. *Phonemaly's* ten cute fan rooms are large and come with comfy beds. Doubles 150,000K

Sengphet Off Chao Fa Ngum Rd ☎071 253534. This clean, family-run affair is a bargain for its location – even its rental bicycles (15,000K) are cheaper than the norm. The price drops a little for rooms (all with TVs) that share a bathroom. Add 30,000K for a/c. Doubles 120,000K

Suan Keo Off Chao Fa Ngum Rd ☎071 254404. Flowery bedspreads enliven the good-sized fan rooms at this peaceful, ever-popular guesthouse. You'll have to be quick to nab one of the two lovely wooden rooms upstairs. Doubles 100,000K

SOUTHEAST OF PHOUSI

Chitlatda Ban Wat Aham ☎071 212227. Behind a bank of internet terminals, the cheapest rooms at this basic but central guesthouse are windowless and musty, but clean and en suite. The wood-floored rooms upstairs are lighter and bigger (with TVs), but almost twice the price. Doubles 60,000K

★**Cold River** Ban Wat Aphay ☎071 252810, ⓦcoldriverluangprabang.com. Run by a welcoming French couple, this sweet riverfront guesthouse has five room types decorated with colourful textiles. Smart eco initiatives include free water refills and refillable shampoo dispensers, and guests rave about the (included) two-course breakfast. Doubles $32

Muena 1989 Guesthouse Ban Wat Aphay ☎020 9170 1061. Budget travellers keen to avoid big dorms will like the intimate four-bedders (with a/c) at this friendly, boho-styled guesthouse. The three private rooms are equally spacious, if a little on the pricey side given that breakfast is not included. Travellers hang out on the colourful patio terrace. Dorms 80,000K

Muong Lao Ban Wat Aphay ☎071 252741. Rooms at this good-value, friendly guesthouse opposite Wat Visoun are simple, but very pleasant, and the old-fashioned, all-wood rooms upstairs have a nice shared balcony looking towards the temple. There's also a little outside restaurant (noodle soup 15,000K). Add 40,000K for a/c. Doubles 120,000K

Vilayvanh Ban Wat Aphay ☎071 252757, ⓦfacebook .com/vilayvanhguesthouse. Nestling among coconut palms down the warren of lanes leading to *Utopia*, this little guesthouse is a real find. Rooms (with TVs) are immaculately maintained; the wood-floored ones at the back feel slightly newer. Free tea and coffee all day. Doubles 120,000K

EATING

Luang Prabang prides itself on its food, and the city boasts more restaurants than anywhere in the country outside of Vientiane. Many of the city's tourist restaurants are located along a 500m strip of Sisavangvong Road that expats sarcastically call "Thang Falang" ("white man's way"), and they tend to be fairly pricey by Lao standards. Cheaper meals can be found at the riverside restaurants along Souliyavongsa Road, and at restaurants outside the old town.

STREET FOOD

Hmong market Sisavangvong Rd/Kitsalat Rd. Baguettes, Lao coffee and fresh fruit shakes are sold throughout the day, and during the evenings you'll also find someone selling delicious *kanom krok* (little coconut and rice pancakes). Daily 9am–10pm.

★ Nang Noy Outside the tourist office gates. The huge, steaming bowls of *khao soi* (a curry-based rice noodle soup with pork and crunchy greens) dished up here (15,000K) are as delicious as they are cheap. Daily 5–10pm.

Night market Off Sisavangvong Rd. Just 15,000K will buy you as much rice, noodles and veg as you can cram onto a plate at the buffet stalls that set up down the narrow side street next to *Indigo House* (grilled meats and Beerlao can be purchased separately), but a word of warning: the food is not as tasty (or hygienic) as it used to be. Daily 5–10pm.

CAFÉS

★ Indigo Café Sisavangvong Rd ☎071 212264, ⓦindigohouse.la. The cool café on the street level of *Indigo House* hotel is a frontrunner for Luang Prabang's best espresso coffees (latte 22,000K). Also has an extensive international menu showcasing produce from *Indigo's* farm, 40km from town, with a tasty selection of meat and dairy-free options. Sweet tooths will love the *Ori Bakery* stand out front. Daily 6.30am–10pm.

Le Banneton Sakkaline Rd ☎030 5788340. Situated just up from Wat Sene, this superb café-boulangerie will transport you to Paris with an excellent choice of patisseries, including the best croissants in town, plus delicious baguettes and good coffee. Breakfast sets from 40,000K. Daily 6.30am–9pm.

Le Café Ban Vat Sene Sakkaline Rd ☎071 252482, ⓦelephant-restau.com. This French-style café is a wonderful place to lose a few hours, whether over a lunchtime baguette (45,000K) or an afternoon coffee

LOCAL SPECIALITIES

You shouldn't miss out on having a traditional Lao meal in Luang Prabang. At the top of the list should be **or lam**, a bittersweet soup, heavy on aubergines and mushrooms. Other local specialities include **phak nâm**, a type of watercress particular to the area and widely used in salads, and **jaew bong**, a condiment of red chillies, shallots, garlic and dried buffalo skin, which is an excellent accompaniment for crispy **khai paen**, a highly nutritious river weed that's first sun-dried with sesame seeds, garlic and chilli, then fried in oil.

★ TREAT YOURSELF

3 Nagas Sakkaline Rd ☎071 253888, ⓦ3-nagas.com. If you can afford to splash out on one meal, it should be at the atmospheric dining room of this gorgeous hotel. You can order à la carte, but it's worth splurging on one of the beautifully presented Lao degustation menus (200,000–250,000K). The wine list is excellent, and the boozy cocktails (lemongrass mojito 50,000K) to die for. Daily 6.30–10.30pm & 11am–10.30pm.

and a heavenly banana tart tatin (25,000K). Daily 6.30am–10pm.

Saffron Souliyavongsa Rd ☎030 5901898, ⓦsaffroncoffee.com. Swing by this hipster spot for a pulse-quickening espresso (10,000K) or sip a cold drip (30,000K) on the terrace overlooking the Mekong. There's a short but good breakfast menu, including a delicious granola bowl (25,000K), with wraps (40,000–45,000K) available later. Daily 7am–8pm.

RESTAURANTS

Amigo's Kitsalat Rd, two blocks south of Dara Market ☎020 5878 0574. Owned by the Aussie-Lao couple behind *Amigo's* in Vang Vieng, Luang Prabang's only Mexican joint will satisfy *larp*-weary travellers with generous servings of burritos, nachos and quesadillas (mains around 40,000K), and obligatory Margaritas (30,000K). Daily 10am–10pm.

Atsalin Manomai Rd, near cnr of Kitsalat Rd ☎020 9999 9933. This unassuming step-up restaurant is great for a cheap feed, with most mains costing a measly 15,000K. There's an English menu with pictures – the heaped bowl of pulled pork served over rice is just as good as it looks. Daily 9am–10pm.

★ Café Toui Sisavangvatthani Rd ☎020 5657 6763. Mr Toui cooks "simply honest food" from the heart. And it shows – the mango and prawn salad (45,000K) is a perfect balance of flavour, texture and zing. Kick off with an inventive cocktail (Mekong martini 40,000K) and order à la carte from the modern-Lao menu (meals 45,000K). Daily 10am–10pm.

★ Dyen Sabai Ban Phan Luang, across the Nam Khan ☎020 5510 4817, ⓦdyensabairestaurant.wordpress.com. One of the most atmospheric places in town, with bamboo "huts" scattered with cushions overlooking the river. The *sin dad* (Lao barbecue, from 70,000K for two) is reason enough to cross the river, but the delicious cocktails (two-for-one noon–7pm) and relaxed vibe will keep you here for much longer. During dry season, cross at the bamboo bridge (7000K 8am–6pm) near Wat Pha Sibhoutthabat; in the wet season a small boat ferries people across from the same point. Daily 11.30am–11pm.

5

Nisha Kitsalat Rd ☎071 900116. A short hop from Dara Market, this no-frills Indian dishes up Luang Prabang's best south Indian veggie curries – try the *malai kofta* (20,000K) or *aloo baingan* (15,000K) – though there's also the obligatory *chicken tikka masala* (28,000K) for the meaty-minded. Daily 7.30am–10pm.

★**Secret Pizza** Ban Nasomphanh, off Rte 13 ☎020 5652 8881, ⒲secret-pizza5.webnode.it. At the end of a bumpy dirt road, this bohemian trattoria run out of an Italian-Lao couple's backyard was never going to stay a secret for long – the wood-fired pizzas (60,000K with Lao ingredients, 80,000K with imported ingredients) are just too good. Book ahead; tuk-tuk drivers know the way. Tues & Fri 6–9.30pm.

Tamarind Kingkitsarat Rd ☎071 213128, ⒲tamarindlaos .com. This Nam Khan-side restaurant has a well-deserved reputation for some of the best modern-Lao food in town. The *mok pa* (45,000K) is melt-in-your-mouth good, but if you can't decide, consider opting for a tasting plate (30,000–70,000K). *Tamarind* also runs a very good cooking school. Mon–Sat 11am–10pm.

View Khem Khong Souliyavongsa Rd ☎071 213032. A lovely outdoor restaurant right on the banks of the Mekong, with candle-lit tables and big umbrellas. The menu is quite extensive and the food inexpensive and delicious (*or lam* 35,000K). One of the best Mekong riverside options. Daily 7.30am–9pm.

DRINKING AND NIGHTLIFE

The main bar area is southeast of the old city, between Phousi and the Nam Khan. Don't expect amazing nightlife – a town curfew sees bars close by 11.30pm.

Bowling Alley 4km southwest of town, past the Southern bus station. Believe it or not, the place to be after the bars close is the ten-pin bowling alley. A game costs 20,000K/ person (after 6pm) but it's more about the Beerlao drinking here. Tuk-tuks wait outside *Lao Lao Garden* and *Utopia* at chucking-out time to take you there. Daily noon–2am.

Icon Klub Off Sisavangvong Rd, near Wat Siphoutthabat ☎071 254905, ⒲iconklub.com. This eclectic bar run by Hungarian poet Lisa packs out most nights. Splurge on delicious cocktails (Absinthe martini 65,000K), and stay for impromptu live music and poetry readings. Lisa closes one night a week, depending which one she fancies taking off, otherwise daily 5–11.30pm.

Lao Lao Garden Ban Aphay ☎020 5678 1169. This tiered garden bar sprawling up the side of Phousi hill is a great place to chill out over "*falang* safe" chicken wings (40,000K) under the lanterns before things pick up later on. The huge drinks menu includes a range of rather potent two-for-one cocktails from 20,000K, and large Beerlao for 14,000K. Daily 8.30am–11.30pm.

★**Utopia** Ban Wat Aphay, by the Nam Khan ☎020 2388 1771, ⒲utopialuangprabang.com. "Zen by day, groovy by night" is *Utopia*'s somewhat naff-sounding philosophy, but

it's actually a real winner. With stunning river views, rustic-tropical decor, and a good food and booze menu, not to mention early morning yoga (see opposite), "beach" volleyball and DJ evenings, there's enough to make your visit last all day. It's on the river, east of Wat Visoun – just follow the signs from the main road. Daily 8am–11.30pm.

ENTERTAINMENT

L'Etranger Books & Tea, just west of *Lao Lao Garden*, shows quality films nightly at 7pm above the bookshop; there's no charge, but you are expected to buy food or a drink. *Ock Pop Tok* (see below) runs a Moonlight Cinema showing new and classic films on Thursday evenings; the 70,000K ticket price includes pick-up from *Joma*'s Chao Fa Ngum branch at 6.45pm, and dinner at its *Silk Road Café*.

Garavek Kounxoau Rd ☎020 9677 7300, ⒲garavek.com. Lao folk legends are brought to life by an animated storyteller during the 1hr production (in English), backed by the haunting strains of a *khene* (bamboo mouth organ), at a tiny neighbourhood theatre. 50,000K. Daily 6.30pm.

Phralak Phralam Theatre Royal Palace Museum ⒲phralakphralam.com. Lao dance performances are held four nights a week (Mon, Wed, Fri & Sat 6pm, from 6.30pm April–Sept); 100,000–150,000K/person). The shows include excerpts from the Lao version of the Ramayana; read the typed introduction (in English) provided at the entrance to help you follow the plot.

SHOPPING

Many of the town's souvenir shops are on Sisavangvong Rd, especially in Ban Jek, near the museum. Textiles are one of the best buys, sold by shops throughout town.

MARKETS

Handicraft market Sisavangvong Road. The city's most famous market is a key souvenir-purchasing stop for most visitors. A lot of what is sold is much of a muchness, and a high proportion is actually from neighbouring countries, but it's fun to browse the range of textiles and trinkets on offer, from indigo-dyed scarves to Lao coffee. Haggling is expected, but do be reasonable (and friendly) throughout, and don't enter into a discussion about price unless you're prepared to buy. Daily 5–10pm.

SHOPS

Monument Books Sathouyaithiao Rd ☎071 254954, ⒲monument-books.com/laos.php. A great little bookshop stocking a good range of magazines, local and international fiction and non-fiction, travel guides, maps and children's books. Mon–Fri 9am–9pm, Sat 9am–6pm.

Ock Pop Tok Two branches on Sakkaline Rd, opposite *3 Nagas*. Though the textiles at its two stores are a little pricey, there's no denying the superb quality of the craftsmanship. All products are made in Laos – either in the shop's Living

Crafts Centre (see p.376) or through their Village Weaver Projects which support local communities. Daily 8am–9pm.

SA Paper Handicrafts Off Souliyavongsa Rd ☎ 020 7777 7613. Tucked down a tiny lane opposite Wat Xieng Mouane, this is one of a number of shops selling colourful traditional mulberry-paper lanterns, including collapsible models, plus books and cards. Daily 8am–9pm.

TAEC Boutique Sakkaline Rd ☎ 030 5377557, ⌨ taeclaos.org. This excellent extension of the TAEC museum shop (see p.374) sells a wonderful collection of reasonably priced fair-trade handicrafts, clothing, textiles and jewellery, with fifty per cent of sales going back to village producers. Daily 9am–9pm.

DIRECTORY

Banks and exchange 24hr ATMs are dotted around all the main tourist areas, and there are several exchange places along Sisavangvong Road, most of which are open until 9 or 10pm.

Hospital The provincial hospital is 4km southwest of town (☎ 071 252026), though for anything serious you'll need to go to Thailand.

Internet Most of the travel agents on Sisavangvong Road have internet connections for around 100K/min. *Thanaboun* (see p.378) has a particularly large number of terminals.

Massage and herbal sauna The Red Cross, opposite Wat Visoun (☎ 071 252856; massage daily 1–8pm), has traditional Lao massage at 50,000K/hr and an excellent sauna (4–8pm) for 15,000K. Proceeds go to help poor villagers. For a wider choice of massages in more comfortable surroundings, try L'Hibiscus (daily 10am–10pm; ☎ 030 920 8358), set in a pretty old building on Sakkaline Rd. Offers traditional Lao massages for 60,000K/1hr and good-value treatment packages.

Post office GPO, Chao Fa Ngum Rd, near the junction with Inthasone Rd (Mon–Fri 8.30am–3.30pm, Sat 8.30am–noon; ☎ 071 212288).

Volunteering Big Brother Mouse, Phayameungchan Rd (☎ 071 254937, ⌨ bigbrothermouse.com) runs programmes to teach and encourage Lao children to read and write. You can visit the centre, help local children with their English (daily 9am & 5pm; 2hr), and buy books and donate them to the cause.

Yoga Luang Prabang Yoga (⌨ luangprabangyoga.org) is a cooperative of yoga teachers who run a variety of classes in several locations around town, including *Utopia* (see opposite) for 40,000K/1hr.

DAY-TRIPS FROM LUANG PRABANG

Luang Prabang's most popular excursions are to the **Pak Ou Caves**, 30km north of

the city, and **Kuang Si waterfall**, around 25km to the southwest – both are typically half-day trips. Tour agencies in town offer a wide variety of trips and activities out of the city (see p.377).

Kuang Si

The best day-trip from Luang Prabang is the picturesque, multi-level **Kuang Si waterfall** (daily 7.30am–5.30pm; 20,000K), tumbling 60m before spilling through a series of aquamarine pools ideal for swimming; there are basic changing facilities at the lower pools. The steep path on the opposite side of the falls leads to the top in about thirty minutes, though it can get quite slippery, so be very careful – and don't attempt it in the wet season. Numerous simple restaurants and food stalls crowd around the entrance to the falls and there are a couple of basic places to eat inside; better still, bring a picnic.

If you're travelling solo, the cheapest option for getting there is by **minibus**, booked via a tour agency or direct with Naluang bus station (daily noon & 2pm; 50min; 60,000K). Taking a **tuk-tuk** can be an economical way to go if you can assemble a group – drivers typically charge 50,000K/person for up to around five people, though you can usually pay a bit less if there's just one or two of you.

Pak Ou Caves and around

Numerous caves punctuate the limestone cliffs around Pak Ou – the confluence of the Mekong and Nam Ou rivers. The best-known caves are the "**Buddha Caves**", Tham Ting and Tham Phoum (daily 8am–sunset; 20,000K). They have been used for centuries as a repository for old and unwanted Buddha images that can no longer be venerated on an altar, and the hundreds upon hundreds of serenely smiling images covered in dust and cobwebs make an eerie scene. **Tham Ting**, the lower cave, just above the water's surface, is light enough to explore without artificial light, but the upper cave is unlit, so bring a torch.

Boat trips (80,000K/person) can be arranged with the boatmen at the bottom

5

THE ELEPHANTS OF LUANG PRABANG

One of the most popular activities outside the city is a visit to one of the numerous **elephant camps**. While these camps provide homes for pachyderms in their retirement from the logging industry, all offer tourist rides, an activity that has been dropped by many international tour providers out of concern for animal welfare. If you must ride one, avoid camps that advertise elephant "shows" and find out how many people the elephant has to carry (more than two small adults – plus mahout – is a no-no), and its workload, which shouldn't total more than four hours per day. Day-trips tend to include an elephant ride along with an opportunity to help bathe the animals, and some camps run courses teaching mahout skills. For information and advice, see Ⓦearsasia.org.

of Inthasone Road – most boats leave around 8.30am. Later in the day you'll need to charter one yourself (300,000K/ six-person boat; be prepared to haggle). It's possible to make the journey by road, but there's little point as the boat trip is half the fun.

Boatmen usually combine a visit to the caves with a stop at Ban Xang Hai, the so-called **Whisky Village**, some 6km back downriver towards the city. This tourist trap is by no means a must-see.

The northeast

Once difficult to reach and still short on proper tourist sites, the remote **northeast** is one of the least-visited parts of Laos. This area was heavily bombed during the Second Indochina War, particularly at the strategic **Plain of Jars**, which takes its name from the fields of ancient, giant funerary urns that are now the northeast's main tourist draw. Relatively few travellers make it here, unless en route to or from Vietnam – either at the crossing near Nong Het, near Phonsavan, or at Na Meo, near Sam Neua.

PHONSAVAN

The capital of **Xieng Khuang province**, **PHONSAVAN** has emerged as the most important town on the Plain of Jars since the total devastation of the region in the Second Indochina War. Hastily rebuilt in the aftermath of decades of fighting, Phonsavan is only now beginning to recover economically, thanks in large part

to international interest in the world-famous **jar sites** scattered around the perimeter of the plain, as well as a raft of mining projects. Although most visitors come only to see these, the Xieng Khuang Plateau is also a place of great natural beauty and its back roads are well worth exploring.

ARRIVAL AND DEPARTURE

BY PLANE

At the time of writing, Lao Airlines (☏ 061 312027) was only operating flights to and from Vientiane (4 weekly; 30min). From the airport, commonly called "Xieng Khuang," you'll need a tuk-tuk (20,000K/person) for the 5km ride into town.

BY BUS AND MINIVAN

Buses arrive at/depart from several different stations. When leaving Phonsavan, it's easier to book your ticket a day in advance from a tour agency (or your guesthouse); you pay a small fee but get a transfer to the bus station.

Inter-provincial bus station The main inter-provincial (or Northern) bus station handling services to/from Vientiane, Luang Prabang and Vang Vieng is 4km west of the centre on Rte 7; tuk-tuks (10,000–15,000K/person) ferry you into town. Buses bound for Vietnam also leave from here, crossing the border at Nong Het–Nam Can; it takes around 10hr to reach Vinh (150,000K), from where you can connect to Hanoi.

Destinations Luang Prabang (2 daily; 8hr); Sam Neua (1 daily; 10hr); Vang Vieng (2 daily; 6hr); Vientiane (4 daily; 9–10hr); Vinh, Vietnam (daily except Mon; 10hr).

Bounmixay bus station The Bounmixay (or Southern) bus station, south of the tourist office on Rte 1D, is where some of the buses travelling from Vientiane come to a stop.

Destinations Pakse (1 daily; 16hr); Vientiane (3 daily; 8hr).

Phoukham bus station Minivans connecting Phonsavan with Laos's three main tourist centres depart (mostly) in the morning from the Phoukham market in the centre of town, just off Rte 7.

Destinations Luang Prabang (1 daily; 7–8hr); Paksan (3 daily; 6hr); Vang Vieng (1 daily; 5hr); Vientiane (3 daily; 8hr).

INFORMATION AND TOURS

Banks There's a BCEL ATM on Rte 7; the main branch, which has currency exchange services, is situated about 1km to the west on the same road (daily 8.30am–3.30pm). Most tour companies and many guesthouses will also change money.

Information The tourist office (daily 8–11.30am & 1.30–4pm; ☎ 061 312217) is inconveniently situated a couple of kilometres south of the town centre. Make sure you check out the collection of old bombs round the back.

Tours The most popular tour, and one offered by every travel agent in Phonsavan, takes in the jar sites (around 150,000–180,000K/person, excluding admission fees). The tours run by Sousath Travel (☎ 020 296 7213, ✉ rasapet _lao@yahoo.com) are particularly recommended.

ACCOMMODATION

Anoulack Khen Lao Just north of Rte 7, on the road leading to the market ☎ 061 213599, ⊛ anoulackkhenlao .com. Aimed at business travellers, but equally good for tourists, this large mid-range hotel is located just off the main road. Its en-suite rooms are big, bright and good value. Doubles 200,000K

Dokkhoune Hotel Just west of *White Orchid* on Rte 7 ☎ 020 234 2555. This monolithic hotel is bang in the centre, and boasts a lobby full of decorative UXO and good views of the mountains from the hallways. The large, but dull, rooms are nothing to write home about, but still pretty good value. Doubles 70,000K

Lao Falang Above *Lao Falang* restaurant, just north of *White Orchid* ☎ 020 2221 2456. The cheapest place to crash for the night, with basic dorm beds above an excellent Italian restaurant (see below). Motorbikes are available to rent, and tours are also offered. Dorms 40,000K

Nice Directly opposite *White Orchid* on Rte 7 ☎ 061 312454. Probably the best budget guesthouse in town, *Nice* has small but comfortable rooms (most with TVs) off a lantern-strung outdoor hallway; they can get chilly in the winter, though. The staff are helpful, too. Doubles 70,000K

White Orchid Cnr Rte 7 & the road leading to the market ☎ 061 312403, ✉ knovahang@yahoo.com. This friendly, family-run place is an excellent choice for budget travellers. Rooms are a little dark, but decent value and very clean. Travel and tour information (and bookings) can be provided by the helpful staff, though prices tend to be a bit higher than other places nearby. Doubles 80,000K

EATING

Bamboozle! Rte 7, just west of *Nisha* ☎ 030 952 3913, ⊛ facebook.com/BamboozleRestaurantBar. Bamboo-bedecked, *falang*-friendly restaurant with a menu that mixes Western dishes with cheaper Asian staples (mains 25,000–68,000K). A great place to meet other travellers over a beer (from 10,000K) and find out about charitable initiatives in the area. Daily 5–10.30pm.

★ **Cranky-T** Rte 7, near MAG ☎ 030 952 3913, ⊛ facebook .com/CrankyTLaos. This hip café-restaurant-bar serves the best coffee (10,000–27,000K) in town, as well as creative all-day breakfasts (including a toothsome banana and Nutella crêpe), New Zealand steaks and lamb chops (135,000K), well-mixed cocktails (20 percent off during the 4–7pm happy hour) and tempting ice creams. Daily 7am–11pm.

Lao Falang Restaurant Just north of the *White Orchid* ☎ 554 06868. This Italian-run restaurant serves the best pizza and pasta in northern Laos, though they don't come cheap (expect to pay 70,000–110,000K for the former, 65,000–120,000K for the latter). There are also tasty barbecued meat dishes, and the desserts – notably the tiramisu – are on point. Daily 6.30am–11.30pm.

Nisha Just east of *Bamboozle!*, Rte 7 ☎ 020 9826 6023. This bare-bones Indian restaurant does not look the most inviting place – spartan doesn't begin to do it justice – but staff are friendly and the food (mains 18,000–30,000K) is top notch: try the butter chicken or the vegetable jalfrezi. Daily 6am–9.30pm.

INTO VIETNAM FROM THE NORTHEAST

There are two official border crossings into Vietnam from northeastern Laos, though both can be long and slow-going. For either you need to have arranged your Vietnam **visa** in advance

NONG HET TO NAM CAN

The easiest way to cross into Vietnam from Phonsavan is on the direct bus to **Vinh**, which leaves Phonsavan's inter-provincial bus station around 6.30am each morning (except Mon), taking around ten hours to reach Vinh (150,000K), from where connections to Hanoi are available. The border is open daily 6am–6pm.

NAM XOI–NA MEO CROSSING FOR THANH HOA PROVINCE

To get to Na Meo from Sam Neua, the nearest big town, catch the daily sawngthaew (3hr) from Sam Neua's Nathong bus station. There's also a daily bus service to Thanh Hoa from Sam Neua's main bus station, which takes nine hours (around 180,000K).

5

THE PLAIN OF JARS

The 15km-wide stretch of grassy meadows and low rolling hills around Phonsavan takes its name from the clusters of chest-high urns found here. Scattered across the **Plain of Jars** and on the hills beyond, the ancient jars, which are thought to be around two thousand years old, testify to the fact that Xieng Khuang province, with its access to key regional trade routes, its wide, flat spaces and temperate climate, has been considered prime real estate in Southeast Asia for centuries. The largest jars measure 2m in height and weigh as much as ten tonnes. Little is known about the Iron Age megalithic civilization that created them, but in the 1930s, bronze and iron tools, as well as coloured glass beads, bronze bracelets and cowrie shells, were found at the sites, leading to the theory that the jars were funerary urns, originally holding cremated remains. More recent discoveries have also revealed underground burial chambers. During the **Second Indochina War**, the region was bombed extensively. American planes levelled towns and forced villagers to take to the forest, as the two sides waged a bitter battle for control of the Plain of Jars, which represented a back door to northern Vietnam. The plain was transformed into a wasteland, the treeless flatlands and low rolling brown hills dramatically pockmarked with craters.

WHAT TO SEE AND DO

Of the dozens of jar sites that give the Plain of Jars its name, three groups have become tourist attractions, largely because they are accessible and have a greater concentration of jars. All three of these sites can be seen in a day, with hotels and tour companies pitching them as a **package** (see p.383). If you're on a tour, check in advance if the entry fee for each site is included in the price. It's also possible to visit independently; you can charter a tuk-tuk (around 150,000–200,000K/half-day), or rent a mountain bike or motorcycle (around 20,000K and 80,000K respectively).

Site 1

Of the three main groups, the closest one, **Thong Hai Hin** ("Stone Jar Plain") – known as Site 1 (15,000K) – just 2km southwest of Phonsavan, has over two hundred jars and is the most visited. Check out the visitor centre first, before following the path (or taking the free golf cart) up to **Hai Cheaum** ("Cheaum Jar"), a massive 2m-high jar named after a Tai Lau hero. Nearby is another group of jars, one of which has a crude human shape carved onto it. In the hill off to the left is a large cave that the Pathet Lao used during the war – and which, according to local legend, was used as a kiln to cast the jars. Erosion has carved two holes in the roof of the cave – natural chimneys that add weight to the kiln theory. It may also have been used as a crematorium.

UXO IN XIENG KHUANG PROVINCE

The countless **mines**, **bombies** (round bomblets) and **bombs** littering Xieng Khuang province remain a huge danger to the local people; when travelling in the province (as elsewhere in Laos), be sure to stick to well-trodden paths. The three main jar sites have been cleared of unexploded ordnance (UXO), but even so it's advisable to stick to the paths. For more information about UXO, visit the Mines Advisory Group (MAG) or the UXO Survivor Information Centre in Phonsavan or the COPE and MAG visitor centres in Vientiane (see p.362).

INFORMATION CENTRES

Mines Advisory Group office (MAG) Rte 7 ⓦ maginternational.org; free. This international NGO has been working in the field to stop the bombs from ruining more lives. The office is a good place to learn about the effects and devastation of the war; films are screened every afternoon/evening. Daily 10am–8pm.

UXO Survivor Information Centre Rte 7; free. Run by a local NGO, this centre acts as a kind of museum, providing visitors with a down-to-earth look at the challenges faced by UXO survivors. Mon–Fri 8am–8pm, Sat & Sun noon–8pm.

Site 2

Site 2 (10,000K) is located about 10km southwest of the village of Lat Houang, which is on the road to Muang Khoun. The site is based on two adjacent hills called Phou Salato. Nearly a hundred jars are scattered across the twin hills here, lending the site the name **Hai Hin Phou Salato** ("Salato Hill Stone Jar").

Site 3

Site 3 (10,000K), the most atmospheric of the three sites, lies 4km up the road from Site 2, just beyond the village of Ban Xieng Di. Here you'll see Wat Xieng Di, a simple wooden monastery that holds a bomb-damaged Buddha. A path at the back of the monastery leads up a hill through several fields to the site, **Hai Hin Lat Khai**, where there are more than a hundred jars on a hillside with sweeping views of the plain below.

The far north

Until recently, decades of war and neglect had kept Laos's isolated **far north** from developing, unwittingly preserving a way of life that has virtually vanished in neighbouring countries. Although inward investment from China is transforming the landscape with large-scale agriculture and dam projects, the hills and mountains up here remain the domain of a scattering of **animist tribal peoples**, including the Hmong, Mien and Akha. It is largely the chance to experience first-hand these near-pristine cultures that draws visitors to the region today.

By far the most popular route out of Luang Prabang is by road to **Nong Khiaw**, perhaps with a side-trip to tiny **Muang Ngoi Neua**, then through **Oudomxai** to **Luang Namtha**, a popular base for trekking, with easy access to Akha, Mien and Tai Dam villages. Travellers en route to **Vietnam** are able to cross at Tay Trang, accessible by bus from Muang Khoua (see box, p.387), and those bound for **China** are able to cross at Boten, reached by bus from Luang Namtha or Oudomxai. From Luang Namtha, it's

just a few hours on a fast road to **Houayxai**, a major border crossing with Thailand. Many travellers entering from Thailand travel straight to Luang Prabang from here, via **slow boat along the Mekong**, but if you've got time, the north rewards further exploration.

NONG KHIAW

Resting at the foot of a striking red-faced cliff, amid towering blue-green limestone escarpments, the touristy town of **NONG KHIAW** on the banks of the Nam Ou River lies smack in the middle of some of the most dramatic scenery in Indochina. Part of Nong Khiaw's attraction are the boat trips that depart from it along the Nam Ou; unfortunately a series of hydroelectric dams means that some routes have already closed and others are under threat.

Although the old town stretches for 1km parallel to the main highway, most of Nong Khiaw's tourist facilities are located by the big bridge over the Nam Ou. At the northern end of the bridge, you'll find the boat mooring, a few guesthouses and the more local side of town. Across the bridge, on the opposite bank, are most guesthouses and restaurants.

A five-minute walk south of the bridge, a path leads off the main road up through thick jungle to the stunning **Nong Khiaw View Point** (daily 6.30am–3.30pm; 20,000K) atop Phou Phadeng, a tough but rewarding ninety-minute climb one-way; bring suitable footwear. A further 2.5km walk or cycle will take you to the atmospheric **Pathok Caves** (daily 7am–5pm; 5000K), where villagers hid during the Second Indochina War – take a torch, as they are very dark.

On the south side of the river, opposite the *Hive* bar (see p.386), is the **New Nong Khiaw View Point** (daily 6.30am–3.30pm; 15,000K). It's wilder, receives fewer visitors and is an easier climb (roughly 45min one-way) than the "old" view point.

ARRIVAL AND DEPARTURE

By bus The bus station is on the northwestern edge of town, a 15min walk from the bridge (tuk-tuk 5000K). All buses depart from here; minibuses come down to the boat

5

landing to meet boats from Muang Ngoi Neua and take passengers up to the bus station.

Destinations Luang Prabang (4 daily; 3–4hr); Oudomxai (usually 1 daily; 4hr); Sam Neua (usually 1 daily; 12hr).

By boat The boat landing is on the north side of the river, a 5–10min walk to most guesthouses. Boats leave for Muang Ngoi Neua at 11am and 2pm (1hr–1hr 20min; 25,000K). If there is enough demand, an 11am boat will also head to Muang Khoua (6hr; 120,000–150,000K, depending on how many people are travelling) for the border (see box, opposite). Tickets should be bought at the ticket office at least 30min beforehand.

INFORMATION AND TOURS

Bicycles and motorbikes Donkham Service (⊕020 30900 5476), south of the river, rents out motorbikes (around 80,000K/day). Tiger Trail rents out regular bikes for 20,000K/day and NK Adventures rents out mountain bikes for 50,000–60,000K/day.

Tours There are three excellent tour operators. Run by forward-thinking local guide Home, ★NK Adventures (⊕020 5868 6068), south of the river, runs good-value cycling, trekking, kayaking and bamboo-rafting trips; note, it's not to be confused with the dubious agency of the same name north of the river. Green Discovery (⊕071 810081, ⊕greendiscoverylaos.com), on the main street, offer all these and more, while opposite, in the same building as *Delilah's*, Tiger Trail (⊕071 252655, ⊕laos-adventures.com) run an excellent 100 Waterfalls trek that involves clambering over the eponymous waterfalls and through paddy fields. There's also a similar good "New 100 Waterfalls" one-day trek. Nong Khiaw Jungle Fly/Laos Outdoor (⊕laosoutdoor.com), 12km east of town, is a zipline centre, also offering canopy walks, abseiling and treks. Half-day trips from $37, full-day trips from $49.

ACCOMMODATION

Bamboo Paradise On the southern side of the bridge; take the first turning (a dirt track) to the right ⊕020 5554 5286. The original bamboo-thatch rooms (60,000K) here each have appealing hammock-slung private balconies at right angles to the river, though they're pretty basic. There are also bigger and more modern – though still simple – rooms in a building further back; they cost 10,000K more. Doubles 60,000K

Delilah's North side of the bridge, on the main street ⊕020 5439 5686. Welcoming, well-run hostel with a comfy seven-bed dorm, plus a double and a triple with shared bathrooms, located above the café-restaurant of the same name (see below). The owner, who runs the neighbouring Tiger Trail agency, is a fount of local knowledge. Dorms 35,000K, doubles/triples 60,000K

Sengdao Chittavong North side of the bridge ⊕030 923 7089. Conveniently located by the bridge, this tranquil

place has big bamboo huts, each with a balcony, neatly arranged around a long, pretty garden. Comfortable a/c bungalows are the latest additions, though at 250,000K they feel rather overpriced. There's also a nice restaurant. Doubles 80,000K

Sunrise On the southern side of the bridge ⊕030 985 3899. *Sunrise* has a collection of simple, clean, bamboo-thatch bungalows on the river, all with hammocks and balconies (shared in the cheapest rooms, which also have squat toilets). Doubles 60,000K

EATING AND DRINKING

★**Coco Home** Main street, just up from the boat landing ⊕020 2367 7818. This restaurant in a leafy setting is a good spot at any time of the day. The short but sweet menu (mains 25,000–40,000K) features red and yellow curries, and there's a range of cocktails if you're after a sundowner. Daily 7am–10.30pm.

Deen South side of the bridge ⊕020 2214 8895. A simple Indian restaurant, offering a vast range of dishes from across the Subcontinent – including tandoori chicken and *masala dosas* (mains $12–40), plus five-course set meals (veg 20,000K, non-veg 25,000K). Fast wi-fi, too. Daily 7am–10.30pm.

★**Delilah's** North side of the bridge, on the main street ⊕020 5439 5686. Attached to the hostel of the same name, this popular travellers' café is a congenial spot for breakfast (15,000–35,000K). There are good lunch and dinner choices too, fine coffees and great desserts. Daily 7.30am–11pm.

Hive Bar North side of the bridge. A 700m walk from the bridge, this cheerful bar draws a mixed crowd of locals and travellers and serves up some potent drinks (from 10,000K). The karaoke lounge is a great place to make friends. Daily 5–11.30pm (or later).

★**TREAT YOURSELF**

Mandala Ou Resort Off the main street, 200m southeast of the bus station ⊕030 537 7332, ⊕mandala-ou.com. Nong Khiaw's most stylish place to stay occupies a gorgeous, tranquil position on the river. Rustic-chic bungalows feature big beds and bathrooms and private terraces. Excellent breakfasts (featuring fresh croissants) are included in the rates; the romantic, lantern-lit restaurant is a great spot for a well-mixed sundowner; and there's nowhere better in town than the infinity pool to soak up the views. There are great off-season offers, yoga retreats (Nov–March), and free bikes for guests to use. Doubles $61

MUANG NGOI NEUA

Hidden away on a peninsula on the Nam Ou about an hour's boat ride from Nong Khiaw, tiny **MUANG NGOI NEUA** is the perfect place for a few days' peace amid beautiful scenery. Most visitors tend just to while away their days sleeping, eating, reading and relaxing by the river, though there are options for the more energetic: excursions to local caves, kayaking down the river, trekking through buffalo-ridden rice fields, and fishing with the locals at sunset.

ARRIVAL AND TOURS

By boat Boats from Nong Khiaw arrive at the landing at the north end of the village, which is strung out along a single dirt track that runs parallel to the river. Leaving Muang Ngoi Neua, boats depart at 9.30am to both Nong Khiaw (25,000K; 1hr) and Muang Khoua (for Vietnam; 100,000–125,000K; around 5hr); for the latter, you'll need to sign up on a board at the ticket office in advance – be prepared to wait a day or two if there aren't enough people travelling.

Services Some guesthouses will change foreign currency (at poor rates), but it's better to bring cash with you.

Tours Lao Youth Travel (☎030 200 5385), near the boat landing, can organize treks, kayaking and homestays.

ACCOMMODATION AND EATING

Muang Ngoi Neua has lots of cheap wood and bamboo bungalows built on stilts, most of which line the strip along the riverbank. Sleepy by day, the village is positively supine by nightfall, and on a quiet night many restaurants will have packed up for bed by 8.30pm.

Lattanavongsa Just up from the boat landing, on the left ☎030 5514 0770. This is a justifiably popular guesthouse, with a clutch of clean, large rooms set in a low wooden bungalow. They also have a number of newer bungalows at *Lattanavongsa 1* set around a palm- and flower-filled compound, just up the road (100,000K), with hot-water

showers, though no river views. Doubles 80,000K

Nicksa's Place 200m south of the boat landing, no phone. If you're on a tight budget, *Nicksa's Place* is one of the best bets. The tiny bungalows are basic, but the setting, among beautiful flowers and with gorgeous views of the river, makes it feel a little special. There's a book exchange, and paddle boats are available to rent. Doubles 60,000K

Riverside 25m south of the boat landing, on the right. It's easy to wile away an afternoon or an evening on the expansive deck at this restaurant-bar, enjoying the views and nursing a beer (10,000–15,000K), cocktail (25,000–40,000K), milkshake or iced coffee. The Lao-Thai food (mains 20,000–50,000K) is good too. Daily 7.30am–10.30pm.

OUDOMXAI

North of Luang Prabang, the bustling administrative town of **OUDOMXAI** is an important transport hub at the junction of Route 1 and Route 4; if you spend any time travelling in the north, you'll most likely need to spend a night here. Though it's not the most exciting of towns, it has an energy about it that you don't often find in Laos. The **fresh market**, 1.5km northwest of the bus station (daily 7am–6pm), is a fascinating place to spend half an hour.

ARRIVAL AND DEPARTURE

By plane Flights are operated between Vientiane and Oudomxai (1–2 daily; 50min) by Lao Airlines and Lao Skyway. The airport is 1km southeast of town; tuk-tuks run into the centre (around 10,000K), though you could easily walk.

By bus Oudomxai has two bus stations. The Northern Bus Station is 1km southeast of the centre, within easy walking distance of most of the town's hotels and guesthouses. It has services to Phongsali, Houayxai, Luang Namtha and Muang Khoua, as well as international connections to Dien Bien Phu

---

INTO VIETNAM: TAY TRANG

Travellers bound for Vietnam can take a direct bus to **Dien Bien Phu**, via the border at Sop Hun–Tay Trang, from the workaday crossroads town of **Muang Khoua**, reached by bus from Oudomxai (see above) or on a spectacular boat journey up the Nam Ou through primeval jungle from Nong Khiaw or Muang Ngoi Neua (see above). At the time of research, the most convenient service left around 9am (around 4hr) from outside Muang Khoua's tourist office; timetables fluctuate, so ask around for the latest. Note that you will already need to have your Vietnamese visa to make this crossing. You can also reach Dien Bien Phu direct from Oudomxai and even Houayxai.

For **accommodation** in Muang Khoua, the most popular backpacker choice is the *Nam Ou Guesthouse* (☎088 210844; doubles 40,000K), right above the boat landing, though the rooms and scruffy and cell-like.

5

in Vietnam (via Tay Trang), and to the Chinese border at Boten. Less conveniently, the Southern bus station is 5km south of the centre. There are services to Luang Prabang, Vientiane, Nong Khiaw and Pakbeng. Aim to arrive at the bus stations around an hour before departure as buses occasionally leave ahead of schedule if they're full.

Destinations Dien Bien Phu, Vietnam (1 daily; 5hr); Houayxai (Bokeo; 2 daily; 7–8hr); Luang Namtha (3 daily; 3hr); Luang Prabang (3 daily; 7hr); Boten (for Mengla, China; 1 daily; 4hr); Muang Khoua (3 daily; 3hr); Nong Khiaw (1 daily, if there's enough demand; 4hr); Pakbeng (2 daily; 3hr 30min); Phongsali (1 daily; 9hr); Vientiane (4 daily; 15hr).

INFORMATION

Tourist information The well-run and very helpful tourist office (Mon–Fri 8am–11.30am & 2–4.30pm; ☏ 081 212483, ⊚ oudomxay.info) is on the northern side of the river, opposite the indoor market. It runs a range of tours, and cookery classes.

Bicycles and motorbikes Mountain bikes (50,000K/day) and motorbikes (from 80,000K) can be rented via the tourist office.

ACCOMMODATION

Litthavixay Main road, 500m north of the Northern Bus Station ☏081 212175, ✉litthavixay@yahoo.com. Probably the best-value deal in town, with bright, very clean rooms, all with TV and attached bathrooms (a/c costs 20,000K extra). Doubles <u>70,000K</u>

Vivanh Just south of the bridge, 900m north of the Northern Bus Station ☏081 212219. A simple but sweet little guesthouse, *Vivanh* offers large rooms with TVs and brightly coloured bedspreads. The staff are very welcoming, too. Doubles <u>70,000K</u>

Xaysana Left off the main road, 400m north of the northern bus station ☏020 251 5737. An attractive, scrupulously well-maintained hotel on a quiet street behind Wat Phu That. The big, bright rooms have high ceilings and pretty curtains. In the same complex, Xaysana 2 has more modern a/c en suites (150,000K). Doubles <u>80,000K</u>

EATING

Mrs Kanya's Right off the main road, 800m north of the bus station ☏020 5568 1110. Ask a local where the best Lao food in Oudomxai is found, and they'll direct you to this bustling restaurant. Grab a seat at one of the shared tables and choose one of the wonderfully hot and sour soups and *larp*, though bear in mind that anything with beef is likely to come with big slabs of tripe (mains 25,000–50,000K). Daily 6am–10pm.

LUANG NAMTHA

Surrounded by forested hills that remain lush even when the rest of the

countryside is a dusty brown in the hot season, **LUANG NAMTHA** is the north's most touristy town after Luang Prabang, though it still has a quiet local charm, away from the travellers' cafés and tour operators. The town is a popular base from which to visit the beautiful **Nam Ha National Biodiversity Conservation Area**, with a whole range of activities available, from rafting and kayaking on the Nam Tha to exploring the surrounding area by bike and trekking to hill-tribe villages.

ARRIVAL AND DEPARTURE

By plane The airport is near the old town, about 6km south of the centre; expect to pay around 10,000K per person in a shared tuk-tuk. There are regular flights to/from Vientiane (1–2 daily; 55min) with Lao Airlines and Lao Skyway.

By bus The main bus station is 11km south of the new town; a shared tuk-tuk to the centre should cost 10,000K. Buses from within the province, including Muang Sing and Muang Long, as well as from Boten, on the Chinese border, arrive at the local bus station, just south of the centre.

Destinations from main bus station Dien Bien Phu, Vietnam (2 daily; 11hr); Houayxai (Bokeo; 3 daily; 4hr); Jinghong, China (1 daily; 8hr); Luang Prabang (1 daily; 9hr); Oudomxai (3 daily; 3–4hr).

Destinations from local bus station Boten, China (6 daily; 2hr); Muang Long (2 daily; 4hr); Muang Sing (5–6 daily; 2hr); Nalae (2 daily; 3hr).

INFORMATION AND GETTING AROUND

Tourist information The tourist office (Mon–Fri 8.30–11.30am & 1.30–4pm; ☏ 086 211534) is one street east of the main road, behind the night market.

Bike and motorbike rental Many of the guesthouses and several shops on the main street rent out bicycles and motorbikes, including Namtha Vehicle Rental Service, just north of *Manychan* (regular bike 10,000K; mountain bike 25,000K; 125cc motorbike 50,000–60,000K).

ACCOMMODATION

Adounsiri One street west of the main road ☏020 2299 1898. Located off the main drag, on a quiet and leafy side street, this little family-run guesthouse has simple but very pleasant rooms, some facing a charming communal terrace. Doubles <u>80,000K</u>

Manychan Opposite the night market ☏020 2292 7878. A decent fall-back if neighbouring *Thoulasith* or *Zuela* are booked up – or too pricey – *Manychan* is situated in a tall building behind the restaurant of the same name and provides simple, tile-floored, en-suite rooms. Doubles <u>60,000K</u>

INTO CHINA: BOTEN

The easiest way for travellers with a valid visa to cross into China is to take the 8am direct bus all the way to Jinghong (8hr), via Mengla (5hr), from Luang Namtha's main bus station. Services also run throughout the morning and early afternoon (every 1hr–1hr 30min, 8am–3.30pm) from the local bus station to the Boten–Mon Han border crossing (daily 7am–4pm), but you'll need to change buses here and at Mengla to reach Jinghong this way.

★**Thoulasith** Main street ☎086 212166. Just off the main street, *Thoulasith* has long been Luang Namtha's top budget choice, with large, bright rooms and arguably the best bathrooms in town; try to get one of the upstairs rooms. The owners have recently built a new wing with smarter a/c rooms and TVs (without English channels), kettles and bath tubs (160,000K). Doubles 80,000K

Zuela Opposite the night market ☎020 5588 6694, ⓦzuela.asia. *Zuela* is one of the most comfortable places to stay in town, with a range of large, terracotta brick-lined or wood-panelled rooms in two gorgeous buildings; standard rooms come with fans; the fancier options are bigger and have a/c ($38). There's also a good restaurant, bike/motobrike rental, and a tour agency. Doubles 160,000K

EATING AND DRINKING

A small night market (daily 5–10pm) sets up in the compound next to the BCEL bank at dusk each evening, where you can pick up grilled meat and cold Beerlao and enjoy it at the tables in the middle.

★**Bamboo Lounge** Main street ☎020 5568 0031, ⓦbambooloungelaos.com. Linked to the Forest Retreat trekking office, this eco-themed bar-restaurant provides training and experience for members of local ethnic minority groups, while profits support a "books for schools" project. Always the busiest place on the strip, its wood-fired pizzas (from 5pm; 60,000–85,000K) are an indulgent treat, while great pastas, risottos, sandwiches and daily specials are also on offer. Daily 7am–11.30pm.

Manikong Bakery Opposite the night market ☎020 2235 4446. This cheerful bakery-café is a great breakfast choice, with an extensive range of sets (20,000–35,000K), plus filled bagels and croissants. The coffee's decent, and the cakes are good – try the coconut muffin or the chocolate cheesecake. Daily 6.30am–10pm.

TREKKING, RAFTING AND KAYAKING AROUND LUANG NAMTHA

Trekking in the **National Biodiversity Conservation Area** (NBCA) must be booked through a licensed agent, or via the tourist office (see opposite). Though Luang Namtha has a few cowboys, there are some excellent outfits running reliably well-organized treks with a strong ethical stance, as well as kayaking, rafting (July–Oct only) and mountain-biking trips. Note that, for all treks and activities, the price you pay is dependent on the number of people on it, and you should make sure that if you're visiting a local village, a percentage of the money you pay goes towards supporting the community.

TREKKING ETIQUETTE

Always **trek in groups**, as there have been assaults on Western tourists in rural areas. If you are approached by armed men and robbery is clearly their intent, do NOT resist.

Most hill-tribe peoples are **animists**. Offerings to the spirits, often bits of food left in what may seem like an odd place, should never be touched or tampered with. The Akha are known for the elaborate gates they construct at the entrances to their villages. These gates have special meaning to the Akha and should also be left alone. Many hill folk are willing to be **photographed**, but old women, particularly of the Hmong and Mien tribes, are not always keen, so ask first. Passing out sweets to village kids is a sure way to generate mobs of young beggars.

TOUR OPERATORS

Forest Retreat ☎020 5568 0031, ⓦforestretreatlaos.com. This operator has a strong reputation for its huge range of trips and activities, from cookery courses to "cultural immersion", plus plenty of rafting, kayaking, biking and "multisport" options.

★**Green Discovery** ☎086 211484, ⓦgreendiscoverylaos.com. The best operation in town (and also the priciest), offering an excellent range of trips and treks, from a two-day trekking-and-kayaking adventure in the Nam Tha valley, to two-day mountain-bike rides to Muang Sing and overnight treks into Nam Ha NBCA.

★**Jungle Eco-Guide Services** ☎086 212025. The best locally owned outfit (and a little cheaper than their competitors), with a network of well-maintained trails through the NBCA, plus kayaking and boating options.

5

Minority Down a small path off the main street ☎020 299 8224. Attached to the Forest Retreat agency, this cute wooden restaurant is run by a Tai Dam family who collect traditional recipes from different tribes in the region, including the Khmu and Akha. Dishes (15,000–45,000K) include rattan-shoot and banana-flower soup, chicken stew with local herbs and Lao-style fried pumpkin. Daily 7am–10pm.

Passion View Just west of the main street ☎030 520 8798. This bar is a fine spot for a sundowner, with a spacious raised deck with views over the town, friendly waitresses, and plenty of two-for-one offers (cocktails from 15,000K). Daily 4–11pm.

HOUAYXAI

The town of **HOUAYXAI**, situated on a hilly stretch of the Mekong River, has long been a favourite crossing point for people moving between Laos and Thailand. Travellers arriving in Houayxai can cruise down the Mekong by boat to Luang Prabang (see box opposite), or take a bus overland up Route 3 to Luang Namtha and beyond. Despite its border-town status, Houayxai is not completely devoid of charm, though the main reason to pause here is to take part in the acclaimed Gibbon Experience (see box, p.392).

Most accommodation and travel services are clustered around the old ferry landing for (locals-only) boats from Chiang Khong.

WHAT TO SEE AND DO

Opposite the old ferry landing, Houayxai's main sight is the hilltop **Wat Chom Khao Manilat**, with a tall, Shan-style drum tower and, to the left of the *sim*, a picturesquely weathered teakwood building now used as a classroom for novice monks. A 1km (signposted) walk south from the temple are the weather-beaten remains of **Fort Carnot**, where you can climb one of the two watchtowers for a fine view across to Thailand.

ARRIVAL AND DEPARTURE

By plane Houayxai's airport is around 5km south of the centre. Flights to/from Vientiane (1 daily; 55min) are operated by Lao Skyway. Chances are you'll need to charter a sawngthaew to town (around 50,000K).

By bus Houayxai has two bus stations, around 1km apart. Domestic "VIP" and international buses, including services

from Chiang Rai, arrive at the private bus (Phetarloun) station, 7km south of the centre. Normal buses arrive at the old (Keo Champa) bus station, 6km south of the centre. Sawngthaews from either bus station cost 10,000K/person to the centre of town. Note that most buses to Houayxai are marked "Bokeo" or "Borkeo".

Destinations from Pheterloun bus station Chiang Khong, Thailand (2 daily; 30min); Chiang Rai, Thailand (2 daily; 3hr); Kunming, China (1 daily; 17hr); Luang Namtha (4 daily; 4–5hr); Luang Prabang (2 daily; 12hr); Mengla, China (1 daily; 8hr); Vang Vieng (1 daily; 17hr); Vientiane (1 daily; 21hr).

Destinations from Keo Champa bus station Luang Namtha (2 daily; 4–5hr); Luang Prabang (2 daily; 13hr); Oudomxai (1 daily; 8hr); Vientiane (1 daily; 23hr).

By boat The slow boat pier is about 1km north of the old ferry landing. Boats depart for Pakbeng (110,000K), midway to Luang Prabang (220,000K), at 11.30am; arrive at least half an hour early to ensure a seat. Tickets can be bought directly from the ticket office at the pier (opens 8am), or from travel agents; the price for the latter will include commission and a tuk-tuk ride to the pier, so anticipate paying a little more. The speedboat pier is 4km downriver of the centre (tuk-tuk 15,000K). Boats for Pakbeng (160,000K) and Luang Prabang (340,000K) theoretically depart at 10.30am, but leave when full – get there well in advance (and be prepared for a wait), or book via an agent in town.

Destinations Luang Prabang (slow boat 1 daily; 2 days; speedboat 1 daily 6–7hr); Pakbeng (slow boat 1 daily; 7hr; speedboat 1 daily; 3–4hr).

INTO THAILAND

Since the opening in 2013 of the grand **Fourth Thai–Lao Friendship Bridge** (daily 6am–10pm), 11km south of Houayxai's old ferry landing, foreigners have been banned from using the river crossing to Chiang Khong. Instead, the easiest way to cross the border is to take a sawngthaew (around 10,000K) to the Phetarloun bus station and pick up one of the "VIP" services direct to Chiang Rai (57,000K), via Chiang Khong, which leave at 9am and 4.30pm. Alternatively, take a sawngthaew to the bridge (25,000K from town, 20,000K for either of the bus stations), from where (after Lao immigration) buses shuttle across to Thai immigration – visas are available on arrival – then a tuk-tuk to Chiang Khong (around B200); from here you can catch direct buses to Chiang Rai and Chiang Mai. There are banks and an information point at the bridge.

INFORMATION AND ACTIVITIES

Tourist information The tourist office (Mon–Fri 8.30am–noon & 1.30–4pm; ☎ 084 211162) is just south of the old ferry landing.

Massage and sauna The Red Cross Sauna (Mon–Fri 1.30–9pm, Sat & Sun 10.30am–9pm) offers traditional massage (from 35,000K/hr) and herbal sauna (10,000K). It's 500m north of the old ferry landing, just beyond the bridge.

ACCOMMODATION

Phonetip At the top of the old ferry landing ☎ 084 211084. If your budget is really tight, and you're only planning to stay a night, *Phonetip* is a reasonable choice. The cheapest rooms here are rather cramped, with shared bathrooms, but an extra 20,000K gets you a bit more space and a private bathroom. Some rooms have views of the river, and there's a communal balcony. Doubles 60,000K

River View Behind *Meuang Neu* restaurant, 100m north of the old ferry landing ☎ 030 903 0993. A popular place with spacious, well-maintained rooms in a long, three-storey block leading down to the river. Shaded by tall palm trees, the raised garden terrace at the back is one of the most atmospheric places to contemplate the sunset. Doubles 100,000K

Sabaydee 200m north of the old ferry landing ☎ 020 5692 9458. The highlight of this hotel is the breezy top-floor terrace, which has terrific views of the Mekong. The rooms (with private bathrooms, TVs and fans or a/c) themselves are fine, if a little starved of care and attention. Doubles 90,000K

EATING AND DRINKING

Bar How? 150m north of the old ferry landing ☎ 020 5516 7220. With its bottle-lined walls, good music and ambient lighting, this relaxed place almost has the feel of a wine bar. It's a favourite with backpackers for its cold Beerlao (from 10,000K), cocktails (25–45,000K) and reasonably priced Lao, Thai and *falang* food. Daily 6am–11pm (or later).

Dream Bakery 100m south of the old ferry landing. An unexpected place to find a Gaggia coffee machine, this cheerful bakery turns out good cappuccinos (10,000K) made from beans from the Bolaven plateau. Their cakes aren't bad either, and it's a good spot for provisions ahead of a slow boat trip. Daily 7am–7pm.

Meuang Neua Riverview Guesthouse, 100m north of the old ferry landing ☎ 020 5568 4257. A long-standing traveller favourite with a rustic feel: steer past the so-so Western dishes and opt for the cheaper and tastier Lao and Thai dishes (from 20,000K). The garden restaurant is a lovely spot at dusk. Daily 6am–11pm.

PAKBENG

Following kilometre after kilometre of lush jungle-clad hills, the river approach to **PAKBENG**, the only sizeable town or roadhead between Houayxai and Luang Prabang, feels rather welcome, even if the town has little more than a ramshackle charm about it. Perched above the water on the hill that rises through the town, Pakbeng has a distinctly northern Laos

---

DOWN THE MEKONG

The two-day journey by **slow boat** (*heua sa*) along the Mekong from Houayxai to the old royal capital of Luang Prabang, stopping overnight at the village of **Pakbeng**, remains a definitive Southeast Asia experience. Originally, these antiquated diesel-powered boats were primarily for cargo and the occasional Lao passengers who relied on them for trade and transport. Although the boats can be incredibly full, these days it's a relatively comfortable journey, with seating generally on cushioned wooden benches (buy a cheap cushion to provide extra comfort) or "airline-style" seating, and enough space to wander around, read and so on. Drinks and snacks are on sale on board – though you'd do better to bring your own provisions; several restaurants in Houayxai and Pakbeng offer sandwiches and packed lunches – and there are Western loos. Big bags are normally stored down in the hold at the back. It can be chilly on board, at least in winter, so bring warm clothing.

Whether you consider taking one of the **speedboats** (*heua wai*) between Houayxai and Luang Prabang, which stop in Pakbeng for lunch, depends on how risk averse you are. Skimming across the water at speeds of up to 60km/hr, or even faster, these cramped eight-seater crafts cut hours off journey times, but there's no doubt that the exhilarating ride is a great deal less comfortable and more dangerous – deaths have occurred, though the vast majority of journeys pass off incident-free. Life vests and crash helmets are provided – the latter most useful as protection against the wind and engine noise.

More comfortable than the public boats are the **cruises** run by Mekong Smile Cruises (☎ 020 5664 9094, ⓦ mekongsmilecruise.com; $130) and Shompoo (☎ 071 213189, ⓦ shompoocruise .com; $150). Prices for both include some meals but not accommodation in Pakbeng.

5

THE GIBBON EXPERIENCE

An ecotourism project 83km from Houayxai, **The Gibbon Experience** (☎ 084 212021, ⓦ gibbonexperience.org) offers both spectacular **treehouse accommodation** and a unique way to explore the Bokeo Nature Reserve – via zipline through the forest canopy. Despite the name, you're highly unlikely to actually spot a gibbon. At around $300 for three nights and $200 for two, the Gibbon Experience is expensive, but worth the splurge. Costs include all meals, accommodation, local guides and transport out to and back from Houayxai. It's very popular, so book well in advance via the website, though in low season it's sometimes possible to walk into the Houayxai office (just north of the old ferry landing; daily 8am–7pm) and join up for the next morning. Bring a torch, good trekking boots, loo roll, a fully charged camera battery (there's no electricity) and plenty of mosquito repellent.

feel about it, and for all its touts and travellers' cafés, beyond the main guesthouse area it still feels very much like somewhere where local people live.

ARRIVAL AND DEPARTURE

By boat Slow boats stop at the landing at the bottom of the port road, a short walk from the guesthouses. Moving on, boats usually depart around 9.30am to Luang Prabang, and about 8.30am to Houayxai – check times locally the night before. Arrive at least 30min early to ensure a seat, particularly heading downriver. Tickets are sold on board. Some captains stop briefly at the caves at Pak Ou (see p.381) before Luang Prabang, charging each passenger who disembarks for a look a few thousand kip extra (this works out cheaper than chartering a boat from Luang Prabang, but leaves little time for exploring). Speedboats pull up to the floating speedboat landing, close to the slow boat landing. Boats heading both up- and downriver normally depart around 9am, though will only leave when full; buy tickets from the booth at the top of the speedboat landing.

Destinations Houayxai (slow boat 1 daily, 8hr; speedboat 1 daily, 3hr); Luang Prabang (slow boat 1 daily, 7hr; speedboat 1 daily, 3hr).

By bus Buses run twice daily to Oudomxai (4hr) from the bus station, 2km northeast of the boat landings (5000K in a shared tuk-tuk).

★ TREAT YOURSELF

Mekong Riverside Lodge 100m west of the boat landings ☎ 020 5517 1068, ⓦ www .mekongriversidelodge.com. Raised on stilts, with bamboo-weave walls and rattan furniture, these stylish wooden bungalows provide a welcome mid-range alternative to Pakbeng's identikit guesthouses. Best of all are the gorgeous private sit-outs, poised right above the water and ideal for a leisurely breakfast (included in rates). Massages are on offer too. Doubles $50

ACCOMMODATION AND EATING

Travellers arriving off the slow boat are usually greeted by countless touts for the town's guesthouses. In the morning, a few stalls lining the road just up from the landings put steaks, sausages and chicken on to grill – a tastier sandwich option for the boat journey than the baguettes sold by the numerous bakeries.

Dockhoun 100m east at the top of the landings ☎ 081 212540. Good-sized rooms with colourful bedspreads in a vivid green building, but the real advantage is the lovely restaurant, bedecked with hanging baskets and boasting superlative views of the river. Doubles 100,000K

Duangpasert Just east at the top of the landings ☎ 081 212624, ⓦ duangpasert.com. Also known as *DP Guesthouse*, this cheerful lodge, owned by Shompoo Cruises (see p.391), is more clued up than most along the port road. For river views go for one of the upstairs rooms, though downstairs you have the advantage of a big (shared) terrace; all rooms have high ceilings and hot showers. There's also a good bakery-café. Doubles $32

Sarika At the top of the speedboat landing ☎ 081 212306. In a plum position very close to the landings, *Sarika* has a big shared terrace with views of the Mekong. The rooms are a little shabby, and lack balconies, but are clean enough. Doubles 120,000K

South central Laos

Few travellers see much of **south central Laos**; most spend just a night or two in the town of Savannakhet before pressing on to the far south or **crossing the border** into Vietnam. The two principal settlements of the region – Thakhek and Savannakhet – both lie on the Mekong River, and both offer straightforward crossings into Thailand. Route 8, branching off Route 13 between Vientiane and Thakhek, is the best and easiest overland route to Vietnam, the paved road snaking through mountains, rainforests and the Phu Pha Man "stone forest" before winding down to the city of Vinh.

Savannakhet has been described as southern Laos's Luang Prabang: this is an overstatement, but its inhabitants do live comfortably among the architectural heirlooms handed down by the French, and it is a pleasant enough place. East from Savannakhet, Route 9 climbs steadily until it eventually bisects another route of more recent vintage: the **Ho Chi Minh Trail**. The trail was used by the North Vietnamese Army to infiltrate and finally subdue its southern neighbour, and is still littered with lots of war junk, some of it highly dangerous. The best way to view these rusting relics is to use the town of **Xepon** as a base. Journeying further east leads to the **Vietnam border crossing** at Dansavanh, popularly known as "Lao Bao".

SAVANNAKHET

Locally known as "Savan", **SAVANNAKHET** is south central Laos's most-visited provincial capital. Its popularity is thanks in part to its central location on the overland routes between Vientiane and Pakse, and Thailand and Vietnam.

Travellers doing the "Indochina loop" – through Cambodia, Vietnam, Laos and Thailand – have the option of taking the 240km-long Route 9 on their way between Laos's two neighbours, hence the presence of both a **Thai** and a **Vietnamese consulate**. But Savannakhet also has its own appeal, with impressive architecture inherited from the French colonial period and narrow streets and shophouses of ochre-coloured stucco reminiscent of parts of Hanoi. A large percentage of the town's population is ethnic Vietnamese, though most have been living here for generations and consider themselves to be Lao in habit and temperament.

WHAT TO SEE AND DO

The town square is dominated by the octagonal spire of **St Teresa Catholic Church**, built in 1930. Check out the old teakwood confessional and, high up on the walls, a set of hardwood plaques with Vietnamese mother-of-pearl inlay work depicting the fourteen Stations of the Cross.

Roads laid out on a neat grid surrounding the square constitute the **Old French Quarter**, and are lined with some fine examples of European-inspired architecture. Aside from wandering about admiring the crumbling buildings and the town's pleasant wats and Chinese temples, there's not much more to do in

---

INTO VIETNAM: NAM PHAO–CAU TREO BORDER CROSSING

Roughly halfway between Paksan and Thakhek at the junction town of **Ban Vieng Kham**, Route 8 heads across central Laos to the Kaew Nua Pass, which marks the border with Vietnam, before switchbacking down to the city of Vinh.

A relatively stress-free way to get across the Nam Phao–Cau Treo crossing is by taking one of the nightly **Vinh-bound buses** from Vientiane or Thakhek. Alternatively, take one of the buses to the frontier town of Lak Xao from Thakhek and Vientiane (1–2 daily; 8hr) and stop at its market. The **Vietnamese border** at Nam Phao–Cau Treo is 35km from Lak Xao and best reached by joining a shared tuk-tuk (about 20,000K/person) from the market. However, you may have to charter it outright (around 100,000K).

Crossing the border (roughly daily 6am–9pm) can be a hassle, so it's best to start your journey early to ensure you don't end up stuck at the frontier. Lao **visas** on arrival are available at this border, but you'll need to arrange Vietnamese visas in advance; there is a Vietnamese embassy in Vientiane (see p.367).

Neither immigration post is near a town of any size; the settlement on the Vietnamese side of the border is **Cau Treo**, 105km west of Vinh on Highway 8. On the Vietnamese side, you'll be greeted by a small army of touts eager to pull you into a minibus headed for Vinh; aim to pay $5–10 for a seat.

5

Savannakhet but watch the sun set over the Mekong.

A bike or motorbike ride in any direction from the centre gives an opportunity to view the difference in lifestyles between the ethnic Vietnamese of the town and the ethnic Lao in the countryside. As you head out, brick and stucco give way to teak and bamboo, while rows of shade trees come to an abrupt halt and fruit trees – mango, guava and papaya – begin to appear in every yard.

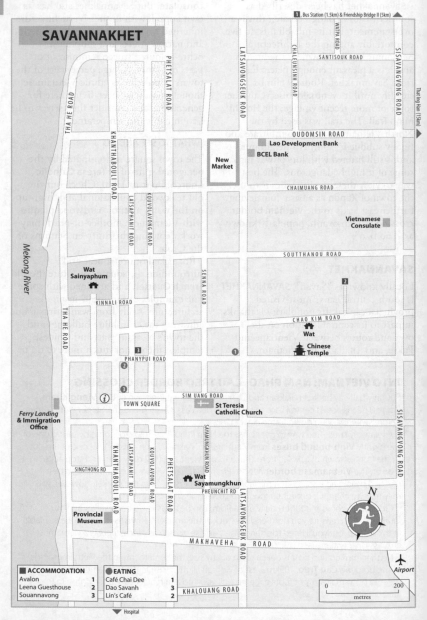

SAVANNAKHET

Bus Station (1.5km) & Friendship Bridge II (5km)

That Ing Han (35km)

WAIPA ROAD

SISAVANGVONG ROAD

SANTISOUK ROAD

CHALEUNSINH ROAD

LATSAVONGSEUK ROAD

PHETSALAT ROAD

KHANTHABOULI ROAD

THA HE ROAD

OUDOMSIN ROAD

New Market

Lao Development Bank

BCEL Bank

CHAIMUANG ROAD

LATSAPHANIT ROAD

KOUVOLAYONG ROAD

Vietnamese Consulate

SOUTTHANOU ROAD

Wat Sainyaphum

SENNA ROAD

KINNALI ROAD

CHAO KIM ROAD

Wat

Chinese Temple

PHANYPUI ROAD

Mekong River

SIM UANG ROAD

St Teresia Catholic Church

Ferry Landing & Immigration Office

TOWN SQUARE

SAYAMUNGKHUN ROAD

SISAVANGVONG ROAD

THA HE ROAD

SINGTHONG RD

KHANTHABOULI ROAD

LATSAPHANIT ROAD

KOUVOLAYONG ROAD

PHETSALAT ROAD

Wat Sayamungkhun

PHEUNCHIT RD

LATSAVONGSEUK ROAD

Provincial Museum

MAKHAVEHA ROAD

N

Airport

■ ACCOMMODATION		● EATING	
Avalon	1	Café Chai Dee	1
Leena Guesthouse	2	Dao Savanh	3
Souannavong	3	Lin's Café	2

KHALOUANG ROAD

0   200
metres

Hospital

That Ing Hang

Outside of town is a much-revered Buddhist stupa, **That Ing Hang** (daily 8am–6pm; 5000K), which can be reached by bicycle, motorbike or tuk-tuk. To get there, follow Route 9 north for 12km, where a sign points to the right; follow this road for another 3.5km. The stuccowork that covers the stupa is crude yet appealing, especially the whimsical rosettes which dot the uppermost spire. Off to one side of the stupa stands an amusing sandstone sculpture of a lion, grinning like a Cheshire cat, which could only have been hauled here from one of the Khmer ruins downriver. The stupa is best visited during its annual festival in February when thousands make the pilgrimage here.

ARRIVAL AND DEPARTURE

By plane The airport is on the southeastern side of town, off Makhaveha Road, a few blocks from the centre. Lao Airlines (T 041 212140, W laoairlines.com) flights connect Savannakhet with Vientiane (10 weekly; 1hr) and Pakse (1 daily; 30min).

By bus Most buses offload at the station on the north side of the town, with tuk-tuks on hand to make the 2km run into the centre (10,000K).

Destinations Attapeu (2 daily; 10hr); Dansavanh–Lao Bao (3–4 daily; 5–6hr); Don Khong, for Si Phan Don (1 daily; 7hr); Pakse (9–10 daily; 5hr); Salavan (1 daily; 8hr); Thakhek (3 daily; 4hr); Vientiane (9 daily; 8–9hr); Xekong (2–3 daily; 5hr).

INFORMATION

Tourist information The tourist office, west of the main square (Mon–Fri 8–11.30am & 1.30–4pm T 041 212755), can help with general enquiries, and has a good series of leaflets with information on local street food and historic buildings.

Tours Green Discovery (W greendiscoverylaos.com), Laos Mood (W laosmood.com) and Exo Travel (W exotravel .com), which all have offices in Vientiane, offer organized tours of the area.

GETTING AROUND

By tuk-tuk As Savannakhet is incredibly spread out, you may find tuk-tuks easier than trying to walk the long blocks outside the old quarter, especially on hot days. Tuk-tuks can be flagged down around town and cost around 10,000K for short distances within the centre.

By bike Bicycles are another excellent way of seeing the town and can be rented at hotels and guesthouses around town, including *Leena Guesthouse* (from 15,000K/day).

ACCOMMODATION

The old French quarter is the most atmospheric part of town to stay in. Many hotels in Savannakhet have their own travel agencies that can organize tours of the Ho Chi Minh Trail (see p.396).

Avalon Sisavanvong Rd T 041 252770, W hotel .avalonbooking.com. A solid, mid-range choice, *Avalon* has rather dowdy – think brown-and-cream decor – but comfortable, clean and good-value rooms. It's a short walk from the bus station, and around 2km from the city centre. Doubles **200,000K**

Leena Guesthouse Head 200m east of the river along Chao Kim Rd, off Latsavongseuk Rd, and follow the signs T 041 212404. Two worn but comfortable buildings in a quiet residential area, offering en-suite rooms, some with a/c (20,000K extra) and TVs. There's a pleasant restaurant serving Western breakfasts downstairs. Doubles **60,000K**

Souannavong Just off Phanypui Rd T 041 212600, W guesthousesouannavong.com. One of the better budget joints in the centre, *Souannavong* is made up of two linked guesthouses: both have simple rooms but #2 is newer and a bit more comfortable – but pricier (doubles 140,000K). Service is a bit slapdash. Doubles **80,000K**

EATING

One famous local noodle dish worth seeking out is *baw bun* (Vietnamese rice noodles served with chopped-up spring rolls and beef). Vietnamese spring rolls are also good here. Other local delights include bamboo shoots and watermelon and *sin Savannakhet* – sweet, dried, roasted beef.

Café Chai Dee Latsavongseuk Rd T 020 5988 6767, W cafechaidee.com. Chilled café-restaurant turning out a mix of Western and Japanese dishes (20,000–50,000K), plus fruit lassis, cold beers, and *lào-láo* mojitos. There's also a book exchange (donate a book and get a free coffee), and

INTO THAILAND: SAVANNAKHET TO MUKDAHAN

Ferries run between Savannakhet and Mukdahan in Thailand, but this crossing is reserved for Thai and Lao nationals only. Tourists must use the 1.6km-long **Friendship Bridge II**, 5km north of Savannakhet. Buses bound for Mukdahan leave Savannakhet's main bus terminal (12 daily; 40min), stopping at Thai immigration, where visas on arrival are available. The bus ride ends at Mukdahan's main bus station, a short ride from the town centre.

5

handmade local crafts are offered for sale. Mon–Sat 9am–3pm & 5–9.30pm.

Dao Savanh On the northwestern side of the town square ☎041 260888. Not to be confused with the hotel of the same name, this restaurant is based in a nicely restored colonial house right in the heart of town. Try the three-course, French-influenced set lunch (70,000K). Mon & Wed–Sun 10am–9.30pm.

★**Lin's Café** Latsaphanit Rd, just north of the town square ☎020 9988 1630. A great spot for a coffee or milkshake, and a flick through the stack of the latest newspapers and wide selection of books about Laos. The globetrotting menu features pizza (50,000–85,000K), green and yellow curries (30,000K) and even T-bone steaks (110,000K). The owner is a good source of information, and upstairs there's a small exhibition about the history of the region. Mon, Tues & Thurs–Sun 8.30am–10pm.

DIRECTORY

Banks and exchange The Lao Development Bank and the BCEL are near the intersection of Latsavongseuk and Oudomsin roads, the former facing Oudomsin Road and the latter facing Latsavongseuk Road.

Consulates Vietnam, Sisavangvong Road (Mon–Fri 7.30–11am & 1.30–4pm; ☎041 212418).

Hospitals The biggest hospital is located on Khanthabouli Road, near the provincial museum.

ROUTE 9: THE HO CHI MINH TRAIL AND THE VIETNAMESE BORDER

Route 9 weaves east through a series of drab towns from Savannakhet to the **Lao Bao border crossing** into Vietnam. While most travellers barrel through on the direct buses, the frontier is not without points of interest, and there are **Ho Chi Minh Trail** sites open for tourism on both sides of the border.

Xepon

A dusty village in the foothills of the Annamite Mountains, 45km from the Vietnamese border, **XEPON** is a pleasant rural stopover between Vietnam and Savannakhet. The old town of Xepon was obliterated during the Second Indochina War – along with every house in the district's two hundred villages – and was later rebuilt here, 6km west of its original location. The old city had become an important outpost on the Ho Chi Minh Trail, and was the target of a joint South Vietnamese and American invasion in 1971, Operation Lam Son 719 (see box below).

ARRIVAL AND DEPARTURE

By bus Buses and sawngthaews arriving from Savannakhet or the Lao Bao border stop at the market. Frequent sawngthaews head west towards Savannakhet (around 40,000K), and east towards Ban Dong (see opposite) and the border with Vietnam (around 20,000K).

ACCOMMODATION

Vieng Xay ☎041 214895. There are a few guesthouses along Rte 9, a short walk east from the market here, including this central one. Rooms are basic, but acceptable for a night, and there's an information folder with bus timetables and so on in the lobby. Doubles 50,000K

OPERATION LAM SON 719

In 1971, US President Richard Nixon ordered an attack on the **Ho Chi Minh Trail** in order to cut off supplies to communist forces. US ground troops were prohibited by law from crossing the border from Vietnam into Laos and Cambodia, but US command saw this as a chance to test the policy of turning the ground war over to the South Vietnamese ("Vietnamization"). During the operation, code-named **Lam Son 719**, ARVN (Army of the Republic of Vietnam) troops were to invade Laos and block the trail with US air support. The objective was **Xepon**, a town straddled by the Trail, which was 30–40km wide at this point. In early February, ARVN troops and tanks pushed across the border into Laos. Like a caterpillar trying to ford a column of red ants, the South Vietnamese troops were soon engulfed by superior numbers of North Vietnamese (NVA) regulars. Halfway to Xepon, the ARVN stopped and engaged the NVA in a **series of battles** that lasted over a month. US air support proved ineffectual, and by mid-March scenes of frightened ARVN troops retreating were being broadcast around the world.

The most tangible relics of Operation Lam Son 719 are two rusting **American tanks** that sit on the outskirts of Ban Dong, on Route 9. Ban Dong is said to have been cleared of UXO, but it's still a good idea to ask a villager to show you the way to any war relics.

INTO VIETNAM: LAO BAO BORDER CROSSING

Crossing the **Dansavanh–Lao Bao border** (daily 7am–7.30pm) can take time, so it pays to head for the Lao immigration post early in the morning if possible. Note that overnight buses from Savannakhet to the border tend to arrive at the border at around 3am, which means you may have to wait for the border to open before crossing. Annoyingly, buses stop around 1km short of the border itself; walk or take a motorcycle taxi. Remember, travellers wanting to enter Vietnam must arrange a visa in advance. On the Vietnamese side, there are motorcycle taxis to take you down the hill to Lao Bao town where buses leave for Khe Sanh and Dong Ha; from here, bus or train connections can be made to Hanoi and Hue.

Ban Dong

Halfway between Xepon and the Vietnam border is the town of **BAN DONG**, the site of one of America's most ignominious defeats during the war and a popular stop on tours of the **Ho Chi Minh Trail**. It is situated in the foothills of the Annamite Mountains, where bomb craters and unexploded ordnance still litter the landscape more than 35 years after the end of the war. If you're travelling by public transport, it's best to visit Ban Dong in the early morning; few late-afternoon sawngthaews ply this stretch of Route 9 and facilities for tourists in Ban Dong are extremely limited.

Dansavanh

Route 9 ends its journey through Laos in the village of **DANSAVANH**, 1km from the Lao immigration office. For a remote border town, Dansavanh is relatively tourist-friendly, with food, accommodation and exchange services. There's a Lao Development Bank in town, as well as a branch at the Lao immigration office on the border. From Dansavanh, you can hire a motorcycle taxi for the final 1km ride to the Lao immigration office, or walk. If you've entered Laos from Vietnam, note that there are three to four buses a day to Savannakhet (4hr) from Dansavanh, and four daily (1hr) buses to Xepon. These buses are supported by much more frequent sawngthaews, which leave when full – or simply at the whim of the driver.

The far south

Bordered by Thailand, Cambodia and Vietnam, the far south conveniently divides into two regions, with **Pakse** – the most

important market town and the access point for the Chong Mek **border crossing** into Thailand – as the hub. In the west, the Mekong River corridor is scattered with ancient Khmer temples, including **Wat Phou**, one of the most important Angkorian ruins outside Cambodia. From the nearby town of **Champasak**, many travellers go with the flow of the river south to **Si Phan Don**, where the Mekong's 1993km journey through Laos rushes to a thundering conclusion in a series of tiny riverine islands hugging the Cambodian border; the waters here are home to a dwindling number of very rare Irrawaddy **dolphins**. In the east of the region, the fertile highlands of the **Bolaven Plateau** separate the Mekong corridor from the Annamite Mountains that form Laos's border with Vietnam. It's possible to get a taste of this remote region on a day-trip from Pakse, but those who venture further afield will be rewarded with waterfall hangouts in the backpacker enclave of **Tad Lo**, and stunning scenery en route to the exotic frontier town of **Attapeu**.

PAKSE

Located at the confluence of the Xe Don and Mekong rivers, roughly halfway between the Thai border and the Bolaven Plateau, **PAKSE** is the far south's biggest city and its commercial and transport hub. For travellers, it is usually a stopover en route to Si Phan Don and Cambodia, and it makes a comfortable base for exploring the Bolaven Plateau (see p.402), with its excellent waterfalls. There is also a border crossing to Thailand just west of Pakse at Chong Mek, making it a logical entry or exit point for travellers doing a north–south tour of Laos.

5

WHAT TO SEE AND DO

Pakse is short on proper tourist attractions. The main (if somewhat underwhelming) sight is the **Champasak Provincial Museum** (Rte 13; Mon–Fri 8.30am–11.30am & 1.30–4pm; 10,000K), which houses some fine examples of ornately carved pre-Angkorian sandstone lintels taken from sites around the province. About 500m west of here on Route 13, the **Champasak Palace Hotel** resembles something of a giant concrete wedding cake. Legend has it that the late Prince Boun Oum na Champasak, a colourful character who was the heir to the Champasak kingdom and one of the most influential southerners of the twentieth century, needed a palace this size so that he could accommodate his many concubines. It is now a hotel.

Wat Luang, the town's main temple (just south of the Xe Don bridge), is worth a look, as is **Chinese Society House** (cnr No. 10 & No. 12 roads), one of Pakse's best-surviving colonial relics. The huge

New Market (Talat Dao Heuang), south of the museum, is also worth a look-in for its nostril-assaulting array of produce, including tea and coffee grown on the Bolaven Plateau.

ARRIVAL AND DEPARTURE

By plane The airport lies 2km northwest of the city on Rte 13. The taxi counter charges a hefty 80,000K (per car) to the centre; tuk-tuks outside can be bartered for less than half. The Lao Airlines office is on No. 11 Rd, near the BCEL Bank (Mon–Fri 8–11.30am & 1.30–4.30pm; ☎ 031 212152).

Destinations Luang Prabang (3 weekly; 1hr 40min); Savannakhet (5 weekly; 30min); Vientiane (1 daily; 75min).

By boat Tourist boats (150,000K each way) run between Pakse and Champasak when demand is strong enough. To book, contact *Pakse Travel* (see p.400).

By bus Long-distance buses pull in at stations around the city. Generally speaking, services to and from the north use the Northern Bus Station, 7km north of the city on Rte 13, while those to and from the south and east pull up at the Southern Bus Station, 8km southeast of town on Rte 13 at the big T-junction; tuk-tuks from either into town cost around 20,000K. The VIP Bus Station, just south of the

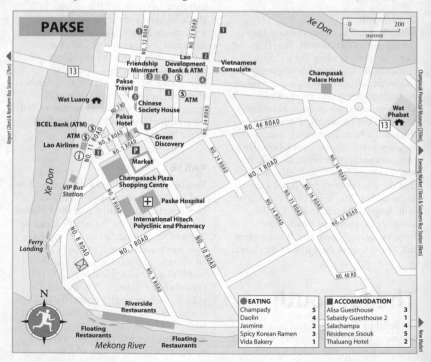

PAKSE

0   200
metres

Xe Don

NO. 12 ROAD
NO. 23 ROAD

13

Lao Development Bank & ATM ⑤
Friendship Minimart ② ③ ⑤
Vietnamese Consulate

Pakse Travel ⑤

Wat Luang ⚐

Chinese Society House
ATM ⑤

NO. 7 RD

Pakse Hotel ④

BCEL Bank (ATM) ⑤
ATM ⑤
Lao Airlines ⓘ ⑤

NO. 11 ROAD
NO. 6 ROAD
NO. 5 ROAD

Green Discovery

P

Market

Champasak Palace Hotel

Wat Phabat ⚐

13

NO. 24 ROAD

NO. 46 ROAD

NO. 1 ROAD

NO. 38 ROAD

NO. 36 ROAD

NO. 33 ROAD

NO. 42 ROAD

Xe Don

VIP Bus Station

Ferry Landing

NO. 8 ROAD

NO. 9 ROAD

NO. 1 ROAD

NO. 10 ROAD

NO. 34 ROAD

NO. 40 RD

Champasak Plaza Shopping Centre

✚ Paske Hospital

International Hitech Polyclinic and Pharmacy

N

Riverside Restaurants

Floating Restaurants

Mekong River

Floating Restaurants

Airport (2km) & Northern Bus Station (7km)

Champasak Provincial Museum (250m)

Evening Market (1km) & Southern Bus Station (8km)

New Market

● EATING	
Champady	5
Daolin	4
Jasmine	2
Spicy Korean Ramen	3
Vida Bakery	1

■ ACCOMMODATION	
Alisa Guesthouse	3
Sabaidy Guesthouse 2	1
Salachampa	4
Résidence Sisouk	5
Thaluang Hotel	2

tourist office on No. 11 Rd, is for buses to Vientiane, Cambodia and Thailand – tour agents (see p.400) in town can book tickets for these services.

Destinations Attapeu (more than 5 daily; 5hr, via Paksong and Xekong); Bangkok, Thailand (1 daily; 15hr); Phnom Penh, Cambodia (1 daily; 16hr); Salavan (9 daily; 3hr, can drop off at the turn-off to Tad Lo); Savannakhet (7 daily; 5hr); Siem Reap, Cambodia (1 daily; 14hr); Si Phan Don (hourly 8am–4pm); 2hr 30min); Thakhek (5 daily; 8hr); Ubon Ratchathani, Thailand (2 daily; 3hr); Vientiane (at least 15 daily; 10–16hr).

By sawngthaew The busy sawngthaew lot on the eastern side of the New Market serves local destinations, including Champasak (2hr; 25,000K) and Vang Tao, where you can cross to the Thai town of Chong Mek. Several sawngthaews to the three main islands of Si Phan Don (3hr; 50,000K) also leave the Southern Bus Station daily; the trip to Si Phan Don includes a boat transfer to the island of your choice.

INFORMATION

Tourist office The Provincial Tourism Office is on No. 11 Road, near the Xe Don River (Mon–Fri 8.30am–noon & 1.30–4pm; ☎031 212021), and has up-to-date bus timetables displayed on the wall.

ACCOMMODATION

Despite the number of travellers who stop in Pakse, the town has a rather disappointing (and largely overpriced) array of accommodation options.

Alisa Guesthouse Rte 13 ☎031 251555, ⚑alisa -guesthouse.com. For what its central, budget, multi-storey guesthouse lacks in character, it makes up for in its large, clean rooms with comfy beds, fridges and TVs – the best in town at this price range. Wi-fi is in the lobby only. Doubles 120,000K

Sabaidy Guesthouse 2 No. 24 Rd ☎031 212992. This budget traveller magnet, sited in a quiet residential area, has clean but spartan rooms (with shared bathrooms) and a dark but cheap dorm. Also has a decent book exchange, and runs good Bolaven Plateau tours. Dorms 35,000K, doubles 80,000K

Salachampa No. 10 Rd, near Champasak Plaza ☎031 212273. Elegant, if showing its age, this French villa has teak floors, verandahs and a sitting room filled with antique furniture. All rooms have bathrooms and a/c;

those in the old building are more spacious, with high ceilings. Doubles 160,000K

Thaluang Hotel Cnr No. 21 & No. 24 rds ☎031 251399. Set behind a wall of plants with a poor caged mynah bird acting as the doorbell, rooms here are a little cramped and cobweb-y, especially at the cheaper end, and beds are quite hard, so it's worth splashing out on a room with a/c, hot shower and TV (110,000K) for a little more comfort. Doubles 70,000K

EATING

Champady 8/1 No. 13 Rd ☎030 5348 999. Set in a French-era building, this simple spot serves tasty Lao fare at refreshingly cheap prices; try the chicken stir-fried with sweet basil (15,000K) washed down with an iced coffee (15,000K). Daily 7am–9pm.

Daolin Cnr Rte 13 & No. 24 Rd ☎020 5573 3199. *Daolin* lures punters in with low prices and reliable backpacker food. Apart from the usual rice and noodle dishes (around 20,000K) and cheese baguettes (15,000K) on the extensive menu, there's decent local coffee, and the Beerlao is ice cold. Daily 6.30am–10pm.

Jasmine Rte 13. Rough and ready *Jasmine* turns out super-tasty halal Indian and Malaysian fare, from mutton rogan josh to chicken *mie goreng*, along with a solid choice of veggie options (mains around 25,000K). Daily 7am–11pm.

Spicy Koren Ramen Rte 13, just east of the Friendship Minimart. The steaming bowls of the Korean noodle soup (from 20,000K) served up at this spot are as delicious as

---

INTO THAILAND: CHONG MEK

The easiest way to cross the border at **Vang Tao–Chong Mek** (daily 6am–8pm) is to board one of the VIP buses bound for Ubon Ratchathani (80,000K), which leave Pakse twice daily. A cheaper, slower and more complex option is to take a sawngthaew from the New Market to the border (20,000K). After you've crossed into Thailand, local sawngthaews will be waiting to shuttle you to the town of Phibun Mangsahan, where you can transfer to buses to Ubon Ratchathani, which has an airport and plentiful road and rail links. Lao and Thai visas are available on arrival at the border.

5

they are good value. There's no English signboard; look for the Korean lanterns dangling beside the street-facing kitchen. Daily 8am–10pm.

Vida Bakery No. 12 Rd ☎ 020 2925 6632. If you've just rolled off a long, overnight bus journey craving croissants, a proper toasted sandwich, or even a bacon and egg roll, follow your nose to this excellent bakery to eat your fill. The espresso coffee is good, too. Lunchtime specials include quiche with salad (20,000K). Daily 6.30am–8pm.

DIRECTORY

Banks and exchange BCEL, on No. 11 Rd, and Lao Development Bank on Rte 13, both with ATMs.

Consulates Vietnam, cnr No. 24 & No. 21 roads (Mon–Fri 7.30–11.30am & 2–4.30pm; ☎ 031 212824).

Hospital South of the shopping centre, accessed via No. 1 Rd. Adjacent on No. 46 Rd, the International Hitech Polyclinic (☎ 031 214712) has higher standards, and a pharmacy.

Massage Opposite *Pakse Hotel* on No. 5 Rd, serene Dok Champa Massage (daily 9am–10pm; ☎ 020 5418 8778) is the place to go for a traditional Lao rub-down (50,000K/1hr).

Tour agencies Green Discovery (ⓦ greendiscovery.org) on No. 10 Rd; Pakse Travel (☎ 020 227 7277) on No. 12 Rd.

CHAMPASAK

An increasingly popular backpacker destination, **CHAMPASAK** serves as the gateway to **Wat Phou** and the **Khmer** ruins, although it is also possible to visit Wat Phou as a day-trip from Pakse. Meandering for 4km along the right bank of the Mekong, Champasak is an unassuming town, but was once the capital of a Lao kingdom whose territory stretched from the Annamite Mountains into present-day Thailand. A former **palace of Prince Boun Oum na Champasak**, the scion of the royal family of Champasak and one-time prime minister, can be seen in the town itself – the first of two pale, old French mansions, if you're coming from the north.

ARRIVAL AND DEPARTURE

By boat If there is sufficient demand, two or three Pakse-bound tourist boats leave the dock, roughly 2km north of town, each day (the first is at 1pm), taking 2hr to reach Pakse (70,000K/person). Travelling to Si Phan Don by boat is a more complicated process. Unless lots of other travellers have the same idea, you'll need to hire the entire boat for the 6hr journey, and stump up around $250. For either of these services, call in at the tourist office.

By bus Sawngthaews from Pakse should let you off at Champasak's tiny roundabout, towards the north of town.

Three sawngthaews run through Champasak each morning (6am, 7am & 8am), charging 20,000K for the journey to Pakse. For bus connections to and from Si Phan Don, you'll need to cross the river to Ban Muang (10,000K). Tickets to Si Phan Don sold at the tourist office in Champasak (70,000K) include a pick-up from your hotel, the ferry crossing and a minibus ride to either Ban Hat Xai Khoun or Nakasang, where you can catch a boat to the islands (15,000K/person).

INFORMATION

Tourist information The tourist office, just off the roundabout (Mon–Fri 8–11.30am & 2–4.30pm; high season also Sat & Sun 8–11.30am & 2–4.30pm) is the best place to arrange onward transport. There's no office phone, but you can try calling Son, the local tourism officer, direct (☎ 020 9740 4986).

Services The Lao Development Bank, 100m to the west of the roundabout, has an ATM and exchange desk. There's a post office just north of the tourist office.

ACCOMMODATION

Dok Champa 200m north of the roundabout ☎ 031 511029. A handful of poky wooden, fan-cooled bungalows face a row of more spacious and bright (and 40,000K more expensive) a/c rooms – all with little balconies – across the leafy driveway of this peaceful riverside spot. Doubles 60,000K

Khamphouy 100m south of the roundabout ☎ 020 2227 9922. None of the furniture matches, but this very welcoming, old-school guesthouse has good-value double and twin rooms in two separate buildings. Free tea, and a little lobby lounge full of books make up for its lack of a river frontage. Doubles 50,000K

Saythong Roughly opposite *Khamphouy*, 100m south of the roundabout ☎ 020 2220 6215. This old-timer offers a handful of plain but clean and comfortable enough en-suite fan rooms in the same compound as its pleasant Mekong-side restaurant (mains around 25,000K). A new block of rooms was being built out front at the time of writing. Doubles 50,000K

Vongpaseud About 500m south of the roundabout, on the riverside ☎ 031 920038. The budget crash pad is looking a little worse for wear these days, but the rates are still temptingly low. Rooms here are dingy but en suite, with hot water costing 20,000K extra per night. Add a/c for 50,000K. Cheap breakfasts are available on the creaking deck out back, which has splendid Mekong views. The friendly owner has a fleet of bicycles (10,000K/day) and motorbikes (60,000K/day) available for rent. Doubles 50,000K

EATING

Champasak With Love 400m north of the roundabout ☎ 030 978 6757. With an inviting riverside patio complete with a tree swing, it's easy to see how most visitors to

Champasak end up whiling away at least one afternoon at this quirky-cool spot. The Lao-international menu (mains from 20,000K) is hit and miss, but after a sweaty bike ride to Wat Phou, the passion fruit shakes (15,000K) go down a treat. Daily 7am–10pm.

★**Nakorn Cafe** Opposite Wat Nakorn ☏020 9817 7964. Run by a hospitable Belgian-Lao couple, this Asian fusion restaurant has a lovely riverside location dotted with thatched *salas*, and a cosy bar and library room. But the real draw is its excellent international menu ranging from duck *larp* to steak and chips (mains from 20,000K). Five guestrooms are planned. Daily 7am–9pm.

ENTERTAINMENT

Champasak Shadow Puppet Theatre and Cinéma Tuk-Tuk Next to the tourist office ☏020 5508 1109, ⓦcinema-tuktuk.org. Fourteen local musicians, artists and singers come together on Tuesday and Friday evenings to perform a lively adaptation of the epic Ramayana with shadow puppets rediscovered after forty years hidden in a local wat. On Wednesdays and Saturdays, the troupe add music and sound effects to *Chang* (1927), a silent movie filmed in Laos by the team behind the original *King Kong* movie. All shows (1hr 30min) start at 8.30pm; admission is 50,000K.

SHOPPING

Chez Maman About 450m south of the roundabout ☏020 9115 5545, ⓦfacebook.com/chezmamanlaos. Delightful French owner Ghislaine proffers an expertly curated collection of textiles, trinkets and woven baskets sourced from hill-tribe artisans around the country. Daily 8am–6pm.

WAT PHOU

The most evocative Khmer ruin outside Cambodia, the UNESCO World Heritage Site of **Wat Phou** (daily 8am–5pm; 50,000K), 10km southwest of Champasak, should be at the top of your southern Laos must-see list. A romantic and rambling complex of pre-Angkorian temples dating from the sixth to the twelfth centuries, Wat Phou occupies a setting of unparalleled beauty in a lush river valley. Unlike ancient Khmer sites of equal size or importance found in neighbouring Thailand, Wat Phou has yet to be over-enthusiastically restored, so walking among the half-buried pieces of sculpted sandstone gives a good idea of what these sites once looked like.

Wat Phou, which in Lao means "Mountain Monastery", is a series of ruined temples and shrines at the foot of Lingaparvata Mountain. Although the site is now associated with Theravada Buddhism, sandstone reliefs indicate that the ruins were once a **Hindu place of worship**. When viewed from the Mekong, it's clear why the site was chosen. A phallic stone outcropping is easily seen among the range's line of forested peaks: this would have made the site especially auspicious to worshippers of Shiva, a Hindu god often symbolized by a phallus.

Archeologists tend to disagree on who the founders of the site were and when it was first consecrated. The oldest parts are thought to date back to the sixth century and were most likely built by the ancient Khmer. The site is highly sacred to the ethnic Lao, and is the focus of an annual festival (in February) that attracts thousands of pilgrims.

WHAT TO SEE AND DO

As you approach from the east, a **stone causeway** – once lined with low stone pillars – leads up to the first set of ruins. On either side of the causeway there would have been reservoirs, which probably represented the oceans that surrounded the mythical Mount Meru, home of the gods of the Hindu pantheon. Just beyond the causeway, on either side of the path, stand two megalithic structures of sandstone and laterite. They may have served as segregated **palaces**, one for men and the other for women.

Continuing up the steep stairs, you come upon a ruined temple containing the finest examples of decorative **stone lintels** in Laos. Although much has been damaged or is missing, sketches done at the end of the nineteenth century show that the temple has changed little since then.

Up the hill behind the temple is a **shallow cave** with a constant drip of water from its ceiling collecting below. This water is considered highly sacred, as it has trickled down from the peak of Lingaparvata. Visitors should resist the temptation to wash with this water.

If you follow the base of the cliff in a northerly direction, a bit of sleuthing will lead you to the enigmatic **crocodile stone** that may have been used as an altar for pre-Angkor-period human sacrifices. A few

5

metres away to the north is the **elephant stone**, a huge, moss-covered boulder carved with the face of an elephant – which is relatively recent, probably dating from the nineteenth century.

ARRIVAL AND DEPARTURE

By tuk-tuk From Champasak tuk-tuks can be hired for the 10km journey to Wat Phou. The drivers charge around 100,000K for up to three passengers, and will wait for you while you visit the ruins.

By bike A much more interesting approach is by bike – bikes can be rented from a number of places along Champasak's main road (10,000–15,000K) – the route is flat and straightforward (just follow the road south through town until you reach Wat Phou, at the end of the road).

THE BOLAVEN PLATEAU AND TAD LO

High above the hot Mekong River valley stands the **Bolaven Plateau** – hilly, roughly circular in shape, and with an average altitude of 600m – dominating eastern Champasak province and overlooking the provinces of Salavan, Xekong and Attapeu to the east. Rivers flow off the high plateau in all directions and then plunge out of lush forests along the Bolaven's edges in a series of spectacular waterfalls.

Tad Lo

In the past few years the area around **Tad Lo**, a 10m-high waterfall on the banks of the Xe Set, has been attracting a growing stream of backpackers. The cheap guesthouses and restaurants in the village just downstream of the main waterfall (there are three along this section of the river) provide everything visitors need for a few days' relaxation. In the hot season, the pools surrounding **Tad Hang**, the falls closest to the guesthouses, are a refreshing escape from the heat. For a long, scenic walk that takes in all three falls, follow the well-marked trail that runs around the back of the *Tad Lo Lodge*. The tourist office on the road to the falls can hook you up with a guide for this walk if you'd prefer not to do it alone. If you do decide to swim, take care and be sure to be clear of the water before darkness, when the floodgates of a dam upstream sometimes unleash a torrent of water without warning.

ARRIVAL AND DEPARTURE

By bus The Tad Lo Falls are 88km northeast of Pakse by bus (about 2hr) and about 30km southwest of Salavan. The turn-off for Tad Lo is just beyond the village of Lao Ngam; buses will drop you at the turn-off, from where it's a 1.5km tuk-tuk ride (10,000K/person) along a dirt road to Tad Hang. Moving on, ask your guesthouse for a lift back to the main road (10,000K), where you can pick up a morning bus to Salavan or Pakse.

ACCOMMODATION AND EATING

Green Garden Just north of *Palamei Guesthouse* ☎ 020 9616 3699. The four (very) basic thatched fan bungalows (all with hammocks) are a little dark, but *Green Garden* really does serve the best breakfasts in town (muesli with fruit and yoghurt and organic Arabica coffee 40,000K). Daily 7am–sunset. Bungalows **35,000K**

Fandee Opposite the tourist office ⓦ fandee-guesthouse .webs.com. Run by a welcoming French couple, *Fandee's* four simple but sturdy en-suite fan bungalows are infused with more character than others at this price range – think bright bedspreads, pebble-floored bathrooms. Dinner tends to be a family-style affair at the sociable communal table, and guests can refill water bottles for free. Doubles **60,000K**

Mama Pap Guesthouse On the road to Tad Hang, no phone. Tetris ten double mattresses onto the first floor of your house, add mozzie nets as "room" dividers and voila: you've got Tad Lo's cheapest dorm. The price is per bed, so it's a better bargain for couples. The friendly family that lives downstairs also runs a decent restaurant (mains 25,000K). Dorms **25,000K**

★ **Palamei Guesthouse** At the T-junction in the middle of the village, just northeast of the tourist office ☎ 030 962 0192. The superb-value rooms at this family-run guesthouse set in a lush garden are very clean and well looked after. Cheaper rooms share a bathroom, while more expensive ones (60,000K) have en-suite facilities (try for room C2, C3, B1 or B2, which overlook an emerald rice paddy). Also has a basic restaurant. Doubles **40,000K**

Sailomyen Guesthouse Next to the river, behind *Siphaseth Guesthouse*, no phone. Sharing a teeny squat toilet bathroom is worth it for the pleasure of swinging in a hammock on your balcony in one of these thatched fan bungalows, gazing at Tad Hang. The guesthouse's basic but good restaurant is set in a lush garden. Doubles **50,000K**

THE XE KONG RIVER VALLEY

The **Xe Kong** is one of Laos's great rivers, starting high in the Annamite Mountains from the eastern flanks of 2500m-high Mount Atouat and flowing southwestward around the southern edge of the Bolaven Plateau and then across the plains of Cambodia to join the Mekong at Stung

WATERFALLS OF THE BOLAVEN PLATEAU

The Bolaven Plateau is Laos's premier coffee- and tea-growing region, but travellers come here just as much for its many **waterfalls** as they do to sample the local brew. The most accessible falls are **Tad Fan** (5000K), a twin cascade more than 100m high, and the swimmable dual cascade of **Tad Yeung** (10,000K). The turn-off to Tad Fan is at the Kilometre 38 marker off Route 23 en route from Pakse to Paksong; 2km east, you'll see the turn-off to Tad Yeung. Day-tours from Pakse typically make stops at Tad Fan, Tad Yeung and the waterfalls of Tad Lo (see opposite), but an increasing number of travellers prefer to take several days to travel this 220km loop by motorbike, overnighting at Tad Lo. If you take this option, factor in a coffee stop at the excellent *Jhai Coffee House* (🌐 jhaicoffeehouse.com) in Paksong.

Treng. The main towns along the Xe Kong in Laos are Xekong (which offers little to interest visitors) and somewhat more happening Attapeu, which are linked by a paved road. Roads into the vast forest interior are still poor, but various tributaries link the Xe Kong to no fewer than four of Laos's most pristine National Biodiversity Conservation Areas.

Attapeu

Occupying a bend in the Xe Kong River, **ATTAPEU** is a cosy settlement of about twenty thousand people, including a sizeable Vietnamese contingent. Despite its name literally translating as "buffalo shit", Attapeu is known throughout southern Laos as the "Garden City" for its abundant trees, which makes for pleasant wandering between coconut palm-shaded wooden houses. Although it was near this distant outpost that the Ho Chi Minh Trail diverged, Attapeu somehow eluded the grave effects of war and remains an easy-going place. This region of Laos has one of the country's highest rates of malaria, so heed the relevant advice (see p.38).

ARRIVAL AND DEPARTURE

By bus Arriving by bus, you'll find yourself on the northwestern outskirts of the city, 4km from the centre. The bus station is served by frequent buses from Pakse, with tuk-tuks generally on hand for the run into town (20,000K). Destinations Pakse (up to 10 daily; 5hr); Salavan (1 daily; 4.5hr); Vientiane (4 daily; 16hr), via Paksong (at least 5 daily; 4hr); Xekong (at least 5 daily; 2hr).

INFORMATION

Services There are several banks and ATMs on Rte 18A. You can change money at the *Dúc Lôc* hotel, and at several exchange booths nearby.

Market Near the bridge. Mostly household goods and food; best in the morning (daily 7am–4pm).

Tourist office The tiny tourism office (Mon–Fri 8am–4.30pm; ☎ 036 211056) is 400m northeast of the water tower on Rte 18A, 2.5km from the centre. Tourism resources – and staff – are limited.

ACCOMMODATION AND EATING

Eating well in Attapeu isn't especially easy: try the market, or the downstairs restaurant at *Dúc Lôc*.

Dúc Lôc On the south side of Rte 18, in the city centre ☎ 020 9982 2334. This Vietnamese-run place is close to the market, and convenient if you're heading to the Bo-Y border crossing (buses leave from right outside the door). The wood-panelled rooms have comfortable mattresses, with TV and a/c to boot. Downstairs there's a restaurant serving good Vietnamese food (a satisfying bowl of pho will cost you 15,000K). Doubles <u>100,000K</u>

Vhang Namyen Hung Heuang Guesthouse South of the centre along the main river road ☎ 020 5579 9498. This lime-green guesthouse is an excellent budget choice. The

INTO VIETNAM: BO Y–PHO KEAU

There's a border crossing with Vietnam at the end of Route 18B, 113km east of Attapeu. Several minibuses leave Attapeu each morning (most on their way from Pakse), crossing the border at **Bo Y** after a winding, three-hour drive. Tickets can be purchased in advance from the **Dúc Lôc hotel** (see above) through to various destinations in Vietnam (70,000K to Kon Tum, though tickets to popular destinations via Bo Y, including Da Nang and Hue, can be bought here, too). To cross into Vietnam, you must have arranged your visa before arrival at the border. Coming from the other direction, Lao visas are available on arrival. Formalities on both sides are relatively quick, as this is not a particularly busy border.

5

purple bedroom walls and floor tiles are a bit extreme, but the rooms (with a/c and TVs) are comfortable enough, and there's a pleasant mango tree-shaded seating area out front. Doubles __100,000K__

SI PHAN DON

In Laos's deepest south, just above the border with Cambodia, the muddy stream of the Mekong is carved into a 14km-wide web of rivulets, creating a landlocked archipelago ripe for exploration. Known as **Si Phan Don**, or "Four Thousand Islands", this labyrinth of islets, rocks and sandbars has acted as a kind of bell jar, preserving traditional southern-lowland Lao culture from outside influences. Local life unravels slowly and peacefully: fishermen head out at sunset silhouetted against the sky's colourful backdrop and cast their nets out across the water, and children play and run about the villages. The archipelago is home to rare flora and fauna, including a species of **freshwater dolphin**. Southeast Asia's largest **waterfalls** are also located here.

Don Khong

The largest of the Four Thousand Islands group, **Don Khong** draws a steady stream of visitors, but has a more laidback feel than popular Don Det (see p.406). It boasts a venerable collection of Buddhist temples and good-value accommodation.

Don Khong has only two settlements of any size: the port town of **Muang Sen** on the island's west coast, and the east-coast town of **Muang Khong**, where the best accommodation and restaurants are. Like all Si Phan Don settlements, both Muang Sen's and Muang Khong's homes and shops cling to the bank of the Mekong for kilometres but barely penetrate the interior, which is reserved for rice fields.

WHAT TO SEE AND DO

The best way to explore the island is to rent a bicycle (see opposite) – the flat terrain and lack of heavy traffic makes it relatively easy to get about, though the potholes can be a little difficult to navigate on a motorbike. Most riders take one of two loops around the island; the **southern loop** (roughly 19km) takes you south of Muang Khong, past the village of **Ban Na**, to the tail of the

island. Continuing west, you'll pass rice paddies and the swishing tails of dusty water buffaloes en route to **Ban Siw**, which has a monastery, Wat Silananthalangsy, that is worth a look. The number of houses lining the road continues to grow until you reach the sleepy port of **Muang Sen** – a good stop for rest and refreshment before heading east via the shadeless 8km stretch of road that leads back to Muang Khong. More ambitious is the 35km **northern loop**. Start by heading due west from Muang Khong on the road that bisects the island, turning north at the intersection as you enter Muang Sen. After almost 7km, look out for the narrow trail on your left that leads up to a ridge of black stone and, on the top of the hill, a large reclining Buddha. Following the trail up another 200m to the right, you'll spot a cluster of monks' quarters that belong to **Wat Phou Khao Kaew**, an evocative little monastery situated atop a river-sculpted stone bluff overlooking the Mekong. If you're not tempted to pedal back the same (slightly shorter) way, you can complete the loop by heading another 6km north to **Ban Houa Khong**, on the outskirts of which stands the modest **residence of Khamtay Siphandone**, former revolutionary and ex-prime minister. Follow the road east to **Ban Dong** and then south to Muang Khong.

ARRIVAL AND DEPARTURE

By boat Taking the boat from Pakse or Champasak sounds romantic but is very expensive to arrange. Boats from other parts of Si Phan Don dock in the middle of Muang Khong, near *Done Khong Guesthouse*. Boats to Don Khon and Don Det depart from the same spot daily at 8.30am (1hr 30min) and cost from 40,000K; arrange through a guesthouse the day before.

By bus and sawngthaew Six public buses to Don Khong, as well as numerous sawngthaews (3hr; 50,000K), leave from Pakse's Southern Bus Station daily, stopping at Ban Hat Xai Khoun to allow passengers to cross the Mekong by boat. For public buses from Ban Hat Xai Khoun back to Pakse, or south to Nakasang for Don Det and Don Khone, cross the river by *pirogue* (15,000K) and wait (potentially for a couple of hours) for one to pass by on Rte 13. A more reliable option is to take one of the tourist buses operated by companies in Pakse and Champasak (both 70,000K). Often, the tickets include the boat transfer from Ban Hat Xai Khoun to Muang Khong, but check when buying. Some buses will drop you off on the highway turn-off to Ban Hat

SI PHAN DON

Pakse & Champasak

Wat Houa Khong

Ban Dong

Don
Het   Don
       Koi

Ban
Houa
Khong

Don
Hinyai

13

N

Don
Khong

Wat Phou Khao Kaew

Muang Khong

Ban Hat Xai Khoun

Don
Khamao

Muang Sen

Ban
Na

Ban Nakhok

LAOS

Wat Silananthalangsy

Ban Siw   Wat
           Thephasourin

Ban Hang Khon

Don
Long

Don
Xang
Phai   Don
        Beng   Don
                Som

Don
Loppadi   Don
           Xemouy

Nakasang

CAMBODIA

Ban Hua Det

Don
Tao

13

Don
Xang

Don
Det   Ban Khon

Khon
Phapheng
Falls

Somphamit
Falls

French
Bridge

Ban Hang
Khon

Cambodia

0   10
kilometres

Don
Sanlat   Don Khon

Dolphins

Xai Khoun, from where it's an 800m walk to the boat dock. Leaving Don Khong is easy; almost every guesthouse in Muang Khong sells tickets to major cities in Laos, Thailand and Cambodia, with prices including boat transfers.

INFORMATION AND GETTING AROUND

Tourist office There's a tourist office just south of *Done Khong Guesthouse* (Mon–Fri 8am–4.30pm).

Money The Agricultural Promotion Bank (daily 8am–3.30pm), at the south end of Muang Khong, exchanges dollars and baht and has an ATM. There's also an ATM on the main road across the island, outside the Lao Telecom building.

Bike and motorbike rental Several of the guesthouses and shops in Muang Khong offer bicycles for rent (10,000K/day); Mr BounKham from *Don Khone Guesthouse* can hook you up with a motorbike (from 60,000K/day).

ACCOMMODATION AND EATING

Don Khong's accommodation is concentrated in Muang Khong. Most guesthouses have riverside restaurants (open

daily 6.30am–10pm) serving the usual array of Asian and international dishes from near-identical menus.

Done Khong Guesthouse Across the road from the ferry landing ☏ 020 9878 9994. This long-established place in a very handy location near the dock has basic en-suite rooms (those at the front share a little terrace). The friendly owner, Mr BounKham, rents bikes and motorbikes and can book tours and transport. Doubles <u>100,000K</u>

Pon's River Guesthouse 100m north of the ferry landing ☏ 020 2227 0037, ⊛ ponarenahotel.com. A great option at the cheaper end, with tidy en-suite rooms and its own riverside restaurant (where the wi-fi signal is strongest). TV and a/c are available for an extra 20,000K. The manager is well connected locally (his brother owns the fancy *Pon Arena Hotel*) and can arrange a variety of tours. Doubles <u>60,000K</u>

Ratana Riverside Guesthouse Between *Done Khong Guesthouse* and *Pon* ☏ 020 2220 1618. The four comfortable river-facing a/c rooms at this two-storey guesthouse all have nice balconies and enormous windows; opt for an upstairs room for more privacy, given the floor-to-ceiling glass window situation. Its riverside

5

restaurant is a cut above the rest. Doubles 100,000K

V Mala Just north of the ATM on the main north—south road ☎ 020 9754 5787. Simple, but surprisingly stylish, these timber-floored rooms are located in a rust-red wooden house one street back from the river. Bathrooms are shared, but there are separate facilities for men and women. Good value. Add breakfast for 50,000K. Doubles 50,000K

Don Khon and Don Det

The tropical islands of **Don Khon** and **Don Det**, 15km downstream from Don Khong, are fringed with swaying coconut palms and planted with jade- and emerald-coloured rice paddies. Besides being a picturesque little haven for backpackers, who come here in ever-increasing numbers, the islands also offer some leisurely walks and bike rides.

The more popular island for backpackers to stay on is the rapidly developing island of Don Det, with Don Khon catering for more mid-range budgets. Despite the explosion of travellers' cafés, many of which openly sell happy shakes and joints, parts of Don Det maintain a rustic charm, though if you're looking for something quieter, head for Don Khon. Simple wooden bungalows with hammocks out front line the coastlines of both islands, coaxing people into staying here for days.

WHAT TO SEE AND DO

A delightfully sleepy place with a timeless feel about it, **BAN KHON**, at the northern end of Don Khon, is the islands' largest settlement. To explore the remnants of Laos's old French railway, head just south of the bridge back behind some houses.

FISH AND WHISKY

Fish is a staple in Si Phan Don. Recipes range from the traditional **larp pa** (a salad of minced fish mixed with garlic, chillies, shallots and fish sauce) to tropical fish steamed in coconut milk. Be sure to try the islands' speciality **mók pa**, fish steamed in banana leaves with zingy Lao herbs, which takes an hour to prepare.

The local **lào-láo** has gained a reputation as one of the best **rice whiskies** in Laos. If Lao white lightning is a little strong for you, ask for a "Lao cocktail", a gentler blend of wild honey and *lào-láo* served over ice.

There you'll find the rusty remains of the locomotive that once hauled French goods and passengers between piers on Don Khon and Don Det, bypassing the rapids that block this stretch of the river.

Most budget travellers head straight for the busy backpacker enclave of **BAN HUA DET**, at the northern end of Don Det. Here, dozens of tourist-friendly **guesthouses**, **bungalows** and **restaurants** have sprung up just a stone's throw from an incongruous industrial structure once used for hoisting cargo from the train onto awaiting boats; it's all that remains of the railroad's northern terminus. In just a few short years the place has grown from a sleepy island community into something resembling Thailand's party islands, and construction continues apace. Needless to say, if you'd rather be woken up by a crowing rooster than the screech of a band saw, stay further south.

Linked by a bridge, Don Khon and Don Det can be easily explored **on foot or by bicycle**. The fee to cross the French Bridge is 35,000K per day; there's a ticket booth at the southern end of the bridge. A short walk west of the bridge on Don Khon stands the village monastery, **Wat Khon Tai**. Taking the southerly path behind the wat for 1.5km, you'll come to a ticket checkpoint, and then a cliff overlooking **Somphamit Falls**, a series of high rapids crashing through a jagged gorge.

ARRIVAL AND DEPARTURE

By boat Boats between Don Khong and Don Det/Don Khon run daily at around 8.30am (1hr 30min; 40,000K) in both directions; the price to Don Khong increases during the rainy season when the current is strong. It's possible to get a boat from either of the islands to Nakasang (15min; 15,000K) for onward connections, though the easiest option is to arrange the whole journey through your guesthouse or a travel agent.

By bus Buses from Pakse and elsewhere in Laos, plus those coming over the Cambodian border, stop at Nakasang, from where boatmen will ferry you across to the islands. To move on from Don Det and Don Khon, it's best to book your bus through one of the travel agents in Ban Hua Det, or at *Pans* on Don Khon; the price will include a boat to Nakasang, and once there, the boatman will direct you to the correct place to pick up your bus. Though most bus departure times are advertised as 11am, this is usually the time of the boat pick-ups from the islands. Alternatively, you could hire a boat to Nakasang yourself and pay for a bus once you're across, but aim to be there by at least 11am to make sure you can get on your desired service.

Destinations Buses run at least once daily to Champasak (2hr 30min); Pakse (3hr); Vientiane (19hr) and beyond; plus Siem Reap (8hr) and other destinations in Cambodia and Thailand.

INFORMATION

Tourist information The *Baba Guesthouse* website (see box, p.408) is the best source of information on the islands.
Bike rental Bicycles are for rent at many guesthouses on each island for 10,000K/day.
Tours A full-day kayaking tour (170,000K), including visits to Don Pa Soi and Khon Phapheng waterfalls, and a shot at spotting Irrawaddy dolphins (see below), can be booked at any of the travel agencies on Don Det's main drag. Guides are hit and miss, as are safety standards. A decent level of fitness is required to navigate wet season currents.
Services The islands still lack a single bank or ATM, so bring cash or factor in a ferry ride to Nakasang. Most guesthouses offer free, if patchy, wi-fi. You'll also find several internet cafés in Ban Hua Det; try Mr Khieo Internet (400K/min).

ACCOMMODATION

DON DET

★ **Crazy Gecko** Sunrise side, south of *Don Det Bungalows* ☎ 020 9719 3565, ⓦ crazygecko.ch. Amid the sea of same-same basic bungalows on Don Det, the *Gecko* feels almost stylish. Clean and comfortable, with just the right amount of decoration, its three thatched rooms share a hammock-strewn terrace on the first floor of the building behind its riverside Lao-international restaurant (daily 7am–9.30pm; mains around 25,000K). There's also a pool table in the reception area. Doubles 90,000K

Don Det Bungalows Sunrise side, around 1.2km south of the centre of Ban Hua Det ☎ 020 2300 4959. For something quiet and relatively classy, try these comfy fan bungalows, which have swooping Lao-style rooflines and cocoon-like hammocks. There's a reasonable restaurant on

the other side of the path. Doubles 140,000K
Green View Sunset side, at the junction with the main trail to sunrise side ☎ 020 9180 3519. Overlooking an emerald rice paddy, this new two-storey concrete guesthouse is super-clean and central, if a little lacking in character (and hammocks). Upgrade to a/c for around 30,000K. Doubles 120,000K
The Last Resort Sunset side, around 750m south of town ⓦ facebook.com/lastresortdondet. This self-styled travellers' community was started by a former banker from the UK. Thatched teepees sleeping two to four people (all share a single, quite decent bathroom) are set around a sociable garden that's home to a fire pit and an open-air cinema. Organic herbs and vegetables grown on site are used in communal meals each night in high season, and there's direct access to secluded beaches. Teepees 100,000K
Mama Leuah Guesthouse and Restaurant Sunrise side, nearly 2km south of Ban Hua Det ☎ 020 5907 8792, ⓦ mamaleuah-dondet.com. Those looking to escape the party scene in Ban Hua Det will find solitude among this collection of basic but ample waterfront bungalows (the cheapest two share a bathroom) managed by affable German expat Lutz and his wife, Pheng. The good on-site restaurant spans Lao favourites to German comfort food staples including a mean schnitzel (47,000K). Doubles 60,000K
Sengthavan1 Just south of the main trail to sunrise side ☎ 020 5613 2696. The four baby blue-walled en-suite fan bungalows here are cleaner and more comfortable than most at this price range. All face the river, but views are obscured by the restaurant: a good enough spot to take in the sunset. 100,000K

DON KHON

Somphamit Just west of *Sala Done Khone* on the main river road ☎ 020 526 2491. Comfortable (albeit windowless) riverside en-suite bamboo bungalows are equipped with fans and wide terraces with decent hammocks. Newer rooms set back from the river have hot

DOLPHIN-SPOTTING FROM BAN HANG KHON

From Ban Khon, follow the path that turns inland near *Chanthounma's Restaurant* through rice paddies and thick forest and eventually, after 4km, you'll reach the village of **Ban Hang Khon**, the jumping-off point for **dolphin-spotting** excursions. The April to May dry season, when the Mekong is at its lowest, is the optimum time of year to catch a glimpse of this highly endangered species (early mornings and late afternoons are best), and boats can be hired out from the village to see them. Boats cost 60,000K for a one-hour trip, depending on the number of people, and you're obliged to pay for the boat regardless of whether you see any *pa kha* (dolphins).

Over the past century, the number of bluish-grey freshwater **Irrawaddy dolphins** (*Orcaella brevirostris*) in the Mekong has dwindled dramatically, from thousands to around 85 today. Sadly, as few as five are thought to remain in Lao waters. Gill-net fishing and, across the border, the use of poison, electricity and explosives, are to blame. A more pressing threat to the dolphins' survival is the vast Don Sahong dam, currently being built south of Don Khon, which scientists believe could change the river's hydrological balance forever.

5

INTO CAMBODIA: NONG NOK KHIENE–TRAPAENG KRIEL

Although buses run to the border, the easiest way to get into Cambodia via the **Nong Nok Khiene–Trapaeng Kriel** (also referred to as **Veun Kham**) crossing is to book through passage from the islands (or Pakse) to your intended destination in Cambodia. The **ferry** to all Cambodian destinations leaves the islands at 8am daily; ticket sellers will tell you the journey takes eight hours to Siem Reap ($38) and ten hours to Phnom Penh ($30), but expect delays. You can save money (and usually also time) by taking the 8am ferry to Nakasang and then the 9.30am bus to the border, and meeting pre-arranged transport on the other side; Asia Van Transfer (Ⓦ asiavantransfer.com) was the most reliable option at the time of writing. Cambodian and Lao visas are available on arrival at this border. Immigration officials on both sides ask for a $2 fee to stamp your passport, in addition to the visa fee. Watch out for scams: refuse help processing your documents, and ignore the "health check" station, neither of which is required.

water and a/c, and there's a small spa on-site (massage 100,000K/60min). Doubles 70,000K

Sunset Paradise Guesthouse The easternmost guesthouse on the main riverside path in Ban Khon, no phone. Spacious and solid, these wooden bungalows face one another across a peaceful garden, just back from the river. There's good food at the restaurant overlooking the water. Doubles 100,000K

EATING AND DRINKING

Most places on the islands serve a fairly predictable mix of Lao and international dishes, and Mekong fish is always on the menu (see p.406). Restaurants on Don Khon serve alcohol, but Ban Hua Det on Don Det is the place to party (in the high season, at least). The handful of similar bars on the main drag wind down towards the semi-official 11.30pm curfew, after which the party often moves to a nearby beach.

DON DET

★**Kea's Backpackers Paradise Restaurant & Bar** Sunset side, opposite *Green View* ☎ 030 9516 715. Never mind that there aren't any beds here yet – Mr Kea's Lao-international restaurant is arguably the best thing to happen to Don Det's dining scene since...forever. Order the beer-battered fish and chips (30,000K) and you'll see. Mr Kea also makes a mean mojito (20,000K). Daily

★TREAT YOURSELF

Baba Guesthouse Don Det, 300m south of the pier ☎ 020 9889 3943, Ⓦ dondet.net. Semi-screened from the busy footpath by a lush grove of banana and papaya trees, the seven smart white rooms (all with balconies, a/c and beautifully crafted wooden furniture) in this newish two-storey guesthouse just south of Ban Hua Det get snapped up fast. Rooms overlook *Baba*'s riverside deck restaurant, a top spot for a Beerlao or two. Doubles 250,000K

6am–9pm, bar until midnight.

Reggae Bar Main drag, Ban Hua Det. It's more about the Rasta-centric beats (sometimes live) than the food at this lazy, sit-down bar, where empty crates of Beerlao prop up the long and sociable tables. There's a diving board into the river for cooling off. Daily 8am–11.30pm.

DON KHON

Chez Fred et Lea Northeast of the bridge, just south of *Somphamit* ☎ 020 2212 8882. This tiny restaurant has taken Don Khon by storm with beautifully presented French and Lao dishes (mains from 30,000K), which reflect the heritage of its owners. The baguettes (from 20,000K) are hearty, and the jams are home-made. Daily 6.30am–10pm.

Pa Kha Northeast of *Chez Fred et Lea* ☎ 031 260 939, Ⓦ bit .ly/pakha. It might not be right on the river, but this raised restaurant attached to the guesthouse of the same name is one of the most pleasant spots on the island to while away an afternoon over a plate of fresh spring rolls (25,000K) and a watermelon shake (10,000K). Don't be shy to ask for your papaya salad (15,000K) "Lao style" (spicy). Daily 7am–10pm.

Khon Phapheng Falls

Despite technically being the largest waterfall in Southeast Asia, **Khon Phapheng** (55,000K), to the east of Don Khon, is not all that spectacular. It's best described as a low but wide cliff that just happens to have a huge volume of water running over it. The vertical drop is highest during the dry season, and a tourist pavilion above the falls provides an ideal place to sit and enjoy the view. Most tourists see the falls as a package from Don Khon or Don Det, but it is also possible to get there by motorbike – get a boat to Ban Hat Xai Khoun (opposite Muang Khong) or Nakasang (where taxi boats connect to Don Det and Don Khon) and head south along Route 13.

Malaysia

HIGHLIGHTS

❶ **George Town** Sample local cuisine at its best in Malaysia's food and art capital. **See p.443**

❷ **Pulau Perhentian** An earthly paradise of palm-fringed white sand and crystal-clear waters. **See p.463**

❸ **Malacca** Explore this colonial city rich in heritage buildings. **See p.470**

❹ **Longhouse stay** Experience traditional Sarawak culture by staying with indigenous tribes. **See p.491**

❺ **Mount Kinabalu** Watch the sunrise from the summit of Borneo's highest mountain. **See p.506**

❻ **Sipadan** Swim with sharks and turtles at one of the world's top diving spots. **See p.516**

HIGHLIGHTS ARE MARKED ON THE MAP ON PP.412–413

ROUGH COSTS

Daily budget Basic RM55/Occasional treat RM80

Drink Beer US$1.50 (pricier in stricter Muslim areas)

Food *Mee goreng* (noodles) US$1.50

Budget hotel US$6.50–18

Travel Bus: Kuala Lumpur–Malacca (144km) US$4; Ferry: Mersing–Pulau Tioman (50km) US$9; Train: Kota Bharu–Jerantut (131km) US$8

FACT FILE

Population 29.2 million

Language Bahasa Malaysia (also English, Tamil, Hokkien, Cantonese and Mandarin)

Currency Malaysian ringgit (RM)

Capital Kuala Lumpur

International phone code ☏ + 60

Time zone GMT + 8hr

6

Introduction

Malaysia has something to offer every traveller – from heady bar- and club-hopping in the capital, historical buildings in towns rich in colonial history and countless regional delicacies, to trekking and wildlife-watching in the world's oldest tropical rainforest and diving at some of the world's best sites off the white-sand beaches of its many islands. The country is full of charm and beauty, and its rich cultural heritage is apparent in both traditional village areas and in its commitment to religious plurality. The dominant cultural force is undoubtedly Islam, but the country's diverse population of Malays, Chinese, Indians and Borneo's indigenous tribes has created a fabulous juxtaposition of mosques, temples and churches, a panoply of festivals, and a wonderful mixture of cuisines. Malaysians insist that their food combines the best flavours and dishes of the surrounding countries – and after a few meals from a sizzling street stall, you're likely to agree.

First impressions of Malaysia's high-tech, fast-growing capital, **Kuala Lumpur (KL)**, are of a vibrant and colourful modern metropolis with gleaming skyscrapers. Less than three hours' journey south lies the birthplace of Malay civilization, **Malacca**. Further up the coast is the first British settlement, the island of **Penang**, and its fascinating historical capital, **George Town**. From here, for a taste of Old England and walks through emerald-green tea plantations, head for the **Cameron Highlands**.

Pulau Langkawi is a popular, palm-fringed, duty-free island north of Penang, while routes down the Peninsula's east coast include stops at the truly stunning islands of **Pulau Perhentian** and **Pulau Tioman**. The state capitals of **Kota Bharu**, in the northeast, and **Kuala Terengganu**, further south, are great stops for soaking up Islam-infused Malay culture, while the unsullied tropical rainforests of **Taman Negara National Park** offer innumerable trails, animal hides, a high canopy walkway and rushing waterfalls.

Across the sea, East Malaysia comprises the Bornean states of **Sarawak** and **Sabah**. **Kuching**, Sarawak's attractive colonial capital, beckons with its mix of the old and the new, but the real attraction lies in the interior: in staying in the **traditional longhouses** of the Iban communities of the Batang Ai and Batang Lupar river systems, or the Bidayuh and Orang-Ulu communities closer to the Kalimantan border. The best time to visit is from late May to early June during the rice harvest festival celebrations. **Sibu**, further to the north, is another starting point for longhouse visits. In the north of the state, **Gunung Mulu National Park** beckons

---

WHEN TO GO

Temperatures in Malaysia constantly hover around 30°C (22°C in highland areas), and humidity is high all year round. The **monsoon season** brings heavy and prolonged downpours to the east coast of Peninsular Malaysia, the northeastern part of Sabah and the western end of Sarawak from November to February; boats to most of the islands stop running. For tropical heat and a buzzing atmosphere, May to September is the time to go, with July and August being the busiest months thanks to holidays in Europe and the US. For those prepared to risk a few showers, the months bordering the monsoon, March–April and October–November, are good options.

with its extraordinary razor-sharp limestone needles providing demanding climbing and its caves among the largest in the world.

There are many reasons for a trip to Sabah: to conquer the 4095m granite peak of **Mount Kinabalu**; to visit the lively modern capital of **Kota Kinabalu**; and to **watch the wildlife**, such as wild orang-utans, proboscis monkeys and hornbills along the Kinabatangan River, not to mention diving at the world-class island destination of **Pulau Sipadan** with its host of sharks, fish and turtles.

CHRONOLOGY

c.2 million BC Evidence of earliest human habitation in Malaysia, and the oldest outside the African continent, based on four archeological sites in the Lenggong Valley.

200 AD onwards Indian traders arrive in the region, bringing Hindu and Buddhist practices. Hindu-Malay kingdom established in what is now Kedah.

Seventh to thirteenth centuries Sumatra-based Buddhist Srivijaya Empire dominates Malaysia, Indonesia and Borneo.

c.1390 Sumatran prince Paramesvara founds the Malacca Sultanate.

Fifteenth century Malacca flourishes as a trading centre. Islam is adopted as the dominant religion, and the Malacca Sultanate expands along the west coast of the Peninsula to Singapore and east-coast Sumatra.

1511 The Portuguese take Malacca and Sultan Mahmud Shah flees.

1526 The Portuguese raze the Sultan's court of Johor on Pulau Bentam. Johor's court moves frequently during a century of assaults by Portugal and Aceh.

1641 The Dutch East India Company take Malacca, which goes into decline. The Johor court ally becomes the predominant Malay kingdom.

Sixteenth to nineteenth centuries Trade with China grows; many Chinese merchants come to Malacca and marry Malay women, creating the unique Baba-Nyonya culture.

1786 The British establish a trading fort at Penang (George Town).

1819 Sir Stamford Raffles establishes a British trading station in Singapore, which weakens both Malacca and Penang, forcing the Dutch to relinquish the former to the British.

1823 The British and Dutch split the territories between them, giving the Dutch Indonesia, and leaving Malaysia to Britain.

1826 The British unify Malacca, Penang and Singapore into one administration, the Straits Settlements, with

Singapore replacing Penang as its capital in 1832.

1839 British explorer James Brooke arrives in Kuching, helps the Sultan of Brunei suppress a rebellion and becomes the first White Rajah.

1874 Struggles between Chinese clan groups are rife and Malay factions frequently become involved, causing a string of civil wars. The British sign the Pangkor Treaty with the Perak Malay chief, Rajah Abdullah, formalizing the control of the British Empire over Peninsular Malaysia.

1880s The name British Malaya comes into use. The Malay sultans' powers are gradually eroded, while the introduction of rubber estates makes British Malaya one of the most productive colonies in the world.

1888 Sarawak, Sabah and Brunei are made British protectorates.

1896 The Peninsula states under British control are given the title the Federated Malay States, with Kuala Lumpur the regional capital.

1909–19 British control in the Peninsula expands to the northern Malay states of Kedah and Perlis (1909), Johor (1914) and Terengganu (1919).

1930s Chinese–Malay tensions increase with Chinese immigration. The Malayan Communist Party is founded in 1930, with significant support in the Chinese community, demanding an end to British rule and the perceived privileges of the Malays. The Singapore Malay Union, formed in response, advocates a Malay supremacist line.

1942–45 Japanese occupation. The British shamefully flee, and up to fifty thousand people – mainly Chinese – are killed in the two weeks following the British surrender of Singapore. Chinese activists in the MCP organize much of the resistance.

1946 The British introduce the Malayan Union, which gives Chinese and Indian inhabitants equal rights to Malays. In response, Malayan nationalists form the United Malays National Organization (UMNO), arguing that Malays should retain special privileges.

1948 The Federation of Malaya replaces the Malay Union. It re-establishes the power of the Malay sultans, and Chinese and Indians only qualify as citizens if they have lived there for fifteen years and speak Malay or English. Sarawak and North Borneo made British Crown Colonies.

1948–60 "The Emergency", with the predominantly Chinese Malayan Communist Party members taking to the jungle and striking at economic targets and at the British in a bid to loosen state control. The violence peaks in 1950–51.

1955 UMNO's leader, Tunku Abdul Rahman, wins the first federal elections by cooperating with moderate Chinese and Indian parties and campaigning for *merdeka* (freedom) – an independent Malaya.

August 31, 1957 Britain grants independence to Malaya, and Rahman becomes the first prime minister. Under the new constitution nine Malay sultans alternate as king.

6

MALAYSIA

THAILAND

SOUTH CHINA SEA

Hat Yai

Kota Bharu

Pulau Langkawi
George Town
Alor Setar
Tumpat
2 Pulau Perhentian
P. Redeng

Penang
Butterworth
Kuala Krai
Kuala Besut
Kuala Terengganu
P. Kapas
Rantau Abang
Dungun

Taiping
Kuala Kangsar
Marang

P. Pangkor
Ipoh
CAMERON HIGHLANDS
TAMAN NEGARA NATIONAL PARK
PENINSULAR MALAYSIA

Strait of Malacca
Tanah Rata
Kuala Lipis
Jerantut
Cherating

Raub
Kuantan

Kuala Selangor
Temerloh

KUALA LUMPUR
Klang
Segamat
P. Tioman

Seremban
Gemas
ENDAU-ROMPIN NATIONAL PARK
Mersing
P. Sibu
Tanjung Leman

SUMATRA
Malacca
3

Dumai
Kukup
Johor Bahru

INDONESIA
SINGAPORE

P. Bunguran

Kep. Anambas (Indonesia)

P. Subi

September 1963 North Borneo (renamed Sabah), Sarawak and Singapore join Malaya to form the Federation of Malaysia. Brunei refuses to join.

August 1965 Following tensions between the Malay-dominated UMNO Alliance Party in KL and Lee Kuan Yew in Singapore, Singapore leaves the Federation.

1969 When the UMNO Alliance loses parliamentary elections, rioting breaks out in Kuala Lumpur. Hundreds of Chinese are killed. The country remains under a state of emergency for nearly two years.

1970 Rahman resigns, handing over to Tun Abdul Razak, also from UMNO, who introduces positive discrimination for ethnic Malays, known as *bumiputra*, which gives them favoured positions in business and professions. This remains a major cause of ethnic tension within Malaysia today.

1981 UMNO leader Dr Mahathir Mohammed becomes prime minister.

2003 Mahathir hands over the premiership to Abdullah Badawi.

2007 Malaysia celebrates fifty years of independence.

March 2008 Badawi and the UMNO scrape to victory in elections.

April 2008 Pakatan Rakyat, an informal Malaysian political coalition party, is formed by the former deputy prime minister, Anwar Ibrahim. It is comprised and collectively managed by the People's Justice Party (PKR),

Democratic Action Party (DAP) and Pan-Malaysian Islamic Party (PAS), following their success in a number of states in the March general election.

July 2009 Thousands of people protest on the streets of Kuala Lumpur against the Internal Security Act, which allows for the arrest and detention without trial of any individual deemed a threat to national security.

2010 A Malaysian court rules that a Roman Catholic newspaper could use the world "Allah" to describe the Christian God in its Malay-language edition. Churches are attacked by protest Muslim groups in Kuala Lumpur, Perak and Sarawak.

2013 The ruling National Front retains power in the national elections.

2015 Prime Minister Najib Tun Razak is accused of channelling over RM2.67 billion from government funds to his personal bank accounts.

ARRIVAL AND DEPARTURE

Malaysia's main **airport** is Kuala Lumpur International Airport (KLIA; ⊛klia.com .my), 57km from the city centre, to which there are international flights from most countries. **Domestic** and **low-cost flights** to other Southeast Asian

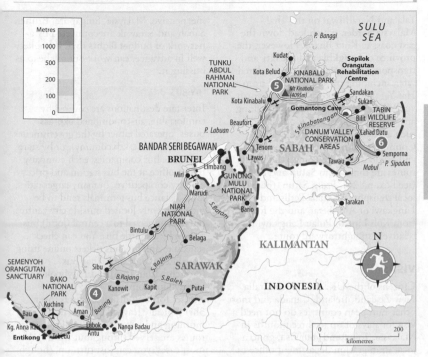

destinations (and beyond) depart from Kuala Lumpur International Airport 2 (KLIA2; ⓦklia2.info), dominated by AirAsia, 2km south. Both terminals are well connected to KL's main transport hub – KL Sentral train station. Low-cost carriers Malindo and Firefly use the smaller Subang Skypark terminal (ⓦsubangskypark.com) thirty minutes west of KL Sentral. Penang, Langkawi, Johor Bahru, Kuching and Kota Kinabalu also receive some international flights. Malaysia's bus and train routes are extremely efficient, and crossing the entire length of the Peninsula can be done overnight.

Malaysia has **land borders** with Thailand, Singapore, Brunei and Kalimantan (Indonesian territory), with frequent long-distance buses crossing all of them, and a variety of possible **sea routes** from Indonesia and Thailand. There is also a twice-weekly ferry (22hr) connecting Sandakan to Zamboanga in the Philippines. However, this crosses the Sulu archipelago, base of separatist Islamic terrorist group Moro Liberation Front; current security advice is to avoid travelling in this region (see box, p.660).

FROM INDONESIA

A variety of ferries and speedboats depart from **Indonesia** to Malaysia (though most travellers now fly): from Dumai, south of Medan, to Malacca; from Pulau Batam, near Pekanbaru, to Johor Bahru; from Tanjung Balai, in Sumatra, to Port Klang; and from Tarakan in northeastern Kalimantan to Tawau in Sabah.

There is a **land border** at Entikong, 100km south of Kuching in Sarawak; buses run from Pontianak in southern Kalimantan through here to Kuching (see p.320).

FROM THAILAND

Ongoing political unrest in Thailand's southern provinces and the threat of terrorism have made travelling from Thailand more dangerous. Visitors are strongly advised against venturing to checkpoints in the provinces of Pattani,

6

Yala and Narathiwat on the Thai–Malaysia border, which lead down the east coast to Kota Bharu. However, the province of Songkhla and the city and transport hub of **Hat Yai** are considered safer, including travelling by rail from Hat Yai (and Bangkok) to Butterworth via Padang Besar. If you plan on taking any of these routes, check official advice, such as that of the Foreign & Commonwealth Office (W fco.gov.uk), and ask locals before going. The safest routes are those from **Satun** and **Ko Lipe** (see box, p.826). From Satun, there is local transport to Kuala Perlis and Pulau Langkawi or Alor Setar, and the ferry from Koh Lipe to Pulau Langkawi is a relatively straightforward route.

VISAS

Citizens of the UK, the US, Australia, New Zealand, Ireland, Canada and most other European countries do not need a **visa** for stays of up to three months in Malaysia. To **extend your visa**, go to a local immigration department office or simply cross into Singapore (or Thailand) and back, but be prepared to show proof of onward travel. Two-month extensions are possible. Citizens of Israel are forbidden to enter Malaysia.

Tourists travelling from the Peninsula to Sarawak and Sabah must be cleared again by immigration and can remain as long as their original three-month stamp is valid; immigration offices in Kuching and Kota Kinabalu can grant one-month extensions.

GETTING AROUND

Public **transport** in Malaysia is very reliable and relatively inexpensive. On the peninsula, buses and the new **ETS trains** (Electric Train Service) connecting the Thai border to Johor Bahru make travelling between major cities a breeze. Most towns in Sarawak (and all towns in Sabah) are connected by road, though to reach the interior you'll have to travel by boat, and while the more out-of-the-way destinations are reachable by rough dirt roads, flying is a far better option, as it's inexpensive. Malaysia, Singapore, Brunei, Sabah and Sarawak are connected by a network of **budget flights** that, if booked well in advance, can work out as cheap as bussing it.

BY BUS

Interstate destinations are covered by comfortable, air-conditioned **express buses**, operated either by the government's Transnasional (W ktb.com.my), or by state or private bus companies; each company has an office at the bus station and prices are very competitive. In many larger cities, long-distance bus terminals tend to be inconveniently located outside city centres, but are connected to a central (local) bus station by a shuttle bus. You can check schedules and buy bus tickets online using a credit card on Catch That Bus (W catchthatbus.com) and Easybook (W easybook.com).

Buses for long-distance routes (over 3hr) typically leave in clusters in the early morning and late evening, while shorter routes are served throughout the day. In most cases, you can just turn up, though on popular routes like KL to Penang (4hr 30min), overnight buses from KK to Semporna, or during public and school holidays, reserve ahead. **Local buses** usually operate from a separate station, serve routes within the state and are cheaper, but also slower, less comfortable and without air-conditioning – except for the Rapid services in KL and Penang (W myrapid.com.my) and Perak Transit (W peraktransit.com.my); buy your ticket on the bus.

Numerous buses run across Sabah, but they're outnumbered by the slightly faster **minibuses** that leave, when full, from the same terminals. Buses in Sarawak ply the trans-state coastal road between Kuching and Kota Kinabalu via Brunei, linked to the two states by convenient direct buses.

Many guesthouses in Peninsular Malaysia offer convenient but more expensive minibus transfers to popular destinations, such as Taman Negara, the Cameron Highlands, and the Perhentian Islands jetty; such transfers also exist between Miri and Brunei and Sandakan and Sukau.

BY TRAIN

The Peninsula's **train** service, operated by Keretapi Tanah Melayu (KTM; ⓦwww .ktmb.com.my), now runs with high-speed electric trains (ETS) – with the exception of the Johor Bahru–Gemas section, which will be completed in 2020. Travelling from KL to the Thai border at Padang Besar now takes only six hours – consequently, there are no more overnight sleeper services. The new ETS trains are very convenient to travel along the west coast, but destinations in the interior are served absurdly early in the morning or late at night. Regardless, they still offer some spectacular scenic views and are the best way to travel in the Peninsula's interior.

There are only **two main lines** through Peninsular Malaysia: one running up from Johor Bahru along the west coast via KL, Ipoh, Tapah Road (for the Cameron Highlands) and Butterworth to Padang Besar, connecting with Thai Railways which then continue to Hat Yai and north to Bangkok. You may have to change trains in KL before continuing up north. The second train line splits off between KL and Johor Bahru at Gemas, 58km northeast of Malacca, running north through the mountainous interior covered in lush vegetation – a section known as the **Jungle Railway** – via Kuala Lipis and skirting Kota Bharu to the northeastern border town of Tumpat. East Malaysia's only rail line is the bone-shaking 55km link between Kota Kinabalu and Tenom in Sabah.

The new **ETS trains** (Electric Train Service) travel up to 140km/hr and have comfortable air-conditioned seats. There are Platinum, Gold and Silver services: Platinum and Gold trains only stop at main stations, while the cheapest Silver services stop at all stations en route. Tickets can be booked at ⓦwww.ktmb .com.my or ⓦeasybook.com.

Malaysian trains no longer travel across the border to Singapore's Woodlands station. If travelling north from Singapore, you can catch the infrequent shuttle train from Woodlands to Johor Bahru Sentral, or one of the direct buses leaving from the Kranji and Woodlands MRT stations.

BY FERRY AND BOAT

Boats sail to all the major islands off Malaysia's coasts, but during the monsoon (Nov–Feb), east-coast services are almost nonexistent. West-coast islands such as Penang and Langkawi are served by passenger/car ferries; reaching the Perhentian Islands requires a bumpy speedboat ride.

In **Sarawak**, regular turbo-charged "flying coffin" express boats ply the mighty Rejang and Baram rivers.

On the smaller tributaries, or during dry season, travel is by **longboat**, which you may have to charter. This mode of travel can get very expensive, as diesel prices multiply alarmingly the further into the interior you travel. Many inland destinations are becoming reachable by 4WD and truck along rough logging tracks, though it's slower and pricier than going by river. **Sabah** has no internal boat transport, but there are ferries **to Brunei** from Labuan island, and **to Indonesia** from Tawau to Nunukan and Tarakan – an alternative to the MASwings' flight.

BY PLANE

The cheapest airline with the most domestic flight routes is **AirAsia** (ⓦairasia .com). Flights are quick and efficient – it is just 55 minutes from KL to Langkawi as opposed to an eleven-hour bus and ferry journey. Other airlines with domestic and Southeast Asian flights include: Malaysia Airlines (ⓦmalaysiaairlines.com); Malindo Airlines (ⓦmalindoair.com), a good alternative to AirAsia; Firefly (ⓦfireflyz .com.my), a budget subsidiary of Malaysia Airlines with flights to Alor Star, Langkawi, Kota Bharu, Kuala Terengganu, Johor Bahru, Ipoh, Penang and Singapore; Silk Air (ⓦsilkair.com), which connects to Singapore; and charter SAS Air (ⓦsassb.com.my), who operates flights to Pulau Tioman and Pulau Pangkor from KL's Subang Skypark.

Flights to East Malaysia operate mainly out of Kuala Lumpur, with Penang and Johor Bahru providing additional services to Kuching, Miri and Kota Kinabalu. Within Sarawak and Sabah, MASwings (ⓦmaswings.com.my) is a subsidiary of

6

Malaysia Airlines, serving Kuching, Miri, Bintulu, KK, Sandakan, Sibu, Bario, Tawau, Lahad Datu and more. AirAsia also flies to all of these destinations, barring Bario, which is only reachable by small aircraft.

VEHICLE RENTAL

Malaysia's main roads tend to be in good condition, though many drivers rarely give way or signal and sometimes don't obey traffic lights or signs. Drivers flash their headlights when they are claiming the right of way, *not* the other way around.

Malaysians drive on the left, and wearing seat belts in the front is compulsory. To rent a vehicle, you must be 23 or over and have held a clean international driving licence for at least a year. Avis, Budget, Hertz and National have offices in major towns and at the airports; **rates** start at RM170 per day or RM800/week. **Motorbike and scooter rental** is offered by guesthouses and shops in touristy areas (around RM30/day). You may need to leave a deposit, but it's unlikely you'll have to show any proof of eligibility – officially, you must be over 21 and have an appropriate driving licence. Wearing helmets is compulsory. **Bicycles** can be rented for about RM10/day.

ACCOMMODATION

Malaysia offers inexpensive **accommodation** to suit all budgets. Besides high season and low season prices, many lodgings have three tariffs: weekday, weekend and holiday, the former being the cheapest and the last the most expensive. Many places offer special deals, particularly in the off-season. Fans of colonial-era architecture will find an abundance of mid-range options with all the amenities but without the shockingly high tariffs.

Room rates rise dramatically during the major holiday periods – Christmas, Easter, Chinese New Year and Hari Raya Haji – but as a general rule it's always worth bargaining.

The mainstays of the travellers' scene in Malaysia are **guesthouses**, located in popular tourist areas. They can range

from simple beachside A-frame huts and chalets to modern multistorey apartment buildings. Most offer dormitory beds (from RM20) and basic double rooms (from RM50, depending on area). At the budget end of the market, you're likely to get a choice of rooms; the cheaper ones will be fan-equipped and share bathrooms, whereas the pricier ones will be en suite with air-conditioning.

The larger, more popular city destinations such as KL and George Town in Penang have international-standard **youth hostels** with all the amenities that globetrotters on a budget have come to expect: clean dorms with lockers and air-conditioning, free wi-fi and a plethora of tours. The most atmospheric accommodation in Malaysia is in stilted **longhouses**, found on the rivers of Sarawak and Sabah. These can house dozens of families, and usually consist of three elevated sections reached by a simple ladder. The snag is that it's difficult to stay in them as an independent traveller as you need to have contacts within the community, but it is possible to stay at longhouses as part of an organized tour or with the help of a local guide.

Electricity in Malaysia is supplied at 220 volts, and plugs have three prongs like British ones.

FOOD AND DRINK

The **cuisine** in Peninsular Malaysia is inspired by the three main communities: Malay, Chinese and Indian. In Borneo, you'll also find many delicious indigenous dishes. Food everywhere is remarkably good value – basic noodle or rice-based meals at a street stall can be bought from around RM5, and a full meal with drinks in a decent restaurant will seldom cost more than RM50 a head. Food hygiene standards are generally quite high; if you're eating from street stalls, it's best to go for the ones with the most customers.

THE CUISINES

Malay cuisine is based on rice, often enriched with *santan* (coconut milk), which is served with a dazzling variety of curries, vegetable stir-fries and sambals, a condiment of chillies and *belacan* (shrimp paste).

The most famous dish is satay – which comprises skewers of barbecued meat dipped in spicy peanut sauce. The classic way to sample Malay curries is to eat *nasi campur*, a buffet (usually served at lunchtime) of steamed rice – supplemented by up to two dozen accompanying dishes, including *lembu* (beef), *kangkong* (greens), fried chicken, fish steaks and curry sauce, and various vegetables. Another popular dish is *nasi goreng* (mixed fried rice with meat, seafood and vegetables). For breakfast, the most popular dishes are *nasi lemak* – rice cooked in coconut milk and served with *sambal ikan bilis* (tiny fried anchovies in hot chilli paste).

In **Sabah**, there's the Murut speciality of *jaruk* – raw wild boar fermented in a bamboo tube (other meats cooked in bamboo tubes are also delicious), and also *hinava*, raw fish pickled in lime juice. Indonesian and Filipino influences are present in places with large immigrant populations, which only enhances the local cuisine. In **Sarawak**, Iban cuisine features many pork dishes, wild boar, *midin* – a curly, crunchy jungle fern commonly found in restaurants (known as "Sabah vegetable" in Sabah) – and sticky rice. A particular favourite in Kuching is bamboo clams – small, pencil-shaped, slivery delicacies that only grow in the wild in mangrove-dense riverine locations.

Typical **Nyonya dishes** (the distinctive fusion cuisine formed by the descendants of Chinese and Malay intermarriage) incorporate elements from Chinese, Malay and Indonesian cooking. Chicken, fish and seafood form the backbone of the cuisine, and, unlike Malay food, pork is used. Noodles (*mee*) flavoured with chillies, and rich curries made from rice flour and coconut cream, are common. A popular breakfast dish is *laksa*, noodles in spicy coconut soup served with seafood and bean sprouts, lemon grass, pineapple, pepper, lime leaves and chilli. Other popular Nyonya dishes include *ayam buah keluak*, chicken cooked with

Indonesian "black" nuts; and *otak-otak*, fish mashed with coconut milk and chilli and steamed in a banana leaf.

Chinese food dominates in Malaysia – fish and seafood is nearly always outstanding, with prawns, crab, squid and a variety of fish on offer almost everywhere. Noodles, too, are ubiquitous, and come in wonderful variations – thin, flat, round, served in soup (wet) or fried (dry). Particular favourites include *hokkien mee*: fat white noodles with *tempe* (a cheese-like food made of the soy residue from tofu-making) in a rich soy sauce, and *kuey teow goreng*, flat rice noodles fried with chicken or seafood and local greens. *Dim sum* make a regular appearance, as does **steamboat**, with thinly sliced meat, fish and vegetables cooked to the desired consistency in a bubbling pot in the middle of the table, with titbits then dunked in soy and chilli sauce.

North Indian food tends to rely more on meat, especially mutton and chicken, and breads – *naan*, *chapatis*, *parathas* and *rotis* – rather than rice. A favourite breakfast is *roti canai* (delicious flaky flat bread) and *dhal*. **Southern Indian food** tends to be spicier and more reliant on vegetables. Its staple is the *dosa* (rice-flour pancake), often served at breakfast as a *masala dosa*, stuffed with onions, vegetables and chutney. Indian Muslims serve *murtabak*, a grilled *roti* stuffed with egg and minced meat. Many South Indian cafés serve *daun pisang* at lunchtime, usually a vegetarian meal where rice is served on banana leaves with vegetable curries.

As for **desserts**, try *ais kacang*, shaved ice with fruit syrup, and often served with sweet red beans and condensed milk. It's deliciously refreshing, particularly in the heat.

WHERE TO EAT

The cheapest places to eat are the ubiquitous **hawker stalls**, often found on the roadside or in hawker centres, and serving standard Malay noodle and rice dishes, satay, Indian fast food such as *roti canai*, plus regional delicacies. Most are scrupulously clean, and the food is cooked in front of you. Some hawker stalls don't have menus and you don't have to sit close

6

6

to the stall you're patronizing: find a free table, and the vendor will track you down when your food is ready. You may find that the meal should be paid for when it reaches your table, but the usual form is to pay when you're finished. Most outdoor stalls open at around 11am and often stay open late – the early ones close around 10pm, while some continue until 2 or 3am.

There are few streets without a *kedai kopi*, a **coffee house** or **café**, usually run by Chinese or Indians. Most open at 7am

or 8am; closing times vary from 6pm to midnight. These places offer more than coffee; basic Chinese coffee houses serve noodle and rice dishes all day, as well as cakes. The culinary standard might not be very high, but a filling one-plate meal only costs a couple of dollars.

Inexpensive **restaurants** are found in all cities. Many offer cheap lunchtime deals. In larger cities – and particularly in Kuala Lumpur – you can find excellent Thai, Italian and other international food.

PEOPLES OF MALAYSIA

With a pivotal position on the maritime trade routes between the Middle East, India and China, Malaysia has always attracted immigration. The region also had many **indigenous tribes**, *Orang Asli* ("the first people"). On the Peninsula, the Malays form just over fifty percent of the population, the Chinese nearly 38 percent, Indians ten percent and the Orang Asli around one percent; in Sarawak and Sabah, the indigenous tribes account for around fifty percent of the population, the Chinese 28 percent, with the other 22 percent divided among Malays, Indians and Eurasians. Although many of Malaysia's ethnic groups are now nominally Christian or Muslim, many of their old **animist** beliefs and ceremonies still survive.

THE MALAYS

The **Malays** first moved to the west coast of the Malaysian Peninsula from Sumatra in early times, but the growth in power of the Malay sultanates from the fifteenth century onwards – coinciding with the arrival of Islam – established Malays as a significant force. They developed an aristocratic tradition, courtly rituals and a social hierarchy that still has an influence today. The main contemporary change for Malays in Malaysia was the introduction after independence of the *bumiputra* policy, which was designed to make it easier for the Malays, the Orang Asli of the Peninsula and other indigenous groups to compete in economic and educational fields against the high-achieving Chinese and Indians. Malays now hold most of the top positions in government and in state companies.

THE CHINESE AND STRAITS CHINESE

The first significant **Chinese** community established itself in Malacca in the fifteenth century. However, the ancestors of the majority of Chinese now living in Peninsular Malaysia emigrated from southern China in the nineteenth century to work in the tin-mining industry. In Sarawak and Sabah, the Chinese played an important part in opening up the interior. Chinatowns developed throughout the region, and Chinese traditions became an integral part of a wider Malayan culture. The Malaysian Chinese are well represented in parliament. One of the few examples of regional intermarrying is displayed in the Peranakan or "Straits-born Chinese" heritage of Malacca and Penang. When male Chinese immigrants married local Malay women, their male offspring were termed "Baba" and the females "Nyonya" (or Nonya).
Baba-Nyonya society adapted elements from both cultures: the descendants of these sixteenth-century liaisons have a unique culinary and architectural style.

THE INDIANS

The first large wave of **Tamil** labourers arrived in the nineteenth century. But an embryonic entrepreneurial class from **North India** soon followed and set up businesses in Penang. Although Indians comprise only ten percent of Malaysia's population, their impact is felt everywhere.

THE ORANG ASLI

The **Orang Asli** are the indigenous peoples of Peninsular Malaysia, thought to have migrated here around fifty thousand years ago. They mostly belong to three distinct groups,

DRINKING

Tap water is said to be safe to drink in Malaysia, though it's wise to stick to bottled water. Using ice for drinks is generally fine. In city centres, look out for the sweetened soy milk, coconut milk and sugar-cane juice touted on street corners.

Malays are big **tea** and **coffee** drinkers; tea is locally grown in the Cameron Highlands, while most of the coffee comes from Indonesia. Coffee tends to be strong and sweetened with condensed milk (as does tea), but you can specify *kurang manis* (less sugar), *tanpa gula* (without sugar) or *kopi kosong* (black, no sugar). Black tea/coffee is *teh/kopi o kosong*.

Drinking alcohol is only outlawed in certain places on the east coast of the Malaysian Peninsula, but there are numerous places where the sale and consumption of alcohol are frowned upon. Elsewhere, alcohol is available in

6

of which there are various tribes. Though most tribes retain some cultural traditions, government drives have encouraged many tribespeople to integrate. The largest group is the **Senoi** (with a population of 40,000), who live in the forested interior of Perak, Pahang and Kelantan states and are divided into two main tribes, the Semiar and the Temiar. They follow animist customs and practise shifting cultivation. The dark-skinned **Semang** (or Negritos; pop. 2000) live in the **northern** areas of the Peninsula and share a traditional nomadic, hunter-gatherer culture. The so-called **Aboriginal Malays** live south of the Kuala Lumpur–Kuantan road.

SARAWAK'S PEOPLES

Nearly fifty percent of **Sarawak's population** is made up of various indigenous Dayak and Orang Ulu groups – including the Iban, Bidayuh, Kayan, Kenyah, Kelabit and Penan tribes, many of whom live in longhouses and maintain a rich cultural legacy. The **Iban**, a stocky, rugged people, make up nearly one-third of Sarawak's population. Iban longhouse communities are found in the Batang Ai river system in the southwest, and along the Rajang, Katibas and Baleh rivers. These communities are quite accessible, their inhabitants always hospitable and keen to show off their traditional dance, music, textile-weaving, blow-piping, fishing and game-playing. In their time, the Iban were infamous head-hunters, but this tradition has been replaced by that of *berjelai*, or "journey", whereby a young man leaves the community to prove himself in the outside world – returning to his longhouse with television sets, generators and outboard motors, rather than heads. The Iban are also famous for their intricate tattoos, each signifying a particular achievement in an individual's life. The southernmost of Sarawak's indigenous groups are the **Bidayuh**, who traditionally lived away from the rivers, building their longhouses on the sides of hills. Most of the other groups in Sarawak are classed as **Orang Ulu** (people of the interior). They inhabit the more remote inland areas, on the upper Rajang, Balui, Baram and Linau rivers, and their most striking features are the elongated earlobes, achieved by wearing exceptionally weighty earrings – a privilege granted only to prominent members of the community. The most numerous, the **Kayan** and the **Kenyah**, are longhouse-dwellers, animists and shifting cultivators. The **Kelabit** live in longhouses on the highland plateau that separates north Sarawak from Kalimantan, and are Christian. The nomadic **Penan** live in the upper Rajang and Limbang areas and rely on hunting and gathering, though the number of true nomads has decreased to a few hundred with government pressure on them to settle.

SABAH'S PEOPLES

The **Dusun**, or Kadazan/Dusun, account for around a third of Sabah's population. Traditionally agriculturists, they inhabit the western coastal plains and the interior. Although most Dusun are now Christians, remnants of their animist past are still evident. The mainly Muslim **Bajau** tribe drifted over from the southern Philippines some two hundred years ago, and now constitute ten percent of Sabah's population, living in the northwest. They are agriculturists and fishermen, noted for their horsemanship and their rearing of buffalo. The **Murut** inhabit the area between Keningau and the Sarawak border, in the southwest.

6

bars, restaurants, Chinese *kedai kopi*, supermarkets and sometimes at hawkers' stalls. Anchor and Tiger **beer** (lager) are locally produced and are probably the best choices. **Wine** is becoming more common and competitively priced, too. Sarawak and Sabah offer their own lethal tipple in the form of *tuak* (fermented rice wine); the young, milky wine isn't particularly strong, but the clear, overproof stuff packs a punch.

There is a thriving bar scene in KL, Penang, Langkawi, Kuching and Kota Kinabalu; less so in other towns. Fierce competition keeps happy hours a regular feature (usually 5–7pm), bringing beer down to around RM5 a glass. Some bars open all day (11am–11pm), but many double as clubs, opening in the evenings until 2 or 3am.

CULTURE AND ETIQUETTE

The Malays like to please and in general are likely to be some of the friendliest and most helpful people you'll come across. The flipside, however, can be that they don't necessarily furnish you with negative information.

The vast majority of Malaysians are Muslims, but there are also significant numbers of Hindus, Buddhists, Confucianists and animists (see p.41) among the population.

Islam in Malaysia today is relatively liberal. Although most Muslim women don headscarves, few wear a veil, and some taboos, like not drinking alcohol, are ignored by a growing number of Malays. There are stricter, more fundamentalist Muslims – in Kelantan the local government is dominated by them – and there's a constant push for replacing state law with sharia law in that province, but in general, Islam here has a moderate and modern outlook. There are hints of other religions within Malaysian tradition as well – the traditional Malay wedding ceremony, for example, has clear **Hindu** influences, and talking to people about their day-to-day beliefs and superstitions often suggests the influence of **Chinese animistic religions**. Just like the cultures, religions tend to overlap

fairly easily in Malaysia. That said, visitors belonging to the Jewish faith would be best advised not to advertise that fact, as anti-Semitism is widespread.

Malaysia shares the same attitudes to dress and social taboos as other Southeast Asian cultures (see p.40).

SPORTS AND OUTDOOR ACTIVITIES

The varied terrain of Malaysia means activities such as **cycling** and **horseriding** are possible across the country. Cycling in towns isn't all that advisable as traffic is fairly unpredictable, but in more regional areas it's a great way to explore. On the islands, **kayaking** is also a great way to go from cove to cove, and kayak rental is usually available from guesthouses for RM15–20 per day.

SNORKELLING AND DIVING

The crystal-clear waters of Malaysia and its abundance of tropical fish and coral make **snorkelling and diving** a must for any underwater enthusiast. This is particularly true of East Sabah's islands, which include Sipadan and Mabul, and the Peninsula's east-coast islands of Perhentian, Kapas and Tioman. Pulau Tioman offers the most choice for schools and dive sites, while the Perhentians offer superb snorkelling, with frequent turtle and shark sightings. Make sure that the dive operator you go with is registered with PADI (Professional Association of Diving Instructors) or equivalent; dive courses cost from around RM1200 for a four-day PADI Open Water course to RM2200 for a Divemaster course. If you're already certified, it's possible to rent all the necessary equipment for a day's worth of diving for RM100–120.

TREKKING

If **trekking** either on the Malaysian Peninsula or in Sarawak and Sabah, you should be prepared for heat, humidity and leeches; also, trails and rivers become much more difficult to negotiate when it rains. That said, although the rainy season (Nov–Feb) undoubtedly slows your progress on some of the trails, conditions are less humid and the parks and adventure tours not oversubscribed. Most visitors trek in the large **national parks** to experience the remaining primary jungle and rainforest at first hand. For these, you often need to be accompanied by a guide, which can either be arranged through tour operators in KL, Kuching, Miri and Kota Kinabalu, or at the parks themselves. For less experienced trekkers, the Cameron Highlands (see p.438) and Taman Negara National Park (see p.456) are probably the best places to start, while Sarawak's Gunung Mulu National Park (see p.497) offers sufficient challenges for most tastes. Few people who make it across to Sabah forego the chance of climbing **Mount Kinabalu** (see p.499).

COMMUNICATIONS

Most hostels, hotels and guesthouses offer free **wi-fi**, mostly for free, and **Internet cafés** are plentiful. By far the easiest and cheapest way to call home is by using **Skype**. Local pre-paid SIM cards cost around RM20 and include at least RM10 of credit; DiGi, Maxis and Celcom networks offer the widest coverage (Celcom is best for Borneo) and inexpensive international calls, and all have affordable data plans. Tune Talk has the cheapest 100MB weekly data package (RM2). Telecom Malaysia (TM) iTalk cards can be used to make international calls on your mobile.

To call **abroad** from Malaysia, dial ⊙00 + IDD country code + area code minus first 0 + subscriber number.

Malaysia's **postal service** is inexpensive and generally reliable; postcards to

MALAYSIA ONLINE
ⓦ **backpackingmalaysia.com** Updated knowledge-base for budget travel in Malaysia and Singapore
ⓦ **expatgo.com** KL-based blog covering Malaysian travel and nightlife
ⓦ **malaysia.my** Tourism Malaysia-sponsored blog focused on local food, nature, culture and arts
ⓦ **malaysiakini.com** The country's longest-running independent news portal.

EMERGENCY NUMBERS
Fire Brigade ⊙**994**
Police/Ambulance ⊙**999**

Europe and the US take ten to fourteen days. Packages are expensive to send, with surface/sea mail taking two months to Europe, longer to the US.

CRIME AND SAFETY

The most common crimes are perpetrated by **pickpockets** and snatch thieves on motorbikes, who grab handbags. Watch your bag in most cities, especially in KL, as motorbike theft is a common occurrence there. **Theft** from dormitories by other tourists is also a relatively common complaint. In the more remote parts of Sarawak or Sabah there is little crime.

If you do need to report a crime in Malaysia, head for the nearest **police station**, where there'll be someone who speaks English – you'll need a copy of the police report for insurance purposes. **Violent crime** against tourists is rare but muggings do occasionally happen after hours in Kuala Lumpur, Penang and in run-down neighbourhoods in general.

Women travelling alone can expect a certain amount of male attention, particularly on the more conservative east coast of Malaysia, so dressing modestly and treating overly friendly strangers with caution is a must.

The penalty for **drug trafficking** is death – foreigners have been executed in the past – and even carrying a small amount on you will earn you a lengthy prison sentence and a caning.

MEDICAL CARE AND EMERGENCIES

Levels of hygiene and **medical care** in Malaysia's larger cities are higher than in much of the rest of Southeast Asia; staff almost everywhere speak good English and use up-to-date techniques. There's always a well-stocked pharmacy in main towns. Oral contraceptives and condoms are sold over the counter, but you won't

6

6

BAHASA MALAYSIA

Although you'll be able to get by with English in all but the most remote areas, the national language of Malaysia, **Bahasa Malaysia**, is simple enough to learn. Nouns have no genders and don't require an article, while the plural form is constructed just by saying the word twice; thus "child" is *anak*, while "children" is *anak anak*. Doubling a word can also indicate "doing"; for example, *jalan jalan* is used to mean "walking". Verbs have no tenses either, so you qualify the verb by saying when you did something. Sentence order is the same as in English, though adjectives usually follow the noun.

PRONUNCIATION

The **pronunciation** of Bahasa Malaysia is broadly the same as the English reading of Roman script, with a few exceptions:

a as in c**u**p
c as in **ch**eap
e as in **e**nd
g as in **g**irl
i as in bout**i**que
j as in **j**oy
k hard, as in English, except at the end of

the word, when you should stop just short of pronouncing it.
o as in g**o**t
u as in b**oo**t
ai as in f**i**ne
au as in h**ow**
sy as in **sh**ut

GREETINGS AND BASIC PHRASES

Selamat is the all-purpose greeting derived from Arabic, which communicates general goodwill.

Good morning	*Selamat pagi*	Bus stop	*Perhentian bas*
Good afternoon	*Selamat petang*	Train station	*Stesen keratapi*
Good evening	*Selamat malam*	Bus station	*Stesen bas*
Goodnight	*Selamat tidur*	Airport	*Lapangan*
Goodbye	*Selamat jalan*		*terbang*
Welcome	*Selamat datang*	Hotel	*Hotel*
Bon appetit	*Selamat makan*	Post office	*Pejabat pos*
Please	*Sila/Tolong*	Restaurant	*Restoran*
Thank you	*Terima kasih*	Shop	*Kedai*
You're welcome	*Sama sama*	Market	*Pasar*
Sorry/excuse me	*Maaf*	Taxi	*Teksi*
Yes	*Ya*	How much is …?	*Berapa harga …?*
No	*Tidak*	Cheap/expensive	*Murah/mahal*
Do you speak English?	*Boleh bercakap*	Good	*Bagus*
	bahasa Inggeris?	Closed	*Tutup*
I don't understand	*Saya tidak*	Ill/sick	*Sakit*
	mengerti	Toilet	*Tandas*
Can you help me, please?	*Bolekah anda*	Water	*Air*
	bantu saya?	Food	*Makanan*
Where is the …?	*Di manakah …?*	Drink	*Minum*

NUMBERS

0	*Kosong*	11, 12, 13, etc	*Sebelas, duabelas,*
1	*Satu*		*tigabelas*
2	*Dua*	20	*Dua-puluh*
3	*Tiga*	21, 22, etc	*Dua-puluh satu,*
4	*Empat*		*dua-puluh dua*
5	*Lima*	30, 40, 50, etc	*Tiga-puluh,*
6	*Enam*		*empat-puluh,*
7	*Tujuh*		*lima-puluh*
8	*Lapan*	100, 200, 300, etc	*Seratus, dua ratus,*
9	*Sembilan*		*tiga ratus*
10	*Sepuluh*	1000	*Seribu*

FOOD AND DRINK GLOSSARY

menu	menu
sejuk	cold
panas	hot (temperature)
pedas	hot (spicy)
saya vegetarian	I am a vegetarian
saya tak makan daging atau ikan	I don't eat meat or fish

Noodles (mee) and noodle dishes

bee hoon	thin rice noodles
char kuey teow	flat rice noodles with prawns, sausage, fishcake, egg, vegetables or chilli
foochow noodles	steamed and served in soy and oyster sauce
hokkien fried mee	yellow noodles fried with pork, prawn and vegetables
kuey teow	flat rice noodles
laksa	noodles, bean sprouts, fishcakes and prawns in a spicy coconut broth
mee	round yellow wheat-flour noodles
mee goreng	spicy fried noodles
mee suah	noodles served dry and crispy
wan ton mee	roast pork, noodles and vegetable soup with dumplings

Rice (nasi) dishes

claypot	rice topped with meat, cooked in an earthenware pot over a fire
daun pisang	banana-leaf curry
nasi campur	rice served with several meat, fish and vegetable dishes
nasi goreng	fried rice with diced meat and veg
nasi putih	plain boiled rice

Meat, fish and basics

ayam	chicken
khinzir	pork
daging	beef
garam	salt
lada hitam	black pepper
gula	sugar
ikan	fish
kambing	mutton
ketam	crab
sup	soup
tahu	tofu (beancurd)
telur	egg
udang	prawn
sotong	squid

Desserts

ais kacang	shaved ice with red beans, rose syrup and evaporated milk
bubor cha cha	sweetened coconut milk with pieces of sweet potato, yam and tapioca balls
cendol	coconut milk, palm syrup and pea-flour noodles poured over shaved ice

Drinks (minum)

air minum	water
bir	beer
jus	fruit juice
kopi	coffee with condensed milk
kopi-o	black coffee
kopi susu/kopi c	coffee with milk
lassi	sweet or sour yoghurt
teh	tea
teh susu	tea with milk
teh tarik	sweet, frothy, milky tea

6

6

find tampons in rural areas, so bring your own. Opening hours are usually Monday to Saturday 9.30am to 7pm; pharmacies in shopping malls stay open later. **Private clinics** are found even in the smallest towns; a visit costs around RM30, excluding medication. The **emergency department** of each town's general hospital will see foreigners for about RM60, and costs rise rapidly if continued treatment or overnight stays are necessary.

Recommended **vaccinations** for Malaysia include hepatitis A, rabies, tetanus and diphtheria; malarial prophylactics are generally not needed anywhere in the country.

INFORMATION AND MAPS

Tourism Malaysia (ⓦtourism.gov.my) operates a **tourist office** in most major towns, but it's not that useful for areas off the beaten track. Their website, however, is a good source of information. Locally run **visitor centres**, found in most major towns, are more geared up to independent travellers' needs. You can also book permits and accommodation for the **national parks** at these centres.

The best general **maps** of Malaysia are Macmillan's 1:2,000,000 *Malaysia Traveller's Map* and the more detailed Nelles 1:650,000 *West Malaysia* (not including Sabah and Sarawak). The best coverage of Sabah is on maps produced by Nelles. **City maps** can usually be picked up in the visitor centres.

MONEY AND BANKS

Malaysia's unit of **currency** is the ringgit, divided into 100 sen. You'll see the ringgit written as "RM" (as it is throughout this chapter), or simply as "$" (M$), and often hear it called a "dollar". Notes come in RM1, RM5, RM10, RM20, RM50, RM100 denominations; coins are minted in 5 sen, 10 sen, 20 sen, 50 sen denominations. At the time of writing, the **exchange rate** was around RM5.1 to £1, RM4.6 to €1 and around RM4.2 to $1.

Major **credit cards** are accepted in many hotels and large shops, but beware of illegal surcharges. Banks will advance cash against major credit cards. **ATMs** are widespread and use Cirrus, Plus and Maestrobank circuits.

Sterling and US dollar **travellers' cheques** can be cashed at Malaysian banks, licensed moneychangers and some hotels. Licensed moneychangers' kiosks in bigger towns tend to open until around 6pm, and sometimes at weekends. It's not difficult to change money in Sabah or Sarawak, though if travelling by river in the interior or outside the larger cities, you should carry a fair bit of cash in small denominations. If travelling to the islands off the coast of Malaysia, a surplus of cash is a necessity, since most of them don't have banks.

OPENING HOURS AND PUBLIC HOLIDAYS

Shops are open daily 9am to 6pm, and shopping centres 10am to 11pm. **Government office** hours are Monday to Thursday 8am to 12.45pm and 2pm to 4.15pm, Friday 8am to 12.15pm and 2.45pm to 4.15pm, Saturday 8am to 12.45pm; however, in the states of Kedah, Kelantan and Terengganu, on Thursday the hours are 8am to 12.45pm; they're closed on Friday and are open with full working hours on Sunday. **Banking hours** are generally Monday to Friday 10am to 3pm and Saturday 9.30am to 11.30am.

Post offices are open Monday to Saturday 8am to 6pm, while on the east coast they're closed on Fridays but open on Sundays.

PUBLIC HOLIDAYS

The Muslim holidays of Hari Raya Haji, which celebrates the end of the annual Muslim pilgrimage to Mecca, and Hari Raya Puasa, which celebrates the end of the Ramadan fast, change from year to year according to the lunar calendar.

January 1 New Year's Day
January/February Chinese New Year (two days)
January/February Thaipusam (depending on the full moon)
February/March Birthday of the Prophet Muhammed
March/April Maal Hijrah (the Muslim New Year)

April Good Friday (Sarawak and Sabah only)
May Pesta Kaamatan – Harvest festival (Sabah only)
May 1 Labour Day
June 1 & 2 Gawai Dayak – Harvest festival (Sarawak only)
June 4 Yang di-Pertuan Agong's (King's) birthday
August 31 National Day
September 16 Malaysia Day (Sabah only)
September/October Hari Raya Puasa (end of Ramadan; two days)
November Deepavali (the Hindu festival more commonly known as Diwali, the Festival of Light)
December 25 Christmas Day

FESTIVALS

Three religions – Islam, Buddhism and Hinduism – are represented in Malaysia, and they play a vital role in the everyday lives of the population. Some religious festivals are celebrated at home or in the mosque or temple. During Ramadan, Muslims fast during the daytime for a whole month, while other festivals are marked with great spectacle. Most of the festivals change annually according to the lunar calendar. It's also worth attending the few art and music festivals that garner international praise.

Chinese New Year Jan–Feb. Chinese operas and lion and dragon dance troupes perform in the streets. The festival is actually fifteen days long, but in general only the first two and the last are observed with actual events – throughout the rest of the time, a general holiday atmosphere abounds but life continues as normal (though in places with a large Chinese population, many services may shut down).

Thaipusam Jan/Feb. Entranced Hindu penitents carry elaborate *kavadis* – which range from the simplest overhead hauling of a jug of milk, to the carrying of more elaborate (and painful) heavy steel canopies mounted over the shoulders, skewers pierced through the tongue and cheeks, or hooks stuck into the wearer's skin – in honour of Murugan, the god of war (especially at KL's Batu Caves and Penang).

Gawai Dayak June. Sarawak's Iban and Bidayuk people hold extravagant feasts to mark the end of the rice harvest, best experienced at the Iban longhouses on the Ai, Skrang and Lemanak rivers near Kuching (June) and in Bidayuh communities around Bau.

Dragon Boat Festival June/July in Penang, Malacca and Kota Kinabalu, where the traditional dragon boats race.

Rainforest Music Festival July/Aug at the Cultural Village near Kuching, Sarawak. Three-day music and art extravaganza with artists from around the world and an emphasis on the indigenous music of Borneo.

George Town Festival Aug. This month-long arts and culture programme is one of Southeast Asia's most celebrated international arts festivals.

Festival of the Hungry Ghosts Late Aug. Known locally as *Yue Lan*, this is a festival for appeasing both ancestors and homeless spirits, by providing them with essentials such as food and drink. The best festivities are held in Penang.

Navarathiri Sept–Oct. Hindu temples devote nine nights to classical dance and music in honour of the deities, and young girls dress as the goddess Kali.

George Town Literary Festival Nov. On the last weekend of November, this gathering of international writers and readers fills George Town's charming heritage lanes.

Kuala Lumpur and around

Founded in the mid-nineteenth century, **KUALA LUMPUR**, or KL, is a vast modern metropolis, a fast-changing super-city with an impressive mix of architectural styles, the most iconic structures being the twin Petronas Towers, which dwarf most other gleaming skyscrapers. As a mix of cultures, KL manages to combine the best of all worlds, being less frenetic than most Indian cities and friendlier and more laidback than a lot of Chinese ones. With a population of nearly two million, it has undeniable energy, but still manages to retain a relaxed old-world charm – and the inhabitants' warmth is hard to beat. There are certainly enough interesting monuments, galleries, markets and museums to keep visitors busy for a while, and its shopping and dining scenes are second to none.

WHAT TO SEE AND DO

The city centre is quite compact, with the **Colonial District** centred on Merdeka Square; close by, across the river and to the north, **Chinatown** and **Little India** are the two main traditional commercial districts. One of the most prominent (and busiest) of KL's central streets, Jalan Tuanku Abdul Rahman, or **Jalan TAR** as it's often known, runs due north from Merdeka Square for 2km to Chow Kit

6

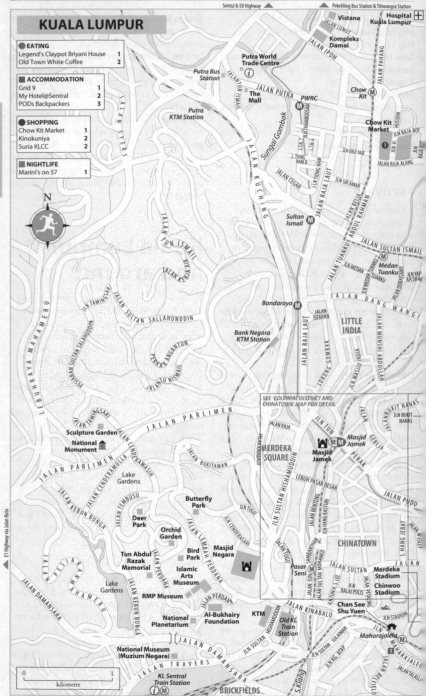

KUALA LUMPUR

● EATING
Legend's Claypot Briyani House	1
Old Town White Coffee	2

■ ACCOMMODATION
Grid 9	1
My Hotel@Sentral	2
PODs Backpackers	3

● SHOPPING
Chow Kit Market	1
Kinokuniya	2
Suria KLCC	2

■ NIGHTLIFE
Marini's on 57	1

N

Sentul & E8 Highway

Pekeliling Bus Station & Titiwangsa Station

Vistana

Hospital Kuala Lumpur

Kompleks Damai

JALAN LUMUT

JALAN IPOH

JALAN PAHANG

Putra World Trade Centre

Putra Bus Station

The Mall

PWRC

Chow Kit

JALAN PUTRA

JALAN UN ISMAIL

Putra KTM Station

JLN TIONG NAM 1

Chow Kit Market

JLN HAJI TAIB

JALAN RAJA ALANG

JALAN CEGAR

Sungai Gombak

JALAN KUCHING

JALAN RAJA LAUT

JALAN TIONG HAM

JLN SIR AMAR

JALAN RAJA ABDUL RAHMAN

Sultan Ismail

JALAN SULTAN ISMAIL

JALAN TUANKU ABDUL RAHMAN

Medan Tuanku

JLN YAP AH SHAK

JALAN DANG WANGI

Bandaraya

JALAN ISFAHAN

LITTLE INDIA

Bank Negara KTM Station

JALAN RAJA LAUT

LOROK GOMBAK

JALAN MUNSHI ABDULLAH

SEE 'COLONIAL DISTRICT AND CHINATOWN' MAP FOR DETAIL

JALAN BUKIT NANAS

JLN BUKIT NANAS

JALAN PARLIMEN

Sculpture Garden

National Monument

JALAN PARLIMEN

JALAN CENDERAWASIH

JALAN RAJA

MERDEKA SQUARE

Masjid Jamek

JALAN GEREJA

PERAK

Masjid Jamek

LEBUH PASAR BESAR

JALAN BENTENG

JLN HANG KASTURI

CHINATOWN

JALAN PUDU

Lake Gardens

JALAN BUKITAMAN

Butterfly Park

JLN TUGU

Deer Park

Orchid Garden

Bird Park

Masjid Negara

JALAN SULTAN

Pasar Seni

Merdeka Stadium

Chinwoo Stadium

Tun Abdul Razak Memorial

Islamic Arts Museum

JALAN PERDANA

Chan See Shu Yuen

RMP Museum

Lake Gardens

KTM

JALAN KINABALU

Old KL Train Station

JLN STADIUM

National Planetarium

Al-Bukhairy Foundation

Maharajalela

National Museum (Muzium Negara)

JALAN DAMANSARA

JALAN TRAVERS

S. Klang

JLN KG. ATAP

0   1
kilometre

KL Sentral Train Station

BRICKFIELDS

2 3 1 2 Bangsar, Midvalley Megamall & E1 Highway via E23

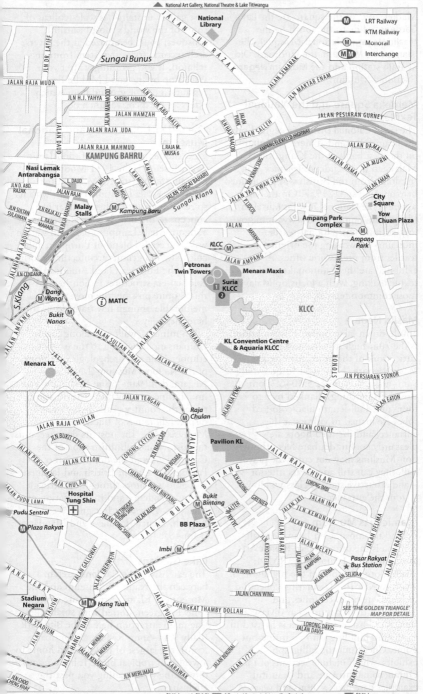

National Art Gallery, National Theatre & Lake Titiwangsa

	LRT Railway
Ⓜ	KTM Railway
Ⓜ	Monorail
ⓂⓂ	Interchange

6

National Library

Sungai Bunus

JALAN TUN RAZAK

JALAN RAJA MUDA

JLN DR. LATIFE

JLN H.J. YAHYA

JLN DATUK ABD. MALIK

SHEIKH AHMAD

JALAN HAMZAH

JALAN RAJA UDA

JALAN DAUD

JALAN RAJA MAHMUD

L.RAJA M. MUSA 6

KAMPUNG BAHRU

JALAN SEMARAK

JLN MAKTAB ENAM

JALAN PESIARAN GURNEY

JALAN DAMAI

JALAN DAMAI

JLN MURNI

JALAN AMAN

JALAN PUNK

JLN HAJI YAACOB

JALAN SALLEH

AMPANG ELEVATED HIGHWAY

Nasi Lemak Antarabangsa

JLN D. ABD. RAZAK

JALAN RAJA

L. DAUD

L.RAMUSA SAID

MUDA MUSA

JALAN SUNGAI BAHARU

L.R.M MUSA 3

Malay Stalls

Ⓜ Kampung Baru

Sungai Klang

JALAN YAP KWAN SENG

VB KWAN SENG

P.UDOCL

City Square

Yow Chuan Plaza

JLN SULTAN SULAIMAN

JLN RAJA ALI

L. RAJA MAHADI

JALAN

MAYANG

Ampang Park Complex

Ⓜ **Ampang Park**

JALAN RAJA ABDULLAH

JLN CENDANA

Dang Wangi Ⓜ

S.Klang

Bukit Nanas Ⓜ

JALAN AMPANG

Ⓜ KLCC

JALAN AMPANG

Petronas Twin Towers

1 **Suria KLCC**
2

Menara Maxis

JALAN BINJAI

JALAN STONOR

KLCC

JALAN AMPANG

ⓘ **MATIC**

JALAN SULTAN ISMAIL

JALAN P. RAMLEE

JALAN PINANG

JALAN PERAK

KL Convention Centre & Aquaria KLCC

JLN PERSIARAN STONOR

Menara KL

JALAN PUNCAK

JALAN TENGAH

Raja Chulan Ⓜ

JALAN KIA PENG

JLN EATON

JALAN RAJA CHULAN

JLN BUKIT CEYLON

LORONG CEYLON

JALAN CONLAY

JALAN PERSIARAN RAJA CHULAN

JALAN CEYLON

JLN NAGASARI

JLN BEDARA

JALAN BERANGAN

Pavilion KL

JALAN RAJA CHULAN

LORONG IMBI

JALAN PUDU LAMA

Hospital Tung Shin ✚

JLN LINGKAR TONG SHIN

JALAN ALOR

CHANGKAT BUKIT BINTANG

JLN GADING

GRENIER

WALTER

JALAN BUKIT BINTANG

Bukit Bintang Ⓜ

JALAN INAI

JLN KEMUNING

JALAN JATI

JALAN UTARA

JALAN MELATI

JALAN DELIMA

Pudu Sentral

Ⓜ **Plaza Rakyat**

JALAN GALLOWAY

JALAN TONG SHIN

BB Plaza

JALAN BARAT

JLN KHIDOTEIKE

JALAN KAMPUNG

JALAN RAWA

Imbi Ⓜ

JALAN HORLEY

JALAN MELUR

JALAN SELATAN

Pasar Rakyat Bus Station ★

JALAN TUN RAZAK

HANG JEBAT

JALAN EBERWEIN

JALAN IMBI

JALAN CHAN WING

JALAN SELATAN

Stadium Negara

ⓂⓂ **Hang Tuah**

JALAN STADIUM

JALAN HANG TUAH

CHANGKAT THAMBY DOLLAH

JALAN PUDU

SEE 'THE GOLDEN TRIANGLE' MAP FOR DETAIL

JLN STADIUM

JLN MERBAU

JLN MERANTI

JALAN KENANGA

JLN CHOO CHENG KHAY

JLN MERLIMAU

JALAN SARAWAK

JALAN BERUNAI

JALAN 1/77C

LORONG DAVIS

JALAN DAVIS

SMART TUNNEL

E2 Highway via E7 & E9 ▼   & Terminal Bersepadu Selatan (Bus Station)   E2 Highway ▼

Market; west of the square are the **Lake Gardens**, while to the south lie the **Masjid Negara** (National Mosque), the **Islamic Arts Museum**, the landmark **Old KL train station** and the **Muzium Negara** (National Museum).

Merdeka Square and the National Textiles Museum

The small **Colonial District** is centred on the beautifully tended **Merdeka Square** on the west bank of the Klang River: Malaysian Independence (*merdeka*, or freedom) from the British was proclaimed here on August 31, 1957. On the same square is the **National Textiles Museum** (daily 9am–6pm; free; ⓦwww.jmm.gov .my/en/museum/national-textiles-museum) showcasing the origins of textiles from prehistoric times. Also exhibited are the traditional techniques of textile making, with a focus on Malaysia's most common textiles.

Masjid Negara

South, down Jalan Sultan Hishamuddin, is the 70m-high minaret and geometric latticework of the unusually angular **Masjid Negara** (National Mosque; daily 9am–noon, 3–4pm & 5.30–6.30pm; closed Fri morning), flanked by a row of fountains. Full-length lilac-coloured robes are loaned to visitors at the entrance, and the tiled floors are pleasantly cool under bare feet. Though non-Muslims may not enter the prayer hall, they can still admire its interior – and attractive stained-glass windows – from the entrance.

Islamic Arts Museum

Behind the mosque on Jalan Lembah Perdana is the ultramodern **Islamic Arts Museum** (daily 10am–6pm; RM14; ⓦiamm.org.my), one of the highlights of a visit to KL. This fascinating collection of Islamic textiles, ceramics and metalwork from countries as diverse as Iran, Kazakhstan and China is housed in a splendid building with an inside-out dome. Check out the calligraphic exhibits, which include sections of the Quran; some intricate and beautiful examples date back a thousand years. A vast gallery upstairs has scale replicas of some of the world's most beautiful mosques; you'll be amazed at the diverse architectural styles that stem from one religion. If you get hungry after your visit, stop by the good Middle Eastern restaurant on the ground floor which offers an inexpensive lunch deal.

The old KL train station and National Museum

One kilometre southeast of the Islamic Arts Museum is the 1911 Moorish-style **KL train station** (the KTM Komuter Railway's Kuala Lumpur station), with its spires, domes and arches. Similar in concept to the British-era train station in Yangon, Kuala Lumpur's old train station was a successful blend of European and culturally indigenous architectural motifs. Of all the European (and American) colonial-era structures in Southeast Asia, this is quite possibly the most memorable, though few trains leave from here these days.

Ten minutes' walk west along Jalan Damansara brings you to the extensive ethnographic and archeological exhibits of the **National Museum** (Muzium Negara; daily 9am–6pm; RM5; ⓦwww .muziumnegara.gov.my). The museum traces the country's early history and displays dioramas of traditional Malaysian life. The upstairs floor recounts the history and administration of the Colonial era and the domination of the Portuguese, Dutch, British and Japanese, and guides visitors through the struggle for independence and the formation of Malaysia. They offer free guided tours in English, French, Japanese and Mandarin (Mon–Sat 10am).

Lake Gardens

The extensive **Lake Gardens** stretch between the National Museum and the Museum of Islamic Art and are a pleasant sprawl of green, dotted with small lakes. The main attraction here is the **Bird Park** (daily 9am–6pm; RM50; ⓦklbirdpark .com), the largest of its kind and home to a wealth of tropical birds. It has a number of walking trails leading you past the enclosures.

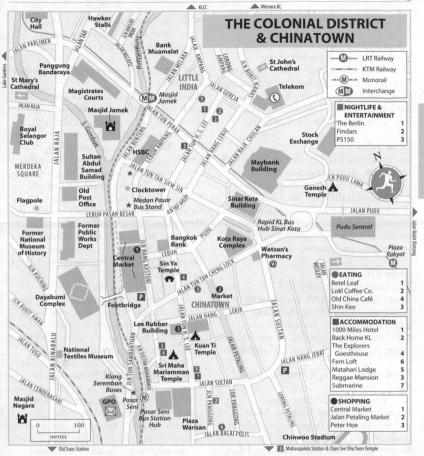

THE COLONIAL DISTRICT & CHINATOWN

NIGHTLIFE & ENTERTAINMENT
The Berlin 1
Findars 2
PS150 3

EATING
Betel Leaf 1
Lokl Coffee Co. 2
Old China Café 4
Shin Kee 3

ACCOMMODATION
1000 Miles Hotel 1
Back Home KL 2
The Explorers
Guesthouse 4
Fern Loft 6
Matahari Lodge 5
Reggae Mansion 3
Submarine 7

SHOPPING
Central Market 1
Jalan Petaling Market 2
Peter Hoe 3

Masjid Jamek

East of Merdeka Square, on a promontory at the confluence of the Klang and Gombak rivers, stands KL's most attractive devotional building, the **Masjid Jamek** (open to visitors outside prayer time; observe conservative dress code, wear long trousers and cover your shoulders and head if female; free). The mosque was completed in 1909, and its pink brick walls, arched colonnades, oval cupolas and squat minarets are inspired by Moghul architecture.

Chinatown

Bordered by **Jalan Tun Perak** to the north and **Jalan Petaling** to the east, **Chinatown**'s narrow lanes are home to the rowdy hubbub of permanent street markets, as well as revealing dilapidated shophouses and Chinese pharmacies. The area's largest temple, **Chan See Shu Yuen**, stands at the far southern end of Jalan Petaling, and displays an ornately painted inner shrine covered in scenes of mythical creatures battling with warriors.

KL's main Hindu place of worship, **Sri Maha Mariamman Temple**, is also located in the heart of Chinatown, on **Jalan Tun H.S. Lee**, between the two main Buddhist temples. Built in 1873, it was radically renovated in the 1960s with a profusion of statues on and around the five-tiered gate tower. On display inside is the silver chariot which makes an annual journey through the street of KL all the way to the Batu Caves during Thaipusam, followed by crowds of the faithful.

Around 100m west of Jalan Tun H.S. Lee lies the **Central Market** (daily 10am–10pm; ⊕centralmarket.com.my). Over a hundred stalls here sell everything from textiles to stationery, fine art to batik clothing and T-shirts, as well as a large array of food on the first floor.

Little India

Just to the north of Chinatown is compact **Little India**, the commercial centre for the city's Indian community. As you turn into Jalan Masjid India from Jalan Tun Perak, it's soon clear that you've entered the Tamil part of the city, with *poori* and *samosa* vendors and cloth salesmen vying for positions on the crowded streets.

Chow Kit

Two kilometres due north of Central Market along Jalan TAR lies **Chow Kit**, a daily market that sells anything and everything. There are excellent hawker stalls here, a great variety of textiles and clothes, as well as fish, meat and vegetables.

The Golden Triangle and Aquaria KLCC

KL's fashionable consumer sector is known as the **Golden Triangle**. Many of the city's expensive hotels, nightclubs and modern malls line the three main boulevards of Jalan Bukit Bintang, Jalan Imbi and Jalan Sultan Ismail, and a visit here is a must.

Apart from some flash shopping and dining in the Golden Triangle's many malls, there's also the impressive **Aquaria KLCC** (daily 10.30am–8pm, last admission 7pm; RM64; ⊕aquariaklcc.com), a state-of-the-art aquarium showcasing more than five thousand denizens of the sea, including sharks, a giant octopus and a touch pool for a closer encounter with rays; it's situated in the Kuala Lumpur Convention Centre on the other side of the KLCC park to the south of the Petronas Twin Towers. Highlights include a moving walkway inside a 90m tunnel, where you can watch sharks and rays swimming around, a hidden shipwreck slowly becoming part of the artificial coral reef, and feeding time, when divers hand-feed sharks, turtles and giant catfish.

The Petronas Towers and the Menara KL Tower

Among the Golden Triangle's main landmarks are the lofty **Petronas Twin Towers**, which, at just over 452m high, were the tallest structures in the world until 2004. They are now the tallest twin structure in the world (quite a few metres shy of the world's tallest building – the 830m-high Burj Khalifa in Dubai) and form part of the **KLCC** (Kuala Lumpur City Centre) development on the northeast of the Golden Triangle. A limited number of tickets are issued daily for the **Skybridge** (170m) connecting the two towers and observation deck (370m) on the 86th floor (Tues–Sun 9am–9pm; last entry 8.15pm; closed 1–2.30pm on Fri; RM85; ⊕petronastwintowers.com.my). It's best to buy tickets online and avoid the first-come-first-served system at the counter in the basement (daily 8.30am–8pm) – queues are long.

Though 69m shorter than the Petronas Towers, the **Menara KL Tower** offers an observation deck (daily 9am–9.30pm; RM52; ⊕menarakl.com.my) at 276m, giving you a great overview of the city; sunset is the best time to visit. The tower is situated to the west of the Petronas Towers, on the other side of Jalan Sultan Ismail.

ARRIVAL AND DEPARTURE

BY PLANE

Kuala Lumpur International Airport (KLIA), the hub for international flights and domestic flights with Malaysia Airlines, is 70km southwest of the centre. The fastest and most efficient way into the city is by KLIA express trains (every 15–20min; 30min; RM55), which terminate at Kuala Lumpur's transportation hub, KL Sentral station, which conveniently connects with LRT and Monorail lines. If you want to halve your fare, take the train (20min) to Putrajaya and then buy a separate ticket to KL Sentral from there. Domestic and low-cost airlines use the AirAsia-dominated Kuala Lumpur International Airport 2 (KLIA2), 2.2km from KLIA. Skybus and Aerobus Airport coaches (6am–midnight, every 30min; RM10) take roughly 1hr 15min to KL Sentral. KLIA and KLIA2 are connected by a 3min KLIA Express train ride (every 15min; RM2). Express coaches connect KLIA and KLIA2 international airports to

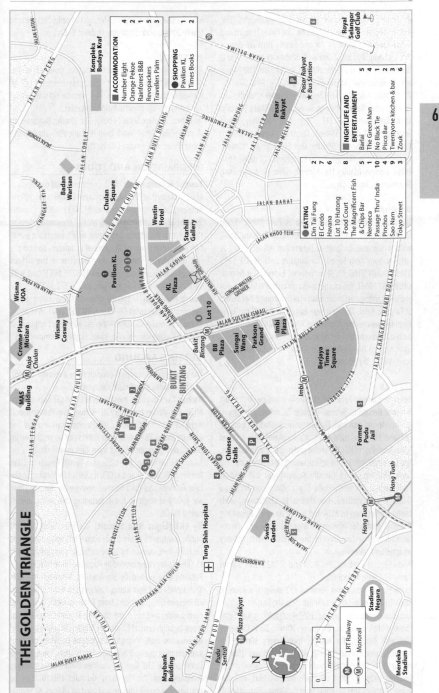

THE GOLDEN TRIANGLE

ACCOMMODATION
Number Eight	4
Orange Pekoe	2
Rainforest B&B	1
Revopackers	5
Travellers Palm	3

SHOPPING
Pavilion KL	1
Times Books	2

NIGHTLIFE AND ENTERTAINMENT
Barfal	5
The Green Man	4
No Black Tie	1
Pisco Bar	2
Twentyone kitchen & bar	3
Zouk	6

EATING
Din Tai Fung	2
El Cerdo	7
Havana	6
Lot 10 Hutong	8
The Magnificent Fish & Chips Bar	5
Neroteca	1
Passage Thru' India	10
Pinchos	4
Sao Nam	9
Tokyo Street	3

Kompleks Budaya Kraf

Royal Selangor Golf Club

Pasar Rakyat Bus Station
Pasar Rakyat

Chulan Square
Westin Hotel
Starhill Gallery
Pavilion KL
KL Plaza
Lot 10
Wisma UOA
Wisma Cosway
Crowne Plaza Mutiara
Raja Chulan
MAS Building
Badan Warisan

BB Plaza
Sungai Wang
Parkson Grand
Imbi Plaza
Bukit Bintang
Berjaya Times Square
Former Pudu Jail
BUKIT BINTANG

Chinese Stalls
Tung Shin Hospital
Swiss Garden
Maybank Building
Pudu Sentral
Plaza Rakyat
Hang Tuah
Stadium Negara
Merdeka Stadium

LRT Railway
Monorail

0   150
metres

N

6

6

KL Sentral station (every 30min, 3am–midnight; 1hr; RM10). Flights with the tiny SAS Air (for Pulau Tioman and Pulau Pangkor), Malindo Air and Firefly Airways depart from Subang Skypark, 24km west of the city centre. Taxi is the quickest option (45min; RM50), or take bus #U81 from outside KL Sentral (hourly, 6am–11pm; 1hr; RM2.50).

Destinations Bandar Seri Begawan, Brunei (2 daily; 2hr 20min); Johor Bahru (4 daily; 50min); Kota Bharu (8 daily; 1hr); Kota Kinabalu (12 daily; 2hr 40min); Kuala Terengganu (3 daily; 55min); Kuantan (4 daily; 40min); Kuching (12 daily; 1hr 50min); Miri (4 daily; 2hr 15min); Penang (hourly; 45min); Pulau Langkawi (11 daily; 1hr); Pulau Tioman (daily; 1hr 15min); Sibu (5 daily; 2hr); Singapore (hourly; 55min).

BY BOAT

The closest port to Kuala Lumpur is Port Klang, 38km southwest of KL, with ferries to Dumai or Tanjung Balai, both in Sumatra, Indonesia. Tickets are available at the jetty, or from Aero Speed (for Tanjung Balai; ☎03 3165 2545 or ☎03 3165 3073) or Indomal Express (for Dumai; ☎03 3167 1058). You can get a visa on arrival at Dumai, but you must arrange an Indonesian visa in advance if entering at Tanjung Balai. The best way to get to Port Klang is by Komuter train (every 30min; 1hr 10min; RM4.80) from KL's train station, which stops opposite the main jetty.

Destinations Dumai (daily 10.30am; 4hr); Tanjung Balai (daily 11am; 3hr 30min).

BY BUS

Buses from all over Peninsular Malaysia converge on the vast Terminal Bersipadu Selatan (Bandar Tasik Selatan station; ⓦ www.tbsbts.com.my). Though connected to KLIA Express, LRT and Komuter train lines, it's inconveniently located 12km southeast of KL's city centre and most accommodation. You can buy tickets online (ⓦ eticketing.tbsbts.com.my).

Some TBS departures (mostly Konsortium) still stop at Pudu Sentral (formerly Pudu Raya) station on Jln Pudu (Plaza Rakyat station), the closest to Chinatown, with useful connections to KLIA and KLIA2 airports; Pekeliling terminal (outside Titiwangsa Monorail station) serves Kuantan and destinations in the interior, most notably Jerantut for Taman Negara.

Pudu Sentral destinations KLIA and KLIA2 (every 30min 3am–12.15am; 1h15min).

Pekeliling destinations Jerantut (12 daily; 3hr 30min); Kuala Lipis (4 daily; 4hr); Kuantan (5 daily; 5hr).

Terminal Bersipadu Selatan (TBS) destinations Alor Setar (hourly; 8hr); Butterworth (every 30min; 5hr); Cameron Highlands (hourly; 4hr 30min); Ipoh (every 30min; 2hr 45min); Johor Bahru (hourly; 4hr); Kota Bharu (hourly except 2.30–9pm; 9hr); Kuala Terengganu (hourly, less frequent 3–9pm; 7hr); Kuala Perlis (6 daily; 9hr); Kuantan (every 30min; 5hr); Lumut (every 30min; 3hr 30min);

Malacca (every 30min; 2hr); Mersing (10 daily; 7hr); Penang (every 30min; 5hr); Singapore (8 daily; 5–6hr).

BY TRAIN

All ETS trains stop at KL Sentral station, from where you can transfer to Kuala Lumpur's city rail systems: the LRT, KL Monorail and KTM Komuter. The website (ⓦ www.ktmb .com.my) has up-to-date train timetables.

Destinations Alor Setar (4 daily; 5hr 30min); Butterworth (5 daily; 3hr 30min–4hr); Ipoh (8 daily; 2hr–2hr 30min); Johor Bahru via Gemas (3 daily; 7hr).

INFORMATION AND TOURS

Tourist information The biggest information centre is MATIC (Malaysian Tourist Information Complex) at 109 Jln Ampang (daily 8am–10pm; ☎03 9235 4800, ⓦ matic .gov.my or ⓦ tourism.gov.my), east of the centre, close to the junction with Jln Sultan Ismail, which hands out useful brochures and maps of KL, as well as information on the rest of Malaysia. There are also branches in the arrivals halls at KLIA (daily 9am–7pm; ☎03 8776 5651) and at KL Sentral station (daily 9am–7pm; ☎03 2272 5823).

Tours Food Tour Malaysia offer "Off the Eaten Track" evening walking tours (7–11pm; RM160; ☎01 7616 5090, ⓦ foodtourmalaysia.com) – a great way to get acquainted with Malaysia's variety of cuisines. Highly recommended.

GETTING AROUND

The city centre is compact enough to be explored on foot, and KL also has an efficient rail system.

By bus The bus you're most likely to use is the hop-on hop-off double-decker bus (every 20–30min; ⓦ myhoponhopoff .com/kl), which includes 42 sightseeing stops and has free wi-fi on board. The 24- or 48hr tickets can be purchased on board, on the website and from designated counters (in Jalan Bukit Bintang, the Malaysian Tourist Centre in Jalan Ampang, KL Sentral and KLCC). It's useful for getting to the Lake Gardens and for a general overview of the city. There are plenty of stops in town, including one by the tourist centre MATIC.

By LRT (Light Rail Transit) KL's reasonably efficient public transport system (daily 6am–midnight) consists of six train lines, owned by three different companies: Rapid KL (Kelana Jaya Line owned by Putraline; Ampang Line & Sri Petaling Line owned by Starline), KL Monorail and KTM Komuter (Sentul Port Klang, Rawang Seremban). These are all inexpensive (fares cost from RM1 upwards, depending on distance) and cover the city (the Monorail in particular loops through central KL and the Golden Triangle area) and its environs well, though connections between different lines are poor due to inadequate integration. You can buy a ticket on one LRT line for another owned by a different company, and the Touch 'n' Go card (RM10) can be purchased at major stations and used on all lines. KL Sentral train station is the hub not just for long-distance train travel, but also for most of the LRT lines; the monorail KL Sentral station is actually a 5min walk away. Besides the LRT lines, there are also the KLIA Transit and KLIA Express, both serving the two international airports.

By taxi Taxis can easily be flagged in the street (fares start at RM3), though you may find that drivers don't speak much English, tend not to use the meter, and are prone to getting lost. Best to stick to recommended companies such as Comfort Taxi (☎ 03 8024 2727), Public Cab (☎ 03 6259 2020) and Sunlight Radio Taxi (☎ 03 9057 5757). Another good option is the app-based services GrabCar (⌨ grab.com/my/car) and Uber (⌨ uber.com/en-MY).

ACCOMMODATION

There are numerous hostels in Chinatown, around the Pudu Raya bus station and in the Golden Triangle. There are also a few budget options near KL Sentral – convenient for onward travel but less so for walking around and sampling the nightlife. Many hotels in KL offer dramatic discounts for on-the-day check-ins.

AROUND KL SENTRAL

★**Grid 9** 9 Jln Maharajalela ☎ 03 9226 2629, ⌨ grid9hotels.com; map pp. 426–427. This great flashpacker joint with a young and vibrant feel offers clean and comfy rooms with private baths, a/c and TV, while dorms all have individual sockets and reading lamps. The pleasant lounge has colourful beanbags, a flatscreen TV and communal computers, as well as a pool table. There's wi-fi throughout and a little café downstairs. Dorms RM45, doubles RM89

My Hotel@Sentral 1, 4 Jln Tun Sanbanthan, Brickfields ☎ 03 2273 8000, ⌨ myhotels.com.my; map pp. 426–427. A great place to stay overnight before catching a train or flight the next day, this hotel offers clean, neat and tidy rooms, all with a/c, wi-fi, TV and coffee-making facilities. Doubles RM180

PODs Backpackers Unit 1–6, 30 Jln Thambipillay, Brickfields ☎ 03 2260 1434, ⌨ podsbackpacker.com; map pp.426–427. Decked out in pea green, PODs offers small but comfy rooms, all with shared bath; there's a chill-out "platform" with beanbags and TV, and a minimart right downstairs. Dorms RM35, doubles RM80

CHINATOWN AND LITTLE INDIA

1000 Miles Hotel 17 & 19 Jln Tun H.S. Lee ☎ 03 2022 3333, ⌨ 1000mileskl.com; map p.429. Friendly staff welcome budget travellers to this artsy place, with yellow and sky-blue facade, stylish common area and a selection of squeaky-clean en-suite doubles. Breakfast is included, and it's very close to super-central Masjid Jamek LRT station. Doubles RM115

★**Back Home KL** 30 Jln Tun H.S. Lee ☎ 03 2022 0788, ⌨ backhome.com.my; map p.429. This leafy hostel has parquet floors, exposed brick walls and comfy modern rooms, all with sinks and wardrobes. Staff are friendly and guests' names are creatively jotted on each door upon arrival. Dorms RM60, doubles RM140

The Explorers Guesthouse 128 & 130 Jln Tun H.S. Lee ☎ 03 2022 2928, ⌨ theexplorersguesthouse.com; map p.429. This calm little oasis in bustling Chinatown features exposed brick walls, recycled wooden furniture and pebble tiles in the bathroom. Rooms are kept neat and tidy, and beds are sturdy. Dorms RM35, doubles RM97

Fern Loft 60A Jln Hang Kasturi ☎ 03 2022 0688, ⌨ fernloft.com; map p.429. The female and mixed dorms here are on the cramped side, but there's a spacious rooftop terrace with kitchenette that makes up for it. Wi-fi, TV area, laundry facilities and pub crawls too. Doubles RM80, dorms RM25

Matahari Lodge 58–1 Jln Hang Kasturi ☎ 03 2070 5570, ⌨ matahari-lodge.kualalumpurhotels.com/en/; map p.429. A well-located cheapie with a plant-filled roof terrace to relax on, a cosy guest lounge and colourful rooms. Simple breakfast included. Dorms RM30, doubles RM60

★**Reggae Mansion** 53 Jln Tun H. S. Lee ☎ 03 2072 6877, ⌨ reggaehostelsmalaysia.com; map p.429. This three-storey white mansion attracts scores of travellers for its cool, welcoming vibe and safe setting. Premises are kept spick-and-span and each dorm bed is fully equipped with privacy curtain, socket, reading light, mirror, shelves and personal locker. There's even a cinema here and the bar on the rooftop terrace is a great spot to mingle. Dorms RM45, doubles RM130

Submarine 1st Floor, 206 Jln Tun H.S. Lee ☎ 03 2022 2259, ⌨ submarinehotels.com; map p.429. Apartment-sized guesthouse with a few simple rooms and tranquil communal area, all with shared bath. Dorm RM25, double RM65

THE GOLDEN TRIANGLE

Number Eight 8–10 Jln Tengkat Tong Shin ☎ 03 2144 2050, ⌨ numbereight.com.my; map p.431. The refurbished dorms and rooms in this traditional shophouse – all with windows – have attractive wooden tiles and a casual-chic ambience. The showers are solar powered, there's a/c and some rooms have private bath. Dorms RM30, doubles RM95

★**Orange Pekoe** 1–1 Jln Angsoka ☎ 03 2110 2000, ⌨ orangepekoe.com.my; map p.431. This welcoming place has clean and tidy rooms with wooden wicker boxes as bedside tables, a/c, wi-fi and private bath. There are splashes of greenery throughout the premises and a lounge area with cable TV and DVDs. Doubles RM119

★**Rainforest B&B** 27 Jln Mesui, off Jln Nagasari ☎ 03 2145 3525, ⌨ rainforestbnbhotel.com; map p.431. This guesthouse does a good job of creating a jungle-lodge ambience with plants everywhere and funky wooden decor in the a/c rooms. There are a couple of single-sex dorms sleeping three. Perks include a library and free breakfast. Dorms RM37, doubles RM115

6

6

Revopackers Level 2, 258 Jln Changkat Thambi Dollah ☎03 9224 7655, ⊛revopackers.com; map p.431. Central and ideal for groups, this clean hostel offers four- to six-bed en-suite a/c dorms or cosy en-suite doubles. Simple breakfast included, and there's a self-catering kitchen - a rarity in KL. Dorms RM33, doubles RM92

Travellers Palm 10 Jln Rembia, off Tengkat Tong Shin ☎03 2145 4745, ⊛travellerspalm-kl.com; map p.431. Staying here is more like staying with a favourite auntie than in a hostel. Dorms are clean, and there's a good range of good-value twin, double and triple rooms to choose from. The lovely owner encourages mingling in the shaded courtyard and is full of helpful advice; inevitably, many backpackers linger longer than originally intended. Dorms RM35, doubles RM90

EATING

The best-value Chinese food in central KL is to be found at the rowdy, chaotic outdoor food stalls of Jln Alor, a couple of streets behind Jln Bukit Bintang. At the top of Jln Alor, Changkat Bukit Bintang serves every national cuisine imaginable, from Thai and Japanese to Russian. A roaring Indian food market can be found on Jln Masjid India. All of the shopping malls have extensive food courts, which serve all manner of cuisine – a good choice for a cheap meal throughout the day. The trendiest area to eat and drink is the expat area of Bangsar, around 4km west of the centre; take the Putra LRT line from KL Sentral to Bangsar and then walk for 10min, or catch bus #822 from the Pasar Seni hub in front of the Central Market and alight at Bangsar Village.

AROUND KL SENTRAL

Legend's Claypot Briyani House 50 Jln Vivekananda; map pp.426–427. Half a block up the street from *PODs*, this canteen-style local favourite specializes in delicious claypot biriyanis (from RM13.50) as well as inexpensive banana-leaf meals (RM9), with lots of vegetarian dishes. Mon–Thurs 11am–11pm, Fri–Sun 8am–11pm.

Old Town White Coffee Jln Tun Sambanthan at Jln Thambipillay; map pp.426–427. Right near *My Hotel*, this popular chain attracts plenty of locals who come here to socialize over the sought-after coffees (RM3.80) and decent grub that includes *nasi lemak* (RM10.50). Daily 24hr.

CHINATOWN AND LITTLE INDIA

Betel Leaf 77A Leboh Ampang ☎03 2032 5932; map p.429. This authentic Indian restaurant serves wonderful curries (RM15) and kebabs (RM16) in an a/c setting. There's plenty on offer for vegetarians, too. Daily 11am–11pm.

Lokl Coffee Co. 30 Jln Tun H.S. Lee ☎03 2072 1188, ⊛loklcoffee.com; map p.429. This cute welcoming café offers a range of savoury dishes, such as southern fried

chicken (RM25) and beef burgers (RM30), as well as a selection of cakes and pastries (RM9). Tues–Sun 8am–8pm.

Old China Café 11 Jln Balai Polis ☎03 2072 5915; map p.429. Step back into the Chinese community's former social life at this old-world café serving succulent Malay and Nyonya traditional dishes such as *rendang* chicken (RM15.90). Daily 11.30am–10.30pm.

Shin Kee 9 Jln Tun Tan Cheng Lock ☎012 6737318; map p.429. This great little place specializes in superb bowls of mixed beef noodles (RM7). Mon, Tues & Thurs–Sun 10.30am–8.30pm.

GOLDEN TRIANGLE

Jln Alor is lined with garrulous Chinese restaurants specializing largely in seafood, and you're guaranteed a good meal at any one that looks popular.

Din Tai Fung Level 6, Pavilion KL; map p.431. Watch the chefs at work as your dumplings (RM10–15) are rolled out and stuffed, then steamed in front of your very eyes. Daily 10am–10pm.

El Cerdo 43 & 45 Changkat Bukit Bintang ☎03 2145 0511; map p.431. Make sure you head to this hugely popular restaurant with a hungry belly; it specializes in pork dishes (its motto is "nose to tail eating"), and the half piglet (RM188) goes down a treat (mains from RM42). Mon–Sat noon–2.30pm & 6–10.30pm. Sun dinner only.

Havana Changkat Bukit Bintang ☎03 2142 7170; map p.431. A great place for meat lovers, with an outdoor courtyard and an open-plan steak and grill bar offering juicy burgers (RM46), tender steaks (RM88) and racks of beef ribs (RM54). The upstairs bar and club really kicks off on weekends. Mon–Fri 4pm–3am, Sat & Sun 4pm–2am.

★ **Lot 10 Hutong Food Court** Lower Ground Floor, Lot 10 Shopping Mall; map p.431. Designed to look like an old Chinese village with narrow alleys linking more than 20 different stalls, this peculiar food court offers a hand-picked selection of award-winning hawkers from KL and Penang. Daily 10am–10pm.

The Magnificent Fish & Chips Bar 28 Changkat Bukit Bintang ☎03 2142 7021; map p.431. This authentic chippie serves excellent fish & chips wrapped in newspaper (RM38) and Sunday roasts (beef, lamb or chicken; RM54) in a cool and stylish setting. Upstairs, there's a balcony and bar with British memorabilia. Daily 9.30am–2am.

Neroteca 8 Lorong Ceylon ☎03 2070 0530; map p.431. This stylish restaurant and wine bar has floor-to-ceiling shelves stacked with wine bottles and offers popular Italian dishes. The deli counter displays meats and cheeses, while the home-made pasta (RM30) is served with exquisite sauces. Daily 11.30am–11.30pm.

Passage Thru' India 4 Jln Delima; map p.431. An Indian experience through and through, with the colourful, kitsch decor matching the fire and flavour of the dishes. The banana-leaf curries stand out and the home-made chutneys are a treat for the palate. Mains from RM21. Daily 11.30am–10.30pm.

Pinchos 18 Changkat Bukit Bintang ☎03 2145 8482; map p.431. This bustling Spanish tapas place is always packed with customers who come for great wine and delicious tapas (RM15–30). Tues–Thurs & Sun 5pm–1am, Fri & Sat 5pm–2am.

Sao Nam 25 Tengkat Tong Shin ☎03 2144 1225; map p.431. Authentic, beautifully presented Vietnamese dishes, with standout mains such as *ga nuong mat ong* (grilled chicken with honey; RM30) and crisp, flavourful spring rolls (RM20). Daily kitchen 12.30–2pm & 7.30–10.30pm, drinks only afterwards.

Tokyo Street Level 6, Pavilion KL; map p.431. Experience Japanese ambience at Tokyo Street, packed with little shops selling Japanese trinkets and places serving great sushi. Mains from RM25. Daily 10am–10pm.

BANGSAR

Alexis 29 Jln Telawi 3 ☎03 2284 2880. This smart coffee shop serves wonderful cakes (RM17), as well as mains (RM24), in an upmarket setting. Mon–Thurs & Sun 11am–1am, Fri & Sat 11am–2am.

Bangsar Fish Head Corner Lorong Ara Kiri 3 ☎03 7593 3616. Malaysians of all backgrounds stand in line at this hugely popular street-food joint serving great fish-head curry, fried fish, and chicken and beansprouts. A meal will set you back RM25–30. Mon–Sat 7am–7pm.

Devi's Corner 14 Jln Telawi 4 ☎012 2676714. This laidback bustling place attracts scores of locals and expats who flock here to feast on all manner of bargain south Indian dishes including great *thosai* (RM2.50) and vegetarian *thalis* (RM7.50). Daily 24hr.

La Bodega 16 Jln Telawi 2 ☎03 2287 0848. The Catalan chef at one of Bangsar's most sought-after restaurants rustles up some great tapas (RM10–28) and paella (RM35). Daily 8am–midnight.

Sri Nirwana Maju 43 Jln Telawi 3 ☎03 2287 8445. A popular local hangout serving excellent banana-leaf meals for just RM8.50. Daily 10am–2am.

Yeast 24G Jln Telawi 2 ☎03 2282 0118. This pleasant restaurant-bakery offers a selection of cakes and pastries (RM4–13), as well as light mains (RM20–32). There's 30 percent off takeaway breads and pastries daily 5–7pm. Mon–Thurs & Sun 8am–10pm, Fri & Sat 8am–10.30pm.

NIGHTLIFE AND ENTERTAINMENT

CHINATOWN AND LITTLE INDIA

The Berlin 208 Jln Tun H.S. Lee ☎03 2022 2111, ⓦtheberlinkl.com; map p.429. This neon-lit call to Berlin's cool in the heart of Chinatown has German graffiti galore on the bathroom walls, a diner-style bar and cocktails, with names like The Brandenburg (RM36), that mix Jagermeister with tropical ingredients. Mon, Wed & Sun 6pm–2am, Thurs–Sat 6pm–3am.

Findars 4th Floor, 8 Jln Panggong ⓦfacebook.com/findars; map p.429. Part artist-run café, part performance venue, this quirky space plays host to indie film screenings, art exhibits and the odd live band, and is a good introduction to KL's alternative scene. Fri–Sun 5pm–midnight, weekdays only during exhibits (check their website).

★ PS150 150 Jln Petaling ☎03 2022 2888, ⓦps150.my; map p.429. Housed in a prewar shop with three seating areas marking three distinct periods in the history of French Indochina, this bar draws from Southeast Asian native ingredients to mix up some of Jln Petaling's most intriguing cocktails. Casual-smart dress code is required at weekends. Tues–Sat 6pm–2am, Sun 4pm–11pm.

GOLDEN TRIANGLE

Barlai 3 Jln Sin Chew Kee ☎016 6810671; map p.431. This artsy retro-styled bar with decaying walls, naked bulbs and wooden picnic tables suits artist and urban types alike. Mon–Fri 5pm–3am, Sat & Sun 3pm–3am.

The Green Man 40 Changkat Bukit Bintang ☎03 2141 9924; map p.431. The congenial atmosphere at one of KL's most popular pubs will ensure a leisurely evening, especially if you linger over the good pub grub. Mon–Fri 10am–1am, Fri & Sat 10am–3am.

No Black Tie 17 Jln Mesui, off Jln Nagasari ☎03 2142 3737; map p.431. This intimate little venue hosts regular jazz, classical and acoustic sessions (with cover price), as well as occasional comedy shows and poetry readings. Pricey Japanese food (set menu RM98) and cocktails (RM25) can be enjoyed as you watch the show. Mon–Sat 5pm–1am.

Pisco Bar 29 Jln Mesui ☎03 2142 2900; map p.431. As the name suggests, pisco sours (RM26) are the drink of choice at this popular bar with exposed brick walls, wooden planks lining the ceiling and upside-down buckets serving as bar lamps. Live bands and open mic on Wednesdays at 9.30pm, while on Fridays and Saturdays DJs spin an eclectic selection of tracks from 10pm. Tues–Thurs & Sun 5pm–1am, Fri & Sat 5pm–3am.

Twentyone kitchen & bar 20–1 Changkat Bukit Bintang ☎03 2142 0021; map p.431. Stylish bar and club

---

★ TREAT YOURSELF

Marini's on 57 57th Floor, Menara 3 Petronas Tower ⓦmarinis57com; map pp.426–427. Instead of paying to go up to Sky Bridge at KLCC, head up to *Marini's* at sunset and soak in the spectacular views, cocktail in hand (from RM30), from this chic 57th-floor bar with floor-to-ceiling glass windows. Dress up or you may be refused entry. Daily 5pm–late.

with delicious modern European food with an Asian touch to complement the excellent cocktails and an open-air area for skyline gazing. Cocktails from RM24. Mon–Tues & Sun noon–1.30am, Wed–Sat noon–3am.

FURTHER AFIELD

Merdekarya 352 Jln 5/57, Bukit Gasing, Petaling Jaya ⓦ merdekarya.com. Run by writer and musician Brian Gomez, this homely blues bar is the best place in town to rub elbows with music-loving locals who, most often, also participate in the night's guitar-strumming and wailing. It's a 10min taxi drive from Bangsar LRT, or catch bus #U75. Ask the driver to point out the Gasing Indah Petronas gas station. Get off a minute later at the shop-lots surrounding a small park to the left. Tues–Sat 7pm till late.

Zouk 436 Jln Tun Razak ⓦ zoukclub.com.my; map p.431. A complete clubbing complex to suit all tastes, this is also one of the biggest nightclubs in Asia. The KL branch of this Singapore-born megaclub comprises eight rooms and lounges, each featuring different genres such as trance, EDM, hip-hop, r'n'b and pop. Entry RM20–50. Mon, Tues & Sun 10pm–3am, Wed 10pm–4am, Thurs–Sat 10pm–5am.

SHOPPING

KL is full of shopping malls, particularly in the Golden Triangle; most are open daily from 10am to 10pm. A wander around KL's many and varied markets is also a great way to soak up some of the atmosphere of the city and perhaps even pick up some bargains.

ENGLISH-LANGUAGE BOOKS

Kinokuniya Level 4, Suria KLCC ☎03 2164 8133; map pp.426–427. Great selection of fiction and travel guidebooks. Daily 10am–10pm.

Times Books Level 6, Pavilion KL ☎03 2148 8813; map p.431. Besides a good fiction and non-fiction selection, there's an extensive array of English-language magazines. Daily 10am–10pm.

HANDICRAFTS AND BATIK

Central Market Jln Hang Kasturi; map p.429. There are numerous batik stalls on the first floor in particular, selling sarongs, colourful shirts and scarves.

Peter Hoe 2nd Floor, Old Lee Rubber Building, Jln Tun H.S. Lee; map p.429. A stone's throw from Central Market, this is a more upmarket outlet specializing in beautiful bags, batik shirts and sarongs, as well as locally made and Indonesian crafts. Mon–Fri 10am–7pm.

MARKETS

Chow Kit Market Jln Haji Hussein, off Jln TAR; map pp.426–427. Quite an experience, with its warren of stalls selling everything from animals' brains to quality batik textiles. Daily 9am–5pm.

Jalan Petaling Market Near Central Market; map p.429. The covered walkways here are crowded and lively and you can pick up anything from tourist trinkets and fake branded backpacks to knock-off designer gear and the usual "I heart MY" T-shirts. Bargaining is a must. Daily 9am–10pm.

SHOPPING MALLS

Bangsar Village 1 Jln Telawi, Bangsar. Chic and shiny, with marble floors and a host of stores that stock international designer labels and draw a yuppie crowd.

Pavilion KL Jln Bukit Bintang; map p.431. Upscale shopping venue with an excellent selection of designer stores and high-street outlets, spas and restaurants.

Suria KLCC Golden Mile; map pp.426–427. If you're on a mission to shop, then this is the place to head to. An awesomely large complex set across six floors, there are plentiful Western brands from designers such as Louis Vuitton to more affordable high-street brands such as Quiksilver and Marks & Spencer, as well as an art gallery and a science discovery centre.

Sunway Pyramid Subang Jaya's biggest mall is guarded by a giant lion-faced Sphynx and a pyramid. It teems with international students and is a great place to experience life in KL's suburbs. To get here, take any Subang or USJ-bound bus from Chinatown (40min).

DIRECTORY

Banks and exchange ATMs and banks can be found throughout the city centre. Major branches include: HSBC, 2 Lebuh Ampang, Little India, and Standard Chartered Bank, 2 Jln Ampang. Official moneychangers, of which there are scores in the main city areas, give better exchange rates than banks.

Embassies and consulates Australia, Jln Yap Kwan Seng (☎03 2146 5555); Brunei, 19th Floor, Menara Tan & Tan, 207 Jln Tun Razak (☎03 2161 2800); Cambodia, 46 Jln U Thant (☎03 4257 3711); Canada, 17th Floor, Menara Tan & Tan, 207 Jln Tun Razak (☎03 2718 3333); China, 1st Floor, Plaza OSK, 25 Jln Ampang (☎03 2163 6815); Indonesia, 233 Jln Tun Razak (☎03 2116 4000); Laos, 25 Jln Damai (☎03 2148

★**TREAT YOURSELF**

Kuala Lumpur is teeming with **masseurs** and Jalan Bukit Bintang is home to a whole host of them, all waiting to soothe your aching muscles. There's usually an assortment of relaxing treatments on offer, including traditional reflexology treatments, body massages, fish spas (where little fish nibble on the dead skin of your feet), body scrubs and facials, all from the comfort of a reclining chair. Prices start from RM40 for a half-hour foot massage.

7059); New Zealand, Menara IMC, 8 Jln Sultan Ismail (☎03 2078 2533); Philippines, 1 Jln Changkat Kia Peng (☎03 2148 4233); Singapore, 209 Jln Tun Razak (☎03 2161 6404); Thailand, 206 Jln Ampang (☎03 2148 8222); UK, 185 Jln Ampang (☎03 2170 2200); US, 376 Jln Tun Razak (☎03 2168 5000); Vietnam, 4 Persiaran Stonor (☎03 2148 4036).

Hospitals and clinics Hospital Kuala Lumpur, Jln Pahang (☎03 2615 5555, ⊛www.hkl.gov.my); Tung Shin Hospital, 102 Jln Pudu (☎03 2037 2288). For less serious ailments, try the Twin Towers Medical Clinic, Level 4, Suria KLCC (Mon–Sat 8.30am–6pm ☎03 2382 3500, ⊛ttmcklcc.com.my; consultation from RM35).

Immigration Level 1–7, 15 Persiaran Perdana (Mon–Fri 8am–5pm; ☎03 8000 8000, ⊛www.imi.gov.my). This office deals with visa extensions.

Internet The tourist office MATIC offers computers with free internet access; Yoshi Connection, Concourse Level of Suria KLCC (daily 10am–10pm; RM8/hr).

Post office The GPO is on Jln Tun Sambanthan (Mon–Fri 8.30am–8pm, Sat 8.30am–5pm).

Tourist police The tourist police station (daily 24hr), where you must report stolen property and claim your insurance form, is within the same complex as the tourist office MATIC at 109 Jln Ampang (☎03 2163 4422).

DAY-TRIPS FROM KL

The biggest attractions **around KL** are north of the city, where limestone peaks rise up out of the forest and the roads narrow as you pass through small kampungs (villages). Amid dramatic scenery just 13km from the city, the vast Hindu shrine at the **Batu Caves** is one of Malaysia's main tourist attractions. Southwest of KL, **Kuala Selangor Nature Park** and the fireflies at **Village Kuantan** appeal to nature lovers.

The Batu Caves

The **Batu Caves**, dark openings in the vast limestone hills, are said to be over 400 million years old, and were once used as shelters by the Orang Asli. Since 1891, the caves have been home to Hindu shrines, and it is one of the biggest shrines outside India. The caves are always packed with visitors, never more so than during the three-day Thaipusam festival held in late January, when more than a million faithful gather here, the skin of many pierced with metal hooks with ropes attached to them; the most devout follow the silver chariot that is taken from the Sri Maha Mariamman temple in the centre of KL (see p.429). If you're lucky enough to be here during Thaipusam, arrive at dawn to have any chance of a place to stand.

Coming out of the train station, you pass a giant statue of the monkey god Hanuman, vendors selling all manner of little trinkets, and the entrance to **Cave Villa** (daily 9am–6.30pm; RM15); the complex here incorporates an Art Gallery Cave, home to dozens of multicoloured deity statues, and a bird and reptile sanctuary. Just beyond is the bottom of the steep 272-step staircase leading up to the main cave, dwarfed by the enormous golden statue of Lord Subramaniam, otherwise known as Muruga, the god of war.

At the top of the main staircase is **Subramaniam Swamy Temple** (daily 7am–9pm; free), set deep in a huge cave, its walls lined with idols representing the six lives of Lord Subramaniam and its interior crowded with the faithful, their shaved heads covered with yellow chalk. The whole place is swarming with macaques, which are not afraid of humans – thanks to those who feed them. Just before the entrance to the main temple, a short path leads to the **Dark Cave** (Tues–Fri 10am–5pm, Sat & Sun 10.30am–5.30pm; RM35); guided excursions are organized at the entrance (45min) and you may see bats and trapdoor spiders.

To get to the caves, take a direct train on the KMT Komuter Line from KL Sentral to the Batu Caves stop (every 15min; 30min).

Kuala Selangor Nature Park and the fireflies

North of Klang is the small **Kuala Selangor Nature Park** (daily 9am–6pm; RM4; ☎03 289 2294, ⊛mns.org.my), set in partial primary rainforest; the trails are short (taking between 15min and 2hr to walk) but lead to hides that make perfect **birdwatching** spots. The park is accessible by bus #141 from behind the Central Market (every 30min 6.30am–7.30pm; 2hr; RM7.30; the last bus back is at 7.45pm).

To view the **fireflies** for which the area is so famous, join one of the tours organized by many of the hostels or take

6

6

a taxi (RM20 return from Kuala Selangor – there's no bus) to **Kuantan** 10km away. It costs RM10 to take a ride in a battery-powered *sampan* (small boat), RM15 in a fibreglass boat, along the river, Sungai Kuantan, at around 8pm, to see the thousands of fireflies glowing on the riverbank.

The west coast

The west coast of the Malaysian Peninsula, from Kuala Lumpur north to the Thai border, is the most industrialized and densely populated part of the country. This is also the area in which the British held most sway, attracted by the political prestige of controlling such a strategic trading region.

The hill stations of the **Cameron Highlands** are a perfect place to relax and escape the heat and humidity, while the UNESCO World Heritage-listed colonial centre of **George Town** on the island of Penang gives another taste of old-world Malaysia with charming old shophouses and fantastic food. From Penang, it's not too far to the pretty white-sand shores of popular **Pulau Langkawi** or tiny **Pulau Pangkor** for a few lazy days on the beach.

CAMERON HIGHLANDS

Amid the lofty peaks of Banjaran Titiwangsa, the various outposts of the **Cameron Highlands** (1524m) form Malaysia's most extensive set of hill stations, which have been used as weekend retreats since the 1920s. The rolling hills are lush and tranquil, and the bright, pure colour of the sky and tea plantations alone is enough to make anybody feel considerably rejuvenated (though during the rainy season you may face torrential rains). While **Brinchang** is the principal settlement for locals, **Tanah Rata** is the backpackers' centre, boasting budget accommodation, travel information, plenty of cheap places to eat and a plethora of tours. Be aware that it's considerably colder here than in the lowlands, so it might be wise to bring a sleeping bag as nights get

chilly. There are direct buses to Tanah Rata from George Town, KL and Taman Negara, and guesthouses in other towns can often arrange minibus transfers.

WHAT TO SEE AND DO

There's plenty to keep you occupied in the Highlands, and activities can either be embarked on alone, armed with the maps and information available at all guesthouses, or as part of a tour – the easiest way to take in all the highlights in one day if you don't have your own transport. There are **strawberry farms** (daily 8.30am–6pm), where you can pick your own (at a price); the **butterfly farm** (daily 8am–6pm; RM5), where you can see leaf insects and cobras; **honey bee farms** (daily 8am–7pm), the BOH (Best Of the Highlands) **tea plantation** and the Buddhist temple **Sam Poh** (daily 7am–7pm).

You can also go **jungle trekking**, taking in some of the most spectacular scenery in Malaysia; day tours of the Cameron Highlands can also include a jungle hike through the mossy forest.

Otherwise, there are a number of trails from Tanah Rata itself; most guesthouses provide rudimentary trail maps with numbered routes, though some of the trails are poorly maintained and are sometimes badly signposted. Always inform someone at your guesthouse where you are going and what time you expect to be back. Take plenty of water, food, a whistle, a torch, a lighter and a jacket; it's advisable to take a guide if you want to do any extensive trekking.

Tanah Rata

Meaning "Flat Land" in Malay, **TANAH RATA** is the one-street travellers' hangout – the location of most hotels, banks and restaurants – and a comfortable base for exploring the highlands. Many walks originate here, and a couple of waterfalls and three reasonably high mountain peaks are all within hiking distance.

ARRIVAL AND DEPARTURE

By bus Local buses go from the bus station, about halfway along the main road. Most guesthouses can arrange direct minibus transfers to popular spots.

Bus destinations Ipoh (10 daily; 2hr); Kuala Lumpur (12

daily; 4hr); Butterworth/Penang (3 daily; 5hr); Johor Bahru (daily at 9.30am; 9hr); Malacca (daily at 9.30am; 6hr); Singapore (daily at 10am; 10hr).

Minibus destinations Taman Negara (daily; 5hr) and the Perhentians (daily; 5hr & 1hr ferry).

TOUR OPERATORS

Cameron Secrets at *Father's Guest House* ☎ 016 566 1111, ⓦ cameronsecrets.com. An established, recommended outfit offering jungle walks, countryside tours, tea plantation trips and Rafflesia tours.

Kang Tours & Travel at *Kang Travellers Lodge* ☎ 05 491 5823, ⓦ kangholiday.com. Not only do these guys arrange daily transfers to George Town, Taman Negara, KL and the Perhentian Islands, but they also have a host of well-organized tours on offer – from the full-day Rainforest Adventure (RM85) and Gunung Irau trekking (RM108) to the less demanding Agro Farm Adventure (RM90).

ACCOMMODATION

Cameronian Inn 16 Jln Mentigi ☎ 05 491 1327, ⓦ thecameronianinn.com. The tidy rooms here are set at the back of a leafy courtyard with a plethora of potted plants; there's a little garden area with seating, an annexe with TV lounge and a hair salon for adventurous types in need of a makeover. Dorms RM25, doubles RM55

Father's Guest House 4 Jln Mentigi ☎ 016 566 1111, ⓦ fathers.cameronhighlands.com. A friendly, welcoming place that buzzes with travellers who come here for the laidback family atmosphere. Rooms are cosy and clean, there's all-day tea and coffee, scooter rental, board games and an attached restaurant. Dorms RM25, doubles RM90

Gerard's Place Carnation Block C9, C10 & C17, Greenhill Resort ☎ 012 588 5454, ⓦ fathers.cameronhighlands.com/gerards/. Under the same management as *Father's Guest House*, Gerard's offers clean, pleasant rooms in a welcoming apartment setting where guests socialize in the comfortable lounge and around the outdoor seating area. Doubles RM80

Hillview Inn 17 Jln Mentigi ☎ 05 491 2915, ⓦ hillview-inn.com. This mock Tudor building with a pleasant garden offers spacious carpeted rooms, most with balcony. There's wi-fi throughout and an on-site café serving freshly baked scones. Doubles RM55

Kang Travellers Lodge 9 Lorong Perdah ☎ 05 491 5823, ⓦ kangholiday.com. This long-standing favourite has a popular, rustic bar that makes for many a sociable night. There are two small attic dorms at the top of a tiny staircase and simple doubles with tacky pictures as decor. Dorms RM18, doubles RM50

EATING AND DRINKING

At night, food stalls set up on Main Road, chiefly opposite the post office; the food is mostly Malay and you're unlikely to spend more than RM10 on a meal. Many restaurants serve steamboat, which involves dipping raw fish, meat, noodles and vegetables in a steaming broth until cooked.

The Jungle Bar Located behind *Kang Travellers Lodge*. Travellers congregate nightly at this laidback, rustic bar made of pine and bamboo. Guests can enjoy drinks (RM6.50) by the crackling bonfire or over a game of pool. Daily 7.30pm–midnight.

Kumar 26 Main Rd. This great Indian place specializes in claypot rice (RM6), tandoori (RM7) and banana-leaf meals (RM7). The combination set is great value at just RM9. *Sri Brinchang* next door offers similar grub. Daily 7am–10.30pm.

May Flower 81A Persiaran Camelli 4. This well-liked restaurant offers a selection of steamboat dishes (including vegetarian; RM15), noodles and fried rice (RM6). Those feeling more adventurous can try the ostrich and deer meat (RM15). Daily 8.30am–3pm & 5.30–10pm.

Ferm Nyonya 78 Persiaran Camellia 4. By the *May Flower*, this restaurant specializes in Chinese and Nyonya dishes; the beef *rendang* (RM13) is among their bestsellers, and there are also Western dishes for those wanting familiar comfort food. Daily 11am–10pm.

IPOH

Eighty kilometres west of the Cameron Highlands in the Kinta Valley, **IPOH** grew rich on the tin trade and is now the third-largest city in Malaysia, scenically set in a valley dotted with dozens of limestone karsts. The muddy **Sungai Kinta** River cuts the centre of Ipoh neatly in two: the **new town**, east of the river, and the **old town**, on the opposite side between Jalan Sultan Idris Shah and Jalan Sultan Iskander. In the past couple of years, thanks to conservation efforts and a budding art scene, Ipoh's old town competes with George Town in terms of cuisine, heritage buildings and old-world charm.

WHAT TO SEE AND DO

The impressive Moorish-style **train station** sits across from the Neoclassical 1914 **Town Hall** and 1928 **Court House**. At the southern end of immaculate lawn **Padang Ipoh**, Jln Dato Maharajalela leads into the **old town**'s collection of colonial and Straits-Chinese architecture. First is the **Birch Memorial Clocktower**, erected in 1909 to commemorate the murder of Perak's first British Resident, James W.W. Birch. Founded in 1929, Hakka miners' club **Han Chin Pet Soo** (Tues–Sun

6

9.30am–5pm; ⓦipohworld.org /reservation) offers free tours that vividly recall Ipoh's tin-mining traditions and Chinese migrant life. Book your slot online.

Tucked along tiny Lorong Panglima, the interesting **Yasmin at Kong Heng** museum (Sat & Sun 10am–4pm; free) celebrates the work of legendary Malaysian trans-gender filmmaker Yasmin Ahmad. Just across the river on Jln Masjid, the two soaring minarets of azure and white **Panglima Kinta Mosque** mark the beginning of the **new town**. Keep walking east after the mosque to find local street art.

Outside the city, the limestone rock formations are home to about thirty impressive Chinese shrines. The most famous are **Sam Poh Tong**, a large and impressive cave temple (daily 8.30am– 4pm) reachable by bus #66, and **Perak Tong**, one of the largest and most striking Chinese temples in Malaysia (daily 8am–5pm). The shrine, 6km north of the city, dates back to 1926 and features over forty Buddha statues and wonderful cave paintings. Follow the steps up and through the cave from where there are views over Ipoh. To get here take bus #35 from Medan Kidd bus terminal.

ARRIVAL AND DEPARTURE

By plane Malindo Air (ⓦmalindoair.com) flies between Johor Bahru and Ipoh (daily; 1hr 20min); Firefly

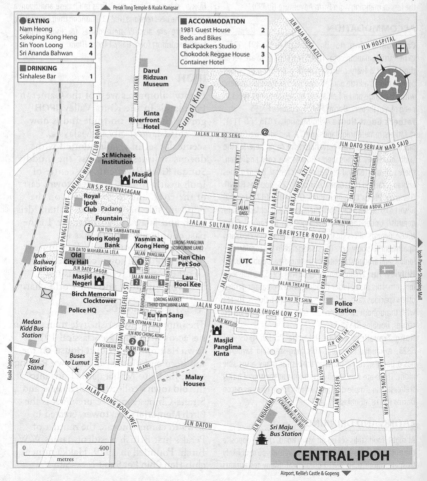

CENTRAL IPOH

● EATING
Nam Heong	3
Sekeping Kong Heng	1
Sin Yoon Loong	2
Sri Ananda Bahwan	4

■ DRINKING
Sinhalese Bar	1

■ ACCOMMODATION
1981 Guest House	2
Beds and Bikes Backpackers Studio	4
Chokodok Reggae House	3
Container Hotel	1

6

(🐱 fireflyz.com.my) and Tigerair (🐱 tigerair.com) connect Ipoh to Singapore (4 daily; 1hr 40min).

By bus There are three bus stations. Medan Kidd, 200m south of the train station, is at the junction with Jln Tun Abdul Razak. Sri Maju station is on Jln Bendahara, a 20min walk from the old town. Buses #116, #T30A and #T30B connect Medan Kidd with Amanjaya – the third, long-distance, bus hub 15km out of town, which serves all main destinations. Sri Maju station has hourly free shuttle bus services connecting to Amanjaya. Buses to the Cameron Highlands leave from Medan Kidd (8am, 11am, 3pm & 6pm; 2hr).

Destinations from Amanjaya Butterworth/George Town (8 daily; 2hr; 30min); KLIA/KLIA2 airport (11 daily; 3hr 30min); Kuala Lumpur (9 daily; 2hr 30min); Lumut (the departure point for Pulau Pangkor; 3 daily; 1hr 30min); Singapore (6 daily; 6hr).

By train The train station is on Jln Panglima Bukit, west of the old town, next to the GPO.

Destinations Butterworth (10 daily; 1hr 40min); Padang Besar (for Thailand; 5 daily; 2hr 40min–3hr 40min); KL (8 daily; 3hr).

INFORMATION

Tourist office The tourist office is on Jln Bandar (Mon–Thurs 8am–1pm & 2–5pm, Fri 8am–12.15pm & 2.45–5pm; ☎ 05 208 3151, 🐱 ipohtourism.mbi.gov.my).

ACCOMMODATION

1981 Guest House 26 Jln Market ☎ 010 965 6991. Right in the heart of the old town, this spick-and-span hostel has nice wooden floors and three big dorms – mixed, male and female – with mosquito nets and personal lockers. Free computers and self-service washing machine available. Dorms RM25

★ **Beds and Bikes Backpackers Studio** 2A-1 Jln Sultan Yusuf ☎ 05 241 1181. An interesting loft-styled hostel divided into large lounge areas fitted with couches, TVs and mini library, and functional dorms with shared bathrooms. Free breakfast and bicycles to scoot around town. Dorms RM24

Chokodok Reggae House 175 Jln Sultan Iskandar ☎ 017 224 5847. This feel-good reggae hostel with recycled wood and corrugated-iron furniture is the cheapest option in town. Rooms and shared bathrooms are really basic, but the chilled atmosphere and colourful bar serving rice-based Asian mains, burgers, nachos and Italian lasagne are attractive. No alcohol is served – the owner is Muslim. Dorms RM15, doubles RM40

Container Hotel 89-91 Jln Sultan Yusuf ☎ 05 243 3311. The smartest flashpacker choice in town, this two-storey industrial-chic hotel offers immaculate personal "pods" in a quirky futuristic container theme. The queen bed pods sleeping two (RM90) are great for couples. Dorms RM50

EATING

Nam Heong 2 Jln Bandar Timah. A no-frills local institution packed with Chinese customers who come here for the great white coffee (RM1.50), noodles and rice, fresh dim sum and Portuguese egg tarts. Daily 6.30am–5pm.

Sekeping Kong Heng 75a Jln Bandar Timah. Come to this traditional *kopitiam* for the rice dumplings, Ipoh's traditional beansprout chicken, and tons of Chinese sweets. Mains from RM6. Daily 6.30am–5pm.

Sin Yoon Loong 17 Jln Bandar Timah. The *kopitiam* that popularized Ipoh's quintessential white coffee still dishes up hearty Chinese delicacies like chicken rice and barbecue pork (4.50RM), curry or mushroom *chee chang fun* (RM4) and toasted bread with *kaya* (coconut jam). Daily 6.30am–5pm.

Sri Ananda Bahwan 7, 9 & 11 Persiaran Bijeh Timah. Popular Indian franchise for hearty and cheap meals, from vegetarian banana-leaf *thalis* (RM5.30) to succulent tandoori chicken and naan bread sets (RM9.50). Daily 7am–11pm.

DRINKING

Sinhalese Bar 2 Jln Bijeh Timah. Push the saloon doors open at the oldest pub in the state of Perak, running non-stop since 1931, and order a chilled Tiger (RM13) to be consumed at the marble-top tables from way back when. Daily 10am–11pm.

PULAU PANGKOR

At only 3km by 9km, **PULAU PANGKOR** is one of the tiniest of the west coast's islands, with some pleasant stretches of beach and where you're guaranteed to spot hornbills. It's only a forty-minute ferry ride from the port of Lumut (85km southwest of Ipoh).

Most villages lie along the east coast, while tourist accommodation and the best beaches are on the west side of the island, at Pasir Bogak and Teluk Nipah. A sealed road runs right round the island, though if you're exploring Pulau Pangkor by motorbike, you do have to be a confident rider, as there are some **steep hairpin bends** between Teluk Dalam on the north coast by the airstrip and the east coast, as well as the stretch between Pasir Bogak and Teluk Nipah.

The west coast

Down the south end of the west coast is **Pasir Bogak**, a beach popular with locals. Halfway along the west coast is **Teluk Nipah**, the most popular place for visitors, with an attractive beach fringed with shade-providing palm trees. Just north of

6

ASIA'S SECRET WORLD HERITAGE SITE

The town of **Lenggong**, 77km north of Ipoh in the midst of the state of Perak's jungle, hosts Malaysia's lesser-known fourth UNESCO World Heritage Site. Inscribed in 2012, Lenggong's open-air and cave sites span from the Paleolithic to the Neolithic and Bronze Age up to 1700 years ago. Hand axes found in nearby Bukit Bunuh, the site of a meteorite impact from 1.83 million years ago, are among the oldest outside of Africa, and suggest that the Lenggong Valley was an extremely early site of hominids' presence in Southeast Asia. Unfortunately, the cave sites can only be accessed by contacting the **Lenggong Archaeological Museum** (daily 9am–6pm; ☎05 767 9700) in Kota Tampan, 9km from Lenggong town, requesting a guided visit two weeks in advance. The museum is worth visiting for a collection of early stone tools, and especially the remains of the mysterious Perak Man, one of Southeast Asia's oldest human skeletons, which is particularly complete. The elaborate burial site where he was unearthed convinced archeologists that the Perak Man was revered as an ancient shaman. The rest of Lenggong Valley's archeological sites – such as the meteorite landing site Bukit Bunuh, or Bukit Jawa's workshop site, with tools dating back to 200,000–100,000 BC – are open to the public and can be visited with your own set of wheels.

To reach Lenggong, catch a **bus** to Kuala Kangsar (every 20min; 1hr 15min) from Ipoh's Medan Kidd station and connect to the frequent services to Lenggong. *Soon Lee Hotel* (31 Jln Besar; ☎ 014 327 6204; doubles RM50) has simple rooms in the heart of town, and amiable owners Mr Ng and Pinky Mok can help with picking up transport in Lenggong.

Teluk Nipah is **Coral Beach**, a perfect cove with crystal-clear sea and smooth white sand, reachable by road; at its north end you'll find the decidedly strange **Lin Je Kong Temple** featuring a devotional figure of Mickey Mouse – Donald Duck was knocked down by vandals. Up from Coral Beach is a lovely stretch of road running through the jungle, passing the airstrip and emerging at Teluk Datam Beach.

There are plenty of independent outfits offering activities and watersports, from kayaking (RM20/hr) to jet skiing (RM70/20min), as well as island-hopping (RM20) and snorkelling trips (RM15).

The east coast

While the east coast's main settlement, pungent-smelling **Pangkor Town**, is unlikely to detain you for long, just north of the centre is a turn-off for the colourful **Foo Lin Kong Temple**, featuring fearsome deities and a miniature version of the Great Wall of China. Three kilometres south of Pangkor Town you'll come across **Kota Belanda**, the Dutch fort originally built in 1670, which looks new because it was rebuilt in the 1980s.

ARRIVAL AND DEPARTURE

By plane Expensive charter Sas Air (ⓦsassb.com.my) flies between Pulau Pangkor and Kuala Lumpur's Subang Airport (daily; 45min).

By boat Pulau Pangkor is served by frequent ferries from Lumut (every 30min, 6.30am–8.30pm; 30min; RM10 round trip), calling at Sungai Pinang Kecil before reaching the main jetty at Pangkor Town.

By bus In Lumut, buses depart from the town's bus station, a 3min walk from the jetty.

Destinations Butterworth (8 daily; 4hr); KL (hourly; 6hr); Kuala Perlis (for Langkawi; 1 daily at 6.30pm; 6hr); Johor Bahru/Singapore (daily 7.30pm; 8hr/9hr); Kota Bharu (2 daily; 10hr); Kuala Terengganu (2 daily; 7hr 30min); Malacca (2 daily; 8hr); Ipoh (hourly; 1hr 30min).

GETTING AROUND

By minibus taxi Pink vehicles meet the ferries from Lumut and charge RM15 from Pangkor Town to Pasir Bogak, RM20 to Teluk Nipah and RM80 for a round-island trip.

By motorbike and bike The best way to explore is by motorbike (RM30 for manual or RM40 for a scooter/day) or bicycle (RM20/day), available from guesthouses in Teluk Nipah or directly at the jetty.

ACCOMMODATION

Try to visit on weekdays as prices rise at weekends and almost double on public holidays.

Nazri Nipah Camp ☎017 604 4942. This well-established reggae-themed backpacker favourite offers tiny A-framed huts sleeping two for RM50, as well as larger, more comfortable rooms with private bath. The dorms are a bit shabby. There's a leafy chill-out area with benches and hammocks, and a kitchen for guests' use. Dorms RM30, doubles RM60

6

★ **Nipah Guesthouse** ☎ 017 506 9259, ⊜ nipah
.guesthouse@gmail.com. This wonderful guesthouse has
four neat A-framed huts surrounding a pleasant pool area
with loungers. Breakfast consists of a continental buffet in the
breezy dining area, where guests are encouraged to rustle up
their own eggs and pancakes. They organize quad-bike jungle
tours in the island's interior (RM80). Doubles **RM120**

Sunset View Chalet ☎ 012 408 2297, ⊚ sunsetviewchalet
.com. Clean rooms with little balconies opening out on to an
avenue charmingly shaded by bougainvillea. The congenial
staff offer full board (three meals including seafood; RM70/
person) and highly photogenic daily hornbill feeding
sessions at 6.30pm. Doubles **RM60**

EATING

Most guesthouses have an attached restaurant serving a
mix of seafood and international dishes.

Daddy's Café On the southern end of Coral Beach. This
beachside restaurant serves fresh Pangkor seafood and
local specialities including fish-head curry (RM19) and
Malaysian crab curry (RM25). Daily 11am–11pm.

Food stalls The northern end of Teluk Nipah beach comes
alive in the evening with informal stalls all doing a roaring
trade in inexpensive fresh seafood and noodles. It's one of
the best places to eat on the island. Seafood mains RM14;
noodles RM5.

Yee Lin 195 Jln Pasir Bogak. Locals from all over the island
head to this popular place for the excellent fish and
seafood dishes. Daily 7pm–midnight.

PENANG AND GEORGE TOWN

On Malaysia's northwestern coast is
PENANG, a large island of 285 square
kilometres, connected to the mainland by
two bridges and frequent ferry services
from Butterworth. It became the first
British settlement in the Malay Peninsula
in 1791, and a major colonial
administrative centre, only declining after
the foundation of Singapore in 1819. Its
capital, **GEORGE TOWN**, was declared a
UNESCO World Heritage Site in 2008
both for its architectural history and for the
distinctive mix of cultures that developed
here. The city has since transformed itself
into one of Southeast Asia's coolest small
cities, which attracts a steady flow of
international artists to its festivals. Today,
the beautiful pastel-coloured buildings that
were once townhouses and shophouses
host a plethora of artsy cafés and boutique
accommodation. The city is also known as
the "Food Capital of Malaysia", offering a
tantalizing range of cuisines that
incorporate the very best of Malay, Chinese
and Indian elements. The city is busy, but
it's a perfect base to explore nearby sights,
including the island's commercialized
north-coast beach of **Batu Ferringhi** where
it's possible to stay overnight.

WHAT TO SEE AND DO

George Town retains more of its cultural
history than virtually anywhere else in the
country, with a host of beautiful colonial
buildings to admire and explore. For a
bird's-eye view, you can proceed to the
top of **KOMTAR** (Kompleks Tun Abdul
Razak; daily 10am–10pm; RM118),
George Town's tallest building, with the
panoramic observatory **Window of the
Top** and thrilling 249m-high glass
walkway **Rainbow Skywalk** on the 65th
and 68th floors respectively.

Fort Cornwallis and around

The site of **Fort Cornwallis** (Mon–Sat
9am–10pm; RM20), on the
northeastern tip of Pulau Penang, marks
the spot where the British fleet under
Captain Francis Light disembarked on
July 16, 1786. For all its significance,
however, it holds little of interest save a
history gallery, the outer walls of the fort
and historic cannons facing the sea.
Southwest from the fort is **Lebuh Pantai**,
which holds some fine colonial
buildings. West of Lebuh Pantai, on
Jalan Masjid Kapitan Kling (or Lebuh
Pitt), stands the Anglican **St George's
Church** (Mon–Thurs 10am–4pm, open
for services only on Sun at 8.30 &
10.30am & Wed at 9.30am; free);
construction started in 1817, making it
one of the oldest buildings in Penang.

6

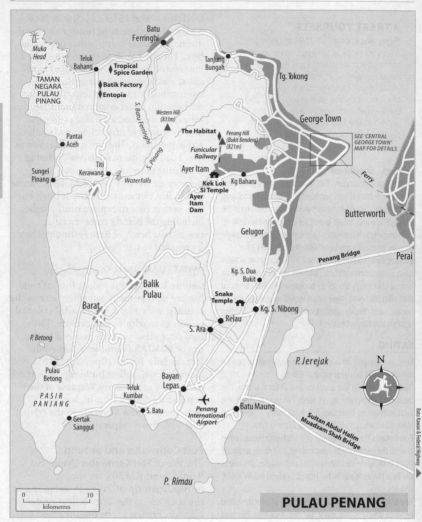

PULAU PENANG

Next to the church on Lebuh Farquhar, **Penang State Museum** (Mon–Thurs, Sat & Sun 9am–5pm; RM1) has an excellent collection of rickshaws, as well as period objects, press cuttings and black-and-white photographs charting the city's history.

Little India

The area enclosed by parallel Lebuh King and Lebuh Queen forms George Town's compact **Little India** district, full of sari and incense shops as well as banana-leaf

curry houses. It is also home to the towering Hindu **Sri Mahamariamman Temple** (main entrance Queen St; daily 8am–noon & 4.30–9pm) on Lebuh Queen, the city's oldest Hindu temple, built in 1833, and one of the starting points for the *kavadi* procession during the Thaipusam festival.

Khoo Kongsi

To the south of Little India, accessed through an archway via Cannon Square, stands the **Khoo Kongsi** (daily 9am–5pm;

RM10), also known as Dragon Mountain Hall – one of many *kongsi*, or traditional "clan-houses", in Penang where Chinese families gather to worship their ancestors, look after the welfare of family members, and settle clan affairs. The building was started in 1894 and meticulously crafted by experts from China, and is now overseen by the 29th generation of the original Leongs. Its three halls boost heavy, intricately carved beams and pillars and bulky mother-of-pearl inlaid furniture, and a shrine to Tua Peh Kong, the god of prosperity.

Pinang Peranakan Mansion

This wonderful mansion, at 29 Lebuh Gereja (daily 9.30am–5pm; RM20; ⓦ pinangperanakanmansion.com.my), re-creates the sumptuous lifestyle of a wealthy Peranakan family, also referred to as Baba and Nyonya, descendants of Chinese migrants who intermarried with Malays. The Peranakans adopted Malay customs while living in line with British colonial traditions. The nineteenth-century stately home displays over a hundred antiques and collectables that embrace a variety of styles, from Chinese carved wooden panels to Scottish ironworks.

Cheong Fatt Tze Mansion

On the western edge of George Town, at 14 Lebuh Leith, is the stunning **Cheong Fatt Tze Mansion** (guided tours daily 11am, 2pm & 3.30pm; 45min; RM17), whose outer walls are painted a striking, rich blue. It's the best example of nineteenth-century Chinese architecture in Penang, and was commissioned by Cheong Fatt Tze, a Hakka businessman,

in 1880. The elaborate halls of ceremony, bedrooms and libraries, separated by courtyards and gardens, have been restored, and tours of the interior give you a fascinating glimpse into the life of the wealthy Straits Chinese at the time.

Kek Lok Si Temple

Bedecked with flags, lanterns, statues and pagodas, the sprawling and exuberant **Kek Lok Si Temple** (daily 9am–6pm; free), also known as the "Temple of Supreme Bliss", to the west of the city, is the largest Buddhist temple complex in Malaysia. On one side, a 30.2m-tall bronze statue of Kua Yin, the Goddess of Mercy, dominates the shrine. On the other side, the "Pagoda of Ten Thousand Buddhas", with its tower of simple Chinese saddle-shaped eaves and more elaborate Thai arched windows, is topped by a golden Burmese stupa. It costs RM5 to climb the 193 steps to the top for a great view of George Town and the bay.

Visit during Chinese New Year and you'll find Kek Lok brightly lit with multicoloured fairy lights and flashing neon. Getting there involves a thirty-minute bus ride west on bus #201, #203, #204 or #502; ask to be let off at Air Itam for the temple. Buses leave around every thirty minutes after 8pm; the last bus is at about 9.30pm.

Penang Hill (Bukit Bendera)

A trip up to the highest peak in Penang (833m) is very worthwhile for the commanding view of the island and the mainland beyond – particularly impressive at sunset. Asia's longest **funicular railway**, with the steepest tunnel track in the world, runs from the base of the hill near the Kek

6

GEORGE TOWN'S ARTISTIC RENAISSANCE

In 2012, young Lithuanian artist Ernest Zacharevic sketched a series of mural installations entitled **Mirrors of George Town** for the George Town Festival. Ever since, Penang has taken off as one of Southeast Asia's street-art capitals. In 2013, Zacharevic's piece depicting two children on a bicycle was selected by *The Guardian* as among the best street art around the world, consolidating the position of the city's murals as a tourist draw. In the wake of this success, Zacharevic has sketched walls in Ipoh, Kuala Lumpur, Johor Bahru and Singapore. Art gallery Hin Bus Depot (31A Jln Gurdwara; ⓦ hinbusdepot.com) has promoted street art in Penang. Today, as well as Zacharevic's pieces, George Town hosts work by local and international artists such as Kenji Chan (Sandakan), Fritilidea (KL), Rone (Melbourne), Elle (New York) and Julia Volchkova (Russia). You can spot the best yourself as you walk around town (see map pp.446–447).

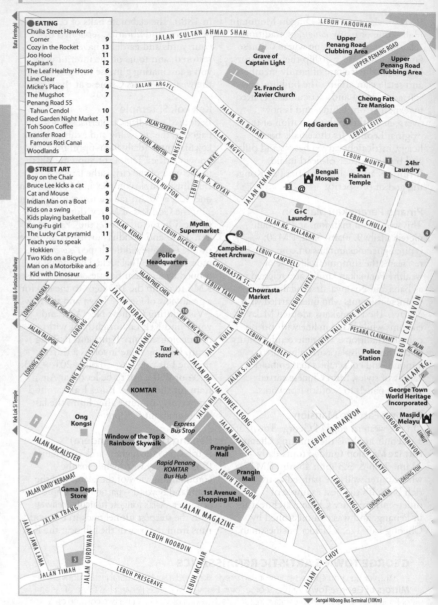

Batu Ferringhi

6

Penang Hill & Funicular Railway

Kek Lok Si Temple

● EATING

Chulia Street Hawker Corner	9
Cozy in the Rocket	13
Joo Hooi	11
Kapitan's	12
The Leaf Healthy House	6
Line Clear	3
Micke's Place	4
The Mugshot	7
Penang Road 55 Tahun Cendol	10
Red Garden Night Market	1
Toh Soon Coffee	5
Transfer Road Famous Roti Canai	2
Woodlands	8

● STREET ART

Boy on the Chair	6
Bruce Lee kicks a cat	4
Cat and Mouse	9
Indian Man on a Boat	2
Kids on a swing	8
Kids playing basketball	10
Kung-Fu girl	1
The Lucky Cat pyramid	11
Teach you to speak Hokkien	3
Two Kids on a Bicycle	7
Man on a Motorbike and Kid with Dinosaur	5

Sungai Nibong Bus Terminal (10Km)

Lok Si Temple (every 30min 6.30am–8am & 6–11pm, every 15min 8am–6pm; RM30 return). At the top, **the Habitat** (RM50; ⓦthehabitat.my) eco-park offers guided walks at the side of primary rainforest, a 700m-long zipline and a 40m-high tree-top walk with views over the island and Andaman Sea. There are several other free walking trails crisscrossing the hill, including the well-signposted 8km hike down to the Moon Gate at the Botanical Gardens. To get here, take bus #204 from Komtar. The last bus back to George Town leaves at 10.40pm.

6

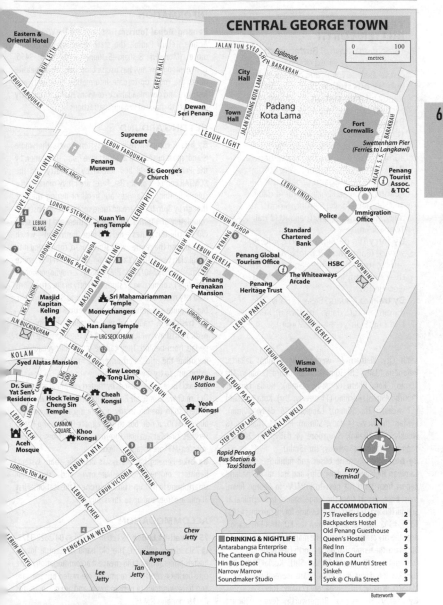

CENTRAL GEORGE TOWN

0   100
metres

ACCOMMODATION

75 Travellers Lodge	2
Backpackers Hostel	6
Old Penang Guesthouse	4
Queen's Hostel	7
Red Inn	5
Red Inn Court	8
Ryokan @ Muntri Street	1
Sinkeh	9
Syok @ Chulia Street	3

DRINKING & NIGHTLIFE

Antarabangsa Enterprise	1
The Canteen @ China House	3
Hin Bus Depot	5
Narrow Marrow	2
Soundmaker Studio	4

Butterworth ▼

ARRIVAL AND DEPARTURE

Arriving at either the bus station, taxi stand or ferry terminal on Pengkalan Weld or nearby Swettenham Pier puts you at the eastern edge of George Town, a 15min walk from the hotels.

By plane Penang International Airport (☏ 04 643 0811) is on the southeastern tip of the island, reachable by buses #401,

#305 and #401E from the Pengkalan Weld or the KOMTAR complex (every 30min 6am–10pm; 40min), or else by taxi (30min; RM45). From Batu Ferringhi catch bus #102. The airport is served by Malaysia Airlines, AirAsia, Cathay Pacific, Firefly, Malindo Air, Thai Airline and Singapore Airlines.

Destinations Banda Aceh, Indonesia (8 weekly; 1hr 30min); Bangkok, Thailand (3 daily; 1hr 50min); Ho Chi

6

TRANSPORT FROM BUTTERWORTH

The industrial town of **Butterworth** is the main port for the island of Penang and its capital, George Town, and a major transport hub. The **bus station**, port complex, taxi stand and **train station** are all next door to each other on the quayside.

By bus to: Bangkok, Thailand (2 daily; 18hr); Cameron Highlands (4 daily; 3hr 30min); Hat Yai, Thailand (5 daily; 5hr 30min); Ipoh (hourly; 3hr); Kota Bharu (2 daily; 6hr); Kuala Lumpur (every 30min; 5hr); Kuala Terengganu (2 daily; 8hr); Kuantan (3 daily; 12hr); Lumut (4 daily; 4hr); Malacca (daily; 6–10hr); Singapore (4 daily; 9hr); Surat Thani, Thailand (2 daily; 10hr 30min).

By ferry The passenger and car ferry service (6am–1am; 20min; RM1.20 return) runs three times an hour from the port complex to Pengkalan Weld in George Town.

By train to: Padang Besar (2 daily; 1hr 45min); Ipoh (5 daily; 1hr 30min); Kuala Lumpur (5 daily; 3hr–4hr 30min).

Minh City, Vietnam (4 weekly; 1hr 45min); Jakarta, Indonesia (daily; 2hr 30min); Johor Bahru (2 daily; 1hr 30min); Kota Bharu (2 daily; 45min); Kuala Lumpur (hourly; 45min); Kuching (11 weekly; 2hr); Kota Kinabalu (11 weekly; 2hr 50min); Langkawi (6 daily; 30min); Medan, Indonesia (4 daily; 50min); Phuket, Thailand (8 weekly; 1hr 10min); Singapore (4 daily; 1hr 20min); Yangon, Myanmar (3 weekly; 2hr 15min).

By bus Although some buses and minibuses from the Cameron Highlands (5 daily; 5hr) and Hat Yai in Thailand depart from Jalan Ria next to KOMTAR in George Town, most buses depart from the long-distance bus terminal at Sungai Nibong, 14km south of George Town; take bus #303, #305, #306, #401 or #401E from the KOMTAR bus station near the city centre. However, the majority of long-distance buses use the terminal at Butterworth (see box above).

Destinations KL (every 15min; 5hr); Kuala Perlis (for Langkawi; 6 daily; 2hr); Kota Bharu (several daily; 6hr); Malacca (8 daily; 7hr); Singapore (7 daily; 10hr).

By ferry Ferries to Butterworth (every 30min; 5.30am–12.30am; RM1.20 from Butterworth, free from Penang to Butterworth) run from the Pengkalan Weld ferry terminal. Ferries to Pulau Langkawi (2 daily; 3hr) depart from Swettenham Pier near Fort Cornwallis. Book ferries a couple of days in advance.

By train Butterworth station is served by ETS trains (see box above).

INFORMATION

Penang Global Tourism First Floor, 8-B The Whiteaways Arcade, Lebuh Pantai. The state government's tourism office (Mon–Fri 8.30am–5.30pm; ☎04 264 3456, ⓦmypenang.gov.my) has useful brochures. Their website offers the most up-to-date information on events and festivals, and downloadable e-coupons that get you entry discounts to many of Penang's attractions.

GETTING AROUND

By bus A comprehensive bus system covers the whole island; most buses stop at (and leave from) the station by the Pengkalan Weld bus station by the jetty and the KOMTAR complex on Jln Ria. Fares are rarely more than a couple of ringgit. Services are frequent during the day, though by 8pm they become more sporadic and most stop completely at 11pm. From KOMTAR, there are two useful CAT shuttle-bus routes – red and blue (both free) – which loop around the centre every 30min or so, connecting it to Pengkalan Weld. There's also a hop-on-hop-off bus service (9am–8pm; RM40/24hr, RM74/48hr, ⓦmyhoponhopoff.com/pg/), connecting 22 stops with fifty major attractions on a city route and a beach route going to Batu Ferringhi, but it's quite expensive compared to normal buses.

By trishaw A traditional way of seeing the city is by pedicab trishaw, which has a seat on the front; the driver pedals from behind. They can be found all over town – negotiate the price in advance. This mode of transport is dying out, so try it while you can.

By taxi There are taxi stands by the ferry terminal and on Jln Dr Lim Chwee Long, off Jln Penang. Drivers rarely use their meters, so fix the fare in advance – a trip across town costs about RM10, a ride out to the airport RM45. App-based services GrabCar (ⓦgrab.com/my/car) and Uber (ⓦuber.com/en-MY) are cheaper options.

By bike Penang has Malaysia's first bike-share system. Register online (ⓦbikeshare.my) and use your smartphone to pick up a bike from one of the stations. First 30min are free, and up to 2hr is only RM2.

ACCOMMODATION

75 Travellers Lodge 75 Lebuh Muntri ☎04 2622 3378, ✉75lodge@gmail.com. The old hand of George Town's hostels offers some of the cheapest accommodation in the core heritage centre. All rooms are renovated but spartan, and have windows (a perk in town) and are clean. Dorms RM18, doubles RM45

Backpackers Hostel 57 Love Lane ☎04 262 6772. This hip hostel offers a/c dorms only; most open onto a balcony and all have privacy curtain, reading lamp and individual power sockets. There's an attached bar with pool table and wi-fi throughout. Dorms RM30

Old Penang Guesthouse 53 Love Lane ☎04 263 8805, ⓦoldpenang.com. This pleasant airy guesthouse has high ceilings and beautiful original tiled floors. It's clean and tidy, and there are just two dorms – one mixed and one (pricier) female only (RM30). Wi-fi throughout. Dorms RM28, doubles RM85

★**Queen's Hostel** 20 & 22 Lebuh Queen ☎013 489 6218, ⍟queenshostel.my. This cute and cosy female and couples-only hostel has a welcoming dorm with painted wooden pods and colourful partition curtains. Each "queen's canopy" has a reading lamp and socket, as well as a painted wooden crate to store possessions. Lovely extra touches such as complementary shampoo, conditioner and nail varnish. Dorms RM59, doubles RM99

Red Inn 55 Love Lane ☎04 261 3931, ⍟redinnpenang .com. Located in a historical building with wonderfully high ceilings, this popular option offers a variety of dorms, from two beds to more spacious six-bed dorms. Travellers can kick back and relax on the raised platform with cushions and beanbags, or at the shaded tables spilling out onto the street. Dorms RM30, doubles RM70

Red Inn Court 35B & 35C Jln Mesjid Kapitan Keling ☎04 261 1144, ⍟redinncourt.com. The premises are spick and span and the spa-type showers are powered by the a/c unit in an effort to be eco-friendly. Dorms are on the small side, though. Dorms RM30, doubles RM88

Ryokan @ Muntri Street 62 Lebuh Muntri ☎04 250 0287, ⍟myryokan.com. This chic flashpacker hostel has a welcoming lounge area and comfortable dorms with a/c, lockers, power sockets and reading lamps. Guests can unwind in the chill-out or reading corners. There's wi-fi throughout and rates include breakfast. Dorms RM39, doubles RM158

★**Syok @ Chulia Street** 458 Lebuh Chulia ☎04 263 2663, ⍟penang-hotels.com/syok-chulia/. This lovely hostel with exposed brick walls has sturdy dorm beds and clean, shared bathrooms with pretty painted wooden doors. There's a pleasant a/c lounge area with beanbags, table footie and DVDs, as well as a sunny terrace with outdoor seating. Guests are encouraged to disclose their deepest darkest secrets on the "confession wall". Dorms RM58, doubles RM110

★**TREAT YOURSELF**

Sinkeh 105 Lebuh Melayu ☎04 261 3966, ⍟sinkeh.com. Run by theatre performers for art lovers, this guesthouse in a nineteenth-century Straits Chinese residence and two additional buildings has private courtyards, an old-meets-new-world charm and rooms with all the expected top-end amenities. What's remarkable is their in-house programme of live performances, movie screenings and talks by international artists. Doubles RM280

EATING

Penang is all about hawker food, with stalls on most street corners, serving cheap and tasty dishes including the local favourite, *Penang laksa* – noodles in thick fish soup garnished with vegetables, pineapple and *belacan* (shrimp paste). Just head to Lebuh Kimberley, Lebuh Cintra, Little India and most lanes off Penang Road – most food is superb.

Chulia Street Hawker Corner Cnr Lebuh Chulia & Cheapside St. These noisy stalls offer Penang's hawker-central smack-bang in the middle of tourist enclave Chulia Street. Being close to hipster cafés and backpacker haunts doesn't make these street stalls and oily metal tables any less authentic: the *wan tan mee*, dim sum, *curry mee*, *laksa, poh piah, lor bak* and fried oyster (food from RM3.60) are served on plastic plates while screaming aunties peddle their drinks. Daily 6pm–midnight.

Cozy in the Rocket 262 & 264 Lebuh Pantai. Arty café with eclectic choice of furniture and a pleasant outdoor garden with little potted plants. The changing menu is scribbled on the board; breakfasts (RM15), great coffees (RM6) and pasta dishes (RM23). Tues–Sun 10am–5pm.

Kapitan's 93 Lebuh Chulia. This 24hr Penang institution is good for post-midnight cravings for tandoori chicken, claypot biryani or curry. Perpetually popular, but service is tediously slow. Mains RM8. Daily 24hr.

The Leaf Healthy House 5 Lebuh Penang. Laidback Chinese veggie café perfect for a healthy pit stop as you explore town; there are Nyonya dishes, noodles, high-fibre rice and spaghetti (RM5.90), as well as exceptional fresh juices. Mon–Fri 11.30am–2.30pm & 5.30–8.45pm, Sat 11.30am–8.45pm.

★**Line Clear** Cnr Chulia & Penang. Hands down one of George Town's best *nasi kandar* (rice with curry) at this no-frills hawker stall where an exceptionally tasty meal will set you back no more than RM10. Daily 24hr.

Micke's Place 94 Love Lane. Travellers scribble their musings all over the walls of this itty-bitty café serving local and Western dishes, from pancakes (RM9) to pastas (RM13). Mon–Sat 4pm–midnight.

★**The Mugshot** 302 Lebuh Chulia. This friendly café offers freshly made yoghurt served in cute glass jars with imaginative toppings, from kiwi and honey to walnuts and raisins, and tasty home-made bagels prepared in the little wood-fired oven. There's a great bakery attached, too, and free wi-fi. Daily 8am–9pm.

Penang Road 55 Tahun Cendol Lebuh Keng Kwee. Penang's quintessential ice-and-sugar-based sweets *cendol* and *ais kacang* (RM2.50) from the original stall that has dished them up for fifty-odd years. Further down the road, their sister operation *Joo Hooi* sells great Penang *Assam laksa*. Daily 8am–5.30pm.

Red Garden Night Market 20 Lebuh Leith. George Town's most central food court boasts an array of

6

6

scrumptious dishes: grilled seafood, claypot noodles, *hokkien mee* (prawn noodles), Indian curries and Thai food – but the karaoke singing shows are slapstick and noisy, and don't facilitate conversation. Mains from RM6. Daily 5.30pm–2am.

Toh Soon Coffee 184 Lebuh Campbell. Locals flock to this back alley filled with metal tables to drink delicious old-school Nanyang *kopi* and gorge on *roti bakar* and boiled eggs. Even current Penang chief minister, Lim Guan Eng, is a habitué. Mon–Sat 8am–6pm.

Transfer Road Famous Roti Canai Transfer Rd between Jln Hutton & Jln Koyah. Sit at the roadside among chatty locals to enjoy Penang's *roti canai mamak* from this eighty-year-strong powerhouse. Whether you want *roti* and curry, a frothy *kopi* or boiled eggs on *roti bakar* – toasted bread smeared with coconut jam and butter – this is a perfect breakfast choice. Daily 6.30am–1pm.

Woodlands 60 Lebuh Penang. This vegetarian South Indian restaurant fills up rapidly at mealtimes, attracting plenty of custom. Try some of their "tongue tickling dishes": the *chenna batura*, large bread served with chickpea stew (RM4.40), or *malai kofta*, potato cooked in ground cashew paste and onion-tomato gravy (RM6.90), are recommended. Daily 8.30am–10pm.

DRINKING AND NIGHTLIFE

Most of George Town's bars are comfortable places to hang out, but try to avoid the shady Chinese karaoke bars renowned for their female "Guest Relation Officers" – a good many turn into meat markets. Usual opening hours are 6pm–2am. Upper Jln Penang is lined with buzzing night venues charging around RM25–50. Wednesday is "ladies' night".

Antarabangsa Enterprise 21 Lorong Stewart. Love it or hate it, this no-frills hole-in-the-wall Chinese-run bar has become a backpacker's favourite thanks to its bargain offer of three beer cans for RM10 and for its loud, quirky, multi-ethnic local characters. Beware: sitting at these sticky tables always results in late, rowdy nights. Daily 5pm–late.

The Canteen @ China House 153 & 155 Lebuh Pantai ☎ 04 263 7299, ⓦ facebook.com/TheCanteenAtChinaHouse. Enjoy a cocktail (RM22) or two at this artsy bar and performance venue which hosts great live music bands, from jazz to folk, on Fridays, Saturdays and Sundays at 9.30pm. Daily 6pm–midnight, Fri & Sat until 1am.

★ **Hin Bus Depot** 31a Jln Gurdwara, ⓦ hinbusdepot .com. Part rotating art gallery, part relaxing cocktail-style open garden filled with cafés, restaurants and arts workshop, this former bus park is one of the liveliest, hippest places to socialize island-wide. The Sunday secondhand pop-up market has plenty of artsy bargains. Mon–Fri noon–8pm, Sat & Sun 11am–9pm.

Narrow Marrow 252 Lebuh Carnarvon ☎ 016 553 6647, ⓦ facebook.com/narrowmarrow. This DIY-furnished, tunnel-like bar with tons of character is great to sip Toddy (palm wine) mojitos (RM12) and rub shoulders with Penang's creatives while indie tunes crackle from vintage speakers. Fri–Sun 2pm–1am.

★ **Soundmaker Studio** 2nd Floor, 62 Pengkalan Weld ⓦ facebook.com/Soundmakerstudio. A welcoming DIY recording studio and bar where most Malaysian, Southeast Asian and international touring punk, metal and alternative rock bands thrash the stage. Check their webpage for gig information, or drop by to meet the scenesters. Daily 2pm–midnight.

DIRECTORY

Banks and exchange Major banks (Mon–Fri 10am–3pm, Sat 9.30–11.30am) with ATMs are along Lebuh Pantai. Licensed moneychangers are on Lebuh Pantai, Lebuh Chulia and Jln Kapitan Kling (daily 8.30am–6pm).

Hospital Penang General Hospital, Jln Residensi (☎ 04 222 5333).

Immigration office Pejabat Imigresen, Lebuh Pantai at Lebuh Light (Mon–Fri 8am–5pm; ☎ 04 250 3413).

Laundry G&C Laundry, 461 Lebuh Chulia (Mon–Sat 9am–8pm; RM5/kg).

Pharmacy There are several pharmacies along Jln Penang, as well as in the KOMTAR complex.

TRAVEL TO THAILAND

There are regular **minibus services** to Thailand, including Bangkok (3 daily; 18hr), Hat Yai (4 daily; 4hr), Krabi (3 daily; 8hr), Koh Lanta (daily; 8hr), Koh Phi Phi (daily; 11hr), Koh Li Pe (daily; 11hr), Koh Samui (3 daily; 12hr), Kho Phangan (3 daily; 16hr), Koh Tao (3 daily; 18hr), Phuket (2 daily; 13hr), Surat Thani (3 daily; 9hr) and Trang (3 daily; 6hr). There's likely to be a change of vehicle in Hat Yai with a fair amount of waiting around, but booking it all as one trip from Penang does at least save you the hassle of having to organize the different legs of the journey yourself. Otherwise, commuter **trains** leave Butterworth at 7.28am and 1.38pm for the border at Padang Besar (1hr 45min; RM12), Here you can buy tickets for overnight Thai Railways train 36 to Bangkok (16hr; RM112), leaving Padang Besar daily at 6.40pm. Hat Yai is the first stop (50min), followed by Surat Thani (for Ko Samui and Ko Tao; 11.54pm), Chumpon (for Ko Tao; 2.34am), Hua Hin (6.29am) and Nakhon Pathom (for Kanchanaburi; 9.03am).

Police station The tourist police is at Lebuh Dickens, just off Jln Penang (☎ 04 899 3222).

Post office The GPO is on Lebuh Downing (Mon–Fri 8.30am–5.30pm, Sat 8.30am–1pm).

Batu Ferringhi

BATU FERRINGHI, a 45-minute bus ride west of George Town on bus #101, is a spread-out one-street village largely populated by flash resorts, but with a decent enough beach and several guesthouses. The road runs more or less straight along the coast for 3km, with all the hotels and restaurants lined up side by side.

Nearby is the peaceful **Tropical Spice Garden** (daily 9am–6pm; RM26), with a range of spices growing among five hundred species of tropical flora and fauna. A few kilometres west is a **batik factory** (daily 9am–5.30pm; free), where you can watch Malaysian-style batik being made and buy the finished product. One kilometre further up the road is **Entopia** (daily 9am–7pm, last entry 5.30pm; RM49; ⓦentopia.com), a re-branding of former Butterfly Farm. This eco-theme park boasts over a hundred species of tropical butterflies. The two storeys of exhibits, plus guided walks, cater to families and nature lovers, and make for a few hours of evergreen entertainment observing and interacting with the insects.

ACCOMMODATION AND EATING

The budget guesthouses face the beach and are all on the same street.

Ali's ☎ 04 881 1316. A welcoming guesthouse with simple rooms set over two floors that open on to a leafy courtyard. Some have private bath and there's a shaded lounge area perfect for a short afternoon kip. Doubles RM80

Baba Guesthouse ☎ 04 881 1686, ⓔbabaguesthouse2000@yahoo.com. Friendly, budget, family-run guesthouse with clean rooms and a welcoming owner who can organize onward domestic travel, as well as buses to Thailand and Singapore. Doubles RM60

Bora Bora ☎ 04 885 1313. This laidback beachside bar with fairy lights and a jungle-like ambience is a popular spot to enjoy a sundowner. There's Western food too, and beach boys lighten up the scene with fire shows. Mains RM13, beer RM15. Mon–Thurs & Sun noon–1am, Fri & Sat noon–3am.

PULAU LANGKAWI

Situated 30km off the coast at the very northwestern tip of the Peninsula is a cluster of 104 tropical islands, the largest of which is **PULAU LANGKAWI**, a resort island popular with travellers and locals alike. Here it's easy to while away a good few days, snorkelling, beach-hopping, taking trips to the mangrove areas and exploring the waters around the island by boat. The name Langkawi combines the Malay words *helang* (eagle) and *kawi* (strong) – hence the eagle is the symbol for the island. Langkawi's principal town is **Kuah**, on the southeastern side of the island, but the main tourist developments have been on the southwest of the island, at **Pantai Tengah** and **Pantai Cenang**.

Langkawi is a large island – almost 500 square kilometres – and to explore it properly you'll need to rent a car or scooter. There is basically one circular road around the island, with the other main road running north and south along with some minor roads branching off from it.

Kuah

Located in the southeastern corner of the island, **Kuah** is the largest town on Langkawi and has a ferry terminal, hotels and duty-free shopping complexes. You'll be passing through here if taking a boat to Penang or Thailand.

Pantai Tengah and Pantai Cenang

A clearly signed junction 18km west from Kuah points you to the popular beaches of **Pantai Cenang** and **Pantai Tengah**. Within walking distance of each other, these two main strips are the best places for cheap accommodation. Overdeveloped Pantai Cenang has numerous bars and restaurants, with Malaysia's largest aquarium, the soulless concrete **Underwater World** (daily 10am–6pm; RM43), lying about half-way down.

The bay itself forms a large sweep of wide, white beach with crisp, sugary sand, and is hugely popular with travellers. Plenty of places offer **watersports** such as jet skiing (RM120/30min), waterskiing (RM120/15min) and parasailing

6

6

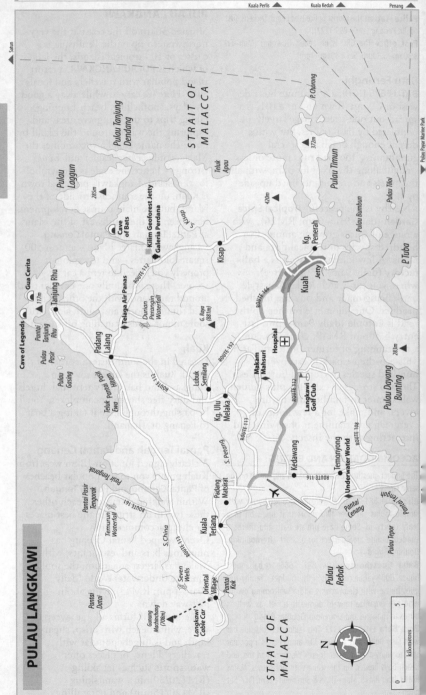

PULAU LANGKAWI

(RM100). **Boat trips** are also easy to arrange (see box, p.455). Animal lovers may also consider volunteering with **Langkawi Animal Shelter & Sanctuary Foundation** (@info@langkawilassie .org.my).

Gunung Machinchang

Head north along the coast past the airport and you'll eventually reach **Mount Machinchang**, the vertiginous hilly jungle (708m high at its peak) scaled by the **Langkawi Cable Car** (daily 10am–7pm, Wed from noon; 15min; RM45) from the touristy shopping complex below. It is allegedly the steepest in the world, and the journey up is pretty spectacular, with the cable cars wobbling up a sheer cliff at an angle of 42 degrees. Avoid weekends and public holidays as you may end up queuing for hours waiting for your ride. From the Skybridge (admission RM5) and the two viewing stations at the top you can see the entirety of the island, as well as some Thai islands. If it's windy, the cable cars won't run.

Telaga Tujuh (Seven Wells)

Shortly before the turn-off for the cable car, a side road leads to **Seven Wells**, a series of natural rock pools connected by a stream gliding over smooth rock, making natural water slides – great, refreshing fun. It's reached via a ten-minute climb up a long staircase leading up from the car park; there is also a signposted 2.5km trail that runs up to the top of Gunung Machinchang, from which you can descend by cable car.

The beaches

The north coast has several attractive **beaches**. Langkawi's loveliest, cleanest beach at **Datai**, reachable by signposted turn-off from Route 113, is accessible only to hotel guests, but on the way you pass a small crescent of white sand with some picnic tables, popular with locals and holidaying Russians, just before the path to the **Temurun waterfall** on the opposite side of the road. With its gorgeous white sand and stunning aquamarine water, Langkawi's northernmost beach – **Tanjung Rhu** – is another attractive option, though it lacks any shade. Though Tanjung Rhu is known for its sunsets, thanks to its location on the west side of the island, the views from Pantai Cenang are actually almost as good.

Gunung Raya

Route 112, which cuts across the middle of the island from Tanjung Rhu to the airport and beyond, has a turn-off to the east halfway along for **Gunung Raya** (881m), Langkawi's tallest mountain. A long, winding and somewhat potholed road leads up to the summit, from where you can enjoy all-encompassing views of the island and beyond.

Galeria Perdana

If you take Route 112 between Padang Lalang and Kuah, you will pass the vastly entertaining **Galeria Perdana** (daily 8.30am–5.30pm; RM15), a private museum dedicated to the splendid gifts that former Malay prime minister, Dr Mohathir Mohammed, received from various heads of state.

ARRIVAL AND DEPARTURE

By plane The airport is 6km north of Pantai Cenang; a taxi will cost RM36 from the prepaid taxi counter in the airport into town.
Destinations Kuala Lumpur (hourly; 1hr); Singapore (2 daily; 1hr 30min); Penang (3 daily; 35min).
By boat Destinations from the Kuah jetty (reachable by taxi only; RM25): Kuala Perlis (hourly; 1hr 15min); Kuala Kedah (hourly; 1hr 45min); Penang (2 daily; 3hr); Satun,

---

BEWARE THE JELLYFISH!

In **jellyfish season** (Feb & March) it's advised not to go swimming, as the **deadly box jellyfish**, responsible for at least three deaths since the 1990s, has been sighted in Langkawi waters, particularly near the mangroves. If you do go for a dip, you're likely to experience a sort of electric shock sensation when you're in the water, which can be a little uncomfortable while swimming. If you notice that you have a visible or particularly painful sting, a splash of vinegar or alcohol (NOT fresh water) should help alleviate it.

6

Thailand (3 daily; 1hr 15min). In high season (Oct–April) there are also boats to Kho Lipe, Thailand (2 daily; 45min).

INFORMATION

Tourist information There are three information points: one at the airport (daily 9am–10pm; ☎04 955 7155); one at the Kuah jetty (daily 9am–5pm; ☎04 966 0494); and one in Jln Persiaran Putra (daily 9am–5pm; ☎04 966 7789).

GETTING AROUND

By car and motorbike Private companies at Kuah jetty, the airport or many guesthouses and hotels offer motorbike and scooter rental (from RM30/day) – the cheapest and most convenient way to explore the island. Take a map, water and plenty of sunscreen. Renting a car will set you back about RM80/day, plus fuel.

By taxis A journey to Pantai Cenang from both the Kuah jetty and from the airport will cost you around RM25/person; from Pantai Cenang to Tanjung Rhu it costs around RM60.

ACCOMMODATION

PANTAI TENGAH

★**Pondok Keladi** Lot 1011, Kg. Padang Putih ☎012 536 9216, ⍟pondok-keladi.com. This wonderful guesthouse has six neat and pleasant a/c, en-suite rooms decked out in Malay and Indonesian furnishings and opening on to the well-manicured garden. There's a lovely chill-out area with kitchenette and plenty of complimentary food, from noodles to eggs. The owner also rents out a fully equipped house sleeping five close to the beach (RM150). Doubles RM120

Zackry Guest House 735 Jln Teluk Baru. Three dogs plod the premises of this family-run place, which has a slightly grubby feel; there's a laidback family vibe, with plenty of day-trips organized with other travellers, frequent communal meals and fun drinking games. A good option for solo travellers. Dorms RM30, doubles RM70

PANTAI CENANG

Gecko Guesthouse Jl Pantai Cenang, turn off opposite *Orkid Ria* ☎019 428 3801. This verdant guesthouse has a series of rooms set around a leafy communal area. There's a bar with cheap drinks that stays open until midnight, and a café serving breakfast too. Dorms RM20, doubles RM45

Langkawi Dormitorio Unit 5, 1556 Jln Pantai Cenang ☎017 236 2587. A good, central choice for clean and airy dorms with individual pods and private bathrooms, or bigger, luminous family rooms that are ideal for groups travelling together. Dorms RM50

Rainbow Inn Kampung Haji Maidin ☎04 955 8103, ⍟rainbowlangkawi.com. As the name suggests, this large place with over fifty rooms is decked out in myriad bright colours; there are fifteen fully furnished houses each

sleeping four, as well as a selection of doubles and a large twenty-bed dorm by the communal area, which has a pool table and café. Dorms RM25, doubles RM55

Sweet Monkey Backpacker 16 Jln Pantai Cenang ☎017 492 1135. This sociable dorm-only hostel (mixed and female) is a good central choice in Cenang. Besides good information, discounted island-hopping tours, a kitchenette for guest use and a relaxing, reggae-themed common living room, they offer muay thai lessons with Malaysian trainers (Tues & Sun 5–7pm; RM30), scooter and car rental. Dorms RM29

EATING AND DRINKING

PANTAI TENGAH

Bam-Boo-Ba End of Sunba Block, Jln Teluk Baru ☎012 566 0254, ⍟facebook.com/bamboobaloungebar. A lively horseshoe-shaped bar with outdoor seating to kick off the night munching on burgers (RM19) and pizzas (RM26). Their "buy two drink three" cocktail happy hour (5–9pm; from RM16) packs a crowd. Tues–Sun 5pm–1am.

La Chocolatine On the northern end of Tengah. All ingredients are imported from France at this French-run café and bakery serving delectable home-baked pastries (RM8), from flaky croissants to warm *pain au chocolat*. There's even goat's cheese salad (RM28) and crêpes (RM10) for a light lunch. Daily 8.30am–7pm.

Sunba On the northern end of Tengah. Located in a large complex, this bar with wooden interiors is set out to resemble a dwelling in a traditional Malay village. There's an in-house band as well as DJs spinning retro tracks from the 1960s to 1980s. You can belt your heart out at the karaoke rooms within the same building, or try your hand at snooker. Daily 11pm–4am.

★**TREAT YOURSELF**

Bon Ton Resort Pantai Cenang ☎04 955 3643, ⍟bontonresort.com. Just a five-minute drive from Cenang's uninspiring concrete strip, *Bon Ton's* eight luxurious Malay stilt houses are the perfect location for tranquillity (doubles RM375). *Nam restaurant* serves a tantalizing range of Asian and Western fusion dishes (mains around RM40). Right next door, sister property *Temple Tree at Bon Ton* (⍟templetree.com.my; doubles RM700) boasts eight restored wooden mansions. Each house, relocated to Langkawi from the Peninsula's most hidden corners, masterfully represents a different Malaysian cultural heritage and architectural style.

LANGKAWI TOURS

The most popular activities on Langkawi are **speedboat trips** to the nearby islands, **diving and snorkelling trips** and **mangrove tours** on the north coast. Most guesthouses can arrange pick-up.

A whole plethora of companies offer half-day speedboat island-hopping tours (RM45), which usually consist of landing on one of the nearby islands for a swim in the freshwater lake, and a stop to feed the sea eagles – not a particularly environmentally sound practice as it can result in food poisoning and makes the birds dependent on handouts.

Dev's Adventure Tours ⓦ langkawi-nature.com. Highly recommended operator leading sea safaris on kayak (RM200), jungle treks (RM140) and nature cycling tours (RM140) around the island.

East Marine ☏ 04 966 3966, ⓦ eastmarine.com.my.

Specializes in diving and snorkelling ventures to Pulau Payar, halfway between Langkawi and Penang; day-trips depart at 9.30am, returning around 4pm; snorkelling RM300, diving RM400.

★ **Yam-Yam Café** On the southern end of Tengah ☏ 012 616 4417, ✉ yamyamlangkawi@gmail.com. With an original Italian espresso machine, this Malaysian–Dutch-run café mixes Western and Asian home-style cuisine, and is perfect for a breakfast or a casual lunch. The non-dairy smoothies, especially the berry blast, are great on any hot day. Mon & Wed–Sun: May–Nov 9am–5pm; Dec–April 9am–2.30pm & 6–10pm.

PANTAI CENANG

There are a few places along the beach at Pantai Cenang that are great for a sundowner or after-dinner cocktails. The area's only club is further south at Pantai Tengah.

★ **Red Tomato** Opposite *McDonald's* ☏ 04 955 4055, ⓦ redtomatorestaurant.com.my. This hugely popular German/Malay-owned place attracts expats and travellers for generous, tasty dishes of international grub such as leafy salads, thin-crust pizzas, saucy pastas, wonderful desserts and mean burgers. All the above also come gluten free. Mains from RM20. Daily 9am–11pm.

Smiling Buffalo 965 Kuala Chenang ☏ 017 364 3319, ⓦ facebook.com/smilingbuffalocafe. Next to the Panji Panji resort, 5min drive from Cenang's main strip, this Malay-style cottage has live blues music matinees and a homey feel. There's good coffee, fresh mango-topped waffles (RM13) and breakfast sets served on a cosy outdoor verandah. Daily 8am–6pm.

Thirstday Lot 1225 Jln Pantai Cenang, behind *Orkid Ria* ☏ 017 515 5395, ✉ thirstdaybarandrestaurant@gmail .com. Cenang's beachside outdoor club pumps r'n'b tunes, serves 35 different cocktails (from RM20) and spills tables on a pretty stretch of beach that's ideal for sundowners and good vibes. Daily 11am–1am.

Yellow Café Towards the south end of Cenang. Commanding a great spot on the beach, this French-owned restaurant offers great steaks, kebabs, salads and seafood barbecue. The cocktails (RM20) complement the

sunset very nicely indeed, and there are occasional live bands. Mains from RM20. Tues–Sun noon–1am.

DIRECTORY

Banks Langkawi's banks are on three parallel streets behind the MAYA shopping complex in Kuah. In Pantai Cenang there is a Maybank with ATM at Cenang Mall; there's also a Maybank ATM at Underwater World and a couple of ATMs and moneychangers at the airport.

Hospital The Langkawi District Hospital is at Jln Bukit Teguh (☏ 04 966 3333).

Laundry On the northern end of Pantai Tengah. Two Seasons Laundry (daily 9am–7pm; RM4.50/kg). Or Cucee (daily 9am–7pm; RM5/kg), on the northern end of Jln Pantai Cenang.

Post offices The GPO is at Jln Kisap in Kuah town; there's also a branch at Padang Matsirat near the airport (daily except Fri 8am–5pm).

The interior

Banjaran Titiwangsa (Main Range) forms the western boundary of the interior; to its east is an H-shaped range of steep sandstone mountains and luxuriant valleys where small towns and villages nestle. The rivers that flow from these mountains – Pahang, Tembeling, Lebir, Nenggiri and Galas – provide the northern interior's indigenous peoples, the Negritos and Senoi, with their main means of transport. Visitors, too, can travel by boat to perhaps the most stunning of all Peninsular Malaysia's delights, **Taman Negara National Park**, with its numerous jungle trails.

6

JERANTUT

JERANTUT, a small grid of streets surrounded by jungle, with only one major street, Jalan Besar, is the gateway to Taman Negara National Park. On Saturday nights, the area next to the new bus station comes alive with a night market. Jerantut also has useful transport links to the Perhentian Islands, Kota Bharu, Kuala Terengganu and Kuantan.

ARRIVAL AND DEPARTURE

By bus and minibus The new bus station is located along Jln Irong 3, right outside the town centre and 10min walk north of the roundabout at the end of Jln Besar.

Long-distance destinations To Kuala Lumpur (7 daily, last at 7pm; 3hr); Jengka/Kuantan (2 daily Mon–Thurs; 3 daily Fri–Sun; 3hr 30min); Dungun/Kuala Terengganu (Mon 5pm; Thurs 8.30am & 5pm; Fri–Sun 7.30pm); Kota Bharu (Mon–Thurs 9.30pm; Fri–Sun 9.30am & 9.30pm). *NKS Hotel & Travel* arranges transport to the Perhentian Islands (9hr), the Cameron Highlands (3hr 30min), Kota Bharu (9hr), Penang (6hr 30min) and Kuala Lumpur (2hr 30min) according to demand.

Local destinations Take a local bus towards Kuala Lipis (daily 6am, 10.30am & 3.30pm; 40min; RM5) and ask the driver to let you off at the Tembeling jetty if you want to approach Taman Negara by river. Otherwise you can take the bus all the way to Kuala Tahan, the village opposite the park headquarters (daily 8am & 1pm; 2hr; RM7), if you prefer to get there quicker. Note that both *NKS Hotel & Travel* and *Greenleaf Travellers Inn* offer a convenient minibus service both to the jetty (daily 8.30am & 1.30pm; 30min; RM5) and the village itself (daily 6.30am, 8.30am & 4.30pm; 1hr; RM25).

By train The train station is off Jln Besar, just behind *Hotel Sri Emas*. Only two trains leave from Jerantut (see box below) in the middle of the night. Check ⓦ ktmb.com.my for the latest schedules.

Destinations Kota Bharu (1 daily at 4.16am; 8hr); Johor Bahru (1 daily at 3.12am; 8hr). For Kuala Lumpur, take the Johor Bahru-bound train and change at Gemas.

ACCOMMODATION AND EATING

Food Court Jln Pasar Besar. Between the train and bus stations there are several open-air restaurants clustered along the side of the road. They're very popular with locals and travellers alike, and serve a mix of Thai, Malay and Chinese food, the special being *tom yam* soup, though there's excellent *roti, nasi goreng* and *kuey teow* too. Mains RM5. Daily 6pm–2am.

Hotel Sri Emas 46 Jln Besar ☏ 09 266 4499. A 5min walk from the train station, this basic hotel has very cheap, decent rooms with shared bathrooms on the top floor. The "dorm" is a bargain, but only has two beds. More expensive, spacious a/c rooms (RM35) dot the other two floors. Dorms RM8, doubles RM15

NKS Hotel & Travel 21–22 Jln Besar ☏ 09 260 1770, ⓦ taman-negara-nks.com. A backpacker favourite, this place is your one-stop shop for organizing your trip to Taman Negara — from transport to accommodation and activity packages. Rooms are pretty spartan and toilet facilities basic, but they are kept clean enough. Double RM48

TAMAN NEGARA NATIONAL PARK

Peninsular Malaysia's largest and most popular national park **Taman Negara** preserves some of the oldest rainforest in the world.

Accommodation ranges from luxury resorts and rustic guesthouses to jungle hides and campsites. The most popular and convenient location to base yourself from is **Kuala Tahan**, the village across the river from the park headquarters. It's best to **visit** the park between February and October, during the "dry" season, although it still rains then. In the wet season (mid-Oct to Feb), there may be restrictions on the trails and boat trips.

THE JUNGLE RAILWAY

Riding the scenic **Jungle Railway** from Johor Bahru to Kota Bharu, 700km to the northeast, through valleys where jungle vines almost envelop the track, used to be a Peninsula highlight and the best way to reach Taman Negara. Unfortunately, in December 2014 the line was interrupted by severe flood damage. With the introduction of the ETS system upgrades in 2016, the line reopened, but current schedules aren't convenient. For Taman Negara, only two direct trains stop in Jerantut: from Kota Bharu, sleeper train #27 leaves Wakaf Bharu at 7.48pm, arriving at 3.12am; from Johor Bahru, train #26 leaves at 7pm, arriving at 4.16am. Besides the ungodly arrival hours, riding the Jungle Railway in the dark defies the purpose. If you want to ride the Jungle Railway, but are not going to Taman Negara, train #26 from Johor Bahru is the best option as it rides in daylight for four hours between Dabong and Wakaf Bharu. Check ⓦ ktmb.com.my for up-to-date schedules.

WHAT TO SEE AND DO

Taman Negara offers a plethora of options for intense **trekking** and **wildlife-spotting**. Attractions include the bat caves of Gua Telinga, the river rapids of Trenggan River, a man-made canopy walkway, night jungle walks, night boat safaris and a lazy boat ride down the Sungai Tahan. You can strike out on multi-day treks staying at off-the-beaten-track jungle camps, or enjoy a relaxed meander through the jungle on plenty of short hikes that loop around the park headquarters.

The hides

Spending a night in one of the park's **hides** (*bumbun*), situated beside salt licks, doesn't guarantee sightings of large mammals, but the sound of the jungle at night does guarantee that it'll be a memorable experience, and you may catch sight of deer, tapir, elephant, leopard or wild ox. The hides offer very (very) basic bunk accommodation in concrete huts for six to eight people and must be booked at the wildlife office in the resort (around RM5/person, depending on the hide). They are sturdily built and sufficiently raised up that you don't have to worry about things creeping up on you during the night, and they do have very basic washing and toilet facilities (except Bumbun Tahan), but no electricity, so bring a torch. Take all the food and drink you will need, a sleeping bag, rain gear and hat – and don't forget to bring your rubbish back.

The closest hide to the park headquarters is the **Bumbun Tahan**, just south of the junction with the Bukit Teresek trail, but it's not possible to stay here overnight. There's also the **Bumbun Tabing**, on the east bank of Sungai Tahan, about 3km from the start of the trail, and **Bumbun Cegar Anjing**, an hour from the Tabing, across the river on the west bank of Sungai Tahan. The most distant hide to the north of the resort is the six-bed **Bumbun Kumbang**, an 11km walk from Kuala Tahan and the best place to catch sight of animals, since the number of visitors to the park scare the wildlife at the hides closer to the park headquarters.

The canopy walkway

The **canopy walkway** (Mon–Thurs, Sat & Sun 9.30am–3.30pm, Fri 9am–noon; RM5), located about thirty minutes' walk east from the park headquarters, is a swaying bridge made from aluminium ladders bound by rope and set 40m above the ground. At 530m, it's one of the longest walkways of its kind in the world – but only 300m were operational at time of research. Particularly in the mornings, it's a good opportunity to rise above the jungle and spot grey-banded leaf monkeys and white-eyed dusky leaf monkeys swinging among the branches. It takes around twenty minutes to cross; from the walkway, you can climb up to the two viewpoints of Bukit Teresek. The first grants panoramic views over the surrounding jungle and Tembeling River, while the second faces Peninsular Malaysia's highest mountain, Gunung Tahan.

The Bukit Indah trail

This is a steep but lovely hill climb, meandering northeast past the canopy. It's a three-hour round trip from the park headquarters. Initially, this follows the riverbank, and you stand a chance of spotting monkeys, various birds, squirrels, shrews, a multitude of insects and perhaps tapir or wild ox. The path to Bukit Indah hill itself leaves the main riverside trail (which continues to Kuala Trenggan, 6km away) and climbs at a slight gradient for 200m to give a view over the jungle and the rapids of Sungai Tembeling.

Gua Telinga Bat Cave

The major Rentis Tenor trail leads south alongside the river, with branches to Gua Telinga. From one of the floating restaurants in Kuala Tahan, take a taxi boat across the Sungai Tahan River. On the other side, the trail continues through a small village into the trees. After 3km, follow the sign north for a further 200m to reach the limestone cave of **Gua Telinga** ("Bat Cave"), which is teeming with tiny roundleaf and fruit bats, as well as giant toads, black-striped frogs and (non-venomous) whip spiders. You can follow a guide rope through the 80m-long cave, and it's weirdly good fun, even

6

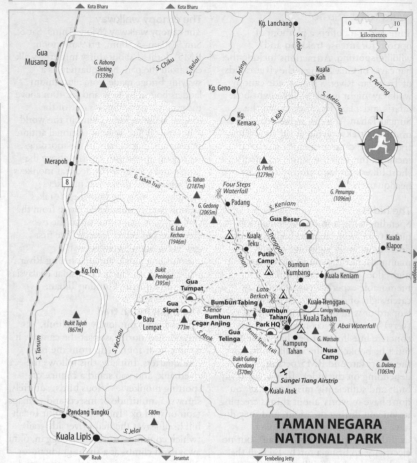

TAMAN NEGARA NATIONAL PARK

though fitting through some of the cavities requires some contortionist action (wear clothes you don't mind ruining).

The rapids of Lata Berkoh

Most people visit the rapids of **Lata Berkoh** by boat, but you could walk the trail there and arrange for a boat to pick you up for the return journey. **Sampans** from Kuala Tahan cost around RM90 for four people and take half an hour. The **trail** from the park headquarters (8.5km; 4hr) starts at the campsite and leads through dense rainforest, then crosses gullies and steep ridges, before reaching the river, which must be forded. The final part of the trail runs north along the west side of Sungei Tahan before reaching the

rapids. The **rapids** themselves are 50m north of *Lata Berkoh* campsite. There's a deep pool for swimming, and you may see kingfishers, large fish eagles, bulbul birds and monitor lizards.

The Keniam trail

From the park headquarters *sampans* travel to Kuala Keniam jetty (1hr 30min), passing Kampung Pagi village along the way. The most popular hike from here is the **Keniam trail** (14km), a major highlight, where there's a small chance of spotting elephants, as well as porcupine, gaur (wild buffalo), clouded leopard, tapir, wild pigs, civets and sun bears. From the jetty a path leads through jungle (5–6hr; 7km) before reaching **Gua Kepayang Besar**

LOVELY LEECHES

Just after the monsoon, the **leeches** come to the surface with even greater wriggling enthusiasm than usual. Leech bites don't hurt at all (unless it's a tiger leech) and leeches are harmless, but if you are determined to avoid them, pick up some leech socks before you leave home and wear long trousers underneath. If you do get leeches on you, you can just gently ease them off; you'll find that locals don't bother with things such as lighters and salt; they tend to wait for the leech to fill its belly with your blood, before leaving satisfied.

cave, where most visitors stay overnight. The following morning, the hike continues to Kuala Trenggan (5–6hr; 7km), from where you can catch a *sampan* back to Kuala Tahan (30min). Alternatively, you can spend an extra night at *Bumbun Kumbang* campsite, about five hours south of the cave, from where you can then trek to Kuala Trenggan.

Gunung Tahan

The park's most rugged trek takes you to Gunung Tahan, Peninsular Malaysia's **highest mountain** (2187m). The mountain is 55km from the park headquarters and the trek is doable in either seven or nine days, depending on the route you take. There are some steep scrambles en route and you have to take everything with you – from a tent, able to withstand torrential rain, to food and water. There are a number of campsites along the way (RM1/person). For this hike, a guide is mandatory (RM1200 for 7 days, maximum of 12 persons; add RM150 for every additional night). The park headquarters can help you organize the hike; get in touch several days in advance.

Other activities

The park headquarters and tour operators such as NKS organize the popular **night jungle walk** (1hr 30min; RM35), with the guide pointing out nocturnal insects and fauna; a **night safari** is similar but involves a 4WD (RM40). It's also possible to ride the **river rapids** on the Trenggan River and combine that with a visit to one of the local Orang Asli communities (both combined RM60), where the tribal elders demonstrate traditional skills such as fire-starting and blowpipe shooting. Most of the fee for visiting goes to the tour company, so purchasing some handicrafts ensures that the community benefits directly.

ARRIVAL AND DEPARTURE

Kuala Tahan is small and everything is within easy walking distance.

By bus/minibus Buses and minibuses pull up opposite the car park just in front of the primary school.

Destinations There are four local buses daily to Jerantut (7.30am, 10am, 3pm & 7pm; 2hr; RM7), from where there are connections to Kuala Lumpur, Kuantan, Kuala Terengganu and Kota Bharu. *NKS* runs three minibuses daily to Jerantut (8am, 10am & 7pm; 1hr 30min; RM25), with onwards minibus connections (see p.456).

By boat Most visitors approach the park by taking a scenic longboat ride from the Tembeling jetty (daily 9am; 3hr; RM35) along the Tahan River to the village of Kuala Tahan; you may well spot monkeys leaping through trees along the way or hornbills sitting on the tallest branches. Boats from the Tembeling jetty dock at the Kuala Tahan jetty just below the village. Regular boats transport ferry passengers across the river to the park headquarters (RM1). Longboats make the return journey to the Tembeling jetty (2hr 30min) at 2pm (double-check times in advance).

INFORMATION

Taman Negara Park Information Centre At the Park Headquarters (Mon–Thurs, Sat & Sun 8am–6pm, Fri 8am–noon & 3–6pm; ☏ 09 266 1122), located at the *Mutiara Taman Negara Resort*, on the opposite bank of the Sungai Tahan from Kuala Tahan, easily reachable by *sampan*, which ferry people across all day (RM1). It deals with all park queries, books you into hides and offers an excellent free site and park map. You can also obtain park entry (RM1) and camera permits (RM5) here; if you come to the park by boat, you pay for the two at the jetty. Hold on to your permit at all times; the penalty for not having a permit is a fine of up to RM10,000 and three years' imprisonment. The park headquarters screen introductory videos on Taman Negara (daily 9.30am, 3pm & 5pm; 25min).

Services There are shops in Kuala Tahan that rent sleeping bags and mats (RM10–15) – though it's best to bring your own. Reliable internet is found at IDD Internet, opposite *Teresek View Motel*.

Trekking in the park The trails are well signposted, but pay attention as several boardwalks are in dire need of

6

maintenance. Most trails do not require guides, though you will get more out of your hikes if accompanied by someone who really knows the jungle and who can point out medicinal and edible plants or spot well-camouflaged wildlife. Guides are licensed by the Ministry of Tourism; the park headquarters can help you to arrange a guide for the day (RM250).

ACCOMMODATION

Most accommodation options besides *Mutiara Taman Negara Resort* are located across the river in Kuala Tahan village.

Mahseer Chalet ☎ 019 383 2633. The neat and tidy wooden chalets here are kept clean; rooms have private bath and a/c, and there's wi-fi too. Dorms RM25, doubles RM90

Mutiara Taman Negara ☎ 09 266 2200, ⓦ mutiarahotels.com. This luxurious resort is by far the best place to camp; you can pitch a tent in the lush grounds shaded by large trees for a very reasonable price (RM15; RM10 if you have your own tent). The location is handy too, as all the park's trails start from here. There are also pricey eight-bed dorms with mosquito nets, ceiling fans, lockers and communal bathrooms. There's a kitchen for campers too, and wi-fi in the lobby area. Dorms RM80, doubles RM320

Rayyan Hostel ☎ 012 679 2637. This simple backpacker pad with great views over the river is run by chilled owners who treat guests like family. It has only two dorms, but the quiet verandah is a perfect spot to strike up a conversation with other travellers, and the pay-as-you-drink mailbox tells a lot about the general good vibes. Dorms RM20

Tahan Guest House ☎ 017 970 2025. This laidback double-storey house 5min walk from the town's main road has a spacious front garden and oozes good vibes thanks to the pastel-coloured, nature-themed murals etched on its walls. The spacious rooms, all with fans, bathrooms and mosquito nets, are a steal. Doubles RM40

Yellow Guest House ☎ 09 266 4243. Run by the warm and welcoming Mohamad, this friendly guesthouse has very spacious tiled rooms with a/c and private bath. There's just one cheap room with shared bath (RM40), while the pricier ones have private balconies. There's all-day tea and coffee, computers for guests' use and free wi-fi. Doubles RM70

EATING AND DRINKING

Floating Restaurants The riverside is lined with floating restaurants serving a samey mix of Malay, Indian and pseudo-Western dishes (mains RM6).

Mutiara Taman Negara Resort Besides being one of the very few places that serves alcohol, this fairly pricey restaurant at the park headquarters offers international dishes, such as pasta, steaks and burgers, welcome to those who've overdosed on noodles and rice. Mains from RM30. Daily noon–10pm.

The east coast

The 400km stretch from the northeastern corner of the Peninsula to Kuantan, roughly halfway down the east coast, is the most "Malay" region in Malaysia, with strong cultural traditions – particularly in **Kota Bharu**, the last major town before the Thai border, with its remarkable blend of Malay and Thai identities. The food on the east coast is some of the most imaginative in Malaysia, and Islamic traditions are strictly followed – the call to prayer may wake you up before sunrise, and on Fridays most businesses shut down. Locals are friendly and very open to travellers. There are some good beaches along the east coast, including laidback **Cherating**. The most beautiful beaches, however, are on **Pulau Perhentian** in the north, with its stunningly clear azure waters and white sands fringed with palm trees. Further south is **Pulau Kapas**, which also boasts fantastic coral reefs and wildlife in idyllic settings. The annual monsoon affects the east coast between November and February (see box, p.410).

KOTA BHARU

At the very northeastern corner of the Peninsula, close to the Thai border, **KOTA BHARU** is the capital of Kelantan State, one of the few **Muslim-governed** states in Malaysia. The town is laidback but growing rapidly, and offers a few interesting sights that will keep you busy for a day. There's an impressive Cultural Centre, lots of craft workshops, museums and a bustling night market. During the holy month of **Ramadan**, majority Muslim Kota Bharu is kept alive by its Chinese community.

WHAT TO SEE AND DO

Small Padang Merdeka in the north part of town is Kota Bharu's historical heart. There's a cluster of museums here (mostly Mon–Thurs, Sat & Sun 8.30am–4.45pm), the best of which is the **Istana Jahar** (daily 8.30am–4.45pm; RM4). It houses the Royal Customs Museum, whose ground floor is given over to a display of exquisite *ikat* and *songket* textiles and ornate gold jewellery. Upstairs, you'll see life size reconstructions of various traditional royal ceremonies, from weddings to circumcisions.

Around the corner to your left is the sky-blue **Istana Batu** (RM2), now the **Kelantan Royal Museum**, in which the sultan's family's rooms have been left in their original state, including photographs of the royal family.

Inside the impressive 1912 Bank Kerapu building, the **War Museum** on Jalan Sultan (RM4) tells the story of World War II in Southeast Asia and the effects of the Japanese occupation on Malaysia.

The octagonal **Siti Khadijah central market** along Jalan Bulu Kubuh is one of the most vibrant in Malaysia; from the first floor there's an extremely photogenic view of the produce stalls below, while the Buluh Kubu complex next door has several floors devoted to **batik** – an excellent place to pick up colourful dresses and shirts. Situated near the central market, the **Kampung Kraftangan** (Handicraft Village) has a small museum (Mon–Thurs & Sun 8.30am–4.45pm; RM1) with exhibits on traditional crafts, as well as **Zecman's** batik workshop (3hr RM50; day course 100RM) and some stalls selling batik and silverware.

The **Gelanggang Seni**, Kota Bharu's **Cultural Centre** on Jalan Mahmood, has free performances (Feb–Sept Mon, Wed & Sat except during Ramadan; free) that feature many of the traditional pastimes of Kelantan, including the vigorous sport of *gasing uri* (top-spinning), the playing of giant 100kg *rebana* drums, *silat* (traditional Malay martial art) displays and *wayang kulit* (shadow puppetry) performances.

ARRIVAL AND DEPARTURE

By plane AirAsia, Firefly, Malindo and Malaysia Airlines operate from Kota Bharu airport, located 9km northeast of the centre. A taxi into town from the airport costs RM30 – buy a coupon from the taxi counter inside.

Destinations KL (hourly; 1hr); Kuching (daily; 2hr); Kota Kinabalu (3 weekly; 2hr 40min); Penang (daily; 1hr).

By bus Transnational buses conveniently serve the Central Bus Station on Jln Hilir Pasar.

Destinations Kuala Besut (for the Perhentian Islands; almost hourly 6.15am–6.30pm; 2hr); Kuala Lumpur (3 daily; 8hr); Malacca (daily; 9hr); Butterworth (2 daily; 8hr); Penang (2 daily; 8hr); Kuala Terengganu (4 daily; 3hr); Kuantan (5 daily; 8hr); Rantau Panjang (Thai border; bus #29; every 30min; 1hr); Singapore (daily; 10–11hr);.

By train The nearest train station to Kota Bharu is 7km to the west at Wakaf Bharu, the penultimate stop on the Jungle Railway (see p.456). It's a 20min taxi ride into town (RM30). To save, get off one stop earlier at Pasir Mas, and catch a bus to Kota Bharu (6.45am–7pm).

Destinations Johor Bahru (daily 7.48pm; 16hr); Kuala Lipis (2 daily; 7hr). Double-check current schedules at ⓦktmb.com.my.

INFORMATION

Tourist information The Tourist Information Centre (Mon–Thurs, Sat & Sun 8am–5pm; ☏ 09 748 5534) on Jln Sultan Ibrahim has useful reading material and can book tours to local craft workshops. There's an information point at the airport, too (daily 6am–midnight; ☏ 09 773 7400).

ACCOMMODATION

KB Backpackers Inn 171–81 Jln Padang Garong ☏ 019 944 5222, ⓦ kbbackpackersinn.blogspot.com. This old-timer hostel has free gym equipment for guests, and ample lounge and rooftop space add value to the basic

TRAVEL TO THAILAND

The **eastern border crossings** are still currently advised against due to political unrest in the southeastern provinces of Thailand (see box, p.826). Nevertheless, a number of travellers keep using these overland routes: check the current travel advice before striking out.

From **Kota Bharu**'s central bus station there are regular buses to Rantau Panjang on the Thai border (every 30min; 1hr). You will pass through customs into Sungai Kolok in Thailand, from where trains travel north to Bangkok. There is a morning departure at 11.30am, calling at Hat Yai (4hr), Surat Thani (for transfers to Ko Tao, Ko Samui and Ko Pha Ngan; 10hr) and Bangkok (22hr), as well as an express train leaving at 2.20pm, calling at the same stations, and partially cutting travel time (although only by about 1–2hr). From the border, there are also plenty of minibuses to these destinations.

6

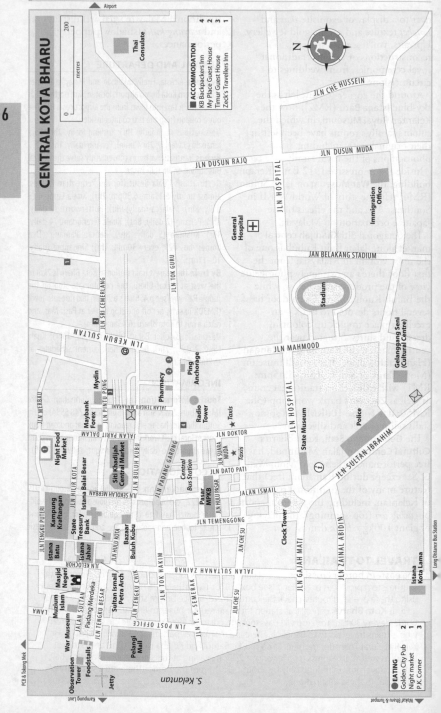

CENTRAL KOTA BHARU

Airport

0 — 200 metres

N

ACCOMMODATION
KB Backpackers Inn 4
My Place Guest House 2
Timur Guest House 3
Zeck's Travellers Inn 1

Thai Consulate

JLN CHE HUSSEIN

JLN DUSUN RAJQ

JLN DUSUN MUDA

Immigration Office

JLN HOSPITAL

General Hospital

JAN BELAKANG STADIUM

Stadium

JLN TOK GURU

JLN SRI CEMERLANG

JLN MAHMOOD

JLN KEBUN SULTAN

Gelanggang Seni (Cultural Centre)

Mydin

Maybank Forex

JLN PINTU PONG

Pharmacy

Ping Anchorage

JLN MERBAU

Radio Tower

JALAN TENGKU MARAANI

Taxis

JALAN PARIT DALAM

Night Food Market

Siti Khadijah Central Market

Istana Balai Besar

JLN HILIR KOTA

State Museum

Police

JLN HOSPITAL

JLN DOKTOR

JLN SUARA MUDA

Taxis

Central Bus Station

JLN BULUH KUBU

JLN PADANG GARONG

JLN DATO PATI

JLN SEKOLAH MERBAU

Kampung Kraftangan

State Treasury Bank

Pasar MPKB

JLN HULU PASAR

JALAN ISMAIL

JLN TENGKU PUTERI

Istana Batu

Istana Jahar

Bazaar Buluh Kubu

JLN HILIR KOTA

JLN TEMENGGONG

Clock Tower

JLN KELOCHOR

Masjid Negeri

Sultan Ismail Petra Arch

JLN TOK HAKIM

JALAN SULTANAH ZAINAB

JLN CHE SU

JLN GAJAH MATI

JLN ZAINAL ABIDIN

Muzium Islam

War Museum

JALAN SULTAN

Padang Merdeka

JLN TENGKU BESAR

JLN T. P. SEMERAK

JLN CHE SU

Istana Kota Lama

LAMA

Observation Tower

Foodstalls

JLN POST OFFICE

Pelangi Mall

Jetty

S. Kelantan

Kampung Laut

PCB & Telong Mek

Wakaf Bharu & Tumpat

Long Distance Bus Station

EATING
Golden City Pub 2
Night market 1
P.K. Corner 3

dorms and rooms. Undergoing renovation at the time of writing. Dorms RM18, doubles RM30

My Place Guest House 4340 R2 Jln Kebun Sultan ☎013 901 1463, ✉myplacekb@yahoo.com. This cosy two-storey townhouse at the edge of Chinatown earns points for its common room decorated with pop-and-Malay-culture memorabilia and a leafy outside verandah. The airy rooms are decked out in wood (a/c rooms RM45), and there's a large common kitchen perfect for those on tight budgets. Doubles RM35

Timur Guest House Lot 284-8, 2nd floor, Jln Tengku Maharni ☎012 922 7597, ✉timurguesthouse@gmail .com. Tucked away in a quiet back lane next to the city centre, *Timur* has wood-tiled floors, a/c dorms and three simple but cosy rooms that open onto a luminous lounge. They offer bicycle tours, free flow of tea and coffee and a wide DVD selection to pick from. Dorms RM25, doubles RM45

★**Zeck's Travellers Inn** 7088 Jln Sri Cemerlang ☎09 743 1613, ⊕zecktravellers.blogspot.com. Located about a 10min walk from the centre, this thirty-year-old backpacker favourite still offers the cheapest dorms in town and basic rooms with shared bathrooms. The friendly owners are a goldmine of information and organize cooking and batik classes. Dorms RM12, doubles RM30

EATING

Golden City Pub 3950-G Jln Padang Garong ☎012 212 8473. As if to prove travellers wrong, Muslim Kota Bharu now has a Western-styled pub serving beer (from RM12) and pork-based, Mexican-styled mains like bacon quesadillas (RM13), bacon burritos (RM12) and pastas (RM15). Mon–Fri & Sun 4pm–midnight.

Night market Jln Pintu Pong. Easily the most exciting place to eat, with a large variety of local dishes. Try the *ayam percik* (barbecued chicken with a creamy coconut sauce) or the delicious *nasi kerabu* (purple, green or blue rice with vegetables, seaweed and grated coconut); finish off with *pisang murtabak* (banana pancake) and you won't have parted with much more than RM12. Daily 6–10pm.

P.K. Corner 1069C Jln Kebun Sultan. It's often hard to get a table at this hugely popular outdoor place featuring local dishes from *tom yam* (RM6) to tempura (RM10), as well as more substantial mains such as crispy sea bass with mango salad (RM30). Daily 1pm–midnight.

BIRD-BARMY

If you hear **birdsong** outside your window at midnight, you're not hallucinating: residents of Kota Bharu are birdsong-crazy, and in some parts of town, birdsong is piped through loudspeakers to attract and encourage birds to nest.

DIRECTORY

Banks and exchange HSBC Bank, Jln Padong Garong; Standard Chartered Bank, Jln Tok Hakim.

Hospital Hospital Kota Bharu, Jln Hospital (☎09 748 5533).

Internet There's an internet café on Jln Kebun Sultan, diagonally opposite the road from *Sri Devi* (Mon–Thurs, Sat & Sun 9.30am–10pm, Fri 3–10pm; RM2/hr).

Post office On Jln Sultan Ibrahim.

Thai visas From the Royal Thai Consulate, 4426 Jln Tok Guru (Mon–Thurs & Sun 9am–noon & 2–3.30pm; ☎09 744 5266). Two-month tourist visas are issued within 24hr.

PULAU PERHENTIAN

Pulau Perhentian, just over 20km off the northeastern coast, is actually two islands – **Perhentian Kecil** (Small Island) and **Perhentian Besar** (Big Island), both less than 4km long. Both have turquoise waters and some of the most attractive white-sand beaches in Malaysia, although the effects of tourism are leaving a mark, with patches of dead coral and litter in evidence. The Perhentians remain a great place to learn to **dive**, though, thanks to some impressive rock formations, good visibility and one of the few wreck dives in the world suitable for relative beginners. But you don't have to dip far below the waves to see some spectacular marine life; most guesthouses offer **snorkelling trips** where you can see reef sharks, turtles and more. There's an excellent choice of budget accommodation (though wi-fi can be patchy and expensive), a good range of cafés and restaurants and a few laidback bars.

There are no banks on the islands; **change money** at Agro or Bank Simpanan Nasional close to Kuala Besut's new bus station before you go.

Perhentian Kecil

Perhentian Kecil is generally considered to be the livelier of the two islands and it is very popular with backpackers, having a slightly more ramshackle atmosphere than its larger neighbour. On the southeastern corner lies the island's only village, **Kampung Pasir Hantu**, with a jetty, police station, school, clinic and littered beach. **Coral Bay** is the most popular west-facing cove

6

on the island, lined with friendly guesthouses and shack restaurants. On the southwestern side, **Rainforest** and **Mira** beaches have inspiring jungle-backed accommodation options. East-facing **Long Beach** has a wide stretch of white beach and a laidback atmosphere, though litter management is currently a problem. The beach is much more exposed to the elements, and the crashing surf forces many of the chalet owners to close up from the end of October through to March.

Coral Bay is usually the first drop-off point when coming from the mainland.

Perhentian Besar

Perhentian Besar is more sedate than its neighbour and more popular with families and a slightly older crowd than with the backpacking set. The pace of life is even more laidback than on Kecil, but Besar's got plenty of budget accommodation and better beaches than its neighbour. The best place on the island for turtle-watching is undoubtedly **Three Coves Bay** on the north coast. A stunning conglomeration of three beaches, it is separated from the main area of accommodation by rocky outcrops and is reached only by speedboat. The bay provides a secluded haven between May and September for green and hawksbill turtles to come ashore and lay their eggs, though sadly, dwindling numbers mean the chances of spotting any are slim.

● EATING	
The Barat	4
Bubu	1
Ewan's Café	2
Mama's	3

■ DRINKING	
Beach Bar	1

■ ACCOMMODATION	
Abdul's	12
Coral View	9
Mama's Chalet	10
Matahari	4
Maya Chalets	7
Mohsin Chalets	6
New Coco Huts & Cozy Chalet	11
Ombak	2
Panorama	1
Rainforest Camping Perhentian	8
Tropicana Inn	3
Villa @ World Café	5

PULAU PERHENTIAN

ARRIVAL AND DEPARTURE

By boat A whole slew of companies run speedboats from the town of Kuala Besut to the islands, weather permitting (every hour or so 7am–5pm; 30min; RM70 return). Tell the boatman which bay you want to be dropped off at when you board; boats from the mainland can't dock at Perhentian Kecil's Long Beach, but stop 50m from shore; from here, you'll have to transfer to a smaller taxi boat (RM2) to take you to the shore. Boat travel is very weather-dependent, so services between the islands and Kuala Besut are virtually nonexistent during the November–February monsoon season. Boats leave the islands at 8am, noon and 4pm; let your guesthouse know the day before which boat you intend to take. There is a RM5 entrance fee to the islands that is paid upon boarding.

By bus From Kota Bharu's central bus station catch bus #629 to Kuala Besut (almost hourly between 6.30am and 6pm; 2hr).

Destinations From Kuala Besut: KL (4 daily; 8hr), Penang (2 daily; 7–8hr); Kuala Perlis (for Langkawi; daily; 8hr); Ipoh (1 daily; 8hr). From Jerteh, 16km away: Cherating (every 2hr; 5hr); Johor Bahru (daily; 8hr); Malacca (daily; 8hr); Mersing (for Tioman; every 2hr; 8hr); Singapore (daily; 9hr). Private minivans leave daily at 10am for Taman Negara, Cameron Highlands and Penang.

By taxi Most guesthouses in Kota Bharu organize shared taxis (1hr 30min; RM60) direct to Kuala Besut.

GETTING AROUND

By boat Taxi boats shuttle visitors between the beaches and two islands. Each bay has at least one clearly signposted taxi-boat point. Prices vary from RM10 to beaches on the same island, RM5 between the Fisherman's Village on Kecil and the point directly opposite on Besar, to RM25 to remoter coves on either island.

DIVE OPERATORS

The pick of the dives are the Three Brothers (Terumbu Tiga), where you go through three seriously impressive rock formations; Temple of the Sea (Tokong Laut), popular on account of its good visibility which enables divers to see an incredible variety of fish; and the Sugar Wreck.

PERHENTIAN KECIL

Quiver Diveschool Coral Bay ☎012 213 8855, ⊛quiver-perhentian.com. This brilliant dive school only operates with small groups and is probably the best bet on either island for friendliness and personal attention. PADI Open Water RM1200, fun dive (3–4 hr) RM80.

Turtle Bay Divers Long Beach ☎09 691 1632, ⊛turtlebaydivers.com. A large, well-kitted-out dive school with friendly staff. PADI Open Water (RM990) and "discover scuba" (RM200) options, and credit cards accepted.

PERHENTIAN BESAR

Flora Bay Divers ☎09 691 1661, ⊛florabaydivers .com. A popular dive outfit that operates dives in small groups. Prices are slightly more expensive than others on the island, but the service and attention from the instructors is exceptional. PADI Open Water RM1150, fun dive RM100.

Universal Diver ⊛universaldiver.net. A well-organized dive centre run by a group of friendly enthusiasts. PADI Open Water RM1180, fun dive RM90.

ACCOMMODATION

PERHENTIAN KECIL

Matahari Long Beach ☎09 691 1740, ⊛mataharichalet .com. Slightly back from the beach, this place has a large cluster of chalets and bungalows set around a pleasant garden. There is a new concrete block with clean a/c rooms, while the cheaper A-frame huts towards the front can get quite loud because of the nearby shop's generator. Doubles RM60

Maya Chalets Coral Bay ☎011 943 0464. All the chalets here have wooden floors and a little balcony, and there are hammocks slung between palm trees to have a little kip in. You can also pitch your own tent in the garden (RM10), or rent one (RM20). Doubles RM80

Mohsin Chalets Long Beach ☎09 691 1363, ⊛facebook .com/mohsinchalet. Nestled on the hillside overlooking Long Beach, the chalets here are basic but functional; the 22-bed dorm has a ward-like feel to it, but the wonderful views over the beach from the breezy restaurant area compensate. You can also try your hand at takraw, a Malay version of volleyball played with your feet. Dorms RM40, doubles RM150

Ombak Coral Bay ☎09 691 1021, ⊛ombak.my. One of the priciest resorts along the beach, but justifiably so – the rooms are welcoming and clean, and there's electricity 24/7. The two dorms with lockers are by far the nicest on the island. There's also a restaurant with comfy cushioned seating and movies screened on the outdoor projector, although the service and food here are pretty mediocre. Dorms RM40, doubles RM150

Panorama Long Beach ☎014 5333 1094. Possibly the most popular choice for backpackers, with rustic chalets and A-frame huts set around a large, verdant area. The vibe is laidback, and there's a pool and nightly films at the welcoming restaurant. Plenty of diving package deals, too. Doubles RM60

★**Rainforest Camping Perhentian** Rainforest Beach, ☎012 308 0425. Feel the nature in these comfy two-person tents set along a jungly slope overlooking the beach. The bamboo and wooden bar offers free breakfast and sees a steady flow of travellers in the evenings who love to sip no-frills cocktails as they glance at the crescent of white sand below. Tents per person RM30

6

Tropicana Inn ☎ 016 266 1333, ⓦ perhentiantropicana .com. Halfway between Coral Bay and Long Beach, this guesthouse has a peaceful jungle location and spotless, freshly painted private rooms and dorms, all en suite and with comfortable beds. There's a café with wi-fi, too. Bring a torch for walking up from either beach in the dark. Dorms RM30, doubles RM120

PERHENTIAN BESAR

Abdul's ☎ 019 912 7303, ⓦ abdulchalet.com. Located on one of the best strips of beach, these cute green-roofed chalets have well-kept a/c rooms with sea views. The restaurant is right on the sand and open until 10pm, after which it's extremely peaceful here. Doubles RM170

★**Coral View** ☎ 09 697 4943, ⓦ perhentianisland .info/c_coralview.php. This wonderful resort has attractive a/c chalets with private terrace and sun loungers, mostly overlooking the sea. A pathway leads to the slightly more economical chalets (twin RM149) at the back, set around a cascading little waterfall. The restaurant serves a good seafood barbecue, there's wi-fi, and the nicest beach on the island lies just a 2min walk away. Doubles RM202

Mama's Chalet ☎ 013 984 0232 or ☎ 019 985 3359, ⓦ mamaschalet.com.my. Run by the friendly Aziz and Jimie, a source of local knowledge, *Mama's* has well-kept chalets, all spotless with wooden floorboards, set around a leafy garden. The more upmarket chalets with a/c and private bath open up onto the beachfront. Doubles RM100

New Coco Huts & Cozy Chalet ☎ 09 691 1811, ⓦ perhentianislandcocohut.com. The spacious green-roofed wooden chalets here with sea views are built on a headland that separates the beach north and south, while the cheaper rooms with garden views are set back from the beach. All rooms have a balcony, cable TV and a fridge. Doubles RM220

EATING

Most of the guesthouses on both islands have a restaurant attached; on Besar, there aren't any stand-alone restaurants, just those at guesthouses. Several places serve alcohol, while others don't mind if you bring your own.

★**TREAT YOURSELF**

Villa @ World Café Long Beach ⓦ theworldcafe.com.my. On the southern end of Long Beach, these six lovely, secluded villas boast huge windows, lots of natural light and beautifully designed interiors, with king-sized beds dominating the spacious rooms. It also has outside power showers set amid sprouting bamboo shoots. Ideal for a romantic getaway. Doubles RM750

PERHENTIAN KECIL

★**Bubu** Long Beach. It may be a tad pricey but it's well worth it: the top-notch Western and Malay dishes here are the best on the island and the beach setting is lovely. The menu includes large salads (RM30), pastas (RM25), burgers and sandwiches (both RM30). Daily 7.30–10.30am & noon–10.30pm.

Ewan's Café Just at the start of the trail from Coral Bay to Long Beach, this laidback restaurant bustles with hungry people dropping by for the inexpensive rice and noodle dishes (RM10). There are also more substantial mains such as fresh fish curry (RM13), and free wi-fi, too. Daily 8am–10pm.

Mama's Coral Bay. The smell of grilled fish wafts down the beach from this laidback place where the day's catch is barbecued before your very eyes. You can feast away for just RM25. Daily 8.30am–11pm.

PERHENTIAN BESAR

The Barat Set along the beach, this restaurant, in the resort of the same name, is a good choice for hearty, albeit a bit pricey, barbecue seafood and meat combo sets. Other classic Western and Asian mains (from RM15) cost less; lively from 7pm onwards. Daily 7am–11pm.

DRINKING AND NIGHTLIFE

Though there aren't many bars on the islands, Perhentian Kecil does have a couple that stay open late and have a bit of a party atmosphere.

Beach Bar Long Beach. This laidback bar seems to close shop more often than not, but when it is open it attracts quite a crowd for the cheap drinks and fire shows on the beach. Opening hours vary.

DIRECTORY

Clinic There's a very basic clinic at Village Pasir Hantu on Perhentian Kecil; the dive centres can offer limited medical care, but you're better off returning to the mainland.

KUALA TERENGGANU

The tiny Muslim metropolis of **KUALA TERENGGANU**, 160km south of Kota Bharu, is a traditional town set on an estuary and a pleasant place for a quick stopover.

At the western end of Kuala Terengganu, Jalan Bandar forms the centre of **Chinatown**, home to vibrant coffee houses and mural art, where you'll find the excellent Teratai, at no. 151, selling local arts and crafts. Kuala Terengganu's **Central Market** (daily

7am–6pm), a little further down on the right, close to the junction with Jalan Kota, also deals in batik, *songkets* and brassware. On the same road, it's also worth taking a peek inside the lavish **Ho Ann Kiong Temple** (daily 7.50am–7.45pm), which was built by Taoist devotees in 1796.

The **State Museum** (Sat–Thurs 9am–5pm, Fri 9am–noon & 3–5pm; RM15), the largest in Malaysia, has a number of galleries dedicated to textiles, crafts, Islam, fisheries, petroleum, and displays of Chinese potteries, traditional garments used in wedding and circumcision ceremonies and weapons. To get here, catch infrequent Heritage bus #C02 from the bus station. It also stops at quirky Islamic theme park **Taman Tamadun Islam** (Mon, Wed, Thurs, Sat & Sun 9am–7pm, Fri 9am–12.45pm & 2.30–7pm; RM21.20), with miniature replicas of some of the world's most famous mosques, including a stunning crystal one (free admission). Heritage bus #C01 stops at the general hospital, 200m from up-and-coming surf spot **Batu Buruk Beach**, and continues to Malaysia's first **Floating Mosque**.

ARRIVAL AND DEPARTURE

By plane Sultan Mohammed Airport is located 13km northeast of the centre, a RM25 taxi ride into town. Kuala Terengganu is served by Malaysia Airlines, Firefly, Malindo and AirAsia, with daily flights to KL (3 daily; 55min) or Subang (6 daily; 1hr 5min).

By bus The bus station is off Jln Tok Lam in the centre of town.

Destinations Butterworth (2 daily; 9–10hr); Ipoh (2 daily; 7hr); Johor Bahru (4 daily; 10hr); Kota Bharu (2 daily; 4hr); Kuala Besut (every 2hr; 2hr); KL (6 daily; 8–9hr); Kuala Perlis (for Langkawi; 3 daily; 10hr); Kuantan (10 daily; 4hr); Malacca (3 daily; 7hr); Lumut (for Pangkor; daily; 10hr); Marang (hourly; 30min); Mersing (2 daily; 7hr); Singapore (daily; 10hr).

INFORMATION

Tourist Information Centre 77A Jln Sultan Zainal Abdin, on the seafront near the GPO (Mon–Thurs & Sun 8am–1pm & 2–5pm, Fri 9am–1pm, Sat 9am–1pm & 2–5pm; ☎09 622 1553, ⓦtourism .terengganu.gov.my). Helpful staff can provide brochures on the area.

ACCOMMODATION

Awi's Yellow House 3576 Kampung Pulau Duyong Besar ☎017 984 0337. This forty-year-old rickety complex of basic stilted huts, built over the water on the tiny island of Duyung, is a local institution. It's a taste of relaxing village life from years past, though a little out of the way. From the bus station, take bus Bandar to Pulau Duyong, and get off at the base of the Sultan Mahmud Bridge, from where Awi's is a short walk. After 6pm, you'll probably have to take a taxi (RM15). Chalets RM35

★ **Rumoh Kayu Bed & Breakfast** 902F Jln Pantai Batu Buruk ☎017 631 4197. This charming wooden house, re-branded as a surfer pad, has one four-bed dorm, two rooms and cosy chalets on stilts sheltered by palm trees. It's 20m from a deserted stretch of beach, and within walking distance of Pantai Batu Buruk's food courts. The self-catering kitchen, breezy verandah and spacious living room-cum-library all help entice you to linger a while. Dorms RM25, doubles RM35

The Space Inn 2nd floor, 12E Jln Engku Pengiran Anom 2 ☎012 928 2997, ⓦfacebook.com/thespaceinn. A 5min walk from Chinatown, this fully a/c, mimimal chic hostel has squeaky-clean cheap dorms with individual lockers, a cosy common room with bean bags, small kitchen and free flow of hot drinks. Rooms, albeit windowless, are clean and good value. Dorms RM25, doubles RM59

EATING AND DRINKING

Batu Buruk Food Court Along Batu Buruk Beach. Famous beachside option for local dishes such as *keropok* (deep-fried fish and seafood rolls with sago flour and pandan leaves with chilli sauce for dipping; RM8) and the incredible fried ice cream. Daily 4pm–midnight.

Madam Bee's Kitchen 177 Jln Kampung Cina. This welcoming little restaurant keeps Peranakan culture and traditions alive – it's allegedly the only place in Terengganu State that serves traditional home-cooked Pernakan dishes. Popular choices include *nasi kerabu* with *curry ayam* (RM8.90) and *laksa Terengganu* (RM7). Mon, Tues & Thurs–Sun 9.30am–5pm.

The Vinum XChange 221 Jln Kampung Cina. This little drinking hole is a truly unusual sight on Malaysia's conservative eastern coast. This café and bar serves beers (RM8), wines from the world over (bottles only; from RM37) and spirits (bottles only; from RM118). Teetotallers can settle for a coffee (RM5) and little pastries (RM1.30). Daily 11am–11pm.

PULAU KAPAS

A fifteen-minute ride by speedboat from the coastal town of Marang takes you to

6

the lovely island of **PULAU KAPAS**, less than 2km in length, where all accommodation options are clustered along the sandy coves along its western side. Kapas is a designated marine park; its white-sand beaches are some of the cleanest in Malaysia, and the aquamarine waters are ideal for sea kayaking and snorkelling. The best snorkelling is around tiny Pulau Raja, just off Kapas, and rocky Pulau Gemia, off the northwestern shore, home to a resort and a turtle sanctuary. The northernmost cove is good for **turtle-spotting**, and turtles and reef sharks have also been spotted at the south side of the island at *Turtle Valley* resort. Besides snorkelling, Kapas has a few good **diving** sites; set on the main beach, Aqua Sport (☎019 379 6808) charge RM130 for a regular dive and RM150 for a night dive. A couple of **jungle trails** cross the island – one from behind *Kapas Island* resort and the other branching off from the trail leading over the promontory to *Turtle Valley* resort; this one is more demanding and there's a certain amount of hauling yourself up using ropes. Both trails end up pretty much at the same spot on the east side of the island. Try to avoid visiting at weekends and during public holidays when the island gets overcrowded with local day-trippers, and people may get turned back at Marang's jetty.

ARRIVAL AND DEPARTURE

The small coastal town of Marang, 18km south of Kuala Terengganu, is the jumping-off point for Pulau Kapas, 6km offshore. You'll find a couple of banks here, as well as onward connections to east-coast destinations.
By bus Any Dungun or Rhu Muda-bound bus (every 30min) from Kuala Terengganu, or Kuala Terengganu-bound bus from Cherating, will drop you on the main road

at Marang, from where the centre is a short walk downhill towards the sea. The bus ticket kiosk is on Jln Tanjung Sulong Musa. To get to Cherating by local bus, catch a Kuala Dungun-bound bus and change there, or take a local bus to Kuala Terengganu's long-distance bus station.
By ferry Ferry company offices are all located by the jetty and there are regular departures for Pulau Kapas – Suria Link is a reliable option, dropping you off right in front of your resort (RM40 return). Most companies do five runs daily to the island (8.30am–5pm); boats can leave before their scheduled departure if full. The last return boat leaves Kapas at 5.30pm. There's practically no service during the monsoon season (Nov–Feb).

ACCOMMODATION AND EATING

Accommodation is arranged along four coves on the west side of the island; all accommodation options have their own restaurant.
Captain's Longhouse ☎012 377 0214. At the southern end of the main beach, this longhouse has a spacious dorm with colourful mosquito nets, local fabrics and clean communal bathrooms. Couples can make use of the darkish doubles, or opt for a double bed within the shared dorm (RM60). There's a chill-out area with hammocks, and nipah carpets are strewn over the wooden floors. Dorms RM40, doubles RM80
Kapas Beach Chalet (KBC) ☎019 343 5606, ✉hans .keune@gmail.com. The friendly and laidback vibes here might tempt you to stay for longer than planned, whiling away your afternoons swinging in a hammock and swimming. The little A-frame chalets with private bath are dotted around a garden, and there are chill-out areas for rainy days and a sociable restaurant. Dorms RM25, doubles RM50
★ **Koko's** ☎010 926 5088. This welcoming English-Malay-run beachside place with coconut beams and rustic wooden furniture serves outstanding Malay dishes – the fresh fish/prawns/squid cooked in a yellow coconut sauce (RM20) is an absolute must. Their new dorms with mosquito nets and fans are basic, but set on a nice patch of beach where you can camp (RM15) when other accommodation is full. Restaurant daily 9am–4pm & 7.30–10.30pm. Dorms RM30

SAVE THE TURTLES

Marang is one of the remaining places in Malaysia where you can see turtles. However, with turtle numbers dwindling, sanctuaries such as the **Ma'Daerah Turtle Sanctuary** (🌐madaerah .blogspot.my) are becoming increasingly important. Volunteering here is a rewarding and worthwhile experience, and can be done for as short a time as a single weekend, or even an afternoon. In April, the beaches are cleaned up ready for the nesting season and any willing hands for this task are gratefully received. A donation of at least RM250 is required, but meals and accommodation are included for your stay, and your money will be going towards the work of the sanctuary. Alternatively, you can adopt a turtle (RM150), or a nest (RM100).

★Longsha Camping ☏ 019 966 2968. If your idea of bliss is camping on a clearing between jungle and sea surrounded by chilled-out budget travellers on hammocks, look no further than this. The shared open-roofed showers, squat toilets and tents with mattresses are basic, but the concept is to be at one with nature. The common kitchen is great to cut costs: bring your own supplies from Marang. Snorkels can be rented for RM15 for two days and are free afterwards. Book ahead by phone only – staff mentioned problems with fraudulent online bookings. Tents RM15

Turtle Valley ☏ 014 809 3083. This intimate, slightly more upmarket, Dutch-owned resort offers bungalows overlooking a quiet bay where turtles come to hatch between April and September. Besides the daily dinner specials, the chef rustles up excellent takes on various cuisines, from burgers to salmon ciabattas, pancakes to *shoarma*. Mains RM35. Daily noon– 1.30pm & 6–8.30pm. Doubles RM190

CHERATING

CHERATING, 47km north of Kuantan, hugs the northern end of a windswept bay, protected from the breeze by the shelter of a rocky cliff. **Surfers**, kitesurfers and windsurfers love this travellers' hangout while many others find the village a bit lacklustre. These days the town has lost some of its laidback kampung vibe due to large resorts popping up all over the place.

The main drag is a tiny surfaced road that runs roughly parallel to the beach; this is where you'll find most of the restaurants and bars, as well as convenience stores and arts and craft shops selling batik, T-shirts and other trinkets. Limbong Art, in particular, has an excellent range of woodcarvings upstairs, and also offers batik classes.

You can rent surfboards from several places from around RM40 per half day; most offer surfing lessons. Windsurfing (RM80/hr), kitesurfing (RM150/hr) and X Sail (RM100/hr) equipment can be rented right on the beach from Kam's Surf Shack (☏ 019 923 8558, ✉ kamsurf007@gmail .com), who also offer surf lessons (RM120/ hr), windsurfing lessons (RM150/hr) and kitesurfing lessons (RM300/hr).

For non-surfers, there are plenty of activities on offer, including firefly and mangrove tours, snorkelling trips, turtle watching (March–Sept), and visiting the local turtle sanctuary.

ARRIVAL AND DEPARTURE

By bus Express and local buses between Kuala Terengganu and Kuantan stop on the main road outside the village. For departures, if you catch a bus south to Kuantan (45min), there's a much greater choice of destinations.

Destinations Ipoh (2 daily; 7hr); Johor Bahru (4 daily; 6hr); Kota Bharu (4 daily; 5hr); Kuala Lumpur (8 daily; 5hr); Kuala Terengganu (4 daily; 3hr); Malacca (2 daily; 6hr); Marang (every 2hr; 4hr); Mersing (3 daily; 3hr 30min); Rantau Panjang (for Thailand; 2 daily; 6hr).

ACCOMMODATION

Matahari ☏ 017 924 7465. The well-kept clean chalets here are cosy and welcoming; cheaper ones have shared bathrooms, while the pricier options have a/c (RM80). There's a communal area and large kitchen for guests' use, as well as free wi-fi. Doubles RM30

Payung ☏ 019 917 1934. Across the road from *Nabil* restaurant, this is a good option, with pleasant chalets giving onto a leafy pathway. The eleven rooms have fan and private bath, while there's one with a/c. Doubles RM60

Tanjung Inn ⊕ tanjunginn.com. The best resort on the beach has excellent budget options: the luxury tents with plush bamboo beds and mosquito nets are a steal (RM70). Budget fan rooms, while pricier, are surrounded by lush vegetation just 50m from the sea. Discounts in off season. Doubles RM120

EATING AND DRINKING

Cherating Beach Bar ☏ 017 674 7015. Happening wooden shack with a huge PA system, perfect for getting tipsy with your toes in the sand. Trance tunes flow as quick as beers (RM10) and spirits (RM15). Owner Mazlam offers surf lessons (100RM/1hr 30min and full-day board rental) and occasional free fish barbecues. Daily 4pm until late.

Duyong This large stilted restaurant at the northern end of the beach offers inexpensive Chinese and Thai dishes, as well as fresh fish sold by weight. Adventurous types can try the chicken-feet salad (RM10). Mains RM10. Thurs–Tues 11am–midnight.

Nabil Popular restaurant serving local seafood dishes as well as Western grub. It's only open in the evenings, but for breakfast and lunch you can head next door to *Warung Ambak*. Mains from RM7. Tues–Sun 6pm–1am.

KUANTAN

Kuantan is the region's transport hub, lying at the junction of routes 2 (which runs across the Peninsula to KL), 3 and 14. Even if it may seem sprawling and busy, it's a worthwile lower-key Malaysian city, and a good stopover between Cherating and KL. Pretty

6

Teluk Cempedak, 5km east of the town centre, makes for a quick beach escape.

ARRIVAL AND DEPARTURE

By plane Kuantan Airport, 15km west of town, is served by several daily Malaysia Airline flights to KL (3 daily; 40min), while Firefly connects it to Singapore (4 weekly; 45min) and KL's Subang airport.

By bus Terminal Sentral is 15min out of town. Buses to Cherating (every 2–3hr; 1hr) leave from the local bus station in Kuantan itself. To get here, catch a taxi
Destinations Butterworth (2 daily; 8hr); Jerantut, for Taman Negara National Park (3 daily; 3hr 30min); Kota Bharu (5 daily; 5hr); Kuala Lipis (2 daily; 5hr); Kuala Lumpur (hourly; 4hr); Kuala Terengganu (5 daily; 3hr 30min); Malacca (2 daily; 5hr); Mersing (6 daily; 3hr); Singapore (2 daily; 6hr).

ACCOMMODATION AND EATING

The hawker stalls near the mosque on Jln Makhota behind the Ocean Shopping Complex on Jln Tun Ismail are a good bet for cheap local dishes, including the local special of *patin* (silver catfish). Catch Rapid Kuantan bus #200 for Teluk Cempedak and its wide array of food options.
Kuantan Backpackers 39 Jln Tun Ismail, 1st floor ☎ 09 513 3830, ⓦ kuantanbackpackers.com. Useful if you have to stay overnight, it has cheap dorms right across the road from Kuantan Rapid Bus Terminal. Dorms RM30

The south

The south of the Malaysian Peninsula, below Kuala Lumpur and Kuantan, has some of the richest history and culture in the country. The west-coast city of **Malacca**, two hours by bus south from KL, retains an enticing charm, with waterside walkways and a stunning mixture of architecture from its Portuguese, Dutch and British colonial days. The relaxed island of **Pulau Tioman** is located on the opposite coast and boasts numerous sandy beaches and good diving opportunities.

MALACCA

When Penang was known only for its oysters and Singapore was just a fishing village, **MALACCA** (**Melaka** in Malay) had already achieved worldwide fame. Under the auspices of the Malacca Sultanate, founded in the early fifteenth century, political and cultural life flourished. The

town grew rich by **trading spices** from the Moluccas in the Indonesian archipelago and textiles from Gujarat in northwest India. A levy on all imported goods made it one of the wealthiest kingdoms in the world, and it gradually expanded its territory to include Singapore and most of east-coast Sumatra. A series of takeovers, beginning in 1511, by the Portuguese, Dutch and British, has also substantially characterized Malacca – the architecture, street plans, churches and overall atmosphere are of an eclectic East-meets-West fusion.

WHAT TO SEE AND DO

Legacies of all phases of Malacca's past remain in the city, constituting the main tourist sights. Of these, the most interesting are the ancestral homes of the **Baba-Nyonya community** (see box, p.418). The centre of Malacca is split in two by the murky **Sungai Malacca**, the western bank of which is occupied by **Chinatown** and **Kampung Morten**, a small collection of stilted houses – free walking tours leave from Villa Sentosa (Mon, Wed & Fri 4pm; 1hr 30min). On the eastern side of the river lies the colonial core with **Stadthuys** (Town Square) at its centre – a favourite gathering point for the tricked-out trishaws. It's overlooked by **Bukit St Paul** (St Paul's Hill), encircled by Jalan Kota. Southeast of here is **Taman Malacca Raya**, a modern area with a good selection of budget hotels, restaurants and bars. A relaxing 45-minute **boat trip** up Sungai Malacca takes you to "**Little Amsterdam**", the old Dutch quarter of red-roofed *godowns*, which back directly onto the water. Boats leave from the jetty behind the Maritime Museum (every 30min, 10am–11pm; 40min; RM15); a night cruise on the river is also recommended.

Around Bukit St Paul

At the eastern side of Bukit St Paul is the **Porta de Santiago** – all that remains of the large Portuguese fort A Famosa. From here, steps lead to the roofless **St Paul's Church**, which was constructed in 1521 by the Portuguese, and visited by the Jesuit missionary St Francis Xavier, whose body was brought here for burial, and later

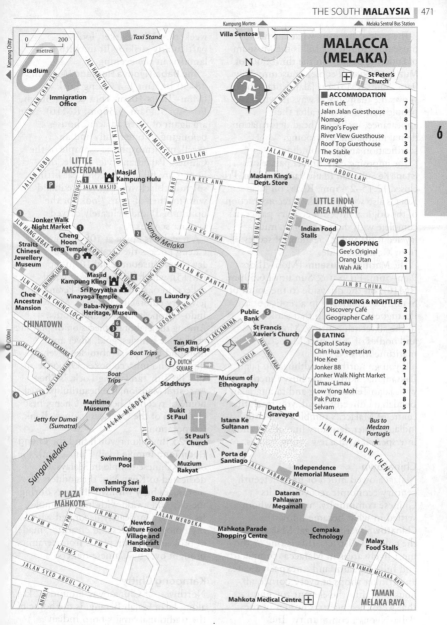

6

moved to Goa in India. Commemorative brass plaques for Dutch and Portuguese dignitaries rest against the church's inner walls. Down a winding path is the sturdy **Stadthuys**, a collection of buildings that dates from 1660 and was used as a town hall during the Dutch and British administrations. It has typically Dutch interior staircases and high windows, and now houses the **Museum of Ethnography** (daily 9am–5.30pm; RM5), which displays Malay and Chinese ceramics and weaponry as well as a blow-by-blow account of Malaccan history.

6

The pick of the somewhat lacklustre museums around the hill is the **Museum of Enduring Beauty** on the third floor of **Muzium Rakyat** (People's Museum; daily 9am–5pm; RM3), on Jalan Kota, which shows the many novel ways in which people have sought to alter their appearance, including head deformation, dental mutilations, tattooing, scarification and foot-binding.

The imposing dark timber palace of **Istana Ke Sultanan** (daily 9am–5.30pm, Fri closed 12.15–2.45pm; RM5) on Jalan Kota is also worth a look. A reconstruction of the original fifteenth-century palace, it's complete with sharply sloping, multi-layered roofs and re-creations of scenes from Malay court life.

The **Maritime Museum** (Mon–Thurs 9am–5pm, Fri, Sat & Sun until 6.30pm; RM10), on the quayside to the south of Stadthuys, is housed in a replica of a Portuguese cargo ship that sank here in the sixteenth century. Model ships and oodles of text chart Malacca's maritime history.

If you go north of Stadthuys up Jalan Laksamana, skirting the busy junction with Jalan Temenggong and taking Jalan Bendahara directly ahead, you reach the centre of Malacca's tumbledown **Little India**, a rather desultory line of sari shops, interspersed with a few eating houses.

Chinatown

Malacca owed much of its nineteenth-century economic recovery to its Chinese community, many of whom settled in what became known as **Chinatown**, across Sungai Malacca from the colonial district. This is one of the most lively areas in Malacca, compact and full of quaint and unexpected cafés and trinket shops at every corner, all housed within the elegant townhouses that were the ancestral homes of the Baba-Nyonya community. The wealthiest and most successful built long, narrow-fronted houses, and minimized the "window tax" by incorporating several internal courtyards. Chinatown's central street, **Jalan Hang Jebat**, known as **Jonker Walk**, famous for its antique shops and weekend night market, looks particularly striking lit up with red lanterns in the evening.

The **Baba-Nyonya Heritage Museum**, 48–50 Jln Tun Tan Cheng Lock (Mon–Thurs 10am–1pm & 2–4.30pm, Fri–Sun 9.45am–4.30pm; RM16), is an amalgam of three adjacent houses belonging to one family and an excellent, atmospheric example of the Chinese Palladian style. Inside, the homes are filled with gold-leaf fittings, splendid blackwood furniture inlaid with mother-of-pearl (look for the opium bed) and delicately carved lacquer screens.

A few doors down at 108 Jln Tun Tan Cheng Lock is the **Straits Chinese Jewellery Museum** (daily 10am–5pm; RM15), which displays a wonderful collection of skilfully crafted Peranakan jewellery embracing Chinese, Malay and Indo-European designs and motifs. Among the elaborate pieces on display are gold ankle bangles, gold, silver and diamond hairpins, embroidered velvet slippers and tobacco boxes. Opposite, at 117 Jln Tun Tan Cheng Lock, is **Chee Ancestral Mansion**, the beautiful palatial home of tycoon Chee Swee Cheng, first chairman of the Overseas Chinese Bank Corporation.

At 25 Jln Tokong you'll find the **Cheng Hoon Teng Temple** (daily 7am–7pm), the oldest Chinese temple in Malaysia dedicated to Kuan Yin, the goddess of mercy. It's busy with worshippers during the day and awash with incense smoke. Its roofs are intricately decorated with mythological figures and creatures, made of broken porcelain pieces from ceramics brought over by Chinese traders.

Kampong Chitty

Northwest of Chinatown, around 1.5km along Jalan Gajah Berang, is the home of the traditional Straits-born Indian community, **Kampung Chitty**. The Chitties pre-date the Baba-Nyonya community, their ancestors having arrived in Malaysia in the 1400s, and the neighbourhood is fun to wander around; look for the archway decorated with elephant sculptures.

6

ARRIVAL AND DEPARTURE

By bus Malacca long-distance bus station is located a 15min bus ride out of town at Meleka Sentral. Bus #17 connects the station to Dutch Square (30min; RM1.50); taxis cost RM20.

Destinations Alor Setar (for Langkawi; 2 daily; 8hr); Butterworth (4 daily; 6hr 30min); Ipoh (6 daily; 4hr); Hat Yai, Thailand (2 daily; 10hr); Jerantut (for Taman Negara; 3 daily; 6hr); Johor Bahru (9 daily; 3hr); Kota Bharu (daily; 9hr); KLIA/KLIA2 airports (12 daily; 2hr); Kuala Lumpur (every 30min until 8pm; 2hr); Kuala Perlis (for Langkawi; 2 daily; 9hr); Kuala Terengganu (2 daily; 8hr); Kuantan (7 daily; 5hr); Mersing (3 daily; 5hr); Penang (4 daily; 7hr); Singapore (2 daily; 4hr).

By ferry The Tunas Rupat ferry (☎06 283 2506) to Dumai in Sumatra docks at the ICQX Complex, close to the historical centre (daily 10am; 2hr 30min; RM130).

INFORMATION AND GETTING AROUND

The compact city centre is best explored on foot.

Tourist information centre On Jln Kota (daily 9am–6pm; ☎06 283 6220, ⓦmelaka.gov.my), just across the roundabout from the Stadthuys. Staff are helpful and there are plenty of brochures on the town's attractions. Free historical walking tours of Malacca leave from here on Tues, Thurs & Sat (9.30am; 2hr 30min).

Trishaws There are trishaws at Padang Pahlawan Square and outside the Mahkota Parade Shopping Centre. A sightseeing tour costs RM40/hr.

ACCOMMODATION

At weekends and during public holidays, all accommodation prices tend to soar to exploit tourist arrivals from Singapore.

Fern Loft 24 Jln Tun Tan Cheng Lock ☎011 1288 3334. Sister hostel to *Fern Loft* in KL, it has just three rooms, all with shared bath: a large sixteen-bed dorm with lockers and clothes racks; a little twin and a family room. There's wi-fi throughout and a/c in the rooms (7pm–9am). Dorms RM25, twin RM70

★ **Jalan Jalan Guesthouse** 8 Jln Tukang Emas ☎06 283 3937. This quiet, laidback guesthouse has a selection of cosy rooms set in two "old" and "new" buildings – both equally charming with sociable communal areas. If you stay in the "new" guesthouse, make sure to choose room no. 5, an airy spacious double. Dorms are welcoming and all have lockers. There's wi-fi throughout and bikes for RM5 per stay. Dorms RM17, doubles RM40

Nomaps 11 Jln Tun Tan Cheng Lock ☎06 283 8311, ⓦthenomaps.com. An upmarket hostel decked out with charming industrial design and mural art by Sabahan artist Kenji Chai. Individual pods have personal foldable tables, reading lights and charging station, and useful backpack-sized lockers. There's a kitchen, TV room with bean bags, and 24hr computer access with free printer. Online bookings get discounts. Dorms RM80

Ringo's Foyer 46A Jln Portugis ☎06 281 6393, ⓦringosfoyer.com. Once a budget traveller party heaven, this long-running guesthouse upgraded to cosy flashpacker place with a good selection of dorms and rooms. The congenial owner, Howard, takes his guests on educational bike tours around the city. There's a rooftop terrace that is a great spot to socialize over an evening beer. Dorms RM35, doubles RM70

★ **River View Guesthouse** 94 & 96 Jln Kampong Pantai ☎012 327 7746, ✉riverviewguesthouse@yahoo.com. Set in a 200-year-old house, this lovely guesthouse with high ceilings and beautiful wooden floorboards has a leafy terrace looking over the river – the views at night are particularly spectacular. There's only one three-bed dorm, while the rest of the rooms are privates. Dorms RM25, doubles RM68

Roof Top Guest House Malacca 39 Jln Kampong Pantai ☎012 327 7746, ✉rooftopguesthouse@yahoo.com. Under the same management as *River View Guesthouse*, this friendly place has a couple of breezy rooftop terraces; most rooms face the interior courtyard and as a result are a bit on the darkish side, but are livened up with a splash of colourful paint. There's a kitchen, living area, book exchange and wi-fi throughout. Dorms RM28, doubles RM63

Voyage 40 Lorong Hang Jebat ☎06 281 5216, ⓦfacebook.com/voyagemalacca/. This laidback place has a lounge area with TV and pool table downstairs, while the first floor has a large fifteen-bed dorm with mosquito nets. There's complimentary bicycle rental, and hearty free breakfasts are served a few doors down at their sister *Voyager Home Café*. Dorms RM18, doubles RM45

EATING

Sampling the spicy dishes of Nyonya cuisine – with its emphasis on sour herbs such as tamarind, tempered by creamy coconut milk – is a must in Malacca.

Capitol Satay 41 Lorong Bukit Cina. The queue at this local institution starts as soon as the shutters are pulled up mid-afternoon – hungry bellies wait in line for satay (RM1 each) of skewered meat and fish, from pork liver to fish balls, cooked in the sizzling peanut sauce pots found at the

6

centre of each table. Daily 5pm–midnight.

★ **Chin Hua Vegetarian** 1/2 Jln Laksamana ☎ 016 646 6366. Self-service Chinese Buddhist buffet with a great selection of vegetable and mock-meat dishes at bargain prices (from RM4). Daily 10am–3pm & 5.30–10pm.

Hoe Kee 4, 6 & 8 Jln Hong Jebat ☎ 06 283 4751. This popular place specializes in one of Malacca's traditional eats: tasty chicken rice balls (RM0.30 each) that go down a treat. Daily 11am–3pm.

Jonker 88 88 Jln Hang Jebat ☎ 019 397 5665. A sweet tooth's delight serving all manner of refreshing desserts including *baba cendol* (RM4). There are plenty of hearty savoury portions too – try the *baba laksa* (noodles with egg, prawn and tuna; RM10.50). Mon–Thurs & Sun 9.30am–5.30pm, Fri & Sat 9.30am–8.30pm.

★ **Jonker Walk Night Market** Jonker Walk. On Friday, Saturday and Sunday evenings, this becomes a pedestrian street, lined with all manner of food stalls – a great way to sample local specialities such as *otak-otak* (spicy fish paste grilled in banana leaf), *popiah* (mega spring roll stuffed with prawns, garlic, carrot, palm sugar and chilli), *cendol* (shaved ice topped with flavoured syrups, coconut milk and jelly) and much more. Snacks from RM3.

Limau-Limau 9 Jln Hang Lekiu ☎ 012 609 9088. Cosy little café set on two floors and dotted with little knick-knacks and mismatched furniture. The light menu includes soups (RM7.90), sandwiches (RM11.90) and focaccia cheese melts (RM20.90), as well as freshly squeezed juices, milkshakes and lassis (from RM8). Mon & Thurs–Sun 9am–5pm.

Low Yong Moh 32 Jln Tukang Emas ☎ 06 282 1235. A great local hangout to refuel with a pork, shrimp or chicken *dim sum* (RM3) as you explore the city. Mon & Wed–Sun 5.30am–noon.

Pak Putra 56 & 58 Jln Laksamana ☎ 012 601 5876. This hugely popular north Indian place with outdoor seating attracts a crowd for its superb chicken tandoori: spicy, crispy and succulent. Mains RM7. Tues–Sun 5.30pm–1am.

Selvam 2 Jln Temenggong ☎ 06 281 9223. This welcoming Indian place serves excellent banana-leaf curries (RM5), all carefully prepared at your table. At weekends there are lunch specials, including tasty veggie biryanis (RM7) and tandoori sets (RM8.50). Daily 7am–10pm, closed Tues every other week.

DRINKING AND NIGHTLIFE

Discovery Café 3 Jln Bunga Raya. Three-litre towers of beer (RM57.90) are on offer for the thirsty at this travellers' hangout; the interior is decorated with old curios, while local and Filipino pop bands take centre stage in the outdoor seating area each day. Daily 9am–1am.

Geographer Café 83 Jln Hang Jebat ☎ 06 281 6813. A local favourite, this leafy café, restaurant and bar offers a large selection of veggie dishes, as well as Asian and Western grub. There are live r'n'b bands on Fridays,

Saturdays and Sundays, while on Mondays the musical flavour is jazz. Daily 10am–midnight.

SHOPPING

Malacca is famed for its antiques, and there are many specialist outlets along Jln Hang Jebat and Jln Tun Tan Cheng Lock, though they are by no means cheap. If it's a genuine antique, check that it can be exported legally and fill in an official clearance form. A number of shops charge RM3 just to browse.

Gee's Original Jln Hang Kasturi ☎ 016 640 4250, ⊕ facebook.com/geesoriginalmelaka/. A shopful of handcrafted wooden clogs that make for great Nyonya-meets-cheeky-modern souvenirs.

Orang Utan House 59 Lorong Hang Jebat ☎ 06 282 6872, ⊕ facebook.com/theorangutanhouse/. Good for modern souvenirs, this is the outlet for local artist Charles Cham's witty cartoon T-shirts and paintings. Daily 10am–6pm.

Wah Aik 92 Jln Tun Tan Cheng Lock ☎ 06 284 9726, ⊕ wahaikshoemakermelaka.webs.com. A third-generation shoemaker selling bound feet silk shoes.

DIRECTORY

Banks and exchange The most central bank is Public Bank on Jln Laksamana; HSBC, Jln Hang Tuah, has a 24hr ATM, as does OCBC bank, in Dataran Pahlawan Megamall. Moneychangers are often more convenient and offer as good rates as the banks: there are a few around town, including on Jonker Street.

Hospital Mahkota Medical Centre, 3 Makhota Malacca, Jln Merdeka (☎ 06 285 2999).

Immigration The Immigration Office is in the Urban Transformation Centre (UTC) on Jln Hang Tuah (☎ 06 333 3333), for on-the-spot visa renewals.

Laundry Clean Clean, Jln Hang Jabat at Jln Kampung Kuli (Mon–Sat 10.30am–12.30pm & 1.30–5.30pm; RM4/kg).

Police The Tourist Police Office (24hr; ☎ 06 288 3732) is on Jln Kota.

Post office On Jln Laksama (Mon–Fri 8.30am–5.30pm, Sat 8.30am–1pm).

MERSING

The small fishing town of **MERSING**, between Kuantan and Johor Bahru, is the gateway both to Pulau Tioman and to the Endau-Rompin National Park and, as such, gets a steady stream of visitors outside the monsoon season. The town centre is grouped around two main streets, Jalan Abu Bakar and Jalan Ismail, both branching off from the main roundabout. You'll most likely find yourself staying here overnight on the way to the island, as boats are far more frequent in the mornings.

ARRIVAL AND DEPARTURE

By bus Long-distance and local buses arrive at the bus station not far from the bridge across the river, a couple of minutes from the roundabout. Mersing is well connected to a number of destinations. You can also get to Singapore by taking a bus to Johor Bahru and changing to one of the frequent connections there.

Destinations Johor Bahru (5 daily; 2hr 30min); Kota Bharu (2 daily; 10hr); Kuala Lumpur (4 daily; 5hr 30min); Kuala Terengganu (2 daily; 6hr); Kuantan (2 daily; 3hr); Malacca (daily; 3hr 30min); Singapore (daily at 1.30pm; 3hr).

By ferry The jetty is about a 10min walk from the roundabout along Jln Abu Bakar. The boat companies that ply the route between Mersing and Tioman have offices inside the R&R Plaza near the jetty; in peak season, get your ticket the day before. Boats for Tioman depart between 7am and 4.30pm, with far more departures in the morning; the journey takes 1hr 30min–2hr. Expect to pay RM70 for a round trip plus the additional RM5 marine conservation fee. There's very little service during the monsoon season (Nov–Feb).

INFORMATION

Tourist information The Mersing Tourist Information Centre along Jln Abu Bakar (☎07 799 5212) keeps erratic opening hours, but has some helpful brochures and photocopied maps of Tioman.

ACCOMMODATION AND EATING

Ee Lo Tepi Jln Dato Mohd Ali. This no-frills restaurant serves tasty Chinese dishes. Daily 10.30am–3pm & 6.30–10pm.

Embassy Hotel 2 Jln Ismail ☎07 799 3545. This large concrete hotel with a central location right near the roundabout offers spacious clean rooms with a/c and cable TV. Boat departure times are posted by the reception and there's wi-fi throughout (though not great on the top floor). Doubles RM55

PULAU TIOMAN

PULAU TIOMAN, 30km east of Mersing, is a popular holiday island scattered with small palm-fringed beach coves. Express boats travel here in less than two hours, and several daily flights arrive from Singapore and Kuala Lumpur.

Damage has unfortunately been inflicted on the surrounding coral and marine life, but Tioman still has some breathtaking natural scenery. Most of the island's facilities are at industrial **Tekek**, on the west coast, and the popular budget places are in the bay of **Ayer Batang** or **Salang**. The east coast's attractive sole settlement, **Juara**, is less developed. One road wide enough for cars spans the length of Tekek, and another stretches along Juara, with a steep, pitted, narrow road connecting the two. Apart from these, the island is crossed by dirt roads and jungle tracks.

Many of Tioman's nearby islets provide excellent opportunities for snorkelling and diving, with numerous dive centres around Tioman. Most of the chalet operations offer day-trips to nearby reefs and around the island, taking in the Asah waterfall on the south coast.

Tekek

TEKEK is the main settlement on Pulau Tioman, with the main jetty and airport both located here as well as most of the island's shops. It's also one of the least attractive places to visit on the island, but this is where you'll find essential services. Situated north of the main jetty at the very end of the bay, the **Marine Centre** (daily 8.30am–4pm; free), set up to protect the coral and marine life around the island, and to patrol the fishing taking place in its waters, contains engaging interactive displays on the marine fauna.

Ayer Batang

AYER BATANG, commonly referred to as ABC, the next beach north of Tekek (jetty to jetty), is the most popular choice for backpackers, and essentially a single concrete track running along the long stretch of beachfront, with some of Tioman's cheapest guesthouses and restaurants spread out along it amid the greenery. There's a good stretch of beach at the southern end, near *Nazri's* (see p.478), a charming series of bridges linking the chalets at the northern end and a pleasant, laidback atmosphere to the whole area. When walking around, you do have to watch out for locals who cruise up and down the concrete path on motorbikes and trundling three-wheelers. It's a twenty-minute walk to here from Tekek, or hitch a ride for RM5.

6

PULAU TIOMAN

P. Chebeh
Gabo Bay
P. Tulai
P. Sepoi
Genting Bay
Tiger Reef
P. Labas
Golden Reef
Tokong Malang
Tokong Magicienne (Reef)
Sparrow Cave
Salang
P. Soyak
Bukit Kerayon Kecil
Monkey Bay
Monkey Beach
Penuba Bay
Air Batang
Tekek
Reef
Bunut
P. Renggis
Paya
Gunung Kajang (1038m)
S. Keliling
Batu Mumbang
Juara
S. Mentawak
Genting
Bukit Nenek Semukut
Bukit Seperok (958m)
S. Nipah
S. Raya
Nipah
Mukut
Asah
P. Jahat
Batu Sepoi (Reef)

Dive sites
Rough trail
Concrete path
Laterite road

N

0   3
kilometres

Salang

North of Ayer Batang, **SALANG** is a pleasant backpacker option with a handful of guesthouses lining the seafront. It's smaller than ABC, although things can get quite lively here too. The northern rocky end of the beach is not ideal for swimming, while the southern end is the more scenic, and Pulau Soyok, the small island off the southern headland, has a pretty reef for snorkelling.

Juara

At **JUARA**, situated across two quiet, spread-out stretches of beach on the east coast, the only entertainments are diving, surfing and sunbathing, and the vibe is more relaxed than on the other side of the island. As the northern (more populated) bay faces out to open sea, it's more susceptible to bad weather but lovely when the weather is good. The southern bay is more secluded, but does have a couple of chalets and a turtle conservation centre.

Hikes around the island

Tioman has a good number of enjoyable and challenging hikes, both along the coast and in the interior. It's very easy to get from ABC to Tekek; there's a

ten-minute path running up and over the promontory. Also from ABC, a fifteen-minute **jungle trail** leads over the headland to the north, which – after an initial scramble – flattens out into an easy walk, ending up at secluded **Penuba Bay**. From here, it's around an hour and a quarter to gorgeous, secluded **Monkey Beach** and then another hour and a half to Salang. This trail involves scrambling over rocky outcrops and is not always easy to follow (follow the power lines overhead).

Another tricky trail is the cross-island one from Tekek to Juara, taking around two or three hours and quite steep in some places. The start of the trail in Tekek (a twenty-minute walk from the airstrip) is the only signposted concrete path that heads off in the direction of the local mosque before hitting virgin jungle after about fifteen minutes; turn right before the gate of the water tank and find the path that snakes around the wall and into the forest. There's no danger of losing your way: cement steps climb steeply through the greenery, tapering off into a smooth, downhill path once you're over the ridge. After an hour or so, there is a **waterfall** – it's forbidden to bathe here, since it supplies Tekek with water. Thirty minutes after the waterfall, the path to Juara village joins the paved road used by cars – continue for another thirty minutes. A five-minute diversion gets you to a second waterfall where you can freshen up. From Juara, the trail starts opposite the jetty.

ARRIVAL AND DEPARTURE

By plane SAS Air (⊗ sassb.com.my) flies from KL's Subang Skypark (weekly; 1hr) and lands at the airstrip in Tekek, from where you'll have to take a boat taxi to the bay of your choice (unless you're staying in ABC, in which case the distance is easily walkable). During monsoon season, flying is the only reliable, albeit expensive, way of getting on and off the island.

By boat You'll have to decide in advance which bay you want to stay in since the boats generally make stops only at the major resorts of Genting, Paya, Tekek, Ayer Batang and Salang (in that order); there are only occasional boats from Mersing to Juara on the east coast. If you book a return boat ticket in Mersing, you have to specify your return time at the time of booking. If you booked a one-way ticket, ask at your guesthouse for the departure times from the particular bay you're staying in – the first boat leaves Salang at 7am, stopping at each jetty in turn, and the last is at mid-afternoon (around 4pm). Bad weather causes delays and the unscrupulous boat companies often pick up more passengers than the boat is designed for, meaning that some end up standing all the way back to Mersing (and it also means that there are not enough life jackets for everyone). There are more frequent boat services between Tekek and Tanjung Gemok, a small port town 20km north of Mersing.

GETTING AROUND

Transport on the island is somewhat limited. In favourable weather, walking and kayaking are good ways to explore the island.

By bike and sea-kayak Several places in Ayer Batang, Salang, Tekek and Juara rent bicycles for around RM5/hr or RM25/day. Navigable routes are limited, since most bays are separated by rocky jungle paths and you'll have to carry your bike over. Sea kayaks are available for rent in most bays for around RM10/hr; be aware of the sea conditions and the tides.

By boat taxi These operate from the majority of guesthouses. Based on a two-person minimum, sample prices from ABC are as follows: Tekek (RM25); Salang (RM30); Juara (RM150). If you're the only passenger, you may have to pay more.

By 4WD taxi Unless you're planning on taking the jungle trail across the island between Tekek and Juara, your only option (besides the expensive boat) is a 4WD taxi, costing around R35/person each way. The narrow cross-island road is very steep and potholed in places, so while it's doable by bike, brakes and tyres have to be in excellent condition and you really have to watch out for vehicles.

DIVE OPERATORS

Many dive centres on Tioman offer the range of PADI certificates, from the four-day Open Water course (usually around RM1000) through to the fourteen-day Divemaster (RM2000); always check that qualified English-speaking instructors are employed, and that the cost includes equipment.

B & J Dive Centre Ayer Batang ☎09 419 1218, ⓦdivetioman.com. This friendly, long-standing outfit on Ayer Batang is a good choice, with the advantage of an open-air pool, so skills don't have to be practised in the unpredictable sea currents. Four-day/three-night PADI Open Water courses from RM1250. They have a sister outfit at Salang beach.

Eco-Divers Ayer Batang ☎09 419 1794, ⓦeco-divers .net. This is a slightly smaller centre, with friendly staff.

Half-day Discover Scuba courses from RM200; Open Water RM1100.

ACCOMMODATION

AYER BATANG

ABC ☎013 922 0263, ⓦabctioman.com. At the far northern end of the bay, with pretty, inexpensive chalets

```
                              ▲ Penuba Bay, Monkey Beach & Salang
  0        250
  ┕━━━━━┙
     metres

              B & J Dive Centre

                                    Eco-Divers
        Ayer Batang                  @

- - - Rough trail
- - - Concrete path
══════ Laterite road

                                              Marine
                                              Centre

■ ACCOMMODATION
ABC                    2
Bamboo Hill Chalets    1
Mokhtar's Place        5
My Friend's Place      4
Nazri's Place          6
YP Chalets             3

● EATING
Aqiss Rock             1
Nazri's Place          2

■ DRINKING & NIGHTLIFE
A Peace Place          3
B&J Bar                2
Hallo Bar              1
Sunset Bar             4

                                              Airport
                                              Terminal

                                    Tekek
                                              Terminal
                                              Complex

                                              Police
                                              Station

                              N

TEKEK &
AYER BATANG
```

6

6

set in a well-tended garden by a nice stretch of beach. All come with mosquito nets and their own bathroom, while the more pricey ones have a/c and tea- and coffee-making facilities. Dorms RM50, doubles RM150

Bamboo Hill Chalets ☎09 419 1339, ⓦbamboohillchalets.com. Nestled on the northernmost tip of the beach, the six wooden chalets here perch on the headland and enjoy great views over the bay. Chalets range from basic with fan to more sophisticated choices with a/c and pretty verandahs. Doubles RM90

Mokhtar's Place ☎09 419 1148. Two regimental rows of clean and airy chalets with little porches, *Mokhtar's* offers booking services for buses on the mainland, water-taxis, fishing and snorkelling trips, for non-guests as well as guests. Doubles RM50

My Friend's Place ☎09 419 1150. A small budget resort, made up of simple chalets in two prim rows, facing each other across a garden, all of which have a fan and attached bathroom. Doubles RM45

Nazri's Place ☎017 490 1384. Opposite the restaurant of the same name, this resort has a selection of accommodation to suit all budgets, from simple A-frame huts (RM40) and dorms, to more expensive en-suite and family rooms set around a quiet garden. Dorms RM20, doubles RM100

YP Chalets One of ABC's cheaper options, *YP* has rows of simple chalets, all with little verandahs, just inland from a decent stretch of beach. Doubles RM40

SALANG

Ella's Place ☎09 419 5004. This welcoming, quiet place at the northern end of the beach is dotted with colourful potted plants and hammocks slung between palm trees, perfect to while the afternoon away. Rooms range from simple huts with private bath to larger a/c rooms facing the beach. Staff are friendly and can organize snorkeling trips too. Doubles RM60

Salang Indah Resort ☎09 419 5015. This large catch-all resort has rooms catering to all budgets, from simple fan huts in various stages of disrepair (have a look at a few) to more upmarket a/c rooms. Doubles RM50

JUARA

Beach Shack Chalet ☎09 419 3106, ⓔbeachshacktioman@gmail.com. This laidback Malay-Ozzie owned place oozes a mellow vibe, with surfers lounging around waiting to catch a good wave. There are tiny A-frame huts with shared bath lining the beach, as well as more spacious doubles all made of recycled timber. Next door, *Driftwood Café* serves traditional Malay food, rents surfboards (25RM/hr) and has a cosy bamboo verandah on the beachfront. Doubles RM60

Bushman Square Chalets ☎09 419 3109, ⓔbushmanchalet@outlook.my. This friendly place offers clean and well-kept chalets on the beach, with sun loungers shaded by palm trees on your doorstep. The attached restaurant serves good food, and they

TRAVEL TO AND FROM JOHOR BAHRU

The big, busy city of Johor Bahru (or JB), right across the border from Singapore, is an excellent transport hub, with bus, train and plane connections to all main destinations in Malaysia and frequent ferries to Indonesia.

By plane There are Malaysia Airlines and AirAsia flights from Senai Airport (☎07 599 4500), 20km north of the city, to: Kota Kinabalu (daily; 2hr 15min); Kuching (3 daily; 1hr 25min); Kuala Lumpur (at least 6 daily; 45min); Penang (2 daily; 1hr 5min); and other destinations. You can stay in Singapore and at the same time take advantage of far cheaper flights to East Malaysia from JB.

By bus Larkin bus station is 4km north of the centre on Jln Geruda. The city transit bus #170 and the Singapore–Johor Bahru Express connect it to Singapore's Queen Street station (every 15min; 30min; RM2.20), and there are long-distance buses to destinations along both coasts of Malaysia, such as Butterworth (at least 2 daily; 14hr); Ipoh (4 daily; 9hr); Kota Bharu (2 daily; 12hr); Kuala Lumpur (every 30min; 4hr 30min); Kuala Terengganu (2 daily; 8hr); Kuantan (6 daily; 5hr); Malacca (5 daily; 2hr 30min);

Mersing (at least 5 daily; 2hr 30min).

By train JB Sentral is slightly east of the city centre, off Jln Tun Abdul Razak. Direct train services to Singapore stopped in July 2015 (take bus #170X to Kranji MRT or the infrequent shuttle train from JB Sentral to Woodlands instead), and you will have to change trains at Gemas: Kuala Lumpur (2 daily; 7hr 10min); Butterworth (1 daily; 11hr 30min). There are no direct trains from JB to Kota Bharu along the Jungle Railway (see p.456), but you can travel north as far as Gemas and change trains there. Check ⓦktmb.com.my for the latest schedules.

By ferry The Zon Ferry Terminal (☎07 221 1677) is 2km east of the Causeway, with departures to the Indonesian destinations of Tanjung Pinang (6 daily; 1hr 30min) and Pulau Batam (hourly; 1hr 30min). There are also boats departing from Kukup, southwest of JB, which go to Tanjung Balai, Sumatra.

also rent out snorkelling equipment for RM10/day. Doubles RM60

Juara Beach ☎ 09 419 3188. The chalets here are set around a large garden that is pleasantly lit up at night. The a/c rooms are spacious and kept clean, and there are tea- and coffee-making facilities too. Doubles RM120

EATING

Most guesthouses and resorts have their own restaurants and usually offer fantastic barbecued seafood.

AYER BATANG

Aqiss Rock A relaxing choice by the beach, with an attractive outdoor seating patio surrounded by palm trees and a wide selection of steaks (from RM30), finger food, Indian curries (from RM15), pastas and barbecue sets (35RM) served from 8 to 11pm. Vegetarians are catered for, too. Daily 10am–2pm & 6pm–midnight.

Nazri's Place This large restaurant with wooden floors and ceilings offers Western, Malaysian and Indian dishes. Daily 7.30am–3pm & 7–11pm.

SALANG

Mini White House Café Confusingly decked out in yellow, this place is where it's at for nightly barbecues (RM20). They also serve pancakes, omelettes and meat dishes. Daily 7–10.30pm.

Salang Beach Restaurant Consistently good Chinese dishes of fish, prawn, chicken, mutton and beef, at one of Salang's best restaurants. Mains RM17. Daily 8am–3pm & 6–10pm.

Salang Indah Restaurant This large restaurant with sea views offers an extensive menu; breakfast includes *roti canai* (RM1.20), while for lunch and dinner the emphasis is on Thai food (RM8). Daily 7.30am–3.30pm & 6.30–10.30pm.

JUARA

Mia Café Located in the midst of Juara, this no-frills and environmentally savvy yellow *warung* is a great budget option for breakfast, cheap burgers (from RM4) and a selection of Malay-style noodle and rice mains (RM8). Daily 8am–10pm.

Paradise Point There's exquisite food at this popular restaurant serving local dishes, from *roti canai* (RM2) to noodles and curries (from RM5). The fresh fish comes grilled, steamed or fried and can be accompanied by all manner of sauces, from sweet and sour to spicy curry. Daily 8am–10pm.

Santai Bistro Right on the waterfront, *Santai* serves refreshing fruit juices and tasty Malaysian and Western dishes – try the garlic prawns (RM25). There are nightly barbecues at 7pm, and there's free wi-fi too. Daily 9am–11pm.

DRINKING AND NIGHTLIFE

Juara is the quietest of the beaches; Ayer Batang and Salang keep their nightlife low-key, although at times things can get pretty lively on both.

AYER BATANG

A Peace Place This friendly and laidback bar prepares sizzling fish and squid barbecues to be washed down with an ice-cold beer. There's unplugged music and open jams, too. Happy hour 4.30–7pm. Tues–Sun 2pm–2am.

B&J Bar This diver hangout opens its doors as divers return to shore, ready to share their underwater tales over a cold beer or two. In the evenings travellers socialize around the beach bonfire, where there are fire poi performances. Happy hour 5–7pm. Daily 5pm–midnight.

Hallo Bar A wonderfully laidback place where you can enjoy a sundowner in one of the open-fronted lime tree cabañas that stretch out into the sea. Beer RM10. Daily 5pm–2am.

Sunset Bar As the name suggests, this bar at the southernmost end of the beach attracts thirsty travellers who come here to watch the last rays disappear over the horizon. Mon, Tues & Thurs–Sun 2pm–midnight.

DIRECTORY

Banks and exchange There are moneychangers in the Terminal Complex (though rates are lousy). *Bank Simpanan Nasional* has an ATM and is located opposite the airport.

Clinic Poliklinik Komuniti Tekek (Mon–Fri 8am–5pm; ☎ 09 419 1800). Situated in a small gated compound 100m south of the jetty in Tekek and deals with minor ailments.

Internet Usually expensive and slow. Try *Featherlight Café* on the first floor of the Terminal Complex by the airport (daily 9am–5pm; RM10; wi-fi RM5). Plenty of restaurants and guesthouses offer wi-fi, sometimes for a fee.

Police station A 10min walk south of the main jetty in Tekek (daily 24hr; ☎ 09 419 1167).

Post office By the ATM opposite the airport (Mon–Fri 9am–4.30pm).

Sarawak

Separated from Peninsular Malaysia by the South China Sea, the two East Malaysian states of Sarawak and Sabah lie on the northern side of the island of Borneo. **SARAWAK** is steeped in indigenous culture, with a large chunk of its population still living in traditional longhouses along Borneo's mighty rivers (even if the legendary head-hunting is no longer practised). Sarawak is the larger of the two states, and, though well

6

developed, is a good deal wilder than its mainland counterpart. Clear rivers spill down the jungle-covered mountains, and the surviving rainforest, plateaux and river communities are inhabited by indigenous peoples – traditionally grouped as Land Dayaks, Sea Dayaks and Orang Ulu.

Most people start their exploration of Sarawak in the capital **Kuching**, from where you can visit Iban longhouses and Bidayuh traditional dwellings. **Bako National Park** is a short day-trip away

from Kuching and is the best place in Sarawak to spot the pot-bellied proboscis monkeys. A four-hour boat ride northeast of Kuching, **Sibu** marks the start of the popular route along **Batang Rajang**, Sarawak's longest river. Most people stop at **Kapit** and make their way up to **Belaga** to explore more of the interior; Belaga can also be accessed directly from the coast from **Bintulu**. Northeast of Bintulu is **Niah National Park**, which boasts a vast cave system and accessible forest hikes. On its way north to the Brunei border,

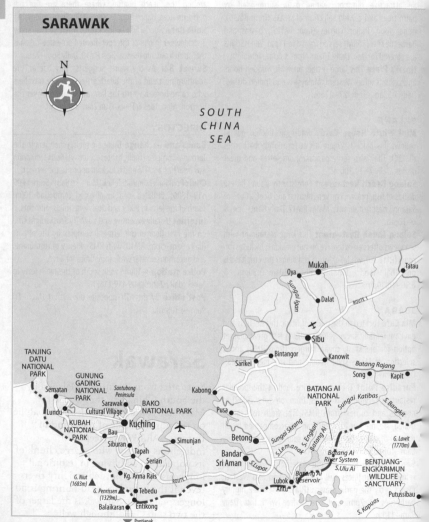

the road goes to Miri, from where you can fly to the spectacular **Gunung Mulu National Park**, Sarawak's chief natural attraction, which features astonishing limestone pinnacles, some of the world's largest caves and a swathe of pristine rainforest for challenging multi-day treks. Also accessible from Miri are the remote **Kelabit Highlands** and their main village of **Bario**, where you can opt for homestays with the Kelabit people and head further into the interior to meet the nomadic Penan.

KUCHING

Sprawled along a lazy waterfront, **KUCHING** has a magnetic charm, with its waterside stalls, antique and trinket markets and some lively bars. Exploring the town's streets on foot is one of its greatest pleasures, and Kuching also makes a great base for trips out into the surrounding area. Kuching's courthouse and fort hark back to the days of the White Rajahs, lending the town a historic air, while the commercial district in the old town is a warren of crowded lanes.

6

6

At weekends, the market off Jalan Satok comes alive with vendors selling mounds of fruit and fresh chillies, pungent dried fish, handicrafts, orchids and all kinds of snacks. Saturday afternoon is the best time to visit.

WHAT TO SEE AND DO

The city sprawls along the banks of the Sungai Sarawak, making the waterfront its main focus. The southern side of the river is flanked by a waterfront promenade, appealing green spaces and numerous food stalls. Facing the waterfront is the **Main Bazaar**, lined with antique and indigenous handicraft shops and still sporting the remains of its original wooden *godowns* (river warehouses). Heading eastwards along the waterfront takes you past Kuching's columned **nineteenth-century courthouse** – now housing chic bistro *ChinaHouse* – with its colonial-Baroque clock tower and Charles Brooke memorial, to the Grand Margherita area, which is full of bars, restaurants and plazas.

The Sarawak museums

The excellent **Sarawak museums** (Mon–Fri 9am–4.45pm; Sat & Sun 10am–4pm; free; ⓦ museum.sarawak.gov.my), spread across opposite sides of Jalan Tun Haji Openg, depict Sarawak in a nutshell. The main building dates from the 1890s and is set in the grounds of the botanical gardens. The ground floor of the museum is a taxidermist's dream, displaying a range of stuffed and pickled Sarawak wildlife. Upstairs, the exceptional ethnographic section includes an authentic wooden Iban longhouse, a Penan hut, traditional tools, musical instruments and weapons. In the same grounds, the **Art Museum** (same hours; free) houses some interesting tribal carvings and hit-and-miss local exhibitions.

Across the bridge is the **Islamic Museum** (same hours; free), which exhibits aspects of Islamic culture, including architecture, weaponry and textiles. On the same side of the road, opposite the post office, the **Textile Museum** (same hours; free) in the Round House displays rich exhibitions of traditional clothing, such as the Iban *pua*

kumbu, Malay *songket* and flamboyant ceremonial headdresses once worn by the Penan, Bidayuh and other tribes.

Chinatown

The grid of streets running eastwards from Jalan Tun Haji Openg, past the main Chinese temple Tua Pek Kong and on to the end of Jalan Padungan, constitutes Kuching's **Chinatown**. On busy Main Bazaar and, one block south, on Jalan Carpenter, there are stores and restaurants operating out of renovated two-storey shophouses, built by Hokkien and Teochew immigrants who arrived in the 1890s. Overlooking the river on Jalan Temple, **Tua Pek Kong** (daily 8am–6pm; free) is the oldest Taoist temple in Sarawak (1876) and attracts a stream of people wanting to pay their respects to Tua Pek Kong, the patron saint of prosperity. You can learn about the history of Sarawak's Chinese community, which dates back to the tenth century, in the insightful **Chinese History Museum** (Mon–Fri 9am–4.45pm, Sat & Sun 10am–4pm; free) across the road.

North of the river

The north side of the river is lined with some stunning buildings, especially eye-catching when they're all lit up at

---

KUCHING: CITY OF CATS

The many cat statues scattered around the centre of Kuching hint at the origin of the city's name, though while "kuching" does indeed mean "cat" in Malay, it's normally spelled "kucing". One theory is that the town was named after the **wild cats** (*kucing hutan*) which were seen along the banks of the river in the nineteenth century, while another suggests that it's a result of James Brooke (an ancestor of Charles) pointing at the original settlement and asking "What's that?" and the person being asked mistakenly thinking that Brooke was pointing at a cat. The most likely theory is that Kuching is a corruption of Cochin (port). In any case, the cats are here to stay.

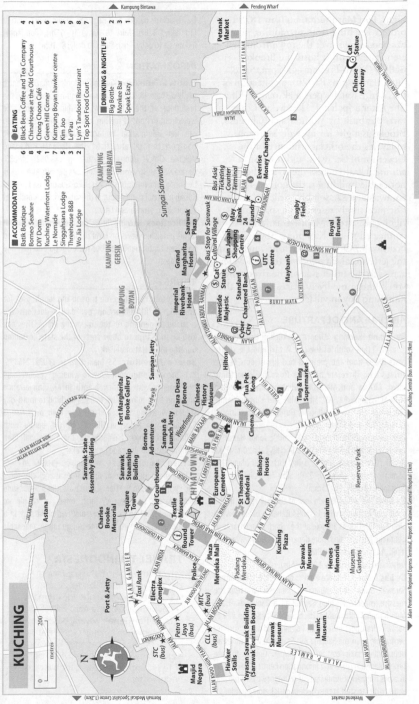

KUCHING

0 ——— 200
metres

ACCOMMODATION

Batik Boutique	6
Borneo Seahare	8
DIY Dorm	4
Kuching Waterfront Lodge	7
Le Nomade	1
Singgahsana Lodge	5
Threehouse B&B	3
Wo Jia Lodge	2

● **EATING**

Black Bean Coffee and Tea Company	4
ChinaHouse at the Old Courthouse	2
Chong Choon Café	5
Green Hill Corner	6
Kampung Boyan hawker centre	1
Kim Joo	3
Le'Pau	9
Lyn's Tandoori Restaurant	8
Top Spot Food Court	7

● **DRINKING & NIGHTLIFE**

Big Bottle	2
Monkee Bar	3
Speak Eazy	1

6

▲ Kampung Bintawa   ▲ Pending Wharf

Sungai Sarawak

KAMPUNG ULU

KAMPUNG SOURABAYA

KAMPUNG GERSIK

KAMPUNG BOYAN

Petanak Market

Cat Statue
Chinese Archway

Sarawak Plaza
Grand Margharita Hotel
Imperial Riverbank Hotel
Riverside Majestic
Cat Statue
Standard Chartered Bank
Cyber City
Hilton

Bus Asia Ticketing Counter
Bus Stop for Sarawak Cultural Village
Tun Jugah Shopping Centre
May Bank
Everrise Money Changer
Laundry
UTC Centre
Maybank

Rugby Field
Royal Brunei

Sampan Jetty
Fort Margharita/Brooke Gallery
Para Desa Borneo
Chinese History Museum
Tua Pek Kong
Ting & Ting Supermarket

Sarawak State Assembly Building
Astana
Charles Brooke Memorial
Square Tower
Old Courthouse
Sarawak Steamship Building
Borneo Adventure
Sampan & Launch Jetty
Waterfront
Main Bazaar
CHINATOWN
Textile Museum
Round Tower
European Cemetery
Bishop's House
St Thomas's Cathedral
Cinema

Port & Jetty
Taxi Rank
Electra Complex
Police
Plaza Merdeka Mall
Padang Merdeka
Kuching Plaza
Sarawak Museum
Heroes Memorial
Museum Gardens
Aquarium
Reservoir Park

Masjid Negara
Hawker Stalls
Yayasan Sarawak Building (Sarawak Tourism Board)
Sarawak Museum
Islamic Museum

Petra Jaya (bus)
MTC (bus)
CLL (bus)
STC (bus)

JALAN ASTANA
JALAN MASUK DUN / JALAN KELUAR DUN
JALAN LITARAN DUN
JALAN TUNKU ABDUL RAHMAN
JALAN BORNEO
JALAN PADUNGAN
JALAN CHAN CHIN ANN
JALAN ABELL
JALAN PADUNGAN
JALAN SONGKRANG
JALAN SONGSONGAN CHEOK
KUCHING
BUKIT MATA
JALAN BAN HOCK
JALAN PELANUK UTARA
JALAN PADUNGAN UTARA
JALAN CENTRAL TIMUR
JALAN PETANAK
JALAN MATHIES
GREEN HILL
JALAN TEMPLE
JALAN WAYANG
JALAN CARPENTER
EBUH CHINA
JLN EWE HAI
BISHOPSGATE
JALAN TUN HAJI OPENG
JALAN MCDOUGALL
JALAN TABUAN
JALAN RESERVOIR
Reservoir Park
JALAN P. RAMLEE
JALAN SATOK
JALAN BADRUDDIN
JALAN GAMBIER
JALAN INDIA
JALAN COURTHOUSE
JALAN BARRACK
JALAN MOSQUE
JALAN KHOO HUN YEANG
LORONG DOCK
JALAN MARKET
JALAN P. RAMLEE
JALAN MASUK DUN

Bordwalk

▼ Normah Medical Specialist Centre (1.2km)

▼ Jalan Penrissen Regional Express Terminal, Airport & Sarawak General Hospital (1km)   Kuching Sentral (bus terminal; 9km)

▼ Weekend market

6

night. **Fort Margherita**, built in 1879 to protect Kuching from marauding pirates, has good views over the town from the crenellated roof; it hosts the **Brooke Gallery** (Mon–Fri 9am–4.45pm, Sat & Sun 10am–4pm; RM20), a collection of the White Rajah's personal memorabilia. The **Astana** (palace), 1km west of the fort, was built by White Rajah Charles Brooke as a gift for his wife Margaret; today, it's the official residence of the Governor of Sarawak, and it's best to admire it from across the river. The most noticeable building is the golden-roofed **Sarawak State Assembly**, which disconcertingly resembles a spaceship, right across from Main Bazaar and connected to the Kampung Boyan by a boardwalk. On the waterfront you'll find the jetty to take a *tambang* (boat; RM1) across to the other side of the river, where you'll find some lively places to eat at the **Kampung Boyan** village.

ARRIVAL AND DEPARTURE

By plane Kuching Airport (Ⓦkuchingairportonline .com) is 11km south of the city. A taxi into the centre costs RM26 from the pre-paid taxi booth outside the arrivals hall. There are no buses from the airport into town. AirAsia and Malaysia Airlines connect Kuching with Singapore, KL, KK, Sibu, Miri and Bintulu, while MASwings also serves Bintulu, Gunung Mulu National Park, Mukah and Sibu.

Destinations Bintulu (4 daily; 55min); Johor Bahru (4 daily; 1hr 30min); Kota Kinabalu (4 daily; 1hr 30min); KL (hourly; 1hr 40min); Miri (5 daily; 1hr); Mulu (daily; 1hr 35min); Penang (3 daily; 2hr); Sibu (8 daily; 45min); Singapore (2 daily; 1hr 25min).

By boat The wharf is 6km east of the city centre in the suburb of Pending, with Ekspress Bahagia boats serving Sibu (RM45). Tickets are sold at the wharf. It's advisable to get to the jetty 30min before departure as they leave early if full. A taxi costs around RM25.

Destinations Sibu (daily 8.30am; 5hr).

By bus All long-distance express buses to destinations in Sarawak, Brunei and Pontianak in Indonesia leave from the massive, modern Kuching Sentral a.k.a. "Six-and-a-Half-Mile-Terminal". City Public Link buses #K3, #K6 and #K9 or Sarawak Transport buses #3A, #6, #4B and #2 to Kuching Sentral run from the Saujana Bus Station several times an hour, while taxis cost around RM30. Get up-to-date timetables from the Visitor Information Centre. Book tickets at a bus company counter, pay at counter two or three and show tickets to staff at the check-in desk before boarding.

Destinations Bandar Seri Begawan (daily; 20hr); Bintulu (10 daily; 12hr); Miri (8 daily; 10–15hr); Pontianak, Indonesia (6 daily; 9hr); Sibu (10 daily; 8–10hr).

INFORMATION

Tourist information Kuching Visitor Information Centre (daily 8.30am–8.30pm, Ⓦsarawaktourism.com) is on the first floor of the UTC Centre, a 5min walk from the waterfront in front of the Tun Jugah shopping centre. You can get information on accommodation and public transport to local attractions. The National Parks and Wildlife Office (Mon–Fri 8am–5pm; ☎082 248088, Ⓦsarawakforestry.com), which issues permits and makes bookings for overnight stays at Bako, Gunung Gading and Kubah national parks, is out in the suburbs. Book online at Ⓦebooking.sarawak.gov.my.

Publications Kuching In & Out (Ⓦkuchinginandout .com) publishes news on local culture and nightlife, and has useful information on bus routes, food and heritage trail maps.

TOURS

Kuching tour operators run trips to the longhouses for upwards of RM200/person per day; reductions are available depending on the size of the group. They can also arrange trips to other parts of the state, including Gunung Mulu National Park.

Borneo Adventure 55 Main Bazaar ☎082 245175, Ⓦborneoadventure.com. Award-winning, professional tour agency with another branch in KK. Can arrange anything from informative tours of Kuching to multi-day wildlife-watching tours and stays in their own Nanga Sampa jungle lodge in Ulu Ai, by the border with Kalimantan, which has links to the traditional Iban community next door and jungle treks.

Borneo Experiences Jln Temple ☎082 241346, Ⓦborneoexperiences.com. Apart from quirky city tours and cycling trips to the Damai peninsula, this *Singgahsana Lodge*-based tour agency also offers a couple of adventurous options – a three-day/two-night stay in a traditional Bidayu village in the Bungu range, reachable

TRAVEL TO INDONESIA

You can travel across the border into Indonesian Kalimantan directly from Kuching. A nine-hour bus ride (from the Kuching Sentral bus station) will take you as far as **Pontianak** (several buses leave either early in the morning or late at night). The border crossing at Entikong issues thirty-day visas on arrival to citizens of 169 countries (see list: Ⓦtopbali.com /indonesia-visa).

only on foot, and homestays in Bario, in the remote Kelabit Highlands (see p.498).

Para Desa Borneo 1 Jln Wayang ☏082 238801, ⓦparadesaborneo.com. This adventure-travel company specializes in off-the-beaten-path bike tours, including Kuching city rides, off-road biking and rafting day-tours, week-long wildlife bike safaris and epic rides into Iban heartland.

ACCOMMODATION

Borneo Seahare 187 Jln Song Thian Cheok ☏082 237945, ⓔseahareguesthouse@gmail.com. Besides a spacious dorm and attractive, pastel-coloured doubles, this hostel has a big common area equipped with dartboard, free computers, TV room and a bar dishing up inexpensive nibbles like French bread pizzas (RM12). Dorms RM20, doubles RM65

★ **DIY Dorm** 64 Jln Carpenter ☏012 810 8580. This airy and light wood-tiled loft houses cosy individual beds with personal wooden lockers and privacy curtains. Everything is cleverly refurbished from secondhand furniture. There's a chill-out balcony, and the *Wrong Place* café downstairs has strong brews, Malaysian staple dishes and industrial-chic, iron-and-wood furnishings. Dorms RM25

Kuching Waterfront Lodge 15 Main Bazaar ☏082 231111, ⓦkuchingwaterfrontlodge.com. Located inside one of the historical houses along the waterfront, it has a beautiful lobby with carved wooden staircase, simple, tastefully decorated rooms, an attractive roof terrace and welcome touches of greenery throughout. Breakfast included. Doubles RM115

Le Nomade 1st Floor, 3 Jln Green Hill ☏082 237831, ⓦlenomadehostel.com. This sociable hostel has a wide variety of rooms, with or without toilet and windows, and functional dorms spread over three colourful storeys. The outdoor patio with barbecue pit and self-catering kitchenettes are nice touches for those wishing to stay longer – ask for long-term rates. Breakfast is included. Dorms RM25, doubles RM55

Singgahsana Lodge 1 Jln Temple ☏082 429277, ⓦsinggahsana.com. *Singgahsana* has a beautiful lounge and on-site café, a lively rooftop bar and walls decorated with vivid photos from the owners' travels. Though downstairs rooms lack natural light, the rest are bright and have comfy beds. If you want to retreat from Kuching's hustle and bustle, ask about *Village House*, the owners' other property out of town. Dorms RM35, doubles RM100

Threehouse B&B 51 Upper China St ☏082 423499, ⓦfacebook.com/threehousebnb. A beautifully decorated hostel with a comfy common area with plenty of books and DVDs. There's a fan-cooled dorm, double (some with a/c) and multi-person rooms. The only downside is that the toilets are practically in the kitchen. Dorms RM20, doubles RM60

(see p.498)

★**TREAT YOURSELF**

Batik Boutique 38 Jln Padungan ☏082 422845, ⓦbatikboutiquehotel.com. With just fifteen rooms – each with a king-sized bed and rain shower – all individually decorated with a batik-style pattern on the wall, this boutique hotel is a splendid central choice. Sip a beer in the courtyard, surrounded by green bamboo shoots, or soak in the jacuzzi. Doubles RM280

6

Wo Jia Lodge 17 Main Bazaar ☏082 251776. This waterfront guesthouse, run by laidback and helpful guys, and featuring a large common area strewn with cushions, has large, sparsely furnished rooms and is great value for money. One of the few places to offer single rooms. Dorms RM20, doubles RM59

EATING

Black Bean Coffee and Tea Company 87 Jln Ewe Hai ☏082 420290. You smell this tiny coffee shop before you reach it, thanks to its wide selection of freshly ground beans from Java, Sumatra and Sarawak itself. The tea list is extensive, too. Mon–Sat 7am–6pm.

★**ChinaHouse at the Old Courthouse** Jln Tun Abang Haji Openg ☏082 417601, ⓦfacebook.com/ChinaHouseK. Come and enjoy the atmosphere of the White Rajah's historical Courthouse turned into chic bistro, cakehouse, restaurant, arts centre and pub with live bands. There are rotating arts exhibits, tables set around the inner courtyard, and all the space you need to enjoy a slice of their delicious cakes (RM10) and Western mains (from RM20). Daily 9am–midnight.

Chong Choon Café Lot 121, Section 3, Jln Abell. Considered by many to be Sarawak's best *laksa* (which is different from mainland *laksa*; RM5) outlet. Get there early before it's all sold out. Mon & Wed–Sun 7–11am.

Green Hill Corner Jln Temple at Jln Green Hill. This Chinese *kopitiam* is legendary among locals for its beef noodle soup. The noodles are handmade, and chicken rice, *laksa* and savoury rice porridge are also on offer. Mains from RM4. Daily 7am–11pm.

Kampung Boyan hawker centre Take one of the regular boats across the river in the evening (RM1) and choose anything from curry to noodles to *tom yam* from the hawker stalls. Behind the food court, there's a restaurant that specializes in fantastic grilled chicken served on a banana leaf. Daily 11.30am–11pm.

Kim Joo 93 Jln Ewe Hai ☏082 243053. This simple *kopitiam* is crowded with locals who come here for big portions of Cantonese specialities in Sarawak style, like tomato-sauce crispy noodles (RM6). Daily 6.30am–2pm.

6

★TREAT YOURSELF

Le'Pau Lot 395, Jln Ban Hock ☎082 233304, ⊛facebook.com/lepaurestaurant. This delightful wooden hall, lit by naked lightbulbs, spills tables out onto an outdoor patio and is manned by Kelabit people. Taste Sarawak's highland dishes while performers put on traditional dances and demonstrate their blowpipe abilities along to the rhythms of the *sape*, the Orang Ulu's traditional lute. It's not just the ambience, but also the food – from veggie *cangkuk manis* with pumpkin and egg, to bamboo-cooked *pansuh* chicken (RM15.90) – that provides a perfectly choreographed immersion in Sarawak's tribal culture. Daily 11am–2pm & 5.30–11pm.

Lyn's Tandoori Restaurant Lot 267, Jln Song Thian Cheok. Not only does Lyn cook up the best *tandoori roti* in town, but the tandoori dishes, curries and freshly baked naan are excellent, too. Lots of veggie options. Mains from RM15. Daily 11.30am–10.30pm.

★**Top Spot Food Court** Jln Bukit Mata. The best food court in town for seafood, located on the roof of a multi-storey car park. Fish and seafood is priced according to weight and includes delicious bamboo clams as well as giant prawns, squid and soft-shell crab. Mains come in small, medium and large; from RM15. Daily noon–11pm.

DRINKING AND NIGHTLIFE

Big Bottle Lot 106 & 107, Jln Abell ☎012 240 8330. An interesting self-service drinking joint: walk to a row of fridges, pick from a wide selection of beers, and pay at a supermarket-style counter. On the opposite side, the spacious drinking lounge fitted with couches and tables has murals and beer-themed aphorisms, or you can sit outside under a covered patio. The huge thin-crust pizzas (from RM17) are recommended. Mon–Thurs 3pm–2.30am, Fri–Sun 2pm–2.30am.

Monkee Bar 12 Padungan Arcade, Jln Song Thian Cheok ☎014 693 9885, ⊛monkeebars.com. This Kuching drinking institution donates one third of its profits to orang-utan and other conservation projects. Beer is cheap (from RM5.5), staff are super-friendly and the eco-themed artworks of Marcus Lim help with the good vibes. There's 25 percent off cocktails on Wednesdays. Mon–Thurs & Sun 4pm–1.30am, Fri & Sat 4pm–2am.

★**Speak Eazy** 63 Jln Ewe Hai ☎012 610 0987, ⊛facebook.com/speakeazykch. Run by brothers fixated with trashy popular culture, this feel-good bar has Darth Vader and Stormtrooper masks on the beer taps, 8-bit videogame art on the walls, and cult-movies playing on the TV while classic rock blasts from the sound system. The home-made flavoured *tuak* selection, ciabatta chilli dogs (RM14) and Dayak food – try the pork steamed inside pitcher plants – are great. Mon–Thurs & Sun 4.30pm–1am & Fri–Sat 4.30pm–2am.

DIRECTORY

Banks and exchange HSBC, Bangunan Binamus, off Jln Padungan; Standard Chartered Bank, Jln Tunku Abdul Rahman. Everise Moneychanger, 199 Jln Pandungan, offers good rates.

Embassies and consulates Australian Honorary Consul, E39, Level 2, Taman Sri Sarawak Mall, Jln Tunku Abdul Rahman (☎082 230777); British Honorary Consul (☎082 250950); Brunei, No. 325 Lorong Seladah 10, Jln Seladah (☎082 456515); Indonesia, No. 21, Lot 16557, Block 11, Jln Stutong (☎082 421734); New Zealand, Lot 8679, Section 64, Pending Commercial Centre (☎082 482177).

SHOPPING IN KUCHING

If you're after **tribal handicrafts**, textiles and more, Kuching offers by far the best selection. **Main Bazaar** along the waterfront is lined with shops selling a mix of mass-produced touristy tat and genuine gems – usually found towards the back of the shops. If you know what you're after, don't be afraid to bargain, but be prepared to pay accordingly for genuine Penan blowpipes, carved Iban shields, longhouse charms and rice paddy guardians. Remember that shipping any part of an endangered animal or bird – hornbill, sun bear, clouded leopard – carries a prison sentence and hefty fine if caught. Not all items you find in the shops are from Sarawak, or, indeed, Borneo; Sarawak crafts are being pushed out of the market by far cheaper Indonesian ones, so if you want to know more about an item's age or origin, ask the sellers and they'll be happy to oblige. Be prepared to spend hours (or even days) just browsing.

The most reputable shops to look out for along Main Bazaar are Kelvin Gallery, Nelson's Antiques and Jewellery, John's Gallery, Bong Gallery and Borneo Tribal Arts.

If you're after some presents to take home, Main Bazaar is also a good spot to pick up Iban *pua kumbu* textiles, Sarawak pepper, sago biscuits, and the ubiquitous *kek lapiz* – colourful, multi-flavoured layer cakes that will survive the journey if you're heading straight home from Kuching.

Hospitals Sarawak General Hospital, Jln Hospital (☎082 276666), has an excellent A&E department and inexpensive consultations, though it can be crowded. For private treatment, go to Normah Medical Specialist Centre, Jln Tun Abdul Rahman (☎082 440055; emergency ☎082 311999).

Immigration Bahagian Visa, 2nd floor, Bangunan Sultan Iskandar, Kompleks Pejabat Persecutuan, Jln Tun Razak at Jln Simpang Tiga (Mon–Thurs 8am–5pm, Fri 8–11.45am & 2.15–5pm; ☎082 245661) for visa extensions; take STC bus #K8 or #K11 from outside Kuching Mosque.

Laundry Mr Clean on Jln Padungan, or 24 Laundry on Jln Padungan at Jln Song Thian Cheok.

Pharmacies Several around the Electra House shopping centre on Jln Power.

Police There is a Tourist Police unit at Kuching Waterfront (☎082 250522); most speak English.

Post office Jln Tun Haji Openg (Mon–Sat 8am–6pm, Sun 10am–1pm).

THE SARAWAK CULTURAL VILLAGE

The **Sarawak Cultural Village** (daily 9am–5pm; RM50; ☎082 846411, ⓦscv.com.my) is picturesquely located on the Santubong Peninsula 35km north of Kuching, and is very much a show for tourists, but a great educational experience nonetheless. A walkway loops around a small lake, passing replicas of traditional dwellings belonging to the Penan, Iban, Melanau, Bidayuh and other indigenous peoples of Sarawak. You can visit all the dwellings, take part in activities such as baking biscuits from sago flour and blowpipe shooting, and shop for traditional crafts such as batik shirts and sarongs. There's an excellent 45-minute dance show at 11.30am and 4pm, featuring dancers in traditional Iban, Melanau and Bidayuh costumes, a hunter demonstrating blowpipe shooting and those five minutes of non-obligatory audience participation. The SCV also hosts the renowned **Sarawak Rainforest World Music Festival** (ⓦrwmf.net), held during three days in July and featuring acts from around the globe. To get here, take the shuttle from the *Singgahsana Lodge* at Jalan Wayang (4 daily from 9.15am; 45min; RM20 return).

SEMENGOH NATURE RESERVE

Semengoh Nature Reserve (daily 8am–5pm; feeding times 9am & 3pm; RM10; ⓦsarawakforestry.com) is home to 25 semi-wild **orang-utans** that have been orphaned or rescued from captivity. Here they are trained in the vital skills to survive in the wild and fend for themselves. Although the main programme has been transferred to Matang Wildlife Centre, Semengoh still has some younger orang-utans which you can see swinging through the trees. They generally spend most of their time roaming the surrounding forest, but some usually come to the main platform for feeding time (though a sighting is not guaranteed during the wet season, when there is plenty of fruit in the forest).

Most hostels offer transfers to and from the nature reserve for RM35, entry included. To get here by public transport, catch bus #K6 to "Semenggok" (at 7.15am, 10.15am, 1pm & 3.30pm, returning at 8.45am, 11.15am, 2.15pm & 4.15pm; 45min; RM4 one-way) from Jalan Masjid. This will drop you at the entrance to the park where you buy your ticket; it's then a 1.3km clearly signed walk through pretty botanical gardens along a tarmac pathway to the feeding area. Taxis cost around RM100 return, including waiting time.

BAKO NATIONAL PARK

BAKO NATIONAL PARK was established in 1957 and is the best place to see wildlife in the state. The rare proboscis monkey, found only in Borneo, is resident here, and most visitors are treated to a sight of its unmistakeable hooter, which has earned it the native nickname "Dutchman". You'll definitely catch sight of cheeky macaques that hang around the visitor centre, and it's not uncommon to see vipers, wild pigs, giant monitor lizards and silver leaf monkeys. Bako can easily be visited as a day-trip from Kuching, but since wildlife is at its most active early in the morning and late in the afternoon, it's far more rewarding to stay overnight.

To get to the park, catch the red bus #1 (hourly 7am–5pm; from Bako, 6.30am–5.30pm; 45min; RM3.50) from 6 Jln Khoo Hun Yeang, across from the Open-Air Market to the jetty at

6

Kampung Bako. From here, you must pay the park fee (RM20), sign in and then take a motorized boat that bounces along the surf all the way to the park headquarters (RM40/person, return at 2pm, 3pm or 4pm; 20min), where you must register. Maps are available from the park headquarters.

The park boasts seventeen **trails**, which all start from park headquarters and are colour-coded with paint splashes every 20m. The trails vary in difficulty and length of time, and you need a guide (RM450/day each 5 people) for trails that are longer than 5 hours or require overnight camping. The easiest and shortest walk (and the best to see proboscis monkeys) is the Telok Paku trail. There's a hike to **Tajor Waterfall** (3.5km; about 2hr), which involves climbing the forested cliff through *kerangas*, with plentiful pitcher plants and peat bogs. As you leave the main trail at the wooden hut you'll see a path that descends to two beautiful beaches, **Telok Pandan Kecil** and **Telok Pandan Besar** (30min), with dramatic karst jutting out of the sea. The longest and most demanding trail is the 13km **Telok Limau** (8hr 30min one-way), which ends on a remote beach where you can camp. Guides can arrange one-way boat transfers (RM165) to or from the park headquarters. Get a **permit** online at ⓦebooking.com.my before you go (see p.484), especially at weekends, as the park is very popular. At the park headquarters, you can camp (RM5), stay in a four-bed dorm (RM15/person or RM40/room) or in one of the lodges (RM50/room with shared bathroom; RM100/three-bed room with private bathroom; RM150/two-room chalet), all of which provide bed linen but no cooking facilities. There's a good cafeteria at headquarters serving rice and noodle dishes (buffet meal RM9) and a provisions shop.

SIBU

SIBU, 60km from the coast up Batang Rajang, is Sarawak's second-largest city and the state's biggest port. If Kuching's symbol is the cat, then Sibu's is the swan, and you'll see plenty of those about. Most of the local population is Foochow Chinese, and its remarkable growth is largely attributed to these enterprising immigrants who came here in the early twentieth century. Sibu is the jump-off point for trips up the Batang Rajang River.

WHAT TO SEE AND DO

The town's most striking landmark is the towering, seven-storey **pagoda** at the back of Tua Pek Kong Temple (daily 6am–8pm; you can climb to the top until 5.30pm) – the oldest Chinese temple in Sibu – beyond the western, waterfront end of Jalan Khoo Peng Loong. The roof and columns are decorated with traditional dragon and holy bird statues, and murals depict Chinese folk tales. Across the road, in the network of streets between Jalan Market, Jalan Channel and Jalan Central, is **Chinatown**. The central artery, **Jalan Market**, runs from Jalan Pulau beside the temple, and forms the hub of possibly the most vibrant and exotic *pasar malam* (night market) in Sarawak. Beside Jalan Channel, the daily **Sibu Central Market** opens before dawn and closes around 5pm; there are hundreds of stalls here, selling anything from mounds of fruit and jungle ferns to rattan baskets, beadwork and charm bracelets.

Along Jalan Central you'll find the **Sibu Heritage Centre**, with an excellent museum (Tues–Sun 9am–5pm; free) on the first floor charting the history of Sibu and Sarawak through a series of photographs and objects associated with each ethnic group – from the Iban and Penan to the Chinese immigrants. Shrunken heads in a wicker harness is a standout exhibit.

ARRIVAL AND DEPARTURE

By plane The airport is 23km east of the city centre. Taxis cost RM55 (via pre-paid coupon at the taxi counter) into the centre. Between them, MASwings and AirAsia connect Sibu to Kuching, KK, Bintulu, Miri and KL.

Destinations Bintulu (2 daily; 35min); Kota Kinabalu (2 daily; 1hr 40min); Kuala Lumpur (7 daily; 2hr); Kuching (6 daily; 40min); Miri (3 daily; 55min).

By boat Boats dock at the River Express Terminal, across the road from the local bus station. The "flying coffin" express boats – thus named because of their oblong shape and accident-prone fame – to Kapit (some via Kanowit and Song; RM25–35) depart once or twice an hour between 5.45am and 2.30pm from the Regional Ferry Terminal, in the same building as the River Express Terminal. If water levels allow, the 5.45am boat continues to Belaga (most regular during the rainy season Oct–April; RM70). Large clocks display the departure time for each boat company; arrive 30min early and, during holidays, buy tickets a day in advance. Express Bahagia (☎084 319228) runs a daily service to Kuching at 11.30am.

Destinations Belaga (daily; 11hr); Kapit (12 daily; 3hr 30min–4hr); Kuching (daily; 5hr).

By bus The local bus and taxi station is on Jln Khoo Peng Loong, opposite the boat terminal. Long-distance buses depart from the Sibu Bus Terminal on Jln Pahlawan, 3.5km northeast of the centre along Jln Pedada. To get there, take the #21 Lanang bus from the city bus station.

Destinations Bintulu (11 daily; 3hr 15min); Kuching (15 daily; 7–8hr); Miri (10 daily; 6hr 30min).

INFORMATION

Tourist information The helpful Sibu Visitors' Information Centre (Mon–Fri 8am–5pm; ☎084 340980, ⓦsarawaktourism.com), located at the ground floor of Sibu Heritage Centre, has plenty of information on how to get upriver and to access the Rajang longhouses, along with a list of recommended local guides which is by no means definitive.

ACCOMMODATION

★ **Eden Inn** 33/35 Jln Maju ☎084 336622. Very good-value, clean en-suite rooms with TVs, only 200m from the jetty and walking distance to all of Sibu's major sights. Singles RM30, doubles RM40

Li Hua Hotel 2 Jln Lanang ☎084 324000, ⓦlihuahotel .com.my. Close to the bus and ferry terminals to the west of town, rooms in this friendly hotel are spotless, spacious and come with river or city views. Free wi-fi. Doubles RM65

River Park Hotel 51–53 Jln Maju ☎084 316688. Comfortable riverfront hotel with friendly staff and river views from some of the a/c rooms (the cheapest are windowless). Wi-fi available. Doubles RM60

EATING AND DRINKING

Jln Maju, by the waterfront, is lined with cheap Chinese *kopitiams*.

★ **Café Café** 10 Jln Chew Geok Lyn. Trendy spot serving wonderful fusion dishes (mains from RM18), oodles of noodles and the likes of tiramisu and black sesame ice cream for dessert. Tues–Sun noon–4pm & 6–11.30pm.

Kian Hock 49 Jln Maju ☎084 324391. The Foochow specialities here, like *kam pua mee* – thin noodles tossed in pork lard and served with roast pork – fried *mee* and charcoal-roasted duck are local favourites (mains from RM5). Daily 8am–10pm.

★ **Night market** Jln Market. Night-time stalls selling everything from Chinese pork and rice to satay, barbecued chicken, grilled fish balls, curry, steam buns and a variety of wonderful unidentifiable fried things (from RM4). Extremely popular with locals. Daily 6–10pm.

Sibu Central Market Pasar Sentral Sibu. Hawker stalls at the Lembangan produce market are the busiest place in the

---

LONGHOUSE VISITS

The interior of Sarawak is home to many tribal groups who still live in their **longhouse communities**, and a visit to one is a true highlight of any trip to this region. Don't go expecting a picturesquely "primitive" lifestyle: today, most longhouses are built of brick and have electricity, radios and satellite TV.

Tour companies in Kuching (see p.484) arrange either day- or overnight trips, but some can be very touristy, with "traditional" dances put on for the visitors. Before you book, establish exactly what the longhouse visit entails and whether the rates cover transport, meals and activities. A good visit should provide a mix of cultural interaction, traditional food and activities such as jungle trekking. If you can only spare time for a day-trip, go to the splendid nineteenth-century **Annah Rais Longhouse** near Tebedu, where you'll notice some shrunken heads in the rafters, left over from the head-hunting days. Here you can also stay overnight at the community-run homestay project (ⓦlonghouseadventure.com).

Visiting independently is more complicated, especially if you don't speak any Malay. It's considered rude to turn up at a longhouse without an invitation, so you either have to go with a tour company or find a local guide with a particular longhouse connection. Taking **presents** for the community is the norm – things that they can use, such as schoolbooks and pencils for the children, are best. During the **Gawai harvest festival** in June, all longhouses welcome visitors and non-stop revelry continues for several days, fuelled by copious amounts of fairly lethal *tuak* (rice wine). If you don't want any, touching your lips with your fingers and then the rim of the glass is a polite way to refuse offers of drunken camaraderie.

6

morning, serving mostly Chinese specialities, such as *kam pua mee* and chicken porridge (mains from RM3); different stalls open at different times. Daily 5am–midnight.

THE BATANG RAJANG

The mighty 560km-long **BATANG RAJANG RIVER** lies at the very heart of Sarawak and a trip into the interior along its cappuccino-coloured waters is one of Borneo's great river journeys. This is a semi-isolated world where the jungle encroaches on both sides, and where people still live in traditional longhouses, though the area has changed greatly since Redmond O'Hanlon's trip, described in *Into the Heart of Borneo*. The communities here are used to visitors, and travel along the river is fairly straightforward. Express "flying coffin" speedboats from Sibu head to **Kapit**, a busy indigenous market town, while further upriver lies little **Belaga**; the latter can be used as springboard for local longhouse visits as well as trips further inland.

Kapit

With the construction of a new road link to Sibu, the busy little trading town of **KAPIT** has lost most of its traditional charm and longhouses. Use it merely as transit point to break the long river journey to Belaga. Close to the jetty is Kapit's main landmark, **Fort Sylvia**, which houses a small museum (Tues–Sun 10am–noon & 2–5pm; free) of tribal artefacts and rice wine jars.

ARRIVAL AND DEPARTURE

By boat Express boats from Sibu dock at the eastern wharf while those Belaga-bound dock 100m away at the western wharf, just off the Kapit town square; both flank the tiny

town centre. Theoretically, you need a (free) permit from the Resident's Office, 9th Floor, Jln Bleteh (☎084 796230) to travel beyond Kapit up the Batang Rajang to Belaga and beyond. However, since permits are never checked and since you don't need one to access Belaga from Bintulu, most travellers don't bother getting one.

Destinations Belaga (daily at around 9.30am; 5–6hr; RM45); Sibu (hourly 6.40am–3.15pm; 3hr; RM20–25).

ACCOMMODATION

Ark Hill Inn Jln Penghulu Gerinang ☎084 796168. Located near the square, with twenty clean en-suite rooms (the singles are tiny) and free wi-fi. Doubles RM90

New Rajang Inn 104 Jln Teo Chow Beng ☎084 796600. This is a real bargain with tiled en-suite a/c rooms with TV, fridge, wi-fi and a Bible for your spiritual needs. Doubles RM88

EATING

Night market Between Jln Teo Chow Beng and Jln Penghulu Berjaya. Mostly Malay dishes, such as satay and *nasi goreng*; also curry and a few Dayak dishes. Mains from RM4. Daily 5–11pm.

Soon Kit Café 13 Jln Tan Sit Liong. Informal place that's locally famous for its chicken rice (RM5) and laksa (RM4). Daily 6am–5pm.

Belaga

Further up the Batang Rajang from Kapit is **BELAGA**, a small, remote village with a laidback atmosphere, filled with crowing roosters and backed by mist-covered mountains. There is one notoriously unreliable ATM, so bring all the cash you need with you. The rivers around Belaga, especially **Sungai Asap**, have a good few Kayan, Kenyah and Orang Ulu **longhouses**, making this one of the better places for a more authentic visit. Independent travel to the longhouses depends on a certain amount of luck and, ultimately, chatting to someone who will

---

RIDING THE "FLYING COFFINS"

The long, swift, closed-top boats that ply the Batang Rajang's waters are a unique experience. Choose between riding in the (mostly) air-conditioned interior, or riding on the roof (hold on tight) to watch nimble-footed boat attendants and passengers disembark at various longhouses carrying anything from roofing material to live chickens in cages. The boats have a reinforced steel walkway along the sides, so you can hang on to the rails and loiter outside. Boating from **Kapit to Belaga** used to be a hair-raising experience during the river stretch encompassing the Pelagus Rapids, as it involved expert manoeuvring in a strong current in between large rocks. Many of those rocks have since been dynamited and the journey is a lot smoother. During dry season, the low water levels sometimes make the Pelagus Rapids section impassible for weeks.

invite you over – try asking around on the boat from Kapit or at one of the cafés, where you're sure to find someone who can help. There are also various treks that take you further into the jungle, past the Bakun Dam area and into the villages beyond; a guide (see box below) is a very good idea.

ARRIVAL AND DEPARTURE

By boat Express boats from Belaga to Kapit leave from the main jetty by the village (daily around 7.30am; RM45). During dry season, boats can't bypass the Pelagus Rapids en route to Kapit and Sibu, but it's still possible to travel upriver to various longhouses.

By 4WD For those who want to travel on to Bintulu (or who are travelling during dry season), there are daily 4WD trips (7.30am departure; 4hr; RM60) using the logging road. Ask Daniel Levoh (see box below) to book transport for you.

ACCOMMODATION AND EATING

Belaga Hotel 14 Main Bazaar ☎ 086 461244. Right on the main drag, this cheapie has fifteen rather battered rooms, all but two of which are fitted out with a/c. No hot water. Doubles RM40

Daniel Levoh's Guesthouse Jln The Ah Kiong ☎ 086 461997 or ☎ 013 848 6351. Two blocks behind the Main Bazaar, off the main road that runs straight from the dock, this guesthouse, run by local guide Daniel Levoh (see box below), has four simple, fan-cooled rooms (a couple without windows) and shared facilities. Wi-fi comes and goes. Dorms RM20, doubles RM40

BINTULU

BINTULU is a coastal boom town grown rich on offshore gas, used as a jumping-off point for the Niah National Park (see p.492) and Belaga; it's also the only place with transport to Belaga (see opposite) during dry season. There are a couple of sights worth visiting, the main one being **Tua Pek Kong** (daily 6am–6pm; free), the large and colourful Chinese temple right on the Main Bazaar. The **daily market** (around 7am–5pm) at the west end of Main Bazaar is filled with colourful mounds of fresh produce; you can also buy bowls of writhing sago grubs – a local speciality. **Tanjung Batu** beach, 6km from the centre, is pleasant enough to while away an afternoon.

ARRIVAL AND DEPARTURE

By plane The airport (☎ 086 339163), served by AirAsia, Malaysia Airlines and MASwings, is 23km out of town. There are no public buses and a taxi to the centre costs around RM40.

Destinations Kota Kinabalu (daily; 1hr 15min); Kuala Lumpur (4 daily; 2hr 5min); Kuching (4 daily; 1hr); Miri (2 daily; 35min); Sibu (daily; 35min).

By bus The long-distance bus station is 5km out of town at Medan Jaya. A taxi to the centre from here will cost RM15, or you can take bus #29 from the local bus station on Lebuh Ray Abang Galau (RM1), which becomes Jln Sri Dagang as it enters town. The long-distance bus station serves Batu Niah, Kuching, Sibu and Miri.

VISITING A LONGHOUSE FROM BELAGA

The tourist office in Sibu keeps a constantly changing list of recommended local guides in Sarawak's interior, and it's best to enquire directly (☎ 084 340980). There are plenty of unlicensed guides who are perfectly knowledgeable; talk to other travellers and local accommodation owners to see whom they recommend. In **Belaga**, *Belaga Hotel* can contact guides for upriver longhouse visits, and Daniel Levoh from *Daniel Levoh's Guesthouse* has lots of contacts in the area, but his services can be expensive and get mixed reviews from travellers.

It's possible to visit longhouses on your own, but don't expect an exotic experience: unless you're coming with a guide/interpreter, there may not be much in the way of activities, as the residents will be busy with their daily lives. Speaking some Malay is also essential, as few longhouses have English-speakers. Independent travellers are expected to bring gifts or donate money, and are typically charged up to RM150 for an overnight stay. Be cautious, for locals are well known to overcharge gullible travellers.

LONGHOUSES AROUND BELAGA

These longhouses are in order of distance from Belaga.

Dong Daah Easily visited Kayan longhouse that's a 10min boat ride upstream.
Lirong Amo Kayan longhouse that's reachable by a 30min walk.

Long Liten Traditional Kejaman longhouse that's around 30min upriver.
Sekapan Pajang Traditional Sekapan longhouse 30min downriver.

6

Destinations Batu Niah (4 daily; 2hr); Kuching (10 daily; 7–10hr); Miri via Niah Junction (every 30min; 4hr); Sibu (10 daily; 3hr 30min).

By 4WD A Belaga resident makes the trip from Belaga to Bintulu and back every day along a paved logging road (4hr). Call Daniel Levoh (see box, p.491) to make arrangements to be picked up from Bintulu. The 4WD tends to head back to Belaga daily at around 2.30pm.

ACCOMMODATION AND EATING

Capitol Hotel 2nd floor, 284 Jln Keppel ☏ 086 339118, ✉ capitolhomestay@gmail.com. The welcoming rooms at this brightly coloured budget guesthouse have a/c, en-suite bathrooms and luminous windows – almost too good for this price range. Doubles RM49

Kintown Inn 93 Jln Keppel ☏ 086 333666. Excellent-value budget hotel with a good view from the upper floors, though the carpeted a/c rooms could do with renovating and wi-fi access. Doubles RM92

Night market Beside Jln Kampung Dadang, off Jln Abang Galau. The night market is a great place for fresh, delicious local dishes and is a good way to mix with locals. Mains from RM4. Daily 4–10pm.

Pasar Utama Main Bazaar, next to the produce market. New Market has a few informal stalls on the first floor, serving the likes of *nasi goreng* and *kueh tiaow* noodles. Mains from RM6. Daily 7am–5pm.

NIAH NATIONAL PARK

Visiting **NIAH NATIONAL PARK** (daily 8am–3pm last entry; RM20) is a highly rewarding experience – in a day you can see one of the largest caves in the world, as well as prehistoric rock graffiti in the remarkable **Painted Cave**, and hike along primary forest trails. This is one of Sarawak's smaller national parks, but it is recognized as one of the most important archeological sites in the world. In the outer area of the present park, deep excavations have revealed human remains and flake stone tools, mortars and shell ornaments that date back forty thousand years – one of the earlier examples of people living in Southeast Asia. The park is roughly halfway between Bintulu and Miri, 11km off the main road and 3km north of Batu Niah, reached either by a half-hour walk or by taxi.

WHAT TO SEE AND DO

Niah National Park is spread over around 31 square kilometres of peat swamp,

forests and gigantic limestone outcrops. The caves are joined by a wooden walkway which takes you through the lowland forest along to all the caves. The marked route takes you into the depths of the cave system; a torch is mandatory (bring your own) and good footwear is a bonus, since the walkway can be slippery; you may also want to wear a hat to protect you from the bat guano. There are a couple of trails and a 400m limestone ridge which you can scale, all of which are clearly signposted from park headquarters.

A small **museum** (Tues–Fri 9am–4.45pm, Sat & Sun 10am–4pm; free) just across the river from the park headquarters covers the geology of the caves and the history of the extremely dangerous profession of collecting birds' nests – a few locals still practise it (see box opposite).

From the park headquarters, it's a thirty-minute walk to the **caves**: take a *sampan* across the river (on demand until 7pm; RM1, RM1.50 after 5.30pm) and then follow a wooden walkway through dense rainforest where you may see monkeys, hornbills, birdwing butterflies, tree squirrels and flying lizards. Inside the caves themselves, you will see bats, swiftlets, cockroaches that feed on the bat guano, and carnivorous crickets.

The caves

The main walkway heads up through the **Traders Cave** (so-called because early nest- and guano-gatherers would congregate here to sell their harvests) to the vast west mouth of the **Great Cave**, its walls stained different shades of green and the small temporary shelters of the birds'-nest collectors dwarfed by the cave's size. From within the immense, draughty darkness, and if you're there during nest-collecting season, you'll hear the voices of the bird's-nest collectors who gather swiftlet nests, and you'll see their tiny lights near the cave ceiling; their thin beanstalk poles snake up from the cave floor like ultra-fragile scaffolding. Once inside, the walkway continues via **Burnt Cave** and then **Moon Cave** for 600m or so in the pitch black before exiting into the jungle again to follow a pathway up to the **Painted Cave**, thirty minutes' walk away. Here, early Sarawak communities buried their dead in boat-shaped coffins, known as "death ships" and arranged around the cave walls; dating of the contents (which have been relocated to the Sarawak Museum) has proved that the caves have been used as a cemetery for tens of thousands of years. The red hematite figures of the wall paintings are fenced off for preservation.

The trails

There are two other colour-coded **trails** in the park. Jalan Madu splits off the main walkway around 800m from the park headquarters and cuts first east then south across a peat swamp forest, where you can see wild orchids, mushrooms and pandanus palms. The trail crosses Sungai Subis and then follows its south bank to its confluence with Sungai Niah, from where you'll have to hail a passing boat to cross over to Batu Niah.

The more spectacular trail to Bukit Kasut starts at the confluence of these two rivers. After crossing the Niah River, the clearly marked trail winds through freshwater swamp forest, round the foothills of Bukit Kasut and up to the summit – a hard one-hour slog, at the end of which there's a view both of the forest canopy and Batu Niah.

ARRIVAL AND DEPARTURE

By bus In Miri take a taxi to the Pujut Bus Terminal, and then any express bus heading towards Bintulu, Sibu or Sarikei. Ask to get off at Niah Junction (2hr; RM15), where taxis wait to take you to park headquarters (30min; RM30), 15km away. From Bintulu bus station there are several buses to

Batu Niah (3hr; RM15). The park office is 3km from Batu Niah, either a taxi ride from the bus station (RM30), or a 30min stroll. The easiest way to reach the caves from Miri is by transfer (RM80) from the *Dillenia Guesthouse* (see p.494).

By taxi Taxis from Miri (1hr 20min) cost around RM150 one-way. A taxi from Bintulu (1hr 40min) costs around RM160.

INFORMATION

Park Headquarters Niah National Park HQ (☎085 737454) is the place to register on arrival. The trails are well signposted.

ACCOMMODATION AND EATING

The park can be visited as a day-trip, but stay overnight if you want to see the "changing of the guard" – swiftlets returning to the cave at sunset and bats flying out (notify park HQ first). Accommodation at the park HQ (☎085 434184) should be booked online in advance through the Sarawak Government Ebooking portal (🌐ebooking .sarawak.gov.my).

Camping There is a campsite with enough pitches for thirty tents. Per person RM5

Canteen There's a café at the park which serves rice and noodle dishes. Mains from RM8. Mon–Sat 9am–6pm.

Forrest Hostel Four simple rooms, each with four beds and attached bathrooms. Bedding provided. Per person RM10

Forrest Lodge Seven chalets, some with fan, some with a/c, consisting of two en-suite rooms with two single beds/room. Bedding provided. Four people from RM100

MIRI

MIRI is a booming oil town with a significant expat community and a strong Chinese character. For tourists, it's the main departure point for independent and organized trips into Gunung Mulu National Park (see p.495), and more local national parks, such as the Niah and

THE PERILOUS LIVES OF BIRDS'-NEST COLLECTORS

The long *belian* (ironwood) wooden poles hanging down from the vast 60m ceiling of the Great Cave are part of the scaffolding used by birds'-nest collectors – men who risk their lives during the short harvesting periods to shimmy up these poles, armed with bamboo sticks with an attached *penyulok* (scraper) to prize **swiftlets' nests** from the ceiling. Men fall to their deaths every year, as no safety equipment is used. Their prize is a delicacy highly valued by the Chinese who consider birds'-nest soup to be an aphrodisiac, and it is the most expensive foodstuff on earth. The male swiftlets make their nests by regurgitating long threads of glutinous saliva that hardens when attached to the cave wall. The nests of the white-nest swiftlets are the most highly prized of all, fetching up to US$2000/kg; black-nest swiftlets' nests are collected as well but require removing dirt and feathers. When cooked, the nests have a gelatinous texture but little taste, making you wonder what all the fuss is about.

6

Lambir Hills National Park, and the route northeast to Brunei and Sabah.

WHAT TO SEE AND DO

Miri's old town around Jalan China to the west has a cluster of cafés, shops and a few cheap hotels. The fish market occupies the top of Jalan China, along with the Tua Pek Kong Chinese Temple, dedicated to a deity well loved by overseas Chinese. **Jalan Brooke** is the main artery through town, with a couple of markets selling fresh fruit and veg, pigs' heads and more. The wide road running east from here and parallel to the river, **Jalan Bendahara**, is the simplest route into the new town area. Directly south of the local bus station is the Padang, on whose border lies **Tamu Muhibbah** (daily 6am–4pm), the town's produce market. There's a better market on Lutong Rd, 3km from the centre (Thurs–Sat 5–10pm), where the Orang Ulu come to sell crafts and jungle produce. Take bus #1, #62, #66 or #68.

For a great **view** of Miri, you can take a taxi up **Canada Hill**. At the top you'll find a lively bar with an outdoor terrace, the well-designed **Petroleum Museum** (daily 9am–5pm; free), detailing the history of oil in Malaysia, and the **Grand Old Lady** – the remnants of the 1910 Shell oil well – the first in the region.

ARRIVAL AND DEPARTURE

By plane The airport (⊕miriairport.com) is 8km west of the town centre; there is no direct bus service, but *Dillenia Guesthouse* can arrange a taxi for RM20. Between them, Malaysia Airlines, Malindo Air and AirAsia cover major destinations such as KL, KK, Kuching and Sibu, while MASwings serves smaller destinations such as Mulu (for Gunung Mulu National Park) and Bario, the latter with 19-person Twin Otters (10km luggage maximum); flights to Bario are weather-dependent.
Destinations Bario (daily; 40min); Bintulu (2 daily; 35min); Mulu (2 daily; 30min); Kota Kinabalu (4 daily; 50min); Kuala Lumpur (10 daily; 2hr 15min); Kuching (5 daily; 1hr); Sibu (3 daily; 1hr); Singapore (4 weekly; 2hr 5min).
By bus Long-distance buses depart from the Pujut Bus Terminal, 4km northeast of the city centre; take bus #33A from the local bus station (10min; RM2.60) or a taxi (RM15). Pujut Bus operates services to Bintulu (RM27), Sibu (RM22) and Kuching (RM90), while Bintang Jaya Express (⊕085 432178) and Borneo Express (⊕085 430420) have services to Kota Kinabalu, Sabah (RM90),

and PHLS bus (⊕085 407175) serves Bandar Seri Begawan, Brunei (RM40).
Destinations Bandar Seri Begawan (2 daily at 8.15am & 3.45pm; 4hr 30min); Bintulu (10 daily; 4hr 30min); Kota Kinabalu (daily at 7.45am except Wed & 8.30am; 12hr); Kuching (8 daily; 14hr); Sibu (13 daily; 8hr).

INFORMATION AND TOURS

Tourist information The ultra-helpful visitor information centre (Lot 452, Jln Melayu; Mon–Fri 9am–5pm, Sat & Sun 10am–3pm; ⊕085 434181) is next to the local bus station. Besides reams of information on Miri and the region, there are up-to-date long-distance bus timetables.
Tours Borneo Jungle Safari, 1st Floor, Centrepoint Commercial Centre, Jln Kubu (⊕085 422595), runs caving and climbing trips, as well as excursions to the Kelabit Highlands.

ACCOMMODATION

★**Dillenia Guesthouse** 1st floor, 846 Jln Sida ⊕085 434204, ⊕dillenia.guesthoouse@gmail.com. Cheerful lime-green a/c rooms presided over by the helpful and friendly Mrs Lee, who is brilliant at anticipating her guests' wishes and has detailed information on all regional attractions. Breakfast includes fresh fruit. Airport pick-up and transfers to Bandar Seri Begawan, Brunei, and Niah National Park can be arranged. Dorms RM30, doubles RM80
My Homestay 2nd floor, Lot 1091, Jln Merpati ⊕085 429091, ⊕staymyhomestay.blogspot.com. The perk at this central hostel is a cosy green and yellow balcony overlooking Miri's most happening strip. Dorms and rooms are clean and functional, but small and windowless. There's breakfast included and a self-catering kitchen for guests. Dorms RM35, doubles RM55
Next Room 1st & 2nd floor, Lot 637 Jln North Yu Seng ⊕085 411422, ⊕nextroomhomestay@gmail.com. This hostel, smack-bang in the centre of town, earns points for its cosy rooftop terrace and classy ambience. Rooms are spacious and modern, and dorms, although quite packed, are good value. Dorms RM32, doubles RM60

EATING

Apollo Seafood Centre 4 Jln South Yu Seng. Local institution specializing in very fresh seafood (just pick your meal from a tank); the crab and prawn dishes stand out (mains from RM16). Accompaniments include *midin belacan*, a delicious, crunchy jungle fern cooked with shrimp paste. Daily noon–10pm.
Bilal Islamic Restaurant Taman Jade Manis, behind the *Mega Hotel*. Informal Indian joint with plastic chairs, some of the best curry in town and a great selection of vegetarian dishes – the okra ones are particularly good. Dishes RM6–17. Daily 10am–10pm.

★**Ming Café** Jln North Yu Seng ☎ 085 422797. This corner establishment is popular both with locals and travellers thanks to a catch-all mix of Malay and Indian food as well as Chinese and Western dishes and barbecued seafood (from RM20), washed down with cold beer or fresh juices. Doubles as a sports bar. Mon & Tues 12.30pm–late, Wed–Sun 10.30am–late.

Summit Café Centre Point Commercial Centre, Jln Melayu. Canteen-style café serving delicious dishes from the Kelabit Highlands, such as jungle fern and shredded fish (mains from RM5). No English spoken, so just point to whatever looks good on display. It's a couple of minutes' walk southwest from the visitor information centre. Mon–Sat 6am–2pm; get here early.

SHOPPING

Miri Handicraft Centre Jln Brooke at Jln Merbau. Indoor craft centre consisting of numerous stalls selling a mix of touristy tat and genuine indigenous craft; the beadwork from the Kelabit Highlands and woven rattan items are particularly good.

DIRECTORY

Banks Maybank, Jln Bendahara; ATMs at the airport. There are also moneychangers and ATMs along Jln China and Jln Melayu.

Hospital Columbia Asia Hospital, Jln Bulan Sabit (☎ 085 437755, ⊛ columbiaasia.com/miri), 4km northeast of *Mega Hotel*, is a private hospital with a 24hr emergency ward favoured by expats.

Immigration (Jabatan Imigresen) 2nd floor, Yu Lan Plaza, Jln Brooke (Mon–Thurs 8am–5pm, Fri 8–11.45am & 2.15–5pm; ☎ 085 442117, ⊛ imi.gov.my); opposite the police station. Does visa extensions.

Post office Jln Post (Mon–Sat 8am–4.30pm).

GUNUNG MULU NATIONAL PARK

GUNUNG MULU NATIONAL PARK is Sarawak's premier natural attraction and home to the second-largest cave on earth. At the last count, Gunung Mulu featured more than three hundred animal species and nearly three thousand plant species, adding incredible natural diversity to the stunning landscape. The park comprises primary rainforest, and is characterized by clear rivers and high-altitude vegetation, supremely accessible caves and three dramatic mountains, including Gunung Mulu itself and 50m-high, razor-sharp limestone spikes known as the **Pinnacles**, which offer some of the most challenging hiking in all of Borneo.

WHAT TO SEE AND DO

It is quite possible to see the four main caves in a day, but if you're considering caving, or one of the treks as well, you'll need to allow three or four days extra. The park is covered in rich primary rainforest and offers a whole range of excellent multi-day **jungle treks** and **mountain hikes**, including the challenging Pinnacles Trail. There are also short, gentle walks along well-marked trails.

The show caves

Only four of the 25 caves so far explored in Mulu are open to casual visitors; they're known as "show caves" and can get quite crowded. Guides are compulsory and tours run in the mornings to Wind and Clearwater caves (65RM), and in the afternoons to Deer and Lang caves (30RM).

Deer Cave

From the headquarters, a well-marked 3km plankway runs to the impressive **Deer Cave**, whose 2km-long and 174m-high cave passage was the largest in the world until the discovery of the Son Doong Cave in Vietnam in May 2009. One of the cave's limestone formations, silhouetted by a cave opening, resembles the profile of Abraham Lincoln. The cave itself takes its name from the deer that used to venture inside to drink from the stream, salty with guano. Inside, it's a vast natural cathedral with streams of water falling from on high; the ground between the boardwalks is covered with enormous mounds of strong-smelling, brown bat guano – nourishment for the cockroaches that live in it. A good guide will point out the paw prints of civets who scour the guano mounds for dead or injured bats and will shine a torchlight into the milky stream to expose blind catfish that have evolved to function in complete darkness. The cave is home to an astonishing twelve species of bat; it is estimated that they consume up to thirty tonnes of insects nightly, which is why there are hardly any mosquitoes in the park. Visits are timed to finish by late afternoon so that you can relax at the outdoor "Bat Observatory" just outside the cave and watch the "changing of the guard": myriads

6

Mentakung & Limbang

GUNUNG MULU
NATIONAL PARK

of swiftlets flying in for the night and three million bats streaming out in long serpentine ribbons across the sky at sunset.

Clearwater Cave and Wind Cave

Probing some 107km through Mulu's substratum, **Clearwater Cave**, thought to be the longest in Southeast Asia, is reached by a fifteen-minute longboat journey (RM65 round trip) along Sungai Melinau from park headquarters.

First, you visit the **Wind Cave**, its several chambers revealing otherworldly sculptures, some resembling a cross between a giant jellyfish and a cauliflower. The **Clearwater Cave** is the grander of the two, reachable by flights of steep steps and bisected by the subterranean river that gives the cave its name. Besides the impressive limestone formations, you may also spot some harmless racer snakes.

Adventure caves

The park is one of the best places in the world for adventure caving, with options ranging from beginner to advanced. If you have no prior spelunking experience, you must start with beginners' circuits like the **Racer Cave** first (RM180; 2hr 30min–3hr 30min), where you'll spot some non-venomous racer snakes that feed on the cave bats. Only after proving their worth, advanced cave-crawlers may wish to try **Clearwater Connection** (RM200; 6–8hr), which involves climbing and a 1.5km river section (you must be able to swim), or the challenging **Sarawak Chamber circuit** (RM280; at least 10hr), a steep traverse which offers a chance to explore the darkness of the world's largest enclosed cave. Both tours require an overnight stop at *Camp 1*.

Short walks from park headquarters

There are plenty of short walks in the park, from the guided walk on the 480m-long **Canopy Skywalk** (RM43) and a full day trek to the **Garden of Eden** (RM140/person for a minimum of three people, including visits to Deer and Lang caves), just beyond the Deer Cave, to the self-guided walk that ends at **Paku Waterfall** (around 4hr return) and the Botanical Trail loop.

The Pinnacles

The first part of the demanding **Pinnacles** trek from park headquarters is by longboat along Sungai Melinau to Kuala Birar (RM406/person including boat transfer, two nights' accommodation and guide fee). From here, it's an easy 9km walk to *Camp 5*, which nestles under Gunung Api (1750m) and Gunung Benarat (1580m). Most climbers spend two nights at *Camp 5*, where there's a large hostel (RM560); bring a sleeping bag.

The ascent up the south face of Gunung Api is only 2.4km, but the climb is unrelentingly steep and the vertical final section requires an actual climb involving ladders and ropes. Climbers make it to the top in two to five hours and the descent also takes up to five hours. If you fail to reach the mini-Pinnacles within one hour, you are not fit enough and will be sent back to *Camp 5*. Bring at least two litres of water, lunch, footwear with good traction and sturdy biking gloves, as you'll be using your hands to scramble up the sharp rock.

Headhunters' Trail

It's possible to hike from *Camp 5* to Limbang along the so-called **Headhunter's Trail**, a route once traced by Kayan war parties. Cross the bridge, turn left and walk along a wide trail passing a large rock (around 4km). From here, a clearly marked flat trail to **Kuala Terikan**, a small Berawan settlement on the banks of Sungai Terikan, takes four hours (11km). To get from Kuala Terikan to Medamit or Lubang Cina, you'll need to organize a guide or boatman in advance via Limbang-based Borneo Touch Ecotour (RM500 for a boat and van in either direction for up to five people; ⓦwalk2mulu.com). Boats run frequently from Limbang to Bandar Seri Begawan, Brunei (hourly until 4.30pm).

Gunung Mulu

The route to the summit of **Gunung Mulu** (2376m) is a straightforward, though very steep and relentless, climb that takes four days and three nights. Park regulations require that you hire a guide (RM506/person). You will have to bring all cooking provisions and sleeping gear. The first stage is from park headquarters to *Camp 1*, an easy three-hour walk on a flat trail. The first night is at the open hut at *Camp 1*, which has cooking facilities. Day two comprises a hard, ten-hour uphill slog, some of it along the southwest ridge, a series of small hills negotiated by a narrow, twisting path. The hut at *Camp 4* is at 1800m; it can be cool here, so bring a sleeping bag. Most climbers set off well before dawn for the hard ninety-minute trek to the summit, to arrive at sunrise.

TREKKING IN THE PARK

If you're trekking independently or travelling on your own, it makes sense to get a group of at least four together to spread the high cost of boat and guide fees in the park; you can post up a note on the board at headquarters. Upon arriving, you need to **register** (if it's after 5.30pm, register for the following day) and pay the RM30 **park fee**, valid for five days. Arranging one of the longer treks with the park office itself (in advance) is considerably cheaper than coming as part of a tour group from KL, Kuching or Miri, though out of peak season you may have trouble making up the numbers (minimum of three people required).

Take plenty of water, decent walking shoes, a sun hat and swimming gear, a poncho or rain sheet, a torch, mosquito repellent, ointment for bites and a basic first-aid kit. Mats and sleeping bags (should you want one) can usually be rented from the park headquarters. Wear shorts and T-shirts on the trails (it'll be easier to spot leeches), and bring long trousers and long-sleeved shirts for the insect assault at dusk.

6

Near the top you have to haul yourself up by ropes onto the cold, windswept, craggy peak. From here, the view, looking down on Gunung Api, is exhilarating.

ARRIVAL AND DEPARTURE

By plane The tiny airport is 2km west of park headquarters; taxis (RM5) meet the planes to take you to the headquarters or accommodation.
Destinations Flights to Miri with MASWings (🖰 maswings.com.my) leave the park twice daily (30min), to Kuching daily (1hr 40min) and to Kota Kinabalu daily (1hr 30min).

INFORMATION

Park Headquarters The Park Headquarters office (daily 8am–5pm; 🕾 085 792300, 🖰 mulupark.com) is the place to sign up for walks, and there are colourful, detailed displays on the park's history, flora and fauna.

ACCOMMODATION

There are several types of accommodation: a dorm and bungalows belonging to the park, and basic guesthouses strewn along the road from the airport and just outside the park entrance. Reserve accommodation inside the park in advance as it fills up fast; prices include a decent breakfast. *Camp 5* is only for hikers doing the Pinnacles (RM160 including boat ride).

PARK ACCOMMODATION

Garden Bungalows The swishest option in the park, with room for up to three people; spacious, attractive a/c rooms and shaded porches. RM230
Hostel There's a large twenty-bed dorm in the hostel with ceiling fans, shared bathrooms, and lockers at extra cost. Dorms RM55
Longhouse Rooms Ten rooms that can sleep up to four people, with ceiling fans and attached bathrooms. From RM250

OUTSIDE THE PARK

D'Cave Homestay 🕾 012 872 9752. The last guesthouse before the turn-off for the park, this homestay gets rave reviews thanks to the warmth and hospitality of its owners, Robert and Dina, and the excellent home-cooked meals. Breakfast is included. Dorms RM40, doubles RM40
Mulu River Lodge 🕾 012 852 7471. Family-run accommodation consisting of a thirty-bed, fan-cooled dorm right outside the park entrance. Electricity 5.30–11.30pm, and breakfast is included. Dorms RM35

EATING

Café Mulu The on-site park café serves a good mixture of Malay and international food; mains from RM10. Daily 7.30am–9pm.

Good Luck Cave'fe Right next to the park's entrance, the cheapest restaurant around (mains RM10) dishes up filling, hearty rice-based meals and is a good spot to have a beer with the local guides. Daily 11.30am–3pm and 5–9.30pm.

KELABIT HIGHLANDS

Sitting between the Indonesian border and the Gunung Mulu National Park, the **KELABIT HIGHLANDS** are inhabited by the Kelabits, and the main attraction of this still-remote part of Sarawak is hiking from longhouse to longhouse along mountain trails and enjoying Kelabit hospitality as part of homestays. There are no banks here, so bring plenty of cash in small denominations.

Bario

Bario is the main settlement, consisting of around a dozen small villages spread out all over the valley. You can visit the **Bario Asal longhouse**, a traditional dwelling where a few of its older residents have earlobes distended down to their shoulders from wearing heavy brass earrings. Not far from the longhouse is a **monument** dedicated to British Major Tom Harrisson who did a parachute drop here behind the Japanese enemy lines in 1945 and lived in Bario after the war. It's also possible to hike up nearby **Prayer Mountain** (2hr each way) for wonderful views of the valley. Jungle treks can be arranged through your accommodation. At the end of July, the three-day food and cultural festival **Pesta Nukenen**

PICNIC WITH THE PENAN

If even the Kelabit Highlands are not remote enough for you, you have the option of staying with the last of Borneo's nomadic **Penan** who live near the Indonesian border and can be reached from the Kelabit Highlands by jungle trek and boat. The website 🖰 picnicwiththepenan.wordpress.com caters to those interested in learning about traditional Penan culture, with jungle treks, camping and survival training thrown in. It helps if you speak some Malay to get the most out of the experience.

offers great insights into Kelabit's cuisine and rituals.

ARRIVAL AND DEPARTURE

By plane The tiny airport is linked to Miri and Ba'kelalan/ Marudi by twice-daily MASwings Twin Otter flights (which are very weather-dependent). The nineteen-person planes have a checked luggage allowance of 10kg, and 5kg carry-on. Passengers are weighed before departure.

ACCOMMODATION AND EATING

Guesthouses and longhouses offer room and board. You can find free wi-fi at the Dewan Serbaguna Bario, a wooden community hall next to the row of shops, a 15min walk from the airport.

Bario Asal Lembaa Longhouse ☎ 019 8259505 or ☎ 019 8549798, ✉ jenetteulun@yahoo.com. At Bario's charming first longhouse, founded in 1958, families rent out rooms and provide meals to guests. An excellent immersion in Kelabit culture. Transport from the airport can be arranged. Per person RM80

Junglebluesdream ☎ 019 8849892, 🌐 junglebluesdream .weebly.com. Combined lodge and art gallery run by local artist Stephen and his Danish wife, Tine, with excellent home-cooked food and four individually decorated rooms. Trekking maps available and kayaking excursions possible. Airport pickup included. Per person RM90

★ **Ngimat Ayu Home Stay** ☎ 013 8406187 (Scott). Run by the son and widow of Bario's last headman and first graduated Kelabit doctor, this gracious wooden home has a huge verandah to soak the views, great home-cooked Kelabit food, and cosy wooden rooms. Per person RM115

Sabah

Bordering Sarawak on the northeastern flank of Borneo, **SABAH**'s beauty lies in its wealth of natural resources and abundant wildlife. You can watch turtles hatch on **Libaran Turtle Island**, see orang-utans at the **Sepilok Orang-utan Rehabilitation Centre**, observe the antics of sun bears at the **Bornean Sun Bear Conservation Centre** and marvel at forest-dwelling proboscis monkeys, macaques and wild orang-utans along the lower reaches of the **Kinabatangan River**. The diving is incredible: **Pulau Sipadan** is rated one of the world's top dive destinations. Sabah's other major attraction is climbing the granite shelves of 4095m-high **Mount Kinabalu**: it's

certainly challenging, but the rewards are spectacular.

As well as its natural beauty, Sabah also has a diverse ethnic heritage. Until European powers gained a foothold here in the nineteenth century, the northern tip of this remote land mass was inhabited by **tribal groups** who had only minimal contact with the outside world. The peoples of the Kadazan and Dusun tribes constitute the largest indigenous racial group, along with the Murut of the southwest and Sabah's so-called "sea gypsies", the Bajau. Recently economic migrants from the Philippines and neighbouring Kalimantan have added to the state's rich ethnic mix.

Travel is more expensive in Sabah than in Peninsular Malaysia and Sarawak. While there are plenty of tour operators, independent travel is completely achievable and a breeze compared to other parts of Borneo.

KOTA KINABALU

Settled on the South China Sea, **KOTA KINABALU** is the thoroughly modern capital of Sabah and the main entry point to the region. Stretching along the waterfront and sporting several large shopping malls, KK offers a range of budget accommodation and plenty of restaurants and bars. Lacking in architectural charm, it's nevertheless pleasant enough to amble around on foot, exploring the various markets, trying local delicacies and soaking up the waterfront atmosphere. KK is also the gateway to the ultra-popular **Kinabalu National Park**, and there's good snorkelling and diving off the **Tunku Abdul Rahman Islands**, a short hop by speedboat from KK's jetty.

WHAT TO SEE AND DO

Downtown KK was almost obliterated by World War II bombs, and only in the northeastern corner of the city centre – an area known as KK Lama, or old KK – are there even the faintest remains of its colonial past, with three notable old buildings: the old **General Post Office**, **Atkinson's Clock Tower** and the **Lands and Surveys building**, now home to the Sabah

6

SABAH

Tourism Board. Jalan Gaya is the most attractive of the central streets, lined with colourful and popular Chinese *kedai kopis*.

The markets

On Sundays, the length of Jalan Gaya comes alive with the **Gaya street market** (6am–2pm) – a great place to buy anything from souvenirs to jungle produce. Along the waterfront you'll find three markets. The **Filipino market** (daily 10am–6pm) on Jalan Tun Fuad Stephens is the best place to buy Sabahan ethnic wares, such as textiles, cultured pearls, bamboo goods and more, as well as Filipino baskets, kampong-wood salad bowls and bags (don't forget to bargain). Next door is the dark and labyrinthine **general market**, selling fresh fruit and vegetables, and behind that is the manic waterfront **fish market**. At the northern end of the central market is the **night market** (daily 5–11pm) – with cheap seafood and many attractive food stalls (see p.504).

Sabah State Museum and Heritage Garden

The **Sabah State Museum** on Jalan Muzium (Mon–Thurs, Sat & Sun 9am–5pm; RM15; ⓦmuseum.sabah.gov .my) is twenty minutes' walk west of the town centre along Jalan Tunku Abdul Rahman. In the main building, its highlight is the **ethnographic collection**, which includes human skulls from Sabah's head-hunting days, Penan blowpipes, traditional costume and musical instruments, carved totem poles and photos of Murut hunters. The **natural history** section showcases a fairly complete collection of stuffed, pickled or pinned examples of Borneo wildlife, but the **Art Museum** is rather hit and miss. Outside, the **Heritage Village** features authentic replicas of Murut- and Rungus-style longhouses and a Chinese farmhouse.

From the museum, a signposted path leads to the rather bland **Museum of Islamic Civilization**, though there are some beautiful ornate swords and Quran pages.

Mari Mari Cultural Village

Even if you've already visited the Sarawak Cultural Village (see p.487), it's still more than worth your while to pay a visit to the **Mari Mari Cultural Village** (ⓦmarimariculturalvillage.com), its counterpart in Sabah, which showcases the traditional dwellings and crafts of Sabah's ethnic groups. It's a very interactive experience; the three-hour tour involves your group being led around by a traditionally attired guide who takes you through the jungle between the Dusun, Lundai, Kajan and other houses, stopping at each one. At each stop, there's an activity for you to try – from cooking in a bamboo tube (you'll get to sample your own efforts after the tour) to blowpipe shooting, *tuak-* (rice wine) making and tasting, fire starting, and jumping on a bamboo trampoline – followed by a spirited traditional dance show and delicious meal. There are three scheduled visits per day, and the price (RM170) includes transport there and back; you can organize the tour directly through Mari Mari, most hostels and the tourist office.

Around 400m beyond the Cultural Village is the **Kiansom Waterfall**, with an appealing swimming hole.

KK Heritage Walk

Those interested in the historical and cultural side of the city should take the informative and highly entertaining **KK Heritage Walk** (Tues & Thurs 9–11.30am; RM120; ⓦkkheritagewalk.com/ heritagewalk.htm), which can be booked through several tour operators and consists of a walking tour that includes visits to the North Borneo War Memorial, the Atkinson Clock Tower, Chinese herbal shops and *kopitiam* (coffee shops), and culminates in a treasure hunt at the *Jesselton Hotel*.

ARRIVAL AND DEPARTURE

By plane KK's airport, served by numerous national and international flights, is 6.5km southwest of the centre in Tanjung Aru. The convenient airport bus (every 45min from 7.30am; 20min; 5RM) shuttles between the arrival hall and the Merdeka Field close to Jln Gaya. The last departure from the city is at 7.15pm, from the airport at 8.30pm. Bus #18C (RM2) also stops opposite the airport and leaves from *Promenade Hotel* at the Api-Api Centre. Taxis from the airport cost RM35; buy a voucher at the pre-paid taxi counter. KK has good connections within Sabah and Sarawak, as well as

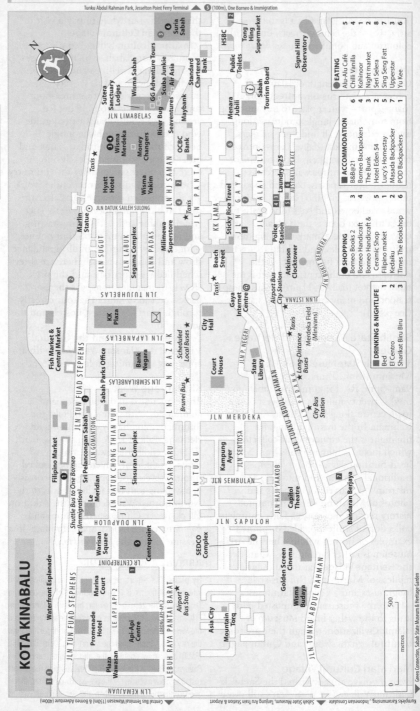

KOTA KINABALU

Tunku Abdul Rahman Park, Jesselton Point Ferry Terminal (100m), One Borneo & Immigration

Central Bus Terminal Wawasan (150m) & Borneo Adventure (400m)

Kampung Karamunsing, Indonesian Consulate

Sabah State Museum, Tanjung Aru Train Station & Airport

Green Connection, Sabah State Museum & Heritage Garden

● SHOPPING
Borneo Books 2	3
Borneo Handicraft	4
Borneo Handicraft & Ceramic Shop	5
Filipino market	1
Kedaiku	2
Times The Bookshop	3

■ ACCOMMODATION
B&B@21	3
Borneo Backpackers	4
The Bunk	1
Hotel Eden 54	2
Lucy's Homestay	5
Masada Backpacker	7
POD Backpackers	6

■ EATING
Alu-Alu Café	5
Chilli Vanilla	4
Kohinoor	1
Night market	2
Seri Selera	8
Sing Seng Fatt	7
Upperstar	3
Yu Kee	6

■ DRINKING & NIGHTLIFE
Bed	1
El Centro	2
Sharikat Biru Biru	3

Waterfront Esplanade
Fish Market & Central Market
Filipino Market
Sabah Parks Office
Plaza Wawasan
Promenade Hotel
Marina Court
Api-Api Centre
Le Meridien
Sri Pelancongan Sabah
Sinsuran Complex
Bank Negara
Warisan Square
Centrepoint
KK Plaza
City Hall
Court House
State Library
Kampung Ayer
Capitol Theatre
SEDCO Complex
Golden Screen Cinema
Wisma Budaya
Asia City
Mountain Torq
City Bus Station
Bandaran Berjaya
Police Station
Atkinson Clocktower
Merdeka Field (Minivans)
Gaya Internet Centre @
Airport Bus City Station
Long-Distance Buses
Scheduled Local Buses
Brunei Bus
Sticky Rice Travel
KK LAMA
Beach Street
Millimewa Superstore
Hyatt Hotel
Wisma Yakim
Wisma Merdeka
Money Changers
Martin Statue
Sutera Sanctuary Lodges
Seaventures
River Bug
Scuba Junkie
GG Adventure Tours
Wisma Sabah
Air Asia
Maybank
OCBC Bank
Standard Chartered Bank
Menara Jubili
Sabah Tourism Board
HSBC
Tong Hing Supermarket
Signal Hill Observatory
Public Toilets
Laundry@25
Australia Place
Segama Complex

JLN LIMABELAS
JLN DATUK SAILEH SULONG
JLN HJ SAMAN
JLN PANTAI
JLN GAYA
JLN BALAI POLIS
JLN SUGUT
JLN LABUK
JLN PADAS
JLN TRUHBELAS
JLN LAPANBELAS
JLN TUN RAZAK
JLN SEMBILANBELAS
JLN TUN FUAD STEPHENS
JLN TUN FUAD STEPHENS
JLN DATUK CHONG THIAN VUN
JLN GOMANTONG
JLN PASAR BARU
JLN TUGU
JLN SEMBULAN
JLN SENTOSA
JLN MERDEKA
JLN P NEGERI
JLN ISTANA
JLN TUNKU ABDUL RAHMAN
JLN PADANG
JLN HAJI YAAKOB
JLN SAPULOH
LEBUH RAYA PANTAI BARAT
LORONG API-API 2
LE API API 2
LORONG API-API
JLN BUKIT BENDERA
JLN KEMAJUAN
LR CENTREPOINT

Taxis

0 500 metres

Shuttle Bus to One Borneo (Immigration)

regular flights to Brunei, Peninsular Malaysia, Indonesia, the Philippines, Thailand, China and Australia.

Destinations Bandar Seri Begawan (3 daily; 40min); Bintulu (5 weekly; 1hr 15min); Johor Bahru (2hr 15min); Kota Bharu (daily; 2hr 40min); Kuala Lumpur (hourly; 2hr 30min); Kuching (4 daily; 1hr 25min); Manila (daily; 2hr); Miri (5 daily; 1hr); Penang (2 daily; 2hr 45min); Sandakan (8 daily; 50min); Singapore (2hr 15min); Tawau (6 daily; 1hr).

By bus Most long-distance buses operate from the bus terminal at Inanam, 9km north of the centre, reachable by local buses from Wawasan central bus station (RM2; 30min) or by taxi (RM25). Buses to Brunei leave from across the street from the courthouse on Jln Pantai. Minivans to take you to Mount Kinabalu National Park congregate around the Merdeka Field area, just off Jln Tunku Abdul Rahman. Generally, buses leave when full; turn up by 7am to ensure a seat. Buses and shared taxis for Kudat, Keningau, Tawau and Kota Belud leave from the Padang Merdeka bus terminal on Jln Padang.

Destinations Bandar Seri Begawan, Brunei (daily; 9hr); Kinabalu National Park (8 daily; 2hr 30min); Kudat (3 daily; 3hr 30min–4hr); Sandakan (15 daily; 6hr); Semporna (4 daily; 9hr); Tawau (3 daily; 9hr).

INFORMATION

The Sabah Tourism Board (Mon–Fri 8am–5pm, Sat & Sun 9am–4pm; ☎ 088 212121, ⓦ sabahtourism.com) is at 51 Jln Gaya and has a range of information on the top tourist destinations in Sabah. Staff are very helpful and provide you with a good map of KK.

TOURS

Borneo Adventure Block E-27-3A, Signature Office, KK Times Square ☎ 088 486800, ⓦ borneoadventure.com. Award-winning operator that organizes anything from multi-day wildlife safaris and trips to Mt Kinabalu to longhouse visits on the northern tip of Sabah. Three-day/two-night Mt Kinabalu tour RM1868.

GG Adventure Tours Lot F-105b, 1st floor, Wisma Sabah ☎ 088 316385, ⓦ gogosabah.com. Very helpful operator that can create pretty much any itinerary you want, as well as organizing offbeat dirt-bike tours and renting motorbikes. Scooter rental RM45/day.

Scuba Junkie Lot G23, ground floor, Wisma Sabah ☎ 088 255816, ⓦ scubajunkiekk.com. A reputable and affordable diving operator offering underwater adventure in the Tunku Abdul Rahman Marine Park (from RM270). Open Water course RM975.

Sticky Rice Travel 4th floor, 134 Jln Gaya ☎ 088 250558, ⓦ stickyricetravel.com. Run by a young and international team and preferred by National Geographic Adventures, they can help you tailor-make any Sabah adventure, including off-the-beaten-track trips with very experienced local guides.

ACCOMMODATION

B&B@21 Lot 21 Lorong Dewan, Australia Place ☎ 088 210632, ⓦ facebook.com/bookingbb21. This new hostel has an attractive backyard garden, where you can relax amid lush greenery. Dorms, rooms and shared toilets are modern and squeaky clean, and the free lockers and two indoor and outdoor self-catering kitchens make it an ideal budget choice. Dorms RM40, doubles RM93

Borneo Backpackers 24 Lorong Dewan, Australia Place ☎ 088 234009, ⓦ borneobackpackers.com; KK's prime backpacker spot has a guest lounge perfect for socializing, friendly staff on hand for booking travel, clean rooms, free breakfast and a great café downstairs. Unfortunately, dorms can get very noisy as they face a heavily trafficked road. Dorms RM30, doubles RM80

★**The Bunk** 113 Jln Gaya ☎ 088 204526, ⓦ thebunk borneo.blogspot.com. Upstairs, two labirynthine storeys of triple bunk-beds equipped with privacy curtains make this dorm-only hostel a great place to socialize. Bring the conversations downstairs, where their dimly lit green-tinted café and secondhand book exchange attracts more people from busy Jln Gaya. Dorms RM30

Lucy's Homestay 25 Lorong Dewan, Australia Place ☎ 088 261495. Like the home of a favourite auntie, hospitable Lucy's place, complete with her cherished cats, has been a traveller favourite – particularly with solo female backpackers – for years. The rooms are simple and clean, there's a cosy library nook and Lucy goes out of her way to help you. Walk-ins preferred. Dorms RM25, doubles RM62

Masada Backpacker 9 Jln Masjid Lama, Pusat Bandar ☎ 088 238494, ⓦ facebook.com/masadabackpackers. Besides the massive cityscapes superimposed on its walls, maps and Mt Kinabalu photos galore, this hostel has good, bed-sized bunks with proper mattresses and other nice touches, such as all the coffee you can guzzle and free washing machine. Dorms RM35, doubles RM80

POD Backpackers 1-1-11, 1st floor, Api-Api Centre, Jln Centre Point ☎ 088 287113, ⓦ podsbackpacker.com. Like its sister hostel in Kuala Lumpur, this small six-room hostel's dominant colour is green. The dorms, with individual sockets and lockers, are a bit cramped but good value. There's free breakfast and 24hr flow of coffee and tea, but the a/c only works at night. Dorms RM35, doubles RM80

★**TREAT YOURSELF**

Hotel Eden54 54 Jln Gaya ☎ 088 266054, ⓦ eden54.com. At this stylish boutique hotel – an absolute bargain at the price – you can expect beds with crisp linen, great showers, urban-chic decor and satellite TV, though the cheapest rooms lack windows. The staff are extremely helpful, too. Doubles RM159

6

EATING

Self-caterers will find many Western foods that they've been missing at the pricey Tong Hing Supermarket on Jln Gaya. Cheaper supermarkets are off Jalan Pantai (Milimewa Superstore), at KK Plaza and Centre Point.

Alu-Alu Café Jesselton Point. Feast on marine dishes such as fish in creamy buttermilk sauce, made from ecologically sourced fish at this bright and breezy spot. Plenty of vegetable dishes here, including Sabah vegetables in oyster sauce. Mains from RM12. Daily 11am–2.30pm & 6.30–10pm.

★ **Chilli Vanilla** 35 Jln Haji Saman. This great little fusion spot serves veggie-friendly dishes – lentil soup, chunky Mediterranean sandwiches with grilled aubergine – as well as home-made chicken liver pâté, washed down with fresh fruit juice, organic coffees, shakes and smoothies. Mains from RM20. Mon–Sat 9am–10.30pm, Sun 5–10.30pm.

Kohinoor Waterfront Esplanade. Large portions of tandoori dishes and curries are on offer at KK's most central Indian restaurant. Plenty of dishes for vegetarians, including okra masala (mains from RM12). Daily 11am–2.30pm & 5.30–11pm.

★ **Night market** Jln Tun Fuad Stephens. Easily the best place for inexpensive seafood, this waterfront market kicks off after 5pm. Pick a stall, order fresh fish and seafood by weight, and specify how you want it prepared (mains from RM13). Accompaniments include rice and "Sabah vegetable" (jungle fern), and sellers from drinks stalls will come by to take your drinks orders. Daily 5–11pm.

Seri Selera SEDCO Complex, off Jln Sapuloh. A restaurant-lined square with outdoor tables; one of the best places in town for fish and seafood – barbecued and Chinese-style. Pick your fresh victims and get some "Sabah vegetable" (midin – jungle fern) on the side. Mains from RM14. Daily 5.30–10.30pm.

Sing Seng Fatt 74 Jln Gaya. Try this very local and gritty kedai kopi for some of the cheapest and tastiest Chinese and Malay food on Jln Gaya. Their rich combinations of nasi campur (from RM4), nasi lemak (from RM2) and noodles are great for filling stomachs on tight budgets. Daily 8am–3am.

Upperstar Ground floor, Suria Sabah shopping mall. When you've had enough of rice, the central outlet of this local franchise is a perfect diversion for the cheapest burgers, tacos, steaks and pastas in town (mains from RM7.90). Daily 4.30pm–2am.

Yu Kee 74 Jln Gaya. This unpretentious Chinese spot serves versatile pork in many delicious forms, from crisp pork belly and pork intestine – an acquired taste – to ribs and barbecue pork and rice (mains from RM7). Daily 10am–10pm.

DRINKING AND NIGHTLIFE

Bed Waterfront Esplanade. Go to Bed to see live Filipino bands lip-synching to the latest hits (from 9pm onwards) and DJs spinning their stuff in between sets. Raucous and best enjoyed in a group, though it's not the place for an intimate conversation. Daily 9pm–late.

★ **El Centro** 32 Jln Haji Saman. Buzzing with expats and travellers, this subtly lit, lively bar pulls in the punters with a mixture of strong drinks and fusion food – from big salads to hummus and tapas. Friday is open-mic night from 9pm, so if you want to sing or recite something, here's your chance. Wednesday is popular pub quiz night. Tues–Sun 5pm–midnight.

Sharikat Biru Biru 24 Lorong Derawan, Australia Place ☎ 011 266 98263, ⚲ facebook.com/birubirucafe. Right below Borneo Backpackers, this cosy café furnished with pan-Asian retro memorabilia – including a vintage bicycle and Vietnamese lanterns – is good for drinks, occasional live music and meeting travellers and KK's expats. The menu includes all-day breakfast (RM17), tacos and salted crêpes (from RM17), and a good list of beers and spirits. Daily 9am–midnight.

SHOPPING

BOOKS

Borneo Books 2 2nd floor, Wisma Merdeka ☎ 088 538689, ⚲ facebook.com/borneobooks. Secondhand bookshop with an excellent range of reference books on Sabah.

Times The Bookshop 2nd floor, Suria Sabah Mall, ☎ 088 487118, ⚲ timesbookstores.com.my. Sells an excellent selection of English books, novels and travel guides. Daily 10am–10pm.

HANDICRAFTS AND SOUVENIRS

Borneo Handicraft 1st floor, Wisma Merdeka ☎ 010 347 2999. Sells a good choice of woodwork, basketry and gongs.

Borneo Handicraft & Ceramic Shop Ground floor, Centrepoint. Stocks ceramics, antiques and primitive sculptures.

Filipino Market Jln Tun Fuad Stephen. A large waterfront market where, besides cheap food, you can bargain for cultured pearls and handicrafts from Borneo, the Philippines and elsewhere. Daily 8am–5pm.

Kedaiku Lot 5, Ground Floor, Block L, Sinsuran Complex. Sabah Tourism's Kedaiku has lots of souvenirs, including toy proboscis monkeys, postcards and many books on the region.

DIRECTORY

Banks and exchange Among the various moneychangers (Mon–Sat 10am–7pm) in Wisma Merdeka are Ban Loong Money Changer and Travellers' Money Changer, both on the ground floor. ATMs are easy to find throughout the centre of KK – HSBC, Jln Gaya; Maybank, Jln Pantai.

Embassies and consulates Australian Honorary Consul, Suite 10.1, Level 10, Wisma Great Eastern Life, 65 Jln Gaya (☎ 088 267151); British Honorary Consul (☎ 08 251755) – contact the High Commission in Kuala Lumpur (see p.436)

for emergency travel documents; Brunei, Lot 8–4, 8th Floor, Api-Api Centre (☎088 236113); Indonesia, Lorong Kemajuan, Karamunsing, Pcti Surat 11595 (☎088 218600).
Hospital KPJ Sabah Specialist Hospital, Lot 2, off Jln Damai, 6km southeast of the city centre (☎088 211333 or ☎088 322000, ⓦkpjsabah.com), offers decent private care.
Immigration office Kompleks Persekutuan Pentadbiran Kerajaan, Jln UMS, 9km south of the centre (Mon–Fri 7am–1pm & 2–5.30pm; ☎088 488700). Take bus #5A from Warisan Square and ask them to drop you off there.
Internet Gaya Internet Centre on Jln Tinku Abdul Rahman (daily 9am–10pm; RM3/hr).
Pharmacy Apex Pharmacy, 2 Jln Pantai, or UMH Pharmacy, 80 Jln Gaya.
Police Balai Polis KK (☎088 241161) is on Jln Dewan.
Post office The general post office (Mon–Sat 8am–4.30pm) is on Jln Tun Razak.

TUNKU ABDUL RAHMAN PARK

Situated within an 8km radius of downtown KK, the five islands of **TUNKU ABDUL RAHMAN PARK** (TAR Park) represent the most westerly ripples of the undulating Crocker mountain range. The largest of the park's islands is **Pulau Gaya**, where a 20km system of trails snakes across the lowland rainforest. Most of these trails start on the southern side of the island at Camp Bay. Wildlife on Gaya includes hornbills, wild pigs, lizards, snakes and macaques, which have been known to swim over to nearby **Pulau Sapi**, a 25-acre islet off the northwestern coast of Gaya that's linked by a sand bar at low tide. It can also be reached by riding the new zipline slung across the two islands (RM65 including return to Gaya by boat). Pulau Sapi has several short hiking trails, a kiosk selling snacks, and decent snorkelling.

The park's other islands cluster together 2.5km west of Gaya. The largest of the three, banana-shaped **Pulau Manukan**, is the most popular island with KK residents and offers a number of hiking trails, as well as good snorkelling, a couple of restaurants and a snack joint – it's the best choice for lunch. Across a channel to the southeast is tiny **Pulau Mamutik**, which can be crossed on foot in fifteen minutes and has excellent sands on either side of its jetty, not to mention the best snorkelling of all the islands and a small café/snack bar.

On Manukan, Mamutik and Sapi it's possible to organize water activities such as banana-boat rides and parasailing. It's cheaper to rent snorkelling equipment at Jesselton Point, though.

THE NORTHWEST COAST

The tip of Borneo on Sabah's northwest coast is growing as a low-key beach destination. Inspired by the pioneering conservation efforts of British-run ecolodge **Tampat do Aman**, several friendly coastal **Rungus villages** opened their largely deserted beaches to tourism. Revenues help keep the area clean of the garbage that washes ashore from as far as the Philippines. The closest town is drowsy **Kudat**, with a colourful Chinese temple near the main square, and a photogenic fish market.

VISITING TUNKU ABDUL RAHMAN PARK

Several boat companies ply the route between KK's Jesselton Ferry Terminal and the islands. Choose which company you're going to go with and decide if you want to visit just one island (RM23 return) or sign up for multi-island hopping (RM33/43/53 for two/three/four islands). **Boats** leave from 8.30am until 4pm, returning between 1pm and 5pm. Since they depart when full, it's better to go earlier in the day when there are more people going. Choose which island you want to go to first, and, once you get there, tell the representative of your boat company when you wish to go on to your next island and they'll arrange pick-up (boats tend to leave hourly). You have to pay a RM7.20 **departure tax** when leaving Jesselton Point, and a RM10 environmental conservation fee is payable upon arrival at your first island (hold on to your receipt). All boat companies can arrange snorkel rental at Jesselton Point (RM10), which is cheaper than renting the gear on the islands.

It is possible to **camp** on Gaya, Manukan and Mamutik for RM5 (bring your own tent); it's worth it to enjoy the islands without the crowds.

6

WHAT TO SEE AND DO

With precipitous cliffs and strong waves that crash onto the northernmost headland of Borneo, the **Tip of Borneo** (Simpangan Mengayau) is a powerful sight. Backtracking south, the coast offers kilometres of empty beaches: long and narrow **Kosohui Beach** is good for surfing, while the next bay, **Bavang Jamal Beach**, has fewer currents and a good reef for snorkelling. It ends with a crest facing tiny islet **Pulau Kulambu**, reachable by walking on a sandbank, which has a few snorkelling and dive sites. **Kulambu Beach** proceeds until the quiet and secluded **Loro Bay**, sheltered by a viridian crest and shallow waters that are perfect for swimming. Sunsets at most beaches colour the sky a stunning purple.

ARRIVAL AND DEPARTURE

By bus There's one daily bus from KK's Padang Merdeka to Kudat (8.30am; 3hr 30min–4hr), but it's quicker to take one of the frequent shared taxis. Shared taxis depart Kudat for KK (3hr; RM30) whenever they fill up and it's easier to get a ride in the mornings. *Tampat Do Aman* runs a shuttle service to/from their affiliated *Tip Top Restaurant* on Kosohui for RM15/person each way. To get around the tip of Borneo, you'll need your own wheels.

ACCOMMODATION AND EATING

In Kudat, there are several inexpensive Indian and Malay joints around the main square. Near the tip of Borneo, Kosohui Beach close to Kampung Marang Parang pretty much has the only eating options. At the time of writing, the community of Loro Kecil village was starting a homestay programme right on Loro Bay's beach. Contact Jackie (☏ 019 5347543) to enquire.

Amat and Sidi Kampung Marang Parang ☏ 014 677 1282 (Sidi). Choose between simple double rooms in wooden chalets right by the sea, or a double room in the longhouse. They also run shack-on-the-beach dive operator Borneo Watersport Surfers (RM1200 for Open Water courses, and RM150 for leisure dives), teach surf lessons (RM80) and rent surfboards (RM30/hr) and scooters (RM80/day). Longhouse doubles RM70, doubles RM100

Bavang Jamal Longhouse Stay Bavang Jamal Beach ☏ 019 812 4577 (Roland). Sleep on floor mats or four tiny private doubles in a traditional stilted Runggus longhouse, sheltered by the forest and a 3min walk to the ochre crescent of Bavang Jamal Beach. At the time of research, they were building private wooden chalets. Prices include breakfast. Longhouse per person RM40

Kafe Tokow Kampung Marang Parang ☏ 013 558 9052. Inexpensive rice and noodle staples and Malay dishes such as *nasi* and *kuey teow goreng* served by friendly locals in a simple open-air restaurant setting. Daily 8am–5pm.
Secret Place Café & Camping ☏ 010 414 5291, ⓦ secretplaceborneo.jimdo.com. Family-run café and campsite surrounded by trees in a beautiful location on Kulambu Beach. You can pitch your own tent (RM20/person) or rent one of their own, but it seems quite overpriced for such a freewheeling concept. Tents per person RM40
★**Tampat Do Aman** ☏ 013 880 8395 (Howard), ⓦ tampatdoaman.com.my. Wonderful ecolodge set amid lush greenery, it has two Rungus-style backpacker longhouses with tiny individual rooms, a Jungle Camp with five attractive en-suite chalets with spacious verandahs, and traditional Rungus huts to offer guests authentic accommodation. The chill-out area overlooking green paddies, Rungus Cultural museum and a restaurant complete these unique grounds. Longhouse rooms/huts per person RM45, chalets RM170

KINABALU NATIONAL PARK

Even after the devastating earthquake that struck the area on June 5, 2015, breaking off one of its peaks, the cloud-encased summit of **Mount Kinabalu** remains one of the most impressive sights in Borneo. Standing at 4095m, Kinabalu's remaning jagged peaks (named Donkey's Ears) look impossibly daunting from a distance, but the mountain is a relatively straightforward – if somewhat exhausting – climb. The well-defined, 8.7km path weaves up the mountain's southern side to the bare granite of the summit, where a 1.6km-deep gully known as Low's Gully cleaves the peak in two. The view from the top is awe-inspiring and the blanket of stars which envelops you until sunrise (not to mention the altitude) will leave you breathless. The aching muscles and creaking joints are well worth the sense of exhilaration you'll achieve at the top.

WHAT TO SEE AND DO

For many, climbing Mount Kinabalu is the main attraction of a visit to Sabah. However, for those not so keen on ascending the 4095m, there are other trails that you can take in the park leading through rich lowland forest to mountain rivers and waterfalls and bringing ample opportunity for birdwatching and nature walks. The park also has its own **botanical garden** and **Poring Hot Springs** – the perfect remedy for aching muscles, post-ascent. Details of all the various walks and trails are available from the park headquarters.

The climb: day one

Climbing to your first night's accommodation brings you to a height of around 3350m, and takes from three to five hours, depending on your fitness. Take your time, as it'll give you a better chance to acclimatize to the high altitude.

The trail is marked out with encouraging signboards every 500m, and there are seven rest shelters with toilets and containers of untreated (but drinkable) water along the Timpohon Trail spread out at regular intervals up until Laban Rata, your stop for the night. The trail is a combination of steep wooden stairs, uneven rock-and-dirt steps and relatively flat sections in between, so it's not all relentlessly uphill. Two or three hours into the climb, incredible views of the hills, sea and clouds below you start to unfold and the trail changes from lowland forest to dense foliage. After about 5km, the surrounding jungle becomes sparse and

6

CLIMBING MOUNT KINABALU

There are various **tour operators** in KK who can organize trips to the summit, but it's possible to make your own way there and sort out guides and accommodation yourself – you should always book as far ahead as possible. After the earthquake, the only active trail is Timpohon Gate, reachable by minivan (RM34/4 people round trip) from park headquarters. Accommodation at Laban Rata, the overnight stop halfway up the mountain, is limited, expensive and fills up fast, so you need to organize it several weeks in advance. The new 25-bed *Lemaing Hostel*, catering for Malaysian nationals, also accepts foreigners (RM200 including meals) in the rare cases when not fully booked. Contact Mr Daikin at the park's operation counter way in advance (☎ 088 889095). In KK, visit the Sutera Sanctuary Lodge's office (Lot G15, Ground Floor, Wisma Sabah; ☎ 088 487 466, ✆ suterasanctuarylodges.com.my) to book a bed on the mountain for the night of the climb. If going with Mountain Torq (see box, p.508), you'll be staying at their *Pendant Hut* (see p.509).

Buses stop about 50m from the park reception office (daily 7am–8pm), which is the check-in point for accommodation and obtaining guides. You'll need to pay the trail fee (RM15), get a climbing permit (RM200/person), mandatory insurance (RM14) and pay for an **obligatory guide** (RM230/five people). It's usually easy to join with others to share the guide fee. The guides do not try to keep everyone walking at the same pace; they walk behind the slowest member, so it's fine if you strike out on your own, as long as you stay on the trail. You can hire a porter (RM130 to Laban Rata/RM160 to Summit, one-way, for no more than 10kg). Aim to be at the park reception by 9am to make it up to the overnight resthouse before nightfall; if going with Mountain Torq, 8am is better, as you'll need to be up at Pendant Hut by 3pm for the briefing; also, by 9am, the headquarters become crowded with hikers.

WHAT TO BRING

You mustn't underestimate the rigours of the climb. There are a few essentials you should not leave KK without, all of which should fit in a small waterproof backpack:

Headlamp (with spare batteries) Essential for the early-morning scramble to the top.
Footwear with good traction
Cash Entrance/guide/miscellaneous fees add up and you can't use credit cards.
Fleece or warm jumper It gets very cold both at Laban Rata at night and at the top of the mountain.
Lightweight windproof and waterproof jacket
Water bottle Or water container.
Long johns To wear at night and/or under

your outer trousers.
Lightweight, breathable trousers For the upper part of the ascent; up to Laban Rata, a pair of shorts will do.
At least two T-shirts
Gloves For holding onto the cold, sodden ropes during the early-morning scramble to the top.
High-energy snacks Snacks sold at the park are extortionate. Bring a packed lunch from KK if you don't wish to fork out at Sutera Lodge.
Collapsible hiking poles

6

you have to cross some steep, exposed rocky ground, where you're most likely to be caught in the rain. The resthouses are located just after 6km at the foot of Panar Laban, from where views of the sun setting over the South China Sea are exquisite.

The climb: day two

Most climbers get up at 2am the next morning in order to make it to the top for sunrise. The gate to the trail is opened from 2.30am to 5.30am, and hikers join the procession snaking their way to the top by the light of their headlamps. This last section is only 2.7km but can seem interminable; the first part consists of an endless climb up steep wooden steps which then give way to exposed rock with ropes strung along it to help you haul yourself up; using your arms will give your legs a bit of a break. The last section is a short, steep scramble to the summit up some large, uneven boulders. If you make it to the summit just before sunrise, you'll have the satisfaction of watching a long line of headlamps making their way up towards you and knowing that when you're heading back down towards a well-deserved hot breakfast, they'll still be struggling up to the summit.

On a clear day, you get a splendid view of the whole valley below, illuminated by the first rays of the sun, as well as the lights of Kota Kinabalu along the coast. On the way down, you'll be able to appreciate the different peaks that you scrambled past in the darkness. If you've chosen to do the via ferrata (see box below), you have to descend to your assigned meeting point before beginning your vertigo-inducing adventure.

After breakfast at Laban Rata, descend at your leisure.

ARRIVAL AND DEPARTURE

By bus A/c express buses from KK to Sandakan (4hr) pass park headquarters (from KK hourly on the hour 7am–noon & at 12.30pm, 2pm, 4.30pm, 6pm, 7pm & 8pm). There are return buses going back to KK (usually until 9pm), which can be flagged down outside the park entrance, and a shuttle bus that heads back to KK at 3.30pm (RM40). Shared jeeps depart when full from the park gates and cost RM150 to KK (for up to five people). For Poring Hot Springs you can take a minivan or taxi for RM55 from park headquarters, hop on the daily shuttle bus from the headquarters at noon, or walk out of the main gate and hail any passing Sandakan-bound bus. They'll drop you off at Ranau (RM8), from where you can take a minibus (RM10) to the springs.

ACCOMMODATION AND EATING

It's worth spending a night at the base of Mt Kinabalu, if only to avoid getting up at an insane hour in KK before catching a bus or a taxi to the park. Most lodging options in the park include meals. Staying at the park headquarters and in Laban Rata is vastly overpriced for what it is, as *Sutera Sanctuary Lodges* have a monopoly on it. At the park headquarters there are a couple of restaurants (daily 6am–10pm, Sat until 11pm) that serve both buffet and à la carte meals, and there's also a (pricey) provisions shop beside reception.

J Residence ☎ 012 869 6969, ⓦ jresidence.com. Just 300m to the right of the park headquarters, the well-maintained and luminous rooms here are housed in six attractive wooden chalets perched on a steep ridge. The surrounding misty forest and covered barbecue area (rental RM30) make up for the lack of mountain views. Prices increase at weekends. Doubles RM88

Laban Rata Resthouse Laban Rata ☎ 088 487466, ⓦ suterasanctuarylodges.com.my. The place where most hikers will stay at the halfway-up-the-mountain point, this rather ordinary lodge offers heated dorms, hot showers and simple twin rooms. The exorbitant prices include all meals and the cafeteria is the only place to eat

---

THE VIA FERRATA

If the precipitous climb to the summit of Mount Kinabalu is not enough of a challenge, you may consider taking the road less travelled and sign up for Mountain Torq's (☎ 088 268126, ⓦ mountaintorq.com) **via ferrata** – the highest in the world. Consisting of metal rungs, bars, steel cables and suspension bridges bolted to the sheer rock face, the via ferrata is an adventure playground for adrenaline junkies. While no prior experience is required, a good level of physical fitness is a must; the enthusiastic English-speaking guides talk you through everything else. You can take part in two circuits: **Low's Peak Circuit** (RM750) or the shorter **Walk the Torq** (RM560; Low's Peak Circuit incorporates Walk the Torq). The former requires a fair amount of abseiling or climbing down a sheer rock face, and the views of the valley from up high are second to none; the latter is far shorter and easier, but still requires traversing a cliff face and wire bridge.

on the mountain. The Gunting Lagadan, Panar Laban and Waras huts around the main lodge have more unheated dorms (and it gets very cold at night) for the same inflated prices. Dorms RM781, doubles RM1572

Mountain Resthouse ☏ 016 837 4060 or ☏ 088 888632. A budget option 300m to the left of the park entrance, this hostel has a simple TV room to socialize in, cheap four-bed dorms and no-frills doubles with en-suite bathrooms that can get damp and cold, but offer the best budget value outside the park. Dorms RM25, doubles RM60

Pendant Hut Laban Rata ☏ 088 268126, ⓦ mountaintorq.com. The one non-*Sutera* option at Laban Rata belongs to Mountain Torq and consists of unheated (though you do get warm sleeping bags) but tidy dorms with superb views. Though the *Pendant Hut* accepts non-via ferrata guests, prices do include the via ferrata experience; meals are taken at the *Laban Rata Resthouse* cafeteria below. One night/two days RM830

Sutera Sanctuary Lodge Park Headquarters ☏ 088 308914, ⓦ suteraharbour.com. If you want to stay at the park headquarters at the base of the mountain, this is the only option, a veritable catch-all consisting of two virtually identical — and overpriced — twenty-bed hostels: *Rock and Grace* and *Hill Lodge* which have semi-detached cabins; hotel rooms at the *Liwagu Suites*; semi-detached two-bedroom units at *Peak Lodge*; and two-storey, two-bedroom units at the priciest *Nepenthes Villa*. Dorms RM310, doubles RM433

Poring Hot Springs and rafflesia sightings

The sulphurous waters of **Poring Hot Springs** are situated on the park's southeastern border. Don't expect a beautiful natural spa location: the springs are man-made, with shared open-air baths (RM15) where you simply slip into a tub and turn on the tap. An additional ticket (RM7) grants admission to 40m-high Poring's **canopy walk** (daily 9am–4pm), which affords you a monkey's-eye view of the surrounding lowland rainforest, and an educational **butterfly farm** (daily 9am–4pm) with a garden, nursery and hatchery housing some spectacular species. A better reason to come here is to spot the world's largest flower, the cabbage-like **rafflesia**. A smelly, parasitic plant whose rubbery, orange-red blooms can reach up to 1m in diameter, it was first catalogued in Sumatra in 1818 by Sir Stamford Raffles and naturalist Dr Joseph Arnold. Rafflesia flowers bloom unpredictably and only last about five days before dying: follow the signs or talk to the private

guides who wait for customers by the roadside. Expect to pay around RM15/30.

ARRIVAL AND DEPARTURE

By bus Regular buses run between KK and nearby Ranau; Poring is a short minivan ride away from Ranau's taxi stand opposite Maybank (RM8). You can also flag down Ranau and KK-bound buses by the entrance to Kinabalu National Park.

ACCOMMODATION AND EATING

At Poring itself, the accommodation scene is limited to overpriced options, so you're better off visiting Poring en route to or from Mt Kinabalu or else staying at *Lupa Masa*. There's a café with a limited menu at the springs, and a couple of restaurants just outside the gates serving Malay food from RM10.

★ **Lupa Masa** ☏ 01 820 8981 or ☏ 012 845 1987. This eco-camp, a 30min trek from Poring Hot Springs, features a covered lounge and open-air kitchen; sleeping arrangements range from tents on a raised platform with a roof, a mattress on a raised platform overlooking the river, with mosquito netting, or a rustic two-person *pondok* (hut) with mattress on the floor. Besides generating its own electricity using a nearby river, *Lupa Masa* also composts organic waste, and meals incorporate organic, locally sourced produce (including various jungle plants). Don't expect wi-fi, and bring a torch to light your way at night. Per person including food (1st night) RM90, 2nd night RM70

TELUPID

Smack in the middle of Sabah and part of the **Heart of Borneo** (ⓦ heartofborneo.org) conservation project, the area around **TELUPID** town is blessed by the forest reserves of **Tawai** and **Ulu Telupid**. In order to safeguard the area from illegal logging and poaching, the Forestry Department and enterprising local villagers have opened these patches of secondary rainforest to ecotourism. At **Tawai Forest Reserve** (RM15; camping RM10/person), a few kilometres off the Telupid roundabout towards Tongod, you can hike along jungle trails filled with several species of nepenthes pitcher plants, or enjoy a dip in the river's swimming holes. Adrenaline junkies should venture into the depths of Ulu Telupid guided by the villagers of KOBEST (Koperasi Kampung Bestaria). It's an adventurous slog through untamed jungle: be prepared for many leeches as you trawl across slippery streams, gape at century-old giant trees, and pull yourself

6

up ropes through the dense thicket leading to the top of **Wasai Kopuron** waterfall. Alternatively, trekking to **Wasai Tunob** waterfall gives you the chance to spot the rare rafflesia species *rhizanthes* and *tengku adlinii*. You can also simply try authentic Dusun village hospitality and have a go at their farming chores.

ARRIVAL AND DEPARTURE

By bus Buses from KK to Sandakan (3hr 30min–4hr) pass the Telupid junction, where KOBEST staff will fetch you. If coming from Poring, Ranau or Mt Kinabalu, you can take one of the minivans that ply the Ranau-Telupid or Sandakan Checkpoint Mile 32-Telupid route several times daily for RM20/25.

ACCOMMODATION AND EATING

Telupid is a cluster of buildings and restaurants offering all amenities, from food to internet, but no accommodation. KOBEST offers transport to and from the junction, guide fees and full-board homestay accommodation in Kampung Bestaria, a 20min drive towards Ranau.

KOBEST ☏ 011 2988 1122. Come as a guest and leave as family by staying with the Dusun residents of tiny Kampung Bestaria, a cluster of concrete and wooden homes at the edge of Ulu Telupid forest reserve. Don't expect wi-fi or many comforts, and come prepared to learn the rhythms of rural Sabah's life by enjoying communal meals on the floor with your host family. Two-days one-night packages per person RM260

SANDAKAN

Sandwiched between sea and cliffs on the northern lip of Sandakan Bay, **SANDAKAN** is a gritty port, founded in 1878 by Englishman William Pryer and spread out around the bay. There's little left of the attractive architecture from its colonial heyday, as it was destroyed by Japanese bombing. During the Japanese occupation between 1942 and 1945, Sandakan was the site of a large prisoner of war camp, and more Australian prisoners died during the death march to Ranau than during the construction of the Burma Railway. Every year on ANZAC Day (April 24), former servicemen and their descendants come to visit the **Australian war memorial** at Mile Seven on Labuk Rd, towards Sepilok (take buses #8, #12 or #14, get off at the "Taman Rimba" signpost and then take Jalan Rimba; taxis cost around RM35).

The **Sandakan Heritage Trail** (ⓦ sabahtourism.com/destination/sandakan-heritage-trail) loops around the town centre, taking in Sandakan's historical buildings, such as the William Pryer monument, the St Michael and All Angels Church, the Chinese World War II memorial and the "100 steps", up to **Agnes Keith's house** (daily 9am–4.45pm; RM15). This beautiful two-storey colonial residence was built on the site of the home of the American author who lived in Sandakan with her English husband between the 1930s and the 1950s. Her first book, *The Land Below The Wind*, gave Sabah an endearing epithet that stuck, while *Three Came Home* told the story of the family's internment in Japanese prisoner of war camps.

Just to the east of Sandakan is **Kampung Buli Sim-Sim**, the water village around which Sandakan expanded in the nineteenth century, its countless photogenic shacks spread like lilies out into the bay – a colourful place to wander around, with some great seafood restaurants.

Most travellers use Sandakan as a base from which to visit or a brief stopover en route to the **Sepilok Orang-utan Rehabilitation Centre** and **Bornean Sun Bear Conservation Centre**, or as a jumping-off point for **wildlife-watching** along the Kinabatangan River and the **Gomantong Caves**, connected to Sandakan by handy transfers.

ARRIVAL AND DEPARTURE

By plane The airport serving Sandakan is 11km north of town and connected by taxis (RM50) to the centre. You can also take bus #7 which stops around 500m from the airport along the main road.

Destinations Kota Kinabalu (4 daily; 50min); Kuala Lumpur (6 daily; 2hr 40min).

By bus Sandakan's local bus station is situated on the waterfront at Jln Pryer. Local buses run along Jln Utara from 6am to 6pm, their number, Batu 7 (Mile 7), telling you the distance they travel from town. A short walk west along Jln Pryer brings you to the minibus area. Most Kinabatangan nature lodges arrange daily pick-ups from Sandakan. The long-distance bus station is at Batu 2.5 (taxis cost RM15).

Destinations from the long-distance station: KK (approximately hourly 6.30am–8pm; 7hr); Lahad Datu (several daily; 2hr 30min); Ranau (3 daily; 4hr); Semporna

(2 daily at 7am & 2pm; 5hr 30min); Tawau (5 daily, hourly 6.30am–10.30am; 5hr 30min).

By long-distance taxi Long-distance taxis operate from the area around the local bus station.

By boat One ferry operated by Aleson Shipping Lines (Mon & Fri; no fixed departure time, check at the jetty; 22hr; RM280; ☏ 089 216996 or ☏ 012 839 1777) connects Sandakan to Zamboanga in the Philippines from the Karamunting Jetty (4km west of town). However, the ferry stops at Tawi Tawi and Jolo islands, infamous hotspots of the Moro Liberation Front, an Islamic separatist group based in the southern Philippines (see box, p.660); currently the security situation in the region means this route is advised against – check the latest advice before considering it.

INFORMATION

Tourist information The only information office in town is privately operated by the staff at *San Da Gen* café, next to *Nak Hotel*. They are a mine of local information, and distribute a self-produced free heritage and food city map.

ACCOMMODATION

Harbourside Backpackers Lot 43, 1st floor, block HS-4, Sandakan Harbour Square ☏ 089 217072, ⓦ harboursidebackpackers.com. A great central location, super-nice staff, a/c-cooled rooms and a lovely TV cum reading lounge make this a top backpacker choice. Breakfast included. Dorms RM30, doubles RM70
★ **Nak Hotel** Jln Pelabuhan Lama at Jln Pryer ☏ 089 272988, ⓦ nakhotel.com. Refurbished, super-central hotel with touches of retro-Chinese decor, helpful staff, spacious rooms with cable TV and sparkling bathrooms, as well as a superb roof lounge, *Balin*. Wi-fi only in lobby or in *Balin*. Breakfast included and singles available. Doubles RM138
Sandakan Backpackers Lot 108, Block SH-11, Sandakan Harbour Square ☏ 089 211213, ⓦ sandakanbackpackers .com. Located right on the waterfront, this hostel has bright dorms and rooms, and a new management that takes good care of travellers. There's a lovely rooftop garden to soak up Sandakan's glowing sunsets, and breakfast is included. Dorms RM18, doubles RM65

EATING AND DRINKING

There are numerous inexpensive restaurants along the waterfront, serving Malay, Chinese and Indian dishes. Central Sandakan is quiet in the evenings; Batu (Mile) 4 is a good place to head for local nightlife and a plethora of food courts serving inexpensive *nasi campur* (RM5).

★ **Balin Roof Garden** At the top of *Nak Hotel*. A chic Balinese-inspired roof lounge with loads of cushions to recline on and a good restaurant and a bar overlooking the sea from the open-air section. The menu is mostly fusion, the thin-and-crispy pizzas are excellent, the fresh fruit juices are better than the cocktails on offer and the staff

are just lovely (mains from RM15). Get there early for incredible sunsets over the sea. Daily 8am–midnight.
The English Tea House and Restaurant Jln Istana. Set up high on a hill overlooking the town, this attractive colonial building is home to an English teahouse. Come for the setting, the views and the scones, clotted cream and tea, but skip the rest of the menu. Also has a good wine list for those in need of more than cake. Daily 10am–midnight.
San Da Gen Cnr Jln Pryor & Jln Pelabuhan Lama ☏ 089 238988, ⓦ facebook.com/tastesandagen. Sandakan's hippest café brings back the city's rich Hakka-Chinese culinary tradition with delicious traditional *ufo* tarts – sweet creamy custard over a crunchy vanilla-flavoured biscuit – and egg tarts (RM2.50) that go down a treat with local brews while vintage vinyls crackle 1960s Malaysian *pop-yeh-yeh* tunes. Their Malaysian staples, like *nasi ayam penyet* (RM12.90), make it a good lunch stop. Daily 8am–5pm.
Sim Sim Seafood restaurants Sim Sim 8. Located at the Sim Sim stilt village's waterfront, there are two restaurants serving some of the best seafood for miles around. *H-90* is the original: pick your choice from a fish tank and they'll do the rest. Take a taxi to Sim Sim Bridge 8. Daily 7.30am–9pm.

SEPILOK

Twenty-five kilometres west of Sandakan lies **SEPILOK**, an area known primarily for the **Sepilok Orang-utan Rehabilitation Centre (SORC)** – the most reliable place in Sabah to see the stunning redhead of the simian world. Nearby is the **Rainforest Discovery Centre**, with nature trails through the jungle and canopy towers for wildlife-watching. The **Bornean Sun Bear Conservation Centre (BSBCC)** has opened right next door to SORC, so you can see two of Borneo's most beguiling mammals during an easy day-trip.

Sepilok Orang-utan Rehabilitation Centre

One of only four orang-utan sanctuaries in the world, the **Sepilok Orang-utan Rehabilitation Centre** (daily 9–11am & 2–4pm; trails 9am–4.15pm; feeding times 10am & 3pm; RM30; camera fee RM10; ☏ 089 531180) is home to semi-wild orang-utans that have been orphaned or rescued from captivity. Young orang-utans learn essential skills – climbing, nesting, finding food – in the "Nursery" before they're allowed into the jungle, and their dependence on

6

humans is decreased until they're ready to be integrated into the wild orang-utan population of Borneo once more. The twenty-minute video screening at the centre (daily at 9am, 10.30am, 11am, noon, 2.10pm & 3.30pm) shows the rescue and rehabilitation of orang-utans.

The orang-utans generally roam the surrounding jungle, but know exactly when **feeding time** is and have their body clocks well tuned to free fruit, so a sighting is pretty much guaranteed. A short boardwalk leads to feeding station A, which is linked to the trees with taut ropes that allow you to see them coming long before they reach the platform, scaring off the long-tail macaques that lurk nearby, waiting to snatch their fill of fruit.

Visitors must leave all their possessions (bar cameras) in the lockers provided, as macaques and orang-utans have been known to snatch items that tickle their fancy.

There are also a number of **pleasant walks** throughout the park ranging from 250m to 4km in length; to gain access, you need to register at the on-site visitor reception centre.

Bornean Sun Bear Conservation Centre

The **sun bear**, named for a vaguely sun-like white crescent on its black chest, is the smallest and least studied of the world's bears (in spite of the fact that it easily rivals the panda for cuteness). An omnivore and an expert climber native to Borneo and other parts of Southeast Asia, it's increasingly under threat due to massive destruction of its natural habitat, competition from other predators, such as leopards, tigers and other bears, illegal hunting for body parts such as the gall bladder, bones and claws used in traditional Chinese medicine, and the illegal pet trade.

The **Bornean Sun Bear Conservation Centre** (daily 9am–5pm; RM31.80; ☎089 534491, ⊛www.bsbcc.org.my) has made it its mission to rescue and rehabilitate orphaned and ex-captive sun bears and to raise awareness locally and worldwide regarding their plight. Currently home to

42 sun bears, the conservation centre has a visitor information centre and several boardwalks (including wheelchair-friendly ramps) leading to viewpoints overlooking the reserve where the bears roam, giving visitors a chance to observe these remarkable mammals in their natural habitat.

For more information on sun bears, see ⊛sunbears.wildlifedirect.org. To help protect them, never buy bear products in markets, and if you see them on sale, report the sellers to the local authorities.

Rainforest Discovery Centre

The **Rainforest Discovery Centre** (daily 8am–5pm; RM15; ☎089 533780, ⊛forest.sabah.gov.my/rdc) – a small nature reserve that's home to flying foxes, gliding lizards, orang-utans and more – is a 1km walk back towards the entrance to Sepilok from SORC. There is a visitor centre by a small lake, from which nature trails branch off into the jungle. One of the longer loops leads you past the Sepilok Giant, an enormous hardwood tree, while just beyond the lake you reach the first of three canopy towers, linked by a metal canopy walk. The best time to see wildlife is early in the morning or later in the afternoon; on Mondays and Fridays from 6 to 8pm you can join guided night walks (RM30/person, minimum four) to experience the jungle's nocturnal sounds and, if lucky, creatures.

Just behind the visitor centre is the **Plant Discovery Garden**, with a maze of short trails showcasing pitcher plants, the ginger family, giant orchids, medicinal plants and cacti.

ARRIVAL AND DEPARTURE

By bus To get to Sepilok from Sandakan take any bus from the central bus station numbering #14 or higher, since Sepilok is located just off "Batu 14" (hourly 9am–4.30pm; 45min; RM5). From Batu 14 it's 2.5km to SORC along a road lined with accommodation options; walk or take one of the taxis that shuttle to and from SORC (RM3/person). To move on to other parts of Sabah, note that the long-distance bus station is en route to Sandakan, so ask the driver to drop you there. Many lodging options along the Kinabatangan River can pick you up from Sepilok if notified in advance.

By taxi Most of the accommodation lodges can arrange taxis to Sandakan. The journey (25min) should cost around RM50.

ACCOMMODATION AND EATING

Most lodging options include breakfast in the price and some offer full board. Otherwise, use the cafeteria at SORC which has inexpensive rice and noodle dishes.

Nature Lodge Sepilok ☏ 089 535889, ⓦ insabah.com/ nature-lodge-sepilok. Set 1.5km from SORC, the newest kid on Sepilok's block boosts six economic chalets that, with spacious a/c rooms, plush beds and en-suite open-air toilets with private garden and jungle views, are hard to pass. The dorms with shared toilets come in the same league of cleanliness and comfort. Dorms RM30, doubles RM159

Paganakan Dii ☏ 012 868 1005, ⓦ paganakandii.com. Beautifully situated on a ridge overlooking the jungle below, this is the only lodging option in Sepilok that's off the other side of the highway from SORC. The dorms have "breathable" walls that keep them cool; the en-suite duplex hut rooms and ridge duplexes have open-air bathrooms and balconies, and there's an on-site café serving simple meals. Two scheduled daily transfers to SORC are included in the price. Dorms RM35, doubles RM155

Sepilok B&B ☏ 089 534050, ⓦ sepilokbedandbreakfast .com. Opposite the Rainforest Discovery Centre, this unpretentious option offers four lodges with various configurations of basic dorms and a/c private rooms, with a communal vibe that draws the backpacker crowd. Dorms RM45, doubles RM68

★ **Sepilok Forest Edge Resort** ☏ 016 523 3190, ⓦ sepilokforestedgeresort.com. Come here for spick-and-span en-suite a/c chalets with open-roofed bathrooms and tree-showers – see to believe – or cosy four-bed dorms with individual tables, reading lights, safety boxes and private toilets. If this wasn't enough, the lush grounds have a jungle trail where orang-utans occasionally come to find fruit trees, a leafy swimming pool, and a restaurant-cum-spacious guest lounge. Dorms RM43, chalets RM245

Uncle Tan's Mile 14, Jln Sepilok ☏ 089 535784 or ☏ 016 824 4749, ⓦ uncletan.com. Run by one of the oldest adventure operators in Sabah, this sociable guesthouse is located 300m from Sepilok Junction and is a firm favourite with backpackers. Although the huts are pretty basic, they include full board. They also arrange cheap wildlife-spotting trips to their jungle camp at Kinabatangan (see p.514). Dorms RM50, doubles RM100

LIBARAN TURTLE ISLAND

Off the northwest coast of Sabah and part of the Sandakan Archipelago, **LIBARAN** is one of the larger islands, easily accessible by boat from Sandakan. The island has a small community of fishermen at one end and a turtle conservation hatchery – part of the **Turtle Conservation Programme** designed to protect endangered green turtles – on the other side of the island. Visitors can stay overnight on the island at beachside accommodation run by *Trekkers Lodge* and Nasalis Larvatus Tours, affiliated with *Nature Lodge* (see above). At night, wildlife guides watch for turtles coming ashore to lay eggs and lead visitors to a nearby spot where they may observe the turtle without disturbing it (flashlights and photography forbidden). The conservation programme works together with locals, discouraging them from poaching turtle eggs by offering them more money for leading them to a nesting turtle (as opposed to RM2–3 per poached turtle egg). Visitors may also participate in setting baby turtles loose from the hatchery. This conservation programme is a better and more affordable way of seeing turtles than the nearby Turtle Islands National Park, visits to which are both hugely expensive and mismanaged.

ARRIVAL AND DEPARTURE

By boat Stays on Libaran Island include boat transfers (by arrangement) from downtown Sandakan (daily in peak season; 45min). During rainy season (Nov–Feb) the *Walai Penyu Resort* on the island may shut down as the seas are too rough for safe passage there and back.

ACCOMMODATION AND EATING

Walai Penyu Resort Booked through Nasalis Larvatus Tours ☏ 088 230534, ⓦ insabah.com. This glamping resort consists of luxury tents with beds inside on a raised platform right by the beach, the best outdoorsy bathrooms you'll ever see, and a shaded verandah where you're served delicious, mostly Malay, meals. Book at least a week in advance as there's only space for sixteen guests. Two days and one night all-inclusive RM445

SUNGAI KINABATANGAN

The wide cappuccino-coloured ribbon that is the Kinabatangan River cuts a long path into the jungle of east Sabah – 560km long, to be precise. The area around, hemmed in by ever-encroaching palm-oil plantations, is one of the best – and most accessible – places to see **wildlife** in Sabah. Pygmy elephants are spotted on the riverbanks during the dry season, and you're likely to see wild orang-utans, proboscis monkeys, gibbons, macaques, wild boar and huge monitor lizards in the

6

forest flanking the river. Swimming is not a good idea, particularly in the river's tributaries, as they're favoured by crocodiles. The resident bird life – four species of hornbill, Brahmin kites, crested serpent eagles, egrets, stork-billed kingfishers and oriental darters – is equally impressive. It's much more difficult to spot the nocturnal dwellers of the forest such as the clouded leopard, slow loris and saucer-eyed tarsier – one of the oldest mammals on earth, though with the tarsiers, you might have better luck in August, the fruit season, when they come to feed on the insects that feed on the fruit.

The best way to appreciate the river is to stay in one of the several jungle camps or lodges on its banks.

ARRIVAL AND DEPARTURE

By bus There are no direct buses from Sabah's bigger towns to Sukau and Bilit, but most jungle lodges can arrange pick-up from Sandakan or from the Sukau Junction. All buses running from KK and Sandakan to Lahad Datu, Semporna and Tawau pass by the junction, so just ask to be let off there. From Sandakan, the junction is around a 1hr 30min drive. All operators can arrange for you to be dropped off at the junction in time for the next bus north or south.

ACCOMMODATION AND EATING

Besides two clusters in the villages of Bilit, closest to the Sukau Junction, and Sukau, further east along the river, jungle lodges are spread out on the upper and lower reaches of the river as far as Batu Puteh and Abai. There's no public transport to or between the villages, but accommodation prices usually include all meals and boat transfers to and from the lodge. Pick-up from Sandakan, Sepilok or Lahad Datu can be arranged. Most riverside lodges offer two longboat river cruises each day – at dawn and at sunset. Depending on the location of the lodge, most also offer short jungle treks and have rubber boots

---

> ## ★ TREAT YOURSELF
>
> **Kinabatangan Wetlands Resort** ☎ 089 211441, ⓦ kwrborneo.com. Tucked in a corner of pristine wetland near Abai village, just 10km from the river mouth, these ten deluxe wooden chalets connected by boardwalks over tropical marshland are perfect for a five-star jungle getaway. The price includes two river cruises, night-walk, full board and return boat transfers. Two days/one night per person RM1050

---

and leech socks for rent. If trekking in the evening, a hand-held torch is better than a headlamp.

The Last Frontier Resort Bilit ☎ 016 676 5922, ⓦ thelastfrontierresort.com. Run by two friendly, knowledgeable guys – one from KL and the other from Belgium – this intimate lodge has just four en-suite doubles. Leech-free jungle treks are guaranteed because of its unique location high up on a ridge, reachable by around 600 steps. The owners can organize a dawn cruise for enthusiastic birdwatchers, and the delicious food is a cut above the rest. Two days/one night per person RM500, three days/two nights RM720

Nature Lodge Kinabatangan Bilit ☎ 013 863 6263, ⓦ naturelodgekinabatangan.com. Diagonally across the river from Bilit, this lodge consists of the budget Civet Wing with dorm-style jungle huts and the pricier a/c-cooled twin-bed, en-suite chalets in the Agamid Wing. Their three-day/two-night packages, with all meals and excursions included, are very good value, and their guides are knowledgeable and friendly. Doubles RM380, chalets RM415

★ **Sukau Greenview B&B** Sukau ☎ 089 212912, ⓦ sukaugreenview.com. Popular with backpackers, this efficient riverside lodge run by a welcoming family consists of nine raised cottage-type, en-suite rooms with fans and a wi-fi-equipped dining area that serves very good buffet meals. There's also a small library for those who want to read up on the local wildlife and price includes transport to/from Sandakan or Sepilok. Two days/one night RM360

★ **MESCOT's Tungog Rainforest Eco Camp (TREC)** ☎ 089 551070, ⓦ mescot.org. Set inside a forest reserve on the shore of marmot-inhabited lake Tungog, these ten elevated A-frame huts set above rustic but charming wood-and-stone toilets with bucket showers are a jewel of eco-sustainability. The area offers 18km of jungle trails and swamp forest boardwalks, and the guides can take you out on river cruises (RM45/person) and night walks. Profits are re-invested in keeping the Tungong lake clear of parasitic *Salvinia molesta*, and fuel KOPEL's other conservation projects. Go before electricity comes to take away the romantic gas lights. Per person RM95

Uncle Tan's Jungle Camp ☎ 089 535784, ⓦ uncletan .com. Runs great tours for backpackers from a proper jungle camp consisting of raised huts with mattresses and mosquito nets. Showers are rustic and will appeal to exhibitionists. Their accommodation in Sepilok can arrange a three-day, two-night per person tour for RM500

GOMANTONG CAVES

The **Gomantong Caves** (daily 8am–noon & 2–4.30pm; RM30, camera RM30), 32km south of Sandakan Bay, just off the road to Sukau, are impressive enough at any time of the year, though you'll get most out of the trip when the edible nests of their resident swiftlets are being harvested (Feb–April & July–Sept). Bird's-nest soup has long been a Chinese culinary delicacy (see box, p.493) and Chinese merchants have been coming to Borneo to trade for birds' nests for at least twelve centuries.

Of the two major caves, **Simud Hitam** is the one you can visit without a guide. It may not be the largest of Borneo's caves, though the ceiling is up to 90m high, but it's certainly the most impressive in terms of the amount of life it supports, and by "life", we mean **cockroaches**. They feed on the mounds of bat guano in the centre of the cave and are absolutely everywhere: bring a torch and wear long trousers, boots and a long-sleeved shirt. Gloves are a great idea, since the handrails are covered in bat guano as well as roaches. The slippery boardwalk loops around the cave and past the flimsy shelters where the birds'-nest collectors sleep, and you'll see a wealth of freshwater crabs in the stream near the exit from the cave. Simud Hitam supports a colony of black-nest swiftlets, whose nests – a mixture of saliva and feathers – sell for around US$100/kg.

Above Simud Hitam, the smaller but less accessible **Simud Putih** is home to the white-nest swiftlet, whose nests are of pure, dried saliva and can fetch prices of over US$2000/kg. During the harvesting season, the birds'-nest collectors live up here for ten days at a time in complete darkness, with supplies lifted up by rope pulley. To reach Simud Putih, you take the left fork, five minutes along the trail behind reception, and start climbing (45min); it's also reachable via a steep and somewhat perilous scramble along some rocks from inside Simud Hitam; ask for a guide at the park headquarters.

You can come to the caves by arranged tour from Sandakan, but many lodges along the Kinabatangan River offer a stopover here as part of their package, or will drop you off here for free at the end of your stay.

SEMPORNA

The Bajau fishing town of **SEMPORNA**, 108km east of Tawau, is the departure point for diving trips to Pulau Sipadan and other neighbouring islands. Semporna's notable feature is the huge water village stretching southwards along the coast from the centre, which incorporates mosques, shops and hundreds of dwellings. Divers and snorkellers tend to stay in Semporna overnight on their way to and from **Mabul** (see p.516).

ARRIVAL AND DEPARTURE

By bus Minivans stop in front of USNO headquarters, a couple of blocks from the waterfront, while buses stop across the road from the waterfront mosque. It's a 7min walk to the waterfront accommodation options along Jln Simunul; when the mosque is in front of you, head right, then left towards the market stalls, then right again. If taking the overnight bus to KK, buy your ticket a day in advance or a few hours before departure, and remember that it gets into KK around 5.30am.

Destinations Kota Kinabalu (daily at 8am & 7.30pm; 10hr); Lahad Datu (4–5 daily; 3hr); Sandakan (daily; 6hr); Tawau (4–5 daily; 1hr 30min).

INFORMATION

All diving outfitters, accommodation options and restaurants are clustered along a couple of blocks of waterfront streets. If heading out to Mabul, get some cash out at Maybank along Jln Jakarullah.

ACCOMMODATION AND EATING

Best Bunk Beds Lot C2, 1st 2nd and 3rd floor, Seafront Newtownship ☎019 851 8039, ✉bestbunkbeds@gmail .com; The loft-like dorms at this new hostel try to fit too many beds, but the bunks are comfy and clean, and next to spacious common areas. The complimentary breakfast is a cut above average. Dorms RM48

Bismillah Semporna Seafront. Curries and *roti canai* go for a song at this Indian cheapie. Mains from RM5. Daily 8am–11pm.

Borneo Global Backpackers Jln Causeway ☎088 270976, ⓦbgbackpackers.com. Located opposite the jetty, this friendly guesthouse still offers cheap a/c dorms and simple twins and doubles (some windowless), but its glory days seem to be over. Dorms RM29, doubles RM99

Dragon Inn Jln Custom ☎089 781088, ⓦdragoninnfloating.com.my. Atmospheric wooden longhouses that extend into the not-too-clean sea, with en-suite a/c rooms with tropical decor and cable TV. The attached restaurant serves decent seafood and Malay noodle dishes. Doubles RM145

Restoran Gembira Ah Loong Lot 17, block C Bandar Baru p/s 124 ☎089 782372. A little removed from the main accommodation strip, this simple Chinese restaurant serves

6

good and inexpensive fish, chicken and beef-over-rice combinations (RM6) including tasty black pepper fish, sweet-and-sour and sweet-and-spicy chicken. Daily 8am–9pm.

Scuba Junkie Dive Lodge 36 Semporna Seafront ☎ 089 782372, ⊛ scuba-junkie.com. A diver-focused hostel with colourful a/c-cooled dorms and rooms, some with own bathrooms. Accommodation for non-divers is twice as expensive. Dorms RM25, doubles RM75

SEMPORNA ARCHIPELAGO

The waters south of Semporna are littered with tiny volcanic islands, which make up the **Semporna Archipelago**. The largest ones are Mabul, Kapalai, Si Amil, Danawan and **Sipadan** – the world-famous diving destination, though the other islands don't lack for diving spots themselves, which range from sunken man-made structures to caves, wrecks and reef walls, the reefs rivalling the Great Barrier Reef for diversity and home to over 200 species of fish (including sharks), as well as rays and turtles.

Mabul

MABUL is an attractive little island, bristling with jetties, where you will be based for your diving and snorkelling. The waters around the island offer the best muck-diving in the archipelago (it involves looking for small marine creatures in shallow waters and the term was coined here). There are a couple of white sandy beaches and two water villages, one Filipino and the one next to the *Scuba Junkie* resort that's home to the Bajau Sea Gypsies, most of whom are stateless and have no rights under Malay law. You'll spot their colourful houseboats and their young children paddling their own sea canoes. It takes twenty minutes or so to walk around the island; the dirt path takes you through the two villages and the expensive *Sipadan Mabul Resort* (you can wander through it, in spite of the "Non-guests Keep Out" sign, as they don't own the beach).

ARRIVAL AND DEPARTURE

By boat Each diving company operates its own speedboats, which tend to leave Semporna every day around 8am and 2pm, arriving in Mabul around 9am and 3pm. Afternoon boats head back to Semporna around 4pm.

DIVING AND SNORKELLING

Each resort tends to offer packages that include three dives per day, with two before lunch and one after, as well as night dives at extra cost; Sipadan day-trips include three dives. Even if you don't dive at Sipadan, there's some spectacular diving to be done off Mabul itself; the man-made structures in front of the *Scuba Junkie* resort attract

---

DIVING IN SIPADAN AND THE SEMPORNA ARCHIPELAGO

There are many operators who arrange dives in Sipadan and the Semporna Archipelago, all of which have offices in Semporna and which also have their own accommodation on Mabul. Once you have chosen an operator, they will take you out to Mabul by boat; you will stay with them, eat with them and go diving with them. Reputable operators include:

Billabong Scuba Lot 28, 1st Floor, Block E, Seafront Newtownship ☎ 089 781866, ⊛ billabongscuba.com. Self-defined as a budget dive operator, they mostly cater to backpackers. Three dives off Mabul/Kapalai RM250; night dive RM90 (minimum three); three-day PADI Open Water course RM1170.

★ **Scuba Junkie** Lot 36 Semporna Seafront ☎ 089 785372, ⊛ scuba-junkie.com. Some of the best-value diving at Mabul and Kapalai (two-day/three-night packages from RM1030) and Sipadan (packages from four days/three nights, including four dives at Sipadan, from RM2380); booking is essential. If you've never dived before, their excellent "Discover Scuba" (RM300) day package introduces you to the underwater world courtesy of their patient, professional diving instructors.

Seaventures 4th floor, Waisma Sabah, Kota Kinabalu ☎ 089 261669, ⊛ seaventuresdive.com. Highly regarded outfit for experienced divers, offering the most unusual lodging option on Mabul – a former oil rig. Four-day/three-night PADI Open Water course RM3686.

Uncle Chang's 36 Semporna Seafront, entrance to *Dragon Inn* ☎ 089 785372, ⊛ ucsipadan.com. Inexpensive dives and snorkelling trips departing from the backpacker-tastic "lodge" on Mabul (two dives Mabul, one dive Kapalai RM270; one-day snorkelling trip RM180). The diving instructors are a bit hit and miss, though. Uncle Chang has a reputation for being able to secure a Sipadan permit if other companies are fully booked.

THE PLIGHT OF SHARKS

If you've come from KK, you may have seen posters around town campaigning against shark's fin soup. In Mabul, *Scuba Junkie* takes the lead in the campaign, pushing for **shark fishing** to be banned altogether and for the Malaysian government to extend protected marine park status beyond Sipadan – one of the world's last strongholds of the scalloped hammerhead shark – to the rest of Semporna Archipelago. The plan is to work together with the local fishing community to ensure that they get alternative sources of income that don't involve shark fishing. Though **shark's fin soup** is a pricey delicacy on the menus of many Chinese restaurants, many consumers don't realize that when the shark is caught, the fin is chopped off straightaway and the shark, still alive, is tossed back into the sea to drown, because it cannot swim, or to bleed to death on the ocean floor, torn apart by other predators. Not only are all shark species now endangered, but since the shark is one of the biggest marine predators, its fin contains a toxic amount of mercury which is detrimental to your health.

6

numerous turtles, the reef at Kapalai Island is home to a great variety of colourful tropical fish, and there are numerous drift dives and wall dives to be done. Snorkellers go out with the diving boats; there's also great snorkelling right off the jetties in Mabul itself.

ACCOMMODATION AND EATING

There are no banks on the island; upmarket resorts accept cards but budget digs don't. All resorts have wi-fi and meals are usually included in the room price. You can buy snacks from shops in the two villages. Rates below are diver rates; non-diver rates are considerably higher.

Mabul Beach Resort ☎ 089 782372, ⦿ scuba-junkie .com. *Scuba Junkie*'s attractive launch pad offers lodging in the form of two rows of appealing a/c or fan-cooled chalets with porches amid sculpted grounds and beach access. The lounge/bar above the dining room is good for socializing over underwater bragging rights. Dorms RM135, doubles RM170

★ **Scuba Jeff** ☎ 019 585 5125, ⦿ scubajeffsipadan.com. Tucked right on the sea at the back of the rickety Filipino stilt village, this reggae-styled, no-frills guesthouse feels homely thanks to gregarious owner Jeff, the relaxed vibe and floor-hammocks slung over the water. Rooms, albeit simple, have rustic open toilets and small verandahs looking out over the sea that are great for chilling. Room price includes full board, dorms only include breakfast. They can organize diving in Sipadan and specialize in underwater photography trips. Dorms RM40, doubles per person RM90

Seaventures ☎ 088 251669, ⦿ seaventuresdive.com. A little way out to sea, this brightly painted, refurbished oil rig is for serious divers only. There are lifts that go right down into the sea, and diving below the rig is amazing. The accommodation is less so, with compact, dated rooms. Four days/three nights RM2880

Uncle Chang's ☎ 017 895 0002 (Mary Jane), ⦿ ucsipadan .com. This lively budget spot, located in the Filipino village, is always popular with backpackers. Rooms vary in type and size, from basic bamboo-tiled en-suite doubles that are

better value than the uninspiring dorms, to newer and more expensive a/c units. At RM750, their Sipadan three-dives package is attractive. Boat transfer RM100 for non-divers; Dorm RM75, doubles per person RM95

Pulau Sipadan

SIPADAN is a name spoken with reverence by divers worldwide, and with good cause. The waters around the tiny island, 36km south of Semporna in the Celebes Sea, which so impressed the venerable marine biologist Jacques Cousteau, teem with green turtles, sharks, barracuda, vast schools of tropical fish, and a huge diversity of coral.

Twenty metres from the shore, the bottom plunges to over 180m, delving to a vast wall of coral. Divers will find themselves face to face with moray eels, large schools of jacks, batfish, parrotfish, and white-tipped and grey reef sharks. The luckiest may catch a glimpse of a hammerhead or two; Sipadan is one of the last strongholds of the scalloped hammerhead and a large school lives around 60m deep.

The reef surrounds nearly ninety percent of the island and the ledges are a common resting point for turtles. In 2016 **Barracuda Point** was voted the world's best dive site by *ScubaTravel*, and is so-called for the vortex of chevron barracuda that lurk in these waters. **South Point** – on the opposite side of the island from Barracuda Point – attracts large pelagic (open sea) species, such as grey reef sharks and (very rarely) manta rays and whale sharks.

Snorkellers accompanying divers to the island can expect to see everything that

6

the divers see (barring hammerheads) without having to leave the surface; in fact, they are more likely than divers to swim among schools of giant parrotfish and jackfish as they tend to congregate in the shallows.

The island is a fully protected conservation zone; numbers are limited to 120 visitors per day, and the dive operators (see box, p.516) are responsible for sorting out who gets to go and when, according to their stipulated number of daily permits; some diving companies are allocated more permits than others. Make reservations several weeks in advance in low season and six months in advance for high season (July & August).

TAWAU

TAWAU, Sabah's southernmost town of any size, is a busy commercial centre and timber port, and you're only likely to stop here en route to or from Semporna (if flying in) or on your way to Kalimantan.

ARRIVAL AND DEPARTURE

By plane The airport (☏ 089 950777) is 31km outside of town and served by frequent flights from Kuala Lumpur and Kota Kinabalu with Malaysian Airlines and AirAsia, and from Sandakan and Tarakan with MASwings. It can be reached by a shuttle bus from the local bus station (6 daily, 45min; RM15) or taxi (RM50) or by transfer from Semporna (RM90).

Destinations Kota Kinabalu (7 daily; 50min); Kuala Lumpur (7 daily; 2hr 45min); Sandakan (2 daily; 40min); Tarakan, Indonesia (daily; 40min).

By bus Most long-distance buses and minibuses terminate at Sabindo Square bus station on the eastern end of Jln Dunlop (which runs parallel to the shore). Buses from KK arrive in front of the public library on Jln Chen Fook. The local bus station, serving the airport, is on Jln Stephen Tan (several blocks west of Sabindo).

Destinations Kota Kinabalu (2 daily at 7.45am & 8pm; 9hr); Lahad Datu (3 daily; 3hr); Sandakan (hourly 7am–2pm; 5hr); Semporna (approximately hourly; 2hr).

ACCOMMODATION AND EATING

The eating scene is the only thing that puts the "wow" in Tawau, with such Indonesian specialities as *soto makassar* (beef soup with cow blood, spices and offal), *gado-gado* (vegetable salad with peanut sauce) and *nasi kuning* (rice cooked with turmeric and coconut milk, served on a banana leaf).

Monaco Hotel Jln Haji Karim at Jln Bunga ☏ 089 769911. A bright-yellow lodging option that has little in common with the glitz of its namesake country, but the spacious, carpeted rooms have a/c, cable TV and private bathrooms. Good location, great value. Doubles RM85

Soon Yee Jln Stephen Tan ☏ 089 772447. This friendly cheapie is very welcoming despite its less-than-inviting exterior. Fan or a/c rooms, most of which have shared bathrooms. Doubles RM40

Taman Selera Jln Waterfront. A 200m stretch of open-air restaurants and hawker stalls, collectively known as Taman Selera, sets up daily two blocks below Jln Dunlop in the Sabindo Complex, with local specials competing with Chinese seafood emporiums. Daily 11am–10pm.

Yassin 1 Sabindo Square. This Indian restaurant serves a delicious range of curries (from RM6), kebabs and vegetable dishes, making it a great choice for vegetarians. Daily 11.30am–9pm.

FISHERMAN AT INLE LAKE

Myanmar (Burma)

HIGHLIGHTS

❶ **Yangon** Explore the city's colonial architecture and the country's most stunning temple. **See p.534**

❷ **Hpa-an** Ride through fields and villages to find Buddhist cave art. **See p.553**

❸ **Bagan** Watch sunset over a plain dotted with thousands of temples. **See p.557**

❹ **Inle Lake** Ride a boat around stilt villages, crafts workshops and traditional markets. **See p.570**

❺ **Mandalay** Magnificent pagodas and palaces surround Myanmar's cultural capital. **See p.574**

❻ **Kyaukme and Hsipaw** Trek through beautiful valleys and sleep in remote ethnic-minority villages. **See p.585**

HIGHLIGHTS ARE MARKED ON THE MAP ON P.521

ROUGH COSTS

Daily budget Basic $25/occasional treat $30–40
Drink Beer 75¢ (draught), $1.50 (bottle)
Food Chicken curry with rice $2.50
Budget hotel $20
Travel Yangon–Mandalay (691km): bus 8–10hr, $11–20; train 15hr, $2.50–10

FACT FILE

Population 53 million
Language Burmese (Myanmar), plus numerous minority languages
Religions Majority Buddhist, with Christian and Muslim minorities
Currency Kyat (K)
Capital Naypyitaw
International phone code ☏ + 95
Time zone GMT + 6hr 30min

Introduction

A beautiful and culturally rich country cursed for decades with a brutally oppressive regime, Myanmar's impressively swift transition to democratic rule has been one of the world's most inspiring stories of recent years. Tourist numbers had already snowballed following the removal of a fifteen-year tourism boycott led by the National League for Democracy (NLD) in 2012, while the NLD's landslide election victory in 2015 confirmed international perceptions that the people of Myanmar are finally achieving a measure of freedom. The country is now firmly on the itineraries of tour groups and independent travellers, while accelerating social, political and economic changes are beginning to reshape the nation. Much of Myanmar's time-warped character survives, however, making this a fascinating time to discover the country's glittering golden stupas, enigmatic ruined temples, picturesque mountain paths and extraordinarily diverse ethnic communities. Most memorable of all, though, are the encounters with people eager to introduce foreigners to their country after decades of isolation.

Although there are affordable flights from Bangkok, Singapore and elsewhere to **Mandalay**, and overland arrivals became possible in 2013 with the opening of four Thai border crossings, most people still start their visit in **Yangon**. This former capital makes a great introduction to the country, with evocative colonial-era buildings, some of the country's best restaurants and the stupendous Shwedagon Pagoda – the holiest Buddhist site in the country.

Highlights of the southeast include the precariously balanced Golden Rock at **Kyaiktiyo**, the limestone scenery around **Hpa-an** and the markets and colonial mansions of **Mawlamyine**, while towns such as **Dawei**, further south, have now opened up for adventurous visitors.

West of Yangon is a handful of beaches, with **Ngapali** the most highly regarded, but **Chaung Tha** and **Ngwe Saung** much more affordable. Most travellers instead hasten north to Mandalay, the hub for "Upper Burma" and the base for visiting the remains of several former capital cities, or to **Bagan** further west for its stunning temple-strewn plains. East of Mandalay is **Kalaw**, the starting point for some great walks. A trek from Kalaw is one way to reach the magnificent **Inle Lake**, with its stilt villages and famous leg-rowing fishermen. If time allows, a trip on the **Ayeyarwady River** around Katha and Bhamo offers a great chance to meet locals, as do the hiking routes around **Kyaukme** and **Hsipaw** in Shan State, which pass through ethnic minority villages.

WHEN TO GO

Myanmar has a tropical **climate**, with the southwest monsoon bringing rain from May to October. Roads can become impassable, particularly from July to September. The central plains, however, receive only a fraction of the rain seen on the coast and in the Ayeyarwady delta. From October onwards the rains subside; **the best time to visit** most of the country is from November to February, when temperatures are relatively manageable. From March to May, the country becomes very hot, particularly the dry zone of the central plains where Bagan and Mandalay often see temperatures in excess of 40°C.

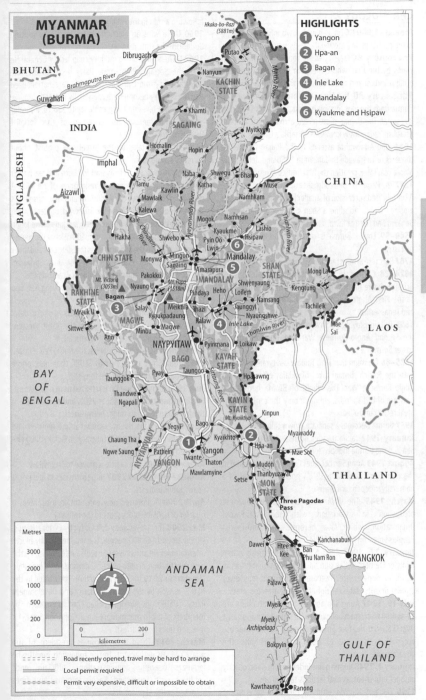

MYANMAR (BURMA)

HIGHLIGHTS

1 Yangon
2 Hpa-an
3 Bagan
4 Inle Lake
5 Mandalay
6 Kyaukme and Hsipaw

7

BHUTAN

Hkaka-bo-Razi (5881m)

Dibrugarh
Putao

Nanyun

INDIA

KACHIN STATE

Guwahati

Brahmaputra River

Khamti

SAGAING

Myitkyina

Homalin

Hopin

Imphal

Myitnge River

Naba Shwegu Bhamo

Tamu Kawlin Katha Muse

Mawlaik Namhkam

CHINA

Kalewa

Hakha Shwebo Mogok Namhsan Lashio

Chindwin River Kale Kyaukme Hsipaw

CHIN STATE Monywa Mingun Pyin Oo Lwin

Irrawaddy River Pakokku Sagaing **Mandalay** 6

Mt. Victoria (3053m) Amarapura

Nyaung U *Mt. Popa (1518m)* **MANDALAY** 5

RAKHINE STATE **Bagan** 3 Salay Pindaya Shwenyaung **SHAN STATE**

Mrauk U **MAGWE** Kyaukpadaung Heho Loilem Mong La

Sittwe Meiktila Thazi Namsang Kengtung

Ann Minbu Magwe Kalaw Taunggyi Tachileik

Nyaungshwe

Thanlwin River **Inle Lake** 4 Mae Sai

LAOS

NAYPYITAW Pyinmana Loikaw

BAY OF BENGAL

BAGO **KAYAH STATE**

Taunggok Pyay Taungoo Hpasawng

Thandwe

Ngapali *Sittaung River*

Gwa Bago **KAYIN STATE** Kinpun

Yegyi *Mt. Kyaiktiyo* Myawaddy

Chaung Tha Kyaikhto 2

Ngwe Saung Pathein 1 **Yangon** **Hpa-an** Mae Sot

YANGON Twante Mudon

Ayeyarwady Thaton Thanbyuzayat **THAILAND**

Mawlamyine

Setse **MON STATE**

Ye **Three Pagodas Pass**

ANDAMAN SEA

Kanchanaburi

Dawei Htee Kee Ban Phu Nam Ron **BANGKOK**

Palaw

TANINTHARYI

Myeik

Myeik Archipelago

Bokpyin **GULF OF THAILAND**

Kawthaung Ranong

Metres
3000
2000
1000
500
200
0

N

0   200
kilometres

- - - - - - - Road recently opened, travel may be hard to arrange
─────── Local permit required
ᴑᴑᴑᴑᴑᴑ Permit very expensive, difficult or impossible to obtain

CHRONOLOGY

Around 11,000 BC The earliest known inhabitants settle in the central plains, around the Ayeyarwady River.

2nd century BC City-states are founded in the central plains by the Pyu, who came from present-day Yunnan (China) and convert to Buddhism in the fourth century AD.

9th century AD The Mon, who originally migrated to Burma from the east, establish a kingdom with Thaton as its capital. The Bamar, more recent arrivals from Yunnan, establish Pagan (now known as Bagan).

1044 King Anawrahta ascends to the Pagan throne. He converts to Theravada Buddhism in 1056 and defeats the Mon a year later, creating the first unified Burmese state.

1287 The Pagan Empire collapses after a Mongol invasion. A complicated succession of smaller kingdoms arises in the empire's wake, including a Shan kingdom based first at Sagaing and then at Inwa.

1540–99 Lower Burma is united under the Toungoo dynasty.

1767 Burmese armies sack the Siamese capital Ayutthaya.

1824–26 Clashes in northeastern India, along with Britain's desire for new markets and raw materials, lead to the First Anglo-Burmese War. Burma cedes Rakhine and Tenasserim.

1852 Britain provokes a naval confrontation, leading to the Second Anglo-Burmese War and the annexing of Lower Burma.

1885–86 Claiming that King Thibaw is a tyrant in league with the French, Britain takes Mandalay after the Third Anglo-Burmese War. The whole of Burma becomes a province of British India, although only the central plains are directly controlled.

1937 Burma becomes a separate crown colony.

January 1942 Japan invades Burma, assisted by Aung San and the Burma Independence Army.

August 1943 Aung San becomes Commander-in-Chief of the Burma National Army (BNA) and War Minister of a nominally independent Burma.

March 1945 The BNA rises up against Japanese occupation in association with the Anti-Fascist Organization, which later becomes the Anti-Fascist People's Freedom League (AFPFL).

January 27, 1947 Aung San and the British prime minister Clement Attlee sign an agreement guaranteeing Burma's independence. A separate agreement later gives ethnic minority states the right to secede after ten years.

July 19, 1947 Aung San and six cabinet members are assassinated by men believed to be linked to nationalist rival U Saw. U Nu, foreign minister during the Japanese occupation, is asked to head the AFPFL and the government.

January 4, 1948 Burma gains independence and quickly plunges into chaos, as rival factions take up arms.

1958 General Ne Win forms a caretaker government following a split in the ruling AFPFL.

1960 U Nu wins an election victory, partly by making Buddhism the state religion.

1962 U Nu is ousted in a military coup led by General Ne Win. The Socialist Programme Party becomes the sole political party, most private businesses are nationalized and the country becomes internationally isolated.

1981 Ne Win gives up the presidency to San Yu, a former general, but remains the chairman of the Socialist Programme Party.

1987 Students take to the streets to protest about currency devaluation.

1988 Pro-democracy protests start in March and reach their peak in August, following the resignation of Ne Win. A general strike begins on August 8 and the army kills thousands of protestors. Aung San Suu Kyi, daughter of Aung San, makes a speech on August 26 at Yangon's Shwedagon Pagoda on behalf of the newly formed National League for Democracy (NLD). The military forms the State Law and Order Restoration Council (SLORC), which abandons socialism, declares martial law and arrests democracy campaigners.

1989 SLORC renames Burma as Myanmar. Aung San Suu Kyi is placed under house arrest.

1990 The NLD wins 82 percent of seats at the general election, but the government ignores the result. Western nations begin sanctions against Myanmar.

1991 Aung San Suu Kyi is awarded the Nobel Peace Prize.

1992 Than Shwe takes over as SLORC chairman, prime minister and head of the armed forces.

July 1995 Aung San Suu Kyi is released from house arrest. She is re-arrested in September 2000, and spends nine of the following ten years under house arrest.

August 2003 Khin Nyunt becomes prime minister and announces a "road map" to democracy. In October 2004 he is placed under house arrest.

November 2005 The capital is moved to Naypyitaw.

August–September 2007 Huge increases in fuel prices spark public protests.

April 2008 A proposed new constitution guarantees a quarter of parliamentary seats to the military.

May 2008 The Ayeyarwady delta is hit by Cyclone Nargis, killing around 140,000 people. The regime initially blocks international aid and presses on with a referendum on the new constitution, claiming that 92 percent voted in favour.

November 2010 The general election – boycotted by the NLD – is won by the Union Solidarity and Development Party (USDP), nominally civilian but dominated by members of the former military junta. Aung San Suu Kyi is released from house arrest.

March 2011 Thein Sein becomes president of the quasi-civilian parliament. In the following months he legalizes peaceful demonstrations, officially ends conflicts with Shan and Kachin groups, and frees selected political prisoners.

April 2012 The NLD wins 43 of 45 by-election seats, with Aung San Suu Kyi taking one. The US and EU begin to ease sanctions.

June 2012 Violence erupts in Rakhine State (see box, p.545), most of it carried out by Buddhists against Muslims of the Rohingya minority. Trouble flares again in October, and sporadically during 2013 and into 2014.

December 2013 A presidential spokesperson announces that all political prisoners have been freed under conditional amnesties. Activists welcome progress but deny that it is complete.

November 2015 NLD wins a landslide victory in the November general elections, although the military retain direct control of a quarter of all seats and several key ministries, while Aung San Suu Kyi herself is barred from becoming president.

ARRIVAL AND DEPARTURE

Most visitors arrive in Myanmar at either **Yangon** or **Mandalay** airports, as the international airport in the capital **Naypyitaw** is used by very few airlines (although there is a handful of flights from Bangkok). The cheapest way to fly to Myanmar from outside the region is usually via a major regional hub such as Bangkok or Singapore, but there are also flights to Yangon from Hanoi, Ho Chi Minh City, Kuala Lumpur, Dubai and Qatar. Airlines have been developing services to Mandalay, including from Kunming, Singapore, Chiang Mai and Bangkok.

The rules about overland border crossings have been in flux recently, so check on the latest information before relying on a particular crossing.

OVERLAND FROM THAILAND

There are five border crossings with Thailand: Ranong–Kawthaung (see p.806); Three Pagodas Pass (Sangkhlaburi–Payathonzu); Phu Nam Ron–Htee Kee (see p.556); Mae Sot–Myawaddy (see p.748); and Mae Sai–Tachileik (see p.770). Of these, Three Pagodas Pass is the least useful as it allows only a day-trip across the border. Thai visas are available at the border but Myanmar visas are not. Myanmar E-visas (see p.524) are valid for entry into Myanmar via all of the above crossing points except for the Three Pagodas Pass and the Phu Nam Ron–Htee Kee **border**.

The Mae Sai–Tachileik crossing offers a useful, if slightly convoluted, way of getting between northern Thailand and eastern Myanmar. Foreigners are allowed to travel overland by bus (5hr) from Tachileik to Kengtung, the next major town heading into Myanmar, but no further. From Kengtung, you'll have to take a flight on to another destination. There are also flights direct from Tachileik to various destinations across Myanmar.

7

THE ETHICS OF VISITING MYANMAR

The question of whether or not it was right to visit Myanmar was for many years an emotive issue. In 1995 Aung San Suu Kyi's National League for Democracy (NLD) called for an international **tourist boycott** of the country, arguing that foreign visitors were putting money directly into the pockets of the regime. Many foreigners respected this call to stay away. Others continued to visit, saying that with care it was possible to minimize the money given to the regime.

With the NLD now in power, the ethical dilemma has reduced significantly, if not entirely vanished. Despite the advent of democracy (or at least something reasonably close) in 2015, the former ruling military elite and their business cronies still control large swathes of the economy. Take a flight, withdraw money from an ATM or stay at an upmarket hotel and you'll be putting money, however indirectly, into their bank accounts.

It's not an ideal situation, obviously, although now not much different from that in, say, neighbouring Cambodia, Laos and Thailand. It's also worth remembering that crony companies employ thousands of ordinary Burmese – indeed, post-democracy some of these companies have been praised for being good employers, paying above-average wages.

As such, the best policy is to follow the usual ground rules of ethical tourism in Asia. Staying in local guesthouses, eating in local restaurants and hiring local guides helps keep your money in the communities you're visiting. Travelling to one or two more off-the-beaten-track destinations also brings money into parts of the country that have yet to enjoy the fruits of the tourism boom.

7

OVERLAND FROM CHINA

The **Myanmar–China** border crossing between Muse in northern Shan State and Ruili in China's Yunnan province is nominally open to foreigners, but you need to hold a permit and to be part of an officially sanctioned tour in order to either enter or leave Myanmar.

VISAS

All foreign nationals apart from citizens of a few Southeast Asian countries require a **visa** to visit Myanmar. Although a visa-on-arrival system does exist, it applies only to business visitors or conference guests who are able to provide documents such as letters of invitation.

You will therefore need to obtain a **tourist visa** before arriving. You can apply for a visa at your nearest Myanmar embassy or consulate, although it's generally easiest to apply online for an e-visa at ⓦevisa.moip.gov.mm. Your passport must be valid for at least six months from your proposed date of arrival. Tourist visas typically last for 28 days from the date of entry, which must be within three months of issue, cost $50 and are usually issued within a couple of days. Note that e-visas are not valid at the Htee Kee–Phu Nam Ron and Three Pagodas Pass border crossings with Thailand.

Tourist visas cannot be extended, but it is possible to overstay them by as much as 90 days (at a cost of $3 per day, payable on departure at the airport). The only possible hitch is that guesthouses occasionally express concern about expired visas.

A special **meditation visa** (see p.529), valid for three months, is also available for people staying at a recognized meditation centre.

GETTING AROUND

Many parts of Myanmar, particularly border areas and regions where the government is in conflict with ethnic minority groups – such as large parts of **Shan** and **Kachin states** – are completely closed to foreign visitors or require **permits**.

There's a list of such areas on the Ministry of Hotels & Tourism website (MTT; ⓦmyanmartourism.org), although it is rarely up to date and closures and requirements can change without warning.

Make sure to plan well in advance if you would like to visit a restricted area. Permits for many of these places take at least a month to arrange, with a private tour operator approved by MTT making the application on your behalf. You will be required to book onto an official tour or – at the bare minimum – hire a guide to make sure you don't misbehave.

BY PLANE

Given the long journey times overland, and the relatively low prices of flight tickets, travelling by plane can be an attractive choice. In a few cases it is the only option as overland routes are closed to foreigners. Many services fly on **circular routes**, stopping at several airports on the way, and it may therefore be easier to make a journey one way than the other way.

In addition to state-owned **Myanmar National Airways** (ⓦflymna.com), which has long had a poor reputation for the condition of its aircraft, though standards and services have improved somewhat in the past few years, an array of **private airlines** – among them Air KBZ (ⓦairkbz.com), Air Mandalay (ⓦairmandalay.com), Air Bagan (ⓦairbagan.com), Apex Airlines (ⓦapexairline.com), Asian Wings (ⓦasianwingsair.com), Golden Myanmar Airlines (ⓦgmairlines.com), Myanmar Airways International (ⓦmaiair.com) and Yangon Airways (ⓦyangonair.com) – run services on domestic routes and have offices in major towns and cities.

BY BUS

Buses are usually faster and cheaper than trains, and are generally the best way to get around on a budget. There are many different bus companies and most are privately owned. Taking buses can be quite tiring, however, since most long-distance services run through the night, stop roughly every three hours for toilet or food breaks and arrive before dawn.

Most long-distance buses are reasonably comfortable, but make sure you bring warm clothes as they tend to crank up the air-conditioning. On major routes, such as Yangon to Mandalay, it's possible to take a more modern and spacious "VIP" bus for a small additional fee. There are also local buses running segments of longer routes, such as Taungoo to Mandalay (rather than the full Yangon to Mandalay trip); these are usually in worse condition but are cheaper for shorter trips, as on long-distance buses you pay the fare for the full journey even if you get on or off partway through. You'll also find smaller, 32-seat buses that should be avoided if possible for long trips, as they tend to be jam-packed with luggage.

It's a good idea to book a day or two ahead for busy routes (such as Bagan to Nyaungshwe), routes where only a few buses run (such as Ngwe Saung to Yangon) or where you're joining a bus partway through its route (such as in Kalaw). Guesthouses can often help book tickets for a small fee, or you can buy them either from bus stations (which in some cases are outside of town) or from in-town bus company offices.

BY TRAIN

The **railway system** in Myanmar is antiquated, slow and generally uncomfortable. On most routes a bus is faster and more reliable, as it is not uncommon for trains to be delayed by several hours. All that said, there are reasons why you might want to take a train at least once during your trip. One is that on a few routes, such as from Mandalay up to Naba and Katha, road transport is closed to foreigners. Another is for the experience itself: many routes run through areas of great beauty, for example the Gokteik viaduct between Pyin Oo Lwin and Kyaukme, and there is the chance to interact with local people.

All express trains have upper- and ordinary-class carriages. The former have reservable reclining seats, although the mechanism is often broken, while the latter have hard seats and no reservations. Some trains also have first-class carriages, which fall somewhere between upper and ordinary. Sleeper carriages, when available, accommodate four passengers and come with blankets and linen.

Long-distance trains may have **restaurant cars**, and food vendors either come on board or carry out transactions

7

MYANMAR OR BURMA?

Controversy has long surrounded the use of the names Myanmar versus Burma, starting in 1989 when the military government renamed the country **Myanmar**. The military argued – albeit on rather shaky linguistic and historical grounds – that **Burma** was an inaccurate name foisted on the country during colonial times, deriving from Bamar (the name of the majority ethnic group), and contending that Myanmar was not only historically and culturally more accurate, but also more politically inclusive as well.

Aung San Suu Kyi's National League for Democracy (NLD) steadfastly opposed the change, however, arguing that the unelected military regime had no right to unilaterally rename the country. The UN recognized the new name, although some governments (including the UK and US) continued to refer to the country as Burma. As such, the use of either Myanmar or Burma was based less on reasoned historical, linguistic and cultural grounds than as a badge of support for either the military or their NLD adversaries.

Emotions surrounding the competing names have cooled significantly since the democratic elections of 2015. The US (for example) has now recognized the name change (Barack Obama diplomatically referred to the country as both Burma and Myanmar during his historic 2012 visit), while Aung San Suu Kyi has begun using the name Myanmar in public speeches.

As such, the whole Myanmar-versus-Burma debate is beginning to feel a bit like yesterday's news. In practice, virtually everyone you're likely to meet in the country will call it Myanmar – although it's fine to use the name Burma. The name Burma is also often used in a historical context when talking about the colonial period, and Burmese is used to describe the food and the language.

through the windows whenever the train stops. The bathrooms on-board are basic and often unclean.

Try to reserve a day or so in advance, or more for sleepers.

BY SHARED TAXI AND VAN

Shared taxis and **shared vans** are available on some routes, and can be arranged either through accommodation or at shared-taxi stands. These vehicles charge separately for each seat, typically around fifty percent more than a seat on an air-conditioned bus. They will usually drop you wherever you like, however, which saves on transfer costs in towns where the bus station is inconveniently located.

CAR, BIKE AND MOTORCYCLE RENTAL

Renting a car is not a realistic option in Myanmar as there is too much red tape involved, but it's easy to arrange a **car and driver** (from around $40 per day) through your accommodation or travel agencies.

Bicycles are available in many places for around K3000 per day. In some parts of the country you can also rent a **motorcycle**, typically for K8000–10,000 a day plus fuel. Before renting a motorbike, check that your travel insurance covers you for riding one.

There are numerous hazards for cyclists and motorcyclists: traffic can be very heavy in the cities, while in rural areas the roads are often in poor condition. Adding to these dangers is the fact that most cars are right-hand drive even though people drive on the right, meaning that cars have large blind spots.

LOCAL TRANSPORT

Local transport in Myanmar is usually some mix of public buses, taxis, pick-ups (adapted pick-up trucks with seating in the covered back portion), motorcycle taxis (where the passenger rides pillion) and cycle rickshaws. **Public buses** run only in the largest cities, including Yangon and Mandalay, and are very cheap. It can be hard to work out the routes, but if you aren't in a rush, then riding on the buses is certainly an experience. The same can be said of **pick-ups**, which cover set routes and pick

up and drop people off on the way; they usually depart when full – which may include passengers riding on the roof. If you want the most comfortable seats, in the cabin, then you can pay a little extra.

Taxis are available in large towns and cities, and range from 1970s Toyotas to occasional new left-hand-drive Chinese imports. There are no meters, but drivers tend not to overcharge as outrageously as in many other Southeast Asian countries. Expect to pay around K1500–3000 for a decent trip, such as from a bus station on the edge of town to a hotel.

Tricycles are still in use in many towns, although they are being edged out by **motorcycle taxis**, which are much faster and normally around the same price (around K1000–1500 for a short ride).

Most of these forms of transport can also be hired for a day including a **driver**, which can be arranged direct, through accommodation or via travel agents; you'll need to bargain to get a good price. Motorcycle taxis may not work out much more expensive than renting a self-drive motorcycle.

In small towns, **horse carts** are used as a key form of transportation, and they also ferry tourists around in a number of places, notably Bagan, Inwa and Pyin Oo Lwin.

ACCOMMODATION

Accommodation is likely to be your major expense, with the average cost of a room significantly higher than in most other parts of Southeast Asia, often even for decidedly lacklustre lodgings – money that would get you a deluxe double in Laos or Cambodia might not even secure you a private bathroom in Myanmar. The good news is that prices are gradually falling (albeit very slowly) as a result of numerous new guesthouse and hotel openings, while a significant number of new **hostels** offering dorm accommodation have also emerged in major tourist centres.

The bottom line, however, is that it's difficult to get a double room in a guesthouse for less than $15, or $20 in Yangon and Mandalay. Most places now at least provide air-conditioning and hot water, and virtually everywhere includes breakfast in their rates, although in cheaper rooms you'll often be sharing a bathroom, and budget rooms (in Yangon particularly) are often little more than windowless boxes. If you're looking for hotel facilities then the prices quickly rise to more than $30. Single rates (where available) are usually around two-thirds to three-quarters the price of a double.

An increasing supply of rooms nationwide has somewhat eased the pressure on accommodation, although it's still wise to **book ahead**, particularly in peak season (November to February).

Power cuts are commonplace in Myanmar, even in Yangon and Mandalay, and many places will have a generator to ensure that fans and air-conditioners work through the night. Avoid leaving gadgets plugged in during a power cut, as there may be a surge when the supply is restored.

FOOD AND DRINK

While people in Myanmar take great pride in their cuisine, if you ask someone for a **restaurant** recommendation then there's a good chance that they will suggest a place serving Chinese food. This is partly because they worry that foreign stomachs can't cope with Burmese food, but also because most people rarely eat at restaurants, so when they do they eat Chinese as a treat. Most towns will have at least a couple of Chinese restaurants, typically with large menus covering unadventurous basics such as sweet-and-sour chicken. Dishes start at around K1500 (vegetables) or K2500 (meat). **Indian restaurants** are also popular, particularly in Yangon, which had a very large Indian population during the British colonial era. In tourist hotspots you'll also find restaurants serving Thai and fairly poor quality Italian dishes.

A visit to a **teahouse** is an unmissable experience: they are hugely popular places to meet friends, family or business associates over tea and affordable snacks, which, depending on the owners, might be Burmese noodles, Indian samosas or Chinese steamed buns. Some teahouses

open for breakfast, while others stay open late into the night.

BURMESE FOOD

As in other Southeast Asian countries, in **Burmese food** it's considered important to balance sour, spicy, bitter and salty flavours; this is generally done across a series of dishes rather than within a single dish. A mild curry, for example, might be accompanied by bitter leaves, dried chilli and a salty condiment such as fish paste.

The typical local **breakfast** is noodle soup, such as the national dish *mohingar* (catfish soup with rice vermicelli, onions, lemongrass, garlic, chilli and lime, with some cooks adding things such as boiled eggs, courgette fritters and fried bean crackers). Alternatives include *oùn-nó k'auq-s'wèh* (coconut chicken soup with noodles, raw onions, coriander and chilli) and *pèh byouq* (fried, boiled beans) served with sticky rice or naan bread. All of these dishes are served in teahouses or available to take away from markets.

Noodles also feature strongly at lunchtime: many locals will have a small bowl at a street café or teahouse. Various Shan noodle dishes are popular, including *mì-she* (rice noodles in a meat sauce accompanied by pickle). Other common dishes include various *ăthouq*, which translates to "salad" but rarely includes vegetables; they are cold dishes, usually with noodles, raw onions, garam flour, chilli and coriander, served with a watery vegetable or bone soup. One variety worth trying is *nàn-gyì thouq*, made with thick rice noodles that look like spaghetti.

Lunchtime is also when you should try **Burmese curries** if you're worried about hygiene, since they are usually cooked in the morning then left in pots all day. Local people, however, would typically have curry in the evening at home. A meat, fish or prawn curry will be accompanied by rice (*t'ămìn*), a watery soup and fried vegetables. A great deal of oil is added to Burmese curries, supposedly to keep bacteria out, but, like locals, you can skim the oil off. At the best restaurants, the meal will also include a selection of up to a dozen small side dishes, plus fresh vegetables and herbs

7

with a dip (such as *ngăpí-ye*, a watery fish sauce). Green tea will usually be thrown in, and sometimes you'll get a "dessert" such as tasty *lăp'eq* (fermented tea leaves with fried garlic, peanuts, toasted sesame and dried shrimp). You may also get *t'ănyeq* (jaggery, unrefined cane sugar).

There are plenty of **regional variations** to discover as you travel: the food of Rakhine State, for example, is influenced by its proximity to Bangladesh, so curries are spicier. They also tend to include fish paste as an ingredient, rather than on the side as a condiment.

Vegetarians should find it reasonably easy to find suitable food throughout the country, since some Buddhists are restrained in their consumption of meat.

DRINKS

Tap water isn't safe to drink in Myanmar; bottled water is available throughout the country for around K300. In many restaurants, free **green tea** (*ye-nwè-gyàn*) is left in jugs on tables and is safe to drink. In teahouses, black tea is usually drunk with plenty of milk and sugar, while coffee is almost always instant, other than in expensive Western-style cafés.

Although there are few places resembling Western bars or pubs outside of Yangon and Mandalay, most towns will have a couple of **beer stations** which look like simple restaurants but with beer adverts on display and a predominantly male clientele. These places usually serve draught beer (around K700 for a glass) as well as bottles (from K1700 for 640ml), with the former usually restricted to the most popular brew, Myanmar Beer (produced by a government joint venture) and sometimes its rival Dagon. Both beers are also available in bottles, as are Mandalay Beer and several Thai and Singaporean beers, including Tiger, Singha and ABC Stout.

Mid-range and upmarket restaurants will often have a list of very expensive imported **wines**. There are a couple of vineyards making wine in Shan State, and it's better than you might expect: look out for Red Mountain (see p.571) and Aythaya. Fruit wines are produced around Pyin Oo Lwin, while local spirits include *t'àn-ye* (toddy or palm wine).

CULTURE AND ETIQUETTE

As in other Southeast Asian countries, **clothing** in Myanmar is usually modest. In some ethnic minority villages it's still the norm to wear traditional dress, and even in cities many men and women wear a skirt-like garment called a *longyi*. These days, though, it is also common for locals to wear Western-style clothes. People will be too polite to say anything, but they may be offended by the sight of tourists wearing revealing clothes. This would include shorts cut above the knee, and – particularly for women – tops that are tight or show the shoulders. It's especially important to **dress conservatively** when visiting temples; some travellers carry a *longyi* for such situations.

Most women and girls, as well as some men and boys, use *thănăk'à* (a paste made from ground bark) on their faces; traditionally thought to improve the skin and act as a sunblock, it is often applied as a circle or stripe on each cheek.

Avoid touching another person's head, as it is considered the most sacred part of the body; feet are unclean, and so when sitting don't point them at anyone or towards images of the Buddha. Remove your **shoes** before entering a Buddhist site or a home. Always use your right hand when shaking hands or passing something to someone, as the left hand is traditionally used for toilet ablutions; however, locals do use their left hand to "support" their right arm when shaking hands.

Most people in the country are **Buddhist**, although there are significant Muslim and Christian minorities. Buddhist men are expected to experience life in a monastery at least once, usually as a child and certainly before they get married. It may only be for a week, although poorer children in particular may become novices and be educated at the monastery. Most Buddhists also believe in *nats*, spirits rooted in older animist traditions, which take an interest in the actions of humans and may need to be propitiated.

Considering the social conservatism of Myanmar's society, it is interesting to note that while in the past most *nat kădaws* (spirit mediums) were women, today most are gay men and many are either trans-gendered or transvestites. A *nat-pwèh* (spirit festival) held, for example, at the start of a new business enterprise is an occasion on which people have licence to sing, cheer and show emotions which would otherwise be repressed in public.

Homosexuality is technically illegal in Myanmar – for tourists as well as locals – and punishable by fines or imprisonment. This is, however, rarely enforced in practice and there is a discreet gay scene in Yangon, but little elsewhere. See ⊚utopia-asia.com/tipsburm.htm for information and advice.

SPORTS AND ACTIVITIES

Outdoor pursuits and **adventure sports** are not yet well developed in Myanmar. With the notable exception of trekking, most activities tend to be arranged through travel agents and are prohibitively expensive.

TREKKING

Opportunities for **treks** are limited by two main factors. One is that many of the most appealing areas are in the mountainous border regions, which tend to be closed to tourists or require expensive permits. The other is that foreigners are generally expected to stay in licensed accommodation for every night of their visit. This means that camping is illegal, as is staying in local houses, in most parts of the country.

As a result, **day-hikes** are the limit in many places. There are exceptions, however, with the most notable all being in Shan State: around Kalaw (see p.567), Nyaungshwe (see p.571), Pindaya (see p.569), Kyaukme (see p.585) and Hsipaw (see p.588). In these areas it's possible to stay in either homes or monasteries, by prior arrangement through a tour agency, and therefore do **multi-day treks**. A guide is either obligatory or strongly recommended for most hiking, but the trails around Hsipaw are sometimes undertaken without one.

BIKING AND MOTORBIKING

Both **mountain biking** and **motorbiking tours** are available in Myanmar, through specialist agencies. There are many advantages to getting around in this way, not least the chance to interact with people in villages and rural areas; disadvantages include the poor state of many roads, plus the requirement to sleep in licensed accommodation. Some cyclists have used camping as a back-up, but it is, strictly speaking, illegal and should not be relied upon. If you cycle off the beaten path, you may be questioned about your plans and even accompanied by immigration or police officers.

SCUBA DIVING

Some affordable dive trips are available from Ngwe Saung (see p.543) and Ngapali (see p.544), though the water clarity and coral aren't all that great. The best diving in Burmese waters is around the Myeik Islands (see box, p.556), reached on a live-aboard out of Thailand, but be prepared to pay some serious money for the pleasure.

MEDITATION

With a strong Buddhist tradition, Myanmar is a good place to learn to **meditate**. There's even a special **meditation visa** available if you have a letter of support from a meditation centre; it lasts for three months and is extendable. Some centres will only take foreigners who commit to staying for several weeks, although shorter options include ten-day courses in Vipassana meditation at the Dhamma Joti Vipassana Centre (☎01 549290, ⊚joti .dhamma.org; donation) in Yangon on Nga Htat Gyi Pagoda Rd, and the nearby Mahasi Meditation Centre at 16 Sasana Yeiktha Rd (☎01 545918, ⊜mahasi .meditationcenter@gmail.com; donation). The Kyunpin Meditation Centre (☎09 421 018 765) in Sagaing, near Mandalay, also has good reports from foreign visitors.

COMMUNICATIONS

Internet cafés (typically charging K400–500/hr) are becoming increasingly thin on the ground, even in larger cities, although **wi-fi** is now pretty much

7

universally available in all hotels, guesthouses and some restaurants (albeit connections can still be unreliable and frustratingly slow).

Many guesthouses will let you make **local calls** from reception (check the price first), or may make the call for you if you're trying to book accommodation for later in your trip. There are also local call stands – often just a table with a telephone – in the streets and in some shops. The cheapest and easiest way to call internationally is online via Skype or similar.

Mobile phones are increasingly big business in Myanmar, with just about everyone in the country seeming to have a couple of Samsung Galaxies or Huaweis stashed away in their *longyis*. Recent relaxations to telecoms regulations mean that foreigners are now allowed to buy Burmese SIM cards. There are three operators, Ooredoo, Telenor and the government's MPT, with SIM cards (and top-up cards) widely available for as little as K1500, although coverage can still be erratic in rural areas. Mobile phone numbers start with 09.

The **postal service** in Myanmar is not known for its efficiency, but many post offices have an EMS (Express Mail Service) counter offering faster and more reliable international delivery.

MYANMAR ONLINE

Ⓦ **burmalibrary.org** A huge collection of text from books and articles about Myanmar, plus relevant links.

Ⓦ **go-myanmar.com** Far and away the best online resource for travellers to Myanmar, crammed with practical information, detailed accommodation and eating listings and other information.

Ⓦ **irrawaddy.org** One of the most reliable sources of up-to-the-minute news on the country.

Ⓦ **myanmartourism.org** This official tourism website has hotel and tour company telephone numbers, plus a list of places that are off-limits or require permits (although this may be out of date).

CRIME AND SAFETY

Very few foreign tourists are victims of **crime** in Myanmar, possibly because the penalties for stealing are severe. There are, however, occasional reports of opportunistic theft such as of cameras left on ferries while the owners wander the decks.

Although the government is engaged in conflict with **ethnic resistance groups** in several parts of the country, if there's any danger in an area then it will be closed to foreigners both for their protection and to keep the violence hidden away from international attention.

In the unlikely event that you fall victim to a crime or theft you'll need to report it to the **police**. There's an extremely patchy tourist police service in Yangon (headquartered at 110 Pansodan Rd in downtown Yangon; ☎ 01 378479) and at a few other major visitor destinations, but it really pays to take along a native Burmese-speaker if at all possible (see if someone from your guesthouse or hotel can accompany you) to explain and expedite matters.

MEDICAL CARE AND EMERGENCIES

The quality of **health care** in Myanmar is generally poor. Routine advice and treatment are available in Yangon and Mandalay, but elsewhere the hospitals often lack basic supplies, and some suffer under corrupt administrations. Avoid surgery and dental work, as hygiene standards cannot be relied upon; if you are seriously ill then contact your embassy for advice, and expect international-quality care to be expensive (and possibly to require payment up front). As always, it is important to travel with **insurance** covering medical care, including emergency evacuation.

Minor injuries and ailments can be dealt with by pharmacists, particularly in major tourist areas where they are more likely to speak English. Pharmacists offer many things over the counter without prescription, although there are serious issues with fake and out-of-date medication.

INFORMATION AND MAPS

The best sources of **information**, besides other travellers and some online resources, are generally the staff at guesthouses. Staff at the country's **state tourist offices**, operated by Myanmar Travels & Tours (MTT), are often helpful for general information, but limited in terms of the services (booking tickets, reserving hotels and so on) which they can provide. The best **map** of the country is the *Reise Know How* 1:1,500,000, printed on unrippable waterproof paper.

MONEY AND BANKS

Myanmar's **currency** is the kyat (pronounced "chet"), usually abbreviated as K, Ks or MMK. Notes are available in denominations of K1, K5, K10, K20, K50, K100, K200, K500, K1000, K5000 and K10,000, although the lowest value you are likely to encounter is the K100 note. At the time of writing the exchange rate was roughly K1360 to $1, K1700 to £1, and K1450 to €1; high-value notes (particularly $100 bills) attract the best exchange rates, so bring those to change. Money can be most easily changed in banks, although there are also a fair number of licensed money-changers offering roughly similar rates. Note also that kyat cannot be bought or sold overseas, so you should change any leftover currency before leaving the country.

Prices are also sometimes quoted in **US dollars** (particularly for more expensive items and services), although in practice it's almost always possible to pay in kyat (although check that the exchange rate being used to convert from dollars to kyat is fair). Equally, some places (including hotels, guesthouses and tourist-oriented shops) will accept payment in dollars for items or services quoted in kyat. Again, check the exchange rate being used and bring some low-denomination dollar notes for these situations.

ATMs accepting foreign-issued Visa and MasterCards are now widespread, and there's likely to be at least one such ATM in any medium-sized town, although you'll pay a commission fee (usually K5000) to withdraw money on top of any charges levied by your home bank or credit-card company. The two biggest ATM networks are those operated by CB Bank and KBZ Bank. As such it's now possible to travel to Myanmar without carrying anything with you but plastic, although it's still a good idea to carry a decent stash of dollars with you just to be safe.

OPENING HOURS AND HOLIDAYS

Standard **business hours** are Monday to Friday 9am to 5pm, with shops staying open a little later (and normally opening on Saturdays). Post office opening times vary but are generally Monday to Friday 9.30am to 4.30pm, with some opening on Saturday mornings. Banks typically open Monday to Friday 9am to 3pm, although some close earlier and currency exchange counters may not open until 11am. Some major pagodas are open 24 hours a day, while others tend to open from early morning until late in the evening. Restaurants are typically open daily from around 9am to 9pm (or slightly later for places aimed at tourists), while many teahouses open much earlier for breakfast but close at around 5/6pm.

THE IMPORTANCE OF PERFECT NOTES

It is essential that any **currency** which you intend to change within Myanmar is pristine, and that US dollars were issued in 2006 or later. Notes that are creased, torn or marked in any way – however minor – may not be accepted by banks, hotels or any other outlets; if they do take them then it is likely to be at a reduced rate. Reject US dollar change unless it is in perfect condition.

PUBLIC HOLIDAYS

Several holidays are based upon the lunar calendar and therefore change date each year.
January 4 Independence Day
February 12 Union Day
March 2 Peasants' Day
March/April Tabaung full moon
March 27 Armed Forces Day

7

BURMESE

Burmese, or Myanmar as it is now officially called, is the country's official language and also the native language of the country's Bamar majority. Burmese is a tonal language that is difficult for Westerners to learn, but local people tend to appreciate even a modest effort.

PRONUNCIATION

There is no universally approved way to Romanize the Burmese language. The system used here is based on the *Burmese By Ear* audio course by John Okell, available as a free download from Ⓦ www.soas.ac.uk/bbe. In the text we give place names and some very common words in their most widely recognized forms. Items on specific restaurant menus are given as printed.

There are five tones which change the meaning of a word: the low tone (syllables with no marker), the plain high tone (spoken with a relaxed throat, marked **à**), the creaky high tone (spoken with a tightened throat, marked **á**), the stopped syllable (high pitch followed by a glottal stop, marked **aq**) and the weak syllable (unstressed, marked **ă**). Aspirated consonants have a short puff of breath expelled after the consonant is pronounced and before the vowel begins; those marked as "whispered" begin with a sound similar to the start of the English "hmm".

ă	as in "about"	**hng**	same as "ng" but whispered
a	as in "car"		
a in aq and an	as in "cat"	**hny**	same as "ny" but aspirated
ai in aiq and ain	as in "site"		
au in auq and aun	"ou" as in "lounge"	**hw**	same as "w" but aspirated
aw	as in "saw"		
e	as in French "café"	**k**	as in French "corps"
e in eh	as in "sell"	**k'**	as in "core" (aspirated)
e in eq	as in "set"		
ei in eiq and ein	"a" as in "late"	**ky**	as in "cello"
i	as in "ravine"	**l**	as in "law"
i in iq and in	as in "sit"	**m**	as in "more"
o	"eau" as in French "peau"	**n**	as in "nor"
		ng	as in "long"
ou in ouq and oun	"o" as in "tone"	**ny**	"gn" as in Italian "gnocchi"
u	as in "Susan"		
u in uq and un	"oo" as in "foot"	**p**	as in French "port"
b	as in "bore"	**p'**	as in "pore" (aspirated)
ch	same as "ky" but aspirated	**q**	glottal stop
		r	as in "raw"
d	as in "door"	**s**	as in "soar"
dh	"th" as in "this"	**s'**	same as "s" but aspirated
g	as in "gore"		
gy	as in "judge"	**sh**	as in "shore"
h	as in "hot"	**t**	as in French "tort"
hl	same as "l" but whispered	**t'**	as in "tore" (aspirated)
hm	same as "m" but whispered	**th**	as in "thaw"
		w	as in "war"
hn	same as "n" but whispered	**y**	as in "your"
		z	as in "zone"

GREETINGS AND BASIC PHRASES

There is no word for a simple "hello" – rather, greetings are nonverbal or based on the situation (e.g. "Where have you been?"). Locals greet foreigners with the very formal *min-gălà-ba*.

Goodbye	*thwà-meh-naw?*	Thank you	*kyè-zù tin-ba-deh*
Excuse me (to get past)	*nèh-nèh-lauq*	Yes	*houq-kéh*
		No	*hín-ìn*
Sorry	*sàw-ri-naw*	Do you speak English?	*Ìn-găleiq sagà*
Please	*kyè-zù pyú-bì*		*pyàw-daq-thălà?*

I don't understand	*nà mǎleh-ba-bù*	Bicycle	*seq-beìn*
Can you help me?	*k'ǎnǎ-lauq louq-pè-ba*	Bank	*ban*
		Post office	*sa-daiq*
Hospital	*s'è-youn*	Passport	*paq-sǎpó*
Police station	*yèh-t'a-ná*	Hotel	*ho-teh*
Where is the…?	*…beh-hma-lèh?*	Restaurant	*sà-thauq-s'ain*
…toilet?	*ein dha…*	Open/closed	*pwín-deh/peiq-teh*
Ticket	*leq-hmaq*	Left/right	*beh-beq/nya-beq*
Airport	*le-zeiq*	Do you have any rooms?	*ǎk'àn à-là?*
Boat (ferry)	*thìn-bàw*		
Bus	*baq-sǎkà*	How much is it?	*beh-lauq kyá-dhǎlèh?*
Bus station	*kà-geiq*		
Train station	*bu-da*	Cheap/expensive	*zè cho-deh/zè kyì-deh*
Taxi	*teq-si*		
Car	*kà*	Air-conditioner	*èh-kun*
		Fan (electric)	*pan-ka*

NUMBERS

0	*thoun-nyá*	10	*tǎs'eh*
1	*tiq*	11, 12, 13, etc	*s'éh-tiq, s'éh-hniq, s'éh-thoùn…*
2	*hniq*		
3	*thoùn*	20, 30, 40, etc	*hnǎs'eh, thoùn-zeh, lè-zeh*
4	*lè*		
5	*ngà*	100, 200, 300, etc	*tǎya, hnǎya, thoùn-ya*
6	*chauq*	1000, 2000, etc	*tǎt'aun, hnǎt'aun…*
7	*k'un(-hniq)*	10,000	*tǎthaùn*
8	*shiq*	100,000	*tǎthèin*
9	*kò*	1,000,000	*tǎthàn*

FOOD AND DRINK

Cheers!	*Chì-yà!*	*ngǎpí*	fish paste
Delicious	*kaùn-laiq-ta*	*ngǎyouq*	chilli
Vegetarian (food)	*theq-thaq-luq*	*paun-moún*	bread
I don't eat meat or fish	*thà-gyì ngà-gyì shaun-deh*	*nan-byà*	Indian naan bread
		pèh-byà	tofu
		s'à	salt
Rice and noodles		*s'ì*	oil
kya-zan	vermicelli	*t'àw-baq*	butter
k'auq-s'wèh	noodles	*thǎgyà*	sugar
nàn-gyì	thick noodles	*thiq-thì*	fruit
t'ǎmìn	rice		
t'ǎmìn-gyaw	fried rice	**Drinks**	
		ǎè	soft drink
Meat, fish and basics		*bi-ya*	beer
ǎthà	meat	*kaw-p'i*	coffee (with milk and sugar)
ngǎshín	eel		
pyi-ji-ngà	squid	*kaw-p'i nwà-nó-néh*	coffee with milk
bèh-ú	duck's egg	*lǎp'eq-ye*	tea
ceq-ú	hen's egg	*p'yaw-ye*	fruit juice
ǎmèh-dhà	beef	*t'àn-ye*	toddy
bǎzun	prawns	*thauq-ye*	drinking water
bèh-dhà	duck	*ye-nwè-gyàn*	green tea
kyeq-thà	chicken	*ye-thán*	purified water
hìn-dhì-hìn-yweq	vegetables	*ye-thán-bù*	bottle of purified water
ngà	fish		
s'eiq-thà	mutton	*nó mǎt'éh-néh*	don't put milk in
weq-thà	pork	*thǎgyà mǎt'éh-néh*	don't put sugar in
chís	cheese	*ye-gèh mǎt'éh-néh*	don't put ice in
hìn	curry		

7

April 13–16 Thingyan (water festival)
April 17 New Year
May 1 Labour Day
May Kasong full moon
July 19 Martyrs' Day
July Waso full moon (beginning of Buddhist "Lent")
October Thadingyut full moon (end of Buddhist "Lent")
November Tazaungmone full moon
Nov 13 National Day
December/January Kayin New Year
December 25 Christmas

FESTIVALS

Most **festivals** in Myanmar are based on the lunar calendar; check the official Ministry of Hotels and Tourism site for a more extensive list (ⓦmyanmartourism .org/index.php/destination/festivals)

Shwedagon Festival Feb/March. The country's biggest *paya pwèh* (temple festival) takes place at Shwedagon Pagoda in Yangon.

Thingyan April 13–16. The water festival is the most popular in the calendar, as crowds take to the streets, celebrating New Year by chucking huge quantities of water all over one another. Good fun, although most businesses close, and it's difficult to go out of doors without being drenched.

Balloon Festival Nov. Daytime parades at this three-day event in Taunggyi, east of Inle Lake, include impressive animal-shaped hot-air balloons. At night, balloons are released with huge gondolas full of fireworks strapped underneath them, with predictably explosive results.

Shan New Year Nov/Dec. Keep an eye open for the different ethnic groups' new year celebrations around Nov and Dec. This one rotates between different Shan towns, and includes live bands, traditional dancing and – on Shan New Year's Eve itself – fireworks.

Ananda Pahto festival Dec/Jan. The *paya pwèh* at Ananda Pahto is the biggest in Bagan, running for the fortnight leading up to the full moon of Pyatho. For the last three days, hundreds of monks chant scriptures.

Yangon

Though no longer the capital, **YANGON** remains Myanmar's commercial heart and also the core of its spiritual life, thanks to the glorious **Shwedagon Pagoda**, while its colonial-era buildings give the downtown area a historical atmosphere that new capital Naypyitaw – and Mandalay for that matter – will never possess. Whether you get lost in the city's animated **markets**, seek out beer and barbecue in **Chinatown**, visit Chinese or Hindu **temples** or take an eye-opening ride on a commuter train, Yangon provides an engaging introduction to the country.

There is a long history of settlement in this part of the delta, but the Mon village of Dagon only grew in size and importance – and was renamed Yangon – after the area was conquered by King Alaungpaya in 1755. In 1852 it was seriously damaged by the invading British, who called the city Rangoon and rebuilt it to their own plans; in 1885 the British made Rangoon their capital.

The city was occupied by the Japanese during World War II, but bomb damage was relatively limited. The decades of international isolation that followed meant that most of the city's heritage buildings were neglected, creating the memorably time-warped colonial streetscapes you see today. Local and international developers have begun to move in following the easing of international sanctions, and the degree to which the city can preserve its extraordinary but largely derelict array of historic buildings in the face of modern economic development remains to be seen.

WHAT TO SEE AND DO

Most travellers on a budget spend most of their time downtown, in the grid of streets north of the Yangon River that has **Sule Pagoda** at its heart. The main reason to head out of the downtown area is **Shwedagon Pagoda**, although there are a number of other attractions further north, including scenic **Kandawgyi Lake** and the enormous marble Buddha at **Kyauk Taw Gyi**.

Sule Pagoda and Mahabandoola Garden

When the British drew up a plan for the city's streets, they put **Sule Pagoda** (daily 5am–9pm; K3000) at the heart; today its golden central stupa, 45m tall and forming a busy roundabout, is still the most striking landmark in downtown Yangon. The inside of the pagoda is surprisingly peaceful, and popular with locals making offerings at the various shrines.

Just southeast of Sule Paya is **Mahabandoola Garden** (daily 6am–6pm; free), centred on the city's soaring Independence Monument and offering an enjoyable respite from downtown's packed pavements.

The colonial core

The streets around Sule Pagoda contain many of Yangon's most interesting colonial-era buildings, including several abandoned by the government when it

moved to Naypyitaw. On the northeast of the roundabout is the imposing **City Hall**, based on a British design but with ornamentation inspired by Bagan's temples. Just east of this is the former **Immigration Department** (now a branch of the AYA Bank), built as a department store and recently restored to its former glory. Further east is the vast **Secretariat**, former seat of the government and the place where General Aung San was assassinated in 1947. Closed to the public since the military coup of 1962 and now semi-derelict, it is due to be restored and redeveloped, although what as remains unclear.

Back towards Sule Paya, bookstall-lined **Pansodan Street** is a treasure-trove of

7

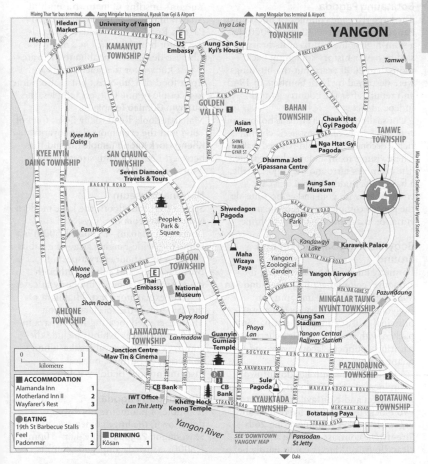

ACCOMMODATION
Alamanda Inn	1
Motherland Inn II	2
Wayfarer's Rest	3

EATING
19th St Barbecue Stalls	3
Feel	1
Padonmar	2

DRINKING
| Kōsan | 1 |

7

colonial buildings including the still-functioning **High Court**, constructed between 1905 and 1911 in a style typical of the British Empire in India. The southern end of Pansodan Street was once home to the most prestigious businesses in Yangon including several in the old **Sofaer's Building**, which was built by two Baghdadi Jewish brothers and housed legal and financial offices, as well as shops selling imported luxury goods.

At the corner with Strand Road are the **Port Authority** and **Yangon Division Court** buildings. A left turn leads to the **Strand Hotel**, built in 1901 and – post-restoration – once again one of the city's best hotels.

Botataung Pagoda

The large riverside complex of **Botataung Pagoda** (daily 5am–9.30pm; K6000) has a 40m-high golden stupa at its heart. It is said to have a history stretching back more than 2000 years, but the buildings were destroyed by RAF bombers in 1943 and rebuilt after the country gained independence.

Unusually, the rebuilt stupa is hollow and contains a series of atmospheric chambers richly decorated with gold-covered walls, where visitors roam and monks meditate. The chambers surround the pagoda's relic, a hair of the Buddha stored in a case embellished with gold and gems. Outside the pagoda complex, opposite the main entrance, is a popular *nat* (spirit) shrine.

Bogyoke Aung San Market and around

Formerly known as Scott Market, the attractive, colonial-era **Bogyoke Aung San Market** (Tues–Sun 10am–5pm) on Bogyoke Aung San Road is the city's principal tourist shopping destination, packed with shops selling jewellery, paintings, puppets, lacquerware and vast quantities of jade.

A block to the south lies downtown's main local market, **Theingyi Zei** (between 25th Street and Konzaydan Road), its two blocks divided by a lively fruit and vegetable market running along **26th Street**. The contrast with the squeaky-clean Bogyoke Market could hardly be

greater, with hundreds of ramshackle stalls packed tightly into every available centimetre of space and crowds of shoppers squeezing their way through the narrow alleyways between.

Just south of Theingyi Zei on 26th Street is the exquisite little **Musmeah Yeshua Synagogue** (Mon–Sat 9.30am–2.30pm; free) of 1896, with a beautifully preserved interior complete with gold-railed *bimah* (the platform from which the Torah is read) flanked by two *menorah* lamps and high arches supporting a pair of wooden balconies – for women – on either side.

Chinatown

On the western side of downtown, Yangon's bustling **Chinatown** (south of Anawrahta Road between Shwedagon Pagoda Road and Lanmadaw Street) is the major home for the city's many Chinese-descended inhabitants. The area is best known for the raucous bars and street food of 19th Street but is also home to a couple of fine Chinese temples, the **Guanyin Gumiao Temple** on Mahabandoola Road (daily 24hr; free) of 1864 and the even more flamboyant **Kheng Hock Keong Temple** (Strand Rd, between 17th and 18th streets; daily 24hr; free) of 1903.

National Museum

Spread over four floors, the large modern **National Museum** on Pyay Road (Tues–Sun 9.30am–4.30pm; K5000) is home to a wide-ranging array of exhibits covering just about every aspect of Burmese crafts and culture, although many exhibits languish in poorly lit cases with no explanatory text. Highlight of the museum is the spectacular Lion Throne, created for King Bodawpaya in 1816, while other exhibits include the country's priceless royal regalia, a fine collection of Burmese musical instruments and Buddhas galore.

Shwedagon Pagoda

A couple of kilometres northwest of downtown, the huge golden stupa of the **Shwedagon Pagoda** (daily 4am–10pm; K8000; ⓦ shwedagonpagoda.com) is

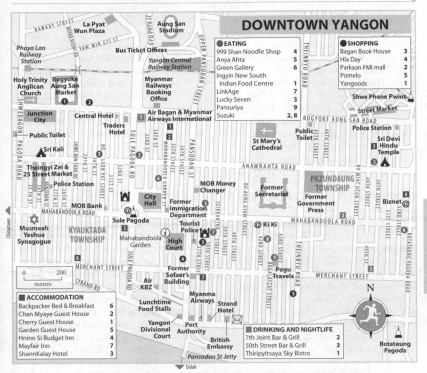

DOWNTOWN YANGON

● EATING

999 Shan Noodle Shop	4
Anya Ahta	5
Green Gallery	6
Ingyin New South Indian Food Centre	1
LinkAge	7
Lucky Seven	3
Pansuriya	5
Suzuki	2, 8

● SHOPPING

Bagan Book House	3
Hla Day	4
Parkson FMI mall	2
Pomelo	5
Yangoods	1

■ ACCOMMODATION

Backpacker Bed & Breakfast	6
Chan Myaye Guest House	2
Cherry Guest House	1
Garden Guest House	5
Hninn Si Budget Inn	4
Mayfair Inn	7
ShannKalay Hotel	3

■ DRINKING AND NIGHTLIFE

7th Joint Bar & Grill	2
50th Street Bar & Grill	3
Thiripyitsaya Sky Bistro	1

visible throughout much of the city. The vibrant heart of Buddhist Myanmar, the shrine was first built (according to legend) during the lifetime of the Buddha to house eight of his hairs, which were brought back by two merchants, although the current structure was rebuilt most recently following an earthquake in 1775.

The shrine can be approached along any of the four covered stairways which climb up to the pagoda from the cardinal directions (or, more easily but less memorably, via one of three lifts). The main stupa may dominate the fourteen-acre platform at the top, but there's a whole host of smaller shrines, stupas and Buddha images surrounding it. For many locals a visit to the pagoda is a social event as well as a religious one, and it's particularly atmospheric in the evenings.

Four greatly revered Buddha images sit in shrines guarding the base of the pagoda at the cardinal points. Arranged around the base of the stupa is a series of eight shrines, each representing a day of the week

(Wednesday is divided into two). Locals visit the shrine relevant to the day on which they were born, offering flowers, lighting a candle and washing the presiding Buddha image with jugs of water.

Look out too for the pagoda's two enormous **bells**, the mighty Tharyarwady Bell, on the northern side, weighing a cool 42 tonnes, and the only slightly smaller Singu Min Bell on the west side – British attempts to make off with the latter in 1825 foundered when the ship carrying it promptly sank in the Yangon River.

Kandawgyi and Inya lakes

Boasting great views of Shwedagon Pagoda to the west, the boardwalk through parkland around pretty **Kandawgyi Lake** is a good place for a walk, particularly towards sunset, when views of the Shwedagon are at their best. Impossible to miss on the east side of the lake is the striking **Karaweik Palace**, a chintzy pagoda-style hall set on a pair of barges pointing out into the water, each

7

with the head of an enormous *karaweik* (a mythical bird) on its prow.

Further north is the larger and less scenic **Inya Lake**, created by the British in 1883. Running along the lake's southern shore, University Avenue is the location of the house in which Aung San Suu Kyi spent some fifteen years under house arrest, although you can't see anything apart from the high perimeter wall, festooned with National League for Democracy flags and a picture of Aung San Suu Kyi's father, General Aung San.

Chauk Htat Gyi and Nga Htat Gyi pagodas

Even in a land of big Buddhas, the giant reclining figure at the **Chauk Htat Gyi Pagoda** on Shwegondaing Road (daily 6am–8pm; free; K3000 by taxi from downtown) is an unquestionable show-stopper: almost 66m long, with a 7.3m-long face, 2.7m worth of nose, and 50cm-high eyes. The figure was begun in 1959 but not completed until 1974, replacing an earlier giant seated Buddha on the same site which was demolished in 1957.

The nearby **Nga Htat Gyi Pagoda** (daily 6am–8pm; free) is home to another of Yangon's supersized Buddhas: a 9m-high seated figure covered in super-intricate, hyperactive decoration complete with riotously decorated golden robes plus a jewel-encrusted crown, the whole thing set against a magnificent wooden backdrop.

Kyauk Taw Gyi

The huge seated Buddha at **Kyauk Taw Gyi** pagoda (daily 6am–6pm; free), around 14km northwest of the centre, is one of Yangon's most impressive religious sites. The statue was carved from a single piece of marble near Mandalay in 1999, then brought to Yangon by boat and train. You can reach it by train yourself – it's close to Insein station on the Circle Line (see opposite) or by taxi (around K6000 from downtown).

Dalah

The easiest way to get a taste of small-town life in the Ayeyarwady delta is to take a ten-minute ferry ride (daily

5.30am–9pm; $2 each way) from the Pansodan Street jetty on Strand Road, straight across the river to **Dalah** township and offering memorable views of Yangon across the water. Motorbike drivers wait on the other side and offer tours into the surrounding countryside, including to the interesting **Baungdawgyoke Pagoda** "snake temple", home to numerous huge Burmese pythons, although they're a cut-throat bunch and you'll need to bargain hard (count on around K6000 for a couple of hours).

ARRIVAL AND DEPARTURE

By plane The airport is around 15km north of downtown Yangon, and has separate domestic and international terminals which are a 5min walk apart. Taxis into town cost K8000 from the taxi counter in the international terminal; independent drivers offer cheaper seats in shared vehicles. The taxi counter at the domestic terminal charges K9000. Crowded buses to Sule Paya (1hr; K300), in downtown Yangon, run during the day but don't stop very close to the airport: turn right out of the international terminal, walk for around 20min to the junction, take a right and then cross the road to catch a south-bound bus. Buses to the airport leave from one block south of Sule Paya.

Destinations Heho (6–7 daily, plus additional services via Mandalay and/or Nyaung U; 45min); Mandalay (around 10 daily; 1hr); Nyaung U (10 daily; 1hr 20min); Sittwe (2–3 daily; 1hr 20min, plus additional services via Thandwe); Thandwe (3–4 daily; 50min).

By bus Yangon has two major bus terminals: Hlaing Thar Yar in the northwest (for the delta region) and Aung Mingalar in the north (for most other destinations). Both are around 20km out of the city centre and should take about 45min–1hr to reach by taxi (K6000–8000) – both stations are huge, so make sure your driver drops you at the appropriate bus company office or you may struggle to find your vehicle. Local buses run from Sule Paya to both Aung Mingalar (at least 1hr; K300) and Hlaing Thar Yar (at least 1hr 30min; K300). Allow plenty of time however you travel, as the traffic can be terrible. Most bus companies have offices on Kun Chan Rd, near the Aung San Stadium, although everything is signed in Burmese and hardly any English is spoken. It's much easier to book bus tickets either through your hotel or through one of the numerous travel agencies which dot the city.

Destinations Bagan (10 daily; 10hr); Bago (8 daily; 2hr); Chaung Tha (2 daily; 6hr); Hpa-an (6 daily; 8hr); Hsipaw (daily; 16hr); Kalaw (6 daily; 10hr); Kinpun for Kyaiktiyo (15 daily; 5hr); Mandalay (18 daily; 8–10hr); Mawlamyine (10 daily; 8hr); Naypyitaw (10 daily; 6hr); Ngwe Saung (2 daily; 6hr); Pyay (6 daily; 6hr); Pathein (4 daily; 4hr);

Shwenyaung for Inle Lake (6 daily; 12hr); Taungoo (4 daily; 5hr); Thandwe for Ngapali Beach (2 daily; 16–18hr).

By train Yangon Central Railway Station is just north of the main grid of downtown streets, most easily reached from Sule Pagoda Rd. There's an information office at the station (daily 9.30am–4pm) – turn right as you go in through the main entrance. Frustratingly, advance tickets can't be bought at the station itself but must be booked at the antiquated (and easily missed) Myanmar Railways Booking Office on Bogyoke Aung San Rd (daily 7am–3pm).

Destinations Bagan (1 daily; 17hr); Bago (3 daily; 2hr); Dawei (1 daily; 23hr); Kyaikhto for Kyaiktiyo (3 daily; 4hr 30min); Mandalay (3 daily; 15hr); Mawlamyine (3 daily; 9hr); Naypyitaw (3 daily; 10hr); Pyay (1 daily; 8hr 30min); Taungoo (3 daily; 6hr 30min).

INFORMATION

Tourist information The official MTT office is centrally located at 118 Mahabandoola Garden St (daily 8.30am–5.30pm; ☎01 252859).

Travel agencies Recommended agencies include: Good News Travels (☎09 595 116 256, ⓦmyanmargood newstravel.com); Myanmar Delight (☎01 651833, ⓦmyanmardelight.com); Myanmar Shalom, 70 31st St (☎01 252814, ⓦmyanmarshalom.com); Pegu Travels, 90 Bogalayzay St (☎09 51 371 937, ⓦpegutravels .com); Santa Maria Travels & Tours (☎01 537191, ⓦmyanmartravels.net); Seven Diamond Travels & Tours (☎01 500712, ⓦsevendiamondtravels.com).

GETTING AROUND

Motorbikes are banned from the city centre.

By bus The bus network covers much of the city, and is very cheap to use, but it is difficult to use if you don't speak Burmese.

By taxi Taxis are plentiful and very good value. Expect to pay K1500 for a short journey, K3000 upwards to travel between different parts of town and at least K6000 to reach the airport (more like K8000 if you book a taxi through your hotel).

By train The Circle Line (around 8 daily in each direction 6am–6pm; 3hr to complete the circuit; K200) carries commuters between central Yangon and the suburbs, stopping at 39 stations as it completes the loop and offering a great way to see daily life, both on and off the train. The easiest place to get on is platforms 6 and 7 at Yangon Central Railway Station.

ACCOMMODATION

Finding an inexpensive bed in Yangon isn't easy, although there's a growing number of good hostels offering affordable dorm accommodation. Budget rooms tend to be small, often bordering on the microscopic, while you'll often have to pay extra for the bonus of a window. Book ahead to stand a chance of finding anything affordable.

Backpacker Bed & Breakfast 2nd floor, 38 Shwe Bon Thar Rd ☎09 263 728 438, ⓦbackpackerbnbyangon.com; map p.537. Smart new hostel offering deluxe dorm accommodation at super-competitive rates. The four-bed a/c dorms come with cosy curtained wooden bunks, each with their own reading light and socket, plus in-dorm bathroom and lockers. Also has a decent selection of private doubles (although most are windowless), plus larger and smarter superior rooms with window for a modest $5 surcharge. Dorms $12, doubles $28

Chan Myaye Guest House 256 Mahabandoola Garden St ☎01 382022, ⓦchanmyaeguesthouse.com; map p.537. Excellent guesthouse right in the thick of the downtown action with professional service and competitive rates. Cheaper rooms are poky, with bunk beds, shared bathroom and no windows; the slightly more expensive en-suite rooms ($30) are relatively spacious, and some even have windows. There are also two state-of-the-art dorms ($10) with individually curtained beds, all with individual a/c units, reading lights and sockets. Staying here will keep you fit too, since rooms are spread between the fourth and eighth floors – and there's no lift. Dorms $10, doubles $25

Cherry Guesthouse 278/300 Mahabandoola Garden St ☎01 255946 or ☎09 534 0623, ⓔcherry.gesthouse @gmail.com; map p.537. One of Yangon's better budget options, on the fourth and fifth floors of a characteristically tall and skinny downtown building with the bonus of an (oversubscribed) lift. Rooms are all en suite, although they're as small as you'd expect in such a central location, while cheaper ones lack windows. Good single rates ($18) too. Doubles $27

Garden Guest House 441–445 Mahabandoola Rd ☎01 253779; map p.537. You'll not get more central than this long-running budget stalwart, right next to Sule Pagoda. Rooms resemble wooden boxes and are shabby but bearable; all are en suite (although with cold water only in cheaper rooms) and rates are as low as almost anywhere,

7

★ TREAT YOURSELF

Alamanda Inn 60b Shwe Taung Gyar Rd ☎01 534513, ⓦhotel-alamanda.com; map p.535. This place is a real find, occupying a colonial-style villa set amid lush gardens in the exclusive Golden Valley area – all very peaceful, and feeling a long way from the hubbub of the city centre. The spacious, old-fashioned rooms are nicely kitted out with colonial-style furniture and the occasional artwork – a little worn around the edges but full of character and charm. There's also a good restaurant in the garden out the front. A taxi from here to Sule Pagoda costs around K3000. Doubles $90

7

although the general air of dinginess and uninterested service doesn't exactly warm the soul. Doubles $18

Hninn Si Budget Inn 213–15 Botataung Pagoda Rd ⊕01 299941, ⊚hninnsibudgetinn.com; map p.537. Neat, clean and quiet little guesthouse (entrance upstairs on the first floor next to some seriously impressive plumbing and crazy wiring). Rooms (all sharing a clean and spacious bathroom) are boxy and mostly windowless, but good value at the price. Doubles $22

Mayfair Inn 57 38th St ⊕01 253454, ⊚mayfair-inn @myanmar.com.mm or ⊚maytinmg@gmail.com; map p.537. Long-running guesthouse in a quiet side street in the heart of Yangon's finest colonial district. Scores highly for its homey atmosphere, peaceful location and spacious – if rather sterile – tiled rooms (all en suite; hot water $5 extra), although service can be haphazard and there's no breakfast. Doubles $25

★**Motherland Inn II** 433 Lower Pazundaung Rd ⊕01 291343, ⊚myanmarmotherlandinn.com; map p.535. One of downtown Yangon's best budget options – if you don't mind the inconvenient location a 20min walk (or short taxi ride) from the centre. Rooms (cheaper ones with fan only and shared bathroom) are unusually large, bright and peaceful, and there's a well-equipped internet café, free airport pick-up for international arrivals (plus free morning and afternoon airport bus shuttles), and an excellent range of travel services. Rates include an excellent breakfast, either Western or Burmese. Doubles $25

ShannKalay Hostel 3rd floor, 166 49th St ⊕01 397627, ⊚shannkalay.com; map p.537. Easy-to-miss little hostel on the quiet eastern side of downtown offering some of the cheapest beds in the city and one of Yangon's prettiest reception areas, stuffed with Burmese artefacts and old photos. Rooms (with shared bathroom only) are simple windowless boxes – basic, but fine at the price (and with single rates from just $15). Only sardines, however, will feel entirely comfortable in the cramped four-bed dorm. Breakfast included. Dorms $9, doubles $20

Wayfarer's Rest 640 Mahabandoola Rd ⊕09 7799 22075, ⊚wayfarerrest@gmail.com; map p.535. In the heart of Chinatown, this top-notch new hostel is one of the city's best budget bargains at present, with a lovely eight-bed dorm featuring curtained teakwood bunks and quality mattresses, plus individual lights and sockets. Includes breakfast. Dorms $12

EATING

One of the most popular places for an outdoor meal is the lively collection of barbecue stalls on 19th St in Chinatown (map p.535), which set up daily from around 5–9pm. Sticks start at around K150 for veg, K300 for meat or K2500 for a whole fish. There's street food available throughout the downtown area, including Indian stalls around Shwe Bon Tha Street.

★**999 Shan Noodle Shop** 130B 34th St ⊕01 389363; map p.537. Shoebox café serving up superb Shan noodles (sticky, flat-rice and wheat) at rock-bottom prices (mains K1500–3000) in a range of soups, salads and stir-fries. Gets packed at lunchtime, so expect to share a table. No alcohol. Daily 6am–7pm.

Anya Ahta 37th St; map p.537 Innovative remake of a traditional beer station, looking like halfway between a drinking den and an art gallery and attracting a mainly local crowd plus occasional tourists thanks to its cheap draught beer and short but excellent selection of traditional Burmese snacks and mains (K1000–3000). Food includes assorted salads (tea-leaf, paratha, pickled green mango) alongside traditional pork sausages, *seik tha lon kyaw* (goat meat and flour-fried meatballs) and a tasty "lad's chicken curry". Daily 8am–10pm.

★**Feel** 124 Pyidaungzu Yeiktha St ⊕09 7320 8132; map p.535. Plenty of Yangonites vote this the city's best place to sample Burmese food, as proven by the queues which form most lunchtimes and evenings outside its doors – arrive early or expect to wait (and don't come at all if you're looking for a quiet romantic meal). The restaurant occupies an attractive bamboo-lined, jungle hut-style construction, with food laid out in a big buffet spread at the back – the helpful, English-speaking staff will explain what's on offer, typically including all sorts of Burmese veg and meat curries. Expect to pay around K6000 for one dish plus vegetables, soup and rice. The main restaurant closes at 8pm, although food is served at the streetside tables outside until 11pm. Daily 6am–8pm.

Green Gallery 52nd St ⊕09 313 15131, ⊚facebook .com/yangongreengallery; map p.537. This rustic little shoebox-sized café is the unlikely home of some of Yangon's finest Thai food, with a short but sweet menu of excellent and authentic salads, soups and flavour-filled curries (mains K4000–6000). Seating is at a premium, so arrive early or expect to wait. Mon–Sat noon–3pm & 6–9pm.

Ingyin New South Indian Food Centre Cnr Bo Sun Pat & Anawratha; map p.537. Lively little place dishing up good, cheap South Indian food. Choose from veg, chicken, mutton, prawn, fish and crab curries served with puri or chapati. They also do a good dosa, although you might wish to steer clear of the "Mutton Fighting Ball", which is just a fancy name for goats' testicles. Mains K1500–3000 (or K5000 for prawn and crab dishes) – and they'll keep on topping up your plate until you can eat no more. Daily 5am–10pm.

LinkAge 1st floor, 141 Seikkantha St ⊕09 451 933 034; map p.537. Brave the treacherously steep stairs to reach this cosy little restaurant, serving up good authentic Burmese food including lots of Myanmar-style fish and seafood curries, salads and soups – the pickled mango with roasted peanut salad is a treat. Most mains K4000–8000. Tues–Sun 11am–2pm & 6–10pm.

★ **Lucky Seven** 130 49 St ☎01 292382; map p.537. One of the few remaining traditional teashops left in downtown Yangon, packed most hours of the day with a lively local crowd enjoying tea, noodles and buns. The big picture menu is full of good things (mains K1000–1500) – an excellent breakfast *mohinga*, noodles and dumplings galore, Indian-style curries with puris or parathas, spare ribs and tasty samosa salads. Seating is either inside or on the pretty little outdoor terrace smothered in plants. Daily 6am–5.30pm.

Padonmar 105/107 Kha Yae Bin Rd ☎01 538895, ⓦ myanmar-restaurantpadonmar.com; map p.535. Enjoyably time-warped restaurant, set in an atmospheric old colonial house and serving a huge selection of Myanmar and Thai food (mains K6000–1000) including traditional dishes like banana bud salad, pork curry with pickled mangoes and so on, plus Myanmar set menus (around K6000). Handy for the National Museum, but can get busy with tour parties. Daily 11am–11pm.

★ **Pansuriya** 102 Bogalayzay St ☎09 778 949 170; map p.537. In a lovely airy whitewashed colonial building with walls covered in artworks and photos, *Pansuriya* has bags of old-world atmosphere backed up by some of the best Burmese food in downtown including a great range of salads, soups and noodle dishes (K3000) plus great Myanmar curries served thali-style on huge white plates. Daily 8am–10pm.

Suzuki 182 Sule Pagoda Rd ☎01 392686; map p.537. A popular backpacker hangout, this long, skinny café squeezed in along Sule Pagoda Rd serves up a good selection of authentic Thai and Chinese food (mains K2500–4000) at bargain prices, with cheapish beer thrown in for good measure. There's a second branch on Bogalayzay St (same hours and menu). Daily 8am–10pm.

DRINKING AND NIGHTLIFE

Yangon's nightlife is getting livelier, but it still has a long way to go before it's anything close to that of somewhere like Phnom Penh, let alone Bangkok. Check out the Myanmore website (ⓦ myanmore.com) for events listings. If you're just looking for a drink then there are plenty of simple "beer stations" around, with those in Chinatown (roughly 18th to 24th streets, and particularly 19th St) typically staying open latest. With a few exceptions, nightclubs in Yangon tend to involve little dancing; many have nightly "fashion shows" (in which fully clothed young women walk up and down on a stage) or karaoke.

7th Joint Bar & Grill Mahabandoola Rd near the corner of 47th St (around the side of *YKKO* restaurant) ☎09 260 600 552; map p.537. Lively reggae bar-cum-restaurant with a party atmosphere most evenings and regular live music. Drinks are reasonably priced (a big bottle of Myanmar beer costs K4000) and there's also a decent menu of grilled meats (including the inevitable jerk chicken) and burgers. Daily 5pm–1am.

50th Street Bar & Grill 50th St ☎01 397060, ⓦ 50thstreetyangon.com; map p.537. This a/c US-style bar is a bit of a surprise coming in from the dusty streets of Botataung district, offering the chance to sit back with a beer (happy hour 6–8pm) and shoot some pool, and there are also regular events including live music on Friday nights. They also serve up a decent, if rather expensive, range of pizzas and other Western-style mains (from around K10,000). Mon–Fri 9am–midnight.

Kôsan 108 19th St; map p.535. Although it serves food, most people come here for a drink before or after eating at one of the 19th St barbecue restaurants. It serves up draught beer and inexpensive mojitos, caiparinhas and other cocktails (from K900). Daily 4pm–midnight.

Thiripyitsaya Sky Bistro 20th floor, Sakura Tower, corner of Sule Paya Rd and Bogyoke Aung San Rd ☎01 255277; map p.537. Worth it for the views of Shwedagon Pagoda and the downtown area. Prices are predictably steep, with a minimum spend of K7000 per person after 7pm, although the 5–7pm happy hour keep prices sensible, with two draught beers for K3000 and discounted cocktails. Daily 10am–10pm.

SHOPPING

The big new Junction City development on Bogyoke Aung San Rd (ⓦ junctioncityyangon.com; not quite open at the time of writing) is likely to provide a home for numerous upscale retail outlets.

Bagan Book House 100 37th St ☎01 377277; map p.537. Stocks the best collection of books about Myanmar. Daily 9am–7pm.

Hla Day 81 Pansodan St ⓦ hladaymyanmar.org; map p.537. Supports local artists and artesans, selling beautiful traditional textiles alongside colourful souvenirs made from recycled materials. Daily 10am–9.30pm.

Parkson FMI mall Bogyoke Aung San Rd; map p.537. Home to a flashy department store and (in the basement) an upmarket supermarket selling imported foodstuffs. Daily 9am–9pm.

Pomelo Above *Monsoon* restaurant, 85–87 Thein Byu Rd ⓦ pomeloformyanmar.org; map p.537. Sells fair-trade products with an emphasis on helping disadvantaged producers to improve their social and economic positions. Daily 9.30am–9.30pm.

Yangoods By the entrance to Bogyoke Aung San Market ⓦ yangoods.com; map p.537. Stocking a quirky selection of colourful bric-a-brac featuring designs from old Myanmar-related prints and posters. Tues–Sun 9am–5pm.

DIRECTORY

Banks and exchange The exchange booths at the international terminal of the airport generally offer good rates, particularly the ones before you exit through customs. Many banks change dollars and euros, and there are also moneychangers around Bogyoke Aung San Market. There are also now numerous ATMs all over the city accepting foreign-issued Visa and MasterCards.

Cinema The Nay Pyi Taw Cinema and the Shae Saung Cinema, either side of *East* hotel on Sule Pagoda Rd, are both modern and central. Tickets cost K1000–4000.

Embassies Thailand, 94 Pyay Rd (Mon–Fri 9am–noon & 1–5pm); ☏ 01 222784; ⓦ thaiembassy.org/yangon/en); UK, 80 Strand Rd (Mon–Thurs 8am–4.30pm, Fri 8am–1pm; ☏ 01 370865, ⓦ gov.uk/government/world/organisations/british-embassy-rangoon); US, 110 University Ave (Mon–Fri 8am–4.30pm; ☏ 01 536509, ⓦ mm.usembassy.gov).

Internet There are several internet cafés in the shops around the base of Sule Pagoda in the heart of downtown. Other places include Ki Ki Network Game on Mahabandoola Rd between 41st and 42nd streets (daily 9am–8pm; K400/hr), and BizNet on Botataung Pagoda Rd (next door to the *Hninn Si* guesthouse; 8am–midnight; K400/hr).

Post office Strand Rd (Mon–Fri 9.30am–4.30pm).

The delta region and western Myanmar

The fertile **delta region** south and west of Yangon has long been of great importance, thanks to its abundant agricultural production and strategic location for trading. It made news headlines around the world in 2008 after being devastated by Cyclone Nargis, when the military regime blocked foreign aid, claiming that they had the situation under control. This worsened an already appalling situation and the official final death toll was 138,000 people, although in reality it was probably much higher.

Most people rush straight through the region's lush green rice fields and sleepy towns on their way to the beaches at **Chaung Tha** and **Ngwe Saung**, though an overnight pause in laidback, work-a-day **Pathein** is recommended.

North of the delta region is the long and thin stretch of Rakhine State, which is separated from the plains to the east by mountains. The most touted destination here is **Ngapali Beach**, but it's a long, hard

journey by bus and rising hotel prices have squeezed out anyone on a strict budget. Of more interest to most budget travellers is temple-dotted **Mrauk U**, capital of Rakhine when it was a separate kingdom.

PATHEIN

The largest settlement in the delta, breezy **PATHEIN** is one of Myanmar's more enjoyable provincial capitals, and although most foreign visitors pass straight through on their way to Chaung Tha and Ngwe Saung beaches, it's well worth an overnight stop for its colourful array of temples, including the landmark **Shwemokhtaw Pagoda**. Inside, the courtyard is one of Myanmar's more architecturally harmonious temple complexes, and while the stupa itself isn't particularly huge, it compensates with its elegantly slender outline.

ARRIVAL AND DEPARTURE

By bus There's no central bus station in Pathein – different services arrive and depart in various places in town. Bus ticket offices are on Pagoda Rd.

Destinations Chaung Tha (6 daily; 2hr); Ngwe Saung (3 daily; 2hr); Yangon (4 daily; 4hr).

ACCOMMODATION

Accommodation in Pathein is generally good value, although few of the cheapies include breakfast in their rates.

Paradise Hotel 14 Zay Chaung Rd ☏ 042 25055. This family-run hotel is set in a compound just back from the road, which makes it quieter than most places, and the small, dark blue rooms are very good value. Even the cheapest rooms have attached bathrooms – but fans. Pricier rooms have a/c. Doubles $15

EATING

There's a decent night market on Strand Rd, although it's rather crammed in alongside the road and not the most relaxing place to eat.

G7 Bakery & Café 28 Min Gyi Rd ☏ 042 25467. A dash of big-city class in little old Pathein, this calm and cool café serves a very passable array of good cakes, including cheesecake, milkshakes, proper coffee, savoury snacks and light meals of the fried-rice variety. Cakes around K800. Daily 9am–9.30pm.

DIRECTORY

Banks The CB and AGD banks have ATMs; there's also a moneychanger at the AGD Bank.

CHAUNG THA BEACH

The sand isn't the whitest you'll see, but **CHAUNG THA BEACH** isn't a bad place to hang out. It gets pretty busy at the weekend and during holidays, but joining the locals at play is a cultural experience in itself. Masses of local tourists bob about in the shallows in huge inner tubes and colourful rubber rings while teenagers kick footballs around the beach and food vendors prowl the foreshore selling grilled crabs and prawns on skewers.

ARRIVAL AND DEPARTURE

The closest large city, and transport hub, is Pathein.
By bus The bus station is towards the southern end of the beach. Tickets should be reserved at least a day in advance, particularly in peak season. There are minibuses to Pathein (5 daily; 2hr 30min) and buses to Yangon (2 daily; 6hr).
By boat A day-trip to Ngwe Saung costs K100,000–150,000 (depending on boat type) for up to five people.
By motorbike The motorbike trip between Chaung Tha and Ngwe Saung beaches (2hr; K20,000) is one of the highlights of a visit to this part of the coast.

INFORMATION AND TOURS

Tourist information The official tourist information office is opposite the bus station. Much more helpful is the private information office run by Mr George (daily 7am–10pm; ☎09 4973 4562, ✉mrgeorgeprince292 @gmail.com), on the main road close to *Shwe Hin Tha* hotel. Services include bus ticket sales, bike (K3000/day) and motorbike (K10,000/day) rental, and snorkelling equipment rental (K3000/day). Also arranges tours and activities including mangrove, river and fishing-village boat trips (K30,000 for up to 5 people); all-day sea-fishing trips (K150,000 for up to 5 people); and cooking classes (K15,000/person).

ACCOMMODATION

Hill Garden Hotel Outside the village ☎09 4957 6072. Peaceful retreat from the beachside hubbub, set amid fields a 10min bike ride from the village. The rustic wooden cabanas come with either shared bathroom (cold water only; $40) or en-suite hot water bathrooms ($55). The more expensive rooms also have a/c. There's a small, and for Chaung Tha quiet, beach nearby. Doubles $15
Shwe Ya Minn Main Rd (opposite the *Belle Resort*) ☎042 42126. Rooms (a/c K10,000 extra) are small and simple but not too hot and perfectly comfortable, with decent mosquito nets, and there's also a good breakfast included in the price. The professional staff can arrange a wide range of boat trips and excursions. Doubles $25

EATING

Shwe Ya Minn *Shwe Ya Minn* hotel, Main Rd ☎042 42126. Chaung Tha's best-looking restaurant, with smooth service, cheap beer and well-prepared versions of all the usual seafood dishes plus one of the village's biggest selections of meat and veg curries, noodles and so on (mains K4000–5000). Daily 7am–11pm.

NGWE SAUNG

The 15km-long stretch of pale, fine sand at **NGWE SAUNG** is more appealing than the beach at Chaung Tha, not least because its length means that it is much less densely developed. There are still plenty of resorts but the beach is cleaner and more laidback; it also has clearer water. The flipside is that Ngwe Saung attracts a lot more foreigners and wealthy locals, meaning that prices are higher and that it's arguably a less interesting experience.

There's a small village with a main street almost entirely devoted to fulfilling tourist needs. If you fancy a wander, then **Lover's Island**, just offshore around 500m south of the two hotels listed, is an easy destination at low tide.

ARRIVAL AND DEPARTURE

The main transport hub is the city of Pathein.
By boat A day-trip to Ngwe Saung from Chaung Tha costs K100,000–150,000 (depending on boat type) for up to five people.
By bus Some buses pick up and drop off at hotels, others stop on the edge of the village.
Destinations Pathein (4 daily; 2hr); Yangon (2 daily; 6hr 30min).
By motorbike The motorbike ride to Chaung Tha (2hr; K20,000 one-way) is an attraction in its own right.

GETTING AROUND AND ACTIVITIES

The beach area is very spread out – it's at least 4km from the village to *Shwe Hin Tha* hotel, for example. Some guesthouses/hotels have bikes for rent, while bikes (K3000/day) and motorbikes (K10,000/day) can also be rented from tour operators. A few motorbike taxis and rickshaws tend to meet arriving buses, but other than this, transport is thin on the ground.
Micheal Kyaw Opposite *Golden Myanmar Restaurant* ☎09 25011 8008. Village bike-rental stall and souvenir shop; organizes tours and boat trips to Bird Island for snorkelling (K25,000) and full-day fishing trips (K150,000).

7

7

Myanmar Dive Centre Next to *Golden Myanmar Restaurant* ☎09 9774 41611, ✉myanmardivecenter @gmail.com. Managed by a PADI dive master with years of experience, they offer Discover Scuba Diving (from $60).
WSE Company Village ☎09 45454 5505. Full range of local tours including snorkelling boat tours to Bird Island and Lover's Island ($35 plus meals for overnight trip). Book through the *Royal Flower* restaurant.

ACCOMMODATION

These two places are next to each other at the very southern end of the beach.
Shwe Hin Tha 4km south of the village ☎042 40340. Ngwe Saung's most popular budget option, towards the southern end of the beach and with Lover's Island rising out of the waters opposite. Choose between the rather plain bungalows ($55) right on the beachfront (with a/c, hot water, TV and fridge) or the cheaper and more characterful but less comfortable wooden cabanas behind (with wall fan and cold water only). Cabanas $33
Silver Coast Beach Hotel 4.5km south of the village ☎042 40324, ✉htoo.maw@mptmail.net.mm. Close to Lover's Island at the sleepy southern end of the beach, this place has a slightly Robinson Crusoe atmosphere, with little to disturb the peace apart from the occasional falling coconut. The simple but large and comfortable bungalows ($40) come with sea views and big verandahs to enjoy them on. There are also some good-value economy rooms (with table fan and cold water only) in a little building at the back. Doubles $30

EATING

Most resorts and hotels have their own restaurant, but it's worth heading into the village where there's much more choice.
Royal Flower Village ☎042 40309. One of the village's most popular hangouts among international visitors thanks to its cooler-than-average decor and ambience. Mains (mostly K5000) feature all the old seafood and meat favourites in generic Chinese style, with a pinch of Thai. Daily 7am–10pm.

NGAPALI BEACH

If you're looking for pristine white sand, clear blue sea and little to do other than kick back with a cocktail and fresh seafood, then **NGAPALI BEACH** is your kind of place. Unfortunately the cost of accommodation has spiralled, plus to get to Ngapali from Yangon requires either a fifty-minute flight or a gruelling eighteen-hour bus journey.

Most of the hotels are strung out between **Lintha** village in the north and **Jade Taw** further south, with **Myabin** village lying in between. Several places on the beach offer **massages** (from K7000/hr), while if you're feeling more active then you can rent bicycles from one of plenty of places (K3000/day) and ride down to Gyeikthaw fishing village – the market is best around 6.30am. You can also arrange **snorkelling** through hotels, although to get to the best sites you need to take a half-day trip (K35,000 including barbecue lunch).

ARRIVAL AND DEPARTURE

The nearest town is Thandwe, located 7km northeast of the beach. Hire of a tuk-tuk between them costs around K7000, or a place in a pick-up costs K500.
By plane Thandwe airport – which has a currency exchange counter – is 6km north of Ngapali Beach; most accommodation will pick you up from the airport by prior arrangement.
Destinations Bagan (daily; 1hr 20min); Sittwe (3 daily; 40min); Yangon (many daily; 40min).
By bus Hotels on Ngapali Beach sell bus tickets, and also act as drop-off and pick-up points.
Destinations Pyay (1 daily; 12hr); Sittwe (1 daily; 12hr); Yangon via Pyay (1 daily; 18hr); Yangon via Gwa (1 daily; 16hr).

ACCOMMODATION

Most of the accommodation in Ngapali is startlingly overpriced, so it's essential to book ahead.
★**Kipling's Bay** 311 Aye Pyar Ye Lan ☎09 2507 56636, ✉paivi.lehtiranta@gmail.com. The Finnish-owned, ten-room *Kipling's Bay* is an old, dark-wood traditional stilted Burmese house (some rooms are in a newer replica block) with thoughtfully decorated rooms with sea shells and other flotsam and jetsam from the beach. It's a 2min walk down a quiet lane to the beach. No wi-fi. Doubles $45
Memento Resort Main Rd ☎09 2508 80852, ✉ngapalimementoresort@gmail.com. The four budget rooms at the back are basic but comfortable enough, and there are also various more expensive rooms along the resort's extensive beachfront (from $60). Doubles $50

EATING AND DRINKING

There are a few shacks on the beach, close to Myabin, typically open from breakfast until 9pm (happy hour usually 4–6pm).
Htay Htay's Kitchen Main road, near Lintha. Customers at this welcoming, family-run restaurant rave about the great seafood – smoked-fish soup through to fishball

RECENT VIOLENCE IN RAKHINE STATE

One of the world's most persecuted minorities (according to the UN), the **Rohingya Muslims** of Myanmar are currently facing a titanic battle not just for basic political rights, but for their very survival. Around 800,000 Rohingya live in Rakhine State, with a further million more spread across Bangladesh, Pakistan, Thailand and Saudi Arabia. Most Burmese regard them, bizarrely, as illegal immigrants (despite the fact that they have been in the country since at least colonial times, possibly much longer) and insist that they should all be sent back to Bangladesh (which doesn't want them, and in which the vast majority of Rohingya have never set foot). They are also **stateless**, having been stripped of their citizenship in 1982 – and, despite their large numbers, the Rohingya ethnicity was not even recognized in the national census of 2014.

Tensions between the Burmese and Rohingya have simmered for decades – particularly since the withdrawal of the British – and the government has routinely discriminated against the Rohingya. As well as stripping them of citizenship, Rohingya have also been forbidden from travelling even locally without permission or from having more than two children. Forced labour, extortion, arbitrary taxation, land seizures and chronic food shortages have also been frequent facts of life.

And then, in 2012, things got even worse with the outbreak of major riots throughout Rakhine State following the rape and murder of a Buddhist woman and the retaliatory killing of ten Rohingya. Dozens, perhaps hundreds, of Rohingya were killed, and thousands displaced – more than 100,000 continue to languish in **camps** in Myanmar (along with many thousands more similarly detained in Bangladesh, and in areas around the Myanmar–Thai border). Efforts by international organizations to ease the plight of those living in the camps have been strongly resisted – the Buddhist clergy have been particularly noisy in condemning organizations working with the Rohingya.

In October 2016, Myanmar border police camps near the Bangladesh–Myanmar frontier were attacked by unknown assailants and nine police were left dead. The Myanmar military responded with an extreme crackdown that by early 2017 had driven thousands more Rohingya into refugee camps. UN and Amnesty International reports (all denied by the Myanmar government) speak of numerous cases of police- and military-committed extrajudicial killings, rape and the burning of villages.

Myanmar's desire to ethnically cleanse itself of the Rohingya appears to permeate all levels of society. Members of the National League for Democracy, while loudly protesting their own lack of political freedom, have been equally dismissive of the Rohingya's plight, while even Aung San Suu Kyi – the one figure in Myanmar with the standing and moral authority to possibly shift entrenched racist attitudes – has been silent on the issue.

salad with lemon leaves and assorted coconut-flavoured curries. Mains K4000–5000. Daily 8am–10pm.

Two Brothers Mya Pyin Village (opposite the *Amata* resort) ☎09 4965 3655. Cute little rattan-roofed restaurant with friendly service and a menu bursting with assorted seafood. Mains K4000–5000. Daily 6am–9pm.

SITTWE

Located at the picturesque point where the Kaladan River meets the Bay of Bengal, **SITTWE** is the main transport hub for visiting Mrauk U (see p.546). The city was off-limits for much of 2012–13 and, although open to tourists again, it has been profoundly changed as Rohingya Muslims – who once formed close to half of the city's population – have almost all been driven into refugee camps. Spend more than a couple of hours here and you will most likely hear locals spout some racist nonsense concerning the brutalized Rohingya minority, which leaves a very sour taste.

WHAT TO SEE AND DO

The town centre is built on a grid pattern, with three main north–south roads. From east to west they are: Minbargyi Road, Main Road and Strand Road (along the shore). Most shops and travel agents are located on Main Road, as is the rather dry **Cultural Museum** (Tues–Sun 10am–4pm; $5).

The most rewarding place for a walk is **Strand Road**, which has a fish market (daily 6am–5pm) at the junction with Merchant Street. It's at its best early in the morning. Around 3km south of here, K2000 return by trishaw, is the **View Point** – a great place to appreciate Sittwe's location on the Bay of Bengal.

ARRIVAL AND DEPARTURE

By plane The airport is 2.5km west of the town, a K3000 ride by tuk-tuk or K5000 by taxi.

By boat Boats to Mrauk U leave from a jetty 3km north of the town. Transport to the jetty costs K3000 (tuk-tuk) or K5000 (taxi). The government ferry (6–7hr; K7000, plus K1000 for a seat) leaves at 7am on Tues and Fri; buy tickets at the jetty from 6am. Two companies run more comfortable private ferries: Shwe Pyi Tan (7am Wed, Fri & Sun; 2hr 30min; K25,000), with an office on Main Rd (daily 7.30am–8pm; ☎ 09 4967 4569); and Aung Kyaw Moe (7am on Mon, Thurs & Sat; 5hr; K10,000), based at the jetty. You can arrange a private boat for up to four people (5–6hr; K170,000 return) at the airport and leave the same day, as long as you arrive by about 2.30pm. Make sure you agree on how many days they will wait for you in Mrauk U.

By bus The bus station is 4km west of town.
Destinations Mandalay (1 daily; 30hr); Mrauk U (3–4 daily; 4hr); Yangon (1 nightly; 30hr).

ACCOMMODATION

Kiss Guesthouse 145 Main Rd ☎ 09 4511 65896. Simple but cheap option, with basic but clean and comfy tiled rooms with attached bathroom (cold water only). The manager speaks brilliant English. Doubles $25

Mya Guesthouse 51/6 Bowdhi St ☎ 043 23315. Sittwe's best-known budget guesthouse has simple rooms, with a/c and attached cold-water bathrooms. Single rooms are a very decent $20. Doubles $30

EATING

River Valley 5 Main Rd ☎ 043 23234. Convivial, foreigner-friendly restaurant with seating in a pleasant garden illuminated with fairy lights after dark, with a long menu of mainstream but well-prepared Chinese dishes (mains K3500–5000). Daily 7.30am–10pm.

DIRECTORY

Bank and exchange KBZ Bank, Main Rd (Mon–Fri 9.30am–3pm), has the town's only ATM and currency exchange desk.

MRAUK U

The many sixteenth- and seventeenth-century temples of **MRAUK U**, some of them as sturdily built as fortresses, make it one of the country's most significant historical sites. Yet it receives only a fraction of the number of tourists who visit Bagan. Certainly Mrauk U is not on the same scale, but it has its own appeal, not least because the temples are located within the town itself – although it is rumoured that, as happened in Old Bagan, the government plans to force inhabitants out of the centre to develop it as a tourist attraction.

It wasn't the first Rakhine capital, but from 1430 onwards Mrauk U was a centre for trade with merchants from as far away as Europe. It was at the height of its powers under King Minbin (who ruled 1531–53), when many of the temples were built, and fell in 1784 when the Konbaung dynasty – which would later go on to found Mandalay – conquered the territory.

WHAT TO SEE AND DO

The heart of modern Mrauk U is its **market**, and immediately to its east lie the remains of the old royal **palace**. The two main concentrations of **temples** are to the north and east of the palace (most daily 7am–5.30pm; most covered by a K5000 entry fee, which is usually collected at Shittaung Paya).

There are great views from temples including Sakya Shwegu, Rathay Thaung and Myan Daw Mu, while for Mrauk U's fabulous **sunsets** the most impressive panorama is the one from the **Discovery Viewpoint** (sunrise–sunset; K500).

The palace and around

There's not much left of the original **palace** complex, bang in the middle of town, apart from its impressively long walls arranged in three concentric squares around a trio of successively rising terraces. There's a **museum** (Tues–Sun 9.30am–4.30pm; $5) as you approach from the south, but many of the objects inside are reproductions.

Northern area

Most visitors start with the temples to the north of the palace, an area that includes the magnificent **Shittaung Paya**. Built in 1536 by King Minbin, its name means "shrine of 80,000 images" but in fact it had 84,000 – some are now missing – representing the number of methods which the Buddha taught to achieve freedom from suffering. On your left as you go up

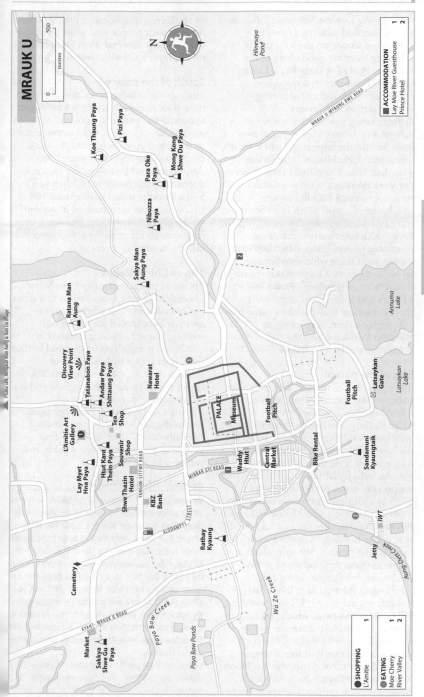

MRAUK U

7

ACCOMMODATION
1 Lay Moe River Guesthouse
2 Prince Hotel

SHOPPING
1 L'Amitie

EATING
1 Moe Cherry
2 River Valley

the steps you'll see the Shittaung Pillar, an obelisk inscribed with royal history.

From the terrace on the west side of Shittaung there are good views of the heavy-set **Htut Kant Thein Paya**. Dating from 1571, it contains a spiral passageway with niches containing Buddha statues and images demonstrating the 64 traditional hairstyles of Mrauk U. The passageway leads up into the large stupa where there's a final seated Buddha. A little further west than Htut Kant Thein is the older **Lay Myek Hna Paya**, a simple circular structure with 28 Buddha images.

Following the road north from Shittaung you pass several temples, including **Andaw Paya**, which contains two octagonal concentric passages, and **Yatanabon Paya** – a big, solid stupa which has been a favourite of treasure hunters as its name means "a lot of jewellery". **Pitaka Taik** was a library and is decorated with flower motifs; it is now protected by a metal roof.

If you have time, keep going to **Mingalar Man Aung** and the hall containing the **Nan Oo Image**.

East of the palace
The largest of the temples east of the palace is **Koe Thaung Paya** ("shrine of 90,000 images"), hurriedly built in 1553 by an ill King Mintaikkha because his astrologers said that otherwise he would die within six months. It was constructed on a grander scale than Shittaung temple, built by Mintaikkha's father, and supposedly it was hit by lightning in 1776 as a punishment for this disrespect.

On a hill to the south of Koe Thaung is **Pizi Paya**, said to contain a testicle (*pizi*) relic of the Buddha. Women are not supposed to climb to the top, which is a shame as there are good views of Koe Thaung and the surrounding fields.

Following the road as it loops back towards central Mrauk U, you pass the hilltop **Para Oke Paya**, which was built by another superstitious king: the people of the kingdom were rebelling, and the astrologer said that building a temple would placate them. Opposite it is **Mong Kong Shwe Du Paya**, which was donated by an intelligent princess who wanted to

be the cleverest in her next life too. It's popular with people who want success, which is why General Than Shwe had a small prayer hall built beside it.

South of the palace
The most interesting attraction south of the palace, across the river, is **Sandamuni Kyaungtaik** monastery. Look out for a metal table-top on the right as you enter its small museum, as it's actually one of the few ceiling tiles that escaped the destruction and looting of the palace. In a separate pink concrete building you'll find a Buddha image dating from 308 BC, which had been covered in cement – possibly to hide it from invaders – then forgotten about until the cement eyes fell off, around twenty years ago.

Trip to Chin villages
The most popular day-trip from Mrauk U heads along the Lemro River to a series of **Chin villages**. This ethnic minority group is best known for having old women whose faces were tattooed in childhood using a mix of soot and buffalo liver. It all feels a little like voyeur tourism, but the women have made a career out of being photographed and it's an interesting day-trip.

A trip can be arranged through hotels or travel agencies in Mrauk U and will typically cost $70–80 for up to four people in a boat, including a guide and transfers to the jetty.

ARRIVAL AND DEPARTURE
By boat The jetty is 1km south of the market. Services to Sittwe all leave at 7am. The fastest is the *Shwe Pyin Tan* (Mon, Thurs & Sat; 2hr 30min; K25,000; buy tickets in advance from the *Hay Mar* restaurant by the jetty); slightly slower is the *Aung Kyaw Moe* (Tues, Fri & Sun; 4–5hr; K10,000; tickets available in advance from their office near the jetty, or buy them as you board the boat); the slow government boat (Wed & Sat; 6hr 30min–7hr 30min; $6 or K7000, plus K1000 for a seat) fills in on the remaining days.
By bus Foreigners are now allowed by road to Mrauk U, although aside from those travelling between here and Sittwe few people brave the long journey times to other parts of Myanmar.
Destinations Magwe (1 daily; 10hr); Mandalay (1–2 nightly; 24hr); Sittwe (3–4 daily; 4hr); Yangon (1–2 nightly; 24hr).

ACCOMMODATION

Lay Myoe River Resort Guesthouse Minbar Gyi Rd
⊕09 2537 70556. One of Mrauk U's cheapest
accommodation options, with simple boxy little rooms
with fan and attached bathroom (cold water only). Basic
but reasonably clean, and at a very fair price. Doubles $15
Prince Hotel Myaung Bwe Rd ⊕09 26070 1079,
ⓦmraukuprince.com. In a pleasant rural setting a 10min
walk from town. The rooms are only so-so but the family
who run the place make up for any discomfort. You'll
barely have time to put your bags down before they're
plying you with tea and snacks. They also have six-bed
dorms which are about as cheap as you'll find in Mrauk U.
Dorms $15, doubles $30

EATING AND DRINKING

There are several teashops and restaurants around
the market.
Moe Cherry Northeast corner of the palace complex
⊕09 4217 33711. Deservedly popular with visiting
foreigners, the Myanmar curries (around K4000) are nicely
cooked and served with a decent selection of vegetable
side dishes, plus soup. Daily 7am–10pm.
River Valley Near the ferry dock. An offshoot of the
popular Sittwe restaurant, set on a pleasant terrace hung
with multicoloured lanterns and serving up an identical
menu (mains K3500–5000) to its Sittwe sister, with a big
and competent if unremarkable selection of Chinese-style
seafood and meat dishes. Daily 7.30am–10pm.

SHOPPING

L'Amitie Just north of the Shittaung Paya ⊖artsmtmu
@yahoo.com. Art gallery that exhibits the work of Shwe
Maung Tha, who has had his work shown overseas, as well
as his son Khine Minn Tun. You're likely to see one or the
other of them around. Daily 7am–after sunset.

DIRECTORY

Bank There's a branch of the KBZ bank with an ATM
opposite the *Shwe Thazin* hotel.

Southeastern Myanmar

Easily overlooked by tourists in the rush
to head north from Yangon, **southeastern
Myanmar** more than justifies a diversion.
With the opening of border crossings
with Thailand (see box, p.555), more
visitors are slowly starting to find their
way down here, and for many of those

people the southeast often ends up being
their favourite part of the country.

The most iconic attraction in Mon State
is the boulder-and-pagoda balancing act
at **Kyaiktiyo**, although the experience of
being among believers is likely to be just
as memorable as the Golden Rock itself.
Further south, you can search out old
colonial buildings and a ridge packed
with pagodas in the former British capital
of **Mawlamyine**.

The mountainous eastern part of the
region, which stretches along the border
with Thailand, has long been a refuge for
ethnic minority resistance groups. Kayin
State, in particular, has seen a great deal
of bloodshed since the country gained
independence, although the Karen
National Union signed a temporary
ceasefire with the government at the start
of 2012. Many Karen, however, complain
that the government has now started
granting their land to foreign investors
such as mining companies. The state
remains largely off-limits apart from
Hpa-an, a town that makes a great base
for day-trips into rice fields overlooked by
imposing Mount Zwegabin, and also
provides access to the border crossing
at Myawaddy.

Other than the opening of the
Myawaddy crossing, the other big news
for tourism here has been the opening up
of the **Tanintharyi Region** further south:
until 2013, it wasn't possible to travel
overland to **Dawei**, **Myeik** or **Kawthaung**,
but now you can travel south all the way
to the Thai border and beyond.

BAGO

A plethora of pagodas, outsized Buddha
statues and monasteries attest to the
historical importance of **BAGO**, which
was at the height of its influence
following the decline of Bagan's empire in
the thirteenth century. Its location at a
major junction, 80km northeast of
Yangon, makes it a convenient stopover
or day-trip destination.

WHAT TO SEE AND DO

Most of Bago's sights are covered by a
$10 government-imposed entrance fee.

7

It's a long walk between them, so ask at accommodation about bicycle rental (around K3000/day) or motorbike tours (around 5hr; K3000) which include the main attractions plus the missable reconstructed palace and a monastery where busloads of tourists intrude on the monks' mealtime.

Shwemawdaw Paya and Hintha Gon

The holiest site in Bago, **Shwemawdaw Paya**, around 2km east of the centre, is at 114m the tallest pagoda in the country. It's said that the original stupa was built here during the lifetime of Gautama Buddha, but it has been destroyed many times and the current one dates back to the 1950s.

A five-minute walk east from Shwemawdaw is a smaller pagoda, **Hintha Gon**, most notable for its *nat* (spirit) shrine in which ceremonies are often performed to bring good luck to worshippers.

Shwethalyaung reclining Buddha and around

To the west of the centre is the elegant **Shwethalyaung reclining Buddha**, over 54m in length and said to have been built by King Miga Depa in 994 to mark his conversion to Buddhism. A ten-minute walk further west is the **Mahazedi Paya**, completed in 1560 under King Bayinnaung, a reformer who is said to have put an end to human and animal sacrifices by animists. It was reconstructed in the 1980s.

Kyaik Pun Paya

The **Kyaik Pun Paya**, located down a road off the main highway, 3.5km south of the centre, consists of four large back-to-back statues representing the four Buddhas who have appeared so far in the current era. This back-to-back arrangement seems to have originated among the Mon before spreading to Bagan and Thailand.

ARRIVAL AND DEPARTURE

By bus You can buy tickets at the bus station, around 1km west of the town centre (K500 by motorbike), at your accommodation, or from the offices on the main road. Most buses will stop at both the bus station and in town by *Three Five* restaurant (where tickets are also sold), but do check this when you buy your ticket.

Destinations Hpa-an (hourly; 6hr); Kinpun (for Kyaiktiyo, hourly; 3hr); Mandalay (3 daily; 10–12hr); Mawlamyine (3 daily; 5hr 30min); Pyin Oo Lwin (2 daily; 10hr 30min); Taunggyi (for Inle Lake, 2 daily; 12hr); Taungoo (3 daily; 4hr); Yangon (4 hourly; 1hr 30min–2hr).

By train The station is centrally located, just north of the main road and most of the cheaper hotels.

Destinations Dawei (daily; 22hr 30min); Kyaikhto (3 daily; 3hr); Mandalay (3 daily; 14hr); Mawlamyine (3 daily; 7–8hr); Naypyitaw (5 daily; 7–8hr); Taungoo (3 daily; 4hr 30min); Thaton (3 daily; 5hr); Thazi (3 daily; 10–11hr); Yangon (8 daily; 2hr); Ye (daily; 14hr).

ACCOMMODATION

San Francisco 14 Main Rd ☎052 22265. With twenty fan-cooled rooms, the cheapest doubles with shared bathrooms, and knowledgeable, helpful staff, *San Francisco* is understandably popular with backpackers. The rooms are acceptable or, in the case of the more expensive rooms, really quite impressive (from $18 for private bathrooms). Breakfast not included. Doubles $14

EATING

★ **Min Htet** Shwetaungyoe Rd, just north of Shwe Taung Yoe Pagoda. Locals flock to this simple restaurant at lunchtime for tasty Burmese-style curries (usually with one vegetarian option on offer), accompanied by the usual trappings of salad, *ngăpí* and vast quantities of rice. Expect to pay K1200 for a meal with tea. Mon–Sat 9am–6pm.
Three Five 10 Main Rd ☎052 22223. Cavernous and popular Chinese restaurant with a long menu that includes interesting dishes (mains K3500–6000) such as chicken with crab. Daily 8am–9pm.

DIRECTORY

Bank CB Bank, Main Rd, has an ATM.

KYAIKTIYO

One of the holiest Buddhist sites in the country, **Kyaiktiyo Paya** draws large numbers of non-believers among its throngs of pilgrims, primarily thanks to its spectacular location. The small pagoda was built atop the Golden Rock, a boulder 15m in circumference and coated in gold leaf, which is itself perched on a larger rock; it's a precarious-looking setup which is supposedly kept in place by one of the Buddha's hairs. On a busy evening, as the sinking sun tinges the sky a fiery orange, the rock glitters and glows and a thousand awed pilgrims whisper prayers to the breeze, Kyaiktiyo becomes one of the most magical places in Myanmar.

The starting point to get up to the rock is the town of **Kinpun** and the full 11km hike takes at least four hours, but almost everyone shortens the walk by cramming into the back of the open trucks (daily 6am–6pm) which depart when full – they are less frequent as the day goes on. Some trucks run only to the old Yathetaung terminal (45min; K1500 each way), from which it's an hour's walk to the top. Most, though, now run all the way to the top (1hr; K2000 each way) so that it's only a ten- to fifteen-minute walk to the rock.

A government fee of K6000 (valid two days) is collected at the top, shortly before the main complex; men can join the pilgrims right beside the **Golden Rock** itself, and even add to its lustre (five sheets of gold leaf K1700), while women must stay a short distance away. Women are not supposed to wear trousers, shorts or miniskirts; men should also dress appropriately.

It's worth pressing on past the rock and the *Yoe Yoe Lay* hotel for fifteen minutes to reach **Kyi Kann Pa Sat**, where you can join locals throwing coins up onto a ledge for good luck. There's also a cave shrine with a very narrow entrance.

ARRIVAL AND DEPARTURE

The transport hub is the town of Kyaikhto – not to be confused with Kyaiktiyo (the name of the mountain and the pagoda) – on the main highway, with Kinpun around 14km to the northeast.

By bus Some buses go right into Kinpun and stop outside *Sea Sar* restaurant; others stop at Kyaikhto and passengers are transferred to Kinpun by truck (usually included in the bus ticket price).

Destinations Bago (hourly; 3hr); Hpa-an (3 daily; 4hr); Mawlamyine (1 daily; 4hr); Yangon (hourly; 5–6hr).

By train The train station is in Kyaikhto.

Destinations Bago (3 daily; 3hr); Mawlamyine (3 daily; 5hr); Yangon (3 daily; 5hr).

ACCOMMODATION

Most backpackers stay in Kinpun, since all the hotels at the top are expensive.

Sea Sar Just off the main road, Kinpun ☎ 09 42535 3566. Tucked away behind *Sea Sar* restaurant and set around a lawn, the bungalows here are clean and decent. The cheapest rooms, though, are in a separate block just down the road. These have fans and cold-water-only bathrooms – and plenty of grime. No discount for single occupancy. Doubles $̶1̶5̶, bungalows $̶2̶5̶

EATING

There are plenty of Chinese and Burmese restaurants on the main road in Kinpun, and cheap eats abound on the mountain itself.

Mya Yeik Nya Overlooking the truck terminal. One of Kinpun's more atmospheric restaurants, with friendly staff and good food. A Burmese curry and rice set costs K3000, with other dishes starting from K2000. Daily 4am–9pm.

DIRECTORY

Bank There is a branch of KBZ Bank with an ATM just southwest of the truck terminal.

7

MAWLAMYINE

Sandwiched between a ridge of pagoda-topped hills and the island-filled estuary of the Thanlyin River, **MAWLAMYINE**, which was the capital of British Lower Burma from 1827 to 1852, when it was known as Moulmein, is an absorbing place to spend a few days. With the town centre dominated by a series of fascinating markets, the neighbourhoods beyond dotted with neat churches and extravagantly crumbling **colonial mansions**, the town is a diverting place to explore. The city is also the base for day-trips to attractions ranging from a colossal Buddha – big enough to walk into – to a sobering war cemetery.

WHAT TO SEE AND DO

The waterside **Strand Road** is the city's most important thoroughfare, and towards its northern end are three busy **markets**. Although locals differentiate between them, for most visitors they merge seamlessly into each other.

Dotted with pagodas, the **central ridge of hills** makes for a great sunset trip. Start at Uzina Paya at the southern end, head north to nearby U Khanti Paya and then continue for about half an hour to the impressive Kyaikthanlan Paya. A covered walkway runs back towards town, but it's worth pressing on to see the mirrored interior of Mahamuni Paya.

Quiet little **Shampoo Island** (Gaungse Kyun), just a few minutes by boat from the city, makes an easy escape from the busy streets. The island is home to a collection of small stupas and is inhabited only by monks, nuns, and their dogs. The boat (K1000 return) runs from a shack beyond the abandoned *Mawylamyine Hotel* at the northern end of town.

Bilu Kyun

Around an hour out of town by ferry, **Bilu Kyun**, or Ogre Island, is home to 200,000 people, most of whom are Mon and none of whom (so far as we know) is an orge. *Breeze Guesthouse* (see below) organizes trips to the island, charging around $30 per person depending on group size, where you visit small workshops making things such as coconut-fibre doormats, rubber bands and walking sticks.

At the time of research a huge new bridge connecting Bilu Kyun with the southern end of Mawlamyine was close to completion. Once finished, change is likely to come fast to the island.

Win Sein Taw Ya

The 170m-long reclining Buddha, **Win Sein Taw Ya**, situated 24km south of Mawlamyine near Mudon, is remarkable both for its scale and for the fact that you can wander around inside it. Still a work in (probably never-ending) progress, and with an even larger counterpart being slowly constructed opposite, it contains dozens of chambers with spectacularly tacky sculptures depicting scenes from the life of Buddha and grisly images from Buddhist hell. There are also several other shrines in the area. A motorbike taxi here will cost K8000 return, while a pick-up from the Zeigyo bus station is K500. It's a twenty-minute walk to the Buddha from the highway, or you could try to hop onto a pick-up.

Thanbyuzayat and around

Thanbyuzayat, 64km south of Mawlamyine, was the end point of the Burma–Siam "death railway", built under appalling conditions for the Japanese army by forced labour, including Allied prisoners of war. There's a locomotive and piece of track on display to commemorate it at the otherwise very lacklustre **Death Railway Museum** (daily 7am–7pm; K5000), and also a well-kept and soberingly low-key war cemetery managed by the Commonwealth War Graves Commission. Buses run to Thanbyuzayat from Mawlamyine's main market (hourly 6am–4pm; 2hr).

The seaside town of **Kyaikkimi**, 9km northwest of Thanbyuzayat, is visited by locals for Yele Paya – a pagoda which is set on stilts over the sea. It can be reached by bus from Mawlamyine, or by pick-up from Thanbyuzayat.

ARRIVAL AND INFORMATION

By boat There is no public ferry to Hpa-an, but private boats (K10,000; 4hr) run daily at 8.30am in season. For some, the boat ride is one of the highlights of their visit to Mawlamyine. Almost any hotel can book a seat.

By bus There are several bus stations in Mawlamyine. Buses to Yangon, Hpa-an and Upper Myanmar leave from the highway bus station on the eastern side of the hills, while southbound services depart from the Zeigyo bus station 6km south of the market. Buses to Thanbyuzayat and Kyaikkami depart from the southern end of the Zeigyi Market on Lower Main Rd until 4pm.

Destinations Bago (5 daily; 5hr 30min); Dawei (11 daily; 9hr); Hpa-an (1–2 hourly until 4pm; 2hr); Kinpun (for Kyaiktiyo, 2 daily; 4hr); Thanbyuzayat (hourly; 2hr); Yangon (3 daily; 8hr).

By shared taxi Minivans depart for Myawaddy (daily; 5hr) from the Zeigyo bus station between 8 and 10am. Book a seat in advance through your accommodation and you'll qualify for a free pick-up.

By train The train station is close to the bus station in the east of the city.

Destinations Bago (3 daily; 7–8hr); Dawei (daily; 15hr); Kyaikhto (for Kyaiktiyo, 3 daily; 5hr); Thaton (3 daily; 2hr 30min–3hr); Yangon (3 daily; 9hr); Ye (daily; 6hr).

ACCOMMODATION

Aurora Guesthouse 277 Lower Main Rd ☏ 057 22785. This lime-green guesthouse has a selection of cheap partitioned rooms (from $7) with shared bathrooms, as well as a few much smarter en-suite rooms. There's a pleasant shared balcony and the owner is gruff but helpful, making this a great budget option. Breakfast not included. Doubles $20

★**Breeze Guesthouse** 6 Strand Rd ☏ 057 21450, ✉ breeze.guesthouse@gmail.com. This backpacker favourite has finally, after many years of wanting, been given a lick of paint and a bit of a renovation. Its cell-like rooms are smart and white though still so small it's like sleeping in a rabbit hutch, and the bathrooms are communal. The most expensive rooms ($30) are large and old-fashioned with shutters that swing open to let in the sea breeze, but these seem to be perennially booked up. The staff are knowledgeable and helpful, and there's always a good crowd of backpackers, flash-packers and throwback hippies staying. Doubles $16

EATING

A series of barbecue stalls sets up in the evening on Strand Rd north of Dawei Jetty in Mawlamyine, selling affordable sticks of chicken, prawns and various innards. However, as atmospheric as it is, food hygiene standards are often left wanting.

Bone Gyi Strand Rd ☏ 057 26528. Dishing up good Chinese food, this popular restaurant is full of well-to-do Mawlamyiners. It's a little more expensive than most Mawlamyine restaurants (mains K4000–7000) but it's worth splashing out on. Daily 9am–9pm.

★ **May South Indian Chetty Restaurant** Strand Rd ☏ 09 4980 4047. This low-key restaurant is at its best (and busiest) around lunchtime, when it fills with market porters and office workers who come for the delicious Indian-inspired curries and biryani, served Burmese-style with fresh vegetables and side dishes. In the evening foreign tourists can outnumber locals, but it hasn't let this international popularity go to its head and it retains a slightly chaotic and grubby feel. You'll pay around K1500 for a filling vegetarian meal and K2500 for a meat-based one. Daily 10am–9pm.

DIRECTORY

Banks and exchange Mawlamyine has plenty of banks and ATMs, with several on Strand Rd just south of the *Mawlamyaing Strand Hotel*, and more just north of *Breeze Guesthouse*.

★ TREAT YOURSELF

Cinderella Hotel 21 Baho St ☏ 057 24411, ⓦ cinderellahotel.com. A few blocks east of Strand Rd, *Cinderella* is one of the best-value hotels in Myanmar. A small army of staff, some in white gloves, provides excellent service, from the welcome drink to the enormous breakfasts. Rooms are spacious and attractively decorated, the beds are comfortable, and the hallways display a treasure-trove of Burmese handicrafts. The huge breakfasts are particularly good. But the *Cinderella* doesn't just do it for mid-range travellers. It also caters to backpackers with spotless, though cramped, eight-bed dorms. Dorms $15, doubles $50

HPA-AN

The riverside town of **HPA-AN** (pronounced "Pa-an") is small and welcoming enough to become familiar quickly, and the limestone hills surrounding it make for a very impressive backdrop to trips taking in pretty villages and caves full of Buddha statues. This has all combined to make it an increasingly popular backpacker hang-out. Many of its main sights can be combined into a day-trip or two, and most hotels provide maps and advice (as well as motorbike rental).

Serene **Kan Thar Yar Lake**, a twenty-minute walk south down Ohn Taw St, is a good spot for sunrise views; at sunset, the riverside **Shweyinhmyaw Paya**, a pagoda in the northwest of town, is particularly atmospheric. Fabulous views of the Thanlwin River and its surrounding fields and limestone hills can also be enjoyed from the pagoda on **Mount Hpa-pu**, reached by taking the ferry (daily 6am–6pm; K500 each way) across the river from near Shweyinhmyaw Paya. Once across, head into the village and follow the sign for the mountain; the path swings right towards the river before curving back around. It's fifteen minutes to the start of the steps up, then thirty minutes to the top.

Mount Zwegabin

From certain angles, the limestone bulk of **Mount Zwegabin** erupts from the landscape like a giant molar tooth. While it may look impossibly steep from downtown Hpa-an, there are two beautiful paths to the summit of the 725m-high mountain, making it a rewarding half-day hike.

Most people ascend the less direct and more scenic western side of the mountain, along a trail starting from **Lumbini Garden** (K1000), 3km east of Kyauk Kalat Pagoda. From here it takes around two hours to climb the steep and winding path to the summit. The trail down the eastern flank of the mountain is more direct, with relentless staircases leading to a small restaurant at the foot of the mountain, from where it's a straight, flat 1km walk to the Myawaddy road.

For many people, staying overnight at the mountaintop monastery to watch sunrise is the highlight of a trip to Hpa-an. The monastery has two twin-bed rooms, which go to the first people to get to the summit, and a hall with sleeping mats. In either case, a payment of K5000 is expected. Simple meals are available at the monastery, but it's best to take snacks and water with you.

Saddan Cave

The vast and atmospheric **Saddan Cave** (K1000), to the south of Mount Zwegabin, is the most dramatic of the region's caverns. A complete golden *zedi* sits inside the cave entrance, but the Buddhist statuary quickly gives way to natural rock formations. Bats roost in the erratically lit main cavern (take a good torch), which takes around fifteen minutes to walk through barefoot. On the far side, the path emerges beside a limpid forest pool, from where (Nov–Feb only) you can take a short boat trip (K1500) back towards the entrance. Note that the entire complex is off limits during the rainy season. A motorbike taxi to Saddan costs K7000 return.

Kawgun and Yathaypyan caves

Over on the other side of the Thanlwin River from Hpa-an and Mount Zwegabin, the **Kawgun** and **Yathaypyan caves** are notable for their Buddhist art, some of which dates back to the seventh century. The most impressive art is at Kawgun (aka Kawthon; K3000), 13km southwest of Hpa-an, where thousands of gold-painted Buddha figures are attached to the walls. Yathaypyan (free), a couple of kilometres further west, is deeper and requires a torch if you want to reach the viewpoint at the far end. A motorbike taxi will charge K7000 to visit the two caves.

Kawka Thawng cave

Kawka Thaung cave is a shallow affair, its single chamber narrowing to a cramped meditation space for monks, with a shrine containing some tiny fragments of bone relic. The area beyond the cave is likely to hold your attention for longer – a photogenic row of monk statues leads to a second Buddhist cave (usually locked), a creepy-looking **nat shrine** and a swimming hole filled with cool, clear spring water, surrounded by teahouses.

A motorbike taxi will charge K2500.

ARRIVAL AND DEPARTURE

By bus The bus station is 4km southeast of the central clocktower on the Myawaddy road. Many buses stop at both the bus station and near the clocktower, but check this when you buy your ticket. Bus tickets are available from the bus station, at the bus company offices near the clocktower, and in most hotels.

Destinations Bago (6 daily; 6hr); Dawei (1 daily; 8hr); Mandalay (1 daily; 15hr); Mawlamyine (1–2 hourly; 2hr); Naypyitaw (2 daily; 9hr); Yangon (6 daily; 9hr).

By boat Private boats (K10,000; 4hr) run daily at 1.30am to Mawlamyine in season. Almost any hotel can book a seat.

By shared taxi Cars to Myawaddy (5–6hr) leave when full from the clocktower.

ACCOMMODATION

★**Galaxy Motel** 2/146 Cnr Thisar Rd & Thida St ☎058 21347. At this wonderfully warm and welcoming town centre hotel it's all about the staff, and in particular the manageress, Kim. Where she gets the energy to keep smiling and answering the same old questions time and again about bus times is beyond us. The rooms themselves are carpeted, well maintained and have boiling-hot water in the bathrooms. Doubles $22

Soe Brothers Guesthouse 2/146 Thitsa St ☎058 21372, ✉hsoebrothers05821372@gmail.com. The rooms are decent in this long-time budget favourite – small but cool and clean – but the main draws are the staff, who are expert at dealing with travellers' needs, and the common areas which add to the fun and friendly atmosphere. Single rooms start at just $7 and doubles with private bathrooms are $25. No breakfast. Doubles $18

EATING AND DRINKING

★**San Ma Tu** Bogyoke Rd ☎058 21802. This place has a well-deserved reputation for great Burmese food, which means that it's often full of foreigners. Choose a vegetarian (K500) or meat (from K1500) curry from their wide selection, and it will be served with at least ten diverse and tasty side dishes, soup and tea. Rice is an additional K500. Daily 10am–9pm.

Shwe Myint Mo 2 Pagoda Rd ☎058 21362. Serving Burmese food with Indian undertones as well as particularly tasty soups and salads, meals at *Shwe Myint Mo* come with numerous enticing side dishes. The tomato salad, lathered in peanut sauce, is simply superb. Plan on K2500 for a full meal. Daily 7am–9pm.

MYAWADDY–MAE SOT BORDER CROSSING

The **Myawaddy–Mae Sot** border crossing is the closest Thai border crossing to Yangon, and since the Myanmar government removed a rule requiring foreigners to leave their passports at the immigration office, numbers of overland travellers using this border have increased dramatically. The Myanmar border post (daily 6am–5.30pm) is on the west side of the Moei River. Foreigners can use a small immigration office, rather than queuing with the locals. From here, it's a short walk over the Friendship Bridge to the Thai side of the border (6.30am–6.30pm Thai time) and a B50 pick-up ride to Mae Sot's bus station, from where there are direct buses to Bangkok and other destinations (see p.748).

DIRECTORY

Banks Both CB Bank on Thitsa Rd and KBZ on Zay Tan St offer currency exchange and have ATMs.

DAWEI AND AROUND

The town of **DAWEI** only opened up to overland travellers in 2013 and the isolated coastline around here conceals some of the region's best **beaches** where, save for the fishermen, there's seldom another person in sight. The only shadow on the horizon for Dawei is the question of how long its temptingly undeveloped shoreline will remain intact. A Myanmar-Thai-Japanese project has started work on what will one day become the largest industrial zone in Myanmar and one of the largest in Southeast Asia. In the meantime the opening of the Thai–Myanmar border at **Htee Kee–Phu Nam Ron** has led to a surge in tourism in Dawei. What was a little-visited backwater just three or four years ago is now an increasingly busy tourist town.

WHAT TO SEE AND DO

It's a pleasant place to wander, but there isn't much to do in Dawei town itself, other than visit the **Shwe Taung Za** pagoda, which is one of those slightly over-the-top Buddhist fantasy-world ensembles at which Myanmar excels. The town is a good base for day-trips. Motorbikes can be rented (K10,000/day) in order to explore the beaches in the vicinity of town.

Maungmagan Beach, a thirty-minute (K2000) motorbike ride away, is the best-known and by far the busiest beach. It's an attractive sweep of sand, once you get away from the litter that blights the main stretch of restaurants.

Some 22km southwest of Dawei, the small town of **Launglon** is the gateway to a string of fantastic beaches that scallop the coastline – if only you can find them. Most of the access roads are little more than sandy or rocky paths leading over the hills to the coast, so be prepared to ask directions and for fairly challenging road conditions.

ARRIVAL AND DEPARTURE

By bus Buses stop at Dawei's Highway bus station, a 15min drive east of the town (K4000 by tuk-tuk or K1500 on a motorbike taxi). Tickets are available from the bus company offices that are concentrated on Ye Rd, just north of the junction with Nibban Rd. Minibuses to the Htee Kee–Phu Nam Ron border crossing depart from Dawei daily (see box, p.556).
Destinations Htee Kee (daily; 3hr); Mawlamyine (11 daily; 6–7hr); Myeik (7 daily; 6–7hr); Yangon (11 daily; 12hr); Ye (11 daily; 4hr).

By train The main train station is just east of the town; there's also another station to the south, but it's less convenient. For all destinations you have to change in the small town of Ye to the north of Dawei.
Destinations Ye (daily; 9hr).

ACCOMMODATION

Coconut Guesthouse Maungmagan village ☏ 09 4237 13681, ✉ cocoguesthouse95@gmail.com. While there are a few places to stay in Maungmagan, this is the pick of the bunch, with ten simple, fan-cooled rooms in bungalows a short walk from the beach. With charming staff and a chilled-out restaurant on-site (breakfast not included), it's a good enough reason to stay in Maungmagan in itself. The beach is a 5min walk away. Doubles $25

★ **Shwe Moung Than** 665 Pakaukku Kyaung St, Dawei ☏ 059 23764, ✉ shwemaungthan22@gmail .com. This smart hotel ticks all the boxes. The comfortable rooms are bright and decently sized, and the staff are terribly helpful. Rooms vary in size, but all are united in their cleanliness and value for money. Doubles $20

THE FAR SOUTH

The town of **Myeik** (Mergui) was previously visited only by high-spending tourists heading out on luxury "live-aboard" boats to the very beautiful **Myeik Archipelago**. While these boats are still by far the best way to see the islands of Myeik, it's now possible to head out on a day-trip to some of the islands (which are frankly far less impressive) nearer the town of Myeik. Two standard trips ($80 per person) are offered, both of which combine snorkelling, village visits and a bit of beach time into one busy day. Trips are sold through most travel agencies and hotels in Myeik, and no matter what the booking agency tells you, clients from all the hotels are likely to end up on the same boat together.

Another reason for travelling through to the far south of Myanmar is for the border crossing from **Kawthaung** to **Ranong** (Thailand), which straddles the Kra Buri or Pakchan River. Boats (B100–150 one-way) cruise from one side to the other while the crossing is open (daily 6am–5.30pm, Myanmar time). There's one short stop close to Kawthaung for Myanmar passport control, and another closer to Ranong for citizens of ASEAN member states, before you reach Thai passport control. Outside the Thai border post, there are ATMs, and it's about a B20 pick-up ride to Ranong bus station.

EATING AND DRINKING

Daw San 506 Hospital Rd ☎09 4987 2584. A low-key Burmese restaurant, which dishes up delicious curries all afternoon. The beef curry is particularly good, but there are plenty of vegetarian options available too. A meal with side dishes will cost around K2500. Daily 11am–8.30pm.

★**Esso Restaurant** Southern end of Maungmagan Beach ☎09 425 073 4865. The *Esso* might be just a simple beach shack restaurant overlooking the sands of Maungmagan, but the curry crab (K7000) they serve and, even more so, the prawns with cashew nuts (K6000) could easily turn out to be one of the best meals you eat in southern Myanmar. Wash them down with the juice of a fresh coconut and you have the making of a meal fit for a beach-bum king. Daily 8am–9pm.

HTEE KEE–PHU NAM RON BORDER CROSSING

Opened in August 2013, the border crossing between **Htee Kee** in Myanmar and **Phu Nam Ron** in Thailand is the closest crossing point to Bangkok and is being increasingly used by tourists as an entry/exit point between Thailand and Myanmar. Minibuses have a monopoly on the route between Dawei and Htee Kee (3hr; K20,000). Once you're stamped out of Myanmar at Htee Kee, it's 5km through no-man's-land to the Thai border post at Phu Nam Ron, which you can cover either on foot or by hitchhiking. From Phu Nam Ron there are buses to Kanchanaburi (2hr), and thence to Bangkok.

Myanmar e-visas are not valid at this border crossing. Get a visa in advance.

DIRECTORY

Banks KBZ Bank (Nibban Rd) and Ayeyarwady Bank (Arzarni Rd) both have ATMs; the former also offers currency exchange. Neither ATM currently accepts MasterCard.

Bagan and the central plains

The **central plains** – the arid lands between the Ayeyarwady River in the west and the Shan hills to the east – have seen many kingdoms rise and fall, including that of the Pyu who were the earliest inhabitants of Myanmar for whom records exist. The ruins of Thayekhittaya, close to the busy trading town of **Pyay**, still hint at the grandeur of the Pyu dynasty, which was at its peak from the fifth to ninth centuries. The mighty sixteenth-century dynasty based further east in **Taungoo**, on the other hand, left fewer tangible traces, but the town is still a rewarding place to spend a day or two exploring off the tourist trail. One of the more surreal and interesting towns in Myanmar is the military junta's twenty-first-century stab at a "royal capital", which is the literal translation of **Naypyitaw**, which is now the official capital of the country.

It's **Bagan**, though, that is the undoubted highlight of central Myanmar. Indeed, few places in the world can offer a spectacle as breathtaking as its vast stupa- and temple-strewn plain. In the eleventh century, King Anawrahta of Bagan became the first to unite the lands that now form Myanmar, and today the legacy of his embrace of Theravada Buddhism exerts a stronger influence on tourist imaginations than anywhere else in the country.

BAGAN

The sheer scale of **BAGAN** (formerly known as Pagan), which covers 67 square kilometres and includes more than two thousand Buddhist structures, is almost impossible to take in. Individual temples, stupas and monasteries impress in different ways – for their evocative frescoes, their imposing bulk or their graceful simplicity – but it's the broader sweep that tends to stay etched in visitors' memories: the spectacle of hot-air balloons rising from behind stupas at dawn, the cool, calm relief of temple interiors in the heat of the day, or grand sunset vistas viewed from terraces.

This stretch of the Ayeyarwady River has a long history of settlement, only rising to prominence in its own right with its 42nd king, Anawrahta, who came to the throne in 1044. He also kick-started the building activity, but it really picked up pace under King Kyansittha (who ruled from 1084–1112): formerly Anawrahta's general, he was exiled for falling in love with a princess who was supposed to marry the king, but he later returned to claim the throne.

WHAT TO SEE AND DO

The main transport hub is **Nyaung U**, which is the nearest thing here to a large town, although once you get off the main roads it quickly feels like a village. It's where most budget travellers base themselves, and has by far the largest range of restaurants.

Southwest from here is **Old Bagan**, an area that includes the site of the old walled palace and has the greatest concentration of must-see temples and pagodas – they're packed in to the extent that you can walk between them, unlike in other parts of Bagan. The government expelled the residents of Old Bagan in 1990, partly so that it could be converted into a tourist zone.

New Bagan, a largely unengaging grid of streets to the south, is where the residents were relocated. It's worth passing through even if you aren't staying in one of its mid-range hotels, though, as there are a few impressive temples in the area.

In addition to these larger settlements, there are a number of smaller villages dotted around the area. The most notable are **Myinkaba**, on the main Old Bagan–New Bagan road and home to many lacquerware shops, and **Wet Kyi Inn**, a village immediately west of Nyaung U, which has several hotels and guesthouses.

Foreign visitors are required to pay a $25 fee on arrival in Bagan, covering entry to all the temples, although the ticket is usually only checked in selected larger ones. Those buildings which can be entered or climbed are normally open during

7

ARCHITECTURE AND DECORATION IN BAGAN

Although there are a few exceptions, most of the ancient structures in Bagan are either stupas (**paya**) or temples (**pahto**). The former are usually placed over relics or Buddha images, and are solid spires or cylinders with pointed or domed tops. The latter are square or rectangular structures that can be entered. The earliest buildings bear evidence of being designed by Mon architects, brought back by Anawrahta after he conquered Thaton: early stupas are simple elongated cylinders while later ones are more elaborate and bell-like; later temples tend to be larger and more complex.

The exterior walls of temples are often decorated with **stucco**; one popular image is the *bălù pàn-zwèh*, the face of an ogre holding garlands of flowers in its mouth. The interior walls of many temples bear **murals** based on the Jataka, stories of the previous reincarnations of the Buddha. Other murals depict mythical creatures such as the *kein-năra* bird-man, a symbol of fidelity. The earliest paintings reflect Indian artistic styles, as many artists were Brahmin. Writing on the walls ranges from records of donations to curses on anyone desecrating the temples.

7

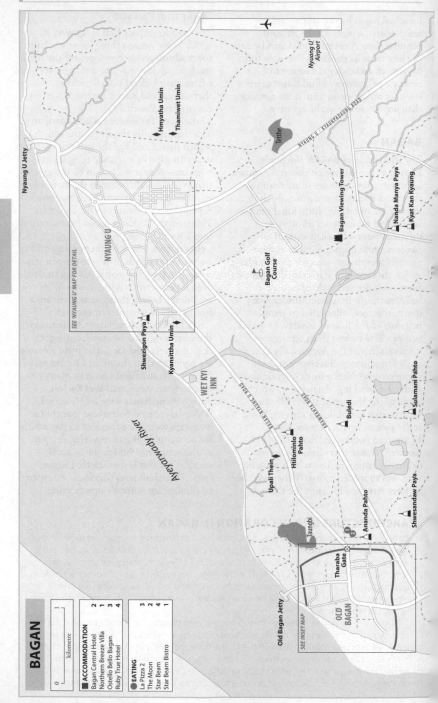

BAGAN

0 ——————— 1
kilometre

■ **ACCOMMODATION**
Bagan Central Hotel   2
Northern Breeze Villa   1
Ostello Bello Bagan   3
Ruby True Hotel   4

● **EATING**
La Pizza 2   3
The Moon   2
Star Beam   4
Star Beam Bistro   1

Nyaung U Airport

Hmyatha Umin
Thamiwet Umin

Tetthe

NYAUNG U – KYAUKPADAUNG ROAD

Bagan Viewing Tower

Nanda Manya Paya
Kyat Kan Kyaung

Nyaung U Jetty

NYAUNG U

SEE 'NYAUNG U' MAP FOR DETAIL

Bagan Golf Course

Shwezigon Paya

Kyansittha Umin

WET KYI INN

Sulamani Pahto

BAGAN-NYAUNG U ROAD

ANAWRAHTA ROAD

Buledi

Ayeyarwady River

Hitlominlo Pahto

Upali Thein

Shwesandaw Paya

Taungbi

Ananda Pahto

Tharaba Gate

OLD BAGAN

SEE INSET MAP

Old Bagan Jetty

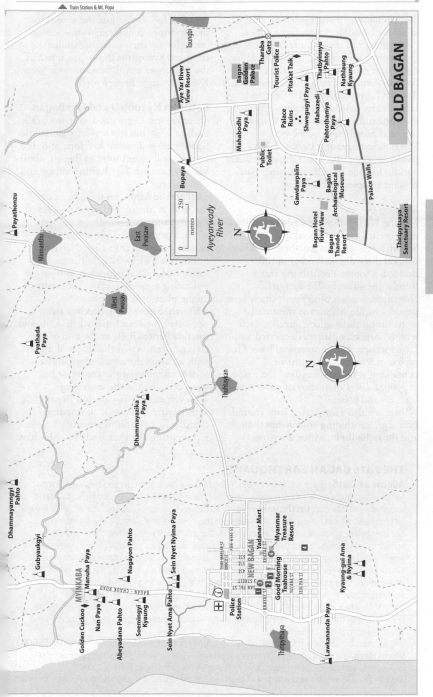

Train Station & Mt. Popa

OLD BAGAN

Taungbi

Tharaba Gate

Bagan Golden Palace

Tourist Police

Aye Yar River View Resort

Pitakat Taik

Thatbyinnyu Pahto

Shwegugyi Paya

Nathlaung Kyaung

Mahabodhi Paya

Palace Ruins

Mahazedi

Pahtothamya Paya

Bupaya

Public Toilet

Gawdawpalin Paya

Bagan Archaeological Museum

Palace Walls

Bagan Hotel River View

Bagan Thande Resort

Thiripyitsaya Sanctuary Resort

Ayeyarwady River

0   250
metres

N

Payathonzu

Minnanthu

East Pwasaw

Pyathada Paya

West Pwasaw

Dhammayazika Paya

Thitahaykan

N

Dhammayanngyi Pahto

Gubyaukgyi

MYINKABA

Golden Cuckoo

Manuha Paya

Nan Paya

Nagayon Pahto

Sein Nyet Nyima Paya

BAGAN - CHAUK ROAD

Abeyadana Pahto

Soeminngyi Kyaung

Sein Nyet Ama Pahto

Thiripyitsaya

NEW BAGAN

THIRI-MINGLA ST
PON-NYA ST

THIRI-MARLAR ST
3 STREET
KHAYAY ST
SAN PAL ST
YUZANA ST
SEIN ST

Police Station

Good Morning Teahouse

Yadanar Mart

Myanmar Treasure Resort

1

2 3

4

Kyaung-gui Ama & Nyima

Lawkananda Paya

7

daylight hours, although you may need to locate the keyholder for smaller temples.

A large part of the pleasure of Bagan lies in exploring and visiting buildings as they catch your eye, but if time really is limited, then don't miss Shwezigon Paya, Ananda Pahto, Shwesandaw Paya and Dhammayangyi Pahto. At sunset everyone rushes to find temples which can be climbed for good views: Shwesandaw Paya and Pyathada Paya are particularly popular, while slightly quieter options include Buledi. The upper parts of some temples are off limits.

Nyaung U

Nyaung U's most important stupa is the early twelfth-century **Shwezigon Paya**. Still an active place of worship, it's said to contain three different relics of the Buddha: a tooth, a collarbone and a frontlet (headband). The design of Shwezigon was a prototype for many later pagodas within Myanmar: the circular stupa sits on three square terraces, each level bearing clay plaques decorated with Jataka scenes, and an octagonal base. On each of the four sides is a shrine containing a 4m standing Buddha made of *pyin-zá-làw-ha* (an alloy of gold, silver, lead, tin and bronze).

There are also a few "cave" sites around Nyaung U, including **Thamiwhet Umin** and **Hmyatha Umin**, which are tunnels designed for meditation and carved into the sandstone hills about 1km southeast of the town. There's another similar complex, **Kyansittha Umin**, just north of the main road as you head towards Wet Kyi Inn village. Bring a torch.

Between Nyaung U and Old Bagan

There are some very good murals, dating back to 1794 but in an older style, in the **Upali Thein** ordination hall (one of only a handful still to be found in Bagan), about halfway between Wet Kyi Inn village and Old Bagan.

Htilominlo Pahto, on the other side of the road, is one of the largest temples in the area, supposedly built on the spot where a prince called Htilominlo was chosen as successor to King Narapati Sithu (ruled 1173–1210). The murals inside include horoscopes, possibly indicating auspicious times for events taking place at the temple.

Shortly before Tharaba Gate (see opposite), you reach the white-and-gold **Ananda Pahto**. Built at the end of the eleventh century in the shape of a cross, with all arms the same length and a square chamber at the centre, it has been described as the crowning achievement of early-period Bagan architecture. A 9.5m teak standing Buddha faces out on each side, representing the four Buddhas who have

---

THE 2016 BAGAN EARTHQUAKE

August 24, 2016 began just like any other Bagan day with tourists drifting between ancient temples and horse and carts clip-clopping down bumpy tracks, but then this peaceful scene was shattered when an **earthquake** measuring 6.8 on the Richter scale hit at a depth of 84km just to the southwest of Bagan. Fortunately, only one person was killed (in nearby Pakokku), but the temples didn't escape so lightly – at least that's how it first appeared. Around 400 temples were damaged and people feared the worst. In the days following, experts started to assess the site and quickly came to the conclusion that much of the damage was not to the valuable, ancient bricks and art but to shoddy and misguided attempts by the former military government to "restore" the temples in the mid-1990s – rebuilding in a manner that often bore little resemblance to how they would have looked originally. The work had been done so badly that, when the quake hit, much of the renovation material simply crumbled and fell to the floor while the original structures, which have already survived countless earthquakes and tremors, stood proud underneath.

The potential silver lining to all this is that Bagan, which has for so long been denied **UNESCO World Heritage** status thanks to this poor-quality restoration work, is now being renovated by real experts and could potentially obtain its World Heritage listing as early as 2018.

While this work takes place, many of the temples are covered in scaffolding.

so far achieved enlightenment in the current era (Gautama Buddha was the fourth – the world awaits a fifth Buddha). Only the northern and southern statues are original.

Old Bagan

The **Tharaba Gate** is the only secular structure surviving from Bagan's glory days and the only remaining entrance to the grounds of the old palace. Just within the gate and to the north is the modern reconstruction of the **Bagan Golden Palace** (daily 6am–8pm; $5), which isn't worth the entry fee. The actual **ruins** of the palaces of Anawrahta and Kyansittha are currently closed to visitors.

Mahabodhi Paya, to the north of the ruins, is notable for being Indian in style.

The main cluster of buildings, though, is to the south of the main road through Old Bagan, including **Thatbyinnyu Pahto**, the highest temple in Bagan. You can't climb up it, but you can climb **Mahazedi**, the bell-shaped stupa opposite, which has good views. Other highlights include single-storey **Pahtothamya**, dimly lit like other Pyu-style temples (later Bamar buildings are typically lighter, with higher ceilings). This does mean that the natural light which enters seems particularly dramatic. Look out also for **Pitakat Taik**, believed to have been built by Anawrahta to house the Buddhist texts that he brought back after conquering the Mon kingdom, and **Nathlaung Kyaung**, where he hid away *nat* animist images as he subsequently imposed Theravada Buddhism.

On the western side of the main road, after it has curved southwards, is imposing two-storey **Gawdawpalin Pahto**. At 55m it's one of the tallest in Bagan.

South of Old Bagan

Not far south of Old Bagan are two of the most popular temples. **Shwesandaw Paya**, just south of Anawrahta Road, is particularly inundated with tour buses at

7

NYAUNG U

ACCOMMODATION
Golden Myanmar Guesthouse	1
May Kha Lar	2
New Park Hotel	3

EATING
Bagan Zay	2
Bibo	3
Weather Spoon's Bagan	1

Ayeyarwady River

IWT Office & Nyaung U Jetty

CB Bank

Market

BAGAN – NYAUNG U ROAD (MAIN ROAD)

Memory Share Taxi Service ★

Police Station

School

Thayaphu Pharmacy

ANAWRAHTA ROAD

Yangon Airways

@

MAB Bank

PYU SAW HTI ST

Thante Hotel

PAGODA ST

OTTAMA ST

Shwezigon Paya

Shwe Pyi Nann

THIRIPITSAYA 1 ST

Sapada Paya

YARMANYA ST

SAPADA ST

T&T

Erawati Bhandagara

THIRIPITSAYA 4 ST

THIRIPITSAYA 2 ST

KYAUKPADAUNG ROAD

Bus Station

BAGAN – NYAUNG U ROAD (MAIN ROAD)

Kyansittha Umin

THIRIPITSAYA 5 ST

AGD Bank

ANAWRAHTA ROAD

Ever Sky

N

0	200
metres	

▼ Wet Kyi Inn, Old Bagan, Myinkaba & New Bagan

▼ Airport & Minnanthu Village

7

sunset; the five-terraced temple has been over-restored but the views of surrounding temples are very good. The sharply tapered spire was a prototype for many others in Bagan and elsewhere in the country.

About 500m east of Shwesandaw Paya is the huge **Dhammayangyi Pahto**, said to have been started by King Narathu in 1166 but left unfinished after he died four years later. He was renowned as a particularly cruel king, and it is said that he had one of his wives – an Indian princess – executed, but he paid for it when her father sent assassins to kill him. The interior decoration is minimal, and nobody really knows why (or when) the inner passageways were bricked up.

Around Myinkaba

To the north of Myinkaba village, **Gubyaukgyi** has some of the best stucco work in Bagan. Further along, **Manuha Paya** is notable for squeezing three large seated Buddhas and one reclining figure into rooms barely big enough to contain them. This sense of confinement is said – with a bit of poetic licence – to reflect the fact that King Manuha of Thaton commissioned the temple while he was imprisoned by Anawrahta.

There are further temples just south of Myinkaba. **Nagayon Pahto** is said to be built on the spot where Kyansittha, who later became king, was protected from his brother Sawlu by a huge *naga* (a serpent – one shelters the largest of the standing Buddha figures). The decorations reflect Theravada Buddhism, while nearby **Abeyadana Pahto** – built at the same time – is said to have been constructed for Kyansittha's wife Abeyadana, who adhered to Mahayana Buddhism. Its murals include deities borrowed from Hinduism, as well as Bodhisattvas.

Soemingyi Kyaung, just a little further along the main road, is the only surviving example in Bagan of a courtyard surrounded by meditation cells.

New Bagan

At the northern edge of New Bagan sit the thirteenth-century **Sein Nyet Ama Pahto** and **Sein Nyet Nyima Paya**. The temple has some fine stucco work, while

the stupa has an unusual ribbed finial. West of the town and with good river views, in a spot that was once an important port, is **Lawkananda Paya**. Built by Anawrahta in the eleventh century to enshrine a replica of a Buddha tooth relic, its bell-shaped dome is more elongated than on later buildings.

Around Minnanthu

The village of Minnanthu is close to the road that runs inland from New Bagan to Nyaung U and the airport. En route to it, the majestic **Dhammayazaka Paya** is visible from the road, although set back from it. Unusually it has pentagonal terraces rather than square ones, and they provide very good sunset views of the temples dotted across the plain.

To the north of Minnanthu lie a number of interesting temples, including **Payathonzu**, which has a distinctive triple-stupa design and some unfinished sketches among the murals inside. Close by is an underground monastery called **Kyat Kan Kyaung**, which is still in use but is pretty bare other than for a small shrine. Back above ground, **Nanda Manya Paya** has well-preserved murals, including images of half-naked women tempting the Buddha to abandon his meditation.

ARRIVAL AND DEPARTURE

Buses will usually stop at a government post so that foreign passengers can pay the $25 Bagan entry fee. It is also collected at the airport and jetties.

By plane Nyaung U airport is around 4km southeast of town. A taxi into Nyaung U is K7000, while New Bagan and Old Bagan are both around K10,000.

Destinations Heho for Inle Lake (7 daily; 40min); Mandalay (4–7 daily; 30min); Ngapali (5 daily; 1hr 20min); Yangon (many daily; 1hr 20min).

By bus The bus station is on the Main Rd in Nyaung U.

Destinations Kalaw (3 daily; 8hr); Magwe (5 daily; 4hr); Mandalay (5–6 daily; 7hr); Meiktila (2 daily; 3hr 30min); Nyaungshwe (2 daily; 8hr 30min); Pyay (1 daily; 8hr); Taunggyi (2 daily; 9hr); Yangon (5 daily; 10hr).

By train The train station is 5.5km southeast of Nyaung U, past the airport (around K7000 by taxi).

Destinations Mandalay (1 daily at 7am; 8hr); Pyay (1 daily at 5pm; 10hr); Yangon (1 daily at 5pm; 19hr).

By boat All services leave from the jetties in either Nyaung U (northeast of the market) or Old Bagan (outside the old walls, to the north), with the departure point depending on water levels. Services leave at around 5.30am, taking roughly 10–12hr to reach Mandalay. The three main operators are Malikha River Cruises (☎09 7314 5748, ⓦmalikha-rivercruises.com), RV Shwe Keinnery (☎09 4027 45566) and Myanmar Golden River Group (MGRG; ⓦmgrgexpress.com); all operators charge $32 from Bagan to Mandalay and $42 going the other way. Prices include breakfast and lunch.

INFORMATION AND GUIDES

Guides Licensed guides can be hired for $35/day from tour agencies or through accommodation. Unlicensed guides cost around $20/day.

Tourist information There are official tourist offices (daily 9.30am–4.30pm) on Anawrahta Rd in Nyaung U and on Main Rd in New Bagan.

TOUR OPERATORS

Ever Sky Thiripyitsaya 5 St, Nyaung U ☎061 60895, ⓔeverskynanda@gmail.com. Helpful and reliable general tour operator.

Tourist Information & Travelling Services (T&T) Thiripyitsaya 4 St, Nyaung U ☎09 4037 19542, ⓔsm.somkiat@gmail.com. Long-established general travel agent and a good place to arrange car rental, bus tickets and local tours.

GETTING AROUND

By bicycle Many places rent out bikes, including most accommodation. Expect to pay around K4000/day. Get a bike with a light, or bring a head torch, if you plan to stay out for sunset – there are few street lights and the main roads can be busy as night falls.

By boat Sunset sightseeing boats depart from Old Bagan jetty around 4.30pm (K10,000 per boat for up to four people; 1hr).

By electric bicycle Foreigners are not allowed to rent motorbikes in Bagan, but enterprising shops and restaurants get around this by renting imported Chinese e-bikes to tourists for K8000/day. It's a fun way to travel, but they aren't especially robust and are very heavy to push if you run out of juice.

By horse and cart A popular option for getting around the temples, although it's generally slower than cycling. Rates start from as little as K25,000/day and K15,000/half day, and you can book either through your hotel or a local tour operator, or approach a driver directly – in Nyaung U they can often be found hanging around at the top end of Thiripyitsaya 4 St and around the bus station.

By taxi For maximum speed and comfort hiring a taxi is the way to explore the temples, although you'll miss out on a lot of the atmosphere of the archeological site while stuck inside a vehicle. Rates are around K35,000/day, or K20,000/half day.

By tourist bus At the time of research the authorities were experimenting with the viability of a hop-on-hop-off tourist bus. The buses run around a dozen times a day and take a circular route around the main temples and hotel areas of Bagan. Buses run to a strict timetable and tend to depart each bus stop bang on time. For more on the service – and to see if it has become a permanent fixture – see ⓦwonderbagan.com.

ACCOMMODATION

Most travellers on a tight budget stay in Nyaung U or Wet Kyi Inn. There are no budget hotels in Old Bagan, and if you do feel like treating yourself then there's better value in New Bagan's mid-range accommodation.

NYAUNG U

Golden Myanmar Guesthouse Main Rd ☎061 60901; map p.561. Long-running and very friendly guesthouse. Rooms are bright and clean but showing their age. There's an in-house travel agency that can organize onward transport and local guides. Doubles $20

May Kha Lar Guesthouse Main Rd ☎061 60304; map p.561. Sky-blue guesthouse with potted plants in the courtyard and wood-panelled, slightly gloomy rooms split between two blocks. It's worth paying $5 extra for a larger, quieter room in the block furthest from the road. It's the best of the budget hotels on Main Rd. Doubles $20

New Park Hotel Off Thiripyitsaya 4 St ☎061 60322, ⓦnewparkmyanmar.com; map p.561. A popular, and very good, budget option in an excellent location on a quiet backstreet. Rooms come in three different classes, but all are spotless, bright and have attached bathrooms. The $30 garden-facing rooms, which have terraces with "sleep-easy chairs", are particularly appealing. The owner has lots of useful travel advice and sells bus tickets and tours. Doubles $25

★ TREAT YOURSELF

Ruby True Hotel Myat Lay Rd, New Bagan ☎061 65065, ⓦrubytruebagan.com; map pp.558–559. Delightful garden hotel with thin-walled, woven bamboo rooms set under the pink and purple blossoms of bougainvillea trees. Rooms are kitted out with desks, fridges, bedside tables and wardrobes, but the real high point of a stay here is the staff, who take the typical Burmese kind, helpful and gentle attitude to new levels of warmth. It's in a quiet area a ten-minute walk from central New Bagan. A great find. $80

7

7

NEW BAGAN

Bagan Central Hotel 15/16 Khayae St ☎092 5713 6019; map pp.558–559. Dated hotel with a design so seriously odd it verges on retro-chic, although somehow it all works. Accommodation is in a cluster of bungalows (faced with knobbly bits of petrified wood) set around a "garden" cobbled with black brick, while rooms come with heaps of gloomy wood panelling and quasi-Victorian furnishings like some kind of Gothic film set. Doubles $35

Northern Breeze Villa 162 Cherry St ☎061 65472, ✉northernbreezehotel.bagan@gmail.com; map pp.558–559. At current rates this place, which has small, clean and modern rooms, is a bargain. It's thoughtful touches like stone-walled showers, art on the walls and a breakfast area strung with weaver-bird nests that really set it apart from similarly priced competition. Doubles $40

★**Ostello Bello Bagan** Main Rd ☎061 65069, ⓦostellobello.com; map pp.558–559. A fabulous new Italian-owned hostel that's in a class above most Southeast Asian hostels. Dorms have between four and eight beds made of nicely faded wood and with good-quality mattresses on them. Each room has its own bathroom. There's a travel desk, tours, bar with happy hour(s), a busy restaurant serving pizzas, party nights and events. Dorms $26, doubles $69

EATING AND DRINKING

NYAUNG U

Bagan Zay Thiripyitsaya 4 St ☎061 246 2057; map p.561. With claret-coloured curtains and a blushing red bar this restaurant doesn't just have the looks to make it stand out from the pack but the food as well, which is described as "modern Myanmar cuisine" and includes dishes such as grilled bull-fish fillets with lentil galettes (mains K4000–6000). Daily 9.30am–11pm.

Bibo Off Thiripyitsaya 4 St ☎09 4025 55241; map p.561. Super-friendly service from owner Thant Zaw Aung and his wife makes eating here a real pleasure. The menu covers Myanmar salads, soup and curries, plus a few Western dishes and a good selection of Thai curries and soups (mains K3000–5000) – not terribly authentic, but tasty enough, and competitively priced. Daily 8am–9pm or until the last customer leaves.

★**Weather Spoon's Bagan** Thiripyitsaya 4 St ☎09 4309 2640; map p.561. This unpretentious and ever busy little café is one of the better places to eat in Bagan. The superb and entirely authentic Thai cuisine (mains K3000–4000) would put many a Bangkok restaurant to shame, while the Western food, including excellent burgers (K4500), is equally good, and there's also an above-average selection of international vegetarian dishes, plus assorted Chinese fare, all at super-competitive prices. Daily 9am–10pm.

OLD BAGAN

There is a clutch of restaurants just outside the Tharaba Gate, north of Ananda Pahto.

The Moon Near Tharaba Gate ☎09 4301 2411; map pp.558–559. The original of the cluster of homespun little vegetarian cafés just outside Tharaba Gate. The veg-only menu (mains K2500–3500) features all sorts of Asian and western options including soups, salads, burgers, curries and stir-fries – anything from mung-bean soup and gazpacho through to deep-fried gourd, tamarind-leaf curry and papaya soup with yoghurt. Daily 9am–9.30pm.

Star Beam Bistro Near Tharaba Gate; map pp.558–559. The original branch of this well-regarded local restaurant, although most people now go to their new premises in New Bagan (see below), while this one has become more of a café than a restaurant. Serves sandwiches, snacks and good coffee. Daily 11am–9pm.

NEW BAGAN

La Pizza 2 Khayae St; map pp.558–559. Colourful Pathein umbrellas welcome you to this very popular pizza restaurant (mains K7000–11,0000) right in the centre of town. Among the standard pizza toppings they have a few local specials such as the tea-leaf pizza. Daily 11.30am–9.30pm.

★**Star Beam** Near New Bagan Market, behind NLD Party Office ☎09 4015 23810; map pp.558–559. Internationally trained chef Myo Myint turns out a short but delicious menu (mains K3500–6000) of superior local and international dishes including Rakhine fish and Myanmar prawn curries alongside a few Western dishes – the freshly baked bread given out with the meals is a tasty touch. Daily 11am–9pm.

DIRECTORY

Banks There are banks with ATMs and foreign exchanges in Nyaung U, including the AGD Bank on Thiripyitsaya 4 St, the CB Bank on Main Rd, and the MAB Bank on Anawrahta Rd.

Pharmacy Thayaphu, Main Rd, Nyaung U (daily 7am–10pm).

Post office Anawrahta Rd, Nyaung U (Mon–Fri 9am–5pm, Sat 9am–noon).

MOUNT POPA

The most popular side-trip from Bagan, **MOUNT POPA** volcano rises 1518m above sea level and is considered to be the home of the 37 *nats* or animist spirits (see p.528). Although a handful of pilgrims do ascend the main peak, most people instead visit a temple on top of a volcanic plug known as **Taungkalat** (737m) on the southwestern flank. There are almost eight hundred steps to climb, and almost as many pick-pocketing monkeys (don't carry any food up with you as they might get aggressive in their demands).

Views from the top are good, but the real interest is in seeing the swarms of local pilgrims. This is a far more colourful, living affair than at most of the Bagan temples. It helps to arrange a guide from Bagan (around $35) who will be able to explain the mountain's religious significance.

ARRIVAL AND DEPARTURE

By pick-up A pick-up leaves the bus station in Nyaung U daily at 8am (2hr 30min) for Taungkalat, returning at 1.30–2pm – although you might have to change to another pick-up at Kyaukpadaung, just over halfway to the mountain, if there aren't enough passengers. It drops you in the village at the foot of the rock.

By car/taxi It's far preferable to either hire your own car with driver (around K35,000; 1hr 30min) or take a seat in a shared taxi. Memory Share Taxi Service (Main Rd, Nyaung U; ☏ 09 204 3579, ✉ kohtaybgn@gmail.com) runs daily shared taxis to Mount Popa at 9am for K10,000/person. Any hotel can book you a seat.

TAUNGOO

TAUNGOO was the centre of a sizeable sixteenth-century empire that defeated Siam and brought the Shan lands under its control. Its king, Bayinnaung, has been much loved by the military junta and the current government. Today the town is a pleasant place to spend a day on the journey between Yangon and Mandalay.

WHAT TO SEE AND DO

The old town is still partially walled and surrounded by a now mainly dry moat. The grandest pagoda in town is **Shwesandaw Paya**, just west of the market, which dates back to 1597. Further west still beyond Kandawgyi Lake, whose shores are a popular leisure spot, is **Kaungmudaw Paya** – a much smaller pagoda with pleasant views over the surrounding fields.

ARRIVAL AND DEPARTURE

Taungoo is located just off the old National Highway 1 that runs between Yangon and Mandalay, and only 10km east of the newer (and faster) Yangon–Mandalay Expressway.

By bus Buses stop at ticket offices either on National Highway 1 or on the Expressway. A motorbike taxi to *Myanmar Beauty II–IV* should cost K1500 from the former, K4000 from the latter.

Destinations Bagan (daily; 5hr 30min); Kalaw (daily; 7hr); Mandalay (2 daily; 7hr); Nay Pyi Taw (5 daily; 2hr); Shwenyaung for Inle Lake (daily; 9hr); Yangon (6 daily; 4hr).

By train The train station is on the edge of town, around 1km west of National Highway 1 and the same distance southeast of the centre of town.

Destinations Bago (3 daily; 4hr 30min); Mandalay (3 daily; 8–10hr); Naypyitaw (frequent; 3–4hr); Thazi (2 daily; 5hr–5hr 30min); Yangon (3 daily; 7hr).

ACCOMMODATION

★**Myanmar Beauty II–IV** 3km south of town, just off the east side of the Yangon–Mandalay Rd ☏ 054 25073 or ☏ 09 78404 0402. Overlooking fields south of town, this lovely guesthouse justifies a stopover in Taungoo all by itself. Rooms are spread over three separate wooden buildings. Those in building *II* (en-suite, cold water only) are simplest and cheapest but perfectly adequate, although they're not always keen to rent them to foreign visitors; those in *III* ($30) are more attractively furnished and have hot water, a/c and little balconies; while those in *IV* ($49) are full of interesting knick-knacks and have beautiful views over rice paddies, far-off hazy mountains and a large pond (and no TVs to spoil the peace). All rates include a spectacular breakfast featuring a huge spread of local fruits, samosas and all sorts of wonderful sticky-rice concoctions. They also have creaky old bikes for rent (K3000/day). Doubles $25

EATING

Aung Moe Hein Off Bo Hmu Po Kun Rd. This cheap, open-fronted beer station-style place is a solidly Burmese affair. The menu is in Burmese only and staff speak little English, which means that for most people it's going to be a point-and-guess ordering experience, which just adds to the fun. Whatever you end up with, though, you can be certain it will taste great and cost very little. Mains mostly K2000–2500. Daily 8.30am–10pm.

NAYPYITAW

It seems strange to say that a country's capital has little to offer visitors, but then **NAYPYITAW** is not an ordinary capital. Its construction was started from scratch in a largely rural area in 2002, with the purpose kept secret until an announcement in 2005 that government offices would move to the new site because Yangon was (supposedly) getting too congested.

7

WHAT TO SEE AND DO

The main reason to visit Naypyitaw is to get a sense of the city's oddness. Its eight-lane highways are almost empty and link a series of grandiose government buildings and vanity projects. The most visible of these is **Uppatasanti Paya**, a huge pagoda paid for by Senior General Than Shwe to atone for his sins.

ARRIVAL AND DEPARTURE

Naypyitaw is very spread out and you're likely to need a taxi or motorcycle taxi if you want to explore. Expect to pay around K10,000 for a half-day tour by motorcycle.

By plane Naypyitaw's shiny new airport is 16km southeast of the centre. A taxi from here into town (there are no buses) will cost around K10,000.

Destinations Heho (1 daily; 40min); Mandalay (3 daily; 50min); Yangon (5 daily; 1hr). Bangkok Air (⊛ bangkokair .com) has flights to and from Bangkok once daily every day except Saturday (2hr).

By bus The main Myoma Bus Station is on Yan Myo Thant Sin Rd, around 6km northwest of the hotel zone. Approaching from the south, you may be able to hop off on Yaza Thingaha Rd, where most of the city's hotels are located.

Destinations Kalaw (1 daily; 5hr); Lashio (daily; 13hr); Mandalay (7 daily; 4hr); Mawlamyine (2 daily; 11–12hr); Meiktila (7 daily; 3hr); Pyin Oo Lwin (2 daily; 8hr); Taungoo (hourly; 2hr 30min); Yangon (10 daily; 6hr).

By train The huge train station is in a massively inconvenient location 14km north of Uppatasanti Pagoda, a $15 taxi journey from town.

Destinations Bago (5 daily; 7–8hr); Mandalay (2 daily; 6–7hr); Taungoo (3 daily; 2hr 30min); Thazi (3 daily; 3hr); Yangon (3 daily; 9–10hr).

ACCOMMODATION AND EATING

All accommodation is located in what is known as the Hotel Zone, which lines Yaza Thingaha Road, and, as with anything to do with Naypyitaw, none of it is small, intimate or subtle. There are no real budget places to stay, although the massive glut of accommodation at least means that most places are excellent value for money, with rooms here going for around half the price or less of equivalent-standard establishments in Yangon.

Golden Lake Yaza Thingaha Rd ☎ 067 434022, ⊛ thegoldenlakehotelnpt@gmail.com. The cheapest option in the city has English-speaking staff and simple but surprisingly smart rooms set in a concrete block overlooking nothing in particular. Even so, it's a good deal, with cheap rooms without bathrooms, and it also has smarter suites and villas. Doubles $22

Maw Kong Nong Golden Hill, near Thabyegone Market. This big and cheery hilltop beer station is one of the few

places in central Naypyitaw resembling a local Burmese restaurant and has decent traditional dishes (with an English menu). Meals K2500–5000. Daily 10am–midnight.

PYAY

The lively port town of **PYAY** (pronounced "pea") boasts an impressive pagoda and provides access to ancient ruins at **Thayekhittaya**. Pyay sees relatively few tourists, since most people rush north on the expressway from Yangon to Mandalay rather than take the more attractive (but longer) western route via Pyay and Magwe.

WHAT TO SEE AND DO

The most obvious attraction in Pyay itself is the hilltop **Shwesandaw Paya** (daily 6am–9pm; K3000), which is said to contain strands of the Buddha's hair and one of his teeth. It's also worth heading south down Strand Road towards the bridge across the river, a pleasant walk past boat jetties and a 1950s Baptist church.

Thayekhittaya

The most interesting day-trip is to **Thayekhittaya** (also known as Sri Ksetra; daily 9am–5pm; $5), an archeological site 8km east of Pyay. It was the capital of a Pyu kingdom from the fifth to the ninth centuries, but its importance had faded by the time it was sacked by Bagan's King Anawrahta in 1057. There's a small government **museum** (daily 9am–4pm; $5) and an 11km path through the site, which includes three pagodas that doubled as watchtowers. A motorbike from Pyay to Thayekhittaya will cost around K3000.

ARRIVAL AND DEPARTURE

By bus The bus station is 4km east of the centre along Bogyoke Rd – to get there from the centre either catch one of the pick-ups that shuttle up and down Bogyoke Rd or catch a motorbike taxi (K1500). The only bus to Bagan currently leaves in the late afternoon; alternatively, catch a bus to Magwe and pick up a connection there.

Destinations Magwe (4 daily; 5hr); Mandalay (2 daily; 13hr); Nyaung U for Bagan (1 daily; 8hr); Ngapali (2 daily 8am & 7pm; 12hr); Sittwe (1 daily; 28hr); Yangon (6 daily; 6–7hr).

By train Nightly services to Yangon leave from the main station right in the middle of town. There's also an overnight service to Bagan departing from Shwethekar station, around 10km east of the centre.

Destinations Bagan (1 nightly; 10hr); Yangon (1 nightly; 8hr 30min).

ACCOMMODATION AND EATING

There is a night market between the main roundabout and the waterfront, where you can fill up on barbecue and noodle dishes for around K1000–2000 per person.

Hotel 3D 1448 Shwe The Tann St ☎ 099 7393 9395. Modern but bland town-centre hotel which is comfortable and has friendly and polite staff. Some of the rooms don't have any windows so it's worth asking to see the room before accepting. Doubles $30

Pan Ga Ba Guesthouse Merchant St ☎ 053 26543. In a wonderful old timber building, this is as much a homestay as a guesthouse, and the family running it will fuss endlessly over you and quite possibly even invite you to eat with them. Rooms are very simple and hot water comes by the bucket. Doubles $16

★ **Wish River View Restaurant** Strand Rd ☎ 09 2524 22828. Lively restaurant enjoying views of the spot-lit river. The sophisticated menu is filled with excellent Thai curries and fresh fish served in imaginative ways – try the prawn kebabs. Mains around K4000–6000. Daily 5–11pm.

DIRECTORY

Banks There are plenty of ATMs around town including the CB Bank, AGD Bank and MOB (the last of these doesn't take MasterCard).

Inle Lake and the east

Covering a huge swathe of Myanmar's far northeast, Shan State epitomizes the country at its most scenically spectacular and ethnically diverse. Large parts of the state remain off limits to foreigners, although the areas which are accessible contain some of Myanmar's unquestioned highlights, including the stilt villages and colourful markets of serene **Inle Lake** and superb trekking through ethnic-minority villages around **Kalaw**.

KALAW

When it got too hot in the lowlands for the British during the colonial era, they retreated to hill stations such as **KALAW**. Today the climate is still part of the appeal,

even if it can get a bit chilly at night in winter, and the town is a base for some excellent treks to ethnic minority villages.

WHAT TO SEE AND DO

Other than the market, which is open every day but spills out into the streets when it's Kalaw's turn to host the rotating market (see box, p.569), there isn't a lot to do in the town itself besides visit its pagodas. These include the mirrored **Aung Chan Tha Zedi** in the centre and small **Thein Taung Pagoda**, uphill from the Union Highway and offering fine views back over the town and into the hills beyond.

7

Trekking

There are many options for one- to three-day treks (or even longer) around Kalaw, following trails through the hills to villages inhabited by Palaung, Danu, Pa-O, Taung Yoe and other ethnic groups. There has been significant deforestation in the area, and the routes mostly run past fields and plantations, but these hikes are nonetheless a great way to get a glimpse of rural life. Prices start at around K10,000 per person per day; the trails can get very muddy during the rainy season (June to October).

The most popular longer trek is to Inle Lake (see p.570), which normally takes three days, although it's possible to shorten it to two (skipping some of the route by car) or lengthen it to four. There are many different routes and finishing points on the western side of the lake, including Khaung Dine and Indein (see p.570), with overnight stays in local villages, although the popularity of the area means you're likely to see several other trekking groups, particularly on the last day as the routes converge on Inle Lake. A typical three-day price is $50–70 for a group of two (cheaper in larger groups), including the cost of a boat from the finishing point to Nyaungshwe and luggage transfer. Always check carefully what is and isn't included in any quoted price, and note that for two-day treks to Inle you'll also have to pay for a car (or other transport) to take you part of the way (around $15 per group). A growing number of operators are also now running cycling tours, or combined trekking and cycling trips, either to Inle Lake or in the countryside around Kalaw.

ARRIVAL AND DEPARTURE

By plane A taxi to Heho airport, around 35km northeast of Kalaw, costs K30,000 and takes an hour. Plane tickets can be arranged through most of the tour and trekking operators around town.

Destinations Mandalay (5 daily; 35min); Nyaung U for Bagan (1–2 daily; 40min); Thandwe (3 daily; 1hr); Yangon (6–7 daily, plus additional services via Mandalay and/or Nyaung U; 45min).

By bus Hardly any buses originate in Kalaw itself, with most passing through en route to or from Taunngyi. Services stop at the various bus company offices along the main road, where you can also buy tickets, although you might find it easier to book either via your hotel or through any of the tour and trekking operators around town. A few minibuses and buses (originating in Mandalay) pass through Kalaw en route to Nyaungshwe, although reserving a seat can be tricky. Alternatively, catch a local pick-up or minibus from the transport stop just southwest of the Aung Chan Tha Zedi to Shwenyaung (1hr 30min), from where you can catch another pick-up or a taxi to Nyaungshwe (30min). To reach Pindaya you'll have to take a pick-up or minibus to Aungban (30min),

and then a second pick-up (1hr) onto Pindaya, although if you're trying to do this as a day-trip from Kalaw note that transport back to Aungban from Pindaya tends to dry up in the afternoon, in which case your only way out will be by taxi.

Destinations Bagan (2 daily; 6–7hr); Mandalay (6 daily; 6hr); Naypyitaw (2–3 daily; 7hr); Taungoo (3–4 daily; 9hr); Thazi (6 daily; 4hr); Yangon (8 daily; 10hr).

By train The train station is less than 1km south of the town centre and is on a line running from Thazi to Shwenyaung (the station for Inle Lake), which is very scenic, particularly on the Thazi–Kalaw stretch. There are connections to Yangon and Mandalay from Thazi.

Destinations Shwenyaung (daily; 3hr 30min); Thazi (daily; 7hr 15min).

By taxi A taxi to Pindaya can be arranged through your guesthouse or any local travel agents. The journey takes around 1hr and costs around K35,000–40,000 (same price one-way or return), or around K55,000 to visit the caves then carry on to Nyaungshwe.

TREKKING AND ACTIVITIES

Reliable trekking guides include:

A1 Trekking Khone Thae St ☎09 4958 5199, ⓦA1trekking.blogspot.com.

Eagle Trekking Aung Chan Tha St ☎09 428 312 678, ✉eagletrekking@gmail.com.

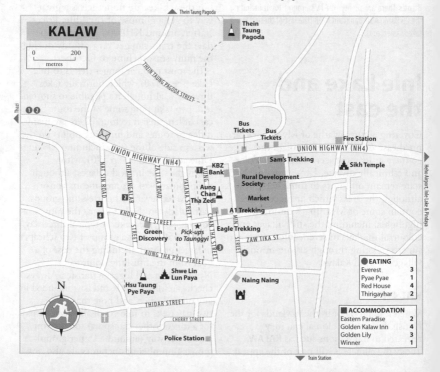

KALAW

0 — 200 metres

Thein Taung Pagoda

Thein Taung Pagoda

THEIN TAUNG PAGODA STREET

Thazi

Bus Tickets
Bus Tickets
Fire Station

UNION HIGHWAY (NH4)
UNION HIGHWAY (NH4)

Sam's Trekking

Sikh Temple

KBZ Bank

NAT SIN ROAD
THIRIMINGALAR
ZA LILA ROAD
YATANA STREET
MIN ROAD
CHAN THA STREET

Rural Development Society

Aung Chan Tha Zedi

Market

KHONE THAE STREET

A1 Trekking

Green Discovery
Pick-ups to Taunggyi
Eagle Trekking

ZAW TIKA ST

AUNG THA PYAY STREET

Shwe Lin Lun Paya

Naing Naing

Hsu Taung Pye Paya

N

THIDAR STREET

CHERRY STREET

Police Station

Heho Airport, Inle Lake & Pindaya

● EATING

Everest	3
Pyae Pyae	1
Red House	4
Thirigayhar	2

■ ACCOMMODATION

Eastern Paradise	2
Golden Kalaw Inn	4
Golden Lily	3
Winner	1

Train Station

Green Discovery Khone Thae St ☎09 428 318 216, ⓦgreendiscoverymyanmar.com. Offer various cycling and cycling-plus-trekking tours.

Naing Naing Min St ☎09 428 312 267. Also does cycling combinations, and has an excellent selection of bikes for rent including gearless runarounds (K3000/day), basic mountain bikes (K5000/day) and "deluxe" bikes ($12/day).

ACCOMMODATION

Accommodation in Kalaw caters to a relatively well-heeled crowd, with a chronic lack of real budget options.

Eastern Paradise Thiri Mangalar St ☎081 50315, ⓔEasternmotel@gmail.com. Dated but acceptable option, although the decor might remind you of childhood visits to an elderly relative and the rooms are a bit gloomy – $5 extra gets you one of the brighter ones upstairs. Doubles $25

Golden Kalaw Inn Nat Sin Rd ☎081 50311, ⓔgoldenkalawinn@gmail.com. Reliable if uninspiring option with smallish but clean and comfortable rooms (those upstairs are brighter, and at the same price), plus good Western and Myanmar-style breakfasts. Doubles $25

Golden Lily Nat Sin Rd ☎081 50108, ⓔaungharri @gmail.com. Long-running backpacker favourite with a mixed bag of rooms. Budget doubles with shared bath – essentially a couple of beds jammed into a small and shabby wooden box – are unquestionably cheap but not at all cheerful. The wood-panelled en-suite rooms are gloomy but otherwise much nicer ($18), opening out onto a grand balcony with sweeping hill views. Doubles $11

Winner Union Highway ☎081 50025, ⓔwinnerhotel .kalaw@gmail.com. Reliable budget option with professional service and a range of rooms including smallish but acceptable fan-only doubles (not that you really need a/c in Kalaw), plus bigger and quieter a/c doubles (from $30) set away from the main road. Doubles $20

EATING

Everest Aung Chan Thar Rd ☎081 50348. Popular North Indian place serving a wide range of meat and veg curries and thalis (mains around K4000) alongside the classic Nepalese-style *dhal bhat* – not the best Indian food you'll ever have, although the attentive service and lively atmosphere make it a nice place for an evening meal. Daily 9am–9pm.

Pyae Pyae Union Highway ☎081 50798. Pint-sized little venue on the main road a short walk west of the centre, popular with tourists and locals alike on account of its excellent Shan noodles (K1000) served in a variety of soups and salad. Daily 6am–9pm.

Red House Min St ☎09 771 357 407. Set in a fine old colonial building (the red house of the name), this stylish new venue has brought a welcome dash of culinary chic to town, with a mainly Italian menu (mains K6600–8800) of pizza, pasta plus real mozzarella, *frittata* and warming bowls of minestrone perfectly suited to chilly Kalaw, plus good coffee. Daily 11am–10pm.

Thirigayhar Union Highway ☎081 50216. Fun restaurant in a creaky and enjoyably time-warped old wooden house next to *Pyae Pyae*. The menu features an eclectic mix of Burmese, Shan, Chinese and European food (mains K6000–7500), including local dishes like *zat byat byat* (spicy minced meat mixed with tomato and basil, K4000) or the curious-tasting peanut soup with mustard leaves. Daily 10am–10pm.

DIRECTORY

Bank KBZ Bank (Mon–Fri 9am–3pm), on Min St, has an ATM and currency exchange.

PINDAYA

The small town of **PINDAYA** is located in the heart of one of the most important agricultural regions in the country. The drive itself is a good reason to make the trip, through a scenic patchwork of red soil, green crops and variously hued flowers – also oddly reminiscent of southern Europe, at least until you see a small Danu child riding on the back of a water buffalo.

WHAT TO SEE AND DO

The main attraction in the town is **Shwe Oo Min** (daily 6am–6pm; K3000), an atmospheric series of caves crammed full

SHAN STATE MARKETS

A number of **markets** in this region operate on a five-day cycle, with three or four markets taking place on each day of that cycle. With the possible exception of the very touristy **Ywama** "floating market", they're fascinating places – particularly early in the morning – where people from remote villages sell their produce or livestock and buy essential goods. At the time of research the cycle was:

Day 1: Kalaw/Shwenyaung/Indein
Day 2: Nyaungshwe/Pindaya/Nampan
Day 3: Than Taung/Heho/Kyone/Taung To
Day 4: Aungban/Taunggyi/Ywama
Day 5: Pwe Hla/Mine Thauth/Phaung Daw Oo Pagoda

The last place listed for each day is on or around Inle Lake.

of Buddha statues – some date back centuries, but the collection is still expanding. It's possible to continue north from here along the hillside via other shrines and the old **Hsin Khaung Taung Kyaung** teak monastery (also accessible by turning left along the first road north of the *Golden Cave* hotel).

ARRIVAL AND DEPARTURE

By bus Buses to Taunggyi (2 daily) depart from close to the town's market and will drop you off at Shwenyaung (2hr), from where it's a 30min ride to Nyaungshwe by taxi or pick-up .

By pick-up Pick-ups run from the market to Aungban (most frequent in the morning; 1hr), from where you can take a taxi or pick-up on to Kalaw.

By taxi Visiting by taxi makes Pindaya a feasible day-trip from either Nyaungshwe (2hr 30min) or Kalaw (1hr 30min), or a stopover on a trip between the two.

TOURS

Guides The hills and villages around Pindaya are visited far less often than those near Kalaw. Hotels and guesthouses can arrange guides, as can U Zaw Min Htike at Pindaya Nature Traveller Trekking (Taxi & Eco-Trekking) on Shwe Oo Min Pagoda Rd just south of *Green Tea* restaurant (☎ 09 431 5490, ✉ naturetravellerpindaya@gmail.com).

ACCOMMODATION AND EATING

Dagon Shwe Oo Min Rd, off northwest corner of lake. Either a restaurant or a beer station, depending upon whether you're looking at the signboard or the menu, but it functions pretty well in both regards. As well as selling draught beer, it's one of the town's more reliable places for food, with simple dishes such as fried rice or noodle soup (mains around K1500). Daily 7am–10pm.

Myit Phyar Zaw Gyi 106 Zaytan Quarter ☎ 081 66325. Centrally located close to the market, lake and several restaurants. Rooms are well past their best but are clean and reasonably well maintained. Rooms facing the lake have nice views, although they can get quite noisy. Good single rates ($15). Doubles $25

INLE LAKE

Vast and serene **Inle Lake** is one of the undoubted highlights of most trips to Myanmar. Its attractions are not just in its considerable natural beauty, however, but also in the stilt villages of the Intha ("Sons of the Lake", descendants of Mon people from the far southeast), for whom it is home.

While the lake is very firmly on the beaten path, it's big enough that you only truly notice just how many other foreigners are around when your boat pulls up at one of the stops. Even now most of the markets are aimed more at villagers of the various ethnic groups that live in the area – among them Shan, Pa-O, Kayah and Danu – than they are at tourists.

Most resorts on the lake cost at least $100 per night, so travellers on a budget usually stay in nearby Nyaungshwe.

WHAT TO SEE AND DO

A typical **day-trip**, taken in a long, narrow boat with a noisy outboard motor, will take in the whole lake. It will include visits to small workshops in stilt villages, such as cheroot making in Tha Lay and lotus fibre weaving in In Paw Khone, plus one or more pagodas and probably a market (see box, p.569). You are also likely to see fishermen using traditional conical nets, propelling their boats using a distinctive leg-rowing technique, and other Intha residents of the lake tending to fruit and vegetables on floating gardens.

You may be offered the chance to see "long-necked" **Padaung women**, so-called because they wear metal rings around their necks (which actually push their collarbones down rather than elongating their necks). These women are often exploited by those within the tourist industry and it's something which some visitors choose to avoid.

Phaung Daw Oo Paya

Boats converge on the tiered lakeside **Phaung Daw Oo Paya**, south of Ywama on the western side of the lake, to the extent that you may need to climb over a log jam of them in order to reach the shore. The pagoda building is nothing special, but men (only) crowd around to add gold leaf to five Buddha figures that are already so coated that they resemble miniature golden boulders rather than anything recognizably human.

Indein

The ride west from Ywama to **Indein**, starting among reed beds before continuing between tree-lined banks, is a striking contrast to the wide-open space of the lake. Just behind Indein village, at the base of a hill, is **Nyaung Oak**, a set of picturesquely overgrown stupas with carvings of Buddhas, *chin-thé* (guardian lions), *devas* (female deities), elephants and peacocks. Head uphill along a covered walkway to reach **Shwe Inn Thein Paya**, a collection of seventeenth- and eighteenth-century stupas which is being slowly and heavy-handedly restored. On the way down, look out for a path on the left which runs through a bamboo forest back to the riverside.

ARRIVAL AND DEPARTURE

By boat The main entry point to the lake is Nyaungshwe (see below), from which dozens of boats run during the tourist season – either depositing tourists in resorts on the lake, or taking them on day-trips. Bring a jumper for the cold morning start, and suntan lotion, since the boats have no cover. Full-day trips cost around K18,000 for a boat capable of seating up to around five people (plus K5000 extra to Indein) and can be arranged through most guesthouses and travel agencies, through the tourist office, or with the freelance boatmen who hang out around the Main Canal.

NYAUNGSHWE

As the most convenient base for trips on Inle Lake, the once-quiet town of **NYAUNGSHWE** has developed into a flourishing tourist town. Things get particularly busy during the Balloon Festival in nearby Taunggyi (see p.534), which takes place in November, and during the Phaung Daw Oo Pagoda Festival (Sept/Oct). At these times, boatmen (and some hotels) tend to increase their prices.

WHAT TO SEE AND DO

Boats to Inle Lake leave from the Main Canal on the western edge of town. Another, much quieter, canal, Mong Li, runs through the centre of Nyaungshwe, and a wander alongside it is a good way to get a sense of local life. There are three sizeable monasteries – **Hlaing Gu Kyaung**, **Shwe Gu Kyaung** and **Kan Gyi Kyaung** – on its eastern bank.

The most holy pagoda in Nyaungshwe is **Yadana Man Aung Paya**, on Phaung Daw Side Road, which has an unusual

Shwenyaung, Highway NH4, Kalaw & Yangon

INLE LAKE

Nyaungshwe

0   2
kilometres

N

Nanthu

Kaung Daing

Red Mountain Winery

Maing Thauk

Inle lake

Than Taung

Thale U

Ywama

Tha Lay

Phaung Daw Oo Paya

Indein

Nyaung Oak

Shwe Inn Thein Paya

In Paw Khone

Nampan

Takhaung Mwetaw Paya,   Taung To, Kyauk Taung & Sankar

7

stepped golden stupa. In the northeast of town is the **Cultural Museum** (Wed–Sun 10am–4pm; K2000), although it's more interesting for its brick-and-teak building (an old Shan palace) than for its ramshackle exhibits.

There are many one- and two-day **treks** around the town, through rice fields, hills and villages, as well as a popular three-day route to Kalaw (see p.567). The roads around the lake are also great for **cycling**, and you can rent a bike through accommodation and travel agencies. They should be able to suggest destinations, but one good bet is the **Red Mountain Winery** (daily 9am–6pm; ☎081 209366, ⊛redmountain-estate.com), around 4km southeast of town and signposted from the main road. It's possible to sample the wines (around $3) and to have lunch in the restaurant.

7

ARRIVAL AND DEPARTURE

Many buses bypass Nyaungshwe, dropping passengers off at Shwenyaung, 12km to the north, where the Nyaungshwe road turns off from the main Taunggyi highway. From Shwenyaung it's 30min to Nyaungshwe by pick-up (K1000) or taxi (K10,000). Trains also terminate at Shwenyaung. A government fee of $10 to enter the Inle Lake area is charged at a permit booth on the northern edge of Nyaungshwe. Leaving Nyaungshwe, pick-ups to Shwenyaung depart from north of the market on the Main Rd.

By plane A taxi to Heho airport (see p.568) costs around K20,000 (1hr).

By bus You can buy tickets from the May Bus Ticket & Taxi Services Centre on the Main Rd, and through most guesthouses and hotels. There are direct buses to Mandalay, Yangon and Bagan, although the short hop to Kalaw can be surprisingly tricky unless you can find a free seat on a long-distance bus (or are prepared to pay the full fare to its final destination). The only other option is to catch a pick-up to Shwenyaung and then try to flag down a passing bus or pick-up on the main road (and you may have to change again at Aungban). Given all this, you might decide just to hire a taxi for the entire journey (around K35,000).

Destinations Bagan (5 daily; 8hr); Bago (3 daily; 10–11hr); Mandalay (5 daily; 8hr); Yangon (8 daily; 12hr).

By train The train line between Shwenyaung and Thazi (which has connections to Yangon and Mandalay) is exceptionally scenic, particularly the final Kalaw–Thazi stretch.

Destinations Kalaw (daily; 3hr 30min); Thazi (daily; 9hr).

INFORMATION AND TOURS

Nyaungshwe is the easiest place to arrange boat trips on Inle Lake (see p.571).

Tourist information The official Directorate of Hotels & Tourism Information Centre is on Strand Rd (daily 9am–5pm).

Bicycle rental Many guesthouses and tour agents have bikes for around K1500/day. Active & Authentic, Kyaunn Taw Shayt St (ⓔaat.toursmyanmar@gmail.com), has mountain bikes for $12/day.

Travel agents and trekking guides Numerous offices in town offer boat trips and transport services. Treks can be arranged through various operators including Sunny Day Tour Services, Main Rd (daily 7am–8pm; ⓣ09 428 372 118; ⓔhtwe.sunny@yahoo .com) and Pyone Cho from *Lotus Restaurant* on Museum Rd (ⓣ09 428 313 717, ⓔpyonecholotus@gmail.com). Most places offer one-day treks in the hills east of the lake (from around K12,000 per person in a group of two) and overnight treks to Kalaw (from around $50/$65 per person for a two/three-day trek including boat and transport fees, and luggage transfer).

ACCOMMODATION

Aquarius 2 Phaung Daw Pyan Rd ⓣ081 209352, ⓔaquarius352@gmail.com. An understandably popular option, set around a lush courtyard stuffed with greenery and a quaint wooden restaurant. The cheaper fan-only rooms are simple but good value, and there are also more modern a/c rooms ($35) in the bright new, vaguely pueblo-style block around the back. Doubles __$20__

Joy Hotel Jetty Rd ⓣ081 209083, ⓔjoyhotelinle@gmail .com. Some of the cheapest beds in town in a canal-side guesthouse, with great people-watching from the upstairs breakfast terrace. Rooms are past their best, but comfortable enough, while shared-bath singles go for just $8, while en-suite doubles are $18. Doubles __$16__

Nawng Kham The Little Inn Phaung Daw Pyan Rd ⓣ081 209195, ⓔnoanhom@gmail.com. Friendly little family-run guesthouse with a few simple but inexpensive fan rooms (plus more expensive a/c doubles, $30) set alongside a little strip of garden. Doubles __$20__

Remember Inn Museum Rd ⓣ081 209257, ⓦrememberinn.jimdo.com. Enduringly popular budget choice with unusually bright and spacious rooms, slightly past their best, but still very comfortable and competitively priced. Breakfast is served on a sunny upstairs terrace, with a choice of Western or various Burmese options, including good *mohingar*. Doubles __$20__

Song of Travel Aung Chan Tha St ⓣ081 209731, ⓦsongoftravel.com. Cool new hostel occupying an utterly bizarre-looking building resembling a gigantic ghetto blaster. Accommodation is in well-equipped fourteen-bed a/c dorms, while guests get free use of a bike and facilities include a neat little café and what staff claim is the "best wi-fi in Nyaungshwe". Doubles __$14__

EATING AND DRINKING

Linn Htet Yone Gyi Rd ⓣ081 209360. Friendly, deceptively simple-looking restaurant that's a favourite with foreigners and locals alike on account of its incredibly

filling curry sets (K3000) – if you can finish the lot you must have been pretty hungry. Daily 11am–9pm.

Live Dim Sum Yone Gyi Rd ☏ 09 428 136 964. This small dim sum restaurant will be a treat to the tastebuds, if you've had one too many bowls of Shan noodles. Try one of their platters (K3500), with a choice between fried (K3700) or steamed (K4000) dim sum; there are also some good Chinese dishes on the menu (around K4000). Daily 10am–9pm.

One Owl Grill Yone Gyi Rd ☏ 09 262 972 841, ⊛ oog.asia. This cool urban-style bistro is the place to come for some excellent (if relatively pricey) meaty Western food (mains K5000–8000), including great burgers and other carnivorous mains. It also does a good range of breakfasts (from K3000), plus cheap happy-hour cocktails from K1500 (2–6pm). Daily 9am–11pm.

Sin Yaw East side of the market ☏ 09 428 338 084. Lively local restaurant with almost manically friendly staff and a great selection of traditional Shan dishes (mains K4000–4500) – Inle lake fish curry, Shan-style chicken with green pepper, long beans and basil, and a lip-smackingly good yellow tofu with lemon coriander sauce. Daily 10am–10.30pm.

★**Thanakha Garden** Thazi St ☏ 09 428 371 552. Attractive garden restaurant serving up quality food from a mainly Asian menu featuring plenty of Burmese and local Shan-style specialities, plus a healthy sprinkling of Western dishes including burgers and fish 'n' chips. Mains K3000–6000. Daily 11am–9.30pm.

TRADITIONAL ENTERTAINMENT

Aung Puppet Show Ahletaung Kyaung Rd. Enjoyable traditional entertainment by a puppeteer who has been performing since 1985, with shows nightly at 7pm & 8.30pm (30min; K5000). They also sell puppets for around K10,000–40,000 (shop open daily 8.30am–9pm).

DIRECTORY

Bank AGD Bank, Yone Gyi Rd, KBZ Bank, Main Rd, and CB Bank, Strand Rd, all have ATMs accepting foreign Visa and MasterCards, and Forex facilities.

Spa and massage Aqua Lilies, Museum Rd (daily 9am–9pm; ☏ 09 428 363 584), offers various treatments, including a traditional *anaite* massage (K14,000/hr). Treatments in more basic surroundings are also available at Win Nyunt Traditional Burmese Massage (daily 8am–8pm; K7000/hr).

Mandalay and around

Thanks partly to Rudyard Kipling's evocative poem *Mandalay*, the name of Myanmar's second city suggests – for many Western visitors, at least – images of a bygone Asia. Arriving in downtown

7

Mandalay tends quickly to dispel such thoughts, however, as visitors find themselves in a grid of congested streets dominated by the walls of the **palace** compound (most of which is taken up by a huge military base).

Despite this, it would be a shame to rush through too quickly without giving the place a chance to grow on you. There's **Mandalay Hill** to climb, memorable both for its views and for the experience of joining throngs of locals doing the same. Then there are day-trips to former Burmese capitals such as the once-mighty **Inwa**, now a sleepy rural backwater, and picturesque **Sagaing**, its rolling hills dotted with myriad pagodas – not to mention the gigantic stump of the unfinished **Mingun Pagoda**, reached via an enjoyable boat ride along the broad Ayeyarwady.

MANDALAY

MANDALAY is a surprisingly young city, founded in 1857 by King Mindon partly to show the British, who were ruling Lower Burma from Rangoon, that his kingdom was still mighty. After being taken by the British in 1885, the city prospered until the Japanese occupation during World War II, which saw many of the old buildings levelled by Allied bombing. Today Mandalay is the commercial hub of northern Myanmar, particularly important for trade with China and with a large Chinese community.

Much of the **downtown area**, including the zone south and southwest of the old royal palace where many budget guesthouses are located, is constantly traffic-choked, and first impressions are rarely positive. Yet even here the backstreets can hold surprises, such as the huddle of mosques and Hindu temples on 82nd and 83rd streets, between 26th and 29th streets. The streets further west, towards the river, are significantly quieter and a popular area for exploring by bicycle.

Mandalay Palace
Built as the residence for King Mindon and the Burmese aristocracy, **Mandalay Palace** is protected by walls and a moat more than 2km long on each side. After the British took the city they used it as a fort, and most of the huge site is still an off-limits military base.

The palace complex itself is right at the centre (daily 7.30am–4.30pm; entrance with K10,000 Mandalay ticket), although the wooden buildings all burned down towards the end of World War II. What you see today is a 1990s reconstruction, which is impressive from a distance – such as from the helter-skelter-like watchtower – but less so up close. Foreigners can only enter the walls through the east gate.

Mandalay Hill
The 45-minute walk up **Mandalay Hill** for sunset is one of the highlights of a visit to the city. The usual starting point is the staircase between a large pair of *chinthé* (mythical lion-like animals) on 10th Street; there is another entrance a little further east. Whichever route you choose, the concrete steps run uphill beneath a corrugated-iron roof, lined with stalls selling drinks and souvenirs. The two routes meet just before **Byar Deik Paya**, from which a large standing Buddha points back towards the city. The story goes that the Buddha visited the hill and foretold that a great city would be built at its foot.

There are numerous other shrines on the way up the hill. As you get higher the crowds become thicker, particularly around sunset, before reaching the wide

---

MANDALAY COMBINED ATTRACTION TICKETS
Several of the city's main attractions are covered by a **K10,000 government ticket**, which is valid for a week and can be bought from any of the relevant attractions – although the ticket isn't always asked for at all the sights it's supposed to cover. There is a separate **K5000 government combined ticket** for Sagaing and Mingun, although chances are you won't be asked to produce or buy this when visiting Sagaing.

terrace of **Sutaungpyi Paya** ("wish-granting pagoda") at the top.

It's also possible to take a pick-up (K500), motorbike (K5000 return) or taxi (K10,000 return) to the top of the hill.

Around Mandalay Hill

There are several temples and monasteries at the base of Mandalay Hill. The most impressive is probably **Shwenandaw Kyaung** (daily 8am–5pm; K10,000 Mandalay ticket), a teak structure built

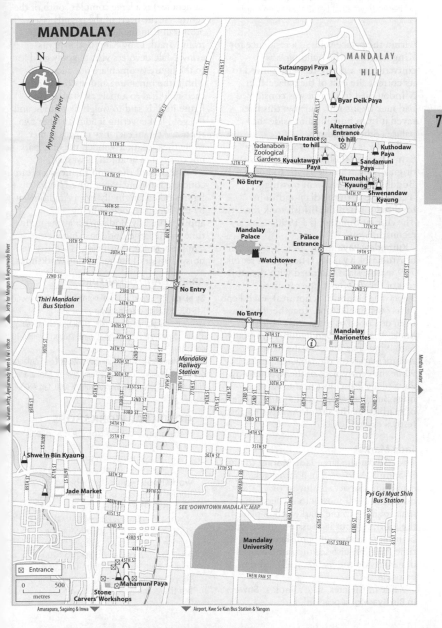

MANDALAY

N

Ayeyarwady River

MANDALAY HILL

Sutaungpyi Paya

Byar Deik Paya

Alternative Entrance to hill

Main Entrance to hill

Kuthodaw Paya

10TH ST

Yadanabon Zoological Gardens

Kyauktawgyi Paya

Sandamuni Paya

11TH ST
12TH ST
13TH ST
14TH ST
15TH ST
16TH ST
17TH ST

12TH ST

Atumashi Kyaung

14TH ST

Shwenandaw Kyaung

15 TH ST

No Entry

17TH ST

18TH ST

Mandalay Palace

Palace Entrance

19TH ST

18TH ST
19TH ST
20TH ST
21ST ST

Watchtower

20TH ST

22ND ST

Thiri Mandalar Bus Station

23RD ST
24TH ST
25TH ST
26TH ST
27TH ST

No Entry

22ND ST

No Entry

Mandalay Marionettes

26TH ST
27TH ST

Jetty for Mingun & Ayeyarwady River

Galwain Jetty, Ayeyarwady River & IWT office

28TH ST
29TH ST
30TH ST

Mandalay Railway Station

28TH ST
29TH ST
30TH ST

Mintha Theater

31ST ST
32ND ST
33RD ST

33RD ST

32N D ST

34TH ST
35TH ST

34TH ST

35TH ST

Shwe In Bin Kyaung

36TH ST

36TH ST
37TH ST

Pyi Gyi Myat Shin Bus Station

38TH ST

38TH ST

AUNG PU RD

Jade Market

39TH ST

MAHA MYAING ST

40TH ST
41ST ST
42ND ST
43RD ST
44TH ST

SEE 'DOWNTOWN MADALAY' MAP

Mandalay University

41ST STREET

⊠ Entrance

0   500
metres

45TH ST

Mahamuni Paya

THEIK PAN ST

Stone Carvers' Workshops

Amarapura, Sagaing & Inwa ▼

▼ Airport, Kwe Se Kan Bus Station & Yangon

7

ADDRESSES IN MANDALAY

The **grid system** makes it easy to find your way around Mandalay. Where **addresses** are given, first comes the street on which the place sits (81st St, for example), and then the cross streets between which it lies (29/30, for example).

within the palace walls as a residence for King Mindon. The building was converted to a monastery and moved to its current site east of the palace after Mindon died in it, as it was considered bad luck by his son, Thibaw; this later saved it from burning alongside the palace's other buildings.

Close by is **Atumashi Kyaung** (daily 8am–5pm; K10,000 Mandalay ticket), originally built in the 1850s to house a Buddha statue that went missing – complete with the diamond in its forehead – when the British took the city. The current building is a 1990s reconstruction.

Kuthodaw Paya (daily 24hr), just north of Atumashi Kyaung, is home to a set of 729 marble slabs inscribed with the entire text of the *Tripitaka* (the canon of Theravada Buddhist scriptures), each kept in its own small stupa. Together they have been described as the world's largest book. The nearby **Sandamuni Paya** (daily 6am–9pm) has marble slabs with commentaries on the same scriptures, while the centrepiece of the **Kyauktawgyi Paya** (daily 24hr) just to the west is a huge Buddha carved from a single piece of marble. It's the site of the city's biggest festival every October.

Jade Market

The stalls in the large **Jade Market** (daily 8–5pm; $1), located in a ramshackle canal-side district southwest of downtown, sell mostly to dealers. The main trading in the market takes place in the morning, but it's possible to see jade being cut, shaped and polished at any time. You can also see the same being done outside the market itself, on the east side.

While in the area, take a look at **Shwe In Bin Kyaung**, a peaceful, late

nineteenth-century teak monastery (junction of 89th & 38th streets; free).

Mahamuni Paya

The most important Buddhist site in the city, **Mahamuni Paya** (open 24hr; K1000 camera fee) is a large complex south of the centre. At the heart of the pagoda is a 3.8m-tall Buddha figure, taken in 1784 from Mrauk U by King Bodawpaya's army. Male devotees visit to apply gold leaf to the figure (women are not allowed within the inner area and instead hand their gold leaf to a male assistant). The figure itself is said to weigh six tonnes, and the gold leaf covering it adds another two tonnes. At 4am each day crowds gather while the face, pretty much the only part not covered in gold leaf, is washed.

Northwest of the main shrine is a cream concrete building containing Hindu figures taken originally from Angkor Wat by the Rakhine, before being appropriated by Bodawpaya at the same time as the large Buddha. Outside the complex, to the southwest, is a dusty and noisy district of **stone-carving workshops**.

ARRIVAL AND DEPARTURE

By plane The airport is 45km south of Mandalay, around K15,000 by taxi to or from town.

Destinations Bhamo (4 weekly; 50min); Heho (5 daily; 35min); Nyaung U (1–2 daily; 30min); Yangon (around 10 daily; 1hr).

By bus Mandalay has three main bus stations. Long-distance departures heading south leave from Kwe Se Kan, around 10km south of town (25min; motorbike K3000, taxi K6000).

GOLD LEAF WORKSHOPS

Pretty much all of the **gold leaf** applied to Buddha images by devotees in Myanmar comes from a small area of Mandalay. There are about fifty gold leaf **workshops**, many of them based in homes, in the blocks around 36th Street, just east of the railway line. King Galon (36th St 77/78; daily 8am–5pm; ☎09 4714 3078) is open to tourists, offering the chance to watch the hammerers at work turning a 12g piece of gold into 1200 sheets, each just 0.0003mm thick. The shops sell gold leaf and other souvenirs, but there's no pressure to buy.

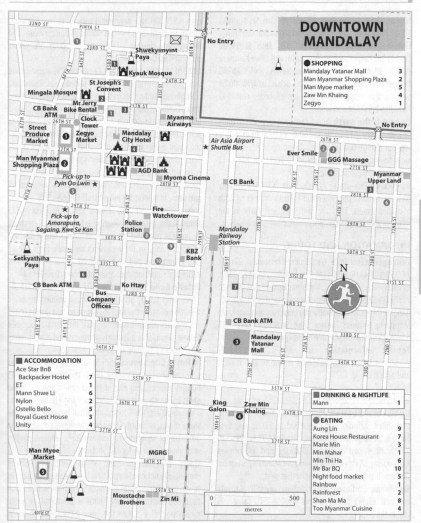

DOWNTOWN MANDALAY

● SHOPPING
Mandalay Yatanar Mall	3
Man Myanmar Shopping Plaza	2
Man Myoe market	5
Zaw Min Khaing	4
Zegyo	1

■ ACCOMMODATION
Ace Star BnB Backpacker Hostel	7
ET	1
Mann Shwe Li	6
Nylon	2
Ostello Bello	5
Royal Guest House	3
Unity	4

■ DRINKING & NIGHTLIFE
Mann	1

● EATING
Aung Lin	9
Korea House Restaurant	7
Marie Min	3
Min Mahar	1
Min Thi Ha	6
Mr Bar BQ	10
Night food market	5
Rainbow	1
Rainforest	2
Shan Ma Ma	8
Too Myanmar Cuisine	4

Pyi Gyi Myat Shin bus station is on 37th St 60/62 (motorbike from downtown K2000, taxi K4000), and has buses running east to Pyin Oo Lwin and Hsipaw. The most central bus station is Thiri Mandalar, 89th St 22/24, although it's of little use to most travellers. Hotels and tour agents can often arrange bus tickets for a small commission, and there are also many bus-company offices and ticket agents in the blocks between 80th to 83rd streets and 30th to 33rd streets; Ko Htay (corner of 32/82) is particular good and sells tickets on most services to most destinations. Some bus companies offer transport from the centre to the appropriate bus station.

Destinations Bago (2 daily; 7–8hr); Hsipaw (2 daily; 6–8hr); Kalaw (6 daily; 6hr); Naypyitaw (8 daily; 4hr); Nyaungshwe (5 daily; 8hr); Nyaung U for Bagan (16 daily; 7–8hr); Pyay (2 daily; 13hr); Taungoo (2 daily; 7–8hr); Yangon (18 daily; 8–10hr).

By train The train station is centrally located on 30th St 78/79. There's a tourist information office as you enter (on your left); tickets are sold upstairs.

Destinations Hsipaw (1 daily; 11hr); Myitkyina (4 daily; 18–21hr); Naba for Katha (3 daily; 10–15hr); Nyaung U for Bagan (2 daily; 8–12hr); Yangon (3 daily; 15hr).

By boat to Bagan Three private companies run tourist services to Bagan (9–10hr), departing at 7am from

Gawain Jetty, at the western end of 35th St: Malikha (☎ 09 731 45748, ⓦ malikha-rivercruises.com); Myanmar Golden River Group/Pioneer (MGRG), 38th St 79/80 (☎ 011 202734, ⓦ mgrgexpress.com); and Shwe Keinnery (☎ 01 294669, ⓦ myanmarrivercruises.com). MGRG Pioneer and Shwe Keinnery services depart daily; Malikha services less frequently. Tickets on all boats cost $42 including breakfast and lunch.

By boat to the north Private fast-boat services run daily to Katha (14hr; $12 on deck, $80 in a cabin) from where you can change boat to Bhamo (see box, p.581). An IWT slow ferry runs to Bhamo (at least 30hr) via Katha (3 weekly on Mon, Thurs & Sat).

By pick-up Pick-ups to Pyin Oo Lwin (K3000) run daily 5am–5pm, departing when full from the corner of 28th and 83rd streets. They are most frequent early in the morning and scarce after 3pm.

INFORMATION AND TOURS

Tour agents Ever Smile, c/o *Rainforest* restaurant, 27th St 74/75 (☎ 09 4316 1551); LM Travel (☎ 09 594 2172 3682, ⓦ lmtravelmyanmar.com); Myanmar Upper Land, 27th St 71/72 (☎ 02 65011, ⓦ myanmarupperland.com); Zin Mi, daughter of Moustache Brother Lu Maw (see opposite); c/o Moustache Brothers Theatre, 39th St 80/81 (☎ 09 431 59591, ⓔ zinmehtunshinshin1987@gmail.com).

Tourist information The MTT office (daily 9.30am–4.30pm; ☎ 02 60356) is on the corner of 68th and 27th sts.

GETTING AROUND

By bike and motorbike Several places rent out bikes and motorbikes, including Mr Jerry, 83rd St 25/26, and Ever Smile at the *Rainforest* restaurant, 27th St 74/75 (☎ 09 4316 1551). Bikes cost around K2000/day and motorbikes K10,000/day . A ride around downtown Mandalay is not for the faint-hearted, but it's quieter further west.

By trishaw Traditional cycle rickshaws are still relatively common. Expect to pay around K1000–1500 for a trip within the centre.

By taxi Motorbike-taxi riders hang out everywhere (particularly around street corners) – it's difficult to walk more than a block without being solicited for custom. Short trips cost around K1000–2000, although sitting on the back of a bike as you weave through the city's often manic traffic can be nerve-jangling. Conventional taxis are harder to come by and relatively expensive, with even quite short rides typically costing around K3000–4000.

ACCOMMODATION

There is a lot of pressure on budget accommodation in Mandalay, so book ahead in high season.

Ace Star BnB Backpacker Hostel Thazin Plaza 31/32 & 77/78 streets ☎ 09 258 411 776, ⓦ acestarbnb.com;

map p.577. Reliable new hostel with functional but well-equipped eight- and ten-bed dorms (including male- and female-only dorms) – although the beds are rather crammed in. Dorms $̲1̲2̲

ET 83rd St 23/24 ☎ 02 65006, ⓔ ethotel129a@gmail.com; map p.577. Central, competitively priced hotel. Rooms are a bit gloomy and nothing special, but well maintained and decent value at the price. Doubles $̲2̲0̲

Mann Shwe Li 84th St 31/32 ☎ 09 258 949 353; map p.577. Tricky to find hotel down an alley off 84th St (look for the small overhead LED sign) but well worth hunting out. The whole place is unusually spacious compared to cramped quarters typical of most city hotels, with good-sized, nicely furnished modern rooms, plus a welcome lift and some of Mandalay's jolliest staff. Doubles $̲2̲5̲

Nylon 83rd St, cnr 25th St ☎ 02 33460, ⓔ nylonhotel25@gmail.com; map p.577. Sharing its lobby with an electrical equipment store, this oddly named hotel is one of the best budget options in the area, with unusually large, clean, nicely furnished and well-equipped rooms with fridge, kettle and surprisingly spacious bathrooms. Doubles $̲2̲0̲

Ostello Bello 28th St 73/74 ☎ 02 64530, ⓦ ostellobello.com; map p.577. Stylish new hostel offering a varied selection of attractive four- to eighteen-bed dorms (rates more expensive in smaller dorms), including a four-bed female dorm, plus a few private rooms and a neat lobby café. Dorms $̲1̲0̲, doubles $̲3̲0̲

★ Royal Guesthouse 25th St 82/83 ☎ 02 31400; map p.577. Intimate and homey, this is the best of the area's budget choices, and one of the cheapest too. Common areas are neatly decorated (perhaps using a Rubik's cube as a colour palette) and rooms are small but cosy, like little ships' cabins, although not all have windows and you'll pay $6 extra for an en-suite room with a/c. Non-a/c singles with shared bath go for just $8. Doubles $̲1̲4̲

Unity 27th St, cnr 82nd St ☎ 02 66583, ⓔ unity@mandalay.net.mm; map p.577. Not the cheapest beds in town, but offering excellent value for money, with a lobby that feels like that of a "real" hotel, a functional lift, and a nice little coffee bar on the ground level. The cheapest rooms lack windows, but all are well equipped, with minibar, safe and kettle, and attractively furnished with modern bathrooms and fittings. Doubles $̲2̲5̲

EATING

One very cheap dinner option, popular with locals, is the night market on 84th St, north of 29th St.

Aung Lin 30th St 80/81 ☎ 02 23151; map p.577. Simple little Chinese restaurant in an airy tiled dining room complete with lucky cats and Chinese characters and landscapes on the walls. Food comprises a good selection of meat, fish, seafood and veggie Chinese standards (mains K4000–5000), with friendly service from the attentive English-speaking owners. Food can sometimes take a while to arrive, but is worth the wait. Daily 11am–10pm.

Korea House Restaurant 27th St 76/77 ☎ 02 71822; map p.577. Run by a Korean–Burmese couple, the pleasingly authentic Korean flavours here can come as a nice change to tired tastebuds. The menu includes favourites such as kimchi, seaweed rolls, ginseng chicken and *bibimbap* (rice topped with beef, vegetables, egg and chilli paste, which you mix together before eating). Mains K3000–4000. Daily 9am–9.30pm.

★ **Marie Min** 27th St 74/75 ☎ 02 36234; map p.577. Cute little vegetarian café on the upstairs balcony of a neat wooden building serving up a good mix of Indian and Burmese cooking ranging from samosas, chappatis and curries through to noodles and salads (mains K3000–3500) plus lassis, juices and probably the best milkshakes in town. Daily 10am–9pm.

Min Mahar Cnr 23rd & 86th streets ☎ 09 508 7882; map p.577. This large, always lively teahouse is a good place for tea and a snack and also serves up excellent Shan noodles at cut-throat prices (K1000). Daily 5am–5.30pm.

Min Thi Ha Cnr 28th & 72nd streets; map p.577. A popular teahouse, part of a small chain known for its mutton curry puffs, which you can nibble while pondering the quote from Samuel Johnson on the wall: "Great works are performed not by strength but by perseverance." Daily 5am–4pm.

Mr Bar BQ 31st 80/81 ☎ 02 73920; map p.577. Cavernous place, somewhere between an upmarket beer station and a Chinese restaurant, serving up a vast selection of tasty Cantonese-style meat, veg and seafood dishes (mains around K5000) to a lively crowd of locals and tourists. Daily 9am–11pm.

Rainbow 84th St 22/23 ☎ 02 23266; map p.577. Set over three floors, the uppermost on the roof, this corner restaurant is a popular spot for cheap draught Myanmar beer. They also have a menu of snacks and a few Chinese basics (mains K4500). Daily 8am–9pm.

Rainforest 27th St 74/75 ☎ 09 4316 1551; map p.577. One of Mandalay's best-looking restaurants – choose between the lovely antique-filled downstairs dining room or the sunny terrace above – serving up good Thai food (mains K4000–6000) including classic dishes like *larb*, tom yum and pad thai. Daily 8am–9pm.

★ **Shan Ma Ma** 81st St 29/30 ☎ 02 71858; map p.577. Usually one of the liveliest places in downtown after dark, with hordes of tourists seated at tables spilling out into the street, tucking into delicious piles of Shan and Chinese-style food. Choose what you want from the vast array of dishes on display – a full spread usually comes in at around K3000–4000. Daily 6am–10pm.

Too Too Myanmar Cuisine 27th St 74/75; map p.577. A good place to fill up on some local fare, if you don't mind the rather dreary dining room, with a big buffet spread of Burmese curries (K3500–5000), all served with at least five side dishes. Daily 10am–9pm.

DRINKING AND NIGHTLIFE

There isn't much nightlife to speak of in Mandalay, beyond the beer stations and a handful of cultural performances put on for tourists (see below).

Mann 83rd St 25/26 ☎ 02 66025; map p.577. Spit-and-sawdust drinking hole attracting an eclectic mix of locals and tourists with cheap beer, Mandalay rum and other cut-price tipples – although the food is best avoided. Daily 10am–10pm.

TRADITIONAL ENTERTAINMENT

Mandalay is considered to be Myanmar's cultural capital, and a handful of regular shows offer foreigners a glimpse into traditional performing arts. Each of the following takes place daily at 8.30pm and lasts for one hour.

Mandalay Marionettes 66th St 26/27 ☎ 02 34446, ⓦ mandalaymarionettes.com. The performance starts with music and dancing, before telling traditional stories using marionettes. It's an entertaining show but without much explanation, so try to read the programme before the lights go down. $8.

Mintha Theater 58th St 29/30 ☎ 09 680 3607, ⓦ minthatheater.com. A great opportunity to see traditional dance with extravagant costumes, accompanied by live music, with ten different performances packed into the show. K14,000.

Moustache Brothers 39th St 80/81 ☎ 09 402 579 799. The only chance you're likely to get to experience *ányeín*, a traditional form of comedy combining political satire and broad slapstick. Two of the performers, Lu Maw and Par Par Lay (who died in 2013), served six years' hard labour after making jokes about the regime in 1996, and their courageous stand against past and present corruption is reason enough to attend, even if the jokes don't always hit the mark. K10,000.

SHOPPING

Mandalay Yatanar Mall Between 77th/78th sts and 33rd/34th sts; map p.577. This vast new shopping mall was in the process of opening at the time of writing. Many of its shops are not yet occupied, although the vast jewellery and gems centre on the top floor is worth a look.

Man Myanmar Shopping Plaza 84th St 27/28; map p.577. Spit-and-sawdust local market immediately to the south of the Zegyo – and even more hectic.

Man Myoe market 84th St 38/39; map p.577. Attractive and completely untouristy little market with many gold dealers, plus a colourful fruit and veg market.

Zaw Min Khaing (aka Shwe Pathein) 36th St 77/78; map p.577. One of several craft shops and workshops in the gold-pounding district around 36th St (see box, p.576). Worth a look for its colourful and inexpensive traditional paper parasols. Daily 7am–6pm.

Zegyo 84th St 26/28; map p.577. Mandalay's biggest market, selling a huge range of everyday goods.

DIRECTORY

Banks and exchange There are foreign exchange counters and ATMs in the arrivals section at the airport. ATMs are dotted all over the centre, and many banks also change foreign currency.

Massage GGG, 27th St 74/75 (daily 10am–11pm; K8000/hr; ☏09 4025 77711), offers traditional Myanmar massages.

Post office 22nd St 80/81 (Mon–Fri 9.30am–4.30pm).

Swimming Non-hotel guests can use the pool at *Mandalay City Hotel*, 26th St 82/83 ($3.50/3hr).

AROUND MANDALAY

Mandalay makes a good base for **day-trips** exploring the surrounding area. Most people opt to combine two or more sights into a day-trip by taxi or motorbike-taxi (with **Mingun** more usually visited by boat as a half-day trip). Accommodation in Mandalay will be able to help with transport, and drivers are likely to approach you in the street. Expect to pay K15,000–20,000 for a motorbike-taxi tour of Amarapura, Sagaing and Inwa, or K20,000–30,000 by taxi.

Amarapura

Amarapura was the capital of Burma from 1783–1823 and again from 1841–57, after which King Mindon moved the seat of power 11km north to the newly founded Mandalay. Although tour buses pull up each morning (10–11am) at Mahaganayon Kyaung monastery so that tourists can watch the monks eat lunch, the real reason to visit Amarapura is for **U Bein's Bridge** – at 1.2km, the longest teak bridge in the world. In theory you need to have a K10,000 Mandalay ticket (see box, p.547) to cross, but nobody seems to check it. The bridge gets particularly busy at sunset, with many tourists hiring boats (45min; around K10,000) in order to get views of the sun setting behind the bridge. It's arguably more atmospheric – and there are certainly fewer tourists – at dawn.

Sagaing

The main reason to visit the town of **Sagaing**, the fourteenth-century capital of a Shan kingdom, is for **Sagaing Hill**, which is dotted with white-and-gold pagodas. It's around 21km from Mandalay, across the Ayeyarwady River; there are two bridges side by side.

You can drive up the hill, but it's really worth making the 25-minute walk. The most common approach on foot is from the south side; the first temple you come to at the top is **Soon U Ponya Shin Paya**, which has fantastic views of the Ayeyarwady River and the surrounding temple-dotted hills. There are several other religious structures on the hill, the most interesting of which is **Umin Thounzeh**, a curved chamber containing 43 seated and two standing Buddha images, a twenty-minute walk from Soon U Ponya Shin.

Inwa

It may be a sleepy rural area nowadays, but **Inwa** – formerly known as Ava – was the site of the Burmese capital for more than 300 years, across three separate periods.

Most people take a tour of Inwa by horse and cart (2hr; K10,000), covering the four main sights in a 5km circuit. The closest to the start is the bulky brick **Maha Aungmye Bonzan** monastery (K10,000 Mandalay ticket), where you should take a look in the bat-filled undercroft. The second attraction, nearby, is the "leaning tower" **Nanmyint**, one of the few structures remaining from King Bagyidaw's palace. Further west you'll find **Yedanasini Paya**, a collection of stupas situated photogenically in fields, and then **Bagaya Kyaung** (K10,000 Mandalay ticket). The highlight of Inwa, this is a wonderfully atmospheric working monastery, built from teak in 1834.

You can visit Inwa as part of a tour, or by public transport: pick-ups from Mandalay (cnr 29th St & 84th St; 30min) can drop you at a junction from which it's a ten-minute walk southwest down a tree-lined road to the jetty. From there, it's a very short ferry ride (daily 6am–6pm; K1200 return, K2000 with a motorbike) to the place where horse-and-cart drivers wait.

Mingun

The village of **Mingun** (K5000 entry), 8km northwest from Mandalay by boat, would not be visited today, were it not for King Bodawpaya, who in 1790 decided to build a gigantic temple here. All that was completed by the time of his death – 29 years later – was the bottom portion, an imposing 70m cube of bricks on top of a huge terrace.

To get an idea of the intended shape for **Mingun Paya**, check out the small **Pondaw Paya** to the southeast of it. The other main attraction in Mingun village is the bronze **Mingun Bell**, just north of Mingun Paya, also commissioned by Bodawpaya; with a circumference of almost 5m, it was the largest ringing bell in the world until eclipsed by one in Henan, China, in 2000. Don't miss **Hsinbyume Paya** a little further north. Its wavy design represents Mount Sumeru, the mountain at the centre of the Buddhist cosmos, and the other mountains that surround it.

Government boats (1hr; K5000; bring your passport) leave for Mingun from the pier on 26th Street in Mandalay at 9am, returning at 12.30pm. It's also possible to visit by road in conjunction with the area's other ancient city sites.

Northern Myanmar

Much of **northern Myanmar** is closed to foreigners, largely because of the history of conflict between the army and ethnic militias in Shan and Kachin states. A preliminary ceasefire was signed in 2013, and negotiations have continued since, but fighting breaks out sporadically, both with the army and between the various militias. For tourists, this has meant some restrictions on travel. Those parts of the north that can be visited, however, are generally safe and offer some of the country's best opportunities to spend time with local people. One way to do this is to take a boat trip on the **Ayeyarwady River** north of Mandalay to **Katha** and **Bhamo** (see box below), where long journey times and a scarcity of foreigners make it easy to get a sense of provincial life. Heading northeast from Mandalay instead, towards the Chinese border, treks from **Kyaukme** or **Hsipaw** offer the opportunity to stay in ethnic minority homes in traditional mountain villages.

7

AYEYARWADY RIVER TRIPS

The stretch of the Ayeyarwady River north of Mandalay is much less frequently travelled by foreigners than the route to Bagan (see p.577). Although the scenery is no more spectacular, other than the brief "second defile" (a narrowing of the river) between Bhamo and Katha, it's more rewarding for the scope it offers for interaction with local people. The route can also provide access to rarely visited towns: midway between Bhamo and Katha boats stop at Shwegu, and a few hours north of Mandalay at Kyaukmyaung, though only the former has accommodation.

The government has closed the river **north of Bhamo** to foreigners. This means that although you can take a train to Myitkina, for example, you can't start a river trip from there. Since the road to Bhamo is also closed, the easiest way to do the whole available route is to fly into Bhamo then take the boat south; the cheapest is to take a train to Katha (via Naba), travel upriver to Bhamo by boat, and then take the boat south again. Upriver travel is, of course, slower than downriver and all travel times depend on the season due to varying water levels (times given here are for November or December). On overnight trips, passengers sleep on the boat, on the bare deck or in spartan cabins.

There are two travel options open to foreigners: government-run IWT ferries, and privately run "special express" fast boats. On the larger, slower IWT ferries you're free to move around the open deck. They travel through the night, so you can make the whole Bhamo-Mandalay trip in one go if you want; it takes at least 30 hours, sometimes longer when water levels are low. On the fast boats you'll be assigned a numbered seat on a wooden bench. The eight-hour Bhamo-Katha and fourteen-hour Katha-Mandalay services run separately, so you'll have to spend a night in Katha en route.

Affordable meals are available aboard the IWT services, or on either boat you can buy a curry for around K1000 at riverside stops. Bring warm clothes as it can be cold in the mornings, plus a sleeping mat and blanket if you will be sleeping on the boat.

7

KATHA

An engagingly low-key place to hang around for a day or two, the small riverside town of **KATHA** was the model for Kyauktada in George Orwell's novel *Burmese Days* (see box below). Although Orwell modified the plan of the town a little, it's possible to seek out several of the colonial buildings that played a part either in the novel or in Orwell's life in the town.

WHAT TO SEE AND DO

At the southern end of the town centre is the British-built **jail**, which is still in use. North of the centre, on the east side of Club Street, is the former **British Club**, which was central to *Burmese Days*. It now functions as an association office and is closed to the public, but the **Tennis Club** beside it is still active. Across the road and further north, the **District Commissioner's House**, a large brick-and-wood building, is being renovated by the Katha Heritage Trust, which hopes to open it as an Orwell museum. Orwell's own house, between the market and *Hotel Katha*, is still a police residence today.

ARRIVAL AND DEPARTURE

Foreigners are not allowed to travel by road between Mandalay and Katha.

GEORGE ORWELL IN BURMA

Eric Blair (1903–50), who would later find fame under his pen name **George Orwell**, arrived in Burma in November 1922 as a youthful member of the Imperial Police. Sent first to Mandalay and Maymyo (now Pyin Oo Lwin), he spent time in the Ayeyarwady delta and Mawlamyine, where his mother had grown up, before being posted to Katha.

Orwell's experiences in Burma convinced him of the wrongs of imperialism, and he gained a reputation as an outsider more interested in spending time with the Burmese than in more "pukka" (appropriate) pursuits for a British officer. In this he resembled **Flory**, the protagonist of his first novel *Burmese Days* (1934), which was set in a thinly disguised Katha. Orwell also wrote about Burma in his essays *A Hanging* (1931) and *Shooting an Elephant* (1936).

By train The nearest mainline train station is at Naba, 30km northwest of Katha. Pick-up trucks between the two take 1hr; in Katha they leave from near the fire station. There are three or four trains daily from Naba to Mandalay (9–13hr).

By boat The IWT office on Riverside Rd, opposite the main jetty, sells tickets for ferries upriver to Bhamo (3 weekly; 10hr; $5 deck or $25 cabin) and downriver to Mandalay (3 weekly; 21hr; $9 or $45). The small fast boat counter (☎ 09 650 1155), also on Riverside Rd, sells tickets to Bhamo (daily 9am; 8hr; K12,000) and Mandalay (daily 5am; 14hr; K25,000).

ACCOMMODATION

Ayarwaddy Guesthouse Riverside Rd ☎ 075 25140. It may not be much, but it's clean and the small rooms with thin plywood partitions are convenient for the early boats. Try to get a room upstairs at the front for a window and river view. Shared bucket shower. Windowless singles $6. No breakfast. No wi-fi. Doubles $12

Hotel Katha Lanmadaw Rd ☎ 075 25390. If you need to recover from a long boat trip, you may prefer this comfortable new hotel in a colonial-style building with singles from $18. Staff are eager to please, and there's an on-site restaurant and bar with occasional live music. Their brochure has an indispensable map of Katha in Orwell's time. Doubles $25

EATING AND DRINKING

The cheapest and most interesting dinner option is the night street market. To get there, take a right out of the *Ayarwaddy Guesthouse* and then the first right.

Shwe Sisa Strand Rd. This otherwise run-of-the-mill beer station has a riverside location ideal for whiling away some time reading *Burmese Days*, perhaps with a draught beer (K750). They also serve dishes including barbecued fish. Daily 9am–10pm.

BHAMO

The pleasant town of **BHAMO** has long profited from its position close to a Chinese border crossing (closed to foreigners). There's a busy market and waterfront, plus a few temples and old teak buildings. The surrounding area is worth exploring too.

WHAT TO SEE AND DO

The most rewarding destination nearby is **Thein Pa Hill**, topped by a stupa and two meditation halls. It has good views but really a visit is all about the journey there: it's an hour's ride by bicycle, and if you're travelling by bike between December and June/July, you'll cross the 400m-long bamboo bridge from Wa Thatar village. Each year the bridge is destroyed by monsoon flooding, and rebuilt by hundreds of villagers; a ferry (K300/person, K200/bike) runs at other times.

Though it's possible to do the trip independently, it's certain to be more interesting and enjoyable if you engage the services of U Sein Win (☎09 2563 50518; K10,000 per person). He's a fascinating character, and you should ask him about the helicopter that he built in his front room (it's still there). He can also arrange a boat to Thein Pa Hill (1hr; K25,000), which from November to January may give you a chance of seeing dolphins.

ARRIVAL AND DEPARTURE

Foreigners are not allowed to travel to Bhamo by road.
By plane The airport is less than 3km east of town.
Destinations Mandalay (4 weekly; 45min); Yangon (6 weekly; 2hr 30min).
By boat IWT boats depart from moorings 4km south of town for most of the year, and from a jetty in the town centre in the rainy season. The IWT office (daily 6am–8pm; ☎074 50117) is in a colonial-era building just north of the main riverfront area. Their slow boat to Mandalay (30hr; deck $12, cabin $60) departs at 7am on Mon, Wed and Fri, stopping at Shwegu (4hr), Katha (9hr) and Kyaukmyaung (26hr). Tickets can also be purchased on board. The fast boat office (daily 6am–6pm) is on Strand Rd. Their boats depart for Katha every morning from the riverfront in town (8.30am; 8hr; K12,000) stopping at Shwegu halfway.

ACCOMMODATION

Hotel Paradise 36 Shwe Kyaung Kone ☎074 50136. A short walk south of the centre, with clean, comfortable rooms and friendly staff. The cheapest rooms have basic shared bathrooms. Doubles $14

EATING AND DRINKING

Blue Sea Off Strand Rd. In a colonnaded building clearly visible at the end of a short road, with Chinese and Kachin dishes, draught beer and stout. Daily 7am–9pm.
Sky Beer Bar Thi Ri St. Young locals pack out this restaurant and bar, around the corner from the *Friendship Hotel*, which isn't surprising given that it serves draught beer and cheap barbecue. There are also standard Chinese and Sagaing dishes for around K3000. Daily 9am–9pm.

PYIN OO LWIN

Founded in 1896 as a British hill station known as Maymyo, **PYIN OO LWIN** (it was renamed on independence) remains a popular escape from the heat of Mandalay. These days, though, most visitors are well-off Burmese who stay in comfortable hotels or holiday homes south of the centre. The town is also the site of the Defence Services Academy, Myanmar's principal military training school, which covers a huge area to the west of the centre.

WHAT TO SEE AND DO

The commercial centre of town, marked by the **Purcell Tower** and nearby **Central Market**, is rather more down-to-earth than the southern suburbs and has a flavour of South Asia thanks to the descendants of Indian and Nepalese workers brought here by the British. Further northeast, the **Shan Market** on the corner of **Circular Road** attracts farmers from surrounding areas and is at its best from 6.30 to 8am.

Circular Road is also one of the richest hunting grounds for the town's **colonial architecture**. Some of the buildings have retained their old function, such as the No. 4 Basic Education High School on Circular Road, and the Myanmar Survey Training Centre on Yone Paung Sone Street. Others have changed: Candacraig on Anawrahta Road, once the residence for unmarried staff of the Bombay Burmah Trading Company, is now being renovated as the *Thiri Myaing Hotel*.

The town's most popular attraction is the **National Kandawgyi Gardens** on Nanda Road (daily 8am–6pm; $5; ☎085 22497), 2.5km south of the centre. Founded in 1915, this large botanical garden includes a short swamp walkway, an orchid nursery and a walk-through aviary. There's an outdoor swimming pool east of the lake (K1000; bring your own towel), while views from the Nan Myint tower on the northwest side give a good sense of the affluent part of town in which the gardens are set.

The most rewarding half-day trip out of Pyin Oo Lwin is to the **Anisakan Falls**, located amid densely forested hills 9km southwest of town. The easiest way to visit is to take a motorbike taxi (K5000 return) from the roundabout on the southwestern edge of town. The walk from the car park to the base of **Dat Taw**

7

PYIN OO LWIN

ACCOMMODATION
Cherry Guest House	1
Grace Hotel I	2
Royal Green Hotel	3

EATING
December	1, 3
Diamond Café and Restaurant	2
Pan Taw Win	4
The Taj	5

Gyaint – the most impressive of the falls – takes 45 minutes, and it's a fairly strenuous hour back. The falls are at their most spectacular in the rainy season.

ARRIVAL AND DEPARTURE

By bus or minibus Buses and minibuses to Hsipaw leave from *San Pya* restaurant, northeast of town on the main highway. A turning close to the restaurant leads to the Thiri Mandala bus station, which is used by most other buses and minibuses. Minibuses or shared taxis for all destinations will pick you up at your accommodation by arrangement.

Destinations Bago (daily; 10hr 30min); Hsipaw (2 daily; 4hr); Mandalay (hourly; 2hr); Naypyitaw (daily; 8hr 30min); Taungoo (daily; 10hr); Yangon (daily; 12hr).

By train The train station is centrally located, 500m north of the Mandalay–Lashio Rd. There's one train daily in each direction.

Destinations Hsipaw (6hr 30min); Kyaukme (5hr); Mandalay (5hr).

By shared taxi or pick-up Shared taxis to Mandalay depart when full from near the *Pin Se Teahouse* on the Mandalay–Lashio road from 6am. Those to Hsipaw (3hr) leave from near the Shan market. Book through your accommodation and shared taxis will come to collect you. The price should be the same. Pick-ups to Mandalay (3hr) run all day, but more frequently early on, from Bogyoke Rd, and from the station when a train arrives.

INFORMATION AND TOURS

Travel agent Seven Diamond Express, Circular Rd (Mon–Sat 8am–8pm, Sun 8am–6pm; ☎ 085 28400).
Motorbike tours Andrew at the *Pin Se Teahouse*, Mandalay–Lashio Rd (☎ 09 4316 7181).
Guide Kyaw Kyaw Oo (☎ 09 7977 81778).

GETTING AROUND

By bike and motorbike You can get around the town's sights on foot, or rent a motorbike (K8000/day) or bicycle (K2000/day) from Crown Bicycle Rental (daily 9am–7pm) near the Purcell Tower on the Mandalay–Lashio road.

By gharry You can take one of the town's iconic *gharries* (horse and carriages) on a short tour for K8000/hr. They wait for customers around Purcell Tower and the Central Market.

ACCOMMODATION

Cherry Guest House 19 Mandalay–Lashio Rd ☎085 21306. It isn't anything fancy, and breakfast isn't included, but this place is one of the best of the cheaper guesthouses. The floors and lower walls are tiled and clean. Most rooms en suite; singles with shared bath are $10. Doubles $20
Grace Hotel I 114 Nan Myaing Rd ☎085 21230. The only budget option in the suburbs, set in spacious grounds, with basic fan-cooled two- to four-bed, en-suite rooms. There's plenty of outdoor space for lounging in the sun, and bikes and motorbikes to rent. $15 for a single guest. Doubles $20
Royal Green Hotel 17 Ziwaka Rd, cnr Pyitawthar 1st St ☎085 28422. You can pay a lot for a room in Pyin Oo Lwin, but this hotel is a mid-range bargain. The standard rooms are comfortable, with fresh new linen, satellite TV and free coffee and tea. Upstairs rooms have more light. Doubles $35

EATING

There's a good café in the National Kandawgyi Gardens.
December Mandalay–Lashio Rd. From a simple K500 glass of milk to extravagant K1800 sundaes, this rather plain shop sells everything dairy, along with a selection of small cakes and juices. There's another branch on Zaygyi St near the Purcell Tower, and a much larger one (with a petting zoo) set among fields a few kilometres out of town. Daily 7am–9pm.
Diamond Café and Restaurant Next to CB Bank, Mandalay–Lashio Rd. Real coffee, cakes, Indian sweets and a menu of standard dishes from around K2000. Free wi-fi. Daily 9am–9pm.
Pan Taw Win Nanda Rd ☎09 8530186. On the road to Kandawgyi Gardens, this is the place to drink locally grown coffee (from K1200). Also cocktails and a wide range of food, from K2000 for noodles up to K7000. Daily 7am–10pm.

★ TREAT YOURSELF

The Taj 26 Nanda Rd ☎09 7840 49880. When you tire of the lukewarm curries and monotonous rice dishes, make your way to the best restaurant in town, on the road to Kandawgyi Gardens. This large lakeside hall, with picture windows and tables neatly divided by screens, offers a range of meticulously prepared and presented Indian food served by well-trained, English-speaking staff. A full meal with dessert and drink will cost around K12,000. Daily 10am–10pm.

DIRECTORY

Bank Many banks have ATMs and currency exchange, including CB Bank, Mandalay–Lashio Rd (Mon–Fri 9.30am–3pm; ATM 24hr).
Internet Green, directly across from the Purcell Tower on Zaygyi St (K400/hr); and Friends, south of the Central Market (24hr; K300/hr).
Post office Just off the Mandalay–Lashio Rd (Mon–Fri 9.30am–4.30pm).

KYAUKME

A larger town than nearby Hsipaw, **KYAUKME** (pronounced "chow-may") is less well known, but it's catching up fast, and provides access to hiking which is arguably even better.

WHAT TO SEE AND DO

Kyaukme's busy **market** is a block south of *Northern Rock* guesthouse. There are hilltop pagodas within easy walking distance, Sunset Hill to the east and Sunrise Hill west of the centre. The primary reason to visit Kyaukme, though, is for the **trekking**. You may need to take a motorbike or tuk-tuk to the trailheads, which makes it more expensive than trekking around Hsipaw, but the ride itself is one of the highlights. The town's handful of guides mostly charge the same sliding scale from K40,000 per day if you're alone, down to K19,000 each for a group of ten. The guesthouse can put you in contact with them; Kyaw Hlaing, known as Joy (☎09 4037 06076, ✉joy .inmyanmar@gmail.com, ⌨shanprinces .webs.com), speaks perfect English and comes recommended. He specializes in motorbike tours and has colleagues who lead walking treks. He can also rent you a motorbike.

ARRIVAL AND DEPARTURE

By bus or minibus The main bus station is off Aung San Rd, just north of the railway line. Buses for Hsipaw and some other destinations also leave from a street southwest of the market.
Destinations Hsipaw (3 daily; 1hr); Mandalay (4 daily; 5hr 30min).
By train The train station is northwest of the town centre. The Gokteik viaduct, between Kyaukme and Pyin Oo Lwin, is an attraction in its own right.

7

Destinations Hsipaw (daily; 1hr 15min); Mandalay (daily; 11hr 15min); Pyin Oo Lwin (daily; 6hr 15min).

ACCOMMODATION

Northern Rock Guesthouse 4/52 Shwe Phe Oo Rd ☎082 40660. A rambling wooden house with small partitioned rooms, and a couple of en-suite rooms behind, which is run by a friendly doctor's family, who also rent bikes and have a detailed map. Doubles $12

One Love Hotel 1/139 Pinlon St ☎082 40943, ✉onelovehotel.kme@gmail.com. There's nothing to fault in this comfortable new hotel with helpful, English-speaking reception staff, a few hundred metres south of the market. Some rooms have balconies, and family rooms have bathtubs. Doubles $30

EATING AND DRINKING

There are noodle shops in the market, and restaurants on the cross street one block south.

Banyan Coffee and Tea 2/418 Aung San Rd, south of the centre. Texan expat David has a strong local clientele for his local coffee (K2000), burgers and K3500 American breakfast. Also a good place to ask for local advice. Mon–Sat 7am–7pm.

Love Village Off Aung San Rd to the east, just before the railway line. Cheap, authentic (and sometimes exotic) Shan dishes served up in a bamboo-fronted hut with open dining area. No English spoken, so you may have to point to order. Take a chance with the K500 stuffed banana leaves, and the K1000 hot mushroom soup is good. Daily 11am–5pm.

Thiripyitsaya 4/54 Shwe Phe Oo Rd. English menu and simple food at this small, friendly place just along from *Northern Rock*. Noodles from K500, plus omelettes, toast and cold juice. Daily 7am–9pm.

HSIPAW

Once considered something of a hidden gem, HSIPAW (sometimes spelt Thibaw) is transforming from a sleepy little backwater into a bustling town, thanks both to trade with China and to a burgeoning tourist industry.

WHAT TO SEE AND DO

Most people visit to go trekking, but Hsipaw itself is an engaging place to wander around. If you get up early enough then visiting the daily **morning market** is particularly interesting when candlelit before dawn.

To learn more about the town and its history, a visit to the **Shan Palace** on the northeastern edge of town (daily 3–5pm;

donation) is a must. The last Shan *saopha* (prince) vanished in 1962, with the military implicated but denying responsibility, and his nephew Sao Oo Kya – aka Mr Donald – was imprisoned for some years on dubious charges. Although released in 2009, he now works in Taunggyi, and his wife Mrs Fern talks visitors through the history of the palace and answers questions.

There are several attractions further north on the edge of town, including **Sao Pu Sao Nai nat shrine**, which is signposted on the left-hand side of Namtu Road. West of the shrine – not far from *Mrs Popcorn's Garden* (see p.588) – is an area known as **Little Bagan**. It's a tongue-in-cheek name, but the decaying stupas are photogenic.

The most popular spot for sunset is **Thein Daung Pagoda**, on a hill 2.5km south of town across the Dokhtawady River. Take a left just after the bridge, then a right at the signposted temple gateway; it's a fifteen-minute walk to the top.

At the southern end of Namtu Road, **Mahamyatmuni Paya** is one of the largest temples in the area.

If you rent a motorbike, several other options open up. One is to ride east out of town to a series of peaceful riverside **Shan villages**. Another is to head in the direction of Lashio, through the village of Su Plan – where the *Song Pinong* restaurant does wonderful barbecued fish with tamarind sauce – and on to an **ice factory** in Pan Hsao which uses ingenious home-made equipment. A little further along is a dragon-fruit plantation with a picturesque viewing platform. Always check with your hotel or with local guides before heading off the main roads.

Another way to explore the area is by **river**. Hotels, and agencies along Namtu Road, can arrange half-day boat trips including visits to a monastery and a Shan village.

ARRIVAL AND DEPARTURE

By bus or minibus Buses pick up and set down passengers at the bus company offices in town, including Duhtawadi, Lanmataw St (who run an a/c bus at 2.30pm), and Yee Shin, Namtu St. There are also several companies on Bogyoke Rd, including Khaing Dhabyay, who also arrange minibuses to Mandalay.

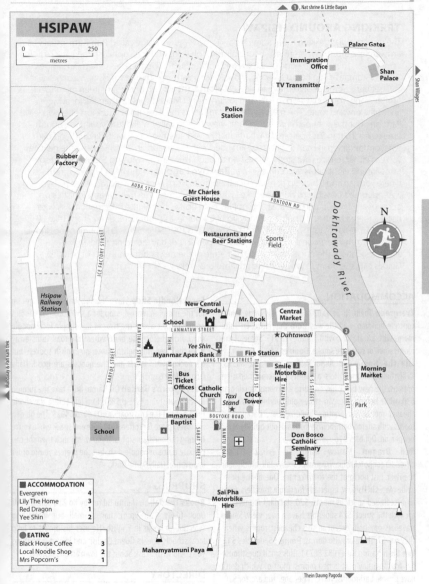

HSIPAW

0 — 250 metres

Nat shrine & Little Bagan

Palace Gates
Immigration Office
TV Transmitter
Shan Palace
Police Station
Rubber Factory
AUBA STREET
Mr Charles Guest House
PONTOON RD
ICE FACTORY STREET
Restaurants and Beer Stations
Sports Field
Dokhtaway River
Hsipaw Railway Station
New Central Pagoda
School
LANMATAW STREET
Mr. Book
Central Market
Duhtawadi
Yee Shin
Myanmar Apex Bank
Fire Station
AUNG THEPYE STREET
Smile Motorbike Hire
Morning Market
TARYOE STREET
KANTRKAW STREET
THEIN NI STREET
Bus Ticket Offices
Catholic Church
Taxi Stand
Clock Tower
THARAPYI ST
THAZIN STREET
HHIN SI STREET
SHWE NYAUNG PIN STREET
Park
Immanuel Baptist
BOGYOKE ROAD
SABAT STREET
NAMTU ROAD
School
Don Bosco Catholic Seminary
School
Sai Pha Motorbike Hire
Mahamyatmuni Paya
Thein Daung Pagoda
Shan Villages
Mandalay & Pan Kam trek
N

ACCOMMODATION
Evergreen — 4
Lily The Home — 3
Red Dragon — 1
Yee Shin — 2

EATING
Black House Coffee — 3
Local Noodle Shop — 2
Mrs Popcorn's — 1

Destinations Kalaw (3 daily; 12hr 30min); Kyaukme (3 daily; 1hr); Lashio (2 daily; 2hr); Mandalay (7 daily; 5hr); Naypyitaw (3 daily; 11hr 30min); Nyaungshwe for Inle Lake (3 daily; 11hr 30min); Pyin Oo Lwin (6 daily; 3hr 30min); Yangon (3 daily; 13hr 30min).

By shared taxi Vehicles to Mandalay (5hr 30min) or Pyin Oo Lwin (3hr 30min) can be booked through your guesthouse or through Khaing Dhabyay, Bogyoke Rd.

By train The train station is on the western side of the town centre, and tickets are only sold on the day of travel. If you're heading for Mandalay it's much quicker to get off at Pyin Oo Lwin and take a bus. This still allows you to see the spectacular Gokteik viaduct (see p.585).

Destinations Kyaukme (daily; 1hr 15min); Lashio (daily; 4hr); Mandalay (daily; 13hr 15min); Pyin Oo Lwin (daily; 6hr 40min).

7

TREKKING AROUND HSIPAW

The most popular trekking route from Hsipaw is to a Palaung village called **Pan Kam**, usually as an overnight trip. It's a four- to five-hour walk through fields and then uphill, starting at a Muslim cemetery on the western edge of Hsipaw and continuing through a series of farming villages.

The headman at Pan Kam, O Maung, works closely with guesthouses in Hsipaw, so the village can get busy. Some people prefer to sleep at **Htan Sant** around one hour fifteen minutes further along. You could stop in Pan Kam for lunch at O Maung's home, then ask for advice about the onward route. The main route to Htan Sant is the left path at a fork just after you leave Pan Kam, but the right path has exceptional views of the valley. Make sure you have enough time to reach Htan Sant before dark, particularly if you take the less-travelled right-hand path.

Accommodation in Htan Sant can be arranged with the headman, Khao San Aye; the next day you can either retrace your steps or press on through Paw Ka, Ohn Mu and Sar Maw. This route takes around eight hours and comes out at **Baw Gyo Pagoda** on the main highway, from where you can find a pick-up or hitch back the 8km to Hsipaw, or call a motorbike to pick you up.

Although it's possible to do these hikes without a guide, bear in mind that skirmishes do occasionally break out in the area and guides have up-to-the-minute information. Ask your hotel if there's been any trouble recently. To hire a guide, ask your hotel or try Than Htike (☎09 3618 6646, ✉lionmanhpw@gmail.com) or Kham Lu (☎09 2506 93985, ✉kyawmoonoo@gmail .com), who charge around K15,000–20,000 per person per day including food and accommodation. The price varies with the nature of the trek and the number of people. Guides can also arrange longer, more adventurous, treks.

ACCOMMODATION

Evergreen Thein Ni St ☎082 80670. This large white concrete building is a little way from the centre. En-suite rooms with a/c are $22; with fan they're $15. Some of the rooms smell of cigarette smoke. Doubles $10

Lily the Home 108 Aung Thapye St ☎082 80318, ⊛lilythehome.com. Offers a variety of accommodation options: the new block has en-suite a/c rooms starting at $30, while behind, the two-storey old building has a few cheaper rooms. Yet another building has "backpacker" rooms with shared bathrooms which sell out quickly at $8 per person. Doubles $16

Red Dragon Mahaw Gani St ☎082 80740, ✉reddragonhotel.hsipaw@gmail.com. A tall block near the river, just north of the town centre. One of the best-value places in Hsipaw, especially for single travellers, with high-ceilinged spacious rooms. $20 standard rooms with a/c face the street, $24 superiors have a river view. Single travellers pay half, except in the cheapest rooms where they pay $7. There are also dorms. Dorms $6, doubles $12

Yee Shin Namtu Rd ☎082 80711. This small guesthouse has fourteen tiny partitioned rooms, most of which don't have private bathrooms; you can get one, and a/c, for $20. On the main road, so it may get noisy. Doubles $12

EATING AND DRINKING

There's a row of restaurants along Namtu Rd, north of the bridge.

Black House Coffee Shwe Nyaung Pin St. An old wooden house with a large, peaceful riverside terrace, owned by a Shan family, serving hot drinks including coffee from K1000, cake at K700 and a few other dishes. Daily around 7am–6pm.

Local Noodle Shop Shwe Nyaung Pin St. If you get up for the morning market, stop for a K500 bowl of noodles on the terrace above the river at this simple local noodle shop, right before the bend where the road turns away from the river. No English name, no English spoken, but it's packed with locals and the noodles are good. Daily from before 6am.

Mrs Popcorn's Garden Off Namtu Rd – take the turning for the *nat* shrine (see p.586), turn left before the shrine then right at the crossroads ☎09 4026 64925. The garden is a lovely place for coffee, fruit juice or a snack while you're touring the northern sights. If you want lunch then she can prepare a rice or noodle dish, but she prefers you to order in advance. Daily 9am–dusk.

SHOPPING

Books The stall on Namtu Rd run by Ko Zaw Tun, aka Mr Book (daily 6am–9pm), has a small but interesting selection of books in English. He uses his profits to help local schools, speaks fluent English and knows everything you could wish to ask about the town and its history.

DIRECTORY

Banks Myanmar Apex bank (Mon–Fri 10am–3pm) has an ATM and currency exchange (plus others).

Bicycle rental Most guesthouses rent bicycles, usually for K2000/day.

Motorbike rental Smile, Aung Thapye St, one block west of *Lily the Home* – no English sign, look for the bikes (daily 7am–7pm; K8000/day). Also Sai Pha, Namtu Rd, at the southern end of town, near Mahamyatmuni Paya (daily 7am–7pm; K8000/day).

BACUIT ARCHIPELAGO, PALAWAN

The Philippines

HIGHLIGHTS

❶ **Vigan** Travel back in time wandering along Vigan's cobbled streets. **See p.617**

❷ **The Cordilleras** Home to Sagada's hanging coffins and Banaue's 2000-year-old rice terraces. See p.619

❸ **Boracay** First stop for sun-worshippers and partygoers is White Beach. **See p.635**

❹ **Malapascua Island** Dive among magnificent thresher sharks at Monad Shoal. **See p.656**

❺ **Bacuit Archipelago** Turquoise waters and hidden beaches amid breathtaking limestone cliffs. **See p.668**

HIGHLIGHTS ARE MARKED ON THE MAP ON P.591

ROUGH COSTS

Daily budget Basic US$25/Occasional treat US$40

Drink San Miguel beer US$1

Food *Adobo* US$3

Hostel/budget hotel US$10/US$15

Travel Bus: Manila–Banaue (9hr) US$10; Fast ferry: Dumaguete–Tagbilaran (2hr) $16; Flight: Manila–Puerto Princesa (1hr 15min) $60

FACT FILE

Population 103 million

Languages Filipino (Tagalog), Visayan, English, with nine other languages and 87 dialects

Currency Peso (P)

Capital Manila

International phone code ☎ + 63

Time zone GMT + 8hr

Introduction

Backpackers on the traditional Asian trails have tended to ignore the Philippines because it involves an extra flight, albeit a short one, across the South China Sea. You won't find the kind of travellers' scene that has come to dominate areas like southern Thailand, though the beaches and islands certainly give Thailand a run for its money. It's this very lack of mass tourism that makes the Philippines such an attractive destination. The world's second-largest archipelago (after Indonesia), with 7107 islands – sixty percent of them uninhabited – and over 36,000km of coastline, it nonetheless has a landmass only roughly the size of Italy. If you're ready to cope with some eccentric infrastructure, a distinctly laidback attitude towards time, and a national obsession with karaoke, the Philippines has plenty to offer.

Most international flights land in the capital, **Manila**, which, though dilapidated and traffic-choked, also has some of the ritziest shopping malls and liveliest nightlife in Asia. For beach connoisseurs, the central **Visayan region** is an island-hopper's paradise. Though Boracay remains the most popular island destination, travellers are discovering quiet islands around Cebu and Bohol; if you're willing to leave the beaten track, it's not hard to find your own deserted tropical beach. **Palawan** is an unforgettable wilderness of diamond-blue lagoons, volcanic lakes and first-rate scuba diving, while the **Cordillera Mountains** of northern Luzon are the country's tribal heartland, populated by the same groups that settled here around 500 BC.

Centuries of **colonial rule** have resulted in a delightfully mixed-up country of potent but conflicting influences. Spain brought Catholicism, European architecture and the *mañana* ethic, while America gave the Philippines its constitution and its passion for basketball, beauty pageants and pizza. In 1946 the Philippines became Asia's first real democracy, a fact most Filipinos remain fiercely proud of.

Despite the political intrigues and the poverty, Filipinos remain enviably optimistic and gregarious. Graciousness and warmth seem to be built into their genes, though they are also passionate,

WHEN TO GO

The Philippines has a tropical marine climate characterized by two distinct seasons: the **wet season** (southwest monsoon, or *habagat*) from May to October and the **dry season** (northeast monsoon, or *amihan*) from November to April, though there can still be quite a lot of rain until February. Between May and December the country is hit directly by at least five or six typhoons. This doesn't necessarily mean the wet season is a bad time to travel, though flights are sometimes cancelled and roads are made impassable by flood waters, even in the capital – but generally this only lasts a few days. The first typhoon can hit as early as May, although typically it is June or July before the rains really start, with August the wettest month. The southern Visayas and Palawan are less prone to typhoons.

Temperatures are fairly constant throughout the year. November through to February are the coolest months, with daytime highs of around 28°C. March, April and May are very hot: expect temperatures to peak at 36°C.

At **Christmas** and **Easter**, the whole of the Philippines hits the road and getting a seat on a bus or plane can be difficult.

sometimes hot-headedly so. They love food, music and romance; and the hundreds of **fiestas** and religious ceremonies that are held throughout the year are an integral part of Filipino life. English is widely spoken and you will be greeted with the honorific "ma'am" or "sir".

The Philippines is a passion play writ large, a country that will turn every notion you ever had of Asia on its head. Even when typhoons devastate entire islands, or when volcanoes erupt, Filipinos remain stoically and passively fatalistic. When dealing with the trials and tribulations of

THE PHILIPPINES

HIGHLIGHTS

1. Vigan
2. The Cordilleras
3. Boracay
4. Malapascua Island
5. Bacuit Archipelago

life in the Philippines, Filipinos' usual reaction is to smile, throw up their hands, and say *bahala-na* – a phrase that loosely translates to "what will be, will be".

CHRONOLOGY

500 BC Trade develops with the archipelago's neighbours – the powerful Hindu empires in Java and Sumatra, and with China.

1380 Arab scholar Makdam arrives in the Sulu Islands.

1475 Muslim leader Sharif Mohammed Kabungsuwan, from Johore, marries a local princess and declares himself the first sultan of Mindanao. Islam becomes established in Mindanao, and influential as far as Luzon.

April 24, 1521 Ferdinand Magellan arrives in Cebu and claims the islands for Spain. He is killed in a skirmish with warriors led by chief Lapu-Lapu.

1565 Miguel Lopez de Legaspi, under orders from King Philip II, establishes a colony in Bohol and erects the first Spanish fort in the Philippines on Cebu.

1571 Legaspi conquers Manila, and a year later the whole country, except the Islamic Sulu Islands and Mindanao. Spanish friars zealously spread Catholicism.

1762 The British occupy Manila for a few months, but hand it back to Spain under the conditions of the Treaty of Paris, signed in 1763.

1892 José Rizal, a lawyer, novelist and poet whose anti-colonial writings portray Spanish friars as unscrupulous and depraved, returns to Manila and founds the reform movement Liga Filipina. He is arrested and exiled to Mindanao. Andres Bonifacio takes over and establishes the revolutionary group Katipunan.

1896 Armed struggle for independence breaks out, and Rizal is arrested and then executed on December 30, in what is now Rizal Park in Manila.

1897 Allied with a young firebrand general, Emilio Aguinaldo, Bonifacio supports violent opposition. Facing all-out insurrection, the Spanish negotiate a truce with Aguinaldo, and Bonifacio is executed.

1898 The US and Spain are at war over Cuba, and the US attack and defeat the Spanish fleet in Manila Bay. The Filipinos fight with the US, and General Aguinaldo declares the Philippines independent. However, the US pays Spain US$20 million for the Philippines, and takes over as a colonizing power.

1898–1902 The Filipino–American War lasts for three years (with skirmishes for another seven), and more than 600,000 Filipinos are killed.

1935 Washington recognizes a new Philippine constitution, making the Philippines a commonwealth of the US. Manuel Quezon wins the country's first presidential elections.

1942 Japanese troops land on Luzon and conquer Manila on January 2. US General MacArthur and Quezon leave the American base on Corregidor, which the Japanese overrun in days; during the Bataan Death March that follows, 10,000 Americans and Filipinos die.

October 1944 MacArthur returns, wading ashore at Leyte and recapturing the archipelago from retreating Japanese forces.

July 4, 1946 The Philippines is granted full independence and Manuel Roxas is sworn in as the first president of the republic.

1965 Ferdinand Edralin Marcos, a brilliant young lawyer and member of the Senate, is elected president, portraying himself as a force for reform. In his first term he embarks on a huge infrastructure programme.

1969 Marcos is re-elected. Poverty and social inequality are still rife, and there is student, labour and peasant unrest, much of it stoked by communists, which Marcos (backed by the US) uses to perpetuate his hold on power.

September 21, 1972 Marcos declares martial law, arresting Senator Ninoy Aquino and other opposition leaders.

August 21, 1983 Aquino, who had been in exile in the US for three years, returns to the Philippines. He is assassinated as he leaves his plane at Manila Airport.

February 7, 1986 At a snap election, the opposition unites behind Aquino's widow, Cory. On February 25, both Marcos and Cory claim victory and are sworn in at separate ceremonies. Archbishop Jaime Sin urges the people to take to the streets and Ferdinand and Imelda Marcos flee into exile in Hawaii; Ferdinand dies in 1989. Conservative estimates of their plunder are around $10 billion.

1986–92 Cory Aquino's presidency is plagued by problems. She backtracks on promises for land reforms, survives seven coup attempts and makes little headway in tackling the widespread poverty.

July 1, 1992 Fidel Ramos is elected president.

1998 Former vice-president Joseph Estrada (known as Erap, a play on the Filipino word for friend, *pare*), a former tough-guy film actor, becomes president.

2000 Estrada is accused of receiving P500 million in illegal gambling payoffs. He is impeached, but the trial falls apart. Following protests of half a million people, the military withdraws its support and Estrada is evicted from Malacañang.

January 20, 2001 Vice-president Gloria Macapagal-Arroyo is sworn in as president.

2004 Macapagal-Arroyo wins the presidential elections against Fernando Poe Jr, a movie star and friend of Estrada. Poe's supporters claim election fraud.

November 2007 An attempted coup in Manila is put down. It is similar to one in 2003, and around a dozen others in the past twenty years.

August 2008 Separatist violence in Mindanao surges after peace talks break down, leaving at least 30 people dead.

November 2009 The slaughter of 57 civilians (at least 34 of them journalists) sends shock waves around the world in what becomes known as the Maguindinao massacre. The massacre underlines the Arroyo administration's tolerance of extra-judicial killings and human rights abuses. Peace talks resume between the government and the Moro Islamic Libration Front.

May 2010 Benigno (Noynoy) Aquino, son of democracy icons Cory and Ninoy, wins the presidency by a landslide, promising to fight corruption.

August 2013 A spate of bombings in Cagayan de Oro and Cotabato City puts Mindanao back in the spotlight. In September separatists occupy the southern city of Zamboanga. Thousands flee.

November 2013 Typhoon Haiyan (known locally as "Yolanda") is recognized as the strongest typhoon to make landfall, with wind speeds in excess of 300km/hr. The death toll is over 6000, while millions are left without food, shelter, electricity or clean drinking water (see box, p.655).

May 2016 Highly controversial Davao mayor Rodrigo Duterte is elected president and sets about fulfilling his campaign promise of a war on drugs by ordering the extra-judicial killings of dealers and addicts, even admitting to personally executing a number of people. He reacts to UN criticism by threatening to withdraw the Philippines and form a new alliance with China and some African nations.

ARRIVAL AND DEPARTURE

Most major Southeast Asian airlines have regular **flights** to Manila and Cebu, with a few also flying to Clark, north of Manila, and Kalibo for Boracay. **Hong Kong** is one of the most convenient gateways; there are also regular flights from many major Asian cities, including Bangkok, Tokyo, Seoul, Shanghai, Beijing, Taipei, Singapore and Kuala Lumpur.

There's a twice-weekly ferry service between Sandakan and Sabah in Malaysia and Zamboanga in Mindanao (22hr). However, the security situation in the Sulu archipelago and much of Mindanao means this route is inadvisable (see box, p.660).

VISAS

Most tourists do not need a visa to enter the Philippines for up to **thirty days**, though you need a passport valid for at least six months and an onward ticket to another country. You can apply for longer visas in advance from a Philippine embassy or consulate. A single-entry visa,

valid for **three months** from the date of issue, costs £76.80/$96, and a multiple-cntry visa, valid for **one year** from the date of issue, around £133.80/$167, though you can only get the latter if you have previously been issued a visa for the Philippines. Apart from a valid passport and a completed application form, downloadable from some Philippine embassy websites (see ⓦ dfa.gov.ph), you will have to present proof that you have enough money for the duration of your stay in the Philippines.

Without a visa in advance, the thirty-day stay you're granted on arrival can be extended at immigration offices in major cities and some key tourist destinations, or through many travel agents. You'll only be granted a month extension the first time, then two months the second time, at which point you'll also have to purchase an **I-Card** (an ID card which should facilitate immigration procedures and allows you to open a bank account in the Philippines). Further extensions of two months will then be granted up to a maximum of sixteen months. Extension fees generally cost P3150 for the first month, then P4900 for the next two months (including a one-off I-Card fee). See ⓦ immigration.gov.ph for information on visa requirements.

GETTING AROUND

The number of **flights** and **ferry services** between major destinations makes it easy to cover the archipelago, even when you're on a budget. One essential, however, is a flexible itinerary. Local road transport is mostly limited to **buses** and **jeepneys**, although in cities such as Manila and Cebu it's still relatively cheap to get around by taxi.

BY PLANE

Air travel is a godsend for island-hoppers, with a number of airlines both large and small linking Manila to most of the country's major destinations. However, while getting from Manila or Cebu to almost any island is straightforward, it can be difficult to fly between islands, meaning some backtracking is hard to

8

AIRLINES

Not all routes appear on the websites, so it's worth phoning to check.

Air Asia ☎ 02 742 2742, **Ⓦ** airasia.com
Cebu Pacific ☎ 02 702 0888,
Ⓦ cebupacificair.com
PAL Express ☎ 02 855 9000,
Ⓦ flypalexpress.com
Philippine Airlines (PAL) ☎ 02 855 8888,
Ⓦ philippineairlines.com
SEAIR ☎ 02 849 0101, **Ⓦ** flyseair.com
Skyjet ☎ 02 823 3366, **Ⓦ** flyskyjetair.com

avoid. Philippine Airlines (PAL), their budget division PAL Express and Cebu Pacific have the most comprehensive schedules, while Air Asia has increased competition on some key routes; Southeast Asian Airlines (SEAIR) and Skyjet are both competitive small airlines offering regular flights to major resort areas and also to interesting destinations often not served by larger airlines. **Airfares** in the Philippines are generally inexpensive, especially if you book more than three days in advance: most flights shouldn't cost more than $75, and are often considerably less when booked much earlier. Budget carriers' base fares are often without check-in luggage, but this is a comparatively cheap add-on. Routes to minor airports which can only take small planes often have maximum **luggage restrictions** of 10kg.

BY BUS

For Filipinos, the journey is as much a part of the experience as the destination. Nowhere is this truer than on the **buses**. Dilapidated contraptions with no air-conditioning compete with bigger bus lines with all mod cons (even wi-fi) on hundreds of routes that span out from Manila. Fares are cheap, but journeys can be long. Manila to Banaue, for instance, costs P450 on an air-conditioned bus, but takes nine hours. You might want to make this type of trip overnight, when traffic is lighter and delays less likely, although night drives can be scary, especially through mountain regions. For longer trips, advance booking is recommended.

BY FERRY

Boats are the bread and butter of Philippine travel, with wooden outrigger boats (*bangkas*) and ferries ready to take you from one destination to the next in varying degrees of comfort and safety. Remember that even in the dry season, the open ocean can get rough, so think carefully about using small boats that look ill-equipped or overcrowded. If it looks a bit dodgy, it probably is. Ferry disasters occur with depressing regularity, often with great loss of life. Since the Chinese government 2012 buyout and amalgamation of Negros Navigation, Cebu Ferries, Supercat and Superferry, 2GO Travel (Ⓦ travel.2go.com.ph) is the country's biggest ferry company. You will still see the old names used on occasion, but all routes are now operated under the 2GO banner. There are daily sailings throughout the country, but even these have not been accident-free. Ferries are cheap but often crowded, although on overnight journeys you can always keep away from the dormitory crowds by sleeping on the deck, or paying extra for a cabin. For an idea of **fares**: Manila to Cagayan de Oro will set you back about P2100, to Cebu City around P2400. Given that airfares are so cheap, there's little appeal in taking long-distance ferries.

LOCAL TRANSPORT

The stalwart of the transport system is the fabled **jeepney**, a legacy of World War II, when American soldiers left behind army jeeps; these were converted by ingenious locals into factotum vehicles, carrying everything from produce to livestock and people. Over the years, they evolved into today's colourful workhorses of the road, with fairy lights and cheesy decor. Provincial jeepneys charge about P10 a ride, while in Manila prices range from P7 for a short hop to P20 for longer distances. Jeepneys ply particular routes, indicated on the side of the vehicle, and stop anywhere, so simply flag one down and hop on. When you want to get off, bang on the roof or shout "*para!*"

In many cities old jeepneys are now being replaced with modern vans or "FXs", cheaper than taxis and more comfortable than jeepneys or buses though still decorated in the same ostentatious manner. The fare is usually P20 for a short trip.

Tricycles are the Filipino equivalent of the Thai tuk-tuk, and while they are not allowed on major roads they can be useful for getting from a bus station to a beach and back again. Most tricycles carry three (or more) passengers, and fares tend to increase dramatically when a tourist approaches, so always reach agreement beforehand. The regular fare is P10 for a quick hop, and fares are lower if you are willing to share the tricycle with anyone else who flags it down and can fit on board. To hire the tricycle exclusively for yourself – or for a small group – P50 is a reasonable fare for a ten-minute journey, or you can charter one for a half day for P350–400.

TAXIS

By international standards, **taxis** in the Philippines are dirt-cheap, making them a viable option for getting around on a daily basis. In larger cities, the flag-down rate is P30 plus P3.50 per 500m. Before you get in, make sure the driver will use his meter or that you have negotiated a reasonable fare. Never use a taxi if the driver has companions and never use one that isn't clearly marked as a taxi. All taxi registration plates have black letters on a yellow background.

ACCOMMODATION

As a budget traveller, this is likely to be your biggest expense. Accommodation is a little more expensive than in other Southeast Asian countries, with quality varying quite dramatically. On the outlying islands the budget rooms are often in the form of a **nipa hut**, made from woven palms, ranging in price from P400 for a simple room with communal bath to P1200 for something a bit more refined with private bath, air-conditioning and TV. In Manila, Cebu and Boracay you can expect to pay up to P1400 at "budget" level. Almost all budget places offer both fan and more expensive air-conditioned rooms.

Electricity is usually supplied at 220V. Plugs have two flat and rectangular pins.

ADDRESSES

It's common in the Philippines for buildings to give an **address** as 122 Legaspi cnr Velasco streets. This means the place you are looking for is at (or near) the junction of Legaspi Street and Velasco Street. Streets are sometimes renamed in honour of new heroes but are often still referred to by their original name. The ground floor of multistorey buildings is referred to as the first floor and the first floor as the second, following US convention.

Power cuts ("brownouts") are common, especially in the more rural areas.

FOOD AND DRINK

The high esteem in which Filipinos hold their **food** is encapsulated by the common greeting "*kain na tayo*" ("Let's eat!"). Filipino food has not been embraced worldwide because it has an unwarranted reputation for being one of Asia's less adventurous cuisines, offering a relatively bland meat and rice diet with little variety or spice. But those willing to experiment will find even the simplest rural dishes can offer an intriguing blend of the familiar and the exotic. Colonization and migration have resulted in Malay, Chinese, Spanish and American culinary influences, sometimes all within the same meal.

Food is something of a comfort blanket for Filipinos, and to be without it is cause for panic. Any Filipino who eats only three meals a day is usually considered unwell because that's simply not thought to be sufficient. A healthy appetite is seen as a sign of a robust constitution, and sundry smaller meals and snacks – **merienda** – are eaten in between every meal. Not to partake when offered can be considered rude. Sampling *balut* (boiled duck embryo in the shell), a popular type of *merienda*, and reputed aphrodisiac, will practically make you an honorary *Pinoy* (Filipino), but whether the admiration of the locals is enough of an incentive is up to you.

Meat dishes, notably of chicken and pork (both cheap and easily available),

8

form the bulk of the Filipino diet. The **national dish** is *adobo*, which is chicken or pork (or both) cooked in soy sauce and vinegar, with pepper and garlic. *Baboy* (pig) is the basis of many coveted dishes such as *pata* (pig's knuckle) and *sisig* (fried chopped pork, liver and onions). At special celebrations, Filipinos are passionate about their *lechon*, roasted pig stuffed with *pandan* (screwpine) leaves and cooked so the skin turns to crackling. *Lechon de leche* is roasted suckling pig. Pork is also the basis of spicy *Bicol Express*, consisting of pork cooked in coconut milk, soy sauce and vinegar, with chillies (a vegetable version is also available). Coconut, soy sauce, vinegar and *patis* (a brown fish sauce, more watery than *bagoong*, a smelly, salty fish paste) are widely used to add flavour. Sweets and desserts are popular throughout the archipelago and make use of a host of local products including cane sugar, coconut and rice.

The **beers** of choice in the Philippines are San Miguel and San Miguel Light (SML), at P40–50 per bottle, some of the world's cheapest. SM's seven percent Red Horse and apple-flavoured beer are also popular, while craft ales are increasingly available, in Manila at least. There are also plenty of cheap Philippine-made spirits such as Tanduay rum and San Miguel *ginebra* (gin), as well as pungent *tapuy* (rice wine). Fresh *buko* (coconut) or *calamansi* (lime) juice are refreshing on a hot day.

CULTURE AND ETIQUETTE

Filipinos tend to be outgoing people who are not afraid to ask **personal questions**

GOOD TO KNOW

Toilets are referred to as CRs (comfort rooms) and more often than not won't have toilet paper, so carry some tissues wherever you go.

Tampons are not displayed on pharmacy shelves; you have to ask for them at the counter.

To ask for **the bill** in a restaurant, make the sign of a rectangle in the air with your thumb and index finger.

---

and certainly don't consider it rude; prepare to be interrogated by everyone you meet. They will want to know where you are from, why you are in the Philippines, how old you are, whether you are married – if not, why not – and so on. Solo travellers are a puzzle to Filipinos, and will be asked with concern why they are alone. They pride themselves on their hospitality and are always ready to share a meal or a few drinks. Don't offend by refusing outright.

A sense of *delicadeza* is also important to Filipinos. This is what you might refer to as propriety, a simple sense of good behaviour, particularly in the presence of elders or women. Filipinos who don't speak good English will often answer any question you ask them with a smile and a nod. Be careful: a smile and a nod doesn't always mean "yes". It can also mean "no", "maybe" or "I have no idea what you are talking about". It's not advisable to **lose your temper** – Filipinos hate to be embarrassed in front of others and so don't respond well to being shouted at. The general rule is to behave in a manner conducive to what the locals refer to as "SIR", or smooth interpersonal relationships. To act otherwise is to invite the worst thing a Filipino can say about another person, that they are *walang hiya* (without shame/propriety).

Filipinos share the same attitudes to **dress** as other Southeast Asian countries (see p.40).

RELIGION

Unlike most of Asia, the Philippines is predominantly Roman Catholic, with over eighty percent of the population professing the faith. This has been the way since the Spanish colonization of the country in the sixteenth century and the older generation especially tend to be rather devout. There are, however, traces of tribal beliefs that sometimes lead to a type of "folk Catholicism" evidenced in certain rituals and practices. Another notable peculiarity is the rather extreme and infamous re-enactments of the crucifixion that still take place every Easter near San Fernando, Pampanga. Recent years have also seen a growth in the number of Protestants. The country's main religious minority, however, are the Muslims, who mostly inhabit Mindanao and the Sulu Archipelago, closer to the Islamic influence of Malaysia and Indonesia.

DIVING

Of the four million tourists who visit the Philippines every year, many come for the diving alone. It's hardly surprising that in a nation made up of 7107 islands there are dive sites all over the place, with the exception perhaps of the far north. An hour from Batangas City by ferry is the hugely popular area around **Puerto Galera**, home to many dive schools and fine beaches (see p.630). The **Visayas** has dive sites in Boracay, Apo Island (near Dumaguete), Cebu, Bohol and other spots. A one-hour flight or twelve-hour ferry journey from the capital takes you to the "last frontier" of **Palawan**, where you can dive at World War II Japanese wrecks in the company of dolphins and manta rays (see p.669).

PADI organizes most scuba tuition in the Philippines. Always pick a PADI dive centre and ask to see their certification. If you haven't been diving before, you can start with a "Discovery Dive" to see if you like it. The full PADI Open Water Diver course takes around four days and costs at least US$380. You might want to consider doing a referral course with PADI at home, which involves doing the pool sessions and written tests before you travel, then doing the final checkout dives with a PADI resort in the Philippines. You'll need to bring your PADI referral documents with you, as your instructor in the Philippines will want to see them.

COCKFIGHTING

Along with basketball, cockfighting (*sabong*), in its legal and illegal forms, is probably the closest thing to a national pastime in the Philippines. It's a bloody business, with knives used and thousands of pesos changing hands on larger fights. If you insist on checking it out for yourself, you're best off going with a Filipino friend.

COMMUNICATIONS

Filipinos love their cell phones and mobile networks provide coverage in areas where landlines are limited. Using them costs next to nothing. If you're planning to be in the country even for a short time, buying a **local SIM card** (P40, including a bundle of free texts) is well worth it, and is convenient for texting reservations to hotels and dive operators. Make sure that your phone is unlocked before you travel, though buying a handset is also pretty cheap. Packages for the country's two largest networks, Smart and Globe, are widely available in malls, and even the tiniest *sari-sari* store (small hut stores selling everything from crackers to shampoo sachets) sells phone credit – look out for the ubiquitous "*Load na dito*" signs. Prepaid cards come in units from P100 to P1000 ("loads"), or more often you'll just give your number to the stall owner, pay the amount and then instantly receive a load balance from the network supplier. Many places only have mobile phone contact numbers, and as such are more likely to change.

International phonecards are sold in convenience stores such as 7-Eleven in P100, P200, P300 and P500 denominations.

Internet cafés are all over Manila, Cebu and the provincial cities (about P15–25/hr), and many establishments offer **wi-fi**. In rural areas internet access is becoming more readily available but connections can be very slow and unreliable.

Letters from the Philippines take at least five days to reach other countries by air, sometimes significantly longer. If you have to post anything valuable, use a

THE PHILIPPINES ONLINE

Ⓦ**divephil.com** An online guide listing the country's best dive spots.
Ⓦ**tourism.gov.ph** The Department of Tourism's official website.
Ⓦ**visitmyphilippines.com** Latest news and events from around the country.
Ⓦ**itsmorefuninthephilippines.co.uk** The DOT's marketing domain showcases the country's most sought-after activities and destinations.

courier or registered mail. Major post offices in Manila and elsewhere have a counter for **poste restante**.

CRIME AND SAFETY

The Philippines has something of an unfair reputation as a dangerous place, often reinforced by Filipinos themselves who are sometimes overzealous in their warnings to travellers. As long as you exercise discretion and common sense, it's no worse than anywhere else. There are a number of insurgent groups in the country fighting for causes that range from an independent Muslim homeland

8

TAGALOG

There are more than 150 languages and dialects in the Philippines. Tagalog, also known as Filipino or Pilipino, is spoken as a first language by 25 million people – mostly on Luzon – and is the national language. Many English words have been adopted by Filipinos, giving rise to a slang known affectionately as Taglish.

Tagalog has formal and informal **forms of address**, the formal usually reserved for people who are significantly older. Honorifics are important to Filipinos; for your elders, use Mr or Mrs/Miss before the surname, or just use Sir/Ma'am/Miss if you don't know their name. It's common to use *kuya/ate* (elder brother/sister) to address people informally. The suffix "po" indicates respect and can be added to almost any word or phrase. The informal form of "I'm fine" is *mabuti* and the formal *mabuti-po*; *o-po* is a respectful "yes" and it's common to hear Filipinos say *sorry-po* for "sorry".

STRESSES

Tagalog sounds staccato to the foreign ear, with clipped vowels and consonants. It has no tones, and most words are spoken as they are written, though working out which syllable to **stress** is tricky. In words of two syllables, the first syllable tends to be stressed, while in words of three or more syllables the stress is almost always on the final or penultimate syllable; thus Boracay is pronounced Bo-**ra**-kay or sometimes Bo-ra-**kay**, but never **Bo**-ra-kay. Sometimes a change in the stress can drastically alter the meaning. Vowels that fall consecutively in a word are always pronounced individually, as is every syllable; for example, *tao* meaning person or people is pronounced ta-o, while *oo* for yes is pronounced oh-oh (with each vowel closer to the "o" in "show" than in "bore").

PRONUNCIATION

a as in "**a**pple"
e as in "m**e**ss"
i as in "d**i**tto", though a little more elongated
o as in "b**o**re"
u as in "p**u**t"
ay as in "b**uy**"
aw as in "m**ou**nt"
iw is the sound **ee** continued into the **u** sound of "p**u**t"
oy as in "n**oi**se"
uw as in "q**ua**rter"
uy produced making the sound **oo** and continuing it to the **i** sound in d**i**tto
c as in "s**k**in"
g as in "**g**et"
k as in "s**k**in" (unaspirated)
mga is pronounced ma**ng**
ng as in "si**nging"**
p as in "s**p**eak" (unaspirated)
t as in "s**t**op" (unaspirated)

GREETINGS AND BASIC PHRASES

Hello/how are you?	*Ka**mu**sta*
Fine, thanks	*Ma**bu**ti, salamat*
Goodbye	Pa**a**lam, or *Bye*
Good evening	*Magandang ga**bi***
Excuse me	*Iskyus* (to get past)
Please	Use the word *paki* before a verb. For example, *upo* means sit, so "please sit" is *paki-upo paki*
Thank you	*Sala**mat***
Yes	*oo (oh-oh)*
No	*Hindi*
My name is …	*Ako si …*

FOOD AND DRINK GLOSSARY

Vegetarian ako	I'm vegetarian

Main dishes

Adobo	Chicken and/or pork simmered in soy sauce and vinegar, with pepper and garlic

in Mindanao to communist rule, and there have been numerous bombings and military stand-offs, as well as isolated cases of tourists being kidnapped in the west and far southwest areas of Mindanao and the Sulu archipelago, to which travel is not recommended. For updates on the situation, you can check foreign ministry, state department and embassy websites (see box, p.45).

You'll find the same **con artists** and hustlers here that you'd find anywhere else, but most Filipinos are amazingly friendly and helpful. The most frequent scams involve changing money on the street (you'd have to be stupid to do this), or an

Beef tapa	Beef marinated in vinegar, sugar and garlic, then dried in the sun, and fried
Bicol Express	Pork ribs cooked in coconut milk, soy sauce, vinegar, *bagoong* and hot chillies
Bistek tagalog	Beef tenderloin with *calamansi* (lime) and onion
Daing na bangus	*Bangus* (milkfish) marinated in vinegar and spices, then fried
Dinuguan	Pork cubes simmered in pig's blood, with garlic, onion and laurel leaves
Lechon (de leche)	Roast whole (suckling) pig, dipped in a liver-paste sauce
Longganisa/longganiza	Small beef or pork sausages, with lots of garlic
Longsilog	*Longganisa* with garlic rice and fried egg
Pinakbet	Vegetable stew with *bagoong*, often with small pieces of meat
Sisig	Fried, chopped pork, liver and onions
Tapsilog	Beef *tapa* with garlic rice and fried egg
Tocino	Marinated fried pork
Tosilog	Marinated fried pork with garlic rice and fried egg

Snacks (*merienda*) and street food

Arroz caldo	Rice porridge with chicken
Chicharon	Fried pork skin, served with a vinegar and chilli dip
Pancit	Noodles
Kanin	Rice (cooked)

Fruit (*fruitas*)

Buko	Coconut
Calamansi	Small lime
Lanzones	Outside, the size and colour of a small potato; inside, sweet translucent flesh with a bitter seed
Mangga	Mango (available in sweet and sour varieties)
Saging	Banana

Desserts

Bibingka	Cake made of ground rice, sugar and coconut milk, baked in a clay stove and served hot, with fresh, salted duck eggs
Halo-halo	Ube ice cream, crushed ice, jelly, beans or sweetcorn and condensed milk
Leche flan	Caramel custard

Drinks (*inumin*)

Buko juice	Coconut water
Chocolate-eh	Thick hot chocolate
Tapuy	Rice wine
Tubig	Water

8

overly keen new pal, often well dressed, buying you a drugged coffee or beer and relieving you of your belongings. Most tourists who find themselves in sticky situations are foreign men looking for local "girlfriends" and falling into honey-trap scams. The country's prostitution scene can be disturbingly overt, especially in certain areas of Manila, and places such as Clark and Puerto Galera, popular with older Western men. The Philippines, sadly, retains its sordid reputation for child prostitution. If you see something suspicious, contact ECPAT Philippines in Manila (☎02 920 8151, ⩎ecpat.net).

Police in the Philippines are not Asia's finest. Successive governments have made some headway in cleaning up the force, but it is still plagued by accusations of corruption, collusion and an alleged willingness to shoot first and ask questions later. If you do get into trouble, contact your embassy immediately (see p.613). It is inadvisable to dabble in any illicit substances – especially given President Duterte's much-publicized "war on drugs".

MEDICAL CARE AND EMERGENCIES

There are pharmacies everywhere in the Philippines, so finding one should not be a problem. The biggest chain is Mercury, which has branches all over the place, but even the smallest village tends to have some sort of store.

In Manila and other major tourist centres, **hospitals** are reasonably well equipped and staffed by English-speaking doctors. Elsewhere your hotels can point you in the direction of a local clinic. Make sure you have arranged **health insurance** before you leave home – if you are hospitalized, you won't be allowed to leave the hospital until the bill is settled.

The 24-hour number for **emergency services** (police, fire and ambulance) throughout the Philippines is ☎117.

INFORMATION AND MAPS

The Philippine **Department of Tourism** (⩎tourism.gov.ph) has offices throughout the Philippines, but outside of the big cities these mostly have small budgets, poorly trained staff and very little in the way of reliable information or brochures. The best sources of information are often guesthouses and hotels that cater to backpackers. Another good source is blogs; Filipinos are enthusiastic tourists of their own country, and you'll find more information online, especially about trekking and diving on a budget, than you will from the tourist offices. A range of maps called *E-Z Map*, covering cities, individual islands and regions, is sold in branches of the National Bookstore (P99) and hotels, and is eminently useful.

MONEY AND BANKS

The Philippine **currency** is the peso (P). It is divided into 100 centavos, with bills in denominations of P20, P50, P100, P200, P500 and P1000. Coins come in 5, 10 and 25 centavos, P1, P5 and P10. Most banks will change sterling, euros and dollars, though the last is preferred, especially outside the cities. If you're likely to be going off the beaten track, you should take a ready supply of cash, and keep small denominations of pesos handy for transport and tips. Breaking anything bigger than a P100 note can be tricky anywhere other than large businesses, so stock up on change. At the time of writing the **exchange rate** was P50 to US$1, P53 to €1 and P62 to £1.

Visa, MasterCard and, to a lesser extent, American Express are widely accepted throughout Manila and other major cities, and also in popular tourist destinations such as Boracay. You can withdraw cash from 24-hour **ATMs** (in the Visa, Plus, MasterCard and Cirrus networks) in all cities and even many smaller towns. Most banks will advance cash against cards for a commission.

OPENING HOURS AND PUBLIC HOLIDAYS

Most **government offices** including **post offices** are open Monday to Friday 8am to 5pm. Businesses generally keep the same hours, with some also open for half a day on Saturday from 9am until noon.

Off the beaten track, hours are less regular. **Banks** open Monday to Friday 9am to 3pm, while **shops** in major shopping centres are usually open 10am to 8pm, seven days a week. **Restaurants** and **cafés** are generally open from early morning until 11pm, seven days a week, although they often close earlier outside of the big cities.

PUBLIC HOLIDAYS

January 1 New Year's Day
February 25 Anniversary of the overthrow of Marcos
March/April Holy Week
April 9 Bataan Day
May 1 Labour Day
June 12 Independence Day
November 1 All Saints' Day
November 30 Bonifacio Day
November/December Eid-ul-Fitr
December 25 Christmas Day
December 26 Public holiday
December 30 Rizal Day

FESTIVALS

It's at the fiestas that you get a chance to see legendary Filipino hospitality at its best. Religious fiestas are a more solemn mixture of devotion, drama and passion.
Feast of the Black Nazarene (Jan 9) Quiapo, Manila. Devotees gather in the plaza outside Quiapo Church to touch a miraculous image of Christ.
Sinulog (Third Sun in Jan) Cebu City. The second city's biggest annual event, in honour of its patron saint, Santo Niño. Huge street parade, live music and plenty of food and drink.
Ati-Atihan (Third week of Jan) Kalibo, Aklan province. Street dancing and wild costumes at arguably the biggest festival in the country.
Dinagyang (Fourth week of Jan) Iloilo, Panay. Relatively modern festival based on Ati-Atihan and including a parade on the Iloilo River.
Baguio Flower Festival (Third week in Feb) Baguio. The summer capital's largest annual event includes parades of floats beautifully decorated with flowers from the Cordillera region.
Lanzones festival (Third week of Oct) Mambajao, Camiguin. Vibrant, good-natured outdoor party giving thanks for the island's *lanzone* crop.
Masskara (Third week of Oct) Bacolod, Negros. Modern festival conceived in 1980 to promote the city. Festivities kick off with food fairs, mask-making contests, brass-band competitions, beauty and talent pageants and so forth.

Manila

The capital of the Philippines, an ever-expanding sprawl of nearly twenty million people, **MANILA** offers an introduction to the country akin to a baptism by fire. Plagued by traffic and pollution, with an infrastructure stretched almost to breaking point, it's not exactly the most traveller-friendly of cities. Many people fly in, spend a day and then get the hell out, only to venture back at the end of their trip. However, once you've acclimatized to the chaos, you'll discover that Manila has a certain shambolic charm. Considering its forbidding reputation, many are surprised by how unthreatening it feels to walk around, how friendly the people are and how (relatively) manageable it all is. Add nightlife unequalled in Asia, cavernous shopping malls and a few historical sights that are worth battling it out with the sea of jeepneys to visit, and you might find yourself lingering.

WHAT TO SEE AND DO

Manila's apparent disorder and relentless growth have been fed by unchecked urban development and an influx of *provincianos* looking for work, most of whom live in shanties on the periphery. To see the major sights you'll have to sweat it out in heavy traffic and be prepared for delays, but at least the main attractions are close to one another, grouped mostly along the crescent sweep of Manila Bay and Roxas Boulevard, taking in the neighbourhoods of **Ermita** and **Malate**, where budget visitors are most likely to want to base themselves. From here it's a relatively short hop to **Rizal Park** and the old town of **Intramuros**. Beyond **Chinatown** (Binondo), the gargantuan **Chinese Cemetery** is morbidly interesting. **Makati**, the Central Business District (CBD), is built around the main thoroughfare of Ayala Avenue and is best known for malls and restaurants. It's now rapidly overtaking Malate as the place to hang out at night.

8

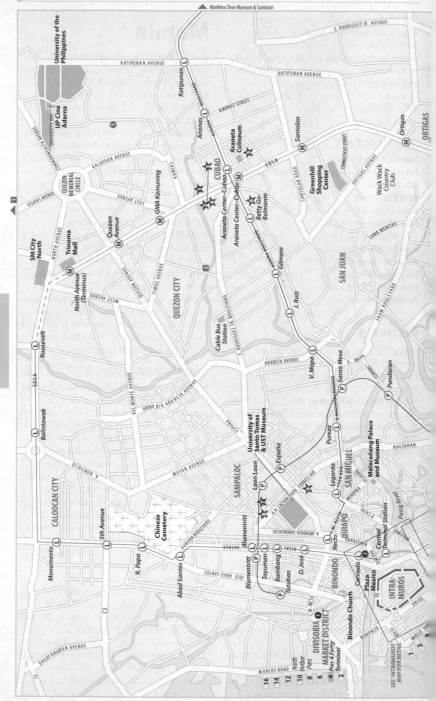

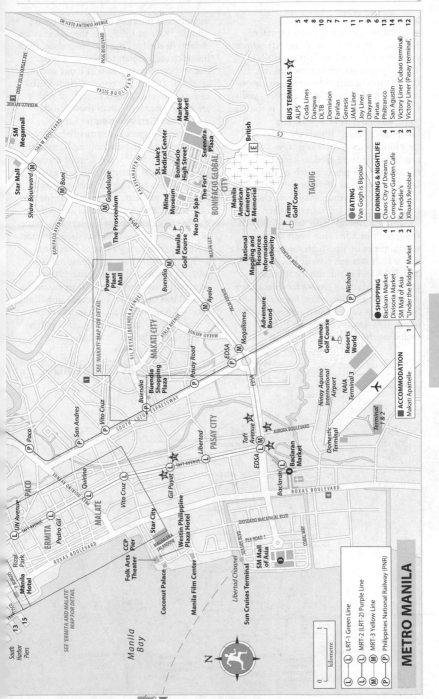

METRO MANILA

L — ⓛ	LRT-1 Green Line
L — ⓛ	MRT-2 (LRT-2) Purple Line
M — Ⓜ	MRT-3 Yellow Line
P — Ⓟ	Philippines National Railway (PNR)

0 ———— 1 kilometre

N

BUS TERMINALS ☆

ALPS	5
Coda Lines	4
Dangwa	8
DLTB	10
Dominion	2
Fariñas	7
Genesis	1
JAM Liner	11
Joy Liner	9
Ohayami	6
Partas	13
Philtranco	14
San Agustin	3
Victory Liner (Cubao terminal)	3
Victory Liner (Pasay terminal)	12

● **EATING**
Van Gogh is Bipolar   1

■ **DRINKING & NIGHTLIFE**

Chaos City of Dreams	4
Conspiracy Garden Cafe	1
Ka Freddie's	2
XRoads Restobar	3

● **SHOPPING**

Baclaran Market	4
Divisoria Market	1
SM Mall of Asia	3
"Under the Bridge" Market	2

■ **ACCOMMODATION**
Makati Apartelle   1

8

Intramuros

Intramuros, the old Spanish capital of Manila, is the one part of the city where you get a real sense of history. Built in 1571, it remains a monumental relic of the Spanish occupation, separated from the rest of Manila by its crumbling walls. Once famous throughout Asia, it featured well-planned streets, plazas, the Governor's Palace, fifteen churches and six monasteries as well as dozens of cannons that were used to keep the natives in their place. Much of this "city within a city" was destroyed in World War II, but Intramuros still lays claim to most of Manila's top tourist sights.

Manila Cathedral (daily 6am–5.30pm; free), built in 1581, has been destroyed several times by fire, typhoon, earthquake and war. It was last rebuilt between 1954 and 1958 and is still the location of choice for Manila's top society weddings.

Continuing southeast on General Luna Street brings you to **San Agustin Church** (daily 8am–noon & 1–5pm; P200 including the monastery), with its magnificent interiors and trompe-l'oeil murals. Built in 1599, it is the oldest stone church in the Philippines. Next door, the historic Augustinian monastery (same hours) houses a **museum** of icons and artefacts, as well as a restored eighteenth-century Spanish pipe organ, all of which are more interesting than they sound.

The **Casa Manila Museum** in the Plaza San Luis Complex is a sympathetically re-created colonial-era house (Tues–Sun 9am–5.45pm; P75), redolent of a grander age. Check out the impressive *sala* (living room) where *tertulias* (soirees) and *bailes* (dances) were held. The family latrine is a two-seater, allowing husband and wife to gossip out of earshot of the servants while simultaneously going about their business.

Nearby, the **Bahay Tsinoy** (Tues–Sun 1–5pm; P100) showcases hundreds of years of Chinese–Filipino integration, an interesting stop before a visit to Binondo. The **Silahis Center** on General Luna (daily 10am–7pm; free) is a craft emporium that's worth a wander. Through a pretty courtyard at the rear is the elegant

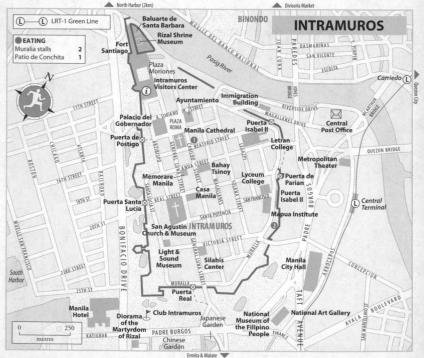

Ilustrado restaurant and its more affordable café, *Kuatro Kantos*.

For more information on the sights or to arrange a walking tour, call into the **Intramuros Visitor Center** (☎02 527 2961), which has a small office in the grounds of Fort Santiago, or take one of Carlos Celdran's Intramuros walking tours (see p.610).

Fort Santiago

The ruins of **Fort Santiago** (daily 8am–6pm; P75) stand at the northernmost end of Intramuros, a five-minute walk from the cathedral. Formerly the seat of the colonial powers of both Spain and the US, it was also a dreaded prison under the Spanish regime and the scene of countless military police atrocities during the Japanese occupation. Inside is the **Rizal Shrine**, which houses the room where José Rizal spent the hours before his infamous execution and the original copy of one of the country's most significant historical documents – Rizal's valedictory poem, *Mi Ultimo Adios*, which was secreted in an oil lamp and smuggled to his family hours before his death.

Rizal Park

Rizal Park (popularly known as the Luneta) was where the colonial-era glitterati used to promenade after church every Sunday. These days, in a city notoriously short of greenery, the park is a refuge for couples and families trying to escape the burning haze of pollution that hangs over much of Manila. People take picnics and lounge under trees, though the park's sundry attractions also include a **planetarium** (Tues–Sat 8am–4.30pm; P50; shows are for large groups only, but you may be able to join one by calling ☎02 527 7889), an open-air auditorium where concerts are held every Friday, Saturday and Sunday at 6pm, a giant relief map of the Philippines, and Chinese and Japanese gardens. At the bay end of the park, close to the *Manila Hotel*, is the **Rizal Memorial** and the flagpole where Manuel Roxas, first President of the third Republic, was sworn in on July 4, 1946. Rizal's execution site is also near here,

close to a memorial commemorating three priests garrotted by the Spanish for alleged complicity in the Cavite uprising of 1872.

The National Museum

At the eastern end of the park lie two branches of the **National Museum of the Philippines** (both Tues–Sun 10am–5pm; free), housed in buildings designed by the American architect Daniel Burnham and well worth a visit. The **National Art Gallery**, in what used to be the Congress Building, houses a comprehensive range of Filipino paintings. Directly opposite is the **National Museum of the Filipino People**, housed in the former Government Finance Building with displays covering geology, zoology, botany, crafts and weapons.

Manila Bay

When the capital was in its heyday, **Manila Bay** must have been a sight to behold, with its sweeping panorama across the South China Sea and its dreamy sunsets. The sunsets are perhaps more vivid than ever, thanks to the ever-present blanket of smog, and Manileños still watch them from the harbour wall, but much of the bay feels as if it's trading on its romantic past. A trip north along the boulevard from its southern end in Pasay takes you past the **Cultural Center of the Philippines** (CCP) and some of Imelda Marcos's other follies from the same era, including the **Coconut Palace**, an insane structure made entirely from coconut products (tours currently suspended, but should be available in the future; contact ☎02 832 6791 or ✉drcomia@ovp.gov.ph). She had it built for the pope's visit in 1981 but he refused to stay there, denouncing her for wasting such vast sums of money while people were starving. Nearby is the **Manila Film Center**, which she hoped would turn the city into the Cannes of the East. Construction was rushed to beat tight deadlines and as a result the building collapsed, allegedly trapping an unknown number of workers inside – an incident that has now passed into local folklore. A great way to see this area is on Carlos Celdran's "Living La Vida Imelda" tour (see p.610).

8

The Met and the Manila Hotel

Just north of the CCP is the **Metropolitan Museum**, usually known as the Met, at the Bangko Sentral ng Pilipinas Complex, Roxas Boulevard (Mon–Sat 10am–5.30pm; P100). This fine arts museum, a Filipino mini-Guggenheim, also houses the Central Bank's collection (Mon–Fri 10am–4.30pm only) of prehistoric jewellery and coins. Roxas Boulevard ends at the atmospheric **Manila Hotel**, home from home over the years for the likes of General Douglas MacArthur (who has a suite named after him), Michael Jackson and Bill Clinton.

Ermita and Malate

Two of the city's oldest neighbourhoods, **Ermita** and **Malate**, are tucked behind Roxas Boulevard, ten minutes' walk east of Manila Bay, and are pretty much the tourist centre for backpackers. Until the late 1980s Ermita was infamous for its go-go bars and massage parlours, but today it's a ragbag of budget hotels, choked streets and fast-food outlets, though convenient for Intramuros and Malate, and the services and restaurants of Robinson's Place mall. Walking southeast along **M. Adriatico Street** brings you into Malate, where things get livelier, with better cafés and bars, centred along Adriatico, Nakpil, Maria Orosa and Remedios streets. A three-minute walk towards the sea from Remedios Circle brings you to **Malate Church**, on M.H. del Pilar Street, where British soldiers took refuge during their ill-advised occupation of the Philippines from 1762 to 1763.

Chinatown (Binondo)

The Chinese–Filipino (Tsinoy) community have created their own niche in **Chinatown** (Binondo), centred around the teeming hubbub of Ongpin Street, where the restaurants serve Soup Number Five, said to cure everything from colds to impotence, and containing who knows what. **Binondo Church**, at the west end of Ongpin, was built in 1614 by the Dominicans, and quickly became the hub of the Catholic Chinese community.

At the eastern end of Chinatown, across Rizal Street, you reach **Quiapo Church**, the nucleus of the Feast of the Black Nazarene on January 9, when crowds of up to three million barefooted faithful crush together to try to touch a crucifix bearing a black figure of Christ.

Two kilometres north is the morbidly impressive **Chinese Cemetery** (Abad Santos LRT station; daily 7.30am–7pm; free). The mausoleums resemble mini-houses, with fountains, balconies, bathrooms and, for at least one, a small swimming pool. It has become a sobering joke that this necropolis, now numbering more than thirty thousand tombs, is packed with amenities that millions in Manila go without. You'll get more out of a visit with one of the guides, who hang around the gates and offer their services for a negotiable fee, usually around P300.

Makati

Makati is Manila's business district, home to most of the city's expats and chock-full of plush hotels, expensive condos and monolithic air-conditioned malls. Though it can feel a bit sterile, in recent years it's seriously begun to rival Malate for nightlife. The main triangle of Makati is delineated by Ayala Avenue, Paseo de Roxas and Makati Avenue, and this is where most of the banks and multinationals are located. In terms of sights, Makati is something of a wasteland, but if all that's on your agenda is shopping, eating and drinking, it's the place to be. The biggest mall by far is the **Ayala Center**, comprising Glorietta and Greenbelt malls and a couple of more downmarket centres such as Landmark (see p.613). Next door, the **Ayala Museum**, on Makati Avenue at the corner of Dela Rosa St (Tues–Sun 9am–6pm; P425), houses original works by Filipino painters and a multimedia "People Power" room that documents the turmoil of the Marcos dictatorship and the restoration of democracy – not to be missed.

On the eastern edge of Makati on McKinley Avenue is the **American Cemetery and Memorial** (daily 9am–5pm; free). Covering a vast area, it contains 17,206 graves of the American military dead of World War II.

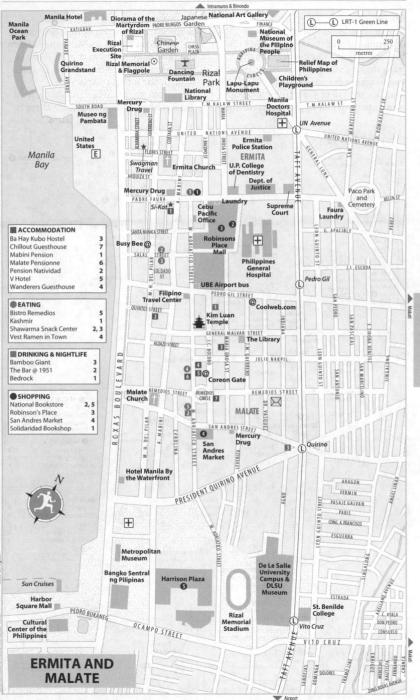

ERMITA AND MALATE

Manila Bay

ACCOMMODATION

Ba Hay Kubo Hostel	3
Chillout Guesthouse	7
Mabini Pension	1
Malate Pensionne	6
Pension Natividad	2
V Hotel	5
Wanderers Guesthouse	4

EATING

Bistro Remedios	5
Kashmir	1
Shawarma Snack Center	2, 3
Vest Ramen in Town	4

DRINKING & NIGHTLIFE

Bamboo Giant	3
The Bar @ 1951	2
Bedrock	1

SHOPPING

National Bookstore	2, 5
Robinson's Place	3
San Andres Market	4
Solidaridad Bookshop	1

8

Corregidor

The small tadpole-shaped island of **Corregidor** lies in the mouth of Manila Bay and makes a fascinating side trip from the city. A visit to the island, which was fought over bitterly during World War II – the fall of Corregidor was to prove instrumental to the success of the Japanese occupation – offers a unique perspective on the Philippine resistance. It's worth including a visit to the **Malinta tunnels** (daily sound-and-light show at 9.30am; P200), where General Douglas MacArthur set up temporary headquarters, and which was the site of vicious hand-to-hand combat. There is

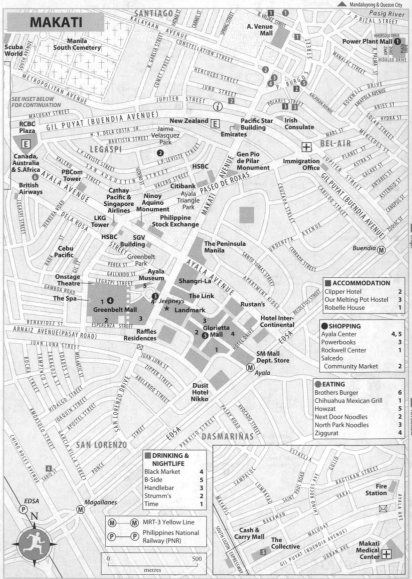

also a Japanese cemetery, a sobering museum and a memorial to the thousands who died here.

Sun Cruises on Seaside Boulevard in Pasay, just north of SM Mall of Asia (☎02 527 5555, ⓦcorregidorphilippines .com), organizes day- and overnight trips every morning at 7am. Packages start at P2350 for a bus tour or P1800 for a walking tour.

ARRIVAL AND DEPARTURE

BY PLANE

Ninoy Aquino International Airport (NAIA) is in Parañaque, on the southern fringes of the city. Most international flights arrive at Terminal 1; Terminal 2, relatively nearby, serves only Philippine Airlines (international and domestic); the tiny Domestic Passenger Airport Terminal (aka Terminal 4) is 3km away on the other side of the airport and serves AirAsia Zest, SkyJet and Tigerair Philippines flights; further around is Terminal 3, serving Cebu Pacific, PAL Express, Cathay Pacific, ANA, KLM, Delta and Emirates (also possibly JAL in the future). Terminal 3 is the best equipped and has a small Department of Tourism (DOT) reception desk, several currency exchanges, ATMs, left luggage, and stalls selling local SIM cards. A shuttle bus connects all the terminals, running frequently throughout the day, but traffic congestion means transfers can take over one hour in some cases – leave plenty of time.

Transport To get into town join the queue to take a yellow airport taxi (P60 flagfall, then P4/500m) or a white ordinary taxi (P30 flagfall, then P3.50/500m) from outside the arrivals hall, which will set you back about P300–400, rather than the fixed-price taxis, which usually have no line, but can cost nearly double.

Destinations Bacolod (12–14 daily; 1hr 15min); Busuanga (8–9 daily; 1hr); Cagayan de Oro (11–13 daily; 1hr 30min); Caticlan (10–11 daily; 55min); Cebu City (28–30 daily; 1hr 15min); Davao (21–24 daily; 1hr 50min); Dumaguete (4–7 daily; 1hr 25min); Iloilo (10–14 daily; 1hr 10min); Kalibo (11–13 daily; 1hr 10min); Laoag (1–3 daily; 1hr); Legaspi: (6–7 daily; 1hr 10min); Puerto Princesa (13–15 daily; 1hr 20min); San José (1–2 daily; 1hr); Surigao (1 daily; 1hr 40min); Tacloban (9–10 daily; 1hr 25min); Tagbilaran (8–9 daily; 1hr 25min).

BY BUS

There's no single bus station for Manila, and timetables are hard to come by and in a constant state of flux, which can make departing Manila by bus a bit of a headache. Often, if you tell your taxi driver your destination, he'll bring you to the right station. An up-to-date resource is the "getting around" section of ⓦ philippines-travel-guide.com.

Bus stations The majority of Manila's plethora of bus stations are located in and around Epifanio de los Santos Avenue (EDSA), in two rough groupings: Pasay (south) and Cubao (north). The MRT runs northeast along EDSA from Pasay to Cubao and on to Quezon City. The closest LRT station to the tourist belt in Malate is Quirino, which runs south to Pasay (EDSA/Taft Ave), where it meets the MRT. There are regular departures to most destinations.

BUS COMPANIES COVERING THE SOUTH
ALPS Araneta Center Bus Terminal, Cubao (☎0923 716 0472, ⓦ alpsthebus.com). Regular departures to Batanga, plus six daily to Legaspi and Sorsogon.
DLTB Taft Ave at Gil Puyat Ave (Gil Puyat/Buendia LRT) (☎0916 123 4567). Regular departures to Naga and Legaspi, four daily to Sorsogon.
JAM Liner Buendia LRT, Taft Ave, Pasay (☎02 541 4409). Hourly to Batangas and various destinations in Laguna.
Philtranco EDSA, Apelo Cruz St, Pasay (☎02 851 8077, ⓦ philtranco.com.ph). Daily runs to Iloilo via Mindoro, and as far afield as Leyte, Samar and Davao, as well as Legaspi and Sorsogon.
San Agustin Park Plaza at the junction of Taft and EDSA in Pasay (Pasay Rotonda). Every 10min to Tagaytay and Nusugbu.
Destinations south Batangas City (at least hourly; 2–3hr); Legaspi (18 daily; 10hr); Sorsogon (14 daily; 12hr); Tagaytay (every 10min 2.30am–11pm; 1hr 30min).

BUS COMPANIES COVERING THE NORTH
Coda Lines HM Terminal, Monte de Piedad St, Cubao (☎0927 559 219). Nightly to Bontoc, Banaue and Sagada.
Dangwa Carola St at Dimasalang Rd, Sampaloc (☎02 731 2879). Overnight service to Banaue, others to Baguio.
Dominion EDSA at East Ave (☎02 741 4146). Roughly every hour to Vigan.
Fariñas Laon Laan St at M. de la Fuente St, Sampaloc (☎02 731 4507, ⓦ farinastrans.com). Regular services to Vigan and Laoag.
Genesis and **Joy Liner** 704 EDSA at New York St, Cubao (☎02 709 0803, ⓦ genesistransport.com.ph). Both firms have hourly departures to Baguio round the clock.
Ohayami Trans J. Fajardo St at Lacson Ave, Sampaloc (☎02 516 0501, ⓦ ohayamitrans.com). Nightly to Banaue.
Partas 816 Aurora Blvd at EDSA, Cubao Terminal (☎02 851 4025, ⓦ partas.com.ph). Regular services to Baguio, Laoag, San Fernando (La Union) and Vigan.
Victory Liner ⓦ victoryliner.com. From 683 EDSA, Cubao Terminal (☎02 727 4688), and 651 EDSA, Pasay Terminal (☎02 833 5019). Hourly services to Baguio.
Destinations north Baguio (3–4 hourly; 6–8hr); Banaue (3 nightly; 9hr); Laoag (17 daily; 10hr); San Fernando (La Union; hourly; 6hr); Vigan (1–2 hourly; 10hr).

8

BY FERRY

There are two main passenger dock areas in Manila: the North Harbor along Marcos Rd, a few kilometres north of Intramuros, and the South Harbor near the *Manila Hotel*. 2GO Travel ferries (ⓦ travel.2go.com.ph) use the passenger terminal at Pier 4, North Harbor. Taxis from North Harbor to Ermita cost about P150.

Destinations Bacolod (4 weekly; 20hr); Cagayan de Oro (4 weekly; 34hr); Cebu City (5 weekly; 23hr); Coron (2 weekly; 15hr); Iloilo (4 weekly; 28hr); Puerto Princesa (2 weekly; 32hr).

INFORMATION AND TOURS

Tourist information The Tourist Information Center is in the Department of Tourism Building, 351 Sen Gil Puyat (Buendia) Ave, Makati (Mon–Fri 7am–6pm, Sat 8am–5pm; ☎02 959 5200 ext 101 or 102, ⓦ visitmyphilippines.com). A useful source of information on Manila is ⓦ clickthecity.com.

Walking tours Walk This Way is run by the highly entertaining Carlos Celdran (☎0920 909 2021 or ☎02 484 4945, ⓦ carlosceldran.com). Carlos leads weekly history-lesson-cum-magical-mystery tours around the old city (P1350, plus P75 Fort Santiago entry; 3hr). Also recommended is Ivan Man Dy of Old Manila Walks (☎0918 962 6452 or ☎02 711 3823, ⓦ oldmanilawalks.com), who conducts fun tours of Binondo and Intramuros.

GETTING AROUND

Manila's roads are in a perpetual state of chaos bordering on gridlock. There are so many vehicles fighting for every centimetre of road space that at peak times it can be a sweaty battle of nerves just to travel a few hundred metres.
By MRT (MetroStar Express; daily 5.30am–11pm; ⓦ dotcmrt3.gov.ph). Runs the length of EDSA from Taft Ave

in the south to North Ave, Quezon City. Key stations are: Taft, from where you can get a taxi, a jeepney or the LRT to Malate; Ayala, which is close to Makati's malls and hotels; and Cubao for bus stations heading north. Fares are P13–28; a prepaid, rechargeable "beep card" costs P100 (including a non-refundable P20 issue fee) and is valid for three months.
By LRT (Light Rail Transit; daily 5am–10pm; ⓦ lrta.gov.ph). An elevated railway that runs from Baclaran in the south (near the airport) to Roosevelt, and due to be extended to North Ave MRT terminus, creating a loop between the MRT and the LRT. Trains run frequently and journeys cost P15–30, and the same "beep card" from the MRT is valid on the LRT. You can use it to get to places in the north of Manila, such as Rizal Park (exit at United Nations station), Intramuros (Central station) and the Chinese Cemetery (Abad Santos station). Pedro Gil station is a 10min walk from Ermita, while Quirino station is closest to Malate. There's also an east-west line, but no through fares.
By jeepney Jeepneys go back and forth all over the city. Fares start at P7 for the shorter journeys and increase by P1.50 for each kilometre thereafter. Pass your fare to the passenger sitting closest to the driver. A useful route runs the length of Taft Avenue from Baclaran in the south to Binondo in the north. From Baclaran, you can get jeepneys to the bus terminals in Pasay. Jeepneys heading to Cubao will take you past a number of bus terminals at the northern end of EDSA, where you can get buses to northern destinations.
By taxi It's extremely cheap and easy to get around Manila by taxi. Many taxi drivers are happy to turn on their meters, while others start even the shortest journey with a long negotiation. Most taxis are a/c and charge an initial P40, then P3.50 for every 300m.
By bus Local buses in Manila grind their way along all major thoroughfares. The destination is written on a sign in the front window, and fares start at P12.

TRAVELLING SAFELY IN MANILA

Like any big city, Manila has a certain level of street crime, but as long as you exercise simple common sense, it shouldn't be a major worry. Armed security guards patrol MRT and LRT platforms, and there are dedicated waiting areas for female passengers, minimizing opportunities for bagsnatchers, though of course it pays to remain alert. Official taxis are safe, but take the precaution of sitting in the back, and lock your doors, as you are likely to sit in traffic for long stretches of any journey. For complaints about taxis, contact LTFRB, the Land Transportation Board (☎1342, ⓔ complaint.ltfrb.gov.ph@gmail.com), or fill in the form at ⓦ taxikick.com.

ACCOMMODATION

Most of Manila's budget accommodation is in Ermita and Malate, which also have a high density of restaurants, bars and tourist services. They are, however, rather insalubrious areas, and some prefer Makati, the modern business area, as a safer option, although budget accommodation is less prevalent.

ERMITA AND MALATE

Ba Hay Kubo Hostel 1717 Maria Orosa St ☎02 243 7537, ⓔ bahaykubohostel@gmail.com; map p.607. Super-friendly, welcoming little hostel in a beautifully done-out traditional Filipino house in a lively location, with free wi-fi and use of the kitchen. Dorms P350, doubles P800
Chillout Guesthouse 612 Remedios St at Remedios Circle ☎02 218 7227, ⓦ chillout-manila.com; map p.607. This hostel, run by an enthusiastic young French crew, has

a choice of fan or a/c en-suite rooms (P1450) and a/c dorms; the back rooms are quieter. There's a common kitchen area for self-caterers, lockers and free wi-fi. Dorms P350, doubles P650

Mabini Pension 1337 A. Mabini St, Ermita ☎02 523 3930, ✉reservations@mabinipension.com; map p.607. Convenient, friendly and well established, with fan and a/c rooms, though in rather close proximity to a number of karaoke joints; get a room at the back. Wi-fi in the restaurant area only. Dorms P680, doubles P1300

Malate Pensionne 1771 M. Adriatico St, Malate ☎02 523 8304, ⓦmalatepensionne.com; map p.607. Cosy rooms delightfully furnished in Spanish-colonial style; there are beautiful parquet floors throughout and the cute little breakfast area is a good spot to start the day. Paid wi-fi. Dorms P490, doubles P950

★**Pension Natividad** 1690 MH del Pilar St, Malate ☎02 521 0524, ⓦpensionnatividad.com; map p.607. A well-liked guesthouse in a quiet old family home with a popular 24hr outdoor terrace café where backpackers mingle. Rooms are clean and spacious and there's free wi-fi in the lobby area. It's one of the best budget places in the area. Single-sex dorms P400, doubles P1000

V Hotel 1766 M. Adriatico St ☎02 328 5553, ⓦvhotelmanila.com; map p.607. Sparkling rooms, but on the small side, and not all have windows. There's wi-fi and a small pool (often out of commission), and breakfast is included. Doubles P1200

Wanderers Guesthouse 1750 M. Adriatico St at Nakpil St ☎02 474 0742; map p.607. The chilled-out balcony bar, bird's-eye view over Malate, low prices and free wi-fi at this backpackers' hostel make it a firm favourite and a great place to hang out. Some rooms have shared bathrooms; some dorms have a/c (P400). Dorms P350, doubles P690

MAKATI

Clipper Hotel 5766 Ebro St ☎02 890 8577, ⓦtheclipperhotel.com; map p.608. Simple but spacious rooms, with cable TV and wi-fi in a wonderful Art Deco building, well located in the most happening part of Makati. Doubles P2688

Makati Apartelle 4411 Montojo St, Brgy. Tejeros ☎02 897 4219, ⓦmakatiapartelle.com; map pp.602–603. This welcoming hotel is decorated with beautiful Chinese artefacts and the odd piece of intricately decorated furniture; all rooms have a/c, kitchenette, living area, private bathroom and cable TV. Great value. Doubles P1085

★**Our Melting Pot Hostel** 3/F Wang Mart Building, 37 Polaris St ☎02 833 4736, ✉mymeltingpotbackpackers @gmail.com; map p.608. In principle two hostels next to each other (*Our Melting Pot* and *The Good Shepherd*), but in reality one large place with spick-and-span dorms and

rooms, spacious public areas, wi-fi throughout, breakfast included, and free use of the gym downstairs. Dorms P500, doubles P1450

Robelle House 4402 Valdez St ☎02 899 8061, ⓦrobellehouse.net; map p.608. Rambling family-run pension, creaking with atmosphere, and it even has a pool, the main downside being its location down a rather desolate back street. Doubles P1750

EATING

INTRAMUROS

Muralla stalls Lining the Intramuros walls; map p.604. The eastern walls of the old Spanish capital are lined with in-built stalls attracting crowds of students for cheap eats. A meal will set you back about P70.

Patio de Conchita 681 Beaterio St ☎02 404 1122; map p.604. This great find is off the beaten path but an excellent place to have lunch, with budget menus at P70–80. Food is served buffet style, with a range of top-notch Filipino dishes; try the *sinigang na baboy* (sour soup with pork; P75) and freshly barbecued squid (P280). Mon–Fri 7am–10pm, Sat 7am–9pm.

ERMITA AND MALATE

Bistro Remedios 1911 M. Adriatico St, just off Remedios Circle; map p.607. Informal and homey restaurant with pretty Filipiniana interior and charming staff. The food is exclusively Filipino, with cholesterol-filled fried pigs' knuckles (P650), beef stew (*kaldaretang baka*, P525) and fried pork in coconut milk (*lechon kawali sa guta*, P190). There's also good fish and prawns, but not a great deal for vegetarians (mains P285–650). Mon–Fri 11am–3pm & 6–11pm, Sat & Sun 11am–3pm & 6pm–midnight.

Kashmir Merchants Center Building, Padre Faura, Ermita; map p.607. Great spot in the middle of Ermita for Indian, Malay and Middle Eastern cuisine; all the meat here is halal and there are plenty of dishes on offer, from kebabs (P250) to tandoori specialities (tandoori chicken P450). Great vegetarian choices (veg curry P280) too. There's another branch at 816 Arnaiz Ave in Makati. Daily 11am–11pm.

★**Shawarma Snack Center** 485 Salas St, Malate; map p.607. This place offers great hummus (P135), *tabouleh* (P185), *shakshouka* (P150) and other Middle Eastern delicacies to be washed down with a zesty fruit shake (P125). There's another branch directly opposite. Free wi-fi. Mains P300–400. Daily 24hr.

Vest Ramen in Town 1755 Adriatico St, Malate; map p.607. This shabby-looking street shack dishes up filling cheap nosh, from ramen noodle soup (P70–100) to pork *sisig* (P170), with cold beer to wash it down. It gets especially lively in the evening when it's more of a bar, plied by hawkers offering anything from peanuts to massages while you eat and drink. Daily 24hr.

MAKATI

Makati is fast becoming the culinary capital of the country, with a dazzling range of world food on offer in the malls and beyond.

Brothers Burgers Unit A, Convergys Building, Ayala Ave; map p.608. Head here to regain your senses after a big night out. If you've really had one too many, note that Manila's best burger joint even delivers (☎02 751 1307). Several other branches including at Greenhills Mall. Burgers from P165. Mon–Fri 8am–11pm, Sat & Sun 9am–9pm.

Chihuahua Mexican Grill 7838 Makati Ave; map p.608. A haven for spicy food lovers with a hot sauce library of over sixty bottles, this great little Mexican place serves large and delicious portions of burritos, tacos (P246–332) and nachos (P235), as well as great margaritas (P195). Mon–Thurs & Sun 11am–midnight, Fri & Sat 11am–2am.

Howzat 8471 Kalayaan Ave cnr. Fermina St; map p.608. Anglo-Aussie pub serving good ol' grub such as fish 'n' chips (P395) and steak-and-kidney pie (P310); there are TV screens to catch up on the latest world sports. Sunday roast buffet (P695 including beer) and a Friday Indian curry lunch buffet (P495 including beer). Mon–Thurs 7am–2am, Fri–Sun 24hr.

Next Door Noodles/North Park Noodles 7876 Makati Ave; map p.608. *Next Door Noodles* sits almost opposite its sister restaurant, *North Park Noodles*, which has a similar menu of Chinese favourites at the same low prices. Fantastic value – almost everything is under P200 (dim sum P58–213, noodles in soup P116–288 and fried rice P188–273). Mon–Thurs & Sun 10am–4pm, Fri & Sat 24hr.

★**Ziggurat** Euphrates St at Tigris St; map p.608. Kick off your shoes, sit back on silky cushions and tuck into exotic curries (P120–380) at this superb restaurant serving delights from India, Africa and the Middle East. Plenty for vegetarians, including a veggie meze combo (P250). Not to be missed. Daily 24hr.

QUEZON CITY

Van Gogh is Bipolar 154H Maginhawa St, Sikatuna Village, Quezon City ☎0922 824 3051, ⊕facebook.com/vgibipolar; map pp.602–603. Cook and travel photographer Jetro lovingly prepares the dishes at this unique place by carefully selecting ingredients, such as honey and black mountain rice, that are supposed to enhance your mood by stimulating your serotonin and dopamine levels. Only twelve diners per night, so it's a good idea to book. Mon & Wed–Sun noon–3pm & 6–11pm.

DRINKING AND NIGHTLIFE

Manila's big clubs have strict dress codes, so leave your T-shirts and flip-flops at home if you're aiming for one of the glitzier venues. Little music bars are a lot less formal, and cheaper, and generally take a lot less getting to

transport-wise, although some of the more interesting ones are up in Quezon. For a bit of casual drinking, you can sign up for Manila's famous Thursday-night pub crawl (☎0905 553 9541, ⊕pubcrawl.ph), which takes in five bars and costs P890 on the spot, or from P590 for women, and P690 for men if you sign up in advance; free T-shirt, shot glass and hangover included.

ERMITA, MALATE AND PASAY

Bamboo Giant 802a San Andres St at Quirino and Taft Ave, Malate; map p.607. Acoustic bands most nights in this beach-bar-style bamboo shack, easy-going, with a chilled vibe, reasonably chilled beers, and food if you want it. Mon–Sat 4pm–2am.

★**The Bar @ 1951** (ex-*Penguin Café*) M. Adriatico St, Malate; map p.607. Legendary 1980s bohemian bar *Penguin Café* has been reborn as this two-floor artsy and congenial space (with a cosy loft upstairs), though locals still refer to it by the old name. Live indie bands play most nights and work from local artists adorns the walls. Tues–Sat 6pm–2am.

Bedrock Unit B, Bellagio Square, J Bacobo St, Ermita; map p.607. A rather nondescript little bar for most of the week, but on Friday and Saturday evenings, it takes over this little square, with live music on stage from around 8.30pm. Daily 3pm–3am.

Chaos City of Dreams Asean Ave at Roxas Blvd, Pasay; map pp.602–603. A luxury club in a prestigious mall, with confetti machines, LED curtains, laser light shows, table reservations, a VIP zone, cage dancers and all the paraphernalia. Sounds vary depending on the evening: Wednesday is band night, Thursday is hip-hop, weekends are party pop. Entry is usually P500 (one drink included), but that may double for special events. Wed–Sat 10pm–6am.

MAKATI AND FORT BONIFACIO

Black Market Warehouse 5, La Fuerza Compound 2, Sabio St, Makati; map p.608. Warehousey club venue opened by the folks at B-Side, with talented resident DJs, emphasis on sounds like hip-hop and r'n'b, a lot of bass, and an eclectic range of guests. Cover usually P300. Wed–Sat 10pm–4am.

★**B-Side** The Collective, 7274 Malugay St, Makati; map p.608. This cool little club in a converted warehouse hosts local and foreign indie gigs and attracts a studenty crowd. Big reggae/ragga sessions on "Irie Sundays". Free entrance, no dress code, but it's a bit out of the way. Wed–Sun 9pm–4am.

Handlebar Warehouse 5, La Fuerza Compound 2, Sabio St, Makati; map p.608. Friendly biker bar with masculine trimmings and live music, sports on TV, draught beer (P70) and some of the best steaks (P659) in Makati. Daily 24hr.

Strumm's 110 Jupiter St, Makati; map p.608. A party-like atmosphere greets nightly bands at this Makati stalwart, which puts on mostly pop and indie but also old-school jazz on Tues. Cover P350 Sun–Thur, P400 Fri & Sat. Daily 8pm–2am.

Time 7840 Makati Ave; map p.608. The centre of the electronic music scene with Filipino and international DJs performing live sets: this is the place for house and techno in Manila. Entry P500. Tues & Thurs–Sat 11pm–4am. Sun 7pm–2am.

XRoads Restobar Unit 108 Food St, Home Depot Complex, Julia Vargas at Meralco, Ortigas Center; map pp.602–603. Pronounced "crossroads", this is Manila's coolest gay and lesbian bar, open to all, with a dedicated Women on Top lesbian space, and a dancefloor, but intimate rather than thumping. Wed–Sun 10pm–6am.

QUEZON CITY
Conspiracy Garden Cafe 59 Visayas Ave ⓦ facebook.com/conspiracy.garden.cafe, map pp.602–603. Performance venue and café set up by the artists who perform there, among them luminaries of the independent Filipino music scene. It's worth checking before you set out here to see who's on. Mon–Sat 5pm–2am.

Ka Freddie's 120 Tomas Morato Ave at Kamuning St ⓦ facebook.com/kafreddiesmusicbarandresto; map pp.602–603. Music bar and restaurant (with pool tables and free wi-fi) opened by Filipino folk legend Freddie Aguilar, who still does weekly shows (Fri). Check out the Facebook page for who's playing. Cover P200–300. Daily 6pm–3am.

SHOPPING
MARKETS
Baclaran Market Southern end of Taft Ave; map pp.602–603. The focus throughout is cheap clothes and shoes of every hue, size and style. The market is crowded, but lots of fun. It's open all week but especially busy on Wed.

Divisoria Market C.M. Recto St, Binondo; map pp.602–603. The grand-daddy of flea markets, where haggling is the order of the day. Fake Converse trainers, pirated DVDs, bags, wallets and household paraphernalia crowd the stalls at this immense and sometimes overwhelming Chinatown market. Dress down and leave valuables at your hotel. Daily dawn–late.

★**Salcedo Community Market** Jaime Velasquez Park, Bel-Air, Makati; map p.608. One of Manila's culinary highlights, Salcedo features a dazzling display of gastronomic delights from all corners of the Philippines and further afield to take away or enjoy at one of the communal tables. Sat 7am–2pm.

San Andres Market San Andres St at M. Adriatico St; map p.607. Offering a wide selection of fruit, this labyrinthine market is home to hundreds of stalls groaning under the weight of mango, pomelo, jackfruit, cantaloupe, watermelon, rambutan and more. Daily 24hr.

"Under the Bridge" Market (*Sa Ilalim ng Tulay*) Quezon Bridge, Quiapo; map pp.602–603. Mainly handicrafts and secondhand clothes, as well as meat, fish, fruit and vegetables. Daily 5am–10pm.

BOOKS
National Bookstore Branches in Harrison Plaza, Robinson's Place and malls city-wide; map p.607. The country's major bookshop chain, selling popular and literary fiction and non-fiction, plus maps and stationery. Harrison Plaza daily 10am–8pm; Robinson's Place Mon–Thurs & Sun 10am–9pm, Fri & Sat 10am–10pm.

Powerbooks Level 2, Greenbelt 4; map p.608. A decent selection of books in a cosy ambience. Daily 10am–10pm.

Solidaridad Bookshop 531 Padre Faura; map p.607. Owned by celebrated Filipino novelist F. Sionil José, this place is a hidden gem, stocking more unusual Filipino titles. Mon–Sat 9am–6pm.

MALLS
Manila's malls loom large in the entertainment of the city, with many of the best restaurants, bars and cinemas inside. You can also do your banking, book travel tickets and stock up on picnic supplies. Opening hours are usually Mon–Fri 10am–9pm, Sat & Sun 10am–10pm.

Ayala Center Makati Ave ⓦ ayalamalls.com.ph; map p.608. Restaurants, boutiques, bars, theatres, cinemas and so on, spread across Greenbelt malls 1–5 (in ascending order of exclusivity). Glorietta, opposite the *Shangri-La Makati*, has a seven-screen cinema complex (ⓣ 02 752 7880), including one dedicated to art-house films, and Landmark has a well-stocked basement supermarket good for self-caterers. There are also plenty of snack chain counters here.

Robinson's Place Adriatico, Pedro Gil and Padre Fauna streets, Ermita ⓦ robinsonsmalls.com; map p.607. Some great restaurants, a multiplex cinema and free wi-fi.

Rockwell Center Rockwell Drive, Makati ⓦ powerplantmall.com; map p.608. Officially called the Power Plant mall, but everyone just refers to it as Rockwell.

SM Mall of Asia Bay Blvd, cnr EDSA extension, Pasay ⓦ smmallofasia.com; map pp.602–603. The largest mall in the Philippines, and fourth largest in the world. Has everything you'd expect and more that you wouldn't, including an Olympic-sized ice-skating rink.

DIRECTORY
Banks and exchange Most major banks have 24hr ATMs. Money changers around Mabini St in Ermita and P. Burgos St in Makati offer better rates than the banks, but shop around; moneychangers that display their rates are more likely to give better ones than those who don't.

Embassies and consulates Australia, Level 23, Tower 2, RCBC Plaza, 6819 Ayala Ave, Makati (ⓣ 02 757 8100, ⓦ philippines.embassy.gov.au); Cambodia, Unit 7A, Country

Space 1 Building, Sen. Gil Puyat Ave, Makati City (☎02 818 9981); Canada, Levels 6–8, Tower 2, RCBC Plaza, 6819 Ayala Ave, Makati (☎02 857 9000, ⓦphilippines.gc.ca); China, 4896 Pasay Rd, Dasmariñas Village, Makati (☎02 848 2395); Indonesia, 185 Salcedo St, Makati (☎02 892 5061); Ireland, 3/F, 70 Jupiter St, Bel-Air 1, Makati (☎02 896 4668); Laos, 14D Chatham House Condominium, 116 Valero St, Salcedo Village, Makati (☎02 865 6566); Malaysia, 107 Tordesillas St., Salcedo Village, Makati (☎02 662 8201); New Zealand, 35/F, Zuellig Building, Makati Ave at Paseo de Roxas, Makati (☎02 234 3800, ⓦnzembassy.com/philippines); Singapore, 505 Rizal Drive, Bonifacio Global City, Taguig (☎02 856 9922, ⓦmfa.gov.sg/manila); South Africa, 29th Floor, Yuchengco Tower, RCBC Plaza, 6819 Ayala Ave, Makati (☎02 889 9383, ⓦwww.dirco.gov.za/manila); Thailand, 107 Rada St, Makati (☎02 810 3833); UK, 120 Upper McKinley Rd, McKinley Hill, Taguig City (☎02 858 2200); US, 1201 Roxas Blvd (☎02 301 2000, ⓦmanila.usembassy. gov); Vietnam, 670 Pablo Ocampo, Malate (☎02 521 6843).

Hospitals and clinics Makati Medical Center, 2 Amorsolo St, Makati (☎02 888 8999, ⓦmakatimed.net.ph), is the largest and one of the most modern hospitals in Manila. Others include: Manila Doctors Hospital, 667 United Nations Ave, Ermita (☎02 558 0888, ⓦmaniladoctors .com.ph); St Luke's Medical Center, 279 E. Rodriguez Sr Blvd, Quezon City (☎02 723 0101, ⓦstluke.com.ph).

Immigration For visa extensions, the Immigration Building is on Magellanes Drive, Intramuros (Mon–Fri 8am–noon & 1–5pm; ☎02 527 3257 or 3280). There's a smaller office (same hours; ☎02 899 3831) in Makati at 385 Gil Puyat Ave, where it's often faster and easier.

Internet Most malls are free wi-fi zones. Internet cafés include: Busy Bee, 1417 M.H. del Pilar St, Malate (daily 24hr; P35/hr); Coolweb.com, 704 Pedro Gil St, Ermita (Mon–Fri 7am–9pm, Sat 8am–8pm, Sun 1–8pm; P20/hr).

Laundry Faura Laundry, 570 Padre Faura St, Ermita (Mon–Sat 9am–7pm; P33/kg; ☎02 526 7519).

Pharmacies You're never far from a Mercury Drug outlet, with 24hr stores on Taft Ave at Apacible St in Ermita and Makati Ave at Eduque St in Makati. Others are listed at ⓦmercurydrug.com.

Police Tourist Police, Department of Tourism Compound, TM Kalaw Ave, Rizal Park (daily 7am–11pm; ☎02 382 6741). For emergencies, dial ☎117.

Post office The main post office is in Intramuros, between Jones Bridge and MacArthur Bridge. In Makati, there is a post office at the junction of Malugay and Ayala avenues. In Malate, there's one at the junction of Remedios and Hidalgo streets. Opening hours are Mon–Fri, 8am–5pm.

Travel agents There are plenty of travel agents around Malate and Ermita. The Filipino Travel Center, 1555 M Adriatico St (☎02 528 4507, ⓦfilipinotravel.com.ph), is one of the best, particularly strong on organizing tours. Also has a branch in Boracay.

Northern Luzon

The provinces of Luzon that lie immediately **northwest of Manila** are so diverse in geographical character that you can go from the volcanic landscape of **Zambales** to the tropical beaches and islands of the **Lingayen Gulf** in a single day. Major attractions of the region include **Mount Pinatubo**, the island-hopper's heaven of **Hundred Islands National Park**, and the chance to surf the breaks of **San Fernando** and **San Juan** on the La Union coast. Further north, the old Spanish-colonial outpost of **Vigan** is a reminder of how much was lost elsewhere in the bombs of World War II.

MOUNT PINATUBO

On April 2, 1991, people on the lower slopes of **Mount Pinatubo** (1780m) saw small explosions followed by steam and the smell of rotten eggs coming from the upper slopes of the supposedly dormant volcano, whose last known eruption was six hundred years ago. Much worse was to follow, and on June 12, the first of several major explosions took place, an eruption so violent that shock waves could be felt in the Visayas. A giant ash cloud rose 35km into the sky, red-hot blasts seared the countryside and nearly twenty million tonnes of sulphur dioxide were blasted into the atmosphere, causing red skies for months afterwards. Ash paralysed Manila, closing the airport for days and turning the capital's streets into an eerie post-apocalyptic landscape. More than 350 people were killed.

Until August 2009, the one- or two-day trek through the resultant moon-like lahar landscape of Pinatubo was one of the country's top activity highlights. However, after heavy landslides that caused the deaths of seven individuals, this longer trail was closed. Organized trips to the volcano now leave from the small town of **Santa Juliana**, about 40km from Clark, where you register. From here, a 4WD takes you for an hour or so across flat lahar beds and over dusty foothills to the start of a gentle hike to

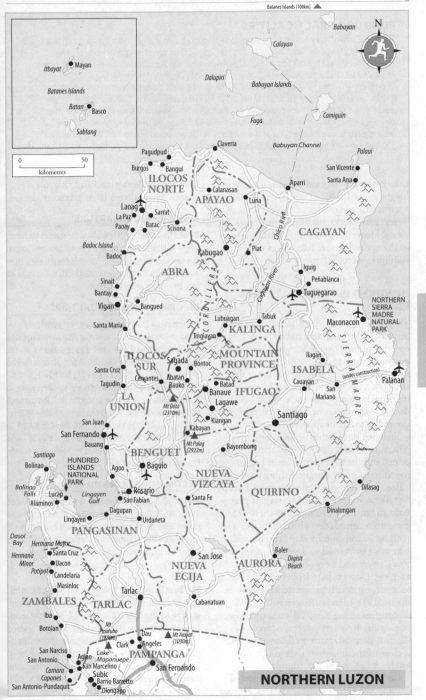

Batanes Islands (100km)

N

Babuyan

Calayan

Itbayat ● Mayan

Batanes Islands

Dalupiri

Babuyan Islands

Fuga

Camiguin

Batan ● Basco

Sabtang

0   50
kilometres

Babuyan Channel

Palaui

Claveria

Pagudpud

Burgos ● Bangui

San Vicente
Santa Ana

ILOCOS
NORTE

APAYAO

Calanasan

Luna

Aparri

Chico River

CAGAYAN

Laoag
La Paz ● Sarrat
Paoay ● Batac ● Scisona

Kabugao

Piat

Badoc Island

Badoc

ABRA

Cagayan River

Iguig

Peñablanca

Tuguegarao

Sinait

Bantay

Vigan ● Bangued

CORDILLERA

Lubuagan

Tabuk

KALINGA

NORTHERN
SIERRA
MADRE
NATURAL
PARK

Maconacon

Santa Maria

Tinglayan

ILOCOS
SUR

Sagada ● Bontoc

MOUNTAIN
PROVINCE

Ilagan

ISABELA

(under construction)

Palanan

Santa Cruz

Tagudin

Cervantes ● Abatan
Bauko

Batad

Banaue

IFUGAO

Cauayan

San
Mariano

LA
UNION

Mt Data
(2370m)

Lagawe

Kiangan

Santiago

San Juan

San Fernando

Bauang

Kabayan

BENGUET

Mt Pulag
(2922m)

Bayombong

SIERRA MADRE

Santiago

Bolinao

HUNDRED
ISLANDS
NATIONAL
PARK

Agoo ● Baguio

NUEVA
VIZCAYA

QUIRINO

Dilasag

Bolinao
Falls

Lucap

Alaminos

Lingayen Gulf

Rosario
San Fabian

Santa Fe

Lingayen ● Dagupan ● Urdaneta

Dinalungan

PANGASINAN

Dasol
Bay

Hermana Mayor

Hermana
Minor ● Santa Cruz
● Uacon

Potipot

Candelaria

San Jose

NUEVA
ECIJA

Baler

AURORA

Digisit
Beach

Masinloc

Tarlac

Cabanatuan

ZAMBALES ● TARLAC

Iba

Botolan

Mt
Pinatubo
(1780m)

Dau ● Mt Arayat
(1030m)

Clark
Angeles

San Narciso
San Antonio

Agno

Lake
Mapanuepe

San Marcelino

PAMPANGA

Camara
Capones ● Subic

Barrio Barretto

San Antonio-Pundaquit

Olongapo

San Fernando

NORTHERN LUZON

8

PINATUBO PRACTICALITIES

The **SCTEX highway** has made getting to Pinatubo much easier, and it's now more feasible as a day-trip from Manila. Trekking Pinatubo (T 02 310 5036; W trekkingpinatubo.com) has day-trips for P3600 per person in a group of five, which include return transport from Manila, entrance fees and a guide. Alternatively, you can stay locally at Alvin's *Mount Pinatubo Guesthouse* in Santa Juliana (T 0919 861 4102, W mt-pinatubo.weebly.com; dorms P500, doubles P1200), and take a trip organized by them, for P2350 per person in a group of five. It's also possible to just get a Tarlac- or Baguio-bound bus from Clark or Manila to Capas, catch a jeepney or tricycle to Paitlin and then one to Santa Juliana, where you'd need to arrive by around 6am to organize a 4WD and guide at the Capas Tourism Satellite Office (T 0999 356 5069, E capastourism@yahoo.com), but it won't work out substantially cheaper to do it this way.

Lake Pinatubo (around 5.5km, with a height gain of 300m; 2–3hr). The lake itself is stunning, with emerald green waters and spectacular surrounding views. However, swimming and boating in the crater lake are banned as the sulphuric water is toxic.

8

HUNDRED ISLANDS NATIONAL PARK

These emerald-like tiny islands (there are actually 123) make up a **national park** covering almost twenty square kilometres, nestled in the Lingayen Gulf. Some islands have beaches, but many are no more than coral outcrops crowned by scrub, and unfortunately much of the coral has been decimated. To prevent further damage, you can only snorkel in approved areas – Taklobos Reef is the nicest, where the government has been reintroducing giant clams, and the underwater life is beginning to return to pre-dynamite fishing levels.

Boat access to the islands is from **Lucap**, but it's far more pleasant to stay in pretty **Bolinao**, an hour away, where there are good accommodation choices. Either way you can island-hop by day (you'll need to take your own food and water), returning to a shower and a comfy bed in the evening. Don't expect Robinson Crusoe solitude, especially at weekends when many of the islands are overrun by day-trippers. You *can* find your own piece of paradise here (try Marta, Marcos or Cuenco islands), but you'll have to make it clear to the boatman that you're not interested in the bigger islands.

The only four islands with any form of development are **Governor's Island**, **Marcos Island**, **Children's Island** and **Quezon Island**, where there's basic accommodation.

ARRIVAL AND DEPARTURE

By bus The closest bus terminal is in the town of Alaminos, where you'll also find ATMs and internet facilities. Several bus companies serve Manila (roughly hourly; 6hr). From Alaminos it's a 15min tricycle ride (P100) to Lucap, or an hour by jeepney or bus to Bolinao.

INFORMATION AND BOAT TRIPS

Information The park is accessible year-round; you have to register and pay a fee (P40/day or P80/overnight, plus a P30 "environmental fee" and P10 insurance) at the National Park/Philippine Tourist Authority office at the end of the pier at Lucap (daily 24hr; T 075 205 0917).

Island-hopping The tourist office is the best place to arrange a boat, as prices are set by the DOT. A motorboat for up to seven people visiting one island is P800–1400 for the day. The latest pick-up time from the islands back to Lucap is 5.30pm. It's more fun to tour the islands by kayak (P350/hr); contact the tourist office or the Hundred Islands Eco-Tours Association (T 075 552 0773).

ACCOMMODATION AND EATING

You can pitch a tent on Children's, Governor's and Quezon islands for P200, payable at the Lucap tourist office. Also enquire here about renting nipa huts on the islands. You'll need to bring all your own food. While there are several places to stay in Lucap, Bolinao is a far more attractive proposition.

LUCAP

The Boat House Great fresh fish and steaks served in this small octagonal building, close to *Maxine*. Fri–Sun 6–10pm.

Maxine by the Sea T 075 696 0964. While the rooms aren't cheap, they are clean, tiled and quiet. The seafood restaurant here is the best in the area and justifiably popular, not least for the romantic views. Doubles **P2950**

Villa Antolin T 075 696 9227, W villa-antolin.com. Homely and friendly option right on the water with small, cosy, comfortable rooms and cable TV. Doubles **P1800**

Villa Milagros ☎075 551 3040, ⊚villamilagros.20m
.com. Simple budget hotel, friendly but thin-walled, with
rooms for two, three or four, and a dorm for backpackers.
Dorms P350, doubles P1400

BOLINAO
Punta Riviera ☎075 696 1350, ⊚puntarivieraresort
.com. Lovely resort right on the beach run by a friendly
Scottish and Filipina couple. Clean, airy rooms and a pool.
Doubles P4704
Rockview Beach ☎0998 805 4878. Simple bamboo and
nipa huts right on the beach, close to some picturesque
coastal rock formations. Doubles P1500

SAN FERNANDO (LA UNION) AND SAN JUAN

SAN FERNANDO, the capital of La Union
province, is a shortish hop up the coast
from Hundred Islands. Quezon Avenue
runs through San Fernando from south
to north, and has a number of internet
cafés and ATMs. Outside the city
limits, Quezon Avenue becomes the
National Highway. The city itself is
nothing out of the ordinary, but in
nearby **San Juan**, 7km to the north,
there are some laidback little beach
resorts stretched along a marvellous
crescent of a beach at Urbiztondo. The
pounding waves here mean that from
October to March this is a prime
destination on the Philippines' surf
scene; it's especially popular with
rookies, as it's an easy, and cheap, place
to learn – lessons average P400 per hour
(board rental only P200).

ARRIVAL AND DEPARTURE
By bus Partas buses from Manila heading north to Vigan
stop along Quezon Ave, from where you can pick up a
jeepney to San Juan (20min; P18). Alternatively, stay on
the bus northbound and ask the driver to let you off at one
of the resorts, which are all signposted along the road.
Frequent buses to and from Baguio (1hr 30min) operate
from San Fernando Plaza.

INFORMATION
Tourist information Municipal tourist office, San
Fernando city hall, F. Ortega Hwy (Mon–Fri 8am–5pm;
☎072 888 6922, ⊚www.sanfernandocity.gov.ph). DOT
office (daily 8am–5pm; ☎072 888 2411, ⊚facebook
.com/DOTRegionOne), *Oasis Country Resort*, 3km south of
San Fernando.

ACCOMMODATION AND EATING
Circle Hostel Urbiztondo ☎0917 832 6253, ⊚launion
.thecirclehostel.com. Hlp budget surf hostel, very sociable,
with good wi-fi but meagre breakfasts. You can stay in a
dorm bed with your own mozzie net, or in a hammock. or
on cushions on the floor of the communal living area.
Dorms P550, hammocks P450
El Union Coffee Opposite *Seabay Surf Resort*, Urbiztondo
⊚facebook.com/elunioncoffee. Cool little café serving
great coffees and wonderful s'mores (toasted marshmallow
and Nutella with crackers; P260). Mon, Wed & Thurs
8am–9pm, Fri–Sun 7am–10pm.
Monaliza Urbiztondo ☎072 607 1396. ⊚facebook.com/
MonalizaSurfResort. This surfer hang-out offering basic
accommodation in fan and a/c concrete cottages (fan
P1200, a/c P1500), some with sea views, has been going
strong since the 1980s. Board rental (P500/half-day) and
lessons (P200/hr) available. Doubles P900
San Juan Surf Resort San Juan ☎072 687 9990,
⊚sanjuansurfresort.ph. Squarely aimed at surfers: there's
a shop selling kit, and surf conditions are posted by the bar.
It's worth paying a bit extra for a deluxe room (P2500) with
free breakfast and more reliable wi-fi. Doubles P1980
Seanymph Café Urbiztondo. Sit back and watch the
surfers ride the waves at this beach restaurant serving a
selection of Western dishes, curries and stir-fries (P160–
180). Daily 7am–10pm.

VIGAN

About 135km north of San Fernando in
La Union lies the old Spanish town of
VIGAN, an unmissable stop on a trip
through the far north for old-world
charm and a flavour of the pre-war
Philippines. It has become a bit of a
cliché to describe Vigan as a living
museum, but it does do some justice to
the tag. One of the country's oldest
towns, it was called Nueva Segovia in
Spanish times and was an important
political, military, cultural and religious
centre. Having narrowly escaped
bombing in World War II, it has retained
its pavements of cobbled stones and
some of the finest **Spanish colonial
architecture** in the country, including
impressive homes that once belonged to
friars, merchants and colonial officials,
now preserved as "Heritage Homes".
Inscribed onto the UNESCO World
Heritage list in 1999, it remains the best
example of a planned Spanish colonial
city in Asia.

WHAT TO SEE AND DO

Vigan's time-capsule ambience is enhanced by the decision to allow only pedestrians and **calesas** (one-pony, two-seat traps) on some streets. A ride in a *calesa* makes for a romantic tour of the town (P150/hr). Vigan is one of the easier Philippine towns to negotiate because its streets follow a fairly regular grid. Crisologo Street runs south from Plaza Burgos and is lined with antique shops and cafés; running parallel to it is the main thoroughfare, Governor A. Reyes Street. On Plaza Salcedo stands **St Paul's Metropolitan Cathedral** (daily 6am–just after 6pm Mass; free), built here in 1790 in "earthquake baroque" style, following the tectonic destruction of the original building on the banks of the river. Across the square is the **Father José Burgos Museum** (daily 9am–5pm; free), a captivating old colonial house that was once home to one of the town's most famous residents, Padre José Burgos, whose martyrdom in 1872 galvanized the revolutionary movement. It houses Burgos memorabilia, as well as fourteen paintings by the artist Villanueva, depicting the violent 1807 Basi Revolt, prompted by a Spanish effort to control the production of *basi* (sugar-cane wine).

Two **Heritage Houses** worth popping into are the Syquia Mansion on Quirino Boulevard (Mon & Wed–Sun 9am–5pm; P50) and the Crisologo Museum on Liberation Boulevard (daily 8.30–11.30am & 1.30–4.30pm; free), which house various colonial artefacts and exhibits on the area. Vigan is also known for its **pottery**. The massive wood-fired kilns at the Pagburnayan Potteries in Rizal Street, at the junction with Liberation Boulevard, turn out huge jars, known as *burnay*, in which northerners store everything from vinegar to fish paste. Carabao (water buffalo) are still used to squash the clay under hoof.

The first week of May is the **Viva Vigan Arts Festival**, one of the biggest cultural events in North Luzon, when the usually staid town lets down its hair with a *calesa* parade and lots of street dancing.

ARRIVAL AND DEPARTURE

By plane Vigan airport, 6km west of the city centre, has no commercial flights at present. The nearest airport with passenger services is at Laoag, a 2hr (P180) bus ride north of Vigan.

By bus Partas buses use their terminal near the Vigan Public Market in Alcantara St at the southern end of town. Dominion buses arrive at and depart from the corner of Quezon Ave (the main street running south to north) and Liberation Blvd. Viron Trans use their terminal in Barangay Ayusan Norte. For the long trip back to Manila, Partas buses offer the most comfort, and three nightly express services. You can also catch a/c buses from the Caltex station on the highway to Laoag. A tricycle between any of the bus terminals and the town centre is P10.

Destinations Baguio (roughly hourly; 5hr); Laoag (every 30min; 2–3hr); Manila (roughly hourly; 10hr); San Fernando (roughly hourly; 3hr).

INFORMATION

Tourist information The provincial tourist office is at Leona Florentino House, 1 Crisologo St (daily 8am–5pm; ☎ 077 644 0315, ✉ sureilocossur@gmail.com). The municipal tourist office on Crisologo St ("Heritage Village Administration Office"; supposedly daily 8am–5pm) is less helpful and often left unstaffed.

ACCOMMODATION

Grandpa's Inn 1 Bonifacio St ☎ 077 722 2118. This cosy heritage house full of old knick-knacks has welcoming rooms, all with lovely wooden floors and most with brick walls. The communal bathrooms are a bit grimy; it's worth paying a little extra for a private bathroom (P980). Free wi-fi. Doubles P730

HEM Apartelle 32 Gov. A. Reyes St ☎ 077 722 2173. This hotel has six sparkling rooms, all with private bath, including singles (P600); staff are helpful and there is free wi-fi. Doubles P1000

★ TREAT YOURSELF

Villa Angela Heritage House 26 Quirino Blvd ☎ 077 722 2914, 🌐 villangela.com. The most charming of all the colonial hotels, this beautiful old Heritage House built in 1870 is a place to wallow in history under the canopy of a four-poster bed, at a still-affordable price. The house is chock-full of old photos and antiques; if you like your history a bit more modern, ask for the room Tom Cruise slept in: he stayed here for a few weeks in 1989 when filming *Born on the Fourth of July* on the sand dunes in nearby Laoag. Doubles P1700

Vigan Hotel Burgos St ☎077 644 0169. A bit run-down but still full of character, this ramshackle family-run hotel in a creaky old colonial building has en-suite a/c rooms (P995), but the cheapest are fan-cooled with shared bathrooms. Doubles P595

EATING AND DRINKING

One of Vigan's specialities is *empanada*, a type of fried pie that you can pick up from one of the many street stalls and small bakeries – try *Irene's* on Salcedo Street.
Café Leona Plaza Burgos. Named after the mother of the Philippines' first labour movement, *Café Leona* is Vigan's most popular restaurant, serving native Ilocano dishes as well as wood-fired pizzas (P285) and Japanese dishes (from P185). Daily 10am–midnight (Japanese dishes until 10pm only).
Uno Grille 2 Bonifacio St. Owned by and opposite to *Grandpa's*, this airy outdoor restaurant offers a variety of sizzling barbecued meats, as well as classic Filipino and European dishes. *Grandpa's* also runs *Café Uno*, an itty-bitty café attached to the hotel serving light meals (pastas from P80), cakes (from P90), cookies (P22), teas and coffees (P60). Free wi-fi. Daily 9am–11pm.

DIRECTORY

Banks and exchange BDO is in Plaza Maestro Mall near Plaza Burgos, and there are several ATMs along Quezon Ave.
Internet Quickline, Bonifacio St (daily 8.30am–9pm; P15/hr); *Café Uno* (see above) has free wi-fi.
Police Rivero St, Brgy 8, south of the city centre (☎077 722 0890).
Post office Governor A. Reyes St, cnr Bonifacio St. (Mon–Fri 8am–5pm).

The Cordilleras

To Filipino lowlanders, brought up on sunshine and beaches, the mountainous north is still seen as a mysterious Shangri-La full of enigmatic tribes and their unfamiliar gods. **Baguio**, the traditional mountain retreat for Manileños during the fierce heat of Easter week, is about as far north as many southerners get. But it's not until you get beyond Baguio into Benguet, Ifugao and Mountain provinces, the **tribal heartlands** of the northern Philippines, that the adventure really begins. There are still towns and valleys where life has changed little in hundreds of years, with traditional customs and values still very much in evidence, but increasingly paved roads are transforming both the physical and cultural landscapes.

A swing through the north shouldn't miss out the mountain village of **Sagada**, with its caves, hanging coffins and backpacker-friendly hostels, and the magnificent **rice terraces at Banaue**. A slightly longer trip might take in **Kabayan**, an Ibaloi village north of Baguio. In the early twentieth century a group of mummies, possibly dating as far back as 2000 BC, was discovered in the caves here, and it's also a base for scaling **Mount Pulag** (2922m), the highest mountain in Luzon.

BAGUIO AND AROUND

BAGUIO is known as "City of Pines", but unchecked development and chronic traffic congestion have greatly diminished its appeal. Lying on a plateau 1400m above sea level, Baguio was built in 1900 by the Americans as a recreational and administrative centre, from where they could preside over their tropical colony

8

TRIBES OF THE CORDILLERAS

The Cordilleras are home to six main indigenous Filipino tribes: the Ibaloi, the Kankana-ey, the Ifugao, the Kalinga, the Apayao and the Bontoc, collectively known as **Igorots**. There are also smaller sub-tribes among these six.

Tribes began to gather in small, isolated communities in the archipelago during pre-Spanish times when lowland Filipinos expanded into the interiors of Luzon, isolating upland tribes into pockets in which they still exist today. Like other Filipinos, these **upland tribes** were a blend of various ethnic origins, ranging from the highly skilled Bontoc and Ifugao to more primitive groups. Some have intermarried with lowlanders for more than a century, but others, like the **Kalinga**, choose to remain isolated from lowland influences. The **Ifugao**, creators of the famous rice terraces, mostly live in and around Banaue and are the tribe with which visitors to the north are most likely to come into contact.

without working up too much of a sweat. Baguio is also etched on the Filipino consciousness as the site of one of the country's worst natural disasters, the earthquake of July 16, 1990, which caused terrible devastation and claimed hundreds of lives.

Although little more than a stopping-off point en route to Sagada and the mountain provinces, Baguio has a few secrets worth discovering, such as its parks, arts enclaves and lovely bohemian cafés.

WHAT TO SEE AND DO

Burnham Park is the city's centrepiece and a nice place for a stroll, with a boating lake and strange little three-wheeled bicycles for rent. The park area was designed by Daniel Burnham, who was also responsible for parts of Chicago, Washington DC, and much of colonial American Manila. On the eastern edge of the park is Harrison Road, and behind that and running almost parallel to it is the city's congested main artery, Session Road, lined with shops and restaurants. Standing hidden above it all, and reached by a flight of a hundred steep steps, is **Baguio Cathedral** (Mon–Sat 5am–7pm, Sun 4.30am–8pm; free), a fine example of "wedding-cake gothic".

The northern end of Session Road leading to Magsaysay Avenue is the least appealing area, the smoky congestion only partly redeemed by the **City Market** (daily 5am–8pm), one of the liveliest and most colourful in the country, which sells

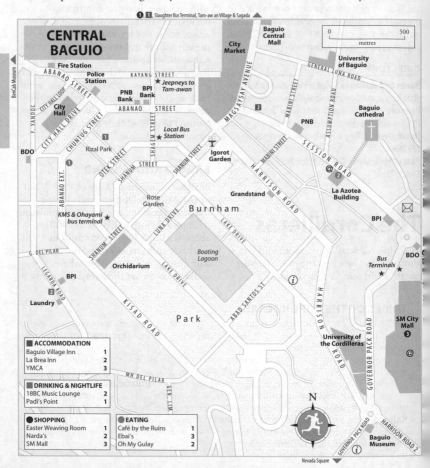

CENTRAL BAGUIO

① ① Slaughter Bus Terminal, Tam-aw an Village & Sagada

8

BenCab Museum

Fire Station
Police Station
City Hall
BDO
ABANAO STREET
CITY HALL LOOP
F. YANDOC
CITY HALL DRIVE
CHUNTUG STREET
ABANAO EXT.
SHANUM STREET
LEGARDA ROAD
BPI
Laundry
G. DEL PILAR
KMS & Ohayami bus terminal
Orchidarium
KISAD ROAD

KAYANG STREET
PNB Bank
BPI Bank
★ Jeepneys to Tam-awan
ABANAO STREET
Rizal Park
OTEK STREET
SHANUM STREET
SHAGEM STREET
SHANUM STREET
Local Bus Station
Rose Garden
LUNA DRIVE
LAKE DRIVE
Boating Lagoon
LAKE DRIVE

City Market
Baguio Central Mall
MAGSAYSAY AVENUE
MABINI STREET
GENERAL LUNA ROAD
University of Baguio
ASSUMPTION ROAD
Baguio Cathedral
PNB
SESSION ROAD
Igorot Garden
HARRISON ROAD
MABINI STREET
Grandstand
La Azotea Building
BPI
Bus Terminals ★
BDO
ABAD SANTOS ST.
HARRISON ROAD
SM City Mall ③
University of the Cordilleras
GOVERNOR PACK ROAD
HARRISON ROAD 2
Baguio Museum

Park

MH DEL PILAR
GEN. LIM

N

0   500
metres

Nevada Square

■ ACCOMMODATION	
Baguio Village Inn	1
La Brea Inn	2
YMCA	3

■ DRINKING & NIGHTLIFE	
18BC Music Lounge	2
Padi's Point	1

● SHOPPING	
Easter Weaving Room	1
Narda's	2
SM Mall	3

● EATING	
Café by the Ruins	1
Ebai's	3
Oh My Gulay	2

strawberries, peanut brittle, sweet wine, honey, textiles, handicrafts and jewellery, all produced in the Cordilleras. A huge *ukay-ukay* night market also sets up along Harrison Road.

The **Baguio Museum** (Tues–Sun 9am–5pm; P40) on Governor Pack Road showcases hundreds of fascinating artefacts from the region, as well as a Kabayan mummy.

Tam-awan Village

On the northwest outskirts of Baguio, **Tam-awan Village** (daily 8am–6pm; P50; ☎074 446 2949, ⊛tam-awanvillage.com) is a replica tribal village comprised of eight Ifugao houses and two Kalinga huts where you can stay and drink rice wine around a traditional Bontoc *dap-ay*, an outdoor meeting place with a fire at its centre. There is also a variety of native craft workshops on offer. Cordilleran food is prepared on site, work by local artists is available to buy, and staff will often perform ceremonies, songs and dances for visitors. An overnight stay here is an experience (P1000 for a small hut for two people with shared toilets and showers). Take a jacket because it can get surprisingly cold. You can reach Tam-awan Village by taxi for less than P100, or take a Tam-awan jeepney (P11) from Kayang Street.

The BenCab Museum

In February 2009, National Artist for the visual arts and longtime Baguio resident Benedicto Cabrera (universally known as BenCab), the driving force behind the Tam-awan Village, opened the **BenCab Museum** (Tues–Sun 9am–6pm; P120). About fifteen minutes outside Baguio, it's home to a mix of contemporary Filipino art and indigenous Cordilleran crafts in a beautiful setting – on a clear day you can even see the South China Sea. The tranquil café is also worth a stop. To get here, catch an Asin-bound jeepney (P10) from Kayang Street, beside the market, and let the driver know where you're going.

ARRIVAL AND DEPARTURE

By bus Buses including Partas, Dagupan, Genesis and Fariña drop passengers on the eastern edge of the city on Governor Pack Rd. KMS and Ohayami buses arrive at the western end

of Burnham Park. Victory Liner services terminate at Governor Park Rd, except for their Manila services, which have a terminal at the south end of Session Rd.

Destinations For Sagada and Bontoc, GL Trans and D'Rising Sun leave from the Slaughterhouse Terminal (Bontoc: D'Rising Sun on the hour 5am–4pm, GL Trans 5 daily; 5–6hr). Several morning A-Liner buses also leave from here for Kabayan (4hr 30min). Buses for Banaue: KMS (Chanum Str) has two departures daily (8am & 9.30pm; 8hr); various companies travel to San Fernando, La Union (hourly; 2hr 30min), leaving from the terminal on Shagem St. Buses for other destinations leave from the terminal in Governor Pack Rd near Session Rd: Manila (at least hourly until 11pm; 6hr); Vigan (Partas, hourly; 5hr).

INFORMATION

Tourist information The department of tourism is in the Baguio Tourism Complex on Governor Pack Rd (Mon–Fri 8am–5pm; ☎074 442 7014, ✉dotregioncar@gmail.com), and there's a smaller city information centre on Lake Drive in Burnham Park (Mon–Fri 8am–5pm; ☎074 446 3434).

ACCOMMODATION

Baguio Village Inn 355 Magsaysay Ave ☎074 442 3901. This spotless place, a 15min walk from the bottom of Session Rd, is friendly and pretty homey, with wooden floors and wood panelling, although the single rooms in particular are rather small. Doubles **P800**

La Brea Inn 23 Lower Session Rd ☎074 446 6061, ⊛labreainn.powersites.ph. Clean and tidy rooms right in the centre of Baguio and just a short stroll from many cafés and restaurants; all rooms have private bath and cable TV. Free wi-fi. Doubles **P1250**

YMCA Post Office Loop ☎074 442 4766. This large, central hostel has spotless twin rooms with flatscreen TVs and single-sex dorms with institutional rows of pine-wood beds crammed in every corner. Dorms **P385**, twins **P1420**

EATING

★**Café by the Ruins** 25 Chuntug St. In a breezy setting with tables dotted around the World War II ruins of the residence of Baguio's first governor, this is one of the city's best restaurants, with excellent organic food prepared with home-grown herbs and served either indoors or in the shady yard. The duck *mami* (noodle soup; P200) is great, and there are home-made breads, pastries, muffins and scones (P88), too. Daily 7am–10pm.

Ebai's Upper Session Rd. The exquisite carrot cake (P68) at this little café was originally baked for the wife of former President Ramos; it's a great little spot to refuel with a slice of that, or a dish of indigenous cuisine such as *bulalo* (P198) or pork *adobo* (P108). Daily 7am–9.30pm.

★**Oh My Gulay** 5th Floor, La Azotea Building, 108 Session Rd. This unique vegetarian café-cum-art gallery

8

translates as "Oh my vegetable" – dishes are light, including salads, sandwiches and pastas (OMG salad P120). The impressive native-wood interior designed by local artist and film-maker Kidlat Tahimik features half a ship's hull and a stream with goldfish. A must-see. Tues–Thurs 11am–8pm, Fri & Sat 11am–9pm, Sun 11am–7pm.

DRINKING AND NIGHTLIFE

18BC Music Lounge Legarda Rd. A fun bar with nightly local bands, popular with students, especially at the weekend, but not to the extent of being overwhelmed with them. Acoustic rock is the mainstay here, but they sometimes have reggae or other sounds too. Daily 6.30pm–2.30am.

Padi's Point Rizal Park. This is one of the most popular places in town, with daily bands playing an eclectic mix of tunes from r'n'b to rock; the DJ then takes over and spins some disco tunes as groups of students gulp "cocktail towers" (three litres). Daily 1pm–4am.

SHOPPING

Easter Weaving Room 2 Easter Rd in Guisad. A huge selection of beautifully crafted woven goods. It's quite touristy but offers the chance to see intricate designs being woven on tablecloths and rugs in the "factory". It's not too far from Tama-awan Village, and can easily be combined with a (taxi) visit. Mon–Sat 8am–5pm.

Narda's 151 Upper Sessions Rd. Fantastic Igorot woven accessories and housewares. Daily 8am–7pm.

SM Mall Luneta Hill, Upper Sessions Rd. There is a supermarket on the lower ground floor, ATMs, a cinema and numerous cafés and restaurants. Mon–Thurs & Sun 10am–9pm, Fri & Sat 10am–10pm.

DIRECTORY

Banks There are plenty of ATMs in the centre; you'll find moneychangers in the City Market at its southern end.

Internet Pat Session Internet Café, 2/F 104 Session Rd (daily 24hr; P15/hr). SM Mall has free wi-fi.

Laundry Laba Ever laundry by 18BC on Legarda Rd (Mon–Sat 9am–9pm; Sun 9am–2pm; P35/kg).

Police The station (☏074 442 4119) is next to the fire station on Abanao St.

Post office On Session Rd opposite Governor Pack Rd.

KABAYAN

The isolated mountain village of **KABAYAN**, 50km or five hours by bus north of Baguio, gained some notoriety in the early twentieth century when a group of mummies was discovered in surrounding caves. The mummies are believed by some scientists to date back as far as 2000 BC. When the Spanish arrived, mummification was discouraged and the practice died out. Controversy still surrounds the Kabayan mummies, some of which have "disappeared" to overseas collectors. Several mummies remain, however, and you can see them in their mountaintop caves and also in the small **Kabayan National Museum** (Mon–Fri 9am–6pm; free).

You have to register at the tourist office and pay a P30 "cultural fee". The tourist office can hitch you up with a guide to trek to the mummy caves, which is obligatory (P1500 for up to seven people) to visit **Timbac Cave** (P30), which is the most impressive, but high on a mountaintop and a strenuous four- to five-hour climb.

ARRIVAL AND DEPARTURE

By bus Access to Kabayan is easiest from Baguio; there are several morning buses (see p.621). If you're continuing north from here, you'll have to hire a vehicle to take you to the Halsema Highway to catch a Bontoc-bound bus.

ACCOMMODATION AND EATING

There are half a dozen sari-sari stores in Kabayan where you can get snacks and basic meals.

Pinecone Lodge ☏0929 327 7749. The best place to stay in Kabayan. As the name suggests, this lodge is decked out in pine and the clean tiled rooms are spacious and all have private bath, plus there's a cosy living area with fireplace. Doubles P550

MOUNT PULAG

Standing 2992m above sea level, **Mount Pulag** is the highest mountain in Luzon and a Level III strenuous climb. Pulag is a challenge: the terrain is steep, there are gorges and ravines and, in the heat of the valleys, it's easy to forget it's bitterly cold on top.

The best **trail** for first-timers starts from nearby Ambangeg, a stop on the Baguio–Kabayan bus route. Note that the park is expected to be closed to visitors on Saturdays starting in 2017, and camping in the park is banned at weekends (Fri–Sun); visitor numbers may also be restricted. The DENR Visitors' Center (☏0919 631 5402, ✉ambangeg@gmail .com) is close to the start of a number of trails, where you must **register** and pay an entrance fee (US$15, or around P750) and heritage fee (P175), plus organize the mandatory guide (P600 for up to five people on the easier trails). The Akiki or Killer Trail starts 2km south of Kabayan on the Baguio–Kabayan road and takes at least two days (P1800 for up to seven people). You will need to get a medical certificate before you set out, signed by a doctor, to certify that you are fit for the climb; you can get a form for this at ⓦpinoymountaineer.com/wp-content/uploads/2015/12/Medical-Certificate-for-Mountaineers-version-1.pdf, which you can take to a doctor to get it filled out; at a pinch there is a health centre in Ambangeg where they should do it for you. The Visitors' Centre can arrange homestay accommodation (P200–2000 depending on facilities). Alternatively, on weekdays (Mon–Thurs), weather allowing, you can take a tent and camp on top for the night (P50 per person); the next morning, wake early to watch the sunrise and marvel at the whole of Luzon at your feet.

SAGADA

In spite of its increasing popularity, the village of **SAGADA**, 151km north of Baguio, at an elevation of over 1500m, still has charm and mystery to spare, much of it connected with the **hanging coffins** that can be seen perched high in the surrounding limestone cliffs. Sagada began to open up as a destination with the arrival of electricity in the early 1970s, and intellectuals flocked here to write and paint. They didn't produce much, perhaps because they are said to have spent much of their time drinking *tapuy,* the local rice wine. European hippies followed, and the artistic influence has left its mark in the form of little boho cafés and inns and a distinctly laidback atmosphere, enhanced by the ready availability of locally grown weed, although a major bust in 2013 may have put paid to this scene for a while. More guesthouses and souvenir shops are springing up as improved roads increase the tourist influx, but for now, Sagada remains one of the country's genuine backpacker enclaves.

It can get very chilly, especially at night, and the streets are poorly lit; bring a sweater, scarf and torch.

WHAT TO SEE AND DO

For insight into Cordilleran culture, call into the small **Ganduyan Museum** (daily 1–6pm, depending on staff availability; P25), opposite the town hall, with a fascinating collection of Igorot artefacts, some of which were still being used in daily life into the 1990s.

A five-minute walk past the hospital on the road to Bontoc takes you to **Sagada Weaving** (daily 7am–6pm), where you can watch distinctive coloured fabrics being produced using tribal designs, and buy souvenirs.

Activities

Sagada's main draw is the outdoors. The area's cool forest paths and extensive cave network make for some great **treks**. One of the most popular hikes, taking two to three hours in all, is a loop around the **hanging coffins** in **Echo Valley**, high on the surrounding limestone cliffs. There are dozens of sinuous paths leading off through deep foliage in all directions, so a guide is essential (see p.624). A typical trek costs P800–1300 for a group of up to ten people.

Caving in Sagada's labyrinthine network of channels and caverns is an exhilarating but potentially risky activity. A small number of tourists have died in these caves, so don't risk going alone. The highlight is **Sumaging Cave**, an old burial cave whose chambers and rock formations are an eerie sight, a 45-minute walk south of town. The set price for a guided tour for up to four people is P500. A more challenging underground adventure is provided by the **Cave Connection**, linking Sumaging and Lumiang, but this is not for the faint of heart or claustrophobics and involves three to four hours of squeezing through narrow crevices and swimming, often to emerge in enormous caverns eerily lit by the glow of the guide's paraffin lamp. Other outdoors options include a visit to pretty nearby waterfalls, rice terraces, and rafting on the Chico River (see ⓦsagadaoutdoors.com).

8

ARRIVAL AND DEPARTURE

By bus Buses and jeepneys terminate by the town hall on the main street. The Halsema Highway to Sagada traverses the highest point on the Philippine highway system (2339m), so bring warm clothing for the trip. GL Lizardo runs buses to Baguio (7 daily; 5–6hr); Coda Lines has a daily bus to Manila (3pm daily; 11hr).

By jeepney Jeepneys leave Sagada for Bontoc (every 30min 6.30am–9am, hourly 9am–1pm; 45min), where you can change for Banaue.

INFORMATION

Tourist information There's a small tourist information centre (daily 7am–5pm; ☎ 0905 513 7626, ⓦ facebook .com/bontoctourisminfocenter) in the old town hall. All visitors must register here and pay an environmental fee (P35; keep the receipt with you as you'll need to show it when visiting the main sights).

Guides The Sagada Environmental Guides Association (SEGA; daily 6am–6pm; ⓦ facebook.com/sega.sagada .guides) are the longest established and fix all guiding prices in the region; Sagada Genuine Guides (daily 6am–7pm; ☎ 0929 556 9553, ⓦ facebook.com/saggas) also provide guides.

ACCOMMODATION

Reservations are advised over holiday periods.

Masferre Inn South Rd, 100m from the centre of the village ☎ 0918 341 6164, ⓦ masferre.blogspot.com. Owned by the family of early twentieth-century photographer Eduardo Masferré, whose historical pictures of local indigenous people decorate the (excellent) restaurant, this friendly place has clean, simple rooms, some with balconies and views. Doubles P1800

★ **Sagada Homestay** Sagada–Besao Rd ☎ 0919 702 8380, ⓔ sagadahomestay@yahoo.com.ph. The smell of fresh pinewood permeates this wonderful family-run guesthouse with an alpine feel. Rooms are clean and cosy and the welcoming family does its utmost to make guests feel at home. Hot water, wi-fi in the main building, and outstanding massages. Doubles P500

St Joseph's Resthouse Sagada–Besao Rd ☎ 0918 559 5934, ⓦ saintjosephresthousesagada.blogspot.com. This friendly place, with great views of the surrounding countryside, has cheap rooms in the main building, and more expensive cottages (P1700) all decked out in local wood in the attractive hilltop garden. Great restaurant, too. Doubles P500

EATING AND DRINKING

Gaia ☎ 0949 137 6777. A kilometre south of town, near Sumaging Cave, this wonderful eco-friendly restaurant, set on a covered patio with views over the rice terraces, offers inventive dishes made largely with organic ingredients,

including *miki mi na* (squash noodles sautéed with green beans, carrots and mushrooms; P125). Daily 7am–7pm.

Lemon Pie House South Rd, at the bottom of the village, past *George Guesthouse*. This laidback café with pillows set around cute pine tables is a great spot for a coffee (P30) and a slice of lemon pie (P30), made with juicy local lemons. Free wi-fi. Daily 6am–8pm.

★ **Log Cabin Café** Sagada–Besao Rd, 100m from the centre of the village ☎ 0920 520 0463. Very popular restaurant which rustles up tasty dishes using different market-fresh produce each day. The setting is cosy, with a crackling fire, and there's a great Saturday-night buffet (P390) whipped up by their French chef at 7pm. Essential to book in advance. Daily 6–9pm.

Yoghurt House South Rd, 300m south of the village centre. Great place in which to soak up the surrounding views from the first-floor balcony and tuck into a creamy home-made yoghurt (P70). Excellent breakfasts and hearty dinners. The chocolate chip cookies are a must. Daily 8am–8.30pm.

DIRECTORY

Banks and exchange There's an ATM in the tourist information centre, and the Rural Bank of Sagada has an ATM (but inside the bank, so only accessible during banking hours Tues–Sat 8.30am–4.30pm); the bank will change dollars and travellers' cheques at an unfavourable rate. There's also a Western Union here.

Internet 5-11-Ten by *Yoghurt House* (daily 8.30am–8pm; P20/hr).

BONTOC

The capital of Mountain province, **BONTOC** is the first major town in the north beyond Baguio. It lies on the banks of the Chico River, 45 minutes east of Sagada by jeepney.

Bontoc is primarily a commercial town used by tourists as a rest-stop on the circuit to Banaue. It is, however, gaining a reputation as a good place for **trekking**; contact the tourism information centre (Mon–Fri 8am–5pm) in the municipal hall, or get in touch directly with provincial tourism officer Francis Degay (☎ 0948 678 7290, ⓔ f_degay@yahoo .com). Guides for up to four people cost around P1500 per day. Don't miss the small but excellent **Bontoc Museum** (Mon–Sat 8am–noon & 1–5pm; P60) behind *Pines Kitchenette and Inn*. It features fascinating black-and-white photos and various artefacts of tribal life in the Cordilleras, plus a decent shop downstairs. Check out the replica village built in the grounds.

ARRIVAL AND DEPARTURE

By bus Hourly to Baguio (5am–4pm; 6–7hr) with D'Rising Sun and 5 daily with GL Trans. Coda Lines buses for Manila (10hr), via Banaue (2hr), usually leave daily at 4pm from the river bridge or the Samoki branch of *Cable Café*.
By van Departures for Banaue from near the tourism information centre leave when they're full, between around 9am and 1.30pm (2hr; P150).

ACCOMMODATION AND EATING

Cable Café Main St, and across the river in Samoki. Daily bands playing an eclectic mix of music hit the little stage at 8pm, keeping Bontoc's liveliest joint up and running. The grub is Filipino, and is better at the Samoki branch, which has chicken or pork meals (P120). Main St supposedly daily 24hr, Samoki daily 8am–11pm.
Churya-a Hotel Main St ☎ 0905 182 1606, ✉ peckley3 @gmail.com. Unremarkable doubles, mostly with attached bathrooms, right in the centre of town; there's a nice balcony eating area with a view over the mountains, which has wi-fi, although the rooms don't. Doubles P500
Pines Kitchenette and Inn Behind the market ☎ 0930 092 0994, ✉ josephinekhayad@yahoo.com. This large family house was originally built to put up adopted World War II war orphans, as photographs in the lobby testify. Rooms are simple and the shared bathrooms (only one room has its own) just about pass muster, but the management is friendly and welcoming. Doubles P400

DIRECTORY

Banks and exchange PNB and Landbank both have ATMs. There's a Western Union on the main street.
Internet Sun Café, by the Banaue van station (daily 8.30am–8pm; P20/hr).
Post office Near the Bontoc Museum.

BANAUE

It's a rugged but spectacular two-and-a-half-hour trip south from Bontoc to **BANAUE** in Ifugao province, along a winding road that leads up into the misty Cordilleras, across a high mountain pass, then down a precipitous mountainside. It may only be 300km north of Manila, but Banaue is a world away, 1300m above sea level and far removed in spirit and topography from the beaches and palm trees of the south. This is the heart of rice-terrace country. The terraces in

Banaue itself are some of the most impressive and well known, although there are hundreds of others in the area, some of the best of which are at nearby **BATAD**, where there are a couple of guesthouses, so you can stay overnight and hike back the next morning.

Banaue itself is a small town centred on a marketplace, with a clutch of guesthouses and some souvenir shops. Two kilometres up the road from the marketplace are the four main **lookout points** for the rice terraces. Tricycle drivers angle constantly to take you there, which can be irritating, but the views are truly superb. A tricycle will cost around P200, but be sure to agree the price beforehand. Ifugao in traditional costume will ask for a small fee if you want to take their photograph, and there's a handful of souvenir stalls surrounding the lookouts selling carved wooden bowls and woven blankets. Don't miss the remarkable little **museum** (daily 8am–4pm; P50) by the *Banaue View Inn*, which documents the extraordinary life of Henry Otley Beyer, an American anthropologist who came to study Ifugao tribes at the beginning of the twentieth century and, after marrying an Ifugao woman, settled and died in the region. The **Museum of Cordilleran Sculpture** (daily 8am–5pm; P100), 1km southwest of town, past the *Banaue Hotel*, houses more than two thousand fascinating Ifugao artefacts, including trophy heads and erotic rice baskets.

ARRIVAL AND DEPARTURES

By bus Buses terminate at the main road above the market place, reached by a flight of steep stone stairs. Destinations Coda Lines, Ohayami and Dangwa all have evening services to Manila (8–9hr); Ohayami and KMS have early evening departures for Baguio (8hr). For Bontoc there are two daily services (2hr).
By van Vans from Bontoc leave when full until about 1pm. For Baguio (6hr) there are six daily vans, best booked a day in advance at the office just below the municipal tourist centre (6hr; P360). For Sagada, change at Bontoc.

INFORMATION

Tourist information The municipal tourist centre is above the market place, where the buses stop (daily 5.30am–5pm; ☎ 0906 770 7969, ✉ elahd_ban@yahoo .com). All visitors must register here and pay the local

8

THE STAIRWAYS TO HEAVEN

The "Stairway to Heaven" **rice terraces** at Banaue are one of the great icons of the Philippines. They were hewn from the land over two thousand years ago by Ifugao tribespeople using primitive tools, an achievement in engineering terms that ranks alongside the building of the pyramids.

The survival of the terraces, added to the United Nations' World Heritage list in 1995, is closely tied to the future of the tribespeople themselves. Part of the problem, it must be said, is tourism, but you can't blame locals, who would otherwise have been toiling on the terraces, for making a much easier buck selling reproduction tribal artefacts. The problem is compounded by the mass migration of many younger tribespeople to the big cities. The result is that the region now only meets a third of its rice requirements, and as you tour the region you'll notice areas where the terraces are clearly in disrepair. Given that the main reason travellers come to the region is to see the terraces, if they disappear then so will the tourist dollars. For now they remain spectacular and are at their most impressive around March, April and May, right before the rice harvest.

environmental fee (P20). They can find you a guide for treks to local Ifugao communities or day-trips to the rice terraces at Batad, and they set rates for each trek (for example, P3450 for up to five people to Batad including guide, transport and local "heritage fee").

ACCOMMODATION AND EATING

Banaue View Inn ☎0916 694 4511, ✉ banaueviewinn_1984@yahoo.com. Friendly, family-run place overlooking town and the terraces beyond, and home to the Banaue Museum. Clean rooms with private hot-water bathrooms. Doubles P1000

People's Lodge and Restaurant Next door to the *Greenview* ☎074 386 4014, ✉ jerwin_t@yahoo.com. Only the relatively pricier rooms here have hot water, while the simple ones have shared bathroom facilities with free cold showers (hot shower P100). There's a terrace with excellent views and a decent restaurant. Doubles P500

★ **Sanafe Lodge and Restaurant** ☎0918 947 7226, ✉ susanmparades@gmail.com. The doubles here are clean and cosy, all with hot water and most with incredible views, but the dorms are quite stuffy with no windows. The fantastic terrace restaurant serves great international food and the views over the terraces are unbeatable. Free speedy wi-fi. Dorms P200, doubles P1000

Uyami's Greenview Lodge and Restaurant ☎0920 540 4225, ⊕ ugreenview.wordpress.com. The cosy doubles here have wooden floors and pine interiors, although the cheaper concrete rooms on the bottom floor aren't as snug, with common bathrooms and cold showers (hot water is an additional P50). The restaurant has wonderful rice-terrace views and wi-fi, and rustles up appetizing local dishes. Doubles P500

DIRECTORY

Banks and exchange W&L moneychangers, 3/F Banaue Building in the main square (daily 8am–5.30pm) don't offer great rates. The ATM by the municipal hall accepts foreign cards, but has been known to swallow them.
Internet Clickers (daily 7am–7pm; P20/hr) and Gamerz (daily 8am–7pm; P20/hr), both on the third floor of the Banaue Building in the main square.
Police In the main square (☎0917 306 7668).
Post office 1km south of town near the *Banaue Hotel*.

BATAD

The 19km trek from Banaue to the remote little village of **BATAD** has become something of a pilgrimage for visitors looking for rural isolation and unforgettable rice-terrace scenery. You'll need to take a tricycle (P800) from Banaue for the first (bumpy) 12km before starting a tiring walk up a steep trail, but the spectacular views more than compensate for any discomfort. A cheaper and less tiring option is to take a public jeepney (P150) to below Saddle, a half-hour walk from Batad. You will have to stay overnight in Batad as there is only one afternoon departure from Banaue at 3pm; you can then catch the 8.30am jeepney back to Banaue. Alternatively, you can hire a private jeepney (P2800); a guide will set you back a further P1200. The tourist information centre can give you more detail on the many different local hikes, or contact Robert's Trekking Adventure (☎0975 450 5609, ✉ robert .immotna@yahoo.com) who organize great hikes of the area.

Batad nestles in a natural amphitheatre, a one-hour hike from the glorious 30m-high

Tappia Waterfall, which has a deep, bracing pool for swimming. Village life in Batad was virtually unchanged for centuries until the development of tourism, but its influence hasn't yet been too insidious; there are just half a dozen basic **guesthouses**. Rooms in Batad, while not as dirt-cheap as they once were, are still very reasonable. Prices and quality are similar (all P250 per person), but *Simon's Inn* has a particularly good restaurant offering the widest choice of dishes in town, including fantastic home-made pitta bread. Rooms fill up quickly in summertime.

South of Manila and Mindoro

Leaving the sprawl of Manila behind and heading south takes you along the South Luzon Expressway (known to Filipinos as the South Luzon Distressway) and into the provinces of Cavite, Laguna and Batangas. Traffic can be grim, particularly at weekends and during holidays, so try to time your journey for a weekday if at all possible. The province of **Batangas** is Manila's weekend playground, with some nice (but rather expensive) beach resorts around Nasugbu and Matabungkay, and alluring **Taal Volcano** to climb. The provincial capital, **Batangas City**, is a polluted port town but its ferry pier offers escape to the island of **Mindoro** and the diving resorts of **Puerto Galera**.

PAGSANJAN FALLS

Francis Ford Coppola chose **PAGSANJAN**, 90km southeast of Manila, as the shooting location for the harrowing final scenes of *Apocalypse Now*, and the sheer drama of the scenery is undeniable. Faded Hollywood associations aside, the real draw here is the chance to shoot down the fourteen rapids of the Bombongan River from **Pagsanjan Falls**. Proceed first of all to the tourist office (see below), who will brief you and get you to the boating stations. The local *bangkeros* are skilled at manoeuvring their canoes between the boulders. The cost of shooting

the rapids is P1250 per person, which includes a round-trip boat ride and a bamboo raft to the main falls, so expect to get wet, and protect your phone and camera. It's customary to tip the boatman, typically P100 per person.

ARRIVAL AND INFORMATION

By bus To get to Pagsanjan from Manila, catch a DLTB or HM bus from the corner of Buendia and Taft Avenue to Santa Cruz, from where you can get a jeepney (P10) to Pagsanjan town.

Pagsanjan Municipal Tourism Office (daily 8am–5pm; ☎ 049 501 3544) in the municipal hall opposite the main church.

ACCOMMODATION

Staying overnight allows you to beat the crowds, but there aren't many accommodation choices.

Pagsanjan Falls Lodge On the Pagsanjan-Cavinti road ☎ 049 501 4251, ☏ pagsanjanfallslodge.com.ph. A resort with a family pool area, a restaurant and a good range of rather ordinary but clean and spacious rooms. Served by jeepneys from General Luna St (south of the river). Doubles P1500

TAAL VOLCANO

Rising majestically from the centre of picturesque Taal lake and perennially popular with day-trippers from Manila, **Taal Volcano** offers gentle trekking, stunning views, and a refreshing change of temperature from the city. **Taal** has had several major eruptions over the centuries and was showing signs of increased activity in 2012. A team of seismologists is permanently based on the lakeshore and continues to monitor the situation, with the authorities occasionally forced to issue evacuation warnings.

Tagaytay, 70km south of Manila, is the nearest town, perched out of harm's way on a 600m-high ridge above the lake. Because of its cool climate – on some days it even gets foggy – Tagaytay is a favourite escape from the city, especially at weekends when it really fills up. Unfortunately it is very spread out, much of the accommodation is overpriced, and the boat touts can wear down your patience. The views from the ridge are admittedly breathtaking, and there are some exceptional restaurants, but staying beside

8

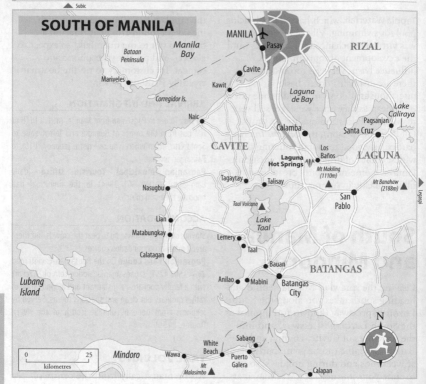

8

the lake in the little *barangay* of **Talisay** is generally a more affordable way to visit.

WHAT TO SEE AND DO

Talisay is the jumping-off point if you want to climb the volcano; you can hire a boat at almost any establishment on the lakeshore for around P2000 per group of up to six (you may be able to bargain this down to P1500 during the week), plus a P50 landing fee per boat and P100 municipal tourist tax per person, and bear in mind that you don't need the offered guide for the hour-long walk. There's not much shade on the volcano and it can get hot, so don't go without sunblock, a good hat, food and plenty of water. There are horses for hire (P500) for the trek if you feel like enjoying the view without expending any energy. Depending on levels of tectonic activity, climbing is sometimes prohibited. Further information can be found at the **Philippine Institute of Volcanology and Seismology**

(PHILVOLCS; Mon–Fri 8am–5pm; ☎043 426 1468, ⓦwww.phivolcs.dost .gov.ph) by the San Roque Beach Resort.

ARRIVAL AND DEPARTURE

By bus San Agustin and BSC buses run from Manila (Pasay) to Olivarez Plaza in Tagaytay (every 15min; 1hr 30min) from where you can get a tricycle to Talisay (P150; 20min). Tagaytay is a stop on the Manila–Lemery route (for Anilao).

INFORMATION

Tourist information Tagaytay City Tourism Office is located in the City Hall (3km west of Tagaytay's central Rotunda; daily 8am–5pm; ☎046 413 1220). The local police have a small tourist information post on the south side of the Rotunda.

GETTING AROUND

Jeepneys mostly terminate at Olivarez Plaza (200m north of the Rotunda). For Talisay, you can take a "People's Park" jeepney to the turn-off (5km east of the Rotunda; P11) and a tricycle (P150) or occasional jeepney from there, or you may be able to negotiate a tricycle for P150 direct from Olivarez Plaza.

ACCOMMODATION

★ **Keni Po** 4km east of the Tagaytay roundabout towards Calamba ☎046 483 0977, ✉keniporooms@yahoo .com.ph. It means "welcome" in the local dialect, which is indeed how you feel at this bright yellow guesthouse with cosy rooms with cable TV and DVD players, plus a pleasant pool in the verdant garden. No restaurant, but the room service is cheap and delicious. Free wi-fi. Doubles P1200
San Roque Beach Resort ☎043 773 0271, ✉sanroquebeachresort@yahoo.com. A welcoming place right on the lakeshore with startling views across to the volcano, owned by a lovely Dutch–Filipina couple Leo and Lita. The spacious rooms have little extra touches such as flowering plants and reading lamps, and there are also great fish meals. Doubles P1500

EATING

Josephine's Aguinaldo Hwy Km 58 (3km west of the Rotunda). An institution among Filipinos since the 1960s, serving good Filipino dishes with great views. They do a weekend lunch buffet for P495. Mains P220–520. Mon–Fri 8am–9pm, Sat & Sun 7am–9pm.
Papa Prito Central roundabout, by the Rotunda. Fast-food diner in the middle of town, nothing fancy, but filling and cheap. A plate of *pancit* noodles (P120) will sort you well out, and if you sit at the back you'll get as good a view as from any of the posh places. Mon–Fri 10am–2am, Sat & Sun 9am–2am.

DIRECTORY

Banks and exchange There's an AUI and a BDO, both with ATMs, at the central Rotunda in Tagaytay. There's a money changer (Tambunking) opposite Olivarez Plaza, but offering very bad rates.
Internet Internet cafés at Olivarez Plaza in Tagaytay include Aiisei Explorer at store 26 opposite *Kubo* restaurant (daily 7am–9pm; P20/hr). Many cafés have wi-fi, including *Josephine's*.

PUERTO GALERA

PUERTO GALERA, on the northern coast of **Mindoro**, is one of the Philippines' top destinations for travellers, especially for snorkellers and divers, with around thirty listed **dive sites**. Easily accessible from Manila (via Batangas City), it has a stunning natural harbour, swathes of quiet sandy beaches and a good range of accommodation options. Backpackers on a budget, however, will find that prices for resorts and restaurants can be on the high side. As well as being the name of a small town, "Puerto Galera" is generally

used to refer to the area between Sabang, 5km to the east, and White Beach, 8km to the west.

WHAT TO SEE AND DO

The area's extensive and diverse coral reefs have been declared a UNESCO Man and the Biosphere Reserve – a marine environment of global importance. The direct protection that comes from such a declaration is minimal, but the reefs remain intact thanks to the efforts of local people, hotel owners and dive operators, who all cooperate to ensure that the undersea riches are not ruined.

Boats and yachts lie at anchor in Muelle Bay, and in the background looms the brooding hulk of **Mount Malasimbo** (1122m), invariably crowned with a ring of cumulus. There's plenty on offer in addition to diving, including dazzling snorkelling, trekking into the mountains and beach-hopping by *bangka*. As if all this weren't enough, thrill-seekers can get their fix at **Puerto Galera X-Treme Sports Adventure Park** (☎0917 552 8114, ⊛extremesportsphilippines.com), where exhilarating activities include paint-balling, go-karting, zorbing and ziplining.

Sabang is by far the busiest area, with lots of accommodation options and dive centres; however, it doesn't have much of a beach, and where it does, it's small and stony and the water is filled with *bangkas*. Towards nightfall the area also becomes quite sleazy, with girlie bars and discos taking centre stage. It's more popular with the older single male crowd, divers and Chinese and Korean tour groups.

Neighbouring **Small La Laguna** and **Big La Laguna** are rather more laidback and quieter. Of the two, Big La Laguna has the better beach. Twenty minutes by jeepney on the other side of Puerto Galera town is **White Beach**, a vast sandy stretch with fewer dive centres, but more affordable local restaurants. It gets busy with weekenders from Manila, and at other peak times, especially Easter, when rates shoot up. Five minutes past White Beach by tricycle are the tranquil areas of **Aninuan** and **Talipanan**, where you'll find Puerto Galera's best beaches. Talipanan has some excellent budget options, while

8

THE PHILIPPINES UNDERWATER

With more than 7000 tropical islands and 40,000 square kilometres of coral reefs, it is no surprise that the Philippines is one of the world's top diving destinations. The archipelago, part of the Coral Triangle, has one of the most productive marine ecosystems on the planet, with an outstanding diversity of marine life. Its waters, enriched by currents from Japan, the South China Sea, the Indian Ocean and the Celebes Sea, abound with rare species of fish, marine invertebrates and more than 500 coral species and organisms. Divers will be overwhelmed by the variety of underwater activity. Those seeking an adrenaline rush can dive at Malapascua, where **thresher sharks** are common. Their large upper caudal fin is used to stun prey and can reach the same length as the shark's body. Docile **whale sharks**, meanwhile, are the world's largest fish and mainly feed on plankton and microscopic plants. Donsol provides the best opportunity to swim with these curious giants. For those wanting to immerse themselves in a bit of history, the renowned Japanese World War II **shipwrecks** off the coast of Coron provide just the opportunity.

Aninuan is home to some of the plushest resorts in the area.

ARRIVAL AND DEPARTURE

By bus and ferry The most convenient way to reach Puerto Galera from Manila is a combined bus-and-ferry service (2hr to Batangas pier, then 1hr by boat; P800 one-way). Si-Kat (☎ 02 708 9628, ⮚ sikatferrybus.com) leaves at 8.30am sharp from the *CityState Tower Hotel* at 1315A Mabini St, Ermita, arriving in Sabang at 12.15pm and Muelle Pier at 1pm. Coming back, the service leaves Puerto Galera at 8.45am, stopping in Sabang at 9am and arriving in Manila at 1.15pm.

By ferry There are numerous ferry departures for Puerto Galera town (Muelle Pier; 1hr), Sabang and White Beach until 5pm. To return, departures begin at 7.30am – the last boat from Puerto Galera leaves at 3.30pm and from Sabang at 1pm. There are also departures from White Beach starting at 7.45am (Sun & Mon at 6.30am), with the last one at 3.30pm (additional trips are scheduled during holidays). Fares are around P230 to Sabang and Muelle Pier and P270 to White Beach. You'll also have to pay a P30 terminal fee and a P50 environmental fee.

INFORMATION

Information and tours There's a tourist information point at Muelle Pier in Puerto Galera (daily 7.30am–5pm; ☎ 043 287 3051). For tours to nearby sights such as the Tamaraw and Talipanan Falls, the Mangyan tribal village and various beaches, your best bet is to hire a private jeepney for the day (around P2000).

GETTING AROUND

Travelling between the tourist areas is relatively easy. From Sabang and White Beach, jeepneys leave regularly for Puerto Galera town (6am–6pm; 15min; P20). A tricycle should cost P30 per person, but you'll be doing well to get this ride for less than P100. A pump boat from Big/Small La Laguna to Sabang costs P200 during the day, P400 at night. Aninuan and Talipanan are harder to access by

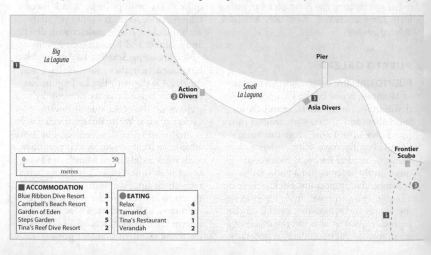

■ ACCOMMODATION	
Blue Ribbon Dive Resort	3
Campbell's Beach Resort	1
Garden of Eden	4
Steps Garden	5
Tina's Reef Dive Resort	2

● EATING	
Relax	4
Tamarind	3
Tina's Restaurant	1
Verandah	2

public transport, but can be reached by tricycle from White Beach. Talipanan is reached via a very rough and steep road – during heavy rains it becomes almost impassable. If you choose to stay here, your best option is to walk along the beach to Aninuan.

DIVE OPERATORS

There are dozens of dive operators, so shop around and get the best deal. You'll find an incredible range of dives to suit all abilities. A single dive is in the region of $30, an Open Water course is about $440.

Action Divers Next to *Out of the Blue Resort* on Small La Laguna (☎043 287 3320, ⓦ actiondivers.com).

Asia Divers Next door to *El Galleon*, Small La Laguna (☎0917 814 5107, ⓦ asiadivers.com).

Badladz Scuba Divers in the hotel of the same name at Muelle Pier (☎043 267 3184, ⓦ badladz.com /badladz-scuba-diving/).

Frontier Scuba Near *Angelyn Beach Resort* in Sabang (☎043 287 3077, ⓦ frontierscuba.com).

ACCOMMODATION

SABANG

★ **Garden of Eden** East of Sabang Pier ☎043 287 3096, ⓦ cocktaildivers.com. One of Sabang's most attractive and relaxed resorts, thatched fan and a/c (P3500) bungalows are set in a tropical garden with a lagoon-shaped pool. There's also a good beachfront restaurant. Doubles P2500

★ **Steps Garden** Just west of Sabang Pier ☎043 287 3046, ⓦ stepsgarden.com. Discreetly tucked into the western end of the cove, Swedish-owned *Steps* has a wide variety of comfortable huts spread through hillside gardens, many of which have great balcony views. There's also an attractive pool, a good restaurant with wi-fi, and friendly staff. Doubles P1600

Tina's Reef Dive Resort Far eastern end of the beach ☎043 287 3046, ⓦ tinasreef.com. Offering some of the cheapest accommodation and food in Sabang, this is a good budget choice. Clean, simple fan rooms with cable TV are scattered up the hillside. Deluxe rooms (P2500) are larger and have the added benefit of a/c. Doubles P1500

PUERTO GALERA

Badladz Right beside Muelle Pier ☎043 287 3693, ⓦ badladz.com. A long-time favourite, this place is more geared up to divers than beach lovers, and has a good dive shop. Rooms are simple and cosy and offer a/c and cable TV, as well as sweeping bay views. Doubles P1490

SMALL LA LAGUNA

Blue Ribbon Dive Resort ☎0917 893 2719, ⓦ blueribbondivers.com. Set in a lush garden a few metres back from the beach, the resort offers a range of thatched poolside rooms and a/c bungalows (P2400). There's also an excellent dive shop. Doubles P2200

BIG LA LAGUNA

Campbell's Beach Resort At the far end of the beach ☎043 287 3466, ⓦ campbellsbeachresort.com. The cosy, well-furnished rooms have a/c, hot water and cable. Backpacker rooms with bunks are also available at their sister resort, *Scandi Divers*, located next door (P700); prices usually quoted in US$. Doubles P2200

WHITE BEACH

Summer Connection At the western edge of the beach ☎043 287 3688 or ☎0915 900 0080, ⓦ www .summerconnection.net. The accommodation here is on the seafront and there are breezy chill-out nipa huts in which to enjoy a cold beer as you watch your fresh catch

8

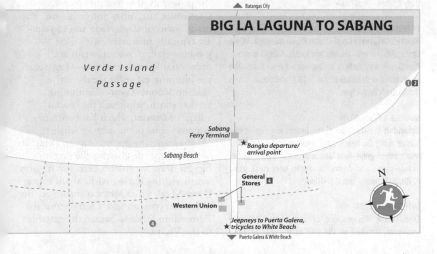

BIG LA LAGUNA TO SABANG

grill on the barbecue. Standard rooms (P2200) are nicely decorated with colourful mosquito nets and lights. There are also a few simple nipa huts at the back. Huts P800

TALIPANAN

★**Luca's** At the far end of the beach ☎0917 792 5263, ⓦlucaphilippines.com. One of the most chilled resorts in the area, its spotless rooms feature bamboo furniture, a/c, fridges and TVs. It also serves authentic Italian cuisine at its beachfront restaurant. Doubles P1500

★**Mountain Beach Resort** In the middle of the beach ☎0906 362 5406, ⓦmountainbeachresort.com. Sitting on one of the loveliest stretches of beach in Puerto Galera, this charming resort offers a good range of rooms, from deluxe with cable (P2500) to a/c beachfront bungalows with kitchens (P3000) and basic nipa huts with fans. There's also a restaurant, beach bar and relaxing hammocks. Huts P1300

EATING

SABANG

Relax Friendly family-run place, hidden down a back alley behind *Big Apple Dive Resort*, serving a range of Filipino, Western and seafood dishes. The chicken *adobo* (P200) and *tanigue* (mackerel) steak (P250) are pretty popular. Daily 6am–3.30am.

Tamarind On the seafront at the western end of the beach. Offering tropical charm, ocean views and tasty Filipino and international dishes, *Tamarind* is one of Sabang's most popular, if pricey, restaurants. They serve everything from seafood to burgers (P350) and steaks (P890). Daily 8am–11pm.

★**Tina's Restaurant** Pleasant little restaurant with chequered tablecloths, bamboo chairs and nice sea views. It serves a range of Filipino, German and Asian dishes at reasonable prices (P150–300). Also good for breakfast. Daily 7.30am–10.30pm.

PUERTO GALERA

Robby's Cafeteria Calpan North Rd, on the way to White Beach. Popular with tourists and locals, *Robby's* is one of Puerto Galera's excellent Italian-owned restaurants. The menu features delicious pizzas (P180) and classic steaks (P600). Daily 8am–9pm.

SMALL LA LAGUNA

Verandah Western end of the beach. High up on the hillside above the beach, the restaurant at *Out of the Blue* resort offers great food and wonderful views. Dishes include pizzas and Australian wagyu beef steak (from P220). Daily noon–3pm & 6–10pm.

WHITE BEACH

Ciao Italia Western end of the beach. This cute restaurant, perched on the side of the cliff, provides wonderful views, as well as tasty Italian dishes. Think home-made pastas and thin-crust pizzas with authentic ingredients such as olives and artichokes (P280–380). Daily 8am–11pm.

TALIPANAN

★**Luca's Cucina Italiana** Far western end of the beach at the resort of the same name. Italian seems to be the order of the day in Puerto Galera, and few places are as good and as relaxed as *Luca's*, a tranquil spot with beachside views and authentic Italian food (mains P200–480). Daily 6am–10pm.

DIRECTORY

Banks and exchange In Sabang there's a Maxbank with an ATM, while in Puerto Galera Town there's an ATM at PNB Bank and a Western Union, both near Muelle Pier.

Southeast Luzon

The region south of Batangas and Quezon (Region V) is commonly known as **South Luzon** or **Bicol**, home of the Philippines' fieriest cuisine, whose staple is the coconut-based *Bicol Express*. It's not very backpacker friendly – there are few budget options and minivans often do not have space for luggage – but if you can find a way to stretch your cash, you'll find soaring volcanoes, idyllic beaches and unique wildlife. From Batangas City, the National Highway meanders through the provinces of Camarines Norte, Camarines Sur, Albay and Sorsogon. The main towns of **Daet**, **Naga** and **Legaspi** are typically provincial, with their jumbled traffic, concrete malls and occasional Spanish-era relics – Legaspi is the jumping-off point for the active volcano **Mount Mayon**. Continuing further south, you reach the coastal village of **Donsol**, which has become famous for its population of whale sharks (*butanding*). The opportunity to swim with these gentle giants is the single biggest draw for visitors here, but it's only worth visiting during whale shark season (Dec–May). From **Matnog** at the very tip of Luzon, you can take a ferry across the Bernardino Strait to Samar, the gateway to the Visayas.

LEGASPI

The port city of **LEGASPI** (often spelt Legazpi), two hours south of Naga and ten hours from Manila, is the place to base yourself if you fancy climbing **Mount Mayon** (2463m). Legaspi would be a fairly charmless provincial town if it weren't for the incredible view of the perfectly conical volcano, looming over the city. It has just one main thoroughfare, Peñaranda Street, which connects the port area (Legaspi city proper) with the district of Albay, where most of the hotels and restaurants are. One place worth seeing is the nearby **Cagsawa Ruins** (daily 8am–6pm; P10), the chilling remains of a church that was buried in the devastating eruption of Mayon in 1814 (although many claim it was not buried, but destroyed by earthquakes and typhoons). The best time to visit is early in the morning before the clouds roll in and obscure the view of the volcano. Take a jeepney bound for Camalig and ask the driver to let you off near the ruins.

ARRIVAL AND DEPARTURE

By plane The airport is about 3km west of the town centre; a tricycle will take you into town for P30.

Destinations Cebu Pacific flies to Cebu (4 weekly, Tues, Thurs, Sat & Sun; 1hr 5min); PAL and Cebu Pacific fly to Manila (daily; 55min).

By bus The bus terminal on Tahao Road, which minivans also use, is 1.5km west of the town centre. Be aware that many of the minivans don't have space for luggage, so will often charge you for an extra person if it takes up a seat.

Destinations Donsol (every 30min; 1hr); Naga (every 30min; 2hr); Sorsogon (every 30min; 1hr 30min). Manila-bound buses depart throughout the day (daily; 10hr). Philtranco goes all the way from Manila to Davao, using ferries where it has to. It stops at Daet, Naga and Legaspi, before heading on to the southernmost tip of South Luzon, for the Samar ferry.

INFORMATION

Tourist information The Legaspi City Tourism Office is in the City Hall (Mon–Fri 8am–5pm; ☎052 481 2698, ✉legazpitourismservices@gmail.com). Enquire here about arranging a guide for Mount Mayon. Call the Regional Tourism Office in the Rawis district (Mon–Fri 8am–5pm; ☎052 418 0250) to check conditions before you set off to see the whale sharks.

Tour operators Donsol EcoTour (✆donsolecotour.com) is one of the best companies to organize a trekking trip up

Mayon. For ATV (all-terrain vehicle) rides up to the lava trail, try Bicol Adventure ATV (☎922 868 2589, ✆bicoladventureatv.com).

ACCOMMODATION

Legazpi Tourist Inn 3rd floor, V&O Building, Quezon Ave, cnr Lapu-Lapu St ☎052 480 6147, ✉legazpitouristinn@yahoo.com.ph. On the second floor of an office block (with no lift), this place occupies a good central location. Standard rooms with a/c are among the cheapest you'll find in Legaspi. Deluxe rooms are in better condition and have cable TVs (P1600). Doubles **P700**

Mayon Backpackers Barangay Maoyod ☎052 742 2613, ✆mayonbackpackers.wordpress.com. Legaspi's only hostel offers a decent collection of brightly painted fan and a/c dorms and doubles (a/c dorms P100 extra). There's a small selection of board games, and the rooftop terrace café has Mount Mayon views. The hostel can also arrange local tours. Dorms **P250**, doubles **P1000**

★**Vista al Mayon** Washington Drive ☎052 481 0308, ✉vistaalmayon@yahoo.com. One of the better budget options, this large pension has spotless rooms with a/c, fridges and cable TV. There's also a central garden with a swimming pool. For the best Mayon views, book one of the larger rooms upstairs in the annexe (P2000). Free wi-fi. Doubles **P1450**

EATING AND DRINKING

Legaspi has a good range of eating options, but not so much in the way of nightlife.

★**Seadog Diner** Legazpi Blvd, Barangay Puro. Cosy little restaurant right on the waterfront, offering brick-oven pizzas and Bicolano classics. Try the set lunchtime menu (P200) of *Bicol Express* with *pinangat* (steamed taro leaves with coconut) and a drink. Daily 7am–midnight.

Small Talk Café 51 D. Aurora St, Albay District. Cute café with old curios and 1950s Bicol photos, serving an exotic range of Italian fusion dishes, such as their famous Bicol-inspired pastas (P105) and the spicy Mayon pizza (P265). Daily 11am–10pm.

Waway's Restaurant Peñaranda St, Bonot. Join the local working crowd for an all-you-can-eat buffet lunch (P250) of native Bicolano specialities. The evening menu is not so good. P150–200. Daily 7am–8pm.

DIRECTORY

Banks and exchange There are a number of banks with ATMs on Quezon Ave and upper Rizal St.

Post office At the northern end of Lapu-Lapu St, cnr Quezon Ave.

Shopping LCC Mall is on Lapu-Lapu St, cnr Quezon Ave. Gaisano Mall and Embarcadero are in the harbour area.

8

8

WHALE SHARK ENCOUNTERS IN DONSOL

After watching a short video, visitors are briefed by a **Butanding Interaction Officer** (BIO), who explains how to behave in the water. The number of snorkellers around any one whale shark is limited to six; flash photography is not permitted, nor is scuba gear, and don't get anywhere near the animal's tail because it's powerful enough to do you some serious damage. Once a whale shark has been sighted, you'll need to get your mask, snorkel and flippers on and get in the water before it dives too deep to be seen – they can move pretty quickly despite their bulk. Boats cost P6000 for up to six people, and there's also a registration fee of P300 per person. Each boat has a crew of three – the captain, the BIO and the spotter – each of whom will expect a token of your appreciation (at least P100 to each person). Renting snorkelling equipment costs P300.

All this makes it an expensive day out by Philippine standards, but take heart from the fact that your money is helping the conservation effort. In Donsol there are very strict rules on whale shark interaction and feeding is prohibited. This isn't the case everywhere – in Oslob in Cebu fishermen feed them, forcing them to change their migration patterns.

MOUNT MAYON

The perfectly triangular cone of **Mount Mayon** (2421m) in Albay province makes it look, from a distance, like a child's drawing of a mountain, but don't be deceived, Mayon has claimed many lives over the years. It is the most active volcano in the country and has erupted more than 47 times in the last four centuries – 1984 and 1993 saw significant eruptions, and in 2006 hundreds were killed by mudslides of volcanic ash loosened by typhoon Durian. Most recently, in May 2013, an eruption caused the death of four German tourists and their guide. Despite the dangers and warnings, when Mayon does erupt, the hotels are often booked up by local tourists wanting to catch a glimpse. Legend has it that Mayon was formed when a beautiful princess eloped with a brave warrior and was pursued by her uncle, Magayon. They prayed to the gods who answered with a terrible landslide that buried Magayon alive. He's said to still be inside the mountain, his irrepressible anger bursting forth in the form of volcanic eruptions.

The only window of opportunity for an ascent is **March to May**, but that's only when the alert level is low. Be prepared for cold nights at altitude and showers, and even if there's no imminent volcanic threat, climbers won't be allowed past 2000m. A guide is essential, arranged at the tourist offices in Legaspi, or through Donsol EcoTour (see p.633). See ⊕www.phivolcs.dost.gov.ph for the latest updates on the status of the volcano.

SORSOGON TOWN AND GUBAT

Near the southeastern tip of Bicol, the provincial capital of **SORSOGON TOWN** makes a good base for visiting Donsol and exploring the beaches of the eastern seaboard, where waves hammer in from the Pacific and surfing is a burgeoning industry. One such gem is **Rizal Beach**, a short trike ride from the barrio of **GUBAT**, half an hour by jeepney (P10) from Sorsogon. There's little development here, but it is wildly beautiful, and there are a couple of basic places to stay. In Sorsogon there are a number of ATMs along Rizal Street.

ARRIVAL AND DEPARTURE

By bus and jeepney Buses, jeepneys and minivans leave from the new Grand Terminal 1km from town along the Maharlika Highway in Balogo. Tricycles can take you into town from here for P10.

Destinations Donsol (every 30min; 1hr); Gubat (every 30min; 30min); Legaspi (every 30min; 1hr 30min); Manila (hourly; 12hr).

ACCOMMODATION

Fernando's Hotel N. Pareja St ☎056 211 1357. At the time of writing, the hotel was undergoing major renovations, including building a swimming pool. As well as their cosy coconut-and-bamboo-clad rooms, they have built deluxe rooms with private balconies (P2000) and simple budget rooms (P1000). The owners are a mine of information and can arrange tours, including hikes and excursions to see the whale sharks. Free wi-fi. Doubles P1600

DONSOL

The area around the peaceful fishing community of **DONSOL**, two hours from either Legaspi or Sorsogon, is best known for one of the greatest concentrations of **whale sharks** (*butanding*) in the world. Your first stop should be the **Donsol Visitors Center** (daily 7am–5pm; ☎0927 483 6735) to register for your whale-shark-watching trip. It's best to arrive early in the morning to secure a place (limited to 500 people per day). The number of sightings varies: the season lasts from December to May, with most facilities closing down out of these months, and during peak season (Feb–May) there's a good chance of seeing ten or fifteen whale sharks a day, but you might be unlucky and see none. In April the town holds its annual *Butanding* festival.

ACCOMMODATION

Most of the accommodation options are in Dancalan Beach, just outside of Donsol town. This is also where you'll find the Donsol Visitors Center. There are no ATMs in Donsol, so bring enough cash to last you – the nearest is in Sorsogon City.

Agualuz San Jose St ☎0918 942 0897. Run by the lovely Pepé and his wife, this welcoming homestay has beautiful *narra* wood floors and a variety of spacious, clean rooms, which once belonged to their six children. Guests can also use the lounge and kitchen, as well as request home-cooked meals. Free wi-fi. Doubles P1700

The Visayas

No one seems entirely sure how many islands there are in **the Visayas**, but it certainly runs into the thousands. Everywhere you turn there's a patch of tropical sand or coral reef, with a vessel to take you there. There are nine main islands or island groups – Panay, Romblon, Guimaras, Negros, Siquijor, Cebu, Bohol, Samar and Leyte – but it's the hundreds of others in between that make this part of the archipelago so irresistible. Indeed, one of the smallest, **Boracay**, is by far the busiest in tourist terms.

No one can accuse the Visayans of being a uniform lot, and a huge variety of dialects is spoken, including Cebuano, Ilonggo, Waray Waray and Aklan. While English is less readily understood in some places, visitors won't find a warmer welcome anywhere.

Getting around is fairly easy. The major islands are accessible by plane from Manila, and, increasingly, from Cebu City, but the **ferry network** is also extensive. The beauty of the Visayas is that there's no need to make formal plans. There's always another beach, another place to stay, another island lost in its own little world.

BORACAY

It may be only 7km long and 1km wide at its narrowest point, but **BORACAY**, 350km south of Manila off the northeastern tip of Panay, is a big tropical island in a small package. **White Beach** grows more commercial and upmarket every year, and caters more and more to Asian package tourists to the point where it's now almost unrecognizable from its backpacker origins, but the beauty of Boracay is that there really is room for everybody. Budget travellers might have to hunt a bit harder for accommodation but there are plenty of compensations, chief among them some of the country's most chilled-out nightlife and its most genuinely breathtaking stretch of beach. The scene around White Beach is what it is, and while some complain about the vendors and the fact that there's hardly a patch of sand not appropriated by the resorts, it's also great fun – and the only place of its kind in the Philippines. Besides, with thirty other beaches and coves to discover around the island and offshore, it's never too difficult to escape the crowds.

Boracay is also a thrill-seekers' paradise, with horseriding, kiteboarding, beach volleyball, mountain biking, motorcycling, kayaking and diving all on offer. There are 24 official **dive sites** in and around the island, and because of the calm waters near the shore outside the rainy season it's a good place to learn. That said, probably the most popular activity here is simply sitting on the beach at dusk with a cocktail watching the sun drift towards the horizon, or having a massage by the sea (P350/hr).

8

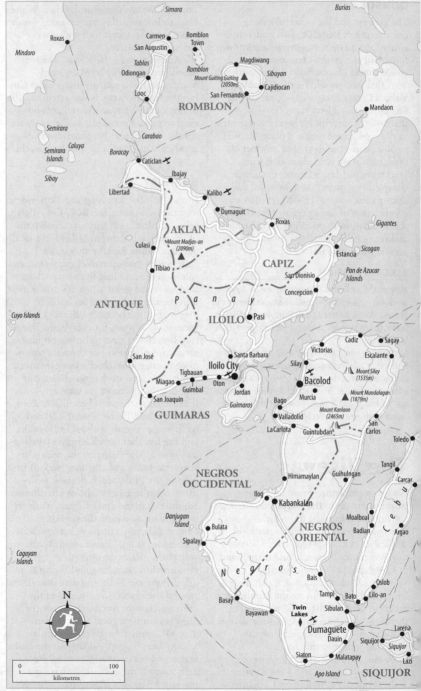

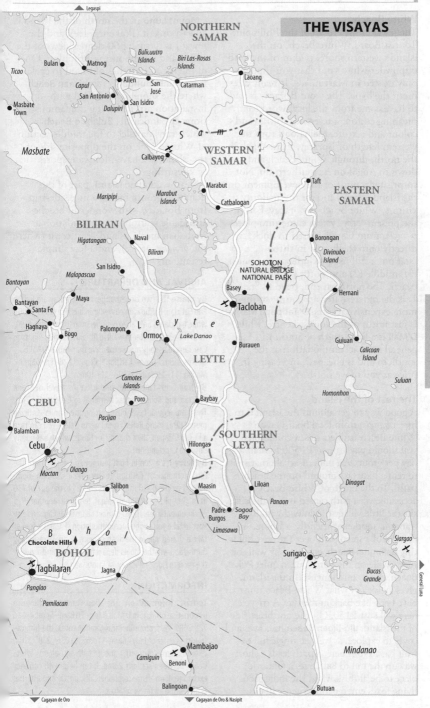

THE VISAYAS

Legaspi

NORTHERN
SAMAR

Ticao

Bulan

Matnog

*Balicuatro
Islands*

*Biri Las-Rosas
Islands*

Allen

San
José

Catarman

Laoang

Capul

San Antonio

San Isidro

Dalupiri

*Masbate
Town*

S   a   m   a   r

Masbate

Calbayog

WESTERN
SAMAR

EASTERN
SAMAR

Maripipi

Marabut

*Marabut
Islands*

Catbalogan

Taft

BILIRAN

Higatangan

Naval

Biliran

Borongan

*Divinubo
Island*

San Isidro

Bantayan

Malapascua

Maya

SOHOTON
NATURAL BRIDGE
NATIONAL PARK

Basey

Hernani

Bantayan

Santa Fe

Hagnaya

Bogo

Palompon

L   e   y   t   e

Ormoc

Lake Danao

Tacloban

Burauen

Guiuan

*Calicoan
Island*

LEYTE

Suluan

CEBU

Danao

*Camotes
Islands*

Poro

Pacijan

Baybay

Homonhon

Balamban

Cebu

Mactan

Olango

Hilongas

SOUTHERN
LEYTE

Talibon

Ubay

Maasin

Liloan

Dinagat

B   o   h   o   l

Chocolate Hills

Carmen

BOHOL

Padre
Burgos

*Sogod
Bay*

Panaon

Tagbilaran

Jagna

Limasawa

Siargao

Surigao

Panglao

Pamilacan

*Bucas
Grande*

General Luna

Mambajao

Camiguin

Benoni

Mindanao

Balingoan

Butuan

Cagayan de Oro

Cagayan de Oro & Nasipit

8

8

White Beach

The jewel in the crown of the Philippine Tourist Board, White Beach, on the island's western shore, is 4km of the kind of powder-white sand that you thought only existed in Martini ads. It really does merit the hype. The word Boracay is said to have come from the local word *borac*, meaning cotton, a reference to the sand's colour and texture. **Main Road** runs the western length of Boracay, from Yapak in the north, through White Beach and down to Angol on its southern tip. Not surprisingly, most of the development on the island is here, and for the majority of visitors, White Beach is Boracay. Before the present ferry system came into place, *bangkas* from Caticlan used to dock directly onto the beach, in three "stations", still used to indicate the south (3), middle (2) and north (1) of the beach. The northern end, beyond Station 1, is the quietest area and home to the more expensive resorts. **D'Talipapa Market** is just north of the tourist centre, while **D'Mall** is a little south of Station 1. As a general rule, accommodation at the southern end is cheapest, increasing in price as you move north.

The rest of the island

A good way to get around the island is to hire a *bangka* from local boatmen on White Beach (subject to sea conditions); you should pay around P1500 for half a day per group. An underused alternative is to rent a bike (ask around on the beach path). To the north of White Beach, accessible via a path carved out of the cliffs, sits the little village of **Diniwid** with its tranquil, snorkeller-friendly seashore. At the end of a steep path over the next hill is tiny **Balinghai Beach**, enclosed by walls of rock, while on the north coast, quiet **Puka Beach**, the second longest on the island, gives an idea of what White Beach must have been like back in the day. A tricycle here will cost P150. On the northeast side of the island, **Ilig-Iligan Beach** has caves and coves to explore, as well as jungle full of fruit bats. From here, a path leads a short way up the hill to **Bat Cave**, a fantastic place to be at dusk when the indigenous flying foxes emerge in immense flocks.

Mount Luho in the north of the island is an easy ascent (P60 entry fee), and the reward is terrific: 360-degree views of the island and neighbouring Romblon. One of the nicest stretches of island to cycle is from **Punta Bunga** to **Tambisaan Beach**, where the shoreline is dotted with installation art, including the famous Boracay Sandcastle. **Bulabog Beach**, which runs parallel to the middle section of White Beach on the opposite side of the island, is a haven for watersports such as kitesurfing.

Nearby **Carabao Island**, part of the **Romblon** group, makes a nice side-trip from Boracay, with wonderful beaches, affordable seafront accommodation at Inobahan on the island's east coast (where the *bangkas* arrive), and a few simple restaurants.

ARRIVAL AND DEPARTURE

By plane The two closest airports to Boracay are Kalibo and Caticlan. Kalibo is an easy 90min bus ride (P111–200), while Caticlan is only an expensive 3min tricycle ride (P50) from the pier – better to walk in little over 5min; flights to Caticlan are usually more expensive than those to Kalibo. Destinations (from Caticlan) Cebu (2 daily; 55min); Manila (11–15 daily; 55min–1hr 10min).

By bus Ceres Liner buses and a/c vans travel between Caticlan and Iloilo's Tagbac terminal to Caticlan (5–7hr). There are regular Ceres buses plying the Manila–Caticlan route (12hr) using RoRo. From Puerto Galera you can take a bus to Calapan, then change for Roxas, which has hourly buses to Caticlan (3hr).

By ferry It's a 20min boat journey to Boracay from the ferry terminal at Caticlan (every 10min 5.30am–6pm, limited service 6–10pm). Tickets are P25 in the day, or P30 at night, plus a P100 terminal fee, and another P75 environmental fee. Tricycles meet all boats at Cagban Jetty Port to take you to your accommodation (P150 flat fee) or take a shared van to the nearest point (P20). Occasionally during bad weather boats depart from Tabon and arrive at the eastern side of Boracay, at Tambisaan.

INFORMATION

Tourist information The Department of Tourism information office is in D'Mall (Mon–Fri 8am–5pm; ☎036 288 3689, ✉deptour6boracay@yahoo.com). The Boracay Tourist Center (daily 8am–11pm; ☎036 288 3704, ✇touristcenter.com.ph), about halfway along White Beach between stations 2 and 3, can help with currency exchange, long-distance phone calls, postal and internet facilities and all travel services.

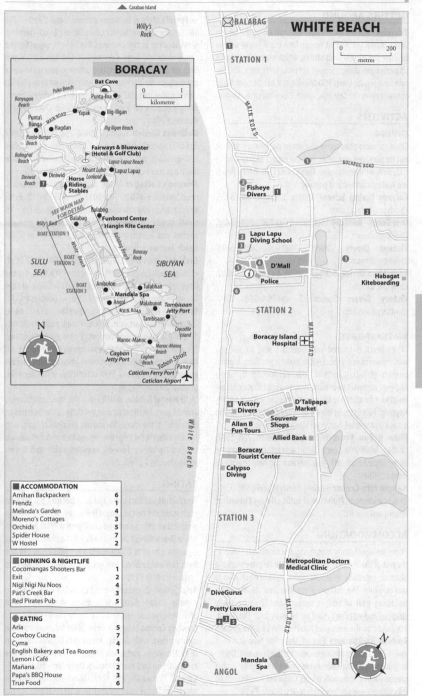

Carabao Island

Willy's Rock

BALABAG

WHITE BEACH

STATION 1

BORACAY

Puka Beach

Bat Cave

Banyugan Beach

Punta-Ina

Ilig-Iligan

Yapak

Punta Bunga

Hagdan

Ilig Iligan Beach

Punta-Bunga Beach

Balinghai Beach

Fairways & Bluewater (Hotel & Golf Club)

Mount Luho Lookout

Lapuz-Lapuz Beach

Diniwid Beach

Diniwid

Horse Riding Stables

Lapuz Lapuz

SEE MAIN MAP FOR DETAIL

Bulabog

Willy's Rock

Balabag

Funboard Center

Hangin Kite Center

BOAT STATION 1

SULU SEA

BOAT STATION 2

White Beach

Bulabog Beach

Boracay Rock

SIBUYAN SEA

BOAT STATION 3

Ambulon

Tulubhan

Mandala Spa

Angol

Malabunot

Tambisaan Jetty Port

MAIN ROAD

Tambisaan

Crocodile Island

Manoc-Manoc

Manoc-Manoc Beach

Cagban Jetty Port

Cagban Beach

Tabon Strait

Panay

Caticlan Ferry Port

Caticlan Airport

N

BULABOG ROAD

Fisheye Divers

Lapu Lapu Diving School

D'Mall

Police

Habagat Kiteboarding

STATION 2

Boracay Island Hospital

White Beach

Victory Divers

D'Talipapa Market

Allan B Fun Tours

Souvenir Shops

Allied Bank

Boracay Tourist Center

Calypso Diving

STATION 3

Metropolitan Doctors Medical Clinic

DiveGurus

Pretty Lavandera

Mandala Spa

ANGOL

N

■ ACCOMMODATION
Amihan Backpackers	6
Frendz	1
Melinda's Garden	4
Moreno's Cottages	3
Orchids	5
Spider House	7
W Hostel	2

■ DRINKING & NIGHTLIFE
Cocomangas Shooters Bar	1
Exit	2
Nigi Nigi Nu Noos	4
Pat's Creek Bar	3
Red Pirates Pub	5

● EATING
Aria	5
Cowboy Cucina	7
Cyma	4
English Bakery and Tea Rooms	1
Lemon í Café	4
Mañana	2
Papa's BBQ House	3
True Food	6

0 200 metres

0 1 kilometre

8

GETTING AROUND

Tricycles Fares for the tricycles that run along the length of the Main Road are P10/person for a trip if you're willing to share the tricycle with others, which means it will pick up passengers along the way. For most foreigners, the flat rate for a private trip is P50/tricycle, not per person. Make sure you agree the fare in advance. Fares increase at night.

ACTIVITIES

DIVING

There are more than thirty dive shops on Boracay, so look out for packages and deals. You can expect to pay around $35/dive, with equipment. These places on White Beach are well established and popular:

Calypso Diving School Station 3 ☎036 288 3206, ⊛calypso-boracay.com.

DiveGurus Boracay Station 3 ☎036 288 5486, ⊛divegurus.com.

Fisheye Divers Station 2 ☎036 288 6090, ⊛fisheyedivers.com.

Lapu Lapu Diving School Station 2 ☎036 288 3302, ⊛lapulapu.com.

Victory Divers Station 2 ☎036 288 3209, ⊛victorydivers.com.

WATERSPORTS

White Beach is littered with agents trying to sell you watersports of every conceivable variety: jetskiing, banana boating, glass-bottom boat rides, parasailing, flyfishing and even mermaid swimming (yes, you read that right) are on offer. One of the most popular trips is a day's island-hopping; P800/person buys a one-day boat trip including a mask and snorkel, barbecue lunch and drinks.

Allan B Fun Tours White Beach ☎036 288 5577, ⊜allan_b68@yahoo.com. With several booths dotted along White Beach path, this operator can help to arrange most activities.

Hangin Kite Center Balabog Beach ☎0998 995 3289, ⊛hanginkite.com. Professional outfit offering kitesurfing lessons and rentals.

ACCOMMODATION

Prices are significantly higher and fluctuate more than in the rest of the Visayas; it's always worth negotiating for a discount, especially outside of high season or if you plan to stay a while. The following are the best of the ever-dwindling pool of budget options, but if you're really strapped and you don't mind being away from the beach, ask around on the main road about renting a private room.

Amihan Backpackers East of Main Rd, near Station 3 ☎036 286 3203, ⊛amihanbackpackersboracay.com. Dorm-only hostel offering unbeatable prices on slightly higher ground about a 5min walk inland. Clean but simple with no frills such as towels or cooking facilities. Dorms P350

★**Frendz** Midway between stations 1 and 2 ☎036 288 3803, ⊛frendzresortboracay.com. Off the beach path in a great location in the centre of the island's nightlife. The comfy male and female dorms (a/c and non-a/c), beach beds for guests' use and buzzing common area make this a great choice for backpackers. There's an authentic 1960s Italian coffee machine for a post-partying caffeine boost. Bring a padlock for your locker. Free wi-fi. Dorms P450, doubles P2000

Melinda's Garden Station 3 ☎036 288 3021 or ☎0907 261 6703, ⊛melindasgarden.com. Lovely nipa-and-bamboo cottages in a garden area off the beach path, all with a private porch and your own wicker hammock. Doubles P1600

Moreno's Cottages At the southern end of the beach, near Station 3 ☎036 288 2031 or ☎0939 118 9616, ⊜boracayjojo29@yahoo.com. A friendly, local option with small, simple fan and a/c rooms set around a pleasant garden, just a 2min walk from a lovely section of White Beach. Free wi-fi. Doubles P1500

Orchids Station 3 ☎036 288 3313 or ☎0917 242 0833, ⊛orchidsboracay.com. Staff are not the friendliest, but the large rooms in the two-storey indigenous building all have hot water and there's paid wi-fi (P50/day). Doubles P915

Spider House Diniwid ☎0918 557 4874, ⊛spiderhouseresort.com. A 10min walk north of Station 1, this is a unique (and romantic) choice on the island. Some of the meandering series of rooms built into the cliff have only two walls, leaving them open to fresh breezes and stunning seascapes. Perfect for those who value their privacy. Doubles P3000

★**W Hostel** Balabag ☎036 288 9059, ⊜whostelboracay @gmail.com. Excellent new hostel close to the beaches on both sides of the island. Decked out in bright colours, with free breakfast in the large kitchen and free wi-fi throughout, this is a top choice. Friendly, knowledgeable staff. Dorms P750, doubles P2500

EATING

Restaurants and bars come and go in Boracay, but the best ones stand the test of time. Choices are so extensive and diverse that you can eat and drink your way up and down White Beach almost 24 hours a day. For a more traditional experience head to D'Talipapa Market where you can buy fresh fish and seafood and get one of the restaurants to prepare it (from P120).

Aria Station 2. Decent-sized pizzas from P410 at this popular D'Mall place which fronts the beach. Great affiliated *gelateria* next door, too. Daily 11am–midnight.

Cowboy Cocina Station 3. Great place for some good old comfort food, with Sunday roasts (P400), fish and chips (P350), bangers and mash (P300), good pizzas and fine cocktails. Pub quiz every Monday. Daily 7am–10.30pm.

Cyma D'Mall ☎036 288 4283. *Cyma's* Boracay branch is smaller and more intimate than in other locations, but the food is every bit as tasty and authentic. Try the *tzatziki* (P175), *horiatiki* (Greek salad; P370) or splash out on some tender *païdakia* (lamb chops; P770). They also do desserts such as baklava (P220). It's very popular and there's limited seating so reserve a table during peak periods. Daily 10am–11pm.

English Bakery and Tea Rooms Bulabog Rd, Balabag, halfway between White Beach and Bulabog Beach. The only remaining branch of the *English Bakery* in Boracay serves up great breakfasts (P135–195), fish and chips (P230), cakes and shakes. Shaded tables looking out over a small lagoon make a great spot to escape the heat and partake in a cup of Lyons English tea and some banana bread. Daily 6am–6pm.

★ **Lemon i Café** D'Mall. Mellow decor creates a soothing ambience at this café-cum-restaurant which continues to turn out some of Boracay's best food. The pan-fried mahi mahi (P420) is a stand-out, as are many of the lemon desserts (from P80) and cocktails. Free wi-fi. Daily 7am–11pm.

Mañana Northern end of Station 2. Colourful interior with sombreros and bright tablecloths at this Mexican place serving good fajitas (P363), chimichangas (from P352), plus exquisite margaritas and daiquiris (from P148). Daily 10am–10pm.

Papa's BBQ House Opposite side of pond from D'Mall. Brightly lit, reliable local joint serving whole roast chicken for P210, as well as meals such as pork adobo and chicken curry (both P150). Open 24hr.

★ **True Food** South of D'Mall. Sit back on puffy yellow cushions and tuck into some of the island's best Indian food – the mouthwatering curries are big enough for two (from P420) and there are plenty of meat-free options to keep vegetarians happy, such as pakora (P230). Daily noon–10.30pm.

DRINKING AND NIGHTLIFE

Nightlife on Boracay starts with drinks at sunset and carries on well into the following morning. You'll find everything from swanky resort bars and chilled-out beach shacks to downright raucous dives.

Cocomangas Shooter Bar Raucous bar on the main road behind *Guilly's Island*, Station 1. Infamous for drinking games involving potent cocktails, it gets rowdier as the night wears on. P100 cover charge on Saturdays. Daily 7pm–3am.

Exit Station 2. Little expat bar on the beach, attracting quite a crowd for its P50–100 drinks; a lively drinking hole to end the evening. There's a pool table too. Daily 4pm–2am.

Nigi Nigi Nu Noos Southern end of Station 2. Hang around at the bar and socialize pub-style at this enduringly popular hangout serving bar food. Happy hour 5–7pm. Free wi-fi. Daily 6am–1am.

★ **Pat's Creek Bar** Just north of D'Mall. At the north end of Station 2. A laidback bar with nightly live bands; it's mainly reggae, to be enjoyed with a chilled beer (P65) or a cocktail (P150) in hand. They share bands with *Bom Bom* next door. Happy hour 5–8pm. Shisha pipes, too. Daily 5pm–1am.

★ **Red Pirates Pub** At the southern end of the beach, Station 3. Enjoy the beats and the sounds of the sea at this chilled-out place with little beach tables in leafy surroundings. Cheap cocktails (from P100) and happy hour 4–7pm. They have their own boat cruises too. Daily 10am–4am.

DIRECTORY

Banks and exchange There are numerous ATMs dotted along the Main Road and at the malls. Many resorts also change money. Credit cards are widely accepted.

Hospitals and clinics The main facility is the Boracay Island Hospital, Main Rd (☎ 036 288 3041). Metropolitan Doctors Medical Clinic is also on Main Rd (☎ 036 288 6357) and is open 24hr. In the event of serious injury, treatment in Kalibo is recommended.

Internet There are dozens of internet cafés on Boracay, most with fast connections (P15–25/hr) – such as the Boracay Tourist Center. Plenty of hotels and restaurants offer wi-fi.

Laundry Pretty Lavandera, Station 3 (daily 9am–7pm; P50/kg).

Pharmacies There are pharmacies selling most necessities in D'Mall, Boracay Tourist Center and D'Talipapa Market.

Police The Philippine National Police (☎ 036 288 3066) are immediately behind the Tourism Information Office in D'Mall.

Post office The post office is in Balabag, the small community halfway along White Beach (Mon–Fri 8am–5pm). The Boracay Tourist Center on White Beach has full postal services, although they charge a small surcharge.

Shopping Dozens of small *sari-sari* stores line White Beach selling the usual range of drinks and snacks, plus beachwear, T-shirts and souvenirs, while at D'Talipapa Market you can buy fruit and fish. D'Mall has an ever-expanding range of shops selling clothes, souvenirs and handicrafts. Boracay Budget Mart at the back of D'Mall is an inexpensive supermarket (by Boracay standards); Heidiland deli in D'Mall is another good, if expensive, option for self-caterers.

PANAY

The big heart-shaped island of **Panay** has been largely bypassed by tourism, perhaps because everyone seems to get sucked

8

towards Boracay off its northern tip instead. Panay comprises four provinces: Antique on the west coast, Aklan in the north, Capiz in the northeast and Iloilo along the east coast to **Iloilo City** in the south. The province of most interest to tourists is Aklan, whose capital **Kalibo** is the home of the big and brash **Ati-Atihan Festival**, held every year in mid-January.

Iloilo City

ILOILO CITY is a useful transit point for Guimaras and other Visayan islands, as well as Kalibo and Boracay if you're coming from the south, but is otherwise of little interest. Apart from some graceful old houses in its side streets, a handful of interesting churches and the splendid new riverfront Esplanade, the city has little to distinguish it from other port cities throughout the archipelago.

West of the city in Molo district is **Molo Church** (daily 8am–7pm except for Mass), a splendid nineteenth-century Gothic Renaissance structure made of coral and egg whites. If you have an hour to spare, the **Museo Iloilo** (Mon–Sat 9.30am–5pm; P50) next door to the tourist office is well worth a browse; it covers the history of Panay through displays of fossils, Stone Age tools, pottery, shells and teeth. The **Dinagyang Festival** on the fourth weekend in January adds some extra frenzy to the city.

The long, traffic-choked artery of General Luna Street is home to banks with ATMs, travel agents, pharmacies, the police and the hospital.

ARRIVAL AND DEPARTURE

By plane Iloilo International Airport is 19km northwest of the city; a taxi to the centre will cost around P400; a cheaper option is to take one of the frequent shuttles (P80) to SM City mall, and then a taxi from there (P100).
Destinations Cebu Pacific and PAL Express have flights to Cebu (5–6 daily; 45min), Davao (1–2 daily; 1hr 5min), Manila (10–12 daily; 1hr) and Puerto Princesa (3 weekly; 1hr).
By bus and jeepney The bus terminal is at Tagbac, 5km north of the centre. Jeepneys marked "Jaro Liko", "Legares" or "Zarraga" all serve the centre of town (P12).
Destinations The terminal serves northern destinations, including Caticlan (hourly; 6hr) and Kalibo (hourly; 5hr) via Concepcion and Roxas. Non-stop minivans from here are

slightly quicker, but more expensive. Both services are most frequent until 1pm. Note that early-morning Ceres buses (until 6am) leave from Tanza Street. Plenty of companies also serve Manila, using the roll-on, roll-off (RoRo) ferries.
By ferry Three terminals serve Iloilo. Ferries to Guimaras are served by Ortiz wharf; ferries serving Bacolod arrive at the Iloilo-Bacolod ferry terminal on Muelle Loney Street, while other domestic services use the nearby wharf off Fort San Pedro Drive, at the eastern end of the city. From Ortiz, walk to the main street and catch a "Baluuarte" or "SM City" jeepney into town; from Fort San Pedro, walk to the main street and catch a "Jaro CPU" jeepney; there are jeepneys just outside the Iloilo-Bacolod terminal.
Destinations Bacolod (every 30min–1hr; 1hr–1hr 30min), Cebu City (7 weekly; 12–14hr); Manila (weekly; 20hr).

INFORMATION

Tourist information The city's tourist information office is on Bonifacio Drive (Mon–Fri 8am–5pm; ☎ 033 337 5411 or ☎ 033 335 0245, ⊚ westernvisayastourism.com.ph).

ACCOMMODATION

★**Highway 21** General Luna St ☎ 033 335 1220 or ☎ 0917 722 4321, ✉ highway21_hotel@yahoo.com. One of three "21" lodgings in Iloilo, this wonderfully efficient hotel is centrally located and has helpful staff. Rooms are modern and spotless, and all have a/c and cable; those in the annexe are slightly smaller and plainer, though cheaper. Free wi-fi in lobby. Doubles P800
Iloilo City Inn 113 Seminario St, Jaro ☎ 033 329 0078. This friendly place enjoys a quiet location and has clean, comfortable a/c rooms at affordable prices. Downstairs, *Bavaria* serves good German food and beer and has wi-fi. The roof deck has views of the nearby cathedral. Doubles P850

EATING AND NIGHTLIFE

Iloilo is known for a number of delicacies, including *pancit molo* soup, a garlicky concoction of pork dumplings and noodles in rich broth, sold at numerous street stalls. *Batchoy*, an artery-hardening combination of liver, pork and beef with thin noodles, is also available everywhere.
Butot Balat Solis St. A haven of tropical tranquillity and greenery in the midst of the downtown mayhem, this popular restaurant offers candlelit dining under thatched cabanas surrounding a small pond. Try chilli shrimps (P295), pork *Bicol Express* (P185), beef *kare-kare* (P325) or fish by weight.
★**Freska** Smallville Boardwalk, Diversion Rd. *Freska* makes Ilonggo dining easy with its mouth-wateringly good-value daily lunch and dinner buffets (P299). Over forty dishes are on offer, including green mango salad, chicken *inasal*

(marinated roast chicken), barbecue pork and a delicious dessert line-up. Your thirst can be quenched by the huge selection of imported beers, and staff are impressively upbeat. Daily 11.30am–2.30pm & 5.30–10.30pm.

Smallville Complex Diversion Rd, just north of the river. This outdoor complex is pretty much the centre of Iloilo nightlife. Popular bars/clubs to look for include *Aura* and *Ice*. All have live bands and/or DJs nightly, usually with a P100 entry fee, and don't get going till about 11pm. Daily 11am–5am.

DIRECTORY

Banks Plenty with ATMs along General Luna St, including BDO.

Internet Netopia at SM City Mall or at Robinson's Mall (both Mon–Fri 9am–8pm, Sat & Sun 10am–8pm; P15/hr); Taven Cyber Café at Riverside Inn (daily 9am–7pm; P15/hr).

Police Opposite the University of San Agustin on General Luna St.

Post office On Muelle Loney St, close to the junction with Guanco St.

Kalibo

KALIBO lies on the well-trodden path to Boracay and for most of the year is an uninteresting town, but on the third Sunday of January it becomes the centre of probably the biggest street party in the country, **Ati-Atihan** (see box below).

Kalibo is a compact place with most amenities within walking distance of each other. The major thoroughfare is Roxas Avenue, which runs into town from the **airport** in the southeast, with most streets leading off it to the southwest.

ARRIVAL AND DEPARTURE

By plane The 10min tricycle ride into town from the airport costs P10/person, or P30 for private hire. There are direct vans and buses from the airport to Caticlan (the jumping-off point for Boracay; P200).

Destinations Cebu (3–4 daily; 50min); Manila (10–12 daily; 1hr 10min).

By bus Cheaper buses serving Caticlan (P111) leave from the terminal on Osmeña Ave, from where there are also regular buses to Iloilo (5hr).

By ferry Dumaguit port is 50min away. There are several 2GO and Moreta Shipping Lines ferries weekly to Manila (16–20hr); Moreta's office is at 19 Martyr's St. Jeepneys run between the port and the town centre.

INFORMATION

Tourist information Kalibo Tourism Office, Magsaysay Park (Mon–Fri 8am–5pm; ☎ 036 262 1020).

ACCOMMODATION

Ati-Atihan Country Inn D. Maagma St ☎036 268 6116. Government-owned place offering good-value rooms with a/c, cable TV and hot showers set around a communal living area with free wi-fi. Dorms ‾P150‾, doubles ‾P700‾

RB Lodge N. Roldan St ☎036 268 5200, ✉ rblodgekalibo@gmail.com. The new branch of this hotel offers clean and simple but stylish a/c rooms with wi-fi, cable TV and free breakfast (new wing rooms P1150). The old wing on Pastrana has simpler fan rooms, an internet café and coffee shop. Doubles ‾P450‾

EATING AND DRINKING

Goto N. Roldan cnr Veteran streets. Chilled-out rooftop restaurant serving burgers, buffalo wings, onion rings and the like for P100–220, plus a range of beers and cocktails.

8

ATI-ATIHAN FESTIVAL

Every January, culminating on the third Sunday, the town of **Kalibo** on the island of Panay erupts into Southeast Asia's biggest street party, **Ati-Atihan**. This exuberant festival celebrates the original inhabitants of the area, the Atis, and culminates with choreographed dances through the streets by locals daubed in black paint (Ati-Atihan means "to make like the Atis"). Thousands dress up in outrageous outfits, blacken their faces with soot (in honour of the aboriginal Ati, whose descendants still live on Panay), and salsa through the streets amid cries of "*hala bira, puera pasma*" ("keep on going, no tiring"). It is said that the festival originated when ten Malay chieftains chanced upon the island and persuaded the Ati to sell it to them; the deal was naturally sealed with a party, where the Malays darkened their faces to emulate their new neighbours. Centuries later, the Spanish incorporated Catholic elements into Ati-Atihan and the modern festival is now dedicated to the Santo Niño (Holy Infant Jesus). The event comes to a climax with a huge Mass in the cathedral, and the three-day party ends with a masquerade ball and prizes for the best dressed.

Good accommodation can be hard to find during the Ati-Atihan and prices increase by up to a hundred percent. Direct flights to Kalibo from Manila are often fully booked.

Simple and inexpensive Filipino cuisine downstairs. Daily 10.45am–1am.

Latte Café Coffee Archbishop Reyes cnr Santa Monica streets. There are two branches of this pleasant coffee shop in Kalibo, both of which sell sandwiches and light meals (P150–350), alongside Havaiana flip-flops. Great coffee and free wi-fi make this place a favourite with students. Daily 7am–9pm.

Mary's G. Pastrana St. Clean, bustling canteen-style place serving huge bowls of noodles (P130), sandwiches, desserts and coffee. Daily 8am–6pm.

DIRECTORY

Banks Several, including BPI and Allied Banking, on Martelino St close to Kalibo Cathedral. There's also a BNP on Pastrana St.

Internet Several internet cafés along Roxas Ave, including *Ed's Video Place* at the junction with Pastrana.

Post office In the Provincial Capitol Building, on Fernandez St.

NEGROS

The island of **Negros** lies at the heart of the Visayas, between Panay to the west and Cebu to the east. Shaped like a boot, it is split diagonally into Negros Occidental and Negros Oriental. The demarcation came when early missionaries decided the central mountain range was too formidable to cross, even in the name of God. It's an island that many tourists skip, yet it has many kilometres of untouched coastline, some relaxed towns – **Dumaguete**, the capital of Negros Oriental, is one of the stateliest in the Philippines – and dormant **volcanoes**. It also has a couple of superb beaches, such as Sugar Beach near Sipilay, whose relative inaccessibility means they have yet to be incorporated into the tourist trail. Negros is known as "Sugarlandia", and produces fifty percent of the country's **sugar**, an industry that has defined its history in sometimes bloody ways. Around **Bacolod**, the capital of Negros Occidental, well-preserved Spanish ancestral homes serve as reminders of the rich sugar barons of the past.

Bacolod

The city of **BACOLOD**, the provincial capital and an important transport hub for the Western Visayas, is big, hot, noisy and lacking much to see or do, although it offers first-rate dining.

The main street is Lacson, which runs almost the entire length of the city. Jeepneys marked "Bata–Libertad" constantly run north–south along Lacson. Backpackers will want to base themselves uptown, in the numbered streets, which benefit from their proximity to the university quarter. The third week of October sees everybody who is anybody joining in with Bacolod's flamboyant **Masskara festival** (see p.601).

WHAT TO SEE AND DO

Though damaged by a storm in 2012, the Old Capitol Building remains one of the few architectural highlights, and is home to the **Negros Museum** (Mon–Sat 9am–6pm; P100), which details five thousand years of local history. Nearby the **Negros Forest and Ecological Foundation** (Mon–Sat 9am–noon & 1.30–4pm; P25) has a selection of rescued Negros' indigenous wildlife including the Visayan warty pig and highly endangered bleeding-heart pigeon and rufous-headed hornbill. In Talisay on the edge of town, **The Ruins** (daily 10am–8pm; P100; ☎034 476 4334) are the remnants of a monumental memorial mansion built by the Lacsons, one of nineteenth-century Negros' pre-eminent sugar families, which also has an excellent restaurant. The cheapest way to visit is to take a tricycle (P50) from the crossroads by the northern bus terminal.

ARRIVAL AND DEPARTURE

By plane The airport is 15km northeast of the city. A taxi to the town centre costs around P500. There are regular shuttles (P150) to SM and Robinson's malls.

Destinations Cebu City (5–7 daily; 45min); Davao (3 weekly; 1hr 10min); Manila (12–15 daily; 1hr 15min).

By bus and jeepney Ceres Liner, which dominates transport in the area, has two bus terminals, one for northern destinations (☎034 433 4993), at Barangay Bata, and one for southern destinations, on Lopez Jaena St (☎034 434 287). Jeepneys run regularly to city plaza, from where you can catch a jeepney uptown (P7).

Destinations Cebu City (7 daily; 9–10hr including ferry); Dumaguete (every 40min–1hr; 5hr 30min–7hr); Sipalay (hourly; 5hr). For destinations north, including Cadiz (1hr) and Sagay, from where you can take a boat to Bantayan, buses run every 15–30min, 6am–6pm.

By ferry Bredco Port, 500m west of the plaza, is the arrival and departure point for most major ferries. Frequent jeepneys into town from Bangko (P7).

Destinations Iloilo City (every 30min–1hr; 1hr–1hr 30min); Manila (3 weekly; 20hr).

INFORMATION

Tourist information Negros Occidental Tourism Center, Provincial Capitol Building (Mon–Fri 9am–5pm; ☎034 432 2881, �ⓦ tourism.negros-occ.gov.ph), is a good source of information on exploring the region's sights.

ACCOMMODATION

11th Street Bed and Breakfast 11th St ☎034 433 9191 or ☎0922 843 3919. Rooms at this friendly pension are set around a leafy garden and parking area; shaded glass windows make the rooms a little dark, but they all have cable TV and rates include free wi-fi and breakfast. Doubles P550

Pension Bacolod 11th St ☎034 433 3377. Not as welcoming as the *11th Street B&B* along the road, this popular cheapie is still great value, though both the walls and mattresses are thin. The cheapest rooms have shared bathrooms. Doubles P290

EATING, DRINKING AND NIGHTLIFE

Bacolod has a well-developed culinary scene and Lacson Street is lined with top-notch restaurants serving local and international food. The city's main nightlife entertainment zone, Goldenfields, is in the far south of the city, and has a few decent clubs, along with a strip of girlie bars, while Lacson Street has a more sophisticated selection.

★**Ading's Pala-Pala** San Juan St, opposite the fish market. Probably Bacolod's best seafood restaurant, serving crabmeat soup (P175), shrimp tempura (P200) and fresh fish at market rates, as well as meat dishes. Daily 11am–3pm & 5–11pm.

> ### ★TREAT YOURSELF
>
> **L'Fisher Chalet** Lacson cnr 14th streets ☎034 433 3731, ⓦ lfisherhotelbacolod .com. You don't have to spend too much extra to buy a little sophisticated urban living at *L'Fisher's* budget wing, *Chalet*. The cheapest "budget" and "economy" rooms are windowless, but the stylish standard twins and doubles (P1850) have all mod cons and balconies looking out over the city. The real reason to stay, though, is for free use of the hotel's trendy rooftop pool with swim-up bar, plus there's a small but well-equipped gym and a decent restaurant. Doubles P1250

Café Bob's 21st and Lacson streets. Super-popular diner which efficiently turns out coffees (P60–140), sandwiches and burgers (P90–200), plus has a huge range of imported goods for sale in the deli (which closes at 9pm). Daily 8am–midnight.

Calea 15th cnr Lacson streets and also in Robinson's Place mall. Hugely popular with a young clientele, this café, decorated in mellow blue and yellow tones, puts all the Negros sugar to good use, with dozens of cakes on offer as well as sandwiches (P120–175) and delectable coffees (P65–100). Mon–Thurs 8am–10pm, Fri–Sun 9am–11pm.

Manokan Country Just outside SM Mall. The name roughly translates as "where you find chicken", and so it is – the dozens of chicken restaurants here are funded by the city government, keeping the locals happy. A meal here will set you back less than P100. Daily 10am–late.

Organic Market Restaurant Behind the Provincial Capitol Building. Fruit-and-veg market with a great organic restaurant serving all sorts of health foods, from organic rice meals to shakes and coffee. Meals for less than P100. Daily 6am–6pm.

DIRECTORY

Banks Numerous banks on Lacson St and around the central Plaza have ATMs.

Internet There's no shortage of cheap internet cafés around the university and in the malls. Try Le Cafenet in Mayfair Plaza, 12th Lacson St (Mon–Fri 8am–8pm, Sat 9am–7pm; P15/hr).

Post office Gatuslao cnr Burgos streets.

Mount Kanlaon National Park

Mount Kanlaon, two hours from Bacolod by jeepney, is the tallest peak and most active volcano in the central Philippines. Climbers have died scaling it, so don't underestimate its fury, especially considering that it has been rumbling ominously since 2006. The surrounding forest helped keep President Manuel Quezon hidden from invading Japanese forces during World War II and contains all manner of wonderful wildlife, including pythons, monitor lizards, tube-nosed bats and the *dahoy pulay*, a venomous green tree snake. The best way to get here is by jeepney via Murcia, southeast of Bacolod.

There are several routes up the volcano; one of the best is from the village of **Guintubdan** on the western slopes, and most involve three tough days of walking and two nights of camping. Before you set out you must visit the Park

Superintendent's office in Bacolod (Penro compound, Abad Santos St, Barangay 39; ☎034 433 3813) to put your name down for a park permit (P700) and a compulsory guide (P700); porters cost P500 per day. Local guide and biologist Angelo (☎0917 301 1410, ✉angelobibar@gmail.com) can arrange everything for you, and tailor the climb to the level of difficulty you're looking for. For up-to-date information about the safety of climbing Kanlaon, contact the tourist office in Bacolod (see p.645).

Sipalay

About halfway between Bacolod and Dumaguete on the island's west coast, the remote town of **SIPALAY** is surrounded by a scattering of islands and some wild and wonderful beaches. Chief among these is **Sugar Beach**, a long stretch of powdery sand that still feels like one of the Philippines' best-kept secrets. Sipalay's historical focal point is the plaza and the church, but these days most activity centres on the main road, where there are numerous canteens, bakeries and a couple of convenience stores. **Buses** will leave you close to *Driftwood City* café (affiliated with the resort of the same name on Sugar Beach) on Poblacion Beach, which has the best **food** in town and is the de facto pick-up point for boats to Sugar Beach.

Sugar Beach and Punto Ballo

The long and lovely **Sugar Beach** has a backdrop of coconut groves and mountains and faces due west, with wonderful sunsets. Though beginning to be discovered by tourists, it's still at its busiest when the kids get out of school and gather there to play in the relative cool of the late afternoon. Nothing more strenuous than sunbathing and beach volleyball are the order of the day here, though a favourite excursion is to the nearby wildlife sanctuary of **Danjugan Island**, which you'll need to reserve in advance (see ⊛prrcf.org for more information). Better diving is to be had at **Punta Ballo**, another clean, quiet and beautiful beach fifteen minutes from Sipalay by tricycle (P150).

ARRIVAL AND DEPARTURE

The easiest way to reach Sugar Beach is to arrange a boat transfer with your resort; they'll send their boatman over to pick you up from Poblacion Beach in Sipilay town, where the bus from Bacolod or Dumaguete will drop you. Rates are P350–400 per boat (4–6 people). A cheaper, more roundabout way of getting to Sugar Beach involves taking a tricycle to Nauhang (P150), where you take a small paddle boat across the creek (P20), and walk around the headland. Ask to be let off the bus in Montilla rather than Sipalay, which is closer to Nauhang and only a P50 tricycle ride away. Coming from Dumaguete, the quickest bus route follows the coast south around the toe of the island and then north through Hinoba-an, but an equally scenic option is to head north and then across the mountains to Kabanklan before travelling south for Sipalay.

ACCOMMODATION AND EATING

Artistic Diving Beach Resort Punto Ballo ☎0905 220 5594, ⊛artisticdiving.com. The beachfront rooms, both fan-cooled and a/c, the cheapest ones with shared bathrooms, are primarily used by divers. There's also a good Swiss/Filipino restaurant. Doubles P550

★ **Driftwood Village** Sugar Beach ☎0920 900 3663, ⊛driftwood-village.com. This welcoming place with eighteen cottages, including one dorm, dotted amid swaying palms and jungle greenery, has an atmospheric chill-out area and restaurant serving great Thai food, plus a lively bar. Free wi-fi. Dorms P250, doubles P450

Sulu Sunset Beach Resort Sugar Beach ☎0919 716 7182, ⊛sulusunset.com. The simple nipa huts right on the beach are good value, and there's table tennis, table football, darts, billiards and hammocks to while away the afternoons. The restaurant is superb, with plenty of veggie dishes (P180), freshly baked wood-oven bread and pizzas (P200). Doubles P650

Takatuka Lodge Sugar Beach ☎0920 230 9174, ⊛takatuka-lodge.com. The wacky world of *Takatuka* has to be seen to be believed. Rooms all feature verandahs and one-of-a-kind furnishings, from the pink Cadillac bed in the Superstar room, to the stereo-controlled microphone lights in Rockadelic. For a/c or hot showers add P300–500 per night. The restaurant serves some of the best food on the beach, and the *Salamizza* (salami *rösti*) is recommended. Wi-fi costs P50 per day. Doubles P1275

Dumaguete and around

DUMAGUETE, the elegant capital of Negros Oriental, lives up to its reputation as "The City of Gentle People". Lying on the southeast coast of Negros, within sight of the most southerly tip of Cebu Island, it's a nicer-than-average port town and the perfect jumping-off point for **Siquijor** and the marine sanctuary of **Apo Island**, where the diving is superb, plus there are plenty of adventurous pursuits to be found in the mountainous hinterlands, from lakes and waterfalls to hot springs and traditional markets. The main street is Perdices Street, which runs north–south, and where you can find plentiful ATMs, travel agents and pharmacies.

ARRIVAL AND DEPARTURE

By plane The airport is a few kilometres northwest of the city centre. Tricycles make the trip for P120. A taxi-van will set you back P250.

Destinations PAL and Cebu Pacific fly to Cebu (4 weekly; 40min) and Manila (4–6 daily; 1hr 25min).

By bus The Ceres Liner terminal is on Governor Perdices St near Robinson's Place mall. A tricycle costs P20. For departures to the north of the island, it's worth making sure that you get on an express bus, shaving a couple of hours from journey times.

Destinations Hourly buses to Sipalay (4–5hr) via Kabankalan or Hinoba-an, and Bacolod (6hr). For Cebu island, take a van (P11, or tricycle P100) north to Sibulan (or Tampi for Bato on Cebu) from where there are boats (every 30min; 30–40min; P40–70) to Lilo-An. From Lilo-An there are buses up the east coast to Cebu City, while from Bato buses go north to Moalboal (and then on to Cebu City).

By ferry The pier is near the northern end of Rizal Blvd, within easy walking distance of the centre. A tricycle costs P20.

Destinations Cagayan de Oro (1 weekly; 7hr 30min); Cebu City (1–2 daily; 6–7hr); Dapitan (on Mindanao; 6–7 daily; 3–4hr); Manila (1 weekly; 19hr); Siquijor (8–10 daily; 45min–1hr 30min); Tagbilaran (1–2 daily; 2hr).

INFORMATION

Tourist information The tourist office has a kiosk in Quezon Park (Mon–Fri 8am–5pm; ☎035 225 0549, ✉tourismdgte@gmail.com) on Santa Catalina St. However, *Harold's Mansion* (see below) is a better source of information for backpackers.

Internet The internet cafés around the Silliman University complex, at the northern end of Hibbard St, are plentiful and cheap (P15/hr).

ACCOMMODATION

DUMAGUETE

★**Harold's Mansion** 205 Hibbard Ave ☎035 225 8000, ✉haroldsmansion.com. Dumaguete's only true hostel has immaculate male and female dorms, plus simple rooms with common or private (P600) bathroom and a/c (P1000), plus a roof-deck coffee shop perfect for meeting other travellers. *Harold's* also has its own dive shop and there's an invaluable information centre from where you can organize excursions. If you want to enjoy some fresh air without venturing too far from the city, ask about their very simple ecolodge up in Valencia (P500). Dorms P300, doubles P500

Hotel Palwa Locsin St ☎035 422 8995. Excellent option at the top end of the budget scale, with small but nicely styled a/c rooms with flatscreen TV. There's a pleasant café with free wi-fi in the lobby. Doubles P1198

SOUTH OF DUMAGUETE

The beach resorts of Dauin are only a 20min drive south of town, and make a pleasant alternative to staying in the centre.

★**Liquid** Barangay Bulak, Dauin ☎0917 314 1778, ✉liquiddumaguete.com. Run by a friendly British-Canadian couple, this low-key dive resort has eight attractive fan-cooled beach huts, all with sea views, and six a/c cottages (P3300). There are also some cheaper concrete rooms (P1000) at the back, which are discounted if you are diving. There's wi-fi, a pool, a bar with great cocktails and the rooftop café serves tasty meals and has a small bakery. Doubles P1600

8

APO ISLAND

The **Apo Island Marine Reserve and Fish Sanctuary** is said by those in the know to be one of the world's top ten diving sites. There are two "resorts" on the island, plus a few budget lodgings. The plush *Apo Island Beach Resort* (☎035 226 3716 or ☎0939 915 5122, ✉apoislandresort.com; dorms P800, doubles P2700) stands on an isolated sandy cove hemmed in by rocks, while cheaper *Liberty Lodge* (☎0920 2385 704, ✉apoisland.com; doubles P1950 including all meals for two) is on the nearby main beach. To get to Apo, take a bus going to Bayawan and ask to get off at Malatapay, where the boats leave, and which also has a fascinating Wednesday-morning market. Small *bangkas* (good for four people) cost P2000 round-trip, while the next size up is P3000 (up to ten people), or alternatively you can arrange a place on one of the four daily *Liberty Lodge* shuttles (P300/person). General admission to the marine sanctuary is P100, which allows you to snorkel with the turtles just offshore. To get the most out of your trip, talk to the guys at *Harold's Mansion* (see above) before you go.

★ TREAT YOURSELF

Casablanca Rizal Blvd ☎ 035 422 4080. The best steaks in town (and probably all of Negros) are worth splashing out for at P500–665, even if you opt for the local beef, rather than imported. The intimate inside is lined with movie posters and has a decent deli, but it's more atmospheric (and noisy) to sit outdoors and watch the world wandering by, to the backdrop of Siquijor across the water. Daily 7am–11pm.

EATING AND DRINKING

Happy hour (4–6pm) is a nice time to watch the promenaders on Rizal Boulevard, though the bars get sleazier as the night wears on.

4TEA2 145 Hibbard Ave. Unique Russian restaurant with a whimsical flying teapot mural in the roadside courtyard. Huge portions of pasta for P130 and pepper beef steak or cheesy giant meatballs for P195. The Saturday Russian buffet costs P295. Daily 9am–10pm.

The Blue Monkey Grill Silliman Ave cnr Rizal Blvd. Set in a pretty torch-lit garden in a prime location for people-watching, *The Blue Monkey Grill* serves tasty food (mostly P100–200) and is popular with college students. Mon–Sat 4pm–2am, Sun 4–11.30pm.

Lantaw Flores Ave, cnr EJ Ianco Drive. It's worth the good 10min hike north of the port for the top-notch seafood at very reasonable prices on offer here. The shrimp *sinigang* soup comes in more of a vat than a bowl, and the sizzling marlin is a steal at P185. Daily 11am–10pm.

Sans Rival Rizal Blvd. The original little cake shop on San Jose St still turns out delicious cakes and coffee, while its larger sister round the corner on Rizal Blvd serves tasty but fairly priced meals (P150–300), including lasagne, tapas, salads, burgers and sandwiches, and stays open later. Daily 9am–9pm.

SIQUIJOR

Siquijor, a laidback little island where life is simple and backpackers are made very welcome, lies slightly apart from the rest of the Visayas off the southern tip of Cebu and about 22km east of Negros. The Spanish sailors nicknamed Siquijor the Isla del Fuego ("Island of Fire") because of eerie luminescence generated by swarms of fireflies at night. Even today, the island is suffused with a lingering sense of mystery, with many Filipinos refusing to visit, believing

Siquijor to be a centre of witchcraft and black magic, a superstition reinforced by the staging of the **Folk Healing Festival** in the mountain village of San Antonio every Easter on Black Saturday. You can circumnavigate Siquijor by tricycle and jeepney along the coastal road, and most resorts can also arrange motorbike rental (P350–500/day) or guided tours to the lush, jungled interior.

SIQUIJOR TOWN is the capital and main port. Nearby is a tricycle terminal that the locals use, a better bet than using the touts around the pier. The town has a couple of ATMs and lies twenty minutes by tricycle (P30) southwest of Larena, which also offers a few facilities.

The most popular beaches on Siquijor are **Sandugan**, where there's also fantastic diving, half an hour north of Larena, and **Paliton** and **San Juan** beaches on the west coast. Multi-cabs and jeepneys run around the island, but stop services early, so if you plan on using them to circumnavigate Siquijor, start in the morning. It's not much more expensive, and far more liberating, to rent a motorbike, or even a mountain bike (P350/day), to explore the island at leisure.

ARRIVAL AND INFORMATION

By ferry Ferries of varying sizes and speeds run daily between Siquijor Town or Larena and Dumaguete (6am–3pm; 45min–1hr 30min).

Tourist office In the provincial capital building near Siquijor Town (Mon–Fri 8am–5pm), but can't do much more than give you a map of the island (handy for motorbike travel).

ACCOMMODATION

★ Coral Cay Resort San Juan Beach ☎ 0919 269 1269, ⓦ coralcayresort.com. The excellent-value seafront cottages here are well worth the extra cost; the budget rooms are set slightly inland. There's a pool, kayaks, gym, pool table, book exchange and a floating raft for those wanting to catch some rays. The laidback restaurant is a good place to mingle over tasty international food. Doubles P1140

JJ's Backpackers Village San Juan Beach ☎ 0918 700 0467, ✉ jiesa26@yahoo.com. Good budget choice owned by a friendly Aussie, where the simple rooms have fans and shared bathrooms. There are also tents for rent and a dorm. Tents P300, dorms P300, doubles P500

★ TREAT YOURSELF

Coco Grove 2km south of San Juan ☎ 035
225 5490, ⓦ cocogrovebeachresort.com.
Towering coconut trees line the 800m
stretch of beach at this welcoming
family-run resort with tropical gardens. The
41 cottages and villas are dotted around
the 15 acres of luscious property and there
are plenty of activities on offer from Hobie
cat sailing to island hopping. The three
pools have natural chlorination and there
are energy-saving lamps in an effort to go
green. There's also a dive shop and three
restaurants with free wi-fi. Doubles **P3500**

Kiwi Dive Resort East end of Sandugan Beach ☎ 0908
889 2283, ⓦ kiwidiveresort.com. Relaxed, laidback Kiwi-
owned place with rustic nipa cottages. There's a pleasant
terrace restaurant with a book swap, and they rent
motorbikes and run island tours, as well as their dive
centre. Free wi-fi. Doubles **P500**

CEBU

The island of **Cebu** is the ninth largest in
the Philippines and is considered as the
beating heart of the Visayas. Any
island-hopping trip will inevitably take
you through **Cebu City**, the Philippines'
second city, which despite its clamour is a
great place to get a fix of shopping and
international restaurants before returning
to lazy tropical living. When you've had
your fill of the city head north to the
idyllic island of **Malapascua**, where the
sand is as fine as Boracay's, or to tranquil
Bantayan off the northwest coast. South
of Cebu City, on the opposite coast, lies
the diving and drinking haven of
Moalboal where the sites around Pescador
Island are rated among the country's best.

Cebu City

The "Queen City of the South", **CEBU
CITY** isn't half as chaotic as Manila, thanks
in part to a one-way traffic system around
much of the city, but it's still pretty
jammed with the usual snarl of polluting
jeepneys. In its favour, Cebu has some
great restaurants, lively nightlife and so
many malls it's a wonder Cebuanos ever
see daylight. The big annual attraction,
however, is the **Sinulog Festival**, which

culminates on the third Sunday of January
with a wild Mardi Gras-style street parade
and outdoor concert at Fuente Osmeña.
The fiesta, in honour of Cebu's patron
saint the Santo Niño, is similar to Kalibo's
Ati-Atihan, and hotels are usually full,
particularly for the climax of the
festivities. Check ⓦ sinulog.ph for details.

WHAT TO SEE AND DO

From a visitor's perspective, Cebu City is
steadily moving northwards, as more
restaurants and amenities appear in the
areas of Lahug and Banilad. These
suburbs and the area around **Fuente
Osmeña**, the large traffic roundabout on
the main north–south drag Osmeña
Boulevard, make up "uptown" Cebu City.

Downtown, or the old part of the city,
meanwhile, is a seething cobweb of
sunless avenues and murky streams; half a
day is enough to see the sights – the only
other reason to come here is to catch a
ferry. **Colon Street** is said to be the oldest
mercantile thoroughfare in the country,
though there's nothing in its appearance
to lend it any kind of historical ambience.
About ten minutes' walk south is **Carbon
Market** (dawn until late), where the range
of goods on offer – edible, sartorial and
unidentifiable – will leave you reeling.

The city's spiritual heart is a small crypt
opposite the city hall containing the **Cross
of Magellan**. It's a modern hollow replica
said to hold fragments of the original
crucifix brought by the infamous
conquistador in 1521. Next to the crypt is
the towering, dusty **Basilica del Santo
Niño**, damaged in the October 2013
Bohol earthquake. It was built from 1735
to 1737, and houses probably the most
famous religious icon in the Philippines, a
statue of the Santo Niño (Christ child),
said to have been presented to Queen
Juana of Cebu by Magellan in 1521. The
succeeding conquistador, Miguel Lopez
de Legaspi, arrived in 1565 and built **Fort
San Pedro** (daily 8am–8pm; P30) near the
port area at the end of Quezon Boulevard.

Two museums are worth a look if you're
interested in Cebuano history and culture:
Casa Gorordo Museum, L. Jaena Street
(Tues–Sun 10am–6pm; P80), is a former
Spanish mansion, which offers a glimpse

8

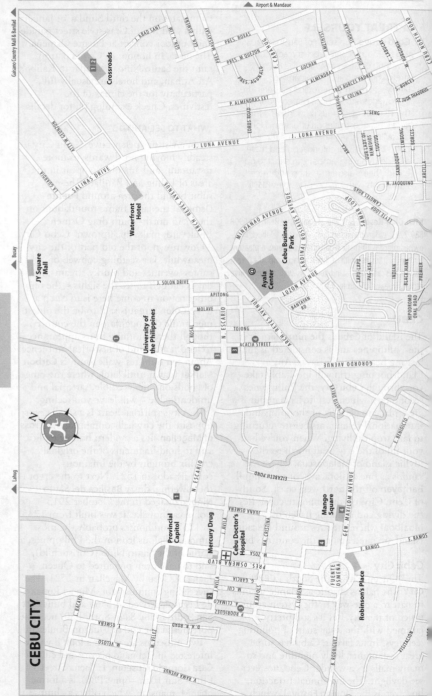

▲ Airport & Mandaue

8

CEBU CITY

◄ Galisano Country Mall & Banilad

◄ Busay

◄ Lahug

Crossroads

J. ABAD SANT
GEN. T. VIL
GEN. J. ESMERA
MT. S. MCLACHAN
PRES. ROXAS
PRES. M QUEZON
PRES. AGUINALDO
F. CABAHUG
F. GOCHAN
P. ALMENDRAS
TRES BORCES PADRES
S. BORCES
ST. JUDE-THADDEUS
R. COLINA
J. SENG

ATTY. M. GEONZON
SALINAS DRIVE
LA GUARDIA

ARCH. REYES AVENUE

EDGRS. ROAD
P. ALMENDRAS EXT

J. LUNA AVENUE
J. LUNA AVENUE

MINDANAO AVENUE
CARDINAL ROSALES AVENUE
LUZON AVENUE

Waterfront
Hotel

JY Square
Mall

Cebu Business
Park

Ayala
Center @

LEYTE LOOP
SAMS LOOP
CANOLS ROAD

H. JAOQUINO
C. TUDTUD
OUR LADY OF
REMEDIOS
T. LIMBONG
SANROQUE
F. BORCES
G. BORCES
F. ARCILLA

J. SOLON DRIVE

APITONG

MOLAVE

C. ROSAL

TOJONG

University of
the Philippines

N. ESCARIO

ARCH. REYES AVENUE

BANTAYAN
RD

BARAYAN
RD

LAPU-LAPU
PAG-ASA
LAPU-LAPU
INDIAN
BLACK HAWK
PREMIER

HIPODROMO
OVAL ROAD

ACACIA STREET

GORORDO AVENUE

N
8

1

2

3

3

4

N. ESCARIO

ELIZABETH POND

E. BENEDICTO

ESOLTO DRIVE
ESOLTO DRIVE

Provincial
Capitol

Mercury Drug

Cebu Doctor's
Hospital

JUANA OSMEÑA
M. AVILA
M. AVILA
MA. CRISTINA
M. ZOSA
PRES. OSMEÑA BLVD
G. GARCIA
JOSEPH
N. BACALSO
L. LLOENTE

Mango
Square

GEN. MAXILOM AVENUE

F. RAMOS
F. RAMOS

1

2

4

4

B. BACAYO
E. OSMEÑA
D. A. R. ROAD
M. YELEZ
M. VELOSO
V. RAMA AVENUE
B. RODRIGUEZ
VISTACION

P. RODRIGUEZ
M. CLIMACO
M CUI

FUENTE
OSMEÑA

Robinson's Place

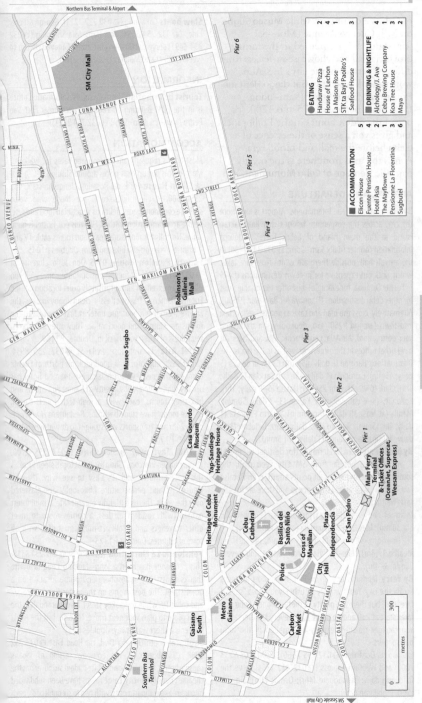

Northern Bus Terminal & Airport ▲

● **EATING**

Handuraw Pizza	2
House of Lechon	4
La Maison Rose	1
STK ta Bayl Paolito's	
Seafood House	3

■ **DRINKING & NIGHTLIFE**

Alchology/J. Ave	4
Cebu Brewing Company	1
Koa Tree House	3
Maya	2

■ **ACCOMMODATION**

Elicon House	5
Fuente Pension House	4
Hotel Asia	2
The Mayflower	1
Pensionne La Florentina	3
Sugbutel	6

8

SM Seaside City Mall ▼

0 — 300 metres

of Cebu's elegant past, while **Museo Sugbo** on M.J. Cuenco Avenue (Mon–Sat 9am–6pm; P75) is housed in the former provincial jail and showcases artefacts from different periods of the city's life. Also worth a look is the **Yap-Sandiego Heritage House** on Mabini Street (9am–noon; P50). Built between 1675 and 1700, it's one of the oldest homes in the Philippines and gives you a sense of the essence of Cebu before the mall and mobile era. Across the road from here is the overtly patriotic **Heritage of Cebu Monument**.

ARRIVAL AND DEPARTURE

By plane Mactan Cebu International Airport is 8km from the city, across the suspension bridges that link Mactan Island to the main island of Cebu. There's a tourist information counter (daily 5am–9pm; ☎ 032 340 2486) in the arrivals hall; outside there are white fixed-fare taxis, which work out expensive for in-town destinations (P475 to Fuente Osmeña, for example), but offer reasonable rates for other Cebu destinations (Hagnaya for Bantayan P2500). Alternatively, cross the road and take a metered yellow taxi into town (around P250–450, depending on traffic and your destination). Air Asia, Cebu Pacific, PAL and Tiger Air have ticket offices at the airport, as well as in the malls.

Destinations Bacolod (8 daily; 45min); Cagayan de Oro (5 daily; 45min); Camiguin (1 daily; 45min); Caticlan (3 daily; 1hr); Clark (6 weekly; 1hr 25min); Davao (6–9 daily; 1hr); Iloilo City (4–6 daily; 50min); Kalibo (3–7 daily; 50min); Manila (at least 30 daily; 1hr 10min); Puerto Princesa (1 daily; 1hr 15min); Siargao (1–2 daily; 1hr); Tacloban (3–4 daily; 45min); Zamboanga (1 daily; 1hr 5min).

By bus The northern bus terminal (for destinations north) is in Mandaue, not far from SM City Cebu mall; the southern bus terminal, for all points south, is on Bacalso Ave. Both are well served by jeepneys and there are usually taxis waiting.

Destinations north Hagnaya, for Bantayan (every 30min; 3hr 30min); Maya, for Malapascua (every 30min; 4hr).

Destinations south Bato (every 30min; 4–5hr) via Moalboal (3hr); Lilo-An, via Carcar and Oslob (every 20min; 3–4hr).

By ferry Jeepneys line up at Pier 1 for short journeys across the city. Touts will try to usher you into a "special fare" taxi, but there are plenty of metered ones. Cebu taxi fares start at P30 and go up by P2.50 every km thereafter. You can get up-to-date ferry information in the local newspapers.

Fast boats OceanJet (☎ 032 255 7560), 2GO (☎ 032 233 7000) and Weesam Express (☎ 032 412 1864) serve the following daily: Dumaguete (4hr); Ormoc (3hr); Siquijor (5hr); Tagbilaran (2hr).

Slow boats Cokaliong (☎ 032 232 7211), George & Peter Lines (☎ 032 254 5154) and Trans-Asia Shipping (☎ 032 254 6491) serve destinations including Cagayan de Oro (4 weekly; 10hr) and Manila (1–2 daily; 21hr).

INFORMATION

Tourist information The main tourist information office is in the LDM Building on Legaspi Street, near Fort San Pedro (Mon–Fri 8am–5pm; ☎ 032 254 2811).

ACCOMMODATION

Most hotels regularly offer discounted rates for walk-ins. Many places put up their prices around Sinulog.

★**Elicon House** Cnr P. del Rosario & Junquera sts ☎ 032 255 0300, ⊚ elicon-house.com. For those who value sociable common spaces, delicious vegetarian food and safe, secure accommodation (with CCTV), this eco-hostel is great value. No-frills a/c rooms are clean, and there's cable TV and – bizarrely – an on-site bike museum. Doubles P1045

Fuente Pension House 0175 Don Julio Llorente St ☎ 032 412 4988, ⊚ fuentepensionhouse.com. Well-run place in an excellent and surprisingly quiet location behind Fuente Osmeña. The spotlessly clean lobby makes the *Fuente* seem like a boutique hotel at first glance, but the rooms are simple and good value. They offer 24hr rates, regardless of when you check in. Doubles P1189

Hotel Asia 11 Don Jose Avila St ☎ 032 255 8534, ⊚ hotelasiacebu.com. In a good location north of Fuente Osmeña, this neat, well-run Japanese-themed hotel has an airy white-tiled lobby, plenty of Mount Fuji motifs and box-sized rooms, each with a high-tech toilet. Larger, deluxe rooms have stone bathtubs. Restaurant *Han-Nya* is open 24hr and transports you straight to downtown Tokyo. Doubles P1950

★**The Mayflower** Villalon Drive ☎ 032 255 2700, ⊚ mayflower-inn.com. "Shop local, eat local, sleep local" is this hotel's motto, and it's easy to see why: its eco-credentials and permaculture philosophy are plastered over the walls. There's a friendly organic café, a mini forest garden (with resident turtles), a games room to meet other travellers and a folk art museum stuffed with all sorts of oddities. Doubles P1375

Pensionne La Florentina 18 Acacia St ☎ 032 231 3318. This *pensionne* has been a long-standing Cebu favourite thanks to its cosy atmosphere and prime location on a quiet street. The best rooms on the upper floors have a/c and cable TV, while the pokey street-level verandah is the ideal place to plan your next move. No café, but the Ayala Center is a short walk away. Doubles P950

Sugbutel South Osmeña Blvd, cnr Road East ☎ 032 232 8888, ⊚ sugbutel.com. The economy version of Japan's capsule hotels, this green-and-white budget stopover has the cheapest beds in the city. Large rooms have been subdivided into train-like compartments, with two to six bunk beds, each of which has an overhead light, small safety box and plug socket. The lobby feels like a station waiting room, but it's functional and cheap. Dorms P265, doubles P1450

EATING

Much of Cebu's best dining and drinking can be found at the malls such as *The Terraces*, built around a garden area in the Ayala Center, Crossroads and Banilad Town Centre mall (BTC).

Handuraw Pizza Gorordo Ave ☎032 231 3398, ⓦhandurawpizza.com. Serving thin-crust concept pizzas with a hearty Cebuano twist, this beloved city-wide franchise has come a long way since opening in 2004. Go local with a Tinapa Delight, topped with smoked milkfish (large P398). Live music most nights. Mon–Thurs & Sun 10am–midnight, Fri & Sat 10am–2am.

House of Lechon Acacia St ☎032 231 0958. If you want to go the full hog in the company of smiling, grease-chinned locals, there's nowhere better in Cebu. With cherry-red, succulent barbecued pig that's been voted the best in the city (no small feat with so much competition), the restaurant prices its secret-recipe *lechon* by weight (250g, P200; or P230 for the spicy version). Daily 10am–10pm.

★**La Maison Rose** 371 Gorordo Ave ☎032 268 5411, ⓦfacebook.com/LaMaisonRoseCebu. Affectionately known as the "Pink Restaurant", this converted villa looks like the French embassy from the street, but is made up of a smart restaurant, outdoor patio and *La Vie Parisienne*, a patisserie and fine-food emporium. In the restaurant, dishes such as duck confit (P650) and escargots (P180) make it a culinary utopia, but with fresh-baked pastries and panini (from P25) the deli is a budget pit stop, too. Daily noon–11pm.

STK ta Bay! Paolito's Seafood House 6 A. Climaco St ☎032 253 4732, ⓦstktabay.com. *STK* stands for Cebu's three most famous cooking methods – *sugba* (grill), *tuwa* (soup) and *kilaw* (ceviche) – while the wall of fame showing a who's-who of Filipino diners underlines the restaurant's credentials. It's set up in Paolo Alcover's home and diners are seated among family heirlooms, including an enormous goatskin drum. Despite the distractions, the food remains the star: try the adobo eel (P150) or black pepper crabs (P295). Daily 9am–2pm & 5–11pm.

DRINKING AND NIGHTLIFE

Alchology/J. Ave Mango Square. It's worth checking out Mango Square, home to some of Cebu's biggest clubs and party places, including these two which play anything and everything with a focus on r'n'b and dance chart hits. They can get a little sleazy at times, but there are plenty of other bars in the precinct to flit between. Both play 9pm–4am.

★**Cebu Brewing Company** Crossroads Mall, Banilad ☎0998 845 2508, ⓦcebubrewing.com. Craft beer lovers are in for a treat. With four draughts on taps, dozens of bottles

from around the world to sample and rotating ale specials, including ones flavoured with mango and coconut (P125), this pokey pub is hop heaven. Tues–Sat 4pm–midnight.

Koa Tree House 55 Gorordo Ave ☎032 318 4853. Little more than a cluster of wooden tables, this open-fronted saloon offers cheap beers, live music and a weekend flea market. *Kukuk's Nest* across the road is a 24hr art-inspired bar where you'll find more of the same. Mon & Sun 6pm–1am, Tues–Sat 6pm–2am.

Maya Crossroads Mall, Banilad ☎032 238 9522, ⓦtheabacagroup.com/maya. The place to whet your sombrero with an exhaustive tequila list (from P210), as well as blue agave tasting tours (P1100). There are also Mexican dishes including burritos and fajitas (from P295) and salsa classes (Wed 8.30pm). Mon–Thurs & Sun 5pm–midnight, Fri–Sat 5pm–2am.

SHOPPING

The main malls are the Ayala Center (Cebu Business Park), Robinson's Galleria (Sergio Osmeña Jr Blvd), SM City (North Reclamation area) and SM Seaside City (Southside Properties area), as well as smaller malls, Robinson's Place (Fuente Osmeña), Gaisano, JY Square and Banilad Town Center (BTC) farther north. All are open 10am to 9pm.

DIRECTORY

Banks and exchange ATMs are everywhere, and there's no shortage of places to change currency, particularly along the main drag of President Osmeña Blvd, where there are branches of HSBC, Citibank and Metrobank.

Immigration Cebu Immigration District Office, P. Burgos St, Mandaue City (Mon–Fri 8am–5pm; ☎032 345 6441).

Internet Internet cafés are everywhere. Try Netopia, top floor of the Ayala Center (daily 10am–9pm; P25/hr).

Medical Care Cebu Doctor's University Hospital, President Osmeña Blvd (☎032 253 7511). There's a branch of Mercury Drug on Fuente Osmeña and other pharmacies in all the malls.

Police Cebu Tourist Police (☎032 412 4138) is located by the Basilica del Santo Niño. For emergencies, call ☎161.

Post office On Quezon Blvd close to the port area. Also at President Osmeña Blvd cnr. R. Landon St.

Moalboal

Almost 90km from Cebu City on the island's southwestern flank lies the small town of **MOALBOAL**, gateway to Pangsama Beach, a relaxed, rather boozy, divers' hangout with cheap accommodation and marvellous sunsets over Negros. The sea is crystal clear, and while many reefs along the mainland coast have been damaged by successive typhoons, the enigmatic Pescador Island has survived, and remains

8

one of the most alluring **dive sites** in the Philippines. Located just a few kilometres offshore, it's a haven for sharks, mantas and moray eels and swirling **vortexes of sardines**. There's also plenty to do on land, from hikes and bike rides to canyoning and horseriding, although sun-worshippers looking for a sandy beach will be better off at White Beach, 5km north.

ARRIVAL AND DEPARTURE

By bus Buses pick up and drop off on the main road in Moalboal, from where a tricycle will take you down the road to Panagsama Beach (15min; P100).
Destinations Bato (every 30min; 2hr); Cebu City (every 30min; 3hr).

DIVE OPERATORS

Dive operators are dotted along the waterfront and most are connected to resorts.
Freediving Philippines ☎0928 263 4646, ⓦfreediving-philippines.com. One of the few freediving centres in the country; teacher Wolfgang Dafert will train you to hold your breath for 2–3 minutes at a time and dive without equipment. Prices start at US$125/day.
Quo Vadis *Located at Quo Vadis* resort ☎032 474 3068, ⓦquovadisresort.com. Swedish-Filipino owned and operated since 1997.
Savedra Dive Center ☎032 474 3132, ⓦsavedra.com. This five-star operation offers plenty of choice for all levels of ability. They also arrange dive safaris to Apo Island, Bohol and Sipalay.

TOUR OPERATORS

Cyan Adventures ☎032 474 3400, ⓦcyan.ph. Highly recommended for jungle tours, with an office beside the *French Coffee Shop*.
Planet Action Adventure Next to *The Last Filling Station* ☎03917 583 0062, ⓦaction-philippines.com). One of the best things about Moalboal, Planet Action Adventure can arrange caving, trekking, canyoning and mountain-biking trips. Adventure day-trips start from P2200.

ACCOMMODATION

★**Chief Mau** ☎0942 742 4535, ⓦfacebook.com /chiefmaumoalboal. Located 50m inland from the beach path's north end, this newcomer knows how to keep backpackers happy. It's set around a sociable bar terrace with a driftwood shack vibe, and you'll find both fan and a/c six- and eight-bed dorms, a handful of private rooms, plus board games and weekly Saturday beer pong. Banana pancake heaven, indeed. Dorms P350, doubles P800

Maya's Native Garden ☎032 474 3053, ⓦmayasnativegarden.com. The most exotic setting in Moalboal, with five thatched, stilted native huts, centred around a rough-and-ready garden (look out for hummingbirds), *Maya's* excels with clean, affordable rooms and friendly service. For local craft beers (P150) and Mexican food, prop up on a stool at the resto-bar out the front. Doubles P800
Moalboal Backpacker's Lodge Along the main beach path ☎09017 751 8902, ⓦmoalboal-backpackerlodge .com. One of the cheapest places to stay, this buzzy hangout has three very simple mixed dorms and four private rooms and cottages. Amenities are basic, but there's a guest kitchen and sun deck. Pride of place in the lobby is an upcycled truck turned breakfast bar. Dorms P300, doubles P950
Quo Vadis Dive Resort At the beach path's southern end ☎032 474 3068, ⓦquovadisresort.com. Attractive place set in coastal gardens with a great pool vibe. Economy rooms are in a block at the back, while more expensive a/c nipa huts and cottages are closer to the front. There's also a bar-restaurant looking straight out to sea and a great dive shop on site. Doubles P1780
Tipolo Beach Resort ☎0917 583 0062, ⓦtipoloresort .com. A slightly pricier option, but well worth the splurge with beautifully built bamboo a/c chalets, all with private balcony and sea views. There's also a small private beach for sun-worshippers and it's owned by the same Filipino-German couple as *The Last Filling Station* and *Planet Action Adventure*. If *Tipolo* is fully booked, ask about its budget property, *Bamboo Inn* (from P950), a 10min walk back towards Moalboal. Chalets P1800

EATING AND DRINKING

Chili Bar ☎0906 353 4315. In spite of legendary Swedish owner Lars's passing, this waterfront bar midway along the beach path remains resolutely popular with divers ("get out of that wet suit and into a dry martini"). Great sea views, two pool tables and cut-price beers to the last man (or woman) standing. Daily 9am–late.
The French Coffee Shop ☎0906 353 4315. Fresh-brewed, bottomless coffee (P80–120), great breakfasts (try the Parisienne, P250), croissants and crêpes (P220), and daily specials. Friendly vibe, right down to the sand on the floor. Free wi-fi. Daily 6am–10pm.
The Last Filling Station At *Tipolo Beach Resort* ☎0917 583 0062, ⓦtipoloresort.com. Right at the heart of the Moalboal scene, this laidback place rustles up tasty international dishes and great wood-fired pizzas (P275), as well as freshly baked bread and heaped breakfasts (P195). Free wi-fi. Daily 6.30am–10pm.
★**The Pleasure Principle** ☎032 474 3988, ⓦpleasureprinciplemoalboal.com. Basque-style fish, Arabic-spiced pizzas, Indian curries and Godzilla-sized shellfish are

SECURITY IN SOUTHERN CEBU

At the time of writing, several governments advised against all but essential travel to **southern Cebu** (up to and including the municipalities of Dalaguete and Badian, immediately south of Moalboal) because of the threat of terrorism. Anticipating kidnapping threats to foreign visitors and attacks by terrorist groups, the US Embassy issued a warning in November 2016, and the UK and Canadian embassies followed suit. This may be a short-term warning, and it has so far not significantly affected tourist numbers. However, if planning to travel anywhere south of Moalboal, check the latest government advice ahead of time (W gov.uk/foreign-travel-advice).

served at this popular jack-of-all-trades fusion restaurant on the main strip. Mains from P200–600. Daily 7am–10pm.

DIRECTORY

Banks and exchange There are a number of ATMs which accept foreign cards in Moalboal, including one opposite SeaQuest Dive Center.

Internet There are several internet cafés (P30/hr) in Moalboal town; most hotels offer free wi-fi.

BANTAYAN ISLAND

Just off the northwest coast of Cebu, this quiet, bucolic and pancake-flat island is the place to go for pleasant, low-key resorts, a smattering of **sparkling beaches** and friendly open armed welcomes. Malapascua takes the lion's share of visitors this far north, which makes **Bantayan** all the quieter: visitors here are occupied by little more than the three "S"s – sand, sunshine and seafood.

But trouble landed in paradise in November 2013, when the island was badly hit by **Typhoon Yolanda**, with few buildings escaping damage. The lack of diving (and therefore diving clientele) meant that it took the island far longer to get back on its feet than its neighbours, but now the resilient community looks nothing like it did immediately post disaster. Visitors are more welcome than ever, though permanent housing remains a problem for many of the island's residents. Working on the long-term recovery effort, Oxfam (W philippines.oxfam.org) welcomes financial and physical aid from volunteers.

Most of the island's resorts stretch north and south of the pier in the attractive little town and main port of **SANTA FE** on Bantayan's southeast coast. A good way to explore is to make like the locals and hop on a bike; almost all the resorts rent bikes (P200/day) and motorbikes (P300/day). Every Easter during **Holy Week**, Bantayan holds

8

TYPHOON YOLANDA

On November 8, 2013, **Typhoon Yolanda** (known internationally as Haiyan) hit the southeastern tip of Samar with wind speeds of up to 315km/hr. The superstorm left a broad band of destruction through northern Leyte, northern Cebu, northeastern Panay and finally Busuanga, in Palawan, before leaving the archipelago. Yolanda made landfall near Guiuan, which was almost completely destroyed, and 2m-plus storm surges wreaked havoc in Tacloban. In spite of a huge **international relief effort**, many of the worst affected areas remained without power, clean water and supplies for weeks. Looting became a major problem, while in unaffected regions businesses and individuals rallied to raise funds and support.

Economically, the recovery period will be counted in years, but for the families of the six thousand dead the losses are clearly irreparable: many remain missing, and allegations surrounding the mismanagement of rehabilitation funds still plague government agencies. While aid groups remained in Tacloban until at least mid-2014, their presence can still be felt in the Leyte capital, particularly because sustained support is still needed to help rebuild homes and repatriate families who continue to live in temporary housing. **Tourism** can have a vital role here, and in popular areas nearby – Bantayan and Malapascua, for example (see above) – much-needed cash injections made a life-changing difference to the speed and scale of recovery, and plenty of local agencies are still working to bring about a positive change.

solemn processions of decorated religious *carozzas* (carriages), each containing a life-sized statue representing the Passion and death of Jesus Christ. Thousands turn out to join in the processions, many setting up camp on the beaches because the resorts are full.

ARRIVAL AND DEPARTURE

By bus Several bus companies compete for business from Cebu's north terminal to the northern port town of Hagnaya (7 daily; 3hr 30min) where you catch the ferry to Bantayan Island. Ceres Liner offers a/c, wi-fi and films, and is the most reliable.

By ferry There are seven scheduled daily crossings to Santa Fe (1hr); the last departures are 5.30pm from Hagnaya and 6pm from Santa Fe. From farther afield, there are several weekly ferries to Bantayan town on the west coast from Cadiz and Sagay on Negros. In good weather, you can also hire a *bangka* to take you directly to Bantayan from Malapascua (P3500).

ACCOMMODATION

There are about a dozen or so resorts in Santa Fe, with the ones on Sugar Beach, the south coast's loveliest stretch of sand, charging significantly more than the budget hotels in town.

Bantayan Cottages Santa Fe ☎032 438 9358, ⊛bantayancottages.com. On the main road into town from the pier, this cut-price option has rooms in the main house and a selection of verandah-fitted deluxe rooms with kingsize beds, a/c and TVs around an orchid-scented garden (P1600). What it lacks in beachfront, it makes up for by being close to town. Doubles P700

Budyong Beach Resort Sante Fe ☎032 438 9285, ⊛budyong.byethost7.com. A good selection of simple beachfront fan and a/c nipa-thatched cottages (P800–2200) set around a well-groomed coconut grove on Santa Fe's loveliest stretch of beach. It's within easy walking distance of town. Doubles P800

★**Kota Beach Resort** ☎032 438 9042, ⊛kotabeachresort.com. Next door to *Budyong*, Kota has a range of tightly packed cottages set in regimented lines on a lovely stretch of beach. The superior cottages (P3400) are right on the sand, while the economy and fan rooms at the back offer decent value. Wi-fi only in the restaurant. Doubles P900

Yooneek Beach Resort West of Santa Fe ☎032 438 9124, ⊛yooneekbeachresort.com. Plonked on a quiet part of Sugar Beach, this laidback nine-room complex has a variety of a/c and fan rooms (some with balconies, fridges and TVs). It's also home to the best backpacker bar on the beach. Doubles P1590

EATING AND DRINKING

The following are all on or just off the Public Market road in Santa Fe. Almost all the resorts have their own restaurants.

Balikbayan ☎0921 438 9216. Friendly restaurant in the Santa Fe back streets with cosy pergolas dotted around a pretty garden. Set grilled seafood and rice menus (P148), good pizza and the house *halo halo* is as good as you'll find anywhere in Cebu. Daily 7am–11pm.

Blue Ice Popular Swedish-owned place with MTV videos, live music and dancing in the evenings. Quieter types can settle for a game of chess on the big wooden board. Salads include "Nick the Greek", and there's an extensive selection of mains including steaks, seafood and pizza (mains around P295). Daily 8am–late.

Caffe del Mare ☎0942 572 2749. Across from *Blue Ice*, this restaurant serves a Mediterranean-influenced menu that is straight from the just-like-Mama-made-it school of Italian cooking, with antipasti, home-made pastas, authentic pizzas and Milanese-flavoured pork. Locals love the generous happy hour, too (1–5pm; San Miguel P40). Daily 7am–midnight.

★**MJ Square** ☎032 438 9013. This community collective of lively, pop-up-style restaurants has a dozen or so choices with everything from Tex-Mex burritos and burgers to cupcakes, coffee and cheap Filipino eats. Two to try are the *Bantayan Burrito Company* and *Cupcake Island Bakery*. Daily 10am–11pm.

MALAPASCUA ISLAND

Eight kilometres off the northern tip of Cebu, the tiny island of **MALAPASCUA** is often erroneously touted as the next Boracay, largely because of **Bounty Beach**, a blindingly white stretch of sand on the island's south coast. This moniker does the island a great injustice because it has more than enough diversions to keep you occupied for at least a week, and locals have no interest in seeing their island gem become a paradise lost.

Malapascua's trump card is its world-class **diving**, with the chance to see thresher sharks congregate in shallow waters. The sting in the tail is that Malapascua was just hitting the big time when **Typhoon Yolanda** struck. Almost every roof on the island was destroyed, and most of the local population was left without shelter. Substantial private contributions helped the island get its groove back and the inhabitants remain

DIVING MALAPASCUA

Although some shallower dive sites were damaged by Yolanda, the major drawcard – the distinctively tailed **thresher sharks** – remain in residence, and anyone staying more than a few days is almost guaranteed a sighting. The vortex of this activity is **Monad Shoal**, the only place in the world where the trident-tailed swimmers can be seen like clockwork. At shallow depths of around 20m, they congregate on the sea plateau in huge numbers, using the seamount as a symbiotic cleaning station for gum-grinding fish to remove and eat parasites from their skin. Long-established dive operators on the island are Evolution (☏ 0917 631 2179, ☒ evolution.com.ph), Malapascua Exotic Island Dive and Beach Resort (☏ 032 516 2990, ☒ malapascua.net) and Sea Explorers (☏ 0917 320 4158, ☒ sea-explorers.com), and all can help with one-off dives and courses.

some of the warmest people you'll meet. They're also renowned for their love of a party, especially during the annual fiesta on May 11–12 when all of Malapascua gets into carnival mode.

You can **walk** the circumference of the island in a few hours, a journey that will take you through sleepy fishing villages lined with mangroves to remote white-sand beaches. **Sunset cruises** involving swimming, snorkelling and cliff jumping are also great fun (P1000/person).

ARRIVAL AND DEPARTURE

By bus Buses run between Cebu City's northern bus terminal and Maya (every 30min; 4hr), but it's best to set off early.

By boat There are hourly *bangkas* to and from Maya and Malapascua from dawn until 4pm (40min; P100, subject to enough passengers on board). When it's low tide, you'll need to transfer to a smaller boat to get you to the shoreline (an additional P20 at each end).

ACCOMMODATION

All the places listed below are on Bounty Beach. As Malapascua is quickly growing in popularity, early booking is advised.

★ **Evolution** ☏ 0917 631 2179, ☒ evolution.com.ph. If only all dive resorts were like this. Run by two of the island's most experienced technical divers – David (Irish) and Matt (English) – this welcoming, sixteen-room hideaway is tucked away on the island's loveliest stretch of real estate. Rooms are split between fabulous bungalows and newly constructed deluxe rooms farther back from the beach, while the personable staff make sure an A–Z of diving needs is taken care of. Doubles P1900

Hiltey's Hideout Beach Resort ☏ 0918 287 0999, ☒ hilteyshideout.com. Cheap, centrally located accommodation run by affable German Volker

Hiltebrandt. Block-built around a garden, the rooms are simple affairs with bamboo furniture, but what keeps it packed is that it's within striking distance of the beach. Long-term discounts are available (from P800 a night). Doubles P1300

Malapascua Exotic Island Dive and Beach Resort ☏ 032 516 2990, ☒ malapascua.net. One of the best established resorts on the island, the motel-style *Exotic* has a huge range to choose from, including standard a/c to pricey beachfront deluxe rooms (P4600). It's Dutch-owned, which explains the in-house European bakery and Heineken on draught. Doubles P2800

Villa Sandra ☏ 926 993 8262, ☒ facebook.com/villasandramalapascua. A rambling place atop the only hill in town, this hideaway is owned by Jonjon, a reggae-dipped Filipino who knows a thing or two about distilling the perfect vibe for travellers. Rooms vary from six-bed dorms with personal fans to thatched bungalows, or, if you want to go really cheap, sling a hammock up in the yard (P200). Also has deliciously cheap vegetarian food. Dorms P350, doubles P800

White Sands Bungalows Logon Beach ☏ 032 318 8666, ☒ whitesand.dk. Overlooking the boat landing, this low-key collection of six fan-cooled nipa huts is as simple as Malapascua gets. The balconies come draped with hammocks, and out front, on a raised wooden platform, is Thai restaurant *Aroi Mak* (seafood from P300). Huts P1200

EATING AND DRINKING

The Craic House In *Evolution* (see above). The kitchen here turns out the island's best breakfasts (P200) and tropical grub including a spicy tuna burger and seafood curries (P325). Happy hour deals (4–7pm) make it the most sociable divers' spot on the island. Daily 7am–11pm.

Kokoy's Maldito Logon Beach ☏ 916 588 4503. The island's prime sunset beach bar, barn-like *Maldito* has pool tables, table football, happy hours, an outdoor screen for sports, and plenty of other reasons to keep you socializing later than planned. Drinks are a bargain P50 for beers, or P40 for rum. Daily 7am–midnight.

BOHOL

It's hard to imagine that sleepy **Bohol**, a two-hour hop south of Cebu by fast ferry, has a bloody past. The only reminder is a memorial stone in the barrio of **Bool**, marking the spot where Rajah Sikatuna and Miguel Lopez de Legaspi concluded hostilities in 1565 by signing a compact in blood. These days, Bohol is largely a dozy sort of place, although the whole island was shaken up by the magnitude 7.2 earthquake that struck on October 15, 2013. More than 200 people died, and thousands of homes and buildings were destroyed, including some of the island's beloved Spanish-era churches. A few of the famed **Chocolate Hills** were also damaged by the quake, but they are still as gorgeous as ever. The main transit hub is the capital, **Tagbilaran**, though there's not a whole lot of reason to base yourself here when you could cross the bridge and be on **Panglao Island** in twenty minutes. The powdery strip of sand on **Alona Beach**, with world-class diving and boozy nightlife, is quickly moving upmarket, but there are still a few places catering to backpackers. Aside from the diving and sights on offer on the main island of Bohol, Alona itself will appeal to some as a mini-Boracay in waiting.

WHAT TO SEE AND DO

Bohol's iconic tourist attraction is the **Chocolate Hills**, which legend says are the calcified tears of a giant, whose heart was broken by the death of a mortal lover. The best time to see them is at dawn, at the end of the dry season when the grass has turned brown, and, with a short stretch of the imagination, the hills really do resemble chocolate drops. Most visitors head for the 360-degree viewpoint at the government-run **Chocolate Hills Main Viewpoint**. Built atop one of the unearthly formations, it's reached by a winding road and a steep climb up 200 or so rough-hewn steps. The site was badly damaged by the October 2013 quake and renovations were ongoing at the time of research. Alternatively, the nearby **Chocolate Hills Adventure Park** (daily 8.30am–5.30pm; P60; ☎0932 667 7098) offers vistas, plus a host of activities, including a canopy walkway, a high-rope challenge course and a bike zipline. The

other natural draw in the interior is the **Philippine tarsier**, one of the world's tiniest primates. The tarsier is simultaneously heart-meltingly cute, with its big eyes, and terrifyingly alien: those eyes are fixed, and instead it rotates its head 180 degrees. Sadly now endangered, its continued survival is thanks in part to the efforts of the **Philippine Tarsier Sanctuary**, and a visit to its centre near Corella (daily 9am–4pm; P50; ☵tarsierfoundation.org), about half an hour from Tagbilaran, is a great way to experience some of Bohol's interior. Most people see this jungle as part of an organized countryside tour, which also includes lunch on a floating restaurant along the lush banks of the Loboc River. Adrenaline-seekers may prefer to join a paddleboarding excursion with **SUP Tours Philippines** (from P1650; ☎038 537 9011), based on a bend of the jade-like river. It's also easy enough to arrange an island tour through your accommodation or rent a motorbike yourself. Otherwise, you can catch a bus to Carmen from the Dao bus terminal in Tagbilaran (hourly; P60).

Other than visiting the interior, the main activities are **beach-based**. There's world-class diving around Panglao; experienced divers shouldn't miss a trip to either the exquisite little island of **Balicasag**, or to **Pamilacan Island**, where it's possible to see short-finned pilot whales and several dolphin species. Any dive operator on Alona Beach can arrange this.

ARRIVAL AND DEPARTURE

By plane Tagbilaran Airport is under 2km from the city and a tricycle will cost P70 to the centre of town. Private taxis will take you to Alona Beach for P500.
Destinations Air Asia, Cebu Pacific and PAL all fly from Tagbilaran to Manila (daily; 1hr 15min).
By bus Dao integrated bus terminal is 10min north of Tagbilaran along Clarin Ave by tricycle (P30) and is the departure point for all other destinations on Bohol. Buses and jeepneys heading for Panglao are marked for Alona. For the Chocolate Hills, catch a bus to Carmen (hourly; 1hr 30min). Buses from Alona to Tagbilaran pick up on the main road, but aren't particularly frequent. Sharing a taxi/private transfer between Alona and Tagbilaran is a more convenient option (P500–600).
By ferry The pier is to the northwest of Tagbilaran off Gallares St, a 10min tricycle ride (P30) to the centre. The terminal fee is P20.

Destinations Daily fast ferries to Cebu City (hourly; 2hr) and Siquijor (3hr 30min) via Dumaguete (2 daily; 2hr).

INFORMATION

Facilities at Alona revolve around the numerous travel agencies, although you can also make most bookings at your resort.

Tourist information The Tagbilaran tourist office (Mon–Fri 8am–5pm; ☎038 412 3666, ⓦboholtourismph.com) is located at Governor's Mansion on CPG Avenue.

Travel agencies In Panglao, Seashine Travel (daily 9am–8pm; ☎038 502 9038, ⓦseashinetravelandtours.com), where the beach path meets the road, can arrange day-trips to the Chocolate Hills and plenty of other adventures. Alternatively, try German-owned Valeroso Travel and Tours (☎038 502 9126, ⓦralleontour.com).

ACCOMMODATION

TAGBILARAN

Nisa Traveller's Hotel 14 CPG Ave ☎038 411 3731, ⓦnisatravellershotel.com. The best budget option in town, featuring good a/c and fan doubles, hot water and clean bathrooms, as well as more expensive rooms with kingsize beds (P1300–1800). Rooms at the front contend with constant traffic noise. Doubles P700

ALONA BEACH

Alona Grove Tourist Inn ☎038 502 4200, ⓦfacebook.com/alonagrovetouristinn. One of a number of off-beach budget resorts with a row of simple thatched huts, some with a/c, fridge and cable TV. Huts P700

Bohol Coco Farm 5km east of Alona Beach ☎0906 807 1869, ⓦfacebook.com/boholcfarm. For those seeking peace, quiet, organic produce and fellow-minded travellers, this Filipino-run eco farm feels like a world apart. The farm features stripped-back nipa huts and mixed dorms, and for getting around motorbikes are a bargain P250 for 3hr. Dorms P350, huts P800

★**Chill-out Guesthouse** ☎038 502 4480, ⓦchillout-panglao.com. Tricky to find on a back road, this delightful French-run guesthouse is all the more rewarding for being away from the beach action. Spotless rooms with private balconies and fan or a/c (P1600) are dotted around a tropical garden, and there's a sociable restaurant serving crêpes and home-made yoghurt. Popular, so book in advance. Doubles P1350

D'Backpackers Barn ☎038 502 4968, ⓦbackpackersbarn.com. This cowboy-themed newcomer is already a firm favourite, despite the obvious lack of beachfront. It's smack by the side of the main road, yet comes up trumps with clean four-bed dorms, fan and a/c rooms, and a common area with hammocks, dartboard and board games. Wi-fi in common areas. Dorms P400, doubles P1200

Peter's House ☎038 502 9056, ⓦgenesisdivers.com. The last genuine budget option on the beach, Peter's is now flanked by luxury pool resorts yet maintains four simple and cosy nipa rooms above its beach bar. Owned by Genesis Divers, the hotel has an in-house, divers-only policy during peak season, but deals are available. Doubles P1200

EATING AND DRINKING

TAGBILARAN

The Garden Café Plaza Rizal ☎038 411 3701. Established by the Bohol Deaf Academy, and providing training for up to forty deaf students, this café has a menu mixing Mexican and Filipino dishes (P150–300). You can communicate with the staff in writing, or with sign language (a few basic signs are listed in the menu). Upstairs, it's very different at Montana Restaurant, a fun-filled Wild West-themed diner with finger-lickin' barbecue (P150–350). Daily 6.30am–10pm, restaurant 11am–10pm.

ALONA BEACH

There's no shortage of restaurants, mainly offering good seafood along the beach and the path leading towards the road inland.

Hayahay ☎038 502 9288, ⓦhayahay.net/restaurant. Promising the best pizza in town, Hayahay lives up to the billing, serving a mean thin-crust on the beach. Try the Balicasag with salmon and tuna (P270). Daily 7am–midnight.

Panglao Birdwatchers Towards the beach's western end ☎0912 710 8328 ⓦpanglaobirdwatchers.com. Aussie-run beachfront bar (hence the super-cold beers) that's big on sunset happy hours, booming tunes and good times. If the quirky staff, cocktails, live sports and zingy tacos from Woody's BBQ Shack next door don't convince you, little else will. Early until late.

T2 Bar, Café & Restaurant At Rona's Corner ☎0908 593 5155, ⓦfacebook.com/pg/t2restaurant. This popular 24hr joint caters for bleary-eyed new arrivals, as well as those who haven't left from the night before. The kitchen dishes up the usual fare (burgers, pizzas and pastas) for a mix of expats and divers, and there are quiz nights every Monday. Daily 24hr.

8

★**TREAT YOURSELF**

Angelina ☎0915 340 4906. Replete with red gingham tablecloths in a sophisticated dining room overlooking pretty Logon Beach, Angelina's turns out the best (and most expensive) food on the island. Delights such as beef carpaccio (P355) and tartar di tonno (P365) are on the menu, but there's no shame in ordering a good old-fashioned wood-fired pizza (from P320). Daily 8am–10pm.

DIRECTORY

Banks In Tagbilaran, there are plenty of banks with ATMs (including BPI and Metrobank) to be found on CPG Ave. There is also a BPI with ATM at Alona Beach.

Internet There are a number of cheap internet cafés in both BQ and ICM malls (daily 10am–9pm; P30/hr).

Police Behind St Joseph's Cathedral. In Alona Beach, there is a Tourist Police outpost at Rona's Corner.

Post office Behind St Joseph's Cathedral. Same complex as the police station.

Mindanao

The signals **Mindanao** sends to the rest of the Philippines and the wider world are nothing if not mixed. This massive island at the foot of the archipelago is a place where tribalism and capitalism clash head-on, and a refuge for those fleeing Manila in search of great surfing and volcanic beaches. All of this has led to something of a cultural and economic boom in cities such as **Davao**, Mindanao's de facto capital and gateway to the southern half of the region, but Mindanao is also a troubled island, with various indigenous Islamic groups agitating, sometimes violently, for autonomy (see box below).

At the centre of this debate is **President Rodrigo Duterte**, who became president in June 2016, a controversial figure who has a reputation for frank – and frankly offensive – speechmaking (he called former President Obama a "son of a whore"). Not only has he made the extrajudicial killing of drug dealers and users the cornerstone of his domestic policy, but as the former mayor of Davao and the first ever Mindanaoan to hold office he has threatened to impose martial law if unrest escalates in the region.

Following continued tensions and violence in 2017, at the time of writing the main island was considered unsafe for visitors and all travel to the area is strongly advised against. We have, therefore, focused on the safe, tourist-friendly satellites of **Camiguin** and **Siargao** – sanctuaries for surfing, diving, volcano climbing and slow-paced beach life – and provided information on **Cagayan de Oro** as a transit hub.

CAGAYAN DE ORO

CAGAYAN DE ORO (CDO) on the north coast of Mindanao is the starting point for many travellers for a trip to dazzling Camiguin Island. The only reason to linger in CDO is to go **whitewater rafting**. Kagay Whitewater Rafting on Corrales Avenue (☎088 852 1021, ⓦkagaycagayandeororafting.com) can organize everything from beginners' courses to night rafting trips.

THE MINDANAO PROBLEM

Mindanao has been a nagging thorn in the side of successive governments, with repeated attempts by the island's Muslims (*Moros*) to establish autonomy on the island, while the indigenous Lumad peoples also assert rights to their traditional lands. The Communist New People's Army (NPA) has also been resurgent in recent years.

The **Moro National Liberation Front** (MNLF) started a war for independence in the 1970s. Meanwhile, a communist-led rebellion spread from the northern Philippines to Mindanao, drawing in many Filipinos. In 1996, the MNLF were recognized by Manila when they co-signed a peace pact granting a certain degree of autonomy to four provinces. This led to the formation of several splinter groups, including the **Moro Islamic Liberation Front** (MILF) and **Abu Sayyaf** ("Bearer of the Sword"), whose centre of operations is largely Basilan Island, part of the Sulu archipelago off Mindanao's southern coast. Abu Sayyaf is widely believed to have ties to al-Qaeda and to have been responsible for the Philippines' deadliest terrorist attack, the bombing of the WG&A *Superferry 14* in February 2004, which claimed 116 lives. Since the **Maguindanao massacre** (see p.593) of November 2009, which led to the president declaring a state of emergency, numerous ceasefires have come and gone.

Today, the unrest continues: at least four Muslim rebel groups operate on the island and there has been an increase in the kidnapping of foreign nationals and tourists. Abu Sayyaf beheaded a Canadian hostage in April 2016, for example, while multiple attacks occurred in November 2016.

ARRIVAL AND DEPARTURE

By plane Laguindingan International Airport is 33km northwest of the city (1hr). The airport is accessible by jeepney (P40 to Laguindingan turn-off, then P20 shuttle to the airport), but the most convenient transfers are with LAX Shuttle (P249), which picks up at the Centrio Ayala Mall, or with Magnum Express, which leaves from Magnum Radio in CM Recto (P249).

Destinations Air Asia, Cebu Pacific and PAL fly to Bacolod (1 weekly; 1hr 10min); Cebu City (6–7 daily; 50min); Davao (1–2 daily; 55min); Iloilo (3 weekly; 55min); Manila (12–13 daily; 1hr 30min); Tagbilaran (1 weekly; 45min).

By bus There are two bus terminals in the city, with eastbound and southbound buses leaving from the one next to the Agora market. Westbound and northbound buses leave from the terminal in barangay Bulua. A jeepney ride to either from the centre is P10–12, or you can take a taxi for around P50.

Destinations Butuan (for Surigao; every 45min until 5pm; 4hr); Davao (every 30min; 6–8hr). The Butuan buses also pass through Balingoan (1hr 45min), the departure point for Camiguin.

By ferry Macabalan Wharf is 5km north of the centre, with regular jeepneys back and forth. 2GO runs three serves to Cebu from CDO, while Trans-Asia has a daily service to Cebu. Super Shuttle Ferry also operates to Cebu every Saturday, while Lite Shipping has services to Cebu, Dumaguete and Jagna on Bohol.

Destinations Bacolod (weekly; 21hr); Cebu City (daily; 10hr); Dumaguete (3 weekly; 7hr); Iloilo (3 weekly; 14hr); Jagna (4 weekly; 6–7hr); Manila (daily; 35hr); and Tagbilaran (3 weekly; 10hr).

INFORMATION

Tourist office The regional tourist office (Mon–Fri 8.30am–5.30pm; ☎ 088 856 4048) is in the Pelaez Sports Centre on A. Velez St, a short walk north of the city centre. The detailed website ⊚ cdoguide.com is also helpful.

Services Besides a supermarket and the usual stores, the Centrio Ayala mall (⊚ ayalamalls.com.ph) is home to several banks, internet cafés and a cinema.

ACCOMMODATION

Budgetel Corrales Ave, north of C.M. Recto ☎ 088 856 4200, ⊚ budgetel.com.ph. Handy for the eastbound bus terminal, this hit-or-miss hotel is the city's cheapest deal. It offers 34 en-suite a/c singles, twins and doubles, as well as enormous sixteen- and eighteen-bed dorms with shared bathroom. There's a laundry, too. Dorms P250, doubles P990

GC Suites Grand Central Building 4th Floor, Hayes St ☎ 088 858 1234, ⊚ gcsuitescdo.com. The closest CDO has to a boutique hotel. There is a variety of a/c single and doubles with TVs and clean bathrooms (P850–1200), and

guests are given a voucher for one free meal, redeemable at one of six restaurants in the same complex. What brings in the locals is the themed rooms dedicated to the likes of The Beatles and Bob Marley. Doubles P1100

★**Red Planet** Claro M. Recto Ave ☎ 063 2519 0888, ⊚ redplanethotels.com. A short stroll to the Centrio Mall and Limketkai Centre, this candy-cane coloured hotel is as switched-on to traveller needs as CDO gets. All rooms have a/c, free high-speed wi-fi, a power shower and a flat-screen TV. Doubles P1400

EATING AND DRINKING

The centre of the action in town is where A. Velez crosses Hayes and Chavez streets. A couple of kilometres east, the Limketkai mall has a good mix of restaurants, with the most bustling area being the Rosario Arcade outside the main entrance.

★**Cucina Higala** 222 Capistrano St ☎ 088 881 1570, ⊚ facebook.com/pg/cucinahigala. This Filipino melting pot mixes Mindanaoan recipes with modern techniques. Try its *sinuglaw* (seafood ceviche with grilled pork) or *humba* (braised pork belly stew) prepared *sous-vide* style. Mains P200–400. Daily 11am–2pm & 5–10pm.

Restaurant Damaso Chavez St ☎ 0935 591 8479, ⊚ facebook.com/restaurantdamaso. A great bet for breakfast, serving up smoked chorizo, beef tapa, eggs, vegetable rice and salads. Also good for Sriracha chicken wings, baby back ribs and grilled wahoo fish. Daily 7am–10pm.

Somewhere Else Corrales Etx. ☎ 0997 536 8175, ⊚ facebook.com/pg/SomewhereElseCDO. CDO's see-to-be-seen party place. DJs are flown in from Manila and Cebu, while the menu features around thirty imported beers (Mindanao's biggest selection). It does bar snacks, too. Mon–Thurs & Sun 5pm–1am, Fri & Sat 5pm–3am.

CAMIGUIN ISLAND

Sitting about 90km north of Cagayan de Oro, the pear-shaped volcanic island of **Camiguin** ("cam-ee-*gin*") is one of the country's highlights, offering ivory beaches, iridescent lagoons and undulating scenery. It's a peaceful, almost spiritual, island, where people are proud of their faith, though there's no shortage of adventure either, with scuba diving and tremendous trekking and climbing in the rugged interior, especially on volcanic **Mount Hibok-Hibok**. Camiguin is home to six other volcanoes, a multitude of hot springs and a submerged cemetery for divers to explore near the town of **Bonbon**. Another major draw is the

8

hugely fun **Lanzones Festival**, held in the third week of October, when everyone dances in the streets as a tribute to this humble fruit, one of Camiguin's major sources of income.

Mambajao, the little capital on the north coast 17km north of the port at Benoni, is the centre for most services, but it doesn't really matter where you stay because you can reach all the sights from anywhere. The **coastal road** is almost 70km long, making it feasible to circle the island in a day, most easily on a motorbike, which are widely available to rent.

ARRIVAL AND DEPARTURE

By plane Cebu Pacific flies to and from Cebu (1–2 daily; 50min). The airport charges a terminal fee of P50.
By ferry Ferries depart roughly hourly (5am–6pm; 1hr) from Balingoan for Benoni on Camiguin's southeast coast. From here, jeepneys run to and from Mambajao. Super Shuttle Ferries leave from Benoni for Jagna on Bohol three times a week at 8am (Mon, Wed, Fri; 3–4hr; ☎ 088 387 4034), returning at 1pm.

INFORMATION

Tourist information The tourist office (Mon–Fri 8am–5pm; ☎ 088 387 1097) is in the Provincial Capitol building, a short tricycle ride from the centre of Mambajao.
Services In Mambajao there's a branch of PNB, an ATM, a couple of internet cafés and a cluster of cheap places to eat around the market.

ACCOMMODATION AND EATING

Most of the beach accommodation is west of Mambajao between the *barangays* of Bug-ong and Yumbing, though the beach itself is coarse dark sand. This stretch also gives easy access to White Island, a dazzling serpentine ribbon of sand that makes a fun, early morning boat excursion.
★ **Guerrera** On the Agohay beach road ☎ 0917 311 9859, ⊛ guerrera.ph. Not even the street-food craze could pass Camiguin by. This ace Asian-flavoured restaurant is set in a beautiful rice paddy and instantly transports you to rural Vietnam or Laos. Dishes like *pad thai* (P250), Viet noodle salads (P275), and *ban xeo* crispy crêpes (P250) are knock outs. Also has a couple of rooms. Daily noon–2.30pm & 5–9pm.
Kurma Yumbing ☎ 0916 469 8912, ⊛ kurmafreedive. com. Run by the friendly Diggi and Valerie, *Kurma* has seven boldly painted fan and a/c rooms (P2300) on the oceanfront. The resort is the headquarters for the couple's freediving and yoga camps, and the veggie-friendly restaurant specializes in fusion cuisine. Doubles P1900

Nypa Style Resort 500m inland from Bug-ong ☎ 0947 181 0196, ⊛ nypastyleresort.jimdo.com. Owned by the hospitable Elena, this gorgeous hilltop resort is centred on a beautiful Indian-almond tree, and features six bungalows, a natural swimming pool and knock-your-socks-off home-made Italian food. Doubles P1600
Paradiso Hillside 1.5km inland from Agoho ☎ 088 387 9037, ⊛ hillside.agoho.ph. Beyond the sigh-triggering views of White Island from the deck, the advantages of staying at this three-room pad in the hills are twofold: first the cooler temperatures, but also the fabulous welcome from Kalen, the Neapolitan owner who makes the island's best brick-oven pizzas (P220–380). Rooms are either in native cottages or smarter doubles. Huts P800, doubles P1200
★ **Volcan Beach Eco Retreat & Dive Resort** Naasag ☎ 088 387 9551, ⊛ camiguinvolcanbeach.com. Though the real standouts at this German-run resort are the bungalows, tropical garden strung with hammocks and great dive centre, the house reef, bamboo yoga deck, and spectacular sunsets are just as welcome. Bungalows P2000

SURIGAO

The busy capital of the province of Surigao del Norte, **SURIGAO** provides nothing more than a jumping-off point for the picture-postcard island of **Siargao**. It's a compact place and easy to negotiate on foot: Rizal Street runs from north to south, while at the northern end is the central plaza, where you'll find a couple of banks with ATMs and fast-food restaurants.

ARRIVAL AND DEPARTURE

By plane The airport is 5km out of town. There are daily flights to Cebu (2 daily; 45min) with Cebu Pacific.
By bus The bus terminal is 4km west of the city. Buses run hourly between 6am and 10pm to Butuan (2hr), where you can connect to Cagayan de Oro or Balingoan (for Camiguin). There are also faster a/c minibuses until 7pm.
By ferry The wharf is at the southern edge of Navarro Street; take a tricycle from here to the city centre. There are daily ferries (4hr) between Surigao and Dapa on Siargao, as well as daily fast crafts (2hr 30min).

ACCOMMODATION

Hotel Tavern Borromeo St ☎ 086 231 7300. Close to the ferry terminal, this is a good place to try if you get stuck here, with comfy a/c rooms, sea views and free breakfast. Doubles P1900
Le Chard Place Km4, National Highway ☎ 0947 890 8891. With a fair amount of designer swagger to it – proof is in the bold orange, green and purple rooms and

the pop art on the walls – this conveniently located B&B manages to squeeze in plenty of goodies. There's free breakfast and free airport transfers, 24hr security, parking and a generator (for those all too common blackouts). Doubles P920

SIARGAO

Off the northeastern tip of Mindanao lies the teardrop-shaped island of **Siargao**, with its secluded white-sand beaches and dramatic coves and lagoons. Siargao has got everything, with a typically tropical coastal landscape of palm trees and dazzling seas, and a lush hinterland of small *barangays* and coconut groves. Some of the first tourists here were **surfers**, who discovered a break at Tuason Point that was so good they called it **Cloud 9**. In recent years, word of mouth has brought an increasing number of surfers from around the world, and today "Crowd 9" is the bona fide capital of surfing in the Philippines. That's led to a boom in seaside resorts along the Pacific coast, concentrated around the island's friendly little capital of **GENERAL LUNA**, known as GL. The Cloud 9 break (see box below) is less than 2km north of GL, an easy *habal-habal* (motorbike taxi) or tricycle ride away (P20).

ON CLOUD 9

The Philippines is not a destination at the forefront of most surfers' minds, although enthusiasts have been riding waves here since the 1960s. Thanks to its location on the Pacific typhoon belt, the country is home to some of the world's greatest swells. The acclaimed reef break **Cloud 9**, with its famed hollow barrel, gained fame in the late 1980s and is today considered one of the world's top surfing waves. It is the site of the annual **Siargao Cup**, an international surfing competition held in late September that draws crowds from all over the globe who come to watch the action from the break's permanent wooden spectator pavilion. The peak surf season is September and October, while things tend to slow down at the end of the year; beginners will find the weaker surf in June and July more manageable.

WHAT TO SEE AND DO

Kayaking is a great way to explore, paddling through mangrove swamps or into hidden coral bays (P250–400/hr). You can also hire a *bangka* to do some serious **island-hopping**, or rent a motorbike for the day and tootle up the dusty coastal road to Alegria and Burgos at the island's northernmost tip, visiting beaches that few travellers see. Don't miss a day-trip to the Dako, Guyam and Naked islands, with superb snorkelling. *Buddha's* (see below) is the best place to organize things, or just ask around.

Surfing remains the main draw, however; you can rent equipment (board rental P750–1000/day) from the resorts, and lessons cost about P400 an hour.

ARRIVAL AND DEPARTURE

By plane Cebu Pacific flies between Siargao and Cebu (1–2 daily; 1hr).
By ferry There are daily ferries (4hr) between Surigao and Dapa, as well as daily fast crafts (2hr 30min).

GETTING AROUND

There are jeepneys between Dapa and GL, but you're much better off getting a ride on a *habal-habal* (motorbike taxi; P100) or arranging pier/airport pick-up through your accommodation (P200–300). The bumpy roads here mean motorbikes are the best way of getting around, and they're widely available for rent (P450/day).

ACCOMMODATION, EATING AND DRINKING

Room prices increase exponentially during the surfing competitions; ask about long-term discounts.
★**Buddha's Surf Resort** At the northern edge of GL ☎0977 802 2144, ⟨w⟩siargaosurf.com. Run by long-term English expat Ashley Charles, *Buddha's* is the beating heart of GL's surf scene, with thatched-roof a/c rooms kitted out with flatscreen TVs, water coolers and balconies. On some nights, this fabulously funky surfers' retreat may resemble an overflowing beer garden, but that's just because of its ace acoustic gigs and burger nights. For all manner of lessons and rentals look no further. Doubles P2500
Harana Surf Resort Midway between GL and Cloud 9 ☎0998 849 5461, ⟨w⟩haranasurf.com. One of the newest surf camps on the strip, with a confident open-plan design, beachfront deck and bespoke surf art. The rooms come in a variety of doubles, while the twelve-bed dorm – or "community hut" – is the nicest on the island. Top it off with appealing hammocks, bean bags and a great cocktail bar, and you're in business. Dorms P700, doubles P2800

8

Kermit Surf Resort 300m off the main GL beach road ☎ 0917 655 0548, ⓦ kermitsiargao.com. In a head-to-head competition with *Buddha's* for the best backpackers in town, this well-run place has a/c and fan cottages, as well as backpacker rooms with shared bathroom. The real draw is its hangout area, with hammocks, ping-pong table, library and sociable bar. Doubles P950, cottages P1400

Paglaom Hostel 200m from *Kermit Surf Resort* ☎ 0999 990 0000, ⓦ paglaomhostel.com. The last genuine budget deal in town, this sociable hostel is justifiably popular with surfers for its free-to-use kitchen, lockers and hangout area. The bunk beds have mosquito nets, and all toilets and showers are shared. Minimum three-night stay in high season. Dorms P300

DIRECTORY

Banks and exchange There is an ATM in Dapa and several places accept credit cards.

Internet access Plenty of resorts have wi-fi and there's internet access in Dapa, GL and Cloud 9 (P30/hr).

8

Palawan

Tourism is becoming increasingly popular on the long, sword-shaped island of **Palawan** to the southwest of Luzon, thanks in part to various world media outlets awarding it accolades such as "Most Beautiful Island in the World" and "World's Best Beach Destination" (**El Nido**). And they're not wrong. Palawan is home to some of the most jaw-dropping scenery – soft powdery beaches, brilliant blue lagoons and razor-sharp limestone cliffs that rise from crystal-clear water. The main tourist spots may be getting crowded, but offshore there's always something new to explore. Palawan province encompasses 1780 islands and islets, many of which are surrounded by a coral shelf that acts as an enormous feeding ground and nursery for marine life. It is sometimes said that Palawan's **Tubbataha Reef** is so ecologically important that, if it dies, the Philippines will perish too. If you're looking for varied and challenging diving, you won't find better anywhere in the world, but there's also plenty to keep non-divers happy.

The capital and main gateway, **Puerto Princesa**, makes a good starting point for exploring the northern half of the island, which is where all the main tourist attractions are. A typical journey through Palawan might take you from Puerto Princesa north to **Honda Bay** and the **Underground River at Sabang**, then onwards up the coast to **Port Barton**, and **El Nido**, before heading across to **Busuanga** and the rest of the Calamian Islands. The southern half of Palawan, from Puerto Princesa downwards, is relatively unexplored, one reason being that during the wet season the southern roads become almost impassable.

PUERTO PRINCESA

Known as "The City in the Forest" or the "City of the Living God", **PUERTO PRINCESA** is the provincial capital and only major town in Palawan. It's the gateway to the beaches, islands and coral reefs of the north. It does, however, have a few good sights of its own, a lively bay area, a handful of exceptionally good restaurants, and is the administrative centre of the island – stock up on cash and arrange Underground River permits while you're here. It also prides itself on being clean and green: seventy percent of it is covered by trees, it's carbon neutral and has enforced fines for littering.

ARRIVAL AND DEPARTURE

By plane The airport is at the eastern end of Rizal Ave, the main drag, within walking distance of most accommodation. Though there are always tricycles waiting (P50), it's cheaper to flag one down outside. At the time of writing, finishing touches were being completed to expand it into Puerto Princesa International Airport.

Destinations Air Asia, Cebu Pacific and Philippine Airlines fly to Manila (12 daily; 1hr 20min). Air Asia and Cebu Pacific also fly to Cebu (2 daily; 1hr 10min).

By bus, van and jeepney All depart from the San José terminal 7km north of the centre. A multi-cab to the centre of town will set you back P15, a tricycle P120. Departures to all points north are most frequent in the early mornings; the times here are guidelines only. Vans are typically 25 percent quicker than buses, leave more frequently and are easier for travellers, but are more expensive, and often less comfortable. Daytripper Palawan (☎ 0917 848 8755, ⓦ daytripperpalawan.com) is a good choice, and is well worth the extra money. They have several daily services from Puerto Princesa to El Nido (P850–950).

Destinations El Nido (10 daily; 6–8hr); Port Barton (5 daily from 7.30am; 3hr); Sabang (8 daily, 6.30am–3pm; 2hr 30min).

By ferry The pier is at the eastern end of Malvar St, a short walk to Rizal Ave. 2GO operates a Puerto Princesa–Coron–Manila service (Sat midnight; 14hr to Coron, 30hr to Manila).

INFORMATION

Tourist information The tourist office (Mon–Fri 9am–5pm; ☎ 048 433 2968, ⓦ visitpuertoprincesa.com) is in the Provincial Capitol Building on Rizal Ave. They have information on the rest of Palawan. There is also a tourist office at airport arrivals (☎ 048 434 4211), which is open for inbound flights.

Tours Plenty of tour companies on Rizal Ave offer day-trips to Honda Bay (P1300); the standard rate for a day-trip to the Underground River is P1500/person. Corazon Travel (☎ 048 433 0508, ⓦ corazontravelandtours.com) is a professional and reputable choice.

ACCOMMODATION

Hibiscus Garden Inn Manalo Extension ☎ 048 434 1273, ⓦ puertoprincesahotel.com. Warmly decorated spacious rooms set around a leafy garden, with a/c, cable TV and fridges. Queen (P2300) and King (P2800) rooms have larger beds and private gardens. Doubles P1800

★**Puerto Pension** 35 Malvar St ☎ 048 433 4148 or ☎ 0917 836 6316, ⓦ puertopension.com. Located at the back of the lively Bay Walk, this triple-decker nipa hut-style building is set in a lush tropical garden. The cosy fan or a/c rooms all have mini fridges and cable TVs, and are decorated with local Palawan artwork. There's also a lovely rooftop restaurant with spectacular bay views and free use of an outdoor hot tub in the evenings. Free wi-fi. Doubles P1946

★**Purple Fountain Inn** 269 Manalo Extension ☎ 048 434 2430 or ☎ 0917 573 2772, ⓦ purplefountaininn.com.ph. Set around a leafy courtyard with a central purple fountain, this quirky inn offers brightly coloured kitsch rooms with stained-glass windows and fun artwork. All have a/c, quality wooden furniture, TVs and hot water. It also has an excellent restaurant – the *White Fence Café*. Free wi-fi. Doubles P1800

EATING AND DRINKING

★**Haim Chicken Inatô** 294 Manalo Extension. Despite sounding like a fast-food chicken chain, this family-run restaurant serves quality local Filipino dishes. Dine on plates such as grilled tuna belly (P175), *Ginataang ubod ng rattan* (young rattan vine with coconut milk and small fish; P117) and vegetable curry (P160). Daily 10am–10pm.

Ima's Gulay Bar 46 Fernandez St. Ima rustles up tasty dishes in the little kitchen at the back of this healthy

vegetarian place with vegan options. The tofu and broccoli with sweet-and-sour sauce is a bestseller (P90); healthy shakes (P60), too. Mon–Thurs & Sun 11am–9pm, Fri 11am–3pm, Sat 6.30–9pm.

★**KaLui** 369 Rizal Ave. This atmospheric restaurant, where everyone goes barefoot and waiters are dressed as indigenous tribes people, is one of the most popular in the city (reservations essential for dinner). Daily set meals (P625 for two) are built around either seafood or meat and come with salad, sweet potato fries and a small portion of fresh, raw seaweed. Mon–Sat 11am–2pm & 6–11pm.

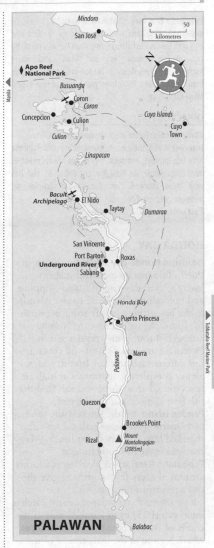

PALAWAN

Palaweño Brewery 28 Manalo St ☎ 048 725 6950 or ☎ 097 559 9109, ✆ palawenobrewery.com. The first and only craft brewery in Palawan, this small bar was set up by two Filipina women, Aya and Malu, and offers microbrewery tours. Beers (P170) use indigenous flavours from Palawan, and P400 buys you a tray of four types. Mon–Sat 1–9pm.

DIRECTORY

Banks All major banks are at the heart of Rizal Ave.
Internet Most of the inns and pensions in Puerto Princesa have free internet, although they're not always reliable. *Itoy's Coffee House*, on Rizal Ave, cnr Baltan St, also has wi-fi (Mon–Thurs & Sun 6am–11pm, Fri–Sat till midnight), and good coffees.
Post office Burgos St, cnr Rizal Ave.

HONDA BAY

Beautiful **Honda Bay** sits 10km north of Puerto Princesa by road and makes a lovely relaxed day-trip of island-hopping and snorkelling. There are twelve islands in the bay, although only some are open to visitors. Most tours (which can be arranged through any travel agent in Puerto for around P1300) will cover a few different islands. **Luli Island**, which almost completely disappears at high tide, has a special area where you can feed the fish (not allowed out on the reef), **Pandan Island** has the finest white sand and **Cowrie Island** has small cabanas and thatched huts to relax in for lunch. Many tours also take in snorkelling at **Tubbataha Reef**, where floating platforms are moved every few months to give the reef a rest from tourism.

If you want to go independently, catch a multi-cab (P25) from Rizal Avenue at the corner of Burgos Street to **Santa Lourdes wharf**. Sign in at the little tourist office and arrange a *bangka* (last departure at 2.30pm), which will cost P1300–1500. There's a P21 terminal fee, and all islands ask visitors to pay a small fee (P25–50).

SABANG AND THE UNDERGROUND RIVER

The **Underground River**, or, to give it its proper name, **Puerto Princesa Subterranean River National Park**, is another UNESCO World Heritage Site and top of the list of wonders for most visitors to central Palawan. One of the longest underground rivers in the world, it meanders for more than 8km through a bewildering array of caverns, chambers and pools, passing stalactites, stalagmites, columns and thousands of bats. The formations are made even more eerie on your ride through by the shadows cast by the boatmen's lamp. An audioguide will give you a rundown of the history and the science as you go, although its suggestions as to what the rocks resemble can sometimes be extremely far-fetched.

Boat trips from Sabang wharf start daily from 8am and the last boat leaves at 3.30pm. Since the site was recognized as one of the "new Seven Wonders of Nature" in 2012, it has become more popular than ever, and the daily quota of 900 visitors is reached every day during peak season. In order to help control visitor numbers you have to arrange your permit (P250) in Puerto Princesa at least one day in advance of your visit. If you join an organized tour this will be done for you, but if not it's easy enough to arrange by visiting the park office in the City Coliseum in San Pedro, Puerto Princesa (☎ 048 433 2983). If you don't pre-arrange a permit, local agents in Sabang (try Green Verde travel centre) can arrange for a visit until 8pm the day before you want to go. The permit will specify the time you need to report to Sabang wharf for the twenty-minute *bangka* ride (around P700 for up to six guests) to the cave. It's easiest to secure a permit for 8am–9am (before the day-trippers arrive), but even if you are issued a different time you can just turn up at the wharf with your permit, pay the P40 terminal fee, and they'll put you on the next boat with space.

Afterwards, if you're feeling energetic, you can hike back from the mouth of the river to **Sabang**, a 5km trip through lush scenery. When you arrive at the park, look out for the famous resident monitor lizards (*bayawak*) and monkeys. The wonders of the Underground River aside, Sabang has a beautiful stretch of beach and is becoming an increasingly popular beach resort in its own right. As well as sunbathing and swimming (pay attention to the flags, though, as currents can be strong), there's an 800m zipline at the far eastern end of the beach (P350) (plus another one 30min away at Ugong Rock), mangrove boat trips (P250; 45min) and jungle trekking (P200/person). Ask at Green Verde travel centre (☎0926 230 9137) for information. Or if this all sounds like too much, there are numerous massage shacks (P500/hr) dotted along the beach.

ARRIVAL AND DEPARTURE

By bus, van and jeepney They make daily morning trips (2–3hr) from the San José terminal in Puerto to Sabang, the jumping-off point for the Underground River. The last departure from Sabang to Puerto is at 6pm (with Lexxus minivans ⓦlexxusshuttle.com), although most services leave in the morning. For El Nido, catch a jeepney to the junction at Salvacion (7am, 10am, noon & 2pm), from where you can change for El Nido services. You can expedite this connection by purchasing a van seat in advance through Lexxus, near the wharf.

Bangkas Unscheduled *bangkas* sometimes do the Sabang–Port Barton route (2hr 30min; P1200/person or P7200 for the whole boat), and might even continue on to El Nido (9hr) if there's demand – ask at the Green Verde travel centre.

ACCOMMODATION AND EATING

There are a growing number of places to stay on Sabang, most aimed at backpackers. All the cheapies only have electricity from around 6 to 11pm and cold-water showers.

Blue Bamboo Restaurant and Sunbird Cottages A 15min walk west from the wharf ☎0910 797 0038. Owned by friendly local Lorena, this place has cottages set up the hillside and is perfect for those looking to escape it all (if you don't mind not being on the beach). The budget backpacker rooms are very simple, but great value, while the family rooms (P1200) are some of the nicest in Sabang (aside from the resorts) and have great views over the bay. The cottages at the front with the best views cost slightly more (P800). Doubles P600

Green Verde Towards the middle of the beach ☎0910 978 4539. Small, clean and simple beach-facing huts, with fans and balconies. The airy restaurant has some good budget meals including spiced ginger pork (P175) and lemongrass tuna (P175). They also have a helpful travel service. Doubles P600

★ **Tangay Tarabidan** This simple, excellent restaurant serves some of the best food in Sabang. They specialize in vegetarian and halal food, although they have lots of meat and fish dishes too. Plates include tofu steak with teriyaki ginger (P130), *aloo gobi masala* (P185) and pad thai (P195). Mon–Thurs & Sun 7am–10pm, Fri 7am–5pm, Sat 6–10pm.

Thalets Beach Cottages East of *Green Verde* ☎0916 237 9599. Basic beach-facing nipa huts with private balconies, bamboo floors and mosquito nets. They also have a popular restaurant. Doubles P500

PORT BARTON AND AROUND

On the northwest coast of Palawan, roughly halfway between Puerto Princesa and El Nido, **Port Barton** has become something of a travellers' rest stop in recent years. There are several white-sand islands in the bay, as well as some excellent snorkelling spots. Port Barton itself is little more than a village, with unpaved roads, and electricity only in the evenings. It has a glorious stretch of beach that is home to half a dozen resorts. Minivans will drop you at the village office as soon as you arrive, so you can register and pay your P50 environmental fee. If going on any island-hopping excursions, remember to take your receipt with you. About 15km north along a rough coastal road from Port Barton is the sleepy fishing village of **San Vicente**, which has a market and a pier where *bangkas* can be chartered to **Long Beach**, an undeveloped (for now) 14km stretch of stunning sand that ranks as one of the most extraordinary beaches in the country. The marvellous beaches around here make a fantastic day-trip. There's a tourist assistance centre (daily 8am–5pm) midway along the beach. Port Barton and San Vicente may not remain untouched for long – an international airport is being built, but with no scheduled completion date.

ARRIVAL AND DEPARTURE

By jeepney Jeepneys leave by *Ayette's Bamboo House*. You can change at Roxas for El Nido. Roxas (daily 7.30am; 1hr); Nido (daily 9am; 5hr); Puerto Princesa (daily 9am; 2hr).

By van Recaro vans will pick up from accommodation and go to Puerto Princesa (daily 6am, 8am, 9am, 11am, 2pm, 4pm; 2hr) and El Nido (daily 8am, 1pm; 5hr). Ask your accommodation to reserve a space for you the day before.

ACCOMMODATION

Internet access is available in the common areas of some of the resorts, but is not very reliable.

8

Ausan Beach Front Cottages Middle of the beach ☎ 0926 707 4154, ⊛ ausanbeachfront.com. Wooden cottages or basic nipa huts, some with colourful murals on the walls and balconies. They are also one of the few places here with a/c rooms (P1950). The treehouse room is particularly popular, but has no private bathroom (P1550). Doubles P1250

Deep Moon Resort Far northern end of the beach ☎ 0919 322 3054. Swiss-style nipa huts right on the beach front with a lovely polished-wood reception area. Those on a budget should ask for one at the back without a sea view (P900). Doubles P1200

Greenviews Resort At the far southern end of the beach ☎ 0929 268 5333, ⊛ palawandg.clara.net. Rustic yet sturdy huts with balconies and modern private bathrooms, set around a tranquil garden. There's also a rooftop restaurant, a separate outdoor lounge area with nightly live music, and free wi-fi. Doubles P1700

EATING

Greenviews Restaurant At the far southern end of the beach, *Greenviews Resort* serves up some of the best food in town, as owner Tina used to cook for presidents and royalty. Chilli con carne (P260). Daily 7am–midnight.

Jambalaya This welcoming Cajun-style café is situated halfway up the beach and is one of the few restaurants not located at the resorts. Its curries (P400) and fish (P400) are overpriced, but its eponymous dish (P270), a Louisiana-style mix of spicy rice, fresh fish and veg, is a bestseller. Daily 8am–9pm.

EL NIDO AND THE BACUIT ARCHIPELAGO

In the far northwest of Palawan is the small coastal town of **EL NIDO**, departure point for excursions to the innumerable islands of the **BACUIT ARCHIPELAGO**, undoubtedly one of the highlights of any trip to the Philippines. This is spectacular limestone-island country, with jaw-dropping formations rising from the sea everywhere you look. These iconic karst cliffs, with their fearsomely jagged rocky outcrops, are believed to have been formed over sixty million years ago, emerging from the sea as a result of India colliding with mainland Asia. Weathering and erosion have produced deep crevices, caves, underground rivers and sinkholes in endlessly strange and wonderful permutations that were allegedly the inspiration for Alex Garland's novel *The Beach*. The result is one of the most

beautiful island seascapes on earth.
El Nido town itself is a bit chaotic and polluted, so many travellers are now heading to the more laidback areas on either side – **Corong Corong** and **Caalan Beach**. Advance reservations are essential if you're on a budget, and especially at Christmas, New Year and Chinese New Year. Prices for all-day island-hopping *bangka* trips are set by the local government and cost P1200–1400 per person depending on the islands visited, plus a P200 ecotourism development fee valid for ten days. There are numerous places offering trips; one of the best is the *El Nido Boutique and Artcafé*.

ARRIVAL AND DEPARTURE

By plane The town is a 6km tricycle ride (P200) from the airport. AirSWIFT (⊛ air-swift.com) flies between Manila and El Nido (4 daily; 1hr 15min), and tickets can be booked online. A 10kg luggage allowance is only included for Premium or Value fares.

By ferry Daily fast-craft ferries (4hr) operated by Montenegro Lines leave for Coron at 6am and cost P1760. Arrange your ticket at least one day in advance from one of the many operators in town or *El Nido Boutique and Artcafé*.

By bangka Daily morning *bangkas* also leave for Coron at 8am and cost P1500 including lunch. However, as they take 8–9hr and are very weather dependent, it's not worth it for the few hundred pesos you'll save.

By bus and van The bus and van "terminal" is in Corong Corong, a 20min walk or P50 tricycle ride from El Nido town. There's a local market here where you can stock up on supplies for your journey. There are regular (P380) and a/c (P480) buses to Puerto Princesa (via Taytay and Roxas) with Roro and Cherry (more comfortable), which take around eight hours. Faster and more expensive, but often more cramped vans (6hr; P700–800) also leave throughout the day. Palawan Daytripper (☎ 0917 848 8755, ⊛ daytripperpalawan.com) is the comfortable alternative. There are more bus and van services in the mornings and last trips leave at 9pm. For Port Barton change in Roxas, and for Sabang jump off at the Salvacion turn-off.

INFORMATION

Tourist information The Municipal Tourist Office (daily 8am–5pm; ☎ 0917 841 7771, ⊛ elnidotourism.com) is near the church; they provide maps, information on the local area and accommodation. *El Nido Boutique and Artcafé* (⊛ elnidoboutiqueandartcafe.com) on Calle Serena is a better resource for tourist information and you can make travel arrangements here.

ACCOMMODATION

Lally and Abet Beach Cottages Northern end of town on the shore, off Calle Hama ☏ 0917 850 2948 or ☏ 02 455 5656, ⓦ lallyandabet.com. Long-established, well-run resort with 35 a/c rooms and lovely wooden cottages (P2400–4500). Doubles P1800

MaryGold Beachfront Inn Calle Hama ☏ 0917 642 7722, ⓦ mgelnido.com. Charming beachfront accommodation with spotless country-cottage and seaside-themed rooms. The more expensive rooms are at the front, with sea views and balconies (P2950). Doubles P2350

★ **Morning Walsh Resort** ☏ 0946 037 5394 or ☏ 0999 548 4336, ⓔ morningwalsh@yahoo.com. A private home, owned by the lovely Nelma, in the middle of laidback Corong Corong Beach. The ten rooms are spacious, individually decorated, and have beautifully carved wooden furniture, private bathrooms and a/c. There's also a large garden filled with quirky sculptures, beachside massage huts, and kayaks for rent. Doubles P2000

★ **Spin Designer Hostel** Cnr Balinsasayaw Rd and Calle Real ☏ 0917 566 7746, ⓦ spinhostel.com. Trendy backpackers' hostel with mixed dorms, female dorms and single or twin privates (P3000). There's also a lounge area with cable TV, basic kitchen equipment for use, self-service laundry and free breakfast. Dorms P1000

EATING AND DRINKING

There's a wide array of places to eat, serving everything from simple Filipino classics to seafood and international cuisine.

Jerace Grill Calle Rizal. Right on the beachfront, this loud and lively restaurant is popular with locals and travellers, and serves up classic Filipino dishes, as well as excellent fresh seafood. Choose your catch of the day and watch it being grilled right in front of you on the shore. Grilled fish comes served with rice and vegetables (P200 depending on the size). Daily 2–11pm.

★ **Lolo Banana** The Bazaar, Calle Rizal. Set in a sandy courtyard, lined with stalls and tropical plants, this cool al-fresco bar and restaurant serves everything from panini (P200) to tapas (P70) and fajitas (P180). Daily 2–11pm.

Odessa Mama Calle Hama. This Ukrainian restaurant is not something you'd expect to find in El Nido, yet its delicious home cooking is popular with travellers, evident from the notes scrawled across the walls. Try the *varenyky* (dumplings stuffed with cottage cheese and honey, P200) and classic *borscht* (red beetroot soup, P150). Daily 7am–11pm.

Purno Bravo Pizza Hauz Calle Real. If you're craving good Italian-style pizza, this is the place to come. Chairs and tables are set around a large wood-fired oven. Try their signature El Nido pizza (P390). They also serve good pastas (P230). Daily 11am–11pm.

Sava Bar In the middle of the beach. This stylish beach bar is one of the liveliest on the beachfront and has a good range of cocktails (P300). Daily 4pm–2am.

★ **V and V Bagel** Calle Hama. This French-owned café serves excellent home-made filled bagels, made to an authentic New York recipe (P240). They also serve giant burgers (P265), iced coffees (P150) and home-made cakes. Daily 7.30am–8.30pm.

DIRECTORY

Banks There are two ATMs in El Nido, one outside the Municipal Hall and the other at the BPI Bank on Calle Real.

Police Calle Hama (daily 24hr; ☏ 0921 255 6368).

THE CALAMIAN ISLANDS

Access to the beautiful Calamian Islands, the largest of which is **Busuanga**, followed in size by **Culion** (where there's spectacular snorkelling) and **Coron**, is through the increasingly popular little fishing port of **CORON TOWN**, which, confusingly, is on Busuanga, not Coron.

Twenty minutes by boat from Coron Town, you'll reach **Coron Island**, surrounded by towering limestone cliffs and coral reefs. Regardless of whether you also plan to dive the area's famous wrecks, you'll find dozens of perfect little coves, hidden in the folds of the mountains, to explore. Tribes, including the Tagbanua, still live in the interior and own much of the land here, including the island's volcanic **Kayangan Lake**, a great place to swim and snorkel. You could spend a lifetime on Coron and still not get to see every hot spring, hidden lake or pristine cove.

Busuanga Island (Coron Town)

Coron Town is home to Busuanga's most backpacker-friendly resorts, and is the place to arrange *bangkas* for island trips (there's no beach in town). Apart from a couple of more expensive resorts dotted around the island, the rest of Busuanga is very rural, with limited electricity and, occasionally, patchy cell-phone coverage. For breathtaking views of the area, climb the 722 steps up to Mount Tapyas in time for sunset, before heading to the 36°C **Maquinit Hot**

Springs (daily 8am–8pm; P150). A fun way to explore the region is to rent a motorbike or hop on a bus from the market to take you west along the **south Busuanga coast** to the villages of Concepcion, Salvacion and Old Busuanga. The presence of several sunken Japanese World War II ships in the bays near Coron Town has made it a point of pilgrimage for **wreck divers**, and the rest of the Calamians have plenty to occupy island-hoppers and regular divers. Plenty of places in town offer island-hopping trips (around P1500, depending on what you want to do), although eco- and socially responsible *Calamines Expeditions & Ecotours* (ⓦcorongaleri.com.ph) are one of the best. They offer day tours as cheap as P650, as well as more adventurous itineraries, including overnight trips.

ARRIVAL AND DEPARTURE

By plane The airport is 30min by van/jeepney (P150) from Coron Town. All the airlines have offices in town, and there are also several travel agencies, including Calamian Islands Travel and Tours on Rosario St.

Destinations Cebu Pacific and Philippine Airlines fly to Manila (9 daily; 1hr). Cebu Pacific also has a flight to Cebu (daily; 1hr 40min).

By ferry Montenegro Lines have a fast craft from Coron Town to El Nido, making travel between the two a lot easier (noon; 3hr 30min; P1760). The 2GO Manila–Coron ferry service leaves Manila at 4pm on Fri, arriving in Coron at 6am on Sat morning; it departs 1hr later for Puerto Princesa, arriving at 9pm on Sat. On the way back, it leaves Puerto at midnight on Sat night/Sun morning, stopping off in Coron at 2pm on Sun, leaving at 3.30pm, and arrives in Manila at 5.30am on Mon morning.

By bangka There is one daily scheduled *bangka* to El Nido (9am; 9hr; around P1500 including lunch), bookable through resorts. With the new ferry service, however, it's not worth taking.

ACCOMMODATION

Coron Village Lodge Busuanga Rd/National Highway ☎0928 202 0819 or ☎0916 420 0252, ⓦcoronvillagelodge .com. A bamboo-fronted lodge, surrounded by lush tropical plants, this former family home has 25 clean and simple rooms with a/c and private bathrooms. There's also a rooftop bar and restaurant. Doubles P950

★**KokusNuss Resort** Busuanga Rd/National Highway, Barangay 6 ☎0919 776 9544 or ☎0919 448 7879, ⓦkokosnuss.info. The first accommodation as you approach Coron Town from the airport, 1km before the town. Accommodation is set around a lovely garden area with hammocks and a small pool. Rooms range from lovely thatched bungalows with a/c (P1980) to eco-rooms with solar-heated showers (P1900) and cave-style rooms with fans. Construction is under way for a range of luxury rooms. Doubles P1740

Marley's Guesthouse Busuanga Rd/National Highway ☎0929 772 5559, ⓦmarleyguesthouse .wixsite.com/marleysguesthouse. A real backpacker hangout, inspired by the owner's love of reggae and Bob Marley, this place has simple fan double rooms with shared bathrooms (some with windows, P500). There's also a communal kitchen, lounge and funky al-fresco bar. Doubles P400

EATING AND DRINKING

★**Brujita** Busuanga Rd/National Highway. Specializing in vegetarian dishes, this is one of the best restaurants in town – arrive early to get a table. The menu includes vegetable curry with coconut milk and chickpea curry with mung beans (P160). It's a hit with meat and seafood eaters too, with plenty of chicken dishes (P190) and fresh fish. Daily 9am–10pm.

Trattoria Altrove Rosario St. This breezy top-floor restaurant has a romantic air and some of the best Italian food you'll find anywhere in the Philippines. The giant thin-crust pizzas (P380–645) are particularly popular. Daily 5–10pm.

DIRECTORY

Banks BPI, Allied Bank and Landbank all have ATMs. There's also a Western Union on Real St. You can change US$ at Bonito Money Changer on Rizal Ave near the junction with Valencia St.

BUDDHA TOOTH RELIC TEMPLE, CHINATOWN

Singapore

HIGHLIGHTS

❶ **Chinatown** Traditional shophouses, fiery red temples and a sprinkling of old-school shops and restaurants. **See p.681**

❷ **Little India** Ornate temples pepper this most atmospheric of Singapore's old districts. **See p.684**

❸ **The Botanic Gardens** Of historic and scientific importance, these gardens boast a fabulous orchid collection and a mini-jungle. **See p.689**

❹ **Night Safari** The nocturnal wing of the zoo lets you get up close and personal with animals in a dimly lit mock twilight. **See p.698**

❺ **Sentosa** A theme-park island that also has beaches and a historic fort. **See p.699**

HIGHLIGHTS ARE MARKED ON THE MAP ON P.673

ROUGH COSTS

Daily budget Basic US$40/Occasional treat US$75

Drink Tiger beer (630ml) US$5

Food Chicken rice US$5

Hostel/budget hotel US$15–30/US$90

Travel Bus and MRT: peak fare on standard services US$2; taxi: airport to downtown US$25

FACT FILE

Population 5.6 million

Languages English, Malay, Mandarin and Tamil

Religions Buddhism, Taoism, Islam, Christianity, Hinduism, Sikhism

Currency Singapore dollar (S$)

International phone code ☎ + 65

Time zone GMT + 8hr

9

Introduction

Linked by two bridges to the southern tip of Malaysia, the vibrant city-state of Singapore makes a gentle gateway for many first-time travellers to Asia, providing Western standards of comfort alongside a taste of Chinese, Malay and Indian cultures. Its downtown areas are dense with towering skyscrapers and gleaming shopping malls, yet the island retains an abundance of nature reserves and lush, tropical greenery.

Singapore is an economically advanced nation, although that success has been achieved via a top-down, centralized approach, which makes the place feel like one of the most micromanaged on Earth: regulations extend to matters as petty as not flushing a public toilet. The government has superficially loosened its grip over the past twenty years; the most obvious spin-off of this for visitors is the island's thriving **arts scene**, in which the state invests heavily.

Although the city is a beacon of modernization and urban planning, its old quarters – **Chinatown**, the **Colonial District** and especially **Little India** – still retain some of their original character. Much of the country's appeal springs from its multicultural residents, who are 74 percent Chinese, thirteen percent Malay, and nine percent Indian. This is also a highly globalized city, with a visible expat community and a significant short-term migrant workforce employed in sectors like construction.

CHRONOLOGY

Third century AD The earliest known mention of Singapore is a Chinese reference to Pu-luo-chung, or "island at the end of a peninsula".

WHEN TO GO

Singapore is just 136km north of the equator, which means that you should be prepared for a hot and sticky time whenever you go; daytime **temperatures** peak around 32°C throughout the year. November, December and January are usually the coolest and wettest months, but rain can fall all year round.

Eleventh century The tiny island is known as "Singa Pura" (Lion City) – according to legend because a prince mistook a local animal for a lion.

Late thirteenth century Marco Polo reports seeing a place called Chiamassie, possibly Singapore, which was known locally as Temasek – "sea town" – and was a minor trading outpost of the Sumatran Srivijaya Empire.

c.1390 A Sumatran prince, Paramesvara, flees to present-day Singapore, murders his host and rules the island until a Javanese offensive forces him to flee north to the Peninsula. He and his son, Iskandar Shah, found the Melaka Sultanate.

1613 A Portuguese account describes the razing of an unnamed Malay outpost at the mouth of Sungei Johor, an event that marks the beginning of two centuries of historical limbo for Singapore.

1819 Thomas Stamford Raffles, lieutenant-governor of Bencoolen (in Sumatra), arrives in Singapore to establish a British trading station.

1822 Raffles draws up the demarcation lines that divide present-day Singapore. South of the Singapore River is earmarked for the Chinese; the commercial district is established on a filled-in swamp at the mouth of the river; and Muslims settle around the Sultan's Palace in today's Kampong Glam.

1824 Singapore is ceded outright to the British, and the island's population reaches ten thousand as Malays, Chinese, Indians and Europeans arrive in search of work.

1826 The fledgling state unites with Penang and Malacca (Meleka; also under British rule) to form the Straits Settlements.

1860 The population reaches eighty thousand. Arabs, Indians, Javanese and Bugis arrive, but most populous of all are the Chinese from the southern provinces of China.

1877 Henry Ridley, director of the Botanic Gardens, introduces the rubber plant into Southeast Asia; Singapore becomes the world centre of rubber exporting, helped as British control of the Malay Peninsula expands, completed in 1913.

1887 The Armenian Sarkies brothers open the *Raffles Hotel*. It becomes the social hub of a booming and cosmopolitan Singapore.

1926 The pro-independence Singapore Malay Union is established.

1942–45 Singapore is occupied by the Japanese during World War II. Thousands of civilians are executed in vicious anti-Chinese purges and Europeans are either herded into Changi Prison, or marched up the Peninsula to work on Thailand's infamous "Death Railway".

1945 Singapore returns to British control.

May 1959 The People's Action Party (PAP), led by Cambridge law graduate Lee Kuan Yew, wins 43 of the 51 seats for the new legislative assembly, which Britain had agreed to two years earlier. Lee becomes Singapore's first prime minister.

1963 Singapore, Sarawak and British North Borneo (now Sabah) join with independent Malaya to form a new country, the Federation of Malaysia.

August 9, 1965 After falling out with Kuala Lumpur, Singapore leaves Malaysia – described by Lee Kuan Yew as "a moment of anguish" – and becomes independent.

1970s Singapore begins to transform into an Asian economic heavyweight, but at the price of heavy-handed state control: the media is censored, the trade unions are co-opted and political opponents suppressed.

1990 Lee retires and is succeeded as prime minister by Goh Chok Tong; Lee remains senior minister.

1997 The Asian economic crisis engulfs Southeast Asia, Singapore included.

2004 Lee Hsien Loong, son of Lee Kuan Yew, becomes prime minister.

September 2008 Singapore hosts its first Formula One night-time Grand Prix.

February 2010 The first of the city-state's two casinos opens on Sentosa Island.

May 2011 Singapore's opposition parties enjoy their best electoral showing since independence, although the ruling People's Action Party retains its virtual monopoly on power.

December 2013 Rioting breaks out in Little India after a migrant worker is killed in a road accident.

March 2015 Lee Kuan Yew dies, aged 91.

ARRIVAL AND DEPARTURE

Singapore is one of the major gateways into Southeast Asia. All touch down at the impressive **Changi International Airport** (see p.690), which is Singapore in microcosm – highly efficient, orderly and with good public transport links. There are plenty of air connections with the rest of Southeast Asia. There are good **road** links with numerous Malaysian cities and southern Thailand, although **train** services are minimal (see box, p.692).

The only international **ferries** serving Singapore link it with the Indonesian Riau islands, notably Batam and

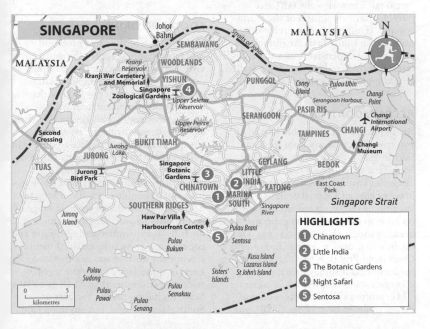

9

Bintan; they use the Singapore Cruise Centre at HarbourFront, south of town, and the Tanah Merah terminal in eastern Singapore.

VISAS

Citizens of Western Europe, Southeast Asia, the US and some Commonwealth countries, including Australia and New Zealand, are automatically given what the Singapore government calls visit passes upon arrival, valid for fourteen to thirty days. Other nationalities will have to apply for visas in advance; details are on the website of the Immigration and Checkpoints Authority (Ⓦ ica.gov.sg).

You can **extend your visit pass** on the ICA's website, which has lots of fine print setting out the details. An alternative option is to do a trip to the Malaysian town of **Johor Bahru** and return the same day.

GETTING AROUND

If you don't mind the heat, getting around **on foot** is the best way to do justice to the downtown area, though the city-state's impressive bus service and metro rail network – the **MRT** (see p.691) – have all corners of the island covered, though expect overcrowding during rush hour. **Taxis** are ubiquitous and not that expensive; bus and MRT **fares**, mostly based on distance travelled, are extremely reasonable.

ACCOMMODATION

Room rates take a noticeable leap when you cross the causeway from Malaysia into Singapore, with prices at Western levels. The good news is that rates in all categories have stagnated and even drifted lower of late, and special deals and last-minute discounts are often advertised on hotel websites as well as general booking sites such as Ⓦ agoda.com. Deals do, however, dry up during the Formula One Grand Prix (late Sept) and can be harder to find if some other sporting event or a major convention is under way.

Many, often stylish, **hostels** offer a choice of dorm beds (from S$20), and

ADDRESSES AND MAPS

With so many of Singapore's shops, restaurants and offices located in vast high-rise buildings and shopping centres, deciphering **addresses** can sometimes be tricky; an address containing #10-08 refers to unit 8 on the tenth floor (ground level is denoted #01). The best online maps of Singapore are at Ⓦ streetdirectory.com, where you can search using street or building names or six-digit postal codes.

some have private doubles too (from S$50); air-conditioning, free wi-fi and internet and private lockers are standard features, and usually a simple self-service breakfast as well. Guesthouses and more upmarket "flashpacker" hostels offer classy decor and designer bathroom fittings, although you can expect to pay around fifty percent more. Otherwise, a decent budget hotel room starts at around S$90, while **mid-range hotels** charge upwards of S$140.

Electricity is supplied at 220 volts; sockets take UK-style plugs.

FOOD AND DRINK

Eating is one of the most profound pleasures that Singapore affords its visitors, and ranks alongside shopping as one of the two main national pastimes. An enormous number of food outlets cater for this obsession, and strict government regulations ensure that they are consistently hygienic. By far the cheapest and most fun place to dine is in a **hawker centre** or **food court**, where scores of stalls let you mix and match Asian dishes, fast-food style, at really low prices; it's possible to eat like a king for S$8. Otherwise, there's a whole range of **restaurants** to visit, ranging from no-frills, open-fronted eating-houses and coffee shops to swanky establishments serving any cuisine you can think of. Even in quite fancy restaurants, you'll seldom spend more than S$40 or S$50 a head, excluding drinks, for East or South Asian cuisine, but anything from

CHINESE FOOD

The majority of the **Chinese** restaurants in Singapore are Cantonese, from Guangdong in southern China, though you'll also come across northern Beijing (or Peking) and western Szechuan cuisines, as well as the Hokkien specialities of the southeastern province of Fujian, and Teochew dishes from the area east of Canton. Whatever the region, it's undoubtedly the real thing – Chinese food as eaten by the Chinese – which means it won't always be particularly appealing to foreigners: the Chinese eat all parts of an animal, from its lips to its undercarriage, and dishes such as "frog porridge" may be an acquired taste.

Fish and seafood are nearly always outstanding, but for something a little more unusual, try a **steamboat**, a Chinese-style fondue filled with boiling stock in which you cook meat, fish, shellfish, eggs and vegetables; or a **claypot** – meat, fish or shellfish cooked over a fire in an earthenware pot. In many Cantonese restaurants (and in other regional restaurants, too), lunch consists of **dim sum** – steamed and fried dumplings served in little bamboo baskets.

further afield will generally command a premium.

All types of cuisine can be found here, from North and South Indian to Malay, Indonesian, Korean, Japanese and Vietnamese. Chinese restaurants are some of the most popular, which reflects the fact that three-quarters of the population is Chinese. As in Penang and Malacca, **Nyonya** (or Nonya) cuisine, a hybrid of Chinese and Malay food developed by the Peranakan community, is popular. However, there are a few quintessentially Singaporean dishes to look out for, such as **chilli crab** (wok-fried crabs cooked in a chilli and tomato sauce).

Vegetarians need to tread carefully, as chicken and seafood will appear in a whole host of dishes unless you make it perfectly clear that you don't want them. The best bets for vegetarians are specialist Chinese and Indian restaurants, as well as international fusion ones; a few stalls at hawker centres serve **vegetarian food** too.

Most restaurants are open daily between 11.30am and 2.30pm and 6 to 10.30pm, though cheaper places tend to open longer hours. Tap **water** is drinkable throughout Singapore except on the rural northeastern island of Pulau Ubin.

CULTURE AND ETIQUETTE

Singaporeans are liberal by Southeast Asian standards but conservative by Western ones, and the state itself is still synonymous with rules and regulations.

All citizens of Singapore are guaranteed housing, but the government enforces strict ethnic quotas per district, ostensibly to prevent ghettos (although critics note that it can also homogenize voting patterns, with electoral implications). Although undoubtedly authoritarian, this approach, together with a stab at meritocracy, does mean that Singapore doesn't suffer from the ethnic tensions simmering in Malaysia.

Public displays of affection may be frowned upon. Sexual activity between men is technically illegal, although the government has essentially declared the law dead (and Singapore has hosted a hugely well-attended **LGBT** rights rally for several years, in June; see ⦿pinkdot .sg). Note that it is also illegal to consume alcohol in public at certain times of day.

When visiting temples and mosques, it may be worth enquiring whether photography is permitted even if there are no signs asking visitors to refrain.

SPORTS AND OUTDOOR ACTIVITIES

Singapore has good sporting facilities, although the oppressive humidity can be a bit of a downer. The easiest and cheapest for visitors to access are the 50m **swimming pools**, which just about every new town and some suburbs boast, with admission costing just S$1; the most central of these is the Jalan Besar complex on Tyrwhitt Road, northeast of Little India (Farrer Park MRT). The rather mundane East Coast Park, a strip of reclaimed land and beach south of the

9

suburbs of Katong, Marine Parade and Bedok, has some beachfront **cycling** and **rollerblading** (rental S$5/hr), plus the cable **ski park**, Ski360 (1206A East Coast Parkway; ⓦski360degree.com), which offers an affordable way to have a go at **wakeboarding** or **waterskiing** (S$38/1hr) while being dragged by an overhead cable instead of a boat. The Bukit Timah Nature Reserve (see p.698) has several rather tame **hiking routes** through the rainforest.

Singapore also hosts some premier international sporting fixtures: the season-ending women's tennis finals (Nov); one leg of the Rugby Sevens tour (April); and – the jewel in the crown – the night-time **Formula One Grand Prix** (late Sept), taking in the Colonial District and Marina Bay, whose roads are temporarily converted to form the race track.

COMMUNICATIONS

Singapore's postal system is predictably efficient (even during Christmas), with letters and cards often reaching international destinations in as little as a week. **Post offices** are scattered across the island, with usual hours of Monday to Friday 8.30am to 5pm and Saturday 8.30am to 1pm; the one on Killiney Road (Somerset MRT) is conveniently placed next to Orchard Road and keeps extended hours.

The easiest way to make **local calls** or access the internet as you sightsee is to pick up a local SIM card; SingTel, StarHub and M1 cards start at around S$10, although note that basic 2G

SINGAPORE ONLINE

ⓦ**yoursingapore.com** The official tourism website with details of most of Singapore's sights.

ⓦ**sg.asia-city.com** The only local listings website worth checking out, with a monthly listings magazine also available for free from some restaurants and malls.

ⓦ**tremeritus.com** One of several independent news websites, offering a fresher take on local affairs than the official media.

---

phones won't work in Singapore. Practically all accommodation offers **free wi-fi** and **internet**. Travellers can also enjoy free wi-fi in certain malls and MRT stations by signing up for the nationwide Wireless@SG service; in theory you can do this on the websites of any of the mobile providers, even if you aren't a customer, but you may find that passwords sent by SMS to foreign mobile numbers fail to arrive.

CRIME AND SAFETY

Singapore is the cleanest, safest city in Southeast Asia for travellers, including single women, though you shouldn't become complacent – muggings have been known to occur, and theft from dormitories by other tourists is a common complaint. The only major outbreak of disorder of recent times was the **Little India** riots of 2013, involving migrant workers.

In theory there are eye-watering fines – seldom meted out – of S$500 for littering, or S$50 for jaywalking – defined as crossing a main road without using a pedestrian crossing or bridge that's less than 50m away. Contrary to rumour, chewing gum isn't illegal in Singapore, only its sale; visitors are perfectly entitled to bring and use their own supplies.

Note that alcohol consumption in public – that is, on the street beyond the bounds of restaurants, bars and hawker centres, or on beaches and in parks – is illegal nightly from 10.30pm to 7am. Within Little India and the suburb of Geylang, an additional ban applies throughout the weekend and until 7am on Mondays. Shops are unable to sell alcohol whenever the ban is in force.

What's most important to keep in mind is that, as in other Southeast Asian countries, the possession of **drugs** – hard or soft – is punishable with a hefty prison sentence and flogging with a rattan cane. Trafficking more than certain designated amounts carries a mandatory **death sentence**.

Singapore's **police**, who wear dark blue, are generally polite and helpful when approached.

EMERGENCY NUMBERS

Police ☎ **999**
Ambulance and Fire Brigade ☎ **995**

MEDICAL CARE

Medical services in Singapore are some of the best in the world. Larger hotels have doctors on call at all times, and your accommodation should be able to recommend a nearby clinic should you need one. There are **emergency services** at the Singapore General Hospital (☎6222 3322; Outram Park or Tiong Bahru MRT) and the Raffles Hospital on North Bridge Road (☎6311 1111; Bugis MRT), among others.

Pharmacies are ubiquitous downtown – some even inside MRT stations – and generally well stocked, although only the largest have pharmacists. As in Malaysia, the Watson's and Guardian chains are ubiquitous.

MONEY AND BANKS

The **currency** is the Singapore dollar, simply denoted as $, though throughout the chapter we have used S$. The Singapore dollar is divided into 100 cents. Notes are issued in denominations of S$2, S$5, S$10, S$50, S$100, S$500, S$1000 and S$10,000; coins are in denominations of 5, 10, 20 and 50 cents, and S$1 (confusingly, the older coinage looks and feels very similar to its Malaysian counterparts, so take care to keep them separate). At the time of writing, the exchange rate was around S$1.80 to £1 and S$1.4 to US$1.

Major **credit and debit cards** are widely accepted in shops and restaurants, and on taxis; they will also work in many Singapore ATMs (those run by DBS/POSB may prove an exception). There are **banks and ATMs** throughout downtown Singapore – MRT stations have ATMs, for example. Licensed moneychangers can be found in Little India, Kampong Glam and Orchard Road's malls, and at hotels.

A seven percent goods and services **tax** (GST) is levied by all businesses except small shops and food outlets. Most prices include GST, but hotel rates are sometimes quoted without it. GST applies on top of the ten percent service charge levied by many hotels, restaurants and bars, making for a total surcharge of 17.7 percent (sometimes denoted ++ after a price). Prices quoted in this chapter include GST and any service charge.

OPENING HOURS AND PUBLIC HOLIDAYS

Banks open at least Monday to Friday 10am to 3pm, Saturday 9.30am to 1pm. In general, Chinese temples open daily from 7am to around 6pm, Hindu temples from 6am to noon and 5 to 9pm, and mosques from 8.30am to noon and 2.30 to 4pm. Opening hours for shops vary widely, but the smallest outlets trade at least from late morning until 7pm, most days. Most malls are open from 9am until 9pm or later, but the stores within keep their own hours.

PUBLIC HOLIDAYS

January 1 New Year's Day
January/February Chinese New Year (two days)
March/April Good Friday
May 1 Labour Day
May Vesak Day
June Hari Raya Puasa
August Hari Raya Haji
August 9 National Day
October/November Deepavali
December 25 Christmas Day

LANGUAGE

English, Mandarin, Malay and Tamil are all official languages, with English used as the main language of education. One intriguing by-product of Singapore's ethnic mix is **Singlish**, or Singaporean English, a patois that blends English with the speech patterns, exclamations and vocabulary of Chinese and Malay. Look out for the Malay suffix "lah" when conversing with Singapore locals – it's added to the end of a reply for emphasis.

9

FESTIVALS

With so many ethnic groups and religions represented in Singapore, you'll be unlucky if your trip doesn't coincide with some sort of **festival**. The timing of most of them depends on the lunar calendar; tourist offices can give you precise dates (see p.690).

Chinese New Year (Jan/Feb; two days) Chinese operas and dragon dances in Chinatown.

Thaipusam (Jan/Feb) Watch Hindu devotees, their flesh pierced within elaborate steel cages, process from Little India's Sri Srinivasa Perumal Temple to the Chettiar Temple near Fort Canning Park.

Singapore Fringe Festival ⓦ singaporefringe.com (Jan/Feb). Theatre, dance and the visual arts; occasional attempts at radicalism sometimes fall foul of the censors.

Hari Raya Puasa (Eid al-Fitr; June). In the run-up to this holiday, marking the end of Ramadan, afternoon food markets are set up outside the Sultan Mosque and in the suburb of Geylang.

Festival of the Hungry Ghosts (July) Catch a free performance of a Chinese opera, or *wayang*, in which characters act out classic Chinese legends.

Singapore International Festival of the Arts ⓦ sifa.sg (Aug/Sept). Theatre, dance, film, concerts – this has it all covered.

Moon Cake Festival or Mid-Autumn Festival (Sept). Celebrate with children's lantern parades after dark in the Chinese Gardens.

Birthday of the Monkey God (Sept). A procession and street opera performance may be staged around the Monkey God Temple on Seng Poh Rd (Tiong Bahru MRT).

Navarathiri (Oct) The Chettiar and Sri Mariamman Hindu Temples stage classical dance and music.

Thimithi (Oct) Watch Hindu devotees running across a pit of hot coals.

Deepavali (Diwali; Oct/Nov) The Hindu festival celebrating the victory of Light over Dark is marked by the lighting of oil lamps outside homes.

Downtown Singapore

Ever since Sir Stamford Raffles first landed on its northern bank, in 1819, the area around the Singapore River, which strikes into the heart of the island from the south coast, has formed the hub of Singapore. All the city's central districts lie within a 3km radius of the mouth of the river – which makes **Downtown Singapore** an extremely convenient place to wander around.

WHAT TO SEE AND DO

The entire state is compact enough to be explored exhaustively in just a few days. Forming the core of downtown Singapore is the **Colonial District**, around whose public buildings and lofty cathedral the island's British residents used to promenade. Each surrounding enclave has its own distinct flavour, from **Little India** with its aromatic spice stores to the tumbledown backstreets of **Chinatown**, where it's still possible to find calligraphers and fortune-tellers, or **Arab Street** (**Kampung Glam**), whose cluttered shops sell fine cloths and perfumes.

The Padang

The vast green rectangle of the **Padang** ("field" in Malay) lies at the heart of what Singapore's city planners mundanely refer to as the civic district, a name that signally fails to evoke its status as the very essence of colonial Singapore. Among reminders of those times are occasional cricket and rugby matches played here.

The National Gallery

The entire west side of the Padang is taken up by Singapore's lavish **National**

SINGAPORE RIVER TRIPS

As Singapore's trade grew, the **Singapore River** – really just a glorified creek – became a major artery, clogged with traditional "bumboats" which ferried coffee, sugar and rice to the adjoining *godowns*, or warehouses. Once highly polluted, it was cleaned up in the 1980s when the bumboats were relocated. **Singapore River Cruises** (ⓣ 6336 6111, ⓦ rivercruise .com.sg) now operates touristy excursions in jazzed-up versions of these boats, setting off from jetties in locations such as Clarke Quay, Boat Quay, Esplanade and Marina Bay (daily roughly 9am–10.30pm; 40min; S$25). The trips take you past the old *godowns* – now mostly converted into bars and restaurants – and antiquated bridges in various styles. A trip by night is particularly atmospheric.

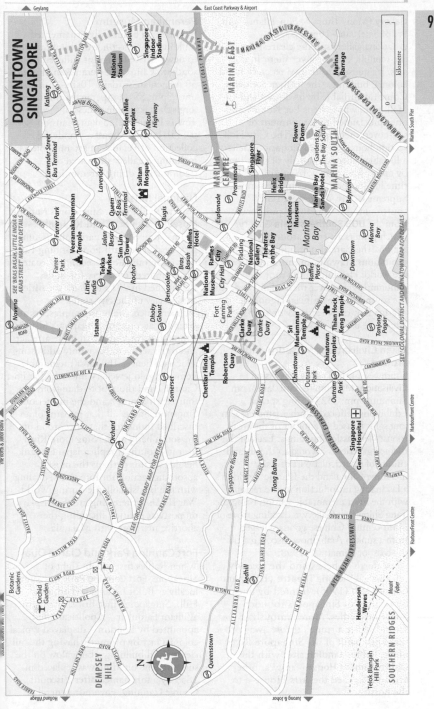

DOWNTOWN SINGAPORE

SEE BRAS BASAH, LITTLE INDIA & ARAB STREET MAP FOR DETAILS

SEE ORCHARD ROAD MAP FOR DETAILS

SEE COLONIAL DISTRICT AND CHINATOWN MAP FOR DETAILS

0   1 kilometre

Places / Landmarks

Geylang
East Coast Parkway & Airport
Stadium
Singapore Indoor Stadium
National Stadium
MARINA EAST
Marina Barrage
MARINA COASTAL EXPRESSWAY
Marina South Pier
Golden Mile Complex
Nicoll Highway
Flower Dome
Gardens By The Bay South
MARINA SOUTH
Lavender Street Bus Terminal
Sultan Mosque
Singapore Flyer
MARINA CENTRE
Helix Bridge
Marina Bay Sands Hotel
Bayfront
Lavender
Queen St Bus Terminal
Bugis
Esplanade
Promenade
Art Science Museum
Marina Boulevard
Farrer Park
Veeramakaliamman Temple
Jalan Besar
Sim Lim Tower
Raffles Hotel
Raffles City
Theatres on the Bay
Marina Bay
Marina Boy
Tekka Market
Bras Basah
City Hall
National Gallery
Padang
Downtown
Little India
Rochor
National Museum
Boat Quay
Raffles Place
Farrer Park
Bencoolen
Fort Canning Park
Clarke Quay
Thian Hock Keng Temple
Tanjong Pagar
Novena
Dhoby Ghaut
Istana
Chettiar Hindu Temple
Robertson Quay
Sri Mariamman Temple
Chinatown Complex
Chinatown
Outram Park
Clemenceau Ave N.
Somerset
Clarke Quay
Cantonment Rd
Newton
Orchard
Singapore General Hospital
Central Expressway
Harbourfront Centre
Tiong Bahru
Botanic Gardens
Orchid Garden
Redhill
Henderson Waves
Telok Blangah Hill Park
SOUTHERN RIDGES
Mount Faber
DEMPSEY HILL
Queenstown
Holland Village
Jurong & Johor
The North & Johor Bahru

9

Gallery (Mon–Thurs & Sun 10am–7pm, Fri & Sat 10am–10pm; S\$20; ⓦnationalgallery.sg), the clearest signal of the republic's major investment in the arts. It's housed inside two recently fused colonial buildings: the former Supreme Court (identifiable by its dome) and City Hall, from whose steps Lee Kuan Yew once proclaimed the attainment of self-government in 1959. The City Hall section houses the **DBS Singapore Gallery**, a likeable collection mostly of paintings by artists who were born in or lived for a time in Singapore. Over in the former Supreme Court, the restored old courtrooms can sometimes pull focus from the **UOB Southeast Asia Gallery**, which gathers art from around the region. There are also temporary exhibitions drawn from museums around the world. Head up to the roof for panoramic views over the Padang and, to the southeast, the artificial lagoon of Marina Bay, crowned by *Marina Bay Sands* (see p.688).

Asian Civilisations Museum and around

Southwest of the Padang, the **Asian Civilisations Museum** (daily 10am–7pm, Sun until 9pm; S\$23 during special exhibitions, reduced at other times; ⓦacm .org.sg) is housed in another of the area's robust Neoclassical buildings. Each of the themed galleries is devoted to the art and culture of a particular part of Asia, including China and the Islamic World. It's a fascinating introduction to the region, with the most memorable section being the Tang Shipwreck Gallery, a dazzling trove of ninth-century Chinese goods salvaged from a sunken Arab dhow discovered off the coast of Sumatra in 1998.

Just north of here stand the recently refurbished **Victoria Theatre** (1862) and **Concert Hall** (1905), fronted by one of two statues of Singapore's founder, Stamford Raffles. More famously, a second statue a stone's throw away on the north bank of the Singapore River marks **Raffles' landing site**, with the **Old Parliament House** – now another arts venue called the Arts House – to the north.

Peranakan Museum

Housed in a beautifully ornamented building that was once a school catering to newly arrived migrant children from southern China, the **Peranakan Museum**, 39 Armenian St (daily 10am–7pm, Fri until 9pm; S\$10; ⓦperanakanmuseum .org.sg), lacks the liveliness of George Town's Pinang Peranakan Mansion (see p.445), but does boast a wonderful collection of Peranakan art and objects, including a gallery dedicated to traditional wedding ceremonies.

National Museum

You can't fail to spot Singapore's **National Museum** at 93 Stamford Rd (daily 10am–7pm; S\$10; ⓦnationalmuseum .sg), nestled beneath Fort Canning Park, its eye-catching dome seemingly coated with hundreds of silvery fish scales. Relaunched in 2015 to mark the fiftieth anniversary of the city-state's independence, the museum presents an extended account of Singapore's history, although it could do with more artefacts and often seems to be mainly addressing a local audience. The most memorable items are gold jewellery unearthed at Fort Canning and thought to date from the fourteenth century, and the mysterious Singapore Stone, all that remains of an inscribed monolith that once stood on the south bank of the Singapore River, near its mouth. A replica Japanese tank heralds what is perhaps the most absorbing section for foreigners, dealing with the British collapse during World War II. Also interesting are the displays on postwar politics, including the abortive marriage with Malaysia.

Fort Canning Park and Clarke Quay

When Raffles first caught sight of Singapore, **Fort Canning Park** was known locally as Bukit Larangan (Forbidden Hill). Singapore's first British Resident, William Farquhar – a political officer appointed by London – displayed typical colonial tact by promptly having the hill cleared and building a bungalow on the summit. The building was replaced in 1859 by a fort named after Viscount George Canning, governor-general of

India, but only a gateway, guardhouse and adjoining wall remain today.

The jumble of relics aside, the park includes some shady walks and a *keramat* ("auspicious place"), the supposed burial site of the semi-mythical Malay ruler Iskandar Shah. Amid more recent and substantial colonial buildings lies the **Battle Box** (entry by guided tour, 3–5 daily; S$18; w battlebox.com.sg), an underground bunker museum which holds dioramas bringing to life the events leading up to the British surrender in February 1942.

On the other side of River Valley Road, which skirts the southwestern slope of Fort Canning Park, lies a clump of nineteenth-century *godowns* which now serve as another of Singapore's popular nightspots, **Clarke Quay**. Further upriver, **Robertson Quay** is similar but quieter.

Raffles Hotel

The lofty halls, restaurants, bars and peaceful gardens of the legendary **Raffles Hotel** at 1 Beach Rd (w raffles. com) all conspire to evoke a sense of the bygone colonial era. It was founded by the Armenian Sarkies brothers, like George Town's *E&O*, and opened for business on December 1, 1887, whereupon it quickly attracted some impressive guests, including Joseph Conrad, Rudyard Kipling and Hermann Hesse. During World War II, the hotel became Japanese officers'

quarters, then a transit camp for liberated Allied prisoners.

Postwar deterioration ended with an expensive facelift in 1991, which controversially added a modern extension. Another renovation was under way at the time of writing, which will see the hotel's theatre converted into a ballroom. *Raffles* remains diminutive compared to its neighbours – the cylindrical *Swissôtel The Stamford* (once the world's tallest hotel) to the southwest, and the gleaming new *Marriott South Beach* development directly opposite. When the hotel reopens in mid-2018, visitors will once again be able to flock to *Raffles'* **Long Bar** – once a favourite watering hole for the likes of Noël Coward and Ernest Hemingway – for the signature Singapore Sling (at least S$37).

Chinatown

The two square kilometres of **Chinatown**, located just south of the Singapore River, once constituted the focal point of Chinese life and culture in Singapore. Now largely gentrified and modernized, it's not a patch on Penang's George Town in terms of atmosphere, but a wander through the surviving nineteenth-century streets can still unearth a few old-fangled shops and clan associations.

A good first port of call is the **Chinatown Heritage Centre** (daily 9am–8pm, closed first Mon of the month; S$15) at 48 Pagoda St. Taking up

---

GETTING HIGH IN SINGAPORE

There are three ways to feel on top of the world on your visit (and we don't mean falling foul of Singapore's draconian laws on drug use).

The Singapore Flyer 30 Raffles Ave w singaporeflyer.com. This observation wheel gets you as high up as the summit of the island's tallest hill, and offers 360-degree views across to the Financial District and distant new towns, although the historical quarters are largely screened by new towers. S$33. Daily 8.30am–10pm.

G-max the Ultimate Bungee Jump & GX-5 Xtreme Swing Clarke Quay w gmaxgx5.sg. Want to see the lights of the big city while upside down at a height of 60m,

having left your stomach somewhere below? Now you can. Next to the bungee catapult is the five-seater swing that catapults you above the Singapore River. S$45. Daily 2pm–late.

1-Altitude 1 Raffles Place T 6438 0410, w 1-altitude.com; map pp.682–683 If you can visit just one fancy watering hole in Singapore, make it this fantastic open-air gastrobar topping a 63-storey building, with some of the best views of any downtown venue; cover charge S$30. Daily at least 6pm–2am.

9

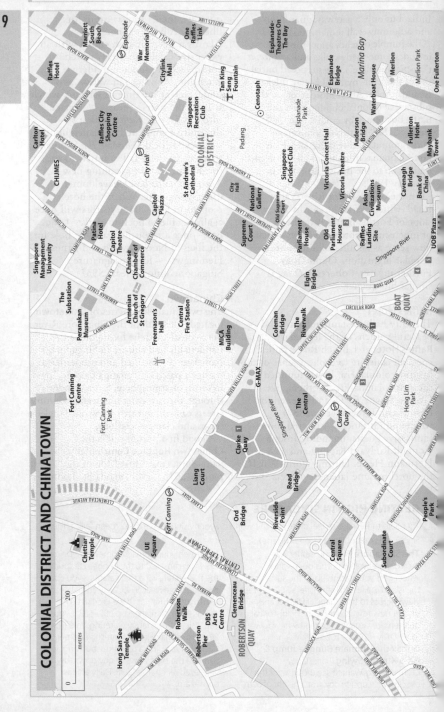

COLONIAL DISTRICT AND CHINATOWN

0 — 200 metres

Marina Bay Sands & Gardens By The Bay ▲

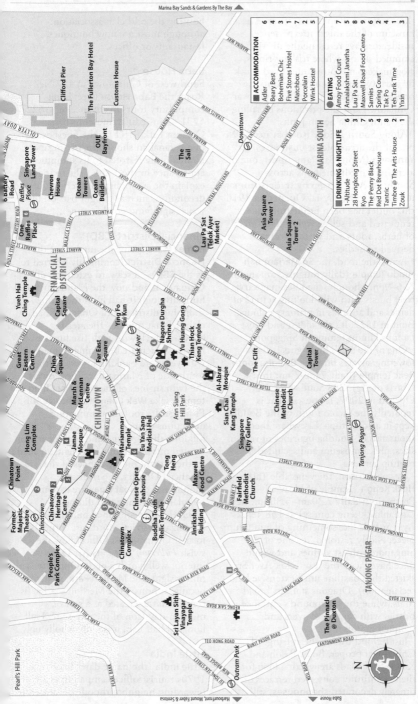

■ ACCOMMODATION	
Adler	6
Beary Best	4
Bohemian Chic	3
Five Stones Hostel	1
Matchbox	7
Porcelain	2
Wink Hostel	5

● EATING	
Amoy Food Court	7
Annalakshmi Janatha	5
Lau Pa Sat	8
Maxwell Road Food Centre	9
Sarnies	6
Spring Court	2
Tak Po	4
Teh Tarik Time	3
Yixin	1

■ DRINKING & NIGHTLIFE	
1-Altitude	6
28 Hongkong Street	3
Kyo	7
The Penny Black	5
Red Dot Brewhouse	4
Tantric	8
Timbre @ The Arts House	2
Zouk	1

MARINA SOUTH

MARINA SOUTH

Downtown

COLLIER QUAY

FINANCIAL DISTRICT

CHINATOWN

TANJONG PAGAR

Pearl's Hill Park

N

▼ Harbourfront, Mount Faber & Sentosa   ▼ Baba House

9

three restored shophouses, it serves as a museum of the migrant experience. Inside, displays re-create the district's cramped slums, where trishaw-riders, clog-makers and prostitutes lived cheek by jowl. Other sections rewind to the now sadly vanished nightlife of postwar Chinatown and the privations of sailing the South China Sea in junks.

Along South Bridge Road at no. 269 is one of the area's oldest businesses, **Eu Yan Sang** (Mon–Sat 9am–6pm), one of a chain of medicine halls across Southeast Asia, set up by traders from near Ipoh in Malaysia. Opened in 1910, this outlet has been beautifully renovated and sells a weird assortment of herbs, roots and various animal-derived remedies.

Across the road, the **Sri Mariamman Hindu Temple** (daily roughly 7am–noon & 6–9pm, though schedules may vary; free) bursts with wild-looking statues of deities and animals in primary colours. Built in 1827, it's the oldest and most famous Hindu temple in Singapore.

One of the area's highlights is the towering, always bustling **Buddha Tooth Relic Temple** (daily 7am–7pm; free; ⊕btrts.org.sg), 288 South Bridge St. Opened in 2007, it houses what is reputedly the sacred tooth of the Buddha, kept in a gold stupa. Elsewhere there are thousands of Buddha figurines of various sizes, plus a museum and secluded rooftop garden.

By comparison, the venerable **Thian Hock Keng** ("Temple of Heavenly Prosperity"; daily 7.30am–5.30pm; free; ⊕thianhockkeng.com.sg) at 158 Telok Ayer St feels like something of a museum piece. Nicely restored, it's one of Singapore's oldest shrines and would once have faced the sea (Telok Ayer St skirted the coastline until extensive land reclamation). Dragons stalk its broad roofs, while the compound's entrance bristles with ceramic flowers and sculpted figures.

Just beyond the southern fringe of Chinatown proper, Bukit Pasoh and Keong Saik roads are worth a look for their beautifully conserved terraces of ornately decorated **shophouses**, still housing the odd clan association, although most are now boutiques, restaurants or offices.

Baba House

Southwest of Chinatown at 157 Neil Road, the **Baba House** (free; book compulsory tours in advance on ☎6227 5731, ⊕nus.edu.sg/museum/baba; Outram Park MRT) is the finest example of a Peranakan shophouse in Singapore, meticulously restored to its sumptuous appearance in the 1920s. The tour guides explain the symbolism of every motif and decoration, such as the gilt bats on the walls (signifying good fortune).

Financial District (CBD)

Raffles Place forms the nucleus of the **Financial District** (commonly referred to as the **CBD**) – a seaward extension of Chinatown and now the island's financial hub, although it had been the prime shopping district until Orchard Road claimed that mantle. The area is chock-a-block with high-rise finance houses, which are beginning to merge with yet more banking towers on the south side of Marina Bay. These dwarf the twin shrines of the **Yueh Hai Ching temple** (aka **Wak Cheng Hai Bio**) at 30B Philip St. Its roofs bear miniature depictions of scenes from Chinese folklore, the figurines and ornamentation created out of ceramic fragments. A shade further north, on the fringes of the Financial District, the riverside shophouses of **Boat Quay** are extremely popular for wining and dining.

The elegant, columned building in the Financial District's northeast corner is the former General Post Office, now the swish *Fullerton Hotel*, its Art Deco interior well worth a peek. Opposite is a minor sight, the **Merlion Park**, so named because it houses the Merlion – a 1970s cement statue created as a sort of modern-day icon of the city-state. Half lion and half fish, it is sadly wholly ugly.

Little India

Little India (the name dates back to a 1970s tourist office campaign) is a rewarding neighbourhood to wander. It immediately feels like the most authentic of Singapore's old quarters, its streets packed with shops selling Indian foods, jewellery and other products, and the sound of Tamil pop music rarely out of earshot.

The district's backbone is the north–south Serangoon Road, east of which sits the lovingly restored block of shophouses comprising the **Little India Conservation Area**, a sort of Little India in microcosm. To the east of here, Dunlop Street's **Abdul Gaffoor Mosque** (no. 41; daily 8.30am–noon & 2.30–4.30pm) has a Mughal fantasy look about it, with numerous ornamented arches and towers. Further up Serangoon, opposite the turning to Veerasamy Road, the photogenic **Sri Veeramakaliamman Temple** is dedicated to the goddess Kali, its interior housing several depictions of her with ten arms.

Further up Serangoon Road, opposite the Angullia mosque, look out for the phenomenon that is the **Mustafa Centre** on Syed Alwi Road. Quite unlike Orchard Road's glitzy outlets, this department store and supermarket stretches over at least two buildings and manages to stay open 24/7 year-round, selling a vast range of everyday items.

It is worth heading up to the **Sri Srinivasa Perumal Temple** at 397 Serangoon Rd to see the five-tiered *gopura* with its sculptures of the manifestations of Lord Vishnu the Preserver. If you are fortunate enough to be in Singapore for the Thaipusam festival (Jan/Feb), you can watch the Hindu devotees parade all the way to the Chettiar Hindu Temple on Tank Road, off Orchard Road, donning huge metal cages fastened to their flesh with hooks and prongs.

Arab Street (Kampung Glam)

Soon after his arrival, Raffles allotted the land north of the Rochor Canal (the canal itself is now largely hidden underground) to the newly installed Sultan Hussein Mohammed Shah and designated the land around it as a Muslim settlement. Soon the zone was attracting Arab traders, as the road names here – Arab, Baghdad and Muscat streets and Haji Lane – suggest. The name **Kampung Glam** is also widely used (*glam* may have been the name of a type of local tree or community of sea gypsies).

Today the area is a hotchpotch of traditional shops and wannabe-hip boutiques and restaurants; so upset has the existing community been by recent gentrification, highly visible on Bussorah Street, plus Haji and Bali lanes, that they have persuaded the authorities to impose a freeze on new bars and diners opening up in the area.

The pavements of **Arab Street** are an obstacle course of carpets, cloths, baskets and bags, though it lacks the hustle and bustle you'd find in a Middle Eastern bazaar. The area's most impressive building is the golden-domed **Sultan Mosque**, or Masjid Sultan, at 3 Muscat St (daily 9.30am–noon & 2–4pm, Fri 2.30–4pm only; free), completed in 1928 and sporting a plush interior (the prayer-hall carpet was a gift from a Saudi prince). Note the decorative band outside, below the dome – it may look to be tilework, but it's actually made up of the bottoms of thousands of glass bottles.

MAXIMUM FUN, MINIMUM BUDGET

Many of Singapore's attractions are undoubtedly costly, but here are four experiences you can enjoy for nothing or next to nothing.

The Botanic Gardens Natural beauty steeped in history, with a terrific orchid section. See p.689

Haw Par Villa and the Southern Ridges A folkloric theme park makes a fun prelude to walk through various hills, linked by bridges. See p.699

The Buddha Tooth Relic Temple One of Singapore's newest and brashest shrines. See opposite

Changi Museum and Beach Visit this museum of wartime remembrance, then chill out at Changi's beach. See p.699

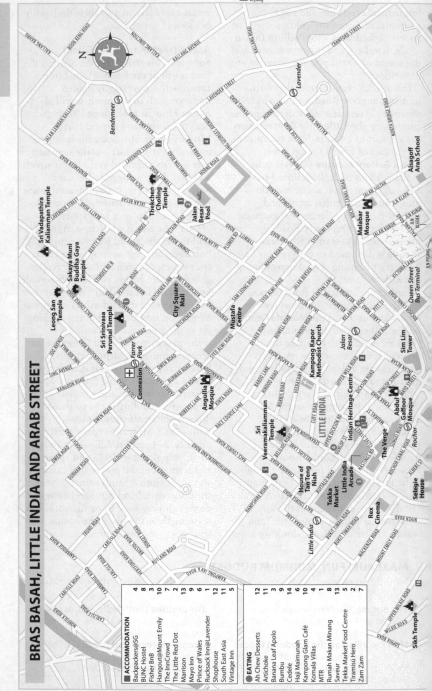

BRAS BASAH, LITTLE INDIA AND ARAB STREET

■ ACCOMMODATION	
Backpackers@SG	4
BUNC Hostel	8
Fisher BnB	3
Hangout@Mount Emily	10
The InnCrowd	7
The Little Red Dot	2
Marrison	13
Mayo Inn	9
Prince of Wales	6
Rucksack Inn@Lavender	1
Shophouse	12
South East Asia	11
Vintage Inn	5

● EATING	
Ah Chew Desserts	12
Artichoke	11
Banana Leaf Apolo	3
Bumbu	9
Cedele	14
Haji Maimunah	6
Kampong Glam Café	10
Komala Villas	4
MTR	1
Rumah Makan Minang	8
Saveur	13
Tekka Market Food Centre	5
Tiramisu Hero	2
Zam Zam	7

9

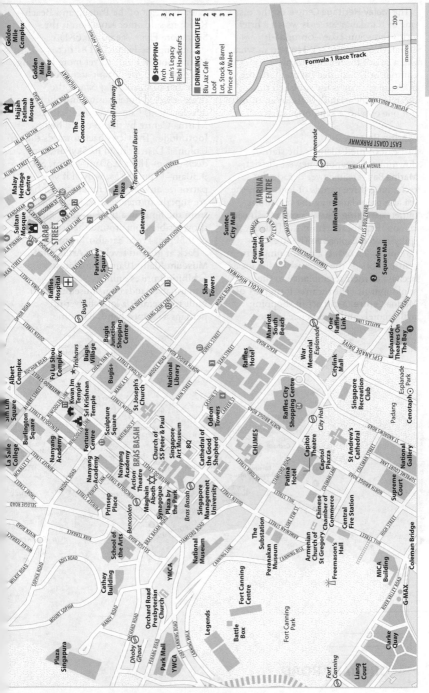

● **SHOPPING**
Arch 3
Lim's Legacy 2
Rishi Handicrafs 1

■ **DRINKING & NIGHTLIFE**
Blu Jaz Café 2
Loof 4
Lot, Stock & Barrel 3
Prince of Wales 1

9

The **Malay Heritage Centre** on the east side of Kandahar Street is worth a brief visit (Tues–Sun 10am–6pm; S$4; ⓦmalayheritage.org.sg). Housed in what was a palace for nobility until compulsorily acquired by the state, the museum enshrines the vanished rural lifestyle of the island's Malay community, not one of whose kampongs survives.

Marina Bay

Just east of the Padang is the start of downtown Singapore's newest district, **Marina Bay**, created over decades by reclaiming three parcels of land from the sea and then damming the remaining outlet, spawning what is now a freshwater lagoon. Unmissable from the Padang, the spiky-roofed **Esplanade Theatres** (ⓦesplanade.com) is a performing arts centre dubbed "the durians" by the locals because of their resemblance to the stinking fruit. The theatres form part of **Marina Centre**, a district of shopping malls, hotels and conference venues extending east of the Padang and Beach Road; its sole other attraction is the Singapore Flyer (see box, p.681).

Abutting the Financial District is **Marina South**, home to yet more banking buildings and the instant architectural icon that is *Marina Bay Sands*, the three-towered hotel, casino and shopping development. Conveniently, it's linked to Marina Centre by the so-called **helix footbridge**. The views back towards the Colonial District from its **SkyPark** top deck (Mon–Thurs 9.30am–10pm, Sat 9.30am–11pm; S$23, waived if you patronize any SkyPark restaurant or bar) are superb. In the evening, lasers splay from the hotel in a fifteen-minute light show visible from around the area (8pm & 9.30pm, Fri & Sat also 11pm).

Back at ground level, the **ArtScience Museum** (daily 10am–7pm; latest exhibition prices online; ⓦmarinabaysands.com/museum.html), built to resemble a lotus flower or perhaps a cupped hand, has some

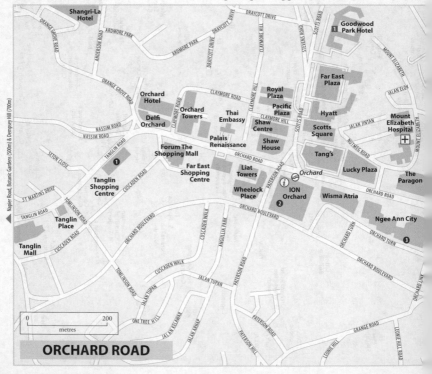

ORCHARD ROAD

tokenistic displays (free) on the interface between science and art; its real purpose is to host pricey travelling exhibitions on anything from the geometrical art of Escher to the special effects used in the Harry Potter films.

Gardens by the Bay

Marina Bay's true highlight is **Gardens By The Bay** (daily 5am–2pm, conservatories 9am–9pm; S$28 for the conservatories, S$8 for the OCBC Skyway, otherwise free; ⓦgardensbythebay.com.sg), intended to serve as the city-state's second botanical gardens. They're most easily accessed using a bridge from *Marina Bay Sands*, or the underpass from Bayfront MRT.

The two giant glass **conservatories** house an impressive range of flora, including cloud forest and African baobabs. The **Supertree Grove** is a collection of golf-tee-shaped towers serving as scaffolding for vertical gardens, linked by the aerial **OCBC Skyway bridge**. Come in the evening to witness them lit in multicoloured hues during a free sound-and-light show (7.45pm & 8.45pm).

Orchard Road and Botanic Gardens

Orchard Road runs through Singapore's glitziest shopping precinct and is lined with huge **malls** featuring everything from high-end designer goods to more everyday household necessities.

A ten-minute walk from the western end of Orchard Road, at the start of Cluny Road, is the main gate to the city-state's sole UNESCO World Heritage Site, the **Singapore Botanic Gardens** (daily 5am–midnight; free; ⓦwww.sbg.org.sg; note, Botanic Gardens MRT is near the newest, least interesting, part of the gardens, furthest from downtown). Founded in 1859, the gardens feature a mini-rainforest, rose garden, topiary, fernery, palm valley and over 10,000 species of plants. Be sure to make for the 1930s bandstand; encircled by eighteen rain trees, it is one of the loveliest spots in all of Singapore.

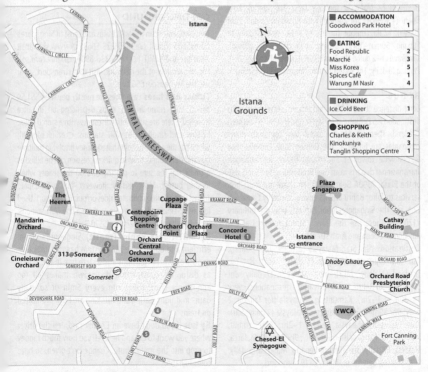

9

The star attraction, however, is the **National Orchid Garden** (daily 8.30am–7pm; S$5), some of its hybrids named after visiting dignitaries and film stars. It also includes the superb Cool House – a greenhouse built to re-create equatorial mountaintop conditions and home to some exquisite slipper orchids.

ARRIVAL AND DEPARTURE

BY PLANE

Changi Airport (☎6595 6868, ⓦchangiairport.com) is located at the far eastern end of Singapore, 16km from the city centre. The cheapest ways to reach downtown are to take the MRT (terminal 2 or 3; around S$1.80) or the #36 bus (all terminals; S$2.50). For taxis from the airport, there are surcharges of S$3–5, plus additional charges at certain times of day. Singapore is one of the busiest hubs in the region, with regular flights all over Southeast Asia and the rest of the world. Airlines connecting Singapore to its neighbours include AirAsia (ⓦairasia.com), Tiger Airways (ⓦtigerairways.com), Jetstar (ⓦjetstar.com), Firefly (ⓦfireflyz.com.my), Malaysia Airlines (ⓦmalaysiaairlines.com) and Singapore Airlines (plus its offshoots Scoot and SilkAir; ⓦsingaporeair.com).

Destinations Malaysia: Ipoh (2 daily; 1hr 30min); Kota Bharu (4 weekly; 1hr 20min); Kota Kinabalu (2 daily; 2hr 30min); Kuala Lumpur (hourly to KLIA, several daily to Subang; 50min–1hr); Kuching (3–4 daily; 1hr 20min); Langkawi (1–2 daily; 1hr 30min); Miri (several weekly; 2hr); Penang (8 daily; 1hr 10min); Pulau Tioman (daily; 45min).

BY BUS

Long-distance buses from Singapore serve numerous destinations in Peninsular Malaysia and Hat Yai in southern Thailand. There is no dedicated bus terminal; many companies are based at the Golden Mile Complex and Golden Mile Tower at 5001/6000 Beach Rd, although Transnasional departs from the Nicoll Highway-facing side of the Plaza, 7500A Beach Rd. Then there are short-hop services to Johor Bahru and its environs, run by Causeway Link and the Singapore-Johor Express, plus the ordinary #170 bus; these use the Queen Street terminal at the junction of Queen and Arab streets.

Destinations Alor Star, Malaysia (2 daily; 12hr 30min); Cameron Highlands, Malaysia (1 daily; 10hr); Hat Yai, Thailand (3 daily; 14hr); Ipoh, Malaysia (7 daily; 8hr 30min); Johor Bahru, Malaysia (various destinations; every 15–30min; 1–2hr); Kamunting, Malaysia (for Taiping; 2 daily; 9hr 30min); Kuala Kangsar, Malaysia (2 daily; 9hr); Kuala Lumpur, Malaysia (every 1–2hr; 6hr); Lumut, Malaysia (for Pangkor island; 1 daily; 9hr 30min); Malacca, Malaysia (9 daily; 3hr 30min); Penang, Malaysia (5 daily; 10hr 30min); Seremban, Malaysia (9 daily; 5hr).

INFORMATION AND TOURS

Tourist offices The Singapore Tourism Board (STB; ☎1800 736 2000, ⓦyoursingapore.com) has three Visitor Centres, the biggest of which is at 216 Orchard Rd (daily 8.30am–9.30pm; Somerset MRT). Besides doling out advice, it sells tickets for some attractions, a service not available at the other, much smaller, tourist offices: level 1, ION Orchard mall (daily 10am–10pm; Orchard MRT); and 2 Banda St (behind Chinatown's Buddha Tooth Relic Temple; daily 9am–9pm; Chinatown MRT).

The Original Singapore Walks ☎6325 1631, ⓦjourneys.com.sg. Guided walks of the historic downtown areas and Changi (the latter with a wartime focus), generally lasting 2hr 30min. From S$32, although the Changi walks are much pricier.

Singapore Footprints ⓦsingaporefootprints.com. Walking tours of the colonial district and Chinatown, run by university student volunteers (so standards vary). Sat & Sun only; free.

Trishaw Uncle Booth on Queen St, close to Bugis MRT ☎6337 7111, ⓦtrishawuncle.com.sg. Unlike in Malaysia, no one in Singapore uses cycle rickshaws to get around any more. Surviving trishaws now do touristy half-hour rides around North Bridge Rd/Little India (S$39, or S$49 with Clarke Quay included). Daily 11am–10pm.

GETTING AROUND

Two companies run the MRT trains and most of Singapore's buses: SBS Transit (☎1800 225 5663, ⓦwww.sbstransit.com.sg) and SMRT (☎1800 336 8900, ⓦsmrt.com.sg). For an overview of the network, visit ⓦmytransport.sg, or use the MyTransport.SG app.

Tickets and fares Cash fares are mostly between S$1.50 and S$2.70, rising in tiny steps depending on distance travelled. There are substantial discounts with a stored-value EZ-Link card (available at MRT stations; ⓦezlink.com.sg), which has the added benefit that a journey involving multiple bus and train connections in quick succession can be billed as a single trip (be sure to tap the card on the reader when leaving buses). Most visitors, however, buy a Singapore Tourist Pass offering unlimited rides on public transport. Used like an EZ-Link card, it's on sale at quite a few MRT stations, including the one at the airport (S$20/3 days).

By MRT (Mass Rapid Transit) Singapore's clean, efficient and good-value MRT system has five lines (see opposite), with extensions and a sixth line in the works, as disruptive construction downtown makes all too annoyingly clear. Trains run every 5min or so, daily 6am–midnight. Eating and drinking are both prohibited on trains.

By bus If you don't have an EZ-Link card, tell the driver where you want to go, and he'll tell you how much money to drop into the metal chute. Change isn't given, so have coins to hand.

THE MRT SYSTEM

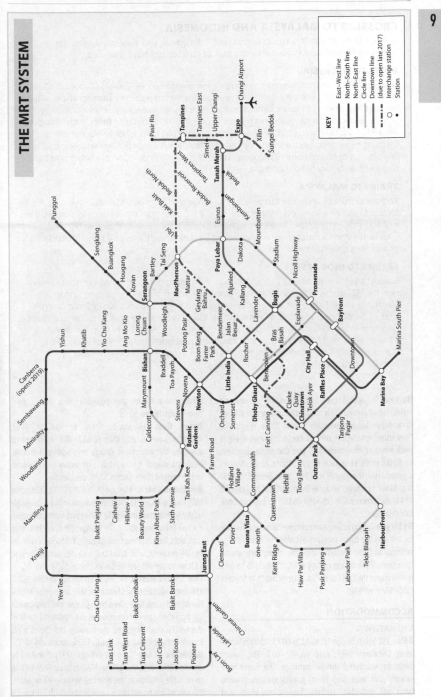

KEY

East–West line
North–South line
North–East line
Circle line
Downtown line
(due to open late 2017)
Interchange station
Station

9

CROSSING TO MALAYSIA AND INDONESIA

To reach East Malaysia and almost everywhere in Indonesia, you must travel by air. For Peninsular Malaysia, buses are the best option as train services have dwindled.

BUSES TO MALAYSIA

Nearly all buses use the Causeway, although a few use the Second Crossing to Johor at Tuas in western Singapore. Long-haul buses will wait for all passengers to clear **immigration**, while on short-hop services to Johor Bahru, you may have to continue your journey on another vehicle serving the same route (just present your ticket). Long-distance **fares** from Singapore are at least double the fare to the same destination starting from Johor Bahru; if you're counting every cent, catch a short-hop bus to Johor Bahru's Larkin bus terminal (see p.478) and attempt to buy an immediate onward ticket from there (a possibly risky strategy at busy times such as before public holidays).

TRAINS TO MALAYSIA

With the closure of Singapore's downtown station several years ago, Malaysian trains have elected to run a meaningless 3min shuttle service (12 daily) from the replacement train station in Woodlands, close to the Causeway, to Johor Bahru's station just on the other side of the Causeway (which is much more easily reached by bus), where there are a handful of onward connections daily (see p.478).

FERRIES TO INDONESIA

Boats to and from the nearby Indonesian Riau archipelago dock at the HarbourFront Centre, near the MRT of the same name, and the Tanah Merah ferry terminal in eastern Singapore (Tanah Merah MRT, then bus #35). For timetables and ferry companies see ⓦ singaporecruise .com.sg. Services include: Batam Centre (Batam island; every 30min from HarbourFront plus 4 daily from Tanah Merah; 40min); Nongsapura (Batam island; every 1–2hr from Tanah Merah; 40min); Sekupang (Batam island; at least hourly from HarbourFront; 45min); Tanjung Balai (Karimun island; 4 daily from HarbourFront; 45min); Tanjung Pinang (Bintan island; every 1–2hr from Tanah Merah; 45min).

By taxi Singapore's taxis come in many colours and styles, but all are relatively affordable and metered. Fares vary depending on whether you're in a regular or "limousine" vehicle, the time of day (surcharges apply at peak times or after midnight) and the route (journeys using toll roads, as in parts of downtown, cost extra). As a general rule, the flagfall is S$3–4, then around S$0.25/km. Major taxi firms include Comfort/CityCab (☎ 6552 1111) and Premier Taxi (☎ 6363 6888), or you can book rides via Uber.

By bicycle Cycling in Singapore requires a major tolerance for not only the sticky weather but also the heavy traffic whizzing along its modern multi-lane roads; there are no cycle lanes. If you do any cycling at all, it's likely to be on a rented bike at the East Coast Park, Changi beach or Sentosa (S$6–10/hr, with ID).

ACCOMMODATION

CHINATOWN

Adler 259 South Bridge Rd ☎ 6226 0173, ⓦ adlerhostel .com; Chinatown MRT; map pp.682–683. This luxury hostel has wonderful antique furniture. The dorms have swanky pods with crisp linen, privacy curtain, reading lamp and individual sockets. Towels, ear-plugs and drinking water are also provided, and there's wi-fi throughout. Dorms S$38

Beary Best 16 Upper Cross St ☎ 6222 4957, ⓦ bearybesthostel.com; map pp.682–683. As the name suggests, this hostel has cuddly toys scattered around, lending a playful feel to what is generally an organized, well-equipped place. Dorms S$28, doubles S$82

Bohemian Chic 40 Mosque St ☎ 8380 0500; Chinatown MRT; map pp.682–683. Not truly Bohemian but appealingly quirky, with glittery masks like something from a Baroque-era ball lining one wall in the lounge. No dorm has more than eight beds (choose from capsules for S$50 or cheaper double-deckers), and breakfast includes sandwiches in addition to the self-service basics. Dorms S$30

Five Stones Hostel 61 South Bridge Rd ☎ 6535 5607, ⓦ fivestoneshostel.com; Chinatown MRT; map pp.682–683. The themed rooms here offer a little glimpse into Singaporean life, from the history of rickshaws to the traditional game of *chapteh*. Polaroid snaps line the hallway and there's a Wii console in the chill-out area. Dorms S$25, doubles S$70

Matchbox 39 Ann Siang Rd ☎ 6423 0237, ⓦ matchbox .sg; Chinatown or Tanjong Pagar MRT; map pp.682–683. In an enviable location in the heart of Singapore's nightlife, this welcoming hostel offers capsule beds with thick walls and little hatch windows to communicate with your neighbour. There's a large attic lounge with parquet floors and TV, as well as wi-fi throughout. Dorms S$35

Porcelain 48 Mosque St ☎ 6645 3131, ⓦ porcelainhotel .com; Chinatown MRT; map pp.682–683. Browns and beiges are the default colours of most Singapore hotels, but *Porcelain* bucks the trend with its calming, Ming pottery motifs in blue and white. A good-value, reliable option. Doubles S$160

Wink Hostel 8A Mosque St ☎ 6222 2940, ⓦ winkhostel .com; Chinatown MRT; map pp.682–683. The original pod hostel in the heart of Chinatown, with spotless dorms named after heritage trees and livened up with a splash of paint. There are also double pods for couples (S$90) – each with a reading light, socket and thick walls for privacy. A relaxed vibe prevails and the staff are among the friendliest in town. Dorms S$50

BRAS BASAH, LITTLE INDIA & ARAB STREET

★**Backpackers@SG** 1st floor, 111J King George's Ave ☎ 6683 2924; Lavender or Bendemeer MRT; map pp.686–687. Exceptionally plain hostel barring a few snazzy murals, but cosier for it, occupying part of a low-rise residential block. Unlike some of its competitors, it doesn't have mega-sized dorms – the largest has eight beds. A great choice if you want a quiet stay and aren't fussed about slickness or a buzzy vibe. If they're full they can put you up at their sister hostel just three doors away. Dorms S$21

★**BUNC Hostel** 15 Upper Weld Rd ☎ 6262 2862, ⓦ bunchostel.com; Rochor or Jalan Besar MRT; map pp.686–687. This bright and airy hostel has it all, from Apple Macs for guests' use to fully equipped dorms with clothes racks, reading lamps, individual sockets, lockers and wi-fi. Guests can make use of the barbecue set by the breezy kitchen, and chill out in the outdoor lounge area with colourful beanbags, an Xbox, a mini football table and even a piano. Dorms S$30, doubles S$50

Fisher BnB 127 Tyrwhitt Rd ☎ 6297 8258, ⓦ fisherbnb .com; Bendemeer or Lavender MRT; map pp.686–687. Unexpectedly smart shophouse-based guesthouse with a twelve-bed women's dorm, a sixteen-bed mixed dorm and a four-bed family room. The bathroom decor is bang up to date – the management is especially proud of the Japanese-built bidets. Dorms S$30, four-bed family room S$140

Hangout@Mount Emily 10A Upper Wilkie Rd ☎ 6438 5588, ⓦ hangouthotels.com; map pp.686–687. An impressive designer guesthouse with a breezy rooftop terrace that's great for chilling out in the evening. The only drawback is that it's 10min walk uphill from Selegie Rd. Dorms S$30, doubles S$120

★**The InnCrowd** 73 Dunlop St ☎ 6296 9169, ⓦ the-inncrowd.com; Rochor or Jalan Besar MRT; map pp.686–687. Perennially excellent, very keenly priced hostel with

dorms and a range of rooms, each with TV. Shared showers and toilets are kept spotless, and there's a comfy lounge, cheap beer and free internet access. They run tours too, including a scooter-powered trip around the old quarters and Gardens by the Bay. Dorms S$20, doubles S$60

The Little Red Dot 125 Lavender St ☎ 6294 7098, ⓦ atthelittlereddot.com; Bendemeer or Lavender MRT; map pp.686–687. The friendly staff at this dorm-only hostel will make you feel right at home. There are dorms with bunks, as well as larger mixed and female dorms with capsule beds – each pod has a privacy curtain, locker and reading lamp. There's also a laidback lounge area with beanbags and sofas, a book exchange, Xbox, and free walking tours, pub crawls and gourmet safaris. S$25

Marrison 103 Beach Rd ☎ 6333 9928, ⓦ marrisonhotel .com; Bugis MRT; map pp.686–687. This hotel is surprisingly comfortable, the rooms done out in neutral hues. A good deal, given the location and that they may include breakfast in the rate when business is slow. S$150

Mayo Inn 9 Jl Besar ☎ 6295 6631, ⓦ mayoinn.com; Jalan Besar or Rochor MRT; map pp.686–687. A partial refurbishment has given a new lease of life to the two dozen rooms at this simple, good-value hotel, which features modern bathrooms and, in some cases, what's billed as a neat Japanese-style "bed" – a wooden dais with a mattress on top. S$110

Prince of Wales 101 Dunlop St ☎ 6299 0130, ⓦ pow .com.sg; Rochor or Jalan Besar MRT; map pp.686–687. Justifiably popular place done out in primary colours, with a/c dorms, a couple of double rooms and cheap beer from their own bar/beer garden. Dorms S$20, doubles S$60

Rucksack Inn@Lavender 280A Lavender St ☎ 6295 2495, ⓦ rucksackinn.com; Bendemeer or Farrer Park MRT; map pp.686–687. This hostel has friendly and informed staff and offers mixed dorms (one with pod-type beds), a female dorm and a handful of private rooms in various sizes. Dorms S$24, doubles S$90

Shophouse 48 Arab St ☎ 6298 8721, ⓦ shophousehostel .com; Bugis MRT; map pp.686–687. The rooftop lounge/ terrace is the standout feature at this slick, bustling hostel,

9

which, given the location, also has some predictably quasi-Arabic decor. There's a women's floor, too. Dorms S$20

South East Asia 190 Waterloo St ☎6338 2394, ⓦseahotel.com.sg; Rochor or Jalan Besar MRT; map pp.686–687. Behind the yellow and white 1950s facade is a reasonable hotel with functional if slightly tired doubles. It's practically next door to the lively Kwan Im Temple. S$100

Vintage Inn 60 Race Course Rd ☎6396 8751, ⓦvintageinn.sg; Little India MRT; map pp.686–687. A swanky affair with arrays of capsule-style beds against the wall, each with a privacy curtain. Breakfast includes local dishes such as roti prata. Dorms S$32, double beds S$65

EATING

THE COLONIAL DISTRICT

Cedele #03-28A Raffles City Shopping Centre ☎6337 8017, ⓦcedelegroup.com; City Hall MRT; map pp.686–687. A café/bakery chain, *Cedele* serves up exemplary sandwiches (S$6–8) and sells a vast variety of specialist breads and rich cakes. Some branches, like this one, also have a restaurant serving soups, pies and inventive light meals. Daily 11am–9.30pm.

CHINATOWN & THE FINANCIAL DISTRICT

Amoy Food Court Telok Ayer St, at Amoy St; Tanjong Pagar or Telok Ayer MRT; map pp.682–683. A huge range of noodle, rice and porridge dishes, all cheap and delicious, is on offer here. Dishes from S$3. Mon–Fri 7am–7pm.

Annalakshmi Janatha 104 Amoy St ☎6223 0809, ⓦannalakshmi.com.sg; Telok Ayer or Tanjong Pagar MRT; map pp.682–683. Volunteers here whip up excellent Indian vegetarian buffet lunches, with no set price – you pay what you feel the meal was worth; profits go to an Indian arts foundation. Mon–Sat 11.30am–3pm.

Lau Pa Sat 18 Raffles Quay; Telok Ayer or Raffles Place MRT; map pp.682–683. Wins the prize for being the most atmospheric of Singapore's old-school hawker centres, housed in a historic market building. There's the full panoply of Singapore hawker food, including Malay satay – vendors set up their barbecues just outside on Boon Tat St in the evenings. Open 24hr.

Maxwell Road Food Centre Maxwell Rd, at the end of South Bridge Rd; Chinatown or Tanjong Pagar MRT; map pp.682–683. Open-sided hawker place with over 100 stalls serving a variety of local and regional dishes; the most celebrated outlet is the Tian Tian chicken rice stall. Daily 8am–10pm.

Sarnies 136 Telok Ayer St; Telok Ayer or Tanjong Pagar MRT; map pp.682–683. This welcoming little café, with the menu casually scribbled on the walls in colourful chalk, serves hearty sandwiches with sourdough or rye bread (S$14). The freshly roasted coffee (S$5) is great too, and there's all-day brunch at the weekend. Mon & Tues 7.30am–10.30pm, Wed–Fri 7.30am–midnight, Sat & Sun 8.30am–4pm.

★**Spring Court** 52–56 Upper Cross St ☎6449 5030, ⓦspringcourt.com.sg; Chinatown or Telok Ayer MRT; map pp.682–683. With a prewar pedigree, this now-gargantuan restaurant is *the* place for a slap-up Chinese meal in Chinatown. Must-tries include the excellent if expensive *popiah* (steamed spring rolls, hand-wrapped at a counter outside; S$9), steamed chicken with Chinese ham and greens, and the braised tofu stuffed with vegetables and crowned by a scallop. Dim sum, too. At least S$30 per person without drinks. Daily 11am–3pm & 6–10.30pm.

Tak Po 42 Smith St ☎6225 0302; Chinatown MRT; map pp.682–683. Compact, almost cafeteria-like Cantonese restaurant with all the usual dim sum favourites, including *siu mai* dumplings, excellent pork ribs with black beans, plus a wide range of savoury rice porridges. For afters, try the custard tarts, which are spot-on. Reckon on S$20 per person, without drinks. Daily 7am–10.30pm.

Teh Tarik Time 43 New Bridge Rd; Clarke Quay MRT; map pp.682–683. Dirt-cheap snack-and-chill joint for those local standards, frothy sweet tea and *roti prata* (Indian griddle bread – aka *roti canai* in Malaysia), which is available in three dozen wacky modern varieties, such as with chocolate or cheese. Also basic rice and noodle meals, and nothing costing more than a few dollars. Daily 24hr.

Yixin 39 Temple St; Chinatown MRT; map pp.682–683. Workaday hole-in-the-wall vegetarian place turning out dishes to order, such as mock Peking duck (S$8), plus rice and noodle standards like *lor mee* (yellow noodles in a tangy, gloopy sauce). It's barely signed in English; look for it by the *Santa Grand Chinatown* hotel. Daily 7.30am–9.30pm.

BRAS BASAH, LITTLE INDIA & ARAB STREET

Ah Chew Desserts #01-11, 1 Liang Seah St; Bugis MRT; map pp.686–687. *Ah Chew* confronts you with nothing but unusual local sweets containing beans or other unexpected ingredients. The cashew-nut paste is not bad if a gloop made of nut butter appeals; also available are the likes of *pulot hitam*, made with black sticky rice. Most bowls cost S$4 or so. Daily at least 1.30–11.30pm.

★**Artichoke** 161 Middle Rd ☎6336 6949; Bras Basah or Rochor MRT; map pp.686–687. Tucked away in a little courtyard just off Middle Rd, this gem of a place, helmed by an idiosyncratic chef, serves creative Middle Eastern-inspired fusion, including meze and sharing platters with eccentric offerings such as pork kebabs or beetroot tzatziki. The only desserts are their home-made "*neh neh pop*" ice creams. A worthwhile treat, with mains around S$30. Tues–Fri 6.30–10.30pm, Sat 11.30am–3.30pm & 6.30–10.30pm, Sun 11.30am–3.30pm.

Banana Leaf Apolo 54 Race Course Rd; Rochor MRT; map pp.686–687. This place has been going strong since

WHERE TO EAT

Old-fashioned "coffee shop" diners – also called **kedai kopi** or **kopitiam** – of the sort still common in Malaysia are thin on the ground here, but inexpensive local cuisine is easily found at **hawker centres** (open either from morning through to dinner or, in a few cases, from around 5pm until late) and their more upmarket counterpart, the mall **food court** (generally noon–10pm). Avoid the peak lunch (12.30–1.30pm) and dining (6–7pm) periods, when they can be rammed.

These and proper restaurants aside, there are any number of moderately priced snack outlet chains and café franchises, specializing in anything from soya milk drinks and *kaya* toast (a classic local breakfast, involving coconut curd jam) through to deli sandwiches, burgers and gourmet ice creams.

1974, specializing in tenderly cooked red snapper fish head curry (from S$25). The "South Indian vegetarian meal" is a huge lunchtime thali and a steal at just S$10. Daily 10.30am–10.30pm.

★**Bumbu** 44 Kandahar St ☎6392 8628, ⓦbumbu.com .sg; Bugis MRT; map pp.686–687. A shophouse restaurant festooned with antique Peranakan tiles and carved wooden screens; the cuisine is a terrific mix of Thai and Indonesian, all fragrantly spiced. Standouts include the inky stir-fried squid, chilli basil chicken and bean sprouts with salted egg yolk, plus traditional desserts such as sago with palm molasses. Around S$25 per person, without drinks. Tues–Sun 11am–3pm & 6–10pm.

★**Haji Maimunah** 11 & 15 Jl Pisang ☎6297 4294, ⓦhjmaimunah.com; Bugis MRT; map pp.686–687. This cosy diner is one of very few places serving authentic, inexpensive Malay food, including delicacies like snails in coconut milk, plus good desserts and snacks. Around S$15 per person. Mon–Sat 7am–8pm (may close during Ramadan).

★**Kampong Glam Café** 17 Bussorah St; Bugis MRT; map pp.686–687. Fantastic roadside diner serving inexpensive rice and noodle dishes, cooked to order, plus curries. Come not just for the food but for a good chinwag with friends over *teh tarik* late into the evening. Daily 8am–3am, but closed every other Mon.

Komala Villas 76–78 Serangoon Rd; Little India MRT; map pp.686–687. A veteran, rather cramped vegetarian establishment with more than a dozen variations of *dosai* at just a few dollars each, plus fresh coconut water to wash it down. They also do more substantial rice-based meals from 11am to 4pm. Daily 7am–10.30pm.

MTR 438 Serangoon Rd; Farrer Park MRT; map pp.686–687. It's small and charmlessly modern, but still has people lining up at peak times for its South Indian vegetarian snack meals: spicy one-bowl rice, lentil and nut combos, plus daily specials. Most items cost between S$4 and S$8. Tues–Sun 8.30am–3pm & 5.30–9.30pm.

★**Rumah Makan Minang** 18A Kandahar St; Bugis MRT; map pp.686–687. A street-corner place serving superb *nasi padang*, including the mildly spiced chicken *balado* and more unusual curries made with tempeh (fermented soybean cakes) or offal. For dessert there are

freshly made sweet pancakes stuffed with peanuts and corn – much better than they sound. Just S$10 per head for a good feed. Mon–Fri 7am–8pm, Sat & Sun 7am–5pm.

Saveur 5 Purvis St; Bugis or Esplanade MRT; map pp.686–687. This casual-chic bistro with minimalist decor serves the most keenly priced French food in town. Try the tasty duck confit. Mains from S$18. Daily noon–2.30pm & 6–9.30pm.

★**Tekka Market Food Centre** Start of Serangoon Rd; Little India MRT; map pp.686–687. One of the best old-school hawker centres on the island, generally steamy hot and busy. The Indian and Malay stalls are especially worthwhile; look out for exceptional Indian *rojak* – assorted fritters with sweet dips. Daily 7am till late.

Tiramisú Hero 121 Tyrwhitt Rd; Bendemeer or Farrer Park MRT map pp.686–687. This mellow café with fairy lights and mismatched furniture is a sweet tooth's delight, offering ten different flavours of tiramisú, from oreo to cinnamon, served in cute glass jars (S$8). Daily 11am–10pm.

Zam Zam 697–699 North Bridge Rd; Bugis MRT; map pp.686–687. An old Indian Muslim diner which draws crowds, especially on Fridays, with its decent enough *murtabak* and *biryani* offerings (there's even a venison version of the latter). Daily 7am–11pm.

ORCHARD ROAD

Food Republic Level 5, 313@Somerset mall, 313 Orchard Rd; Somerset MRT; map pp.688–689. Singapore has taken food courts to the level of franchises, some claiming to hand-pick the hawker tenants for quality. This spacious, comfortable example has a wealth of decent stalls. Daily 8am–10pm.

Marché Ground floor and basement, 313@Somerset mall, 313 Orchard Rd; Somerset MRT; map pp.688–689. Mövenpick's *Marché* restaurants are formulaic, but what a formula, when you can have rösti, sausages or crêpes cooked to order in front of you, or help yourself to the superb salad bar. Daily lunch specials offer a meal and drink for S$12, while the bakery counter does takeaway sandwiches (from S$5). Mon–Fri 11am–11pm, Sat & Sun 10am–11pm; bakery from 7.30am.

Miss Korea 87 Killiney Rd; Somerset MRT; map pp.688–689. Cosy, great-value place with tasty one-plate meals

9

and snacks such as *bibimbap* (rice with vegetables, a meat or egg topping and spicy sauce) starting at S$8, plus pork, chicken and beef buffets cooked at your table (lunch S$24, dinner S$30). Mon–Fri noon–2.30pm & 6–10.30pm, Sat 6–11pm, Sun 6–10.30pm.

Spices Café *Concorde Hotel*, 100 Orchard Rd ☎ 6739 8370; Somerset MRT; map pp.688–689. Elaborate buffets galore, the best value of which is the spread of Peranakan and other local cooking for lunch on weekdays (S$42). Daily 6am–11pm.

Warung M Nasir 69 Killiney Rd; Somerset MRT; map pp.688–689. Tiny, venerable Indonesian *nasi Padang* joint, with standards such as fried chicken *balado*, beef and chicken *rendang* and tofu or beans fried with sambal, plus one or two sticky dessert options. Daily 10am–10pm.

DRINKING AND NIGHTLIFE

Bars are sprinkled throughout downtown, especially where gentrified shophouse properties are to hand, such as Boat Quay (popular with tourists and expats alike) and Ann Siang Hill off South Bridge Road (very much a hangout for expat bank staff). There's also a penchant for bars to nestle on rooftops, for the views and seclusion, best of which is *1-Altitude* (see box, p.681).

BARS AND PUBS

It's possible to buy a small glass of beer in most bars and pubs for around S$15, but prices are much higher at posh outlets. During happy hour in the early evening, bars offer local beers or a "house pour" (a cocktail) either at half price, or "one for one" – you get two of whatever you order, but one is held back for later.

28 Hongkong Street 28 Hongkong St, Chinatown ☎ 6533 2001; Clarke Quay MRT; map pp.682–683. The atmosphere is bustling and the innovative cocktails (S$18) will ensure you stay for more than one. The reason you won't find it signed at all is that the management are obsessed with their imagined "underground" status. Book ahead. Mon–Thurs 5.30pm–1am, Fri & Sat 6pm–3am.

Ice Cold Beer 9 Emerald Hill Rd, off Orchard Rd ☎ 6735 9929; Somerset MRT; map pp.682–683. One of several happening places on this period shophouse terrace, with beers kept in ice tanks under the glass-topped bar. Mon–Thurs & Sun 5pm–2am, Fri & Sat 5pm–3am.

Loof Top of the Odeon Towers Extension, 391 North Bridge Rd #03-07 ☎ 9773 9304, ⊛ loof.com.sg; Esplanade or City Hall MRT; map pp.682–683. This rooftop garden bar is an elegant place to chill out, with views into the back of the *Raffles* hotel opposite. There's a strong local flavour too, in the form of cocktails and bar snacks that use lots of Southeast Asian ingredients. Mon–Thurs & Sun 5pm–1am, Fri & Sat 5pm–3am.

Lot, Stock and Barrel 30 Seah St ☎ 6338 5540; Esplanade MRT; map pp.686–687. Cheerful, unpretentious

venue frequented by a post-work crowd in the early evening, with some backpackers making their presence felt later on, drawn partly by a jukebox featuring everyone from Sinatra to Beyoncé. Happy hour until 9pm. Daily 4pm–3am.

The Penny Black 26–27 Boat Quay; Raffles Place MRT; map pp.682–683. Named after the world's oldest stamp, this Victorian London pub was built in Britain and painstakingly reassembled on the busy waterfront. The outdoor area is a great spot for people-watching over an Old Speckled Hen or for watching a Premiership game. Mon–Thurs 11.30am–1am, Fri & Sat 11.30am–2am, Sun 11.30am–midnight.

Prince of Wales 101 Dunlop St, Little India ☎ 6299 0130; Rochor MRT; map pp.686–687. The ground floor of this hostel is taken up by a buzzing travellers' bar with frequent live acoustic sets, plus Australian and New Zealand beers, among many others, at keen prices. Mon–Thurs & Sun 9am– midnight, Fri & Sat 9am–2am.

Red Dot Brewhouse 33 & 34 Boat Quay ☎ 6535 4500; Raffles Place MRT; map pp.682–683. Many of Singapore's slicker bars are expat-run, but not the *Red Dot Brewhouse*, the brainchild of one local who got bitten by the homebrew bug. Among their range of beers and ales, the most radical is the Monster Green Lager, rich in blue-green algae regarded by some as a superfood. Mon–Thurs noon–midnight, Fri noon–2am, Sat 3pm–1am.

Tantric 78 Neil Rd, Tanjong Pagar ⊛ homeofthebluespin .com; Outram Park MRT; map pp.682–683. This likeable shophouse bar is one of several gay nightspots, with outdoor seating on a slick terrace and, upstairs, a nominally separate bar that's a mini-shrine to the prewar American Chinese actress Anna May Wong. Mon–Fri & Sun 8pm–3am, Sat until 4am.

CLUBS

Singapore's clubbing scene has come off the boil in recent years, although big-name DJs continue to play at a couple of establishments. A cover charge of S$20–40 may apply, covering entrance plus one drink; women may be able to get in free on Wednesday, often deemed "ladies' night".

Kyo #B1–02 Keck Seng Tower, 133 Cecil St, Financial District ☎ 8299 8735; Telok Ayer or Raffles Place MRT; map pp.682–683. Highly rated basement venue with progressive dance sounds. Wed & Thurs 9pm–3am, Fri 9pm–3.30am, Sat 10.30pm–4.30am.

Zouk The Cannery, Clarke Quay ⊛ zoukclub.com; Clarke Quay or Fort Canning MRT; map pp.682–683. *Zouk* has proven itself the most enduring and sometimes boundary-pushing dance venue in town, with occasional big-name DJ sets, although it remains to be seen if it can re-create the magic at its new Clarke Quay premises. Cover charge from S$25 but free on Thursdays, when only its hip-hop sub-venue *Phuture* is open. Wed & Fri 9pm–3am, Thurs 9pm–2am, Sat 9pm–4am.

LIVE MUSIC

Singapore is an established stop for big-name and indie bands touring east Asia and Australia, so expect performances at stadiums or at festivals such as Laneway (Jan; ⓦsingapore.lanewayfestival.com). Some bars have house bands playing rock covers or blues, while local indie bands do play at assorted low-key venues and the annual Sundown Festival (ⓦsundownfestival.sg). There are also performances of Western and Chinese classical music at high-profile venues such as the Esplanade Theatres and the Victoria Concert Hall, although there are also occasional free shows at the Botanic Gardens or Gardens by the Bay.

Blu Jaz Café 12 Bali Lane, Kampong Glam ⓦblujazcafe .net; Bugis MRT; map pp.686–687. Raucous café serving reasonably priced beer with live jazz some nights. Mon–Thurs noon–1am, Fri noon–2am, Sat 2pm–4am.

Timbre @ The Arts House 1 Old Parliament Lane, Colonial District #01-04 ⓦtimbregroup.asia; Raffles Place or City Hall MRT; map pp.682–683. Close to the Singapore River, this popular joint is a good spot to sit back and enjoy acoustic sets. Mon–Thurs 6pm–1am, Fri & Sat 6pm–2am.

ENTERTAINMENT

CINEMA

Singapore has more than fifty cinemas, most of which belong to the Cathay (ⓦwww.cathay.com.sg) and Shaw (ⓦshaw.sg) chains; all show a mixture of Hollywood blockbusters and Hong Kong cinema, with occasional art-house flicks. The highlight of the cinematic year is the Singapore International Film Festival (late Nov/early Dec; ⓦsgiff.com).

The Projector Level 5, Golden Mile Tower, 6001 Beach Rd ⓦtheprojector.sg; Nicoll Highway MRT. Lurking within a concrete parking deck is the island's best cinema, an unmodernized 1970s affair lovingly revived with just some fresh coats of paint and cool murals. Devoted to independent films from around the world, it also hosts regular film mini-festivals and sports two bars.

THEATRE AND DANCE

Among local companies to watch out for are the Necessary Stage (ⓦnecessary.org), Theatreworks (ⓦtheatreworks.org.sg) and the Singapore Dance Theatre (ⓦsingaporedancetheatre.com), whose performances may take place at their own premises or other arts centres.

SHOPPING

Don't assume the shopping scene is dominated by the Orchard Road malls – it's worth checking out small shops in areas like Little India and Chinatown, and Chinatown's shopping centres are refreshing because they're totally workaday. Wherever you shop, you'll find that the perennial strength of the Singapore dollar means prices of products such as electronic gear and clothes are on a par with those in the West; some good deals on Asian arts and crafts might be available, but they're likely to be imports. Haggling is the exception, not the rule, and is only expected at small, independent retailers. Tourists can reclaim the 7 percent GST on purchases worth more than S$100, provided the retailer is participating in the scheme, in which case they will display a "Tax Free" sign. It's quite an involved process, however, and some of the refund may be swallowed up by an administrative charge; for the ins and outs, check the "Tourist Refund Scheme" section of ⓦiras.gov.sg.

BOOKS

Kinokuniya Level 4, Ngee Ann City, 391 Orchard Rd; Orchard MRT; map pp.688–689. The island's biggest and by far the best bookshop. Daily 10.30am–9.30pm.

FABRICS AND SILK

On Arab St (see p.685), you'll find some worthwhile textiles and batiks, and the occasional decent Persian carpet amid a mass of Chinese knock-offs. Little India has some silk stores (see p.684).

FASHION AND JEWELLERY

Chinatown has some established jewellery shops, especially worth a visit if you share the Chinese passion for jade. More jewellery shops and goldsmiths can be found at the start of Serangoon Rd in Little India. One classic item (although viewed as a cliché locally) is the gold-plated Risis orchids sold at the National Orchid Garden (see p.690).

CHINESE OPERA

If you walk around Singapore's streets for long enough, you're likely to come across a **wayang**, or Chinese opera, played out on outdoor stages next to temples; downtown, a promising spot is Waterloo St, near the Kwan Im Temple. Wayangs are highly dramatic and stylized affairs, in which garishly made-up and costumed characters enact popular Chinese legends to the accompaniment of the crashes of cymbals and gongs. They take place throughout the year, especially around the time of Chinese/Buddhist festivals; during the Festival of the Hungry Ghosts (see p.678) they are held to entertain passing spooks. An alternative is to pop along to the **Chinese opera teahouse**, 5 Smith St, near the Chinatown Complex (☎6323 4862, ⓦctcopera.com), where S$25 buys you Chinese tea, snacks and an abridged opera performance with English subtitles.

9

Charles & Keith #B3-58 ION Orchard mall, above Orchard MRT; map pp.688–689. Elegant women's footwear by Singapore's answer to Penang's Jimmy Choo. Daily 10.30am–10pm.

SOUVENIRS

Touristy outlets in Chinatown sell everything from multicoloured chops to lacquered bowls. On Bussorah St in Kampong Glam, a couple of outlets selling Peranakan and Malay crafts are clinging on amid the tide of Middle Eastern restaurants.

Arch Esplanade Mall (part of Esplanade Theatres); Esplanade or City Hall MRT; map pp.686–687. Delightful wooden images and models bearing detailed etchings of, say, Marina Bay Sands or shophouse terraces. Daily 10.30am–7.30pm.

Lim's Legacy #02-324 Marina Square mall; Esplanade or City Hall MRT; map pp.686–687. Good for Asian-themed homeware and knick-knacks, sometimes tacky but priced accordingly. Daily 11am–9.30pm.

Rishi Handicrafts 5 Baghdad St ☎6298 2408; Bugis MRT; map pp.686–687. Sells basketware made from rattan, bamboo and other materials. Mon–Sat 10am–5.30pm & Sun 1–5pm.

Tanglin Shopping Centre 19 Tanglin Rd (the western extension of Orchard Rd); Orchard MRT then a short walk; map pp.688–689. For artwork and antiques from around the region.

DIRECTORY

Embassies and consulates Australia, 25 Napier Rd (☎6836 4100); Brunei, 325 Tanglin Rd (☎6733 9055); Cambodia #10-03 Orchard Towers, 400 Orchard Rd (☎6341 9785); Canada, 1 George St, #11-01 (☎6854 5900); Indonesia, 7 Chatsworth Rd (☎6737 7422); Ireland, #08-00 Liat Towers, 541 Orchard Rd (☎6238 7616); Laos, 51 Goldhill Plaza, #13-04 (☎6250 6044); Malaysia, 301 Jervois Rd (☎6235 0111); New Zealand, 1 George St, #21-04 (☎6235 9966); Philippines, 20 Nassim Rd (☎6737 3977); South Africa, #15-01 Odeon Towers, 331 North Bridge Rd (☎6339 3319); Thailand, 370 Orchard Rd (☎6737 2644); UK, 100 Tanglin Rd (☎6424 4200); US, 27 Napier Rd (☎6476 9100); Vietnam, 10 Leedon Park (☎6462 5938). A database of all international representatives in Singapore can be found at ⓦmfa.gov.sg.

Excursions

Wherever you head beyond the downtown area, you're never far from suburbia or ranks of tower blocks in the many new towns. It is worth venturing out, though, as the rest of Singapore's

main island holds quite a few attractions. The **night safari** – the zoo's evening attraction – is on most visitors' lists; less obvious draws include the kitsch Chinese folklore fantasy that is **Haw Par Villa**, and the **Changi Museum**, which commemorates the wartime prison camp where Allied troops and civilians were interned. Many people also dart south across to **Sentosa Island**, now developed into a sort of gargantuan theme park; the big attractions here are **Universal Studios** and the superb **S.E.A. Aquarium**.

BUKIT TIMAH NATURE RESERVE

Singapore's centre remains forested, and there's a family-friendly sliver of primary rainforest on show at the **Bukit Timah Nature Reserve**, Hindhede Drive, a short walk from Beauty World MRT (daily 7am–7pm; free). Many visitors simply walk up the windy road to the top of Bukit Timah, the island's highest point at 170m above sea level, but there are three other colour-coded trails to explore. Expect to see long-tailed macaques, although thankfully no leeches.

THE ZOO, NIGHT SAFARI AND RIVER SAFARI

In the Mandai area of northern Singapore, bordering on a reservoir, nestle three significant zoos (combination tickets available; ⓦzoo.com.sg). All have an "open" philosophy, putting animals in naturalistic enclosures rather than cages. The original is the **Singapore Zoo** (daily 8.30am–6pm; S$33), a substantial affair with numerous highlights, such as the Fragile Forest biodome – a magical zone where you can walk among ring-tailed lemurs, sloths and fruit bats – and Frozen Tundra, featuring, naturally enough, polar bears.

Popular as the zoo is, it's overshadowed by its younger, nocturnal sibling, the **Night Safari** (daily 7.15pm–midnight; S$45), where you get to see animals in spooky, muted lighting, including giant fruit bats, Asian elephants and incredibly cute (but shy) fishing cats. Most visitors line up to catch a tram ride that takes you around two-thirds of the site; seeing it on foot gets you closer to the animals, but quite a few zones can't be accessed this way. Be sure to catch the **Creatures of the Night** show (hourly 7.30–9.30pm, plus Fri & Sat 10.30pm, included in ticket), touching on the importance of conservation and recycling, and starring raccoons, owls and wolves, among others.

Newest of the trio is **River Safari** (daily 10am–7pm; S$30, plus S$5 for Amazon River Quest). Part zoo, part aquarium, it celebrates the fauna of the world's great river basins and the lands they flow through, so covers everything from catfish to giant pandas. One popular attraction is Amazon River Quest, a sluiceway-based theme park ride taking you past scarlet ibis and spider monkeys.

Many hotels and guesthouses sell tickets for private bus transfers to the zoo, which are convenient especially if you're returning late from the night safari. To reach the area by public transport, take the MRT to Ang Mo Kio, then bus #138; or the MRT to Choa Chu Kang, then bus #927.

CHANGI MUSEUM AND CHANGI BEACH

Bus #2 from Tanah Merah MRT drops you right outside the **Changi Museum**, near the site of an infamous World War II POW camp in which Allied prisoners were subjected to the harshest of treatment by their Japanese jailers. The hugely moving prison **museum** (daily 9.30am–5pm; free; ⓦchangimuseum.sg) has sketches and photographs that plot the Japanese invasion of Singapore and the fate of the soldiers and civilians subsequently incarcerated here and elsewhere. Pride of place is given to reproductions of Stanley Warren's so-called Changi Murals, depicting New Testament scenes (the originals are housed within an army camp nearby where Warren was interned). A replica of a simple wooden chapel includes a board of remembrance where visitors can contribute their own thoughts.

From here, it's a ten-minute ride on bus #2 to Changi Point and its **beach**.

Singapore's oldest surviving beach spot (others have been affected by land reclamation and remodelling), it's an indifferent but still relaxing stretch of sand, where you can bask while watching planes descend towards the airport.

HAW PAR VILLA AND THE SOUTHERN RIDGES

The southwest coast of Singapore is lined by a series of ridges and hills billed as the **Southern Ridges**. With the MRT's Circle line running alongside, they offer a decent walk and hilltop views south to the sea and Sentosa, and occasionally east over downtown. If you take the route from west to east, you end up at the HarbourFront Centre, effectively the gateway to Sentosa – making this a possible prelude to an afternoon/evening there.

The one sight at the Southern Ridges is **Haw Par Villa** at 262 Pasir Panjang Rd (daily 10am–7pm; free; Haw Par Villa MRT), an endearing collection of lifesize, occasionally bizarre statuary of scenes from Chinese folklore. Its centrepiece is the **Ten Courts of Hell**, a tunnel that depicts, with both gore and perhaps unwitting humour, the punishments meted out to deceased sinners.

The best starting point for part of the **Southern Ridges walk** is at Pasir Panjang MRT. A short stroll east of here, Pepys Road leads uphill into a ribbon of parkland that continues eastwards, punctuated by the occasional aerial bridge over a highway, through Telok Blangah Hill Park and then Mount Faber, served by the Sentosa cable car; reckon on 1hr 30min. From here it's a steep descent to the HarbourFront Centre, where the VivoCity mall has numerous places to grab food and drink.

SENTOSA

Covering five square kilometres, **Sentosa** (ⓦsentosa.com.sg) was once the sinisterly named Pulau Blaking Mati ("Island of Death Behind"), a jungled affair housing some British military facilities. Thirty

9

VISITING SENTOSA

The **HarbourFront Centre** (HarbourFront MRT), housing VivoCity mall, is the gateway to Sentosa. From there, you can simply stroll the **Sentosa Boardwalk** to reach the island (S$1), although many visitors prefer to head to the top floor of the mall, where the **Sentosa Express monorail** departs (daily 7am–midnight; S$4 from VivoCity, but free from any other station). The most spectacular way there, however, is by **cable car** from HarbourFront Tower II or Mount Faber (daily 8.45am–10pm; S$29 one-way, or S$33 return).

Within Sentosa, all travel is free other than the new cable-car branch line west to Fort Siloso (S$13). There's a colour-coded system of three **bus** lines (daily at least 7.30am–10.30pm) and a beach **tram** that link the island's attractions.

years of intensive development have endowed it with dozens of rides, museums and other attractions, plus a golf course, marina, three beaches and luxury hotels and apartments. Think twice about visiting Sentosa at the weekend and during public or school holidays, when the place can be madly busy.

Resorts World

Two of the island's most high-profile attractions are close to Sentosa's north shore at **Resorts World** (ⓦrwsentosa.com), one of Singapore's two casino resorts; its website advertises occasional ticket deals. Most visitors make a beeline for **Universal Studios** (daily 10am–7pm, with extended hours at peak times; S$74), a blend of massive re-creations of film sets (think ancient Egypt, fairy-tale castles or sci-fi) and corresponding high-tech rides. It is the single most expensive attraction in Singapore, but it can be worth shelling out for the full-on theme park experience, though some rides attract long queues.

The overlooked gem here is the stunning **S.E.A. Aquarium**, simply one of the finest examples of its kind (daily 10am–7pm; S$32). Entered via a middling maritime museum (included in ticket), it has ten tanks superbly covering the marine life of the Indian and Western Pacific oceans. The largest of these, the monster Ocean Gallery, is 36m long.

Fort Siloso

Fort Siloso (daily 10am–6pm; free, S$4.50 for the Surrender Chambers), on the far western tip of the island, serves as a lonely reminder of Sentosa's historical defensive role; with gun emplacements, lookout posts and tunnels, it guarded Singapore's western approaches from the 1880s until 1956. The Surrender Chambers are considered the main attraction, telling the story of the British and Japanese surrenders of 1942 and 1945, respectively, using waxwork figures and commentary.

Beaches and activities

Those wanting a bit more action can learn to surf on the artificial waves of **Wave House Sentosa** (daily 10.30am–10.30pm; from S$35), race down a paved track on the **Sentosa Luge** (daily 10am till late; S$18), or slide down to an islet while suspended from an aerial cable at **Megazip** (daily 11am–7pm; S$45), among many others.

There are also three south-coast **beaches**, which benefit from plenty of imported beige sand, less so from the shipping constantly chugging past; **Siloso** and **Palawan** beaches are central and popular with families, while the more distant **Tanjong** is quieter unless you happen to be there during one of the occasional ticketed beach party events.

Sentosa is generally pretty quiet after dark. If you do linger, you can take in **Crane Dance** (nightly at 8pm; free) on the north shore close to the boardwalk – it's a sound, light and water show involving the courtship of two giant mechanical birds.

AYUTTHAYA

Thailand

HIGHLIGHTS

❶ **The Grand Palace, Bangkok** Home of the country's holiest temple. **See p.717**

❷ **Ayutthaya** Crumbling relics of an ancient kingdom. **See p.739**

❸ **Chiang Mai** Thailand's adventure tourism capital. **See p.750**

❹ **Ko Pha Ngan** Choose between quiet island beaches and the infamous full-moon parties. See p.797

❺ **Khao Sok National Park** Mist-clad cliffs and whooping gibbons make for a memorable stay. See p.808

❻ **Krabi region** Home to stunning islands, lovely beaches and great diving. See p.814

HIGHLIGHTS ARE MARKED ON THE MAP ON PP.704–705

ROUGH COSTS

Daily budget Basic US$20, occasional treat US$50

Drink Singha beer (large) US$2.50

Food Pad thai US$1

Hostel/Budget hotel US$6–15

Travel Bangkok–Chiang Mai (713km): bus 10hr, US$11–27; train 12hr, US$7–42

FACT FILE

Population 68 million
Language Thai
Religions Buddhism and Islam
Currency Baht (B)
Capital Bangkok
International phone code ☎66
Time zone GMT + 7hr

Introduction

With thirty million foreigners visiting the country each year, Thailand is Asia's primary holiday destination and a useful and popular first stop on any overland journey through Southeast Asia. Despite the influx of tourist cash and influence, Thailand's cultural integrity remains largely undamaged. Some ninety percent of Thais practise Theravada Buddhism, and the monarchy is a revered institution. The country is still mainly traditional and rural, and though some cities boast modern high-rises and neon lights, tiered temple rooftops and saffron-robed monks still predominate.

10

Most journeys start in **Bangkok**, which can be an overwhelming introduction to Southeast Asia, but there are traveller-oriented guesthouses and hostels aplenty, as well as heaps of spectacular temples to visit. A popular side-trip is to **Kanchanaburi**, home of the infamous Bridge over the River Kwai. After Bangkok, most travellers head north, sometimes via the ancient capitals of **Ayutthaya** and **Sukhothai**, to the enjoyably laidback city of **Chiang Mai**, where they organize all manner of outdoor activities. To the northwest of Chiang Mai, the beautiful highlands around **Mae Hong Son** and **Pai** are idyllic, while Thailand's **northeast** (Isaan), its least-visited region, offers ancient Khmer ruins at **Phimai** and **Phanom Rung** and is home to the

country's most accessible national park, **Khao Yai**.

After trekking and temples in the north, most visitors head for the **beach**. Thailand's **eastern and southern coasts** are lined with gorgeous white-sand shores, aquamarine seas and kaleidoscopic reefs. The most popular resorts for backpackers are the east-coast islands of **Ko Samet** and **Ko Chang**, the **Gulf coast islands** of Ko Samui, Ko Pha Ngan and Ko Tao, and the **Andaman coast** centres of Laem Phra Nang, Ko Phi Phi, Ko Lanta and Ko Lipe; on this coast, Ko Chang and Ko Phayam offer quieter scenes.

CHRONOLOGY

c. Third or second century BC Buddhism is introduced to the region by Indian missionaries.

c. Sixth century AD The Theravada Buddhist Dvaravati civilization emerges in central Thailand.

Eighth century Peninsular Thailand comes under the sway of the Srivijaya Empire, a Mahayana Buddhist state centred on Sumatra.

Ninth century The Khmer Empire, based at Angkor, takes control of much of Thailand. Their administrative centre is at modern-day Lopburi.

1238 The Thais capture the Khmer outpost at Sukhothai.

1278–99 The reign of King Ramkhamhaeng. He seizes control of the Chao Phraya Valley and develops Sukhothai as the capital of the first major Thai kingdom. Following his death the empire declines.

1351 King Ramathibodi founds the city of Ayutthaya and adopts Angkor's elaborate court rituals. Ayutthaya prospers and by 1540 it rules most of the area of modern-day Thailand.

1568 The Burmese occupy for twenty years.

Seventeenth century Ayutthaya makes a spectacular comeback, as its foreign trade booms, first with Portugal, then Spain, England, France and Holland.

WHEN TO GO

The **climate** of most of Thailand is governed by three seasons: rainy (roughly June–Oct), caused by the southwest monsoon; cool (Nov–Feb); and hot (March–May). The cool season is the most pleasant time to visit and the most popular; during the hot season, temperatures can rise to 40°C. The rainy season hits the Andaman coast harder than anywhere else in the country – heavy rainfall often starts in May and persists until November. The Gulf coast gets much less rain from the southwest monsoon, but is also hit by the northeast monsoon, which brings rain between October and December.

1767 Ayutthaya is recaptured by the Burmese, who raze it to the ground, take tens of thousands of prisoners and abandon the city to the jungle.

1768 Phraya Taksin, a charismatic general, emerges out of the lawless mess, and is crowned king at Thonburi, on the opposite bank to modern-day Bangkok. He conquers all of Ayutthaya's territories, plus Cambodia and Laos.

1782 Taksin is ousted in a coup led by his military commander, Chao Phraya Chakri.

1782–1809 Chakri – reigning as Rama I – moves the capital across the river to Bangkok and builds a new royal palace in Ratanakosin.

1809 Rama I's son, Rama II, succeeds the throne, securing the Chakri dynasty, still in place today.

1851–68 The reign of Rama IV, known as Mongkut. Signs trade treaties with the British, French and the US. By avoiding a close relationship with one power, he protects Thailand from annexation.

1868 Mongkut's son, fifteen-year-old Chulalongkorn (who had been educated by Mrs Anna Leonowens, subject of *The King and I*), takes the throne as Rama V.

1893 Thailand comes under pressure from Western powers, most notably during the Franco–Siamese Crisis when the French send gunboats as far as Bangkok. Chulalongkorn cedes Laos and parts of Cambodia to France.

June 24, 1932 Lawyer Pridi Phanomyong and an army major, Luang Phibunsongkhram (Phibun), lead a coup. Siam's absolute monarchy comes to an end as King Rama VII is sidelined to a symbolic position.

1938 Phibun is elected prime minister. A year later he renames the country Thailand.

December 8, 1941 The Japanese invade, and, after initially resisting, Phibun's government allies with Japan. Pridi secretly coordinates the resistance movement. More than 100,000 people (POWs and Asian labourers) die constructing the notorious Death Railway linking Thailand and Burma.

January 1946 Pridi is elected prime minister.

June 1946 Rama VII's successor, King Ananda, is shot dead in his bed. Three palace servants are convicted, but the murder has never been satisfactorily explained. He is succeeded by King Bhumibol (Rama IX).

1948 Phibun becomes prime minister, and allies with the US against the communist threat.

1957 Phibun narrowly wins a general election, but only by vote-rigging and coercion. He is overthrown by army chief General Sarit, who encourages the monarchy into a more active role.

1963 Sarit dies and is succeeded by General Thanom. The Thais, with US backing, conduct covert military operations in Laos. By 1968, around 45,000 US military personnel are in Thailand, and the economy swells with dollars. Prostitution proliferates, especially in Bangkok's Patpong district.

October 1973 Bloody student demonstrations bring the downfall of Thanom.

October 1976 Students demonstrate again, and hundreds are beaten by police; the military take control and suspend the constitution.

1980 General Prem Tinsulanonda becomes prime minister, with broad popular and parliamentary support, and rules with a unique mixture of dictatorship and democracy. He stands down in 1988 to allow for a democratic prime minister.

1991 Prem's successor, Chatichai Choonhavan, is overthrown in a coup. General Suchinda becomes premier.

1992 Mass demonstrations against Suchinda are brutally crushed, with hundreds killed or injured, but Suchinda is forced to resign when King Bhumibol expresses his disapproval.

1997 Foreign-exchange dealers mount speculative attacks on the baht and the currency collapses, causing a currency crisis across the region.

2001 One of Thailand's wealthiest men, telecoms tycoon Thaksin Shinawatra, and his new party, Thai Rak Thai (Thai Loves Thai), win the elections.

2004 Violence in the Islamic southern provinces escalates sharply, with frequent attacks on police, soldiers, and also Buddhist monks.

September 2006 Thaksin's government is overthrown in a bloodless army coup and Thaksin goes into self-imposed exile.

December 2007 The pro-Thaksin People Power Party wins parliamentary elections, supported by the "Red Shirts", but opposed by the royalist, nationalist "Yellow Shirts".

May 2011 The pro-Thaksin party, now called Pheua Thai, again wins the general election, with Thaksin's sister, Yingluck, as prime minister.

May 2014 The army, led by General Prayut, stages another coup and seizes the reins of power; initially they talk about staging elections in 2015, but the most recent estimate is late 2018, and counting.

October 2016 The much-revered King Bhumibol dies, to be succeeded by his son, Vajiralongkorn (Rama X).

ARRIVAL AND DEPARTURE

Thailand has **land borders** with Myanmar (Burma), Laos, Cambodia and Malaysia, and all these countries have embassies in Bangkok. Bangkok is a major transport hub in Southeast Asia and there are **flights** in from all over the world. There are also international airports at Phuket, Chiang Mai, Ko Samui and Krabi with flights from regional hubs, including Kuala Lumpur and Singapore.

10

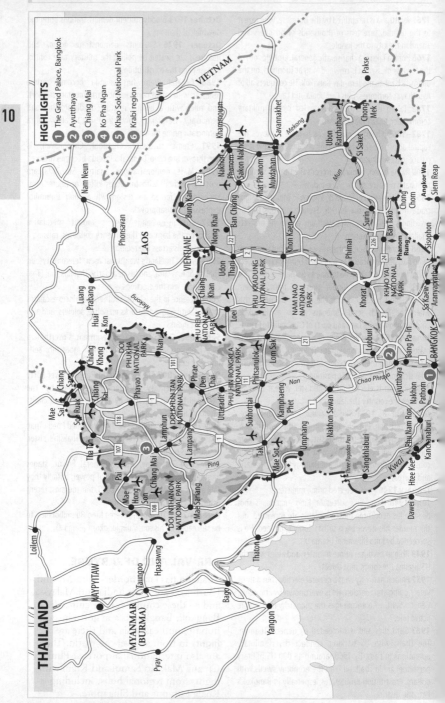

HIGHLIGHTS
1 The Grand Palace, Bangkok
2 Ayutthaya
3 Chiang Mai
4 Ko Pha Ngan
5 Khao Sok National Park
6 Krabi region

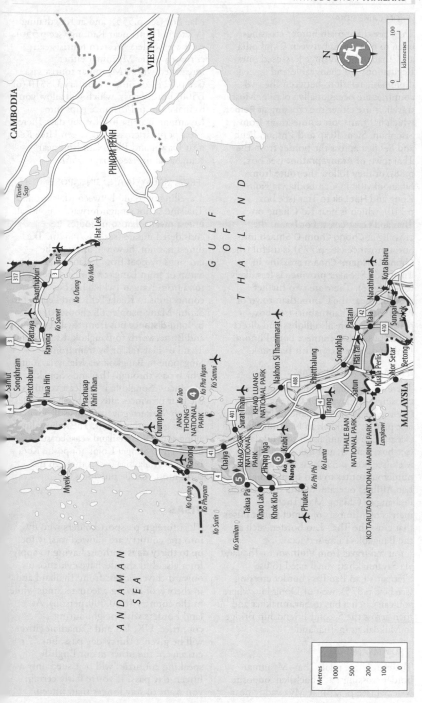

10

FROM CAMBODIA

There are three main border crossings open to non-Thais between Cambodia and Thailand (and three less-used ones). Regulations are changeable and diplomatic relations between the two countries are occasionally volatile. Most travellers use either the crossing at **Poipet**, which has transport connections from Sisophon, Siem Reap and Phnom Penh and lies just across the border from the Thai town of **Aranyaprathet** (see box, p.88); or they follow the route from Sihanoukville in Cambodia via Koh Kong and **Hat Lek** to Trat (see box, p.110), which is near Ko Chang on Thailand's east coast. For Isaan, the crossing at **Chong Chom-O'Smach** into Surin province (see p.775) is useful (the **Chong Sa Ngam–Choam** crossing in Thailand's Si Saket province is less likely to be of use). There are two further crossings near the Cambodian town of **Pailin** east of Chanthaburi (see box, p.104). There are also **flights** and **direct public buses** that connect both Phnom Penh and Siem Reap with Bangkok.

FROM LAOS AND VIETNAM

There are five main Thai–Lao border crossings: Houayxai for Chiang Khong (see box, p.390); Vientiane to Nong Khai (see p.365); Thakhek to Nakhon Phanom (see p.777); Savannakhet to Mukdahan (see box, p.395); and Pakse for Chong Mek (see box, p.399). As well as the numerous routes to and from Bangkok, Lao Airlines operates **flights** from Luang Prabang to Chiang Mai. There are increasing numbers of **direct public buses** that cross the Thai–Lao border, such as the Bangkok–Pakse service.

You can travel from **Vietnam** to Thailand via Savannakhet; you'll need to use Vietnam's Lao Bao Pass border crossing (see box, p.875), west of Dong Ha, where you can catch a bus to Savannakhet and then across the Second Friendship Bridge to Mukdahan in Thailand.

FROM MYANMAR

There are three main Thai–Myanmar border crossings: at Thachileik opposite Mae Sai (see p.523); at Myawaddy near Mae Sot (see p.555); and at Kawthaung (Victoria Point) near Ranong (see p.556). At these borders Western tourists can currently enter Myanmar either forearmed with a Myanmar tourist visa (see p.524), or on a temporary US$10 (or B500) border pass, which will allow you to make limited-distance trips into Myanmar, usually just for the day. There's a less popular crossing between Htee Kee near Dawei and Phu Nam Ron near Kanchanaburi (see box, p.556).

FROM MALAYSIA AND SINGAPORE

Travelling overland between Malaysia and Thailand is not straightforward – political unrest means that some routes are considered unsafe (see box, p.826). The unrest has not, however, affected the crossings by **boat** from Pulau Langkawi to Satun or from Langkawi to Ko Lipe, or by **road** from Kangar (which has bus connections to Kuala Perlis and Penang) to Satun. Many people still choose to travel by **long-distance bus** from Kuala Lumpur and Butterworth to Bangkok, Krabi, Surat Thani or Hat Yai, or by **train** from Singapore to Bangkok via Malaysia, routes which pass through Thailand's Songkhla province – Songkhla is the least volatile of the four provinces affected by the troubles, though Western governments still advise against going through it. The railway line along southern Thailand's east coast, however, to Sungai Kolok (opposite Kota Bahru in Malaysia) passes through the three most volatile provinces.

VISAS

Most foreign passport holders who fly into the country are allowed to stay **for up to thirty days** without having to apply for a visa, but should have evidence of onward travel tickets from Thailand and, in theory, of having adequate funds while in the country (B10,000/person). At land borders with neighbouring countries, UK, US and Canadian citizens will be given a thirty-day pass, but citizens of the other major English-speaking countries will be issued only a fifteen-day pass. If you're fairly certain you want to stay longer than fifteen/

thirty days, you may wish to apply for a **sixty-day tourist visa** at a Thai embassy or consulate in advance (B1000). Your application – which generally takes several days to process – must be accompanied by your passport, one or two passport photos and sometimes by evidence of travel on from Thailand.

It's not a good idea to **overstay** your visa limits. Once at the airport or the border, you'll be required to pay a fine of B500 per day before you leave. And if you get involved with police or immigration officials while in possession of an expired visa, they're obliged to take you to court, possibly imprison you, and deport you.

Sixty-day tourist visas and fifteen- and thirty-day stays can be **extended** in Thailand for a further thirty days, at the discretion of officials; extensions cost B1900 and are issued over the counter at immigration offices (*kaan khao muang*) in nearly every provincial capital – most offices ask for one or two photos as well, plus one or two photocopies of the main pages of your passport, including your Thai departure card, arrival stamp and/or visa; you may be asked for proof of tickets to leave Thailand and evidence of where you're staying. Many tour agents on Bangkok's Thanon Khao San offer to get visa extensions for you, but beware: they are reputedly faking the stamps. Immigration offices also issue **re-entry permits** (B1000 single re-entry) if you want to leave the country and come back again while maintaining the validity of your existing visa.

For the latest information, see the Thai Ministry of Foreign Affairs' **website** at Ⓦmfa.go.th; for further, unofficial details, such as the perils of overstaying your visa, see Ⓦthaivisa.com.

If you need a visa for China or India, you might want to apply at the consulates in Chiang Mai. Laos and Vietnam have consulates in Khon Kaen as well as in Bangkok.

GETTING AROUND

The wide range of efficient **transport** options makes travelling around Thailand very easy and inexpensive.

BUSES, SONGTHAEWS AND MINIBUSES

Ordinary (not a/c) orange buses (*rot thammadaa*) are now found mostly in more remote areas, covering short distances between towns. They've generally been replaced as the workhorses of the bus system by blue, **second-class** (*baw sawng*), air-conditioned buses (*rot air*), which are state-run and inexpensive, but can get packed and are usually quite slow because they stop fairly frequently.

The state-run, blue, **first-class** (*baw neung*), air-conditioned buses are faster and more comfortable, but tend to depart less frequently and don't cover as many routes. In a lot of cases they're indistinguishable from **privately owned air-conditioned buses** (often known as *rot thua*), which ply the most popular long-distance routes and often operate out of government bus terminals.

On some longer routes, there are also more expensive **VIP buses**, with fewer seats and more legroom. Major private companies, such as Nakorn Chai and Win Tour, are generally reliable, but many smaller companies on the main travellers' routes, especially from Thanon Khao San to Chiang Mai and Surat Thani, have a poor reputation for service and comfort despite attracting customers with bargain fares and convenient timetables. Travellers have reported a frightening lack of safety awareness and frequent thefts from luggage on these routes, too (see p.713).

On departure, it's best to **reserve** seats on long-distance a/c bus services ahead, either online at Ⓦwww.pns-allthai.com, the official website, or at Ⓦthaiticketmajor.com, or in person at the relevant bus station or at major post offices. As a rough indication of **prices**, a trip from Bangkok to Chiang Mai (713km) costs up to B900 VIP, around B500 first-class and B400 second-class.

In rural areas, the bus network may be supplemented or replaced by **songthaews** (see p.708). Usually cramped and crazily fast, **air-conditioned minibuses** (*rot tuu*) increasingly feature on popular short- and medium-distance inter-town routes all over the country. They now generally depart from main bus stations, often to a written

10

10

timetable, but sometimes they operate like share taxis, only leaving when they are full.

TRAINS

Managed by the State Railway of Thailand (SRT; ⓦ www.railway.co.th), the **rail network** consists of four main lines and a few branch lines. **Fares** depend on the class of seat, whether or not you want air-conditioning and on the speed of the train – always slow, and usually late. Hard, wooden, third-class seats are very cheap (Bangkok–Chiang Mai B231); in second class, you can often choose between reclining seats and berths, with or without air-conditioning, on long journeys (Bangkok–Chiang Mai B391–881); and in first class (B1253–1453) you'll be in a one- or two-person air-conditioned sleeping compartment. Nearly all long-distance trains have dining cars. **Advance booking** of at least one day is strongly recommended for second-class seats on all lengthy journeys, and for sleepers, book as far in advance as possible. Make bookings at the station in any major town, through the SRT's booking website (ⓦ www.thairailwayticket .com) or through a travel agent such as 12Go Asia (ⓦ 12go.asia). The SRT has a 24-hour hotline (☎ 1690) and publishes free **timetables**; the best place to get hold of one is over the counter at Bangkok's Hualamphong Station (see p.725).

BOATS

Plenty of **boats**, in all shapes and sizes, connect the islands of southern Thailand to the mainland and each other. Large **ferries** with interior seating and decks often jammed with sunbathers serve the bigger islands, and vehicle ferries, catamarans and speedboats are also common. The most pleasurable water vessels to travel in for short journeys, however, are the traditional **longtail boats**, so named for their long-stick propellers that make shallow coastal navigation a doddle.

PLANES

Thai Airways (ⓦ www.thaiair.com) and Bangkok Airways (ⓦ bangkokair.com) are the major full-service airlines on the internal **flight** network, which extends to all parts of the country, using some two dozen airports; Thai Smile (ⓦ thaismileair .com) is Thai Airways' low-cost but often barely distinguishable arm. AirAsia (ⓦ airasia.com) and Nok Air (ⓦ nokair .com) provide the main low-cost competition; look out also for Thai Lion Air (ⓦ lionairthai.com), Vietjet (ⓦ vietjetair.com) and, mostly out of Chiang Mai, Kan Airlines (ⓦ kanairlines .com). Book early if possible – you can reserve online with all companies – as fares fluctuate wildly. For a fully flexible economy ticket, Bangkok to Chiang Mai costs around B4000 with Thai Airways, but you'll find flights on the same route with the low-cost carriers for less than B1000 (with restrictions on changes), if you book far enough in advance.

CAR AND MOTORBIKE RENTAL

Nearly all tourist centres rent **cars** (B800–1500/day) and **motorbikes** (B150–400/day), for which a national driver's licence is usually acceptable; helmets are obligatory on bikes. Thais drive on the left, and the speed limit is 60km/hr within built-up areas and 90km/hr outside them; in practice, a major road doesn't necessarily have right of way over a minor, but the bigger vehicle always has right of way. Avoid driving at night, which can be very dangerous.

LOCAL TRANSPORT

Most sizeable towns have some kind of fixed-fare transport network of **local buses**, **songthaews** or even **longtail boats**, often with set routes, but never with rigid timetabling; within towns songthaews tend to act as communal taxis, picking up people heading in the same direction and usually taking them to their destination, with set prices (around B10–30). It's possible to charter a whole songthaew as a private taxi (notably in Chiang Mai), though this makes it much more expensive. In most towns, you'll find the songthaew "terminal" near the market; to pick one up between destinations, just flag it down, and to indicate to the driver that you want to get out, press the bell, shout, or rap hard with a coin on the ceiling.

Named after the noise of its excruciatingly unsilenced engine, the three-wheeled open-sided **tuk-tuk** is the classic Thai vehicle. They are fast and fun, with fares starting at around B40 (B60 or more in Bangkok), regardless of the number of passengers. Even faster and more precarious than tuk-tuks, **motorbike taxis** feature both in big towns and out-of-the-way places; prices are lower than tuk-tuks and they can halve journey times during rush hour. Motorbike taxis should come with helmets for the pillion passenger. Around the country, these are supplemented by a wonderful variety of jerry-built, hybrid vehicles, including a dwindling band of tricycle rickshaws (*samlor*).

With all types of taxi, bar Bangkok's metered taxis, always establish the fare before you get in.

ACCOMMODATION

It is possible in most places to find simple double rooms with shared bathrooms for B200–350. If you're travelling on your own, expect to pay anything between sixty and one hundred percent of the double-room price. Checkout time is usually noon, so during high season (roughly Nov–Feb, July & Aug) you should try to arrive to check in at about 11.30am.

Most of Thailand's **budget accommodation** is in traveller-friendly **guesthouses** and, at the beach, **bungalows**, which nearly always include an inexpensive restaurant and often also have a tour desk. Many offer a spread of options: their cheapest rooms will often be furnished with nothing more than a double bed, a blanket and a fan (window optional, private bathroom extra) and might cost around B200–300 for two people. For a room with air-conditioning and a hot shower, and perhaps a TV and fridge as well, you're looking at B350–1500. In the major tourist centres, smart, sociable, Western-style **hostels** are increasingly common, charging B200–600 for a dorm bed.

Few Thais use guesthouses, opting instead for Chinese–Thai-run **budget hotels**, often located near bus stations, with rooms in the B200–600 range. They're generally clean and en suite, but usually lack any communal area. Beds are usually large enough for a couple, and it's quite acceptable for two people to ask and pay for a single room (*hong diaw*). **Mid-range hotels** (B600–1200) are often much more comfortable and come equipped with extras such as TV, fridge, air-conditioning, hot showers and perhaps a pool; they generally work out to be good value.

With private rooms so cheap, there's little point in lugging a tent around, unless you're planning an extensive tour of national parks (which often rent out fully equipped tents). Many **national parks** offer basic bungalow accommodation: they aren't always cheap, but advance booking is usually unnecessary except at weekends and during holidays; book online at ⊛nps.dnp.go.th.

Electricity is supplied at 220 volts AC and available at all but the most remote and basic beach huts. Several **plug** types are commonly in use, most usually with two round pins, but also with two flat-blade pins, and sometimes with both options.

FOOD AND DRINK

Thai **food** is renowned for its fiery but fragrant dishes, flavoured with lemongrass, holy basil and chilli, and you can eat well and cheaply even in the smallest provincial towns. **Hygiene** is a consideration when eating anywhere in Thailand, but there's no need to be too cautious: wean your stomach gently by avoiding excessive amounts of chilli and too much fresh fruit in the first few days and always drink bottled water. You can be pretty sure that any noodle stall or curry shop that's permanently packed with customers is a safe bet.

WHERE TO EAT

Throughout the country most inexpensive Thai **restaurants** specialize in one type of food – a "noodle shop" might do fried noodles and noodle soups plus a basic fried rice, but nothing else; a

10

restaurant displaying whole roast chickens and ducks will offer these sliced or with chillies and sauces served over rice; and "curry shops" serve just that. The best and most entertaining places to eat are the local **night markets** (*talaat yen*), where pushcart kitchens congregate from about 6pm (sometimes until 6am), often close to the fruit and vegetable market or the bus station. Each stall is fronted by tables and stools, and you can choose your food from wherever you like.

At a cheap café, you'll get a main course for less than B60, while upmarket restaurants can charge more than B130. Nearly all restaurants open every day for lunch and dinner, often closing around 9pm.

WHAT TO EAT AND DRINK

Thais eat **noodles** when Westerners would dig into a sandwich – for lunch or as a late-night snack – and at around B30–40 they're the cheapest hot meal you'll find anywhere. They come in assorted varieties (wide and flat, thin and transparent, made with eggs, soy-bean flour or rice flour) and get boiled up as soups, doused in sauces, or stir-fried. The most popular noodle dish is pad thai, a delicious combination of fried noodles, spring onions and egg, sprinkled with ground peanuts and lime juice, and often spiked with dried shrimps. Fried **rice** is the other faithful standby. Although very few Thais are **vegetarian** (*mangsàwirat*), you can nearly always ask for a vegetable-only fried rice or noodle dish – though many places will routinely add fish sauce as a salt substitute. All traveller-oriented restaurants are veggie-friendly.

Aside from fiery **curries** and **stir-fries**, restaurant menus often include spicy Thai **soup**, which is eaten with other dishes, not as a starter. Two favourites are *tôm khàa kài*, a creamy coconut chicken soup, and *tôm yam kûng*, a prawn soup without coconut milk. Food from the northeastern **Isaan** region is popular throughout the country, particularly sticky rice, which is rolled up into balls and dipped into chilli sauces, and *sôm tam*, a spicy green-papaya salad with garlic, raw chillies, green beans, tomatoes,

peanuts and dried shrimps. Barbecued chicken on a stick (*kai yaang*) is the classic accompaniment. Raw minced pork is the basis for *larb*, subtly flavoured with mint and served with vegetables.

Sweets (*khanom*) don't really figure on most restaurant menus, but a few places offer bowls of *luk taan cheum*, a jellied concoction of lotus seeds floating in syrup, and coconut custard (*sangkaya*) often cooked inside a small pumpkin. Sweets are more likely to be sold on the street, alongside sticky cakes made from glutinous rice and coconut cream pressed into squares and wrapped in banana leaves.

Thais don't drink **water** straight from the tap, and nor should you: plastic bottles of drinking water are sold countrywide, and in some towns you'll find blue-and-white roadside machines that dispense drinking water at B1 for 1 or 2 litres (bring your own bottle). Night markets, guesthouses and restaurants do a good line in freshly squeezed **fruit juices** and shakes, as well as fresh coconut water and freshly squeezed sugar-cane juice, which is sickeningly sweet.

Beer costs around B35 for a 330ml bottle in a shop, more in a restaurant or bar; the most famous beer is the locally brewed Singha, though many people prefer Leo or Heineken. At about B60 for a 375ml bottle, the local **whisky** is a lot better value and Thais think nothing of consuming a bottle a night. The most drinkable of these is the 35 percent proof Mekhong. Sang Som is an even stronger **rum**. Bars aren't an indigenous feature, as Thais rarely drink out without eating, but you'll find a fair number in Bangkok and the tourist centres.

CULTURE AND ETIQUETTE

Tourist literature has so successfully marketed Thailand as the "Land of Smiles" that a lot of tourists arrive in the country expecting to be forgiven any outrageous behaviour. This is just not the case: there are some things so universally sacred in Thailand that even a hint of disrespect will cause deep offence. The worst thing you can possibly do is to bad-mouth the revered **royal family**. The king's anthem is always played before every film screening in the cinema, during which the audience is expected to stand up.

Thais rarely shake hands, using the **wai**, a prayer-like gesture made with raised hands, to greet and say goodbye and to acknowledge respect, gratitude or apology. The *wai* changes according to the relative status of the two people involved, and as a *farang* (foreigner) it's best to wait for the other person to initiate before responding: raise your hands close to your chest, bow your head and place your fingertips by your nose. Although all Thais have a first name and a family name, everyone is addressed by their first name – even when meeting strangers – prefixed by the title **Khun** (Mr/Ms).

Thailand shares the same attitudes to dress and social taboos as other Southeast Asian cultures (see p.40).

SPORTS AND OUTDOOR ACTIVITIES

Thailand's natural environment is well exploited by numerous tour agencies cashing in on the tourist dollar. While this can sometimes lead to dodgy, often dangerous, practices, the range of outdoor activities available – from snorkelling and scuba diving, river rafting and inner-tube riding, sea kayaking, jet skiing, waterskiing, kiteboarding and stand-up paddleboarding to rock climbing, caving, bungee jumping, elephant trekking, jungle trekking and bike riding – is astonishing. Always choose your tour operator carefully, however, and ask for advice from other travellers.

TREKKING

Trekking is concentrated in the north around Chiang Mai (see p.751) and Chiang Rai (see p.768) but there are smaller, less touristy trekking operations in Kanchanaburi (see p.734), Mae Hong Son (see p.763), Pai (see p.764) and Umphang (see p.749), all of which are worth considering. Treks in the north usually include overnight stays in hill-tribe villages (see box, p.756), a visit to a hot spring or waterfall, elephant

THAI BOXING

Thai boxing (*muay thai*) enjoys a following similar to football in Europe: every province has a stadium, and whenever it's shown on TV you can be sure that large noisy crowds will gather round the sets in streetside restaurants and noodle shops. The best place to see live Thai boxing is at one of Bangkok's two stadiums (see box, p.732). There's a strong spiritual and ritualistic dimension to *muay thai*, adding grace to an otherwise brutal sport. Any part of the body except the head may be used as an offensive weapon, and all parts except the groin are fair targets. Kicks to the head are the blows that cause most knockouts.

riding and bamboo rafting, plus around three hours' walking per day (see box, p.751). A few **national parks**, such as Khao Yai (see p.772) and Khao Sok (see p.808), offer shorter trails for unguided walks; most national parks charge a B200–400 entrance fee.

DIVING

You can **dive** all year round in Thailand, as the coasts are subject to different monsoon seasons: the diving seasons are from November to April along the Andaman coast, from December or January to October on the Gulf coast, and all year round on the east coast.

Major dive centres include Ko Chang (see p.785) on the east coast; Phuket (see p.813), Ao Nang near Krabi (see p.816), Ko Phi Phi (see p.817) and Ko Lanta (see p.819) on the Andaman coast; and Ko Tao (see p.803), Ko Samui (see p.792) and Ko Pha Ngan (see p.797) on the Gulf coast. The diving off the Similan islands, which are accessible from Khao Lak (see p.809), is widely considered to be the most spectacular in the country, and the seas around Ko Tarutao National Marine Park (see p.824) are also impressive. You can organize dive expeditions and undertake a certificated diving course at all these places; Ko Tao dive centres offer the cheapest courses, charging B9000–10,500 for a four-day PADI Open Water course. Always verify the dive instructors'

10

MEDITATION CENTRES AND RETREATS

Of the hundreds of **meditation** temples in Thailand, a few cater specifically for foreigners by holding meditation sessions and retreats in English. The meditation is mostly Vipassana, or "insight", which emphasizes the minute observation of internal physical sensation. Novices and practised meditators alike are welcome. Longer retreats are for the serious-minded only: there's usually around eight hours of meditation per day; tobacco, alcohol, drugs and sex are forbidden; there's generally no eating after midday and no talking; and conditions are spartan. In the south, the most famous retreat centre for foreigners is at Wat Suan Mokkh (ⓦ suanmokkh-idh.org), an hour north of Surat Thani, with a branch on Ko Samui (ⓦ dipabhavan.org). For options in the north, head to the Northern Insight Meditation Centre at Wat Ram Poeng, the Vipassana Meditation Centre at Doi Suthep or, for a gentler introduction to meditation, Wat Suan Dork, all in Chiang Mai (see p.756).

PADI or equivalent credentials, as this guarantees a certain level of professionalism. There are currently **recompression chambers** in Bangkok, Pattaya, on Ko Samui and on Phuket.

OTHER OUTDOOR ACTIVITIES

Thailand's other major outdoor activities are **snorkelling**, which is so widespread that you may want to buy your own equipment rather than rent the often-ropey local gear; and **sea kayaking** – most famous are the guided tours among Krabi and Phang Nga's lagoon caves (see box, p.815), but you'll find kayaks to rent (or sometimes free at your resort) on scores of beaches. **Mountain-bike** rental is sometimes available, but most islands are considerably mountainous, so be prepared for a workout and bring lots of water. At Railay, in the south, you will find one of the best **rock-climbing** destinations in the world, with towering limestone cliffs. **Stand-up paddleboarding** and **kiteboarding** courses and rental are offered on most of the main islands, and **fishing tours** are also plentiful. But to truly appreciate your surroundings while working up a sweat there's **beach volleyball** and **football**, a sunset phenomenon on most island beaches and great way to make new friends; there's truly nothing like freshening up after a big game with a sunset swim in the ocean.

COMMUNICATIONS

Most foreign **mobile-phone** networks have links with Thai networks, but you might want to check roaming rates, which are often exorbitant, before you leave home. You can purchase a Thai pre-paid SIM card for as little as B50 (sometimes free at airports) and refillable at 7-Elevens around the country They offer very cheap calls, both domestically and internationally, and data packages; AIS is the biggest network with the best coverage, including 3G just about everywhere and 4G in many cities. Note that Thai area codes have been incorporated into the subscriber number so even when phoning from the same city, you must dial the entire number.

Wi-fi is now offered free at nearly all guesthouses, hostels and hotels, as well as at many cafés and restaurants. Most travellers now use 3G or wi-fi with their own smartphones, and internet cafés are becoming an endangered species.

International **mail** takes around a week from Bangkok, longer (up to two weeks) from more isolated areas. Almost all main post offices across the country operate a **poste restante** service and will hold letters for two to three months. Surface packages take three months or more.

CRIME AND SAFETY

As long as you keep your wits about you and follow the usual precautions, you shouldn't encounter much trouble in Thailand. **Theft** and **pickpocketing** are two of the main problems, but the most common cause for concern is the **con-artists** who dupe gullible tourists into parting with their cash: be suspicious of anyone who makes an unnatural effort to befriend you, never buy anything from a tout, and heed specific warnings given throughout this chapter. The most notorious scam entails flogging low-grade **gems** at vastly inflated prices: don't be tempted to get involved in gem-dealing unless you know a lot about precious stones.

Theft from some long-distance **overnight buses** is also a problem, with the majority of reported incidents taking place on the temptingly cheap buses run by private companies direct from Bangkok's Khao San Road (as opposed to those that depart from the government bus stations) to destinations such as Chiang Mai and the southern beach resorts. The best solution is to travel direct from the bus stations. On any bus or train, be wary of accepting food or drink from strangers, especially on long overnight journeys: it may be drugged so as to knock you out while your bags are stolen. Violent crime against tourists is not common but it does occur.

There have been several serious attacks on **women travellers** in the past few years, but bearing in mind the millions of tourists visiting the country every year, the statistical likelihood of becoming a victim is extremely small. Unfortunately, it's also necessary for female tourists to think twice about spending time alone with a monk, as there have been rapes and murders committed by men wearing the saffron robes of the monkhood.

Drug smuggling carries a maximum penalty of death in Thailand, **dealing** will get you anything from four years to life in a Thai prison, and **possession** of Category 1 drugs (heroin, amphetamines, LSD and ecstasy) for personal use can result in a life sentence; travellers caught with even the smallest amount of drugs at airports and international borders are prosecuted for trafficking. Away from international borders, most foreigners arrested in possession of small amounts of cannabis are fined and deported, but the law is complex and prison sentences are possible.

MEDICAL CARE AND EMERGENCIES

Thai **pharmacies** (*raan khai yaa*; typically daily 8.30am–8pm) are well stocked with local and international branded medicaments, and most pharmacists speak English. All provincial capitals have at least one **hospital** (*rong phayaabahn*). Cleanliness and efficiency vary, but generally hygiene and healthcare standards are good; most doctors speak English. In the event of a major health crisis, get someone to contact your embassy or insurance company – it may be best to get yourself flown to Bangkok or even home.

INFORMATION AND MAPS

For impartial but often limited **information** on local attractions and transport, call in at the **Tourism Authority of Thailand** (**TAT**; ⓦ tourismthailand.org), which has offices in Bangkok and dozens of regional towns, all open daily 8.30am to 4.30pm. You can also contact the TAT Call Centre from anywhere in the country on ⓣ 1672 (daily 8am–8pm). For a decent **map** of the country, try the 1:1,500,000 maps produced by Nelles and Bartholomew. In addition, Nancy Chandler's maps of Bangkok and Chiang Mai are interesting and quirky; they are available from bookshops.

MONEY AND BANKS

Thailand's unit of **currency** is the baht (abbreviated to "B"), which is divided into 100 satang. Notes come in B20, B50, B100, B500 and B1000 denominations. At the time of writing, the **exchange rate** was B45 to £1 and B35 to US$1. You should be able to withdraw cash from hundreds of **ATMs**, though you'll be charged a fee of B200 at most of them.

10

EMERGENCY NUMBERS

In any emergency, contact the English-speaking **tourist police** who maintain a 24-hour toll-free nationwide line (ⓣ**1155**) and have offices in most tourist centres.

10

THAI LANGUAGE

Most Thais who deal with tourists speak some English, but off the beaten track you'll probably need a few words of **Thai**. Thai is extremely tonal and difficult for Westerners to master. Five different tones are used – low (syllables marked `` ` ``), middle (unmarked), high (marked ´), falling (marked ^), and rising (marked ~). Thus, using four of the five tones, you can make a sentence from just one syllable: mái mài mâi māi – "New wood burns, doesn't it?"

Street signs in tourist areas are nearly always written in Roman script as well as Thai. Because there's no standard system of transliteration of Thai script into Roman, Thai words and names in this book will not always match the versions written elsewhere. Ubon Ratchathani, for example, could come out as Ubol Rajatani, while Ayutthaya is synonymous with Ayudhia.

PRONUNCIATION

a as in "dad"
aa is pronounced as it looks, with the vowel elongated
ae as in "there"
ai as in "buy"
ao as in "now"
aw as in "awe"
ay as in "pay"
e as in "pen"
eu as in "sir", but heavily nasalized
i as in "tip"
ii as in "feet"
o as in "knock"
oe as in "hurt", but more closed

oh as in "toe"
u as in "loot"
uu as in "pool"
r as in "rip"; often pronounced like "l"
kh as in "keep"
ph as in "put"
th as in "time"
k is unaspirated and unvoiced, and closer to "g"
p is also unaspirated and unvoiced, and closer to "b"
t is also unaspirated and unvoiced, and closer to "d"

GREETINGS AND BASIC PHRASES

Whenever you speak to a stranger in Thailand, it's polite to end your sentence in khráp if you're a man, khâ if you're a woman. Khráp and khâ are also often used to answer "yes" to a question, though the most common way is to repeat the verb of the question (preceded by mâi for "no").

Hello	sawàt dii	My name is …	phŏm (men)/ diichān (women) chêu …
Where are you?	pai nǎi? (used as a general greeting)		
I'm out having fun /I'm travelling	pai thîaw (answer to pai nǎi)	I don't understand	mâi khâo jai
Goodbye	sawàt dii/la kàwn	Do you speak English?	khun phûut phasǎa angkrìt dâi mǎi?
Excuse me	khǎw thâwt	Can you help me?	chûay phŏm/ diichān dâi mǎi?
Thank you	khàwp khun		
What's your name?	khun chêu arai?		

GETTING AROUND

Where is the …?	… yùu thîi nǎi?	Boat	reua
How far?	klai thâo rai?	How much is … ?	… thâo rai?/kìi bàat?
I would like to go to …	yàak jà pai …		
When will the bus leave?	rót jà àwk mêua rai?	Cheap/expensive	thùuk/phaeng
		A/c room	hâwng ae
Train station	sathǎanii rót fai	Bathroom/toilet	hâwng nám
Bus station	sathǎanii rót meh	Telephone	thohrásàp
Airport	sanǎam bin	Today	wan níi
Ticket	tǔa	Tomorrow	phrûng níi
Hotel	rohng raem	Yesterday	mêua wan
Restaurant	raan ahǎan	Now	diǎw níi
Market	talàat	Morning	cháo
Hospital	rohng pha-yaabaan	Afternoon	bài
Motorbike	rót mohtoesai	Evening	yen
Taxi	rót táksîi	Night	kheun

10

NUMBERS

0	*sŭn*	10	*sìp*
1	*nèung*	11	*sìp èt*
2	*săwng*	12, 13, etc	*sìp săwng, sìp săam*
3	*săam*	20	*yîi sìp/yiip*
4	*sìi*	21, 22, etc	*yîi sìp èt, yîi sìp săwng*
5	*hâa*		
6	*hòk*	30, 40, etc	*săam sìp, sìi sìp*
7	*jèt*	100, 200, etc	*nèung rói, săwng rói*
8	*pàet*		
9	*kâo*	1000	*nèung phan*

FOOD AND DRINK GLOSSARY

Khăw…	I would like …
Khăw check bin?	Can I have the bill please?
kin ahăan mangsàwirát /jeh	I am vegetarian/vegan

Basic ingredients

kài	chicken
mŭu	pork
néua	beef, meat
pèt	duck
ahăan thalay	seafood
plaa	fish
kûng	prawn, shrimp
puu	crab
khài	egg
phàk	vegetables

Noodle dishes

ba mìi	egg noodles
ba mìi kràwp	crisp fried egg noodles
kwáy tiăw	white rice noodles
… haêng	… fried with egg, meat and vegetables
… nám (mŭu)	… with chicken broth (and pork balls) …
… rât nâ (mŭu)	… fried in sauce with vegetables (and pork)
pad thai	thin noodles fried with egg and spring onions, topped with ground peanuts

Rice (khâo) dishes

khâo màn kài	rice with chicken and chicken broth
khâo nâ kài/pèt	rice with chicken/ duck with sauce
khâo rât kaeng	rice with curry
khâo niăw	sticky rice
khâo pàt kài/muŭ /kûng/néua/phàk	fried rice with chicken/pork/ shrimp/beef/ vegetables
khâo tôm	rice soup

Curries, soups and other dishes

kaeng phèt	hot, red curry
kaeng phánaeng	thick, savoury curry
kaeng khiăw wan	green curry
kài pàt nàw mái	chicken with bamboo shoots
kài pàt mét mámûang	chicken with cashew nuts
kài pàt khĭˉng	chicken with ginger
mŭu prîaw wăan	sweet and sour pork
néua pàt krathiam phrík thai	beef fried with garlic and pepper
néua pàt nám man hŏy	beef in oyster sauce
pàt phàk lăi yang	stir-fried vegetables
plaa rât phrík	whole fish cooked with chillies
plaa thâwt	fried whole fish
sôm tam	spicy papaya salad
tôm khàa kài	chicken coconut soup
tôm yam kûng	hot and sour prawn soup
yam néua	spicy beef salad

Drinks (khreûang deùm)

bia	beer
chaa ráwn	hot tea
chaa yen	iced tea
kaafae ráwn	hot coffee
nám klûay	banana shake
nám maprao	fresh coconut water
nám awy	fresh sugar-cane juice
nám plaò	drinking water

10

OPENING HOURS AND HOLIDAYS

Most **shops** open daily from about 8am to 8pm, though a few close on Sunday. **Banking hours** are Monday to Friday 8.30am to 3.30 or 4.30pm, though bank exchange booths in tourist areas will stay open much later. **Post offices** are generally open Monday to Friday 8.30am to 4.30pm, Saturday 9am to noon. **Private office** hours are generally Monday to Friday 8am to 5pm and Saturday 8am to noon, though in tourist areas these hours are longer, with weekends worked like any other day. **Government offices** work Monday to Friday 8.30am to noon and 1pm to 4.30pm, and national **museums** tend to stick to these hours, too, but some close on Mondays and Tuesdays rather than at weekends. Most shops and tourist-oriented businesses, including TAT, stay open on national holidays. The only time an inconvenient number of shops, restaurants and hotels do close is during **Chinese New Year**, which, though not marked as an official national holiday, brings many businesses to a standstill for several days in late January or early February.

Among official public holidays, the late king Bhumibol's coronation day anniversary (May 5) and birthday (December 5) look set to remain as public holidays for the time being, and the new king Vajiralongkorn's birthday (July 28) may well be added (his coronation will probably take place some time in 2018).

PUBLIC HOLIDAYS

January 1 International New Year's Day.
February/March (day of full moon) Maha Puja.
April 6 Chakri Day.
April (usually 13–15) Songkhran. Thai New Year.
May 1 Labour Day.
May 5 Coronation Day.
May/June (day of full moon) Visakha Puja. The holiest of all Buddhist holidays, celebrating the birth, enlightenment and death of the Buddha.
July/August (day of full moon) Asanha Puja.
August 12 Queen's Birthday/Mothers' Day.
October 23 Chulalongkorn Day. The anniversary of Rama V's death.
December 5 King Bhumibol's Birthday/Fathers' Day.
December 10 Constitution Day.
December 31 Western New Year's Eve.

FESTIVALS

Thais use both the Western Gregorian **calendar** and a Buddhist calendar – the Buddha is said to have died in the year 543 BC, so Thai dates start from that point: thus 2017 AD becomes 2560 BE (Buddhist Era). The most spectacular festivals include:

Songkhran (usually April 13–15) Thai New Year is welcomed in with massive public water fights in the street, at their most exuberant in Chiang Mai and on Bangkok's Th Khao San.

Candle Festival (July/Aug) For three days around the full moon, enormous wax sculptures are paraded through Ubon Ratchathani to mark the beginning of the annual Buddhist retreat period.

Vegetarian Festival (Oct/Nov) Chinese devotees in Phuket and Trang become vegetarian for a nine-day period and then parade through town performing acts of self-mortification.

Loy Krathong (late Oct or early Nov) Baskets of flowers and lighted candles are floated on rivers and ponds to celebrate the end of the rainy season. Best in Sukhothai and Chiang Mai.

Elephant Roundup (third weekend of Nov) The main tourist-oriented festival is in Surin: two hundred elephants play team games, and parade in battle dress.

Bangkok and around

Manic, thrilling, dynamic, exhausting, overpowering, titillating – the one thing **BANGKOK** (Krung Thep in Thai; the "City of Angels") is not, is boring. Whether you spend two days here or two weeks, you'll always find something to invigorate your senses, kick-start your enthusiasm and drive you crazy: frenetic markets and bustling temples, zinging curries and cutting-edge clubs. Bring patience, a sense of adventure and comfy shoes; leave your Western expectation of aesthetics behind and you'll not be disappointed.

Bangkok began life as a largely amphibious city in 1782 after the Burmese sacked the former capital of Ayutthaya. The first king of the new dynasty, Rama I, built his palace at Ratanakosin, which remains the city's spiritual heart. The capital was modernized along European lines in the late nineteenth century, and since World War II has undergone a dramatic transformation. Most of the city's waterways have been concreted over, its citizens no longer live on floating bamboo rafts and the charmless urban sprawl is spiked by skyscrapers. Yet in among the chaotic jumble of modern Bangkok there remains a city fiercely proud of its traditions. As such it is a perfect microcosm of Southeast Asia, and the perfect place to begin your adventures.

WHAT TO SEE AND DO

Bangkok's traveller heart is **Banglamphu**, with its myriad guesthouses, bars and restaurants. From here, it's a short walk to **Ratanakosin**, the royal island on the east bank of the Chao Phraya that is home to the **Grand Palace**, **Wat Pho** and the **National Museum**. To the east, **Chinatown** is noteworthy for its markets and street food, while across the river **Thonburi**'s appeal lies in its traditional canal-side life and boat rides. The amorphous sprawl of **downtown** Bangkok offers several impressive historical residences among its rampant commercialism, though it's primarily a shopper's paradise. At weekends, don't miss the enormous **Chatuchak Weekend Market**, on the city's outskirts, which sells just about everything under the sun.

Wat Phra Kaeo and the Grand Palace

Built as a private royal temple in 1782, the dazzling and sumptuous **Wat Phra Kaeo** is the holiest site in the country and houses its most important icon, the Emerald Buddha. The temple is located within the eighteenth-century **Grand Palace**, now used solely for state functions. The main entrance is on Thanon Na Phra Lan, near to Banglamphu and Tha Chang express-boat pier. Admission (daily 8.30am–4pm, last admission 3.30pm; B500, 2hr audioguide B200, with passport or credit card as deposit) includes entry to the Queen Sirikit Textiles Museum, just to the right of the main gate (daily 9am–4.30pm, last admission 3.30pm), and to Vimanmek Palace (see p.722). There's a strict dress code (legs and shoulders must be covered) but suitable garments and shoes are available just inside the main entrance (free, B200 deposit).

Most visitors head straight for the bot (main sanctuary), which contains the sacred Emerald Buddha, a tiny, jadeite Buddha image, which is just 75cm high. The king ceremonially changes the statue's costume and jewellery seasonally. At the western end of the upper terrace, the eye-boggling gold Phra Si Ratana Chedi enshrines a piece of the Buddha's breastbone. Worth looking out for here are the well-preserved murals of the Ramayana, which stretch for more than 1km inside the wat walls and depict every blow of this ancient Hindu story of the triumph of good over evil in 178 panels.

Wat Pho

Lying south of the Grand Palace, close to the Tha Thien express-boat pier, the seventeenth-century **Wat Pho** (daily 8am–6.30pm; B200), Bangkok's oldest temple, is most famous for housing an enormous statue of the **reclining Buddha**. In 1832, Rama turned the temple into "Thailand's first university" by decorating the walls with diagrams on history,

10

A WORD OF WARNING

If you're heading for the major sights, beware of **scams**. Tuk-tuk drivers or well-dressed people pretending to be students or officials may lie and tell you that the sight is closed, because they want to lead you on a shopping trip, invariably to purchase gems or silk that are often fake or on sale at vastly inflated prices (for which they'll receive a hefty commission). Major sights are rarely closed for national holidays or state occasions, so play it safe and check it out for yourself (you can check closing days for the Grand Palace, for example, at ⓦ palaces.thai.net). Similarly, steer clear of tuk-tuk or taxi drivers who offer to take you on a ridiculously cheap tour of the city; gem shops are often in the itinerary.

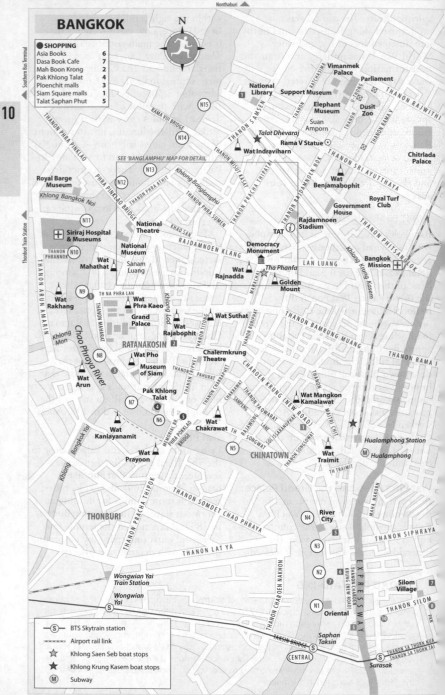

BANGKOK

10

● SHOPPING

Asia Books	6
Dasa Book Cafe	7
Mah Boon Krong	2
Pak Khlong Talat	4
Ploenchit malls	3
Siam Square malls	1
Talat Saphan Phut	5

N

Nonthaburi ▲

Southern Bus Terminal ◀
Thonburi Train Station ◀

THANON PHRA PINKLAO

RAMA VIII BRIDGE

N15
N14

SEE 'BANGLAMPHU' MAP FOR DETAIL

N13
N12
N11

Royal Barge Museum

Khlong Bangkok Noi

PHRA PINKLAO BRIDGE

THANON PHRA ATHIT

National Theatre

Siriraj Hospital & Museums

THANON PHRANNOK

N10
N9

Wat Mahathat

Wat Rakhang

Chao Phraya River

Khlong Mon

THANON ARUN AMARIN

N8

Wat Arun

Khlong Bangkok Yai

N7
N6
N5

Wat Kanlayanamit

Wat Prayoon

THONBURI

THANON PRACHA THIPOK

MEMORIAL BR.

PHRA PHOKKLAO BRIDGE

THANON SOMDET CHAO PHRAYA

THANON LAT YA

Wongwian Yai Train Station

Wongwian Yai

THANON CHAROEN NAKHON

National Library

National Museum

Sanam Luang

TH NA PHRA LAN

Wat Phra Kaeo

Grand Palace

RATANAKOSIN

Wat Pho

Museum of Siam

Pak Khlong Talat

THANON TRIPHET

THANON MAHARAT

THANON SAMSEN

THANON WISUT KASAT

Talat Dhevaraj

★ Rama V Statue ⊙

Wat Indraviharn

Khlong Banglamphu

THANON PHRA SUMEN

KHAO SAN

RAJDAMNOEN KLANG

Wat Rajnadda

THANON PRACHA TIPATAN

THANON RAJDAMNOEN NAI

Democracy Monument

Tha Phanfa ☆

Golden Mount

Wat Suthat

Wat Rajabophit

THANON TI THONG

THANON BURIPHAT

Chalermkrung Theatre

THANON PAHURAT

THANON CHAKRAPHET

CHAROEN KRUNG (NEW ROAD)

Wat Chakrawat

THANON CHAKRAWAT

THANON YAOWARAT

SAMPENG

SOI ISSARANUPHAP

RAJWONG LANE

TH SONGWAT

N5

CHINATOWN

Wat Traimit

THANON SONGWAT

THANON BAMRUNG MUANG

THANON RAMA I

Wat Mangkon Kamalawat

THANON MAITRI CHIT

THANON CHAROEN KRUNG (NEW ROAD)

Hualamphong Station

Ⓜ Hualamphong

MAHA NAKHON

TH TRAIMIT

River City

N4
N3
N2
N1

THANON SIPHRAYA

E X P R E S S W A Y

Silom Village

THANON SILOM

7

10

8

Oriental

Saphan Taksin

TAKSIN BRIDGE

Ⓢ CENTRAL

THANON SA THON NUA

THANON SA THON TAI

Surasak Ⓢ

Vimanmek Palace

Parliament

THANON RAJWITHI

National Library

Support Museum

Elephant Museum

Suan Amporn

Dusit Zoo

THANON RAMA V

THANON SRI AYUTTHAYA

Chitrlada Palace

Wat Benjamabophit

Royal Turf Club

Government House

THANON PHITSANULOK

Rajdamnoen Stadium ⓘ TAT

LAN LUANG

Khlong Krung Kasem

Bangkok Mission ✚

N1

—Ⓢ— BTS Skytrain station

‧‧‧‧‧‧ Airport rail link

☆ Khlong Saen Seb boat stops

★ Khlong Krung Kasem boat stops

Ⓜ Subway

▼ Krung Thep Bridge

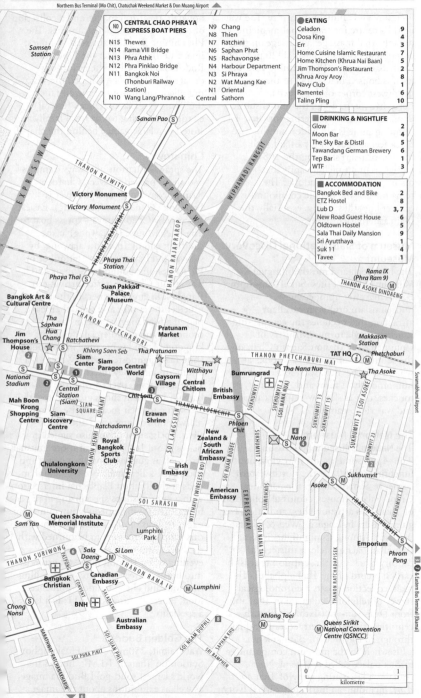

Northern Bus Terminal (Mo Chit), Chatuchak Weekend Market & Don Muang Airport

N0	CENTRAL CHAO PHRAYA EXPRESS BOAT PIERS		
N15	Thewes	N9	Chang
N14	Rama VIII Bridge	N8	Thien
N13	Phra Athit	N7	Ratchini
N12	Phra Pinklao Bridge	N6	Saphan Phut
N11	Bangkok Noi (Thonburi Railway Station)	N5	Rachavongse
		N4	Harbour Department
		N3	Si Phraya
N10	Wang Lang/Phrannok	N2	Wat Muang Kae
		N1	Oriental
		Central	Sathorn

● EATING

Celadon	9
Dosa King	4
Err	3
Home Cuisine Islamic Restaurant	7
Home Kitchen (Khrua Nai Baan)	5
Jim Thompson's Restaurant	2
Khrua Aroy Aroy	8
Navy Club	1
Ramentei	6
Taling Pling	10

■ DRINKING & NIGHTLIFE

Glow	2
Moon Bar	4
The Sky Bar & Distil	5
Tawandang German Brewery	6
Tep Bar	1
WTF	3

■ ACCOMMODATION

Bangkok Bed and Bike	2
ETZ Hostel	8
Lub D	3, 7
New Road Guest House	6
Oldtown Hostel	5
Sala Thai Daily Mansion	9
Sri Ayutthaya	1
Suk 11	4
Tavee	1

10

literature and animal husbandry. The wat is still a centre for traditional medicine, notably Thai massage: a massage on the compound's east side costs B420 per hour (daily 8am–6pm). The reclining Buddha itself is housed in a chapel in the northwest corner of the courtyard. Forty-five metres long, the gilded statue depicts the Buddha entering nirvana. The beaming smile is 5m wide, and the vast black feet are beautifully inlaid with mother-of-pearl showing the 108 lakshanas or auspicious signs that distinguish the true Buddha. The remainder of the temple compound is quieter but still striking, especially the main sanctuary or bot.

Museum of Siam (National Discovery Museum)
The high-tech and mostly bilingual **Museum of Siam** (Tues–Sun 10am–6pm; B200, free after 4pm; ⓦwww .museumsiam.org) is an excellent attraction that occupies the century-old, European-style former Ministry of Commerce on Thanon Sanam Chai, on the south side of Wat Pho. It looks at what it is to be Thai, with lots of humorous short films and imaginative touches such as shadow-puppet cartoons and war video games.

The National Museum
The **National Museum** (Wed–Sun 9am–4pm, some rooms may close at lunchtime; B200), at the northwestern corner of Sanam Luang, the park near the Grand Palace, houses a colossal collection of Thailand's artistic riches, and offers free guided tours in English (Wed & Thurs 9.30am). Among its highlights is King Ramkhamhaeng's stele, a thirteenth-century black stone inscription that is the earliest record of the Thai alphabet. The main collection boasts a chronological survey of religious sculpture in Thailand, from Dvaravati-era (sixth to eleventh centuries) stone and terracotta Buddhas through to the modern Bangkok era.

Elsewhere in the museum compound, a former palace called the Wang Na contains a fascinating array of Thai *objets d'art*, including an intricately carved ivory howdah, theatrical masks, and a collection of traditional musical instruments. The Phra Sihing Buddha, the second-holiest image in Thailand after the Emerald Buddha, is housed in the beautifully ornate Buddhaisawan Chapel, the vast, muralled hall in front of the entrance to the Wang Na. Elaborate teak funeral chariots belonging to the royal family are stored in a large garage behind the chapel.

Chinatown
The sprawl of narrow alleyways, temples and shops packed between Charoen Krung (New Road) and the river is Bangkok's **Chinatown** (Sampeng). Easiest access is by Chao Phraya Express boat to Tha Rachavongse (Rajawong) at the southern end of Thanon Rajawong, by subway to Hualamphong Station, or by Hualamphong-bound bus #53 or #507. The ethnic Chinese started arriving in Bangkok in large numbers in the early nineteenth century and since then have played a fundamental role in the economic and commercial life of the kingdom. Spend some time in **Sampeng Lane** (also signposted as Soi Wanit 1), a kilometre-long alley off Thanon Songsawat that's packed with tiny, bargain-basement shops grouped together according to their merchandise. About halfway down Sampeng Lane on the right, **Soi Issaranuphap** (also signed in places as Soi 16) is good for more unusual fare such as ginseng roots, fish heads and cockroach-killer chalk. Soi Issaranuphap ends at the Thanon Plaplachai intersection with a knot of shops specializing in paper funeral art: Chinese people buy miniature paper replicas of necessities (like houses, cars, suits and money) to be burned with the body. Aim to be here in the early evening when **Thanon Yaowarat** explodes into life and street stalls are set up selling delicious and cheap Chinese-influenced food, especially around Soi 11; fish is a speciality.

The Golden Buddha
Wat Traimit, 250m west of Hualamphong Station on Thanon Tri Mit, houses the world's largest solid-gold Buddha image, as well as exhibitions about the image's

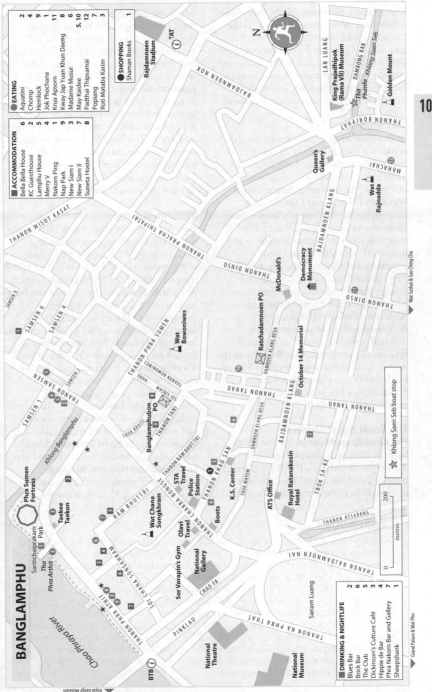

BANGLAMPHU

ACCOMMODATION

Bella Bella House	6
KC Guesthouse	2
Lamphu House	5
Merry V	4
Nakorn Ping	1
Nap Park	9
New Siam I	3
New Siam II	7
Suneta Hostel	8

● EATING

Aquatini	2
Chomp	4
Hemlock	9
Jok Phochana	1
Krua Apsorn	11
Kway Jap Yuan Khun Daeng	8
Madame Musur	6
May Kaidee	5, 10
Padthai Thipsamai	12
Popiang	7
Roti Mataba Karim	3

● SHOPPING

Shaman Books	1

■ DRINKING & NIGHTLIFE

Blues Bar	2
Brick Bar	6
The Club	5
Dickinson's Culture Café	3
Hippie de Bar	4
Phra Nakorn Bar and Gallery	7
Sheepshank	1

10

history and Chinatown (daily 8am–5pm, exhibitions closed Mon; B40, or B100 including exhibitions). More than 3m tall and weighing five and a half tonnes, the **Golden Buddha** was cast in the thirteenth century and completely encased in stucco for several hundred years, probably to protect it from the marauding Burmese.

Wat Arun

In the **Thonburi** district, almost directly across the river from Wat Pho and reached by a cross-river ferry from Tha Thien, rises Bangkok's most distinctive landmark, the enormous five-pranged **Wat Arun** ("Temple of Dawn"; daily 8am–6pm; B100; currently undergoing extensive renovations – some of the temple is likely to be inaccessible at any one time). The temple has been reconstructed numerous times, but Wat Arun today contains a classic central prang (tower) built as a representation of Mount Meru, the home of the gods in Khmer mythology. The prangs are decorated with flowers made from donated porcelain as well as mythical figures. The terrace depicts Buddha at the four most important stages of his life: at birth (north), in meditation (east), preaching his first sermon (south) and entering nirvana (west).

The Royal Barge Museum

The Royal Barge Museum on the north bank of Khlong Bangkok Noi (daily 9am–5pm; B100, plus B100 fee to take photos, B200 for video) houses eight intricately lacquered and gilded vessels which are used every few years for major royal processions. The largest barges require fifty navy oarsmen, and a full procession comprises 52 boats. Photos and drawings give an idea both of the splendour of the barges, and of their practical use and importance; similar boats were used to defend Ayutthaya against the Burmese invasion in 1767. To get to the museum, cross the river, either by ferry to Tha Phra Pinklao or by bus across Phra Pinklao Bridge, and then turn south down Soi Wat Dusitaram, which leads, via winding alleys, to the museum, about a ten-minute walk away.

Vimanmek Palace

Believed to be the largest teak building in the world, the **Vimanmek Palace** was commissioned by Rama V (the whole complex was closed for renovations at the time of writing; see ⓦvimanmek.com). The palace stands in the heart of the leafy royal district of Dusit, northeast of Banglamphu. The entire building was constructed without a single nail, and was home to Thailand's first light bulb and indoor plumbing. Today it holds Rama V's collection of artefacts from all over the world including bencharong ceramics, European furniture and bejewelled Thai betel-nut sets. The whole complex, known as **Dusit Park**, shelters half a dozen other small museums, including the **Support Museum**, filled with exquisite traditional crafts, and the **Royal Elephant National Museum**.

The main entrance to the Vimanmek compound is on Thanon Rajwithi, but

---

CANAL TOURS

One of the most popular ways of seeing Wat Arun and the traditional riverine neighbourhoods of Thonburi is to embark on a **canal tour**. Licensed by TAT, with fixed prices, Mitchaopaya Travel Service (☏02 623 6169) operates out of Tha Chang (on the left at the start of the pier, if you're walking). They offer a one-hour trip for B1000 per boat (max. 6 people) or B450 per person, passing Wat Arun and the barge museum without stopping; or two hours with time to stop at both and an orchid farm thrown in for B1500. On Saturday and Sunday, you could get to Taling Chan floating market on the two-hour trip.

It's also possible to organize your own longtail-boat trip around Thonburi from other piers, including Central Pier (Saphan Taksin Skytrain station), Tha Thien and the small piers between Tha Phra Athit and the Phra Pinklao Bridge. Pandan Tour (☏087 109 8873, ⓦthaicanaltour.com) runs several full-day tours of the canals and floating markets in an eco-friendly teak boat, starting from B2400/person, including lunch.

there's also a ticket gate opposite Dusit Zoo on Thanon U-Thong; Grand Palace dress rules apply (see p.717). The #70 bus runs from Thanon Rajdamnoen Klang near Banglamphu to Thanon U-Thong, or take the express boat to Tha Thewes and then walk (15min).

Wat Benjamabophit

Located on Thanon Sri Ayutthaya, about 600m southeast from Vimanmek's U-Thong gate, **Wat Benjamabophit** (daily 8am–5.30pm; B20) was commissioned by Rama V in the early 1900s. The style blends classical Thai and nineteenth-century European design – the Carrara-marble walls, which gleam in the midday sun, are complemented by unusual stained-glass windows. The courtyard behind the bot houses a gallery of Buddha images from all over Asia. Wat Ben is also the best place to see the daily early-morning ritual alms-giving ceremony (between about 6am and 7.30am); in contrast to the usual parade of monks around the locality, the temple's monks line up and await donations from local citizens.

Wat Indraviharn

The temple complex of **Wat Indraviharn** is dominated by an enormous standing Buddha, 32m high. The striking image, commissioned in the mid-nineteenth century and covered in gold mirror-mosaic, is the tallest representation in the world of the Buddha holding an alms bowl from beneath his robes. His toes peep out through flower garlands, and you can climb the stairs supporting the statue to get a decent view over the area. The temple compound is an interesting amalgam of religious architectural styles and includes a Chinese shrine. Wat Indraviharn is an easy ten-minute walk north of Banglamphu, along Thanon Samsen; bus #53 stops nearby on Thanon Samsen. Be aware that the complex has become a favourite hangout for con-artists (see box, p.717).

Jim Thompson's House

Decades after his death, Jim Thompson remains Thailand's most famous *farang* (foreigner). A former agent of the OSS (later to become the CIA), Thompson moved to Bangkok after World War II and later disappeared mysteriously in Malaysia's Cameron Highlands in 1967. He is most famous for introducing Thai silk to the world and for his collection of traditional art, much of which is now displayed at his former home, **Jim Thompson's House**, which can be seen by compulsory guided tour (daily 9am–6pm; B150; ⊚jimthompsonhouse.com; National Stadium or Siam Central Skytrain stations or on the Khlong Saen Seb canal boat), near Siam Square at 6 Soi Kasemsan 2, Thanon Rama I. The grand, rambling house was constructed – without nails – from six two-hundred-year-old teak houses that Thompson shipped to Bangkok from around the kingdom. The tasteful interior has been left as it was during Thompson's life. There's an appealing restaurant (see p.730) on site, as well as fascinating exhibitions at the Jim Thompson Centre for the Arts.

Bangkok Art and Cultural Centre

A striking, white hunk of modernity at the junction of Rama I and Phrayathai roads, the prestigious **Bangkok Art and Cultural Centre** (Tues–Sun 10am–9pm; free; ⊚bacc.or.th) houses several galleries on its upper floors, connected by spiralling ramps like New York's Guggenheim, as well as performance spaces. There's always something interesting among its temporary shows, which are by contemporary artists from Thailand and abroad across all media. To get here, catch the Skytrain to National Stadium or Siam (Central).

Erawan Shrine

Located on the congested corner of Ploenchit and Rajdamri roads, sitting conspicuously next to the *Grand Hyatt Erawan*, the garishly ornate **Erawan Shrine** is well worth a visit. It is dedicated to Brahma, the Hindu creation god, and Buddhists, including many from Singapore, Hong Kong and Taiwan, come in droves to pray and offer thanks to each of Brahma's heads – luckily for the flower and incense hawkers. Thai dance troops can be hired to perform thanksgiving

10

10

routines here when a prayer has been answered; the number of dancers depends on the magnitude of the wish fulfilled.

Suan Pakkad Palace Museum

The **Suan Pakkad Palace Museum** (daily 9am–4pm; B100), five minutes' walk from Phaya Thai train station at 352–4 Thanon Sri Ayutthaya, is the former palace of Prince and Princess Chumbhot, and visitors can view their private collection of antiquities. The palace is constructed of groups of individual buildings clustered around a garden. Highlights include four-thousand-year-old pottery and jewellery, and the interior of the Lacquer Pavilion, which is decorated with Ramayana panels in gilt on black lacquer. Elsewhere you'll find Thai and Khmer sculptures, ceramics and some fine theatrical *khon* masks.

Chatuchak Weekend Market

With eight thousand open-air stalls to peruse, the enormous **Chatuchak Weekend Market** (Sat & Sun roughly 7am–6pm), about 5km north of Banglamphu, is Bangkok's most enjoyable shopping experience. It's the place to make for if you want to get handicrafts and cheap northern and northeastern textiles and products, including axe pillows, silk, farmers' shirts, musical instruments, jeans, jewellery and designer T-shirts. The market occupies a huge patch of ground adjacent to Mo Chit Skytrain station and Chatuchak Park and Kamphaeng Phet subway stations, and can also be reached by air-conditioned bus #509 from Rajdamnoen Klang in Banglamphu (1hr). By far the best map of the market is on Nancy Chandler's *Map of Bangkok* (see p.713), but boards with maps are also posted at various points around the market, including in the subway stations. You can change money in the market building, and there are ATMs here, too.

ARRIVAL AND DEPARTURE

BY PLANE

Suvarnabhumi Airport Bangkok's main airport (pronounced su-wan-na-poom; BKK; ⓦ suvarnabhumiairport.com) is 30km east of central Bangkok. The airport is well stocked with 24hr exchange booths, ATMs and places to eat, and there are two TAT tourist information counters on the arrivals floor (Floor 2). There's an airport rail link from here to the city centre every 12–15min (30min; B45), where the most useful stops are Makkasan, which is within walking distance of Phetchaburi subway station, and the terminus at Phraya Thai, which is connected to Phraya Thai Skytrain station and is served by bus #59 to Th Rajadamnoen Klang in Banglamphu. An air-conditioned, metered public taxi to central Bangkok, from clearly signposted counters outside Gates 4 and 7 on Level 1, should cost around B300–400 (depending on traffic), including expressway tolls and B50 airport fee. Never take an unlicensed taxi, as robberies are not unknown. From the airport, there are direct buses for Khorat, Khon Kaen, Nong Khai, Rayong (for Ko Samet) and the ferry to Ko Chang (see ⓦ suvarnabhumiairport.com or contact the bus information counter near Gate 7 on Floor 1 of the terminal). To get back out to the airport, guesthouses and travel agents in Banglamphu can book tickets on hourly private minibuses for around B140.

Don Muang Airport Don Muang Airport (DMK; ⓦ donmueangairportthai.com), 25km and a B300–400 taxi ride north of the city, handles low-cost flights operated by the likes of Air Asia, Nok Air and Thai Lion Air; facilities include currency exchange booths, ATMs and restaurants. Shuttle buses from outside arrivals run to Suvarnabhumi (every 20min–1hr; free with a boarding pass) or to Mo Chit Skytrain station, Chatuchak Park subway station and Mo Chit Bus Station (every 12min; B30). There are also Limo Bus Express services to Banglamphu and to Th Silom (every 30min–1hr; B150; ⓦ limobus.co.th), while Don Muang Station, served by trains from Hualamphong Station to the north and northeast, is 5min walk from the airport.

Destinations Chiang Mai (30 daily; 1hr); Chiang Rai (20 daily; 1hr 20min); Chumphon (2 daily; 1hr 10min); Khon Kaen (7 daily; 55min); Ko Samui (20 daily; 1hr 20min); Krabi (20 daily; 1hr 20min); Lampang (7 daily; 1hr); Mae Sot (3–4 daily; 1hr 15min); Nakhon Phanom (4 daily; 1hr 5min); Nakhon Si Thammarat (13 daily; 1hr 15min); Nan (5 daily; 1hr 30min); Phitsanulok (5 daily; 45min); Phuket (30 daily; 1hr 25min); Ranong (2 daily; 1hr 10min–1hr 35min); Sukhothai (3 daily; 1hr 10min); Surat Thani (10 daily; 1hr 15min); Trang (8 daily; 1hr 30min); Trat (3 daily; 1hr); Ubon Ratchathani (10 daily; 1hr 5min).

BY BUS

Bangkok has three long-distance bus terminals. Most services from Malaysia and the south, and from places west of Bangkok, come in at the Sai Tai Mai (Southern) Bus Terminal, about 10km into Thonburi (a few of these services also use the Northern Bus Terminal). City buses serving this terminal include #511 for Banglamphu and Th Sukhumvit, and #30 and #516 for Banglamphu and Thewet. Services from the north and northeast use the Mo Chit (Northern and Northeastern) Bus Terminal on Th Kamphaeng Phet 2, near Chatuchak Weekend Market; either take a short taxi or motorbike taxi ride to Mo Chit Skytrain station or Kamphaeng Phet subway station, or use buses #3, #157 or #159 to Banglamphu. Most buses from the east coast pull into the Ekamai (Eastern) Bus Terminal at Soi 40, Th Sukhumvit (a few east-coast services also use the Northern and Southern Bus Terminal), which is right next to Ekamai Skytrain Station and is connected to Banglamphu by bus #511. On departure, seats on long-distance a/c bus services should be reserved ahead, either online at ⓦpns-allthai .com, the official website, or at ⓦthaiticketmajor.com, or in person at the relevant bus station, at major post offices or at the ATS (Advance Technology System; Mon–Fri 8.30am–5pm; ☎02 872 1777) office near the *Royal Ratanakosin Hotel* on Th Rajdamnoen Klang in Banglamphu, the official seller of government a/c bus tickets.

Eastern Bus Terminal Ban Phe (for Ko Samet; hourly; 3hr); Rayong (every 30min; 2hr 30min–3hr); Trat (roughly hourly; 5hr).

Northern Bus Terminal Aranyaprathet (hourly; 4hr); Ayutthaya (every 20–30min; 1–2hr); Chiang Khong (10 daily; 13–14hr); Chiang Mai (30 daily; 9–11hr); Chiang Rai (at least 20 daily; 12hr); Chong Mek (daily; 11hr); Kanchanaburi (hourly; 2hr 30min); Khon Kaen (every 30min; 6–7hr); Khorat (every 20min; 3hr); Lampang (at least hourly; 8hr); Lopburi (every 20min; 3hr); Mae Hong Son (2 daily; 16hr); Mae Sai (13 daily; 13hr); Mae Sot (13 daily; 8hr); Mukdahan (20 daily; 11hr); Nakhon Phanom (12 daily; 12hr); Nan (13 daily; 11–12hr); Nong Khai (12 daily; 10–11hr); Pak Chong (every 15min; 3hr); Pakse, Laos (2 daily; 12hr); Phitsanulok (50 daily; 5–6hr); Phnom Penh, Cambodia (1 daily; 14hr); Siem Reap, Cambodia (2 daily; 8hr); Sukhothai (every 30min; 6–7hr); Surin (roughly hourly; 8hr); Trat (roughly hourly; 5hr); Ubon Ratchathani (hourly; 10–12hr); Vientiane, Laos (1 daily; 12hr).

Southern Bus Terminal Chumphon (roughly hourly; 7–9hr); Damnoen Saduak (every 40min; 2hr); Kanchanaburi (every 20min; 2hr–2hr 30min); Ko Pha Ngan (2 daily; 14hr); Ko Samui (5 daily; 13hr); Krabi (12 daily; 12–14hr); Nakhon Pathom (every 10min; 40min–1hr 20min); Nakhon Si Thammarat (10 daily; 12hr); Phang Nga (8 daily; 11hr–12hr 30min); Phetchaburi (hourly; 2hr); Phuket (20 daily; 14hr); Ranong (13 daily; 8hr); Surat Thani (12 daily; 10–12hr).

BY BUDGET TRANSPORT

Many Bangkok outfits offer budget transport on small and large buses to Chiang Mai, Surat Thani, Krabi, Ko Samet and Ko Chang. This often works out cheaper than a public a/c bus, and is often handier as departures are usually from Th Khao San. However, many of the buses are cramped and airless, drivers often race, and drop-off points can be far from the town centre, despite adverts to the contrary.

Security on large buses is also a big problem, so keep everything of value on your person at all times and lock other luggage. If you're heading for an island, check whether your bus ticket covers the ferry ride. Consult other travellers before booking any budget transport – all in all, it's better to take the train or a public a/c bus instead.

BY TRAIN

All trains use centrally placed Hualamphong Station except services to Kanchanaburi (plus a few, very slow trains to the south), which leave from Thonburi (Bangkok Noi) Station, about an 850m walk west of the Bangkok Noi express-boat pier. Hualamphong is on the subway line and served by buses #53 to Banglamphu and Thewes, #159 which runs between the Southern and Northern bus terminals, and #507 to Banglamphu. State Railways of Thailand (SRT) operate a special "Ticket Office for Foreigners" (daily 6am–8pm; bring your passport if you're buying tickets) to the left of the main ticket counters in the concourse at Hualamphong Station, as well as a 24-hour information booth in front of the main ticket counters on the right that keeps English-language timetables.

Destinations from Hualamphong Station Aranyaprathet (2 daily; 6hr); Ayutthaya (20 daily; 1hr 30min–2hr); Butterworth, Malaysia (1 daily; 23hr); Chiang Mai (5 daily; 12–15hr); Chumphon (10 daily; 7hr–9hr 30min); Khon Kaen (6 daily; 8–10hr); Khorat (14 daily; 4–5hr); Lampang (5 daily; 10–13hr); Lopburi (16 daily; 2hr 30min–3hr); Nakhon Pathom (12 daily; 1hr 30min); Nakhon Si Thammarat (2 daily; 15–16hr); Nong Khai (4 daily; 11–13hr); Pak Chong (11 daily; 3hr 30min–4hr 45min); Phetchaburi (11 daily; 2hr 45min–3hr 45min); Phitsanulok (11 daily; 5hr 40min–8hr); Surat Thani (10 daily; 9–12hr); Surin (9 daily; 7–10hr); Trang (2 daily; 16hr); Ubon Ratchathani (7 daily; 8hr 30min–12hr).

Destinations from Thonburi (Bangkok Noi) Station Kanchanaburi (2 daily; 3hr); Nakhon Pathom (2 daily; 1hr 30min); Nam Tok (2 daily; 5hr).

GETTING AROUND

BY BOAT

Bangkok's network of waterways is the most interesting means of getting around the city.

Express boats The Chao Phraya Express (ⓦchaophrayaexpressboat.com) runs large river buses in daylight hours between Krung Thep Bridge in the south and Nonthaburi in the north, stopping at numbered piers (*tha*) all along its course, including several useful central ones (see box, p.726). "Local" boats with no flag stop at every landing, but only operate during rush hours (Mon–Fri roughly 6.30–8am & 3–5.30pm; every 20–25min; B10–14). The only boats to run all day (6am–7pm) every day are on the limited-stop orange-flag service (every 5–20min; B15). Other limited-stop, express services run only during rush

10

hours, flying either a yellow (B20–29) or green (B13–32) flag; a sign on each pier shows which service stops there.

Tourist boats Chao Phraya Express tourist boats, distinguished by light-blue flags, with on-board guides, run every 30min between Phra Athit (departs 10am–6pm) and Sathorn (departs 9.30am–5.30pm), stopping at all piers close to tourist attractions, on both sides of the river. A one-day ticket with unlimited stops costs B150; one-way tickets are also available, costing B40.

Khlong Saen Seb boats Passenger boats (ⓦ khlongsaensaep.com) run every 15min or so during daylight hours along Khlong Saen Seb canal from Tha Phanfa, near Democracy Monument (within walking distance of Banglamphu and Ratanakosin), and head way out east, with useful stops at Th Phrayathai, aka Saphan Hua Chang (for Jim Thompson's House and Ratchathevi Skytrain stop), Pratunam (for the Erawan Shrine; everyone has to change boats here because of low bridges) and Soi Asoke (Soi 21, for Phetchaburi subway stop) off Th Sukhumvit. This is your quickest and most interesting way of getting across town, if you can stand the stench of the canal; fares cost B10–20.

Khlong Krung Kasem boats This new service (every 20–30min; free) runs along the canal between Hualamphong Station and the pier at Talat Dhevaraj (Thewes Market), which is 10min walk from the Thewes guesthouses and the express-boat pier at Tha Thewet.

BY BUS

There are two main types of bus services in the city: ordinary (non-a/c; B6.50–8.50, though some are currently free), which come in various colours and run either from around 5am to 10pm or 24hr; and blue, yellow or orange a/c buses (B10–23), most of which run from around 5am to 10pm. Some routes are of use to visitors (see box opposite). For route descriptions, maps and a route planning function, go to ⓦ transitbangkok.com. Of the several bus maps sold at bookshops and hotels, the best and most useful is *Bangkok Guide's Bus Routes & Map*.

BY SKYTRAIN

Although their networks are limited, the BTS Skytrain and the subway provide much faster alternatives to the bus. There are two Skytrain lines (ⓦ bts.co.th) that interconnect at Siam Square (Central Station), both running daily every few minutes from 6am to midnight, with fares B15–52/ trip depending on distance travelled. The Sukhumvit Line heads to the centre from Mo Chit in the northern suburbs, before heading east along Th Sukhumvit to Bearing. The Silom Line runs south from National Stadium, then across the river into Thonburi via Saphan Taksin station, which links up with express boats at Central pier.

BY SUBWAY

The single-line subway (aka the MRT Blue Line) runs frequently (up to every 2min in rush hour; daily 6am–midnight; ⓦ bangkokmetro.co.th). Fares are B16–42. From Hualamphong Station, the line loops round, via Silom, Sukhumvit and Chatuchak Park (each of these three stations is a short walk from a Skytrain station), to Bang Sue in the northern suburbs. Work is under way (scheduled to complete in 2019) to continue the line from Hualamphong, through Chinatown and Ratanakosin, to Thonburi.

BY TAXI

Fares in Bangkok's metered, a/c taxi cabs start at B35 (look out for the "TAXI METER" sign on the roof, and a red light in the windscreen by the passenger seat, which means that the cab is free). Insist that the taxi use its meter; some taxis refuse, especially for late-night or inconvenient journeys. Try to have change with you as cabs tend not to carry a lot

---

CENTRAL STOPS FOR THE CHAO PHRAYA EXPRESS BOAT

N15 Thewes (all express boats) – for Thewes guesthouses.

N14 Rama VIII Bridge (no flag) – for Samsen Soi 5.

N13 Phra Athit (no flag and orange flag) – for Th Khao San and Banglamphu.

N12 Phra Pinklao Bridge (all boats) – for Royal Barge Museum.

N11 Bangkok Noi (Thonburi Railway Station; all boats) – for Kanchanaburi trains.

N10 Wang Lang (or Prannok; all boats) – for Siriraj Hospital.

N9 Tha Chang (no flag, green flag and orange flag) – for the Grand Palace.

N8 Thien (no flag and orange flag) – for Wat Pho, and the ferry to Wat Arun.

N7 Ratchini (no flag).

N6 Saphan Phut (Memorial Bridge; boats stop either here or at the adjacent N6/1, Yodpiman; no flag and orange flag) – for Pak Khlong Talat.

N5 Rachavongse (all boats) – for Chinatown.

N4 Harbour Department (no flag and orange flag).

N3 Si Phraya (all boats) – for River City.

N2 Wat Muang Kae (no flag).

N1 Oriental (no flag and orange flag) – for Th Silom.

Central Sathorn (all boats) – for the Skytrain and Th Sathorn.

10

USEFUL BUS ROUTES

#3 (ordinary and a/c): Northern Bus Terminal–Chatuchak Weekend Market–Th Samsen–Th Phra Athit/Th Chakrabongse–Sanam Luang–Grand Palace–Wat Pho–Memorial Bridge–Wong Wian Yai.

#25 (ordinary, 24hr): Eastern Bus Terminal–Th Sukhumvit–Siam Square–Hualamphong Station–Th Yaowarat (for Chinatown and Wat Traimit)–Wat Pho–Tha Chang (for the Grand Palace).

#53 circular (also anticlockwise; ordinary): Thewes–Th Krung Kasem–Hualamphong Station–Th Yaowarat–Th Maharat (for Wat Pho and the Grand Palace)–Sanam

Luang–Th Phra Athit and Th Samsen (for Banglamphu guesthouses)–Thewes.

#159 (ordinary): Southern Bus Terminal–Phra Pinklao Bridge–Democracy Monument–Hualamphong Station–MBK Shopping Centre–Th Ratchaprarop–Victory Monument–Chatuchak Weekend Market–Northern Bus Terminal.

#511 (a/c): Southern Bus Terminal–Phra Pinklao Bridge–Rajdamnoen Klang–Democracy Monument–Th Lan Luang–Th Phetchaburi–Th Sukhumvit–Eastern Bus Terminal–Pak Nam (for Muang Boran Ancient City buses).

of money. The Uber app has recently come to Bangkok, alongside its Southeast Asian rival, Grab, which offers rides in both cars and motorbikes.

BY TUK-TUK

The unmetered buggies known as tuk-tuks have very little to recommend them (see p.717). The drivers prey on rookie tourists and often overcharge; always agree a price before you set off, and don't forget to barter. Also, there have been cases of robberies and attacks on solo women in tuk-tuks late at night. It's always cheaper (and more pleasant) to use a taxi.

BY MOTORBIKE TAXI

Motorbike taxis, which can only carry one passenger, generally do short local journeys down into the side streets (from B10) but can also be hired to go out onto the main streets (around B40 from Th Samsen to the National Museum). The riders wear numbered, coloured vests; crash helmets are now compulsory. Always agree a price before you set off.

INFORMATION

Tourist information Bangkok Tourism Division, 17/1 Th Phra Athit next to Phra Pinklao Bridge in Banglamphu (Mon–Fri 8am–7pm, Sat & Sun 9am–5pm; ☎02 225 7612, ⓦbangkoktourist.com), provides a decent information service and has thirty or so booths around the capital. Tourism Authority of Thailand (TAT), 4 Th Rajdamnoen Nok (daily 8.30am–4.30pm; national tourist hotline daily 8am–8pm ☎1672), covers destinations further afield.

ACCOMMODATION

Banglamphu, with Thanon Khao San (better known as Khao San Rd) at its heart, remains the city's travellers' ghetto and is home to most of its cheapest accommodation. Th Khao San itself, however, has become progressively

more upmarket and budget accommodation is no longer plentiful. Downtown accommodation is well placed for Bangkok's shopping districts and nightlife.

BANGLAMPHU AND RATANAKOSIN

★**Bangkok Bed and Bike** 19/6 Th Charoen Krung ☎094 487 8058, ⓦbangkokbedandbike.com; map pp.718–719. Excellent hostel with a smart urban look, close to Wat Pho and the Grand Palace. Women's, men's and mixed dorms are a/c with hot showers, and there are bicycle tours, bikes for rent (with great hand-drawn maps of the area) and an impressive array of amenities, including a washing machine and drier. Good breakfast included. Dorms B650, doubles B1600

Bella Bella House 74 Soi Chana Songkhram ☎02 629 3090 1; map p.721. Above a plant-strewn café, the pastel-coloured rooms here are no frills but well priced, and a few boast lovely views over Wat Chana Songkhram. The cheapest share cold-water bathrooms, a notch up gets you an en-suite hot shower, while the most expensive have a/c. Good prices for single rooms, especially the en-suite ones. Doubles B320

KC Guesthouse 64 Trok Kai Chae, corner of Th Phra Sumen ☎02 282 0618, ⓦkc64guesthouse.com; map p.721. Friendly, family-run guesthouse offering exceptionally clean, colourful fan and a/c rooms, with or without private bathrooms, though some rooms suffer from street noise. Doubles B450

Lamphu House 75 Soi Ram Bhuttri ☎02 629 5861–2, ⓦlamphuhouse.com; map p.721. With smart bamboo beds, coconut-wood clothes rails, and elegant rattan lamps, this travellers' hotel set round a quiet courtyard has a calm, modern feel. The cheapest fan rooms share facilities and have no outside view. Doubles B480

Merry V Soi Ram Bhuttri ☎02 282 9267 8, ⓔmerryvguesthouse@gmail.com; map p.721. Large, utterly plain but efficiently run guesthouse offering some of

10

the cheapest accommodation in Banglamphu (small, with shared bathrooms). Better en-suites with hot showers and a/c also available. Good rates for singles. Doubles B300

Nakorn Ping 9/1 Soi 6, Th Samsen ☎02 281 6574, ⓦnakornpinghotel.com; map p.721. In a low-rise, orange building dotted with plants on a fairly quiet soi, this classic Thai-Chinese hotel is efficiently run and good value, offering fridges, cable TV and bathrooms in all rooms. Doubles B490

Nap Park 5 Th Tani ☎02 282 2324, ⓦnappark.com; map p.721. On a surprisingly untouristed street just north of Th Khao San, this lively hostel shelters smart dorm beds with free wi-fi, lockers and hot showers (some with personal TVs), as well as plenty of space for lounging, either inside in front of the TV or outside in the tamarind-shaded front yard. Women-only dorm and laundry available. Dorms B400

New Siam I Soi Chana Songkhram ☎02 629 0101, ⓦnewsiam.net; map p.721. Above a pleasant terrace restaurant, the cheaper options here are well-kept tiled-floor rooms (doubles, twins and singles), all with windows and shared cold showers. Doubles B400

New Siam II 50 Trok Rong Mai, off Th Phra Athit ☎02 282 2795, ⓦnewsiam.net; map p.721. Tastefully decorated fan or a/c en-suite rooms in a quiet, clean, modern guesthouse, with a small swimming pool. Doubles B790

Suneta Hostel 209–11 Trok Kraisi ☎02 629 0150, ⓦsunetahostel.com; map p.721. Welcoming, well-equipped place, 5min walk from Th Khao San, done out with acres of wood to give a retro look; the top-end "cabin" dorm beds have personal TVs. Light breakfast included. Dorms B440

THEWES

The guesthouses clustered behind the National Library on Th Sri Ayutthaya, close to the lively Thewes market, are more charming than their Banglamphu counterparts, appealing to a mixed crowd of travellers and families.

Sri Ayutthaya Soi 14, 23/11 Th Sri Ayutthaya ☎02 282 5942, ⓔsriayuttaya@yahoo.com; map pp.718–719. The most attractive guesthouse in Thewes, with elegant, wood-panelled rooms, ranging from fan-cooled with shared hot shower to en-suite with a/c. There's a great restaurant downstairs which serves delicious vegetarian food. Doubles B500

★**Tavee** 83 Soi 14, Th Sri Ayutthaya ☎02 280 1447, ⓔtaveethai@yahoo.com; map pp.718–719. Down a pedestrian alley behind *Sri Ayutthaya Guesthouse* and owned by the same family, but quieter and friendlier. Fan rooms sport attractive wood floors and share hot-water bathrooms, while the a/c options are en-suite. Doubles B500

DOWNTOWN

The following are away from the main sights of Ratanakosin, but handy for nightlife and shopping.

ETZ Hostel 5/3 Soi Ngam Duphli, off Th Rama IV ☎02 286 9424, ⓦetzhostel.com; map pp.718–719. Above a branch of the recommended ETC travel agent, and handy for Lumphini subway. Helpful, modern and clean, with a roof terrace and a lounge with free computers. A/c dorms sharing hot showers include a six-bed women's room. Dorms B220, doubles B900

Lub D 4 Th Decho (near Chong Nonsi Skytrain) ☎02 634 7999, & 925/9 Th Rama I (National Stadium Skytrain) ☎02 612 4999, ⓦlubd.com; map pp.718–719. Two great hostels with a chilled-out vibe, big, funky, a/c dorms and bedrooms with swish, hot-water bathrooms. The communal areas have an open layout and a friendly feel. Dorms B400, doubles B1000

★**New Road Guest House** 1216/1 Th Charoen Krung, between sois 34 and 36 ☎02 630 9371, ⓦnewroadguesthouse.com; map pp.718–719. Thai headquarters of a Danish backpacker tour operator, with a helpful travel agent and interesting Thailand tours. On offer are comfortable a/c dorms, fan twins and doubles (some with shared bathrooms) and attractive a/c rooms, set around a quiet courtyard off New Rd. Dorms B350, doubles B640

Oldtown Hostel 1048 Th Charoen Krung ☎02 639 4879, ⓦoldtownhostelbkk.com; map pp.718–719. Handy for Hualamphong Station, this hundred-bed hostel features spruce a/c bunk beds and double beds, shared hot showers and extensive common areas, including a ground-floor café and pool table. Dorms B230, doubles B800

Sala Thai Daily Mansion 15 Soi Saphan Khu ☎02 287 1436; map pp.718–719. The last and best of several budget guesthouses on a quiet, narrow alleyway off Soi Saphan Khu, which runs south off Th Rama IV (handy for the subway). Clean, cheerful rooms with wall fans share hot showers and a large, leafy roof garden. B400

Suk 11 1/33 Soi 11, Th Sukhumvit ☎02 253 5927, ⓦsuk11.com; map pp.718–719. The most backpacker-oriented guesthouse on Sukhumvit Rd, whose interior resembles a village of traditional wooden houses, with a wide variety of guest rooms, terraces and lounging areas. The rooms themselves are simple but comfortable, all with a/c and some are en-suite; all showers are hot. Decent rates for singles. Doubles B700

EATING

Bangkok boasts an astonishing fifty thousand places to eat, ranging from chicken on a stick to world-class haute cuisine. There are food stalls on almost every corner (expect to pay B30–50), so you could easily spend a week here without setting foot inside a restaurant.

BANGLAMPHU AND RATANAKOSIN

Aquatini *Navalai River Resort*, 45/1 Th Phra Arthit ☎02 280 9955; map p.721. Occupying a nice wooden deck in a breezy riverfront spot, this hotel restaurant does exceptionally good Thai food at quite reasonable prices.

★ TREAT YOURSELF

A great way to see Bangkok's beautifully illuminated riverside temples at night is on a dinner cruise. Chomping on Thai green curry while gliding past the Grand Palace is an experience you'll never forget. Cruises usually last two hours. Always book in advance; some cruises may not run during the rainy season.

Loy Nava ☎02 437 4932, ⓦloynava.com. The original, forty-year-old converted rice-barge service still departs Si Phraya pier twice nightly, at 6pm and 8.10pm, with pick-ups at Tha Sathorn possible. Live traditional music and dancing. B1550, including hotel pick-up in central Bangkok.

Manohra ☎02 476 0022, ⓦbangkok -riverside.anantara.com. Beautiful converted rice-barge operated by the *Anantara Riverside Resort*, south of Taksin Bridge in Thonburi. Departs at 7.30pm from the hotel, which has a free shuttle boat from Tha Sathorn. From B2300.

Seafood's the speciality, with most mains around B300. Daily 6.30am–midnight.

Chomp Cnr Soi 1, Th Samsen ⓦfacebook.com/ chompcafe; map p.721. Cool café and social hub offering tasty comfort food, such as Western breakfasts and pasta mushroom alfredo (B160), and activities such as yoga and art exhibitions. Daily 9am–11pm.

Err Soi Maharat, Th Maharat ☎02 622 2291, ⓦerrbkk .com; map pp.718–719. A more basic offshoot of *Bolan*, one of Bangkok's finest restaurants, *Err* rustles up "urban rustic" dishes such as delicious *moo hong*, braised pork belly with pepper (B230), in a chic, retro space; wash it down with rice whisky. Tues–Sun 11am–10pm.

Hemlock 56 Th Phra Athit ☎02 282 7507; map p.721. Small, stylish restaurant that offers a long, mid-priced menu, including delicious *tom yam* and green and *phanaeng* curries (around B150). Good veggie selection; worth reserving on Fri and Sat nights. Mon–Sat 5–11pm.

Jok Phochana On a side soi running between Soi 2 and Soi 4, Th Samsen; map p.721. This bare-basics, forty-year-old restaurant, which has featured on national TV, is about as real as you're going to get near Th Khao San (green curry B80). The day's ingredients are colourfully displayed at the front of the shop, and the quiet pavement tables get more crowded as the night wears on. Daily 4pm–midnight.

Krua Apsorn Th Dinso ☎02 685 4531; map p.721. Very good, spicy and authentic food and a genteel welcome. Try the green fish-ball curry (B120) and put the fire in your mouth out with home-made coconut sorbet. Mon–Sat 10.30am–8pm.

Kway Jap Yuan Khun Daeng Th Phra Athit ☎085 246 0111; map p.721. Bustling canteen serving delicious *kway jap yuan* (noodle soup) – go for the "extra" version with egg (B65) and you're set up for the day. Find it in an historic wooden shophouse, unmistakeably painted white and green. Mon–Sat 11am–9.30pm.

Madame Musur Soi Ram Bhuttri; map p.721. Mellow bar-restaurant festooned with vines and paper lanterns with good people-watching tables on the alley, serving a wide range of drinks, including good espressos, and authentic northern Thai food – try the *khantoke*, two kinds of chilli dip with pork scratchings and organic vegetables (B150). Daily 9am–midnight.

★ **May Kaidee** Off Th Tanao & 33 Th Samsen, opposite Soi 2 ⓦmaykaidee.com; map p.721. May Kaidee is something of a Bangkok institution and now operates at two locations, as well as running cookery courses (from B1000). The main restaurant, on a lane off the east side of Th Tanao, serves a full menu of excellent Thai vegetarian food and a popular buffet on Saturday evenings (B150), while *May Kaidee 2* at 33 Th Samsen is an a/c café serving juices, salads and raw food. Daily 9am–10pm (*May Kaidee 2* closed Sun).

Navy Club (Krua Khun Kung) Tha Chang ☎02 222 0081; map pp.718–719. The real draw here is the shaded terrace built right over the river, immediately on the south side of the express-boat pier (though you have to walk around, through the navy compound, with its entrance about 50m south on Th Maharat, to get to it), where you can enjoy excellent dried prawn and lemongrass salad (B130) and other marine delights. Daily 11am–10pm; Mon–Fri kitchen closes 3–4pm, terrace closes from 2pm (last orders) to 6pm.

Padthai Thipsamai 313 Th Mahachai ☎02 221 6280; map p.721. The most famous pad thai in Bangkok, flash-fried by the same husband-and-wife team since 1966. The "special" option is huge, comes with especially juicy prawns, and is wrapped in a translucent, paper-thin omelette. Daily 5pm–2am.

Popiang Soi Ram Bhuttri; map p.721. Popular place specializing in freshly cooked seafood at reasonable prices, such as barbecued whole red snapper for B250. Testament to the rule that the worse the decor is, the better the food. Daily 7am–midnight.

Roti Mataba Karim 136 Th Phra Athit; map p.721. Famous outlet for very cheap fried Indian breads, or rotis, served here in lots of sweet and savoury varieties, including stuffed with meat and vegetables (*mataba*; from B39), served with vegetable and meat curries, or with bananas and condensed milk. A good place to watch the world go by. Tues–Sun 10am–9pm.

DOWNTOWN

Celadon *Sukhothai Hotel*, 13/3 Th Sathorn Tai ☎02 344 8888, ⓦsukhothai.com; map pp.718–719. Consistently rated as the best Thai hotel restaurant in Bangkok, in an

10

10

elegant setting among lotus ponds; well worth a splurge. Try the pomelo salad (B350) and the red curry with duck (B450). Daily noon–2.30pm & 6.30–10.30pm.

Dosa King Soi 11/1, Th Sukhumvit ☎ 02 651 1700; map pp.718–719. Usually busy with expat Indian diners, this vegetarian Indian restaurant serves delicious food from both north and south, including more than a dozen different dosa (southern pancake) dishes, tandooris and the like. Most dishes B100–200. Daily 11am–11pm.

Home Cuisine Islamic Restaurant 186 Soi 36, Th Charoen Krung ☎ 02 234 7911; map pp.718–719. A short, cheap menu of very good Indian and southern Thai dishes, including delicious *khao mok kai* (B85), a kind of chicken biryani, served with aubergine curry. Mon–Sat 11am–9.30pm, Sun 6–9.30pm.

Home Kitchen (Khrua Nai Baan) 94 Soi Lang Suan; map pp.718–719. Congenial, unpretentious restaurant on whose inexpensive Thai and Chinese picture menu you're bound to find something delicious, such as *kaeng som*, a curried soup with shrimp and acacia-shoot omelette (B200). Daily 8am–midnight.

Jim Thompson's Restaurant Jim Thompson's House, 6 Soi Kasemsan 2, Th Rama I ☎ 02 612 3601; map pp.718–719. A civilized, moderately priced haven with delicious Thai dishes (around B250) such as grilled mushroom salad, as well as desserts, cakes and other Western food. Daily 10am–4.30pm & 6–9.30pm.

Khrua Aroy Aroy 3/1 Th Pan; map pp.718–719. In a fruitful area for street food (there's also a night market across Th Silom on Soi 20), this simple shophouse stands out for its choice of cheap, tasty dishes from around the country, such as chicken massaman curry (B90). Daily 10am till about 6pm, or when the food runs out.

★**Ramentei** 23/8–9 Soi Thaniya, Th Silom; map pp.718–719. Excellent Japanese noodle café, bright, clean and welcoming. The open kitchen turns out especially good, huge bowls of miso ramen (B230), which goes very well with the gyoza dumplings (B130). Daily 11am–2am.

★**Taling Pling** Baan Silom Arcade, corner of Th Silom and Soi 19 ☎ 02 236 4829; map pp.718–719. One of the best Thai restaurants in the city outside of the big hotels. The green beef curry (B145) is toothsome and delicious, and goes well with roti bread and the house deep-fried fish salad. Branches in Siam Paragon and Central World shopping centres. Daily 11am–10pm.

DRINKING AND NIGHTLIFE

The lively, teeming venues of backpacker-oriented Banglamphu are a great place to meet other travellers and enjoy live music. Elsewhere, Silom 2 (Soi 2, at the east end of Th Silom) and Silom 4 are the focus of the city's gay scene.

BANGLAMPHU

Blues Bar (aka Ad Here the 13th) 13 Th Samsen; map p.721. Small, chilled-out bar where you can relax with musos and enjoy popular live jazz and blues from about 9.30pm onwards. Good cocktails too. Daily 6pm–midnight.

Brick Bar Buddy Village complex, 265 Th Khao San; map p.721. Funky live-music bar that offers reggae, ska, rock'n'roll and Thai pop. Popular with locals and gets rammed at weekends, when there's sometimes an entry charge, depending on who's on. Daily 7pm–1.30am.

The Club Th Khao San; map p.721. If all the Chang beer's gone straight to your feet, grab your dancing shoes and head to *The Club*. Resident DJs pump thumping house tunes through the two bars and relatively spacious dance-floor until late. Daily 9pm–3am.

Dickinson's Culture Café 64 Th Phra Athit; map p.721. Grungy shophouse café decorated with a mess of empty picture frames and traffic cones, which hosts some great DJs playing techno, underground house and trance. Sip on cocktails (including dozens of martinis) or buckets. Mon–Fri noon–2am, Sat & Sun 5pm–2am.

★**Hippie de Bar** 46 Th Khao San; map p.721. Inviting courtyard bar set away from the main fray, attracting a mixed studenty/arty/high-society, mostly Thai crowd, to drink at its wrought-iron tables and park benches. Indoors is totally kitsch. Daily 4pm–2am.

Sheepshank Tha Phra Arthit express-boat pier ⓦ sheepshankpublichouse.com; map p.721. Set in a former boat-repair yard overlooking the river and sporting an industrial look, *Sheepshank* offers a wide selection of bottled craft beers, as well as imaginative bar snacks and a long menu of more substantial gastropub dishes. Tues–Sun 5pm–1am.

DOWNTOWN

Glow 96/4–5 Soi 23, Th Sukhumvit ⓦ facebook.com /glowbkk; map pp.718–719. This small, unpretentious three-storey venue with a great sound system attracts an interesting roster of Thai and international DJs to play house and techno. Wed–Sun 9pm–2.30am.

RED-LIGHT BANGKOK

More than a thousand sex-related businesses operate in Bangkok: they dominate Thanon Sukhumvit's Soi Cowboy (between sois 21 and 23) and Soi Nana (Soi 4), but the city's most notorious zone is **Patpong**, between the eastern ends of Silom and Suriwong roads. If you do end up at a sex show, be warned that you'll be charged exorbitant prices for drinks, and will have to face a menacing bouncer if you refuse to pay.

10

★**Tawandang German Brewery** 462/61 Th Rama III ☎02 678 1114–6, ⓦfacebook.com/tawandang; map pp.718–719. A taxi ride south of Chong Nonsi Skytrain down Th Narathiwat Ratchanakharin – and best to book a table in advance – but this vast, good-time all-rounder is well worth the effort: good food, great microbrewed German beer and a hugely entertaining cabaret, featuring Thai and Western music, magic shows and ballet. Daily 5pm–1am.

Tep Bar Soi Nana, off Th Charoen Krung ⓦfacebook.com/tepbarth; map pp.718–719. On Chinatown's artsy Soi Nana, *Tep* offers Thai herbal whisky, grilled meats and other tasty food, and weekend performances of Thai music. Tues–Sun 5pm–midnight.

WTF 7 Soi 51, Th Sukhumvit, 5min walk west of BTS Thong Lo ☎02 662 6246, ⓦwtfbangkok.com; map pp.718–719. Small Spanish-influenced bar-café and art gallery, which hosts occasional poetry nights, left-field DJs and gigs. It offers tapas, a tempting variety of cocktails and wines, and a great soundtrack. Tues–Sun 6pm–1am.

SHOPPING

Department stores, shopping malls and tourist-oriented shops in the city open at 10 or 11am and close at about 9pm.

BOOKS

Asia Books ⓦasiabooks.com; map pp.718–719. English-language bookshop with many branches including: on Th Sukhumvit between sois 15 and 19; in Siam Paragon on Th Rama I; in Central Chitlom on Th Ploenchit; and in Thaniya Plaza on Soi Thaniya off Th Silom.

Dasa Book Cafe Between sois 26 and 28, Th Sukhumvit ⓦdasabookcafe.com; map pp.718–719. Bangkok's best secondhand bookshop: browse its stock online, or enjoy coffee and cakes *in situ*. Daily 10am–8pm.

Shaman Books 71 Th Khao San; map p.721. One of Banglamphu's main outlets for secondhand books. Daily 8am–11pm.

MALLS

Mah Boon Krong (MBK) Rama I/Phrayathai intersection; National Stadium Skytrain stop; map pp.718–719. Labyrinthine shopping centre that houses hundreds of small, mostly inexpensive outlets. It's great for cheap flip-flops, handbags and clothes, and there are numerous opticians as well as stalls selling cut-price beauty products. Floor 3 is the best place to buy anything to do with mobile phones; floors 5 and 6 have extensive food courts and floor 7 has a cinema with daily English-language film showings.

Ploenchit map pp.718–719. Around Ploenchit you'll find yet more upmarket malls, including the unclassifiably huge Central World and the small but ever so chi-chi

★**TREAT YOURSELF**

Bangkok can be monstrously ugly by day, but as the sun sets and the smog dissolves, the city can reveal a magical charm. The best way to take advantage of this is to treat yourself to a pricey drink at one of the enormously tall skyscraper hotels that have rooftop bars.

Moon Bar *Banyan Tree Hotel*, Th Sathorn Tai ⓦbanyantree.com; map pp.718–719. Almost as high as *Sky Bar*, but not as crowded, *Moon Bar* offers fabulous views and an awesome cocktail menu. Daily 5pm–1am.

Phra Nakorn Bar and Gallery 58/2 Soi Damnoen Klang Tai ⓦfacebook.com/phranakornbarandgallery; map p.721. Popular with artists and art students, who can admire the floodlit view of the Golden Mount chedi from the candlelit rooftop terrace, tuck into good food and browse one of the regular exhibitions. Nothing like as stunning as the lofty hotel bars, but then again the drinks are about a quarter of the price. Daily 6pm–1am.

The Sky Bar & Distil Floor 63, State Tower, 1055 Th Silom, corner of Th Charoen Krung ⓦlebua.com; map pp.718–719. Come at opening time to enjoy the stunning panoramas in both the light and the dark. It's standing-only at the circular *Sky Bar*, on the edge of the building with almost 360° views, but for the sunset itself, you're better off on the outside terrace of *Distil* on the other side of the building, which has huge couches to recline on. Very popular since *Hangover II* was filmed here, and they have introduced a smart-casual dress code. Daily: *Sky Bar* 6pm–1am, *Distil* 5pm–1am.

Gaysorn Village, as well as Central Chitlom, the city's best department store.

Siam Square map pp.718–719. The area around Siam Square is packed full of malls; check out Siam Center and Siam Discovery Centre, the former of which is especially good for trendy local labels. In Siam Square, head to what's styled as the area's "Centerpoint" between sois 3 and 4, around which hundreds of inexpensive boutiques sell colourful street-gear. Siam Paragon houses the most expensive shops in Bangkok in a luxurious mall and has an incredible food centre in the basement.

MARKETS
Chatuchak Weekend Market See p.724.

10

THAI BOXING

Thai boxing (*muay thai*) can be very violent, but also very entertaining. Sessions usually feature around ten bouts of five three-minute rounds and are held at Rajdamnoen Stadium, next to the TAT office on Thanon Rajdamnoen Nok (Mon, Wed & Thurs 6.30pm, Sun 5pm & 8.30pm; ⓦ rajadamnern.com), and Lumphini Stadium, in its new location on Thanon Ram Intra way out near Don Muang Airport (Tues & Fri 6.30pm, Sat 4.30pm; ⓦ muaythailumpinee.net). Tickets range from B1000 to B2000. To partake in *muay thai* yourself, head to Sor Vorapin's Gym at 13 Trok Kasap, off Thanon Chakrabongse in Banglamphu (B500 per session; ☎02 282 3551, ⓦ thaiboxings.com).

Pak Khlong Talat map pp.718–719. Sprawling 24hr flower and vegetable market in Chinatown that's been in business since the nineteenth century.

Talat Saphan Phut map pp.718–719. Night bazaar around the base of Memorial Bridge, Chinatown, purveying cheap and idiosyncratic fashions. Tues–Sun 8pm–midnight.

DIRECTORY

Embassies and consulates Australia, 37 Th Sathorn Tai, due to move to Th Witthayu in early 2018 (☎02 344 6300, ⓦ thailand.embassy.gov.au); Cambodia, 518/4 Th Pracha Uthit (☎02 957 5851–2); Canada, 15th floor, Abdulrahim Place, 990 Th Rama IV (☎02 646 4300, ⓦ thailand.gc.ca); Ireland, 12th Floor, 208 Th Witthayu (☎02 016 1360, ⓦ dfa.ie); Laos, 502/1–3 Soi Sahakarnpramoon, Th Pracha Uthit (☎02 539 6667 8); Myanmar (Burma), 132 Th Sathorn Nua (☎02 234 4789); New Zealand, 14th Floor, M Thai Tower, All Seasons Place, 87 Th Witthayu (☎02 254 2530, ⓦ nzembassy.com/thailand); South Africa, Floor 12A, M Thai Tower, All Seasons Place, 87 Th Witthayu (☎02 659 2900, ⓦ saembbangkok.com); UK, 14 Th Witthayu (☎02 305 8333); US, 120 Th Witthayu (☎02 205 4000); Vietnam, 83/1 Th Witthayu (☎02 650 8979).

Emergencies For English-speaking help in any emergency, call the tourist police on their free 24hr phoneline ☎1155. The tourist police are based on the grounds of Suvarnabhumi Airport (☎02 134 0521), or drop in at the more convenient Chana Songkhram Police Station at the west end of Th Khao San in Banglamphu (☎02 282 2323). In the evenings, you'll also find tourist police at the Silom end of Patpong 1.

Exchange The Suvarnabhumi Airport exchange desks are open 24hr, while many other exchange booths stay open till 8pm or later, especially along Khao San, Sukhumvit and Silom roads and in the major shopping malls. You can withdraw cash from hundreds of ATMs around the city and at the airports.

Hospitals, clinics and dentists Most expats rate the private Bumrungrad Hospital, 33 Soi 3, Th Sukhumvit (☎02 667 1000, emergency ☎02 667 2999, ⓦ bumrungrad.com), as the best and most comfortable in the city; also has a dental department (☎02 667 2300).

Immigration office North of the centre off Th Wiphawadi Rangsit at Floor 2, B Building, Government Complex, Soi 7, Th Chaengwattana (Mon–Fri 8.30am–noon & 1–4.30pm; ☎02 141 9889, ⓦ bangkok .immigration.go.th). Be very wary of any Khao San tour agents who offer to organize a visa extension for you: some are reportedly faking the relevant stamps.

Laundry Nearly all guesthouses offer a one-day turnaround laundry service for around B40/kg (including ironing).

Left luggage At Suvarnabhumi Airport (B100/day); Don Muang Airport (B75/day); Hualamphong Station (B20–80/day); the bus terminals, and at most hotels and guesthouses.

Pharmacies There are English-speaking staff at most pharmacies, including the citywide branches of Boots the Chemist (most usefully on Th Khao San and in the Mah Boon Krong Centre on Th Rama I), which are also the easiest places to buy tampons.

Post office If you're staying in Banglamphu, it's probably most convenient to use the postal, packing and poste restante services at Banglamphubon PO, Soi Sibsam Hang, Bangkok 10203.

Telephones SIM cards can be bought at all 7-Elevens, starting from around B100 for connection and credit. For anything more complicated, the best place is the Mah Boon Krong Centre (see above).

Travel agents Banglamphu is a notorious centre of fly-by-night operations, some of which have indeed been known to flee with travellers' money overnight. Head instead for Olavi Travel, opposite the west end of Th Khao San at 53 Th Chakrabongse (☎02 629 4710, ⓦ olavi.com); or STA Travel, *Baan Chart Hotel*, Th Chakrabongse, near the corner of Th Ram Buttri (☎02 160 5200, ⓦ statravel.co.th), one of three Bangkok branches of the worldwide travel agent.

DAY-TRIPS FROM BANGKOK

There are a few day-trips out of Bangkok that provide a happy respite from the smog and mayhem.

Muang Boran Ancient City

A day-trip out to the **Muang Boran Ancient City** open-air museum (daily 9am–7pm; B700, B600 if booked online, B350 after 4pm; ⓦ ancientcitygroup.net/ancientsiam/en), 33km southeast of

Bangkok, is a great way to explore Thailand's history and architecture. There are 116 immaculately reproduced or restored traditional Thai buildings dotted around the Thailand-shaped 320 acres of landscaped grounds, ranging from a copy of the Grand Palace and a reconstruction of the lost palace of Ayutthaya to a rare and original scripture library from Samut Songkhram. The best way to do the site justice is to hop on a bike (free).

ARRIVAL AND DEPARTURE

To get here, take (a/c) bus #511 from Banglamphu or Th Sukhumvit to Samut Prakan on the edge of Greater Bangkok (about 1hr 30min), then change onto songthaew (pick-up) #36 for Muang Boran. Alternatively, take the Skytrain to the Sukhumvit Line terminus at Bearing, then bus #511, then songthaew #36; at weekends, there's a free shuttle bus once a day from Bearing Skytrain station to Muang Boran.

Damnoen Saduak floating markets

To get an idea of what shopping in Bangkok used to be like before all the canals were tarmacked over, many people take an early-morning trip to the floating markets of **Damnoen Saduak** (daily 6–11am), 109km southwest. Vineyards and orchards back onto a labyrinth of narrow canals thick with paddle boats, and floating farmers in traditional dress sell fresh fruit and vegetables as well as touristy souvenirs. It's picturesque but feels increasingly manufactured; there are hordes of tour groups and some visitors have complained of seeing more tourists than vendors. The target for most groups is the main **Talat Khlong Ton Kem**, 2km west of the tiny town centre at the intersection of Khlong Damnoen Saduak and Khlong Thong Lang. However, **Talat Khlong Hia Kui** (a little further south down Khlong Thong Lang) should be a little less crowded. Touts congregate at the Ton Kem pier to sell longtail- or rowing-boat trips (hourly rates from B300/person), or you can explore on foot along the canalside walkways and bridges.

ARRIVAL AND DEPARTURE

By bus To make a trip worthwhile you'll need to catch an early bus from Bangkok's Southern Bus Terminal (every 40min from 6am; 2hr). Frequent yellow songthaews will carry you the 2km to Ton Kem.

On an organized tour Nearly all Bangkok travel agents (see opposite) run half-day tours to Damnoen Saduak, usually leaving at 7am (B250 including a longtail-boat ride, B150 extra for a paddle-boat ride).

Nakhon Pathom

NAKHON PATHOM, 56km west of Bangkok, has little of interest to most travellers, but if you're into temple chedis, this is the *crème de la crème*. Measuring a staggering 120m – the same height as St Paul's Cathedral in London – **Phra Pathom Chedi** (daily 7am–5pm; B60) is the tallest in the world. Legend has it that the Buddha rested in Nakhon Pathom, and the original Indian-style chedi may have been erected to commemorate this. It was rebuilt with a Khmer prang (tower) between the eighth and twelfth centuries, which was later encased in the enormous plunger-shaped chedi that exists today. The inner and outer chambers at the cardinal points each contain a tableau of the life of the Buddha, and there are two **museums** within the chedi compound: the newer Phra Pathom Chedi National Museum (Wed–Sun 9am–noon & 1–4pm; B100), which is clearly signposted from the bottom of the chedi's south staircase, displays historical artefacts excavated nearby, while the Phra Pathom Chedi Museum (same hours; free), halfway up the steps near the east viharn, contains a beguiling selection of curios.

For inexpensive Thai food, head for the market in front of the train station, where you'll find some of the tastiest *khao laam* (bamboo cylinders filled with steamed rice and coconut) in Thailand.

ARRIVAL AND DEPARTURE

By train Nakhon Pathom's station (12 daily from Bangkok Hualamphong, 2 daily from Thonburi Station; 1hr 30min) is served by trains heading for southern Thailand and for Kanchanaburi. From the station, a 200m walk south across the canal and past the market will get you to the chedi's north gate.

By bus Buses from Bangkok's Southern Bus Terminal (every 10min; 40min–1hr 20min) stop at the bus station, 1km east of the town centre, but most will drop you off near the chedi first.

10

The central plains

10

North and west of the capital, the unwieldy urban mass of Greater Bangkok peters out into the vast, well-watered **central plains**, a region that for centuries has grown the bulk of the nation's food and been an irresistible temptation for neighbouring power-mongers. The riverside town of **Kanchanaburi** has long attracted visitors to the notorious Bridge over the River Kwai and is now well established as a budget travellers' hangout. Few tourists venture further west except to travel on the Death Railway, but the tiny hilltop town of **Sangkhlaburi** is worth the trip for its idyllic remoteness. On the plains north of Bangkok, the historic heartland of the country, the major sites are the ruined ancient cities of **Ayutthaya**, **Lopburi** and **Sukhothai**. **Mae Sot** makes a therapeutic change from old monuments and is the departure point for **Umphang**, a remote border region that's popular for trekking and rafting.

KANCHANABURI AND AROUND

Nestled among limestone hills 121km northwest of Bangkok, the peaceful riverside guesthouses of **KANCHANABURI** make it a popular and pleasant travellers' hangout. Aside from the main historical sights – the Bridge over the River Kwai and several moving memorials to the area's role in World War II – there are caves and waterfalls to explore. A very popular commemorative *son-et-lumière*

River Kwai Bridge Festival is held here for ten days every November or December.

WHAT TO SEE AND DO

Kanchanaburi's commercial heart is a dusty, frenetic place, while the northern part of town is full of package tourists snapping photos of the bridge. The main tourist street, Thanon Maenam Kwai, is lined with guesthouses and expat bars, and, despite the tragic history, there's an upbeat feel to the place. But Kanchanaburi's real charm lies in the natural sights out of town, especially the seven-tiered Erawan Falls, and the unusual cave temples across the river. The Death Railway itself makes a fascinating day-trip as it winds through rugged terrain towards the tiny town of Nam Tok.

The museum and cemeteries

The excellent **Thailand–Burma Railway Centre** (daily 9am–5pm; B140; Ⓦtbrconline.com), west of the train station, gives a clear and successfully impartial introduction to the horrifying history of this line, and features some extraordinary original photographs and film footage shot by Japanese engineers, as well as interviews with surviving labourers and POWs.

Thirty-eight POWs died for each kilometre of track laid on the Death Railway, and many of them are buried in Kanchanaburi's two war cemeteries. Next to the Thailand–Burma Railway Centre, the **Kanchanaburi War Cemetery**, also known as Don Rak (daily dawn–dusk; free), is the bigger of the two, with 6982 POW graves laid out in straight lines amid immaculately kept lawns.

THE DEATH RAILWAY

In spite of the almost impenetrable terrain, Japanese military leaders chose the River Kwai basin as the route for the construction of the 415km **Thailand–Burma Railway**, which was to be a crucial link between Japan's newly acquired territories in Singapore and Burma. Work began in June 1942, and Kanchanaburi became a POW camp and base for construction work on the railway. About 60,000 Allied POWs and 200,000 conscripted Asian labourers worked on the line. With little else but picks and shovels, dynamite and pulleys, they shifted three million cubic metres of rock and built more than 14km of bridges. By the time the line was completed, fifteen months later, it had more than earned its nickname, the Death Railway: an estimated 16,000 POWs and 100,000 Asian labourers died while working on it.

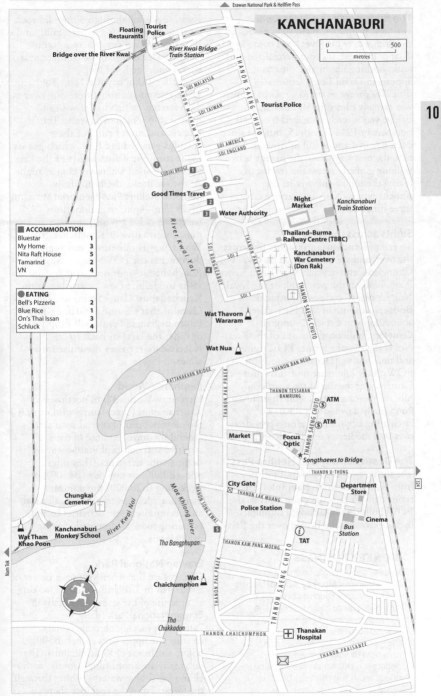

Erawan National Park & Hellfire Pass

KANCHANABURI

0 _____ 500
metres

10

Floating Restaurants
Tourist Police
River Kwai Bridge Train Station
Bridge over the River Kwai
SOI MALAYSIA
SOI TAIWAN
THANON MAENAM KWAI
THANON SAENG CHUTO
Tourist Police
SOI AMERICA
SOI ENGLAND
SUDJAI BRIDGE
Good Times Travel
Water Authority
Night Market
Kanchanaburi Train Station
River Kwai Yai

ACCOMMODATION
Bluestar	1
My Home	3
Nita Raft House	5
Tamarind	2
VN	4

Thailand–Burma Railway Centre (TBRC)
Kanchanaburi War Cemetery (Don Rak)
SOI RONGHEABOY
SOI 2
SOI 1
THANON PAK PRAEK
THANON SAENG CHUTO

EATING
Bell's Pizzeria	2
Blue Rice	1
On's Thai Issan	3
Schluck	4

Wat Thavorn Wararam
Wat Nua
RATTANAKARN BRIDGE
THANON BAN NEUA
THANON TESSABAN BAMRUNG
THANON PAK PRAEK
ATM
ATM
Market
Focus Optic
Songthaews to Bridge
THANON SAENG CHUTO
THANON U-THONG
Chungkai Cemetery
City Gate
THANON LAK MUANG
Department Store
Kanchanaburi Monkey School
Police Station
Cinema
Wat Tham Khao Poon
Mae Khlong River
Bus Station
River Kwai Noi
Tha Bangphupan
THANON SONG KWAI
THANON KAM PANG MOENG
TAT
Nam Tok
N
THANON PAK PRAEK
Wat Chaichumphon
Tha Chukkadon
THANON CHAICHUMPHON
THANON SAENG CHUTO
Thanakan Hospital
THANON PRAISANEE

10

The Bridge over the River Kwai
For most people the plain steel arches of the **Bridge over the River Kwai** come as a disappointment: it's commercialized and looks nothing like as awesome as it appears in David Lean's famous 1957 film, *The Bridge on the River Kwai* (which was actually filmed in Sri Lanka). The Bridge was severely damaged by Allied bombers in 1944 and 1945, but has since been repaired and is still in use today. In fact, the best way to see the bridge is by walking gingerly across the tracks, or taking the train right over it: the Kanchanaburi–Nam Tok service crosses it three times a day.

Sights across the river
Several of Kanchanaburi's sights lie **across the river**, and are best reached by bike. For Chungkai Cemetery and Wat Tham Khao Poon, both on the west bank of the Kwai Noi, it's best to cycle over Rattanakarn Bridge, just south of Wat Nua. After about 2km you'll reach **Chungkai Cemetery**, built on the banks of the Kwai Noi at the site of a former POW camp, and final resting place for some 1750 POWs. One kilometre on from Chungkai Cemetery, at the top of the road's only hill, sits the cave temple **Wat Tham Khao Poon** (daily dawn–dusk; B30), a fascinating labyrinthine grotto presided over by a medley of religious icons.

The Death Railway and Hellfire Pass
The scenic two-hour-plus rail journey from Kanchanaburi to **Nam Tok** (three trains daily in each direction) travels the POW-built **Death Railway**. Highlights include crossing the Bridge over the River Kwai, squeezing through 30m solid rock cuttings at Wang Sing (Arrow Hill), and the Wang Po viaduct, where a 300m trestle bridge clings to the cliff face as it curves with the Kwai Noi.

Starting 18km beyond Nam Tok, seven separate cuttings were dug over a 3km stretch, which has now been turned into a memorial walk. The longest and most brutal of these cuttings was Hellfire Pass, which got its name from the hellish lights of the fires the POWs used when working at night. At the trailhead, the beautifully designed **Hellfire Pass Memorial Museum** (daily 9am–4pm; free, donations welcome; ⓦdva.gov.au), the best and most informative of Kanchanaburi's World War II museums, movingly documents the POWs' story. Most Kanchanaburi tour operators feature visits to Hellfire Pass, or any bus from Kanchanaburi (1hr 15min) or Nam Tok (20min) that's bound for Thong Pha Phum or Sangkhlaburi will drop you outside; the last bus back to Kanchanaburi passes the museum at about 4.45pm.

Elephants' World
Elephants' World, 32km northwest of Kanchanaburi (ⓦelephantsworld.org), is the most popular of several such camps around the town, because of their sensitive and non-exploitative way of dealing with elephants. They offer one- (B2500) or two-day (B4500), or week-long (B20,000) programmes, including pick-ups from town, all meals and accommodation; activities include preparing food, feeding and bathing the pachyderms.

Erawan National Park
Chances are that when you see a poster of a waterfall in Thailand, you'll be looking at a picture of the seven-tiered falls in **Erawan National Park** (daily 7am–4.30pm, though rangers start clearing the upper tiers earlier; B300), 65km northwest of Kanchanaburi. The falls really are astonishingly lovely, with clear, glacial-blue waters gushing through the forest. From the entrance there's a

---

MONKEY BUSINESS
If you're given the opportunity to visit Kanchanaburi's "**Monkey School**" as part of a tour around Kanchanaburi, you're strongly advised to turn it down. The monkeys here are said to have been rescued from abusive owners, but now they spend their days chained up by the neck until they are coerced into performing circus tricks like shooting hoops and riding children's bicycles.

progressively more difficult trail up to the seventh tier (2km; wear strong shoes). The best pools for swimming are at levels two (often crowded), five and, during the rainy season, seven; food and drink are not permitted beyond level two, apart from bottles of water on which you must pay a deposit of B20, returnable on your way back down.

Buses run from Kanchanaburi's bus station to the national park visitor centre near the base of the falls (#8170; roughly every hour; 1hr 30min; the last bus back to Kanchanaburi departs at around 4pm). However, the majority of foreign tourists charter return transport from Kanchanaburi (around B1500 per car) through the guesthouses. The falls are about 40km from Nam Tok so are also commonly combined with a ride on the Death Railway.

ARRIVAL AND DEPARTURE

By train Trains are the most scenic way to get to Kanchanaburi from Bangkok (daily 7.50am & 1.55pm, both continuing via the River Kwai Bridge Station to Nam Tok), though they're often late.
Destinations Bangkok Thonburi (2 daily; 2hr 30min); Nakhon Pathom (2 daily; 1hr 40min–2hr); Nam Tok (3 daily; 2hr 20min).
By bus and minibus As well as the public services detailed here, there are tourist minibuses to Ayutthaya and Suvarnabhumi Airport that can be booked through guesthouses.
Destinations Bangkok (Northern Bus Terminal; hourly; 2hr 30min); Bangkok (Southern Bus Terminal; every 20min; 2hr–2hr 30min); Chiang Mai (2 daily; 10–11hr); Erawan (roughly hourly; 1hr 30min); Nakhon Pathom (every 20min; 1hr 30min–2hr); Nam Tok (every 30min; 1hr 30min); Sangkhlaburi (every 30min; 3hr 30min–4hr 30min).

GETTING AROUND

As well as songthaews and tuk-tuks (about B50/journey in town), there are bicycles (B50/day) and motorbikes (about B200/day) available for rent from guesthouses and tour agencies.
By songthaews Public songthaews run a fairly fixed route up and down Th Saeng Chuto, originating from outside the Focus Optic optician's, three blocks north of the bus station, and travelling north via the Kanchanaburi War Cemetery, Thailand–Burma Railway Centre, train station and access road to the bridge (roughly every 15min until 6pm; about 15min to the bridge; B10).

INFORMATION AND TOURS

Tourist information The TAT office (daily 8.30am–4.30pm; ☎034 511200, ✉tatkan@tat.or.th) is on Th Saeng Chuto near the bus station and keeps up-to-date bus timetables.
Tour operators Many tour operators offer reasonably priced day-trips and overnight excursions to local caves, waterfalls and sights, plus elephant-riding, trekking, boat rides and bamboo rafting. Operators include: Good Times Travel, 63/1 Th Maenam Kwai (☎034 915484, ⊕good-times-travel.com), which does all the standard trips; and Safarine, outside of town in Ban Puksakan (☎086 049 1662, ⊕safarine.com), which offers a wide variety of trips, including kayaking.

ACCOMMODATION

The stretch of river along Soi Rongheaboy and Th Maenam Kwai is the most popular area for backpacker accommodation. Many of the guesthouses have cheaper floating raft rooms, though boat noise can be a problem during the day.
Bluestar 241 Th Maenam Kwai ☎034 512161, ⊕bluestar-guesthouse.com. Popular and clued-up, with a wide range of good-value accommodation, including very cheap, basic fan bungalows with en-suite cold showers, in a quiet garden that runs down to the riverside. Doubles B150
My Home 1/16–18 Th Maenam Kwai, signposted down an unnamed soi just north of the Water Authority building ☎034 521511, ⊕myhomekan.com. Clean, smart, fairly central place on a quiet soi between Th Maenam Kwai and the river, where the cheapest rooms are sparsely furnished with shared bathrooms. Doubles B250
Nita Raft House Th Pak Praek ☎034 514521, ✉nita_rafthouse@yahoo.com. Away from the Th Maenam Kwai fray, a friendly, laidback, old-school guesthouse, whose simple floating rooms, some en-suite with river views, are among the cheapest in town; the very cheapest share bathrooms and face inland. Also does great food. Doubles B200
Tamarind 29/1 Th Maenam Kwai ☎034 518790, ✉tamarind_guesthouse@yahoo.co.th. At this clean, friendly place, sleep either in the two-storey house or in one of the spacious rafthouse rooms (all en-suite with hot showers), which share a breezy, orchid-strewn terrace. No restaurant. Doubles B350
VN 44 Soi Rongheaboy ☎034 514082, ⊕vnguesthouse.net. A quiet, pretty place just south of the Maenam Kwai hub, with good food and decent raft-house rooms: they're large and come with terraces, en-suite hot showers and either fan or a/c. Doubles B350

EATING AND DRINKING

At dusk, a night market sets up alongside Th Saeng Chuto on the west side of the train station, offering a huge range of food, though mostly to take away. Drinking haunts are

10

not hard to come by either, with plenty of bars along Th Maenam Kwai, many of which show sport and serve basic Western food.

Bell's Pizzeria 24/5 Th Maenam Kwai. Lively, Swiss-run place with pavement tables that's justly popular for its great pizzas (from B170). Also offers pastas, salads and a handful of Thai dishes (*tom yam* soup B120). Daily 4–11pm or later.

★ **Blue Rice** *Apple's Retreat*, on the west bank of the Kwai Yai, across Sudjai Bridge ☎034 512017. In a lovely riverside guesthouse restaurant, delicious mid-priced Thai food, including veggie options and mouthwatering curries – *massaman* is the signature dish (B135). Cookery classes available (B1990 for a one-day course). Daily noon–2pm & 6–9.30pm.

On's Thai Issan 36 Th Maenam Kwai ⓦonsthaiissan .com. Simple, friendly place with a picture menu that serves only vegetarian dishes (B60 each), such as seaweed soup and pad thai. Two-hour daytime cookery classes available (B600 for three dishes). Daily 10am–9pm.

Schluck Th Maenam Kwai. Cosy a/c restaurant serving salads, pizzas and steaks (from B150) as well as Thai food, but what really makes it stand out are its mouthwatering, home-made cakes such as vanilla choux buns and lemon meringue tart. Tues–Sun 4–10pm.

DIRECTORY

Banks and exchange There are several banks with ATMs and money-changing facilities on Th Saeng Chuto and Th Maenam Kwai.

Hospitals The private Thanakan Hospital is at 20/20 Th Saeng Chuto (☎034 622358).

Tourist police Main office on Th Saeng Chuto (☎1155 or ☎034 512795), with handy booths by the bridge and at the bus station.

SANGKHLABURI

Located right at the northernmost tip of the 73km-long Vajiralongkorn Reservoir, the tiny hilltop town of **SANGKHLABURI**, 220km north of Kanchanaburi, is a charming if uneventful hangout. It lies close to the border with Myanmar, though at the time of writing the crossing

at the Three Pagodas Pass had been closed to foreign tourists for several years.

WHAT TO SEE AND DO

You can boat across the reservoir to see the submerged temple **Wat Sam Phrasop** in canoes rented from *P* guesthouse (see opposite), dependent on water levels (in dry years, during the cool and hot seasons it fully emerges from the water). Alternatively, join a sunset longtail boat trip (B400–500/boat).

Across the reservoir stands the Mon village of Ban Waeng Ka, which grew up in the late 1940s after the outbreak of civil war in Myanmar forced the country's ethnic minorities to flee across the border. To reach it, walk across the lake via what's said to be the longest handmade wooden bridge in the world, at nearly 400m, which is reputedly visible from space. Dramatic **Wat Wang Wiwekaram** stands 2km from the bridge at the edge of Ban Waeng Ka; its massive, golden chedi is modelled on the centrepiece of India's Bodh Gaya, the sacred site of the Buddha's enlightenment.

ARRIVAL AND DEPARTURE

By bus Frequent a/c minibuses from Kanchanaburi terminate about 100m east of the market, about 2 or 3km north of the accommodation near the lake listed here; less frequent, larger buses stop directly in front of the market. Motorbike taxis will take you to the guesthouses for B20–30.

Destinations Bangkok (Northern Bus Terminal; 1–2 daily; 7hr); Kanchanaburi (every 30min; 3hr 30min–4hr 30min).

ACCOMMODATION AND EATING

The food stalls at the market are great for cheap eats, but otherwise the restaurant at *P* guesthouse, with fine lake views from its large terrace, is your best bet for a full Thai (or Burmese) meal.

Baan Unrak Bakery Th Si Suwan Khiri. Part of the Baan Unrak project, this sociable café and bookstore serves hot

---

BAAN UNRAK

Baan Unrak ("House of Joy"; ⓦbaanunrak.org) is a local charity that supports destitute women and children in the community, many of whom are Burmese refugees. The charity runs a children's home, primary school, bakery, bookstore and a project that encompasses a weaving and sewing centre to help women learn skills that enable them to earn money. If you want to make a worthwhile contribution while on your travels, note that Baan Unrak offers a number of volunteering opportunities, including teaching English.

vegetarian meals (B60–100) and great cakes, as well as selling their woven products. Mon–Sat 8am–8pm.

J Family 17/1 Soi 2, Th Si Suwan Khiri ☎ 034 595511. A genuine homestay offering big rooms with fan and shared cold-water bathroom in a large family home. Very welcoming and good English spoken. Dorms B200, doubles B300

P ☎ 034 595061, ⓦ p-guesthouse.com. Spacious rooms, a garden leading down to the lake and stunning views across the water make this a worthwhile choice. The fan rooms have great shared bathrooms (cold showers); the large, bright a/c rooms are en-suite (hot showers; B950), but unless it's really hot, they're not worth splashing out on. Motorbikes (B200/day), bicycles (B100/day) and canoes (B150/half-day) can be rented. Doubles B400

DIRECTORY

Bank The Siam Commercial Bank behind the market has an ATM and exchange facilities.
Internet Wi-fi and computers at the *Baan Unrak Bakery*.
Post office Just south of the bus station.

AYUTTHAYA

The city of **AYUTTHAYA**, 80km north of Bangkok, was founded in 1351 by King U-Thong and rapidly became the pre-eminent city-state in Thailand. By 1685 it had a population of one million people – roughly double the population of London at the same time – living largely on houseboats in a 140km network of waterways. In 1767, the city was sacked by the Burmese and today its ruins are a designated UNESCO World Heritage Site. Over a week in mid-December, this status is celebrated with nightly *son-et-lumière* shows.

WHAT TO SEE AND DO

The heart of this ancient city was a 4km-wide river island, and the majority of the ancient remains – some of which are floodlit in the evening – are spread among the grassy spaces of its western half; the hub of the modern town occupies its northeast corner. The only way to do justice to the ruins is to rent a bicycle (B40–60/day) or motorbike (B200–250/day), available from guesthouses. Otherwise, there are plenty of tuk-tuks around (about B50 for short journeys on the island).

Wat Phra Mahathat and Wat Ratburana

Built in the fourteenth century to enshrine relics of the Buddha himself, the overgrown **Wat Phra Mahathat** (daily 8am–5pm; B50) is the epitome of Ayutthaya's atmospheric decay, and the home of an oft-photographed Buddha head serenely trapped in gnarled tree roots. Across the road is towering, fifteenth-century **Wat Ratburana** (daily 8am–5pm; B50), which retains some original stuccowork, including fine statues of garudas (large, mythical birds) swooping down on nagas. It's possible to go down steep steps inside the prang (central tower) to the crypt, where you can make out fragmentary murals of the early Ayutthaya period.

Wat Phra Si Sanphet and Viharn Phra Mongkol Bopit

Further west is the grand, well-preserved **Wat Phra Si Sanphet** (daily 8am–5pm; B50), which was built in 1448 as a private royal chapel; its three grey chedis have become the most hackneyed image of Ayutthaya. Save for a few bricks in the grass, the wat is all that remains of the huge walled complex of the royal palace that extended north as far as the Lopburi River.

Viharn Phra Mongkol Bopit (Mon–Fri 8.30am–4.30pm, Sat & Sun 8.30am–5.30pm; free), on the south side of Wat Phra Si Sanphet, is a replica of a typical Ayutthayan viharn (assembly hall), complete with characteristic chunky lotus-capped columns. It was built in 1956, with help from the Burmese to atone for their flattening of the city two centuries earlier, in order to shelter the still-much-revered Phra Mongkol Bopit. This powerfully austere bronze statue, with its flashing mother-of-pearl eyes, was cast in the fifteenth century, then sat exposed to the elements from the time of the Burmese invasion until its new home was built.

Wat Na Phra Mane

Across on the north bank of the Lopburi River, **Wat Na Phra Mane** (aka Wat Na Phra Meru; daily 8am–6pm;

10

10

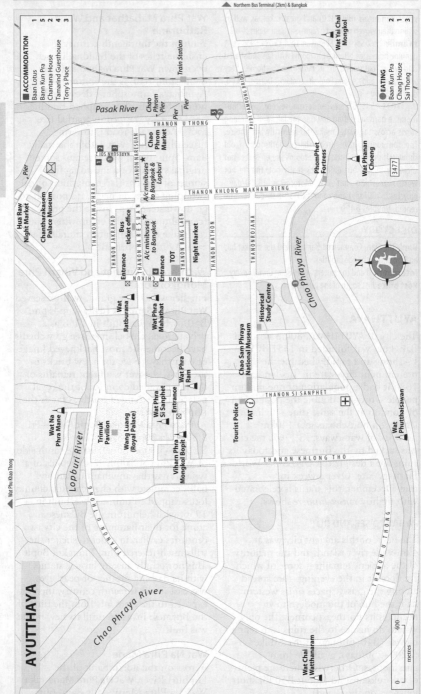

Northern Bus Terminal (2km) & Bangkok

ACCOMMODATION	
Baan Lotus	1
Baan Kun Pra	5
Chantana House	2
Tamarind Guesthouse	4
Tony's Place	3

● EATING	
Baan Kun Pra	2
Chang House	1
Sai Thong	3

AYUTTHAYA

Pasak River

Chao Phrom Pier

Train Station

PRIDI DAMRONG BRIDGE

Wat Yai Chai Mongkol

THANON U THONG

Chao Phrom Market

Hua Raw Night Market

Chantharakasem Palace Museum

Pier

THANON NARESUAN

NARESUAN SOI 2

A/c minibuses to Bangkok & Lopburi

PhomPhet Fortress

Wat Phanan Choeng

3477

THANON PAMAPRAO

THANON JAKRAPAD

THANON KHLONG MAKHAM RIENG

THANON NARESUAN

A/c minibuses to Bangkok

TOT

THANON BANG LAEN

Night Market

THANON PATHON

THANON ROJANA

Chao Phraya River

Bus ticket office

Entrance

THANON CHIKUN

Entrance

Wat Phra Mahathat

Wat Ratburana

Wat Phra Ram

Historical Study Centre

Chao Sam Phraya National Museum

Wat Na Phra Mane

Lopburi River

Trimuk Pavilion

Wang Luang (Royal Palace)

Wat Phra Si Sanphet

Entrance

Viharn Phra Mongkol Bopit

THANON SI SANPHET

Tourist Police

TAT ℹ

Wat Phutthaisawan

THANON KHLONG THO

THANON U THONG

Wat Phu Khao Thong

Chao Phraya River

THANON U THONG

Wat Chai Watthanaram

N

0   400
metres

B20) is Ayutthaya's most rewarding temple, as it's the only one from the town's golden age that survived the ravages of the Burmese. The main bot (ordination hall), built in 1503, is typically Ayutthayan: its outside columns are topped with lotus cups, and there are slits in the walls instead of windows to let the wind pass through. Inside, underneath a rich red-and-gold coffered ceiling representing the stars around the moon, sits a powerful 6m-high Buddha in the disdainful, overdecorated style characteristic of the later Ayutthaya period.

Museums

Ten minutes' walk south of Viharn Phra Mongkol Bopit, the large **Chao Sam Phraya National Museum** (Wed–Sun 9am–4pm; B150) holds numerous Ayutthaya-era Buddhas, some fine woodcarving and gold treasures such as the original relic casket from Wat Mahathat. The **Historical Study Centre** (daily 9am–5pm; B100), a few minutes' walk away along Thanon Rojana, dramatically presents a broad social history of Ayutthaya with the help of videos and reconstructions.

Wat Yai Chai Mongkol and Wat Phanan Choeng

The colossal and celebrated chedi of the ancient but still functioning **Wat Yai Chai Mongkol** (daily 8am–5pm; B20), across the bridge to the southeast of the island, was built by the greatest Ayutthayan king, Naresuan, to mark his decisive victory over the Burmese in 1593. By the entrance, a reclining Buddha, gleamingly restored to toothpaste white, dates from the same time.

To the west of Wat Yai Chai Mongkol, at the confluence of the Chao Phraya and Pasak rivers, stands the city's oldest and liveliest working temple, **Wat Phanan Choeng** (daily 8am–5pm; B20), whose main Buddha image has survived since 1324, and is said to have wept when Ayutthaya was sacked by the Burmese. The stunning murals in the ordination hall have been beautifully restored.

ARRIVAL AND DEPARTURE

By bus and minibus Buses to and from the north stop at Ayutthaya's Northern Bus Terminal, 5km to the east of the centre, from where you'll need a tuk-tuk (B100–150); for most of these services, you can make bookings at the Public Transport Company's handy ticket office on Th Naresuan. Licensed, a/c minibuses to and from Bangkok's Northern and Southern Bus Terminals can be found at two places on Th Naresuan near the main accommodation area; the more easterly stop is also home to a/c minibuses to Lopburi. Tourist minibuses to Kanchanaburi and Suvarnabhumi Airport can be booked through guesthouses.

Destinations Bangkok (every 20–30min; 1–2hr); Chiang Mai (15 daily; 10hr); Chiang Rai (5 daily; 12hr); Lampang (15 daily; 8hr); Lopburi (every 20min; 1hr 30min–2hr); Phitsanulok (20 daily; 5hr); Sukhothai (11 daily; 6hr).

By train From the pier 100m west of the train station, take the ferry (B6; last ferry around 8pm) up to Chao Phrom pier, then walk five minutes to the junction of U-Thong and Naresuan (Chao Phrom) roads, to reach the centre. (If you're staying at *Bann Kun Pra*, however, take the ferry from the neighbouring jetty, which runs directly across the river.) The station has a left-luggage service (24hr; B30/piece/day).

Destinations Bangkok Hualamphong (around 20 daily; 1hr 30min–2hr); Chiang Mai (5 daily; 10–13hr); Lopburi (16 daily; 45min–1hr 30min); Nong Khai (4 daily; 9hr 30min); Phitsanulok (10 daily; 3hr 30min–6hr 20min); Ubon Ratchathani (8 daily; 7hr 20min–10hr 30min).

INFORMATION

Tourist information TAT, in the former city hall, Th Si Sanphet (daily 8.30am–4.30pm; ☎035 246076 7, ✉ tatyutya@tat.or.th); it's well worth heading upstairs to the free, smartly presented multimedia exhibition on Ayutthaya (same hours).

ACCOMMODATION

Most of the guesthouses and tourist amenities are crowded into an area that's become known as "Soi Farang" (Th Naresuan Soi 2), which runs north from Chao Prom market.

Baan Lotus Th Pamaprao ☎035 251988. Two tranquil old houses with polished wooden floors and large, plain, but clean rooms, with either shared or en-suite hot showers, at the end of a long garden with a lotus pond at the back. Doubles B350

Bann Kun Pra Th U Thong, just north of Pridi Damrong Bridge ☎035 241978, ✇bannkunpra.com. A gorgeous riverside complex of hundred-year-old teak buildings, with four-bed, single-sex dorm rooms that have hot showers and individual lockable tin trunks. Most of the luxurious private rooms have river views, some share bathrooms. Road noise can be a problem here. Dorms B250, doubles B500

10

Chantana House Naresuan Soi 2 ☎035 323200, ✉chantanahouse@yahoo.com. At the quieter end of the travellers' soi, this low-key guesthouse has simple but spotlessly clean fan and a/c rooms with hot showers in a spacious, two-storey house. Doubles B400

★**Tamarind Guesthouse** On a lane off Th Chikun in front of the entrance to Wat Phra Mahathat ☎081 655 7937. Tranquil, helpful old wooden house with bags of character, where the stylish rooms have attractive polished floors and en-suite hot showers. Free coffee, tea, fruit and biscuits. Doubles B650

Tony's Place Naresuan Soi 2 ☎035 252578. More than thirty cheap to mid-priced rooms, all clean and with shared or en-suite hot showers, set around a convivial restaurant with a pool table and a good selection of Thai and Western food. Doubles B200

EATING

The Chao Prom market is good for food during the day, and there are a couple of good night markets: on Th Bang Laen near Wat Mahathat, and a smaller one at Hua Raw at the northeastern corner of the island. Otherwise the choice isn't great, and many travellers end up eating Thai-Western food and listening to live music on Naresuan Soi 2.

Baan Kun Pra Th U Thong, just north of Pridi Damrong Bridge. Beneath the guesthouse of the same name, this peaceful and atmospheric riverside restaurant has an interesting menu including lots of seafood, Ayutthaya's famous river prawns, spicy salads and delicious fruit smoothies. Mains B70–200. Daily 7am–9.30pm.

Chang House Naresuan Soi 2. Lively bar-restaurant serving tasty burgers, Thai standards, and lots of veggie-friendly Indian dishes (mains around B100), while the drinks menu includes imported wine and cocktails. Daily 7.30am–12.30am.

★**Sai Thong** Th U Thong. On the south side of the island, this excellent traditional restaurant has an attractive riverside terrace and is especially popular among locals for its seafood (most dishes around B150). Daily 10am–9.30pm.

LOPBURI

LOPBURI, 150km north of Bangkok, is famous for its seventeenth-century palace, its historically important but rather unimpressive Khmer ruins – and the large pack of tourist-baiting monkeys that swarm all over them. Many of the ruins date back to the eleventh century, when Lopburi was the local capital for the extensive Khmer Empire. The town was later used as a second capital both by King Narai of Ayutthaya and Rama IV of Bangkok because its remoteness from the

sea made it less vulnerable to European expansionists. Lopburi works best as a half-day stopoff; the railway runs north–south through the town and everything of interest lies to the west of the line, within walking distance.

On the last weekend of November Lopburi puts on a banquet for its monkeys, which swarm over trestle tables laden with fresh fruit in the centre of town. Lopburi's main festival is the five-day King Narai Reign Fair in February, with costumed processions and a *son et lumière*.

WHAT TO SEE AND DO

Exiting the train station, you'll see the sprawled ruins of **Wat Phra Si Ratana Mahathat** (daily 8.30am–4.30pm; B50), whose impressive centrepiece is a laterite prang in the Khmer style of the twelfth century, decorated with finely detailed stuccowork and surrounded by a ruined cloister.

The heavily fortified palace of **Phra Narai Ratchanivet** (Wed–Sun 8.30am–4pm; B150), a short walk northwest of Wat Mahathat on Thanon Sorasak, was built by King Narai in 1666 and lavishly restored by Rama IV in 1856. The shady grounds house ruined elephant stables, throne halls and treasure warehouses, but the best feature is the **Narai National Museum**. The museum contains fine examples of Khmer-influenced, Lopburi-style Buddha images, and the Chanthara Phisan Pavilion alongside boasts an excellent exhibition on Narai's reign and international relations.

About 200m north of the palace complex along rue de France is **Ban Vichayen** (daily 8.30am–4pm; B50), the home of King Narai's Greek minister (*vichayen*), Constantine Phaulkon. Originally built as a residence for foreign ambassadors, its Christian chapel is incongruously stuccoed with Buddhist motifs. Around 150m east along Thanon Vichayen, past the three red-brick towers of Prang Khaek, an eighth-century shrine to Shiva sitting on a traffic island, is the striking **Phra Prang Sam Yod** (daily 8am–6pm; B50), a Hindu temple later converted to Buddhism under the

Khmers. The three chunky prangs, made
of dark laterite with some restored
stuccowork, are a favourite haunt of
Lopburi's fierce monkeys. Just east at San
Phra Karn, there's even a monkeys'
adventure playground beside the ruins of
a huge Khmer prang.

ARRIVAL AND INFORMATION

By bus and minibus The main bus and minibus station
is 2km east of the town centre: a blue or green bus or a
songthaew will save you the walk. Fast a/c minibuses
between Bangkok's Northern Bus Terminal and Lopburi are
based at two offices on Th Na Phra Karn, north of the train
station towards Phra Prang Sam Yod.
Destinations Ayutthaya (every 20min; 1hr 30min–
2hr); Bangkok (every 20min; 3hr); Chiang Mai (4 daily;
9hr); Khorat (hourly; 3hr–3hr 30min); Phitsanulok (4
daily; 4hr).
By train The train station is directly opposite Wat Phra Si
Ratana Mahathat; there are left-luggage facilities.
Destinations Ayutthaya (16 daily; 45min–1hr 30min);
Bangkok Hualamphong (16 daily; 2hr 30min–3hr); Chiang
Mai (5 daily; 9–11hr); Phitsanulok (11 daily; 3hr–5hr
15min).
Tourist information TAT's office (daily 8.30am–4.30pm;
☎036 770096, ✉tatlobri@tat.or.th) is 5km east of San
Phra Karn on Th Narai Maharat in the city hall.

ACCOMMODATION AND EATING

There are food stalls dotted around the centre of Lopburi,
especially on Th Ratchadamnern between the northeast
corner of Phra Narai Ratchanivet and the railway. A good
night market sets up along the west side of the tracks on
Th Na Phra Karn; this is the best place for dinner, with a
wide variety of dishes from B30, and it is a great place to sit
and people-watch.
Nett Hotel One block east of Phra Narai Ratchanivet at
17/1–2 Soi 2, Th Ratchadamnern ☎036 411738.
Announced by a three-storey mural of a cockerel and a
snake, the *Nett* is slightly sterile but clean and friendly,
offering plain fan or a/c rooms with en-suite bathrooms.
Doubles B250
★**Noom Guest House** Two blocks east of Phra Narai
Ratchanivet on Th Praya Kumjud ☎036 427693,
✆noomguesthouse.com. Teak-floored rooms with shared
hot showers (and decent rates for singles), above a very
good bar-restaurant in the main wooden house, or
en-suite a/c bungalows in the back garden. The friendly
staff can organize rock climbing, caving, trekking and
motorbike rental. Doubles B300
Pae Ban Rim Nam Soi Wat Choeng Tha, off Th Phetracha,
5min walk southwest of Phra Narai Ratchanivet. Popular
floating restaurant on the Lopburi River, offering huge

portions of classics such as green curry and seafood (mains
from B100). Daily 10am–10pm.
Pelaplearn Th Ratchadamnern. Stylish little a/c café
serving cakes, snacks and a good range of espresso coffees
(latte B35). Tues–Sun 11am–8pm.

PHITSANULOK

10

Pleasantly located on the banks of the
Nan River, PHITSANULOK (locally called
"Phitlok") is a major transport hub and a
handy base for exploring the Sukhothai
area (see p.745), but only holds a couple
of sights itself.

WHAT TO SEE AND DO

Dating from the fourteenth century,
Wat Phra Si Ratana Mahathat (aka Wat
Mahathat or Wat Yai; dress
conservatively) draws a constant stream
of worshippers to view the country's
second most important Buddha image.
The holy statue itself, Phra Buddha
Chinnarat, is a lovely example of late
Sukhothai style, and boasts an unusual
flame-like halo around its upper body;
it is said to have wept tears of blood
when Ayutthayan princes arrived to
oust the last Sukhothai king in the
fifteenth century.
Across town on Thanon Wisut Kasat,
southeast of the train station (bus #1
will drop you close by or it's about B60
in a tuk-tuk), is the small **Sergeant
Major Thawee Folk Museum** (daily
8.30am–4.30pm; B50), one of the best
ethnology museums in the country; it
includes a reconstruction of a typical
village house, as well as traditional toys
and animal traps. About 50m south of
the museum, at 26/43 Th Wisut Kasat,
is the **Buranathai Buddha Bronze-
Casting Foundry** (daily roughly
8am–5pm; free). The foundry gives you
a rare chance to see Buddha images
being forged; anyone can drop in to
watch the stages involved in moulding
and casting an image.

ARRIVAL AND INFORMATION

By plane Nok Air and Air Asia run flights to Bangkok (Don
Muang; 5 daily; 50min), Kan Airlines to Chiang Mai (1
weekly; 1hr), from Phitsanulok Airport, 7km south of the
centre and about B150 by tuk-tuk.

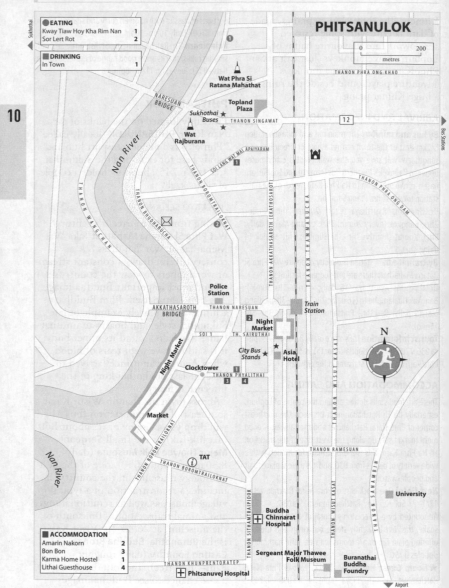

EATING
Kway Tiaw Hoy Kha Rim Nan	1
Sor Lert Rot	2

DRINKING
In Town	1

PHITSANULOK

0 ____ 200
metres

THANON PHRA ONG KHAO

Wat Phra Si
Ratana Mahathat

Topland
Plaza

NARESUAN
BRIDGE

Sukhothai
Buses

THANON SINGAWAT

12

Wat
Rajburana

SOI LANG WAT MAI APAIYARAM

THANON BOROMTRAILOKNAT

THANON PHRA ONG DAM

Nan River

THANON WANG CHAN

THANON BUDDHABUCHA

THANON AKKATHASAROTH (EKATHOSAROT)

THANON THAMMABUCHA

Police
Station

AKKATHASAROTH
BRIDGE

THANON NARESUAN

Train
Station

Night
Market

TH. SAIRUTHAI

N

City Bus
Stands

SOI 1

Asia
Hotel

THANON WISUT KASAT

Night Market

Clocktower

THANON PHYALITHAI

Market

THANON BOROMTRAILOKNAT

THANON BOROMTRAILOKNAT

TAT

THANON RAMESUAN

THANON WISUT KASAT

THANON SANAMBIN

University

Nan River

THANON SITHAMTRAIPIDOK

Buddha
Chinnarat
Hospital

Sergeant Major Thawee
Folk Museum

Buranathai
Buddha
Foundry

ACCOMMODATION
Amarin Nakorn	2
Bon Bon	3
Karma Home Hostel	1
Lithai Guesthouse	4

THANON KHUNPRENTORATEP

Phitsanuvej Hospital

Airport

By bus Buses for Sukhothai and other adjacent provinces use the old bus station, 2km east of the city centre; Sukhothai buses also make useful stops in the centre near Topland Plaza. Long-distance buses use the new bus station, which is about 7km east of the centre near Indochina Junction, where highways 11 and 12 meet. Shared songthaews (B15–30) shuttle between the new bus station and the centre of town, via the old bus station.

Destinations Bangkok (50 daily; 5–6hr); Chiang Mai (40 daily; 5–6hr); Chiang Rai (30 daily; 7–8hr); Khon Kaen (16 daily; 5–6hr); Khorat (14 daily; 6–7hr); Mae Sot (4 daily; 4hr); Nan (3 daily; 6hr); Sukhothai (at least every 40min; 1hr–1hr 30min).

By train The train station is in the town centre, less than 500m from accommodation. Left-luggage costs B30 (daily 7am–11pm).

Destinations Ayutthaya (11 daily; 4hr 30min–6hr 20min);
Bangkok Hualamphong (11 daily; 5hr 30min–8hr); Chiang
Mai (6 daily; 6–8hr); Lopburi (11 daily; 3hr–5hr 15min).
Tourist information The TAT office is on the eastern arm
of Th Boromtrailoknat (daily 8.30am–4.30pm; ☎055
252742 3, ✉ tatphlok@tat.or.th).

GETTING AROUND

By bus Many city buses (mostly B10–13) start their routes
at the bus stops 150m south of the train station, where
southbound buses pick up outside the *Asia Hotel*, and
northbound ones from across the road. Useful routes
include: #1, from the old bus station to Wat Mahathat, the
train station and the Folk Museum; and #11, via the train
station, Topland Plaza and Wat Mahathat.

ACCOMMODATION

Amarin Nakorn 3/1 Th Chao Phraya ☎055 219069. Very
central, good value but dated, this hotel has compact a/c
rooms, all with hot showers; the upper floors enjoy
panoramic views of the city. Doubles B380
Bon Bon 77 Th Phayalithai ☎055 219058 or ☎081 707
7649. The only genuine guesthouse in town, welcoming
and set back from the road around a small yard. The rooms
are kept nice and clean and have en-suite hot showers and
TVs; pay B50 extra for a/c. Doubles B350
Karma Home Hostel 26/54 Soi Lang Wat Mai Apaiyaram
☎088 814 1268, ⬡facebook.com/karmahomehostel.
Welcoming and informative hostel-cum-homestay in the
centre of town, with fan-cooled bunk beds and hammocks
for chilling on the roof terrace; light breakfast included.
Dorms B200
Lithai Guesthouse 73/1–5 Th Phayalithai ☎055
219629, ✉lithaiphs@yahoo.com. Good but bland option,
used mainly by salespeople so not especially cosy and
much more of a hotel than a guesthouse. The clean, bright
rooms come with hot shower, TV and either fan or a/c.
Doubles B300

EATING AND DRINKING

Along the east bank of the river, south of Akkathasaroth
Bridge, there's a good night market, where the most
famous dish is "flying vegetables" – morning glory is stir-
fried before being tossed flamboyantly in the air to the
plate-wielding waiter.
Kway Tiaw Hoy Kha Rim Nan 100m north of Wat
Mahathat. The noodles here (B30–50) – Sukhothai
noodles with red pork in a sweet and spicy broth, pad thai
or *tom yam* soup with noodles – are so famously tasty
they've been on all the local TV channels. You sit on the
raised floor with legs dangling (*hoy kha*) under the table.
There's no English sign, but it's got a brown awning and is
always packed. Daily 9am–4pm.
Sor Lert Rot Th Boromtrailoknat, immediately south of

the *Pailyn Hotel*. It doesn't look much, but this basic, rather
untidy, Thai-Chinese restaurant cooks up some of the best
food in town. Try the fried chicken (B120) and the salted
fish with Chinese kale (*khana pla khem*; B50). Mon–Sat
8am–9/10pm.

DRINKING

In Town 50–52 Th Phayalithai. Lively and welcoming,
Phitlok's first craft beer bar is a big hit with locals, serving
Belgian, Japanese and British brews on tap and in bottles.
Daily 6pm–midnight.

DIRECTORY

Hospital Buddha Chinnarat Hospital, Th Sithamtraipidok
(☎055 219844–52).
Tourist police In the far northern suburbs near the
stadium (☎1155).

SUKHOTHAI

For a brief but brilliant hundred and
forty years (1238–1376), the walled city
of **SUKHOTHAI** presided as the capital of
Thailand. Now an impressive assembly of
elegant ruins, Muang Kao Sukhothai
(Old Sukhothai), 58km northwest of
Phitsanulok, has been designated a
historical park. It's one of Thailand's
most visited sites and is the most famous
place to celebrate the **Loy Krathong
Festival** in October/November. Most
travellers stay in lively "New" Sukhothai,
12km to the east, which has good travel
links and a broader range of
accommodation and restaurants.

WHAT TO SEE AND DO

Cycling around **Old Sukhothai** is a great
way to spend a day; its collapsed ruins
are evocative of a glorious time gone by.
Some of its temples are exquisitely
restored, while others have been left to
crumble. In its prime, Old Sukhothai
boasted some forty separate temple
complexes and covered an area of about
seventy square kilometres. At its heart
stood the walled royal city, protected by
a series of moats and ramparts.
Sukhothai Historical Park covers all this
area and is divided into five zones, with
all the most important temples in the
central zone. There's free access to the
east and south zones, but the central
(daily 6.30am–7pm, Sat until 9pm,

10

NEW SUKHOTHAI

when it's floodlit), north (daily 8am–6pm) and west zones (daily 8am–4pm) each charge B100/person.

The central zone

Just outside the entrance to the central zone is the well-presented **Ramkhamhaeng National Museum** (daily 9am–4pm; B150), named after Sukhothai's most important king. As well as several illuminating exhibitions and some of the finest sculptures and reliefs found among the ruins, it contains a copy of Ramkhamhaeng's famous stele – essentially an advertisement for a utopian land of plenty, aimed at prospective traders and settlers.

Turn left inside the gate to the central zone for Sukhothai's most important site, the enormous **Wat Mahathat** compound, packed with the remains of scores of monuments and surrounded, like a city within a city, by a moat. It was the spiritual heart of the city, the king's temple and symbol of his power.

A few hundred metres southwest, the triple corn-cob-shaped prangs of **Wat Sri Sawai** indicate that this was a pre-Sukhothai Hindu shrine for the Khmers, which was later pressed into

Buddhist service; the square base inside the central prang originally supported the Shiva lingam (phallus). Just west, the ordination hall of **Wat Trapang Ngoen** rises gracefully from an island in the middle of the eponymous "silver pond". On the pond's west bank, north of the graceful lotus-bud chedi, notice the fluid lines of the walking Buddha mounted onto a brick wall – a classic example of Sukhothai sculpture. Taking the water feature one step further, **Wat Sra Sri** commands a fine position on two connecting islands north of Wat Trapang Ngoen; its bell-shaped chedi with a tapering spire and square base shows a strong Sri Lankan influence.

The outer zones

There are interesting outlying temples in the north, west and east zones, but there's little worth seeing in the south zone. Continuing north of Wat Sra Sri, cross the city walls into the north zone and you'll find **Wat Sri Chum**, which boasts Sukhothai's largest surviving Buddha image. The enormous brick-and-stucco seated Buddha, measuring over 11m from knee to knee and almost 15m high, peers through the slit in its tightly fitting, custom-made building.

Around 5km west of the city walls, lonely **Wat Saphan Hin** sits atop a hill, affording decent views of the surrounding countryside and the distant ruins. About 1km east of the city walls, the best temple in the east zone is **Wat Chang Lom**, by a canal just off the road to New Sukhothai. Chang Lom translates as "surrounded by elephants": the main feature here is a large, Sri Lankan-style, bell-shaped chedi encircled by a frieze of pachyderms.

ARRIVAL AND INFORMATION

By plane You can fly between Bangkok's Suvarnabhumi Airport and Sukhothai with Bangkok Airways (3 daily; 1hr 15min), although fares are quite high. The airport is about 25km north of New Sukhothai; flights are met by shuttle buses that head into the centre (B180/person).

By bus Buses use the terminal 3km northwest of New Sukhothai's town centre on the bypass. A tuk-tuk from here to the centre costs B60–80.

Destinations Ayutthaya (11 daily; 6hr); Bangkok (every 30min; 6–7hr); Chiang Mai (roughly hourly; 5–6hr); Chiang Rai (3–4 daily; 8–9hr); Khon Kaen (10–11 daily; 6–7hr); Lampang (roughly hourly; 3–4hr); Mae Sot (4 daily; 2hr 30min–3hr); Nan (1 daily; 4–5hr); Phitsanulok (at least every 40min; 1hr–1hr 30min).

Tourist information The TAT office is on Th Charodvithong (daily 8.30am–4.30pm; ☏055 616228–9, ✉tatsukho@tat.or.th).

GETTING AROUND

By songthaew Big songthaews (every 15–30min; 20–30min) run between New Sukhothai and the historical park; they leave from 200m west of TAT on Th Charodvithong, and some also stop at the main bus station. They pull into Old Sukhothai near the central zone entrance point.

By bike Most guesthouses in New Sukhothai rent out bicycles for B30/day (also available at the historical park for the same price) and motorcycles for B200–250/day.

ACCOMMODATION

OLD SUKHOTHAI

Old Sukhothai only has a handful of restaurants, but it is laidback and staying here allows you to take your time with the sights – and catch them deserted at sunrise and sunset when the light's at its most spectacular.

Old City Guest House Th Charodvithong, opposite the museum ☏055 697515. Within spitting distance of the ruins, a wide range of options mostly in two-storey wooden buildings around a yard, set back from the road. The cheapest are small, rather dark rooms with shared cold-water bathrooms. Doubles `B200`

★**Siam Villa** Route 1272, about 1km southeast of the museum ☏055 019956, ✇siamvillasukhothai.com. Excellent-value choice with oodles of charm: a/c rooms with hot showers in traditional Thai-style villas with steep roofs and wood-panelled walls, set around a lotus pond in a leafy garden. Doubles `B720`

NEW SUKHOTHAI

Ban Thai 38 Th Pravetnakorn ☏055 610163, ✇banthaiguesthouse.wixsite.com/banthaiguesthouse. A friendly guesthouse, where clean, comfortable but small wood-floored rooms sharing hot-water bathrooms are set in a small garden, which also has some smart wooden en-suite bungalows (from B400). The restaurant is a good place to meet people and does tasty Thai food tamed for the *farang* palate. Doubles `B250`

Blue House & Green House 295/34 Soi Sri Samarang ☏055 614863, ✇sukhothaibluehouse.wordpress.com. Two houses at the end of a quiet lane, operated by the same welcoming family. *Green* is a more basic wooden house, sheltering tightly packed fan dorms and private rooms with shared, cold or en-suite, hot showers. A gleaming modern house, *Blue* provides a/c rooms with comfortable wooden beds and en-suite hot water (from B600). Dorms `B120`, doubles `B240`

Hang Jeng Soi Meakaphut, signposted off Th Pravetnakorn just beyond *Ban Thai Guesthouse* ☏055 610585 or ☏081 972 4345. Down a short, quiet lane, this sprawling concrete house with big balconies offers bright rooms with parquet floors and en-suite hot showers, sharing plentiful toilets; add just B100 for a/c. Doubles `B250`

★**TR** 27/5 Th Pravetnakorn ☏055 611663, ✇sukhothaibudgetguesthouse.com. This friendly family-run guesthouse with en-suite hot showers throughout offers a little restaurant, neat rooms in a hotel-style building, plus some slightly more expensive, charming wooden bungalows (B450, or B600 with a/c) with verandahs overlooking the small back garden. Doubles `B300`

EATING

OLD SUKHOTHAI

The Coffee Cup Th Charodvithong, opposite the museum. At this clean and airy café, the menu of Thai, Western and fusion dishes is huge (with photos to help), including bagels, baguettes, *massaman* chicken curry (B100) and delicious fruit shakes. Daily 7am–10pm.

NEW SUKHOTHAI

Food carts set up every evening in front of Wat Ratchathani on Th Charodvithong, while Saturday night sees a busy market selling food and all sorts on Th Nikhon Kasem.

Dream Café 88/1 Th Singhawat. Cosy, wood-panelled restaurant with an artsy atmosphere and walls full of curios. It has a great mid-priced menu (most dishes above

10

10

B100) featuring delicious green curry, *tom yam* with pork ribs and tamarind leaves, fiery wing-bean salad – and gin and tonics. Daily 5–11pm.

Poo Restaurant 26 Th Charodvithitong. Although the surroundings aren't up to much, the cheap curries are tasty (around B60), and you can wash them down with a nice Belgian beer in front of big-screen sports. See how many toilet humour fans you see snapping pictures by the sign. Daily 8am or later–11pm.

Ton Krachee Th Charodvithitong, about 500m west of the bridge. One of the best places to try the very more-ish Sukhothai noodle soup – laced with palm sugar, it's sour, spicy and sweet (B30). English menu but no English sign – it's the old one-storey wooden building next to Saijo Denki a/c shop. Daily 8am–4pm.

DRINKING

Chopper Bar Th Pravetnakorn. This popular balcony bar with nightly live acoustic music, cheap beer and a vague biker theme is a great place to watch the world go by. Daily 3pm–midnight.

DIRECTORY

Hospital Sukhothai Hospital (☎055 616403) is west of New Sukhothai on the road to Old Sukhothai.

Post office Th Nikhon Kasem, about 1km south of the bridge (Mon–Fri 8.30am–4.30pm, Sat & Sun 9am–noon).

MAE SOT

Located only 6km from the Burmese border, **MAE SOT** boasts a thriving trade in gems and teak and a rich ethnic mix of Burmese, Karen, Hmong and Thai, plus a lively injection of committed NGO expats working with the thousands of refugees from Myanmar. It's a relaxed place to hang out before heading down to Umphang for some trekking (see box opposite) – treks can be arranged from Mae Sot – and chances are you'll meet some interesting people at one of several good places to eat. Most of the aid organizations that work in the Burmese refugee camps welcome donations, and some are happy to receive visitors and even short-term volunteers; ask at *Borderline* or *Krua Canadian* or *Bai Fern* restaurants (see opposite).

WHAT TO SEE AND DO

There's little to see in the small town apart from several glittering Burmese-style temples, an ornate Chinese temple

and a bustling, Burmese-influenced day market with interesting delicacies such as eels, live toads, tiny tortoises and a range of insects. Frequent songthaews (B20) run from Thanon Banthung near the south end of the market to the Burmese border at **Rim Moei**, 6km from Mae Sot, where a large, slightly tacky market for Burmese handicrafts such as woodcarving and other goods crowds the banks of the River Moei.

ARRIVAL AND DEPARTURE

By plane Nok Air (⦿nokair.com) operates flights from Bangkok (Don Muang; 3–4 daily; 1hr 10min), and Kan Airlines (⦿kanairlines.com) flies from Chiang Mai (4 weekly; 40min) to Mae Sot's airport, 3km west of town. Taxis and motorbike taxis await arrivals.

By bus, songthaew and a/c minibus Buses, minibuses and long-distance songthaews use the government bus station, about 2km west of town at the intersection of Highway 105 and the main east–west street, Th Indharakiri, with motorbike taxis shuttling passengers to the guesthouses.

Destinations Bangkok (13 daily; 8hr); Chiang Mai (3 daily; 6hr); Chiang Rai (2 daily; 9hr); Lampang (2 daily; 4–5hr); Mae Sai (2 daily; 10hr); Mae Sariang (songthaew; roughly hourly in the morning; 6hr; change onto a bus or minibus to Mae Hong Son); Phitsanulok (9 daily; 4hr); Sukhothai (9 daily; 2hr 30min–3hr); Umphang (roughly hourly 7.30am–2pm; 4–5hr).

ACCOMMODATION

Bai Fern 660 Th Indharakiri ☎055 531349. A popular, well-run and helpful guesthouse, offering simple rooms with shared hot-water bathrooms, and very good rates for singles; it's in the centre of town, behind a good restaurant of the same name. Doubles B250

Ban Thai Down a short lane off the north side of Th Indharakiri, beyond Wat Arunyaket on the west side of town ☎055 531590. The most appealing guesthouse in town

---

> ### INTO MYANMAR: THE MAE SOT–MYAWADDY BORDER
>
> It's now possible to cross the **Thai–Myanmar Friendship Bridge** at Rim Moei (see above) to the Burmese village of Myawaddy on the opposite bank of the River Moei: if you already have a Burmese visa, you can travel on to popular destinations such as Mawlmayine and Hpa-an; if you don't have a visa, you can pay B500 to visit Myawaddy for the day.

occupies several traditional-style, wooden-floor houses in a peaceful garden compound; the cheapest rooms in the main house share hot-water bathrooms. Doubles B280

Duang Kamol (DK) Hotel 298/2 Th Indharakiri, near the post office ☎ 055 531699. Great-value town-centre hotel offering huge, clean rooms with hot showers, many of them with little balconies and some with a/c. The entrance is on the first floor, above a series of shops. Doubles B250

EATING AND DRINKING

Borderline Tea Garden Th Indharakiri, behind the Borderline crafts shop and arts gallery ⓦ borderlinecollective.org. Cheap Burmese dishes (mostly B35–50), including tea-leaf salad and potato curry, Burmese tea, lemon-grass juice and other healthy drinks, are sold at this simple, relaxed tea garden; profits go to refugee women's groups. Also runs cookery classes (B500–1000 depending on group size). Tues–Sun 7.30am–9pm.

Casa Mia Th Don Kaew, off Th Indharakiri, 5min walk west of *Ban Thai Guesthouse*. Delicious home-made pastas at rock-bottom prices (under B100), as well as pizzas, Thai food, veggie options and great cakes. Daily except Sat 8am–9.30pm.

Krua Canadian 3 Th Sriphanit, off Th Indharakiri diagonally across from the police station. Huge menu of tasty dishes (mostly around B100), including Thai, Mexican, vegetarian, Western breakfasts and deli sandwiches. Also a good source of local information. Daily 7am–2pm & 5–9.30pm.

DIRECTORY

Banks There are banks dotted all about Mae Sot, especially on Th Indharakiri and Th Prasat Vithi.

Bike and motorbike rental Available at many guesthouses: bikes around B50/day, motorbikes around B250/day.

Post office To the east of the police station on Th Indharakiri.

UMPHANG

Even if you don't fancy joining a trek, it's worth considering making the spectacular 164km trip south from Mae Sot through over a thousand bends to the village of **UMPHANG**, both for the fine mountain scenery and for the buzz of being in such an isolated part of Thailand. Chances are your songthaew will be crammed full of people from varied ethnic and tribal backgrounds. About halfway, the road goes past Umpiem Mai, a refugee camp for fifteen thousand or so Burmese.

Surrounded by mountains and sited at the confluence of the Mae Khlong and Umphang rivers, Umphang itself is small and quiet; it takes no more than twenty minutes to walk from one end to the other. It has few signposted roads, but the two main points of orientation are the River Umphang at the far western end of the village, and the wat – about 500m east of the river bridge – that marks its centre.

10

TREKKING AROUND UMPHANG

The focus of most treks from Umphang is beautiful, three-tiered **Tee Lor Su Waterfall**. It's at its most thunderous, with a drop of around 200m and a width of around 400m, just after the rainy season in November, when you can also swim in the beautifully blue lower pool, though trails can still be muddy at this time. During the dry season (Dec–April or later), it's usually possible to climb up to one of the upper tiers. A typical trek lasts three days and features rafting, hot springs, two to four hours' walking per day, a night in a Karen village and an optional elephant ride. Bring a fleece as nights can get chilly. Many itineraries now include transport from and to Mae Sot and accommodation in Umphang, with prices starting at around B5500 for a three-day trek, though you can save money by making your own way to Umphang and shopping around there (around B4000 for a three-day trek). In the rainy season (roughly June–Oct), trips focus on whitewater rafting.

TREKKING OPERATORS

Max One Tour In the DK Hotel plaza, 296/2 Th Indharakiri, Mae Sot ☎ 055 542942, ⓦ maxonetour .com. Outlet for Umphang Hill (see below).

Mr Boonchuay 360 Th Pravitpaiwan, southeast of the main songthaew stop ☎ 055 561020, ⓦ boonchuaytour .net. Umphang-born and bred, Mr Boonchuay knows the area well and has a good reputation; his English is not perfect, but he has English-speaking guides.

Umphang Hill Resort By the bridge in Umphang ☎ 055 561063, ⓦ umphanghill.com. The biggest outfit in the area is efficiently run and offers eleven different itineraries.

10

ARRIVAL AND DEPARTURE

By songthaew Songthaews stop at the northern end of Th Pravitpaiwan, at the top of the town; most places are within walking distance, though there are also motorbike taxis. In terms of public transport, Umphang is effectively a dead end, so you'll need to return to Mae Sot (roughly hourly until noon; 4–5hr) before continuing on to other destinations.

ACCOMMODATION

Phu Doi Campsite Resort Soi 4, off the east side of Th Pravitpaiwan ☎055 561049, ⓦphudoi.com. Dark wood-panelled fan or a/c rooms with hot-water bathrooms and verandahs, in log buildings overlooking a lotus pond. Also has a popular restaurant with an English-language menu and does treks to Tee Lor Su. Doubles B400
Tu Ka Su Cottage West of the river, up the hill ☎055 561295, ⓦtukasu.webs.com. In a spacious, pretty garden, this attractive place offers nicely designed wooden cabins with large verandahs, a/c and hot showers, as well as treks to Tee Lor Su. Doubles B600

The north

In the northern uplands, the climate becomes more temperate, nurturing the fertile land that gave the old kingdom of **the north** the name of **Lanna**, "the land of a million rice fields". Until the beginning of the last century, Lanna was a largely independent region, with its own styles of art and architecture. Its capital, the pleasant, 700-year-old city of **Chiang Mai**, is now a major centre for travellers' activities and courses and the most popular base from which to organize treks to nearby hill-tribe villages. Another great way of exploring the scenic countryside up here is to rent a jeep or motorbike and make the 600km loop over the forested western mountains, via the backpackers' honeypot of **Pai**, to **Mae Hong Son** and back. Heading north from Chiang Mai towards the Burmese border brings you to the smaller town of **Chiang Rai**, a base for trekking and river trips, and then on to the frontier settlement of **Mae Sai**, the so-called "**Golden Triangle**" at Sop Ruak, and the atmospheric ruined temples of **Chiang Saen**. **Chiang Khong**, on the Mekong River, is an important crossing point to Laos.

CHIANG MAI

Despite becoming a fixture on the package-tourist itinerary, **CHIANG MAI** – Thailand's second city – manages to preserve a little of the atmosphere of an overgrown village and a laidback traveller vibe, especially in the traditional old quarter, set within a two-kilometre-square moat. Chiang Mai is a fun and historic city, packed with culture and bustling markets, but its real charm lies in the staggering range of tours, treks, courses and activities available. You can easily spend a week in Chiang Mai and do something completely different every day: visiting elephant parks, walking to hill-tribe villages, waterfalls, massage, cooking classes, mountain biking, rock climbing, bungee jumping, river cruises, unlimited shopping experiences and national parks. On top of that, there are fabulous temples, delicious food, unparalleled evening markets and an energetic nightlife that caters to everyone. It's impossible to get bored here.

WHAT TO SEE AND DO

The main sights are mostly situated within the ancient city walls, which are surrounded by a moat, and intersected at the cardinal points by elaborate gates. Tha Pae Gate, on the east side of old Chiang Mai, leads out to the town's commercial centre and the river. Just 16km west of town, the striking Wat Phra That Doi Suthep is set on a mist-shrouded mountain.

Wat Phra Singh

If you see only one temple in Chiang Mai it should be **Wat Phra Singh**, at the far western end of Thanon Ratchdamnoen in the old town. Just inside the gate to the right, the wooden library is the best example of its kind in the north, inlaid with glass mosaic and set high on a base decorated with stucco angels. The temple's largest structure, a colourful modern viharn (congregation hall) fronted by naga (serpent) balustrades, hides from view the beautiful Viharn Lai Kam, a wooden gem of early nineteenth-century Lanna

TREKKING

Trekking in the mountains of northern Thailand differs from trekking in most other parts of the world, in that the emphasis is not primarily on the scenery but on the region's inhabitants. More than a hundred thousand travellers now trek each year, most heading to well-trodden areas such as the Mae Tang Valley, 40km northwest of Chiang Mai, and the hills around the Kok River west of Chiang Rai. This steady flow of trekkers creates pressures for the traditionally insular hill tribes. Foreigners unfamiliar with hill-tribe customs can easily cause grave offence, especially those who go looking for drugs. Most tribespeople are genuinely welcoming to foreigners; nonetheless, it is important to take a responsible attitude.

    The hill tribes are big business in northern Thailand. **Chiang Rai** is the second-biggest trekking centre after Chiang Mai, and agencies can also be found in Nan, **Mae Hong Son** and **Pai**, although these usually arrange treks only to the villages in their immediate area. Guided trekking on a much smaller scale than in the north is available in **Umphang** (see p.749).

10

THE BASICS

On any trek, you'll need walking boots or training shoes, long trousers (against thorns and wet-season leeches), a hat, a sarong or towel, a sweater or fleece, plus insect repellent and, if possible, a mosquito net. On an organized trek, water, blankets or a sleeping bag, and possibly a small backpack, should be supplied. It's wise not to take anything valuable with you; most guesthouses in Chiang Mai have safes, but check their reputation with other travellers, and sign an inventory – theft and credit-card abuse are not uncommon.

TREKKING ETIQUETTE

As guests, it's up to *farangs* to adapt to the customs of the hill tribes and not to make a nuisance of themselves.
* Dress modestly and wear a sarong when showering; no bikinis or swim suits.
* Before entering a hill-tribe village, look out for taboo signs of woven bamboo strips on the ground outside the village entrance, which mean a special ceremony is taking place and that you should not enter. Be careful about what you touch. In Akha villages, keep your hands off cult structures such as the entrance gates and the giant swing. Do not touch or photograph any shrines, or sit underneath them. You'll have to pay a fine for any violation of local customs.
* Most villagers do not like to be photographed, in keeping with their spiritualist and animist beliefs. Be particularly careful with pregnant women and babies – most tribes believe cameras affect the soul of the foetus or newborn. Always ask first, and accept that you may have to offer a "donation" for any photos taken.
* Offering gifts is dubious practice: ask your guide what the village actually *needs* and follow their advice; clothes are always useful, but avoid sweets and cigarettes, as they may encourage begging.

ORGANIZED TREKS

Organized treks can last for anything from one to seven days, and follow a route regularly used by the agency. There will be a few hours' walking every day, plus the possibility of an elephant ride and a trip on a bamboo raft. The group usually sleeps on the floor of the village headman's hut, and the guide cooks communal meals. A typical three-day trek costs B1500–3000 in Chiang Mai, sometimes less in other towns, and much less without rafting and elephant rides.

    Word of mouth is often the best way to choose a trekking agency. If you want to trek with a small group, get an assurance that you won't be tagged onto a larger group. Meet the guides, who should speak reasonable English, know about hill-tribe culture and have a certificate from the Tourism Authority of Thailand (TAT). Check how much walking is involved per day, and ask about the menu. Also enquire about transport from base at the beginning and end of the trek, which sometimes entails a long public bus ride. Before setting off, each trek should be registered with the tourist police.

---

architecture, with its squat, multi-tiered roof and exquisitely carved and gilded pediment. Inside sits the Phra Singh Buddha image, a portly, radiant and much-revered bronze in fifteenth-century Lanna style. The walls are enlivened by murals depicting daily life in the north a hundred years ago.

10

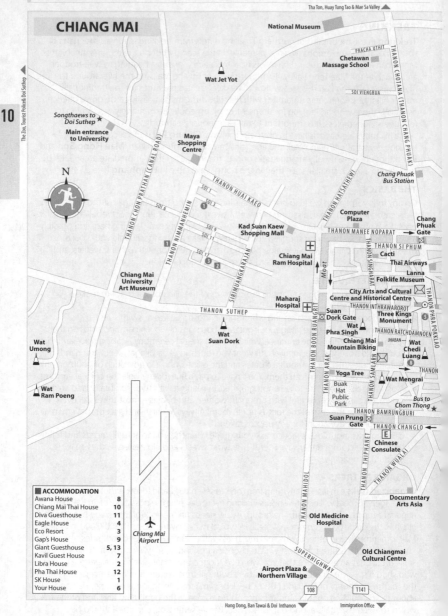

Wat Chedi Luang

Wat Chedi Luang (main entrance on Thanon Phra Pokklao) is named after an enormous crumbling pink-brick fifteenth-century chedi, which was reduced to its present height of 60m by an earthquake in 1545. It once housed the Emerald Buddha in the niche on its eastern side (now in Bangkok's Wat Phra Kaeo), but now has to make do with an oversized replica. On the northeast side of the chedi, "Monk Chat" is advertised (daily 9am–6pm), giving you a chance to

10

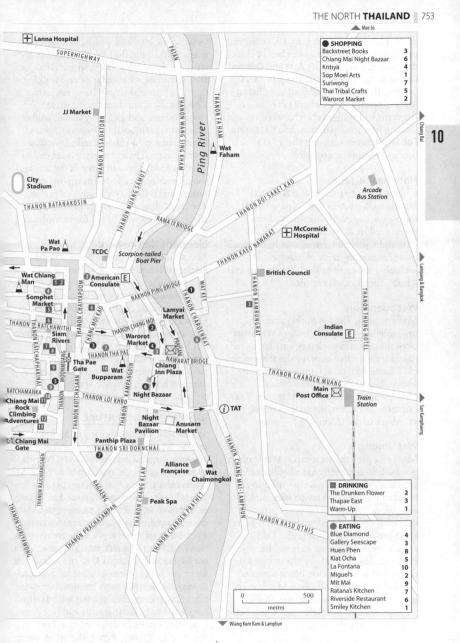

Mae Jo

Chiang Rai

Lampang & Bangkok

San Kamphaeng

● SHOPPING

Backstreet Books	3
Chiang Mai Night Bazaar	6
Kritiya	4
Sop Moei Arts	1
Suriwong	7
Thai Tribal Crafts	5
Warorot Market	2

Lanna Hospital

SUPERHIGHWAY

THANON ASSADATORN

THANON MUANG SAMUT

THANON WANG SING KHAM

THANON FA HAM

PATAN

Ping River

Wat Faham

JJ Market

City Stadium

THANON RATANAKOSIN

RAMA IX BRIDGE

THANON DOI SAKET KAO

Arcade Bus Station

Wat Pa Pao

TCDC

Scorpion-tailed Boat Pier

THANON KAEO NAWARAT

McCormick Hospital

THANON BAMRUNGRAT

British Council

THANON THUNG HOTEL

Wat Chiang Man

American Consulate E

NAKHON PING BRIDGE

WAT KET

Somphet Market

THANON CHAIYAPOOM

CHANG MOI KAO

Lamyai Market

THANON CHAROENRAT

Indian Consulate E

THANON RATCHAWITHI

Siam Rivers

THANON CHANG MOI

THANON RATCHAPHAKINAI

THANON MOONMUANG

Warorot Market

THANON THA PAE

PRASAN

NAWARAT BRIDGE

THANON CHAROEN MUANG

Tha Pae Gate

Wat Bupparam

THANON KAMPANGDIN

Chiang Inn Plaza

Main Post Office

Train Station

RATCHAMANKA

THANON KOTCHASARN

THANON LOI KHRO

Night Bazaar

Chiang Mai Rock Climbing Adventures

Chiang Mai Gate

THANON RATCHAMANKA

Night Bazaar Pavilion

Anusarn Market

(i) TAT

THANON RATCHIANGSAEN

THANON SURIYAWONG

Panthip Plaza

THANON SRI DORNCHAI

Alliance Française

Wat Chaimongkol

THANON CHANG KLAN

RAGAENG

Peak Spa

THANON CHAROEN PRATHET

THANON PRACHASAMPAN

THANON CHANG MAI–LAMPHUN

THANON RASD UTHIS

■ DRINKING

The Drunken Flower	2
Thapae East	3
Warm-Up	1

● EATING

Blue Diamond	4
Gallery Seescape	3
Huen Phen	8
Kiat Ocha	5
La Fontana	10
Miguel's	2
Mit Mai	9
Ratana's Kitchen	7
Riverside Restaurant	6
Smiley Kitchen	1

0   500
metres

▼ Wiang Kum Kam & Lamphun

meet and talk to the monks in English. An
impressive new building in traditional
Lanna style to the left of the main entrance
enshrines the Sao Inthakin, Chiang Mai's
city pillar, which is celebrated with a major
festival in late May or early June.

The city museums
Three adjacent museums provide an
informative overview of the history,
customs and culture of the city and the
region and are well worth a visit (Tues–
Sun 8.30am–5pm; B90 each, or B180 for

10

all 3). Housed in the elegant 1920s former provincial office on Thanon Phra Pokklao, the main **Chiang Mai City Arts and Cultural Centre** focuses on the city's identity and culture. Behind it, you'll find the **Chiang Mai Historical Centre**, where you can see the excavated walls of the chapel of the old Chiang Mai royal palace, while the **Lanna Folklife Museum** occupies the 1920s former courthouse opposite.

National Museum

Chiang Mai's branch of the **National Museum** (Wed–Sun 9am–4pm; B100), on the northwestern outskirts of town, doesn't tell its story as well as the City Arts and Cultural Centre, but has a much more interesting array of artefacts, including a wealth of Buddha images and a fine collection of ceramics.

Wat Suan Dork

Midway along Thanon Suthep, the brilliantly whitewashed chedi of **Wat Suan Dork** sits next to a garden of smaller, equally dazzling chedis that contain the ashes of the old Chiang Mai royal family – framed by Doi Suthep to the west, this makes a photogenic sight, especially at sunset. You can meet and talk to the monks in English at "Monk Chat" (Mon–Fri 5–7pm).

Wat Umong

More of a park than a temple, **Wat Umong** was built in the 1380s for a brilliant monk who was prone to wandering off into the forest to meditate. To try to keep him in one place, the tunnels (*umong*) beneath the chedi were painted with trees, flowers and birds to simulate his favourite environment, and some can still be explored. Above them, by the overgrown chedi, stands a grotesque black statue of the fasting Buddha, all ribs and veins. To get to the wat, head west along Thanon Suthep for 2km, turn left after Wang Nam Gan and follow the signs for about 1km.

Doi Suthep

A jaunt up **Doi Suthep**, the mountain that rises steeply at Chiang Mai's western edge, is the best short outing you can make from the city, chiefly on account of beautiful **Wat Phra That Doi Suthep**, which gives fine views of the city, and which, because of a magic relic of the Buddha enshrined in its chedi, is the north's holiest shrine (B30, or B50 including a funicular to save walking up three hundred steps). Its upper terrace is a breathtaking combination of carved wood, filigree and gleaming metal, whose altars and ceremonial umbrellas surround the dazzling gold-plated chedi. **Songthaews** leave when full from the northwest end of Thanon Huai Kaeo, in front of the zoo and the university, for the 16km trip up the mountain (B40–50 each way per person). The road, although steep in places, is paved all the way and well suited for motorbikes.

Elephant Nature Park

About an hour north of Chiang Mai, the **Elephant Nature Park** (city office at 1 Th Ratchamanka ☎053 818932, ⓦelephantnaturepark.org) is essentially a hospital for sick elephants, but hands-on pre-arranged educational – and recreational – visits by the public are encouraged. Either opt for a full-day trip (B2500, including pick-up from Chiang Mai), or sign up as a paying volunteer for up to a week. Ensure that you book in advance as the park is quite often oversubscribed for weeks.

ARRIVAL AND DEPARTURE

On arrival at the train station or one of the bus stations, you can either flag down a red songthaew on the road or charter a tuk-tuk or songthaew (see opposite) to get to the centre.

By plane The airport, 3km southwest of the centre, has currency exchange booths, ATMs, cafés and a post office. Taxis (from B150) and a/c minibuses (B40/person, from the south end of the terminal) await arriving passengers; tuk-tuks and chartered songthaews can bring departing passengers to the airport, but are not allowed to pick up. The airport's busiest route, Bangkok, is served by all the main carriers, among which only Thai, Thai Smile and Bangkok Airways use Suvarnabhumi Airport. Kan Airlines (ⓦkanairlines.com) has a constantly changing schedule of local routes. International destinations include Luang Prabang (Lao Airlines), Yangon, Mandalay (both Bangkok Airways) and Kuala Lumpur (Air Asia).

Destinations Bangkok (30 daily; 1hr); Krabi (2 daily; 2hr); Mae Hong Son (3 daily; 35min); Mae Sot (4 weekly; 50min); Phuket (5 daily; 2hr); Samui (1 daily; 1hr 50min).

By bus The long-distance Arcade bus station on Th Kaeo Nawarat is 3km northeast of the centre. The main Chiang Mai bus company, Green Bus (ⓦgreenbusthailand.com), maintains a ticket office in the centre of town, on the corner of Th Ratchdamnoen and Th Samlarn in front of Wat Phra Singh.

Tha Ton buses use the much more central Chang Puak bus station, just off Th Chotana on the north side of the old town.
Destinations Bangkok (30 daily; 9–11hr); Chiang Khong (2 daily; 5–6hr); Chiang Rai (20 daily; 3hr); Chiang Saen (2 daily; 4hr); Khon Kaen (12 daily; 10–12hr); Khorat (10 daily; 11–12hr); Lampang (roughly hourly; 2hr); Mae Hong Son (7 daily; 8hr); Mae Sai (6–8 daily; 4hr); Mae Sot (2 daily; 6hr 30min); Nan (9–11 daily; 6hr); Pai (at least hourly; 3–4hr); Phitsanulok (40 daily; 5–6hr); Sukhothai (roughly hourly; 5–6hr); Tha Ton (4 daily; 4hr); Ubon Ratchathani (6 daily; 14hr); Udon Thani (for Nong Khai; 4 daily; 11–12hr).
By train The train station is on Th Charoen Muang, just over 2km east of Tha Pae Gate, and has a left-luggage office.
Destinations Ayutthaya (5 daily; 10–13hr); Bangkok (5 daily; 12–14hr); Lampang (6 daily; 2hr 30min); Lopburi (5 daily; 9–11hr); Phitsanulok (6 daily; 6–8hr).

GETTING AROUND

By bike Some guesthouses rent bicycles for around B50/day, and you can also pick them up around Tha Pae Gate.
By car or motorbike Many places around Tha Pae Gate rent out motorbikes (from B150) and cars (from B800). The latter should come with insurance included: check before you set off.
By songthaew Red trucks (songthaews) act as shared taxis within the city, picking up people heading in roughly the same direction and taking each to their specific destination; fares to most places should cost B20 during the day. They sometimes also operate as chartered taxis for about the same price as tuk-tuks.
By tuk-tuk The city is stuffed with tuk-tuks, ready to take advantage of tourists – haggle hard. Expect to pay around B60 for a short journey from the Night Bazaar to Tha Pae Gate.

INFORMATION

Tourist information The TAT office (daily 8.30am–4.30pm; T 053 248604) is at 105/1 Th Chiang Mai–Lamphun on the east bank of the river near Nawarat Bridge. It's not to be confused with TAD Travel and Tours on Th Ratchaphakinai, or several other outlets around town, which pretend to be government information offices but are in fact private travel agents.
Maps Nancy Chandler's *Map of Chiang Mai* (B290) is very handy for a detailed exploration.

CHIANG MAI BOAT TRIPS

One of the most leisurely ways to explore the surrounding countryside is to take a river cruise with **Mae Ping River Cruise** (Wat Chaimongkol, Th Charoenprathet; T 053 274822, W maepingrivercruise.com; minimum two people; transfers from your accommodation included), who offer two-hour cruises through lush countryside, with a stop at a local farmer's house and herbal drink and snack included (B550 per person), as well as popular trips to the ruined city of Wiang Kum Kam, by boat and horse-and-carriage (B800). They also offer evening dinner cruises (7.30pm; B650).

TREKKING AND ADVENTURE TOURS

In Chiang Mai, treks (see box, p.751) are usually arranged through one of the guesthouses, among which *Eagle House*, which passes on a proportion of its revenue towards funding projects in hill-tribe villages, and *Your House* have particularly good reputations. The choice of other adventure activities on offer is staggering.

TOUR OPERATORS

Active Thailand Based at Tasala, east of Chiang Mai T 053 850160, W activethailand.com. Offers treks, river- and lake-kayaking, cycling and whitewater rafting.
Chiang Mai Mountain Biking 1 Th Samlarn, 50m south of Wat Phra Singh T 081 024 7046, W mountainbikingchiangmai.com. A wide range of routes for all levels of fitness and experience, ranging from single-track downhill rides, mostly on Doi Suthep, to cross-country leisure trips.
Chiang Mai Rock Climbing Adventures 55/3 Th Ratchapakhinai T 053 207102, W thailandclimbing.com. Climbing trips at the striking Crazy Horse Buttress, 35km from Chiang Mai, plus caving and bouldering trips. Also runs climbing and caving courses, with extensive equipment for rent or to buy, and a partner-finding service. Its in-town bouldering wall is a good place to meet and train.
Click and Travel 158/40 Th Chiang Mai–Hod T 053 281553, W clickandtravelonline.com. Belgian-Thai company that runs cycling tours of Chiang Mai and the north, lasting from a few hours to four days, and maintains a useful website, W chiangmaicycling.org, full of all manner of information for cyclists.
Flight of the Gibbon T 053 010660, W treetopasia.com. Zoom through the tropical rainforest on zipwires and sky bridges in this exhilarating trip high above the jungle floor.
Siam Rivers 17 Th Ratchawithi T 089 515 1917, W siamrivers.com. Chiang Mai's longest-standing whitewater rafting outfit, with high standards of safety (trips run roughly late May to Feb/March), which also offers full-moon trips and whitewater kayaking.

COURSES

The courses listed below are only a taster of the huge range on offer.

COOKERY

Basil Cookery School 22/4 Soi 5, Th Sirimuangkarajan T 083 320 7693, W basilcookery.com. Highly recommended school with interesting menu choices and small class sizes. You'll visit a market and learn to cook six dishes (B1000).

10

THE HILL TRIBES

There are at least ten different **hill tribes** in northern Thailand, many of them divided into distinct subgroups. Migrating from various parts of China and Southeast Asia, most arrived in Thailand in the twentieth century and many have tribal relatives in other parts of Southeast Asia. The tribes have sophisticated systems of customs, laws and beliefs, and are predominantly animists. They often have exquisitely crafted costumes, though many men and children now adopt Western clothes for everyday wear. To learn more about the tribes, visit the hill-tribe museum in Chiang Rai (see p.768).

KAREN

The largest hill-tribe group (pop.500,000), the **Karen** began to arrive in the seventeenth century, though many are recent refugees from Myanmar. Most of them live west of Chiang Mai, stretching all the way down to Kanchanaburi. Unmarried Karen women wear loose V-necked shift dresses, often decorated with grass seeds at the seams. Married women wear blouses and skirts in bold red or blue. Perhaps the most famous of all hill-tribe groups are the **Padaung**, a small subgroup of the Karen. Padaung women wear columns of heavy brass rings around their necks (see p.763).

HMONG

The **Hmong** (or Meo; pop.110,000) are found widely in northern Thailand, and are also the most widespread minority group in south China. The Blue Hmong subgroup live to the west of Chiang Mai, while the White Hmong are found to the east. Most Hmong live in extended families in traditional houses with a roof descending almost to ground level. Blue Hmong women wear intricately embroidered pleated skirts decorated with bands of red, pink, blue and white. White Hmong women wear white skirts for special occasions and black baggy trousers for everyday use. All the Hmong are famous for their chunky silver jewellery.

LAHU

The **Lahu** (pop.80,000) originated in the Tibetan highlands. The Lahu language has become the lingua franca of the hill tribes, since the Lahu often hire out their labour. About one-third of Lahu have been converted to Christianity. The remaining animist Lahu believe in a village guardian spirit, who is often worshipped at a central temple. Houses are built on high stilts and

★**Chiang Mai Thai Farm Cooking School** 38 Soi 9, Th Moonmuang ☎081 288 5989, ⓦthaifarmcooking.com. A good way to escape the city: you can pick your own organic vegetables, herbs and fruits for cooking on their farm, a 30min drive from town (B1500/day, transport provided).

MASSAGE

Massages in Thailand are considered a healthy part of daily life rather than a luxurious pampering treat so they're readily available all over Chiang Mai, with prices starting around B150/hr.

Old Medicine Hospital 78/1 Soi Mo Shivagakomarpaj, off Th Wualai ☎053 275085, ⓦthaimassageschool.ac.th. Highly respected week-long courses (B5000) with dorm accommodation available; foot, oil and herbal compress courses are also available. Also the best place in Chiang Mai to get a massage (B300/90min).

Thai Massage School of Chiang Mai 203/6 Th Mae Jo ☎053 854330, ⓦtmcschool.com. Five-day courses (B8500) fully accredited by the Ministry of Education, as well as longer professional courses.

MEDITATION

Most meditation courses are serious undertakings: conditions are sparse, the routine is strict and there's often no reading or music, and speaking must be kept to a minimum.

Wat Phra That Doi Suthep (see p.754) Vipassana Meditation Centre ☎053 295012, ⓦfivethousandyears.org. A variety of meditation courses for beginners and experienced students, from 4 to 21 days. Registration must be made in advance (courses are often full).

Wat Ram Poeng Northern Insight Meditation Centre, off Th Chon Prathan near Wat Umong ☎053 278620, ⓦpalikanon.com/vipassana/tapotaram/tapotaram.htm. Disciplined courses (with a rule of no food after noon and respectful silence), taught by Thai monks with translators. The basic course is 26 days but the meditation practice can be "tried out" for ten days with special permission.

Wat Suan Dork (see p.754) Mahachulalongkorn Buddhist University ⓦmonkchat.net. Introductory one- and two-day meditation courses; the latter is a retreat at a training centre on Doi Suthep, including chanting and

thatched with grass. Some Lahu women wear a distinctive black cloak with diagonal white stripes, decorated in bold red and yellow on the sleeve, but many now wear ordinary clothes. The tribe is famous for its richly embroidered shoulder bags.

AKHA

The poorest of the hill tribes is the **Akha** (pop.50,000). Every Akha village is entered through ceremonial gates decorated with carvings of human attributes – even cars and aeroplanes – to indicate to the spirit world that only humans should pass. Akha houses are recognizable by their low stilts and steeply pitched roofs. Women wear elaborate headgear consisting of a conical wedge of white beads interspersed with silver coins, topped with plumes of red taffeta and framed by dangling silver balls.

MIEN

The **Mien** (or Yao; pop.42,000) consider themselves the aristocrats of the hill tribes. Originating in central China, and widely scattered throughout the north, they are the only people to have a written language, and a codified religion, based on medieval Chinese Taoism, although many have converted to Christianity and Buddhism. Mien women wear long black jackets with bright scarlet lapels, and heavily embroidered, loose trousers and turbans.

LISU

The **Lisu** (pop.30,000), who originated in eastern Tibet, are found mostly in the west, particularly between Chiang Mai and Mae Hong Son. They are organized into patriarchal clans, and their strong sense of clan rivalry often results in public violence. The Lisu live in extended families in bamboo houses. The women wear a blue or green knee-length tunic, with a wide black belt and blue or green trousers. Men wear green, pink or yellow baggy trousers and a blue jacket.

LAWA

The **Lawa** people (pop.17,000) have inhabited Thailand since at least the eighth century and most Lawa villages look no different from Thai settlements. But between Hot, Mae Sariang and Mae Hong Son, the Lawa still live a largely traditional life. Unmarried Lawa women wear strings of orange and yellow beads, white blouses edged with pink, and tight skirts in parallel bands of blue, black, yellow and pink. All the women wear their hair tied in a turban.

---

alms-giving (B500 requested to cover food and transportation). Participants need to wear white clothes, available for B300.

ACCOMMODATION

The main concentrations of guesthouses are in the surprisingly quiet sois around the eastern side of the moat, close to all the sights and amid a proliferation of restaurants. Some guesthouses make their bread and butter from trekking and will encourage you to use their service; though this can be convenient, it's always worth shopping around. None of the places listed should hassle you to trek.

Awana House 7 Soi 1, Th Ratchadamnoen ☎ 053 419005, ⓦ awanahouse.com. This helpful, Thai-Dutch guesthouse has a tiny pool, fan rooms sharing hot-water bathrooms and large, nicely furnished, en-suite, a/c rooms. Doubles B400

Chiang Mai Thai House 5/1 Soi 5, Th Tha Pae ☎ 053 904110, ⓦ chiangmaithaihouse.com. There's a choice of smallish but well-furnished rooms with fan, hot shower and TV or bigger ones with a/c in this centrally located place, which also has an outdoor jacuzzi pool. Doubles B600

Diva Guesthouse 84/13 Th Ratchaphakinai ☎ 053 273851, ⓦ divaguesthouse.com. Helpful spot with richly coloured murals on the walls, a sociable ground-floor café and a wide choice of clean rooms with en-suite hot showers: six-bed, fan-cooled or a/c dorms and fan or a/c private rooms of all sizes. Dorms B120, doubles B300

★ **Eagle House** 16 Soi 3, Th Chang Moi Kao ☎ 053 235387, ⓦ eaglehouse.com. Friendly, well-maintained Thai-Irish guesthouse with a good garden café and en-suite doubles with cold or hot showers; well-organized treks and cookery courses are on offer. Doubles B300

★ **Eco Resort** 109 Th Bamrungrat ☎ 053 247111, ⓦ ecoresortchiangmai.com. This former school in huge, lush, quiet gardens has been tastefully transformed into a modern, eco-friendly hostel-cum-hotel, with a/c and hot water throughout. There's a lovely, 25m pool surrounded by hanging plants and stylish common rooms. Breakfast included. Dorms B530, doubles B1160

★ **Gap's House** 3 Soi 4, Th Ratchdamnoen ☎ 053 278140, ⓦ gaps-house.com. Set around a relaxing, leafy compound strewn with objets d'art is a wide range of a/c rooms with antique furniture and hot showers. The room price includes

10

a simple cooked breakfast, and a vegetarian buffet is served in the evening (not Sun); cookery courses available. No reservations are taken, though you can call on your proposed arrival date to check availability. Decent rates for singles. Doubles B500

Giant Guesthouse Soi 6, Th Moonmuang ☎053 227338, ⓦgiantguesthouse.com. This popular option is right next to the market and has its own kitchen – ideal if you fancy practising your Thai cooking. The staff are helpful and put on films in their comfortable lounge; coffee, tea and bottled water are free. Rooms come with fan (shared or en-suite bathrooms) or a/c. There's another branch at the bottom of Th Ratchaphakinai with three- or four-bed dorms (B120). Doubles B240

Kavil Guest House 10/1 Soi 5, Th Ratchdamnoen, near Somphet Market ☎053 224740. Smallish, friendly, well-run place in a quiet soi with tastefully renovated fan and a/c rooms; all have hot-water bathrooms. Doubles B550

Libra House 28 Soi 9, Th Moonmuang ☎053 210687, ⓦlibrahousechiangmai.com. Excellent, family-run, trekking-oriented guesthouse with 24hr check-in. All of the fifty-plus rooms are en suite with hot water, some with a/c. Free pick-ups during the day if booked in advance. Decent rates for singles. Doubles B400

Pha Thai House 48/1 Th Ratchaphakinai ☎053 278013 or ☎081 998 6933, ⓦphathaihouse.com. A wide variety of a/c rooms, all en suite with hot showers, and an attractive pool in a leafy garden setting. Doubles B700

SK House 30 Soi 9, Th Moonmuang ☎053 210690, ⓦtheskhouse.com. Efficient, brick-built high-rise with a small, shaded swimming pool. Fan and fancier a/c rooms come with hot-water bathrooms. Free pick-ups from the train station. Doubles B250

Your House 8 Soi 2, Th Ratchawithi ☎053 217492, ⓦyourhouseguesthouse.com. Welcoming old-town teak house. Big rooms with shared hot-water bathrooms, plus some smarter en-suite ones in two modern annexes; optional a/c in most. Fabulous, inexpensive breakfasts. Good for treks and day-trips; free pick-ups are sometimes possible from train and bus stations or the airport. Doubles B250

EATING

There are several night markets with good street-food stalls, including by Chiang Mai Gate on Th Bamrungburi. Several stalls set up in the evenings on Th Moonmuang in front of Somphet Market, handy for the main guesthouse area.

Blue Diamond Soi 9, Th Moonmuang. Popular, mostly vegetarian restaurant with a pleasant garden, serving very good Thai dishes, Western breakfasts (sets from B140), home-made bread, shakes, herbal teas and espresso coffee. Mon–Sat 7am–8.30pm.

NORTHERN FOOD

Northern food has been strongly influenced by Burmese cuisine, especially in curries such as the spicy **kaeng hang lay**, made with pork, ginger and tamarind. Another favourite local dish, especially for lunch, is **khao soi**, a thick broth of curry and coconut cream, with meat and both soft and crispy egg noodles.

Gallery Seescape Soi 17, Th Nimmanhemin ⓦfacebook .com/galleryseescape. Gallery, design shop and café run by a famous local artist, offering shady garden tables, very good espressos and creative, attractively presented Western breakfasts and lunches (around B150). Tues–Sat 8am–6pm.

Huen Phen 112 Th Ratchamanka. Probably Chiang Mai's most authentic northern restaurant. Try local specialities such as *sai oua* (sausage), *kaeng hang lay* (pork curry) and *khao soi* (noodle curry; B40). The more attractive evening restaurant around the back is pricier but also serves good northern Thai food. Daily 8am–4pm & 5–10pm.

Kiat Ocha 41–43 Th Inthrawarorot, off Th Phra Pokklao (the English sign says "Hainanese chicken"). Delicious and very popular satay and *khao man kai* – boiled chicken breast served with dipping sauces, broth and rice – at around B40 a dish. Daily 6am–3pm, or until the food runs out.

La Fontana 39/7–8 Th Ratchamanka. Chiang Mai's best Italian, dishing up great home-made pastas (B150–200), authentic pizzas and delicious Italian desserts. Daily 11am–11pm; sometimes closed Tues and at lunchtimes in low season.

Miguel's Th Chaiyapoom. Warm welcome, a relaxing terrace and great Mexican food: feast on the *nachos grande* for B180. Daily 10am–11pm.

Mit Mai 42/2 Th Ratchamanka. Excellent food in large portions from Yunnan province in southwest China, including a zesty chicken salad and delicious snow peas with Yunnanese ham (B90). Daily 10am–10pm.

Ratana's Kitchen 320–322 Th Tha Pae. A favourite among locals both for northern specialities, such as *kaeng hang lay* and *khao soi*, and for tasty Western breakfasts, sandwiches and steaks, all at good prices (B50–150). Daily 7.30am–11.30pm.

Riverside Restaurant 9 Th Charoenrat ☎053 243239. Candlelit terraces by the water and an often heaving, lively bar for gigs, and, on the other side of the road, a spacious complex of rooms, including a craft beer bar with tapas and live music. Various soloists and bands perform nightly on the two stages, with the tempo increasing as the night wears on. Long, high-quality menu of Western, Thai and northern Thai food and drinks on offer (*tom yam kung* B160). For an extra

B150, you can eat on their boat, which cruises up the Ping River each evening at 8pm (boarding 7.15pm). Daily 10am–1am.

Smiley Kitchen Soi 3, Th Nimmanhemin. Excellent restaurant serving authentic Japanese home-style cooking, such as a *tonkatsu* (pork cutlet) set for B190. Mon–Sat 11.30am–2.30pm & 5.30–9pm.

DRINKING

Chiang Mai has a huge number of bars, most of which serve food; *Riverside* (see opposite) is also a great place just for a drink. There's a clutch of hostess bars along Th Loi Khro, but the town generally avoids Bangkok's sexual excesses.

The Drunken Flower (Mao Dok Mai) Soi 17, Th Nimmanhaemin. Laidback and congenial, this quirky venue is a favourite among twenty-somethings, both Thai and *farang*. Reasonable prices for drink and an eclectic range of background music. Wed–Sat 5pm–midnight.

Thapae East 88 Th Tha Pae ⓦ facebook.com/thapaeeast. Set in atmospheric red-brick houses and a garden of half-constructed buildings, this "venue for the creative arts" serves craft beers and usually has something interesting on, notably live music. Mon–Sat 6–11pm.

Warm-Up Th Nimmanhemin. Hugely popular bar-club hosting both DJs and live bands, where girls in short skirts dance around their handbags to pulsating techno beats. Either chill out at the tables out front or tackle the madness of the masses within. Daily 6pm–1am.

SHOPPING

Chiang Mai is a shopper's paradise, selling everything from touristy slogan T-shirts to unique hill-tribe handicrafts. It's worth shopping around as quality and prices vary, and don't forget to haggle in the night market, but be prepared to pay out for quality handmade products.

BOOKS

Backstreet Books Th Chang Moi Kao (just off Th Tha Pae). Sells a huge range of secondhand books in a well-organized display.

Suriwong 54/1 Th Sri Dornchai. The best place for new books, and also sells maps.

CRAFTS AND FABRICS

The road to San Kamphaeng, which extends due east for 13km from the end of Th Charoen Muang, is lined with craft shops and factories, including silverware, lacquerware, ceramics, woodcarving and jade. The biggest concentrations are at Bo Sang, the "umbrella village", 9km from town, and at San Kamphaeng itself, dedicated chiefly to silk-weaving. Frequent white songthaews to San Kamphaeng leave Chiang Mai from the central Lamyai market. In Chiang Mai itself, the biggest selections of local crafts are at the Night Bazaar and the Walking Streets.

There are several stylish outlets for clothes and interior design around Sop Moei Arts on Th Charoenrat, and at the northern end of Th Nimmanhaemin around Soi 1.

Kritiya 46 Th Khwang Men. In the atmospheric lanes to the south of Warorot Market, this small shop is probably the best place in town to buy bolts of high-quality local silk at competitive prices. Closed Sun.

Sop Moei Arts 150/10 Th Charoenrat ⓦ sopmoeiarts .com. Gorgeous fabrics – scarves, wall-hangings, bags and cushion covers – and stylish basketware, with part of the profits going back to the Karen refugee camp where they're made.

Thai Tribal Crafts (Fair Trade Shop) 25/9 Th Moonmuang, near Th Ratchamanka. Non-profit shop with a wide range of products made by seven hill tribes, from bags and silverware to musical instruments. Closed Sun.

MARKETS

Chiang Mai Night Bazaar Spread expansively around the junction of Chang Klan and Loi Khro roads, this is the main shopper's playground, where bumper-to-bumper street stalls and shops sell just about anything produced in Chiang Mai; for less hectic scenes duck into Anusarn Market, where the stalls are set in an open square. Highlights are the hill-tribe jewellery and bags, and buffalo-hide shadow puppets. Daily from 5pm.

Walking Streets Th Ratchdamnoen turns into a huge, pedestrianized market on Sunday evenings, spreading west from Tha Pae Gate as far as Wat Phra Singh and into the side streets; on offer are typical northern Thai items such as clothes and musical instruments, lots of cheap street food and music. There's a smaller version on Saturday night on Th Wualai.

Warorot Market Bustling daytime market selling food, cheap cotton, linen and ceramics; there's a pungent and colourful flower market on its east side.

DIRECTORY

Banks and exchange There are banks all over Chiang Mai, most of which offer exchange facilities and ATMs.

Consulates Canada, 151 Superhighway (ⓣ 053 850147); US, 387 Th Witchayanon (ⓣ 053 252629).

Hospital 24hr emergency service (and dentistry) at Lanna Hospital, 103 Superhighway (ⓣ 053 999777, ⓦ lanna-hospital.com), east of Th Chotana.

Immigration office Promenada Shopping Mall, 5km southeast of the old city (ⓣ 053 142788).

Laundry Laundry is available at most guesthouses (around B40/kg) or at small shops and hairdressers across town.

Post office Probably the most convenient is on Th Samlarn near Wat Phra Singh (Mon–Fri 8.30am–4.30pm, Sat 9am–noon; extended opening until 8pm on weekdays is planned).

10

10

LAMPANG

The north's second-largest town and an important transport hub, **LAMPANG**, 100km southeast of Chiang Mai, has a sedate, traditional charm and a few key attractions, such as temples and an elephant conservation centre.

The majority of the town is south of the river, which curls west to east; the clock tower is considered the central point, while Thanon Tipchang and Thanon Talat Kao run along the south bank just northeast of here. Lampang is unique in Thailand for its horse-drawn carriages, which give charming, if bumpy, tours of town (from B200 for a 3km ride).

Wat Phra Kaeo Don Tao

The imposing, Burmese-influenced **Wat Phra Kaeo Don Tao** on Thanon Phra Kaeo, northeast of the river, about 3km from the clock tower, is noteworthy for its bronze Mandalay Buddha, housed in a Burmese-style building with a high, gilded roof. From 1436 to 1468 the temple was home to the Emerald Buddha, now housed in Bangkok at Wat Phra Kaeo (see p.717).

Wat Si Rong Muang

West of the clock tower on Thanon Takrao Noi, **Wat Si Rong Muang** is a Burmese-style temple built in 1905. Its wooden viharn has a beautifully tiered roof, and its interior is elaborately decorated with coloured glass in patterns of animals, flowers, leaves and guardian angels. The nine spires represent the nine families who donated generously for the building of the temple.

Wat Phra That Lampang Luang

It's also well worth heading 18km southwest of town to **Wat Phra That Lampang Luang**, a grand and well-preserved capsule of beautiful Lanna art and architecture. Its main, open-sided, wooden viharn is one of the oldest in Thailand, dating back to 1486, and features attractive nineteenth-century

painted panels. To get here, take a blue songthaew from Thanon Robwiang and be sure to ask for Wat Phra That Lampang Luang (roughly hourly; 45min); or rent a motorbike from the *Riverside Guest House* (B200/day).

Thai Elephant Conservation Centre

Run by the Thai government, the **Thai Elephant Conservation Centre** (shows daily 10am, 11am & 1.30pm; bathing at 9.40am and 1.10pm; B200; ☎ 054 228034, ⓦ thailandelephant.org), 30km northwest of Lampang on Highway 11 towards Chiang Mai, is the most authentic place to see elephants displaying their skills; it also cares for abandoned and sick elephants in its elephant hospital. The interpretive centre has exhibits on the history of the elephant in Thailand, elephant rides are available and there is a full-day package on offer combining a show, bathing your elephant and bareback riding with the chance to meet the staff and see the hospital, plus lunch (B4000); two- and three-day packages and mahout training courses are also available. The centre is best visited en route between Chiang Mai and Lampang: any Chiang Mai-bound bus will drop you off on Highway 11 at the main entrance to the centre; from the gates there are regular shuttle buses to the elephant showground 2km away.

ARRIVAL AND INFORMATION

By plane Bangkok Airways runs flights from Bangkok's Suvarnabhumi Airport (3 daily; 1hr), Nok Air from Don Muang (4 daily; 1hr). The airport is just south of town, and songthaews and taxis are on hand for the short ride to the centre (about B100).

By bus The bus station is around 1km southwest of the city, though many buses also stop on Th Phaholyothin in the centre. Shared yellow-and-green songthaews will drop you off at your destination (B20).

Destinations Bangkok (at least hourly; 8hr); Chiang Mai (roughly hourly; 2hr); Chiang Rai (every 30min; 4hr); Mae Sot (2 daily; 4–5hr); Nan (9–11 daily; 4hr).

By train The train station is about 500m further west than the bus station, on Th Prasaanmaitri, and is also served by shared songthaews (B20).

Destinations Bangkok (5 daily; 10–12hr); Chiang Mai (6 daily; 2–3hr).

Information There's a small municipal tourist information centre (Mon–Fri 9am–4.30pm, plus Sat in high season 10am–4pm; ☏ 054 237229, ⊛ lampangcity .go.th), just west of the clocktower, next to the fire station on Th Takrao Noi.

ACCOMMODATION AND EATING

The stretch of Th Takrao Noi west of the clock tower is lively after dark, featuring many simple restaurants and the Atsawin night market running off it to the south, as well as pubs and karaoke bars. On Saturday and Sunday evenings, Th Talat Kao comes to life as a "walking street", similar to though not as interesting as those in Chiang Mai, with food and crafts for sale.

★ **Aroy One Baht** Th Tipchang ☏ 089 700 9444. Cheap eats in a nice old wooden house staffed by happy young Thais. The spicy snakehead fish soup, served in coconut milk, is a bargain at B40. Highly recommended. Daily 4.30pm–midnight.

R Lampang Th Talat Kao, just east of *Riverside Guest House* ☏ 054 225278, ⊛ r-lampang.com. Part guesthouse, part doll's house, with shades of green and pink providing the backdrop for a weird and wonderful collection of curios. Occupying a prime spot on the riverfront, its cheapest offerings are small fan rooms with mattresses on the floor and shared bathrooms. Bicycles for rent. Doubles B350

Riverside Guest House 286 Th Talat Kao ☏ 054 227005, ⊛ theriverside-lampang.com. Traditional garden compound of elegant, mostly en-suite rooms in two teak houses; the helpful owner also rents out bikes and motorbikes. Doubles B400

Riverside Restaurant 328 Th Tipchang. This relaxing bar-restaurant-bakery on rustic wooden terraces overlooking the water offers a wide variety of excellent Thai dishes, including northern specialities (from B70), as well as Western food and live music at weekends. Daily 10am–midnight.

NAN

Ringed by high mountains, the small but prosperous provincial capital of **NAN**, 225km northeast of Lampang, rests on the grassy west bank of the Nan River. Few visitors make it out this far, but it's a likeable place with a thriving handicraft tradition, a good museum and some superb temple murals at Wat Phumin.

The National Museum

The best place to start a tour of Nan is at the **National Museum**, just off Thanon Phakong in the southwest part of town, which occupies the century-old palace of the former lords of Nan with its superb teak floors. Its informative, user-friendly displays give a bite-sized introduction to Nan, its history and its peoples. Most of the museum was closed for renovation at the time of writing (due to reopen early 2018), but its prize exhibit, a talismanic elephant tusk with a bad case of brown tooth decay, which is claimed to be magic black ivory, is still open to the public (Wed–Sun 9am–4pm, though sometimes inaccessible due to the renovation works; currently free).

Wat Phumin

With a five-hundred-year-old cruciform building as its centrepiece, bisected by two giant nagas, **Wat Phumin**, a five-minute walk south of the museum down Thanon Phakong, will please even the most over-templed traveller. What really sets this temple apart are its murals, the bright, simple colours of which seem to jump off the walls of the bot. Executed in the late nineteenth century – though retouched in recent years – the paintings take you on a whirlwind tour of heaven, hell, the Buddha's previous incarnations, local legends and incidents from Nan's history, and include stacks of vivacious, sometimes bawdy, detail, which provides a valuable pictorial record of that era.

ARRIVAL AND INFORMATION

By plane The airport is 2km northwest of town, served by Nok Air (3 daily) and Air Asia (2 daily) flights from Bangkok (1hr 30min) and Kan Airlines from Chiang Mai (2 weekly; 45min). A/c minibuses and taxis run between here and the centre of town.

TOURS AROUND NAN

★ **Fhu Travel** 453/4 Th Sumondhevaraj ☏ 081 287 7209, ⊛ facebook.com/fhutravel. Fhu can organize treks of one day (around B1500/person, based on two sharing) and longer, which head west through tough terrain of thick jungle and high mountains, visiting Mrabri, Htin, Hmong and Mien villages. Other options include cycling tours around town, one- or two-day whitewater-rafting excursions and kayaking. Fhu can also advise about getting to Luang Prabang in Laos, via the little-used border crossing at Huai Kon in the north of Nan province, which is open to foreigners.

10

By bus The bus station is in the southwest corner of town, off the main road to Phrae; songthaews to the centre cost B20.
Destinations Bangkok (13 daily; 11–12hr); Chiang Mai (9–11 daily; 6hr); Chiang Rai (1 daily; 6–7hr); Den Chai (on the Bangkok–Chiang Mai railway; roughly hourly; 2hr 30min); Phitsanulok (5 daily; 6hr).

Information There's a municipal tourist information booth opposite Wat Phumin (daily 8.30am–4.30pm, usually closing 1hr for lunch; ☏ 054 751169 or ☏ 054 750247), or visit helpful Fhu Travel (see p.761).

ACCOMMODATION AND EATING

When it comes to eating, there's a small night market, about 500m north of the museum on Th Phakong.

Heuan Jao Nang East bank of the Nan River, about 500m north of the main bridge. The attractive tables on an embankment above the river are good for sunset-watching, and the food's great, too, including lots of northern specialities (most dishes B150–250) – try the *pla khang patcha*, fish stir-fried with green peppercorns, lady-finger roots and other herbs. It's the last of several restaurants in all price ranges to the north of the bridge. Daily noon–11pm.

SP Guest House 233 Th Sumondhevaraj ☏ 054 774897. Actually on Trok Hua Wiangtai, a narrow alley off the main road, this well-maintained, friendly and very helpful guesthouse offers spacious a/c rooms, with hot-water bathrooms, fridges and TVs. The owners are extremely helpful, and there are big family rooms available. Doubles B500

DOI INTHANON NATIONAL PARK

Covering a huge area to the southwest of Chiang Mai, **Doi Inthanon National Park** (B300, plus B20–30 per vehicle), with its hill-tribe villages, dramatic waterfalls and fine panoramas, is a popular destination for naturalists and trekkers. The park supports about 380 bird species and, near the summit of Doi Inthanon itself, the highest mountain in Thailand, the only red rhododendrons in the country (in bloom Dec–Feb). Night-time temperatures occasionally drop below freezing, so bring warm clothing. The park is best explored as a day-trip from Chiang Mai using private transport, but set out early because there's a lot to see and the distances are deceptive.

WHAT TO SEE AND DO

Three sets of **waterfalls** provide the main roadside attractions on the way to the

park headquarters: overrated and overcrowded Mae Klang Falls, 8km from Chom Thong; Vachiratharn Falls, a long misty drop 11km beyond; and the twin cascades of Siriphum Falls, behind the park headquarters. The more beautiful **Mae Ya Falls**, believed to be the highest in Thailand, are accessed by a road that heads west off the main park road 3km north of Chom Thong.

Beyond the headquarters, the paved road down to Mae Chaem skirts yet more waterfalls: 7km after the turn-off from the summit road, look for a steep, unpaved road to the right, leading down to a ranger station and, just to the east, the dramatic long drop of **Huai Sai Luaeng Falls**. A circular 2.5km **walking trail** from the ranger station takes in some smaller waterfalls, such as Mae Pan Falls.

For the most spectacular views in the park, head for the twin chedis on the summit road. Just above the chedis lies the trailhead of **Kew Mae Pan Trail**, an easy two-hour circular walk (closed June–Oct) through beautiful forest and savannah – home of the red rhododendrons – around the steep, western edge of **Doi Inthanon**; you need to hire a guide at the trailhead (B200/guide). Doi Inthanon's summit (2565m), 6km beyond the chedis, is a disappointment.

ARRIVAL AND INFORMATION

By private transport The best way to access Doi Inthanon is by using private transport rented in Chiang Mai; the roads, though winding, are well paved and the views are stunning.

By bus and songthaew If you want to use public transport you'll need to get to the village of Chom Thong, 58km southwest of Chiang Mai on Highway 108. Frequent buses run from Chang Puak bus station, via Chiang Mai Gate, in Chiang Mai to Chom Thong, from where you can catch a songthaew towards Mae Chaem through the park, leaving you to hitch the last 10km to the summit, or you can charter a whole songthaew from Chom Thong's temple (around B1500 round trip). The main road through the park leaves Highway 108 1km north of Chom Thong, winding northwestwards for 48km to the top of Doi Inthanon.

Information The park's visitor centre is 9km up the main park road from Chom Thong, while the park headquarters are 22km further on. Both sell park maps.

ACCOMMODATION AND EATING

You can stay in the national park bungalows (☎053 286728–9, ⊕nps.dnp.go.th; from B1000) near the headquarters, or camp near the headquarters and at Huai Sai Luaeng Falls (B30/person). Two- to three-person tents (B225, bedding extra) can be rented at the headquarters. Food stalls operate at Mae Klang, Vachiratharn and Mae Ya Falls (daytime only) and at the park headquarters.

MAE HONG SON AND AROUND

Set deep in a mountain valley, **MAE HONG SON** is often billed as the "Switzerland of Thailand", and has enjoyed a boost in tourism due in part to the zoo-like villages of "long-necked" Padaung women nearby. Most travellers come here to trek in the beautiful countryside and cool climate, but crowds are also drawn here over the first weekend in April for the spectacular parades of the **Poy Sang Long Festival**, which celebrates local Thai Yai/Shan boys' temporary ordination into the monkhood.

WHAT TO SEE AND DO

Mae Hong Son's main Thanon Khunlumprapas, lined with shops and businesses, runs north–south and is intersected by Singhanat Bamrung at the traffic lights in the centre of town.

To the southeast of the traffic lights, the town's classic picture-postcard view is of its twin nineteenth-century Burmese-style temples, **Wat Chong Kham** and **Wat Chong Klang**, from the opposite bank of Jong Kham Lake. The latter temple is famous for its paintings on glass, depicting stories from the lives of the Buddha.

The town's vibrant, smelly **morning market** is a magnet for hill-tribe traders and worth getting up at dawn for. Next door, the many-gabled viharn of **Wat Hua Wiang** shelters the beautiful bronze Burmese-style Buddha image, Chao Palakeng. For a godlike overview of the area, especially at sunset, climb up to **Wat Doi Kong Mu** on the steep hill to the west.

Local treks

Trekking up and down Mae Hong Son's steep inclines is tough, but the hill-tribe villages are generally unspoilt and the scenery is magnificent. To the west, trekking routes tend to snake along the Burmese border and can sometimes get a little crowded; the villages to the east are more traditional. Plenty of guesthouses and travel agencies run treks out of Mae Hong Son (see p.764).

Pha Sua Falls and Mae Aw

North of Mae Hong Son, a trip to **Pha Sua Falls** and the border village of Mae Aw takes in some spectacular and varied countryside, best visited by motorbike (around B200/day from guesthouses) or on a tour (B1100/person) from Rose Garden Tours (see p.764). Head north for 17km on Highway 1095 (ignore the first signpost for Pha Sua, after 10km) and then, after a long, steep descent, turn left onto a side road, paved at first, which passes through the village of Ban Bok Shampae. About 9km from the turn-off, you'll reach the wild, untidy Pha Sua Falls; take care when swimming, as several people have been swept to their deaths here.

Above the falls, the paved road climbs 11km to the village of Naphapak, from where it's another 7km to **Mae Aw** (aka Ban Ruk Thai), a settlement of Kuomintang (anti-communist Chinese) refugees. It's the highest point on the Burmese border that visitors can reach, and provides a fascinating window on Kuomintang life. Bright-green tea bushes line the slopes, and Chinese ponies wander past long bamboo houses. In the central marketplace on the north side of the village reservoir, shops sell Oolong and Chian Chian tea, and dried mushrooms.

ARRIVAL AND DEPARTURE

By plane Mae Hong Son airport is towards the northeast of town. Bangkok Airways and Kan Airlines run direct flights to and from Chiang Mai (5 daily; 35min). From the airport terminal tuk-tuks (about B80) run into the centre.
By bus and minibus Buses to Mae Hong Son depart from Chiang Mai's Arcade bus station, travelling via Mae Sariang or Pai. There are also hourly a/c minibuses between Pai's bus station and Mae Hong Son. Minibuses go past the Khunlumprapas–Singhanat Bamrung crossroads, so ask the driver to stop there if you're staying in town. From the bus station, south of the centre, tuk-tuks (about B80) run into the centre.

10

10

Destinations Bangkok (2 daily; 16hr); Chiang Mai via Mae Sariang (4 daily; 8–9hr); Chiang Mai via Pai (1 daily; 8hr); Pai (hourly; 3hr).

INFORMATION AND TOURS

Information TAT, Th Ratchathumpitak, towards the northeast of the city centre (daily 8.30am–4.30pm; ☎053 612982–3, ✉tatmhs@tat.or.th).

Tour operators Day tours from Mae Hong Son might include elephant riding and bamboo rafting on the babbling Pai River. Rose Garden Tours at 86/4 Th Khunlumprapas (☎053 611681, ⓦrosegarden-tours.com) has day-long excursions starting from B1100. Tour Merng Tai at 89 Th Khunlumprapas (☎053 611979, ⓦtourmerngtai.com) offers community-based tourism programmes including cycling tours, treks and homestays, employing village guides and cooks and contributing part of the profits to local communities. Trekking Thailand (☎083 153 2566, ⓦtrekkingthailand.com), a highly recommended independent group of Mae Hong Son guides, offers one- to six-day treks; contact them by phone, email or Facebook.

ACCOMMODATION

Baan Mai Guesthouse Th Chamnansathit, northeast of the lake ☎080 499 1975, ⓦfacebook.com /baanmaiguesthouse. Welcoming homestay in a cosy, plant-strewn, traditional wooden house with shared hot-water bathrooms. Good breakfast included. Doubles B600
Jonnie House 5/1 Th U-Domchaonitesh ☎053 611667. In a small compound on the north side of the lake, this clean, friendly place has airy rooms, sharing hot showers, in a nice, old, wooden house, as well as bright, concrete affairs with en-suite hot-water bathrooms. Doubles B200
Romtai House 22 Th Chamnansathit ☎053 612437. Southeast of the lake, beyond the twin temples, this tranquil place offers a wide choice of spacious, well-kept rooms and bungalows with hot showers, set around a rambling garden. Doubles B350

EATING AND DRINKING

Alawaa South side of Jong Kham Lake, across from Wat Chong Klang. Stylish, a/c, polished-concrete café with a small garden patio, serving good espresso coffees, teas, smoothies and cakes. Mon–Sat 8.30am–5.30pm.
Fern 87 Th Khunlumprapas, south of the central traffic lights. Justly popular restaurant, with a nice terrace and a good reputation for its varied Thai and Western food (from B80). Daily 10.30am–10pm.
★**Salween River** 23 Th Praditjongkham. Welcoming English- and Thai-run restaurant and bar, on the west side of the lake, with wi-fi and a book exchange. There's a big selection of Western grub (main dishes from B100), including home-made bread, plus Thai, Shan and Burmese dishes and local coffee. Mon–Fri 8am–11pm, Sat & Sun 9am–10pm.

PAI

Once just a stopover on the tiring journey to Mae Hong Son, **PAI**, set in a broad, lush, upland valley 135km from Chiang Mai, is now a major tourist hub. It has retained some of the laidback, New Age feel that draws certain travellers in for weeks, but has also become a honeypot for Thai tourists. There's all manner of **outdoor activities** to tempt you, plus courses – there's even a circus school – and therapies, not to mention retail therapy at the art studios, leather and jewellery shops. It's very pleasant to stroll through the stalls that set up along the "walking street" of Thanon Chaisongkhram every evening.

WHAT TO SEE AND DO

Pai itself is a cute but rambling town. Most points of interest lie west of the Pai River, although the most tranquil guesthouses are east of the river.

Towards Mo Pang Falls

To the west of town, the continuation of Wat Chaisongkhram will bring you, after about 4km, to the Kuomintang Chinese village of **Ban Santichon**. Here you'll find a Chinese theme park of thatched adobe buildings, housing tea and souvenir shops and several popular Yunnanese restaurants. As you continue, the road gradually climbs through Thai Yai, Lisu and Lahu village to **Mo Pang Falls**, with a pool for swimming, about 10km west of Pai.

Swimming and hot springs

On the east side of town is Fluid, a large open-air **swimming pool** in an attractive garden setting with a popular bar-restaurant (daily 9am–6.30pm; closed in the rainy season; B60). About 7km southeast of town, down the minor road beyond the swimming pool, the **hot springs** (B300) aren't up to much, but nearby spas put the piped hot water to much better use. *Pai Hotsprings Spa Resort* (☎053 065748, ⓦpaihotspringssparesort .com), down a side road about 1km north of the springs, has a large hot-spring pool and a swimming pool (B100 for use of both) and offers massages and other treatments.

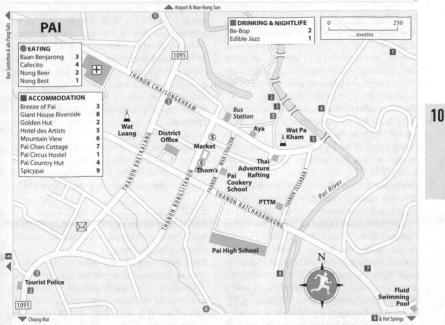

Airport & Mae Hong Son

PAI

Ban Santichon & alo Pang Falls

DRINKING & NIGHTLIFE
Be-Bop	2
Edible Jazz	1

0   250
metres

EATING
Baan Benjarong	3
Cafecito	4
Nong Beer	2
Nong Best	1

ACCOMMODATION
Breeze of Pai	3
Giant House Riverside	8
Golden Hut	2
Hotel des Artists	5
Mountain View	6
Pai Chan Cottage	7
Pai Circus Hostel	1
Pai Country Hut	4
Spicypai	9

THANON CHAISONGKHRAM

Bus Station

Wat Luang   District Office   Market

Aya   Wat Pa Kham

THANON KHETKALANG

THANON WAN CHALERM

Thom's   Pai Cookery School

Thai Adventure Rafting

THANON RUNGSIYANON

PTTM

THANON RATCHADAMRONG

THANON TESSABAN 1

Pai River

Pai High School

N

Tourist Police

1095

Chiang Mai

Fluid Swimming Pool

& Hot Springs

10

Elephants, rafting and trekking

Among several **elephant camps** about 5km south of town on the hot springs road, Thom's maintains an office in town on Thanon Runsiyanon (☎053 065778, ⓦthomelephant.com). Here you can arrange tours that include trekking with the elephants (either walking with them or riding bareback), bathing and feeding them, as well as one-day and longer mahout training courses; hot springs and bamboo rafting are also available. From early June to mid-February you can take an impressive two-day **rubber-raft trip** down the Pai River to Mae Hong Son with the reliable, French-run Thai Adventure Rafting, Thanon Chaisongkhram (☎053 699111, ⓦthairafting.com; B3500), who also offer one-day rafting trips and other tours such as mountain-biking. Pai is a centre both for undemanding valley walks and for **trekking** (around B800–1000/day, depending on numbers, plus extra for bamboo rafting and elephant-riding) through varied terrain to Karen, Lisu and Lahu villages. These can be arranged either through guesthouses such as *Duang* opposite the bus station on the corner of Rungsiyanon and Chaisongkhram (☎053

699101) or with Thai Adventure Rafting. Agencies in town can also arrange bamboo-rafting, kayaking and tubing on the Pai River.

ARRIVAL AND INFORMATION

By plane Domestic airline Kan Airlines (ⓦkanairlines .com) flies to Pai from Chiang Mai (2 daily; 25min), landing at the airstrip on the north side of town.

By bus and minibus There's only one bus a day (non-a/c) between Chiang Mai and Mae Hong Son via Pai. A/c minibuses cover the route at least hourly, through either Prempracha at the bus station (who also cover the Pai–Mae Hong Son route) or Aya, a nearby travel agent.

Destinations Chiang Mai (hourly; 3–4hr); Mae Hong Son (hourly; 3–4hr).

Information The free, monthly, English-language *Pai Events Planner* has news about what's on.

COURSES

Cookery classes Pai Cookery School, Th Wan Chalerm (☎081 706 3799, ⓦpaicookeryschool.com), holds Thai cooking courses of two hours in the morning (B600), or four hours in the afternoon (B750), which includes a trip to the market to learn about ingredients; vegetarians catered for.

Massages and massage courses Pai Traditional Thai Massage on Th Wangtai (PTTM; ☎083 577 0498) teaches a three-day massage course (B3000) and gives excellent massages (B200/1hr).

10

ACCOMMODATION

Breeze of Pai Just off Th Chaisongkhram near Wat Pa Kham ☎081 998 4597, ⓦfacebook.com/breezeofpai. Congenial, well-maintained place with large, simple but chic, ochre bungalows and rooms with nice parquet floors and hot showers. The compound's a little crowded but lent privacy by plenty of rich foliage. Doubles B500

Giant House Riverside Just south of the Th Ratchadamrong bridge ☎087 182 1611, ⓦgiantguesthouse.com. Mellow, old-style branch of the Chiang Mai *Giant* guesthouses, offering a range of thatched bungalows in a lovely garden on the river bank. Free coffee, tea and drinking water. Doubles B200

Golden Hut North of *Edible Jazz*, next to the river ☎053 699949, ⓦgoldenhut.wordpress.com. Very cheap bamboo fan rooms with shared hot showers, in a quiet garden set back from the river, or riverside bungalows on stilts. Doubles B150

Mountain View 500m up a side road by the tourist police at the south end of town ☎086 180 5998, ⓦthemountainviewpai.com. Laidback resort of wood and woven bamboo bungalows, most with private bathrooms, on ten acres of hilltop land. Free pick-ups if you call, and free access to Fluid swimming pool (see p.764). Doubles B200

★**Pai Chan Cottage** About 300m east of the bridge ☎081 180 3064, ⓦpaichan.com. Overlooking paddy fields and the resort's attractive swimming pool, the thatched wooden bungalows here are colourful and tasteful, with en-suite hot showers and mosquito nets. Free pick-ups from town. Good rates for singles. Doubles B600

★**Pai Circus Hostel** East side of the river ☎099 273 3678, ⓦpaicircushostel.com. Free fire-juggling lessons and a slack line give this spacious, popular resort its name, but there's also a swimming pool with great views of the valley, free yoga and a great party vibe. The cheapest dorms have bamboo bunks with mosquito nets, while the

---

★TREAT YOURSELF

Hotel des Artists (Rose of Pai) Th Chaisongkhram ☎053 699539, ⓦhotelartists.com. On a corner plot near the river and centred around an attractive glass-sided living room, this stylish hotel has just fourteen bedrooms, the best of which have fantastic terraces that face out across the water. In the spacious rooms, bell-shaped lanterns illuminate the beds (which are raised off the ground on platforms made from local wood) while facilities include a/c, TVs, DVD players, minibars and artfully tiled en-suite bathrooms. Rates, which include breakfast, are significantly lower between April and mid-October. Doubles B4000

---

cheapest doubles are basic A-frames with shared bathrooms, but there's a wide range in both categories. Free pick-ups from town. Dorms B200, doubles B380

★**Pai Country Hut** East side of the river ☎087 779 6541, ⓦpaicountryhut.com. Friendly guesthouse in a lovely garden surrounded by very attractive bamboo bungalows thatched with leaves in the local style; the cheapest share hot showers. Free pick-ups from town. Doubles B300

Spicypai Around 700m east of the bridge; keep right at the junctions you pass along the way and then follow the signs to the hostel ☎052 040177. Ultra-cheap and ultra-sociable dorm beds with mosquito nets in a series of lofty, thatched, bamboo huts surrounded by vivid green paddy fields. Simple breakfast and hot showers included. Dorms B180

EATING

Because of the thriving international expat community in Pai it's easy to get food from all over the world, including Mexican, Italian and French.

Baan Benjarong Th Rungsiyanon, to the south of town. An understandably popular restaurant overlooking rice fields that serves some of the best Thai food in town, on a varied and imaginative menu (dishes around B100). Daily 11am–2pm & 5–8pm, though hours are temperamental.

★**Cafecito** South side of town ⓦfacebook.com/cafecitopai. It's well worth the trek out to this café for excellent home-roasted coffee, scrummy home-baked cakes and great Mexican food such as tacos (B110). Daily except Thurs 9am–5pm.

Nong Beer Cnr Chaisongkhram and Khetkalang. One of Pai's longest-standing and most popular places for cheap eats, dishing up great *khao soi* (northern curry noodle soup; B40), pork satay and a wide array of buffet stir-fries and curries. Daily 8am–9pm.

Nong Best Th Khetkalang, just south of *Pai Flora Resort*. Bare-bones restaurant with an open streetside kitchen that's very popular with locals, and you can taste why – excellent pork with basil and chillies (B50) and crispy pork with snow peas (B60). Daily 9am–9pm.

DRINKING AND NIGHTLIFE

Pai is no Khao San Rd; its nightlife scene is more laidback and music-oriented, so don't expect too much drunken revelry.

Be-Bop Th Rungsiyanon, at the south end of town. A popular travellers' bar that hosts live jazz, funk, blues and rock most evenings (from about 10pm). Daily 8pm–1am.

★**Edible Jazz** Just off Th Chaisongkhram near Wat Pa Kham ⓦfacebook.com/ediblejazz. This ramshackle and laid-way-back garden café-bar on a quiet, leafy lane hosts live jazz and other music every night (roughly 7–11pm), including an open mike night on Sun. Daily roughly noon–midnight.

DIRECTORY

Banks There are a few banks dotted along Th Chaisongkhram and Th Rungsiyanon with ATM and exchange facilities.

Hospital Th Chaisongkhram ☏ 053 699211.

Motorbikes These can be rented from Aya Service on Th Chaisongkhram (☏ 053 699888; B100/day), who also offer one-way rentals to Chiang Mai for B300.

Post office At the southern end of Th Khetkalang.

Tourist police South end of town on the road to Chiang Mai (☏ 1155).

THA TON AND THE KOK RIVER

Leafy **THA TON**, 176km north of Chiang Mai, sits clustered either side of the **Kok River**, which flows out of Myanmar, 4km upstream. The main attractions here are boat and raft rides, which offer a novel way of getting to Chiang Rai (though they may not run in the hot season, when the river's low). There are also magnificent panoramic views of the river and the surrounding landscape from the top of the hill on the west bank where you'll find **Wat Tha Ton**, with its over-the-top ornamental gardens and colossal Buddhist statues.

Travelling down the 100km stretch of the Kok River to Chiang Rai gives you the chance to soak up a rich diversity of typical northern landscapes, through rice fields and orchards, past riverside wats and over rapids. Noisy, canopied longtail boats leave from the south side of the bridge in Tha Ton every day at 12.30pm, if they have enough takers (4hr; B400). Slower, return boats from Chiang Rai leave at 10.30am (☏ 053 750009). If you have more time, choose the peaceful bamboo rafts, which glide downriver to Chiang Rai in two or three days. These can be organized via *Garden Home Nature Resort* (B8000/raft for 2 days, B9000 for 3 days, for 2 people, including food and soft drinks), visiting hill-tribe villages and the hot springs on the way.

ARRIVAL AND DEPARTURE

By bus Regular buses (roughly every 2hr) between Chiang Mai's Chang Phuak bus station and Tha Ton take about 4hr. Otherwise, take one of the more frequent buses or a/c minibuses to Fang and change onto a yellow songthaew for the last 40min to Tha Ton.

ACCOMMODATION

Garden Home Nature Resort 300m north of the bridge on the east bank of the river ☏ 053 373015. By far the best accommodation option in town, with attractive bungalows and rooms, all with en-suite hot showers, in a spacious lychee orchard. They also rent out motorbikes. Doubles B300

CHIANG RAI

CHIANG RAI lives in the shadow of the local capital, Chiang Mai, but offers a good choice of accommodation, some splendid temples and a variety of treks and tours in the surrounding countryside.

WHAT TO SEE AND DO

Sprawled untidily over the south bank of the Kok River, Chiang Rai's main daytime focus is the bustling market on Thanon Tanalai. At weekends, the town's **walking streets**, similar to those in Chiang Mai, come alive with musicians and all manner of stalls, including lots of food and local crafts and products. There's one on **Thanon Tanalai**, around the junction with Wisetwiang, on Saturday evening, and another on Thanon San Khong Noi, to the southwest of the centre, on Sunday evening (aka "Happy Street").

Doi Tong

A walk up to **Doi Tong**, the hill to the northwest of the centre, offers a fine view up the Kok River. On the highest part of the hill stands a kind of phallic Stonehenge centred on the town's new **Lak Muang** (the city pillar), representing the Buddhist layout of the universe. The old wooden Lak Muang can be seen in the viharn of **Wat Phra That Doi Tong**, the city's first temple, which sprawls shambolically over the eastern side of the hill.

Wat Phra Kaeo

The Emerald Buddha, Thailand's most important image, now housed in Bangkok (see p.717), resided at **Wat Phra Kaeo** on Thanon Trairat for 44 years from 1390. A beautiful replica, millimetres smaller than the actual statue, which was carved in China from 300kg of milky green jade, can now be seen here. There's

10

10

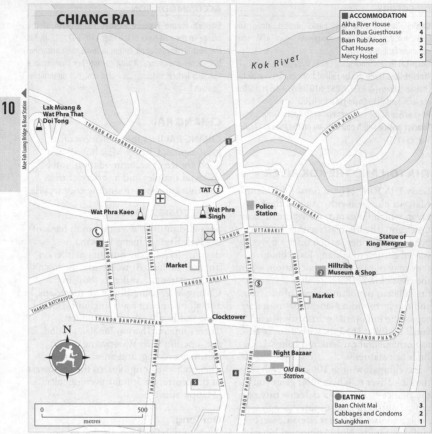

CHIANG RAI

■ ACCOMMODATION
Akha River House	1
Baan Bua Guesthouse	4
Baan Rub Aroon	3
Chat House	2
Mercy Hostel	5

Kok River

Mae Fah Luang Bridge & Boat Station

Lak Muang &
Wat Phra That
Doi Tong

THANON KAISORNRASIT

THANON KAOLOI

TAT (i)

THANON SINGHAKAI

Wat Phra Kaeo

Wat Phra
Singh

Police
Station

THANON UTTARAKIT

Statue of
King Mengrai

Airport, Mae Sai & Chiang Saen

THANON NGAM MUANG

THANON TRAIRAT

THANON RATTANAKHET

THANON WISITWIANG

Hilltribe
Museum & Shop

THANON PHAHOLYOTHIN

Market

THANON TANALAI

Market

THANON RATCHAYOTA

THANON BANPHAPRAKAN

Clocktower

N

THANON SANAMBIN

THANON JET YOI

THANON PHAHOLYOTHIN

Night Bazaar

Old Bus
Station

0   500
metres

●EATING
Baan Chivit Mai	3
Cabbages and Condoms	2
Salungkham	1

New Bus Station, Wat Rong Khun & Chiang Mai ▼

also an impressive museum of Buddhist paraphernalia, the Sangkaew Hall (daily 9am–5pm; free), with informative English labels on religious practice.

Wat Rong Khun
It's well worth heading out to the stunning **Wat Rong Khun** (Mon–Fri 8am–noon & 1–5pm, Sat & Sun 8am–noon & 1–5.30pm; B50), 13km southwest of Chiang Rai on the west side of Highway 1, where a zealous, renowned local artist has dedicated his life to building a dazzling all-white stucco temple with fragments of reflective glass that sparkle in the sun. Check out the disturbing mural artwork inside the viharn. To get there, catch a Phayao-bound bus from the old bus station or a light-blue songthaew from the day market on Thanon Uttarakit.

Treks and tours
The Chiang Rai region offers a range of **treks**, from gentle walking trails near the Kok River to tough mountain slopes further north towards the Burmese border. Most treks include staying in hill-tribe villages, elephant riding, hot springs and waterfalls. An average three-day trek, with an elephant ride, costs B2500–4000. The museum (Mon–Fri 8.30am–6pm, Sat & Sun 10am–6pm; B50) at the Population and Community Development Association (PDA), 620/25 Thanon Tanalai (☎053 719167, ⓦpdacr.org), is a good place to find out about the local hill tribes before

AKHA HILL HOUSE

An authentic and rewarding way of spending time in a hill-tribe village is offered by the **Akha Hill House** (☎ 091 747 9499, ⓦ akhahill.com; B300), situated just 23km southwest of Chiang Rai (with free pick-up) among stunning mountain scenery and within walking distance of waterfalls, hot springs and other hill-tribe villages. There's a wide variety of bamboo, wooden and adobe-style bungalows, most with view-filled balconies and some with charming open-air bathrooms; all have access to hot showers, whether en suite or shared. From here you can either trek independently or take an organized tour. It's also possible to get here from the Tha Ton–Chiang Rai boat (see p.767), disembarking at the hot springs on the south bank of the river near Huai Kaeo waterfall and walking for 3km.

10

going on a trek; there's a non-profit-making handicrafts shop here, too. The PDA also offers treks and tours, as does *Chat House* (see below).

ARRIVAL AND INFORMATION

By plane Thai Smile, Bangkok Airways, Nok Air, Thai Lion Air and Air Asia fly from Bangkok to Chiang Rai's airport (20 daily; 1hr 15min), from where taxis run into town (8km south), for about B200.

By bus Chiang Rai's new Bus Station 2 is about 6km south of the centre on Highway 1. It handles inter-provincial routes, while the old Bus Station 1 off Th Phaholyothin in the centre serves Chiang Rai province (Mae Sai, Chiang Saen and Chiang Khong buses); some long-distance services stop at both, however. Shared songthaews shuttle between the two bus stations for B20.

Destinations Bangkok (at least 20 daily; 11–12hr); Chiang Khong (every 30min; 2–3hr); Chiang Mai (every 30min; 3–4hr); Chiang Saen (every 30min; 1hr 30min); Khon Kaen (6 daily; 11hr–12hr 30min); Khorat (6 daily; 12–13hr); Lampang (every 30min; 4hr); Mae Sai (every 20min; 1hr 30min); Mae Sot (2 daily; 10hr); Nan (1 daily; 6–7hr); Phitsanulok (30 daily; 7–8hr); Sukhothai (3–4 daily; 8–9hr).

By boat Longtails to and from Tha Ton dock on the north side of the Mae Fah Luang Bridge, northwest of town, from which tuk-tuks cost around B60 to the centre.

Tourist information TAT, 448/16 Th Singhakai (daily 8.30am–4.30pm; ☎ 053 717433, ⓔ tatchrai@tat.or.th).

ACCOMMODATION

Akha River House Just west of Th Ratannakhet, on the south bank of the Kok River ☎ 063 290 5662, ⓦ akhahill .com. Under the same Akha ownership as *Akha Hill House* (see above), with part of the profits going to an educational project. The cheapest rooms share bathrooms in an old building, but you might well be tempted to cough up (B800) for their smart, a/c, en-suite offerings with terraces overlooking the lawn and the river channel. Doubles **B200**

Baan Bua Guesthouse 879/2 Th Jet Yot ☎ 053 718880, ⓦ baanbua-guesthouse.com. Congenial and well-run establishment arrayed around a surprisingly large, quiet

and shady garden, set back off the road. The very clean and attractive single-storey rooms come with hot showers. Doubles **B300**

★ **Baan Rub Aroon Guesthouse** 65 Th Ngam Muang ☎ 053 711827, ⓦ baanrubaroon.com. In a quiet, pretty garden, this lovely early twentieth-century mansion has polished teak floors and immaculate rooms with a/c and hot showers, either shared or en suite. Breakfast included. Doubles **B650**

Chat House 3/2 Soi Sangkaew, Th Trairat ☎ 053 711481, ⓦ chatguesthouse.com. Behind its own garden café-bakery on a quiet soi, Chiang Rai's longest-running travellers' hangout has a laidback atmosphere and fantastic staff. The cheaper rooms are in an old, mostly wooden house with shared hot showers. Dorms **B100**, doubles **B200**

Mercy Hostel 1005/22 Th Jet Yot ☎ 053 711075, ⓦ mercyhostelchiangrai.com. At this friendly new hostel and coffee shop, arrayed around a small but attractive pool on a quiet soi, smart a/c dorms and private rooms come with hot showers. Dorms **B250**, doubles **B800**

EATING

There's a food court with a wide selection of stalls and live traditional music and dancing in the night bazaar off Th Phaholyothin. You need never go without a good coffee fix in Chiang Rai: the stuff grown on the nearby mountains of Doi Wawee, Doi Chaang and Doi Salong is served up at eponymous cafés around the main Rattanakhet–Phaholyothin junction.

Baan Chivit Mai 172 Th Prasobsuk, opposite the old bus station ⓦ bcmthai.com. Bakery run by a Swedish charity that helps children in Chiang Rai and Bangkok slums. Very clean a/c café, serving excellent sandwiches, cakes (chocolate cake B45) and espresso coffees, plus Scandinavian meatballs and simple Thai dishes. Mon–Sat 8am–9pm.

Cabbages and Condoms 620/25 Th Tanalai. Proclaiming "our food is guaranteed not to cause pregnancy", this popular restaurant is run by the Population and Community Development Association in the same building as the hill-tribe museum (see opposite). It serves traditional northern and veggie dishes (B70–200) and hosts regular live music. Daily 10am–midnight.

10

INTO MYANMAR: THE MAE SAI–TACHILEIK BORDER CROSSING

Armed with a Burmese visa, you can cross over into Myanmar at Mae Sai, though the frontier is occasionally closed during disputes. It's also possible to make a day-trip across to the Burmese border town of **Tachileik**: Thai immigration on the bridge will give you an exit stamp; Burmese immigration will hang on to your passport and charge you B500 or US$10 for a one-day stay; and on return to Thailand – unless you already have a multiple-entry Thai visa or re-entry permit – you'll automatically be given a new fifteen-day entry stamp (thirty days for British, US and Canadian citizens).

From Tachileik you can travel by bus to Kengtung, though from here you have to fly to other destinations in Myanmar, as road travel is closed to visitors.

Salungkham 834/3 Th Phaholyothin, between King Mengrai's statue and the river ☎053 717192. By far the best Thai and northern Thai food in town (mains from B80), with a garden for evening dining; try the superb banana-flower salad with fresh prawns. There's no sign in English, but look out for the Cosmo petrol station opposite. Daily 10.30am–10pm.

DIRECTORY

Cooking classes *Chat House* runs one-day cookery classes (B950) including transfers from your accommodation and a trip to the local market.

Motorbike and bicycle rental Guesthouses rent out motorbikes (around B200/day) and bicycles (B50–100).

Tourist police South of town near Wat Rong Khun (☎1155).

MAE SAI

MAE SAI, with its bustling border crossing, is Thailand's northernmost town, 61km from Chiang Rai. Thanon Phaholyothin is the town's single north–south street, which ends at a bridge over the Mae Sai River, the frontier with Myanmar.

ARRIVAL AND INFORMATION

By bus Buses to Mae Sai stop 4km south of the frontier at the bus station, from where frequent songthaews (B15) run into town.

Information There's a tourist police booth (☎1155) at the frontier bridge.

ACCOMMODATION

Navy Home About 1km south of the bridge on the east side of Th Phaholyothin ☎053 732929, ⊛navyhome.com. Owned by a retired admiral, this hotel greets guests with a gangway over a pond, a display of his ceremonial uniforms and "Welcome aboard" signs. It's even shaped like a ship and, although some of the rooms are cabin-like in size, they're all neat, clean and, well, ship-shape, with a/c and hot showers. Doubles <u>B500</u>

SOP RUAK

For the benefit of tourists, the "**Golden Triangle**" (see box opposite) has been artificially concentrated into the precise spot where the Thai, Lao and Burmese borders meet, at the confluence of the Ruak and Mekong rivers, 70km northeast of Chiang Rai: **SOP RUAK**. Don't expect to run into sinister drug-runners or poppy fields here – instead, you'll find souvenir stalls, tacky shrines and much-photographed "Golden Triangle" signs. The ambitious **Hall of Opium**, about 2km out of the village towards Mae Sai (Tues–Sun 8.30am–5.30pm, last entry 4pm; B200; ⊛maefahluang.org; not to be confused with the "House of Opium" in the village), gives an imaginatively presented, balanced picture of the use and abuse of opium, and its history over five thousand years. For uninterrupted views of the meeting of the rivers and of Myanmar and Laos beyond, climb up to **Wat Phra That Phu Khao**, a 1200-year-old temple perched on a small hill above the village.

ARRIVAL AND DEPARTURE

Hourly a/c minibuses run to Sop Ruak from Chiang Rai (1hr–1hr 30min). From Chiang Saen, you have a choice of regular blue songthaew in the morning or rented bicycle (an easy 10km ride on a paved road). From Mae Sai, blue songthaews make the 45min trip in the morning from Th Phaholyothin, about 300m south of the bridge near Soi 8.

CHIANG SAEN

Combining the tumbledown ruins of an ancient trading post with sweeping Mekong River scenery, **CHIANG SAEN**, 60km northeast of Chiang Rai, makes a

INTO LAOS AT CHIANG KHONG

Chiang Khong, 70km downriver from Chiang Saen, is the only crossing point into Laos in this part of Thailand. The journey **from Chiang Saen** is convoluted and time-consuming: green songthaews run when they're full and you usually have to change to a red songthaew halfway at the village of Ban Hat Bai. The journey can take up to four hours. Regular buses run to Chiang Khong **from Chiang Rai** (every 30min; 2–3hr), and there are twice-daily direct buses **from Chiang Mai** (ⓦgreenbusthailand.com); there are also four daily buses from Chiang Rai across the border to Houayxai. Chiang Khong's best guesthouse is the helpful, easy-going *Baan Tam-Mi-La*, down a riverside lane off the main street 1km north of the bus station (ⓣ053 791234; B450). It has an excellent restaurant (daily 7am–6pm) with awesome views across into Laos.

Tourists cross the border via the Fourth Thai-Lao Friendship Bridge, 8km downstream from Chiang Khong (daily 6am–10pm), where thirty-day **visas for Laos** (see p.349) are available on arrival. From the Lao town opposite Chiang Khong, Houayxai (see p.390), you can get passenger boats down the Mekong to Luang Prabang, and buses to elsewhere in northern Laos.

From Chiang Khong, catch a songthaew to the bridge (B60; *Baan Tam-Mi-La* are currently offering free lifts once a day to guests, at 8.30am). Then there are shuttle buses across the bridge (B25–40), and songthaews on the Lao side to the piers for Luang Prabang boats (about B100). You can buy in advance a boat ticket to Luang Prabang through *Baan Tam-Mi-La* in Chiang Khong for B1350, which will include all transport from your guesthouse to the pier in Houayxai.

relaxing base camp for the border region east of Mae Sai. Armed with a Chinese visa, it should also be possible to move on from here to Jing Hong, by either cargo boat or irregular passenger boat – contact *Gin's Maekhong View Resort* on riverside Thanon Rim Khong about 2km north of the T-junction (ⓣ053 650847, ⓦginmaekhongview.com).

WHAT TO SEE AND DO

The informative **National Museum** on the main east–west street, Thanon Phaholyothin (Wed–Sun 8.30am–4.30pm; B100), houses some impressive, locally cast Buddha images and architectural features rescued from the ruins. Originally the town's main temple, **Wat Phra That Chedi Luang** next door is worth looking in on for its imposing, overgrown octagonal chedi, said to contain a relic of the Buddha's breastbone. Outside the town's ramparts just to the northwest, **Wat Pa Sak** (open access; B50 admission fee if the custodian's around) is the most impressive of Chiang Saen's many temple ruins. Enshrining relics of the Buddha's right ankle, the central, square-based chedi owes its eclectic shape largely to the grand temples of Bagan in Myanmar and displays some beautiful carved stucco decoration.

ARRIVAL AND DEPARTURE

Buses from Chiang Rai and Chiang Mai and songthaews from Sop Ruak and Mae Sai stop just west of the T-junction of the main Th Phaholyothin and the river road. Songthaews from Ban Hat Bai and Chiang Khong stop on the river road to the south of the T-junction.

THE GOLDEN TRIANGLE

Opium growing has been illegal in Thailand since 1959, but during the 1960s and 70s, rampant production and refining of the crop in the lawless region on the borders of Thailand, Myanmar and Laos earned the area the nickname the **"Golden Triangle"**. Two "armies" operated most of the trade within this area: the Shan United Army from Myanmar, led by the notorious warlord Khun Sa, and the Kuomintang (KMT) refugees from communist China. The Thai government's concerted attempt to eliminate opium growing within its borders has been successful, but Thailand still has a vital role to play as a conduit for heroin; most of the production and refinement of opium has simply moved over the borders into Myanmar and Laos. More worryingly for the Thai authorities, factories just across the Burmese border are now also producing vast quantities of methamphetamines, either **ya baa** or "ice" (crystal meth), destined for consumption in Thailand itself.

10

ACCOMMODATION AND EATING

At night, street stalls set up on the illuminated riverfront promenade north of the T-junction, where you can sprawl on mats at low tables. Throughout the day, and in the evenings, a range of street stalls set up on Th Phaholyothin. **Jay Nai** Just off the riverside Th Rim Khong, north of the T-junction ☏ 081 960 7551. The prominent *Chiang Saen Guesthouse* has gone downhill, but nearby *Jay Nai* offers clean, simple, modern rooms with a/c, hot showers and TV. Doubles B̲4̲0̲0̲

The northeast: Isaan

Bordered by Laos and Cambodia on three sides, the tableland of **northeast** Thailand, known as **Isaan**, is the least-visited region of the kingdom and the poorest, but also its most traditional. Most northeasterners speak a dialect that's more comprehensible to residents of Vientiane than Bangkok, and Isaan's historic allegiances have tied it more closely to Laos and Cambodia than to Thailand. Between the eleventh and thirteenth centuries, the all-powerful Khmers covered the northeast in magnificent stone temple complexes, which can still be admired at **Phimai** and **Phanom Rung**. The mighty **Mekong River** forms 750km of the border between Isaan and Laos, and there are four main points along it where foreigners can cross the border; there's also a little-used border crossing into Cambodia from Isaan (see box, p.775). The river provides an awesome backdrop to explorations in this region, not least at **Nong Khai** with its laidback waterfront guesthouses. Inland scenery is rewarding too, with good hiking trails at **Khao Yai National Park**.

KHAO YAI NATIONAL PARK

Only 120km northeast of Bangkok, **Khao Yai** is Thailand's most popular national park. It offers a realistic chance of seeing wild elephants, white-handed (lar) gibbons, pig-tailed macaques, hornbills, civets and barking deer, plus the very slim possibility of sighting a tiger. The park has lots of waterfalls and several undemanding walking trails. The best way to see Khao Yai is to stay in the park, or in the nearby town of **Pak Chong**. You have the choice of exploring the trails yourself or joining a backpackers' tour; bring warm clothes as it gets cool at night.

WHAT TO SEE AND DO

You're most likely to spot the animals if you join a tour with an expert guide, but if you're short of time or money you can always take your chances and follow the trails. Several **trails** radiate from the area around the park's visitor centre and headquarters (at kilometre stone 37), and a few more branch off from the roads that cross the park. The most popular include the paths to lakeside Nong Pak Chee observation tower (4.5km one-way; 2hr 30min); and to beautiful, 25m-high Haew Suwat Falls (8.3km one-way; 3–4hr), which featured in the 1999 film, *The Beach*. Brochures with maps are available at the visitor centre.

ARRIVAL AND DEPARTURE

There are two access roads to the park – one from the south and another from the north, Route 2090 – with checkpoints on both. Everyone travelling by public transport approaches the park from Pak Chong, about 25km north of the northern entrance, and around 4hr from Bangkok by train, 2–3hr by bus or a/c minibus.

By songthaew Public songthaews leave from outside the 7-Eleven shop in Pak Chong, 200m west of the footbridge on the north side of the main road near Soi 21 (Mon–Sat every 30min roughly 6am–4.30pm, less frequently on Sun; 30–45min; B40). Songthaews cannot enter the park itself, so you'll be dropped at the park checkpoint, about 14km short of the Khao Yai visitor centre. At the checkpoint (where you pay the B400 national park entrance fee) park rangers will flag down passing cars and get them to give you a ride up to the visitor centre; this is common practice here. A quicker but more expensive option is to charter a songthaew from the corner of Soi 19 in Pak Chong (B1500 for a return trip, including several hours in the park).

GUIDED TOURS

The good thing about joining a tour of Khao Yai is that you're accompanied by an expert wildlife-spotter, and you have transport between the major sights of the park; book ahead if possible. Beware, however, that Khao Yai has problems with unscrupulous, fly-by-night tour operators. Two recommended companies run the standard tours and charge the same prices: half a day on the fringes of the park (B500), so avoiding the steep national park fee; a full day in the park (B1300, including the national park fee); and a combination of the two lasting a day and a half (B1500), with the middle night spent outside the park; accommodation is extra.

Bobby's Apartments and Jungle Tours South end of Pak Chong, near the turning for Route 2090 ☎ 086 262 7006, ⓦ bobbysjungletourkhaoyai.com. As well as the standard tours, they can organize two-and-a-half-day tours, including camping in the park (B3500). The "apartments" are actually day-glo a/c cabins with hot showers (B600) or you can stay in the fan dorm for B100. Call for free transfer from Pak Chong bus or train station.

Green Leaf Tour At kilometre stone 7.5 on the park road, 12.5km out of Pak Chong ☎ 044 936361, ⓦ greenleaftour .com. The staff here go out of their way to make sure your stay runs smoothly, and will pick you up from Pak Chong if you're booked on a full-day tour or longer. They also offer private tours including wildlife photography and birding. Sparse though brightly decorated en-suite rooms (B300) and decent Thai meals.

NIGHT SAFARIS

A much-touted park attraction is the hour-long night safaris that take truckloads of tourists round Khao Yai's main roads in the hope of sighting wildlife in the glare of specially fitted searchlights. You can book a place on one of the trucks at the national park headquarters; they leave from here every night at 7pm and 8pm and cost B500 for up to eight people.

ACCOMMODATION AND EATING

INSIDE THE PARK

To stay at the national park lodges in high season, you'll probably need to reserve ahead through the National Parks website (ⓦ nps.dnp.go.th), though there may be availability for walk-ins on weekdays. Advance booking is not usually necessary if camping, but is advisable at weekends. Tents and bedding can be rented for around B250 for two people. There's a cafeteria complex opposite the HQ and visitor centre.

PAK CHONG

Pak Chong's exceptionally good night market sets up on the edge of the main road, between Tesaban sois 17 and 19.
At Home Hostel 27 Tesaban Soi 16/1, opposite the night market ☎ 095 609 6719, ⓦ facebook.com/athomepakchong. Stylish new a/c hostel done out with polished concrete, bamboo and exposed brickwork, offering hot showers, laundry facilities and tours of the park. Dorms B300, doubles B640

KHORAT (NAKHON RATCHASIMA)

Ninety kilometres northeast of Pak Chong, bustling and non-touristy **KHORAT** (officially known as Nakhon Ratchasima) is Isaan's largest city and a major transport hub, where you may have to change buses. It can be used as a base for exploring Phimai and Phanom Rung, though you'll be better off for budget accommodation in Phimai itself and in Surin (for Phanom Rung).

The town's most important statue is of **Thao Suranari** (Ya Mo), the deputy governor's feisty wife whose bravery and cunning were an inspiration to the people of Khorat when it was attacked by Laos in 1826. People come in their droves in the evening to lay flowers at her feet, and some even dance around her. From March 23 to April 3, the town holds a festival in her honour.

ARRIVAL AND INFORMATION

By bus Most buses from other provinces arrive at the main Bus Terminal 2, north of the city on Highway 2 and connected to it by city buses #7 and #15, as well as tuk-tuks and metered taxis (around B70). Bus Terminal 1, just off Th Suranari, is closer to the town centre and runs local services as well as a few buses to Bangkok.
Destinations Ayutthaya (every 30min; 3hr); Bangkok (every 20min; 3–4hr); Ban Tako (for Phanom Rung; every 30min; 2hr); Chanthaburi (5 daily; 6hr); Chiang Mai (10 daily; 11–12hr); Khon Kaen (every 30min; 2hr 30min–3hr); Lopburi (roughly hourly; 3hr 30min); Nakhon Phanom (2 daily; 8hr); Nong Khai (10 daily; 6–8hr); Pak Chong (every 30min; 1hr 30min); Phimai (every 30min; 1hr); Phitsanulok (10 daily; 6–7hr); Rayong (for Ko Samet; at least 8 daily; 6–8hr); Surin (every 30min; 4–5hr); Ubon Ratchathani (hourly; 5–7hr); Vientiane (Laos; 1 daily; 8hr).
By train The train station on Th Mukkhamontri, towards the west of town, is served by city bus routes #1, #2 and #3.
Destinations Ayutthaya (14 daily; 3hr 30min); Bangkok (14 daily; 4hr–6hr 40min); Khon Kaen (8 daily; 3hr 20min); Nong Khai (2 daily; 5–6hr); Surin (14 daily; 2hr–3hr 20min); Ubon Ratchathani (11 daily; 4hr–6hr 10min); Udon Thani (7 daily; 5hr–5hr 40min).
Tourist information The TAT office (daily 8.30am–4.30pm; ☎ 044 213666, ⓔ tatsima@tat.or.th) is on the western edge of town on Th Mitraphap. Take city bus #1, #2 or #3 to reach it.

GETTING AROUND

Khorat is sprawling and clogged with traffic, so walking is rarely the best option.

10

10

By bus and songthaew Local buses and songthaews (B8–15) travel most of Khorat's main roads. The most useful routes are #2, which runs between the TAT office in the west, via the train station, and Suranari and Assadang roads to the east; and #3, which also runs right across the city, via Mahathai and Jomsurangyat roads, past the train station.

By tuk-tuk and taxi Tuk-tuks and motorcycle and metered taxis swarm the streets.

ACCOMMODATION AND EATING

There are night markets about 400m east of *Siri Hotel* on Th Pho Klang (corner of Th Yota) and on the east side of the centre near the *Iyara Hotel* on Th Chumphon.

Cabbages and Condoms 86/1 Th Suebsiri (north–south road just east of TAT). Excellent Thai and Isaan food at this cosy, mid-priced restaurant (most dishes around B100), with all proceeds going to the Population and Community Development Association. Daily 10am–10pm.

Siri Hotel 688 Th Pho Klang, 500m northeast of the train station ☎044 341822, ⓦsirihotelkorat.com. A modern and comfortable choice with very smart, spacious and quiet rooms, all with a/c, hot showers and cable TV. Breakfast included. Doubles B660

★ **Urban Bamboo** 111 Th Watcharasrit, a block east of the Thao Suranari statue ☎044 268800, ⓦurban-bamboo.com. Design B&B with twelve different, artistically created rooms (all a/c with TVs and hot showers) and a great roof terrace for chilling. Good breakfasts included. Doubles B640

DIRECTORY

Hospital Expats favour the private Bangkok Hospital at 1308/9 Th Mittraphap (Highway 2; ☎044 429999).

Tourist police Opposite Bus Terminal 2 ☎044 341777 9 or ☎1155.

PHIMAI

A more appealing overnight stop than Khorat is tiny **PHIMAI**, 60km to the northeast. It's particularly attractive during its main festival over a long weekend in early November, which includes longboat races, *son-et-lumière* and classical dance performances.

Prasat Hin Phimai

The town is dominated by the exquisitely restored eleventh- or twelfth-century Khmer temple complex of **Prasat Hin Phimai** (Phimai Historical Park; daily 7.30am–6pm; B100), which is reminiscent of Angkor Wat. Built mainly of dusky pink and greyish-white sandstone, it was oriented southeast

towards, and connected by a direct road to, the Khmer capital of Angkor and follows the classic symbolic precepts of Khmer temple design: the moat represented the cosmic ocean, the surrounding walls the mountains, and the main prang (sanctuary tower) Mount Meru, the mythological axis of the world according to Hindu cosmology.

Phimai's magnificent main prang has been restored to its original cruciform ground plan, complete with an almost full set of carvings, mostly picking out episodes from the Ramayana. Those around the outside of the prang depict predominantly Hindu themes: Shiva – the Destroyer – dances above the main entrance to the southeast antechamber heralding the end of the world and the creation of a new order. By the early thirteenth century, Prasat Hin Phimai had been turned into a Buddhist temple, and the main prang now houses Phimai's most important image – the Buddha sheltered by a seven-headed naga (snake).

Phimai National Museum

Many other stonecarvings, notably an exceptionally fine sandstone statue of twelfth-century Khmer king Jayavarman VII rescued from the main prang, can be seen at the well-presented **Phimai National Museum** (Wed–Sun 9am–4pm; B100), ten minutes' walk north of the ruins by the river.

ARRIVAL AND DEPARTURE

By bus Buses to and from Khorat's Bus Terminal 2 (every 20min; 1hr–1hr 30min) stop near the ruins and the museum; the last return bus departs Phimai around 7pm. If coming from the north (Khon Kaen or Nong Khai), take any bus towards Bangkok and get off at the Highway 2–Highway 206 junction, where you can change to the Khorat–Phimai service for the last 10km.

ACCOMMODATION AND EATING

The cheapest place to eat is the night market just east of the entrance to the ruins on Th Anantajinda.

Boonsiri Guest House 228 Th Chomsudasadet, 50m south of the ruins ☎044 471159, ⓦboonsiri.net. Clean, ten-bed dorms at great prices, plus private rooms with hot showers (only B100 extra for a/c) and a nice planted roof terrace with seating. Bicycle rental. Dorms B150, doubles B400

10

INTO CAMBODIA: CHONG CHOM–O'SMACH

A/c minibuses (every 30min; 1hr 30min) travel to the **Chong Chom border pass**, 70km south of Surin, mostly to service the casinos on the Cambodian side. Cambodian visas are issued on arrival at the Chong Chom–O'Smach checkpoint (daily 7am–8pm; US$20, although you may be asked for B1000), from where you can get taxis to Siem Reap, 150km from the border crossing (reckon on B1500 per car).

Nom Noey On the north side of Prasat Hin Phimai. This small bakery-café does good cakes and coffee, as well as Western breakfasts and Thai dishes (around B100). Daily 8am–5pm or later.

PHANOM RUNG AND MUANG TAM

Built during the same period as Phimai, the temple complexes of **Prasat Hin Khao Phanom Rung** (often shortened to just Phanom Rung) and **Prasat Muang Tam** form two more links in the chain that once connected the Khmer capital, Angkor, with the limits of its empire. It's best to visit the ruins as a day-trip from either Khorat (see p.773) or Surin (see below).

Prasat Hin Khao Phanom Rung

Prasat Hin Khao Phanom Rung (daily 6am–6pm; B100, or B150 for a joint ticket with Muang Tam) dates back to the tenth century and stands as the finest example of Khmer architecture in Thailand, its every surface ornamented with exquisite carvings and its buildings so perfectly aligned that on the morning of the full-moon day of the fifth lunar month (usually April) you can stand at the westernmost gateway and see the rising sun through all fifteen doors. This event is celebrated with a day-long festival of huge parades.

Before entering the temple, it's well worth visiting the excellent, museum-like **Phanom Rung Tourist Information Centre** (daily 9am–4.30pm; free) by the main entrance to learn more about its symbolism and background. You approach the temple compound along a dramatic 200m-long avenue flanked with lotus-bud pillars, going over the first of three naga bridges, and past four small purification ponds. This constitutes the symbolic crossing of the abyss between earth and heaven. Part of the gallery that runs right round the inner

compound has been restored to its original covered design, with arched roofs, small chambers inside and false windows. Above the entrance to the main prang are carvings of a dancing ten-armed Shiva, and of a reclining Vishnu, who is dreaming up a new universe.

Prasat Muang Tam

Down on the well-watered plains 8km to the southeast of Phanom Rung, and accessed via a scenic minor road that cuts through a swathe of rice fields, lies the small but elegant temple complex of **Prasat Muang Tam** (daily 6am–6pm; B100, or B150 for a joint ticket with Phanom Rung). It sits behind a huge kilometre-long *baray* (Khmer reservoir), which was probably constructed at the same time as the main part of the temple, in the early eleventh century. Like Phanom Rung, Muang Tam is based on the classic Khmer design of a central prang, flanked by minor prangs and encircled by a gallery punctuated with gateways. The four stone-rimmed L-shaped ponds between the gallery and the outer wall may have been used to purify worshippers as they entered the complex.

ARRIVAL AND DEPARTURE

To get to the ruins, you first need to take a bus to the small town of Ban Tako, located on Highway 24, 115km southeast of Khorat or 83km southwest of Surin; bus #274 travels between the two provincial capitals (every 30min). From Ban Tako, it's 12km south to Phanom Rung and another 8km south to Muang Tham, so you'll either have to hitch or rent a motorbike taxi (B400–500/person round trip). The last bus back to Khorat from Ban Tako leaves around 5pm.

SURIN

The quiet, typically northeastern town of **SURIN** is best known for the much-hyped elephant roundup held here every year on

10

the third weekend of November when hundreds of elephants congregate from the surrounding countryside (contact TAT for details and tickets). Situated about 150km east of Khorat, Surin makes a good base for Phanom Rung and has a fine guesthouse. It's also an excellent place to buy silk, either from the women around the Tannasarn–Krungsrinai intersection, or from one of the town's silk shops.

ARRIVAL AND INFORMATION

By bus Buses stop one block east of the train station.
Destinations Bangkok (at least hourly in the morning and evening; 7–8hr); Khon Kaen (roughly hourly; 4hr–5hr 30min); Khorat (every 30min; 4–5hr) and Ubon Ratchathani (6 daily; 3–4hr).
By train Trains from Bangkok (9 daily; 6hr 30min–9hr 30min) and Ubon (11 daily; 2hr 30min) pull in at the northern edge of town.
Tourist information The TAT office is just east of the centre at 355/3–6 Th Tessaban 1 (daily 8.30am–4.30pm; ☎ 044 514447 8, ✉ tatsurin@tat.or.th).

ACCOMMODATION AND EATING

For fiery Isaan food, you can't beat Surin's lively night market, which occupies the eastern end of Th Krungsrinai.
Pirom and Aree's Guest House 55-326 Soi Arunee, Th Thung Poh, about 1.5km northwest of the train station ☎ 089 355 4140. Quiet, laidback and super-clean guesthouse with shared cold showers, run by Pirom, a knowledgeable ex-social worker, and his friendly wife, Aree; they also serve food on request. Their fascinating tours give tourists an unusual glimpse into rural northeastern life; most itineraries feature the Ban Ta Klang elephant trainers' village. Doubles B200

UBON RATCHATHANI

Almost always referred to simply as Ubon, **UBON RATCHATHANI**, 168km east of Surin, is Thailand's fifth-largest city, but only really worth stopping at en route to the Lao border. If you're here in early July, though, drop by for the **Ubon Candle Festival**, when huge beeswax sculptures are paraded through the streets to celebrate the anniversary of the Buddha's first sermon.

Wat Thung Si Muang, 200m east of the central Thung Si Muang Park along Thanon Sri Narong, is noteworthy for its well-preserved teak library – raised on stilts over an artificial pond to keep book-devouring insects at bay – and its murals in the bot, to the left of the library, which display lively scenes of nineteenth-century life. The **Ubon Ratchathani National Museum** (Wed–Sun 9am–4pm; B100), on Thanon Kheunthani on the south side of the park, has decent displays on the region's geology, history and folk crafts.

ARRIVAL AND INFORMATION

By plane Ubon airport is just north of the town centre, with frequent flights to and from Bangkok; a metered taxi to the centre costs about B80.
By bus The main long-distance bus terminal is about 3km northwest of Ubon city centre on Th Chayangkun, from where songthaews #2, #3 and #10 run into town.
Destinations Bangkok (hourly; 10hr); Chiang Mai (6 daily; 14hr); Chong Mek (roughly hourly; 1hr–1hr 30min); Khon Kaen (at least hourly; 4–5hr); Khorat (hourly; 5–7hr); Mukdahan (every 30min; 2hr 30min–3hr); Pakse, Laos (2 daily; 3hr); Rayong (for Ko Samet; 7 daily; 12–13hr); Surin (6 daily; 3–4hr).
By train The train station is in Warinchamrab, south across the Mun River. Songthaew #2 (B10) runs from the train station across the river into central Ubon; a taxi or tuk-tuk costs around B80.
Destinations Ayutthaya (7 daily; 7hr–10hr 40min); Bangkok (7 daily; 8hr 30min–12hr 15min); Khorat (11 daily; 3hr 45min–6hr); Surin (11 daily; 1hr 50min–2hr 40min).
Tourist information The TAT office on Th Khuenthani can provide maps showing the city songthaew routes (daily 8.30am–4.30pm; ☎ 045 243770, ✉ tatubon@tat .or.th).

ACCOMMODATION AND EATING

Ubon's night market on Th Khuenthani, just west of TAT, is a great place to eat, selling a wide variety of food, including the Isaan classics, grilled chicken, sticky rice and *som tam* (papaya salad).
★ **The Outside Inn** 11 Th Suriyat, about 2km northeast of Thung Si Muang park (catch songthaew #10 from the bus station) ☎ 088 581 2069, ⊛ theoutsideinnubon.com. This welcoming and clued-up guesthouse in a quiet part of town provides tasteful, spacious rooms with a/c, hot showers, fridges and TVs, as well as very good Mexican, American and Thai food in the garden restaurant (closed Tues) and bicycle and motorbike rental. Full breakfast included. Doubles B650
Sakhon 66 Th Pha Daeng, 2min walk north of the northeast corner of Thung Si Muang park. One of the best places in Ubon to sample Isaan food, particularly

recommended for its more unusual seasonal dishes, like *tom yam* soup with fish eggs. Most dishes around B80. Daily 10am–10pm.

Tokyo Hotel 178 Th Upparat ☏045 241739. Basic but acceptable and welcoming hotel, where large, bright fan rooms have hot showers and TV, and it's only an extra B90 if you want a/c. It's about a 10min walk north of the museum. Doubles B360

DIRECTORY

Hospital Ubonrak-Thonburi Hospital, Th Burapanai (☏045 260285), to the east of the town centre.
Tourist police Th Suriyat (☏1155 or ☏045 245505).

NAKHON PHANOM

NAKHON PHANOM, 100km north of Mukdahan and 313km east of Nong Khai, affords stunning views of the Mekong and the mountains behind but is chiefly of interest as a point of access to Laos (see box, below).

ARRIVAL AND INFORMATION

By plane AirAsia and Nok Air each fly twice daily from Bangkok (Don Muang) to Nakhon Phanom; the airport is 15km from town, and served by a/c minibuses (B100/person).

By bus The bus station is about 2km west of the centre; buses arrive here from Nong Khai (2 daily; 6hr), Mukdahan (every 30min; 2hr) and Bangkok (12 daily; 12hr).

Tourist information There's a TAT office 700m north of the ferry pier at 184/1 Th Sunthon Vichit, on the corner with Th Salaklang (daily 8.30am–4.30pm; ☏042 513490, ✉tatphnom@tat.or.th).

INTO LAOS FROM NORTHEAST THAILAND

There are four border crossings to Laos from Isaan province.

CHONG MEK

Ninety-nine kilometres east of Ubon Ratchathani, Highway 217 hits the Lao border at Chong Mek, site of a Thai–Lao market, and one of the legal border crossings for foreigners.

There are a/c minibuses roughly hourly to Chong Mek from the main bus terminal, but the fastest and easiest way to get across is to take the a/c bus all the way to **Pakse**, the main town on the other side of the border (2 daily, 9.30am & 3.30pm; 3hr); the bus will wait at Vongtao, on the Lao side of the border, while you get a visa on arrival for Laos (see p.349).

NAKHON PHANOM–THAKHEK

Eight daily buses from Nakhon Phanom's bus station run across the third Thai–Lao Friendship Bridge, 8km north of the town centre, to Khammouan (**Thakhek**) in Laos; they'll wait while you get a Lao visa on arrival (see p.349). The passenger ferry across the Mekong is for Lao and Thai people only.

MUKDAHAN

Buses run to **Mukdahan**, 170km north of Ubon Ratchathani, from Bangkok (20 daily; 11hr), Khon Kaen (every 30min; 3–4hr), Nakhon Phanom (every 30min; 2hr) and Ubon (every 30min; 2hr 30min–3hr). Tourists can cross to Laos here by catching one of the Savannakhet buses from Mukdahan bus station over the Second Friendship Bridge, 7km north of town (roughly hourly from 7.30am to 7pm); you can get a thirty-day Lao visa on arrival (see p.349).

NONG KHAI

The border crossing at Nong Khai is the **First Friendship Bridge** (daily 6am–10pm, although the shuttle buses across the bridge stop around 9pm, sometimes earlier), where you can get a thirty-day Lao visa on arrival (see p.349); expect to pay $1 extra if you arrive after 6pm or at the weekend. It's possible to pay in baht, rather than dollars for your visa, though at B1500 their exchange rate is poor. From Nong Khai's bus station, you can take one of the six daily buses that run all the way through to Vientiane (B55), but only if you have arranged your Lao visa in advance. If you need a visa on arrival, take a tuk-tuk to the foot of the bridge (about B50 from the train station), then a shuttle bus (B20–30) across the span itself; on the other side you can catch a shared a/c minibus, tuk-tuk or bus to Vientiane, 24km away.

At Nong Khai train station it is possible to switch to the international train for the quick hop across to Tha Naleng (2 daily), but as the tracks stop here (around 20km from downtown Vientiane) you'll need to charter a tuk-tuk, car or minibus for the rest of the journey.

ACCOMMODATION

P Hometel 508 Th Sri Thep ☎ 042 512508. The best budget place to stay is the central *P Hometel*, a block back from the river just north of the ferry pier near the clock tower, with large, bright a/c rooms with en-suite hot showers and balconies above a café. Doubles B500

10 NONG KHAI

The major border town in these parts is **NONG KHAI**, the terminus of the rail line from Bangkok and the easiest place to cross overland into Laos, whose capital Vientiane is just 24km away. The town is reasonably tranquil and still retains a backwater charm, but has been developing fast since the construction of the huge First Thai–Lao Friendship Bridge over the Mekong to its west (see box, p.777). As with most of the towns along this part of the Mekong, the thing to do in Nong Khai is just to take it easy, enjoying the peaceful atmosphere and the stunning sunsets.

WHAT TO SEE AND DO

Nong Khai stretches 4km along the south bank of the Mekong. Running from east to west, Thanon Meechai dominates activity, with the main shops and businesses plumb in the middle around the post office and the main pier and Thai–Lao market at Tha Sadet. The town is famous for the **Bang Fai Phaya Nak (naga fireballs)**, pink balls of light that rise noiselessly from the river after dusk on the last day of Buddhist Lent on October's full-moon night. Despite eager attempts to disprove it as a hoax, no evidence of misdoing has been found and thousands of people amass every year to gawp at this mysterious phenomenon, especially as it coincides with the annual long-boat races on the Mekong. One of the best ways to see Nong Khai's famous sunset is on a cruise run by *Mut Mee* guesthouse (daily 5pm, if there are enough takers; about 1hr; B100) on their floating restaurant, *Nagarina*, which docks at the pier beneath (food is available at extra cost).

Just off the main highway, 5km east of Nong Khai, **Sala Kaeo Kou** (aka Wat Khaek; daily 8am–6pm; B20) is best

known for its bizarre sculpture garden, which looks like the work of a giant artist on acid. The temple was founded by the unconventional and charismatic holy man, Luang Phu Boonlua Surirat, who believed, somewhat controversially, in a fusion of the teachings from all religions. The garden bristles with Buddhist, Hindu, Christian and secular figures, all executed in concrete with imaginative abandon by unskilled followers under Luang Phu's direction, and continued after his death in 1996. He also established a similarly weird "Buddha Park" (Xieng Khouan) across the Mekong near Vientiane in Laos (see p.368). The best way to get here is to rent a bike (around B50/day) or motorbike (around B200) from your guesthouse, but return trips in a tuk-tuk (around B150) are also possible.

ARRIVAL AND INFORMATION

By bus The bus terminal is on the east side of the centre off Th Prajak; tuk-tuks abound, and guideline rates for common trips are posted within the terminal. You could easily walk from here to *Sawasdee* but not to the other guesthouses listed here.
Destinations Bangkok (12 daily; 11hr); Khon Kaen (hourly; 3hr 30min); Khorat (10 daily; 6hr 30min); Nakhon Phanom (2 daily; 6hr); Vientiane (Laos; 6 daily; 1hr–1hr 30min).
By train The train station is 3km west of the town centre towards the Friendship Bridge; tuk-tuks wait around to ferry passengers into town.
Destinations Ayutthaya (4 daily; 9hr 30min–11hr); Bangkok (4 daily; 11–13hr); Khon Kaen (5 daily; 2hr 45min); Khorat (2 daily; 5–6hr); Tha Naleng, Laos (2 daily; 15min).

ACCOMMODATION

Ban Sabai Rimkhong 168 Th Rimkhong ☎ 042 413545. In an attractive new building on the river bank to the west of Tha Sadet market, smart a/c rooms with hot showers, some with sweeping views of the Mekong, and big balconies. Doubles B490
★ **Mut Mee** 1111 Th Kaeworawut, on the west side of town ☎ 042 460717, ⊛ mutmee.com. A magnet for travellers with its huge range of well-kept rooms in an attractive riverside garden, friendly, informative staff, yoga, reiki and massage sessions, and mountain bikes. It's always busy, so aim to arrive early. Doubles B300
Sawasdee Guest House 402 Th Meechai ☎ 042 412502, ⊛ sawasdeeguesthouse.com. A grand old wooden shophouse set around a pleasant courtyard east of the centre, with cheap fan rooms that share bathrooms (try to

avoid those overlooking the noisy main road). A/c rooms with en-suite hot-water bathrooms also available. Doubles B250

EATING AND DRINKING

★**Daeng Namnuang** Th Rimkhong, near Tha Sadet. Delicious, inexpensive Vietnamese food at this stupendously popular place with a lovely riverside terrace. Specialities include deep-fried prawns on sugar-cane skewers (B130) and the eponymous *nam nuang*, make-them-yourself fresh spring rolls with sausage. Daily 8am–8pm.

Nagarina As well as cruising on the river (see opposite), *Mut Mee's* floating restaurant serves tasty authentic Thai food in an atmospheric setting, specializing in seafood and Isaan dishes (main dishes B80–1200). There's also a floating bar, *Gaia*, with live music and a laidback atmosphere. Meanwhile, under bamboo shelters back on dry land, the main guesthouse restaurant offers lots of Thai vegetarian dishes and apple pie. Daily 10am–9pm.

SHOPPING

Hornbill Bookshop Th Kaeworawut, on the access road to *Mut Mee Guest House*. Stocks new and secondhand books and offers internet access. Mon–Sat 10am–7pm.

KHON KAEN

The lively, studenty city of **KHON KAEN**, 213km south of Nong Khai, makes a decent resting point on the Bangkok–Nong Khai rail line and has both a Lao and a Vietnamese consulate, the only ones outside Bangkok.

In keeping with its status as a university town, the **Khon Kaen National Museum**, on Thanon Lung Soon Rachakarn (Wed–Sun 9am–4pm; B100), boasts several fine collections including Bronze Age pots, Buddha images and local folk art. South of the centre, the striking, modern, nine-tiered pagoda at **Wat Nongwang**, resplendent in red, white and gold, is also well worth a visit. It offers good views of Beung Kaen Nakhon, the adjacent lake in a park.

ARRIVAL AND INFORMATION

By plane The airport, 10km west of the city centre, has hour-long flights to Bangkok with Thai (Suvarnabhumi Airport), Nok Air and Air Asia (both Don Muang). Many hotels send a/c minibuses out to pick up guests; otherwise, a taxi will cost around B100.

By bus Khon Kaen has recently opened a huge new bus station southwest of the centre near the junction of the city ring road and Highway 2; the former a/c bus station in the city centre off Th Klang Muang is currently used only by local a/c minibuses, while the old non-a/c bus station on Th Prachasamoson has been closed. The situation remains a bit fluid (the new bus station is not popular locally); a free shuttle bus runs between the new terminal and the old Th Klang Muang terminal.

Destinations Bangkok (every 30min; 6–7hr); Chiang Mai (12 daily; 10–12hr); Khorat (every 30min; 2hr 30min–3hr); Nong Khai (hourly; 3hr 30min); Phitsanulok (16 daily; 5–6hr); Sukhothai (10–11 daily; 6–7hr); Surin (roughly hourly; 4hr–5hr 30min); Ubon Ratchathani (at least hourly; 4–5hr).

By train Khon Kaen's train station is on the southwest edge of the centre.

Destinations Ayutthaya (6 daily; 7hr–7hr 30min); Bangkok (6 daily; 8hr 30min–9hr 45min); Khorat (8 daily; 3hr–3hr 30min); Nong Khai (5 daily; 2hr 25min–3hr 30min).

Tourist information The TAT office is south of the centre on Th Klang Muang (daily 8.30am–4.30pm; ☎ 043 227144 5, ✉ tatkhkn@tat.or.th).

ACCOMMODATION

Eco Place 27/9 Th Robmuang ☎ 043 246959. In a reasonably quiet central location, this eco-friendly hotel is great value, offering bright white a/c rooms with hot showers and TVs. Doubles B600

Saen Sumran 55 Th Klang Muang ☎ 043 239611. The most traveller-oriented hotel in town has spacious, if slightly dilapidated, rooms with en-suite cold showers in an old-fashioned whitewashed wooden building. Doubles B220

EATING

Khon Kaen has a reputation for very spicy food, particularly delicious sausages (*sai krog isaan*). Food stalls pop up across town at dusk, with a particular concentration at the night bazaar on Th Ruen Rom and, on Saturday evenings, at the lively weekly "Walking Street" market on Thanon Na Soon Rachakarn near City Hall. Nightlife is focused on Th Prachasamran, behind the *Pullman Hotel*.

Didines Th Prachasamran. Welcoming Canadian-run bar-restaurant offering tasty Thai, Mexican and Western food (main dishes around B200), as well as craft beers and a wide selection of wines. Daily 5pm–midnight.

Naem Nuang Lab Lae Down a lane off Th Klang Muang, next door but one to the *Saen Sumran Hotel*. Justifiably popular place that serves good Vietnamese food, including *naem nuang*, do-it-yourself fresh spring rolls with pork

10

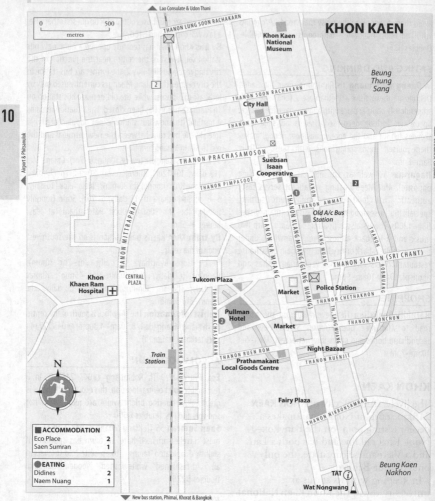

10

Airport & Phitsanulok

▲ Lao Consulate & Udon Thani

Vietnamese Consulate

KHON KAEN

0 — 500 metres

THANON LUNG SOON RACHAKARN

Khon Kaen National Museum

Beung Thung Sang

THANON SOON RACHAKARN

City Hall

THANON NA SOON RACHAKARN

THANON PRACHASAMOSON

Suebsan Isaan Cooperative

THANON PIMPASOOT

THANON AMMAT

Old A/c Bus Station

THANON KLANG MUANG (GLANG MUANG)

THANON NA MUANG

THANON MITTRAPHAP

THANON SI CHAN (SRI CHANT)

LANG MUANG

ROBMUANG

CENTRAL PLAZA

Khon Khaen Ram Hospital

Tukcom Plaza

Market

Police Station

THANON CHETHAKHON

THANON PRACHASAMRAN

Pullman Hotel

Market

TH. LANG MUANG

THANON CHONCHUN

Night Bazaar

THANON RUEN ROM

THANON RUENJIT

Train Station

Prathamakant Local Goods Centre

THANON DAMRONGSAMRAN

Fairy Plaza

THANON NIKRONSAMRAN

Beung Kaen Nakhon

N

TAT ⓘ

Wat Nongwang

■ **ACCOMMODATION**
Eco Place	2
Saen Sumran	1

● **EATING**
Didines	2
Naem Nuang	1

▼ New bus station, Phimai, Khorat & Bangkok

sausage (sets from B130); also has an a/c buffet-only branch opposite. Daily 9am–8.30pm.

DIRECTORY

Consulates The Lao consulate is on the east side of Highway 2 towards Udon Thani, 8km north of town and accessible on most #4 city songthaews (Mon–Fri 8am–noon & 1–4pm; ☏ 043 393402). The Vietnamese consulate is off the east end of Th Prachasamoson at 65/6 Th Chataphadung (Mon–Fri 8.30–11.30am & 1.30–4.30pm; ☏ 043 242190; city songthaew #10 can save you a long walk).

Hospital Khon Kaen Ram Hospital, on the far western end of Th Si Chan (☏ 043 333900, ⊕ khonkaenram.com).

Tourist police Southwest of town on Th Mittraphap (Highway 2; ☏ 043 220337 or ☏ 1155).

The east coast

Thailand's **east coast** is a 500km string of fairly dull beaches and over-packaged resorts, the largest and most notorious of which is eminently missable Pattaya. Offshore, the tiny island of **Ko Samet** with its pretty white-sand beaches attracts weekending Bangkokians and an increasing number of package-holiday-makers. Further east are the much larger, forested island of **Ko Chang**, whose long, fine beaches have made it Thailand's latest major resort destination; and the small, much less developed **Ko Mak**. East of Ko Chang lies the Cambodian border post of Hat Lek, one of two points in this region – the other being Aranyaprathet, a little way north – where it's possible to **cross overland into Cambodia** (see box below).

KO SAMET

Pretty little **Ko Samet** attracts big crowds these days, drawn mostly from Bangkok's middle classes and expats, especially at weekends and on national holidays. Despite being declared a national park in 1981 (B200; payable at the checkpoint near Hat Sai Kaew or at Ao Wong Duan pier), a building ban has had little effect and the island is now weighed down with more than fifty sprawling, albeit low-rise, resorts. The shady beaches, however, are still blessed with squeaky white sand, and there's plentiful plant and animal life.

At just 6km long, the island's size means you can easily walk to most destinations, along the mostly well-marked paths that link the east-coast beaches. There are also motorbikes and bicycles for rent on nearly every beach, and the main road

down the spine of the island is now paved. Green songthaews wait for fares at the pier in the main village of **Na Dan** and half a dozen other stands around the island, charging from B20/person, depending on distance and the number of other passengers; chartering a songthaew will cost anything up to B400.

The beaches

Hat Sai Kaew (Diamond Beach), so-called after its beautiful long stretch of luxuriant sand, lies on the south side of Na Dan village, ten minutes' walk down the village high street from the main pier. It's the busiest beach on Samet, packed with resorts and restaurants.

Separated from Hat Sai Kaew by a low promontory, **Ao Hin Kok** has equally fine sand. It's much smaller than its neighbour and has more of a travellers' vibe, with some backpacker-oriented budget choices for accommodation.

Past the next rocky divide is **Ao Phai**, one of the livelier places to stay on the island. By day, a relaxed beach-life atmosphere pervades, but in the evening *Silver Sand*'s nightly parties thump out bland dance music.

10

INTO CAMBODIA: ARANYAPRATHET

The most commonly used overland crossing into Cambodia from Thailand is at **Poipet**, which lies just across the border from the Thai town of **Aranyaprathet**, 210km due east of Bangkok. It's best to arm yourself in advance with an e-visa for Cambodia (see p.67) and to make the journey to Aranyaprathet – or through to Siem Reap or Phnom Phenh – by regular public transport, but it's also possible to buy a combination ticket from a travel agent through to Siem Reap and to get a thirty-day visa on arrival at the border, though both of the latter options are more likely to open you up to the many **scams on this route**, including a fake "Cambodian Consulate/Immigration" in Aranyaprathet and rip-off currency exchange (it's not compulsory to buy riel before entering Cambodia, despite what some touts may say).

Once you've walked across the border and entered Cambodia, it's about two hours in a taxi or bus to Siem Reap, 150km away. If you have the deep misfortune of getting stuck in dusty, dirty Aranyaprathet, where local transport comes in the form of tuk-tuks, try the comfortable fan and a/c rooms at *Inter Hotel* at 108/7 Th Chatasingh (☏037 231291, ⊛ourweb.info/ interhotel; B300).

From **Bangkok**, you can travel to Aranyaprathet Station, 4km from the border post, by **train** (2 daily; at least 6hr); you'll need to catch the 5.55am if you want to get across the border the same day. Alternatively, take a **bus** or a/c minibus from Bangkok's Northern (Mo Chit) Bus Terminal to Aranyaprathet (at least hourly; 3hr 30min–4hr 30min). There are also regular public buses from Bangkok's Northern Bus Terminal through to Siem Reap (2 daily; 8hr) and Phnom Penh (1 daily; 14hr).

To reach Aranyaprathet from east-coast towns, the easiest route is to take a bus from **Chanthaburi** to the town of **Sa Kaew**, 130km to the northeast, and then change to one of the frequent buses for the 55km ride east to Aranyaprathet.

10

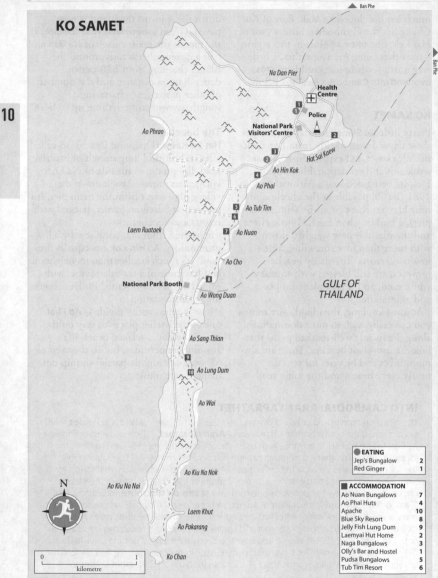

KO SAMET

Ban Phe

Ban Phe

Na Dan Pier

Health Centre

1
1

Police

National Park Visitors' Centre

2

Ao Phrao

3

Hat Sai Kaew

4

Ao Hin Kok

Ao Phai

5

Ao Tub Tim

6

Laem Ruataek

7

Ao Nuan

Ao Cho

8

National Park Booth

Ao Wong Duan

GULF OF THAILAND

Ao Sang Thian

9

Ao Lung Dum

10

Ao Wai

N

Ao Kiu Na Nok

Ao Kiu Na Nai

Laem Khut

Ao Pakarang

Ko Chan

0   1
kilometre

● **EATING**
Jep's Bungalow   2
Red Ginger   1

■ **ACCOMMODATION**
Ao Nuan Bungalows   7
Ao Phai Huts   4
Apache   10
Blue Sky Resort   8
Jelly Fish Lung Dum   9
Laemyai Hut Home   2
Naga Bungalows   3
Olly's Bar and Hostel   1
Pudsa Bungalows   5
Tub Tim Resort   6

Further south is **Ao Tub Tim**, also known as Ao Pudsa, a small white-sand bay sandwiched between rocky promontories. It has just two bungalow operations, shaded by plentiful trees.

Clamber up over the headland from Ao Tub Tim (which gives you a fine panorama over Hat Sai Kaew) to reach Samet's

smallest and most laidback beach, the secluded **Ao Nuan**, effectively the private domain of *Ao Nuan Bungalows*. Because it's some way off the main track, the beach gets hardly any through-traffic and feels quiet and private. Although not brilliant for swimming, the rocky shore reveals a good patch of sand when the tide withdraws.

A ten-minute walk south along the track from Ao Nuan brings you to the horseshoe bay of **Ao Wong Duan**, the second most popular beach on the island and dominated by pricey bungalow resorts. Unfortunately its sand, while white and fine, is almost lost under a plethora of deck-chairs, stalls and crowds of sunbathers.

Ao Sang Thian (also known as Candlelight Beach), a couple of minutes' walk over the hill, has almost none of the commerce of Wong Duan, though its lovely, scenic shorefront is fronted by an unbroken line of bungalows and little restaurants. At its southern end, Ao Sang Thian becomes **Ao Lung Dum**, where the cheaper bungalow outfits in this area are located.

ARRIVAL AND DEPARTURE

The mainland departure point for Ko Samet is the fishing port of Ban Phe, about 200km from Bangkok. Boats leave from half a dozen piers, including the central Nuan Thip pier (Nov–Feb approximately hourly 8am–6pm; 40min; B70) and back again to roughly the same schedule. Most go to Na Dan pier, but if you're headed for Ao Nuan or Ao Sang Thian, it might be more convenient to take the boat to Ao Wong Duan (around 3 daily, depending on demand; 1hr; B90). In low season, there should be up to four boats daily to Na Dan.
To Ban Phe Buses and a/c minibuses from Bangkok's Eastern Bus Terminal run hourly to Ban Phe (3–4hr), or you can take a bus to Rayong instead (roughly every 30min) and then change onto a songthaew to Ban Phe (30min). Coming by bus from Chanthaburi or Trat, you'll be dropped at a T-junction on Highway 3, from where a songthaew or motorbike taxi will take you the remaining 5km to the Ban Phe piers.

ACCOMMODATION

The trend across the island is upmarket, and in high season you'll be hard pressed to secure an en-suite bungalow for less than B800. The cheapest budget accommodation is located on the high street in Na Dan village – numerous restaurants and shops double up as guesthouses, though they have only a few rooms each for B500 or so; the beach is a short walk.

NA DAN
Olly's Bar and Hostel On the west side of the high street ☎086 349 0064, ⊛ollyskohsamed.com. English-run hostel with niftily designed pods – some big enough for two – in a colourful, mixed a/c dorm and with hot showers. Dorms B400, doubles B600

HAT SAI KAEW
Laemyai Hut Home North end of Hat Sai Kaew ☎038 644282. The bungalows here are the best of the budget options on this beach, not least because they're dotted widely around a shaded, sandy, plant-filled garden in one of the prettiest spots, under the Laem Yai headland at the quieter northern end. Most of the bungalows have been upgraded to a/c (B1500), though one or two dishevelled but colourfully painted en-suite fan options remain. Doubles B800

AO HIN KOK AND AO PHAI
Ao Phai Huts North end of Ao Phai ☎038 644075. Cheap white bungalows with verandahs and cold-water bathrooms spread out over a shady hillside. Doubles B600
Naga Bungalows Ao Hin Kok ☎038 644035. Long-running, somewhat jaded resort, with a lively beachfront bar, post office, currency exchange and internet shop. Simple, scrappy wooden huts are stacked in tiers up the slope, with decks, mosquito nets and shared bathrooms, as well as pricier concrete a/c rooms with their own adjacent cold-water bathroom. Doubles B600

AO TUB TIM AND AO NUAN
Ao Nuan Bungalows ☎038 644334. Birdsong provides the soundtrack for a variety of idiosyncratic but sturdy wooden huts that dot the forested hillside. The cheaper choices have a mattress on the floor, a mosquito net and a shared cold-water bathroom, but the view of the beach from the balconies is great. Doubles B800
Pudsa Bungalows Ao Tub Tim ☎038 644030. Laidback place on the beach, offering a range of sturdy but rather battered huts, all en suite, the cheapest with cold-water shower only. There's a beachside restaurant that does barbecues. Doubles B800
Tub Tim Resort Ao Tub Tim ☎038 644025, ⊛www.tubtimresort.com. The most popular place to stay here is a sprawling, well-run resort with over a hundred handsome chalet-style wooden bungalows of various sizes and designs, plus a good restaurant. The cheapest bungalows sport cold showers, ceiling fans and small verandah. Doubles B800

AO WONG DUAN
Blue Sky Resort Northern Ao Wong Duan ☎089 936 0842. Perched high above the beach, this somewhat tatty resort has fan huts with mosquito nets and a/c bungalows, all en suite with sea views, as well as a popular restaurant in a lofty position. Doubles B600

AO LUNG DUM
Apache Ao Lung Dum ☎081 452 9472. This laid-way-back resort takes up most of the beachfront in Ao Lung Dum with its rustic, creatively designed bungalows and rooms and appealing restaurant. Doubles B800

10

10

Jelly Fish Lung Dum Ao Lung Dum ☏ 081 652 8056. Friendly spot under the bougainvillaea where many of the bungalows with hot showers are right on the rocky shore, practically overhanging the water; a few cheaper rooms and bungalows at the back are also available. Doubles **B900**

EATING

Most visitors to Ko Samet just eat at their resorts, and in truth there are few restaurants worth making an effort to get to.

Jep's Bungalow South-central Ao Hin Kok. Popular all-rounder serving a great menu of authentic Thai dishes (from around B100), as well as Indian and other international food, at its tables on the sand, set under trees strung with fairy lights and given extra atmosphere by mellow music. Also does cappuccino and cakes, and evening barbecues. Daily 7am–10pm.

Red Ginger On the west side of the high street in Na Dan village, but planning to move premises at the time of writing ☏ 084 383 4917, ✆ redgingersamed.com. This cosy and welcoming Thai–Canadian place is well worth seeking out for its great Western dishes such as oven-baked ribs (B385) as well as much cheaper Thai dishes (around B100–150). Daily noon–around 10pm, depending on who's in.

DIRECTORY

Banks and exchange There are ATMs in the village and on most of the main beaches, and currency exchange booths in the village.

Emergencies Ko Samet's health centre and police station (☏ 038 644111) are on Na Dan high street, but for any serious medical problem you should go to the Bangkok Hospital in Rayong (☏ 038 921999, ✆ bangkokrayong .com).

CHANTHABURI

There's not a lot to see in **CHANTHABURI**, a provincial capital 80km east of Ban Phe that's famous for its gem trade and its high-quality fruit, but you may find yourself stranded here, as this is a transit point for many Rayong–Trat buses and a handy terminus for services to and from the northeast.

ARRIVAL AND DEPARTURE

By bus Five daily buses make the scenic six-hour Chanthaburi–Sa Kaew–Khorat journey in both directions, with Sa Kaew (3hr) being a useful interchange for buses to Aranyaprathet and the Cambodian border (see box opposite). Buses to and from all these places, as well as

Bangkok's Eastern and Northern bus terminals, use the Chanthaburi bus station on Th Saritidech, a 10min walk northwest of the town centre.

ACCOMMODATION

River Guest House 3/5–8 Th Srichan ☏ 039 328211. In the centre, by one of the main river bridges, you'll find the traveller-oriented *River Guest House*, which has fan and a/c rooms with private or shared facilities, some with hot showers and river-view balconies. Doubles **B250**

TRAT

The small, engaging market town of **TRAT**, 68km east of Chanthaburi, with its charming historic neighbourhood of narrow lanes, old wooden shophouses and lively bars, cafés and restaurants, is a good place to while away time and stock up on essentials before heading, via local ports, to Ko Chang or Ko Mak, or moving on to Cambodia.

ARRIVAL AND INFORMATION

By plane The airport is about 30km west of the centre; a taxi will cost B500/person.

Destinations Bangkok (Suvarnabhumi; 3 daily with Bangkok Airways; 1hr).

By bus The bus station is 1.5km northeast of Trat centre. Songthaews charge B20/person into Trat's centre and around B60 (B250–300/vehicle) to the island ferry ports near Laem Ngop.

Destinations Bangkok Eastern Bus Terminal (at least hourly; 5hr); Bangkok Northern Bus Terminal (hourly; 5hr); Bangkok Suvarnabhumi Airport (2 daily; 4hr 10min); Chanthaburi (hourly; 1hr–1hr 30min); Hat Lek (hourly; 1hr 30min).

Information TAT have a Trat office, but it's inconveniently located in the village of Laem Ngop, about 20km southwest of town (daily 8.30am–4.30pm; ☏ 039 597259, ✉ tattrat@tat.or.th).

ACCOMMODATION AND EATING

The best places to eat in Trat are the day market, on the ground floor of the Th Sukhumvit shopping centre, and the atmospheric night market, north of the historic centre, on Soi Vijit Junya (east of Th Sukhumvit).

★**Ban Jaidee** 67–69 Th Chaimongkon, about 200m southeast of the market ☏ 083 589 0839. Very calm, inviting and rather stylish guesthouse with a pleasant seating area downstairs and simple bedrooms sharing hot-water bathrooms. The nicest rooms are in the original building and have polished wood floors. Doubles **B200**

Residang House 87/1–2 Th Thoncharoen, about 500m

INTO CAMBODIA: HAT LEK

Many travellers use the **Hat Lek–Koh Kong border crossing** for overland travel into Cambodia. It's best to arm yourself in advance with an e-visa for Cambodia (see p.67) and to make the journey by regular public transport, but it's also possible to buy a package all the way through to Sihanoukville or Phnom Penh and to get a thirty-day visa on arrival at the border, though both of the latter options are more likely to open you up to the many **scams on this route**.

The only way to get to **Hat Lek** under your own steam is by minibus from Trat bus station, 91km northwest (hourly; 1hr–1hr 30min). Hat Lek (on the Thai side) and Koh Kong (in Cambodia) are on opposite sides of the Dong Tong River estuary, but a bridge connects the two. Once through immigration, taxis or motorcycle taxis ferry you into **Koh Kong** town for onward transport to Sihanoukville and Phnom Penh or for guesthouses should you arrive too late for connections (mid-afternoon onwards). **Vans, buses and share-taxis** to Phnom Penh and Sihanoukville should take around 4–5hr.

10

southeast off the main Th Sukhumvit ☎ 089 224 1866, ⓦ trat-hotel-residang.com. Comfortably appointed, good-value German–Thai-managed guesthouse. Rooms are large, light and clean, and all have thick mattresses and hot-water bathrooms. Doubles B350

KO CHANG

The focal point of a national marine park archipelago of 52 islands, **Ko Chang** is Thailand's second-largest island (after Phuket) and an increasingly popular destination, drawing crowds to its beautiful white-sand beaches, which are backed by a mountainous interior of dense jungle. During peak season, accommodation on the west coast fills up very fast, but it gets quieter (and cheaper) from May to October, when fierce storms can make the sea too rough for swimming.

Hat Sai Khao (White Sand Beach)

Framed by a broad band of fine white sand at low tide, **Hat Sai Khao** (White Sand Beach) is the island's longest beach but also its most commercial, with scores of unattractive hotel-style developments and bungalow operations squashed in between the road and the shore. The atmosphere is more laidback and traveller-oriented at the northern end of the beach, however, where through a maze of haphazard boardwalks (a high-tide necessity) you'll find the most budget-priced accommodation. Currents can get very strong on Hat Sai Khao, so be careful when swimming.

Hat Khlong Phrao and Hat Kai Bae

Just south of the khlong fed by **Khlong Phu Waterfall** (B200 entry) is the long sandy beach of central **Hat Khlong Phrao**, which remains a beauty. Behind a thin line of casuarinas there's a scattering of cheap and charming bungalow operations nestled in a huge coconut grove. About 5km further south, the narrow, once-beautiful beach at **Hat Kai Bae**, while almost ruined by breakneck development, remains quaint at its southern extremity.

Hat Tha Nam (Lonely Beach)

Around the southern headland from Hat Kai Bae is the long curve of white-sand bay at **Hat Tha Nam** – dubbed **Lonely Beach** before it became the backpackers' haven – which is lovely, if slightly sullied by a few ugly developments. There's a youthful atmosphere, cheapish accommodation and raucous parties every evening. Be extremely careful when swimming here, however, especially around *Siam Beach Resort* at the far northern end, as the steep shelf and dangerous current result in a sobering number of **drownings** every year; do your swimming further south and don't go out at all when the waves are high.

Bang Bao

Almost at the end of the west-coast road, the southern harbour village of **Bang Bao**, much of it built on stilts off a kilometre-long central jetty, is the departure point for boats to the outer islands, has several famous seafood restaurants and is also an

10

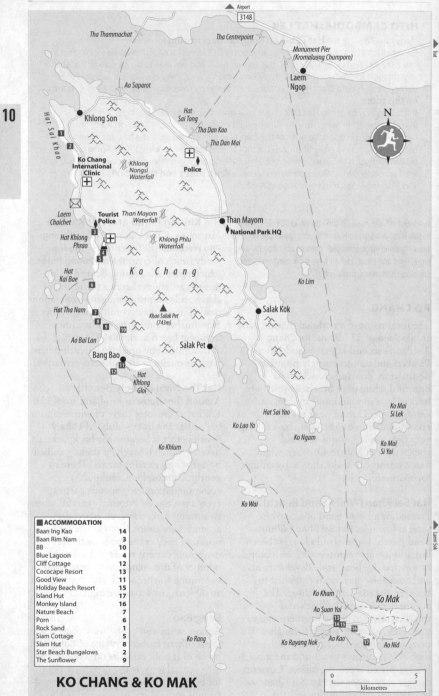

ACCOMMODATION

Baan Ing Kao	14
Baan Rim Nam	3
BB	10
Blue Lagoon	4
Cliff Cottage	12
Cococape Resort	13
Good View	11
Holiday Beach Resort	15
Island Hut	17
Monkey Island	16
Nature Beach	7
Porn	6
Rock Sand	1
Siam Cottage	5
Siam Hut	8
Star Beach Bungalows	2
The Sunflower	9

KO CHANG & KO MAK

increasingly popular place to stay. Bang Bao has no beach of its own, but it's only 2km east to long, sandy and little-developed Hat Khlong Gloi, which offers great views from its small beach cafés.

ARRIVAL AND DEPARTURE

By boat The main piers for Ko Chang are near Laem Ngop, about 20km southwest of Trat. The main services to Ko Chang are the car ferries (both B80/person), which operate from two piers, Tha Centrepoint (to Tha Dan Kao; hourly; 45min) and Tha Thammachat (to Ao Saparot; every 45min; 25min). White songthaews meet the boats and deliver passengers to the main beaches (B50–150 per person). Tickets on tourist buses and minibuses to Ko Chang (notably from Suvarnabhumi Airport, for B600/person, and the shuttle from Trat Airport, for B500/person) usually include the ferry crossing and often transport to your accommodation.

To Laem Ngop The piers are served by share-taxi songthaews from Trat bus station and Th Sukhumvit (allow 60–90min before your boat leaves for the vehicle to fill up and get you to the pier). There are also plenty of long-distance buses and minibuses direct from Bangkok's Eastern Bus Terminal (Ekamai) to Laem Ngop, bypassing Trat town.

GETTING AROUND

A paved road, precipitously steep in places, runs almost all the way round the island, served – between Tha Dan Kao and Bang Bao – by frequent public songthaews; you can also rent cars and motorbikes on most beaches.

INFORMATION AND TOURS

Tourist information The free maps and guides published by Whitesands Publications (ⓦkoh-chang-guide.com) are a handy source of information, but for better insights and advice, check out ⓦiamkohchang .com, compiled by a British Ko Chang resident.

Tours Tour agents or your accommodation can book you on popular snorkelling trips, jungle walks or a visit to an elephant camp. Among dive outfits, long-running BB Divers, a PADI Five-Star Centre with offices at Bang Bao, Lonely Beach and Hat Sai Khao (ⓣ039 558040, ⓦbbdivers-koh-chang.com), charges B3000 for certified diver day-expeditions (2 dives) and B14,500 for the four-day PADI Open Water course. Well-organized Kayak Chang at *Emerald Cove Resort*, Hat Khlong Phrao (ⓣ093 532 7241, ⓦkayakchang.com), offers one-day kayaking trips (B3200, return transport from your accommodation and lunch included), as well as expeditions of up to 12 days.

ACCOMMODATION

HAT SAI KHAO (WHITE SAND BEACH)

It is only possible to walk along the beach to the listings below, just two of ten or so similar resorts in the same area; enter via the walkway by the *KC Grande Resort* and walk a few hundred metres north.

Rock Sand ⓣ084 781 0550, ⓦrocksand-resort.com. With a smart restaurant jutting over the water below, and ten percent discount for single travellers, this is great value as prices also include breakfast. The fan rooms with shared bathrooms (cold showers) are in a brick building, and another couple of hundred baht gets you either a sea-view terrace or a bungalow with hot shower. Doubles B700

Star Beach Bungalows ⓣ089 574 9486, ⓦstarbeach-kohchang.com. Breezy, cheerily painted plywood huts, with good mattresses and hot showers, perch precariously on a steep rocky hillside, above a decent beachside restaurant. No advance reservations taken, though you can call or text ahead to see if a room is available. Doubles B500

HAT KHLONG PHRAO AND HAT KAI BAE

Baan Rim Nam Hat Khlong Phrao ⓣ087 005 8575, ⓦiamkohchang.com. Peaceful, scenic and unusual, this converted fishing family's house is built on stilts over the wide, attractive khlong at the end of a walkway through the mangroves. Run by the British author of the best Ko Chang website, it has just five comfortable a/c rooms with good hot-water bathrooms, plus decks for soaking up views of the khlongside village, but no restaurant (breakfast is available). You can borrow kayaks and it's a couple of minutes' walk to the beach. Doubles B1000

★**Blue Lagoon** Khlong Phrao ⓣ089 515 4617, ⓦkohchang-bungalows-bluelagoon.com. Overlooking a scenic stretch of river 100m walk from an equally appealing part of the beach, this friendly French–Thai resort offers artist-designed bungalows with hot showers, fridges, large decks and bamboo hammocks, as well as tents (B250), a good restaurant, a cooking school and yoga. Doubles B700

Porn's At the southern end of the beach, Hat Kai Bae ⓣ080 613 9266, ⓦpornsbungalows-kohchang.com (no advance reservations). The most famous of the dwindling number of budget accommodation options on Hat Kai Bae, laidback *Porn's* has scores of fan bungalows in various styles, well spaced out under the trees along a huge expanse of the shorefront. The cheapest are concrete huts with cold showers at the back. Also has a great two-storey restaurant and bar on the beach. Doubles B600

Siam Cottage Northern Hat Kai Bae ⓣ089 153 6664, ⓦfacebook.com/siamcottagekohchang. With cheerily painted interiors, partly outdoor bathrooms and decks, the wooden bungalows here face each other across a narrow but well-watered, flowery lot that runs down to the sea, and a cute restaurant. Doubles B650

10

HAT THA NAM (LONELY BEACH)

BB On the main road, towards the south end of Lonely Beach ☎039 611690, ⓦ bblonelybeach.com. Behind a good bar-restaurant and a tiny swimming pool, the garden shelters small but smart fan rooms, mostly en suite, half with hot showers. The complex, which also has four-bed fan dorms, is owned by BB Divers (see p.787), who have a gym with yoga classes next door. Dorms <u>B250</u>, doubles <u>B450</u>

Nature Beach Central Lonely Beach ☎081 803 8933. Largely responsible for Lonely Beach's party reputation, this place's rooms, bar-restaurant (with built-in DJ station) and the beach out front are all hugely popular. The cheapest of its shady, closely set bungalows are attractive, fan-cooled log cabins with verandahs, some with hot showers. Doubles <u>B600</u>

Siam Hut Central Lonely Beach ☎086 609 7772. Row upon row of flimsy, primitive, bamboo huts, all of which are en suite. It is, however, one of the few remaining budget options that's right on the beach. There's a swimming pool and big restaurant/bar deck that's great for watching the sunset and hosts barbecues and regular parties. Doubles <u>B480</u>

The Sunflower Soi Sunset ☎084 017 9960, ⓦ the-sunflower.com. Run by a genial German and his Thai family, the bungalows here are set under palm and banana trees 200m or so from the roadside village and equidistant from the rocky coast at *Sunset Hut*, a 5min walk south of the sandy beach. Choose between wooden fan bungalows with mosquito nets and cold- or hot-water bathrooms, and concrete bungalows with a/c; all have good thick mattresses and are kept very clean. The restaurant is also good. Doubles <u>B500</u>

BANG BAO

★**Cliff Cottage** West side of Bang Bao bay ☎080 823 5495, ⓦ cliff-cottage.com. British-run resort and dive company with a nice deck restaurant on a west-facing cove, and kayaks and snorkels for rent. Bell tents on wooden platforms with decent mattresses, electricity, fans, shared bathrooms and good sunset views sit up on a small, dusty, shady rise (available high season only); there are also reasonably priced a/c rooms and bungalows with hot showers. Doubles <u>B600</u>

Good View Bang Bao jetty ☎089 108 0429, ⓦ goodviewbangbao.wordpress.com. Built over the water halfway down the east side of the jetty, the good views from this guesthouse take in the shoreline opposite. Lovely, clean, bright, large, wooden-floored bedrooms come with huge hot-water bathrooms, big balconies and a/c – try to snag an upstairs room. There's a very large, attractive ground-floor deck with a book corner. Doubles <u>B1000</u>

DIRECTORY

Banks Most beaches offer ATMs and currency exchange.
Clinic The 24hr Ko Chang International Clinic, beyond the south end of White Sand Beach (☎039 551555), is a branch of the Bangkok Hospital in Trat (☎039 552777, ⓦ bangkoktrathospital.com), where you'll be evacuated for anything major.
Post office On the road between Sai Khao and Khlong Phrao (Mon–Fri 10am–noon & 1–5pm, Sat 10am–1pm).
Tourist police At the north end of Hat Klong Phrao (☎1155).

KO MAK

Tiny **Ko Mak** (sometimes spelt "Maak") is 20km southeast of Ko Chang and offers a slow-paced, peaceful alternative. An interior of palm and rubber plantations makes road journeys a pleasure, and the colourful reefs and fishes of nearby islands are a treat for scuba divers and snorkellers (contact Koh Mak Divers on Ao Kao, ☎083 297 7724, ⓦ kohmakdivers.com). The palm-fringed, white-sand and shallow **Ao Kao** on the southwest coast is the most developed beach, with plush resorts and a couple of budget options. Long, curvy **Ao Suan Yai**, on the northwest coast, also has fine sand and a pretty outlook. Most bungalows offer, or can arrange, motorbike (B300–350/day) or mountain-bike (B150/day) rental, and there's a small clinic off the Ao Nid road, though no banks or ATMs.

ARRIVAL AND INFORMATION

From Trat/Laem Ngop/Laem Sok In high season, up to eight speedboats a day run from Kromaluang (Monument) pier in Laem Ngop, to either Ao Kao or Ao Suan Yai on Ko Mak (50min; B450). Buses and a/c minibuses to Laem Ngop from Bangkok, for example, will sometimes only go as far as the Thammachat or Centrepoint Ko Chang piers, however – check exactly which piers are served when you buy your ticket, or you may be able to pay the driver a little extra to go on to Kromaluang. Meanwhile, Boonsiri operates a catamaran from Laem Sok pier, 30km south of Trat, to Ao Nid on Ko Mak twice daily in high season (1hr; B400 including transfer from Trat town), as well as connecting buses from Banglamphu in Bangkok.
From Ko Chang The main company is Bang Bao Boat (☎087 054 4300, ⓦ kohchangbangbaoboat.com), which in high season runs a slow boat once daily (2hr; B400) and

★ **TREAT YOURSELF**

Cococape Resort Southern end of Ao Suan Yai ☏ 081 810 2679, ⓦ kohmakcococape.com. Individually designed rooms, bungalows and converted boats situated on a rocky cliffside offering stunning views over the bay or around a lotus pond. *Cococape* has direct access to good snorkelling via a small wooden pier with a sun deck and a cocktail bar as well as easy access to the lovely Ko Pee across the water. The beach is a short walk away and there's an attractive swimming pool. Doubles B1200

a speedboat twice daily (1hr; B600) from Bang Bao pier in the south of Ko Chang to Ao Suan Yai on Ko Mak. Koh Chang Boats (Kaibae Hut) operates high-season speedboats from Hat Kai Bae to Ao Kao on Ko Mak once daily (1hr; B600; ☏ 090 506 0020, ⓦ kohchangboat.com). All of these prices include transfers to or from the west coast of Ko Chang.

Information Whitesand produces an annual free map of the island (ⓦ koh-chang-guide.com); ⓦ kohmak.com is also useful, especially for boats to the island.

ACCOMMODATION

It is best to book accommodation in advance for free pick-up transfers from the piers.

Baan Ing Kao Ao Kao ☏ 087 053 9553, ⓦ baaningkao .com. Located among trees on a steep hill at the western end of the beach, this secluded resort of thatched bamboo en-suite bungalows with verandahs exudes a quaint, village-like atmosphere. Snorkels are free for guests and kayaks can be rented to explore the islands close by. Doubles B350

Holiday Beach Resort Ao Kao ☏ 086 751 7668, ⓦ holidaykohmak.com. Friendly, well-maintained place, strewn with flowers, where a good restaurant and white clapboard cottages (the cheapest with cold showers) face a large, beachside lawn with deckchairs and tables. Doubles B800

Island Hut Ao Kao ☏ 087 139 5537. The cheapest option on the island, offering en-suite rough-hewn timber huts, many with idiosyncratic driftwood artwork, on a quiet stretch of beach. Doubles B250

Monkey Island Ao Kao ☏ 089 501 6030, ⓦ monkeyislandkohmak.com. A laidback, monkey-themed resort with a small pool which has a wide range of accommodation, starting with nice, thatched wooden huts with shared facilities and hammocks. There's also a beach bar a little way along the beach with live reggae and Thai folk every evening. Doubles B400

Southern Thailand: the Gulf coast

Southern Thailand's Gulf coast is famous chiefly for the three fine islands of the Samui archipelago: large and increasingly upmarket **Ko Samui**, laidback **Ko Pha Ngan**, site of monthly full-moon parties at **Hat Rin**, and tiny **Ko Tao**, which is encircled by some of Thailand's best dive sites. Other attractions seem minor by comparison, but the historic town of **Phetchaburi** has a certain charm, and the grand old temples in **Nakhon Si Thammarat** are worth a detour.

The Gulf coast has a slightly different **climate** from the rest of Thailand, being hit heavily by the northeast monsoon's rains, especially in November, when it's best to avoid this part of the country altogether. Most times during the rest of the year should see pleasant, if changeable, weather, with some effects of the southwest monsoon felt between May and October.

PHETCHABURI

Straddling the River Phet about 120km south of Bangkok, the provincial capital of **PHETCHABURI** flourished as a seventeenth-century trading post. Now a centre for sweet manufacturing, it retains much of its old-world charm, with fine historic wats, wooden shophouses and a nineteenth-century hilltop palace.

WHAT TO SEE AND DO

The town's central sights cluster around Chomrut Bridge (**Saphaan Chomrut**) and the River Phet. About 700m east of the bridge is the still-functioning seventeenth-century **Wat Yai Suwannaram**, which contains a remarkable set of faded old murals, depicting divinities ranged in rows of ascending importance in its ordination hall, and a well-preserved scripture library built on stilts over a pond. A further five minutes' walk east, and then ten minutes' walk south, takes

10

you to the five crumbling stone prangs of **Wat Kamphaeng Laeng**, elegant structures of weathered earth-tone beauty. Built to enshrine Hindu deities, they were later adapted for Buddhist use. A short way southwest of Chomrut Bridge stands Phetchaburi's most fully restored and important temple, **Wat Mahathat**, probably founded in the fourteenth century. The five landmark prangs at its heart are adorned with stucco figures of mythical creatures, while miniature angels and gods embellish the roofs of the main viharn and bot.

About thirty minutes' walk west of Chomrut Bridge is **Khao Wang**, the hill on which stands Rama IV's palace – a great place to explore. Quaint brick paths wind through a forest of gnarled frangipanis, some covered in brilliant flowering vines, to reveal whitewashed – now peeling and pleasingly mottled – chedis and gazebos, as well as the king's summer house, Phra Nakhon Khiri, and observatory, now a **museum** (daily 8.30am–4pm; B150). It's reached on foot from near the western end of Thanon Rajwithi or by cable car from the western base of the hill off Highway 4 (daily 8.30am–4.30pm; B200 including admission to the palace); songthaews from Chomrut Bridge should drop you close to either access point. The hill is populated by a large number of monkeys, which can be aggressive, so keep your distance and don't carry food.

ARRIVAL AND DEPARTURE

By bus Several companies run roughly hourly a/c minibuses between Phetchaburi and Bangkok's Southern Bus Terminal (2hr), including one on Thanon Rot Fai about 500m southeast of the train station near the night market; from here, it's an easy 10min walk south to Chomrut Bridge. Otherwise, Phetchaburi is served by through-buses on their way to or from Bangkok – Highway 4, carrying all services between the capital and southern Thailand, passes right through the west side of town. The best place to board or disembark is "Sii Yaek Phetcharat", the crossroads by Phetcharat Hospital, about 2km southwest of Chomrut Bridge (catch a songthaew or motorbike taxi); otherwise you might be put off at the Big C department store, 5km south of town.
By train The train station is about 1km northwest of Chomrut Bridge.

Destinations Bangkok (Hualamphong 11 daily, Thonburi Station 2 daily; 3hr); Chumphon (12 daily; 4hr–6hr 30min); Nakhon Pathom (13 daily; 1hr 30min–2hr); Nakhon Si Thammarat (2 daily; 12–13hr); Surat Thani (9 daily; 6hr 45min–9hr).

ACCOMMODATION AND EATING

Decent, cheap accommodation is in short supply in Phetchaburi.
Rabieng Rimnum Guest House Beside Chomrut Bridge at 1 Th Chisa-in ☏ 032 425707. Situated in a century-old teak house, this guesthouse offers very simple rooms with hard mattresses and shared facilities; it can get noisy, so ask for a room away from the road. The staff are helpful and can provide a town map, and the riverside restaurant serves a range of excellent Thai food (from B60) accompanied by a blues and Americana soundtrack. Doubles B240

CHUMPHON

CHUMPHON is the main departure point for Ko Tao, and can also give access to the more distant islands of Ko Pha Ngan and Ko Samui, but is otherwise of little interest. Thanon Sala Daeng, running north–south, is the city's main stem, a good place to orient yourself, and the place to head to for most amenities. If you do find yourself stuck here and hungry, then follow the smells to the night market on east–west Thanon Kromluang Chumphon.

ARRIVAL AND DEPARTURE

BY PLANE
Nok Air (2 daily; 1hr 10min) flies from Don Muang to Chumphon Airport, which is 40km north of town, and sells through-tickets to Ko Tao with Lomprayah. *Fame* (see opposite) run a/c minibuses between the airport and hotels in Chumphon for B150/person.

BY BOAT
Tickets for all boats are sold by travel agents and guesthouses in Chumphon and should include transport to the pier from town, though it's worth checking. As well as the services below, there are several different night boats (B300–450 depending on quality), which take about 6hr to reach Ko Tao. The overnight train from Bangkok that arrives around 4am is a popular choice for catching the early Lomprayah and Songserm boats.
Lomprayah Catamaran Office at the train station ☏ 081 956 5644, ⊛ lomprayah.com. Reliable twice-daily service from Ao Thung Makham Noi, 27km south of

Chumphon; 1hr 45min to Ko Tao (B600); around 3hr 30min to Ko Pha Ngan (B1000); around 4hr to Maenam, Ko Samui (B1100).

Songserm Express Office at the train station ☏077 506205, ⓦsongserm.co.th. Once daily from Pak Nam, about 20km south of Chumphon; 3hr to Ko Tao (B500); around 5hr to Ko Pha Ngan (B800); around 6hr 30min to Nathon, Ko Samui (B900).

BY BUS AND MINIBUS

The government bus station is 11km south of town on Highway 4, where buses to all points north and south will call in; it's connected to the centre by songthaews (B50/person), though long-distance services will sometimes drop off in town. Among private bus services from the centre, Chokeanan Tour buses to Bangkok (4 daily; 8hr) and some Rungkit buses to Phuket (5 daily; 7hr), via Ranong and Khao Lak, start from Th Pracha Uthit, which runs southeast from Th Sala Daeng. Ask at TAT or your guesthouse about a/c minibuses from Chumphon to places such as Ranong, Krabi, Ko Lanta and Surat Thani, most of which are tourist services organized by travel agents; *Fame* runs an a/c minibus to and from Bangkok's Th Khao San to connect with the Ko Tao night boat.

BY TRAIN

The train station is 100m west of Th Sala Daeng on Th Kromluang Chumphon.

Destinations Bangkok (10 daily to Hualamphong, 2 daily to Thonburi; 7hr–9hr 30min); Butterworth (Malaysia; 1 daily; 14hr); Phetchaburi (12 daily; 4hr–6hr 30min); Surat Thani (11 daily; 2–4hr).

INFORMATION

The TAT office is down a short soi at 111 Th Tawee Sinka, which runs northwest off Th Sala Daeng (daily 8.30am–4.30pm; ☏077 501831, ⓔtatchumphon@tat.or.th).

ACCOMMODATION

Fame 188/20–21 Th Sala Daeng ☏077 571077, ⓦchumphon-kohtao.com. Above a good travellers' restaurant, specializing in Italian food, and a reliable tour agency, both of the same name, this place has good-sized and very clean rooms (some with mattresses on the floor), with fans and hot water in either shared or en-suite bathrooms. Doubles B150

Retro Box About 1km east of the train station, just off Th Kromluang Chumphon on Soi 3 ☏077 510333, ⓦretroboxhotel.com. Colourful a/c dorms and rooms with hot showers in salvaged shipping containers stacked up around an inviting swimming pool; some of the rooms have balconies, some of which give direct access to the pool. Dorms B300, doubles B690

SURAT THANI

Uninspiring **SURAT THANI** is of use only as a jumping-off point for trips to Ko Samui, Ko Pha Ngan and, at a pinch, more distant Ko Tao. On Thanon Ban Don, which hugs the River Tapi on the northwest side of the town centre, you'll find Ban Don pier and an atmospheric night market. To the south, east–west Thanon Namuang bustles with retail trade, while multi-laned Thanon Taladmai, the next block south, is the town's main thoroughfare; the central bus terminals, Talat Kaset I and Talat Kaset II, are here, a few hundred metres east of the main post office.

ARRIVAL AND DEPARTURE

BY PLANE

Air Asia, Nok Air and Thai Lion Air fly to Surat Airport, 27km northwest of town, from Bangkok's Don Muang, Thai Smile from Suvarnabhumi Airport; Air Asia and Thai Lion Air also serve Chiang Mai, and Air Asia serve Kuala Lumpur. A minibus (B100) operated by Phantip (see p.792) connects with the town centre, or you can buy a bus-boat combination ticket to Ko Samui (from B400) or Ko Pha Ngan (from B500).

Destinations Bangkok (17 daily; 1hr 15min); Chiang Mai (2 daily; 2hr); Kuala Lumpur, Malaysia (4 weekly; 1hr 35min).

BY BOAT

Details of boats to Ko Samui, Ko Pha Ngan and Ko Tao, most of which leave from Don Sak pier, 68km east of Surat, are given in the account of each island. Phunphin and the bus stations are teeming with touts, with transport waiting to escort you to their employer's bus-and-boat service to the islands – they're generally reliable, but make sure you don't get talked onto the wrong boat. Otherwise, head for Phantip travel agency (see p.792), whose services include buses to Don Sak to connect with the cheap vehicle ferries to Ko Samui and Ko Pha Ngan. You'll have to sort out the night boats to Samui, Pha Ngan and Tao yourself: barely glorified cargo boats, they line up during the day at Ban Don Pier in the centre of Surat; turn up and buy a ticket as early as you can to snag a bed.

BY BUS

Buses use three different locations, two of which are on Th Taladmai in the centre of town: Talat Kaset I on the north side of the road (Phunphin train station via the Bangkok bus terminal and other local buses) and opposite at Talat Kaset II (regional buses and a/c minibuses, including those for Krabi, Nakhon Si Thammarat, Phuket and Ranong). The

10

BKS (Baw Khaw Saw) terminal, about 5km southwest of town on the road towards Phunphin, handles mostly Bangkok services. Many buses heading west out of Surat also make a stop at Phunphin train station.

Destinations Bangkok (12 daily; 10–12hr); Chumphon (roughly hourly; 3hr); Khao Sok (7 daily; 2hr 30min); Krabi (at least hourly; 3hr); Nakhon Si Thammarat (every 30min; 2hr); Phuket (hourly; 4–5hr); Ranong (10 daily; 4hr).

BY TRAIN

The train station is at Phunphin, 13km to the west. Here you can buy a boat ticket to Ko Samui, Ko Pha Ngan and Ko Tao, including a connecting bus to the relevant pier. Otherwise, buses run into town every 40min or so during the day.

Destinations Bangkok (10 daily; 9–12hr); Butterworth, Malaysia (1 daily; 10hr 30min); Nakhon Si Thammarat (2 daily; 4hr); Trang (2 daily; 4hr 30min).

GETTING AROUND

Small share-songthaews buzz around town, charging around B15–20/person for most journeys.

INFORMATION

Tourist information TAT (daily 8.30am–4.30pm; ☎077 288817–8, ✉ tatsurat@tat.or.th) is at the western end of town at 5 Th Taladmai.

Phantip travel agency Surat's best travel agency is the reliable Phantip, in front of Talat Kaset I at 293/6–8 Th Taladmai (☎077 272230, ✪ phantiptravel.com), where you can book bus-and-boat, train and plane tickets; they also have a branch opposite Phunphin train station and a booth at the airport.

ACCOMMODATION AND EATING

There's a large night market on Th Ton Pho between Th Si Namuang and Th Ban Don, which displays an eye-catching range of dishes; a smaller offshoot by Ban Don pier offers less choice but is handy if you're taking a night boat.

Ban Don Hotel 268/2 Th Namuang ☎077 272167. Set above a basic but good Thai-Chinese restaurant, most of the very clean rooms here, with en-suite cold-water bathrooms, TV and fans or a/c, are set back from the noise of the main road. Doubles B250

Milano Opposite the night-boat piers on Th Ban Don. This place has an authentic oven turning out very tasty and reasonably priced pizzas, though its home-made pasta is less successful. Also serves espresso coffee. Daily 11am–10pm.

My Place 247/5 Th Namuang ☎077 272288, ✪ myplacesurat.com. A welcoming spot with a café near the night market in the town centre, which also sells boat tickets to the islands. The cheapest rooms have shared cold showers and plusher en-suite options are available for B160 more. Doubles B199

KO SAMUI

An ever-widening cross section of visitors, from globetrotting backpackers to suitcase-toting fortnighters, comes to southern Thailand just for the beautiful beaches of **Ko Samui**, 80km from Surat Thani. At 15km across and down, Samui is generally large enough to cope with this diversity, except during the Christmas and New Year rush. The island was once *the* destination for paradise sands fringed with palm trees, but development behind the beaches is extensive and often thoughtless, with girly bars by the main beaches beginning to rival those of Phuket. At least there's a local bylaw limiting construction to the height of a coconut palm (about three storeys), and there are still a few pockets of bungalows for backpackers.

Na Thon

The island capital, **NA THON** is a frenetic half-built town that most travellers use only for stocking up with supplies en route to the beaches. The three piers come to land at the promenade, Thanon Chonvithi, which is paralleled by Thanon Taweeratpakdee (or Route 4169), the round-island road.

Maenam

The 4km bay of **Maenam**, 13km from Na Thon, with its leafy, relatively unadulterated beachfront set well away from the ugly round-island road, is an attractive location for a day or two of swimming and relaxation. Here, a number of quiet, cheap beachside accommodations, offering great views, make Maenam a popular destination for budget travellers. On Thursday evenings, the pier road at the centre of Ban Maenam village becomes a pleasant **walking street**, with performances, cheap souvenirs and lots of food stalls.

Bophut, Bangrak and Choeng Mon

The next beach east of Maenam is 2km-long **Bophut**. The beach here is wider and has welcoming clear water, but the area is becoming steadily more upmarket and now has hardly any budget accommodation. Its narrow beach road is surprisingly quaint, however, with a

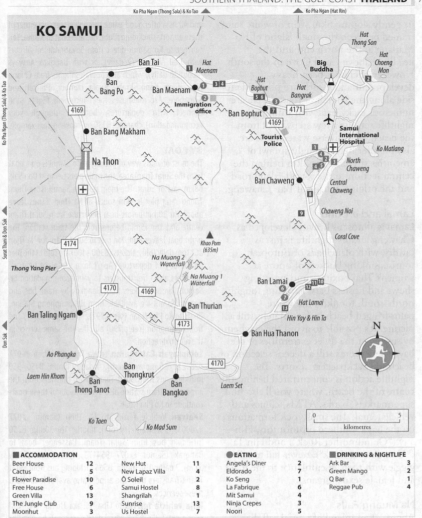

KO SAMUI

Ko Pha Ngan (Thong Sala) & Ko Tao

Ko Pha Ngan (Hat Rin)

Ban Tai

Hat Maenam

Big Buddha

Hat Thong Son

Hat Choeng Mon

Ban Bang Po

Ban Maenam

Hat Bophut

Hat Bangrak

Immigration office

Ban Bophut

Ban Bang Makham

4169

Tourist Police

Samui International Hospital

Na Thon

Ko Matlang

Ban Chaweng

North Chaweng

Central Chaweng

4174

Khao Pom (635m)

Chaweng Noi

Na Muang 2 Waterfall

Coral Cove

Na Muang 1 Waterfall

Thong Yang Pier

4170

4169

Ban Lamai

Ban Thurian

Hat Lamai

Ban Taling Ngam

4173

Hin Yay & Hin Ta

Ban Hua Thanon

N

Ao Phangka

4170

Laem Hin Khom

Ban Thongkrut

Ban Thong Tanot

Ban Bangkao

Laem Set

Ko Taen

Ko Mad Sum

0   5
kilometres

■ ACCOMMODATION				● EATING		■ DRINKING & NIGHTLIFE	
Beer House	12	New Hut	11	Angela's Diner	2	Ark Bar	3
Cactus	5	New Lapaz Villa	4	Eldorado	7	Green Mango	2
Flower Paradise	10	Ô Soleil	2	Ko Seng	1	Q Bar	1
Free House	6	Samui Hostel	8	La Fabrique	6	Reggae Pub	4
Green Villa	13	Shangrilah	1	Mit Samui	4		
The Jungle Club	9	Sunrise	13	Ninja Crepes	3		
Moonhut	3	Us Hostel	7	Noori	5		

number of attractive, traditional Thai wooden buildings in what's now tagged "**Fisherman's Village**". At night, the village is a pleasant place for a stroll, with a concentration of good upmarket restaurants; on Friday evenings, it hosts a **walking street** very similar to Maenam's.

Bangrak is also known as Big Buddha Beach, after the huge **Big Buddha** statue on a small island at the east end of the bay, which gazes down on the sunbathers populating its less-than-perfect beach. A short causeway leads to a clump of

souvenir shops and food stalls in front of the temple, and ceremonial dragon-steps take you to the terrace around the statue, from where there's a fine view of the sweeping north coast.

After Bangrak comes the northeastern cape and beautiful, laidback **Choeng Mon**, whose white sandy beach is lined with casuarina trees.

Chaweng

For sheer natural beauty, none of the other beaches can match **Chaweng**, with

10

its gently sloping 6km strip of white sand framed between the small island of Ko Matlang at the north end and the headland above Coral Cove in the south. However, there has been heavy development and resorts are piled side to side along the stretch of road. There are numerous tacky bars with thumping nightlife set just a few steps back from the beach, and diverse watersports are also on offer here. An ugly sprawl of amenities stretches for 2km behind the central section to the round-island road and the original village of Ban Chaweng.

Lamai and around

Lamai is almost as heavily developed as Chaweng and its nightlife is just as tawdry, with planeloads of European tourists sinking buckets of booze at women's Thai boxing, mud-wrestling shows and hostess bars. Running roughly north–south for 4km, the white palm-fringed beach is, fortunately, still a picture. It's possible to avoid the mayhem by staying at the quiet extremities of the bay, where there's still a decent selection of beachside backpackers' resorts. The nightlife action is concentrated behind the centre of the beach, where you'll also find supermarkets, banks, ATMs, clinics and vehicle rental. The small rock formations on the bay's southern promontory, Hin Yay ("Grandmother Rock") and Hin Ta ("Grandfather Rock"), never fail to raise a giggle with their resemblance to the male and female sexual organs.

Na Muang Falls

About 10km inland of Lamai, off the round-island road, lie **Na Muang Falls**. Each of the two main falls has its own kilometre-long paved access road off Route 4169: the lower falls splash down a 20m wall of rock into a large pool, while Na Muang 2, upstream, is a more spectacular cascade that requires a bit of foot-slogging from the car park (about 15min uphill).

ARRIVAL AND DEPARTURE

BY PLANE
Flights to Samui are among the most expensive in Thailand, so you might want to consider flying from Bangkok to Surat Thani or Nakhon Si Thammarat; Nok Air

and Air Asia offer good-value through-tickets via either of these airports, including flight, bus and boat to Samui. You can get to Ko Samui direct from Suvarnabhumi Airport with Thai Airways (2 daily), or with Bangkok Airways (about 20 daily), which also operates flights from Chiang Mai, Hong Kong, Krabi, Kuala Lumpur, Phuket and Singapore. A/c minibuses meet incoming flights (and connect with departures, bookable through your accommodation), charging B130 to Chaweng, for example.

BY BOAT
The most obvious way of getting to Ko Samui is on a boat from the Surat Thani area, the main piers being at Don Sak, 68km east of Surat. The main port on Samui is Na Thon; Thong Yang pier is 9km south of Na Thon. Buses leave about 1hr 30min before boat departure from Surat Thani centre and 1hr 45min before from the train station. The night boat leaves Ban Don pier in Surat Thani for Na Thon at 11pm daily (6hr); tickets (B300–400) are sold at the pier on the day of departure. Apart from the night boat, all operators also offer transfers to your accommodation on Samui. Through-tickets from Bangkok by train, bus and boat to Samui are available from Hualamphong Station. Boats to Ko Pha Ngan (see p.797), Ko Tao (see p.801) and from Chumphon (see p.790) all offer the same service in the return direction.

Lomprayah Catamaran to Na Thon (Na Thon ☎077 420121, ⓦ lomprayah.com): 4 daily; 45min; B450–550 including bus from Surat Thani town; transfers from the airport and train station also available. All of these boats continue to Ko Pha Ngan.

Seatran Vehicle ferries to Na Thon (Samui ☎077 426001, ⓦ seatranferry.com): hourly; 1hr 30min; B250 including bus from Surat Thani. Passenger boat to Bangrak (Samui ☎077 954171, ⓦ seatrandiscovery .com): 2 daily; 1hr 30min; B565 including bus from Surat Thani. Transfers from the airport also available for both these services.

Raja vehicle ferries to Lipa Noi aka Thong Yang (Call centre ☎02 276 8211, ⓦ rajaferryport.com): hourly; 1hr 30min; B310 including bus from Surat Thani; transfers from the airport and train station also available.

BY LONG-DISTANCE BUS
Ko Samui's government bus terminal (Baw Khaw Saw) is on Th Taweeratpakdee towards the north end of Na Thon (☎077 421125 or ☎077 420765). It handles bus-and-boat services (via Don Sak and Lipa Noi), for example from Bangkok's Southern Terminal (some also stopping at Mo Chit bus terminal; at least 5 daily; 13hr), which cost from B656 on a basic a/c bus to B898 on a VIP bus – these are far preferable to the deals offered by dodgy travel agents on Th Khao San, as the vehicles used on the latter services are often substandard and many thefts have been

reported. The Baw Khaw Saw also sells through-tickets to Nakhon Si Thammarat (roughly hourly; 4hr), which involve catching the ferry to Don Sak, then changing on to an a/c minibus.

GETTING AROUND

By car and motorbike You can rent motorbikes (from B200/day) at all the main beaches, though note that dozens are killed on Samui's roads each year, so go with extreme caution and wear a helmet. You can also rent 4WDs (from B800).

By songthaew Songthaews, which congregate at the car park near the southerly pier in Na Thon, cover a variety of set routes during the daytime, either heading off clockwise or anticlockwise on Route 4169, to serve all the beaches; destinations are marked in English and fares range from B50 to Maenam to B80–100 to Chaweng or Lamai. In the evening, they tend to operate more like taxis and you'll have to negotiate a fare to get them to take you exactly where you want to go.

By taxi Ko Samui sports dozens of a/c taxis. Although they all have meters, you'd be wasting your breath trying to persuade any driver to use his; instead, you're looking at a flat fare of around B500 from Na Thon to Chaweng, for example.

INFORMATION

Tourist information TAT runs a small but helpful office (daily 8.30am–noon & 1–4.30pm; ☎077 420504, ✉tatsamui@tat.or.th), tucked away on an unnamed side road in Na Thon, north of the pier and inland from the post office. Here, and at many other places on Samui, you can pick up Siam Map Company's detailed map of the island.

ACTIVITIES

Samui has around a dozen scuba-diving companies, offering trips for divers and snorkellers and courses throughout the year, and there's a decompression chamber at Bangrak (☎081 081 9555, ⊛sssnetwork.com). Most trips for experienced divers, however, head for the waters around Ko Tao (see p.803); a day's outing costs around B4000, but of course if you can make your own way to Ko Tao you'll save money. Other popular activities, besides trips to Ang Thong Marine Park (see p.797), include kiteboarding and cookery courses.

Easy Divers Head office on Highway 4269 opposite *Sandsea Resort*, Lamai ☎077 231190, ⊛easydivers-thailand.com. PADI Five-Star dive centre, with branches in Chaweng and Bangrak.

Kiteboarding Asia ☎083 643 1627, ⊛kiteboardingasia .com. Instruction in kiteboarding (B4000 for one day), either from the beach south of Ban Hua Thanon or from Nathon, depending on the time of year, as well as rentals and stand-up paddleboarding.

Planet Scuba Head office next to the Seatran pier on Bangrak ☎077 413050, ⊛planetscuba.net. PADI Five-Star dive centre, with a branch on Chaweng.

Samui Institute of Thai Culinary Arts (SITCA) Soi Colibri, opposite Centara Grand Resort in Chaweng ☎077 413172, ⊛sitca.com. This highly recommended outfit runs 3hr cookery classes in the morning and afternoon (B1850), plus fruit-carving classes.

ACCOMMODATION

Budget accommodation is increasingly scarce on Ko Samui, with very little left for less than B600. All the accommodation prices given are for high season, but dramatic reductions are possible out of season (roughly April–June, Oct & Nov).

MAENAM

Moonhut On the east side of the village ☎077 425247, ⊛moonhutsamui.com. Welcoming English-run place on a large, sandy, shady plot, with a lively restaurant and beach bar. The colourful, substantial and very clean bungalows all have en-suite bathrooms, and some have hot water and a/c. Kayaking, water-skiing and stand-up paddleboarding available. Doubles B650

New Lapaz Villa Down a 1km access road, east of the village centre but just west of the post office ☎077 425296, ⊛newlapaz.com. Enjoying plenty of shade, the lush, spacious grounds here shelter a small swimming pool and fifty diverse bungalows on stilts, with verandahs and hot showers, many in bright pastel colours – maintenance could be better but they're clean enough. Doubles B550

Shangrilah On an access road 500m west of the village ☎077 425189. In this huge compound that sprawls onto the nicest, widest stretch of sand along Maenam, the main area of shoulder-to-shoulder bungalows sports beautiful flowers, trees and carefully tended topiary. All rooms are en suite, with verandahs on stilts, ceiling fans and sturdy furniture. The restaurant serves good Thai food. Breakfast included. Doubles B1100

BOPHUT, BANGRAK AND CHOENG MON

Cactus Access from the highway, west Bophut ☎077 245565, ⊛cactus-bungalow.com. Ochre cottages with attractive bed platforms, large French windows and stylish, earth-tone bathrooms stand in two shady rows, running down to the inviting beachfront restaurant with a wood-fired pizza oven. Choose either fan and cold shower or a/c and hot shower. Doubles B800

Free House West of Bophut village ☎077 427517. On a quiet plot that's shaded by a thick canopy of trees, running back from the popular beachfront bar-restaurant, the tasteful en-suite bungalows here are very well designed and maintained, with plenty of natural light. Made either of white-painted concrete or slatted dark wood, they

10

10

feature mosquito nets, hammocks, hot showers and verandahs. Doubles B700

Ô Soleil Choeng Mon ☎077 425232, ⊕osoleilbungalow .com. Lovely, orderly, Belgian-run place in a tranquil, pretty garden dotted with ponds. Among the well-built, clean bungalows, the cheapest are fan-cooled, with cold showers, at the back, while the elegant beachside restaurant has a nice shaded deck area and serves 600 cocktails. Doubles B600

Us Hostel Off Route 4169 at the east end of Bophut ☎098 696 6358, ⊕ushostel-samui.com. Friendly new hostel with smart bunks in a/c recycled shipping containers, hot showers, a pool and wooden chill-out decks scattered with beanbags. Dorms B350, doubles B1000

CHAWENG

Budget travellers have largely been priced off Chaweng and there's nothing cheap left on the beachfront itself.

The Jungle Club 2km up a steep, partly paved road from the south end of Chaweng ☎081 894 2327, ⊕jungleclubsamui.com. Breezy, French–Thai antidote to Chaweng's commercial clutter: a huge, grassy, shady plot with a small pool on the edge of the slope to catch the towering views of Ko Pha Ngan and beyond. A chic bar-restaurant has been built into the rocks, while the accommodation – nearly all thatched, with mosquito nets and fans – includes coconut-wood huts with cold showers. Free pick-ups twice a day. Doubles B800

Samui Hostel South end of Chaweng ☎089 874 3737, ⊕facebook.com/samuihostelthailand. On a side road off the main beach road near the *Mercure Hotel*, this neat, welcoming hostel has fan or a/c six- to twelve-bed mixed dorms, as well as a/c doubles or twins with hot showers, TVs and fridges. Dorms B200, doubles B600

LAMAI

Lamai's budget accommodation is concentrated around the beach's northern and southern ends.

Beer House In the central section of the northern part of the beach ☎077 256591, ⊕beerhousebungalow.com. Appealing bungalows with fans, hot showers, verandahs and hammocks in a lush, shaded compound – try to bag one of the four on the beachfront, which are only B50 extra. Doubles B600

Flower Paradise On the bay's northern headland ☎077 270675, ⊕samuiroestiland.com. Just a short walk from the beach, a friendly, well-run German-Swiss place in a small but beautiful garden. All the attractive, well-tended bungalows of varying sizes have verandahs and hot water. Doubles B400

Green Villa Southern end of the bay ☎077 424296 or ☎081 893 7227, ⊕greenvillasamui.com. Though set back from the beach towards the main road, this resort enjoys a spacious, leafy garden among palm trees, and a small

swimming pool. Clean, simple, en-suite, wooden bungalows with fans and hot showers, or grand, a/c villas. Doubles B700

New Hut *Beer House*'s northern neighbour ☎077 230437, ✉newhutlamai@yahoo.co.th. These rustic A-frames are close together, but cheap, brightly coloured and located right on the beach. They consist of nothing more than a mattress, fan and mosquito net, and have shared cold-water bathrooms, but there's a good restaurant attached and you can't beat the location. More expensive en suites (B600–800) with a/c are also available. Doubles B400

Sunrise On the Hin Yay Hin Ta access road ☎077 424433, ⊕sunrisebungalow.com. Welcoming and clued-up establishment on the far southern end of the beach, with a decent restaurant and a gym. In a quiet, shady garden amid coconut palms, choose between clean fan rooms with cold or hot showers and larger a/c bungalows. Doubles B600

EATING

MAENAM

Angela's Diner Almost opposite the police station on the main through-road, east of the pier ☎077 427396. American-style, a/c diner, offering great all-day breakfasts and a wide choice of sandwiches, salads, soups and Western main courses, as well as home-made cakes and apple pie (B100). Daily 7.30am–4pm.

Ko Seng On the road parallel to and just east of the pier road ☎077 425365. At this locally famous seafood restaurant that's been on national TV, you buy your seafood according to weight, or plump for noodles (B80) or dishes such as *kaeng som plaa* (B200), a thin fish curry with tamarind paste that can be spiced to order. Daily 10am–9pm.

BOPHUT

Ninja Crêpes Far east end of the bay, on the road towards Bangrak. Newly relocated to a beachfront location with nice tables on a terrace by the sea, this is a popular option for cheap, good-quality Western and Thai meals along with breakfasts and sweet and savoury crêpes. Main dishes around B80. Daily 9am–8pm.

CHAWENG

For cheap Thai food, join local workers at the evening food stalls of Laem Din market, on the road between the heart of central Chaweng and Ban Chaweng, or there's another good night market just south of Central Festival shopping mall, running west off the main beach road.

Mit Samui On the road between north Chaweng and Ban Chaweng. Very popular with both locals and tourists, this large, bustling, simple restaurant specializes in pick-your-own seafood (priced by weight), but also serves tasty stir-fried squid with salted egg (B200). Daily 11am–midnight.

Noori Opposite *Chaweng Buri Resort* towards the north end of central Chaweng ☎ 077 300757, ⊚ nooriindiasamui .com. Superior Indian food (around B200/dish) in relatively basic surroundings, including all the old favourites such as chicken tikka masala, as well as plenty of seafood and vegetarian options. Also offers cookery courses. Daily 11.30am–11.30pm.

LAMAI

Eldorado Just west of the central crossroads. Good-value Swedish restaurant, serving a few Thai favourites and all manner of tasty international mains. All-you-can-eat barbecue on Wednesday (B290). Mon–Sat 3pm–midnight.

La Fabrique Route 4169, just south of the temple in Lamai village. Authentic French patisserie-café, a civilized retreat from the busy road. As well as superb cakes such as custard tarts (B80), it serves great breakfasts and omelettes, pizzas, salads and sandwiches for lunch. Daily 7am–6pm.

DRINKING AND NIGHTLIFE

All of the beaches have relaxing places to drink on the sands, but the main bars and clubs are on Chaweng.

Ark Bar North-central Chaweng. This resort hosts popular beach parties with international and Thai house DJs, fire shows and a swim-up pool bar. Parties Wed & Fri 2pm–2am.

Green Mango Soi Green Mango, north-central Chaweng. Now surrounded by bars (including lively *Sweet Soul* across the soi, under the same ownership), a long-standing megaclub in a massive multi-zoned shed with tropical-garden touches. Daily 9pm–3am.

Q Bar North off the Ban Chaweng road ⓦ facebook.com/ qbarsamui. Sleek, futuristic decor, great views over the lake from high on its north shore and cutting-edge music from local and international DJs. Daily 6pm–2am.

Reggae Pub Inland from Central Chaweng across the lake. Chaweng's oldest nightclub is a venerable Samui institution – with a memorabilia shop to prove it. It does time now as an unpretentious, good-time party venue, with pool tables, big-screen sports, DJs and live reggae bands every night. Daily 6pm–late.

DIRECTORY

Books Bookazine sells English-language books, newspapers and magazines at stores in central Chaweng and the airport. Island Books (ⓦ island-books-samui .com), on Highway 4169 towards the north end of Lamai, is a good secondhand bookshop.

Hospitals The state hospital (☎ 077 421230 2), 3km south of Na Thon off Route 4169, plus several private ones in Chaweng.

Immigration office Soi 1, Maenam (☎ 077 421069).

Post office At the northern end of the promenade, Na Thon (Mon–Fri 8.30am–4.30pm, Sat & Sun 9am–noon), with international telephones upstairs (closed Sat & Sun). Dotted along Route 4169, there are further post offices at Maenam, Chaweng and Lamai.

Tourist police On the Route 4169 ring road between Bophut and Chaweng, north of Big C supermarket on the same side of the road (☎ 1155 or ☎ 077 430018).

10

ANG THONG NATIONAL MARINE PARK

It's possible to buy tickets at any of the beaches on Samui for boat trips to **Ang Thong National Marine Park** (B1400 including hotel transfers, entry to the national park, snorkelling, lunch; park closed Nov and early Dec), a gorgeous group of 42 small islands, 30km west of Samui. Boats generally leave Na Thon at 8.30am and return at 4.30–5pm; there are also regular trips from Ko Pha Ngan. First stop on any boat tour is usually **Ko Wua Talab**, site of the park headquarters, from where it's a steep 430m climb (1–2hr return; bring walking sandals or shoes) to the island's peak and fine panoramic views. The feature that gives the park the name Ang Thong, meaning "Golden Bowl", is a steep-sided lake, 250m in diameter, on Ko Mae Ko to the north of Ko Wua Talab; it was the inspiration for the setting of Alex Garland's cult bestseller, *The Beach*. Steps (30min return) lead up from the beach to the rim of the cliff wall encircling the lake, which is connected to the sea by an underground tunnel. If you want to get away from it all, you could rent a bungalow (from B500) or tent (around B200) at park headquarters (ⓦ nps.dnp.go.th) and catch a return boat to Samui on another day. Blue Stars, based on Chaweng, lead highly recommended kayak day-trips to the park (☎ 077 300615, ⓦ bluestars.info; B2100–2500/person).

KO PHA NGAN

In the last decade or so, backpackers have tended to move over to Ko Samui's fun-loving little sibling, **Ko Pha Ngan**, 20km to the north, which generally has a simpler atmosphere, mostly because

10

the poor road system has been an impediment to the developers. With dense jungle covering its inland mountains and rugged granite outcrops along the coast, Pha Ngan lacks sweeping beaches, but it does have some coral and a few beautiful, sheltered bays. The legendary pilgrimage site for ravers, Hat Rin, is where the infamous **full-moon parties** are held, which see swarms of visitors descend upon the island. Several smaller outdoor parties have now got in on the act, all at Ban Tai on the south coast, including the **Half Moon Festival** (twice monthly, about a week before and after the full moon; ⓦhalfmoonfestival.com) and the monthly **Black Moon Culture** (ⓦblackmoon-culture.com).

Thong Sala

THONG SALA is a port of entrance and little more. In front of the piers, transport to the rest of the island (songthaews, jeeps and a/c minibuses) congregates by an assortment of banks, restaurants, supermarkets, dive centres, and motorbike and jeep rental places.

Hat Rin

Hat Rin's **full-moon parties** (see box opposite) have established it as the major party venue in Southeast Asia. Comprising two back-to-back beaches, joined by transverse roads at the north and south ends and a whole mess of chaotic development, Hat Rin's geography is ideally suited to an intense party town. The main, eastern beach,

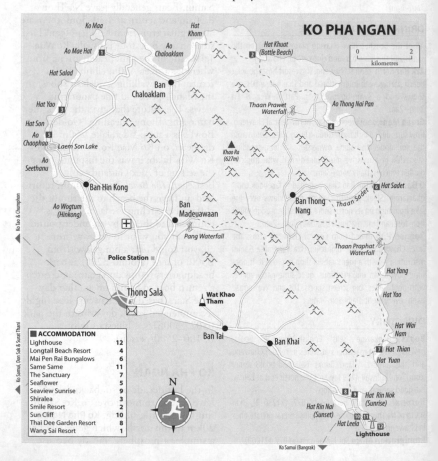

KO PHA NGAN

Ko Maa
Hat Khom
Ao Mae Hat 〔1〕
Ao Chaloaklam
Hat Khuat (Bottle Beach) 〔2〕

0 — kilometres — 2

Hat Salad

Ban Chaloaklam

Hat Yao 〔3〕

Thaan Prawet Waterfall
Ao Thong Nai Pan

Hat Son
Ao Chaophao 〔5〕
Laem Son Lake
〔4〕

Khao Ra (627m)

Ao Seethanu

Ban Hin Kong

Hat Sadet 〔6〕

Ao Wogtum (Hinkong)

Ban Madeuawaan

Ban Thong Nang
Thaan Sadet

Pang Waterfall

Thaan Praphat Waterfall

Police Station

Hat Yang

Thong Sala

Wat Khao Tham

Hat Yao

Hat Wai Nam

Ban Tai

Ban Khai

〔7〕 Hat Thian
Hat Yuan

N

〔8〕〔9〕 Hat Rin Nok (Sunrise)

Hat Rin Nai (Sunset)
〔10〕〔11〕 Hat Leela
〔12〕 Lighthouse

Ko Tao & Chumphon ◀

Ko Samui, Don Sak & Surat Thani ◀

Ko Samui (Bangrak) ▼

ACCOMMODATION	
Lighthouse	12
Longtail Beach Resort	4
Mai Pen Rai Bungalows	6
Same Same	11
The Sanctuary	7
Seaflower	5
Seaview Sunrise	9
Shiralea	3
Smile Resort	2
Sun Cliff	10
Thai Dee Garden Resort	8
Wang Sai Resort	1

usually referred to as **Sunrise** or Hat Rin Nok, is a classic curve of fine sand between two rocky slopes, but with so much boat traffic and its role as a public urinal at full-moon time, these days its waters are far from limpid. **Sunset Beach** (Hat Rin Nai) is often littered with flotsam, but has plenty of quieter accommodation.

The east coast
North of Hat Rin, no roads run along the rocky, exposed **east coast**. Accessible in ten to fifteen minutes by longtail boats from Sunrise are the picturesque bays of Hat Yuan and the small, sandy **Hat Thian**, which make a quiet alternative to Hat Rin.

Inland, a paved road winds for 12km from Ban Tai on the south coast to Ao Thong Nai Pan, at the island's northeast corner. A side road forks east to the gorgeous small bay of **Hat Sadet**, which is framed by large boulders and within walking distance of the beautiful Thaan Sadet waterfall, a favourite of King Rama V and a great place to unwind.

Ao Thong Nai Pan is a beautiful, two-part sandy bay, good for swimming and backed by steep, green hills; it has decent budget accommodation, a few shops, ATMs, dive outfits and restaurants. Songthaews connect with boats at Thong Sala every day.

The north coast
Ao Chaloaklam, the largest bay on the **north coast** with a vibrant fishing village, can easily be reached by songthaew from Thong Sala, 10km away. If the sea is not too rough and there are enough takers, longtail boats run several times a day for most of the year from the village of **Ban Chaloaklam** to the lovely, secluded **Hat Khuat** (Bottle Beach); you could also walk there in about ninety minutes along a testing trail from Hat Khom.

THE FULL MOONERS

The **full-moon parties** on Hat Rin (ⓦfullmoonpartykohphangan.com for dates) attract up to thirty thousand revellers a time to the beach. As there are only around five thousand rooms in Hat Rin, you should book or arrive early. Note that many accommodations insist on a minimum stay of five nights during full-moon period (all sorts of foam, pool and other parties are now organized on the nights around full moon to keep people occupied), up to ten nights for the big Christmas and New Year parties. Alternatively, you can forget about sleep altogether and take the *Had Rin Queen* over from Bangrak on Ko Samui and back in the morning (see p.800); plenty of party boats from Ko Samui are advertised (around B900), but they're often dangerously overcrowded. There's also transport from all the other beaches on Ko Pha Ngan. Partygoers not staying on Hat Rin are charged an admission fee of B100.

On the night, *Paradise* at the south end of Sunrise Beach styles itself as the party host, but the mayhem spreads along most of the beach, fuelled by hastily erected drinks stalls and sound systems. The *Back Yard* club, up the hill behind the southern end of Sunrise, hosts the morning-after.

Drug-related horror stories are common currency in Hat Rin, and some of them are even true: dodgy MDMA, ice and *ya baa* (Burmese-manufactured methamphetamines) and all manner of other concoctions put several *farangs* a month into hospital for psychiatric treatment. The police box at Hat Rin conducts bungalow and personal searches for drugs, pays dealers, bungalow and restaurant owners to inform on travellers whom they've sold drugs to, and drafts in scores of extra officers (both uniformed and plain-clothes) on full-moon nights. Not only that, but the "bucket" sellers on Sunrise Beach replace brand-name spirits with dodgy, illegal, home-brewed alcohol, which can really mess with your head.

Other **tips** for surviving the full moon are mostly common sense: leave your valuables in your resort's safe – it's a bad night for bungalow break-ins – and don't take a bag out with you; keep an eye on your drink to make sure it's not spiked; watch out for broken bottles and anchors on the beach; and do not go swimming while under the influence – there have been several deaths by drowning at previous full-moon parties. There have also been several reports of sexual assaults on women and of unprovoked, late-night gang attacks in Hat Rin, especially around full-moon night.

10

The west coast

Pha Ngan's **west coast** is lush and hilly with good sunset views over the islands to the west; reefs, enclosing most of the bays, keep the sea too shallow for a decent swim, however, especially between May and October.

Ao Chaophao, with its narrow strand and densely foliaged beachfront, is a nice place to relax. Beyond, the long, gently curved beach of **Hat Yao** boasts soft white sand and clear waters, and is becoming deservedly busier and more popular. On the northwest tip of the island, the broad, coarse-sand bay of **Ao Mae Hat** is good for swimming and snorkelling among the coral that lines the sandy causeway to the islet of **Ko Maa**.

ARRIVAL AND DEPARTURE

Kan Airlines (w kanairlines.com) are still hoping to open their much-delayed airport in the northeast corner of the island.

BY BOAT

From Surat Thani A basic overnight boat, with mattresses on the floor, leaves Ban Don pier in Surat Thani at 11pm every night for Thong Sala (7hr; B450); tickets are available from the pier on the day of departure. It returns at 10pm from Thong Sala.

From Don Sak There are five Raja vehicle ferries daily (4hr 30min, B375, including transfer from Surat Thani; w rajaferryport.com), four Lomprayah catamaran sailings (via Ko Samui; 3hr–3hr 30min, B550–650, including transfer from Surat Thani; w lomprayah.com) and two Seatran Discovery sailings (4hr, B680, including transfer from Surat Thani; w seatrandiscovery.com).

From Ko Samui Lomprayah catamarans sail both from Na Thon (4 daily) and from Wat Na Phra Larn at the west end of Maenam (2 daily) to Thong Sala (both 30min; B300). From Bangrak (Big Buddha Beach), the *Had Rin Queen* has four sailings a day to Hat Rin (50min; B200), while Seatran Discovery sails three times a day to Thong Sala (30min; B340). Outside of the rainy season, if there are enough takers, one small boat a day crosses from the pier in Ban Maenam at noon to Hat Rin, before sailing up Pha Ngan's east coast, via Hat Thian and Hat Sadet, to Thong Nai Pan (about 3hr; B400).

From Ko Tao Three Lomprayah catamarans a day (1hr 15min; B500–600) and three Seatran Discovery ferries (1hr 30min; B540) sail to Thong Sala.

From Chumphon Boat services also run from Chumphon (see p.790).

INFORMATION

The free, regularly updated *Phangan Info* guide is available at many outlets, including travel agents. On their website, w phangan.info, you can book accommodation and download their app. The excellent English-Thai travel agency, Backpackers Information Centre, towards the south end of Hat Rin Sunrise, also has a very useful website (w backpackersthailand .com).

ACTIVITIES

Diving Lotus Diving has a dive resort on Ao Chaloaklam (t 077 374142, w lotusdiving.com). A PADI Five-Star centre, it offers frequent courses and trips to Sail Rock, halfway between Pha Ngan and Tao.

Kiteboarding Kiteboarding Asia, just west of Ban Tai (t 080 600 0573, w kiteboardingasia.com), offers kiteboarding, stand-up paddleboarding and wakeboarding.

ACCOMMODATION

HAT RIN

Beachside budget accommodation is gradually being replaced by more upmarket resorts, but dormitory guesthouses – most open only during full moon – are found in the road network between the two beaches (as well as in the village of Ban Tai to the west).

Lighthouse On the tip of the Hat Rin peninsula, beyond Leela Beach t 084 911 3454. At this friendly haven, fan-cooled wooden and concrete en-suite bungalows, sturdily built into the rock to withstand the wind, are priced according to size and comfort; all have good-sized balconies with hammocks. The restaurant food is varied and tasty. Phone for a pick-up from Sunset pier or Thong Sala, or do the 30min walk from *Chicken Corner* in the centre of Hat Rin, the last section along a wooden walkway over the rocky shoreline. Doubles B600

Same Same Above the south end of Sunrise at the start of the road to Leela Beach t 077 375200, w same-same .com. A sociable and well-run Danish guesthouse offering good-value rooms, all en suite, colourful and clean, some with a/c (including the dorms). There's a decent restaurant downstairs with a bar and a long list of excuses to party to a mainstream soundtrack. Dorms B500, doubles B550

Seaview Sunrise Northern end of Sunrise t 077 375160, w seaviewsunrise.com. On a big plot of shady, flower-strewn land at the quieter end of the beach, this clean, friendly, orderly old-timer with a good restaurant offers more than forty bungalows and rooms. The bungalows on the beachfront are all fan-cooled with hot showers. Further back are a/c versions, as well as the cheapest rooms with cold showers. Comparatively small price rise at full moon. Minimum stay two nights (five at full moon). Doubles B500

Sun Cliff High up on the tree-lined slope above the south end of Sunset Beach ☎077 375134 or ☎077 375463, ✉rsvnsuncliff@hotmail.com. Friendly, spacious place with great views of the south coast and Ko Samui, especially from its heart-shaped pool by the restaurant. Among a wide range of fan and a/c bungalows that are a bit rough around the edges, you'll find some quirky architectural features such as rock-built bathrooms and fountains; some have huge decks for partying. Doubles B500

Thai Dee Garden Resort Northern transverse ☎098 701 8898, ⓦthaideegarden.com. Pleasant staff and a range of smart concrete and white clapboard bungalows, on a broad, grassy slope strewn with trees and plants and set back from the road. Choose either fan and cold water or a/c and hot. Not on the beach, so one of the last places to fill at full moon. Doubles B950

THE EAST AND NORTH COASTS

Many of the resorts here provide shuttles at B200/person from or to Thong Sala Pier.

Longtail Beach Resort At the far southern end of Thong Nai Pan ☎077 445018, ⓦlongtailbeachresort.com. In quiet, leafy rows on either side of two long strips of lawn that run down to the attractive beachfront restaurant and small swimming pool, these wooden en-suite bungalows are well designed and maintained; all have verandahs and hammocks, most have hot showers and a/c. Doubles B690

★**Mai Pen Rai Bungalows** Hat Sadet ☎080 719 0700, ⓦthansadet.com. On the beach within a short walk of the waterfalls, this welcoming spot has a wide variety of attractive accommodation with airy bathrooms, fans and hammocks (some with big upstairs terraces), either on the beach at the stream mouth or scattered around the rocks for good views. Doubles B580

★**The Sanctuary** Hat Thian ☎081 271 3614, ⓦthesanctuarythailand.com. This magical fairyland, connected by a labyrinth of dirt paths, offers a huge range of basic and luxury en-suite bungalows built into the lush promontory. It also hosts courses in yoga and meditation, and has a spa and a wellness and detox centre. The beautiful timber restaurant serves up healthy plates with a great selection of vegetarian food. Dorms B350, doubles B950

Smile Resort Western end of Bottle Beach ☎085 429 4995, ⓦsmilebungalows.com. Set on a rocky slope strewn with flowers and trees on the western side of the beach, with fun owners, a sociable bar-restaurant area and kayaks for paddling around the bay. The basic en-suite bungalows come with wall fans and mosquito nets. Doubles B520

THE WEST COAST

★**Seaflower** Ao Chaophao ☎077 349090, ⓦseaflowerbungalows.com. Quiet spot, set in a lush garden, with good veggie and non-veggie food. Smart,

large bungalows with a/c and hot-water bathrooms vary in price according to their size and distance from the beach. Kayaks are available, as well as free pick-ups from Thong Sala with advance notice. Doubles B1200

Shiralea Hat Yao ☎077 349217, ⓦshiralea.com. On a broad, grassy bank beneath coconut trees behind the north end of the beach, the spacious, very attractive thatched bungalows here all come with hot water and verandahs with hammocks, and there's a seductive pool, smart a/c dormitories and a sociable atmosphere. Dorms B250, doubles B600

Wang Sai Resort Ao Mae Hat ☎077 374238, ⓦwangsairesort.com. Popular, friendly spot by a shady creek at the south end of the bay. On a huge plot of land, most of the en-suite bungalows are set back from the beach, including the cheapest options, with fans and cold showers, which are set on a slope with great sunset views. On-site dive school and kayaks and snorkels for rent. Doubles B1200

DIRECTORY

In the dense tourist village of Hat Rin you will easily find supermarkets, travel agents, motorbike rental places (from B200/day), plenty of ATMs and currency exchange booths.

Hospital 3km north of Thong Sala, on the road towards Mae Hat (☎077 377034), plus plenty of private clinics in Hat Rin and a 24hr volunteer emergency rescue service (☎077 377500), but for anything serious you'll need to be transferred to Ko Samui.

Police The main station is 2km up the Ban Chaloaklam road from Thong Sala (☎077 377114), and there's a sub-station on Hat Rin.

Post office About 500m southeast of the piers on Thong Sala's old main street (Mon–Fri 8.30am–noon & 1–4.30pm, Sat 9am–noon).

KO TAO

Forty kilometres north of Ko Pha Ngan, small, forested **Ko Tao** is the last and most remote island of the archipelago, with a long curve of classic beach on its west side, **Hat Sai Ree**, and secluded rocky coves along its east coast. It's a popular travellers' destination, especially from December to March. Ko Tao feels the southwest monsoon more than Samui and Pha Ngan, so June to October can have strong winds and rain.

Blessed with clear seas (visibility up to 35m), a wide range of coral species and other marine life, and deep water

10

10

relatively close to shore, Ko Tao is one of Thailand's premier **diving** locations. Diving is possible year-round, but visibility is best from April to July, and in September (usually best of all) and October; November, during the northeast monsoon, is the worst time.

If you're just arriving and want to stay on one of the less accessible beaches, it might be a good idea to hook up with one of the touts who meet the ferries at **Mae Hat**, the island's main village, with pick-up or longtail boat on hand; otherwise call ahead, as most bungalow owners come to market once a day (pick-ups are either free or B50–150/person). Note that some resorts with attached scuba-diving operations have been known to refuse guests who don't sign up for diving trips or courses.

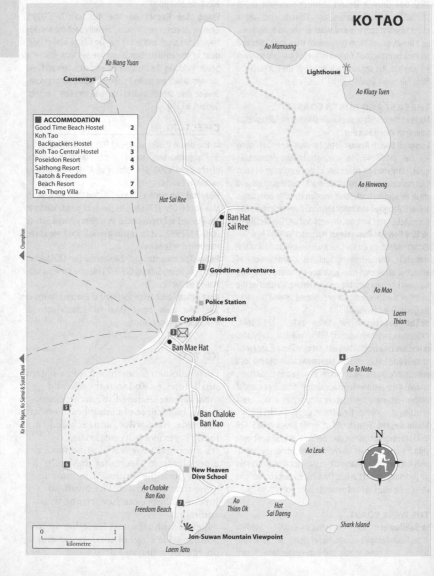

KO TAO

Ao Mamuang

Ko Nang Yuan

Lighthouse

Ao Kluay Tuen

Causeways

ACCOMMODATION
Good Time Beach Hostel	2
Koh Tao Backpackers Hostel	1
Koh Tao Central Hostel	3
Poseidon Resort	4
Saithong Resort	5
Taatoh & Freedom Beach Resort	7
Tao Thong Villa	6

Ao Hinwong

Hat Sai Ree

Chumphon

1 Ban Hat Sai Ree

2 Goodtime Adventures

Ao Mao

Police Station

Laem Thian

Crystal Dive Resort

3 Ban Mae Hat

Ko Pha Ngan, Ko Samui & Surat Thani

4 Ao Ta Note

5

Ban Chaloke Ban Kao

6

Ao Leuk

New Heaven Dive School

N

Ao Chaloke Ban Kao

7

Freedom Beach

Ao Thian Ok

Hat Sai Daeng

Shark Island

Jon-Suwan Mountain Viewpoint

Laem Tato

0 ___ 1
kilometre

The west coast

All boats to the island dock at **BAN MAE HAT**, a small, lively village with the most facilities on the island. On the roads leading inland from the main pier and the neighbouring Seatran pier, and on the narrow coastal road that extends north and south of them, you'll find bars, restaurants, bakeries, motorbike rental, banks and more.

To the north of Mae Hat, **Hat Sai Ree** is Ko Tao's only long beach. The strip of white sand stretches for 2km in a gentle curve, backed by a smattering of coconut palms and scores of bungalow resorts. Goodtime Adventures, towards the southern end of the beach (☎087 275 3604, ⓦgoodtimethailand.com), are the main organizers of land- and water-based activities on the island, offering **rock-climbing**, **abseiling** and **hiking**, as well as snorkelling, diving and other watersports. Around the northerly end of the beach spreads **BAN HAT SAI REE**, a village of supermarkets, clinics, pharmacies, ATMs, currency exchange booths, restaurants and bars.

Ko Nang Yuan

One kilometre off the northwest of Ko Tao are the three tiny islands of **Ko Nang Yuan**. Encircled by a ring of coral and joined by a causeway of fine white sand, these are arguably one of the most beautiful sights in Thailand, though they do get very crowded. You can easily swim off the east side of the causeway to snorkel over the Japanese Gardens, which feature hundreds of hard and soft coral formations. Longtail taxis from Mae Hat

charge B200/person each way; day-trippers are charged B100 to land on the island, and cans, plastic bottles and fins are banned.

The east and south coasts

The sheltered inlets of the **east coast**, most of them containing at least one or two sets of bungalows, can be reached by boat, pick-up or four-wheel-drive. **Ao Ta Note**, a horseshoe inlet with half a dozen resorts, is a good option for watersports and relaxation. It's sprinkled with boulders and plenty of coarse sand, with excellent snorkelling just north of the bay's mouth.

On the **south coast**, the main bay, deeply indented **Ao Chaloke Ban Kao**, is protected from the worst of both monsoons. Consequently it has seen a fair amount of development, with several dive resorts taking advantage of the sheltered, shallow bay which sometimes gets muddy at low tide.

ARRIVAL AND DEPARTURE

BY BOAT

Boat services and prices fluctuate according to demand, and in high season extra boats may appear.

From Chumphon and Bangkok The main jumping-off point for boats to Ko Tao is Chumphon (see p.790), which is connected to Bangkok by train, bus and plane. The two main Chumphon–Tao boat companies both offer through-tickets from Bangkok; with Lomprayah (on Ko Tao ☎077 456176, ⓦlomprayah.com), for example, this costs B1100, including a VIP bus from their office on Th Ram Bhuttri in Banglamphu (☎02 629 2569–70).

From Ko Pha Ngan and Ko Samui Boats between Thong Sala on Ko Pha Ngan and Ko Tao are operated by Lomprayah (see above) and Seatran (on Ko Tao ☎077

DIVING ON KO TAO

Ko Tao has fifty or so **dive companies**, making this the largest training centre in Southeast Asia. **Operators** include Crystal (☎077 456106, ⓦcrystaldive.com), a large, sociable PADI Five-Star Career Development Centre on the north side of Ban Mae Hat; and at the other end of the scale, small, personal and laidback New Heaven on Chaloke Ban Kao (☎077 457045, ⓦnewheavendiveschool.com). Both of these companies have a strong commitment to marine conservation (also check out Crystal's marine conservation website, ⓦecokohtao.com).

COSTS

PADI's four-day Open Water course for beginners costs B9000–10,500; you can usually get reduced-cost accommodation and insurance with your diving school. For qualified divers, one dive typically costs B1000, a ten-dive package around B7000.

10

10

456907, ⓦ seatrandiscovery.com), who cover the ground in about 1hr 30min (both 3 daily; B500–600). The Lomprayah catamaran originates at Maenam, Seatran at Bangrak, on Ko Samui (total journey time to Ko Tao on either is about 2hr–2hr 30min; B600–700).

From Surat Thani Lomprayah's catamarans sail from Don Sak pier twice daily via Samui and Pha Ngan, usually with a change of boat at Pha Ngan (total journey time from Surat about 5hr; B700–800 including bus to the pier from Surat Thani). There's a night boat from Ban Don pier in Surat Thani town, departing at around 10pm (ⓣ 077 284928; 8hr; B550); in the opposite direction, this leaves Ko Tao at around 9pm.

GETTING AROUND

You can get around easily enough on foot, but there are roads of sorts now to most of the resorts, though many are still very rough, steep tracks, suitable for four-wheel-drive only. A paved road extends down the west coast from north to south (ending at Ao Chaloke), and the road eastwards to Ao Ta Note is mostly paved.

By taxi Pick-up taxis are available in Mae Hat (B100–150/person to Chaloke Ban Kao, for example, minimum 2 people; rates are higher at night, or for a 4WD to somewhere more remote).

By motorbike Rental motorbikes are available from B150/day. If you can, resist the temptation to rent a quad bike, or ATV – not only do they have a disproportionate number of accidents, but they're also very polluting. There have been lots of reports of travellers being charged exorbitant amounts if they bring the vehicle back with even the most minor damage – rent from your bungalow or someone reliable like Island Travel (see below).

By boat Round-island boat tours are available at Mae Hat or through your bungalow, with stops for snorkelling and swimming (from B650/person, including lunch and pick-ups, or around B2000 to rent your own longtail boat for the day).

INFORMATION

Tourist information The regularly updated and widely available free booklet, *Ko Tao Info*, is a useful source of information, along with its associated website, ⓦ kohtaoonline.com, which features online accommodation booking.

ACCOMMODATION

Most dive schools now have their own accommodation and will often throw in a discounted or free room with a dive course.

WEST COAST

Good Time Beach Hostel South end of Hat Sai Ree ⓣ 061 461 0933, ⓦ goodtimethailand.com. Sociable hostel run by the island's adventure specialists (see

p.803), who offer Sunday booze cruises and monthly parties. Smart, well-equipped six- to ten-person dorms, some with balconies on the beach, have a/c and hot showers. Dorms B500

Koh Tao Backpackers Hostel Middle of Sai Ree village, inland from *Silver Sands Resort* ⓣ 088 447 7921, ⓦ kohtaobackpackers.com. A popular choice offering four- to eight-bed dormitories with a/c and hot showers in good, shared facilities. There are security lockers, a swimming pool and a bar/restaurant. Dorms B300

Koh Tao Central Hostel On the Seatran road in Ban Mae Hat ⓣ 077 456925, ⓦ kohtaohostel.com. English-run hostel – look for the London Underground logo – attached to the Island Travel travel agency and *The Reef* sports bar and restaurant and very handy for the piers. Smart, partitioned dorm beds with a/c and hot showers. Dorms B340

Saithong Resort Sai Nuan beach, 1hr walk south of Mae Hat pier ⓣ 077 456868. An isolated, shady place, with soft sand on two small beaches, offering various types of bungalows with cold showers and mosquito nets, either in gardens or perched on the rocks – the latter with stunning sea views. Free snorkels. Doubles B500

Tao Thong Villa 1hr walk south of Mae Hat, or get there by pick-up or boat taxi ⓣ 077 456078. Sturdy, en-suite bungalows dotted around the rocky outcrop of Cape Jeda Gang and the slope behind, with a breezy restaurant on the tiny, grassy isthmus with two small beaches in between. Plenty of shady seclusion, great views and good snorkelling and swimming. Doubles B500

EAST COAST

Poseidon Resort Ao Ta Note ⓣ 077 456734, ⓦ poseidontao.atspace.com. Basic en-suite bungalows with balconies and hammocks, set back a little from the beach on the flower-strewn, rocky slopes. There is a traveller vibe, a stargazing cocktail bar above a restaurant and kayaks and snorkels for rent. Doubles B600

SOUTH COAST

Taatoh & Freedom Beach Resort Ao Chaloke Ban Kao ⓣ 077 456596, ⓦ taatoh.com. Two combined resorts with their own private beaches; white-sand *Freedom Beach* is a particularly lovely spot. The cheaper en-suite, balconied bungalows here are perched on the hillside above, some offering beautiful views. Doubles B900

DIRECTORY

Health Mae Hat has a small government health centre (halfway up the high street from the main pier, turn right), plus several private clinics, pharmacies and diving medicine clinics.

Police A 5min walk on the narrow coast path heading north from Mae Hat (ⓣ 077 456631).

Post office At the top of the road leading inland from the Seatran pier in Ban Mae Hat (Mon–Fri 9am–noon & 1–5pm, Sat 9am–noon).

Travel agent Reliable, English-run Island Travel is on the Seatran road in Ban Mae Hat (parallel to and north of the high street; ☎ 077 456769, ⌨ islandtravelkohtao.com).

NAKHON SI THAMMARAT

NAKHON SI THAMMARAT, a seldom-visited but bustling town, is the south's religious capital. A major Buddhist pilgrimage site, it is also well known for its traditional handicrafts, shadow plays and especially its festivals. The biggest of these is Tamboon Deuan Sip every September/October, which is marked by a ten-day fair at Thung Talaat park on the north side of town, as well as processions, shadow plays and other theatrical shows.

WHAT TO SEE AND DO

The town runs 7km from north to south, to either side of Thanon Ratchadamnoen (the third parallel street, east of the rail line), which is served by frequent blue share-songthaews. The south's most important temple, **Wat Mahathat**, is on this road, about 2km south of the town centre. Its courtyard is dominated by the huge Sri Lankan-style chedi enshrining relics of the Buddha, around which are arrayed row upon row of smaller chedis, an Aladdin's cave of a temple museum, and local handicraft stalls. A few minutes' walk south of Wat Mahathat on the same road is the **National Museum** (Wed–Sun 9am–noon & 1–4pm; B150), which houses a small but diverse collection covering prehistoric finds, Buddha images and ceramics.

For the best possible introduction to southern Thailand's **shadow puppet theatre**, head for 110/18 Soi 3, Th Si Thammasok (☎075 346394), ten minutes' walk and two blocks east of Wat Mahathat – the easiest way is to walk north, turn right along Thanon Panyom, turn right again onto Thanon Si Thammasok, then left into Soi 3. Here at Ban Suchart Subsin, you can visit a museum of puppetry and watch excerpts from a shadow play (B50/person). You can also buy puppets and see them being made.

ARRIVAL AND INFORMATION

By plane The airport is around 20km northwest of Nakhon, costing around B300 in a taxi. There are five flights daily from Bangkok (1hr 10min) with Nok Air, four with AirAsia, four with Thai Lion Air; Nok Air and Air Asia offer through-tickets to Ko Samui and Ko Pha Ngan, via the nearby piers at Don Sak.

By bus Nakhon's bus and a/c minibus terminal, southwest of the train station on the other side of the river, is a cheap songthaew or motorbike taxi ride from town.

Destinations Bangkok (10 daily; 12hr); Don Sak (hourly; 2hr); Krabi (hourly; 3–4hr); Phuket (hourly; 6hr); Surat Thani (every 30min; 2hr–2hr 30min); Trang (hourly; 3hr).

By train Nakhon's train station is on the west side of the town centre. There are two trains to Bangkok daily (14–16hr).

Tourist information The very helpful TAT office is south of the centre, just off Th Ratchadamnoen in Sanam Na Muang park (daily 8.30am–4.30pm; ☎075 346515 6, ✉ tatnksri@tat.or.th).

ACCOMMODATION AND EATING

There's a busy, colourful night market on Th Chamroenwithi south of the train station.

★**Krua Thale** Th Pak Nakhon, opposite the *Nakorn Garden Inn* (no English sign – look for the Coke sign). The town's best restaurant, renowned among locals for its excellent, varied and inexpensive seafood. Plain and very clean, with an open kitchen and the day's catch displayed out front, and relaxing patio tables at the back. Recommended dishes include very good *yam plaa duk foo*, shredded and deep-fried catfish with a mango salad dip (B120). Daily 4–10pm.

★**Nakorn Garden Inn** 1/4 Th Pak Nakhon (the road running east from the train station, about 500m along) ☎075 313333. Large, nicely appointed rooms set on three floors in red-brick buildings overlooking a tree-shaded courtyard. All have a/c, hot water, cable TV and minibars. Doubles B445

The Andaman coast

The landscape along the Andaman coast is lushly tropical and spiked with dramatic limestone crags, best appreciated by staying in **Khao Sok National Park** or taking a boat trip around the bizarre **Ao Phang Nga Bay**. Most people, however, come here for the beaches and the coral reefs. **Phuket** is

10

10

Thailand's largest island, though it's overdeveloped and hugely commercial. **Ko Phi Phi** and **Ao Nang** are heading the same way, but retain their great natural beauty. The **Similan Islands**, located further north, are among the best dive sites in Thailand. Meanwhile, **Ko Chang**, **Ko Phayam**, **Laem Phra Nang** and **Ko Lanta** have great beaches and a laidback vibe where you can kick back for weeks on end. The Andaman coast is hit by the southwest monsoon from May to October, when the rain and high seas render some of the outer islands inaccessible and litter many beaches with debris, so prices drop significantly during this period.

RANONG

The multi-ethnic provincial capital of **RANONG** is chiefly of interest as a stepping-off point for boats to Ko Chang and Ko Phayam. It's well linked to major towns, being on the bus route from Bangkok to Phuket.

ARRIVAL AND INFORMATION

By plane Nok Air fly to Ranong from Bangkok's Don Muang Airport (2 daily; 1hr 10min–1hr 35min). *Pon's Place* organize a/c minibuses from the airport to town or the pier (B200/person).

By bus Most services between Bangkok (13 daily) and Phuket (8 daily) or other points south stop at the bus terminal, 1.5km southeast of the centre on Highway 4, Th Phetkasem. Hourly a/c minibuses to and from Chumphon and Surat Thani also use the bus terminal. Songthaew #2 or #6 can take you to the main street, Th Ruangrat (B15).

By boat To get to the islands pier, take songthaew #3 or #6 (B20) from the market on Th Ruangrat, or #6 from the bus station, to Saphan Pla 5km southwest, then it's a 500m walk south from the main road to the pier.

INTO MYANMAR: KAWTHAUNG

Kawthaung, which lies across the Chan River estuary from Ranong, can be used as an entry point for travelling in Myanmar if you already have a Burmese visa (though its position in the far south doesn't make it the most convenient option), or for a visa run; in either case, it's best to arrange the complex practicalities at *Pon's Place* (see below).

Tourist information There is no official TAT office in town, but *Pon's Place* restaurant and travel agency offers good information on the islands and sells transport tickets.

ACCOMMODATION AND EATING

Madinah Hostel 11/8 Th Kamlangsap ⊕077 984791. Friendly new hostel on the east side of town, with smart a/c dorms and en-suite private rooms, all with hot showers. Dorms B250, doubles B550

Pon's Place North of the market at 92/1 Th Ruangrat ⊕081 597 4549 or ⊕077 823344. The obvious place to eat while you plan your next move, offering Western breakfasts, Thai food, traditional coffee and free wi-fi. Daily 8am–7pm.

KO CHANG

Not to be confused with the much larger Ko Chang on Thailand's east coast (see p.785), Ranong's **Ko Chang** is an ultra-laidback forested island about 5km offshore, with a charmingly low-key atmosphere and many long-stay Europeans. The beaches are connected by tracks through the trees; there are only a couple of cars on the island and sporadic electricity. At the moment, there's barely any commercial activity on Ko Chang save for a couple of local mini-markets and a dive operator, Aladdin, at *Cashew Resort* on Ao Yai (also at the island's pier in Saphan Pla; ⊕087 274 7601, ⦿aladdindivesafari.com), who organize Surin, Similan Islands and Myanmar live-aboards and PADI courses, as well as day-trips. The prettiest (and longest) beach on the island is **Ao Yai**, which arches its way along the mid-west coast.

ARRIVAL AND DEPARTURE

By boat In high season, roughly from early November to late April, from Saphan Pla (see above), there are two daily boat departures to Ko Chang's west coast, stopping at most resorts (1hr 30min; B200), and at least two daily speedboats to the pier on Ko Chang's east coast (30min; B350, including transfer to your resort). In low season, though it's sometimes cancelled in the rainy season, a daily boat runs from Saphan Pla to the pier on Ko Chang's east coast (1hr; B150), from where a motorbike taxi can take you to your resort.

ACCOMMODATION

The dozen or so family-run bungalow operations are mostly scattered along the west coast, many of them hidden among the shore-front trees on Ao Yai; they nearly all close May–Oct. Most of them are simple constructions with mosquito nets on the beds; you shouldn't necessarily expect flush toilets (buckets and dippers are provided). Though the bungalow resorts nearly all have their own generators (which usually only operate in the evenings), some stick to candles and paraffin lamps so you should bring a torch; very few bungalows have fans.

Cashew Resort North end of Ao Yai ☎081 485 6002, ⓦfacebook.com/cashewresort. The largest outfit, *Cashew* feels like a tiny village, with its forty en-suite, sea-view bungalows spread among the cashew trees along 700m of prime beachfront. The resort offers the most facilities on the island, including foreign exchange and bus reservations, and its restaurant bakes bread and serves Thai and a few German dishes. Doubles B300

★**Crocodile Rock** ☎081 370 1434, ⓦfacebook.com /crocodilerockbungalows. In a shady, elevated position at the start of Ao Yai's southern headland, with great views of the whole bay, on which the friendly owners have capitalized, with attractive decks at the restaurant, hammocks on every bungalow and picture windows in some of the bathrooms. Bungalows, some of which have nice pebbledash bathrooms, have a touch more style than the Ko Chang average. The restaurant bakes its own bread, and serves espresso coffee. Doubles B400

Sawasdee Resort By a stream at the far southern end of Ao Yai ☎084 846 5828, ⓦsawasdeekohchang.com. This welcoming place has twelve thoughtfully designed, even stylish wooden bungalows with big decks and good bathrooms. There's an attractive restaurant, serving a wide variety of Thai dishes and plenty of vegetarian options, with decks and terraces under the shady trees. Doubles B350

KO PHAYAM

Diminutive **KO PHAYAM**, measuring just 5 by 8km, is home to some fine white-sand beaches and relaxing beachfront bungalows connected by a network of winding concrete paths. Behind the beaches, the island is covered in rubber, cashew and palm plantations. Slightly more developed than Ko Chang (though it, too, has no ATMs), it has 24hr electricity and wi-fi at most resorts, a fledgling though still very low-key bar scene, several dive shops, including a branch of Aladdin (see opposite), and a **village** at the port comprising several small shops, restaurants and a clinic. Motorbike rental (from B200) is available in the village or at the bungalows, many of which close down during the wet season (June–Oct).

Ko Phayam's nicest beach is the 3km-long **Ao Yai** on the southwest coast, a beautiful sweep of soft white sand that occasionally gets pounded by large waves. Across on the northwest coast, the prettiest stretch of beach is the northern part of **Ao Kao Kwai** (also known as Ao Kao Fai, or Buffalo Horn Bay).

ARRIVAL AND DEPARTURE

By boat There are slow boats (1–3 daily; 2hr; B200) to Ko Phayam from Saphan Pla (see opposite). In high season, roughly from November to May, there are also between four and eight daily speedboat services (45min; B310–350). Motorbike taxis meet incoming boats at the pier in Ko Phayam village and charge B80 to most bungalows.

ACCOMMODATION

Aow Yai Bungalow Southern end of Ao Yai ☎098 313 1777, ⓦaowyaibungalows.com. French–Thai resort with more than twenty good-quality en-suite bungalows of various styles, dotted around an extensive garden of flowers, fruit trees and palms. Body boards, surfboards and kayaks available. Doubles B700

Bamboo Bungalows Central Ao Yai ☎077 820012, ⓦbamboo-bungalows.com. Israeli–Thai managed and very traveller-savvy, with kayaks, snorkels, surf- and boogie-boards, and currency exchange. Its en-suite bungalows are set under the trees in a well-tended flower garden and all have fans. Doubles B600

Coconut Beach Resort Ao Yai ☎089 920 8145, ⓦkoh-phayam.com. Occupying a great spot in the centre of the bay and run by a Ko Phayam family, the en-suite bungalows here are of a high standard, each set in its own tiny garden, and there's a good restaurant. Kayaks and snorkels available. Doubles B300

★**PP Land** East coast, 10min walk north of the village ☎081 678 4310, ⓦppland-heavenbeach.com. Fronting a small beach, this eco-friendly Belgian–Thai place has tasteful thatched bungalows with polished wood floors, nice bathrooms and big decks, as well as an attractive swimming pool. Doubles B900

Starlight Bungalows Northern end of Ao Kao Kwai ☎081 978 5301, ⓦphayambooking.com. Not the cheapest on Kao Kwai, but very laidback and peaceful at the best stretch of beach. There is a restaurant with a fabulous stargazing deck, tasty food and bamboo and wood or brick en-suite bungalows. Doubles B700

EATING AND DRINKING

Most visitors eat and drink at their resort, but there are several laidback little beach-bars, including *Rasta Baby* at the north end of Ao Yai and *Hippie Bar* at the north end of Ao Kao Khwai, that put on fireshows and occasional parties.

10

10

Bamboo Bungalows Central Ao Yai. Tasty pasta, schnitzels, sandwiches and breakfasts at this beachfront restaurant (Western dishes around B150–200), as well as home-baked wholewheat bread and lots of Thai standards. Daily 7.45am–10pm.

KHAO SOK NATIONAL PARK

Whether you're heading down the Andaman or the Gulf coast, the stunning jungle-clad limestone crags of **Khao Sok National Park** (B300, valid for 24hr) are well worth veering inland for.

WHAT TO SEE AND DO

Much of the park is carpeted in impenetrable rainforest, home to gaurs, leopard cats and tigers among others – and up to 155 species of bird – but it offers a number of easy trails. The park has two centres: the **tourist village** that has grown up on the access road to the park headquarters, which offers ATMs and currency exchange; and the dam, 65km further east, at the head of **Cheow Lan Lake**, which has some scenic rafthouse accommodation. Most visitors stay in the tourist village and organize their lake trips from there.

The trails

Seven of the park's nine attractions (waterfalls, pools, gorges and viewpoints) branch off the clearly signed main **trail** that runs west of the park headquarters, along the Sok River (sketch map available from the park checkpoint). Most people walk to **Ton Kloi waterfall**, 7km from headquarters (allow 3hr each way), which tumbles into a pool that's good for swimming.

Cheow Lan Lake

With photogenic karst islands and mist-clad mountains encircling jade-coloured waters, the vast **Cheow Lan Lake** (aka **Ratchabrapa Dam**) is Khao Sok's most famous feature. Tours generally combine a longtail trip on the reservoir with a trek through the nearby flooded cave system and a night on a floating rafthouse.

For many people, the highlight of the park is the three-hour hike through **Nam Talu cave**. The **trek** is not for everyone, however, as the cave section entails an hour-long wade through the river and there will be at least one 20m section where you have to swim. Never attempt the cave without an authorized park guide; in October 2007 a flash flood caused nine fatalities here. Wear sandals with decent grip and check if the tour leader will provide a torch.

ARRIVAL AND DEPARTURE

Khao Sok Track & Trail in the tourist village (☏ 081 958 0629, ⊛ khaosoktrackandtrail.com) sells bus (including a VIP bus to Bangkok) and boat tickets, as well as tickets for a/c minibuses to destinations that include Krabi (2hr 30min) and Surat Thani (2hr), its airport and the train station at Phunphin.

By bus All buses between the west-coast junction town of Takua Pa and Surat Thani pass the main park entrance, including some Surat Thani services to and from Khao Lak and Phuket. If you're coming by bus from Bangkok or Chumphon, take a Surat Thani-bound bus, but ask to be dropped off at the junction with the Takua Pa road, about 20km before Surat Thani, and then change onto a Takua Pa bus. At the start of the access road to the tourist village and headquarters (less than 2km away), guesthouse staff usually meet bus passengers and offer free lifts to their accommodation; otherwise, call your guesthouse for a pick-up or walk.

Destinations Bangkok (1 daily; 10hr 30min); Khao Lak (3 daily; 1hr 30min); Surat Thani (every 90min; 2hr); Takua Pa (every 90min; 1hr).

GUIDED TREKS AND TOURS OF KHAO SOK

Most visitors join one of their guesthouse's **guided treks** at some point during their stay, as they're fun, informative and inexpensive. The usual **day trek** (B700–900) goes to Ton Kloi waterfall, and from about December to March there's a special route that takes in the blooming of the world's second-biggest flower, the **rafflesia kerrii meier**; it's also known as "stinking corpse lily" because of its smell. **Night safaris** along the main park trails (B500–800 for 2–4hr) are also popular. You get to stay out in the jungle on the **overnight camping trips** (about B2500), usually around Tan Sawan falls. Khao Sok guesthouses charge around B1500 for a day-trip to Cheow Lan Lake and B2500 for two-day, one-night trips.

ACCOMMODATION

As well as guided treks and trips to Cheow Lan Lake, guesthouses can arrange elephant rides and fix you up with equipment and transfers for tubing, bamboo rafting and canoeing trips along the Sok River. Just north of the river, a side road leads east off the north–south access road to many guesthouses, including *Nung House*.

Khao Sok Jungle Huts East off the north–south access road, south of the river ☎077 395160, ⓦ khaosokjunglehuts.com. You're bound to find a hut you like at this family-run spot in a large garden by the river, among a huge range of en-suite accommodation with verandahs on stilts, most with hot showers; there's a decent restaurant, too. Doubles B400

★**Morning Mist Resort** On the north–south access road, just south of the river ☎089 971 8794. Built within a profuse riverside garden, this well-run place offers large, immaculate rooms in variously styled wooden and concrete bungalows, all with hot water. Small swimming pool and excellent restaurant. Doubles B650

Nung House ☎077 380723, ⓦ nunghouse.com. Friendly place known for its trekking options, with very good huts set around an attractive grassy garden full of rambutan trees. Choose either simple but sturdy bamboo and wood constructions with en-suite facilities, or brick and concrete bungalows; some have hot showers. Attached are a good Thai and Western restaurant and the chilled *Nirvana Bar*. Doubles B300

KHAO LAK AND KO SIMILAN

Just an hour north of Phuket International Airport, **KHAO LAK** has established itself as a mid-market beach resort, with opportunities for diving and snorkelling at the supreme national park reefs of **Ko Similan**, and a style that is determinedly unseedy. It is mostly a bit pricey for backpackers, but is extremely popular with northern European tourists.

The area usually referred to as Khao Lak is in fact a string of beaches west off Highway 4. **Khao Lak** proper is the southernmost and least developed, 5km from the most commercial part of the resort, **Nang Thong** (aka Bang La On), which throngs with restaurants, dive centres, banks, ATMs, clinics, a post office (at its north end) and countless places to stay, both on the beachfront and inland from Highway 4. North again about 3km is lower-key **Bang Niang**, a lovely long stretch of golden sand that's backed by a developing tourist village with a network of sois and mostly upmarket accommodation.

There is little obvious evidence these days of the December 2004 **tsunami**, when the undersea earthquake off Sumatra sent a series of waves on to Khao Lak's shores, vaporizing almost every shorefront home and hotel here and killing thousands.

ARRIVAL AND DEPARTURE

By bus All buses running from Phuket to Takua Pa and Ranong (and vice versa) pass through Khao Lak and can drop you anywhere along Highway 4; coming from Krabi or Phang Nga, you'll generally need to change buses in Khokkloi; from Khao Sok, in Takua Pa. On departure, you can flag down most buses on the main road, but the Bangkok services use a bus station at the far north end of Bang Niang. A/c tourist minibuses to Krabi, Surat Thani and elsewhere can be arranged with any local tour company.

Destinations Bangkok (4 daily; 12hr); Phuket (20 daily; 2hr 30min); Ranong (8 daily; 2hr 30min–3hr); Takua Pa (20 daily; 30min).

GETTING AROUND

By songthaew A few public songthaews shuttle between Nang Thong and Bang Niang (where they have a base in

10

TSUNAMI MEMORIALS

In Bang Niang, set back on the east side of Highway 4, a **beached police boat** stands as a memorial to the tsunami's power – it was propelled up here, 2km inland, while patrolling the waters in front of *La Flora* resort, where Princess Ubolrat and her children, one of whom perished in the disaster, were staying.

The main local tsunami memorial is on the beach at **Ban Nam Khem**, the worst-hit village in Thailand, where half of the four thousand inhabitants died in the waves; it lies 25km north of Bang Niang up Highway 4, then left for a signposted 3km. Built by the Thai army, it's an evocative installation: you walk down a path between a curling, 4m-high, concrete "wave" and a grassy bank, representing the land, on which plaques commemorate individual victims. Through a window in the concrete wave, a fishing boat looms over you – this "miracle boat" was swept inland but stopped just short of devastating a house and its occupants.

10

front of the market), charging around B20, but mostly they act as private taxis instead and charge B100 or more.

By motorbike Motorbikes are available for rent on all beaches and through guesthouses (from B250/day).

DIVING AND SNORKELLING

There are plenty of snorkelling and diving trips to the spectacular reefs off Ko Similan (roughly Nov–April), 2hr away by speedboat. This archipelago of nine islands offers visibility of up to 30m and an enormous diversity of underwater species. The prices here include the national park fees.

IQ Dive Nang Thong, opposite *McDonald's* ☎076 485614, ⓦ iq-dive.com. Swiss–Thai-run dive centre that specializes in one-day dive trips to the Similans, on a big dive boat (B5200; B3200 for snorkellers).

Sea Dragon Dive Center Across from Nang Thong supermarket ☎076 485420, ⓦ seadragondivecenter .com. Highly regarded and the longest-running Khao Lak dive operator, Sea Dragon operate both budget and deluxe live-aboard dive trips to the islands (3 days from B12,000). PADI Openwater B10,500, or B15,700 with one day spent diving the Similans.

Similan Tour At *Poseidon Bungalows*, 7km south of central Nang Thong, in Khao Lak ☎087 895 9204, ⓦ similantour.com. Highly recommended three-day live-aboard snorkelling trips to the Similans (B9200).

ACCOMMODATION

NANG THONG

Khao Lak Banana Soi Bang La-on, which runs east off Highway 4 towards the south end of the beach ☎076 485889, ⓦ khaolakbanana.com. Dozens of thoughtfully designed fan and a/c bungalows packed into a garden of banana trees and tropical flowers. All have a safety box and hot shower and there's a small swimming pool. Doubles B700

Phu Khao Lak Resort Towards the south end, east side of Highway 4 ☎076 485141, ⓦ phukhaolak.com. There's a luxurious amount of space at this well-run place with a swimming pool, where the large, spotlessly clean bungalows sit prettily amid a grassy park-style coconut plantation. Fan rooms have tiled floors, verandahs and hot-water bathrooms. About 500m walk from the beach. Doubles B600

★**Walkers Inn** South end, on Highway 4 ☎084 840 2689, ⓦ walkersinn.com. The single dorm beds with hot showers here are the best budget option in town. Also has a/c, en-suite private rooms, a good bar-restaurant with a pool table, sports on TV and a decent cup of tea. Dorms B200, doubles B600

KHAO LAK

★**Poseidon Bungalows** 7km south of central Nang Thong ☎087 895 9204, ⓦ similantour.com. Surrounded

by rubber plantations and set above its own mostly sandy, partly rocky shore, the fifteen bungalows at this Swedish– Thai-run guesthouse have generous amounts of space, hot showers and balconies, some enjoying sea views; there's also a swimming pool and motorbike rental. Get off the bus at the *Poseidon* sign between kilometre-stones 53 and 54, then phone for a pick-up or walk 1km. Doubles B950

EATING AND DRINKING

BANG NIANG

Khao Niau Behind 7–11 by the market. Rustic, open-sided restaurant dishing up very good northeastern Thai food, including loads of salads (from B60) such as *som tam* (green papaya salad), as well as seafood and central Thai food. Daily 1–10pm; closed 9th and 23rd of each month.

NANG THONG

Happy Snapper Towards the north end, east side of Highway 4. Khao Lak's most famous dive-staff hangout has a folksy lounge ambience, good burgers (B120) and a drinks menu that runs to over a hundred cocktails. There's live music every night, kicking off with an acoustic set in the beer garden at 5.30pm and including a jam session on Wednesdays. Daily 5pm–2am.

PHUKET

Thailand's largest island and a province in its own right, **Phuket** (pronounced "Poo-ket") ranks second in tourist popularity only to Pattaya. Thoughtless developments have scarred much of the island, particularly along the central west coast, and the trend on all the beaches is to cater very much for package tours, with very few budget resorts left.

WHAT TO SEE AND DO

Phuket is Thailand's most important **diving** centre, offering access to some of the most spectacular reefs in the world. The sea gets quite rough during monsoon season (May–Oct), when diving is less rewarding and swimming can be dangerous. Aside from the beaches and the reefs, the island's main attractions include the dramatic headland of **Laem Promthep** at Phuket's southernmost tip – a popular coach-tour stop for sunset – and the **Gibbon Rehabilitation Centre** (daily 9am–4.30pm, closes 3pm on Sat; B200 national park admission fee; ⓦ gibbonproject.org), which is in Phra Taew National Park, 10km northeast of the Heroines' Monument, off

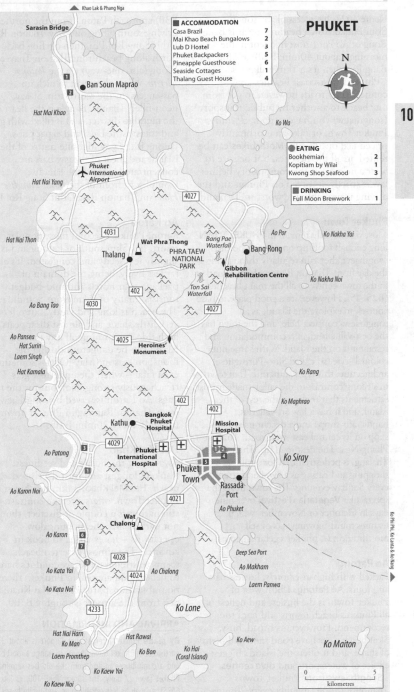

PHUKET

N

10

■ ACCOMMODATION	
Casa Brazil	7
Mai Khao Beach Bungalows	2
Lub D Hostel	3
Phuket Backpackers	5
Pineapple Guesthouse	6
Seaside Cottages	1
Thalang Guest House	4

● EATING	
Bookhemian	2
Kopitiam by Wilai	1
Kwong Shop Seafood	3

■ DRINKING	
Full Moon Brewwork	1

Khao Lak & Phang Nga

Sarasin Bridge

Ban Soun Maprao

Hat Mai Khao

Ko Wa

Phuket International Airport

Hat Nai Yang

Hat Nai Thon

4027

4031

Wat Phra Thong

Thalang

Bang Pae Waterfall

PHRA TAEW NATIONAL PARK

Gibbon Rehabilitation Centre

Ao Por

Ko Nakha Yai

Bang Rong

Ko Nakha Noi

Ton Sai Waterfall

402

4027

Ao Bang Tao

4030

4025

Heroines' Monument

Ao Pansea
Hat Surin
Laem Singh

Hat Kamala

Ko Rang

402

402

Ko Maphrao

Bangkok Phuket Hospital

Kathu

Mission Hospital

Ko Siray

4029

Phuket International Hospital

Ao Patong

Phuket Town

Rassada Port

Ao Karon Noi

Ao Phuket

4021

Wat Chalong

Ao Karon

4028

Deep Sea Port

Ao Makham

Ao Chalong

Laem Panwa

Ao Kata Yai

4024

Ao Kata Nai

Ko Lone

4233

Hat Nai Harn
Ko Man

Hat Rawai

Ko Aew

Ko Maiton

Laem Promthep

Ko Bon

Ko Hai (Coral Island)

Ko Kaew Yai

Ko Kaew Noi

Ko Phi Phi, Ko Lanta & Ao Nang

0   5
kilometres

10

Route 4027. It's accessible by songthaew from Phuket Town heading towards Bang Rong or Ao Por (most frequent in the mornings; about 40min; B40); ask for Bang Pae, then it's a 1km walk.

Phuket's west-coast beaches are connected by road; however, to get from one beach to another by public transport (songthaew) you have to go back into Phuket Town, or take an exorbitantly priced taxi or tuk-tuk. **Motorbikes** can be rented on all the beaches, but be sure to wear a helmet, as the compulsory helmet law is strictly enforced on Phuket and the driving is probably the worst in Thailand.

Phuket Town

Most visitors only remain in **PHUKET TOWN** long enough to jump on a beach-bound songthaew; they run regularly throughout the day from Thanon Ranong by the market in the town centre to all the main beaches (B25–45). However, it's a good place to base yourself to explore the island, as all songthaews connect here, and the town has the best-value budget accommodation and restaurants on the island. With some fine colonial-style (so-called Sino-Portuguese) architecture, this is an authentic Thai town, in striking contrast to the tailor-made tourist settlements that make up the rest of the island, and it has a few art galleries, handicrafts shops and a decent used-book shop on its central east–west road, Thanon Phang Nga. The next road up, Thanon Thalang, is pedestrianized for strolling, shopping and eating as a "**walking street**" every Sunday evening. The town hosts the spectacular **Vegetarian Festival** over nine days in October or November, which features mind-blowing acts of self-mortification (Ⓦ phuketvegetarian.com).

Ao Patong

Packed with high-rise hotels, hostess bars and touts, **Ao Patong**, 15km west of Phuket Town, is the busiest and ugliest of all Phuket's beach resorts and hard to recommend. However, its broad, busy, 3km beach does have good sand and plenty of shade, and it offers the island's biggest choice of watersports and **dive centres**.

Songthaews from Phuket Town's Thanon Ranong (roughly every 20min;

B30) approach Patong from the northeast, driving south along one-way Thanon Raja Uthit Song Roi Phi, then circling back north along beachfront Thanon Thavee Wong (also one-way) via the *Patong Merlin*, where they wait to pick up passengers for the return trip. Sleazy, neon-filled Thanon Bangla is the heart of the **nightlife** district, and is filled with girly and transvestite bars, and expat pubs. Patong is the **gay** nightlife centre of the island, and most of the gay bars are concentrated around the Paradise Complex in front of the *Royal Paradise Hotel* on Thanon Raja Uthit Song Roi Phi.

Ao Karon

Karon, Phuket's second most popular resort, lies 5km south of Patong and is slightly less seedy and congested. It's also far less lively, being the domain of package-tour hotels and mid-budget tourists, many of them from Scandinavia. The beach is long and sandy, but offers very little shade and almost disappears at high tide. Swimming off any part of Karon can be dangerous during the monsoon season (May–Oct) – sometimes even fatal – when the undertow gets treacherously strong; look out for the red flags. Ao Karon is served by songthaews from Thanon Ranong in Phuket Town (roughly every 20min; B40).

Hat Mai Khao

Away from the hustle and seediness, Phuket's longest and least developed beach, **Hat Mai Khao**, 34km northwest of Phuket Town, offers a serene contrast. It still harbours a couple of discreet, though not particularly cheap, bungalow operations – it's essential to book in advance. The almost deserted beach seems to stretch on forever and it's hard to believe you are still in Phuket. There's no public transport to Hat Mai Khao; a taxi from the airport is roughly B300.

ARRIVAL AND INFORMATION

By plane Phuket International Airport is about 32km northwest of Phuket Town. There are orange airport buses and a/c minibuses to and from the old bus terminal in Phuket Town (7 daily; 1hr 30min; B90–100; Ⓣ 086 470 6675), as well as less reliable blue-and-white buses and

DIVING IN PHUKET

See ⓦphuket.com/diving/sites/index.htm for information about dive sites around Phuket. All dive shops offer day-trips for certified divers (B3400–5600) and diving courses (B14,000–16,000 for a four-day PADI Open Water). Always check the equipment and staff credentials carefully and ask whether the dive centre has membership for one of Phuket's recompression chambers. Reliable **dive centres**, all of which offer live-aboards, include:

Dive Asia 23/6 Th Karon, Kata/Karon headland ☎076 330598, ⓦdiveasia.com.

Santana 74/26 Soi Banzaan, behind Jung Ceylon shopping centre, Patong ☎086 802 0615,

ⓦsantanadiving.com.

Scuba Cat Soi Wattana, Th Thavee Wong (the beachfront road), Patong ☎076 293120, ⓦscubacat .com. Also offers snorkelling trips.

a/c minibuses (roughly hourly; 1hr 15min; ☎076 328291) to and from Patong (B150) and Karon (B200). Travel agents in the arrivals hall organize a/c minibuses, which leave when they're full, to Phuket town (B150/person), Rassada pier (B150) and Patong (B180). Taxis charge about B500–600 to Phuket Town, for example.

By bus Phuket is served by dozens of bus and a/c minibus services to and from Bangkok and southern Thai destinations. Nearly all terminate at the new bus station, about 5km north of Phuket Town up Th Thepkasatri (Route 402); none serves the beaches. Some a/c minibuses still use the old bus station on Th Phang Nga, on the east side of the centre. A pink city bus/songthaew (B10) runs into town from the new bus station, skirting the east and south sides of the centre and passing the old bus station.

By boat Ferries connect Phuket with Ko Phi Phi, Ko Lanta and Ao Nang, usually docking at Rassada Port; minibuses meet the ferries and charge B100 per person for transfers to Phuket Town and B150 for the west-coast beaches, or B200 to the airport. On departure, transport from Phuket Town or beaches to the port is usually included in your ferry ticket.

Tourist information TAT, 191 Th Thalang, Phuket Town (daily 8.30am–4.30pm; ☎076 212213, ⓔtatphket @tat.or.th).

ACCOMMODATION

PHUKET TOWN

Phuket Backpackers 167 Th Ranong Rd ☎076 256680. Probably the best-value budget option in Phuket, with a lively bar-restaurant downstairs and lots of tours and information available. The hostel has hot showers, a kitchen available for use and a huge TV with a well-stocked DVD library. Dorms B250, doubles B600

Thalang Guest House 37 Th Thalang ☎076 214225. Housed in a 1940s, Sino-Portuguese, wood-floored shophouse in one of the Old Town's most attractive streets, this place is fairly simple but full of character, traveller-friendly and good value. The fourteen fan rooms (in some of which you can pay a B100 surcharge

for a/c) are large and en suite; rates include a simple breakfast. Doubles B460

AO PATONG

Lub D Hostel 5/5 Th Sawatdirak, 200m from the beach in central Patong ☎076 530100, ⓦlubd.com. New branch of the creative Bangkok hostels (see p.728), featuring a co-working space, a lovely pool and Thai boxing classes. Great, thoughtfully designed, a/c, four-bed dorms, including women-only options, share smart hot-water bathrooms. Dorms B630, doubles B2250

AO KARON

★**Casa Brazil** 9 Soi 1 (Soi Bangla), Th Luang Po Chuan ☎076 396317, ⓦphukethomestay.com. Appealingly arty little hotel, designed in Santa Fe style, with adobe-look walls and cool decor. All rooms have hot showers and balconies, with breakfast included. Doubles B1200

Pineapple Guesthouse Karon Plaza, off Patak and Luang Pho Chuan rds ☎076 396223, ⓦpineapplephuket .com. Good-value British–Thai guesthouse offering sprucely kept, tiled-floor rooms, all with fridges, TV, a/c and hot water, plus a ten-bed mixed dorm, with lockers, a fridge and a/c (for most of the year). Minimum stay two nights. Dorms B250, doubles B800

HAT MAI KHAO

Mai Khao Beach Bungalows ☎081 895 1233, ⓦmaikhaobeach.wordpress.com. Sturdy but simple en-suite bungalows sit in spacious, grassy grounds just behind the shore, beneath coconut palms hung with hammocks. There's a nice restaurant and a massage sala here too. Closed Aug, sometimes longer, during the rainy season. Doubles B1000

Seaside Cottages ☎094 805 9318, ⓦmai-khao-beach .com. A peaceful spot in a large and colourful beachfront garden with brick-built en-suite bungalows, more expensive thatched round cottages and a decent restaurant. In high season, they have tents for rent (B300 for two people). Rates for their cheaper rooms come down to B1000/night if you book three nights or more through their website. Doubles B1500

10

EATING

PHUKET TOWN

Bookhemian 61 Th Thalang ⓦ facebook.com/bookhemian. Cool bookstore and hangout for cappuccinos (B65), cakes, film screenings and other art events. Daily 9am–8.30pm.

Kopitiam by Wilai 14 & 18 Th Thalang ⓣ 083 606 9776. Traditional coffee shop (plus an a/c room two doors away) that's been cleverly updated and made accessible to foreigners by broadening its menu. Alongside tasty Phuket specialities such as *muu hong* (pork belly simmered with Chinese spices; B100), you can get breakfasts, sandwiches, salads and afternoon tea with plates of Phuket sweets (B150). Mon–Sat 11am–5.30pm & 6.30–9pm.

PATONG AND KARON

Kwong Shop Seafood 114 Th Taina, Karon. Unassuming but very popular, friendly, family-run institution sporting gingham tablecloths that's famous for its well-priced fresh seafood cooked to order, including big oysters for B50 and whole seabass for B300. Daily 8am–midnight.

DRINKING

Full Moon Brewwork Port Zone (next to the replica junk), Jung Ceylon shopping centre, Patong. The best of this award-winning microbrewery's offerings is their dark ale, and there's good food too, including Thai dishes (around B150) and classic pub fare such as fish'n'chips. Daily 11am–11.30pm.

DIRECTORY

Banks and exchange Banks and ATMs are plentiful in Phuket Town, Patong and Karon.

Books South Wind Books, Th Phang Nga, Phuket Town, has a big, sprawling range of secondhand books (Mon–Sat 9am–6pm, Sun 10am–3pm).

Hospital Phuket International Hospital (ⓣ 076 361888, emergencies ⓣ 076 210935, ⓦ phuketinternationalhospital .com), north of Central Festival shopping centre on Highway 402, just west of Phuket town, is considered to have the best facilities.

Immigration office At the southern end of Th Phuket, Phuket Town, near Ao Makham (Mon–Fri 8.30am–4.30pm; ⓣ 076 221905).

Post office On Th Montri, near the corner of Th Phang Nga, Phuket Town; on Th Patak, just south of Th Taina, in Karon; and on beachfront Th Thavee Wong, south of its intersection with Th Bang La, in Patong.

Tourist police For all emergencies, contact the tourist police, either on the free, 24hr phone line (ⓣ 1155), at their main office at 327 Th Yaowarat on the north side of Phuket town or at their beachfront office on Th Tavee Wong in Patong.

AO PHANG NGA

Covering some four hundred square kilometres of coast between Phuket and Krabi, the mangrove-lined bay of **Ao Phang Nga** is dotted with dramatic limestone karst formations up to 300m in height.

WHAT TO SEE AND DO

The best, and most affordable, way of seeing the bay is to join one of the longtail **boat trips** arranged from the nearby town of **Phang Nga**. There are half-day tours (daily at about 8.30am & 2pm; about 4hr; B800) and full-day tours (B1100). Overnight trips with a stay in the Muslim stilt village of Ko Panyi, including dinner and breakfast, cost an extra B850. **Kayaks** can be rented along the way for an extra B350. The standard itinerary follows a circular or figure-of-eight route around the bay, passing weirdly shaped karst silhouettes including "James Bond Island", which was Scaramanga's hideaway in *The Man With the Golden Gun*. Most boats return to the mainland via Ko Panyi.

ARRIVAL AND DEPARTURE

By bus The bus station is centrally placed on Th Phetkasem, a few minutes' walk from the hotels, banks (with ATMs and exchange) and restaurants along the same road. Phang Nga town has bus connections to Phuket, Krabi and Trang at least hourly, and four daily to Surat Thani.

TOURS

Sayan Tour (ⓣ 076 430348, ⓦ sayantour.com) and Mr Kean Tour (ⓣ 076 430619 or ⓣ 089 871 6092) in Phang Nga town both have offices inside the bus station and offer similar waterborne itineraries. They will also store your baggage for a few hours and sell bus and boat tickets to Ko Phi Phi and Ko Samui, for example.

ACCOMMODATION AND EATING

Baan Phang Nga 100/2 Th Phetkasem ⓣ 076 413276 or ⓣ 061 642 6226. Friendly guesthouse, offering a/c rooms with TVs, hot-water bathrooms and a few touches of kitsch contemporary decor. The popular ground-floor restaurant and bakery does everything from Western breakfasts, cakes and pizzas to seafood fried rice. Doubles B650

KRABI

The small estuary town of **KRABI** is a major transport hub for the islands of Ko Phi Phi and Ko Lanta and makes a nice spot to stay for a night. Although the town has no beaches of its own, Ao Nang and Laem Phra Nang (Railay) are only 45 minutes away. Every Krabi travel agent sells **sea-kayaking** expeditions (see box below) and snorkelling trips, and many also offer tours of Krabi's mangrove swamps and trips to Wat Tham Seua, dramatically sited inland amid limestone cliffs. Krabi River runs north to south on the eastern flank of the town. North–south Thanon Utrakit provides a lot of the town's restaurants and tourist facilities; the longtail-boat pier and night market are just off it to the east.

ARRIVAL AND DEPARTURE

From Bangkok, one of the most comfortable options is to get an overnight sleeper train to Surat Thani and then pick up a Krabi bus.

By plane Krabi Airport is 18km east of town, just off Highway 4. Flights are met by shuttle buses to Krabi (B90) and Ao Nang (B150). AirAsia, Bangkok Airways, Nok Air, Thai Airways, Thai Lion Air and Thai Smile supply numerous hour-long flights to Bangkok each day. Bangkok Airways also has flights to Samui (1 daily), while AirAsia flies to Chiang Mai (2 daily) as well as to Kuala Lumpur (3 daily); AirAsia and Tiger each fly to Singapore once daily.

By bus and minibus The bus and a/c minibus station is just off Highway 4, 5km north of Krabi Town at Talat Kao, from where there's a frequent songthaew service (B15) to the town centre.

Destinations Bangkok (12 daily; 12hr); Ko Lanta (hourly; 2hr 30min–3hr 30min); Nakhon Si Thammarat (roughly hourly; 3–4hr); Phang Nga (every 30min; 2hr); Phuket (hourly; 3–5hr); Ranong (2 daily; 5hr); Satun (4 daily; 5hr); Surat Thani (5 daily; 3hr); Trang (hourly; 3hr).

By boat There are boats to Ko Phi Phi (year-round; 2–4 daily; 2hr) and Ko Lanta (roughly mid-Nov to mid-April;

1–2 daily; 2hr 30min), either from Tha Chao Fa in the centre of Krabi Town or from Krabi Passenger Port (Tha Khlong Jilad), 2km southwest of town; ferry tickets bought from tour operators in town should include a free transfer to Tha Khlong Jilad. There are also boat services from Hat Nopparat Thara, next to Ao Nang, some of which call at Railay, to Ko Phi Phi Don (1 daily; 2hr) and to Phuket (1–2 daily; 2hr 30min), both year-round in theory though they sometimes don't run in the monsoon season; and to Ko Lanta (2hr 30min) from roughly November to April. Transfers from Ao Nang hotels are included in the ticket price.

INFORMATION

Tourist information The unhelpful TAT office (daily 8.30am–4.30pm; ☎075 622163, ✉tatkrabi@tat.or.th) is 3km north of the centre on Maharat Rd.

ACCOMMODATION

★**Chan-Cha-Lay** 55 Th Utrakit ☎075 620952, ⊛lovechanchalay.com. With its stylish blue-and-white theme throughout, this is the most charming and arty place to stay in Krabi. The en suites in the garden are by far the nicest option; rooms in the main building share bathrooms and some don't have windows. Doubles B400
K Guest House 15–25 Th Chao Fa, just southwest off Th Utrakit ☎075 623166, ✉kguesthouse@yahoo.com. Deservedly popular, well run and recently renovated, this long, timber-clad row house sits in a peaceful but central spot. The nicest bedrooms are upstairs, with wooden floors, streetside balconies and hot showers, but there are also cheaper rooms with shared hot-water bathrooms downstairs. Doubles B400
Pak-up Hostel 87 Th Utrakit ☎075 611955, ⊛pakuphostel.com. Colourful, modern hostel in a short tower block on Krabi's busiest corner, with smart, a/c, four-to ten-bed dorms and doubles with shared bathrooms, self-service laundry and a roof terrace. This is the place to come to meet people, with lots of common areas and an adjacent garden bar. Dorms B380, doubles B800

SEA-KAYAKING IN THE KRABI AREA

By far the most enjoyable way of exploring the glories of the Krabi coastline is by **sea kayak**. Paddling into the mangrove swamps and secret tidal lagoons, or **hongs**, hidden inside the limestone karsts is a fantastic experience and gives you close-up views of birds, animals and plants that would be impossible from a roaring longtail.

The most popular kayaking destination is **Ao Thalen** (also called Ao Talin or Talane), about 25km northwest of Krabi Town, where you can paddle out to the *hongs* and beaches of Ko Hong and Ko Bileh. Another 25km north up the Krabi coast, the Ban Bor Tor (aka Ban Bho Tho) area of **Ao Luk** bay is famous for its caves, in particular Tham Lod, which has a long tunnel hung with stalactites, and Tham Phi Hua Toe, whose walls display around a hundred prehistoric cave paintings.

Kayaking **trips** usually cost about B2000–2500 for a full day or B1000 for half a day. Trips can be arranged through any tour operator in Krabi Town, Laem Phra Nang or Ao Nang, or with reputable, though more expensive, kayaking operators such as John Gray Sea Canoe (☎076 254505, ⊛johngray-seacanoe.com) in Phuket Town.

10

EATING

Try either the riverside night market near the longtail-boat pier on Th Kong Ka, or the inland night market on Soi 10, Th Maharat, off the northern end of Th Utrakit. On Wednesday, Saturday and Sunday, the pedestrianized night bazaar on Soi 8 offers cheap eats in a lively atmosphere.

Chalita Th Chao Fa, west of the longtail-boat pier. Congenial Italian–Thai restaurant that serves mostly Thai food, but also pastas (from B120), pizzas, steaks and burgers. Mon–Sat 4–10.30pm.

Ko Tung Th Maharat. About 4km north of the centre near the bus station, this place fully justifies the journey, with superb southern Thai seafood dishes such as *nam phrik kung siab* (chilli dip with dried prawns; B120) and crab curry with rice noodles. Daily 11am–10pm.

DIRECTORY

Hospital Krabi International Hospital, Soi Pisanpop, about 2km north of the town centre off Th Maharat (☎075 626555, ⓦ krabinakharin.co.th).

Immigration office In the compound of government offices on the way to Krabi Passenger Port (Mon–Fri 8.30am–4.30pm; ☎075 611097).

Post office About 100m south of *Chan-Cha-Lay* on Th Utrakit (Mon–Fri 8.30am–4.30pm, Sat 9am–noon).

AO NANG AND HAT NOPPARAT THARA

AO NANG, 22km west of Krabi Town, is a busy, commercial resort that has seen mass development over the years and caters mainly for package tourists. Most travellers who stop here do so in order to take a longtail boat to nearby Laem Phra Nang (Railay). Though the beach in Ao Nang is no great shakes, the less-developed western beach, **Hat Nopparat Thara**, part of which comes under the protection of a marine national park, is prettier and more peaceful; here, Kiteboarding Asia (☎084 628 5786, ⓦ kiteboardingasia.com) offers kiteboarding and stand-up paddleboarding lessons and rental.

Ao Nang is Krabi's main hub for snorkelling trips and **dive shops** – most diving expeditions head to the reefs around Ko Phi Phi and Ko Ha (near Ko Lanta). A reputable firm is Poseidon, about 3km from the beach off the main Krabi Town road (☎098 071 9035, ⓦ poseidon-diving.com), who offer local two-dive trips for B2800, and Openwater courses for B14,900.

ARRIVAL AND DEPARTURE

By songthaew To reach Ao Nang, take a white songthaew from Krabi bus station or town centre, passing eastern Nopparat Thara en route (roughly 45min; B50–60).

ACCOMMODATION AND EATING

With package holidays taking over, budget accommodation is becoming increasingly hard to find. There's a small night market in front of *Krabi Resort*, on the main road about 200m from the main beachfront, heading towards Nopparat Thara. Locals eat at the seafood restaurants in the national park visitors' centre car park, which is at the west end of Nopparat Thara's eastern beach.

Glur Hostel Soi 11/1, 1.5km from the beach just off the main access road, Ao Nang ☎075 695297, ⓦ krabiglurhostel.com. Designed and run by an architect, this very stylish hostel offers dorms and twins done out in white, orange and aquamarine, as well as a garden swimming pool. Light breakfast included. Dorms B600, doubles B1300

Laughing Gecko Soi Hat Nopparat Thara 13 ☎081 270 5028, ⓦ laughinggeckobungalows.com. Perhaps the last of the old-style bungalows left in the Ao Nang area, this is an easy-going and exceptionally traveller-friendly haven run by a Thai–Canadian couple, with nightly all-you-can-eat Thai buffets. Choose from a range of simple, thatched, fan-cooled, en-suite bamboo huts set around a garden dotted with cashew trees, including four-person dorms. It's about a 10min walk from the beach at Hat Nopparat Thara East. Dorms B180, doubles B500

Wang Sai Beside the bridge at the far eastern end of Hat Nopparat Thara ☎075 638128. There are no reasonably priced, authentic Thai restaurants left on Ao Nang proper, but fortunately this place is just around the corner on the main road, where you can get fried rice for as little as B80. It offers good sunset views from its beachfront tables, an enormous range of the freshest seafood and lots of southern Thai specialities. Daily 11am–9.20pm.

LAEM PHRA NANG (RAILAY)

The stunning headland of **Laem Phra Nang** is accessible only by boat, so staying on one of its four beaches feels like being on an island. The sheer limestone cliffs, pure-white sand and emerald waters make it a spectacular spot, though bungalows have now been built in all the prime spots so the whole place feels a little congested.

Furthest out on the headland, **Ao Phra Nang** is the prettiest beach, with luxuriously soft sand, reefs close to shore, and luxury hotels. It's reached by a short path from the southern end of **East Railay**, which is not suitable for swimming because of its fairly dense mangrove growth and a tide that goes out for miles, but has some cheap accommodation. Five minutes' walk away on the opposite side of the headland, **West Railay** enjoys impressive karst scenery, crystal-clear water and a much longer stretch of good sand. On the other side of a rocky promontory from northern West Railay (take a longtail or walk along the path from East Railay in 20min), the beach at **Ao Ton Sai** is coarse and littered with rocks that make it impossible to swim at low tide. Leafy and wedged between towering limestone cliffs, this is the travellers' beach, with budget bungalows set among the palms a couple of hundred metres uphill from the shore.

ARRIVAL AND DEPARTURE

By boat Longtail boats to the cape depart when full from the pier on Th Kong Ka in Krabi Town and dock at East Railay (roughly 45min), from where it's easy to cut across to West Railay along any of the through-tracks. Krabi boats do run during the rainy season, but it's safer to go via Ao Nang instead. Ao Nang is much closer to Laem Phra Nang, and longtails run from the beachfront here to West Railay and Ao Ton Sai (10min) year-round.

ACTIVITIES

Laem Phra Nang is Thailand's premier rock-climbing centre, with seven hundred bolted sport-climbing routes around Ton Sai and Railay (see ⓦ railay.com for a full rundown). Of the many climbing schools that rent out equipment and lead guided climbs, the most established include King Climbers, just behind *Flame Tree* restaurant on West Railay (ⓦ railay.com/railay/climbing/climbing_king_climbers.shtml), and Basecamp Tonsai on Ton Sai (ⓣ 081 149 9745, ⓦ basecamptonsai.com). A typical half-day introduction costs from B1000.

ACCOMMODATION

During high season (Nov–Feb), it's essential to arrive on the beaches as early in the morning as possible to get a room. Most accommodation options have attached restaurants.
Chill Out Bar and Bungalows Ao Ton Sai, on the inland road above and parallel to the beach ⓣ 062 943 9288. This mellow, friendly outfit has recently moved inland to offer rough-hewn timber bungalows on stilts among the trees, with mossie nets, fans, verandahs and cold-water bathrooms decorated with artworks. The bar still features fire shows and reggae but has been joined by a coffee bar. Dorms B250, doubles B600

The Forest Resort Ao Ton Sai, 2min walk along the path towards East Railay ⓣ 081 149 9745, ⓦ basecamptonsai.com. Run by Basecamp Tonsai climbing school, who also have some bungalows at their nearby office, this spot offers a wide variety of basic accommodation (some bookable online, some walk-in only) in wood and bamboo bungalows with mosquito nets and less appealing concrete rooms, all en suite with balconies. Dorms B250, doubles B600
Pasook Resort Ao Ton Sai, on the inland road above and parallel to the beach ⓣ 089 645 3013. Friendly, welcoming spot, set on sloping lawns amid flowers and small trees, offering simple, en-suite, fan-cooled concrete rooms and bigger clapboard bungalows. Prices change frequently, according to demand. Doubles B600
Railay Cabana ⓣ 075 621733. In a spacious, grassy, tree-filled amphitheatre of majestic karst cliffs, a 5min walk from East Railay beach on the track to Ton Sai, this friendly and quiet family-run place offers simple wooden bungalows with mosquito nets, fans, cold-water bathrooms and big verandahs. Doubles B500

KO PHI PHI

One of southern Thailand's most famous destinations, the two spectacular **Ko Phi Phi** islands, 40km south of Krabi and 48km east of southern Phuket, leapt to international notoriety as the location for the 1999 film, *The Beach*. Then, in December 2004, they became headline news again as the tsunami wreaked inconceivable destruction on the two main beaches of the larger island, **Ko Phi Phi Don**, and on the densely packed tourist village connecting them. The island made a fast recovery, however, and Ko Phi Phi is very much a thriving tourist hub, perhaps too crowded for its own good; budget accommodation is sparse, particularly in peak season. Phi Phi Don's sister island, **Ko Phi Phi Leh**, home to the magnificent Maya Bay, is an uninhabited national marine park and can only be visited on day-trips.

Detailed **maps** are available at travel agents and dive shops in the village.

Ao Ton Sai, Laem Hin and Ao Loh Dalum

Ko Phi Phi Don would itself be two islands were it not for the narrow isthmus that connects the hilly expanses to the east and west, separating the stunningly symmetrical double bays of **Ao Ton Sai** to

10

10

the south and Ao Loh Dalum to the north.
The land between the two bays is occupied
by a commercial tourist village, crammed
with guesthouses, tour operators,
restaurants, bars, cafés and dive centres.

East along the coast from the pier on
Ao Ton Sai, about ten minutes' walk
down the main track is the **Laem Hin**
promontory, which overlooks a quieter
patch of swimmable beach. Just a few
minutes' walk north through Ton Sai
village, seductively curvaceous **Ao Loh
Dalum** is much better for swimming and
sunbathing, though the tide here goes out
for miles. The **viewpoint** that overlooks
eastern Ao Loh Dalum affords a
magnificent panorama over the twin
bays, and every evening a stream of
people makes the steep fifteen-minute
climb up the steps for sunset shots;
admission is B30, though there are good,
free views just metres before the entrance.

Hat Yao (Long Beach)

With its luxurious white sand and large
reefs just 20m offshore, **Hat Yao** (Long
Beach), east along the coast from Ao Ton
Sai, is the best of Phi Phi's main beaches,
though it is extremely crowded. Longtail
boats do the ten-minute shuttle from Hat
Yao to Ao Ton Sai during daylight hours
(B100 per person, minimum 2 people),
and from Ao Ton Sai to Hat Yao till all
hours of the morning, but it's also
possible to walk between the two in half
an hour. At low tide you can get to Hat
Yao along the rocky shore, from Laem
Hin, past many quaint secluded beaches.
The island's single road follows an inland
route to the east end of Hat Yao from *The
Rock* junction in the village; it's a hot,
hilly and unshaded forty-minute walk.

Ao Toh Koh

For those wishing to escape the madding
crowds, the bays on the east coast such as
Ao Toh Koh offer tranquillity and beaches
of fine, white sand, though little in the way
of budget digs. Transfers from Ao Ton Sai
cost B800 by longtail boat.

ARRIVAL AND DEPARTURE

By boat Scheduled ferries connect Ao Ton Sai on Ko Phi
Phi Don with Ao Nang and Railay (1 daily; 2hr; B450); Ko

Lanta (1–3 daily; 1hr 30min; B300–400); Krabi (2–4 daily;
1hr 30min–2hr; B350); and Phuket (3–5 daily; 1hr
30min–2hr 30min; B350).

ACTIVITIES

Diving and snorkelling As well as responsible, small-
group dive trips (B2500 for two dives) and courses
(B13,800 for the PADI Openwater), Phi Phi Adventure Club
in Ao Ton Sai (☎081 895 1334, ⌨phi-phi-adventures
.com) offers half-day snorkelling trips to swim with sharks
or to Phi Phi Leh (from B1000).

Rock climbing Phi Phi Travel and Tours, Ao Ton Sai
(☎093 732 4804, ⌨phiphitravelandtours.com), does
introductory climbing classes (B1400 for a half-day).

ACCOMMODATION

Ko Phi Phi is one of Thailand's most expensive locations,
with Hat Yao the most exorbitant.

AO TON SAI AND AO LOH DALUM

Blanco East end of Ao Loh Dalum ☎075 601400,
⌨blancodorm.com. Hardcore party hostel (no over-35s)
with tightly packed, bunk-bedded dorms and hot showers
behind a rollicking beach bar that organizes daily booze
cruises. Dorms **B480**

Coco's Close to the base of the viewpoint access steps
☎075 601400, ⌨ppcocos.com. Reminiscent of a city
guesthouse, with a main two-storey block and diverse
other rooms, all painted bright white, clean and well
organized. All rooms are en suite, some have a/c.
Doubles **B900**

Oasis East end of Ton Sai village, north of the mosque
☎075 601207. A hill stands between this place and the
main bar zone, so noise shouldn't be a problem. Set in a
colourful wooden house, rooms are comfortable and en
suite. Doubles **B600**

The Rock Ton Sai village ☎081 607 3897. Traveller-
oriented hangout behind a landmark boat-shaped bar-
restaurant, offering some of the cheapest beds on the
island, in large mixed-sex dorms; up to seventeen bunk
beds are crammed in each, but there are fans and lockers.
Also has doubles with shared, cold-water bathrooms.
Dorms **B250**, doubles **B600**

Sunflower Boathouse East end of Ao Loh Dalum ☎080
038 3374. Spacious dark-wood rooms with en-suite hot
showers, mosquito nets and bags of character, in a
thatched, boat-shaped building with sociable, wraparound balconies, right on the beach. Doubles **B1500**

Tara Inn Ton Sai village, south of *The Rock* ☎075
601021. A budget favourite for many years; fan rooms
are spacious if a little on the tired side. Most bungalows
have large balconies and views over the bay, with more
expensive a/c options (B1300) having the better views.
Doubles **B800**

HAT YAO

Phi Phi Long Beach Resort ☎075 818741, ⓦ pplongbeachresort.com. The least expensive place to stay on Long Beach, on a great stretch of beach with a swimming pool and an attached dive shop (ⓦ longbeachdivers.com). The cheapest of the tightly packed rooms have fans and cold-water bathrooms, while the dorms are a/c. Dorms <u>B600</u>, doubles <u>B900</u>

Viking Natures Resort ☎075 819399, ⓦ vikingnaturesresort.com. Tucked away on two private sandy coves just west of Hat Yao, this is a very stylish take on the classic beach bungalow. It's all wood and bamboo here, with no a/c, but interiors are decorated with Asian boho-chic artefacts. Doubles <u>B1500</u>

AO TOH KO

Ao Toh Ko Beach Resort ☎081 537 0528, ⓦ tohkobeachresort.com. The exceptionally welcoming family who run this place keep people staying and returning – and they're great cooks too. The comfortable range of accommodation kicks off with attractive, breezy, en-suite, bamboo huts with mossie nets, some sitting right over the sea on the rocks. Doubles <u>B2500</u>

EATING

Ao Ton Sai is the best place to eat on the island and offers the most choice.

Papaya Northeast of the pier in Ton Sai village. With two nearby branches, *Papaya* offers good, reasonably priced Thai and Indian standard dishes, including tasty chicken with cashew nuts (B130). Daily 8.30am–10pm.

Patcharee Bakery On the main alley running east from the pier. This place and *Pee Pee Bakery* square up to each other across the narrow alley, vying for trade. Croissants – plain, chocolate (B35), almond or savoury – are the thing here, washed down with espresso, but it also does delicious grilled baguettes with mozzarella, tomato and ham (B100). Daily 7am–11pm.

NIGHTLIFE

Ko Phi Phi is a major party island. In high season, Ao Ton Sai and Ao Loh Dolum teem with young Westerners out for a good time.

Reggae Bar Northeast of the pier in Ton Sai village, on the main route heading towards *The Rock*. A Phi Phi institution that's been running for years in various incarnations. These days it offers free buckets to anyone willing to take part in *muay thai* in its boxing ring at around 9.30pm and has pool tables and a bar around the sides. Daily 9am–1am.

Slinky Towards the east end of Loh Dalum, where the left fork just before *The Rock* hits the beach. The messy, throbbing heart of Phi Phi nightlife, with a booming sound system, fire shows and buckets and buckets of booze. Daily 6pm–2am.

Sunflower Bar On the beach at the east end of Loh Dalum. Timber-built chill-out spot with tables, axe cushions and plants strewn around the garden, plus great views, good music and a pool table. Daily roughly 11am–2am.

KO LANTA

At 25km long, **Ko Lanta** (actually two islands, Ko Lanta Yai and adjacent, untouristed Ko Lanta Noi) offers plenty of fine sandy beaches all along its west coast and is a deservedly popular destination. It's also within easy day-tripping distance of the stunning beaches and reefs of Ko Rok Nai and Ko Rok Nok, 47km south (B1300, including lunch and snorkelling, through any tour agent).

Though Lanta has plenty of boat connections, most people arrive on air-conditioned minibuses from the mainland – either Krabi, Phuket or Trang – which take a car ferry to Ko Lanta Noi (a new bridge is planned here), then cross the bridge to Ko Lanta Yai. A road runs the entire length of Ko Lanta's west coast, serviced by plenty of tuk-tuks; many bungalows rent out **motorbikes** (B200–300). Most beaches have some facilities, but to be sure of getting what you want, head to the commercial centre and port at the north end of the island, **Ban Sala Dan**, which is jammed full of clothing stalls, banks, restaurants, travel agents, and arts and crafts shops.

Hat Khlong Dao and Ao Phra-Ae (Long Beach)

Ko Lanta's most developed beach, **Hat Khlong Dao**, is broad and nice, but no longer has any decent budget accommodation. A couple of kilometres south of Khlong Dao, **Ao Phra-Ae** (also known as **Long Beach**) boasts a beautiful long strip of white sand and an enjoyably youthful ambience. Traveller-oriented bamboo huts are fairly plentiful here, as are beach-shack **bars** with mats on the sand.

Hat Khlong Khong, Hat Khlong Nin and Ao Kantiang

The lovely long beach at **Hat Khlong Khong**, south of Ao Phra-Ae, is peppered with rocks and you can only really swim

10

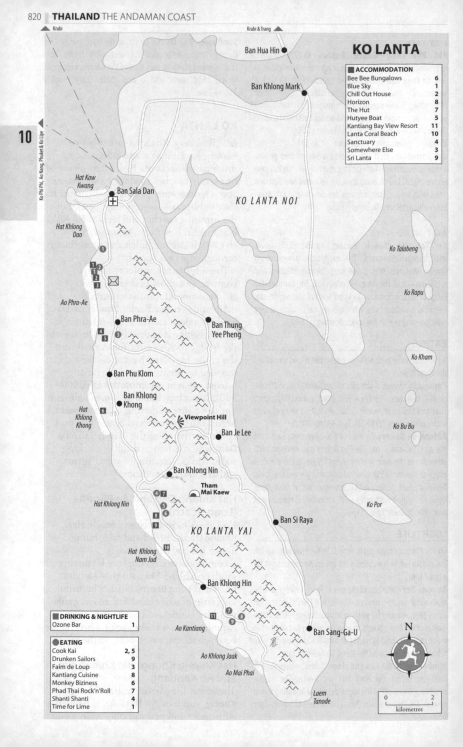

KO LANTA

ACCOMMODATION

Bee Bee Bungalows	6
Blue Sky	1
Chill Out House	2
Horizon	8
The Hut	7
Hutyee Boat	5
Kantiang Bay View Resort	11
Lanta Coral Beach	10
Sanctuary	4
Somewhere Else	3
Sri Lanta	9

Ban Hua Hin

Ban Khlong Mark

10

Ko Phi Phi, Ao Nang, Phuket & Ko Lipe

Hat Kaw Kwang

Ban Sala Dan

KO LANTA NOI

Hat Khlong Dao

Ko Talabeng

Ko Rapu

Ao Phra-Ae

Ban Phra-Ae

Ban Thung Yee Pheng

Ko Kham

Ban Phu Klom

Ban Khlong Khong

Hat Khlong Khong

Viewpoint Hill

Ko Bu Bu

Ban Je Lee

Ban Khlong Nin

Tham Mai Kaew

Hat Khlong Nin

Ko Por

KO LANTA YAI

Ban Si Raya

Hat Khlong Nam Jud

Ban Khlong Hin

DRINKING & NIGHTLIFE

Ozone Bar	1

Ao Kantiang

Ban Sang-Ga-U

EATING

Cook Kai	2, 5
Drunken Sailors	9
Faim de Loup	3
Kantiang Cuisine	8
Monkey Biziness	6
Phad Thai Rock'n'Roll	7
Shanti Shanti	4
Time for Lime	1

Ao Khlong Jaak

Ao Mai Phai

Laem Tanode

N

0   2
kilometres

at high tide. There are lots of beautiful places to stay and a number of colourful beachfront bars that host regular parties.

About 4km south of Hat Khlong Khong, the road forks, with the left-hand, east-bound arm running across to Ko Lanta Yai's east coast, via Tham Mai Kaew caves and Viewpoint Hill, and the right-hand fork running south to long, sandy, laidback **Hat Khlong Nin**, a great spot for swimming. About 8km further south, **Ao Kantiang** has a lovely beach in a sheltered bay, where swimming is possible year-round.

ARRIVAL AND DEPARTURE

Bungalow touts meet the boats at Ban Sala Dan and will usually transport you to the beach of your choice. If you need to use the motorbike sidecar taxi or white songthaew services instead, be warned that drivers will try and charge arrivals way over the normal fares; walk 250m from the pier head to the main road to get a ride at more reasonable rates. For the a/c minibuses, the price often depends on how far south on Ko Lanta you want to go.

From Krabi Ferries run from Krabi, either from the Passenger Port at Khlong Jilad or from Tha Chao Fa in the centre of town (roughly mid-Nov to mid-April 2 daily; 2hr 30min; B400). There are also year-round a/c minibuses from Krabi bus station (hourly; 2hr 30min–3hr; B250–400); if booked in advance, they'll pick you up from your hotel in Krabi Town. On departure from Lanta, the Krabi minibuses will drop you off at Krabi Airport; on arrival, you'll need to call ☎ 081 606 3591 to ask them to pick you up on the main road in front of the airport.

From Phuket and Ko Phi Phi Ferries run from Rassada Port (1–3 daily; 4hr; B600–900), usually with a change of boat at Ko Phi Phi (1hr 30min; B300–400). There are also a/c minibuses from Phuket to Hat Khlong Dao (roughly hourly; 6hr; B400).

From Hat Nopparat Thara (near Ao Nang) Ferries usually travel via Laem Phra Nang (1 daily; 2hr 30min; B500).

From Ko Lipe In high season, there's one daily ferry (5hr 30min; B1700) and two daily speedboat services (3–4hr; B2000).

From Trang A/c minibuses run year-round (5–6 daily; 2hr 30min–3hr; B320–420).

ACTIVITIES

Cooking classes Cooking classes are provided by Time for Lime, at the south end of Hat Khlong Dao (☎ 075 684590, ⓦ timeforlime.net).

Diving Among reliable diving centres, Lanta Diver, in the centre of Ban Sala Dan (☎ 087 891 4141, ⓦ lantadiver .com), with branches around the island, is a

Swedish-owned, PADI Five-star Centre, charging from B3300 for two dives, excluding equipment, and B14,400 for the Openwater course.

Yoga Oasis, Hat Khlong Dao (☎ 085 115 4067, ⓦ oasisyoga-lanta.com).

ACCOMMODATION

Accommodation prices listed here are for high season; many places increase their rates for "peak season", usually between mid-December and mid-January, while in the rainy season (May–Oct) rates are vastly discounted and some bungalows close down.

AO PHRA-AE (LONG BEACH)

Blue Sky North Long Beach (☎ 081 906 7577, ⓦ blueskylanta.com. This place has it all: decent, cheap, en-suite, fan bungalows, beachside restaurant and bar, massage platform, coffee bar and a bookshop. Doubles B500

★**Chill Out House** North Long Beach, same road as to *Ozone* (☎ 082 183 2258, ⓦ chillouthouselanta.com). Hand-built using recycled materials, bamboo and driftwood, this is a fabulous place with a dormitory in a treehouse and a relaxed bar. The dorm beds and the private rooms share hot and cold showers, while the private bungalows have en-suite cold showers. There's a laidback common area with big-screen TV. Dorms B230, doubles B310

Hutyee Boat South Long Beach, opposite and south of *Faim de Loup* restaurant (☎ 083 633 9723). These large, sturdy, stilted bungalows stand in a grove of tall, shady trees less than 50m from the beach, have en-suite bathrooms and fridges – and the owner's a real character. Doubles B500

Sanctuary Southern Long Beach (☎ 081 891 3055, ⓦ sanctuarykohlanta.com). In a spacious garden setting, cheap A-frames with shared facilities at the back and elegant bamboo-clad bungalows with open-air bathrooms at the front, some with a/c and hot showers. The restaurant serves Indian and vegetarian food, and there's a cute bar hut on the beachfront. Doubles B350

Somewhere Else North Long Beach (☎ 081 536 0858. Located in the heart of the liveliest part of Ao Phra-ae, with bars to the left and right, this cheap, congenial place on a beachside lawn is one of the main travellers' centres on the beach. Its spacious, unusually designed hexagonal bungalows made of tightly woven bamboo come with pretty bathrooms with hot showers. Doubles B500

HAT KHLONG KHONG, HAT KHLONG NIN AND AO KANTIANG

★**Bee Bee Bungalows** Hat Khlong Khong (☎ 081 537 9932, ⓔ beebeepiya02@hotmail.com. This place stands out for its highly individual huts, each one a charming experiment in bamboo architecture. All are simple but comfortably furnished, given style with batik fabric

10

10

★TREAT YOURSELF

Sri Lanta Hat Khlong Nin ☎ 075 662688, ⓦ srilanta.com. On a lengthy beachfront here, the restaurants, bar, two pools and sea-view spa sit in beautiful gardens, adorned with ponds, fountains and a huge lawn. Meanwhile, running up the lush, shady slope across the road, the large, attractive cottages enjoy plenty of space, as well as all the facilities you need. Service is tip-top and breakfast is included. Doubles **B3720**

flourishes, and have fans, mosquito nets and partially open-air bathrooms. There's a very good bar-restaurant, too, with similarly experimental but lovely wood and thatch salas. Doubles **B700**

Horizon Hat Khlong Nin ☎ 087 626 4493, ⓦ lantahorizon .com. A wide cross section of comfortable accommodation includes four- and six-bed a/c dorms and small rooms with mosquito nets and shared bathrooms, and there's a relaxing bar-restaurant with deckchairs and nightly fire shows on the beach. Dorms **B500**, doubles **B600**

The Hut Hat Khlong Nin ☎ 084 446 5585. A small, laidback and friendly place, just across the road from *Otto's Bar & Grill*, with clean, simple bungalows packed tightly together in a small garden, and a tasty restaurant (mains from B80). Doubles **B500**

Kantiang Bay View Resort Ao Kantiang ☎ 075 665049, ⓦ kantiangbay.net. At this diverse, family-run resort, the sturdy, woven-bamboo, en-suite bungalows in the garden near the beach are about the only budget choices left on Ao Kantiang. Also home to *Why Not* beach bar with live music and fire shows nightly. Doubles **B600**

Lanta Coral Beach Hat Khlong Nam Jud, a tiny bay between Hat Khlong Nin and Ao Kantiang ☎ 075 662535, ⓦ lantacoralresort.com. Friendly resort with a lovely, lofty restaurant – especially nice at sunset – up on the rocky point. The plain but very clean and en-suite bamboo and concrete huts are scattered over a lawn among the palms (some of which are hung with hammocks); the concrete options, whether fan or a/c, boast hot showers. Doubles **B600**

EATING

HAT KHLONG DAO AND AO PHRA-AE (LONG BEACH)

On the road towards the north end of the beach, there's a branch of the good Hat Khlong Nin restaurant, *Cook Kai* (see below).

★**Faim de Loup** On the main road towards the south end of Long Beach. Very good French bakery, where the

croissants, pains au chocolat, fruit tarts and excellent espressos just hit the spot. Also does sandwiches and quiches (B200 with salad). Daily 7.30am–5pm.

Time for Lime Hat Khlong Dao (see p.821). At its beach bar, this cooking school serves delicious six-course tasting menus of Thai and fusion food (B540, vegetarian B480), which can be shared between two people; happy hour on cocktails until 6.30pm. Mon–Sat 5–9.30pm.

HAT KHLONG KHONG, HAT KHLONG NIN AND AO KANTIANG

Cook Kai Hat Khlong Nin. Popular restaurant hung with shell mobiles and lamps, dishing up hearty portions of all the Thai classics (from B100), including good salads, and a few Western dishes including breakfast. Daily 8am–10.30pm.

Drunken Sailors Ao Kantiang ⓦ facebook.com/ drunkensailors. Mellow café scattered with beanbags and hammocks, dishing up delicious Thai, Western and fusion food (main courses around B150), as well as cakes, espressos and shakes. Daily 9am–4pm & 6.30–9pm.

★**Kantiang Cuisine** Ao Kantiang. This place serves central Thai and Western dishes but stands out as one of the few places on the island where you can get good southern Thai food, including *khua kling* (B100), a dry curry with chicken or pork, and excellent *pla thawt khamin*, deep-fried snapper with turmeric. Daily 9am–9/10pm, depending on how busy they are.

Monkey Biziness Hat Khlong Nin. Friendly, relaxing café for good cappuccinos (B70), smoothies, cakes, ice cream and simple breakfasts and lunches, plus nice clothes, accessories and gifts for sale. Daily except Tues 9am–5pm.

Phad Thai Rock'n'Roll North end of Ao Kantiang. Delicious shrimp, chicken or veg pad thai (B90), expertly prepared by a famous local bass player, before he goes off to play with his band every evening. Daily 11am–4pm & 6–9pm.

Shanti Shanti Hat Khlong Nin. This unpretentious, roadside, French–Thai restaurant dishes up very good gourmet burgers with chips (B370), simple French main courses, crêpes and Western breakfasts, as well as superb home-made ice creams and espresso coffees. Also has a beachfront branch 2km north on Hat Khlong Tob serving Thai food. Mon–Sat 9am–noon & 6–10pm.

DRINKING AND NIGHTLIFE

On Long Beach, bars take turns putting on parties so there's usually something going on somewhere, as advertised on posters and fliers.

Ozone Bar On Ao Phra-Ae beach, north of *Somewhere Else* bungalows, ⓦ facebook.com/ozonebar. One of the most famous bars on the beach, especially for its weekly DJ parties on Thursday, which usually draw a lively crowd. Daily roughly 10am–2am.

DIRECTORY

Clinic Just south of Sala Dan town centre is South Lanta Medical Clinic (☎ 075 656134), with a branch at the south end of Khlong Khong (☎ 075 656843).
Police Sala Dan ☎ 075 668192.
Post office On the main road towards the north end of Ao Phra-Ae, just north of Andaman International Clinic.

The deep south

As Thailand drops down to meet Malaysia, the cultures of the two countries begin to merge. Many inhabitants of the **deep south** are ethnically more akin to the Malaysians, and a significant proportion of the 1,500,000 followers of Islam here speak a dialect of Malay. Some also yearn for secession from Thailand; since 2004 there has been continuing violence in the region, leading the Thai government to introduce special security measures in certain parts of Songkhla, Pattani, Yala and Narathiwat provinces – currently all but essential travel is advised against. For up-to-the-minute advice, consult your government travel advisory. The safest border crossings to Malaysia are detailed below.

TRANG AND AROUND

TRANG hosts a **vegetarian festival** every October that's similar to but smaller than Phuket's (see p.812), but is chiefly of interest for the string of gorgeous **beaches and islands** nearby. Travel agents offer snorkelling day-trips to the islands of Ko Hai, Ko Mook and Ko Kradan, which provide a perfect getaway and also have some accommodation. Trang province's coastline, from Ban Pak Meng down to Ban Chao Mai, offers some exceptional beaches, well worth exploring on a motorbike, by car or as part of a tour. Trang town's main thoroughfare is Thanon Rama VI, where you'll find restaurants, accommodation, banks and travel agents – most cluster near the train station at its western extremity.

ARRIVAL AND INFORMATION

By plane Trang Airport, around 3km south of town, is served by 1hr 30min flights from Bangkok's Don Muang Airport with AirAsia, Nok Air (both 3 daily) and Thai Lion Air (2 daily). On arrival, a/c minibuses bring passengers downtown (B90/person), while on departure you can charter a tuk-tuk or book a taxi through a travel agent (about B200/vehicle).
By bus and minibus All buses arrive at the terminal on Th Phatthalung (Highway 4), about 3km northeast of the centre; take a blue local bus or songthaew to the train station in the centre (both B12/person) or charter a tuk-tuk (about B80). Travel agents sell tickets for a/c minibus services to Ko Lanta (6 daily; 2hr 30min) and Pak Bara (at least 1 daily; 1hr 30min–2hr) in high season.
Destinations Bangkok (10 daily; 12–14hr); Krabi (roughly every 30min; 2–3hr); Nakhon Si Thammarat (hourly; 3hr); Phuket (hourly; 5hr); Satun (roughly hourly; 2–3hr).
By train From the train station at the western end of Th Rama VI, two trains depart for Bangkok daily (14–16hr).
Tourist information TAT have a helpful office on Th Huay Yod, about 2km north of the train station (daily 8.30am–4.30pm; ☎ 075 215867, ✉ tattrang@tat.or.th). The best travel agent in town is the helpful and clued-up Trang Island Hopping Tour, directly opposite the station at 28/2 Th Sathanee (☎ 082 804 0583, ☺ tour-in-trang.com), a great source of impartial information on the area.

ACCOMMODATION AND EATING

For a cheap feed, head for the very good night market on Th Ruenrom (100m up Th Rama VI from the clocktower, turn left).
Ban Aothong 25/28–31 Th Sathanee, less than 50m south of the station ☎ 086 479 5466. Multi-tiered roofs and gables announce this guesthouse, which sports chunky wooden furniture and canopied beds. Some rooms have no window, but all have a/c, hot water, fridges and cable TV. Light breakfast included. Doubles B650
Fatimah 28/2 Th Sathanee, directly opposite the station. Simple, popular halal restaurant attached to Trang Island Hopping Tour that serves a buffet of southern Thai curries, tasty pad thai (B40), tom yam, fried rice, local filtered coffee and tea. Tues–Sun 9am–9pm.
Sri Trang Hotel 22 Th Sathanee, 50m straight ahead from the station on the left ☎ 075 218122. Welcoming, thoroughly updated 1950s hotel offering a/c rooms with some colourful decorative touches, hot water, cable TV and fridges above a cool café. Doubles B600
Yamawa 94 Th Visetkul, north from the clocktower on Th Rama VI ☎ 075 216617, ☺ yamawaguesthouse.com. Around a stairwell decorated with hanging vines and pot plants, the rooms are en suite with cable TV, fridges, a/c and hot shower. Doubles B480

10

KO TARUTAO NATIONAL MARINE PARK

Ko Tarutao National Marine Park (B200 admission fee, valid for 5 days) is perhaps the most beautiful of all Thailand's accessible beach destinations. The park covers 51 mostly uninhabited islands, of which three – Tarutao, Adang and the more heavily developed and increasingly expensive Lipe – are easy to reach and have accommodation. The port of **Pak Bara**, towards the north end of Satun province, is the main jumping-off point for the park, and houses the main **national park visitor centre** (☎074 783485, ⊕nps.dnp.go.th), near the pier. There are several ATMs on Ko Lipe (including at the 7–11 near the middle of Walking Street), but none on Tarutao or Adang.

The park's forests and seas support a fascinating array of wildlife, including about 25 percent of the world's tropical fish species, as well as dugongs, sperm whales, dolphins and a dwindling population of turtles. Snorkelling gear can be rented on Tarutao (though there's little coral there) or Adang for B50 per day, and is widely available from the private bungalow outfits or dive shops on Ko Lipe. The park amenities on Tarutao and Adang are closed to tourists from mid-May to mid-October, while getting to Lipe at the height of the monsoon in September and early October is an unlikely – or at the very least unappealing – proposition.

Ko Tarutao

Hilly **Ko Tarutao**, the largest of the islands, is wild and covered in rainforest and has perfect beaches all along its 26km west coast. Boats dock at **Ao Pante**, on the northwestern side (see opposite), where you'll find the park headquarters, a visitor centre, a restaurant and a small shop, all of which have a slightly institutional feel; there is, in fact, an old prison on the island, now being reclaimed by the jungle. You can stay in the national park bungalows (B600–1000), more basic longhouses (B500, sleeps four), or tents (B225; bedding and pillows B50/person), or pitch your own tent (B30/person/night); kayaks and mountain bikes are available. Behind the settlement, the steep, half-hour

Tolkienesque climb to **To-Boo Cliff** is a must, especially at sunset, for its fine views. Boat trips, arranged at the park headquarters (1hr–1hr 30min; B500/boat; fits 8 people), venture up a bird-filled, mangrove-lined canal to Crocodile Cave. A half-hour walk south from Ao Pante brings you to the quiet, white-sand bays of **Ao Jak** and **Ao Molae**, the latter with bungalows (B600) and a good restaurant; beyond (2hr from Ao Pante; look out for the road behind the house at the south end of Ao Molae) lies **Ao Sone**, backed by a steep forested escarpment, with rooms (B300–800) and a simple restaurant. The Ao Pante visitor centre can arrange transport by road, usually in an open truck, to several of the island's beaches, charging B50/person to Ao Molae and around B800/vehicle for a return trip to Ao Sone.

Ko Adang

Ko Adang, an untamed island covered in rainforest where you really can get away from it all, has a **national park station** at Laem Sone beach, the luxurious white-sand curve of its southeast coast. Facilities include an inexpensive cafeteria-style restaurant, a visitor centre, and great-value en-suite bungalows overlooking the sea (B600). There are also tents for rent (B225; bedding and pillows B50/person), which can be pitched in a pleasant casuarina grove fronting the beach (pitch your own for B30/person). Should you wish to venture further afield, the visitor centre can give information on forest trails and waterfalls, and can organize excellent snorkelling trips to nearby islands (from B1500 for up to 8 people).

Ko Lipe

Home to around a thousand *chao ley* or sea gypsies (a traditionally nomadic group, with animistic beliefs and their own language), tiny **Ko Lipe**, just 2km south of Ko Adang, is something of a frontier maverick. It attracts ever more travellers with one dazzling beach – **Hat Pattaya**, a southwesterly crescent of squeaky-soft white sand, though sometimes clogged with longtails – a relaxed, anything-goes atmosphere and mellow nightlife.

Lipe's main drag is **Walking Street**, a paved path lined with tourist businesses between the eastern end of Hat Pattaya and the south end of the island village, which lies on east-facing **Sunrise**, an exposed, largely featureless beach that gives access to some good snorkelling around Ko Gra. Paved tracks run both from here and from the far west end of Pattaya across to **Sunset** beach, a shady, attractive spot with good views northwest to Ko Adang.

ARRIVAL AND DEPARTURE

By bus to Pak Bara To get to Pak Bara from Trang, either take the direct high-season a/c minibus opposite the train station (1hr 30min–2hr), or catch a Satun-bound bus (2hr–2hr 30min) to Langu and change to a red songthaew for the 10km hop to the port. From Satun, frequent buses and a/c minibuses travel the 50km to Langu.

By boat to the islands From Pak Bara, boats (mostly speedboats; 1hr 30min; B600–650) leave for Lipe (from where you'd need to take a longtail if heading for Ko Adang) up to six times daily in high season, once or twice daily in low season. Generally, they'll call in at Tarutao upon request (B400 from Pak Bara, B400–500 from Lipe). In high season, there's one daily ferry (5hr 30min; B1700; with a connection from Phuket and Ko Phi Phi) and two daily speedboat services (3–4hr; B2000) to Lipe from Ko Lanta, as well as boats from Langkawi (see p.453). There's no pier at Ko Lipe, but speedboats often run up onto the beach (Sunrise in the rainy season, Hat Pattaya at other times); otherwise, you'll be transferred onto a longtail – check if it's included in your ticket, but if not it's B50 to Ko Lipe shore, up to B200 to Ko Adang.

INFORMATION AND ACTIVITIES

Tourist information The best travel agent and source of information on Ko Lipe is Koh Lipe Thailand (Boi's Travel; ☎089 464 5854, ⌨ kohlipethailand.com), which has two outlets on Walking Street, with the main one hard by Hat Pattaya.

Activities The prime diving and snorkelling sites around Ko Lipe are around Ko Adang, Ko Rawi and Ko Dong, just to the north and west in Ko Tarutao National Marine Park, where encounters with reef and even whale sharks, dolphins and stingrays are not uncommon. Koh Lipe Thailand (☎089 464 5854, ⌨ kohlipethailand.com) run snorkelling day-trips and sunset trips for B300–800 per person. The well-regarded dive shop Lotus (at Pooh's on Walking Street between Sunrise and Hat Pattaya; ☎074 750345, ⌨ lotusdive.com) offers daily trips (from B2800 for two dives) and PADI courses (from B13,400 for the Openwater), as well as snorkelling equipment rental (B100/day).

ACCOMMODATION

PATTAYA BEACH

Café Lipe West of Walking Street, central Pattaya ☎086 969 9472, ⌨ cafe-lipe.com. Eco-conscious place in a great location, offering large, old-style bamboo bungalows that are nicely spaced out under a thick canopy of teak and fruit trees. Each has a partly outdoor, cold-water bathroom, fan and mosquito net. Good Western and Thai daytime restaurant. Doubles B800

Daya West end ☎081 542 9866 or ☎089 466 7318. This locally run resort with a popular seafood-barbecue restaurant on the beach provides colourful but basic en-suite accommodation in a large, shady, flower-strewn garden, ranging from concrete rooms to clapboard bungalows in a great position on the beach. Kayaks and snorkels available. Doubles B600

Gecko Lipe Resort Off the north side of Walking Street, 5min walk from Hat Pattaya ☎087 810 7257, ⌨ geckolipe.com. Set on a shady slope, these en-suite bamboo bungalows have shaggy thatched roofs, mosquito nets and a modicum of style; upgrade to deluxe for an indoor-outdoor hot shower, a large balcony and a bit more space. Doubles B1250

Koh Lipe Backpackers Hostel On the beach just east of Daya ☎085 361 7923, ⌨ kohlipebackpackers.com. Part of Davy Jones' Locker diving centre, this place has two a/c dorms in plain concrete rooms with thick mattresses, hot showers and lockers, as well as smart, en-suite private rooms. Dorms B700, doubles B2500

Seaside Near the midpoint ☎087 398 7932. Basic but sturdy woven-bamboo bungalows with large bathrooms and mosquito nets, in plenty of space on a grassy patch and mostly under shade, behind the popular Family restaurant. Doubles B600

SUNRISE BEACH

Adang Sea Divers and Eco Lodge Central beachfront ☎090 070 0233 85, ⌨ adangseadivers.com. Set among tamarind trees, this eco-friendly resort offers smart, clean and well-maintained accommodation, as well as free drinking water, tea and coffee. Choose either a room with

★TREAT YOURSELF

Castaway Beach Resort Sunrise beach, south of the village ☎083 138 7472, ⌨ castaway-resorts.com. The perfect place to splurge. The thatched, hardwood one- and two-storey bungalows are spacious and elegant, with large decks and hammocks, and the multi-tiered bar-restaurant fronting the beach is charming. There's also a dive shop and massage spa. Doubles B2700

10

10

INTO MALAYSIA FROM SOUTHERN THAILAND

Because of ongoing violence in parts of the deep south, all major Western governments are currently advising **against all but essential travel** through the Thai provinces of **Songkhla, Pattani, Yala and Narathiwat**. With violent attacks happening almost on a daily basis, it's important to check your country's foreign office advice (see box, p.45) for up-to-date information. The city and transport hub of **Hat Yai** and several of the main border crossings to Malaysia are included in the no-go zones, though trains do still run from Hat Yai (and Bangkok) to Butterworth via Padang Besar. Unaffected by the troubles, the safest routes into Malaysia are the border crossings from Satun and Ko Lipe.

FROM SATUN

Remote Satun, in the last wedge of Thailand's west coast, has boat and overland passages to Malaysia. Satun's bus terminal is at the town's southeastern periphery, but many buses also make a detour through the town centre. Should you need to stay here, head for helpful *On's Guesthouse* (☎074 724133; dorms B250, doubles B350), 36 Th Bureewanit, near the central Mambang Mosque; On is the main fixer for transport tickets and tourist information in town. **Ferries** to the Malaysian island of Langkawi depart from Thammalang pier, 10km south of town (2–3 daily; 1hr 15min; B350; ⌨langkawi-ferry.com); songthaews (B40) to Thammalang leave from near the 7-Eleven on Th Sulakanukul. Longtail boats no longer run from Thammalang to Kuala Perlis but there is an irregular a/c minibus from Satun to Malaysia's Kangar (which has bus connections to Penang and Kuala Lumpur) – contact On (see above) to book tickets.

FROM KO LIPE

In high season, there are at least two boats a day between Langkawi and Lipe (1hr 30min; B1050–1200), serviced by an immigration office box on Lipe's Pattaya Beach.

FROM HAT YAI

It is not recommended to travel to Hat Yai, but being a major transport hub and stop-off point to or from Malaysia, you might find yourself stuck here. If so, make your way to *Cathay Guest House* (93/1 Th Niphat Uthit 2; ☎074 243815; B240), a short walk east of the train station, which has a small café, basic en-suite rooms and a useful travel agency downstairs.

mosquito screens in a concrete longhouse at right angles to the beach, or a cheaper bamboo bungalow with a mosquito net on the bed. Doubles B1150

SUNSET BEACH

Bila Beach 5min walk down the coast from Sunset Beach and 5min over the hill from the west end of Pattaya ☎097 359 7946, ⌨bilabeach.weebly.com. This hideaway resort has its own small, white-sand beach, where the bar-restaurant serves good Thai and Western food. On the slopes behind, the bungalows are old-school, made entirely from bamboo (even the beds and verandahs), with outdoor bathrooms, mosquito nets and thatched roofs. Doubles B1650

EATING AND DRINKING

The east end of Pattaya has Lipe's biggest concentration of bars, with low candlelit tables and cushions sprawled on the sand, fire shows and names like *Peace and Love*.

Elephant Walking Street, 100m inland from Pattaya ☎083 169 1216. Mellow restaurant and secondhand bookshop with live music every night, where you can tuck into delicious burgers made with Australian beef (B300), as well as pizzas, sandwiches, salads, breakfasts, cakes and espressos. Daily 7am–1am.

Pooh's On Walking Street between Sunrise and Hat Pattaya ☎087 392 3838. This welcoming, long-standing bar-restaurant is a popular hive of activity, offering tasty Thai food, including vegetarian dishes (around B150), as well as sandwiches, evening barbecues, DJs and live music. Daily roughly 7am–10.30pm.

FLOATING MARKET NEAR CAN THO

Vietnam

HIGHLIGHTS

❶ Hanoi Sample the street food of the captivating capital city. **See p.842**

❷ Sa Pa and around Hike amid rice terraces and stay in minority tribe villages. **See p.863**

❸ Phong Nha–Ke Bang National Park Go caving or jungle trekking. **See p.870**

❹ Hoi An Admire beautifully preserved historical houses and feast on great food. **See p.883**

❺ Nha Trang Vietnam's beach central is perfect for partying and snorkelling. **See p.889**

❻ HCMC Eat, drink and party in Vietnam's liveliest city. **See p.903**

❼ Mekong Delta Cycle through the lush countryside and cruise the waterways. **See p.912**

HIGHLIGHTS ARE MARKED ON THE MAP ON P.829

ROUGH COSTS

Daily budget Basic US$25–30/Occasional treat US$45

Drink Bottle of beer US$1

Food Pho (noodle soup) US$1.50

Hostel/Budget hotel US$6/US$12–20

Travel Hanoi to Hue (660km): train 14hr, hard sleeper US$26; tourist bus 12hr, US$26

FACT FILE

Population 94.4 million

Language Vietnamese

Religion Mahayana Buddhism, Catholicism, animism, Protestantism, Hoa Hao, Cao Dai

Currency Vietnamese dong (VND) or US$

Capital Hanoi

International phone code ☏ +84

Time zone GMT + 7hr

Introduction

One has to admire Vietnam – despite some rather heavy recent history, the country has bounced back to become a fully-fledged big-hitter, and occasional firm favourite, on the Southeast Asia travel circuit. As one would expect from a country so long and skinny, there's plenty of variety on offer – a land of shimmering paddy fields and white-sand beaches, historical cities and venerable pagodas, vast caves, craggy mountains and friendly minority tribes. Visitors are generally met with warmth, curiosity and a seemingly irrepressible desire to connect; add in some of the region's most nuanced cuisine, and you're onto a winner.

For many visitors, venerable **Hanoi** – Vietnam's capital for close on a thousand years – provides a full-on introduction to Vietnam, its mad traffic clashing with its colonial buildings, pagodas and dynastic temples. From here, many strike out east to the labyrinth of limestone outcrops and karst jutting out of the azure **Ha Long Bay**. The market town of **Sa Pa**, set in spectacular uplands close to the Chinese border in the far northwest, makes a good base for exploring nearby ethnic minority villages. Heading south, **Phang Nha Ke Banh National Park** is home to the world's largest cave, with one of the most picturesque parts of the **Ho Chi Minh Trail** winding its way through the beautiful countryside. Further south still, beyond the wartime memorials of the **DMZ**, is aristocratic **Hue**, with its temples, palaces and imperial mausoleums. Next up comes the most beautiful city in Vietnam: **Hoi An**, its city centre full of beautifully preserved wooden shophouses and some of the best food in the country. If you then head further south, the quaint hill station of **Da Lat** provides a good place to cool down, but some travellers eschew the highlands for the **beaches** of **Mui Ne** or **Nha Trang**. The southern gateway to Vietnam is the furiously commercial city of **Ho Chi Minh City** (**HCMC**, formerly Saigon), where memories of the Vietnam War are immortalized in one of the country's best museums. In contrast, the southernmost part of the country, the **Mekong Delta** – rice fields and orchards bisected by canals and the slow-moving river – provides an antidote to the high-octane cities, with its slow pace of life and **cycling trails** running through the lush greenery.

CHRONOLOGY

2789 BC Vang Lang kingdom – the first independent Vietnamese state – is founded by the Hung Vuong kings.

WHEN TO GO

Vietnam has a tropical **monsoon climate**, dominated by the south or southwesterly monsoon from May to September and the northeast monsoon from October to April. Overall, late September to December and March and April are the best times if you're covering the whole country, but there are distinct regional variations. In **southern Vietnam and the Central Highlands** the dry season lasts from December to April, and daytime temperatures rarely drop below 20°C in the lowlands, averaging 30°C during March, April and May. Along the **Central Coast** the wet season runs from September to February, though even the dry season brings a fair quantity of rain; temperatures average 30°C from June to August. Typhoons can hit the coast around Hue in April and May and the northern coast from July to November, when flooding is a regular occurrence. **Hanoi and northern Vietnam** are generally hot (30°C) and very wet during the summer, warm and sunny from October to December, then cool and misty until March.

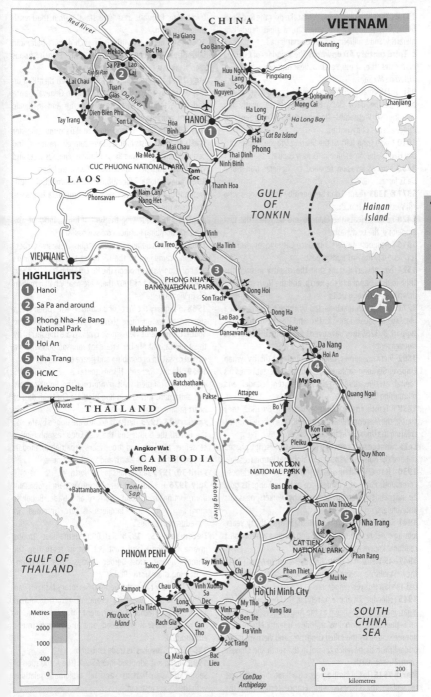

VIETNAM

11

HIGHLIGHTS

1 Hanoi
2 Sa Pa and around
3 Phong Nha–Ke Bang
   National Park
4 Hoi An
5 Nha Trang
6 HCMC
7 Mekong Delta

CHINA

Red River

Ha Giang
Cao Bang
Nanning
Bac Ha
Hekou
Fan Si Pan
Sa Pa   Lao
          Cai
Lai Chau
          Tuan
          Gias   Da River
Dien Bien Phu
Tay Trang   Son La
                  Hoa
                  Binh
          Mai Chau
Na Meo
CUC PHUONG NATIONAL PARK
                  Tam
                  Coc
LAOS
Phonsavan   Nam Can/
             Nong Het
VIENTIANE
          Cau Treo
                  Ha Tinh
Huu Nghi
Thai   Lang
Nguyen   Son   Pingxiang
                  Dongxing
                  Mong Cai   Zhanjiang
Ha Long
City   Ha Long Bay
            Cat Ba Island
HANOI
1
          Hai
          Phong
Thai Binh
Ninh Binh
Thanh Hoa
          GULF
          OF
          TONKIN
                  Hainan
                  Island
Vinh

3
PHONG NHA-KE BANG NATIONAL PARK
          Dong Hoi
Son Trach
          Dong Ha
Lao Bao
Mukdahan   Savannakhet
            Dansavanh   Hue
                              Da Nang
                              Hoi An
                         4
                         My Son
Ubon
Ratchathani   Quang Ngai
          Attapeu
          Pakse   Bo Y
Khorat   Kon Tum
THAILAND   Pleiku
                              Quy Nhon
          Angkor Wat
CAMBODIA   YOK DON
               NATIONAL PARK
Siem Reap
          Tonle
          Sap   Ban Don
Battambang   Buon Ma Thuot
          Mekong River   5   Nha Trang
                         Da
                         Lat
                    CAT TIEN
                    NATIONAL PARK
PHNOM PENH   Phan Rang
          Tay Ninh
Takeo   Cu   Phan Thiet
          Chi   Mui Ne
                    6
Kampot   Chau Doc Ho Chi Minh City
          Vinh Xuong
          Long Sa   Vung Tau
Ha Tien   Xuyen Dec
                    My Tho
Phu Quoc Rach Gia Vinh
Island   Long Ben Tre
          Can   SOUTH
          Tho   7   Tra Vinh   CHINA
                    Soc Trang   SEA
GULF
OF   Ca Mau   Bac
THAILAND   Lieu
          Con Dao
          Archipelago

N

Metres
2000
1000
400
0

0   200
kilometres

11

111 BC The Chinese Han emperors take over the Red River Delta; they introduce Confucianism, a rigid, feudalistic hierarchy, and a millennium of occupation.

c. Third century AD onwards The kingdom of Champa dominates the south, and builds numerous temples, including My Son.

938 AD Vietnamese forces defeat the Chinese at the battle of the Bach Dang River, heralding nearly ten centuries of Vietnamese independence (in the north) under a series of dynasties.

1010 Thanh Long (City of the Soaring Dragon) – present-day Hanoi – becomes Vietnam's new capital.

1288 Mongol invasion repelled by General Tran Hung Dao's forces.

1377 & 1383 Thanh Long besieged by Cham forces who kill Viet emperor Tran Due.

1428 Le Loi defeats the Chinese and becomes the first emperor of the Le dynasty.

1516 Portuguese traders introduce Catholicism via Faifo (present-day Hoi An) trading post.

1524 Two powerful clans split the country in two: the Trinh lords in Hanoi and the north, and the Nguyen in Hue down to the Mekong Delta.

1771 The Tay Son rebellion, led by three brothers with a message of equal rights, justice and liberty, gains broad support. By 1788 they have overthrown both the Trinh and Nguyen lords.

1802 Vietnam comes under a single authority when Emperor Gia Long captures the throne and establishes his capital at Hue, building its magnificent citadel and reimposing feudal order.

1858 A French armada captures Da Nang. By 1862, they control the Mekong Delta, and by 1887 the whole country, creating the Union of Indochina.

Late nineteenth century Chinese-style script phased out and the Romanized *quoc ngu* alphabet introduced.

1930 Ho Chi Minh establishes the Indochinese Communist Party at a conference in Hong Kong, its goal an independent Vietnam governed by workers, peasants and soldiers.

1941 Ho Chi Minh returns to Vietnam after thirty years, joining other resistance leaders and forging a nationalist coalition, known as the Viet Minh.

1941–45 Vietnam is controlled by Japan; in March 1945 they establish a nominally independent state under Bao Dai, the last Nguyen emperor.

1945 Following Japanese surrender, Ho Chi Minh calls for a national uprising, known as the August Revolution, and on September 2 proclaims an independent Vietnam. It is not recognized by the Allied countries, and Vietnam is put under British then French control in the south and Chinese control in the north.

March 1946 Ho Chi Minh agrees on a limited French force to replace the Chinese, with France recognizing the

Democratic Republic as a "free state" within the French Union in return.

1946–54 The treaty with the French doesn't hold, and skirmishes between Vietnamese and French troops escalate into war (the First Indochina War).

May 1954 The French are defeated at Dien Bien Phu on May 7, just as peace discussions begin in Geneva. France and the Viet Minh agree to a ceasefire and to divide Vietnam, pending elections.

July 1954 In Saigon, Emperor Bao Dai's prime minister Ngo Dinh Diem ousts him, declares himself President, and begins silencing his enemies, including religious sects and Viet Minh dissidents – more than 50,000 are killed.

1960 The National Liberation Front is formed in South Vietnam to oppose Diem's regime; its guerrilla forces are known as the Viet Cong.

August 1964 Following the Gulf of Tonkin incident, the US starts bombing northern coastal bases.

1965 Operation Rolling Thunder begins, a massive carpet-bombing campaign by the US to try to stop the North's lines of supply south, along the Ho Chi Minh Trail (see box, p.902). By the end of 1967 there are nearly half a million GIs in Vietnam.

1968 In January the Viet Cong launch the Tet Offensive, a surprise attack on more than a hundred towns in the South. Hundreds of Vietnamese civilians are massacred by the Americans at My Lai. President Johnson announces a virtual cessation of bombing and peace talks begin.

1969 Under Richard Nixon there is a gradual US withdrawal coupled with reinforcing the South's army and a dramatic increase in bombing. Ho Chi Minh dies of heart failure.

January 27, 1973 The Paris Accords are signed by the US, the North, the South and the Viet Cong, establishing a ceasefire; all American troops are repatriated, though fighting between the North and South continues.

April 30, 1975 Saigon falls to the North.

July 1976 The Socialist Republic of Vietnam is officially born, nationalizing land, industry and trade. Buddhist monks, priests and intellectuals are interned in "re-education camps".

December 25, 1978 120,000 Vietnamese troops invade Cambodia and oust Pol Pot in retaliation for Khmer Rouge cross-border forays into Vietnam, remaining there until 1989.

1986 The new reformist General Secretary Nguyen Van Linh introduces sweeping economic reforms, known as *doi moi*, Vietnam's equivalent of perestroika. A market economy is embraced, and foreign investment encouraged.

1994 The US revokes its trade embargo.

1995 Vietnam is admitted into ASEAN (the Association of Southeast Asian Nations), and full diplomatic relations with the US are restored.

2007 Vietnam joins the WTO.

2008–9 The global economic crisis rocks Vietnam, as the stock market loses seventy percent of its value.

2009 The world's largest cave – Son Doong – is found in Vietnam's Phong Nha region.

2013 Hundreds of thousands evacuated in preparation for Typhoon Haiyan, which made landfall near Haiphong, killing three people.

2018 Estimated date of completion of the Ho Chi Minh City metro – the country's first subway system.

ARRIVAL AND DEPARTURE

Vietnam has three main **international airports**: Noi Bai in Hanoi, Tan Son Nhat in HCMC and Da Nang in central Vietnam. The national airline is Vietnam Airlines, with flights to and from Asia, Europe, Australia and the US. The cheapest option to get to Vietnam from outside Asia is usually to take a flight to Bangkok, Kuala Lumpur or Singapore, and take a budget connecting flight.

The main airports in Hanoi and HCMC both handle flights to major cities (and some more minor bases) all across East and Southeast Asia, and plenty more beyond. Low-cost airfares are offered by many of the regional players (see p.34).

A large number of travellers, especially backpackers, arrive overland through one of Vietnam's **borders** with Cambodia, Laos and China. **Visas** for Vietnam must be arranged in advance (see below).

OVERLAND FROM CAMBODIA

Tourist buses ply the route between Phnom Penh and **HCMC**, via the **Moc Bai–Bavet** border crossing (see box, p.86). Foreigners can also cross at a popular border crossing at **Vinh Xuong–Kaam Samnor**, near Chau Doc in the Mekong Delta; some tour operators run boats from Phnom Penh down the Mekong River through to Chau Doc in Vietnam (see box, p.86). There is another border checkpoint near Chau Doc at **Tinh Bien–Phnom Den** (see box, p.916), or at **Xa Xia–Prek Chak** (see box, p.113) near Kep and Kampot on the Cambodian side, and just 10km from Ha Tien in Vietnam.

OVERLAND FROM LAOS

Travellers can choose from six border crossings between **Laos** and Vietnam. **Lao Bao–Dansavanh** (see box, p.397), roughly 240km from Savannakhet, is the most popular, though the international bus link between Savannakhet and Da Nang can take up to 24 hours.

There are also border crossings open at **Bo Y–Pho Keau** near Kon Tum in the Central Highlands (see box, p.403) and **Tay Trang–Sop Hun** near Dien Bien Phu in the far northwest (see box, p.387), which offer two interesting but challenging routes. There are additional crossings close to the Vietnamese city of Vinh at **Cau Treo–Nam Phao** (see box, p.393); **Na Maew–Nam Xoi**, near Sam Neua in northeastern Laos; and **Nong Het–Nam Can**, east of Phonsavan in Laos (see box, p.383).

OVERLAND FROM CHINA

At the time of writing, the Chinese border was open to foreigners at three points: **Lao Cai–Hekou** from Kunming (see box, p.863), the little-used **Mong Cai–Dongxing** from Guangzhou (see box, p.858) and, busiest of all, at **Youyiguan–Huu Nghi Quan** from Pingxiang or Nanning (see box, p.855). There is one **direct train service** between China and Vietnam from Beijing to Hanoi (see box, p.855). The Kunming–Hanoi service was suspended in 2004; the Chinese side of the line finally reopened in 2014, though there are still no direct services, and you'll need to use taxis or buses to bridge the gap over the border.

VISAS

Most foreign nationals need a **visa** to enter Vietnam – citizens of some Asian and Nordic nations get 15–30 days visa-free, and from 2016–17 the government allowed the same of passport-holders from the UK, France, Germany, Italy and Spain (retracted in mid-2017, though potentially to be reintroduced). **Tourist visas** are generally valid for **thirty days** from your specified arrival date and cost $25–90, depending on where you apply (Bangkok, Phnom

11

Penh and Jakarta are at the cheap and speedy end of the spectrum). **Three-month visas** are also available for $100 to $145; both types take three to ten days to process, though some agencies and consulates offer an express one-day service.

There are a growing number of **authorized agents** in Vietnam – including Ann Tours and STA in HCMC and Hanoi – who can issue **visas on arrival** (contact the agent five days in advance to secure paperwork; costs start at $20 plus $25 "stamp fee"). Though in reality more "pre-arranged" than "on-arrival", they can be helpful for people with no Vietnamese consulate in their home country, or those strapped for time – note that they can only be picked up at Hanoi, HCMC or Da Nang airports, not at land border crossings. The agent will email you a special clearance document, which you'll need to print out to hand it in upon arrival at one of Vietnam's international airports, along with a passport-sized photo and a completed application form (available at the airport) in order to be granted a visas. A number of online agencies offer visas on arrival; some are scams while others are reliable; the latter include Vietnam Evisa (ⓦvietnam-evisa.org) and Vietnam Visa Center (ⓦvietnamvisacenter.org).

At the time of writing, **thirty-day visa extensions** were being issued through tour agents and travellers' cafés in HCMC, Da Lat, Nha Trang, Hoi An, Hue, Da Nang and Hanoi (from $25; 1–5 working days, depending on where you apply), but the situation changes frequently, so check with the embassy before you leave. The **fine** for overstaying your visa can also vary; fines cannot be paid at the airport, so if you do overstay make sure to visit an immigration office before trying to board your plane.

GETTING AROUND

Vietnam's main thoroughfare is Highway 1, which runs from Hanoi to HCMC and is shadowed by the country's main rail line. **Public transport** is comprehensive and inexpensive; in addition to the north-south rail line, various buses and minibuses connect all towns and cities, while domestic flights are now also a cheap, viable means of transport. Fast passenger ferries connect the mainland to outlying islands such as Phu Quoc in the south and Cat Ba in the north. There's still room for improvement, however: buses are at the mercy of slow traffic that clogs up Vietnam's main roads, while trains get booked up weeks in advance before Tet New Year celebrations in January/February.

PLANES

There are four airlines offering **domestic flights**; Vietnam Airlines (ⓦvietnamairlines.com) is the flag-carrier, and has the most comprehensive network from Hanoi and HCMC, though these days budget carriers Jetstar (ⓦjetstar.com) and VietJet Air (ⓦvietjetair.com) run many of the same routes too, and new ones have sprung up linking some provincial cities directly. Vasco (ⓦvasco.com.vn) links Ho Chi Minh City with destinations around the Mekong Delta. Even if you're on a budget, flights can be quite affordable – the two-hour ones linking Hanoi and HCMC, for instance, can cost as little as $20.

BUSES, MINIBUSES AND OPEN-TOUR BUSES

Vietnam's **national bus network** offers daily services between all major towns, served by a mixture of ancient, jam-packed local buses and minibuses that leave when full, and deluxe air-conditioned buses.

For longer journeys, tickets are best bought a day in advance, since many routes are heavily over-subscribed. Most bus stations (there is often more than one in major cities) have boards displaying timetables and departures.

Most foreigners – and, these days, the majority of locals too – travel from city to city on high-quality **air-conditioned buses**, some of which are **sleeping buses** with fully reclined seats. They're run by a bunch of private transport companies, including the recognizable white-and-green Mai Linh Express (ⓦmailinh.vn) buses, and the bright orange Futa Express (⊚futabus.vn) ones; these big companies occasionally use their own dedicated terminals. Services run according to set timetables, and many companies also offer free pick-up and drop-off, effectively taking you from door to door. In addition, your accommodation may well agree to call for a ticket reservation and pick-up – tremendously convenient, all in all, though note that there are no toilets on board, with rest breaks occurring every few hours.

Part of this air-conditioned fleet are "**open-tour**" buses shuttling two or three times daily between major tourist destinations. For those with a good idea of their route, one-way open tickets can be a good idea – for example, from HCMC to Hue ($32) or Hanoi ($45), stopping off at specified destinations en route, usually Mui Ne, Da Lat, Nha Trang, Hoi An, Da Nang and Hue. Sinh Tourist (⊚thesinhtourist.vn) was the first company to offer this service, and is still among the best. Tickets and onward reservations are available from agents in each town; book a day in advance.

Rarely used by travellers these days, **local buses** are good for short journeys, as are local **minibuses**; both pick up passengers en route and can be flagged down along roads.

Watch your **luggage** at stops, and don't accept drinks from strangers as there's a chance of being drugged and robbed.

BOATS

Frequent ferries and boats run between the mainland and Phu Quoc Island, as well as between Nha Trang and outlying islands and Hoi An and the Cham Islands. Boats also used to be one of the best ways of traversing the Mekong Delta, though services are now limited to cross-river hops, and recreational river tours.

TRAINS

Though Vietnamese **trains** (⊚dsvn.vn) can be slow on some services, they generally provide the most comfortable and pleasant way to travel the country. The website ⊚seat61.com is a useful resource.

The main line shadows Highway 1 on its way from **HCMC to Hanoi** (1726km), passing through Nha Trang, Da Nang and Hue en route. **From Hanoi**, one branch goes northwest to Lao Cai; another runs north to Dong Dang, which is the route taken by the two weekly trains from **Hanoi to Beijing**; and the third goes to **Hai Phong**.

The most popular lines with tourists are the shuttle from Da Nang to Hue, which offers some of the most stunning views in the country, and the overnighters from Hue to Hanoi and from Hanoi up to Lao Cai, for Sa Pa. Four "**Reunification Express**" trains, labelled SE1 to SE8, depart each day from Hanoi to HCMC and vice versa, taking 33–37 hours; there are also cheaper commuter trains, which stop at nearly every station.

There are four main ticket **classes** of travel: hard seat, soft seat, hard sleeper and soft sleeper. It's worth paying extra for more comfort. Hard seats are packed wooden benches in smoky carriages with trash on the floor; they're gradually being phased out. Soft seats are regular coach-style seats. On overnight journeys, you should go for a **berth**: cramped hard-sleeper berth compartments have three tiers of bunks (six bunks in total, the cheapest at the top), while soft-sleeper berths have only four bunks. Bed linen is provided, but you may have to ask the carriage attendant for fresh sheets if you get on anywhere besides the initial boarding station, as they don't get changed automatically.

On the express trains, all compartments bar cattle-class have air-conditioning, and reclining soft seats are located in new double-decker carriages; they have free wi-fi. Several private companies have designated first-class "tourist carriages" attached to the night trains between Hanoi and Lao Cai (for Sa Pa). Booking ahead for sleeper berths is essential, and it's possible to book tickets online (though there have been teething problems with the system); you'll need to enter your passport number, and to show the document itself if buying tickets at the station.

Fares vary according to class, and also slightly by train number. A soft seat from

11

Hanoi to HCMC will generally cost around 905,000VND, a hard sleeper from 985,000VND, and a soft sleeper from 1,335,000VND. Fares on slower trains tend to be cheaper.

VEHICLE RENTAL

Bicycles are available from hotels and tour agencies in most towns for around 50,000VND per day. Small **motorbike** rental (150,000–200,000/day) is possible in most major destinations, but you have to be confident to cope with the hazardous conditions on Vietnam's roads and be aware that the risk of an accident is very real (see box below). Organized motorbike tours can be a better option (see p.838); trail bikes rent for around 500,000VND/day, and comprehensive travel insurance is essential. If you go it alone, check everything carefully, especially brakes, lights, horn and the small print on your **insurance** policy, and carry a repair kit. **Repair shops** are ubiquitous – look for a Honda sign or ask for *sua chua xe may* (motorbike repairs). Fuel (*xang*) is around 18,000VND/l and widely available.

The theory is that you **drive on the right**, though in practice motorists and cyclists swerve and dodge wherever they want, using their **horn** instead of a brake. **Right of way** invariably goes to the biggest vehicle on the road; pull over onto the hard shoulder to avoid them. Road conditions can be extremely poor in rural areas; watch out for livestock, giant potholes, children and landslides. Police frequently fine motorists for real and imagined offences, including speeding. If you are involved in an **accident** and it is deemed to be your fault, the penalties can involve major fines.

LOCAL TRANSPORT

Taxis are common in big cities, and inexpensive by Western standards, charging around 10,000–15,000VND/km. Most branded companies are fine, though it's still prudent to use well-known ones such as Mai Linh, as some taxis have been known to use rigged meters that run at lightning pace – check that the meter is reset at the start of your journey. Travellers on very tight budgets may use some local city **bus** services, which can be handy for transport between major bus stations and shuttling to and from the airports, though it can be extremely time-consuming. Other modes of transport include the ubiquitous *xe om* (pronounced: zay-ohm) or motorbike taxi. Drivers loiter at bus stations and cruise along the roads to solicit custom. Negotiate the price before getting on; a short ride should cost around 10,000–15,000VND, a longer (more than 2km) ride or night ride 20,000–25,000VND.

ACCOMMODATION

Compared to some Southeast Asian countries, such as Indonesia, **accommodation** in Vietnam is more expensive but generally of good quality. Free wi-fi is pretty much ubiquitous, even in budget accommodation. The cheapest option is a bed in a **dormitory**; an increasing number of budget guesthouses (*nha khach* or *nha nghi*) and rooms for rent in Hanoi, HCMC and other tourist centres offer dorms at around $5–9 per bed per night. Genuine youth hostels (mostly foreign-run) exist only in a few cities, such as Hanoi, HCMC, Mui Ne and Hue, and a full range of services is on offer – tours, guest lounge, bar and so on. Next up is a

---

WEAR A HELMET

A shocking 11,000 people or so die every year on Vietnamese roads, and a further 30,000 are seriously injured. **Traffic accidents** are the leading cause of death, severe injury and evacuation for foreigners. Insist on a helmet before renting a motorbike or getting on the back of a *xe om*, and check that the chin straps are properly adjusted and fastened before taking off. Wearing a helmet is compulsory, though the law doesn't specify the type of helmet, as a result of which many wear nothing more than glorified eggshells. Cheap plastic helmets can be bought in nearly every town for as little as 50,000VND; for more serious protection, you can pick up a sturdier imported helmet in Hanoi and HCMC for 700,000VND or so.

ADDRESSES

Where two numbers are separated by a slash, such as 110/5, you simply make for number 110, where an alley will lead off to a further batch of buildings – you want the fifth one. Where a number is followed by a letter, as in 117a, you're looking for a single block encompassing several addresses, of which one will be 117a.

simple en-suite fan room in either a **state-run hotel** (*khach san*) or (usually family-run) **guesthouse** for around $8–12. In the main tourist destinations, **mini-hotels** (a modest, privately owned hotel) and **hotels** offer decent en-suite rooms, with fans and hot water, for around $10–15; add air-conditioning and satellite TV and they can range from $15 to $35; both are very good value and some throw in a free breakfast. **Rates** are sometimes negotiable in budget hotels in rural areas, and during low season prices can drop by up to fifty percent.

Hotel **security** can be a problem – it's generally fine at proper hotels, but at budget guesthouses (or, of course, dorms) never leave valuables in your room.

On the whole there's little need to book ahead, not even during the festival of Tet (Jan/Feb), as most destinations have plentiful budget accommodation.

Upon check-in, you're required to hand in your passport; lodgings tend to hold on to it until your departure, in lieu of a deposit.

FOOD AND DRINK

The cheapest and most fun places to eat are the **street kitchens**, which range from makeshift food stalls set up on the street to open-fronted eating houses. They are permanent, with an address if not a name, and most serve one type of local speciality, generally indicated on a signboard. **Com binh dan**, "people's meals", comprise an array of prepared dishes like stuffed tomatoes, fried fish, tofu, pickles and eggs, plus rice; expect to pay from 30,000VND for a good plateful. Outside the major cities, street kitchens rarely stay open beyond 8pm.

Western-style **Vietnamese restaurants** (*nha hang*) serve a wide range of meat and fish dishes. Most restaurants aimed at tourists serve a range of Vietnamese and Western dishes; large cities and tourist hotspots such as Hanoi, HCMC and Nha Trang also have good international food, with Indian, French and Italian the easiest to track down. A modest meal can cost anywhere from 70,000VND, though at pricier places mains are around 200,000VND. Catering primarily to budget travellers, **travellers' cafés** tend to serve reasonably priced Western and Vietnamese dishes – from banana pancakes to steak and chips or fried noodles.

VIETNAMESE FOOD

Vietnamese food is distinctive, using plenty of fresh herbs, though flavours and dishes vary depending on the region. The cuisine relies on a balance of salty, sweet, sour and hot flavours, achieved through use of *nuoc mam*, a fermented **fish sauce**, cane sugar, the juice of kalamansi citrus fruit or tamarind, and chilli peppers. Vietnamese food tends not to be overly spicy, as chilli sauces are served separately, but pepper is used liberally; Vietnamese pepper is some of the most flavourful in the world.

The staple of Vietnamese meals is **rice** (*com*), with **noodles** (*mi*) a popular alternative, and potatoes eaten in the northern highlands. Typically, rice will be accompanied by a fish or meat dish, a vegetable dish and a soup. The other great staple is **pho** (its approximate pronunciation akin to the British "fur"), a noodle soup eaten at any time of day but primarily at breakfast. The basic bowl of pho consists of a light beef or chicken broth flavoured with ginger and coriander, to which are added broad, flat rice noodles, spring onions and slivers of chicken, pork or beef; there are regional variations.

Spring rolls (*nem*) are ubiquitous throughout Vietnam. Various combinations of minced pork, shrimp or crab, rice vermicelli, onions, straw mushroom, catfish and dill, bean sprouts and fragrant herbs are rolled in rice-paper

11

11

wrappers, and then eaten fresh or deep-fried, usually dipped in the ubiquitous chilli-fish sauce, or a dark peanut sauce. **Steamboat** (*lau*) is the Vietnamese take on the Chinese hotpot, with groups of diners cooking slices of meat and seafood in the communal pot, and then afterwards drinking the flavourful liquid that's left.

Vietnam is a great country for **seafood**, with clams, crab, prawns, squid, and all manner of fish (including snake-head and elephant-ear fish in the Mekong Delta). Meats consumed include beef, chicken and pork; less conventional sources of protein include freshwater snails, rat, dog, snake and frogs.

Most restaurants offer a few **meat-free dishes**, such as stewed spinach or similar greens, or a mix of onion, tomato, bean sprouts, various mushrooms and peppers (*rau xao cac loai*); places used to foreigners may do **vegetarian** spring rolls (*nem an chay* or *nem khong co thit*). The phrase to remember is *nguoi an chay* (vegetarian), or seek out a vegetarian rice-shop (*tiem com chay*) – Buddhist restaurants that serve faux-meat dishes.

Regional specialities not to miss in the south include: *bahn mi* (baguette sandwiches with fillings including sausage, pâté and omelette), *canh chua ca* (a hearty Mekong Delta soup with snakehead fish, pineapple and taro in a tamarind broth), and *banh xeo* (chewy rice crepe with pork, shrimp and mung bean filling). Central Vietnam is famous for *bun bo hue* (rice noodle soup with chilli, lemongrass, beef, pork and herbs), *com hen* (rice served with tiny clams and broth, garnished with rice crackers, pork crackling, herbs and vegetables), and *bahn khoai* (crepes filled with shrimp, pork, bean sprouts, star fruit and green banana, dunked in a fermented soybean sauce). In Hoi An and further north you'll find claypot dishes featuring smoky charred aubergine, while northern dishes include *bahn cuon* (steamed rice rolls filled with pork, mushrooms and dried shrimp, garnished with crispy shallots), *bun cha* (barbecued pork patties with rice, vermicelli and fresh herbs, dipped in fish sauce with pickled vegetables) and

pho bo (beef noodle soup made with shallot, black cardamom, star anise and fish sauce).

Vietnam is blessed with dozens of tropical and temperate **fruits**. Pineapple, coconut, papaya, mango, longan and mangosteen flourish in the south. A fruit that people either love or hate is the **durian**, a spiky, yellow-green football-sized fruit with an unmistakeably pungent odour and a strong taste. Vegetables such as aubergines and potatoes are widely used, particularly in northern cooking; look out also for wonderful salads that use banana blossoms and green papaya.

DRINKS

Don't drink the **tap water** in Vietnam; bottled water and carbonated drinks are ubiquitous throughout the country.

Good thirst-quenchers include fresh coconut milk, orange, lime and other fruit **juices**, and sugar-cane juice (*mia da*). Somewhere between a drink and a snack is **chè**, sold in glasses at the markets. Made from taro flour and green bean, it's served over ice with chunks of fruit, coloured jellies and even sweetcorn or potato.

Vietnam is one of the world's leading exporters of **coffee**; domestically it's usually taken strong in small, espresso-like doses. Locals tend to have it black with sugar (*ca phé den*), iced (*ca phé da*), or with a dollop of sweetened condensed milk (*ca phé sua*); foreigners may prefer it made unsweetened, with actual milk (*ca phé tuoi*). Green tea is also widely available.

Several foreign **beers** are brewed under licence in Vietnam, but good local brews include 333, Halida and Saigon; **craft beer** is now also a very big deal in Hanoi and HCMC. On the other end of the quality and price scale, **bia hoi** ("fresh" or draught beer) is super-cheap, served warm from the keg and then poured over ice – it has a 24-hour shelf life, so the better places sell out by early evening, and most offer snacks of some sort. You'll also come across rice wine (*ruou*), a strong (and often foul) spirit often flavoured with herbs, fruit and spices. In the northern part of the country, locals drink it through long bamboo straws from communal clay vessels. Avoid buying *ruou ran* (snake wine with pickled cobras inside); this elixir is allegedly good for male virility but bad news for the endangered cobra population.

CULTURE AND ETIQUETTE

Vietnam shares similar **attitudes to dress and social taboos** (see p.40) as other Southeast Asian cultures. In a pagoda or temple you are also expected to leave a small **donation**; taking photos inside a temple is a sign of disrespect, though these days even locals are doing it. If you have been invited to dinner, always wait for your host to be seated first, and never refuse food that is placed in your bowl during the meal; it will be taken as a sign of ingratitude.

Tipping is not expected, but greatly appreciated; some upmarket restaurants will automatically add a service charge. It's good practice to tip good tour guides; $5 for a day's work is a reasonable amount.

Although officially deemed a "social evil" on a par with drug use and prostitution, **homosexuality** is largely ignored in Vietnam, though discretion is advised. The gay scene is slowly emerging in Hanoi and HCMC; visit ⓦutopia-asia .com for more information and advice.

SPORTS AND ACTIVITIES

Outdoor pursuits and adventure sports have taken off in Vietnam in recent years, and specialist tour agencies offer a wide range of options for adventurous travellers.

TREKKING AND ROCK CLIMBING

Compared to other countries in Asia, **trekking** in Vietnam remains relatively low-key, but one-day hikes and longer treks incorporating overnight stays in minority villages are a popular way to explore the countryside. Sa Pa and Mai Chau in the north, and to a lesser extent Da Lat and Kon Tum in the Central Highlands, provide good bases for treks. A guide is essential for longer treks into more remote areas, especially if you intend to stay the night, as many places are sensitive to the presence of foreigners, and some require a permit or may even be out of bounds altogether: unexploded ordnance still litters Vietnam (see box, p.874). As the tallest mountain in the country, Mount Fansipan (see p.864) offers one of the most challenging hikes, but easier, very pleasant treks can be taken around the country's national parks, including Cat Ba (see p.859), Cuc Phuong (see p.856) and Yok Don. Multi-day hikes that incorporate jungle trekking, caving (and camping in caves) and crossing rivers are available in Phong Nha–Ke Bang National Park (see p.870).

11

VIETNAM'S MINORITY TRIBES

Vietnam's culture is far from homogeneous and the Vietnamese government recognizes 54 different minority tribes that number around 12 million people. Each tribe has its own language, culture, spiritual beliefs and elaborate, beautifully embroidered traditional dress, though the latter is largely worn by tribes in the northern highlands, while many others have reverted to wearing regular, mass-produced clothing, at least outside special events. Most make a living from subsistence agriculture, though enterprising tribeswomen act as guides in the mountains around Sa Pa (see p.865) or sell traditional embroidery to visitors; many practise animism and ancestor worship. The relationship of the hill tribes with the government has always been fraught with tension; during the war with the French, many tribesmen fought on the French side, and were then recruited as US Special Forces during the Vietnam War, for which the tribes have paid dearly since, their languages, customs and clamours for religious freedom reportedly violently suppressed. Though the Vietnamese government limits contact between foreigners and tribes people by placing visiting restrictions on certain villages and regions, you can visit Dao and H'mong villages in the valleys around Sa Pa (p.865), see the Flower H'mong in Bac Ha (p.867), meet the White Tay in Mai Chau (p.868) and stay in Bahnar villages around Kon Tum (p.896), among other places.

11

The rivers and waterfalls around Da Lat provide good conditions for **canyoning** and **rock-climbing**, and the limestone karsts and caves around Ha Long Bay are attracting international attention for their climbing, deep-water soloing and bouldering opportunities.

CYCLING, MOUNTAIN BIKING AND MOTORBIKING

Cycling, **mountain biking** and **motorbiking** are very popular means of travel for tourists visiting Vietnam. The most popular motorbiking routes include Hanoi to HCMC through the Central Highlands along the scenic Ho Chi Minh Highway, and the Northwestern circuit (see p.862), while the pancake-flat Mekong Delta, and numerous mountain-to-coast routes starting in Da Lat and ending in Mui Ne, Nha Trang or Hoi An are particularly popular with cyclists. You can rent a bike or motorbike, but be sure to take out adequate insurance cover; a guide is highly recommended but not essential. Motorbike **tours** can be booked with independent guides, travel agencies or outfits such as the legendary Easy Riders in Da Lat (see p.902) and several in Hanoi (see p.850).

DIVING AND WATERSPORTS

A number of **watersports** operators have opened up along Vietnam's 3000km coastline, though classes and equipment rental aren't cheap. Mui Ne is the country's premier **kitesurfing** and **windsurfing** destination, hosting an international kitesurfing competition every spring (usually February); paddle-boarding and surfing are also on offer. Several operators in Nha Trang and Hoi An can organize **wakeboarding**, **waterskiing**, **kitesurfing** and **sea kayaking**, while the surf is up on China Beach near Da Nang from September to December. **Sea kayaking** between the karsts around Cat Ba Island is one of the most rewarding ways to experience Ha Long Bay.

The waters around Phu Quoc, Nha Trang and Hoi An are popular places for **scuba diving** and **snorkelling**; established outfits in all three locations offer certified courses to suit all levels as well as discovery dives.

COMMUNICATIONS

Internet cafés are still found in most towns and cities, although they are becoming obsolete with the ever-increasing number of free **wi-fi** hotspots. The vast majority of hotels and guesthouses provide free wi-fi, as do most restaurants and cafés.

The cheapest way to make **international calls** is via Skype. Alternatively, it's well worth getting a local SIM card from Viettel, Vinaphone or Mobifone. SIM cards can be purchased at the airports and from company stores (around 160,000VND per package; top-up packages 20,000–100,000VND).

The general enquiries numbers are: International Operator ☎110; Directory Enquiries ☎116.

Regular mail can take anywhere from four days to four weeks in or out of Vietnam; from major towns, eight to ten days is the norm, though express mail service (EMS), available in larger cities, is twice as fast and everything is sent by recorded delivery. When **sending a parcel**, take it unwrapped to the post office parcel counter (often open mornings only; take your passport as well). After inspection, and a good deal of form-filling, the parcel will be wrapped for you.

VIETNAM ONLINE

Ⓦ**vietnamtourism.com** Government tourist information site, listing basic information about the country and its main tourist attractions, and also offering an expensive hotel and tour-booking service.
Ⓦ**vietnamnews.vn** Online version of the national English-language daily newspaper, with brief snippets of local and international news.
Ⓦ**saigoneer.com** News, events and travel advice, not just pertaining to Saigon, but the whole of Vietnam.

CRIME AND SAFETY

Violent **crime** against tourists in Vietnam is extremely rare, but some tourist destinations (such as HCMC, Hanoi and Nha Trang) have more than their fair share of pickpockets, and some cases of **bag snatching** – day or night – are occasionally reported. Always take care when carrying valuables and money, and wherever possible leave them in a hotel safe.

Penalties for buying and using drugs are severe.

Vietnam is generally a safe country for **women** to travel around alone; that said, it pays to take the normal precautions, especially late at night, when you should avoid taking a *xe om* by yourself – take a taxi instead, and try to let someone know where you're headed.

If you have anything valuable **stolen**, go to the nearest **police** station and ask for a report for your insurance company; it can help immensely to have a Vietnamese speaker come along with you.

Undetonated explosives still pose a serious threat throughout Vietnam (see box, p.874): the problem is most acute in the Demilitarized Zone. Always stick to well-trodden paths and never touch any shells or half-buried chunks of metal.

MEDICAL CARE AND EMERGENCIES

Pharmacies can generally help with minor injuries or ailments, and provide some medication without prescription, though fake medicines and out-of-date drugs are common, so it pays to bring anything you know you're likely to need from home.

Local **hospitals** will treat minor problems, but are overcrowded and not many have a licence to treat foreigners. In a real emergency head for Hanoi, Da Nang or HCMC, where excellent

international medical centres can provide diagnosis and treatment.

INFORMATION AND MAPS

There is no such thing as an impartial tourist office in Vietnam; government-owned enterprises such as Vietnam Tourist are travel agencies looking to make a profit, so your best bet for **information** may be your fellow travellers, plus the savvier tourist accommodation.

The best **maps** of Vietnam are online – the country is well covered on Google Maps (and perhaps even better on local site ⓦdiadiem.com), as well as offline smartphone apps such as the excellent Maps.me.

MONEY AND BANKS

Vietnam's **currency** is the **dong**, usually abbreviated as "VND" or "d". Notes come in denominations of 500VND, 1000VND, 2000VND, 5000VND, 10,000VND, 20,000VND, 50,000VND, 100,000VND, 200,000VND and 500,000VND – a lot of zeroes there, so first-timers should be very careful with the notes that they give and receive. Dong are not available outside the country, but the **US dollar** can often be used as unofficial tender – prices are often quoted as such for accommodation and tours. If changing money, go for large denomination bills (US$50 and $100 get better rates than if you exchange $1, $5, $10 or $20). At the end of your trip, try to use up your dong, as few countries outside Vietnam will exchange their own currencies for it. At the time of writing, the **exchange rate** was 22,600VND to $1; 27,600VND to £1; and 24,100VND to €1.

Major **credit cards** are accepted in many hotels and upmarket restaurants and shops throughout the country. ATMs are ubiquitous in larger cities, and even smaller ones will have a couple.

PRICES AND BARGAINING

The Vietnamese have a reputation for being particularly voracious when it comes to making money, so be mindful

11

EMERGENCY NUMBERS

Try to get a Vietnamese-speaker to phone for you.
Police ☎ 113
Fire ☎ 114
Ambulance ☎ 115

11

VIETNAMESE

Vietnamese is tonal and is extremely tricky for Westerners to master – luckily the script is Romanized, and English is increasingly spoken in tourist areas. Vietnam's minority peoples have their own languages, and may not understand standard Vietnamese.

PRONUNCIATION

Six tones are used, which change the meaning of a word: the mid-level tone (syllables with no marker), the low falling tone (marked ă), the low rising tone (marked à), the high broken tone (marked ã), the high rising tone (marked á) and the low broken tone (marked a).

a "a" as in father	**o'i** "uh-i"
ă "u" as in hut (slight "u" as in unstressed English "a")	**ua** "waw"
	uê "weh"
â "uh" sound as above only longer	**uô** "waw"
e "e" as in bed	**uy** "wee"
ê "ay" as in pay	**u'a** "oo-a"
I "i" as in -ing	**u.u** "er-oo"
o "o" as in hot	**u'o'I** "oo-uh-i"
ô "aw" as in awe	**c** "g"
o' "ur" as in fur	**ch** "j" as in jar
u "oo" as in boo	**d** "y" as in young
u' "oo" closest to French "u"	**v** "d" as in day
y "i" as in -ing	**g** "g" as in goat
ai "ai" as in Thai	**gh** "g" as in goat
ao "ao" as in Mao	**gi** "y" as in young
au "a-oo"	**k** "g" as in goat
âu "oh" as in oh!	**kh** "k" as in keep
ay "ay" as in hay	**ng/ngh** "ng" as in sing
ây "ay-i" (as in "ay" above but longer)	**nh** "n-y" as in canyon
eo "eh-ao"	**ph** "f"
êu "ay-oo"	**q** "g" as in goat
iu "ew" as in few	**t** "d" as in day
iêu "i-yoh"	**th** "t"
oa "wa"	**tr** "j" as in jar
oe "weh"	**x** "s"
ôi "oy"	

GREETINGS AND BASIC PHRASES

How you speak to somebody depends on their gender, age and social standing. Addressing a man as *ông*, and a woman as *bà*, is being polite. With someone of about your age, you can use *anh* (for a man) and *chi* (for a woman).

Hello	*Chào ông/bà*	ticket	*vé*
Goodbye	*Chào, tạm biệt*	aeroplane	*máy bay*
Excuse me	*Xin lôi*	airport	*sân bay*
Excuse me (to get past)	*Xin ông/bà hú' lôi*	boat	*tàu bè*
Please	*Làm o'n*	bus	*xe buýt*
Thank you	*Cám o'n ông/bà*	bus station	*bê'n xe buýt*
Do you speak English?	*Ông/bà biê't nói tiê'ng không?*	train station	*bê'n xe lù'a*
		taxi	*tắc xi*
I don't understand	*Tôi không hiê'u*	car	*xe hoî*
Yes	*Vâng (N); da (S)*	bicycle	*xe đap*
No	*Không*	bank	*nhà băng*
Can you help me?	*Ông/bà có thê' giúp tôi không?*	post office	*sô bu' điên*
		passport	*hô chiê'u*
hospital	*bê'nh viê'n*	hotel	*khách san*
police station	*don cong an*	restaurant	*nhà hàng*
Where is the…?	*…ò' đâu?*	left/right	*bên trái/bên phài*

Do you have any rooms?	*Ông/bà có phòng không?*	air conditioner	*máy lanh*
How much is it?	*Bao nhiêu tiên?*	fan (electric)	*quat máy*
cheap/expensive	*rè/đàt*	open/closed	*mò' cù'a/vòng cù'a*

NUMBERS

For numbers ending in 5, from 15 onwards, *lăm* is used in the north and *nhăm* in the south, rather than the written *nam*. An alternative for numbers that are multiples of 10 is *chayc* – so, 10 can be *môt chục* etc.

0	*không*	8	*tám*
1	*môt*	9	*chín*
2	*hai*	10	*mùòi*
3	*ba*	11, 12, 13 etc	*mù'òi môt, mu'òi hai, mu'òi ba*
4	*bôn*		
5	*năm*	20, 30 etc	*hai mu'òi, ba mu'òi*
6	*sáu*	100	*mot trăm*
7	*bày*	1000	*mot ngàn*

11

FOOD AND DRINK GLOSSARY

Some names differ in the north (N) and south (S).

Useful phrases

bát (N); chén (S)	bowl
can chén (N); can ly (S)	cheers!
đá	ice
đūa	chopsticks
chay	vegetarian
tôi không ăn thit	I don't eat meat

Rice and noodles

bún	round rice noodles
bún bò	beef with bun noodles
bún cha	vermicelli noodles with pork and vegetables
bún gà	chicken with bun noodles
com	cooked rice
com rang (N); com chiên (S)	fried rice
com trang	boiled rice
cháo	rice porridge
mì xào	fried noodles
pho	flat rice noodle soup
pho bò	noodle soup with beef

Fish, meat and vegetables

cá	fish
cá rán (N); cá chiên (S)	fried fish
cua	crab
con luon	eel
muc	squid
tôm	shrimp or prawn
tôm hùm	lobster
bò	beef

gà	chicken
lon (N); heo (S)	pork
vit	duck
rau co or rau các loai	vegetables
xà lách	salad
trái cây	fruit

Miscellaneous

bánh	cake (sweet or savoury)
bánh mì	bread
bo	butter
pho mát	cheese
lac (N); đau phong (S)	peanuts (groundnuts)
muoi	salt
ot	chilli
tiêu	pepper
tàu hū (N); đau phu (S)	tofu
trung	egg

Drinks

bia	beer
cà phê	coffee
cà phê đá	iced coffee
cà phê đen	black coffee
cà phê sua	coffee with milk
trà	tea
trà voi chanh	tea with lemon
trà voi sua	tea with milk
không đá	no ice
nuoc	water
nuoc khoáng	mineral water
nuoc cam	orange juice
nuoc chanh	lime juice
nuoc dua	coconut milk
ruou ran	snake wine

11

of overcharging – much more of an issue in tourist areas, though one in general decline. Accommodation prices can be negotiable, especially outside high season – ask for a "discount" when checking in. If shopping, **bargain** hard but with a smile and good humour, as anger and unpleasantness constitutes a major loss of face. The idea is to agree on a price that both you and seller are happy with.

OPENING HOURS AND HOLIDAYS

State-run **banks** and government offices usually open Monday to Friday, closing at weekends. **Banking hours** are usually Monday to Friday 7.30 to 11.30am and 1 to 4pm, though most ATMs are 24hr. Most main **post offices** are open daily from 6.30am to 8pm or 9pm. **Museums** are open daily from 7 or 8am to 5pm; some Hanoi museums tend to close on Monday or Friday. Temples and pagodas tend to be open from 5 or 6am until 8 or 9pm, though many close for an hour or two at lunchtime. **Restaurants** tend to open around 8am and stay open right through until 10pm. Bars are generally open until 11pm, with later opening hours common in the bigger cities and tourist hotspots.

PUBLIC HOLIDAYS

January 1 New Year's Day
Late January/mid-February (dates vary each year). Tet, Vietnamese New Year (three days, though businesses and restaurants tend to close down for a full week)
February 3 Founding of the Vietnamese Communist Party
March/April (tenth day of the third lunar month) Commemoration of the Hung Kings (celebration of modern Vietnam)
April 30 Liberation of Saigon, 1975
May 1 International Labour Day

May 19 Ho Chi Minh's birthday
June Buddha's birthday (Phat Dan); eighth day of the fourth lunar month
September 2 National Day

FESTIVALS

Most Vietnamese **festivals** are fixed by the lunar calendar. On the eve of the full moon, every month, Hoi An celebrates a **Full-Moon Festival**. Electricity is switched off, silk lanterns light up traffic-free streets, and traditional games, dance and music are performed in the streets.

Tet Nguyen Dan Or simply Tet ("festival"). Seven days between the last week of January and the third week of February, when families get together to celebrate the New Year. Ancestral spirits are welcomed back to the household, offerings are made to Ong Tau, the Taoist god of the hearth, and everyone in Vietnam becomes a year older. The eve of Tet explodes into a cacophony of drums and percussion, and the subsequent week is marked by feasting on special foods.

Water Puppet Festival At Thay Pagoda, west of Hanoi, as part of Tet.

Buddhist full-moon festival (March–April). Two-week festival at the Perfume Pagoda, west of Hanoi (see box, p.854).

Buon Ma Thuot Coffee Festival (March). A great time for caffeine addicts to head for the highlands.

Tet Doan Ngo (late May to early June). Summer solstice, marked by offerings to spirits and dragon boat races.

Hue Festival (June 2018, 2020, 2022). This biennial festival is the biggest cultural event in Vietnam, held in Hue every two years.

Trung Nguyen (Wandering Souls Day) Huge food offerings are made to spirits on the fifteenth day of the seventh lunar month.

Children's or Mid-Autumn Festival (Sept–Oct). Dragon dances take place in Hoi An and children are given lanterns in the shape of stars, carp or dragons.

Hanoi

Vietnam's elegant capital, **HANOI**, lies in the heart of the northern delta. Given the political and historical importance of this thousand-year-old city and its burgeoning population of more than seven million, parts of it are surprisingly low-key. Its narrow streets and colonial buildings of the Old Quarter are steeped in history,

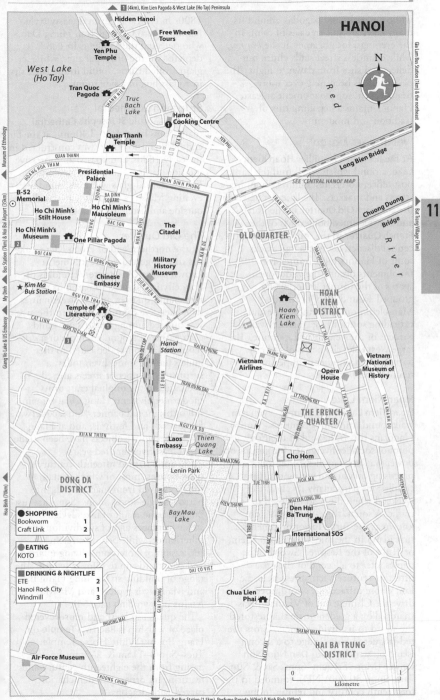

HANOI

West Lake (Ho Tay)

11

SEE 'CENTRAL HANOI' MAP

Hidden Hanoi
Free Wheelin Tours
Yen Phu Temple
Tran Quoc Pagoda
Hanoi Cooking Centre
Quan Thanh Temple
Presidential Palace
B-52 Memorial
Ho Chi Minh's Stilt House
Ho Chi Minh's Museum
Ho Chi Minh's Mausoleum
One Pillar Pagoda
The Citadel
Military History Museum
Chinese Embassy
Kim Ma Bus Station
Temple of Literature
Hanoi Station
Vietnam Airlines
Laos Embassy
Thien Quang Lake
Lenin Park
Bay Mau Lake
Den Hai Ba Trung
International SOS
Chua Lien Phai
Air Force Museum
Cho Hom
Opera House
Vietnam National Museum of History
Hoan Kiem Lake
OLD QUARTER
HOAN KIEM DISTRICT
THE FRENCH QUARTER
DONG DA DISTRICT
HAI BA TRUNG DISTRICT

Truc Bach Lake
Ba Dinh Square

Long Bien Bridge
Chuong Duong Bridge
Red River

Museum of Ethnology
Bus Station (7km) & Noi Bai Airport (35km)
My Dinh Bus Station (1km) & the northeast
Gia Lam Bus Station (1km) & the northeast
Bat Trang Village (7km)
Giang Vo Lake & US Embassy
Hoa Binh (70km)

(4km), Kim Lien Pagoda & West Lake (Ho Tay) Peninsula

Giap Bat Bus Station (1.5km), Perfume Pagoda (60km) & Ninh Binh (90km)

● SHOPPING
Bookworm	1
Craft Link	2

● EATING
KOTO	1

■ DRINKING & NIGHTLIFE
ETE	2
Hanoi Rock City	1
Windmill	3

0 — 1 kilometre

while the parks and pagodas around its many lakes are still an oasis of calm. In the evenings, locals gather at the *bia hoi*, while countless street stalls churn out delicious dishes from dawn to night. The pace of life is becoming ever more frenetic, but, for the moment at least, Hanoi remains a beguiling mix of tradition and modernity.

WHAT TO SEE AND DO

At the heart of Hanoi lies **Hoan Kiem Lake**, around which you'll find the banks, post office, hotels, restaurants, shopping streets and markets. The lake lies between the compact **Old Quarter** in the north, and the tree-lined boulevards of the **French Quarter** to the south. West of this central district, across the rail tracks, some of Hanoi's most impressive monuments occupy the wide, open spaces of the former **Imperial City**, grouped around Ho Chi Minh's Mausoleum on Ba Dinh Square and extending south to the ancient, walled gardens of the Temple of Literature. The large **West Lake** sits north of the city, harbouring a number of appealing temples and pagodas.

Hoan Kiem Lake
Hoan Kiem Lake itself is small – you can walk round it in thirty minutes – but to Hanoians this is the soul of their city, a point of social convergence for groups of power-walkers, families, older folk practising tai chi and young courting couples; it's particularly lovely at the weekend when the road is closed to traffic. A squat, three-tiered pavilion known as the **Turtle Tower** ornaments a tiny island in the middle of Hoan Kiem, or "Lake of the Restored Sword". The names refer to a legend of the great fifteenth-century Vietnamese hero, Le Loi, whose miraculous sword, used to drive the Chinese out of Vietnam, was snatched by a golden turtle that restored the sword to its divine owners. Cross the red-lacquered Huc Bridge to a second island on which stands **Den Ngoc Son** temple (Mon–Fri 7am–6pm, Sat & Sun 7am–9pm; 30,000VND), founded in the fourteenth century and rebuilt in the

1800s in typical Nguyen dynasty style. National hero General Tran Hung Dao, who defeated the Mongols in 1288, is depicted on the principal altar, while a giant stuffed turtle, found in the lake, sits in a glass box in a side room.

St Joseph's Cathedral
The neo-Gothic **St Joseph's Cathedral** (daily 5am–noon & 2–7.30pm), at the far end of Nha Tho Street, was constructed in the early 1880s, and boasts an impressive interior featuring an ornate altar and French stained-glass windows. Sunday-evening Mass is a good time to dawdle outside and listen to the singing.

The Old Quarter
At the northern end of Hoan Kiem Lake lies the congested square kilometre known as the **Old Quarter**. Hanoi is the only city in Vietnam to retain its ancient merchants' quarter, and its street names date back five centuries to when the area was divided among 36 artisans' guilds, each gathered around a temple or a *dinh* (communal house) dedicated to the guild's patron spirit. Even today, a surprising number of streets are still dedicated to the original craft or its modern equivalent: Hang Quat remains full of bright red banners and lacquerware for funerals and festivals, and at Hang Ma, paper votive objects have been made for at least five hundred years.

The aptly named fifteenth-century **tube-houses**, most of which remain today, evolved from market stalls into narrow single-storey shops. Some are just 2m wide, the result of taxes levied on street-frontages and of subdivision for inheritance, while behind stretches a succession of storerooms, living quarters and courtyards up to 60m in length. The range of building styles along Hang Bac and Ma May is typical, and Ma May even retains its own **dinh** (no. 64).

The quarter's oldest and most revered place of worship is **Bach Ma Temple** on Hang Buom (White Horse Temple; Tues–Sun 8–11am & 2–5pm; free), dating from the eighteenth century and featuring an ornate wooden chariot carved with dragons.

The city's largest covered market, **Cho Dong Xuan** (daily from 7am), occupies a whole block behind its original 1889 facade, and is packed with stalls selling cheap clothing, souvenirs and fresh and dried food.

The French Quarter

The first French concession was granted in 1874, and gradually elegant villas filled plots along the grid of tree-lined avenues to the south and east of Hoan Kiem Lake. The jewel in the crown was

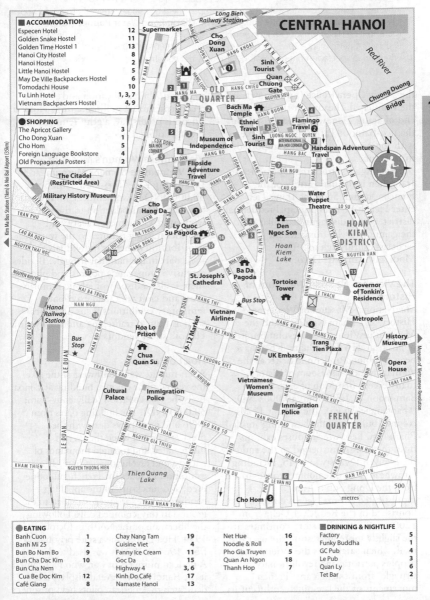

CENTRAL HANOI

■ **ACCOMMODATION**

Espesen Hotel	12
Golden Snake Hostel	11
Golden Time Hostel 1	13
Hanoi City Hostel	8
Hanoi Hostel	2
Little Hanoi Hostel	5
May De Ville Backpackers Hostel	6
Tomodachi House	10
Tu Linh Hotel	1, 3, 7
Vietnam Backpackers Hostel	4, 9

● **SHOPPING**

The Apricot Gallery	3
Cho Dong Xuan	1
Cho Hom	5
Foreign Language Bookstore	4
Old Propaganda Posters	2

● EATING						■ DRINKING & NIGHTLIFE	
Banh Cuon	1	Chay Nang Tam	19	Net Hue	16	Factory	5
Banh Mi 25	2	Cuisine Viet	4	Noodle & Roll	14	Funky Buddha	1
Bun Bo Nam Bo	9	Fanny Ice Cream	11	Pho Gia Truyen	5	GC Pub	4
Bun Cha Dac Kim	10	Goc Da	15	Quan An Ngon	18	Le Pub	3
Bun Cha Nem		Highway 4	3, 6	Thanh Hop	7	Quan Ly	6
Cua Be Doc Kim	12	Kinh Do Café	17			Tet Bar	2
Café Giang	8	Namaste Hanoi	13				

WATER PUPPETRY

Traditional **water puppetry**, *mua roi nuoc* – literally, puppets that dance on the water – is a northern Vietnamese art form that originated in the Red River Delta over one thousand years ago. Traditional performances consist of short scenes depicting rural life or historic events accompanied by musical narration. Puppeteers stand waist-deep in murky water, behind a bamboo screen, manipulating the heavy, colourfully painted wooden puppets (that only last for three months of continuous use, hence the puppet-making villages outside Hanoi), attached to long underwater poles, to the accompaniment of a single-stringed zither, bamboo xylophones, drums, wooden flutes and gongs. The **Thang Long Water Puppet Troupe** give tourist-oriented performances on the north corner of Hoan Kiem Lake at 57b Dinh Tien Hoang (5 daily, first performance 3pm; last performance 8pm; 70,000–120,000VND). It's an entertaining spectacle; front row seats occasionally get splashed.

11

the stately **Opera House** (now known as the Municipal Theatre), at the eastern end of Trang Tien, which was based on the neo-Baroque Paris Opéra, complete with Ionic columns and tiles imported from France.

Stretching west from the Opera House, **Trang Tien** is the main artery of the French Quarter. South of Trang Tien you enter French Hanoi's principal residential district, whose distinguished villas run the gamut of styles from elegant Neoclassical through to 1930s Modernism and Art Deco.

The Vietnam National Museum of History

The National Museum of Vietnamese History, at 1 Pham Ngu Lao, and the Museum of Vietnamese Revolution, just opposite at 216 Tran Quang Khai, have been combined under one ticket as the **Vietnam National Museum of History** (daily except first Mon of each month 8am–noon & 1.30–5pm; 40,000VND; ⓦbaotanglichsu.vn). The elegant 1920s colonial building is the best thing about 1 Pham Ngu Lao, which houses exhibits from the prehistoric period to the end of the Nguyen Dynasty in 1945, including arrowheads and ceremonial bronze drums from the Dong Son culture, a sophisticated Bronze Age civilization that flourished in the Red River Delta from 1200 to 200 BC. The story continues at the slightly more interesting site over the road, which catalogues the "Vietnamese people's patriotic and revolutionary struggle" from the first anti-French movements of the late nineteenth century

to post-1975 reunification and reconstruction. A guillotine from Hoa Lu prison is on display, a grim reminder of French colonial rule.

Vietnamese Women's Museum

The **Vietnamese Women's Museum**, at 36 Ly Thuong Kiet (Tues–Sun 8am–5pm; 30,000VND; ⓦwomenmuseum.org.vn), is a fantastic introduction to the role of women in Vietnamese society, and includes moving tributes to the wartime contribution of heroic individuals and their part in the national struggle. Besides extensive propaganda posters and photos, there is also a display of ethnic minority dress and craftwork, and excellent temporary exhibitions focus on topics such as human trafficking and the lives of Hanoi's street vendors.

Hoa Lo Prison

A ten-minute walk southwest of the lake, the yellow stone colonial building at 1 Hoa Lo is the **Hoa Lo Prison** (daily 8am–5pm; 30,000VND). The building dates from 1896 and its displays deal with the pre-1954 period when the French incarcerated and tortured thousands of patriots and revolutionaries here. The exhibition includes the French guillotine used, and mock-ups of the appalling conditions here, prisoners shackled to the ground in tiny, cramped cells. Following the liberation of the North in October 1954, Hoa Lo became a state prison, and from 1964 to 1973 it was used to detain American prisoners of war, who nicknamed it the **Hanoi Hilton**; several displays are dedicated to American pilots held prisoner here, including John McCain. The photographs of American POWs playing volleyball, designed to convey a holiday camp atmosphere, should be taken with a pinch of salt; the experience of McCain and others included torture.

Ho Chi Minh Mausoleum complex

The wide, open spaces of **Ba Dinh Square**, their multiple flagpoles flying the red banners festooned with hammer and sickle, 2km west of Hoan Kiem Lake, are the nation's ceremonial centre. It was here that Ho Chi Minh read out the Declaration of Independence to half a million people on September 2, 1945, and here that independence is commemorated each National Day with military parades. Cyclos and *xe om* will bring you to Ba Dinh Square from the centre for 20,000–25,000VND. The square's west side is dominated by **Ho Chi Minh's Mausoleum** (all year Tues–Thurs 8am–noon; Dec–Sept also Sat & Sun 8am–noon; free). In the tradition of great communist leaders, Ho Chi Minh's compact, embalmed body is displayed under glass in a cold, dark room, with four guards of honour in crisp white standing to attention around the glass sarcophagus. Huge crowds come here to pay their respects to "Uncle Ho", especially at weekends: sober behaviour and appropriate dress are required (no shorts or vests, preferably full-length skirts or trousers) and nothing can be taken inside; storage is provided for your belongings. Note that "Uncle Ho" takes a two-month "holiday" to Russia each year to be touched up by those responsible for Lenin's upkeep.

Nearby is **Ho Chi Minh's stilt house**, 3 Ngoc Ha (daily 8am–noon, Tues–Thurs, Sat & Sun also 2–4.30pm; 40,000VND, free guide on request), built by the president in 1954 and modelled on an ethnic minority stilt house. The ground-level meeting area was used by Ho and the politburo; upstairs, his study and bedroom are austere, with a simple bed, desk and bookcase on display. Ho Chi Minh's cars, including a Soviet ZIL, are parked nearby and the Presidential Palace – a restored grand colonial building

– stands in stark contrast to the leader's humble lodgings. **Ho Chi Minh's Museum** (daily 8am–noon, Tues–Thurs, Sat & Sun also 2–4.30pm; 40,000VND) contains many photographic displays, a collection of "feudal and imperialist" objects and symbolic art installations celebrating Ho Chi Minh's life and the pivotal role he played in the nation's history.

Close by the mausoleum is the tiny **One Pillar Pagoda**, which rivals the Tortoise Tower as a symbol of Hanoi and represents a flowering of Vietnamese art. Founded in the eleventh century (and reconstructed in 1954), it is supported on a single column rising from the middle of a lake; the whole structure is designed to resemble a lotus blossom, the Buddhist symbol of enlightenment.

Vietnam Military History Museum

The **Vietnam Military History Museum**, 28 Dien Bien Phu (Tues–Thurs, Sat & Sun 8–11.30am & 1–4.30pm; 40,000VND; ⓦbtlsqsvn.org.vn), chronicles military history from the 1930s to the present day, a period dominated by the French and American wars, well documented in two separate halls, and with a supporting cast of weaponry from both wars as well as a Soviet-built MiG-21 jet fighter. Unlike HCMC's War Remnants Museum, the captions here are still clogged with outdated communist rhetoric – "spies", "bandits" and "puppet-regime soldiers" are everywhere. Speaking of outdated relics, there is a Lenin statue in the small park opposite the museum.

Temple of Literature

The **Temple of Literature**, or **Van Mieu**, west of the centre in a park off Nguyen Thai Hoc, is Vietnam's principal Confucian sanctuary and its historical centre of learning (daily 8am–6pm, Sat until 9pm; 30,000VND). The temple is one of the few remnants of Thang Long, the Ly kings' original eleventh-century city, and consists of five walled courtyards, modelled on that of Confucius's birthplace in Qufu, China. As you enter the third courtyard, via an imposing double-roofed gateway, you'll see the central Well of Heavenly Clarity (a walled pond), flanked by the temple's most valuable relics: 82 stone **stelae** mounted on tortoises. Each stele records the results of a state examination held at the National Academy between 1442 and 1779, and gives biographical details of successful candidates. The fourth courtyard leads to the **ceremonial hall**, a long, low building whose sweeping, tiled roof is crowned by two lithe dragons bracketing a full moon. Here, the king and his mandarins would make sacrifices before the altar of Confucius. Directly behind the ceremonial hall lies the temple sanctuary, where Confucius sits with his four principal disciples. The fifth courtyard was formerly the site of the National Academy, Vietnam's first university, which was destroyed by French bombs in 1947.

11

West Lake (Ho Tay)

North of the city, cool breezes drift off **West Lake (Ho Tay)**. In the seventeenth century, villagers built a causeway across the lake's southeast corner, creating a small fishing lake still in use today and now called **Truc Bach**. The eleventh-century **Quan Thanh Temple** (daily 8am–5pm; 5000VND) stands on the lake's southeast bank, and is dedicated to the Guardian of the North, Tran Vo, whose statue, cast in black bronze in 1677, is nearly 4m high and weighs 4 tonnes. The shrine room also boasts a valuable collection of seventeenth- and eighteenth-century poems and parallel sentences (boards inscribed with wise maxims and hung in pairs). The gate of Quan Thanh is just a few paces south of the causeway, Thanh Nien, which leads to Hanoi's oldest religious foundation, **Tran Quoc Pagoda**, occupying a tiny island in West Lake (daily 7.30–11.30am & 1.30–6.30pm). The pagoda probably dates back to the sixth century, and the sanctuary's restrained interior, part of which was under renovation at the time of writing, is typical of northern Vietnamese pagodas. West of Quan Thanh in Ngoc Ha (Flower Village), down the alley next to 55 Hoang Hoa Tham, lies the **B-52 Memorial**. The remains of the downed bomber,

half-submerged in a lake, form a poignant memorial to the victims of the 1972 "Christmas Bombing" raids.

Museum of Ethnology

The highly recommended **Museum of Ethnology**, or Bao Tang Toc Hoc Viet Nam, situated on the western outskirts of Hanoi in the Cau Giay district along Nguyen Van Huyen (Tues–Sun 8.30am–5.30pm; 40,000VND; ⓦvme .org.vn), is a bit of a trek out of town, but worth the effort for its fantastic exhibitions on all the country's major ethnic groups. Musical instruments, games, traditional dress and other items of daily life fill the showcases, alongside excellent life-size displays on funerary ceremonies, conical-hat production and traditional sacrificial spears. Outside in the museum grounds there are detailed replicas of various ethnic dwellings and burial statues; standout exhibits include a thatch-roofed Giarai tomb and stilt village houses. The museum is 7km from the centre, signposted left off Hoang Quoc Viet. A taxi from the Old Quarter will set you back around 130,000VND, or hop on city bus #14 (4000VND) from the west side of Hoan Kiem Lake to the Hoang Quoc Viet stop, from where it's a 500m walk.

ARRIVAL AND DEPARTURE

By plane It's a 45min ride into central Hanoi from Noi Bai Airport (ⓦhanoiairportonline.com), 35km away. The cheapest option upon arrival is to take the bright orange city bus #86 to Hanoi train station (6.20am–10.30pm every 20–30min; 30,000VND), which stops en route at the north of Hoan Kiem Lake. Just outside the international and domestic arrival terminals, you'll find Vietnam Airlines minibuses (40,000VND) that bring you to their office at the corner of Trang Phi and Quang Trung. Airport taxis should be around 350,000VND for a door-to-door ride and it's usually $20 if you've booked transport with your accommodation. In the airport arrivals hall, there are ATMs and exchange bureaux. To get to the airport, you can take the Vietnam Airlines minibus from their office (daily 6am–7pm), which leaves every 30min 4.30am–11.30am and every hour noon–6pm, or the #86 bus (5am–9.40pm every 20–30min; 30,000VND).

Destinations Da Lat (4 daily; 1hr 40min); Da Nang (14 daily; 1hr 15min); Dien Bien Phu (daily; 1hr); HCMC (36 daily; 2hr); Hue (4 daily; 1hr 10min); Nha Trang (4 daily; 1hr 40min); Phu Quoc (daily; 2hr 15min).

SCAMS IN HANOI

Hanoi plays host to a large number of **hotel racketeers**, phoney tour operators and con artists determined to part you from your cash. Check the authenticity of any establishment before booking a tour (check the real address using a guidebook or the internet), as names of good and popular hotels, taxi companies and tour agencies are shamelessly copied, and be very sceptical of taxi drivers telling you that a hotel or restaurant has closed down or relocated. Many **taxis** that loiter outside the bus and train stations have rigged meters, so try and get a taxi with a reputable company (see below) or be aware how far you're travelling and how much you should be paying (prices per km are displayed on the sides of taxis). If you take a **cyclo**, firmly agree on a price and be aware that some cyclo drivers try to add an extra zero when you come to pay ("I said 200,000, not 20,000") or try to charge double for two people. Also be wary of "students" who approach you around Hoan Kiem Lake wishing to practise their English – it is a renowned scam that could land you with a restaurant or bar bill of a few hundred dollars. Such incidents should be reported to the Vietnam National Administration of Tourism, 3 Tran Phu (☎024 3356 0789, ⊕hanoitourism.gov.vn).

11

By open-tour bus For tickets and information on long-distance open-tour buses that stop at popular cities between Hanoi and HCMC, contact reliable operators such as Sinh Tourist (see p.850). Direct one-way (and hugely uncomfortable) overnight buses run to Vientiane (daily; 16hr; $30), departing from Hanoi at 7pm, crossing the border at Cau Treo.

By public bus Hanoi has three main bus stations. Giap Bat bus station, 6km south of the Old Quarter, serves the south and the east, including Ninh Binh, Hue, Da Lat, Nha Trang and HCMC. Northeast services to Hai Phong and Bai Chay/Ha Long Bay and Lao Cai operate from Gia Lam station, 3km northeast of the centre on the east bank of the Red River. My Dinh bus station (Pham Hung), 7km west of the city, serves northern and western destinations, such as Dien Bien Phu and Mai Chau, with onwards sleeper buses to Laos from Dien Bien Phu (see p.869). Xe om rides from these bus stations to the centre vary between 40,000–70,000VND. For popular destinations, it's best to buy tickets the day before.

Destinations Bai Chay (2 hourly; 3hr 30min); Da Lat (2 daily at 11am & 6pm; 24hr); Da Nang (hourly 2–6pm; 13hr); Hai Phong (2 hourly; 2hr); HCMC (3 daily at 11am, 3pm & 6pm; 36hr); Hue (hourly 2–6pm; 12hr); Lao Cai (daily at 1 & 7pm; 9hr); Mai Chau (2 daily at 6.30am & 2.30pm; 2hr); Nha Trang (2 daily at 10am & 6pm; 22hr); Ninh Binh (2 hourly; 2hr 30min).

By train Trains to and from the south use the main station (Ga Hanoi) at 120 Le Duan, 1km southwest of the Old Quarter. If you're arriving by train, you'll exit onto Le Duan (exit A). Trains for Lao Cai (for Sa Pa) and China leave from the separate Tran Quy Cap station, just behind the main train station (exit B). Eastbound trains to Hai Phong run either from the Gia Lam station, on the east side of Song Hong River, or from Long Bien, on the west side of the river. A taxi from the main train station to the Old Quarter should be no more than 40,000VND, and a xe om

25,000VND. Book tickets early, especially for sleeping berths to Hue and HCMC.

Destinations Beijing (Tues & Fri at 6.30pm; 42hr); Da Nang (5 daily; 14–18hr); Hai Phong (daily; 2hr 30min); HCMC (5 daily; 30–41hr); Hue (6 daily; 13–15hr); Lao Cai (5 daily; 8hr 30min–10hr 15min); Nha Trang (5 daily; 23–31hr); Ninh Binh (4 daily; 2hr–2hr 30min); Vinh (7 daily; 5hr–6hr 40min).

GETTING AROUND

By cyclo Cyclos are banned from some roads in central Hanoi, notably around Hoan Kiem Lake and in some parts of the Old Quarter, so don't be surprised if you seem to be taking a circuitous route; city authorities are threatening to ban them altogether. Always agree on a price in advance (about 30,000VND for a short journey) and avoid using cyclos at night.

By taxi Metered taxis wait outside the more upmarket hotels and at the north end of Hoan Kiem Lake and cost about 15,000VND/km; prices are displayed on the side of the taxi. Reputable companies include Mai Linh Taxis ☎024 3861 6161 and Thang Nga Taxis ☎024 3821 5215.

By bike Bicycles can be rented for around $3/day from many hotels and tour agencies in the Old Quarter. It's best to pay the minuscule charge at a supervised bike park (gui xe dap), located on most main roads. Parking is banned on Trang Tien and Hang Khay; elsewhere, it's only allowed within designated areas. Motorbikes are available from guesthouses and small tour agencies for about $7–10/day. Park in supervised motorbike parks (gui xe may).

By bus Hanoi's a/c city buses are useful for transport between the long-distance bus stations (every 15min 5am–5.30pm; 7000–10,000VND one-way). A map showing the bus routes is on sale at the Foreign Language Bookstore (see p.853), or see ⊕hanoibus.com.vn. There's a much talked about new BRT (Bus Rapid Transport; ⊕hanoibrt.vn) in the city, but the route between Kim Ma and the suburbs is more useful for locals than for tourists.

INFORMATION AND ACTIVITIES

It's best to go to one of the reliable tour operators (see box below) for information on visas, tours and transport. State-run "tourist offices" such as Vietnam Tourism are only interested in selling substandard tours, as are the batch of duplicate-name travel agencies, such as the plethora of fake "Sinh Cafés" in the Old Quarter, trading on the reputation of the original.

Cookery classes Hidden Hanoi, 147 Nghi Tam (☎091 225 4045, ⌨hiddenhanoi.com.vn), holds 3hr hands-on classes (11am Mon–Sat) for $45/person. It's an extra $10 to do the market tour before the class and you'll need to get a taxi here from the Old Quarter. Hanoi Cooking Centre at 44 Chau Long (☎024 3715 3277, ⌨hanoicookingcentre.com) is another professional outfit near West Lake (about a 25min walk from the Old Quarter). A tour of the market and wine or beer as you eat is included in the $59 cost. Twice-daily classes.

Walking tours Hidden Hanoi (see above) organizes several excellent walking tours ($25/hr) in the Old Quarter and French Quarter, as well as a street-food tour and temple tour on the fringes of Hanoi. Hanoi Street Foods (⌨hanoistreetfoods.com), at 137 Hang Bac, organize enjoyable daily tours (11am, 5pm & 6.30pm; 3hr) of local street food venues for $20/person; you get to sample five or so local dishes as your guide explains each one, finishing off with a strong Vietnamese coffee.

ACCOMMODATION

Have the exact address of your lodgings written down for taxi drivers and insist on being taken to the hotel of your choice.

Especen Hotel 28 Tho Xuong ☎024 3824 4401, ⌨especen.vn; map p.845. This well-run budget operation is located just a stone's throw from St Joseph's Cathedral. The rooms are spacious and bright, some have balconies, and all come with satellite TV, wi-fi and a/c. They might also put you up a few doors down at no.38, but note that any other *Especen Hotels* aren't legit. Doubles $25

Golden Snake Hostel 45 Ngo Huyen ☎024 6273 0110, ✉goldensnake.hostel@gmail.com; map p.845. The new kid on the backpackers' block, the rooms here might not quite live up to the cool industrial feel of the reception, but the young staff are friendly and the rooms super clean. The teeny tiny cubicles for showers and toilets are challenging to anyone over 5ft. Dorms $7, doubles $16

Golden Time Hostel 1 43 Ly Thai To ☎024 3935 1091, ⌨goldentimehostel.com; map p.845. Fair-sized rooms with flat-screen TVs, welcome drinks for guests and other nice touches, such as the huge breakfast, earn this original *Golden Time* hostel rave reviews, as does the helpfulness of the staff. Doubles $18

Hanoi City Hostel 95B Hang Ga ☎024 3828 1379, ⌨hanoicityhostel.com; map p.845. Efficient, well-located and well-run place with a/c rooms, decked out in pastel shades. Some staff members go out of their way to make you feel welcome. Doubles $16

Hanoi Hostel 91C Hang Ma ☎024 6270 0006, ⌨vietnam-hostel.com; map p.845. Peaceful lilac rooms with crisp sheets, comfortable dorm beds and sweet, helpful staff make this a great backpacker choice. Friendly vibe without it being a party hostel. Dorms $5.50, doubles $18

(see p.861) ... (see p.865)

TOUR OPERATORS

The following are tour operators, rather than travel agents; most of the booking offices you see in the Old Quarter are simply acting as middle men and taking a commission. Always try to establish who is operating the tour and exactly what is included. Most places organize bargain-basement tours to the Perfume Pagoda ($20), Ha Long Bay (2 days; $55–110) and the Sa Pa area (3–4 days; $100–150), though for the last two, it's far better to organize tours from Cat Ba Island (see p.861) and Sa Pa (see p.865), respectively.

Ethnic Travel 35 Hang Giay ☎091 3926 1951, ⌨ethnictravel.com.vn. It has a good reputation for small-group, off-the-beaten-track tours of the north, trekking, cycling and cooking tours.

Flamingo Travel 66 Dao Duy Tu ☎091 9221 4554, ⌨flamingotravel.com.vn. Highly regarded for their inexpensive motorcycle tours across the country, plus great-value rentals.

Flipside Adventure Travel 23 Bat Dan ☎04 3923 1040, ⌨flipsideadventuretravel.com. A reliable Kiwi-run operator who gets rave reviews for its budget three-day motorbike tours of Ha Giang, as well as tours to Ninh Binh and Sa Pa, and Ha Long Bay cruises.

Free Wheelin' Tours 6th Floor, 62 Duong Yen Phu ☎04 3932 6743, ⌨freewheelin-tours.com. Guided motorbike tours around the north of Vietnam, ranging from four to fourteen days.

Handspan Adventure Travel 78 Ma May ☎091 3926 2828, ⌨handspan.com. These guys specialize in community-based tourism in northern Vietnam, sea kayaking in Ha Long Bay, mountain biking and trekking tours.

Sinh Tourist 52 Luong Ngoc Quyen ☎04 3926 1568, ⌨thesinhtourist.vn. The original Sinh is still the pick of the bunch – good for open-tour bus journeys. Also at 64 Tran Nhat Duat (☎04 3929 0394).

Little Hanoi Hostel 48 Hang Ga ⊕024 3828 4461, ⓦ littlehanoihostel.com; map p.845. This friendly mini-hotel has modern superior rooms with baths and balconies, and cheaper, windowless doubles. The six-bed a/c dormitory is excellent value, including breakfast and free coffee all day long. Dorm $8, double $20

May De Ville Backpackers Hostel 1 Hai Tuong ⊕024 3935 2468, ⓦ maydeville.com; map p.845. Luxury for a budget price, this is more like a hotel than a hostel, with spacious rooms (private ones come with laptops you can borrow and plasma-screen TVs) and a vast buffet breakfast. The tinted glass in the dorm bathrooms doesn't give much privacy, though. Dorms $5, doubles $30

★**Tomodachi House** 5A Tong Duy Tan ⊕092 271 9999, ⓦ tomodachihouse.com; map p.845. Japanese-themed "home sweet home" for backpackers, this small minimalist hotel is a great find. Staff are eager to help, breakfast is delicious and filling, and rooms are clean and quiet (even the dorm, which has two bathrooms). Dorms $8, doubles $40

Tu Linh Hotel 58 Hang Cot ⊕024 3828 2626, ⓦ tulinhpalacehotels.com; map p.845. Not quite a palace, but neither a hovel: large, sparklingly clean rooms come with mod cons such as satellite TV, electronic safes and comfortable beds, and the staff's attitude gets rave reviews also. Equally popular sister hotels at 2B Hang Ga and 86 Ma May have virtually identical decor, facilities and equally congenial staff. Doubles $28

★**Vietnam Backpackers Hostel – Original** 48 Ngo Huyen ⊕024 3828 5372, ⓦ vietnambackpackershostel .com; map p.845. Australian-run, standard-setting hostel west of Hoan Kiem Lake, offering bunks in mixed or women-only dorms and private doubles. Lockers, breakfast and internet access are included, and the rooftop bar hosts regular barbecues and parties. The sociable vibe makes it a great place for solo travellers, and their tour service runs high-octane trips to Ha Long Bay that include tubing and paddleboarding. The second ("Downtown") branch at 9 Ma May (⊕024 3935 1890) is particularly well located, with a lively on-site bar and spacious dorms and rooms. Dorms $5, doubles $20

EATING

Hanoi has exploded with coffee shops and cafés; you'll find the usual chains such as *Starbucks* and Vietnam's own *Highlands Coffee*, but cool young locals will tell you that *Cong Caphe* (ⓦ congcaphe.com) is the best.

Banh Mi 25 25 Hang Ca; map p.845. Your sandwich might take a little longer than at other places, but the warm fresh bread oozing with tofu, honey-grilled chicken or pork (15,000–25,000VND), presented in cute baskets, is worth the wait at the little tables and stools on the roadside. Mon–Sat 7am–7pm, Sun 7am–5pm.

Bun Bo Nam Bo 67 Hang Dieu; map p.845. Deservedly popular place serving generous portions of rice noodles

topped with lean beef, mint, roasted peanuts and garlic, all swimming in a delicious broth, for 60,000VND. Daily 7.30am–10.30pm.

Bun Cha Dac Kim 1 Hang Manh; map p.845. This local restaurant draws crowds of locals for its excellent *bun cha* (grilled pork over flat rice noodles) and *nem cua be* (crabmeat spring rolls), from 20,000VND. Daily 9.30am–9pm.

Café Giang 39 Nguyen Huu Huang ⓦ giangcafehanoi .com; map p.845. Pop down a narrow lane to this very local café, and perch on a stool to sample some of Hanoi's best coffee. Go for *caphe trung da* – coffee topped with a frothy beaten egg white. Daily 10am–10pm.

Chay Nang Tam 79a Tran Hung Dao ⓦ nangtam.com.vn; map p.845. Small Buddhist vegetarian restaurant down a quiet alleyway off Tran Hung Dao, which specializes in making veggie dishes that look like meat. *Nom hoa chuoi*, a salad of banana flower, star fruit and pineapple, is recommended, or try one of the well-priced set menus (60,000VND or 100,000VND). Daily 11am–11pm.

Cuisine Viet 80 Ma May ⓦ facebook.com/ Cuisineviet.80mamay; map p.845. A cut above most vegetarian restaurants, serving innovative food with a Taiwanese-Vietnamese slant; dishes such as the veggie "Tower of Babel" (85,000VND) are excellent. Wash it all down with fresh juices or a selection of lassis. Daily 8am–11pm.

Fanny Ice Cream 48 Le Thai To; map p.845. Snigger at the name if you must, but this is the best place in town for French-style local ice cream, and the more unusual flavours include *com* (young sticky rice). One scoop 20,000VND. Daily 10am–8pm.

★**Highway 4** 3 Hang Tre ⓦ highway4.com/en; map p.845. On a wide street at the edge of the Old Quarter, this atmospheric bar-restaurant has a warren of rooms on three floors culminating in a great rooftop terrace. Known for its excellent array of northern Vietnamese dishes (mains from 80,000VND), such as catfish and dill spring rolls, glass noodles with crab and jicama salad, as well as liquor made from glutinous rice. Another branch at 25 Bat Su. Daily 10am–midnight.

11

11

Kinh Do Café 252 Hang Bong; map p.845. Follow in Catherine Deneuve's footsteps and have a strong coffee at this ageing landmark café, like she did during the filming of *Indochine*. The French pastries and toasted sandwiches are delicious, too. Also serves noodles and other mains from 40,000VND. Daily 8am–8pm.

KOTO 59 Van Mieu ⊚koto.com.au; map p.843. "*Know One Teach One*" restaurant, overlooking the Temple of Literature, has bright seating areas strewn with cushions and the menu runs the gamut from expertly prepared Vietnamese dishes (snakehead fish soup, fresh spring rolls and honey prawns) to Western offerings, such as cheeseburgers, fettuccine and fish and chips. The staff are disadvantaged children and former street kids being trained by an Australian-run charity. Mains from 130,000VND. Daily 7am–10pm.

Namaste Hanoi 47 Lo Su ⊚namastehanoi.com; map p.845. One of the best Indian restaurants in the country, this reasonably priced place serves up a huge range of dishes from across the Subcontinent, with an emphasis on northern Indian (mains from 70,000VND), along with ample options for vegetarians. The fantastic ice cream is the one non-Indian item on the dessert menu, but we're not complaining. Daily 11am–2.30pm & 6–10.30pm.

Net Hue 198 Hang Bong ⊚nethue.com.vn; map p.845. If you don't make it to Hue, there's no reason why you should miss out on its exceptional cuisine. This family-run restaurant serves great takes on the likes of *banh nam* (steamed rice pancake with minced shrimp filling) and *bun bo hue* (noodle dish with a multitude of toppings). Mains from 40,000VND. Daily 7am–10.30pm.

Noodle & Roll 39C Ly Quoc Su; map p.845. Travellers return here day after day for cheap and filling Vietnam staples. Most mains are around 40,000VND. Try the *bun nem cua be*: rice noodles with crab spring rolls – and orders in this laidback place are yelled upstairs. Daily 10am–10pm.

DRINKING AND NIGHTLIFE

Venues open and close quickly and popularity wavers, so check the English-language press such as *Vietnam Pathfinder* (⊚pathfinder.com.vn) for the latest information and consult ⊚beervn.com for the best beer and microbreweries in Hanoi (and elsewhere in Vietnam). Ta Hien is home to most of the bars catering to expats and backpackers.

BARS

ETE 95 Giang Van Minh; map p.843. Microbrewery serving its "special" beer in unmarked bottles. This spot is popular with expats in the know, has friendly English-speaking staff and excellent hamburgers. Daily 11am–midnight.

GC Pub 3 Bao Khanh; map p.845. Friendly gay bar with a good mix of locals and foreigners; a good place to make enquiries about other LGBT venues. Daily noon–late.

Le Pub 25 Hang Be; map p.845. Relaxed and welcoming by day, atmospheric and crowded by night, this tavern-like bar with streetside seating draws a regular crowd of backpackers and expats, with nightly drinks specials and the coldest beer in the capital. You can pick your own music too. Daily noon–late.

Quan Ly 82 Le Van Hu; map p.845. This traditional *ruou* (Vietnamese liquor) bar has been around for a long time, and the English menu can help you get acquainted with the many varieties on offer – from ginseng to ones with life forms in them. If that's too exotic for you, stick to the *bia hoi* and the good Vietnamese bar food. Daily 4pm–late.

Tet Bar 2a Ta Hien; map p.845. Multi-level yet intimate and smoky bar, popular with expats and doubling as a very small dance venue as the night drags on. Daily 5pm–late.

Windmill 31 Dang Tran Con; map p.843. This is a lovely courtyard spot not far from the Temple of Literature. It's

---

STREET EATS

Hanoi's street food scene is legendary, and for sheer value for money and atmosphere it's hard to beat the rock-bottom, stove-and-stool **food stalls** or the slightly more upmarket **street kitchens**. Pho Cam Chi is a narrow lane around 500m northeast of the main train station, packed with cheap places; streets such as Mai Hac De, Hang Dieu and Duong Thanh are also a good bet. If you're after specific Hanoi specialities, pop into one of the following:

Banh Cuon 12 Hang Ga; map p.845. An excellent spot for just thin steamed rice crêpes filled with mushrooms, minced pork and ground shrimp and topped with crispy shallots. Daily 5–11pm.

Bun Cha Nem Cua Be Doc Kim 67 Duong Thanh; map p.845. Look no further than here for *bun cha*, barbecued pork served over a bowl of rice noodles and minty greens. Daily 10am–8.30pm.

Goc Da 52 Ly Quoc Su; map p.845. This basic streetside shack that spills out onto the pavement is excellent for

banh goi (Vietnamese-style empanadas filled with minced pork and glass noodles), as well as deep-fried spring rolls.

Pho Gia Truyen 49 Bat Dan; map p.845. For the ubiquitous pho noodle soup, this is one of the best places in town. Daily 6am–10pm.

Thanh Hop 12 Dinh Liet; map p.845. Small and admittedly a bit grubby-looking, but with delicious chicken or beef pho for 40,000VND. Daily noon–10pm.

THE OTHER BIA HOI CORNER

Enjoyed more for their atmosphere than for the quality of the brew, Hanoi's local **bia hoi** outlets are fun, friendly and extremely cheap (usually 5000–10,000VND). The four small *bia hoi* joints at the crossroads of Ta Hien and Luong Ngoc Quyen are known as **International Bia Hoi Corner** (map p.845), and draw crowds of backpackers, expats and out-of-towners. For a more authentic experience head to the **Bia Hoi Corner** at Bat Dan and Duong Thanh, where local men sip warm draught beer and nibble traditional Vietnamese food.

one of the few good microbreweries in the city and serves up Czech-style draught lager, with tasty Vietnamese dishes on offer too. Daily 11am–11pm.

CLUBS AND LIVE MUSIC

Factory 11a Bao Khanh; map p.845. This funky multi-level drinking venue has an appealing roof terrace, decorated with socialist art; sit back with a hookah and enjoy the live music or snack on the edible goodies at the bar. Daily noon–late.

Funky Buddha 2 Ta Hien; map p.845. Crowded bar-cum-club, with a small dancefloor, drinks specials and trippy disco lights. Backpackers tend to haunt the L-shaped bar. Daily 5pm–late.

Hanoi Rock City 27/52 To Ngoc Van Ⓦ hanoirockcity.com; map p.843. The 7km journey north of the centre is worth making for the excellent live music – from hip-hop and punk to electronica and DJ mixes (check online to see what's on). Daily until 10pm; much later most weekend nights.

SHOPPING

The best areas to browse for clothing and souvenirs are Hang Gai and around the cathedral in the Old Quarter, but for high-end shopping visit the French Quarter and Trang Tien Plaza, on the southeastern edge of Hoan Kiem Lake. Look out for the Made in Vietnam stores, which stock end-of-the-line designer gear at rock-bottom prices. The city has more than fifty markets, selling predominantly foodstuffs: there is a large supermarket at the north corner of Ly Nam De, and small 24hr Circle K convenience stores are dotted everywhere in the Old Quarter.

The Apricot Gallery 40b Hang Bong Ⓦ apricotgallery.com.vn; map p.845. A well-established gallery with a range of works by local contemporary and traditional artists. Daily 8am–8pm.

Bookworm 44 Chau Long Ⓦ bookwormhanoi.com; map p.843. This comforting little bookshop has new and

secondhand fiction and non-fiction (the latter is upstairs) and they buy used books too. It's a bit of a trek from the Old Quarter, but worth it. They're tucked behind the Hanoi Cooking Centre. Daily 9am–7pm.

Cho Dong Xuan Dong Xuan; map p.845. Hanoi's largest covered market is a good place to buy cheap bags, shoes, hats and materials. Daily 8am–5pm.

Cho Hom 81 Pho Hue; map p.845. A bit of a walk from the Old Quarter, but it's good for purchasing fabrics if you're looking to get some clothes tailored. There's fresh produce for sale here too. Daily 6am–5pm.

Craft Link 43–45 Van Mieu Ⓦ craftlink.com.vn; map p.843. A not-for-profit business selling traditional crafts made by ethnic minorities, including lacquerware, paper goods, baskets and clothes. Daily 9am–6pm.

Foreign Language Bookstore 64 Trang Tien; map p.845. The small shop is the best place for English-language books, with a good selection of cookery and history titles, as well as maps and bus timetables for sale. There are a couple more bookshops along the same street. Daily 9am–7pm.

Old Propaganda Posters 16 Hang Bac; map p.845. If you're keen on Communist memorabilia, make a beeline for here for brightly coloured original – though these are hard to verify – and replica propaganda prints and paintings. Officially it's "Thang Long Gallery", and over the road at #5 is "Hanoi Art Gallery", with more of the same. Daily 8.30am–10pm.

DIRECTORY

Banks and exchange Vietcombank's main branch is at 198 Tran Quang Khai; there's another branch at 78 Nguyen Du. 24hr ATMs are widespread.

Embassies and consulates Australia, 8 Dao Tan, Ba Dinh (☎ 024 3774 0100); Canada, 31 Hung Vuong (☎ 024 3734 5000); China, 46 Hoang Dieu (☎ 024 3845 3736);

11

WHAT'S ON IN HANOI

A number of resources carry **listings** information for Hanoi and the surrounding area, including *Hanoi Grapevine* (Ⓦ hanoigrapevine.com), which has information about art exhibitions and concerts. Others include *TNH* (previously *New Hanoian*; Ⓦ tnhvietnam.xemzi.com) – with a wealth of information for visitors and expats, including restaurant and bar reviews; *The Word* (Ⓦ wordhanoi.com) – the online version of the free monthly expat magazine filled with local lifestyle articles and restaurant listings. *Sticky Rice* (Ⓦ stickyrice.typepad.com) is a great resource for foodies.

Ireland, Vincom City Towers, 8th floor, 191 Ba Trieu (☎ 024 3974 3291); New Zealand, 5th floor, 63 Ly Thai To (☎ 024 3824 1481); UK, 5th Floor, 31 Hai Ba Trung (☎ 024 3936 0500); US, The American Center, 1st floor, Rose Garden Tower, 170 Ngoc Khanh (☎ 024 3850 5000).

Medical care Hanoi Family Medical Practice and Dental Surgery in Van Phuc, 109–112 Kim Ma (Mon–Fri 8.30am–5.30pm, Sat 8.30am–noon; ☎ 024 3843 0748, ⓦ vietnammedicalpractice.com), and SOS International Clinic, 51 Xuan Dieu (☎ 024 3934 0666, ⓦ internationalsos .com), both have English-speaking doctors, and provide 24hr emergency care. Make sure your travel insurance will cover the high costs.

Pharmacies 119 Hang Gai and 3 Trang Thi. There's also a 24hr pharmacy at 87 Phu Doan.

Post office The main post office occupies a whole block at 75 Dinh Tien Hoang (Mon–Sat 8am–7pm, Sun 9am–6pm).

Around Hanoi

The fertile and densely populated landscape of the Red River Delta that surrounds Hanoi is crisscrossed by massive ancient dykes and studded with temples and pagodas, including the **Perfume Pagoda** – the city's most popular day-trip. The magnificent karst scenery at **Tam Coc**, 90km south of Hanoi, can also be visited as a day-trip from the capital, but many travellers choose to explore the area at a more leisurely pace: the sleepy town of **Ninh Binh** makes an excellent base for Tam Coc, the nearby ancient capital of **Hoa Lu** and trips to **Cuc Phuong National Park**.

THE PERFUME PAGODA

Sixty kilometres southwest of Hanoi, a forested spur shelters north Vietnam's most famous Buddhist pilgrimage site, the **Perfume Pagoda** (Chua Huong) – a pagoda and shrine complex built into the cliffs of Huong Tich Mountain, and said to be named after spring blossoms that scent the air.

The pagoda occupies a grotto more than 50m high; the journey there begins with a pleasant, hour-long sampan ride up a flooded valley among karst hills, then a path brings you to the seventeenth-century Chua Thien Chu ("Pagoda Leading to Heaven"), in front of which stands a magnificent, triple-roofed bell pavilion. Quan Am, Goddess of Mercy, takes pride of place on the pagoda's main altar. To the right, a slippery 3km path leads steeply uphill (1–2hr), at the end of which a gaping cavern is revealed beneath the inscription "supreme cave under the southern sky". The Perfume Pagoda is also dedicated to Quan Am and a flight of 120 steps descends into the dragon's-mouth-like entrance, where gilded Buddhas emerge from dark recesses wreathed in clouds of incense (bring a torch). You must wear long trousers and long-sleeve shirts to visit Chua Thien Chu, and shoes with good grip are highly recommended. If you don't want to hike to the top, you can take the **cable car** (one-way/return 80,000/120,000VND) to the summit.

This is a popular destination for Vietnamese tourists, day-trippers from Hanoi and Buddhist pilgrims; to avoid the worst of the crowds, don't come on the even dates of the third lunar month (March or April), avoid weekends and expect to be pursued by hawkers throughout the experience. The easiest way to visit the pagoda is on an all-inclusive tour from Hanoi (approx $20–30).

NINH BINH AND AROUND

The dusty provincial capital of **NINH BINH**, 90km from Hanoi, has little to detain you, but serves as a good base for exploring the beautiful countryside that surrounds it. There's a burgeoning backpacker area behind the bus station, converging on Hoang Hoa Tham.

WHAT TO SEE AND DO

The most rewarding way to see the area is by **renting a bicycle** ($2–3/day from any Nimh Binh guesthouse); the surrounding landscape, with giant limestone karsts dramatically rising from glistening rice paddies, makes the journey to **Tam Coc** worthwhile; it can be combined with the temples of **Hoa Lu** in a day-trip. **Trang An Grottoes** are another option, but it's a little further

INTO CHINA

THE TRAIN TO CHINA

Tickets should be booked well in advance for the direct train service from Hanoi to China, and you'll need your passport with a valid China visa when you buy them. The **Hanoi–Beijing** service (42hr; around 7,000,000VND) leaves Hanoi main station on Tuesdays and Fridays at 9.20pm and cannot be boarded anywhere other than Hanoi; it stops in Dong Dang, Pingxiang, Nanning, Guilin and Beijing. The Hanoi–Kunming service runs daily and there is a daily connection for Guilin and Beijing, but for this, you will need to purchase two tickets. You can also take the train to Lao Cai, and take a bus from there to Kunming (see box, p.863). See ⓦ seat61.com for up-to-date details of train journeys between Vietnam and China.

HUU NGHI AND ON TO NANNING

The road crossing known as the **Huu Nghi ("Friendship") Gate** is 164km northeast of Hanoi at the end of Highway 1 and is the most popular border crossing in the north. Local trains from Hanoi (hard seat only) terminate at Dong Dang station, 800m south of the main town, from where you can take a *xe om* up to the border (40,000VND). The Huu Nghi border (daily 7am–5.30pm) has no exchange facilities; there's a walk of less than 1km between the two checkpoints. On the Chinese side, shared taxis and buses (from ¥20–40) will take you to **Pingxiang**, 15km away, for the nearest accommodation and the trains to **Nanning** (3 daily; 4hr–5hr 30min; $7). If entering Vietnam here, ignore the touts and get on a minibus at the Dong Dang minibus terminal, with frequent services to Hanoi (2 hourly; 3hr 15min).

11

and is best visited by motorbike ($6–8/ day). It's a longer sampan ride (3hr) and costs 200,000VND.

Tam Coc

It's hard not to be won over by the mystical, watery beauty of the Tam Coc region, a miniature, landlocked version of Ha Long Bay. Journey's end for the two-hour sampan ride through the flooded landscape is **Tam Coc**, three long, dark tunnel-caves eroded through the limestone hills with, in places, barely sufficient clearance for the sampan.

The starting point is the dock in Van Lam village. **Boats** leave here between 7am and 5pm (go early or late to avoid the crowds), and cost 150,000VND; each boat carries two people, plus there's an additional 120,000VND entry per person. A *xe om* from Ninh Binh will cost about 100,000VND all-in. However, many tourists complain of constant hassle to buy refreshments and handicrafts; be firm from the outset.

Follow the road another 2km beyond the boat dock to visit the cave-pagoda of **Bich Dong** (free), where stone-cut steps lead up a cliff face peppered with shrines to the cave entrance. Three Buddhas sit unperturbed on their lotus thrones beside

a head-shaped rock, which bestows longevity if touched.

If your next stop is Hoa Lu, you can take a back road for a spectacular 10km ride through rice fields, karst scenery and villages; the 30km round trip is easily done in a day. This route starts in the village halfway down the road between Highway 1 and the boat landing; follow the signs for Troung Yen village to reach Hoa Lu.

Hoa Lu

Thirteen kilometres northwest of Ninh Binh stands **Hoa Lu** (20,000VND), site of the tenth-century capital of an early, independent Vietnamese kingdom called Dai Co Viet. The fortified royal palaces of the Dinh and Le kings are now in ruins, but their dynastic temples, seventeenth-century copies of eleventh-century originals, still rest quietly in a narrow valley surrounded by hills. Opposite the temples, steps lead up "Saddle Mountain" for a panoramic view of Hoa Lu.

The quickest way out to Hoa Lu is by *xe om* (260,000VND or so round trip), but going by **bicycle** is another option. Follow Highway 1 for 6km, then it's a pleasant ride on paved back roads west of the highway, following signs to Truong

11

Yen village and Hoa Lu (13km in total). You can cycle back along the Sao Khe River: take the paved road heading east directly in front of the temples, turn right over the bridge and follow the dirt track for about 4km to the first village. Here, a left turn leading to a concrete bridge will take you back to Ninh Binh, while the road straight ahead continues for another 6km to Tam Coc.

ARRIVAL AND INFORMATION

By bus The central bus station is on Le Dai Hanh, east of the Van River. From here, public buses depart every 20min for Hanoi's Giap Bat and Luong Yen stations. Open-tour buses en route between Hanoi and points south, including Hue, Da Nang, Hoi An and HCMC (all 2 daily), pick up and drop off at their associated hotels – public buses south stop on the new bypass.

Destinations Hai Phong (several daily; 3hr); Hanoi (every 20min; 2hr 30min).

By train The station is east of the Van River on Hang Hoa Tham.

Destinations Da Nang (5 daily; 14hr); Hanoi (4 daily; 2hr 30min); HCMC (5 daily; 40hr); Hue (5 daily; 12hr 30min); Nha Trang (5 daily; 24hr).

Services The Vietcombank, on the main strip on Tran Hung Dao, has an ATM.

ACCOMMODATION AND EATING

A string of goat meat (*thit de*) restaurants lines the road 3km out of town; this local speciality is served with rice paper and herbs. Atmospheric *bia hoi* stands line the riverside just north of Hong Phong. All these hotels can assist with tours, car and motorbike rental, as well as onward transport.

Go Ninhbinh Hostel 1 Hoang Hoa Thamg ☏0229 387 1186, ⓦgoninhbinhhostel.com. Close to the bus station (the building was originally the train station), this colourful place is at the centre of the town's small backpacker "scene". The double rooms and eight- or ten-bed dorms are a little dark – and can be noisy – but the hostel is popular for its cheap beer, decent menu and pool table. Dorms $\overline{\$5}$, doubles $\overline{\$20}$

Hoa Lu Eco Backpackers Hostel Trang An Village, 8km from Ninh Binh ☏090 439 6779, ⓦhoaluecohomestay .com. The real reason to come to Ninh Binh is the landscape, and this backpacker-friendly place along a bumpy track is right by Trang An Grottoes. Ideal if you have your own transport, otherwise the remote location means you'll pay a lot more for services such as onward travel or food and drink. The dorm is twelve-bed. Dorms $\overline{\$8}$, doubles $\overline{\$22}$

Kim Lien Guest House 54 Van Thanh Phuc Thinh ☏030 6250800, ⓦguesthousekimlien.com. Friendly, family-run guesthouse that makes a great base due to the owner's knowledge of the area (a book's been compiled for the guests' perusal). Rooms are clean and perfectly comfortable. Doubles $\overline{\$17}$

Than Thuy's Guesthouse 53 Le Hong Phong ☏0229 387 1811. Good spot for meeting other travellers, with decent older rooms in the guesthouse ($15), and spacious, fully equipped rooms in the newer hotel at the back ($30). Their tailor-made motorbike tours to outlying villages are popular. Doubles $\overline{\$10}$

Trung Tuyet 14 Hoang Hoa Tham. Quite possibly the best restaurant in town, with large portions of inexpensive Vietnamese dishes such as vegetable spring rolls and fried noodle with egg. A "small" is plenty for one person; only go for "large" if there's a ravenous group of you. Mains from 60,000VND. Daily 11.30am–9pm.

CUC PHUONG NATIONAL PARK

Established as Vietnam's first national park in 1962, **Cuc Phuong**, 200 square kilometres of tropical evergreen forest surrounded by limestone mountains, spreads over three provinces and two mountain ranges. The myriad species of wildlife that live among the forest's ancient trees – some of which are more than a thousand years old – include rare butterflies, more than three hundred bird and ninety mammal species, including bats, bears, leopards, and one of the world's most endangered monkeys, Delacour's langur. At the entrance gate (60,000VND), the reception (daily 6am–10pm; ⓦwww .cucphuongtourism.com) can organize biking, hiking, birdwatching, night-time wildlife spotting and overnight accommodation either in the park headquarters, bamboo bungalows or stilt houses in a Muong village in the park ($7–15 per person).

Beyond the visitors' centre stands the **Endangered Primate Rescue Center** (daily 9–11am & 1.30–4pm, 60,000VND/two people), where you can see the park's research, conservation and breeding programmes to save endangered langurs, lorises and gibbons and learn about the threats to this unique environment in the form of illegal logging and poaching. There's also good hiking to be done here; a couple of well-trodden trails lead to thousand-year-old trees, and there's a tougher 11km walk to Silver Cloud Peak (3hr, 500,000VND per group), as well as a fairly tough 16km (5hr; 770,000VND one-way per group) hike to the Muong village of Kanh; park staff can provide basic maps, but you must hire a guide for longer hikes.

ARRIVAL AND DEPARTURE

On a tour Tourist agencies in Hanoi arrange day-trips to Cuc Phuong for about $35 per person (not including entrance fees).

By bus A morning bus runs from Giap Bat bus station in Hanoi directly to the park at 9am, returning at 3pm. If coming from Ninh Binh, take the public bus (20,000VND).

By bike From Ninh Binh you can rent a motorbike or hire a *xe om* (about 250,000VND return including waiting time). Head north along Highway 1 for about 10km, and take the left at the sign for Cuc Phuong. From here it's another 18km to the park entrance.

Ha Long Bay

Nearly two thousand bizarrely shaped limestone outcrops jut out of the emerald **Ha Long Bay**, its hidden coves, echoing caves and needle-sharp ridges providing the inspiration for dozens of local legends and poems. Navigating the watery channels and scrambling through caves is a hugely popular activity, justifiably so, but some may be put off by the numerous boats that congregate in the bay and the queues to get into caves. If you want to go off the beaten track and experience true beauty without the crowds, it's well worth taking a small-group tour with Cat Ba Ventures (see p.861) on Cat Ba Island or heading out to the remote Bai Tu Long Bay (see box below). Bear in mind also that the **weather** from January to March can be overcast and even cold.

The vast majority of visitors to Ha Long Bay come on **organized tours** from Hanoi (two days/one night; from $110); a good alternative is to go from Cat Ba Island as these tours take a quieter route and also visit the beaches of Lan Ha Bay. If you're planning on visiting Ha Long Bay from Cat Ba Island and are travelling up from the south, it's possible to bypass Hanoi and go via the port city of **Hai Phong** instead.

HA LONG CITY

The gateway to Ha Long Bay is **HA LONG CITY**, an amalgamation of two towns – Hong Gai and Bai Chay. Although it's popular with Chinese and Korean tourists, staying here isn't really appealing or necessary. Some independent travellers stay overnight in Bai Chay so they can

HA LONG BAY CRUISES

Cruises around Ha Long Bay are peddled by every hotel and travel agency in Hanoi, but despite the undeniable beauty of the karst-studded bay, complaints abound about the tours and the service provided, particularly on budget tours. You tend to get what you pay for, so, if you're only being charged $50 for a two-day-one-night trip, expect a dirty, unsafe boat and being shuttled from one commission-paying place to another. That said, even paying doesn't always help; travel agencies seldom own their own boats, merely acting as agents for boat operators in Ha Long and Cat Ba (white boats are from Ha Long, brown from Cat Ba), who shift passengers mid-tour from boat to boat to cram as many on board as possible. Day-trips from Hanoi to Ha Long Bay are not worth it, as you spend a great deal of time on the bus; **overnight trips** that throw in some kayaking and swimming are a better way to go, and if you can spare three days and venture as far as the remote **Bai Tu Long Bay**, even better. A great way to see Ha Long Bay is to base yourself on **Cat Ba Island** and do an unhurried small-group tour with the highly professional Cat Ba Ventures (see p.861) who take you kayaking to more remote lagoons where you're not constantly paddling through floating garbage left in the wake of numerous tour boats. If booking from Hanoi, the high-octane adventure that includes tubing and waterboarding as well as cruising is organized by *Vietnam Backpackers* (see p.851). Otherwise, ask as many questions as you can about what's included before booking, and request a written itinerary detailing the size of the group, standard of accommodation, and planned activities, so you have some comeback at the end if the tour fails to live up to what was promised. Report any unsatisfactory experiences to the Administration of Tourism in Hanoi (see box, p.849). There are several recommended **tour companies** in Hanoi (see p.850).

11

organize their own Ha Long Bay cruise from **Tuan Chau Island**, the new marina 10km west of the city where all boats for Ha Long Bay now embark. You can get to Bai Tu Long Bay's remote Quan Lan island from Ben Tau pier in Hong Gai (2 daily; 1hr 30min; 200,000VND), and the atmospheric market and fishing harbour close to the pier definitely warrant a wander for an hour or two.

HA LONG BAY AND BAI TU LONG BAY

Ha Long Bay and Bai Tu Long Bay, to the northeast, are separated by a wide channel running north–south: the larger, western portion contains dramatic scenery and most of the caves, while to the northeast lies an even more attractive collection of smaller islands, known as Bai Tu Long and part of the Bai Tu Long National Park; this bay is still relatively untouristy and unpolluted, making for a more laidback experience than Ha Long Bay.

The bay's most famous cave is **Hang Dau Go** ("Grotto of the Wooden Stakes"). In 1288, General Tran Hung Dao amassed hundreds of wooden stakes here; these were driven into the Bach Dang River estuary mud, skewering the boats of Kublai Khan's Mongol army as the tide went out. The same island also boasts the beautiful **Hang Thien Cung** cave, whose rectangular chamber, 250m long and 20m high, holds a textbook display of sparkling stalactites and stalagmites. To the south, you should single out **Ho Dong Tien** ("Grotto of the Fairy Lake") and the enchanting **Dong Me Cung** ("Grotto of the Labyrinth").

Of the far-flung sights, **Hang Hanh** is one of the more adventurous day-trips from Cat Ba Island: the tide must be exactly right (at half-tide) to allow a coracle ($15 extra, or $2 per person) access to the 2km-long tunnel-cave; a powerful torch is very useful. Dau Bo Island, on the southeastern edge of Ha Long Bay, encloses **Ho Ba Ham** ("Three Tunnel Lake"), a shallow lagoon wrapped round with limestone walls and connected to the sea by three low-ceilinged tunnels that are only navigable by sampan or kayak at low tide. This cave can be included in a one- or two-day excursion from Cat Ba Island.

HAI PHONG

Located 100km east of Hanoi, **HAI PHONG** is north Vietnam's principal port – a small, orderly city of broad avenues, with hydrofoil and ferry links to Cat Ba Island (for Ha Long Bay). Given the frequency of transport connections to and from Hai Phong, there's little reason to linger en route either to Hanoi or the south.

ARRIVAL AND DEPARTURE

By plane Cat Bi airport is 6km southeast of the city, around 130,000VND by taxi.

Destinations Da Nang (3 daily; 1hr 20min); HCMC (5 daily; 2hr).

By bus Lac Long bus station is centrally located on Cu Chinh Lan (convenient for Ben Binh Harbour) and receives buses from the northeast. Buses serving the south and west (including Ninh Binh) operate from Niem Nghia bus

---

INTO CHINA: MONG CAI

Buses from Hanoi (8hr; 230,000VND) arrive at Mong Cai bus station, 500m west of the centre. The blue, space-age building northwest of the roundabout identifies Mong Cai's focal point, the covered market. The **Chinese border** is 1km away: walk north along Tran Phu and turn left at the end of the road to reach the border gate (daily 7am–7pm; visas must be arranged in advance). Once in Dongxing on the Chinese side, take a *xe om* to the bus station, from where regular buses depart for Nanning and Guilin.

For somewhere to stay in Mong Cai, try *Truong Minh*, 36 Trieu Duong (☎0203 388 3368), or *Thanh Tam* down the street at no. 71 (☎0203 377 0181); both have clean, pleasant rooms for around $15. Streets near the market turn into open-air food stalls in the evening. Vietcombank has a branch with a 24hr ATM north of the market, on Van Don.

For those arriving **in Mong Cai**, there are numerous buses to Hai Phong (every 2hr; 4hr); Hanoi (at least hourly; 8hr) and Ha Long City (2 hourly; 4hr).

station, 3km from the centre on Tran Nguyen Han. Some Hanoi services use Tam Bac bus station, near the west end of Tam Bac Lake, though Hanoi-bound minibuses also hang around the Ben Binh harbour and can be flagged down on the riverfront south of Dien Bien Phu.

Destinations Da Nang (15hr); Hanoi (2hr 30min); HCMC (38hr); Hue (14hr); Nha Trang (10hr); Ninh Binh (3hr).

By train Hai Phong train station is on the southeast side of town on Luong Khanh Thien.

Destinations Hanoi (2 daily; 2hr 30min).

By boat Ben Binh harbour is on the Cua Cam River, a short walk from the Lac Long bus station. A fast boat runs from Ben Binh to Cat Ba's Cai Vieng harbour at 7am and 10am, with a bus connection waiting in Cat Ba to take you to Cat Ba Town; return buses leave Cat Ba Town at 2pm and 4pm (1hr 30min). Another option is to take a bus from Hai Phong's Ben Binh harbour to Dinh Vu port to catch another hydrofoil to Cat Ba's Cai Vieng harbour, as departures from Dinh Vu are more frequent (6 daily; 2hr).

Destinations Cat Ba Island (hydrofoils 8 daily; 45min–1hr).

CAT BA ISLAND

Dragon-back mountain ranges loom on the horizon 20km out of Hai Phong as boats approach **Cat Ba Island**, the largest member of an archipelago sitting to the west of Ha Long Bay.

WHAT TO SEE AND DO

The island's main settlement is **CAT BA TOWN**, an old fishing village, but the main strip along the waterfront is now lined with countless budget hotels and restaurants. The hydrofoil from Hai Phong docks here, within walking distance of most accommodation. A fifteen-minute walk along a steep road just east of the waterfront leads to a small, sandy **beach**, **Cat Co 1**; from here, follow a scenic, cliff-hugging boardwalk south to reach **Cat Co 3**, which is dominated by the low-slung *Sunrise Resort*. Cat Co 2 – north of Cat Co 1 – is a lovely and quiet stretch of sand, but is also owned by a resort. Overlooking the Cat Co 1 and Cat Co 2 beaches is **Fort Cannon** (daily sunrise–sunset; 40,000VND), its guns and underground tunnels first used by the Japanese in World War II, and later by the French and the Vietnamese. The sunsets from this spot are fantastic. The entrance gate is a steep fifteen-minute walk from

Cat Ba Town; if you don't want to trudge uphill you can hire a waiting *xe om* from the waterfront (around 30,000VND).

Almost half the island and adjacent waters are part of **Cat Ba National Park** (40,000VND), home to over seventy species of bird, and mammals such as civets, deer, wild boar and the world's most endangered primate – the golden-headed or Cat Ba langur – with only sixty or so remaining. The park entrance is 13km along the road from Cat Ba Town. Companies such as Cat Ba Ventures and Asia Outdoors (see p.861) run half- and full-day hiking tours of the park; otherwise it's worth hiring an experienced and English-speaking guide to explore the park (around 270,000VND for a full day) from the ranger station to point out the wildlife. There are several short hikes in the park, including one to **Trung Trang Cave** and a rewarding 18km hike up one of the peaks. Many guided hikes either finish at or stop for lunch at the remote minority village of **Viet Hai**, where *Whisper of Nature* (see p.861) is located. You'll need good boots, lots of water and mosquito repellent. The going can be quite tough, and trekking should be avoided after heavy rains, when the paths can be slippery and treacherous. You can reach the park independently via the green QH public buses that depart from the hydrofoil dock in Cat Ba Town (at 8am, 11am & 3pm; 20min; 30,000VND) or by your own rented motorbike or scooter.

En route to the park, 10km north of Cat Ba Town, is the **Hospital Cave** (daily 8am–4.30pm; 40,000VND), a three-storey construction within a natural cave that served as a hospital and shelter for Viet Cong leaders from 1965 to 1975. The entrance fee includes a guide who'll point out where the cinema and swimming pool used to be and explain what each of the seventeen spartan bunker rooms was used for. *Kim Ba* restaurant is just over the road from the entrance and is a nice shady spot for a cheap lunch.

ARRIVAL AND INFORMATION

A bridge via Cat Hai Island is slated to join Cat Ba to the mainland in 2017, but at the time of writing it was unclear if this would mean changes to ferry and hydrofoil services.

11

11

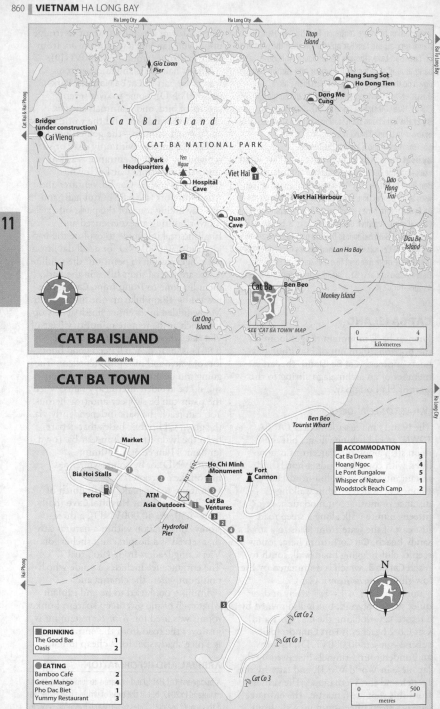

Ha Long City

Ha Long City

Ba Tu Long Bay

Titop Island

Gia Luan Pier

Hang Sung Sot
Ho Dong Tien

Dong Me Cung

Cat Ha & Hai Phong

C a t   B a   I s l a n d

Bridge
(under construction)
Cai Vieng

CAT BA NATIONAL PARK

Dao Hong Trai

Park Headquarters
Yen Ngua

Hospital Cave
Viet Hai 1

Viet Hai Harbour

Quan Cave

Dau Be Island

2

Lan Ha Bay

Cat Ba   **Ben Beo**

Cat Ong Island

SEE 'CAT BA TOWN' MAP

Monkey Island

N

CAT BA ISLAND

0   kilometres   4

National Park

CAT BA TOWN

Ha Long City

Ben Beo Tourist Wharf

Market

ACCOMMODATION
Cat Ba Dream	3
Hoang Ngoc	4
Le Pont Bungalow	5
Whisper of Nature	1
Woodstock Beach Camp	2

Ho Chi Minh Monument

Fort Cannon

Bia Hoi Stalls 1

2

Petrol

ATM
Asia Outdoors

Cat Ba Ventures 1

3

3

2

4

4

Hydrofoil Pier

Hai Phong

N

5

Cat Co 2

Cat Co 1

DRINKING
| The Good Bar | 1 |
| Oasis | 2 |

Cat Co 3

EATING
Bamboo Café	2
Green Mango	4
Pho Dac Biet	1
Yummy Restaurant	3

0   metres   500

By ferry Coming from Hai Phong, ferries via Cat Hai Island pull in at Cai Vieng harbour at the island's western point, about 20km from town, and are met by a bus that whisks passengers to Cat Ba Town. Ferries from Tuan Chau (accessed from Ha Long City) land at the Gia Luan pier, in the north of the island, 40km from Cat Ba Town. Public QH Green Buses leave Gia Luan at 9am, noon and 4pm (30,000VND) for Cat Ba Town, and despite what some unscrupulous locals might tell you, foreigners are very much allowed to take the bus. Minibuses at the same price are usually there to meet ferries too.

Destinations Hai Phong (hourly; 1hr 30min); Tuan Chau, Ha Long City (3 daily; 50min); boat and bus to Hanoi (7 daily; 3hr 30min–4hr 30min).

By hydrofoil The hydrofoil is the quickest way to travel between Hai Phong and Cat Ba (4 daily; 45min), and docks in town within walking distance of most accommodation.

Services There are several ATMs in town, including an Agribank at no. 209 on the waterfront. There's also a petrol station across the small bridge at the far end of the waterfront.

GETTING AROUND

By bus QH Green Buses run between Cat Ba Town and Gia Luan pier (3 daily; 30,000VND); for the latest timetables, check with the tourist office at the hydrofoil pier.

By motorbike The most efficient way to get around is by renting a motorbike or scooter from most hotels; rental is around US$5 per day, and although Cat Ba's roads have very little traffic, construction work and blind bends can make them tricky to negotiate.

TOURS AND ACTIVITIES

Popular tours include full-day treks through the national park, with lunch in Viet Hai village, and a boat trip back to Cat Ba Town via Lan Ha Bay ($18 including lunch and kayaking). A day venture into Lan Ha and Ha Long Bay, including kayaking, swimming and a visit to one of the bay's most dramatic caves, Ho Ba Ham, costs $28–31, food included. Some shops and hotels near the seafront can rent out two-person sea kayaks ($10/day) for self-powered paddling around the bay.

Asia Outdoors No. 222 (above *The Noble House*) ☏ 091 368 8450, ⓦ asiaoutdoors.com.vn. The limestone outcrops in Lan Ha Bay and Ha Long Bay are internationally renowned sites for amateur and professional climbers. Set up by two experienced American climbers, Asia Outdoors has developed an extensive network of rock-climbing routes and bouldering sites in the area suitable for all skill levels. They can also incorporate boat trips (necessary to access some of the climbing sites), deep-water soloing, kayaking, trekking and the occasional beach party into their highly recommended, tailor-made packages. Daily 9am–8pm.

Cat Ba Ventures No. 223 along the main waterfront ☏ 0225 388 8755, ☏ 091 246 7016, ⓦ catbaventures.com. Hands down the best operator when it comes to small-group cruises, with their highly professional management, English-speaking guides and well-organized tours that don't feel rushed or whisk you off to commission-paying pearl farms. Daily 7.30am–8pm.

ACCOMMODATION

The summer months get very busy with domestic tourists – book in advance and be aware that the prices quoted here will more than triple. For hotels located along the main waterfront strip, we give the street number in brackets.

Cat Ba Dream (226) ☏ 0225 388 8274, ⓦ catba-dream-vn .book.direct. A central location, good sea views from the top floors of this seven-storey building, and friendly management make this hotel a solid bet. Doubles $10

Hoang Ngoc (245) ☏ 0225 368 8788. One of the nicest of the budget options along the waterfront, at the quieter south end. Family run, with fresh and pleasant rooms and a communal balcony on every floor. Nab a seaview room if you can. Doubles $10

Le Pont Bungalow Cat Co 3 Street. About a 10min uphill stroll west of the waterfront, *Le Pont Bungalow* has a backpacker vibe, a beautiful view, a decent breakfast and paper-thin walls. Rooms are comfortable enough and you have a choice of en suite or shared bathrooms. There's also a cheap, fourteen-bed rooftop dorm. Dorms $7, doubles $19

★ **Whisper of Nature** Viet Hai Village ☏ 024 3923 3706, ⓦ vietbungalow.com. Located in the tiny village of Viet Hai, in the Cat Ba National Park, this cluster of thatch-roofed bungalows sits by a stream on the edge of the forest; most house private en-suite rooms, with one large bungalow acting as a dorm room. The setting is unbeatable and getting there is part of the fun; contact the management before you set off. Dorms $15, doubles $30

Woodstock Beach Camp 9km north of Cat Ba Town ☏ 031 388 8599, ⓔ woodstockbeachcamp@gmail.com. Turning the island vibe up a notch, this chilled-out hostel has a bar and some dorms (plus tents) right on the beach, with another block set a bit back. Murals decorate the place and backpackers stay for weeks, swinging in hammocks and strumming guitars. Dorms $8, doubles $20

EATING

At night, you'll find a cluster of *bia hoi* stands at the western end of the strip and in front of the pier – an atmospheric place for a cheap beer (25,000VND) or a sugar-cane juice. The floating restaurants south of the pier are best avoided as they are renowned for ripping tourists off.

Bamboo Café (199). Delicious, reasonably priced fresh seafood, including crab spring rolls (70,000VND) and mains such as steamed clams with lemongrass (90,000VND) or garlic prawns (125,000VND). Daily 8am–10pm.

Green Mango (231). The ambitious menu of Western and Asian dishes at this trendy restaurant can be a bit hit and miss, but the coffee (Lavazza 55,000VND) is excellent and the breakfast a cut above elsewhere (eggs Benedict 100,000VND). Daily 7am–11pm.

Pho Dac Biet (184) Busy local joint with plastic chairs and sticky menus, serving ample portions of pho (from 30,000VND), deep-fried spring rolls (50,000VND) and noodle dishes (30,000–60,000VND). Daily 7am–10pm.

Yummy Restaurant 180 Nui Ngoc. New on the scene and cooking up a storm, this cheap local spot is tucked away on a road behind the waterfront. Delicious plates of freshly cooked Vietnamese and Thai dishes are served – splash out for fish hotpot between two for 250,000VND. Get here early to nab a table. Daily 7am–10pm.

DRINKING

The Good Bar (231). Popular with visitors thanks to its laidback vibe, cheap beer and sizeable portions of Western and Vietnamese grub. The banana and pineapple pancakes (40,000VND) make a great breakfast, too. Daily 7.30am–late.

Oasis (228). At the centre of Cat Ba's nightlife scene, this busy place keeps pouring drinks and playing music until the last patron stumbles out. The staff actually seem to love working here, and the service is spot-on. Daily 7.30am–late.

The far north

Vietnam fans out above Hanoi, the majority of it a mountainous zone wrapped around the Red River Delta. The region is mostly wild and inaccessible, sparsely populated by a fascinating mosaic of **minority tribes** whose presence is the chief tourist attraction in the area. The popular hill station of **Sa Pa** is the main departure point for treks to minority villages, although **Mai Chau** and **Bac Ha** are worthy of a visit too, not least for Bac Ha's famous Sunday market. To get far off the beaten track, the **northwestern circuit** is a difficult but hugely rewarding trip, and some adventurous travellers choose to push onto Laos via Dien Bien Phu, or China via Lao Cai. Northern Vietnam's final frontier is the **Ha Giang province** that borders China, with remote, spectacular mountain scenery; travel here requires permits (easily acquired in Hanoi) because of its proximity to the border.

THE NORTHWESTERN CIRCUIT

Highway 6 loops around Vietnam's northwest, skimming the borders of Laos and China, and passing through some of the country's most dramatic landscapes. The journey from Hanoi typically passes through **Mai Chau**, **Moc Chau**, **Son La**, **Dien Bien Phu** and **Muong Lay** before finishing in **Sa Pa** or **Lao Cai**. Terraced rice paddies, tropical rainforests, stilt-house minority villages and markets bursting with colour make a journey around the northwestern circuit one of the most spectacular in Southeast Asia. However, there is a reason why the route attracts so few tourists: the bumpy, unpaved road swerves around hairpin bends, and landslides are common, causing serious delays even after a short spell of rain. Public transport takes the form of rickety old minivans crowded to twice their capacity, so the best way to travel is by motorbike. You can then detour off Highway 6 and on to smaller back roads, with even more stunning scenery and many Hmong, Black and White Thai, Dao and Muong villages, where it is usually possible to stay overnight in a local house. It takes at least a week to make the journey, and ten days to do so comfortably. **Guided motorbike** and **mountain-bike tours** of the region are offered by agents in Hanoi (see p.850) for between $100 and $125 per day all-inclusive.

LAO CAI

The Red River Valley runs northwest from Hanoi, and after 300km, pushing ever deeper into the mountains, you eventually reach the border town of **LAO CAI**, renowned for cross-border trade and all manner of illegal smuggling. Travellers tend to pass through en route to Sa Pa or if catching the bus **into China** en route to Kunming.

ARRIVAL AND DEPARTURE

By train Most people arrive on the night train from Hanoi; the train station is on the east bank of the Red River, just 3km south of the Chinese border. Several travel agents hook their own a/c, soft-berth carriages up to the three nightly trains between Hanoi and Lao Cai (from $32/berth;

INTO CHINA: LAO CAI

The border crossing from Lao Cai into China is via the **Hekou border gate** (daily 7am–10pm), on the east bank of the Red River, 3km from the train station (around 25,000VND by *xe om*). Queues at immigration are longest in the early morning. Inside the Vietnamese border post building, there's an exchange desk that deals in dong, dollars and yuan. There's a bank across the street, and plenty of women hanging around eager to change cash. Across on the Chinese side, several high-quality a/c buses depart for **Kunming**, 520km away, from Hekou bus station, 100m from the border crossing (three in the morning, two sleeper services in the evening around 7pm; 12hr; $25). Visas for both countries must be arranged in advance. China is one hour ahead of Vietnam.

W et-pumpkin.com, W fanxipantrain.com or W livitrans .com). Vietnam Railways' (VR) carriages are almost as good; buy your tickets (hard a/c sleeper 295,000VND, soft a/c sleeper 400,000VND) in Hanoi, purchasing the return ticket at Sa Pa's VR office, or at the train station in Lao Cai. **By bus** Minibuses to Sa Pa (1hr; 50,000VND) meet the morning Hanoi trains; bear in mind that drivers have been known to overcharge foreign tourists, so if possible, double check with a local how much they're paying. Many hotels in Sa Pa offer pick-up if you've booked a room with them.

ACCOMMODATION AND EATING

Unless you arrive in the evening there's no need to stay in Lao Cai. The road outside the train station is lined with mediocre, overpriced restaurants.
Lao Cai Galaxy Hotel 268 Minh Khai ☎ 098 408 5828. Clean, spacious rooms at this business-style hotel a 5min walk from the train station. Rate includes breakfast. Doubles $22
Terminus Restaurant Opposite the main train station building. A reasonably priced Vietnamese joint serving a mix of noodle, rice, meat and fish dishes. Mains from 70,000VND. Daily 10am–10pm.

SA PA AND AROUND

Forty kilometres from Lao Cai, the small market town of **SA PA** perches dramatically on the western edge of a high plateau, overshadowed by imposing **Fansipan**, Vietnam's highest peak. A former hilltop retreat for French rulers, Sa Pa enjoys a refreshing climate and magnificent scenery, with vertiginous mountains plunging into lush green valleys terraced with rice paddies. Sadly, the never-ending hotel construction and stream of minibuses through town can mar its beauty, but from here it is possible to visit the outlying **minority villages** of H'mong, Dao, Tay and Giay peoples. The area around Sa Pa is loveliest between July

and September, when the rice terraces are green with crops, but is also busiest at that time; winter can be cold, but at least the town doesn't feel overcrowded. Weekdays throughout the year are quieter than weekends.

WHAT TO SEE AND DO

As part of the Vietnamese government's policy is to limit the minority tribes' contact with outsiders in order to isolate them, tourists are only allowed to visit the area around Sa Pa (including Ta Phin, Hoang Lien valley and Fansipan) with a **permit and guide**; only Cat Cat village can be explored solo. Permits are free and arranged by licensed tour agents for guided hikes in the area (see p.865). There's a 40,000VND entrance fee to most villages, but bear in mind that this is charged by a private company and none of the money goes to the community.

Sa Pa market

In Sa Pa, the Hmong minority are a majority, and the **market**, busiest on Saturdays, draws in villagers from all around, with the women clad in their colourful finery. The evening "love market" sees local youths come to Sa Pa to try and find a love interest. However, tourists often outnumber locals and the market is more modest than those in Can Cau (see p.868) and Bac Ha (see p.868).

Cat Cat village

A steep, lovely 3km walk leads down into the valley from the western end of Fansipan road, reaching **CAT CAT** village, a huddle of wooden houses hidden among fruit trees and bamboo. The hike offers

11

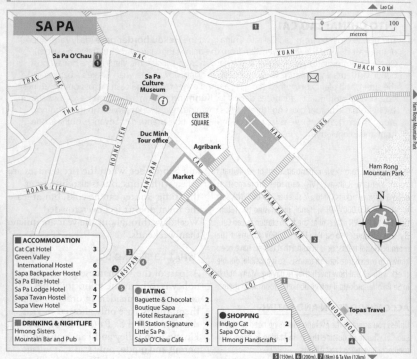

SA PA

0 100
metres

Sa Pa O'Chau

Sa Pa Culture Museum

BAC

XUAN

THAC SON

THAC

BAC

THAC

HOANG LIEN

Duc Minh Tour office

CENTER SQUARE

Agribank

FANSIPAN

CAU

Market

HAM

RONG

Ham Rong Mountain Park

HOANG LIEN

MAY

PHAM XUAN HUAN

N

ACCOMMODATION
Cat Cat Hotel	3
Green Valley International Hostel	6
Sapa Backpacker Hostel	2
Sa Pa Elite Hotel	1
Sa Pa Lodge Hotel	4
Sapa Tavan Hostel	7
Sapa View Hotel	5

FANSIPAN

DONG

LOI

MUONG HOA

EATING
Baguette & Chocolat	2
Boutique Sapa Hotel Restaurant	5
Hill Station Signature	4
Little Sa Pa	3
Sapa O'Chau Café	1

SHOPPING
Indigo Cat	2
Sapa O'Chau Hmong Handicrafts	1

Topas Travel

DRINKING & NIGHTLIFE
Hmong Sisters	2
Mountain Bar and Pub	1

5 (150m), 6 (200m), 7 (8km) & Ta Van (12km)

Ham Rong Mountain Park

spectacular views over the valley's terraced rice paddies. Look out for tubs of indigo dye outside the houses, used to colour the hemp cloth typical of Hmong dress. **Cat Cat waterfall** is just below the village.

Ta Phin

Some of the most enjoyable guided treks in the area take you into the valley north of Sa Pa. The most popular is a gentle hike that skirts rice terraces and small villages, with pot-bellied pigs rooting around in the dirt. You get great views of the valley during the walk, which culminates in a homestay in the Red Dao village of **TA PHIN**. Sapa O'Chau (see box, p.866) work with a particularly welcoming family who live in a traditional house with earthen floors and with smoked meat hanging above the fire. Don't miss the chance to try a traditional herbal bath, which involves soaking in a wooden tub; the fumes make you feel wonderfully relaxed and a little light-headed. From Ta Phin, treks take you to the Hmong village of **TRUNG**

CHAI where hikers get picked up and taken back to Sa Pa.

Ta Van and Lao Chai

The most spectacular scenery in the area is in the Muong Hoa valley south of Sa Pa, with expansive views of rice terraces and villages below. The best of the guided treks takes you down into the valley into the Hmong village of **LAO CHAI**, from where you follow the road that meanders through the fields to **TA VAN**, a Dao village uphill from a Giay community. From here, treks either cross the river and join the main road for a pick-up back to Sa Pa, or carry on down the valley to stay overnight in the Tay village of **BAN HO**. Note that some tour groups do the well-trodden hike to Ta Van along the main road, where they have to contend with traffic.

Fansipan

Rising dramatically above the rest of the Hoang Lien Son mountain range is **Mount Fansipan**, Vietnam's highest peak at 3143m. The mountain lies within Hoang Lien Son Nature Reserve, a thirty-square-kilometre national park established in 1986 to protect the forest habitat. Fansipan's summit is 19km from Sa Pa and the view on a clear day takes in the whole mountain range of northwest Vietnam, south to Son La province, and north to the peaks of Yunnan in China. Previously only accessible to a few thousand hikers a year, in 2016 a cable car opened (daily 7.30am–5.30pm; 20min; 600,000VND; ⓦfansipanlegend .com.vn) and now many people can visit in an hour; a new development of restaurants and souvenir shops aimed squarely at wealthy Chinese and domestic tourists stands testament to its popularity.

To tackle Fansipan on foot, an experienced **local guide** is essential; organized group excursions with all equipment can be arranged by reputable operators such as Sapa O'Chau (see box, p.866). It is not a technical climb, but a strenuous one, and day-trippers have to get up before sunrise to make it to the summit and back before dark.

ARRIVAL AND DEPARTURE

By bus Vietbus (ⓣ024 3627 2727) runs two daily sleeper buses directly to Hanoi (7.30am & 5.30pm; 10hr) from the Sa Pa bus station, a 30,000VND *xe om* ride from the centre. Minibuses also run from Sa Pa to Dien Bien Phu (7.30am; 9hr; from 190,000VND).

By train Minibuses from Lao Cai (connecting from the Hanoi train) drop you along the main street, Cau May. To return to Lao Cai, minibuses congregate all day from near the church on the main square; your hotel can also arrange for you to be picked up from your lodgings. Tickets for the night trains from Lao Cai to Hanoi are in short supply, so book as far ahead as possible, either at the Lao Cai Railway Station Office in Sa Pa across from the bus station off Ngu Chi Son (daily 7am–4pm; ⓣ0214 387 1480), or (more expensively) through your guesthouse.

INFORMATION AND TOURS

Information The Tourism Information Centre of Sa Pa, 2 Fansipan (daily 7.30–11.30am & 1.30–5.30pm; ⓣ0214 387 1975, ⓦsapa-tourism.com), is unusually helpful, with good maps and a small selection of handicrafts for sale at fixed prices.

Tours Sapa O'Chau (see box p.866) are one of the best tour operators in and around Sa Pa. The Sapa Sisters – four Hmong girls who speak excellent English (as well as some French and Spanish) – offer guided day treks and longer treks with overnight stays in surrounding villages (ⓦsapasisters.com); email them in advance. Sa Pa-based Topas Travel at 21 Muong Hoa (ⓣ0214 387 1331, ⓦtopastravel.vn) offer hiking, biking and homestays, as well as sojourns at their highly regarded *Topas Eco Lodge*.

Motorbike rental Can be arranged through most hotels for around $10/day. Keep in mind that roads around Sa Pa

HIKING AROUND SA PA

Historically, all the peoples of northern Vietnam migrated from southern China at various times throughout history: those who arrived first, notably the Tay and Thai, settled in the fertile valleys, where they now lead a relatively prosperous existence, whereas late arrivals, such as groups of Hmong and Dao, were left to eke out a living on the inhospitable higher slopes. More than five million minority people (nearly two-thirds of Vietnam's total minority population) now live in the northern uplands, mostly in isolated villages. The largest ethnic groups are **Thai** and **Muong** in the northwest, **Tay** and **Nung** in the northeast, and **Hmong** and **Dao** dispersed throughout the region. Despite government efforts to forcibly integrate them into the Vietnamese community, many of the minorities in these remote areas continue to follow a way of life little changed over the centuries.

It is easy to arrive in Sa Pa independently and organize a local guide from there, rather than in Hanoi; it's of greater benefit to the local community and yourself if you have a guide from one of the surrounding villages. While throngs of Hmong women wait outside Sa Pa guesthouses to escort visitors to the surrounding villages, they only speak a smattering of English, and while all hotels can also arrange guides, many pay them poorly and send guests on the well-trodden trek along a main road to Ta Van (see opposite). Your best option is to join a small-group tour with Sapa O'Chau, Sapa Sisters, or Topas Travel – reputable operators that take you off the beaten track, have English-speaking guides and pay them fairly. Expect to pay from $25 per person for a day hike, from $60 for 2D1N, and from $100 for 2D3N. If you have four days to spare, you can stay with three different minority tribes during the course of your hike. Meals and accommodation are included; bring sunblock and plenty of water.

SAPA O'CHAU

The brainchild of local Hmong girl, Shu Tan, **Sapa O'Chau** (8 Thac Bac; ☎0214 377 1166, Ⓦ sapaochau.org) was created to empower and educate the local Hmong youth, an endeavour in which Shu is ably assisted by local women. Shu Tan herself started out by selling handicrafts to tourists as a child – many local children are kept out of school so that they can earn a living that way, or as tour guides. Alcoholism, domestic violence, marriage at a very young age and virtual illiteracy are also commonplace. Sapa O'Chau aims to educate the young Hmong generation to reduce the prevalence of such practices, providing education at the Sapa O'Chau Learning Centre – a live-in school where children learn English and Vietnamese to improve employment opportunities. Sapa O'Chau welcome volunteers and do some of the best trek-and-homestay combinations in the region; expect to pay from $95 for a one-day Fansipan trek, to $213 for a couple of days trekking around Sa Pa (including transfers from Hanoi and a night in a minority village).

11

are narrow and winding, landslides are common, fog can make visibility extremely poor and alcohol-induced accidents are also common.

Services The Agribank at 1 Cau May can exchange cash and travellers' cheques. There are a few ATMs in town. There are several pharmacies on Cau May, and the Post Office is at 6 Thach Son (daily 7am–9pm).

ACCOMMODATION

Sa Pa is generally busy all year round, especially at weekends. Rooms can be in short supply in high season (March, April & Sept–Nov). Homestays in the surrounding villages don't need to be booked in advance; just show up and ask around.

Cat Cat Hotel 42 Fansipan ☎0214 350 2681, Ⓦ hotelcatcat.com. A popular terraced guesthouse just below the market, offering budget and mid-range rooms with fireplaces and panoramic views of Fansipan from the spacious balconies. There's also a decent restaurant. Doubles $24

Green Valley International Hostel 45 Muong Hoa ☎0214 387 1449. Somewhat grungy dorm rooms that have electric blankets and good showers in spite of being

the cheapest beds in town, plus decent private rooms with stunning views of the valley below. Dorms $6, doubles $14

Sapa Backpacker Hostel 3 Pham Xuan Huan ☎0163 659 2370. Not to be confused with *Sapa Backpackers*, this hostel is run by a friendly family and is one of the cheapest spots in town. Rooms could be cleaner, and walls thicker, but it does the job – ask for a mountain view. Note that although it's called a hostel, they no longer have a dorm. Doubles $16

Sa Pa Elite Hotel 12 Hoang Dieu ☎0214 388 8368, Ⓦ sapaelitehotel.com. Great central location, spacious rooms with king-sized beds, wooden floors, electric blankets and a choice of breakfasts make this a good option. On the downside, the staff don't speak much English. Doubles $28

Sa Pa Lodge Hotel 18A Muong Hoa ☎0214 377 2885, Ⓦ sapalodgehotel.com. Though only some have incredible views of the valley below ($20), all rooms here are spacious and have a/c that doubles as a heater. Staff are very helpful. Doubles $10

Sapa Tavan Hostel Ta Van, 8km east of Sa Pa ☎098 304 8166, Ⓦ sapahostel.net. A homestay that's easily accessible by road, but in a quiet minority village away from built-up Sa Pa. Views from the terrace here are beautiful and there's plenty of common space to chill out in. You can rent the entire house (the price depends on the group size) or just a bed in the comfy dorm, plus it's easy to arrange trekking in the area. Dorms $5, doubles $13

EATING

For local barbecued meat, pho and rice dishes, try the food stalls on Pham Xuan Huan, parallel to Cau May. Stalls also pop up in the evenings by the market and along Ngu Chi Son, by Sa Pa Lake.

Baguette & Chocolat Thac Bac. For delicious breakfasts, bakery snacks, pizzas and Vietnamese favourites, look no further than this cosy branch of a Hanoian-based training school for disadvantaged youth. They also sell gourmet lunch packets for hikers. Mains 75,000VND. Daily 7am–9.30pm.

ETIQUETTE

There's a whole debate about the **ethics of cultural tourism** and its negative impact on traditional ways of life. Most villagers are genuinely welcoming, appreciating contact with Westerners. Nonetheless, it's important to take a responsible attitude, and try not to cause offence. It's preferable to visit the minority villages as part of a **small group**, ideally four people or fewer, as this causes least disruption and allows for greater communication. Dress modestly (no shorts or vests), never take photographs without asking and only enter a house when invited, removing your shoes first and carrying your backpack in your hands; don't ever enter homes with leaves, bones or feathers hanging above the entrance. If you're staying overnight, remember that your hosts go to bed early and get up early. Respect religious rituals and symbols. To avoid fostering a culture of begging, rather than bringing gifts, see if you can contribute to the community in a meaningful way by donating to a local school, hiring a local guide and purchasing local crafts. Take all your litter with you.

Boutique Sa Pa Hotel Restaurant 41 Fansipan. Beautifully presented dishes made from local ingredients – try the buffalo steak with pepper sauce (195,000VND) and other Hmong-themed delights. Daily 11.30am–10pm.

★ **Hill Station Signature** 37 Fansipan ⑩ thehillstation .com. This former hill station, flooded with natural light and boasting unusual decor, specializes in traditional cuisine from the region, so expect the likes of sweet potato cooked over hot coals, dried buffalo meat, fresh spring rolls with raw trout and smoked pork belly – all meant for sharing. Not to be confused with *Hill Station* on Muong Hoa, which is a deli. Mains from 95,000VND. Daily noon–10pm.

Little Sa Pa 18 Cau May. The best bet for Vietnamese food, right in the middle of Sa Pa, the menu running the gamut from curries, pho and spring rolls to filled pancakes, enormous hotpots and mulled wine – perfect for warming your cockles on a cold evening. Mains from 60,000VND. Daily 11am–10pm.

Sapa O'Chau Café 8 Thac Bac ⑩ sapaochau.org. A gathering point for hikers and homesick travellers, this cheerful café, part of the Sapa O'Chau tour agency, serves scrumptious beer-battered fish and chips, full English breakfasts, and a range of warming soups. Great coffee, too. Mains from 60,000VND. Daily 8am–6pm.

DRINKING

There's a *bia hoi* on the corner of Cau May and Fansipan.

Hmong Sisters 31 Muong Hoa. Cosy little bar with thumping music, a good mix of locals and visitors, and a pool table to while away the evening. Daily 4pm–late.

Mountain Bar and Pub 2 Muong Hoa. Very popular night spot with lethal cocktails, raucous games of table football, shishas, massive hamburgers and pick-me-up warm apple wine. Daily 5pm–1am.

SHOPPING

Sa Pa and the surrounding villages are a great place to pick up Hmong or Dao embroidered items – from clothing to

bags and more; however, many sellers also peddle mass-produced Chinese items, so you need to be able to tell the difference. The lovely but very persistent Red Dao and Hmong ladies will find you the minute you set foot on Cau May, and they do have some quality items for sale (if you don't mind the hard sell). If you wish to try and re-create the Red Dao herbal bath (see p.864) at home, you can buy pre-packed bags of herbs at the market.

Indigo Cat 46 Phan Xi Pang. If you're after somewhere just to browse hassle free, head to this little place for its quality hand-made Hmong items at fixed prices. Daily 9am–7pm.

Sapa O'Chau Hmong Handicrafts 8 Thac Bac. There's a lovely showroom right next door to the café, with contemporary and traditional Hmong handicrafts for sale. All proceeds support local women (see box opposite). Daily 7am–10pm.

BAC HA AND AROUND

The small, untouristy town of **BAC HA**, nestling in a high valley 40km northeast of Highway 7, is a good base for exploring nearby minority villages. Numerous travellers also come here on a long day-excursion from Sa Pa, especially on Sunday for the lively and colourful local market.

WHAT TO SEE AND DO

Bac Ha is a far less commercial town than Sa Pa, and makes for a peaceful alternative, if you're looking to interact with local minority tribes without the hard sell employed by some of Sa Pa's tour agencies. Guided treks and trips around Bac Ha can be arranged through the accommodation recommended.

11

11

Bac Ha Sunday Market

Bac Ha's **Sunday market** (6am–2pm) sees villagers of the Tay, Dao, Thai, Thulao, Xa Fang, Lachi, Fula, Nung, Giay and Flower Hmong ethnic minorities converging on the town, transforming the otherwise rather drab centre into a mass of colour and activity. Everything – from haircuts to suits, vats of rice wine and corn liquor to bundles of incense, and of course the usual vegetables, meat and dried fish – is on sale. The stunningly adorned Flower Hmong women trade embroidery, cloth and silver, and there's a large livestock fair to the rear of the market. Hotels in Sa Pa can organize a long day-trip to the Sunday market for about $15 per person, but it's far better to stay overnight in Bac Ha and visit the market early to avoid the Sunday crowds.

Hiking around Bac Ha

The picturesque Flower Hmong hamlet of **BAN PHO**, 3km from town, makes a pleasant stroll. Take the road half left at the hammer-and-sickle sign and head down past the *Sao Mai Hotel*, turning left immediately after the next big building, which is the local hospital. The road continues up the hill for 2km after the village and affords good views of the valley; you can carry on to the nearby village of **Na Kheo**. Other good day hikes include an 8km return walk to the village of **Tireu Cai** and a 6km return walk to **Na Ang** village; both are best done with a local guide.

Can Cau market

The village of **CAN CAU**, 19km north of Bac Ha, hosts a market each Saturday, which is well worth visiting. The emphasis is on livestock, especially buffalo, with traders trekking in from as far afield as China in search of bargains. Relatively few visitors get here, and the fair retains much of its authenticity; you may well be invited to drink some *ruou* with the locals. It's possible to arrange guided trips from Bac Ha that take in the market and include an afternoon trek to the nearby Fula village; there's a daily public bus from Bac Ha to Can Cau, so ask around for the latest timetable.

ARRIVAL AND INFORMATION

By bus Local buses terminate at Bac Ha's bus station, near the market's south entrance in the centre of town. Tourist buses running directly to Sa Pa depart from the main square outside the post office (Sun 1–2pm); regular minibuses depart for Sa Pa from Lao Cai. To get to Bac Ha from Sa Pa, it's easier and quicker to join a tour ($15), which will include the market and a short trek, with the option of being dropped off at Lao Cai on the way back if catching a night train to Hanoi. A motorbike from Sa Pa takes 3hr and costs $30–35, from Lao Cai $25.

Information and guides Operating out of *Hoang Vu Hotel*, Mr Nghe is by far the best source of information on the area, and his website ⓦ bachatourist.com is a great starting point for planning your trip.

ACCOMMODATION AND EATING

The town's hotels and restaurants are clustered around the square near the post office.

Bac Ha Homestay 2.5km from Bac Ha market ☎091 468 3833, ⓦ bachahomestay.com. In a small village an easy walk from town, this welcoming homestay is a gem; Mr Son will collect you from town and organize any tours or treks you'd like to do in the area. Choose between the shared stilt house or a private room in the modern house next door – either way it's the same price and includes dinner and breakfast. Dorm or double per person $17

Cong Fu Hotel ☎0214 388 0254. Smart mini-hotel offering the most modern accommodation in Bac Ha; some rooms have huge windows overlooking the livestock market. The restaurant (daily 11am–9pm) is popular with the Sunday tourists for its cheap rice and noodle dishes (from 50,0000VND). Doubles $25

Hoang Vu Hotel ☎0214 880 264, ⓦ bachatourist.com. Basic but friendly hotel with ten large en-suite rooms: look at a few before choosing. The owner, Mr Nghe, knows everything there is to know about the surrounding area and can arrange all manner of tours and transport, and rent out motorbikes. Doubles $10

Ngan Nga Bac Ha Hotel 115–117 Ngoc Uyen ☎0214 388 0286, ⓦngannngabachahotel.com. The rooms are spacious though a little worn, and the family that runs this place is friendly and helpful; you can even sweet-talk them into making you a picnic lunch for your hike. The restaurant fills with day-trippers on Sundays, with an enormous selection of Vietnamese food and set menus for 115,000VND. Doubles $20

MAI CHAU

The minority villages of the fertile **Mai Chau Valley**, inhabited mainly by White Thai people, related to tribes in Thailand,

Laos and China, are close enough to Hanoi (150km) to make this a popular destination, particularly at weekends. The valley is still largely unspoilt, a peaceful scene of rice fields and jagged mountains. **MAI CHAU** is the valley's main town, a friendly, quiet place that is liveliest on a Sunday, when minority people – who, unlike in Sa Pa, have largely forsaken their traditional dress (though the women still produce beautifully embroidered clothing) – trek in for a produce and bric-a-brac **market** (7am–3pm). You can stay overnight in Mai Chau, but it's more interesting to head for the outlying villages.

The most accessible village is **BAN LAC**, a White Thai settlement where you can buy hand-woven textiles (polite bargaining is the norm here, rather than the hard sell), watch performances of traditional dancing and sleep overnight in a stilt house; expect to pay around 130,000VND per person per night, including breakfast. If it's a little touristy for your tastes, push on to **Na Phon** village. There are some lovely day treks that can be done from Ban Lac, including to the villages of Na Meo, Na Mo and Xam Pa. It's also a good base to visit Pu Luong Nature Reserve.

INTO LAOS: TAY TRANG

A relatively straightforward border crossing operates at **Tay Trang** (daily 7am–7pm), 31km from Dien Bien Phu. Local buses depart from the bus station in **Dien Bien Phu** (daily 5.30am; 8hr; 100,000VND; buy ticket the day before) to the town of Muang Khoua on the Laos side, from where you can catch a boat down the Nam Ou River to Muang Ngoi or Nong Khiaw. Several daily buses depart from Muang Khoua for elsewhere in the region; for onward travel to Luang Prabang, take a bus to Oudomxai and from there a bus to Luang Prabang. One-month Lao visas are available on arrival for $40–50; you'll need two passport photos. If you need to stay in Dien Bien Phu, the *Viet Hoang Hotel* opposite the bus station (67 Tran Dang Ninh; ☎0214 373 5046; $15) will do in a pinch.

ARRIVAL AND INFORMATION

By tourist bus Most people arrive on an organized tour from Hanoi, but you can book the tourist bus to pick you up from your hotel (7.30am or 1pm; 250,000VND).
By public bus From Hanoi's My Dinh bus station (several 8am–2pm; 3hr 45min; 80,000VND) to Mai Chau town, from where it's an easy walk to Ban Lac or Na Phon.

ACCOMMODATION

Stilt-house accommodation (split-level thatched-roof houses with bamboo floors, electricity and Western toilets) is easy to find and needn't be booked in advance. **Maichau Hostel** Ban Lac ☎0123 585 8688, ✉namsppt @yahoo.com. Little English is spoken in most Mai Chau homestays, so if you're after conversation and the company of other backpackers, this is a good place to book. A traditional stilt house with a comfy dorm, but with the added bonus of a woodburning stove for great pizza – and a pool table. Dorms $6

The central provinces

Vietnam's narrow waist comprises a string of provinces squeezed between the long, sandy coastline and the formidable barrier of the Truong Son Mountains, which mark the border between Vietnam and Laos. The most heavily bombed area during the war, this is also one of the most beautiful parts of Vietnam. The province of Quang Binh is increasingly on the traveller radar, including the quietly engaging capital **Dong Hoi** and **Phong Nha–Ke Bang National Park**, an as yet unspoilt part of the country, with the world's largest cave, lush green countryside, friendly village life and dramatic karst its main attractions. In 1954, Vietnam was divided at the Seventeenth Parallel, only 100km or so south of here, where the **Demilitarized Zone** (**DMZ**) marked the border between North and South Vietnam until reunification in 1975. The desolate battlefields of the DMZ and the extraordinary complex of residential tunnels at nearby **Vinh Moc** are a poignant memorial to those who fought on both sides, and to the civilians who lost their lives in the bitter conflict. Further south

11

lies the city of **Hue**, its central role in imperial Vietnam evident in an immense citadel and wealth of royal tombs. The coastal city of **Da Nang** boasts some spectacular cave temples, while further south still, the riverside town of **Hoi An** is one of Vietnam's most charming destinations. Renowned for its hundreds of tailor shops, crafts, traditional Chinese merchants' houses and temples, and some of the best food in the country, it also makes a good base for exploring the fine ruins of the Cham temple complex at nearby **My Son**.

DONG HOI

Flattened in the American War, Quang Binh's provincial capital, **DONG HOI**, today is a prosperous and buzzing city that's particularly attractive where the Nhat Le River reaches the sea and the long swathe of beach stretches northwest. It has the closest airport and train station to **Phong Nha–Ke Bang National Park** and is a great place to base yourself for forays into the park.

ARRIVAL AND DEPARTURE

By plane The airport is 6km north of Dong Hoi; taxis to Dong Hoi cost 120VND and to Phong Nha Town around 500VND.
Destinations Hanoi (4 weekly; 1hr 20min); HCMC (4 weekly; 1hr 45min).
By train The train station is 3km west of the centre.
Destinations Hanoi (7 daily; 9hr–12hr 30min); Hue (9 daily; 2hr 30min–6hr); HCMC (5 daily; 22hr–25hr 30min).
By bus The bus station is 1km west of the centre at the junction of Tran Hung Dao and Nguyen Huu Canh.
Destinations Da Nang (17 daily; 5hr); Dong Ha (27 daily; 2hr); Hue (27 daily; 4hr); Phong Nha Town (hourly; 1hr 30min); Vinh (19 daily; 4hr).

TOURS

Phong Nha Discovery 63 Ly Thuong Kiet ☎ 093 259 4126, ☹ phongnhadiscovery.com. The best tour operator in Dong Hoi for guided trips into the national park (from $50).

ACCOMMODATION

Beachside Backpackers Truong Phap ☎ 091 892 1015 or ☎ 016 8533 4345, ☹ beachsidebackpackers.com. Owned and run by Anh and his Irish wife, Michaella, this new hostel is right on the beach. It's a blissful, chilled-out place with a big outdoor communal area dotted with hammocks. You could easily spend a few days here, using the free bicycles to get into town or to visit the nearby sand dunes, and drinking beer by the campfire in the evening. Dorms $6.50, doubles $20

Nam Long Plus 28a Phan Chu Trinh ☎ 091 892 3595, ☹ namlonghotels.com. Nga and Sy originally opened *Nam Long* on Ho Xuang Huong and now have this smarter hotel too. It's kept immaculately clean, and the rooms, including the dorms, are quiet and comfortable. You can organize any onward travel plans here, including visits to the park. Dorms $6, doubles $25

EATING

Buffalo 4 Nguyen Du. If you're after a burger and a few cold beers or cocktails, this place is on point. A friendly vibe and Western menu – plus the Wild West theme – keeps the place busy into the night. Burgers and sandwiches from 60,000VND. Daily 11am–midnight.

Tree Hugger Café 30 Nguyen Du. This German-owned coffeeshop with an eco-conscience uses fresh, local ingredients for everything on the simple menu. Great smoothies from 30,000VND, plus local handicrafts on sale and all the information on the area you could ever need. Daily 7am–10pm.

PHONG NHA–KE BANG NATIONAL PARK

Consisting of 885 square kilometres of unspoilt jungle, the mountainous **PHONG NHA-KE BANG NATIONAL PARK** stretches up to the border with Laos and is an area of incredible biodiversity. A UNESCO World Heritage Site since 2003, its ancient karst mountains hide extensive cave systems, many of which haven't yet been explored, and are home to more than one hundred species of mammal, including tigers, elephants and monkeys, as well as more than three hundred species of bird. The subterranean highlights are **Phong Nha Cave**, one of the longest in the world, and **Son Doong**, the world's largest cave, properly explored for the first time in 2009 (see box, p.872).

WHAT TO SEE AND DO

As this was the most heavily shelled region of Vietnam during the American War, there is no question of solo treks into the jungle, though guided jungle treks combined with caving are available (see p.872). A loop of the park from town is around 65km and takes in a spectacular and sometimes steep section of the Ho Chi Minh Trail (see p.902) – but only experienced motorbike drivers should go it alone.

Phong Nha Town

The largest village in the park is **PHONG NHA TOWN** (also called Son Trach), a spread-out, mostly one-street settlement that sits along the slow-flowing Song Con River, surrounded by karst mountains covered in lush vegetation. This is where you find the boat dock, a smattering of budget hotels and restaurants and a local market which is an interesting place to wander in the early morning. Life here runs at a sedate pace, apart from evening fun at local hangout *Easy Tiger* (see p.873). It's an easy bicycle or motorbike ride to Bong Lai Valley or Farmstay Village.

Phong Nha Cave

Discovered in 2005, **Phong Nha Cave** (daily 7.30am–4pm) is the park's most popular attraction, reached via a 45-minute ride in a dragon boat from Phong Nha Town's dock. "Phong Nha" means "dragon's breath", and the "teeth", or stalagmites, are indeed numerous, illuminated along with the turrets and stony cascades of myriad other rock formations. Visitors may only access a 1km section of the cave, though the cave is actually a staggering 55km long. As the boat enters the cave mouth, the boatman turns off the engine and switches to oars, rowing silently as you watch the subtly lit rock formations pass by in the semi-gloom. You're then deposited on a sandy beach, from where you make your way out of the cave on foot to the boat landing.

Outside, a steep flight of 330 steps leads up to the smaller **Tien Son Cave**, used as a makeshift hospital by the Viet Cong during the American War. The climb is worth it for the expansive views over the countryside; the pools of water in the fields are former bomb craters.

You'll need to purchase tickets for the two caves (150,000VND for Phong Nha and 80,000VND for Tien Son) and for the boat (400,000VND if you want to visit

both) at the jetty; if you can get other people to share your boat, it works out significantly cheaper per person – but keep in mind that every boat that goes out is an income for a local family. Seasonal flooding means that Phong Nha Cave may be closed in November and December, and at weekends, especially in summer, both caves tend to be mobbed by local tourists.

Paradise Cave

The third-largest cave in the park, and reputedly the world's biggest cave without any water source, **Paradise Cave** (daily 7.30am–4pm; 250,000VND) is greater than 31km in length, though visitors are only allowed access to a small part of it. To reach the cave, which is fairly high up, you either have to take a steep set of steps or else a more circuitous trail up the side of the small mountain. Uneven steps lead down into the deceptively small entrance, but as soon as you enter, you immediately feel like the Hobbit in the lair of Smaug – tiny and insignificant compared to the sheer size of the cavern, its twisted and sculpted rock formations glimmering with quartz fragments in the subtle light (signs in Vietnamese indicate "the rabbit", "reach for the sky" and so on). A boardwalk takes you into the bowels of the earth, with numerous viewpoints along the way.

Paradise Cave lies around 14km southwest of Phong Nha Town. There are a couple of restaurants at the car park and buggies will ferry you the 1.5km to the steps that lead up to the cave (around 150,000VND return per buggy; buy ticket along with entry ticket).

Dark Cave and Nuoc Mooc Eco-Trail

These two sights are just a couple of kilometres apart on the Ho Chi Minh Highway West, 6km north of Paradise Cave. The **Nuoc Mooc Eco-Trail** (daily 7am–5pm; 180,000VND) consists of a set of wooden walkways next to a turquoise waterhole fed by a subterranean river. You can swim and sunbathe here, but it's not the wonderful isolated spot it once was. **Dark Cave** (daily 7.30am–4pm; 450VND for all activities) is best explored early, before the tour groups arrive. It's a

11

11

THE WORLD'S LARGEST CAVE

Found by local hunter Ho Khanh in 1991 and explored for the first time by British cavers, led by Howard Limbert, in 2009, **Son Doong cave** (Ⓦ sondoongcave.org) is a natural phenomenon. It is the world's largest cave – almost double the size of the second largest, Malaysia's Deer Cave. It is 449m tall at its highest point, its caverns are big enough to accommodate an entire city, and where the roof has collapsed, enormous skylights have allowed two separate jungles to flourish, with 50m-tall trees home to monkeys, eagles, hornbills and other wildlife.

Access to the cave is very limited, with a view to preserving the pristine environment. Oxalis Adventure Tours (see below) have permission to take a total of around 500 visitors into the cave during the course of a year in small groups. The ultimate caving adventure, the six-day expedition involves more than two dozen porters and expert guides. Everything is carried back out of the cave, even the composting toilets. At the time of writing, the cost of this expedition was $3000 per person, with at least $1000 going to the national park; tickets are snapped up almost instantly on release.

beautiful cave, but the 400m zipline, pitch-black squelch through thigh-deep mud, and mandatory kayak and swim means it's only for the adventurous. Leave all valuables in the lockers.

Highway 20

Part of the Ho Chi Minh Trail, **Highway 20** (also known as Victory Road 20) is a beautiful stretch of road that includes **Eight Ladies' Cave**, in which eight young locals died when they took shelter during an American bombing. The bombs dislodged a rock that sealed the cave, making it their tomb, and the cave entrance and temple make a poignant stop. On the same road, closer to town, is the **botanical gardens** (40,000VND), which are worth visiting after rainy season to scramble down to Gio Waterfall.

ARRIVAL AND DEPARTURE

By bus A public bus runs out here hourly from Dong Hoi, 50km southeast. Phong Nha itself is also a stop on the open-tour bus route. Easy Tiger (see opposite) is a good source of information.

Destinations Dong Hoi (hourly; 1hr 30min); Hanoi (10hr–12hr 30min); Hue (4hr 30min–6hr).

INFORMATION AND TOURS

Tour operators Oxalis Adventure Tours (Ⓦ oxalis .com.vn) run extremely professional, well-organized caving and trekking tours to the main caves, as well as the Tu Lan cave system and Hang En cave. Oxalis is also the only operator that has permission to lead five-day adventure tours into Son Doong cave (see box, above). Jungle Boss (Ⓦ junglebosshomestay.com) are a fantastic company who organize one- or two-day treks out to

Abandoned Valley and Ma Da Valley, as well as the recently opened and pristine Tra Ang Cave. If you're interested in conservation and wildlife, get in touch with Hai at *Bamboo Café* (see opposite) or online at Ⓔ ecophongnha.com.

Services The cash machine by the Phong Nha jetty works most of the time, but bring plenty of cash just in case. Bicycles ($3–5/day) and motorbikes ($7–10/day) can be rented from guesthouses and hotels.

ACCOMMODATION

Great-value homestays dot the countryside around town and there's no need to book in advance. Turn up and ask around.

THE BONG LAI VALLEY

Bong Lai is a beautiful unspoiled valley just 10km east of Phong Nha Town that's only now opening to tourism. It's an easy half-day loop by bicycle or motorbike on the valley's dirt roads – arm yourself with a map from your homestay and be warned that it can get pretty treacherous in the rainy season. At any of the small businesses out here you'll get a friendly welcome, cold beer and menus in English. At the legendary **Pub with Cold Beer** you can fling yourself into a hammock, and if you're hungry, the owner will kill and cook a chicken (for around 200,000VND). Quynh at **The Duck Stop** will give you a "duck massage" and show you round his family's pepper plantation, **Moi Moi's** speciality is slow-cooked pork in bamboo tubes (100,000VND), and finally, the remote **Wild Boar Eco Farm** has yet more river views and spit-roasted chicken. Don't forget swimwear in the summer as Bong River is great for a dip, and avoid biking back to town in the dark.

★TREAT YOURSELF

Phong Nha Farmstay 8km from Phong Nha Town ☎ 094 475 9864, ⓦ phong-nha-cave.com. Phong Nha's most luxurious accommodation is this lodge, with its tall ceilings and dark-wood accents, delicious Asian and Western food, a pool table and bar, and bicycles to borrow. Cosy en-suite rooms offer great sunset views over the rice paddies and there's a swimming pool for dipping. Helpful owners Ben and Bich can advise you on the surrounding attractions, and also arrange excellent tours of the park. Doubles $40

Easy Tiger Phong Nha Town ☎ 0232 367 7844, ⓔ easytigerphongnha@gmail.com. Orange, Aussie-run multistorey backpacker magnet, with clean, comfortable dorms and staff who know their stuff. All manner of local adventures are organized, and a great on-site restaurant morphs into a late-night bar. Breakfast not included. Dorms $8

Phong Nha Lake House 7km east of Phong Nha Town ☎ 0232 367 5999, ⓦ phongnhalakehouse.com. Besides the most luxurious dorms that you're likely to see in Vietnam, with proper two-tiered beds and mosquito nets, this Australian-run guesthouse, owned by husband-and-wife team Tony and Tham, has expansive views over a lake from the terrace, a lively bar and restaurant and spacious en-suite "rustic chic" villas and bungalows, the latter with their own garden areas. Tony has motorbikes for rent ($10/day). Dorms $8, doubles $35

Phong Nha Rustic Home 3km west of Phong Nha Town, ☎ 016 4659 00719, ⓦ phongnharustichome.com. At the far end of town where it still has a feel of rural Vietnam, the comfortable rooms here are all en suite. The friendly family also own Thang's Riders, so they are a great contact for motorbike tours in Phong Nha and beyond. Doubles $25

EATING

Bamboo Café Opposite *Easy Tiger* ☎ 0232 367 8777, ⓦ phong-nha-bamboo-cafe.com. Comfy sofas, strong coffee and friendly local staff make this cool café-restaurant a great place to chill for a few hours – and Western and Vietnamese dishes including mouth-watering browned pork and rice (80,000VND) will keep you here for dinner. They do cooking classes too (400,000VND). Daily 7am–10pm.

The Best Spit Roast Pork & Noodle Shop in the World (Probably) Phong Nha. Close to the ferry dock, this long-standing local's favourite really does do the best barbecued pork in the world (probably). It's a cheap eat and the owner is super-friendly. Daily 7am–10pm.

THE DMZ

Under the terms of the 1954 Geneva Accords, Vietnam was split in two along the Seventeenth Parallel. The demarcation line ran along the Ben Hai River and was sealed by a strip of no-man's-land 5km wide on each side, known as the **Demilitarized Zone**, or **DMZ**. The two provinces either side of the DMZ were the most heavily bombed and saw the highest casualties, civilian and military, American and Vietnamese, during the American War. So much firepower was unleashed over this area, including napalm and herbicides, that for years nothing would grow in the chemical-laden soil. Now, the region's low, rolling hills are mostly reforested and green. There's not that much to see here, besides the **museums** at Ben Hai, Vinh Moc and Khe Sanh, but Quang Tri, Hamburger Hill and other names live on in infamy because of the bloody battles fought there, so visiting the locations alone is meaningful for those interested in the country's recent history.

WHAT TO SEE AND DO

You can explore the DMZ independently, but it's highly recommended to take a local **guide** who will be able to show you the unmarked sites and will know which paths are free from **unexploded mines** (see box, p.874). Most one-day tours take in the Highway 1 sights, and you can also visit the **Rockpile**, a 230m-high karst used by the US as an artillery base and lookout, **Hamburger Hill**, where a massive infantry battle took place in May 1969 (though you'll need a permit for anything more than a sixty-second stop), or the touristy **Van Kieu Bru minority village.** Your understanding of the area depends a great deal on how good your guide is – contact one of the recommended companies in Hue (see p.879) or *Tam's Café* (☎ 090 542 5912, ⓦ tamscafe.jimdo.com) in the town of Dong Ha, a former US Marine command post 70km north of Hue that some use as a base for exploring the DMZ.

Vinh Moc tunnels

The creation of the **Vinh Moc** tunnels was an impressive feat and they're the highlight of the DMZ. To provide shelter

11

UNEXPLODED ORDNANCE

Casualties of the American War persist to this day, due to an estimated 350,000 to 800,000 tonnes of unexploded ordnance (UXO) and more than 3 million mines that remain uncleared. From 1975 to the present day, unexploded ordnance in Vietnam has resulted in more than 100,000 injuries and 45,000 deaths. Each year, around 1000 people die and almost twice as many are injured, mainly in the countryside; the number of children and members of minority tribes is disproportionately high. Don't stray from marked paths when hiking and check out the work of the Mines Advisory Group (🌐 maginternational.org), an NGO working to dispose of the ordnance and help survivors of landmine and UXO accidents through various community projects. **The Mine Action Visitor Center** in Dong Ha at 185 Ly Thuong Kiet has more information (Mon–Fri 8am–5pm; free; ☎ 0233 356 7338, 🌐 landmines.org.vn).

from constant American air raids, from 1966 villagers spent two years digging more than fifty tunnels. All were constructed on three levels at 10, 15 and 20–23m deep, with freshwater wells, a generator and lights. The underground village had a school, clinics and a maternity room where seventeen children were born. Families of up to five people were each allocated a tiny cavern and were only able to emerge at night; the lack of fresh air and the smoke from the kerosene lamps and cooking caused respiratory problems, and the lack of sunlight also impacted on the villagers' health. In 1972, the villagers finally abandoned their tunnels and rebuilt their homes above ground. A section of the tunnels has been restored and opened to visitors, with a small museum on-site (daily 7am–5pm; 60,000VND).

Doc Mieu Firebase

The American front line comprised a string of firebases looking north across the DMZ. The most accessible of these is **Doc Mieu Firebase**, where a number of bunkers built by the North Vietnamese Army (NVA) still stand amid a landscape pocked with craters. Before the NVA overran Doc Mieu in 1972, the base played a pivotal role in the South's defence, and for a while this was the command post for calling in airstrikes along the Ho Chi Minh Trail.

Con Thien Firebase

The largest American installation along the DMZ was **Con Thien Firebase**, which, in the lead-up to the 1968 Tet Offensive, became the target of prolonged shelling.

The Americans replied with everything in their arsenal, but the NVA finally overran the base in the summer of 1972. From the single remaining US-built bunker in the ruined lookout post on Con Thien's highest point you get a great view over the DMZ and directly north to former enemy positions on the opposite bank of the Ben Hai River.

The Ben Hai River

Right next to Highway 1, a footbridge lined with Vietnam's flags spans the Ben Hai River. On the south bank there is a grandiose reunification monument, the heroic figure holding stylized palm leaves. On the north bank, there's a reconstructed flag tower with Socialist mosaics around its base. The museum (daily 7am–5pm; 20,000VND) across the road features wartime photos and mementoes.

The Truong Son Cemetery

The **Truong Son War Martyr Cemetery** is dedicated to the estimated 25,000 men, women and children – some soldiers were as young as twelve – who died on the Truong Son Trail, better known in the West as the Ho Chi Minh Trail. Around 300,000 North Vietnamese soldiers were missing in action – far, far more than a total of 10,036 graves lie in this cemetery; each simple headstone announces *liet si* ("martyr").

Khe Sanh

The **battle of Khe Sanh** attracted worldwide media attention and, along with the simultaneous Tet Offensive, demonstrated the futility of the US's efforts to contain its enemy. The North Vietnam Army's (NVA) attack on the US base at Khe Sanh began in the early hours of January 21, 1968, and the battle lasted nine weeks, during which time the US pounded the area with nearly 100,000 tonnes of bombs, averaging one airstrike every five minutes, backed up by napalm and defoliants. The NVA were so well dug in that they continued to return fire, despite horrendous casualties. By the middle of March, the NVA had all but gone, having successfully diverted American resources away from southern cities prior to the Tet Offensive. The battle cost 500 American, 10,000 North Vietnamese and uncounted civilian lives. Three months later, the Americans also withdrew, leaving a plateau that resembled a lunar landscape, contaminated for years to come with chemicals and explosives;

gazing at the lush greenery and coffee plantations that cover the place now, it's difficult to imagine.

HUE

A UNESCO World Heritage Site since 1993, **HUE** is the city of the Nguyen emperors. The city has suffered extensive damage, both when the French destroyed much of the once-magnificent Imperial City, and during the 1968 **Tet Offensive**, when the North Vietnamese Army (NVA) held Hue for 25 days, and the city was all but levelled in the ensuing counter-assault.

Nevertheless, some magnificent historical sights remain – including the nineteenth-century walled citadel, and seven palatial royal mausoleums in the city's outskirts.

11

INTO LAOS: LAO BAO, CAU TREO AND NAM CAN

It's possible to cross into Laos at three border crossings in the central provinces. Long-distance tourist buses depart from Vinh, Hue and Hanoi (they also skirt Dong Ha, where it's possible to board if you've booked in advance). Thirty-day tourist visas for Laos are available at all three crossings (about $35, depending on your nationality).

THE LAO BAO BORDER CROSSING

The **Lao Bao** border crossing (daily 7am–6pm) is the most popular of Vietnam's overland routes into Laos. There are daily buses from Hue to **Savannakhet** in Laos, leaving between 6am and 8am, arriving at around 5pm, and you can also opt for Sinh Tourist (see p.879) buses (from 600,000VND), which leave Hue every day at 7am and arrive in **Savannakhet** in Laos at around 5pm; in Hue, you can also buy tickets for sleeper buses all the way to Vientiane, but this journey is at least twenty hours and isn't recommended.

THE CAU TREO BORDER CROSSING

It is also possible to cross the border at **Cau Treo** (daily 7am–6pm), 95km west of the city of **Vinh** on Highway 8, though overcharging and delays are common. From Vinh's provincial bus station (Ben Xe Cho Vinh), about 500m from Vinh's market, several morning buses depart for Tay Son (formerly Trung Tam) from 6am, the last settlement of any size before the border. There are morning buses from Tay Son to Lak Sao, but you have to get there mid-morning in order to make the connection. From here, you'll either have to pick up a motorbike taxi for the last 35km to Cau Treo, or catch one of the regular shuttle buses that ferry locals to the border. Alternatively, hotels in Vinh can arrange a share taxi all the way to the border for around $50, or a *xe om* for $25. An easier option is the Laos-bound buses, booked in Hanoi (see p.849), that trundle through this border en route to Vientiane. Facilities at Cau Treo amount to about half a dozen pho stalls, so sort out money (carrying dollars is best) and anything else you need before leaving.

THE NAM CAN–NONG HET BORDER CROSSING

The **Nam Can** border crossing (daily 7am–5pm) is also accessible from Vinh, and near Nong Het in Laos, convenient for Phonsavan and the Plain of Jars (see p.382). Direct buses depart from Vinh to Phonsavan (Tues– Sun at 6am; 300,000VND; 13hr); going the other way, buses that claim to take passengers all the way to Hanoi can leave them in Vinh.

Hue is the main starting point for day-tours of the DMZ, as well as a springboard for buses to Savannakhet in Laos, via the Lao Bao border (see box p.875), and a handy connection to Phong Nha National Park.

Built astride the wide, slow-flowing **Perfume River**, with its pleasant, tree-lined boulevards, abundance of historic sights, beautiful buildings and picturesque surrounding countryside, Hue repays exploration at a leisurely pace. The imperial **citadel** stands on the northern bank of the river, while the southern bank hosts the majority of the city's hotels and restaurants. The city is easily navigated on foot, while the best way to visit outlying **temples** and **mausoleums** and enjoy the surrounding countryside is by renting a bicycle or motorbike, or on the back of a *xe om* (though you'll be charged 5000VND – or asked to buy a drink – for parking at most sites).

11

The citadel

Hue's days of glory kicked off in the early nineteenth century when Emperor Gia Long, founder of the **Nguyen dynasty**, moved the capital here and laid out a vast **citadel**, comprising three concentric enclosures. The city must have been truly awe-inspiring in its heyday; today, only twenty of the original 148 buildings survive, though the citadel is as imposing as ever, with a large chunk of Hue's residents still living within its 10km-long, 2m-thick walls.

Ten gates pierce the citadel wall: you enter through Ngan Gate, east of the flag tower. A second moat and defensive wall inside the citadel guard the **Imperial City** (daily 8am–5pm; 150,000VND), which follows the same symmetrical layout along a north–south axis as Beijing's Forbidden City, though on a much smaller scale. By far the most impressive of its four gates is south-facing **Ngo Mon**, the Imperial City's principal entrance and a masterpiece of Nguyen architecture. The gate itself has five entrances: the central one for the emperor, two for civil

and military mandarins, and two for the royal elephants. Perched on top is an elegant pavilion called the **Five Phoenix Watchtower** as its nine roofs are said to resemble five birds in flight. Facing Ngo Mon, **Thai Hoa Palace**, dating from 1883, boasts a spectacular interior glowing with sumptuous red and gold lacquers. This was where major imperial ceremonies were held; it's well worth watching the introduction video for the digital reconstruction of the citadel.

The **Forbidden Purple City**, enclosed by a low wall, was the personal domain of the emperor; only eunuch servants and concubines were allowed in. Many of the residential palaces are nothing but grass-covered stone outlines today, thanks to the damage inflicted by the French as they attempted to retake the city in 1947. The **Royal Reading Pavilion**, an appealing, two-tier structure surrounded by bonsai, and the nearby Royal Theatre are all that remain intact; the latter holds music performances (9am, 10am, 2.30pm, 3.30pm; 100,000VND). The beautifully restored dynastic **Mieu temple**, a decorous low, red-lacquerwork building in the south corner of the citadel complex, has a row of thirteen altar tables dedicated to the Nguyen royal emperors. Behind it is the partially ruined **Dien Tho Residence** where the queen mothers resided, followed by the **Truong San Residence** with its splendid dragon-and-phoenix gate.

Thien Mu Pagoda

Founded in 1601 by Nguyen Hoang, **Thien Mu Pagoda** (daily 7am–5pm; free), 4km from Hue, is the oldest in **Hue** and has long been a hotbed of Buddhist protest against repression. In 1963, it hit international headlines when one of its monks, Thich Quang Duc, immolated himself in Saigon in protest at the excesses of President Diem's repressive regime. The monk's powder-blue Austin car is now on display here, with a copy of the famous photograph that shocked the world. The seven tiers of the octagonal, brick stupa each represent one of Buddha's incarnations on earth. Thien Mu Pagoda is included on most boat trips along the river (see box p.878), but

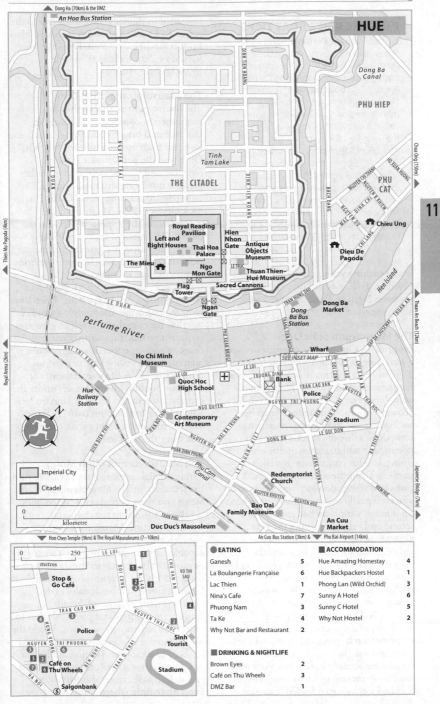

HUE

Dong Ha (70km) & the DMZ
An Hoa Bus Station

Dong Ba Canal

PHU HIEP

THE CITADEL

Tinh Tam Lake

PHU CAT

Chieu Ung

Dieu De Pagoda

Royal Reading Pavilion
Left and Right Houses
Thai Hoa Palace
Hien Nhon Gate
Antique Objects Museum
The Mieu
Ngo Mon Gate
Thuan Thien–Hué Museum
Flag Tower
Sacred Cannons
Ngan Gate
Dong Ba Bus Station
Dong Ba Market

Hen Island

Perfume River

Wharf

SEE INSET MAP

Ho Chi Minh Museum

Quoc Hoc High School
Bank

Hue Railway Station

Contemporary Art Museum

Police
Stadium

Redemptorist Church

Bao Dai Family Museum

Duc Duc's Mausoleum

An Cuu Market

Imperial City
Citadel

0   1
kilometre

Hon Chen Temple (9km) & The Royal Mausoleums (7–10km)

An Cuu Bus Station (3km)   Phu Bai Airport (14km)

0   250
metres

Stop & Go Café

Police
Sinh Tourist

Café on Thu Wheels

Stadium

Saigonbank

●EATING	
Ganesh	5
La Boulangerie Française	6
Lac Thien	1
Nina's Cafe	7
Phuong Nam	3
Ta Ke	4
Why Not Bar and Restaurant	2

■DRINKING & NIGHTLIFE	
Brown Eyes	2
Café on Thu Wheels	3
DMZ Bar	1

■ ACCOMMODATION	
Hue Amazing Homestay	4
Hue Backpackers Hostel	1
Phong Lan (Wild Orchid)	3
Sunny A Hotel	6
Sunny C Hotel	5
Why Not Hostel	2

11

11

PERFUME RIVER BOAT TRIPS

A boat trip on the **Perfume River** is in theory one of the city's highlights, puttering in front of the citadel, past rowing boats heading for Dong Ba market. The standard **boat trip** takes you to Thien Mu Pagoda, Hon Chen Temple and the most rewarding royal mausoleums. You can enquire directly at the wharf east of the Trang Tien Bridge, rather than going through middleman tour agents; be prepared to barter hard. Hotels, travellers' cafés and tour agents offer group tours that tend to last from around 8am to 4pm and cost around $10 per person (this does not include entrance to the tombs or Hon Chen Temple). Agents can also arrange charter boats at $25–30 for the day.

is also within **cycling** distance of Hue (30min). Follow Kim Long (which becomes Nguyen Phuc Nguyen) west along the river.

The Mausoleum of Tu Duc

Emperor Tu Duc was a romantic poet and a weak king, who ruled Vietnam from 1847 to 1883. His mausoleum is the most harmonious of all those in Hue. It took only three years to complete (1864–67), allowing Tu Duc a full sixteen years here for boating and fishing, meditation and composing some of the four thousand poems he is said to have written, while sitting with his concubines in a lakeside pavilion. From the southern gate, brick paths lead alongside a lake and a couple of waterside pavilions, from where steps head up through a triple-arched gateway to a second enclosure containing the **Hoa Khiem temple**, which Tu Duc used as a palace. Behind the temple stands the colourful royal theatre, where you can play dress-up in traditional Vietnamese clothing, and the austere, dark wood **Luong Khiem temple** dedicated to Tu Duc's mother, Tu Du. The second group of buildings, to the north, is centred on the **emperor's tomb**, preceded by the salutation court and stele-house. The imperial remains are actually buried in an unknown location to prevent grave robbing; the two hundred servants who buried him were beheaded to (literally) take the secret to the grave. Tu Duc's Mausoleum is around 5km from central Hue by road. From the boat jetty, it's a 2km walk or *xe om* ride (30,000VND return).

The Mausoleum of Khai Dinh

The **Mausoleum of Khai Dinh** is a monumental confection of European Baroque and ornamental Sino-Vietnamese style, set high up on a wooded hill. Khai Dinh was the penultimate Nguyen emperor and his mausoleum has neither gardens nor living quarters. Though he only reigned for nine years (1916–25), it took eleven (1920–31) to complete his mausoleum. The approach is via a series of dragon-ornamented stairways leading through an imposing gate first to the **Honour Courtyard**, watched over by stone mandarin honour guards, and the stele-house. Climbing up a further four terraces brings you to the main **Thien Dinh temple**, with a jaw-droppingly splendid interior, decorated to the hilt in glass and porcelain mosaic that writhes with dragons and is peppered with symbolic references; the ceilings are covered in dragon murals. A life-size statue of the emperor holding his sceptre sits under the canopy, his remains interred 18m under. Khai Dinh's Mausoleum is 10km from Hue by road, or a 1.5km walk or *xe om* ride from the boat jetty.

The Mausoleum of Minh Mang

Court officials took fourteen years to find the location for the **Mausoleum of Minh Mang** and then only three years to build it (1841–43), using ten thousand workmen. Minh Mang, the second Nguyen emperor (1820–41), was a capable, authoritarian monarch who was passionate about architecture, and he designed his mausoleum along traditional Chinese lines, in a beautiful wooded location, with 37 acres of superb landscaped gardens and plentiful lakes to reflect the red-roofed pavilions. Inside the mausoleum, a processional way links the series of low mounds bearing all the main buildings. After the salutation courtyard and stele-house comes the crumbling **Sung An temple** where Minh Mang and

VISITING THE ROYAL MAUSOLEUMS

The Nguyens built magnificent **royal mausoleums** in the valley of the Perfume River among low, forested hills to the south of Hue. Each one is a unique expression of the monarch's personality, usually planned in detail during his lifetime to serve as his palace in death. Though details vary, all the mausoleums consist of three elements: the **main temple** is dedicated to the worship of the deceased emperor and his queen, and houses their funeral tablets and possessions; a large, stone **stele** records details of his reign, in front of which spreads a paved courtyard, where ranks of stone mandarins line up to honour their emperor; and the royal **tomb** itself is enclosed within a wall.

The contrasting mausoleums of Tu Duc, Khai Dinh and Minh Mang are the most attractive and well preserved, and are easily accessible, though they can be crowded – particularly Tu Duc, which is the most popular. **Entry** to the mausoleums (daily 7am–5.30pm) is 100,000VND each for the main three; most of the others are free. To **get to the mausoleums** you can either rent a bicycle (not advised to Minh Mang – the roads have some heavy traffic) or motorbike, or take a Perfume River boat trip (see box opposite), which entails a couple of longish walks or *xe om* rides; the best way to avoid the crowds is to go early in the morning by *xe om*; you can negotiate your custom tour stops with the likes of *Café on Thu Wheels* (see p.880). If cycling, take plenty of water and a good map.

11

his queen are worshipped. Continuing west, you reach **Minh Lau**, the elegant, two-storey "Pavilion of Pure Light" standing among frangipani trees, symbols of longevity. A stone bridge leads across the Tan Nguyet Lake to the gate of the emperor's sepulchre, opened only on the anniversary of his death.

You can reach Minh Mang's Mausoleum from Khai Dinh's by following the **road** west for 1.5km and crossing the bridge over the Perfume River. The entrance is then 200m on the left.

ARRIVAL AND DEPARTURE

By plane Flights into Hue's Phu Bai Airport, 15km southeast of the city, are met by an airport bus run by Vietnam Airlines ($2.50), which goes to central hotels, and by metered taxis (about $15). Going to the airport, the bus departs from the Vietnam Airlines branch office at 23 Nguyen Van Cu (☎ 054 382 4709), or you can arrange a pick-up from your hotel reception.
Destinations Hanoi (3 daily; 2hr); HCMC (8 daily; 1hr 20min).

By bus Hue is one of the stops on the open-tour bus routes; buses stop at the cluster of travel agents and hotels along Hung Vuong or the northern end of Le Loi. Southbound bus services operate from An Cuu station (sometimes called Phia Nam station), 4km southeast of the centre along Highway 1; northbound buses for Hanoi and other destinations run from An Hoa station, 4km northwest on Highway 1.
Destinations Da Nang (3hr); Dong Ha (1hr 30min); Hanoi (16–17hr); HCMC (22hr); Phong Nha (4hr 30min).

By train The train station lies 1.5km from the centre at the far western end of Le Loi.
Destinations Da Nang (8 daily; 2hr 30min–4hr); Dong Hoi (8 daily; 3hr–5hr 30min); Hanoi (5 daily; 12hr–16hr 30min); HCMC (4 daily; 19–22hr); Nha Trang (4 daily; 11hr–15hr 30min); Ninh Binh (5 daily; 10–13hr).

TOURS

Tour operators Sinh Tourist, 37 Nguyen Thai Hoc (daily 6.30am–10pm; ☎ 0234 382 3309, ⓦ thesinhtourist .vn), arranges Perfume River boat trips and DMZ tours, as well as tickets for buses to Savannakhet in Laos. The *Café on Thu Wheels* (see p.880) and the *Stop & Go Café* at 3 Hung Vuong (☎ 0234 382 7051, ⓦ stopandgo-hue.com) are recommended for their motorcycle tours around the area ($10–20) as well as car tours of the DMZ (around $45 per person).

ACCOMMODATION

Hue Amazing Homestay 2/10 Vo Thi Sau ☎ 091 263 0219, ⓔ hueamazinghomestay@gmail.com. The cheapest dorms in town might not be spacious, but they are comfy and clean. Mr Duyen and his family are on hand for advice – especially motorbike-related – and you're close to everything but away from the touts on the main strip. Breakfast is decent, too. Dorms $5̄, doubles $1̄2

Hue Backpackers Hostel 10 Pham Ngu Lao ☎ 0234 382 6567, ⓦ vietnambackpackershostel.com. Branch of the perennially popular *Vietnam Backpacker* hostel (see p.851), with simple yet smart a/c dorms (with queen-sized beds on request), private rooms and lots of activities on offer – from the Top Gear motorbike tour to cooking classes. Rates include breakfast, and the busy bar downstairs is a good spot for happy hour (5–6pm). Dorms $8̄, doubles $2̄0

★**Phong Lan (Wild Orchid)** 12/66 Le Loi ☎0234 382 6255, ✉phonglanhue@gmail.com. Tucked away at the end of a quiet cul-de-sac with several other guesthouses, this cheerful place offers pleasant, warmly decorated rooms, has the friendliest, most helpful staff and pretty balconies hung with orchids. Breakfast included. Doubles $14

Sunny A Hotel 17/34 Nguyen Tri Phuong ☎0234 382 9990. The budget rooms in this bright and friendly mini-hotel are outstanding value, equipped with satellite TV and a/c, and all but the cheapest have their own computer with internet access. The *Sunny C Hotel* (4/34 Nguyen Tri Phuong; ☎0234 383 0145; $15) has larger rooms, also equipped with all mod cons. Doubles $12

Why Not Hostel 26 Pham Ngu Lao ☎0234 393 8855, ⓦwhynot.com.vn. Rooms here are exceptional for a backpackers' joint. The dorms, doubles and triples are roomy and clean – dorms have solid wooden partitions. You get a free beer in the bar every night, a good breakfast each morning, and staff go out of their way to be helpful. Dorms $7, doubles $17

EATING

Hue is renowned for its imperial cuisine, thanks to the fussy Emperor Tu Duc, and local specialities to try include *bun bo hue* (a spicy rice noodle soup with lemongrass, shrimp paste and plenty of fresh herbs), *banh hoai* (a small, crispy yellow pancake, fried up with shrimp, pork and bean sprouts, and served with peanut and sesame sauce, star fruit, green banana, lettuce and mint), *bahn nam* and *bahn beo* (steamed royal rice cakes), *com hen* (rice with steamed clams, green banana, salted shredded meat and chilli), and *che* (a sweet dessert soup). Find these (from 7000VND) and more at the *Dong Ba Market* on Tran Hung Dao (daily 6.30am–8pm), just north of the Trang Tien Bridge.

Ganesh 34 Nguyen Tri Phuong. This restaurant is deservedly popular for its north Indian menu, which includes numerous vegetarian dishes, biryanis, curries, naan and thali. Mains from 90,000VND, thalis from 140,000VND. Daily noon–10pm.

La Boulangerie Française 46 Nguyen Tri Phuong. Sells fresh croissants, brown bread, pastries and cakes for 8000–30,000VND – perfect for that early bus departure. Profits go to local charities. Daily 7am–8.30pm.

★**Lac Thien** 6 Dinh Tien Hoang. This is one of Hue's more interesting restaurants, run by a family with several deaf members and popular both with locals and visitors. The food is excellent, taking in the Hue staples, including steamed fish (mains from 20,000VND). Order a beer to get a special bottle opener made by the owner. The two other similarly named restaurants along this street are owned by the proprietor's brothers. Daily 11am–9pm.

Nina's Cafe 16/134 Nguyen Tri Phuong ☎0234 383 8636. Simple, cheap and friendly, *Nina's* is tucked away in a small covered courtyard. It's great for spring rolls, soups, meat

and vegetarian dishes (around 40,000–60,000VND), and set menus at 140,000–200,000VND. Its cooler younger sister, *Nook*, has opened around the corner, but is pricier. Daily 7.30am–10.30pm.

Phuong Nam 38 Tran Cao Van. Perch yourself on a plastic chair at this friendly, family-run spot and order deep-fried spring rolls with mushrooms (from 30,000VND), Vietnamese mains (from 40,000VND), salads and delectable fruit shakes (15,000VND). Daily 10.30am–8pm.

Ta Ke 34 Tran Cao Van. Austere Japanese restaurant with traditional seating and wonderfully affordable sushi sets (from 50,000VND), as well as tonkatsu, gyoza, noodle dishes and more. Wash it down with an avocado shake or sweetened cucumber juice. Daily 10.30am–10pm.

Why Not Bar and Restaurant 26 Pham Ngu Lao. Western food (including some good veggie pizzas), football on the big screen, a pool table, good deals on beer and streetside seating are the draws here. Daily 8am–late.

DRINKING AND NIGHTLIFE

Brown Eyes 56 Chu Van An. Late-night bar-club playing rock and punk, with a pool table and happy crowds comprising mostly inebriated backpackers. Cocktails are two-for-one 5–10pm. Daily 5pm–late.

Café on Thu Wheels 10/2 Nguyen Tri Phuong. This tiny bar-café has friendly staff, cheap beer and a laidback backpacker vibe. They run excellent motorbike tours – attested to by the recommendations scribbled on the walls – and serve a mix of Vietnamese and Western dishes. Daily 7.30am–10pm.

DMZ Bar 44 Le Loi. The hottest spot in town, crowded with a mix of locals and backpackers on any given night, with a free pool table, nightly drinks specials and an extensive food selection, including pizza (from 70,000VND). Cocktails from 55,000VND. Daily 7am–2.30am (food served until midnight).

DIRECTORY

Bank Saigon Bank, 50 Hung Vuong; Vietcombank, 30 Le Loi.
Bike rental Bicycles ($2–3/day) and motorbikes ($5–7/day) can be rented from most hotels, guesthouses and cafés.
Hospital Hue Central Hospital, 16 Le Loi ☎0234 382 2325.
Pharmacies 33 and 36 Hung Vuong.
Post office 8 Hoang Hoa Tham.

DA NANG

DA NANG is Central Vietnam's dominant port and its fifth-largest city. Though there are few sights in the city itself, greater attractions lie just outside. Da Nang is also a major transport hub with air connections as well as road and rail links, and it's the main access point for

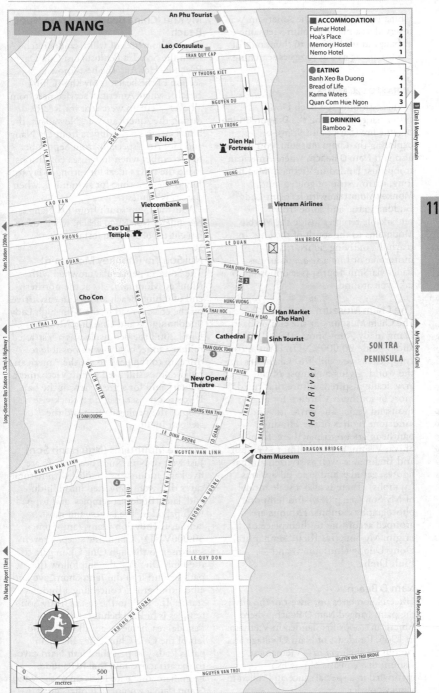

DA NANG

An Phu Tourist

Lao Consulate

TRAN QUY CAP

LY THUONG KIET

NGUYEN DU

LY TU TRONG

Police

Dien Hai Fortress

TRUNG

Vietcombank

Vietnam Airlines

Cao Dai Temple

HAI PHONG

LE DUAN

LE DUAN

HAN BRIDGE

PHAN DINH PHUNG

YEN BAY

Cho Con

HUNG VUONG

NG THAI HOC

TRAN H DAO

Han Market (Cho Han)

LY THAI TO

Cathedral

Sinh Tourist

TRAN QUOC TOAN

SON TRA PENINSULA

THAI PHIEN

New Opera/ Theatre

Han River

HOANG VAN THU

LE DINH DUONG

LE DINH DUONG

CO GIANG

BACH DANG

NGUYEN VAN LINH

DRAGON BRIDGE

NGUYEN VAN LINH

Cham Museum

HOANG DIEU

PHAN CHU TRINH

TRUONG NU VUONG

LE QUY DON

N

NGUYEN VAN TROI BRIDGE

0   500
metres

ONG ICH KHIEM

CAO VAN

DONG DA

LE LOI

QUANG

NGUYEN THI MINH KHAI

NGUYEN CHI THANH

NGO GIA TU

ONG ICH KHIEM

TRUONG NU VUONG

TRUONG DIEU

NGUYEN VAN TROI

ACCOMMODATION
Fulmar Hotel	2
Hoa's Place	4
Memory Hostel	3
Nemo Hotel	1

EATING
Banh Xeo Ba Duong	4
Bread of Life	1
Karma Waters	2
Quan Com Hue Ngon	3

DRINKING
Bamboo 2	1

Train Station (200m)

Long-distance Bus Station (1.5km) & Highway 1

Da Nang Airport (1km)

(2m) & Monkey Mountain

My Khe Beach (2km)

My Khe Beach (3km)

4 (9km), Marble Mountains (15km), Non Nuoc Beach & Hoi An (32km)

11

China Beach. During the American War it served as a massive South Vietnamese airbase and played host to thousands of US troops, as well as refugees searching for work.

WHAT TO SEE AND DO

Besides strolling the Bach Dong promenade and seeing the **Dragon Bridge** breathe fire (Sat & Sun 9pm), or exploring the **Cham Museum**, you can also visit **Nam O Beach**, where American troops first landed in Vietnam, **My Khe**, a long, narrow strip of golden sand, **Monkey Mountain** with its giant Lady Buddha statue and some truly remarkable temples inside the **Marble Mountains** to the south of the city. To reach the outlying sights, rent a motorbike or hire a *xe om* or an Easy Rider via Sinh Tourist (see opposite) to take you around.

The Cham Museum

The Cham Museum, at the end of Bach Dang (daily 7am–5pm; 40,000VND, audio-guide 20,000VND), is the most comprehensive exhibit of Cham art in the world, giving a glimpse of the artistically inspired culture that ruled most of southern Vietnam for a thousand years. The terracotta and sandstone figures of the Hindu pantheon are on display here, from Shiva, Vishnu and Lakshmi to Ganesh and Brahma, as well as stylized animal figures, garudas and graceful apsaras (nymphs). There is also a scale model of My Son (see p.888) and temporary photography exhibits. Exhibits are grouped according to their place of origin: My Son, Tra Kieu (Simhapura), Dong Duong (Indrapura) and Binh Dinh.

Nam O Beach

Fifteen kilometres northwest of the city is the palm-fringed **Nam O Beach**, where American troops first landed in Vietnam in 1965. Residents of Nam O village are famous for their *goi ca* – Vietnamese sashimi that consists of raw fish marinated in a special sauce and rolled in a spicy powder.

My Khe (China Beach) and Non Nuoc Beach

Thirty kilometres of white sand stretch from the Son Tra Peninsula to Cua Dai Beach in Hoi An. The best-known section of the beach is **My Khe** (China Beach), where American servicemen from all over Vietnam were sent for R&R during the American War. Nowadays, the beach attracts day-trippers from Da Nang and Hoi An, especially from September to December when rough sea conditions make the waves ideal for surfing. May to July is the best time for swimming, when the sea is calmest.

A further 3km south from Da Nang is the quieter **Non Nuoc** beach, where there is a cluster of **seafood restaurants**.

Nui Son Tra (Monkey Mountain)

The Son Tra peninsula, crowned with Monkey Mountain, sits at the northern end of China Beach and it's an easy drive on the coastal road to the 67m-high **Lady Buddha** statue and **Ling Ung** Monastery. Until 2008 the peninsula was a restricted military zone, but now it's possible to drive up to the peak to see the American radar domes still used by the Vietnamese military and for a great view of the bay. If you're on a scooter, do a clockwise loop of the peninsula to avoid the steepest inclines.

Marble Mountains (Ngu Hanh Son)

Just west of Non Nuoc beach there are five karst mountains, riddled with natural caves that were converted into Hindu and, later, Buddhist temples, and topped with pagodas. The largest and most famous is **Thuy Son** (daily 7am–5pm; 40,000VND). Climb the steep, uneven staircase, go through Ong Chon gate to the Linh Ong Pagoda, and follow the path behind it to the **Tang Chon Cave** and a beautiful grotto concealing a Buddha statue. The path to the rest of Thuy Son's temples is hidden behind the Xa Loi Pagoda, reachable by a walkway to the left of the Ong Chon gate. The main paths leads you past the Limh Nam cave to the attractive **Tam Thai Tu Pagoda**. From here, one path leads up to the **Vong Giang Dai** viewpoint that offers great views of the other Marble Mountains. Another path branches off towards the large **Huyen Khong Cave** guarded by statues of mandarins; the chamber on the right was used as a Viet Cong hospital. Another steep, winding path leads you down from the Tam Thai Tu Pagoda to the main road.

Near the infrequently working elevator is the sometimes overlooked **Am Phu Cave** (20,000VND). The entrance is guarded by the animals from the Chinese zodiac and the vast, dark caverns are scented with incense and guano. Head right, descend the crumbling, steep steps then squeeze through a narrow passage and you'll find yourself in another cavern where green-skinned devils are torturing sinners, two of them sawing a figure in half – a creepy and compelling spectacle.

ARRIVAL AND DEPARTURE

By plane Da Nang's international airport (ⓦdanangairportonline.com) is 3km southwest of the centre and served by taxis (100,000VND).
Destinations Buon Ma Thuot (daily; 1hr 10min); Da Lat (daily; 1hr 20min); Hanoi (8 daily; 1hr 10min); HCMC (15 daily; 1hr 10min); Hong Kong (3 daily; 3hr 30min); Nha Trang (daily; 1hr 20min); Siem Reap (daily; 1hr 45min); Singapore (3 daily; 3hr 45min).
By bus Long-distance buses operate from the Lien Tinh bus station 2.5km from town. Take a *xe om* (25,000VND) to get there. Open-tour buses generally drop off passengers at the Cham Museum on Bach Dang.
Destinations Da Lat (14–17hr); Hanoi (19hr); HCMC (24hr); Hoi An (45min–1hr); Hue (3hr); Kon Tum (6hr); Nha Trang (13hr).
By train The train station is 1.5km west of town at 128 Hai Phong. A *xe om* into town will cost you 25,000VND. The train journey from Da Nang to Hue, hugging the cliff over the dramatic Hai Van Pass with the vast expanse of the ocean to your right, is one of the most impressive stretches of railway in Vietnam, a journey well worth taking in itself.
Destinations Hanoi (5 daily; 15–21hr); HCMC (5 daily; 17–23hr); Hue (8 daily; 2hr 30min–4hr); Nha Trang (5 daily; 9–12hr).

INFORMATION AND TOURS

Tour operators For tickets and information, Sinh Tourist, 154 Bach Dang (daily 7am–9pm; ☎0236 384 3259, ⓦthesinhtourist.vn), is your best bet.
Services Vietcombank, 140 Le Loi, has exchange facilities and an ATM.

ACCOMMODATION

Fulmar Hotel 11 Yen Bai ☎0236 3810809, ⓦfulmarhotel .com. Friendly four-storey hotel with compact, bright rooms and helpful management. Central location is a boon, and there are plenty of single rooms for solo travellers. Doubles $20
★**Hoa's Place** 9km south of Da Nang ☎090 564 0542, ⓔhoasplace@gmail.com. The genial Hoa and his wife have opened a new hotel just a stone's throw from Non Nuoc Beach and Marble Mountain; nightly communal dinners (80,000VND), cheap beer and friendly conversation make it the kind of place where days slip leisurely into weeks. All four rooms are en suite. Doubles $20
Memory Hostel 3 Tran Quoc Toan ☎0236 374 7797, ⓦmemoryhostel.com. Cool hostel just off Bach Dang. Rooms are quiet and comfortable and dorms have privacy curtains and secure lockers. Staff are super-helpful but there's not much communal space for mingling. Dorms $8, doubles $18
Nemo Hotel 100/2 Nguyen Van Thoai ☎0236 395 1951, ⓦdanangnemohotel.com. Quiet hotel near My Khe Beach and some great seafood restaurants. Expect spacious doubles and helpful owners. Doubles $18

EATING

Banh Xeo Ba Duong K280/23 Hoang Dieu. Hidden at the end of an alley, in the evening this place buzzes with local families – and the occasional tourist – here for the cheap and delicious meat skewers and *banh xeo* (literally "sizzling cakes") stuffed with pork and shrimp. Daily 4–10pm.
Bread of Life 4 Dong Da. Excellent bakery and café employing members of the deaf community, where you can enjoy cakes, gourmet sandwiches and Italian coffee. The English breakfast (145,000VND) will set you up for the day, and the pizzas are also good. Daily 7.30am–10.30pm.
Karma Waters 34 Nguyen Chi Thanh. Vegetarians and vegans, rejoice, for this Indian restaurant prides itself on the best vegetable dishes in town and fresh juices, as well as bakery items. Daily 9am–9pm.
Quan Com Hue Ngon 65 Tran Quoc Toan. This is a friendly and very local spot that does some of the best Vietnamese barbecue (meat and fish) in town as well as noodle dishes. Mains from 50,000VND. Daily 11am–11pm.

DRINKING

Bamboo 2 216 Bach Dang. Nineties tunes, happy hour (5.30–7pm), live sport on TV and a Western menu ensure this place is packed out until the small hours. Daily 10am–late.

HOI AN

The ancient core of seductive, charming **HOI AN** – recognized as a UNESCO World Cultural Heritage Site in 1999 – is a rich architectural fusion of Chinese, Japanese, Vietnamese and European influences dating back to the sixteenth century. In its heyday the port town attracted vessels from the world's great trading nations, and many Chinese merchants stayed on. Today its charming two-hundred-year-old wooden-fronted shophouses are among its chief attractions, as is the city's dining scene.

WHAT TO SEE AND DO

The **historic core** of Hoi An consists of just three short parallel streets: Tran Phu is the oldest and, even today, the principal commercial street, with plenty of crafts shops and galleries; one block south, Nguyen Thai Hoc has many wooden townhouses and some galleries, while riverfront Bach Dang holds the market and several waterside cafés. There are also a couple of attractive **beaches** nearby, and a cluster of **islands** that make for excellent day-trips from the town.

Japanese Covered Bridge

The western end of Tran Phu is marked by a small arched bridge known as the **Japanese Covered Bridge**, which used to connect the Japanese community to the Chinese one in the sixteenth century and has been adopted as Hoi An's emblem since. It has been reconstructed several times throughout its existence to the same simple design. Inside the bridge's narrow span are a collection of stelae and four statues, two dogs and two monkeys, usually said to record that work began in the year of the monkey and ended in that of the dog. You need a ticket to enter the

chapel in which a monster called Cu is said to have lived.

The Chinese Assembly Halls

Historically, Hoi An's ethnic Chinese population organized themselves according to their place of origin (Fujian, Guangdong, Chaozhou or Hainan), and each group maintained its own assembly hall as both community centre and house of worship. The most populous group hails from Fujian, and their **Phuoc Kien Assembly Hall**, at 46 Tran Phu (daily 7am–5.30pm), is an imposing edifice with an ostentatious, triple-arched gateway. The hall is dedicated to Thien Hau, Goddess of the Sea and protector of sailors. She stands, fashioned in 200-year-old papier-mâché, on the main altar flanked by her green- and red-faced assistants. It is said that they can see or hear any boat in distress over a range of 1600km.

Trieu Chau Assembly Hall, on the far eastern edge of town at 157 Nguyen Duy Hieu (daily 7.30am–5.30pm), was built in 1776 by Chinese from Chaozhou and has a remarkable display of woodcarving. In the altar-niche sits Ong Bon, a general in the Chinese Navy, surrounded by a frieze teeming with bird, animal and insect life; the altar table also depicts life on land and in the ocean.

The merchants' houses

Most of Hoi An's original wooden buildings are on Tran Phu and south towards the river, which is where you'll see the best-known merchants' house, at 101 Nguyen Thai Hoc. The **Tan Ky House** (daily 8am–noon & 2–4.30pm) is a beautifully preserved example of a two-storey, late eighteenth-century shophouse, all dark wood and dimly lit, with shop space at the front, a tiny central courtyard, and access to the river at the back. It is wonderfully cluttered with the property of seven generations grown wealthy from trading silk, tea and rice, and boasts two exceptionally fine hanging poem-boards and a wall devoted to photos of Hoi An's floods. The house gets very crowded and is best visited early or late in the day.

TICKETS FOR SIGHTS IN THE OLD TOWN

More than eight hundred historical buildings have been preserved in Hoi An, thanks to UNESCO, and you'll need to buy a **ticket** to access the most important sights (ⓦ hoianworldheritage.org.vn). There are several **ticket booths** (daily 7am–5pm) scattered throughout the Old Town where you can buy strips of five tickets (120,000VND), each one valid for a UNESCO site of your choice.

11

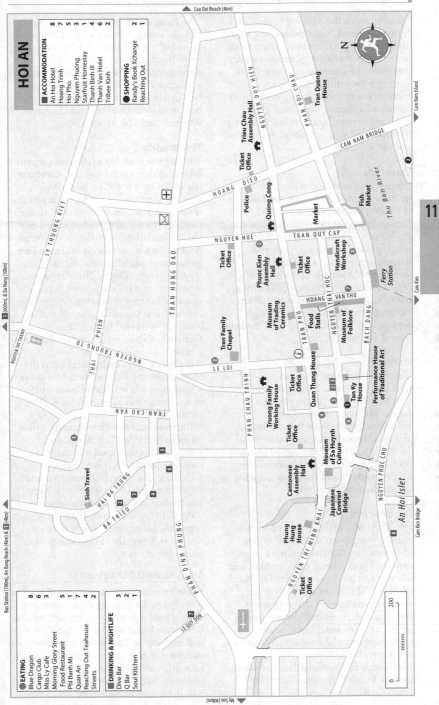

HOI AN

▲ Cua Dai Beach (4km)

■ ACCOMMODATION
An Hoi Hotel	8
Hoang Trinh	7
Hoi Pho	5
Nguyen Phuong	3
Starfruit Homestay	1
Thanh Binh III	4
Thanh Van Hotel	6
Tribee Kinh	2

● SHOPPING
Randy's Book Xchange	2
Reaching Out	1

● EATING
Blue Dragon	8
Cargo Club	6
Miss Ly Cafe	3
Morning Glory Street	5
Food Restaurant	1
Phi Banh Mi	7
Quan An	4
Reaching Out Teahouse	2
Streets	

■ DRINKING & NIGHTLIFE
Dive Bar	3
Q Bar	2
Soul Kitchen	1

Bus Station (700m), An Bang Beach (4km) & ▲ 1 (4km)
▲ 1 (600m), & Da Nang (30m)

Thu Bon River

Cam Nam Island
Cam Kim
Cam Nam Bridge
Ferry Station
Cam Kim

Fish Market

Trieu Chau Assembly Hall
Tran Duong House
Ticket Office
Police
Quong Cong
Market
Hoang Dieu
Tran Quy Cap
Nguyen Hue
Phuoc Kien Assembly Hall
Ticket Office
Handicraft Workshop
Ticket Office
Museum of Trading Ceramics
Food Stalls
Museum of Folklore
Hoang Van Thu
Nguyen Thai Hoc
Tran Phu
Bach Dang
Performance House of Traditional Art
Tran Family Chapel
Quan Thang House
Tan Ky House
Ticket Office
Le Loi
Truong Family Working House
Phan Chau Trinh
Ticket Office
Museum of Sa Huynh Culture
Tran Cao Van
Cantonese Assembly Hall
Hai Ba Trung
Ba Trieu
Sinh Travel
Nguyen Tat Thanh
Nguyen Truong To
Thai Phien
Tran Hung Dao
Ly Thuong Kiet
Japanese Covered Bridge
Phung Hung House
Nguyen Thi Minh Khai
Phan Dinh Phung
Nguyen Phuc Chu
An Hoi Islet
Cam Kim Bridge
Le Qui Don
Ticket Office

N

▼ My Son (40km)

metres
0   200

11

Just up from the covered bridge, at 4 Nguyen Minh Khai, **Phung Hung House** (daily 8am–7pm) has been home to the same family for eight generations since they moved from **Hue** in about 1780. The large two-storey house is Vietnamese in style although its eighty ironwood columns and small glass skylights denote Japanese influence, and it's decorated with beautiful embroidery and elaborate lanterns.

Museums

Housed in a traditional timber residence-cum-warehouse, the **Museum of Trading Ceramics** (daily 7am–5.30pm) at 80 Tran Phu showcases the history of Hoi An's ceramics trade, which peaked in the fifteenth and sixteenth centuries. The smaller **Museum of Sa Huynh Culture** at 149 Tran Phu (daily 7am–5.30pm) displays artefacts found in Sa Huynh, 130km south of Hoi An, which flourished between the second century BC and the second century AD.

Markets

The produce **market** at the east end of Tran Phu retains the atmosphere of a typical, traditional country market despite the tourist contingent.

The bustling riverside **fish market** (6–7am), opposite the southern end of the market, is worth setting the alarm clock for; it's a hive of early-morning activity, as dozens of fishwives gather to sell the catch of the night.

The beaches

The 30km of coastline between Hoi An and Da Nang boast some of Vietnam's finest beaches. **Cua Dai Beach** – a 3km stretch of sand – lies a pleasant 5km bike ride east of Hoi An along Cua Dai Road (30,000VND by *xe om*). Sadly it has some ugly cement sea defences and a problem with litter, and the vendors go for the hard sell here, but a number of restaurants near the road are a worthwhile stop for seafood. Windsurfers, bodyboards and surfboards are available for rent from the five-star *Palm Gardens Beach Resort*.

An Bang Beach, 4km from town along Hai Ba Trung, is much quieter and more beautiful – a wide stretch of golden palm-lined sand as yet unspoilt by development, though small restaurants and some charming homestays line the beach. There's a small backpacker scene here in summer and you can choose to stay here and visit Hoi An.

The islands

Touring the outlying islands on a rented bicycle makes a good day out. **Cam Nam Island** lies over the Cam Nam Bridge, offering a great view of Hoi An across the water. The waterfront restaurants to the south of the island specialize in *hen tron* (fried fresh clams). On the southwest of An Hoi Islet there's a new bridge to **Cam Kim**, a large island famous for its specialist craft villages. The island's woodcarving workshops are a popular stopover for tourist boats returning from My Son, but the maze of sandy tracks, bamboo "monkey" bridges and picturesque little villages makes the island a beautiful place to explore independently. A main road bisects the island from the western to eastern shore, where there is a small jetty from where you can take a boat back to Bach Dang (20,000VND).

The mountainous **Cham Islands**, 10km offshore from Cua Dai Beach, are renowned for their swallows' nests, a culinary delicacy that can fetch up to $2500/kg. The islands' main attraction for tourists, however, is the coral reefs and marine life in the surrounding waters; diving and snorkelling (see opposite) are possible mainly between April and September as the seas get too rough out of season.

ARRIVAL AND DEPARTURE

By bus Once-daily open-tour buses drop off at central hotels. They provide the easiest and quickest way out of Hoi An, stopping at all major destinations north and south. Tickets can be booked from Sinh Tourist or in your hotel. Local buses stop at the main bus station about 1km northwest of the town centre at 96 Hung Vuong; these are notorious for overcharging tourists.

Destinations Da Lat (18hr); Da Nang (1hr); Hanoi (21hr); HCMC (22hr); Hue (4hr); Mui Ne (17hr).

INFORMATION AND ACTIVITIES

Tours Hoi An has plenty of agencies offering tours, visas, open-tour bus, train and air tickets, Sinh Tourist, 587 Hai Ba Trung (daily 6am–10pm; ☎0235 386 3948, ⓦ thesinhtourist.vn), being a particularly reliable option.

Cooking Many restaurants teach you how to make Hoi An specialities during their half-day (around $30) and full-day (around $50) cooking courses. Taste Vietnam outgrew their original premises at *Morning Glory* (see below) and now operate from a professional kitchen on An Hoi Islet at 3 Nguyen Hoang (☎0235 224 1555, ⓦ msvy-tastevietnam .com). Red Bridge Cooking School (☎0235 393 3222, ⓦ visithoian.com) teaches small groups at their school, reachable by 4km boat cruise down the river; the full-day course is particularly worthwhile.

Diving Blue Coral Diving (33 Tran Hung Dao; ☎0235 627 9297, ⓦ divehoian.com) is run by experienced dive masters and offers snorkelling and diving trips around the Cham Islands; a one-day trip including two dives costs 1,800,000VND (PADI certification required); snorkelling day-trips cost 950,000VND.

ACCOMMODATION

An Hoi Hotel 69 Nguyen Phuc Chu ☎0235 391 1888, ⓦ anhoihotel.com.vn. Decent a/c rooms in a perfect location for the Old Town, on An Hoi Islet. Perks include a swimming pool and breakfast. Doubles $20

Hoang Trinh 45 Le Quy Don ☎0235 391 6579, ⓦ hoianhoangtrinhhotel.com. All rooms in this friendly place have a bath and a balcony, and even the cheapest are given the sorts of personal touches you'd expect from a much more expensive hotel. Rooms at the front ($30) have views of the Confucius Temple, and the communal rooftop terrace is a great spot for breakfast. Double $20

Hoi Pho 627 Hai Ba Trung ☎0235 391 6382, ⓔ hoipho .hotel@yahoo.com. The bright, unfussy rooms in this quiet little hotel are good value, the staff are helpful and you can play PS4 in the lobby. Double $18

Nguyen Phuong 109 Ba Trieu ☎0235 391 6588, ⓔ nguyenphuonghotel1@gmail.com. Polished, spotlessly clean little a/c rooms, a short walk from the Old Town. Doubles $20

★**Starfruit Homestay** 26A Dinh Tien Hoang ☎0235 626 0026, ⓦ starfruithomestay.com. Run by a wonderfully friendly family, this beautiful guesthouse, a 20min walk from the Old Town, offers luxurious rooms in both the original and new block; the more expensive rooms ($40) have proper bathtubs. Free bicycles available for guest use, plus a swimming pool. Doubles $20

Thanh Binh III 98 Ba Trieu ☎0235 391 6777, ⓔ thanhbinhserenehotel@gmail.com. One of several similar hotels in the Hai Ba Trung cluster, with spacious a/c rooms and a swimming pool. All rooms have a private balcony or patio. Doubles $25

Thanh Van Hotel 78 Tran Hung Dao ☎0235 391 6916, ⓦ thanhvanhotel.com. Great location on the fringe of the Old Town, with comfortable rooms, plus a pool to lounge around and breakfast is included. Doubles $25

Tribee Kinh 103 Ba Trieu ☎0235 386 3153, ⓔ tribeekinh@gmail.com. New hostel offering simple doubles and twins and three-bed or four-bed dorms (not bunks) in the attic. Rooms are clean, and it's a nice place to meet fellow travellers. Dorms $8.50, doubles $18

EATING

Blue Dragon 46 Bach Dang. A percentage of the profits made at this restaurant goes to the Blue Dragon Foundation, assisting street kids in Hoi An. There are more than a hundred inexpensive dishes to choose from, including Hoi An specialities such as *banh bao vac* (30,000VND). Cookery classes are also available ($15). Mains 40,000–80,000VND. Daily 11am–10pm.

Cargo Club 107 Nguyen Thai Hoc. A colonial-style Vietnamese and international restaurant, executing Western breakfasts, speciality dumplings, grilled sea bass and gnocchi with equal ease. Next door the bakery section serves delicious home-made cakes, ice cream and pastries (from 30,000VND). Mains from 90,000VND. Daily 7.30am–11pm.

Miss Ly Cafe 22 Nguyen Hue. This well-established restaurant is run by a delightful family who take great pride in the Hoi An specialities they serve, such as *cao lau* (50,000VND). The taster plate (160,000VND) is a great introductoin to four local dishes. Daily 11.30am–10pm.

★**Morning Glory Street Food Restaurant** 106 Nguyen Thai Hoc ☎0235 224 1555. The king of the dining scene, featuring an incredible array of street-food dishes – from squid stuffed with pork and a smoky aubergine claypot dish, to fragrant spring rolls and mackerel steamed in banana leaf. Get here early or make a reservation. Mains 70,000–120,000VND. Daily 11am–11pm.

Phi Banh Mi 88 Thai Phien. Look no further for the best *banh mi* in Hoi An (you'll spot the queue before you see the tiny street-food restaurant). Veggies rave about the cheese and tofu option (20,000VND). Daily 7am–8pm.

Quan An 19 Hoang Van Thu. The guestbook testifies to the popularity of this little restaurant, with outside seating, friendly service and cold *bia hoi* for just 5000VND/glass. The chilli duck (70,000VND), prawn spring rolls, vegetarian *cao lao* and pork hotpot all get rave reviews. Daily 11.30am–11pm.

Reaching Out Teahouse 131 Tran Phu. A wonderfully tranquil spot for tea and coffee (they've got quite a selection), this café is dedicated to providing fair treatment and wages to servers who are hearing- and speech-impaired. Daily 9am–7pm.

Streets 17 Le Loi. This beautifully restored shophouse provides a wonderful setting for the equally wonderful

11

food: try the squid salad with tamarind or the crispy rice pancake with shrimp and pork, or grab a sandwich with pear and grilled cheese. Mains from 65,000VND. Daily 11am–10pm.

DRINKING AND NIGHTLIFE

The Old Town gets sleepy around 11pm and the backpacker action moves across the Thu Bon River to An Hoi Islet.

Dive Bar 88 Nguyen Thai Hoc. British-run bar that's also home to the Cham Islands Diving Center, with a lovely cocktail garden, great mix of tunes and extensive cocktail list. Learn to make your own in their mixology classes ($30). Daily 10am–midnight.

Q Bar 94 Nguyen Thai Hoc. Trendy, gay-friendly bar that's usually busy with a good mix of locals and travellers, thanks to its expertly mixed cocktails and chilled-out electronica on the stereo. A little pricier than elsewhere. Daily 5–11.30pm.

Soul Kitchen An Bang Beach ☎09 0644 0320, ⓦsoulkitchen.sitew.com. This phenomenally popular bar and restaurant is at the centre of the beach scene on An Bang. Laidback, with a decent menu (noodles from 80,000VND, Western dishes a bit pricier) and the perfect view to enjoy over a cold beer (Larue is 20,000VND). Daily 8am–11pm; Mon closes early.

SHOPPING

The trio of streets running parallel to the river – Bach Dang, Nguyen Thai Hoc and Tran Phu – are the best places to search for lacquerware, original and copied artwork, pottery and ceramics, and shops selling colourful silk lanterns, a Hoi An speciality.

Randy's Book Xchange Cam Nam Island ⓦbookshoian.com. A huge selection in English, and, as the name suggests, you can exchange your old books for

---

HOI AN TAILORS

Tailors are a dime a dozen in Hoi An and some will approach you as soon as you set foot in town. Those who offer to make your clothes in 24 hours are ones to avoid, as it allows no time for alterations and presumably involves sweatshop labour to carry out your order in such a short space of time. Recommended places include: **Thu Thuy** (ⓦthuthuysilk .com) at 23 Tran Hung Dao, **Yaly** (ⓦyalycouture.com) at 47 Nguyen Thai Hoc, 47 Tran Phu and 358 Nguyen Duy Hieu, and **Kimmy Custom Tailor** (ⓦkimmytailor.com) at 70 Tran Hung Dao. It's possible to arrange for your clothing order to be shipped to your country.

---

credit. The owner is a great source of local information. Daily 8am–7pm.

Reaching Out 103 Nguyen Thai Hoc, ⓦreachingoutvietnam .com. A particularly good fair-trade handicrafts shop that employs artisans with disabilities. Ask about workshop tours. Mon–Fri 8.30am–9.30pm, Sat & Sun 9.30am–8.30pm.

DIRECTORY

Bank Agribank, 12 Tran Hung Dao, has an ATM. The post office has a Vietcombank ATM.

Bike rental Bicycles (30,000VND/day) and motorbikes ($7–10/day) are available for rent from most guesthouses.

Hospital Dr Ho Huu Phuoc Practice, 74 Le Loi ☎0235 386 1419; daily 11am–12.30pm & 5–9.30pm. Local doctor who speaks English.

Pharmacy Bac Ali, 68 Nguyen Thai Hoc.

Post office 4b Tran Hung Dao (daily 6.30am–9pm).

MY SON

The mouldering, overgrown World Heritage-listed ruins of Vietnam's most evocative Cham site, **MY SON** (daily 6.30am–4pm; 70,000VND), lie 40km southwest of Hoi An in a bowl of lushly wooded hills.

The kingdom of Champa existed between the second and fifteenth centuries, and Cham kings were buried here as early as the fourth century, but the ruined sanctuaries you see today were erected between the seventh and thirteenth centuries. My Son was considered the domain of gods and god-kings, and, in its prime, comprised some seventy buildings, which weathered well until the 1960s when the Viet Cong based themselves here and were pounded by American B52s. There are **unexploded mines** in the area, so don't stray from main paths.

Archeologists regard **Group B** as the spiritual centre of My Son. Of the eleventh-century central *kalan* (sanctuary), **B1**, only the base remains; stone epitaphs reveal that it was dedicated to the god-king Bhadresvara, a hybrid of Shiva and King Bhadravarman. **B5**, the impressive **repository room**, boasts a bowed, boat-shaped roof still in reasonably good shape. The outer walls support ornate columns and statues of deities, and, on the western side, a crumbling bas-relief depicting two elephants with their trunks entwined around a coconut tree. Next door in **Group C**, the central *kalan*, **C1**, is fairly well preserved; statues of gods stand around the walls and a carved lintel runs across the entrance.

East of B and C, the two long, windowed meditation halls that comprise **Group D** now house modest galleries: **D1** contains a lingam, the remains of a carving of Nandi, Shiva's Bull; **D2** houses a fine frieze depicting many-armed Shiva dancing, and, below the steps up to its eastern entrance, stands a statue of Garuda. Bomb damage was particularly cruel near **Group A**, reducing the once-spectacular *kalan*, **A1**, to a heap of toppled columns and lintels. Within, a huge lingam base is ringed by a number of detailed, small figures at prayer. Group A is reached by crossing the stream north of Group D and turning right.

The path from here loops past groups G, E and F, where restoration work is ongoing, before reaching the car park.

ARRIVAL AND DEPARTURE

Tour Most visitors come on tours from Hoi An; there's a choice of sunrise tours (departing at 5am, returning at 11am; 180,000VND) and regular tours (departing at 9am, returning at 1pm; 120,000VND); for both tours there's the option to return by boat, visiting traditional villages along the river; allow a couple of extra hours and around 40,000VND more.

The south-central coast

Extending from the central provinces all the way down to the wetlands of the Mekong Delta, Vietnam's south-central coast was, from the seventh to the twelfth century, the domain of the Indianized trading empire of Champa. A few communities of Cham people still live in the area, and there are some fine relics of their ancestors' temple complexes near the seaside city of **Nha Trang**. The other beach resort along this stretch of coast is the one-street **Mui Ne**, a 21km-long arc of fine sand lapped by aquamarine waters that's a big destination for kitesurfers. At both resorts the majority of tourists are sun-seeking Russians; Chinese travellers are also now arriving in droves, making for quite a cosmopolitan scene.

NHA TRANG

Some 508km south of Hoi An, **NHA TRANG**'s main features are its fine municipal beach, and some excellent examples of **Cham architecture**. In addition, the plentiful marine life and coral reefs found around its outlying islands make it the top **diving** destination in Vietnam, though avoid the **rainy season** (Nov–early Jan), when the sea becomes choppy, the beach windy and rather dirty, and the waters too murky to dive.

11

WHAT TO SEE AND DO

The centre of the city itself has a decent nightlife scene, with scores of bars catering to sozzled Russian tourists and Western backpackers. Most new arrivals make a beeline for the **municipal beach**, a grand 6km scythe of soft yellow sand lined with some decent restaurants and high-end resorts. If the sea is too rough for swimming, you can rent a bodyboard on the beach instead.

Alexandre Yersin Museum

The Pasteur Institute at the top of Tran Phu, which runs parallel to the beach, houses the **Alexandre Yersin Museum** (Mon–Fri 7.30–11am & 2–4.30pm, Sat 8–11am; 30,000VND). It profiles the Swiss-French scientist who settled in Nha Trang in 1893, discovered the cause of the bubonic plague in 1894, and became a local hero, thanks to his educational work and his ability to predict typhoons.

Long Thanh Gallery

The work of internationally acclaimed photographer Long Thanh is on display at **Long Thanh Gallery**, 126 Hoang Van Thu (Mon–Sat 8am–5.30pm; free;

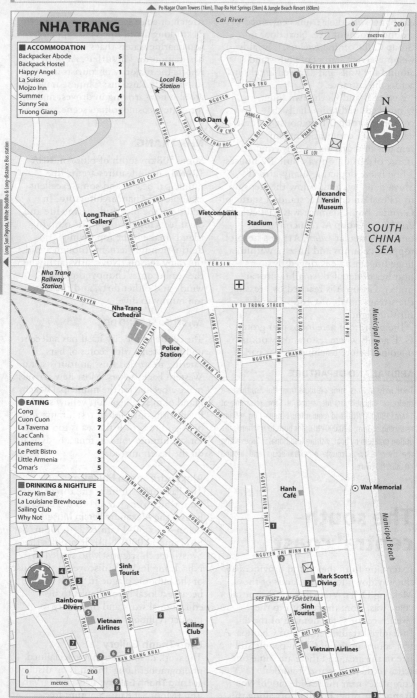

Po Nagar Cham Towers (1km), Thap Ba Hot Springs (3km) & Jungle Beach Resort (60km)

Cai River

NHA TRANG

0   200
metres

■ **ACCOMMODATION**
Backpacker Abode	5
Backpack Hostel	2
Happy Angel	1
La Suisse	8
Mojzo Inn	7
Summer	4
Sunny Sea	6
Truong Giang	3

● **EATING**
Cong	2
Cuon Cuon	8
La Taverna	7
Lac Canh	1
Lanterns	4
Le Petit Bistro	6
Little Armenia	3
Omar's	5

■ **DRINKING & NIGHTLIFE**
Crazy Kim Bar	2
La Louisiane Brewhouse	1
Sailing Club	3
Why Not	4

11

Long Son Pagoda, White Buddha & Long-distance Bus station

HA RA
Local Bus Station
NGUYEN BINH KHIEM
NGO QUYEN
CONG TRU
NGUYEN
QUANG TRUNG
SINH TRUNG
NGUYEN THAI HOC
Cho Dam
BEN CHO
HANG CA
PHAN BOI CHAU
HAM THUYEN
PHAN CHU TRINH
LE LOI
TRAN QUI CAP
THONG NHAT
LE THANH PHUONG
HOANG VAN THU
PHUONG SAI
Long Thanh Gallery
Vietcombank
TRANG NU VUONG
Alexandre Yersin Museum
Stadium
PASTEUR
SOUTH CHINA SEA
Nha Trang Railway Station
THAI NGUYEN
Nha Trang Cathedral
YERSIN
NGUYEN TRAI
Police Station
QUANG TRUNG
LY TU TRONG STREET
TO HIEN THANH
HOANG HOA THAM
TRAN HUNG DAO
TRAN PHU
Municipal Beach
LE THANH TON
NGUYEN THAI
CHANH
LE QUY DON
MAC DINH CHI
HUYNH TUC KHANG
VO TRU
NGUYEN THIEN THUAT
Hanh Café
War Memorial
TRINH PHONG
TRAN NGUYEN HAN
DONG DA
HONG BANG
NGO DUC KE
NGUYEN THI MINH KHAI
Mark Scott's Diving
Municipal Beach

SEE INSET MAP FOR DETAILS
Sinh Tourist
NGUYEN THIEN THUAT
BIET THU
HUNG VUONG
TRAN PHU
Vietnam Airlines
TRAN QUANG KHAI

N
NGUYEN THIEN
Sinh Tourist
Rainbow Divers
BIET THU
HUNG VUONG
Vietnam Airlines
THUAT
TRAN PHU
Sailing Club
TRAN QUANG KHAI
0   200
metres

(500m), Cau Da Wharf, Vinpearl Land, Bai Dai Beach (19km) & Cam Ranh Airport (30km)

ⓦlongthanhart.com). Mr Thanh, whose black-and-white photographs capture poignant vignettes of Vietnamese life, is often on-hand to talk to visitors, and prints are available for purchase.

The Po Nagar Cham towers

Nha Trang's most gripping attraction, the **Po Nagar Cham towers** (daily 6am–6pm; 22,000VND), stand 1.5km north of the city centre along Duong 2/4 (a 30,000VND *xe om* ride). The Hindu Cham probably built ten towers, or *kalan*, here on Cu Lao Hill between the seventh and twelfth centuries, but only four remain. The largest and most impressive is the 23m-high northern tower, built in 817 and dedicated to Yang Ino Po Nagar, Goddess Mother of the Kingdom and a manifestation of Uma, Shiva's consort. Time has taken its toll on this square-shaped tower, but the lotus-petal and spearhead motifs are still intact, as is the lintel over the outer door, on which four-armed Shiva dances. Inside, the dark and smoky main chamber holds a black stone statue of ten-armed Uma. To go inside the towers, scented with incense and used as places of worship, you need to don one of the "lab coats" provided if you're not appropriately attired.

The islands

Perhaps the single greatest pleasure of a stay in Nha Trang is an excursion to one of the nearby **islands**, easiest reached on one of the popular day-trips from around $8/person (see below). Morning trips include a tour of the islands, snorkelling and lunch on board, while in the afternoon the booze-cruise party boats come out.

The closest island, **Hon Mieu**, is also served by a local ferry from Cau Da wharf, 5km south of the centre (15min; 20,000VND), which docks at the fishing village of Tri Nguyen.

The shallows that ring **Hon Tam**, 2km southeast of Hon Mieu, are good for snorkelling. **Hon Tre** is the largest of Nha Trang's islands, endowed with dramatic cliffs and a fine, white-sand beach, Bai Tru – perhaps the best beach in the area. Two smaller isles hover off Hon Tre's

11

southern coast: **Hon Mot** has a stony beach which is popular with snorkellers, and while there's no beach to speak of on **Hon Mun**, there's some great coral.

ARRIVAL AND DEPARTURE

By plane Cam Ranh Airport (ⓦnhatrangairport.com) is 28km south of town; Vietnam Airlines runs buses to and from its pick-up point at 86 Tran Phu (60,000VND) 2hr before scheduled departure times; metered taxis cost about 350,000VND.

Destinations Da Nang (1–2 daily; 1hr 15min); Hanoi (7–10 daily; 1hr 50min); HCMC (10–12 daily; 55min).

By bus Nha Trang is a major stop for open-tour buses, which terminate at their respective agencies' offices in the centre. They run to HCMC (9hr) and Mui Ne (4hr 30min), and less frequently to Da Lat (5hr), Hoi An (11hr), Hue (17hr) and Hanoi (32hr). The Phia Nam Nha Trang long-distance bus station is 500m west of the train station on Thai Nguyen. Mai Linh runs buses from here to Buon Ma Thuot (several daily; 4hr), Da Lat (several daily; 5hr) and HCMC (hourly; 9hr); book through your accommodation, and free pick-up should be available.

By train Nha Trang's train station is just west of the centre along Thai Nguyen. The ticket office is open daily 7–11.30am, 1.30–6pm & 7–9pm, or you can book online, or (for a commission) at agencies in town.

Destinations Da Nang (15 daily; 9–13hrs); Hanoi (13 daily; 24–31hrs); HCMC (16 daily; 7–12hrs); Hue (15 daily; 11hr 30min–16hr).

INFORMATION AND TOURS

Services Vietcombank is at 17 Quang Trung. There are pharmacies at 23d Biet Thu & 21 Quang Trung, and the post office is at 24 Hung Vuong.

Tour operators Tour operators can arrange motorbike tours ($20–60/day, depending on distance), open-tour

11

buses, tours of the region, and boat trips to nearby islands. Reputable operators include Sinh Tourist, 130 Hung Vuong (☎ 0258 352 4329, ⊛ thesinhtourist.vn).

ACTIVITIES

Diving During the rainy season, visibility can be low, and dives are often cancelled. The most reliable and professional operators are Rainbow Divers, 19 Biet Thu (☎ 0258 352 4351, ⊛ divevietnam.com); Mark Scott's Diving, 24/4 Hung Vuong (☎ 012 2903 7795, ⊛ divingvietnam.com); and Sailing Club, 72–74 Tran Phu (☎ 0258 352 2788, ⊛ sailingclubnhatrang .com). Expect to pay $85 for two dives ($65 for certified divers), including lunch on the boat. All offer PADI Open Water beginner and advanced courses ($310).

Watersports Various outfits along the beach, including one by La Louisiane Brewhouse (see opposite), organize wakeboarding, water-skiing, windsurfing, catamaran sailing, kitesurfing and kayaking.

ACCOMMODATION

Backpacker Abode 79 Nguyen Thien Thuat ☎ 0258 352 9139. Though it may look a little grubby from the outside, this hostel is a cut above the norm here – curtains on the beds add that little bit of privacy to the dorms, and evenings often see a keg of free beer opened for guests. Dorms $6, doubles $14

Backpack Hostel 92/12 Hung Vuong ☎ 0258 352 1140, ⊛ backpackhostel.net. Smart hostel option tucked into a relatively quiet side-street just a couple of blocks from the beach. The staff go out of their way to help, though private rooms are rather overpriced. Dorms $5, doubles $40

Happy Angel 11a/3 Nguyen Thien Thuat ☎ 0258 352 5006. A little way north of the hubbub, and set into a quiet back alley, this is a good place for those looking to escape Nha Trang's noise – though the bars and beach are just a short walk away, if you need them. Doubles $12

La Suisse 34 Tran Quang Khai ☎ 0258 352 4353, ⊛ lasuissehotel.com. Perhaps the most popular budget hotel in the city, combining great service with cheap but well-appointed rooms. The semi-secluded location is also a bonus. Doubles $15

CRIME IN NHA TRANG

Nha Trang seems to have more **petty crime** than elsewhere, so leave surplus cash in the hotel safe when heading out. There have been reports of attacks on young men coming back alone late at night, as well as drive-by bag snatchings and laced drinks in nightclubs – this most often happens with large "bucket" cocktails. Check prices on tickets to avoid being overcharged at tourist sites.

★**Mojzo Inn** 120/36 Nguyen Thien Thuat ☎ 0258 625 5568, ⊛ facebook.com/MojzoInn. The staff here are a lot of fun, plus the good location, free breakfasts, particularly comfortable bunk beds and thoughtful touches such as storage cages and individual power sockets make this a top backpacker choice. Dorms $6, doubles $19

Summer 34 Nguyen Thien Thuat ☎ 0258 352 2186, ⊛ thesummerhotel.com.vn. Good if you want to splash out a little – perhaps in a literal sense, since there's a small pool on the rooftop. Rooms are modern and comfy, though the cheapest ones are small and windowless. Doubles $32

Sunny Sea 64b/9 Tran Phu ☎ 0258 352 2286. Set at the end of an alley teeming with cheap places to stay, this is a popular choice, with rooms that are excellent value, if occasionally a little musty. Doubles $12

Truong Giang 3/8 Tran Quang Khai ☎ 0258 352 2125, ⊛ truonggianghotel.hostel.com. With professional service and clean, attractive rooms featuring small TVs, minibars and colourful bedspreads, this is a great option in a competitive price category. Doubles $13

EATING

Cong 27 Nguyen Thien Thuat. If you're in the mood for coffee, give this artistically designed place a try – split over three levels and popular with young locals, its main wall features a retro Socialist Realist-style mural. Daily 7am–11pm.

Cuon Cuon 3/9 Trang Quang Khai. Tucked away down a side street, this friendly restaurant, decorated with colourful prints and carnival masks, serves roll-your-own fresh spring rolls (75,000VND), fragrant curries (105,000VND), pho and other delicious Vietnamese dishes. Daily 11.30am–10pm.

La Taverna 115 Nguyen Thien Thuat. Excellent pizza, pasta, steaks and Vietnamese dishes made using imported ingredients are served up by the Italian–Swiss owner in an atmospheric, trattoria-style setting. Pizzas from 100,000VND. Daily 11.30am–11pm.

Lac Canh 44 Nguyen Binh Khiem. Set north of the centre in the quiet streets east of Cho Dam, Lac Canh is locally renowned for its mouth- and eye-watering cooked-at-the-table barbecues from around 60,000VND/person. Daily 11.30am–11pm.

Lanterns 72 Nguyen Thien Thuat. Pleasant little restaurant offering a range of Vietnamese and Western dishes; the claypot dishes are particularly good (from 80,000VND). Some of the profits go to a local orphanage, and cookery classes are also available. Daily noon–11pm.

★**Le Petit Bistro** 26b Tran Quang Khai. Come here for a cheap breakfast of great coffee and pain au chocolat (25,000VND), or an eggs Benedict (60,000VND), or try something more adventurous like the delicious onion soup (110,000VND), or their expensive meat dishes. Daily 8am–10.30pm.

★**Little Armenia** 3/12 Tran Quang Khai. Join the Russian tourists at this super place, which sells an array of food from across the former Soviet Union, as well as some Vietnamese staples. Best are the Georgian dishes – try the soup-filled *khinkali* dumplings (25,000VND each), or the Adjarian *khachapuri*, a deliciously unhealthy meal that's something like a pizza filled with butter, egg and cheese (120,000VND). Daily 10am–midnight.

Omar's 89b Nguyen Thien Thuat. The best target if you're up for a curry – authentic Indian dishes from both north and south, accompanied by superb lassis. The thali set meals (150,000VND) are a real belly-filler; mains otherwise from 85,000VND. Daily 7am–10pm.

DRINKING AND NIGHTLIFE

Crazy Kim Bar 19 Biet Thu. Enjoy the huge cocktails during the 4.30–10.30pm happy "hour", or drop by for a hangover breakfast (45,000VND). A percentage of the profits goes towards Kim's campaign to assist vulnerable street children, and accommodation is offered to volunteers who wish to teach English in her free education scheme. Daily 6am–1am.

La Louisiane Brewhouse 29 Tran Phu. Beach club with a free pool and private beach; the microbrewery offers a range of beers (large beer 80,000VND) made with all-natural ingredients, and there's an eclectic menu of Japanese, Vietnamese, Thai and international dishes. Daily 7am–1am.

Sailing Club 7 Tran Phu. Draws a well-heeled expat crowd and hordes of tourists to its refined beachfront bar and dancefloor – rowdy travellers and drunks not welcome. Monthly full-moon parties are held on the beach, with live DJ sets. Admission costs 150,000VND after 8pm (7pm at weekends), including one drink. Daily 7am–2am.

Why Not 24 Tran Quang Khai. Highly popular venue with seating both inside and out, a dance floor, cheap booze, and shishas to suck on. Happy hour is so happy that it lasts for six hours (4–10pm). Daily 2pm–late.

MUI NE

What started out as a pristine 10km-long stretch of sand with a small fishing village at the end of it is now lined cheek by jowl with beachside accommodation – mostly upmarket resorts, though some budget places survive. Low-key **MUI NE** is a prime place for adrenaline junkies: the waves between August and December attract surfers, while the strong, consistent winds and relatively low rainfall mean that kitesurfers and windsurfers thrive

year-round, particularly from late October to late April.

WHAT TO SEE AND DO

Mui Ne is justifiably famous for its impressive Sahara-esque red and white **sand dunes**, best seen in late afternoon, which can be visited as part of a guided tour or independently by bicycle or motorbike. The white-sand dunes are quite far out and neither the white nor the red is pristine, unfortunately; a steady stream of visitors brings a steady stream of rubbish, and quad bikes erode the fragile landscape. En route to the dunes, it is worth a stop at **Mui Ne village** for a scenic vantage point from the road, high over the bevy of blue fishing boats jostling in the harbour, as the fishmongers prepare their wares on the sand below. Another worthy stop is at the **Fairy Springs**, 5km east of the centre of Mui Ne, a shallow stream that runs through a beautiful red rock and sand dune canyon. Ignore the young men who offer to be guides; you can hardly get lost here.

ARRIVAL AND DEPARTURE

By bus Open-tour buses from both north and south pass through around noon and, less conveniently, around 2am. Sinh Tourist buses operate from their office at *Mui Ne Resort*, 144 Nguyen Dinh Chieu (☎0252 847542) near Mui Ne village.

Destinations Da Lat (5hr); HCMC (5hr); Nha Trang (5hr).

By train From Ho Chi Minh City, a/c trains head as far as Phan Thiet (departing 6.40am; 3hr 50min), a pleasant town just 50,000VND from Mui Ne by *xe om* – far comfier than the bus. The train heads back to HCMC at 1.10pm.

INFORMATION

Tours Sinh Tourist, all other tour operators on the strip and lodgings offer almost identical sunset tours to the red and white dunes ($7–10) that also tend to take in the Fairy Springs.

Services There are numerous ATMs scattered along the length of Nguyen Dinh Chieu. The area is best seen independently by bicycle (50,000VND/day) or motorbike (200,000VND/day), rentable from numerous lodgings and tour operators.

ACTIVITIES

Watersports C2Sky (16 Nguyen Dinh Chieu; ☎091 665 5241, ⓦc2skykitecenter.com) offer a 2hr taster kitesurfing course for $100, and their 7hr beginner course costs $385. *Jibes* (90 Nguyen Dinh Chieu; ☎0252 384 7008,

11

11

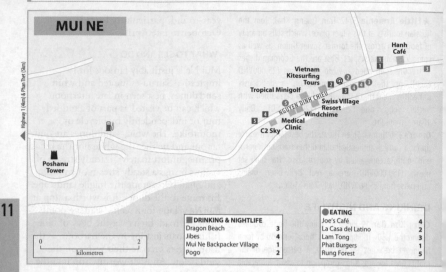

■ DRINKING & NIGHTLIFE		● EATING	
Dragon Beach	3	Joe's Café	4
Jibes	4	La Casa del Latino	2
Mui Ne Backpacker Village	1	Lam Tong	3
Pogo	2	Phat Burgers	1
		Rung Forest	5

ⓦ windsurf-vietnam.com) rent windsurfers, surfboards, kitesurf equipment, paddleboards and kayaks and offer lessons ($60–70/hr). Vietnam Kitesurfing Tours (68 Nguyen Dinh Chieu; ☎ 090 946 9803, ⓦ vietnamkitesurfingtours .com) specialize in kitesurfing only, with a team of expat and local riders as instructors, taking you to great spots further out of Mui Ne; day-trips from $90.

Mini golf The course at Tropical Minigolf (97 Nguyen Dinh Chieu; 100,000VND) is very good fun – and even more so if you grab a beer to swan around the place with.

ACCOMMODATION

The western end of the beach is home to the luxury resorts, while budget places are clustered at the centre. In low season (May–Oct), rates drop by up to thirty percent. Most lodgings have decent restaurants attached.

Herbal 21 Nguyen Dinh Chieu ☎ 0942 427911, ⓦ herbalhotelmuinevietnam.com. Fourteen spacious bungalows sleeping up to four, overlooking a calm garden area – highly pleasant, and in a nice area. They also offer cheap spa treatments. Doubles $19

Hiep Hoa 80 Nguyen Dinh Chieu ☎ 0252 384 7262. There are only eight rooms and a handful of bungalows at this small place, some with fan and others a/c. Very good value for money. Doubles $20

★ **Mui Ne Backpacker Village** 137 Nguyen Dinh Chieu ☎ 0252 384 7047, ⓦ muinebackpackers.com. This friendly, Aussie-run place proved so popular that they upped sticks and moved to a far larger location. The atmosphere is loungey, rather than scroungey – comfy a/c dorm rooms (with proper beds; no bunks) and a bunch of beach loungers are set around a large swimming pool, which is backed at one end by an awesome bar (see opposite).

Great for organizing tours, and helpful when it comes to local information. Dorms $7, doubles $40

Nam Hai 25 Nguyen Dinh Chieu ☎ 0252 374 1789. A good option if you want something approximating a hotel room – moderate luxury at a moderate price, and there are super views from the upper-floor rooms. You'll save almost $10 if you choose to do without breakfast, too. Doubles $33

Sand Dune 117 Nguyen Dinh Chieu ☎ 0252 384 9849. Neat and fairly large place with small but cheery rooms, right in the thick of things. There's a good travel agency on the ground floor, though the hotel reception is actually hidden away upstairs. Doubles $20

EATING

★ **Joe's Café** 86 Nguyen Dinh Chieu. The best Western food on the strip, with a range of great burgers (around 140,000VND) – have them stuffed with mushroom and mozzarella, or beetroot, egg and cheese. At 5.30pm they turn on the barbecue, and the resultant grills are rather slurp-worthy. Beach-side seating, too. Daily noon–11pm.

La Casa del Latino 117 Nguyen Dinh Chieu. A neat addition to Mui Ne's culinary scene – Mexican cuisine including breakfast burritos and tasty quesadillas (100,000VND). Eat them by the pool with a passion-fruit mojito (40,000VND). Daily 8am–11pm.

★ **Lam Tong** 92 Nguyen Dinh Chieu. Great-value fresh seafood and other local specialities served on a simple, extremely popular open-air terrace right on the beach. Try the fried fish with lemon grass and chilli (70,000VND) or their flavourful take on *pho bo*, with tiny peppery meatballs (29,000VND). Daily 7.30am–10pm.

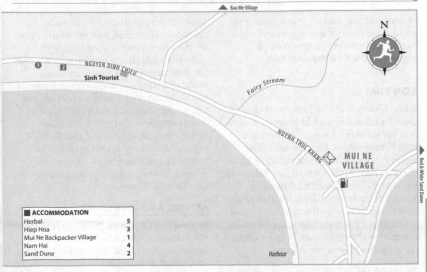

ACCOMMODATION

Herbal	5
Hiep Hoa	3
Mui Ne Backpacker Village	1
Nam Hai	4
Sand Dune	2

11

Phat Burgers 253 Nguyen Dinh Chieu. This bright little place serves some of the best burgers in the country; choose from "phat phish", "baby phat" (if not too hungry) or the enormous, 1.25kg "king of Mui Ne" (if ravenous). Burgers 70,000–300,000VND. Daily 11.30am–11pm.

Rung Forest 65 Nguyen Dinh Chieu. Rainforest-themed restaurant decorated with banana leaves, bark, oil lamps and ethnic carvings – an atmospheric setting to enjoy tasty dishes like seafood and rice in a coconut (avoid the endangered snake and turtle) and to listen to regular live Cham music. Mains from 80,000VND. Daily noon–10pm.

DRINKING AND NIGHTLIFE

You'll find several surfy beach-bars along the strip, and monthly full-moon parties are popular – look out for billboards along the road. Many of the town's bars stay open into the early hours of the morning, or until the crowd thins out.

Dragon Beach 120/1 Nguyen Dinh Chieu. The best party-spot in town, with a slew of taxis and bikes picking up and dropping off through the night – it's east of the main strip, but well worth the trip for those in a dancing mood. Daily noon–late.

Jibes 90 Nguyen Dinh Chieu. Casual surfer bar overlooking the beach, with surfboards on the walls, beer from 25,000VND, and a mixed menu of international and Vietnamese offerings. Daily 10am–11pm.

Mui Ne Backpacker Village 137 Nguyen Dinh Chieu ☎ 062 384 7047, ⬤ muinebackpackers.com. This hostel (see opposite) is also a great drinking hole, whether you're staying here or not. They don't so much have a happy hour as an entire happy afternoon and evening, and if you can

find space between downing cocktails, there are pool and ping pong tables, and a slouch space where people zone out watching films. Daily 7am–late.

★**Pogo** 138 Nguyen Dinh Chieu. Popular beach bar with an atmosphere that oscillates between mellow and hectic, depending upon who's in town. It's a lovely place to drain cheap beer or suck on a shisha pipe while squashing sand in between your toes; they often do great all-you-can-drink specials. Daily 8am–2am.

The southern and central highlands

After a hot and sticky stint in the Delta or by the coast, you'll find that the **southern and central highlands**, with their host of ethnic minorities, mist-laden mountains, vast plantations and trickling waterfalls, provide an enjoyable contrast. Many of the highlands' inhabitants are *montagnards* ("mountain folk") from Bahnar, E De, Jarai, Sedang, Koho and Mnong **ethnic minorities**, but visiting their villages independently can be difficult and is best done by basing yourself in the highland towns of **Buon Ma Thuot** and **Kon Tum**. For most tourists, the main target is the former French mountain retreat of **Da Lat**, with its refreshingly cool climate, an abundance of fruit and veg, and its prime setting for motorcycle tours of the region and visits to one of Vietnam's biggest natural treasures – **Cat Tien National Park**.

KON TUM

Some 174km south of Hoi An as the crow flies, southbound Highway 14 runs into the northern limits of diminutive **KON TUM**, a sleepy, friendly town that serves as a springboard for jaunts to its outlying **Bahnar villages**, or as a brief stop en route to Laos. You'll find some of Vietnam's most beautiful Christian places of worship in this far-flung location, and it feels like a place that deserves far more international visitors than it gets – come see what the crowds are missing.

WHAT TO SEE AND DO

Kon Tum's calm air betrays the hardships endured during the American War: a major battle was fought here between the North and South Vietnamese in 1972, which ended in defeat for the South, the soldiers joined by many civilians in the "Convoy of Tears". Going back further in time, a stroll along Nguyen Hue reveals red-tile terraces of shophouses left over from the French era. At the base of Tran Phu stands the grand, whitewashed bulk of Tan Huong Church. Further east is the so-called **Wooden Church**, built by the French in 1913. In the grounds, there's a scale model of a communal house.

Kon Harachot

There are dozens of Bahnar villages encircling Kon Tum, but one of the most accessible is **Kon Harachot**, south of the road linking the two churches. Their impressive high-roofed *rong* (communal house) is among the best in the area, facing a football field often used for all-Bahnar games.

Kon Ko Tu

The most visited village in the area is **Kon Ko Tu**, a relatively timeless community 5km east of town. Follow Tran Hung Dao east until you cross the Dakbla River; turn left at the first crossing after the bridge and continue for 3 to 4km to reach the village.

Many of the dwellings are still made of bamboo and secured with rattan string, but it's the village's immaculate *rong*, with its impossibly tall thatch roof, that commands the most attention. Constructed with wood and bamboo, and without the use of any nails, the *rong* is used for festivals and village meetings, and as a village court at which anyone found guilty of a tribal offence must apologize and ritually kill a pig and a chicken. Tourist agencies (see below) can organize homestays in local villages, as well as day-trips to those further out (from $25/person).

ARRIVAL AND DEPARTURE

By plane There's an airport in Pleiku, a city just 1hr south of Kon Tum by bus, taxi or *xe om*.

Destinations Da Nang (1 daily; 45min); Hanoi (3–4 daily; 1hr 30min); HCMC (4 daily; 1hr).

By bus Kon Tum's bus station is 3km north of the main bridge along Phan Dinh Phung. Take a *xe om* into the centre (around 30,000VND), or if coming from the south, ask the driver to let you off at the bridge over the river, which is far closer to the town centre.

Destinations Buon Ma Thuot (5 daily; 5hr); Da Lat (2 daily at 4.30am & 5.30am; 8hr); Da Nang (15 daily; 4hr); Nha Trang (daily; 9hr).

INFORMATION

Tours The *Eva Café* (see opposite) runs various tours, including a two-day tour combining a jungle trek with a night in a Bahnar village stilt house, and a riverboat trip.

INTO LAOS: BO Y

The easiest option to cross to Attapeu or Pakse in Laos is to take a direct bus across the border, crossing at **Bo Y**, 86km northwest of Kon Tum. There are daily buses; however, companies servicing this route have been in flux for some time, and there's no set pick-up spot in Kon Tum, since all buses start an hour south in Pleiku. It's best to get your accommodation to call for a ticket, and to arrange a pick-up time and place – buses usually pass through Kon Tum daily around 9–10am, hitting Attapeu after 5–7hr depending upon where the lunch stop is (170,000VND), and then continuing on to Pakse (12hr; 330,000VND). One-month Lao visas are available at the border for about $40, depending on your nationality.

ACCOMMODATION AND EATING

Benz's House 53 Nguyen Trai. If you've made it as far as Kon Tum, you'd be forgiven for wanting something a little different in your diet. Step forward this cheery Korean restaurant, serving cheap and passably authentic "Seoul" food such as *bibimbap* (veggies and egg on rice; 29,000VND). You could also give *soju*, Korea's favourite alcohol, a try. Daily 8am–11pm.

★ **Eva Café** 1 Phan Chu Trinh. Designed and built by the owner, this treehouse-like café is a wonderfully relaxed spot to munch on inexpensive local dishes that use locally grown vegetables, and try a speciality drink, such as coffee with whipped egg. Mains from 60,000VND. Daily 10.30am–9pm.

Hoang Van 1a Hoang Van Thu ☎0260 391 7555. Superb value, this guesthouse's lobby gives off the feel of a "real" hotel – a little luxury for no extra cost. Rooms are basic but more than adequate; the cheapest have no windows, but all have small tubs and a TV. Double $14

★ **Konklor** 155 Bac Can ☎0260 386 1555. The bad news first: this hotel is pretty far from the centre, a 25,000VND *xe om* ride to the east (though also walkable with light luggage). The good news is pretty much everything else – it's set in a quiet area by a totally tourist-free Bahnar village (also called Kon Klor), rooms are astonishingly attractive for the price, the grounds are green and pretty, and staff are just lovely. Breakfast extra. Double $16

BUON MA THUOT

In recent years coffee production in the highlands has grown rapidly, making Vietnam the second-largest coffee producer in the world after Brazil. The highland town of **BUON MA THUOT** holds a deserved reputation for the best (and strongest) coffee in Vietnam, and the town boasts many **streetside cafés** serving cups of the syrupy brew. Though the town is not terribly appealing, it makes a good base for visiting Yok Don National Park and the outlying **minority villages** – the province is home to 44 different tribes.

WHAT TO SEE AND DO

The one ethnic minority village you can easily visit from Buon Ma Thuot is the E De village of **Ban Don**. It's very touristy, though you can witness gong performances and participate in drinking rice wine through long bamboo straws from communal jars.

If you need to while away a few hours in town, try the adventurously designed

Ethnographic Museum on Le Duan (entrance 4 Y Ngong; daily 9am–5pm; 20,000VND), with its exhibits about local minority peoples, including a scale model of an E De longhouse, rice-wine jars and instruments for taming elephants.

The Dray Sap and Trinh Nu Falls

The splendid crescent-shaped **Dray Sap Falls** (daily 7am–5pm; 30,000VND) and neighbouring **Dray Nur Falls** lie 30km from Buon Ma Thuot, and can be reached by heading southwest out of town along Chu Jut – rent a scooter, or take the local buses plying the route from Nguyen Tat Thanh near the Victory Monument (hourly; 30,000VND). Almost 15m high and more than 100m wide, the "waterfall of smoke" can be reached by clambering through bamboo groves, across suspension bridges and over rocks to the right of the pool formed by the falls. From here, a 5km walk through the jungle and past a good swimming hole brings you to **Trinh Nu Falls**, smaller than the other two but quite pretty nonetheless. To get there, turn left off the road to Dray Sap at the sign for "Trinh Nu" and continue along a dirt track for about 2km.

Yok Don National Park

The entrance to Vietnam's largest wildlife reserve – the 1155-square-kilometre **Yok Don National Park** (⟨w⟩yokdon nationalpark.vn) – lies 45km west of Buon Ma Thuot. More than sixty species of animals, including tigers, leopards and red wolves, and around two hundred types of birds, from peacocks to hornbills, populate the park, but many are visitor-shy; you're likely to spot some monkeys, though. Four minority villages, populated by the Mnong, Lao and Ede people, are found within the park boundaries; the Mnong are renowned for their skill at capturing wild elephants.

One-day walking tours, overnight safaris, elephant rides (240,000VND/hr) and boat tours down the Serepok River are available, as are longer tours penetrating deeper into the forest. The park is best visited in the dry season (Aug–March) when wildlife is more visible. For

11

enquiries, check the park website, or arrange through a tour operator (see below), who can organize transport and combined day-tours to visit the park and Ban Don. There's also a range of basic **accommodation** available by the park entrance (doubles 200,000VND), and it's possible to stay overnight in the park at the forest stations (basic wooden huts; $5).

Ban Don

The three sub-hamlets that comprise the much-visited village of **BAN DON** lie 2km beyond Yok Don's park headquarters on the bank of the crocodile-infested Serepok River. Khmer, Thai, Lao, Jarai and Mnong live in the vicinity, as do the **E De**, who adhere to a matriarchal social system and build their houses on stilts. As you explore, you may be invited to share tea or rice wine.

Both the Ban Don Tourist Centre (daily 7am–5pm; ☎0262 378 3082), in the centre of the village, and the Yok Don park headquarters can organize an overnight stay in a nearby longhouse ($10).

ARRIVAL AND DEPARTURE

By plane The airport is 8km east of town; a taxi costs around 150,000VND.

Destinations Da Nang (1 daily; 1hr 10min); Hanoi (1 daily; 1hr 40min); HCMC (4 daily; 55min).

By bus Buon Ma Thuot's bus station is 4km north of town at 71 Nguyen Tat Thanh. Regular local buses run to elsewhere in the Highlands, Nha Trang and HCMC. Buses to and from Lak Lake and Dray Sap Falls stop near the Victory Monument in the centre of town.

Destinations Da Lat (4hr); Da Nang (12hr); Kon Tum (5hr); Lak Lake (1hr 30min); HCMC (9hr); Nha Trang (5hr).

INFORMATION

Travel agents Dak Lak Tourist, 51 Ly Thuong Kiet (☎0262 385 8243, ⌨daklaktourist.com.vn), can arrange tours and treks in the surrounding hills and jungles.

Services Agribank is at 37 Phan Boi Chau.

ACCOMMODATION AND EATING

For budget cuisine, try the street kitchens lining the western end of Ly Thuong Kiet; the dish of choice is *com tam* (broken rice served with barbecued pork and an egg).

An Thai Café 18 Hai Ba Trung. Pleasant and popular café, where you can sample the region's finest brew (12,000VND) on a leafy terrace. Daily noon–10pm.

Eden 228 Nguyen Cong Tru ☎0262 384 0055, ⌨edenhotel bmt.com.vn. The town's default Easy Rider base at the time of writing, and as such quite a focus of traveller activity when there's a group staying – the small table outside often groans under the weight of copious beer bottles. Rooms are passable, but service is good. Doubles $18

Nem Viet 24 Ly Thuong Kiet. One of several friendly family-run restaurants on Ly Thuong Kiet serving excellent *nem* (fresh spring rolls) for 35,000VND in bright, acceptably clean surroundings. Daily 8am–10pm.

Ngoc Mai Guesthouse 14b Dien Bien Phu ☎0262 385 3406. The owner at this pleasant, centrally located guesthouse speaks both English and French and is happy to share his knowledge of the area. Rooms come with firm beds and balconies; wi-fi comes and goes. Doubles $9

LAK LAKE AND AROUND

Fifty-two kilometres south of Buon Ma Thuot, Highway 27 passes **Lak Lake**, a beautiful and peaceful spot. Along the lake's shoreline, Emperor Bao Dai's palace, which has been converted into a three-star resort, enjoys a prime vantage point. Beyond this sits **JUN VILLAGE**, a thriving Mnong community, whose impressive longhouses clustered on the shore have remained practically unchanged, although numerous tourists detract slightly from the tableau.

Dak Lak Tourist (see above) has one branch by the lake and one inside the village gate, both of which organize homestays with a family at a Jun longhouse in the village ($12), gong shows and rice-wine feasts ($60/group), guided treks or elephant rides around the lake ($30/hr for two).

On the southwestern shore is a Mnong village, which can be reachable by boat or by elephant; consult Dak Lak Tourist.

ARRIVAL AND DEPARTURE

By xe om and bus It's possible to get to Lak Lake independently by *xe om* from Buon Ma Thuot (around 220,000VND for a day-trip), and there are hourly buses.

On a tour Lak Lake is part of many Easy Rider (see p.900) tours of the region.

DA LAT AND AROUND

Standing at an elevation of around 1500m, the city of **DA LAT** is Vietnam's premier hill station, an amalgam of maze-like streets and picturesque churches, and French colonial buildings spliced with less appealing new constructions – all arranged around a pretty lake fringed with sculpted parkland. In 1897, the governor-general of Indochina ordered the founding of a convalescent hill station here, where Saigon's hot-under-the-collar *colons* could recharge their batteries. By tacit agreement during the American War, both Hanoi and Saigon refrained from bombing the city; many of the old buildings remain.

WHAT TO SEE AND DO

Da Lat's major attractions can all easily be seen in one day by bicycle. **Day-trips** to outlying attractions, best seen on the back of a *xe om* with a good guide (see p.900), usually take in a minority village, silk-worm hamlet and factory, Lien Khuong and Prenn waterfalls, a rice-wine factory and a cut-flower farm. It's well worth making Da Lat your base for an extra day to do a motorbike tour to **Cat Tien National Park** – great for hiking, birdwatching and mountain biking.

Hang Nga's Crazy House
One of Vietnam's more unusual attractions, **Hang Nga's Crazy House** (3 Huynh Thuc Khang; daily 8.30am–7pm; 40,000VND) is the brainchild of a local architect – Mra Dang Viet Nga, the daughter of Ho Chi Minh's right-hand man, who studied architecture in Soviet Moscow. Not that that's evident in her creation – a bizarre, Gaudí-meets-*Lord-of-the-Rings* construction of intertwining buildings joined by seemingly organic, tangled walkways and drowning in bougainvillea, with the gingerbread cottage in the little garden peeking from behind giant cobwebs and oversized mushrooms.

Lake Xuan Huong and Ga Da Lat
Cycling or walking the 7km path around **Lake Xuan Huong** is a pleasant pastime, and takes in Da Lat's **flower gardens** (daily 7.30am–5pm; 30,000VND) to the north. From there you have the option of striking east to **Ga Da Lat**, the city's Art

Deco train station off Quang Trung, built in 1938. A tourist train runs along the restored section of the cog railway (5 daily, according to demand; 30min; 124,000VND return) to the village of **Trai Mat**, 7km away. The train idles for thirty minutes – time enough to take a look at **Linh Phuoc Pagoda** – before returning to Da Lat. Back at the southwest corner of the lake on Tran Phu, Da Lat's charming pink Venetian-style **cathedral**, completed in 1942, is dedicated to St Nicholas, protector of the poor.

Dinh III
On a wooded hillock just off Le Hong Phong sits the oddly shaped **Dinh III** (daily 7am–5pm; 20,000VND), erstwhile summer palace of Emperor Bao Dai, erected between 1933 and 1938 to provide him with a bolt hole between elephant-slaughtering sessions. The palace has nautical portholes punched into its walls and a mast-like pole sprouting from its roof, giving it the distinct look of a ship's bridge. Inside, you have the chance to peek into the emperor's working room, festivities room and imperial bedrooms, which are surprisingly modest.

Waterfalls
There are several waterfalls located around Da Lat, most of which are modest cascades but nevertheless make for a pleasant stop. The closest one is **Datanla Falls** (20,000VND), 7km south of Da Lat, off Highway 20, just past the turn-off to Tuyen Lam Lake; nearby you'll also be able to ride an odd go-kart-like rail through the trees (50,000VND). The impressive **Elephant Falls**, 30km west of Da Lat, are best admired from below after you scramble up the hazardous path to the base of the falls.

ARRIVAL AND DEPARTURE

By plane Lien Khuong Airport is 29km south of the city, off the road to HCMC. Shuttle buses (45,000VND) run from here to the *Ngoc Phat* hotel, off the southern flank of the lake, 2hr before scheduled flights; a transfer to your hotel is often provided, and for the return journey, your accommodation may be able to organize a free pick-up service. Alternatively, a taxi or *xe om* will cost about 340,000VND or 240,000VND, respectively.

11

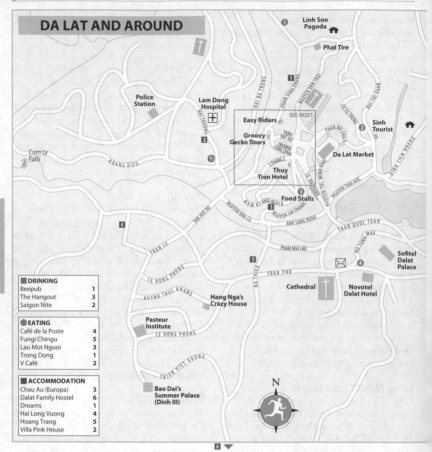

DA LAT AND AROUND

DRINKING
Beepub	1
The Hangout	3
Saigon Nite	2

EATING
Café de la Poste	4
Fungi Chingu	5
Lau Mot Nguoi	3
Trong Dong	1
V Café	2

ACCOMMODATION
Chau Au (Europa)	3
Dalat Family Hostel	6
Dreams	1
Hai Long Vuong	4
Hoang Trang	5
Villa Pink House	2

Destinations Da Nang (5 weekly; 1hr 15min); Hanoi (6 daily; 1hr 45min); HCMC (5–6 daily; 50min).

By bus Buses arrive at Da Lat's long-distance bus station, about 2km south of the centre, and most public buses leave early in the morning from here. Open-tour buses will drop you off at their respective offices. You can buy tickets for daily open-tour bus departures to HCMC, Mui Ne and Nha Trang from Sinh Tourist inside the *Trung Cang Hotel* at 4a Bui Thi Xuan (☎0263 382 2663, ⓦthesinhtourist.vn) or most hotels.

Destinations Buon Ma Thuot (5hr); HCMC (7hr); Hoi An (16hr); Mui Ne (5hr); Nha Trang (4hr).

INFORMATION AND TOURS

Motorbike tours *Xe om* drivers charge $20–25 for a day-long tour to local pagodas, waterfalls and ethnic villages. If they don't find you first, look for the Easy Riders (70 Phan Dinh Phung; ⓦdalat-easyrider.com), a group of war veterans who have been conducting highly rated tours of the area for the past twenty years. English-, French- and German-speaking guides are available, and their local knowledge is unrivalled. Each Easy Rider carries identification and wears a black-and-blue jacket to distinguish them from the many impersonators in town, but membership is not as exclusive as it once was and some say standards have dropped. Many other *xe om* drivers are decent too – discuss your itinerary before you set off to ensure that your guide is knowledgeable and speaks good English. Trips through the Central Highlands, ending up in Hoi An, HCMC, Nha Trang, Mui Ne or even Hanoi, are all possible (approx. $70/day, including accommodation).

Activities Phat Tire Ventures, 109 Nguyen Van Troi (☎0263 382 9422, ⓦphattireventures.com), and Groovy Gecko Tours, 65 Trong Cong Dinh (☎0263 383 6521, ⓦgroovygeckotours.net), both organize recommended adventure trips including hiking, mountain biking, climbing and canyoning; prices start at $30 for a day's hike to $170 for a two-day all-included off-road mountain-bike trip.

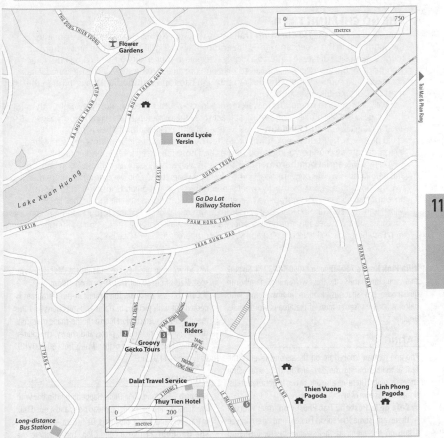

▼ Highway 20, Airport (29km), Datanla Falls & Lake Tuyen Lam

ACCOMMODATION

Check that your accommodation has hot water and heating – necessities in Da Lat during the colder months.

Chau Au (Europa) 76 Nguyen Chi Thanh ☎ 0263 382 2870. Popular, well-run mid-range hotel, with an English- and French-speaking owner. Rooms are simply decorated but homey and clean; some come with balconies ($20). Doubles $15

★ **Dalat Family Hostel** 19a Trieu Viet Vuong ☎ 0263 360 8086. The most popular hostel of the many dotted around town – largely thanks to owners who try to ramp up the party aspect with drinking games and the like. Rooms are comfy, and even the dorms and the private rooms are something of a steal. It's a little way south of the centre, though staff run free walking tours around town most days. Dorms $5, doubles $12

★ **Dreams** 151 Phan Dinh Phung ☎ 0263 383 3748, ⓦ dreamshoteldalat.com. Mini-hotel with well-equipped and spotlessly clean en-suite rooms, all with massaging power-showers and some with jacuzzi bathtubs. Generous free breakfasts (complete with Marmite, peanut butter and fresh passion fruit juice) and friendly staff have made it a hit with travellers – and that's without mentioning the sauna, steam room and communal jacuzzi on the rooftop. They also have another location down the road, with slightly larger rooms. Doubles $25

★ **Hai Long Vuong** Log 6, Tran Le ☎ 090 986 2901, ⓔ phuonghanhhotel@gmail.com. The friendliest guesthouse in town, a 10min walk from the centre. The English-speaking owner is always on hand to advise and most rooms have great views over Da Lat. Doubles $18

Hoang Trang 5/3 Ba Trieu ☎ 0987 639053. Also known as the *Happy Hostel*, this is another excellent option, though only with private rooms and no dorms. Still, it's cheap as chips, especially if you're travelling as a pair; they're also great at arranging tours and giving general travel advice. Doubles $12

11

THE HO CHI MINH TRAIL

Conceived in 1959, the **Ho Chi Minh Trail** was a vital supply route from North Vietnam into the South during the American War. By the end of its "working" life the trail had grown from a rough assemblage of jungle paths to a highly effective logistical network stretching from near Vinh, north of the Seventeenth Parallel, to Tay Ninh province on the edge of the Mekong Delta. For much of its southerly route the trail ran through **Laos** and **Cambodia**, always through the most difficult, mountainous terrain.

Initially, it took up to six months to walk from north to south, travelling mostly by night, but by 1975, the Ho Chi Minh Trail – comprising at least three main arteries plus several feeder roads and totalling more than **15,000km** – was wide enough to take tanks and heavy trucks, and could be driven in just one week. It was protected by anti-aircraft emplacements and supported by fuel depots, ammunition dumps, food stores and hospitals, often located underground.

By early 1965, **aerial bombardment** by American planes had begun in earnest, using napalm and defoliants as well as conventional bombs. In eight years the US Air Force dropped more than two million tonnes of bombs, mostly over Laos and the Central Highlands, in an effort to cut the flow. But the trail was never completely severed, and you can ride parts of it today. The Ho Chi Minh Highway is a stunning road that runs from south of Hanoi and passes through some of the country's most picturesque mountain scenery along the way. Motorbike tours can be arranged with Easy Riders in Da Lat (see p.900) and several companies in Hanoi (see p.850).

Villa Pink House 7 Hai Thuong ⊙ 090 588 3224. So pink that you can't miss it, this welcoming, family-run guesthouse has spacious, modern rooms, some with balcony. Mr Rot's "secret tour" of the area is worthwhile. Doubles $18

EATING

Pho and *com* are cooked up on the second level of the central market during the day, and in the surrounding streets at night. There are also one or two vegetarian stalls, signposted as *com chay*.

★ **Café de la Poste** 12 Tran Phu. Go on, treat yourself – there are some cheapish French and Vietnamese dishes on the menu at this swanky bistro, including afternoon tea for a knockdown 90,000VND. You can't miss the large display of affordable cakes and pastries, laid out just in from the entrance, and therefore making it very hard to leave without trying some. Daily 8am–10pm.

Fungi Chingu Nguyen Thi Minh Khai. A great recent addition to Da Lat's culinary scene is this Korean-style barbecue hall – the place is almost always packed at mealtimes, which is no surprise since portions of meat (you do your own grilling at the table) can cost as little as 55,000VND. Daily 11am–2pm & 5–10pm.

Lau Mot Nguoi 16b Nguyen Chi Thanh. You'll see "Single Hot Pot" on the sign, and that's just what you'll get (59,000VND) – a broth for one (various flavours available; best is the Thai lemongrass), which can be a real treat if you've turned up in Da Lat on a chilly evening, and only have flip-flops and a T-shirt for warmth. Daily 8am–10pm.

★ **Trong Dong** 220 Phan Dinh Phung. Feast on eel and rabbit dishes – this restaurant's specialities – as well as

less adventurous noodles, rice and soups at this bistro-type spot. Mains from 60,000VND. Daily noon–10pm.

V Café 1/1 Bui Thi Xuan. This American-run restaurant is decked out with pictures of trains and musicians and the menu features such comfort food as home-made macaroni cheese, spinach cannelloni, pizza, and chewy, chocolatey brownies. Live music most nights. Mains from 80,000VND. Daily noon–11.30pm.

DRINKING

Beepub 74 Truong Cong Dinh. Happening little bar with live music almost every night, cheap beer, and a good mix of travellers and young, hip locals. Daily 8am–10pm.

The Hangout 71 Truong Cong Dinh. This is where the Easy Rider set hang out – the drivers, the passengers and customers-to-be. Drinks can sometimes taste a little nasty, but it's a fun mingling spot. Daily 8am–10pm.

Saigon Nite 11a/1 Hai Ba Trung. This bar has been here for decades, and is so laidback that one wonders how the place is still in business. Games of pool can be fun – space is so tight that you might need to borrow a chopstick to play certain shots. Daily 3pm–midnight.

DIRECTORY

Banks Vietin Bank, 1 Le Dai Hanh, and Agribank at 36 Hoa Binh. There are plenty of ATMs south of the market, and all around town.

Bike rental Hotels and tourist offices rent bicycles and mountain bikes (from 50,000VND/day).

Hospital Hoan My hospital, south of the centre off Mimosa St (⊙ 0263 357 7633), is by far the best place to be sick in provincial Vietnam.

Pharmacy 34 Khu Hoa Binh.

Post office 14 Tran Phu.

Ho Chi Minh City

Above the Mekong Delta, some 40km north of the South China Sea, **HO CHI MINH CITY** (**HCMC**, also known as **Saigon**) is Vietnam at its frenetic best, with the city's colonial villas and elegant pagodas sitting alongside glitzy malls, stylish restaurants and towering skyscrapers, and never-ceasing ribbons of crazy traffic lubricating the city's veins. Perched on the west bank of the Saigon River, HCMC has gone through many changes – serving first as the capital of French Indochina as Saigon, and then as the capital of the Republic of Vietnam before it fell to the northern Vietnamese forces in 1975. It was renamed Ho Chi Minh City in 1976, a year after the communists rolled through the gates of the Presidential Palace and took control of the city, but the evocative old name lives on.

WHAT TO SEE AND DO

Ho Chi Minh City is divided into eighteen districts, though tourists rarely travel beyond districts 1, 3 and 5. The city hugs the west bank of the Saigon River, and its central area, District 1, nestles in the hinge formed by the confluence of the river with the silty Ben Nghe Channel; traditionally the French Quarter of the city, this area is still widely known as **Saigon**. Dong Khoi is its backbone, and around the T-shape it forms with Le Duan are scattered most of the city's museums and colonial remnants. Except for **Cho Lon**, HCMC's frenetic Chinatown, the city doesn't carve up into homogeneous districts, so visitors have to do a dot-to-dot between sights. These are almost invariably places that relate to the American War, but there are some religious sights too, most notably the **Jade Emperor Pagoda**.

The Ho Chi Minh City Museum

Of all the stones of empire thrown up in Vietnam by the French during their rule, few are more eye-catching than the former **Gia Long Palace**, 65 Ly Tu Trong, built in 1886. Ngo Dinh Diem – the president of the Republic of South Vietnam – decamped here in 1962, and it was in the

tunnels under the building that he spent his last hours of office, before fleeing to the church in Cho Lon, and meeting his death nearby. It houses the **Ho Chi Minh City Museum** (daily 8am–5pm; 15,000VND; ⊛hcmc-museum.edu.vn), which traces the history of the city. The ground floor focuses on archeology and the environment, and there's also a gallery dedicated to HCMC's ethnic communities. Displays devoted to anti-French and anti-American resistance in the twentieth century take up all of the upstairs section.

The Reunification Palace

A red flag billows proudly above the **Reunification Palace** (135 Nam Ky Khoi Nghia; daily 7.30am–noon & 1.30–5pm; 40,000VND), which occupies the site of the Norodom Palace, a colonial mansion erected in 1871 to house the governor-general of Indochina. With the French departure in 1954, Ngo Dinh Diem commandeered this extravagant monument as his presidential palace, but after the February 1962 assassination attempt by his own air force, it was pulled down. The palace, known as Independence Palace, was reconstructed in 1966, and remained the home and office of the president. On April 30, 1975, a North Vietnamese tank stormed the gates, an act that became the defining moment in the fall of Saigon; it was then renamed Reunification Hall. A replica of the tank stands just inside the entrance and serves as an imposing reminder of the victory. Spookily unchanged from its working days, much of the building's interior is a time capsule of 1960s and 1970s kitsch. Most interesting is the third floor, with its presidential library, projection room and entertainment lounge, as well as rooftop nightclub and helipad. The basement served as the former command centre and displays archaic radio equipment and vast, strategic wall maps; here you can watch a video about the palace's history.

The War Remnants Museum

The **War Remnants Museum** at 28 Vo Van Tan (daily 7.30am–noon & 1.30–5pm; 15,000VND) is the city's most significant

11

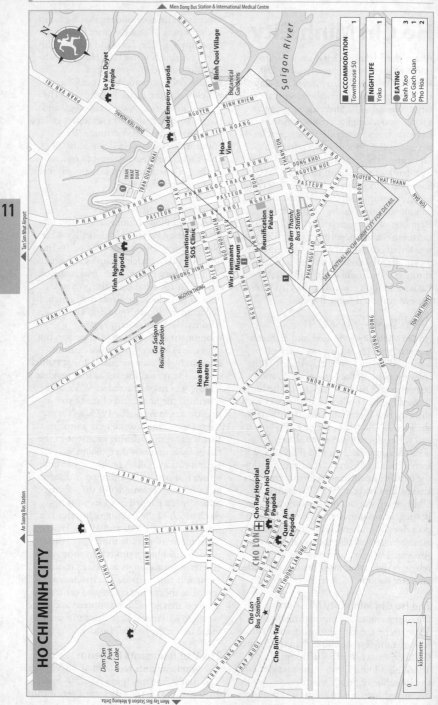

HO CHI MINH CITY

Mien Dong Bus Station & International Medical Centre

Saigon River

ACCOMMODATION	
Townhouse 50	1

NIGHTLIFE	
Yoko	1

EATING	
Banh Xeo	3
Cuc Gach Quan	1
Pho Hoa	2

Le Van Duyet Temple

Binh Quoi Village

Jade Emperor Pagoda

Botanical Gardens

Binh Khiem

Nguyen

Dinh Tien Hoang

Hoa Vien

Hai Ba Trung

Phan Dinh Phung

Pasteur

Dong Khoi

Nguyen Hue

Pasteur

Vinh Nghiem Pagoda

International SOS Clinic

War Remnants Museum

Reunification Palace

Cho Ben Thanh / Bus Station

SEE CENTRAL HO CHI MINH CITY FOR DETAIL

Le Van Sy

Nguyen Van Troi

Truong Dinh

Nguyen Thong

Ga Saigon Railway Station

Cach Mang Thang Tam

Hoa Binh Theatre

3 Thang 2

Ly That To

Cho Ray Hospital

Phuoc An Hoi Quan Pagoda

Quan Am Pagoda

CHO LON

Le Dai Hanh

Cho Lon Bus Station

Cho Binh Tay

Dam Sen Park and Lake

Tan Son Nhat Airport

An Suong Bus Station

Mien Tay Bus Station & Mekong Delta

0	1
	kilometre

11

museum and one that relentlessly drives home the message that war is brutal and ultimately it's the civilians who suffer terribly. In Vietnam's case, out of its three million dead, two thirds were non-combatants. A series of halls presents a hard-hitting portfolio of photographs of mutilation, napalm burns, torture and massacres. One gallery details the effects of the 75 million litres of defoliant sprays dumped across the country; another displays photographs of victims of Agent Orange; another still looks at international opposition to the war as well as the American peace movement. There's also a moving exhibition of children's artwork and an excellent display of war photographs taken by the countless photojournalists who lost their lives working during the French and American wars. On display in the courtyard outside are a 28-tonne howitzer, a ghoulish collection of bomb parts and a renovated Douglas Skyraider plane. The museum rounds off with a grisly mock-up of the "tiger cages", the prison cells of Con Son Island in which Viet Cong prisoners were held.

The History Museum

An attractive, pagoda-style roof crowns the city's **History Museum** (Tues–Sun 8–11am & 1.30–4.30pm; 15,000VND), whose main entrance is tucked just inside the gateway to the Botanical Gardens. To visit the museum only, use the side entrance at 2 Nguyen Binh Khiem. The museum houses a series of galleries illuminating Vietnam's past from the rise of the Bronze Age Dong Son civilization, followed by the Funan civilization, then the Cham, the Khmer and the Vietnamese, through to the end of French rule by means of a thorough collection of artefacts and pictures.

Jade Emperor Pagoda

The spectacular **Jade Emperor Pagoda**, 73 Mai Thi Lu (daily 7am–6pm; free), was built by the city's Cantonese community in around 1900. It captivates with its exquisite panels of carved gilt woodwork and a panoply of Taoist and Buddhist deities beneath a roof that groans under the weight of dragons, birds and animals. Inside, a statue of the Jade Emperor lords it over the main hall's central altar, amid clouds of joss-stick smoke, monitoring entry into Heaven, and his two keepers – one holding a lamp to light the way for the virtuous, the other wielding an ominous-looking axe – are on hand to aid him. To the right of the main hall, a rickety flight of steps runs up to a balcony, behind which is set a neon-haloed statue of Quan Am, a female saint in Buddhist tradition, known as Quan Yin in Chinese. Left out of the main hall stands Kim Hua, to whom women pray for children, and in the larger chamber behind you'll find the Chief of Hell alongside ten dark-wood reliefs depicting all sorts of punishments awaiting evil people in the Ten Regions of Hell. If you're lucky, you may spot black-clad acolytes playing xylophones.

Cho Lon

The dense cluster of streets comprising the Chinese ghetto of **Cho Lon** is linked to the city centre by 5km-long Tran Hung Dao and best reached by cyclo or a bus to Huynh Thoai Yen, on Cho Lon's western border. The full-tilt mercantile mania here is breathtaking, and from its beehive of stores, goods spill exuberantly out onto the pavements. If any one place epitomizes Cho Lon's vibrant commercialism, it's **Cho Binh Tay** on Thap Muoi Binh Tay, near the bus terminus – under reconstruction at the time of writing, but soon to be abuzz once more with stalls offering everything from dried fish and chilli paste to pottery and bonnets.

Quan Am Pagoda, on tiny Lao Tu, has ridged roofs encrusted with "glove-puppet" figurines and gilt panels at the doorway depicting scenes from traditional Chinese court life. Nearby at 184 Hung Vuong is **Phuoc An Hoi Quan Temple**, which has menacing dragons and sea monsters on its roof, and a superb woodcarving of jousters and minstrels over the entrance.

ARRIVAL AND DEPARTURE

By plane Tan Son Nhat Airport (ⓦ tsnairport .hochiminhcity.gov.vn) is 7km northwest of the centre. There are several currency exchange counters as you exit

11

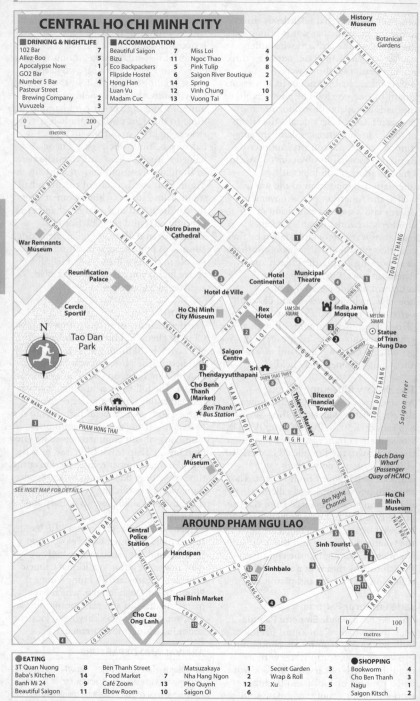

CENTRAL HO CHI MINH CITY

DRINKING & NIGHTLIFE

102 Bar	7
Allez-Boo	5
Apocalypse Now	1
GO2 Bar	6
Number 5 Bar	4
Pasteur Street Brewing Company	2
Vuvuzela	3

ACCOMMODATION

Beautiful Saigon	7	Miss Loi	4
Bizu	11	Ngoc Thao	9
Eco Backpackers	5	Pink Tulip	8
Flipside Hostel	6	Saigon River Boutique	2
Hong Han	14	Spring	1
Luan Vu	12	Vinh Chung	10
Madam Cuc	13	Vuong Tai	3

0 ——— 200
metres

Labels on map

History Museum
Botanical Gardens
War Remnants Museum
Notre Dame Cathedral
Reunification Palace
Cercle Sportif
Tao Dan Park
Ho Chi Minh City Museum
Hotel de Ville
Hotel Continental
Municipal Theatre
Rex Hotel
LAM SON SQUARE
India Jamia Mosque
MEI LINH SQUARE
Statue of Tran Hung Dao
Saigon Centre
Sri Thendayyutthapani
Cho Benh Thanh (Market)
Sri Mariamman
Ben Thanh Bus Station
Bitexco Financial Tower
Thieves' Market
Saigon River
Art Museum
Ben Nghe Channel
Bach Dang Wharf (Passenger Quay of HCMC)
Ho Chi Minh Museum
Central Police Station
Handspan
Sinhbalo
Sinh Tourist
Thai Binh Market
Cho Cau Ong Lanh
SEE INSET MAP FOR DETAILS

AROUND PHAM NGU LAO

EATING

3T Quan Nuong	8	Ben Thanh Street Food Market	7	Matsuzakaya	1	Secret Garden	3
Baba's Kitchen	14			Nha Hang Ngon	2	Wrap & Roll	4
Banh Mi 24	9	Café Zoom	13	Pho Quynh	12	Xu	5
Beautiful Saigon	11	Elbow Room	10	Saigon Oi	6		

SHOPPING

Bookworm	4
Cho Ben Thanh	3
Nagu	1
Saigon Kitsch	2

0 ——— 100
metres

the arrivals hall, and counters where you can purchase local pre-paid SIM cards. ATMs are all over the place, and taxis jostle for position outside both terminals – it's still prudent to go with a reputable firm such as Vinasun or Mai Linh, but almost all outfits are fine, so long as you go to the proper taxi rank, and ignore the touts. It'll be 70,000–130,000VND on the meter, depending on your destination; if you book with the taxi counters inside the arrivals halls, it'll cost more. A cheaper option is to get a *xe om* (50,000–100,000VND) from outside the airport gates; there are also shuttle buses (20,000VND) or old city buses (5000VND) which head into the centre.

Destinations Buon Ma Thuot (3 daily; 1hr); Da Lat (2–3 daily; 50min); Da Nang (1–2 hourly; 1hr 10min); Hanoi (2–3 hourly; 2hr); Hue (1–2 hourly; 1hr 20min); Nha Trang (1–2 hourly; 1hr); Phu Quoc (1–2 hourly; 1hr); Rach Gia (1 daily; 40min).

By bus There are three large intercity bus terminals. Buses for the north (Da Lat, Nha Trang, Buon Ma Thuot) run from Mien Dong bus station, 5km north of the city on Quoc Lo 13. Express buses depart from the east side and local ones from the west. Most buses from the Mekong Delta (My Tho, Can Tho, Chau Doc, Ha Tien, Rach Gia) use Mien Tay bus station, 10km west of the centre. Buses to Cu Chi depart from An Suong bus station in District 12 but are not worth using as there are competitively priced tour buses departing from District 1.

The vast majority of travellers opt for open-tour buses that have scheduled daily departures from budget travel companies in District 1. All stop at the main tourist destinations north of HCMC such as Da Lat, Mui Ne, Nha Trang, Hoi An, Da Nang, Hue and Hanoi.

Destinations Buon Ma Thuot (9hr); Can Tho (4hr); Chau Doc (6–7hr); Da Lat (7hr); Da Nang (21hr); Hanoi (42hr); Ha Tien (8hr); Hue (27hr); Mui Ne (5hr); My Tho (1hr 30min); Nha Trang (10hr); Rach Gia (6hr).

By train The train station, Ga Saigon, is 3km northwest of town at 1 Nguyen Thong in District 3. A *xe om* will take you to or from District 1 for around 40,000VND (10min); a taxi is about 60,000VND. Always book train tickets as far ahead as possible, through a travel agent, online, or in person at counters no. 9–16 on the first floor of the train station (daily 7am–9pm).

Destinations Da Nang (15 daily; 15–20hr); Hanoi (11 daily; 30–41hr); Hue (15 daily; 18–24hr); Nha Trang (15 daily; 6hr 20min–8hr 30min); Phan Thiet (for Mui Ne; 1 daily; 4hr).

GETTING AROUND

Taxis Get your lodgings to call Mai Linh taxis (☎028 3838 3838) or Vinasun taxis (☎028 3827 2727) to avoid dodgy taxis with rigged super-fast meters. Rates should be approximately 15,000VND/km, meaning that it's around 30,000VND for a short ride, up to 75,000VND to somewhere like Cho.

CRIME IN HCMC

HCMC has more than its fair share of people for whom progress hasn't yet translated into food, lodgings and employment, so begging, stealing and prostitution are all facts of life here. **Petty crime** is a fairly regular occurrence and drive-by bag snatching can occur. Keep a tight grip on your belongings while walking the streets, or travelling on cyclos and motorbikes – especially after dark and around tourist nightspots.

Xe om Motorbike taxis (*xe om*) are ubiquitous, with drivers hanging around street corners. Agree on a price before setting off; short hops are around 20,000VND.

Cyclo Cyclos are nowhere as plentiful as they once were and are banned from many streets, having to take circuitous routes as a result. Some drivers were South Vietnamese soldiers and speak fluent English as a result. You should always agree a price before setting off, writing down numbers or holding up the exact number of bills to avoid frequent "misunderstandings". Short hops cost from 30,000VND.

Bike and motorbike rental Most rental places are around Pham Ngu Lao; prices per day average around 60,000VND for a bicycle and 200,000VND for a moped or medium-sized motorbike. Traffic in HCMC is chaotic, and road accidents are common.

INFORMATION AND TOURS

The best sources of information are hotels, tour agencies and travellers' cafés, which also offer open-tour buses, motorbike and car rental, guide services and day-trips; some also do longer tours and visa services.

Listings Several publications carry listings information and travel tips, both online and off: try *Word HCMC* (🌐wordhcmc.com), *Oi* (🌐oivietnam.com) or *Saigoneer* (🌐saigoneer.com). Paper versions are widely available in bars, hotels and backpacker cafés.

Tour agencies Recommended agencies include: Sinh Tourist, 246–248 De Tham (☎028 3838 9593, 🌐thesinhtourist.vn); Sinhbalo, 283/20 Pham Ngu Lao (☎028 3837 6766, 🌐sinhbalo.com); and Handspan, 7th floor, Titan Building, 18 Nam Quoc Cang, District 1 (☎028 3925 7605, 🌐handspan.com).

ACCOMMODATION

HCMC's budget enclave centres are Pham Ngu Lao, Bui Vien and De Tham, 1km west of the city centre. The charming alleyways between Co Giang and Co Bac offer excellent family-run budget options a 10min walk away. The most pleasant area to stay in is around Dong Khoi, though there are few budget establishments here.

PHAM NGU LAO AND AROUND

Beautiful Saigon 62 Bui Vien ☎028 3836 4852; map p.906. Not cheap, but this place may well tempt you to splash out in a most literal sense – it's got a great pool downstairs by the excellent restaurant (see opposite). Rooms are comfy affairs with swish bathrooms; call them up, rather than booking online, and you can sometimes get good discounts. Doubles $43

Bizu 183 De Tham ☎028 3920 8986, ⓦbizuboutiquehotel.com; map p.906. Spotless, spacious, tiled rooms with crisp sheets in a fantastic central location. The receptionists are particularly helpful. Doubles $32

Eco Backpackers 264 De Tham ☎028 3836 5836; map p.906. We're not sure where the "eco" bit comes in, but the individual pods in the dorms give some measure of privacy, the location is as central as can be and the private rooms, though dark, are clean and spacious. Dorms $7, doubles $20

★Flipside Hostel 175/24 Pham Ngu Lao ☎028 3920 5656, ⓦflipsideadventuretravel.com; map p.906. Kiwi-owned hostel which has been a real backpacker hit, thanks to decent dorms, a buzzing atmosphere, great service (if rather pricey tours; compare prices elsewhere), and that hostel holy of holies... a rooftop pool. Dorms $6, doubles $30

Hong Han 238 Bui Vien ☎028 3836 1927, ⓦhonghanhotelhcm.com; map p.906. Huge, well-furnished rooms, a great central location, helpful staff and good view of the city from the top floor are all pros. On the downside, there's no lift. Doubles $30

★Luan Vu 35/2 Bui Vien ☎028 3837 7185; map p.906. Located down an alley away from the traffic, this hotel has pleasantly furnished rooms, awesome breakfasts and helpful staff – the attention to detail places this amiable establishment a cut above the rest. Doubles $22

Madam Cuc 127 Cong Quynh ☎028 3836 8761, ⓦmadamcuchotels.com; map p.906. Hugely popular, this guesthouse and its satellite locations offer a range of comfortable rooms, some sleeping up to four ($35), with satellite TV and fridges, plus free breakfast and airport transfers. Doubles $22

Miss Loi 178/20 Co Giang ☎028 3837 9589, ⓔmissloi@hcm.fpt.vn; map p.906. This charmingly old-fashioned multistorey guesthouse, with a communal dining area complete with colourful statuettes and welcoming staff, is a local institution. However, lack of lift is a disadvantage, and the breakfast is nothing to write home about. Doubles $16

Ngoc Thao 241/4 Pham Ngu Lao ☎028 3837 0273, ⓦngocthaoguesthouse.hostel.com; map p.906. Family-run hotel, offering quiet and smart double, triple and family rooms with all the amenities. The owner, Mr Tuan, runs tours to the Mekong Delta and the staff are friendly and helpful. Dorms $7, doubles $17

Pink Tulip 40/11 Bui Vien ☎028 3837 3567, ⓦpinktuliphotel.com; map p.906. This family-run establishment is just about the cheapest place in town to boast a functional lift – a nice little surprise, as are the pleasantly decorated rooms, amiable staff and excellent breakfasts. Doubles $25

★Townhouse 50 50e Bui Thi Xuan ☎028 3925 0210; map p.904. This is a super little spot, and one that gives off a "flashpacker" ibe. It's a little way north and west of the action at the end of a tiny alley – still within easy walking distance of the bars. On entry you'll be wondering whether you're at the right place, or a fancy café – rows of backpacks betray the clientele, who stay in a series of immaculate dorms and private rooms. Sells out quickly. Dorms $10, doubles $32

★Vinh Chung 283/26 Pham Ngu Lao ☎028 3837 9865, ⓦvinhchunghotel.com; map p.906. The owner of this hotel bends over backwards to accommodate her guests, some rooms come with balcony, some come with cable TV and the beds are a tad softer than the usual hard-as-rock variety. Doubles $20

DONG KHOI AND AROUND

Saigon River Boutique 58 Mac Thi Buoi ☎028 3822 2828, ⓦsaigonriverhotel.com; map p.906. With budget-boutiquey flourishes from top to toe, this is a popular budget spot in pricey Dong Khoi. Rooms are large for the price, and some have balconies; also check out the wonderful rooftop bar area. Doubles $35

★Spring 44–46 Le Thanh Ton ☎028 3829 2738, ⓦspringhotelvietnam.com; map p.906. With its spiral staircase, and Roman-style statuary and columns, this place is the epitome of budget chic; throw in top-quality services, a convenient location and carpeted rooms, and this is a relative Dong Khoi steal. Doubles $45

Vuong Tai 20 Luu Van Lang ☎028 3521 8597, ⓦvuongtaihotel.com; map p.906. Small hotel set on a shoeshop-lined street east of the market – you can't miss its gleaming, gold-coloured lobby. Rooms are less ostentatious, with nice bathrooms; some of the cheaper ones have smaller windows, yet (ironically) better views. Doubles $40

EATING

The culinary capital of Vietnam, HCMC offers everything from fine French cuisine in the Dong Khoi area, to noodle soups and fresh spring rolls at the makeshift street kitchens scattered around the city. Cho Lon has the best Chinese restaurants, and average but reasonably priced backpacker cafés predominate around Pham Ngu Lao. Where phone numbers are given, it's best to book ahead.

PHAM NGU LAO AND AROUND

Baba's Kitchen 164 Bui Vien; map p.906. The best of several Indian options hereabouts, with curries hovering around the 100,000VND mark; pay a little more at lunchtime and you'll get a full thali set. Daily 10.30am–10.30pm.

Beautiful Saigon 62 Bui Vien; map p.906. Eat by the pool at this hotel restaurant – and you can jump in for 100,000VND. The food's surprisingly affordable, too, mostly Vietnamese staples – try the DIY spring rolls (89,000VND). Daily 6am–11pm.

★**Ben Thanh Street Food Market** 26–30 Thu Khoa Huan; map p.906. It was going to take something special to lure backpackers north of their Bui Vien comfort zone, and this place *is* that good – hordes of foreigners and young Vietnamese descend on this covered, market-like venue to have a crack at street food from over twenty stalls. Cheap, tasty and fun, with cheap beer and occasional live music –a superb addition to the HCMC dining scene. Daily 9am–11pm.

Café Zoom 169a De Tham; map p.906. This Vespa and Lambretta hangout is the best café in the area, with cheap Vietnamese coffee (from 25,000VND), plus Western yummies such as sourdough toast and Tex-Mex. Daily 7am–2am.

Pho Quynh 323 Pham Ngu Lao; map p.906. Considering its location in backpacker central, this pho spot gets a large amount of local custom – proof that the noodle soup (65,000VND) is of excellent quality. Daily 7am–11pm.

Wrap & Roll 62 Hai Ba Trung; map p.906. Excellent chain that specializes in different types of rolls (steamed rice with minced pork, mustard lettuce rolls with prawns, fresh and fried spring rolls), as well as hotpots, claypot dishes, salads and noodle dishes, all served in cheerful yellow-and-white surroundings. Mains from 68,000VND. Daily 11.30am–10.30pm.

DONG KHOI AND AROUND

3T Quan Nuong 29–31 Thon That Thiep; map p.906. Convivial rooftop restaurant, where groups of locals, expats and visitors alike barbecue their own seafood, beef, pork and vegetables on individual tabletop grills

STREET FOOD

Informal local eating-houses, makeshift **street kitchens** and market **food stalls** offer the cheapest, most authentic dining experience; those packed with locals are your best bet. At night, the stalls around Ben Thanh Market buzz with life, as locals and foreigners alike tuck into steaming bowls of soup, barbecued meat skewers and delectable seafood dishes. If you'd like similar food but in slightly more formal surroundings, try *Nha Hang Ngon* (see above), or even the *Ben Thanh Street Food Market* (see above).

★**TREAT YOURSELF**

Xu 75 Hai Ba Trung ☎028 3824 8468, ⓦxusaigon.com; map p.906. Its name meaning "coin", this dark and stylish resto-lounge with impeccable service specializes in Vietnamese fusion. Delight your senses with the likes of dragon-fruit salad with crab, seabass spring rolls, braised pork belly and chicken rice and save some room for durian tiramisu. Dinner dishes are designed for sharing. Mains from 200,000VND. Daily 11.30am–2.30pm & 6.30–11pm.

(120,000–180,000VND/person). Round off your meal with a sundae from *Fanny* on the ground floor. Daily 5–11pm.

Banh Mi 24 31 Hai Trieu; map p.906. Tiny place serving novel takes on the humble *banh mi*, all freshly made to order, with a heated bun to boot – try the beef Philly cheese one for 22,000VND. Daily 6am–10pm.

Elbow Room 52 Pasteur; map p.906. Elbow room can be difficult to find at this popular American-style bistro, serving ample breakfasts of pancakes, bacon, eggs and more. If you're homesick, the giant burritos, hot dogs, pizza and burgers may dull your pain. Mains from 120,000VND. Mon–Sat 8am–10pm, to 5pm Sun.

Matsuzakaya 17/34a Te Thanh Ton; map p.906. A little secret largely kept to the local Japanese expat community – cheap, authentic ramen and curry-rice served at rock-bottom prices, down an atmospheric alley. Daily 11am–10pm.

★**Nha Hang Ngon** 160 Pasteur; map p.906. For street food in refined surroundings, this is the perfect place to sample local specialities; pick and choose your dishes from the dozens of food stalls scattered through the leafy courtyard of this lovely old colonial villa, and they'll be delivered to your table; alternatively, you can order off the extensive menu. Mains 75,000–100,000VND. Daily 7.30am–10.30pm.

Saigon Oi 42 Nguyen Hue; map p.906. The best of the many, many trendy cafés to have sprung up in this gentrified residential block, filled with stylish young locals from morning to night. Try a coffee (45,000VND) or flavoured yoghurt (35,000VND) and soak up views that are even more spectacular at sunset. Daily 7am–9pm.

Secret Garden 158 Pasteur; map p.906. Secret indeed – this surprisingly stylish place is located on the rooftop of an elevator-less building, down a hard-to-spot alley filled with motorbikes. The menu is filled with fantastic Vietnamese home-cooking, and most mains are just 75,000VND, though regular (genuine) cock-a-doodle-doos may dissuade you from ordering chicken. Daily 8am–10pm.

11

NORTH OF THE CENTRE

Banh Xeo 46a Dinh Cong Trang; map p.904. Enormous, cheap and filling *banh xeo* (Vietnamese pancakes) stuffed with shrimp, pork, beans and egg for around 75,000VND are the speciality at this streetside place off Hai Ba Trung. Daily 10am–9pm.

★**Cuc Gach Quan** 10 Dang Tat ⓦ cucgachquan.com; map p.904. The food at this French colonial house is beautiful Vietnamese, with an emphasis on local and organic ingredients and eco-friendly practices. Try sea bass in passion-fruit sauce, aubergine sautéed with pork, lotus-shoot salad or clams steamed with lemongrass, and don't run off without trying the home-made durian or black-bean ice cream. Mains from 80,000VND. Daily noon–10.30pm.

★**Pho Hoa** 260c Pasteur; map p.904. Heaving with locals, this restaurant serves up generous portions of pho (65,000VND) with bigger-than-usual slices of beef or chicken, and piles of fresh greens – it's by far the best you'll find in HCMC. Daily 7am–10pm.

DRINKING AND NIGHTLIFE

The area around Pham Ngu Lao is lined with lively, cheap bars, while Dong Khoi and around plays host to most of the city's nightclubs, which shut in the early hours of the morning; take care of your bag when leaving, and be aware that quite a few bars have upfront prostitution.

★**102 Bar** 102 Bui Vien; map p.906. For many backpackers, this is *the* abiding memory of HCMC – sitting on a tiny plastic chair outside this shop pretending to be a bar, with motorbikes zooming way too close, and a bottle of 15,000VND beer in hand. Daily 5pm–late.

Allez-Boo 187 Pham Ngu Lao; map p.906. Pham Ngu Lao's busiest bar, popular for its classic tunes, Thai food and selection of cocktails; there's seating on the street outside and backpackers show what they're made of on the dancefloor upstairs. Daily 7am–late.

Apocalypse Now 2c Thi Sach; map p.906. One of the original Saigon nightspots, attracting travellers, locals and expats (and a few working girls) with its party atmosphere and eclectic mix of music. Always heaving and apocalyptically busy at weekends. Daily 9pm–late.

GO2 Bar 187 De Tham; map p.906. Fabulously cheesy backpacker hangout, with Vietnamese and Western snacks served late into the night in the neon-lit downstairs bar to a soundtrack of classic pop tunes. The upstairs dancefloor hosts a nightly DJ and you can chill out with a hookah on the roof terrace. Open 24hr.

Number 5 Bar 44 Pasteur; map p.906. When is 130,000VND for a beer a good deal? When it's free-flowing for four hours, that's when – swing by between 3 and 7pm and you can drink as much San Miguel as you like. Daily 3pm–midnight.

★**Pasteur Street Brewing Company** 67 Pasteur; map p.906. The best of the many new microbreweries in town, with creations including beer flavoured with jasmine, passion fruit, jackfruit and other local ingredients. Daily 11am–11pm.

Vuvuzela 54 Nguyen Trai; map p.906. One of nine branches (and counting), this bar atop Zen Plaza has commanding views from its outdoor seats, and the beer isn't all that pricey (from 37,000VND). It may be a bit weird to say this, but guys… you'll love the views from the urinals. Daily 10am–midnight.

Yoko 22a Nguyen Thi Dieu; map p.904. Leave the backpackers behind and join Saigon's student population to see local rock bands perform – there's a pleasing variety to the music roster (nightly from 9pm), and they've Pasteur craft beer (see above) on tap. Daily 8am–midnight.

TRADITIONAL ENTERTAINMENT

Hoa Binh Theatre 3 Thang 2 ☎028 3865 3353, ⓦ nhahathoabinh.com.vn. Regular performances of modern and traditional Vietnamese music, as well as traditional theatre and dance.

Saigon Water Puppet Theatre History Museum, Nguyen Binh Khiem. This very Vietnamese form of entertainment is way more fun than Punch and Judy, with the watery stage adding a measure of magic to the show performed with beautifully carved wooden puppets (daily at 9am, 10am, 11am, noon, 2pm, 3pm and 4pm; 20min; 100,000VND).

SHOPPING

Galleries specializing in replicas of famous originals abound in HCMC, especially along De Tham and Nguyen Hue.

Bookworm 4 Do Quang Dao; map p.906. Has a decent selection of secondhand books, in a variety of languages. Daily 7am–10pm.

Cho Ben Thanh Junction of Tran Hung Dao, Le Loi and Ham Nghi; map p.906. The city's biggest market, with everything from conical hats, basket-ware bags, Da Lat coffee and Vietnam T-shirts to buckets of eels and pigs' ears and snouts. Daily sunrise–sunset.

Nagu 155 Dong Khoi; map p.906. Sells small teddies made from traditionally patterned fabric, sporting dinky conical hats – fantastic presents, and yours from 220,000VND. Daily 9am–10pm.

Saigon Kitsch 43 Mac Thi Buoi; map p.906. Humorous souvenirs including Mr Binh and iPho T-shirts, cups and the like. Daily 8am–9pm.

DIRECTORY

Banks and exchange ATMs are everywhere. For banks, try ANZ, 11 Me Linh Square; HSBC, 235 Dong Khoi; or Vietcombank, 29 Chuong Duong. You can exchange money at most hotels, but you'll get better rates at the exchange bureaux dotted around the city.

Embassies and consulates Australia, Landmark Building, 5b Ton Duc Thanh (☎ 028 3521 8100); Canada, 9th floor, The Metropolitan, 235 Dong Khoi (☎ 028 3827 9899); China, 39 Nguyen Thi Minh Khai (☎ 028 3829 2457); USA, 4 Le Duan (☎ 028 3520 4200).

Hospitals and clinics International SOS Clinic, 65 Nguyen Du (☎ 028 3829 8520; ⓦ internationalsos.com), has a 24hr emergency service, and international doctors who speak English; they also have a dental clinic. International Medical Centre, 1 Han Thuyen (☎ 028 3827 2366, ⓦ cmi-vietnam.com), is a non-profit hospitalization centre staffed by English-speaking French doctors, with a 24hr emergency service and profits subsidizing operations for underprivileged children.

Pharmacies Several around the Pham Ngu Lao area, including at 65 Bui Vien. Also at 156 Pasteur and 105 Nguyen Hue.

DAY-TRIPS FROM HO CHI MINH CITY

The most popular trips out of the city take in two of Vietnam's most memorable sights: the **Cu Chi tunnels**, for twenty years a bolt hole, first for Viet Minh agents, and later for Viet Cong cadres; and the weird and wonderful **Cao Dai Holy See** at Tay Ninh, the fulcrum of the country's most charismatic indigenous religion. Most HCMC travel agents combine these two sights into a day-trip, with tours costing as little as $8 (not including entrance to the tunnels).

The Cu Chi tunnels

During the American War, the villages around the district of Cu Chi supported a substantial Viet Cong (VC) presence. Faced with American attempts to neutralize them, they quite literally dug themselves out of harm's way, and the legendary **Cu Chi tunnels** were the result.

By 1965, 250km of tunnels crisscrossed Cu Chi and the surrounding areas. The tunnels could be as small as 80cm wide and 80cm high, and were sometimes four levels deep; there were latrines, wells, meeting rooms and dorms here, as well as rudimentary hospitals, where operations were carried out by torchlight using instruments fashioned from shards of ordnance. At times inhabitants stayed below ground for weeks on end, and they often had to lie on the floor to get

enough oxygen to breathe. American attempts to flush out the tunnels proved ineffective. They evacuated villagers into strategic hamlets and then used defoliant sprays and bulldozers to rob the VC of cover, in "scorched earth" operations. A special GI unit known as tunnel rats was faced with the task of infiltrating the tunnels themselves, which involved crawling in complete darkness with a partner, facing all manner of booby traps, as well as bombs and fire from the Viet Cong. Some sections of tunnels were deliberately flooded and the casualty rate was very high.

Today, the tunnels have been widened to allow passage for tourists, but it's still a dark, claustrophobic experience, as it's very warm inside the tunnels and you can go down as far as the third level during the 50m stretch of tunnel that visitors are allowed to access. To unwittingly add a touch of authenticity, there are occasional power cuts that leave you briefly in complete darkness. Before entering the tunnel, you are led around by guides in army greens who demonstrate various crude but effective pit traps used by the Viet Cong, as well as a bomb crater and an M-41 tank. There are two sites, Ben Duoc and Ben Dinh, the most popular being **Ben Dinh** (daily 7.30am–4.30pm; 110,000VND), around 50km from HCMC and easiest visited on a tour organized through your lodgings (from $6, not including tickets).

The Cao Dai Holy See

Northwest of Cu Chi at Tay Ninh lies the fantastical confection of styles that is the **Cao Dai Holy See** (24hr; free). The Cao Dai religion was founded in October 1926 as a fusion of oriental and occidental religions. Though its beliefs centre on a universal god and it borrows the structure and terminology of the Catholic Church, Cao Dai is primarily influenced by Buddhism, Taoism and Confucianism, and looks to hasten the evolution of the soul through reincarnation.

The cathedral's central portico is topped by a bowed, first-floor balcony and a Divine Eye, the most recurrent motif in the building. Two figures in semi-relief

11

INTO CAMBODIA: MOC BAI

The main overland entry and exit point between Cambodia and Vietnam for foreigners is at **Moc Bai**, northwest of HCMC. The Moc Bai border is open daily 7am–5pm. Sinh Tourist, Kim Travel (see p.907) and a number of other operators around Pham Ngu Lao run daily a/c buses **to Phnom Penh** from their offices, leaving hourly from 6am–2pm ($12; 6–7hr). Some, such as Mekong Express at 275F Pham Ngu Lao (ⓦ catmekongexpress.com), also have direct daily services to Sihanoukville ($22; 10–11hr) and Siem Reap ($22; 13–14hr). Bus tickets can be bought in advance or on the day. Another option is to sign up with a tour operator for a **share taxi** in Pham Ngu Lao (around $40 for a full car); this will take you as far as the Moc Bai border crossing, from where you can walk over the border into the duty-free shopping zone and negotiate onward transport to Phnom Penh. One-month Cambodian visas are available on the border for $35 including the "processing fee".

11

emerge from either side of the towers: Cao Dai's first female cardinal, Lam Huong Thanh, on the left; and on the right, Le Van Trung, Cao Dai's first pope. Men enter through an entrance in the right wall, women by a door to the left. Tourists can wander through the nave as long as they remain in the aisles and don't stray between the rows of pink pillars, entwined by green dragons. The papal chair stands at the head of the chamber, its arms carved into dragons. Dominating the chamber, and guarded by eight silver dragons, a vast, duck-egg-blue sphere, speckled with stars, rests on a polished, eight-sided dais. **Services** are held daily at 6am, noon, 6pm and midnight, and tours usually arrive in time to catch the noon service. A traditional band plays as robed worshippers chant, pray and sing. Dressing modestly is a must and photographing worshippers without their permission is a no-no; however, it's possible to photograph the colourfully robed adherents from the balconies above.

The Mekong Delta

The orchards, paddy fields and swamplands of the **Mekong Delta** stretch from Ho Chi Minh City's limits southwest to the Gulf of Thailand, crisscrossed by nine channels of the Mekong River – Asia's third-longest river after the Yangtze and Yellow rivers. Here in the delta, not only does the Mekong water "Vietnam's rice bowl", but it also serves as a crucial transportation artery, teeming with rowing boats, sampans, ferries and floating markets.

The most enjoyable way to experience delta life is by boat: most travellers come by tour from HCMC, with boat trips organized for them, taking in laidback **Ben Tre** and the famous floating markets near **Can Tho**. From here, a road runs to the Cambodian border towns of **Chau Doc** and **Ha Tien**; the latter is a gateway to beach resort **Phu Quoc island**, as is the port town of **Rach Gia**.

BEN TRE

The travellers who head into river-locked **Ben Tre province** – nearly all of whom do so as part of organized tours – are rewarded with breathtaking scenery of fruit orchards and coconut groves. **BEN TRE TOWN** itself is a pleasant place, famous for its *keo dua* (coconut candy); stop at a riverside candy workshop to watch the sticky mixture swirled around in a cauldron, then hardened and wrapped in rice paper.

Beyond the buzzing **market** in the centre, the town itself offers little to see. From the channel's more rustic south bank, where scores of boats moor in front of thatch houses, you can explore the maze of dirt tracks and visit the riverside **wine factory**, 450m west of the bridge, where *ruou trang* (rice wine) fizzes away in earthenware jars; bicycles are available for rent at the *Hung Vuong* hotel or at Ben Tre Tourist.

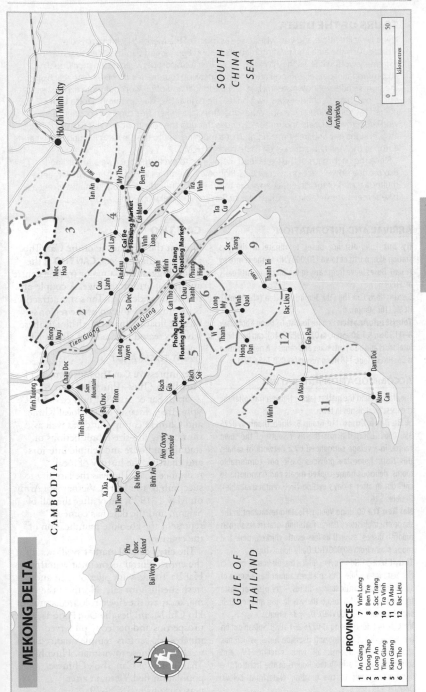

MEKONG DELTA

SOUTH CHINA SEA

Con Dao Archipelago

0   50
kilometres

Ho Chi Minh City

Tan An
My Tho
Ben Tre
Cai Mon
Tra Vinh
Tra Cu

Cai Lay
Cai Be Floating Market
Vinh Long
Moc Hoa
Cao Lanh
An Huu
Binh Minh
Cai Rang Floating Market
Phung Hiep
Soc Trang
Thanh Tri
Sa Dec
Can Tho
Chau Thanh
Hong Ngu
Long Xuyen
Phong Dien Floating Market
Long My
Vinh Quoi
Bac Lieu
Vi Thanh
Gia Rai
Chau Doc
Sam Mountain
Rach Gia
Rach Soi
Hong Dan
Dam Doi
Vinh Xuong
Tinh Bien
Ba Chuc
Tri Ton
U Minh
Ca Mau
Nam Can
Xa Xia
Ba Hon
Binh An
Hon Chong Peninsula

CAMBODIA

Ha Tien

Phu Quoc Island

Bai Vong

GULF OF THAILAND

Tien Giang
Hau Giang

N

PROVINCES

1	An Giang	7 Vinh Long
2	Dong Thap	8 Ben Tre
3	Long An	9 Soc Trang
4	Tien Giang	10 Tra Vinh
5	Kien Giang	11 Ca Mau
6	Can Tho	12 Bac Lieu

11

TOURS OF THE DELTA

If you have little time and you wish to see as much of the Mekong Delta as possible – particularly the area and floating markets around Ben Tre and Can Tho, then tours can be extremely worthwhile, as they provide hassle-free transport between destinations, quality accommodation, excellent food and English-speaking tour guides. It's possible to reach all of the sights under your own steam, but it'll take longer and often work out more expensive, since you'll have to charter your own boats. The regular two-day-one-night **Delta tours** offered by Sinh Tourist and many other operators take in Ben Tre's canals, a coconut candy workshop, rowing boats and motor-cart rides through the countryside, a visit to fruit orchards, an overnight stay and free time in Can Tho, a morning visit to the Cai Rang floating market and a stop at the Vinh Long market en route back to HCMC.

Since the back roads of the Delta lend themselves to **cycling**, it's also very rewarding to explore at a slower pace on two wheels. Sinhbalo Adventures in HCMC (see p.907) organize multi-day tours of the green, sleepy countryside and its friendly villages; alternatively, rent a bike somewhere suitable like Chau Doc or Ben Tre, and make up your own tour.

11

ARRIVAL AND INFORMATION

By bus Long-distance buses terminate at the bus station 4km north of town (30,000VND to the centre by *xe om*). Buses leave from early in the morning until early afternoon.

Destinations Can Tho (1hr 30min); Ha Tien (4hr 30min); HCMC (1hr 30min).

Tourist information Ben Tre Tourist, 65 Dong Khoi (daily 8–11.30am & 1.30–5pm; ☎ 0275 382 9618), can help with local tours and also rents bikes and canoes. A newer option is Din Ho Eco Tour, 148 Hung Vuong (☎ 090 745 6791).

ACCOMMODATION AND EATING

The stalls around the market (along Nguyen Trai) offer the cheapest local dishes in town.

★ **Ba Danh Home** 11d Group 3, Nhon Thanh ☎ 0275 356 0561. Located across the river south of the town centre, in a village surrounded by a network of canals, this rustic homestay provides basic but comfortable rooms, delicious home-cooked meals and hammocks to chill out in after a day's cycling (free rental available). Doubles $16

Noi Ben Tre 60 Hung Vuong. Floating restaurant in the shape of a multistorey barge, featuring local treats such as mudfish dishes, as well as less exotic chicken, pork and soups. Mains from 60,000VND. Daily noon–10pm.

Thuy Pizza 51 Ngo Quyen. A nice treat if you've been in the delta for a while, this small restaurant has a range of surprisingly authentic Italian dishes – try pizza or pasta from just 35,000VND, or go the whole hog and try their superb lasagne (50,000VND). Daily 3–11pm.

Viet Uc 144 Hung Vuong ☎ 0275 251 1888. Splash out on a room at this smart-looking riverside hotel, which has spotlessly clean rooms, all with satellite TV, and sometimes with bathtub too. Rooms at the front of the hotel offer views of the bustling waterfront below. Doubles $25

CAN THO

Sited at the confluence of the Can Tho and Hau Giang rivers, **CAN THO** is the delta's biggest city, a major trading centre and transport interchange. A couple of museums aside, Can Tho's star attraction is its proximity to two of the region's biggest floating markets, although these have decreased markedly in size of late.

WHAT TO SEE AND DO

The impressive **Can Tho Museum**, at 11 Hoa Binh (Tues–Thurs 8–11am & 2–5pm, Sat & Sun 8–11am & 6.30–9pm; free), focuses on the local Khmer and Chinese communities, as well as showcasing life-size reproductions of traditional house and temple interiors and charting the history of local resistance. Can Tho was the last city to succumb to the North Vietnamese Army, on May 1, 1975, a day after the fall of Saigon, and the date has come to represent the absolute reunification of the country.

The city's **central market** swallows up the entire central segment of waterfront Hai Ba Trung, with piles of fruit and fresh shellfish for sale. North of the market, past the silver-coloured statue of Ho Chi Minh, lies the **Ong Pagoda**, a prosperous and perfectly preserved nineteenth-century temple financed by a wealthy Chinese townsman, Huynh An Thai; much of Can Tho's Chinese population fled Vietnam after persecutions in 1978–79.

ARRIVAL AND DEPARTURE

By bus Can Tho's bus station is around 1km from the waterfront. Mai Linh express minibuses to Chau Doc and HCMC depart from here (or ask your hotel to arrange pick-up). Futa Express luxury buses have their own bus station further out of town, though again they will pick up for free if you book a ticket through your accommodation.
Destinations Chau Doc (2hr 30min); Ha Tien (6hr); HCMC (4hr); My Tho (3hr); Rach Gia (3hr).

INFORMATION

Tourist information Can Tho Tourist, 50 Hai Ba Trung (daily 7am–5pm; ☏ 0292 0382 1852, ⊛ canthotourist.vn), give out maps and can arrange boat tours and terrestrial transport.

ACCOMMODATION

Kim Long 9 Chau Van Liem ☏ 0292 389 9909. One of the best deals in the city centre, with plush rooms (all including cable TV, minibar and piping-hot showers), excellent breakfasts, and super views from the top-floor balcony. Doubles $18
★ **Nguyen Shack** 185c Ong Tim, Thanh My ☏ 0292 628 8688, ⊛ nguyenshack.com. It's a little far from the centre, but this is a good thing – this homey place is tucked into a canal-surrounded village, which provides far more of a delta feel than central Can Tho. They arrange all the regular boat tours and rent out bikes, while the rooms are pleasingly rustic – even the dorm has a riverside balcony. Dorms $9, doubles $25
Thao An 1/79 Ly Tu Trong ☏ 093 927 5114. About as cheap as you can get in Can Tho, and not too far of a walk from the city centre, if a little tricky to find on your first visit. The very cheapest rooms have no a/c. Doubles $10

EATING AND DRINKING

For a local dining experience, head to the eastern end of Nam Ky Khoi Nghia, where there are plenty of stalls serving barbecued fish, pork, frog and snake (a local speciality).

★ **L'Escale** 1 Ngo Quyen. Treat yourself to some of the cheaper items on the menu at this colonial-style restaurant, on top of the *Nam Bo* boutique hotel, and boasting superb views over the river. Vietnamese mains are as little as 100,000VND, with French dishes a fair bit more; save room for the delectable crème brûlée (65,000VND). Daily 7am–10pm.
Mekong Restaurant 38 Hai Ba Trung. This established favourite is hard to top for its extensive menu of cheap, flavoursome Vietnamese and international meals; the pork *bun xao* noodles (35,000VND) are recommended, or go for something more fun like a soft-shell taco (35,000VND). Daily 8am–2pm & 4–10pm.
★ **Sao Hom** Off Hai Ba Trung. Munch on snake curry as part of a good-value set menu ("snake menu" 220,000VND), or go for cheaper dishes such as stuffed pumpkin flowers (70,000VND) or tofu with lemongrass and chilli (60,000VND) at this wonderful riverside location. Daily 6am–11pm.
Viva Green 26 Hai Ba Trung. Resembling a cavern for hobbits, this riverfront bar is typically packed; perhaps it's something to do with the two-for-one beer promotion before 6pm. Daily noon–4am.

CHAU DOC

Snuggled against the west bank of the Hau Giang River, next to the Cambodian border (see box, p.916), **CHAU DOC** was under Cambodian rule until the mid-eighteenth century and still sustains a large Khmer community. Forays by Pol Pot's genocidal Khmer Rouge into this corner of the delta led to the Vietnamese invasion of Cambodia in 1978 and put an end to Pol Pot's regime. Today Chau Doc is home to a mix of Khmer, Cham, Vietnamese and Chinese communities, with a cluster of interesting sights to boot.

MEKONG DELTA'S FLOATING MARKETS

Every morning an armada of boats takes to the web of waterways spun across Can Tho province, heading for the famed **floating markets** – these are slowly dying, but for now they still provide unbeatable snapshots of Mekong life. Everything your average villager could need is for sale, from haircuts to coffins, though fruit and vegetables make up the lion's share of the wares. Each boat's produce is identifiable by a sample hanging off a bamboo mast in its bow. Of the major markets in the province, **Cai Rang** (6km from Can Tho) is the busiest and largest, while **Phong Dien** (20km southwest of Can Tho) is visited mostly by traditional rowing boats rather than motorized craft. They are at their best and busiest between 6am and 8am, with customers whizzing around in small boats and docking for supplies at whichever large boat takes their fancy. From Can Tho, tours can be organized through your hotel or at the Can Tho Tourist Office (see above) for $25–50 per boat, depending on the route and the number of people in your group, or else you can negotiate with any of the many touts along the waterfront, where you should pay no more than $15 per boat for a three-hour tour.

WHAT TO SEE AND DO

The town's lively produce **market**, roughly between Quang Trung, Doc Phu Thu, Tran Hung Dao and Nguyen Van Thoi, makes for a good spectacle. A grand, four-tiered gateway deep in the belly of the market announces **Quan Cong Temple**, ornamented with two rooftop dragons and some vivid murals.

River communities

Northwest up Tran Hung Dao, long boardwalks lead to sizeable stilt-house communities, and from here, at the junction with Thuong Dang Le, you can take a ferry across the Hau Giang River to the stilt houses of **Con Tien Island**. Best visited during morning floating-market time (either as part of a tour, or with a self-commandeered boatperson), most houses here have mini fish farms underneath.

Sam Mountain

Arid, brooding **Sam Mountain** rises dramatically from an ocean of paddy fields 5km southwest of Chau Doc, and Buddhist visitors flock here to worship at its clutch of pagodas and shrines. From town, a road runs straight to the foot of the mountain, reached by moto or taxi, or easily covered by bicycle. A winding, bumpy road leads **up the mountain** for 1km in a generally clockwise direction; the turn is on the right, just after a large temple. If you don't fancy walking, motorbikes can take you up for around 25,000VND, or all the way from town for double that. From the summit, you're rewarded with spectacular views of the patchwork of fields below.

ARRIVAL AND DEPARTURE

By boat Boats to/from Phnom Penh dock at a small jetty at the northern end of Tran Hung Dao, 1km from the centre.
By bus Buses offload 2km southeast of town, en route to the bus station on Le Loi, from where *xe om* run into town for about 20,000VND; some buses and minibuses drop off in the centre, on or around Thu Khoa Nghia. Public buses to HCMC depart hourly from the bus station; regular Mai Linh express minibuses to elsewhere in the delta can be booked through your hotel. Futa Express buses offer free minibus drop-off from their bus station to your guesthouse.
Destinations Can Tho (2hr 30min); Ha Tien (3hr); HCMC (hourly; 6–7hr).

INFORMATION

Tourist information Mekong Tours at 14 Nguyen Huu Canh (daily 8am–9pm; ☏ 0296 356 2828) offer half-day trips to a fish farm and Cham village (around $18 for two people) as well as longer trips through the delta, and can assist with onward travel arrangements to Cambodia (see box below).
Services Agribank, 4–5 Quang Trung, has an ATM. *Trung Nguyen Hotel* offers bike rental for 50,000VND/day, and motorbikes for 200,000VND.

ACCOMMODATION

Dong Bao 21 Phan Van Vang ☏ 0296 356 9789. The best budget choice in town, scoring above-average marks for cleanliness (you have to remove your footwear on entering), and also room quality – nice little numbers with cream walls and dark-wood furnishings. The cheapest are windowless, and breakfast costs extra. Doubles **$11**
Murray Guesthouse 11–15 Truong Dinh ☏ 0296 356 2108, ⌨ www.murrayguesthouse.com. A 10min walk

---

INTO CAMBODIA: VINH XUONG AND TINH BIEN

VINH XUONG

Arguably the nicest crossing into Cambodia is the **Vinh Xuong border crossing** (daily 8am–8pm), 30km north of Chau Doc, as it's done by boat. Sinh Tourist in HCMC (p.907) incorporate it into their Exit to Cambodia tour, and you can also take a daily boat with Hang Chau (⌨ hangchautourist.com.vn), departing at 7.30am from a pier at 18 Tran Hung Dao, returning from Phnom Penh at noon (4hr; $25 one-way). Cambodian visas are available at the border for $30, plus a near-obligatory $5 bribe.

TINH BIEN

A less convenient border crossing near Chau Doc is at **Tinh Bien**, 25km west of Sam Mountain. The road from Chau Doc to Tinh Bien is poor, but local buses from Chau Doc make the trip direct to Phnom Penh daily, departing at 7.30am (5hr; $22); tickets can be booked through Mekong Tours (see above).

from the town centre and less from the river, this budget boutique choice comes with spacious a/c rooms, a rooftop relaxation space with pool table, and drinks on an honour system. Onward transport organized. Doubles $\overline{\underline{\$32}}$

Trung Nguyen 86 Bach Dang ⊕ 0296 356 1561. Bustling, conveniently located mini-hotel popular with tour groups. Rooms are modern and spacious, with balconies overlooking the market. Rates include free breakfast, internet and wi-fi. Doubles $\overline{\underline{\$17}}$

EATING AND DRINKING

Stalls at the market offer heaped bowls of pho, fresh spring rolls and other Vietnamese dishes for around 20,000VND. At night, different vendors set up food stalls in the surrounding streets.

★ **Bassac Restaurant** 32 Le Loi. The pleasure of eating at Chau Doc's finest doesn't come cheap, but what a pleasure it is. The stir-fried squid with green peppercorn is superb, and both the Vietnamese and French mains (from 180,000VND) are beautifully executed. Daily 9am–11pm.

Bay Bong 22 Thuong Dang Le. This informal, nondescript-looking place serves a particularly good take on the local speciality of pork or stewed fish cooked in a clay pot (*ca kho to*) for 60,000VND, and chunky, fragrant sweet-and-sour soup, as well as other delta dishes. Daily noon–10pm.

Mekong 41 Le Loi. The brash neon exterior belies the delicacy of the local dishes on offer within. The caramelized fish claypot (70,000VND) hits the spot and there are noodle dishes and more. Daily noon–10pm.

RACH GIA

Teetering precariously over the Gulf of Thailand, **RACH GIA** is a booming farming and fishing community. A small islet in the mouth of the Cai Lon River forms the hub of town, its central area shoehorned tightly between Le Loi and Tran Phu. Most visitors simply pass through on their way to or from Phu Quoc island, but it's worth visiting the **Nguyen Trung Truc Temple** at 18 Nguyen Cong Tru; it's dedicated to the leader of a resistance campaign against the French in the 1860s who turned himself in and was then executed when they took some civilians hostage, including his mother, and threatened to kill them.

ARRIVAL AND DEPARTURE

By plane Flights from HCMC (1 daily; 45min) and Phu Quoc (3 weekly; 40min) arrive 7km south of Rach Gia. From the airport, you can take a *xe om* (50,000VND) or taxi (around 90,000VND) direct to the centre.

By boat Superdong boats (2–4 daily; 2hr 20min; 250,000VND; ⓦ superdong.com.vn) to Phu Quoc depart from Ben Tau Khach Bien quay on Nguyen Cong Tru, a 10min walk from the centre. Tickets can be bought in advance from offices along Nguyen Cong Tru, or from the dock.

By bus Local buses depart when full from the central bus station along Nguyen Binh Khiem, 500m north of town, at Nguyen Binh Khiem. Some larger scheduled departures (including Can Tho and HCMC) use a bigger terminal 8km south, past the airport; book with Futa through your accommodation, and they'll pick up and drop off for free.

Destinations Can Tho (3hr); Ha Tien (3hr); HCMC (7hr).

ACCOMMODATION

11

Kim Co Hotel 141 Nguyen Hung Son ⊕ 0297 387 9610. Central hotel offering clean, brightly painted doubles with a/c; most face the corridor. Doubles $\overline{\underline{\$15}}$

My Nhung 27–29 Dinh Liet ⊕ 0297 396 2624. Good new option in the thick of things, an easy walk from the Phu Quoc ferries. All rooms have a/c, the wi-fi and showers are strong – sometimes that's all you need. Double $\overline{\underline{\$18}}$

EATING

Gio Bien Ton Duch Thang A little way south of the centre (take a *xe om*, or walk along the shore), this pier-cum-restaurant is a prime spot for seafood. Prices can be sky-high but many fishy mains go for just 70,000VND; it's also by far the most atmospheric place in town for a beer. Daily 24hr, in theory.

Hoa Binh-Rach Gia 3–7 Co Bac. The riverside restaurant at this fancy hotel, just south of the centre, is a prime spot for eating – they've a whole slew of Vietnamese dishes to choose from, and they aren't all that pricey, considering the relatively luxurious environment (many mains under 100,000VND). Daily 10am–10pm.

HA TIEN

Right near the Cambodian border and lapped by the Gulf of Thailand, **HA TIEN**, with its riverfront promenade and crumbling colonial buildings, is the most appealing town in the delta, and preferable to Rach Gia if you're heading to Phu Quoc.

WHAT TO DO AND SEE

Ha Tien is big on atmosphere, and beyond the lively waterfront **market** there are a couple of appealing pagodas, as well as elaborate tombs and a good stretch of

INTO CAMBODIA: XA XIA

Ha Tien offers an easy crossing to Kep and Kampot on Cambodia's south coast; for travellers coming from Cambodia, it's an easy way of visiting Phu Quoc, and many operators will arrange combined bus and ferry tickets. Buses leave Ha Tien at noon and 4pm daily for Kep (1hr; 200,000VND,), Kampot (1hr 30min; 250,000VND), Sihanoukville (4hr; 450,000VND) and Phnom Penh (4hr; 430,000VND); Ha Tien Tourism arrange bus tickets, and visas for most nationalities are available at the border ($30, plus $5 bribe). For Kep and Kampot, it doesn't end up costing much more to arrange a direct xe om ride – you'll potentially save a lot of time at the border (there's always one foreigner who slows things down by refusing to pay the extra $5), the route they take on the Cambodian side is far prettier, and you can go from door to door with consummate ease.

white beach – all of which can be explored by bicycle or motorbike.

Mac Cuu family tombs

West along Mac Cuu, which branches off the main Phuong Thanh, you'll find Nui Lang, or the Hill of Tombs. Here **Mac Cuu**, the eighteenth-century feudal lord who founded Ha Tien, is buried with his relatives in peaceful, wooded grounds in semicircular Chinese graves. Mac Cuu's grave is uppermost on the hill, daubed with a yin and yang symbol, and guarded by two swordsmen, a white tiger and a blue dragon.

Thach Dong Cave Pagoda and Mui Nai Beach

A pleasant circular cycling route takes in Ha Tien's outlying attractions. Strike off west along Lam Son, through rice fields, coconut groves and water palm, past a war cemetery (2.5km from town), from where it's 1.5km to the first of three marked turnings – all with toll gates (10,000VND) – to **Mui Nai** peninsula, a relatively peaceful, dark-sand cove, with numerous cafés and restaurants.

Set inland from Mui Nai, and a little north, you'll see the 48m-high granite outcrop housing **Thach Dong** cave long before you reach it. A monument shaped like a clenched fist and commemorating the 130 Vietnamese killed by the Khmer Rouge near here in 1978 marks its entrance (daily 7am–5pm; 10,000VND), beyond which steps lead up to several Buddhist shrines hidden inside a network of caves, which are also home to a colony of bats. From here, another 3km along the circular road brings you back to Ha Tien.

ARRIVAL AND INFORMATION

By boat Superdong (ⓦ superdong.com.vn) hydrofoils depart for Ham Ninh port on Phu Quoc (3–4 daily; 1hr 15min; 230,000VND) from the south bank of the To Chau River; tickets can be booked at many offices around town. There are also boats run by Ngoc Thanh, which run to similar schedules and have the same prices.

By bus Buses terminate at the station, across the bridge about 2km south of town, though some drop off or pick up in the centre, often with the aid of shuttle services.

Destinations Can Tho (5–6hr); Chau Doc (3hr); HCMC (8hr); Rach Gia (2hr 30min).

Services There's an ATM at Agribank, 37 Lam Son. For bike or motorbike rental, ask at *Oasis* (see opposite) or the large *River* hotel, on the riverfront on Dang Thuy Tram.

ACCOMMODATION

Hai Phuong So 52, Dong Thuy Tram ☎ 0297 385 2240. The biggest international traveller magnet in town, this basic multi-storey hotel features large, spotless, tiled, a/c rooms. They'll often discount from the rack rate. Doubles $18

Hai Van 55 Lam Son ☎ 0297 385 2872. A convivial choice offering immaculate, spacious rooms with satellite TV. Superior doubles, costing around double, are available in the mid-range annexe. Doubles $10

Hai Yen 15 Duong To Chau ☎ 0297 385 1580. The staff here are not going to win any prizes for congeniality, but the rooms are spacious and finished in wood, some with waterfront views. Doubles $13

Happy 13–14 Hoang Van Thu ☎ 0297 396 6688. Also known as the *Hanh Phuc*, this is a good cheap choice, just a stone's throw from the river bridge, and maybe two or three hefty throws of said stone from the night market. Some rooms are a bit musty, but they're all en suite and pretty comfortable; little English is spoken, so it's best booked online. Doubles $11

EATING AND DRINKING

A slew of seafood stalls opens up by the river around sundown – atmospheric, and the food's usually good, though be sure to clarify prices on ordering, since there are occasional stories of foreigners being ripped off.

5 Lua 36 Dang Thuy Tram. The most popular place in town with locals themselves; most come for the hotpots (not that pricey if you're in a small group), but you can select simpler Vietnamese staples (from 75,000VND) from the English-language menu. Can get a little boozy, too. Daily 9am–midnight.

★**Oasis** 30 Tran Hau. Run by an English-Vietnamese couple, this little restaurant-bar draws hungry foreigners like moths to a flame, thanks to Western options such as hearty English breakfasts (90,000VND; black pudding 20,000VND extra), breakfast dishes such as muesli and omelettes, and cheap-as-chips beer (from 12,000VND). The owner, Andy, is a treasure-trove of local information and can help arrange motorbike tours of the area. Daily 9am–9pm, sometimes closes for lunch.

Thuy Tien Dong Ho. This little café, built on a floating river raft, is the perfect place to enjoy an iced coffee (15,000VND) or beer. Daily noon–9pm.

PHU QUOC

Lying in the Gulf of Thailand 45km west of Ha Tien and just 15km from the coast of Cambodia, **PHU QUOC** is a tropical island of almost six hundred square kilometres, much of which is part of a UNESCO Biosphere Reserve. Fringed with golden and powder-white sandy beaches, with lively Duong Dong town halfway along the west coast, a tropical forested interior, and an archipelago of fifteen small islands off the southern tip – perfect for diving, snorkelling and fishing – the place is a relatively low-key alternative to the beach resorts along Vietnam's south coast, though recent years have seen a fair bit of development.

WHAT TO SEE AND DO

Besides the island's main beaches and the islets offering **diving** and **snorkelling** opportunities, the network of partially paved but mostly dirt tracks throughout the island makes for bumpy exploration of Phu Quoc's protected forest, waterfalls, and deserted stretches of sand by **motorbike** or **bicycle**.

Duong Dong

The island's only town, **DUONG DONG**, is a congested little place with fishing boats bobbing in the harbour and a bustling port-side market, just over the Nguyen Trung Truc bridge. Phu Quoc is famous for its **fish sauce** (*nuoc mam*), and you can check out the enormous vats of fermenting fish at the Hung Thanh factory on Nguyen Van Troi (daily 8–11am & 1–5pm; free). At sunset, locals congregate at **Cau Castle** – a cross between a lighthouse and a temple on Bach Dang – while foreigners do likewise at the **night market** nearby, and at restaurants and bars all along the strip.

The beaches

The palm-fringed, 20km stretch of golden grainy sand sweeping down the island's west coast, aptly named **Bai Truong** (Long Beach), is the most accessible of Phu Quoc's beaches. Though the northern end is crammed with hotels and luxury resorts, the southern 10km is relatively deserted.

While lacking the palm fringes of Long Beach, **Bai Ong Lang**, north of Duong Dong town, offers more privacy and seclusion, and its rocky shore is good for snorkelling. To the northeast and northwest, **Bai Thom**, **Bai Cua Can**, **Bai Vung Bao** and **Bai Dai** offer similarly rocky coves; all can be reached by motorbike along dirt paths.

The blindingly white, powdery sand, clean turquoise waters and excellent palm-shaded seafood restaurants make **Bai Sao** (Star Beach) popular for a day-trip; the road leading down there is pleasantly rough and gravelly. Further north of Bai Sao on the island's east coast, **Bai Vong** has more white sand, good shade and shallow waters suitable for paddling.

Phu Quoc National Park

Seventy percent of the island is cloaked in tropical forest. The north is mountainous and heavily forested, while in the south much of the land has been cleared for pepper plantations; visitors are welcome to have a closer look in places like **Khu Tuong**, inland from Ong Lang Beach – ask permission first.

ARRIVAL AND DEPARTURE

By plane The international airport lies south of Duong Dong, a 60,000–120,000VND cab ride depending upon how far along the strip you want to go.

Destinations Can Tho (1 daily; 45min); Hanoi (4–5 daily; 3hr); HCMC (1–2 hourly; 1hr); Rach Gia (3 weekly; 40min).

11

11

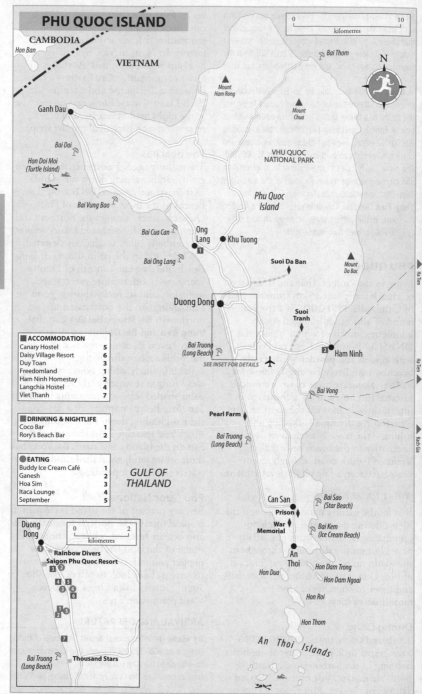

PHU QUOC ISLAND

CAMBODIA

Hon Ban

VIETNAM

Ganh Dau

Bai Dai

Hon Doi Moi
(Turtle Island)

Bai Vung Bao

Bai Cua Can

Bai Thom

Mount
Ham Rong

Mount
Chua

VHU QUOC
NATIONAL PARK

Phu Quoc
Island

Ong
Lang   Khu Tuong

Bai Ong Lang

Suoi Da Ban

Mount
Da Bac

Duong Dong

Suoi
Tranh

Bai Truong
(Long Beach)

SEE INSET FOR DETAILS

Ham Ninh

Bai Vong

Pearl Farm

Bai Truong
(Long Beach)

GULF
OF
THAILAND

Can San

Prison

War
Memorial

Bai Sao
(Star Beach)

Bai Kem
(Ice Cream Beach)

An
Thoi

Hon Dua

Hon Dam Trong

Hon Dam Ngoai

Hon Roi

Hon Thom

An Thoi Islands

0   10
kilometres

N

Ha Tien

Ha Tien

Rach Gia

ACCOMMODATION
Canary Hostel	5
Daisy Village Resort	6
Duy Toan	3
Freedomland	1
Ham Ninh Homestay	2
Langchia Hostel	4
Viet Thanh	7

DRINKING & NIGHTLIFE
Coco Bar	1
Rory's Beach Bar	2

EATING
Buddy Ice Cream Café	1
Ganesh	2
Hoa Sim	3
Itaca Lounge	4
September	5

Duong
Dong

0   2
kilometres

Rainbow Divers
Saigon Phu Quoc Resort

Bai Truong
(Long Beach)   Thousand Stars

DIVING AND SNORKELLING AROUND PHU QUOC

When Nha Trang's waters become too murky to dive, Phu Quoc's dive centres are open (Oct–April), ferrying divers and snorkellers to **Turtle Island** to the northwest and the **An Thoi** archipelago to the south, where you can see hard and soft corals, and a spectacular array of reef fish including scorpion fish, butterfly fish, parrot fish, fairy basslets, damsel fish and huge sea urchins. Rainbow Divers, 17A Tran Hung Dao (☎091 340 0964, ⊛divevietnam .com), offers well-organized and highly recommended diving and snorkelling trips; a day-trip with two boat dives and lunch costs $95 ($35 for snorkellers). They also offer full-day "discover diving" beginners' courses ($130), and PADI certification courses for all levels. Their office is on the main roundabout coming into Duong Dong from the south (Long Beach road). Flipper Diving Club (60 Tran Hung Dao; ☎0297 399 4924, ⊛flipperdiving.com) is another reputable dive operator.

By boat Superdong (⊛superdong.com.vn) runs hydrofoils from the east coast to Rach Gia (2–3 daily; 250,000VND; 2hr 20min) and Ha Tien (3–4 daily; 230,000VND; 1hr 10min); the latter link up with buses to Cambodia and HCMC. Private minivans ply the route to the resorts (from 30,000VND/person), but are notorious for overcharging. Hydrofoil tickets for the trip back to the mainland can be booked through your hotel; you may well get a free drop-off too.

INFORMATION

Information and tours Resorts and hotels can organize all manner of tours; most can organize motorbike rental (ask for a map of the island), and assist with booking onward transport. Many work with John's Tours, 4 & 92 Tran Hung Dao (daily 6am–9pm; ☎091 910 7086, ⊛johnsislandtours .com), who organize all-inclusive fishing and snorkelling day-trips for $17/person; *Langchia Hostel* (see below) also run tours, many of them revolving around beer.

Services There are a number of ATMs dotted along the length of Tran Hung Dao, and an Agribank at 2 Trang Hung Dao in Duong Dong. There are several pharmacies near the market on Ngo Quyen in Duong Dong. The post office is at Thang 4 in Duong Dong (daily 7am–7pm).

ACCOMMODATION

Prices skyrocket around Dec and Jan, but during low season (May–Sept), prices are slashed by up to two-thirds, making some budget and mid-range resorts fantastic value.

LONG BEACH

Canary Hostel 170 Tran Hung Dao ☎0297 399 6772, ⊛canary-hostel.com. One of the best of the many hostels to have opened in recent years – the sizeable pool encourages mingling and daytime boozing, while Dorm and private rooms are comfy affairs. Dorms $10, doubles $30

Daisy Village Resort ☎0297 384 4412, ⊛daisyresort .com. If you're willing to splash out a bit, rooms here can

often be a steal – especially when off-season discounts kick in. Of their two adjoining resorts, the *Daisy Village* is cheaper, with candy-coloured bungalows set around a highly attractive swimming pool; it's just a little bit of a walk out, though this makes for quiet at night. Breakfast is awesome too. Doubles $50

Duy Toan 91/6a Tran Hung Dao ☎0297 384 7666. Some of the cheapest private rooms in the Dong Duong area; they're spick and span with small TVs and private facilities. A great deal. Doubles $12

★**Langchia Hostel** 84 Tran Hung Dao ☎09 3913 2603, ✉info@langchia-hostel.com. This hostel's popularity has meant it has expanded in recent years; the large dorm is comfortable, and they have fairly pricey private rooms too. It's fronted by a large bar-like area with pool table, and backed by a small pool, while staff run regular tours, movie nights and the like. Dorms $7, doubles $30

Viet Thanh 118/14 Tran Hung Dao ☎0122 986 6542, ⊛vietthanhbungalow.com. Spacious bungalows with porches and hammocks in a friendly family-run compound on the beach. There are also simple rooms on offer in a concrete building out back. Doubles $25, bungalows $50

11

★**TREAT YOURSELF**

Freedomland ☎0297 399 4891, ⊛freedomlandphuquoc.com. Drowning in greenery down one of the winding dirt paths near Ong Lang Beach, this is a hippie-esque retreat. Accommodation is rustic: fan-cooled bungalows with mosquito nets, cold showers, and no wi-fi, but travellers end up lingering here for days because of the friendly vibe. You're likely to make new friends here over communal dinner, and the beach is 5min away. Minimum two-night stay (three nights Dec–Feb). Doubles $70

★**TREAT YOURSELF**

Itaca Lounge 125 Tran Hung Dao ☎0297 399 2022, ⊛itacalounge.com. Lanterns in the trees and strings of tiny lights subtly illuminate this open-air lounge, with comfy couches and tables scattered around. The menu is creative international, with an emphasis on Spanish food – try chorizo-and-egg pizza (210,000VND), Andalucian fried squid (160,000VND) or paella (310,000VND per person). The service is super-attentive and the ambience just lovely. Daily 6–11pm.

HAM NINH

Ham Ninh Homestay ☎090 675 8797. For something a little different, head to this cosy little homestay, just a short walk away from where the ferries set down. It's a little far from the beaches, but the friendly owners can help you to get a rental motorbike in no time. Doubles $14

EATING

Most resorts have decent bar-restaurants. Places close fairly early; little is open past 10pm, even at weekends. For the island's best, cheapest seafood, head for the vendor stalls by the lighthouse and the open-air eateries at the night market along Vo Thi Sau in Duong Dong (daily from 5pm, mains from 80,000VND). The basic restaurants on Bai Sao are locally famous for their barbecued seafood and grilled fish.

Buddy Ice Cream Café 6 Bach Dang. This congenial café upped sticks to a new location in recent years – and is all the better for it. It's a highly attractive place where locals pop by for an extended coffee- or lunch-break. What hasn't changed is the menu: imported New Zealand ice cream (40,000VND/scoop), sublime fruit shakes, fish and chips and toasted sandwiches. Daily 7.30am–11pm.

Ganesh 97 Tran Hung Dao. Large Indian restaurant specializing mostly in northern Indian cuisine, such as tandoori dishes. Plenty of vegetarian options, and the thalis (veggie or seafood; 180,000VND) make for a gut-busting meal. Daily 11am–10pm.

Hoa Sim 92 Tran Hung Dao. Sometimes you just want good Vietnamese food at regular Vietnamese prices. If that's you, head straight to this family place, which whips up rice and noodle staples from just 30,000VND, and fancier curries for a little more. Daily 9am–10pm.

September Tran Hung Dao. A lovely, lovely new option near the south end of the strip – veggie food served in a simple but elegant environment. Follow your nose to the source of the tantalizing aromas emanating from the open kitchen and try yummy mains such as sweet pumpkin and peanut curry (75,000VND), or claypot tofu with bitter melon (70,000VND). Daily 1–10pm.

DRINKING AND NIGHTLIFE

Coco Bar 118/3 Tran Hung Dao. Popular watering hole with cheaper booze than its exterior may hint at (including some good home-made rum), as well as shisha pipes to suck on – loads of flavours available. Daily 9am–midnight.

Rory's Beach Bar By *La Veranda Resort*, Long Beach. Aussie-owned beach venue that's without doubt the best, and most popular, nightlife option in Phu Quoc. Think chairs on the beach, campfires, a pool table and decent beer… what more could you want? Daily 9am–midnight, often later.

Small print and index

A ROUGH GUIDE TO ROUGH GUIDES

Published in 1982, the first Rough Guide – to Greece – was a student scheme that became a publishing phenomenon. Mark Ellingham, a recent graduate in English from Bristol University, had been travelling in Greece the previous summer and couldn't find the right guidebook. With a small group of friends he wrote his own guide, combining a contemporary, journalistic style with a thoroughly practical approach to travellers' needs.

The immediate success of the book spawned a series that rapidly covered dozens of destinations. And, in addition to impecunious backpackers, Rough Guides soon acquired a much broader readership that relished the guides' wit and inquisitiveness as much as their enthusiastic, critical approach and value-for-money ethos. These days, Rough Guides include recommendations from budget to luxury and cover more than 120 destinations around the globe, from Amsterdam to Zanzibar, all regularly updated by our team of roaming writers.

Browse all our latest guides, read inspirational features and book your trip at **roughguides.com**.

Help us update

We've gone to a lot of effort to ensure that the fifth edition of **The Rough Guide to Southeast Asia on a Budget** is accurate and up-to-date. However, things change – places get "discovered", opening hours are notoriously fickle, restaurants and rooms raise prices or lower standards. If you feel we've got it wrong or left something out, we'd like to know, and if you can remember the address, the price, the hours, the phone number, so much the better.

Please send your comments with the subject line "**Rough Guide Southeast Asia on a Budget Update**" to mail@uk.roughguides.com. We'll credit all contributions and send a copy of the next edition (or any other Rough Guide if you prefer) for the very best emails.

Readers' updates

Thanks to all the readers who have taken the time to write in with comments and suggestions (and apologies if we've inadvertently omitted or misspelt anyone's name):

Joseph Andrews; Russ Austin; Evgeny Bobrov; Natalie Braine; Mike Burnett; Helen Clutton; David Cunningham; Bethan Davies; Sandra De Bastos; Frédéric De Rycke; Friedel Geeraert; Maria Gotzner; Julia Hanson-Abbott; Sarah Harris; Posy Harvey; Oliver Heard; Andrew J. Hebert; Bronya James; Stephen Jones; Johannes Kellner; Monica Mackaness and John Garratt; Julia MacKenzie; Siegfried Olbrich; Mila Rodriguez; Heather Rogers; Lee Seldon; Andrew Slater; Verstuurd Vanaf; Dennis Vervlossen; Wade and Sarah; Jeff Waistell; Franziska Wellenzoh; David Whitling.

Rough Guide credits

Editor: Alice Park
Layout: Ankur Guha
Cartography: Ashutosh Bharti, Richard Marchi
Picture editor: Marta Bescos
Proofreader: Jan McCann
Managing editor: Andy Turner
Assistant editor: Divya Grace Mathew

Production: Jimmy Lao
Cover photo research: Marta Bescos
Editorial assistant: Aimee White
Senior DTP coordinator: Dan May
Programme manager: Gareth Lowe
Publishing director: Georgina Dee

Publishing information

This fifth edition published October 2017 by
Rough Guides Ltd,
80 Strand, London WC2R 0RL
11, Community Centre, Panchsheel Park,
New Delhi 110017, India
Distributed by Penguin Random House
Penguin Books Ltd, 80 Strand, London WC2R 0RL
Penguin Group (USA), 345 Hudson Street, NY 10014, USA
Penguin Group (Australia), 250 Camberwell Road,
Camberwell, Victoria 3124, Australia
Penguin Group (NZ), 67 Apollo Drive, Mairangi Bay,
Auckland 1310, New Zealand
Penguin Group (South Africa), Block D, Rosebank Office
Park, 181 Jan Smuts Avenue, Parktown North, Gauteng,
South Africa 2193
Rough Guides is represented in Canada by DK Canada, 320
Front Street West, Suite 1400, Toronto, Ontario M5V 3B6
Printed in Singapore
© Rough Guides 2017
Maps © Rough Guides

944pp includes index
A catalogue record for this book is available from the
British Library
ISBN: 978-0-24127-922-9
The publishers and authors have done their best to ensure
the accuracy and currency of all the information in
The Rough Guide to Southeast Asia on a Budget,
however, they can accept no responsibility for any loss,
injury, or inconvenience sustained by any traveller as a
result of information or advice contained in the guide.
1 3 5 7 9 8 6 4 2

MIX
Paper from
responsible sources
FSC™ C018179
www.fsc.org

Photo credits

All photos © Rough Guides, except the following:
(Key: t-top; c-centre; b-bottom; l-left; r-right)

1 Getty Images: John W Banagan
2 Alamy Stock Photo: David Noton
4 AWL Images: Gavin Hellier
5 AWL Images: Michele Falzone
9 Alamy Stock Photo: Karin De Winter (t). **Getty Images**:
Christian Aslund (b)
10 Alamy Stock Photo: Dino Geromella
11 123RF.com: freeartist (t). **Alamy Stock Photo**:
robertharding (b). **AWL Images**: Katja Kreder (c)
13 Alamy Stock Photo: Blend Images
14 AWL Images: Michele Falzone (t); AWL Images: Travel Pix
Collection (b); Robert Harding Picture Library: Olaf Protze (c)
15 AWL Images: Peter Adams (tl & br)
16 Alamy Stock Photo: Eitan Simanor (c), Aroon
Thaewchatturat (b). **AWL Images**: Gavin Hellier (tr)
17 Alamy Stock Photo: Simon Reddy (t)
18 Alamy Stock Photo: Paul Kennedy (t); WaterFrame (b).
Getty Images: 117 Imagery (cl); Ed Norton (cr)
19 Alamy Stock Photo: Khaled Kassem (cl), Jan
Wlodarczyk (b). **Dreamstime.com**: Sinseeho (t)

20 Alamy Stock Photo: Robert Harding World Imagery (t)
21 Alamy Stock Photo: Hemis (b). **Robert Harding
Picture Library**: Aurora Photos (cl)
28 AWL Images: Andrew Watson / John Warburton-Lee
Photography Ltd
51 Alamy Stock Photo: Tibor Bognar
121 Corbis: Calle Montes
161 Robert Harding Picture Library: Matthew Williams-
Ellis
409 Dreamstime.com: Rodrigolab
589 Getty Images: Peter Adams
671 Dreamstime.com: Chrishowey
701 Getty Images: Flickr RM

Front cover, spine and back cover: *Decorative umbrellas
drying after hand painting by local artists at Umbrella
Making Center, Bo Sang, Chiang Mai, Thailand*
AWL Images: Danita Delimont

Acknowledgements

Stuart Butler: In Myanmar I would like to thank William Myatwunna from Good News Travels for his huge help, Marcus Allender from Pegu Travels and go-mynamar.com for his help and also Phone Kyaw Moe Myint in Ngwe Saung and the staff at *Motherland Inn II* in Yangon. Finally, but most importantly, I must thank my wife Heather and children, Jake and Grace, for their endless patience and understanding while I was away from home working on this project.

Tom Deas: Thanks to my father, John Deas.

Nick Edwards: I would like to thank the following for invaluable help and/or great hospitality: in London Gerry Panga and Richard de Villa of the DoT; Archie at *W Hostel*, Boracay; Kaila Ledesma in Bacolod and Dave Albao on Danjugan Island; Peter and Daisy of *Driftwood Village* on Sugar Beac; Zoe at Liquid Dumaguete; and finally to Camille and Mike Butler at *Coco Grove Beach Resort*, Siquijor. Last but not least, thanks to Maria for arranging the great do back home.

Marco Ferrarese: The mammoth task of updating the whole of Malaysia and Brunei chapters would have never been possible without the help of many great people. First and foremost, I wish to thank my wife, Kit Yeng Chan, who followed me for three months of research, helping immensely with taking pictures and keeping up the good vibes. At home in Penang, thanks to Gareth Richards, Yew Kuok Cheong, the Chan family and all my friends who taught me everything about my second home. In Langkawi, kudos to Narelle McMurtrie, Kay Mohlman and Richard Krause – always a pleasure. On the East Coast, thanks to Tan Swee Leong in Kota Bharu and Hakim in Kuala Terengganu for the good times and food galore. In Kuching, I kowtow to Robin and Rudolph Landau, Jacqueline Fong, Marvin Gayle, Phillip Yong and Borneo Adventures, Paradesa Borneo, and Kevin Nila Nangai at Sarawak Tourism. In Sibu, many thanks to Golda Mowe and Jason Tai Hee – without your careful suggestions, the whole Sarawak research trip would have been so much less interesting. Thanks also to Scott Apoi and his mom at Ngimat Ayu homestay in Bario, and Alec "Elvis" Leong in Miri. In Brunei, thanks to Nikie – the Sultan should make you minister of tourism. And last, in the Land below the Wind, thanks to Charles Ryan and Sticky Rice Travel, Eddie Chua and family in Kampung Bestaria, Simon and Itisha in Lahad Datu, the Scuba Junkie team in Semporna, Mabul and Sipadan, Rizo Leong and Pangrok Sulap in Ranau, and Richard and Virgil Gunting in Sapulot. Terima kasih kamu semua kawan-kawanku.

Esme Fox: I would like to thank Rahul Aggarwal from Travel The Unknown for all his help with the Southern Luzon area; Philippine Tourism Attaché Gerard O. Panga for all his contacts; tourism officer Andrew Zuniga for his help researching Legaspi and Donsol; tour guide Bryan Ocampo for all his invaluable knowledge and useful contacts; and tour guide Donna Gunn from Corazon Travel for all her help in Palawan. I would also like to thank my editors Andy Turner, Helen Abramson and Alice Park. Lastly, I would like to thank Dan Convey for being a great travel companion.

Anthon Jackson: Thanks to Iman in Bandaneira, Muhammad in Ternate, Tommy in Bukittinggi and Firman in Banda Aceh; Alice Park for excellent editing, Andy Turner for the opportunity, and Joanna, Bodil and WKJ for company at various points along the way.

Daniel Jacobs: Thanks to Jane Manibog, Gabby de Leon, Iryn Camtan and everyone at *Pension Natividad* in Manila, Buonna at the DoT office in Vigan, Imee Awichen and Jovi Lopez at Bontoc Municipal Tourism, Jake at Banaue Tourism, and Ronette Masferré at *Pines Kitchenette* in Bontoc.

Richard Lim: Thanks to Susanah Toh; Kee Beng; John; Tony C; the Bukit Brown posse; and to my family.

Mike MacEacheran: Thanks all those who helped out and provided assistance along the way, in particular: Jason Keall at KLM; Juliet Fallowfield, Cassandra Cuevas and Lesley Tan at Shangri-La; David Joyce and Matt Reed at Evolution on Malapascua; Ashley Charles at Buddha's Surf Camp on Siargao; and everyone at Bohol Tourism who really went out of their way to help at the very last minute. Thanks also to my fellow authors and ever-patient editor Alice Park.

Shafik Meghji: Many thanks to all the locals, readers and travellers who helped me out along the way. A special thanks must go to: Alice Park for her sterling editing work; Helen Abramson at RG HQ; Kati Taylor and Huw Owen at Travel Local; Jason Rolan of Exo Travel; Kai Saythong of Laos Mood; Ross Corbett of NZ Aid; Dennis Ulstrup of Green Discovery; Claire Boobbyer; Jean, Nizar and Nina Meghji; and Sioned Jones.

Rachel Mills: Thanks to: Ben and Bich at *Phong Nha Farmstay*, Tonkin Travel in Hanoi, TravelLocal.com, *Tam's Cafe* in Dong Ha, Anh and Michaella at *Beachside Backpackers* in Dong Hoi, and to Michael Yates for bringing the sunshine.

Sarah Reid: Thanks firstly to the Rough Guides team: to Andy for the opportunity to work on this book, to Helen and Ed for your support along the way, and to Alice for stellar editing. Thanks also to the lovely Mr Bounxou at the *Residence Sisouk* for your hospitality in Pakse, and to excellent operator Rickshaw Travel for an authentic insight into the ancient royal capital. I will forever be in debt to my amazing friend Laura, who saved me both from drowning in the Mekong and from dying of shame after being attacked by bedbugs, and I'm grateful to the other travellers who shared tips (and Beerlaos) with me along the way. A special thank you to the locals and expats who welcomed me into their business and homes, and a final nod to my new husband Tim, who was missed on this great adventure.

Daniel Stables: Many thanks to everyone who helped me out before, during and after my time in Indonesia, in particular Iain Stewart and Anthon Jackson for their advice; Sian, Andy and Lizzie Stables; and Andy Turner at Rough Guides for sending me there in the first place.

Martin Zatko: Thanks to Mark at the Vietnam Visa Center, Felix in Nha Trang, Mia and Kim in HCMC, and the staff at the Hoan My hospital in Da Lat.

OUR WRITERS

Stuart Butler
Myanmar (Burma)

Meera Dattani
Cambodia

Tom Deas
Myanmar (Burma)

Nick Edwards
The Philippines

Marco Ferrarese
Brunei and Malaysia

Esme Fox
The Philippines

Paul Gray
Thailand

Anthon Jackson
Indonesia

Daniel Jacobs
The Philippines

Joanna James
Hong Kong and Macau

Richard Lim
Singapore

Mike MacEacheran
The Philippines

Shafik Meghji
Laos

Rachel Mills
Vietnam

Sarah Reid
Laos

Daniel Stables
Indonesia

Iain Stewart
Indonesia

Gavin Thomas
Cambodia and
Myanmar (Burma)

Martin Zatko
Vietnam

Index

Maps are marked in grey

Map symbols

The symbols below are used on maps throughout the book

International boundary	Embassy	Monastery	Shipwreck
Province boundary	ATM	Tower	Viewpoint
Chapter boundary	Gate	Monument	Spring
Motorway	Statue	Fortress	Surfing
Major road	Point of interest	Stately home	Snorkelling
Minor road	Internet access	Mountain refuge/lodge	Swimming pool
Pedestrian road	Garden	Cave	Waterfall
Steps	Golf course	Volcano	Lighthouse
Footpath	Bridge	Mountain peak	Church (regional maps)
Railway	Ruins	Mountain range	Church/cathedral
Ferry route	Border crossing	Petrol station	Building
River/coastline	Museum	Helipad	Market
Wall	Chinese temple	International airport	Stadium
Cable car	Synagogue	Domestic airport	Park/forest
Post office	Campsite	Bus/taxi stop	Beach
Information office	Pagoda	Parking	Cemetery
Telephone	Buddhist temple	Boat/ship	Swamp/marsh
Hospital	Thai temple/stupa		

Listings key

- ■ Accommodation
- ● Eating
- ■ Drinking/nightlife/entertainment
- ● Shopping

Long bus journey?
Phone run out of juice?

1 Denim, the pencil, the stethoscope and the hot-air balloon were all invented in which country?

a. Italy
b. France
c. Germany
d. Switzerland

2 What is the currency of Vietnam?

a. Dong
b. Yuan
c. Baht
d. Kip

3 In which city would you find the Majorelle Garden?

a. Marseille
b. Marrakesh
c. Tunis
d. Malaga

4 What is the busiest airport in the world?

a. London Heathrow
b. Tokyo International
c. Chicago O'Hare
d. Hartsfield-Jackson Atlanta International

5 Which of these countries does not have the equator running through it?

a. Brazil
b. Tanzania
c. Indonesia
d. Colombia

6 Which country has the most UNESCO World Heritage Sites?

a. Mexico
b. France
c. Italy
d. India

7 What is the principal religion of Japan?

a. Confucianism
b. Buddhism
c. Jainism
d. Shinto

8 Every July in Sonkajärvi, central Finland, contestants gather for the World Championships of which sport?

a. Zorbing
b. Wife-carrying
c. Chess-boxing
d. Extreme ironing

9 What colour are post boxes in Germany?

a. Red
b. Green
c. Blue
d. Yellow

10 For three days each April during Songkran festival in Thailand, people take to the streets to throw what at each other?

a. Water
b. Oranges
c. Tomatoes
d. Underwear

1:b / 2:a / 3:b / 4:d / 5:b / 6:c / 7:d / 8:b / 9:d / 10:a

Welcome
to a World
of Good

When you travel with G Adventures,
you get more than the adventure of a
lifetime. You become part of a global
social enterprise that connects you
with people and places in a way you
never could on your own.

**Making the world a better place is
easy. All you have to do is have the
time of your life.**

0344 272 2010
gadventures.co.uk

G·Adventures

of   trips

BORNEO

meaningful adventures
STICKY RICE
TRAVEL

134 Jalan Gaya, 3rd Floor | 88000 Kota Kinabalu | Sabah, Malaysia
www.stickyricetravel.com | info@stickyricetravel.com
phone: (60) 88 250 588 | 250 177 | 251 654